Preface

In this second edition we have radically revised both the text and the supporting materials. The extent of the text is now such that we have retitled the book *Text with Materials*. The many changes have been occasioned by the great volume of legal activity in England and other common-law jurisdictions since the first edition appeared. Indeed, further structural changes are in the offing from April 1994 when, for example, a reduction in the number of regions will take place. These changes were announced too late for inclusion in Chapter 2. We have also sought to take account of and benefit from the many helpful comments offered by reviewers, colleagues and students (not least as regards the layout). We have not, however, acceded to all the suggestions made by the commentators. For example, the book remains firmly embedded in English law. Where there is no or little law or where analogies or comparisons are called for, we have looked to other common-law jurisdictions. European legal developments, therefore, are noticed when they materially touch on English law. After all, there is very little in the way of European Community law which yet affects medical law. And, as regards the particular legal regimes of various European countries, since we do not have the necessary expertise to do other than describe at one remove (at best) what is the living law, we resist this temptation. Equally, we have continued to concentrate on medical law. We recognise, of course, the wider issues of health and the extent of the relationship between medicine and health. But, health law, touching on matters as diverse as public sanitation, industrial health and safety, and the regulation of the food and drug industry, is a subject, if indeed it is one, for a separate work.

We are acutely aware of the fact that the book is long – longer even than the previous edition. The explanation is that medical law is still a young subject and the materials are still diffuse. Furthermore many, indeed the majority of, students and practitioners may not yet have access to the rich variety of sources needed to understand how the subject has developed and will do so in the future. In time, libraries will develop. But until that time we feel it incumbent on us to bring together as much as we can so that the reader has the opportunity to choose what to read and rely on.

Finally, the reader should note that footnotes to material have not been included except in odd instances where they provide references to matters in the body of the extract.

Since AG moved from Cambridge to King's College, London, any sense of nostalgia on the completion of this edition is confined to memories of the Pineapple pub and the Italian sandwich bar in Kentish Town. Nevertheless, the collaboration remained great fun. Once again, Josie, AG's dog, slept or chewed contentedly on discarded drafts throughout our work.

We record our thanks once again to Butterworths' editorial staff for the patience shown to us. We thank also Cathy Hargreaves and Clive Pugh who helped to collate the huge volume of material we sent them in search of. Stephanie Lawson typed the whole manuscript and we are forever in her debt.

The law is stated as of 1 August 1993, although a few subsequent developments have been included where possible.

IK
AG
31 December 1993

Contents

PART III
MEDICAL LAW IN ACTION

B : DURING LIFE

PART III
MEDICAL LAW IN ACTION

C: THE END(ING) OF LIFE

Chapter 16 The end(ing) of life: the incompetent patient 1179

Acknowledgments

The publishers and authors wish to thank the following for permission to reprint material from the sources indicated.

American Psychiatric Association: Roth, Meisel & Lidz: 'Tests of Competency to Consent to Treatment' (March 1977) American Journal of Psychiatry.

American Society of Law and Medicine: Battin: 'Voluntary Euthanasia and the Risk of Abuse: Can We Learn Anything from the Netherlands?' (1992) 20 Law, Med & Health Care 133; Mady: 'Surrogate Mothers: The Legal Issues' (1981) Am J Law & Med 324, pp 332-339; 'A Moment in Human Development: Legal Protection, Ethical Standards and Social Policy on the Selective Non-treatment of Handicapped Neonates' American Journal of Law and Medicine, Vol 3 no 1 (1988), pp 39-41; Weir: 'The Morality of Physician Assisted Suicide' (1992) 20 Law, Med & Health Care 116.

Arnold (Edward) (Publishers) Ltd: 'Report of Working Party on Living Wills', King's College/Age Concern.

Blackwell Scientific Publications Ltd: Raymond: 'The Employment Rights of the NHS Hospital Doctor' in *Doctors, Patients and the Law* (ed Dyer) (1992), pp 197-205.

Blackwell (Basil) Ltd: 'The Report to the Committee of Inquiry into Human Fertilisation and Embryology' (Cmnd 9314) (1984) (The Warnock Report), paras 2.5, 2.13, 3.3, 3.4, 4.4, 4.7-4.9, 4.17, 4.19, 4.22, 4.25, 5.1-5.5, 6.8, 8.10, 8.12, 10.11, 10.12, 11.8, 11.9, 11.11-11.50, 12.5, 13.13; Mary Warnock: *A Question of Life*, pp 642, 700.

British Medical Association: Gillon: (1981) 7 JME 56; Gillon: 'Ethics of Fetal Brain Cell Transplants', BMJ (1988) 30 April; 'Impaired Autonomy and Rejection of Treatment', JME 1983, Vol 9, no 3, pp 131-132; Pallis: *ABC of Brain Stem Death*, pp 1-9, 17, 23, 28-32; 'Diagnosis of Death, Code of Practice' (1976) 2 BMJ 1187-1188, (1979) 1 BMJ 332; Tunkel: 'Abortion: How Early, How Late and How Legal?' (1979) BMJ 253.

Cambridge University Press: Matthews: 'Freedom, Unrequested Improvements and Lord Denning' [1981] CLJ 340.

Canada Government Publishing Centre: Keyserlinck: 'Sanctity of Life or Quality of Life', study written for the Law Reform Commission of Canada (1979) pp 50-51, 57-60, 70-72; Canadian Law Reform Commission: 'Human Dignity and Genetic Heritage' (Study Paper) (1991), 48-51; Canadian Law Reform Commission: 'Medically Assisted Procreation' (Paper No 65) (1992); Canadian Law Reform Commission: 'Procurement and Transfer of Human Tissues and Organs' (Paper No 66) (1992).

Canada Law Books Incorporated: Anderson v Chasney (1949) 4 DLR 71, (1950) 4 DLR 223; Girard v Royal Columbian Hospital (1976) 66 DLR (3d) 676; Hopp v Lepp (1980) 112 DLR (3d) 67; Johnson v Wellesley Hospital (1970) 17 DLR (3d) 139, 144-145; Kelly v Hazlett (1976) 75 DLR (3d) 536, 562-563; Lawson v Laferrière (1991) 78 DLR (4th) 609; McInerney v MacDonald (1992) 93 DLR (4th) 415; Malette v Shulman (1990) 67 DLR (4th) 421; R v Maurantonio (1967) 65 DLR (2d) 674; Reibl v Hughes (1978) 114 DLR (3d) 10-11, 12-13, 15-17, 494-495; Snell v Farrell (1990) 72 DLR (4th) 289; Re Superintendent of Family and Child Services and Dawson (1983) 145 DLR (3d) 610, 611-612, 620, 622-624; Urbanski v Patel (1978) 84 DLR (3d) 650; White v Turner (1981) 120 DLR (3d) 264, 285; Yepremian v Scarborough General Hospital (1980) 110 DLR (3d) 513; Zimmer v Ringrose (1981) 124 DLR (3d) 215.

Carswell Company Ltd: Halushka v University of Saskatchewan (1965) 52 WWR 608, 616; Picard: *Legal Liability of Doctors and Hospitals in Canada* (2nd edn, 1984), pp 45-46, 141, 143, 146-147, 243-247, 260-261, 308-311, 313-314; Rodriguez v British Columbia (Attorney General) (1993) 82 BCLR (2d) 273.

Cass (Frank) & Co Ltd: Brazier: 'Sterilisation: Down the Slippery Slope?' (1960) 6 Prof Neg 25; Brazier: 'Liability of Ethics Committees and their Members' (1990) Prof Neg 186; Dugdale: 'Diverse Reports, Canadian Professional Negligence Cases' (1986) 2 Prof Neg 108 at 109-110; Jones: 'Arbitration for Medical Claims in the NHS' (1992) 8 Prof Neg 142; Terry: 'The Malpractice Crisis in the United States, A Dispatch from the Trenches' (1986) 2 Prof Neg 145-150.

Clarendon Press: Skegg: *Law, Ethics and Medicine* (1984), pp 30-31, 36-37, 43-46, 51-52, 60-62, 72-73, 79-80, 107-109, 128-131, 135-136, 213-223.

Columbia Law Review: Robertson: 'Organ Donations by Incompetents and Substituted Judgment Doctrine' 76 Columbia L Rev 48 (1976), © 1976 by the Directors of the Columbia Law Review Association Inc. All Rights Reserved. Reprinted by permission.

Croom Helm: Lamb: *Death, Brain Death and Ethics*, pp 11-16.

Danish Council of Ethics: 'Ethics and Mapping the Human Gene', Danish Council of Ethics Report (1993).

DoH Publications: Conference of the Medical Royal Colleges and their Faculties of the UK, Working Paper Report (Hoffenberg) 'On the Supply of Donor Organs for Transplantation' (1987), p 6; HM(88)37 (Government Circular); 'Claims of Medical Negligence against NHS Hospitals and Community Doctors and Dentists' (HC(89)34); 'A Guide to Consent for Examination or Treatment' Consent Form (HC(90)22, App A(1)); NHS Management Executive Letter accompanying 'Local Research Ethics Committees' (HSG(91)5); 'Guidance on Partner Notification for HIV Infection' (PLICO(92)5).

Foundation Press Incorporated: Kaimowitz v Department of Mental Health for the State of Michigan (1973) 42 US LW 2063; Little v Little (1979) 576 SW (2d) 493.

General Medical Council: 'Professional Conduct and Discipline: Fitness to Practise' (January 1993), paras 9-30.

Hastings Center: Annas: 'From Canada with Love' (December 1987), pp 36-39; Caplan: 'Organ Procurement: It's not in the cards' (1984); Capron: 'Anencephalic Donors: Separate the Dead from the Dying' (February 1987).

IME Publications Ltd: Bulletin of the Institute of Medical Ethics, February 1986, pp 8-9.

Infertility Center of New York: 'Surrogate Parenting Agreement'.

Institute of Law Research and Reform, Alberta, Canada: 'Competence and Human Reproduction' (Report No 25, February 1989).

Jordan & Sons Ltd: A v C (1985) FLR 445; Re C (A Minor) (1985) FLR 846; Gold v Haringey Health Authority (1987) FLR 137-140; Re P (Minors) (1987) 2 FLR 421.

King's College, Centre of Medical Law and Ethics: Schylter: 'Advance Directives and AIDS' (1992).

King's Fund Publishing and Press Office: Capron: 'A National Commission on Medical Ethics', in *Health, Rights and Resources* (1988), pp 188-190; Ham, Dingwall et al: *Medical Negligence, Compensation and Accountability* (1988), pp 8-17, 26-34.

Kluwer Publishing: Lanham: 'Transplants and the Human Tissue Act 1961' (1971) 11 Med Sci Law 16, 17-18, 18-20, 21-22; Skegg: 'Human Tissue Act 1961' (1976) 16 Med Sci Law 197-199; Skegg: 'Liability for the Unauthorised Removal of Cadaveric Transplant Materials' (1974) 14 Med Sci Law 53, 55-56.

The Law Book Company Ltd: Department of Health and Community Services (NT) v JWB and SMB (1992) 88 ALJR 300; Ellis v Wallsend District Hospital (1989) 17 NSWLR 553; Rogers v Whitaker (1992) 67 ALJR 47; X and Y v Pal (1991) 23 NSWLR 26.

Lloyds of London Press Ltd: Wimpey Construction UK Ltd v DV Poole (1984) 2 Lloyds Rep 498.

Longman Professional & Business Communications Division: Clarke v Adams (1950) 94 SJ 599; Landau v Werner (1961) 105 SJ 1008.

McGill Law Journal: Picard: 'The Liability of Hospitals in Common Law Canada' (1981) 26 McGill LJ 997; Somerville: 'Structuring the Issues in Informed Consent' (1981) 26 McGill LJ 740.

Michegan Law Review Association: Dukeminier: 'Supplying Organs for Transplantation' 68 Mich L Rev, pp 811-866 (April 1970).

Monash University: 'Law and Medical Experimentation' (1987) 13 Monash Univ LR 189, pp 198-203, 200, 204.

New England Journal of Medicine: 'Ethics and Clinical Research' 274 New Eng J Med 1354 (1966); 'Incidence of Adverse Events and Negligence in Hospitalized Patients' 324 New Eng J Med (1991); 'The Nature of Adverse Events in Hospitalized Patients' 324 New Eng J Med (1991); 'Relation between Malpractice Claims and Adverse Events Due to Negligence' New Eng J Med (1991).

New Zealand Government Printing Office: Crimes Act 1961, s 61A, s 182A.

Ontario Law Reform Commission: 'Report on Human Artificial Reproduction and Related Matters' (1984), pp 102-104, 106-107, 118-120, 123-130,

153-159, 185-190. Reprinted with permission from the Queen's Printer for Ontario.

Oxford University Press: Annas: *Standard of Care* (1993), pp 149-159; Nicholson: *Medical Research with Children* (1986), pp 24-26, 119-120, 154; Singer & Wells: *New Ways of Making Babies, Reproduction Revolution* (1984), pp 107-108, 114-120.

Penguin Books Ltd: Brazier: *Medicine, Patients and the Law*, pp 11-12, 53-54, 70, 90, 128-134; Scott: *The Body as Property* (1981), pp 127-134, 136.

Royal College of Physicians: Hodges: 'Harmonisation of European Controls over Research: Ethics Committees, Consent, Compensation and Indemnity' in *Pharmaceutical Medicine and the Law* (eds Goldberg and Dodds-Smith) (1991).

Russell Sage Foundation: Katz: *Experimentation with Human Beings* (1972), pp 292-306.

Stevens & Sons Ltd: Brushett v Cowan [1991] 2 Med LR 271; Blyth v Bloomsbury Health Authority [1993] 4 Med LR 151; Dworkin: 'The Law Relating to Organ Transplantation' Med LR Vol 33, July 1970; Glanville Williams: *Textbook of Criminal Law* (2nd edn), pp 148-149, 285, 289, 294-301, 378, 579, 589-591; Hughes: 'The Reorganisation of the NHS: The Rhetoric and Reality of the Internal Market' (1991) 54 Med LR 88; Keown: 'The Law and Practice of Euthanasia in the Netherlands' LQR; Montrose: 'Is Negligence an Ethical or Sociological Concept?' (1958) 21 Med LR 259; Pace: 'Civil Liability for Pre-Natal Injuries' (1977) Med LR 141, pp 141-147, 150-153; Whitfield: 'Common Law Duties to Unborn Children' (1993) 1 Med LR 28.

Sweet & Maxwell Ltd: Douglas: *Law, Fertility and Reproduction* (1991); Eekelaar & Dingwall: 'Some Legal Issues in Obstetric Practice', Journal of Social Welfare (1984), p 258; *Encyclopaedia of Health Services and Medical Law*, ed Jacobs & Davies, paras 1.031-1.044; Keown: 'Miscarriage, A Medico-Legal Analysis' (1984) Crim LR 605, 608-611; R v Bodkin Adams (1957) CLR 365; R v Lennox-Wright (1973) Crim LR.

The Terrence Higgins Trust and the Centre of Medical Law and Ethics, King's College: 'The Living Will' (form).

UC Davis Law Review: Capron: 'Alternative Birth Technologies: Legal Challenges' (1987) UC Davis LR, pp 679, 682, 697-701.

US Government Printing Office: President's Commission for the Study of Ethical Problems in Medicine and Biomedical and Behavioral Research: 'Deciding to Forego Life Sustaining Treatment' (1983), pp 78-81, 82-88, 136-139, 139-141, 217-223; 'Making Health Care Decisions' (1983), pp 31-35, 32, 35-36, 38-40, 52-62, 63-67, 63-67, 68-69, 70-72, 82-88, 136-138, 139, 141, 172-173.

University of California: Rhoden: 'The Judge in the Delivery Room: The Emergency of Court-Ordered Caesareans' (1986) 74 Cal LR 1951.

University of Toronto: Dickens: 'The Control of Living Body Materials' (1977) 27 Univ Toronto Law J 142; Dickens: 'Reproduction Law and Medical Consent' 35 Univ Toronto Law J (1985), pp 255-286.

West Publishing Co: Furrow, Jost & Schwartz: *Health Law* (1987), pp 276-285, 310-315.

Table of statutes

References in this Table to *Statutes* are to Halsbury's Statutes of England (Fourth Edition) showing the volume and page at which the annotated text of an Act may be found. Page references printed in **bold** type indicate where the section of an Act is set out in part or in full.

List of cases

Part I

Introduction

Chapter 1

Introduction

Medical law is still a comparatively young subject. It has emerged in English law over the last decade or so as a distinct subject, both as an area of increasing importance in legal practice and as an academic discipline. As with all areas of English law, the central core of medical law is easier to identify than its boundaries. We see it as essentially concerned with the relationship between doctors (and to a lesser extent hospitals or other institutions) and patients. It is made up of, borrows from and reflects other areas of law, in particular tort, crime and family law. It is, however, more than the sum of these parts. It is not, in our view, a subject defined merely by reference to a set of factual circumstances. This is, of course, the traditional approach of the pragmatic common law, but it is an approach which is always intellectually unsatisfying. This is not least because it leaves unstated the criteria for deciding whether any particular factual circumstance falls within or outside a given subject area. Thus, typically, the borders of common law subjects routinely overlap and arguments about how to respond to problems at the edges are commonplace.

There are common issues which permeate all the problems which arise: respect for autonomy, consent, truth-telling, confidentiality, respect for personhood and persons, respect for dignity and respect for justice. All of these ethical issues run throughout the field. Until these common themes are recognised and reflected in legal thinking and analysis, a coherent approach to the emerging problems in medical law will be difficult. Thus, we see medical law as having some conceptual unity. The unifying legal theme is, to us, that of human rights. In our view, therefore, medical law is a subset of human rights law. This is what provides its intellectual coherence. This is not to say that we will not address discrete factual issues such as transplantation or IVF. Rather, we do it after, and in the light of, a close examination of the general principles of, for example, consent, which inform the analysis of particular areas of medical practice.

In this brief introductory chapter we can illustrate these central thematic points, ie the rich diversity of the legal issues, the factual complexity and yet the underlying symmetry of the subject, by noticing developments in the field of genetics.

It is trite to observe that developments in genetics have implications which go far wider than the practice of medicine and the doctor-patient relationship. The pursuit of knowledge which goes to the very essence of being is bound both to inspire and to trouble all of us. But even within the relatively limited confines of medical law, developments in genetics pose challenging questions for the application of traditional legal principles.

A massive scientific project, known as the Human Genome Initiative, is underway worldwide to map and sequence the approximately three billion base pairs that make up the 23 human chromosomes. Let us begin with an overview of this important area of medical science and its implications for society. The social impact of the HGI and the legal and ethical problems it raises are discussed by George Annas in the following extract.

G Annas *Standard of Care* (1993) pp 149-159

For the purposes of a preliminary exploration of the social policy issues raised by the project, it is only necessary to know a few basic definitions and facts. The first is that the term genome refers to the entire complement of genetic material in the set of chromosomes of a particular organism. Chromosomes are composed of genes (50,000 to 100,000 in a human being), which in turn are composed of deoxyribonucleic acid (DNA), the chemical carrier of genetic information. DNA is made of nucleotides, which are found in two linear strands wrapped around each other in the form of a double helix. The DNA strands are themselves composed of four nucleotides: adenosine (A), guanosine (G), cytidine (C), and thymidine (T). The two strands of DNA are bound together by weak bonds between base pairs of the nucleotide: A's only bind with T's, and G's only bind with C's. The size of the genome is usually expressed as the total of such base pairs; approximately 3 billion in the twenty-three chromosome (haploid) human genome.

Genetic mapping is the process of assigning genes to specific chromosomes; genetic linkage maps determine where one genetic locus is relative to another on the basis of how often they are inherited together. A genetic locus is an identifiable area, or 'marker,' on a chromosome, the presence of which indicates that a specific trait (such as eye color or blood type) will be expressed by the gene. The physical map of greatest interest to scientists is one that has the highest possible resolution. This is the complete nucleotide sequence of the human genome, and is why the project is often referred to as 'mapping and sequencing' the human genome. Current methods of sequencing remain laborious, and the complete sequencing of the human genome will almost certainly require major innovations in sequencing technology . . . .

The uniqueness of the Human Genome Project is not its quest for knowledge. The history of science is filled with little else. What is unique is an understanding at the outset that serious policy and ethical issues are raised by the research, and that steps ought to be taken now to try to assure that the benefits of the project are maximized and the potential dark side is minimized.

THE LEGAL AND ETHICAL ISSUES RAISED BY THE HUMAN GENOME PROJECT

To oversimplify somewhat, there are three levels of issues that the Human Genome Project raises: individual/family, society, and species. Almost all of our work on genetics to date has involved the individual/family level, where questions of genetic screening and counseling have center stage. Negligence in failing to offer or to properly perform these tests has resulted in lawsuits for wrongful birth and wrongful life, and standards for genetic screening and counseling have been set by professional organizations.

Issues at the second level implicate society more directly. In the Human Genome Project there are three major societal issues: population-based genetic screening, resource allocation and commercialization, and eugenics. More specifically: To what uses should the fruits of the project be put in screening groups of people, such as applicants for the military, government workers, immigrants, and others? What priority should the genome project have to federal funding, and what role should patenting laws play? Should we attempt to use the new genetics to improve our citizens, either by trying to eliminate specific genetic diseases or by enhancing desirable traits?

Issues at the third level are somewhat more speculative and involve how a genetic view of ourselves could change the way we think about ourselves. This level raises recurrent philosophical questions involving determinism, reductionism, normalcy, and the meaning of health and disease.

This brief cataloging of the major issues raised on each level suggests that there probably are no unique issues raised by the Human Genome Project. On the other hand, this project raises all of the issues in a much more focused manner (certainly a difference in degree if not in kind), and the fact that all of these issues are implicated in the genome project may itself make the project societally unique.

Individual/Family Issues

Genetic screening and counseling are techniques that have been in widespread use in the United States for more than two decades. Stated concisely: 'Genetic counseling is the process whereby an individual or family obtains information about a real or possible genetic problem.' Counseling is usually primarily directed toward couples deciding whether or not to have children based on their risk of having a child with a genetic handicap, counseling pregnant women about the existence of genetic tests to determine the status of the fetus, and counseling parents of newborns about the genetic condition of their child.

Genetic screening bridges level one and level two issues because it is primarily a public health endeavor that actively seeks out asymptomatic people, many of whom would not otherwise seek medical care or discover their condition. It is primarily a 'search in a population for persons possessing certain genotypes that (1) are already associated with disease or predisposed to disease, (2) may lead to disease in their descendants, or (3) may produce other variations not known to be associated with disease.' Individuals in the first category are identified for treatment, the second can receive counseling about their reproductive options, and the third are primarily identified for research purposes to help determine the genetic make-up of populations. Screening may target groups, such as married couples planning to have children, pregnant women, or newborns.

Since we have had a number of large-scale genetic screening and counseling programs (including Tay-Sachs, sickle cell disease, PKU [phenylketonuria], and neural tube defects) it might be supposed that we have solved the major social policy issues raised by such screening. This would be incorrect. Partly this is due to the fact that each genetic disease has unique characteristics, and thus each poses some unique issues. For example, some diseases occur most frequently in specific racial or ethnic groups, raising potential issues of discrimination and stigmatization. Other screening tests, such as those for neural tube defects, can only be done on pregnant women, and abortion is the only 'treatment'. Still others can only be performed on newborns, and screening for conditions, such as PKU, that require immediate treatment to prevent harm, has been made mandatory by almost all states in this context.

Although we have not solved any of the major issues raised by past genetic screening and counseling cases, we have been able to identify the major factors to be considered before initiating a screening program: (1) the frequency and severity of the condition, (2) the availability of treatment of documented efficacy, (3) the extent to which detection by screening improves the outcome, (4) the validity and safety of the screening test, (5) the adequacy of resources to assure effective screening and counseling follow-up, (6) the costs of the program, and (7) the acceptance of the screening program by the community, including both physicians and the public.

This list primarily relates to the scientific validity and a cost/benefit analysis of the testing procedure. In addition, two major legal issues are implicit in all genetic screening programs: autonomy and confidentiality. Autonomy requires that all screening programs be voluntary, and that consent to them is sought only after full information concerning the implications of a positive finding is disclosed and understood. Confidentiality requires that the finding not be disclosed to anyone else without the individual's consent. While not a genetic disease, HIV infection has provided us with an opportunity to see how discrimination against individuals with a particular condition demands that testing be voluntary and that the results be kept confidential to protect the rights of individuals.

Provided that testing remains voluntary, and that the results are only disclosed with the individual's permission, genetic testing based on one's genome raises questions only of degree rather than kind. The degree is that instead of one or even hundreds of conditions that can be screened for, there may be thousands. Perhaps even more important, we may find that certain genes predispose a person to specific illnesses, such as breast cancer or Alzheimer disease. This information may be very troubling to individuals, but it will be of great interest to health insurance companies and employers.

In the employment setting, for example, it has already been suggested that five principles should guide legislators, regulators, and professional groups in setting guidelines for medical screening: (1) medical inquiries of employees should be limited to job-related information; (2) only tests that are safe and of proven efficacy should be used; (3) applicants and employees should be informed of all medical tests in advance, given the results, and told when any employment decision will be based on test results; (4) intracompany and extracompany disclosure of medical records must be controlled and confidentiality assured; (5) comprehensive, consistent, and predictable handicap discrimination legislation should be enacted. These worthy principles should be supplemented with three others directed at employers: (1) ethical issues involving screening should be fully explored *before* a screening program commences; (2) screening should only be done on an individual with the individual's informed consent; and (3) counseling should be available both before and after screening, and the resources for any reasonable intervention that can benefit the individuals screened should be in place and available to him or her before screening is offered.

We have so far managed to develop genetic screening and counseling as tools that we have permitted individuals and families to use or not use as they see fit. This has followed the medical model of the beneficent doctor-patient relationship: a model of mutuality in which decisions are made for the benefit of the patient. This model has served us well to date in expanding the reproductive options of individuals. Level two concerns move us away from concern with the individual to concern with society itself.

Societal Issues

Societal issues involved in the genome cluster in three areas: population-based screening, resource allocation and commercialism, and eugenics. Of these the first overlaps level one concerns (since population screening can be used to identify individuals to help them), and the last is the most unique and troubling. All merit discussion.

Population-based screening has already been discussed in level one. It can be aimed at the attempted elimination of a genetic condition, at simply identifying the incidence of a genetic condition in a population, or at identifying the presence of a genetic condition in an applicant for a particular benefit (such as employment, insurance, and immigration). As previously discussed, autonomy and confidentiality are the major legal issues involved, and this type of screening becomes problematic primarily when it is mandatory and the results are made known to others without consent. The other two areas are more uniquely societal.

The issue of resource allocation itself has its own three aspects. The first is the obvious one: What percentage of the nation's research budget should be devoted to the Human Genome Project? Answering this question requires us to consider how research priorities are set in science and who should set them. With the federal government making a major commitment to this program (currently approximately $100 million annually each to NIH [National Institute of Health] and DOE [Department of Energy]), should Congress appropriate funds directly to the genome project (as it is currently doing) or should the program compete directly with other proposed research projects, and be peer-reviewed?

The second aspect involves making the fruits of the genome project available to all those who want them. This involves at least two questions. The first is the issue of commercialism, and who 'owns' and can patent the products that are produced by the genome project. Should the fact that much of this research is federally funded mean that its fruits should be in the public domain? Or should individual companies and scientists be able to patent or copyright maps and sequences of specific areas of the human genome in order to encourage them to become involved in mapping research? Patent issues have proven the most controversial at the outset of the project, and an international agreement on patenting (or not patenting) genes and gene fragments (cDNA) may be a prerequisite to effective international cooperation. The other issue can be summed up in three words: national health financing. Specifically, should the genetic tests and their follow-up procedures be made part of a 'minimum benefit package' under a national health financing program (or some other scheme for universal access), or should they only be available to those who can pay for them privately? This, of course, is also not a question unique to the genome project, but one that society must confront with every new medical technology.

The third aspect of the resource allocation issue is probably the most intrinsically interesting. It involves determining the balance of resource priorities between how much we should spend on identifying and treating genetic diseases, as opposed to how much we should spend directly on *other* conditions that cause disease, such as poverty, drug and alcohol addiction, lack of housing, poor education, and lack of access to reasonable medical care. In a country like the United States, it is ethical or rational to develop medical technologies that large segments of the population would not have access to today if they were available, or to develop technologies that even if universally available, would only be useful to a few individuals?

What is the social impact of putting the spotlight on an endeavor like the Human Genome Project? Could the fact that we are vigorously pursuing this project lead us to downplay environmental pollution, worksite hazards, and other major social problems that cause disease based on the hope that we will someday find a 'genetic fix' to permit humans to 'cope' with these unhealthy conditions? It has been unpersuasively and bizarrely suggested, for example, that the fruits of the Human Genome Project may help solve society's homelessness problem on the basis that many of the homeless are mentally ill, and their condition may be genetically determined and genetically treatable. Finally, what role does or should international economic competition play in deciding how much federal funding should go to the genome project?

The third societal issue, and the most important one, is the issue of eugenics. This issue is perhaps the most difficult to address because of the highly emotional reaction many individuals have to even mentioning the racist genocide of the Nazis, which was based on a eugenic program founded on a theory of 'racial hygiene.' Although repugnant, the Nazi experience and legacy demands careful study to determine what led to it, why scientists and physicians supported it and collaborated on developing its theory and making possible its execution, and how it was implemented by a totalitarian state. In this regard our own national experience with racism, sterilization, and immigration quotas will have to be reexamined. In so doing, we are likely to rediscover the powerful role of economics in driving our own views of evolution (in the form of social Darwinism) and who should propagate.

The U.S. Supreme Court, for example, wrote in 1927, with clear reference to World War I, that eugenics by involuntary sterilization of the mentally retarded was constitutionally acceptable based on utilitarianism:

> We have seen more than once that the public welfare may call upon the best citizens for their lives. It would be strange if it could not call upon those who already sap the strength of the State for these lesser sacrifices often not felt to be such by those concerned, in order to prevent our being swamped with incompetence. It is better for all the world, if instead of waiting to execute degenerate offspring for crime, or to let them starve for their imbecility, society can prevent those who are manifestly unfit from continuing their kind [*Buck v Bell* (1927) 274 US 200, 207].

That may seem ancient history, but in 1988 the U.S. Congress's Office of Technology Assessment (OTA), in discussing the 'Social and Ethical Considerations' raised by the Human Genome Project, developed a similar theme:

> Human mating that proceeds without the use of genetic data about the risks of transmitting diseases will produce greater mortality and medical costs than if carriers of potentially deleterious genes are alerted to their status and encouraged to mate with noncarriers or to use artificial insemination or other reproductive strategies.

The likely primary reproductive strategy, mentioned only in passing in the report, will be genetic screening of human embryos, already technically feasible, but not nearly to the extent possible once the genome is understood. Such screening need not be governmentally-imposed; people will want it, even insist on it as their right. As OTA notes: 'New technologies for identifying traits and altering genes make it *possible for eugenic goals to be achieved through technological as opposed to social control*' (emphasis added). Huxley's *Brave New World*, rather than George Orwell's *Nineteen Eighty-Four*, seems to be in our future.

Much excellent work is under way on the history of medicine and its linkage to the eugenics movement. This scholarship should be made an integral part of any effort to understand the eugenics movement in the 20th century. It will also be necessary to decide whether or not to use genetics to *improve* the species, and to articulate the philosophical and moral concerns that a change in the direction of genetics from prevention and treatment to enhancement and improvement would entail.

So far most writers have insisted that it is at least premature to follow the example of Moreau and try to improve upon the species, either by enhancing certain genetic characteristics, such as height, or by altering sex cells so that characteristics modified in an individual can be passed on to future generations. Just as population-based screening provided a bridge between levels one and two, enhancing genetic traits provides a bridge between levels two and three.

Species Issues

Species issues relate to the fact that powerful new technologies do not just change what human beings can do, they change the way we think, especially about ourselves. In this respect, maps may become particularly powerful thought transformers. Maps model reality to help us understand it. Columbus changed the shape of the world's map forever – from a flat chart to a spherical globe. Monsters could no longer either prowl or guard the edge of the world because there was no edge of the world. . . .

What new human perspectives, or what new perspectives on humans, will a sequential map of the 3 billion base pairs of the human genome bring? The most obvious is that breaking 'human beings' down into 6 billion 'parts' is the ultimate in reductionism. James

Watson [a co-discover of DNA] himself has used such reductionist language in promoting the Human Genome Project. In his words, the project will provide 'the ultimate tool for understanding at the molecular level.' Just what this means is unclear, but Watson continues: 'How can we not do it? We used to think our fate is in our stars. Now we know, in large measure, our fate is in our genes.' Seeing our fate in our genes, of course, resonates with level two concerns: if genes determine our fate, then we can alter our fate by altering our genes. Maybe we really will come to believe the unlikely prospect that we can look forward to the day that mental illness, and therefore at least some homelessness, can be prevented by a genetic manipulation. Such a view suggests most of the species concerns.

The first is the consequence of viewing humans as an assemblage of molecules, arranged in a certain way. The almost inevitable tendency in such a view is that expressed in *Brave New World*. People could view themselves and each other as products that can be manufactured, and thus subject to quality control measures. People could be 'made to measure,' both literally and figuratively. If people are so seen, we might not only try to manipulate them as embryos and fetuses, but we might also see the resulting children as products themselves. This raises the current stakes in the debates about frozen embryos and surrogate mothers to a new height: if children are seen as products, the purchase and sale of the resulting children themselves, not only embryos, may be seen as reasonable.

The second concern is that, to the extent that genes are seen as more important than environment, our actions may be viewed as genetically determined, rather than as a result of free will. We have already witnessed an early example with this type of reasoning in the use of the 'XYY defense.' Those possessing the 47, XYY karyotype were thought to be more prone to commit crime. Individuals accused of crime who also had an extra Y chromosome consequently argued that their genetic composition predisposed them to crime and therefore they should not be held criminally responsible for their actions. This defense was generally rejected, and in the few cases where it was accepted, the defendant was confined to a mental institution until 'cured.' Of course, since it is impossible to remove the extra Y chromosome from any cell, let alone every cell, in one's body, a cure is not possible.

In addition to use by the criminal law, perhaps in the form of genetic screening followed by monitoring or 'predelinquency detention,' such genetic predispositions are likely to be used in education, and perhaps job placement and military assignments. For example, if intelligence in mathematics is found to be genetic, should schools use this information to track, grade, and promote the genetically gifted in math classes?

Finally, we know that most diseases and abnormalities are social constructs, not facts of nature. Myopia, for example, is well accepted, whereas obesity is not. We won't discover a 'normal' or 'standard' human genome, but we may invent one. If we do, what variation will society view as permissible before an individual's genome is labeled substandard or abnormal? And what impact will such a construct of genetic normalcy have on society and on substandard individuals? For example, what variation in a fetus should prompt a couple to opt for abortion, or a genetic counselor to suggest abortion? What variation should prompt a counselor to suggest sterilization? What interventions will society deem acceptable in an individual's life based on his or her genetic composition? Should health care insurance companies, for example, be able to disclaim financial responsibility for the medical needs of a child whose parents knew prior to conception or birth that the child would be born with a seriously abnormal genome? Should employers be able to screen out workers on the basis of their genomes? These and many other similar issues exist today based on screening for single genes. But the magnitude of the screening possibilities that may result from analysis of the map of the human genome will raise these issues to new heights and will almost inevitably change the way we think about ourselves and what it means to be human.

As regards the specific legal problems, we can begin, for example, by noticing access to and control over genetic information. How would this information become available?

The Danish Council of Ethics in its 1993 Report, *Ethics and Mapping of the Human Genome*, explains the nature of genetic screening and the kinds of genetic information which can (or will in the future) be obtained.

Ethics and Mapping of the Human Genome (1993)

The genome, i.e. the combination of genes acquired from one's biological parents, is of key importance to a person's development. Genomic changes, in the form of modifications of specific genes or of the chromosomal make-up, may be pathogenic per se or in combination with certain environmental factors. Such diseases, in which the composition of the genome is of decisive importance to the development of disease, are termed *genetic diseases*. Genetic screening targets this category of disease. . . .

What is genetic screening?

Genetic screening in the widest sense is understood to mean a study of the occurrence of persons with a specific gene or chromosome composition in a population or population group. In terms of disease and health, on which the present report focuses, such an investigation may have the following aims:

- to trace persons with a gene or chromosome composition which may result in, or predispose the persons concerned, to develop a disease;
- to trace persons with a gene or chromosome composition which may result in, or predispose the descendants of the persons concerned, to develop a disease;
- to illuminate the frequency of a given genetic disease, a specific disposition, a specific chromosomal rearrangement or possibly a specific combination of genes in the population.

Examples of screening for genetic disease

The Danish national health service offers routine fetal screening for chromosomal disorders to expectant women over the age of 35 and others, as well as screening of neonates for the metabolic dysfunctions Folling's disease (also called PKU, phenylketonuria) and hypothyroidism (impaired function of the thyroid gland).

In practice, these forms of screening do not differ materially from screening for non-genetic diseases. The rationale behind them is that, by screening, the relevant disease or disposition to disease can be detected sufficiently early on to allow for action to be taken, in the form of either abortion (fetal screening) or dietetic or medical treatment (neonatal screening), enabling parents to avoid giving birth to children who have or will develop the diseases concerned.

The hereditary aspect. The concept of genetic carrier

One of the peculiar aspects of genetic screening is that the things being screened for – gene and chromosome changes – can be passed down from one generation to the next. As a corollary to this, the detection of such a change means immediately having to regard the parents and any siblings or children of the person concerned (so-called first-degree relatives) as belonging to a high-risk group, concerning the same modification. Therefore, genetic screening can very easily affect relatives of the people in question, genes being shared with relatives.

The import of this is reinforced by the fact that genetic or chromosomal changes can be carried without the individual showing any sign of disease, but with a risk of the disease in one's progeny and possibly oneself later on in life.

Many disease genes do not manifest if they occur together with a correspondingly normal gene (recessively inherited disease) or do manifest despite occurring with a correspondingly normal gene (dominantly transmitted disease), though in this case maybe not until adulthood and after the person concerned has brought children into the world, with the resultant risk of the progeny developing the disease.

By the same token, chromosomal aberrations can occur in a so-called balanced form, which is to say that the cellular genome functions normally, even if – as detectable by microscopy – it is distributed abnormally between the chromosomes. This may lead to chromosomal disorders in children, as the change can be passed on in unbalanced form, the parent in question being capable of transmitting either too much or too little genetic material, owing to the chromosomal arrangement.

A fit person carrying a pathological (disease) gene or a balanced chromosomal mutation is labelled a (genetic) carrier.

Carrier screening

Genetic carrier screening is generally understood to mean screening for carriers of a recessive disease gene. However, screening for healthy carriers of dominant disease genes as well as for carriers of balanced chromosomal mutations will also fall under this category.

The purpose of carrier screening is to find those persons (at-risk individuals) or couples (at-risk couples) who by virtue of being healthy carriers have an undetected risk of giving birth to children destined or predisposed to develop a genetic disease. These at-risk individuals/couples can then be offered genetic counselling, including fetal diagnosis in the event of pregnancy.

When screening for carriers of dominant disease genes which do not manifest until an advanced stage, the result will also be of direct significance to the future health prospect of the relevant person, sometimes allowing the option of exerting an active influence on this factor.

Carrier screening is currently practised in certain population groups in which a particular severe hereditary disease is frequent enough to motivate screening action. Examples of this are carrier screening for the serious Tay-Sachs disease among American Ashkenazi Jews and for the haemoglobin disease B-thalassaemia in the Mediterranean region.

In Denmark, pilot projects have been carried out with carrier screening of neonates for familial hypercholesterolaemia and of pregnant women for cystic fibrosis.

Time of screening

Unlike 'general' screening, genetic screening – and this is another special feature – can by definition be undertaken at any time whatsoever; in principle, from the initial stages of division of the fertilized ovum onwards. The gene and chromosome composition generally remains unchanged from conception to death.

The optimal point for screening depends partly on purpose and partly on technical facilities. For example, the development of more and more sensitive analytical methods may allow fetal screening to be carried out by analysing fetal cells in the blood of the pregnant woman, or by replacing fetal screening with screening of early embryos, i.e. at the very early stage when the fertilized egg has divided only a few times. This is rendered even more topical by the continuing spread of test-tube fertilization (more correctly: IVF or in vitro fertilization). . . .

Future prospects

Given the large-scale research programmes being conducted in the USA, Japan and Europe, the detailed mapping of the human genome can be expected to have been completed within about 15 years. As the individual genes are mapped, this also increases the possibilities of detecting disposition to disease, i.e. making diagnoses and pinpointing genetic carriers, including the detection of disposition to diseases which may not develop until a much later juncture and possibly only if the person concerned is exposed to certain environmental determinants.

To this can be added methodological advances which will enable a vast array of different genetic examinations to be conducted at relatively little expense on minute volumes of specimen, i.e. very early on in a person's development and on pre-existing biological material such as deposited blood and tissue samples.

The existence of biomaterial collections at hospitals and other institutions, combined with the above-mentioned developments in methodologies and the sharp increase anticipated in analytical capabilities for genetically determined *predisposition to disease* and *normal attributes*, raises special questions in connection with genetic screening and the treatment of data thus obtained.

Perhaps, not unnaturally, a patient may well wish to know about his own genetic makeup. It may affect decisions about marriage, children, employment. It may go further and indicate the likely course his life could run, with a crippling disease and, death (for example, in the case of Huntington's disease) the prospect to be faced. The claim to know about oneself once information exists, ie to have access to it, comes up against the desire (perhaps need) of others, especially doctors, to protect us from information which may have devastating effects. We shall see how this clash between competing claims over access to information is currently dealt with by the law in Chapter 8. The principles found there are those which must steer us through the new uncharted waters of genetic information.

Patients may not only want access to information about themselves, they may also wish to prevent their doctors from disclosing it to others. This is the familiar territory of the law of confidentiality. Developments in genetics give the traditional arguments a new impetus. Spouses or children may wish (again, some would say need) to know a patient's genetic makeup despite the prohibition of the patient. We discuss the general issue of whether a doctor may (or, perhaps must) disclose confidential information to another in Chapter 9.

The dilemma the doctor faces here is both familiar and startlingly novel. It is familiar in that the question of when, if ever, a doctor may tell others about the patient's condition has been with us since Hippocrates. The greater the commitment to keeping a patient's confidences, the more the interests of others may be placed in jeopardy. On the other hand, the more the law requires a doctor to tell others information which he has acquired in confidence, the greater the threat to the trust a patient may place in his doctor, and trust is at the heart of everything.

The availability of genetic testing may also result in a demand for such tests to be used. Patients may well demand to know whether a child that may be conceived, or which is already *in utero*, will suffer from a particular genetic disability. Failure to detect the genetic abnormality will increasingly expose doctors to claims by parents and disabled children for negligent genetic screening or counselling. We discuss in Chapter 13 how these claims for 'wrongful birth' and 'wrongful life' have developed in English law. Their importance can only increase.

Equally, as the detection of genetic abnormalities becomes more sophisticated, pre-natal diagnosis will enable decisions about termination of pregnancy on the grounds of fetal disability to be made more accurately and for a wider range of conditions. We discuss in Chapter 12 the law of abortion. No doubt the degree of disability which justifies a termination will be tested as less severe disabilities become detectable through genetic testing.

Of course, beyond these issues there are great dangers in these advances if we do not remain vigilant. Discrimination on genetic grounds is a danger that should not be ignored. In a study paper written by Professor Bartha Knoppers, the Canadian Law Reform Commission draws attention to the dangers in the areas of employment, insurance and reproductive choices (the latter we have already mentioned).

Canadian Law Reform Commission *Human Dignity and Genetic Heritage* (Study Paper), 1991

Discrimination as to genotype can be seen as either a means of informing one's personal decisions, or as a means of imposing the decisions of others. We will look at three areas in which genetic disposition may be used to discriminate against the individual: testing in the workplace, testing for access to insurance and testing for reproduction.

A. Workplace Testing

The purposes of genetic screening in the workplace include the determination of the cause of an illness (for example, to what degree it is genetic or environmental in origin), and the prevention of illness by the detection of genetic susceptibility. This could be of benefit to both the employee and the employer. Since genetic information demonstrates individuality, it can provide the employee or the potential employee with information to make occupational, environmental or life-style choices that are in his or her own interests. Such information also provides the employer who has access to it with the power to control or exclude the person tested. At the same time, it gives the employer a greater responsibility for employee health and safety, based on that information.

Genetic screening may be lawful if directly related to qualifications for doing a task or if necessary for employee safety. It could be argued, however, that refusal or termination of employment should only be permitted on the basis of the employee's current capabilities and not on predicted future incapacities.

Furthermore, while the employee should have a right to any information obtained about himself or herself, workplace testing poses a special problem with regard to medical confidentiality. The employer is privy to information that is usually confined to the physician-patient relationship. The potential for breaches of confidentiality may be of special concern where personnel data are computerized.

In 1982, the United States Office of Technology Assessment conducted a nationwide survey on genetic testing in the workplace. Its report revealed that such testing, used by many employers, may be scientifically unfounded. This was the case, for example, with sickle cell testing. Sickle cell anaemia is a life-threatening autosomal recessive disorder with a high frequency among blacks. Those who carry only one of the two mutant alleles are said to have the sickle cell trait. Even though there was, and is, no evidence that having the trait affects work performance, blacks were often screened for it and were excluded from some occupations on that basis.

It could be asked whether protection against discrimination on the basis of mental or physical disability as provided by the *Charter* [*of Rights and Freedoms*], or by provincial human rights codes, would be broad enough to include genetic discrimination.

While awaiting the diffusion of genetic education at all levels of society, the balance to be struck between workplace safety, individual rights and employer or public health care costs is a delicate one. In the absence of widespread genetic education, we may need a specific legal prohibition on genetic discrimination.

B. Insurance Testing

The issue of genetic testing as a prerequisite for insurance raises similar concerns. The Canadian health care system, with its universal coverage of the costs of illness, gives greater protection to Canadians than does the American system to their counterparts. Nonetheless, private disability insurance, life insurance policies and employer-sponsored programs share similar problems with the United States of rating persons 'at risk.' Parallels could be made with current insurance practices of HIV seropositivity where high-risk individuals pay a higher rate or may be denied coverage altogether. Unlike the situation in employment testing, testing for insurance usually does not directly benefit insurance applicants; moreover, knowledge derived from such testing could be just as easily acquired through one's personal physician without the above consequences.

For personal policies, the insurance company must be privy to sensitive health information concerning an individual. Best test reliability and validity, as well as the unjustifiable discriminatory exclusion of those persons with a high risk of disease, are factors to be considered in the development of future legislative policies. The very nature of private insurance legitimates discrimination. However, a basic disability or life insurance for all applicants with 'no questions asked' could provide minimum coverage to everyone and avoid problems of discrimination. Additional coverage could be dependent on an agreement by the applicant to be tested for genetic disorders.

C. Reproductive Testing

Certain legal and canonic rules have always imposed restrictions on consanguineous marriages (that is, between genetically related individuals). Nevertheless, genetic screening is not a legal requirement for marriage. Unlike blood testing for rhesus compatibility, which is generally mentioned to prospective couples by their physician, other genetic testing is not. However, as family linkage studies develop and expand, and as individuals become genetically informed and sensitized, voluntary recourse to genetic testing before marriage or reproduction will be more frequent. Yet, even for certain populations at identifiably high risk, the state should have to justify mandatory screening that interferes with such a personal decision as marriage or procreation.

In Chapter Three, we discussed a proposal by the Parliamentary Assembly of the Council of Europe to legislate a right to an unaltered genetic heritage. A genome could be considered 'altered' if it would result in one of a list of serious illnesses. It was suggested that the right of an individual with such an 'altered' genome to have children might be tied to the individual's agreeing to undergo engineering. Available and accessible genetic testing would be more effective and less intrusive routes of health policy, by allowing carriers to make their own choices with respect to such risks, that is, whether to marry, have children and use prenatal testing where available.

In the field of reproductive technologies, physicians are advised to offer donor gametes or embryos to couples at genetic risk or to follow up those persons (or their progeny) found to be at genetic risk. Furthermore, the risk of transmitting serious genetic disease is generally accepted as one of the criteria for the use of reproductive technology. Will the availability of the technology and the choices for the selection of 'healthy' gametes or embryos bring us one step closer to striving for genetic perfectionism?

The scholarly literature on the impact of the HGI is immense. The following articles, written from an American perspective, identify the underlying social, moral and legal issues in *three* principal areas which are relevant to all societies: A Lippman 'Parental Genetic Testing and Screening: Constructing Needs and Reinforcing Inequities' (1991) 17 American Journal of Law and Medicine 15 (screening); L Andrews and A Jaeger 'Confidentiality of Genetic Information in the Workplace' (1991) 17 American Journal of Law and Medicine 75 (employment); L Gostin 'Genetic Discrimination: The Use of Genetically Based Diagnostic and Prognostic Tests by Employers and Insurers' (1991) 17 American Journal of Law and Medicine 109 (insurance).

When we turn to *gene therapy* we meet a further set of issues for medical law. The background to gene therapy and the distinction between somatic cell therapy and germ line therapy is discussed in the Report of a Government Committee chaired by Sir Cecil Clothier QC.

Report of the Committee on the Ethics of Gene Therapy (Cm 1788) 1992 paras 2.14-2.27

2.14. The prospect of gene therapy is obviously attractive if it can make good the genetic defects responsible, and thereby cure or alleviate disorders in which the outcomes are so dismal. Moreover, the effective introduction of gene therapy into medical practice would also serve to augment and enhance the choices that may face parents who are at high risk of transmitting a serious disorder to their children.

2.15. Gene therapy has wider possibilities for medical practice than the correction of single gene disorders. For example, it is being investigated as a possible new approach to the management of a wide spectrum of diseases, ranging from infections such as AIDS to cancer, and it is being studied as a means of strengthening the body's immune response to viral infections. Various approaches are being used which require the insertion of genes into particular cell populations in an attempt to counter some of the basic changes in cells which lead to them becoming cancerous. Gene therapy is also being explored for the management of chronic diseases such as diabetes. The requirements for demonstration of the effectiveness of this approach in animal systems, and the clear demonstration of its safety, will follow the same principles as those set out for the use of gene therapy to correct single gene disorders.

Normal human characteristics

2.16. Normal variations in human characteristics such as personality, intelligence and physique may also be explained by the inheritance of multiple genes and their interaction, together with environmental influences. We are alert to the profound ethical issues that would arise were the aim of gene modification ever to be directed to the enhancement of normal human rights.

Gene therapy

2.17. Some genes have been isolated, together with the associated DNA sequences which are required to regulate their working in the cell. They have been replicated and their structures and functions studied. Such isolated genes have been inserted into living cells cultivated in the laboratory, which then produce the protein for which the inserted gene carries the code (ie the gene is *expressed*). Isolated genes have also been inserted experimentally into animals and shown to work. This has been applied for practical purposes; for example, human genes have been used in sheep to achieve production of the protein needed to treat haemophilia. It is now possible to insert appropriate human genes into selected cells of patients with specific genetic disorders. These developments have opened the way to gene therapy.

Scientific requirements for gene therapy

2.18. If gene therapy of a particular disorder is to be achieved a number of requirements must be met:
(a)   The gene must have been isolated and be available for therapeutic use.
(b)   Something must be known of the function of the gene, so that treatment can be sensibly designed.
(c)   It must be known which tissues and cell types need to express the gene and when, during development, its expression is required.
(d)   The genetic sequences that control the function of the gene, for example by switching it on and off, must be known and have been isolated. If gene therapy is to work it is clearly important that the product of the gene is made in the right cells, in the right amounts and at the right time. Too much or too little of the gene product, or its production in the wrong cells, or at the wrong time during development, could be harmful.
(e)   There must be means available for getting the gene, and its controlling elements, into the right cells and under the right control. Conversely, the gene must be prevented from getting into the wrong cells, or to the wrong place within a cell, or from spreading to other tissues, or even to other individuals, any of which might cause harm.
(f)   Means must be available for monitoring the efficacy and safety of the treatment, for a long time.
These requirements are discussed in more detail in the following paragraphs.

2.19. As we said, genes contain the recipes that cells use to make particular proteins. It is obviously important that the genetic recipe should be correct, so that the right protein is made; and just as important that the gene should be expressed at the right time. There are elaborate genetic signals, not yet well understood, which regulate whether particular genes are switched on or off at particular times of development and in particular cells or tissues. This 'gene control' must be satisfactorily preserved if a transplanted gene is to work effectively.

2.20. For a transferred gene to do any good it must clearly be targeted into the cells which need it. If a particular gene is essential for the proper function of the liver there is little point in placing it into the hair root cells. It is necessary, therefore, to know in which tissues the gene is required and how to ensure that it gets there.

2.21. Gene therapy could be attempted by seeking to correct part of an abnormal gene to make it functional again; or by removing the abnormal gene and replacing it with a normal one; or by simply inserting a normal gene, so that the necessary gene product is made, while leaving the abnormal gene in place within the cells. At this very early stage of gene therapy research, the last of these approaches, although the least elegant, is likely to be the most practicable, because the technical means for inserting genes into cells are already at hand whereas the means for removing existing genes from cells are much less advanced.

2.22. The inserted gene must be integrated somewhere within the cells being treated, in such a way that it becomes part of the genetic constitution of those cells and is transmitted to the cellular progeny each time the cells divide. Ideally it should be inserted precisely in place of the abnormal gene, and be subject to the same cellular environment and cellular controls as in the natural state. In practice this may be very difficult to achieve, current methods merely allowing the gene to be inserted at any random site within the genetic material of the cell. The majority of genes apparently function satisfactorily following insertion in this way. There is, however, the danger that such random insertion may lead to inappropriate control of the gene – of where, when and how much of the gene product is expressed. It is also possible that the random insertion may actually disrupt some other genetic function, with unwanted consequences.

2.23. Even within a single tissue there are many different types of cell. For example, in blood are red blood cells and many different kinds of white blood cell. Normally these cells undergo constant replacement and renewal. This biological maintenance programme depends upon the presence of a very small number of *stem cells* whose function it is to generate new cells. If genes are placed in cells other than stem cells their effect will last only for as long as those treated cells survive. As they are replaced the effect of gene therapy will be lost. To avoid this it is necessary to target gene therapy at the stem cells, so that the new cells being formed have the correcting gene in place. This is made difficult because stem cells are few and in many tissues they cannot be easily identified.

Somatic cell gene therapy

2.24. Making good a defective gene in the body cells where it is needed is known as somatic cell gene therapy. The aim is to provide the right genetic information, under proper control, in precisely those cells which need it for their normal function. Ideally, the effect should be permanent so that no further therapy is required. It should also be permanent in the sense that the inserted gene is securely lodged. If successful, therapy would make good the genetic defect in the treated cells and tissues of the individual, although the abnormal gene would still be present in other tissues. This is unlikely to matter provided the abnormal gene product has no effect, or, if it is actually harmful, is not used. However, the germ cells, which give rise to sperm or ova, would retain the defective form of the gene, with the possibility of its transmission to future generations.

Methods of gene therapy

2.25. Our interest in the methods available for inserting genes into living cells turns on their safety and effectiveness. Genes can be inserted into cells directly by physical techniques or by using a biological vehicle for delivery. At present, delivery employing suitably modified viruses seems most promising. Viruses are fashioned by nature to enter cells and to insert their own genetic material. Some viruses can be modified to carry genetic material different from their own, and insert it into host cells, and thus provide a technique for gene modification therapy. So far it has been possible only to supplement a defective gene, not to replace it; neither is it yet possible to lodge a gene precisely where it would naturally be. Nonetheless, this approach may well be effective in selective disorders. In time it may be feasible to harness the natural process of *recombination* which allows formation of new combinations of genes.

Germ line gene therapy

2.26. In order to remove the threat to future generations of a defective gene it would be necessary to correct the defect in the germ cells, which give rise to ova and sperm. This is known as germ line gene therapy. Because little is known about the possible consequences and hazards, and any harm to future generations would take a long time to discover and deal with, this application of gene therapy needs to be considered quite separately from somatic cell gene therapy.

Possible dangers of gene therapy

2.27. Among the possible dangers of gene therapy are, therefore, that:
(a) It might not work, in which case the patient will have undergone the procedure without benefit.
(b) The correcting gene might be inserted into the wrong cell type, or be expressed inappropriately, either in the wrong amount or at the wrong time during development. The therapy might then do more harm than good.
(c) The gene might be inserted in such a way as to cause a new mutation, by disrupting some other gene or its means of control. This might initiate a new genetic disease, or perhaps an uncontrolled multiplication of cells which could lead to cancer.

(d) If the means of inserting the gene were faulty, it is conceivable although in the present state of knowledge improbable, that the gene, or parts of it, might emerge from the cells and be "infective", moving to other somatic cells or germ line cells, or even to other individuals. This might cause harm to the treated patient and to others.

These factors which bear on the effectiveness and safety of gene therapy must all be taken carefully into account when proposals for gene therapy are considered.

The techniques of gene therapy are undoubtedly new. New therapeutic procedures need to be rigorously tested in order to ensure that they are beneficial and safe. Research on human subjects raises its own concerns about the rights of patients and others who are being used as 'guinea pigs'. We discuss these in Chapter 14. The Clothier Committee considered whether gene therapy was research, (*op cit*) paras 3.9-3.10:

3.9. The initial use of gene therapy will clearly be a digression of this sort from ordinary medical practice. Indeed, the establishment of this Committee acknowledged concerns that gene therapy is perceived as different, both in its nature and possible consequences, from treatments used hitherto in medical practice, including those already applied to the treatment of genetic disorders. The prospect has raised the question whether gene therapy should be subject to more than the usual constraints which direct ordinary medical practice and innovation, or even those which at present govern medical research.

3.10. Our discussions and enquiries confirmed our tentative view that, notwithstanding the primary intention to benefit an individual patient, gene therapy should initially be regarded as research involving human subjects, and governed by requirements at least as exacting as those which at present applied to that kind of research. Accordingly, any proposal to conduct gene therapy should be subject to approval following authoritative ethical review, which includes critical scrutiny of its medical and scientific merit, the legal implications, and wider public concerns. It should also be subject to conditions laid down for the conduct and oversight of therapy and evaluation and reporting of the outcome. In what follows we consider the detailed basis of this view and the means by which it may be given force. This position is in keeping with the general view that any marked change in medical practice should be subject to the discipline of scientific, medical and ethical appraisal before its introduction.

As we have seen, the Clothier Report identified a number of dangers inherent in gene therapy. The committee considered whether gene therapy of either kind should be permitted and, if so, how it should be regulated. The committee recommended that germ line therapy should be banned. By contrast, the committee recommended a regulatory framework for permitting somatic cell therapy. Many of the recurring themes of medical law were considered by the committee in their deliberations, (*op cit*) paras 4.1-6.4:

Purpose of somatic cell gene therapy

4.1. The purpose of somatic cell gene therapy in an individual patient is to alleviate disease in that individual, and that individual alone. There would be no intention to modify the gene in the germ line. We consider that the development of safe and effective means of gene modification for this purpose is a proper goal for medical science, and we **recommend** that the necessary research should continue.

Initial application of somatic cell gene therapy

4.2. A new treatment yet unproven in human subjects should only be contemplated when the potential benefits outweigh possible harm, including inadvertent harm, to the patient, and to others, and any discomfort and distress that might accompany treatment. It is evident that this position is now being reached in respect of gene therapy for a number of serious genetic disorders. Somatic cell gene therapy may hold great potential benefit for some patients, but it may also carry risks which are more than minimal. Therefore, to ensure that the benefits are assessed and the risks are identified as expeditiously as possible, we **recommend** that somatic cell gene therapy should, for the present, be conducted according to the discipline of research.

4.3. The first candidates for gene therapy should be patients who are suffering from a disorder which is life-threatening, or causes serious handicap, and for which treatment is unavailable or unsatisfactory; but which has not already progressed so far as to reduce significantly the potential for benefit. Therapy should hold promise of bringing about a remission in the advance of the disorder whilst sparing the patient any unduly adverse consequences of treatment. To achieve most benefit, by preventing suffering, impaired development and irreversible damage, gene therapy should be considered at the earliest possible stage in the course of the disorder. A patient who had already suffered irreversible tissue and organ damage would be subject at best to only partial relief by gene therapy. Among those disorders to which gene therapy might be applicable are some which lead to irreversible and cumulative effects from early childhood, and even before birth. In such instances therapy must be given correspondingly early in life.

4.4. The basic structures and organs of the body are formed during the first few weeks after fertilisation. If, because of a genetic defect (or, indeed, any other adverse influence), this early development has been impaired it is unlikely that any resulting structural fault could be corrected except by surgery. This state of affairs naturally leads to the consideration of interventions that might be possible in the very earliest stages of life, soon after fertilisation. There are many technical problems to be overcome, and there would need to be clear safeguards for the mother; but we see no objection in principle to such a procedure provided it takes place after differentiation of the germ line cells, which has occurred by five weeks after fertilisation.

Somatic cell gene therapy research

4.5. The normal rules which govern research in human subjects and the requirements for prior ethical approval of research and its subsequent oversight, which have been considered . . . should apply to somatic cell gene therapy. When a patient who is the subject of such research stands to benefit directly from participation it is properly described as therapeutic research.

4.6. A decision on whether gene therapy research should proceed must depend on the careful prior assessment of the balance of potential benefits and risks for the individual patient. This assessment must draw on knowledge of the genetic basis of the disorder, its pathological effects and clinical course. It will call for evidence of adequate experience of gene modification in experimental systems using isolated cells and laboratory animals, and must incorporate a judgment on the possible consequences of the proposed treatment. The risks to the patient will largely depend on the safety of procedures for introducing genes into cells therapeutically, and the effects, both immediately and in the long term. Safety must be a foremost consideration when proposals to conduct gene therapy are made. Intrusions on privacy, too, are an inevitable accompaniment of such pioneering procedures and the long term follow-up that is necessary.

4.7. In their joint statement the European Medical Research Councils brought out clearly the technical complexity of the procedures used in gene modification. Undesirable consequences (to which we have drawn attention . . .) might include genetic modification of the germ line, and its effects in progeny; modification of somatic cells other than those which have been targeted; interference with the normal working of modified cells; cancerous changes in cells of the population modified; and changes induced by the insertion process.

4.8. The crucial first step in ethical review is a careful assessment of the scientific merits of the proposal, the competence of those wishing to carry out gene therapy, and the potential benefits and risks in each particular instance for which a proposal is made. This assessment should include a critical examination of the arrangements to be made for the conduct of therapy and subsequent monitoring. It will necessarily call upon an uncommon degree and range of scientific and medical expertise, encompassing a deep knowledge of molecular biology, of experimental work in gene manipulation, and close familiarity with the molecular basis and clinical features of the disorder under consideration. No existing body is constituted for these tasks. Accordingly we **recommend** that a supervisory body with the necessary collective expertise, experience and authority be set up, having the responsibility for making such assessments in conjunction with ethical review. We also **recommend** that any proposal for gene therapy must be approved by this body as well as by a properly constituted local research ethics committee (LREC).

4.9. There is a duty to identify and assess promptly any adverse consequence of gene therapy for the patient, both in the aftermath of treatment and in the long term. This duty does not end with the death of the patient. To verify that therapy has not inadvertently affected offspring and successive generations monitoring should extend at least into the next generation. Indeed, insofar as it is possible, monitoring should continue over several generations. Therefore, those conducting such research have a duty not only to maintain adequate records but also to ensure that an effective monitoring system is in place. It will require that a register be set up, and carefully maintained, with safeguards to protect confidentiality. We **recommend** that the necessary arrangements are made before the therapy begins. A complementary duty is to obtain the reliable commitment of patients, and their families, to participate in extended follow-up. During the process of informing and counselling, and obtaining consent, the patient should learn of the need for such follow-up and understand the reasons for it. The patient should also be made aware that although follow-up might be intrusive and burdensome the doctors accept a duty to minimise these effects.

4.10. Accordingly, the conditions which must be satisfied when gene therapy research is proposed are that:
(a) There must be sufficient scientific and medical knowledge, together with knowledge of those proposing to undertake the research, to make sound judgments on:
    (i)   the scientific merit of the research;
    (ii) its probable efficacy and safety;
    (iii) the competence of those who wish to undertake the research; and
    (iv) the requirements for effective monitoring.
(b) The clinical course of the disorder must be known sufficiently well for the investigators and those entrusted with counselling to:
    (i)   give accurate information and advice; and
    (ii) assess the outcomes of therapy.

Consent to research

4.11. A prior ethical requirement of research involving patients is the consent of the individual subject. Consent implies that sufficient information has been given, in a form that is understood, to enable that individual to make a voluntary decision to participate or not. Because gene therapy has novel, complex and possibly far-reaching aspects we are concerned to ensure that the patient is enabled to take these fully into account when giving consent. It is important that serious attention be given not only to the content of the information given to the patient but also to the way in which it is conveyed. Above all, care must be taken to ensure that the patient has understood the risks, benefits and obligations, and has the fullest possible information. Independent advice, not aimed at obtaining consent, should ideally be provided by someone unconnected with the research or therapeutic team and well versed in the implications of gene therapy.

4.12. We foresee the possibility that a competent adult, in whom the disorder had progressed to a stage at which there was little prospect of direct benefit from therapy, might nevertheless consent to participate in non-therapeutic research – for the collective human benefit that the research should be designed to yield. For such research to be ethical it must be to assess the consequences of the procedure, by measurement or detection of changes within the body, or their absence, even if there were to be no discernible clinical benefit. We conclude that participation by a competent adult in such research is acceptable.

4.13. Children with genetic diseases are likely to be among the first candidates for gene therapy. The special problems to be faced when children are the subjects of research have been examined in existing guidelines. The foremost consideration must be the best interests of the child, and in this respect somatic cell gene therapy raises no new ethical issue.

Confidentiality of genetic information

4.14. Clear principles govern the confidentiality of personal health information obtained within the National Health Service (NHS), the use of such information, and the circumstances in which it might be disclosed. They are set out in guidance *'Confidentiality, Use and Disclosure of NHS Information'* which is to be issued shortly. The guidance takes account of the ethical obligations of health professionals towards protecting the confidentiality of personal health information.

4.15. The duty of confidentiality is by no means absolute; it is balanced by a duty of disclosure. The tension is heightened when the special qualities of genes and genetic events give rise to different, and possibly conflicting, interests of kindred, including those yet unborn, who share, or might share, the same genes. For example, an individual might be the source of genetic information which is important to relatives. It might be important to their health care, decisions on parenthood, or like plans which might be influenced by known health risks. Conversely, information which is important to a particular individual might only be obtainable from relatives. These factors have a bearing on the confidentiality of such information and the circumstances in which it might be disclosed. Similar considerations also lead to the question of just what genetic information should be sought from any individual. These issues are already familiar to clinical geneticists, who are guided in their practice by evolving codes on the circumstances in which the boundaries of confidentiality may be extended beyond the individual to include kindred. Therefore, when consent to treatment is sought, which in the case of a child will be from the parents or guardians or other persons who may legally be in a position to give consent on behalf of the child, the possible need for subsequent disclosure of personal health information should be discussed.

4.16. In the case of a child, the parents or others giving consent should first be told that the duty of confidentiality is to the child and, whatever their wishes, that it is in the child's best interests, at the proper time, to know its own clinical history. There might also be a duty, as stated above, to disclose the information to others, including those of subsequent generations.

Gene therapy and the essence of humanity

4.17. The total complement of genes which are found in the human population, the human *gene pool*, is the source of human genetic variability. From it is drawn the parental contribution to the unique endowment of genes possessed by each individual human being, or by identical twins. The interaction of these genes and external influences throughout life confers the quality of humanness, a quality that in each individual is characterised, in part, by variants which determine human differences, and contributes to the collective quality we call humanity.

4.18. This is the background against which we have considered the origin of material that might be used in gene therapy. So far as we can see the genes used in therapy will come from a human source. Should it ever become clinically necessary to use genes which have been derived from any species other than man we believe that such use would in no way impair the humanness of an individual who received the gene. The change conferred would be no different in kind from that resulting from any medical intervention which introduced tissue from other individuals; for example, an organ transplantation, or blood transfusion; or, indeed, from another species, as in the case of pig's [sic] heart valves, which are commonly used to replace defective valves in the human heart.

Preclinical experimental procedures

4.19. We are sensitive to issues raised by the use of laboratory animals in genetic experiments that precede therapy in patients. These issues are common to all experimentation in animals. They concern the welfare of such animals, which is a responsibility of the Home Office. However, the types of procedures used in preclinical genetic studies raise no new problem either in substance or scale.

4.20. The safety of procedures for gene manipulation is a responsibility of the Advisory Committee on Gene Manipulation (ACGM). ACGM was established in 1984 by the Health and Safety Commission and is primarily responsible for advising on health and safety at work issues, for which the Health and Safety Commission is responsible to the Secretary of State for Employment. ACGM is also able to advise the Health, Agriculture, Environment, Industry and Northern Ireland Ministers on such other matters relating to genetic manipulation as may be referred to those ministers, and to offer comment on the technical or scientific aspects of any new developments in genetic manipulation which may have implications for their departments. We do not foresee any new problems in this respect but, nevertheless, we **recommend** that the attention of ACGM be drawn to our report.

Costs

4.21. We are not charged with concern for the allocation of national resources as between different kinds of illness, groups of patients, or particular therapies. These are political questions, and the priorities, when resources are limited, must be decided by those entrusted with the provision of health care, guided by the national will as expressed through Parliament. We do, however, draw attention to the high costs of treatment and care of patients who are afflicted with chronic disorders of genetic origin which are severely disabling. These financial and human costs are not borne by health services alone, but also by other agencies, and by families themselves. In the event of the potential benefits of gene therapy being realised, these costs should be set against the costs of therapy and the provision of services and access to them, and savings that alleviation of these diseases may bring.

Limits to somatic cell gene therapy

4.22. We are firmly of the opinion that gene therapy should at present be directed to alleviating disease in individual patients, although wider applications may soon call for attention (see 2.15). In the current state of knowledge it would not be acceptable to use gene modification to attempt to change human traits not associated with disease. In addition, whilst we recognise that many selective influences, whether random, accidental, or caused by medical interventions, result in changes to the total human gene pool, we hold the general view that human genetic variability and diversity are precious and should be protected.

Conclusion

4.23. We conclude that the development and introduction of safe and effective means of somatic cell gene modification, directed to alleviating disease in individual patients, is a proper goal for medical science. Somatic cell gene therapy should be regarded, at first, as research involving human subjects and we **recommend** that its use be conditional upon satisfactory scientific, medical and ethical review. Although the prospect of this new therapy heightens the familiar ethical concerns which attend the introduction of any new treatment, we conclude that it poses no new ethical problems. However, in view of the scientific and medical complexity of this treatment and the need for a most careful assessment of the therapy proposed in each instance, and subsequent long term monitoring, we **recommend** that a new supervisory body should be set up and charged with these tasks . . .

Germ Line Gene Therapy

5.1. The purpose of gene modification of sperm or ova or cells which produce them would be to prevent the transmission of defective genes to subsequent generations. Gene modification at an early stage of embryonic development, before differentiation of the germ line, might be a way of correcting gene defects in both the germ line and somatic cells. However, we share the view of others that there is at present insufficient knowledge to evaluate the risks to future generations, to which we have already pointed.

5.2. We **recommend**, therefore, that gene modification of the germ line should not yet be attempted. For couples identified as being at risk of bearing a child with a serious genetic disorder, embryonic diagnosis and selective implantation of an unaffected embryo would provide another way of achieving the same end without incurring the unknown risks of germ line modification. (See 4.3-4.4.) Moreover, this approach offers the prospect of avoiding genetic disorders which result in structural fetal abnormalities.

Supervision of Gene Therapy

Expert Supervisory Body

6.1. Among our tasks were: to invite and consider proposals from doctors wishing to use such treatment on individual patients; and to provide advice to United Kingdom Health Ministers on scientific and medical developments which bear on the safety and efficacy of human gene modification. An assessment of the safety and efficacy of gene therapy, and of the design, content and conduct of research involving patients, depends upon technical, scientific and medical expertise which only a minority of members of this Committee possess. Similar expertise is required in this field to provide advice to Ministers. During consultation we encountered much support for the setting up of a new expert group. Local research ethics committees (LRECs), in particular, wished for a national body to which they could look for advice when proposals to conduct gene therapy research were submitted to them for ethical review. Moreover, we have come to the conclusion that continuing supervision of gene therapy is necessary. No existing body is constituted for these tasks. Consideration of particular proposals for research is excluded from the tasks envisaged for the Nuffield Bioethics Council which was set up during 1991. Therefore, to discharge the second part of our remit, we **recommend** the establishment of a new expert supervisory body [4.8].

6.2. We **recommend** that this supervisory body should be of sufficient standing to command the confidence of LRECs, and of the public, the professions and of Parliament. It should have a responsibility for:
(1)   advising on the content of proposals, including the details of protocols, for therapeutic research in somatic cell gene modification;
(2)   advising on the design and conduct of the research;
(3)   advising on the facilities and service arrangements necessary for the proper conduct of the research;
(4)   advising on the arrangements necessary for the long term surveillance and follow-up of treated patients;
(5)   receiving proposals from doctors who wish to conduct gene therapy in individual patients and making an assessment of:
    (a)   the clinical status of the patient;
    (b)   the scientific quality of the proposal, with particular regard to the technical competence and scientific requirements for achieving therapy effectively and safely;
    (c)   whether the clinical course of the particular disorder is known sufficiently well
      –   for sound information, counselling and advice to be given to the patient (or those acting on behalf of the patient)
      –   for the outcomes of therapy to be assessable;
    (d)   the potential benefits and risks for the patient of what is proposed;
    (e)   the ethical acceptability of the proposal.
In the light of this assessment the expert supervisory body should make a recommendation on whether the proposal should be approved, and if so on what, if any, conditions. The supervisory body should also have a responsibility for:
(6)   acting in co-ordination with LRECs;
(7)   acting as a repository of up-to-date information on research in gene therapy internationally;
(8)   setting up and maintaining a confidential register of patients who have been the subjects of gene therapy;
(9)   oversight and monitoring of the research;
(10) providing advice to Health Ministers in the United Kingdom, on scientific and medical developments which bear on the safety and efficacy of human gene modification.

6.3. We **recommend** that any proposal for gene therapy must be approved by this body as well as by a properly constituted LREC.

6.4. Decisions on a therapeutic intervention for an individual should be made promptly, and the new arrangements should not cause unnecessary delay to the consideration of proposals. Therefore, we **recommend** that anyone wishing to conduct such research should submit proposals simultaneously to LRECs and the new supervisory body.

Subsequently, the government acted to create the expert advisory body, as the committee recommended, and it subsequently approved somatic cell therapy for cystic fibrosis.

We should now turn our attention away from the specific area of genetics and consider one or two matters of general importance for medical law: the role of the law and its relationship with moral philosophy; the role of the courts and the form of regulation that should be employed.

Medical law, as you will come to see on reading further, is a complex subject. It co-exists with any equally intricate and important areas of study that sheds light on the issues – medical ethics. This is a specialist sub-discipline of moral philosophy. Here is not the place to attempt any detailed examination of medical ethics. That is a task for others. In the first edition of this book we attempted to give an overview of medical ethics and its approaches to analysis. The reader is referred to those materials (pp 33-74).

The morality of a particular course of conduct may help to inform us of how the law should respond to the same situation. But it need not. Law and morality may not always march hand in hand. Importantly, not everything that is immoral need or should be illegal. The law may stay its hand and leave the field to moral censure. Defining when the immoral should be transformed into the illegal is an issue that has long challenged scholars. The Hart/Devlin debate will no doubt be familiar. Although not concerned with medical ethics and medical law, that debate has great importance for us. It surfaced in the debates concerning regulation of infertility treatments and embryo research in the mid-1980s. Baroness Warnock (the Chairman of the Government Committee on such matters) commented on this.

M Warnock *A Question of Life* (1985)

The relation between morality and the law has been a central issue in jurisprudence for very many years. There is a distinction between the way we approached this issue in the two parts of our report, that concerned with the treatment of infertility and that concerned with research. If the question is what measures to remedy infertility should be permitted in this country, the problem may be put in the following form: Why should the law intervene to prevent people using whatever methods are possible to enable them to have children? Why should not everybody be entitled to whatever is currently the best and most efficient treatment for infertility? The issues here are quite closely parallel to the issues raised in the 1960s by the Wolfenden Report on homosexuality between consenting males. Ought the law to intervene to make such conduct criminal or ought it not? The famous view of Lord Devlin (*The Enforcement of Morals*, Oxford, 1959) was that where there is a consensus of opinion against a certain practice among members of the general public (exemplified by the notorious 'man on the Clapham omnibus') then the law must intervene to prevent conduct which is repellent to that public. A shared moral view, Lord Devlin argued, was the cement that bound society together. If such shared views were not reflected in law, if law did not enforce what society held to be morally right and wrong, then society itself would disintegrate. A society is characterised by a shared moral view; without it there would be no society. Therefore to act against such a shared view should be tantamount to treason. The law could no more permit acts contrary to the shared morality than it could permit treason.

The drawback with Devlin's view is that, increasingly, we are compelled to accept that 'common morality' is a myth. There is no agreed set of principles which everyone, or the majority, or any representative person, believes to be absolutely binding, and especially is this so in areas of moral concern which are radically and genuinely new. We saw that the concept of a 'rule' breaks down, in novel and hitherto unthought-of cases, and the notion that there is a consensus morality in such cases is equally untenable. The question must be recast: In situations where people disagree with each other as to the rights and wrongs of a specific form of behaviour, how do we decide whether or not the law is to intervene?

H L A Hart (*Law, Liberty and Morality*, Oxford, 1963) identified two moral problems, one 'primary' and the other 'critical'. At the first level the question is whether a certain practice (homosexual acts between consenting males, or AID) is morally right or wrong; at the second level the question is whether, if the law intervened on this matter, the infringement of liberty involved would itself be morally right or wrong. If we consider a case that concerned the Inquiry, the case of AID, it is plain that moral opinions about it vary through the whole spectrum, from those who think it absolutely wrong (like members of the Jewish Community, who think that it is 'bringing orphans into the world', and therefore necessarily wrong) through those who are doubtful, because of the possible risk to AID children, to those who regard it as an absolute right that anyone should have access to AID, whether they are married or single, hetero- or homosexual.

Furthermore, any law enacted to render AID a criminal offence, besides going against the moral views of a fair number of the community, would involve, in itself, a disagreeable intrusiveness, for AID is something that can relatively easily be carried out at home, without any medical intervention. For a law to be enforceable, there would need to be a band of snoopers or people ready to pry into the private lives of others, which might well itself constitute a moral wrong.

Similarly, in the controversial matter of surrogate mothers, the Inquiry agreed unanimously that they disapproved of the practice (largely because of possible consequences for the child); but they also agreed that it could not be prevented by law, because of the intrusiveness of any law that would be enforceable. The Inquiry therefore concentrated on how surrogacy for commercial purposes might be checked, leaving on one side the question whether surrogacy was intrinsically morally right or wrong. We might all of us have answered the primary moral question in a way which made surrogacy wrong. This did not pre-empt the answer to the second-order moral question. Should the law be invoked to stop surrogacy? We all agreed that it would be morally wrong to envisage a law which would intrusively curtail human freedom, and which would in addition be impossible to enforce (how could the law tell whether the child whom Abraham claimed as his own was born to Sara, or to a servant girl who happened to be more fertile?) The Inquiry, then, while unanimously answering the first-order question negatively, holding that surrogacy was wrong, nevertheless held that legislation should not be invoked to prevent it. We did however by a majority recommend that the commercial use of surrogacy arrangements, as a way of making money for an agency, could and should be made a criminal offence. For not only was the wrongness of surrogacy compounded by its being exploited for money, but also a law against agencies would not be intrusive into the private lives of those who were actually engaged in setting up a family.

. . . in some cases it was necessary to distinguish the issue of moral right or wrong, as we saw it, from a further, also moral question, whether it would be right to enforce a moral view, even it such a view were agreed. There was, however, a more testing kind of question, infinitely more important, in my opinion. This was the question of research using human embryos . . . No-one felt inclined to argue that the decision whether or not to embark on research with the use of human embryos was a matter of personal conscience, as they might in the case of AID, surrogacy, or, for that matter, homosexuality between adults. Everyone agreed that this was a matter on which there must be legislation, and that whether and to what extent embryos should be used must be a decision for the law.

The reason for this uncertainty, for the distinction, that is, between what might be thought a private matter and one which was *necessarily* public was somewhat obscure. Nor did the Inquiry draw the distinction explicitly or clearly. But the grounds for it are something like this: research is largely publicly funded. Therefore society, from whom ultimately funding comes, is entitled to know, and even to some extent to control, what research methods are used . . . There is a strong feeling that certain possible experiments and research should be subject to criminal law and made a criminal offence, wherever undertaken. . . .

All members of the Committee wanted the criminal law to be invoked in this matter.

A further issue arises. Once it is considered that law has a role to play, who should make that law? Given the often controversial nature of many issues in medical law, are the courts the appropriate forum to resolve (and adjudicate upon) questions of morality and public policy in this area? Clearly the answer must be 'sometimes'. But, of course, these questions are also for others. Perhaps the most obvious alternative to the courts is Parliament.

As Lord Bridge pointed out in *Gillick v West Norfolk and Wisbech AHA* [1985] 3 All ER 402 the courts should be cautious about becoming involved in these areas (at 427):

> . . . the occasion of a departmental non-statutory publication raising, as in that case, a clearly defined issue of law, unclouded by political, social or moral overtones, will be rare. In cases where any proposition of law implicit in a departmental advisory document is interwoven with questions of social and ethical controversy, the court should, in my opinion, exercise its jurisdiction with the utmost restraint, confine itself to deciding whether the proposition of law is erroneous and avoid either expressing ex cathedra opinions in areas of social and ethical controversy in which it has no claim to speak with authority or proffering answers to hypothetical questions of law which do not strictly arise for decision.

If we look to Parliament, it is unlikely that help will be forthcoming. There are as many votes to be lost as won in trying to resolve such charged issues. The delay in dealing with the Warnock Report bears witness to this. If any legislation were to be forthcoming, it would probably be couched in the most general terms and therefore of only limited value to those who must make particular decisions in particular contexts.

The concerns of the judges were focused in the 1993 case of *Airedale NHS Trust v Bland* [1993] 1 All ER 821. This case will be considered in detail in Chapter 16. It concerned the legality of withdrawing artificial hydration and nutrition from a permanently unconscious patient in a condition known as a 'persistent vegetative state'. For some, the case raised the issue of the legality of euthanasia and all that is entailed. While all the judges (nine in all) agreed that it would be lawful to withdraw treatment, two of the judges in the House of Lords expressed concerns about whether these were not more appropriately matters for Parliament to give the courts guidance upon.

Airedale NHS Trust v Bland [1993] 1 All ER 821 (HL)

> **Lord Browne-Wilkinson**: I have no doubt that it is for Parliament, not the courts, to decide the broader issues which this case raises. . . .
> Where a case raises wholly new moral and social issues, in my judgment it is not for the judges to seek to develop new, all-embracing, principles of law in a way which reflects the individual judges' moral stance when society as a whole is substantially divided on the relevant moral issues. Moreover, it is not legitimate for a judge in reaching a view as to what is for the benefit of the one individual whose life is in issue to take into account the wider practical issues as to allocation of limited financial resources or the impact on third parties of altering the time at which death occurs.
> For these reasons, it seems to me imperative that the moral, social and legal issues raised by this case should be considered by Parliament. The judges' function in this area of the law should be to apply the principles which society, through the democratic process, adopts, not to impose their standards on society. If Parliament fails to act, then judge-made law will of necessity through a gradual and uncertain process provide a legal answer to each new question as it arises. But in my judgment that is not the best way to proceed.

> **Lord Mustill**: The formulation of the necessary broad social and moral policy is an enterprise which the courts have neither the means nor in my opinion the right to perform. This can only be achieved by democratic process through the medium of Parliament.

Given the limitations, however, of all the possible institutional methods for responding to the sort of questions we have been considering, is there any better approach? In 1980 in the United States President Carter established the President's Commission for the Study of Ethical Problems in Medicine and Biomedical and Behavioral Research. In the five years of its existence (it was 'defunded' by President Reagan in 1985) the Commission produced sixteen reports which have already become classics. Professor Alexander Capron, who was the Executive Director of the Commission, explains the Commission's functions and evaluates its impact on medical law and ethics in the US. He does so in the context of an examination of the four model approaches which could be adopted, if it were thought that some sort of commission should, in fact, be set up.

A Capron, 'A National Commission on Medical Ethics' in *Health, Rights and Resources* (ed P Byrne), 1988

Types of commissions

Ad hoc panels

My first task, then, is to explain what I have in mind as the four types of commissions on medical ethics. The first is the ad hoc panel. This has been, as I understand it, the approach taken here in the United Kingdom, where commissions such as the Warnock committee on alternative methods of human reproduction have functioned successfully. In the United States, too, ad hoc panels have been used; indeed, the first major forays into this general field were of this sort. For example, the Department of Health, Education, and Welfare (DHEW) during the late 1960s and early 1970s established several ad hoc bodies to examine the implications of transplanted and artificial organs, such as the totally implantable artificial heart. I think it is noteworthy that such bodies returned several times to this same topic and yet their recommendations did not seem to have much impact on the activities of the Department nor on the development of public policy generally. The absence of follow-through is a decided risk of ad hoc groups when the topic is not one that can be disposed of in a single legislative or administrative stroke.

In 1972, a journalist uncovered a research project that had been going on for 40 years among black men in rural Alabama. Several hundred men had been involved in this government-sponsored study of untreated syphilis. The study was begun in 1932 prior to the development of effective therapies of syphilis, but it continued up until the time that it was revealed to the public, which was plainly shocked to discover that scientific curiosity had apparently won out over medical care in the treatment of the victims of this disease in the study group. As a consequence, the DHEW established the Tuskegee syphilis Ad Hoc Advisory Panel made up of distinguished physicians, ethicists, lawyers, and others. Within a few months they issued a report directed both at the particular problems caused by this study and at the larger issue of government regulation of scientific research conducted under government auspices.

It is characteristic of this first type of committee that groups, usually of about a dozen people from medicine, law, economics, ethics, and often a few with prior government service, attempt to reach fairly concrete recommendations and conclusions on a specific subject. Further, such groups are usually staffed by the agency that set them up, which is usually interested in specific fact-finding and recommendations on an immediate problem. Sometimes larger recommendations about the general process may also emerge, as they did from Tuskegee panel. That body was effective in clarifying most of the facts, though some crucial facts about the degree of intentional deception of the participants were not uncovered. One panel member has now publicly stated that he believes these facts may have been intentionally suppressed and kept from the panel.

Single-subject standing bodies

The broader recommendations of the Tuskegee panel were quickly overshadowed, however, by the creation of another governmental commission in 1974 – the National Commission for the Protection of Human Subjects of Biomedical and Behavioral Research. I will use this group to illustrate the second category in my list – a standing body with authority to study and make recommendations on a narrow field within medical ethics.

The creation of the National Commission had the same provocation as the Tuskegee panel: namely, revelations about human experimentation run amok. In 1972 and 1973 the Congress of the United States took special interest in this subject. In particular, Senator Edward Kennedy, then the Chairman of the Senate Health Subcommittee, held hearings on this topic, during which a number of troubling cases, in addition to the Tuskegee study, were disclosed, particularly research in prisons and mental hospitals and research on human fetuses. As a result, provisions were included in the National Research Act of 1974: namely, that each institution conducting federally-supported research with human subjects was required to create an institutional review board (IRB); and an eleven-member commission drawn from medicine, research, law, ethics, and related fields was to be appointed by the Secretary of Health, Education, and Welfare. As a result, the National Commission for the Protection of Human Subjects was appointed by Secretary Caspar W Weinberger on 3 December 1974, and was lodged within the National Institute of Health, a subdivision of the Department, under the chairmanship of Dr Kenneth Ryan, head of obstetrics and gynaecology at Harvard Medical School.

Most of the topics assigned by the National Research Act to the Commission dealt with experiments on humans; in particular, the Commission was instructed to prepare a report within four months on the subject of fetal experiments, to be followed by other reports on psychosurgery and on various groups of experimental subjects, such as prisoners, children, and persons institutionalised as mentally disabled. (In addition, the Commission was asked to study the social implications of developments in biomedical research, a rather open-ended topic on which the Commission made little headway compared to its thorough treatment of the topics centrally related to experiments on humans.) To draw together its work and provide guidance to IRBs the Commission also prepared a brief summary report – called the 'Belmont Report' after the federal meeting center at which its conclusions were first debated – in which it set forth several basic principles of bioethics on which it had attempted to base its conclusions.

The staff of the National Commission was a mixed group: some career civil servants mostly from DHEW, and some outside experts from academic medicine and ethics. In addition, consultants from a wide variety of fields were commissioned to write advisory papers. The Commission held open monthly meetings which included an opportunity for public testimony. In some ways the National Commission seems similar to what I know of the Comité National Consultatif d'Ethique, although the French group has only one annual open meeting, includes government officials, and is much larger in size, consisting of about 35 people.

Broad-based standing bodies

As the National Commission was completing its statutory mandate in 1978, Senator Kennedy recommended raising it to the level of a Presidential Commission to look at issues in human research across the entire federal government. In the House of Representatives, however, the view arose that any successive commission should have a broader mandate, encompassing issues in medical practice as well as in research on human subjects. Through the agreements reached by Senator Kennedy and Representative Paul Rogers, Chairman of the House Health Subcommittee, a provision was attached to a statute passed in 1978 authorising the creation of the President's Commission.

I will use this group to illustrate my third type of governmental bioethics committee. The mandate of such a group is general in nature, including potentially all topics in bioethics. The President's Commission was required by its statute to conduct studies of a number of topics – including access to health care, informed consent in treatment as well as in research, genetic screening and counselling, and the definition of death – but the topics could be increased at the request of the President. (President Jimmy Carter, through his Science Advisor, Dr Frank Press, did add a topic – human genetic engineering – to the Commission's mandate.) The topics could also be increased at the option of the Commission itself, and this course was also followed when the Commission chose to add the topic of foregoing life sustaining treatment to its list of studies.

What are the salient characteristics of this third type of commission? Like the National Commission, the President's Commission consisted of eleven members from law, ethics and public affairs, under the chairmanship of Morris B Abrams, a New York lawyer and former President of Brandeis University. Unlike the National Commission, the President's Commission was conceived as a permanent body whose members would serve in groups with staggered terms. Since the Commissioners were not named by the President until the summer of 1979 (and were not sworn in until January 1980), the terms served by the first group of Commissioners expired two years later in the summer of 1981. By the conclusion of the Commission's work, eight of the eleven members were appointees of President Ronald Reagan.

Although the Commission was established in a fashion that contemplated a continuing life (as, for example, the limitation of service to two consecutive four-year terms for any Commissioner), the inclusion of a 'sunset clause' meant that the Commission was scheduled to go out of business in December 1982. The purpose of this clause was to allow the legislature to review the group's work and then, by a simple action, to extend its work. Despite the termination date, I still believe that it makes sense to describe such groups as 'standing committees', both because their lives are of indefinite duration (if the termination date is postponed) and because during the three or four years that the President's Commission functioned, it felt free to range quite widely in the field of bioethics. It is true, nonetheless, that the termination date – with the deadlines it imposed for the completion of reports – was an effective, if somewhat oppressive stimulus for Commissioners and staff alike. It might well be that without this goad, some of the intensity that characterised the Commission would have been lacking. The limited time period also made it sensible to bring in staff from outside government, while a truly permanent body might be more heavily staffed by career civil servants. This is not to condemn such a body as a hopeless bureaucracy, but it has been my experience, especially when part of the subject under scrutiny is the performance of the government itself (as it was in our work), that outsiders are more likely to take a fresh look at an issue and are less likely to temper their findings and recommendations out of a need to be gentle with their fellow civil servants.

Like the National Commission, the President's Commission had to 'do ethics in public', because its work was governed by the Federal Advisory Committee Act which requires that such groups hold their meetings in public unless they make a strong case for the need to hold specific private sessions. Despite the prediction of some people that sensitive subjects of the sort being dealt with by the President's Commission could not usefully be discussed in public (lest there be a great deal of posturing and pointless rhetoric on all sides), the requirement that the meetings were open to the public did not prove an impediment to the effective functioning of the Commission. Indeed, the requirement seems to me to have had mostly salutary effects. All those who spoke, especially Commissioners and staff members, were mindful of the need for responsible comments and thoughtful deliberations. Further, the fact that a stenographic record was being made of the proceedings encouraged witnesses to aim for a high degree of accuracy and emphasised the importance of pointed comments rather than rambling dissertations. Finally, the fact that the sessions were public served to underline that the subject matter before the Commission was not esoteric but was a matter of concern and interest to all citizens; and their interest was furthered by the general press coverage of many of the meetings, particularly those at which reports and conclusions were set forth.

Another characteristic of the President's Commission – actually one of the most important – was that the Commission had no power to regulate. Its only real power was that of persuasion. In 1978, philosopher Ruth Macklin told the House Committee holding hearings on the bill that established the President's Commission, that to have any clout, the work of a commission must be 'clear and understandable to a concerned public as well as satisfying to those of us who work professionally in the field of biomedical ethics and health policy'. Therefore, the Commission made its minutes widely available to thousands of people across the country who requested to be on its mailing list, and members of the Commission and its staff testified frequently before Congressional committees holding hearings on topics germane to the Commission's work and held briefings for Congressional members and their staff. One measure of the effectiveness of the Commission was the frequency with which it was asked to present its work to legislative bodies, as well as the number of times its reports received front-page coverage in the newspapers and were featured on the major news and discussion programmes on radio and television.

Because of the need to persuade, there was a strong drive towards consensus, since a divided body would be unlikely to find its conclusions well respected. Although this may not seem remarkable, it should be remembered that in the eyes of many people the field of bioethics is regarded as highly polarised and subject to political polemics. Yet the only major topic that the Commission chose to avoid was abortion, on which its opinions had not been sought and on which it could add little to the already well-developed medical and ethical arguments on both sides. Otherwise, the Commission tackled many difficult issues. Rather than leading to timid reports, however, the search for consensus actually pushed the Commission's reports further and made them more influential. The Commissioners worked inductively from specific examples to general principles; that is, they moved outwards from a common core of agreement to the point where agreement was no longer possible. This form of deliberation helped to show that the sphere of consensus was quite large.

Action-oriented panels

Let me describe the fourth type of governmental group on medical ethics with which we have had experience in the United States, namely a standing body with direct involvement in binding decisions. As a result of the work of the National Commission, new regulations were issued by what is now known as the Department of Health and Human Services in 1978. Among the provisions of these regulations was the requirement that research involving certain highly sensitive groups be approved at a national level by an Ethics Advisory Board (EAB) appointed by the Secretary as well as review and approval by the IRB of the institution at which the research is to be conducted.

The Secretary of the Department of Health, Education, and Welfare, Joseph Califano, established an EAB in 1978. Its first task was to review the acceptability of *in vitro* fertilisation (IVF) because of a protocol submitted by Dr Pierre Soupart of Vanderbilt University. After one year of hearings and commissioned papers, the EAB issued a report in May 1979 recommending that the Secretary permit research on embryos up to two weeks after fertilisation in the laboratory, provided there was to be no implantation of the embryo thereafter. That report has sat on the table for the past eight years without having a definitive response from Secretary Califano or any of his successors, and, ironically, Dr Soupart has since died while waiting for action by the federal government. With the onset of the President's Commission, the EAB was dissolved. Although the President's Commission and EAB had different functions, with no necessary overlap, the EAB did not have the necessary bureaucratic support to continue.

Structure, functions, and accomplishments of the President's Commission

. . . The work of the President's Commission was carried out by a staff of about 25 people, mostly professionals, with a small support staff. The Commission was housed independently of any government department or agency and was not part of a standing bureaucracy. Most members of the support staff and one senior professional came from careers in government service but all the rest of the staff were outsiders to government. For example, I took leave from the University of Pennsylvania to run the Commission, and other senior staff members, who included a physician, two of the lawyers, two sociologists, an expert in public health, one economist and a succession of philosophers, plus various research assistants, were drawn from academic settings. The Commission met monthly. During the first several years of its work these meetings took the form primarily of hearings at which experts and other interested parties testified on particular topics that were under study by the Commission and were questioned by the Commissioners and senior staff members. Furthermore, the Commission staff themselves were sometimes in the witness chair, to engage in a dialogue with the Commissioners and attempt to convey the results of their studies and to learn from the Commissioners, in general form, the directions that should be taken by the Commission's reports. Although many of the witnesses were invited – and included the consultants who were writing papers for the Commission – time was always allotted for other experts and members of the general public who wished to appear and make statements.

After the initial phase during which background was provided to the Commissioners, the primary work of the staff was to prepare drafts of the Commission's reports. After these had been reviewed by the Commissioners they were rewritten by the staff. Commissioners who had special expertise in an area under study took a more active hand in the process of revision of these reports. In the end, there was unanimity on all the Commission's ten reports except one, on which there was one dissent. In addition to the ten reports there was one report of the Commission's work in commissioning papers and convening a workshop on *Whistleblowing in Biomedical Research*. The reports were released as finished; the work amounted to 16 volumes because the background papers were published as separate appendix volumes for some of the reports.

Rather than review all of these, I will characterise the results in four ways: (1) laying to rest, (2) the crucible, (3) the watchdog, and (4) the small rock (sometimes called the lightning rod or, less charitably, the dumping ground) but I prefer to think of this last role in Homer's terms when, in *The Odyssey*, he says 'a small rock holds back a great wave'.

Laying to rest

The first category is probably best illustrated by the first report the Commission issued in July 1981 on the 'definition' of death. This topic has been a matter of public concern since December 1967 when Dr Christiaan Barnard performed the first human-to-human heart transplant. In 1968 an ad hoc committee at the Harvard Medical School promulgated criteria for diagnosing death in comatose bodies whose breathing was being artificially maintained. By 1980 when the President's Commission began, many states had laws recognising criteria of the type promulgated by the Harvard Committee and there was general medical agreement although no up-to-date guidelines had been agreed upon.

Given the fact that the subject was already well advanced, it seemed to the Commission that the major impediment to its mandate – to consider the advisability of legislation on the subject – was the very multiplicity of statutory proposals that had been made by groups such as the American Medical Association, the American Bar Association, and the National Conference of Commissioners on Uniform State Laws. Most of the legislative 'definitions' had been adopted by states in the early 1970s, but the process had slowed to a trickle, and the few that were legislating tended to write their own bills (with all the confusion and imprecision one would expect) rather than choose among the competing laws. Therefore, the Commission concluded that the best way to avoid simply adding to the multiplicity of proposals was to develop a proposal on which all the major proponents could agree. The result was the Uniform Determination of Death Act (UDDA) which was endorsed by the AMA, the ABA and the NCCUSL, as well as the Commission, when its report *Defining Death* was issued in July 1981. The UDDA has since become law in many states. It recognises that death occurs when there is a total and irreversible cessation of circulatory and respiratory functions, or a total and irreversible cessation of all functions of the brain including the brain stem. Equally important to the provision of a statute was the drafting of a set of medical guidelines by a group of the leading medical experts convened by the Commission. When these guidelines were published in the *Journal of the American Medical Association* they were hailed as a landmark, and today they provide a reliable statement on medical techniques for determining that death has occurred either on cardiopulmonary or neurological grounds.

To summarise, the 'laying to rest' function of a commission seems to be to develop recommendations for action, in this case for legislation and for professional action, and to bring together a broad coalition of people in the field to ensure that the recommendations will be so broadly accepted that the topic will no longer be a matter of division or contention.

The crucible

I refer to the second category as that of the crucible, thinking of it as a place of publicly grinding out conclusions on controversial issues when a consensus is not yet apparent. In the case of the President's Commission, three of its reports probably fall into this category: the one on informed consent, *Making Health Care Decisions*; on 'pulling the plug'; *Deciding to Forego Life-Sustaining Treatment*; and on equitable access to health care, *Securing Access to Health Care*. These are all topics which had been approached by divergent groups in the previous decade. The Commission's role here was threefold. First, it had to identify those elements underlying the apparently disparate views expressed in previous discussions. Second, it had to correct misunderstanding or errors, particularly as those were responsible for the divisions in the public debates; and finally, it had to articulate the implications for public policy and ethical behaviour in a way that would be broadly acceptable. Plainly these objectives involved the Commission in processes of analysis and synthesis; as such it required more original scholarship than the first ('laying to rest') function because there was less existing agreement. These topics did not in the view of the Commission always lead to recommendations for legislation. In some cases the objective of the Commission was to frame the thinking on the subject of public officials, such as judges and legislators, and to attempt to push the academic experts forward so that the Commission's findings and recommendations could become the starting point for future discussions. This would reduce some of the jagged pieces that had prevented public understanding and the advancement of conclusions.

A good example of this second category was the work of the Commission on patient autonomy, and the necessity for and the means for its preservation in the face of patient incompetence contained in the reports on making health-care decisions and on deciding to forego life-sustaining treatment. These conclusions have been widely influential. For example, in the past year a California Appellate court and the Supreme Court in 'landmark opinions' have placed heavy reliance on the report, *Deciding to Forego Life-Sustaining Treatment*. The weight accorded to this report illustrates that those who perform ethical and social analysis need a clear understanding of the realities of the practice they are scrutinising. Such an understanding was provided for the Commission by its members, its staff and expert consultants who all insisted that the realities be well attended to rather than solely being concerned with ethical or philosophical discourse. A great deal of effort was placed on the clarification of facts as they illuminate issues, such as 'active' versus 'passive' euthanasia – something that can become a matter of heated, but nonetheless rather abstract, discussion until it is grounded in understanding of the realities of hospital practices and nursing home procedures, the means of dealing with pain, and the psychology of physicians and nurses.

Watchdog

The third function of the Commission is well illustrated by its work in the areas of federal regulation of human subject research. This is a topic that had been thoroughly studied by our predecessor, the National Commission for the Protection of Human Subjects. The Commission therefore placed particular emphasis on the portion of its mandate to report biennially on the adequacy and uniformity of the federal oversight of research conducted or funded by the government. Although this was perhaps the least exciting topic assigned to the President's Commission, it was very important for several reasons. First, the government's efforts in this area are plainly a matter of great public concern; indeed, the process of governmental commissions and study panels in biomedical ethics was begun because of what was perceived as abuses of human subjects in research. Second, since the National Commission had gone out of existence there was a strong possibility that some of its conclusions and recommendations would simply fall between the cracks of the federal bureaucracy if the President's Commission did not vigilantly monitor the response of federal agencies. Third, the National Commission had primarily studied the work of what is now the Department of Health and Human Services, the largest sponsor of research with human subjects, but the President's Commission had a broader mandate. It was to examine research issues throughout the federal government, and one of the principal recommendations in this area in the first biennial report on research in 1981 was that the government should adopt a single set of regulatory requirements for all federally sponsored human subject research to simplify the burdens placed on researchers and the local IRBs.

A small rock

The final function that a standing ethics group can serve is illustrated, I believe, by the work of the President's Commission on a very controversial topic – namely, genetic engineering. In 1980, shortly after the Commission began its work, leaders of the Catholic, Protestant, and Jewish congregations in the United States voiced cries of alarm over the prospect that genetic engineering techniques would be soon extended to human beings. Their concerns, which were addressed to President Carter, led his science advisor to request that the President's Commission add the subject of human genetic engineering to its mandate.

In its report, *Splicing Life*, the Commission took a scientific and a philosophical and religious view of the topic. It attempted to place the concerns in historical context and to show that many forms of manipulation of the genetic basis of human disease were no different from conventional, accepted treatment. But treatment that went beyond the somatic cells to alter the human germ line cells raised moral as well as medical concerns. By the time the Commission had completed its work, a number of newspaper reporters had become interested enough in the topic to write thoughtfully about it for their publications and the Commission's conclusions were greeted with general support by editorial writers. In three days of Congressional hearings, when the report was issued in November 1982, the conclusions of the Commission were accepted by a wide variety of scientific and ethical experts and by representatives of the religious groups that had initially provoked the study.

We will see that England has been slow to develop any institutional framework for analysing issues of medical law and ethics and formulating public policy. The Warnock Committee reviewed the areas of infertility treatment and embryo research but was *ad hoc*. The Law Commission is engaged on a review of the law relating to medical treatment and incapacitated adults. The Human Fertilisation and Embryology Authority has a statutory remit within its particular terms of reference to keep issues of ethics and law under review: see, for example, Consultation Paper on *Sex Selection* (1993). But still the government has not sought to create a national commission, unlike many other countries, for example, France and Denmark.

However, in the summer of 1991 the Trustees of the Nuffield Foundation established the Nuffield Council of Bioethics. Its terms of reference are as follows:

1   to identify and define ethical questions raised by recent advances in biological and medical research in order to respond to, and to anticipate public concern;

2   to make arrangements for examining and reporting on such questions with a view to promoting public understanding and discussion; this may lead, where needed, to the formulation of new guidelines by the appropriate regulatory or other body; and

3   in the light of the outcome of its work, to publish reports; and to make representations, as the Council may judge appropriate.

At present, the Council has undertaken two studies, through the mechanism of multi-disciplinary working parties, on the use of *Human Tissue* and *Genetic Screening*. The report on *Genetic Screening* was published in December 1993 and the report on *Human Tissue* will be published in 1994.

In the result, of course, medical law remains in large part a matter for the judges. In particular, the principles of medical law, to which we refer at the outset of this chapter and which we will consider in detail in the general part of this book, are judge-made. However, before we consider those principles, in the next chapter we consider the structure of the health service in England.

Chapter 2

Doctors and patients: the provision of medical care

Many providers of health care may become involved in the management of a patient. Doctors and nurses obviously come to mind and, in most cases, it will primarily be they who will take care of the patient. But others too may well have a role to play, for example, physiotherapists, pharmacists, health visitors and, in the case of pregnant women, midwives. The organisation and regulation of these various professions are to be found in a complicated collection of primary and secondary legislation. For our part, we intend to focus our attention upon the doctor. Hence we examine who may describe himself as a doctor, the institutional framework within which doctors work, what services they provide and to whom they provide these services. This is not to underplay the role of other professionals. (The legislation which you should refer to in the case of these other professions is, for example, the Dentists Act 1984 (dentists); Pharmacy Act 1954 (chemists); Nurses, Midwives and Health Visitors Act 1979 (nurses etc) and the statutory instruments made thereunder.) A brief summary of the regulation of the health care professions can be found in the following account.

***Encyclopedia of Health Services and Medical Law* (eds J Jacob and J Montgomery)**

1-031: Many of the health-care occupations have been recognised by statute. They are: the doctors' profession now in the Medical Act 1983; the dentists now in the Dentists Act 1984; the chemists now in the Pharmacy Act 1954; the nurses and allied professions now in the Nurses, Midwives and Health Visitors Act 1979; a variety of other occupations in the Professions Supplementary to Medicine Act 1960 (speech therapists are outside the Act but some of its forms are applied to them); the opticians in the Opticians Act 1989 and the suppliers of hearing aids in the Hearing Aid Council Act 1968.

1-032: The basic function of this type of professional regulation is the maintenance of registers of practitioners deemed competent. Occasionally, particularly in its older forms, the Council may be given, or assume, a policing function. *Pharmaceutical Society of Great Britain v Storkwain Ltd* [1985] 3 All ER 4. Today the structure most commonly used to achieve this is the establishment of a Council with duties (for example, to register those who satisfy the 'statutory' criteria) and powers (for example, to determine the criteria). The efficacy of the registers is supported by the creation of certain monopolies (which might be shared with specified other groups) and which are protected by provisions preventing the recovery of fees (or limitations on the right to take appointments which might yield an income) by the unregistered, and by the use of the criminal law to protect professional titles. *Younghusband v Luftig* [1949] 2 KB 354, [1949] 2 All ER 72; *Wilson v Inyang* [1951] 2 KB 799. It is to be noted that the monopolies of dentists, Dentists Act 1984, s 38 (practice), section 39 (titles), and section 41 (business of dentistry) the monopolies of opticians, Opticians Act 1989 ss 24-27, and the monopolies of pharmacists, Medicines Act 1968, are shared with registered medical practitioners. . . .

1-033: It is worth pausing to compare the various schemes. The model, both historically and today, is that provided under the Medical Acts. The General Medical Council consists of some 100 members. Fifty-four are elected by the profession, thirty-five are appointed by the teaching institutions and 'not more than' thirteen are nominated by Her Majesty on the advice of the Privy Council. All, except a majority of this thirteen, must be 'registered medical practitioners'. (It is the custom to appoint the fourth Chief Medical Officers for each of the countries of the United Kingdom.) Thus the lay representation on the General Council cannot be large and the Merrison Report suggested (Committee of Inquiry into the Regulation of the Medical Profession, Cmnd 6018, 1975, para 383) that 'lay' meant non-medical which might include nurses and other health care professionals. Some part of the work of the GMC is conducted by Branch Councils for each of the countries of the United Kingdom.

So it is with other professions. The General Dental Council consists of representatives of the 'Dental Authorities', ie the dental schools, together with eighteen elected by the profession and the four Chief Dental Officers for each of the Departments for the countries of the United Kingdom. One dental auxiliary is elected by the Dental Auxiliaries Committee. (A dental auxiliary performs functions in dentistry roughly corresponding to nurses in medicine.) Six persons who are not registered dentists are appointed by the Privy Council. The pattern is largely reflected in the General Optical Council where (Opticians Act 1989 Sch 1 paras 1-5) registered opticians provide ten members, the examining bodies six, the registered medical practitioners six, of whom four are nominated by the Faculty of Ophthalmologists (a part of the Royal College of Surgeons) and two by the Privy Council (one after consultation with the medical profession to represent it and one who shall engage in pre-clinical training of doctors). There are six lay members (here 'lay' excludes doctors as well as opticians).

The Pharmaceutical Society of Great Britain is incorporated by Charter from the Crown. It is therefore subjected to the legal rules applicable to such incorporation, *Jenkin v Pharmaceutical Society of Great Britain* [1921] 1 Ch 392 (the 1843 Charter was substantially replaced by the Supplemental Charter of 1953) and its constitution is to be found in its Byelaws. However these Byelaws are themselves subject to the approval of the Privy Council (Pharmacy Act 1954 s 16. Some of the Byelaws grant discretions not subject to the approval of the Privy Council.) Its organisational form is thus markedly different from others. That is, it is closer to the Royal Colleges than other professional councils and boards which are incorporated by statute. The Charter is however recognised by Act of Parliament and in some of its most important functions and powers it is directly comparable to those councils. . . . This [organisational] form was adopted in both the grant of the Charter (1843) and its first statutory recognition (1852) prior to the first Medical Act (1858). The Council of the Society consists of twenty-one registered pharmaceutical chemists and three persons appointed by the Privy Council whose qualifications are not specified.

1-034: This pattern of occupational dominance in the governing councils is repeated in the other statutes regulating the professions. The regulation of nursing and its allied professions is now to be found in the Nurses, Midwives and Health Visitors Act 1979. The professions are governed by the Central Council committees of the Central Council, National Boards (for each of the countries of the United Kingdom) and committees of the National Boards. The Central Council consists of forty-five members, seven nominated by each of the National Boards and seventeen appointed by the Secretary of State. There is a complex electoral scheme for election to the National Boards, see United Kingdom Central Council for Nurses, Midwives and Health Visitors (Electoral Scheme) Order 1982 (SI 1982 No 1104). Each of the three professions form separate constituencies within the National Boards, and the persons they each may nominate must include, by virtue of the Act, Sched 1, para 1, each profession and also at least one person engaged in the teaching of nurses, midwives or health visiting. The Secretary of State makes appointments, section 1(4), (5), and section 5(4), (5), to both the Central Council and to the National Boards. His appointments are made from practitioners of each of the professions or from registered medical practitioners or persons who have 'such qualifications and experience in education or other fields as . . . will be of value to the Council in the performance of its functions'. The committees of the Central Council and the National Boards include a Midwifery Committee. Further, joint committees between the Central Council and the National Boards may be appointed.

1-035: Somewhat similar provision is to be found in the Professions Supplementary to Medicine Act 1960, although the specific occupations as such are relatively badly represented. Once more there is a Council and Boards for each of the occupations under its wing – they are now chiropodists, dietitians, medical laboratory technicians, occupational therapists, physiotherapists, radiographers and remedial gymnasts and orthopists. The Council consists of twenty-one members. Each profession has only one. Of the others six are doctors (appointed variously by the 'English Colleges', ie The Royal College of Physicians, of Surgeons and Obstetricians and Gynaecologists, the Scottish Corporations and the GMC). Three persons, of whom only one may be a doctor and none can belong to a profession regulated by the Act, are appointed jointly by Secretaries of State. Five other persons are appointed by the Privy Council (and the Secretary of State for Northern Ireland) none of whom may belong to any of the professions or the medical profession. The Boards each contain a majority of practitioners in their respective professions but repeat the general pattern by including doctors. The representative character of the Boards is shown eg in the requirement that the Radiographers Board shall include both diagnostic and radiotherapeutic radiographers.

1-036: The only exception to the pattern of occupational control is to be found in a possibility under the Hearing Aid Council Act 1968. Under that Act again there is a professional council regulating the occupation of 'dispensers of hearing aids'. It has twelve members, four of whom either are dispensers or employ dispensers, four of whom are not within these categories but who have relevant specialised knowledge and four who represent the interest of those with impaired hearing. The Chairman must not represent any of these interests. Under this Act therefore there is some change of a significant consumer representation in the management of the occupation. Of note also, the jurisdiction of the Disciplinary Committee is unusually restricted; see *R v Hearing Aid Disciplinary Committee, ex p Douglas and Brown (1989) Times* 30 January, and see note to Hearing Aid Council Act 1968, s 7.

1-037: To generalise, the State involvement with the functioning of each of these professional councils is limited to those matters which might involve the use of its wider machinery. Thus the GMC 'may make regulations with respect to the form and keeping of the registers, and the making of entries, alterations and corrections in them'. The only regulations made under this provision which require the approval of the Privy Council are those relating to overseas registration and to restoration to a particular list in the register. The principal significance of these matters is that they concern the level of registration or retention fee which is payable. Other matters do not concern the Privy Council. It is incidentally worth noting that overseas registration does not include those who hold primary European qualification. Under the 1858 Act, overseas qualifications were not recognised at all, see *Younghusband v Luftig* [1949] 2 KB 354, [1949] 2 All ER 72. The GMC was given power exercisable by order of the Privy Council to recognise such qualifications on a country by country basis by the 1886 Act. The far more flexible provisions were introduced by the 1978 Act. As regards the EEC, domestic policy was overtaken by the First and Second Medical Directives.

1-038: Some of the most important functions of the professional councils are reserved by statute to their Education Committees. In the case of the GMC this committee must be chosen. Medical Act 1983, Sched 1 para 19 (but note also para 25(2) relating to powers of co-option) ' . . . as to ensure that the number of appointed members exceeds the number of elected and nominated members . . . .' ie teachers of medicine must form the majority. It is possible that no nominated members may be chosen. In accord with the scheme of the 1858 Act, the GMC engages in no teaching or examining. It does however prescribe, section 5, the knowledge, skill and standard of proficiency required for registration. It has powers, section 6, to require information as to the requisites for obtaining qualifications and to appoint inspectors at examinations and, section 7, to appoint visitors to medical schools. With the approval of the Privy Council, it may, section 8, add to the list of approved medical schools or, section 9, delete one already there. In order to become fully registered a practitioner must have acquired a pattern of experience prescribed by the Education Committee, sections 5 and 10.

1-039: The change effected by the Medical Act 1969 from clinical experience in 'medicine and surgery' to 'prescribed branches of medicine' reflected a much older recognition of the increases in the specialisation of medicine. The doctor acquires it, section 10, at an institution approved by his examining body, but the institution itself is, section 12, subject to visitation by representatives of the Education Committee. Institutional academic freedom is therefore displaced by what is largely the collective academic freedom of the teaching side of the profession as a whole.

1-040: In the other professions there are similar forms for the regulation of education but with the same reservation as before: in education, as in the structure of their councils, the other occupations maintain a dominance but also generally utilise the patronage of doctors. With dentists, all the members of the Education Committee are registered dentists or doctors. As with doctors, the GDC engages in no teaching. That function is carried out by the 'dental authorities' which are defined as 'any medical authority', ie Dentists Act 1984, s 3(3), 'any of the universities or other bodies who choose appointed members of the General Medical Council'. Section 3, and see section 5, authorise the Royal College of Surgeons to continue to hold examinations etc in dentistry.

Again, as with the doctors, the GDC, with the advice, section 2 and Sched 1, of its Education Committee has powers, section 9, regarding the supervision of courses and examinations and, section 10, to appoint visitors and to recommend, section 11, in appropriate cases, that particular degrees or licences in dentistry are not sufficient. The Act maintains a provision, in section 12, which corresponded to one in the old Medical Acts that the General Council shall prevent any degree granting authority from requiring, or preventing, candidates having particular theories. As regards medicine, the Medical Act 1858 s 23 (which became Medical Act 1956 s 14 and was repealed by Medical Act 1978) made similar provision. In both *Allison v GMC* [semble] [1894] 1 QB 750, and *R v GMC* [semble] *ex p Kynaston* [1930] 1 KB 562, it appears that the practitioners fell foul of their professional brethren because of difference in 'theory'. In the one case it was over the use of drug therapy and in the other over the use of tonsillotomy. In neither case did the court appear concerned at any restriction on liberty. They upheld the GMC on grounds relating to the way in which the heterodoxy was expressed. *Allbutt v General Council of Medical Education and Registration* (1889) 23 QBD 400, is perhaps an even stronger case. There the doctor published a book discussing contraception which he sold at a low price. The GMC appear to have taken the view that the price made it available to 'the youth of both sexes to the detriment of public morals' and that was infamous conduct, and see also *Ex p La Mert* [1863] 33 LJQB 69 4 B & S 582.

1-041: As regards opticians, the Education Committee consists of, Opticians Act 1989, s 2 and its Education Committee Rules 1974 (SI 1974 No 149), one general educationalist, nine persons involved in the education of opticians, one in the education of doctors, an ophthalmic optician, a dispensing optician, two ophthalmologists and a person appointed by the Secretary of State for Education and Science. The GOC has, sections 12, 13, powers similar in relation to education to those of the GMC and GDC. It is also so with the Professions Supplementary to Medicine. The Boards (whose corporation is described above but without the statutory formation of an Education Committee) under their Council approve and supervise, sections 4 and 5, courses, qualifications, institutions, and examinations.

1-042: A break in the pattern appears in the Pharmacy Act (and see also Hearing Aid Council Act). True there is provision, in section 4, for the recognition of university degrees in pharmacy but also provision is made, section 3, for the Society itself to conduct examinations. Besides this, the intermediate status of the profession is also illustrated by the Privy Council control of the examiners, section 3(1)(a), and the statutory definition of the syllabus, section 3(4). Among other things, it still includes 'the Latin language' (although this is no longer insisted on) and excludes 'the theory and practice of medicine, surgery and midwifery'.

1-043: With the nurses and allied professions, the Educational Policy Advisory Committee includes eight members of the Central Council engaged in teaching nursing, midwifery or health visiting, and four more who can advise on professional education generally. The practice side of the profession is represented by seven specialised nurses (in midwifery, health visiting, district nursing, the nursing of children and of the mentally ill and handicapped, and occupational nursing). The control of education is, as is to be expected from both the number of nurses and their variety, more complex: there are eleven Parts of the Register having different educational requirements under The Nurses, Midwives and Health Visitors Rules. Generally, however, the Central Council and the National Boards have similar powers to the other professional councils but their exercise is more formal, being contained in a statutory instrument, Nurses, Midwives and Health Visitors Rules Approval Order 1983 (SI 1983 No 873).

1-044: The Privy Council has reserve powers under some of these Acts. Typical of them is the provision as regards doctors (Medical Act 1983, s 50), which it may use where it considers the GMC or the Education Committee to have failed to secure the prescribed proficiency or do anything which they ought to have done (except appoint visitors to medical schools or to prescribe the period and branches of medicine for the requisite post-clinical experience). There are no corresponding default powers of the Privy Council in the Dentists, the Pharmacy, the Nurses, Midwives and Health Visitors, or the Hearing Aid Council Acts. It does not appear open to the Privy Council to use its default powers merely where it disagrees with the prescriptions of a professional council or its education committee.

One important matter not touched upon in this extract is the *disciplinary* role played by the various regulatory bodies. Since we shall concentrate on doctors, we shall have to return later to consider the role of the General Medical Council in this context (Chapter 7).

The doctor

Who is a doctor? Anyone can call himself a doctor. Curiously, medical practitioners do not ordinarily have doctorates and therefore, the attribution to them of the title 'doctor' is wholly a convention. Thus, when we talk of a doctor we are really concerned with a medical practitioner. The answer to the question 'Who is a medical practitioner?' can be discovered by examining the Medical Act 1983 which is now the governing legislation. As regards a 'registered medical practitioner', section 3 provides (and notice the role of the Education Committee of the GMC which has already been referred to):

3. Subject to the provisions of this Act any person who –
(a)   holds one or more primary United Kingdom qualifications and has passed a qualifying examination and satisfied the requirements of this Part of this Act as to experience; or
(b)   being a national of any member State of the Communities, holds one or more primary European qualifications;
is entitled to be registered under this section as a fully registered medical practitioner.

Section 4 defines what amounts to a 'primary United Kingdom qualification' and a 'qualifying examination'. Section 17 (and Schedule 2) defines 'primary European qualification'.

The Education Committee of the GMC has a specific statutory duty to promote 'high standards of medical education' and co-ordinate 'all stages of medical education' (s 5). In performing its duty, the Education Committee has to ensure that medical education provides appropriate 'knowledge and skill', 'standard of proficiency' and 'experience'. In addition the Medical Act contemplates other types of registration: 'provisional', 'limited' and 'temporary full' registration.

'Provisional' registration allows those who have graduated from medical school to work as doctors in 'a resident medical capacity' so as to complete their training prior to full registration (s 1).

There are also provisions to allow those trained abroad to be registered so as to practice in the UK. They are: 'provisional' registration (s 21), allowing a doctor to work in a 'resident medical capacity'; 'limited' registration (s 22), whereby the GMC may place limits on the period of registration and the type of work to be undertaken; and 'temporary full' registration (s 27), which allows 'visiting overseas specialists' to provide specialist medical services for a period up to 12 months.

Being registered as a 'fully registered medical practitioner' has certain consequences for an individual. The most important, perhaps, is that although the legislation does not prevent a person from practising medicine if his name is not on the medical register, he cannot hold himself out as being a registered medical practitioner. Section 49 of the Medical Act 1983 provides, *inter alia*:

> **49.** (1) Subject to subsection (2) below, any person who wilfully and falsely pretends to be or takes or uses the name or title of physician, doctor of medicine, licentiate in medicine and surgery, bachelor of medicine, surgeon, general practitioner or apothecary, or any name, title, addition or description implying that he is registered under any provision of this Act, or that he is recognised by law as a physician or surgeon or licentiate in medicine and surgery or a practitioner in medicine or an apothecary, shall be liable on summary conviction to a fine.

On the other hand, being a fully registered medical practitioner confers certain privileges on a doctor. For example, in relation to the recovery of his fees, section 46 of the 1983 Act provides, *inter alia*:

> **46.** (1) Except as provided in subsection (2) below, no person shall be entitled to recover any charge in any court of law for any medical advice or attendance, or for the performance of any operation, or for any medicine which he has both prescribed and supplied unless he proves that he is fully registered.

Is the effect of this section that, for example, a physiotherapist providing medical advice or attendance under a contract could not sue for the fees? On its face, it would seem that the physiotherapists could not recover the fees.

But Jacob and Montgomery in *Encyclopedia of Health Services and Medical Law* provide a useful gloss on section 46. They note: 'The section is historic. Subject to the provision in subsection (2) relating to visiting European practitioners it has three parts representing the ancient divisions of medicine. The reference to "any medical advice or attendance" is to the practice of physicians; that to "any operation" to the practice of surgeons; and that to "any medicine which he has both prescribed and supplied" to the practice of apothecaries.' Seen in this light, section 46 only applies to those holding themselves out as registered medical practitioners performing the functions previously associated with the ancient divisions in medicine. Thus, the physiotherapist would be able to recover fees providing there was no representation of being a registered medical practitioner. The section's effect is merely to give the registered medical practitioner a competitive edge in providing services because he alone can describe himself as such and, thereafter, recover any fees.

Similarly, registration allows a doctor to hold certain appointments which he otherwise could not, the most important example being those within the National Health Service. Section 47 of the 1983 Act provides:

> **47.** (1) Subject to subsection (2) below, no person who is not fully registered shall hold any appointment as physician, surgeon or other medical officer –
> (a) in the naval, military or air service,
> (b) in any hospital or other place for the reception of persons suffering from mental disorder, or in any other hospital, infirmary or dispensary not supported wholly by voluntary contributions,

(c)   in any prison, or

(d)   in any other public establishment, body or institution, or to any friendly or other society for providing mutual relief in sickness, infirmity or old age.

More generally, being a fully registered medical practitioner confers on a doctor as a matter of public policy the privilege of doing certain things to other people which would otherwise be prima facie unlawful. (It is no surprise, therefore, that the law should wish to hold the doctor to account for what he does in the exercise of this privilege.)

Registered medical practitioners will usually work either within the NHS, as general practitioners or hospital doctors, or in private practice. These are not mutually exclusive. It is often the case that a particular doctor working in a hospital as a consultant will undertake some private work as well as fulfilling his NHS duties.

Institutional framework within which doctors work

Doctors work in many areas of public service such as the prison medical service and within the medical service of the armed forces. Here, however, we are interested in the provision of medical services within the National Health Service. Of course, medical services are provided outside the framework of publicly funded medical care, ie private medical care. While the provision of private care is the subject of some statutory regulation particularly as regards licensing, eg Registered Homes Act 1984 in respect of nursing homes, for the most part the organisation of private health care providers is not specifically regulated and their relationship with their patients is a matter for the general law.

A. GENERAL PRACTITIONERS

The statutory provisions relating to the provision of general medical services by general practitioners within the NHS is complex. The principal Act is the National Health Service Act 1977. More recently, the National Health Service and Community Care Act 1990 introduced further statutory provisions. Many of the details of the legal framework are to be found in the National Health Service (General Medical Services) Regulations 1992 (SI 1992 No 635) as amended by SI 1992 No 2412 and SI 1993 No 540 and the National Health Service (Pharmaceutical Services) Regulations 1992 (SI 1992 No 662) together with a host of other statutory instruments. Here we set out only in general terms the legislative scheme.

Section 29 of the 1977 Act places upon every Family Health Service Authority (FHSA) (previously called a Family Practitioner Committee (FPC)) a duty 'to arrange as respects their locality with medical practitioners to provide personal medical services for all persons in the locality who wish to take advantage of the arrangement'. Prior to the 1990 Act, this duty was placed upon District Health Authorities (DHA). In fulfilment of this statutory duty each FHSA is required to prepare and publish a list of general medical practitioners who undertake to provide general medical services and additional services such as maternity medical services (see below). This list is known as 'the medical list' (reg 4 of the National Health Service (General Medical Services) Regulations 1992) ('the Medical Regulations').

A doctor who wishes to be included on the list of a particular FHSA must apply to the FHSA for inclusion (1977 Act, s 30; reg 5(1) of the Medical Regulations). The FHSA must then refer the application, together with a report containing certain information specified in Part III of Schedule 3 to the Medical Regulations, to the Medical Practices Committee (MPC). The MPC determines applications made under section 30 in accordance with sections 31-34 of the 1977 Act and regulation 14 of the Medical Regulations. In particular, regulation 15 allows the MPC to specify the conditions under which general medical services may be provided by a GP.

The GP undertakes to abide by 'terms of service' contained in Schedule 2 to the Medical Regulations. What is the legal nature of the relationship between a GP and the FHSA? There are a number of options. First, the relationship is one of contract which, in this situation, would undoubtedly be a contract for services since the GP could never be viewed as a employee of an FHSA. Secondly, the relationship is one which is *sui generis* defined by statute and lying in the realm of public law. Thirdly, their relationship may be a hybrid, being a creature in part of private law (though not contract) and in part of public law.

Roy v Kensington & Chelsea FPC [1990] 1 Med LR 328 (CA), [1992] 1 AC 624 (HL)

On October 25, 1984, the defendant Kensington and Chelsea and Westminster Family Practitioner Committee decided that the plaintiff medical practitioner, Dr Roy, was not devoting a substantial amount of time to his general practice under the National Health Service. The committee reduced his practice allowance by 20 per cent from January 1, 1985. It was not disputed that Dr Roy had been absent from his practice, for reasons of family, sickness or holiday, for lengthy spells over a period of years. During his absence Dr Roy employed a locum who acted as his practice manager when he was not there. There have been no complaints from individual patients of the service that Dr Roy had provided.

Dr Roy claimed that he had a contractual relationship with the committee to provide general medical services to National Health Service patients. He contended that he had fulfilled his obligation by providing a locum during his periods of absence. Other disputes arose between Dr Roy and the committee in respect of, inter alia, payments for ancillary staff. He brought an action against the committee contending inter alia that, by reducing his practice allowance, the committee were in breach of contract.

On an application by the committee to strike out those paragraphs in Dr Roy's statement of claim which claimed to recover the moneys deducted by the committee from his allowance on the ground that they were an abuse of the process of the court, His Honour Judge White held ([1989] 1 Med LR 10), as a preliminary issue, that to allow Dr Roy to proceed would be an abuse of the process of the court because, although there were contractual echoes in the relationship between the doctor and the committee those were deceptive. The rights and duties of the parties were dependent on statute and the duty which the committee discharged was a public law function, an administrative decision, and the court would not substitute its decision for that of the committee. Accordingly, Dr Roy could only proceed on that part of his claim concerned with deductions from his practice allowance by way of an action for judicial review.

Balcombe LJ: In my judgment, the application by a general practitioner in the form prescribed in part II of Schedule 1 to the 1974 Regulations constitutes an offer in writing to perform general medical services in the FPC's locality upon the terms as defined above. When that application is accepted by the FPC and the acceptance is communicated to the applicant (either by letter or by the inclusion of his name in the medical list) a contract between the applicant and the FPC for the performance of services by the applicant is constituted. All the indicia of a contract are present. There is consideration consisting of the promise by the applicant to perform general medical services under the terms of service, in return for the promise by the FPC to pay for those services in accordance with the Statement of Fees and Allowances. The 1974 Regulations also provide for the termination of the relationship: Regulation 5 sets out the circumstances in which the FPC may remove a doctor's name from the medical list, while Regulation 6 enables the doctor to withdraw his name from the list.

Both a general practitioner and a FPC have complete freedom whether and with whom to contract, subject only to the monopoly position of each FPC as the National Health Service employer within its locality, and to the statutory duty of the FPC (under sections 15 and 29 of the 1977 Act) to make arrangements for the provision of general medical services within its locality. The fact that neither the FPC nor the doctor has freedom of contract in relation to the terms of service, which are laid down by the 1977 Act and the 1974 Regulations, is quite immaterial.

If the relationship were not contractual it is difficult to see what else it could be ... I am satisfied that the judge was wrong and that the relationship between Dr Roy and the committee was contractual.

Nourse and Neill LJJ agreed with Balcombe LJ's analysis of the relationship between Dr Roy and the FPC.

Curiously, the Court of Appeal in *Roy* was not referred to the earlier case of *Wadi v Cornwall & Isles of Scilly FPC* [1985] ICR 492 where the Employment Appeal Tribunal held that the relationship was not one of contract. On appeal in *Roy*, the House of Lords was asked to resolve this conflict. Lord Lowry set out the relevant parts of the judgment of the Employment Appeal Tribunal in *Wadi* as follows:

It is clear from the Act of 1977 and the Regulations of 1974 that the family practitioner committee's designated role in the statutory scheme is merely to administer on behalf of the district health authority the arrangements which it is the duty of the district health authority to make with medical practitioners.

And

There is in our view little to support Mr Susman's suggestion that the family practitioner committee, still less the medical committee, enters into a contract with the doctor who successfully applies for a vacancy. The family practitioner committee is obliged to cause payments to be made to doctors, but it is a mere conduit pipe for such moneys which the Secretary of State must pay to it and which it must pass on to the doctors. It has no discretion in the amounts or the circumstances of the payments. Nor does the 'light supervision' (to use the industrial tribunal's words) which it exercises over the doctors signify a contract. Still less is there anything to indicate that the medical committee has a contract with the doctor, there being no continuing relationship between them. In summary, our view is that under the statutory arrangements the doctor on the one side and each of the family practitioner committee and the medical committee on the other have rights and obligations conferred by statute rather than by contract. It is not necessary and we think it wrong to seek to import a contract into a scheme of things which is governed by the very detailed statutory arrangements made by neither the family practitioner committee nor the medical committee.

The House of Lords ([1992] 1 AC 624, [1992] 1 All ER 705) chose not to resolve the difference between the Court of Appeal in *Roy* and the Employment Appeal Tribunal in *Wadi*. Instead, the House of Lords decided that Dr Roy's action by writ was properly brought since, whatever the general nature of their relationship in law may be, the statutory framework conferred private rights upon Dr Roy at least as regards payment.

Lord Lowry (with whom the other Law Lords agreed) stated:

[T]he actual or possible absence of a contract is not decisive against Dr Roy. He has in my opinion a bundle of rights which should be regarded as his individual private law rights against the Committee, arising from the statute and regulations and including the very important private law right to be paid for the work that he has done.

Lord Bridge was content to assume no contract existed and stated:

I do not think the issue in the appeal turns on whether the doctor provides services pursuant to a contract with the Family Practitioner Committee. I doubt if he does and am content to assume that there is no contract. Nevertheless, the terms which govern the obligations of the doctor on the one hand, as to the services he is to provide, and of the Family Practitioner Committee on the other hand, as to the payments which it is required to make to the doctor, are all prescribed in the relevant legislation and it seems to me that the statutory terms are just as effective as they would be if they were contractual to confer upon the doctor an enforceable right in private law to receive the remuneration to which the terms entitle him. It must follow, in my view, that in any case of dispute the doctor is entitled to claim and recover in an action commenced by writ the amount of remuneration which he is able to prove as being due to him. Whatever remuneration he is entitled to under the Statement is remuneration he has duly earned by the services he has rendered. The circumstances that the quantum of that remuneration, in the case of a particular dispute, is affected by a discretionary decision made by the Committee cannot deny the doctor his private law right of recovery or subject him to the constraints which the necessity to seek judicial review would impose upon that right.

Will it ever be crucial whether or not a GP works under a contract for services? Arguably, as a matter of remedy no procedural problem need necessarily arise. A GP who wishes to dispute some aspect of his relationship with the FHSA will either have a specific remedy (by, for example, appealing to the Secretary of State) or he could bring an application for judicial review under RSC Ord 53. The latter should be the remedy of first resort (once the statutory remedies have been exhausted) for two reasons: first, challenges to public decision are appropriately pursued under Ord 53 and secondly, the GP could take advantage of the 'cross-over' provision of Ord 53 r 9(5) which allows the court to regard his action as if it had been begun by writ. This approach would not, however, have assisted Dr Wadi. Judicial review was unavailable since the FPC's decision not to employ him did not lie within the realm of public law. Instead, his only right (if any) not to be discriminated against, lay under the Race Relations Act 1976. A pre-condition to such rights accruing would be that he was seeking 'employment' which, as defined in the Act, requires that had he been successful he would have had a *contract* with the FHSA. Therefore, the nature of the relationship between the GP and FHSA is crucial and could not be avoided by the court.

We describe below the services which the doctor undertakes to provide. In this section, we describe some of the more important *conditions* upon which all GPs undertake to provide general medical services. The first matter to notice is that by paragraph 19(1) of the terms of service (contained in Schedule 2 to the Medical Regulations) 'a doctor shall give treatment personally' but, as regards general medical services, he is permitted to use a deputy providing 'reasonable steps are taken to ensure the continuity of the patient's treatment' (paragraph 19(2)). Further, 'before employing any person [ie another doctor] to assist him in the provision of general medical services' paragraph 28(1) provides that the doctor shall 'take reasonable care to satisfy himself that the person in question is both suitably qualified and competent to discharge the duties for which he is to be employed'. It must be noticed, however, that by paragraph 20(1):

a doctor is responsible for all acts and omissions of –
(a)   any doctor acting as his deputy;
(b)   any deputising service while acting on his behalf; and
(c)   any person employed by, or acting on behalf of, his or such a deputy or deputising service . . .

Also notice that by paragraph 22(1) 'before entering into arrangements with a deputising service for the provision of any deputy', a doctor shall obtain the consent of the FHSA. Where a deputy acts on behalf of a doctor, paragraph 20(1) states that 'In relation to his obligations under these terms of service, a doctor is responsible for all acts and omissions' of his deputy, any deputising service or anyone employed by him or them. This liability only applies, however, to a deputy who is not also on the medical list of the FHSA. If the deputy is on the medical list then *he* alone is 'responsible for his own acts and omissions' under the terms of service (paragraph 20(2)).

By paragraph 29(1) a doctor whose name is included in the medical list 'shall . . . normally be available at such times and places as shall have been approved by the FHSA . . . and . . . inform his patients about his availability in such manner as the FHSA may require'. Furthermore, by paragraph 47 a doctor 'whose name is included in the medical list of an FHSA shall compile in relation to his practice a document . . . called a "practice leaflet"'. The information which the practice leaflet should contain is set out in Schedule 12 and includes such matters as the personal and professional details of the doctor, times of availability, whether an appointment system is operated and whether he provides special services such as 'maternity medical services' or 'contraceptive services'.

A further duty imposed upon a doctor under the terms of service is to keep adequate records of the illnesses and treatments of his patients (paragraph 36). Finally notice that a doctor may not demand nor accept payment for the provision of general medical services to, or any other treatment of, patients on his list or who are otherwise his patients under the terms of service (paragraph 38). This general prohibition is subject to a number of exceptions, for example, when attending and examining a patient at a police station (paragraph 38(d)).

Another feature of the statutory framework is that there is a limit placed upon the number of persons who may appear on a doctor's list which is generally '3,500 for a doctor carrying on practice otherwise than as an assistant or in a partnership' or '4,500 for a doctor carrying on practice in partnership, subject to a maximum average of 3,500 for each of the partners in the practice' (reg 24(2)).

In addition to being on the medical list, a general practitioner may also apply to the FHSA to have his name placed upon one of the specialist lists maintained by the FHSA namely, the obstetric list (reg 30) (and, therefore, he will provide maternity services), the child health surveillance list (reg 27) and the minor surgery list (reg 32). We will discuss below what is entailed in each of these special services.

As regards all the matters upon which the approval of the FHSA is required, a doctor may, by regulation 17, appeal on a point of law to the Secretary of State. By virtue of the National Health Service (Appellate and Other Functions) Regulations 1992 (SI 1992 No 660) appeals relating to matters of his practice are delegated to the Yorkshire Regional Health Authority.

Finally, we should notice that the FHSA may permit a doctor to withdraw his name from any of the lists maintained by the FHSA on giving three months' notice (reg 6).

The FHSA may remove a doctor's name from a list where, for example, he is dead, he has ceased to be a registered medical practitioner or he is subject to a direction from the Professional Conduct Committee of the General Medical Council that his name be erased or subject to immediate suspension (reg 7). In addition, the FHSA must remove the name of any GP from its list who has reached the age of 70 (reg 7(11)).

Another way in which a GP may be removed from the medical list is in the context of disciplinary proceedings for breach of the terms of service under Schedule 2 to the Medical Regulations. As we will see (Chapter 7), the disciplinary machinery is part of the complaints procedure under the legislation. Here, it suffices to note that where a GP is found to be in breach of his terms of service and where continued inclusion would, in the opinion of the FHSA, 'be prejudicial to the efficiency of the [various] services' provided under the regulations, the FHSA may refer his case to a statutory Tribunal set up under section 46 (and Schedule 9) of the National Health Service Act 1977 (National Health Service (Service Committees and Tribunal) Regulations 1992 (SI 1992 No 664), reg 24). It appears that the FHSA *must* remove the GP's name from the medical list if directed to do so by the Tribunal. This was previously explicit in the 1974 Regulations (reg 5(1)(d)) but was omitted in the Medical Regulations 1992 presumably because it is implied that a direction under section 46 of the 1977 Act by the Tribunal effects removal without more (see the wording of section 47: 'Any person whose name *has been removed by a direction* . . . ').

One further matter arises relating to the statutory framework within which GPs function. The National Health Service and Community Care Act 1990 introduced a novel method through which GPs can organise their practice known as 'fund-holding practices' (ss 14-17 of the 1990 Act). These provisions do not formally affect the relationship between the GP and his patient. Instead, they create a new relationship between the practice and the relevant Regional Health Authority (or the Secretary of State in the case of Wales where there are no Regional Health Authorities). They allow a 'fund-holding practice' to be a 'purchaser' of services within the internal market of the NHS created by the 1990 Act.

Under section 14 of the 1990 Act, one or more medical practitioners may apply to the Regional Health Authority (or the Secretary of Sate in the case of Wales) for recognition as a 'fund-holding practice'. The conditions for obtaining recognition are contained in the National Health Service (Fund-holding Practices) (Applications and Recognition) Regulations 1990 (SI 1990 No 1753). The conditions include, for example, that the practice should have a minimum number of patients (currently 7,000) and that the Regional Health Authority is satisfied that the practice is able to manage its allotted budget 'effectively and efficiently'.

B. HOSPITAL DOCTORS

A doctor working in an NHS hospital is not subject to the statutory framework which applies to GPs. Instead, the doctor's legal relationship is with the health authority (or NHS Trust) responsible for the hospital within which he works. He is employed by the health authority (or NHS Trust) under a contract of service.

The conditions of service are, at least in theory, a matter of agreement between the doctor and the health authority. In practice, they are not. There are two reasons. First, Parliament has laid down some matters which are no longer open to negotiation, for example, relating to the process of appointment of consultants. Secondly, a hospital doctor's terms of employment are negotiated nationally ('Terms and Conditions of Service of Hospital Medical and Dental Staff (England and Wales)' – the 'red book'). By virtue of certain statutory provisions (which we will see shortly) a doctor may not be employed on less (or indeed more) favourable terms than these. In addition to these statutory provisions, there are a number of government circulars dealing particularly with disciplinary proceedings (eg HC (90)9). Unless these are expressly incorporated into the contract of a particular doctor it is unlikely that, as a matter of law, they will be incorporated by implication (*Higgs v Northern RHA* [1989] 1 Med LR 1).

The National Health Service Act 1977, Schedule 5, paragraph 10 provides:

10. (1) Subject to and in accordance with regulations and such directions as may be given by the Secretary of State, an authority [. . .] may employ such officers as it may determine at such remuneration and on such conditions of service as it may determine; and regulations and directions under this sub-paragraph may contain provision –
(a)   with respect to the qualifications of persons who may be employed as officers of an authority;
(b)   requiring an authority to employ, for the purpose of performing prescribed functions of the authority or any other body, officers having prescribed qualifications or experience; and
(c)   as to the manner in which any officers of an authority are to be appointed.
. . .
      (4) Regulations made in pursuance of this paragraph shall not require that all consultants employed by an authority are to be so employed whole-time.

The hospital doctor's conditions of employment are regulated by the National Health Service (Remuneration and Conditions of Service) Regulations 1991 (SI 1991 No 481). Regulation 3 provides:

3. Subject to any directions, the conditions of service –
(a)   of an officer who belongs to a class of officer in respect of which conditions of service have been agreed in negotiations and approved by the Secretary of State, shall include the conditions so agreed and approved;
(b)   of an officer for whom, or for whose class, the Secretary of State has determined any other conditions of service, shall include the conditions of service so determined, whether or not they also include conditions agreed in negotiation and approved by the Secretary of State.

Notice that in relation to consultants, but not other grades of hospital doctors, there is a statutory procedure for appointment under the National Health Service (Appointment of Consultants) Regulations 1982 (SI 1982 No 276). These regulations lay down, for example, (i) a requirement that a consultant post be advertised (reg 5); (ii) the constitution of the appointments committee (reg 6); (iii) rules relating to the selection procedure (reg 7); (iv) rules relating to who may be appointed (reg 8).

As we shall see in detail later, the National Health Service and Community Care Act 1990 provides for the creation of a new species of NHS body, namely the National Health Service Trust (section 5). While not so limited, most Trusts are, in fact, hospitals. What is the position of an employee of an NHS Trust? Two solicitors specialising in health service law discuss this issue.

Brian Raymond 'Employment Rights of the NHS Hospital Doctor' in *Doctors, Patients and the Law* (ed C Dyer) (1992)

> Section 6 of the NHS and Community Care Act 1990 makes it clear that on day one of their existence the trusts take over all the employment duties and liabilities of the health authority, which must therefore include the disciplinary apparatus set out above. On the other hand, it has been stated repeatedly that trusts have the power to determine their own terms and conditions of service for staff and it is therefore open to a trust to introduce different systems by following the appropriate procedures for variation of contracts of employment. The net position for doctors employed by trusts is therefore that they are covered by the mainstream NHS procedures unless their own trust has introduced different procedures, in which case the latter are applicable.

As Raymond points out, the terms of an NHS employee may change once a Trust is created. Mary Siddall considers the implications of this.

Mary Siddall 'Not as Well as Can be Expected' (1992) 142 New LJ 763

> Prior to the creation of the Trusts, all Health Service employees had the benefit of any nationally negotiated terms and conditions set by the Whitley Council for their particular staff group. Any such terms took automatic effect in their contracts of employment on approval by the Secretary of State for Health (by virtue of SI 1974/296).
>
> Following the transfer to the Trust, the current Whitley Council terms and conditions are preserved. What is the effect of subsequent changes to Whitley terms? Once a Trust employee has accepted a new contract with the Trust, then both employer and employee have effectively 'opted out' of Whitley. If no new contract has been agreed, or if there have been only piecemeal changes in the employment contract (eg the introduction of a new pay structure) then the majority of Whitley Council provisions continue to apply. However, such provisions are subject to renegotiation at national level.
>
> It appears to be the Department of Health's view that Trust employees will enjoy any change in Whitley terms and conditions unless and until they agree new terms. How this can be so, is problematic. It is stated in s 5(5)(a) of the 1990 Act that Trusts shall be a 'body corporate', autonomous in that they hold their own budgets, can run hospitals and other Health Service units without direct control by the Health Authority and can set their own terms and conditions of contract for staff.
>
> It is therefore difficult to see how the 'self-governing' Trusts can still be subject to changes in Whitley. Whitley Council terms take effect in the contracts of Health Authority employees by order of the Secretary of State, as noted above. However, Trust employees are *not* the employees of a Health Authority (as defined by s 128 National Health Service Act 1977). That would suggest that the terms are not incorporated. Possibly the changes can take effect as collective agreements incorporated into individual contracts, although the extent to which Whitley Councils can be said to represent Trusts must be very limited. In some cases, Trust employees may have an express clause in their original contract with the Health Authority that they are subject to Whitley Council terms. It is perhaps arguable that there is an implied term to this effect in any case. However, whatever the legal position, the end result must be that the contractual position of Trust employees is very uncertain, and may have to be settled by the courts.
>
> This is particularly so where Trusts introduce minor changes to contractual terms, but leave the existing contractual position intact, at least for the time being. Does this then mean that if, for example, a Trust introduces a new pay structure, the terms of the contract as to pay are 'frozen' as between the Trust and its employees, but that other contractual terms are subject to change by Whitley Councils?
>
> An even greater problem is the fact that large portions of Whitley Council terms and conditions are completely inappropriate to the organisational structures of the Trust. Whitley provisions are lengthy and extremely complicated; there are separate provisions for

different groups of staff and there is constant reference to officers, Tribunals, Boards and other administrative bodies which are found throughout the Health Service. The extent of the bureaucracy accentuates the 'teething' difficulties which are usually found following any transfer or merger of a business. Disciplinary procedures are a case in point. Many will have to be substantially revised. At present, for example, many employees have the right of appeal against dismissal from their employing Authority to the Regional Health Authority. Following the creation of a Trust, Regional Authorities have 'discretion' as to whether to consider to hear some appeals. Until new procedures are introduced, an employee who wishes to raise a grievance, or who is facing disciplinary action, is going to have grave difficulty in establishing what action to take – as indeed his or her employer will have even greater difficulty in deciding what procedure to apply. Such cases are already causing problems in the first wave of Trusts.

The position is even more complicated in relation to employees who, prior to the setting up of the Trust, work at more than one Health Authority location – for example, one hospital which is due to become a Trust, and another which is not. Section 6(1)(b) of the 1990 Act says that a 'special scheme' must be made in relation to these employees if their employment rights are to be protected, and envisages that they will have 'split' contracts, one with the Health Authority and one with the Trust. This will create huge difficulties in managing the very large number of Health Service employees whom this will affect and in administering matters such as holidays, sickness, use of cars etc. These factors must be an incentive, if any be needed, for Trusts to create their own contracts of employment with their staff as soon as possible, so as to 'contract out' of the Whitley Council and Health Authority terms of employment.

Health Authority employees working in those parts of the Health Service which have become, or are due to become, Trusts are in a vulnerable position. Their employment is transferred (without any requirement for their consent) to a body which is autonomous from the Health Service in general and is not bound by nationally negotiated terms and conditions. Although many Trusts have consulted fully with their employees prior to the transfer, if they do not consult, the possibilities of an employee obtaining a remedy are extremely limited. Following the transfer, the terms of their contracts are uncertain and may be difficult to enforce. This means that even the most conscientious manager may find great difficulty in applying existing contractual arrangements to the circumstances of the Trust, and that could lead to the employee being seriously disadvantaged. It seems certain that Trusts will begin to move towards developing their own contracts of employment, on their own terms, even if they have not done so already. Of course, no variation in a contract of employment can be brought about without the consent of the employee but, should the employee not consent then he or she will face the possibility of dismissal.

It is too early to say if the fears of employees and their representatives concerning the new Trusts will be realised. Certainly, the majority of managers working for the Trusts whom I have spoken to are concerned, not only to keep their employees fully informed of what is occurring, but also to offer them a good deal when it comes to talking about new terms and conditions. However, the Trusts are also looking increasingly to the principles of personnel management in the private sector. There is talk of killing the 'sacred cows of Britain's Health Service' (see *The Independent*, December 2, 1991). The matter of Union recognition is still very much up in the air. Deprived of the bulwark of the Whitley Councils, Trust employees face an uncertain future.

In order to understand the relationship between a doctor and his patient, and in particular, the medical services provided, it is essential to have in mind the institutional framework within which hospital services are provided.

Until the National Health Service and Community Care Act 1990, these services were provided by Regional and District Health Authorities which performed (as delegates) the statutory functions of the Secretary of State pursuant to the National Health Service Act 1977 and managed the resources allocated to them. The 1990 Act radically altered the structure for the provision of services (for a thorough discussion of the reforms including some intriguing matters of competition law, see F Miller, 'Competition Law and Anti-competitive Professional Behaviour Affecting Health Care' (1992) 55 MLR 453).

As we shall see shortly, the Secretary of State's statutory duty to provide a 'comprehensive health service' (s 1(1) of the NHS Act 1977), is delegated to the

Regional Health Authorities, which in turn delegate most of their functions to the District Health Authorities (see *infra*). However, under the 1990 Act District Health Authorities may now make arrangements for providing these services in a variety of ways. The 1990 Act distinguishes between 'acquirers' of medical services and 'providers' of those services (s 4 of the 1990 Act). In essence the scheme of the 1990 Act creates what has become known as the 'internal market' whereby 'acquirers' to fulfil their statutory duties purchase medical services from others, the 'providers'. The following diagrams describe in outline the arrangements for allocating financial resources within the NHS at the various levels of the structure.

Figure 1:

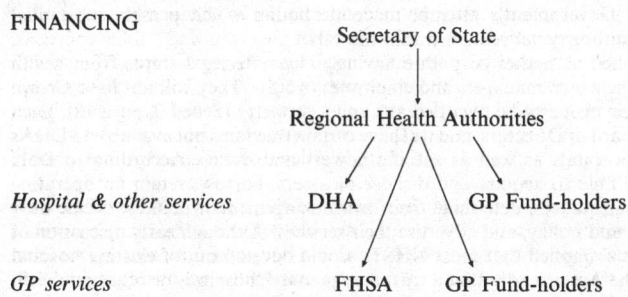

FINANCING

Secretary of State

Regional Health Authorities

Hospital & other services   DHA   GP Fund-holders

GP services   FHSA   GP Fund-holders

[In Wales there are no RHAs and their functions are performed by the DHAs.]

The 'internal market' relates to the provision of hospital and other non-GP services. As this diagram shows the sources of money for paying for these services are the DHAs (in relation to the residents of the area for which they have responsibility) and GP 'fund-holders' (in respect of their patients). In the language of the 1990 Act these are 'acquirers'.

There are a number of possible 'providers' from whom an 'acquirer' may purchase these services. The following diagram describes in outline the arrangements that may be made.

Figure 2:

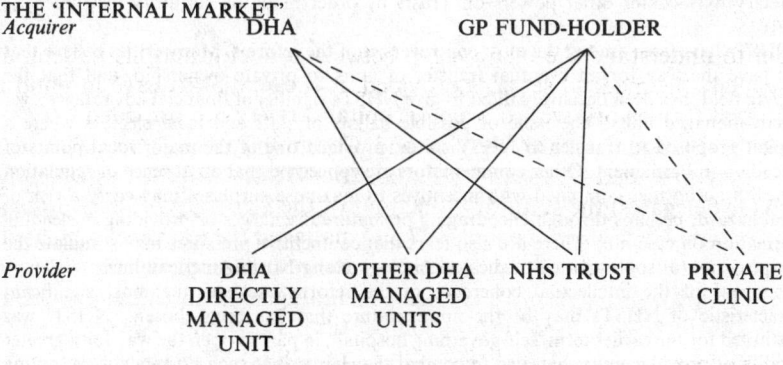

THE 'INTERNAL MARKET'
Acquirer   DHA   GP FUND-HOLDER

Provider   DHA   OTHER DHA   NHS TRUST   PRIVATE
           DIRECTLY   MANAGED   CLINIC
           MANAGED   UNITS
           UNIT

[—— NHS contract; – – – contract; .... internal accounting procedure]

This diagram introduces two new entities as 'providers', although, in fact, one of them previously existed under a different name. A DHA directly managed unit is a hospital or other service previously provided by a DHA which since 1990 the DHA has continued itself to provide. It is, therefore, both 'acquirer' and 'provider' in these circumstances and financing is a matter of internal accounting within the DHA. The second entity is, however, decidedly novel and is known as the 'NHS Trust'. David Hughes explains the nature, and the place in the system of, the NHS Trust.

D Hughes 'The Reorganisation of the National Health Service: The Rhetoric and Reality of the Internal Market' (1991) 54 MLR 88

NHSTs represent the Government's attempt to create bodies which possess substantial devolved managerial authority yet remain within the NHS. . . .

NHSTs are established as bodies corporate having a separate legal status from health authorities and from their own managers and employees (s 5(5)). They will not have Crown immunity, nor will their property be regarded as Crown property (Sched 2, para 18). Each trust will be run by a Board of Directors, and will have certain freedoms not available to DHAs or directly-managed hospitals as well as specific powers and duties. According to DoH guidance, they will be able to acquire and dispose of assets, borrow, retain an operating surplus in normal circumstances, determine their own management structures, decide their own staffing structure and policy, and advertise their services. Although early discussion of 'self-governing hospitals' implied that most NHSTs would develop out of existing hospital units, section 5(1) of the Act provides that a trust may manage 'hospitals or other establishments or facilities', and thus opens up the possibility of a future growth of larger, more comprehensive, provider units. The capital charging scheme will apply to NHSTs as well as to other NHS bodies; however, the originating capital debt of a trust will be divided between an interest-bearing loan and public dividend capital (PDC). The latter carries no fixed repayment obligations but is expected in the long run to yield dividends to the Consolidated Fund at a rate at least equal to the interest that would have been paid. The possibility of deferring payment with respect to PDC for the foreseeable future has been seen by some critics as one of the major financial advantages of NHSTs over directly-managed units.

A NHST will have functions conferred by the Secretary of State under order. While the Act gives little indication of what may be involved, a NHST will have a statutory duty to carry out these functions 'effectively, efficiently and economically' (Sched 2, para 6). The powers vested with [sic] a NHST in furtherance of its functions are specified in more detail. A Trust will be able to enter NHS contracts, to commission research and provide training, to charge private patients for accommodation and services, and to generate income under the terms of the Health and Medicines Act 1988 (Sched 2, paras 10, 11, 12, 14, 15). There are also general powers to acquire and dispose of land, to enter contracts with non-NHS bodies necessary or expedient for the discharge of the Trust's functions, to accept gifts and to determine terms of employment of staff (Sched 2, para 16). Additionally, the Health Secretary may confer other powers on Trusts by order made by statutory instrument (s 5(10)).

NHSTs have been among the most controversial of the reforms. Many critics believe that they pave the way for an eventual transfer of units to private ownership, and that the 'playing field' has been decisively tilted to give NHSTs significant financial advantages over directly-managed units. The issue of possible ballots of staff and local electors where a hospital proposed to transfer to NHST status, provided one of the major focal points of opposition in Parliament. Other commentators are concerned that an absence of regulation by health authorities combined with incentives to maximise surpluses may carry a risk of moral hazard, perhaps through encouraging premature discharges or providing misleading information on case-mix. There are also fears that competitive pressures may stimulate the over-provision of sophisticated medical technology along North American lines.

In terms of the intellectual coherence of the reform package, the most significant characteristic of NHSTs may be the nomenclature that has been chosen. 'NHST' was substituted for the earlier term 'self-governing hospital', in part to open the way for a greater plurality of provider units, but also to combat the charge that such hospitals were 'opting out' of the NHS. Clearly, the major *symbolic* advantage of the term is the connotation of public benefit and the absence of the profit motive. But in what sense may NHSTs be regarded as trusts? Section 90 of the National Health Service Act 1977 provides for a health authority to accept, hold and administer any property on trust for all or any purpose relating to the health service. The 1990 Act enables the Secretary of State to appoint trustees for a NHST, with analogous powers to administer property on behalf of the NHST (s 11). However, this capacity to hold assets on trust hardly resolves the question of overall status. NHSTs are corporations established by statute and run by a Board of Directors appointed by the Health Secretary, which is a separate body from any trustees appointed. Could it be argued that the corporation itself functions as a trust for a beneficiary or beneficiaries?

The trust is a notoriously imprecise and diffuse concept. It is surrounded by a grey area in which, in the absence of any clear determination of status some, though not all of the provisions of trust law – such as a fiduciary duty – may be imposed. Where the specification of a NHST's powers and duties in the Statute leaves gaps, it might be that the title 'trust' would encourage the courts to seek analogies from trust law. However, it seems doubtful, in the case of the NHST, that close parallels will be found. First, although the 1990 Act provides for the transfer of assets to a NHST, it does not specify that these are to be held on trust and, in fact, the newly-established NHST is deemed to have an originating capital debt equal to the assets transferred (s 9). Second, a NHST has uncertain longevity: it may be dissolved if the Secretary of State 'considers it appropriate in the interests of the health service' and its assets transferred to the Secretary or another NHS body, to be used for unspecified purposes (Sched 2, paras 29-30). Third, if the NHST is to be regarded as a public trust, there may be difficulties in establishing charitable status. While it has been assumed that the general purposes of hospitals within the NHS are charitable, it seems unlikely that NHSTs will have this status. A trust is only a charity if it is exclusively for charitable purposes. For example, it must not distribute profits or dividends to individuals. This does not mean that charges cannot be made, but they must be applied for the purposes of the trust. It may be that a NHST's powers to charge private patients would cause problems here; certainly, there is the theoretical possibility that an operating surplus might be transferred to the Consolidated Fund and thus removed from the 'trust' (Sched 3, para 6).

Even more importantly, there is the issue of the independence of the NHST. While one may argue that the statute is effectively a charter or deed for the trust, declaring its rights and prescribing its duties, there is nothing to stop these definitions being varied by order. The open-ended nature of the primary legislation means that the NHST is subject to a degree of direct Government control that no ordinary trust or corporation experiences. Thus the Health Secretary may give the NHST such functions as he may specify, and he may determine the membership of NHST boards and the form of proceedings (ss 5(5), 5(7)). NHSTs must achieve the financial objectives set by the Secretary with the consent of the Treasury (s 10(2)). They must comply with the Health Secretary's directions on such matters as officers' qualifications, their appointment and employment, the retention of assets, and (subject to certain caveats) with directions and circulars to health authorities (Sched 2, para 6(2)). With respect to the financing of NHSTs, the Secretary has significant powers to regulate the terms and upper limits of borrowing, and he may direct the transfer of monies judged to be surplus to requirements to the Consolidated Fund (Sched 3, para 1, 3, 6). Finally – as already noted – the Health Secretary may dissolve a NHST and transfer its assets to another body. Against the background of these considerable executive powers, the term 'trust' would seem to be a misnomer. Had the Act used the style 'NHS Corporation' the powers and duties of the body would be the same. Of course, the *symbolic* connotations, in terms of the wider policy debate, might be significantly different.

The arrangements which exist between 'acquirers' and 'providers' differ depending upon who are the parties to the arrangement. Where a 'provider' is outside the NHS, the arrangement will be a contract between a DHA or 'fund-holder' and the private 'provider' and like any other commercial contract for the provision of services will be enforceable at law.

When the parties are within the NHS, arrangements will be formed by an entirely new regime which is, perhaps, the key feature of the 'internal market'. This is the 'NHS Contract'. David Hughes (*supra*) describes the nature of these 'NHS contracts' and identifies some problems which may arise.

Under the present Government, contract has emerged as a key concept in policies designed to establish the primacy of market forces in the provision of public services. The implementation of contractual relations in the NHS is a central plank of the reforms, but this is less straightforward than it seems. One of the most significant features of the 1990 Act is the creation of a new species of contract – here manifested in the form of the *NHS contract* – which may come to have increasing importance in those areas of public provision not amenable to privatisation.

The nature of the contracts to be employed in the re-organised service was one of the most difficult issues in the policy debate that preceded legislation. The outline description in the White Paper and Working Paper 2 has been considerably elaborated in further DoH guidance and discussion papers. Contracts will fall under three major headings. Those between DHAs and private sector providers will take a conventional legal form and be enforceable through the courts in the usual way. This involves very little change from the present situation, although it is expected that the number of such contracts will increase. DHAs and providers within the NHS will, however, stand in quite a different legal relationship, subject to different dispute-resolution mechanisms. The financial arrangements for DHA-managed hospitals will be structured as contracts, but will continue to be enforced through normal management processes. Here, contract seems to be essentially a metaphor, intended to signify a shift in the organisational culture rather than to have a direct practical effect. The 'contracts' to be placed between NHS bodies which have no direct management relationship do not, however, seem to fit either of these forms. These will cover arrangements such as those between a fund-holding GP and a hospital, or between a DHA and a NHST or a directly-managed hospital in another District. The latter, which are to be known as *NHS contracts*, imply a significant departure from the concept of contract in English law and are the subject of section 4 of the 1990 Act.

The classical model on which English contract law is based defines the contract as a voluntary agreement through which parties make legally binding promises. Each is free to enter other transactions and there is an absence of constraints affecting the operation of ordinary market forces. But *NHS contracts* will fail to meet all these conditions and frequently will meet none of them. First, the introduction of *NHS contracts* will itself be the outcome of central regulation; the product of legislation rather than the market. Public bodies entering such contracts will do so because it is a statutory requirement rather than necessarily because of the inherent economic advantages. Second, the internal market is – on closer inspection – a poor marketplace. Given the inescapable need to provide a range of key services locally and the DoH requirement that the services bought by DHAs reflect general practitioners' existing referral patterns, district general hospitals are likely to continue to be the only realistic contractors for a wide range of services in their local areas. Initially, at least, real choice over contract placement is likely to occur only in those areas of elective surgery where some hospitals have waiting lists and others do not – a rather small proportion of total activity in the health field.

Third, and most significantly, NHS contracts will not be enforceable in the courts in the usual way. In the immediate aftermath of the White Paper the legal status of contracts between NHS bodies was uncertain, but the greater rigour of the Parliamentary drafting process has clearly exposed the inherent difficulties of the *NHS contract* as a legal concept. The 1990 Act defines the *NHS contract* as an 'arrangement under which one health service body (the 'acquirer') arranges for the provision to it by another health service body (the 'provider') of goods and services which it reasonably requires for the purposes of its functions' (s 4(1)). Critically the Act provides that: 'Whether or not an arrangement which constitutes an NHS contract would, apart from this subsection, be a contract in law, it shall not be regarded for any purpose as giving rise to contractual rights or liabilities, but if any dispute arises with respect to such an arrangement, either party may refer the matter to the Secretary of State for determination under the following provisions of this section' (s 4(3)).

As an alternative to litigation or negotiation in the shadow of litigation, the DoH intends to create a special regime of conciliation and arbitration. Use of the courts is ruled out because a system of imposed public sector contracts violates the basic assumptions of contract law, and gives rise to problems – notably the pre-contractual dispute – with which ordinary contract law does not deal. Where parties to a proposed *NHS contract* cannot agree terms, or where collusion, unfair practice or false information is alleged, they will be required to submit to mandatory conciliation by Regional Health Authorities, followed, if necessary, by binding arbitration by the Secretary of State or his appointee. Disputes over alleged breach of contract will also be subject to arbitration. Here the arbitrator will normally be appointed by the parties, but either party retains the right to refer the matter to the Secretary of State for determination. The option of third party enforcement, perhaps through an independent arbitration agency, attracted considerable support in the discussions that followed publication of the White Paper. In the event the Act gives the Health Secretary maximum discretion to deal with disputes that are referred to him: he 'may determine the matter himself or, if he considers it appropriate, appoint a person to consider and determine it in accordance with regulations' (s 4(5)).

These dispute-resolution arrangements are undergirded by a range of reserve powers which appear to go well beyond what a narrow arbitration rule would require. As indicated above, the Health Secretary is empowered to deal not only with disputes over alleged breach (s 4(3)), but also disputes arising out of negotiations regarding a proposed contract (s 4(4)). Since the Secretary may specify terms to be included in a proposed contract and direct that it is proceeded with (s 4(6)), he can effectively impose a contract. With regard to disputes over existing contracts, the Secretary may vary the terms of an arrangement or bring it to an end (s 4(7)). He has power to impose 'directions' (including directions regarding payments) needed to give effect to variation or termination, and these are to be treated as if they were the result of agreement between the parties themselves. This power, of course, significantly exceeds the powers of judges in contract cases. While it is relatively common for judges to imply terms or interpret terms so as to rectify ambiguity or omissions in contracts, the imposition of terms without reference to the original intentions of the parties amounts to a very significant shift from traditional law. It is but one of a very substantial range of powers placed with the Health Secretary by the Act.

Recent DoH guidance suggests that recourse to arbitration may be limited by building 'clear disincentives to non-performance' into the contract itself. Thus a provider which fails to carry out contractual obligations might be required to subcontract the work to another provider at its own expense; or contract prices might be reduced *pro rata* to reflect unsatisfactory performance. However, the use of penalty clauses in a public sector environment is not without difficulties. Monetary penalties simply involve transferring funds between different pockets of the public purse, and are largely ineffective in situations where local monopoly suppliers cannot be allowed to go bankrupt.

NHS contracts will be enforced primarily through an administrative process. They will amount to a system of imposed, public sector contracts which has no obvious precedent in English contract law, and bears little resemblance to the North American system on which it is said to be modelled. As I have argued elsewhere, there may be unexpected and closer parallels with contracts in the planned economies of Eastern Europe. Certainly, problems that have arisen with these contracts – the proliferation of pre-contract disputes, the need to shift the emphasis in remedy from monetary damages to specific performance, and the tendency to blur legal and administrative controls – are also likely to surface in the NHS.

You will notice the point made by David Hughes that 'NHS contracts' are by virtue of section 4(3) not to be regarded 'as giving rise to contractual rights or liabilities'. Instead, any dispute is to be resolved by a mechanism of conciliation and arbitration by the Secretary of State (s 4(3)). This process includes not only disputes over existing contracts but also in relation to negotiations over the formation of NHS contracts. The dispute resolution mechanism, therefore, goes further than the general law which only deals with the former. The procedure is set out in the National Health Service Contracts (Dispute Resolution) Regulations 1991 (SI 1991 No 725).

Two points arise out of section 4(3). First, whilst NHS contracts are not contracts enforceable by the courts, the courts may, nevertheless, be called upon in certain circumstances to consider (or take account of) their terms. All the potential parties to an NHS contract are public bodies and, as a consequence, are amenable to judicial review if they exceed their statutory powers. As Hughes (*op cit*) points out:

> Since a trust's functions will be defined by the terms of the order by which it is established, any contract placed by it would need to be within the scope of the powers vested in the trust, or it might be subject to a public law action for judicial review seeking to show that the contract is *ultra vires*.

A similar argument could be made in relation to a DHA or GP fund-holder.

Another circumstance in which a court may be called upon to take account of the terms of an NHS contract would be in the context of an action in negligence against a 'provider' (or even, possibly, an 'acquirer') of services by an injured patient. A court might have to look to the terms of the NHS contract to determine the scope of any duty owed to the patient. This is a complex issue which we consider in Chapter 5 on medical malpractice.

Secondly, the definition of an 'NHS Contract' in section 4(1) may give rise to difficulties. Joe Jacob raises the point as follows.

J Jacob 'Lawyers Go to Hospital' [1990] PL 255

[S]ection 4(1) of the 1990 Act says that it is an arrangement under which an acquiring health service body arranges for the provision to it 'of goods or services which it reasonably requires for the purposes of its functions'. That is, an arrangement is not an *NHS contract* if the acquirer did not *reasonably* require the goods or services. If the goods or services were not reasonably required, the arrangement cannot be an *NHS contract* and the rest of the section making provision for such *contracts* does not apply. It is not difficult to imagine situations where goods or services may not be reasonably required but nevertheless their acquisition may not be *ultra vires* the corporation. Suppose an NHS body decided to acquire more goods than it reasonably needed for a particular year in order to dispose of a cash surplus (for example, to prevent it committing itself to recurrent expenditure or to guard against projected price rises or to be able to sell them out of a dominant market position). It is perhaps important that these last may be caught by European Community competition rules, and their application may itself depend on whether the arrangement was enforceable as a contract, that is, was not *reasonably required* so as to prevent it becoming an *NHS contract*.

If Jacob is correct, there is, however, a further point to notice. Arguably, the parties will not have an intention to create legal relations (and hence a legally enforceable contract) since they (erroneously) believed that they were creating an NHS contract. The arrangement, as a consequence, would not be subject to the dispute resolution procedure nor amenable to enforcement or interpretation by the courts. This does not seem to have been a situation anticipated by Parliament.

Services provided within the NHS

We need to examine here the legal framework within which a registered medical practitioner works as a GP or hospital doctor. We need to consider one general question first: is the legal relationship between a doctor and his patient who is being treated within the NHS contractual in nature? The answer would seem to be no.

A P Bell 'The Doctor and the Supply of Goods and Services Act 1982' (1984) 4 LS 175

The common law draws an important distinction between treatment under the National Health Service and private treatment. The House of Lords has held [*Pfizer Corpn v Ministry of Health* [1965] AC 512] that where services are provided pursuant to a statutory obligation there is no contractual relationship, for the element of compulsion is inconsistent with the consensual basis of contract. The fact that the patient makes some payment is irrelevant. Thus, the NHS patient can only sue in tort.

The Royal Commission on *Civil Liability and Compensation for Personal Injury* chaired by Lord Pearson in their 1978 Report (Cmnd 7054) take the same view.

Breach of contract
1313 Private patients may sue their doctors for a breach of contract if inadequate or faulty services have been provided, for example, if a swab has been left in the abdomen after an operation or if blood of the wrong blood group has been used in a transfusion. Under the National Health Service, however, there is no contract between patient and doctor and a plaintiff must rely on an action in tort. But the National Health Service patient is in no worse position than the private patient, because the same considerations determine if there has been a breach of duty whether the case is brought in contract or in tort.

Bell's position represents the orthodox view. The contrary, however, is not completely unarguable, on two bases. First, that the existence of a statutory duty to provide services by A may also serve as consideration for an agreement to provide the same services. The statutory duty may not be inconsistent with a contract based upon valuable consideration by the doctor. Secondly, consideration may actually move from the patient for whom the doctor promises to provide medical services, in that he agrees to have his name entered upon the medical list of the doctor in the knowledge that the doctor will be remunerated by the Family Health Service Authority. As a consequence, the patient provides good consideration.

A. BY GENERAL PRACTITIONERS

As part of the reform of the NHS presaged in the government's White Paper, *Working for Patients*, the terms of service of a GP, originally set out in the National Health Service (General Medical and Pharmaceutical Services) Regulations (SI 1974, No 160) were substantially amended in 1990. In particular the GP's role in health promotions and preventive health care was embodied in the new terms of service. Finally, in 1992 the Regulations were consolidated with amendments. They were also divided between 'general medical services' (National Health Service (General Medical Services) Regulations 1992 (SI 1992 No 635): hereafter the 'Medical Regulations'); and 'pharmaceutical services' (National Health Service (Pharmaceutical Services) Regulations 1992 (SI 1992 No 662): hereafter the 'Pharmaceutical Regulations'). A GP's terms of service are now set out in Schedule 2 to each of the respective Regulations. In essence, the GP is required to provide 'personal medical services' which are defined in paragraph 12(1) of Schedule 2 to the Medical Regulations as follows:

12. (1) Subject to paragraphs 3, 13 and 44, a doctor shall render to his patients all necessary and appropriate personal medical services of the type usually provided by general medical practitioners.

Paragraph 12(2) goes on to state:

12. (2) The services which a doctor is required by sub-paragraph (1) to render shall include the following –
(a) giving advice, where appropriate, to a patient in connection with the patient's general health, and in particular about the significance of diet, exercise, the use of tobacco, the consumption of alcohol and the misuse of drugs or solvents;
(b) offering to patients consultations and, where appropriate, physical examinations for the purpose of identifying, or reducing the risk of disease or injury;

   (c)   offering to patients, where appropriate, vaccination or immunisation against measles, mumps, rubella, pertussis, poliomyelitis, diphtheria and tetanus;

   (d)   arranging for the referral of patients, as appropriate, for the provision of any other services under the National Health Service Act 1977; and

   (e)   giving advice, as appropriate, to enable patients to avail themselves of services by a local social services authority.

In the new terms of service additional duties are imposed upon a GP as regards three specific classes of patient: *the newly registered patient, the patient who has not been seen for three years* and *the patient who is 75 or over.*

As regards 'newly registered patients', paragraph 14(1) provides that ' . . . Where a patient has been accepted on a doctor's list . . . , the doctor shall, in addition to and without prejudice to, his other obligations in respect of that patient under these terms of service, within 28 days . . . invite the patient to participate in a consultation . . . '. Paragraph 14(2) sets out the detailed obligations of a doctor, during the consultation:

14.(2)(a) seek details from the patient as to his medical history and, so far as may be relevant to the patient's medical history, as to that of his consanguineous family, in respect of –
   (i)   illnesses, immunisations, allergies, hereditary conditions, medication and tests carried out for breast or cervical cancer;
   (ii)   social factors (including employment, housing and family circumstances) which may affect his health;
   (iii)   factors of his lifestyle (including diet, exercise, use of tobacco, consumption of alcohol, and misuse of drugs or solvents) which may affect his health; and
   (iv)   the current state of his health;
   (b)   offer to undertake a physical examination of the patient, comprising –
   (i)   the measurement of his height, weight and blood pressure; and
   (ii)   the taking of a urine sample and its analysis to identify the presence of albumen and glucose;
   (c)   record, in the patient's medical records, his findings arising out of the details supplied by, and any examination of, the patient under this sub-paragraph;
   (d)   assess whether and, if so, in what manner and to what extent he should render personal medical services to the patient;
   (e)   in so far as it would not, in the opinion of the doctor, be likely to cause serious damage to the physical or mental health of the patient to do so, offer to discuss with the patient (or, where the patient is a child, the parent) the conclusions the doctor has drawn as a result of the consultation as to the state of the patient's health.

(Paragraph 14(4) sets out some exceptions to the duty under paragraph 14(1), for example, where the patient is a child under 5 years of age, or a patient who has had such a consultation within the preceding 12 months with another doctor in the partnership.)

As regards 'patients not seen within 3 years', the Medical Regulations until 1993 required the doctor to offer each patient on his list between the ages of 16 and 75 an opportunity to participate in a consultation with him. In 1993 the terms of service were amended (by SI 1993 No 540) so as to remove this obligation and only to require a consultation if the patient requested it. Paragraph 15(1) now provides that:

15. (1) . . . a doctor shall, in addition to and without prejudice to any other obligation under these terms of service, invite each patient on his list who appears to him –
   (a)   to have attained the age of 16 years but who has not attained the age of 75 years; and
   (b)   within the preceding 3 years have attended neither a consultation with, nor a clinic provided by, any doctor in the course of his provision of general medical services, requests a consultation for the purpose of assessing whether he needs personal medical services, a doctor shall in addition to and without prejudice to any other obligation under these terms of service, provide such a consultation.

Paragraph 15(4) specifies that:

15. (4) . . . the doctor shall, in the course of that consultation;
(a) where appropriate, seek details from the patient as to his medical history and, so far as may be relevant to the patient's medical history, as to that of his consanguineous family, in respect of –
  (i) illnesses, immunisations, allergies, hereditary diseases, medication and tests carried out for breast or cervical cancer;
  (ii) social factors (including employment, housing and family circumstances) which may affect his health;
  (iii) factors of his lifestyle (including diet, exercise, use of tobacco, consumption of alcohol, and misuse of drugs or solvents) which may affect his health; and
  (iv) the current state of his health;
(b) offer to undertake a physical examination of the patient, comprising –
  (i) the measurement of his blood pressure; and
  (ii) the taking of a urine sample and its analysis to identify the presence of albumen and glucose; and
  (iii) the measurement necessary to detect any changes in his body mass;
(c) record, in the patient's medical records, his findings arising out of the details supplied by, and any examination of, the patient under this sub-paragraph;
(d) assess whether and, if so, in what manner and to what extent he should render personal medical services to the patient; and
(e) in so far as it would not, in the opinion of the doctor, be likely to cause serious damage to the physical or mental health of the patient to do so, offer to discuss with the patient the conclusions the doctor has drawn as a result of the consultation as to the state of the patient's health.

As regards 'patients aged 75 and over', paragraph 16(1) provides that:

16. (1) . . . a doctor shall, in addition to and without prejudice to any other obligations under these terms of service, in each period of 12 months beginning on 1 April in each year –
(a) invite each patient on his list who has attained the age of 75 years to participate in a consultation; and
(b) offer to make a domiciliary visit to each such patient,
for the purpose of assessing whether he needs to render personal medical services to that patient.

In making the assessment following the consultation under sub-paragraph (1), paragraph 16(5) provides that the doctor shall:

16. (5) . . . record in the patient's medical records the observations made of any matter which appears to him to be affecting the patient's general health, including where appropriate the patient's –
(a) sensory functions;
(b) mobility;
(c) mental condition;
(d) physical condition including continence;
(e) social environment;
(f) use of medicines.

Paragraph 16(8) goes on to provide that:

16. (8) Where a patient has participated in a consultation pursuant to subparagraph (1), the doctor shall offer to discuss with him the conclusions he has drawn, as a result of the consultation, as to the state of the patient's health, unless to do so would, in the opinion of the doctor, be likely to cause serious harm to the physical or mental health of the patient.

As a consequence of providing the services already outlined, the Regulations impose on the doctor the duty to prescribe drugs or appliances and to issue certain certificates in appropriate circumstances. In certain exceptional circumstances a doctor is even under a duty to *dispense* drugs or appliances.

As regards *prescribing*, paragraph 43 provides:

43. . . . a doctor shall order any drugs or appliances which are needed for the treatment of any patient to whom he is providing treatment under these terms of service by issuing to that patient a prescription form, and such a form shall not be used in any other circumstances.

Under paragraph 44 a doctor is not ordinarily permitted to prescribe, for supply to a patient under his terms of service, a drug specified in Schedule 10 to the Medical Regulations. This Schedule set out those drugs or other substances which, in the view of the Government, should be obtained at the patient's expense rather than be a charge on the National Health Service.

As regards *certification*, paragraph 37(1) provides –

37. (1) A doctor shall issue free of charge to a patient or his personal representative any medical certificate of a description prescribed in . . . Schedule 9, which is reasonably required [for the purposes specified in that Schedule], except where, for the condition to which the certificate relates, the patient –
(a) is being attended by another doctor (other than a partner, assistant or other deputy of the first named doctor); or
(b) is not being treated by, or under the supervision of, a doctor.

As regards *dispensing*, the relevant obligations are not set out in the Medical Regulations but are contained in the Pharmaceutical Regulations. Regulation 19 of the Pharmaceutical Regulations provides –

19. A doctor –
(a) *shall provide* to a patient any appliance or drug, not being a Scheduled drug, where such provision is needed for the immediate treatment of that patient before a provision can be otherwise obtained; and
(b) *may provide* to a patient any appliance or drug, not being a Scheduled drug, which he personally administers or applies to that patient [our emphasis].

A 'Scheduled drug' is one listed in Schedule 10 to the Medical Regulations as being a drug which a doctor is not ordinarily permitted to prescribe for supply under his terms of service as we saw above. Notice in relation to regulation 19 only regulation 19(a) is mandatory, obviously by reason of the circumstances contemplated therein. Further, regulation 20(1) provides for the situations in which a patient either:

20. (1) (a) satisfies an FHSA that he would have serious difficulty in obtaining any necessary drugs or appliances from a pharmacy by reason of distance or inadequacy of means of communication; or
(b) is resident in a controlled locality [ie certain rural areas], at a distance of more than one mile from any pharmacy, and [subject to certain detailed provisions, see paragraph 20(2)]
he may at any time request in writing the doctor on whose list he is included to provide him with pharmaceutical services.

If, following a request under regulation 20(1), the doctor agrees to provide pharmaceutical services to this patient, the FHSA will then authorise the doctor on his application to do so (reg 20(3)(a)). If, however, the doctor does not agree to provide the services and so does not apply to the FHSA for permission to provide them, the FHSA may, nevertheless, require him to do so (reg 20(3)(b)) subject to the doctor demonstrating that he should not be required to provide such services on one of the grounds specified in regulation 20(5).

In addition to the services we have seen so far which every GP is *required* to offer there are *four* further services which a GP *may* undertake to the FHSA to offer to his patients (though this does not entail that he will undertake to provide them to each patient). Paragraph 12(3)(a) of the terms of service contained in Schedule 2 to the Medical Regulations provides that:

12. (3) A doctor is not required . . .
(a) to provide to any person child health surveillance services, contraceptive services, minor surgery services nor, except in an emergency, maternity medical services, unless he has previously undertaken to the FHSA to provide such services to that person.

This paragraph makes it clear, however, that in an emergency a doctor must provide maternity medical services regardless of whether he has previously undertaken to the FHSA to offer them.

The undertaking referred to in paragraph 12(3)(a) is to the FHSA since regulation 4 requires that the FHSA 'shall prepare a list, to be called the medical list' (regs 4(1)) and 4(4) goes on to provide:

4. (4) In respect of any doctor whose name is included in it, the medical list shall indicate –
(a) if he is on any of the child health surveillance list, the obstetric list or the minor surgery list;
(b) if the general medical services he has undertaken to provide include, exclude or are limited to maternity medical services;
(c) except in the case of a doctor who has requested otherwise, if he has undertaken to provide contraceptive services, and if so –
  (i)   whether he has so undertaken in respect only of patients for whom he or his partners have also undertaken to provide other general medical services, or
  (ii) whether he has so undertaken without such restriction . . .

As regards the provision of 'maternity medical services', paragraph 7 of the terms of service provides that a doctor *may* 'undertake to provide maternity services to a woman who has made an arrangement with him in accordance with regulation 31(2)'. Regulation 31(2) provides that –

31. (2) A woman who, after a doctor has diagnosed that she is pregnant, requires the provision of maternity medical services may arrange for the provision of any or all of the services . . . with –
(a) any doctor in the obstetric list;
(b) the doctor on whose list she is included; or
(c) any doctor who has accepted her as a temporary resident.

What this means is that where a woman's doctor does not agree to offer maternity medical services, or the woman would prefer to go to another doctor other than her regular GP, she may obtain these services alone from another doctor who is on the obstetric list and who has agreed to make an arrangement with her for their provision. This is also the case as regards the provision of 'contraceptive services'. Under paragraph 7 of the terms of service a doctor may 'undertake to provide contraceptive services to a woman who has applied to him in accordance with regulation 29'. Regulation 29 provides that –

29. (1) Whether or not she is included in his list for provision of other personal medical services, a woman may apply to a doctor who has undertaken to provide contraceptive services to be accepted by him for the provision of those services.

Where a doctor has made such an undertaking that fact will be indicated on the FHSA's medical list (reg 4(4)).

As regards 'child health surveillance services', which were introduced by the 1990 amendments to the (then) 1974 Regulations, regulation 28(1) and (2) of the 1992 Medical Regulations provides that:

28. (1) A parent may, in relation to a child of his who is under the age of 5 years, apply to a doctor –
(a) who is –
    (i)   the doctor on whose list the child is included (in this paragraph referred to as 'the child's doctor'),
    (ii) a doctor with whom the child's doctor is in partnership, or
    (iii) a doctor with whom the child's doctor is associated in a group practice; and
(b) whose name is included in any medical list and in the child health surveillance list of the FHSA,
for the provision of child health surveillance services in respect of that child for a period ending on the date on which that child attains the age of 5 years.
   (2) A doctor whose name is included in the medical list may, in respect of any person on his list or on the list of a doctor with whom he is in partnership or with whom he is associated in a group practice, undertake to provide child health surveillance services provided that –
(a) his name is also included in the child health surveillance list, and
(b) the person in question is a child who is under the age of 5 years.

As regards 'minor surgery services', which were also introduced in 1990, regulation 33(1) and (2) of the Medical Regulations provides that:

33. (1) A person may apply either in writing or in person to a doctor –
(a) who is –
    (i)   the doctor in whose list he is included (in this paragraph referred to as 'his own doctor'),
    (ii) a doctor with whom his own doctor is in partnership, or
    (iii) a doctor with whom his own doctor is associated in a group practice; and
(b) whose name is included in the medical list and the minor surgery list of the FHSA, for the provision of [minor surgery services] . . .
(2) A doctor whose name is included in the medical list may, in respect of any person on his list or on the list of a doctor with whom he is in partnership or with whom he is associated in group practice, undertake to provide minor surgery services, provided that his name is included in the minor surgery list.

You will notice that the opportunity to select, enjoyed by a woman as regards maternity medical services and contraceptive services, does not apply as regards the latter two services.

Further, the relevance of all these provisions is that a doctor may not provide the further optional services to persons who are not his patients unless his name appears on the relevant list maintained by the FHSA as offering them. Of course, there is nothing to stop a doctor carrying out these services for *his patients* as part of the provision to them of 'personal medical services'. If he does so, however, he will not qualify for payment by the FHSA specifically associated with the provision of these optional services. This is because he would not be supplying these further services within the terms of the regulations not least because he will not have demonstrated his fitness to do so as called for by the regulations (ie the regulations, as regards these further services, operate *inter alia* as a quality control mechanism).

What then are these four further services a GP may offer?

Maternity medical services are defined in regulation 31(1) as –

31. (1) Maternity medical services shall comprise –

(a) the provision of personal medical services to a woman during the ante-natal period;
(b) the provision of personal medical services to a woman during labour;
(c) the provision of personal medical services to a woman and to her baby . . . during the post-natal period; and
(d) the provision of a full post-natal examination.

(These services are further particularised in Part II of Schedule 5.)
Contraceptive services are defined in regulation 3(1)(c) as follows:

(i)   the giving of advice to women on contraception;
(ii)   the medical examination of women seeking such advice;
(iii) the contraceptive treatment of such women; and
(iv)   the supply to such women of contraceptive substances and appliances.

Child health surveillance services are described in regulation 28(3) and Schedule 4. Schedule 4 provides in paragraph 1 that:

1. The services . . . shall comprise –
(a) the monitoring –
   (i)   by the consideration of information concerning the child received by or on behalf of the doctor, and
   (ii) on any occasion when the child is examined or observed by or on behalf of the doctor (whether pursuant to sub-paragraph (b) or otherwise),
of the health, well-being and physical, mental and social development (all of which characteristics are referred to in this Schedule as 'development') of the child while under the age of 5 years with a view to detecting any deviations from normal development;
(b) the examination of the child by or on behalf of the doctor on so many occasions and at such intervals as shall have been agreed between the FHSA and the health authority in whose district the child resides (in this Schedule called 'the relevant health authority') for the purposes of the provision of child health surveillance services generally in that district.

Paragraphs 2 and 3 go on to specify the record of the child's development which must be compiled and information which must be made available to the relevant health authority.

Minor surgery services are described in regulation 33 of the 1992 Medical Regulations and Schedule 6 thereto; for example, these services include the excision of warts, the incision of abscesses and the removal of foreign bodies.

B. BY HOSPITALS AND OTHER NHS FACILITIES

What we are principally concerned with here is those functions which we have seen are delegated by the Secretary of State under the National Health Service Functions (Directions to Authorities and Administration Arrangements) Regulations 1991 (SI 1991 No 554) (as amended by SI 1992 No 659). As we saw, the Secretary of State is empowered to delegate his statutory duties, in effect, to provide for a National Health Service under sections 1-5 of the National Health Service Act 1977 by virtue of section 13 of the Act. In essence, these duties relate to the provision of hospitals and other NHS facilities not relating to GPs. The 1991 Regulations delegate his powers in England to the Regional Health Authorities (reg 3) and, in turn, the Regional Health Authorities are empowered (section 14 of the 1977 Act and reg 5) to delegate by instrument in writing, with some exceptions, their powers to the District Health Authorities. (In Wales the Secretary of State delegates his powers directly to the Districts (reg 7).) The exceptions relate, for example, to the supply of human blood (s 25 of the 1977 Act and reg 5(2)(b)). The powers (and, therefore, functions delegated) to the Regions are set out in the Schedule to the regulations which provides as follows:

SCHEDULE

ENACTMENTS CONFERRING FUNCTIONS EXERCISABLE BY REGIONAL AND DISTRICT AUTHORITIES

Enactment	Subject Matter
Health Services and Public Health Act 1968 – sections 63(1), (3), (5) and (6)	Providing for instruction of officers of health authorities and other persons employed or contemplating employment by health authorities connected with health or welfare.
section 64	Giving financial assistance to voluntary organisations.
Chronically Sick and Disabled Persons Act 1970 –	
section 17	Provision with respect to persons under 65.
The Act [ie National Health Service Act 1977] –	
section 2	Providing services considered appropriate for discharging duties imposed on the Secretary of State and doing other things calculated to facilitate the discharge of any such duty.
section 3(1)(a) and (b)	Providing hospital and other accommodation.
section 3(1)(c)	Providing medical, dental, nursing and ambulance services.
section 3(1)(d)	Providing facilities for the care of expectant and nursing mothers and young children.
section 3(1)(e)	Providing facilities for the prevention of illness, the care of persons suffering from illness and the aftercare of persons who have suffered from illness.
section 3(1)(f)	Providing other services required for the diagnosis and treatment of illness.
section 5(1), (1A) and paragraph 1 of Schedule 1	Providing for the medical inspection and treatment of pupils, their dental inspection and treatment and their education in dental health.
section 5(1)(b)	Arranging for the giving of advice on contraception, for the medical examination of persons seeking such advice, for the treatment of such persons and for the supply of contraceptive substances and appliances.

Enactment	Subject Matter
section 5(2)(d)	Conducting or assisting, by grants or otherwise, persons to conduct research into matters relating to illness or other matters connected with a service provided under the Act.
section 19(1), (2) and (3) and paragraphs 1, 2 and 3 of Schedule 6	Recognising regional and district advisory committees.
section 23(1)	Arranging with any person or body (including a voluntary organisation) for that person or body to provide or assist in providing any service under the Act.
section 23(2)	Making available to certain persons or bodies (including voluntary organisations) facilities and services of persons employed in connection with such facilities.
section 23(3)	Agreeing terms and making payments in respect of facilities or services provided under section 23 of the Act.
section 25 other than paragraphs (b) and (c)	Making available supplies of human blood.
section 26(1)	Supplying goods, services and other facilities to local authorities and other public bodies and carrying out maintenance work in connection with any land or building the maintenance of which is a local authority responsibility.
section 26(2)	Supplying prescribed goods, materials or other facilities to persons providing general medical services, general dental services, general ophthalmic services or pharmaceutical services.
section 26(3)	Making available to local authorities any services or other facilities and the services of employed persons to enable local authorities to discharge their function relating to social services, education and public health.
section 26(4)	Making available to local authorities the services of contractors to enable such authorities to discharge their functions relating to social services, education and public health.
section 27(1) and (2)	Providing for consultation before the services of any officer of a health authority are made available to a local authority.
section 27(4)	Agreeing terms and charging for services and facilities provided.
section 51	Making available facilities for university clinical teaching and research.
section 52	Making accommodation available.

Enactment	Subject Matter
section 63	Authorising use of hospital accommodation, determining the extent to which it is to be made available and determining and recovering charges in respect of the use of such accommodation.
section 72(1), (3), (4) and (5)	Making available health service accommodation or facilities for the purpose of providing medical, dental, pharmaceutical, ophthalmic or chiropody services to non-resident private patients.
section 81(a)	Charging and recovering the charges for more expensive supplies.
section 82(a)	Charging for replacement or repair of appliances and vehicles in certain circumstances.
section 83A(1)(b)	Paying travelling expenses.
section 87(1) and (2)	Acquiring land or other property required for the purpose of the Act and the use or maintenance of any property belonging to the Secretary of State by virtue of the Act.
section 121	Determining charges for prescribed services provided in respect of prescribed non-residents.
Mental Health Act 1983 – section 12(2)	Approving medical practitioners as having special experience in the diagnosis and treatment of mental disorder.
Registered Homes Act 1984 – section 23(3), (4) and (5)	Registration of nursing homes and mental nursing homes.
section 25	Refusal of registration.
section 26	Conduct of homes.
section 27	Supplementary.
section 28	Cancellation or registration.
section 29(1), (2) and (3)	Additional registration conditions.
section 30	Urgent procedure for registration, cancellation, variation of conditions and additional conditions.
section 32	Representations.
section 33(1) and (2)	Decisions.
section 34(2) and (7)	Appeals.
section 35(1), (3) and (4)	Authorisation of persons to inspect mental nursing homes.
section 37	Exemption of Christian Science homes.
section 53(1)	Criminal proceedings.

In addition to the general duties and functions of the Secretary of State which have been delegated to the Regional Health Authorities and District Health Authorities, the 1977 Act allows the Secretary of State to create special bodies for 'the purpose of performing any function which he may direct the body to perform on his behalf . . . ' (s 11). These are known as 'special health authorities' (s 11(3)). There are a number of these created by statute. For our purposes two are of interest: the National Blood Authority established to manufacture blood products (see the National Blood Authority (Establishment and Constitution) Order 1993 (SI 1993 No 585)); and the United Kingdom Transplant Support Service Authority responsible for maintaining a service for the collection and supply of human organs (see the United Kingdom Transplant Support Service Authority (Establishment and Constitution) Order 1991 (SI 1991 No 407) and the United Kingdom Transplant Support Service Authority Regulations 1991 (SI 1991 No 408)).

The Secretary of State must also 'provide and maintain establishments [. . . "special hospitals"] for persons subject to detention under the Mental Health Act 1983 who, in his opinion, require treatment under conditions of special security on account of their dangerous, violent or criminal propensities' (s 4 of the 1977 Act). The duty contained in this section is now discharged by a 'special health authority' established in 1989 under section 11, called the 'Special Hospitals Service Authority' which provides and maintains special hospitals at Broadmoor, Rampton, Moss Side and Park Lane (see the Special Hospitals Service Authority (Establishment and Constitution) Order 1989 (SI 1989 No 948) and the Special Hospitals Service Authority (Functions and Membership) Regulations 1989 (SI 1989 No 949)).

One final example of a statutory function placed upon the Secretary of State under the 1977 Act which is not delegated to the Regional Health Authorities and the District Health Authorities is contained in section 5(2)(c) of the 1977 Act. This provides that the Secretary of State may 'provide a microbiological service, which may include the provision of laboratories, for the control of the spread of infectious diseases . . . '. Pursuant to section 5(4) and (5) such of these functions as are allocated to it by the Secretary of State are carried out by the Public Health Laboratory Service Board constituted by section 5(5) of and Schedule 3 to the 1977 Act as a body corporate.

C. BY NHS TRUSTS

Paragraph 6(1) of Schedule 2 to the National Health Service and Community Care Act 1990 provides that:

> . . . an NHS trust shall carry out effectively, efficiently and economically the functions for the time being conferred on it by an order [made by the Secretary of State] under section 5(1) of this Act . . .

Clearly, therefore, in general terms, the services offered by an NHS Trust will be those contained in the Order. These will relate to services which previously fell within the duties and powers of the Secretary of State and through him health authorities under the 1977 Act. The specific services which will be provided to any particular patient will be determined by the 'NHS contract' made between the Trust as 'provider' and the 'purchaser' of the service on behalf of the patient.

There is nothing more that needs to be said in general terms. There is, however, one point of general importance which arises. Notwithstanding the fact that an NHS contract would purport to determine the services that must be provided by an NHS Trust in any given case, it could well be argued that, in the case of any particular patient, the Trust must meet a minimum standard of reasonable care regardless of the terms of the NHS contract. In legal terms, this is properly to be understood as a question relating to the scope of the Trust's primary liability (see Chapter 5).

The patient

It may seem blindingly obvious who are a doctor's patients. However, the relevant law may not be quite as straightforward. As we shall see, who is a patient analytically turns upon there being an agreement (usually not express) between a doctor and an individual. What is involved in this agreement is a request for medical services by an individual and a consequent undertaking by a doctor to provide these services. Out of this factual request and undertaking, the law forges the legal relationship of doctor and patient. For us the key significance of this legal consequence is that the doctor will, as a matter of law, owe the individual (now, his patient) a duty of care. Given that the law does impose this duty upon a doctor it is, obviously, of critical importance to determine *when* the relationship of doctor and patient is legally created.

While the coincidence of a 'request' by an individual and a resulting 'undertaking' by a doctor adequately captures the normal case, in fact there are situations in which the legal relationship will come into existence without there having been a 'request' on the part of the individual. The doctor, however, must always have given an undertaking of some sort or other to provide medical care before the law will recognise the legal relationship and his duty which flows from it. Examples of these latter situations are where a parent seeks medical care on behalf of a young child or where an emergency arises and the individual is unconscious. We can consider these situations later.

A. REQUEST BY THE INDIVIDUAL

Let us now consider the circumstances in which the law recognises that a doctor-patient relationship exists between an individual and the various kinds of doctor.

1. The general practitioner

(a) Creation of the relationship

An individual becomes a patient (in a formal sense) of a GP through a mechanism created under the National Health Service (General Medical Services) Regulations (SI 1992 No 635) 1992 (the 'Medical Regulations'). In essence, the procedure requires the individuals to apply to be included on a particular GP's list (reg 20). The doctor may then accept the individual on his list(s) as a patient (paragraph 6(1) of the terms of service).

The consequence of this is that the GP, by virtue of his terms of service, undertakes to provide the relevant medical services to the patient. In other words, what is involved is a general request followed by a general undertaking upon acceptance, but a *duty* between the GP and the individual only concretises when the GP is requested to provide, or becomes aware of the need for, the medical services.

The qualifying conditions whereby an individual may become a GP's patient in the formal sense require an understanding of the 1992 Medical Regulations. Whether thereafter a patient (in the formal sense) is actually owed a duty by the GP is largely a factual matter turning upon whether a request for services has been made or whether the GP is aware of the possible need for such services.

Regulation 20 sets out the basic mechanism of application by an individual to become a GP's patient.

> 20. (1) An application to a doctor for inclusion in his list for the provision of general medical services shall be made by delivering to the doctor a medical card or a form of application signed (in either case) by the applicant or a person authorised on his behalf.

You will recall that a woman may apply to a doctor other than the one on whose list she is included for the provision of 'maternity medical services' providing the doctor is on the obstetric list (reg 31(2)), or for 'contraceptive services' (reg 29(1)). In either case, the doctor may undertake to provide those services to the woman (paragraph 7 of the terms of service).

Exceptionally, as regulation 21 indicates, a patient may be assigned to a GP, ie the GP has no option but to undertake to provide services. Regulation 21 provides:

> 21. (1) Where –
> (a) a person who is not on the list of any doctor has been refused acceptance by a doctor for inclusion in his list; or
> (b) a person has been refused acceptance by a doctor as a temporary resident,
> he may apply to the FHSA for assignment to a doctor, and the provisions of this regulation shall apply in relation to that application.
>
> (2) An application under paragraph (1) shall be made in writing and shall be considered by the FHSA, which shall assign the applicant to such doctor in its medical list as it thinks fit, having regard to –
> (a) the respective distances between the person's residence and the practice premises of the doctors in the part of the locality in question;
> (b) whether within the previous six months the person has been removed from the list of any doctor in that part of the locality at the request of that doctor; and
> (c) such other circumstances, including those concerning the doctors in that part of the locality and their practices, as the FHSA think relevant,
> and shall notify the doctor accordingly.
>
> (3) Nothing in paragraph (2) shall –
> (a) require a doctor to provide child health surveillance services, contraceptive services, maternity medical services or minor surgery services for a patient who is assigned to him unless, pursuant to regulation 28, 29, 31 or 33, as the case may be, he has accepted that patient for the provision of such services; or
> (b) enable the FHSA to assign any person to a doctor whose list is at or exceeds the maximum permitted by regulation 24, without the consent of the Secretary of State.
> . . .
> (11) The FHSA may exempt from the liability to have persons assigned to him under this regulation any doctor who applies to the FHSA for that purpose, and in considering such an application shall have regard to the doctor's age, state of health and the number of persons on his list and the FHSA shall notify any such doctor in writing of any decision under this paragraph.

Paragraph 4 of the terms of service in summary form lists those individuals who are a GP's patients.

> 4. (1) . . . a doctor's patients are –
> (a) persons who are recorded by the FHSA as being on his list;

   (b)   persons whom he has accepted or agreed to accept on his list, whether or not notification of that acceptance has been received by the FHSA, and who have not been notified to him by the FHSA as having ceased to be on his list;

   (c)   for the limited period specified in sub-paragraph (4), persons whom he has refused to accept;

   (d)   persons who have been assigned to him under regulation 21;

   (e)   for the limited period specified in sub-paragraph (5), persons in respect of whom he has been notified that an application has been made for assignment to him in a case to which regulation 21(3)(b) applies;

   (f)   persons whom he has accepted as temporary residents;

   (g)   in respect of [*inter alia*, cervical smears, vaccinations, child health surveillance services and minor surgery services] persons to whom he has agreed to provide those services;

   (h)   persons to whom he may be requested to give treatment which is immediately required owing to an accident or other emergency at any place in his practice area, provided that –

       (i)   he is not, at the time of the request, relieved of liability to give treatment under paragraph 5, [ie is elderly or infirm] and

      (ii)   he is not, at the time of the request, relieved, under paragraph 19(2), of his obligation to give treatment personally, [ie by reason of having employed a deputy] and

     (iii)   he is available to provide such treatment,

and any persons by whom he is requested, and agrees, to give treatment which is immediately required owing to an accident or other emergency at any place in the locality of any FHSA in whose medical list he is included, provided there is no doctor who, at the time of the request, is under an obligation otherwise than under this head to give treatment to that person, or there is such a doctor but, after being requested to attend, he is unable to attend and give treatment immediately required;

   (i)   persons in relation to whom he is acting as deputy for another doctor under these terms of service;

   (j)   during the period [when a doctor is temporarily providing services] under regulation 25, persons whom he has been appointed to treat temporarily;

   (k)   in respect of child health surveillance services, contraceptive services, maternity medical services, or minor surgery services persons for whom he has undertaken to provide such services; and

   (l)   during the hours arranged with the FHSA, any person whose own doctor has been relieved of responsibility during those hours . . . and for whom he has accepted responsibility . . .

   (2) Except in a case to which head (h), (i) or (j) of sub-paragraph (1) applies, no person shall be a patient for the purposes of that sub-paragraph if the doctor has been notified by the FHSA that he is no longer responsible for the treatment of that person.

   (3) Where a person applies to a doctor for treatment and claims to be on that doctor's list, but fails to produce his medical card on request and the doctor has reasonable doubts about that person's claim, the doctor shall give any necessary treatment and shall be entitled to demand and accept a fee . . .

   (4) Where a doctor refuses to accept for inclusion on his list a person who lives in his practice area and who is not on the list of another doctor practising in that area, or refuses to accept as a temporary resident a person to whom regulation 26 [relating to temporary residents] applies, he shall on request give that person any immediately necessary treatment for one period not exceeding 14 days from the date when that person was refused acceptance or until that person has been accepted by or assigned to another doctor, whichever period is the shorter.

   (5) Where the FHSA has notified a doctor that it is applying for the Secretary of State's consent under regulation 21(3)(b) [see above], the doctor shall give the person proposed for assignment any immediately necessary treatment until the FHSA has notified him that –

   (a)   the Secretary of State has determined whether or not the person is to be assigned to that doctor; and

   (b)   either the person has been accepted by, or assigned to, another doctor or another doctor has been notified that an application has been made, in a case to which regulation 21(3)(b) applies, to assign that person to him.

As paragraph 4 makes plain, the existence of a GP-patient relationship is normally characterised by the twin features of 'request' by the individual and 'undertaking' by the doctor. There are, however, a number of exceptions to this. The most significant relates to the provision of care in emergencies which we will deal with later (see *infra*). The other exceptions we can conveniently notice here. They relate to the circumstances contemplated, first in paragraph 4(4) above and secondly in regulation 25 and paragraph 4(1)(j) above where the patient's previous GP has died, retired or whose registration has been suspended.

(b) Termination of the relationship

The formal relationship between a GP and a patient may be brought to an end when the GP withdraws his undertaking in the manner prescribed in paragraphs 9-11 of the terms of service.

9. (1) A doctor may have any person removed from his list and shall notify the FHSA in writing that he wishes to have a person removed from his list and, subject to sub-paragraph (2), the removal shall take effect –
(a) on the date on which the person is accepted by or assigned to another doctor; or
(b) on the eighth day after the FHSA receives the notice,
whichever is the sooner.
(2) Where, at the date when the removal would take effect under sub-paragraph (1), the doctor is treating the person at intervals of less than 7 days, the doctor shall inform the FHSA in writing of the fact and the removal shall take effect –
(a) on the eighth day after the FHSA receives notification from the doctor that the person no longer needs such treatment; or
(b) on the date on which the person is accepted by or assigned to another doctor,
whichever is the sooner.
10. Where a doctor informs the FHSA in writing that he wishes to terminate his responsibility for a temporary resident, his responsibility for that person shall cease in accordance with paragraph 9, as if the temporary resident were a person on his list.
11. (1) A doctor with whom an arrangement has been made for the provision of any or all of the maternity medical services mentioned in regulation 31(1)(a) may agree with the woman concerned to terminate the arrangement, and in default of agreement the doctor may apply to the FHSA for permission to terminate the arrangement.
(2) On an application under paragraph (1), the FHSA, after considering any representations made by either party and after consulting the Local Medical Committee, may terminate the arrangement.
(3) Where a doctor ceases to provide any or all of the maternity medical services mentioned in regulation 31(1)(a), he shall inform any woman for whom he has arranged to provide such services that he is ceasing to provide them and that she may make a fresh arrangement to receive those services from another doctor.

Merely by complying with this procedure, a doctor may not necessarily cease to be responsible for the individual. First, until the individual is accepted by (or assigned to) another GP, the formal relationship may come into being once more under paragraph 4(a) if the individual requests treatment which is 'immediately necessary'. Secondly, irrespective of the formal relationship, the doctor may continue to owe any individual who is currently receiving treatment a duty of care until such time as it is reasonable for that treatment to be taken over by another doctor; in other words, whatever the terms of service may say, the doctor may not abandon an individual whom he is treating.

2. The hospital doctor

When a patient attends a hospital whether as an in-patient or out-patient, at least two distinct legal relationships call for analysis: the relationship between doctor and patient and between the hospital and the patient. (We use the word 'patient' in the context of this second relationship for convenience only. We take the view that a person can only be the patient *stricto sensu* of a doctor, although a hospital may owe him a duty of care under the law of negligence, as we shall see.) Here we are concerned with the relationship between the hospital doctor and the patient.

In the classic (though now dated) work by Lord Nathan, *Medical Negligence* (1957), the underlying explanation of how and why the doctor-patient relationship exists is stated (pp 8 and 10):

> The medical man's duty of care arises . . . quite independently of any contract with his patient. It is based simply upon the fact that the medical man has undertaken the care and treatment of the patient.

Later Nathan continues:

> It is clear then that the duty of care which is imposed upon the medical man arises quite independently of contract. It is a duty in tort which is based upon the relationship between the medical man and his patient, owing its existence to the fact that the medical man has assumed responsibility for the care, treatment or examination of the patient, as the case may be.

This, in our view, properly reflects the position in English law, as far as it goes, as regards the hospital doctor. Of course, it needs some rather more rigorous analysis. At what point can we determine that the doctor has undertaken the care and treatment of the patient? Put another way, when has the doctor 'assumed responsibility' for the patient?

A patient is admitted to an NHS hospital through a formal procedure of reference by a GP and acceptance by a consultant after consultation with the hospital's manager. The admission is to occupy a bed assigned to the relevant consultant within the hospital. The question immediately arises as to the point at which the doctor-patient relationship is created. You will realise immediately that for the medical lawyer the importance of this is to determine when, if at all, a duty is owed by a doctor to a particular person.

If the principle is that the doctor must have undertaken to care for the person, the question is when, in fact, will that undertaking be judged to have been given in law. It will arise somewhere along the continuum which begins with the patient being at home and ends with the doctor embarking on the first 'laying on of hands'. It is important to remember we are concerned with the *doctor's* undertaking and consequent duty. Others, such as nurses or the hospital itself, may owe a patient their own duty from a different point in time.

Ordinarily, it will be clear in any given case whether a doctor has or has not undertaken to care for someone. At the margins, however, there could be a doubt. For example, it may not always be obvious in a case where the doctor has not yet met (nor is aware of the presence of) the person who has been admitted to the hospital under his care. The patient may meanwhile have been put in the wrong bed or have received inappropriate care such as being given a meal when he should not have been.

In determining whether in these situations at the margin there will be an 'undertaking', it may be helpful to bear in mind the following considerations. First, the admitting consultant could be said to have undertaken to make all appropriate arrangements for the individual to be admitted and what follows thereafter. It is unlikely, however, that the doctor will be regarded as having undertaken (absent an express statement to that effect) to be on hand at all times to deal with every eventuality that may arise.

Returning to the general theme of 'undertaking', a patient, in the context of hospital care will be in the care of a team of doctors headed by the consultant. Of course, there will be other teams of professionals not necessarily led by the consultant but our concern here is only with the position of the doctors. Ordinarily each member of the team of doctors will be deemed to have separately undertaken the care of the patient when so assigned by the responsible consultant. However, the consultant as leader of the team remains responsible throughout because his undertaking of the care of the patient continues throughout the care of the patient.

If determining when an undertaking arises is sometimes difficult even *after* admission, it may be equally difficult when the individual is in the hospital but has not yet gone through the formal process of admission. Take, for example, the situation where a person walks into a hospital and suffers an unexpected heart attack requiring immediate care. Here, only in very exceptional circumstances will the admitting doctor be said to have undertaken to care for the person. It does not follow, however, that no duty is owed to the individual. The *hospital* may be judged to have undertaken to care for all those who enter once one of its employees has knowledge that a person needs, or may be in need of, medical attention. In this situation, the hospital could be exposed to primary liability for breach (if established) of its own duty to the individual (see Chapter 5).

The last area of difficulty concerning 'undertaking' arises where the doctor is *prima facie* a stranger to a patient who is under the care of another doctor. Take, for example, the situation where a doctor in one team is asked by a nurse to help to care for a patient under the care of another consultant (and he is not part of that consultant's team). The solution to the question whether he becomes that patient's doctor lies in the principle that the law does not require a doctor to act as a good Samaritan towards any person in the absence of an undertaking by the doctor to take care of that person. It is problematic whether the law would deem there to be an undertaking here, but the presence of the doctor and the existence of a need could well lead the law to reach that conclusion.

3. Doctors outside the NHS

(a) Introduction

Outside the NHS the same analytical model, of a 'request' by the individual and 'undertaking' by a doctor, applies so as to determine when someone is owed a duty as a patient. Ordinarily, there will be a contract between the parties which will set out the nature and scope of the undertaking. It may be that in emergencies, as we shall see, a duty of care arises as much in private practice as within the NHS such that the doctor by virtue of holding himself out as being engaged, at a particular time, in doing what doctors do may be deemed to have undertaken to render necessary care.

Curiously, although the coming into existence of a contract between a doctor and patient is critical, there is little guidance to be found in the law as to when the contract is formed. Given that there must be an offer and acceptance (together with consideration), who is it who offers and who accepts? Is it the patient who offers to pay if the doctor agrees to treat, or the patient who accepts the doctor's offer to treat by agreeing to pay? Ellen Picard, in *Legal*

Liability of Doctors and Hospitals in Canada (2nd edn 1984) (at pp 1-2), writes: 'The offer could be found [in law] in the patient's request for treatment and the acceptance in the doctor's commencement of care. Consideration [is] not a problem unless the patient [is] unable to pay. In such circumstances the law of contract [is] that the patient's submission to treatment [is] sufficient consideration for the doctor's services' (citing *Coggs v Bernard* (1703) 2 Ld Raym 909 and *Banbury v Bank of Montreal* [1918] AC 626).

The law of contract, of course, has limited application in regulating the relationship between doctor and patient in England and Wales because most doctor-patient contacts are within the NHS, to which the law of contract does not apply, as we have seen. It is therefore in the context of private practice that the law of contract operates.

(b) Terms

(i) EXPRESS TERMS

This is entirely a matter of what the parties agree amongst themselves, for example, as to payment or who may carry out a particular procedure. A consent form is an example of an agreement containing express terms (see *Thake v Maurice* [1986] 1 All ER 497 and *Eyre v Measday* [1986] 1 All ER 488).

There are, of course, limits to what the parties may purport to agree through express terms. They cannot, for example, agree to do that which would be regarded as contrary to public policy, for example, selling an organ (see *infra*), nor to waive those obligations implied by law.

(ii) IMPLIED TERMS

I. Reasonable care and skill. In two cases in 1986 involving a sterilisation procedure which failed, the Court of Appeal analysed the legal obligations of the doctor to his patient with whom he had contracted to carry out the procedure. In *Eyre v Measday* [1986] 1 All ER 488, Slade LJ said:

> Applying the *Moorcock* principle, I think there is no doubt that the plaintiff would have been entitled reasonably to assume that the defendant was warranting that the operation would be performed with reasonable care and skill. That, I think, would have been the inevitable inference to be drawn, from an objective standpoint . . . The contract did, in my opinion, include an implied warranty of *that* nature.

Similarly, in the later case of *Thake v Maurice* [1986] 1 All ER 497, Nourse LJ observed:

> The particular concern of this court in *Eyre v Measday* was to decide whether there had been an implied guarantee that the operation would succeed. But the approach of Slade LJ in testing that question objectively is of equal value in a case where it is said that there has been an express guarantee. Valuable too are the observations of Lord Denning MR in *Greaves & Co (Contractors) Ltd v Baynham, Meikle & Partners* [1975] 3 All ER 99 at 103-104, [1975] 1 WLR 1095 at 1100 which I now quote in full:
>
> > Apply this to the employment of a professional man. The law does not usually imply a warranty that he will achieve the desired result, but only a term that he will use reasonable care and skill. The surgeon does not warrant that he will cure the patient. Nor does the solicitor warrant that he will win the case.

Neill LJ in the same case said: 'It is common ground that the defendant contracted to perform a vasectomy operation on Mr Thake and that in the performance of that contract he was subject to the duty implied by law to carry out the operation with reasonable skill and care.'

But notice that Oliver J (as he then was), when talking about the nature of a professional person's obligations, in *Midland Bank Trust Co Ltd v Hett, Stubbs & Kemp* [1979] Ch 384, makes it clear that the implied term that the professional person will use reasonable care and skill is a less than complete description of his obligations.

> **Oliver J:** The classical formulation of the claim in this sort of case as 'damages for negligence and breach of professional duty' tends to be a mesmeric phrase. It concentrates attention on the implied obligation to devote to the client's business that reasonable care and skill to be expected from a normally competent and careful practitioner as if that obligation were not only a compendious, but also an exhaustive, definition of all the duties assumed under the contract created by the retainer and its acceptance. But, of course, it is not. A contract gives rise to a complex of rights and duties of which the duty to exercise reasonable care and skill is but one.
>
> If I employ a carpenter to supply and put up a good quality oak shelf for me, the acceptance by him of that employment involves the assumption of a number of contractual duties. He must supply wood of an adequate quality and it must be oak. He must fix the shelf. And he must carry out the fashioning and fixing with the reasonable care and skill which I am entitled to expect of a skilled craftsman. If he fixes the brackets but fails to supply the shelf or if he supplies and fixes a shelf of unseasoned pine, my complaint against him is not that he has failed to exercise reasonable care and skill in carrying out the work but that he has failed to supply what was contracted for.

Rupert Jackson and John Powell in *Professional Negligence* (3rd edn 1992) comment on Oliver J's views (para 1.10):

> The particular illustration chosen by Oliver J . . . must be used with caution, since the obligations of a carpenter to his employer are generally of a different nature to those owed by a professional man to his client. Nevertheless in every contract between a professional man and his client there will be express or implied terms defining the nature of the engagement. Thus if a surveyor is instructed to produce a report on certain property, there is an express or implied obligation to inspect it. If a surgeon agrees with his patient to perform a particular operation, there may be an implied term that he will 'give the necessary supervision thereafter until the discharge of the patient'. If a solicitor is instructed to effect the grant of an option, there are implied terms that he will draw up the option agreement and effect registration. The importance of specific terms such as these is that a professional man will be liable if he breaks them, quite irrespective of the amount of skill and care which he has exercised.

An example of an implied term other than to exercise care and skill arises, for example, in the case of a doctor fitting a prosthesis. In such a case the question arises as to whether the terms implied by law by virtue of the Supply of Goods and Services Act 1982 as to the fitness for the purpose of the goods supplied or their merchantable quality apply (see generally, Bell (1984) 4 LS 175). Similarly, a contract will have implied into it an obligation to keep the patient's medical information confidential (*Furniss v Fitchett* [1958] NZLR 396).

II. Guarantee of success. It is one thing for the law to expect a contract to be performed properly, it is quite another to demand of the doctor that he guarantee success unless he has expressly agreed to do so. As Nourse LJ stated in *Thake v Maurice* (*supra*):

> Lord Denning MR thought [in *Greaves v Baynham, Meikle & Partners*], and I respectfully agree with him, that a professional man is not usually regarded as warranting that he will achieve the desired result. Indeed, it seems that that would not fit well with the universal

warranty of reasonable care and skill, which tends to affirm the inexactness of the science which is professed. I do not intend to go beyond the case of a doctor. Of all sciences medicine is one of the least exact. In my view a doctor cannot be objectively regarded as guaranteeing the success of any operation or treatment unless he says as much in clear and unequivocal terms. The defendant did not do that in the present case.

Courts in other jurisdictions have been prepared to find that a doctor has guaranteed a particular result and when he has failed to achieve it, they have allowed the patient to succeed in an action for breach of contract. Two cases involving cosmetic surgery illustrate this. In *Sullivan v O'Connor* (1973) 296 NE 2d 183 (Cal Sup Ct) the plaintiff, a professional entertainer, sued the defendant because of the condition of her nose after he had operated. Justice Kaplan described the plaintiff's condition as follows:

> ... judging from exhibits, the plaintiff's nose had been straight, but long and prominent; the defendant undertook by two operations to reduce its prominence and somewhat to shorten it, thus making it more pleasing in relation to the plaintiff's other features. Actually the plaintiff was obliged to undergo three operations, and her appearance was worsened. Her nose now had a concave line to about the midpoint, at which it became bulbous; viewed frontally, the nose from bridge to midpoint was flattened and broadened, and the two sides of the tip had lost symmetry. This configuration evidently could not be improved by further surgery.

The court allowed the plaintiff to recover for breach of contract. The court went on, however, to warn of the difficulties facing plaintiffs who allege that a doctor guaranteed success:

> It is not hard to see why the courts should be unenthusiastic or skeptical about the contract theory. Considering the uncertainties of medical science and the variations in the physical and psychological conditions of individual patients, doctors can seldom in good faith promise specific results. Therefore it is unlikely that physicians of even average integrity will in fact make such promises. Statements of opinion by the physician with some optimistic coloring are a different thing, and may indeed have therapeutic value. But patients may transform such statements into firm promises in their own minds, especially when they have been disappointed in the event, and testify in that sense to sympathetic juries. If actions for breach of promise can be readily maintained, doctors, so it is said, will be frightened into practising 'defensive medicine'. On the other hand, if these actions were outlawed, leaving only the possibility of suits for malpractice, there is fear that the public might be exposed to the enticements of charlatans, and confidence in the profession might ultimately be shaken.
> ... The law has taken the middle of the road position of allowing actions based on alleged contract, but insisting on clear proof. Instructions to the jury may well stress this requirement and point to tests of truth, such as the complexity or difficulty of an operation as bearing on the probability that a given result was promised.

In the Canadian case of *LaFleur v Cornelis* (1979) 28 NBR (2d) 569 (New Brunswick), the defendant, a cosmetic surgeon, performed a procedure to reduce the size of the plaintiff's nose. He failed to inform her that there was a 10 per cent risk of scarring. She, in fact, was scarred. In addition to succeeding in an action in negligence, the plaintiff established a breach of contract.

Barry J: A cosmetic surgeon is in a different position than the ordinary physician. He is selling a special service and he is more akin to a businessman. Therefore, this is not the ordinary malpractice case. Normally a doctor contracts to use the best skill he possesses and he is expected to exercise at least the methods ordinarily employed by similarly trained professionals. If he does not do so, he may be guilty of negligence in carrying out his contract, as I have found the defendant was in this case.

In the instant case, that was not the kind of a contract which the defendant entered into with the plaintiff. The latter told the defendant what she wanted, namely, a smaller nose. The defendant drew a sketch on his notes to show the changes he would make if the plaintiff paid him a fee of $600.00. There was no misunderstanding whatever. Both parties were *ad idem* as to what each was to do. The plaintiff paid the fee and the defendant failed to carry out his part of the contract. Negligence is not a factor in a straight breach of contract action. There is no law preventing a doctor from contracting to do that which he is paid to do. I appreciate that usually there is no implied warranty of success, in the absence of special circumstances. In this case, the defendant stated to the plaintiff – 'no problem. You will be very happy.' He made an express agreement, which he was not required to, without explaining the risk.

I find that the parties made a contract, and the defendant breached it, leaving the plaintiff with a scarred nose with a minimal deformity.

4. Doctors engaged by others

There may be a number of situations in which a person may see a doctor in circumstances which do not seem to be those of the normal doctor-patient relationship but rather where the doctor is employed by a third party to give a medical opinion on the individual. Two common examples of this are the occupational physician who examines an employee (or prospective employee) for the employer's purposes and the doctor who is engaged by an insurance company to carry out a medical examination. The question for us in determining whether there is a doctor-patient relationship is, again, what has the doctor undertaken to do or what duty, if any, he owes the individual. Obviously, the doctor owes the person a duty to exercise care in performing the specific procedures he uses when examining the person. If he were to injure the person by, for example, negligently taking a blood sample, he would be liable for the harm. The more difficult question concerns whether he has a wider duty. Has he undertaken, and therefore does he owe the individual a duty, to inform the person of his findings to the extent that they may have significance for the individual's health?

Green v Walker (1990) 910 F 2d 291 (5th Circ, CA)

Background

Sidney Green was employed as an offshore cook by ARA/GSI International. As a condition of continued employment ARA/GSI required that its employees undergo an annual physical examination that included a thorough examination of the physical systems, a urine test, and x-rays of the chest and spine. ARA/GSI contracted with Dr Walker to conduct these examinations in accordance with an outlined protocol. Green submitted to his annual employment physical with Dr Walker on May 6, 1985. According to the report submitted . . . to ARA/GSI, Dr Walker found all test results normal and classified Green as 'employable without restriction', the best possible rating on the report. Approximately one year later Green was diagnosed with lung cancer, necessitating extensive diagnostic and surgical procedures.

Sidney and Joni Green, individually and on behalf of their minor daughter, filed suit against Dr Walker, claiming that he had negligently failed to diagnose the beginnings of the cancer at the time of the May 1985 physical examination, and had failed to disclose these findings timely, thus lessening Sidney Green's chances of survival and reducing his life expectancy. Sidney Green has since died. Dr Walker moved for summary judgment contending that his examination of Green had been conducted pursuant to a contract with Green's employer and that therefore no physician-patient relationship, on which a malpractice claim could be based, existed between him and Green. The district court granted summary judgment and Joni Green timely appealed. The sole question posed on appeal may be stated thus: Did Dr Walker have a duty to Sidney Green to perform the prescribed examination with due care, consistent with the medical skills he held out to the public, and to report his finding, particularly any finding which appeared to pose a threat to the physical or mental health of Sidney Green? The district court answered this question in the negative. We now answer it affirmatively . . .

Analysis

The traditional malpractice paradigm
It is a long-established principle of law that liability for malpractice is dependent on the existence of a physician-patient relationship . . . .

Emphasizing a distinction between treatment and a consultative physical examination conducted at the request and for the benefit of a third party, state courts addressing the issue generally have held that no physician-patient relationship exists between '(a) a prospective or actual insured and the physician who examines him for the insurance company; or (b) a prospective or actual employee and the doctor who examines him for the employer.' *Hoover v Williamson* 236 Md 250, 203 A 2d 861 (1964); see *Ervin v American Guardian Life Assur Co* 376 Pa Super 132, 545 A 2d 354(1988); *LoDico v Caputi* 129 AD 2d 361, 517 NYS 2d 640 (1987); *Thomas v Kenton* 425 So 2d 396 (La App 1982); *Keene v Wiggins* 69 Cal App 3d 308, 138 Cal Rptr 3 (D Ct App 1977); *Rogers v Horvath* 65 Mich App 644, 237 NW 2d 595 (1975); *Wilcox v Salt Lake City Corpn* 26 Utah 2d 78, 484 P 2d 1200 (1971); *Lotspeich v Chance Vought Aircraft* 369 SW 2d 705 (Tex Civ App 1963). . . .

Mrs Green contends that we must reverse the district court, citing the decision of the Louisiana Supreme Court in *Ducote v Albert* 521 So 2d 399 (La 1988). Dr Walker counters that we are bound to follow the lead of an intermediate appellate court in *Thomas v Kenton* 425 So 2d 396 (La App 1982), and affirm the district court.

Albeit persuasive, and of some guidance as we walk a dimly blazed trail, neither case is truly dispositive. In *Ducote* the Louisiana Supreme Court adopted the 'dual capacity' doctrine, holding that the Louisiana Worker's Compensation Law does not provide a company doctor with immunity from civil liability for medical malpractice. As Dr Walker points out, however, *Ducote* involved a situation in which the plaintiff-employee had seen the company physician for treatment of his injured hand; whether the physician had rendered 'treatment', thereby creating a physician-patient relationship in the traditional sense, was not in dispute. *Ducote*, therefore, arguably may stand merely for the proposition that a company physician committing malpractice may not raise his co-employee status as a defence to a malpractice claim.

Alternatively, *Thomas v Kenton* arguably is on all fours with the case at bar. Thomas's employer had retained a physician to conduct annual or biennial physical examinations of its employees to assess their continued employability; the examinations were neither initiated by Thomas nor conducted to diagnose and treat a particular ailment. Thomas sued the examining physician, claiming that he had failed in the course of the examination to diagnose and disclose a condition from which Thomas suffered, thus allowing the condition to progress without Thomas's knowledge.

Adopting the reasoning of other jurisdictions that had considered 'strikingly similar' situations, such as *Hoover* and *Lotspeich*, the *Thomas* court held that there was no physician-patient relationship between a prospective or actual employee and the doctor conducting an examination at the employer's request. In the absence of such a relationship, the *Thomas* court concluded, there could be no liability for malpractice. Above all, the *Thomas* court was impressed that it was the employer, not the employee, who was the intended beneficiary of the doctor's contractual obligations:

> The doctor was hired by the company for their benefit and any benefit that their employees receive from having a doctor there to conduct these examinations was only secondary in nature.
> (*Thomas*, 425 F 2d at 400.)

Duty of care – physicians

Like any person, a physician 'is responsible for the damage he occasions not merely by his act, but by his negligence, his imprudence, or his want of skill.' La Civ Code art 2316. As the Louisiana Supreme Court acknowledged in *Pitre* however, the Louisiana Legislature has expressly provided that a physician's professional status carries with it additional legal obligations. A physician practicing as a general practitioner must possess the degree of knowledge or skill possessed and exercise the degree of care ordinarily exercised by physicians in active practice in a similar community under similar circumstances: La R S 9:2794 (A) (1), *Pitre* [*v Opelousas General Hosp*] 530 So 2d at 1156.

The issue presented by the instant case is whether Louisiana jurisprudence supports an extension of the traditional physician-patient relationship to admit of a legal relationship between examining physician and examinee, thus imposing the physician's duty of due care in that situation. The Louisiana Supreme Court's recent enunciation of the principles underlying article 2315, as applied to physicians in *Pitre*, convinces us that the Civil Code permits the articulation of a duty of care that would protect physical examinees, if they are to be deemed other than 'patients', a position we do not here concede:

> The persons at whose disposal society has placed the potent implements of technology owe a heavy moral obligation to use them carefully and to avoid foreseeable harm to present or future generations. In the field of medicine, as in that of manufacturing, the need for compensation of innocent victims of defective products and negligently delivered services is a powerful factor influencing tort law. Typically in these areas also the defendants' capacity to bear and distribute the losses is far superior to that of consumers. Additionally these defendants are in a much better position than the victims to analyze the risks involved in the defendants' activities and to either take precautions to avoid them or to insure against them. Consequently, a much stronger and more effective incentive to prevent the occurrence of future harm will be created by placing the burden of foreseeable losses on the defendant than upon the disorganized, uninformed victims.
> *Pitre*, 530 So 2d at 1157.

. . . it . . . supports a duty between an examining physician and the person present and consenting to the examination, notwithstanding the claim that the examination is being conducted ostensibly for the benefit of another.

We live in an age in which the drive for an increasingly productive workforce has led employers increasingly to require that employees subject their bodies (and minds) to inspection in order to obtain or maintain employment. See Rothstein, 'Employee Selection Based on Susceptibility to Occupational Illness', 81 Mich L Rev 1379 (1983) (common procedures include blood tests, urine analysis, pulmonary function tests, and x-rays). In placing oneself in the hands of a person held out to the world as skilled in a medical profession, albeit at the request of one's employer, one justifiably has the reasonable expectation that the expert will warn of 'any incidental dangers of which he is cognizant due to his peculiar knowledge of his specialization' (*American Manufacturers Mutual Insurance Co v United Gas Corpn* 159 So 2d 592, 595 (La App 1964)).

We therefore now hold that when an individual is required, as a condition of future or continued employment, to submit to a medical examination, that examination creates a relationship between the examining physician and the examinee, at least to the extent of the tests conducted. This relationship imposes upon the examining physician a duty to conduct the requested tests and diagnose the results thereof, exercising the level of care consistent with the doctor's professional training and expertise, and to take reasonable steps to make information available timely to the examinee of any findings that pose an imminent danger to the examinee's physical or mental well-being. To impose a duty upon the doctor who performs such tests to do so in accordance with the degree of care expected of his/her profession for the benefit of the employee-examinee, as well as the employer, is fully consistent with the very essence of Civil Code article 2315.

The decision of the district court is REVERSED and the matter is REMANDED for further proceedings consistent herewith.

(See also *Thomsen v Davison* [1975] Qd R 91 especially at p 97.)

This issue has not been considered by the English courts. However, the English courts should, in our view, find the reasoning in *Green v Walker* persuasive.

What, however, would be the legal position if (as sometimes happens) a doctor purports expressly to *restrict* any undertaking he is giving, and therefore any duty he owes, by stating that his only obligation is to carry out his instructions from, for example, the insurance company, and that he will only impart information to the insurance company and not to the individual he is examining? On the face of it, his undertaking (and, therefore, his duty) is of a very limited nature. It would mean that if he discovered a condition of significance to the individual's health he would be under no obligation to reveal it even though the person suffers as a consequence of not knowing.

However, in English law the ability to exclude or restrict liability for death or personal injury resulting from negligence is severely curtailed by the Unfair Contract Terms Act 1977. Section 2(1) provides that:

2. (1) A person cannot by reference to any contract term or to a notice given to persons generally or to particular persons exclude or restrict his liability for death or personal injury resulting from negligence.

By section 14, 'notice' is defined to include 'an announcement, whether or not in writing, and any other communication or pretended communication'. The Act only applies in respect of a person's 'business liability'. Section 1(3) provides that the Act applies:

only to business liability, that is liability for breach of obligations or duties arising –
(a)   from things done or to be done by a person in the course of a business (whether his own business or another's) . . .

Section 14 defines 'business' to include 'a profession . . . '. On the face of it, these provisions would extend to any purported 'exclusion' or 'restriction' of liability by a doctor in private practice (semble, within the NHS also in that section 14's definition of a 'business' refers also to the activities of a 'public authority').

One problem, however, remains. It could be argued that a purported restriction by a doctor of his undertaking to the individual prevents any duty arising and hence, is not an 'exclusion' or 'restriction' of liability that has arisen within section 2(1). This argument was considered and rejected by the House of Lords in *Smith v Eric S Bush (a firm)* [1989] 2 All ER 514. Lord Griffiths stated that 'I read [the provisions of the 1977 Act] as introducing a "but for" test in relation to the notice excluding liability. They indicate that the existence of the common law duty to take reasonable care . . . is to be judged by considering whether it would exist "but for" the notice excluding liability' (at p 530). As we have already suggested, if the doctor did not purport to restrict his obligation to the person he is examining, he would, as a matter of law, be held to have undertaken a minimum degree of responsibility *qua* doctor which would include, for example, advising the person of any significant matters which might affect his health. Consequently, any purported restriction of a doctor's duty, at least as regards this obligation of a minimum degree of responsibility, will be ineffective.

B. REQUEST BY ANOTHER

In the case of a child who is too immature to enter into the relationship of doctor and patient, the request for medical services must come from another. In most circumstances, this would be a parent (section 2 of the Children Act 1989). It may, however, be that parental responsibility, as regards medical care, has been acquired by the local authority (under Parts IV and V of the Children Act 1989) to the exclusion of the parents (s 33(3) of the Children Act 1989) or is vested in the court because the child is a ward of court (section 41 of the Supreme Court Act 1981 and RSC Ord 90). In all of these cases the request is made on behalf of another. We are not concerned here with a request by just anyone. The request must be by someone who has the legal authority to act on that other's behalf to bring the relationship of doctor and patient into existence. Of course, that other, ie the child, may well dissent. Assuming (as we are) that the child is incompetent to make decisions on his own by reason of his immaturity, such dissent would have no *legal* force.

To whom does the doctor give his undertaking? The answer must be that the undertaking is given as a matter of fact to the parents or other who acts on behalf of the child. Of course, what flows from this undertaking is the legal duty to care for the child which is owed to the child and no one else.

So far we have been concerned with the issue as a matter of principle. As regards the child's becoming a patient of a GP, the formal creation of the relationship is dealt with in the Medical Regulations. Regulation 20 describes the procedure whereby a child *may* become a GP's patient.

> 20. (2) An application to a doctor for inclusion in his list may be made (otherwise than by the person concerned) –
> (a)   on behalf of any child, by either parent, or in the absence of both parents, the guardian or other adult person who has the care of the child; or . . .
> (c)   on behalf of any person under 18 years of age who is –
> (i)   in the care of an authority to whose care he has been committed under the provisions of the Children Act 1989, by a person duly authorised by that authority,
> (ii)   in the care of a voluntary organisation, by that organisation or a person duly authorised by it.

Of course, it does not follow that a child (defined in regulation 2 as a person under the age of 16) cannot apply for inclusion on a GP's list. This would turn upon whether the child was competent to do so.

The discussion so far has been concerned with the incompetent child; legal orthodoxy would have it that when a child becomes competent (as defined by law) only that child may request medical treatment. No one else can request on the child's behalf and, *ex hypothesi*, no one can request medical services when the child has refused. The Court of Appeal, in the cases of *Re R* [1991] 4 All ER 177 and *Re W* [1992] 4 All ER 627 has suggested that both a court, in the exercise of its inherent jurisdiction, and a parent may request medical services (enter their consent) even in the case of a competent child and even in the face of the child's refusal of those services (for an analysis of this judicial development, see Chapter 4).

C. WHERE THERE IS NO REQUEST

The person we are primarily concerned with here is the adult who is unconscious or is otherwise mentally incompetent to request medical treatment. There is, of course, regulation 20(2)(b) of the Medical Regulations which as regards a GP provides for the inclusion on his list of a 'person who is incapable of making . . . an application' on the application of a 'relative or other adult person who has the care of [that] person'. This allows for the formal creation of the doctor-patient relationship but no more. As we shall see, there is no one who is authorised in law to request medical treatment on behalf of such a person (Chapter 4). Thus, the law must have a mechanism by which treatment which the person needs can lawfully be administered. Curiously, until the decision of the House of Lords in *Re F (mental patient: sterilisation)* [1989] 2 All ER 545 (HL) and [1990] 2 AC 1, there had been no authoritative statement by the courts or in legislation recognising the legality of such treatment except in the case of mental illness (see Mental Health Act 1983). It had been assumed (or argued) that, in appropriate circumstances, such treatment would be lawful (see eg P D

G Skegg, *Law, Ethics and Medicine* (1988) ch 5 and *Wilson v Pringle* [1986] 2 All ER 440 at 447 per Croom-Johnson LJ).

Re F (a mental patient: sterilisation) [1990] 2 AC 1, [1989] 2 All ER 545 (HL)

Lord Goff: We are searching for a principle upon which, in limited circumstances, recognition may be given to a need, in the interests of the patient, that treatment should be given to him in circumstances where he is (temporarily or permanently) disabled from consenting to it. It is this criterion of a need which points to the principle of necessity as providing justification.

That there exists in the common law a principle of necessity which may justify action which would otherwise be unlawful is not in doubt. . . .

We are concerned here with action taken to preserve life, health or well-being of another who is unable to consent to it. Such action is sometimes said to be justified as arising from an emergency; in *Prosser and Keeton, Hornbook on Torts*, 5th edn (1984), p 117, the action is said to be privileged by the emergency. Doubtless, in the case of a person of sound mind, there will ordinarily have to be an emergency before such action taken without consent can be lawful; for otherwise there would be an opportunity to communicate with the assisted person and to seek his consent. But this is not always so; and indeed the historical origins of the principle of necessity do not point to emergency as such as providing the criterion of lawful intervention without consent. . . . when a person is rendered incapable of communication either permanently or over a considerable period of time (through illness or accident or mental disorder), it would be an unusual use of language to describe the case as one of 'permanent emergency' – if indeed such a state of affairs can properly be said to exist. In truth, the relevance of an emergency is that it may give rise to a necessity to act in the interests of the assisted person, without first obtaining his consent. Emergency is however not the criterion or even a pre-requisite; it is simply a frequent origin of the necessity which impels intervention. The principle is one of necessity, not of emergency.

[The legal principle is] not only (1) must there be a necessity to act when it is not practicable to communicate with the assisted person, but also (2) the action taken must be such as a reasonable person would in all the circumstances take, acting in the best interests of the assisted person . . .

. . . Take the example of an elderly person who suffers a stroke which renders him incapable of speech or movement. It is by virtue of this principle that the doctor who treats him, the nurse who cares for him, even the relative or friend or neighbour who comes in to look after him, will commit no wrong when he or she touches his body.

[This illustrates an example of] a permanent or semi-permanent state of affairs. Another example of the latter kind is that of a mentally disordered person who is disabled from giving consent. I can see no good reason why the principle of necessity should not be applicable in his case as it is in the case of the victim of a stroke. Furthermore, in the case of a mentally disordered person, as in the case of a stroke victim, the permanent state of affairs calls for a wider range of care than may be requisite in an emergency which arises from accidental injury. When the state of affairs is permanent, or semi-permanent, action properly taken to preserve the life, health or well-being of the assisted person may well transcend such measures as surgical operation or substantial medical treatment and may extend to include such humdrum matters as routine medical or dental treatment, even simple care such as dressing and undressing and putting to bed.

Re F establishes that a doctor-patient relationship may arise without any request by the patient but for it to do so there must still be an undertaking of care by the doctor.

D. SPECIAL CASES

1. Emergencies

You will have noticed Lord Goff's reference in *Re F* to 'emergency' cases. These may involve a request for care or circumstances in which a person is unable to make one. What is important to notice is that even in an emergency the doctor must still have undertaken the care of the individual before any duty in law will arise. Obviously, if the emergency occurs when the individual is already in the care of the doctor, for example, in a hospital, the undertaking will already exist and be deemed to continue. Equally, when a doctor has held himself out as undertaking to treat individuals requiring emergency care, for example, by being on duty in an Accident and Emergency Department of a hospital, he will be deemed to have undertaken to provide emergency care once he is aware of the need for it. No case in England has touched upon this matter but in principle this is the correct approach. Some reliance can be placed upon the only relevant English decision in *Barnett v Chelsea and Kensington HMC* [1968] 1 All ER 1068.

> **Nield J:** At about 5 am on Jan 1, 1966, three night watchmen drank some tea. Soon afterwards all three men started vomiting. At about 8 am the men walked to the casualty department of the defendant's hospital, which was open. One of them, the deceased, when he was in the room in the hospital, lay on some armless chairs. He appeared ill. Another of the men told the nurse that they had been vomiting after drinking tea. The nurse telephoned the casualty officer, a doctor, to tell him of the men's complaint. The casualty officer, who was himself unwell, did not see them, but said that they should go home and call in their own doctors. The men went away, and the deceased died some hours later from what was found to be arsenical poisoning. Cases of arsenical poisoning were rare, and, even if the deceased had been examined and admitted to the hospital and treated, there was little or no chance that the only effective antidote would have been administered to him before the time at which he died.

Nield J then asked himself the following question: 'Is there, on these facts, shown to be created a relationship between the three watchmen and the hospital staff such as gives rise to a duty of care in the defendants which they owe to the three men?' The answer he gave was ' . . . I have no doubt that [the nurse] and [the doctor] were under a duty to the deceased . . .'

This case is, in one sense, an obvious one for us since by giving advice over the telephone the doctor had clearly embarked upon the care of the three watchmen, albeit inadequately. The difficult question is what if the three watchmen had come into the casualty department and the doctor on seeing them declined to treat them despite their apparent need for treatment for no good reason? The position must be that the law would deem there to be an undertaking because of the coincidence of an open Accident and Emergency Department, a doctor on duty and a person apparently in need of emergency care.

However, in general an undertaking will not be held to exist in law merely because of the coincidence of an emergency and a doctor nearby. In general, the law does not impose an obligation upon a doctor to act as a 'good Samaritan', ie to act as a rescuer in an emergency. However, there is an exception in the case of a GP. Paragraph 4(1)(h) of the terms of service provides as follows:

> 4. (1)(h) . . . persons to whom he may be requested to give treatment which is immediately required owing to an accident or other emergency at any place in his practice area, provided that –
> (i)   he is not, at the time of the request, relieved of liability to give treatment under paragraph 5 [ie elderly or infirm], and
> (ii) he is not, at the time of the request, relieved, under paragraph 19(2), of his obligation to give treatment personally [ie by reason of having employed a deputy], and
> (iii) he is available to provide such treatment,
> and any persons by whom he is requested, and agrees, to give treatment which is immediately required owing to an accident or other emergency at any place in the locality of

any FHSA in whose medical list he is included, provided there is no doctor who, at the time of the request, is under an obligation otherwise than under this head to give treatment to that person, or there is such a doctor but, after being requested to attend, he is unable to attend and give treatment immediately required . . .

Paragraph 4(1)(h) contemplates two types of situation: first, an emergency which arises in his practice area; and secondly, an emergency outside this area but within the area covered by the FHSA on whose medical list he appears. As regards the latter, he has to agree to provide the emergency medical care once he has been requested to provide it. As regards the former, however, providing the three requirements in (i) to (iii) are satisfied, he has no choice but to render emergency care if requested.

There is one final situation we should consider which may be a further exception to the principle that a doctor need not act as a good Samaritan, ie as a rescuer in an emergency. It is clear that when a call is made in a theatre 'is there a doctor in the house?', a doctor by his mere presence gives no undertaking and can, as a matter of law, ignore the call. However, if the call occurs not in a social setting, but in a professional context the answer is not so clear. Consider the following two examples. First, a hospital doctor leaving for home at the end of his period of duty is confronted by someone who has just entered the hospital and has collapsed. Secondly, a worker carrying out repairs at the offices of a Harley Street physician collapses and is in need of immediate medical attention. Can it be said that the law would deem there to be an undertaking on the part of the doctors in the two cases by virtue of the incident occurring in the context in which the doctor ordinarily acts as a doctor? Arguably, the law would determine that the doctor was not entitled to ignore the call for help in these limited circumstances. In other words, the court would find that the doctor, because what has happened took place in a context where he is practising his profession, is deemed to undertake to render emergency medical care.

2. Legislative provisions

There are a number of legislative provisions which recognise that the normal requirement of a request and undertaking need not exist for there to be a doctor-patient relationship. The effect of these provisions is that the relationship may arise not only without the person's request but also in the face of his refusal providing the doctor undertakes to provide treatment. The two clearest examples are the Mental Health Act 1983 and the Public Health (Control of Disease) Act 1984. The Mental Health Act 1983 authorises the compulsory admission to a hospital of an individual for assessment and for treatment. The original justification was represented as being the need to protect the public. Today although this justification may persist in some cases, the justification advanced is a therapeutic one; the desire to promote, in so far as possible, the well-being of the mentally disordered patient.

The relevant provisions are in sections 2-4 of the Act.

MENTAL HEALTH ACT 1983

Admission for assessment
2. (1) A patient may be admitted to hospital and detained there for the period allowed by subsection (4) below in pursuance of an application (in this Act referred to as 'an application

for admission for assessment') made in accordance with subsections (2) and (3) below.

(2) An application for admission for assessment may be made in respect of a patient on the grounds that –

(a) he is suffering from mental disorder of a nature or degree which warrants the detention of the patient in a hospital for assessment (or for assessment followed by medical treatment) for at least a limited period; and

(b) he ought to be so detained in the interests of his own health or safety or with a view to the protection of other persons.

(3) An application for admission for assessment shall be founded on the written recommendations in the prescribed form of two registered medical practitioners, including in each case a statement that in the opinion of the practitioner the conditions set out in subsection (2) above are complied with.

(4) Subject to the provisions of section 29(4) [which provides for the extension of the period of detention in specified circumstances] below, a patient admitted to hospital in pursuance of an application for admission for assessment may be detained for a period not exceeding 28 days beginning with the day on which he is admitted, but shall not be detained after the expiration of that period unless before it has expired he has become liable to be detained by virtue of a subsequent application, order or direction under the following provisions of this Act.

Admission for treatment

3. (1) A patient may be admitted to a hospital and detained there for the period allowed by the following provisions of this Act in pursuance of an application (in this Act referred to as 'an application for admission for treatment') made in accordance with this section.

(2) An application for admission for treatment may be made in respect of a patient on the grounds that –

(a) he is suffering from mental illness, severe mental impairment, psychopathic disorder or mental impairment and his mental disorder is of a nature or degree which makes it appropriate for him to receive medical treatment in a hospital; and

(b) in the case of psychopathic disorder or mental impairment, such treatment is likely to alleviate or prevent a deterioration of his condition; and

(c) it is necessary for the health or safety of the patient or for the protection of other persons that he should receive such treatment and it cannot be provided unless he is detained under this section.

(3) An application for admission for treatment shall be founded on the written recommendations in the prescribed form of two registered medical practitioners, including in each case a statement that in the opinion of the practitioner the conditions set out in subsection (2) above are complied with; and each such recommendation shall include –

(a) such particulars as may be prescribed of the grounds for that opinion so far as it relates to the conditions set out in paragraphs (*a*) and (*b*) of that subsection; and

(b) a statement of the reasons for that opinion so far as it relates to the conditions set out in paragraph (*c*) of that subsection, specifying whether other methods of dealing with the patient are available and, if so, why they are not appropriate.

Admission for assessment in cases of emergency

4. (1) In any case of urgent necessity, an application for admission for assessment may be made in respect of a patient in accordance with the following provisions of this section, and any application so made is in this Act referred to as 'an emergency application'.

(2) An emergency application may be made either by an approved social worker or by the nearest relative of the patient; and every such application shall include a statement that it is of urgent necessity for the patient to be admitted and detained under section 2 above, and that compliance with the provisions of this Part of this Act relating to applications under that section would involve undesirable delay.

(3) An emergency application shall be sufficient in the first instance if founded on one of the medical recommendations required by section 2 above, given, if practicable, by a practitioner who has previous acquaintance with the patient and otherwise complying with the requirements of section 12 [which sets out the procedure to be followed in making 'medical recommendations'] below so far as applicable to a single recommendation, and verifying the statement referred to in subsection (2) above.

(4) An emergency application shall cease to have effect on the expiration of a period of 72 hours from the time when the patient is admitted to the hospital unless –

(a) the second medical recommendation required by section 2 above is given and received by the managers within that period; and

(b)   that recommendation and the recommendation referred to in subsection (3) above together comply with all the requirements of section 12 below (other than the requirement as to the time of signature of the second recommendation).

These provisions provide for the relationship of doctor and patient to come into being without the need for the agreement of the patient. Once the patient is admitted for assessment or treatment a doctor may then carry these out without more. In some circumstances, however, the Act expressly limits what the doctor may do as regards particular forms of treatment (see Part IV which we consider in Chapter 4).

The second example can be found in the Public Health (Control of Disease) Act 1984 which provides for the medical examination, removal to hospital and detention in hospital of those who are (or are believed to be) suffering from a 'notifiable disease'. Section 10 of the Act defines 'notifiable disease' as meaning cholera, plague, relapsing fever, smallpox and typhus.

PUBLIC HEALTH (CONTROL OF DISEASE) ACT 1984

Medical examination
35. (1) If a justice of the peace (acting, if he deems it necessary, ex parte) is satisfied, on a written certificate issued by a registered medical practitioner nominated by the local authority for a district –
(a)   that there is reason to believe that some person in the district –
  (i)   is or has been suffering from a notifiable disease, or
  (ii)   though not suffering from such a disease, is carrying an organism that is capable of causing it, and
(b)   that in his own interest, or in the interest of his family, or in the public interest, it is expedient that he should be medically examined, and
(c)   that he is not under the treatment of a registered medical practitioner or that the registered medical practitioner who is treating him consents to the making of an order under this section,
the justice may order him to be medically examined by a registered medical practitioner so nominated.

(2) An order under this section may be combined with a warrant under subsection (3) of section 61 below authorising a registered medical practitioner nominated by the local authority to enter any premises, and for the purposes of that subsection that practitioner shall, if not an officer of the local authority, be treated as one.

(3) In this section, references to a person's being medically examined shall be construed as including references to his being submitted to bacteriological and radiological tests and similar investigations.

Medical examinations of group of persons believed to comprise carrier of notifiable disease
36. (1) If a justice of the peace (acting, if he deems it necessary, ex parte) is satisfied, on a written certificate issued by the proper officer of the local authority for a district –
(a)   that there is reason to believe that one of a group of persons, though not suffering from a notifiable disease, is carrying an organism that is capable of causing it, and
(b)   that in the interest of those persons or their families, or in the public interest, it is expedient that those persons should be medically examined,
the justice may order them to be medically examined by a registered medical practitioner nominated by the local authority for that district.

(2) Subsections (2) and (3) of section 35 above apply in relation to subsection (1) above as they apply in relation to subsection (1) of that section.

Removal to hospital of person with notifiable disease
37. (1) Where a justice of the peace (acting, if he deems it necessary, ex parte) is satisfied, on the application of the local authority, that a person is suffering from a notifiable disease and –
(a)   that his circumstances are such that proper precautions to prevent the spread of infection cannot be taken, or that such precautions are not being taken, and

(b)   that serious risk of infection is thereby caused to other persons, and
(c)   that accommodation for him is available in a suitable hospital vested in the Secretary of State or, pursuant to arrangements made by a District Health Authority (whether under an NHS contract or otherwise), in a suitable hospital vested in a NHS trust or other person,

the justice may, with the consent of the Area or District Health Authority in whose district lies the area, or the greater part of the area, of the local authority, order him to be removed to it.

(2) An order under this section may be addressed to such officer of the local authority as the justice may think expedient, and that officer and any officer of the hospital may do all acts necessary for giving effect to the order.

Detention in hospital of person with notifiable disease
38. (1) Where a justice of the peace (acting, if he deems it necessary, ex parte) in and for the place in which a hospital for infectious diseases is situated is satisfied, on the application of any local authority, that an inmate of the hospital who is suffering from a notifiable disease would not on leaving the hospital be provided with lodging or accommodation in which proper precautions could be taken to prevent the spread of the disease by him, the justice may order him to be detained in the hospital.

(2) An order made under subsection (1) above may direct detention for a period specified in the order, but any justice of the peace acting in and for the same place may extend a period so specified as often as it appears to him to be necessary to do so.

(3) Any person who leaves a hospital contrary to an order made under this section for his detention there shall be liable on summary conviction to a fine not exceeding level 1 on the standard scale, and the court may order him to be taken back to the hospital.

(4) An order under this section may be addressed –
(a)   in the case of an order for a person's detention, to such officer of the hospital, and
(b)   in the case of an order made under subsection (3) above, to such officer of the local authority on whose application the order for detention was made,

as the justice may think expedient, and that officer and any officer of the hospital may do all acts necessary for giving effect to the order.

In 1985 the Secretary of State promulgated (pursuant to the 1984 Act) the Public Health (Infectious Diseases) Regulations 1985 (SI 1985 No 434). Subsequently, these were replaced by the Public Health (Infectious Diseases) Regulations 1988 (SI 1988 No 1546). Regulation 3 and Schedule 1 of the regulations apply sections 35, 37, 38 (as modified by regulation 5), 43 and 44 of the 1984 Act) to acquired immune deficiency syndrome (AIDS).

Regulations 5 and 13 provide as follows:

Modification of section 38 of the Act as it is applied to acquired immune deficiency syndrome
5. (1) In its application to acquired immune deficiency syndrome section 38(1) of the Act shall be modified in accordance with paragraph (2) below.

(2) The said section 38(1) shall in addition to the circumstances specified in that section apply so that a justice of the peace may on the application of any local authority (acting if he deems it necessary ex parte) make an order for the detention in hospital of an inmate of that hospital suffering from acquired immune deficiency syndrome if the justice is satisfied that on his leaving the hospital proper precautions to prevent the spread of that disease would not be taken by him –
(a)   in his lodging or accommodation, or
(b)   in other places to which he may be expected to go if not detained in the hospital.

It is a curious feature of these regulations that for the most part they apply only to patients with AIDS. Arguably, the public health risk arises, if at all, more commonly from the person with HIV infection rather than from the person with AIDS. Thus, if there is to be some police power vested in the state directed against the spread of AIDS (something which is itself problematic), the regulations to be coherent should have specifically referred to a person infected with HIV. The regulations when read with the Act do this in only one respect, namely as regards medical examination under section 35 which refers to a person 'carrying an organism that is capable of causing [AIDS]'. The more important public health provisions under sections 37 and 38 are limited to AIDS. Furthermore, the Act and the regulation make no reference to treatment and thereby appear to be oppressive without any saving therapeutic grace.

Part II

Medical law: the general part

Chapter 3
Consent

Introduction

The ethical principle that each person has a right to self-determination finds its expression in law through the concept of consent. Thus, the law relating to consent is of the utmost importance in medical law, serving as it does as the means of protecting and preserving the right of a patient to decide what is to happen to him. Robins JA in *Malette v Shulman* (1990) 67 DLR (4th) 321 in the Ontario Court of Appeal examines its importance (see *infra*, p 1331 for the facts).

Malette v Shulman (1990) 67 DLR (4th) 321 (Ont CA)

Robins JA: The right of a person to control his or her own body is a concept that has long been recognized at common law. The tort of battery has traditionally protected the interest in bodily security from unwanted physical interference. Basically, any intentional nonconsensual touching which is harmful or offensive to a person's reasonable sense of dignity is actionable. Of course, a person may choose to waive this protection and consent to the intentional invasion of this interest, in which case an action for battery will not be maintainable. No special exceptions are made for medical care, other than in emergency situations, and the general rules governing actions for battery are applicable to the doctor-patient relationship. Thus, as a matter of common law, a medical intervention in which a doctor touches the body of a patient would constitute a battery if the patient did not consent to the intervention. Patients have the decisive role in the medical decision-making process. Their right of self-determination is recognized and protected by the law. As Justice Cardozo proclaimed in his classic statement:

> Every human being of adult years and sound mind has a right to determine what shall be done with his own body; and a surgeon who performs an operation without his patient's consent commits an assault, for which he is liable in damages.

[*Schloendoff v Society of New York Hospital* 211 NY 125 (1914). See also *Videto v Kennedy* (1981) 33 OR (2d) 497, 125 DLR (3d) 127, 17 CCLT (CA); Linden, *Canadian Tort Law*, 4th edn (1988) at pp 40-3 and p 59 et seq; Prosser & Keeton, *The Law of Torts*, 5th edn (1984) at pp 39-42; and Fleming, *The Law of Torts*, 7th edn (1987) at pp 23-4.] . . .

The right of self-determination . . . obviously encompasses the right to refuse medical treatment. A competent adult is generally entitled to reject a specific treatment or all treatment, or to select an alternate form of treatment, even if the decision may entail risks as serious as death and may appear mistaken in the eyes of the medical profession or of the community. Regardless of the doctor's opinion, it is the patient who has the final say on whether to undergo the treatment. The patient is free to decide, for instance, not to be operated on or not to undergo therapy or, by the same token, not to have a blood transfusion. If a doctor were to proceed in the face of a decision to reject the treatment, he would be civilly liable for his unauthorized conduct notwithstanding his justifiable belief that what he did was necessary to preserve the patient's life or health. The doctrine of informed consent is plainly intended to ensure the freedom of individuals to make choices concerning their medical care. For this freedom to be meaningful, people must have the right to make choices that accord with their own values regardless of how unwise or foolish those choices may appear to others: see generally, Prosser & Keeton, *op cit* p 112 et seq; Harper, James & Gray, *The Law of Torts*, 2nd edn (1986), cIII; Linden, *op cit* p 64 et seq; and *Reibl v Hughes* (1980) 114 DLR (3d) 1; [1980] 2 SCR 880; 14 CCLT 1.

In England, the House of Lords has endorsed this understanding of the role and significance of consent in *Sidaway v Governors of Royal Bethlem Hospital* [1985] AC 871, *Re F (a mental patient: sterilisation* [1990] 2 AC 1 and *Airedale NHS Trust v Bland* [1993] 1 All ER 821. In *Re F*, Lord Goff expanded on the views he had expressed earlier concerning the inviolability of every person's body in the absence of their consent.

> **Lord Goff:** I start with the fundamental principle, now long established, that every person's body is inviolate. As to this, I do not wish to depart from what I myself said in the judgment of the Divisional Court in *Collins v Wilcock* [1984] 3 All ER 374, [1984] 1 WLR 1172, and in particular from the statement that the effect of this principle is that everybody is protected not only against injury but against any form of physical molestation (see [1984] 3 All ER 374 at 378, [1984] 1 WLR 1172 at 1177). . . .
>
> In the old days it used to be said that, for a touching of another's person to amount to a battery, it had to be a touching 'in anger' (see *Cole v Turner* (1704) Holt KB 108, 90 ER 958 per Holt CJ); and it has recently been said that the touching must be 'hostile' to have that effect (see *Wilson v Pringle* [1986] 2 All ER 440 at 447, [1987] QB 237 at 253). I respectfully doubt whether that is correct. A prank that gets out of hand, an over-friendly slap on the back, surgical treatment by a surgeon who mistakenly thinks that the patient has consented to it, all these things may transcend the bounds of lawfulness, without being characterised as hostile. Indeed, the suggested qualification is difficult to reconcile with the principle that any touching of another's body is, in the absence of lawful excuse, capable of amounting to a battery and a trespass. Furthermore, in the case of medical treatment, we have to bear well in mind the libertarian principle of self-determination which, to adopt the words of Cardozo J (in *Schloendorff v Society of New York Hospital* (1914) 211 NY 125 at 126), recognises that –
>
>> Every human being of adult years and sound mind has a right to determine what shall be done with his own body; and a surgeon who performs an operation without his patient's consent, commits an assault . . .
>
> . . . In *Wilson v Pringle* the Court of Appeal considered that treatment or care of such persons may be regarded as lawful, as falling within the exception relating to physical contact which is generally acceptable in the ordinary conduct of everyday life. Again, I am with respect unable to agree. That exception is concerned with the ordinary events of everyday life, jostling in public places and such like, and affects all persons, whether or not they are capable of giving their consent. Medical treatment, even treatment for minor ailments, does not fall within that category of events. The general rule is that consent is necessary to render such treatment lawful. If such treatment administered without consent is not to be unlawful, it has to be justified on some other principle.

After referring to Goff LJ's remarks in *Collins v Wilcock*, Brennan J in the Australian High Court case of *Department of Health v JWB and SMB* (1992) 66 ALJR 300 at 317-8 emphasised the breadth of the law's protection.

> **Brennan J:** Blackstone declared the right to personal security to be an absolute, or individual, right vested in each person by 'the immutable laws of nature' (Blackstone, ibid, vol 1, pp 124, 129; vol 3, p 119). Blackstone's reason for the rule which forbids any form of molestation, namely, that 'every man's person [is] sacred', points to the value which underlies and informs the law: each person has a unique dignity which the law respects and which it will protect.
>
> Human dignity is a value common to our municipal law and to international instruments relating to human rights. (The inherent dignity of *all* members of the human family is commonly proclaimed in the preambles to international instruments relating to human rights: see the United Nations Charter, the International Covenant on Civil and Political Rights (which declares 'the right to . . . security of person': Art 9), the Universal Declaration of Human Rights, the International Covenant on Economic, Social and Cultural Rights and the Convention on the Rights of the Child.) The law will protect equally the dignity of the

hale and hearty and the dignity of the weak and lame; of the frail baby and of the frail aged; of the intellectually able and of the intellectually disabled. Thus municipal law satisfies the requirement of the first paragraph of the 1971 United Nations Declaration on the Rights of Mentally Retarded Persons which reads:

> The mentally retarded person has, to the maximum degree of feasibility, the same rights as other human beings.

Our law admits of no discrimination against the weak and disadvantaged in their human dignity. Intellectual disability justifies no impairment of human dignity, no invasion of the right to personal integrity. . . .

Human dignity requires that the whole personality be respected: the right to physical integrity is a condition of human dignity but the gravity of any invasion of physical integrity depends on its effect not only on the body but also upon the mind and on self-perception.

In *Re T (adult: refusal of treatment)* [1992] 4 All ER 649 all three judges in the Court of Appeal based their analysis on this fundamental principle.

Re T (adult: refusal of treatment) [1992] 4 All ER 649, (1992) 9 BMLR 46 (CA)

Lord Donaldson MR: An adult patient who, like Miss T, suffers from no mental incapacity has an absolute right to choose whether to consent to medical treatment, to refuse it or to choose one rather than another of the treatments being offered . . . This right of choice is not limited to decisions which others might regard as sensible. It exists notwithstanding that the reasons for making the choice are rational, irrational , unknown or even non-existent (*Sidaway v Board of Governors of the Bethlem Royal Hospital and Maudsley Hospital* [1985] AC 871 at 904F-905A). . . .

The fact that, 'emergency cases' apart, no medical treatment of an adult patient of full capacity can be undertaken without his consent, creates a situation in which the absence of consent has much the same effect as a refusal. . . .

Butler-Sloss LJ: A man or woman of full age and sound understanding may choose to reject medical advice and medical or surgical treatment either partially or in its entirety. A decision to refuse medical treatment by a patient capable of making the decision does not have to be sensible, rational or well-considered (see *Sidaway v Governors of Bethlem Royal Hospital* [1985] AC 871 at 904-5). I agree with the reasoning of the Court of Appeal in Ontario in their decision in *Malette v Shulman* (1990) 67 DLR (4th) 321 (a blood transfusion given to an unconscious card-carrying Jehovah's Witness). Mr Justice Robins JA said . . .

> At issue here is the freedom of the patient as an individual to exercise her right to refuse treatment and accept the consequences of her own decision. Competent adults, as I have sought to demonstrate, are generally at liberty to refuse medical treatment even at the risk of death. The right to determine what shall be done with one's own body is a fundamental right in our society. The concepts inherent in this right are the bedrock upon which the principles of self-determination and individual autonomy are based. Free individual choice in matters affecting this right should, in my opinion, be accorded very high priority. . . .

He excluded from consideration the interest of the state in protecting innocent third parties and preventing suicide. I agree with the principles set out above.

Staughton LJ: An adult whose mental capacity is unimpaired has the right to decide for herself whether she will or will not receive medical or surgical treatment, even in circumstances where she is likely or even certain to die in the absence of treatment. Thus far the law is clear.

Issues of consent in the doctor-patient relationship arise in three main contexts: (i) in the crime of battery; (ii) in the tort of battery; and (iii) in the tort of negligence. In reality, consent or lack of it is only an issue in the civil law of torts. Although theoretically, a doctor who ordinarily acts without obtaining a patient's consent may not only be exposed to liability in tort, but also runs the risk of facing a criminal prosecution for the crime of battery, there is little or no chance that this will actually happen in the context of the ordinary practice of medicine in good faith. Obviously there are many circumstances where a doctor can be guilty of a crime involving lack of consent. For example, he may obtain his patient's consent to intercourse by representing it as a legitimate examination (*R v Williams* [1923] 1 KB 340) or he may fraudulently represent that a particular medical procedure is essential and thereby gain financial reward from a private patient by deception. But these are matters which do not concern us here since our concern is with the ordinary practice of medicine in good faith.

The scope of the crime of battery, should it ever arise, is likely to be held by the courts to be the same as the tort of battery, apart from the fact that the doctor's intention will be relevant in determining whether he has the necessary *mens rea* for the crime. (See, P D G Skegg *Law, Ethics and Medicine* (1984) at pages 79-80).

As regards the tort of battery, Professor Fleming in his *Law of Torts* (8th edn, 1992) defines a battery as follows (at p 24):

> Of the various forms of trespass to the person the most common is the tort known as battery, which is committed by intentionally bringing about a harmful or offensive contact with the person of another. The action, therefore, serves the dual purpose of affording protection to the individual not only against bodily harm but also against any interference with his person which is offensive to a reasonable sense of honour and dignity. The insult in being touched without consent has been traditionally regarded as sufficient, even though the interference is only trivial and not attended with actual physical harm.

There have been relatively few cases in England in which a patient has successfully sued his doctor for battery on the ground that he had not consented to being touched. However, there are a few examples – *Hamilton v Birmingham RHB* (1969) 2 BMJ 456 (sterilisation without consent during the performance of a Caesarean section); *Michael v Molesworth* (1950) 2 BMJ 171 (operation performed by a different surgeon from the one agreed); *Cull v Royal Surrey County Hospital* (1932) 1 BMJ 1195 (patient consented to an abortion and the doctor carried out a different procedure, a hysterectomy); *Devi v West Midlands RHA* [1981] (CA Transcript 491) (patient consented to an operation to repair a perforation of the uterus, the surgeon performed a sterilisation operation as well). This does not mean that the tort of battery is unimportant. Its greatest significance lies in the fact that it represents a statement by the law of the importance of an individual patient's right to determine what should or should not be done to his body. Further proof of this is, of course, the fact that, as regards the tort of battery, the plaintiff need not prove that he has suffered harm so as to recover damages. Harm is assumed, since the tort protects the plaintiff from harm which is symbolic as well as that which results in injury. It is clear that a battery will be committed by a doctor even if he acts only out of what he sees as the best interests of his patient.

Mohr v Williams (1905) 104 NW 12 (Sup Ct Minn)

> Plaintiff consulted defendant, an ear specialist, concerning trouble with her right ear. On examining her, he found a diseased condition of the right ear, and she consented to an operation upon it. When she was unconscious under the anaesthetic, defendant concluded that the condition of the right ear was not serious enough to require an operation; but he found a more serious condition of the left ear, which he decided required an operation.

Without reviving the plaintiff to ask her permission, he operated on the left ear. The operation was skillfully performed, and was successful. Plaintiff nevertheless brought an action for battery and succeeded.

Brown J: The last contention of defendant is that the act complained of did not amount to an assault and battery. This is based upon the theory that, as plaintiff's left ear was in fact diseased, in a condition dangerous and threatening to her health, the operation was necessary, and having been skillfully performed at a time when plaintiff has requested a like operation on the other ear, the charge of assault and battery cannot be sustained: that, in view of these conditions, and the claim that there was no negligence on the part of defendant, and an entire absence of any evidence tending to show an evil intent, the court should say, as a matter of law, that no assault and battery was committed, even though she did not consent to the operation. In other words, that the absence of a showing that defendant was actuated by a wrongful intent, or guilty of negligence, relieves the act of defendant from the charge of an unlawful assault and battery.

We are unable to reach that conclusion, though the contention is not without merit. It would seen to follow from what has been said on the other features of the case that the act of defendant amounted at least to a technical assault and battery. If the operation was performed without plaintiff's consent, and the circumstances were not such as to justify its performance without, it was wrongful; and, if it was wrongful, it was unlawful. As remarked in *1 Jaggard on Torts*, 437, every person has a right to complete immunity of his person from physical interference of others, except in so far as contact may be necessary under the general doctrine of privilege: and any unlawful or unauthorised touching of the person of another, except it be in the spirit of pleasantry, constitutes an assault and battery. In the case at bar, as we have already seen, the question whether defendant's act in performing the operation upon plaintiff was authorised was a question for the jury to determine. If it was unauthorised, then it was, within what we have said, unlawful. It was a violent assault, not a mere pleasantry: and, even though no negligence is shown, it was wrongful and unlawful.

(For a similar case in Canada, see *Murray v McMurchy* [1949] 2 DLR 442 Supreme Court of British Columbia.) You will also remember Lord Goff's reference in *Re F*: 'surgical treatment by a surgeon who mistakenly thinks that the patient has consented to it . . . may transcend the bounds of lawfulness'.

The variety of situations in which a battery action may be brought is explored by Allan McCoid in his seminal article.

A McCoid 'A Reappraisal of Liability for Unauthorised Medical Treatment' (1957) 41 Minnesota LR 381

The study of cases involving unauthorised operations or medical treatment indicates the existence of a great diversity of factual situations ranging from a case such as *Schloendorff v Society of New York Hospital* [105 NE 92 (NY, 1914)] in which the doctor operated in direct violation of express prohibitions of the patient and the operation resulted in serious physical injury, to cases such as *Mohr v Williams* [104 NW 12 (1905)] or *Pratt v Davis* [(1906) 79 NE 562], in which the operation was done without the express consent of the patient but probably caused no serious harm to the patient and in point of fact may have conferred some benefit. Between these two extremes lie cases in which there was only a limitation upon a general scope of consent the violation of which did not seriously injure the patient, as in *Rolater v Strain* [(1913) 39 Okla 572] and cases in which there was no express prohibition but substantial harm resulted to the patient from an operation which went beyond the scope of express consent, as in *Wall v Brim* [138 F 2d 478 (5th Circ, 1943)] or *Paulsen v Gundersen* [218 Wis 578, 260 NW 448 (1935)]. Yet the courts tend to group together all of these diverse fact situations under the category of 'assault and battery' and rely upon any one of the early cases as authority for imposing liability upon the doctor which may differ substantially from the nature and scope of liability in a general malpractice action. . . .

Traditionally the distinction between an 'assault and battery' and a 'negligent tort' has been drawn on the basis of the existence or nonexistence of 'intent', that state of mind in which the actor acts for the purpose of accomplishing a given consequence or acts with knowledge that such a consequence is substantially certain to occur, although there need be no showing of a hostile or malicious purpose or of an intent to do harm. In all of the cases discussed in this article, the physician knew what he was doing; he knew that he was performing a certain operation or that he was rendering certain treatment affecting the body of the patient. In all but a few of the cases it is to be inferred that he also knew that there was no specific assent to such operation or treatment, and in some of those few the lack of such knowledge was the result of mistake as to the identity of the patient or the identity of a particular portion of the body to be treated, neither of which would constitute a defense. In each of the cases there has been a legal 'harm' in the sense of a physically harmful invasion of the body of the plaintiff-patient or an interference with the patient's personal integrity or right to determine what shall and shall not be done with his body. Following these traditional lines of analysis, one would conclude that except in a very rare case, such as a true emergency, the doctor who acts without the consent of a patient is guilty of an assault and battery.

What appears to distinguish the case of the unauthorized operation from traditional assault and battery cases is the fact that in almost all of the cases, the doctor is acting in relative good faith for the benefit of the patient. It is true that in some cases the results are not in fact beneficial, but the courts have stated repeatedly that doctors are not insurers. The traditional assault and battery, on the other hand, involves a defendant who is acting for the most part out of malice or in a manner which is generally considered as 'anti-social'. And in general the assaulter and batterer is not seeking to confer any benefit upon the plaintiff, even though he may believe, as Dean Prosser has suggested, that he is complimenting the plaintiff by his amatory advances. This leads to the conclusion that there is some basis for separating most of the cases discussed in this paper from the traditional assault and battery. At the same time, there appears to be justification for retaining the 'assault and battery' classification for such situations as occurred in *Bryan v Grace* [(1940) 11 SE 2d 241], *Wellman v Drake* [(1947) 43 SE 2d 57] and *Keen v Coleman* [(1942) 20 SE 2d 175] as well as the 'fraud' cases. Operations, declared to be anti-social in their very nature by statutes making their performance a crime, deserve specialized treatment.

So, the central issue for the medical lawyer here is the legal concept of consent. A legally valid, or real, consent consists of the following elements: (a) it is given by a competent person; (b) it is given voluntarily; (c) it is an informed consent.

For the present it is important to notice the move away from the tort of battery to negligence, reflected in the courts' concern less with the question whether the touching was consented to at all and more with the quality of the information imparted to gain the consent.

Reibl v Hughes (1980) 114 DLR (3d) 1 (Can Sup Ct)

Laskin CJ: The tort [of battery] is an intentional one, consisting of an unprivileged and unconsented to invasion of one's bodily security. True enough, it has some advantages for a plaintiff over an action of negligence since it does not require proof of causation and it casts upon the defendant the burden of proving consent to what was done. Again, it does not require the adducing of medical evidence, although it seems to me that if battery is to be available for certain kinds of failure to meet the duty of disclosure there would necessarily have to be some such evidence brought before the Court as an element in determining whether there has been such a failure. . . .

The well-known statement of Cardozo J in *Schloendorff v Society of New York Hospital* 211 NY 125 at 129, 105 NE 92 at 93 (1914) that 'every human being of adult years and sound mind has a right to determine what shall be done with his own body; and a surgeon who performs an operation without his patient's consent commits an assault, for which he is liable in damages' cannot be taken beyond the compass of its words to support an action of battery where there has been consent to the very surgical procedure carried out upon a patient but there has been a breach of the duty of disclosure of attendant risks. In my opinion, actions of battery in respect of surgical or other medical treatment should be confined to cases where surgery or treatment has been performed or given to which there has been no consent at all where, emergency situations aside, surgery or treatment has been performed or given beyond that to which there was consent. . . .

In situations where the allegation is that attendant risks which should have been disclosed were not communicated to the patient and yet the surgery or other medical treatment carried out was that to which the plaintiff consented (there being no negligence basis of liability for the recommended surgery or treatment to deal with the patient's condition), I do not understand how it can be said that the consent was vitiated by the failure of disclosure so as to make the surgery or other treatment an unprivileged, unconsented to and intentional invasion of the patient's bodily integrity. I can appreciate the temptation to say that the genuineness of consent to medical treatment depends on proper disclosure of the risks which it entails, but in my view, unless there has been misrepresentation or fraud to secure consent to the treatment, a failure to disclose the attendant risks, however serious, should go to negligence rather than to battery. Although such a failure relates to an informed choice of submitting to or refusing recommended and appropriate treatment, it arises as the breach of an anterior duty of due care, comparable in legal obligation to the duty of due care in carrying out the particular treatment to which the patient has consented. It is not a test of the validity of the consent.

You will see from this extract from the leading Canadian case, that the Chief Justice considered that the scope of battery in medical law is restricted. Failure of the doctor to provide information will only in exceptional circumstances mean that the patient has not consented to a particular procedure. It is another matter, as we will see, whether an action in negligence may lie for the non-disclosure.

It is clear that the English courts do not favour the action in battery in the context of medical treatment. In *Hills v Potter* [1983] 3 All ER 716 Hirst J said:

I should add that I respectfully agree with Bristow J [in *Chatterton v Gerson*] in deploring reliance on these torts in medical cases of this kind; the proper cause of action, if any, is negligence.

Lord Scarman expressly agreed with these remarks in *Sidaway* (*supra*) when the case reached the House of Lords. Why should this be so? Consider the following remarks of Justice Mosk in the Californian case of *Cobbs v Grant* (1972) 502 P 2d 1.

Mosk J: [M]ost jurisdictions have permitted a doctor in an informed consent action to interpose a defense that the disclosure he omitted to make was not required within his medical community. However, expert opinion as to community standard is not required in a battery count, in which the patient must merely prove failure to give informed consent and a mere touching absent consent. Moreover a doctor could be held liable for punitive damages under a battery count, and if held liable for the intentional tort of battery he might not be covered by his malpractice insurance. Comment, 'Informed Consent in Medical Malpractice', 55 Cal L Rev 1396 (1967). Additionally, in some jurisdictions the patient has a longer statute of limitations if he sues in negligence.

Do any or all of these reasons apply in England?

G Robertson 'Informed Consent to Medical Treatment' (1981) 97 LQR 102

It is submitted that there are two principal reasons for the judicial policy evident in *Chatterton* [*v Gerson* [1981] QB 432] . . . against trespass claims in informed consent litigation. First, as can be seen from the decisions in *Fowler v Lanning* [[1959] 1 QB 426] and *Letang v Cooper* [[1965] 1 QB 232] judicial policy appears to be in favour of restricting claims in battery to situations involving deliberate, hostile acts, a situation which most judges would regard as foreign to the doctor-patient relationship. Coupled with this is the stigma and damage to professional reputation which courts repeatedly emphasise are an inevitable by-product of a successful claim against a doctor. These consequences are probably seen as even more serious in an action for battery than in an action for negligence. The second reason stems from the view expressed in the concluding section of this article, namely, that courts in this country will attempt to restrict the scope of the doctrine of informed consent, principally by means of the requirement of causation, the use of expert evidence as to accepted medical practice, and emphasis on the 'best interests of the patient' principle [on which we now have the House of Lords' decision in the *Sidaway* case: *infra*]. Restriction of the doctrine of informed consent in this way would not be possible if it were to be accepted that failure to inform of inherent risks of proposed treatment could ground an action for trespass. As was outlined above, the plaintiff in such an action would not be required to prove, by way of causation, that he would not have consented to the treatment had he been informed of the risks. Similarly, evidence of accepted medical practice has no place in an action for trespass; if failure to disclose a particular risk were to be regarded as vitiating consent, the fact that a reasonable doctor would not have disclosed the risk cannot absolve the defendant from liability for battery. Finally, although the point is not entirely clear, it would seem that a doctor cannot avoid liability for battery simply on the grounds that he was acting in the best interests of his patient. Thus it can be seen that the three principal ways in which the doctrine of informed consent is likely to be restricted would not be available to a court dealing with a case based in trespass.

As we will see, the Crown Indemnity Scheme whereby health authorities pay any damages awarded against doctors in their employment is restricted to claims in negligence (see *infra* p 499). It remains uncertain whether a doctor would be covered for a battery claim if he remained a member of a defence organisation.

A final, and by no means trivial point, concerns the juridical basis of the plea of consent: is it for the plaintiff to prove its absence or for the defendant to prove that the plaintiff consented? In *Freeman v Home Office (No 2)* [1984] QB 524 at 539 McCowan J asserted that it was for the plaintiff to prove lack of consent. There is little or no English case law to determine this issue. In principle, however, consent should be seen as a defence. Given the importance the law places on the bodily integrity of the individual, it is for the defendant to justify the interference. This is the law in other Commonwealth jurisdictions and was convincingly supported by McHugh J in the Australian High Court case of *Department of Health v JWB and SMB* (1992) 66 ALJR 300 at 337.

McHugh J: Consent is not necessary, however, where a surgical procedure or medical treatment must be performed in an emergency and the patient does not have the capacity to consent and no legally authorised representative is available to give consent on his or her behalf.

In England, the onus is on the plaintiff to prove lack of consent *(Freeman v Home Office (No 2)* [1984] QB 524 at 539). That view has the support of some academic writers in Australia (See Balkin and Davis, *Law of Torts*, (1991) pp 38-39; Luntz and Hambly, *Torts: Cases and Commentary* (3rd edn, 1992), pp 680-681; Blay, 'Onus of Proof of Consent in an Action for Trespass to the Person' (1987) 61 *Australian Law Journal 25*), but it is opposed by other academic writers in Australia. (See Fleming, *The Law of Torts* (7th edn, 1987), p 72; Trindade and Cane, *The Law of Torts in Australia,* (1985), pp 39-40.) It is opposed by Canadian Authority *(Hambley v Shepley* (1967) 63 DLR (2d) 94 at 95; *Kelly v Hazlett* (1976) 75 DLR (3d) 536 at 556; *Allan v New Mount Sinai Hospital* (1980) 109 DLR (3d) 634). It is also opposed by Australian authority *(Hart v Herron* [1984] Aust Torts Reports 80-201; *Sibley v Milutinovic* [1990] Aust Torts Reports 81-013). Notwithstanding the English view, I think that the onus is on the defendant to prove consent. Consent is a claim of 'leave and licence'. Such a claim must be pleaded and proved by the defendant in an action for trespass to land *(Kavanagh v Gudge* (1844) Ad & ER 7 Man & G 316, 135 ER 132; *Wood v Manley* (1839) 11 Ad & El 34, [1835-42] All ER Rep 128; *Plenty v Dillon* (1991) 171 CLR 635 at 647). It must be pleaded in a defamation action when the defendant claims that the plaintiff consented to the publication. (See *Loveday v Sun Newspapers Ltd* (1938) 59 CLR 503 at 525.) The Common Law Procedure Act 1852 (15 & 16 Vict c 76) (Sch B 44) also required any 'defence' of leave and licence to be pleaded and proved. However, those who contend that the plaintiff must negative consent in an action for trespass to the person deny that consent is a matter of leave and licence. They contend that lack of consent is an essential element of the action for trespass to a person. I do not accept that this is so. The essential element of the tort is an intentional or reckless, direct act of the defendant which makes or has the effect of causing contact with the body of the plaintiff. Consent may make the act lawful, but, if there is no evidence on the issue, the tort is made out. The contrary view is inconsistent with a person's right of bodily integrity. Other persons do not have the right to interfere with an individual's body unless he or she proves lack of consent to the interference.

For a discussion of this issue in the context of the crimes of assault and battery see *R v Brown* [1993] 2 All ER 75 HL; contrast Lord Jauncey at 92 and Lord Slynn at 119. Cf Lord Mustill at 103.

Form of consent

A. EXPRESS

Consent is express when the patient explicitly agrees to what is proposed by the doctor. It need not have been set out in any specific form and it need not be in writing: see *Re T (adult: refusal of treatment)* [1992] 4 All ER 649 at 653 per Lord Donaldson MR). Indeed, the vast majority of occasions when patients are touched by doctors take place in a GP's surgery where none of the apparatus of formal consent is present.

Consent forms have, however, long been a part of hospital procedure. The Department of Health (DOH) has published specimen forms in its *A Guide to Consent for Examination or Treatment* (NHS Management Executive, 1990) (HC (90) 22).

CONSENT FORM   **APPENDIX A(1)**
For medical or dental investigation, treatment or operation

Health Authority .... Patient's Surname ....

Hospital .... Other Names....................................

Unit Number .... Date of Birth...................................

Sex: (*Please tick*) Male   Female

DOCTORS OR DENTISTS (*This part to be completed by doctor or dentist.*)
                                                           See notes on the reverse
Type of operation, investigation or treatment for which written evidence of consent is considered appropriate

I confirm that I have explained the operation, investigation or treatment, and such appropriate options as are available and the type of anaesthetic, if any (general/local/ sedation) proposed, to the patient in terms which in my judgment are suited to the understanding of the patient and/or to one of the parents or guardians of the patient.

Signature .... Date..

Name of doctor or dentist...
PATIENT/PARENT/GUARDIAN
1.   Please read this form and the notes overleaf very carefully.
2.   If there is anything that you don't understand about the explanation, or if you want more information, you should ask the doctor or dentist.
3.   Please check that all the information on the form is correct. If it is, and you understand the explanation, then sign the form.
I am the patient/parent/guardian (*delete as necessary*).
I agree   ■ to what is proposed which has been explained to me by the doctor/ dentist named on this form.
               ■ to the use of the type of anaesthetic that I have been told about.

I understand	■ that the procedure may not be done by the doctor/dentist who has been treating me so far.
	■ that any procedure in addition to the investigation or treatment described on this form will only be carried out if it is necessary and in my best interests and can be justified for medical reasons.
I have told	■ the doctor or dentist about the procedures listed below I would *not* wish to be carried out straightaway without my having the opportunity to consider them first.

....

....

Signature   ....

Name   ....

Address   ....

(if not the patient)   ....

In addition to this general form, the DOH provides specimen consent forms, *inter alia*, for use in case of sterilisations and as regards treatment of the mentally disordered.

There is no specific form prescribed by law to which the document must conform. It need only record faithfully that which was agreed between the parties and not contemplate that which is unlawful. Indeed, there is no requirement in law that consent be reduced to writing. The written consent form is merely therefore evidence of what was agreed. Notice the words of Bristow J in *Chatterton v Gerson* [1981] 1 All ER 257 at 265:

> I should add that getting the patient to sign a pro forma expressing consent to undergo the operation 'the effect and nature of which have been explained to me', as was done here in each case, should be a valuable reminder to everyone of the need for explanation and consent. But it would be no defence to an action based on trespass to the person if no explanation had in fact been given. The consent would have been expressed in form only, not in reality.

In commenting upon the DOH's form, Margaret Brazier expressed the following views.

M Brazier 'Revised Consent Forms in the NHS' (1991) 6 Professional Negligence 148

The experienced cynic might well conclude that the new form is longer than its predecessor but how does the extra verbiage actually reinforce patients' rights?

Nothing on the face of the form prevents the doctor scrawling unhelpfully 'D & C' under type of operation and hustling the patient through filling out his part of the form. Note how the doctor certifies that in his judgment the explanation of the proposed treatment is suited to the understanding of the patient. Paternalism enshrined in *Sidaway* is given further official blessing. But the Department of Health was not responsible for *Sidaway*. The House of Lords retains that dubious honour. The new form does seek to focus the attention of professional and patient on some of the matters their consultation should cover. At a most banal level more room is made on the form for the explanation of the type of operation, investigation or treatment. The doctor is required to confirm that he has canvassed alternative options available and discussed with the patient the type of anaesthetic. The form prompts the patient to ask questions. In a sense the 'official' form gives the patient express 'permission' to question the doctor. And the patient is offered a specific opportunity to state what additional procedures she would not wish to be carried out straightaway without an opportunity to consider them first. Those instances where a woman goes into hospital for minor gynaecological surgery and wakes up sterilised 'in her best interests' ought not now to recur.

You will notice that the form states that:

> I understand that any procedure in addition to the investigation or treatment described on this form will only be carried out if it is necessary and in my best interests and can be justified for medical reasons.

Two Canadian cases illustrate the questions that can arise from such a clause.

Brushett v Cowan [1991] 2 Med LR 271 (Newfoundland CA)

Marshall JA: On June 25, 1984 [Miss Brushett] entered hospital to undergo that procedure. Prior to the operation she signed a consent which read as follows:

> I Brushett Sheila of 198 Pleasant St hereby consent to the submission of myself to the operation or special procedure of Muscle Biopsy Right Distal Thigh the nature and purpose of which have been explained to me by Dr Cowan.
>
> I also consent to such further or alternative measures as may be found to be necessary during the course of the operation or special procedure and to the administration of a general, local or other anaesthetic for any of these purposes.
>
> I further agree that in his discretion Dr Cowan may make use of the assistance of other surgeons, physicians, and hospital staff and may permit them to order or perform all or part of the treatment, special procedure or operative procedure and they shall have the same discretion in my treatment and in the execution of any procedure as Dr Cowan.

After Dr Cowan had excised a portion of the muscle, he went down to the bone and, having observed an area that appeared abnormal he biopsied a portion of it. Miss Brushett was discharged from hospital that same day. No instructions were given to her at that time relating to the use of crutches nor were any provided to her.

Two days later she visited Dr Cowan at his clinic in the hospital for consultation and examination. While arrangements were then made to supply her with crutches, Miss Brushett testified no one advised her to be non-weight bearing. She also maintained she was not made aware that a biopsy had been taken from her bone as well as her muscle and remained unaware of that fact until so advised by a Dr Perkins prior to operating upon her on July 7, 1984, to repair a fracture to her leg. On the other hand, Dr Cowan maintained that during the course of the examination on June 22, 1984, he had advised Miss Brushett of the bone biopsy and instructed her to be non-weight bearing. In support of this contention a letter was produced bearing the same date from the doctor to the Workers Compensation Board relative to Miss Brushett in which he stated:

> Today I gave her crutches and advised her to be non-weight bearing.

Miss Brushett testified that she used the crutches intermittently for mobilization, getting in and out of chairs or climbing stairs. She stated that she never used them otherwise inside her home but generally used them outside. However, she was not using them on 6 July 1984, when, in the course of a visit to Old Perlican, she fell and broke her right leg at the site of the bone biopsy. She was subsequently conveyed to the General Hospital in St John's where Dr Perkins operated upon her on 7 July to repair the fracture.

Later Miss Brushett took action against Dr Cowan, the General Hospital and a resident physician at the hospital. Her claim against Dr Cowan was founded in battery arising from the bone biopsy allegedly performed without her knowledge and consent and in negligence primarily related to her post-operative care.

The action against the hospital was discontinued at the commencement of the trial. The claim against the resident physician was dismissed by the trial judge. . . . However, the learned trial judge found Dr Cowan liable in battery and in negligence in failing to advise his patient to be non-weight bearing and of the possible effects of normal use of her leg. . . .

Citing *Reibl*, the trial judge focused her assessment entirely upon the formal consent signed by Miss Brushett. In so doing, she found para 3 inapplicable and para 2 too vague to permit an interpretation expanding Miss Brushett's consent beyond the muscle biopsy to which she specifically consented in the initial part of the document. As a result she found that the bone biopsy amounted to a battery.

In my respectful opinion the learned trial judge erred in confining her assessment to the formal written consent form. It is noted that Laskin CJC in *Reibl* held that battery should be confined to cases where there has been 'no consent at all' or where medical procedures go 'beyond that to which there was consent'. He did not state that one's inquiry must be limited to the specific formal consent. On the contrary, the statement that battery is predicated upon the absence of any consent 'at all' implies that one must examine all aspects of the situation to determine if the patient had agreed to the medical procedure in respect of which complaint is laid.

Therefore, all relevant circumstances leading up to the surgery should be considered when determining what the patient agreed to when he or she submitted to the procedure. Any written consent will bear obvious weight upon such an assessment. However, inasmuch as many formal consents are signed – as was the one in the case at bar – immediately before the surgery, on the threshold as it were of the operating room, when a patient is experiencing a certain degree of trauma and stress, the circumstances leading up to his or her presence at the hospital are relevant to the patient's intent and the consent form ought to be read in light of them.

In the present case, the circumstances show Miss Brushett to have been referred to Dr Cowan for the purpose of investigating persistent problems associated with an injury which she had sustained. Within a relatively short period of time Miss Brushett had a number of consultations and underwent several investigative procedures at Dr Cowan's instigation, all of which were aimed at determining the cause of her symptoms. Indeed, the biopsy was part of the ongoing investigative process.

It is true that the consent form made specific reference to a muscle biopsy and that the patient must have entered hospital contemplating a part of her muscle was to be excised. However, this was because the bone scan indicated that certain abnormalities detected by it were due to muscle damage. Submission to the surgical procedure was for the purpose of determining the cause of her persistent problem with her right thigh and to achieve this she agreed to undergo a procedure that would enable a portion of her body inside the thigh to be excised for investigation. While the scan caused, at that juncture, both the doctor, Miss Brushett and the written consent to focus upon the muscle in her right thigh, the overriding general purpose and intent must be taken to remain investigatory to determine the cause of the medical problem for which she had first consulted the specialist.

Had the scan signalled potential bone as well as muscle disorders, it is reasonable to assume specific reference would have been made in the consent to bone biopsy and that Miss Brushett would have agreed to it as well. In fact the trial judge, while addressing the doctor's negligence in relation to pre-operative advice, concluded that upon discovery of the discoloured bone and possible malignancy, Miss Brushett as a reasonable patient would have consented to the procedure.

It is, therefore, against the background of these circumstances that the formal consent must be viewed. In doing so the perceived vagueness which the trial judge felt rendered para 2 ineffective becomes clearer. Likewise para 3 acquires a relevance.

Considered from that perspective of the circumstances, the authorization in the second paragraph consenting

> . . . to such further or alternate measures as may be found to be necessary during the course of the operation or special procedure . . .

may be construed, in my opinion, as consenting to the removal of a necessary sample of the bone adjacent to the muscle in pursuit of the continuing investigative process. The discretion which para 3 records to have been given to the operating surgeon supports this view.

The law has always clearly recognized the individual's right to determine medical treatment upon his or her person: see *Allan v New Mount Sinai Hospital* (1980) 109 DLR (3d) 634, 28 OR (2d) 356; 11 CCLT 299 (HCJ), per Linden J at 642-3. It may not be abridged by considerations of medical convenience. However, this inviolable right must be interpreted in relation to the overall social interest of precluding undue hindrance of the physician legitimately acting within the scope of the consent actually given by adopting too narrow a view of its ambit. The full extent of that consent must be gained by looking at all of the circumstances arising from the relation of doctor and patient, against the background of which the formal consent will be viewed.

In summary, I conclude, with respect, that the trial judge erred in looking exclusively to the signed consent form without regard to all of the factors. Considering all of these circumstances, I am of the opinion that the bone biopsy performed upon Miss Brushett by Dr Cowan did not go beyond the consent given by her to him and, hence, there was no battery.

In the following case the judge also found that the procedure fell within the express consent given.

Pridham v Nash (1986) 33 DLR (4th) 304 (Ontario High Court)

R E Holland J: This medical malpractice case raises issues of consent to treatment.

Facts
Patricia Pridham is a 39-year-old married woman with four children who works as a driver for Canada Post. The late Dr Nash was an obstetrician and gynaecologist practising in Toronto. Dr Nash delivered three of Mrs. Pridham's children and also performed a tubal ligation and a partial hysterectomy prior to the operation that has given rise to this action.

For about two years before February of 1980, Mrs Pridham had been suffering from periodic pain in the pelvic area. She consulted Dr Nash on 14 February 1980, and told him about her complaints. He then examined her.

Dr Nash's note of the consultation reads as follows:

Feb 14/80 —   Had an operation in Etobicoke General in November 1977 for adhesions.

Took out her tube on left side.

Still having left sided pain. Has been on antibiotics.

Pelvis negative. Pap smear.

To have laparoscopy as out patient.

Mrs Pridham testified that after the examination Dr Nash recommended a laparoscopy to find out what was wrong. A laparoscopy is an examination of the abdominal structures within the peritoneum by means of a tubular instrument passed through the abdominal wall. Dr Nash explained there would be a small incision in the area of the navel. A scope would be inserted so that he could look around and he would then let her know what he had found. The procedure was to take place in the hospital under a general anesthetic and a date was fixed for the operation.

Following the consultation Mrs. Pridham signed a consent to treatment which was filled out by Dr Nash and reads, in part, as follows:

TO: MOUNT SINAI HOSPITAL, TORONTO, ONTARIO.

1. I Patricia Pridham consent to the following procedure being performed upon me/upon me
    General Nature of the Treatment: laparoscopy
2. The anticipated nature and effect of such procedures have been explained to me.
3. I confirm that I understand the explanations about the nature and effect of the procedures that will be performed upon me.
4. I consent to all preliminary and related procedures and to the administration of general and other anaesthetics and to additional or alternative procedures as may be necessary or medically advisable during the course of such procedures.
5. I understand that Mount Sinai Hospital is a teaching hospital and that various medical care personnel may be involved in the procedures.
    '*Patricia Pridham*'
Signature of Patient, Parent or Guardian.

PHYSICIAN'S STATEMENT

On the above date I explained the general nature of the procedure specified above to the person who signed this form and I was witness to that signing.

'*S S Nash*'
Signature of Physician.

Mrs Pridham had undergone a laparoscopic examination before at Etobicoke General Hospital. She said that a similar explanation of the procedure had been given to her at that time. Following that laparoscopic examination there had been a further consultation with her doctor and she had consented to a further operation that had been performed the next day.

On Friday, 29 February 1980, Mrs Pridham was admitted to Mount Sinai Hospital and the operation was performed in the afternoon. Dr Nash's operative report, which is part of the hospital records, reads, in part, as follows:

Surgeon: Dr S Nash.
Anesthetic: General.
Pre-operative Diagnosis: PELVIC PAIN
Post-operative Diagnosis: ADHESION IN PELVIS
Procedure: LAPAROSCOPY AND LYSES OF ADHESIONS

Procedure: Under general anesthesia, a stab wound was made in the lower end of the umbilicus. The Verres needle was introduced and 8.5(?) litres of (?) carbon dioxide gas was insufflated. The stab wound was increased, and the trocar was pushed through. The laparoscope was put through the sleeve of the trocar.

Evaluation of the pelvis showed no evidence of any uterus. It was difficult to see the ovaries, since they were in the cul-de-sac. There was an adhesive band going from the pelvis to the anterior abdominal wall, and this, I believe, could cause recurrent phases of subacute bowel obstruction.

What was decided was to lyse these two adhesions. A coagulating forceps was then put in, and the two adhesions were lysed using the cutting current. The gas and instruments were removed, and the incision in the umbilicus was closed.

The patient withstood the procedure well, and left the operating room in good condition.

The term lyse used in the report means to cut or divide.

Dr Nash spoke to Mrs Pridham in the recovery room following the procedure and told her that he had found some adhesions, that she would be all right, and that she could go home that day. She said that she just assumed that what was done had to be done and she made no complaint.

After Mrs Pridham returned home she experienced pain in the abdomen. The pain grew in intensity over the week-end and she was admitted, through the emergency department, to Scarborough General Hospital on Monday, 3 March. She came under the care of Dr O'Dwyer, a general surgeon. He diagnosed pelvic peritonitis – inflammation of the peritoneum. He operated and found a perforation of the ileum from which intestinal content leaked readily. There was a surrounding necrotic area (area of dead tissue) which he presumed was the result of cautery. Dr O'Dwyer resected about a three-inch segment of ileum. Mrs Pridham tolerated the operation well and was discharged from the hospital on 21 March.

Mrs Pridham appeared to me to be a hard working, well-motivated person and she was able to get back to work within a reasonable time. She has been left with an unsightly scar on the abdomen and still has some minor complaints.

Issues
The issues raised are as follows:
1.   Did Mrs Pridham expressly or by implication consent to the lyseing of the adhesions since it was during this procedure that the damage was caused to the ileum which resulted in peritonitis . . .

Was there consent, express or implied, to lyse the adhesions?
Counsel for Mrs Pridham submits that although there was consent to an investigative procedure, there was no consent to lyse or cut adhesions during such procedure.

Dr Scott Russell, an obstetrician and gynaecologist, was called as a defence witness. He explained the procedure known as laparoscopy. It is a surgical procedure usually performed under a general anesthetic. A small incision is made in the abdomen and the abdomen is then inflated with carbon dioxide. A trocar is then inserted. A trocar used for such a procedure in 1980 looks like a stainless steel spike about eight inches and one centimetre in diameter. The trocar is covered by a stainless steel sleeve. Once the trocar and sleeve are in place the trocar is withdrawn leaving the sleeve extending through the wall of the abdomen. An optical tube, a laparoscope, is then placed through the sleeve and the surgeon can observe the contents of the abdomen. The laparoscope is about 15 ins long. It is rigid and slightly less than one centimetre in diameter.

Should the surgeon wish to move an internal organ, because it obstructs his view, or wish to cut tissue, or take tissue for biopsy, the surgeon may make a second incision at the pubic hair-line and, through a trocar, introduce a cutting and coagulating forceps. The forceps may also be introduced through the original incision, using another trocar and sleeve, and this latter procedure was apparently followed in this case.

Laparoscopy is frequently performed and is possibly performed on one in 12 women of child-bearing age in Toronto.

The cutting of adhesions is generally not considered to be serious. Dr Russell said that adhesions can look like cobwebs or can be thicker, like pieces of butchers' cord. Dr Nash apparently thought that Mrs Pridham was well enough following the operation to go home that same afternoon.

The consent form, above-quoted . . . , reads in part as follows:

4. I consent to . . . additional . . . procedures as may be necessary or medically advisable during the course of such procedures.

If the laparoscopic examination, an investigative procedure, had revealed a major problem requiring surgery then, in my view, the surgeon would not be entitled to rely on the original consent and the general words of the consent, as quoted above, to carry out the major surgery. The surgeon would have been required to consult further with the patient and obtain a further consent to the major operation. However, this case, in my view, is different.

From a practical point of view it would have been foolish for Dr Nash to wait for Mrs Pridham to come out of the anesthetic and then seek her consent to go through the same incision again to cut the two adhesions. The additional curative surgery was of such a minor nature that it falls practically in the same category as taking a sample for biopsy.

It was Dr Russell's opinion that he would consider it part of Dr Nash's mandate to move and clear away obstructions that were in the way and, for this purpose, to introduce a second trocar. Further, in the process of dividing adhesions the doctor would have to cut and coagulate them. Dr Russell testified that if Dr Nash discovered a solitary or simple situation during a laparoscopy it would be reasonable for him to deal with such a situation as a simple curative act undertaken in the process of having the problem discovered. Dr Russell was of the view that Dr Nash properly considered what he did as within his mandate.

In my opinion what happened here came within the wording of the consent and there was, therefore, express consent to this surgery.

(See also *Davis v Barking, Havering and Brentwood HA* [1993] 4 Med LR 85 (McCullough J) on relevance of a consent form where unexpected procedure performed.)

B. IMPLIED

In *Sidaway v Bethlem Royal Hospital Governors* [1985] AC 871 Lord Diplock reminded us that 'consent to battery is a state of mind personal to the victim of the battery . . .' This being so, if the patient does not explicitly express what is in his mind, a question arises as to whether it is proper to imply from his conduct what his state of mind is. On one view, it is said that the law implies consent from the patient's conduct ie deduces his state of mind. Another view which we think more tenable would describe implied consent as something of a fiction. Without express agreement no one may know what was in the patient's mind but it may be thought appropriate to prevent him complaining after the event that he did not consent. On this view, implied consent properly analysed becomes a form of estoppel whereby a patient, although he may not actually have agreed to some intervention, is estopped from denying that he did so.

Professor John Fleming in his authoritative text, *Law of Torts* (8th edn, 1993) illustrates the kind of situations in which implied consent arises.

J Fleming *Law of Torts* (8th edn, 1993)

Consent may be given expressly, as when a patient authorises a surgeon to perform an operation, but it may just as well be implied: Actions often speak louder than words. Holding up one's bare arm to a doctor at a vaccination point is as clear an assent as if it were expressed in words. Similarly, acquiescence by a landowner in the use by the public of a shortcut across his property permits the inference of an implied licence and prevents him from treating such intruders as trespassers until he has made it clear that further entry is prohibited. Participants in games or sports involving a likelihood of bodily contact, such as wrestling or boxing, consent to all the risks ordinarily incidental, though not to undue violence or unfair play. Even silence and inaction may in some circumstances be interpreted as an expression of willingness. Failure to resist or protest indicates consent if a reasonable person who is aware of the consequences and capable of protest or resistance would voice his objection. A girl who is silent to an amorous proposal cannot afterwards capriciously complain of assault.

The best known case in which consent was implied in a medical law context is the following.

O'Brien v Cunard SS Co (1891) 28 NE 266 (Mass Sup Jud Ct)

Knowlton J: . . . To sustain the first count, which was for an alleged assault, the plaintiff relied on the fact that the surgeon who was employed by the defendant vaccinated her on ship-board while she was on her passage from Queenstown to Boston. On this branch of the case the question is whether there was any evidence that the surgeon used force upon the plaintiff against her will. In determining whether the act was lawful or unlawful, the surgeon's conduct must be considered in connection with the surrounding circumstances. If the plaintiff's behavior was such as to indicate consent on her part, he was justified in his act, whatever her unexpressed feelings may have been. In determining whether she consented, he could be guided only by her overt acts and the manifestations of her feelings. . . . It is undisputed that at Boston there are strict quarantine regulations in regard to the examination of emigrants, to see that they are protected from small-pox by vaccination, and that only those persons who hold a certificate from the medical officer of the steamship, stating that they are so protected, are permitted to land without detention in quarantine, or vaccination by the port physician. It appears that the defendant is accustomed to have its surgeons vaccinate all emigrants who desire it, and who are not protected by previous vaccination, and give them a certificate which is accepted at quarantine as evidence of their protection. Notices of the regulations at quarantine, and of the willingness of the ship's medical officer to vaccinate such as needed vaccination, were posted about the ship in various languages, and on the day when the operation was performed the surgeon had a right to presume that she and the other women who were vaccinated understood the importance and purpose of vaccination for those who bore no marks to show that they were protected. By the plaintiff's testimony, which, in this particular, is undisputed, it appears that about 200 women passengers were assembled below, and she understood from conversation with them that they were to be vaccinated; that she stood about 15 feet from the surgeon, and saw them form up in a line, and pass in turn before him; that he 'examined their arms, and, passing some of them by, proceeded to vaccinate those that had no mark'; that she did not hear him say anything to any of them; that upon being passed by they each received a card, and went on deck; that when her turn came she showed him her arm; he looked at it, and said there was no mark, and that she should be vaccinated; that she told him she had been vaccinated before, and it left no mark; 'that he then said nothing; that he should vaccinate her again'; that she held up her arm to be vaccinated; that no one touched her; that she did not tell him she did not want to be vaccinated; and that she took the ticket which he gave her, certifying that he had vaccinated her, and used it at quarantine. She was one of a large number of women who were vaccinated on that occasion, without, so far as appears, a word of objection from any of them. They all indicated by their conduct that they desired to avail themselves of the provisions made for their benefit. There was nothing in the conduct of the plaintiff to indicate to the surgeon that she did not wish to obtain a card which would save her from detention at quarantine, and to be vaccinated, if necessary, for that purpose. Viewing his conduct in the light of the surrounding circumstances, it was lawful; and there was no evidence tending to show that it was not. The ruling of the court on this part of the case was correct. . . .

One situation in which it has been said that implied consent justifies intervention is the case of the unconscious patient who is brought in to the emergency department of a hospital. Express consent is impossible, but it is argued the patient would agree to treatment which is in his 'best interests' if he were conscious. The consent may, therefore, be implied (see Skegg, 'A Justification For Medical Procedures Performed without Consent' (1974) 90 LQR 512).

Mohr v Williams (1905) 104 NW 12 (Sup Ct Minn)

Brown J: It is not, however, contended by defendant that under ordinary circumstances consent is unnecessary, but that, under the particular circumstances of this case, consent was implied; that it was an emergency case, such as to authorize the operation without express consent or permission. The medical profession has made signal progress in solving the problems of health and disease, and they may justly point with pride to the advancement made in supplementing nature and correcting deformities, and relieving pain and suffering. The physician impliedly contracts that he possesses, and will exercise in the treatment of patients, skill and learning, and that he will exercise reasonable care and exert his best judgment to bring about favorable results. The methods of treatment are committed almost exclusively to his judgment, but we are aware of no rule or principle of law which would extend to him free license respecting surgical operations. Reasonable latitude must, however, be allowed the physician in a particular case; and we would not lay down any rule which would unreasonably interfere with the exercise of his discretion, or prevent him from taking such measures as his judgment dictated for the welfare of the patient in a case of emergency. If a person should be injured to the extent of rendering him unconscious, and his injuries were of such a nature as to require prompt surgical attention, a physician called to attend him would be justified in applying such medical or surgical treatment as might reasonably be necessary for the preservation of his life or limb, and consent on the part of the injured person would be implied.

And again, if, in the course of an operation to which the patient consented, the physician should discover conditions not anticipated before the operation was commenced, and which, if not removed, would endanger the life or health of the patient, he would, though no express consent was obtained or given, be justified in extending the operation to remove and overcome them. But such is not the case at bar. The diseased condition of plaintiff's left ear was not discovered in the course of an operation on the right, which was authorized, but upon an independent examination of that organ, made after the authorized operation was found unnecessary. Nor is the evidence such as to justify the court in holding, as a matter of law, that it was such an affection [sic] as would result immediately in the serious injury of plaintiff, or such an emergency as to justify proceeding without her consent. She had experienced no particular difficulty with that ear, and the questions as to when its diseased condition would become alarming or fatal, and whether there was an immediate necessity for an operation, were, under the evidence, questions of fact for the jury.

While implied consent is one possible justification for the intervention, it is not, we would suggest, the most appropriate. Instead, the doctor's justification for treating an unconscious patient must, if at all, rest in the doctrine of necessity recognised by the House of Lords in *Re F (a mental patient: sterilisation)* [1990] 2 AC 1 which we will see in detail later (*infra*, pp 317 *et seq*).

This explanation also applies when the patient's incompetence to consent is permanent, for example, due to intellectual disability. Here, the notion of implying consent when the patient never had, nor will have, capacity to consent is legerdemain. In *Re F* Lord Goff said that to imply consent 'can be regarded as artificial; and in particular, it is difficult to impute consent to those who, by reason of their youth or mental disorder, are unable to give their consent' (at 72). Hence, in *Re F* the legal justification for treating the permanently incompetent was seen as the principle of necessity.

If, as has been argued, the true nature of implied consent is a form of estoppel, what are the criteria which give rise to the estoppel? It could be said that a patient will be estopped from denying that he consented to a procedure in circumstances in which a reasonable person looking at the situation would reach the conclusion that consent had been given in the light of all the circumstances. Of course, the reasonable onlooker would not necessarily possess all the knowledge, nor make all the assumptions, of a doctor. Thus, it is not appropriate to judge whether the patient is consenting from the vantage point of the doctor. Equally, to look at the circumstances from the subjective position of the patient would be unduly harsh and unfair to the medical profession. Thus, a middle position employing the common law stalwart of the 'reasonable person' suggests itself. Much then will depend upon the circumstances and the court's view of what can fairly be said to be the impression left by the patient's conduct.

An example which tests the application of this approach is the oft-cited proposition that any patient admitted to a teaching hospital thereby consents to being touched by students in the course of their training. Let us be clear about this example to avoid misunderstanding. There are two situations in which it may be proposed that the problems of implied consent arise. The first is where a patient agrees to be touched, for example, for the purpose of taking a blood sample and, without her knowledge, it is done by a student. In such a case there is no problem of implied consent. This is not to say there is no legal issue but the issue is whether the express consent given to the procedure is valid given the identity of the person carrying out the procedure (see *infra*). The second situation is where additional, and for the patient, unnecessary procedures are carried out without her knowledge for the purpose of furthering students' training. The paradigm is the vaginal examination of a woman whilst she is under anaesthetic awaiting surgery. This is a case where the legality of the touching turns upon whether consent can be implied. Arguably, without express knowledge that she was in a teaching hospital a reasonable person would not conclude that by consenting to treatment she had thereby impliedly consented to the vaginal examination. Further, even with such knowledge a court should insist that the patient gives express consent particularly bearing in mind the vulnerability of any person who finds herself in a hospital. [For an express recognition of the *ethical* validity of this argument see, *Medical Students in Hospital* (HC (91) 18 (April 1991).]

Perhaps the most controversial recourse to the law of implied consent (or as we would argue, estoppel) has been in the area of HIV testing. It has been argued that testing blood taken from a patient for other purposes with the secret intention of testing for HIV is entirely lawful as merely being an example of implied consent (see the discussion in Keown, 'The Ashes of Aids and the Phoenix of Informed Consent' (1989) 52 MLR 790). As we shall see, the issue is by no means as simple as this. The analysis requires a two-stage approach. The first stage is a consideration of whether the individual expressly, and with sufficient understanding of what is involved, consents to the taking of the blood for testing for HIV. Secondly, if it is the case that there was no express consent, does the patient's conduct amount to implied consent? Since consideration of the question of implied consent entails examining the question of the 'nature and purpose' of the allegedly express consent, we defer consideration until later (see *infra* pp 147-166).

The nature of consent

There are three relevant issues which fall to be determined: (1) Did the patient have *capacity* in law (was the patient competent to give consent?); (2) Was the person giving consent appropriately *informed* beforehand?; and (3) Was the consent *voluntarily* given?

Each of these issues may be analysed by reference to the nature and extent of the doctor's duty, ie to inform or to ensure voluntariness and competence.

What is the function of the legal requirement of consent? As we saw at the beginning of this chapter, the need for consent derives from the law's respect for the patient's right to decide. Consent, therefore, has a positive and negative property, ie it is as much the exercise of the right to make one's own decision to say 'yes' (consent) or to say 'no' (refuse). An alternative and more limited view of the true role of consent emerged in the early 1990s in cases concerned with medical treatment and children. In these cases – *Re R (a minor) (wardship: consent to treatment)* [1992] Fam 11 and *Re W (a minor) (medical treatment)* [1992] 4 All ER 627 – the Court of Appeal developed a more restrictive role for consent. In *Re R* Lord Donaldson stated:

> . . . Consent by itself creates no obligation to treat. It is merely a key which unlocks a door. Furthermore, whilst in the case of an adult of full capacity there will usually only be one keyholder, namely the patient, in the ordinary family unit where a young child is the patient there will be two keyholders, namely the parents, with a several as well as a joint right to turn the key and unlock the door. If the parents disagree, one consenting and the other refusing, the doctor will be presented with a professional and ethical, but not with a legal, problem because, if he has the consent of one authorised person, treatment will not without more constitute a trespass or a criminal assault.

In *Re W* Lord Donaldson MR returned to the issue.

> **Lord Donaldson MR:** There seems to be some confusion in the minds of some as to the purpose of seeking consent from a patient (whether adult or child) or from someone with authority to give that consent on behalf of the patient. It has two purposes, the one clinical and the other legal. The clinical purpose stems from the fact that in many instances the cooperation of the patient and the patient's faith or at least confidence in the efficiency of the treatment is a major factor contributing to the treatment's success. Failure to obtain such consent will not only deprive the patient and the medical staff of this advantage, but will usually make it much more difficult to administer the treatment. I appreciate that this purpose may not be served if consent is given on behalf of, rather than by the patient. However, in the case of young children knowledge of the fact that the parent had consented may help. The legal purpose is quite different. It is to provide those concerned in the treatment with a defence to a criminal charge of assault or battery or a civil claim for damages for trespass to the person. It does not, however, provide them with any defence to a claim that they negligently advised a particular treatment or negligently carried it out. . . .
>
> On reflection I regret my use in *Re R* of the keyholder analogy . . . because keys can lock as well as unlock. I now prefer the analogy of the legal 'flak jacket' which protects from claims by the litigious whether he acquires it from his patient who may be a minor over the age of 16, or a 'Gillick competent' child under that age or from another person having parental responsibilities which include a right to consent to treatment of the minor. Anyone who gives him a flak jacket (ie consent) may take it back, but the doctor only needs one and so long as he continues to have one he has the legal right to proceed.

Of course, as far as it goes Lord Donaldson's analysis is right: consent does provide an answer to a claim in battery. But, as these cases show, at least where children are concerned, Lord Donaldson MR was anxious to assert that competent children do not have an *exclusive* right to determine their own treatment. We will examine this controversial development later (*infra* p 378 *et seq*). For now it suffices to notice the legal implications of consent given by a child, though not an adult: consent to treatment is effective unless and until the court is involved, refusal of treatment may not be.

Even this statement may need qualification in this somewhat confused area of law. There is, at least, one plausible reading of Lord Fraser's speech in *Gillick v West Norfolk and Wisbech AHA* [1985] 3 All ER 402, (1985) 2 BMLR

11 (HL). It suggests that while a competent child's consent is effective as against any view of the parents as to the child's best interest, it may not be sufficient in that Lord Fraser leaves the final decision whether to treat to the doctor. *Gillick* is, of course, a case concerned with young persons and where young persons are involved the court may be saying that capacity to consent, while being a necessary condition, *may* not be a sufficient one for justifying any doctor's action based on an expression of will. The law may demand that the doctor's action also be in the best interests of the girl as judged by someone other than the young person, ie the doctor. This would, of course, run counter to the thesis contained in the notion of capacity that it is the legal reflection of the ethical principle of respect for autonomy. It may, however, be that Lord Fraser believes this to be the law: (p 412f) 'Nobody doubts, certainly I do not doubt, that in the overwhelming majority of cases the best judges of a child's welfare are his or her parents'; (p 413a) 'The only practical course is, in my opinion, to entrust the doctor with a discretion to act in accordance with his view of what is best in the interests of the girl who is his patient.' Lord Scarman, however, does not subscribe to this view and it is submitted his view is to be preferred.

But, there is another (and better) view of Lord Fraser's speech. Lord Fraser's observations need not be read as undermining the principle that an autonomous person is the best judge of his own interest. An alternative interpretation would be that Lord Fraser is making a far more commonplace point that in any context where a patient seeks medical care from a doctor it is the doctor who has the final word on whether treatment *is* called for. On this reading, Lord Fraser's speech does not detract from the thesis developed by him and Lord Scarman concerning the capacity of young persons to decide for themselves once they have sufficient maturity and understanding.

A. CAPACITY

1. What is capacity?

This first question calls for an inquiry into what factors the law regards as important before attaching any significance to any expression of will by the patient. It is a secondary question (which we will consider later) what particular criteria, if any, must be satisfied before the law recognises in the particular case that the abstract notion of capacity has been satisfied.

There may in essence be two alternative approaches to capacity: (1) status; (2) understanding; but traditional scholarship has not always reflected this. The traditional approach has tended to confuse that which goes to the notion of capacity and that which goes to demonstrate its presence in a particular case. This misunderstanding can be found in the otherwise excellent analysis offered by the President's Commission in their 'Making Health Care Decisions' report in 1983, at pp 169-171.

President's Commission 'Making Health Care Decisions' (1983)

Identification of incapacity
In the light of the presumption that most patients have the capacity to make health care decisions, on what grounds might a person be found to lack such a capacity? Three general

criteria have been followed: the outcome of the decision, the status or category of the patient, and the patient's functional ability as a decisionmaker.

The outcome approach – which the Commission expressly rejects – bases a determination of incapacity primarily on the content of a patient's decision. Under this standard, a patient who makes a health care decision that reflects values not widely held or that rejects conventional wisdom about proper health care is found to be incapacitated.

Using the status approach, certain categories of patients have traditionally been deemed incapable of making treatment decisions without regard to their actual capabilities. Some of these categories of patients – such as the unconscious – correspond closely with actual incapacity. But other patients who are presumed to be incapacitated on the basis of their status may actually be capable of making particular health care decisions. Many older children, for example, can make at least some health care decisions, mildly or moderately retarded individuals hold understandable preferences about health care, and the same may be true in varying degrees among psychotic persons.

The third approach to the determination of incapacity focuses on an individual's actual functioning in decisionmaking situations rather than on the individual's status. This approach is particularly germane for children above a certain age (variously described as from seven to mid-teens). For example, rather than considering children under the age of majority incompetent to decide unless they come within one of the exceptions created by the statutory and common law, these patients could be regarded as competent unless shown to lack decisionmaking capacity. Similarly, a senile person may have been declared incompetent by a court and a guardian may have been appointed to manage the person's financial affairs, but the functional standard would not foreclose the need to determine whether the senility also negated the individual's capacity to make health care decisions. What is relevant is whether someone is in fact capable of making a particular decision as judged by the consistency between the person's choice and the individual's underlying values and by the extent to which the choice promotes the individual's well-being as he or she sees it.

The misunderstanding lies in regarding the first 'outcome approach' as being relevant to determining what is capacity. The better view must be that the outcome approach, if it has any significance at all, can only serve as a possible criterion for establishing capacity.

Thus, the debate concerning capacity must revolve around number 2, status, and number 3, understanding, and it is to these that we must now turn.

(a) Status

The appropriateness or otherwise of a status approach to capacity can, perhaps, best be judged by reminding ourselves of the very simple question, what are we concerned about here? The answer in short is a patient's expression of will and the question whether that expression of will ought to be respected. The customary answer given is that it ought to be respected in those circumstances where the patient is capable of acting autonomously, ie in exercising self-determination. It is in the words 'autonomy' and 'self-determination' that the key is to be found. These words tell us that the concern of both the law and ethics is with the individual.

It should follow therefore, that any notion of capacity should be individual-orientated. It should not consist in mere membership of a group to whom a general classification or status is applied, regardless of the individual's particular circumstances, save where the clearest reasons of public policy demand. Any notion of capacity which did adopt such an approach would, by so doing, undermine the commitment to individual rights which it is the central concern of law and ethics to advance.

Some of the candidates proposed for the appropriate status are as follows.

(i) MAJORITY

Professor Skegg, in *Law, Ethics and Medicine,* at pp 51-52 sets the scene.

> The view that at common law all minors are incapable of consenting to medical procedures results from a fundamental misconception of the position of such procedures in relation to the criminal and the civil law. Medical procedures are not in a different category from other bodily touchings. If minors are incapable by reason of their age alone of consenting to medical procedures, it would follow that they were incapable of consenting to other touchings. This would have interesting consequences. There would not have been any need for the Tattooing of Minors Act 1969, for a tattooist who tattooed a minor with only that minor's consent would commit a battery. So, too, would anyone who embraced a girl who had not attained her majority – unless, on one view, the consent of one of her parents had first been obtained. Furthermore, a minor would not be able to give a legally effective consent to a haircut. There is no reason to believe that this is so, and cases have been decided on the assumption that minors can consent to medical touchings, and to other applications of force.

The status approach in the guise of majority was rejected by Addy J in *Johnston v Wellesley Hospital* (1970) 17 DLR (3d) 139 at 144-5 in the Ontario High Court.

> **Addy J:** The plaintiff sues for damage allegedly caused to the skin on his cheeks and forehead as a result of being treated by the defendant Dr Williams at the outpatient department of the defendant hospital. The treatment was administered in order to remove certain marks, scars and pitting caused by acne.
>
> . . . I can find nothing in any of the old reported cases, except where infants of tender age or young children were involved, where the courts have found that a person under 21 years of age was legally incapable of consenting to medical treatment. If a person under 21 years were unable to consent to medical treatment, he would also be incapable of consenting to other types of bodily interference. A proposition purporting to establish that any bodily interference acquiesced in by a youth of 20 years would nevertheless constitute an assault would be absurd. If such were the case, sexual intercourse with a girl under 21 years would constitute rape. . . .
>
> I feel that the law on this point is well expressed in the volume on *Medical Negligence* (1957), by Lord Nathan, p 16:
>
>> It is suggested that the most satisfactory solution of the problem is to rule that an infant who is capable of appreciating fully the nature and consequences of a particular operation or of particular treatment can give an effective consent thereto, and in such cases the consent of the guardian is unnecessary; but that where the infact is without that capacity, any apparent consent by him or her will be a nullity, the sole right to consent being vested in the guardian.

(ii) 16 YEARS OF AGE

In 1969, section 8(1) of the Family Law Reform Act made it clear (if it was not clear before) that majority, whether 21, or 18 as it was reduced to by the same Act, was not relevant when determining capacity to consent to medical treatment.

> FAMILY LAW REFORM ACT 1969
> 8. (1) The consent of a minor who has attained the age of sixteen years to any surgical, medical or dental treatment which, in the absence of consent, would constitute a trespass to his person, shall be as effective as it would be if he were of full age; and where a minor has by virtue of this section given an effective consent to any treatment it shall not be necessary to obtain any consent for it from his parent or guardian.
>
> (2) In this section 'surgical, medical or dental treatment' includes any procedure undertaken for the purposes of diagnosis, and this section applies to any procedure (including, in particular, the administration of an anaesthetic) which is ancillary to any treatment as it applies to that treatment.

The first and indeed the only occasion upon which this statute has been judicially considered in detail was in *Re W (a minor) (medical treatment)* [1992] 4 All ER 627. Nolan LJ pointed out that:

> [T]he effect of section 8 is to make it clear that a child of 16 or 17 years of age has the same capacity as an adult to consent to surgical, medical or dental treatment which would otherwise constitute a trespass. The phrase 'surgical, medical or dental treatment' is evidently used in a fairly narrow sense otherwise it would not have been necessary for Parliament to provide, by section 8(2), that the expression includes diagnostic procedures, and ancillary procedures such as the administration of an anaesthetic. The section does not cover, for example, the giving of blood. It does not even include the taking of a blood sample. Separate provision for that is made by section 21 of the Act.

Also organ donation would not be included because it is neither 'treatment' nor 'diagnosis' (per Lord Donaldson MR). Contrast the wording of section 2(4) of the Age of Legal Capacity (Scotland) Act 1991 which, in relation to children under 16, provides that they may consent to 'any surgical, medical or dental *procedure* or treatment' (our emphasis). Arguably, by virtue of the word 'procedure', Lord Donaldson MR's proposed limitation would not apply in Scotland. Indeed, this was the intention of the Scottish Law Commission whose Report in 1990 led to the 1991 Act (see *Report on the Legal Capacity and Responsibility of Minors and Pupils* (No 110)).

But section 8 left unclear whether another age, this time the age of 16, had replaced the age of majority. Subsection 3 states:

> (3) Nothing in this shall be construed as making ineffective any consent which would have been effective if this section had not been enacted.

The case of *Gillick v West Norfolk and Wisbech AHA* [1986] AC 112, [1985] 3 All ER 402 provided the first opportunity for the court to examine the issue. Mrs Gillick sought a declaration that a Government circular which contemplated that contraceptive advice and treatment might, in exceptional circumstances, be given to girls under the age of 16 without parental consent was unlawful. *Inter alia*, she asserted that the Circular encouraged that which was unlawful because children under 16 were unable in law to give effective consent such that without parental consent the doctor would commit a battery. The Court of Appeal, reversing the decision of Woolf J, agreed with Mrs Gillick's argument. In the Court of Appeal [1985] 1 All ER 533, Fox LJ stated that:

> In the final analysis the position is in my view as follows. (1) It is clearly established that a parent or guardian has, as such, a parcel of rights in relation to children in his custody. (2) By statute, subject to an exception, such rights can be neither abandoned nor transferred. (3) Such rights include the right to control the manner in which and the place at which the child spends his or her time. (4) Those rights will be enforced by the courts subject to the right of the court to override the parental rights in the interests of the child. (5) There is no authority of any kind to suggest that anyone other than the court can interfere with the parents' rights otherwise than by resort to the courts, or pursuant statutory exceptions. (6) It is clearly recognised that there is some age below which a child is incapable as a matter of law of giving any valid consent or making any valid decision for itself in regard to its custody or upbringing. (7) The authorities indicate that this age is 16 in the case of girls and 14 in the case of boys, at all events for the purposes of habeas corpus. (8) So far as girls are concerned, the provisions of the criminal law show that Parliament has taken the view that the consent of a girl under 16 in the matter of sexual intercourse is a nullity.
>
> In the light of the above, I conclude that as a matter of law a girl under 16 can give no valid consent to anything in the areas under consideration which apart from consent would constitute an assault, whether civil or criminal, and can impose no valid prohibition on a doctor against seeking parental consent.

I conclude further that any doctor who advises a girl under 16 as to contraceptive steps to be taken or affords contraceptive or abortion treatment to such a girl without the knowledge and consent of the parent, save in an emergency which would render consent in any event unnecessary, infringes the legal rights of the parent or guardian. Save in emergency, his proper course is to seek parental consent or apply to the court.

Parker LJ introduced his own requirement by drawing on the alleged common law principle of the 'age of discretion' to guide him in solving the problem posed by s 8(3). This somewhat mysterious principle, thought by some family lawyers to have been buried, was given a brief moment of after-life before being suitably laid to rest again by the House of Lords.

Gillick v West Norfolk and Wisbech AHA [1986] AC 112, [1985] 3 All ER 402, (1985) 2 BMLR 11 (HL)

Lord Fraser: *1. The legal capacity of a girl under 16 to consent to contraceptive advice, examination and treatment*

There are some indications in statutory provisions to which we were referred that a girl under 16 years of age in England and Wales does not have the capacity to give valid consent to contraceptive advice and treatment. If she does not have the capacity, then any physical examination or touching of her body without her parents' consent would be an assault by the examiner . . .

[A] statutory provision which was referred to in this connection is the National Health Service (General Medical and Pharmaceutical Services) Regulations 1974, SI 1974/160, as amended by the National Health Service (General Medical and Pharmaceutical Services) Amendment Regulations 1975, SI 1975/719. The regulations prescribe the mechanism by which the relationship of doctor and patient under the NHS is created. Contraceptive services, along with maternity medical services, are treated as somewhat apart from other medical services in respect that only a doctor who specially offers to provide contraceptive or maternity medical services is obliged to provide them: see the definition of 'medical care' and 'treatment' in reg 2(1); see also regs 6(1)(a) and Sch 1, para 13. But nothing turns on this fact. Two points in those regulations have a bearing on the present question although, in my opinion, only an indirect bearing. The first is that by reg 14 any 'woman' may apply to a doctor to be accepted by him for the provision of contraceptive services. The word 'woman' is not defined so as to exclude a girl under 16 or under any other age. But reg 32 provides as follows:

> An application to a doctor for inclusion on his list . . . may be made, either – (a) on behalf of any person under 16 years of age, by the mother, or in her absence, the father, or in the absence of both parents the guardian or other adult person who has the care of the child; or (b) on behalf of *any other person who is incapable* of making such an application by a relative or other adult person who has the care of such person . . .

The words in para (b) which I have emphasised are said, by counsel for Mrs Gillick, to imply that a person under 16 years of age is incapable of applying to a doctor for services and therefore give some support to the argument on behalf of Mrs Gillick. But I do not regard the implication as a strong one because the provision is merely that an application 'may' be made by the mother or other parent or guardian and it applies to the doctor's list for the provision of all ordinary medical services as well as to his list for the provision of contraceptive services. I do not believe that a person aged 15, who may be living away from home, is incapable of applying on his own behalf for inclusion in the list of a doctor for medical services of an ordinary kind not connected with contraception.

Another provision, in a different branch of medicine, which is said to carry a similar implication is contained in the Mental Health Act 1983, s 131, which provides for informal admission of patients to mental hospitals. It provides by sub-s (2):

> In the case of a minor who has attained the age of 16 years and is capable of expressing his own wishes, any such arrangements as are mentioned in subsection (1) above [for informal admission] may be made, carried out and determined

notwithstanding any right of custody or control vested by law in his parent or guardian.

That provision has only a remote bearing on the present question because there is no doubt that a minor under the age of 16 is in the custody of his or her parents. The question is whether such custody necessarily involves the right to veto contraceptive advice or treatment being given to the girl.

Reference was also made to the Education Act 1944, s 48, which dealt with medical inspection and treatment of pupils at state schools. Section 48(3), which imposed on the local education authority a duty to provide for medical and dental inspection of pupils, was repealed and superseded by the National Health Service Reorganisation Act 1973, s 3 and Sch 5. The 1973 Act in turn was replaced by the National Health Service Act 1977, s 5(1)(a). Section 48(4) of the Education Act 1944, which has not been repealed, imposes a duty on the local education authority to arrange for encouraging pupils to take advantage of any medical treatment so provided, but it includes a proviso in the following terms:

> Provided that if the parent of any pupil gives to the authority notice that he objects to the pupil availing himself of any of the provision [for medical treatment etc] so made the pupil shall not be encouraged . . . so to do.

I do not regard that provision as throwing light on the present question. It does not prohibit a child under the stipulated age from availing himself of medical treatment or an education authority from providing it for him. If the child, without encouragement from the education authority, 'wishes to avail himself of medical treatment' the section imposes no obstacle in his way. Accordingly, in my opinion, the proviso gives no support to the contention from Mrs Gillick, but on the contrary points in the opposite direction.

The statutory provisions to which I have referred do not differentiate so far as the capacity of a minor under 16 is concerned between contraceptive advice and treatment and other forms of medical advice and treatment. It would, therefore, appear that, if the inference which Mrs Gillick's advisers seek to draw from the provisions is justified, a minor under the age of 16 has no capacity to authorise any kind of medical advice or treatment or examination of his own body. That seems to me to so surprising that I cannot accept it in the absence of clear provisions to that effect. It seems to me verging on the absurd to suggest that a girl or a boy aged 15 could not effectively consent, for example, to have a medical examination of some trivial injury to his body or even to have a broken arm set. Of course the consent of the parents should normally be asked, but they may not be immediately available.

Provided the patient, whether a boy or girl, is capable of understanding what is proposed, and of expressing his or her own wishes, I see no good reason for holding that he or she lacks the capacity to express them validly and effectively and to authorise the medical man to make the examination or give the treatment which he advises. After all, a minor under the age of 16 can, within certain limits, enter into a contract. He or she can also sue and be sued, and can give evidence on oath. Moreover, a girl under 16 can give sufficiently effective consent to sexual intercourse to lead to the legal result that the man involved does not commit the crime of rape: see *R v Howard* [1965] 3 All ER 684 at 685, [1986] 1 WLR 13 at 15, when Lord Parker CJ said:

> . . . in the case of a girl under sixteen, the prosecution, in order to prove rape, must prove either that she physically resisted, or if she did not, that her understanding and knowledge were such that she was not in a position to decide whether to consent or resist . . . there are many girls under sixteen who know full well what it is all about and can properly consent.

Accordingly, I am not disposed to hold now, for the first time, that a girl aged less than 16 lacks the power to give valid consent to contraceptive advice or treatment, merely on account of her age.

Lord Scarman: The law has . . . to be found by a search in the judge-made law for the true principle. The legal difficulty is that in our search we find ourselves in a field of medical practice where parental right and a doctor's duty may point us in different directions. This is not surprising. Three features have emerged in today's society which were not known to our predecessors: (1) contraception as a subject for medical advice and treatment; (2) the increasing independence of young people; and (3) the changed status of women. In time past contraception was rarely a matter for the doctor; but with the development of the contraceptive pill for women it has become part and parcel of everyday medical practice, as is made clear by the department's *Handbook of Contraceptive Practice* (1984 revision) esp para 1.2. Family planning services are now available under statutory powers to all without any express limitations as to age or marital status. Young people, once they have attained the age of 16, are capable of consenting to contraceptive treatment, since it is medical treatment; and, however extensive be parental right in the care and upbringing of children, it cannot prevail so as to nullify the 16-year-old's capacity to consent which is now conferred by statute. Furthermore, women have obtained by the availability of the pill a choice of life-style with a degree of independence and of opportunity undreamed of until this generation and greater, I would add, than any law of equal opportunity could by itself effect.

The law ignores these developments at its peril. The House's task, therefore, as the supreme court in a legal system largely based on rules of law evolved over the years by the judicial process is to search the overfull and cluttered shelves of the law reports for a principle or set of principles recognised by the judges over the years but stripped of the detail which, however appropriate in their day, would, if applied today, lay the judges open to a justified criticism for failing to keep the law abreast of the society in which they live and work.

It is, of course, a judicial commonplace to proclaim the adaptability and flexibility of the judge-made common law. But this is more frequently proclaimed than acted on. The mark of the great judge from Coke through Mansfield to our day has been the capacity and the will to search out principle, to discard the detail appropriate (perhaps) to earlier times and to apply principle in such a way as to satisfy the needs of his own time. If judge-made law is to survive as a living and relevant body of law, we must make the effort, however inadequately, to follow the lead of the great masters of the judicial art.

In this appeal, therefore, there is much in the earlier case law which the House must discard; almost everything I would say but its principle. For example, the horrendous *Agar-Ellis* decisions (see *Re Agar-Ellis, Agar-Ellis v Lascelles* (1878) 10 Ch D 49, (1883) 24 Ch D 317) of the late nineteenth century asserting the power of the father over his child were rightly remaindered to the history books by the Court of Appeal in *Hewer v Bryant* [1969] 3 All ER 578, [1970] 1 QB 357, an important case to which I shall return later. Yet the decisions of earlier generations may well afford clues to the true principle of the law: eg *R v Howes* (1860) 3 E & E 332 at 336, 121 ER 467 at 468, which I also later quote. It is the duty of this House to look at, through and past decisions of earlier generations so that it may identify the principle which lies behind them. Even Lord Eldon (no legal revolutionary) once remarked, when invited to study precedent (the strength of which he never underrated):

> . . . all law ought to stand upon principle, and unless decision has removed out of the way all argument and all principle, so as to make it impossible to apply them to the case before you, you must find out what is the principle upon which it must be decided.

(*See Queensberry Leases Case* (1819) 1 Bligh 339 at 486-487, 4 ER 127 at 179, quoted by Lord Campbell *Lives of the Lord Chancellors* (4th edn, 1857) vol 10, ch 213, p 244.)

Approaching the earlier law in this way, one finds plenty of indications as to the principles governing the law's approach to parental right and the child's right to make his or her own decision. Parental rights clearly do exist, and they do not wholly disappear until the age of majority. Parental rights relate to both the person and the property of the child: custody, care and control of the person and guardianship of the property of the child. But the common law has never treated such rights as sovereign or beyond review and control. Nor has our law ever treated the child as other than a person with capacities and rights recognised by law. The principle of the law, as I shall endeavour to show, is that parental rights are derived from parental duty and exist only so long as they are needed for the protection of the person and property of the child. The principle has been subjected to certain age limits set by statute for certain purposes; and in some cases the courts have declared an age of discretion at which a child acquires before the age of majority the right to make his (or her) own decision. But these limitations in no way undermine the principle of the law, and should not be allowed to obscure it.

Let me make good, quite shortly, the proposition of principle.

First, the guardianship legislation. Section 5 of the Guardianship of Infants Act 1886 began the process which is now complete of establishing the equal rights of mother and father. In doing so the legislation, which is currently embodied in s 1 of the Guardianship of Minors Act 1971 [now repealed], took over from the Chancery courts a rule which they had long followed (it was certainly applied by Lord Eldon during his quarter of a century as Lord Chancellor, as Parker LJ in this case (see [1985] 1 All ER 533 at 541, [1985] 2 WLR 413 at 424), quoting Heilbron J, reminds us) that when a court has before it a question as to the care and upbringing of a child it must treat the welfare of the child as the paramount consideration in determining the order to be made. There is here a principle which limits and governs the exercise of parental rights of custody, care and control. It is a principle perfectly consistent with the law's recognition of the parent as the natural guardian of the child; but it is also a warning that parental right must be exercised in accordance with the welfare principle and can be challenged, even overridden, if it be not.

Second, there is the common law's understanding of the nature of parental right. We are not concerned in this appeal to catalogue all that is contained in what Sachs LJ has felicitously described as the 'bundle of rights' which together constitute the rights of custody, care and control (see *Hewer v Bryant* [1969] 3 All ER 578 at 585, [1970] 1 QB 357 at 373). It is abundantly plain that the law recognises that there is a right and a duty of parents to determine whether or not to seek medical advice in respect of their child, and, having received advice, to give or withhold consent to medical treatment. The question in the appeal is as to the extent and duration of the right and the circumstances in which outside the two admitted exceptions to which I have earlier referred it can be overridden by the exercise of medical judgment.

As Parker and Fox LJJ noted in the Court of Appeal, the modern statute law recognises the existence of parental right: eg ss 85 and 86 of the Children Act 1975 and ss 2, 3 and 4 of the Child Care Act 1980 [both Acts now repealed]. It is derived from parental duty. A most illuminating discussion of parental right is to be found in *Blackstone's Commentaries* (1 Bl Com (17th edn, 1830) vol 1, chs 16 and 17). He analyses the duty of the parent as the 'maintenance . . . protection, and . . . education' of the child (at 446). He declares that the power of parents over their children is derived from their duty and exists 'to enable the parent more effectually to perform his duty, and partly as a recompense for his care and trouble in the faithful discharge of it' (at 452). In ch 17 he discusses the relation of guardian and ward. It is, he points out, a relation 'derived of [the relation of parent and child]: the guardian being only a temporary parent, that is, for so long a time as the ward is an infant, or under age' (at 460). A little later in the same chapter he again emphasises that the power and reciprocal duty of a guardian and ward are the same, pro tempore, as that of a father and child and adds that the guardian, when the ward comes of age (as also the father who becomes guardian 'at common law' if an estate be left to his child), must account to the child for all that he has transacted on his behalf (at 462-463). He then embarks on a discussion of the different ages at which for different purposes a child comes of sufficient age to make his own decision; and he cites examples, viz a boy might at 12 years old take the oath of allegiance; at 14 he might consent to marriage or choose his guardian 'and, if his discretion be actually proved, may make his testament of his personal estate'; at 18 he could be an executor: all these rights and responsibilities being capable of his acquiring before reaching the age of majority at 21 (at 463).

The two chapters provide a valuable insight into the principle and flexibility of the common law. The principle is that parental right or power of control of the person and property of his child exists primarily to enable the parent to discharge his duty of maintenance, protection and education until he reaches such an age as to be able to look after himself and make his own decisions. Blackstone does suggest that there was a further justification for parental right, viz as a recompense for the faithful discharge of parental duty; but the right of the father to the exclusion of the mother and the reward element as one of the reasons for the existence of the right have been swept away by the guardianship of minors legislation to which I have already referred. He also accepts that by statute and by case law varying ages of discretion have been fixed for various purposes. But it is clear that this was done to achieve certainty where it was considered necessary and in no way limits the principle that parental right endures only so long as it is needed for the protection of the child.

Although statute has intervened in respect of a child's capacity to consent to medical treatment from the age of 16 onwards, neither statute nor the case law has ruled on the extent and duration of parental right in respect of children under the age of 16. More specifically, there is no rule yet applied to contraceptive treatment, which has special problems of its own and is a late comer in medical practice. It is open, therefore, to the House to formulate a rule. The Court of Appeal favoured a fixed age limit of 16, basing itself on a view of the statute law which I do not share and on its view of the effect of the older case law which for the reasons already given I cannot accept. It sought to justify the limit by the public interest in the law being certain. Certainty is always an advantage in the law; and in some branches of the law it is a necessity. But it brings with it an inflexibility and a rigidity which in some branches of the law can obstruct justice, impede the law's development and stamp on the law the mark of obsolescence where what is needed is the capacity for development. The law relating to parent and child is concerned with the problems of the growth and maturity of the human personality. If the law should impose on the process of 'growing up' fixed limits where nature knows only a continuous process, the price would be artificiality and a lack of realism in an area where the law must be sensitive to human development and social change. If certainty be thought desirable, it is better that the rigid demarcations necessary to achieve it should be laid down by legislation after a full consideration of all the relevant factors than by the courts, confined as they are by the forensic process to the evidence adduced by the parties and to whatever may properly fall within the judicial notice of judges. Unless and until Parliament should think fit to intervene, the courts should establish a principle flexible enough to enable justice to be achieved by its application to the particular circumstances proved by the evidence placed before them.

The underlying principle of the law was exposed by Blackstone and can be seen to have been acknowledged in the case law. It is that parental right yields to the child's right to make his own decisions when he reaches a sufficient understanding and intelligence to be capable of making up his own mind on the matter requiring decision. Lord Denning MR captured the spirit and principle of the law when he said in *Hewer v Bryant* [1969] 3 All ER 578 at 582, [1970] 1 QB 337 at 369:

> I would get rid of the rule in *Re Agar-Ellis* ((1883) 24 Ch D 317) and of the suggested exceptions to it. That case was decided in the year 1883. It reflects the attitude of a Victorian parent towards his children. He expected unquestioning obedience to his commands. If a son disobeyed, his father would cut him off with 1s. If a daughter had an illegitimate child, he would turn her out of the house. His power only ceased when the child became 21. I decline to accept a view so much out of date. The common law can, and should, keep pace with the times. It should declare, in conformity with the recent report on the Age of Majority (Report of the Committee on the Age of Majority (Cmnd 3342) under the chairmanship of Latey J, published in July 1967), that the legal right of a parent to the custody of a child ends at the eighteenth birthday; and even up till then, it is a dwindling right which the courts will hesitate to enforce against the wishes of the child, the older he is. It starts with a right of control and ends with little more than advice.

But his is by no means a solitary voice. It is consistent with the opinion expressed by the House in *J v C* [1969] 1 All ER 788, [1970] AC 668, where their Lordships clearly recognised as out of place the assertion in the *Agar-Ellis* cases (1878) 10 Ch D 49, (1883) 24 Ch D 317 of a father's power bordering on 'patria potestas'. It is consistent with the view of Lord Parker CJ in *R v Howard* [1965] 3 All ER 684 at 685, [1966] 1 WLR 13 at 15, where he ruled that in the case of a prosecution charging rape of a girl under 16 the Crown must *prove* either lack of her consent or that she was not in a position to decide whether to consent or resist and added the comment that 'there are many girls who know full well what it is all about and can properly consent'. And it is consistent with the views of the House in the recent criminal case where a father was accused of kidnapping his own child, *R v D* [1984] 2 All ER 449 [1984] AC 778, a case to which I shall return.

For the reasons which I have endeavoured to develop, the case law of the nineteenth and earlier centuries is no guide to the application of the law in the conditions of today. The *Agar-Ellis* cases (the power of the father) cannot live with the modern statute law. The habeas corpus 'age of discretion' cases are also no guide as to the limits which should be accepted today in marking out the bounds of parental right, of a child's capacity to make his or her own decision and of a doctor's duty to his patient. Nevertheless the 'age of discretion' cases are helpful in that they do reveal the judges as accepting that a minor can in law achieve an age of discretion before coming of full age. The 'age of discretion' cases are cases in which a parent or guardian (usually the father) has applied for habeas corpus to secure the return of his child who has left without his consent. The courts would refuse an order if the child had attained the age of discretion, which came to be regarded as 14 for boys and 16 for girls, and did not wish to return. The principle underlying them was plainly that an order would be refused if the child had sufficient intelligence and understanding to make up his own mind. A passage from the judgment of Cockburn CJ in *R v Howes* (1860) 3 E & E 332 at 336-337, 121 ER 467 at 468-469, which Parker LJ quoted in the Court of Appeal, illustrates their reasoning and shows how a fixed age was used as a working rule to establish an age at which the requisite 'discretion' could be held to be achieved by the child. Cockburn CJ said:

> Now the cases which have been decided on this subject shew that, although a father is entitled to the custody of his children till they attain the age of twenty-one, this Court

will not grant a habeas corpus to hand a child which is below that age over to its father, provided that it has attained an age of sufficient discretion to enable it to exercise a wise choice for its own interests. The whole question is, what is the age of discretion? We repudiate utterly, as most dangerous, the notion that any intellectual precocity in an individual female child can hasten the period which appears to have been fixed by statute for the arrival of the age of discretion; for that very precocity, if uncontrolled, might very probably lead to her irreparable injury. The legislature has given us a guide, which we may safely follow, in pointing out sixteen as the age gap up to which the father's right to the custody of his female child is to continue; and short of which such a child has no discretion to consent to leaving him.

The principle is clear; and a fixed age of discretion was accepted by the courts by analogy from the Abduction Acts (the first being the Act 4 & 5 Ph & M c 8 (1557)). While it is unrealistic today to treat a sixteenth century Act as a safe guide in the matter of a girl's discretion, and while no modern judge would dismiss the intelligence of a teenage girl as 'intellectual precocity', we can agree with Cockburn CJ as to the principle of the law: the attainment by a child of an age of sufficient discretion to enable him or her to exercise a wise choice in his or her own interests.

The modern law governing parental right and a child's capacity to make his own decisions was considered in *R v D* [1984] 2 All ER 449, [1984] AC 778. The House must, in my view, be understood as having in that case accepted that, save where statute otherwise provides, a minor's capacity to make his or her own decision depends on the minor having sufficient understanding and intelligence to make the decision and is not to be determined by reference to any judicially fixed age limit. The House was faced with a submission that a father, even if he had taken his child away by force or fraud, could not be guilty of a criminal offence of any kind. Lord Brandon, with whom their other Lordships agreed, commented that this might well have been the view of the legislature and the courts in the nineteenth century, but had this to say about parental right and a child's capacity in our time to give or withhold a valid consent ([1984] 2 All ER 449 at 456, [1984] AC 778 at 804-805):

> This is because in those times both the generally accepted conventions of society and the courts by which such conventions were buttressed and enforced, regarded a father as having absolute and paramount authority, as against all the world, over any children of his who were still under the age or majority (then 21), except for a married daughter. The nature of this view of a father's rights appears clearly from various reported cases, including, as a typical example, *Re Agar-Ellis, Agar-Ellis v Lascelles* (1883) 24 Ch D 317. The common law, however, while generally immutable in its principles, unless different principles are laid down by statute, is not immutable in the way in which it adapts, develops and applies those principles in a radically changing world and against the background of radically changed social conventions and conditions.

Later he said ([1984] 2 All ER 449 at 457, [1984] AC 778 at 806):

> I see no good reason why, in relation to the kidnapping of a child, it should not in all cases be the absence of the child's consent which is material, whatever its age may be. In the case of a very young child, it would not have the understanding or the intelligence to give its consent, so that absence of consent would be a necessary inference from its age. In the case of an older child, however, it must, I think, be a question of fact for a jury whether the child concerned has sufficient understanding and intelligence to give its consent; if, but only if, the jury considers that a child has these qualities, it must then go on to consider whether it has been proved that the child did not give its consent. While the matter will always be for the jury alone to decide, I should not expect a jury to find at all frequently that a child under 14 had sufficient understanding and intelligence to give its consent.

In the light of the foregoing I would hold that as a matter of law the parental right to determine whether or not their minor child below the age of 16 will have medical treatment terminates if and when the child achieves a sufficient understanding and intelligence to enable him or her to understand fully what is proposed. It will be a question of fact whether a child seeking advice has sufficient understanding of what is involved to give a consent valid in law. Until the child achieves the capacity to consent, the parental right to make the decision continues save only in exceptional circumstances. Emergency, parental neglect, abandonment of the child or inability to find the parent are examples of exceptional situations justifying the doctor proceeding to treat the child without parental knowledge and consent; but there will arise, no doubt, other exceptional situations in which it will be reasonable for the doctor to proceed without the parent's consent.

Lord Bridge fully agreed with Lords Fraser and Scarman and added nothing further on the issue of consent.

Lord Brandon dealt with the case on the prior question of whether a doctor, by complying with the circular, would act unlawfully by reference to the criminal law or public policy (for which see *infra*, p 680) irrespective of the consent of the child or indeed the parents.

Lord Templeman, however, did address the issue of consent by children and in general agreed with the others. As we shall see in chapter 10, in the context of contraception, however, he took the somewhat idiosyncratic view that contraceptive treatment or advice is special and thus something to which a child could not consent.

Subsequently, the Alberta Court of Appeal applied Lord Scarman's analysis of the law.

C v Wren (1987) 35 DLR (4th) 419 (Alta CA)

Kerans JA: A 16-year-old girl became pregnant by her boyfriend while she was living at home. Several weeks later, she abruptly left home and went elsewhere and has since avoided contact with her parents. She also attended on a physician and surgeon with a view to an abortion and has received approval for it by the statutory committee provided under the *Criminal Code*. The urgency of the matter is that a statutory deadline looms. . . .

The ground of appeal is that the learned chambers judge erred in finding that the expectant mother had given informed consent to the proposed surgical procedure.

The law in Alberta is that a surgeon may proceed with a surgical procedure immune from suits for assault if she or he has informed consent from the patient. That test was applied by the learned trial judge, and he found on the evidence before him that this child was capable of giving informed consent and had done so. . . .

The law and the development of the law in this respect was analyzed in detail by Lord Scarman in the *Gillick* case. . . .

What is the application of the principle [outlined in *Gillick*] in this case? We infer from the circumstances detailed in argument here that this expectant mother and her parents had fully discussed the ethical issues involved and, most regrettably, disagreed. We cannot infer from that disagreement that this expectant mother did not have sufficient intelligence and understanding to make up her own mind. Meanwhile, it is conceded that she is a 'normal intelligent 16-year-old'. We infer that she did have sufficient intelligence and understanding to make up her own mind and did so. At her age and level of understanding, the law is that she is to be permitted to do so.

(iii) THE MENTALLY DISORDERED

It could be suggested that a person who is mentally disordered, by virtue of that status, is *ipso facto* incompetent. Professor Skegg rightly dismisses this approach in his book *Law, Ethics and Medicine* (1984) (pp 56-7):

The fact that a person is suffering from a mental disorder, as defined in the Mental Health Act 1983, does not of itself preclude that person from giving a legally effective consent. Whether the person is capable of doing so depends upon whether that person can understand and come to a decision upon what is involved. Most patients in mental hospitals are capable of giving a legally effective consent, including many who are compulsorily detained. Doctors are sometimes free to proceed without consent, but even then a patient will sometimes have the capacity to give a legally effective consent, which would of itself prevent the doctor's conduct from amounting to the tort or crime of battery.

Re C (1993) Independent, 15 October (discussed briefly *infra*, p 139) confirms Professor Skegg's view. Also, in Part IV of the Mental Health Act 1983, which deals with 'Consent to Treatment', it is explicitly recognised that a person suffering from 'mental disorder' may none the less have the capacity in law to consent to or refuse treatment for mental disorder if 'the patient is capable of understanding . . .'.

MENTAL HEALTH ACT 1983
57. (2) Subject to section 62 below, a patient shall not be given any form of treatment to which this section applies unless he has consented to it and -
(a) a registered medical practitioner appointed for the purposes of this Part of this Act by the Secretary of State (not being the responsible medical officer) and two other persons appointed for the purposes of this paragraph by the Secretary of State (not being registered medical practitioners) have certified in writing that the patient is capable of understanding the nature, purpose and likely effects of the treatment in question and has consented to it:

[Section 57 applies to a surgical operation for destroying brain tissue or its capacity to function and surgical implantation of hormones for the purpose of reducing male sexual drive.]

58. (3) Subject to section 62 below, a patient shall not be given any form of treatment to which this section applies unless -
(a) he has consented to that treatment and either the responsible medical officer or a registered medical practitioner appointed for the purposes of this Part of this Act by the Secretary of State has certified in writing that the patient is capable of understanding its nature, purpose and likely effects and has consented to it.

[Section 58 applies to electro-convulsive therapy (ECT) and the administration of medicine to treat the mental disorder for more than three months.]

Contrast the position taken in a Michigan circuit court in the well-known case of *Kaimowitz v Michigan Department of Mental Health* (1973) 42 USLW 2063 (Mich Cir Ct). In that case the court considered whether a person compulsorily detained in a mental hospital could validly consent to take part in a trial involving psychosurgery as a form of treatment. The court held:

To advance scientific knowledge, it is true that doctors may desire to experiment on human beings, but the need for scientific inquiry must be reconciled with the inviolability which our society provides for a person's mind and body. Under a free government, one of a person's greatest rights is the right to inviolability of his person, and it is axiomatic that this right necessarily forbids the physician or surgeon from violating, without permission, the bodily integrity of his patient.

Generally, individuals are allowed free choice about whether to undergo experimental medical procedures. But the State has the power to modify this free choice concerning experimental medical procedures when it cannot be freely given, or when the result would be contrary to public policy. For example, it is obvious that a person may not consent to acts that will constitute murder, manslaughter, or mayhem upon himself. In short, there are times when the State for good reason should withhold a person's ability to consent to certain medical procedures. . . .

We must first look to the competency of the involuntarily detained mental patient to consent. Competency requires the ability of the subject to understand rationally the nature of the procedure, its risks, and other relevant information. The standard governing required disclosure by a doctor is what a reasonable patient needs to know in order to make an intelligent decision. See Waltz and Scheuneman, 'Informed Consent to Therapy', 64 Northwestern Law Review 628 (1969). . . .

Although an involuntarily detained mental patient may have a sufficient IQ to intellectually comprehend his circumstance (in Dr Rodin's experiment, a person was required to have at least an IQ of 80), the very nature of his incarceration diminishes the capacity to consent to psychosurgery. He is particularly vulnerable as a result of his mental condition, the deprivation stemming from involuntary confinement, and the effects of the phenomenon of 'institutionalisation'. . . .

Institutionalisation tends to strip the individual of the support which permits him to maintain his sense of self-worth and the value of his own physical and mental integrity. An involuntarily confined mental patient clearly has diminished capacity for making a decision about irreversible experimental psychosurgery.

Here is a case where the court appears to be using the status approach. The patient was compulsorily detained and mentally disordered. The court appears to be saying that because of that fact he was incapable of giving a valid consent. The court was using this approach to protect the patient from himself.

The conclusion must be that as a matter of principle and in the light of the law as stated by Parliament and the House of Lords the status approach to capacity to consent to medical treatment is not the law. This is not to say that in all circumstances a status approach is unjustified. A fixed and certain age may be appropriate as indicating the capacity, eg to vote, enlist in the armed forces or marry.

(b) Understanding

As has been seen, both Lord Fraser and Lord Scarman in their rejection of the status approach in *Gillick* opt for a notion of capacity centred on understanding. This reflects the view expressed by Addy J in *Johnston v Wellesley Hospital* (1970) 17 DLR (3d) 139 at 144-5. Indeed, it reflects the general approach of the law, see, *Re Beaney* [1978] 1 WLR 770 (*inter vivos* gift and will); *Re K* [1988] Ch 310 (enduring power of attorney). In their two Consultation Papers, entitled 'Mentally Incapacitated Adults and Decision-Making: A New Jurisdiction' (No 128, 1993) and 'Mentally Incapacitated Adults and Decision-Making: Medical Treatment and Research' (No 129, 1993), the Law Commission provisionally proposes what is called a 'cognitive functioning test', ie understanding as the legal test for capacity to consent (see paras 3.19-3.35 and 2.3-2.21 respectively).

Returning to *Gillick*, unfortunately, however, the news is both good and bad. In *Gillick* the majority in the House of Lords made it clear that capacity is centred on 'understanding'. The words used to express this view, however, pose problems for the future as to what is involved in the concept of understanding. Let us repeat here the views of Lords Fraser and Scarman before we analyse them.

Lord Fraser: The solution depends on a judgment of what is best for the welfare of the particular child. Nobody doubts, certainly I do not doubt, that in the overwhelming majority of cases the best judges of a child's welfare are his or her parents. Nor do I doubt that any important medical treatment of a child under 16 would normally only be carried out with the parents' approval. That is why it would and should be 'most unusual' for a doctor to advise a child without the knowledge and consent of the parents on contraceptive matters. But, as I have already pointed out, Mrs Gillick has to go further if she is to obtain the first declaration that she seeks. She has to justify the absolute right of veto in a parent. But there may be circumstances in which a doctor is a better judge of the medical advice and treatment which will conduce to a girl's welfare than her parents. It is notorious that children of both sexes are often reluctant to confide in their parents about sexual matters, and the DHSS guidance under consideration shows that to abandon the principle of confidentiality for contraceptive advice to girls under 16 might cause some of them not to seek professional advice at all, with the consequence of exposing them to 'the immediate risks of pregnancy and of sexually-transmitted diseases'. No doubt the risk could be avoided if the patient were to abstain from sexual intercourse, and one of the doctor's responsibilities will be to decide whether a particular patient can reasonably be expected to act on advice to abstain. We were told that in a significant number of cases such abstinence could not reasonably be expected. An example is *Re P (a minor)* (1986) 80 LGR 301, in which Butler-Sloss J ordered that a girl aged 15 who had been pregnant for the second time and who was in the care of a local authority should be fitted with a contraceptive appliance because, as the judge is reported to have said (at 312) –

> I assume that it is impossible for this local authority to monitor her sexual activities, and therefore, contraception appears to be the only alternative.

There may well be other cases where the doctor feels that because the girl is under the influence of her sexual partner or for some other reason there is no realistic prospect of her abstaining from intercourse. If that is right it points strongly to the desirability of the doctor being entitled in some cases, in the girl's best interest, to give her contraceptive advice and treatment if necessary without the consent or even the knowledge of her parents. The only practicable course is, in my opinion, to entrust the doctor with a discretion to act in accordance with his view of what is best in the interests of the girl who is his patient. He should, of course, always seek to persuade her to tell her parents that she is seeking contraceptive advice, and the nature of the advice that she receives. At least he should seek to persuade her to agree to the doctor's informing the parents. But there may well be cases, and I think there will be some cases, where the girl refuses either to tell the parents herself or to permit the doctor to do so and in such cases the doctor will, in my opinion, be justified in proceeding without her parents' consent or even knowledge provided he is satisfied on the following matters: (1) that the girl (although under 16 years of age) will understand his advice; (2) that he cannot persuade her to inform her parents or to allow him to inform the parents that she is seeking contraceptive advice; (3) that she is very likely to begin or to continue having sexual intercourse with or without contraceptive treatment; (4) that unless she receives contraceptive advice or treatment her physical or mental health or both are likely to suffer; (5) that her best interests require him to give her contraceptive advice, treatment or both without the parental consent.

That result ought not to be regarded as a licence for doctors to disregard the wishes of parents on this matter whenever they find it convenient to do so. Any doctor who behaves in such a way would, in my opinion, be failing to discharge his professional responsibilities, and I would expect him to be disciplined by his own professional body accordingly. The medical profession have in modern times come to be entrusted with very wide discretionary powers going beyond the strict limits of clinical judgment and, in my opinion, there is nothing strange about entrusting them with this further responsibility which they alone are in a position to discharge satisfactorily.

Lord Scarman: In the light of the foregoing I would hold that as a matter of law the parental right to determine whether or not the minor child below the age of 16 will have medical treatment terminated if and when the child achieves a sufficient understanding and intelligence to enable him or her to understand fully what is proposed. It will be a question of fact whether a child seeking advice has sufficient understanding of what is involved in give a consent valid in law. Until the child achieves the capacity to consent, the parental right to make the decision continues save only in exceptional circumstances. Emergency, parental neglect, abandonment of the child or inability to find the parent are examples of exceptional situations justifying the doctor proceeding to treat the child without parental knowledge and consent; but there will arise, no doubt, other exceptional situations in which it will be reasonable for the doctor to proceed without the parent's consent.

When applying these conclusions to contraceptive advice and treatment it has to be borne in mind that there is much that has to be understood by a girl under the age of 16 if she is to have legal capacity to consent to such treatment. It is not enough that she should understand the nature of the advice which is being given: she must also have a sufficient maturity to understand what is involved. There are moral and family questions, especially her relationship with her parents; long-term problems associated with the emotional impact of pregnancy and its termination; and there are the risks to health of sexual intercourse at her age, risks which contraception may diminish but cannot eliminate. It follows that a doctor will have to satisfy himself that she is able to appraise these factors before he can safely proceed on the basis that she has at law capacity to consent to contraceptive treatment. And it further follows that ordinarily the proper course will be for him, as the guidance lays down, first to seek to persuade the girl to bring her parents into consultation, and, if she refuses, not to prescribe contraceptive treatment unless he is satisfied that her circumstances are such that he ought to proceed without parental knowledge and consent.

Like Woolf J, I find illuminating and helpful the judgment of Addy J of the Ontario High Court in *Johnston v Wellesley Hospital* (1970) 17 DLR (3d) 139, a passage from which he quotes in his judgment in this case ([1984] 1 All ER 365 at 374, [1984] QB 581 at 597). The key passage bears repetition (17 DLR (3d) 139 at 144-145):

> But, regardless of modern trends, I can find nothing in any of the old reported cases, except where infants of tender age or young children were involved, where the Courts have found that a person under 21 years of age was legally incapable of consenting to medical treatment. If a person under 21 years were unable to consent to medical treatment, he would also be incapable of consenting to other types of bodily interference. A proposition purporting to establish that any bodily interference acquiesced in by a youth of 20 years would nevertheless constitute an assault would be absurd. If such were the case, sexual intercourse with a girl under 21 years would constitute rape. Until the minimum age of consent to sexual acts was fixed at 14 years by a statute, the Courts often held that infants were capable of consenting at a considerably earlier age than 14 years. I feel that the law on this point is well expressed in the volume on *Medical Negligence* (1957) by Lord Nathan (p 176): 'It is suggested that the most satisfactory solution of the problem is to rule that an infant who is capable of appreciating fully the nature and consequences of a particular operation or of particular treatment can give an effective consent thereto, and in such cases the consent of the guardian is unnecessary; but that where the infant is without that capacity, any apparent consent by him or her will be a nullity, the sole right to consent being vested in the guardian.'

Lord Templeman in his speech does not dissent from this view in general though he makes an exception for contraceptive treatment for young girls.

> **Lord Templeman**: I accept also that a doctor may lawfully carry out some forms of treatment with the consent of an infant patient and against the opposition of a parent based on religious or any other grounds. The effect of the consent of the infant depends on the nature of the treatment and the age and understanding of the infant. For example, a doctor with the consent of an intelligent boy or girl of 15 could in my opinion safely remove tonsils or a troublesome appendix.

(i) ACTUALLY UNDERSTANDS VERSUS CAPABLE OF UNDERSTANDING

The problem is as follows: does a test which stipulates that the patient understands mean that the doctor must satisfy himself (a) that the patient *does in fact* understand what is involved, or (b) that the patient is *capable* generally of understanding though, as it may subsequently transpire, he did not understand in the particular case, or (c) that the patient as a *reasonable patient is capable* of understanding or would have understood. Let us assume that (c) can be discounted since it is not concerned with the circumstances of the particular patient which, as we have seen, ought to be the central concern of the law.

While agreeing on the general direction of the law in favour of some notion of 'understanding', neither Lord Fraser nor Lord Scarman appears to choose his language with precision or indeed consistency on whether (a) or (b) represents the law. At a number of points in their speeches the judges use language consistent with (a). So, for example, Lord Fraser requires 'that the girl . . . *will* understand' the doctor's advice. Similarly, Lord Scarman states that 'a doctor will have to satisfy himself that she *is* able to appraise' those matters involved in the procedure and its consequences. This is a somewhat equivocal statement by Lord Scarman but on one reading he is saying that the girl must *in fact* understand. The weight of the dicta in *Gillick* is, however, in favour of (b). Consider the following statements.

Lord Fraser: Provided the patient, whether a boy or a girl, is *capable of understanding* what is proposed, and of expressing his or her own wishes, I see no good reason for holding that he or she lacks the capacity to express them validly and effectively and to authorise the medical man to make the examination or give the treatment which he advises [our emphasis].

Lord Scarman: It is that parental right yields to the child's right to make his own decisions when he reaches a sufficient understanding and intelligence to be *capable of making* up his own mind on the matter requiring decision [our emphasis].

Lord Scarman: It follows that a doctor will have to satisfy himself that she *is able to appraise* these factors before he can safely proceed on the basis that she has at law capacity to consent to contraceptive treatment [our emphasis].

Notice also the reference by Lord Scarman in the extract set out earlier to *Johnston v Wellesley Hospital* (1970) 17 DLR (3d) 139, where Addy J speaks of the child being 'capable' of understanding.

In his judgment in *Re R (a minor) (wardship: medical treatment)* [1992] Fam 11, [1991] 4 All ER 177 however, Lord Donaldson MR demonstrated how easy it is to use language without the precision which is essential here. In *Re R* the doctor had given evidence that at times R was capable of understanding what was involved in the proposed treatment for her mental illness. Latching onto this, Lord Donaldson MR stated that

> . . . it is far from certain that [the doctor] was saying that R understood the implications of treatment being withheld, as distinct from understanding what was proposed to be done by way of treatment . . . But, even if she was capable on a good day of a sufficient degree of understanding to meet the *Gillick* criteria, her mental disability, to the cure or an alleviation of which the proposed treatment as directed, was such that on other ways she was not only '*Gillick* incompetent' but actually sectionable.

The importance of precision here lies in the following. If the test of understanding is *actual understanding* ie (a), then whether or not the girl understands *and therefore is competent* to consent may turn on what she is told. Indeed, this seems to have been Lord Donaldson's approach in *Re R* in the quotation above. If the girl is not given certain information she may not understand enough but this would not be the product of any lack of competence but merely that she decided in relative ignorance. It would be an unsatisfactory state of law if doctors could by controlling the information given to a patient thereby grant or deny her competence. Competence or incompetence is a state inherent in the individual patient which cannot depend how much the doctor tells the patient. It must, therefore, be the law that competence is determined by reference to the unvarying conceptual standard of *capacity* or *ability* to understand. Whether, thereafter a patient who is judged competent because she has the capacity or ability to understand, in fact consented, is a distinct question turning upon the reality of the consent based upon legally adequate information (see *infra*, p 147 *et seq*).

Finally, can we find any guidance in legislation? Not surprisingly, there are few statutes which address this question. The Mental Health Act 1983 in its provisions in sections 57 and 58 (set out *supra*, p 117 *et seq*) clearly endorsed approach (b). Similarly, the relevant provisions of the Children Act 1989 dealing with medical or psychiatric examination or treatment follow this approach (ss 38(6), 43(8) 44(7) and Sch 3, paragraphs 4(4)(a) and 5(5)(a)).

By contrast the Human Organ Transplants (Unrelated Persons) Regulations 1989 (SI 1989 No 2480) made pursuant to section 2 of the Human Organ Transplants Act 1989 seem to adopt approach (a), since one of the conditions for approving donations between unrelated persons is that the 'donor *understands* the nature of the medical procedure and risks and consents to the removal of the organ' (reg 2(2)(b)) (our emphasis). Unless it can be argued organ donation between unrelated persons is a special case, it may be that this is merely an example of imprecise drafting.

The most pertinent statutory provision, though only applicable to Scotland, is the Age of Legal Capacity (Scotland) Act 1991. This Act seeks to clarify the law, *inter alia*, in relation to the competence of children to consent to medical treatment in Scotland. Section 2(4) provides:

> 2. (4) A person under the age of 16 years shall have legal capacity to consent on his own behalf to any surgical, medical or dental procedure or treatment where, in the opinion of a qualified medical practitioner attending him, he is *capable* of understanding the nature and possible consequences of the procedure or treatment [our emphasis].

This gives statutory expression to the decision in *Gillick*. For our purposes it is important to notice that Parliament adopted approach (b) ie that the child should be 'capable of understanding' what is involved.

(ii) UNDERSTAND WHAT?

In *Gillick*, the House of Lords required that the patient to be competent must, in the words of Lord Scarman, 'have sufficient maturity to understand *what is involved*' (our emphasis). Crucially, therefore, we must determine what it is that a patient must be capable of understanding ie what is meant by 'what is involved'? Clearly, 'what is involved' must relate to that information which the law stipulates a patient should be aware of before a valid consent may be given. (In large part, it will be the doctor's duty to disclose this information. There may be circumstances in which the patient is aware of 'what is involved' without the need to be told but even here the doctor will have a duty to assess the accuracy of the patient's beliefs.)

Put this way, it will be clear that what the patient needs to understand is largely that which the doctor as a matter of law is obliged to inform the patient of. This conclusion does not, however, resolve the problem since, as we shall see, there are two levels of duty imposed upon the doctor by the law. The first, and more fundamental, concerns information that must be disclosed to avoid a claim in battery. What the law requires here is, as we shall see, merely that the doctor inform the patient of the *broad nature and purpose* of the procedure (see *Re C* (1993) NLJR 1642: 'understand the nature, purpose and effects of the proposed treatment', per Thorpe J). This would give to 'what is involved' a very limited content. It is, of course, consistent with Lord Donaldson MR's view that, as we saw above, consent is merely an aspect of the law of battery. However, the better view is that the law of consent goes further and encompasses what we shall see as the more extensive duty (albeit in negligence) to disclose information beyond that minimal level required to avoid a battery claim. Logically, the capacity or ability to understand 'what is involved' must embrace this further information since the basis for requiring disclosure is to allow the patient to make an informed choice and this can only be achieved if the patient is able to understand that further information.

Notice, for example, that in the Age of Legal Capacity (Scotland) Act 1991, section 2(4) requires that the child be capable of understanding the 'nature and *possible consequences* of the procedure or treatment' (our emphasis). This clearly goes beyond the information which a patient must understand in order for the doctor to avoid a claim in battery. (Contrast the Mental Health Act 1983, sections 57(2) and 58(3) referring to the 'nature, purpose and *likely effects* of the treatment' (our emphasis). Perhaps the latter wording *is* more consistent with the individual having a capacity to understand the more limited information necessary for the doctor to avoid a claim in battery.)

(The Law Commission in their 1993 Consultation Papers *op cit* adopts a somewhat confusing approach though appearing to accept the wider approach suggested here: see paras 3.19-3.24 and 2.8-2.12 respectively.)

Lord Scarman in *Gillick* defined 'what is involved' even more extensively.

> There are moral and family questions, especially her relationship with her parents; long-term problems associated with the emotional impact of pregnancy and its termination; and there are the risks to health of sexual intercourse at her age. . .

As can be seen, Lord Scarman was concerned with contraceptive advice and treatment involving young girls. Perhaps his remarks should be understood to be limited to this context not only in their precise detail but also their reference to wider issues such as 'moral . . . questions'. Indeed, in *C v Wren* (1987) 35 DLR (4th) 419, the Alberta Court of Appeal described the obligation as an ethical one but not a legal one in a case concerned with the termination of the pregnancy of a young girl. Kerans JA said:

> It is argued before us today that informed consent means consent after consideration of issues like the ethics of an abortion and the ethics of obligation by children to parents. It may be, as Lord Fraser has said in *Gillick v West Norfolk & Wisbech Area Health Authority* [1985] 3 All ER 402, that doctors have an ethical obligation in circumstances like this to discuss issues of that sort with young patients. If so, the doctor would account to the College of Physicians and Surgeons for the performance of that obligation. That is not the issue before us today. Rather, the issue is whether these issues relate to the defence of consent to assault. In our view, they do not.

2. Establishing capacity

As has been seen, concern about the establishment of capacity arises out of the two propositions: (1) that a doctor ought to respect his patient's autonomy, but (2) he need only do so when the patient who expresses his will is capable of behaving autonomously. It follows that autonomy is, in effect, a status granted by others, in this case, the doctor. It also follows that in granting the status, it is the doctor's assessment of capacity which is crucial. Thus, capacity is a state of affairs granted by the doctor. In determining capacity, the doctor both as a matter of ethics and law must (ie has a duty to) behave with integrity and satisfy himself that the criteria deemed relevant to determine capacity are present in the particular case. The obverse of this proposition is that if these criteria are present, on any objective assessment, the doctor may not (ie is under a duty not to) impose his own views so as to regard the patient as incapable of understanding and thus, of making his own decisions.

An initial point we should notice is that as Lord Donaldson MR pointed out in *Re T* (*supra*) '[e]very adult is presumed to have . . . capacity [to consent], but it is a presumption which can be rebutted.' We shall return shortly to examine the circumstances in which the presumption may be rebutted. Similarly, as a result of section 8 of the Family Law Reform Act 1969 a child aged between 16 and 18 is presumed to be competent in respect of 'surgical, medical or dental treatment'.

Curiously, Lord Donaldson MR in *Re W* (*supra*) stated that section 8 'conclusively presumed' a 16- or 17-year-old to be competent. Section 8 clearly does not do this since it merely puts the child patient in the same position as an adult patient. Hence, as he himself asserted in *Re T*, the presumption is rebuttable. Further, as to section 8, he stated that 'alternatively, the test of *"Gillick* competence" is bypassed and has no relevance'. This view is somewhat idiosyncratic and the better view is that expressed by Balcombe and Nolan LJJ that the child is merely presumed to be competent as if an adult. As regards a child under 16 or in circumstances where section 8 is inapplicable, then the child is presumed to be incompetent at common law although this presumption is rebuttable as *Gillick* establishes.

What in law are the criteria for establishing capacity? It is critical to notice here that when we talk of the doctor making a decision as to capacity, there are in fact *two* stages to the process. The first is the reference to the relevant criteria. As will be made clear, these criteria are not for doctors to determine but are a matter for the law. The second stage is the doctor's application of these general criteria. That clearly is a decision for him alone. In theory it would be subject to review but in practice it would be hard to challenge it; hence our insistence upon integrity.

(a) The scholarly writing

What we intend to do now is first to notice the contribution by scholarly writing and then, in the light of this, examine the limited case law that exists. Perhaps the best-known work in this area is that of the American writers Loren Roth, Alan Meisel and Charles Lidz. Their work is extensive and much of it is brought together in *Informed Consent: Legal Theory and Clinical Practice* by P Appelbaum, C Lidz and A Meisel. However, the seminal piece is the following.

Roth, Meisel and Lidz, 'Tests of Competency to Consent to Treatment' (1977) 134 Am J Psychiatry 279

The concept of competency, like the concept of dangerousness, is social and legal and not merely psychiatric or medical. Law and, at times, psychiatry are concerned with an individual's competency to stand trial, to make a will, and to contract. The test of competency varies from one context to another. In general, to be considered competent an individual must be able to comprehend the nature of the particular conduct in question and to understand its quality and its consequences. For example, in *Dusky v United States* [362 US 405 (1960) (per curiam)] the court held that to be considered competent to stand trial an individual must have 'sufficient present ability to consult with his lawyer with a reasonable degree of rational understanding – and . . . a rational as well as a factual understanding of the proceedings against him'. A person may be considered competent for some legal purposes and incompetent for others at the same time. An individual is not judged incompetent merely because he or she is mentally ill.

There is a dearth of legal guidance illuminating the concept of competency to consent to medical treatment. Nevertheless, competency plays an important role in determining the validity of a patient's decision to undergo or forego treatment. The decision of a person who is incompetent does not validly authorise a physician to perform medical treatment. Conversely, a physician who withholds treatment from an incompetent patient who refuses treatment may be held liable to that patient if the physician does not take reasonable steps to obtain some other legally valid authorisation for treatment.

In psychiatry the entire edifice of involuntary treatment is erected on the supposed incompetency of some people voluntarily to seek and consent to needed treatment. In addition, the acceptability of behaviour modification for the patient who is considered dangerous, the resolution of ethical issues in family planning (ie, sterilisation), and the right to refuse psychoactive medications – to cite only a few of the more prominent examples – turn in part on the concept of competency.

As we explain in our companion paper in this issue of the *Journal* [(1977) 134 Am J Psychiatry 285], competency is theoretically one of the independent variables that is determinative in part of the legal validity of a patient's consent to or refusal of treatment. There is therefore a need to specify how competency can be determined. Related questions include the following: Who raises the question of competency? When is this question raised? and Who makes the determination? Answers to these questions are beyond the scope of this paper.

The objective of the present inquiry is to make sense of various tests of competency, to analyse their applicability to patients' decisions to accept or refuse psychiatric treatment, and to illustrate the problems of applying these tests by clinical case examples from the consultation service of the Law and Psychiatry Program of Western Psychiatric Institute and Clinic.

In a brief presentation it is impossible to provide any serious linguistic analysis of a number of words that are frequently used in discussions of competency – words such as 'responsible', 'rational' or 'irrational', 'knowing', 'knowingly', 'understandingly', or 'capable'. These words are often used interchangeably without sufficient explanation or clear behavioural references. Only the rare scholarly article attempts to explain with precision what is meant by such terms; judicial decisions or statutes generally do not.

In evaluating tests for competency several criteria should be considered. A useful test for competency is one that, first, can be reliably applied; second, is mutually acceptable or at least comprehensible to physicians, lawyers, and judges; and third, is set at a level capable of striking an acceptable balance between preserving individual autonomy and providing needed medical care. Reliability is enhanced to the extent that a competency test depends on manifest and objectively ascertainable patient behaviour rather than on inferred and probably unknowable mental status.

Tests for competency

Several tests for competency have been proposed in the literature; others are readily inferable from judicial commentary. Although there is some overlap, they basically fall into five categories: 1) evidencing a choice, 2) 'reasonable' outcome of choice, 3) choice based on 'rational' reasons, 4) ability to understand, and 5) actual understanding.

Evidencing a choice

This test for competency is set at a very low level and is the most respectful of the autonomy of patient decision-making. Under this test the competent patient is one who evidences a preference for or against treatment. This test focuses not on the quality of the patient's decision but on the presence or absence of a decision. This preference may be a yes, a no, or even the desire that the physician make the decision for the patient. Only the patient who does not evidence a preference either verbally or through his or her behaviour is considered incompetent. This test of competency encompasses at a minimum the unconscious patient; in psychiatry it encompasses the mute patient who cannot or will not express opinion.

Even such arch-defenders of individual autonomy as Szasz have agreed that patients who do not formulate and express a preference as to treatment are incompetent. In answer to a question about the right to intervene against a patient's will, Szasz has stated:

> It is quite obvious, and I make this abundantly clear, that I have no objection to medical intervention vis-à-vis persons who are not protesting, . . . [for example,] somebody who is lying in bed catatonic and the mother wants to get him to the hospital and the ambulance shows up and he just lies there.

The following case example illustrates the use of the test of evidencing a choice:

> *Case 1.* A 41-year-old depressed woman was interviewed in the admission unit. She rarely answered yes or no to direct questions. Admission was proposed; she said and did nothing, but looked apprehensive. When asked about admission, she did not sign herself into the hospital, protest, or walk away. She was guided to the in-patient ward by her husband and her doctor after being given the opportunity to walk the other way.

This test may be what one court had in mind when, with respect to sterilisation of residents of state schools, it rules that even legally incompetent and possibly noncomprehending residents may not be sterilised unless they have formed a genuine desire to undergo the procedure.

The guidelines proposed by the US Department of Health, Education and Welfare concerning experimentation with institutionalised mentally ill people also point in this direction by requiring even the legally incompetent person's 'assent to such participation . . . when . . . he has sufficient mental capacity to understand what is proposed and to express an opinion as to his or her participation'. Although this low test of competency does not fully assure patients' understanding of the nature of what they consent to or what they refuse, it is behavioural in orientation and therefore more reliable in application; it also guards against excessive paternalism.

'Reasonable' outcome of choice

This test of competency entails evaluating the patient's capacity to reach the 'reasonable', the 'right', or the 'responsible' decision. The emphasis in this test is on outcome rather than on the mere fact of a decision or how it has been reached. The patient who fails to make a decision that is roughly congruent with the decision that a 'reasonable' person in like circumstances would make is viewed as incompetent.

This test is probably used more often than might be admitted by both physicians and courts. Judicial decisions to override the desire of patients with certain religious beliefs not to receive blood transfusions may rest in part on the court's view that the patient's decision is not reasonable. When life is at stake and a court believes that the patient's decision is unreasonable, the court may focus on even the smallest ambiguity in the patient's thinking to cast doubt on the patient's competency so that it may issue an order that will preserve life or health. For example, one judge issued an order to allow amputation of the leg of an elderly moribund man even though the man had clearly told his daughter before his condition deteriorated not to permit an amputation.

Mental health laws that allow for involuntary treatment on the basis of 'need for care and treatment' without requiring a formal adjudication of incompetency in effect use an unstated reasonable outcome test in abridging the patient's common-law right not to be treated without giving his or her consent. These laws are premised on the following syllogism: the patient needs treatment; the patient has not obtained treatment on his or her own initiative; therefore, the patient's decision is incorrect, which means that he or she is incompetent, thus justifying the involuntary imposition of treatment.

The benefits and costs of this test are that social goals and individual health are promoted at considerable expense to personal autonomy. The reasonable outcome test is useful in alerting physicians and courts to the fact that the patient's decision-making process may be, but not necessarily is, awry. Ultimately, because the test rests on the congruence between the patient's decision and that of a reasonable person or that of the physician, it is biased in favour of decisions to accept treatment, even when such decisions are made by people who are incapable of weighting the risks and benefits of treatment. In other words, if patients do not decide the 'wrong' way, the issue of competency will probably not arise.

Choice based on 'rational' reasons

Another test is whether the reasons for the patient's decision are 'rational', that is, whether the patient's decision is due to or is a product of mental illness. As in the reasonable outcome test, if the patient decides in favour of treatment the issue of the patient's competency (in this case, whether the decision is the product of mental illness) seldom if ever arises because of the medical profession's bias towards consent to treatment and against refusal of treatment.

In this test the quality of the patient's thinking is what counts. The following case example illustrates the use of the test of rational reasons:

> *Case 2.* A 70-year-old widow who was living alone in a condemned dilapidated house with no heat was brought against her will to the hospital. Her thinking was tangential and fragmented. Although she did not appear to be hallucinating, she seemed delusional. She refused blood tests, saying 'You just want my blood to spread it all over Pittsburgh. No, I'm not giving it.' Her choice was respected. Later in the day, however, when her blood pressure was found to be dangerously elevated (250 over 135 in both arms), blood was withdrawn against her will.

The test of rational reasons, although it has clinical appeal and is probably much in clinical use, poses considerable conceptual problems; as a legal test it is probably defective. The problems include the difficulty of distinguishing rational from irrational reasons and drawing inferences of causation between any irrationality believed present and the valence (yes or no) of the patient's decision. Even if the patient's reasons seem irrational, it is not possible to prove that the patient's actual decisionmaking has been the product of such irrationality. The patient's decision might well be the same even if his or her cognitive processes were less impaired. For example, a delusional patient may refuse ECT not because he or she is delusional but because he or she is afraid of it, which is considered a normal reaction. The emphasis on rational reasons can too easily become a global indictment of the competency of mentally disordered individuals, justifying widespread substitute decision making for this group.

The ability to understand

This test – the ability of the patient to understand the risks, benefits and alternatives to treatment (including no treatment) – is probably the most consistent with the law of informed consent. Decision making need not be rational in either process or outcome; unwise choices are permitted. Nevertheless, at a minimum the patient must manifest sufficient ability to understand information about treatment, even if in fact he or she weights this information differently from the attending physician. What matters in this test is that the patient is able to comprehend the elements that are presumed by law to be a part of treatment decisionmaking. How the patient weights these elements, values them, or puts them together to reach a decision is not important.

The patient's capacity for understanding may be tested by asking the patient a series of questions concerning risks, benefits, and alternatives to treatment. By providing further information or explanation to the patient, the physician may find deficiencies in understanding to be remediable or not. The following case examples illustrate the use of the test of the ability to understand:

> *Case 3.* A 28-year-old woman who was unresponsive to medication was approached for consent to ECT. She initially appeared to be unaware of the examiner. Following an explanation of ECT, she responded to the request to explain its purposes and why it was being recommended in her case with the statement, 'Maul McCartney, nothing to zero'. She was shown a consent form for ECT that she signed without reading. Further attempts to educate her were unsuccessful. It was decided not to perform the ECT without seeking court approval.

> *Case 4.* A 44-year-old woman who was diagnosed as having chronic schizophrenia refused amputation of her frostbitten toes. She was nonpsychotic. Although her condition was evaluated psychiatrically as manifesting extreme denial, she understood what was proposed and that there was some risk of infection without surgery. Nevertheless, she declined. She stated, 'You want to take my toes off; I want to keep them.' Her decision was respected. She agreed to return to the hospital if things got worse. A month later she returned, having suffered an auto-amputation of the toes. There was no infection; she was rebandaged and sent home.

Some of the questions raised by this test of competency are, What is to be done if the patient can understand the risks but not the benefits or vice versa? Alternatively, what if the patient views the risks as the benefits? The following case example illustrates this problem:

> *Case 5.* A 49-year-old woman whose understanding of treatment was otherwise intact, when informed that there was a 1 in 3,000 chance of dying from ECT, replied, 'I hope I am the one.'

Furthermore, how potentially sophisticated must understanding be in order that the patient be viewed as competent? There are considerable barriers, conscious and unconscious and intellectual and emotional, to understanding proposed treatment. Presumably the potential understanding required is only that which would be manifested by a reasonable person provided with a similar amount of information. A few attempts to rank degrees of understanding have been made. However, this matter is highly complex and beyond the scope of the present inquiry. Certainly, at least with respect to nonexperimental treatment, the patient's potential understanding does not have to be perfect or near perfect for him or her to be considered competent, although one court seemed to imply this with respect to experimental psycho-surgery. A final problem with this test is that its application depends on unobservable and inferential mental processes rather than on concrete and observable elements of behaviour.

Actual understanding

Rather than focusing on competency as a construct or intervening variable in the decision-making process, the test of actual understanding reduces competency to an epiphenomenon of this process. The competent patient is by definition one who has provided a knowledgeable consent to treatment. Under this test the physician has an obligation to educate the patient and directly ascertain whether he or she has in fact understood. If not, according to this test the patient may not have provided informed consent. Depending on how sophisticated a level of understanding is to be required, this test delineates a potentially high level of competency, one that may be difficult to achieve.

The provisional decision of DHEW to mandate the creation of consent committees to oversee the decisions of experimental subjects implicitly adopts this test, as does the California law requiring the review of patient consent to ECT. Controversial as these requirements may be, they require physicians to make reasonable efforts to ascertain that their patients understand what they are told and encourage active patient participation in treatment selection.

The practical and conceptual limitations of this test are similar to those of the ability-to-understand test. What constitutes adequate understanding is vague, and deficient understanding may be attributable in whole or in part to physician behaviour as well as to the patient's behaviour or character. An advantage that this test has over the ability-to-understand test, assuming the necessary level of understanding can be specified a priori, is its greater reliability. Unlike the ability-to-understand test, in which the patient's comprehension of material of a certain complexity is used as the basis for an assumption of comprehension of other material of equivalent complexity (even if this other material is not actually tested), the actual understanding test makes no such assumption. It tests the very issues central to patient decisionmaking about treatment.

Discussion

It has been our experience that competency is presumed as long as the patient modulates his or her behaviour, talks in a comprehensible way, remembers what he or she is told, dresses and acts so as to appear to be in meaningful communication with the environment, and has not been declared legally incompetent. In other words, if patients have their wits about them in a layman's sense it is assumed that they will understand what they are told about treatment, including its risks, benefits, and alternatives. This is the equivalent of saying that the legal presumption is one of competency until found otherwise. The Pandora's box of the question of whether and to what extent the patient is able to understand or has understood what has been disclosed is therefore never opened.

In effect, the test that is actually applied combines elements of all of the tests described above. However, the circumstances in which competency becomes an issue determine which elements of which tests are stressed and which are underplayed. Although in theory competency is an independent variable that determines whether or not the patient's decision to accept or refuse treatment is to be honoured, in practice it seems to be dependent on the interplay of two other variables, the risk/benefit ratio of treatment and the valence of the patient's decision, ie, whether he or she consents to or refuses treatment.

The phrase 'risk/benefit ratio of treatment' issued here in a shorthand way to express the fact that people who determine patient competency make this decision partly on the basis of the risks of the particular treatment being considered and the benefits of that treatment. We do not mean to imply that any formal calculation is made or that any given ratio is determinative of competency. The problems of who decides what is a risk and what is a benefit, the relative weights to be attached to risks and benefits, and who bears the risks and to whom the benefits accrue (eg, the patient, the clinician, society), are beyond the scope of the present inquiry.

Table 1 illustrates the interplay of the valence of the patient's decision and the risk/benefit ratio of treatment. When there is a favourable risk/benefit ratio to the proposed treatment in the opinion of the person determining competency and the patient consents to the treatment, there does not seem to be any reason to stand in the way of administering treatment. To accomplish this, a test employing a low threshold of competency may be applied to find even a marginal patient competent so that his or her decision may be honoured (cell A). This is what happens daily when uncomprehending patients are permitted to sign themselves into the hospital. Similarly when the risk/benefit ratio is favourable and the patient refuses treatment, a test employing a higher threshold of competency may be applied (cell B). Under such a test even a somewhat knowledgeable patient may be found incompetent so that consent may be sought from a substitute decision-maker and treatment administered despite the patient's refusal. An example would be the patient withdrawing from alcohol who, although intermittently resistive, is nevertheless administered sedative medication. In both of these cases, in which the risk/benefit ratio is favourable, the bias of physicians, other health professionals, and judges is usually skewed towards providing treatment. Therefore, a test of competency is applied that will permit the treatment to be administered irrespective of the patient's actual or potential understanding.

However, there is a growing reluctance on the part of our society to permit patients to undergo treatments that are extremely risky or for which the benefits are highly speculative. Thus if the risk/benefit ratio is unfavourable or questionable and the patient refuses treatment, a test employing a low threshold of competency may be selected so that the patient will be found competent and his or her refusal honoured (cell C). This is what happens in the area of sterilisation of mentally retarded people, in which, at least from the perspective of the retarded individual, the risk/benefit ratio is questionable. On the other hand, when the risk/benefit ratio is unfavourable or questionable and the patient consents to treatment, a test using a higher threshold of competency may be applied (cell D), preventing even some fairly knowledgeable patients from undergoing treatment. The judicial opinion in the well-known *Kaimowitz* psychosurgery case delineated a high test of competency to be employed in that experimental setting [*Kaimowitz v Michigan Department of Mental Health* 42 USLW 2063 (Mich Cir Ct, (1973))].

Of course, some grossly impaired patients cannot be determined to be competent under any conceivable test, nor can most normally functioning people be found incompetent merely by selective application of a test of competency. However, within limits and when the patient's competency is not absolutely clear-cut, a test of competency that will achieve the desired medical or social end despite the actual condition of the patient may be selected. We do not imply that this is done maliciously either by physicians or by the courts; rather, we believe that it occurs as a consequence of the strong societal bias in favour of treating treatable patients so long as it does not expose them to serious risks.

Conclusions
The search for a single test of competency is a search for a Holy Grail. Unless it is recognised that there is no magical definition of competency to make decisions about treatment, the search for an acceptable test will never end. 'Getting the words just right' is only part of the problem. In practice, judgments of competency go beyond semantics or straightforward applications of legal rules; such judgments reflect social considerations and societal biases as much as they reflect matters of law and medicine.

TABLE 1
Factors in selection of competency tests

Patient's decision	Risk/benefit ratio of treatment	
	Favourable	Unfavourable or questionable
Consent	Low test of competency (cell A)	High test of competency (cell D)
Refusal	High test of competency (cell B)	Low test of competency (cell C)

You will notice the running together of the concept of capacity and the criteria for establishing it in any given case.

President's Commission for the Study of Ethical Problems in Medicine and Biomedical and Behavioural Research: 'Making Health Care Decisions' (1983)

Assessments of incapacity
The objective of any assessment of decisional incapacity is to diminish errors of mistakenly preventing competent persons from directing the course of their own treatment or of failing to protect the incapacitated from the harmful effects of their decisions. Health care professionals will probably play a substantial role, if not the entire one, in the initial assessment and the finding may never be reviewed by outside authorities. Nonetheless, since assessment of an individual's capacity is largely a matter of common sense, there is no inherent reason why a health care professional must play this role.

'Decision making incapacity' is not a medical or a psychiatric diagnostic category; it rests on a judgment of the type that an informed layperson might make – that a patient lacks the ability to understand a situation and to make a choice in light of that understanding. Indeed, if a dispute arises or a legal determination of a patient's competence is required, the judge empowered to make the determination will consider the situation not as a medical expert but as a layperson. On the basis of the testimony of health care personnel and others who know the individual well, and possibly from personal observation of the patient, the judge must decide whether the patient is capable of making informed decisions that adequately protect his or her own interests.

Health care professionals are called upon to make these assessments because the question of incapacity to make health care decisions usually arises while a person is under their care. Particularly within institutions such as hospitals, a treating physician often involves colleagues from psychiatry, psychology, and neurology who have ways to accumulate, organise, and analyse information relevant to such assessments. These examinations can yield considerable information about the patient's capabilities. The sources of useful information to be collected include discussions of the situation with relatives and other care-givers, particularly those in close contact with the patient, such as nurses. Ultimately, whether a patient's capabilities are sufficiently limited and the inadequacies sufficiently extensive for the person to be considered incapacitated is a matter for careful judgment in light of the demand of the situation. If the patient improves (or worsens) or if the decision to be made has different consequences, a reassessment of the individual's capacity may be required.

Finally, in any assessment of capacity due care should be paid to the reasons for a particular patient's impaired capacity, not because the reasons play any role in determining whether the patient's judgment is to be honoured but because identification of the causes of incapacity may assist in their remedy or removal. The Commission urges that those responsible for assessing capacity not be content with providing an answer to the question of whether or not a particular patient is incapacitated. Rather, in conjunction with the patient's health care team (of which the assessor may be a member), they should to the extent feasible attempt to remove barriers to decisional capacity.

Earlier, the President's Commission stated:

Elements of capacity. In the view of the Commission, any determination of the capacity to decide on a course of treatment must relate to the individual abilities of a patient, the requirements of the task at hand, and the consequences likely to flow from the decision. Decision-making capacity requires, to greater or lesser degree: (1) possession of a set of values and goals; (2) the ability to communicate and to understand information; (3) the ability to reason and to deliberate about one's choices.

The first, a framework for comparing options is needed if the person is to evaluate possible outcomes as good or bad. The framework, and the values that it embodies, must be reasonably stable; that is, the patient must be able to make reasonably consistent choices. Reliance on a patient's decision would be difficult or impossible if the patient's values were so unstable that the patient could not reach or adhere to a choice at least long enough for a course of therapy to be initiated with some prospect of being completed.

The second element includes the ability to give and receive information, as well as the possession of various linguistic and conceptual skills needed for at least a basic understanding of the relevant information. These abilities can be evaluated only as they relate to the task at hand and are not solely cognitive, as they ordinarily include emotive elements. To use them, a person also needs sufficient life experience to appreciate the meaning of potential alternatives; what it would probably be like to undergo various medical procedures, for example, or to live in a new way required by a medical condition or intervention.

Some critics of the doctrine of informed consent have argued that patients simply lack the ability to understand medical information relevant to decisions about their care. Indeed, some empirical studies purport to have demonstrated this by showing that the lay public often does not know the meaning of common medical terms, or by showing that, following an encounter with a physician, patients are unable to report what the physician said about their illness and treatment. Neither type of study establishes the fact that patients cannot understand. The first merely finds that they do not currently know the right definitions of some terms; the second, which usually fails to discover what the physician actually did say, rests its conclusions on an assumption that information was provided that was subsequently not understood. In the Commission's own survey, physicians were asked: 'What percentage of your patients would you say are able to understand most aspects of their treatment and condition if reasonable time and effort are devoted to explanation?' Overall, 48% of physicians reported that 90-100% of their patients could understand and an additional 34% said that 70-89% could understand.

The third element of decision-making capacity – reasoning and deliberation – includes the ability to compare the impact of alternative outcomes on personal goals and life plans. Some ability to employ probabilistic reasoning about uncertain outcomes is usually necessary, as well as the ability to give appropriate weight in a present decision to various future outcomes.

Standards for assessing capacity. The actual measurement of these various abilities is by no means simple. Virtually all conscious adults can perform some tasks but not others. In the context of informed consent, what is critical is a patient's capacity to make a specific medical decision. An assessment of an individual's capacity must consider the nature of the particular decision-making process in light of these developments: Does the patient possess the ability to understand the relevant facts and alternatives? Is the patient weighting the decision within a framework of values and goals? Is the patient able to reason and deliberate about this information? Can the patient give reasons for the decision, in light of the facts, the alternatives, and the impact of the decision on the patient's own goals and values?

To be sure, a patient may possess these abilities but fail to exercise them well; that is, the decision may be the result of a mistaken understanding of the facts or a defective reasoning process. In such instances, the obligation of the professional is not to declare, on the basis of a 'wrong' decision, that the patient lacks decision-making capacity, but rather to work with the patient towards a fuller and more accurate understanding of the facts and a sound reasoning process.

How deficient must a decision-making process be to justify the assessment that a patient lacks the capacity to make a particular decision? Since the assessment must balance possibly competing considerations of well-being and self-determination, the prudent course is to take into account the potential consequences of the patient's decision. When the consequences for well-being are substantial, there is a greater need to be certain that the patient possesses the necessary level of capacity. When little turns on the decision, the level of decision-making capacity required may be appropriately reduced (even though the constituent elements remain the same) and less scrutiny may be required about whether the patient possesses even the reduced level of capacity. Thus a particular patient may be capable of deciding about a relatively inconsequential medication, but not about the amputation of a gangrenous limb.

This formulation has significant implications. First, it denies that simply by expressing a preference about a treatment decision an individual demonstrates the capacity to make that decision. The 'expressed preference' standard does nothing to preclude the presence of a serious defect or mistake in a patient's reasoning process. Consequently, it cannot ensure that the patient's expressed preference accords with the patient's conception of future well-being. Although it gives what appears to be great deference to self-determination, the expressed preference standard may actually fail to promote the values underlying self-administration, which include the achievement of personal values and goals. For these reasons, the Commission rejects the expressed preference standard for decisions that might compromise the patient's well-being.

The Commission also rejects as the standard of capacity any test that looks solely to the content of the patient's decision. Any standard based on 'objectively correct' decisions would allow a health professional (or other third party) to declare that a patient lacks decision-making capacity whenever a decision appears 'wrong', 'irrational', or otherwise incompatible with the evaluator's view of what is best for the patient. Use of such a standard is in sharp conflict with most of the values that support self-determination: it would take the decision away from the patient and place it with another, and it would inadequately reflect the subjective nature of each individual's conception of what's good. Further, its imprecision opens the door to manipulation of health care decision-making through selective application.

Logically, just as a patient's disagreement with a health care professional's recommendation does not prove a lack of decision-making capacity, concurrence with the recommendation would not establish the patient's capacity. Yet, as testimony before the Commission made clear, coherent adults are seldom said to lack capacity (except, perhaps, in the mental health context) when they acquiesce in the course of treatment recommended by their physicians. (Challenges to patients' capacity are rarer still when family members expressly concur in the decision.) This divergence between theory and reality is less significant than it might appear, however, since neither the self-determination nor the well-being of a patient would usually be advanced by insisting upon an inquiry into the patient's decision-making capacity (or lack thereof) when patient, physicians, and family all agree on a course of treatment. Even if the course being adopted might not, in fact, best match the patient's long-term view of his or her own welfare, a declaration of lack of capacity will lead to a substitute making a decision for the patient (which means full self-determination will not occur), yet will rarely result in a different health care decision being made (which means no change in well-being). Substitution of a third party for an acquiescent patient will lead to a different outcome only if the new decision-maker has a strong commitment to promoting previously expressed values of the patient that differ significantly from those that guided the physician. If, as would usually be the case, the substitute would be a family member or other individual who would defer to the physician's recommendation, there would be little reason to initiate an inquiry into capacity. The existing practice thus seems generally satisfactory.

Questions of patient capacity in decision-making typically arise only when a patient chooses a course – often a refusal of treatment – other than the one the health professional finds most reasonable. A practitioner's belief that a decision is not 'reasonable' is the beginning – not the end – of an inquiry into the patient's capacity to decide. If every patient decision that a health professional disagreed with were grounds for a declaration of lack of capacity, self-determination would have little meaning. Even when disagreement occurs, an assessment of the patient's decision-making capacity begins with a presumption of such capacity. Nonetheless, a serious disagreement about a decision with substantial consequences for the patient's welfare may appropriately trigger a more careful evaluation. When that process indicates that the patient understands the situation and is capable of reasoning soundly about it, the patient's choice should be accepted. When it does not, further evaluation may be required, and in some instances a determination of lack of capacity will be appropriate.

Professor Margaret Somerville addresses the particular and troubling issue of rationality.

M Somerville 'Structuring the Issues in Informed Consent' (1981) 26 McGill LJ 740

Does the law require rationality of the patient's decision as a substantive element of a valid consent?

The first consideration is the relationship between understanding and rationality. If the law requires that the patient apparently understand the required disclosure of information in order to give a valid consent, does this mean that the law is seeking to promote rationality of the patient's decision and, further, if his decision is adjudged irrational, may it be ignored or overridden on this basis?

Even if it is accepted that understanding of the required disclosed information is being mandated in order to promote rationality, it must be asked whether this means rationality of the decision-making process or rationality of the decision itself or both. Although understanding may promote rationality in both of these respects, it is usually only the rationality of the decision outcome that is relevant to the law, and understanding may not be an essential condition for this. It is quite possible for a decision to be judged rational by an objective bystander, when the reasons on which it was based were quite irrational. Moreover, the law's requirement of understanding of information by the patient may be seen as promoting autonomy rather than rationality. In this case, to require rationality either of the patient's decision-making process or its outcome would be to contradict directly the value of self-determination which is being promoted by requiring understanding, because self-determination requires recognition of the competent patient's right, for no matter what reason or on what basis, to determine what shall be done to himself.

It is submitted that the preferable approach is to view understanding as promoting autonomy, rather than rationality. Any legal limits to irrationality of a decision-making process or decision outcome should then be set by declaring the person factually or legally incompetent. Thus, the right to autonomy would mean that the competent patient could make irrational decisions concerning himself without the law overriding such decisions. Further, in order to give proper scope to such a rule, it is necessary to recognise that irrationality of the decision-making process or of decision outcomes does not of itself indicate incompetence, although in some circumstances it may be evidence of this.

The issue of irrationality of the patient's decision was considered in *Kelly v Hazlett* [(1976) 75 DLR (3rd) 536]. The defendant surgeon gave evidence that he considered the plaintiff 'irrational', that is, 'irrational from the point of view of not being able to think the way that [he, the doctor] was thinking, which [he] thought was more rational'. The actual irrationality referred to was the patient's decision to undergo the operation only if the cosmetic procedure were included. In the result the Court held that the patient's 'apparent consent' was insufficient to protect the surgeon from liability in negligence on the basis of failure to obtain informed consent. It is not exactly clear how much the irrationality of the patient's decision influenced his holding, but it seems that such irrationality should at least put the physician on notice that the patient's 'decision was not based upon any knowledge or appreciation of the risk', in which case the physician may not rely on the consent as being valid. This case is probably a demonstration of a court looking to the rationality of the patient's decision to indicate both whether the patient had the required understanding of the risks that must be understood in order to give informed consent, and whether the physician had, or ought to have had, knowledge of any lack of understanding on the part of the patient.

In summary, the question of rationality in matters of consent is difficult. To allow (or even more so, require) second-guessing of the patient's decision according to whether that decision is rational may seriously detract from autonomy (which it is the purpose of consent to protect). The more a person's decision deviates from what the person assessing that decision would decide in the same circumstances, and the more serious the consequences of that decision, the more likely it is that the person making the decision will be labelled incompetent and his decision irrational. Rather than judging the rationality of a patient's decision and validating or invalidating consent on that basis, the better solution (which was probably the approach of the Court in *Kelly v Hazlett*) is to adopt understanding by the patient of the information required to be disclosed as the necessary safeguard. Pursuant to such an approach, provided the patient is otherwise judged to be competent, if the physician has no subjective knowledge that the patient lacks understanding and the reasonable physician would have believed that the patient apparently understood the information disclosed, the resulting consent may be relied upon as valid whether or not the patient's decision is considered rational.

In a paternalistic physician-patient relationship, consent was often the *imprimatur* of the doctor's rational decision-making on the patient's behalf. Under a doctrine of informed consent the aim is to enable the patient to make a decision on his own behalf. A remaining question is how far the physician is justified in carrying out a patient's informed, irrational decisions. The physician is far less likely to be acting within legal or ethical limits when implementing such a decision requires a positive intervention on his part, than when it is a situation in which he must desist from violating the patient's physical or mental integrity against his will. More explicitly, a patient's irrational refusal of treatment should be accorded greater respect than his irrational demand for it.

Dr Raanon Gillon in an editorial in the *Journal of Medical Ethics* considers the relevance of delusion and misperception of facts.

R Gillon (1983) 9 Journal of Medical Ethics 131

Impaired autonomy and rejection of treatment
Two important moral principles can, and occasionally do, come into conflict in the context of medical practice: the first is the principle of helping others who are in need (beneficence), presumably the basic moral principle motivating the caring professions; the second is respect for people's autonomy – acknowledgment of their right to make their own deliberated decision within the context of their own life plan and preferences, so far as this does not harm others. Normally, of course, these two principles do not conflict – people consult doctors because they have medical problems which they want the doctors to do their best to abolish or ameliorate. In a minority of cases, however, the patient rejects the course of action proposed by the doctor and the doctor's dilemma is generated.

The polar cases are relatively uncontroversial. Thus when a patient is clearly competent to make his own decisions and rejects his doctor's advice despite understanding it and the anticipated consequences of rejecting it, then a consensus probably exists in favour of respecting the patient's decision. Hence contemporary medical respect for life-threatening decisions by Jehovah's Witnesses to refuse blood transfusions and by hunger strikers to refuse food and medical attention.

At the other pole, when a patient is clearly incompetent to make autonomous decisions it is widely agreed that beneficent decisions must be taken on his or her behalf, overriding, if this seems desirable, the incompetent patient's protests. A young child is operated on for appendicitis even if he refuses most volubly; a severely mentally handicapped patient is treated with antibiotic injections for his meningitis even if he does hate needles. A patient in a severe confusional state is treated against his will when this is judged necessary. All this is relatively uncontroversial. More controversial is who should make the decisions and on what basis, though once again a consensus is apparently emerging that next of kin and/or the patient's loved ones are presumed to be best placed to make such decisions, in the context of medical advice and where possible on the basis of what the patient would decide autonomously, but failing that, on the basis of the patient's best interests. The presumption that the next of kin should decide on behalf of the incompetent patient is always defeasible and if the doctors or others believe that particular decisions are *not* what the patient would have autonomously wished or not in the patient's best interests, and if agreement between them and the relatives is impossible it is open to them to obtain a judicial assessment.

What, however, differentiates the patient who is competent to make his own deliberated decisions and thus is to have his autonomy respected from the patient who is not? The symposium in this issue of the journal and the paper in the *American Journal of Psychiatry* which provoked it analyse this issue of competence (or competency – the final 'y' is sometimes added where the term has a legal connotation) in the context of 'competent but irrational' refusal of electroconvulsive therapy (ECT) as treatment for depression.

The first important point to emerge from the symposium is that information is essential for autonomous and therefore rational decision-making. One cannot reason or deliberate about alternative courses of action if one has no information about them, and as Dr Taylor, a forensic psychiatrist, points out, patients are likely to make irrational decisions if their doctors give them inadequate information. She explains in detail the clinical importance of ensuring that patients are given adequate information, and given it personally and with care. Nonetheless, as Dr Taylor also points out, the amount of information which patients actually retain is often likely to be fairly limited. How much is necessary for competent decision-making by the patient? Dr Culver and his colleagues recommend a 'minimalist' requirement – a patient should be regarded as competent to reject or accept medical treatment if he knows the doctor believes he is ill and in need of treatment, knows the doctor believes the treatment may help his illness and knows he is expected to decide whether or not to have the treatment. The grounds for this minimalism are that others should not make decisions for patients unless 'it is abundantly clear that the patient is simply unable to represent his or her own interest'.

One problem with this requirement is, as Dr Taylor points out, that patients may meet the cognitive standards set by Culver *et al*, manifest impeccable logical reasoning ability, and yet, because of their seriously distorted perception of the world, base much of their reasoning on false premises. If a patient 'knows' that guns are pointing at him wherever he goes it makes good sense for him to run away or hit back – and it makes good sense to pity and scorn the doctor for not being able to see the guns, or hear the voices, and for diagnosing him as a paranoid psychotic. But is that sort of reasoning to be regarded as *competent*? By the minimal criteria of Culver *et al* presumably, it may be; and rejection of medication, however irrational it may be, would therefore be accepted. Many, clinicians and non-clinicians alike, would not accept such decisions as being competently made, nor would they want them respected if they led to actions which harmed others or the patient himself. Thus while Culver *et al* are surely right – in the interests of respecting patients' autonomy – to insist on a 'minimalist' criterion for competence to reject treatment it seems necessary to allow that if a patient's perception of reality is *sufficiently* distorted by delusions, illusions and hallucinations, then his competence to reject treatment may properly be questioned even if he meets Culver and his colleagues' criteria.

However, Professor Sherlock is surely right to criticise the Culver criteria on the grounds that they are only cognitive whereas informed consent and rejection require not only adequate information but also what Sherlock calls voluntariness, by which he means 'an uncoerced consent'. And Dr Taylor raises similar doubts in relation to common psychiatric conditions in which patients show no sign of being able to make free decisions of any kind: the patient who just does not know what to do; the patient who sits in the corner wringing his hands and saying nothing; the patient who has 'more important things to think about' – all manifest grossly impaired volition (still these days philosophically a fishy concept but an unshakably real phenomenon to most clinicians). Their cognitive status, however, may be well up to the standards required by Culver *et al* for recognition of competence. Once again it seems sensible to modify their minimalist cognitive criteria by adding a criterion of voluntariness – a requirement that the patient is in a state of mind in which he can make ordinary voluntary decisions.

Here, however, great care is needed – in the interests of justice – to make sure that the criteria for voluntariness required of patients are no more stringent than those required of anyone else in society for his autonomy to be recognised. Sherlock suggests that an irrational refusal to have ECT can *in itself* be grounds for classifying a patient as incompetent. Somewhat contentiously classifying this as a 'phobia' he says that the patient 'is not more free to decide *vis-à-vis* the dreaded object than he would be were he faced with severe hardship for failure to comply with a command to consent'. This doctrine that the presence of a phobia is sufficient for a patient to be judged incompetent to reject treatment has only to be universalised to be shown to be far too demanding. Thus, according to the doctrine, if a patient consults her psychiatrist about an admitted phobia to do with, say, spiders or flying or open spaces, and the doctor confirms the diagnosis he immediately is justified in deeming her incompetent to decide about her treatment (because she has a phobia) and in instituting against her will any standard treatment he happens to favour.

Voluntariness and autonomy can be greatly impaired in ordinary life without a person's right to make his own decision being overridden; similar minimalist standards should in justice be set for patients. Thus, while recognition should be given to the fact that mental and other illness can on occasion impair the patient's competence to give any sort of voluntary decision (even if he meets the cognitive standards proposed) the mere presence of a psychiatric or other disorder cannot in itself justify an assessment of incompetence to decide on treatment.

Finally, Professor Sherlock's justification of paternalistic intervention to force a depressed patient to have ECT against his will on the grounds that by doing so he would actually be respecting the patient's autonomy by seeking to increase it requires critical consideration. In the recent issue of the journal an editorial criticised Dr Komrad's argument that illness always represented a state of diminished autonomy and that this justified paternalistic medical interventions imposed in order to restore or increase the patient's autonomy by ameliorating the effects of the illness. Professor Sherlock's argument is similar. To respect a patient's irrational decision to refuse ECT is, he writes, to respect only a 'limited autonomy' and it is better to override that decision in the interests of restoring the patient's full autonomy. 'If we do value autonomy we ought to pursue it in its fullest possible form, not in the truncated one-dimensional case of refusal of ECT. If autonomy is a good then I submit that the morally appropriate course of action is to foster the autonomy of patients by relieving to the best of our abilities the impediments to autonomy such as major depression'.

There can be no objection to this when the patient consents. But when such 'relief of impediments' is imposed against the competent patient's will, then this benign paternalism represents, as Lesser points out, a serious threat to personal freedom. Autonomy is not an all or nothing phenomenon. People are autonomous to different degrees, their autonomy varying with time and circumstances. If mere evidence of impairment of autonomy (or even of serious impairment) is to be used to justify compulsory intervention by others in order to increase people's autonomy then all standard concepts of respect for autonomy and respect for individual liberty will have taken on new, and to many, somewhat sinister meanings.

(b) The law

In the light of these analyses, we must now examine the limited case law in England and elsewhere. You will notice from the cases a number of criteria for establishing that a patient is competent, ie that he is capable of understanding what is involved. These criteria are, as we shall see, of varying plausibility. The *first* criterion, in the language of the Roth *et al* article, is that of 'evidencing a choice'. This is clearly wrong even though it has never been judicially considered in a medical law case in England since making a choice demonstrates nothing about the patient's 'understanding'. *Secondly*, there is the criterion of 'reasonable outcome'. This, arguably, is equally untenable since it makes capacity to understand turn upon the agreement of others with the decision reached. Again this does not help to determine the patient's 'understanding'. Such judicial statements as there are support this conclusion.

Smith v Auckland Hospital Board [1965] NZLR 191 (NZCA)

> **T A Greeson J:** An individual patient must, in my view, always retain the right to decline operative investigation or treatment however unreasonable or foolish this may appear in the eyes of his medical advisers.

The issue of capacity did not arise directly in this case but Greeson J's remark appears to be authority for the proposition that capacity is not to be doubted simply on the ground that the decision is unreasonable in the eyes of others.

Hopp v Lepp (1979) 98 DLR (3d) 464 (Alta CA)

> **Prowse JA:** Each patient is entitled to make his own decision even though it may not accord with the decision knowledgeable members of the profession would make. *The patient has a right to be wrong.* When specific questions are directed to a surgeon he must make a full and fair disclosure in response to them. This duty requires a surgeon to disclose risks which are mere possibilities if the patient's questions reasonably direct the surgeon's attention to risks of that nature and if they are such that the surgeon, in all of the circumstances, could reasonably foresee would affect the patient's decision.

Further, as Butler-Sloss LJ observed in *Re T* (*supra*) '[a] decision to refuse medical treatment does not have to be sensible . . . or well-considered'.

The *third* criterion is that of 'rationality'. By this is meant that the patient has applied a process of reasoning to the issue and that the conclusion arrived at can be justified by reference to that process. This is an immensely difficult criterion to deploy. Are we not entitled to be irrational? See, for example, decisions about whom we marry, the job we take, the house we buy, the political party we support. Arguably a distinction must be drawn between a decision based upon beliefs or values not commonly held or accepted (eg a Jehovah's Witness's refusal of a blood transfusion) and a decision based upon a misperception of reality (eg that blood is a poison because it is red). In both cases the decisions are based upon premises which most find unintelligible and, therefore, we may be prepared to regard the decisions as irrational. There is, however, an important distinction. The premise of the Jehovah's Witness, for example, is one derived from the individual's value system. Provided the decision is consistent with those values, the decision can only be challenged by refusing to accept (by merely asserting) that the basic premise is wrong. By contrast, in the case of the patient who thinks blood is a poison, the decision can be demonstrated to be based upon a false premise of fact. The individual, unlike the Jehovah's Witness, does not understand what is involved in the treatment. The Jehovah's Witness does understand but rejects the treatment for his own reasons based upon his value system. For the sake of completeness, it is of no consequence that the misapprehension that blood is a poison is a result of a temporary delusion, eg in the case of a schizophrenic, or is a long-held view based upon a perverse understanding of the world.

The criterion of rationality more than any other highlights the clash between respect for autonomy and beneficence which is often at the root of decisions about competence. Of course, to talk of beneficence as being in conflict with respect for autonomy is to a certain extent to beg an important question. One of the major drawbacks in appeals to beneficence is that to urge that one should seek to do good does not answer the questions 'What is good?' and 'Who decides?'. Furthermore, on a closer analysis, respect for autonomy maybe the most highly prized form of doing good which would mean that the alleged clash between respect for autonomy and beneficence does not materialise. It would also follow that the guiding principle in determining the criteria of competence ought, therefore, to be respect for autonomy.

Lord Templeman in *Sidaway v Governors of Bethlem Royal Hospital* [1985] AC 871 indicated that approach the courts must take:

> If the doctor making a balanced judgment advises the patient to submit to the operation, the patient is entitled to reject that advice for reasons which are rational or irrational, or for no reason. The duty of the doctor in these circumstances . . . is to provide the patient with information which will enable the patient to make a balanced judgment if the patient chooses to make a balanced judgment.

But, as we have seen, the courts need to proceed more carefully than Lord Templeman's aphorism would suggest. The courts, in respecting autonomy, must be aware of those circumstances in which the patient's views are the product of a belief or value system or a misperception of reality. Clearly for a court to accept (and to allow the patient to act upon) a decision derived from the latter is not to respect a patient's autonomy but to undermine it. In such a case a court could well take the view that the patient is unable to understand what is involved and is, therefore, incompetent (see the discussion of 'rationality' in Law Commission Consultation Paper No 129, *op cit*, paras 2.14-2.16).

(i) BELIEFS AND VALUE SYSTEMS

R v Blaue [1975] 1 WLR 1411 (CA) was one of the first cases in which an English court addressed the issue of the relevance of an individual's beliefs in determining competence to decide. In this case, the victim of an assault died after refusing a blood transfusion. She did so because she was a Jehovah's Witness. The defendant argued that this decision by the victim broke the chain of causation such that he was exonerated from liability for homicide. Clearly, if a court were to decide that the victim was entitled to refuse medical treatment, and that she was competent to do so, this argument would fail. The Court of Appeal rejected the defendant's argument which in essence was that no one in her right mind would refuse life-saving treatment.

R v Blaue [1975] 1 WLR 1411 (CA)

> Lawson LJ: Counsel for the appellant . . . submitt[ed] that the jury should have been directed that if they thought the girl's decision not to have a blood transfusion was an unreasonable one, then the chain of causation would have been broken. At once the question arises – reasonably by whose standards? Those of Jehovah's Witnesses? Humanists? Roman Catholics? Protestants of Anglo-Saxon descent? The man on the Clapham omnibus? But he might well be an admirer of Eleazar who suffered death rather than eat the flesh of swine or of Sir Thomas More who unlike nearly all his contemporaries, was unwilling to accept Henry VIII as Head of the Church in England. Those brought up in the Hebraic and Christian traditions would probably be reluctant to accept that these martyrs caused their own deaths.
>
> As was pointed out to counsel for the appellant in the course of argument, two cases, each raising the same issue of reasonableness because of religious beliefs, could produce different verdicts depending on where the cases were tried. A jury drawn from Preston, sometimes said to be the most Catholic town in England, might have different views about martyrdom to one drawn from the inner suburbs of London.

The point arose directly in *Re T (adult: refusal of treatment)* [1992] 4 All ER 649 (CA) in which an adult woman, apparently a Jehovah's Witness, refused a life-saving blood transfusion. On the facts, the Court of Appeal held that her decision was invalid because it was based solely upon the persuasion, ie undue influence of her mother who was a Jehovah's Witness (see *infra*, p 233). Nevertheless, the judges squarely faced up to whether, if she had been a Jehovah's Witness, her decision would have been legally effective. In deciding that it would have been, the court accepted that she would have been competent (ie would have understood what was involved) even though she came to a decision most would find unreasonable and irrational.

Lord Donaldson MR stated that:

[A patient's] right of choice is not limited to decisions which others might regard as sensible. It exists notwithstanding that the reasons for making the choice are rational, irrational, unknown or even non-existent . . .

Later he pointed out:

That [the patient's] choice is contrary to what is to be expected of the vast majority of adults is only relevant if there are other reasons for doubting his capacity to decide. The nature of his choice or the terms in which it is expressed may then tip the balance.

Similarly, Butler-Sloss LJ stated:

A man or woman of full age and sound understanding may choose to reject medical advice and medical or surgical treatment either partially or in its entirety. A decision to refuse medical treatment by a patient capable of making the decision does not have to be sensible, rational or well-considered . . .

Subsequently, Lord Donaldson MR in *Re W (a minor) (medical treatment)* [1992] 4 All ER 627 stated that:

I personally consider that religious or other beliefs which bar any medical treatment or treatment of particular kinds are irrational, but that does not make minors who hold beliefs any the less 'Gillick competent' [*a fortiori* adults]. They may well have sufficient intelligence and understanding fully to appreciate the treatment proposed and the consequences of their refusal to accept that treatment.

It is clear that most of the cases in which the understanding of the patient will be questioned on the grounds that the beliefs giving rise to it are irrational will involve religious beliefs. Jehovah's Witnesses and Christian Scientists are two classic examples. It is possible, however, to postulate decisions being based upon beliefs unrelated to religion. The case of *Re Maida Yetter* provides an illustration.

Re Maida Yetter (1973) 96 D & C 2d 619 (CP Northampton County PA)

Williams J: This matter involves the appointment of a guardian of the person for Maida Yetter, an alleged incompetent, under the Incompetents' Estates Act of February 28, 1956, PL (1955) 1154, as amended, 50 PS $3101, et seq. The petition was filed by Russell C Stauffer, her brother, a citation issued on May 10, 1973. The citation was served on the alleged incompetent by a deputy sheriff of Lehigh County at Allentown State Hospital, Lehigh County Pa, on May 15, 1973. A hearing was held on May 30, 1973, as specified in the petition. Present at the hearing were petitioner and his counsel, Dr Ellen Bischoff, a psychiatrist on the staff of the hospital; Mrs Marilou Perhac, a caseworker at the hospital assigned to Mrs Yetter's ward; the alleged incompetent and her counsel. Mrs Yetter is married, although she has been separated from, and has had no contact with, her husband since 1947.

From the petition and the testimony it appears that the primary purpose of the appointment of a guardian of the person is to give consent to the performance of diagnostic and corrective surgery.

Mrs Yetter was committed to Allentown State Hospital in June 1971, by the Courts of Northampton County after hearings held pursuant to section 406 of the Mental Health and Mental Retardation Act of October 20, 1966, Sp Sess, PL 96, 50 PS $4406. Her diagnosis at that time was schizophrenia, chronic undifferentiated. It appears that late in 1972, in connection with a routine physical examination, Mrs Yetter was discovered to have a breast discharge indicating the possible presence of carcinoma. The doctors recommended that a surgical biopsy be performed together with any additional corrective surgery that would be indicated by the pathology of the biopsy. When this recommendation was first discussed with Mrs Yetter in December of 1972 by her caseworker, Mrs Perhac, who had weekly counselling sessions with Mrs Yetter for more than a year, Mrs Yetter indicated that she would not give her consent to the surgery. Her stated reasons were that she was afraid because of the death of her aunt which followed such surgery and that it was her own body and she did not desire the operation. The caseworker indicated that at this time Mrs Yetter was lucid, rational and appeared to understand that the possible consequences of her refusal included death.

Mr Stauffer, who indicated that he visits his sister regularly, and Dr Bischoff, whose direct contacts with Mrs Yetter have been since March 1973, testified that in the last three or four months it has been impossible to discuss the proposed surgery with Mrs Yetter in that, in addition to expressing fear of the operation, she has become delusional in her reasons for not consenting to surgery. Her tendency to become delusional concerning this problem, although no others, was confirmed by Mrs Perhac. The present delusional nature of Mrs Yetter's reasoning concerning the problem was demonstrated at the hearing when Mrs Yetter, in response to questions by the court and counsel, indicated that the operation would interfere with her genital system, affecting her ability to have babies, and would prohibit a movie career. Mrs Yetter is 60 years of age and without children.

Dr Bischoff testified that Mrs Yetter is oriented as to time, place and her personal environment, and that her present delusions are consistent with the diagnosis and evaluation of her mental illness upon admission to the hospital in 1971. The doctor indicated that, in her opinion, at the present time Mrs Yetter is unable, by reasons of her mental illness, to arrive at a considered judgment as to whether to undergo surgery.

Mr Stauffer testified that the aunt referred to by Mrs Yetter, although she underwent a similar operation, died of unrelated causes some 15 years after surgery.

He further indicated that he has been apprised by the physicians of the nature of the proposed procedures and their probable consequences as well as the probable consequences if the procedures are not performed. He indicated that if he is appointed guardian of the person for his sister he would consent to the surgical procedures recommended.

At the hearing Mrs Yetter was alert, interested and obviously meticulous about her personal appearance. She stated that she was afraid of surgery, that the best course of action for her would be to leave her body alone, that surgery might hasten the spread of the disease and do further harm, and she reiterated her fears due to the death of her aunt. On several occasions during the hearing she interjected the statements that she would die if surgery were performed. It is clear that mere commitment to a state hospital for treatment of mental illness does not destroy a person's competency or require the appointment of a guardian of the estate or person. Ryman's Case, 139 Pa Superior Ct 212. Mental capacity must be examined on a case by case basis.

In our opinion, the constitutional right of privacy included the right of a mature competent adult to refuse to accept medical recommendations that may prolong one's life and which, to a third person at least, appear to be in his best interests; in short, that the right of privacy includes a right to die with which the State should not interfere where there are no minor or unborn children and no clear and present danger to public health, welfare or morals. If the person was competent while being presented with the decision and in making the decision which she did, the court should not interfere even though the decision might be considered unwise, foolish or ridiculous.

While many philosophical articles have been published relating to this subject there are few appellate court decisions and none in Pennsylvania to our knowledge. The cases are collected in an annotation in 9 ALR 3d 1391. Considering other factors which have influenced the various courts, the present case does not involve a patient who sought medical attention from a hospital and then attempted to restrict the institution and physicians from rendering proper medical care. The State hospital as Mrs Yetter's custodian certainly has acted properly in initiating the present proceeding through the patient's brother and cannot be said to have either overridden the patient's wishes or merely allowed her to die for lack of treatment.

The testimony of the caseworker with respect to her conversations with Mrs Yetter in December 1972, convinces us that at that time her refusal was informed, conscious of the consequences and would not have been superseded by this court. The ordinary person's refusal to accept medical advice based upon fear is commonly known and while the refusal may be irrational and foolish to an outside observer, it cannot be said to be incompetent in order to permit the State to override the decision.

The obvious difficulty in this proceeding is that in recent months Mrs Yetter's steadfast refusal has been accompanied by delusions which create doubt that her decision is the product of competent, reasoned judgment. However, she has been consistent in expressing the fear that she would die if surgery were performed. The delusions do not appear to us to be her primary reason for rejecting surgery. Are we then to force her to submit to medical treatment because some of her present reasons for refusal are delusional and the result of mental illness? Should we now override her original understanding but irrational decision?

There is no indication that Mrs Yetter's condition is critical or that she is in the waning hours of life, although we recognise the advice of medical experts as to the need for early detection and treatment of cancer symptoms. Upon reflection, balancing the risk involved in our refusal to act in favour of compulsory treatment against giving the greatest possible protection to the individual in furtherance of his own desires, we are unwilling now to overrule Mrs Yetter's original irrational but competent decision.

Mrs Yetter's delusion that she had a prospect of becoming a movie star and having babies was judged an irrational delusion which provided strong evidence that she was unable to understand what was being proposed. On the other hand, her aversion to surgery based upon the death of her aunt fifteen years earlier, was not regarded as evidencing an inability to understand though obviously many would regard it as irrational. She had held this view for some time, had lived by it and ordered her life by it. It is of no consequence that others may disagree with it (see also *Re Quackenbush* 383 A 2d 785 (1978) – where a person with a conscientious objection to medical treatment and had shunned treatment for forty years was held competent to refuse life-sustaining surgery).

(ii) MISPERCEPTION OF REALITY

Here the issue is clearer. Someone who is deluded about the world – in our context they do not accept what is happening to them or what treatment may offer for them – is not capable of understanding what is involved.

State of Tennessee v Northern (1978) 563 SW 2d 197 (Tenn Ct App)

Judge Todd: On January 24, 1978, the Tennessee Department of Human Services filed this suit alleging that Mary C Northern was 72 years old, with no available help from relatives; that Miss Northern resided alone under unsatisfactory conditions as a result of which she had been admitted to and was a patient in Nashville General Hospital; that the patient suffered from gangrene of both feet which required the removal of her feet to save her life; that the patient lacked the capacity to appreciate her condition or to consent to necessary surgery.

Attached to the complaint are identified letters from Drs Amos D Tackett and R Benton Adkins which read as follows:

Mrs Mary Northern is a patient under our care at Nashville General Hospital. She has gangrene of both feet probably secondary to frost bite and then thermal burning of the feet. She has developed infection along with the gangrene of her feet. This is placing her life in danger. Mrs Northern does not understand the severity or consequences of her disease process and does not appear to understand that failure to amputate the feet at this time would probably result in her death. It is our recommendation as the physicians in charge of her case, that she undergo amputation of both feet as soon as possible.

The judge then turned to consider whether Miss Northern had capacity to refuse the treatment.

> . . . Capacity means mental ability to make a rational decision, which includes the ability to perceive, appreciate all relevant facts and to reach a rational judgment upon such facts.
>
> Capacity is not necessarily synonymous with sanity. A blind person may be perfectly capable of observing the shape of small articles by handling them, but not capable of observing the shape of a cloud in the sky.
>
> A person may have 'capacity' as to some matters and may lack 'capacity' as to others. . . .
>
> In the present case, this Court has found the patient to be lucid and apparently of sound mind generally. However, on the subjects of death and amputation of her feet, her comprehension is blocked, blinded or dimmed to the extent that she is incapable of recognising facts which would be obvious to a person of normal perception.
>
> For example, in the presence of this Court, the patient looked at her feet and refused to recognise the obvious facts that the flesh was dead, black, shrivelled, rotting and stinking.
>
> The record also discloses that the patient refuses to consider the eventuality of death which is or ought to be obvious in the face of such dire bodily deterioration.
>
> As described by the doctors and observed by this Court, the patient wants to live and keep her dead feet, too, and refuses to consider the impossibility of such a desire. In order to avoid the unpleasant experience of facing death and/or loss of feet, her mind or emotions have resorted to the device of denying the unpleasant reality so that, to the patient, the unpleasant reality does not exist. This is the 'delusion' which renders the patient incapable of making a rational decision as to whether to undergo surgery to save her life or to forego surgery and forfeit her life.
>
> The physicians speak of probabilities of death without amputation as 90% to 95% and the probability of death with surgery as 50-50 (1 in 2). Such probabilities are not facts, but the existence and expression of such opinions are facts which the patient is unwilling or unable to recognise or discuss.
>
> If as repeatedly stated, this patient could and would give evidence of a comprehension of the facts of her condition and could and would express her unequivocal desire in the face of such comprehended facts, then her decision, however unreasonable to others, would be accepted and honoured by the Courts and by her doctors. The difficulty is that she cannot or will not comprehend the facts.

The court was clearly influenced by Miss Northern's refusal to comprehend the facts of her situation. In a concurring judgment, Judge Drowota emphasises this important factor in *Northern*.

> **Drowota J:** In the instant case, the Court found that Miss Northern does not have the capacity to decide whether her feet should or should not be amputated. This finding is not based on any belief by this Court that a competent adult should not be permitted to reject lifesaving treatment. It is *not*, as has been argued to us, based on any idea of this Court that any person who refuses treatment we subjectively think a 'normal' or 'rational' person would choose is 'incompetent' merely because of that refusal. It is based on the Court's finding that Miss Northern is unable or unwilling to comprehend even dimly certain very basic *facts*, without which no one, whether elderly lady, doctor, or judge, would be competent to make such a decision. These facts include the appearance of her feet, which are disfigured, coal black, crusty, cracking, oozing, and rancid. Yet, Miss Northern looks at them and insists that nothing is wrong. Also included was the fact that her doctors are of the opinion that her life is in danger, yet she has expressed no understanding of either the gravity or the consequences of her medical condition. Again, this Court respects Miss Northern's right to disagree with medical opinions and advice. Again, if this Court in good faith could find that she perceived as facts that her feet *do* look and smell as they do, and that her doctors *are* telling her that she needs surgery to save her life, we would not interfere with whatever decision she made regardless of how much it conflicted with the substance of her medical advice or with what we ourselves might have chosen. But from our honest evaluation of the facts and evidence of this case, we have been forced to conclude that Miss Northern does not comprehend such basic facts and hence is currently incompetent to decide this particular question. While this finding was made more difficult by Miss Northern's apparent ability to grasp facts not related to the condition of her feet, it is nonetheless correct.
>
> Since Miss Northern was not competent to decide the question of amputation, it fell . . . to this Court to do so. Again, the question for me is what would Miss Northern decide if she

understood the facts. The presumption with any person must be that he would want surgery that would increase the chance of life from 5-10% to 50% unless some statement made or attitude held while the patient was competent contradicts the presumption. No such contradiction exists in Miss Northern's case. Further, the presumption is strengthened, if anything, by Miss Northern's assertion that she does not want to die. Medically, her feet are dead and lost to her whether or not they are amputated. Psychotic effects are likely if surgery is done, but are quite possible even if Miss Northern survives and loses her feet without surgery. Her prognosis is poor either way, but there is a substantially better chance of life if the surgery is performed. In these circumstances, this Court simply could not find that Miss Northern, if she had a basic understanding of the situation, would not choose the substantially greater chance of life that surgery offers. Our Decision has been made accordingly . . .

But it is important to distinguish a case such as *Northern,* where the irrationality of the patient's decision affects his understanding, and one in which (albeit rarely) the court takes the view that his understanding remains unimpaired despite the surrounding irrationality.

Lane v Candura (1978) 376 NE 2d 1232 (Mass App Ct)

This case concerns a 77-year-old widow, Mrs Rosaria Candura, of Arlington, who is presently a patient at the Symmes Hospital in Arlington suffering from gangrene in the right foot and lower leg. Her attending physicians recommended in April that the leg be amputated without delay. After some vacillation, she refused to consent to the operation, and she persists in that refusal. . .

The principal question arising on the record before us, therefore, is whether Mrs Candura has the legally requisite competence of mind and will to make the choice for herself . . .

A person is presumed to be competent unless shown by the evidence not to be competent . . . Such evidence is lacking in this case. We recognise that Dr Kelly, one of two psychiatrists who testified, did state that in his opinion Mrs Candura was incompetent to make a rational choice whether to consent to the operation. His opinion appears to have been based upon (1) his inference from her unwillingness to discuss the problem with him that she was unable to face up to the problem or to understand that her refusal constituted a choice; (2) his characterisation of an unwilling[ness], for whatever reason, to consent to life saving treatment . . . as suicidal; and (3) a possibility, not established by evidence as a reasonable probability, that her mind might be impaired by toxicity caused by the gangrenous condition. His testimony, read closely, and in the context of the questions put to him, indicates that his opinion is not one of incompetency in the legal sense, but rather that her ability to make a rational choice (by which he means the *medically* rational choice) is impaired by the confusions existing in her mind by virtue of her consideration of irrational and emotional factors.

A careful analysis of the evidence in this case, including the superficially conflicting psychiatric testimony, indicates that there is no real conflict as to the underlying facts. Certainly, the evidence presents no issue of credibility. The principal question is whether the facts established by the evidence justify a conclusion of legal incompetence. The panel are unanimous in the opinion that they do not.

The decision of the judge, as well as the opinion of Dr Kelly, predicates the necessity for the appointment of a guardian chiefly on the irrationality (in medical terms) of Mrs Candura's decision to reject the amputation. Until she changed her original decision and withdrew her consent to the amputation, her competence was not questioned. But the irrationality of her decision does not justify a conclusion that Mrs Candura is incompetent in the legal sense. The law protects her right to make her own decision to accept or reject treatment, whether that decision is wise or unwise. . . .

Similarly, the fact that she has vacillated in her resolve not to submit to the operation does not justify a conclusion that her capacity to make the decision is impaired to the point of legal incompetence. Indeed, her reaction may be readily understandable in the light of her prior surgical experience and the prospect of living the remainder of her life nonambulatory. Senile symptoms, in the abstract, may, of course, justify a finding of incompetence, but the inquiry must be more particular. What is lacking in this case is evidence that Mrs Candura's areas of forgetfulness and confusion cause, or relate in any way to, impairment of her ability to understand that in rejecting the amputation she is, in effect, choosing death over life.

. . . this case is like *Re Quackenbush*, 156 NJ Super 282, 383 A 2d 785 (Morris County Ct

1978), in which an elderly person, although subject (like Mrs Candura) to fluctuations in mental lucidity and to occasional losses of his train of thought, was held to be competent to reject a proposed operation to amputate gangrenous legs because he was capable of appreciating the nature and consequences of his decision. . . .

Mrs Candura's decision may be regarded by most as unfortunate, but on the record in this case it is not the uninformed decision of a person incapable of appreciating the nature and consequences of her act. We cannot anticipate whether she will reconsider and will consent to the operation, but we are all of the opinion that the operation may not be forced on her against her will.

The case of *Re C* (1993) NLJR 1642 illustrates the point that a mentally-ill patient may have the capacity to consent or refuse consent even if he suffers from delusions, providing the patient is capable of understanding what is proposed. C was 68 years old and developed gangrene in his right foot. He refused to consent to an amputation of his right leg below the knee. He sought an injunction to restrain his doctors from amputating the leg without his express consent. In granting the injunction, Thorpe J held that C sufficiently understood the 'nature, purpose and effects' of the proposed amputation despite the fact that C was a chronic paranoid schizophrenic and suffered from delusions of grandeur, for example that he had an international medical practice. Thorpe J concluded that C comprehended and retained the relevant information, he believed it and he was able to weigh the information, balance the risks and needs, and arrive at a choice. He was, therefore, competent to refuse the medical intervention.

There is another circumstance in which a patient may fail to understand what is involved. The patient's illness may be of such a type as to impair understanding of their condition (ie induce a misperception of reality) though in other respects they retain the ability to manage their lives. The paradigms in such cases are the person *suffering from anorexia nervosa*, the person of *fluctuating lucidity* (in particular the manic depressive) and the *drug addict*.

Let us first consider the case of the person suffering from anorexia nervosa. In *Re W (a minor) (medical treatment)* [1992] 4 All ER 627, (1992) 9 BMLR 22 (CA), W, a girl aged 16, was suffering from anorexia nervosa. Her condition was such that it was felt by those caring for her that she should be cared for at a specialist institution and that the doctors should have the option, if they considered it necessary, to force feed her as a last resort. She, however, refused to be moved or treated in this way. The court was asked to decide whether it could authorise her removal and treatment against her stated wishes in the exercise of its inherent jurisdiction. Central to this question, as we shall see later, was whether W was competent to decide about her medical treatment. The trial judge (Thorpe J) held that she was on the basis that '. . . there is no doubt at all that W is a child of sufficient understanding to make an informed decision'. The Court of Appeal accepted this finding but held, as we shall see, that the court nevertheless could override her competent refusal (*infra*, p 383). Lord Donaldson MR expressed the view, however, that W could have been considered incompetent. He stated:

[W]ith all respect I do not think that Thorpe J took sufficiently into account (perhaps because the point did not emerge as clearly before him as it did before us). . . that it is a feature of anorexia nervosa that it is capable of destroying the ability to make an informed choice. It creates a compulsion to refuse treatment or only to accept treatment which is likely to be ineffective. This attitude is part and parcel of the disease and the more advanced the illness, the more compelling it may become. Where the wishes of the minor are themselves something which the doctors reasonably consider need to be treated in the minor's own best interests, those wishes clearly have a much reduced significance.

Balcombe LJ also noted that 'it is a feature of anorexia nervosa that it is capable of destroying the ability to make an informed choice', but, unlike Lord Donaldson MR, he did not cast any doubt on Thorpe J's finding that she was competent. Nolan LJ simply accepted Thorpe J's view. In our view, Lord Donaldson MR was correct to doubt W's competence given the effect of anorexia upon a patient's capacity to understand her condition and hence what is involved (see the Law Commission's Consultation Paper No 129, *op cit*, paras 2.18-2.20 – patient incompetent if unable to make a 'true choice' due to mental disorder). Had this been the basis for the court's authorising treatment, the very problematic issue of the court's power to override a competent minor's refusal of treatment would have been avoided.

The case of a patient with what we have called fluctuating lucidity is also particularly problematical. Between periods of depressive illness or manic moods the patient may experience spells of normality. During such a spell, he may deny that he is ill and refuse the medication which has produced the current spell of normality and is prescribed to prevent the onset of another period of illness, in the mistaken view that he is cured. Once the illness begins to take hold again, the patient becomes unable to understand that he is ill and may have to be restrained so as to be treated. The dilemma for the law is whether to regard the decision to refuse medication while lucid as a valid refusal or whether to regard it as the product of a syndrome the total effect of which is to undermine the patient's capacity to understand what is involved. The latter view allows the patient to be treated before the onset of illness albeit contrary to the apparent will of the patient.

The law is probably otherwise if the patient while lucid does not deny that he suffers swings in mood but simply insists that now that he feels better he will not take the prescribed medication. In our view, in this case the patient is competent in that he is capable of understanding what is involved. Any attempt to save him from himself by averting the onset of another period of illness may only be achieved lawfully (unless he is a child) by treating him under Part IV of the Mental Health Act 1983 which provides for treatment of mental illness or disorder without consent in certain circumstances.

It would, of course, be helpful if the 1983 Act gave us some clear guidance in this sort of case. Not surprisingly, however, the Act speaks in terms of a patient (in order to be competent) being 'capable of understanding the nature, purpose and likely effects of ... treatment' (see ss 57(2)(a) and 58(3)(a)). This, of course, leads nowhere in the difficult cases, except that in relation to some treatments for mental illness the Act permits treatment even if the patient is competent and is refusing treatment (s 58).

A case which illustrates the mental conditions we have called fluctuating lucidity is *Re R (a minor) (wardship medical treatment)*.

Re R (a minor)(wardship: medical treatment) [1992] Fam 11, (1991) 7 BMLR 147 (CA)

Lord Donaldson MR: R was born on 15 September 1975 and is therefore 15 years and 10 months old. Her family had been known to the social services for over 12 years and at an earlier stage she had been on the local authority's at-risk register as one who was thought to be a possible victim of emotional abuse. She was a child who gave rise to anxiety because of poor and sometimes violent parental relationships and difficulties generally in establishing boundaries in her life.

Those worries became more acute this year when, on 8 March 1991, she was received into voluntary care after a fight with her father. She claimed she felt it was unsafe to stay in the house with him. She was placed first with emergency foster parents and then at a children's home maintained by the local authority.

While in care she asked not to see her father and showed some ambivalence about her wish to return to live in the care of either parent. Anxiety developed about her mental health. She seemed often flat and expressionless and resistant to being touched by anyone. She appeared to experience visual and auditory hallucinations and sometimes suicidal thoughts. She was accordingly referred to a consultant child psychiatrist, Dr R.

Early in May 1991 her mother went to the children's home and cancelled the voluntary care order under which she had been admitted. R went back home but stayed only a few minutes and then ran off. She was found and returned to the children's home but then ran off again and was found by the police on a bridge over the River Thames threatening suicide. In these circumstances the local authority sought and was granted a five-day place of safety order. R was then placed in a small children's home from which she absconded that night, being found by police the following day at her parents' home.

An interim care order was granted on 24 May and R was persuaded to return to the general children's home to which she had originally been admitted. Her behaviour however was increasingly disturbed. On the same night she had to be the subject of an emergency psychiatric assessment due to her increasingly paranoid and disturbed behaviour.

The psychiatrist who saw her on that occasion was of the opinion that she was ill enough to be the subject of an application under ss 2 and 3 of the Mental Health Act 1983. This view was confirmed by R's subsequent behaviour. She absconded from the children's home and went back to her own house where she ran amok doing serious damage to the building and furniture. She made a most savage attack on her father and also assaulted her mother. Thereafter she calmed down but her behaviour remained highly variable with substantial swings of mood. The downward swings became serious enough for an application to be made on 2 June 1991 for her admission under s 2 of the Mental Health Act 1983. She at once again absconded and attacked her parents, but this time in the presence of an emergency social worker and two psychiatrists.

She was placed in the psychiatric ward of a general hospital and remained there for one week. On 7 June 1991 she was discharged to a more suitable centre for the treatment of someone of her age, namely an adolescent psychiatric unit (the unit) which specialises in disturbance problems in young people of her age.

When the social worker principally concerned with R attended a case review at the unit she was further given a disturbing account of R's progress there. The senior registrar and director of child psychiatry stated that concern was growing over R's mental health to the extent that serious thought was being given to the use of compulsory medication because she was becoming increasingly defiant. Furthermore she was denying her past experience of hallucinations and voices, alleging that she had made it all up. The social worker was advised by the staff of the unit that they had been using sedation from time to time whenever they felt the situation warranted it, but that had always been done with R's consent. When the social worker asked R about this, she replied that she had given her consent because she felt she had no choice, since if she had refused they would have injected her with drugs anyway.

Eventually matters came to a head in events which gave rise to R becoming a ward of court and to the application granted by Waite J. On 28 June 1991 the social worker received a telephone call from a senior consultant at the unit stating that he believed R to be in a psychotic state and that he wanted the permission of the local authority, as the body exercising legal responsibility for R under the care order, to administer anti-psychotic medication to her. The consultant assured the social worker that this was not a decision taken out of the blue, advising her that R was acting extremely paranoid, becoming extremely argumentative, hostile and accusative.

After consulting higher authority within the social services, the social worker telephoned back to the unit giving the local authority's consent to the administration of such medication as the medical authorities of the unit might think necessary.

Later that evening R herself telephoned the social services night duty department. She advised the duty social worker (who happened to be experienced in problems of this kind, being an approved social worker under the Mental Health Act) that the unit were trying to give her drugs. She said she did not need them and she did not want to take them. It was a very long conversation indeed, lasting some three hours. The social worker decided that R sounded lucid and rational and he did not regard her as 'sectionable', ie liable to be made the subject of an application under s 2 and s 3 of the Mental Health Act 1983. Urgent consultation took place within the social services department and as a result a decision was taken that, on reflection, the local authority could not give the necessary permission for R to have the drugs administered to her against her will.

On 3 July 1991 R was again seen by Dr R, the consultant child psychiatrist. R admitted to him that she had been suffering from labile mood swings, fewer suicidal ideas than previously and visual and auditory hallucinations, although not so frequent or persecuting as before. She behaved calmly and was rational.

Dr R reported that:

> I believe that she still requires treatment as an in-patient but that she has improved sufficiently for the Mental Health Act not to be relevant. (She also needs to be involved in later, planned assessment for care proceedings.) She is of sufficient maturity and understanding to comprehend the treatment being recommended and is currently rational. Should she not continue with the [unit] treatment, her more florid psychotic behaviour is likely to return, and she might become a serious suicidal risk. I do not believe that out-patient treatment is adequate for her at this time. I also believe that her family situation is too chaotic for her to be able to return home at this time.

The unit had by then made it clear that it was essential, if R was to remain a patient in its care, that it should have an entirely free hand in regard to the administration of medication to her, whether she was willing or not. Accordingly on 5 July the local authority decided to have recourse to wardship proceedings.

Dr R gave evidence both in the form of report and orally. He explained the nature and functions of the unit. It operated, he said, a very carefully thought out procedure. If an adolescent patient behaved disturbingly, there was first a meeting of the whole community. Then that may have to be followed by exclusion of the adolescent to his or her bedroom and, finally, and only as a last resort, tranquillising medication is administered which is, or often may be, medication of the same nature and effects as drugs prescribed for anti-psychotic purposes. That step was only taken if it was absolutely necessary to enable the staff to cope.

He confirmed that the unit could only continue to accept responsibility for R if their regime was acceptable to whoever had parental responsibility for her. The message from the local authority that they could not give consent to medication administered against her will had the result that, unless that could be changed, the unit would be unable to continue to care for her.

Dr R stated that, if R were to lapse into a fully psychotic state, she would be a serious suicidal risk. She would be potentially very violent and unpredictable in her behaviour and liable to hear persecuting voices. It would be likely, he said, that she would return within some days or weeks to a state of mind in which ss 2 or 3 of the Mental Health Act would have to be invoked. He was asked whether he was familiar with the decision in *Gillick*'s case and said that he was and that he had applied the principles there considered to the circumstances of R's case. He expressed his conclusion in the following answers to questions during his oral examination:

> Q. I think there are two elements we should perhaps look at, and the first of them is whether the proposed treatment is for the benefit and protection of a minor. Could you just comment on that limb for us? *A*. Yes, I think, as I have described, that if [R] were to receive the treatment that has been recommended I think it is highly likely that her condition would improve significantly.
>
> Q. The second matter we must consider is whether, having regard to her development and maturity, she understands the nature and the implications of the treatment proposed. Can you comment on that? *A*. Yes, I felt that she is mature enough to understand the nature of the proposal. When I saw her on [4 July] she was rational and, I thought, of sufficient understanding to be able to make a decision in her own right.
>
> Q. Have you actually seen for yourself when she has been in a condition displaying mental illness? *A*. No, not a florid state where, for example, at the time she needed to be admitted under a section, but I have seen her when I was extremely concerned about her killing herself and experiencing hallucinations and feeling persecuted, but her behaviour was not as floridly excitable or unpredictable at that time.
>
> Q. When was that that you saw her in that condition, just approximately? *A*. This was the beginning of May.
>
> Q. Would your comments about her understanding and consent be any different when applied to [R] in that condition? *A*. Yes. I also recall that I saw her at the

[meeting to assess her suitability for admission to the unit] while she was [in the adult psychiatric ward at the general hospital] when she was behaving very aggressively and, yes, I felt in those circumstances her rationality and capacity to understand recommendations was severely impaired.

Q. When she is in that condition would your assessment of her be one when she is or is not capable of giving an important consent about treatment? *A.* In a florid psychotic stage I think she is unable to give informed consent and therefore I agreed with my colleagues, who decided to section her under the Mental Health Act, even though that is extremely rare in our practice.

Gillick competence
The test of 'Gillick competence', although not decisive in this case is nevertheless of general importance and the evidence of Dr R suggests that it is capable of being misunderstood. The House of Lords in that case was quite clearly considering the staged development of a normal child. For example, at one age it will be quite incapable of deciding whether or not to consent to a dental examination, let alone treatment. At a later stage it will be quite capable of both, but incapable of deciding whether to consent to more serious treatment. But there is no suggestion that the extent of this competence can fluctuate upon a day-to-day or week-to-week basis. What is really being looked at is an assessment of mental and emotional age, as contrasted with chronological age, but even this test needs to be modified in the case of fluctuating mental disability to take account of that misfortune. It should be added that in any event what is involved is not merely an ability to understand the nature of the proposed treatment – in this case compulsory medication – but a full understanding and appreciation of the consequences both of the treatment in terms of intended and possible side effects and equally important, the anticipated consequences of a failure to treat.

On the evidence in the present case it is far from certain that Dr R was saying that R understood the implication of treatment being withheld, as distinct from understanding what was proposed to be done by way of treatment – 'the nature of the proposal' which I take to have been intended as a paraphrase of Lord Scarman's 'to understand fully what is proposed'. But, even if she was capable on a good day of a sufficient degree of understanding to meet the *Gillick* criteria, her mental disability, to the cure or amelioration of which the proposed treatment was directed, was such that on other days she was not only 'Gillick incompetent', but actually sectionable. No child in that situation can be regarded as 'Gillick competent' and the judge was wholly right in so finding in relation to R. . . .

'Gillick competence' is a developmental concept and will not be lost or acquired on a day-to-day or week-to-week basis. In the case of mental disability, that disability must also be taken into account, particularly where it is fluctuating in its effect.

Farquharson LJ: Counsel for the Official Solicitor, Mr Munby QC, submitted that the court should determine the application on the *Gillick* principle (see *Gillick v West Norfolk and Wisbech Area Health Authority* [1985] 3 All ER 402, [1986] AC 112). Counsel argued on that authority that the parental right to determine whether a child should have medical treatment terminates if and when the child achieves a sufficient understanding and intelligence to enable him or her to understand fully what is proposed. If the child has the capacity to give a consent valid in law it is not for the court to substitute its own different view. On the other hand, if the child is shown not to have that capacity, then the court has the power and duty to substitute its own decisions if it is different from that of the child.

The learned judge accepted this analysis of the position in law, but came to the conclusion on the evidence available to him that R had not the necessary capacity to make this decision. She was in his judgment a deeply disturbed and unhappy child, who in making her decision had been the victim of her own immaturity. He accordingly granted the application.

The Official Solicitor then brought the present appeal because as counsel informs us it involves important questions of principle. So far as R is concerned however, it seems that the decision of this court will have little impact, as she is likely to be subjected to the medication whether the appeal succeeds or not. If Waite J's decision is upheld, as I think it should be, she will be treated at the unit, otherwise she will receive the medication, at any rate in Dr R's opinion, at an adult hospital.

Mr Munby of course supports the learned judge's statement of the law but complains that there was no evidence upon which he could find that R lacked the capacity to make a decision about her treatment. Counsel relied on the evidence of Dr R about R's state of mind of 3 July which was the most recent account of her condition. Dr R had found on 3 July, just a few days before the judge heard the application, that R was rational and of sufficient understanding to be able to make a decision in her own right. In the face of that evidence counsel submits there was no room for the judge to come to what in effect was the opposite conclusion.

In my judgment, this submission cannot be sustained. It involves assessing the mental state and capacity of the patient at a particular moment in time, isolated from the medical history and background. It is clear from Dr R's evidence and indeed from the evidence of the three-hour telephone conversation that from time to time R had clear intervals when her mental illness was in recession. It is equally clear from Dr R's evidence that this state was neither permanent nor even long term. The prognosis was that if the medication was not given to R she would return to her earlier florid psychotic state. It would be dangerous indeed if the learned judge, or for that matter this court, refused to authorise the medication because on a particular day R passed the *Gillick* test when the likely consequences were so serious. In deciding whether the court's decision is to be substituted for that of the patient it is the task of the court to consider the whole of the medical background of the case as well as the doctor's opinion of the effect of its decision upon the patient's mental state. On the facts of this case, I am clearly of the opinion that the judge's decision was correct.

Staughton LJ agreed that R was incompetent and that, therefore, treatment could be authorised in her best interests.

Although the court undoubtedly arrived at the right result the reasons deployed for doing so are open to criticism. As you will have seen, the court arrived at its decision by concluding that *Gillick* did not apply. This is a somewhat perverse reading of *Gillick*. *Gillick* establishes a concept of competence – ie ability to understand what is involved – which is applicable to children and adults alike. The House of Lords in *Gillick* developed a general legal concept of competence albeit that the case concerned consent to, and not refusal of, treatment. The key to the concept is 'understanding'. In children it is appropriate to see this in the context of maturity, ie as reflecting a process of development. But such an approach, though helpful as regards children, has nothing to do with the key concept of 'understanding'. Hence, the issue in *Re R*, as in all cases, was simply put, if not simply determined, 'Was R able to understand what was involved?' On the evidence, it is arguable that R (like W) was unable to understand by virtue of her denial that she had suffered a 'past experience of hallucinations and voices' which she claimed she had just made up (contrast the Law Commission's view in Consultation Paper No 129, *op cit*, at para 2.17).

Our conclusion as regards these difficult cases that test the meaning and application of the legal concept of competence is that it is more respectful of patients' autonomy to interpret *incompetence* so as to include the manic depressive and the anorexic (where appropriate) rather than regard them as apparently competent and then do wholesale violence to the law's commitment to the rights of decision-making of the competent.

(iii) FULL AND MATURE

As we have seen judges have referred to understanding as having to be 'full' (see *Johnston v Wellesley Hospital* (1970) 17 DLR (3d) 139 per Addy J; *Gillick* per Lord Scarman) or 'mature' (*Gillick* per Lord Scarman). As regards the need for 'full' understanding, Lord Scarman in *Gillick* may simply have been concentrating too closely on the correct approach which the law should adopt towards children. He may have meant that the law should be slow to reach a view that a child is competent, by setting a high level of understanding. If Lord Scarman intended to make a point which is not specific to children it is not clear what the word 'full' adds to 'understanding'. If Lord Scarman meant 'total' or 'complete' understanding this would be an impossible standard for the patient to reach since it is doubtful whether even the most experienced doctor would be likely to claim that he understood in that sense what was involved. A parallel may be drawn with the duty of the doctor to inform his patient where a distinction is made between 'adequate' information and 'full' understanding. Just as the law does not require the patient to be fully informed (see *infra*, pp 147-212) – an impossible goal – so it cannot require that the patient is only competent if he is capable of full understanding.

As regards maturity, the suggestion is that to be competent the patient must be able to weigh and balance relevant facts and arguments before arriving at a decision. Once again this may be a qualification introduced in *Gillick* because the case concerned a child. If it is to be applied to adults, as well, there is a danger that 'maturity' will come to be interpreted by the courts as synonymous with 'wise' (indeed this was the conclusion reached by Professor Glanville Williams in a commentary on *Gillick*, see, (1985) NLJ 1179 at 1180). In our view the law should not judge patients to be incompetent based upon the unwisdom of their decision since this would be to usher in the 'outcome approach' (and reopen the question of who sets the criteria of wisdom).

(iv) THE CIRCUMSTANCES OF THE PATIENT

Apart from beliefs that some may find strange or misperceptions of reality, the circumstances in which decisions are made by patients must never be forgotten. Patients are usually under stress and may well be in pain or under the influence of medication. In such circumstances their powers of reasoning may be affected. This is not to argue that these patients are necessarily unable to understand what is involved but merely to suggest that great care must be taken in responding to requests and decisions in each case. As Lord Donaldson MR pointed out in *Re T* (*op cit*):

> Others who would normally have . . . capacity may be deprived of it or have it reduced by reason of temporary factors, such as unconsciousness or confusion or other effects of shock, severe fatigue, pain or drugs being used in their treatment.

Two cases illustrate this point.

Application of President and Directors of Georgetown College, Inc (1964) 331 F 2d 1000 (DC Cir)

Skelly Wright J: Attorneys for Georgetown Hospital applied for an emergency writ at 4.00pm, September 17, 1963, seeking relief from the action of the United States District Court for the District of Columbia denying the hospital's application for permission to administer blood transfusions to an emergency patient. The application recited that 'Mrs Jesse E Jones is presently a patient at Georgetown University Hospital', 'she is in extremis' according to the attending physician 'blood transfusions are necessary immediately in order to save her life', and 'consent to the administration thereof can be obtained neither from the patient nor her husband'. The patient and her husband based their refusal on their religious beliefs as Jehovah's Witnesses. The order sought provided that the attending physicians 'may' administer such transfusions to Mrs Jones as might be 'necessary to save her life'. After the proceedings detailed [below], I signed the order at 5.20pm. . . .

Mrs Jones was brought to the hospital by her husband for emergency care, having lost two thirds of her body's blood supply from a ruptured ulcer. She had no personal physician, and relied solely on the hospital staff. She was a total hospital responsibility. It appeared that the patient, age 25, mother of a seven-month-old child, and her husband were both Jehovah's Witnesses, the teachings of which sect, according to their interpretation, prohibited the injection of blood into the body. When death without blood became imminent, the hospital sought the advice of counsel, who applied to the District Court in the name of the hospital for permission to administer blood. Judge Tamm of the District Court denied the application, and counsel immediately applied to me, as a member of the Court of Appeals, for an appropriate writ.

I called the hospital by telephone and spoke with Dr Westura, Chief Medical Resident, who confirmed the representations made by counsel. I thereupon proceeded with counsel to the hospital, where I spoke to Mr Jones, the husband of the patient. He advised me that, on religious grounds, he would not approve a blood transfusion for his wife. He said, however, that if the court ordered the transfusion, the responsibility was not his . . .

I asked permission of Mr Jones to see his wife. This he readily granted. Prior to going into the patient's room, I again conferred with Dr Westura and several other doctors assigned to the case. All confirmed that the patient would die without blood and that there was a better than 50 per cent chance of saving her life with it. Unanimously they strongly recommended it. I then went inside the patient's room. Her appearance confirmed the urgency which had been represented to me. I tried to communicate with her, advising her again as to what the doctors had said. The only audible reply I could hear was 'Against my will'. It was obvious that the woman was not in a mental condition to make a decision. I was reluctant to press her because of the seriousness of her condition and because I felt that to suggest repeatedly the imminence of death without blood might place a strain on her religious convictions. I asked her whether she would oppose the blood transfusion if the court allowed it. She indicated, as best I could make out, that it would not then be her responsibility.

Kelly v Hazlett (1976) 75 DLR (3d) 536 (Ontario H Ct)

Morden J: I have found that on July 28th the plaintiff was told that to straighten the crooked elbow would require the breaking of the bone in her arm followed by a period of time in a cast. The risk of stiffness may have been 'mentioned' but certainly no more than that. The matter was then closed by the mutual decision that the ulcer nerve transplant and the joint clean-out only would be performed. On the following day when the plaintiff was under sedation as the result of an injection of 100mg of pethidine (a matter to which I shall return), and just prior to the intended operation, she demanded of the defendant that he not operate on her unless her crooked elbow was straightened. According to the defendant, and this was his view at that time, she was 'a little more undependable' than she was previously, 'irrational', 'foolish' and 'silly'. In saying 'irrational' the defendant meant 'irrational from the point of view of not being able to think the way I was thinking which, I think, was more rational'. He further elaborated on this. He said: 'I thought that it was rational to be concerned about her paralysed, weak hand. She was only interested in the appearance of her elbow.' It may thus be seen that the defendant was concerned with her choice of priorities – between curing the paralysis and straightening the arm – and was not so much concerned with the risks of the osteotomy. I repeat his key evidence on his understanding of her state of mind just prior to the signing of the consent to the osteotomy operation:

> Q. Did you have any other discussions with her that morning as to the effects of either operation?
> A. Well, I think I probably tried to point out to her that she was being foolish and silly and that it wasn't a wise way for her to act, and it was unwise for her to demand something about which she didn't know the consequences, and I sensed that I was not communicating the consequences to her in a way, or I could sense that she was not understanding what I was attempting to communicate with her by words . . .

If her state of mind was such that at the point of her conversation with the defendant she did not know the basic nature of the operation required to straighten her arm, and it may be noted that all she was asking for was a *result*, not a procedure, and she manifested this lack of knowledge to the defendant, then her apparent consent to the operation, notwithstanding her clear desire for the result, would be ineffective.

The plaintiff was calm but more irrational than the day before. I do not think that it could be suggested otherwise than that the giving of a consent under such circumstances, at the very least, leaves the validity of the consent open to question (Rozovsky, *Canadian Hospital Law* (1974), p 36, and *Beausoleil v La Communaute des Soeurs de la Charité de la Providence* (1963) 53 DLR (2d) 65, [1965] Que QB 37) and that it would be incumbent on the defendant to prove affirmatively that the effect of the sedation probably did not adversely affect the patient's understanding of the basic nature of the contemplated operation. Notwithstanding these frailties in the defendant's position, I do find that, taking the conversation of the day before into account, the defendant could reasonably have thought that the plaintiff, in asking to have her elbow straightened on July 29th, was aware that this

involved the fracture and resetting of her arm under general anaesthetic. In other words –
that the combination of the sedation, and her labile condition, had not blotted the
information when she made her demand. In such circumstances he has shown a sufficient
consent to avoid liability on the basis of battery.

B. INFORMED CONSENT

The aphorism 'informed consent' has entered the language as being
synonymous with valid consent. This is, of course, not so and is in fact unhelpful. It gives only a partial view. The requirement that consent be informed is
only one, albeit a very important, ingredient of valid consent. Furthermore, the
expression informed consent begs all the necessary questions which are the
subject of the following section; for example, how informed is informed? It is
helpful to consider the law of battery and that of negligence separately.

1. Battery

(a) Nature and purpose

The approach of the English courts was established by Bristow J in the
following case in which, for the first time, an English court considered the
scope of battery in a medical case.

Chatterton v Gerson [1981] QB 432, [1981] 1 All ER 257 (QBD)

The plaintiff was treated by the defendant, a specialist for chronic pain around the area of
an operation scar following a hernia operation. The first treatment was only partially
successful. The plaintiff then had a second injection. This also failed to relieve her pain but
rendered her right leg completely numb thereby impairing her mobility. The plaintiff alleged
that her consent to the treatment was vitiated because she had not been informed of the risk
of numbness as a side-effect and that the defendant was, therefore, liable in battery. In
dismissing her claim in battery (her claim in negligence was also dismissed) the judge stated
the law as follows.

Bristow J: In my judgment what the court has to do in each case is to look at all the
circumstances and say, 'Was there a real consent?' I think justice requires that in order to
vitiate the reality of consent there must be a greater failure of communication between
doctor and patient than that involved in a breach of duty if the claim is based on negligence.
When the claim is based on negligence the plaintiff must prove not only the breach of duty
to inform but that had the duty not been broken she would not have chosen to have the
operation. Where the claim is based on the trespass to the person, once it is shown that the
consent is unreal, then what the plaintiff would have decided if she had been given the
information which would have prevented vitiation of the reality of her consent is irrelevant.
   In my judgment once the patient is informed in broad terms of the nature of the
procedure which is intended, and gives her consent, that consent is real, and the cause of the
action on which to base a claim for failure to go into risks and implications is negligence, not
trespass. Of course, if information is withheld in bad faith, the consent will be vitiated by
fraud. Of course, if by some accident, as in a case in the 1940s in the Salford Hundred Court,
where a boy was admitted to hospital for tonsillectomy and due to administrative error was
circumcised instead, trespass would be the appropriate cause of action against the doctor,
though he was as much the victim of the error as the boy. But in my judgment it would be
very much against the interests of justice if actions which are really based on a failure by the
doctor to perform his duty adequately to inform were pleaded in trespass.

In *Hills v Potter* [1983] 3 All ER 716, Hirst J approved *Chatterton,* in a case in
which the plaintiff alleged non-disclosure of a risk of injury inherent in a

medical procedure and claimed that non-disclosure gave rise to an action both
in battery and negligence. The judge rejected the battery claim stating:

> As to the claim for assault and battery, the plaintiff's undoubted consent to the operation
> which was in fact performed negatives any possibility of liability under this head: see
> *Chatterton v Gerson* [1981] QB 432, [1981] 1 All ER 257. I should add that I respectfully
> agree with Bristow J in deploring reliance on these torts in medical cases of this kind. The
> proper cause of action, if any, is negligence.

The leading English case is *Sidaway v Bethlem Royal Hospital Governors* [1984]
1 All ER 1018 (CA) [1985] AC 871, [1985] 1 All ER 643 (HL). This case
concerned a woman who underwent an operation to relieve pain in her neck
and shoulders. The surgeon told her of the possibility of disturbing a nerve root
and the consequences of this. However, she alleged that he did not tell her that
there was a risk of damaging the spinal cord and the possibly catastrophic
consequences if that transpired. In fact, this did occur and the plaintiff sued.
She brought her action in negligence, no doubt in light of *Chatterton* and *Hills*.
Her action failed, but the Court of Appeal chose to state its view of the scope
and application of the tort of battery. In what circumstances, if any, could
failure to disclose information give rise to an action in battery?

> **Sir John Donaldson MR:** I am wholly satisfied that as a matter of English law a consent is
> not vitiated by a failure on the part of the doctor to give the patient sufficient information
> before the consent is given. It is only if the consent is obtained by fraud or by
> misrepresentation of the nature of what is to be done that it can be said that an apparent
> consent is not a true consent. This is the position in the criminal law (*R v Clarence* (1888) 22
> QBD 23, 43) and the cause of action based upon trespass to the person is closely analogous.
> I should add that the contrary was not argued upon this appeal.

> **Dunn LJ:** The first argument was that unless the patient's consent to the operation was a
> fully informed consent the performance of the operation would constitute a battery on the
> patient by the surgeon. This is not the law of England. If there is consent to the nature of the
> act, then there is no trespass to the person. So in *R v Clarence* (1888) 22 QBD 23, a
> conviction of rape [*sic*] was quashed where the woman did not know that the prisoner was
> suffering from a venereal disease which he communicated to her. If she had known, she
> would not have consented to sexual intercourse, even though without knowledge of the
> probable risk of infection, there was no rape. On the other hand, in *R v Flattery* (1877) 2
> QBD 410 where a doctor had had sexual intercourse with a patient under pretence of
> performing a surgical operation, his conviction of rape was upheld because the patient had
> only consented to an operation and not the act of sexual intercourse. As Bristow J said in
> *Chatterton v Gerson* [1981] QB 432, 443: 'once the patient is informed in broad terms of the
> nature of the procedure which is intended, and gives her consent, that consent is real' so that
> it affords a defence to a battery.

In dismissing Mrs Sidaway's appeal, the only comment made in the House of
Lords on this aspect of the case was by Lord Scarman, who agreed that 'it
would be deplorable to base the law in medical cases of this kind on the torts of
assault and battery' (at 650).

Finally, in *Freeman v Home Office (No 2)* [1984] 1 All ER 1036, Sir John
Donaldson MR reiterated his earlier views in *Sidaway*:

> If there was real consent to the treatment, it mattered not whether the doctor was in breach
> of his duty to give the patient the appropriate information before that consent was given.
> Real consent provides a complete defence to a claim based on the tort of trespass to the
> person. Consent would not be real if procured by fraud or misrepresentation but, subject to
> this and subject to the patient having been informed in broad terms of the nature of the
> treatment, consent in fact amounts to consent in law.

You will notice that we refer to the need to know the 'nature *and purpose*' of the touching whereas the courts tend to restrict themselves to the word 'nature'. In our view there is no conflict here. The word 'nature' as used by the judges is intended to connote 'nature' and 'purpose' (see, eg, *Re C* (1993) NLJR 1642: Thorpe J stated that the patient must understand 'the nature, purpose and effect' of the treatment).

Since the House of Lords' apparent endorsement in *Sidaway* of the narrow view that consent means only consent sufficient to avoid an action in battery, the argument that battery may also lie where the consent is given in ignorance of relevant material facts seems to have no place in English law. Although the law is unlikely to change, the counter view is both intellectually respectable and, in the light of the interests at stake, may be regarded by some as desirable. The argument is made in the following article.

M A Somerville, 'Structuring the Issues in Informed Consent' (1981) 26 McGill Law Journal 740

Battery or negligence?
The proper cause of action when a defective consent is alleged may be either battery or negligence. The difference is significant because:

> It will have important bearing on such matters as the incidence of the onus of proof, causation, the importance of expert medical evidence, the significance of medical judgment, proof of damage and, most important, of course, the substantive basis upon which liability may be found.

While each of these factors will not be discussed in detail here, it is necessary to be aware of them.

Common law courts in Canada have taken the traditional approach that the consent that is both necessary and sufficient for avoiding a cause of action in battery in medical cases is consent to 'the basic nature and character of the operation or the procedure'. The difficulty in applying this rule is determining which factors form part of the basic nature and character of an act and which do not. Such determinations have been made by judges on a case-by-case basis, with no more definite guidelines than the rule itself. But some judges have tried to formulate a clearer, more objective rule, which would help determine when non-disclosure of information or failure to obtain consent should give rise to a cause of action in battery.

The situation facing the judges can be represented diagrammatically:

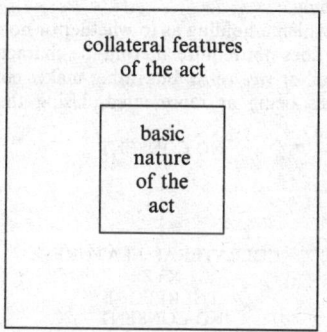

The outer square represents all the consequences or risks to which the patient must consent if liability in tort (battery or negligence) for failure to obtain consent is to be avoided. The inner square represents the factors that make up the basic nature and character of the act of touching. Failure to obtain consent to these factors will give rise to a cause of action in battery. Thus, whether or not battery lies depends on where the inner line is drawn.

That judges will vary in drawing this line, even with respect to the same facts, can be seen by comparing the decision of the majority of the Supreme Court of Canada in *R v Bolduc and Bird* [(1967) 63 DLR (2d) 82] with that of the dissent and that of the Court of Appeal of British Columbia in the same case. Likewise, the judgment of the majority of the Court of Appeal of Ontario in *R v Maurantonio* [(1967) 65 DLR (2d) 674] can be compared with that of the dissent. These are criminal assault (battery) cases, but the rules governing consent in criminal law and in the tort of battery not only have common origins but are directly comparable. Such cases demonstrate that because criminal assault (or battery) will not lie if there is consent as to the basic nature and character of the act, liability will depend on whether or not the feature to which consent has *not* been obtained forms part of the act's basic nature and character. Thus, to the extent that there is discretion involved in determining whether or not a particular feature forms part of the basic nature and character of the act ('basic features'), there is discretion as to the imposition of liability. The two possible alternative analyses of any given fact situation that gives rise to this discretion may be represented as [follows].

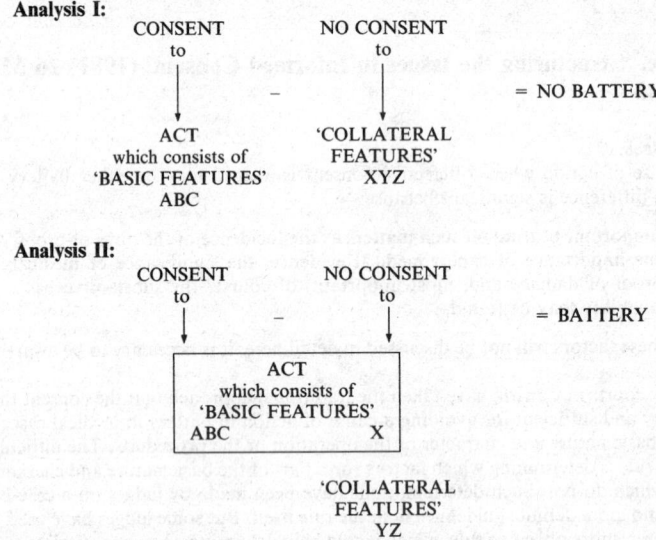

From this diagram it can be seen that, depending on whether or not X is held to be a 'collateral feature' or a 'basic feature' of the act alleged to constitute criminal assault or the tort of battery, the necessary consent will or will not be present, respectively, and liability will be determined accordingly.

There is another way in which a holding as to whether or not battery-avoiding consent is present can be varied. This does not require altering the characterisation of a feature of the act from 'basic' to 'collateral' or *vice versa*, but rather makes consent to the act conditional upon the collateral features being as represented. Using the same model this can be represented as follows:

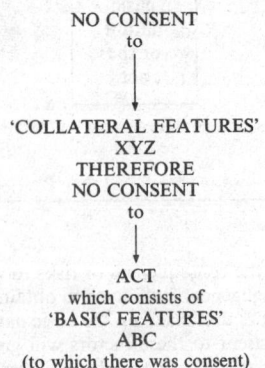

Pursuant to this analysis, it is irrelevant whether X is characterised as a 'basic' or 'collateral' feature, as even if X is a 'collateral' feature, if X is not as represented, the consent will fail to 'flow through' as a valid consent to the act. *R v Williams* ([1923] 1 KB 340), in which the accused, a choir-master, persuaded a young woman that sexual intercourse was therapy for her voice, is probably an example of a court taking such an approach. Depending on the circumstances, whether an act is therapeutic for the patient could be regarded as a 'collateral' feature of the act or could relate to the basic nature of the act. However, accepting that in the particular circumstances characterisation of an act as therapy is a collateral feature, battery could still lie when there is fraud or misrepresentation in this respect. For instance, if, as in the *Williams* case, a collateral feature of an act was not as represented (that is the act of sexual intercourse was not voice therapy), then despite the consent to the act itself (having sexual intercourse), that consent would be invalid, as the Court held, because consent to the act was conditional on the collateral feature (that the act was therapy) being as represented. Although this example may seem very far removed from a normal medical context, it may have important applications. For instance, if a patient were misled to the effect that a particular procedure was therapeutic when in fact it was performed for the purposes of non-therapeutic research, battery-avoiding consent could similarly be vitiated.

How has the law outlined above been applied in the medical relationship? The requirement that there be consent to the basic nature and character of the operation or procedure means that a physician must disclose all inevitable consequences of a proposed procedure in order to obtain battery-avoiding consent. Consequently, all courts faced with the issue have held that there will be a cause of action in battery when a physician does something to which the patient has not consented at all, or which the patient has expressly requested not be done or has refused. Battery could also be established where the physician's act was essentially different in nature from that to which the patient consented. For instance, if the patient was told that the purpose of the operation was to relieve pain, but not told that the consequences would include sterility, any consent given would be invalidated and a cause of action in battery would be available.

Some courts have also held that knowledge of certain risks could be so material to understanding of the basic nature and character of an operation that failure to disclose them would vitiate battery-avoiding consent. In other words, it has been held that not only non-disclosure of inevitable results of a procedure can vitiate battery-avoiding consent, but also non-disclosure of risks of which knowledge was 'essential to an informed decision to undergo the operation'. It is with respect to failures to disclose a risk, as compared with an inevitable consequence, that the Supreme Court of Canada has probably restricted the availability of an action in battery.

It is not easy to decide, from a policy point of view, whether or not a cause of action in battery should be allowed for non-disclosure of certain risks. The argument that it should be allowed is that some risks are so serious that they necessarily relate to the basic nature and character of an operation and, therefore, their non-disclosure should give rise to a battery action. The difficulty is that as only some risks have this effect, how is the line to be drawn between those that do and those that do not? The alternative solution, which may be the position adopted by the Supreme Court of Canada in *Reibl v Hughes,* [(1980) 114 DLR (3d) 1] is that any liability for non-disclosure of a risk can only lie in negligence and not in battery.

> [A]ctions of battery in respect of surgical or other medical treatment should be confined to cases where surgery or treatment has been performed or given to which there has been no consent at all or where, emergency situations aside, surgery or treatment has been performed or given beyond that to which there was consent . . . [U]nless there has been misrepresentation or fraud to secure consent to the treatment, a failure to disclose the attendant risks, however serious, should go to negligence rather than to battery. Although such a failure relates to an informed choice of submitting to or refusing recommended and appropriate treatment, it arises as the breach of an anterior duty of due care, comparable in legal obligation to the duty of due care in carrying out the particular treatment to which the patient has consented. It is not a test of the validity of the consent.

That is, non-disclosure of a risk will not give rise to a cause of action in battery except when there has been a 'misrepresentation or fraud to secure consent to . . . treatment'. But what can constitute misrepresentation within this rule, and why does such misrepresentation allow non-disclosure of a risk to give rise to an action in battery whereas without such misrepresentation it does not?

In exploring these issues it is necessary to determine the basis of the holding of the Supreme Court referred to above. Is it, first, that non-disclosure of a risk does not amount to misrepresentation (although that of an inevitable consequence can); or, second, that information about risks can never relate to the basic nature and character of an operation and thus cannot vitiate battery-avoiding consent; or both propositions; or neither? Presumably, the Court has established the second proposition rather than the first, as it is difficult to draw a distinction between one type of non-disclosure (non-disclosure of inevitable consequences) constituting misrepresentation, and the other (non-disclosure of risks) not doing so. It may be argued that because there is a pre-existing duty to disclose inevitable consequences, but not risks, non-disclosure of inevitable consequences constitutes a misrepresentation, while that of risks does not. But this pre-empts the question to which an answer is sought, that is, just what information is there a duty to disclose so as to avoid an action in battery? Moreover, reliance on a rule that total non-disclosure of a risk does not give rise to a cause of action in battery, because a total non-disclosure cannot constitute misrepresentation, would not exclude a *partial disclosure*. But an approach that recognises partial but not total non-disclosure of risks as misrepresentation would be artificial and could give rise to fortuitous results. Further, the distinction between nonfeasance and misfeasance has no place when there is a pre-existing duty relationship, as there is between physician and patient.

If the Court has not relied on a rule that a non-disclosure is unable to constitute misrepresentation, has it held that the risks of a procedure cannot relate to its basic nature and character? This question can be explored by asking what the situation would be where a significant and serious risk was grossly misrepresented, rather than undisclosed. This could, arguably, give rise to a cause of action in battery within the Court's ruling. However, the fact that misrepresentation of a risk could give rise to a cause of action in battery means, by definition, that the misrepresentation must relate to the basic nature and character of the act. If this is true it shows that the action in battery is not excluded because of the nature of the misrepresentation, that is, because the misrepresentation related to a risk and a risk cannot relate to the basic nature and character of a procedure, but that battery is excluded on some other basis.

If the above analysis is accepted the basis of the Supreme Court's holding is not that total non-disclosure of risks cannot constitute misrepresentation, nor that risks cannot relate to the basic nature and character of a medical procedure. This leaves the question which reveals the key to the basis of the Supreme Court's ruling still unanswered. Why does 'misrepresentation or fraud to secure consent to the treatment' cause non-disclosure of a risk to give rise to a cause of action in battery, where it would not do so if the elements in misrepresentation or fraud were not present?

The true test of whether or not a cause of action in battery will lie for non-disclosure of a risk, provided the risk is serious and sufficiently likely of occurrence to relate to the basic nature and character of the act carried out, depends on the *nature of the physician's conduct with respect to the non-disclosure*. Not only the nature of the undisclosed information is significant, but also the nature of the *failure* to disclose. It is not proposed that, if the physician negligently (ie, unintentionally) fails to disclose or misrepresents a risk, he will be liable in negligence. If he intentionally does either of these things the action will also lie in battery, provided that the risk which is not disclosed or is misrepresented is fundamental enough to relate to the basic nature and character of the procedure. Thus the presence or absence of intention with respect to the non-disclosure of a risk which relates to the basic nature and character of an intervention will determine the cause of action available for failure to obtain consent to that risk. By contrast, when the non-disclosure relates to an inevitable consequence of an intervention, intention or lack of it in relation to the non-disclosure is irrelevant to establishing a cause of action in battery. This is true because the intention necessary to support a cause of action for battery arising from an intentional, non-consensual touching of the kind which occurs is present in carrying out the act which has those inevitable consequences, regardless of the presence or absence of intention with respect to the non-disclosure.

Hence, what is being suggested is that the intention necessary to support an intentional tort will be found in relation to a different element of the tortious act (that is, either the touching or the non-disclosure) depending on whether the failure in obtaining consent relates to failure to inform of risks or of inevitable consequences, but in both cases, the necessary intention may be present.

In relation to determining whether the touching itself was intentional, there is a key concept: the question which must be asked is not simply whether there was consent to a touching, which in most cases there will be, but whether there was consent to touching *of that kind* or *in that manner*. Likewise, it is relevant to ask not only whether there was intention to touch, but whether there was intention to touch *in that manner*. The concept of intention 'to touch in that manner' is broader and more precise than the concept of just touching. It includes the inevitable consequences and purposes of an intervention, as well as the touching itself. Because risks, by definition, may not occur, it is not possible to find the required intention to touch in the manner which results from risks occurring simply by demonstrating their crystallisation. Any proof of intention relates, rather, to the act of non-disclosure of these risks. By contrast, when what occurs is an inevitable consequence of an intervention it can be presumed that this was intended, as in tort a reasonable person is presumed to intend the inevitable consequences of his acts. Consequently, in the latter case, the necessary intention to support intentional touching in that manner and a *prima facie* tort of battery is established by proving the touching, and the only question is whether or not there was sufficient consent.

An objection could be raised here that two different entities are being compared: in one case the question asked is whether or not there is *intentional non-disclosure of information* to which the patient is entitled: that is, is there intentional failure to obtain consent? In the other case the question is whether there is *intentional touching* in a situation where the failure to obtain consent to that touching may have been intentional or unintentional. It is submitted that there is no contradiction between these two approaches. Battery is an intentional tort, which may be established through the intention 'to touch in that manner' or the intentional failure to obtain the necessary consent. It is just that demonstrating the latter is superfluous when it can be shown that there was an intention to touch in a certain manner to which there was no consent.

There is one further problem with the Supreme Court's approach to actions in battery for failure to obtain adequate consent. Some risks are so important that most people would regard them as an essential part of any description of the basic nature and character of a procedure. For instance, the fact that an operation carries a substantial risk of death would cause most persons to characterise that operation as being of a serious nature. Further, can any real distinction be drawn between failure to disclose, for instance, that as a result of an operation a person will certainly be rendered sterile, and failure to disclose that there is a substantial risk of this occurring? It is submitted that the law should not try to draw distinctions that do not accord with generally held views as to what factors constitute the basic nature and character of an act, no matter how conceptually pleasing and easy of application the resulting rule may be.

Thus, with all respect, it is submitted that to the extent that the Supreme Court has limited the availability of an action in battery by stating the law to be that risks do not relate to the basic nature and character of an act and, consequently, their non-disclosure cannot vitiate battery-avoiding consent, the ruling may not be desirable. However, as shown above, the effect of the Supreme Court's ruling on the availability of a battery action will vary, depending on how it is analysed. The analysis suggested accepts the Supreme Court's ruling but minimises its effect of making unavailable a battery action that otherwise would have been available under Canadian common law.

The approach suggested may be summarised as follows: in all cases where lack of consent is alleged, one is arguing either that there was no consent at all to the touching or to touching in that manner. The first question is whether the touching itself and in that manner was intentional. It is highly unlikely that the touching itself will be unintentional, but this is not true of the manner of the touching. The manner of the touching includes two types of consequences: inevitable consequences and risks which eventuate. When the feature of the touching to which it is alleged there was no consent is an inevitable consequence, then there will necessarily have been an *intention* to touch *in that manner*. When, on the other hand, the touching is of that manner because of the crystallisation of a risk, touching *in that manner is unintentional* (unless, possibly, the risk which eventuates was of very high probability, but this case will not be considered here). In the second case, it may initially seem that battery should not lie for non-disclosure of a risk, as the act of which the plaintiff complains – that he was touched in a manner to which he did not consent – was unintentional. However, a second question is relevant: whether the failure to obtain consent was intentional. It is suggested that where it is intentional, and provided the non-disclosure is of a sufficiently serious and probable risk that the risk can be said to form part of the basic nature and character of the intervention, the necessary intention for a cause of action in battery will exist. Such an approach would allow non-disclosure of certain risks because of 'misrepresentation or fraud' to give rise to a cause of action in battery, as the Supreme Court suggests. It would include within the notion of misrepresentation some total non-disclosures; that is, intentional concealment of certain risks would suffice. Thus, only the unintentional non-disclosure of a risk that relates to the basic nature and character of an act would not be actionable in battery. The suggested approach and the correlation of the variables it includes can be demonstrated in the following way:

Non-disclosure:	of inevitable consequence	of 'sufficiently serious and probable' risk
INTENTIONAL	Battery	Battery
UNINTENTIONAL	Battery	Negligence

Defects in consent which do not give rise to a cause of action in battery will be either actionable in negligence (or possibly in contract) or will not be actionable at all. The dividing line between those that are actionable in negligence and those that are not actionable at all is determined by whether or not the physician has breached the standard of care required of him by the law relating to negligence with respect to obtaining the patient's consent . . .

Finally, it is appropriate here to note that some confusion may be caused because two doctrines 'consent' and 'informed consent' are not distinguished. It is suggested that the word 'consent' be reserved to refer to the substantive entity which must be present to avoid liability in battery and similarly for the term 'informed consent' in relation to negligence. It is proposed that with respect to the substantive content of consent the traditional notion should be retained. This means that consent will be present when there is consent to the basic nature and character of the act. Informed consent is a more extensive concept that also comprehends consent to certain consequences or risks of consequences. But, as further discussion will show, there has not always been consensus as to its requirements. It necessarily includes all elements of the consent doctrine, but the reverse is not true. Thus a physician may have obtained sufficient consent to avoid liability in battery, but not in negligence.

Notwithstanding Somerville's cogent argument, the law in England and Wales undoubtedly reflects a less subtle view of the law. The distinction is clearly made between information going to the 'nature and purpose' of the proposed procedure and information concerning risks attending it. As regards the latter, action lies, if at all, in the tort of negligence rather than battery. Laskin CJ put it as follows in *Reibl v Hughes* (1980) 114 DLR (3d) 1.

Laskin CJ: In situations where the allegation is that attendant risks which should have been disclosed were not communicated to the patient and yet the surgery or other medical treatment carried out was that to which the plaintiff consented (there being no negligence basis of liability for the recommended surgery or treatment to deal with the patient's condition), I do not understand how it can be said that the consent was vitiated by the failure to disclose so as to make the surgery or other treatment an unprivileged, unconsented to and intentional invasion of the patient's bodily integrity. I can appreciate the temptation to say that the genuineness of consent to medical treatment depends on proper disclosure of the risks which it entails, but in my view . . . a failure to disclose the attendant risks, however serious, should go to negligence rather than to battery. Although such a failure relates to an informed choice of submitting to or refusing recommended and appropriate treatment, it arises as the breach of an anterior duty of due care, comparable in legal obligation to the duty of due care in carrying out the particular treatment to which the patient has consented. It is not a test of the validity of the consent.

For the purposes of the tort of battery, the crucial issue is what facts or information must a patient be aware of in order to be able to understand the 'nature and purpose' of the touching by the doctor so that the patient's consent is valid. Obviously, any analysis of such an indeterminate phrase as this invites judgments of policy which others may not accept. Cases involving fraudulently obtained consent are instructive here since they address the question whether the defendant's fraud denied the plaintiff information crucial to understanding the nature and purpose of the conduct.

The cases fall into three broad categories where the person touched is misled: (i) as to what is being done; (ii) as to who is doing it; and (iii) as to the risks and consequences of the conduct.

(i) WHAT IS BEING DONE

Two criminal law cases illustrate the extent to which an awareness of what is being done may amount to ignorance of the 'nature and purpose' of the touching and vitiate the consent.

R v Williams [1923] 1 KB 340 (CCA)

The appellant, who was engaged to give lessons in singing and voice production to a girl of sixteen years of age, had sexual intercourse with her under the pretence that her breathing was not quite right and that he had to perform an operation to enable her to produce her voice properly. The girl submitted to what was done under the belief, wilfully and fraudulently induced by the appellant, that she was being medically and surgically treated by the appellant and not with any intention that he should have sexual intercourse with her. Lord Hewart CJ adopted the statement of the law of the trial judge (Branson J) in dismissing the appeal.

Lord Hewart CJ: Branson J stated the law in the course of the summing up in the present case in accurate terms. He said:

> The law has laid it down that where a girl's consent is procured by the means which the girl says this prisoner adopted, that is to say, where she is persuaded that what is being done to her is not the ordinary act of sexual intercourse but is some medical or surgical operation in order to give her relief from some disability from which she is suffering, then that is rape although the actual thing that was done was done with her consent, because she never consented to the act of sexual intercourse. She was persuaded to consent to what he did because she thought it was not sexual intercourse and because she thought it was a surgical operation.

In the second case, *R v Flattery* (1877) 2 QBD 410 the victim's ignorance was not about the fact that she was having sexual intercourse (the nature of the touching) but its purpose.

R v Flattery (1877) 2 QBD 410 (Court of Crown Cases Reserved)

The prisoner professed to give medical and surgical advice for money. The prosecutrix, a girl of nineteen, consulted him with respect to illness from which she was suffering. He advised that a surgical operation should be performed, and under pretence of performing it, had carnal connection with the prosecutrix. She submitted to what was done, not with any intention that he should have sexual connection with her, but under the belief that he was merely treating her medically and performing a surgical operation, that belief being wilfully and fraudulently induced by the prisoner.

Kelly CB: I think this conviction ought to be affirmed. Counsel for the defendant has ably argued that there was consent on the part of the prosecutrix, and therefore no rape. But, on the case as stated, it is plain that the girl only submitted to the plaintiff's touching her person in consequence of the fraud and false pretences of the prisoner, and that the only thing she consented to was the performance of a surgical operation. Up to the time when she and the prisoner went into the room alone, it is clearly found on the case that the only thing contemplated either by the girl or her mother was the operation which had been advised; sexual connection was never thought of by either of them. And after she was in the room alone with the prisoner, what the case expressly states is that the girl made but feeble resistance, believing that she was being treated medically, and that what was taking place was a surgical operation. In other words, she submitted to a surgical operation and nothing else.

Mellor J: I am of the same opinion . . . it is said that submission is consent, and that here there was submission. But submission to what? Not to carnal connection. The case is exactly within the words of Wilde, CJ, in *R v Case* [(1850) 1 Den 580]: 'She consented to one thing, he did another materially different, on which she had been prevented by his fraud from exercising her judgment and will.'

Denman and Field JJ and Huddleston B agreed.

Importantly, in *Sidaway* Dunn LJ in the Court of Appeal (see above) approved *Flattery* as a case in which the consent was not valid.

Applying the reasoning in these cases to the context of medical practice may, in many instances, not give rise to difficulties. It will be obvious what is the nature of the procedure, ie what is being done and whether the patient is aware of it. Some cases, however, will remain problematical where it will be difficult to determine precisely what is meant by 'what is being done' for these purposes and hence whether the patient has been adequately informed so as to give a valid consent.

Consider, for example, the facts of *R v Bolduc and Bird* (1967) 63 DLR (2d) 82.

R v Bolduc and Bird (1967) 63 DLR (2d) 82 (Can Sup Ct)

[Bolduc, a] physician, about to conduct a vaginal examination and, if necessary, perform a medical procedure in the area to be examined, falsely introduced a lay friend [Bird] of his to the patient as a medical intern and asked if the friend, who, in fact, was present for his own gratification, might observe the examination. The patient consented to the friend's presence and the physician proceeded with the examination during which he touched the patient's private parts and inserted an instrument therein for the purposes of the examination while the friend looked on but at no time touched the patient. Both [Bolduc] and [Bird] were convicted of indecent assault on the patient and their conviction was affirmed by the Court of Appeal.

Hall J: The question for decision is whether on those facts and in the circumstances so described the appellants Bolduc and Bird were guilty of an indecent assault upon the person of the complainant contrary to s 141 of the Criminal Code which reads:

141(1) Every one who indecently assaults a female person is guilty of an indictable offence and is liable to imprisonment for five years and to be whipped.

(2) An accused who is charged with an offence under subsection (1) may be convicted if the evidence establishes that the accused did anything to the female person with her consent that, but for her consent, would have been an indecent assault, if her consent was obtained by false and fraudulent representations as to the nature and quality of the act.

With respect, I do not agree that an indecent assault was committed within the meaning of this section. What Bolduc did was unethical and reprehensible in the extreme and was something no reputable medical practitioner would have countenanced. However, Bolduc's unethical conduct and the fraud practised upon the complainant do not of themselves necessarily imply an infraction of s 141. It is common ground that the examination and treatment, including the insertion of the speculum, were consented to by the complainant. The question is: 'Was her consent obtained by false and fraudulent representations as to the nature and quality of the act?' Bolduc did exactly what the complainant understood he would do and intended that he should do, namely, to examine the vaginal tract and to cauterize the affected parts. Inserting the speculum was necessary for these purposes. There was no fraud on his part as to what he was supposed to do and in what he actually did. The complainant knew that Bird was present and consented to his presence. The fraud that was practised on her was not as to the nature and quality of what was to be done but was as to Bird's identity as a medical intern. His presence as distinct from some overt act by him was not an assault. . . .

This case differs from *R v Harms*, 81 CCC 4, [1944] 2 DLR 61, [1944] 1 WWR 12, where the accused was charged with rape following carnal knowledge of an Indian girl, her consent to the intercourse having been obtained by false and fraudulent misrepresentations as to the nature and quality of the act. In that case Harms falsely represented himself to be a medical doctor, and although the complainant in that case knew that he was proposing sexual intercourse, she consented thereto because of his representations that the intercourse was in the nature of a medical treatment necessitated by a condition which he said he had diagnosed. Harms was not a medical man at all. He had no medical qualifications. The Court of Appeal affirmed the conviction by the jury that the Indian girl's consent had been obtained by false and fraudulent representations as to the nature and quality of the act.

The question of fraud vitiating a woman's consent in the case of rape or indecent assault was fully canvassed by Stephen J in *R v Clarence* (1888) 22 QBD 23, and by the High Court of Australia in *Papadimitropoulos v R* (1957) 98 CLR 249, where the court, in concluding a full review of the relevant law and cases decided up to that time, including the *Harms* case, supra, said [at 261]:

> To return to the central point; rape is carnal knowledge of a woman without her consent: carnal knowledge is the physical fact of penetration; it is the consent to that which is in question; such a consent demands a perception as to what is about to take place, as to the identity of the man and the character of what he is doing. But once the consent is comprehending and actual the inducing causes cannot destroy its reality ...

The complainant here knew what Bolduc was proposing to do to her, for this was one in a series of such treatments.

Her consent to the examination and treatment was real and comprehending and it cannot, therefore, be said that her consent was obtained by false or fraudulent representations as to the nature and quality of the act to be done, for that was not the fraud practised on her. The fraud was as to Bird being a medical intern and it was not represented that he would do anything but observe. It was intended that the examination and treatment would be done by Bolduc and this he did without assistance or participation by Bird.

Spence J (dissenting): Let us examine for a moment what was the consent obtained from the complainant. Surely upon the evidence to which I have referred above, it was a consent to the examination of her private parts and the touching of them in the course of treatment in the presence of a doctor, and not a mere medical student or a mere layman who was in some vague fashion considering becoming a medical student.

There was no evidence whatsoever that the complainant knew the accused Bird at all. The name Bird meant nothing to her. She only gave this consent to such a serious invasion of her privacy on the basis that Bird was a doctor intending to commence practice and who desired practical experience in such matters as Bolduc was proposing to engage in. That was the consent which the complainant granted. The indecent assault upon her was not the act to which she consented and therefore I am of the opinion that the two accused were guilty under the provisions of s 141(1).

If it were needed, this case clearly illustrates the inherently uncertain meaning which can be ascribed to 'nature and purpose'. The difference between the judges lies in the degree of specificity ascribed to the term in the particular context. Consider the example of medical research. Blood is taken from the finger of a patient who is otherwise healthy but has a broken leg. He is led to believe or assumes that the taking of the blood is related to the general treatment he is receiving for his leg. In fact, it is to be used for research unrelated to his care. Does his ignorance of the purpose for which the blood is taken mean that he had not validly consented to its being taken? Certainly he understands that blood is being taken. Is this enough or must he also know the reason why? *Flattery* would suggest that he must know the reason why before his consent is real and valid.

One of the most problematical situations in which this question has arisen involves taking blood for the purposes of testing for the presence of HIV. If a patient has consented to blood being taken in the context of treatment or diagnosis, is this consent sufficient to permit the testing of the blood for the presence of HIV where the context does not suggest that this was called for? Or, is it essential that testing for HIV may only be carried out with the explicit agreement of the patient? Again, the degree of specificity entailed in the words 'nature and purpose' determines these questions. If all that is required is that the patient should agree to the physical touching for consent to be valid, then the subsequent testing for HIV without awareness does not make the touching unlawful. If, on the other hand, 'nature and purpose' is defined in a more general way, it is arguable that an awareness that the blood is to be tested for HIV is necessary before the touching would be lawful. In our view this latter approach more properly reflects the law. The reason is ultimately one of policy. The significance to a patient of being tested for HIV (whatever the result of the test) is so great in terms of possible stigma, discrimination and personal anxiety that the law must insist that the patient must expressly agree to the test. (For a more extended discussion see our 'Testing for HIV Infection: The Legal Framework' (1989) 86(7) LSG 32 and 86(9) LSG 30 and J Keown, 'The Ashes of AIDS and the Phoenix of Informed Consent' (1989) 52 MLR 790.)

(ii) WHO IS DOING IT?

An old American mid-West case illustrates the issue of whether the identity of the person touching can effect the validity of the patient's consent.

De May v Roberts (1881) 9 NW 146 (Sup Ct Mich)

Martson CJ: The declaration in this case in the first count sets forth that the plaintiff was at a time and place named a poor married woman, and being confined in child-bed and a stranger, employed in a professional capacity defendant De May who was a physician; that the defendant visited the plaintiff as such, and against her desire and intending to deceive her wrongfully, etc, introduced and caused to be present at the house and lying-in room of the plaintiff and while she was in the pains of parturition the defendant Scattergood, who intruded upon the privacy of the plaintiff, indecently, wrongfully and unlawfully laid hands upon her and assaulted her, the said Scattergood, which was well known to defendant De May, being a young unmarried man, a stranger to the plaintiff and utterly ignorant of the practice of medicine, while the plaintiff believed that he was an assistant physician, a competent and proper person to be present and to aid her in her extremity. . . .

The evidence on the part of the plaintiff tended to prove the allegations of the declaration. On the part of the defendants evidence was given tending to prove that Scattergood very reluctantly accompanied Dr De May at the urgent request of the latter; that the night was a dark and stormy one, the roads over which they had to travel in getting to the house of the plaintiff were so bad that a horse could not be ridden or driven over them; that the doctor was sick and very much fatigued from overwork, and therefore asked the defendant Scattergood to accompany and assist him in carrying a lantern, umbrella and certain articles deemed necessary upon such occasions; that upon arriving at the house of the plaintiff the doctor knocked, and when the door was opened by the husband of the plaintiff, De May said to him 'that I had fetched a friend along to help carry my things;' he, plaintiff's husband, said all right, and seemed to be perfectly satisfied. They were bid to enter, treated kindly and no objection whatever made to the presence of defendant Scattergood. That while there Scattergood, at Dr De May's request, took hold of plaintiff's hand and held her during a paroxysm of pain, and that both of the defendants in all respects throughout acted in a proper and becoming manner actuated by a sense of duty and kindness. . . .

Dr De May therefore took an unprofessional young unmarried man with him, introduced and permitted him to remain in the house of the plaintiff when it was apparent that he could hear at least, if not see all that was said and done, and as the jury must have found, under the instructions given, without either the plaintiff or her husband having any knowledge or reason to believe the true character of such third party. It would be shocking to our sense of right, justice and propriety to doubt even but that for such an act the law would afford an ample remedy. To the plaintiff the occasion was a most sacred one and no one had a right to intrude unless invited or because of some real and pressing necessity which it is not pretended existed in this case. The plaintiff had a legal right to the privacy of her apartment at such a time, and the law secures to her this right by requiring others to observe it, and to abstain from its violation. The fact that at the time, she consented to the presence of Scattergood supposing him to be a physician, does not preclude her from maintaining an action and recovering substantial damages upon afterwards ascertaining his true character. In obtaining admission at such a time and under such circumstances without fully disclosing his true character, both parties were guilty of deceit, and the wrong thus done entitles the injured party to recover the damages afterwards sustained, from shame and mortification upon discovering the true character of the defendants.

Judgment for plaintiff affirmed.

You may think it harsh that a man who went to assist the doctor and comforted the woman during her labour should be held to have committed a battery. But, battery clearly is concerned in part with protecting a person's interest in dignity and undoubtedly the plaintiff's privacy and dignity were invaded. The identity of the defendant, Scattergood was, therefore, crucial in the context of the times since a woman would be affronted if any man other than a doctor assisted her in confinement.

A modern Canadian criminal law case echoes this approach.

R v Maurantonio (1967) 65 DLR (2d) 674 (Ontario CA)

Hartt J: The appellant, Antonio Maurantonio, was convicted by WFB Rogers, Co Ct J, on six counts of indecent assault contrary to s 141 of the Criminal Code, [which we saw earlier in *Bolduc and Bird*] and sentenced to be imprisoned for a period of two years less one day on each count, the sentences to run concurrently. The appeal is from both conviction and sentence.

The convictions arose out of circumstances associated with the attendance of the six female persons upon the appellant at various times while he was allegedly engaged in the practice of medicine for a period of some six months in the City of Toronto.

At the outset of the trial the appellant made the following factual admissions as he is entitled to do pursuant to s 562 of the Criminal Code:

(a) that he was not a medical doctor and did not have any formal education or training and was not entitled to practise medicine;

(b) that he represented to the public and specifically to the complainants that he was a doctor of medicine and licensed to practise medicine; and

(c) that the complainants consented to being treated or examined by the accused only because they believed he was a doctor and that they would not have consented to being examined or treated had they known he was not a doctor.

The evidence called during the course of the trial established the facts covered by these admissions. Clearly, the appellant was not entitled to practise medicine in Ontario or any other jurisdiction and each of the complainants sought his services in the belief that he was a qualified medical practitioner. . . .

There is no doubt but that each of the complainants consented to the intimate incidents associated with their own particular examination or treatment and that, but for their consent, the physical activity involved would have clearly constituted an indecent assault. Several grounds of appeal were advanced and disposed of adversely to the appellant during the course of oral argument. The sole point which remains to be determined involves the interpretation of s 141(2), that is, was the consent in each case obtained by 'false and fraudulent representations as to the nature and quality of the act'.

Any consideration of the relationship of fraud to the presence or absence of consent must be prefaced by an appreciation of the distinction between two different kinds of fraud. The general rule is that if deception causes a misunderstanding as to the nature of the act itself there is no legally recognized consent because what happened is not that for which consent was given, whereas consent induced by fraud is as effective as any other consent, if the deceit relates not to the thing done but merely to some collateral matter.

It is urged by counsel for the appellant that the words 'nature and quality of the act' as used in s 141(2) have reference only to the physical touching, that such contact was known to the complainants to be part of the alleged treatment or examination and that each complainant did, in fact, consent to what actually took place. The admitted false representation of the appellant that he was a licensed and duly qualified medical practitioner then becomes only fraud in the inducement and not fraud in the factum. That is, that although the appellant may have fraudulently induced them to submit to the examination or treatment upon the false representation that he was a physician, nevertheless there was no misrepresentation as to the nature and quality of the act to be performed. Therefore, each complainant having consented to the actual physical contact involved, the appellant, despite the admitted fraudulent misrepresentation as to his status, could not be convicted under s 141 of the Criminal Code.

Although superficially appealing, this argument cannot prevail. In my opinion, the words 'nature and quality of the act' as used in s 141(2) should not be so narrowly construed as to include only the physical action but rather must be interpreted to encompass those concomitant circumstances which give meaning to the particular physical activity in question. Here the physical touching was essentially bound up with, and consented to, as part of the medical treatment or examination. It was only to a medical examination or medical treatment, including the reasonable intimate physical contact necessary thereto, that each complainant consented. If that to which they were subjected was not in fact of the nature of a *bona fide* medical examination or treatment then it was something entirely different from that to which they consented. The physical contact in issue here being of an equivocal nature in the circumstances, the question whether or not the complainants received *bona fide* medical attention was dependent upon the intent with which it was carried out and, as such, became a question of fact to be determined on all the evidence by the trial tribunal. On the six counts upon which convictions were registered that issue was found adversely to the appellant by the trial Judge and there is ample evidence to support that finding.

The fraudulent misrepresentation of the appellant that he was a duly qualified and licensed physician was not what induced the complainants to submit to the physical acts entailing the touching of their persons. The false representation which led to consent was that what the appellant was about to do was to conduct a medical examination or administer medical treatment. Since the representation went to the very nature and quality of the act to be performed the consent of each of the complainants, even if given in the full understanding of what physical acts the appellant was about to perform, 'was obtained by false and fraudulent representations as to the nature and quality of the act'. The question is not whether the appellant was a duly qualified and licensed physician but rather an issue of fact as to whether or not the physical touching was a necessary part of a *bona fide* medical examination or treatment, because it was to that and that alone that consent was given. In deciding this issue of fact the trial tribunal would, of course, be entitled to consider the lack of professional qualifications. The weight to be given to this and other relevant facts would depend on the circumstances of a particular case. The authorities, both English and Canadian, dealing with the question of fraud and its relationship to consent are clearly and succinctly reviewed by the High Court of Australia in *Papadimitropoulos v R* (1957) 98 CLR 249, and little would be gained by repeating them here.

In the result, the appeal against the convictions will be dismissed.

Kelly JA agreed.

Laskin JA (dissenting): The sole argument of the Crown to show that consent was obtained 'by false and fraudulent representations as to the nature and quality of the acts' done to the female patients is that these women gave their consent to a medical examination or treatment and this they did not get because of the accused's misrepresentation of his character or qualification. . . .

It might just as well be argued that a medically trained person would be guilty of indecent assault if he ministered as did the accused to female patients without being registered as a qualified physician. Crown counsel's admission, previously referred to, makes the question of professional qualification in the present case external to the issue to be decided under s 141(2).

In this state of the matter, it was incumbent on the Crown to prove deceit by the accused as to the 'nature and quality' of the very acts charged against him; whether or not they constituted medical treatment in the abstract would be merely a refined way of challenging professional qualification, and to raise this in the context of s 141(2) would, in my opinion, be begging the question to be decided. The Crown failed completely to show any deceit in this respect.

The plain fact is that the women patients involved in the charges herein against the accused were fully aware of what was being done to them, accepted what was done as medical treatment, and the accused did not delude them into accepting something other than what they expected or sought. I adopt the principle and some of the words of the High Court of Australia in *Papadimitropoulos v R* (1957) 98 CLR 249, when it said (at 261) '... once the consent is comprehending and actual the inducing causes cannot destroy its reality.'

I also find support for my view of the law applicable to this case in the recent judgment of the Supreme Court in *R v Bolduc and Bird* [1967] 3 CCC 294, 2 CRNS 40, present case is *a fortiori*; and I would say of the accused here as was said of the doctor there that [p 295 CCC]: 'There was no fraud on his part as to what he was supposed to do and in what he actually did.'

It follows that the convictions cannot stand, and I would accordingly set them aside and enter verdicts of acquittal.

It could be argued that this case is really a case about 'what's being done' and lack of consent thereto. Certainly, *De May* is a case which turns upon 'who is doing' the touching. But is this true of *Maurantonio*? The explanation of *Maurantonio* which warrants its inclusion alongside *De May* is that the character of what was being done was (for the majority) clearly affected by who was doing it; ie the actor's identity was critical in determining the nature and purpose of the touching. Laskin JA (dissenting), you will notice, was not impressed by the majority's view of the facts.

Further examples of the relevance of 'who is doing' the touching can be found in the criminal cases of rape concerned with the identity of the person with whom the woman is having sexual intercourse. These cases are helpfully reviewed by the Australian High Court in *Papadimitropoulos v R* (1957) 98 CLR 249.

Papadimitropoulos v R (1957) 98 CLR 249 (Australian High Court)

There has been some judicial resistance to the idea that an actual consent to an act of sexual intercourse can be no consent because it is vitiated by fraud or mistake. The key to the difficulty may perhaps be found in a brief sentence of Cussen J in *R v Lambert* [[1919] VLR 205]: 'Now, carnal knowledge is merely the physical fact of penetration, though, of course, there cannot be consent even to that without some perception of what is about to take place.'

In 1822 Bayley J reserved for the consideration of the twelve judges the case of one Jackson who had been convicted before him of burglary with intent to commit rape. Jackson had entered a dwelling house by night in the absence of the householder with the intention of personating him and deceiving his wife into submitting to sexual intercourse with him. As he was proceeding to his purpose she discovered the deception and he made off; 'four judges thought, that having carnal knowledge of a woman whilst she was under the belief of its being her husband would be a rape, but the other eight judges thought it would not: and Dallas CJ pointed out forcibly the difference between compelling a woman against her will, when the abhorrence which would naturally arise in her mind was called into action, and beguiling her into consent and co-operation; but several of the eight judges intimated that if the case should occur again they would advise the jury to find a special verdict': *R v Jackson* [(1822) Russ & Ry 487]. The case did occur again. In *R v Saunders* [(1838) 8 C & P 265] it appeared that the person had got into a married woman's bed and by personating her husband had connexion with her. Bayley J directed the jury that he was bound to tell them that the charge of rape was not made out 'as the crime was not committed against the will of the prosecutrix, as she consented believing it to be her husband'. Alderson B applied the same law in a similar case in the same year: *R v Williams* [(1838) 8 C & P 286]. Twelve years later a case arose for the consideration of the judges in which a prisoner who was a medical man had been convicted of assault on evidence that he had induced a girl of fourteen years of age to submit to his having connexion with her by leading her to believe that it was but 'medical treatment for the ailment under which she laboured': the conviction was affirmed: *R v Case* [(1850) 1 Den 580]. In 1854 another case was reserved for the judges in which a prisoner had been convicted of a rape on evidence that he impersonated the woman's husband and so obtained her assent to sexual intercourse. The judges declined to permit the question to be re-opened and followed *Jackson's Case*: *R v Clarke* [(1854) Dears CC 397].

In 1868 the Court of Crown Cases Reserved quashed a conviction of rape based on a similar impersonation. 'It falls', said Bovill CJ for the judges, 'within the class of cases which decide that, when consent is obtained by fraud, the act does not amount to rape': *R v Barrow* [(1868) LR 1 CCR 156]. In *R v Young* [(1878) 38 LT 540] the court upheld a conviction of a man who had connexion with a sleeping woman who, when she first woke, thought the man was her husband, and then discovering it was not threw him off. In the course of the reasons doubts were raised about the decisions beginning with *Jackson's Case*. In Ireland the court refused to follow the reasoning: *R v Dee* [(1884) 15 Cox CC 579]. In the meantime the Court of Crown Cases Reserved in *R v Flattery* [(1877) 2 QBD 410] had questioned the decision in *Barrow's Case*. The facts resembled those in *R v Case* except that the prisoner was not a medical man but a quack, and the representations about his giving some form of treatment were put to the mother as well as the girl, and in a form which might well have excited the mother's suspicions. Field J said: 'The question is one of consent, or not consent; but the consent must be to sexual connection. There was no such consent.' This decision was strongly criticised by Sir James Fitzjames Stephen in his *Digest of the Criminal Law*, 3rd edn (1833), at p 185, on the ground that it almost overruled the principle 'that where consent is obtained by fraud the act does not amount to rape'. At this point a declaration of the law was made by statute. Section 4 of the Criminal Law Amendment Act 1885 (48 & 49 Vict c 69) (Imp) after reciting that doubts had been entertained whether a man who induces a married woman to permit him to have connexion with her by personating her husband is or is not guilty of rape, enacted and declared that every such offender should be deemed to be guilty of rape (cf now Sexual Offences Act 1956 (4 & 5 Eliz II c 69), s 1(2)).

The next judicial step was taken in the case of *R v Clarence* [(1888) 22 QBD 23]. The decision was simply that a husband who infects his wife with venereal disease is not thereby guilty of inflicting grievous bodily harm. But this led to the judges' giving much consideration to what was involved in the wife's consent, ignorant as she was of her husband's condition. The judgments contain many observations which are pertinent to the distinction upon which this case turns. For example, in the judgment of Willis J there is to be found, to say the least of it, a dyslogistic description of a fraud that will afford no basis for treating the woman's consent as a nullity and the act of intercourse as rape. 'Take, for example,' said his Lordship, 'the case of a man without a single good quality, a gaol-bird, heartless, mean and cruel, without the smallest intention of doing anything but possessing himself of the person of his victim, but successfully representing himself as a man of good family and connections prevented by some temporary obstacle from contracting an immediate marriage, and with conscious hypocrisy acting the part of a devoted lover, and in this fashion, or perhaps under the guise of affected religious fervour, effecting the ruin of his victim.' The conception which Willis J had of what sufficed to vitiate consent is expressed as follows: 'The essence of rape is, to my mind, the penetration of the woman's person without her consent. In other words it is, roughly speaking, where the woman does not intend that the sexual act shall be done upon her either at all, or, what is pretty much the same thing, by the particular individual doing it, and an assault which includes penetration does not seem to me under such circumstances to be anything else but rape.' Stephen J refers to the conflict between the decision in *R v Barrow* and the Irish decision in *R v Dee* and remarks that the decisions were examined minutely in the latter case. Stephen J proceeded: 'I think they justify the observation that the only sorts of fraud which so far destroy the effect of a woman's consent as to convert a connection consented to in fact into a rape are frauds as to the nature of the act itself, or as to the identity of the person who does the act.' Field J speaks of the woman's consenting to the act of intercourse yet not consenting to it in its actual nature and conditions, and he again says that a consent obtained to one act is not a consent to an act of a different nature.

In *R v Williams* [[1923] 1 KB 340] a new version of the 'medical treatment' cases was dealt with by the Court of Criminal Appeal. This time it was a singing master and the pretence was that the treatment was for breathing. Possibly the case went a little further than *R v Case* and *R v Flattery* but, if so, that is only with reference to the complexion the facts were given. The materiality of the case lies only in a broad statement which Lord Hewart CJ quoted from a text book. '"A consent or submission obtained by fraud is, it would seem, not a defence to rape or cognate offences".' It is interesting to notice that this statement is the contradictory of that of Sir James Fitzjames Stephen in the note in his *Digest* quoted above, in which he describes the principle to be 'that where consent is obtained by fraud the act does not amount to rape'. It is the contradictory too of that made by Bovill CJ in *R v Barrow* also quoted above. From what has been said already, however, it should be clear enough that the truth lies between the two opposing generalisations.

In the language of a note to the Canadian decision of *R v Harms* [[1944] 2 DLR 61] fraud in the inducement does not destroy the reality of the apparent consent; fraud in the factum does. The note distinguishes 'between the type of fraud which induces a consent that would not otherwise have been obtained but which is non the less a valid consent and the type of fraud which prevents any real consent from existing'. The same distinction exists in relation to fraud inducing marriage itself. In *Moss v Moss* [[1897] P 263], Lord St Helier, as he afterwards became, said: 'It has been repeatedly stated that a marriage may be declared null on the ground of fraud or duress. But, on examination, it will be found that this is only a way of amplifying the proposition long ago laid down (*Fulwood's Case* [(1637) Cro Car 482]) that the voluntary consent of the parties is required. In the case of duress with regard to the marriage contract, as with regard to any other, it is obvious that there is an absence of a consenting will. But when in English law fraud is spoken of as a ground for avoiding a marriage, this does not include such fraud as induces a consent, but is limited to such fraud as procures the appearance without the reality of consent.' . . .

It must be noted that in considering whether an apparent consent is unreal it is the mistake of misapprehension that makes it so. It is not the fraud producing the mistake which is material so much as the mistake itself. But if the mistake or misapprehension is not produced by the fraud of the man, there is logically room for the possibility that he was unaware of the woman's mistake so that a question of his *mens rea* may arise. For that reason it is easy to understand why the stress has been on the fraud. But that stress tends to distract the attention from the essential inquiry, namely, whether the consent is no consent because it is not directed to the nature and character of the act. The identity of the man and the character of the physical act that is done or proposed seem now clearly to be regarded as forming part of the nature and character of the act to which the woman's consent is directed. That accords with the principles governing mistake vitiating apparent manifestations of will in other chapters of the law.

In the present case the decision of the majority of the Full Court extends this conception beyond the identity of the physical act and the immediate conditions affecting its nature to an antecedent including cause – the existence of a valid marriage. In the history of bigamy that has never been done. The most heartless bigamist has not been considered guilty of rape. Mock marriages are no new thing. Before the Hardwicke Marriage Act it was a fraud easily devised and readily carried out. But there is no reported instance of an indictment for rape based on the fraudulent character of the ceremony. No indictment of rape was founded on such a fraud. Rape, as a capital felony, was defined with exactness, and although there has been some extension over the centuries in the ambit of the crime, it is quite wrong to bring within its operation forms of evil conduct because they wear some analogy to aspects of the crime and deserve punishment. The judgment of the majority of the Full Court of the Supreme Court goes upon the moral differences between marital intercourse and sexual relations without marriage. The difference is indeed so radical that it is apt to draw the mind away from the real question which is carnal knowledge without consent. It may well be true that the woman in the present case never intended to consent to the latter relationship. But, as was said before, the key to such a case as the present lies in remembering that it is the penetration of the woman's body without her consent to such penetration that makes the felony. The capital felony was not directed to fraudulent conduct inducing her consent. Frauds of that kind must be punished under other heads of the criminal law or not at all: they are not rape. To say that in the present case the facts which the jury must be taken to have found amount to wicked and heartless conduct on the part of the applicant is not enough to establish that he committed rape. To say that in having intercourse with him she supposed that she was concerned in a perfectly moral act is not to say that the intercourse was without her consent. To return to the central point; rape is carnal knowledge of a woman without her consent; carnal knowledge is the physical fact of penetration; it is the consent to that which is in question; such a consent demands a perception as to what is about to take place, as to the identity of the man and the character of what he is doing. But once the consent is comprehending and actual the inducing causes cannot destroy its reality and leave the man guilty of rape.

Regardless of whether the decision is right on the facts, the upshot of this case is clearly that the identity of the person who is doing the touching has some legal relevance. In our view, the best way to understand these cases in the context of medical law is to say that where the identity of the person affects the understanding of what is being done then the patient who misapprehends does not validly consent.

A common everyday practice in teaching hospitals offers a troubling example of the relevance to consent of the identity of the person touching. Medical students routinely, as part of their training, lay hands on patients. Obviously, when the patient knows that the student is a student, and consents to being touched, no problem will ordinarily arise. There are at least two factual situations, however, which do give rise to legal difficulties if the patient is *unaware* that the person is a student.

First, a student may, in fact, examine (ie touch) a patient solely so as to acquire knowledge or experience for himself. The touching plays no part in the care of the patient. In such a circumstance, the consent given by the patient is probably invalid since the identity of the person touching affects the nature of what is being done to the patient, ie training rather than caring.

Secondly, a student may touch a patient as part of the patient's care. Does the lack of awareness by the patient of the identity of the person touching (identity being status here) affect the validity of the patient's consent? You will recall that Laskin JA in *Maurantonio* thought that if the patient got what he was bargaining for, the identity of the carer was irrelevant. The difficulty, as the majority pointed out, is that the patient may have bargained for a doctor. In our view, the majority's position is correct in principle. It is a nice question as to what conclusion the majority would have reached in the situation posed. It could be said that the difference between a lay person and a doctor is material whereas the difference between a medical student (presumably supervised) and a doctor is not. In our view, unless the patient suffered harm and could establish that the medical student was negligent, an English court would reject any claim by a patient.

Hence, an action in battery would not lie or reverting to the analysis we have adopted: this level of mistake as to identity would not invalidate the consent of the patient. (The need for the explicit consent of the patient to being touched by students as part of their training is recognised in the Government Circular: *Medical Students in Hospitals* (HC (91) 18, April 1991).)

A case which appears to challenge this view is *Perna v Pirozzi* 457 A 2d 431 (1983). In this case, a patient brought an action in battery when she discovered that she had not been operated upon by the doctor whom she had specifically requested when agreeing to the operation.

Perna v Pirozzi (1983) 457 A 2d 431 (New Jersey Sup Ct)

Pollock J: On the advice of his family physician, Thomas Perna entered St Joseph's Hospital on 8 May 1977 for tests and a urological consultation. Mr Perna consulted Dr Pirozzi, a specialist in urology, who examined Mr Perna and recommended that he undergo surgery for the removal of kidney stones.

Dr Pirozzi was associated with a medical group that also included Drs Del Gaizo and Ciccone. The doctors testified at trial that their medical group customarily shared patients; no doctor had individual patients, and each doctor was familiar with all cases under care of the group. Further, it was not the practice of the group to inform patients which member would operate; the physicians operated as a 'team', and their regular practice was to decide just prior to the operation who was to operate. If, however, a patient requested a specific member of the group as his surgeon, that surgeon would perform the operation. Nothing indicated that Mr Perna was aware of the group's custom of sharing patients or of their methods for assigning surgical duties.

Although Mr Perna had never consulted with Dr Del Gaizo or Dr Ciccone, he had been treated by Dr Pirozzi previously in conjunction with a bladder infection. According to Mr Perna, he specifically requested Dr Pirozzi to perform the operation. None of the defendants directly contradicted Mr Perna's testimony. However, Dr Ciccone testified that he met with Mr Perna on May 16 and, without discussing who would operate, explained that two members of the medical group would be present during the operation. The following day, in the presence of a urological resident, Mr Perna executed a consent form that named Dr Pirozzi as the operating surgeon and authorized him, with the aid of unnamed 'assistants', to perform the surgery . . .

The operation was performed on 18 May by Dr Del Gaizo assisted by Dr Ciccone. Dr Pirozzi was not present during the operation; in fact, he was not on duty that day. At the time of surgery, Dr Del Gaizo and Dr Ciccone were unaware that only Dr Pirozzi's name appeared on the consent form.

Mr Perna first learned of the identities of the operating surgeons when he was readmitted to the hospital on June 11 because of post-surgical complications. . .

[The plaintiffs] alleged that there was a failure to obtain Mr Perna's informed consent to the operation performed by Dr Del Gaizo. That is, plaintiffs claimed that Mr Perna's consent to the operation was conditioned upon his belief that Dr Pirozzi would be the surgeon . . .

. . . if an operation is properly performed, albeit by a surgeon operating without the consent of the patient, and the patient suffers no injuries except those which foreseeably follow from the operation, then a jury could find that the substitution of surgeons did not cause any compensable injury. Even there, however, a jury could award damages for mental anguish resulting from the belated knowledge that the operation was performed by a doctor to whom the patient had not given consent . . .

A nonconsensual operation remains a battery even if performed skillfully and to the benefit of the patient. The medical profession itself recognizes that it is unethical to mislead a patient as to the identity of the doctor who performs the operation. American College of Surgeons, Statements on Principles, § IA (June 1981). Participation in such a deception is a recognized cause for discipline by the medical profession. See American College of Surgeons, Bylaws, art VII, § 1(c) (as amended June 1976). By statute, the State Board of Medical Examiners is empowered to prevent the professional certification or future professional practice of a person who '[h]as engaged in the use or employment of dishonesty, fraud, deception, misrepresentation, false promise or false pretense ...' *NJSA* 45: 1-21. Consequently, a statutory, as well as a moral, imperative compels doctors to be honest with their patients.

Few decisions bespeak greater trust and confidence than the decision of a patient to proceed with surgery. Implicit in that decision is a willingness of the patient to put his or her life in the hands of a known and trusted medical doctor. Sometimes circumstances will arise in which, because of an emergency, the limited capacity of the patient, or some other valid reason, the doctor cannot obtain the express consent of the patient to a surrogate surgeon. Other times, doctors who practice in a medical group may explain to a patient that any one of them may perform a medical procedure. In that situation, the patient may accept any or all the members of the group as his surgeon. In still other circumstances, the patient may consent to an operation performed by a resident under the supervision of the attending physician. The point is that a patient has the right to know who will operate and the consent form should reflect the patient's decision. Where a competent patient consents to surgery by a specific surgeon of his choice, the patient has every right to expect that surgeon, not another, to operate.

In our view an English court would be unlikely to adopt the approach in this case for a number of reasons. First, the quality of the touching does not change simply because a different doctor carries out the procedure. Second, and in any event, the standard NHS consent form (which we have already seen) specifically appraises the patient that there is no guarantee that a particular doctor will carry out the procedure. This is not to say that a claim in contract (if one existed) could not be brought where it was an express term of the contract that a particular doctor and no other would carry out the procedure (*Michael v Molesworth* (1950) 2 BMJ 171 (£1 damages awarded)).

(iii) RISKS AND CONSEQUENCES

The question here is whether the lack of awareness of risks inherent in a medical procedure or possible consequences of undergoing it, can affect the validity of the patient's consent. As we have seen from cases such as *Chatterton, Sidaway* and *Reibl*, the approach of the courts is that knowledge or ignorance of risks or possible consequences are properly to be dealt with by the tort of negligence. Consent for the purposes of the tort of battery is not affected. This modern legal position reflects the view of the law taken in the well-known nineteenth-century cases of *R v Clarence* (1888) 22 QBD 23 and *Hegarty v Shine* (1878) 4 LR Ir 288. In both cases a woman had sexual intercourse with a man as a consequence of which she was infected with a venereal disease. In neither case was her consent held to have been vitiated by her lack of awareness of the risk she ran and the consequences of having intercourse. As we have seen, Professor Somerville argues that some consequences and some risks are so intrinsically a feature of the procedure that the patient must be aware of them in order to understand the 'nature and purpose' of the procedure and therefore give a valid consent for the purposes of an action in battery. Although this does not appear to be English law, it may well be that lack of awareness of some *inevitable consequences* of the proposed procedure could render any consent invalid, eg, being unaware that radiation treatment for testicular cancer will result in the patient being sterile.

(b) Revisiting the fraud exception

In *Reibl* Laskin CJ stated that a failure to disclose the attendant risks should go to negligence rather than battery 'unless there has been misrepresentation or fraud to secure consent to the treatment . . . '. This would suggest, on its face, that where fraud or misrepresentation were involved consent may be vitiated *even* if the patient understood the nature and purpose of the procedure, ie the fraud or misrepresentation went to other things.

The Canadian medical law scholar Ellen Picard analyses Laskin CJ's view in *Reibl*.

E Picard *Legal Liability of Doctors and Hospitals in Canada* (2nd edn 1984)

One area of great concern springs from the comments of the Supreme Court of Canada on misrepresentation and fraud. Professor Klar has said that the Chief Justice 'was not clear as to what the misrepresentation or fraud must relate or how it will operate' [(1982) 3 SCLR 385]. Professors Gochnauer and Fleming [(1981) 15 UBCL Rev 475] find an internal inconsistency in the Chief Justice's words and asks whether by them he meant to give an illustration of or an exception to the test for battery. Professor Somerville raises a number of concerns about the step taken by the Supreme Court of Canada and says a basic question is: 'Why does "misrepresentation or fraud to secure consent to the treatment" cause non-disclosure of a risk to give rise to a cause of action in battery, where it would not do so if the elements of misrepresentation or fraud were not present?' [(1981) 26 McGill LJ 740] She suggests an analysis that minimises the Supreme Court ruling and its consequence of making a battery unavailable where it would in the past have been available.

At the bottom of the reservations expressed by a number of commentators is the apparent attempt by the Supreme Court of Canada to separate risks and consent. The criticism is strong. As Professor Somerville has summarised it:

. . . it is submitted that to the extent that the Supreme Court has limited the availability of an action in battery by stating the law to be that *risks do not relate to the basic nature and character of an act and, consequently, their non-disclosure cannot vitiate battery-avoiding consent*, the ruling may not be desirable [emphasis supplied].

Professors Gochnauer and Fleming say:

> The Court's position separating risk and consent is a distortion of our ordinary understanding of the concepts and in a number of cases will defeat our normal, reasonable expectations.

They are critical of the failure of the Supreme Court of Canada to give any policy considerations to justify its position and say:

> By cutting us off from our ordinary intuitions in these matters without setting up signposts of policy the decision fails to clarify wholly the applicability of battery and negligence when there has been a breach of the duty to disclose risks of medical treatment.

The parameters of the new battery action have not yet been fully tested by litigation. Although the number of cases where fraud or 'serious' misrepresentation (such as negligent or fraudulent misrepresentation as contrasted with innocent misrepresentation) will be alleged and proven will likely be few, there may be some confusion in the 'grey' areas. For example, in a case where a person is told he will be given an anaesthetic but is not told this will be done by moving a needle into his heart would there be misrepresentation? Would there be misrepresentation if a tonsillectomy was described as a minor, routine and safe procedure when for that patient it was not? What about the prescription of tranquillisers for emotional complaints given without a description of the risks of addiction and misuse? Hopefully future judicial review of battery will provide answers if not an assuagement of the critics.

Communication between the health care professional and the patient is the means by which a valid consent to treatment is given. It is also part of the therapy of good medicine. The absence of good communication is the reason for most lawsuits against health care professionals and hospitals.

On the other hand, in *Sidaway* Sir John Donaldson MR (in the Court of Appeal) specifically rejected the view that fraud going to matters other than 'nature and purpose' invalidated consent for the purposes of the tort of battery. In doing so, he approved *R v Clarence*. In our view, Sir John Donaldson MR is correct. The so-called 'fraud exception' is in fact not an exception at all. At all times the issue in a battery case is whether the patient understood the 'nature and purpose' of the procedure. If he misunderstands, in principle the reason for that is irrelevant. If he understands, fraud as to other matters cannot affect this understanding and cannot give rise to an action in battery. It may, of course, (as with a negligent misrepresentation) give rise to liability in the tort of negligence.

A fortiori, therefore, it will be clear that Laskin CJ's reference to a misrepresentation vitiating consent is not the law in England.

(c) The place of battery in modern medical law

What we have seen is a determined effort by the courts whether in England or elsewhere severely to limit the scope of the tort of battery. The role left for it is virtually vestigial. As a mechanism for compensating injured patients, however, it remains a powerful symbolic and actual deterrent against doctors ignoring the right of autonomy of their patients. We can conclude by reminding ourselves of Professor Gerald Robertson's explanation of the decline in the tort of battery in the context of medical law.

G Robertson, 'Informed Consent to Medical Treatment' (1981) 97 LQR 102

It is submitted that there are two principal reasons for the judicial policy evident in *Chatterton v Gerson* [[1981] QB 432] against trespass claims in informed consent litigation. First, as can be seen from the decisions in *Fowler v Lanning* [1959] 1 QB 426 and *Letang v*

Cooper [1965] 1 QB 232, judicial policy appears to be in favour of restricting claims in battery to situations involving deliberate, hostile acts, a situation which most judges would regard as foreign to the doctor-patient relationship. Coupled with this is the stigma and damage to professional reputation which courts repeatedly emphasise are an inevitable by-product of a successful claim against a doctor. These consequences are probably seen as even more serious in an action for battery than in an action for negligence. The second reason stems from the view expressed in the concluding section of this article, namely, that courts in this country will attempt to restrict the scope of the doctrine of informed consent, principally by means of the requirement of causation, the use of expert evidence as to accepted medical practice, and emphasis on the 'best interests of the patient' principle. [On which we now have the House of Lords decision in the *Sidaway case*; see *infra*.] Restriction of the doctrine of informed consent in this way would not be possible if it were to be accepted that failure to inform of inherent risks of proposed treatment could ground an action for trespass. As was outlined above, the plaintiff in such an action would not be required to prove, by way of causation, that he would not have consented to the treatment had he been informed of the risks. Similarly, evidence of accepted medical practice has no place in an action for trespass; if failure to disclose a particular risk were to be regarded as vitiating consent, the fact that a reasonable doctor would not have disclosed the risk cannot absolve the defendant from liability for battery. Finally, although the point is not entirely clear, it would seem that a doctor cannot avoid liability for battery simply on the grounds that he was acting in the best interests of his patient. Thus it can be seen that the three principal ways in which the doctrine of informed consent is likely to be restricted would not be available to a court dealing with a case based in trespass.

2. Negligence

(For a detailed discussion of the social and ethical background to the legal debate about 'informed consent' and the duty of a doctor to inform his patient, see the first edition of this book at pages 229-242.)

Prior to 1984 a series of decisions at first instance addressed the issue of a doctor's duty in negligence to disclose information to his patient: *O'Malley-Williams v Board of Governors of the National Hospital for Nervous Disease* (1974) (7 October, Bridge J); *Wells v Surrey AHA* Times (29 July 1978, unreported) (Croom-Johnson J); *Sankey v Kensington and Chelsea and Westminster AHA* (2 April 1982, unreported) (Tudor Evans J). These cases, however, left the matter open as Professor Gerald Robertson points out in his paper 'Informed Consent to Medical Treatment' (1981) 97 LQR 102 at 116.

> Thus . . . the courts in this country, while suggesting that there was no positive legal duty incumbent on the doctor to warn his patient of the risks inherent in proposed treatment, at the same time displayed an obvious reluctance to discuss this important issue in anything approaching adequate detail. As the legal correspondent to the British Medical Journal commented, in discussing the *O'Malley-Williams* [(1975) 1 BMJ 635, 636] decision:
>
>> [w]hether there is a positive duty on doctors to keep their patients informed of all aspects of their treatment, even when they pose no queries, is an issue of some importance to the [medical] profession and one that some day will have to be faced head-on.

It was not until the cases of *Chatterton v Gerson* [1981] QB 432 and *Hills v Potter* [1984] 1 WLR 641n (still at first instance) that the English courts had to face the issue head on. Hirst J summarised the position in *Hills v Potter*.

Hills v Potter [1984] 1 WLR 641n

Hirst J: My conclusions are as follows: 1. In my judgment, McNair J in *Bolam v Friern Barnet Hospital Management Committee* [1957] 1 WLR 582 applied the medical standard to advice prior to an operation, as well as to diagnosis and to treatment. This standard is clearly applied without differentiation to all three aspects of the case which McNair J described as 'the three major points': see pp 586-587, 590. The fact that the plaintiff was mentally sick did not affect the legal principle, but might of course affect its application to the facts of the particular case, as McNair J himself said, at p 590.

2. Although the House of Lords in *Maynard v West Midlands Regional Health Authority* [1984] 1 WLR 634, did not specifically affirm McNair J in relation to advice as such, the general and unqualified approval given to *Bolam's* case in the House of Lords makes it quite impossible for me to depart from McNair J's decision, especially as it has been applied to advice in the other three first instance cases which I have cited. Indeed I respectfully agree with, and would have thought it right to follow, these first instance cases even without the authoritative guidance contained in *Maynard's* case, which they preceded. I for my part doubt whether the distinction in the medical context between advice on the one hand and diagnosis and treatment on the other is really so clear or so stark as [was] forcefully submitted.

3. . . . I hold that the proper standard is the medical standard in accordance with *Bolam v Friern Hospital Management Committee* [1957] 1 WLR 582 and the other first instance cases.
. . .

I do not accept [the] argument that by adopting the *Bolam* principle, the court in effect abdicates its power of decision to the doctors. In every case the court must be satisfied that the standard contended for on their behalf accords with that upheld by a substantial body of medical opinion, and that this body of medical opinion is both respectable and responsible, and experienced in this particular field of medicine.

In 1985, the doctor's duty to disclose was finally considered by the House of Lords in the well-known case of *Sidaway*.

Sidaway v Board of Governors of the Bethlem Royal Hospital [1985] AC 871, [1985] 1 All ER 643

The plaintiff, who had suffered recurrent pain in her neck, right shoulder and arms, underwent an operation in 1974 which was performed by a senior neuro-surgeon at the first defendant's hospital. The operation, even if performed with proper care and skill, carried an inherent risk, which was put at between one and two per cent, of damage to the spinal column and the nerve roots. The risk of damage to the spinal column was substantially less than to a nerve root but the consequences were much more serious. In consequence of the operation the plaintiff was severely disabled. Her monetary loss was assessed at £67,500.

The plaintiff claimed damages for negligence against the hospital and the executors of the deceased surgeon, the second defendants. She relied solely on the alleged failure of the surgeon to disclose or explain to her the risks inherent in, or special to, the operation which he had advised. Skinner J found that the surgeon did not tell the plaintiff that it was an operation of choice rather than necessity; that whilst he had told her of the possibility of disturbing a nerve root and the consequences, he did not refer to the danger of damage to the spinal cord; that in refraining from informing her of those two factors he was following a practice which in 1974 would have been accepted as proper by a responsible body of skilled and experienced neuro-surgeons; and applying the test formulated in *Bolam v Friern Barnet Management Committee* [1957] 1 WLR 582 that the standard of care was that of the ordinary skilled man exercising and professing to have that special skill and that a doctor was not negligent if he acted in accordance with the practice accepted at the time as proper by a responsible body of medical opinion, notwithstanding that other doctors adopted different practices, the judge dismissed the plaintiff's claim. The Court of Appeal affirmed Skinner J's decision. On further appeal to the House of Lords, the majority view was given by Lords Bridge, Templeman and Keith.

Lord Bridge: Broadly, a doctor's professional functions may be divided into three phases: diagnosis, advice and treatment. In performing his functions of diagnosis and treatment, the standard by which English law measures the doctor's duty of care to his patient is not open to doubt. 'The test is the standard of the ordinary skilled man exercising and professing to have that special skill.' These are the words of McNair J in *Bolam v Friern Hospital Management Committee* [1957] 1 WLR 582 at 586, approved by this House in *Whitehouse v Jordan* [1981] 1 WLR 246 at 258, *per* Lord Edmund-Davies and in *Maynard v West*

Midlands Regional Health Authority [1984] 1 WLR 634 at 638 *per* Lord Scarman. The test is conveniently referred to as the *Bolam* test. In *Maynard's* case, Lord Scarman, with whose speech the other four members of the Appellate Committee agreed, further cited with approval, at 638 the words of Lord President Clyde in *Hunter v Hanley* 1955 SLT 213 at 217:

> In the realm of diagnosis and treatment there is ample scope for genuine difference of opinion and one man clearly is not negligent merely because his conclusion differs from that of other professional men . . . The true test for establishing negligence in diagnosis or treatment on the part of a doctor is whether he has been proved to be guilty of such failure as no doctor of ordinary skill would be guilty of if acting with ordinary care . . .

The language of the *Bolam* test clearly requires a different degree of skill from a specialist in his own special field than from a general practitioner. In the field of neuro-surgery it would be necessary to substitute for Lord President Clyde's phrase 'no doctor of ordinary skill', the phrase 'no neuro-surgeon of ordinary skill'. All this is elementary and, in the light of the two recent decisions of this House referred to, firmly established law.

The important question which this appeal raises is whether the law imposes any, and if so what, different criterion as the measure of the medical man's duty of care to his patient when giving advice with respect to a proposed course of treatment. It is clearly right to recognise that a conscious adult patient of sound mind is entitled to decide for himself whether or not he will submit to a particular course of treatment proposed by the doctor, most significantly surgical treatment under general anaesthesia. This entitlement is the foundation of the doctrine of 'informed consent' which has led in certain American jurisdictions to decisions, and in the Supreme Court of Canada, to dicta, on which the appellant relies, which would oust the *Bolam* test and substitute an 'objective' test of a doctor's duty to advise the patient of the advantages and disadvantages of undergoing the treatment proposed and more particularly to advise the patient of the risks involved.

There are, it appears to me, at least theoretically, two extreme positions which could be taken. It could be argued that, if the patient's consent is to be fully informed, the doctor must specifically warn him of *all* risks involved in the treatment offered, unless he has some sound clinical reason not to do so. Logically, this would seem to be the extreme to which a truly objective criterion of the doctor's duty would lead. Yet this position finds no support from any authority, to which we have been referred, in any jurisdiction. It seems to be generally accepted that there is no need to warn of the risks inherent in all surgery under general anaesthesia. This is variously explained on the ground that the patient may be expected to be aware of such risks or that they are relatively remote. If the law is to impose on the medical profession a duty to warn of risks to secure 'informed consent' independently of accepted medical opinion of what is appropriate, neither of these explanations for confining the duty to special as opposed to general surgical risks seems to me wholly convincing.

At the other extreme it could be argued that, once the doctor has decided what treatment is, on balance of advantages and disadvantages, in the patient's best interest, he should not alarm the patient by volunteering a warning of any risk involved, however grave and substantial, unless specifically asked by the patient. I cannot believe that contemporary medical opinion would support this view, which would effectively exclude the patient's right to decide in the very type of case where it is most important that he should be in a position to exercise that right and, perhaps even more significantly, to seek a second opinion as to whether he should submit himself to the significant risk which has been drawn to his attention. I should perhaps add at this point, although the issue does not strictly arise in this appeal, that, when questioned specifically by a patient of apparently sound mind about risks involved in a particular treatment proposed, the doctor's duty must, in my opinion, be to answer both truthfully and as fully as the questioner requires.

The decision mainly relied on to establish a criterion of the doctor's duty to disclose the risks inherent in a proposed treatment which is prescribed by the law and can be applied independently of any medical opinion or practice is that of the District of Columbia Circuit Court of Appeals in *Canterbury v Spence* 464 F 2d 772 (DC, 1972). The judgment of the Court (Wright, Leventhal and Robinson JJ), delivered by Robinson J, expounds the view that an objective criterion of what is a sufficient disclosure of risk is necessary to ensure that the patient is enabled to make an intelligent decision and cannot be left to be determined by the doctors. He said, at 784:

> Respect for the patient's right of self-determination on particular therapy demands a standard set by law for physicians rather than one which physicians may or may not impose upon themselves.

In an attempt to define the objective criterion it is said, at 787, that 'the issue on non-disclosure must be approached from the view point of the reasonableness of the physician's informational needs'. A risk is required to be disclosed 'when a reasonable person, in what the physician knows or should know to be the patient's position, would be likely to attach significance to the risk or cluster of risks in deciding whether or not to forgo the proposed therapy': 464 F 2d 772 at 787. The judgment adds, at 788: 'Whenever non-disclosure of particular risk information is open to debate by reasonable-minded men, the issue is for the finder of facts.'

The court naturally recognises exceptions from the duty laid down in the case of an unconscious patient, an immediate emergency, or a case where the doctor can establish that disclosure would be harmful to the patient.

Expert medical evidence will be needed to indicate the nature and extent of the risks and benefits involved in the treatment (and presumably of any alternative course). But the court affirms, at 792: 'Experts are unnecessary to a showing of the materiality of a risk to a patient's decision on treatment, or to the reasonable, expectable effect of risk disclosure on the decision.' In English law, if this doctrine were adopted, expert medical opinion as to whether a particular risk should or should not have been disclosed would presumably be inadmissible in evidence.

I recognise the logical force of the *Canterbury* doctrine, proceeding from the premise that the patient's right to make his own decision must at all costs be safeguarded against the kind of medical paternalism which assumes that 'doctor knows best'. But, with all respect, I regard the doctrine as quite impractical in application for three principal reasons. First, it gives insufficient weight to the realities of the doctor-patient relationship. A very wide variety of factors must enter into a doctor's clinical judgment not only as to what treatment is appropriate for a particular patient, but also as to how best to communicate to the patient the significant factors necessary to enable the patient to make an informed decision whether to undergo the treatment. The doctor cannot set out to educate the patient to his own standard of medical knowledge of all the relevant factors involved. He may take the view, certainly with some patients, that the very fact of this volunteering, without being asked, information of some remote risk involved in the treatment proposed, even though he describes it as remote, may lead to that risk assuming an undue significance in the patient's calculations. Secondly, it would seem to me quite unrealistic in any medical negligence action to confine the expert medical evidence to an explanation of the primary medical factors involved and to deny the court the benefit of evidence of medical opinion and practice on the particular issue of disclosure which is under consideration. Thirdly, the objective test which *Canterbury* propounds seems to me to be so imprecise as to be almost meaningless. If it is to be left to individual judges to decide for themselves what 'a reasonable person in the patient's position' would consider a risk of sufficient significance that he should be told about it, the outcome of litigation in this field is likely to be quite unpredictable.

I note with interest from a learned article entitled 'Informed Consent to Medical Treatment' by Mr Gerald Robertson, Lecturer in Law, University of Leicester (1981) 97 LQR 102, 108, that only a minority of states in the United States of America have chosen to follow *Canterbury* and that since 1975 'there has been a growing tendency for individual States to enact legislation which severely curtails the operation of the doctrine of informed consent'. I should also add that I find particularly cogent and convincing the reasons given for declining to follow *Canterbury* by the Supreme Court of Virginia in *Bly v Rhoads* 222 SE 2d 783 (1976).

Having rejected the *Canterbury* doctrine as a solution to the problem of safeguarding the patient's right to decide whether he will undergo a particular treatment advised by his doctor, the question remains whether that right is sufficiently safeguarded by the application of the *Bolam* test without qualification to the determination of the question what risks inherent in a proposed treatment should be disclosed. The case against a simple application of the *Bolam* test is cogently stated by Laskin CJC, giving the judgment of the Supreme Court of Canada in *Reibl v Hughes* (1980) 114 DLR (3d) 1 at 13.

> To allow expert medical evidence to determine what risks are material and, hence, should be disclosed and, correlatively, what risks are not material is to hand over to the medical profession the entire question of the scope of the duty of disclosure, including the question whether there has been a breach of that duty. Expert medical evidence is, of course, relevant to findings as to the risks that reside in or are a result of recommended surgery or other treatment. It will also have a bearing on their materiality but this is not a question that is to be concluded on the basis of the expert medical evidence alone. The issue under consideration is a different issue from that

involved where the question is whether the doctor carried out his professional activities by applicable professional standards. What is under consideration here is the patient's right to know what risks are involved in undergoing or foregoing certain surgery or other treatment.

I fully appreciate the force of this reasoning but can only accept it subject to the important qualification that a decision what degree of disclosure of risks is best calculated to assist a particular patient to make a rational choice as to whether or not to undergo a particular treatment must primarily be a matter of clinical judgment. It would follow from this that the issue whether non-disclosure in a particular case should be condemned as a breach of the doctor's duty of care is an issue to be decided primarily on the basis of expert medical evidence, applying the *Bolam* test. But I do not see that this approach involves the necessity 'to hand over to the medical profession the entire question of the scope of the duty of disclosure, including the question whether there has been a breach of that duty'. Of course, if there is a conflict of evidence as to whether a responsible body of medical opinion approves of non-disclosure in a particular case, the judge will have to resolve that conflict. But even in a case where, as here, no expert witness in the relevant medical field condemns the non-disclosure as being in conflict with accepted and responsible medical practice, I am of opinion that the judge might in certain circumstances come to the conclusion that disclosure of a particular risk was so obviously necessary to an informed choice on the part of the patient that no reasonably prudent medical man would fail to make it. The kind of case I have in mind would be an operation involving a substantial risk of grave adverse consequences, as, for example, the ten per cent risk of a stroke from the operation which was the subject of the Canadian case of *Reibl v Hughes* (1980) 114 DLR (3d) 1. In such a case, in the absence of some cogent clinical reason why the patient should not be informed, a doctor, recognising and respecting his patient's right of decision, could hardly fail to appreciate the necessity for an appropriate warning.

In the instant case I can see no reasonable ground on which the judge could properly reject the conclusion to which the unchallenged medical evidence led in the application of the *Bolam* test. The trial judge's assessment of the risk at one to two per cent covered both nerve root and spinal cord damage and covered a spectrum of possible ill effects 'ranging from the mild to the catastrophic'. In so far as it is possible and appropriate to measure such risks in percentage terms – some of the expert medical witnesses called expressed a marked and understandable reluctance to do so – the risk of damage to the spinal cord of such severity as the appellant in fact suffered was, it would appear, certainly less than one per cent. But there is no yardstick either in the judge's findings or in the evidence to measure what fraction of one per cent that risk represented. In these circumstances, the appellant's expert witness's agreement that the non-disclosure complained of accorded with a practice accepted as proper by a responsible body of neuro-surgical opinion afforded the respondents a complete defence to the appellant's claim.

Lord Templeman: In my opinion a simple and general explanation of the nature of the operation should have been sufficient to alert Mrs Sidaway to the fact that a major operation was to be performed and to the possibility that something might go wrong at or near the site of the spinal cord or the site of the nerve root causing serious injury. If, as the judge held, Mr Falconer probably referred expressly to the possibility of damage to a nerve root and to the consequences of such damage, this warning could only have reinforced the possibility of something going wrong in the course of a delicate operation performed in a vital area with resultant damage. In view of the fact that Mr Falconer recommended the operation, Mrs Sidaway must have been told or could have assumed that Mr Falconer considered that the possibilities of damage were sufficiently remote to be ignored. Mrs Sidaway could have asked questions. If she had done so, she could and should have been informed that there was an aggregate risk of between one per cent and two per cent risk of some damage either to the spinal cord or to a nerve root resulting in injury which might vary from irritation to paralysis. But to my mind this further information would only have reinforced the obvious, with the assurance that the maximum risk of damage, slight or serious, did not exceed two per cent. Mr Falconer may reasonably have taken the view that Mrs Sidaway might be confused, frightened or misled by more detailed information which she was unable to evaluate at a time when she was suffering from stress, pain and anxiety. A patient may prefer that the doctor should not thrust too much detail at the patient. We do not know how Mr Falconer explained the operation to Mrs Sidaway and we do not know the reasons for the terms in which he couched his explanation.

On the assumption that Mr Falconer explained that it was necessary to remove bone and free a nerve root from pressure near the spinal cord, it seems to me that the possibility of damage to a nerve root or to the spinal cord was obvious. The operation was skilfully performed but by mishap the remote risk of damage to the spinal cord unfortunately caused the disability from which Mrs Sidaway is now suffering. However much sympathy may be felt for Mrs Sidaway and however much in hindsight the operation may be regretted by her, the question now is whether Mr Falconer was negligent in the explanation which he gave.

In my opinion if a patient knows that a major operation may entail serious consequences, the patient cannot complain of lack of information unless the patient asks in vain for more information or unless there is some danger which by its nature or magnitude or for some other reason requires to be separately taken into account by the patient in order to reach a balanced judgment in deciding whether or not to submit to the operation. To make Mr Falconer liable for damages for negligence, in not expressly drawing Mrs Sidaway's attention to the risk of damage to the spinal cord and its consequences, Mrs Sidaway must show and fails to show that Mr Falconer was not entitled to assume, in the absence of questions from Mrs Sidaway, that his explanation of the nature of the operation was sufficient to alert Mrs Sidaway to the general danger of unavoidable and serious damage inherent in the operation but sufficiently remote to justify the operation. There is no reason to think that Mr Falconer was aware that, as Mrs Sidaway deposed, a specific warning and assessment of the risk of spinal cord damage would have influenced Mrs Sidaway to decline the operation although the general explanation which she was given resulted in her consenting to the operation.

There is no doubt that a doctor ought to draw the attention of a patient to a danger which may be special in kind or magnitude or special to the patient. In *Reibl v Hughes* (1980) 114 DLR (3d) 1, a surgeon advised an operation on the brain to avoid a threatened stroke. The surgeon knew or ought to have known that there was a four per cent chance that the operation might cause death and a ten per cent chance that the operation might precipitate the very stroke which the operation was designed to prevent. The patient ought to have been informed of these specific risks in order to be able to form a balanced judgment in deciding whether or not to submit to the operation.

When a patient complains of lack of information, the court must decide whether the patient has suffered harm from a general danger inherent in the operation or from some special danger. In the case of a general danger the court must decide whether the information afforded to the patient was sufficient to alert the patient to the possibility of serious harm of the kind in fact suffered. If the practice of the medical profession is to make express mention of a particular kind of danger, the court will have no difficulty in coming to the conclusion that the doctor ought to have referred expressly to this danger as a special danger unless the doctor can give reasons to justify the form or absence of warning adopted by him. Where the practice of the medical profession is divided or does not include express mention, it will be for the court to determine whether the harm suffered is an example of a general danger inherent in the nature of the operation and if so whether the explanation afforded to the patient was sufficient to alert the patient to the general dangers of which the harm suffered is an example. If a doctor conscientiously endeavours to explain the arguments for and against a major operation and the possibilities of benefiting and the dangers, the court will be slow to conclude that the doctor has been guilty of a breach of duty owed to the patient merely because the doctor omits some specific item of information. It is for the court to decide, after hearing the doctor's explanation, whether the doctor has in fact been guilty of a breach of duty with regard to information.

A doctor offers a patient diagnosis, advice and treatment. The objectives, sometimes conflicting, sometimes unattainable, of the doctor's services are the prolongation of life, the restoration of the patient to full physical and mental health and the alleviation of pain. Where there are dangers that treatment may produce results, direct or indirect, which are harmful to the patient, those dangers must be weighed by the doctor before he recommends the treatment. The patient is entitled to consider and reject the recommended treatment and for that purpose to understand the doctor's advice and the possibility of harm resulting from the treatment.

I do not subscribe to the theory that the patient is entitled to know everything nor to the theory that the doctor is entitled to decide everything. The relationship between doctor and patient is contractual in origin, the doctor performing services in consideration for fees payable by the patient. The doctor, obedient to the high standards set by the medical profession impliedly contracts to act at all times in the best interests of the patient. No doctor in his senses would impliedly contract at the same time to give to the patient all the information available to the doctor as a result of the doctor's training and experience and as a result of the doctor's diagnosis of the patient. An obligation to give a patient all the information available to the doctor would often be inconsistent with the doctor's contractual obligation to have regard to the patient's best interests. Some information might confuse, other information might alarm a particular patient. Whenever the occasion arises for the doctor to tell the patient the results of the doctor's diagnosis, the possible methods of treatment and the advantages and disadvantages of the recommended treatment, the doctor must decide in the light of his training and experience and in the light of his knowledge of the patient what should be said and how it should be said. At the same time the doctor is not entitled to make the final decision with regard to treatment which may have disadvantages or dangers. Where the patient's health and future are at stake, the patient must make the final decision. The patient is free to decide whether or not to submit to treatment recommended by the doctor and therefore the doctor impliedly contracts to provide information which is adequate to enable the patient to reach a balanced judgment, subject always to the doctor's own obligation to say and do nothing which the doctor is satisfied will be harmful to the patient. When the doctor himself is considering the possibility of a major operation the doctor is able, with his medical training, with his knowledge of the patient's medical history and with his objective position to make a balanced judgment as to whether the operation should be performed or not. If the doctor making a balanced judgment advises the patient to submit to the operation, the patient is entitled to reject that advice for reasons which are rational, or irrational, or for no reason. The duty of the doctor in these circumstances, subject to his overriding duty to have regard to the best interests of the patient, is to provide the patient with information which will enable the patient to make a balanced judgment if the patient chooses to make a balanced judgment. A patient may make an unbalanced judgment because he is deprived of adequate information. A patient may also make an unbalanced judgment if he is provided with too much information and is made aware of possibilities which he is not capable of assessing because of his lack of medical training, his prejudices or his personality. Thus the provision of too much information may prejudice the attainment of the objective of restoring the patient's health. The obligation of the doctor to have regard to the best interests of the patient but at the same time to make available to the patient sufficient information to enable the patient to reach a balanced judgment if he chooses to do so has not altered because those obligations have ceased or may have ceased to be contractual and become a matter of duty of care. In order to make a balanced judgment if he chooses to do so, the patient needs to be aware of the general dangers and of any special dangers in each case without exaggeration or concealment. At the end of the day, the doctor, bearing in mind the best interests of the patient and bearing in mind the patient's right of information which will enable the patient to make a balanced judgment must decide what information should be given to the patient and in what terms that information should be couched. The court will award damages against the doctor if the court is satisfied that the doctor blundered and that the patient was deprived of information which was necessary for the purposes I have outlined. In the present case on the judge's findings I am satisfied that adequate information was made available to Mrs Sidaway and that the appeal should therefore be dismissed.

Lord Keith concurred with Lord Bridge.

By contrast, Lord Diplock, while concurring in the result, differed significantly in his analysis of the doctor's duty to disclose.

Lord Diplock: The merit of the *Bolam* test is that the criterion of the duty of care owed by a doctor to his patient is whether he has acted in accordance with a practice accepted as proper by a body of responsible and skilled medical opinion. There may be a number of different practices which are likely to alter with advances in medical knowledge. Experience shows that, to the great benefit of human kind, they have done so, particularly in the recent past. That is why fatal diseases such as smallpox and tuberculosis have within living memory become virtually extinct in countries where modern medical care is generally available.

In English jurisprudence the doctor's relationship with his patient which gives rise to the normal duty of care to exercise his skill and judgment to improve the patient's health in any particular respect in which the patient has sought his aid, has hitherto been treated as a single comprehensive duty covering all the ways in which a doctor is called upon to exercise his skill and judgment in the improvement of the physical or mental condition of the patient for which his services either as a general practitioner or specialist have been engaged. This general duty is not subject to dissection into a number of component parts to which different criteria of what satisfy the duty of care apply, such as diagnosis, treatment, advice (including warning of any risks of something going wrong however skilfully the treatment advised is carried out). The *Bolam* case itself embraced failure to advise the patient of the risk involved in the electric shock treatment as one of the allegations of negligence against the surgeon as well as negligence in the actual carrying out of treatment in which that risk did result in injury to the patient. The same criteria were applied to both these aspects of the surgeon's duty of care. In modern medicine and surgery such dissection of the various things a doctor has to do in the exercise of his whole duty of care owed to his patient is neither legally meaningful nor medically practicable. Diagnosis itself may involve exploratory surgery, the insertion of drugs by injection (or vaccination) involves intrusion upon the body of the patient and oral treatment by drugs although it involves no physical intrusion by the doctor on the patient's body may in the case of particular patients involve serious and unforeseen risks.

My Lords, no convincing reason has in my view been advanced before your Lordships that would justify treating the *Bolam* test as doing anything less than laying down a principle of English law that is comprehensive and applicable to every aspect of the duty of care owed by a doctor to his patient in the exercise of his healing functions as respects that patient.

Lord Scarman also differed markedly from the majority in his analysis.

Lord Scarman: The *Bolam* principle has been accepted by your Lordships' House as applicable to diagnosis and treatment: see *Whitehouse v Jordan* [1981] 1 All ER 267, [1981] 1 WLR 246 (treatment) and *Maynard v West Midlands Regional Health Authority* [1985] 1 All ER 635 (diagnosis). It is also recognised in Scots law as applicable to diagnosis and treatment; indeed, McNair J in the *Bolam* case cited a Scottish decision to that effect, *Hunter v Hanley* 1955 SLT 213 at 217 per the Lord President (Clyde).

But was the judge correct in treating the 'standard of competent professional opinion' as the criterion in determining whether a doctor is under a duty to warn his patient of the risk, or risks, inherent in the treatment which he recommends? Skinner J and the Court of Appeal have in the instant case held that he was correct. Bristow J adopted the same criterion in *Chatterton v Gerson* [1981] 1 All ER 257, [1981] QB 432. The implications of this view of the law are disturbing. It leaves the determination of a legal duty to the judgment of doctors. Responsible medical judgment may, indeed, provide the law with an acceptable standard in determining whether a doctor in diagnosis or treatment has complied with his duty. But is it right that medical judgment should determine whether there exists a duty to warn of risk and its scope? It would be a strange conclusion if the courts should be led to conclude that our law, which undoubtedly recognises a right in the patient to decide whether he will accept or reject the treatment proposed, should permit the doctors to determine whether and in what circumstances a duty arises requiring the doctor to warn his patient of the risks inherent in the treatment which he proposes.

The right of 'self-determination' – the description applied by some to what is no more and no less than the right of a patient to determine for himself whether he will or will not accept the doctor's advice – is vividly illustrated where the treatment recommended is surgery. A doctor who operates without consent of his patient is, save in cases of emergency or mental disability, guilty of the civil wrong of trespass to the person: he is also guilty of the criminal offence of assault. The existence of the patient's right to make his own decision, which may be seen as a basic human right protected by the common law, is the reason why a doctrine embodying a right of the patient to be informed of the risks of surgical treatment has been developed in some jurisdictions in the USA and has found favour with the Supreme Court of Canada. Known as the 'doctrine of informed consent', it amounts to this: where there is a 'real' or a 'material' risk inherent in the proposed operation (however competently and skilfully performed) the question whether and to what extent a patient should be warned before he gives his consent is to be answered not by reference to medical practice but by accepting as a matter of law that, subject to all proper exceptions (of which the court, not the profession, is the judge), a patient has a right to be informed of the risks inherent in the treatment which is proposed. The profession, it is said, should not be judge in its own cause: or, less emotively but more correctly, the courts should not allow medical opinion as to what is best for the patient to override the patient's right to decide for himself whether he will submit to the treatment offered him. It will be necessary for the House to consider in this appeal what is involved in the doctrine and whether it, or any modification of it, has any place in English law.

The appellant's submissions
The appellant's first submission is that, even if (which she does not accept) the *Bolam* principle determines whether a warning of risk should or should not be given, the facts

found establish liability. My Lords, the submission is untenable. It is not possible to hold that the appellant has shown negligence in the *Bolam* sense on the part of Mr Falconer in advising or treating her. His decision not to warn her of the danger of damage to the spinal cord and of its possible consequences was one which the medical witnesses were agreed to be in accordance with a practice accepted as proper by a responsible body of opinion among neuro-surgeons. Further, the medical evidence also emphasised that in reaching a decision whether or not to warn his patient a competent and careful surgeon would attach especial importance to his assessment of the character and emotional condition of his patient, it being accepted that a doctor acting in the best interests of his patient would be concerned lest a warning might frighten the patient into refusing an operation which in his view was the best treatment in the circumstances. Nobody knows what Mr Falconer's assessment of Mrs Sidaway's character, state of mind and emotion was before her operation. There is no evidence to justify an inference that this careful and compassionate man (the history of the case, which I have related, shows that he merited both adjectives) would have failed to consider what was in the best interests of his patient. He could well have concluded that a warning might have deterred her from agreeing to an operation which he believed to be the best treatment for her.

The appellant's second submission is that she has a cause of action which is independent of negligence in the *Bolam* sense. The submission is based on her right to decide for herself whether she should submit to the operation proposed. In effect, she invokes the transatlantic doctrine of informed consent.

The law

The doctrine is new ground in so far as English law is concerned. Apart from the judgment of Bristow J in *Chatterton v Gerson* [1981] 1 All ER 257, [1981] QB 432, I know of only one case prior to the present appeal in which an English court has discussed it. In *Hills v Potter* [1983] 3 All ER 716, [1984] 1 WLR 641 Hirst J followed Skinner J in this case, adding a comment, with which I respectfully agree, that it would be deplorable to base the law in medical cases of this kind on the torts of assault and battery. He did, however, carefully and helpfully devote part of his judgment to a consideration of the transatlantic cases which accept a doctrine of informed consent. He was, if I may say so, right to refuse to follow them: he was sitting at first instance and was faced with formidable English authority accepting the *Bolam* test (Skinner J in the present case and Bristol J in respect of advice: and this House in respect of diagnosis and treatment). But the circumstance that this House is now called on to explore new ground is no reason why a rule of informed consent should not be recognised and developed by our courts. The common law is adaptable; it would not otherwise have survived over the centuries of its existence. The concept of negligence itself is a development of the law by the judges over the last hundred years or so. The legal ancestry of the tort of negligence is to be found in the use made by the judges of the action on the case. Damage is the gist of the action. The action on the case was sufficiently flexible to enable the judges to extend it to cover situations where damage was suffered in circumstances which they judged to call for a remedy. It would be irony indeed if a judicial development for which the opportunity was the presence in the law of a flexible remedy should result now in rigidly confining the law's remedy to situations and relationships already ruled on by the judges.

Counsel for the appellant referred to *Nocton v Lord Ashburton* [1914] AC 932, [1914-15] All ER Rep 45 in an attempt to persuade your Lordships that the relationship between a doctor and patient is of a fiduciary character entitling a patient to equitable relief in the event of a breach of fiduciary duty by the doctor. The attempt fails: there is no comparison to be made between the relationship of doctor and patient with that of solicitor and client, trustee and cestui qui trust or the other relationships treated in equity as of a fiduciary character. Nevertheless, the relationship of doctor and patient is a very special one, the patient putting his health and his life in the doctor's hands. Where *Nocton v Lord Ashburton* does throw light is on the approach of our law to new or special situations and relationships not previously considered by the judges. In that case the House had to consider the field covered by *Derry v Peek* (1889) 14 App Cas 337, [1889-90] All ER Rep 1, the famous case in which the House had held that in an action of deceit it is necessary to prove actual fraud. Viscount Haldane LC had this to say ([1914] AC 932 at 947, [1914-15] All ER Rep 45 at 49):

> My Lords, the discussion of the case by the noble and learned Lords who took part in the decision appears to me to exclude the hypothesis that they considered any other question to be before them than what was the necessary foundation of an ordinary action for deceit. They must indeed be taken to have thought that the facts

proved as to the relationship of the parties in *Derry v. Peek* were not enough to establish any special duty arising out of that relationship other than the general duty of honesty. But they do not say that where a different sort of relationship ought to be inferred from the circumstances the case is to be concluded by asking whether an action for deceit will lie. I think that the authorities subsequent to the decision of the House of Lords shew a tendency to assume that it was intended to mean more than it did. In reality the judgment covered only a part of the field in which liabilities may arise. There are other obligations besides that of honesty the breach of which may give a right to damages. These obligations depend on principles which the judges have worked out in the fashion that is characteristic of a system where much of the law has always been judge-made and unwritten.

This remains the approach of the judges to new or as yet unconsidered situations.

Unless statute has intervened to restrict the range of judge-made law, the common law enables the judges, when faced with a situation where a right recognised by law is not adequately protected, either to extend existing principles to cover the situation or to apply an existing remedy to redress the injustice. There is here no novelty: but merely the application of the principle ubi jus ibi remedium. If, therefore, the failure to warn a patient of the risks inherent in the operation which is recommended does constitute a failure to respect the patient's right to make his own decision, I can see no reason in principle why, if the risk materialises and injury or damage is caused, the law should not recognise and enforce a right in the patient to compensation by way of damages.

For the reasons already given, the *Bolam* principle does not cover the situation. The facts of this very case expose its limitation. Mr Falconer lacked neither care for his patient's health and well-being nor professional skill in the advice and treatment which he offered. But did he overlook or disregard his patient's right to determine for herself whether or not to have the operation? Did he fail to provide her with the information necessary for her to make a prudent decision? There is, in truth, no evidence to answer these questions. Mrs Sidaway's evidence was not accepted: and Mr Falconer was dead. Assume, however, that he did overlook this aspect of his patient's situation. Since neither his advice nor his treatment could be faulted on the *Bolam* test, his patient may have been deprived of the opportunity to exercise her right of decision in the light of information which she, had she received it, might reasonably have considered to be of importance in making up her mind. On the *Bolam* view of the law, therefore, even if she established that she was so deprived by the lack of a warning, she would have no remedy in negligence unless she could also prove that there was no competent and respected body of medical opinion which was in favour of no warning. Moreover, the tort of trespass to the person would not provide her with a remedy: for Mrs Sidaway did consent to the operation. Her complaint is that her consent resulted from ignorance of a risk, known by the doctor but not made known by him to her, inherent in the operation. Nor would the law of contract offer her a sure way forward. Medical treatment, as in her case, is frequently given today under arrangements outside the control of the law of contract.

One point is clear, however. If failure to warn of risk is actionable in English law, it must be because it is in the circumstances a breach of the doctor's duty of care: in other words, the doctor must be shown to be negligent. English law has not accepted a 'no-fault' basis for the liability of a doctor to compensate a patient for injury arising in the course of medical treatment. If, however, the *Bolam* principle is to be applied to the exclusion of any other test to advice and warning, there will be cases in which a patient who suffers injury through ignorance or a risk known to the doctor has no remedy. Is there any difficulty in holding that the doctor's duty of care is sufficiently extensive to afford a patient in that situation a remedy, if as a result she suffers injury or damage? I think not. The root principle of common law negligence is to 'take reasonable care to avoid acts or omissions which you can reasonably foresee would be likely to injure your neighbour': *Donoghue v Stevenson* [1932] AC 562 at 580 *per* Lord Atkin. If it be recognised that a doctor's duty of care extends not only to the health and well-being of his patient but also to a proper respect for his patient's rights, the duty to warn can be seen to be a part of the doctor's duty of care.

It is, I suggest, a sound and reasonable proposition that the doctor should be required to exercise care in respecting the patient's right of decision. He must acknowledge that in very many cases factors other than the purely medical will play a significant part in his patient's decision-making process. The doctor's concern is with health and the relief of pain. These are the medical objectives. But a patient may well have in mind circumstances, objectives, and values which he may reasonably not make known to the doctor but which may lead him to a different decision from that suggested by a purely medical opinion. The doctor's duty can be seen, therefore, to be one which requires him not only to advise as to medical treatment but also to provide his patient with the information needed to enable the patient to consider and balance the medical advantages and risks alongside other relevant matters, such as, for example, his family, business or social responsibilities of which the doctor may be only partially, if at all, informed.

I conclude, therefore, that there is room in our law for a legal duty to warn a patient of the risks inherent in the treatment proposed, and that, if such a duty be held to exist, its proper place is as an aspect of the duty of care owed by the doctor to his patient. I turn, therefore, to consider whether a duty to warn does exist in our law and, if it does, its proper formulation and the conditions and exceptions to which it must be subject.

Some American courts have recognised such a duty. They have seen it as arising from the patient's right to know of material risks, which itself is seen to arise from the patient's right to decide for himself whether or not to submit to the medical treatment proposed. This is the doctrine of informed consent, to which I have already briefly referred.

The landmark case is a decision of the United States Court of Appeals, District of Columbia Circuit, *Canterbury v Spence* 464 F 2d 772 (DC, 1972). This case . . . has now been approved by the District of Columbia Appeal Court in *Crain v Allison* 443 A 2d 558 (1982)
. . .

It is necessary before discussing the doctrine to bear in mind that it is far from being universally accepted in the United States of America, or indeed elsewhere . . .

There can be little doubt that policy explains the divergence of view. The proliferation of medical malpractice suits in the USA has led some courts and some legislatures to curtail or even to reject the operation of the doctrine in an endeavour to restrict the liability of the doctor and so discourage the practice of 'defensive medicine' – by which is meant the practice of doctors advising and undertaking the treatment which they think is legally safe even though they may believe that it is not the best for their patient.

The danger of defensive medicine developing in this country clearly exists though absence of the lawyer's 'contingency fee' (a percentage of the damages for him as his fee if he wins the case but nothing if he loses) may make it more remote. However that may be, in matters of civil wrong or tort, courts are concerned with legal principle: if policy problems emerge, they are best left to the legislature: *McLoughlin v O'Brian* [1983] 1 AC 410.

In *Canterbury v Spence* the court enunciated four propositions. (1) The root premise is the concept that every human being of adult years and of sound mind has a right to determine what shall be done with his own body. (2) The consent is the informed exercise of a choice, and that entails an opportunity to evaluate knowledgeably the options available and the risks attendant on each. (3) The doctor must, therefore, disclose all 'material risks'; what risks are 'material' is determined by the 'prudent patient' test, which was formulated by the court (464 F 2d 772 at 787):

> [a] risk is . . . material when a *reasonable person*, in what the physician knows or should know to be the patient's position, would be likely to attach significance to the risk or cluster of risks in deciding whether or not to forgo the proposed therapy. (My emphasis.)

(4) The doctor, however, has what the court called a 'therapeutic privilege'. This exception is that a reasonable medical assessment of the patient would have indicated to the doctor that disclosure would have posed a serious threat of psychological detriment to the patient.

In Canada, in *Reibl v Hughes* (1980) 114 DLR (3d) 1, Laskin CJC expressed broad approval of the doctrine as enunciated in *Canterbury v Spence*, though it would seem that approval of the doctrine was not necessary to a decision in the case. I find no difficulty in accepting the four propositions enunciated in *Canterbury*'s case. But with two notable exceptions they have not yet been considered, so far as I am aware, by an English court. In *Chatterton v Gerson* [1981] 1 All ER 257, [1981] QB 432 Bristow J did consider whether there is any rule in English law comparable with the doctrine of informed consent. He held that a doctor ought to warn of what may happen by misfortune however well the operation may be carried out 'if there is a *real* risk of a misfortune inherent in the procedure' (see [1981] 1 All ER 257 at 266, [1981] QB 432 at 444; my emphasis). He held that whether or not a warning should have been given depended on what a reasonable doctor would have done in the circumstances; and he applied the *Bolam* test to determine the reasonableness of what the doctor did. In *Hills v Potter* [1984] 3 All ER 716, [1984] 1 WLR 641 Hirst J, after discussing the doctrine, also applied the *Bolam* test.

In my judgment the merit of the propositions enunciated in *Canterbury v Spence* 464 F 2d 772 (DC, 1972) is that without excluding medical evidence they set a standard and formulate a test of the doctor's duty the effect of which is that the court determines the scope of the duty and decides whether the doctor has acted in breach of his duty. This result is achieved first by emphasis on the patient's 'right of self-determination' and secondly by the 'prudent patient' test. If the doctor omits to warn where the risk is such that in the court's view a prudent person in the patient's situation would have regarded it as significant, the doctor is liable.

The *Canterbury* propositions do indeed attach great importance to medical evidence, though judgment is for the court. First, medical evidence is needed in determining whether the risk is material, ie one which the doctor should make known to his patient. The two aspects of the risk, namely the degree of likelihood of it occurring and the seriousness of the possible injury if it should occur, can in most, if not all, cases be assessed only with the help of medical evidence. And secondly, medical evidence would be needed to assist the court in determining whether the doctor was justified on his assessment of his patient in withholding the warning.

My Lords, I think the *Canterbury* propositions reflect a legal truth which too much judicial reliance on medical judgment tends to obscure. In a medical negligence case where the issue is as to the advice and information given to the patient as to the treatment proposed, the available options, and the risk, the court is concerned primarily with a patient's right. The doctor's duty arises from his patient's right. If one considers the scope of the doctor's duty by beginning with the right of the patient to make his own decision whether he will or will not undergo the treatment proposed, the right to be informed of significant risk and the doctor's corresponding duty are easy to understand: for the proper implementation of the right requires that the doctor be under a duty to inform his patient of the material risks inherent in the treatment. And it is plainly right that a doctor may avoid liability for failure to warn of a material risk if he can show that he reasonably believed that communication to the patient of the existence of the risk would be detrimental to the health (including, of course, the mental health) of his patient.

Ideally, the court should ask itself whether in the particular circumstances the risk was such that this particular patient would think it significant if he was told it existed. I would think that, as a matter of ethics, this is the test of the doctor's duty. The law, however, operates not in Utopia but in the world as it is: and such an inquiry would prove in practice to be frustrated by the subjectivity of its aim and purpose. The law can, however, do the next best thing, and require the court to answer the question, what would a reasonably prudent patient think significant if in the situation of this patient. The 'prudent patient' cannot, however, always provide the answer for the obvious reason that he is a norm (like the man on the Clapham omnibus), not a real person: and certainly not the patient himself. Hence there is the need that the doctor should have the opportunity of proving that he reasonably believed that disclosure of the risk would be damaging to his patient or contrary to his best interest. This is what the Americans call the doctor's 'therapeutic privilege'. Its true analysis is that it is a defence available to the doctor which, if he invokes it, he must prove. On both the test and the defence medical evidence will, of course, be of great importance.

The 'prudent patient' test calls for medical evidence. The materiality of the risk is a question for the court to decide upon all the evidence. Many factors call for consideration. The two critically important medical factors are the degree of probability of the risk materialising and the seriousness of possible injury, if it does. Medical evidence will be necessary so that the court may assess the degree of probability and the seriousness of possible injury. Another medical factor, upon which expert evidence will also be required, is the character of the risk. In the event of an operation is the risk common to all surgery, eg sepsis, cardiac arrest, and the other risks associated with surgery and the administration of an anaesthetic? Or is it specific to the particular operation under consideration? With the worldwide development and use of surgical treatment in modern times the court may well take the view that a reasonable person in the patient's situation would be unlikely to attach significance to the general risks; but it is not difficult to foresee circumstances particular to a patient in which even the general risks of surgery should be the subject of a warning by his doctor: eg a heart or lung or blood condition. Special risks inherent in a recommended operation procedure are more likely to be material. The risk of partial paralysis, as in this case where the purpose of the operation was not to save life but merely to relieve pain, illustrates the sort of question which may face first the doctor and later the court. Clearly medical evidence will be of the utmost importance in determining whether such a risk is material: but the question for the court is ultimately legal, not medical in character.

If the doctor admits or the court finds that on the prudent patient test he should have disclosed the risk, he has available the defence that he reasonably believed it to be against the best interest of his patient to disclose it. Here also medical evidence, including the evidence of the doctor himself, will be vital. The doctor himself will normally be an essential witness: and the reasonableness of his assessment may well need the support of independent medical testimony.

My conclusion as to the law is therefore this. To the extent that I have indicated I think that English law must recognise a duty of the doctor to warn his patient of risk inherent in the treatment which he is proposing: and especially so, if the treatment be surgery. The critical limitation is that the duty is confined to material risk. The test of materiality is whether in the circumstances of the particular case the court is satisfied that a reasonable person in the patient's position would be likely to attach significance to the risk. Even if the risk be material, the doctor will not be liable if upon a reasonable assessment of his patient's condition he takes the view that a warning would be detrimental to his patient's health.

Conclusion

Applying these principles to the present case, I ask first: has the appellant shown the risk of damage to the spinal cord to have been a material risk? The risk was slight – less than one per cent – but, if it were to materialise, it could result in severe injury. It was for the appellant, as plaintiff, to establish that the risk was so great that the doctor should have appreciated that it would be considered a significant factor by a prudent patient in the appellant's situation deciding whether or not to have the operation. The medical evidence even of Mr Uttley, the appellant's expert witness, gets nowhere near establishing the materiality of the risk in the sense just outlined. It is, or course, possible that Mr Uttley's evidence was not directed to anything other than negligence in the *Bolam* sense. If so, the appellant, who now relies on the principle of informed consent, must accept the consequences: it was up to her to prove such a case, if she were seeking to establish it. Further, we do not know Mr Falconer's assessment of his patient. It is possible that, had he lived, he could have enlightened the court on much that would have been relevant. After an anxious consideration of the evidence I do not find it possible to say that it has been proved that Mr Falconer failed in his duty when he omitted – as we must assume that he did – to warn his patient of the risk of injury to the spinal cord.

At the end of the day, therefore, the substitution of the *Canterbury*, 464 F 2d 772 (DC, 1972) propositions for the *Bolam* [1957] 1 WLR 582 test of duty and breach of duty does not avail the appellant because the evidence does not enable her to prove that Mr Falconer was in breach of his duty when he omitted the warning. Lack of evidence was always her difficulty; and it remains so, even though, contrary to the submission of the respondents, the law, in my view, recognises a right of a patient of sound understanding to be warned of material risks in the exceptional circumstances to which I have referred. Accordingly, I would dismiss this appeal.

(a) Understanding Sidaway

(i) BOLAM OR MORE?

Lord Scarman authoritatively restated in *Sidaway* how English law has come to see the decision in *Bolam*.

The *Bolam* principle may be formulated as a rule that a doctor is not negligent if he acts in accordance with a practice accepted at the time as proper by a responsible body of medical opinion even though other doctors adopt a different practice. In short, the law imposes the duty of care; but the standard of care is a matter of medical judgment.

(We shall see *infra*, ch 5, that other common law jurisdictions take a different view.) With Lord Scarman's statement in mind, the only judge in *Sidaway* to apply the *Bolam* test unequivocally was Lord Diplock. Certainly this was the view of Lord Scarman speaking extra-judicially in a lecture to the Royal Society of Medicine in 1986:

We can ignore Lord Diplock's opinion, as he was in a minority of one; the other three opinions were perhaps truer to the spirit of English law ('Consent, Communication and Responsibility' (1986) 79 J Roy Soc Med 697)

We must therefore turn to the speeches of the other Law Lords. What place does *Bolam* have in the analysis of the law which they severally offer. Certainly

Lord Scarman rejected *Bolam* as we saw. We are left, therefore, with Lord Bridge (with whom Lord Keith concurred) and Lord Templeman. Neither judge went so far as to reject *Bolam* explicitly nor did they join Lord Diplock in relying wholly upon it as setting the standard of the duty to disclose.

The key words are those of Lord Bridge:

> . . . the issue whether non-disclosure in a particular case should be condemned as a breach of the doctor's duty of care is an issue to be decided primarily on the basis of expert medical evidence, applying the *Bolam* test.

What can Lord Bridge mean by the qualifying adverb 'primarily'? Can it be the same as 'rightly'? Sir John Donaldson MR said in the Court of Appeal in *Sidaway*:

> . . . I think that, in an appropriate case, a judge would be entitled to reject a unanimous medical view if he were satisfied that it was manifestly wrong and that the doctors must have been misdirecting themselves as to their duty in law.
>
> Another way of expressing my view of the test is to add just one qualifying word (which I have emphasised) to the law as Skinner J summarised it so that it would read:
>
>> The duty is fulfilled if the doctor acts in accordance with a practice *rightly* accepted as proper by a body of skilled and experienced medical men.

If so, what do either or both of them mean? Without referring explicitly to *Bolam*, Lord Templeman distances himself from the *Bolam* approach when he states that:

> I do not subscribe to the theory that the patient is entitled to know everything *nor* to the theory that the doctor is entitled to decide everything [our emphasis].

And later when he states that:

> At the end of the day, the doctor, bearing in mind the best interests of the patient and bearing in mind the patient's right of information which will enable the patient to make a balanced judgment must decide what information should be given to the patient and in what terms that information should be couched. The court will award damages against the doctor if the court is satisfied that the doctor blundered and that the patient was deprived of information which was necessary for the purposes I have outlined.

Presumably a doctor 'blunders' when he does not behave 'rightly', ie the rule is a matter of law and not medical practice. If *Bolam simpliciter* does not represent the law of England this must mean that the views of the medical profession are not conclusive on disclosure. (This is not to say they are irrelevant.)

The validity of the analysis suggested here is called into question however by the surprising decision of the Court of Appeal in *Gold v Haringey HA* [1987] 2 All ER 888.

Gold v Haringey HA [1987] 2 All ER 888, [1988] QB 481 (CA)

> In 1979 the plaintiff, who already had two children, became pregnant and agreed with her husband that they would not have any more children. She was referred to a hospital run by the defendant health authority, where the consultant obstetrician suggested sterilisation but made no reference to the alternative of the plaintiff's husband having a vasectomy and gave no warning of the risk of the sterilisation operation failing. The failure rate for sterilisation (20-60 per 10,000) was higher than that for vasectomy (5 per 10,000). The sterilisation

operation was performed on the day after the birth of the child but was not a success, with the result that the plaintiff subsequently became pregnant again and gave birth to a fourth child. She brought an action for damages for negligence against the health authority alleging, inter alia, that it had been negligent in not warning her of the risk of failure of the operation and that a statement made to her that the operation would be 'irreversible' amounted to a negligent misrepresentation. The judge held that the operation itself had not been negligently performed but that, having regard to the fact that the contraceptive advice had been given in a non-therapeutic context, the defendants had been negligent in failing to warn the plaintiff of the possibility of failure of the operation. He awarded the plaintiff damages of £19,000. The defendants appealed.

Lloyd LJ: How then, I ask again, did it come about that the judge found the defendants guilty of negligence, when he accepted that there was a substantial body of responsible medical opinion in 1979 who would not have given any warning? The answer is that he drew a distinction between advice or warning in a therapeutic context and advice or warning in a contraceptive context. In a therapeutic context there was a body of responsible medical opinion which would not have warned of the failure rate. But in a contraceptive context there was no such body of responsible medical opinion. Even if there had been, he would still have found the defendants negligent, since in his view the *Bolam* test does not apply to advice given in a non-therapeutic context. He said:

> I accept that it was the view of the majority of the House of Lords that in the therapeutic context of that case [*Sidaway*] the duty to give advice was subject to the same test as the duty to diagnose and treat, and that this test, known as the *Bolam* test after an earlier case, was that a doctor is not negligent if he acts in accordance with a practice accepted as proper by a responsible body of medical opinion even though other doctors adopt a different practice. This test is different from the one generally applied in actions in respect of negligent advice. I see nothing in the reasons given for adopting the *Bolam* test in the sort of circumstances under consideration in *Sidaway* which compels me to widen the application of this exceptional rule so as to cause it to apply to contraceptive counselling.

So the judge decided against the defendant on two grounds. First, he held that the *Bolam* test did not apply at all in a contraceptive context. Instead he applied his own judgment as to what should have been mentioned in that context. Second, if the *Bolam* test did apply, then he found as a fact that there was no body of responsible medical opinion which would not, in a contraceptive context, have warned of the risk of failure. I have reversed these two grounds, since the first ground raises a question of considerable general importance.

Was the judge right when he held that the *Bolam* test is an exception to the ordinary rule in actions for negligence? If by an 'exceptional rule' the judge meant that the *Bolam* test is confined to actions against doctors, then I would respectfully disagree. I have already quoted a passage from McNair J's summing up in *Bolam*'s case. In an earlier passage he had said ([1957] 2 All ER 118 at 121, [1957] 1 WLR 582 at 586):

> . . . where you get a situation which involves the use of some special skill or competence, then the test whether there has been negligence or not is not the test of the man on top of a Clapham omnibus, because he has not got this special skill. The test is the standard of the ordinary skilled man exercising and professing to have that special skill.

So far as I know that passage has always been treated as being of general application whenever a defendant professes any special skill. It is so treated in *Charlesworth on Negligence* (7th edn, 1983) para 6-17. The *Bolam* test is not confined to a defendant exercising or professing the particular skill of medicine. If there had been any doubt on the question, which I do not think there was, it was removed by the speech of Lord Diplock in the *Sidaway* case [1985] 1 All ER 643 at 657, [1985] AC 871 at 892 where Lord Diplock made it clear that the *Bolam* test is rooted in an ancient rule of common law applicable to all artificers. In *Saif Ali v Sydney Mitchell & Co (a firm)* [1978] 3 All ER 1033 at 1043, [1980] AC 198 at 220 Lord Diplock treated the same test as applicable to barristers, although he did not mention the *Bolam* case by name. The question in that case was whether a barrister is immune from an action in negligence in relation to advice given out of court. It was held that he is not. Lord Diplock said:

> No matter what profession it may be, the common law does not impose on those who practise it any liability for damage resulting from what in the result turned out to

have been errors of judgment, unless the error was such as no reasonably well informed and competent member of that profession could have made.

Counsel for the plaintiff did his best to argue that the *Bolam* test is confined to doctors. For the reasons I have given, I cannot accept that argument. I can see no possible ground for distinguishing between doctors and any other profession or calling which requires special skill, knowledge or experience. To be fair to the judge, it was not, I think, on this ground that he regarded the *Bolam* test as exceptional.

In passing, I should mention that the *Bolam* test is often thought of as limiting the duty of care. So in one sense it does. But it also extends the duty of care, as the second of the two passages I have quoted from McNair J's summing up in the *Bolam* case makes clear. The standard is not that of the man on the top of the Clapham omnibus, as in other fields of negligence, but the higher standard of the man skilled in the particular profession or calling.

Why then did the judge think that it would be an extension of the *Bolam* test to apply it in the present case? The reason can only have been that which I have already mentioned, namely the distinction between therapeutic and non-therapeutic advice. Counsel for the plaintiff took us through the *Sidaway* case speech by speech, and paragraph by paragraph, in order to point the distinction. But I remain unconvinced. In the first place the line between therapeutic and non-therapeutic medicine is elusive. A plastic surgeon carrying out a skin graft is presumably engaged in therapeutic surgery; but what if he is carrying out a facelift, or some other cosmetic operation? Counsel found it hard to say.

In the second place, a distinction between advice given in a therapeutic context and advice given in a non-therapeutic context would be a departure from the principle on which the *Bolam* test is itself grounded. The principle does not depend on the context in which any act is performed, or any advice given. It depends on a man professing skill or competence in a field beyond that possessed by the man on the Clapham omnibus. If the giving of contraceptive advice required no special skill, then I could see an argument that the *Bolam* test should not apply. But that was not, and could not have been, suggested. The fact (if it be the fact) that giving contraceptive advice involves a different sort of skill and competence from carrying out a surgical operation does not mean that the *Bolam* test ceases to be applicable. It is clear from Lord Diplock's speech in *Sidaway* that a doctor's duty of care in relation to diagnosis, treatment and advice, whether the doctor be a specialist or general practitioner, is not to be dissected into its component parts. To dissect a doctor's advice into that given in a therapeutic context and that given in a contraceptive context would be to go against the whole thrust of the decision of the majority of the House of Lords in that case. So I would reject the argument of counsel for the plaintiff under this head, and hold that the judge was not free, as he thought, to form his own view of what warning and information ought to have been given, irrespective of any body of responsible medical opinion to the contrary.

Watkins and Stephen Brown LJJ agreed.

Although the decision in *Gold* offers an unambiguous interpretation of *Sidaway*, it has to be said that it is difficult, at best, to reconcile it with the speeches of *any* of the judges in *Sidaway* apart from Lord Diplock. Significantly, Lloyd LJ only referred to (and relied upon) Lord Diplock's speech. Subsequently, in a number of cases, the view taken in *Gold* has been regarded as the authoritative interpretation of *Sidaway*: *Palmer v Eadie* (18 May 1987, unreported), CA; *Blyth v Bloomsbury HA* [1993] 4 Med LR 151 (CA); *Moyes v Lothian Health Board* [1990] 1 Med LR 463 (Court of Session (Outer House)).

Despite the fact that the House of Lords refused leave to appeal in *Gold*, it should not be assumed that *Gold* has settled the law in England. For example, the Department of Health in its *A Guide to Consent for Examination or Treatment* (HC (90)22), specifically directs the reader's attention to the speeches of Lord Bridge and Lord Templeman (but not of Lord Diplock) in seeking to clarify the duty to disclose established in *Sidaway*. In our view, *Gold* will not (and should not) constitute the last word on the meaning of *Sidaway*. So, with this in mind is it possible to be more specific about what, in the view of Lord Bridge and Lord Templeman the law looks for, to determine whether or not a doctor has complied with his legal obligation of disclosure?

(ii) WHAT MORE?

There are two indications.

I. 'Substantial risk of grave adverse consequence'. Lord Bridge considered that the court might regard as negligent non-disclosure in accordance with accepted medical practice if in the court's opinion: 'disclosure of a particular risk was so obviously necessary to an informed choice on the part of the patient that no reasonably prudent medical man would fail to make it'. His Lordship gave the example of an operation involving a substantial risk of grave adverse consequences, citing the 10% risk of a stroke in *Reibl v Hughes*. What can 'substantial' mean here? If it is to be regarded in terms of percentage of risks this must carry with it certain difficulties for the law's development. It has at least two drawbacks. The first is that it represents what is really a normative exercise (of what *ought* to be disclosed) as if it were an empirical matter. The danger is that this will suggest that the law's approach is a simplistic and arithmetical one, merely concerned with expert evidence on percentages.

The second objection lies in the danger that reference to percentage risks will merely provoke disagreements among experts as to what is the precise percentage in any particular case. Furthermore, it leaves undecided what percentage is the percentage beyond which a risk is regarded as substantial. Would the law not run the risk of having experts give evidence (hand on heart) that a particular risk has only a 3½% chance of occurring if 4% had become the magic legal limit? A court would have no criteria by which to chose amongst conflicting expert views. The consequence could be that in effect the law would be handed back to the medical profession through experts.

In any event, discussion of the size of risk in isolation overlooks the fact that in matters of risk calculation it is not only whether a risk exists but of what happens if the risk eventuates which are relevant in determining whether a patient is prepared to run that risk. For example, if an operation may bring benefits but carries a high risk of causing a long-term irritating rash, the patient may decide to run that risk whereas he may not decide to run what is represented as a low risk of having a permanent limp as a consequence of the same operation. It is all well and good to refer to 'grave adverse consequences'. The above example tends to suggest that the only judge of what is 'grave' or 'adverse' can be the patient.

II. General and special risks. Lord Templeman draws a distinction between risks that are *general* and ones which are *special*. The *former* ordinarily would be known to the patient and no duty to disclose would arise. The latter may call for specific mention by the doctor. Lord Templeman seems to derive this distinction from the Canadian cases. In so doing, however, it is submitted, with respect, he may have read them in a way which others would not. The Canadian cases, particularly *Reibl v Hughes* and *White v Turner* (1981) 120 DLR (3d) 269 are concerned with 'material risks': 'materiality' depending on what a reasonable patient would want to know. The distinction between 'general' and 'special' risks may be relevant to 'materiality' but is not determinative of it. For, ordinarily, a 'general' risk would not be 'material' because the 'reasonable patient' would be presumed to know it. By contrast, a 'special' risk may be 'material' but need not be. Thus, to categorise a risk as 'general' or 'special' is only tangentially relevant to the question of whether the doctor must disclose it.

White v Turner (1981) 120 DLR (3d) 269 (Ont High Ct)

Linden J: The meaning of 'material risks' and 'unusual or special risks' should now be considered. In my view, *material* risks are significant risks that pose a real threat to the patient's life, health or comfort. In considering whether a risk is material or immaterial, one must balance the severity of the potential result and the likelihood of its occurring. Even if there is only a small chance of serious injury or death, the risk may be considered material. On the other hand, if there is a significant chance of slight injury this too may be held to be material. As always in negligence law, what is a material risk will have to depend on the specific facts of each case.

As for 'unusual or special risks' these are those that are not ordinary, common, everyday matters. These are risks that are somewhat extraordinary, uncommon and not encountered every day, but they are known to occur occasionally. Though rare occurrences, because of their unusual or special character, the Supreme Court has declared that they should be described to a reasonable patient, even though they may not be 'material'. There may, of course, be an overlap between 'material risks' and 'unusual or special risks'. If a special or unusual risk is quite dangerous and fairly frequently encountered, it could be classified as a material risk. But even if it is not very dangerous or common, an unusual or special risk must be disclosed.

Even if it be the case that Lord Templeman has reinterpreted Canadian law, the distinction he draws is at least for the time being part of English law for him. It must therefore be asked what are 'general' and 'special' risks in law? One tenable distinction (though as we have seen *prima facie* irrelevant to the issue of 'materiality') could be that a 'general' risk is one that attends all medical procedures, eg risks from anaesthesia in operations. The reasonable patient would, in law, be expected to be aware of these. On this theory the doctor would not be under a specific duty to volunteer information, though he may do if especially questioned (cf Lord Scarman *infra*).

A 'special' risk, on the other hand, would be one inherent in the particular procedure either because of the nature of the procedure itself or because of some circumstances particular to the patient. This is the Canadian view. Is it Lord Templeman's? It may be his view. But even if it is, the distinction is unhelpful unless understood in the context of 'materiality' and the 'reasonable patient' which, as we shall see, Lord Templeman appears to reject.

The difficulty is, however, that what Lord Templeman says, suggests it is not his view:

When a patient complains of lack of information, the court must decide whether the patient has suffered harm from a general danger inherent in the operation or from some special danger.

It is difficult to know how there can be a 'general danger' inherent in the operation as distinct from all operations. Indeed, on the basis of the words used by Lord Templeman the distinction between 'general' and 'special' becomes a distinction without a difference.

The important question then becomes, what is a 'special risk', because whatever else Lord Templeman means he seems to suggest that there may be a duty to disclose such a risk. He defines a special risk as one which may be 'special in kind or magnitude or special to the patient'. Obviously what is 'special to the patient' can *only* be determined by this patient. The reference to 'kind' or 'magnitude' does not seem to take us very far. This is because it is at least arguable that the only judge of what is special here can be the patient himself also. This would mean that Lord Templeman is embracing a legal rule which requires that the doctor must disclose that which the specific patient would need to know, a position expressed nowhere except in Oklahoma (*Scott v Bradford* 606 P 2d 554 (1979)) and, of course, rejected elsewhere in the speech of Lord Templeman himself. This is a legal test going beyond the 'reasonable patient', which again Lord Templeman purports to reject in another part of his speech. The meaning attributed to 'special' is further rendered imprecise by Lord Templeman's reference to *Reibl v Hughes* and the recourse to percentage risks. Reference to percentage risks may be helpful as regards the issue of 'magnitude' but seems to offer no assistance, without more, in determining whether the risk is 'special'.

The conclusion must be that Lord Templeman either embraces a test based upon what the particular patient would wish to know (though he rejects this) or his speech suffers from a degree of internal inconsistency.

(iii) THE REASONABLE PATIENT TEST

The majority opted for a duty of disclosure which, while rejecting the *Bolam* test *simpliciter*, leaves the exact nature of the duty somewhat obscure. Lord Scarman declares his commitment to 'the right of his patient to determine for himself whether he will or will not accept the doctor's advice concerning any proposed medical procedure'. This commitment could have led Lord Scarman to opt for either of two positions concerning the legal duty to disclose: the 'reasonable patient' test or the 'particular patient' test. As for the latter, as we have seen Lord Scarman concedes its validity in theory but regards it as Utopian. It may also be logically impossible to satisfy as a test since it may contemplate an infinite regression of question, answer and subsequent question:

Dr: 'So that is what happens. Is there anything else you need to know?'
Patient: 'I don't know, is there any more I can know?'
Dr: 'Yes, the following happens . . . now is there anything else you would like to know?'
Patient: 'I'm not sure, is there anything else you can tell me?'

Lord Scarman therefore opted for the 'reasonable' or 'prudent patient' test as 'the next best thing' to give effect to the patient's right to self-determination. Crucial for the 'reasonable' or 'prudent patient' test in all the jurisdictions in which it has been adopted is the notion of 'materiality', since it is only *material risks* which the doctor must disclose.

How does Lord Scarman define what risks are material? He states 'the test of materiality is whether in the circumstances of the particular case the court is satisfied that a reasonable person in the patient's position would be likely to attach significance to the risk'. As we have seen, Lord Scarman states that this 'is a question for the court to decide upon all the evidence'. Notice that Lord Scarman rejects the distinction between 'general' and 'special' risks as being relevant to 'materiality'. He states:

> With the worldwide development and use of surgical treatment in modern times the court may well take the view that a reasonable person in the patient's situation would be unlikely to attach significance to the general risks; but it is not difficult to foresee circumstances particular to a patient in which even the general risks of surgery should be the subject of a warning by his doctor, eg a heart or lung or blood condition. Special risks inherent in a recommended operational procedure are more likely to be material.

In reaching his view of the law, Lord Scarman draws heavily upon the American decision of *Canterbury v Spence* and the language of rights which is so much more familiar to American courts.

Canterbury v Spence (1972) 464 F 2d 772 (DC Cir)

The plaintiff consulted the defendant because of severe pain between his shoulder blades. After x-rays and a myelogram, surgery was recommended to establish the true nature of the problem identified in the region of the fourth thorasic vertebra. The defendant carried out a laminectomy – the excision of the posteria arch of the vertebra. The plaintiff, who was 19-years-old, did not raise any objection or ask about the procedure's implications. The plaintiff's mother was told that the operation was 'not any more [serious] than any other operation'. The laminectomy revealed a number of problems which the defendant sought to deal with. Subsequently, the plaintiff suffered a number of disabilities of a permanent nature which it was claimed arose from the laminectomy including urological problems, incontinence, and difficulties in walking. The plaintiff alleged that the doctor failed to warn of the risk of serious disability inherent in the laminectomy. In reversing the lower court's judgment that the defendant had no case to answer, Judge Robinson developed the 'prudent patient' (ie 'reasonable patient') test of disclosure.

Robinson J: The context in which the duty of risk-disclosure arises is invariably the occasion for decision as to whether a particular treatment procedure is to be undertaken. To the physician, whose training enables a self-satisfying evaluation, the answer may seem clear, but it is the prerogative of the patient, not the physician, to determine for himself the direction in which his interests seem to lie. To enable the patient to chart his course understandably, some familiarity with the therapeutic alternatives and their hazards becomes essential.

A reasonable revelation in these respects is not only a necessity, but as we see it, is as much a matter of the physician's duty. It is a duty to warn of the dangers lurking in the proposed treatment, and that is surely a facet of due care. It is, too, a duty to impart information which the patient has every right to expect. The patient's reliance upon the physician is a trust of the kind which traditionally has exacted obligations beyond those associated with arms-length transactions. His dependence upon the physician for information affecting his well-being, in terms of contemplated treatment, is well-nigh abject. As earlier noted, long before the instant litigation arose, courts had recognised that the physician had the responsibility of satisfying the vital information needs of the patient. More recently, we ourselves have found 'in the fiducial qualities of [the physician-patient] relationship the physician's duty to reveal to the patient that which in his best interests it is important that he should know'. We now find, as a part of the physician's overall obligation to the patient, a similar duty of reasonable disclosure of the choices with respect to proposed therapy and the dangers inherently and potentially involved.

This disclosure requirement, on analysis, reflects much more of a change in doctrinal emphasis than a substantive addition to malpractice law. It is well established that the physician must seek and secure his patient's consent before commencing an operation or other course of treatment. It is also clear that the consent, to be efficacious, must be free from imposition upon the patient. It is the settled rule that therapy not authorised by the patient may amount to a tort – a common law battery – by the physician. And it is evident that it is normally impossible to obtain a consent worthy of the name unless the physician first elucidates the options and the perils for the patient's edification. The physician has long borne a duty, on pain of liability for unauthorised treatment, to make adequate disclosure to the patient. The evolution of the obligation to communicate for the patient's benefit as well as the physician's protection has hardly involved an extraordinary restructuring of the law.

There are, in our view, formidable obstacles to acceptance of the notion that the physician's obligation to disclose is either germinated or limited by medical practice. To begin with, the reality of any discernible custom reflecting a professional consensus on communication of option and risk information to patients is open to serious doubt. We sense the danger that what in fact is no custom at all may be taken as an affirmative custom to maintain silence, and that physician-witnesses to the so-called custom may state merely their personal opinions as to what they or others would do under given conditions. We cannot gloss over the inconsistency between reliance on a general practice respecting divulgence and, on the other hand, realisation that the myriad of variables among patients makes each case so differing that its omission can rationally be justified only by the effect of its individual circumstances. Nor can we ignore the fact that to bind the disclosure obligation to medical usage is to arrogate the decision on revelation to the physician alone. Respect for the patient's right of self-determination on particular therapy demands a standard set by law for physicians rather than one which physicians may or may not impose upon themselves.

More fundamentally, the majority rule overlooks the gradation of reasonable-care demands in Anglo-American jurisprudence and the position of professional custom in the hierarchy. The calibre of the performance exacted by the reasonable-care standard varies between the professional and non-professional worlds, and so also the role of professional custom. 'With but few exceptions', we recently declared, 'society demands that everyone under a duty to use care observe minimally a general standard'. 'Familiarly expressed judicially', we added, 'the yardstick is that degree of care which a reasonably prudent person would have exercised under the same or similar circumstances'. 'Beyond this', however, we emphasised, 'the law requires those engaging in activities requiring unique knowledge and ability to give a performance commensurate with the undertaking'. Thus physicians treating the sick must perform at higher levels than non-physicians in order to meet the reasonable-care standard in its special application to physicians – 'that degree of care and skill ordinarily exercised by the profession in [the physician's] own or similar localities'. And practices adopted by the profession have indispensable value as evidence tending to establish just what that degree of care and skill is.

We have admonished, however, that '[t]he special medical standards are but adaptions of the general standard to a group who are required to act as reasonable men possessing their medical talents presumably would'. There is, by the same token, no basis for operation of the special medical standard where the physician's activity does not bring his medical knowledge and skills peculiarly into play. And where the challenge to the physician's conduct is not to be gauged by the special standard, it follows that medical custom cannot furnish the test of its propriety, whatever its relevance under the proper test may be. The decision to unveil the patient's condition and the chances as to remediation, as we shall see, is oft times a non-medical judgment and, if so, is a decision outside the ambit of the special standard. Where that is the situation, professional custom hardly furnishes the legal criterion for measuring the physician's responsibility to reasonably inform his patient of the options and the hazards as to treatment . . .

Prevailing medical practice, we have maintained, has evidentiary value in determinations as to what the specific criteria measuring challenged professional conduct are and whether they have been met, but does not itself define the standard. That has been our position in treatment cases, where the physician's performance is ordinarily to be adjudicated by the special medical standard of due care. We see no logic in a different rule for nondisclosure cases, where the governing standard is much more largely divorced from professional considerations. And surely in nondisclosure cases the fact-finder is not invariably functioning in an area of such technical complexity that it must be bound to medical custom as an inexorable application of the community standard of reasonable care.

Thus we distinguished, for purposes of duty to disclose, the special – and general – standard aspects of the physician-patient relationship. When medical judgment enters the picture and for that reason the special standard controls, prevailing medical practice must be given its just due. In all other instances, however, the general standard exacting ordinary care applies, and that standard is set by law. In sum, the physician's duty to disclose is governed by the same legal principles applicable to others in comparable situations, with modifications only to the extent that medical judgment enters the picture. We hold that the standard measuring performance of that duty by physicians, as by others, is conduct which is reasonable under the circumstances.

Once the circumstances give rise to a duty on the physician's part to inform his patient, the next inquiry is the scope of the disclosure the physician is legally obliged to make. The courts have frequently confronted this problem but no uniform standard defining the adequacy of the divulgence emerges from the decisions. Some have said 'full' disclosure, a norm we are unwilling to adopt literally. It seems obviously prohibitive and unrealistic to expect physicians to discuss with their patient every risk of proposed treatment – no matter how small or remote – and generally unnecessary from the patient's viewpoint as well. Indeed, the cases speaking in terms of 'full' disclosure appear to envision something less than total disclosure, leaving unanswered the question of just how much.

The larger number of courts, as might be expected, have applied tests framed with reference to prevailing fashion within the medical profession. Some have measured the disclosure by 'good medical practice', others by what a reasonable practitioner would have bared under the circumstances, and still others by what medical custom in the community would demand. We have explored this rather considerable body of law but are unprepared to follow it. The duty to disclose, we have reasoned, arises from phenomena apart from medical custom and practice. The latter, we think, should no more establish the scope of the duty than its existence. Any definition of scope in terms purely of a professional standard is at odds with the patient's prerogative to decide on projected therapy himself. That prerogative, we have said, is at the very foundation of the duty to disclose, and both the patient's right to know and the physician's correlative obligation to tell him are diluted to the extent that its compass is dictated by the medical profession.

In our view, the patient's right of self-decision shapes the boundaries of the duty to reveal. That right can be effectively exercised only if the patient possesses enough information to enable an intelligent choice. The scope of the physician's communications to the patient, then, must be measured by the patient's need, and that need is the information material to the decision. Thus the test for determining whether a particular peril must be divulged is its materiality to the patient's decision: all risks potentially affecting the decision must be unmasked. And to safeguard the patient's interest in achieving his own determination on treatment, the law must itself set the standard for adequate disclosure.

Optimally for the patient, exposure of a risk would be mandatory whenever the patient would deem it significant to his decision, either singly or in combination with other risks. Such a requirement, however, would summon the physician to second-guess the patient, whose ideas on materiality could hardly be known to the physician. That would make an undue demand upon medical practitioners, whose conduct, like that of others, is to be measured in terms of reasonableness. Constantly with orthodox negligence doctrine, the physician's liability for nondisclosure is to be determined on the basis of foresight, not hindsight; no less than any other aspect of negligence, the issue on nondisclosure must be approached from the viewpoint of the reasonableness of the physician's divulgence in terms of what he knows or should know to be the patient's informational needs. If, but only if, the fact-finder can say that the physician's communication was unreasonably inadequate is an imposition of liability legally or morally justified.

Of necessity, the content of the disclosure rests in the first instance with the physician. Ordinarily it is only he who is in position to identify particular dangers; always he must make a judgment, in terms of materiality, as to whether and to what extent revelation to the patient is called for. He cannot know with complete exactitude what the patient would consider important to his decision, but on the basis of his medical training and experience he can sense how the average, reasonable patient expectably would react. Indeed, with knowledge of, or ability to learn, his patient's background and current condition, he is in a position superior to that of most others – attorneys, for example – who are called upon to make judgments on pain of liability in damages for unreasonable miscalculation.

From these considerations we derive the breadth of the disclosure of risks legally to be required. The scope of the standard is not subjective as to either the physician or the patient; it remains objective with due regard for the patient's informational needs and with suitable leeway for the physician's situation. In broad outline, we agree that '[a] risk is thus material when a reasonable person in what the physician knows or should know to be the patient's position would be likely to attach significance to the risks or cluster of risks in deciding whether or not to forego the proposed therapy'.

The topics importantly demanding a communication of information are the inherent and potential hazards of the proposed treatment, the alternatives to that treatment, if any, and the results likely if the patient remains untreated. The factors contributing significance to the dangerousness of a medical technique are, of course, the incidence of injury and the degree of the harm threatened. A very small chance of death or serious disablement may well be significant; a potential disability which dramatically outweighs the potential benefit of the therapy or the detriments of the existing malady may summons discussion with the patient.

There is no bright line separating the significant from the insignificant; the answer in any case must abide a rule of reason. Some dangers – infection, for example – are inherent in any operation; there is no obligation to communicate those of which persons of average sophistication are aware. Even more clearly, the physician bears no responsibility for discussion of hazards the patient has already discovered, or those having no apparent materiality to patients' decision on therapy. The disclosure doctrine, like others marking lines between permissible and impermissible behaviour in medical practice, is in essence a requirement of conduct prudent under the circumstances. Whenever nondisclosure of particular risk information is open to debate by reasonable-minded men, the issue is for the finder of the facts.

Two exceptions to the general rule of disclosure have been noted by the courts. Each is in the nature of a physician's privilege not to disclose, and the reasoning underlying them is appealing. Each, indeed, is but a recognition that, as important as is the patient's right to know, it is greatly outweighed by the magnitudinous circumstances giving rise to the privilege. The first comes into play when the patient is unconscious or otherwise incapable of consenting, and harm from a failure to treat is imminent and outweighs any harm threatened by the proposed treatment. When a genuine emergency of that sort arises, it is settled that the impracticality of conferring with the patient dispenses with need for it. Even in situations of that character the physician should, as current law requires, attempt to secure a relative's consent if possible. But if time is too short to accommodate discussion, obviously the physician should proceed with the treatment.

The second exception obtains when risk-disclosure poses such a threat of detriment to the patient as to become unfeasible or contraindicated from a medical point of view. It is recognised that patients occasionally become so ill or emotionally distraught on disclosure as to foreclose a rational decision, or complicate or hinder the treatment, or perhaps even pose psychological damage to the patient. Where that is so, the cases have generally held that the physician is armed with a privilege to keep the information from the patient, and we think it clear that portents of that type may justify the physician in action he deems medically warranted. The critical inquiry is whether the physician responded to a sound medical judgment that communication of the risk information would present a threat to the patient's well-being.

The physician's privilege to withhold information for therapeutic reasons must be carefully circumscribed, however, for otherwise it might devour the disclosure rule itself. The privilege does not accept the paternalistic notion that the physician may remain silent simply because divulgence might prompt the patient to forego therapy the physician feels the patient really needs. That attitude presumes instability or perversity for even the normal patient, and runs counter to the foundation principle that the patient should and ordinarily can make the choice for himself. Nor does the privilege contemplate operation save where the patient's reaction to risk information, as reasonably foreseen by the physician, is menacing. And even in a situation of that kind, disclosure to a close relative with a view to securing consent to the proposed treatment may be the only alternative open to the physician.

Lord Scarman's approach relying, as it does, on the language of rights and the North American experience, has clearly not endeared itself to the English courts. There remains an obvious deference to the medical profession.

You will recall Lord Scarman's attempt to pay proper regard to medical evidence but, at the same time, to seek to put it into proper place. The Australian High Court faced up to this issue in a landmark decision in 1992.

Rogers v Whitaker (1992) 67 ALJR 47 (Australian High Court)

Mason CJ, Brennan, Dawson, Toohey and McHugh JJ: The appellant, Christopher Rogers, is an ophthalmic surgeon. The respondent, Maree Lynette Whitaker, was a patient of the appellant who became almost totally blind after he had conducted surgery upon her right eye. The respondent commenced proceedings against the appellant for negligence in the Supreme Court of New South Wales and obtained judgment in the amount of $808,564.38. After an unsuccessful appeal to the Court of Appeal of New South Wales (1991) 23 NSWLR 600, the appellant now appeals to this Court.

There is no question that the appellant conducted the operation with the required skill and care. The basis upon which the trial judge, Campbell J, found the appellant liable was that he had failed to warn the respondent that, as a result of surgery on her right eye, she might develop a condition known as sympathetic ophthalmia in her left eye. The development of this condition after the operation and the consequent loss of sight in her left eye were particularly devastating for the respondent as she had been almost totally blind in her right eye since a penetrating injury to it at the age of nine. Despite this early misfortune, she had continued to lead a substantially normal life, completing her schooling, entering the workforce, marrying and raising a family. In 1983, nearly forty years after the initial injury to her right eye and in preparation for a return to the paid workforce after a three-year period during which she had looked after her injured son, the respondent decided to have an eye examination. Her general practitioner referred her to Dr Cohen, an ophthalmic surgeon, who prescribed reading glasses and referred her to the appellant for possible surgery on her right eye.

The respondent did not follow up the referral until 22 May 1984 when she was examined by the appellant for the first time. The appellant advised her that an operation on the right eye would not only improve its appearance, by removing scar tissue, but would probably restore significant sight to that eye. At a second consultation approximately three weeks later, the respondent agreed to submit to surgery. The surgical procedure was carried out on 1 August 1984. After the operation, it appeared that there had been no improvement in the right eye but, more importantly, the respondent developed inflammation in the left eye as an element of sympathetic ophthalmia. Evidence at the trial was that this condition occurred once in approximately 14,000 such procedures, although there was also evidence that the chance of occurrence was slightly greater when, as here, there had been an earlier penetrating injury to the eye operated upon. The condition does not always lead to loss of vision but, in this case, the respondent ultimately lost all sight in her left eye. As the sight in her right eye had not been restored in any degree by the surgery, the respondent was thus almost totally blind.

In the proceedings commenced by the respondent, numerous heads of negligence were alleged. Campbell J rejected all save the allegation that the appellant's failure to warn of the risk of sympathetic ophthalmia was negligent and resulted in the respondent's condition. While his Honour was not satisfied that proper medical practice required that the appellant warn the respondent of the risk of sympathetic ophthalmia if she expressed no desire for information, he concluded that a warning was necessary in the light of her desire for such relevant information. The Court of Appeal (Mahoney, Priestley and Handley JJA) dismissed all grounds of the appellant's appeal from the judgment of $808,564.38 on both liability and damages, the Court also dismissed a cross-appeal by the respondent on the question of general damages. The respondent does not pursue the latter issue in this Court but the appellant has appealed on the questions of breach of duty and causation.

Breach of duty

Neither before the Court of Appeal nor before this Court was there any dispute as to the existence of a duty of care on the part of the appellant to the respondent. The law imposes on a medical practitioner a duty to exercise reasonable care and skill in the provision of professional advice and treatment. That duty is a 'single comprehensive duty covering all the ways in which a doctor is called upon to exercise his skill and judgment' [*Sidaway v Governors of Bethlem Royal Hospital* [1985] AC 871 per Lord Diplock at 893]; it extends to the examination, diagnosis and treatment of the patient and the provision of information in an appropriate case. It is of course necessary to give content to the duty in the given case.

The standard of reasonable care and skill required is that of the ordinary skilled person exercising and professing to have that special skill [*Bolam*], in this case the skill of an ophthalmic surgeon specializing in corneal and anterior segment surgery. As we have stated, the failure of the appellant to observe this standard, which the respondent successfully alleged before the primary judge, consisted of the appellant's failure to acquaint the respondent with the danger of sympathetic ophthalmia as a possible result of the surgical procedure to be carried out. The appellant's evidence was that 'sympathetic ophthalmia was not something that came to my mind to mention to her'.

The principal issue in this case related to the scope and content of the appellant's duty of care; did the appellant's failure to advise and warn the respondent of the risks inherent in the operation constitute a beach of this duty? The appellant argues that this issue should be resolved by application of the so-called *Bolam* principle, derived from the direction given by McNair J to the jury in the case of *Bolam v Friern Hospital Management Committee*. . . .

Before the primary judge there was evidence from a body of reputable medical practitioners that, in the circumstances of the present case, they would not have warned the respondent of the danger of sympathetic ophthalmia; there was also, however, evidence from similarly reputable medical practitioners that they would have given such a warning. The respondent, for her part, argues that the *Bolam* principle should not be applied if it entails courts deferring to the medical experts in medical negligence cases and that, in any event, the primary judge was correct in the circumstances of this case in not deferring to the views of those medical practitioners who gave evidence that they would not have warned the respondent . . .

In *Sidaway*, the House of Lords considered whether the *Bolam* principle should be applied in cases of alleged negligence in providing information and advice relevant to medical treatment. . . .

As the speeches in the House of Lords make clear, the action was destined to fail because there was no reliable evidence in support of the plaintiff's central pleading that the surgeon had given no advice or warning. Nevertheless, the majority of the Court (Lord Scarman dissenting) held that the question whether an omission to warn a patient of inherent risks of proposed treatment constituted a breach of a doctor's duty of care was to be determined by applying the *Bolam* principle. However, the members of the majority took different views of the *Bolam* principle. Lord Diplock gave the principle a wide application; he concluded that, as a decision as to which risks the plaintiff should be warned of was as much an exercise of professional skill and judgment as any other part of the doctor's comprehensive duty of care to the individual patient, expert evidence on this matter should be treated in just the same way as expert evidence on appropriate medical treatment. Lord Bridge of Harwich (with whom Lord Keith of Kinkel agreed) accepted that the issue was 'to be decided primarily on the basis of expert medical evidence, applying the *Bolam* test' but concluded that, irrespective of the existence of a responsible body of medical opinion which approved of non-disclosure in a particular case, a trial judge might in certain circumstances come to the conclusion that disclosure of a particular risk was so obviously necessary to an informed choice on the part of the patient that no reasonably prudent medical practitioner would fail to make it. Lord Templeman appeared even less inclined to allow medical opinion to determine this issue. He stated:

> [T]he Court must decide whether the information afforded to the patient was sufficient to alert the patient to the possibility of serious harm of the kind in fact suffered.

However, at the same time, his Lordship gave quite substantial scope to a doctor to decide that providing all available information to a patient would be inconsistent with the doctor's obligation to have regard to the patient's best interests. This is the doctor's so-called therapeutic privilege, an opportunity afforded to the doctor to prove that he or she reasonably believed that disclosure of a risk would prove damaging to a patient.

In dissent, Lord Scarman refused to apply the *Bolam* principle to cases involving the provision of advice or information . . .

His Lordship referred to American authorities, such as the decision of the United States Court of Appeals, District of Columbia Circuit, in *Canterbury v Spence*, and to the decision of the Supreme Court of Canada in *Reibl v Hughes*, which held that the 'duty to warn' arises from the patient's right to know of material risks, a right which in turn arises from the patient's right to decide for himself or herself whether or not to submit to the medical treatment proposed.

One consequence of the application of the *Bolam* principle to cases involving the provision of advice or information is that, even if a patient asks a direct question about the possible risks or complications, the making of that inquiry would logically be of little or no significance; medical opinion determines whether the risk should or should not be disclosed and the express desire of a particular patient for information or advice does not alter that opinion or the legal significance of that opinion. The fact that the various majority opinions in *Sidaway*, for example, suggest that, over and above the opinion of a respectable body of medical practitioners, the questions of a patient should truthfully be answered (subject to the therapeutic privilege) indicates a shortcoming in the *Bolam* approach. The existence of the shortcoming suggests that an acceptable approach in point of principle should recognize and attach significance to the relevance of a patient's questions. Even if a court were satisfied that a reasonable person in the patient's position would be unlikely to attach significance to a particular risk, the fact that the patient asked questions revealing concern about the risk would make the doctor aware that *this patient* did in fact attach significance to the risk. Subject to the therapeutic privilege, the question would therefore require a truthful answer.

In Australia, it has been accepted that the standard of care to be observed by a person with some special skill or competence is that of the ordinary skilled person exercising and professing to have that special skill. But, that standard is not determined solely or even primarily by reference to the practice followed or supported by a responsible body of opinion in the relevant profession or trade. Even in the sphere of diagnosis and treatment, the heartland of the skilled medical practitioner, the *Bolam* principle has not always been applied. Further, and more importantly, particularly in the field on non-disclosure of risk and the provision of advice and information, the *Bolam* principle has been discarded and, instead, the courts have adopted the principle that, while evidence of acceptable medical practice is a useful guide for the courts, it is for the courts to adjudicate on what is the appropriate standard of care after giving weight to 'the paramount consideration that a person is entitled to make his own decisions about his life'.

In *F v R* [(1983) 33 SASR 189], which was decided by the Full Court of the Supreme Court of South Australia two years before *Sidaway* in the House of Lords, a woman who had become pregnant after an unsuccessful tubal ligation brought an action in negligence alleging failure by the medical practitioner to warn her of the failure rate of the procedure. The failure rate was assessed at less than 1 per cent for that particular form of sterilization. The Court refused to apply the *Bolam* principle. King CJ said:

> The ultimate question, however, is not whether the defendant's conduct accords with the practices of his profession or some part of it, but whether it conforms to the standard of reasonable care demanded by the law. That is a question for the court and the duty of deciding it cannot be delegated to any profession or group in the community.

King CJ considered that the amount of information or advice which a careful and responsible doctor would disclose depended upon a complex of factors: the nature of the matter to be disclosed; the nature of the treatment; the desire of the patient for information; the temperament and health of the patient; and the general surrounding circumstances. His Honour agreed with the following passage from the judgment of the Supreme Court of Canada in *Reibl v Hughes*:

> To allow expert medical evidence to determine what risks are material and, hence, should be disclosed and, correlatively, what risks are not material is to hand over to the medical profession the entire question of the scope of the duty of disclosure, including the question whether there has been a breach of that duty. Expert medical evidence is, of course, relevant to findings as to the risks that reside in or are a result of recommended surgery or other treatment. It will also have a bearing on their materiality but this is not a question that is to be concluded on the basis of the expert medical evidence alone. The issue under consideration is a different issue from that involved where the question is whether the doctor carried out his professional activities by applicable professional standards. What is under consideration here is the patient's right to know what risks are involved in undergoing or foregoing certain surgery or other treatment.

The approach adopted by King CJ is similar to that subsequently taken by Lord Scarman in *Sidaway* and has been followed in subsequent cases. In our view, it is correct.

Acceptance of this approach does not entail an artificial division or itemization of specific, individual duties, carved out of the overall duty of care. The duty of a medical practitioner to exercise reasonable care and skill in the provision of professional advice and treatment is a single comprehensive duty. However, the factors according to which a court determines whether a medical practitioner is in breach of the requisite standard of care will vary according to whether it is a case involving diagnosis, treatment or the provision of information or advice; the different cases raise varying difficulties which require consideration of different factors. Examination of the nature of a doctor-patient relationship compels this conclusion. There is a fundamental difference between, on the one hand, diagnosis and treatment and, on the other hand, the provision of advice or information to a patient.

In diagnosis and treatment, the patient's contribution is limited to the narration of symptoms and relevant history; the medical practitioner provides diagnosis and treatment according to his or her level of skill. However, except in cases of emergency or necessity, all medical treatment is preceded by the patient's choice to undergo it. In legal terms, the patient's consent to the treatment may be valid once he or she is informed in broad terms of the nature of the procedure which is intended. But the choice is, in reality, meaningless unless it is made on the basis of relevant information and advice. Because the choice to be made calls for a decision by the patient on information known to the medical practitioner but not to the patient, it would be illogical to hold that the amount of information to be provided by the medical practitioner can be determined from the perspective of the practitioner alone or, for that matter, of the medical profession. *Whether* a medical practitioner carries out a particular form of treatment in accordance with the appropriate standard of care is a question in the resolution of which responsible professional opinion will have an influential, often a decisive, role to play; *whether* the patient has been given all the relevant information to choose between undergoing and not undergoing the treatment is a question of a different order. Generally speaking, it is not a question the answer to which depends upon medical standards or practices. Except in those cases where there is a particular danger that the provision of all relevant information will harm an unusually nervous, disturbed or volatile patient, no special medical skill is involved in disclosing the information, including the risks attending the proposed treatment. Rather, the skill is in communicating the relevant information to the patient in terms which are reasonably adequate for that purpose having regard to the patient's apprehended capacity to understand that information.

In this context, nothing is to be gained by reiterating the expressions used in American authorities, such as 'the patient's right of self-determination' or even the oft-used and somewhat amorphous phrase 'informed consent'. The right of self-determination is an expression which is, perhaps, suitable to cases where the issue is whether a person has agreed to the general surgical procedure or treatment, but is of little assistance in the balancing process that is involved in the determination of whether there has been a breach of the duty of disclosure. Likewise, the phrase 'informed consent' is apt to mislead as it suggests a test of the validity of a patient's consent. Moreover, consent is relevant to actions framed in trespass, not in negligence. Anglo-Australian law has rightly taken the view that an allegation that the risks inherent in a medical procedure have not been disclosed to the patient can only found an action in negligence and not in trespass; the consent necessary to negative the offence of battery is satisfied by the patient being advised in broad terms of the nature of the procedure to be performed. In *Reibl v Hughes* the Supreme Court of Canada was cautious in its use of the term 'informed consent'.

We agree that the factors referred to in *F v R* by King CJ must all be considered by a medical practitioner in deciding whether to disclose or advise of some risk in a proposed procedure. The law should recognize that a doctor has a duty to warn a patient of a material risk inherent in the proposed treatment; a risk is material if, in the circumstances of the particular case, a reasonable person in the patient's position, if warned of the risk, would be likely to attach significance to it or if the medical practitioner is or should reasonably be aware that the particular patient, if warned of the risk, would be likely to attach significance to it. This duty is subject to the therapeutic privilege.

The appellant in this case was treating and advising a woman who was almost totally blind in one eye. As with all surgical procedures, the operation recommended by the appellant to the respondent involved various risks, such as retinal detachment and haemorrhage infection, both of which are more common than sympathetic ophthalmia, but sympathetic ophthalmia was the only danger whereby both eyes might be rendered sightless. Experts for both parties described it as a devastating disability, the appellant acknowledging that, except for death under anaesthetic, it was the worst possible outcome for the respondent. According to the findings of the trial judge, the respondent 'incessantly' questioned the appellant as to, amongst other things, possible complications. She was, to the appellant's knowledge, keenly interested in the outcome of the suggested procedure, including the danger of unintended or accidental interference with her 'good', left eye. On the day before the operation, the respondent asked the appellant whether something could be put over her good eye to ensure that nothing happened to it; an entry was made in the hospital notes to the effect that she was apprehensive that the wrong eye would be operated on. She did not, however, ask a specific question as to whether the operation on her right eye could affect her left eye.

The evidence established that there was a body of opinion in the medical profession at the time which considered that an inquiry should only have elicited a reply dealing with sympathetic ophthalmia if specifically directed to the possibility of the left eye being affected by the operation on the right eye. While the opinion that the respondent should have been told of the dangers of sympathetic ophthalmia only if she had been sufficiently learned to ask the precise question seems curious, it is unnecessary for us to examine it further, save to say that it demonstrates vividly the dangers of applying the *Bolam* principle in the area of advice and information. The respondent may not have asked the right question, yet she made clear her great concern that no injury should befall her one good eye. The trial judge was not satisfied that, if the respondent had expressed no desire for information, proper practice required that the respondent be warned of the relevant risk. But it could be argued, within the terms of the relevant principle as we have stated it, that the risk was material, in the sense that a reasonable person in the patient's position would be likely to attach significance to the risk, and thus required a warning. It would be reasonable for a person with one good eye to be concerned about the possibility of injury to it from a procedure which was elective. However, the respondent did not challenge on appeal that particular finding.

For these reasons, we would reject the appellant's argument on the issue of breach of duty. . . .

For the foregoing reasons, we would dismiss the appeal.

Gaudron J: There is no difficulty in analysing the duty of care of medical practitioners on the basis of a 'single comprehensive duty' covering diagnosis, treatment and the provision of information and advice, provided that it is stated in terms of sufficient generality. Thus, the general duty may be stated as a duty to exercise reasonable professional skill and judgment. But the difficulty with that approach is that a statement of that kind says practically nothing – certainly, nothing worthwhile – as to the content of the duty. And it fails to take account of the considerable conceptual and practical differences between diagnosis and treatment, on the one hand, and the provision of information and advice, on the other.

The duty involved in diagnosis and treatment is to exercise the ordinary skill of a doctor practising in the area concerned. To ascertain the precise content of this duty in any particular case it is necessary to determine, amongst other issues, what, in the circumstances, constitutes reasonable care and what constitutes ordinary skill in the relevant area of medical practice. These are issues which necessarily direct attention to the practice or practices of medical practitioners. And, of course, the current state of medical knowledge will often be relevant in determining the nature of the risk which is said to attract the precise duty in question, including the foreseeability of that risk.

The matters to which reference has been made indicate that the evidence of medical practitioners is of very considerable significance in cases where negligence is alleged in diagnosis or treatment. However, even in cases of that kind, the nature of particular risks and their foreseeability are not matters exclusively within the province of medical knowledge or expertise. Indeed, and notwithstanding that these questions arise in a medical context, they are often matters of simple commonsense. And, at least in some situations, questions as to the reasonableness of particular precautionary measures are also matters of commonsense. Accordingly, even in the area of diagnosis and treatment there is, in my view, no legal basis for limiting liability in terms of the rule known as 'the *Bolam* test' which is to the effect that a doctor is not guilty of negligence if he or she acts in accordance with a practice accepted as proper by a responsible body of doctors skilled in the relevant field of practice. That is not to deny that, having regard to the onus of proof, 'the *Bolam* test' may be a convenient statement of the approach dictated by the state of the evidence in some cases. As such, it may have some utility as a rule-of-thumb in some jury cases, but it can serve no other useful function.

Diagnosis and treatment are but particular duties which arise in the doctor-patient relationship. That relationship also gives rise to a duty to provide information and advice. That duty takes its precise content, in terms of the nature and detail of the information to be provided, from the needs, concerns and circumstances of the patient. A patient may have special needs or concerns which, if known to the doctor, will indicate that special or additional information is required. In a case of that kind, the information to be provided will depend on the individual patient concerned. In other cases, where, for example, no specific inquiry is made, the duty is to provide the information that would reasonably be required by a person in the position of the patient.

Whether the position is considered from the perspective of the individual patient or from that of the hypothetical prudent patient and unless there is some medical emergency or something special about the circumstances of the patient, there is simply no occasion to consider the practice or practices of medical practitioners in determining what information should be supplied. However, there is some scope for a consideration of those practices where the question is whether, by reason of emergency or the special circumstances of the patient, there is no immediate duty or its content is different from that which would ordinarily be the case.

Leaving aside cases involving an emergency or circumstances which are special to the patient, the duty of disclosure which arises out of the doctor-patient relationship extends, at the very least, to information that is relevant to a decision or course of action which is taken or pursued, entails a risk of the kind that would, in other cases, found a duty to warn. A risk is one of that kind if it is real and foreseeable, but not if it is 'far-fetched or fanciful'. Certainly, the duty to warn extends to risks of that kind involved in the treatment or procedures proposed.

Although on the facts the plaintiff's questioning of her doctor was of central importance, the High Court makes it clear that their judgment is concerned with the doctor's duty to disclose information as a matter of general principle. As to the precise nature of the duty it appears clear that the court adopts the 'reasonable patient' test paying due regard to the circumstances of the particular patient. On one reading, the court could be said to have gone further and endorsed, albeit elliptically, the 'particular patient' test rejected by Lord Scarman in *Sidaway*. The joint judgment stated:

A risk is material if in the circumstances of the particular case, a reasonable person in the patient's position, if warned of the risk, would be likely to attach significance to it *or* if the medical practitioner is or should reasonably be aware that the particular patient, if warned of the risk, would be likely to attach significance to it [our emphasis].

It all depends upon the meaning of 'or'. An alternative interpretation would be that the court is merely stating 'the reasonable patient' test in alternative forms. As can be seen, the Australian High Court's decision represents another common law jurisdiction's emphatic rejection of *Bolam* and its application in *Sidaway*. It must now only be a matter of time before English law adopts the 'reasonable patient' test. The often expressed fears of the courts as to what would follow the adoption of the 'reasonable patient' test would seem to be ill-founded. For example, there is no evidence in Canada that following *Reibl* the floodgates opened and the courts were swamped with cases alleging breaches of a doctor's duty to disclose. Indeed, Professor Robertson, in a careful empirical study of the cases in Canada involving informed consent since *Reibl*, shows that there were only 117 in the following ten years throughout Canada (excluding Quebec), half of them unreported. Moreover, the plaintiff failed in his action in 82% of the cases in which he relied upon a breach of duty to disclose (Robertson, 'Informed Consent Ten Years Later: The Impact of *Reibl v Hughes*' (1991) 70 Canadian Bar Review 423). Significantly, in only 13 of the 117 cases (ie about 11%) did the plaintiff rely *solely* upon an alleged failure to disclose information. Thus, although the importance of the legal development in *Reibl* and *Rogers* cannot be overstated its effect on litigation (rather than on the practice of medicine) is minimal (see, Robertson, 'Informed Consent in Canada: An Empirical Study' (1984) 22 Osgoode Hall LJ 139).

Equally, the concern expressed by the House of Lords in *Sidaway*, particularly by Lord Bridge, that the adoption of the 'reasonable patient' test would mean that the courts could not hear medical evidence and take proper account of medical practice has been shown to be unfounded. Medical evidence remains of relevance, as Lord Scarman pointed out in *Sidaway*. Indeed, it must be determinative of the factual questions of what risks and alternatives exist. Furthermore, it remains of significant persuasive importance when the court comes to decide whether a breach of duty has been established. Finally, if the 'reasonable patient' test is accompanied by an exception based upon the 'therapeutic privilege' (see below), medical evidence again becomes crucial.

In predicting the eventual abandonment of the *Bolam* approach and *Sidaway* in the context of duty to disclose, account must be taken of a recent development crafted by the Canadian Supreme Court which may offer an alternative and even more radical analysis of the doctor-patient relationship and the duties following therefrom. We refer to the characterisation of the duty owed by a doctor to his patient as being a *fiduciary* duty. If adopted in England it could extend the doctor's duty to disclose information even beyond that contemplated by the 'reasonable patient' test quite apart from its impact on the other aspects of the doctor's duty to his patient. If English law wishes to resist this far-reaching development, English law may well have to concede the validity of the less radical approach in *Reibl* and *Rogers*.

Norberg v Wynrib (1992) 92 DLR (4th) 449 (Can Sup Ct)

A doctor supplied drugs (Fiorinal) to a female patient, after he discovered she was addicted, in exchange for sexual favours, including simulated sexual intercourse. The patient brought an action for damages against the doctor for the tort of battery (sexual assault), negligence and breach of fiduciary duty.

The British Columbia Supreme Court dismissed the sexual assault claim on the ground that the patient consented. The trial judge dismissed the negligence action, because although the doctor breached his duty to the patient by continuing to prescribe drugs to an addict, the patient was not injured by this conduct. The trial judge dismissed the breach of fiduciary duty claim on the bases of ex turpi causa non oritur actio, where both parties voluntarily participated in an illicit relationship. The patient appealed.

The British Columbia Court of Appeal, Locke JA dissenting, dismissed the appeal. The trial judge was correct in dismissing the sexual assault claim on the basis of consent. The court also rejected the claim of breach of fiduciary duty. The court agreed that the doctor breached his duty of care to the patient, but the damage claim was barred by the application of the maxim ex turpi causa non oritur actio. Locke JA agreed that the claims in battery and fiduciary duty failed, but would have awarded $1,000 nominal damages for breach of duty, because the maxim ex turpi causa non oritur actio did not apply. The patient appealed.

The Supreme Court of Canada allowed the appeal. La Forest J (Gonthier and Cory JJ concurring), found the doctor liable solely under the tort of battery (sexual assault) on the ground that the consent was ineffective and the maxim ex turpi causa non oritur actio did not bar relief.

McLachlin J (L'Heureux-Dubé J concurring), found the doctor liable for breaching his fiduciary duty to his patient.

Sopikna J found the doctor liable for breaching his duty to treat the patient arising out of the doctor-patient relationship. Sopinka J agreed that the battery claim failed because of consent.

For us the important judgment is that of McLachlin J (with whom L'Heureux-Dubé J agreed) relying on the unanimous decision of the court in *McInerney v MacDonald* (1992) 93 DLR (4th) 415 (discussed *infra* ch 8).

McLachlin J: Perhaps the most fundamental characteristic of the doctor-patient relationship is its fiduciary nature. All the authorities agree that the relationship of physician to patient also falls into that special category of relationships which the law calls fiduciary.

The recent judgment of La Forest, J, in *McInerney v MacDonald* (1992) 137 NR 35 (SCC), at pp 46 and 47, a case recognizing a patient's right of access to her medical records, canvasses those authorities and confirms the fiduciary nature of the doctor-patient relationship. I can do no better than to quote the following passage from his judgment:

> A physician begins compiling a medical file when a patient chooses to share intimate details about his or her life in the course of medical consultation. The patient 'entrusts' this personal information to the physician for medical purposes. It is important to keep in mind the nature of the physician-patient relationship within which the information is confided. In *Kenny v Lockwood*, [1932] OR 141 (CA), Hodgins JA stated, at p 155, that the relationship between physician and patient is one in which 'trust and confidence' must be placed in the physician. This statement was referred to with approval by LeBel J in *Henderson v Johnston* [1956] OR 789, who himself characterized the physician-patient relationship as 'fiduciary and confidential', and went on to say: 'It is the same relationship as that which exists in equity between a parent and his child, a man and his wife, an attorney and his client, a confessor and his penitent, and a guardian and his ward' (p 799). Several academic writers have similarly defined the physician-patient relationship as a fiduciary or trust relationship: see, for example, E I Picard, *Legal Liability of Doctors and Hospitals in Canada* (2nd ed. 1984), at p 3; A Hopper, *The Medical Man's Fiduciary Duty* (1939), 7 Law Teacher 73; A J Meaghers, P J Marr & R A Meagher, *Doctors and Hospitals: Legal Duties* (1991), at p 2; M V Ellis *Fiduciary Duties in Canada* (1988), at pp 10-11. I agree with this characterization.

So do I. I think it is readily apparent that the doctor-patient relationship shares the peculiar hallmark of the fiduciary relationship – trust, the trust of a person with inferior power that another person who has assumed superior power and responsibility will exercise that power for his or her good and only for his or her good and in his or her best interests. Recognizing the fiduciary nature of the doctor-patient relationship provided the law with an analytic model by which physicians can be held to high standards of dealing with their patients which the trust accorded them requires. . . .

The foundation and ambit of the fiduciary obligations are conceptually distinct from the foundation and ambit of contract and tort. Sometimes the doctrines may overlap in their application, but that does not destroy their conceptual and functional uniqueness. In negligence and contract the parties are taken to be independent and equal actors, concerned primarily with their own self-interest. Consequently, the law seeks a balance between enforcing obligations by awarding compensation when those obligations are breached, and preserving optimum freedom for those involved in the relationship in question. The essence of a fiduciary relationship, by contract, is that one party exercises power on behalf of another and pledges himself or herself to act in the best interests of the other. . . .

The fiduciary relationship has trust, not self-interest, as its core, and when breach occurs, the balance favours the person wronged. The freedom of the fiduciary is limited by the obligation he or she has undertaken – an obligation which 'betokens loyalty, good faith and avoidance of a conflict of duty and self-interest'. *Canadian Aero Services Ltd v O'Malley*, [1974] SCR 592 at p 606. . . .

Wilson J in *Frame v Smith and Smith* [1987] 2 SCR 99 . . . attributed the following characteristics to a fiduciary relationship: '(1) the fiduciary has scope for the exercise of some discretion or power; (2) the fiduciary can unilaterally exercise that power or discretion so as to affect the beneficiary's legal or practical interests; and (3) the beneficiary is peculiarly vulnerable or at the mercy of the fiduciary holding the discretion or power.'

(iv) DISCLOSING ALTERNATIVES

You will recall that the House of Lords in *Sidaway* spoke of the doctor's duty to disclose only in terms of a duty to disclose risks. None of their Lordships referred to any concomitant duty to advise patients of alternatives to any contemplated treatment, including the alternative not to be treated at all. That this should be an intrinsic element in the duty to disclose is beyond doubt. As a matter of principle if it is intended to empower the patient by informing him, knowledge of alternatives may well be as significant as knowledge of risks. This being so, the courts must regard the types or classes of information that form part of the duty to disclose as a matter of law for them. Of course, while *Bolam* prevails it will largely (wholly?) be a matter of medical evidence whether in a particular case a doctor has breached his duty (see, eg, *Gold v Haringey HA* [1987] 2 All ER 888).

The Canadian case of *Haughian v Paine* (1987) 37 DLR (4th) 624 (Sask CA) illustrates that the doctor's duty extends in principle to disclose alternative forms of treatment. There, a failure to advise a patient that a more conservative treatment was available than that advocated by the doctor was held by the Saskatchewan Court of Appeal to be a breach of the doctor's duty to the patient. The Californian case of *Truman v Thomas* (1980) 611 P 2d 902 (Cal Sup Ct) illustrates that, again in principle, the doctor's duty may extend to advising the patient of non-treatment (and its dangers). There, the California Supreme Court found that a failure to advise a female patient of the consequences of refusing a pap smear could constitute a breach of duty by the doctor, when she subsequently died from cancer of the cervix.

(b) Duty to answer questions

Hatcher v Black (1954) Times, 2 July (QBD)

Mrs Hatcher was a lady who occasionally broadcast for the BBC. She went into St Bartholomew's Hospital suffering from a toxic thyroid gland. An operation was advised. She asked if there was any risk to her voice. She was reassured by the doctors. The operation was performed. In the course of it, the nerve was so badly damaged that she could not speak properly. She could not broadcast again. Mrs Hatcher had asked her doctor whether there was any risk to her voice.

Denning LJ: What should the doctor tell his patient? Mr Tuckwell admitted that on the evening before the operation he told the plaintiff that there was no risk to her voice, when he knew that there was some slight risk, but that he did it for her own good because it was of vital importance that she should not worry. In short, he told a lie, but he did it because he thought in the circumstances it was justifiable. If this were a court of morals, that would raise a nice question on which moralists and theologians have differed for centuries. Some hold that it is never permissible to tell a lie even for a just cause: a good end, they say, does not justify a bad means. You must not do a little wrong in order to do a great right. Others, however, hold that it is permissible, if the justification is strong enough, and they point to the stratagems used in war to deceive the enemy. This, however, is not a court of morals but a court of law, and the law leaves this question of morals to the conscience of the doctor himself – though I may perhaps remark that if doctors have too easy a conscience on this matter they may in time lose the confidence of the patient, which is the basis of all good medicine. But so far as the law is concerned, it does not condemn the doctor when he only does that which many a wise and good doctor so placed would do. It only condemns him when he falls short of the accepted standards of a great profession: in short, when he is deserving of censure. Not one of the doctors that have been called before you has suggested that Mr Tuckwell did wrong. All agree that it was a matter for his own judgment. They did not condemn him; nor should we.

This case was, of course, decided in 1954. It might be thought that social attitudes and therefore the law have changed since then. In the *Sidaway* case it was stated (*obiter*) that the doctor has a duty both to answer questions and to do so truthfully.

Lord Bridge: When questioned specifically by a patient of apparently sound mind about risks involved in a particular treatment proposed, the doctor's duty must, in my opinion, be to answer both truthfully and as fully as the questioner requires.

Lords Diplock and Templeman agreed. Notice that Lord Bridge recognises the touchstone of the duty as being to answer 'fully'. What does 'fully' mean? For a long time the leading case was *Smith v Auckland Hospital Board* [1965] NZLR 191.

Smith v Auckland Hospital Board [1965] NZLR 191 (NZ CA)

The appellant had entered the respondent board's hospital at Green Lane, Auckland, for an examination, and, if necessary, for surgical treatment for a suspected aortic aneurism. In the course of the proper preliminary investigations he was subjected to a procedure known as aortography, wherein a catheter is inserted into the femoral artery and guided upwards through the arterial passage towards the aorta, into which ultimately an opaque fluid is injected through the catheter, enabling the aorta to be outlined satisfactorily for the proposes of X-ray photography. In the course of this procedure the appellant suffered a surgical mishap through the catheter accidentally dislodging a plaque of atheromatous material from the interior wall of the artery. A condition of clotting supervened, and notwithstanding all due efforts by the surgeons, the appellant's right leg degenerated into a gangrenous condition and ultimately had to be amputated below the knee. Negligence was pleaded in a number of respects, but the jury found for the defence on all issues of negligence alleged in respect of the conduct of the aortogram procedure on the part of the operating radiographer or any members of his team. But it was also alleged that, the risk of the mishap being a reasonably foreseeable one, albeit in only a low percentage of cases, it should have been the subject of a warning to the patient in the circumstances of this case; for the appellant gave evidence, which was uncontradicted, that he had made a specific inquiry as to the risk involved in the procedure, and alleged that the answer given was equivalent to an assurance that there was none. It was contended on his behalf that these facts gave rise to a cause of action in negligence, and an issue was put to the jury accordingly in these terms:

Was the defendant by its servants or agents negligent so as to involve the plaintiff in the loss of his leg in . . . (d), failing to inform the plaintiff adequately of the risks of conducting a femoral aortogram upon him?

to which the jury answered 'Yes'.

Woodhouse J, on an application by the respondent for judgment for the defendant *non obstante veredicto*, upheld the respondent's submissions, and gave judgment for it notwithstanding the jury's finding, holding that there was no evidence on which the jury could find any breach of duty, and alternatively that, even if there had been such evidence, the answer given by the surgeon could not reasonably be found causative of the damage suffered by the appellant. Both these conclusions were attacked in the appeal. Gresson J in the New Zealand Court of Appeal examined what the duty of the doctor was when asked the question 'is there any risk?'

Gresson J: In these circumstances either a refusal to answer at all, which would have carried its own clear implications, or a suggested reference back to Mr Barratt-Boyes, or an honest and reasonably complete and accurate answer was required, and the circumstances did not warrant – as they sometimes may do – *a suppressio veri . . .* Here again the distinction lies in the fact that Mr Windsor did not reply to the appellant's question in accordance with what other competent medical men stated was their practice in a similar situation. After all, it was the appellant's prerogative to decide for himself whether he would submit to the proposed procedures, and this placed the doctor under a duty to give a careful and reasonably accurate reply to the appellant's direct inquiry as to the risk involved.

Two comments can be made. First, that Gresson J considers that the duty is, in part, at least, determined by reference to the practice of reasonable doctors and secondly, that this might allow for a range of answers from the *wholly* truthful to the partially truthful to the somewhat deceptive to the '*suppressio veri*'. In the Canadian case of *Hopp v Lepp* (1980) 112 DLR (3d) 67, Laskin CJ found otherwise.

Apart from situations of this kind, a surgeon need not go into every conceivable detail of a proposed operation so long as he describes its nature, unless the patient asks specific questions not by way of merely general inquiry, and, if so, those questions must be answered, although they invite answers to merely possible risks. If no specific questions are put as to possible risks, the surgeon is under no obligation (although he may do so) to tell the patient that there are possible risks since there are such risks in any operation. It becomes a question of fact of how specific are any questions that are put.

Hopp v Lepp may be reconciled with *Smith* on the basis that in *Smith* the question asked was a '*general*' question and not a '*specific*' one. *Hopp v Lepp* would suggest that where the question is *specific* the doctor has no discretion but to answer and tell the truth. It could be said, therefore, that 'fully' (per Lord Bridge) must mean what Laskin CJ sets out in *Hopp* when the question is *specific*. But can 'fully' be what Gresson J states when the question is a general one? Given that Gresson J contemplates '*suppressio veri*' as a permissible response, it would appear not. It may be, therefore, that Lord Bridge's definition of the doctor's duty, ie that he must answer truthfully and fully (as we have defined it), must be understood as applying to all cases where it is clear to the doctor that the patient is expressly seeking information whether the question be general *or* specific. *How* the doctor will respond will depend upon the content of the question. A hard and fast distinction between general and specific questions is consequently unhelpful.

There is some suggestion that a doctor may be justified in withholding information (or perhaps in not telling the truth) when to do so could reasonably be regarded as injurious to his patient's health, applying in effect the doctrine of therapeutic privilege (see later).

Lee v South West Thames Regional Health Authority [1985] 2 All ER 385 (CA)

Sir John Donaldson MR: The recent decision of the House of Lords in *Sidaway v Bethlem Royal Hospital Governors* [1985] AC 871, [1985] 1 All ER 643 affirms that a doctor is under a duty to answer his patient's questions as to the treatment proposed. . . . This duty is subject to the exercise of clinical judgment as to the terms in which the information is given and the extent to which, in the patient's interests, information should be withheld.

It may be open to question whether leaving the doctor with this discretion is either ethical or should properly be the law. However, when the issue of answering questions arose immediately after *Sidaway*, the Court of Appeal took a surprising stance.

Blyth v Bloomsbury Health Authority [1993] 4 Med LR 151 (CA)

Kerr LJ: This is an appeal by the defendant health authority against part of a judgment given by Mr Justice Leonard on 23rd May 1985 after a trial lasting some 10 days. The action had been brought by the plaintiff, Mrs Blyth, against ... the health authority on the ground that negligent advice or information had been given to the plaintiff in December 1978 by a member of staff of University College Hospital ('UCH') in relation to a contraceptive drug called Depo-Provera, which was then injected and had allegedly caused the plaintiff unpleasant side effects after her discharge from the hospital.

The plaintiff, Mrs Blyth, qualified as a nurse in New Zealand. She came here in 1973 and began to take a contraceptive called Minilyn, which caused her considerable problems. It was a combined pill, containing oestrogen and progesterone, and she subsequently gave it up.

She returned to New Zealand in 1975 to nurse her mother, who was unfortunately ill with cancer and died in November of that year. In 1976 she married and returned here; and in 1977 she began to work as a health worker in Hackney. In 1978 she became pregnant, and in May of that year she was referred to UCH for ante-natal care.

In that connection she saw a Miss Aileen Dickins, a consultant at UCH, who gave evidence at this trial. It was then established that she had no, or insufficient immunity to rubella, but fortunately this had no adverse effects on the subsequent history.

However, two consequences followed. First, although it was of course too late to vaccinate her against rubella at that stage of her pregnancy, it was necessary to do so after the birth of her baby in order to protect her and the baby against the risk of infection. Secondly, since the vaccine could itself cause adverse symptoms to a foetus if she were to become pregnant again within three months, it was necessary that she should have some contraceptive protection during this period, since that was certainly her wish.

The general practice at UCH in that regard at that time was to use Depo-Provera for this purpose in many cases unless there were countervailing factors, or the patient did not want it. The judge found that since 1975, when the drug was introduced, it had been administered to about 100 patients a year.

In the result, when Mrs Blyth was admitted to UCH in December 1978 for the birth of her baby, she received (i) a vaccination against rubella and (ii) an injection of the contraceptive Depo-Provera, which was designed to provide her with contraceptive cover for three months. Depo-Provera was a progesterone-only contraceptive and it was therefore thought that it would not have the same adverse consequences for her as the Minilyn which she had used for some years previously.

It is important to bear in mind throughout that there is no complaint in this case about the prescription or administration of the rubella vaccine; nor of the prescription or administration of the Depo-Provera. An allegation to that effect about the latter drug was abandoned at the beginning of the trial.

The remaining complaints of the plaintiff can be summarised as follows: (1) She was insufficiently informed and advised about the possible side effects of Depo-Provera when she was in hospital, and the hospital staff were negligent in that respect. That is the issue raised on this appeal. (2) If she had been informed about the possible side effects more fully than she was, she would not have agreed to have the Depo-Provera injection. This was found by the judge and is not contested. (3) She suffered from manifold side effects, allegedly due to Depo-Provera, for which she claimed damages. All her allegations in that connection were rejected, with the exception of bleeding and menstrual irregularity. The judge held that on the balance of probability these consequences could be attributed to Depo-Provera for some time after her discharge, but that they had certainly disappeared by February 1980, and on one view by July 1979.

An appeal against the award of £3,500 general damages having been abandoned, we are therefore now only concerned with the first of the three issues which I have mentioned . . .

I must turn to certain parts of the pleadings. The amended statement of claim included the following paragraphs 6 to 9:

6. The Plaintiff agreed to have the said drug after being assured by Dr Burt, a member of the staff of the said hospital:

(a) that the only known side effects of Depo-Provera were occasional spotting and one or two irregular periods;

(b) that all effects contraceptive and otherwise ceased after 3/4 months;

(c) that the drug would not affect breast feeding or pass through to the baby.

7. The said assurances were wrong and inaccurate in the following respects:

(a) that the only known side effects of Depo-Provera included menstrual irregularity, bodyweight changes, mood changes, depression of sexual drive and changes to nails and hair, such side effects lasting for up to a year.

(b) It was known that Depo-Provera would be likely to pass in the milk but it was unknown what effects this would be likely to have on the baby.

8. The Plaintiff would not have agreed to administration of the said drug if she had been told of the possible side effects.

9. As a result of the said drugs the Plaintiff suffered menstrual irregularity, mood changes, loss of sexual drive, eczema, 'galacthorrea' – that is, over-production of milk – 'loss of sleep, loss of weight and hormonal changes including changes in her skin colour and texture, loss of hair, change in hair colour and reduced resistance to infection'.

As will be seen, virtually all of these allegations were rejected by the judge. The only symptoms which he accepted she had after discharge were irregular bleeding and menstruation.

In the particulars of negligence the plaintiff included an allegation that the defendants were negligent by '(iv) failing to answer the Plaintiff's enquiries concerning Depo-Provera accurately and of failing to obtain answers to her questions before attempting to give her the said assurances about the said drug'.

She was asked to supply further and better particulars of that allegation, as to the enquiries she had made, to whom they were addressed and full particulars of the answers that were given and that should have been given, and her reply was as follows:

The Plaintiff informed the Certified Midwife, Sister Nixon, and a Staff Midwife that she was not prepared to have an injection of Depo-Provera until she had discussed the possible consequences of such an injection with a Specialist. The first defendants arranged for Dr Burt to see the Plaintiff. The Plaintiff was able to put various questions to Dr Burt. The relevant questions and answers given by Dr Burt are recorded in the Plaintiff's diary, see under (b) below.

Then it gives the questions and answers as recorded by the plaintiff in her diary, as follows:

1. What is in the drug? A. Progesterone only.

2. Are there any side effects? A. Only occasional spotting.

and then she was asked: 'Does it affect breast feeding? Does it pass in the milk? Does it have an effect on the baby? Are there any known reactions or upsets in anyone at all? All those questions were answered with the word 'No'. 'How long does it take for all effects to wear off: (a) completely, (b) contraceptive, (c) side?', and the answer is: 'All effects completely over within three months.' Then: 'Does it upset periods? (A) Not after three to four months. How does Depo-Provera work in and on the body? (A) Prevention of ovulation.'

There was added: 'The plaintiff should have been told of the known possible side effects of the said drug.'

That alleged record of questions and answers in the plaintiff's diary was rejected by the judge . . . he said this at p 26D:

For reasons which are inherent in the passages I have cited, it seems to me important to consider whether the plaintiff asked the nursing and medical staff for information and advice about the drug or not. The plaintiff says that she asked the questions which are set out in her diary. The entry is headed 'For Tony' – that is her husband – 'tonight, re DP' – and an abbreviation for 'contraceptive'. In conjunction with the question as to whether the drug would affect breast-feeding the plaintiff has written in brackets '(intend 6/12' – that is six months – 'at least)'. I find an artificial flavour to those two entries, particularly the first, if all of the writing, with minor possible exceptions, was done at the same time as the plaintiff maintains. As I have already indicated, I do not regard it as in any way probable that Dr (Burt) would have answered the question in the form 'Any known reactions, upsets in anyone at all' with a simple negative. Moreover, I do not believe that a person with the plaintiff's professional training would in fact ask such a question. I therefore doubt the accuracy of the plaintiff's evidence as to how precisely the document came to be written. If she had really been writing the answers, or most of them, down at the time, I think that fact would have been sufficiently unusual to stick in Dr (Burt's) memory, but it does not.

That speaks for itself.

In an earlier part of his judgment he found the following facts about the discussions concerning Depo-Provera between the plaintiff and, first, Sister Nixon, and thereafter Dr Burt. At p 10C the judge said:

Sister Nixon is an experienced midwifery sister. I accept her evidence that she would not have withheld information about the titre reading if she had been asked (that was a reference to the degree of immunity to rubella).

It was she, of course, who administered both injections. She told me that it was her practice to tell the patient the possible side effects of Depo-Provera. She would have warned of spotting or irregular bleeding which might be light or heavy. If the patient had expressed concern about the injections, it would have been noted in the record and the vaccination would not have been carried out. If the patient requested further advice that would have been recorded and the appropriate arrangements made. The usual practice was to give the vaccine and the Depo-Provera consecutively. As in this case they were administered with an interval of two days the explanation might well be that the plaintiff had been offered the contraceptive injection, for example, by Dr Beatles but was not happy about it initially. Having seen Sister Nixon in the witness box, I am satisfied that she would not have tried to over-persuade the plaintiff into accepting the injection when she did not want it.

He then turns at p 10H to the important discussion about Depo-Provera which the plaintiff had with Dr Burt:

Dr Burt was practising in 1978 under her maiden name of Burt. She had qualified in 1974 and was fully registered in July 1975. She had obtained the Diploma of Child Health in 1977, and in 1981, of course subsequently to the events with which this case is concerned, she obtained her Membership of the Royal College of Obstetricians and Gynaecologists by examination. Membership is the senior qualification by examination given by the college. In 1978 Dr (Burt) was reading for that examination. She had previously held senior house office posts before becoming a senior house officer in obstetrics and gynaecology at University College Hospital on 1st December. It was in the context of this case that she first came across the use of Depo-Provera as a contraceptive, though she had some experience of it in the treatment of cancer. Although she has some memory of a patient who may have been the plaintiff, Dr (Burt) had to accept that she has no memory of events connected with her seeing the plaintiff, apart from what the record contains. This shows that she prescribed the Depo-Provera on 23rd December – that was the Saturday shortly before Christmas. She was then responsible for the obstetric wards and on call for the labour ward and the gynaecological emergencies. Her purpose in seeing the plaintiff was to check her condition prior to discharge. She thinks it was in the course of writing up her notes that she saw that the vaccine had been prescribed and, therefore, appreciated the need for advice that contraceptive action should be taken. The discharge sheet has a section which is headed 'Contraception'. It contains provision for recording whether advice has been requested or offered. That provision has not been used, but the doctor has simply recorded 'Depo-Provera to cover rubella vaccination'. She thought that her suggesting Depo-Provera came about because the sister said that it was often used in these circumstances. She would have referred to the data sheet compendium for the proper dosage and in order to see whether there was any other information which she ought to know. The compendium is a book which contains the manufacturer's information about various drugs. At this time the only relevant comment on side effects relating to a single (injection) was as follows: 'Clinically Depo-Provera is well tolerated. No significant untoward effects have been reported.' However, because of her reading, particularly in preparation for her membership examination, Dr (Burt) was aware that there might be a problem with irregular bleeding. It was her evidence that she would have told the patient of the need for contraception and would have discussed alternative methods. She would have described Depo-Provera as effective, and convenient, and having the appropriate duration of protection, that is to say 90 days. She would have said that it was in common use at the hospital. She would have warned that there might be the problem of irregular bleeding. She would not, she says, have used the word 'spotting' which is attributed to her by the plaintiff. She would have told the plaintiff that the drug was generally acceptable and had no serious or significant side effects. She might have added that progesterone was less associated with side effects than oestrogen and that it would have no adverse effects on the baby. If she had been asked the question postulated by the plaintiff 'Are there any known reactions or upsets in anyone at all?' she would have replied that there might be reactions of which she was not aware, and her answer would have been that she did not know. It was the plaintiff's evidence that she prepared a number of questions before she was seen by the doctor. They were recorded in a diary in which she wrote, at any rate, most of the answers as they were given. Dr (Burt) has no memory of this. The doctor accepted that the delay between the prescribing of the vaccine and the Depo-Provera suggests that there may have been some discussion about the latter. She also accepted that she may have been told that the plaintiff wanted to discuss the drug. She agreed that she would have conveyed the impression to the plaintiff that there were no significant side effects other than bleeding.

The judgment contains no adverse conclusion of any kind concerning Dr Burt, or about her discussion with the plaintiff. Furthermore, none of the medical witnesses criticised her conduct or the information which she gave, as summarised in this account by the judge, other than Professor Huntingford, whose evidence was not accepted as to what was known and required to be disclosed about Depo-Provera in December 1978. On the contrary, the effect of the evidence of all three doctors called by the defendants was to approve the conduct of Dr Burt on the basis of her evidence, which the judge clearly accepted, ie Miss Dickins, Dr Law and an independent highly qualified expert, Dame Josephine Barnes. The judge also clearly accepted the evidence of all these witnesses, and I shall be returning to some short passages in that connection later on.

In effect, therefore, Dr Burt was absolved from any allegation of negligence – indeed, as appears hereafter, not only by the judge but also by counsel for the plaintiff. Nevertheless, somewhat surprisingly in the circumstances, the judge concluded that the defendants had been negligent . . . I must refer to some passages in the speeches in the House of Lords in *Sidaway*, on which the judge relied . . . there were . . . a number of remarks, *obiter* in their context, on the duty to reply to questions. For present purposes I need only refer to two passages. At p 895B Lord Diplock mentioned the natural tendency of many people to want to decide for themselves whether anything should be done to their bodies and whether or not to consent to any treatment which might be advised. In that connection he said:

> No doubt if the plaintiff in fact manifested this attitude by means of questioning, the doctor would tell him whatever it was the patient wanted to know.

Lord Bridge, with whom Lord Keith agreed, said at p 898B:

> I should perhaps add at this point, although the issue does not strictly arise on this appeal, that, when questioned specifically by a patient of apparently sound mind about risks involved in a particular treatment proposed, a doctor's duty must, in my opinion, be to answer both truthfully and as fully as the question requires.

The judge referred to these passages and to another passage in the speech of Lord Bridge before dealing with the questions and answers which appear in the plaintiff's diary, to which I have already referred.

Kerr LJ cited further the judgment of Mr Justice Leonard, and continued:

(1) It confirms, as I have already mentioned, that the judge absolved Dr Burt from all blame; indeed, he appears to have commended her conduct.

(2) The judge does not find anywhere what enquiries the plaintiff in fact made about Depo-Provera, let alone that she made any specific enquiry. On the contrary, he had already rejected her evidence that she made the specific enquiries recorded in her diary and in the pleading. All that he said in that connection was that it was more probable than not that she asked for some information and advice, and that she had expressed some sort of reservation

about Depo-Provera and had made some form of request for reassurances about it. That, so far as it goes, is of course a finding which the defendants accept, as they must, and it is fully in accordance with the probabilities on the rest of the evidence.

(3) On that assumption, what were the defendants obliged to tell the plaintiff in response, and did they fail in their duty in that regard? In that connection it must be borne in mind that there was no medical evidence on which the judge could properly conclude that the defendants had been negligent by not having given any more information to the plaintiff than what she was told by Dr Burt.

(4) In my view the judge overstated the position on the evidence when he said, at p 28C:

> As Miss Dickins said in evidence, if the patient is making a specific enquiry, it would be right to tell her the whole picture.

The expression 'the full picture' was used by counsel in his cross-examination of Miss Dickins. Her assent to it, at the end of a question occupying nearly eight lines, cannot properly be divorced from the context of her evidence as a whole, and I set out later on the judge's own summary of it.

(5) In the passage which I have read the judge referred to 'such information as is available to the hospital', and to the retrieval of information 'from the files'. What he appears to have had in mind was information, case studies, statistics and other literature which had been collated by Dr Law as part of a piece of research of her own, but which was also available for consultation by others; and he may also have had this in mind when he referred twice to 'the full picture'. . . .

For present purposes it is sufficient to take the judge's summary of [the experts'] evidence, thought in my view its effect was a good deal stronger and more favourable to the defendants than the summary suggests.

In relation to Miss Dickins, the judge said at p 20:

> Miss Dickins, who was the consultant obstetrician and gynaecologist in charge of the plaintiff from the time of her referral, preceding Daniel's birth, described Depo-Provera as being 'convenient and useful for suitable patients who needed to be without anxiety about becoming pregnant for a period of three months'. Presented with a summary of the answers said to have been by Dr Burt

and I interpolate 'according to Dr Burt's account of the interview (which the judge accepted) and not according to what the plaintiff claims to have been recorded in her diary'

> she was of the opinion that they contained sufficient information for the patient, in the light of the material which was available in 1978. In her view there was no need to mention the other symptoms which were rare, though she thought that it would be necessary to mention them now because of the public discussion. It was common practice to tell the patient about irregular bleeding, but not the minor side effects. However, she added that, if the patient made a specific enquiry, then it would be proper to tell her the full picture.

I have already dealt with the point made again in the last sentence.

Then in relation to Dame Josephine Barnes, the judge said:

> (She) is an obstetrician and gynaecologist of formidable reputation. In addition to her academic and institutional distinctions she is a consultant to the Charing Cross and Elizabeth Garrett-Anderson Hospitals. She regards Depo-Provera as useful in certain applications, including cases in which a woman has been vaccinated against rubella and, therefore, needs to avoid pregnancy for three months. Her evidence was that in 1978 all that was known was that the main side effect of the drug was irregular bleeding. The patient should have been told about it; it was probably unnecessary to warn her of other comparatively trivial side effects of which complaint had been made.

(6) In the light of these comments I conclude that the judge was in error in holding that there was any obligation to pass on to the plaintiff all the information available to the hospital; that is to say in this case the information contained in Dr Law's files. That conclusion could not properly be based upon the evidence. As regards the judge's repeated reference to the need to give a full picture in answer to a specific enquiry, it must be borne in mind, apart from the other matters already mentioned in that regard, that no specific enquiry was found to have been made in this case.

Secondly, I think the judge's conclusions equally cannot properly be based on the remarks of Lord Diplock and Lord Bridge in *Sidaway*. The question of what a plaintiff should be told in answer to a general enquiry cannot be divorced from the *Bolam* test, any more than when no such enquiry is made. In both cases the answer must depend upon the circumstances, the nature of the enquiry, the nature of the information which is available, its reliability, relevance, the condition of the patient, and so forth. Any medical evidence directed to what would be the proper answer in the light of responsible medical opinion and practice – that is to say, the *Bolam* test – must in my view equally be placed in the balance in cases where the patient makes some enquiry, in order to decide whether the response was negligent or not.

In that connection, apart from what was said by Lords Diplock and Bridge, I would also draw attention to the speech of Lord Templeman at p 903D onwards, which suggests to me that the *Bolam* test is all-pervasive in this context. Indeed I am not convinced that the *Bolam* test is irrelevant even in relation to the question of what answers are properly to be given to specific enquiries, or that Lord Diplock or Lord Bridge intended to hold otherwise. It seems to me that there must always be grey areas, with differences of opinion, as to what are the proper answers to be given to any enquiry, even a specific one, in the particular circumstances of any case. However, on the evidence in the present case this point does not arise, since no specific enquiry was found to have been made.

(7) Accordingly, I conclude that the judge erred in finding negligence in relation to what the plaintiff was not told by Dr Burt, whether he relied on the medical evidence or on the *obiter* remarks in *Sidaway*, or both . . .

Neill LJ: I do not understand that in the decision of the House of Lords in *Sidaway v Board of Governors of the Bethlem Royal Hospital* [1985] AC 871, [1985] 1 All ER 643, in the passages to which my Lord has already drawn attention that Lord Diplock or Lord Bridge were laying down any rule of law to the effect that where questions are asked by a patient, or doubts are expressed, a doctor is under an obligation to put the patient in possession of all the information on the subject which may be available in the files of a consultant, who may have made a special study of the subject. The amount of information to be given must depend upon the circumstances, and as a general proposition it is governed by what is called the *Bolam* test. In 1978 irregular bleeding was the side-effect which was known and recognised. The plaintiff was told about it. In my judgment it was not established, either by means of evidence of some usual system, which broke down in this particular, or by the application of some rule of law, that the plaintiff would, or should, have been put in possession of the material, or the bulk of the material, then in Dr Law's files.

With the utmost respect to the judge, I think he fell into error. Accordingly, I too would allow this appeal.

Balcombe LJ agreed with both judgments.

On one reading of the Court of Appeal's decision it would appear that not much has changed since *Hatcher v Black*, ie that it is still open to the doctor in the exercise of his judgment to decide what information to give even if asked direct questions and that he will be judged by the standards of the profession. There is, however, an alternative and more subtle interpretation of at least the judgment of Neill LJ. While it flies in the face of the conventional view taken of *Blyth*, it merits attention. It is as follows. A close examination of the facts of *Blyth* suggests that the doctor caring for Mrs Blyth did not know the contents of the research in the consultant's (Dr Law's) files. Thus, *Blyth* is not a case of a doctor failing to answer questions of which she knows the answers. Rather, it is a case of whether she should have known the answers (and the court held that she need not have this extra knowledge). Interpreted in this way it is possible to preserve intact the legal force of the views advanced by Lords Diplock, Bridge and Templeman in *Sidaway* by pointing out that *Blyth* is concerned with an entirely different issue.

An additional virtue of this view of *Blyth* is that it prompts a more careful analysis of what may be entailed in their Lordships' views in *Sidaway*. The process of question and answer from a legal point of view involves the following steps, assuming a question is asked.

- *There must be a determination by the doctor of what information the patient is seeking or inquiring about.*

A specific question will clearly identify for the doctor the area to be discussed. A general question will require the doctor to assess what he thinks the patient is interested in. His assessment may lead him to the conclusion that what looks like a general question is, in fact, a request for certain specific information, ie is a specific question.

In determining whether a doctor is in breach of duty by misunderstanding the nature of the patient's request, the law must look to the *Bolam* test since it cannot be doubted that this is a matter, largely, of the exercise of professional skill and judgment.

- *Having reached a view as to what the patient wishes to know, the doctor must give his mind to what he knows in order to answer the question.*

In determining whether a doctor is in breach of duty here, again *Bolam* ought to apply; ie is the doctor's lack of awareness reasonable in the circumstances? (this reflects the alternative view of Neill LJ's judgment in *Blyth* advanced above).

- *Once the doctor has reflected on what he knows, he must decide whether, and if so to what extent, to inform his patient.*

It is at this stage that the legal test for breach of duty need not be the *Bolam* test. Rather it can be as expressed by the judges in *Sidaway*. Indeed, the Australian High Court in *Rogers v Whitaker* (1992) 67 ALJR 47 at 50, went further and stated:

> an acceptable approach in point of principle should be recognized and attach significance to the relevance of a patient's questions. Even if a court were satisfied that a reasonable person in the patient's position would be unlikely to attach significance to a particular risk, the fact that the patient asked questions revealing concern about the risk would make the doctor aware that this patient did in fact attach significance to the risk. Subject to the therapeutic privilege, the question would therefore require a truthful answer.

- *As a variant of the previous situation, the doctor may wish to withhold information because he considers it harmful, ie rely on what we will see is known as the 'therapeutic privilege'.*

Here again evidence from the medical profession must be significant in determining the possible effects on the patient and thus, *Bolam* is again relevant. (Of course, when we refer to the *Bolam* test and its application we are seeking to describe the prevailing English interpretation of *Bolam* notwithstanding our view that ultimately the criticisms of courts in the Commonwealth that *Bolam* is too deferential to the ways of the profession, will gain favour.)

(c) Therapeutic privilege

As long as a doctor's duty to disclose information in English law is as stated by the House of Lords in *Sidaway*, with the exception of Lord Scarman (and perhaps, Lord Templeman), there is no need for a doctrine of therapeutic privilege. According to this doctrine, a doctor need not disclose information to a patient, whatever his *prima facie* obligation to do so, if by doing so he may do more harm to the patient than any benefit to be gained from the treatment. English law's continued reliance on the *Bolam* approach avoids the need to establish such an exception since *Bolam* entails that the doctor may exercise appropriate discretion in choosing whether and what to disclose.

Against the day when the current understanding of *Sidaway* undergoes revision, it may be helpful, however, to offer some analysis of the therapeutic privilege. We can begin with the words of Lord Scarman in *Sidaway*. In keeping with all judicial statements which adopt the 'reasonable patient' test, Lord Scarman seeks to make it clear that the law does not make the duty to disclose absolute, but leaves the doctor with some discretion. This is the discretion which has become known as the 'therapeutic privilege'. He states:

> Even if the risk be material, the doctor will not be liable if upon a reasonable assessment of his patient's condition he takes the view that a warning would be detrimental to his patient's health.

Two points must be made. The first is to ask whether in the result the 'reasonable patient' test plus 'therapeutic privilege' is any different from the test advanced in *Sidaway* by Lord Bridge. The answer must be that it is not the same. The difference lies in the fact that under Lord Scarman's (and the North American) view, the doctor has a *prima facie* duty to disclose, and must justify non-disclosure by reference to medical evidence concerning the particular patient's circumstances. Thus, it is for the doctor to advance and prove this justification.

More significantly for a general understanding of *Sidaway*, it is clear from the way Lord Scarman expresses the 'therapeutic privilege' that the doctor may not justify non-disclosure simply by stating that the patient fell into a *class* of patient whom a *responsible body* of medical opinion would not have informed. Lord Scarman appears to reject the relevance of evidence referring to the patient as a member of a particular *class* of patient, and any reliance upon what a responsible body of medical opinion might have done. He states:

> . . . it is plainly right that a doctor may avoid liability for failure to warn of a material risk if he can show that he reasonably believed that communication to the patient of the existence of the risk would be detrimental to the health (including, of course, the mental health) of his patient.

The second point which arises concerns the potential implications of adopting the justification of therapeutic privilege. It needs tight control, otherwise, as the President's Commission argues in 'Making Health Care Decisions' (*op cit*) (pp 95-96):

> The obvious danger with such an exception is the ease with which it can swallow the rule, thereby legitimating wholesale noncompliance with the general obligation of disclosure. Accordingly, some courts and commentators hold that the scope of therapeutic privilege should be severely circumscribed, and that, at the least, the privilege should not apply in situations when the potential harm to the patient from full disclosure would result not from the disclosure itself, but from a treatment decision the practitioner fears the patient might make as a result of the information disclosed. More plausible claims of therapeutic privilege might involve certain disclosures to patients previously known to be suicidal or those susceptible to serious physiological effects of stress, and in situations where there is strong reason to believe that a particular disclosure is likely to result in serious self-destructive behaviour that could not be justified in terms of the patient's own long-term values and goals.
>
> Despite all the anecdotes about patients who committed suicide, suffered heart attacks, or plunged into prolonged depression upon being told 'bad news', little documentation exists for claims that informing patients is more dangerous to their health than not informing them, particularly when the informing is done in a sensitive and tactful fashion. On the contrary . . . there is much to suggest that the therapeutic privilege has been vastly overused

as an excuse for not informing patients of facts they are entitled to know. In light of the values at stake, the burden of justification should fall upon those who allege that the informing process is dangerous to patient health, and information should be withheld on therapeutic grounds only when the harm of its disclosure is both highly probably and seriously disproportionate to the affront to self-determination.

One of the few cases which applies the 'therapeutic privilege' is the following Australian case.

Battersby v Tottman (1985) 37 SASR 524 (South Australia Sup Ct)

A doctor at a public hospital prescribed a prolonged course of high doses of a particular drug for a patient suffering from mental illness. The doctor was aware that there was a risk of the drug causing serious and permanent eye damage to the patient, but he was of the opinion that the advantages to be derived by the patient from treatment with the drug outweighed the risk of damage to the eyes. The doctor did not warn either the patient or the patient's relatives of the risk of damage to the eyes, or arrange for the patient's eyes to be regularly monitored by an eye specialist, because he was of the opinion that this would have an adverse effect upon the patient. The doctor kept a look out for signs of incipient eye trouble, but the patient nevertheless developed permanent eye damage, and sued the doctor and the hospital for damages for negligence.

There was evidence which the trial Judge (Cox J) accepted that the severe mental illness from which the patient was suffering had responded only to the high doses of the drug in question, that without the prescribed treatment her life was in danger, and that by means of her mental illness the doctor reasonably believed that the patient could not make a rational choice if confronted with the risks to which his treatment exposed her.

The trial judge held on the facts, that it had not been established that the doctor or the hospital had been guilty of any negligence. King CJ (with whom Jacobs J concurred) regarded the facts as justifying the doctor's exercise of the therapeutic privilege.

King CJ: In *F v R* [(1983) 33 SASR, 189, 193] I referred to 'the paramount consideration that a person is entitled to make his own decisions about his life'. The doctor would be in breach of his duty to the patient, in my opinion, if he withheld from a mentally normal and emotionally sound patient information as to a material risk simply because he found that the patient might make an unwise decision, perhaps based upon unreasonable considerations, not to undergo the treatment.

I adhere to what I said in the same case at p 193:

> Even where all other considerations indicate full disclosure of risks, a doctor is justified in withholding information, and in particular refraining from volunteering information, when he judges on reasonable grounds that the patient's health, physical or mental, might be seriously harmed by the information. Justification may also exist for not imparting information when the doctor reasonably judges that a patient's temperament or emotional state is such that he would be unable to make the information a basis for a rational decision.

I think that the appellant's mental and emotional condition as understood by Dr Tottman and as found by the learned trial Judge, placed the doctor in the position of having to make the decision for her for two reasons. First, merely knowledge of the risk to her vision would be sufficient to give rise to a real risk of hysterical blindness. Second, she was quite incapable by reason of her abnormal mental condition of using the information as the basis for calm or rational decision. She was likely to react hysterically and irrationally and to refuse treatment not on rational grounds or as a result of calm deliberation but as a result of distorted mental processes produced by her mental illness. The result of refusal of the treatment, in the belief of the doctor formed on reasonable grounds, was likely to be indeterminate close confinement in a mental institution with a high risk of suicide. I agree with the learned trial Judge that in the circumstances the doctor's decision not to acquaint the patient with the risk to her vision attendant upon the treatment was not negligent.

As if to prove the problematical nature of this concept, Zelling J saw the facts in a different way and dissented.

Zelling J: As the Chief Justice said in *F v R* a doctor may be justified in withholding information where the doctor judges on reasonable grounds that the plaintiff's health, physical or mental, might be seriously harmed by the information. In my opinion, this indicates a balancing test where one has to balance the seriousness of the risk of telling her, against the likelihood of, in this case, serious eye damage, to the plaintiff. My view is, that the balance comes down heavily in favour of telling the patient something as serious as this. After all, as I commented during argument, a doctor could hardly chop off a patient's leg without discussing it with the patient first. I see no reason why a doctor should be able to send a patient blind and be excused by saying 'I thought it was in your best interests for you to be blinded rather than have your treatment hampered'. The matter can easily be tested from the evidence of Dr Cotton, one of the witnesses whom the trial Judge accepted. Dr Cotton said that the most severe side-effect of melleril was not melleri retinopathy but death by cardiac arrest from taking melleril. Surely it could not be put to a court that it was better for the patient to die from cardiac arrest due to the administration of the drug, rather than to tell her of the drug's side-effects and risk a possible suicide. When one deals with effects as serious as the ones I have detailed, and in particular in this case blindness or near blindness or very serious damage which could have led to blindness if persisted in, the patient must be allowed to make her own decision, whether the doctor thinks she is well enough to do so or not, except in the case of a person who is too young to make decisions or is, by reason of mental infirmity, unable to consider and weight the risks inherent in the treatment. Despite the plaintiff's mental troubles, she was not in that position. The case would have been different if melleril had only been used for a short time, in moderate doses, to stabilize the position.

Battersby deals with only one aspect of the doctrine of therapeutic privilege, *viz* that the doctor may withhold information if his disclosing it to the patient would probably cause actual physical (or mental) harm to the patient (hysterical blindness in this case). There is another situation which gives rise to the privilege which must not be overlooked. As Robinson J put it in *Canterbury v Spence* 464 F 2d 772 (DC, 1972): 'It is recognized that patients occasionally become so ill or emotionally distraught on disclosure as to foreclose a rational decision. . . . the physician is armed with a privilege to keep the information from the patient . . .'.

If these two cases both offer valid meanings of 'therapeutic privilege', it is important immediately to reject a third meaning which is sometimes advanced. It may be argued that a doctor may invoke the 'therapeutic privilege' out of a concern for the patient's wider interests as he sees them.

In *Nishi v Hartwell* (1970) 473 P 2d 116 (Haw Sup Ct) it was stated that:

the doctrine [of informed consent] recognizes that the primary duty of a physician is to do what is best for his patient . . . a physician may withhold disclosure of information regarding any untoward consequences of a treatment where full disclosure will be detrimental to the patient's total care and best interest.

It will be obvious that if this is accepted as being within the scope of the privilege, it would as Robinson J remarked in *Canterbury v Spence* 'devour the disclosure rule itself' (at 789).

While the view taken in *Nishi v Hartwell* is clearly bad law, so equally there is a need to avoid responding to such a view by throwing the 'baby out with the bath water' and declaring that where the 'reasonable patient' test is applied there can never be a situation of therapeutic privilege. Such a view has been expressed in the Canadian case of *Meyer Estate v Rogers* (1991) 2 OR (3d) 356 (Ontario High Ct) but must be wrong. It is easy, however, to sympathise with Maloney J in the *Meyers* case since he reached his decision as a reaction against what he saw as the never-ending extension of the doctrine of the 'therapeutic privilege' in the United States.

(d) The 'reasonable patient' test in practice

If, as we have suggested, the English courts will ultimately adopt the 'reasonable patient' test now applied in Canada and Australia it may be of benefit to consider briefly how the test would come to be applied by a court in practice. In their joint report, *Informed Decisions About Medical Procedures* (1989) the Victorian, New South Wales and Australian Law Reform Commissions most helpfully identify the factors relevant to a court's determination of the central issue of the 'reasonable patient' test, ie whether a particular risk is 'material'.

Informed Decisions About Medical Procedures (1989)

Relevant factors in determining reasonable risks. In all jurisdictions, the question whether a particular risk is material must be determined in each case as a matter of fact in all the circumstances. The factors that may be relevant in deciding whether a particular risk is material include the following (which obviously overlap):

— *the personality and temperament of the patient and the patient's attitude.* As Mr Justice Cox said in *Gover v State of South Australia and Perriam*: '[A doctor] is obliged to act reasonably in the circumstances, and the circumstances will include a fair appraisal of [the] patient's intelligence and temperament and apparent understanding, made in the light of the simplicity or complexity of the recommendation [the doctor] is making [(1985) 39 SASR 543 at 558].'

— *whether the patient wants information.* If a patient is apparently keen to be given more information, rather than seeking reassurance, more information should generally be given. If, on the other had, the patient does not want information, the doctor is obviously not required to force it upon the patient: 'Many people are prepared to place themselves in the hands of their doctors and leave all decisions to them [*F v R* (1983) 33 SASR 189 at 193 per King CJ].' The patient can be said to be exercising autonomy by requesting not to be given information and by accepting the decision of the doctor. However, doctors are nevertheless still required to give patients basic information and, in some cases, they may have difficulty in deciding how much to tell a patient who does not want fuller information. For example, if the choice for the patient is between a lumpectomy and a mastectomy, how much information should the doctor give about the two operations if the patient says 'I'll leave it to you Doctor'? In deciding whether the patient wants information, as in other matters, the doctor must exercise reasonable care and judgment.

— *whether the patient asks questions.* North American courts have said that a doctor's duty to give information is not altered by the patient asking questions. A doctor is an expert and should therefore be required to give all the relevant information whether it is specifically requested or not. Many patients may be unable to identify the relevant questions to ask and 'a rule which presumes a degree of sophistication which many members of society lack is likely to breed gross inequities [*Canterbury v Spence* 464 F 2d 772, 783, n 36 (DC, 1972)'. In addition to not knowing the relevant questions to ask, patients may not wish to show their ignorance or they may be too ill or overawed by their situation to ask questions. In Australia and England, however, courts have said that more information should be given if patients ask questions. The patient's questions indicate to the doctor additional information that is 'material' for that patient in deciding whether to undertake the recommended procedure and 'A direct question would have called for an answer telling of the risk, however slight [*F v R, supra* per Bollen J at 207].'

— *the patient's level of understanding.* A doctor need not 'cross-examine his patient exhaustively to ensure that she both understands and will remember his advice' but should give information that the doctor thinks that the patient will understand after 'a fair appraisal of his patient's intelligence and temperament and apparent under-standing, made in the light of the simplicity or complexity of the recommendation he is making' [*Gover, supra* per Cox J at 558]'.

— *the nature of the treatment.* More drastic treatment (such as major surgery) requires more information. If the treatment is necessary to preserve the patient's life or health, however, it may require less explanation than less urgent treatment, even if it is relatively serious. Thus, in the South Australian case *Gover v State of South Australia and Perriam*, a patient undertook eye surgery, principally for cosmetic reasons, to reduce her 'baggy' eyelids. One factor that was held to be relevant in deciding what information she should have been given was that eye drops or ointment were alternative treatments so far as the medical condition of the eye was concerned. The 'bagginess' of her eyelids was not unduly gross and if she had known that her medical condition could be treated non-surgically, that might have influenced her decision whether to agree to surgery. Similarly, in the Canadian case *Haughian v Paine* [(1987) 37 DLR (4th) 624] a patient agreed to a laminectomy and discotomy recommended by his surgeon to relieve pain and disability in his right arm. This operation was not immediately necessary and an alternative, at least for the time being, was 'conservative management' – supervised rest, traction, muscle therapy and analgesic medication. The court held that as the operation was not essential to preserve the patient's life or health, he should have been given this information and allowed to decide for himself.

— *the magnitude of the possible harm.* There is a greater duty to provide information about the possibility of serious harm even if the chance of it occurring is slight. A doctor should discuss a risk of death, stroke, paralysis, blindness or other serious complication with a patient even if there is only a slight chance of the risk eventuating. Thus, in the eye surgery case referred to above, the court said that the risk that the operation might cause blindness should have been mentioned to the patient; the risk of blindness was very small indeed, but the magnitude of such a complication meant that the decision should properly have been left to the patient herself. Similarly, Mr Justice Zelling said in [*Battersby v Tottman* (1985) 37 SASR 524 at 534] in which the patient suffered eye damage as a result of a drug to treat severe mental illness: 'In my view, no doctor is entitled to give a patient treatment which may blind or seriously damage her eyesight without first discussing it with the patient and obtaining her consent to the treatment.' However, if the chance of the risk eventuating is so slight that no reasonable person would be influenced by it, the risk need not be mentioned to the patient.

— *the likelihood of the risk.* There is a greater obligation to discuss risks that are more likely to occur than those that are rare. This applies even if the harm is relatively slight. However, it is probably not generally necessary for a doctor to discuss with a patient risks that are inherent in any operation, such as the general risks of anaesthesia or infection after surgery, because patients are assumed to know these risks or to consider them too remote to be significant.

— *the general surrounding circumstances.* The extent of the duty to give information may be affected by emergency conditions, or the absence of the opportunity for detached reflection or calm counselling, and the existence of alternative sources of advice. A doctor may proceed to treat a patient without giving information or obtaining consent if it is an emergency. The courts have not defined what constitutes an emergency, in particular whether it must be threatening to the patient's life or whether it is sufficient that there is a risk of grave physical or mental injury to the patient, or both. In practice, doctors often face difficult decisions in situations which might not be life-threatening. In judging the doctor's conduct in such circumstances, the principal question will be whether the doctor's actions accorded with what a reasonable doctor would have done in similar circumstances.

(e) Causation: much ado about nothing

The plaintiff may establish a breach of duty properly to inform but will only succeed in the action if he can also show that the breach of duty caused him some injury. It would appear that injury here must mean more than a sense of grievance at not being told or of being misinformed. It must mean physical injury or nervous shock as understood in the law of torts (economic loss would be recoverable but would usually arise as a consequence of the physical injury of which complaints had already been made).

(i) FACTUAL CAUSATION

Some would say that the need to prove causation makes much of the heart-searching over the duty to inform irrelevant, since the patient may win the argument over the duty to inform yet lose the action because he cannot show causation. This is because it may be hard for him to say that if he were a 'reasonable person' he would still have refused the treatment concerned even with knowledge of the material (but undisclosed) risks, since evidence may well have been given by doctors that the treatment involved was, all things being equal, medically desirable.

The question is, of course, whether the test of causation is based upon what the 'reasonable patient' would have consented to had he been properly informed or what the 'particular patient' would have consented to if informed. That the test for the duty to inform may be the 'reasonable patient' standard in some jurisdictions and edging towards it in English law, does not necessarily mean that causation should also be governed by a criterion of reasonableness.

The leading reported English case is *Chatterton v Gerson* [1981] QB 432 in which Bristow J adopted (*obiter*) a subjective test of causation.

> When the claim is based on negligence the plaintiff must prove not only the breach of duty to inform but had the duty been broken *she* would not have chosen to have the operation [our emphasis].

He regarded as relevant what the patient would have decided. As it happens, however, even in the face of her evidence as to what she felt she would have done, the judge determined that she would have consented because she was 'a lady desperate for pain relief'. This approach is no more than using the 'reasonable patient' test as a yardstick by which to assess the particular patient's evidence. If this is so, it means that the plaintiff faces a considerable difficulty in succeeding in his action even if he can show a breach of duty to inform. He could, of course, show that he was not a reasonable patient, but some type of eccentric. In such a case he would win but it may be hard to satisfy the judge on the facts.

The following case illustrates the English court's approach.

Smith v Barking, Havering & Brentwood HA (unreported) (29 July 1989) (QBD)

Hutchinson J: Miss Sharon Smith, whose twenty-eighth birthday fell on the first day of the hearing, claims damages against the Barking, Havering and Brentwood Health Authority in respect of alleged negligent surgical treatment in January 1981. The defendants are sued on the basis that they are responsible for the alleged negligence of Mr Fairburn, the neurosurgeon who carried out an operation on the plaintiff's cervical spinal cord. Mr Fairburn died on 12 October 1984 . . .

In March 1970, when she was nine-years-old, the plaintiff was admitted to Oldchurch Hospital in Romford under the care of Mr Fairburn, with complaints of pain in the cervical spine associated with mild quadriparesis and upper motor neurone signs in all limbs, particularly the legs. There was also some hypoaesthesia in the upper limbs. X-rays showed widening of the upper cervical canal. A myelogram was carried out – the report has been lost – and in April an operation was undertaken for what was described as 'drainage of hydromyelia'. There has been some suggestion that this was a wrong diagnosis, but nothing turns on that. There is no doubt about the nature of the problem that was discovered, which I shall briefly describe.

The operation involved an incision above the cervical spine, with exposure of the spines. Portions of bone were then removed to expose the covering of the spinal cord, which was opened to reveal the cord itself. Within the cord a thin-walled cyst was found occupying two-thirds of the transverse diameter of the cord. The cyst had been caused by the access of cerebro-spinal fluid into the vestigial central canal in the spinal cord and its accumulation there. At the operation Mr Fairburn drained the cyst and, discovering a mid-line funnel-shaped opening at the apex of the obex, thought to be responsible for this condition, he took steps to close it.

The operation was successful in the sense that, after an initial and quite long recovery period, the plaintiff's symptoms abated and she was able to live a more or less normal life for some nine years. Over that period she made regular visits of decreasing frequency to the hospital where she was seen by Mr Fairburn, and ultimately, when the plaintiff was eighteen, she was discharged.

By that time she was working as a clerk for an export business and was living an independent life away from home. However, very shortly after her discharge from medical care she began again to experience symptoms. First she noticed tingling in the fingers with some loss of sensation at the ends, and this was followed by weakness in the arms of gradual onset. She had trouble picking things up and came to be unable to distinguish between hot and cold. Ultimately her legs became so weak that it took her a very long time to get up the two flights of stairs to her home, she had difficulty walking, she could only comb her hair if she supported one arm with the other, and she was quite severely disabled.

Of course, once the symptoms began, Miss Smith consulted her doctor and again attended Oldchurch Hospital under the care of Mr Fairburn. The view was taken that she was experiencing a recurrence of the condition which had led to the operation nine years previously. It will be appreciated – and I do not need to go into great detail because it is not a matter of controversy – that the effect of an internal cyst in the spinal cord is that the cord is expanded and becomes compressed against adjacent structures. This leads to interference with the nerve pathways leading from the spinal cord, and they quite quickly sustain irreversible degeneration. The opinion of Dr Turner, the neurologist called on behalf of the defendants, was that had nothing been done the plaintiff's condition would have continued to deteriorate quite rapidly, so that within about three months of 20 January 1981, the date of the operation I am about to describe, she would have been in a wheelchair and within a further six months she would have been tetraplegic. [Counsel for the plaintiff] ultimately accepted that this opinion was correct.

Mr Fairburn considered that a further operation was advisable. What he had hoped to achieve was the location and drainage of the cyst which he believed had re-formed in the hope that this would arrest the progress of the condition, as had happened before. The documents that survive show, however, that Mr Fairburn regarded such an operation as a very difficult one and that he was to some extent reluctant to undertake it. . . .

Mr Fairburn carried out the second operation on 20 January 1981, and it was unsuccessful. The plaintiff suffered immediate and permanent tetraplegia. It is unnecessary that I should describe why that came about – nor indeed is it positively known. It is sufficient to say that it is believed to have resulted from some damage to the spinal cord occurring during the second operation . . . The plaintiff's claim, and the only matter with which this action is concerned, arises out of Mr Fairburn's failure to warn her of the risks inherent in the operation or to afford her any opportunity to reach an informed decision as to whether to submit to it.

 . . . it was common ground that Mr Fairburn should have given the plaintiff some advice as to the risks involved and the desirability of submitting to the operation and that her evidence that he had not done so must be accepted . . .

Given the admitted necessity for such an explanation and the fact, as I find, that there was none, the only significant issue in this case has been whether the plaintiff, had she been given proper advice, would have elected against the operation . . .

There was some discussion as to whether the issue of causation would be approached on what was called the objective or the subjective basis – ie, was the question to be resolved by deciding what a reasonable person in the plaintiff's position would have chosen to do or by deciding what the plaintiff herself would have chosen to do. In support of the former approach I was referred to the Canadian authority of *Reibl v Hughes* [1980] 2 SCR 880 and in support of the latter to the decision of Hirst J in *Hills v Potter* [1983] 3 All ER 716, [1984] 1 WLR 641n. Both counsel invited me to accept that in the end the matter must be one for decision on a subjective basis. This must plainly as a matter of principle be right, because the question must be: if this plaintiff had been given the advice that she would have been given, would she have decided to undergo the operation or not?

However, there is a peculiar difficulty involved in this sort of case – not least for the plaintiff herself – in giving, after the adverse outcome of the operation is known, reliable answers as to what she would have decided before the operation had she been given proper advice as to the risks inherent in it. Accordingly, it would, in my judgment, be right in the ordinary case to give particular weight to the objective assessment. If everything points to the fact that a reasonable plaintiff, properly informed, would have assented to the operation, the assertion from the witness box, made after the adverse outcome is known, in a wholly artificial situation and in the knowledge that the outcome of the case depends upon that assertion being maintained, does not carry great weight unless there are extraneous or additional factors to substantiate it. By extraneous or additional factors I mean, and I am not doing more than giving examples, religious or some other firmly held convictions; particular social or domestic considerations justifying a decision not in accordance with what, objectively, seems the right one; assertions in the immediate aftermath of the operation made in a context other than that of a possible claim for damages; in other words, some particular factor which suggests that the plaintiff had grounds for not doing what a reasonable person in her situation might be expected to have done. Of course, the less confidently the judge reaches the conclusions as to what objectively the reasonable patient might be expected to have decided, the more readily will he be persuaded by her subjective evidence.

I should make it clear that nothing I have said is intended to reflect adversely on the plaintiff or to suggest that I have any doubts as to her honesty; but as I listened to her grappling with the different hypothetical questions which were put to her, I felt the greatest sympathy for her and reflected that one would need almost to be a saint to answer such questions objectively – ie, without allowing one's reaction to be influenced by the knowledge of what had, in fact, happened and appreciation of the vital significance of the question. Hence the importance of giving proper weight to an objective assessment of what a reasonable patient could be expected to decide in the light of such proper advice as should have been given. . . .

The plaintiff was first asked [when giving evidence] what would have been her reaction had Mr Fairburn told her that if she had the operation there was a chance that it might stop her getting worse coupled with a remote possibility that it would actually produce some improvement, and a risk that if unsuccessful she would be paralysed. She responded, sensibly, that she would have wanted some assurance that the risk of being paralysed was balanced with the risk of not being paralysed: she would have wanted to know the degree of risk. She said that if she had been told that the risk of paralysis was substantial, she would not have had the operation. She was asked, in anticipation of Mr Galbraith's evidence, what her response would have been had she been told that the risk of paralysis was one in four, and she said that she would not have had the operation. She was asked what would have been her response had Mr Fairburn brought together all the material factors. By that counsel meant the hope on the one hand of arresting the progress of the disease for a significant time and on the other hand the risk of making her condition worse or perhaps even causing total paralysis. She said, echoing her earlier answers, that she would have wanted to know what the risk of success was as compared with the risk of failure and that she might have discussed the matter with her parents but would, ultimately, have made up her own mind. She was asked to consider her response to advice to the effect that if she had the operation and it was successful, the condition was in any event likely to recur sooner or later, whereas if she did not have it she would be paralysed within at most two years. She said that she would have wished to wait for a time to see how things worked out. As to this, the evidence shows that if anything was going to be done it was a matter of urgency, because of the speed at which she was deteriorating, and that accordingly she could not sensibly have postponed the decision for more than a week or two. She was asked whether she would have questioned Mr Fairburn and she said that she did not think that she would have done unless invited to do so.

In cross-examination the ground was covered again. [Counsel for the defendant], in a question which attempted to include all the relevant factors on each side, asked her what she would have said, and she responded again that she would have wished to know the risk of paralysis. If she had been told that it was a quarter and that the doctor nevertheless recommended the operation what would she have said, [counsel] asked. She said that if it was a great risk she wouldn't have had the operation.

I have to say that as a means of resolving the all-important question as to what the plaintiff would have decided in January 1981 I found these questions and answers of little assistance. I did, however, derive from her evidence certain material conclusions which are as follows:

(a)   The plaintiff was not somebody imbued with any particular views or prejudices on the subject of operations. On the contrary, like most people, she was temperamentally disposed to follow the advice of her doctors – a tendency which would be particularly strong in the case of Mr Fairburn whom she knew and in whom she must have had considerable trust as a result of the long period of their association.

(b)   The plaintiff plainly found it, as it seemed to me, extremely difficult to imagine herself back into the situation as it was in January 1981, and I had the impression that in the main, though doing her best, she was not really convinced of her own answers. In truth, I think, she just did not know what she would have done.

(c)   There were not, so far as I can discover, any pressing personal or social considerations which would have made her tend to decide one way or the other.

In submitting that I should conclude that the plaintiff would have chosen not to have the operation, [counsel for the plaintiff] invited me to have regard to the circumstances as they were at the time and, in particular, to the following factors. First, he submitted, and I accept, that the plaintiff was a reasonably intelligent young woman capable of independent judgment, shown by the medical records to be cheerful and not depressed and well able to make up her own mind. He submitted, furthermore, that her condition, though grave in fact, might not have appeared so to her. This I cannot accept, because it seems to me inescapable that the degree of disability which she suffered in the period immediately preceding the operation would have been perceived by anyone to be serious. Moreover, part of the advice that she ought to have been given would have involved an explanation about continued and quite rapid deterioration. He invited me to give full weight to the plaintiff's attitude towards operations and desire to be assured that the risk balanced the expected benefits and also to remember how unpleasant she had found the myelogram which had preceded the first operation. Finally, he reminded me that there were no immediate family responsibilities such as a husband or child and no factors connected with her work or economic circumstances which would have impelled her to elect for an operation: although as to that I have already implied that that fact is neutral in the sense that there was nothing of this sort militating in favour of a decision against the operation.

Turning to the appreciation of the operation from the doctors' side, [counsel for the plaintiff] invited me to remember that it was very definitely an elective rather than an essential operation; that it was very rare and that the reason for the risks and benefits were self-evidently difficult to assess and that the doctors recommended it reluctantly. He further submitted that, while it had ultimately been agreed that the proper view was that the plaintiff would have been tetraplegic within nine months, I should not assume that this was the advice she would have necessarily been given at the time. He instanced Mr Galbraith's view that she might have survived a year or even possibly two before reaching that state. He asked me not to confuse the advice with influence and again emphasised that, as Mr Garfield plainly accepted, this was not the sort of decision where the doctor would feel that a plaintiff was necessarily wrong to elect against surgery. He suggested that there is a danger that lawyers tend to weight the choices in a legal as opposed to a human way and argued that the proper approach was to concentrate on the fact that there was a substantial risk up to 25% of total paralysis and that in that situation the plaintiff's approach would have been that she would require to be persuaded of the advisability of the operation, which was by no means an obvious solution. I must, he submitted, give full weight to the plaintiff's own evidence.

Nothing that [counsel for the plaintiff] said in the course of his submissions suggested that there was anything about the plaintiff or her views of reactions which differentiated her from an ordinary reasonable patient. This does not, of course, mean that the response which it is assumed she would have given to a question which she was never asked must be predicted on a purely objective basis, but it does again emphasise the importance to be attached in this difficult field to an objective assessment of what a reasonable patient might be expected to have decided if properly acquainted with all the relevant factors.

It seems to me that in the light of the evidence I have heard from three distinguished neurosurgeons, it is not possible to say with absolute certainty what ought to have been said. Plainly different doctors approach the matter in different ways and further uncertainty is introduced by the possibility that the patient will respond by asking questions to a greater or lesser extent. However, there are some things that I can in the light of their evidence say with confidence. First, there is no doubt that the plaintiff should have had a full and careful explanation of the risks and benefits inherent in the operation. Secondly, I have no doubt that she should have been told in general terms as to the prognosis if she did not have an operation. Thirdly, as I have already said, I accept Mr Garfield's and Professor Hankinson's view that part of the advice she should have been given should have included a clear indication that the surgeon, weighing all the consideration as best he could, had reached the view that an operation was in her best interests. It may be, as [counsel for the defendant] indicated, that Mr Fairburn was reluctant to carry out the operation because of its difficulties, but he had plainly decided that despite that reluctance it was an operation to be recommended, and it is not to be supposed that he would then have undermined the plaintiff's confidence in his decision and abilities by leaving her with the impression that he did not want to do it.

I consider that what Mr Fairburn ought to have told the plaintiff was something along the following lines. He should have explained to her that the indications were that the condition from which she had previously suffered had recurred and that it was getting worse quickly. He should have explained that if nothing was done she would be totally disabled within quite a short period. If he had been pressed for an estimate, he would, I think, have been talking in terms of less than rather than more than a year. If he had been questioned further, he would have indicated that in the course of that deterioration the plaintiff would very soon be in a wheelchair even though not at that stage tetraplegic. He should then have gone on to explain that the operation held out a reasonable chance of arresting the progress of the disease for a significant period – possibly a few years. If questioned, he would have made it clear that this benefit could not be expected to be anything like as great as that achieved by the first operation. Against that reasonable chance of benefit, however, he should have explained that there was a significant risk that her condition would be made worse and that, instead of postponing the onset of total disability, the operation might even markedly accelerate it. He should have made it clear to the plaintiff that, while in his expert view the operation was one which, because it presented a worthwhile chance of significant benefit, she should undergo, the decision was very much for her to take and that in taking it she should bear in mind the risks which he had explained. He should have suggested that she might like to discuss the matter with her parents or her boyfriend and indicated that he would answer any questions that she had so as to assist her to make up her mind.

It seems to me that if, after such a discussion, the plaintiff had quietly considered what to do, the factors which would principally have weighed with her were the following:
(a) First and most important, that if nothing was done she would quite quickly be more or less totally disabled.
(b) Second, that the risk to which the operation exposed her, if it were unsuccessful, was not a risk of something worse than she was going to have to experience anyway but merely of the earlier onset of a condition which she was going to experience anyway.
(c) Third, that while the operation did not hold out any hope of a permanent cure, it would, if successful, result in the postponement of total disability for a significant period.
(d) Finally, and hardly of less significance than the first factor, the plaintiff would inevitably in my view have been much influenced by the reflection that the surgeon in whom she had cause to repose her trust had himself concluded that the chances of success were such as to justify attempting the operation.
Looking at the matter objectively, I cannot escape the conclusion that these factors pointed very strongly towards agreeing to have the operation. Reflection on what she was told would have led a reasonable patient to say to herself: 'Well, it seems I'm going to be paralysed anyway in a very short time. This operation gives me a reasonable chance of avoiding that condition perhaps for a few years. True, there is a real risk the operation will not be successful and I'll then be paralysed even sooner, but the possible benefits clearly considerably outweigh the possible detriment and the chance is one well worth taking.'

In the light of these conclusions I ask myself what the plaintiff would have decided, had she been given advice along the lines I have indicated. For reasons already foreshadowed in this judgment I unhesitatingly conclude that the strong probability is that the plaintiff would have agreed to have the operation. While, of course, there is no certainty about matters of this sort, and the possibility must remain that the plaintiff would have refused, it seems to me in the highest degree unlikely that she would have done so.

One consequence of this blending of the objective to the subjective approach may be that a plaintiff would be more believable when the treatment was not urgently pressing but rather was in a real sense something the patient could take or leave, for example, certain forms of cosmetic surgery.

Given the acceptance of a subjective test (but with an objective ingredient) in England albeit by trial court judges who have not analysed in depth the alternative objective test, it would be useful to look to decisions in Commonwealth jurisdictions where the merits of the two tests have been examined.

Reibl v Hughes (1980) 114 DLR (3d) 1 (Can Sup Ct)

Laskin CJC: In saying that the test is based on the decision that a reasonable person in the patient's position would have made, I should make it clear that the patient's particular concerns must also be reasonably based; otherwise, there would be more subjectivity than would be warranted under an objective test. Thus, for example, fears which are not related to the material risks which should have been but were not disclosed would not be causative factors. However, economic considerations could reasonably go to causation where, for example, the loss of an eye as a result of non-disclosure of a material risk brings about the loss of a job for which good eyesight is required. In short, although account must be taken of a patient's particular position, a position which will vary with the patient, it must be objectively assessed in terms of reasonableness.

However, a vexing problem raised by the objective standard is whether causation could ever be established if the surgeon has recommended surgery which is warranted by the patient's condition. Can it be said that a reasonable person in the patient's position, to whom proper disclosure of attendant risks has been made, would decide against the surgery, that is, against the surgeon's recommendation that it be undergone? The objective standard of what a reasonable person in the patient's position would do would seem to put a premium on the surgeon's assessment of the relative need for the surgery and on supporting medical evidence of that need. Could it be reasonably refused? Brooke JA [in the court below] appeared to be sensitive to this problem by suggesting a combined objective-subjective test.

I doubt that this will solve the problem. It could hardly be expected that the patient who is suing would admit that he would have agreed to have the surgery, even knowing all the accompanying risks. His suit would indicate that, having suffered serious disablement because of the surgery, he is convinced that he would not have permitted it if there had been proper disclosure of the risks, balanced by the risks of refusing the surgery. Yet, to apply a subjective test to causation would, correlatively, put a premium on hindsight, even more of a premium than would be put on medical evidence in assessing causation by an objective standard.

I think it is the safer course on the issue of causation to consider objectively how far the balance in the risks of surgery or no surgery is in favour of undergoing surgery. The failure of proper disclosure pro and con becomes therefore very material. And so too are any special considerations affecting the particular patient. For example, the patient may have asked specific questions which were either brushed aside or were not fully answered or were answered wrongly. In the present case, the anticipation of a full pension would be a special consideration, and, while it would have to be viewed objectively, it emerges from the patient's particular circumstances. So too, other aspects of the objective standard would have to be geared to what the average prudent person, the reasonable person in the patient's particular position, would agree to or not agree to, if all material and special risks of going ahead with the surgery or foregoing it were made known to him. Far from making the patient's own testimony irrelevant, it is essential to his case that he put his own position forward.

The adoption of an objective standard does not mean that the issue of causation is completely in the hands of the surgeon. Merely because medical evidence establishes the reasonableness of a recommended operation does not mean that a reasonable person in the patient's position would necessarily agree to it, if proper disclosure had been made of the risks attendant upon it, balanced by those against it. The patient's particular situation and the degree to which the risks of surgery or no surgery are balanced would reduce the force, on an objective appraisal of the surgeon's recommendation. Admittedly, if the risk of foregoing the surgery would be considerably graver to a patient than the risks attendant upon it, the objective standard would favour exoneration of the surgeon who has not made the required disclosure. Since liability rests only in negligence, in a failure to disclose material risks, the issue of causation would be in the patient's hands on a subjective test, and would if his evidence was accepted, result inevitably in liability unless, of course, there was a finding that there was no breach of the duty of disclosure. In my view, therefore, the objective standard is the preferable one on the issue of causation.

Professor Dugdale in discussing the Canadian cases since *Reibl* illustrates the difficulty faced by plaintiffs where the 'reasonable patient' test is used for causation.

A Dugdale 'Diverse Reports: Canadian Professional Negligence Cases' (1984) 2 Professional Negligence 108

Three Canadian cases illustrate such low level risk situations where an English court might well have found no duty of disclosure but it seems that the *Reibl* approach would require disclosure.

In *Considine v Camp Hill Hospital* (1982) 133 DLR (3d) 11, the patient was not warned of the 1 per cent risk of permanent incontinence resulting from a prostate operation. It was not the practice of the surgeons involved to warn of such a risk because it was rare and the approach taken was 'not to dwell on death and serious complications'. Although Clarke J does not expressly state that there was a breach of the duty to disclose a material risk, the tenor of his judgment suggests that this was indeed his view. 'The evidence persuades me that prior to the operation (the patient) was not told the full story with respect to the risk of permanent incontinence', he commented and later added that he 'was not impressed by the manner by which (the surgeons) failed to deal with the risk'. In *Ferguson v Hamilton Civic Hospitals* (1983) 144 DLR (3d) 214, Krever J was quite clear that a failure to warn of a 2 per cent risk of a stroke following an arteriogram was a breach of duty. Such limited risk explanation as there was in the case, he regarded as being given at an inappropriate time, namely whilst the patient was affected by valium.

The most striking of the three decisions is that of *Casey v Provan* (1984) 11 DLR (4th) 708. There the surgeon failed to warn the patient of a 2 per cent risk of injury to his vocal cord resulting from an endarterectomy. Despite the fact that the expert evidence showed that 'in the medical profession there is room for differences of opinion and practice' on whether to warn of such a risk, Callaghan J held that the loss of the ability to communicate should be treated as a material risk and that there was a breach of duty.

In all three cases the risk in question materialised and the patients claimed respectively for the incontinence, stroke and loss of voice they had suffered. In all three cases the claims failed for the same reason: the breach of duty had not caused the loss.

To prove causation the patient must show that *but for* the breach of duty there would have been no loss, in other words, that but for the lack of warning there would have been no treatment of the kind proposed and no resulting stroke etc. In *Reibl* Laskin CJ held that this issue of causation had to be tested objectively: a patient has to prove not that he personally, subjectively would have declined the treatment if properly warned, but that a reasonable patient in his position would not have proceeded with the treatment if fully informed. What would the reasonable patient have chosen to do in the *Casey* situation, if advised of the 2 per cent voice risk and of the 30 per cent risk of suffering a future stroke were the operation to be declined? In all three cases it was clear that without treatment the patient would be running much higher risks of illness or death than he was in undergoing the treatment. The reasonable patient in that situation will obviously opt for the treatment even if fully warned. It was for that reason that the patients lost in the three cases considered. Indeed, it may be doubted whether a subjective test would have made much difference in these cases: in both *Ferguson* and *Casey* the court noted the confidence of the patient in his surgeon and concluded that the surgeon's advice would have been followed in any event.

Does this suggest that where the recommended treatment is reasonable, causation will always prevent recovery for a failure to warn of the risks? That only where there is an unreasonable recommendation will causation and liability be established – in which case might not the liability be more simply based on the negligent selection of the treatment? That this is the consequence of the *Reibl* approach to causation was denied by Laskin CJ. 'Merely because medical evidence establishes the reasonableness of a recommended operation does not mean that a reasonable person in the patient's position would necessarily agree to it, if proper disclosure had been made of the risks attendant upon it . . . the patient's particular situation and the degree to which the risks of surgery or no surgery are balanced would reduce the force, on an objective appraisal, of the surgeon's recommendation.' However, he went on to add a qualification: 'The patient's particular concerns must be reasonably based . . . thus for example, fears which are not related to the material risks would not be causative factors.' However, economic considerations could reasonably go to causation where, for example, the loss of an eye as a result of non-disclosure of a material risk brings about the loss of a job for which good eyesight is required.

Despite Laskin's denial that 'the adoption of an objective standard (means) that the issue of causation is completely in the hands of the surgeon' ie a surgeon reasonably recommending treatment would be able to show that a full warning would not have influenced a reasonable patient, one is left with the feeling that this will normally be the case unless the treatment is purely elective. It is not surprising that it is in this category of case where the Canadian courts have found causation to be established.

The leading elective treatment case is perhaps *White v Turner* [(1981) 120 DLR (3d) 269], the case concerning breast reduction surgery. Linden J had no doubt that a reasonable person in the position of the patient, if she were warned of the possible scarring 'would probably not have undergone the operation, except in rare circumstances'. As Linden J noted, 'after all, she did live most of her life with large breasts and managed quite well'. Arguments along these lines are likely to be applicable in many cosmetic surgery cases. It is also arguable that the doctor's advice may be less influential in the elective surgery case.

(Professor Gerald Robertson points out that a significant consequence of adopting the objective test is that in 56% of cases decided in the 10 years since *Reibl*, the plaintiff failed to meet the test of causation notwithstanding that there was a breach of duty to inform by the doctor: Robertson, 'Informed Consent 10 Years Later: The Impact of *Reibl v Hughes*' (1991) 70 Canadian Bar Review 423 at 428.)

When an appelate court in England has to determine the test of causation it is unlikely that it will follow the approach adopted in Canada. There will be two questions for the court, as we suggested in the discussion of *Chatterton* above: (i) What is the correct test of causation? (ii) How is that to be established: what evidentiary burden should be cast upon the plaintiff? The court may adopt a subjective test of causation but may demand that in seeking to establish that he would not have consented, the plaintiff must meet a standard of evidence which incorporates an element of reasonableness. This approach was, in fact, adopted by the New South Wales Court of Appeal in 1989. *Reibl* was rejected.

Ellis v Wallsend District Hospital (1989) 17 NSWLR 553 (NSW CA)

In 1975 the plaintiff, Mrs Marie Ellis, consulted Dr A W Chambers, a neurosurgeon who had treated her on several occasions in the previous years, at his consulting room. Mrs Ellis, who had a background of intractable and very severe neck pain, drug dependence, drug overdoses, and failure of other treatment, was interested in having five-nerve separation microsurgery which Dr Chambers had already mentioned to her. Dr Chambers advised that the only concern that she need have was the risk of slight numbness in her right hand. Mrs Ellis agreed to have the operation.

There was evidence that the operation carried a remote risk of paralysis and a more substantial risk of failure to relieve pain. Mrs Ellis gave evidence that if she had been warned of those risks she would not have undergone the operation.

On June 18, 1975, Dr Chambers performed a laminectomey and a cervical posterior rhizotomy of the nerve roots at the cervical vertebrae 2 to 6. During the operation there was haemorrhage which was controlled; numerous adhesions surrounding the spinal cord were noted; Dr Chambers did not use magnification available. Six days after the operation Mrs Ellis developed quadriplegia.

In 1981 Mrs Ellis commenced proceedings in the New South Wales court against Dr Chambers alleging that Dr Chambers had been negligent in (1) advising her to have the operation; (2) failing to warn her of the risks involved; (3) failing to obtain her consent to the operation; (4) in the performance of the operation. She also alleged breach of contract and assault.

Dr Chambers died in 1986. On June 6, 1988, Mrs Ellis settled her claim against his estate for A$500,000. She then claimed against the hospital on the grounds that (1) the hospital was vicariously liable for Dr Chambers' negligence; (2) that the hospital was in breach of its independent and nondelegable duty to her as its patient to ensure that she received proper medical treatment and was warned of all material risks involved in the surgery.

The hospital contended that Mrs Ellis was not its patient but that of Dr Chambers.

In dismissing Mrs Ellis's claim, Cole J held inter alia that:
(1)   Dr Chambers negligently failed to warn Mrs Ellis of the risk of developing paraplegia and low prospect of achieving pain relief;
(2)   applying a subjective test, Mrs Ellis had failed to establish a causative link between that negligence and her damage.

Samuels JA: The test by which causation is determined in cases of medical negligence has not yet been established in Australia by any decision of the High Court. In *Gover v State of South Australia* (1985) 39 SASR 543 at 564, Cox J summarized the possible views thus:

... if a doctor negligently fails to notify his patient of a particular risk of treatment, and the treatment is given and things do in fact go wrong, will the patient, on suing for damages, have to satisfy the Court that he would not have accepted the treatment had the warning been given? Or is it a matter of what a reasonable man would have done in the patient's situation? Or is there no causation element of this sort at all to be proved before a patient can recover?

On the assumption that there is a burden upon the plaintiff to establish a 'causation element' the contest is between the response to the information which the plaintiff would have made had it been furnished (which has been called the subjective test) and the response which a reasonable person in the plaintiff's situation would have made (which has been called the objective test). As Cox J's review of the authorities indicates, the subjective test has been adopted by single judges in England in *Bolam v Friern Hospital Management Committee* [1957] 1 WLR 582 at 590, [1957] 2 All ER 118, by McNair J, and in *Chatterton v Gerson* [1981] QB 432 at 442 and at 445, by Bristow J. Although *Sidaway* was directed to a different question, that of the nature and extent of any warning which a surgeon should give his patient about the possible risks inherent in the proposed procedure, it contains dicta which tend both to favour and deny the subjective test. For example (at 887) Lord Scarman, summarizing the plaintiff's case, said: '... and that, had she been warned, she would not have consented to the operation.'

... [I]n the judgments in *Smith v Auckland Hospital Board* [1965] NZLR 191 as Cox J pointed out in *Gover* (at 565) a majority of the judges favoured the subjective test.

The objective test has been applied in two cases, one in the United States and one in Canada, which are commonly regarded as conveying the leading exegesis of that view. One is *Canterbury v Spence* 464 F 2d 772 (1972), a decision of the United States Court of Appeals for the District of Columbia, and the other *Reibl v Hughes* (1980) 114 DLR (3d) 1, a decision of the Supreme Court of Canada delivered by Laskin CJC. Both these cases dealt primarily with the doctrine of 'informed consent', but each prefers, to quote from *Canterbury* (at 791):

... to resolve the causality issue on an objective basis: in terms of what a prudent person in the patient's position would have decided if suitably informed of all perils bearing significance.

The subjective test was regarded in *Reibl* (in which *Canterbury* was applied) as 'hypothetical and thus unreliable' and, as Laskin CJC observed (at 16) calculated to 'put a premium on hindsight, even more of a premium than would be put on medical evidence in assessing causation by an objective standard'.

I do not myself find these objections to the subjective test persuasive. I respectfully agree with Cox J in *Gover* (at 566) when he said:

... At any rate the basic causation principle governing actions in negligence plainly supports, in my opinion, the subjective test. ...

It is, of course, true that a patient's evidence about what he or she would have done if told of certain risks may be coloured by the fact that the risks did in fact eventuate; but it is open to a court to disbelieve evidence found to be tainted by hindsight: Manderson, 'Following Doctors' Orders: Informed Consent in Australia' (1988) 62 ALJ 430 at 434. Obviously, in endeavouring to ascertain what the plaintiff's response would have been to adequate information had it been conveyed at the appropriate time, a court will be greatly assisted by evidence of the plaintiff's temperament, the course of any prior treatment for the same or a like condition, the nature of the relationship between patient and doctor including pre-eminently, so far as it can be established, the degree of trust reposed in the doctor by the patient. The extent to which the procedure was elective or imposed by circumstantial exigency and the nature and degree of risk involved will all be matters of considerable importance: see Robertson, 'Informed Consent to Medical Treatment' (1981) 97 LQR 102 at 122.

Despite these practical difficulties I agree with the learned judge that the subjective test is the correct one to apply. It is supported by persuasive authority and is consistent with the principle by which proof of causation is governed in other areas of the law of negligence. To the extent that there may be a choice open to be determined upon grounds of policy (there being no decision of any appellate court in Australia upon the point), while there are difficulties inherent in both tests, I would more readily accept the threat of hindsight than adopt medical practice as the determinant. As Manderson (*op cit* at 434) points out the causation question, on the objective view:

. . . resolves itself into a consideration of whether reasonable persons would have refused treatment if they had known the information concealed from them. The answer must be that reasonable persons would have gone ahead with the proposed treatment despite the risks, if it was likely to be beneficial to their health. Yet how is the court to determine whether medical risks are, in short, worth taking, except by asking the opinion of the medical profession?

And the learned author quotes the comment of Laskin CJC in *Reibl* (at 15):

The objective standard of what a reasonable person in the patient's position would do would seem to put a premium on the surgeon's assessment . . .

As I have indicated, Cole J favoured the subjective test but found that, whichever test he applied, he was not satisfied on the balance of probabilities that had the appellant been told that there was a slight risk that the operation might cause paralysis, she would have declined to proceed. This conclusion involved rejection of the following evidence of the appellant:

Q: Was anything ever suggested to you at that stage as to paralysis or possible paralysis as the outcome? A: Definitely not, if he had mentioned anything, I would have run to Bourke.

It is true that, as his Honour points out, adequate information upon this aspect would have been to the effect that there was a slight risk of paralysis coupled with a recommendation that the operation should be performed. Furthermore, it is plain that the appellant had faith in Dr Chambers with whom she was on friendly and comfortable terms, and her probable response to the warning she should have been given must be considered, as the judge indicated, against the background of intractable and very severe pain, drug dependence, the occasions of drug overdoses and the failure of all other treatment. Moreover, it was correct for the judge to take heed, as he did, of the likelihood that the appellant's account of her hypothetical response must be coloured by the catastrophe which the operation brought in its wake.

It was therefore essential for his Honour to examine with great care the evidence which the appellant gave upon this critical point. This attention was all the more necessary since Dr Chambers' death deprived the court of a witness whose evidence would have been highly relevant to this issue. I do not doubt that his Honour did consider the evidence closely although he does not analyze it at any length in his judgment. As I have said, he mentions the background factors which I have summarized above. He refers to the appellant's evidence that had the risk of paralysis been suggested she 'would have run to Bourke'; and he adds the comment: 'A very real question arises as to whether this evidence should be accepted.' It is evident that his doubt about its credibility arises from what I have called the background factors coupled with the undoubted element that the subjective test necessarily entails the risk of distortion by hindsight. Ultimately, Cole J expressed his material findings thus:

Applying the subjective test, I am satisfied, on the balance of probabilities, that Mrs Ellis would not have rejected the operation if the slight risk of paralysis had been mentioned. I find that her position was such, all else having been tried and failed, she would have accepted the advice of Dr Chambers in whom she had such faith and on whom she placed such reliance, had he recommended the rhizotomy operation yet coupled it with a warning that there was a slight risk of paralysis.

. . . Cole J did not explicitly say that he derived assistance from the appellant's demeanour; nor did he offer any other general assessment of her credibility. Certainly, he seems to have accepted everything she said concerning her dealings with Dr Chambers, and no attack was made upon her credit in any particular. Nevertheless, it seems to me inescapable that in arriving at a conclusion as to what the appellant was likely to have done in 1975 if faced with warnings about the possible consequences of a surgical procedure which had been in fact represented to her in an almost entirely favourable light, he must have taken account of how the witness presented herself to him. The question which the learned judge had to decide, which, to me, is a very difficult one, did not only depend upon his view of the appellant's truthfulness, but also upon her capacity, assuming that she was endeavouring to be honest, to restore herself in recollection to the situation in which she stood when the critical decision had to be made. Indeed, it would have been necessary for her to attribute to that decision a significance far greater than any that it could have assumed at the time.

Examining merely the written record, there seems to me much to be said in favour of our view that the circumstances that the appellant hesitated for as long as she did, and sought assurance as often as she did, about a procedure which, so far as she knew, offered only the most minor risk, suggest that her reaction to the true state of affairs would probably have been retreat. Moreover, on the face of it, she appeared to minimize to some extent the gravity of the pain and to diminish its influence upon her decision. But, no doubt, his Honour considered all these matters and was able to do so with the advantage of having seen the appellant in the witness-box. . . .

There are . . . cogent reasons for concluding that it is not open to an appellate court to differ from this critical finding.

However, there are powerful considerations in this case which make in the contrary direction. First, his Honour does not appear to have considered the fact that this crucial passage in the appellant's evidence stood unchallenged; certainly, he makes no mention of it. . . . There was, so far as I can see, no other evidence in contradiction of the appellant's statement. . . .

Secondly, the judge evidently took the view that the appellant's failure to offer any evidence as to how she would have reacted to information about the low prospect of success put her out of court on this issue. I do not consider that that was a justifiable view. The omission to offer the evidence was of considerable materiality. But it did not follow that a likely hypothetical response could not have been inferred from the appellant's evidence as a whole, taking advantage of the light which that cast upon her character and likely attitudes. I do not think, therefore, that it is correct to say, as the learned judge did, that in the 'absence of any evidence which permits a determination on a subjective basis whether she would have proceeded or not' the plaintiff failed to prove the necessary link. The absence of direct evidence as to how she thought she would have behaved at the time did not preclude consideration of the issue on a subjective basis.

Additionally, the learned judge did not give any attention to the possible subjective response which the appellant might have made had the information conveyed to her contained both a warning about possible paralysis and an accurate assessment of the likely prospects of success. This is curious, if I may say so, because he found that Dr Chambers' negligence involved failure to warn about both these matters. But he took this course, I would judge, because of the way in which he eliminated from consideration the possible influence of the low rate of statistical success. But, in my respectful opinion, he was not only bound to consider that matter alone from a subjective standpoint, but bound also to consider it from the same standpoint as one of two combined elements in the warning which the appellant should have received.

For these reasons, it is my opinion that the finding that the appellant failed to establish any causative link cannot stand.

Kirby P: I consider that Cole J was correct in applying the 'subjective' test rather than an 'objective' one to the question whether Mrs Ellis would have undergone the operation had she been more fully informed of its risks both of paralysis (remote) and failure to relieve her pain (more substantial). For the reasons given by Samuels JA, I consider that the question to be asked is whether, in the particular circumstances, the risk was such that the particular patient should have been told and, if told, would not have accepted the treatment. It is not whether a hypothetical 'reasonable' patient or even the hybrid 'reasonable patient in the position of the particular patient' would have accepted or rejected the treatment if fully and properly informed of the risks involved in it: cf Cox J in *Gover v South Australia* (1985) 39 SASR 543 at 564; *Smith v Auckland Hospital Board* [1965] NZLR 191; *Bolam v Friern Hospital Management Committee* [1957] 1 WLR 582; [1957] 2 All ER 118; cf *Sykes v Midland Bank Executor and Trustee Co Ltd* [1971] 1 QB 113 at 127, 131 (CA); see also *Sidaway v Bethlem Royal Hospital and Maudsley Hospital Board of Governors* [1985] AC 871 at 894 (HL).

It is true that in Canada and the United States an 'objective' test of 'what a prudent [or reasonable] person in the patient's position would have decided if suitably informed of all perils bearing significance' has been adopted: see *Reibl v Hughes* (1978) 89 DLR (3d) 112 (SCC); *Haughian v Paine* (1987) 37 DLR (4th) 624 (Sask CA); *Schanilec Estate v Harris* (1987) 39 CCLT 279 (BCCA) and *Canterbury v Spence* 464 F 2d 772 at 791 (1972). However, that approach was trenchantly criticized by Lord Diplock in *Sidaway* (ibid at 894). It has also been criticized in Canadian academic literature: see, eg. M A Somerville, 'Structuring the Issues in Informed Consent' (1981) 26 McGill LJ 740. The courts in Canada, whilst remaining loyal to the language of the Supreme Court in *Reibl*, have sought to develop the notion of the hybrid: see eg. *White v Turner* (1981) 120 DLR (3d) 269. We are under no such compulsion to conform to *Reibl*. Deference to respect for the integrity of the patient as an individual, entitled to have command over his or her body, suggests that the common law should uphold the right of the patient to

> ... decline operative investigation or treatment however unreasonably or foolish this may appear in the eyes of his [or her] medical advisers ... [*Smith v Auckland Hospital Board* at p 210]

The same approach has been adopted in civil law jurisdictions: see discussion. D Giesen, International Medical Malpractice Law, Martinus Nijhoff, London, (1988) at 345. It is the one which I would apply.

Although Cole J stated that he would reach the same conclusion whether the 'subjective' or 'objective' test were applied, his correct specification of the 'subjective' test made all the more important the accurate ascertainment of what Mrs Ellis, herself, would have done, had she been properly advised of the risks involved in the operation.

It is true that answering the question involves an exercise in retrospective reasoning. The patient cannot, when the mishap leading to damage and litigation has occurred, determine the answer authoritatively by the response in court to the question of what he or she would have done had only full and proper advice been given. However honest the patient may try to be, self-interest and the knowledge of the misfortunes that have followed the treatment will necessarily colour the patient's response to that question. Nonetheless, the answer remains an important ingredient in the decision by the fact finding tribunal as to what it thinks the patient, subjectively and at the time before operation, would have done if properly and fully advised.

Mrs Ellis (in the passages incorporated in Samuels JA's judgment) gave clear evidence on this point. Had she known that paralysis or possible paralysis was an outcome of the operation she would 'definitely not' have had the operation: 'If he had mentioned anything, I would have run to Bourke.' This colloquial expression, poignant in the case of a quadriplegic, envisaging as it does a race to one of the most remote outback towns of Australia, leaves in no doubt what Mrs Ellis was asserting to be (albeit retrospectively) the stance she would have taken at the time.

Other evidence tends to support her assertion. She emerges from the written testimony as a somewhat obsessive person, with strong views, for example, on the taking of tablets. Her step-daughter, according to the evidence, specifically pressed Dr Chambers in her presence to an assurance about the risks of the operation. Once before she had been admitted to hospital in 1971 for an operation but she elected not to have it. Far from assisting the hospital's case, this answer, secured in cross-examination, suggests to my mind that she was the kind of person who would have thought carefully about the risks of the operation as they were explained to her. It is true that she was suffering pain. But according to her, Dr Chambers built the operation up, describing it as 'terrific'. In these circumstances she was certainly entitled, in modern conditions, to be given a more detailed, candid and balanced statement of the risks of the operation. Not, perhaps, remote or fanciful risks or those minuscule, freak, unpredictable risks that can sometimes occur. But the bigger the devastation of the possible risk, the greater is the obligation to lay it before the patient so that he or she can make an informed decision.

Cole J found (in terms which are not challenged and appear anyway to be manifestly right) that Dr Chambers did not warn Mrs Ellis that there was a high chance that the operation would not relieve her from pain and that there was a small, but not fanciful, risk of a resultant paralysis. The two risks are obviously inter-related. An operation with a very high success rate and a very low risk of paralysis may, rationally, be accepted much more readily than one where the prospects of success were more circumscribed, though the risk of paralysis was still slight. Dr Chambers undoubtedly thought it in the best interests of Mrs Ellis that she should undergo the operation, but the decision was hers, not his (or the hospital's) to make.

Despite Mrs Ellis' emphatic evidence, Cole J concluded as he did. He had the advantage of seeing Mrs Ellis give her testimony. No doubt this entered into his evaluation of the issue. Mrs Ellis was not cross-examined directly on her statement. Nor was it put to her, specifically, that she would have undergone the operation, contrary to her assertion. The death of Dr Chambers and his consequent absence from the trial did not, in my view, explain or justify the failure of the hospital to challenge Mrs Ellis' direct assertion and to do so in plain terms so that she might meet the challenge ... Mrs Ellis' evidence not being 'inherently incredible' or 'inherently improbable', I am of the opinion that an error has occurred in Cole J's reasoning which is of critical importance. It is one sufficiently serious to require relief from this court. No other explanation is given by Cole J as to why he rejected Mrs Ellis' unchallenged statement. There is no express reference to her demeanour. ... But in the face of emphatic, unchallenged evidence which had support from several objective or unchallenged facts, the conclusion by his Honour to the contrary without adequate or any explanation demands correction.

Meagher JA agreed with Samuels JA.

(ii) LEGAL CAUSATION: REMOTENESS

Generally speaking, no particular problems arise specific to informed consent involving remoteness of damage. One problem which we ought to notice, however, is what we can call the problem of the 'unrelated risk'. This involves the following. A patient is advised by his doctor of risk 'X' but not of risk 'Y' and, thereafter, consents to the treatment, ie agrees to run risk 'X'. Let us assume, for these purposes, that the failure to disclose risk 'Y' is a breach of the doctor's duty to his patient. Further, let us assume it can be proved that the patient would not have undergone the procedure had he been informed of risk 'Y'. During the treatment risk 'X' eventuates and the patient is injured. The patient brings an action against the doctor alleging a breach of duty in failing to warn of risk 'Y' relying upon the harm suffered unrelated to risk 'Y' since risk 'Y' has not eventuated.

This issue was considered by the Court of Session (Outer House) in the following case.

Moyes v Lothian Health Board [1990] 1 Med LR 463 (CS(OH))

A patient was advised to undergo angiography. She was informed of the risk of suffering a stroke inherent in such a procedure. She was not, however, informed that the risk was increased given her particular medical condition of hypersensitivity to the contrast medium used in the procedure and the fact that she had a history of migraine. In the event she suffered a stroke. It was not associated with her hypersensitivity but with the standard risk of suffering a stroke about which she had been informed. In her action in negligence, Lord Caplan at one stage assumed that not warning her of the increased risk associated with her hypersensitivity constituted a breach of duty to inform. On this basis he addressed the question whether she could claim where the harm she suffered was unrelated to the breach of duty.

Lord Caplan: The ordinary person who has to consider whether or not to have an operation is not interested in the exact pathological genesis of the various complications which can occur but rather in the nature and extent of the risk. The patient would want to know what chance there was of the operation going wrong and if it did what would happen. If we were to suppose a situation where an operation would give rise to a 1 per cent risk of serious complication in the ordinary case but where there could be four other special factors each adding a further 1 per cent to the risk, a patient to whom all five factors applied might have a 5 per cent risk rather than the 1 per cent risk of the average person. It is perfectly conceivable that a patient might be prepared to accept the risk of one in 100 but not be prepared to face up to a risk of one in 20. If a doctor contrary to established practice failed to warn the patient of the four special risks but did warn the patient of the standard risk and then the patient suffered complication caused physiologically by the standard risk factor rather than by one or other of the four special risks factors I do not think the doctor should escape the consequences of not having warned the patient of the added risks which that patient was exposed to. A patient might well with perfect reason consider that if there were five risk factors rather than one then the chance of one or other of these factors materializing was much greater. The coincidence that the damage which occurred was due to the particular factor in respect of which a warning was given does not alter the fact that the patient was not properly warned of the total risks inherent in the operation and thus could not make an informed decision as to whether or not to go through with it. In the example I give, by going through an operation with five risk factors rather than one the patient was exposed to a degree of risk materially in excess of what the patient had been warned about and was prepared to accept. If he had been given due warning he would have not risked suffering adverse complication from that particular operation and the fact that such complication occurred is causal connection enough to found a claim against the doctor.

While Lord Caplan's judgment is correct as far as it goes, it treats the issue wholly in terms of *factual* causation. Lord Caplan, however, did not recognise that there was also an issue of legal causation, ie remoteness of damage. It is axiomatic in the law of torts that not every factual cause founds a claim even though harm is produced. The issue which Lord Caplan should have addressed is whether the patient's harm was too remote from the breach of duty. It may well be that Lord Caplan would still have held the doctor liable assuming as he did there was a breach of duty to inform. Other cases may arise, however, where the result of the case may be different depending on whether the question is recognised to be one of factual or legal causation. In other words, if the court chooses to address this issue as a question of remoteness, a claim by a plaintiff may be less likely to succeed. This is because a court may have an intuitive sense that liability should not arise for a harm which is *unrelated* to the doctor's breach of duty to inform and so organise the legal test to achieve this result.

(f) Post-treatment disclosure

Robertson 'Fraudulent Concealment and the Duty to Disclose Medical Mistakes' (1987) 25 Alberta LR 215

In recent years a great deal of attention has focused on the duty of a doctor to provide the patient with information prior to performing medical treatment: the concept of 'informed consent'. Very little, however, has been said about a related issue – how much information must a doctor give a patient after the treatment has been performed? In particular, if a mistake is made in the course of treatment (especially surgical treatment), is the doctor under a legal duty to inform the patient of this?

Where a mistake is made in the course of a surgical operation, the doctor's duty to provide reasonable post-operative care requires that proper corrective measures be taken. This will often involve having to inform the patient that something has gone wrong, if this is not already apparent, in order to make the patient aware of the need for further treatment. If the patient is not told, and suffers injury as a result, the doctor is clearly liable. For example, in *Melvin v Graham* [[1973] DRS 659 (Ont HC)] a surgeon who cut into the patient's bladder during a herniotomy was held to have been negligent in not providing proper post-operative care to deal with potential complications arising from his mistake. Similarly, it has been held that failure to inform a patient that a sterilization operation has been unsuccessful [*Cryderman v Ringrose* (1978) 3 WWR 481 (Alta CA)] or that the tip of a hypodermic syringe has broken off during an injection and remains lodged in the patient's body [*Gerber v Pines* (1934) 79 Sol Jo 13 (KB); but see *Daniels v Heskin* [1954] IR 73 (SC) (doctor not negligent in failing to inform patient of presence of broken needle)], renders the doctor liable for any additional injuries suffered as a result of the patient not undergoing corrective treatment. [In *Kueper v McMullin* (1986) 37 CCLT 318 (NBCA), the tip of a dental drill accidentally broke off and lodged in the patient's tooth while the defendant-dentist was performing a root canal. The dentist tried unsuccessfully to remove the drill tip, and decided to seal the tooth. He did not inform the patient of what had happened. The patient's subsequent claim for damages was dismissed. The court held that the dentist ought to have informed the patient of what had happened, and discussed with her the alternative methods of dealing with the problem. However, the court concluded that, even if she had been told, the patient would have consented to having the tooth sealed with the drill tip inside.]

A much more problematic situation arises where the doctor's failure to tell the patient what has happened does not cause any additional physical injury, but merely keeps the patient ignorant of a possible cause of action against the doctor. In many instances a patient who suffers injury during a surgical operation may only discover this (if at all) several years later. In view of the applicable limitation period in Alberta, it becomes especially important to consider whether the law imposes a duty on the doctor to inform the patient of what went wrong in the course of the operation. The recent decision of the English Court of Appeal in *Lee v South West Thames Regional Health Authority* [[1985] 2 All ER 385 (CA)], and the Ontario case of *Stamos v Davies* [(1985) 21 DLR (4th) 507 (Ont HC)] which follows it, suggests that a duty to disclose medical mistakes does exist.

Let us consider in turn the two cases referred to by Robertson at the end of the extract and the further case of *Naylor v Preston AHA* [1987] 2 All ER 353.

Lee v South West Thames Regional Health Authority [1985] 2 All ER 385 (CA)

Sir John Donaldson MR: It should never be forgotten that we are here concerned with a hospital-patient relationship. The recent decision of the House of Lords in *Sidaway v Bethlem Royal Hospital Governors* [1985] 1 All ER 643, [1985] 2 WLR 480 affirms that a doctor is under a duty to answer his patient's questions as to the treatment proposed. We see no reason why there should not be a similar duty in relation to hospital staff. This duty is subject to the exercise of clinical judgment as to the terms in which the information is given and the extent to which, in the patient's interests, information should be withheld. Why, we ask ourselves, is the position any different if the patient asks what treatment he has in fact had? Let us suppose that a blood transfusion is in contemplation. The patient asks what is involved. He is told that a quantity of blood from a donor will be introduced into his system. He may ask about the risk of AIDS and so forth and will be entitled to straight answers. He consents. Suppose that, by accident, he is given a quantity of air as well as blood and suffers serious ill effects. Is he not entitled to ask what treatment he in fact received, and is the doctor and hospital authority not obliged to tell him, 'in the event you did not only get a blood transfusion. You also got an air transfusion'? Why is the duty different before the treatment from what it is afterwards?

If the duty is the same, then if the patient is refused information to which he is entitled, it must be for consideration whether he could not bring an action for breach of contract claiming specific performance of the duty to inform. In other words, whether the patient could not bring an action for discovery, albeit on a novel basis.

We consider that some thought should be given to what is the duty of disclosure owed by a doctor and a hospital to a patient after treatment, but that is not an issue in this appeal.

Mustill LJ agreed.

Naylor v Preston Area Health Authority [1987] 2 All ER 353, [1987] 1 WLR 958 (CA)

Sir John Donaldson MR: I personally think that in professional negligence cases, and in particular in medical negligence cases, there is a duty of candour resting on the professional man. This is recognised by the legal professions in their ethical rules requiring their members to refer the client to other advisers, if it appears that the client has a valid claim for negligence. This also appears to be recognised by the Medical Defence Union, whose view is that 'the patient is entitled to a prompt, sympathetic and above all truthful account of what has occurred' (*Journal of the MDU* (1986) vol 2, no 2, p 2). It was also the view (admittedly *obiter*) of myself and Mustill LJ, as expressed in our judgment in *Lee v South West Thames Regional Health Authority* [1985] 2 All ER 385 at 389-390, [1985] 1 WLR 845 at 850. In this context I was disturbed to be told during the argument of the present appeals that the view was held in some quarters that whilst the duty of candid disclosure, to which we there referred, might give rise to a contractual implied term and so benefit private fee-paying patients, it did not translate into a legal or equitable right for the benefit of national health service patients. This I would entirely repudiate. In my judgment, still admittedly and regretfully *obiter*, it is but one aspect of the general duty of care, arising out of the patient/ medical practitioner or hospital authority relationship and gives rise to rights both in contract and in tort.

Professor Robertson (*op cit*) goes on:

It is interesting to note that in *Lee* Sir John Donaldson was repeating what he had said extra-judicially two months earlier, in an address to the Medico-Legal Society [(1985) 53

Medico-Legal J 148]. In that address he admitted that he was simply 'flying a kite' with respect to his views on the duty to disclose medical mistakes. When asked by a member of the audience whether the law does say that doctors must inform their patients if something goes wrong, he replied, 'the law does not say so yet'. Two months later it did.

As was predicted by a leading English barrister [Whitfield (1985) 54 Medico-Legal J 11 at 21], the kite flown by the Master of the Rolls did not stay in the air indefinitely. It landed in Ontario, in the judgment of Mr Justice Kreever in *Stamos v Davies*.

Stamos v Davies (1985) 21 DLR (4th) 507 (Ontario High Ct)

While performing a lung biopsy on the plaintiff, the defendant internist accidentally punctured the plaintiff's spleen. As a result, the spleen had to be removed surgically at a later time. Following the biopsy the defendant did not tell the plaintiff that his spleen had been biopsied and not his lung. The defendant told the plaintiff that he had no result from the biopsy because he had not obtained what he wanted. When asked by the plaintiff what, in fact, he had obtained his reply was simply that he had obtained 'something else' and that there would have to be another biopsy.

Krever J: I hold that, in law, there was a duty on the defendant to inform the plaintiff that he had entered his spleen. The plaintiff asked the defendant what he had obtained at the biopsy. The defendant's failure to be candid with the plaintiff was a breach of duty.

Again, however, the defendant's breach of duty to disclose does not lead to liability. There is no causal connection between the failure to inform the plaintiff about the splenic injury (or, for that matter, the failure to order an ultrasound study or the early discharge from hospital, if I am wrong in my opinion that they did not amount to a breach of duty) and the loss of the spleen. No other conclusion can be drawn from the evidence than that the spleen, in this case, was doomed from the moment it was injured. There is no suggestion in the evidence that anything the plaintiff did at home caused the spleen to rebleed and thus cause its removal. As the defendant's breach of duty to inform the plaintiff of what had happened to his spleen did not cause the damage suffered by the plaintiff, that is, his pain and suffering or the loss of his spleen, the breach of duty was not negligence. The term, negligence, imports the existence of a duty to the plaintiff, a breach of that duty by the defendant and resulting damage to the plaintiff.

Arguably, the legal difficulty identified by Krever J in *Stamos*, ie the inability to show harm *flowing from the breach of duty to disclose post-treatment*, will be common to most cases. Thus, while the Master of the Rolls' comments may have significant ethical force, they are unlikely to take the law any further.

3. Waiver

The question here is whether a patient may (expressly or impliedly) absolve a doctor from his duty to inform, assuming the situation to be one in which this duty *prima facie* exists. The answer is probably sometimes but not always. Regrettably it is difficult to be much more precise than this. In their 1983 Report the President's Commission 'Making Health Care Decisions' (1983) address the issue (at p 94):

The modest attention paid to the fourth exception – waiver – in the courts and scholarly literature is regrettable given its interesting relationship to the value of self-determination that underlies the doctrine of informed consent . . . self-determination encompasses both the moral right to formal control over a decision and the ideal of active participation in the decisionmaking process. Although these two senses of self-determination often go hand in hand, sometimes they do not, as in the case of a waiver, when a patient asks not to be informed of certain matters and/or delegates decisional authority to another person.

The impact of the waiver exception is that if a waiver is properly obtained the patient remains the ultimate decisionmaker, but the content of his decision is shifted from the decisional level to the metadecisional level – from the equivalent of 'I want this treatment (or that treatment or no treatment)' to 'I don't want any information about the treatment' [Meisel (1979) Wis L Rev 413 at 459].

The legal requirements for effective waiver in the context of informed consent have never been clearly articulated by the courts. There is substantial reason to believe that the courts would respect waivers of certain information (for example, the disclosure of particular risks) or the delegation of certain decisions to others. Yet it is questionable whether patients should be permitted to waive the professional's obligation to disclose fundamental information about the nature and implications of certain procedures (such as, 'when you wake up, you will learn that your limb has been amputated' or 'that you are irreversibly sterile'). In the absence of explicit legal guidance, health care professionals should be quite circumspect about allowing or disallowing, encouraging or discouraging, a patient's use of waiver.

Obviously the court must be satisfied that there was in truth a waiver in that the doctor was prepared to inform and the patient willingly declined. The suggestion is that there is a public policy limitation as to which the extent a patient may waive a doctor's duty.

In our view, while the patient may waive the right to information as to risks or whatever, it would be against public policy to allow him to waive the right to be informed of the 'nature and purpose' of the proposed procedure. In other words, it could be argued that the law recognises that a patient has a duty to inform himself of what is proposed which he cannot waive.

C. VOLUNTARINESS

The third element of consent is that it be voluntarily and freely given.

Winfield & Jolowicz on Tort (13th edn 1989) at 691

The consent must be freely given
The main point to notice here is that 'a man cannot be said to be truly "willing" unless he is in a position to choose freely, and freedom of choice predicates, not only full knowledge of the circumstances on which the exercise of choice is conditional, so that he may be able to choose wisely, but the absence of any feeling of constraint so that nothing shall interfere with the freedom of his will' [*Bowater v Rowley Regis Corpn* [1944] KB 476 at 479 per Scott LJ].

In the context of medical law detailed consideration of the issue was given by the President's Commission in its 1983 Report.

President's Commission 'Making Health Care Decisions' (1983)

Voluntariness in decisionmaking
The patient's participation in the decisionmaking process and ultimate decision regarding care must be voluntary. A choice that has been coerced, or that resulted from serious manipulation of a person's ability to make an intelligent and informed decision, is not the person's own free choice. This has long been recognised in law: a consent forced by threats or induced by fraud or misrepresentation is legally viewed as no consent at all. From the perspective of ethics, a consent that is substantially involuntary does not provide moral authorisation for treatment because it does not respect the patient's dignity and may not reflect the aims of the patient.

Of course, the facts of disease and the limited capabilities of medicine often constrict the choices available to patient and physician alike. In that sense, the condition of illness itself is sometimes spoken of as 'coercive' or involuntary. But the fact that no available alternative may be desirable in itself, and that the preferred course is, at best, only the least bad among a bad lot, does not render a choice coerced in the sense employed here. No change in human behaviour or institutional structure could remove this limitation. Such constraints are merely facts of life that should not be regarded as making a patient's choice involuntary.

Voluntariness is best regarded as a matter of degree, rather than as a quality that is wholly present or absent in particular cases. Forced treatment – the embodiment of coercive, involuntary action – appears to be rare in the American health care system. Health care professionals do, however, make limited intrusions on voluntary choice through subtle, or even overt, manipulations of patients' wills when they believe that patients would otherwise make incorrect decisions.

Forced treatment. The most overt forms of involuntariness in health care settings involve interventions forced on patients without their consent (and sometimes over their express objection) and those based on coerced consent. Although rare in mainstream American health care, such situations do arise in certain special settings, and therefore require brief discussion. Society currently legitimates certain forced medical interventions to serve important social goals such as promoting the public health (with, for example, compulsory vaccination laws), enforcing the criminal law (removing bullets needed as evidence for criminal prosecutions), or otherwise promoting the well-being of others (sedating uncontrollable inmates of mental institutions on an emergency basis, for example, to protect other inmates or staff).

Although it is typically not viewed as forced treatment, a good deal of routine care in hospitals, nursing homes, and other health care settings is provided (usually by health professionals such as nurses) without explicit and voluntary consent by patients. The expectation on the part of professionals is that patients, once in such a setting, will simply go along with such routine care. However, the Commission's study of treatment refusals found that in a hospital setting it was the routine tests that were most likely to be refused. At least some patients expected that participation was voluntary and refused tests and medications ordered without their knowledge until adequate information was provided about the nature, purpose, and risks of these undertakings. Lack of information in such cases may not only preclude voluntary participation but also raises questions about a patient's rationality, and hence competence.

When a situation offers the patient an opportunity to refuse care, then patient compliance or acquiescence may be viewed as implicit consent. But when the tacit communication accompanying such care is that there is no choice for the patient to make, and compliance is expected and enforced (at least in the absence of vigorous objections), the treatment can be properly termed 'forced'. The following conversation between a nurse and a patient regarding postoperative care, obtained in one of the Commission's observational studies, illustrates forced treatment that follows routinely from another decision (surgery) that was made voluntarily.

Nurse: Did they mention anything about a tube through your nose?
Patient: Yes, I'm gonna have a tube in my nose.
Nurse: You're going to have the tube down for a couple of days or longer. It depends. So you're going to NPO, nothing by mouth, and also you're going to have IV fluid.
Patient: I know. For three or four days they told me that already. I don't like it, though.
Nurse: You don't have any choice.
Patient: Yes, I don't have any choice, I know.
Nurse: Like it or not, you don't have any choice (laughter). After you come back, we'll ask you to do a lot of coughing and deep breathing to exercise your lungs.
Patient: Oh, we'll see how I feel.
Nurse: (Emphasis) No matter how you feel, you have to do that!

The interview ended a few minutes later with the patient still disputing whether he was going to co-operate with the postoperative care.

Coerced treatment. Unlike forced treatment, for which no consent is given, coerced treatment proceeds on the basis of a consent that was not freely given. As used in this sense, a patient's decision is coerced when the person is credibly threatened by another individual, either explicitly or by implication, with unwanted and avoidable consequences unless the patient accedes to the specified course of action. Concern about coercion is accordingly greatest when a disproportion in power or other significant inequality between a patient and another individual lends credibility to the threat of harm and when the perceived interests of the individuals diverge.

The disparity in power between patient and health care professional may be slight or substantial, depending on the nature of the patient's illness, the institutional setting, the personalities of the individuals involved, and several other factors. In nonemergency settings, a patient typically can change practitioners or simply forego treatment, thus avoiding the potential for coercion. Further, although health care professionals do have interests distinct from and sometimes in conflict with those of their patients, strong social and professional norms usually ensure that priority is accorded to patients' welfare. To be sure, coercion can be exercised with benevolent motives if practitioner and patient differ in their assessments of how the patient's welfare is best served. Nonetheless, there is little reason to believe that blatant forms of coercion are a problem in mainstream American health care. When isolated instances of abuse do arise, the law provides suitable remedies.

A patient's family and other concerned persons may often play a useful role in the decisionmaking process. Sometimes, however, they may try to coerce a particular decision, either because of what they perceive to be in the patient's best interests or because of a desire to advance their own interests. In such instances, since the health care professional's first loyalty is to the patient, he or she should attempt to enhance the patient's ability to make a voluntary, uncoerced decision and to overcome any coercive pressures.

Manipulation. Blatant coercion may be of so little concern in professional-patient relationships because, as physicians so often proclaim, it is so easy for health professionals to elicit a desired decision through more subtle means. Indeed, some physicians are critical of the legal requirement for informed consent on the grounds that it must be mere window dressing since 'patients will, if they trust their doctor, accede to almost any request he cares to make'. On some occasions, to be sure, this result can be achieved by rational persuasion, since the professional presumably has good reasons for preferring a recommended course of action. But the tone of such critics suggests they have something else in mind: an ability to package and present the facts in a way that leaves the patient with no real choice. Such conduct, capitalising on disparities in knowledge, position, and influence, is manipulative in character and impairs the voluntariness of the patient's choice.

Manipulation has more and less extreme forms. At one end of the spectrum is behaviour amounting to misrepresentation or fraud. Of particular concern in health care contexts is the withholding or distortion of information in order to affect the patient's beliefs and decisions. The patient might not be told about alternatives to the recommended course of action, for example, or the risks of other negative characteristics of the recommended treatment might be minimised. Such behaviour is justly criticised on two grounds: first, that it interferes with the patient's voluntary choice (and thus negates consent) and, second, that it interferes with the patient's ability to make an informed decision. At the other end of the spectrum are far more subtle instances: a professional's careful choice of words or nuances of tone and emphasis might present the situation in a manner calculated to heighten the appeal of a particular course of action.

It is well known that the way information is presented can powerfully affect the recipient's response to it. The tone of voice and other aspects of the practitioner's manner of presentation can indicate whether a risk of a particular kind with a particular incidence should be considered serious. Information can be emphasised or played down without altering the content. And it can be framed in a way that affects the listener – for example, 'this procedure succeeds most of the time' versus 'this procedure has a 40 per cent failure rate'. Health professionals who are aware of the effects of such minor variations can choose their language with care; if, during discussions, they can adjust their presentation of information accordingly.

Because many patients are often fearful and unequal to their physicians in status, knowledge, and power, they may be particularly susceptible to manipulations of this type. Health care professionals should, therefore, present information in a form that fosters understanding. Patients should be helped to understand the prognosis for their situation and the implications of different courses of treatment. The difficult distinction, both in theory and in practice, is between acceptable forms of informing, discussion, and rational persuasion on the one hand, and objectionable forms of influence or manipulation on the other.

Since voluntariness is one of the foundation stones of . . . consent, professionals have a high ethical obligation to avoid coercion and manipulation of their patients. The law penalises those who ignore the requirements of consent or who directly coerce it. But it can do little about subtle manipulations without incurring severe disruptions of private relationships by intrusive policing, and so the duty is best thought of primarily in ethical terms.

We now turn to consider the extent to which this analysis is reflected in English law.

A case in the last century adopted a view which would undoubtedly be regarded now as out of sympathy with the times.

Latter v Braddell (1881) 50 LJQB 448

The plaintiff's mistress requested a doctor to examine the plaintiff, who was a domestic servant, in order to ascertain whether she was pregnant. The plaintiff objected to the examination, but undressed by the doctor's orders, and submitted to be examined. The doctor examined her, and ascertained that she was not pregnant. He used no violence or threats and did nothing more than was necessary for the examination. The mistress was not present.

The plaintiff sued her master and mistress and the doctor for assault. At the trial the Judge directed a verdict for the master and mistress, and the jury found a verdict for the doctor.

Held (affirming the order of the Common Pleas Division), that there was no evidence against the master and mistress, that the verdict in favour of the doctor was right, and that a rule for a new trial was rightly discharged.

The plaintiff appealed.

Bramwell LJ: I am of opinion that Mr Justice Lindley was right; in fact, I may almost say that he was more than right, for it seems to me that he might have directed a verdict for the defendant, Dr Sutcliffe; but if there was any evidence, his direction to the jury was right, and their finding was right, although it may be a practical hardship. Very likely the plaintiff thought the defendants had a right to have her examined; but the truth is, she submitted to it, and it is impossible to say the jury were wrong in finding that she submitted. She may have submitted under an erroneous notion of law, but it was not through fear of violence. It seems to follow that if the verdict for Dr Sutcliffe was right the other defendants are entitled to a verdict. I think Mr Justice Lindley was right in telling the jury that there was no evidence against Captain and Mrs Braddell. There could only be evidence against them if the plaintiff submitted through fear of violence, and if what was done was done by their order.

Baggallay LJ: I am of the same opinion. The argument for the plaintiff is on the ground of misdirection in withdrawing the case against Captain and Mrs Braddell from the jury, and on the ground that the verdict in favour of Dr Sutcliffe was against the weight of evidence. I think the verdict as to Dr Sutcliffe was right. As to Mrs Braddell I am not satisfied that she did more than tell Dr Sutcliffe to do what might be necessary and proper. Order XXXIX rule 3 would be fatal to the appeal, for no wrong was occasioned, even if there was misdirection.

Brett LJ: I am of opinion that Mr Justice Lindley was right. The doctor could only be liable if he did what he did without the consent or submission of the plaintiff; and Captain and Mrs Braddell could only be liable if they authorised the doctor to do what he did, and he did it, without such consent or submission. I think there was no evidence against Captain and Mrs Braddell. As to the doctor, there might be a case against him, though there was not a case against the other defendants. Then, was there any case for the jury as against Dr Sutcliffe? I think Mr Justice Lindley would have been justified in withdrawing the case from the jury. To make out an assault by Dr Sutcliffe, the plaintiff must shew that he used violence, or that she had reasonable cause to believe that he was threatening violence. I think the law laid down in the judgment of Mr Justice Lindley in the Court below is correct. Even if there was any evidence against Dr Sutcliffe I think there was no misdirection; and if the verdict as to him was right the withdrawal from the jury of the case against Captain and Mrs Braddell was immaterial, because, if Dr Sutcliffe did not assault the plaintiff, it does not matter if they authorised him.

The judgment was affirmed.

Should such facts arise today, there can be little doubt that the plaintiff would have succeeded.

In *Re T (adult: refusal of medical treatment)* [1992] 4 All ER 649 the Court of Appeal sought to establish the legal context in which voluntariness should be placed. The court went beyond the identification of involuntariness with the more usual examples of duress and instead analysed it in terms of the more general legal concept of undue influence. In so doing, the court potentially broadened the scope of the factors which could vitiate a patient's consent or, as in the case itself, a refusal of consent.

Re T (adult: refusal of medical treatment) [1992] 4 All ER 649, (1992) 9 BMLR 46 (CA)

On July 1 1992, Miss T, an adult then 34 weeks pregnant, was involved in a road traffic accident. On July 4 she was admitted to hospital complaining of chest pains. She was diagnosed as suffering from pleurisy or pneumonia and was prescribed antibiotics and analgesics and given oxygen.

Although brought up by her mother, a fervent Jehovah's Witness, Miss T was not a member of that faith. Her paternal family was opposed to the sect.

On the evening of July 5, when she was in considerable pain, coughing up sputum, on various drugs and suffering contractions in the first stage of labour Miss T said that she did not want a blood transfusion. Shortly before this she had been alone with her mother. Miss T did ask whether there was a substitute treatment and was told that there was.

A decision was made that the delivery should be by caesarean section. A form of refusal of consent to blood transfusions was signed by Miss T. Contrary to what was stated on the form, it was not explained to Miss T that it might be necessary to give a blood transfusion so as to prevent injury to her health, or even to preserve her life, nor was the form read or its contents explained to her.

The caesarean section was performed on July 6, but the baby was stillborn. That night Miss T's condition deteriorated and she was transferred to intensive care. It appeared that an abscess had developed in Miss T's lungs. Miss T remained in a critical condition throughout July 7.

On July 8 Ward J granted a declaration that in the circumstances which were then prevailing, it would not be unlawful for the hospital to administer a blood transfusion to Miss T despite the absence of her consent because that appeared manifestly to be in her best interests.

Thereupon Miss T received a transfusion of blood or plasma.

Lord Donaldson MR: In essence Ward J found that the physical and mental state of Miss T on the Sunday afternoon and evening were such that although she was undoubtedly under the influence of her mother, she was capable of reaching and did reach a decision as to her own treatment . . .

A special problem may arise if at the time the decision is made the patient has been subjected to the influence of some third party. This is by no means to say that the patient is not entitled to receive and indeed invite advice and assistance from others in reaching a decision, particularly from members of the family. But the doctors have to consider whether the decision is really that of the patient. It is wholly acceptable that the patient should have been persuaded by others of the merits of such a decision and have decided accordingly. It matters not how strong the persuasion was, so long as it did not overbear the independence of the patient's decision. The real question in each such case is 'Does the patient really mean what he says or is he merely saying it for a quiet life, to satisfy someone else or because the advice and persuasion to which he has been subjected is such that he can no longer think and decide for himself?' In other words 'Is it a decision expressed in form only, not in reality?'

When considering the effect of outside influences, two aspects can be of crucial importance. First, the strength of the will of the patient. One who is very tired, in pain or depressed will be much less able to resist having his will overborne than one who is rested, free from pain and cheerful. Second, the relationship of the 'persuader' to the patient may be of crucial importance. The influence of parents on their children or of one spouse on the other can be, but is by no means necessarily, much stronger than would be the case in other relationships. Persuasion based upon religious beliefs can also be much more compelling and the fact that arguments based upon religious beliefs are being deployed by someone in a very close relationship with the patient will give them added force and should alert the doctors to the possibility – no more – that the patient's capacity or will to decide has been overborne. In other words the patient may not mean what he says.

Butler-Sloss LJ: A most relevant factor in this appeal is the extent and effect of the intervention of the mother who was alone with her daughter immediately before each of the two occasions that Miss T indicated her rejection of a blood transfusion. It is an irresistible inference that before 5 pm the mother had discussed the question of blood transfusions with her daughter because Miss T 'out of the blue' according to the nurse raised the subject. The mother was also alone in the ambulance with her daughter when she was transferred about 11 pm to the labour ward in another part of the hospital shortly before she signed the refusal form. The judge referred to the 'mother's fervent belief in the sin of blood transfusion' and that Miss T had reached her decision under the influence of her mother, but nonetheless found that Miss T's decision was not vitiated by any undue influence. . . . both at law and in equity it has long been recognized that an influence may be subtle, insidious, pervasive and where religious beliefs are involved especially powerful. It may also be powerful between close relatives where one may be in a dominant position vis a vis the other. In this case Miss T had been during her childhood subjected to the religious beliefs of her mother and in her weakened medical condition, in pain, and under the influence of the drugs administered to assist her, the pressure from her mother was likely to have a considerably enhanced effect. I find it difficult to reconcile the facts found by the judge with his conclusion that the influence of the mother did not sap her will or destroy her volition. The degree of pressure to turn persuasion or appeals to affection into undue influence may . . . be very little. In my view the trial judge, dealing as he was with a most difficult and distressing case under the necessity to give a decision immediately, did not sufficiently take into account the degree of pressure required to constitute undue influence in the case of a patient in the position of Miss T. I agree with the Master of the Rolls that there is abundant evidence that she was subjected to the undue influence of her mother which vitiated her decision.

Staughton LJ: It is, I think, misleading to ask whether [the patient's refusal] was made of the patient's own free will, or even whether it was voluntary. Every decision is made of a person's free will, and is voluntary, unless it is effected by compulsion. Likewise every decision is made as a result of some influence: a patient's decision to consent to an operation will normally be influenced by the surgeon's advice as to what will happen if the operation does not take place. In order for an apparent consent or refusal of consent to be less than a true consent or refusal, there must be such a degree of external influence as to persuade the patient to depart from her own wishes, to an extent that the law regards it as undue. I can suggest no more precise test than that. The cases on undue influence in the law of property and contract are not, in my opinion, applicable in the different context of consent to medical or surgical treatment. The wife who guarantees her husband's debts, or the widower who leaves all his property to his housekeeper, are not in the same situation as a patient faced with the need for medical treatment. There are many different ways of expressing the concept that what a person says may not be binding upon him: a Greek poet wrote 'my tongue has sworn, but no oath binds my mind'. . . .

As is clear, *Re T* was a case in which a patient refused treatment. Perhaps the court adopted the undue influence approach out of its desire that the patient should not die. In fact, of course, most questions involving voluntariness arise in the converse situation, ie when it appears that the patient consented but the patient asserts that the consent was not freely given. In such a case any resort to the argument that the consent was involuntary would be so as to protect the patient from unwanted treatment. It could be argued that here the courts would be more reluctant to make a finding of involuntariness since to do so would be to render a doctor liable in battery. But, now that the test has been developed, it cannot be limited to refusals only. Of course, since everything turns on the facts, a court may simply prefer to believe 'refusals' are unreliable while being less doubting of 'consents'.

This last point is, perhaps, illustrated by the following case.

Freeman v Home Office (No 2) [1984] QB 524, [1984] 1 All ER 1036 (CA)

By writ of 15 October 1979 the plaintiff, David Freeman, who at all material times was serving a sentence of life imprisonment at HM Prison, Wakefield, claimed damages for assault and for battery and for trespass to the person by the administration to him of certain drugs, namely Stelazin and/or Modecate and/or Serenace by or under the direction of Dr Cedric Melville Xavier, the servant or agent of the defendants, the Home Office and/or certain prison officers at HM Prison, Wakefield, being also servants or agents of the defendants, between in or about September 1972 and in or about December 1972 against the plaintiff's will and/or without his consent. By paragraph 4 of the statement of claim it was alleged that the plaintiff had not consented to the administration of the drugs or any of them and had 'actively resisted it, but was overcome forcibly by the said medical officer and/or prison officers'.

Stephen Brown LJ: Mr Blom-Cooper submits not only should the judge have inferred the absence of consent by reference to the documentary evidence but, furthermore, that it is impossible within the prison context as between a prisoner and a prison medical officer for free and voluntary consent to exist, at least, he added, in the absence of any written consent form. The prison medical officer is not merely a doctor, he is, submits Mr Blom-Cooper, a prison officer within the meaning of the Prison Rules and accordingly is a person who can influence a prisoner's life and his prospects of release on licence. There must inevitably be an atmosphere of constraint upon an inmate in such circumstances. He cited the well-known passage from the judgment of Scott LJ in *Bowater v Rowley Regis Corpn* [1944] KB 476 at 479:

> With regard to the doctrine 'volenti non fit injuria' I would add one reflection of a general kind. That general maxim has to be applied with specially careful regard to the varying facts of human affairs and human nature in any particular case just because it is concerned with the intangible factors of mind and will. For the purpose of the rule, it if be a rule, a man cannot be said to be truly 'willing' unless he is in a position to choose freely, and freedom of choice predicates, not only full knowledge of the circumstances on which the exercise of choice is conditioned, so that he may be able to choose wisely, but the absence from his mind of any feeling of constraint so that nothing shall interfere with the freedom of his will.

He also cited the American case of *Kaimowitz v Michigan Department of Mental Health* 42 USLW 2063 (1973) Cir Ct Wayne Co, Mich the decision of a circuit court in the County of Michigan in 1973 which is the subject of a learned article: *Law, Psychiatry and the Mental Health System* (1974), by Alexander Brooks, p 902. The judgment appears in the course of the article. The case concerned an inmate of a state hospital who had been committed to that institution as a criminal sexual psychopath and had signed what was termed an 'informed consent form' to become an experimental subject for experimental surgery and he later withdrew his consent. The court had to consider the nature of a legally adequate 'informed consent'. Although Mr Blom-Cooper recognised that having regard to recent authority 'informed consent' as such does not apply to the law of this country, he nevertheless placed reliance upon a passage of the judgment which appears at p 914 of the article:

> We turn now to the third element of an informed consent, that of voluntariness. It is obvious that the most important thing to a large number of involuntarily detained mental patients incarcerated for an unknown length of time, is freedom.
> The Nuremberg Standards require that the experimental subjects be so situated as to exercise free power of choice without the intervention of an element of force, fraud, deceit, duress, overreaching, or other ulterior form of constraint or coercion. It is impossible for an involuntarily detained mental patient to be free of ulterior forms of restraint or coercion when his very release from the institution may depend upon his co-operating with the institutional authorities and giving consent to experimental surgery.

At p 915:

> Involuntarily confined mental patients live in an inherently coercive institutional environment. Indirect and subtle psychological coercion has profound effect upon the patient population. Involuntarily confined patients cannot reason as equals with the doctors and administrators over whether they should undergo psycho-surgery. They are not able to voluntarily give informed consent because of the inherent inequality in their position.

Mr Blom-Cooper seeks to apply those considerations and that reasoning to the position of the plaintiff in this present case, and he argues that in fact a valid free and voluntary consent cannot be given by a person such as the plaintiff, who is in prison, to a prison medical officer who is an officer of the prison having a disciplinary role in relation to him. Mr Blom-Cooper also drew the court's attention to the statutory provisions of the Mental Health Act 1983 which relate to detained and voluntary patients. The provisions are to be found in sections 57 and 58 of the Act and relate to the question of consent and impose certain statutory safeguards which have to be fulfilled. He submits that a prisoner like the plaintiff is in a similar situation and accordingly that the court should bear in mind such safeguards in considering whether consent is established.

It was Mr Blom-Cooper's intention to argue additionally that even if contrary to his submission a prisoner can give a legally valid consent to treatment by a prison medical officer, such consent must be 'informed consent'. Having regard to the decision of this court in *Sidaway v Board of Governors of the Bethlem Royal Hospital and the Maudsley Hospital* [1984] QB 493, [1984] 1 All ER 1018, in respect of which judgment was delivered on 23 February 1984, it is not open to him to argue that 'informed consent' is a consideration which can be entertained by the courts of this country. Nevertheless, he submitted to the court that in psychiatric treatment the test of consent should be that which is required by sections 57 and 58 of the Mental Health Act 1983.

Although the circumstances and the facts giving rise to the allegations made in this action afford an opportunity for interesting matters of principle and policy to be raised and considered, nevertheless I find myself in complete agreement with the trial judge that the sole issue raised at the trial, that is to say whether the plaintiff had consented to the administration of the drugs injected into his body, was essentially one of fact. The judge considered with care all the evidence, both oral and documentary, and it is clear from his careful judgment that he took into account the various submissions which Mr Blom-Cooper made as to the nature and effect of the documentary evidence and the setting in which the events occurred. The judge said [1984] 2 WLR 130 at 145C-D:

> The right approach, in my judgment, is to say that where, in a prison setting, a doctor has the power to influence a prisoner's situation and prospects a court must be alive to the risk that what may appear, on the face of it, to be real consent is not in fact so. I have borne that in mind throughout the case.

Essentially, however, the matter is one of fact. The judge made the positive finding that the plaintiff consented. He rejected Mr Blom-Cooper's submission that the plaintiff was entitled to judgment because he was incapable in law of giving his consent to the treatment by Dr Xavier in question. In my judgment he was right so to do. There was ample evidence to justify his finding of fact and accordingly the decision to which he came. It is not for this court to consider and decide this appeal upon the basis of an alternative and hypothetical set of facts and circumstances.

I would dismiss this appeal.

Sir John Donaldson MR and Fox LJ agreed.

The significance of *Freeman*'s case is that it goes beyond the more obvious proposition that voluntariness turns on the facts, to state a more challenging hypothesis: that what the President's Commission called the 'institutional setting' may make apparent consent invalid. In *Freeman* counsel for the plaintiff's argument was that by virtue of his being in prison, Freeman was *ipso facto* incapable of exercising a free choice. The Court of Appeal rejected this, merely commenting that the 'institutional setting' should put doctors and others on notice that they should be especially careful to satisfy themselves that the consent was freely given.

By contrast, in the well-known case of *Kaimowitz v Michigan Department of Mental Health* (1973) 42 USLW 2063 the Michigan Circuit Court saw the institutional setting as crucial.

Kaimowitz v Michigan Department of Mental Health (1973) 42 USLW 2063 (Mich Cir Ct)

We turn now to the third element of informed consent, that of voluntariness. It is obvious that the most important thing to a large number of involuntarily detained mental patients incarcerated for an unknown length of time, is freedom.

The Nuremberg Standards require that the experimental subjects be so situated as to exercise free power of choice without the intervention of an element of force, fraud, deceit, duress, overreaching, or other *ulterior form of constraint or coercion*. It is impossible for an involuntarily detained mental patient to be free of ulterior forms of restraint or coercion when his very release from the institution may depend upon his co-operating with the institutional authorities and giving consent to experimental surgery.

As pointed out in the testimony in this case, John Doe consented to this psycho-surgery partly because of his effort to show the doctors in the hospital that he was a co-operative patient. Even Dr Yudashkin, in his testimony, pointed out that involuntarily confined patients tend to tell their doctors what the patient thinks these people want to hear.

The inherently coercive atmosphere to which the involuntarily detained mental patient is subjected has bearing upon the voluntariness of his consent.

Involuntarily confined mental patients live in an inherently coercive institutional environment. Indirect and subtle psychological coercion has profound effect upon the patient population. Involuntarily confined patients cannot reason as equals with the doctors and administrators over whether they should undergo psycho-surgery. They are not able to voluntarily give informed consent because of the inherent inequality in their position.

Footnote: [It should be emphasised that once John Doe was released in this case and returned to the community he withdrew all consent to the performance of the proposed experiment. His withdrawal of consent under these circumstances should be compared with his response on January 12, 1973, to questions placed to him by Prof Slovenko, one of the members of the Human Rights Committee. These answers are part of exhibit 22 and were given after extensive publicity about this case, and while John Doe was in Lafayette Clinic waiting the implantation of depth electrodes. The significant questions and answers are as follows:

1. Would you seek psycho-surgery if you were not confined in an institution?
A. Yes, if after testing this showed it would be of help.
2. Do you believe that psycho-surgery is a way to obtain your release from the institution?
A. No, but it would be a step in obtaining my release. It is like any other therapy or program to help persons to function again.
3. Would you seek psycho-surgery if there were other ways to obtain your release?
A. Yes, if psycho-surgery were the only means of helping my physical problem after a period of testing.]

You may think that neither *Kaimowitz* nor *Freeman* is entirely satisfactory. In *Kaimowitz* the court could be said to have been over-protective. In *Freeman* it could be said that the court dismissed the argument that the 'institutional setting' deprived him of his free will too readily.

D. MISTAKE

1. As to capacity

What if a doctor reaches a view concerning a patient's competence that is objectively unjustified on the evidence and then goes on to act on the purported consent of the patient to treat him? What if any cause of action would lie against the doctor? For example, what if a doctor in good faith, but wrongly, should determine that an elderly confused patient agrees to treatment?

Obviously if there were an action it is important to establish which action, that is negligence or battery, since in the latter action a patient would not need to prove, in order to maintain the action, that he had suffered injury as a result of the doctor's conduct. Whichever action can be brought, there is no doubt that any mistake made by the doctor must be reasonable before the law will (if at all) excuse him. An *unreasonable mistake* would seem to give rise *prima facie* to a negligence action and *a fortiori* would not excuse the doctor even if battery was relied upon (*Fletcher v Fletcher* (1859) 1 E & E 420).

Let us therefore assume we are only concerned with *reasonable* mistakes. Deciding which action may be brought is by no means simple: the difficulty lies in whether the mistaken view of the doctor is as to a matter of fact or of opinion; ie that whether a patient is competent or not is a matter exclusively of fact or one of opinion. If it is a mistake of fact, then on first principles an action in battery would lie since mistake is not ordinarily a defence to such an intentional tort (see *John & Co Ltd Lewis v Tims* [1952] AC 676). There are however exceptions where a mistake may be a defence. For example, a policeman making an arrest in the mistaken belief, based on reasonable grounds, that a crime has been committed, would at common law quite apart from statute be excused.

Since the House of Lords' decision in *Re F (Mental Patient: Sterilisation)* [1990] 2 AC 1, the doctor will have a defence based upon necessity if on the facts the treatment was in the incompetent patient's best interests. Of course, *Re F* would not apply in the converse position where the doctor decides in good faith that a patient is *incompetent* when this is not so. *Prima facie* the law in these circumstances would consider the doctor to have committed a battery if he treats the patient in the face of a refusal. In *Re T* Staughton LJ stated:

> Some will say that, when there is doubt whether an apparent refusal of consent is valid in circumstances of urgent necessity, the decision of a doctor acting in good faith ought to be conclusive . . . However, I cannot find authority that the decision of a doctor as to the existence or refusal of consent is sufficient protection, if the law subsequently decides otherwise. So the medical profession, in the future as in the past, must bear the responsibility unless it is possible to obtain a decision from the courts.

If, by contrast, in law the mistaken view of the doctor as to the patient's understanding is regarded as relating to a matter of *opinion*, assuming the doctor acts in good faith, then the answer may be different. Will the law excuse the doctor from liability in battery when he has formed a judgment which is mistaken, in that the consensus of informed opinion is otherwise? On grounds of public policy it may be desirable that the law should recognise a legal excuse for the doctor in these circumstances.

That the law should as a matter of policy recognise that a doctor should have a defence of mistake, is illustrated by section 2(4) of the Age of Legal Capacity (Scotland) Act 1991.

> s. 2(4) A person under the age of 16 years shall have legal capacity to consent on his own behalf to any surgical, medical or dental procedure or treatment where, in the opinion of a qualified medical practitioner attending him, he is capable of understanding the nature and possible consequences of the procedure or treatment.

As is clear this provision was intended by the Scottish Law Commission precisely to cover the case in which a doctor makes a wrong but honest assessment of a child's capacity (see the Report on the Legal Capacity and Responsibility of Minors and Pupils (No 110), 1988, paras 3.72-3.77). Indeed, section 2(4) may go even further than we would anticipate the common law to go by excusing even an unreasonable but honest mistake. (Notice the Law Commission in its Consultation Paper No 129 (April 1993) proposes that only if the mistake is reasonable would the doctor have an excuse: see, para 3.72.)

2. As to information

Here we are concerned with the situation in which a doctor is mistaken as to the extent (if at all) to which a patient is informed or understands the information. It is important here to differentiate between a doctor's possible liability in battery and in negligence.

As for *battery*, if the patient is not informed about, or does not understand, the 'nature and purpose' of the procedure, on the face of it the doctor should be liable in battery since the touching of the patient is not consented to even though the doctor thinks it is.

However, an exception to this may be the circumstances where, as Lord Diplock put it in *Sidaway*, 'the patient is estopped from denying that he possessed the relevant information, because he so acted towards the defendant as to lead the latter reasonably to assume the relevant information was known to him' ([1985] 1 All ER 643 at 658).

As for *negligence*, the position of the doctor is explored by Professor Margaret Somerville.

Margaret Somerville 'Structuring the Issues in Informed Consent' (1981) 26 McGill LJ 740 at 776-9

Must the patient understand the information given by the physician in order to give consent or informed consent? This question was raised in *Kelly v Hazlett* [(1976) 75 DLR (3d) 536] and was dealt with separately in relation to battery and negligence.

The plaintiff-patient, in that case, had been given 100 mg of pethidine just before she purportedly gave consent. In relation to battery-avoiding consent the judge did not believe

that it could be suggested otherwise than that the giving of the consent under such circumstances, at the very least, leaves the validity of the consent open to question . . . and that it would be incumbent on the defendant to prove affirmatively that the effect of this sedation probably did not adversely affect the patient's understanding *of the basic nature of the contemplated operation.*

In other words, the surgeon must show

that the combination of sedation, and . . . [the patient's] labile condition, had not blotted the information from her mind, respecting the basic nature and character of the operation when she made her demand. In such circumstances he has shown a sufficient consent to avoid liability on the basis of battery.

But, if the plaintiff

did not know the basic nature of the operation . . . and . . . all she was asking for was a result *not a procedure, and she manifested this lack of knowledge to the defendant, then her apparent consent to the operation, notwithstanding her clear desire for the result, would be ineffective.*

In other words, if the doctor *knows* or if he ought to know that the plaintiff does not understand the basic nature of the operation, the doctor is, in the absence of other justification, liable in battery if he performs the operation. Moreover, proof of battery-avoiding consent by the physician will require proof of the necessary degree of understanding of the information by the patient.

With respect to the patient's understanding of any collateral risks that the physician must disclose in order to avoid liability in negligence, the defendant surgeon in *Kelly v Hazlett* admitted that he 'could sense that . . . [the plaintiff] was *not understanding* what . . . [he] was attempting to communicate with her by words'. That is, in this particular case, the surgeon had subjective knowledge of the patient's lack of understanding. The Court held that it is the doctor's 'duty to be satisfied that . . . [the risk] had been brought home to the patient before he could reasonably regard her apparent consent as being valid.' The consent needed to avoid liability in negligence, that is the consent required in relation to collateral risks, 'involves both *awareness* and assent'. However, 'it would be quite unreasonable, and the law does not call for it, to expect the doctor to see into the mind of the patient to satisfy himself that the patient not only understands the risks but also puts the degree of emphasis on them which the doctor considers to be reasonable'.

Although the remarks of the Court in *Kelly v Hazlett* in both the battery and negligence contexts could be read as requiring actual subjective understanding by the patient of the disclosed information, it is clear that this is not the case, as the physician may rely on the patient's consent if he could reasonably have thought at that time that she was aware of the basic nature and character of the special risks of the operation. Hence the physician may rely on the patient's consent if it is given pursuant to *apparent subjective understanding* by the patient of the information disclosed. It is submitted that this is the most satisfactory approach. A fully subjective standard requiring actual understanding by the patient is too onerous for physicians and may not be in the best interests of patients, as the patient may not want to understand the information, or to make the intellectual effort to understand it, or have the physician bothering him to ensure that he does understand. Thus a physician may rely on the consent of a patient as a defence to an action in battery if the physician shows that a reasonable physician in those circumstances would have thought that this patient apparently understood the basic nature and character of the operation, provided, always, that the particular physician had no subjective knowledge that this patient did not understand. When a patient sues in negligence for breach of a physician's duty to inform him and alleges that the breach consists in the physician's failure to ensure that he, the patient, understood the information, the plaintiff-patient must prove on the balance of probabilities that a reasonable patient in the same circumstances as those in which the plaintiff found himself would not have understood the information communicated to him, or that he did not understand the information, and the physician knew this.

This approach can be examined in view of *Reibl v Hughes*. At the trial level the test of when the requirement of understanding of information by the patient will be fulfilled was formulated in different terms with respect to battery and negligence. It was held that 'the law of battery in effect places on a physician a strict duty to explain to his patient, in language which the patient can *understand*, the essential nature and quality of the treatment he is to undergo'. To avoid negligence liability, on the other hand, the doctor must have 'take[n] sufficient care to convey to the plaintiff and *assure* that the plaintiff *understood* the gravity, nature and extent of risks specifically attendant on the [procedure]'. It is not exactly clear what standard of care is being required of the physician here in order to avoid negligence liability for non-disclosure, but it seems to vacillate between one of taking all reasonable means that a reasonable physician would take to ensure understanding and one of actually requiring that this result be achieved. In comparison, it is much clearer that actual understanding by the patient of the information is necessary to obtain battery-avoiding consent.

This approach should be contrasted with that of the majority of the Court of Appeal in the same case. In discussing whether the patient understood the *purpose* for which the surgery was being undertaken, a matter which would relate to battery-avoiding consent, it was held that '[i]f as the patient said, the doctor did his best to tell him about the surgery, and the patient had some difficulty in understanding it, there was some obligation to have told the doctor what troubled him'. This approach is acceptable to the extent that it maintains that the test for validity of the patient's consent, as far as non-understanding of information is concerned, should be determined in the absence of subjective knowledge on the part of the physician that the patient does not understand, on the basis of whether the reasonable physician, taking all the circumstances into account, would have thought the patient understood. But, to the extent that it establishes only an obligation on the physician to ensure understanding by the patient if the patient expressly indicates that he does not understand, it should not be accepted. To make the content of the physician's duty depend on the patient fulfilling some obligation, such as asking questions,

> may overlook the power and status differential in the doctor-patient relationship. From a practical point of view, such a power imbalance both makes the patient less likely to ask questions or to understand what he is told and makes him reluctant to disclose this to the doctor. Further, the patient may not even know enough to ask appropriate questions, or to know he does not understand the answers, or he may be too emotionally upset to realize this.

The proposed test requiring 'apparent understanding' of information by the patient avoids such difficulties, as it would require the physician to assess at least, as a reasonable doctor would, whether the patient apparently understands the information he has been given, and to act accordingly.

More recently, Professor Robertson has observed that some Canadian courts have imposed 'a potentially onerous duty' on a doctor.

Robertson, 'Informed Consent Ten Years Later: The Impact of Reibl v Hughes' (1991) 70 Canadian Bar Review 424 at 430-1

> There is . . . some indication of courts interpreting *Reibl v Hughes* as requiring physicians to satisfy themselves that the patient understands the information which is given, a potentially onerous duty in light of studies which indicate that many patients understand little of what their doctors tell them and remember even less. For example, in finding a surgeon liable for failing to disclose material risk to a 75-year-old patient, the trial judge in *Kellett v Griesdale* commented that [(BCS Ct) 26 June 1985, unreported]:
>
> > It may very well be that the defendant gave a warning but, if so, it did not make a sufficient impression on the plaintiff. The defendant was aware of the problem I mentioned earlier about patients tending to push aside any considerations of risk. That being so, *it was incumbent on him to ensure that the plaintiff clearly understood the risk of significant hearing loss* . . .
>
> Likewise, in *Schanczl v Singh* [[1988] 2 WWR 465] the Alberta Court of Queen's Bench imposed liability on a physician for failure to disclose material risks, and in so doing emphasized the plaintiff's difficulty in understanding English. The court stated that this difficulty 'placed a special duty on . . . [the defendant] to be certain that his patient understood the alternatives available to him'.

This latter view has now been approved by the Canadian Supreme Court in *Ciarlariello v Schacter* (1993) 100 DLR (4th) 609 at 622-3 per Cory J. There is no English case law which addresses this specific point. Michael Jones in his book, *Medical Negligence* (1991) at para 6.88 argues as follows:

> The doctor does not have to make the patient understand; it is a duty to make a reasonable effort to communicate information to the patient. It is not an answer, for the doctor to say that he does not have the time to give seminars in medicine or that the information is too complicated or technical for the patient to understand. The duty must be to give an explanation in terms which are reasonably comprehensible to a layman, although there can be no guarantee that the patient will in fact understand the information. Where it is quite apparent to the doctor that the patient has not understood he may have to make further efforts. The Canadian courts, for example, have taken the view that where the patient has language difficulties the doctor is under a special duty to be sure that the patient has understood.

3. As to voluntariness

Where it is alleged that the doctor was mistaken that the patient's consent (or refusal) was freely given, the legal analysis mirrors that which we saw above in relation to mistakes concerning a patient's capacity.

E. LIMITS ON CONSENT

The final question to be addressed in an analysis of the law relating to consent is whether the law places any limits on what a competent person may consent to. Lord Griffiths in *Re F*, a case concerned with the sterilisation of a mentally incapacitated adult woman (discussed *infra*, ch1 10), states the nature of the enquiry.

Re F (a mental patient: sterilisation) [1990] 2 AC 1, (1989) 4 BMLR 1 (HL)

> **Lord Griffiths:** I cannot agree that it is satisfactory to leave this grave decision with all its social implications in the hands of those having the care of the patient with only the expectation that they will have the wisdom to obtain a declaration of lawfulness before the operation is performed. In my view the law ought to be that they must obtain the approval

of the court before they sterilise a woman incapable of giving consent and that it is unlawful to sterilise without that consent. I believe that it is open to your Lordships to develop a common law rule to this effect. Although the general rule is that the individual is the master of his own fate the judges through the common law have, in the public interest, imposed certain constraints on the harm that people may consent to being inflicted on their own bodies. Thus although boxing is a legal sport a bare knuckle prize fight in which more grievous injury may be inflicted is unlawful (*R v Coney* (1882) 8 QBD 534), and so is fighting which may result in actual bodily harm: see *A-G's Reference (No 6 of 1980)* [1981] QB 715. So also is it unlawful to consent to the infliction of serious injury on the body in the course of the practice of sexual perversion: *R v Donovan* [1934] 2 KB 498. Suicide was unlawful at common law until Parliament intervened by the Suicide Act 1961.

The common law has, in the public interest, been developed to forbid the infliction of injury on those who are fully capable of consenting to it. The time has now come for a further development to forbid, again in the public interest, the sterilisation of a woman with healthy reproductive organs who, either through mental incompetence or youth, is incapable of giving her fully informed consent unless such an operation has been inquired into and sanctioned by the High Court. Such a common law rule would provide a more effective protection than the exercise of parens patriae jurisdiction which is dependent upon some interested party coming forward to invoke the jurisdiction of the court. The parens patriae jurisdiction is in any event now only available in the case of minors through their being made wards of court. I would myself declare that on grounds of public interest an operation to sterilise a woman incapable of giving consent either on grounds of age or mental incapacity is unlawful if performed without the consent of the High Court. I fully recognise that in so doing I would be making new law. However the need for such a development has been identified in a number of recent cases and in the absence of any Parliamentary response to the problem it is my view that the judges can and should accept responsibility to recognise the need and to adapt the common law to meet it. If such a development did not meet with public approval it would always be open to Parliament to reverse it or to alter it by perhaps substituting for the opinion of the High Court judge the second opinion of another doctor as urged by counsel for the Mental Health Tribunal.

In *A-G's Reference (No 6 of 1980)* [1981] 2 All ER 1057, Lord Lane CJ, speaking for the court, held:

We think that it can be taken as a starting point it is an essential element of an assault that the act is done contrary to the will and without the consent of the victim: and it is doubtless for this reason that the burden lies on the prosecution to negative consent. Ordinarily, then, if the victim consents, the assailant is not guilty.
. . . The question is: at what point does the public interest require the court to hold otherwise?
. . . The answer to this question, in our judgment, is that it is not in the public interest that people should try to cause or should cause each other actual bodily harm for no good reason.

However, Lord Lane then went on:

Nothing which we have said is intended to cast doubt on the accepted legality of properly conducted games and sports, lawful chastisement or correction, *reasonable surgical interference,* dangerous exhibitions etc. These apparent exceptions can be justified as involving the exercise of a legal right, in the case of chastisement or correction, or as needed in the public interest, in the other cases [our emphasis].

Presumably, Lord Lane would include *any* medical intervention, surgical or otherwise, which might otherwise constitute a battery.

What then is the explanation for this medical exception to the general rule? In *Airedale NHS Trust v Bland* [1993] 1 All ER 821 Lord Mustill (at 889) offered the following view.

1. *Consent to bodily invasion.* Any invasion of the body of one person by another is potentially both a crime and a tort. At the bottom end of the scale consent is a defence both

to a charge of common assault and to a claim in tort. . . . How is it that, consistently with [this proposition] . . . a doctor can with immunity perform on a consenting patient an act which would be a very serious crime if done by someone else? The answer must be that bodily invasions in the course of proper medical treatment stand completely outside the criminal law. The reason why the consent of the patient is so important is not that it furnishes a defence in itself, but because it is usually essential to the propriety of medical treatment. Thus, if the consent is absent, and is not dispensed with in special circumstances by operation of law, the acts of the doctor lose their immunity.

Lord Mustill makes the question turn upon whether the touching amounts to 'proper medical treatment'. With respect, of course, this may not take us very far. It still leaves open the central question of what is 'proper' and what constitutes 'medical treatment' (ie who decides).

If these judicial pronouncements do not take us very far, let us turn to the views of Professor Glanville Williams.

G Williams *Textbook of Criminal law* (2nd edn 1983) pp 589-91

. . . the validity of consent to harm is a grey area in the law. It is sufficiently uncertain to have given rise to the opinion that the judges have a commission to pronounce upon the legality of all forms of surgery; and certainly the pronouncement in *A-G's Reference*, conferring the benediction of the judges on 'reasonable surgical interference', seems to confirm that opinion. In practice, of course, the courts would find in favour of such 'interference', if the question ever arose, almost as a matter of routine.

There have been doubts about sterilisation 'of convenience', ie as a form of birth control. However, medical practice came to accept the operation after counsel advised the BMA that it might be performed without fear of legal repercussions. For some time there was less certainty about castration, which, unlike sterilisation, is a de-sexing operation. It may occasionally be recommended as the only way of obtaining relief from abnormalities in the sexual urge, and in these cases the judges would certainly regard it as lawful. Moreover, the so-called sex-change operation has come to be accepted as lawful. A change from male to pseudo-female sex organs involves castration: the penis and testicles are removed and a pseudo-vagina constructed from the scrotum. Now castration was regarded as a maim at common law, because it was thought to reduce the will to fight. Yet the male-'female' sex-change is performed openly by reputable surgeons. If the issue were raised, the operation could be supported as conducive to the patient's mental health; and Ormrod J [in *Corbett v Corbett* [1971] P 83] accepted its legality on this ground. Again, no one has ever doubted the legality of the operation of prefrontal leucotomy, which, by severing the frontal lobes of the brain, changes the personality of the patient in certain cases of mental illness. Therapy also gives moral support to some cosmetic surgery, but not all. The justification for padding bosoms, chiselling noses, and restoring hymens lost in premarital encounters, is that the patient is pleased and may be socially or maritally advantages, rather than that the operation is a psychiatric necessity.

A more serious interference with the body is in taking an organ for transplant, such as a kidney. Nevertheless, no serious legal doubts have been expressed about such operations upon adult donors, where a paired organ is surrendered for the benefit of another.

It may be questioned whether the criminal law has any acceptable place in controlling operations performed by qualified practitioners upon adults of sound mind with their consent . . .

In a civil case relating to an operation changing a male to a pseudo-female, Ormrod J said:

> There is obviously room for differences of opinion on the ethical aspects of such operations but, if they are undertaken for genuine therapeutic purposes, it is a matter for the decision of the patient and the doctors concerned in his case. The passing of section 1 of the Sexual Offences Act 1967 seems to have removed any legal objections which there might have been to such procedures [*Corbett v Corbett* (otherwise Ashley) [1971] P 83 at 99].

There is no reason why the same view should not be taken for all medical procedures, assuming that the patient has capacity to consent. The law would still play a part in determining legal capacity in the case of the young and the mentally abnormal.

If this is so, the only threat presented by the law in respect of operations on the body is to those who are not medically qualified.

Professor Skegg after discussing the 'medical exception' referred to in the *A-G's Reference* offers the following analysis of the limits of consent.

P D G Skegg *Law, Ethics and Medicine* (1984)

Many touchings which occur in the course of medical practice do not involve 'any hurt or injury calculated to interfere with health or comfort'. In these cases, consent can prevent liability in battery, even if there is 'no good reason' for the touching. Surgery, and some other medical procedures, could be said to involve 'hurt or injury calculated to interfere with health or comfort' in a manner which is 'more than merely transient and trifling'. As has already been suggested, conduct which benefits bodily health should not be regarded as causing bodily harm. But even if it were regarded as causing bodily harm, there could be absolutely no doubt that it was possible to give a legally effective consent to such procedures. There is clearly a good reason for them.

Sometimes medical procedures which were intended to benefit the patient will fail in their object, and will cause what is undoubtedly bodily harm. If an application of force was not intended to cause bodily harm, and the person responsible did not take an unjustifiable risk as to the causing of bodily harm, then the undesired consequence should not render ineffective consent which would otherwise have been effective. In the course of medical practice there is often good reason to attempts to benefit a patient's health, even though there is a risk of harm resulting. Here, too, consent will undoubtedly prevent liability being incurred.

Some medical procedures are not intended to benefit the person on whom they are performed. Indeed, sometimes a procedure is performed on a person in the knowledge that it will certainly be to that person's bodily detriment. This is the case when a kidney is removed from a healthy person, for transplantation into someone who is in need of it. The operation is a major one, and is not without risks. But it is not unreasonably dangerous, and the probable benefit to the recipient far outweighs the probable detriment to the donor. Hence, if called upon to deal with a case in which a kidney had been removed from a consenting adult, for transplantation into someone in need of it, the courts may confidently be expected to take the view that the operation did not amount to the offence of battery. Even though the operation causes serious bodily harm, there is clearly a good reason for it. There is also a good reason for some non-therapeutic medical experimentation, even if it may cause bodily harm.

Where judges regard an activity as socially acceptable they are unlikely to question the reasons for it. In the *A-G's Reference (No 6 of 1980)* the court spoke of the 'accepted legality' of properly conducted games and sports, of dangerous exhibitions, and of 'reasonable surgical interference'. The need for these 'apparent exceptions' only arises where an application of force is intended to cause, or does in fact cause, bodily harm. As the Court of Appeal was prepared to accept that dangerous exhibitions are needed in the public interest, it would be extraordinary if a later court took a restrictive view of the scope of permissible medical interventions. A court is not likely to inquire closely into whether there are good reasons for a particular intervention. There is no danger of a court attempting to decide whether there were good reasons for removing a kidney from a living donor, instead of keeping the patient on dialysis in the hope that a suitable cadaver kidney would become available. And there is now very little danger of a court seeking to manipulate the offence of battery so as to prevent individuals reaching their own decisions about whether to be sterilised, or undergo cosmetic surgery. Opinions vary as to the desirability of such operations in particular circumstances. But it is doubtful whether judges would regard these operations as sufficiently against the public interest to warrant their being regarded as constituting the offence of battery, despite the presence of consent.

Were a patient to consent to having his limbs amputated, for no good reason, his consent would not prevent the amputation from amounting to the offence of battery. But the judges' insistence that there are some applications of force to which consent cannot be given, for the purpose of the offence of battery, should not hinder modern medical practice.

One long-standing limit to consent is to be found in the ancient crime of mayhem (maim). Stephen in his *Digest of the Criminal Law* (1878) defines the crime of maim as follows (p 145):

A maim is bodily harm whereby a man is deprived of the use of any member of his body, or of any sense which he can use in fighting, or by the loss of which he is generally and permanently weakened; but bodily injury is not a maim merely because it is a disfigurement.

Does this affect the practice of medicine? Professor Skegg (*op cit*) in his book argues as follows (pp 43-46):

In practice, the common law offence of maim has long been supplanted by statutory offences. But is has not been expressly abolished, and a judge has made an extrajudicial statement which suggests that there is at least a theoretical possibility of the offence of maim applying to operations in which a kidney is removed from a healthy living donor, for transplantation into a person who is in need of it [R Ormrod 'Medical Ethics' (1968) 2 BMJ 7 at 9]. It is therefore desirable to consider the extent to which the offence of maim would apply to medical procedures, and the related issue of whether consent would be effective to prevent liability.

The [institutional] authorities have long distinguished between acts which permanently disable and weaken a man, rendering him less able in fighting; and acts which simply disfigure. The former are maims, the latter are not. There is no shortage of examples of injuries which fall within one category rather than the other. Over many centuries, it has been agreed that it is a maim to cut off, disable, or weaken an arm or foot. It has also been agreed that it is a maim to deprive a man of an eye, foretooth, or 'those parts, the loss of which in all animals abates their courage' [4 BL Com 205]. However, it has also long been accepted that it is not a maim to cut off an ear or nose, as such injuries are said not to affect a man's capacity for fighting. . . .

Most medical procedures do not permanently disable a person and render that person less able in fighting. They therefore fall outside even the potential scope of any offence of maim. This is as true of the removal of a healthy kidney for transplantation as it is of the removal of a diseased appendix. But even if a medical procedure did come within the potential scope of an offence of maim, it would not follow that a doctor would commit an offence of maim in going ahead with it. Just as the infliction of maim was sometimes permitted in self-defence, so a maiming operation would not amount to the offence of maim if there was a good reason for it. Hence, even if castration could still be regarded as coming within the potential scope of maim, it would be justified if performed for a therapeutic purpose.

The offence of maim would very rarely apply to any procedure performed in the course of medical practice, even if consent had not been given. But if something was done which did come within the potential scope of maim - as where a member of the armed forces persuaded a friend to cut off his trigger finger for him, in an attempt to obtain a discharge - consent would normally be irrelevant.

(In *R v Brown* [1993] 2 All ER 75, Lord Mustill (dissenting) stated that the crime of maim was now 'obsolete' (at 106) and, in any event, was no part of English Law since it had been omitted from the crimes of violence in the Offences Against the Person Act 1861. The other Law Lords did not regard the key to the limits of consent to be contained within the four corners of the crime of maim.)

An example of a medical intervention which tests the limits of the law is sex reassignment surgery. David Meyers examines the public policy considerations in the first edition of his book *The Human Body and the Law* (1970) at p 66.

The enquiry is concerned fundamentally with the extent to which an individual's consent will insulate the performing surgeon from criminal liability for the surgical invasion that is repugnant or unjustified to many.

It may eventually be resolved that consent to such operations will only negate their criminality when their purpose is considered to be therapeutic. The question then to be resolved will be: what is therapeutic?

While conversion surgery for transsexuals involves a more severe, more repugnant bodily infringement, it is also sought to be justified on wider, rather atypical therapeutic grounds. The practice is often advocated not so much to ease the torment and suffering of the transsexual as it is to serve as a therapeutic measure to prevent him from harming himself either physically or mentally. The therapeutic effect then of the surgery is indirect, in deterring the patient from subsequently injuring himself. This is an extension of traditional interpretations of therapeutic motive and it remains to be seen whether public policy will accept such an extension in this controversial context.

If full, knowing consent has been given by the patient and medical opinion feels conversion surgery in some degree to be irrefutably indicated, then, it is submitted, the public has no interest in denying the acute transsexual the only means currently known to medical science for relief of his severe, self-endangering condition by threatening the performing surgeon with criminal prosecution.

Sex reassignment operations are now available within the National Health Service. Their legality was probably established by the case of *Corbett v Corbett (otherwise Ashley)* [1970] 2 All ER 33. Although this case concerned the validity of a purported marriage between a man and another who had undergone a sex reassignment operation and so the legality of the operation did not specifically arise, Ormrod J clearly did not regard it as unlawful. He said (at p 43):

There is, obviously, room for differences of opinion on the ethical aspects of such operations but, if they are undertaken for genuine therapeutic purposes, it is a matter for the decision of the patient and the doctors concerned in his case. The passing of the Sexual Offences Act 1967, s 1, seems to have removed any legal objections which there might have been to such procedures.

His reference to the Sexual Offences Act 1967 is, perhaps, a little curious since this legalises sexual intercourse between consenting male adults over the age of 21. Since then, however, public policy, and the legality of the procedure, have never been questioned again (eg *R v Tan* [1983] QB 1053, (CA), *Rees v United Kingdom* [1987] 2 FLR 111 ECt HR and *Cossey v United Kingdom* (1990) 13 EHRR 622 (ECt HR)).

In addition to the common law there are examples of statutes which limit consent. One such statute is the Prohibition of Female Circumcision Act 1985.

Prohibition of Female Circumcision Act 1985

1. (1) Subject to section 2 below, it shall be an offence for any person –
   (a)   to excise, infibulate or otherwise mutilate the whole or any part of the labia majora or labia minora or clitoris of another person; or
   (b)   to aid, abet, counsel or procure the performance by another person of any of those acts on that other person's own body.
2. (1) Subsection (1)(a) of section 1 shall not render unlawful the performance of a surgical operation if that operation –
   (a)   is necessary for the physical or mental health of the person on whom it is performed and is performed by a registered medical practitioner; or
   (b)   is performed on a person who is in any stage of labour or has just given birth and if so performed for purposes connected with that labour or birth by –
      (i)   a registered medical practitioner or a registered midwife; or
      (ii)   a person undergoing a course of training with a view to becoming a registered medical practitioner or a registered midwife.

   (2) In determining for the purposes of this section whether an operation is necessary for the health of a person, no account shall be taken of the effect on that person of any belief on the part of that or any other person that the operation is required as a matter of custom or ritual.

You will notice section 2(1)(a). Does this give the clue as to what separates the permissible from the impermissible, ie touching is permissible when it is intended to benefit the person in a therapeutic context and is done by a doctor? The insistence that the touching must be by a doctor does not mean the

Parliament has endorsed the view that anything done by doctors is *ipso facto* 'proper medical treatment'. Rather, Parliament has accepted that the involvement of a doctor is a necessary though not a sufficient condition for legitimising certain kinds of touching.

In *R v Brown* [1993] 2 All ER 75, the House of Lords examined the extent to which an individual could consent to physical interference by another. Regardless of their differences over the law relating to violence, their Lordships agreed that surgical (*semble* medical) treatment is justified in law provided it is consented to or is otherwise justified in law. It is to this second basis for lawful treatment that we turn in the next chapter.

Chapter 4

Consent by others

In this chapter we are concerned with two issues. First, we consider the extent to which treatment may be lawfully given to an individual who is incompetent, ie lacks the capacity to consent. In particular, we will consider who (if any) may consent on behalf of that individual, ie parents, spouses and the court. Also, we will consider whether a doctor may lawfully treat an incompetent patient without seeking any consent from another. Secondly, we consider the circumstances, if any, in which treatment may be lawfully given to a competent individual in the face of a refusal of consent by that individual, whether a child or an adult, and, if so, who may validly consent to the treatment or indeed whether consent is required.

Treating without consent: the incompetent

The incompetent include those, whether children or adults, who fail to meet the criteria discussed above – *supra*, ch 3 – in relation to *Gillick* in that they lack the capacity to consent in law by reason of lack of understanding, those who by reason of mental illness also lack understanding and those who are unconscious. Obviously in these cases, *if the law requires consent* it must look to someone other than the patient, ie the consent of a proxy.

A. PROXIES

1. In respect of children

We consider here two issues: (a) who may act as a proxy; and (b) the scope and limits, if any, of a proxy's power.

(a) Who may act as a proxy?

A parent is the most obvious proxy in the case of a child. A parent who has 'parental responsibility' under the Children Act 1989 in respect of a child may consent to medical treatment on behalf of that child (until majority) where the child is incompetent.

Others, such as a local authority, may acquire parental responsibility under Part IV of the Children Act 1989 and, thus, be empowered to consent. It should be noticed, however, that in such a case the child's parents will retain 'parental responsibility' and hence the power to consent unless the local authority restricts their powers as parents (s 33(3) and (4)).

That the power to consent to medical treatment is an aspect of 'all the rights, duties, powers, responsibilities and authority which by a law a parent of a child has in relation to the child' (s 3(1)), ie 'parental responsibility' can be clearly deduced from the *Gillick* decision.

The Children Act 1989 introduced a further possible proxy. Section 3(5) provides that:

> 3. (5) A person who –
> (*a*) does not have parental responsibility for a particular child; but
> (*b*) has care of the child.
> may (subject to the provisions of this Act) do what is reasonable in all the circumstances of the case for the purpose of safeguarding or promoting the child's welfare.

Teachers and child-minders are the sorts of person contemplated by this provision. It is clear from the Law Commission's Report which led to s 3(5) that the provision was intended to extend, in principle, to medical care (see *Report on Guardianship and Custody* (1988) (Law Commission Report No 172 paragraph 2.16)). However, it is unlikely that s 3(5) has much relevance as regards medical treatment. This is because it will rarely (if ever) be 'reasonable . . . for the purpose of safeguarding or promoting the child's welfare' for someone temporarily caring for the child to consent to medical treatment without first consulting the parents. The only circumstance in which it may be 'reasonable' would be in an emergency. But in an emergency, as we shall see, a doctor would be entitled to treat the child without consent in any event.

Another possible proxy decision-maker is, of course, the court itself. The court's jurisdiction may take a variety of forms – in *wardship*, under its *inherent jurisdiction* or under *s 8* of the Children Act 1989.

Latey J described the wardship jurisdiction in *Re X (a minor) (wardship: restriction on publication)* [1975] 1 All ER 697 at 700-701 as follows:

> What then are the origin and function of the wardship jurisdiction? In my understanding they are these. All subjects owe allegiance to the Crown. The Crown has a duty to protect its subjects. This is and always has been especially so towards minors, that is to say now, the young under the age of 18. And it is so because children are especially vulnerable. They have not formed the defences inside themselves which older people have, and therefore, need especial protection. They are also a country's most valuable asset for the future. So the Crown as parents patriae delegated its powers and duty of protection to the courts.

In a medical case, Lord Donaldson MR put it as follows in *Re C (a minor) (wardship: medical treatment) (No 2)* [1989] 2 All ER 791 at 793-794:

> The origin of the wardship jurisdiction is the duty of the Crown to protect its subjects and particularly children who are the generation of the future. It is exercised by the courts on behalf of the Crown (see Latey J in *Re X (a minor) (wardship: restriction on publication)* [1975] 1 All ER 697 at 700-701, [1975] Fam 47 at 52). The machinery for its exercise is an application to make the child a ward of court. Thereafter, the court is entitled and bound in appropriate cases to make decisions in the interests of the child which override the rights of its parents. Furthermore, the court is entitled, and bound in appropriate cases, to make orders affecting third parties which the parents could not themselves have made. Obvious examples are orders forbidding the publication of information about the ward or the ward's family circumstances.

For a detailed discussion of the origins of the jurisdiction see Lowe and White *Wards of Court* (2nd edn 1986), Chapter 1. Three points are worth noticing.

First, the wardship jurisdiction is vested in the court under s 41 of the Supreme Court Act 1981 (and RSC Ord 90) and ends when a child ceases to be a minor, ie at 18 (Family Law Reform Act 1969, s 1). Secondly, the use of wardship has been severely curtailed by s 100 of the Children Act 1989. In particular, wardship may not be used when a child is in the care of a local authority (s 100(2)(c)). Nor may the jurisdiction be invoked by a local authority even where the child is not in care because the court would not grant leave to the local authority under s 100(3). Leave could only be granted if no other court order could be made (s 100(4)(a)) and, as we shall see, the local authority could apply for a section 8 order under the Children Act 1989. Wardship is still available, however, where the child is not in care, to other interested parties including a health authority (which is not a local authority under the Children Act 1989; see s 105(1)).

Thirdly, it is important to notice that if the court's wardship jurisdiction is invoked then 'no important step in the life of that child, can be taken without the consent of the Court . . . ' (see Heilbron J in *Re D (a minor) (wardship: sterilisation)* [1976] Fam 185). Few, if any, forms of medical treatment could therefore be properly embarked upon where the child is a ward without first seeking the authorisation of the court.

More common today in medical law cases will be the use of the court's inherent jurisdiction. This jurisdiction which, by contrast with wardship, *may* be invoked by a local authority even in the case of a child in care, was described in *Re W (a minor) (refusal of treatment)* [1992] 4 All ER 627, CA.

Lord Donaldson MR: . . . Before the coming into force of the Children Act 1989 the appropriate step would have been an application to make W a ward of court. Since that Act came into force, a child who is the subject of a care order, as W was and is, cannot be made a ward of court (see s 100(2)(*c*) of that Act). Instead the appropriate procedure is for the authority to apply to the court for leave under s 100(3) to make an application for the exercise by the court of the inherent jurisdiction of the High Court.

Since there seems to be some doubt about the matter, it should be made clear that the High Court's jurisdiction in relation to children – the parens patriae jurisdiction – is equally exercisable whether the child is or is not a ward of court (see *Re M and N (minors) (wardship: freedom of publication)* [1990] 1 All ER 205 at 210, [1990] Fam 211 at 223). Indeed the only additional effect of a child being a ward of court stems from its status as such and not from the inherent jurisdiction, eg a ward of court cannot marry or leave the jurisdiction without the consent of the court and no 'important' or 'major' step in a ward's life can be taken without that consent.

Balcombe LJ: [E]ven before the 1989 Act made the distinction [between wardship and the court's inherent jurisdiction] clear for all to see, it had long been recognised that wardship was only machinery and that the court's inherent jurisdiction could be exercised whether or not the child was a ward – see eg *Re L* [1968] 1 All ER 20 at 25, [1968] P 119 at 157. The inherent jurisdiction is the exercise by the High Court of the powers of the Crown as parens patriae and is theoretically without limit – see *Re X (a minor) (wardship: restriction on publication)*[1975] 1 All ER 697 at 706, [1975] Fam 47 at 61.

Unlike wardship, the inherent jurisdiction does not result in the court taking to itself all decisions relating to the life of the child. Instead, the court will only determine certain issues in respect of the child's upbringing, for example medical care, but it is not part of this jurisdiction to seek to superintend any other decision about the child's welfare.

The final jurisdiction of the court in this context is that set out in s 8 of the Children Act 1989, in particular the power to make 'specific issue orders' and 'prohibited steps orders'. These are defined as follows in s 8(1):

8. (1) In this Act –

. . .

'a prohibited steps order' means an order that no step which could be taken by a parent in
meeting his parental responsibility for a child, and which is of a kind specified in the
order, shall be taken by any person without the consent of the court; . . .

'a specific issue order' means an order giving directions for the purpose of determining a
specific question which has arisen, or which may arise, in connection with any aspect of
parental responsibility for a child.

Again, these orders may not be made when a child is in the care of a local
authority. The inherent jurisdiction will remain the most common means of
access to the court in that situation. One difficulty may be that a 'section 8
order' may not be obtained ex parte in an emergency whilst the court's inherent
jurisdiction may be invoked (see *Re O (a minor) (medical treatment)* [1993] 4
Med LR 272 (Johnson J). Contrast the obiter remarks of Booth J in *Re R (a
minor)* [1993] 2 FLR 5. Also, it should be noted that only 'exceptionally' can a
section 8 order be made if the child has reached 16 or if the order would
otherwise run beyond the child's 16th birthday (s 9(6) and (7)).

(b) The scope and limits of a proxy's power

The central question which we must answer is what is the *scope* of a proxy's
power in making decisions and what, if any, *limits* are there?

(i) 'BEST INTERESTS'

It is relatively straightforward to state the scope of a proxy's power in
principle. Both Parliament and the courts have repeatedly asserted that the
guiding principle is that the proxy must act out of a concern for the child's
welfare. The principle is customarily represented by the phrase 'acting in the
best interests of the child' – the 'best interests' test (but for other views see *infra*,
p 256 et seq).

The current parliamentary statement of the proxy's power is contained in
s 1(1) of the Children Act 1989 (though it first appeared in the Guardianship of
Infants Act 1925, but see also the earlier Act of 1886). It is on its face addressed
to the court.

1. (1) When a court determines any question with respect to –
(a) the upbringing of a child; or
(b) the administration of a child's property or the application of any income arising from
it,
the child's welfare shall be the court's paramount consideration.

The court for its part has insisted that all proxies must adopt the same
approach, ie act in the child's best interests. Hence, in *Gillick* Lord Scarman
was able, having referred to the legislation, to state that:

There is here a principle which limits and governs the exercise of parental rights of custody,
care and control. It is a principle perfectly consistent with the law's recognition of the parent
as the natural guardian of the child; but it is also a warning that parental right must be
exercised in accordance with the welfare principle and can be challenged, even overridden, if
it be not.

(See also Lord Hailsham in *Re B (a minor) (wardship: sterilisation)* [1987] 2
All ER 206 at 212.)

At the outset it is fair to state that inherent in the notion of 'best interests' is that the medical intervention must be *therapeutic*, ie intended to benefit the particular individual. The law's equating 'best interests' with therapy causes problems, as we shall see, when dispute exists as to whether a particular intervention (or class of interventions) is indeed therapeutic. Examples exist in the concern over the legality of a proxy's consent to the involvement of a child in non-therapeutic medical research, organ or blood donation and sterilisation. As regards these difficult cases, the courts could choose from three options: (1) absolute prohibition; (2) the adoption of different and less rigorous tests (with safeguards); and (3) prohibit them in all circumstances other than when the court authorises the intervention. We will consider this third option in some detail later. Here we need to notice, in the rare cases in which this has arisen, how the courts have chosen between option (1) and option (2).

S v S, W v Official Solicitor (or W) [1972] AC 24, [1970] 3 All ER 107 (HL)

In the two appeals heard together, the court was concerned with the paternity of children born to the parties of marriages. During divorce proceedings, the husbands of the children's mothers denied paternity. In each case the parent who had control of the child consented to a blood test. In each case the House of Lords ordered that a blood test should be taken.

Lord Reid: The Official Solicitor argues on behalf of these children that no blood test of any child ought ever to be ordered unless it can be shown to be in the interest of the child that there should be a test . . .

I must now examine the present legal position with regard to blood tests. There is no doubt that a person of full age and capacity cannot be ordered to undergo a blood test against his will. In my view, the reason is not that he ought to be required to furnish evidence which may tell against him. By discovery of documents and in other ways the law often does this. The real reason is that English law goes to great lengths to protect a person of full age and capacity from interference with his personal liberty. We have too often seen freedom disappear in other countries not only by coups d'état but by gradual erosion; and often it is the first step that counts. So it would be unwise to make even minor concessions. It is true that the matter is regarded differently in the United States. We were referred to a number of State enactments authorising the courts to order adults to submit to blood tests. They may feel that this is safe because of their geographical position, size, power or resources or because they have a written Constitution. But here Parliament has clearly endorsed our view by the provision of s 21(1) of the 1969 Act [Family Law Reform Act].

But the position is very different with regard to young children. It is a legal wrong to use constraint on an adult beyond what is authorised by statute or ancient common law powers connected with crime and the like. But it is not and could not be a legal wrong for a parent or person authorised by him to use constraint to his young child provided it is not cruel or excessive. There are differences of opinion as to the age beyond which it is unwise to use constraint, but that cannot apply to infants or young children. So it seems to me to be impossible to deny that a parent can lawfully require that his young child should submit to a blood test. And if the parent can require that, why not the court? There is here no overriding requirement of public policy as there is with an adult.

I shall not refer in detail to the authorities. They were all discussed at some length in argument. But I venture to think that there has been some error in applying to this subject principles and authorities which deal with the custody of children. There the question is simple, though a decision may be very difficult – to whom shall the custody be entrusted? There is no competing question of general public interest, and it has long been well recognised that the paramount question is what is in the best interests of the child. But here there is or may be a conflict between the interests of the child and the general requirements of justice. Justice requires that available evidence should not be suppressed but it may be against the interests of the child to produce it.

The argument, as I understand it, is that a court can only order a blood test of a child in the exercise of the old Chancery jurisdiction acting on behalf of the Sovereign as parens patriae, and that when exercising that jurisdiction a court must act solely in the interests of the child disregarding all more general considerations. I greatly doubt that line of argument.

Every court in any litigation must see that the interests of a child are not neglected. I am not at all certain that it is accurate to say that a court orders a blood test. What happens is that by appointing guardians ad litem and by a *Practice Direction* of the Probate Divorce and Admiralty Division of 21st October 1968, the court prevents parents who retain care and control of their children from exercising their right to have blood tests. Then, when an order for a test is sought the true position appears to me to be that the court is being asked to lift this ban. I do not see why any special jurisdiction is necessary either to impose the ban or lift it, and if, in defiance of the ban, a parent should have his child's blood tested, he might incur penalties, but, if it is the law that evidence is admissible though obtained by unlawful means, the court could not refuse to receive the result of such a test in evidence. No case has yet occurred in which a court has ordered a blood test to be carried out against the will of the parent who has the care and control of the child, and I am not at all certain that it would be proper to do that or that it will be possible to do that after Part III of the 1969 Act comes into operation.

But even if one accepts the view that in ordering, directing or permitting a blood test the court should go no further than a reasonable parent would go, surely a reasonable parent would have some regard to the general public interest and would not refuse a blood test unless he thought that would clearly be against the interests of the child? I cannot assume that in the present cases the husbands are acting in selfish disregard of these children's interests in asking for blood tests.

Lord MacDermott: . . . Must the court, before exercising its jurisdiction to order a blood test to be taken of an infant, be satisfied that it is in the best interests of the infant that it should do so?

The duty of the High Court as respects the affairs and welfare of infants falls into two broad categories. There is, first of all, the duty to *protect* the infant, particularly when engaged or involved in litigation. This duty is of a general nature and derives from the Court of Chancery and to some extent also, I believe, from the common law courts which were merged along with the Court of Chancery in the High Court of Justice by the Act of 1873. It recognises that the infant, as one not sui juris may stand in need of aid. He must not be allowed to suffer because of his incapacity. But the aim is to ensure that he gets his rights rather than to place him above the law and make his rights superior to those of others. I shall refer to this duty and the powers of the court relative thereto as the 'protective jurisdiction'. Exercising it the court will be alert to see that the infant is separately represented where his interest so requires, and to change his next friend or guardian *ad litem* if not acting with due diligence and in a proper manner. Other examples of the protective jurisdiction are – the payment into court and investment of moneys recovered by an infant in litigation, the appointment of the Official Solicitor to act on his behalf in matters of special difficulty, and the approval of compromises and settlements entered into on the infant's behalf.

In exercising what I have called the ancillary jurisdiction in relation to infants the court must also observe and, if need be, exercise its protective jurisdiction. For instance, if the court were satisfied that – as might possibly be the case on rare occasions – a blood test would prejudicially affect the health of the infant it would, no doubt, exercise its discretion against ordering the test. And, again, if the court had reason to believe that the application for a blood test was of a fishing nature, designed for some ulterior motive to call in question the legitimacy, otherwise unimpeached, of a child who had enjoyed a legitimate status, it may well be that the court, acting under its protective rather than its ancillary jurisdiction, would be justified in refusing the application. I need not, however, pursue such instances as they do not arise on these appeals. The point to be made is that the protective jurisdiction, if of the nature I have described, would not ordinarily afford ground for refusing a blood test merely because it might, in revealing the truth, prove the infant's illegitimacy in duly constituted paternity proceedings.

This case has importance beyond its particular facts which are now covered, in any event, by ss 20-22 of the Family Law Reform Act 1969 (see *Re F (a minor) (blood tests : parental rights)* [1993] 3 All ER 596 (CA) for the court's approach to its powers under s 20). It is the only English authority which offers guidance on the legality of medical interventions which are not, on their face, therapeutic. The House of Lords held that such interventions would be lawful providing that they were not 'against the interests' of the child. In other words, the House of

Lords changed the test – ie adopted option (2). They justified doing so on the basis that there was a public interest in a child's paternity being known and the intervention involved, at worst, a minimal risk of harm to the child. As we shall see later (in chapter 14) this analysis has been adopted by those commenting on the law of research, and its application is crucial to the question of the legality of such research.

A difficulty in this view is that it requires some creative reading of the speeches. On its face the case could be said to be limited to ordering (or giving consent to) a blood test in the course of litigation so as to ensure that the court has before it the best evidence to ensure a fair trial. This is expressed particularly by Lords MacDermott and Hodson as being in exercise of the court's 'inherent' or 'ancillary' 'jurisdiction to make interlocutory orders for the purpose of promoting a fair and satisfactory trial' (per Lord MacDermott at 114). Thus, a narrow reading of the case could be that the test of 'not against the interests' is not the law except where it is applied by the *court* in these limited circumstances. If this narrow view were right, it would follow that the test would have no relevance generally for determining the legality of non-therapeutic interventions so as, for example, to permit a parent to volunteer a child for non-therapeutic research.

Of course, the court could make these 'difficult cases' go away by simply fudging the distinction between that which is therapeutic and that which is not. This seems to be an approach which has appealed to some American courts in the context of organ donation by incompetent children.

In the early case of *Bonner v Moran* (1941) 126 F 2d 121 (USCA DC) a traditional approach was taken.

Bonner v Moran (1941) 126 F 2d 121 (USCA DC)

Groner CJ: The facts are these. Appellant, a colored boy residing in Washington city, was at the time of the events about to be stated fifteen years of age. His cousin, Clara Howard, who lived in North Carolina, had been so severely burned that she had become a hopeless cripple. She was brought to Washington by her aunt, who was also the aunt of appellant, and taken to the charity clinic in the Episcopal Hospital, where she was seen by appellee, a physician specializing in plastic surgery. Appellee advised that a skin graft would help her, provided the blood of the donor matched. After a number of unsuccessful efforts to match her blood, the aunt persuaded appellant, then a student in junior high school, to go with her to the hospital for the purpose of having a blood test. His blood matched, and the aunt telephoned appellee, who came to the hospital and performed the first operation on appellant's side. His mother, with whom he lived, was ill at the time and knew nothing about the arrangement.

After the operation, appellant returned home and while there advised his mother that he was going back to the hospital to have his side 'fixed up.' Instead, he remained and in the subsequent operations a tube of flesh was cut and formed from his arm pit to his waist line, and at the proper time one end of the tube was attached to his cousin in the effort to accomplish her relief. The result was unsatisfactory because of improper circulation of the blood through the tube. Accordingly, the tube was severed, after appellant had lost a considerable amount of blood and himself required transfusions. The tube of flesh was later removed and appellant was released from the hospital. From beginning to end, he was there nearly two months . . . [I]n all such cases the basic consideration is whether the proposed operation is for the benefit of the child and is done with a purpose of saving his life or limb. The circumstances in the instant case are wholly without the compass of any of these exceptions. Here the operation was entirely for the benefit of another and involved sacrifice on the part of the infant of fully two months of schooling, in addition to serious physical pain and possible results affecting his future life. This immature colored boy was subjected several times to treatment involving anesthesia, blood letting, and the removal of skin from his body, with at least some permanent marks of disfigurement.

With the advent of organ transplantation in the late 1950s the courts were tempted to take a different line. A number of American cases considered the issue of transplantation and incompetents in the ensuing years. They do not adopt a uniform approach and are helpfully drawn together in the following case.

Curran v Bosze (1990) 566 NE 2d 1319 (Illinois Sup Ct)

Calvo J: Allison and James Curran are 3½-year-old twins. Their mother is Nancy Curran. The twins have lived with Ms Curran and their maternal grandmother since their birth on January 27, 1987.

The twins' father is Tamas Bosze. Ms Curran and Mr Bosze have never been married. As a result of an action brought by Ms Curran against Mr Bosze concerning the paternity of the twins, both Mr Bosze and the twins underwent a blood test in November of 1987. The blood test confirmed that Mr Bosze is the father of the twins. . . .

Mr Bosze is the father of three other children: a son, age 23; Jean Pierre Bosze, age 12; and a one-year-old daughter. Ms Curran is not the mother of any of these children. Each of these children has a different mother. Jean Pierre and the twins are half-siblings. The twins have met Jean Pierre on two occasions. Each meeting lasted approximately two hours.

Jean Pierre is suffering from acute undifferentiated leukemia (AUL), also known as mixed lineage leukemia. Mixed lineage leukemia is a rare form of leukemia which is difficult to treat. Jean Pierre was initially misdiagnosed as having acute lymphocytic leukemia (ALL) in June 1988, in Colombia, South America. Jean Pierre was brought to American in August 1988, and has been treated by Dr Jong Kwon since that time. Jean Pierre was treated with chemotherapy and went into remission. Jean Pierre experienced a testicular relapse in January 1990, and a bone marrow relapse in mid-June 1990. Dr Kwon has recommended a bone marrow transplant for Jean Pierre.

Mr Bosze asked Ms Curran to consent to a blood test for the twins in order to determine whether the twins were compatible to serve as bone marrow donors for a transplant to Jean Pierre. Mr Bosze asked Ms Curran to consent to the twins' undergoing a bone marrow harvesting procedure if the twins were found to be compatible. After consulting with the twins' pediatrician, family members, parents of bone marrow donors and bone marrow donors, Ms Curran refused to give consent to the twins' undergoing either the blood test or the bone marrow harvesting procedure.

On June 28, 1990, Mr Bosze filed an emergency petition in the circuit of Cook County. The petition informed the court that Jean Pierre 'suffers from leukemia and urgently requires a [bone] marrow transplant from a compatible donor. Without the transplant he will die in a short period of time, thereby creating an emergency involving life and death.' The petition stated that persons usually compatible for serving as donors are parents or siblings of the recipient, and Jean Pierre's father, mother, and older brother had been tested and rejected as compatible donors.

According to the petition, '[t]he only siblings who have potential to be donors and who have not been tested are the children, James and Allison.' The petition stated Ms Curran refused to discuss with Mr Bosze the matter of submitting the twins to a blood test to determine their compatibility as potential bone marrow donors for Jean Pierre. The petition stated the blood test 'is minimally invasive and harmless, and no more difficult than the paternity blood testing which the children have already undergone.' According to the petition, there would be no expense involved to Ms Curran.

In the petition, Mr Bosze requested the court find a medical emergency to exist and order and direct Ms Curran to 'forthwith produce the parties' minor children . . . at Lutheran General Hospital . . . for the purpose of compatibility blood testing.' Further, Mr Bosze requested in the petition that 'if the children, or either of them, are compatible as donors, that the Court order and direct that [Ms Curran] produce the children, or whichever one may be compatible, for the purpose of donating bone marrow to their sibling.' . . . [T]he court ruled on July 18, 1990, that it did not have authority to grant Mr Bosze's petition. . . .

Several courts from sister jurisdictions have addressed the issue whether the consent of a court, parent or guardian, for the removal of a kidney from an incompetent person for transplantation to a sibling, may be legally effective. These cases have been addressed by the parties. While not mandatory authority to this court, these cases are illustrative of the complexities involved when otherwise healthy minors or incompetent persons, who lack the legal capacity to give consent, are asked to undergo an invasive surgical procedure for the benefit of a sibling. . . .

Having considered the well known case of *Strunk v Strunk* (1969) 445 SW 2d 145 (Ky CA) (*infra*, p 306), Justice Calvo continued:

In *Hart v Brown* (Super 1972), 29 Conn Supp 368, 289 A 2d 386, the parents of identical twins, age 7 years and 10 months, sought permission to have a kidney from the healthy twin transplanted into the body of the seriously ill twin who was suffering from a kidney disease. The parents brought a declaratory judgment action, as parents and natural guardians of the twins, seeking a declaration that they had the right to consent to the proposed operation. Guardians *ad litem* for each of the twins were appointed. Defendants in the declaratory judgment action were the physicians and the hospital at which the proposed kidney transplantation operation was to take place; the defendants had refused to use their facilities unless the court 'declare[d] that the parents and/or guardians ad litem of the minors have the right to give their consent to the operation upon the minor twins.' *Hart* 29 Conn Supp at 369, 289 A 2d 387.

The court in *Hart* concluded it had the power to determine that the parents have the right to consent to the operation 'using the doctrines of law as stated in the *Strunk* case, in the *Bonner* case, and in the Massachusetts cases.' (*Hart*, 29 Conn Supp at 377, 289 A 2d at 391.) The Massachusetts cases referred to by the *Hart* court were unreported cases where the 'commonwealth of Massachusetts ruled that a court of equity does have the power to permit the natural parents of minor twins to give their consent to a procedure such as is being contemplated by this court.' (*Hart*, 29 Conn Supp at 370-71, 289 A 2d at 387.) The *Hart* court stated *Bonner v Moran* (DC Cir 1941), 126 F 2d 121, was 'authority . . . that nontherapeutic operations can be legally permitted on a minor as long as the parents or other guardians consent to the procedure.' (*Hart*, 29 Conn Supp at 376, 289 A 2d at 390.) In *Bonner*, a 15-year-old minor child's consent to removal of a skin patch for the benefit of his cousin was held legally ineffective.

The court in *Hart* noted it was 'not being asked to act where a person is legally incompetent. The matter, however, does involve two minors who do not have the legal capacity to consent.' (*Hart*, 29 Conn Supp at 370, 289 A 2d at 387.) The *Hart* court referred to the *Strunk* court's decision that a court of equity has the power to permit the natural parent of a 27-year-old mental incompetent to give her consent, using the doctrine of substituted judgment, to a kidney transplantation operation. The court in *Hart* stated:

> 'The court [in *Strunk*] held that a court of equity does have such power, applying also the 'doctrine of substituted judgment.'
> Therefore, this court is of the opinion that it has the power to act in this matter.'
> *Hart*, 29 Conn Supp at 371, 289 A 2d at 388.

The *Hart* court reviewed the medical testimony presented concerning the kidney transplant which 'indicate[d] that scientifically this type of procedure is a "perfect" transplant.' (*Hart*, 29 Conn Supp at 375, 289 A 2d at 389.) The court also noted that a psychiatrist examined the proposed donor and testified the proposed donor 'has a strong identification with her twin sister.' (*Hart*, 29 Conn Supp at 374, 289 A 2d at 389.) Further, the psychiatrist testified 'that if the expected successful results are achieved they would be of immense benefit to the donor in that the donor would be better off in a family that was happy than in a family that was distressed and in that it would be a very great loss to the donor if the donee were to die from her illness.' (*Hart*, 29 Conn Supp at 374-75, 289 A 2d at 389.) The court in *Hart* considered the testimony of the psychiatrist to be 'of limited value only because of the ages of the minors.' *Hart*, 29 Conn Supp at 375, 289 A 2d at 390.

Both guardians *ad litem* gave their consent to the procedure. Both parents gave their consent to the procedure. A clergy person testified that the natural parents were 'making a morally sound decision.' (*Hart*, 29 Conn Supp at 375, 289 A 2d at 390.) The *Hart* court found the testimony of the parents showed they reached their decision to consent 'only after many hours of agonizing consideration.' (*Hart*, 29 Conn Supp at 375, 289 A 2d at 390.) The twin who would serve as the kidney donor 'ha[d] been informed of the operation and insofar as she may be capable of understanding she desires to donate her kidney so that her sister may return to her.' *Hart*, 29 Conn Supp at 375, 289 A 2d at 389.

The *Hart* court stated:

To prohibit the natural parents and the guardians ad litem of the minor children the right to give their consent under these circumstances, where there is supervision by this court and other persons in examining their judgment, would be most unjust, inequitable and injudicious. Therefore, natural parents of a minor should have the right to give their consent to an isograft kidney transplantation procedure when their motivation and reasoning are favorably reviewed by a community representation which includes a court of equity.

It is the judgment of this court that [the parents] have the right, under the particular facts and circumstances of this matter, to give their consent to the operations. (*Hart*, 29 Conn Supp at 378, 289 A 2d at 391.)

Although purporting to apply the doctrine of substituted judgment, the *Hart* court did not inquire as to what the 7½-year-old minors would do if the minors were competent. The *Hart* court instead determined that 'the natural parents would be able to substitute their consent for that of their minor children after a close, independent and objective investigation of their motivation and reasoning.' *Hart*, 29 Conn Supp at 375, 289 A 2d at 390.

In *Little v Little* (Tex Civ 1979), 576 SW 2d 493, the mother of a 14-year-old mentally incompetent daughter petitioned the court to authorize the mother's consent to the removal of a kidney from her daughter for transplantation into her younger son, who suffered from a kidney disease. The mother had been appointed guardian of her mentally incompetent minor daughter. An attorney *ad litem* was appointed by the court to represent the proposed donor. The attorney *ad litem* argued there was no constitutional or statutory provision empowering the probate court to authorize the removal of an incompetent's kidney for the purpose of benefiting another person.

The mother relied on *Strunk*. The *Little* court discussed the doctrine of substituted judgment as it was applied in *Strunk*. The *Little* court also discussed two cases where the court refused to authorize a transplant, *In Re Guardianship of Pescinski* (1975), 67 Wis 2d 4, 226 NW 2d 180, and *In Re Richardson* (La App 1973), 284 So 2d 185.

The court in *Little* stated:

It is clear in transplant cases that courts, whether they use the term 'substituted judgment' or not, will consider the benefits to the donor as a basis for permitting an incompetent to donate an organ. Although in *Strunk* the Kentucky Court discussed the substituted judgment doctrine in some detail, the conclusion of the majority there was based on the benefits that the incompetent donor would derive, rather than on the theory that the incompetent would have consented to the transplant if he were competent. We adopt this approach. *Little* 576 SW 2d at 498.

The *Little* court determined that 'the testimony . . . conclusively establish[ed] the existence of a close relationship between [the proposed donor] and [her brother], a genuine concern by each for the welfare of the other and, at the very least, an awareness by [the proposed donor] of the nature of [her brother's] plight and an awareness of the fact that she is in a position to ameliorate [her brother's] burden.' (*Little*, 576 SW 2d at 498.) Both parents of the incompetent minor consented to the kidney donation; there was no evidence that the incompetent minor had been subjected to family pressure; and there were no medically preferable alternatives to the kidney transplant. The *Little* court also found that the dangers of the operation were minimal and there was evidence the incompetent minor would not suffer psychological harm. The kidney transplant would probably be substantially beneficial to the proposed recipient, and the trial court's decision was made 'only after a full judicial proceeding in which the interests of [the incompetent minor] were championed by an attorney ad litem.' (*Little*, 576 SW 2d at 499.) The *Little* court concluded:

Given the presence of all the factors and circumstances outlined above, and limiting our decision to such facts and circumstances, we conclude that the trial court did not exceed its authority by authorizing the participation of [the incompetent minor] in the kidney transplant as a donor, since there is strong evidence to the effect that she will receive substantial psychological benefits from such participation. Nothing in this opinion is to be construed as being applicable to a situation where the proposed [recipient] is not a parent or sibling of the incompetent. *Little* 576 SW 2d at 500.

In *Pescinski*, the sister and guardian of an adult incompetent 39-year-old man petitioned the court for permission for the incompetent brother to donate a kidney to another sister suffering from a kidney disease. The incompetent, 'classified as a schizophrenic, chronic, catatonic type' (*Pescinski*, 67 Wis 2d at 6, 226 NW 2d at 180) for over 17 years, was a mental patient at a State hospital. A physician testified that the ward had a mental capacity of a 12-year-old child. The guardian *ad litem* for the incompetent person would not consent to the procedure.

In *Pescinski*, the supreme court of Wisconsin addressed the issue: 'Does a county court have the power to order an operation to be performed to remove a kidney of an incompetent ward, under guardianship of the person, and transfer it to a sister where the dire need of the transfer is established but where no consent has been given by the incompetent or his guardian *ad litem*, nor has any benefit to the ward been shown?' (*Pescinski*, 67 Wis 2d at 5, 226 NW 2d at 180.) The court answered that it did not.

The *Pescinski* court noted that 'no statutory authority [is] given the county court to authorize a kidney transplant or any other surgical procedure on a living person.' (*Pescinski*, 67 Wis 2d at 7, 226 NW 2d at 181.) The court in *Pescinski* discussed the doctrine of substituted judgment approved by the court in *Strunk*. The *Pescinski* court declined to adopt the doctrine of substituted judgment.

> An incompetent particularly should have his own interests protected. Certainly no advantage should be taken of him. In the absence of real consent on his part, and in a situation where no benefit to him has been established, we fail to find any authority for the county court, or this court, to approve this operation. *Pescinski*, 67 Wis 2d at 8-9, 226 NW 2d at 182.

In *In Re Guardianship of Eberhardy* (1981), 102 Wis 2d 539, 307 NW 2d 881, the supreme court of Wisconsin discussed its decision in *Pescinski* and clarified that *Pescinski* 'should not be read as a ruling of want of jurisdiction.' (*Eberhardy*, 102 Wis 2d at 565 n 13, 307 NW 2d at 893 n 13.) On the part of a court to authorize the kidney transplant therein considered, the court in *Eberhardy* stated:

> *Pescinski* represents the exercise of judicial restraint under particular circumstances. Those circumstances included the lack of consent of the guardian *ad litem*, no showing of benefit to the ward, and an absence of legislative guidance. *Pescinski* should not be read as a ruling of want of jurisdiction, and, insofar as it may, we disavow that conclusion. *Eberhardy*, 102 Wis 2d at 565 n 13, 307 NW 2d at 893 n 13.

The Louisiana Court of Appeal in *In Re Richardson* (La App 1973), 284 So 2d 185, declined to adopt the doctrine of substituted judgment announced in *Strunk*. Both parents of a 17-year-old incompetent son with a mental age of three or four years consented to a kidney transplant from the son to his sister. As a procedural vehicle to bring the issue before the court, the father filed suit against the mother to compel her to consent to the kidney transplant. The *Richardson* court distinguished the case before it from the case in *Strunk*:

> We find the facts in [*Strunk*], particularly the conclusion relative to the 'best interest' of the incompetent, are not similar to the facts in the instant case and we also find that both the procedural and the substantive aspects of the majority opinion are not in accord with Louisiana law. *Richardson*, 284 So 2d at 187.

The *Richardson* court stated that the law of its State 'is designed to protect and promote the ultimate best interest of a minor.' (*Richardson*, 284, So 2d at 187.) Louisiana law did not provide for the *inter vivos* donations of a minor's property either by the minor or by the minor's tutor (guardian). The *Richardson* court stated:

> Since our law affords this unqualified protection against intrusion [*sic*] into a comparatively mere property right, it is inconceivable to us that it affords less protection to a minor's right to be free in his person from bodily intrusion to the extent of loss of an organ unless such loss be in the best interest of the minor. Of course, that statement and our conclusion are restricted to the facts of the present case. *Richardson*, 284 So 2d at 187.

In the concurring opinion in *Richardson*, it was stated:

> The majority, in my opinion, rightfully assumes that the court is empowered to authorize the transplant of the kidney from the minor, provided certain standards are met, ie, the best interests of the minor. However, I am of the opinion that before the court might exercise its *awesome* authority in such an instance and before it considers the question of the best interests of the child, certain requirements must be met. I am of the opinion that it must be clearly established that the surgical intrusion is urgent, that there are no reasonable alternatives, and that the contingencies are minimal. These requirements of prerequisites are not met in this case. Having so determined,

we are not confronted with the question of the best interests of the child. (Emphasis in original.) *Richardson*, 284 So 2d at 188 (Gulotta, J, concurring).

In each of the foregoing cases where consent to the kidney transplant was authorized, regardless whether the authority to consent was to be exercised by the court, a parent or a guardian, the key inquiry was the presence or absence of a benefit to the potential donor. Notwithstanding the language used by the courts in reaching their determination that a transplant may or may not occur, the standard by which the determination was made was whether the transplant would be in the best interest of the child or incompetent person.

The primary benefit to the donor in these cases arises from the relationship existing between the donor and recipient. In *Strunk*, the donor lived in a State institution. The recipient was a brother who served as the donor's only connection with the outside world. In both *Hart* and *Little*, there was evidence that the sibling relationship between the donor and recipient was close. In each of these cases, both parents had given their consent.

We hold that a parent or guardian may give consent on behalf of a minor daughter or son for the child to donate bone marrow to a sibling, only when to do so would be in the minor's best interest.

As sole custodian of the twins, Ms Curran 'may determine the child[ren]'s upbringing, including but not limited to, [the] education, health care and religious training, unless the court, after hearing, finds, upon motion by the noncustodial parent, that the absence of a specific limitation of the custodian's authority would clearly be contrary to the best interests of the child[ren].' Ill Rec Stat 1987, Ch 40, par. 608(a). . . .

The evidence reveals three critical factors which are necessary to a determination that it will be in the best interests of a child to donate bone marrow to a sibling. First, the parent who consents on behalf of the child must be informed of the risks and benefits inherent in the bone marrow harvesting procedure to the child.

Second, there must be emotional support available to the child from the person or persons who take care of the child. The testimony reveals that a child who is to undergo general anesthesia and the bone marrow harvesting procedure needs the emotional support of a person whom the child loves and trusts. A child who is to donate bone marrow is required to go to an unfamiliar place and meet with unfamiliar people. Depending upon the age of the child, he or she may or may not understand what is to happen. The evidence establishes that the presence and emotional support by the child's caretaker is important to ease the fears associated with such an unfamiliar procedure.

Third, there must be an existing, close relationship between the donor and recipient. The evidence clearly shows that there is no physical benefit to a donor child. If there is any benefit to a child who donates bone marrow to a sibling it will be a psychological benefit. According to the evidence, the psychological benefit is not simply one of personal, individual altruism in an abstract theoretical sense, although that may be a factor.

The psychological benefit is grounded firmly in the fact that the donor and recipient are known to each other as family. Only where there is an existing relationship between a healthy child and his or her ill sister or brother may a psychological benefit to the child from donating bone marrow to a sibling realistically be found to exist. The evidence establishes that it is the existing sibling relationship, as well as the potential for a continuing sibling relationship, which forms the context in which it may be determined that it will be in the best interests of the child to undergo a bone marrow harvesting procedure for a sibling.

Both Mr Bosze and Ms Curran are informed of the risks inherent in a bone marrow harvesting procedure performed on a child. Mr Bosze has consulted with Dr Kwon, Jean Pierre's treating physician, Ms Curran has consulted with the twins' pediatrician, parents of bone marrow donors, and bone marrow donors. Both Ms Curran and Mr Bosze listened to Drs Johnson, Kwon, Leventhal, Lechtor, Camitta, and Kohrman.

The primary risk to a bone marrow donor is the risk associated with undergoing general anesthesia. The risk of a life-threatening complication occurring from undergoing general anesthesia is 1 in 10,000. As noted by the circuit court, the risks associated with general anesthesia include, but are not limited to, 'brain damage as a result of oxygen deprivation, stroke, cardiac arrest and death.'

The pain following the harvesting procedure is usually easily controlled with post-operative medication. Although there is a risk of infection at the needle puncture site, this is rare.

Ms Curran has refused consent on behalf of the twins to the bone marrow transplant because she does not think it is in their best interests to subject them to the risks and pains involved in undergoing general anesthesia and the harvesting procedure. While Ms Curran is aware that the risks involved in donating bone marrow and undergoing general anesthesia are small, she also is aware that when such risk occurs, it may be life-threatening.

On February 16, 1989, Mr Bosze and Ms Curran agreed in the parentage order that Ms Curran would have sole custody of the twins. Allison and James have lived with Ms Curran and their maternal grandmother since their birth. Mr Bosze and Ms Curran also agreed that Mr Bosze would have visitation rights with the twins. Until the twins reached the age of five years, Mr Bosze would have visitation once a week. Ms Curran was to be present during the visitation.

Between February 16, 1989, and February 14, 1990, Mr Bosze exercised his visitation rights 15 times. On two of these occasions, Jean Pierre was present. Before Mr Bosze ever requested Ms Curran to consent to the twins' donating bone marrow to Jean Pierre, Ms Curran requested that Mr Bosze not tell the twins that Jean Pierre was their half-brother. Ms Curran thought that it would be confusing to the twins to be told that they have two half-brothers and a half-sister, each of whom had a different mother. Mr Bosze honored this request.

It is a fact that the twins and Jean Pierre share the same biological father. There was no evidence produced, however, to indicate that the twins and Jean Pierre are known to each other as family.

Allison and James would need the emotional support of their primary caregiver if they were to donate bone marrow. The evidence establishes that it would not be in a 3½-year-old child's best interests if he or she were required to go to a hospital and undergo all that is involved with the bone marrow harvesting procedure without the constant reassurances and support by a familiar adult known and trusted by the child.

Not only is Ms Curran presently the twins' primary caretaker, the evidence establishes she is the only caretaker the twins have ever known. Ms Curran has refused to consent to the twins' participation in donating bone marrow to Jean Pierre. It appears that Mr Bosze would be unable to substitute his support for the procedure for that of Ms Curran because his involvement in the lives of Allison and James has, to this point, been a limited one. . . .

This court shares the opinion of the circuit court that Jean Pierre's situation 'evokes sympathy from all who've heard [it].' No matter how small the hope that a bone marrow transplant will cure Jean Pierre, the fact remains that without the transplant, Jean Pierre will almost certainly die. The sympathy felt by this court, the circuit court, and all those who have learned of Jean Pierre's tragic situation cannot, however, obscure the fact that, under the circumstances presented in the case at bar, it neither would be proper under existing law nor in the best interests of the 3½-year-old twins for the twins to participate in the bone marrow harvesting procedure.

(ii) THE COURT AND THE MEANING OF THE TEST

It is important to realise, though it may appear trite to say, that the scope of the proxy's power is a matter for the law. The importance of stating this lies in the fact that as the law sets the scope so it necessarily sets the boundaries of the power and thereby imposes limits. At one level, it could be argued that the boundaries established by the court are essentially, indeed inherently, *ad hoc*. The court merely determines whether in the particular case before it a proxy's decision is, or is not, in the child's best interests. This, of course, atomises the legal approach and prevents the emergence of any general outline of the boundaries of the proxy's power by reference to which proxies in the future may be guided or held to account. If it is accepted that a court's role, indeed obligation, is to offer such an outline it would seem that the court has been slow to undertake this quasi-legislative role. Even when the court begins to undertake this responsibility it is in the nature of the judicial process working from case to case that it will take some time before general criteria begin to emerge.

Because, as we have seen, the meaning of 'best interests' is to some extent conditioned by the context and that, therefore, more general criteria take time to emerge, we can notice how the court applies the test of 'best interests' by looking at the leading case in one particular factual area – the treatment of the severely handicapped baby (see, *infra*, ch 16 for a full discussion). It is fair to say that even in this area there are very few cases – a phenomenon which bedevils English medical law generally – but that said, the court's slow progress towards developing general criteria so as to give substance to the words 'best interests' can be discerned.

Re J (a minor) (wardship: medical treatment) [1991] Fam 33, [1990] 3 All ER 930 (CA)

J was a ward of court who had been born very prematurely. He suffered very severe and permanent brain damage at the time of his birth, the brain tissue then lost being irreplaceable. He was epileptic and the medical evidence was that he was likely to develop serious spastic quadriplegia, would be blind and deaf and was unlikely ever to be able to speak or to develop even limited intellectual abilities, but it was likely that he would feel pain to the same extent as a normal baby. His life expectancy was uncertain but he was expected to die before late adolescence, although he could survive for a few years. He had been ventilated twice for long periods when his breathing stopped, that treatment being both painful and hazardous. The medical prognosis was that any further collapse which required ventilation would be fatal. However he was neither on the point of death nor dying. The question arose whether if he suffered a further collapse the medical staff at the hospital where he was being cared for should reventilate him in the event of his breathing stopping. . . .

Lord Donaldson MR: The issue here is whether it would be in the best interests of the child to put him on a mechanical ventilator and subject him to all the associated processes of intensive care, if at some future time he could not continue breathing unaided. Let me say at once that I can understand the doctors wishing to ascertain the court's wishes at this stage, because it is an eventuality which could occur at any time, and, if it did, an immediate decision might well have to be made. However, the situation is significantly different from being asked whether or not to consent on behalf of the child to particular treatment which is more or less immediately in prospect. The judge has found that the odds are about even whether the need for artificial ventilation, whether mechanical or manual, will ever arise. If it does arise, the very fact that it has arisen will mean that the more optimistic end of the range of prognoses, pessimistic though the whole range is, will have been falsified. On the other hand, the child's state of health might change at any time for the better as well as for the worse, even though there are distinct limits to what could be hoped for, let alone anticipated.

The doctors were unanimous in recommending that there should be no mechanical reventilation in the event of his stopping breathing, subject only to the qualifications injected by Dr W and accepted by the judge that in the event of a chest infection short term manual ventilation would be justified and that in the event of the child stopping breathing the provisional decision to abstain from mechanical ventilation could and should be revised, if this seemed appropriate to the doctors caring for him in the then prevailing clinical situation.

There can be no criticism of the judge for endorsing this approach on the footing that he was thereby abdicating his responsibility and leaving it to the doctors to decide. He had reviewed and considered the basis of the doctors' views and recommendations in the greatest detail and with the greatest care. Nothing could be more inimical to the interest of the child than that the judge should make an order which restricted the doctors' freedom to revise their present view in favour of more active means to preserve the life of the child, if the situation changed and this then seemed to them to be appropriate.

The basis of the doctors' recommendations, approved by the judge, was that mechanical ventilation is itself an invasive procedure which, together with its essential accompaniments, such as the introduction of a naso-gastric tube, drips which have to be resited and constant blood sampling, would cause the child distress. Furthermore, the procedures involve taking active measures which carry their own hazards, not only to life but in terms of causing even greater brain damage. This had to be balanced against what could possibly be achieved by the adoption of such active treatment. The chances of preserving the child's life might be improved, although even this was not certain and account had to be taken of the extremely poor quality of life at present enjoyed by the child, the fact that he had already been ventilated for exceptionally long periods, the unfavourable prognosis with or without ventilation and a recognition that if the question of reventilation ever arose, his situation would have deteriorated still further.

I can detect no error in the judge's approach and in principle would affirm his decision. This is subject to two qualifications. (i) Although all concerned have, as they know, liberty to apply to the judge at any time and he had arranged to review his decision in December, I think that he should have asked for periodic reports meanwhile on J's condition, so that he could, if he thought it appropriate, review the matter before then of his own motion. (ii) I do not think that his order should have been in the form of 'The [local authority] shall direct the relevant health authority to continue to treat . . . ' because neither the court in wardship proceedings nor, I think, a local authority having care and control of the baby is able to require the authority to follow a particular course of treatment. What the court can do is to withhold consent to treatment of which it disapproves and it can express its approval of other treatment proposed by the authority and its doctors. There is ample precedent for the judge's formula, but I think that it is wrong and obscures the co-operative nature of the relationship between court and medical authorities. I would prefer 'Approval is given to the continuance of the treatment of . . . '

Balcombe LJ: . . . In deciding in any given case what is in the best interests of the ward, the court adopts the same attitude as a responsible parent would do in the case of his or her own child; the court, exercising the duties of the sovereign as parens patriae, is not expected to adopt any higher or different standards than that which, viewed objectively, a reasonable and responsible parent would do.

I turn now to consider the two submissions of counsel for the Official Solicitor.

(1) *The 'absolute' submission* This submission was based on the following proposition. (a) The court is unable to evaluate the consequence of death, ie non-existence: see *McKay v Essex Area Health Authority* [1982] 2 All ER 771 at 781-782, 790, [1982] QB 1166, 1181, 1189, 1192-1193 per Stephenson, Ackner and Griffiths LJJ. But this was said in the context of a claim for damages by a child born disabled as the result of an infection of German measles suffered by the mother while the child was in the womb. The basis of the claim was that the defendants were negligent in allowing the child to be born alive, ie that in the circumstances of the case the doctors should have performed an abortion and terminated the life of the foetus. This court decided that the child's claim was contrary to public policy as being a violation of the sanctity of human life and a claim which could not be recognised and enforced because the court could not evaluate non-existence *for the purpose of awarding damages for the denial of it*. In my judgment, the facts of that case, and the issues to which those facts gave rise, are wholly different from the facts and issues in the present case, and the views expressed by the members of that court do not assist us in dealing with a wholly different problem; in particular, it cannot be too firmly stressed that, notwithstanding the somewhat emotive language used by Templeman LJ in *Re B (a minor: wardship: medical treatment)* (1981) [1990] 3 All ER 927 at 929, [1981] 1 WLR 1421 at 1424, for example 'condemned to die', in none of the wardship cases has there ever been, as there was in *McKay*'s case, a proposal that a positive step should be taken to terminate a life: the issue in every case is whether or not treatment which might save or prolong a life should be withheld. (b) Respect for the sanctity of human life and the requirements of public policy preclude attempts by the court to evaluate the quality of a disabled person's life. This submission also was supported by citations from *McKay's* case and from the judgment of McKenzie J in the Canadian case of *Re Superintendent of Family and Child Service and Dawson* (1983) 145 DLR (3d) 610. (c) The 'slippery slope' argument that it is unsafe to permit any erosion in the principle of the absolute sanctity of human life.

Both the submissions summarised under paras (b) and (c) above depend on the assertion that public policy precludes any inroad on the sanctity of human life. I have already cited the passage from the speech of Lord Hailsham LC in *Re B (a minor) (wardship: sterilisation)* [1987] 2 All ER 206 at 212, [1988] AC 199 at 202 which established that issues of public policy, as such, cannot prevail over the interest of the ward. In my judgment there is no warrant, either on principle or authority, for the absolute submission. There is only the one test: that the interests of the ward are paramount. Of course the court will approach those interests with a strong predilection in favour of the preservation of life, because of the sanctity of human life. But there neither is, nor should there be, any absolute rule that, save where the ward is already terminally ill, ie dying, neither the court nor any responsible parent can approve the withholding of life-saving treatment on the basis of the quality of the ward's life. (For my part I would not accept that the so-called 'cabbage' cases could be treated as an exception to this suggested rule, since in deciding that a child whose faculties have been destroyed is a 'cabbage' of itself involves making a judgment about the quality of that child's life.) I say that there is no such rule because there is no authority to that effect: indeed the judgments in *Re B (a minor) (wardship: medical treatment)* (1981) [1990] 3 All ER 927, [1981] 1 WLR 1421 are consistent only with there being no 'absolute' rule. I say that there should be no such rule because it could in certain circumstances be inimical to the interests of the ward that there should be such a requirement: to preserve life at all costs, whatever the quality of the life to be preserved, and however distressing to the ward may be the nature of the treatment necessary to preserve life, may not be in the interests of the ward.

(2) *The 'qualified' submission* Here again I cannot accept the submission in the terms in which it was framed, which treats the language used by Templeman and Dunn LJJ in *Re B (a minor) (wardship: medical treatment)* [1990] 3 All ER 927 at 929-930, [1981] 1 WLR 1421 at 1424 as if they had intended to lay down a test applicable to all circumstances, which clearly they did not. Further, I would deprecate any attempt by this court to lay down such an all-embracing test since the circumstances of these tragic cases are so infinitely various. I do not know of any demand by the judges who have to deal with these cases at first instance for this court to assist them by laying down any test beyond that which is already the law: that the interests of the ward are the first and paramount consideration, subject to the gloss on that test which I suggest, that in determining where those interests lie the court adopts the standpoint of the reasonable and responsible parent who has his or her child's best interests at heart.

Taylor LJ: . . . Three preliminary principles are not in dispute. First, it is settled law that the court's prime and paramount consideration must be the best interests of the child. That is easily said but not so easily applied. What it does involve is that the views of the parents, although they should be heeded and weighed, cannot prevail over the court's view of the ward's best interests. In the present case the parents, finding themselves in a hideous dilemma, have not taken a strong view so that no conflict arises.

Second, the court's high respect for the sanctity of human life imposes a strong presumption in favour of taking all steps capable of preserving it, save in exceptional circumstances. The problem is to define those circumstances.

Third, and as a corollary to the second principle, it cannot be too strongly emphasised that the court never sanctions steps to terminate life. That would be unlawful. There is no question of approving, even in a case of the most horrendous disability, a course aimed at terminating life or accelerating death. The court is concerned only with the circumstances in which steps should not be taken to prolong life.

Two decisions of this court have dealt with cases at the extremes of the spectrum of affliction. *Re C (a minor) (wardship: medical treatment)* [1989] 2 All ER 782, [1990] Fam 26 was a case in which a child had severe irreversible brain damage such that she was hopelessly and terminally ill. The court held that the best interests of the child required approval of recommendations designed to ease her suffering and permit her life to come to an end peacefully with dignity rather than seek to prolong her life.

By contrast, in the earlier case of *Re B (a minor) (wardship: medical treatment)* (1981) [1990] 3 All ER 927, [1981] 1 WLR 1421, the court was concerned with a child suffering from Down's syndrome, who quite separately was born with an intestinal obstruction. Without an operation this intestinal condition would quickly have been fatal. On the other hand, the operation had a good chance of successfully removing the obstruction, once and for all, thereby affording the child a life expectation of some 20 to 30 years as a mongol. The parents genuinely believed it was in the child's interests to refrain from operating and allow her to die. The court took a different view. Templeman LJ said that the court had to decide –

> whether the life of this child is demonstrably going to be so awful that in effect the child must be condemned to die, or whether the life of this child is still so imponderable that it would be wrong for her to be condemned to die. There may be cases, I know not, of severe proved damage where the future is so certain and where the life of the child is bound to be full of pain and suffering that the court might be driven to a different conclusion, but in the present case the choice which lies before the court is this: whether to allow an operation to take place which may result in the child living for 20 to 30 years as a mongoloid or whether (and I think this must be brutally the result) to terminate the life of a mongoloid child because she also has an intestinal complaint. Faced with that choice I have no doubt that it is the duty of this court to decide that the child must live . . . The evidence in this case only goes to show that if the operation takes place and is successful then the child may live the normal span of a mongoloid child with the handicaps and defects and life of a mongol child, and it is not for this court to say that life of that description ought to be extinguished.

(See [1990] 3 All ER 927 at 929, [1981] 1 WLR 1421 at 1424.)

Dunn LJ said ([1990] 3 All ER 927 at 930, [1981] 1 WLR 1421 at 1424-1425):

. . . there is no evidence that this child's short life is likely to be an intolerable one. There is no evidence at all as to the quality of life which the child may expect. As counsel for the Official Solicitor said, the child should be put into the same position as any other mongol child and must be given the chance to live an existence. I accept that way of putting it.

Those two cases thus decide that where the child is terminally ill the court will not require treatment to prolong life; but where, at the other extreme, the child is severely handicapped although not intolerably so and treatment for a discrete condition can enable life to continue for an appreciable period, albeit subject to that severe handicap, the treatment should be given.

I should say that, in my view, the phrase 'condemned to die' which occurs twice in the passage cited from the judgment of Templeman LJ is more emotive than accurate. As already indicated, the court in these cases has to decide, not whether to end life, but whether to prolong it by treatment without which death would ensue from natural causes.

It is to be noted that Templeman LJ did not say, even obiter, that where the child's life would be bound to be full of pain and suffering there would come a point at which the court should rule against prolonging life by treatment. He went no further than to say there may be cases where the court might take that view.

This leads to the arguments presented by counsel for the Official Solicitor. His first submission propounded an absolute test, that, except where the ward is terminally ill, the court's approach should always be to prolong life by treatment if this is possible, regardless of the quality of life being preserved and regardless of any added suffering caused by the treatment itself. I cannot accept this test which in my view is so hard as to be inconsistent at its extreme with the best interests of the child. Counsel for the Official Solicitor submits that the court cannot play God and decide whether the quality of life which the treatment would give the child is better or worse than death. He referred to dicta in *McKay v Essex Area Health Authority* [1982] 2 All ER 771, [1982] QB 1166. That case involved a quite different situation since a claim was being made for damages for negligence against doctors for allowing a gravely damaged infant plaintiff to be born at all after his mother had contracted German measles. The exercise of weighing the disability against the alternative of not being born at all was, therefore, in a damages context. But Stephenson LJ said ([1982] 2 All ER 771 at 781, [1982] QB 1166 at 1180):

> Like this court when it had to consider the interests of a child born with Down's syndrome in *Re B (a minor) (wardship: medical treatment)* ([1990] 3 All ER 927, [1981] 1 WLR 1421), I would not answer until it is necessary to do so the question whether the life of a child could be so certainly 'awful' and 'intolerable' that it would be in its best interests to end it and it might be considered that it had a right to be put to death.

Again there is reference in that passage to the possibility of a child being 'put to death'. I repeat, because of its importance, the debate here is not about terminating life but solely whether to withhold treatment designed to prevent death from natural causes.

Ackner LJ said ([1982] 2 All ER 771 at 787, [1982] QB 1166 at 1189):

> But how can a court begin to evaluate non-existence, 'The undiscovered country from whose bourn no traveller returns?' No comparison is possible and therefore no damage can be established which a court could recognise.

Despite the court's inability to compare a life afflicted by the most severe disability with death, the unknown, I am of the view that there must be extreme cases in which the court is entitled to say: 'The life which this treatment would prolong would be so cruel as to be intolerable.' If, for example, a child was so damaged as to have negligible use of its faculties and the only way of preserving its life was by the continuous administration of extremely painful treatment such that the child either would be in continuous agony or would have to be so sedated continuously as to have no conscious life at all, I cannot think counsel's absolute test should apply to require the treatment to be given. In those circumstances, without there being any question of deliberately ending the life or shortening it, I consider the court is entitled in the best interests of the child to say that deliberate steps should not be taken artificially to prolong its miserable life span.

Once the absolute test is rejected, the proper criteria must be a matter of degree. At what point in the scale of disability and suffering ought the court to hold that the best interests of the child do not require further endurance to be imposed by positive treatment to prolong its life? Clearly, to justify withholding treatment, the circumstances would have to be extreme.

Counsel for the Official Solicitor submitted that if the court rejected his absolute test, then at least it would have 'to be certain that the life of the child, were the treatment to be given, would be intolerably awful'.

I consider that the correct approach is for the court to judge the quality of life the child would have to endure if given the treatment and decide whether in all the circumstances such a life would be so afflicted as to be intolerable to that child. I say 'to that child' because the test should not be whether the life would be tolerable to the decider. The test must be whether the child in question, if capable of exercising sound judgment, would consider the life tolerable. This is the approach adopted by McKenzie in *Re Superintendent of Family and Child Service and Dawson* (1983) 145 DLR (3d) 610 at 620-621 in the passage cited with approval by Lord Donaldson MR. It takes account of the strong instinct to preserve one's life even in circumstances which an outsider, not himself at risk of death, might consider unacceptable. The circumstances to be considered would, in appropriate cases, include the degree of existing disability and any additional suffering or aggravation of the disability which the treatment itself would superimpose. In an accident case, as opposed to one involving disablement from birth, the child's pre-accident quality of life and its perception of what has been lost may also be factors relevant to whether the residual life would be intolerable to that child.

Counsel for the Official Solicitor argued that, before deciding against treatment, the court would have to be *certain* that the circumstances of the child's future would comply with the extreme requirements to justify that decision. Certainty as to the future is beyond human judgment. The courts have not, even in the trial of capital offences, required certainty of proof. But, clearly, the court must be satisfied to a high degree of probability.

In the present case, the doctors were unanimous that in his present condition, J should not be put back on to a mechanical ventilator. That condition is very grave indeed. I do no repeat the description of it given by Lord Donaldson MR. In reaching his conclusion, the judge no doubt had three factors in mind. First, the severe lack of capacity of the child in all his faculties which even without any further complication would make his existence barely sentient. Second, that, if further mechanical ventilation were to be required, that very fact would involve the risk of a deterioration in B's condition, because of further brain damage flowing from the interruption of breathing. Third, all the doctors drew attention to the invasive nature of mechanical ventilation and the intensive care required to accompany it. They stressed the unpleasant and distressing nature of that treatment. To add such distress and the risk of further deterioration to an already appalling catalogue of disabilities was clearly capable in my judgment of producing a quality of life which justified the stance of the doctors and the judge's conclusion. I therefore agree that, subject to the minor variations to the judge's order proposed by Lord Donaldson MR, this appeal should be dismissed.

Notice, we use the handicapped baby only as an example. It is not the only area of medical law in which the courts have sought to establish more clearly the meaning of 'best interests' (see the sterilisation cases *infra*, ch 10).

So far we have identified the test which is to guide the proxy decision-maker and we have noticed an example of the way in which the courts have begun to give substance to that test. There remains a further and crucially important issue. Undoubtedly, the court has taken to itself a quasi-legislative role in articulating the 'best interests' test. In this way it seeks to set the general criteria to be applied by proxies.

(iii) THE ROLE OF THE COURT: DECISION-MAKER OR REVIEWER?

What, however, is the court doing when the decision of a proxy about the best interests of a child is challenged before the court? In situations when the criteria have to be applied in a particular case, there are a number of possible roles which a court might choose to play. The court could become the proxy decision-maker and impose its own view, *de novo*, of the child's best interests. Alternatively, the court could inquire whether the decision-maker had given his mind to, and taken account of, the relevant criteria set by the law and further, if he had, that he had not applied them capriciously. If the court adopts the former role is it not setting itself up as a kind of 'super-parent' all wise and knowing? Leaving aside the factual issue of why a judge should be a better parent than the parent(s) in question, is there any legal basis for this role? That the courts do it is, of course, a legal basis of a sort in itself. At a deeper level, when the question is 'are they entitled to do it?' it can at least be argued that they have no right to substitute their view for that of the parent. This is because at the level of political philosophy the law makes the assumption that parents are *prima facie* the decision-makers. It is not a good ground for interfering with the parents' decision to say you disagree with it. Lord MacKay LC can be seen reflecting this in his comment on the Children Bill (later the Children Act 1989) when he said:

> The integrity and independence of the family is the basic building block of a free and democratic society and the need to defend it should be clearly perceivable in the law. [Perceptions of the Children Bill and Beyond (1989) 139 New LJ 505 at 505.]

So what of the other role where the court acts to *review* the parents' decision? This is similar to the court's role in public law when a public body's decision is challenged. The legal basis as well as the attractions of this role are that the court does not usurp the function of the *prima facie* decision-maker. Rather, it stands back from the outcome of the particular decision while ensuring that the process of decision-making is legitimate.

In our view the court's proper role is to *review* but not usurp. An inevitable consequence of adopting this role is that the courts must establish the criteria by reference to which the *prima facie* decision-maker must be guided. This quasi-legislative function in turn demands that in the sorts of cases we are considering the courts must begin to give substance to such general expressions as 'best interests'. This is precisely what we have seen the courts, albeit reluctantly, move towards in the cases concerning handicapped babies. A similar development can be seen in the cases concerned with sterilising the intellectually disabled (see *infra*, ch 10).

One feature of the development of criteria is that the court will begin to identify factors which the proxy may *not* have regard to, such that if he does his decision cannot stand. One example may be where a proxy bases his decision on his particular religious creed. Regard may, of course, be paid to a religious view of a proxy when the effect on the child is not significant (eg male circumcision). The moment the child's life or limb is at risk the court will have regard to the well-known aphorism of Rutledge J in *Prince v Massachusetts* (1944) 321 US 158 at 170):

> Parents may be free to become martyrs themselves, but it does not follow that they are free in identical circumstances to make martyrs of their children before they have reached the age of full and legal discretion when they can make the choices for themselves.

A classic example is, of course, the refusal of a life-saving blood transfusion for a child of a Jehovah's Witness. The following case illustrates the approach of the English courts.

Re S (a minor) (medical treatment) [1993] 1 FLR 376 (Fam Div)

> S, aged 4½, had recently been diagnosed as suffering from T-cell leukaemia with a high risk of death. The condition was able to be treated by intensified chemotherapy treatment which had four phases. The transfusion of blood or blood products was an essential supplement. S's parents were dedicated Jehovah's Witnesses and the family records and instructions had

always opposed blood transfusions. A case conference had explored the irreconcilable gulf between the consultant's need to include transfusion in the range of treatments available and the parents' conscientious objection to consent to the treatment. The local authority had sought leave to invoke the inherent jurisdiction under s 100 of the Children Act 1989, which had been granted, and for an order permitting a blood transfusion. The following day the parents had issued an application under the Children Act 1989 for a prohibited steps order. The consultant paediatrician had given evidence of the medical need to administer a transfusion in emergency and non-emergency categories. He had been of the opinion that it would have been impossible for him to treat S intensively without the discretion to administer blood. The consultant had already varied the conventional treatment of S's condition to reflect the convictions of the parents. A senior lecturer in paediatric oncology who had a shared responsibility for major decisions with the consultant in relation to S's treatment had also given evidence on behalf of the local authority. He had stated that either the consultant had the authority to treat S intensively with the discretion to administer blood or there was no medical treatment which held any prospect of cure. The father had been fully supportive of any form of medical or scientific intervention provided it did not breach the veto upon the use of blood. Thorpe J granted the local authority the order it sought.

Thorpe J: The case for the defendants rested on the evidence of the father. He is a young man, but impressive in his emotional control and in the sincerity and simplicity with which he states his convictions. He is fully supportive of any form of medical or scientific intervention providing it does not breach the veto upon the use of blood. There was no impression of the bigot, of the closed mind, or of unreasonable obstinacy. His acceptance of the inevitability of life and death coupled with his faith seemed to make it easy for him to conclude that faith comes first and is not to be abandoned simply because it leads to awful decisions.

At the end of his evidence, Mr Daniel, on his behalf, sought to argue that regard should be had to the risk factor inherent in the use of blood in the course of medical treatment. He specified the risks as falling into the following categories: mismatch of blood types; samples which had been carelessly stored; samples which had been taken from an HIV positive; samples that were contaminated with hepatitis virus and, finally, samples contaminated with diverse other diseases.

It seems to me that that argument is of little weight beside the argument of conviction advanced by the father, although it is accepted by both doctors that there is a theoretical risk in the use of blood in treatment. It is statistically absolutely tiny, so tiny as to be almost minimal. As the second doctor said, it is impossible to say that any medical treatment is absolutely free of risk. In respect of any medical treatment it is necessary for the practitioner to balance the risks against the advantages, and that exercise in the case of the use of blood invariably results in the conclusion that the advantages enormously outweigh the risks.

Then, Mr Daniel relies upon a statement contained in an American publication which is at p 27 and following in the second exhibit to his client's affidavit. It is issued by the Counsel of Judges in America and is headed, 'Guides to the Judge in Medical Orders Affecting Children'. The passage relied upon by Mr Daniel appears at p 39. It reads thus:

> If there is a choice of procedures, if, for example, a doctor recommends a procedure which had an 80% chance of success but of which the parents disapprove, and the parents have no objection to a procedure which has only a 40% chance of success the doctor must take the medically riskier but parentally unobjectionable course.

Well, in relation to that passage I make the general observation that the proposition that it states is not one which seems to me to apply in child cases in which this court exercises its inherent jurisdiction. In this court, the test must remain the welfare of the child as the paramount consideration. Specifically, in this case, the choice is not between two medical procedures with similar, if differing, prospects of success. Here the stark choice is between one medical procedure with no prospect of success and one medical treatment with a prospect of success which is put at even.

So, as I put to Mr Daniel in argument: are the religious convictions of the parents to deny their child a 50% chance of survival? Are those convictions to deny him that 50% chance and condemn him to inevitable and early death? Mr Daniel realistically saw that this was an extreme case and one in which it is difficult to pursue the argument that the religious convictions of the parents should deny the child the chance of treatment.

Finally, Mr Daniel invites the court to look ahead to the later years of childhood. If this treatment is applied in the face of parental opposition what would be the difficulties and stresses for S in years to come – parented by parents who believe that his life was prolonged by an ungodly act? Well, that consideration seems to me one that has little foundation in reality. The reality seems to me to be that family reaction will recognise that the responsibility for consent was taken from them and, as a judicial act, absolved their conscience of responsibility.

(For other such cases see *Re E (a minor)* (1990) 9 BMLR 1 (Ward J); *Re O (a minor) (medical treatment)* [1993] 4 Med LR 272 (Johnson J); *Re R (a minor)*, [1993] 2 FLR 5 (Booth J)).

You will notice that in *Re S*, and indeed in the other cases, the evidence established that there was only one treatment which carried any hope for the child. This may not always be the case. Indeed, Thorpe J refers to the situation where two therapies are available with differing chances of success but, perhaps, equally with differing risks or side-effects.

What should be the court's approach if the parents elect for the treatment with the lower chance of success because of the less severe side-effects? The following American case provides some guidance. It suggests that some cases will arise in which the proxy's decision does not fall outside the permitted bounds (by reason of taking account of inappropriate factors) nor is it capricious but is one with which others may disagree, perhaps vehemently. The New York case of *Re Hofbauer* (1979) 395 NE 2d 1109 (NY CA) provides an example. The case involved the use of laetrile (a natural substance derived from apricot pits) as a treatment for a child's leukaemia.

Re Hofbauer (1979) 395 NE 2d 1109 (NY CA)

Jason J: [I]t is important to stress that a parent, in making the sensitive decision as to how the child should be treated, may rely upon the recommendations and competency of the attending physician if he or she is duly licensed to practise medicine in this State, for '[i]f a physician is licensed by the State, he is recognised by the State as capable of exercising acceptable clinical judgment.' (*Doe v Bolton* 410 US 179 at 199, 93 S Ct 739 at 751, 35 L Ed 2d 201 at 217, reh den 410 US 959, 93 S Ct 1410, 35 L Ed 2d 694.) Obviously, for all practical purposes, the average parent must rely upon the recommendations and competency of the attending physician since the physician is both trained and in the best position to evaluate the medical needs of the child.

Ultimately, however, the most significant factor in determining whether a child is being deprived of adequate medical care, and, thus, a neglected child within the meaning of the statute, is whether the parents have provided an acceptable course of medical treatment for their child in light of all the surrounding circumstances. This inquiry cannot be posed in terms of whether the parent has made a 'right' or a 'wrong' decision, for the present state of the practice of medicine, despite its vast advances, very seldom permits such definitive conclusions. Nor can a court assume the role of surrogate parent and establish as the objective criteria with which to evaluate a parent's decision its own judgment as to the exact method or degree of medical treatment which should be provided, for such standard is fraught with subjectivity. Rather, in our view, the court's inquiry should be whether the parents, once having sought accredited medical assistance and having been made aware of the seriousness of their child's affliction and the possibility of cure if a certain mode of treatment is undertaken, have provided for their child a treatment which is recommended by their physician and which has not been totally rejected by all responsible medical authority.

With these considerations in mind and cognisant that the State has the burden of demonstrating neglect (see *Re C Children* 55 AD 2d 646, 390 NYS 2d 10), we now examine the facts of this case. It is abundantly clear that this is not a case where the parents, for religious reasons, refused necessary medical procedures for their child (eg *Re Sampson* 37 AD 2d 668, 323 NE 2d 253; affd 29 NY 2d 900, 326 NYS 2d 398; *Re Gregory* S 85 Misc 2d 846, 380 NE 2d 620), nor is this a case where the parents have made an irreversible decision to deprive their child of a certain mode of treatment (*Custody of a Minor* 379 NE 2d 1053 [Mass]). Indeed, this is not a case where the child is receiving no medical treatment, for the record discloses that Joseph's mother and father were concerned and loving parents who sought qualified medical assistance for their child.

Rather, appellants predicate their charge of neglect upon the basis that Joseph's parents have selected for their child a mode of treatment which is inadequate and ineffective. Both courts below found, however – and we conclude that these findings are supported by the record – that numerous qualified doctors have been consulted by Dr Schachter and have contributed to the child's care; that the parents have both serious and justifiable concerns about the deleterious effects of radiation treatments and chemotherapy; that there is medical proof that the nutritional treatment being administered Joseph was controlling his condition and that such treatment is not as toxic as is the conventional treatment; and that conventional treatments will be administered to the child if his condition so warrants. In light of these affirmed findings of fact, we are unable to conclude, as a matter of law, that Joseph's parents have not undertaken reasonable efforts to ensure that acceptable medical treatment is being provided their child.

(Cf *Custody of a Minor* (1979) 393 NE 2d 836 (Mass Sup Jud Ct) and *Re Hamilton* (1983) 657 SW 2d 425 (Tenn CA), discussed in 1st edition at pp 970–5).

The question in English law is whether a court would stay its hand or feel compelled to take its own view. Our view is that the court should stay its hand both because the parents are *prima facie* entitled to form a judgment within the permissible limits, and because the court has no real basis for claiming to be a better parent.

(iv) THE ROLE OF THE COURT: AUTHORISE OR ORDER?

What is the precise power which the court exercises? It is sometimes said (somewhat carelessly) that a court *orders* that a specific form of treatment be carried out. It may be better analytically to describe the court's power as one of *authorisation* only. For example, Templeman LJ stated that: ' . . . the local authority must be authorised themselves to authorise and direct the operation to be carried out . . . ' (*Re B (a minor) (wardship: medical treatment)* (1981) [1990] 3 All ER 927).

This is because first, courts do not make orders which they cannot supervise and secondly, in the context of medical treatment the last word must, save in the most exceptional circumstances, remain with the doctor. As Margaret Somerville put it in her article, 'Refusal of Medical Treatment in "Captive" Circumstances' (1985) 63 Canadian Bar Review 59 at 89:

> Consequently, if the treating physician thought that treatment were contra-indicated, because, for instance, the circumstances had suddenly changed (and there was no negligence involved in holding such an opinion, in that a reasonable and competent physician in the same circumstances could be of the same opinion), the physician would not only have no duty to treat, but would have a duty not to treat, breach of which would constitute medical negligence or malpractice.

The point arose directly in the following case.

Re J (a minor) (wardship: medical treatment) **[1993] Fam 15, [1992] 4 All ER 614 (CA)**

J, a 16-month-old child, was profoundly handicapped, both mentally and physically, as a result of hitting his head in an accidental fall when he was one month old. He was severely microcephalic, his brain not having grown sufficiently following the injury, and he suffered from a severe form of cerebral palsy. He had cortical blindness and severe epilepsy. He was largely fed by a nasogastric tube. Medical opinion was unanimous that J was unlikely to develop much beyond his present level of functioning, that that level might well deteriorate and that his expectation of life, although uncertain, would inevitably be short. He required constant attention day and night. He had been placed with foster parents by the local authority, which shared parental responsibility for him. In December 1991 the consultant paediatrician in charge of J, Dr I, wrote a report in which she expressed the view that 'it would not be medically appropriate to intervene with intensive therapeutic measures such as artificial ventilation if [J] were to suffer a life-threatening event' and that although it 'would be appropriate to offer ordinary resuscitation with suction, physiotherapy and antibiotics [it] would not, however, be appropriate to subject [J] to the more intensive measures that would be required if he was unable to breathe spontaneously'. In a further report Dr I stated that if J was unable to breathe spontaneously it would be cruel to subject him to intensive care to prolong his life artificially, that he would be unlikely to survive positive pressure ventilation and that all that such treatment would achieve would be artificially to prolong his vegetative state. Dr N, a consultant paediatrician and paediatric cardiologist with a London teaching hospital who had been consulted by the Official Solicitor, broadly agreed with Dr I. On 30 March 1992 the local authority sought and was granted leave under s 100 of the Children Act 1989 to invoke the inherent jurisdiction of the High Court to determine whether artificial ventilation and/or other life-saving measures should be given to J if he suffered a life-threatening event and sought an order requiring the health authority to continue to provide all available treatment to J including 'intensive resuscitation'. The judge made an interim order and injunction to that effect requiring the health authority to use intensive therapeutic measures including artificial ventilation for so long as they were capable of prolonging his life. The health authority, supported by the Official Solicitor as the guardian ad litem and the local authority, which had changed its view, appealed against the order. J's natural mother sought to uphold the order, relying on a report by Professor B, an expert in child health at another London teaching hospital who did not regard artificial ventilation as being a 'cruel treatment' and took a much more optimistic view than Dr I as to the likelihood of it being possible to wean J from such ventilation if it were ever undertaken. The judge's order was stayed pending the appeal.

Lord Donaldson MR: The fundamental issue in this appeal is whether the court in the exercise of its inherent power to protect the interests of minors should ever require a medical practitioner or health authority acting by a medical practitioner to adopt a course of treatment which in the bona fide clinical judgment of the practitioner concerned is contra-indicated as not being in the best interests of the patient. I have to say that I cannot at present conceive of any circumstances in which this would be other than an abuse of power as directly or indirectly requiring the practitioner to act contrary to the fundamental duty which he owes to his patient. This, subject to obtaining any necessary consent, is to treat the patient in accordance with his own best clinical judgment, notwithstanding that other practitioners who are not called upon to treat the patient may have formed a quite different judgment or that the court, acting on expert evidence, may disagree with him.

It is said that the views which I expressed in my judgments in *Re J (a minor) (wardship: medical treatment)* [1990] 3 All ER 930, [1991] Fam 33 and *Re R (a minor) (wardship: medical treatment)* [1991] 4 All ER 177, [1992] Fam 11 which are relevant to this were obiter and did not receive the express assent of those sitting with me. So be it but, remaining as I am of the view that they were a correct expression of the law, I repeat them as part of the ratio of my decision in this case. From *Re J* [1990] 3 All ER 930 at 934, [1991] Fam 33 at 41:

> No one can *dictate* the treatment to be given to the child, neither court, parents nor doctors. There are checks and balances. The doctors can recommend treatment A in preference to treatment B. They can also refuse to adopt treatment C on the grounds that it is medically contra-indicated or for some other reason is a treatment which they could not conscientiously administer. The court or parents for their part can refuse to consent to treatment A or B or both, but cannot insist on treatment C. The inevitable and desirable result is that choice of treatment is in some measure a joint decision of the doctors and the court or parents. This co-operation is reinforced by another consideration. Doctors nowadays recognise that their function is not a limited technical one of repairing or servicing a body. They are treating people in a real life context. This at once enhances the contribution which the court or parents can make towards reaching the best possible decision in all the circumstances. (My original emphasis.)

From *Re R* [1991] 4 All ER 177 at 184, 187, [1992] Fam 11 at 22, 26:

> It is trite law that in general a doctor is not entitled to treat a patient without the consent of someone who is authorised to give that consent . . . However consent by itself creates no obligation to treat. It is merely a key which unlocks the door . . . No

doctor can be required to treat a child, whether by the court in the exercise of its wardship jurisdiction, by the parents, by the child or anyone else. The decision whether to treat is dependent upon an exercise of his own professional judgment, subject only to the threshold requirement that, save in exceptional cases usually of emergency, he has the consent of someone who has authority to give that consent.

The order of Waite J was wholly inconsistent with the law as so stated and cannot be justified upon the basis of any authority known to me. Furthermore it was, in my judgment, erroneous on two other substantial grounds, only slightly less fundamental than that to which I have just adverted. The first is its lack of certainty as to what was required of the health authority. The second is that it does not adequately take account of the sad fact of life that health authorities may on occasion find that they have too few resources, either human or material or both, to treat all the patients whom they would like to treat in the way in which they would like to treat them. It is then their duty to make choices.

The court when considering what course to adopt in relation to a particular child has no knowledge of competing claims to a health authority's resources and is in no position to express any view as to how it should elect to deploy them. Although the order is subject to the condition precedent that 'the required drugs and equipment are or could reasonably be made available', it makes no reference to the availability of staff and it has to be borne in mind that artificial ventilation of a young child in an intensive care unit is highly intensive of highly skilled staff. It gives no guidance as to what is meant by the concept of being reasonably available, yet it is not difficult to imagine circumstances in which there could be bona fida differences of opinion as to whether equipment or staff was reasonably available. The health authority is entitled to object and does object to being subject to an order of the court with penal consequences in the event of disobedience when it does not know precisely what is required of it.

Balcombe LJ: So recognising that there are limits to the exercise of this inherent jurisdiction, I agree with Lord Donaldson MR that I can conceive of no situation where it would be a proper exercise of the jurisdiction to make such an order as was made in the present case: that is to order a doctor, whether directly or indirectly, to treat a child in a manner contrary to his or her clinical judgment. I would go further, I find it difficult to conceive of a situation where it would be a proper exercise of the jurisdiction to make an order positively requiring a doctor to adopt a particular course of treatment in relation to a child, unless the doctor himself or herself was asking the court to make such an order. Usually all the court is asked, or needs, to do is to authorise a particular course of treatment where the person or body whose consent is requisite is unable or unwilling to do so.

It will be apparent from what I have already said that I agree with the views expressed by Lord Donaldson MR in *Re J (a minor) (wardship: medical treatment)* [1990] 3 All ER 930 at 934-935, [1991] Fam 33 at 41-42. Since the point has now been taken that in my judgment in that case I did not support that particular passage from Lord Donaldson MR's judgment, I should state that the reason was because I did not find it necessary to do so in the particular circumstances of the case. I did then, and do now, agree with what is there stated as well as with the passages to the like effect in *Re R (a minor) (wardship: medical treatment)* [1991] 4 All ER 177 at 184, 187, [1992] Fam 11 at 22, 26.

Apart from the obvious reasons for this limitation of the exercise of the jurisdiction, there is one other matter which should not be overlooked. The court is not, or certainly should not be, in the habit of making orders unless it is prepared to enforce them. If the court orders a doctor to treat a child in a manner contrary to his or her clinical judgment it would place a conscientious doctor in an impossible position. To perform the court's order could require a doctor to act in a manner which he or she genuinely believed not to be in the patient's best interests; to fail to treat the child as ordered would amount to a contempt of court. Any judge would be most reluctant to punish the doctor for such a contempt, which seems to me to be a very strong indication that such an order should not be made.

I would also stress the absolute undesirability of the court making an order which may have the effect of compelling a doctor or health authority to make available scarce resources (both human and material) to a particular child, without knowing whether or not there are other patients to whom those resources might more advantageously be devoted. Lord Donaldson MR has set out in his reasons the condition of J and his very limited future prospects. The effect of the order of Waite J, had it not been immediately stayed by this court, might have been to require the health authority to put J on a ventilator in an intensive care unit, and thereby possibly to deny the benefit of those limited resources to a child who was much more likely than J to benefit from them. At the very least it would in those circumstances have required the health authority to make a further application to the court to vary or discharge the injunction.

Leggatt LJ agreed.

It may be thought that *Re J* goes too far. Perhaps courts should be reluctant to say 'never'. For example, a court should *order* treatment if what they are really saying is that the child should not be neglected and left to die. In exceptional circumstances a court would be entitled to take the view that a doctor is under a duty to provide certain treatment notwithstanding the medical opinion to the contrary. This might arise, for example, if the denial of treatment was based upon a moral or religious belief which the court does not accept as being in the child's 'best interests' (see the view of Thomas J in *Auckland AHA v A-G* [1993] 1 NZLR 235 at 252).

2. In respect of adults

(a) No proxy?

Can anyone consent to medical treatment on behalf of an incompetent adult?

Professor Skegg puts the issue well in his book *Law, Ethics and Medicine*, at pp 72, 73:

> It is sometimes stated or assumed that, where a patient is incapable of consenting, an effective consent may be given by his spouse, or by some near relative. Unfortunately, those who hold this view do not indicate the grounds on which it is based . . .
>
> The better view is that there is no general doctrine whereby a spouse or near relative is empowered to give a legally effective consent to medical procedures to be carried out on an adult. Of course, doctors are sometimes justified in proceeding without the consent of the patient. But this is not because the consent of others justifies a doctor in proceeding without the patient's consent, but because in the circumstances the doctor is justified in proceeding despite the absence of legally effective consent.

Sometimes the contrary claim is made in America. However, those who make it have difficulty in pointing to authority in support. They sometimes find refuge in the dictum in *Canterbury v Spence* (1972) 464 F 2d 772 at 789 of Judge Robinson: 'even in situations of that character where the patient is unconscious or otherwise incapable of consenting the physician should, as current law requires, attempt to secure a relative's consent if possible'. The authority cited to support this proposition is *Bonner v Moran* (1941) 126 F 2d 121 at 122-23, but this is a case of an aunt consenting on behalf of a child.

The same mistaken reasoning can be seen in the judgment of Croom-Johnson LJ in *Wilson v Pringle* [1987] QB 237, where he assumes that in the case of an unconscious patient, who is, therefore, unable to consent, the next-of-kin may validly consent on the patient's behalf. But, like the other judges before him, he cites no authority for this assumption.

Sometimes, in the case of mentally ill patients, a spouse or relative may be appointed a guardian under s 7 of the Mental Health Act 1983. In *T v T* [1988] Fam 52, Wood J considered whether a guardian could consent to medical treatment. The case concerned a 19-year old incompetent woman whom it was thought should undergo an abortion and a sterilisation operation in her own best interests.

Wood J: . . . I pose myself the question – is there anyone who can consent on behalf of this defendant? It is submitted that the answer is 'No'.

This defendant is clearly suffering from a mental disorder within section 1 of the Mental Health Act 1983, and I therefore turn to the possibility of a guardianship application and an order under section 7. The procedure for such an application can be cumberous, and it was not suggested that an application *ex parte* on notice, as in the present case, could properly be made. The effect of a guardianship application is set out in section 8 where the relevant words read:

> Where a guardianship application, duly made . . . is accepted by that authority, the application shall, subject to regulations by the Secretary of State, confer on the authority or person named in the application as guardian, to the exclusion of any other person . . . (*b*) the power to require the patient to attend at places and times so specified for the purpose of medical treatment, occupation, education or training.

Section 145 of the Mental Health Act 1983, which is the definition section, provides: "medical treatment" includes nursing, and also includes care, habilitation and rehabilitation under medical supervision'.

Section 8 replaces section 34(1) of the Mental Health Act of 1959, where subsection (1) reads, materially:

> Where a guardianship application, duly made under the foregoing provisions of this Act and forwarded to the local authority within the period allowed by subsection (2) of this section, is accepted by that authority, the application shall . . . confer on the authority or person therein named as guardian, to the exclusion of any other person – and here is the important point – all such powers as would be exercisable by them or him in relation to the patient if they or he were the father of the patient and the patient were under the age of 14 years.

The wording of section 8 of the Mental Health Act 1983 will be seen to be much more restricted than the wider powers of the guardian under section 34 of the Act of 1959. One important effect is to remove the guardian's implicit power to consent to treatment on behalf of the patient. In my judgment there is no power to consent to the present operation to be found in section 8 of the Mental Health Act 1983, and indeed, on a construction of the statute as a whole I am satisfied that medical treatment in this context means psychiatric treatment.

If spouses and relatives have no authority to consent, does the court?

It is clear that the court's protective wardship jurisdiction comes to an end when a child reaches majority. Until recently, it was thought that thereafter the court had no power to authorise medical treatment on an incompetent adult, however beneficial or necessary the treatment might be (see *Re B* [1987] 2 All ER 206 at 210, CA per Dillon LJ). However, in the Canadian case of *Re Eve*, the Supreme Court 'rediscovered' the Crown's ancient prerogative jurisdiction (originally vested in the Lord Chancellor) over 'lunatics, idiots and others of unsound mind'. La Forest J set out the history of the *parens patriae* jurisdiction.

Re Eve [1986] 2 SCR 388 (Supreme Court of Canada)

La Forest J: The origin of the Crown's *parens patriae* jurisdiction over the mentally incompetent, Sir Henry Theobald tells us, is lost in the mists of antiquity; see H Theobald, *The Law Relating to Lunacy* (1924). *De Prerogatica Regis*, an instrument regarded as a statute that dates from the thirteenth or early fourteenth century, recognised and restricted it, but did not create it. Theobald speculates that 'the most probable theory [of its origin] is that either by general assent or by some statute, now lost, the care of persons of unsound mind was by Edw I taken from the feudal lords, who would naturally take possession of the land of a tenant unable to perform his feudal duties'; see Theobald, *supra*, p 1.

In the 1540s the *parens patriae* jurisdiction was transferred from officials in the royal household to the Court of Wards and Liveries, where it remained until that court was wound up in 1660. Thereafter the Crown exercised its jurisdiction through the Lord Chancellor to whom by letters patent under the Sign Manual it granted the care and custody of the persons and the estates of persons of unsound mind so found by inquisition, ie, an examination to determine soundness or unsoundness of mind.

Wardship of children had a quite separate origin as a property right arising out of the feudal system of tenures. The original purpose of the wardship jurisdiction was to protect the rights of the guardian rather than the ward. Until 1660 this jurisdiction was also administered by the Court of Wards and Liveries which had been created for the purpose.

When tenures and the Court of Wards were abolished, the concept of wardship should, in theory, have disappeared. It was kept alive, however, by the Court of Chancery, which justified it as an aspect of its *parens patriae* jurisdiction; see, for example, *Cary v Bertie* (1696) 2 Vern 333 at 342, 23 ER 814 at 818; *Morgan v Dillon* (1724) 9 Mod Rep 135 at 139, 88 ER 361 at 364. In time wardship became substantively and procedurally assimilated to the *parens patriae* jurisdiction, lost its connection with property, and became purely protective in nature. Wardship thus is merely a device by means of which Chancery exercises its *parens patriae* jurisdiction over children. Today the care of children constitutes the bulk of the courts' work involving the exercise of the *parens patriae* jurisdiction.

It follows from what I have said that the wardship cases constitute a solid guide to the exercise of the *parens patriae* power even in the case of adults . . . But proof of incompetence must, of course, be made.

This marks a difference between wardship and *parens patriae* jurisdiction over adults. In the case of children, Chancery has a custodial jurisdiction as well, and thus has inherent jurisdiction to make them its wards; this is not so of adult mentally incompetent persons (see *Beall v Smith* (1873) 9 Ch App 85 at 92). Since, however, the Chancellor had been vested by letters patent under the Sign Manual with power to exercise the Crown's *parens patriae* jurisdiction for the protection of persons so found by inquisition, this difference between the two procedures has no importance for present purposes.

By the early part of the nineteenth century, the work arising out of the Lord Chancellor's jurisdiction became more than one judge could handle and the Chancery Court was reorganised and the work assigned to several justices including the Master of the Rolls. In 1852 (by 15 & 16 Vict, c 87, s 15 (UK)) the jurisdiction of the Chancellor regarding the 'Custody of the Persons and Estates of Persons found idiot, lunatic or of unsound Mind', was authorised to be exercised by anyone for the time being entrusted by virtue of the Sign Manual.

Since historically the law respecting the mentally incompetent has been almost exclusively focused on their estates, the law on guardianship of their persons is 'pitifully unclear with respect to some basic issues'; see P McLaughlin, *Guardianship of the Person* (Downsview 1979), p 35. Despite this vagueness, however, it seems clear that the *parens patriae* jurisdiction was never limited solely to the management and care of the estate of a mentally retarded or defective person. As early as 1603, Sir Edward Coke in *Beverley's Case* (1603) 4 Co Rep 123 b at 126 a, 126 b, 76 ER 1118 at 1124, stated that 'in the case of an idiot or fool natural, for whom there is no expectation, but that he, during his life, will remain without discretion and use of reason, the law has given the custody of *him*, and all that he has, to the King' (emphasis added). Later at the bottom of the page he adds:

> 2. Although the state says, *custodian terrarum*, yet the King shall have as well the custody of the body, and of their goods and chattels, as of the lands and other hereditaments, and as well those which he has by purchase, as those which he has as heirs by the common law.

At 4 Co Rep p 126 b, 76 ER 1125, he cites Fitzherbert's *Natura brevium* to the same effect. Theobald (*supra*, pp 7-8, 362) appears to be quite right when he tells us that the Crown's prerogative 'has never been limited by definition'. The Crown has an inherent jurisdiction to do what is for the benefit of the incompetent. Its limits (or scope) have not, and cannot, be defined . . .

It was argued before us, however, that there was no precedent where the Lord Chancellor had exercised the *parens patriae* jurisdiction to order medical procedures of any kind. As to this, I would say that lack of precedent in earlier times is scarcely surprising having regard to the state of medical science at the time. Nonetheless, it seems clear from *Wellesley v Wellesley* [(1828) 2 B/i NS 124, 4 ER 1078], that the situations in which the courts can act where it is necessary to do so for the protection of mental incompetents and children have never been, and indeed cannot, be defined. I have already referred to the remarks of Lord Redesdale. To these may be added those of Lord Manners who, at Bli pp 142-42 and 1085, respectively, expressed the view that 'It is . . . impossible to say what are the limits of that jurisdiction; every case must depend upon its own circumstances.'

Even if *Eve* is correct that it was part of English common law (and it seems to have been), the important question for the English lawyer is whether it remains part of *English* law after the mental health legislation of the twentieth century? This issue was, of course, not relevant, nor discussed in *Eve*. The legislation does not expressly remove the power of the courts which was delegated to the Lord Chancellor and the judges of the Court of Chancery. Instead, the argument must be that since the legislation vests that part of the *parens patriae* power dealing with the 'property and other affairs' of the incompetent in the Court of Protection, the remaining power over the 'person' has impliedly been taken away. This argument does seem to be in direct conflict with the usual approach of constitutional law to see the prerogative as only taken away expressly or by *necessary* implication. Arguably, that does not seem to have occurred here. Even if the power remains, the last delegation to the judges was revoked in 1960 when the Mental Health Act 1959 became law. A new delegation of the Crown's power to the judges would be necessary today.

In *Re B (a minor) (wardship: sterilisation)* [1988] AC 199 the House of Lords left the existence of the *parens patriae* power unresolved because its existence was irrelevant to the case since it concerned a child. The House of Lords finally was required to confront the issue in the case of *Re F (mental patient: sterilisation)* [1990] 2 AC 1, which involved the legality of the proposed sterilisation of a 36-year-old mentally handicapped woman. Lord Brandon expressed the following view:

> **Lord Brandon:** I consider first the parens patriae jurisdiction. This is an ancient prerogative jurisdiction of the Crown going back as far perhaps as the 13th century. Under it the Crown as parens patriae had both the power and the duty to protect the persons and property of those unable to do so for themselves, a category which included both minors (formerly described as infants) and persons of unsound mind (formerly described as lunatics or idiots). While the history of that jurisdiction and the manner of its exercise from its inception until the present day is of the greatest interest, I do not consider that it would serve any useful purpose to recount it here. I say that because it was accepted by the Court of Appeal and not challenged by any of the parties to the appeal before your Lordships, that the present situation with regard to the parens patriae jurisdiction was as follows. First, so much of the parens patriae jurisdiction as related to minors survives now in the form of the wardship jurisdiction of the High Court, Family Division. Secondly, so much of the parens patriae jurisdiction as related to persons of unsound mind no longer exists. It ceased to exist as a result of two events both of which took place on 1 November 1960. The first event was the coming into force of the Mental Health Act 1959, section 1 of which provided:
>
> > Subject to the transitional provisions contained in this Act, the Lunacy and Mental Treatment Acts, 1890 to 1930, and the Mental Deficiency Acts, 1913 to 1938, shall cease to have effect, and the following provisions of this Act shall have effect in lieu of those enactments with respect to the reception, care and treatment of mentally disordered patients, the management of their property, and other matters related thereto.
>
> The second event was the revocation by Warrant under the Sign Manual of the last Warrant dated 10 April 1956, by which the jurisdiction of the Crown over the persons and property of those found to be of unsound mind by inquisition had been assigned to the Lord Chancellor and the judges of the High Court, Chancery Division.
>
> The effect of section 1 of the Act of 1959, together with the Warrant of revocation referred to above, was to sweep away the previous statutory and prerogative jurisdiction in lunacy, leaving the law relating to persons of unsound mind to be governed solely, so far as statutory enactments are concerned, by the provisions of that Act. So far as matters not governed by those provisions are concerned, the common law relating to persons of unsound mind continued to apply. It follows that the parens patriae jurisdiction with respect to persons of unsound mind is not now available to be invoked in order to involve the court or a judge in the decision about the sterilisation of F.

The 1959 Act contained a provision which allowed guardians (properly appointed) a wide range of powers extending, it appears, to consent to medical treatment (see *T v T* discussed earlier referring to ss 7-8 of the 1959 Act). As a consequence of this provision it was thought that after 1959 the pre-existing common law power of the court was no longer required. The mechanism for bringing this power into effect was therefore revoked in 1960. Unhappily, the Mental Health (Amendment) Act 1982 abolished the power of the guardian to consent to medical treatment but did not, perhaps by oversight, put anything else back into the law in its place.

It is an interesting point of some constitutional importance whether the *parens patriae* power fell into abeyance when the 1959 Act came into effect, ie the statute was necessarily inconsistent with the continued existence of the prerogative and it could only be re-activated if the statute were amended or repealed. Alternatively, the prerogative was only lost by the courts through the procedural device of the revocation of the warrant under the Sign Manual. In that case there can be no question in constitutional law of the power being lost for ever.

Brenda Hoggett 'The Royal Prerogative in Relation to the Mentally Disordered: Resurrection, Resuscitation or Rejection', in *Medicine, Ethics and the Law* (ed M D A Freeman) (1988)

... [T]he 1959 Act established the jurisdiction and powers of the Court of Protection to deal with the property and affairs of a patient who was adjudged incapable of managing them for himself. There is clearly some overlap between property and personal affairs, for example where the court may direct the use of the patient's assets to maintain him in a particular home or hospital, or where the court may conduct divorce or other proceedings on his behalf. Generally, however, issues relating to the care and treatment of the patient are dealt with under the quite different compulsory procedures for hospital admission or guardianship.

The provisions of the 1959 (and now the 1983) Act dealing with the jurisdiction and powers of the Court of Protection do appear to be a complete code. They no longer refer to or assume the existence of any royal prerogative. All the previous legislation dealing with it, including the relevant parts of 'The Statute Praerogativa Regis' (for which no date is given) is repealed. There is no provision (akin to section 104 of the Children Act 1975) expressly preserving it. Such a provision might have proved hard to explain. Stripped of centuries of legislation and case law based on *praerogativa regis*, what exactly were the Crown's powers? They would certainly contrast oddly with the generally liberal tone of the rest of the Act. Neither is there any provision expressly abrogating the prerogative. Most probably it was felt that it would still exist, but that the legislation had covered all the necessary ground. That being so, the Royal Warrant under which the prerogative was delegated was revoked in 1960.

There are at least two reasons why it might appear in 1959 that the Mental Health Act had made any use of the prerogative, even in relation to the person, unnecessary. First, it did indeed look as though the Act had provided comprehensively for all kinds of decisions to be made on behalf of permanently or seriously disordered patients. The definition of mental disorder may have left some gaps, but long term powers could be exercised over the mentally ill and the severely handicapped. Those powers included long term admission to hospital or reception into guardianship. A guardian enjoyed the same powers over the patient as did the father of a child under 14. This would certainly be adequate to provide consent to medical treatment in most cases. Secondly, however, the legislation was strangely silent on the question of consent to treatment. It was probably assumed that compulsorily admitted patients could be treated without consent, at least if they had been admitted 'for treatment' under the Act. It was probably also assumed that non-protesting patients could be treated without formality. The whole aim of the Act was to keep formalities to a minimum, as these were regarded as both inconvenient and stigmatising, and to allow the professionals to proceed on the basis of their professional judgment wherever possible. However strange this may seem to rights-minded lawyers, we should not underestimate the strength and persuasiveness of the view that this is indeed a preferable approach.

The amendments made in 1982 and then consolidated in the Mental Health Act 1983 represented something of a return to the rights-based lawyers' approach. They restricted the scope of compulsory powers, they increased the protection involved in the procedures, and they dealt expressly with the question of consent to treatment for those compulsorily admitted to hospital. However, at the same time, they reduced the scope of long term procedures in relation to mentally handicapped people, they reduced the powers of guardians, and they did nothing to deal with the question of consent to treatment for the informal incapable patient. Whereas the 1959 Act would have provided some solution to the problems in *Re B* [[1988] AC 199] and *T v T* [[1988] Fam 52], supposing that they had at that stage been perceived, the 1983 Act provided no solution at all.

The Prerogative Dead or Dormant?

It is tempting to argue that, as the 1959 Act appeared to cover all the ground which had been covered by the prerogative, and in a manner which was then thought preferable, the prerogative itself has been abrogated and could not be revived by the modifications in the 1983 Act.

Parliament can no doubt legislate to abolish a prerogative in this way, but did not do so expressly in this case. Alternatively, it may retain the prerogative but regulate how it is to be exercised. The nineteenth and twentieth century legislation referred to earlier regulated the exercise of the prerogative, expanded or clarified the powers available, and conferred analagous powers in relation to wider categories of people. Yet again, Parliament may replace the prerogative with a statutory scheme which supersedes and may therefore curtail or expand it. This would now appear to be the position with respect to the 'property and affairs' of a mentally disordered person. Part VII of the 1983 Act has all the appearance of falling within the principle enunciated by Lord Parmoor in *A-G v De Keyser's Royal Hotel* [[1920] AC 508]:

> The constitutional principle is that when the power of the executive to interfere with the property or liberty of subjects has been placed under Parliamentary control, and directly regulated by statute, the executive no longer derives its authority from the Royal Prerogative of the Crown but from Parliament, and that in exercising such authority the executive is bound to observe the restrictions which Parliament has imposed in favour of the subject.

At first sight, that principle appears equally applicable to the Act's scheme of compulsory powers over the person, for these are undoubtedly thought to deal with the 'liberty of the subject'. There is no longer any suggestion, as there was with the earlier legislation, that they exist alongside an alternative prerogative jurisdiction. When, for example, Parliament carefully prescribed the conditions under which psycho-surgery could be performed, could it seriously be said to have intended to leave open some alternative power to authorise it under the Royal Prerogative?

This line of reasoning seems highly persuasive in relation to particular issues which are dealt with in the Act. Once we turn to matters which quite clearly are *not* dealt with in the Act, we are faced with the problem of deciding whether Parliament intended to limit the executive's powers to what was there or whether it intended to leave open an alternative source of power. The 'Catch 22' is obvious. If the statute gives power to do all that the prerogative allows, then the statute may prevail; but if it does not, then the prerogative still survives. However, the 'Catch 22' is only so alarming if this is looked upon as a matter of civil rights and the 'liberty of the subject'. It could be argued that the prerogative was concerned with people who had been found (after inquisition) not to be ordinary subjects, endowed with the usual legal rights and duties, at all. Such an argument, if accepted, could form some theoretical basis for distinguishing these quasi-parental prerogative powers from others. Although their origin, scope and nature were quite different, they have been likened to the court's inherent powers over children. These were described by Lord Eldon in the well-known case of *Wellesley v Duke of Beaufort* [(1827) 2 Russ 1] as belonging to the Crown as *parens patriae*, and 'founded on the obvious necessity that the law should place somewhere the care of individuals who cannot take care of themselves'. The case had nothing to do with the prerogative relating to mental disorder, but clearly the rationale for both could be the same, even if the content and machinery were not.

That being so, the courts might well be tempted to apply similar reasoning to the relationship between statute and prerogative. The cases dealing with the relationship between the statutory powers of local authorities and the prerogative jurisdiction over wards of court have reached the following position. The statutory powers of local authorities do not use the prerogative jurisdiction. Nevertheless, the courts should decline to exercise that jurisdiction in a manner which conflicts with the statutory powers. If, therefore, the local authority objects to the court's intervention in a matter which is within its control, the court should decline to proceed. If, however, the local authority does not object, or actively seeks the court's assistance in the exercise of its powers, or invokes the jurisdiction in order to fill the gaps in its statutory powers, the court may proceed. This reasoning does not permit the court to use the jurisdiction in order to supply any gaps which the statutes have left in the rights of children, parents or relatives. It is entirely possible that a similar position would develop were the prerogative in relation to the mentally disordered to be revived: the jurisdiction might be used to fill the gaps in the statutory powers of the mental health authorities but not to improve the position of the patient or his family under those statutes.

This in itself would give rise to controversy, for the same reasons that the present imbalance in the availability of the wardship jurisdiction has done so. In relation to mentally disordered people, there is perhaps even more reason for concern. The statutory definitions of mental disorder, the procedures to be invoked, and the powers which those procedures allow, have all been quite carefully thought about. The notion that the restrictions could be circumvented, the procedures replaced, and the powers increased because of the revival of an ancient prerogative created for quite different reasons raises serious constitutional issues, quite apart from the more mundane questions which follow.

The absence of a formal proxy presents a legal and practical problem. If treatment is necessary, a decision has to be made to do it. The law must accommodate the need to treat in such circumstances. The House of Lords recognised this in *Re F* [1990] 2 AC 1 and, as we shall see, laid the basis for a justification of treating an incompetent adult in the absence of consent (see *infra*, p 317 et seq). The practical problem was, in effect, solved by making the doctor a 'quasi-proxy', ie the doctor was the person empowered to carry out treatment. The House of Lords recognised the need to indicate the criteria to be followed by the doctor. In deciding whether to treat, Lord Goff (with whom the other Law Lords concurred on this point) identified the test as follows (at 77): ' . . . the doctor must . . . act in the best interests of his patient, just as if he had received his patient's consent so to do'.

(b) The test: 'best interests' v substituted judgment

Of course, *Re F* concerned a woman who had never been competent to make decisions about medical treatment. What if an adult (or even, for that matter, a mature child) had previously been competent such that he would have had views about the proposed treatment? We are not concerned here with the situation where the person has, in fact, expressly stated his view with the intention of anticipating the situation in which he is now placed (for this *infra*, ch 17). Instead, we are concerned with the following issue. To what, if any, extent should the views and values of a patient find expression in the test to be used by the quasi-proxy decision-maker? Concern to reflect the views and values of a patient has led to the development of the so-called 'substituted judgment' test. This test requires that the decision-maker who acts as proxy (who is the substitute decision-maker) should seek to make that judgment which the incompetent patient would have made, by reference to the patient's known views and values.

In its Report of 1988 on 'Sterilisation Decisions: Minors and Mentally Incompetent Adults', the Alberta Institute of Law Research and Reform described the test of substituted judgment as follows:

'Substituted judgment' test
9.35 The 'substituted judgment' test has been employed by some American courts in recent years as an alternative to the best interests test. Under the substituted judgment test the

decision is to be the one that would be made by the mentally incompetent person if she were mentally competent. The test requires the application of the subjective values of the individual insofar as they can be known. To apply it, an attempt must be made to ascertain the mentally incompetent person's actual preference for or against such matters as sterilisation, other means of contraception and parenthood.

9.36 The substituted judgment test was developed in terminal illness cases involving decisions about the use or removal of life support systems. The Supreme Judicial Court of Massachusetts used it as the basis for a sterilisation decision in the case of *Re Moe* [(1982) 432 NE 2d 712]. This court found that the substituted judgment test best protects the mentally *incompetent* person by recognising the dignity, worth and integrity of the person and affording him the same personal rights and choices that are afforded to persons in the mainstream of society.

In his article 'Law and Medical Experimentation' (1987) 13 Monash University Law Review 189, at 200, Professor Gerald Dworkin comments on the 'substituted judgment' test:

> Another concept which is creeping into American case-law in contrast to the traditional 'best interests' approach to proxy consent is that of 'substituted judgment'. The proxy, or court, does not attempt to decide what is in the 'best interests' of the patient, but rather what decision would be made by the individual if he were competent. The court 'dons the mental mantle of the incompetent and substitutes itself as nearly as possible for the individual in the decision-making process'. [*Superintendent of Belchertown State School v Saikewicz* 370 NE 2d 417 (1977)]. It is one of those strange doctrines which was used in England in the early nineteenth century in connection with the administration of the estates of incompetent persons, [*Re Hinde, Ex p Whitbread* (1816) 2 Mer 99, 35 ER 878] forgotten, and then rediscovered recently by American courts. It has been raised in cases involving incompetent persons to help establish whether, for example, to consent to the withdrawal of life support systems or to certain unusual or controversial types of medical treatment, such as shock therapy or psychosurgery.
>
> It is a controversial concept, not the least because of the inherent difficulties of attempting to assess what an incompetent patient would have decided were he competent, whether that assessment should be subjective or objective and, if objective, how it can really differ from a 'best interests' approach.

Professor Dworkin rightly questions the relationship between the 'best interests' and 'substituted judgment'. On one view, 'substituted judgment' could be thought to be merely an application of the 'best interests', in that if a person's views are known, and, assuming that a person is the best judge of his own interests, the 'best interests' test would require compliance with his views, ie 'substituted judgment'. The accepted view, however, is that the two tests are different and that the 'best interests' test trumps any concern for the views and values of a patient since 'best interests' contemplates that others must be free to reach a judgment in the light of *their view* of the patient's interests and condition.

The origins of the test and some of its difficulties are also discussed by John Robertson in his article 'Organ Donations by Incompetents and the Substituted Judgment Doctrine' (1976) 76 Columbia LR 48:

> Under the substituted judgment doctrine – at least since the 1816 case of *Re Hinde, ex p Whitbread* [(1816) 2 Mer 99] – courts have authorised gifts from the incompetent's estate to persons to whom the incompetent owes no duty of support. The substituted judgment doctrine requires the court to 'don the mental mantle of the incompetent' and to 'substitute itself as nearly as may be for the incompetent, and to act upon the same motives and considerations as would have moved her'. Motives of charity and altruism, self-interest, and even the desire to minimise estate taxes have all been imputed to an incompetent on this basis. To determine whether the incompetent, if sane, would have made a gift, the courts look to several factors that would move one in the incompetent's situation – the needs of the donee, the relationship to the incompetent, the degree of intimacy both before and during

incompetency, the ward's past expressions or manifestations of concern or gift-giving, the present and future requirements of the incompetent himself, the extent of others' dependency upon him, and the size and condition of the estate – 'giving to these and any other pertinent matters such weight as the incompetent, if sane, probably would have given'.

The decisions have had little difficulty squaring the concept with a duty to act in the best interests of the incompetent. The justifications asserted include benefit to the incompetent, his likely ratification of the imputed choice upon recovery, or the satisfaction of intentions and patterns of conduct commenced before the period of incompetency. A notion of respect for persons has been implicit in the doctrine: it is in the incompetent's best interests to be treated as nearly as possible as the person he would be if his incompetence had never occurred. As an early commentator on the doctrine put it:

> Acting for the general welfare and advantage of a person does not mean merely supplying his or her physical wants or investing his or her money wisely. It is as much to the general advantage and welfare of a mother, for example, that the health of her children be preserved and that they be cared for in sickness, as it is that she herself be provided with a proper means of support.

> . . . Although the substituted judgment doctrine is recognised in most American and British jurisdictions either in judicial or statutory form, there is wide variation in the facts and circumstances upon which courts find that an incompetent, if competent, would make a gift. The varying results reveal internal tensions which limit the scope of the substituted judgment doctrine in the estate area and its applicability to other situations. The main tension stems from attempting to discern what in fact the incompetent would have done, if competent. The courts invariably focus on the desires and preferences which the incompetent would have had if he never had become incompetent, or if he had, if he recovered and essentially retained his pre-incompetency preference schedule. But there is an alternative approach. The courts could ask what a person in the incompetent's situation would do if he had legal capacity; that is, the courts could act to maximise the present subjective interests of the incompetent.

Professor Robertson justifies the substituted judgment test in the following ways at pp 63-68:

> If a person because of age or mental disability cannot select or communicate his preferences, respect for persons requires that the integrity of the person still be maintained. As stated by Rawls [*A Theory of Justice*] maintaining the integrity of the person means that we act toward him 'as we have reason to believe [he] would choose for [himself] if [he] were [capable] of reason and deciding rationally'. It does not provide a license to impute to him preferences he never had or to ignore previous preferences.

>> Paternalistic decisions are to be guided by the individual's own settled preferences and interests insofar as they are not irrational, or failing a knowledge of these, by the theory of primary goods.

> If preferences are unknown, we must act with respect to the preferences a reasonable competent person in the incompetent's situation would have.

> There are several reasons for treating incompetents in this way. One is that if the person recovered or became competent, and was informed of our actions, he would be most likely to ratify a decision that attempted to ascertain and do that which from the circumstances it appeared that he would have wanted done. For such an attempt would continue to regard him, even during his incapacity, as an individual with free choice and moral dignity, and not as someone whose preferences no longer mattered. Even if we were mistaken in ascertaining his preferences, the person could still agree that he had been fairly treated, if we had a good reason for thinking he would have made the choices imputed to him.

> In addition, if a person were to decide in advance how he would want to be treated if he lost his rational faculties, he would be likely to choose a scheme that, to the extent possible, approximated what he would do if rational. His moral worth is recognised since he is treated as the person he was, that is, as a person with the final ends and beliefs he previously expressed. Moreover, since incompetents are treated as persons in other important respects, consistency requires that, when questions arise concerning their treatment in particular situations, they also be treated as persons with wants and preferences. By failing to treat them as we treat competent persons, in similar situations, ascertaining and respecting their lawful choices, we might undercut respect for the incompetent persons in other situations, and eventually diminish respect for all persons.

In most situations respect for the person of incompetents will result in actions which benefit or are in the best interest of the incompetent. A competent person will ordinarily satisfy his wants and preferences. To the extent that the benefits rule advances the incompetent's previously expressed preferences, or procures him more of the primary goods if his preferences are unknown, there is a firm basis for ascribing to him choices which yield a net benefit.

If the incompetent's apparent best interests conflict with the choice he would make if competent, respect for persons requires that his imputed choice have priority. Thus, the fact that a Jehovah's Witness is unconscious does not justify transfusing blood to save his life, if he has previously made it clear that under no circumstances would he want a transfusion and he would not be required to accept a transfusion if conscious. Nor should an unconscious person be maintained on an artificial life-support system contrary to previously expressed preference if he would have been permitted to refuse treatment when conscious. By a parity of reasoning, the absence of benefit to the incompetent should not prevent an intervention when a choice in favor of the intervention can be imputed to the incompetent. In short, if respect for persons dictates honoring the wishes of competents even when their objective interests are impaired, a like rule should apply to incompetents.

One objection to this approach might be that it is absurd to treat an incompetent as he would choose to be treated if he were competent, when he is not competent, perhaps never has been, and may never be. The actual situation of the incompetent diverges from how he is treated or regarded under the substituted judgment doctrine. But it is precisely such a divergence that respect for persons requires and which generally confers benefits on the incompetent. Eliminating this divergence would mean that we treat the incompetents in all respects as a non-thinking, non-choosing, irrational being – in short, as a non-person.

A more substantial problem is specifying precisely what it means to 'choose as the incompetent would, if competent'. It could mean what the person would have chosen if he had never become incompetent – if he had remained in possession of his faculties. But what if the incompetency is congenital, or the person is a child? Alternatively, it could mean the choice made by the incompetent if his incompetency were suddenly lifted for a moment, only to have the clouds of unreason later descend. Or it could mean the person's choice if he were permanently to recover competency. This latter interpretation would be appropriate in the situation of children who will develop the faculty of reason or persons temporarily psychotic; but not in that of the retarded, the senile, or the chronically insane. Proper application of the substituted judgment test depends on specifying the precise characteristics of the situation into which competency is projected when the court substitutes its judgment for that of the incompetent.

If respect for persons means that we accede to a person's choice of ends and means, respect for incompetent persons requires that they be similarly treated. It must be determined what choices a competent person with the characteristics, tastes, preferences, history and prospects of the incompetent would make to maximise his interests or wants – both those he presently has and those he is likely to have in the future. These characteristics might include present incompetency, a period of previous incompetency, and the possibility of future incompetency. His interests or wants will thus vary with the length of the incompetency; his preferences as an incompetent; the identity and preferences established before becoming incompetent; and the likelihood of regaining competency. A competent person with the characteristics of this incompetent cannot very well maximise satisfaction of his preferences if he ignores factors such as present incompetency and future institutionalisation which will determine present and future preferences as an incompetent. To assign the incompetent characteristics as if he had never become incompetent would be to misdescribe him. The divergence between the wants thus assigned him and his actual wants is, in fact, of greater significance than the divergence between his actually being incompetent and the treatment of him as competent for the purposes of the substituted judgment doctrine. The latter divergence merely enable us to respect and honor the wants of the incompetent by treating him like a competent person who would try to maximise his wants. The former distorts what his wants are and thus risks abusing his person by never recognising or satisfying his wants. It acts not to advance his interests, but to advance the interests of a person who superficially resembles the incompetent.

The extent to which the preferences to be maximised depend on recognition of present, past and future incompetency will of course vary with particular situations. A 30-year-old man experiencing a transient psychosis has reasonable prospects of resuming his former social role upon recovery and thus maintaining his prior preferences. To maximise his wants during his incompetency we must take into account the fact that previous preferences will soon be reasserted. The fact of incompetency alters some of his present wants, but it does not allow us to ignore altogether his past preferences.

Suppose, however, that the prognosis for recovery of the 30-year-old man is nil. He faces an indefinite future of incompetency and institutionalisation, in which he will be unable to advance his own interests as an incompetent. The fact of future incompetency has significantly altered his situation and thus his present interest. If he had been an avid mountain-climber while competent and would be likely to continue this sport upon recovery, it would be pertinent to whether a kidney transplant, which would limit such activity, should occur. But the fact that a kidney transplant would interfere with his climbing would not be relevant if he had no chance of climbing again. Choosing for him on the basis of a set of preferences which would exist only if he were competent would thus be inappropriate. Respect for persons only demands that we make the best and most reasonable choice for a person given his wants and preferences in the circumstances he is presently and likely to be in, and not the circumstances in which we, if omnipotent, would like to place him.

A third situation is that of a child or a person with a long history of incompetency who will attain competency in the future. This case resembles the first, in that the incompetent's preferences must take account of future competency, but differs from the first two situations in that no preferences have been established during a prior period of competency. The interests to be maximised include the incompetent's existing tastes and preferences and the tastes or preferences the person is likely to have in the future when competent. Since the latter are unknowable, it would be in his interest to preserve maximum flexibility.

The fourth situation is that of one who has only a brief history of competency or none at all and no expectation of competency in the future. Severely mentally retarded persons and persons who become incurably insane or incur brain damage at an early age, *inter alia*, fall into this category. To respect the dignity and integrity of such a person the task of substituted judgment will be to ascertain his actual interests and preferences, which will be circumscribed by his present and future incompetency.

In each of these situations the wants or interests of a person in the incompetent's situation will include his present wants in the state of incompetency. But how do we ascertain the wants of an incompetent? Should they be granted any validity at all? If the incompetent lacks the capacity to communicate his preferences in the ways that people ordinarily do, it may be more difficult or perhaps impossible to know them. If he somehow communicates preferences, his very incompetency means that his preferences are not necessarily to be honored. But it would be erroneous to conclude that none of the expressed wants of incompetents should be satisfied. Incompetency encompasses several types of mental impairment, including the inability to have certain wants, the possession of bizarre wants, or the inability to choose among or satisfy conflicting preferences. Thus some expressed wants, if they appear irrational and indicative of his incompetency (such as a desire to fly) need not be honored. Expressed wants not in this category, however, should be satisfied. Clearly, they define, in part, his interests, of which respect for persons must take account.

Respect for persons, as argued above, requires that previously expressed preferences, or preferences we think the incompetent has or would have, should also be honored. What if a past preference conflicts with a present preference? The present preference should be honored if so doing will have a favorable or trivial impact on the attainment of other wants, present or future, attributed to the incompetent. Present preferences should not be respected if they will foreclose achieving other expressed wants or wants the incompetent would be presumed to have if competent. Overriding a present want in order to satisfy an imputed want is justified especially if it permits the satisfaction of other present wants. Substituted judgment thus combines subjective and objective elements. The subjective elements are the present tastes and preferences of the incompetent and those which he might have if competent, if he has a reasonable chance of becoming so. The objective aspect is the determination of what a reasonable person with the characteristics and present and future wants of the incompetent would choose to maximise his interest.

Substituted judgment has had its greatest impact on the law in cases having to do with dying, as we shall see in Chapter 16. For present purposes the following decision illustrates the application of the substituted judgment test in the case of an incompetent patient whose religious beliefs suggested that she would have refused treatment had she been competent.

Re Lucille Boyd (1979) 403 A 2d 744 (DC Cir)

Ferren Associate Judge: This appeal presents one question: whether – in a nonemergency situation – the court may authorise a hospital to administer psychotropic drugs to a patient adjudicated mentally ill and incompetent, when that patient, before her illness and incompetency, had rejected any use of medication on religious grounds.

. . . She contends that the court, in deciding whether to force medical treatment on an unwilling incompetent, should apply the 'substituted judgment' rule; ie the court should attempt to ascertain, as nearly as possible, the choice which that individual would make if competent. It follows, according to appellant, that if an individual has clearly expressed a religious objection to medical treatment immediately prior to incompetency, that objection must control the trial court's decision . . .

As appellant has pointed out, in nonemergency situations a number of courts have adopted the 'substituted judgment' approach. The court, as surrogate for the incompetent, is to determine as best it can what choice that individual, if competent, would make with respect to medical procedures . . . We believe this approach is sound, whether religious preference or other factors are involved, for it is the only way to pay full respect to the individuality and dignity of a person who has expressed clear, deeply felt, even sacred preferences while competent, but no longer has the capacity to decide. The Supreme Judicial Court of Massachusetts recently developed this rationale in *Superintendent of Belchertown State School v Saikewicz*, 370 NE 2d 417, 428 (1977):

> The 'best interests' of an incompetent person are not necessarily served by imposing on such persons results not mandated as to competent persons similarly situated. It does not advance the interest of the State or the ward to treat the ward as a person of lesser status or dignity than others . . . Nor do statistical factors indicating that a majority of competent persons similarly situated choose treatment resolve the issue. The significant decisions of life are more complex than statistical determinations. Individual choice is determined not by the vote of the majority but by the complexities of the singular situation viewed from the unique perspective of the person called on to make the decision. To presume that the incompetent person must always be subjected to what many rational and intelligent persons may decline is to downgrade the status of the incompetent person by placing a lesser value on his intrinsic human worth and vitality.

Obviously, in attempting to make such a subjective evaluation, in contrast with an objective, 'reasonable person' analysis, the court will be engaging, at best, in approximation; any imputation of a preference to an incompetent person will, to some extent, be fictional. But that inherent limitation does not make the 'substituted judgment' analysis less valid than one which purports to be wholly objective, for *any* analysis presupposes the court's judgment as to what a human being would decide for oneself under the circumstances. There is no reason to believe that the court's use of a hypothetical, reasonable person as the role model for its decision is preferable to an approach which attempts, however imperfectly, to account for the particular qualities of mind and preference known about the individual before the court . . .

With this said, we should underscore that inevitably the substituted judgment approach, because of its obvious limitations, will result in a synthesis of (1) factors known to be true about the incompetent and (2) other considerations which necessarily suggest themselves when the court cannot be sure about an incompetent's actual wishes. Thus, in trying to decide what choice the individual would make if competent, the court is not precluded from filling the gaps in its knowledge about the incompetent by taking into account what most persons are likely to do in a similar situation. See *Saikewicz, supra*, 370 NE 2d at 430 . . .

We turn now, in greater detail, to how the court should construct the 'substituted judgment' synthesis, particularly as it attempts to account for religious views. With respect to a situation in which an individual's life itself is not at stake, we conclude that (a) when an individual, prior to incompetence, has objected, absolutely, to medical care on religious grounds, (b) the evidence demonstrates a strong adherence to the tenets of that faith, and (c) there is no countervailing evidence of vacillation, the court should conclude that the individual would reject medical treatment . . .

More specifically, as to the previously-expressed objection itself, several factors are important: whether the objection, if religious, is a recognisable, established one, such as the well-known views of a Jehovah's Witness or Christian Scientist; whether the individual has acted upon these views that demonstrate they have been deeply felt; and whether these views have been long held, perhaps as a matter of family tradition, or if more recently adopted, have been the result of demonstrable experience, such as a religious conversion, which would justify a court's conclusion that the views are unequivocal.

Second, the possibility of detrimental side effects may be especially relevant in a case, such as this, concerning psychotropic drugs. Materials filed with the trial court indicate that such medication may produce side effects which commonly motivate even competent patients to reject their use on nonreligious, as well as religious grounds. See *Rennie v Klein* 462 F Supp 1131 (DNJ, 1978).

Third, the likelihood of cure or improvement with or without treatment is likely to have a bearing on one's decision. It may be, as we stated in [*Re Osborne* (1972) 294 A 2d 372] at 374, that absent a conviction as strong as Mr Osborne's when life is threatened and can only be saved with prompt medical assistance, one's 'instinct for survival' may overtake a lifelong conviction that medical care is wrong. But when life cannot be saved – when death is not far off in any event – a patient may be less likely to accept treatment merely to prolong life, . . . especially when the treatment is likely to cause severe pain. . . . It follows that where the prospect of imminent death is a marginal or nonexistent factor, as in Mrs Boyd's case, there may be even less incentive for one to compromise religious or other principles to accept medication.

. . . it does not appear that the court gave sufficient consideration, under the 'substituted judgment' concept, to Mrs Boyd's previously expressed religious views. . . . The court should inquire whether the hospital still seeks authorisation for psychotropic medication. If it does, the court should then take the 'substituted judgment' approach by attempting to determine what course of action Mrs Boyd would choose now. If the court decides that Mrs Boyd would reject psychotropic drugs on religious grounds if presently competent and fully aware of her situation, it must refuse to authorise such treatment unless the government can demonstrate that a particular, 'compelling state interest' would justify overriding Mrs Boyd's putative choice . . .

Do the English cases recognise the 'substituted judgment' test? In *Re T (adult: refusal of treatment)* [1992] 4 All ER 649, (1992) 9 BMLR 46 the Court of Appeal directly addressed the question of substituted judgment. Lord Donaldson MR remarked that:

Consultation with the next of kin has a further advantage in that it may reveal information as to the personal circumstances of the patient and as to the choice which the patient might have made, if he or she had been in a position to make it. Neither the personal circumstances of the patient nor a speculative answer to the question 'What would the patient have chosen?' can bind the practitioner in his choice of whether or not to treat or how to treat or justify him in acting contrary to a clearly established anticipatory refusal to accept treatment but they are factors to be taken into account by him in forming a clinical judgment as to what is in the best interests of the patient.

It appears that Lord Donaldson considers 'substituted judgment' merely to be an aspect of the 'best interests' test, ie as evidence, but not determinative, of what should be done. It can be argued that if substituted judgment is taken seriously as a test, the view of the Master of the Rolls must be doubted. Once a patient's views and values have been identified any decision should be based upon them and should, in England, be binding upon the doctor.

Some doubt has been cast upon the place in English law of the substituted judgment test by the speeches in *Airedale NHS Trust v Bland* [1993] 1 All ER 821 of Lords Goff and Mustill:

Lord Goff: I wish however to refer at this stage to the approach in most American courts under which the court seeks, in a case in which the patient is incapacitated from expressing any view on the question whether life-prolonging treatment should be withheld in the relevant circumstances, to determine what decision the patient himself would have made had he been able to do so. This is called the substituted judgment test, and it generally involves a detailed inquiry into the patient's views and preferences: see eg *Re Quinlan* 70 NJ 10 (1976) and *Belchertown State School Superintendent v Saikewicz* 373 Mass 728 (1977). In later cases concerned with PVS patients it has been held that, in the absence of clear and convincing evidence of the patient's wishes, the surrogate decision-maker has to implement as far as possible the decision which the incompetent patient would make if he was competent. However, accepting on this point the submission of Mr Lester, I do not consider that any such test forms part of English law in relation to incompetent adults, on whose behalf nobody has power to give consent to medical treatment. Certainly, in *F v West Berkshire Health Authority* your Lordships' House adopted a straightforward test based on the best interests of the patient; and I myself do not see why the same test should not be applied in the case of PVS patients, where the question is whether life-prolonging treatment should be withheld.

Lord Mustill: [Substituted judgment] involved the appointment of a surrogate to make on behalf of the patient the choice which he believes the patient would now make if able to do so. For this purpose the surrogate builds up a picture of the patient's former character, feelings, convictions and so on from which the putative choice is deduced. This process may perhaps have some justification where the patient is sentient but unable to communicate a choice, but it breaks down totally in a case such as the present. To postulate a patient who is in such condition that he cannot know that there is a choice to be made, or indeed know anything at all, and then ask whether he would have chosen to terminate his life because that condition made it no longer worth living is surely meaningless, as is very clearly shown by the lengths to which the court was driven in *Belchertown State School Superintendent v Saikewicz* 373 Mass 728 (1977). The idea is simply a fiction, which I would not be willing to adopt even if there were in the case of Anthony Bland any materials upon which a surrogate could act, which as far as I can see there are not.

Is it not the case that their Lordships misunderstand the true nature of substituted judgment? As regards Lord Goff two points are worth noting. First, the premise for his view is the decision in *Re F*. But, of course, as we shall see shortly, substituted judgment was inappropriate in *Re F* as F had never been in a position to form competent views. Secondly, the House of Lords in *Re F* never, therefore, gave any consideration to whether the substituted judgment test could ever be a part of English law. As for Lord Mustill, his distinction between the patient who is sentient and one who is not sentient seems odd. Substituted judgment does not involve the patient deciding, but somebody else 'stepping into the patient's shoes' to decide for the patient. Lord Mustill relies on the unsatisfactory nature of the *Saikewicz* case to demonstrate the inappropriateness of substituted judgment. Saikewicz, however, had never been competent to form a competent view and, therefore, substituted judgment was legally inappropriate in that case. (*Saikewicz* is one of a series of cases in which the Massachusetts Supreme Judicial Court has misunderstood and misapplied the substituted judgment test: *Re Moe* (1982) 432 NE 2d 712 (sterilisation of mentally disabled woman) and *Re Jane Doe* (1992) 583 NE 2d 1263 (a PVS case).)

This last point allows us to reiterate the circumstances in which 'substituted judgment' is inappropriate. It is inappropriate in any case in which the patient has *never* been competent to form views or hold values. Examples include the immature minor and the mentally disabled adult.

The impossibility faced by a court or other proxy in applying the substituted judgment test in these situations was recognised in the Institute of Law Research and Reform of Alberta's Report (*op cit*):

9.37 The obvious difficulty with the application of the substituted judgment standard relates to persons who have been mentally incompetent from birth and who may therefore never have been able to express their values or desires. It may also be difficult to determine the values and desires of a person who was once competent but has been made incompetent by a supervening injury or disease.

Consequently, in *Re Eve* (*op cit*) the Supreme Court of Canada rejected the application of the test to Eve who had been incompetent from birth. The reasoning would also apply in the case of an incompetent child.

La Forest J: Counsel for the respondent strongly contended, however, that the Court should adopt the substituted judgment test recently developed by a number of state courts in the United States. That test, he submitted, is to be preferred to the best interests test because it places a higher value on the individuality of the mentally incompetent person. It affords that person the same right, he contended, as a competent person to choose whether to procreate or not.

There is an obvious logical lapse in this argument . . . it is obviously fiction to suggest that a decision so made is that of the mental incompetent, however much the court may try to put itself in her place. What the incompetent would do if she or he could make the choice is simply a matter of speculation. The sophistry embodied in the argument favouring substituted judgment has been fully revealed in [*Re Eberhardy's Guardianship*, 307 NW 2d 881 (1981)] at p 893 where in discussing [*Matter of Grady* 426 A 2d 467 (1981)], the court stated:

> The fault we find in the New Jersey case is the *ratio decidendi* of first concluding, correctly we believe, that the right to sterilisation is a personal choice, but then equating a decision made by others with the choice of the person to be sterilised. It clearly is not a personal choice, and no amount of legal legerdemain can make it so.

. . . We conclude the question is not choice because it is sophistry to refer to it as such, but rather the question is whether there is a method by which others, acting in behalf of the person's best interests and in the interests, such as they may be, of the state, can exercise the decision. Any governmentally sanctioned (or ordered) procedure to sterilise a person who is incapable of giving consent must be denominated for what it is, that is, the state's intrusion into the determination of whether or not a person who makes no choice shall be allowed to procreate.

In *Curran v Bosze* (1990) 566 NE 2d 1319 (the facts of which are set out *supra*, p 259) the Illinois Supreme Court rejected the application of the 'substituted judgment' test in the case of an incompetent child.

Curran v Bosze (1990) 566 NE 2d 1319 (Illinois Sup Ct)

Justice Calvo: Mr Bosze and the guardian *ad litem* for Jean Pierre strenuously argue that the doctrine of substituted judgment, recognized by this court in *In Re Estate of Longeway*, 133 Ill 2d 33, 139 Ill Dec 780, 549 NE 2d 292 (1989), and *In Re Estate of Greenspan*, 137 Ill 2d 1, 146 Ill Dec 860, 558 NE 2d 1194 (1990), should be applied in this case to determine whether or not the twins would consent, if they were competent to do so, to the bone marrow donation if they, or either of them, were compatible with Jean Pierre. The doctrine of substituted judgment requires a surrogate decision-maker to 'attempt to establish, with as much accuracy as possible, what decision the patient would make if [the patient] were competent to do so.' (*Longeway*, 133 Ill 2d at 49, 139 Ill Dec 780, 549 NE 2d 292.) Mr Bosze and the guardian *ad litem* for Jean Pierre contend the evidence clearly and convincingly establishes that the twins, if competent, would consent to the bone marrow harvesting procedure.

Ms Curran and the guardian *ad litem* for the twins vigorously object to the application of the doctrine of substituted judgment in this case. It is the position of Ms Curran and the guardian *ad litem* for the twins that it is not possible to establish by clear and convincing evidence whether the 3½-year-old twins, if they were competent – that is, if they were not minors but were adults with the legal capacity to consent – would consent or refuse to consent to the proposed bone marrow harvesting procedure. According to Ms Curran and the guardian *ad litem* for the twins, the decision whether or not to give or withhold consent to the procedure must be determined by the best-interests-of-the-child standard. Ms Curran and the guardian *ad litem* for the twins argue that the evidence reveals it is not in the best interests of the children to require them to submit to the bone marrow harvesting procedure.

This court recognized the doctrine of substituted judgment in *Longeway*. The issue addressed by this court in *Longeway* was whether the guardian of a formerly competent, now incompetent, seriously ill adult patient may exercise a right to refuse artificial nutrition and hydration on behalf of his or her ward and, if so, how this right may be exercised . . .

In *Longeway*, this court held that a guardian may exercise the right to refuse artificial sustenance on behalf of a ward in accordance with certain guidelines. This court determined that the doctrine of substituted judgment had been implicitly adopted by the General

Assembly in the Powers of Attorney for Health Case Law, which states: '[Y]our agent will have authority . . . to obtain or terminate any type of health care, including withdrawal of food and water . . . if your agent believes such action would be consistent with your intent and desires.' Ill Rev Stat 1987, ch 1101/2, par. 804-10.

This court recognized two sources of appropriate evidence by which a guardian may be guided in determining whether a formerly competent, now incompetent, patient would choose to refuse artificial nutrition and hydration. The first source requires the surrogate to 'determine if the patient had expressed explicit intent regarding this type of medical treatment prior to becoming incompetent.' (*Longeway*, 133 Ill 2d at 49, 139 Ill Dec 780, 549 NE 2d 292.) If there is no clear evidence of such intent, then the patient's personal value system must guide the surrogate:

> [E]ven if no prior specific statements were made, in the context of the individual's entire prior mental life, including his or her philosophical, religious and moral views, life goals, values about the purpose of life and the way it should be lived, and attitudes toward sickness, medical procedures, suffering and death, that individual's likely treatment/nontreatment preferences can be discovered. Family members are most familiar with this entire life context. Articulating such knowledge is a formidable task, requiring a literary skill beyond the capacity of many, perhaps most, families. But the family's knowledge exists nevertheless, intuitively felt by them and available as an important decisionmaking tool. [*In Re*] *Jobes*, 108 NJ [394] at 415, 529 A 2d [434] at 445 [(1987)] quoting Newman, *Treatment Refusals for the Critically Ill: Proposed Rules for the Family, the Physician and the State*, 3 NYL Sch Hum Rts Ann 45-46 (1985). (*Longeway*, 133 Ill 2d at 49-50, 139 Ill Dec 780, 549 NE 2d 292.)

The guardian is required to prove by clear and convincing evidence whether the incompetent patient, if competent, would choose to terminate artificial nutrition and hydration if the guardian is to be allowed to substitute his or her judgment for the incompetent's judgment. *Longeway*, 133 Ill 2d at 50-51, 139 Ill Dec 780, 549 NE 2d 292.

The best-interests standard, by which a guardian, in the exercise of his or her judgment, determines what is best for the ward, was rejected by this court in *Longeway* as an inappropriate vehicle by which a guardian may be guided in determining whether an incompetent patient, in either an irreversible coma or a persistent vegetative state, should have artificial nutrition and hydration withdrawn. This court rejected the best-interests standard because 'it lets another make a determination of a patient's quality of life, thereby undermining the foundation of self-determination and inviolability of the person upon which the right to refuse medical treatment stands.' (*Longeway*, 133 Ill 2d at 49, 139 Ill Dec 780, 549 NE 2d 292.) By requiring a guardian to proceed under the doctrine of substituted judgment instead of the best-interests standard, the inquiry is necessarily focused on whether the formerly competent, now incompetent, patient had ever manifested an intent as to whether he or she would consent or refuse to consent to artificial nutrition and hydration.

In *Greenspan*, this court addressed the issue of the use of the doctrine of substituted judgment by a guardian of an incompetent person in a chronic vegetative state. The guardian of Mr Greenspan requested leave of court to order the withdrawal of artificial nutrition and hydration as 'Mr Greenspan's surrogate and in order to give effect to what are represented as Mr Greenspan's own wishes.' (*Greenspan*, 137 Ill 2d at 15, 146 Ill Dec 860, 558 NE 2d 1194.) . . .

In *Greenspan*, this court stated: 'though a guardian's duty is to act in a ward's best interest, such a standard is necessarily general and must be adapted to particular circumstances. One such circumstance is a ward's wish to exercise common law, statutory, or constitutional rights, which may sometimes influence or even override a guardian's own perception of best interests.' . . .

Mr Bosze argues that the twins, if they had the legal capacity, would have the right to consent or refuse to consent to the proposed bone marrow harvesting procedure. Mr Bosze argues that if the doctrine of substituted judgment is not applied in this case, the twins' right to consent or refuse to consent to medical treatment, which they would have if they were competent, would be violated. Since the twins are without legal capacity to consent or refuse to consent to the proposed bone marrow harvesting procedure, and since the parents do not agree, Mr Bosze argues that both his and Ms Curran's opinions regarding whether the twins should serve as bone marrow donors should be read out of the equation, and the court, applying the doctrine of substituted judgment, should look solely to what the twins would decide to do if they were competent . . .

Concerning the use of the doctrine of substituted judgment, this court in *Longeway* recognized that '[a] dilemma [exists] . . . when the patient is an infant or life-long incompetent who never could have made a reasoned judgment about his [or her] quality of life.' (*Longeway*, 133 Ill 2d at 49, 139 Ill Dec 780, 549 NE 2d 292.) Mr Bosze argues that this dilemma was resolved by this court in *Longeway* when it stated that 'although actual, specific express intent would be helpful and compelling, the same is not necessary for the exercise of substituted judgment by a surrogate.' *Longeway*, 133 Ill 2d at 50, 139 Ill Dec 780, 549 NE 2d 292.

Immediately following this statement in *Longeway*, however, this court stated: 'In this case, Mrs Longeway's guardian must substitute her judgment for that of Longeway's, based upon *other* clear and convincing evidence of Longeway's intent.' (Emphasis added.) (*Longeway*, 133 Ill 2d at 50-51, 139 Ill Dec 780, 549 NE 2d 292.) This language addressed the instance where a formerly competent, now incompetent, patient had never 'expressed explicit intent regarding [the] type of medical treatment prior to becoming incompetent.' (*Longeway*, 133 Ill 2d at 49, Ill Dec 780, 549 NE 2d 292.) This language did not address the dilemma of a guardian substituting the judgment of one who never has been able to make 'a reasoned judgment about his [or her] quality of life.' (*Longeway*, 133 Ill 2d at 49, 139 Ill Dec 780, 549 NE 2d 292.) In applying the doctrine of substituted judgment, 'the key element in deciding to refuse or withdraw artificial sustenance is determining the patient's intent.' *Longeway*, 133 Ill 2d at 51, 139 Ill Dec 780, 549 NE 2d 292.

Under the doctrine of substituted judgment, a guardian of a formerly competent, now incompetent, person may look to the person's life history, in all of its diverse complexity, to ascertain the intentions and attitudes which the incompetent person once held. There must be clear and convincing evidence that the formerly competent, now incompetent, person had expressed his or her intentions and attitudes with regard to the termination of artificial nutrition and hydration before a guardian may be authorized to exercise, on behalf of the incompetent person, the right to terminate artificial sustenance.

If the doctrine of substituted judgment were to be applied in this case, the guardian of the 3½-year-old twins would have to substitute his or her judgment for that of the twins, based upon clear and convincing evidence of the twins' intent. (*Longeway*, 133 Ill 2d at 50-51, 139 Ill Dec 780, 549 NE 2d 292.) Because each twin is only 3½ years of age, neither has yet had the opportunity to develop 'actual, specific express intent,' or any other form of intent, with regard to serving as a bone marrow donor. We agree with Ms Curran and the guardian *ad litem* for the twins that it is not possible to determine the intent of a 3½-year-old child with regard to consenting to a bone marrow harvesting procedure by examining the child's personal value system. It is not possible to discover the child's 'likely treatment/ nontreatment preferences' by examining the child's 'philosophical, religious and moral views, life goals, values about the purpose of life and the way it should be lived, and attitudes toward sickness, medical procedures, suffering and death.' (*Longeway*, 133 Ill 2d at 50, 139 Ill Dec 780, 549 NE 2d 292, quoting *In Re Jobes* (1987), 108 NJ 394, 529 A 2d 434.) The twins have not yet developed the power of self-determination and are not yet capable of making an informed, rational decision based upon all the available information concerning the risks and benefits associated with serving as bone marrow donors. There is no evidence by which a guardian may be guided in ascertaining whether these 3½-year-old children, if they were adults, would or would not consent to a bone marrow harvesting procedure for another child, their half-brother whom they have met only twice.

The doctrine of substituted judgment requires clear and convincing proof of the incompetent person's intent before a court may authorize a surrogate to substitute his or her judgment for that of the incompetent. Any lesser standard would 'undermin[e] the foundation of self-determination and inviolability of the person upon which the right to refuse medical treatment stands.' (*Longeway*, 133 Ill 2d at 49, 139 Ill Dec 780 549 NE 2d 292.) A guardian attempting to prove what a 3½-year-old child would or would not do in a given set of circumstances at a given time in the distant future would have to rely on speculation and conjecture.

Neither justice nor reality is served by ordering a 3½-year-old child to submit to a bone marrow harvesting procedure for the benefit of another by a purported application of the doctrine of substituted judgment. Since it is not possible to discover that which does not exist, specifically, whether the 3½-year-old twins would consent or refuse to consent to the proposed bone marrow harvesting procedures if they were competent, the doctrine of substituted judgment is not relevant and may not be applied in this case.

Curiously, however, in *Re J (a minor) (wardship: medical treatment)* [1990] 3 All ER 930, [1991] Fam 33, which concerned the treatment of a severely handicapped baby, two judges in the Court of Appeal adopted a test which could be thought by some to be that of 'substituted judgment'. Taylor LJ stated that:

> I consider that the correct approach is for the court to judge the quality of life the child would have to endure if given the treatment and decide whether in all the circumstances such a life would be so afflicted as to be intolerable to that child. I say 'to that child' because the test should not be whether the life would be tolerable to the decider. The test must be whether the child in question, if capable of exercising sound judgment, would consider the life tolerable. This is the approach adopted by McKenzie J in *Re Superintendent of Family and Child Service and Dawson* (1983) 145 DLR (3d) 610 at 620-621 in the passage cited with approval by Lord Donaldson MR. It takes account of the strong instinct to preserve one's life even in circumstances which an outsider, not himself at risk of death, might consider unacceptable. The circumstances to be considered would, in appropriate cases, include the degree of existing disability and any additional suffering or aggravation of the disability which the treatment itself would superimpose. In an accident case, as opposed to one involving disablement from birth, the child's pre-accident quality of life and its perception of what has been lost may also be factors relevant to whether the residual life would be intolerable to that child.

Similarly, Lord Donaldson MR approved the British Columbia case of *Re Superintendent of Family and Child Service and Dawson* (1983) 145 DLR (3d) 610 where McKenzie J stated:

> it is not appropriate for an external decision maker to apply his standards of what constitutes a liveable life and exercise the right to impose death if that standard is not met in his estimation. The decision can only be made in the context of the disabled person – and in that context he would not compare his life with that of a person enjoying normal advantages. He would know nothing of a normal person's life having never experienced it.

Commenting, Lord Donaldson MR said:

> He was considering the best interests of a severely handicapped child, not of a normal child, and the latter's feelings and interests were irrelevant.

Properly interpreted, as Lord Donaldson MR's remarks make clear, the Court of Appeal in *Re J* was in fact merely asserting that the 'best interest' test requires the decision-maker to seek to take account of the actual circumstances of the patient. Thus, neither Taylor LJ's nor the Master of Rolls' judgments should be taken as legitimising an application of the 'substituted judgment' test in a case where the patient has never been competent.

(c) Changing the law

Arguably, the current position regarding the decision-making process in the case of incompetent adults is unsatisfactory. At best the courts have fashioned a quasi-proxy, ie the doctor. But it is not clear that doctors should be left to make these sorts of decisions, if only because the doctor may genuinely feel torn between his desire to respect the interests of the patient and his desire to intervene and render assistance from a general commitment to doing good. Further, if the goal of the law is to seek to ensure, so far as is practicable, that a proxy decision conforms to the views and values of the patient, is the doctor generally best placed to reach such a determination? Of course, in some cases he may be. However, usually such a decision would be better made by someone close to the patient. To this end, therefore, three options present themselves. *First*, the law should allow a patient to appoint his chosen health care proxy. *Secondly*, in default of this, the law should presume those close to the patient to be proxies best able to know the patient's likely choice of health case. *Thirdly*, if there is no one then the law should recognise that the doctor must of necessity act as he sees fit in the patient's 'best interests'. A number of options have been considered by the Law Commission against the background of the experience abroad in its Consultation Paper *Mentally Incapacitated Adults and Decision-Making: An Overview* (No 119, 1991). It examined the merit of advance directives (on which see *infra*, ch 17), the improvement of existing procedures, establishment of a system of patient advocacy, and the establishment of a formal decision-making body. In the context of our discussion here it is worth while to notice more fully the other option examined, namely that of a designated decision-maker, ie a proxy.

6.17 In some areas, it would be possible to clarify and regularise mechanisms for taking certain decisions without any prior certification or commitment of the mentally incapacitated person. In its simplest form, this would be akin to the way the intestacy laws automatically prescribe who shall inherit the estate of someone who has not made a will. It would prescribe who should make certain decisions for someone unable to make them for himself. The choice of decision-maker could vary according to the type of decision, and might be a single individual, or a combination of people. Possible alternative decision-makers include the following.

6.18 *A decision-maker previously nominated by the person concerned.* This would allow many of the options discussed above, principally refinements of the enduring power of attorney, to be combined with this system. A representative personally chosen by the mentally incapacitated person could be given first priority, with the statutory scheme only coming into operation if no prior choice has been made.

6.19 *A representative already formally appointed such as a guardian or receiver.* Where a guardian or receiver has been appointed he may well be an appropriate person to make some decisions, but not necessarily all. Most people will not have or need a guardian or receiver.

6.20 *A responsible professional.* Examples might be the doctor proposing certain medical treatment, or the social services department wishing to admit someone to residential care. There are obvious objections to resting the decision-making power with any single individual who is proposing a course of action, but it would be possible to include safeguards, such as requiring a second opinion or consultation with a multi-disciplinary team.

6.21 *The primary carer.* This may, or may not be a relative of the mentally incapacitated adult. This would, in many cases, be recognising the status quo and giving legitimacy to the substitute decision-making which already occurs on a day to day basis on everyday matters. There are many good reasons for this. The person caring for a mentally incapacitated adult generally has his well-being at heart and will be in the best position to know what his wishes and preferences are likely to be. However, there are some drawbacks. The carer's personal involvement may make it difficult to be objective and dispassionate. Long experience of looking after the person concerned may make the carer over-protective, and create a tendency to stifle, rather than encourage self-determination. There will be an occasional carer who acts in bad faith, and through motives of self-interest.

6.22 *The family.* This would include at least spouses, parents, adult children and siblings. Some method of ranking might be appropriate in the event of disputes, but a close family can often reach a consensus; this may deserve recognition as a substitute decision-maker on behalf of one of its members. However, many people do not have any close family, or any family at all, or are estranged from them. Problems can also arise if family members are very closely involved emotionally in a particular situation, and they lack the professional skills and training which can aid dispassionate judgment.

6.23 *A combination of professional, primary carer and family.* In practice, many more serious decisions about health care or residence are taken by a combination of the relevant professional and the primary carer who is often a close relative. Indeed, this is the model upon which the Mental Health Act procedures have long been based, the only distinction being the degree of formality (or as it might be thought, regularity) involved.

6.24 *A court, tribunal or other authority.* Some decisions may be thought so serious that they should only be carried out with the prior approval of an independent court or tribunal. A common example is the approval of the High Court to the non-therapeutic sterilisation of mentally handicapped young women. It would be possible for legislation to provide that certain decisions could only be made by a specialist tribunal or court. Examples in addition to sterilisation might be abortion or other serious medical procedures, the transfer or disposal of property over a certain value or the giving of consent in divorce proceedings. This would also provide a forum for resolving any disputes arising between joint decision-makers. . . . The choice between a court or tribunal would depend, not only upon the degree of formality and procedural safeguards felt to be desirable, but also upon whether inquisitorial or adversarial procedures were most appropriate. In the former, the tribunal might make its own inquiries and use its own expertise in making a decision, whereas in the latter it would rely upon the evidence and arguments presented by opposing parties. One problem with the adversarial approach in this area is that, for many decisions in which an independent safeguard might be desirable, there are no opposing parties.

6.25 A further refinement, suggested in the USA in the context of medical treatment, is that someone (i.e. the doctor) is designated to choose a substitute decision-maker for a particular matter. In 1982, the President's Commission recommended that decisions about incapacity should be made at institutional level whenever possible, and that the validity of such determinations should be recognised by law. The Commission considered it impossible to draw up a formula for selecting a substitute decision-maker which would be capable of capturing the complexities involved. Accordingly, they recommended that it should be the responsibility of the medical practitioner in each case to decide who knows the patient best and has his best interests in view, or to decide that there is no appropriate person and to apply to the court for the appointment of a guardian.

Subsequently, the Law Commission produced a further Consultation Paper: *Mentally Incapacitated Adults and Decision-Making: Medical Treatment and Research* (No 129 1993). This contains detailed proposals which carry forward the options explored in their earlier paper. The Consultation Paper addresses a number of issues: (i) the nature of incapacity; (ii) the effect of 'anticipatory decisions' of patients; (iii) the role of doctors or decision-makers; (iv) the role of relatives in decision-making; (v) the role of the court; (vi) the creation of a statutory scheme for the appointment of proxies and (vii) the development of enduring powers of attorney in medical cases. For our purposes here we draw attention to a number of these issues. We shall take account of their views on anticipatory decisions and enduring powers of attorney in ch 17. We have already referred to the material on incapacity in the previous chapter.

The Scheme proposed by the Law Commission to enable decisions to be made on behalf of incompetents consists of the following. As you will see, these are still provisional proposals (pp 125-133):

PART III . . .
8. A treatment provider should be given a statutory authority (subject to the other proposals contained in this paper) to carry out treatment which is reasonable in all the circumstances to safeguard and promote the best interests of an incapacitated person [or a person whom he or she has reasonable grounds for believing to be incapacitated].
We invite views on whether a health care provider should only be required to have reasonable grounds for believing the person to be incapacitated (paragraph 3.40).
9. Unless it is essential to prevent loss of life or irreversible deterioration of health while an issue is referred to a relevant judicial forum, the statutory authority should not permit the carrying out of any treatment contrary to a valid anticipatory refusal by the person who is now incapacitated, a refusal of consent by a person with the authority to do so, or a prohibition by a judicial forum.
10. The statutory authority should not permit the taking of any step for which the approval of the judicial forum or some other person is required (see Part VI below) unless that approval has been obtained.
11. The statutory authority should not permit the carrying out of any treatment to which the incapacitated person objects, unless such treatment is essential to prevent an immediate risk of serious harm to that person or others.

A best interests criterion
12. In deciding whether a proposed medical treatment is in the best interests of an incapacitated person, consideration should be given to:

    (1)   the ascertainable past and present wishes and feelings (considered in the light of his or her understanding at the time) of the incapacitated person;

    (2)   whether there is an alternative to the proposed treatment, and in particular whether there is an alternative which is more conservative or which is less intrusive or restrictive;

    (3)   the factors which the incapacitated person might be expected to consider if able to do so, including the likely effect of the treatment on the person's life expectancy, health, happiness, freedom and dignity.

13.   The interests of people other than the incapacitated person should not be considered except to the extent that they have a bearing on the incapacitated person's individual interests.

The involvement of relatives and others

14.   A treatment provider should be under a duty to consult the incapacitated person's 'nearest relative' (as defined in the Mental Health Act 1983, section 26) so far as is reasonably practicable, to give that person sufficient information (including information about the patient's condition, the proposed treatment and the reasonably foreseeable consequences of providing or not providing treatment) and to have regard to the views of that person.

15.   If the nearest relative is not reasonably available, or is incapacitated, or is unwilling to be consulted, that person should be disregarded for the purpose of determining the identity of the nearest relative.

16.   Where the patient has named another person to be consulted about treatment decisions should he or she become incapacitated, the person named should be the 'nearest relative' for the purpose of the duty to consult.

17.   Any suitable person who consents to perform the functions of a 'nearest relative' for the purpose of the duty to consult may be appointed if the incapacitated person has no 'nearest relative', or it is not reasonably practicable to ascertain whether he or she has such a relative, or who that relative is.

18.   There should be no duty to obtain the consent of another person to the medical treatment of an incapacitated person simply on the basis of a family relationship.

We invite comment on whether there should be any other grounds for appointing an acting nearest relative (paragraph 3.66) . . .

PART IV
A new jurisdiction

1.   There should be a judicial forum with a statutory jurisdiction:

    (1)   to make orders approving or disapproving the medical treatment of incapacitated patients; and

    (2)   to make declarations as to the patient's capacity or the scope or validity of the patient's own decisions.

We invite comment on the nature of the judicial forum (paragraph 4.5), and on whether there are any situations where the existence of a separate forum for medical decisions, and other decisions, would cause practical problems (paragraph 4.6). We also invite comment on the relationship of the judicial forum with the High Court (paragraph 4.7).

2.   The judicial forum must be satisfied that the making of an order will bring greater benefit to the incapacitated person than making no order at all.

We welcome comments on the likely number of applications to the judicial forum (paragraph 4.8).

3.   Any order made should be in the best interests of the incapacitated person, taking into account:

    (1)   the ascertainable past and present wishes and feelings (considered in the light of his or her understanding at the time) of the incapacitated person;

    (2)   whether there is an alternative to the proposed treatment, and in particular whether there is an alternative which is more conservative or which is less intrusive or restrictive;

    (3)   the factors which the incapacitated person might be expected to consider if able to do so, including the likely effect of the treatment on the person's life expectancy, health, happiness, freedom and dignity, but not the interests of other people except to the extent that they have a bearing on the incapacitated person's individual interests.

4. An order dealing with a specific issue is to be preferred to the appointment of a proxy, unless there is a need for a continuing authority, and any order should be as limited in scope as possible.

A range of orders
5. The judicial forum may make an order giving or withholding approval to the giving, withholding or withdrawal of particular medical treatment in respect of an incapacitated person.
6. The judicial forum may make recommendations instead of, or as well as, making an order.
7. The judicial forum may make an order requiring the person or persons responsible for the medical care of an incapacitated person to allow some other person, who agrees to take over the care of the incapacitated person, to do so.

A declaratory jurisdiction
8. The judicial forum may declare that the person concerned is not incapacitated, either in general or in relation to a particular matter.
9. The judicial forum may make a declaration as to whether or not an apparent decision by the patient concerned is 'clearly established' and 'applicable in the circumstances'.
We invite comment on whether any restrictions should be imposed on the availability of declarations under this jurisdiction (paragraph 4.18).

Appointment of medical treatment proxies
10. If the judicial forum finds that a single issue order will not be sufficient to benefit the incapacitated person, it may appoint any suitable person who agrees to discharge the duties of a medical treatment proxy for that person. The proxy will have such powers in relation to that person's medical treatment as are specified in the order making the appointment.
We invite views on what powers a medical treatment proxy might be granted other than an authority to give or refuse consent to medical treatment, or particular types of medical treatment (paragraph 4.20).
We invite comments on whether it should be possible to appoint a public official as a proxy of last resort (paragraph 4.21).
11. If a medical treatment proxy has been appointed, a person proposing to provide treatment which is within the scope of the proxy's authority should be under a duty to obtain the proxy's consent, or the approval of the judicial forum, before that treatment is given. There should be no duty to consult the incapacitated person's 'nearest relative' in relation to treatments within the authority of the proxy.
12. The judicial forum may appoint joint, joint and several, alternative or successive medical treatment proxies.
13. The maximum duration of any order or appointment by the judicial forum should be [six or] twelve months in the first instance. Appointments should be renewable for [six or] twelve months at a time.
We invite comment on the need for a supervisory body, such as the Mental Health Act Commission, in relation to those for whom a medical treatment proxy has been appointed (paragraph 4.23).
14. A medical treatment proxy must act in the best interests of the incapacitated person, taking into account:
    (1) the ascertainable past and present wishes and feelings (considered in the light of his or her understanding at the time) of the incapacitated person;
    (2) whether there is an alternative to the proposed treatment, and in particular whether there is an alternative which is more conservative or which is less intrusive or restrictive;
    (3) the factors which the incapacitated person might be expected to consider if able to do so, including the likely effect of the treatment on the person's life expectancy, health, happiness, freedom and dignity, but not the interests of other people except to the extent that they have a bearing on the incapacitated person's individual interests.
15. A medical treatment proxy should be able to recover the expenses of acting.
16. A medical treatment proxy should be able to exercise the rights of the incapacitated person to apply for access to health records under the Access to Health Care Records Act 1990 [sic] and the Data Protection Act 1984, unless this possibility is specifically excluded by the judicial forum.

17. A medical treatment proxy should have no authority to refuse pain relief or 'basic care', including nursing care and spoon-feeding.
18. A medical treatment proxy should have no authority to consent to the carrying out of any treatment contrary to a valid anticipatory refusal by the person who is now incapacitated, or a prohibition by the judicial forum.
19. A medical treatment proxy should have no authority to consent to the taking of any step for which the approval of the judicial forum or some other person is required (see Part VI).
20. A medical treatment proxy should have no authority, unless granted explicitly by the judicial forum, to consent to the carrying out of any treatment to which the incapacitated person objects.

Applicants
21. Close relatives, people with whom the incapacitated person has resided, medical treatment proxies or attorneys, personal welfare managers or attorneys, and the person himself or herself, should have a right to apply for an order. The health authority or any person responsible for the incapacitated person's health care should also have a right to apply. Other persons might apply with leave of the judicial forum.

The authorisation of treatment to which the incapacitated person objects
We invite views on whether any additional procedures or criteria should be included before treatment to which the person objects is authorised (paragraph 4.31).

3. Court as sole proxy?

The question to be considered here is whether there are circumstances in which the courts have or will reserve to themselves the exclusive right to decide whether a child or adult shall undergo certain treatment. Obviously, if a child is already a ward of court, the court thereafter has exclusive power to make all significant decisions concerning medical treatment, ie those that involve a 'serious step' in the upbringing of the child (*Re D (a minor) (wardship; sterilisation)* [1976] 1 All ER 326 at 335 per Heilbron J). We, however, are concerned with whether in principle a parent or other (as proxy) or doctor (as quasi-proxy) may *not* have the power to consent to medical intervention in certain classes of case. If such cases exist, it means that only the court (if anyone) may give consent. In England and elsewhere this issue has arisen in the context of the controversial cases of sterilising mentally disabled girls and women. In *Re B (a minor) (wardship: sterilisation)* [1988] AC 199, Lord Templeman (at 205-206) expressed the following views:

Lord Templeman: In my opinion sterilisation of a girl under 18 should only be carried out with the leave of a High Court judge. A doctor performing a sterilisation operation with the consent of the parents might still be liable in criminal, civil or professional proceedings. A court exercising the wardship jurisdiction emanating from the Crown is the only authority which is empowered to authorise such a drastic step as sterilisation after a full and informed investigation. The girl will be represented by the Official Solicitor or some other appropriate guardian: the parents will be made parties if they wish to appear and where appropriate the local authority will also appear. Expert evidence will be adduced setting out the reasons for the application, the history, conditions, circumstances and foreseeable future of the girl, the risks and consequences of pregnancy, the risks and consequences of sterilisation, the practicability of alternative precautions against pregnancy and any other relevant information. The judge may order additional evidence to be obtained. In my opinion, a decision should only be made by a High Court judge. In the Family Division a judge is selected for his or her experience, ability and compassion. No one has suggested a more satisfactory tribunal or a more satisfactory method of reaching a decision which vitally concerns an individual but also involves principles of law, ethics and medical practice. Applications for sterilisation will be rare. Sometimes the judge will conclude that a sufficiently overwhelming case has not been established to justify interference with the fundamental right of a girl to bear a child; this was the case in *Re D (a minor) (wardship: sterilisation)* [1976] 1 All ER 326, [1976] Fam 185. But in the present case the judge was satisfied that it would be cruel to expose the girl to an unacceptable risk of pregnancy which could only be obviated by sterilisation in order to prevent child bearing and childbirth in circumstances of uncomprehending fear and pain and risk of physical injury. In such a case the judge was under a duty and had the courage to authorise sterilisation.

It is important to notice that in *Re B* only Lord Templeman took this view. When the issue surfaced again in the case of a mentally disabled adult in *Re F (mental patient: sterilisation)* [1990] 2 AC 1, a majority of the House of Lords did not adopt Lord Templeman's view. It could, of course, be that their view was pre-conditioned by the fact, as we have seen, that the court has no *parens patriae* jurisdiction over adults. However, the better view is that this is irrelevant and that the real issue is simply whether the proxy or quasi-proxy other than the court has the power to decide. Only one of the judges, Lord Griffiths, adopted Lord Templeman's robust view.

Lord Griffiths: I cannot agree that it is satisfactory to leave this grave decision with all its social implications in the hands of those having the care of the patient with only the expectation that they will have the wisdom to obtain a declaration of lawfulness before the operation is performed. In my view the law ought to be that they must obtain the approval of the court before they sterilise a woman incapable of giving consent and that it is unlawful to sterilise without that consent. I believe that it is open to your Lordships to develop a common law rule to this effect. Although the general rule is that the individual is the master of his own fate through the common law the judges have, in the public interest, imposed certain constraints on the harm that people may consent to being inflicted on their own bodies. Thus although boxing is a legal sport a bare knuckle prize fight in which more grievous injury may be inflicted is unlawful (*R v Coney* (1882) 8 QBD 534), and so is fighting which may result in actual bodily harm: see *A-G's Reference (No 6 of 1980)* [1981] QB 715. So also is it unlawful to consent to the infliction of serious injury on the body in the course of the practice of sexual perversion: *R v Donovan* [1934] 2 KB 498. Suicide was unlawful at common law until Parliament intervened by the Suicide Act 1961.

The common law has, in the public interest, been developed to forbid the infliction of injury on those who are fully capable of consenting to it. The time has now come for a further development to forbid, again in the public interest, the sterilisation of a woman with healthy reproductive organs who, either through mental incompetence or youth, is incapable of giving her fully informed consent unless such an operation has been inquired into and sanctioned by the High Court. Such a common law rule would provide a more effective protection than the exercise of parens patriae jurisdiction which is dependent upon some interested party coming forward to invoke the jurisdiction of the court. The parens patriae jurisdiction is in any event now only available in the case of minors through their being made wards of court. I would myself declare that on grounds of public interest an operation to sterilise a woman incapable of giving consent either on grounds of age or mental incapacity is unlawful if performed without the consent of the High Court. I fully recognise that in so doing I would be making new law. However the need for such a development has been identified in a number of recent cases and in the absence of any Parliamentary response to the problem it is my view that the judges can and should accept responsibility to recognise the need and to adapt the common law to meet it. If such a development did not meet with public approval it would always be open to Parliament to reverse it or to alter it by perhaps substituting for the opinion of the High Court judge the second opinion of another doctor as urged by counsel for the Mental Health [Act Commission].

A number of issues arise:

- Is Lord Griffiths correct that the involvement of the courts in some circumstances is mandatory?
- If the involvement of the courts is not mandatory, is it ever desirable?
- What is the appropriate role of the courts in sterilisation, abortion and other cases?

(a) Is Lord Griffiths correct?

Subsequent to *Re F*, there is no English case that has considered this issue. The Australian High Court in addressed the question in some detail.

Department of Health v JWB and SMB (1992) 66 ALJR 300 (Aust High Ct)

Mason CJ, Gaudron, Toohey and Dawson JJ:

Can parents, as guardians, consent to sterilisation? Conclusion

There are, in our opinion, features of a sterilisation procedure or, more accurately, factors involved in a decision to authorise sterilisation of another person which indicate that, in order to ensure the best protection of the interests of a child, such a decision should not come within the ordinary scope of parental power to consent to medical treatment. Court authorisation is necessary and is, in essence, a procedural safeguard. Our reasons for arriving at this conclusion, however, do not correspond precisely with any of the judgments considered. We shall give our reasons. But first it is necessary to make clear that, in speaking of sterilisation in this context, we are not referring to sterilisation which is a by-product of surgery appropriately carried out to treat some malfunction or disease. We hesitate to use the expressions 'therapeutic' and 'non-therapeutic', because of their uncertainty. But it is necessary to make the distinction, however unclear the dividing line may be.

As a starting point, sterilisation requires invasive, irreversible and major surgery. But so do, for example, an appendectomy and some cosmetic surgery, both of which, in our opinion, come within the ordinary scope of parental power to consent to medical treatment. However, other factors exist which have the combined effect of marking out the decision to authorise sterilisation as a special case. Court authorisation is required, first, because of the significant risk of making the wrong decision, either as to a child's present or future capacity to consent or about what are the best interests of a child who cannot consent, and secondly, because the consequences of a wrong decision are particularly grave.

The factors which contribute to the significant risk of a wrong decision being made are:

(i)   The complexity of the question of consent. Although there are some cases, of which the facts in *Re X* [[1991] 2 NZLR 365] are an example, in which the parents can give an informed consent to an operation of sterilisation on an intellectually disabled child and in which that operation is clearly for the benefit of the child, there is no unproblematic view of what constitutes informed consent . . . And, even given a settled psychological or legal rule, its application in many cases is fraught with difficulty. The fact that a child is disabled does not of itself mean that he or she cannot give informed consent or, indeed, make a meaningful refusal. And there is no reason to assume that those attempting to determine the capacity of an intellectually disabled child, including doctors, may not be affected by commonly held misconceptions about the abilities of those with intellectual disabilities. . . . There is no doubt that some sterilisation operations have been performed too readily and that the capacity of a child to give consent (and, later, to care for a child) has been wrongly assessed both here and overseas, historically and at the present time. . . .

(ii)   The medical profession very often plays a central role in the decision to sterilise as well as in the procedure itself. Indeed the question has been 'medicalised' to a great degree. (See, for example, *Re a Teenager* (1988) 94 FLR, at 221-222, 223-224; *In Re F* [1990] 2 AC, per Lord Goff, at 78; *Re Eve* [1986] 2 SCR, at 399; (1986) 31 DLR (4th), at 7-8, citing from the judgment of the provincial Supreme Court in that case.) Two concerns emerge from this. It is hard to share the view of Cook J in *Re a Teenager* (1988) 94 FLR, at 223 that absolute faith in the integrity of all medical practitioners is warranted. We agree with Nicholson CJ in *Re Jane* (1988) 94 FLR, at 26 that, as with all professions, there are those who act with impropriety as well as those who act bona fide within a limited frame of reference. And the situation with which they are concerned is one in which incorrect assessments may be made. (See, for example, *In Re D (A Minor)* [1976] Fam 185; [1976] 1 All ER 326; *Re Jane* (1988) 94 FLR 1; *In Re F* [1990] 2 AC 1.) The second concern is that the decision to sterilise, at least where it is to be carried out for contraceptive purposes, and especially now when technology and expertise make the procedure relatively safe, is not merely a *medical* issue. This is also reflected in the concern raised in several of the cases reviewed, that the consequences of sterilisation are not merely biological but also social and psychological. The requirement of a court authorisation ensures a hearing from those experienced in different ways in the care of those with intellectual disability and from those with experience of the long term social and psychological effects of sterilisation.

(iii) The decision by a parent that an intellectually disabled child be sterilised may involve not only the interests of the child, but also the independent and possibly conflicting (though legitimate) interests of the parents and other family members. (See, for example, *Re Jane* (1988) 94 FLR, at 27, 30; *Re K and Public Trustee* [1985] 3 WWR 204, per Wood J, at 224, at first instance and (1985) 19 DLR (4th) 255, per Anderson JA, at 279, cited with approval by Cook J in *Re a Teenager* (1988) 94 FLR, at 208.) There is no doubt that caring for a seriously handicapped child adds a significant burden to the ordinarily demanding task of caring for children. . . . Subject to the overriding criterion of the child's welfare, the interests of other family members, particularly primary care-givers, are relevant to a court's decision whether to authorise sterilisation. However, court involvement ensures, in the case of conflict, that the child's interests prevail.

The gravity of the consequences of wrongly authorising a sterilisation flows both from the resulting inability to reproduce and from the fact of being acted upon contrary to one's wishes or best interests. The fact of violation is likely to have social and psychological implications concerning the person's sense of identity, social place and self-esteem. As the Court said in *In Re Grady* (1981) 85 NJ 235 426 A 2d at 471-472, a decision to sterilise involves serious questions of a person's 'social and biological identity'. As with anyone, reactions to sterilisation vary among those with intellectual disabilities but it has been said (The Canadian Law Reform Commission Report, *Sterilization*, (1979) p 50, reporting on Sabagh and Edgerton, 'Sterilized Mental Defectives Look at Eugenic Sterilization' (1962) 9 *Eugenics Quarterly* 213) that 'sterilised mentally retarded persons tend to perceive sterilisation as a symbol of *reduced* or *degraded* status'. Another study found (Roos, 'Psychological Impact of Sterilization on the Individual' (1975) *Law and Psychology Review* 45 at 54, in the Canadian Report, pp 50-51 and see generally pp 49-52) that:

Essential anxieties commonly associated with mental retardation are likely to be seriously reinforced by coercive sterilisation of those who have had no children. Common sources of these anxieties include low self-esteem, feelings of helplessness, and need to avoid failure, loneliness, concern over body integrity and the threat of death.

The far-reaching consequences of a general rule of law allowing guardians to consent to all kinds of medical treatment, as well as the consequences of a wrong decision in any particular case, are also relevant. As Nicholson CJ pointed out in *Re Jane* in the passage quoted earlier ((1988) 94 FLR, at 26), such a rule may be used to justify other procedures such as a clitoridectomy or the removal of a healthy organ for transplant to another child.

For the above reasons, which look to the risks involved in the decision, particularly in relation to the threshold question of competence and in relation to the consequences of a wrong assessment, our conclusion is that the decision to sterilise a minor in circumstances such as the present falls outside the ordinary scope of parental powers . ´ . . This is not a case where sterilisation is an incidental result of surgery performed to cure a disease or correct some malfunction. Court authorisation in the present case is required. Where profound permanent incapacity is indisputable, where all psychological and social implications have in fact been canvassed by a variety of care-givers and where the child's guardians are, in fact, only considering the interests of the child or where their own interests do not conflict with those of the child, court authorisation will ordinarily reproduce the wishes of the guardian. But it is not possible to formulate a rule which distinguishes these cases. Given the widely varying circumstances, it is impossible to apply a single rule to determine what are, in the respondents' words, the 'clear cases'.

Children with intellectual disabilities are particularly vulnerable, both because of their minority and their disability, and we agree with Nicholson CJ (at 27) that there is less likelihood of (intentional or unintentional) abuse of the rights of children if an application to a court is mandatory, than if the decision in all cases could be made by a guardian alone. In saying this we acknowledge that it is too costly for most parents to fund court proceedings, that delay is likely to cause painful inconvenience and that the strictly adversarial process of the court is very often unsuitable for arriving at this kind of decision. These are clear indications of the need for legislative reform, since a more appropriate process for decision-making can only be introduced in that way. The burden of the cost of proceedings for parents would in the meantime, of course, be alleviated by the application being made by a relevant public body pursuant to s 63C(1) of the *Family Law Act*. (See generally Blackwood, 'Sterilisation of the Intellectually Disabled: The Need for Legislative Reform' (1991) 5 *Australian Journal of Family Law* 138.)

One more thing should be said about the basis upon which we have concluded that sterilisation is a special case with respect to parental powers. As we have indicated, the conclusion relies on a fundamental right to personal inviolability existing in the common law, a right which underscores the principles of assault, both criminal and civil, as well as on the practical exigencies accompanying this kind of decision which have been discussed. Our conclusion does not, however, rely on a finding which underpins many of the judgments discussed; namely, that there exists in the common law a fundamental right to reproduce which is independent of the right to personal inviolability. We leave that question open. It is debatable whether the former is a useful concept, when couched in terms of a basic right, and how fundamental such a right can be said to be. (See Kingdom, 'The Right to Reproduce' in Ockelton (ed), *Medicine, Ethics and Law*, (1986), 55; cf Freeman, 'Sterilising the Mentally Handicapped' in Freeman (ed), *Medicine, Ethics and the Law*, (1988) 55.) For example, there cannot be said to be an absolute right in a man to reproduce (except where a woman consents to bear a child), unless it can be contended that the right to bodily integrity yields to the former right, and that cannot be so. That is to say, if there is an absolute right to reproduce, is there a duty to bear children? But if the so-called right to reproduce comprises a right not to be prevented from being biologically capable of reproducing, that is a right to bodily integrity. The same applies, though in a different way, to a woman's 'right to reproduce'. Again, if the right is, in fact, a right to do with one's person what one chooses, it is saying no more than that there is a right to bodily and personal integrity. Furthermore, it is quite impossible to spell out all the implications which may flow from saying that there is a right to reproduce, expressed in absolute terms and independent from a right to personal inviolability. We think it is important, in the terms of this judgment, to make it quite clear that it is inviolability that is protected, not more.

You will notice that the majority of the court emphasised three aspects of decision-making in this area which called for the mandatory involvement of the court: (1) the potential for abuse by the proxy; (2) the danger of the proxy making a wrong decision and (3) the seriousness of the decision in question for the patient. The judges in the minority disagreed although their views differ somewhat *inter se*. We set out here extracts from the judgments of Deane and McHugh JJ.

Deane J: [t]he preferable course will ordinarily be to appoint a guardian of the child for the limited period necessary for the authorisation and performance of the surgery. If, however, circumstances were to arise in which there was no appropriate person prepared to accept appointment as such a temporary guardian, the court could, in my view, itself directly authorise it. (See, eg, *Re L (An Infant)* [1968] P 119, per Denning MR, at 157; *K v Minister for Youth and Community Services* [1982] 1 NSWLR at 323; *Rolands v Rolands* (1983) 9 Fam LR, at 330, 322; [1984] FLC, at 79, 203, 79, 204.) More important for present purposes, the jurisdiction extends to granting, at the suit of a parent or interested party, declaratory or other relief in relation to the existence and proper exercise of parental authority. That jurisdiction extends to the making of a declaration that a parent or the parents of an incapable child would or would not, in the particular circumstances of a case, be justified in authorising surgery involving irreversible sterilisation.

In *In Re B (A Minor)* [1988] AC, at 205, Lord Templeman expressed the opinion that, in England, 'sterilisation of a girl under 18 should only be carried out with the leave' of a judge of the Family Division of the English High Court. The other members of the House of Lords in that case did not express any opinion on that question but a similar view was expressed by Lord Goff of Chieveley in the case of an operation for the sterilisation of an intellectually disabled adult woman who lacked the capacity to consent (*In Re F (Mental Patient: Sterilisation)* [1990] 2 AC, at 79). There are powerful considerations which support those views, including the grave consequences, both physical and psychological, of irreversible sterilisation and the need to protect the weak and vulnerable from eugenic and utilitarian theories which discount the importance of human integrity and complete personality and which are repugnant to the standards of our community. Those considerations also include the fact that there may well exist a divergence or conflict – sometimes unappreciated – between the interests of the incapable child and the interests of those who are or will be responsible for looking after her or him and for caring for any offspring. In a context where the factors militating against surgery involving sterilisation will not be confined to medical considerations, the courts are likely to be better able than medical practitioners, even acting as members of a multidisciplinary team, to ensure that due regard is paid to, and only to, relevant factors in ascertaining what is truly in the interests of the welfare of the child. All these considerations strongly support a conclusion that the effect of the requirement that parental authority be exercised only after due inquiry and adequate consideration is that, in the absence of any applicable statutory procedure or jurisdiction in any other competent tribunal, the parents of an incapable child must obtain a declaratory order from the Family Court (or some other court vested with applicable welfare jurisdiction) before they can validly authorise surgery involving irreversible sterilisation for a purpose other than the conventional medical ones of preserving life and treating or preventing grave physical illness.

On the other hand, one cannot but be conscious of the undeniable fact that a general requirement that the parents of an incapable child maintain proceedings for declaratory relief in the Family Court before authorising such surgery would represent an extraordinarily onerous burden upon them. Proceedings in the superior courts of this country are commonly protracted (For example, *Re a Teenager* (1988) 94 FLR 181; *Re Jane* (1988) 94 FLR 1; *Re Elizabeth* (1989) 13 Fam LR 47; [1989] FLC 92-023 and *A-G (Qld) v Parents (In Re S)* (1989) 98 FLR 41) and, at least in the many cases where legal aid is not provided, oppressively expensive. (See, eg, *Re Marion* (1990) 14 Fam LR, at 462; [1991] FLC, at 78, 312-78, 313; *Re K and Public Trustee* (1985) 19 DLR (4th), at 278; Professor T W Church, 'A Consumer's Perspective on the Courts', The Second Annual Oration in Judicial Administration, 31 October 1990, pp 6-7.) The delays which are likely to be involved in such litigation are notorious. Inevitably, proceedings about whether surgery involving irreversible sterilisation is in the interests of the welfare of an incapable child will impose a heavy and additional load of anxiety upon the shoulders of caring parents. A consequence of such a general requirement would be that the understandable reluctance of parents to become involved in such legal proceedings would prevent such surgery taking place in at least some cases where it was obviously for the welfare of an incapable child.

What then is the legal resolution of the different considerations favouring and militating against a conclusion that the common law requirement of due inquiry and adequate consideration can only be satisfied by recourse to the Family Court (or to the Supreme Court exercising cross-vested or any residual jurisdiction) in the case of surgery involving the irreversible sterilisation of an incapable child in the Northern Territory? That question arises in this Court as a question of law. The processes of legal reasoning by induction and deduction from legal principle are, however, inadequate to provide an answer to it. The reason why that is so is that, while the question arises in a legal context, the issues which it involves are as much social or moral as they are legal and the answer to it is inevitably affected by personal perceptions of current social conditions, standards and demands. The answer which I would give to it is that the reconciliation of the conflicting considerations requires that a distinction be drawn between those cases where the need for such surgery in the interests of the welfare of the child is, according to general community standards, obvious and those cases where it is not. In a case where such surgery is obviously necessary, a requirement of court approval would impose an unjustifiable burden upon the parents of an incapable child. More important, the requirement would itself be undesirable in that its only significant effect would be to prevent parents, who were not prepared to subject themselves and their families to the expense, inconvenience and anxiety of court proceedings, from authorising surgery which was obviously in the interests of the welfare of the child. In a case where such surgery is not obviously necessary, the need to protect an incapable child from unjustified surgery involving irreversible sterilisation outweighs all other considerations. Notwithstanding the expense, inconvenience and other disadvantages of court proceedings, it appears to me that, in the absence of some special statutory procedure, such proceedings represent the only adequate protection.

McHugh J: In principle, no reason exists for denying to parents the power to consent to the sterilisation of a child in their custody. Public policy does not prevent a person from consenting to an operation which will irreversibly sterilise that person *(Thake v Maurice* [1986] QB 644). Since the parent is the person whom the law entrusts with the power and authority to consent to surgical and medical treatment for the welfare of a child, logically the parent must have the power and authority to consent to any operation or treatment for the welfare of the child which is not contrary to law or public policy.

In the United States, however, courts have consistently held that parents do not possess the authority to consent to the sterilisation of their children (*AL v GRH* 325 NE 2d 501

(Indiana Court of Appeals, (1975)); *Ruby v Massey* (1978) 452 F Supp 361 (United States District Court); *In Re Grady* (1981) 85 NJ 235 426 A 2d 467 (New Jersey Supreme Court); *Matter of Moe* (1982) 432 NE 2d 712 (Massachusetts Supreme Judicial Court)). Moreover, in *Stump v Sparkman* (1978) 435 US 349 at 358-359 the United States Supreme Court appeared to approve the decision of the Indiana Court of Appeals in *AL v GRH* which held that parents had no authority to consent to the sterilisation of their child. The reasons given for rejecting parental consent as sufficient authority for sterilising a child include the history of abuse of sterilising the intellectually disabled – particularly the fear that they will be sterilised for the convenience of the guardians; the destruction of 'an important part of a person's social and biological identity – the ability to reproduce'; and the irreversibility of the procedure. The effect of the blanket rule applied in the United States, however, is that parents cannot consent to an operation which results in the sterilisation of a child even though the procedure is necessary to remove or treat a diseased reproductive organ.

Understandable as the United States approach is, as a matter of principle, a line cannot be drawn between sterilisation procedures and other forms of surgical and medical treatment. It is true, as Holmes said (*The Common Law,* (1881), p 5):

> The life of the law has not been logic: it has been experience. The felt necessities of the time, the prevalent moral and political theories, intuitions of public policy, avowed or unconscious, even the prejudices which judges share with their fellow-men, have had a good deal more to do than syllogism in determining the rules by which men should be governed.

But none of these matters provides any sure ground, in my respectful opinion, for a court to hold that sterilisation procedures should be treated as an exception to the rule that parents can consent to medical treatment and surgical procedures involving their child. If the consensus of the community was that parents ought not to have an unsupervised right to consent to the sterilisation of children, it might be proper to mould common law doctrine to give effect to that consensus, even though the demands of legal principle suggest a contrary course. It might be proper, therefore, to hold that parents cannot give consent to such a procedure without the consent of a court. But as no community consensus on the issue exists, and as the subject of sterilisation 'gives rise to moral and emotional considerations to which many people attach great importance' (*In Re F* [1990] 2 AC, at 56), the proper course for a court is to give effect to established principle instead of laying down a rule which gives effect to what that court thinks is the best social solution to the issue.

In any event, the social utility of requiring the consent of the court in all cases of sterilisation is debatable. Beneficial as such a course may prove to be in some cases, it would require a depressing view of the discharge of the responsibilities of parents and doctors to conclude that the unnecessary sterilisation of children is so widespread that a blanket rule is the only remedy which can protect children from the abuse of their right to bodily integrity. This is especially true in an era when litigation is always expensive and frequently protracted with the result that, in cases where sterilisation is warranted, applications for consent might not be made. Moreover, as Lord Brandon of Oakbrook pointed out in *In Re F* (at 56), if every sterilisation operation required curial consent 'the whole process of medical care for such patients would grind to a halt'. A better remedy for the protection of children than requiring curial consent in all cases of sterilisation is the development of objective standards which the courts can supervise and enforce where necessary. Such standards will promote certainty and consistency in decision making. They will also enable parents to give a valid consent to an operation which will sterilise their child without the cost and trauma associated with litigation.

It follows that, as a matter of principle, a parent has authority to consent to the sterilisation of a child in his or her custody if it will advance or protect the welfare of the child. What is in the best interests of the child is conventionally seen as being synonymous with the welfare of the child. To say that a medical or surgical procedure is in the best interests of the child, however, is merely to record a result. Before the best interests of the child can be determined, some principle, rule or standard must be applied to the facts and circumstances of the case (cf Kennedy, 'Patients, Doctors, and Human Rights', Blackburn and Taylor (eds), *Human Rights for the 1990s* (1991), pp 90-91).

Since sterilisation has grave consequences for a person's adult life, it cannot be in the best interests of a child to pre-empt a choice about the procedure which the child would otherwise have as an adult person. If there is any real possibility that, at some future time, the child will acquire the capacity and maturity to choose whether he or she should be sterilised, the carrying out of that procedure cannot be in the best interests of the child unless, of course, protection of the child's health urgently requires that the procedure be carried out during incompetency. Moreover, it must not be assumed that, simply because the child is intellectually disabled, he or she does not have or cannot acquire the capacity to consent to sterilisation. Intellectually disabled persons will frequently have the capacity to make the choice as to whether they should be sterilised (Committee on Rights of Persons with Handicaps (SA), *The Law and Persons with Handicaps*, vol 2: *Intellectual Handicaps*, (1981), p 125). Furthermore, sterilisation involves invasive procedures resulting in the permanent deprivation of a person's right or liberty to reproduce, with the potentiality for psychological harm including the lowering – perhaps the destruction – of self-esteem and, in the case of the intellectually disabled, the reinforcement of anxieties which are commonly the result of intellectual disability. (See Law Reform Commission of Canada, (Working Paper No 24 1979), *Sterilization: Implications for Mentally Retarded and Mentally Ill Persons*, pp 49-52.)

So grave are the certain and potential effects of sterilisation that that procedure can only be for the welfare of the child if the circumstances are so compelling and so likely to endure that they justify the invasive surgery or procedure involved in sterilisation. The circumstances may be compelling if the failure to carry out the procedure is likely to result in the child's physical or mental health being seriously jeopardised or if it is likely to result in the suffering of pain, fear or discomfort of such severity and duration or regularity that it is not reasonable to expect the child to suffer that pain, fear or discomfort. In these cases, the right of the incompetent person to have his or her body protected against invasive procedures resulting in removal or destruction of reproductive organs is outweighed by the necessity for appropriate 'treatment'. The circumstances may also be compelling if the failure to carry out the procedure is likely to result in a real risk that an intellectually disabled child will become pregnant and she does not, and never will, have any real understanding of sexual relationships or pregnancy. In such a case, to speak of a fundamental right of reproduction is meaningless. The human dignity of an intellectually disabled child is not advanced, and indeed is denied, by allowing her (by, what is in point of law, rape) to become pregnant and to give birth in circumstances which she cannot understand and which may result in a frightening ordeal for her not only at the time of birth, but for many months prior thereto.

What constitutes sufficiently compelling circumstances to justify sterilisation will have to be worked out on a case by case basis. But, unless the case falls within one of the above categories or a category analogous thereto, it should be held that the sterilisation of a child is not for his or her welfare. In particular, it is not for the welfare of an intellectually disabled child to sterilise that child merely to avoid pregnancy or to give effect to eugenic policies. Nor is it for the welfare of the child to sterilise her merely because of the hygiene problems associated with menstruation. As the Law Reform Commission of Canada has pointed out, intellectually disabled females who require a great deal of assistance in managing their menstruation are already likely to require assistance with urinary and faecal control, problems which are much more troublesome in terms of personal hygiene (at 34). Moreover, even if the case falls within one of the three categories which I have mentioned or an analogous category, it is not in the best interests of a child to sterilise him or her if the harm can reasonably be avoided by means less drastic than sterilisation.

Furthermore, as I have indicated, sterilisation is one area where the potential for conflict between the parent's interests and the child's interests exists. As Justice Horowitz pointed out in *Matter of Guardianship of Hayes* (1980) Wash 608 p 2d 635 at 640:

> unlike the situation of a normal and necessary medical procedure, in the question of sterilisation the interests of the parent of a retarded person cannot be presumed to be identical to those of the child.

Thus, parents may see sterilisation as relieving them of the worry and distress of the child becoming pregnant or of the burden of caring for a grandchild whom the child would not be able or fully able to care for. If a decision to consent is actuated by interests such as these, a conflict of interest arises. In such a case, the parents have no authority to consent to the sterilisation of their child. However, since parents have authority to consent to a sterilisation procedure only in cases where the grounds for the procedure are compelling it is unlikely that, in practice, conflict will arise. If it does, a court of general jurisdiction invested with the parens patriae jurisdiction or the Family Court may give consent in substitution for the parents.

The principles which apply to the sterilisation of children, as I have adumbrated them, fall somewhere between the approach of the Supreme Court of Canada in *Re Eve* (*E* (*Mrs*) *v Eve* ('*Re Eve*') [1986] 2 SCR 388; 31 DLR (4th) 1) and the approach of the House of Lords in *In Re F*. In *Re Eve*, the Supreme Court held that, in the exercise of the parens patriae jurisdiction, a court should not give consent to a non-therapeutic sterilisation. The distinction between therapeutic and non-therapeutic treatment was strongly criticised by members of the House of Lords in *In Re B (A Minor)* [1988] AC 199 at 203-204, 205. I agree with Professor Kennedy, in the article to which I have earlier referred, where he said (Kennedy, op cit, p 102) that, although 'there are problems at the edges' of the two concepts, '[a]n intervention is therapeutic if treatment (therapy) is intended thereby'. This definition would include the first two categories of justification to which I have referred but exclude the third category. However, for the reasons that I have already given, I think that, where the child has no real understanding of sexual relationships or pregnancy, sterilisation may be justified if no method of contraception is reasonably feasible. In that respect, I would go beyond the approach of the Supreme Court in *Re Eve*. Moreover, it would be inconsistent with the historical development of common law principles to close the categories to which they apply. Consequently, unlike the Supreme Court of Canada, I would hold that sterilisation may also be carried out for purposes which are analogous to the three categories to which I have referred. Such an approach allows the law to develop incrementally, guided by the overarching principle that the circumstances must be so compelling that they justify such an invasive procedure as sterilisation.

In *In Re F*, the House of Lords held that sterilisation of an incompetent child was justified if it was necessary or in the public interest and that it would be in the public interest if the procedure was in the best interests of the child. Their Lordships held that it will be in the best interests of the patient if a doctor has formed the opinion that sterilisation should be carried out provided that that opinion corresponds with a respectable body of medical opinion among those experienced in the field. Their Lordships (Lord Griffith dissenting on this point) held that the involvement of a court was highly desirable as a matter of good practice although it was not necessary as a matter of law. The approach of their Lordships goes well beyond what I consider is the proper view of the common law, even when the decision to sterilise is ultimately made by a court.

A similar view to that of the majority in *JMB* was expressed in the well-known Kentucky case of *Strunk v Strunk*.

Strunk v Strunk (1969) 445 SW 2d 145 (Ky CA)

Osborne J: The facts of the case are as follows: Arthur L Strunk, 54 years of age, and Ava Strunk, 52 years of age, of Williamstown, Kentucky, are the parents of two sons. Tommy Strunk is 28 years of age, married, an employee of the Penn State Railroad and a part-time student at the University of Cincinnati. Tommy is now suffering from chronic glomerulus nephritis, a fatal kidney disease. He is now being kept alive by frequent treatment on an artificial kidney, a procedure which cannot be continued much longer.

Jerry Strunk is 27 years of age, incompetent, and through proper legal proceedings has been committed to the Frankfort State Hospital and School, which is a state institution maintained for the feeble-minded. He has an IQ of approximately 35, which corresponds with the mental age of approximately six years. He is further handicapped by a speech defect, which makes it difficult for him to communicate with persons who are not well acquainted with him. When it was determined that Tommy, in order to survive, would have to have a kidney the doctors considered the possibility of using a kidney from a cadaver if and when one became available or one from a live donor if this could be made available. The entire family, his mother, father and a number of collateral relatives were tested. Because of incompatibility of blood type or tissue none were [sic] medically acceptable as live donors. As a last resort, Jerry was tested and found to be highly acceptable. This immediately presented the legal problem as to what, if anything, could be done by the family, especially the mother and the father to procure a transplant from Jerry to Tommy. The mother as a committee petitioned the county court for authority to proceed with the operation. The court found that the operation was necessary, that under the peculiar circumstances of this case it would not only be beneficial to Tommy but also beneficial to Jerry because Jerry was greatly dependent upon Tommy, emotionally and psychologically, and that his well-being would be jeopardised more severely by the loss of his brother than by the removal of a kidney.

A psychiatrist, in attendance to Jerry, who testified in the case, stated in his opinion the death of Tommy under these circumstances would have 'an extremely traumatic effect upon him' (Jerry).

The Department of Mental Health of this Commonwealth has entered the case as *amicus curiae* and on the basis of its evaluation of the seriousness of the operation as opposed to the traumatic effect upon Jerry as a result of the loss to Tommy, recommended to the court that Jerry be permitted to undergo the surgery. Its recommendations are as follows:

> It is difficult for the mental defective to establish a firm sense of identity with another person and the acquisition of this necessary identity is dependent upon a person whom one can conveniently accept as a model and who at the same time is sufficiently flexible to allow the defective to detach himself with reassurances of continuity. His need to be social is not so much the necessity of a formal and mechanical contact with other human beings as it is the necessity of a close intimacy with other men, the desirability of a real community of feeling, an urgent need for a unity of understanding. Purely mechanical and formal contact with other men does not offer any treatment for the behaviour of a mental defective; only those who are able to communicate intimately are of value to hospital treatment in these cases. And this generally is a member of the family.
>
> In view of this knowledge, we now have particular interest in this case. Jerry Strunk, a mental defective, has emotions and reactions on a scale comparable to that of a normal person. He identifies with his brother Tom; Tom is his model, his tie with his family. Tom's life is vital to the continuity of Jerry's improvement at Frankfort State Hospital and School. The testimony of the hospital representative reflected the importance to Jerry of his visits with his family and the constant inquiries Jerry made about Tom's coming to see him. Jerry is aware he plays a role in the relief of this tension. We the Department of Mental Health must take all possible steps to prevent the occurrence of any guilt feelings Jerry would have if Tom were to die.
>
> The necessity of Tom's life to Jerry's treatment and eventual rehabilitation is clearer in view of the fact that Tom is his only living sibling and at the death of their parents, now in their fifties, Jerry will have no concerned, intimate communication so necessary to his stability and optimal functioning.
>
> The evidence shows that at the present level of medical knowledge, it is quite remote that Tom would be able to survive several cadaver transplants. Tom has a much better chance of survival if the kidney transplant from Jerry takes place.

Upon this appeal we are faced with the fact that all members of the immediate family have recommended the transplant. The Department of Mental Health has likewise made its recommendation. The county court has given its approval. The circuit court has found that it would be to the best interest of the ward of the state that the procedure be carried out. Throughout the legal proceedings, Jerry has been represented by a guardian *ad litem*, who has continually questioned the power of the state to authorise the removal of an organ from the body of an incompetent who is a ward of the state. We are fully cognisant of the fact that the question before us is unique. Insofar as we have been able to learn, no similar set of facts has come before the highest court of any of the states of this nation or the federal courts. The English courts have apparently taken a broad view of the inherent power of the equity courts with regard to incompetents. *Ex p Whitbread* (1816) 2 Mer 99, 35 ER 878, LC holds that courts of equity have the inherent power to make provisions for a needy brother out of the estate of an incompetent. This was first followed in this country in New York, *Re Willoughby, a Lunatic* 11 Paige 257 (NY 1844). The inherent rule in these cases is that the chancellor has the power to deal with the estate of the incompetent in the same manner as the incompetent would if he had his faculties. This rule has been extended to cover not only matters of property but also to cover the personal affairs of the incompetent. . . .

The right to act for the incompetent in all cases has become recognised in this country as the doctrine of substituted judgment and is broad enough not only to cover property but also to cover all matters touching on the well-being of the ward. The doctrine has been recognised in American courts since 1844.

Review of our case law leads us to believe that the power given to a committee under KRS 387.230 would not extend so far as to allow a committee to subject its ward to the serious surgical techniques here under consideration unless the life of his ward be in jeopardy. Nor do we believe the powers delegated to the county court by virtue of the above statutes would reach so far as to permit the procedure which we are dealing with here.

We are of the opinion that a chancery court does have sufficient inherent power to authorise the operation. The circuit court having found that the operative procedures in this instance are to the best interest of Jerry Strunk and this finding having been based upon substantial evidence, we are of the opinion the judgment should be affirmed. We do not deem it significant that this case reached the circuit court by way of appeal as opposed to a direct proceeding in that court.

Notably, also as in the *JMB and SWB* case, a strong dissent was registered in *Strunk*:

Steinfeld J: Apparently because of my indelible recollection of a government which, to the everlasting shame of its citizens, embarked on a programme of genocide and experimentation with human bodies, I have been more troubled in reaching a decision in this case than in any other. My sympathies and emotions are torn between a compassion to aid an ailing young man and a duty to fully protect unfortunate members of society.

The opinion of the majority is predicated upon the authority of an equity court to speak for one who cannot speak for himself. However, it is my opinion that in considering such right in this instance we must first look to the power and authority vested in the committee, the appellee herein. KRS 387.060 and KRS 387.230 do nothing more than give the committee the power to take custody of the incompetent and the possession, care and management of his property. Courts have restricted the activities of the committee to that which is for the best interest of the incompetent. *Harding's Administrator v Harding's Executor* 140 Ky 277, 130 SW 1098 (1910); *Miller v Keown* 176 Ky 117, 195 SW 430 (1912) and 3 ALR 3d 18. The authority and duty have to protect and maintain the ward, to secure that to which he is entitled and preserve that which he has. *Ramsay's Executor v Ramsey* 243 Ky 202, 47 SW 2d 1059 (1932); *Aaronson v State of New York* 34 Misc 2d 827, 229 NYS 2d 550, 557 (1962) and *Young v State* 32 Misc 2d 965, 225 NYS 2d 549 (1962). The wishes of the members of the family or the desires of the guardian to be helpful to the apparent objects of the ward's bounty have not been a criterion. 'A curator or guardian cannot dispose of his ward's property by donation, even though authorised to do so by the court on advice of a family meeting, unless a gift by the guardian is authorised by statute.' 44 CJS Insane Persons para 81, p 191.

Two Kentucky cases decided many years ago reveal judicial policy. In *WT Sistrunk & Co v Navarra's Committee* 268 Ky 753, 105 SW 2d 1039 (1937), this court held that a committee was without right to continue a business which the incompetent had operated prior to his having been declared a person of unsound mind. More analogous is *Baker v Thomas* 272 Ky 605, 114 SW 2d 1113 (1938), in which a man and woman had lived together out of wedlock. Two children were born to them. After the man was adjudged incompetent, his committee, acting for him, together with his paramour, instituted proceedings to adopt the two children. In rejecting the application and refusing to speak for the incompetent the opinion stated:

> The statute does not contemplate that the committee of a lunatic may exercise any other power than to have the possession, care, and management of the lunatic's or incompetent's estate. No authority is given by any statute to which our attention has been called, or that we have been by careful research able to locate, giving the committee of a lunatic or an incompetent authority to petition any court for the adoption of a person as heirs capable of the inheritance of his or her estate.

The same result was reached in *Re Bourgeois* 144 La 501, 80 So 673 (1919), in which the husband of an incompetent wife sought to change the beneficiary of her insurance policy so that her children would receive the proceeds. *Grady v Dashiell* 24 Wash 2d 272, 163 P 2d 922 (1945), stands for the proposition that a loan to the ward's adult insolvent son made at a time when it was thought that the ward was incurably insane constituted an improper depletion of the ward's estate.

The majority opinion is predicated upon the finding of the circuit court that there will be psychological benefits to the ward but points out that the incompetent has the mentality of a six-year-old child. It is common knowledge beyond dispute that the loss of a close relative or a friend to a six-year-old child is not of major impact. Opinions concerning psychological trauma are at best most nebulous. Furthermore, there are no guarantees that the transplant will become a surgical success, it being well known that body rejection of transplanted organs is frequent. The life of the incompetent is not in danger, but the surgical procedure advocated creates some peril.

It is written in *Prince v Massachusetts* 321 US 158, 64 S Ct 438, 88 L Ed 645 (1944), that 'Parents may be free to become martyrs themselves. But it does not follow they are free, in identical circumstances, to make martyrs of their children before they have reached the age of full and legal discretion when they can make that choice for themselves.' The ability to fully understand and consent is a prerequisite to the donation of a part of the human body. Cf *Bonner v Moran* 75 US App DC 156, 126 F 2d 121, 139 ALR 1366 (1941), in which a fifteen-year-old infant's consent to removal of a skin patch for the benefit of another was held legally ineffective.

Unquestionably the attitudes and attempts of the committee and members of the family of the two young men whose critical problems now confront us are commendable, natural and beyond reproach. However, they refer us to nothing indicating that they are privileged to authorise the removal of one of the kidneys of the incompetent for the purpose of donation, and they cite no statutory or other authority vesting such right in the courts. The proof shows that less compatible donors are available and that the kidney of a cadaver could be used, although the odds of operational success are not as great in such case as they would be with the fully compatible donor brother.

I am unwilling to hold that the gates should be open to permit the removal of an organ from an incompetent for transplant, at least until such time as it is conclusively demonstrated that it will be of significant benefit to the incompetent. The evidence here does not rise to that pinnacle. To hold that committees, guardians or courts have such awesome power even in the persuasive case before us, could establish legal precedent, the dire result of which we cannot fathom. Regretfully I must say no.

In the *JMB and SWB* case in Australia, Brennan J perceptively remarked:

Leaving aside for the moment the possibility of statutory investiture of a specific jurisdiction . . . the only legal explanation advanced is that a court, in exercising its parens patriae jurisdiction, enjoys a wider power than parents or guardians possess in respect of the personal integrity of their children. That proposition, in my respectful view, is erroneous in law and disturbing in its social implications.

In our view, Brennan J's remark is well made. There can be no circumstances in which a court should have exclusive power (short of legislation) to make decisions that proxies should not. As we have seen, in our view the court's function is to legislate legitimate criteria for decision-making and thereafter to review particular decisions *of others*.

(b) Desirable if not mandatory?

Although it may be argued that it would be helpful or desirable if certain types of case were routinely brought before the courts, the court cannot, of course, insist upon this. If it were to try to do so, it would be making involvement of the courts, in effect, mandatory. Regardless of the logic of this, the courts have succumbed to the temptation of getting involved. Thus in *Re F*, having rejected a mandatory role for the court, Lord Brandon stated that:

. . . although involvement of the court is not strictly necessary as a matter of law, it is nevertheless highly desirable as a matter of good practice. In considering that question, it is necessary to have regard to the special features of such an operation. These features are: first, the operation will in most cases be irreversible; secondly, by reason of the general irreversibility of the operation, the almost certain result of it will be to deprive the woman concerned of what is widely, and as I think rightly, regarded as one of the fundamental rights of a woman, namely, the right to bear children; thirdly, the deprivation of that right gives rise to moral and emotional considerations to which many people attach great importance; fourthly, if the question whether the operation is in the best interests of the woman is left to be decided without the involvement of the court there may be a greater risk of it being decided wrongly, or at least of it being thought to have been decided wrongly; fifthly, if there is no involvement of the court, there is a risk of the operation being carried out for improper reasons or with improper motives; and, sixthly, involvement of the court in the decision to operate, if that is the decision reached, should serve to protect the doctor or doctors who perform the operation, and any others who may be concerned in it from subsequent adverse criticisms or claims.

Having regard to all these matters, I am clearly of the opinion that, although in the case of an operation of the kind under discussion involvement of the court is not strictly necessary as a matter of law, it is nevertheless highly desirable as a matter of good practice.

There may be cases of other special operations to which similar considerations would apply. I think it best, however, to leave such other cases to be examined as and when they arise.

Further, Lord Goff expressed a similar view:

Although the parens patriae jurisdiction in the case of adults of unsound mind is no longer vested in courts in this country, the approach adopted by the courts in the United States and in Australia provides, in my opinion, strong support for the view that, as a matter of practice, the operation of sterilisation should not be performed on an adult person who lacks the capacity to consent to it without first obtaining the opinion of the court that the operation is, in the circumstances, in the best interests of the person concerned, by seeking a declaration that the operation is lawful. (I shall return later in this speech to the appropriateness of the declaratory remedy in cases such as these.) In my opinion, that guidance should be sought in order to obtain an independent, objective and authoritative view of the lawfulness of the procedure in the particular circumstances of the relevant case, after a hearing at which it can be ensured that there is independent representation on behalf of the person upon whom it is proposed to perform the operation. This approach is consistent with the opinion expressed by Lord Templeman in *Re B (A Minor) (Wardship: Sterilisation)* [1988] AC 199, 205-206, that, in the case of a girl who is still a minor, sterilisation should not be performed upon her unless she has first been made a ward of court and the court has, in the exercise of its wardship jurisdiction, given its authority to such a step. He said:

> No one has suggested a more satisfactory tribunal or a more satisfactory method of reaching a decision which vitally concerns an individual but also involves principles of law, ethics and medical practice.

Despite the logical untenability of this approach, subsequent cases have explored the range of its application. In three cases decided by Sir Stephen Brown, the President of the Family Division, his Lordship had to decide whether the approval of the court was desirable when it was proposed to perform an abortion (*Re SG (a patient)* (1990) 6 BMLR 95), a hysterectomy for serious menorrhagia in a severely disabled adult (*F v F* (1991) 7 BMLR 135) and in a girl (*Re E (a minor) (medical treatment)* (1991) 7 BMLR 117).

In all three cases, the judge distinguished *Re F* and did not deem the involvement of the court desirable.

Re E (a minor) (medical treatment) (1991) 7 BMLR 117 (Fam Div)

Sir Stephen Brown P: This is an application to the court, formally made as an interlocutory application in wardship proceedings by the Official Solicitor, who is the guardian and litem of a mentally handicapped minor called J, who was born on 6 August 1973. J, now 17 years old, sadly, suffers from a severe mental handicap and is unable to make decisions on her own account. Her parents are very concerned for her welfare. They undertake her full-time care, but they are particularly concerned because she suffers from serious menorrhagia, which is excessive menstruation. This has serious effects upon J. I need not enlarge upon them because they are fully set out in a statement which has been submitted to the court by Mr Robinson, a consultant surgeon at Addenbrooke's hospital in Cambridge. He is the consultant gynaecologist who has been responsible for treating J. He has not sworn an affidavit because of a cautionary position recommended to him by the Medical Defence Union, which is concerned about the effects of carrying out medical treatment on mentally handicapped persons. However, there is no doubt that his statement sets out very clearly and fully the medical position so far as J is concerned. She is severely overweight, and an attempt to treat her menstrual conditions by hormones would exacerbate the obesity factor. No effective method of treating her unfortunate physical condition is possible which does not involve surgery. The consultant says in terms that the best treatment and, indeed, the only effective treatment in this case would be to perform a hysterectomy. In this case this would involve sterilising J.

I emphasise at once that it would not be the purpose of such an operation to sterilise J. It would be the inevitable and incidental result, however, of the hysterectomy operation which is recommended by the consultant gynaecologist.

J's parents are quite certain that they should accept the medical advice given to them. They are represented before me, and I am very grateful for the assistance of Mr Lane who appears for them. He makes it quite clear that as parents, so far as it rests within their power, they would consider it appropriate and, indeed, essential that they should responsibly grant their consent for such an operation to be carried out in the interests of the health of their daughter. She has been made the subject of a wardship summons solely in order that the matter can come before the court. I say at once that in the light of the evidence before me and the very careful analysis of her position by the Official Solicitor, who is her guardian ad litem, it is clearly in the interests of J that this operation should be carried out. I have no doubt whatsoever about the fact, and if it is necessary for the court to grant its formal consent to the doctors and her parents for that operation to be carried out, the court will very willingly grant that consent.

However, the issue which has been brought before the court is a somewhat different one. Mr Nicholls, for the Official Solicitor, submits that it is not necessary for the formal consent of the court to be granted in this case in order that the operation in question can be carried out. In a detailed skeleton argument, he has analysed what he submits is the correct legal position. This is a case where the operation is required for therapeutic reasons; it is in order to treat J therapeutically that the operation is said to be required. This is not a case where the objective is sterilisation. This is not a case where the doctors are saying that this young girl should be sterilised because it would be wrong for her to become pregnant. That is not the issue in this case, and I make that very clear. In this case, the submission is made to the court that it ought not to be necessary for a responsible doctor to have to seek the formal consent of the court for the carrying out of an operation which is required in order to treat the patient therapeutically.

It is quite clear that, in recent times, the medical profession has become very anxious about its legal position and possible legal liabilities. It was because of this climate of concern, if I may so describe it, that the Medical Defence Union advised Mr Robinson, the consultant in this case, that he should not swear an affidavit or take any step in this matter unless the court made an order in the wardship proceedings. Mr Nicholls, in an attempt to clarify the legal position of doctors and, indeed of parents placed in a similar position to the parents of J, decided that this matter should be clarified by an application to the court.

The case of *Re F* (1989) 4 BMLR 1, [1990] 2 AC 1, recently decided in the House of Lords, is, of course, the basis of the Medical Defence Union's position in this matter. However, that was a wholly different case on its facts, and it is to be observed that the House of Lords did not rule that the consent of the court was required by law. It stated that, as a matter of good practice, it would be wise for consent to be sought.

It is important that the medical profession should be clear about the position in such cases. I am satisfied, after the careful analysis which Mr Nicholls has presented to the court, that there is a clear distinction to be made between cases where an operation is required for genuine therapeutic reasons and those where the operation is designed to achieve sterilisation. That position was recognised by Lord Bridge in *Re F,* and I believe that it is the correct position in the present case. I think that J's parents are in a position to give a valid consent to the proposed operation. I am not dealing in this instance with the case of an adult; I am dealing with the case of a minor, and it is plainly desirable that in order to relieve the particular symptoms of her distressing condition, J should undergo this particular treatment. Accordingly, in this case, I rule that the consent of the court is not required for this operation to be carried out. It is necessary for therapeutic reasons. In any event, if it were to be considered necessary, I would have no hesitation in granting the court's consent.

This is a case where, after careful deliberation and consideration of all the medical factors, the consultant has come to the conclusion that this treatment is necessary for the relief of the condition from which this unfortunate girl suffers. Accordingly the court will rule and declare that on the facts of this case no formal consent is necessary.

F v F (1991) 7 BMLR 135 (Fam Div)

Sir Stephen Brown P: The court has before it a summons issued by the mother of a 29-year-old mentally handicapped woman. The Official Solicitor appears by counsel as the guardian ad litem of the woman in question.

The situation of the woman, to whom I shall refer by the initial G, is a sad one. She has been seriously disabled from birth. Although she is 29 years of age she has the mental age of a five-year-old. She has no sense of balance and is largely confined to a wheelchair. She lives with her parents, who are husband and wife, and it is her mother who had issued the summons before this court.

Unhappily she has suffered for many years from a distressing condition which in ordinary terms may be described as excessively heavy 'periods'. She is unable to take care of her own menstrual hygiene or basic sanitary care. She dreads having her period and is embarrassed and humiliated by the experience. The general practitioner who has been responsible for her care for many years became increasingly concerned about the effect upon G of this distressing condition. At the instance of her general practitioner she has consulted a consultant gynaecologist, who has also discussed the case with a colleague who is a consultant obstetrician and gynaecologist. The position is that her condition cannot be satisfactorily treated in order to provide relief by hormone treatment. In the opinion of all the doctors the only practicable method of treating this condition is by performing a hysterectomy with ovarian conservation. This would in fact have the incidental effect of sterilising the patient. However, the purpose of such treatment is not to achieve sterilisation; it is in order to treat her therapeutically for a condition which is becoming increasingly distressing and disturbing to this unfortunate young woman.

The mother has issued a summons seeking a declaration that the operation may lawfully be carried out. The Official Solicitor, who appears by counsel, has considered the situation with great care, having regard to the desirability of informing the medical profession of the legal position which arises in a case such as this. In a careful skeleton argument further developed orally by counsel before the court, the Official Solicitor has traced the cases on sterilisation, and submits that in this particular case, and in similar cases, where the purpose of the treatment is essentially therapeutic but which may incidentally result in sterilisation, the approval of the court is not necessary provided that two medical practitioners are satisfied that the operation in question is necessary for therapeutic purposes, and that it is in the best interests of the patient. Further, that there is no practicable less intrusive means of treating the condition from which the patient suffers. The Official Solicitor submits that if these criteria are satisfied then the treatment should be capable of being carried out without specific recourse to the court.

In the present case it is clear from the affidavit evidence of the general practitioner, together with the evidence of the consultant gynaecologist and the consultant obstetrician and gynaecologist, that hysterectomy with ovarian conservation is in the best interests of G, and that there does not exist any practicable less intrusive alternative means of treating her condition. It is clear, therefore, that the purpose of the proposed operation is essentially therapeutic and is not designed to achieve sterilisation.

I have no doubt that in this case if the law were to require the approval of the court for the carrying out of such an operation, that approval should be given, and I would make a declaration to that effect in the terms sought by the summons issued by the plaintiff mother. However, it appears to me that the submission of the Official Solicitor is validly made. That is to say, that in a case where the operation is necessary in order to treat the condition in question, it may be lawfully carried out even though it may have the incidental effect of sterilisation. It is appropriate, however, to indicate that the criteria to which I have already referred should be satisfied in any such case. I take the view that no application for leave to carry out such an operation needs to be made in cases where two medical practitioners are satisfied that the operation is, (1) necessary for therapeutic purposes, (2) is in the best interests of the patient, and (3) that there is no practicable less intrusive means of treating the condition.

I propose, therefore, to make a declaration at the invitation of the Official Solicitor in the following terms: that no application to the court is necessary as a matter of good medical practice for a declaration as to the lawfulness of a proposed therapeutic operation which would have the incidental effect of sterilisation of a woman who cannot consent thereto by reason of mental disability, where the operation is necessary in order to ensure the improvement of the health of the patient, or to prevent deterioration in her health.

In the present circumstances, therefore, the declaration sought by the plaintiff is not necessary, but I have in any event indicated that if I were wrong about that then I would have no hesitation in this case in making a declaration in the terms sought. It is quite clear that this operation should be carried out in order to safeguard the health of this unfortunate young woman.

You will notice that in *F v F* the judge imposed the requirement that the opinions of *two* doctors be sought. The basis for this is unclear unless it reflects the need to establish that a body of medical opinion approves of the procedure and hence that the *Bolam* test is satisfied. The final case involved an abortion rather than a procedure with the consequence of sterilising the young woman or girl.

Re SG (a minor) (1991) 6 BMLR 95 (Fam Div)

Sir Stephen Brown P: The court has before it two summons. Firstly there is an originating summons of 4 December 1990 issued by a young woman, Miss SG, by her father and next friend, Mr RG. The unhappy situation is that Miss SG is a 26 year old severely mentally handicapped woman with a mental age equivalent to a seven or eight year old child. She is looked after at home by her mother and father with assistance and attends an adult training centre for the mentally handicapped. The family is unfortunately further burdened with two other children who suffer from various degrees of mental handicap.

It became apparent recently that Miss SG was pregnant; and she is presently believed to be some 17 weeks pregnant. The general practitioner referred her to a consultant gynaecologist and both he and the general practitioner took the view that it would be in the best interests of Miss SG that her pregnancy should be terminated. It is necessary that any termination should be carried out at a specialist institution, and provisional arrangements have been made for it to be carried out next week on 11 December. The evidence before me is that if there were any delay beyond 11 December there might very well be complications causing pain, distress and other trauma to the applicant, Miss SG. It is therefore a matter of urgency.

Because of concern in the medical profession generally arising principally as a result of the recent decision of the House of Lords in the case of *F v West Berkshire Health Authority (Mental Health Act Commission intervening)* (1989) 4 BMLR 1, sub nom *Re F (mental patient: sterilisation)* [1990] 2 AC 1, the applicant by her father and next friend has felt it desirable to apply to the court for a declaration that it would be lawful in the existing circumstances to terminate the pregnancy of Miss SG despite her inability to give her personal consent to it by reason of her mental incapacity. The applicant appears to take the view that in law it may be necessary in the case of a proposed termination of pregnancy to obtain such a declaration. The medical termination of pregnancy is, however, regulated by the Abortion Act 1967. Section 1(1) provides for two conditions to be fulfilled if a pregnancy is to be terminated:

> Subject to the provisions of this section, a person shall not be guilty of an offence under the law relating to abortion when a pregnancy is terminated by a registered medical practitioner if two registered medical practitioners are of the opinion, formed in good faith – (a) that the continuance of the pregnancy would involve risk to the life of the pregnant woman or of injury to the physical or mental health of the pregnant woman or any existing children of her family, greater than if the pregnancy were terminated; or (b) that there is a substantial risk that if the child were born it would suffer from such physical or mental abnormalities as to be seriously handicapped.

Counsel has indicated to me that both those conditions are capable of being met in this case. Accordingly, the submission is made that that being so and having regard to the strict safeguards of the Abortion Act 1967, this is not a situation which should require a formal declaration from the High Court before the treatment can be carried out. It will be understood by those who have made themselves familiar with this branch of the law that it is a developing branch of the law; and I say that advisedly, because at present the Law Commission is considering the position generally in relation to the medical treatment of such persons and there is an extensive debate about the medical treatment of 'incapable' adults within the medical profession. The Medical Ethics Committee and the Mental Health Committee of the British Medical Association are currently considering their representations to the Law Commission.

In the case of *F v West Berkshire HA*, Lord Brandon, while dealing with a case of sterilisation – a very different type of operation – said in the course of his speech that, provided that the operation or treatment concerned is in the best interests of the patient, it may be lawfully carried out and that the common law would permit that to be done. However, as a matter of good practice, said Lord Brandon, the High Court should be asked to declare the lawfulness of proposed medical treatment which falls within a 'special category'. He indicated that sterilisation would fall within such a special category. The termination of pregnancy, on the other hand, has not been described by the House of Lords as being within a special category. I am told that the Master of the Rolls has indicated that he would be prepared so to describe it, but there is no decision about this particular matter.

The court has been assisted in this case by the Official Solicitor. Mr Nicholls has appeared upon this application and has made submissions, supported by an excellent skeleton argument, as to the position in law of the termination of pregnancy. The Official Solicitor submits that since the termination of pregnancy is already so closely regulated by statute, it is not essential as a matter of practice to seek a declaration from the High Court before carrying out such treatment. He emphasises that this is a very different form of treatment from sterilisation. Abortion, of course, raises emotive and sensitive issues. Having regard no doubt to these sensitivities this application has been made to this court for a declaration. However, the applicant, supported by the views of the Official Solicitor, has also issued a summons seeking alternatively a declaration that such a declaration as is envisaged in the case of a 'special category', is not required by this applicant in this case.

I have no doubt on the facts of this case that, if a declaration such as was considered in the case of *F v West Berkshire HA* is required as a matter of good practice, I should make it, but in the light of the present state of the law I accept the submissions of the Official Solicitor that it is not necessary that the specific approval of the High Court should be a condition precedent to the carrying out of a termination of pregnancy. I consider that the Abortion Act 1967 provides fully adequate safeguards for the doctors who are to undertake this treatment. Accordingly, I am prepared to indicate that in my judgment a formal declaration is not required for this particular treatment. However, it is important that I should also make it clear that the conditions of s 1 of the Abortion Act 1967 must be complied with.

I would add that it has to be borne in mind that in *F v West Berkshire HA* the view of the House of Lords was that such a declaration was desirable in cases falling within a 'special category' as a matter of good practice. No doubt the particular situation arising in cases of the termination of pregnancy will be considered in the Law Commission's current investigation and it may be that further guidelines will be issued by the Medical Ethics Committee of the British Medical Association in addition to recommendations which may be made by the Law Commission. For the time being, however, I express my view that a formal declaration is not required in this case such as was considered to be desirable in the case of *F v West Berkshire HA*. However, I also say that on the facts of this case if such a declaration were to be considered necessary I would be prepared to make it.

The net effect of these decisions, if they survive any future attack in the Court of Appeal, is that the court has resiled from any direct involvement in decision-making in any cases other than those with which Stephen Brown P describes as 'non-therapeutic' (see also, *Re H (mental patient)* (1992) 9 BMLR 71 (Fam Div) – declaration not necessary or desirable before carrying out a diagnostic procedure). The most obvious example of a non-therapeutic procedure is that of contraceptive sterilisation, but you will recall that Lord Brandon asked whether there might not be others in a 'special category'. One example of such case may be the removal of tissue from a healthy incompetent person (see, for example Neill LJ in *Re F* [1990] 2 AC 1 at 33 and Lord Bridge at 52).

(A similar concern for the proper role of the court, ie the desirability or otherwise of bringing a case to court has been expressed by some courts in the United States, particularly in the context of the care of the dying: see 1st edn, pp 963-967. See also the approach of the House of Lords in *Airedale NHS Trust v Bland* [1993] 1 All ER 821, (1993) 12 BMLR 64 discussed *infra*, ch 16.)

By contrast to our approach, the Law Commission in its Consultation Paper (no 129) of April 1993 (*op cit*) advances the view that certain medical procedures should be placed in a 'special category' and, as such, could *only* be authorised by the court.

Treatments in a 'special category'
1.   There should be a 'special category' of steps which require the approval of the judicial forum before they are taken in relation to an incapacitated person, except where the step is essential to prevent an immediate risk of serious harm to that person.

(i) Sterilisation operations
2.   Sterilisation operations, for the purpose of contraception or menstrual management, should be included in the special category.

(ii) Donation of tissue
3.   An operation to allow donation of non-regenerative tissue, or bone marrow, should be included in the special category.

(iii) Abortion
We invite views on whether abortion should be included in the special category (paragraph 6.10).

(iv) Withdrawals of nutrition and hydration
4.   The withdrawal of nutrition or hydration necessary for continuation of the patient's life should be included in the special category.

(v) Medical research
We invite views on whether some types of research should be included in the special category (paragraph 6.14).

(vi) Other decisions
We invite comment on whether any other treatments or any other decisions to withdraw treatment should be included in the special category (paragraph 6.15).

We doubt that the proposals should invest the courts with powers even greater than they have granted themselves, bearing in mind the controversial nature of the issues at stake and the proper reluctance of judges to be drawn into these issues. You will recall the remark of Brennan J in the *JWB* case that to require court intervention was 'disturbing in its social implications'.

(c) The appropriate role?

If the conclusion is accepted that the courts should not make it mandatory, and cannot make it desirable, that particular cases be brought before them for decision-making, what should be the court's role?

As we have seen, the first role is to establish the legal criteria which must inform a proxy's decision. Also, the second role is to review or exercise a supervisory jurisdiction over (within the strict limits which we have seen) the proxy's decision. What needs to be explored further, here, is the nature of the first role mentioned above. It is our view that in addition to setting criteria to govern a proxy's decision, the court has a further role. It must define areas of decision-making which do not fall within any proxy's power to decide. An obvious example of this would be that a proxy may not authorise the killing of the patient (see, *Re J (a minor) (wardship: medical treatment)* [1990] 3 All ER 930 at 936, per Lord Donaldson MR).

Perhaps the most distinctive device for indicating the outer limit placed upon a proxy's decision-making lies in the contrast between interventions which are *therapeutic* and those which are *non-therapeutic*. We would argue that, ordinarily, interventions which are non-therapeutic are impermissible in law. This is subject to certain exceptions, for example, in some cases of research (see *infra*, ch 14). The distinction was considered in the House of Lords in *Re B* and robustly rejected. Lord Hailsham remarked:

I find the distinction . . . between 'therapeutic' and 'non-therapeutic' purposes of this operation in relation to the facts of the present case above as totally meaningless, and, if meaningful, quite irrelevant to the correct application of the welfare principle.

Lord Bridge put it as follows:

To say that the court can never authorise sterilisation of a ward as being in her best interests would be patently wrong. To say that it can only do so if the operation is 'therapeutic' as opposed to 'non-therapeutic' is to divert attention from the true issue, which is whether the operation is in the ward's best interest, and remove it to an area of arid semantic debate as to where the line is to be drawn between 'therapeutic' and 'non-therapeutic' treatment.

Lord Oliver remarked:

Something was sought to be made of the description of the operation for which authority was sought in *Re D* as 'non-therapeutic', using the word 'therapeutic' as connoting the treatment of some malfunction or disease. The description was, no doubt, apt enough in that case, but I do not, for my part, find the distinction between 'therapeutic' and 'non-therapeutic' measures helpful in the context of the instant case, for it seems to me entirely immaterial whether measures undertaken for the protection against future and foreseeable injury are properly described as 'therapeutic'. The primary and paramount question is only whether they are for the welfare and benefit of this particular young woman situate as she is situate in this case.

In these speeches, their Lordships choose to turn their backs on the considered analysis of La Forest in *Re Eve* (1986) 31 DLR (4th) 1 (Canadian Sup Ct).

The validity of the distinction between therapeutic and non-therapeutic interventions was subsequently accepted by the Australian High Court in the *JWB and SMB* case. As we saw above, the majority of the court, though they thought the line between them was imprecise, nevertheless found it 'necessary to make the distinction'. (See also the judgment of McHugh J, set out *supra*, p 303 et seq.)

To say that the distinction between therapeutic and non-therapeutic exists and should be the basis of legal analysis is not to say that simply by relying on it, all problems are solved. If 'therapy' means that which is intended to produce benefit, the word 'benefit' then becomes the focus of attention. Some would say that it is not significantly different from acting in the 'best interests'. Furthermore, particularly in the context of alleged psychological benefit, benefit is capable of widely differing interpretations, as we saw above when discussing the US cases of *Bonner v Moran* (1941) 126 F 2d 121 (USCA DC); *Strunk v Strunk* (1969) 445 SW 2d 145; and *Curran v Bosze* (1990) 566 NE 2d 1319 (Illinois Sup Ct).

In the light of the views expressed by the Canadian Supreme Court and Australian High Court, it could therefore be argued that the House of Lords' rejection of the distinction is out of step. It could be said that the distinction is rejected out of a misunderstanding of its true basis. It is not entirely a descriptive distinction to be applied or not mechanistically to any particular intervention. This is because the distinction is also, in part, normative reflecting prior value judgments as to what types of medical interventions are legitimate and acceptable to society. A differing set of values are at the heart of the different results in *Re B* and *Re Eve*. The misunderstanding of the House of Lords in *Re B* is that they applied the simplistic 'best interests' approach, instead of proceeding in two stages. First, the court must determine in general terms the permissible limits of medical interventions. Secondly, the court must then determine whether the particular doctor did what he did with the intention of producing those permissible ends. The value of the distinction between therapeutic and non-therapeutic interventions is that ordinarily, *ex hypothesi*, the court will regard a therapeutic intervention as legitimate. By contrast the court will need to be persuaded that an intervention which has no therapeutic purpose is legitimate. (See the judgment of Brennan J in the *JWB and SMB* case, in which he emphasises the point that the issue is really a matter of judicial choice applying societal values rather than one of identifying the correct descriptive category into which the particular intervention falls without understanding the underlying basis for the categorisation. See further Chapter 10.)

It may be that the insistence of the Australian High Court on the distinction need not *in fact* produce any different result in any particular case from an application of the 'best interests' test. This is because the 'best interests' test also proceeds from judicial and societal values. The question then has to be put, if the result may be the same why should we be concerned? The answer is that the criterion of 'best interests' contains within it, as Brennan J is anxious to point out, virtually no explicit guidelines as to the values it embraces and thereby allows the court free rein and provides no guidance to proxy decision-makers. By contrast, the distinction between therapeutic and non-therapeutic causes the court to identify the values underlying the notion of treatment and then places a not inconsiderable burden on those who would engage in a non-therapeutic intervention to justify it. Finally, we may speculate that the true reason for the House of Lords' preference for the 'best interests' test rested on pragmatic rather than theoretical grounds. It may well be that their Lordships thought that the therapeutic/non-therapeutic distinction limited them to a consideration of medical matters whereas the 'best interests' test allowed a consideration of wider matters. Wanting the freedom to take account of non-medical factors, their Lordships opted for the 'best interests' approach. We have concentrated here on the sterilisation cases because these have been the cases in which the courts have, on the whole, sought to struggle with the question of the role of the court and that of others, for example parents. We will return to these, and other cases, in Chapter 10 when we consider the legality of sterilising incapable women and girls.

B. COMMON LAW JUSTIFICATION

We have been considering so far the role and authority of proxies or the court and the criteria to be applied by them in making decisions. We turn now to consider the situation in which, as regards the law as it stands, no one has authority to decide on behalf of an *incompetent adult*. If treatment is to be carried out, we must find some legal justification. It is a matter of commonsense, though until recently the law had not shown its hand, that it must be lawful to give medical treatment to an incompetent person in appropriate circumstances. Otherwise, the mentally disabled adult patient suffering from severe toothache would have to be left to suffer. Since 'the common law is commonsense under a wig' (per Lord Donaldson MR in *Re F (mental patient: sterilisation)* [1990] 2 AC 1 at 17), the question for the law is not *whether* treatment of the incompetent adult is lawful but *how it is to be justified*. It was not until 1989 that the House of Lords addressed this question of principle.

Re F (Mental Patient: Sterilisation) [1990] 2 AC 1, (1989) 4 BMLR 1 (HL)

A 36-year-old mentally handicapped woman, F, who resided as a voluntary in-patient in a mental hospital and who had the mental age of a small child, had formed a sexual relationship with a male patient. The hospital staff considered that she would be unable to cope with the effects of pregnancy and giving birth, and that, since all other forms of contraception were unsuitable and it was considered undesirable to further curtail F's limited freedom of movement in order to prevent sexual activity, it would be in her best interests to be sterilised. F's mother, who for the same reasons also wished her to be sterilised, issued an originating summons seeking a declaration from the court under RSC, Ord 15, R 16, that such an operation would not amount to an unlawful act by reason only of the absence of F's consent.

The judge granted the declaration sought. On appeal by the Official Solicitor, the Court of Appeal upheld the judge's order. In upholding the grant of the declaration Lord Goff explored the position at common law.

Lord Goff: I turn to consider the question whether, and if so when, medical treatment or care of a mentally disordered person who is, by reason of his incapacity, incapable of giving his consent, can be regarded as lawful. As is recognised in Cardozo J's statement of principle, and elsewhere (see eg *Sidaway v Board of Governors of the Bethlem Royal Hospital and the Maudsley Hospital* [1985] AC 871, 882, per Lord Scarman), some relaxation of the law is required to accommodate persons of unsound mind. In *Wilson v Pringle* [1987] QB 237, the Court of Appeal considered the treatment or care of such persons may be regarded as lawful, as falling within the exception relating to physical contact which is generally acceptable in the ordinary conduct of everyday life. Again, I am with respect unable to agree. That exception is concerned with the ordinary events of everyday life – jostling in public places and such like – and affects all persons, whether or not they are capable of giving their consent. Medical treatment – even treatment for minor ailments – does not fall within that category of events. The general rule is that consent is necessary to render such treatment lawful. If such treatment administered without consent is not to be unlawful, it has to be justified on some other principle.

Upon what principle can medical treatment be justified when given without consent? We are searching for a principle upon which, in limited circumstances, recognition may be given to a need, in the interests of the patient, that treatment should be given to him in circumstances where he is (temporarily or permanently) disabled from consenting to it. It is this criterion of a need which points to the principle of necessity as providing justification.

That there exists in the common law a principle of necessity which may justify action which would otherwise be unlawful is not in doubt. But historically the principle has been seen to be restricted to two cases of private necessity. The former occurred when a man interfered with another man's property in the public interest – for example (in the days before we could dial 999 for the fire brigade) the destruction of another man's house to prevent the spread of a catastrophic fire, and indeed occurred in the Great Fire of London in 1666. The latter cases occurred when a man interfered with another's property to save his own person or property from imminent danger – for example when he entered upon his neighbour's land without his consent, in order to prevent the spread of fire onto his own land.

There is, however, a third group of cases, which is also properly described as founded upon the principle of necessity and which is more pertinent to the resolution of the problem in the present case. These cases are concerned with action taken as a matter of necessity to assist another person without his consent. To give a simple example, a man who seizes another and forcibly drags him from the path of an oncoming vehicle, thereby saving him from injury or even death, commits no wrong. But there are many emanations of this principle, to be found scattered through the books. These are concerned not only with the preservation of the life or health of the assisted person, but also with the preservation of his property (sometimes an animal, sometimes an ordinary chattel) and even with certain conduct on his behalf in the administration of his affairs. Where there is a pre-existing relationship between the parties, the intervenor is usually said to act as an agent of necessity on behalf of the principal in whose interests he acts, and his action can often, with not too much artificiality, be referred to the pre-existing relationship between them. Whether the intervenor may be entitled either to reimbursement or to remuneration raises separate questions which are not relevant in the present case.

We are concerned here with action taken to preserve the life, health or well-being of another who is unable to consent to it. Such action is sometimes said to be justified as arising from emergency; in *Prosser and Keeton, Handbook on Torts,* 5th ed. (1984), p.117, the action is said to be privileged by the emergency. Doubtless, in the case of a person of sound mind, there will ordinarily have to be an emergency before such action taken without consent can be lawful for otherwise there would be an opportunity to communicate with the assisted person and to seek his consent. But this is not always so; and indeed the historical origins of the principle of necessity do not point to emergency as such as providing the criterion of lawful intervention without consent. The old Roman doctrine of negotiorum gestio presupposed not so much an emergency as a prolonged absence of the dominus from home as justifying intervention by the gestor to administer his affairs. The most ancient group of cases in the common law, concerned with action taken by the master of a ship in distant parts in the interests of the shipowner, likewise found its origin in the difficulty of communication with the owner over a prolonged period of time – a difficulty overcome today by modern means of communication. In those cases, it was said that there had to be an emergency before the master could act as agent of necessity; though the emergency could well be of some duration. But when a person is rendered incapable of communication either permanently or over a considerable period of time (through illness or accident or mental disorder), it would be an unusual use of language to describe the case as one of 'permanent emergency' – if indeed such a state of affairs can properly be said to exist. In truth, the relevance of an emergency is that it may give rise to a necessity to act in the interests of the assisted person, without first obtaining his consent. Emergency is however not the criterion or even a pre-requisite; it is simply a frequent origin of the necessity which impels intervention. The principle is one of necessity, not of emergency.

We can derive some guidance as to the nature of the principle of necessity from the cases on agency of necessity in mercantile law. When reading those cases, however, we have to bear in mind that it was (since there was a pre-existing relationship between the parties) there was a duty on the part of the agent to act on his principal's behalf in an emergency. From these cases it appears that the principle of necessity connotes that circumstances have arisen in which there is a necessity for the agent to act on his principle's behalf at a time when it is in practice not possible for him to obtain his principal's instructions so to do. In such cases, it has been said that the agent must act bona fide in the interests of his principal: see *Prager v Blatspiel Stamp & Heacock Ltd* [1924] 1 KB 566, 572 *per* McCardie J. A broader statement of the principle is to be found in the advice of the Privy Council delivered by Sir Montague Smith in *Australasian Steam Navigation Co v Morse* (1872) LR 4 PC 222, 230, in which he said:

> when by the force of circumstances a man has the duty cast upon him of taking some action for another, and under that obligation, adopts the course which, to the judgment of a wise and prudent man, is apparently the best for the interest of the persons for whom he acts in a given emergency, it may properly be said of the course so taken, that it was, in a mercantile sense, necessary to take it.

In a sense, these statements overlap. But from them can be derived the basic requirements, applicable in these cases of necessity, that, to fall within the principle, not only (1) must there be a necessity to act when it is not practicable to communicate with the assisted person, but also (2) the action taken must be such as a reasonable person would in all the circumstances take, acting in the best interests of the assisted person.

On this statement of principle, I wish to observe that officious intervention cannot be justified by the principle of necessity. So intervention cannot be justified when another more appropriate person is available and willing to act; nor can it be justified when it is contrary to the known wishes of the assisted person, to the extent that he is capable of rationally forming such a wish. On the second limb of the principle, the introduction of the standard of a reasonable man should not in the present context be regarded as materially different from that of Sir Montague Smith's 'wise and prudent man', because a reasonable man would, in the time available to him, proceed with wisdom and prudence before taking action in relation to another man's person or property without his consent. I shall have more to say on this point later. Subject to that, I hesitate at present to indulge in any greater refinement of the principle, being well aware of many problems which may arise in its application – problems which it is not necessary, for present purposes, to examine. But as a general rule, if the above criteria are fulfilled, interference with the assisted person's person or property (as the case may be) will not be unlawful. Take the example of a railway accident, in which injured passengers are trapped in the wreckage. It is this principle which may render lawful the actions of other citizens – railway staff, passengers or outsiders – who rush to give aid and comfort to the victims: the surgeon who amputates the limb of an unconscious passenger to free him from the wreckage; the ambulance man who conveys him to hospital; the doctors and nurses who treat him and care for him while he is still unconscious. Take the example of an elderly person who suffers a stroke which renders him incapable of speech or movement. It is by virtue of this principle that the doctor who treats him, the nurse who cares for him, even the relative or friend or neighbour who comes in to look after him, will commit no wrong when he or she touches his body.

The two examples I have given illustrate, in the one case, an emergency, and in the other, a permanent or semi-permanent state of affairs. Another example of the latter kind is that of a mentally disordered person who is disabled from giving consent. I can see no good reason why the principle of necessity should not be applicable in his case as it is in the case of the victim of a stroke. Furthermore, in the case of a mentally disordered person, as in the case of a stroke victim, the permanent state of affairs calls for a wider range of care than may be requisite in an emergency which arises from accidental injury. When the state of affairs is permanent, or semi-permanent, action properly taken to preserve the life, health or well-being of the assisted person may well transcend and may extend to include such humdrum matters as routine medical or dental treatment, even simple care such as dressing and undressing and putting to bed.

The distinction I have drawn between cases of emergency, and cases where the state of affairs is (more or less) permanent, is relevant in another respect. We are here concerned with medical treatment, and I limit myself to cases of that kind. Where, for example, a surgeon performs an operation without his consent on a patient temporarily rendered unconscious in an accident, he should do no more than is reasonably required, in the best interests of the patient, before he recovers consciousness. I can see no practical difficulty arising from this requirement, which derives from the fact that the patient is expected before long to regain consciousness and can then be consulted about longer term measures. The point has however arisen in a more acute form where a surgeon, in the course of an operation, discovers some other condition which, in his opinion, requires operative treatment for which he has not received the patient's consent. In what circumstances he should operate forthwith, and in what circumstances he should postpone the further treatment until he has received the patient's consent, is a difficult matter which has troubled the Canadian Courts (see *Marshall v Curry* [1933] 3 DLR 260, and *Murray v McMurchy* [1949] 2 DLR 442), but which it is not necessary for your Lordships to consider in the present case.

But where the state of affairs is permanent or semi-permanent, as may be so in the case of a mentally disordered person, there is no point in waiting to obtain the patient's consent. The need to care for him is obvious; and the doctor must then act in the best interests of his patient, just as if he had received his patient's consent so to do. Were this not so, much useful treatment and care could, in theory at least, be denied to the unfortunate. It follows that, on this point, I am unable to accept the view expressed by Neill LJ in the Court of Appeal, at 32C-H that the treatment must be shown to have been necessary. Moreover, in such a case, as my noble and learned friend Lord Brandon of Oakbrook has pointed out, a doctor who has assumed responsibility for the care of a patient may not only be treated as having the patient's consent to act, but may also be under a duty so to act. I find myself to be respectfully in agreement with Lord Donaldson of Lymington MR, when he said, at 18D-E:

> I see nothing incongruous in doctors and others who have a caring responsibility being required to act in relation to an adult who is incompetent to exercise a right of choice in exactly the same way as would the court or reasonable parents in relation to a child, making due allowance of course for the fact that the patient is not a child, and I am satisfied that that is what the law does in fact require.

In these circumstances, it is natural to treat the deemed authority and the duty as interrelated. But I feel bound to express my opinion that, in principle, the lawfulness of the doctor's action is, at least in its origin, to be found in the principle of necessity. This can perhaps be seen most clearly in cases where there is no continuing relationship between doctor and patient. The 'doctor in the house' who volunteers to assist a lady in the audience who, overcome by the drama or by the heat in the theatre, has fainted away, is impelled to act by no greater duty than that imposed by his own Hippocratic oath. Furthermore, intervention can be justified in the case of a non-professional, as well as a professional, man or woman who has no pre-existing relationship with the assisted person – as in the case of a stranger who rushes to assist an injured man after an accident. In my opinion, it is the necessity itself which provides the justification for the intervention.

I have said that the doctor has to act in the best interests of the assisted person. In the case of routine treatment of mentally disordered persons, there should be little difficulty in applying this principle. In the case of more serious treatment, I recognise that its application may create problems for the medical profession; however, in making decisions about treatment, the doctor must act in accordance with a responsible and competent body of relevant professional opinion, on the principles set down in *Bolam v Friern Hospital Management Committee* [1957] 1 WLR 582. No doubt, in practice, a decision may involve others besides the doctor. It must surely be good practice to consult relatives and others who are concerned with the care of the patient. Sometimes, of course, consultation with a specialist or specialists will be required; and in others, especially where the decision involves more than a purely medical opinion, an inter-disciplinary team will in practice participate in the decision. It is very difficult, and would be unwise for a court to do more than to stress that, for those who are involved in these important and sometimes difficult decisions, the overriding consideration is that they should act in the best interests of the person who suffers from the misfortune of being prevented by incapacity from deciding for himself what should be done to his own body, in his own best interests.

Lords Bridge, Brandon and Jauncey concurred with Lord Goff. Lord Griffiths also concurred on this point.

If the legal justification is the principle of necessity, what test did Lord Goff lay down as the means of determining when treatment would be lawful? Lord Goff decided that the test should be the 'best interests' of the patient. You will notice that Lord Goff decided that a doctor would act 'in the best interests' of a patient if 'a responsible and competent body of relevant professional opinion' would support the doctor's conduct, ie the *Bolam* test. What Lord Goff means by this is that a doctor will behave reasonably when he intervenes to treat an incompetent patient if the *Bolam* test is satisfied. It should be added, however, that Lord Goff placed a gloss upon the *Bolam* test by setting the criteria which must inform the view of the 'responsible and competent body' of medical opinion. Lord Goff identified the criteria as being the 'life, health or well-being' of the patient.

Even more clearly Lord Brandon stated that:

> The operation or other treatment will be in their best interests if, but only if, it is carried out in order either to save their lives, or to ensure improvement or prevent deterioration in their physical or mental health.

Before proceeding to examine how this test of 'best interests' is to be applied in particular circumstances of incompetence, it may be worthwhile to enquire whether Lord Goff's decision to found his judgment on the *Bolam* principle is satisfactory. As we shall see, it can be said that the *Bolam* test hands over to doctors power to establish the legal duty a doctor owes to his patient (*Sidaway v Governors of Bethlem Royal Hospital* [1985] 1 All ER 643 at 649 per Lord Scarman). At the heart of the *Bolam* test is the flawed assumption that the court is concerned with a matter of purely medical judgment. Expert opinion of proper professional practice thus resolves the issue of what a reasonable doctor should do. Arguably, when the issue is whether a reasonable doctor *should* have a lawful justification for treating an adult patient who is incapable of consenting, more than a purely medical judgment is called for. Professional opinion is certainly relevant but should not be determinative (see *infra*, ch 5). Arguably, the court should reserve to itself the ultimate role of determining whether intervention is justified and should, therefore, set a legal test which is less deferential to professional practice.

Lord Mustill put it as follows in *Airedale NHS Trust v Bland* [1993] 1 All ER 821 at 898, when examining the weight to be given to the views of doctors in determining when treatment should end.

> **Lord Mustill:** . . . I venture to feel some reservations about the application of the principle of civil liability in negligence laid down in [*Bolam*] to decisions on 'best interests' in a field dominated by the criminal law. I accept without difficulty that this principle applies to the ascertainment of the medical raw material such as diagnosis, prognosis and appraisal and patient's cognitive functions. Beyond this point, however, it may be said that the decision is ethical, not medical, and there is no reason in logic why on such a decision the opinions of doctors should be decisive.

(Lord Goff (with whom the others agreed) applied *Re F*.)

Curiously, given his acceptance of *Bolam*, Lord Goff in *Re F*, at the same time, seemed to recognise that the court did indeed have a role:

> **Lord Goff:** It was urged before your Lordships by Mr Ouseley, on behalf of the Mental Health Act Commission (the Commission having been given leave to intervene in the proceedings), that a court vested with the responsibility of making a decision in such a case, having first ensured that an independent second opinion has been obtained from an

appropriate consultant of the appropriate speciality, should not, if that second opinion supports the proposal that sterilisation should take place, exercise any independent judgment but should simply follow the opinion so expressed. For my part, I do not think that it is possible or desirable for a court so to exercise its jurisdiction. In all proceedings where expert opinions are expressed, those opinions are listened to with great respect; but, in the end, the validity of the opinion has to be weighed and judged by the court. This applies as much in cases where the opinion involves a question of judgment as it does in those where it is expressed on a purely scientific matter. For a court automatically to accept an expert opinion, simply because it is concurred in by another appropriate expert, would be a denial of the function of the court. Furthermore, the proposal of the Commission is impossible to reconcile with the American and Australian authorities which stress the need for a court decision after a hearing which involves separate representation on behalf of the person upon whom it is proposed to perform the operation. Having said this, I do not feel that the Commission need fear that the opinions of the experts will in any way be discounted. On the contrary, they will be heard with the greatest respect; and, as the present case shows, there is a high degree of likelihood that they will be accepted.

In the Court of Appeal, Neill LJ (with whom Butler-Sloss LJ agreed) also recognised what to him were the drawbacks of applying *Bolam* here:

Neill LJ: With respect, I do not consider that this test is sufficiently stringent. A doctor may defeat a claim of negligence if he establishes that he acted in accordance with a practice accepted at the time as proper by a responsible body of medical opinion skilled in the particular form of treatment in question. This is the test laid down in *Bolam v Friern Hospital Management Committee* [1957] 1 WLR 582. But to say that it is not negligent to carry out a particular form of treatment does not mean that that treatment is necessary. I would define necessary in this context as that which the general body of medical opinion in the particular specialty would consider to be in the best interests of the patient in order to maintain the health and to secure the well-being of the patient. One cannot expect unanimity but it should be possible to say of an operation which is necessary in the relevant sense that it would be unreasonable in the opinion of most experts in the field not to make the operation available to the patient. One must consider the alternatives to an operation and the dangers or disadvantages to which the patient may be exposed if no action is taken. The question becomes: what action does the patient's health and welfare require?

You will notice that Neill LJ still looks to professional practice though, for him, the 'general body' of medical opinion must approve of the intervention rather than 'a' body of medical opinion.

A test even less deferential to medical opinion was suggested in the first case to consider the legality of medical intervention and incompetent adults. In *T v T* [1988] Fam 52 the test which Wood J opted for was whether good medical practice 'demands' intervention. The case concerned the legality of a sterilisation and abortion to be performed on a 19-year-old severely mentally disabled woman.

Wood J: In the light of an inability to obtain consent from anyone, a surgeon who performs an operation without his patient's express or implied consent would be liable for trespass to the person – an assault and battery – a tortious remedy. . . I pose myself the question: is there any basis upon which the court can declare such an assault to be justified? . . . I prefer to approach the problem in this way. This defendant is never going to be able to consent – we are not dealing with a temporary inability such as a person under an anaesthetic. I compare the Canadian cases *Marshall v Curry* [1933] 3 DLR 260 and *Murry v McMurchy* [1949] 2 DLR 442, and there is no one in a position to consent. A medical adviser must therefore consider what decisions should be reached in the best interests of his patient's health. What does medical practice demand?

I use the word 'demand' because I envisage a situation where based upon good medical practice there are really no two views of what course is for the best. Upon the facts of this case I accept the medical evidence that not only would it be contrary to the defendant's best interests to postpone these proposed procedures, but it is positively in her best interests to proceed with due despatch.

It might be argued that the sterilisation could reasonably be postponed for further consideration, and indeed, that was my own first reaction, but after hearing argument I am quite satisfied that the risks to the defendant of a second operation, coupled with the doubts whether it could in fact be achieved in the light of her strength and inability to understand, are such as to be unacceptable, and I have no doubt that her best interests demand that all appropriate procedures to this end are carried out at the same time as the termination. . . .

I am convinced, as are all the lay and professional persons involved in this case, that it is in the best interests of the first defendant that these procedures should be carried through and I have made the declarations which were sought. I am content to rely upon the principle that in these exceptional circumstances where there is no provision in law for consent to be given and therefore there is no one who can give the consent, and where the patient is suffering from such mental abnormality as never to be able to give such consent, a medical adviser is justified in taking such steps as good medical practice 'demands' in the sense that I have set it out above and on that basis it is that I have made the declaration sought.

Whatever the merits of departing to some extent from the *Bolam* test, Lord Goff's flirtation with this approach was not indulged in by the other members of the House of Lords. The four other Law Lords tested the legality of an intervention solely on the basis of the *Bolam* test (*per* Lord Bridge at 52; Lord Brandon at 66-67; Lord Griffiths at 69; Lord Jauncey at 83-84).

An explanation of this reluctance to go beyond *Bolam* lies in the judges' desire to link the scope of a doctor's duty to his incompetent patient with the scope of the legal justification for *treating* an incompetent patient. Since the former is to be judged on the basis of the *Bolam* test, so must the latter. Lord Brandon put it thus:

In many cases, however, it will not only be lawful for doctors, on the ground of necessity, to operate on or give other medical treatment to adult patients disabled from giving their consent; it will also be their common law duty to do so.

In the case of adult patients made unconscious by an accident or otherwise, they will normally be received into the casualty department of a hospital, which thereby undertakes the care of them. It will then be the duty of the doctors at that hospital to use their best endeavours to do, by way of either an operation or other treatment, that which is in the best interests of such patients.

Reiterating this approach of mirroring the doctor's duty to his patient in the test for judging the legality of the intervention, Lord Bridge stated:

It would be intolerable for members of the medical, nursing and other professions devoted to the care of the sick that, in caring for those lacking the capacity to consent to treatment they should be put in the dilemma that, if they administer the treatment which they believe to be in the patient's best interests, acting with due skill and care, they run the risk of being held guilty of trespass to the person, but if they withhold that treatment, they may be in breach of a duty of care owed to the patient. If those who undertake responsibility for the care of incompetent or unconscious patients administer curative or prophylactic treatment which they believe to be appropriate to the patient's existing condition of disease, injury or bodily malfunction or susceptibility to such a condition in the future, the lawfulness of that treatment should be judged by one standard, not two. It follows that if the professionals in question have acted with due skill and care, judged by the well known test laid down in *Bolam v Friern Hospital Management Committee* [1957] 1 WLR 582, they should be immune from liability in trespass, just as they are immune from liability in negligence.

There are a number of objections to this view. First, it presumes that there is a pre-existing duty owed by a doctor to the incompetent person. Although usually such a duty will be owed, there are circumstances in which this will not be the case, as Lord Goff pointed out:

. . . I feel bound to express my opinion that, in principle, the lawfulness of the doctor's action is, at least in its origin, to be found in the principle of necessity. This can perhaps be seen most clearly in cases where there is no continuing relationship between doctor and patient. The 'doctor in the house' who volunteers to assist a lady in the audience who, overcome by the drama or by the heat in the theatre, has fainted away, is impelled to act by no greater duty than that imposed by his own Hippocratic oath. Furthermore, intervention can be justified in the case of a non-professional, as well as a professional, man or woman who has no pre-existing relationship with the assisted person – as in the case of a stranger who rushes to assist an injured man after an accident. In my opinion, it is the necessity itself which provides the justification for the intervention.

Thus, to define the scope of the justification for intervention in terms of the pre-existing duty would be to limit the justification too narrowly.

Secondly, whatever the position as regards duty, to express the scope of the justification in terms of *Bolam* effectively makes what is an issue of legal principle become a matter of medical evidence. That is to say that whether conduct is justified must rest on principle not on professional practice.

Thirdly, it could be argued that the judges were unduly blinded by the language of duty. The primary issue should be, first, whether the intervention is legal and, secondly, whether the doctor is in breach of his duty to the patient. So, if the patient were competent a precondition would be the need for the patient's consent. Here, given that the patient is incompetent, his consent cannot be a precondition. Nevertheless, some other legal criterion could be necessary in lieu of the patient's consent to reflect a respect for the patient's rights, for example, that the treatment is 'demanded' or supported by a *substantial* body of medical opinion. In any event, some criterion which goes beyond the *Bolam* test should be employed.

Having considered the principles on which the justification for intervention may be based it is helpful to refer to the three types of situation in which medical intervention may take place: (1) emergencies; (2) the temporarily incompetent; (3) the permanently incompetent. While the principle remains the same in each of these, the application may vary in the sense that greater intervention may be justified in, for instance, the case of the permanently incompetent than the temporarily incompetent.

1. Emergencies

As Lord Goff states in *Re F*:

> Emergency is however not the criterion or even a pre-requisite; it is simply a frequent origin of the necessity which impels intervention. The principle is one of necessity, not of emergency.

Lord Goff gave examples of the situations in which an emergency would justify medical intervention:

> Take the example of a railway accident, in which injured passengers are trapped in the wreckage. It is this principle which may render lawful the actions of other citizens – railway staff, passengers or outsiders – who rush to give aid and comfort to the victims: the surgeon who amputates the limb of an unconscious passenger to free him from the wreckage; the ambulance man who conveys him to hospital; the doctors and nurses who treat him and care for him while he is still unconscious.

In the Court of Appeal in *Re F*, Butler-Sloss LJ explained the emergency situation as follows:

> **Butler-Sloss LJ:** Logically the well known exception of emergency or necessity might be difficult to justify. It is, however, well-established by decisions both in the United States and Canada. In *Pratt v Davis* (1906) 224 Ill 300, 309, Scott CJ said:

Emergencies arise, and when a surgeon is called it is sometimes found that some action must be taken immediately for the preservation of the life or health of the patient, where it is impracticable to obtain the consent of the ailing or injured one or of anyone authorised to speak for him. In such event, the surgeon may lawfully, and it is his duty to, perform such operation as good surgery demands, without such consent.

Chisholm CJ in *Marshall v Curry* [1933] 3 DLR 260, 275, ruled:

it is the surgeon's duty to act in order to save the life or preserve the health of the patient; and that in the honest execution of that duty he should not be exposed to legal liability.

He found that the removal of a diseased testicle by the surgeon was:

in the interest of his patient and for the protection of his health and possibly his life. The removal I find was in that sense necessary, and it would be unreasonable to postpone the removal to a later date.

In *Murray v McMurchy* [1949] 2 DLR 442, where the decision went the other way, Macfarlane J said at pp.443-444:

I think the law is clear that if that [sterilisation operation] were necessary as opposed to being convenient, for the protection of the life or even for the preservation of the health of the patient, the surgeon would be entitled to take the intended procedure.

The Court of Appeal in *Wilson v Pringle* [1987] QB 237 interpreted the category formulated by Robert Goff LJ of 'all physical contact which is generally acceptable in the ordinary conduct of daily life' to include an emergency operation on an unconscious patient. I find difficulty in accepting that interpretation and would prefer to see the emergency cases as a separate category based on the American approach that, in situations where a patient of full mental competence is unable to give consent, an operation necessary for the preservation of life or for the preservation of health of the patient not only can but should be performed. It does not appear to me to be based on implied consent but on public policy that it is in the public interest that unconscious patients requiring emergency treatment should be able to receive it and that doctors giving it should not be liable in tort.

Neill LJ also considered emergencies.

Neill LJ: To the general rule that the patient's consent must be obtained before an operation can be carried out there is one well-recognised exception. Thus, if a patient is unconscious and therefore unable to give or to withhold his consent, emergency medical treatment which may include surgical procedures can be lawfully carried out. Indeed, once the care of the patient has been assumed by, for example, admission into hospital, a failure to give necessary treatment may well be a ground for complaint. The treatment which can be so given, however, is, within broad limits, confined to such treatment as is necessary to meet the emergency and such as needs to be carried out at once and before the patient is likely to be in a position to make a decision for himself . . .

For my part, I would prefer to explain the emergency cases on the basis that it is in the public interest that an unconscious patient who requires treatment should be able to receive it and that those who give this treatment in an emergency should be free from any threat of an action for trespass to the person.

You will notice that Neill LJ is careful to identify the limits to that which may be justified in an emergency, ie that it is both *necessary* and *cannot be reasonably delayed*.

2. The temporarily incompetent

In a sense, the analysis of this category may be no different from emergencies, namely that a temporarily incompetent may only be treated to the extent that it is both necessary and cannot reasonably be delayed. Lord Goff considered (though left open) this category in *Re F*.

Lord Goff: Where, for example, a surgeon performs an operation without his consent on a patient temporarily rendered unconscious in an accident, he should do no more than is reasonably required, in the best interests of the patient, before he recovers consciousness. I can see no practical difficulty arising from this requirement, which derives from the fact that the patient is expected before long to regain consciousness and can then be consulted about longer term measures. The point has however arisen in a more acute form where a surgeon, in the course of an operation, discovers some other condition which, in his opinion, requires operative treatment for which he has not received the patient's consent. In what circumstances he should operate forthwith, and in what circumstances he should postpone the further treatment until he has received the patient's consent, is a difficult matter which has troubled the Canadian Courts (see *Marshall v Curry* [1933] 3 DLR 260, and *Murray v McMurchy* [1949] 2 DLR 442), but which it is not necessary for your Lordships to consider in the present case.

The Canadian cases referred to by Lord Goff and Butler Sloss LJ (above) probably reflect English law. Ellen Picard explains the Canadian law in her textbook *Legal Liability of Doctors and Hospitals in Canada* (2nd edn, 1984) (pp 45-46):

In *Marshall v Curry* [1933] 3 DLR 260, the doctor discovered a grossly diseased testicle in the course of a hernia repair operation. He removed the testicle, firstly because it was necessary for the hernia repair, and secondly because he judged it potentially gangrenous and therefore a menace to the patient's life and health. Because the patient was under general anaesthetic, the doctor proceeded without consent, and subsequently was sued for battery. Prior to this case it had been held that in emergencies, the doctor became the patient's representative with authority to give his consent on the patient's behalf. Here the court refused to employ this reasoning and instead justified the doctor's action in emergency circumstances on 'the higher ground of duty'. The Chief Justice of Nova Scotia said that 'where a great emergency which could not be anticipated arises' a doctor can act without consent in order to save the life or preserve the health of the patient. The action against the doctor was dismissed.

However, in *Murray v McMurchy* [1949] 2 DLR 442 (BCSC), a doctor who tied a patient's fallopian tubes because he had discovered fibroid tumours in the uterine wall during a Caesarian section, and was concerned about the hazards of a second pregnancy, was held liable. The trial judge found that while it was convenient to carry out the procedure at that time, there was no evidence that the tumours were an immediate danger to the patient's life or health.

Similarly, in *Parmley v Parmley and Yule* [1945] 4 DLR 81 (SCC), in which a patient requested the removal of two teeth and the defendant dentist extracted all of her upper teeth because he found advanced tooth decay and pyorrhoea in the gums, the court held the dentist liable. Again there was no evidence of emergency and thus no basis for proceeding without consent. However, an important *obiter* comment was made in the case:

There are times under circumstances of emergency when both doctors and dentists must exercise their professional skill and ability without the consent which is required in the ordinary case. Upon such occasions *great latitude may be given to the doctor or dentist* [emphasis supplied].

A reconciliation of these cases leads to the principle that consent is unnecessary only where the procedure or treatment is required in order to save life or preserve health. Consent is required on all other occasions and it is no answer for the doctor to say that it was more convenient to perform the unauthorised procedure at that time or that he believed it was then that the patient would have wanted it done.

In short, our Canadian courts differentiate between a procedure that is 'necessary' and one that is 'convenient'.

3. The permanently incompetent

Here, the very situation considered in *Re F*, the range of interventions justified in law may be greater because the doctor cannot wait and see what the patient may subsequently be prepared to consent to. In *Re F* Lord Goff acknowledged this.

Lord Goff: Take the example of an elderly person who suffers a stroke which renders him incapable of speech or movement. It is by virtue of this principle that the doctor who treats him, the nurse who cares for him, even the relative or friend or neighbour who comes in to look after him, will commit no wrong when he or she touches his body . . .

Another example . . . is that of a mentally disordered person who is disabled from giving consent. I can see no good reason why the principle of necessity should not be applicable in his case as it is in the case of the victim of a stroke. Furthermore, in the case of a mentally disordered person, as in the case of a stroke victim, the permanent state of affairs calls for a wider range of care than may be requisite in an emergency which arises from accidental injury. When the state of affairs is permanent, or semi-permanent, action properly taken to preserve the life, health or well-being of the assisted person may well transcend such measures as surgical operation or substantial medical treatment and may extend to include such humdrum matters as routine medical or dental treatment, even simple care such as dressing and undressing and putting to bed . . . where the state of affairs is permanent or semi-permanent, as may be so in the case of a mentally disordered person, there is no point in waiting to obtain the patient's consent. The need to care for him is obvious; and the doctor must then act in the best interests of his patient, just as if he had received his patient's consent so to do. Were this not so, much useful treatment and care could, in theory at least, be denied to the unfortunate.

Importantly, you may notice an inconsistency between the court's apparent adoption of the *Bolam* test as setting the scope of the justification and what the court says as regards intervention in an emergency and where the patient is only temporarily incompetent. As regards the later situations, *the court* sets limits as to what is permissible. By so doing, the court enumerates the criteria which determine the legality of intervention. In any particular case, medical opinion will determine whether these criteria were in fact met, ie whether it was proper for the doctor to consider that the patient's life was threatened or that the treatment could be delayed. The onus, therefore, is thrust upon the doctor to demonstrate that there was an emergency in the sense defined by the courts. By contrast, as regards the permanently incompetent, arguably Lord Goff relies entirely upon the *Bolam* test.

Before we leave this discussion of *Re F*, there is one point of general importance that we should deal with.

The analysis so far has proceeded upon the basis of the language used by the court in *Re F*: the language of *necessity*. Arguably, it is possible to understand this area of law by recourse to a more general, but at the same time, more familiar justification, namely that of the *public interest*. The significance of seeing the justification of medical interventions on the incompetent adult as depending on the public interest is that it focuses attention upon the need to balance conflicting interests. These must not be seen as the interests of the individual (private interests) as against the interests of society (public interests). Rather, the conflict or tension must be seen as being between competing *public* interests, ie the public interest in protecting the bodily integrity of a patient as against the public interest in caring for a patient who cannot care for himself. Neill LJ's judgment in *Re F* is significant here.

Neill LJ: For my part, I would prefer to explain the emergency cases on the basis that it is in the public interest that an unconscious patient who requires treatment should be able to receive it and that those who give this treatment in an emergency should be free from any threat of an action for trespass to the person . . .

The law in this field is concerned to achieve a balance between different rights and duties. The doctor who has undertaken the care of a patient is under a duty to offer such appropriate treatment as is available. The patient has the right to be offered that treatment, though the conscious patient over the age of 16 has the right, certainly in the vast majority of cases, either to accept or to refuse it. Where, however, the patient is unconscious, the right either to accept or to refuse the treatment is valueless. Moreover, except in the case of a child, there is in the ordinary way no one who is able to exercise the right on the patient's behalf. In such circumstances the public interest in my judgment provides the justification for the treatment.

Of course, others may argue for another set of general principles – those of human rights. These do not so readily allow for balancing, although some balancing at some point cannot be avoided. Reliance on human rights alerts us to the danger intrinsic in the process of balancing whereby the balance will be struck in a way which gives inadequate weight to the individual patient's interests.

Balancing of interests is unavoidable in the case of treating the incompetent. If the overarching principle is that of regard for the *public interest*, involving a balancing of competing interests, there is a real danger that *the same balancing process*, used in the context of the incompetent patient, may be prayed in aid also in the case of the *competent patient*. The consequences could be that a competent patient who is refusing treatment could be required to submit to treatment on the grounds that it was in the public interest that the treatment be given. Lord Donaldson MR adopted this approach in *Re T (refusal of treatment)* [1992] 4 All ER 649 (see *infra*, p 342).

C. UNDER STATUTE

By way of example, the Mental Health Act 1983 and the National Assistance Act 1948 are briefly discussed here.

1. Mental Health Act 1983

The Mental Health Act 1983, s 63 reads as follows:

Treatment not requiring consent
63. The consent of a patient shall not be required for any medical treatment given to him for the mental disorder from which he is suffering, not being treatment falling within section 57 or 58 above, if the treatment is given by or under the direction of the responsible medical officer.

Notice that treatment is limited to medical treatment 'for the mental disorder from which he is suffering' and is limited to patients 'liable to be detained' under the MHA 1983 (see *T v T* [1988] 1 All ER 613 at 617, [1988] Fam 52 at 57, per Wood J).

Any treatment falling within s 57 may only be given with the consent of the patient and a 'second opinion'. Consequently, it may not be carried out on the incompetent, subject to its not being 'urgent treatment' under s 62. The treatments covered by s 57 are psychosurgery and, by Regulation, the surgical implantation of hormones to reduce male sexual drive (Mental Health (Hospital, Guardianship and Consent to Treatment) Regulations 1983, SI 1983 No 893, Reg 16): see discussion in *R v Mental Health Act Commission, ex p X* (1988) 9 BMLR 77 (QBD). Section 58 covers the administration of medicines for longer than three months and, by the above Regulations, electro-convulsive therapy (ECT). As regards these treatments, s 58 does permit them to be administered to the incompetent provided that (by s 58(3)(b)) a second medical opinion confirms that:

the patient is not capable of understanding the nature, purpose and likely effects of that treatment . . . but that, having regard to the likelihood of its alleviating or preventing a deterioration of his condition, the treatment should be given.

Further, the Mental Health Act 1983 also includes a provision which represents a statutory example of the principle of necessity. Section 62 provides that:

Urgent treatment
62.(1) Sections 57 and 58 above shall not apply to any treatment–
(a) which is immediately necessary to save the patient's life; or
(b) which (not being irreversible or hazardous) is immediately necessary to prevent a serious deterioration in his condition; or
(c) which (not being irreversible) is immediately necessary to alleviate serious suffering by the patient; or
(d) which (not being irreversible or hazardous) is immediately necessary and represents the minimum interference necessary to prevent the patient from behaving violently or being a danger to himself or to others.
(2) Sections 60 and 61(3) above shall not preclude the continuation of any treatment or of treatment under any plan pending compliance with section 57 or 58 above if the responsible medical officer considers that the discontinuance of the treatment or of treatment under the plan would cause serious suffering to the patient.
(3) For the purposes of this section treatment is irreversible if it has unfavourable irreversible physical or psychological consequences and hazardous if it entails significant physical hazard.

(For a detailed discussion of the 1983 Act see B Hoggett *Mental Health Law* (3rd edn) (1990) and L Gostin *Mental Health Services: Law and Practice* (1986) passim.)

2. National Assistance Act 1948

Removal to suitable premises of persons in need of care and attention

47. (1) The following provisions of this section shall have effect for the purposes of securing the necessary care and attention for persons who –
(a) are suffering from grave chronic disease or, being aged, infirm or physically incapacitated, are living in insanitary conditions, and
(b) are unable to devote to themselves, and are not receiving from other persons, proper care and attention.
(2) If the medical officer of health certifies in writing to the appropriate authority that he is satisfied after thorough inquiry and consideration that in the interests of any such person as aforesaid residing in the area of the authority, or for preventing injury to the health of, or serious nuisances to, other persons, it is necessary to remove any such person as aforesaid from the premises in which he is residing, the appropriate authority may apply to a court of summary jurisdiction having jurisdiction in the place where the premises are situated for an order under the next following subsection.
(3) On any such application the court may, if satisfied on oral evidence of the allegations in the certificate, and that it is expedient so to do, order the removal of the person to whom the application relates, by such officer of the appropriate authority, as may be specified in the order, to a suitable hospital or other place in, or within convenient distance of, the area of the appropriate authority, and his detention and maintenance therein.
Provided that the court shall not order the removal of a person to any premises, unless either the person managing the premises has been heard in the proceedings or seven clear days' notice has been given to him of the intended application and of the time and place at which it is proposed to be made.
(4) An order under the last foregoing subsection may be made so as to authorise a person's detention for any period not exceeding three months, and the court may from time to time by order extend that period for such further period, not exceeding three months, as the court may determine.

(5) An order under subsection (3) of this section may be varied by an order of the court so as to substitute for the place referred to in that subsection such other suitable place in, or within convenient distance of, the area of the appropriate authority as the court may determine, so however that the proviso to the said subsection (3) shall with the necessary modification apply to any proceedings under this subsection.

(6) At any time after the expiration of six clear weeks from the making of an order under subsection (3) or (4) of this section an application may be made to the court by or on behalf of the person in respect of whom the order was made, and on any such application the court may, if in the circumstances it appears expedient so to do, revoke the order.

(7) No application under this section shall be entertained by the court unless, seven clear days before the making of the application, notice has been given of the intended application and of the time and place at which it is proposed to be made –

(a)   where the application is for an order under subsection (3) or (4) of this section, to the person in respect of whom the application is made or to some person in charge of him,

(b)   where the application is for the revocation of such an order, to the medical officer of health.

(8) Where in pursuance of an order under this section a person is maintained neither in hospital accommodation provided by the Minister of Health under the National Health Service Act 1977 or by the Secretary of State under the National Health Service (Scotland) Act 1978, nor in premises where accommodation is provided by, or by arrangement with, a local authority under Part III of this Act, the cost of his maintenance shall be borne by the appropriate authority.

(9) Any expenditure incurred under the last foregoing subsection shall be recoverable from the person maintained or from any person who for the purposes of this Act is liable to maintain that person; and any expenditure incurred by virtue of this section in connection with the maintenance of a person in premises where accommodation is provided under Part III of this Act shall be recoverable in like manner as expenditure incurred in providing accommodation under the said Part III.

(10) [*Repealed for England and Wales by the National Health Service Reorganisation Act 1973, s 57, Sched 5.*]

(11) Any person who wilfully disobeys, or obstructs the execution of an order under this section shall be guilty of an offence and liable on summary conviction to a fine not exceeding ten pounds.

(12) For the purposes of this section, the appropriate authorities shall be the councils of districts and London boroughs and the Common Council of the City London [. . .], and in Scotland the councils of [regions and islands areas].

(13) The foregoing provisions of this section shall have effect in substitution for any provisions for the like purposes contained in, or having effect under, any public general or local Act passed before the passing of this Act:

Provided that nothing in this subsection shall be construed as affecting any enactment providing for the removal to, or detention in, hospital of persons suffering from notifiable or infectious diseases.

(14) Any notice under this section may be served by post.

The first question is, does s 47 extend to the *incompetent* person? Secondly, does it allow for medical treatment of a person coming within this section? Brenda Hoggett writes in her *Mental Health Law* (3rd edn) at 133:

What does an order allow?
The Acts are by no means clear about what may be done with the person once he has been removed. Section 47(1) of the 1948 Act declares that the purpose of the provisions is to secure 'the necessary care and attention' for the people concerned; and section 47(3) provides that the court may order their removal to the hospital or home, and their 'detention and maintenance therein'. It seems that the [amending] 1951 Act was expressly passed because a doctor had been unable to persuade a person with a broken leg to go to hospital for treatment. Yet the Acts say nothing about imposing medical treatment, as opposed to care, attention and maintenance, without the patient's consent. In this they are very like the Mental Health Act 1959, which seems to have assumed that getting the patient to hospital was the only problem; what happened once he was there could safely be left to the clinical judgment of the doctors. Nowadays, however, we are very much less inclined to read such powers into statutes which do not expressly contain them . . . and it would be most unwise to go beyond the limits of what is permitted by these Acts and by the common law.

(Reform of this area of law is proposed by the Law Commission in its Consultation Paper No 130 (1993): *Mentally Incapacitated Adults and Decision-Making: Public Law.*)

Treating without consent: the competent

Given the law's concern to protect the individual from unwanted invasion of his body and given the law's recognition that consent in the case of the competent patient is the legal safeguard to protect his interest, it could be argued that treatment of a *competent* patient without consent is only lawful if specifically provided for by statute (and then, perhaps, subject to the overarching provisions of the European Convention of Human Rights and Fundamental Freedoms). That being the case, we should examine the law, particularly the extent to which the *common law* may in fact permit treatment without consent.

A. BY STATUTE

Let us first see what (if any) statutory provisions allow for treatment without consent (compulsory treatment) of the competent. We consider three significant examples of legislative action.

1. Mental Health Act 1983

As regards this Act, two preliminary points must be noticed when the question is raised concerning the treatment of competent persons without their consent. First, not all those who are 'liable to be detained' (and who are subject to detention) under the Act, are by that reason alone incompetent. Secondly, it is clear from the Act that if indeed treatment can be given without consent, it can only under the Act be treatment for the relevant mental disorder, and not for other conditions requiring medical treatment.

Section 63 of the Act allows any treatment, not being within ss 57 and 58, to be given without the consent of the patient. Presumably, this envisages the giving of treatment *against the refusal* of even a competent patient. Section 63 of the Mental Health Act 1983 provides:

> *Treatment not requiring consent*
> 63. The consent of a patient shall not be required for any medical treatment given to him for the mental disorder from which he is suffering, not being treatment falling within section 57 or 58 above, if the treatment is given by or under the direction of the responsible medical officer.

Section 57 (dealing with psychosurgery and by Regulation, the surgical implantation of hormones to reduce male sexual drive, is not relevant here since it does require consent) need not detain us. By s 58, however, treatment in the form of the long-term administration of medicine, that is beyond three months, or electro-convulsive therapy, may be administered either with the consent of the patient or – importantly for our purposes here – without consent (presumably again in the face of dissent) in the following circumstances:

> S. 58 (3) Subject to section 62 below, a patient shall not be given any form of treatment to which this section applies unless –
>
> . . .
>
> (b) a registered medical practitioner appointed as aforesaid (not being the responsible medical officer) has certified in writing that the patient is not capable of understanding the nature, purpose and likely effects of that treatment or has not consented to it but that, having regard to the likelihood of its alleviating or preventing a deterioration of his condition, the treatment should be given.

2. Public Health (Control of Diseases) Act 1984

As its name suggests, this Act is concerned with the control of disease rather than with treatment. It is concerned primarily with the interests of the public who are not ill rather than with any particular person who may be ill. Section 37 provides as follows:

> *Removal to hospital of person with notifiable disease*
> **37.** (1) Where a justice of the peace (acting, if he deems it necessary, *ex parte*) is satisfied, on the application of the local authority, that a person is suffering from a notifiable disease and –
> (a) that his circumstances are such that proper precautions to prevent the spread of infection cannot be taken, or that such precautions are not being taken, and
> (b) that serious risk of infection is thereby caused to other persons, and
> (c) that accommodation for him is available in a suitable hospital vested in the Secretary of State or, pursuant to arrangements made by a District Health Authority (whether under an NHS contract or otherwise), in a suitable hospital vested in a NHS Trust or other person,
> the justice may, with the consent of the District Health Authority in whose district lies the area, or the greater part of the area, of the local authority, order him to be removed to it.
>   (2) An order under this section may be addressed to such officer of the local authority as the justice may think expedient, and that officer and any officer of the hospital may do all acts necessary for giving effect to the order.

Similarly, s 38 provides power to detain someone already in hospital and suffering from a notifiable disease, if on leaving the hospital they would not have accommodation in which proper precautions could be taken to prevent the spread of the disease. (Notifiable diseases are cholera, plague, relapsing fever, smallpox and typhus: s 10.)

You will notice that s 37 does not specifically authorise treatment without consent. Arguably, such a power to treat without consent must be expressly given since such a power would override the basic principles of the common law having to do with the inviolability of the person, but notice s 13 of the 1984 Act:

> *Regulations for control of certain diseases*
> **13.** (1) Subject to the provisions of this section, the Secretary of State may, as respects the whole or any part of England and Wales, including coastal waters, make regulations –
> (a) with a view to the treatment of persons affected with any epidemic, endemic or infectious disease and for preventing the spread of such diseases.

Again, arguably, these Regulations, if they were to provide for compulsory treatment, would be *ultra vires* given that the Act is ambiguous and therefore must be read not to affect fundamental rights (see *R v Hallstram, ex p W (No 2)* [1986] QB 1090, (1985) 2 BMLR 73 at 83 per McCullough J).

The Act also makes provision for the *examination* of any person found in [a common lodging-house] with a view to ascertaining whether he is suffering, or has recently suffered, from a notifiable disease (s 40). The section is restricted to granting a power to *examine*; this should not be interpreted as authorising *treatment* without consent. Regulations were promulgated by the Secretary of State under the Public Health (Control of Diseases) Act 1984 so as to apply s 37 to those suffering from AIDS as if it were a notifiable disease (see now Public Health (Infectious Diseases) Regulations 1988, SI 1988 No 1546).

The same question arises here as we saw earlier: does this authorise compulsory treatment of the person suffering from AIDS? This particular provision is curious in at least two respects. First, it refers to those only suffering from AIDS and not to those infected with HIV. *If* a police power under the Public Health Regulations were needed, it is rather odd that it does not extend to the person who potentially poses a greater threat than the actual suffer from AIDS, ie the still healthy HIV-infected person. Secondly, the provision may be a response to hysteria since the threat possessed by AIDS to public health is of a different order calling for different responses.

For an extended discussion of the issues of policy in England and the USA concerning HIV and AIDS, see I Kennedy and A Grubb 'HIV and AIDS: Discrimination and the Challenge For Human Rights', in A Grubb (ed) *Challenges in Medical Care* (1992) and Sullivan and Field, 'AIDS and the Coercive Power of the State' (1988) 23 Harv CR – CLLRev 139 and see *supra*, ch 2.

3. National Assistance Act 1948, s 47

Removal to suitable premises of persons in need of care and attention

47. (1) The following provisions of this section shall have effect for the purposes of securing the necessary care and attention for persons who –
(a) are suffering from grave chronic disease or, being aged, infirm or physically incapacitated, are living in insanitary conditions, and
(b) are unable to devote to themselves, and are not receiving from other persons, proper care and attention.
(2) If the medical officer of health certifies in writing to the appropriate authority that he is satisfied after thorough inquiry and consideration that in the interests of any such person as aforesaid residing in the area of the authority, or for preventing injury to the health of, or serious nuisance to, other people, it is necessary to remove any such person as aforesaid from the premises in which he is residing, the appropriate authority may apply to a court of summary jurisdiction having jurisdiction in the place where the premises are situated for an order under the next following subsection.
(3) On any such application the court may, if satisfied on oral evidence of the allegations in the certificate, and that it is expedient so to do, order the removal of the person to whom the application relates, by such officer of the appropriate authority, as may be specified in the order, to a suitable hospital or other place in, or within convenient distance of, the area of the appropriate authority, and his detention and maintenance therein;
Provided that the court shall not order the removal of a person to any premises, unless either the person managing the premises has been heard in the proceedings or seven clear days' notice has been given to him of the intended application and of the time and place at which it is proposed to be made.
(4) An order under the last foregoing subsection may be made so as to authorise a person's detention for any period not exceeding three months, and the court may from time to time by order extend that period for such further period, not exceeding three months, as the court may determine.

Again, this statute does not appear to authorise the treatment of a person to whom the section has been applied, without that person's consent (see *supra*, p 330).

For a discussion of the 1948 Act see B Hoggett *Mental Health Law* (3rd edn, 1990). For proposals for reform in this area see Law Commission, Consultation

Paper No 130, *Mentally Incapacitated Adults and Decision-Making: Public Law* (1993).

B. THE COMMON LAW: ADULTS

1. The general principle

The traditional view must be that if a person is competent he may refuse treatment and it would then be unlawful to attempt to treat him because this would amount to the tort of battery and a crime. It would appear to follow that there is no public policy justifying the treatment of the competent against their wishes. This may, however, be easier to accept where the person is obviously competent and/or his condition is not one which is life- (?limb-) threatening. There is, however, a tendency in all of us, and perhaps more so in doctors, to want to treat even though the person refusing is apparently competent, when it is clear that the person's life is threatened or there is very grave risk to his health. How has the law responded to this? In a few early cases there was a tendency in the courts to avoid attacking head on the principle of the inviolability of the person and instead choosing, by and large, to cast doubt on the competence of the person whose *decision* is in question. This had the purported merit of preserving the principle while acting beneficently towards the individual. If, however, it constitutes an improper manipulation of the concept of competence it does the law no credit (see *supra*, ch 3). Let us consider first the case of *Leigh v Gladstone*.

Leigh v Gladstone (1909) 26 TLR 139 (King's Bench Div Ct)

Lord Alverstone CJ: This was an action claiming damages for assault and for an injunction to restrain a repetition of the acts complained of, brought by Mrs Marie Leigh against the Right Hon Herbert Gladstone, MP (the Home Secretary), Captain Percy Green, Governor of Winson-Green Prison, Birmingham, and Dr Ernest Haslar Helby, the Medical Officer of the same prison. The defence was that the acts complained of were necessary in order to save the plaintiff's life, and that the *minimum* of force necessary was used. The matter arose out of the forcible feeding in prison of the plaintiff, who had been convicted of resisting the police and disturbing a meeting held by Mr Asquith, in connexion with the woman's franchise movement.

. . . . It was the duty, both under the rules and apart from the rules, of the officials to preserve the health and lives of the prisoners, who were in the custody of the Crown. If they forcibly fed the plaintiff when it was not necessary, the defendants ought to pay damages. The plaintiff did not complain – and it did her credit – of any undue violence being used towards her. The medical evidence was that at the time she was first fed it had become dangerous to allow her to abstain from food any longer.

You many think that this is a product of its time and its circumstances, namely suffragettes seeking to gain the vote in the early part of the twentieth century. Even if its authority is restricted to those who are imprisoned, it can be doubted whether it still represents the law (see 877 HC Debs Col 451, 17 July 1974). A more recent Canadian case has added its weight to the general disapproval of *Leigh v Gladstone*. In *A-G of British Columbia v Astaforoff* [1983] 6 WWR 322, Bouck J (at first instance), in factual circumstances similar to *Leigh* held that:

As I see it, my responsibility is to decide whether, under the particular circumstances of this case, there is a legal duty cast upon the province to force-feed the respondent against her will in order to prevent her from committing suicide. If there is this duty, then should I make the order compelling the prison to carry it out?

I am aware of the responsibility of the court to preserve the sanctity of life. It is a moral as well as a legal duty. However, in the circumstances of this case the facts are against the motion of the Attorney General for Canada. The prisoner has a long history of fasting. Her health is very poor. There is the danger that she might die by the applying of the procedure necessary to get nutrients into the stomach. She is free to leave the prison, but chooses to remain there and starve herself to death. Given these facts, I cannot find that it is reasonable that the Attorney General for British Columbia and the prison authorities under his direction should force-feed her in order to prevent her suicide.

If she becomes unconscious or incapable of making a rational decision, that is another matter. Then she will be unable to make a free choice. But while she is lucid no law compels the provincial officers to apply force to her against her will.

On appeal, the British Columbia Court of Appeal ([1984] 4 WWR 385), in upholding Bouck J, found that there was no duty to feed the prisoner. The court left open, however, whether there was a power to treat such that in any subsequent action brought by the prisoner, there might have been a defence justifying the intervention.

Although the *Astaforoff* case undercuts the reasoning of *Leigh v Gladstone*, it still leaves the argument that a doctor *may* act to save a patient's life without consent. However, in *Airedale NHS Trust v Bland* [1993] 1 All ER 821, Lord Keith (at 861) appears to have rejected the proposition when he stated that the principle of the sanctity of life 'does not authorise forcible feeding of prisoners on hunger strike'.

The duty to treat postulated in *Leigh v Gladstone* seems to have surfaced in *R v Stone* [1977] QB 354, [1977] 2 All ER 341, (CA). In his book, *Law, Ethics and Medicine*, at 113-114 Professor Skegg comments on this case:

The deceased, who lived with the defendants, suffered from anorexia nervosa. She made it clear that she did not want any medical assistance, and there was no reason to believe that she would have consented to medical treatment. The jury found that the defendants had assumed a duty of care for the deceased, and that a failure to fulfil this duty resulted in the death. In upholding the conviction for manslaughter, the Court of Appeal appears to have assumed that it was open to the defendants, or to a doctor, to disregard the wishes of the 'victim'. But in this and the other prosecutions there does not appear to have been any consideration of what a coroner once spoke of as 'an absolute principle that a person of full age and consciousness is entitled to refuse treatment by a doctor'.

It does not follow from the fact that a doctor, or anyone else, is under a duty to provide medical treatment (or food) that there is an entitlement – much less, an obligation – to administer that treatment (or feed) irrespective of the views of the patient. The doctor who was responsible for the victim in *R v Blaue* ([1975] 1 WLR 1411) undoubtedly owed her a duty of care, and in the circumstances would have been in breach of that duty if he had not given her the opportunity of having a blood transfusion. But there was no suggestion that he was therefore obliged, or even permitted, to administer it without consent.

Skegg goes on to discuss in a footnote the later case of *R v Smith* [1979] Crim LR 251, where he says (at 114):

'Griffiths J did at least recognise that the wishes of the deceased might be relevant. But he left it to the jury 'to balance the weight that it is right to give to his wife's wish to avoid calling in a doctor against her capacity to make rational decisions', and added 'if she does not appear too ill it may be reasonable to abide by her wishes. On the other hand, if she appeared desperately ill then whatever she may say it may be right to override.'

Griffiths J's emphasis upon Mrs Smith's state of mind and consequent capacity may offer the true explanation of *Stone*. It can be said that the deceased in *Stone* relied upon the defendants to care for her and they assumed the duty to do so, thereafter, she became incompetent and so her protests could not absolve them of their duty (see in support of this approach Lord Keith in *Airedale NHS Trust v Bland* [1993] 1 All ER 821 at 861).

Peter Skegg in *Law, Medicine and Ethics (op cit)* goes on to examine cases involving suicide in which the courts have considered whether a duty to prevent suicidal behaviour exists.

> In all but the most exceptional circumstances, a doctor may not carry out treatment involving the bodily touching of a patient who is capable of consenting, if the patient's consent has not been sought, or if the patient has refused to give consent. The fact that, without the treatment, the patient's health will suffer will not of itself justify a doctor in overriding the patient's refusal. Indeed, in many circumstances, even the certainty that the patient will die if treatment is not given will not justify a doctor in proceeding without consent.
>
> However, there is at least one exception to the general rule that consent is required. Where someone has done something in an apparent attempt to kill himself, doctors will often be justified in taking action to avert the consequences of the action. Prior to the abolition of the offence of suicide, there was no difficulty in explaining the legal basis for a doctor acting to prevent a person from attempting to commit suicide, or to avoid death resulting from such an attempt. Suicide was a felony, so the doctor was simply exercising the general liberty to prevent a felony. [*R v Duffy* [1967] 1 QB 63 at 67] Doctors were not only free to prevent someone from committing suicide; they were sometimes under a duty to do so. [*Thorne v Northern Group Management Committee* (1964) 108 Sol Jo 484] However, since the enactment of the Suicide Act 1961 it has continued to be accepted that doctors are sometimes free – sometimes, indeed, under a duty* – to prevent patients from committing suicide.
>
> In some cases, the person who has apparently attempted to commit suicide will be suffering from a mental disorder which prevents the giving or withholding of consent. But in many cases the person will have a sufficient understanding to give, or withhold, consent. This is so, even though the act will often result from a passing impulse or temporary depression, rather than from a rational and fixed decision. If restrained and given assistance, the majority are glad that their action did not result in death. Hence, even if it is accepted that a person should not be prevented from carrying out a calm or a reasoned decision to terminate his own life, there is an overwhelming case for intervention where there is reason to believe that, if given help, the person will be glad he did not kill, or seriously injure, himself. Doctors are constantly intervening in these circumstances and there can be little doubt that, were their conduct to be questioned, the courts would hold it justified.
>
> Where the need for life-saving treatment does not result from any act of the patient taken with a view to ending his own life, it is normally accepted that a doctor is bound by the patient's refusal of consent. Hence in *R v Blaue* [[1975] 1 WLR 1411] where the assailant's victim was a Jehovah's Witness who refused to consent to the blood transfusion that was necessary to save her life, there was no suggestion that the doctor would have been justified in overriding her refusal of consent. In one case a patient recovered nominal damages from a doctor who performed a life-saving operation on her, despite her refusal of consent. Such conduct would often amount to a criminal assault, and there would be the possibility of obtaining an injunction restraining further treatment.

> *   *Selfe v Ilford and District Hospital Management Committee* (1970) 114 Sol Jo 935, (1970) *Times,* 26 November, [1970] 4 *Br Med J* 754. In *Hyde v Tameside Area Health Authority,* [1981] CLY 1854, CA, (1981) 282 *Med J* 1716-17, the plaintiff had attempted to commit suicide while a patient in hospital. He became a tetraplegic in consequence of the attempt, and Anthony Lincoln J awarded him damages of £200,000. The Court of Appeal allowed the defendant's appeal, Lord Denning MR, Watkins LJ, and O'Connor LJ, all agreeing that on the evidence no breach of duty had been established. No member of the court suggested that there was never a duty to prevent suicide, although Lord Denning MR was of the view that on grounds of public policy the personal representative of someone who had committed suicide, or the person himself if his attempt does not succeed, should not be permitted to claim damages. The other members of the court did not express such a view. See also *Hopital Notre-Dame v Dame Villemure* [1970] Que SC 528 revsd: *sub nom Villemure v L'Hopital Notre-Dame* (1972) 31 DLR (3d) 454: *Haines v Bellissimo* (1977) 82 DLR (3d) 215. [See now *Kirkham v Chief Constable of Greater Manchester* [1990] 2 QB 283.]

Surely Professor Skegg is not right in asserting that a doctor is '. . . under a duty . . . to prevent patients from committing suicide . . .'. Unless his proposition is limited to the incompetent, he contradicts himself when he goes on to say:

> If, from the fact that a doctor had a duty of care to a patient, it followed that he was entitled to administer necessary treatment without consent, the right to refuse treatment would be severely curtailed. Although some cases appear to have proceeded on the assumption that there is such an entitlement, the courts are unlikely to adopt expressly so undesirable a doctrine. For the most part doctors should not administer even life-saving treatment if the patient refuses consent and no one else is authorised to give it.

Not surprisingly, courts in the United States have had to consider the legality of treating a competent patient who refuses to consent. As we will see later in Chapter 17, this issue often arises in the context of a dying patient. Here, it is important to identify the general principles, and, in the main, we will consider cases concerned with situations where the patient's life is only at risk because of his refusal of the particular treatment (but he is not otherwise dying), for example, a blood transfusion refused upon religious grounds. These cases, in fact, test the strength of the legal principles because the law is faced with a patient whose life *could* be saved.

Bouvia v Superior Court (1986) 225 Cal Rptr 297 (Cal CA)

Associate Justice Beach:. . . Petitioner is a 28-year-old woman. Since birth she has been afflicted with and suffered from severe cerebral palsy. She is quadriplegic. She is now a patient at a public hospital maintained by one of the real parties in interest, the County of Los Angeles. Other parties are physicians, nurses and the medical and support staff employed by the County of Los Angeles. Petitioner's physical handicaps of palsy and quadriplegia have progressed to the point where she is completely bedridden. Except for a few fingers of one hand and some slight head and facial movements, she is immobile. She is physically helpless and wholly unable to care for herself. She is totally dependent upon others for all of her needs. These include feeding, washing, cleaning, toileting, turning, and helping her with elimination and other bodily functions. She cannot stand or sit upright in bed or in a wheelchair. She lies flat in bed and must do so the rest of her life. She suffers also from degenerative and severely crippling arthritis. She is in continual pain. Another tube permanently attached to her chest automatically injects her with periodic doses of morphine which relieves some, but not all of her physical pain and discomfort.

She is intelligent, very mentally competent. She earned a college degree. She was married but her husband has left her. She suffered a miscarriage. She lived with her parents until her father told her that they could no longer care for her. She has stayed intermittently with friends and at public facilities. A search for a permanent place to live where she might receive the constant care which she needs has been unsuccessful. She is without financial means to support herself and, therefore, must accept public assistance for medical and other care.

She has on several occasions expressed the desire to die. In 1983 she sought the right to be cared for in a public hospital in Riverside County while she intentionally 'starved herself to death'. A court in that county denied her assistance to accomplish that goal. She later abandoned an appeal from that ruling. Thereafter, friends took her to several different facilities, both public and private, arriving finally at her present location. Efforts by the staff of real party in interest County of Los Angeles and its social workers to find her an apartment of her own with publicly paid live-in help or regular visiting nurses to care for her, or some other suitable facility have proved fruitless.

Petitioner must be spoon fed in order to eat. Her present medical and dietary staff have determined that she is not consuming a sufficient amount of nutrients. Petitioner stops eating when she feels she cannot orally swallow more, without nausea and vomiting. As she cannot now retain solids, she is fed soft liquid-like food. Because of her previously announced resolve to starve herself, the medical staff feared her weight loss might reach a life-threatening level. Her weight since admission to real parties' facility seems to hover between 65 and 70 pounds. Accordingly, they inserted the subject tube against her will and contrary to her express written instructions.

. . . a patient has the right to refuse *any* medical treatment, even that which may save or prolong her life. (*Barber v Superior Court* 147 Cal App 3d 1006, 195 Cal Rptr 484 (1983); *Bartling v Superior Court* 163 Cal App 3d 186, 209 Cal Rptr 220 (1984).) In our view the foregoing authorities are dispositive of the case at bench. Nonetheless, the county and its medical staff contend that for reasons unique to this case, Elizabeth Bouvia may not exercise the right available to others. Accordingly, we again briefly discuss the rule in the light of real parties' contentions.

The right to refuse medical treatment is basic and fundamental. It is recognised as a part of the right of privacy protected by both the state and federal constitutions. (Calif Const, art I, para 1; *Griswold v Connecticut* 381 US 479, 484, 85 S Ct 1678, 1681, 14 L Ed 2d 510 (1965); *Bartling v Superior Court, supra,* 163 Cal App 3d 186, 209 Cal Rptr 220.) Its exercise requires no one's approval. It is not merely one vote subject to being overridden by medical opinion.

In *Barber v Superior Court, supra,* 17 Cal App 3d 1006, 195 Cal Rptr 484, we considered this same issue although in a different context. Writing on behalf of this division, Justice Compton thoroughly analysed and reviewed the issue of withdrawal of life-support systems beginning with the seminal case of *Quinlan* 355 A 2d 647, *cert den* 429 US 922, 97 S Ct 319, L Ed 2d 289, (NJ, 1976) and continuing on to the then recent enactment of the California Natural Death Act (Health & Saf Code. ss 7185-7195). His opinion clearly and repeatedly stresses the fundamental underpinning of its conclusion, ie, the patient's right to decide: 147 Cal App 3d at page 1015, 195 Cal Rptr 484. 'In this state a clearly recognised legal right to control one's own medical treatment predated the Natural Death Act. A long line of cases, approved by the Supreme Court in *Cobbs v Grant* 8 Cal 3d 229 [104 Cal Rptr 505, 502 P 2d 1 (1972)] . . . have held that where a doctor performs treatment in the absence of an informed consent, there is an actionable battery. The obvious corollary to this principle is that *a competent adult patient has the legal right to refuse medical treatment*' (emphasis added); 147 Cal App 3d at page 1019, 195 Cal Rptr 484, '[T]he *patient's interests and desires are the key* ingredients of the decision-making process' (emphasis added); at page 1020, 105 Cal Rptr 484, 'Given the general standards for determining when there is a duty to provide medical treatment of debatable value, the question still remains as to who should make these vital decisions. Clearly, the medical diagnoses and prognoses must be determined by the treating and consulting physicians under the generally accepted standards of medical practice in the community and, *whenever possible, the patient himself should then be the ultimate decisionmaker*' (emphasis added); at page 1021, 195 Cal Rptr 484, 'The authorities are in agreement that any surrogate, court appointed or otherwise, ought to be guided in his or her decisions first by his knowledge of *the patient's own desires* and feelings, to the extent that they were expressed before the patient became incompetent.' (Emphasis added.)

Bartling v Superior Court, supra, 163 Cal App 3d 186, 209 Cal Rptr 220, was factually much like the case at bench. Although not totally identical in all respects, the issue there centred on the same question here present: ie, 'May the patient refuse even life continuing treatment?' Justice Hastings, writing for another division of this court, explained: 'In this case we are called upon to decide whether a competent adult patient, with serious illnesses which are probably incurable but have not been diagnosed as terminal, has the right, over the objection of his physicians and the hospital, to have life-support equipment disconnected despite the fact that withdrawal of such devices will surely hasten his death.' (At p 189, 209 Cal Rptr 220.) '(1) Mr Bartling's illnesses were serious but not terminal, and had not been diagnosed as such; (2) although Mr Bartling was attached to a respirator to facilitate breathing, he was not in a vegetative state and was not comatose; and (3) Mr Bartling was competent in the legal sense. . . . The court below concluded that as long as there was some potential for restoring Mr Bartling to a "cognitive, sapient life", it would not be appropriate to issue an injunction in this case. We conclude that the trial court was incorrect when it held that the right to have life-support equipment disconnected was limited to comatose, terminally ill patients, or representatives acting on their behalf.' (At p 193, 209 Cal Rptr 220.)

The description of Mr Bartling's condition fits that of Elizabeth Bouvia. The holding of that case applies here and compels real parties to respect her decision even though she is not 'terminally' ill. The trilogy of *Cobbs v Grant, supra* 8 Cal 3d 229, 104 Cal Rptr 505, 502 P 2d 1, *Barber v Superior Court, supra,* 147 Cal App 3d 1006, 195 Cal Rptr 484, and *Bartling v Superior Court, supra,* 163 Cal App 3d 186, 209 Cal Rptr 220, with their thorough explanation and discussion, are authority enough and in reality provides a complete answer to the position and assertions of real parties' medical personnel.

But if additional persuasion be needed, there is ample. As indicated by the discussion in *Bartling* and *Barber*, substantial and respectable authority throughout the country recognises the right which petitioner seeks to exercise. Indeed, it is neither radical nor startlingly new . . .

Further recognition that this right is paramount to even medical recommendation, is evidenced by several declarations of public and professional policy which were noted in both the *Barber* and *Bartling* cases.

For example, addressing one part of the problem, California passed the 'Natural Death Act', Health and Safety Code sections 7185 et seq. Although addressed to terminally ill patients, the significance of this legislation is its expression as state policy 'that adult persons have the fundamental right to control the decisions relating to the rendering of their own medical care . . .'. (Health & Saf Code, s 7186.) Section 7188 provides the method whereby an adult person may execute a directive for the withholding or withdrawal of life-sustaining procedures. Recognition of the right of other persons who may not be terminally ill and may wish to give other forms of direction concerning their medical care is expressed in section 7193: 'Nothing in this chapter shall impair or supersede any legal right or legal responsibility which any person may have to effect withholding or withdrawal of life-sustaining procedures in any lawful manner. In such respect the provisions of this chapter are cumulative.'

Moreover, as the *Bartling* decision holds, there is no practical or logical reason to limit the exercise of this right to 'terminal' patients. The right to refuse treatment does not need the sanction or approval by any legislative act, directing how and when it shall be exercised.

In large measure the courts have sought to protect and insulate medical providers from criminal and tort liability. (Eg, *Barber v Superior Court, supra*, 147 Cal App 3d 1006, 195 Cal Rptr 484.) The California Natural Death Act also illustrates this approach. Nonetheless, as indicated it too recognises, even if inferentially, the existence of the right, even in a non-terminal patient, which overrides the concern for protecting the medical profession.

This right is again reflected in the statute concerning execution of a power of attorney for health care (Civ Code, s 2500), which states in pertinent part: 'Notwithstanding this document, you have the right to make medical and other health care decisions for yourself so long as you can give informed consent with respect to the particular decision. In addition, no treatment may be given to you over your objection at the time . . .'.

A recent Presidential Commission for the Study of Ethical Problems in Medicine and Biomedical and Behavioral Research concluded in part: 'The voluntary choice of a competent and informed patient should determine whether or not life-sustaining therapy will be undertaken, just as such choices provide the basis for other decisions about medical treatment. Health care institutions and professionals should try to enhance patients' abilities to make decisions on their own behalf and to promote understanding of the available treatment options . . . Health care professionals serve patients best by maintaining a presumption in favor of sustaining life, while recognizing that competent patients are entitled to choose to forego any treatments, including those that sustain life.' (*Deciding to Forego Life-Sustaining Treatment*, at pp 3, 5 (US Govt Printing Office 1983) (Report of the President's Commission for the Study of Ethical Problems in Medicine and Biomedical and Behavioral Research).) . . .

We do not believe that all of the foregoing case law and statements of policy and statutory recognition are mere lip service to a fictitious right. As noted in *Bartling*, 'We do not doubt the sincerity of '[the hospital and medical personnel's] moral and ethical beliefs, or their sincere belief in the position they have taken in this case. However, if the right of the patient to self-determination as to his own medical treatment is to have any meaning at all, it must be paramount to the interests of the patient's hospital and doctors. . . . The right of a competent adult patient to refuse medical treatment is a constitutionally guaranteed right which must not be abridged.' (Fn omitted, 163 Cal App 3d at p 195, 209 Cal Rptr 220.)

It is indisputable that petitioner is mentally competent. She is not comatose. She is quite intelligent, alert and understands the risks involved . . .

Here, if force fed, petitioner faces 15 to 20 years of a painful existence, endurable only by the constant administrations of morphine. Her condition is irreversible. There is no cure for her palsy or arthritis. Petitioner would have to be fed, cleaned, turned, bedded, toileted by others for 15 to 20 years! Although alert, bright, sensitive, perhaps even brave and feisty, she must lie immobile, unable to exist except through physical acts of others. Her mind and spirit may be free to take great flights but she herself is imprisoned and must lie physically helpless subject to the ignominy, embarrassment, humiliation and dehumanising aspects created by her helplessness. We do not believe it is the policy of this State that all and every life must be preserved against the will of the sufferer. It is incongruous, if not monstrous, for medical practitioners to assert their right to preserve a life that someone else must live, or, more accurately, endure, for '15 to 20 years'. We cannot conceive it to be the policy of this State to inflict such an ordeal upon anyone.

It is, therefore, immaterial that the removal of the nasogastric tube will hasten or cause Bouvia's eventual death. Being competent she has the right to live out the remainder of her natural life in dignity and peace. It is precisely the aim and purpose of the many decisions upholding the withdrawal of life-support systems to accord and provide as large a measure of dignity, respect and comfort as possible to every patient for the remainder of his days, whatever be their number. This goal is not to hasten death, though its earlier arrival may be an expected and understood likelihood.

Real parties assert that what petitioner really wants is to 'commit suicide' by starvation at their facility. The trial court in its statement of decision said:

> It is fairly clear from the evidence and the court cannot close its eyes to the fact that [petitioner] during her stay in defendant hospital, and for some time prior thereto, has formed an intent to die. She has voiced this desire to a member of the staff of defendant hospital. She claims, however, she does not wish to commit suicide. On the evidence, this is but a semantic distinction. The reasonable inference to be drawn from the evidence is that [petitioner] in defendant facility has purposefully engaged in a selective rejection of medical treatment and nutritional intake to accomplish her objective and accept only treatment which gives her some degree of comfort pending her demise. Stated another way, [petitioner's] refusal of medical treatment and nutritional intake is motivated not by a *bona fide* exercise of her right of privacy but by a desire to terminate her life . . . Here [petitioner] wishes to pursue her objective to die by the use of public facilities with staff standing by to furnish her medical treatment to which she consents and to refrain from that which she refuses.

Overlooking the fact that a desire to terminate one's life is probably the ultimate exercise of one's right to privacy, we find no substantial evidence to support the court's conclusion. Even if petitioner had the specific intent to commit suicide in 1983, while at Riverside, she did not carry out that plan. Then she apparently had the ability without artificial aids, to consume sufficient nutrients to sustain herself, now she does not. That is to say, the trial court here made the following express finding, 'Plaintiff, when she chooses, can orally ingest food by masticating "finger food" *though additional nutritional intake is required intravenously and by nasogastric tube* . . . (emphasis added).' As a consequence of her changed condition, it is clear she has now merely resigned herself to accept an earlier death, if necessary, rather than live by feedings forced upon her by means of nasogastric tube. Her decision to allow nature to take its course is not equivalent to an election to commit suicide with real parties aiding and abetting therein. (*Bartling v Superior Court, supra,* 163 Cal App 3d 186, 209 Cal Rptr 220; *Lane v Candura,* (1978) 376 NE 2d 1232.)

Moreover, the trial court seriously erred by basing its decision on the 'motives' behind Elizabeth Bouvia's decision to exercise her rights. If a right exists, it matters not what 'motivates' its exercise. We find nothing in the law to suggest the right to refuse medical treatment may be exercised only if the patient's *motives* meet someone else's approval. It certainly is not illegal or immoral to prefer a natural, albeit sooner, death than a drugged life attached to a mechanical device.

It is not necessary to here define or dwell at length upon what constitutes suicide. Our Supreme Court dealt with the matter in the case of *Re Joseph G* 34 Cal 3d 429, 194 Cal Rptr 163, 667 P 2d 1176 (1983), wherein declaring that the State has an interest in preserving and recognising the sanctity of life, it observed that it is a crime to aid suicide. But it is significant that the instances and the means there discussed all involved affirmative, assertive, proximate, direct conduct such as furnishing a gun, poison, knife, or other instrumentality or usable means by which another could physically and immediately inflict some death producing injury upon himself. Such situations are far different than the mere presence of a doctor during the exercise of his patient's constitutional rights.

This is the teaching of *Bartling* and *Barber*. No criminal or civil liability attaches to honouring a competent, informed patient's refusal of medical service.

We do not purport to establish what will constitute proper medical practice in all other cases or even other aspects of the care to be provided . . . petitioner. We hold only that her right to refuse medical treatment even of the life-sustaining variety, entitles her to the immediate removal of the nasogastric tube that has been involuntarily inserted into her body. The hospital and medical staff are still free to perform a substantial, if not the greater part of their duty, ie, that of trying to alleviate Bouvia's pain and suffering.

(The decision was approved by the California Supreme Court in *Thor v Superior Court* (1993) 855 P 2d 375 – recognising right of competent adult prisoner who was a quadriplegic to refuse artificial feeding and medication.) We can deduce the following from the *Bouvia* decision. First, a competent adult has a legal right to refuse medical intervention even if this will lead to his death. Secondly, such a refusal does not amount to suicide because the patient does not in law cause his own death. Thirdly, the court drew no distinction between withholding or withdrawing artificial hydration and nutrition and other medical interventions. Fourthly, however, the patient's enjoyment of this right may be subject to the law's obligation to consider other interests of society which may conflict with those of the patient. For example, in *Bouvia* the court referred to society's interest in preventing suicide. In certain cases *Bouvia* would suggest that society's interests may prevail over those of the patient.

At last in 1992 in *Re I (adult: refusal of medical treatment)* [1992] 4 All ER 649, the Court of Appeal confronted the issue of the right of a competent patient to refuse life-sustaining treatment. As we have seen, the court held that on the facts the patient's refusal of treatment was invalid by virtue of the undue influence of her mother (discussed *supra*, ch 3). Nevertheless, all three judges in the Court of Appeal addressed the central issue. You will recall that the case concerned a young woman in need of a blood transfusion following the stillbirth of her baby. She had been brought up by her mother who was a 'fervent Jehovah's Witness'. T was not a member of that faith. After T became unconscious her father, who was opposed to her holding these beliefs along with her boyfriend sought a declaration from the court that it would be lawful for the doctors to give a blood transfusion notwithstanding her prior refusal.

Re T (adult: refusal of medical treatment) [1992] 4 All ER 649, (1992) 9 BMLR 46 (CA)

Lord Donaldson MR: An adult patient who like Miss T suffers from no mental incapacity has an absolute right to choose whether to consent to medical treatment, to refuse it or to choose one rather than another of the treatments being offered. The only possible qualification is a case in which the choice may lead to the death of a viable foetus. That is not this case and if and when it arises, the courts will be faced with a novel problem of consideration legal and ethical complexity. This right of choice is not limited to decisions which others might regard as sensible. It exists notwithstanding that the reasons for making the choice are rational, irrational, unknown or even non-existent (see *Sidaway v Bethlem Royal Hospital Governors* [1985] 1 All ER 643 at 666, [1985] AC 871, at 904-905). . .

The law requires that an adult patient who is mentally and physically capable of exercising a choice *must* consent if medical treatment of him is to be lawful, although the consent need not be in writing and may sometimes be inferred from the patient's conduct in the context of the surrounding circumstances. Treating him without his consent or despite a refusal of consent will constitute the civil wrong of trespass to the person and may constitute a crime . . .

[A refusal of treatment in] this situation gives rise to a conflict between two interests, that of the patient and that of the society in which he lives. The patient's interest consists of his right to self determination – his right to live his own life how he wishes, even if it will damage his health or lead to his premature death. Society's interest is in upholding the concept that all human life is sacred and that it should be preserved if at all possible. It is well established that the ultimate the right of the individual is paramount. But this merely shifts the problem where the conflict occurs and calls for a very careful examination of whether, and if so the way in which, the individual is exercising that right. In case of doubt, that doubt falls to be resolved in favour of the preservation of life, for if the individual is to override the public interest he must do so in clear terms . . .

Butler-Sloss LJ: A man or woman of full age and sound understanding may choose to reject medical advice and medical or surgical treatment either partially or in its entirety. A decision to refuse medical treatment by a patient capable of making the decision does not have to be sensible, rational or well-considered (see *Sidaway v Bethlem Royal Hospital Governors* [1985] 1 All ER 643 at 666, [1985] AC 871 at 904-905). I agree with the reasoning of the Court of Appeal in Ontario in their decision in *Malette v Shulman* (1990) 72 OR (2d) 417 [2 Med LR 162] (a blood transfusion given to an unconscious card-carrying Jehovah's Witness). Robins JA said (at 432):

> At issue here is the freedom of the patient as an individual to exercise her right to refuse treatment and accept the consequences of her own decision. Competent adults, as I have sought to demonstrate, are generally at liberty to refuse medical treatment even at the risk of death. The right to determine what shall be done with one's own body is a fundamental right in our society. The concepts inherent in this right are the bedrock upon which the principles of self-determination and individual autonomy are based. Free individual choice in matters affecting this right should, in my opinion, be accorded very high priority.

He excluded from consideration the interests of the state in protecting innocent third parties and preventing suicide. I agree with the principles set out above . . .

Staughton LJ: An adult whose mental capacity is unimpaired has the right to decide for herself whether she will or will not receive medical or surgical treatment, even in circumstances where she is likely or even certain to die in the absence of treatment. Thus far the law is clear.

2. Balancing competing interests

It is possible to discern in the case of *Re T* two distinct (and perhaps inconsistent) approaches. Lord Donaldson MR initially describes the right of a patient to refuse treatment as an 'absolute' right, albeit possibly subject to an exception when the patient is pregnant. Later in his conclusion he describes the right of the patient as being a '*prima facie*' right, the enjoyment of which is to be balanced against possibly countervailing societal interests. The latter view, that there are interests which need to be balanced against each other, is also reflected in the judgment of Butler-Sloss LJ.

In the subsequent case of *Airedale NHS Trust v Bland* [1993] 1 All ER 821, in one of a number of asides dealing with general principles of medical law, the Law Lords endorsed the right of a patient to refuse life-sustaining treatment:

Lord Keith: It is unlawful, so as to constitute both a tort and the crime of battery, to administer medical treatment to an adult, who is conscious and of sound mind, without his consent: see *F v West Berkshire Health Authority (Mental Health Act Commission intervening)* [1989] 2 All ER 545, [1990] 2 AC 1. Such a person is completely at liberty to decline to undergo treatment, even if the result of his doing so will be that he will die . . .

Lord Goff: The fundamental principle is the principle of the sanctity of human life – a principle long recognised not only in our society but also in most, if not all, civilised societies throughout the modern world, as is indeed evidenced by its recognition both in art 2 of the European Convention on Human Rights (Convention for the Protection of Human Rights and Fundamental Freedoms (Rome, 4 November 1950; TS 71 (1953); Cmd 8969)) and in art 6 of the International Covenant on Civil and Political Rights (New York, 19 December 1966; TS 6 (1977); Cmnd 6702).

But this principle, fundamental though it is, is not absolute. Indeed there are circumstances in which it is lawful to take another man's life, for example by a lawful act of self-defence, or (in the days when capital punishment was acceptable in our society) by lawful execution. We are not however concerned with cases such as these. We are concerned with circumstances in which it may be lawful to withhold from a patient medical treatment or care by means of which his life may be prolonged. But here too there is no absolute rule that the patient's life must be prolonged by such treatment or care, if available, regardless of the circumstances . . .

Lord Mustill: If the patient is capable of making a decision on whether to permit treatment and decides not to permit it his choice must be obeyed, even if on any objective view it is contrary to his best interests. A doctor has no right to proceed in the face of objection, even if it is plain to all, including the patient, that adverse consequences and even death will or may ensue . . .

Thus it is that the patient who is undergoing life-maintaining treatment and decides that it would be preferable to die must be allowed to die, provided that all necessary steps have been taken to be sure that this is what he or she really desires.

Lords Lowry and Browne-Wilkinson also recognised a competent adult patient's right to refuse medical treatment.

You will recall the two distinct approaches in *Re T*. In *Bland* the judges, on the face of it, adopt an 'absolute' approach espoused by Lord Donaldson MR in *Re T*. However, it could be said that their Lordships do accept that the law involves a balancing exercise. What they do is that, as a matter of principle, they resolve the balance where the conflict is between sanctity of life and self-determination in favour of the latter as we saw explicitly in the speech of Lord Goff (see also Lord Keith at 861).

The classic example of the balancing approach is the New Jersey case of *In the Matter of Claire Conroy* (1985) 486 A 2d 1209.

Schrieber J: Whether based on common-law doctrines or on constitutional theory, the right to decline life-sustaining medical treatment is not absolute. In some cases, it may yield to countervailing societal interests in sustaining the person's life. Courts and commentators have commonly identified four state interests that may limit a person's right to refuse medical treatment: preserving life, preventing suicide, safeguarding the integrity of the medical profession, and protecting innocent third parties. *See, eg, Satz v Perlmutter, supra,* 362 *So* 2d at 162; *Re Spring,* 380 *Mass* 629, 640, 405 *NE* 2d 115, 123 (1980); *Comr of Correction v Myers,* 379 *Mass* 255, 261, 399 *NE* 2d 452, 456 (1979); *Saikewicz, supra,* 373 *Mass* at 728, 370 *NE* 2d at 425; *Re Torres,* 357 *NW* 2d 322, 339 (Minn 1984); *Re Colyer,* 99 *Wash* 2d 114, 121, 660 *P* 2d 738, 743 (1983); *President's Commission Report, Deciding to Forego Life-Sustaining Treatment* (1983) at 31-32: Note, '*Re Storar:* The Right to Die and Incompetent Patients', 43 *U Pitt L Rev* 1087, 1092 (1982).

The state's interest in preserving life is commonly considered the most significant of the four state interests. *See, eg, Spring, supra,* 380 *Mass* at 633, 405 *NE* 2d at 119; *Saikewicz, supra,* 373 *Mass* at 740, 370 *NE* 2d at 425; *President's Commission Report, supra,* at 32. It may be seen as embracing two separate but related concerns: an interest in preserving the life of the particular patient, and an interest in preserving the sanctity of life. Cantor, '*Quinlan,* Privacy, and the Handling of Incompetent Dying Patients,' 30 *Rutgers L Rev* 239, 249 (1977); *see* Annas 'In Re Quinlan: Legal Comfort for Doctors,' *Hastings Center Rep,* June 1976, at 29.

While both of these state interests in life are certainly strong, in themselves they will usually not foreclose a competent person from declining life-sustaining medical treatment for himself. This is because the life that the state is seeking to protect in such a situation is the life of the same person who has competently decided to forego the medical intervention; it is not some other actual or potential life that cannot adequately protect itself. *Cf Roe v Wade, supra,* 410 *US* 113, 93 *S Ct* 705, 35 *L Ed* 2d 147 (authorising state restrictions or proscriptions of woman's right to abortion in final trimester of pregnancy to protect viable fetal life); *State v Perricone,* 37 *NJ* 463, 181 *A* 2d 751, *cert* denied, 371 *US* 890, 83 *S Ct* 189, 9 *L Ed* 2d 124 (1962) (affirming trial court's appointment of guardian with authority to consent to blood transfusion for infant over parents' religious objections); *Muhlenberg Hosp v Patterson,* 128 *NJ Super* 498, 320 *A* 2d 518 (Law Div 1974) (authorising blood transfusion to save infant's life over parents' religious objections).

In cases that do not involve the protection of the actual or potential life of someone other than the decisionmaker, the state's indirect and abstract interest in preserving the life of the competent patient generally gives way to the patient's much stronger personal interest in directing the course of his own life. *See, eg, Quackenbush, supra,* 156 *NJ Super* at 290, 383 *A* 2d 785; Cantor, *supra,* 30 *Rutgers L Rev* at 249-50. Indeed, insofar as the 'sanctity of individual free choice and self-determination [are] fundamental constituents of life,' the value of life may be lessened rather than increased 'by the failure to allow a competent human being the right of choice.' *Saikewicz, supra,* 373 *Mass* at 742, 370 *NE* 2d at 426; *see also* Cantor, *supra,* 30 *Rutgers L Rev* at 250 ('Government tolerance of the choice to resist treatment reflects concern for individual self-determination, bodily integrity, and avoidance of suffering, rather than a depreciation of life's value.')

It may be contended that in conjunction with its general interest in preserving life, this state has a particular legislative policy of preventing suicide. *See NJSA* 30: 4-26.3a (subjecting any person who attempts suicide to temporary hospitalisation when the person's behavior suggests the existence of mental illness and constitutes a peril to life, person, or property); see also NJSA 2C:11-6 ('A person who purposely aids another to commit suicide is guilty of a crime of the second degree if his conduct causes such suicide or an attempted suicide, and otherwise of a crime of the fourth degree.') This state interest in protecting people from direct and purposeful self-destruction is motivated by, if not encompassed within, the state's more basic interest in preserving life. Thus, it is questionable whether it is a distinct state interest worthy of independent consideration.

In any event, declining life-sustaining medical treatment may not properly be viewed as an attempt to commit suicide. Refusing medical intervention merely allows the disease to take its natural course; if death were eventually to occur, it would be the result, primarily, of the underlying disease, and not the result of a self-inflicted injury. See *Satz v Perlmutter, supra,* 362 *So* 2d at 162; *Saikewicz, supra,* 373 *Mass* at 743 n 11, 370 *NE* 2d at 426 n 11; *Colyer, supra,* 99 *Wash* 2d at 121, 660 *P* 2d at 743; *see also President's Commission Report, supra,* at 38 (summarising case law on the subject). But cf *Caulk,* NH 480 *A* 2d 93, 96-97 (1984) (stating that attempt of an otherwise healthy prisoner to starve himself to death because he preferred death to life in prison was tantamount to attempted suicide, and that the state, to prevent such suicide, could force him to eat). In addition, people who refuse life-sustaining medical treatment may not harbor a specific intent to die, *Saikewicz, supra,* 373 *Mass* at 743, n 11, 370 *NE* 2d at 426 n 11; rather, they may fervently wish to live, but to do so free of unwanted medical technology, surgery, or drugs, and without protracted suffering, see *Satz v Perlmutter, supra,* 362 *So* 2d at 162-63 ('The testimony of Mr Perlmutter . . . is that he really wants to live, but [to] do so, God and Mother Nature willing, under his own power.').

Recognizing the right of a terminally ill person to reject treatment respects that person's intent, not to die, but to suspend medical intervention at a point consonant with the 'individual's view respecting a personally preferred manner of concluding life.' Note, 'The Tragic Choice: Termination of Care for Patients in a Permanent Vegetative State', 51 *NYUL Rev* 285, 310 (1976). The difference is between self-infliction or self-destruction and self-determination. See Byrn, 'Compulsory Lifesaving Treatment for the Competent Adult', 44 *Fordham L Rev* 1, 16-23 (1975). To the extent that our decision in *John F Kennedy Memorial Hosp v Heston,* 58 *NJ* 576, 581-82, 279 *A* 2d 670 (1971), implies the contrary, we now overrule it.

The third state interest that is frequently asserted as a limitation on a competent patient's right to refuse medical treatment is the interest in safeguarding the integrity of the medical profession. This interest, like the interest in preventing suicide, is not particularly threatened by permitting competent patients to refuse life-sustaining medical treatment. Medical ethics do not require medical intervention in disease at all costs. As long ago as 1624, Francis Bacon wrote, 'I esteem it the office of a physician not only to restore health, but to mitigate pain and dolours; and not only when such mitigation may conduce to recovery, but when it may serve to make a fair and easy passage.' *F Bacon, New Atlantis,* quoted in Mannes, 'Euthanasia vs The Right to Life', 27 *Baylor L Rev* 68, 69 (1975). More recently, we wrote in *Quinlan, supra,* 70 *NJ* at 47, 355 *A* 2d 647, that modern-day 'physicians distinguish between curing the ill and comforting and easing the dying; that they refuse to treat the curable as if they were dying or ought to die, and that they have sometimes refused to treat the hopeless and dying as if they were curable.' Indeed, recent surveys have suggested that a majority of practicing doctors now approve of passive euthanasia and believe that it is being practiced by members of the profession. See sources cited in *Storar, supra NY* 2d at 385-386 n 3, 420 *NE* 2d at 75-76 n 3, 438 *NYS* 2d at 277-78 n 3 (Jones, J, dissenting), and in Collester, 'Death, Dying and the Law: A Prosecutorial View of the *Quinlan* Case', 30 *Rutgers L Rev* 304, n 3 312 & n 27.

Moreover, even if doctors were exhorted to attempt to cure or sustain their patients under all circumstances, that moral and professional imperative, at least in cases of patients who were clearly competent, presumably would not require doctors to go beyond advising the patient of the risks of foregoing treatment and urging the patient to accept the medical intervention. *Storar, supra,* 52 *NY* 2d at 377, 420 *NE* 2d at 71, 438 *NYS* 2d at 273; see *Colyer, supra,* 99 *Wash* 2d at 121-23, 660 *P* 2d at 743-44, citing *Saikewicz, supra,* 373 *Mass* at

743-44, 370 *NE* 2d at 417. If the patient rejected the doctor's advice, the onus of that decision would rest on the patient, not the doctor. Indeed, if the patient's right to informed consent is to have any meaning at all, it must be accorded respect even when it conflicts with the advice of the doctor or the values of the medical profession as a whole.

The fourth asserted state interest in overriding a patient's decision about his medical treatment is the interest in protecting innocent third parties who may be harmed by the patient's treatment decision. When the patient's exercise of his free choice could adversely and directly affect the health, safety, or security of others, the patient's right of self-determination must frequently give way. Thus, for example, courts have required competent adults to undergo medical procedures against their will if necessary to protect the public health, *Jacobson v Massachusetts*, 197 *US* 11, 25 *S Ct* 358, 49 *L Ed* 643 (1905) (recognising enforceability of compulsory smallpox vaccination law); to prevent a serious risk to prison security, *Myers*, *supra*, 379 *Mass* at 263, 265, 399 *NE* 2d at 457, 458 (compelling prisoner with kidney disease to submit to dialysis over his protest rather than acquiescing in his demand to be transferred to a lower-security prison); *accord Caulk*, *supra*, 480 *A* 2d at 96; or to prevent the emotional and financial abandonment of the patient's minor children, *Application of President & Directors of Georgetown College, Inc*, 331 *F* 2d 1000, 1008 (DC Cir), *cert* denied, 377 *US* 978, 84 *S Ct* 1883, 12 *L Ed* 2d 746 (1964) (ordering mother of seven-month-old infant to submit to blood transfusion over her religious objections because of the mother's 'responsibility to the community to care for her infant'); *Holmes v Silver Cross Hosp*, 340 *F Supp* 125, 130 (ND Ill 1972) (indicating that patient's status as father of minor child might justify authorizing blood transfusion to save his life despite his religious objections).

On balance, the right to self-determination ordinarily outweighs any countervailing state interests, and competent persons generally are permitted to refuse medical treatment, even at the risk of death. Most of the cases that have held otherwise, unless they involved the interest in protecting innocent third parties, have concerned the patient's competency to make a rational and considered choice of treatment. See Annot, 93 *ALR* 3d 67, at 80-85 (1979) ('Patient's Right to Refuse Treatment Allegedly Necessary to Sustain Life'). For example, in *Heston*, *supra*, 58 *NJ* 576, 279 *A* 2d 670, this Court approved a blood transfusion to save the life of a twenty-two-year-old Jehovah's Witness who had been severely injured and was rushed to the hospital for treatment, despite the fact that a tenet of her faith forbade blood transfusions. The evidence indicated that she was in shock on admittance to the hospital and was then or soon became disorientated and incoherent. Part of the Court's rationale was that hospitals, upon which patient's case is thrust, 'exist to aid the sick and the injured', *id* 58 *NJ* at 582, 279 *A* 2d 670, and that it is difficult for them to assess a patient's intent in an emergency and to determine whether a desire to refuse treatment is firmly and competently held, *id* 58 *NJ* at 581, 582, 279 *A* 2d 670. Similarly, courts in other states have authorized blood transfusions over the objections of Jehovah's Witnesses when the patient's opposition to the treatment was expressed in equivocal terms. *Compare Georgetown College*, *supra*, 331 F 2d at 1006-07 (authorizing transfusion to save life of patient who said that for religious reasons she would not consent to the transfusion, but who seemed to indicate that she would not oppose the transfusion if court ordered it since it would not then be her responsibility), *and United States v George*, 239 *F Supp* 752, 753, (D Conn 1965) (transfusion was authorised for patient who told court that he would not agree to the transfusion, but volunteered that if the court ordered it he would not resist in any way since it would be the court's will and not his), *with Re Osborne*, 294 *A* 2d 372, 374, 375 (DC 1972) (stating that guardian should not be appointed to consent to transfusion on behalf of man who told court that he would be deprived of 'everlasting life' if compelled by a court to submit to the transfusion, and who explained, 'it is between me and Jehovah; not the courts . . . I'm willing to take my chances. My faith is that strong.').

In our view, the balancing approach whereby a patient's rights are understood as being only *prima facie* rights which must be weighted against the interests of society more properly states the English law. That being so, what does the court in *Re T* and *Bland* say about the four societal interests identified in *Conroy*, ie (1) the preservation of life ; (2) preventing suicide; (3) preserving the integrity of the medical profession; (4) protection of an innocent third party. As regards the first, clearly by preferring the patient's right to refuse, the courts in *Re T* and *Bland* reached a conclusion that this societal interest could not outweigh the patient's right. As regards the second, again clearly the court in

Re T does not consider that any interest that society has in preventing suicide transcends the right of the patient, though it is doubtful whether a patient's conduct in such circumstances amounts to suicide (see, on similar facts, *Fosmire v Nicoleau* (1990) 551 NE 2d 77 (NY CA) held by majority of the court that refusing a blood transfusion is not suicide. Contrast the judgment of Hancock and Simons JJ, concurring).

In *Bland* Lord Goff stated (at 866):

> I wish to add that, in cases of this kind, there is no question of the patient having committed suicide, nor therefore of the doctor having aided or abetted him in doing so. It is simply that the patient has, as he is entitled to do, declined to consent to treatment which might or would have the effect of prolonging his life, and the doctor has, in accordance with his duty, complied with his patient's wishes.

As regards the third societal interest, although there are a number of American cases which give some weight to concern for the interests of the medical profession (eg *Brophy v New England Sinai Hospital* (1986) 497 NE 2d 626 (Mass Sup Jud Ct)), it is clear that English law would not consider these interests overreaching. Thus, the first three interests identified in *Conroy* do not outweigh the right of the competent adult patient to refuse treatment.

It is the fourth societal interest which is problematic. There are two situations to consider here: *first*, where the patient's child has been born and it is suggested that its interests will be compromised by the death of the patient; *secondly*, where the patient is pregnant and the refusal of treatment may (or will) deleteriously affect the unborn child, for example, lead to its death.

(a) The pregnant woman and the fetus

Re T recognises only the fourth category of interest as potentially capable of outweighing the right of the adult patient to decide for herself. Subsequently, the High Court in some haste was called upon to consider this potential exception to the patient's right to refuse treatment.

Re S (adult: refusal of medical treatment) [1992] 4 All ER 671, (1992) 9 BMLR 69

> **Sir Stephen Brown P:** This is an application by a health authority for a declaration to authorise the surgeons and staff of a hospital to carry out an emergency Caesarian operation upon a patient, who I shall refer to as 'Mrs S'.
>
> Mrs S is 30 years of age. She is in labour with her third pregnancy. She was admitted to a hospital last Saturday with ruptured membranes and in spontaneous labour. She has continued in labour since. She is already six days overdue beyond the expected date of birth, which was 6 October, and she has now refused, on religious grounds, to submit herself to a Caesarian section operation. She is supported in this by her husband. They are described as 'born-again Christians' and are clearly quite sincere in their beliefs.
>
> I have heard the evidence of P, a Fellow of the Royal College of Surgeons who is in charge of this patient at the hospital. He has given, succinctly and graphically, a description of the condition of this patient. Her situation is desperately serious, as is also the situation of the as yet unborn child. The child is in what is described as a position of 'transverse lie', with the elbow projecting through the cervix and the head being on the right side. There is the gravest risk of a rupture of the uterus if the section is not carried out and the natural labour process is permitted to continue. The evidence of P is that we are concerned with 'minutes rather than hours' and that it is a 'life and death' situation. He has done his best, as have other surgeons and doctors at the hospital, to persuade the mother that the only means of saving her life, and also I emphasise the life of her unborn child, is to carry out a Caesarian section operation. P is emphatic. He says it is absolutely the case that the baby cannot be

born alive if a Caesarian operation is not carried out. He has described the medical condition. I am not going to go into it in detail because of the pressure of time.

I have been assisted by Mr Munby QC appearing for the Official Solicitor as amicus curiae. The Official Solicitor answered the call of the court within minutes and, although this application only came to the notice of the court officials at 1.30 pm, it has come on for hearing just before 2 o'clock and now at 2.18 pm I propose to make the declaration which is sought. I do so in the knowledge that the fundamental question appears to have been left open by Lord Donaldson MR in *Re T (adult: refusal of medical treatment)* [1992] 4 All ER 649, heard earlier this year in the Court of Appeal, and in the knowledge that there is no English authority which is directly in point. There is, however, some American authority which suggests that if this case were being heard in the American courts the answer would be likely to be in favour of granting a declaration in these circumstances: see *Re AC* (1990) 573 A 2d 1235 at 1240, 1246-1248, 1252.

I do not propose to say more at this stage, except that I wholly accept the evidence of P as to the desperate nature of this situation, and that I grant the declaration as sought.

Can the view of Stephen Brown P be reconciled with the decision in *Re T*? In so far as the court's declaration was based upon its determination of what it saw as the 'vital interests of the mother', then this is quite inconsistent with *Re T*. A medical procedure refused by a competent adult cannot be lawfully carried out due to concern for that individual's interest. The patient determines his own interests. In so far as the judgment in *Re S* prefers the interests of the unborn child to those of the mother, should these interests prevail?

(i) THE EARLY US CASES

It may be instructive to look to the United States, where there is much more jurisprudence and scholarship on this issue. The early cases demonstrated a preparedness to override the refusal of the pregnant woman in circumstances where the unborn child would be put at great risk of death.

Raleigh Fitkin – Paul Morgan Memorial Hospital v Anderson (1964) 201 A 2d 537 (NJ Sup Ct)

Per curiam: The plaintiff hospital brought an action in the Chancery Division of the Superior Court seeking authority to administer blood transfusion to the defendant Willimina Anderson in the event that such transfusions should be necessary to save her life and the life of her unborn child. The child is quick, the pregnancy being beyond the 32nd week. Mrs Anderson had notified the hospital that she did not wish blood transfusions for the reason that they would be contrary to her religious conviction as a Jehovah's Witness. The evidence establishes a probability that at some point in the pregnancy Mrs Anderson will haemorrhage severely and that both she and the unborn child will die unless a blood transfusion is administered.

The trial court held that the judiciary could not thus intervene in the case of an adult or with respect to an unborn child. Because of the likely emergency we directed immediate argument of the hospital's appeal. At the argument we were advised that Mrs Anderson left the hospital yesterday against the advice of the attending physician and the hospital. It is doubtful whether the hospital has a remaining interest but the parties request the court to determine the issues and since it is likely that the matter would arise again at the instance of an interested party we have decided to do so.

In *State v Perricone*, 37 NJ 463, 181 A 2d 751 (1962), we held that the State's concern for the welfare of an infant justified blood transfusions notwithstanding the objection of its parents who were also Jehovah's Witnesses, and in *Smith v Brennan*, 31 NJ 353, 157 A 2d 497 (1960), we held that a child could sue for injuries negligently inflicted upon it prior to birth. We are satisfied that the unborn child is entitled to the law's protection and that an appropriate order should be made to insure blood transfusions to the mother in the event that they are necessary in the opinion of the physician in charge at the time.

We have no difficulty in so deciding with respect to the infant child. The more difficult question is whether an adult may be compelled to submit to such medical procedures when necessary to save his life. Here we think it is unnecessary to decide that question in broad terms because the welfare of the child and the mother are so intertwined and inseparable that it would be impracticable to attempt to distinguish between them with respect to the sundry factual patterns which may develop. The blood transfusions (including transfusions made necessary by the delivery) may be administered if necessary to save her life or the life of her child, as the physician in charge at the time may determine.

The intervention in this case, a blood transfusion, was intrusive but not as intrusive as in the next case.

Jefferson v Griffin Spalding County Hospital Authority (1981) 274 SE 2d 457 (Sup Ct Georgia)

Per curiam: On Thursday, January 22, 1981, the Griffin Spalding County Hospital Authority petitioned the Superior Court of Butts County, as a court of equity, for an order authorizing it to perform a caesarean section and any necessary blood transfusions upon the defendant, an out-patient resident of Butts County, in the event she presented herself to the hospital for delivery of her unborn child, which was due on or about Monday, January 26. The superior court conducted an emergency hearing on Thursday, January 22, and entered the following order:

> This petition and rule nisi were filed and served on defendant today. When the Court convened at the appointed hour, defendant did not appear, in spite of the fact that both she and her husband had notice of the hearing.
>
> Defendant is in the thirty-ninth week of pregnancy. In the past few weeks she has presented herself to Griffin Spalding Hospital for pre-natal care. The examining physician has found and defendant has been advised that she has a complete placenta previa; that the afterbirth is between the baby and the birth canal; that it is virtually impossible that this condition will correct itself prior to delivery; and that it is a 99% certainty that the child cannot survive natural childbirth (vaginal delivery). The chances of defendant surviving vaginal delivery are not better than 50%.
>
> The examining physician is of the opinion that a delivery by caesarean section prior to labor beginning would have an almost 100% chance of preserving the life of the child, along with that of defendant.
>
> On the basis of religious beliefs, defendant has advised the Hospital that she does not need surgical removal of the child and will not submit to it. Further she refuses to take any transfusion of blood.
>
> The Hospital is required by its own policies to treat any patient seeking emergency treatment. It seeks authority of the Court to administer medical treatment to defendant to save the life of herself and her unborn child.
>
> The child is, as a matter of fact, viable and fully capable of sustaining life independent of the mother (defendant). The issue is whether this unborn child has any legal right to the protection of the Court . . .
>
> Because the life of defendant and of the unborn child are, at the moment, inseparable, the Court deems it appropriate to infringe upon the wishes of the mother to the extent it is necessary to give the child an opportunity to live.
>
> Accordingly, the plaintiff hospitals are hereby authorized to administer to defendant all medical procedures deemed necessary by the attending physician to preserve the life of defendant's unborn child. This authority shall be effective only if defendant voluntarily seeks admission to either of plaintiff's hospitals for the emergency delivery of the child.
>
> The Court has been requested to order defendant to submit to surgery before the natural childbirth process (labor) begins. The Court is reluctant to grant this request and does not do so at this time. However, should some agency of the State seek such relief through intervention in this suit or in a separate proceeding, the Court will promptly consider such request.

On Friday, January 23, the Georgia Department of Human Resources, acting through the Butts County Department of Family and Children Services, petitioned the Juvenile Court of Butts County for temporary custody of the unborn child, alleging that the child was a deprived child without proper parental care necessary for his or her physical health . . . and praying for an order requiring the mother to submit to a caesarean section. After appointing counsel for the parents and for the child, the court conducted a joint hearing in both the superior court and juvenile court cases and entered the following order on the afternoon of January 23:

> This action in the Superior Court of Butts County was heard and decided yesterday, January 22, 1981.
>
> This morning, the Georgia Department of Human Resources, acting through the Butts County Department of Family and Children Services, filed a complaint in the Juvenile Court of Butts County alleging deprivation and seeking temporary custody of Jessie Mae Jefferson's unborn child.
>
> Because of the unusual nature of the relief sought in these cases and because the Juvenile Court of Butts County may not have the authority needed effectively to grant the relief sought, the Court consolidates these cases and renders the following judgment both as a Juvenile Court and under the broad powers of the Superior Court of Butts County. The Court readopts its findings contained in the Order dated January 22, 1981.
>
> At the proceeding held today, Jessie Mae Jefferson and her husband, John W Jefferson were present and represented by counsel, Hugh Glidewell, Jr. Richard Milam, Attorney at Law, represented the interests of the unborn child.
>
> Based on the evidence presented, the Court finds that Jessie Mae Jefferson is due to begin labor at any moment. There is a 99 to 100 percent certainty that the unborn child will die if she attempts to have the child by vaginal delivery. There is a 99 to 100 percent chance that the child will live if the baby is delivered by Caesarean section prior to the beginning of labor. There is a 50 percent chance that Mrs Jefferson herself will die if vaginal delivery is attempted. There is an almost 100 percent chance that Mrs Jefferson will survive if a delivery by Caesarean section is done prior to the beginning of labor. The Court finds that as a matter of fact the child is a human being fully capable of sustaining life independent of the mother.
>
> Mrs Jefferson and her husband have refused and continue to refuse to give consent to a Caesarean section. This refusal is based entirely on the religious beliefs of Mr and Mrs Jefferson. They are of the view that the Lord has healed her body and that whatever happens to the child will be the Lord's will.
>
> Based on these findings, the Court concludes and finds as a matter of law that this child is a viable human being and entitled to the protection of the Juvenile Court Code of Georgia. The Court concludes that this child is without the proper parental care and subsistence necessary for his or her physical life and health.
>
> Temporary custody of the unborn child is hereby granted to the State of Georgia Department of Human Resources and the Butts County Department of Family and Children Services. The Department shall have full authority to make all decisions, including giving consent to the surgical delivery appertaining to the birth of this child. The temporary custody of the Department shall terminate when the child has been successfully brought from its mother's body into the world or until the child dies, whichever shall happen.
>
> Because of the unique nature of these cases, the powers of the Superior Court of Butts County are invoked and the defendant, Jessie Mae Jefferson, is hereby Ordered to submit to a sonogram (ultrasound) at the Griffin Spalding County Hospital or some other place which may be chosen by her where such procedure can be given. Should said sonogram indicate to the attending physician that the complete placenta previa is still blocking the child's passage into the world, Jessie Mae Jefferson is Ordered to submit to a Caesarean section and related procedures considered necessary by the attending physician to sustain the life of this child.
>
> The Court finds that the State has an interest in the life of this unborn, living human being. The Court finds that the intrusion involved into the life of Jessie Mae Jefferson and her husband, John W Jefferson, is outweighed by the duty of the State to protect a living, unborn human being from meeting his or her death before being given the opportunity to live.
>
> This Order shall be effective at 10:00 a.m. on Saturday, January 24, 1981, unless a stay is granted by the Supreme Court of Georgia or some other Court having the authority to stay an Order of this Court.

The parents filed their motion for stay in this court at about 5:30 p.m. on January 23 . . . [T]his court entered the following order on the evening of January 23:

It is ordered that the Motion for Stay filed in this matter is hereby denied. The trial court's orders are effective immediately . . .

Motion for stay denied.

Hill, Presiding Justice: The power of a court to order a competent adult to submit to surgery is exceedingly limited. Indeed, until this unique case arose, I would have thought such power to be nonexistent. Research shows that the courts generally have held that a competent adult has the right to refuse necessary lifesaving surgery and medical treatment (ie, has the right to die) where no state interest other than saving the life of the patient is involved . . .

On the other hand, one court has held that an expectant mother in the last weeks of pregnancy lacks the right to refuse necessary lifesaving surgery and medical treatment where the life of the unborn child is at stake. *Raleigh Fitkin-Paul Morgan Memorial Hospital v Anderson*, [42 NJ 421, 201 A 2d 537, cert den 377 US 985, 84 SCt 1894, 12 LEd 2d 1032 (1964)]; see also *Re Melideo*, 88 Misc 2d 974, 390 NYS 2d 523 (1976); *Re Yetter*, 62 Pa D&C 2d 619, 623 (1973).

The Supreme Court has recognized that the state has an interest in protecting the lives of unborn, viable children (viability usually occurring at about 7 months, or 28 weeks) . . .

The mother here was in her last week of normal pregnancy (the 39th week). She has diligently sought parental care for her child herself, except for her refusal to consent to a caesarean section. She was due to deliver on Monday, January 26, and the medical testimony showed that the birth could occur at any time within 2 weeks of that date. . . .

In denying the stay of the trial court's order and thereby clearing the way for immediate reexamination by sonogram and probably surgery, we weighed the right of the mother to practice her religion and to refuse surgery on herself, against her unborn child's right to live. We found in favor of her child's right to live.

Justice Smith agreed and added:

. . . In the instant case, it appears that there is no less burdensome alternative for preserving the life of a fully developed fetus than requiring its mother to undergo surgery against her religious convictions. Such an intrusion by the state would be extraordinary, presenting some medical risk to both the mother and the fetus. However, the state's compelling interest in preserving the life of this fetus is beyond dispute. Moreover, the medical evidence indicates that the risk to the fetus *and* the mother presented by a Caesarean section would be minimal, whereas, in the absence of surgery, the fetus would almost certainly die and the mother's chance of survival would be no better than 50 percent. Under these circumstances, I must conclude that the trial court's order is not violative of the First Amendment, notwithstanding that it may require the mother to submit to surgery against her religious beliefs. See *Raleigh Fitkin-Paul Memorial Hospital v Anderson, supra*; see also *Green v Green*, 448 Pa 338, 292 A 2d 387 (1972).

(ii) *RE AC* AND *RE MADYUN*

Perhaps the most significant decision in the United States is the case of *Re AC*.

Re AC (1990) 573 A 2d 1253 (DC CA)

Terry JA: We are confronted here with two profoundly difficult and complex issues. First, we must determine who has the right to decide the course of medical treatment for a patient who, although near death, is pregnant with a viable fetus. Second, we must establish how that decision should be made if the patient cannot make it for herself – more specifically, how a court should proceed when faced with a pregnant patient, *in extremis*, who is apparently incapable of making an informed decision regarding medical care for herself and her fetus. We hold that in virtually all cases the question of what is to be done is to be decided by the patient – the pregnant woman – on behalf of herself and the fetus. If the patient is incompetent or otherwise unable to give an informed consent to a proposed course of medical treatment, then her decision must be ascertained through the procedure known as substituted judgment. Because the trial court did not follow that procedure, we vacate its order and remand the case for further proceedings . . .

This case came before the trial court when George Washington University Hospital petitioned the emergency judge in chambers for declaratory relief as to how it should treat its patient, AC, who was close to death from cancer and was twenty six and one-half weeks pregnant with a viable fetus. After a hearing lasting approximately three hours, which was held at the hospital (though not in AC's room), the court ordered that a caesarean section be performed on AC to deliver the fetus. Counsel for AC immediately sought a stay in this court, which was unanimously denied by a hastily assembled division of three judges. *In Re AC* 533 A 2d 611 (DC 1987). The caesarean was performed, and a baby girl, LMC, was delivered. Tragically, the child died within two and one-half hours, and the mother died two days later.

Counsel for AC now maintain that AC was competent and that she made an informed choice not to have the caesarean performed. Given this view of the facts, they argue that it was error for the trial court to weigh the state's interest in preserving the potential life of a viable fetus against AC's interest in having her decision respected. They argue further that, even if the substituted judgment procedure had been followed, the evidence would necessarily show that AC would not have wanted the caesarean section. Under either analysis, according to these arguments, the trial court erred in subordinating AC's right to bodily integrity in favor of the state's interest in potential life. Counsel for the hospital and for LMC contend, on the other hand, that AC was incompetent to make her own medical decisions and that, under the substituted judgment procedure, the evidence clearly established that AC would have consented to the caesarean. In the alternative, counsel for LMC argues that even if LMC's interests and those of the state were in conflict with AC's wishes, it was proper for the trial court to balance their interests and resolve the conflict in favour of surgical intervention.

We do not accept any of these arguments because the evidence, realistically viewed, does not support them . . .

[T]he trial court made oral findings of fact. It found, first, that AC would probably die, according to uncontroverted medical testimony, 'within the next twenty-four to forty-eight hours'; second, that AC was 'pregnant with a twenty-six and a half week viable fetus who, based upon controverted medical testimony, has approximately a fifty to sixty percent chance to survive if a caesarean section is performed as soon as possible'; third, that because the fetus was viable, 'the state has [an] important and legitimate interest in protecting the potentiality of human life'; and fourth, that there had been some testimony that the operation 'may very well hasten the death of [AC],' but that there had also been testimony that delay would greatly increase the risk to the fetus and that 'the prognosis is not great for the fetus to be delivered post-mortem . . .' Most significantly, the court found:

> The court is of the view that it does not clearly know what [AC's] present views are with respect to the issue of whether or not the child should live or die. She's presently unconscious. As late as Friday of last week, she wanted the baby to live. As late as yesterday, she did not know for sure.

Having made these findings of fact and conclusions of law, and expressly relying on *In Re Madyun,* 114 Daily Wash L Rptr 2233 (DC Super Ct July 26, 1986), the court ordered that a caesarean section be performed to deliver AC's child . . . there is only one published decision from an appellate court that deals with the question of when, or even whether, a court may order a caesarean section: *Jefferson v Griffin Spalding County Hospital Authority*, 247 Ga 86, 274 SE 2d 457 (1981).

Jefferson is of limited relevance, if any at all, to the present case. In *Jefferson* there was a competent refusal by the mother to undergo the proposed surgery, but the evidence showed that performance of the caesarean was in the medical interests of both the mother and the fetus. In the instant case, by contrast, the evidence is unclear as to whether AC was competent when she mouthed her apparent refusal of the caesarean ('I don't want it done'), and it was generally assumed that while the surgery would most likely be highly beneficial to the fetus, it would be dangerous for the mother. Thus there was no clear maternal-fetal conflict in this case arising from a competent decision by the mother to forego a procedure for the benefit of the fetus. The procedure may well have been against AC's medical interest, but if she was competent and given the choice, she may well have consented to an operation of significant risk to herself in order to maximize her fetus' chance for survival. From the evidence, however, we simply cannot tell whether she would have consented or not.

Thus our analysis of this case begins with the tenet common to all medical treatment cases: that any person has the right to make an informed choice, if competent to do so, to accept or forego medical treatment. The doctrine of informed consent, based on this principle and rooted in the concept of bodily integrity, is ingrained in our common law. *See Crain v Allison*, 443 A 2d 558, 561-562 (DC 1982); *Canterbury v Spence*, 150 US App DC 263, 271, 464 F 2d 772, 780, *cert denied*, 409 US 1064, 93 S Ct 560, 34 L Ed 2d 518 (1972);

Schloendorff v Society of New York Hospital 211 NY 125, 127, 105 NE 92, 93 (1914). Under the doctrine of informed consent, a physician must inform the patient 'at a minimum' of the 'nature of the proposed treatment, any alternative treatment procedures, and the nature and degree of risks and benefits inherent in undergoing and in abstaining from the proposed treatment.' *Crain v Allison, supra,* 443 A 2d at 562 (footnote omitted). To protect the right of every person to bodily integrity, courts uniformly hold that a surgeon who performs an operation without the patient's consent may be guilty of a battery, *Canterbury v Spence, supra,* 150 US App DC at 274, 464 F 2d at 783, or that if the surgeon obtains an insufficiently informed consent, he or she may be liable for negligence. *Crain v Allison, supra,* 443, A 2d at 561-562. Furthermore, the right to informed consent 'also encompassed a right to informed refusal.' *In Re Conroy,* 98 NJ 321, 336, 486 A 2d 1209, 1222 (1985) (citation omitted).

In the same vein, courts do not compel one person to permit a significant intrusion upon his or her bodily integrity for the benefit of another person's health. *See, eg Bonner v Moran,* 75 US App DC 156, 157, 126 F 2d 121, 122 (1941) (parental consent required for skin graft from fifteen-year-old for benefit of cousin who had been severely burned); *McFall v Shimp,* 10 Pa D & C 3d 90 (Allegheny County Ct 1978). In *McFall* the court refused to order Shimp to donate bone marrow which was necessary to save the life of his cousin, McFall.

> The common law has consistently held to a rule which provides that one human being is under no legal compulsion to give aid or to take action to save another human being or to rescue. . . . For our law to *compel* defendant to submit to an intrusion of his body would change every concept and principle upon which our society is founded. To do so would defeat the sanctity of the individual, and would impose a rule which would know no limits, and one could not imagine where the line would be drawn.

Id at 91 (emphasis in original). Even though Shimp's refusal would mean death for McFall, the court would not order Shimp to allow his body to be invaded. It has been suggested that fetal cases are different because a woman who 'has chosen to lend her body to bring [a] child into the world' has an enhanced duty to assure the welfare of the fetus, sufficient even to require her to undergo caesarean surgery. Robertson, *Procreative Liberty,* 69 Va L Rev at 456. Surely, however, a fetus cannot have rights in this respect superior to those of a person who has already been born.[8] . . .

This court and others, while recognizing the right to accept or reject medical treatment, have consistently held that the right is not absolute. *Eg, In Re Boyd, supra,* 403 A 2d at 749-750; *In Re Osborne, supra,* 294 A 2d at 374; *In Re President & Directors of Georgetown College, Inc,* 118 US App D C 80, 331 F 2d 1000, *cert denied,* 377 US 978, 84 S Ct 1883, 12 L Ed 2d 746 (1964); *Rasmussen ex rel Mitchell v Fleming, supra,* 154 Ariz at 216, 741 P 2d at 683; *In Re Conroy, supra,* 98 NJ at 337, 486 A 2d at 1223; *cf Hughes v United States,* 429 A 2d 1339 (DC 1981) (upholding as reasonable a minor surgical intrusion to remove bullets from a criminal suspect), *United States v Crowder,* 177 US App DC 165, 543 F 2d 312 (1976) (same), *cert denied,* 429 US 1062, 97 S Ct 788, 50 L Ed 2d 779 (1977). In some cases, especially those involving life-or-death situations or incompetent patients, the courts have recognized four countervailing interests that may involve the state as *parens patriae*: preserving life, preventing suicide, maintaining the ethical integrity of the medical profession, and protecting third parties. *See, eg, In Re Boyd, supra,* 403 A 2d at 748 n 9; *Brophy v New England Sinai Hospital, Inc,* 398 Mass 417, 431-433, 497 NE 2d 626, 634 (1986); *Saikewicz, supra,* 373 Mass at 737, 370 NE 2d at 425; *In Re Farrell, supra,* 108 NJ at 350, 529 A 2d at 410-411. Neither the prevention of suicide nor the integrity of the medical profession has any bearing on this case. Further, the state's interest in preserving life must be truly compelling to justify overriding a competent person's right to refuse medical treatment. *In Re Osborne, supra,* 294 A 2d at 374-375; *Tune v Walter Reed Army Medical Hospital, supra,* 602 F Supp at 1455-1456. This is equally true for incompetent patients, who have just as much right as competent patients to have their decisions made while competent respected, even in a substituted judgment framework. *See In Re Boyd, supra,* 403 A 2d at 750; *John F Kennedy Memorial Hospital, Inc v Bludworth, supra,* 452 So 2d at 923-924; *Saikewicz, supra,* 373 Mass at 739, 370 NE 2d at 427-428; *In Re Conroy, supra,* 98 NJ at 343, 486 A 2d at 1229.

In those rare cases in which a patient's right to decide her own course of treatment has been judicially overridden, courts have usually acted to vindicate the state's interest in protecting third parties, even if in fetal state. *See Jefferson v Griffin Spalding County Hospital Authority, supra* (ordering that caesarean section be performed on a woman in her thirty-ninth week of pregnancy to save both the mother and the fetus); *Raleigh Fitkin-Paul*

Morgan Memorial Hospital v Anderson, 42 NJ 421, 201 A 2d 537 (ordering blood transfusions over the objection of a Jehovah's Witness, in her thirty-second week of pregnancy, to save her life and that of the fetus). *cert denied*, 377 US 985, 84 S Ct 1894, 12 L Ed 2d 1032 (1964); *In Re Jamaica Hospital*, 128 Misc 2d 1006, 491 NY S 2d 898 (Sup Ct 1985) (ordering the transfusion of blood to a Jehovah's Witness eighteen weeks pregnant, who objected on religious grounds, and finding that the state's interest in the not-yet-viable fetus outweighed the patient's interests); *Crouse Irving Memorial Hospital, Inc v Paddock*, 127 Misc 2d 101, 485 NYS 2d 443 (Sup Ct 1985) (ordering transfusions as necessary over religious objections to save the mother and a fetus that was to be prematurely delivered); *cf In Re President & Directors of Georgetown College, Inc, supra*, 118 US App DC at 88, 331 F 2d at 1008 (ordering a transfusion, *inter alia*, because of a mother's parental duty to her living minor children). *But see Taft v Taft*, 388 Mass 331, 446 NE 2d 395 (1983) (vacating an order which required a woman in her fourth month of pregnancy to undergo a 'purse-string' operation, on the ground that there were no compelling circumstances to justify overriding her religious objections and her constitutional right of privacy).

What we distill from the cases discussed in this section is that every person has the right, under the common law and the Constitution, to accept or refuse medical treatment. This right of bodily integrity belongs equally to persons who are competent and persons who are not. Further, it matters not what the quality of a patient's life may be; the right of bodily integrity is not extinguished simply because someone is ill, or even at death's door. To protect that right against intrusion by others – family members, doctors, hospitals, or anyone else, however well-intentioned – we hold that a court must determine the patient's wishes by any means available, and must abide by those wishes unless there are truly extraordinary or compelling reasons to override them. *In Re Osborne, supra*. When the patient is incompetent, or when the court is unable to determine competency, the substituted judgment procedure must be followed.

From the record before us, we simply cannot tell whether AC was ever competent, after being sedated, to make an informed decision one way or the other regarding the proposed caesarean section. The trial court never made any finding about AC's competency to decide. Undoubtedly, during most of the proceedings below, AC was incompetent to make a treatment decision; that is, she was unable to give an informed consent based on her assessment of the risks and benefits of the contemplated surgery. The court knew from the evidence that AC was sedated and unconscious, and thus it could reasonably have found her incompetent to render an informed consent; however, it made no such finding. On the other hand, there was no clear evidence that AC was competent to render an informed consent after the trial court's initial order was communicated to her.

We think it is incumbent on any trial judge in a case like this, unless it is impossible to do so, to ascertain whether a patient is competent to make her own medical decisions. Whenever possible, the judge should personally attempt to speak with the patient and ascertain her wishes directly, rather than relying exclusively on hearsay evidence, even from doctors. *See In Re Osborne, supra*, 294 A 2d at 374; *In Re President & Directors of Georgetown College, Inc, supra*, 118 US App DC at 87, 331 F 2d at 1007. It is improper to presume that a patient is incompetent. *United States v Charters, supra*, 829 F 2d at 495. We have no reason to believe that, if competent, AC would or would not have refused consent to a caesarean. We hold, however, that without a competent refusal from AC to go forward with the surgery, and without a finding through substituted judgment that AC would not have consented to the surgery, it was error for the trial court to proceed to a balancing analysis, weighing the rights of AC against the interests of the state.

There are two additional arguments against overriding AC's objections to caesarean surgery. First, as the American Public Health Association cogently states in its *amicus curiae* brief:

> Rather than protecting the health of women and children, court-ordered caesareans erode the element of trust that permits a pregnant woman to communicate to her physician – without fear of reprisal – all information relevant to her proper diagnosis and treatment. An even more serious consequence of court-ordered interventions is that it drives women at high risk of complications during pregnancy and childbirth out of the health care system to avoid coerced treatment.

Second, and even more compellingly, any judicial proceeding in a case such as this will ordinarily take place – like the one before us here – under time constraints so pressing that it is difficult or impossible for the mother to communicate adequately with counsel, or for counsel to organize an effective factual and legal presentation in defense of her liberty and privacy interests and bodily integrity. Any intrusion implicating such basic values ought not to be lightly undertaken when the mother not only is precluded from conducting pre-trial discovery (to which she would be entitled as a matter of course in any controversy over even a modest amount of money) but also is in no position to prepare meaningfully for trial. As one commentator has noted:

> The procedural shortcomings rampant in these cases are not mere technical deficiencies. They undermine the authority of the decisions themselves, posing serious questions as to whether judges can, in the absence of genuine notice, adequate representation, explicit standards of proof, and right of appeal, realistically frame principled and useful legal responses to the dilemmas with which they are being confronted. Certainly courts dealing with other kinds of medical decision-making conflicts have insisted both upon much more rigorous procedural standards and upon significantly more information.

Gallagher, *Parental Invasions and Interventions: What's Wrong with Fetal Rights*, 10 Harv Women's LJ 9, 49 (1987).

In this case AC's court-appointed attorney was unable even to meet with his client before the hearing. By the time the case was heard, AC's condition did not allow her to be present, nor was it reasonably possible for the judge to hear from her directly. The factual record, moreover, was significantly flawed because AC's medical records were not before the court and because Dr Jeffrey Moscow, the physician who had been treating AC for many years, was not even contacted and hence did not testify. Finally, the time for legal preparation was so minimal that neither the court nor counsel mentioned the doctrine of substituted judgment, which – with benefit of briefs, oral arguments, and above all, time – we now deem critical to the outcome of this case. We cannot be at all certain that the trial judge would have reached the same decision if the testimony of Dr Moscow and the abundant legal scholarship filed in this court had been meaningfully available to him, and if there had been enough time for him to consider and reflect on these matters as a judge optimally should do.

B. Substituted Judgment

In the previous section we discussed the right of an individual to accept or reject medical treatment. We concluded that if a patient is competent and has made an informed decision regarding the course of her medical treatment, that decision will control in virtually all cases. Sometimes, however, as our analysis presupposes here, a once competent patient will be unable to render an informed decision. In such a case, we hold that the court must make a substituted judgment on behalf of the patient, based on all the evidence. This means that the duty of the court, 'as surrogate for the incompetent, is to determine as best it can what choice that individual, if competent, would make with respect to medical procedures.' *In Re Boyd, supra,* 403 A 2d at 750 (citation omitted).

. . . [T]o determine the subjective desires of the patient, the court must consider the totality of the evidence, focusing particularly on written or oral directions concerning treatment to family, friends, and health-care professionals. The court should also take into account the patient's past decisions regarding medical treatment, and attempt to ascertain from what is known about the patient's value system, goals, and desires what the patient would decide if competent. *See In Re Conroy, supra,* 98 NJ at 343-44, 486 A 2d at 1229-1230; *In Re Dorone, supra,* 349 Pa Super at 68, 502 A 2d at 1278.

After considering the patient's prior statements, if any, the previous medical decisions of the patient, and the values held by the patient, the court may still be unsure what course the patient would choose. In such circumstances the court may supplement its knowledge about the patient by determining what most persons would likely do in a similar situation. *In Re Boyd, supra,* 403 A 2d at 751, citing *Saikewicz, supra,* 373 Mass, at 343, 370 NE 2d at 430; *accord,* 1983 President's Commission Report, *Deciding to Forego Life-Sustaining Treatment* at 135; 1982 President's Commission Report, *Making Health Care Decisions* at 180-181. When the patient is pregnant, however, she may not be concerned exclusively with her own welfare. Thus it is proper for the court, in a case such as this, to weigh (along with all the other factors) the mother's prognosis, the viability of the fetus, the probable result of treatment or non-treatment for both mother and fetus, and the mother's likely interest in avoiding impairment for her child together with her own instincts for survival. *Cf In Re Roe, supra,* 383 Mass at 431, 421 NE 2d at 57 . . .

The [trial] court did not go on, as it should have done, to make a finding as to what AC would have chosen to do if she were competent. Instead, the court undertook to balance the state's and LMC's interests in surgical interventions against AC's perceived interest is not having the caesarean performed . . .

What a trial court must do in a case such as this is to determine, if possible whether the patient is capable of making an informed decision about the course of her medical treatment. If she is, and if she makes such a decision, her wishes will control in virtually all cases. If the court finds that the patient is incapable of making an informed consent (and thus incompetent), then the court must make a substituted judgment. This means that the court must ascertain as best it can what the patient would do if faced with the particular treatment question. Again, in virtually all cases the decisions of the patient, albeit discerned through the mechanism of substituted judgment, will control. We do not quite foreclose the possibility that a conflicting state interest may be so compelling that the patient's wishes must yield but we anticipate that such cases will be extremely rare and truly exceptional. This is not such a case.

Having said that, we go no further. We need not decide whether, or in what circumstances, the state's interests can ever prevail over the interests of a pregnant patient. We emphasize, nevertheless, that it would be an extraordinary case indeed in which a court might ever be justified in overriding the patient's wishes and authorizing a major surgical procedure such as a caesarean section. Throughout this opinion we have stressed that the patient's wishes, once they are ascertained, must be followed in 'virtually all cases,' *ante* at 1249, unless there are 'truly extraordinary or compelling reasons to override them,' *ante* at 1247. Indeed, some may doubt that there could ever be a situation extraordinary or compelling enough to justify a massive intrusion into a person's body, such as a caesarean section, against that person's will. Whether such a situation may someday present itself is a question that we need not strive to answer here. We see no need to reach out and decide an issue that is not presented on the record before us; this case is difficult enough as it is. We think it sufficient for now to chart the course for future cases resembling this one, and to express the hope that we shall not be presented with a case in the foreseeable future that requires us to sail off the chart into the unknown.[23]

Footnotes to majority opinion

8.   There are also practical consequences to consider. What if AC had refused to comply with a court order that she submit to a caesarean? Under the circumstances, she obviously could not have been held in civil contempt and imprisoned or required to pay a daily fine until compliance. *Cf United States v United Mine Workers,* 330 US 258, 304-306, 67 S Ct 677, 701002. 91 LEd 884 (1947); *DD v MT* 550 A 2d 37, 43 (DC 1988). Enforcement could be accomplished only through physical force or its equivalent. AC would have to be fastened with restraints to the operating table, or perhaps involuntarily rendered unconscious by force injecting her with an anesthetic, and then subjected to unwanted major surgery. Such situations would surely give one pause in a civil society, especially when AC had done no wrong. *Cf Rochin v California,* 72 S Ct 205, 208.

23.   In particular, we stress that nothing in this opinion should be read as either approving or disapproving the holding in *In Re Madyun, supra.* There are substantial factual differences between *Madyun* and the present case. In this case, for instance, the medical interests of the mother and the fetus were in sharp conflict: what was good for one would have been harmful to the other. In *Madyun,* however, there was no real conflict between the interests of mother and fetus; on the contrary, there was strong evidence that the proposed caesarean would be beneficial to both. Moreover, in *Madyun* the pregnancy was at full term, and Mrs Madyun had been in labor for two and a half days; in this case, however, AC was barely two-thirds of the way through her pregnancy and there were no signs of labor. If another *Madyun* type case ever comes before this court, its result may well depend on facts that we cannot now foresee. For that reason (among others), we defer until another day any discussion of whether *Madyun* was rightly or wrongly decided.

Belson, Associate Judge: I agree with much of the majority opinion, but I disagree with its ultimate ruling that the trial court's order must be set aside, and with the narrow view it takes of the state's interest in preserving life and the unborn child's interest in life.

More specifically, I agree with the guidance the opinion affords trial judges as to how to approach a case like this, first determining the mother's competency to make an informed decision whether to have a caesarean delivery and, if the mother is not competent, then making a substituted judgment for the mother. I also agree that, with respect to surgical procedures, the pregnant woman's wishes, either as stated expressly or as discerned through substituted judgment, should ordinarily be respected and carried out unless there are compelling reasons to override them . . .

[An] aspect of the majority opinion deserves comment. Having determined that the trial court must be reversed, the majority goes on to opine, in dictum, that this particular case is not one of those 'extremely rare and truly exceptional' cases in which a patient's wishes regarding the proposed medical treatment can be overruled by reason of a compelling state interest (here, the interest in protecting the life of the viable unborn child). This is dictum because, as the majority points out, '[w]e have no reason to believe that, if competent, AC would or would not have refused consent to a caesarean.' Majority opinion at 1247. That being the case, and the actual application of the standard the majority adopts to the facts of this case not being necessary to the majority's determination to reverse, one must regard as dictum the majority's statement that this would not be one of those rare cases in which compelling interest might warrant overriding a mother's decision not to consent.

I think it appropriate, nevertheless, to state my disagreement with the very limited view the majority opinion takes of the circumstances in which the interests of a viable unborn child can afford such compelling reasons. The state's interest in preserving human life and the viable unborn child's interest in survival are entitled, I think, to more weight than I find them assigned by the majority when it states that 'in virtually all cases the decision of the patient . . . will control.' Majority opinion at 1252. I would hold that in those instances, fortunately rare, in which the viable unborn child's interest in living and the state's parallel interest in protecting human life come into conflict with the mother's decision to forgo a procedure such as a caesarean section, a balancing should be struck in which the unborn child's and the state's interests are entitled to substantial weight . . .

. . . for the purposes that are, at least, relevant to this case, a viable unborn child is a *person* at common law who has legal rights that are entitled to the protection of the courts. In a case like the one before us, the unborn child is a patient of both the hospital and any treating physician, and the hospital or physician may be liable to the child for the child's prenatal injury or death if caused by their negligence . . .

Without going into the difficult question of the extent to which an unborn viable child may be entitled to protection under the Fifth, the Fourteenth, or other Amendments to the Constitution, the already recognized rights and interests mentioned above are sufficient to indicate the need for a balancing process in which the rights of the viable unborn child are assigned substantial weight. This view is consistent with the decision of the only appellate court which has heretofore considered this issue . . .

The balancing test should be applied in instances in which women become pregnant and carry an unborn child to the point of viability. This is not an unreasonable classification because, I submit, a woman who carries a child to viability is in fact a member of a unique category of persons. Her circumstances differ fundamentally from those of other potential patients for medical procedures that will aid another person, for example, a potential donor of bone marrow for transplant. This is so because she has undertaken to bear another human being, and has carried an unborn child to viability. Another unique feature of the situation we address arises from the singular nature of the dependency of the unborn child upon the mother. A woman carrying a viable unborn child is not in the same category as a relative, friend, or stranger called upon to donate bone marrow or an organ for transplant. Rather, the expectant mother has placed herself in a special class of persons who are bringing another person into existence, and upon whom that other person's life is totally dependent. Also, uniquely, the viable unborn child is literally captive within the mother's body. No other potential beneficiary of a surgical procedure on another is in that position.

For all of these reasons, a balancing becomes appropriate in those few cases where the interests we are discussing come into conflict. To so state is in no sense to fail to recognize the extremely strong interest of each individual person, including of course the expectant mother, in her bodily integrity, her privacy, and, where involved, her religious beliefs.

Thus, I cannot agree with the conclusion of the majority opinion that while we 'do not quite foreclose the possibility that a conflicting state interest may be so compelling that the patient's wishes must yield . . . we anticipate that such cases will be extremely rare and truly exceptional.' Majority opinion at 1252. While it is, fortunately, true that such cases will be rare in the sense that such conflicts between mother and viable unborn child are rare, I cannot agree that in cases where a viable unborn child is in the picture, it would be extremely rare, within that universe, to require that the mother accede to the vital needs of the viable unborn child.[8] . . .

Despite the majority's admonition that 'nothing in this opinion should be read as either approving or disapproving the holding in *In Re Madyun*,' 114 Daily Wash L Rptr 2233 (DC Super Ct July 26, 1986), majority opinion at 1252-1253 n 23, I am concerned that the majority's emphasis on the 'extremely rare and truly exceptional' nature of the circumstances in which the unborn child's rights may prevail may move the law toward the extinguishment of the rights of unborn children in cases like *In Re Madyun*. In that case, the trial court was faced with a situation in which an expectant mother refused on religious grounds to consent to a caesarean section even though she was already in labor, and sixty hours had passed since her membrane had ruptured. Although the heavy risk of infection and possible death to the fetus in the absence of a caesarean section were explained to both parents, they refused consent to the caesarean section. Because the child could not be delivered through the birth canal, the child faced a serious and increasing danger of death or brain damage, and the mother's health was endangered as well.

After considering the facts and applicable law, the Superior Court granted the hospital's request for authorization to deliver the baby by the most expedient means – a caesarean section. Counsel appointed to represent the unborn child had also joined the hospital's request. A motions division of this court denied a stay of the trial court's order. Pursuant of the trial court's order, the caesarean section was performed, and a healthy child was born and survives.

I next address the sensitive question of how to balance the competing rights and interests of the viable unborn child and the state against those of the rare expectant mother who elects not to have a caesarean section necessary to save her life or her child. The indisputable view that a woman carrying a viable child has an extremely strong interest in her own life, health, bodily integrity, privacy, and religious beliefs necessarily requires that her election be given correspondingly great weight in the balancing process. In a case, however, where the court in an exercise of a substituted judgment has concluded that the patient would probably opt against a caesarean section, the court should vary the weight to be given this factor in proportion to the confidence the court has in the accuracy of its conclusion. Thus, in a case where the indicia of the incompetent patient's judgment are equivocal, the court should accord this factor correspondingly less weight. The appropriate weight to be given other factors will have to be worked out by the development of law in this area, and cannot be prescribed in a single court opinion. Some considerations obviously merit special attention in the balancing process. One such consideration is any danger to the mother's life or health, physical or mental, including the relatively small but still significant danger that necessarily inheres in any caesarean delivery, and including especially any danger that exceeds that level. The mother's religious beliefs as they relate to the operation would appear to deserve inclusion in the balancing process.

On the other side of the analysis, it is appropriate to look to the relative likelihood of the unborn child's survival. This could range from the situation in *Madyun* where the full-term child's chances for survival were apparently excellent, through a case like the one before us where the unborn child's chances of survival were from fifty to sixty percent, and on to cases where the child's chances for survival are less than even. The child's interest in being born with as little impairment as possible should be considered. This may weigh in favor of a delivery sooner rather than later. The most important factor on this side of the scale, however, is life itself, because the viable unborn child that dies because of the mother's refusal to have a caesarean delivery is deprived, entirely and irrevocably, of the life on which the child was about to embark.

Turning to the specifics of this case . . . [w]eighed in the balance against ordering the procedure were two considerations that were central to the entire proceeding: the invasive and serious nature of the proposed surgery and the fact that such surgery cannot ordinarily be performed without the consent of the patient. Under the peculiar circumstances of this case, the influence of these factors was diminished by the fact that it was not clear whether AC would have consented to the surgery or not. Before events began to close in on her, AC had agreed to a caesarean at twenty-eight weeks. Thus, she was not averse, in principle, to having that particular type of surgery. What was unresolved was whether she would consent to that surgery at twenty-six and one-half weeks, when the unborn child's chances of survival were somewhat reduced and the chances of impairment to the child somewhat enhanced. It was clear that she had intended all along to carry her unborn child until the point the child could be successfully delivered, and she persevered in that intention even when she knew she would not live long, if at all, after her child was born. Even in the tragically difficult circumstances in which AC found herself at the very time of the court's proceedings, she first appeared in her sedated state to agree to the procedure and then apparently to disagree. Under the circumstances, the court could deem these matters, usually most pertinent to a determination of substituted judgment, to lessen the net weight of the factors that weighed against the performance of the surgery. Also to be considered in the balance was the rather minimal, but nevertheless undisputable, additional risk that caesarean delivery presented for the mother.[15]

Turning to the interest of the unborn child in living and the parallel interest of the state in protecting that life, the evidence indicated that the child had a fifty to sixty percent chance of survival and a less than twenty percent chance of entering life with a serious handicap such as cerebral palsy or mental retardation. The evidence also showed that a delay in delivering the child would have increased the likelihood of a handicap. In view of the record before [the trial judge], and on the basis that there had been no plain error in not applying the sort of substituted judgment analysis that we for the first time mandate in today's ruling, I think it cannot be said that he abused his discretion in the way he struck the balance between the considerations that favored the procedure and those that went against it.

Footnotes to dissenting opinion
8.   To the contrary, it appears that a majority of courts faced with this issue have found that the state's compelling interest in protection of the unborn child should prevail. *See* Noble-Allgire, *Court-Ordered Caesarean Sections,* 10 J Legal Med 211, 236 (1989). I added that in mapping this uncharted area of the law, we can draw lines and a line I would draw would be to preclude the use of physical force to perform an operation. The force of the court order itself as well as the use of the contempt power would, I think, be adequate in most cases. *See id,* at 243.
15.   I note that there was no evidence in this case that the caesarean procedure was likely to shorten AC's life. Although the trial judge alluded in his findings to testimony to that effect, he was apparently referring to argument of counsel rather than testimony. After the judge's findings were made, the record was reopened to receive information from Dr Hamner who had just spoken to AC. In reporting that she seemed more lucid and had three times answered that she assented to a caesarean delivery, he said he had asked her if she realized that she 'may not survive the surgical procedure.' Because Dr Hammer had already testified that in his opinion AC had less than twenty-four hours to live, and because he presumably was concerned with obtaining the consent of a patient informed of even those risks that were less than probable, this cannot be deemed the statement of an opinion that the surgery would probably shorten AC's life.

In effect, this case appears to have stemmed the tide of decision authorising caesarian sections and other compulsory treatments against the wishes of a competent mother. The majority view reflects the position that the patient's right to refuse treatment is determinative even if she is pregnant. In other words, as a matter of law her right outweighs any conflicting interest of the unborn child. On the other hand, the majority leave open the possibility that if there are 'truly extraordinary or compelling reasons' the patient's right must give way. However, such cases (if they exist) will be rare since the majority contemplate that the patient's refusal will be effective in 'virtually all cases'. Thus *Re AC* rejects, *exceptional cases apart,* the fourth societal interest advanced in *Conroy* as potentially outweighing the patient's right.

What then, if anything, amounts to an exceptional case? In *Re AC,* in footnote 23 to their judgment, the majority refer to the earlier decision in Washington DC of *Re Madyun* (1990) 573 A 2d 1259 appended to the judgment in *Re AC.*

What is the difference between the facts of *Re AC* and *Madyun* which justifies the different outcomes? In *Madyun* the intervention carried no risk of harm to the pregnant woman beyond that inherent in the procedure itself. By contrast, in *Re AC* the procedure did carry an additional risk, namely of accelerating AC's death because of her weakened physical condition. Of course, this makes the facts of *Re AC* unusual and the situation in *Madyun* the norm. On this basis, the 'exceptional case' recognised by the majority in *Re AC* based upon *Madyun* (where intervention is justified against the pregnant woman's wishes) is *in fact* the usual case, ie the result in *Madyun* would be more common than that in *Re AC.*

Clearly this was not contemplated in *Re AC,* since it would produce the result that in most cases the mother's right to refuse would be made to give way to the claims of the unborn child; the exact opposite of what the majority intended.

As you will have noticed, the judge in *Re S* relied upon the 'exceptional case' left open in *Re AC*. If we are right that the DC court misstates what is the exception and what is the norm, then the decision in *Re S* cannot be sustained.

(iii) WHAT SHOULD A COURT DO?

Having doubted the juridical basis for the decision in *Re S* we must now confront the question of policy: is it right for a court to engage in a balancing exercise so as deny a pregnant woman the right to refuse treatment? Certainly there are circumstances in which the law has given some recognition to the claims of an unborn child (eg *McKay v Essex Area Health Authority* [1982] 2 All ER 771, [1982] QB 1166, CA; *Burton v Islington Health Authority* [1993] QB 204, [1992] 3 All ER 833, CA; Congenital Disabilities (Civil Liability) Act 1976). This recognition has not been at the expense of the rights of the pregnant woman to control her own body (see the general exclusion of a mother as defendant in a pre-natal injury claim under the 1976 Act). There are, of course, moral arguments which could suggest that the unborn child, particularly as it develops, may have a legitimate *moral* claim on the mother so as to limit her freedom of action. But there is a world of difference between moral claims and legal claims enforceable by the courts – ie between what one *ought* to do and what one *must* do and can be made to do by the state. In our view, it is inappropriate for the law to seek to recognise and give effect to what is even at the realm of moral argument a problematic claim on behalf of the unborn child. The arguments are well made in the following seminal paper.

Nancy Rhoden, 'The Judge in the Delivery Room: The Emergency of Court-Ordered Caesareans' (1986) 74 Cal LR 1951

Not surprisingly, very few cases involve performing a medical procedure on one person in order to save the life of another. This dearth of precedent is partially explained by the highly factual circumstances such cases require – that an organ or bodily substance of *A*, and only *A*, may potentially save *B*, yet *A* refuses to donate it. Additionally, few people in even such desparate straits as *B* are likely to try to compel donation by *A*, because this goes so strongly against the grain of American insistence on bodily integrity, autonomy, and nonsubordination. The general law concerning the duty (or lack of duty) to rescue illustrates this. The following discussion will first briefly review the principles of Samaritan law and then will examine the few cases that consider bodily interventions intended to aid a third party.

With limited exceptions, Anglo-American law imposes no duty to come to the assistance of a person in distress. One exception provides that one who injures or imperils another has a duty to render aid. Another exception requires that a person who begins a rescue attempt perform it with reasonable care, and that she not abandon the effort if doing so will leave the imperiled person in a worse position than before. For our purposes, the most important exception is that some special relationships between the parties justify imposing a duty to rescue. Special relationships clearly include those such as innkeeper to guest, common carrier to passenger, and jailer to prisoner. They also include such fundamental relationships as parent and child, and it has been suggested that other fundamental relationships, such as husband and wife, should also be recognized as giving rise to a duty to rescue. These exceptions mitigate the harshness of the general principle that one may be a 'bad Samaritan,' a controversial principle that many commentators have long criticized as being callous and indifferent both to moral duties and to human life.

Whatever one's view about the general rule, one feature of the law of rescue is quite uncontroversial: even when rescue is required, rescues that risk life and limb are, and should remain, optional. Persons to whom the various exceptions apply have an obligation to take only rather minimal action, such as warning of danger or calling a doctor or other proper authorities. The few states that have statutorily created a duty to rescue require only such assistance as can be rendered without danger to the rescuer. It would, therefore, be an extraordinary revision of American law to require risky rescues, even by a spouse or parent.

In *McFall v Shimp* [10 Pa D and C 3d 90 (1978)] the court wisely recognized that a plaintiff's claim to mandatory medical intrusion on another so that the plaintiff's life might be saved fell under the rubric of Samaritan law. Robert McFall was a victim of aplastic anemia who sought to force David Shimp, his cousin, to donate bone marrow to him. Although bone marrow extraction is far less risky than major surgery, it is painful and invasive, requiring multiple insertions of a curved needle into the iliac bones while the donor is under anesthesia. Shimp underwent initial tests to determine bone marrow compatibility, and was found to be the only family member with potentially compatible bone marrow. He then refused to undergo further testing. Although the court found the defendant's conduct morally reprehensible, it refused to order him to complete the testing and, if found compatible, to donate. The court emphasized that there is no legal duty to rescue others, and stated that to require this Samaritan act 'would change every concept and principle upon which our society is founded.' It continued:

> For a society which respects the rights of *one* individual, to sink its teeth into the jug-ular vein or neck of one of its members and suck from it sustenance for *another* member, is revolting to our hard-wrought concepts of jurisprudence. Forceable extraction of living body tissue causes revulsion to the judicial mind. Such would raise the spectre of the swastika and the Inquisition, reminiscent of the horrors this portends.

Thus, the court would not order this invasion of Shimp's body even though Shimp's refusal to donate meant death for McFall.

McFall is a sad case, but it was not, as the court's strong and even lurid language indicates, a hard one. The principle of privacy, autonomy, and bodily integrity compel the conclusion that however repugnant the refusal to aid may be, the courts cannot mandate assistance of this nature and magnitude. This conclusion almost certainly would not differ had the case involved a father and child. Mandatory organ donation is a standard scholarly example of a practice that would unquestionably lie beyond the limits of the law. As Angela Holder states, 'In no case is an adult ever ordered to surrender a kidney, bone marrow, or any other part of his body for donation to his child, to another relative, or to anyone else.' Likewise, Donald Regan asks rhetorically, 'Would a court impose criminal liability on anyone, even the child's parent, who did not attempt to save the child at the risk of second-degree burns over one or two per cent of his or her body?' Because risky rescues have never been required, even of parents, we must conclude with Holder and Regan that courts would not compel a parent to donate bone marrow to a dying child.

This conclusion is supported by *In Re George* [630 SW 2d 614 (Mo Ct App 1982)] another sad case in which a thirty-three-year-old adoptee suffering from chronic myelocytic leukemia sought a court order to open his adoption records so that he could locate a compatible bone marrow donor. The judge consulted the man's natural mother, who was tested but found not compatible. The judge then contacted the alleged natural father, whose name was obtained from the adoption records. The man denied paternity and was unwilling to be tested for compatibility. The matter stopped there; the court refused to give the dying man his natural father's name.

Ordering a Cesarean to save the fetus is just as extraordinary as ordering a parent to donate bone marrow to save a child. Even so, courts faced with these cases have not recognized this. This is probably because the Cesarean cases *seem* different. The woman is going to give birth anyway – if she just agrees to a surgical delivery rather than insisting on a vaginal one, the baby will survive unharmed. If she refuses, the harm to the baby will be both immediate and in the same location as the woman (literally). In contrast, the victim who is refused a bone marrow donation will succumb more slowly and, perhaps, out of sight. In addition, it is the doctor, with his or her persuasive professional authority, who seeks the Cesarean rather than the individual victim.

These differences may affect the emotional responses of participants and judges. They do not, however, legally distinguish the refusals. In each case, a parent is refusing an invasive and somewhat risky procedure without which his or her child will die or suffer severe harm. John Robertson, a proponent of mandatory Cesareans in certain circumstances, accepts this equivalency, and hence supports compulsory parental 'donations' of blood, bone marrow, and perhaps even organs, depending upon the degree of risk. Robertson's consistency of approach helps to demonstrate the equivalency of the two situations. Once equated, however, the degree to which a court-ordered Cesarean violates fundamental tenets of American law also becomes clear: logical consistency demands that if Cesareans can be required, American law concerning duties to rescue must be radically restructured.

It might be objected that a pregnant woman is a special case because the voluntary act of continuing a pregnancy creates special obligations over and above the duty to rescue imposed upon all parents. A further objection might claim that carrying a fetus to term but refusing a Cesarean may cause the child to be far worse off – profoundly retarded, for example – than if it had never been conceived. If construed as suggesting that the woman fits into an additional exception to the 'bad Samaritan' principle as someone who has begun a rescue, these arguments are still insufficient to create a legal duty to run physical risks for the sake of the fetus. Even if one takes the position that a woman who has carried a pregnancy to term has embarked upon a course of action vis-à-vis the fetus that may be viewed as a rescue and that may arguably allow certain demands to be placed upon her, compulsory surgery goes far beyond demands imposed on other voluntary rescuers. For example, the person who begins to rescue a child trapped in a burning building but then realizes it is far more dangerous than he thought, would not have a duty to continue the rescue despite the change in circumstances. In the Cesarean context the mother's act of nurturing the fetus through pregnancy would not require that she undergo additional risks to ensure its safe passage into the world.

Perhaps, though, this legalistic interpretation does not do justice to the claim that the woman has assumed special obligations. Surely what is meant by the claim is not completely captured by the argument that at the time of delivery multiple exceptions to the 'bad Samaritan' principle may apply. Rather, the real thrust of this objection seems to be that the woman is physically and morally responsible for the life within her, and she ought to do more than the minimum to promote its welfare. The extent of a pregnant woman's moral obligations to her developing fetus merits serious consideration, especially as we learn more about substances that may harm the fetus. Fortunately, most women in our society take these obligations very seriously, even subordinating their desires for such things as alcohol, cigarettes, or caffeine to the interests of the fetus. But in this very private and bodily sphere, the issue of moral obligations, even very compelling ones, must be kept distinct from the issue of legal coercion of individuals to meet their moral obligations. The law of rescue condones many omissions that are morally reprehensible. For that matter, refusal to undertake risk rescues does not normally even invoke moral opprobrium. Morally, we seem to have a different standard for pregnant women. But this moral standard does not justify an unparalleled level of legal constraint.

Although there are no other cases involving *refusal* to donate a bodily organ, in a number of cases parents have sought court permission to authorize an incompetent sibling to donate a kidney to a sibling suffering from renal failure. Some courts have granted this permission. One commentator has suggested, in an extraordinary interpretation of these decisions, 'that there is a rather stringent duty to prevent or remove harm, or both, to a member of one's immediate family, a duty that involves significant risk to oneself and is shared by members of the family who are incompetent to shoulder other types of obligations.' She concludes that cases authorizing donation by incompetents can constitute a legal precedent for compelling parents to undergo invasive medical procedures, including organ donation, for the sake of their children and, of course, for analogous forms of parental compulsion.

Cases authorizing donation from incompetents have not even hinted that the incompetent has a moral or legally enforceable obligation to donate. In fact, there is little doubt that even an incompetent refusal would be sacrosanct. The problem is that could he or she understand the issue, the potential donor might, or might not, wish to donate. Many courts faced with these cases have used the substituted judgment test, which asks what the incompetent would most likely want. When courts have permitted donation, they have stressed the incompetent's probable anguish at the sibling's death. Other courts have rejected the claim that the proper test is whether the incompetent would consent to donate if he could do so, and have simply refused to authorize the transplant on the grounds that it is not in the best interest of the incompetent. Some might argue that in the cases that authorize donation, the imputation of devotion and altruism to the incompetent is somewhat suspect. But even if some courts exaggerate notions of filial devotion to allow donation, the focus of the substituted judgment test on the incompetent's probable desires demonstrates that refusal would also be honored.

The law of donations from the dead also reflects the absence of a legal obligation to donate. The current law is that organs cannot be removed unless either the person had, when alive, indicated his donative intent, or consent from the family is obtained. A person opposed to donation may refuse to donate both for 'good' reasons – religious beliefs, for example – and for 'bad' ones ('if I can't live, I don't want to help someone else to live'). Proposals to revise the law to increase the supply of available organs would merely reverse this presumption; routine removal would be allowed unless this individual had previously indicated opposition, or the family objected when informed of this practice. In other words, such proposals still would not violate the prior choices of the deceased by nonconsensual organ removal. Certainly, by way of comparison, an organ taken from a cadaver can save a life just as an emergency Cesarean can. Yet, respect for individual choice extends even to those decisions that can be exercised only after a person's death. In this way, forcing women to undergo major surgery emerges as an anomalous and inconsistent derogation of individual choice . . .

Why should law allow these tragedies?
We have seen that legal principles support respecting maternal refusals of surgery. This is an extraordinarily complex and troubling area, however. It surely merits something beyond narrowly legal analysis. A taxonomy of woman's moral obligations to the developing fetus is far beyond this Article's scope. Yet, I suspect that most people would find a woman who refused a Cesarean for a frivolous reason such as abhorring abdominal scars to be acting in an immoral manner. They might wonder what is wrong with judicial intervention to prevent the tragic consequences of her reprehensible conduct. After all, pregnancy *is* unique, and the woman in labor is uniquely able to prevent irreparable harm to a vulnerable being by undergoing a quite routine surgical procedure. In these unusual cases, why should not a court hold that the principles of autonomy, nonsubordination, and bodily integrity exemplified in the law of treatment refusal, rescue, and abortion are weighty, but are not weighty enough to justify the predicted harm?

There are broad societal grounds that favor paying this tragic price for maternal freedom. First, court-ordered Cesareans may start us down that 'slippery slope' toward controlling and coercing pregnant women in the name of fetal well-being. In addition . . . physicians may be overly alarmist in their predictions, causing judges to order unnecessary surgery. But let us hold both 'slippery slope' fears and medical realities in abeyance a bit longer. Assuming that medical predictions are accurate, and that at least some maternal refusals may evoke justifiable moral condemnation, can we argue, at the level of ethical or legal theory, that upholding maternal refusals is the best general policy?

. . . I argue that despite the strong impulse to save the baby in an individual case, courts that respond to this temptation behave far more problematically than those that resist. My argument seeks to make explicit what is implicit in the *McFall* holding: that in some cases it is wrong for courts to pursue admittedly better consequences because this pursuit involves such significant invasions of individual rights and autonomy that they compromise the integrity of the court and the humanity of those subject to its rulings. In other words, I suggest that in these cases, courts should not decide on the basis of consequences, but rather upon the primacy of individual rights and upon principles that limit the way in which a person (or state) may legitimately treat another.

My argument inevitably has its limitations. These cases are true dilemmas, pitting certain of our most fundamental intuitions against one another. I do not show that upholding refusals is morally unproblematic – no solution here will be ideal . . . the problems inherent in elevating consequences above rights are extremely serious, and that courts violate our fundamental ethical intuitions and societal precepts when they intervene to compel one individual to assume risks for the sake of another.

It is virtually a truism to say that the issue of court-ordered Cesareans could arise only within a medical system in which Cesareans had become safe and relatively routine. I suspect that few doctors would even consider seeking a court order if the recalcitrant woman faced unusually high surgical risks – for example, if she had a severe bleeding disorder or a family history of unexplained death or paralysis from anesthesia. Analyzing why surgery should not be imposed if there is a significant risk of serious maternal harm, albeit a lesser risk than the fetus would face in a vaginal delivery, may help show why a proper appreciation of the import of harm suggests that even relatively safe major surgery should not be imposed.

Theories of moral and legal obligation uniformly recognize the fundamental fact that human beings tend to value their own lives above those of others, making it unrealistic to expect them to sacrifice themselves for other persons. Hence, using lethal force in self-defence is lawful, even if the attacker is himself innocent. A person under attack by several others can kill all of them, even though the end result is the death of several persons rather than one. Objectively, this result is worse, but an individual is not expected to take an objective stance when his own life is threatened. Likewise, even in countries where rescue is required, no one is under a legal duty to risk his life in a rescue. This is simply too much to demand of a person, in the light of the ingrained human drive for self-preservation.

Needless to say, persons in the position of making decisions about others must respect the fact that an individual's life is, to him, invaluable. This is another reason why it would be unthinkable for a surgeon unilaterally to decide to distribute one person's organs to five other patients who desperately need just those organs. The almost primal revulsion we feel at a person's or government's sacrificing one person to benefit others applies to lesser bodily invasions as well. As Laurence Tribe states, 'That one person's two good eyes, distributed to two blind neighbours, might yield a net increase in happiness on the theory that one blind person will experience less misery than two, cannot justify a governmental decision to compel the exchange.' Were there a serious risk of the woman's suffering permanent harm from the surgery, requiring it would seem too much like these examples, where our intuitions strongly tell us that such decisions are ethically impermissible.

The intuition that it is impermissible to harm one person to aid another is derived from two closely related principles. The first is that any duty to help must be viewed as less weighty or stringent than a duty not to harm, such that if helping A requires harming B, it is better that we forego helping A. The second principle is that, contrary to the consequentialist's views, it is significant that A's injury will occur through natural forces or the malevolent act of a third person, but that the harm to B, if you choose to aid A, will be of your own doing. It is tragic that persons are harmed, but it is wrong that you harm them. These principles explain why physicians and courts would be so unlikely to impose surgery upon, for example, a woman who would be rendered sterile by it; it would be too clear that the fetus could not be rescued without harming her.

But how does all this apply to the typical Cesarean case, given the general safety of surgical delivery? First, we should note that there is at least a risk, albeit a small one, of lasting physical harm. The mortality rate for Cesareans is very low, approximately 4 in 10,000. For the individual woman, however, there is no way to determine the precise risk of death imposed, because statistics apply to groups, not individuals. Nor can the court foresee the extent to which the risk might be increased by the fact that the surgery will often be done on an emergency basis and will be nonconsensual as well. Thus, the court necessarily imposes some small chance of death or permanent damage upon the woman. More importantly, if our society adopts a general policy of mandating Cesarean delivery when the fetus is imperiled, some women, albeit a very small number, will eventually be sacrificed in order to save some much larger number of babies. Thus, although the chances of sacrifice in any individual case are very small, when we view compulsory Cesareans as a general policy, we see that it imposes the very trade-offs between maternal and fetal health that the Supreme Court disallowed in the abortion cases. Although the Court did not provide an ethical analysis of why trade-offs were impermissible, abortion doctrine reflects the view that a woman should not be used without her consent as means to enhanced fetal health.

We need not, however, rely on the potential for death or lasting disability to hold that forced Cesarean delivery constitutes a harm. Returning to Nagel's example:

> You have an auto accident one winter night on a lonely road. The other passengers are badly injured, the car is out of commission, and the road is deserted, so you run along it till you find an isolated house. The house turns out to be occupied by an old woman who is looking after her small grandchild. There is no phone, but there is a car in the garage, and you ask desperately to borrow it and explain the situation. She doesn't believe you. Terrified by your desperation, she runs upstairs and locks herself in the bathroom, leaving you alone with the child. You pound ineffectively on the door and search without success for the car keys. Then it occurs to you that she might be persuaded to tell you where they are if you were to twist the child's arm outside the bathroom door. Should you do it?

. . . someone who objected to a pure deontological [ie, rights-based] ethic could readily feel that twisting the child's arm was justifiable because the wrong was de mimimus and the harm it would prevent severe. But how about breaking his arm? If the distraught driver goes this far, he will not only violate the boy's rights but will also cause him significant, though presumably not permanent, physical harm. It is safe to say that most people, except for thoroughgoing consequentialists, would feel this was going too far, because harming the boy to this degree, even in the pursuit of good consequences, transcends the bounds of moral permissibility. The reason it does, of course, hearkens back to the principle that one should not breach the (stringent) duty not to harm in order to comply with the (weaker) duty to do good.

Performing a Cesarean, I submit, imposes harm that is on the order of breaking the child's arm to benefit the passengers. Neither performing a Cesarean nor breaking an arm is likely to have permanent consequences, but they both involve substantial pain, bodily invasion, and subsequent recovery time. Similarly, the *McFall* court's revulsion at imposing the (lesser) harm of bone marrow extraction can be explained by the unwillingness to treat a human being as a means to another's end, especially when doing so entails physical harm.

Just as the *McFall* court implied that its judicial integrity would be compromised by 'sinking its teeth' into one citizen to aid another, courts ordering Cesareans compromise their integrity by plunging knives into unconsenting women.

Of course, the court merely authorizes the surgery, it does not perform it. But this only obscures the violence lurking within the court order, violence that can be highlighted by practical realities. For example what are the limits on force that may be imposed on women . . . who refuse to return to the hospital? Can the police be sent to get them? Or, if a woman is present but resisting, can the doctors hold her down and forcibly anesthetize her? Concerned physicians inevitably raise these issues; they abhor the thought of doing violence to patients. These issues are much more than mere practical problems in enforcement. Rather, they illustrate how, in a very real sense, the state is assaulting the woman even though her compliance in the face of a court order may often obscure this. The court order muffles the disturbing overtones of violence because the court authorizes but does not act, while the doctor acts but can tell himself that the court has given a superior authorization. But even if, in our variant on Nagel's example, someone else gave the driver permission to break the child's arm, or did the actual breaking at the driver's request, the moral responsibility for the broken arm would still be the driver's. Likewise, when the court authorizes nonconsensual surgery, it becomes responsible for the violence it is approving.

The court that orders surgery may also be responsible for real harm. Suppose that the nonconsensual surgery is performed, and despite all due care by the doctors, the woman dies or suffers irreparable injury. Absent negligence, the physicians would not be legally liable, and of course the court would not be legally liable in any case. But, intuitively, the court seems to bear moral responsibility here, just as the man in Nagel's example would be morally responsible if he twisted the child's arm and it broke. The court seems responsible because it imposed the risk and set in motion the harmful series of events, that is, the nonconsensual surgery. The court is heavily involved when it imposes surgery; it takes on responsibility for rescuing the fetus and must therefore be responsible if the woman is ever harmed seriously or even less substantially.

It might be objected that if the court does not order surgery it sacrifices the fetus and will bear responsibility for this. Initially, a decision not to order surgery may appear this way. But the degree of state responsibility is very different when the court orders surgery and when it does not. Because individuals ordinarily make their own medical choices and assume moral responsibility for them, the woman who refuses surgery despite predictions of harm to her baby may be morally to blame if such a result materializes. It may be appropriate to say that, morally speaking, if surgery could have prevented the harm, its occurrence is the woman's responsibility. But the state is not ordinarily so involved. Only if the state overrides the woman's choice does it become a sufficiently active participant to acquire moral responsibility for the outcome. Surely the driver in our variant of Nagel's example would not be responsible for the passengers' deaths if he failed to break the child's arm to secure the car. No duty to rescue could encompass inflicting such harm. Similarly, it is unlikely that the state has a duty to rescue when doing so requires imposing major surgery upon an unwilling citizen. Therefore, the state is not responsible for the consequences, however tragic, to the fetus, in the same way that it will be responsible for any harm that befalls a woman whom it coerces to have surgery. . .

It could be objected that while doctors may recommend surgery in questionable cases, thus giving rise to unnecessary Cesareans, they will not seek to mandate it in any but the most clearcut cases – those where, without surgery, disaster will unquestionably ensue. Indeed, two of the Cesarean cases, *Jefferson* and *Jeffries*, involved women with placenta previa, one of the most clearcut and uncontroversial indications for a Cesarean. The successful vaginal deliveries in those two cases were surprising and unexpected, and these are not the sorts of situations in which critics of obstetrical interventionism would claim that the doctors were excessively alarmed. Nonetheless, these cases illustrate a very crucial point here: that physicians *feel certain* that disaster will ensue does not mean that it will.

Physicians' subjective feelings of certainty will be even less likely to translate into objective certainty in situations in which they are relying on technology with inherent limitations such as EFM [Electronic Fetal Monitoring]. As one expert stressed, when doctors can legitimately feel certain about the ominous import of monitor tracings, such as when the monitor shows a late terminal heart pattern, there is no time to go to court. If the baby is to be saved at all, immediate action is necessary. At that point, however, surgery might either fail to prevent death or save a severely brain damaged infant. In other words, where there is certainty as to peril, it may sometimes be too late to prevent the damage.

A situation that almost became a court-ordered Cesarean illustrates the danger that unnecessary surgery will on occasion be ordered. An African woman failed to progress in labor satisfactorily, and the internal fetal monitor revealed repetitive late decelerations in the fetal heart rate. No fetal scalp blood sampling was done, even though the woman was between five and six centimeters dilated. The physician advised a Cesarean, but the woman and her husband adamantly refused. They argued that after they returned to Africa, there would be no available facilities for a repeat Cesarean. Consequently, the Cesarean would place the woman at significant risk in future pregnancies. They also noted that doctors recommended a Cesarean for failure to progress during her first pregnancy, but she nonetheless delivered vaginally. In this case a judge was contacted and indicated his willingness to order a Cesarean. Before any order could be issued, however, the woman progressed rapidly to the second stage of labor and delivered an infant with excellent Apgar scores – scores that were not suggestive of fetal distress. Had the labor taken even a little more time, this woman might have been subjected to an unnecessary operation – in her case one that would have greatly increased her future reproductive risks.

Naturally, the above discussion is not meant to suggest that the physician will not be right in a great many cases. Moreover, physicians are surely right when they stress that because the goal of gathering data about such things as fetal heart rate is to *prevent* damage before it can occur, achieving a good outcome despite ominous data does not necessarily mean that the data or the approach taken were wrong – only that doctors discovered the problem in time. Certainly, many or most women would want their doctors to use this conservative and time-honored medical strategy. But there are serious problems with courts' *requiring* a woman to abide by this approach, inasmuch as it does mean that some unnecessary operations will be judicially mandated.

One problem with courts' essentially requiring a maximum approach to obstetrical risks is that whether or not the physician's degree of alarm is warranted, a very prompt judicial decision is almost always required. Hence, judges who hear these cases will typically hear only the doctor's side and will learn little or nothing of the risks of surgical delivery or the ambiguity of many fetal diagnostic procedures. If they attempt to balance the maternal and fetal risks, judges will have no choice but to accept the physician's assessment and, therefore, to implement his or her recommendations. This is analogous to holding a civil commitment proceeding without the potential in-patient present or represented. Unlike a civil commitment proceeding, however, where a short delay is seldom a life-or-death matter, here the time needed to provide the woman even marginally adequate representation may render the proceeding futile (the damage having already been done), moot (the baby having already been born vaginally), or both. Given the very real time constraints, there is no solution to this. Thus, a court that tries to balance risks and benefits will almost inevitably have to base its decision on a one-sided presentation of factors. Courts can avoid this only by limiting their inquiry to an evaluation of competency (if it is in question) and firmly refusing to overturn competent refusals.

Along with one-sided decisionmaking is the threat that nonconsensual Cesareans will lead to other intrusions into pregnant women's lives. The Cesarean cases themselves do not always involve surgery alone. For example, the chief of obstetrics at North Central Bronx Hospital was made guardian ad litem for Mrs Headley and her fetus, with authority to consent to whatever diagnostic and therapeutic procedures were necessary for the fetus's health. The police were sent to locate Mrs Jeffries and bring her forcibly to the hospital. If a high-risk woman cannot refuse a Cesarean, it is hard to see how she can refuse the diagnostic procedures that will determine if a Cesarean is necessary. As doctors define 'high risk' to include more and more women, freedom for any woman to opt out of this country's technologically intensive obstetrics may be threatened.

As we learn more about fetal development and the impact of maternal conduct on the fetus, diagnostic procedures and restrictions on women's conduct could be ordered earlier in pregnancy. Already, some courts have ordered transfusions for pregnant Jehovah's Witnesses, and one court has done so even before the fetus was viable. At least one court has involuntarily committed a schizophrenic woman in the last trimester of pregnancy in order to protect the fetus; another has ordered a pregnant heroin addict to report for drug testing; and yet another has required a pregnant diabetic to take insulin despite her religious beliefs. A criminal prosecution was brought against a California woman for the death of her infant son, who was born with brain damage allegedly resulting from her failure to seek immediate medical attention when she began to hemorrhage from placenta previa, though the action was dismissed. Interventions such as brief involuntary hospitalization, testing, or surveillance to control drinking, drug use, diet, etc, may be viewed by some courts as less intrusive than major surgery – though longer lasting, such interventions are, after all, much less risky. Visions of a 'slippery slope' progression appear very real when one begins with mandatory major surgery.

The potential for far-reaching state control of pregnant women also is suggested by the frightening array of prenatal interventions that some proponents of fetal protection advocate. For example, John Robertson states that pregnant women

> may also be prohibited from using alcohol or other substances harmful to the fetus during pregnancy, or be kept from the workplace because of toxic effects on the fetus. They could be ordered to take drugs, such as insulin for diabetes, medications for fetal deficiencies, or intrauterine blood transfusions for Rh factor. Pregnant anorexic teenagers could be force fed. Parental screening and diagnostic procedures, from amniocentesis to sonography or even fetoscopy could be made mandatory. And, in utero surgery for the fetus to shunt cerebroventricular fluids from the brain to relieve hydrocephalus, or to relieve the urethral obstruction of bilateral hydronephrosis could also be ordered. Indeed, even extra-uterine fetal surgery, if it becomes an established procedure, could be ordered, if the risks to the mother were small and it were a last resort to save the life or prevent severe disability in a viable fetus. [Robertson, 'The Right to Procreate and In Utero Fetal Therapy' 3 J Legal Med (1982)]

Margery Shaw goes even further, approving of breathalyzer tests for pregnant women suspected of alcohol abuse, and seeming to countenance mandatory prenatal diagnosis and even abortion in cases of fetal defects so severe that abortion may be deemed in the fetus's best interest.

The civil liberties implications of all this are staggering, as are the equal protection problems, since pregnant women are the only candidates for this unprecedented state control. A more subtle problem is the potential for prenatal coercion to do fetuses as much harm as good. In the *North Central Bronx* case, Mrs Headley never returned to the hospital and, despite the risk, had a home birth. Mrs Jeffries went into hiding, and the police search for her was unsuccessful. Women of strong religious beliefs may forego care entirely rather than violate their principles, a course that puts the women and their babies at even greater risk. Pregnant women who take illicit drugs or engage in other types of conduct that may cause fetal harm may avoid prenatal care for fear of involuntary hospitalization or treatment. Thus, ironically, efforts at fetal protection may instead increase fetal peril. Moreover, the coercion necessary to prevent 'maternal flight' – surveillance, reporting requirements (as with child neglect), or sending out the 'obstetrics police' – has mind-boggling implications for individual rights in this country.

A final point is that although coercion to protect a fetus may seem tempting in the individual case when the fetus is imperiled, on a societal scale this is an extraordinarily inefficient way to reduce perinatal mortality and morbidity. In this country, many women are still unable to obtain any, or adequate, prenatal care even though good nutrition and basic care can vastly improve the outcome in many pregnancies. The societal tendency to take all measures possible to rescue an identified individual, while foregoing precautions that could prevent many more deaths (though to unidentifiable persons) is perhaps understandable. But in this area, it is irrational to fail to provide prenatal care to all, thus risking *many* mothers and babies, and at the same time make women with atypical religious or medical beliefs choose between accepting care that violates their most cherished beliefs and foregoing care altogether. How much wiser it would be instead to ensure that caregivers work with these women to provide the best medical care possible within the limitations of their belief systems.

Rhoden's argument that the court should stay its hand seems to us to be extremely persuasive. Furthermore if compulsory intervention upon pregnant women were ever to be legally sanctioned, only Parliament should do so. In a case decided before *Re S* the Court of Appeal made this quite clear. In *Re F (in utero)* [1988] Fam 122; [1988] 2 All ER 193 the Court of Appeal rejected the view that an unborn child could be made a ward of court. The case concerned a 36-year-old woman who suffered from mental disturbance accompanied by drug abuse. Very late in her pregnancy she went missing. The local authority were concerned about the welfare of the unborn child. It sought to make the unborn child a ward of court so that the mother could be found and ordered to reside in a certain place and attend a particular hospital. In deciding that the court did not have jurisdiction to ward an unborn child, the court accepted the earlier cases of *C v S* [1988] QB 135, [1987] 1 All ER 1230 and *Paton v British Pregnancy Advisory Service Trustees* [1979] QB 276, [1978] 2 All ER 987, which had held that an unborn child has no legal existence until it is physically independent of its mother (ie it has been born): on which, see *infra*, ch 13. However, the court also accepted the overwhelming practical problems that might arise if wardship were available because of a possible conflict between mother and unborn child.

Re F (in utero) [1988] 2 All ER 193, [1988] Fam 122 (CA)

May LJ: I have considerable sympathy with the local authority in their position on the facts of the instant case, but I am driven to the conclusion that the judge was right and that the court has no jurisdiction to ward an unborn child. If the courts are to have this jurisdiction in a sensitive situation such as the present, I think that this is a matter for Parliament and not for the courts themselves.

Balcombe LJ: Approaching the question as one of principle, in my judgment there is no jurisdiction to make an unborn child a ward of court. Since an unborn child has, ex hypothesi, no existence independent of its mother, the only purpose of extending the jurisdiction to include a foetus is to enable the mother's actions to be controlled. Indeed, that is the purpose of the present application. In the articles already cited Lowe gives examples of how this might operate in practice [Lowe 'Wardship and Abortion Prevention – Further Observations' (1980) 96 LQR 29 at 30]:

> It would mean, for example, that the mother would be unable to leave the jurisdiction without the court's consent. The court being charged to protect the foetus's welfare would surely have to order the mother to stop smoking, imbibing alcohol and indeed any activity which might be hazardous to the child. Taking it to the extreme were the court to be faced with saving the baby's life or the mother's it would surely have to protect the baby's.

Another possibility is that the court might be asked to order that the baby be delivered by Caesarian section: in this connection see Fortin 'Legal Protection for the Unborn Child' (1988) 51 MLR 54 at 81 and the US cases cited in note 16, in particular *Jefferson v Griffin Spalding County Hospital Authority* (1981) 274 SE 2d 457. Whilst I do not accept that the priorities mentioned in the last sentence of the passage cited above are necessarily correct, it would be intolerable to place a judge in the position of having to make such a decision without any guidance as to the principles upon which his decision should be based. If the law is to be extended in this manner, so as to impose control over the mother of an unborn child where such control may be necessary for the benefit of that child, then under our system of Parliamentary democracy it is for Parliament to decide whether such controls can be imposed and, if so, subject to what limitations or conditions. Thus, under the Mental Health Act 1983, to which we were also referred, there are elaborate provisions to ensure that persons suffering from mental disorder or other similar conditions are not compulsorily admitted to hospital for assessment or treatment without proper safeguards: see s 2, 3 and 4 of that Act. If Parliament were to think it appropriate that a pregnant woman should be subject to controls for the benefit of her unborn child, then doubtless it will stipulate the circumstances in which such controls may be applied and the safeguards appropriate for the mother's protection. In such a sensitive field, affecting as it does the liberty of the individual, it is not for the judiciary to extend the law.

Staughton LJ: When the wardship jurisdiction of the High Court is exercised, the rights, duties and powers of the natural parents are taken over or superseded by the orders of the court. Until a child is delivered it is not, in my judgment, possible for that to happen. The court cannot care for a child, or order that others should do so, until the child is born; only the mother can. The orders sought by the local authority are not by their nature such as the court can make in caring for the child; they are orders which seek directly to control the life of both mother and child. As was said by the European Commission of Human Rights in *Paton v UK* (1980) 3 EHRR 408 at 415 (para 19): 'The "life" of the foetus is intimately connected with, and cannot be regarded in isolation from, the life of the pregnant woman.'

We were urged by counsel to extend the wardship jurisdiction; but, in my judgment, we are being asked to create a new, perhaps similar, jurisdiction to care for mother and foetus together. I can see that there may be arguments that the court should have such powers. One would hope that they would be needed very rarely, but a need may well exist. I do not think that it is for this court to create that jurisdiction. The exercise of it would, in this case, directly impinge on the liberty of the mother. Where Parliament has granted similar powers, for example in the Mental Health Act 1983, safeguards and limits have been provided; there have to be certificates of qualified doctors who have examined the patient, and such like. No doubt that was done after careful consideration of the topic, and of the circumstances in which a person's liberty should be taken away.

This court is in no position to inquire into the problem of mothers who may neglect or harm their children before birth, or to decide in what circumstances and with what safeguards there should be power to restrict the liberty of the mother in order to prevent that happening. Even if the court were entitled to extend the jurisdiction, as counsel puts it, in that way, it is not a power which the court should exercise.

In our view on a proper analysis English law is (and should remain) more consistent with the sentiments expressed by Professor George Annas in his book *Judging Medicine* (1989) than by Judge Levie in the *Madyun* case. Annas writes:

No mother has ever been legally required to undergo surgery or general anesthesia (eg, bone marrow aspiration) to save the life of her dying child. It would be ironic and unfair if she could be forced to submit to more invasive surgical procedures for the sake of her fetus than of her child.

By contrast, Judge Levie writes:

All that stood between the Madyun fetus and its independent existence, separate from its mother, was, put simply, a doctor's scalpel. In these circumstances, the life of the infant inside its mother's womb was entitled to be protected.

For a further discussion of court-ordered interventions in the United States see, for example, Gallagher, 'Pre-natal Invasions and Interventions: What's Wrong with Fetal Rights' (1987) 10 Harvard Women's LJ 9; Johnsen, 'The Creation of Fetal Rights: Conflicts with Women's Constitutional Rights to Liberty, Privacy, and Equal Protection' (1986) 95 Yale LJ 599; Field, 'Controlling the Woman to Protect the Fetus' (1989) 17 Law, Medicine and Health Care 114; Robertson and Schulman, 'Pregnancy and Prenatal Harm to Offspring: The Case of Mothers with PKU' (1987) 17 Hastings Center Report 23 (Aug/Sept).

(b) The parent and child

So far we have been concerned with a competent adult making a decision which affects her unborn child. There is another strand of authority which is concerned with the situation where existing children of the patient's family may be affected by the patient's refusal of life-sustaining treatment. It could be said that since the decision of the patient here will not lead to the death of the child (unlike the situation where the patient is pregnant) *a fortiori* the court should not compel treatment when it is refused. In the first case of its kind in America, however, the court seems to have taken a different view.

Application of the President and Director of Georgetown College (1964) 331 F 2d 1000 and (on rehearing) 331 F 2d 1010 (USCA DCC)

J Skelly Wright, Circuit Judge: Attorneys for Georgetown Hospital applied for an emergency writ at 4:00 pm, September 17, 1963, seeking relief from the action of the United

States District Court for the District of Columbia denying the hospital's application for permission to administer blood transfusions to an emergency patient. The application recited that 'Mrs Jesse E Jones is presently a patient at Georgetown University Hospital,' 'she is in extremis,' according to the attending physician 'blood transfusions are necessary immediately in order to save her life,' and 'consent to the administration thereof can be obtained neither from the patient nor her husband.' The patient and her husband based their refusal on their religious beliefs as Jehovah's Witnesses. The order sought provided that the attending physicians 'may' administer such transfusions to Mrs Jones as might be 'necessary to save her life.' After the proceedings detailed in Part IV of this opinion, I signed the order at 5:20 pm. . . .

Mrs Jones subsequently appeared in the cause, in this court, as respondent to the application. The treatment proposed by the hospital in its application was not a single transfusion, but a series of transfusions. The hospital doctors sought a court determination before undertaking either this course of action or some alternative. The temporary order issued was more limited than the order proposed in the original application, in that the phrase 'to save her life' was added, thus limiting the transfusions in both time and number. Such a temporary order to preserve the life of the patient was necessary if the cause were not to be mooted by the death of the patient . . .

Mrs Jones was brought to the hospital by her husband for emergency care, having lost two thirds of her body's blood supply from a ruptured ulcer. She had no personal physician, and relied solely on the hospital staff. She was a total hospital responsibility. It appeared that the patient, age 25, mother of a seven-month-old child, and her husband were both Jehovah's Witnesses, the teachings of which sect, according to their interpretation, prohibited the injection of blood into the body. When death without blood became imminent, the hospital sought the advice of counsel, who applied to the District Court in the name of the hospital for permission to administer blood. Judge Tamm of the District Court denied the application, and counsel immediately applied to me, as a member of the Court of Appeals, for an appropriate writ.

I called the hospital by telephone and spoke with Dr Westura, Chief Medical Resident, who confirmed the representations made by counsel. I thereupon proceeded with counsel to the hospital, where I spoke to Mr Jones, the husband of the patient. He advised me that, on religious grounds, he would not approve a blood transfusion for his wife. He said, however, that if the court ordered the transfusion, the responsibility was not his. I advised Mr Jones to obtain counsel immediately. He thereupon went to the telephone and returned in 10 or 15 minutes to advise that he had taken the matter up with his church and that he had decided that he did not want counsel.

I asked permission of Mr Jones to see his wife. This he readily granted. Prior to going into the patient's room, I again conferred with Dr Westura and several other doctors assigned to the case. All confirmed that the patient would die without blood and that there was a better than 50 percent chance of saving her life with it. Unanimously they strongly recommended it. I then went inside the patient's room. Her appearance confirmed the urgency which had been represented to me. I tried to communicate with her, advising her again as to what the doctors had said. The only audible reply I could hear was 'Against my will.' It was obvious that the woman was not in a mental condition to make a decision. I was reluctant to press her because of the seriousness of her condition and because I felt that to suggest repeatedly the imminence of death without blood might place a strain on her religious convictions. I asked her whether she would oppose the blood transfusion if the court allowed it. She indicated, as best I could make out, that it would not then be her responsibility.

I returned to the doctors' room where some 10 to 12 doctors were congregated, along with the husband and counsel for the hospital. The President of Georgetown University, Father Bunn, appeared and pleaded with Mr Jones to authorize the hospital to save his wife's life with a blood transfusion. Mr Jones replied that the Scriptures say that we should not drink blood, and consequently his religion prohibited transfusions. The doctors explained to Mr Jones that a blood transfusion is totally different from drinking blood in that the blood physically goes into a different part and through a different process in the body. Mr Jones was unmoved. I thereupon signed the order allowing the hospital to administer such transfusions as the doctors should determine were necessary to save her life . . .

This opinion is being written solely in connection with the emergency order authorizing the blood transfusions 'to save her life.' It should be made clear that no attempt is being made here to determine the merits of the underlying controversy. Actually, the issue on the merits is res nova. Because of the demonstrated imminence of death from loss of blood, signing the order was necessary to maintain the status quo and prevent the issue respecting the rights of the parties in the premises from becoming moot before full consideration was possible. But maintaining the status quo is not the only consideration in determining whether an emergency writ should issue. The likelihood of eventual success on appeal is of primary importance, and thus must be here considered.

Before proceeding with this inquiry, it may be useful to state what this case does not involve. This case does not involve a person who, for religious or other reasons, has refused to seek medical attention. It does not involve a disputed medical judgment or a dangerous or crippling operation. Nor does it involve the delicate question of saving the newborn in preference to the mother. Mrs Jones sought medical attention and placed on the hospital the legal responsibility for her proper care. In its dilemma, not of its own making, the hospital sought judicial direction.

It has been firmly established that the courts can order compulsory medical treatment of children for any serious illness or injury, eg, *People ex rel Wallace v Labrenz*, 411 Ill 618, 104 NE 2d 769, cert denied, 344 US 824, 73 S Ct 24, 97 L Ed 642 (1952); *Morrison v State*, Mo App, 252 SW 2d 97 (1952); *Mitchell v Davis*, Tex Civ App, 205 SW 2d 812 (1947), and that adults, sick or well, can be required to submit to compulsory treatment or prophylaxis, at least for contagious diseases, eg, *Jacobson v Massachusetts*, 107 US 11, 25 S Ct 358, 49 L Ed 643 (1905). An there are no religious exemptions from these orders, eg, *People ex rel Wallace v Labrenz, supra*; cf *Hamilton v Regents*, 293 US 245, 55 S Ct 197, 79 L Ed 343 (1934), rehearing denied, 293 US 633, 55 S Ct 345, 79 L Ed 717 (1935). These principles were restated by the Supreme Court in *Prince v Massachusetts*, 321 US 158, 166-167, 64 S Ct 438, 442, 88 L Ed 645, 652, 653 (1944):

> . . . Acting to guard the general interest in youth's well being, the state as parens patriae may restrict the parents' control. . . . Its authority is not nullified merely because the parent grounds his claim to control the child's course of conduct on religion or conscience. Thus, he cannot claim freedom from compulsory vaccination for the child more than for himself on religious grounds. [*Jacobson v Massachusetts*, 197 US 11, 25 S Ct 358, 49 L Ed 643.] The right to practice religion freely does not include liberty to expose the community or the child to communicable disease or the latter to ill health or death. *People v Pierson*, 176 NY 201, 68 NE 243 [63 LRA 187] [see also *State v Chenoweth*, 163 Ind, 94, 71 NE 197; *Owens v State*, 6 Okl Cr 110, 116 P 345, 36 LRA, NS, 633] . . .

Of course, there is here no sick child or contagious disease. However, the sick child cases may provide persuasive analogies because Mrs Jones was in extremis and hardly compos mentis at the time in question; she was as little able competently to decide for herself as any child would be. Under the circumstances, it may well be the duty of a court of general jurisdiction, such as the United States District Court for the District of Columbia, to assume the responsibility of guardianship for her, as for a child, at least to the extent of authorizing treatment to save her life. And if, as shown above, a parent has no power to forbid the saving of his child's life, a fortiori the husband of the patient here had no right to order the doctors to treat his wife in a way so that she would die.

The child cases point up another consideration. The patient, 25 years old, was the mother of a seven-month-old child. The state, as parens patriae, will not allow a parent to abandon a child, and so it should not allow this most ultimate of voluntary abandonments. The patient had a responsibility to the community to care for her infant. Thus the people had an interest in preserving the life of this mother.

Apart from the child cases, a second range of factors may be considered. It is suggested that an individual's liberty to control himself and his life extends even to the liberty to end his life. Thus, 'in those states where attempted suicide has been made lawful by statute (or the lack of one), the refusal of necessary medical aid [to one's self], whether equal to or less than attempted suicide, must be conceded to be lawful.' Cawley, Criminal Liability in Faith Healing, 39 Minn L Rev 48, 68 (1954). And, conversely, it would follow that where attempted suicide is illegal by the common law or by statute, a person may not be allowed to refuse necessary medical assistance when death is likely to ensue without it. Only quibbles about the distinction between misfeasance and nonfeasance, or the specific intent necessary to be guilty of attempted suicide, could be raised against this latter conclusion.

If self-homicide is a crime, there is no exception to the law's command for those who believe the crime to be divinely ordained. The Mormon cases in the Supreme Court establish that there is no religious exception to criminal laws, and state obiter the very example that a religiously-inspired suicide attempt would be within the law's authority to prevent. *Reynolds v United States*, 98 US (8 Otto) 145, 166, 25 L Ed 244, 250 (1878); *Late Corporation of the Church of Jesus Christ of Latter-Day Saints v United States (Romney v United States)*, 136

US 1, 49-50, 10 S Ct 792, 34 L Ed 478, 493 (1890). But whether attempted suicide is a crime is in doubt in some jurisdictions, including the District of Colombia.

The Gordian knot of this suicide question may be cut by the simple fact that Mrs Jones did not want to die. Her voluntary presence in the hospital as a patient seeking medical help testified to this. Death, to Mrs Jones, was not a religiously-commanded goal, but an unwanted side effect of a religious scruple. There is no question here of interfering with one whose religious convictions counsel his death, like the Buddhist monks who set themselves afire. Nor are we faced with the question of whether the state should intervene to reweigh the relative values of life and death, after the individual has weighed them for himself and found life wanting. Mrs Jones wanted to live.

A third set of considerations involved the position of the doctors and the hospital. Mrs Jones was their responsibility to treat. The hospital doctors had the choice of administering the proper treatment or letting Mrs Jones die in the hospital bed, thus exposing themselves, and the hospital, to the risk of civil and criminal liability in either case. It is not certain that Mrs Jones had any authority to put the hospital and its doctors to this impossible choice. The normal principle that an adult patient directs her doctors is based on notions of commercial contract which may have less relevance to life-or-death emergencies. It is not clear just where a patient would derive her authority to command her doctor to treat her under limitations which would produce death. The patient's counsel suggests that this authority is part of constitutionally protected liberty. But neither the principle that life and liberty are inalienable rights, nor the principle of liberty of religion, provides an easy answer to the question whether the state can prevent martyrdom. Moreover, Mrs Jones had no wish to be a martyr. And her religion merely prevented her consent to a transfusion. If the law undertook the responsibility of authorizing the transfusion without her consent, no problem would be raised with respect to her religious practice. Thus, the effect of the order was to preserve for Mrs Jones the life she wanted without sacrifice of her religious beliefs.

The final, and compelling, reason for granting the emergency writ was that a life hung in the balance. There was no time for research and reflection. Death could have mooted the cause in a matter of minutes, if action were not taken to preserve the status quo. To refuse to act, only to find later that the law required action, was a risk I was unwilling to accept. I determined to act on the side of life.

[On rehearing before Bazelon, Ch J and Wilbur K Miller, Fahy, Washington, Danaher, Bastian, Burger, Wright, and McGowan, Circuit Judges, en banc, in Chambers
. . .
Per Curiam. Upon consideration of a pleading styled 'Petition for Rehearing En Banc' in the above-cited matter and an opposition thereto, it is
Ordered by the court en banc that said petition is denied.]

Burger, Circuit Judge: We can assume first that a hospital, like a doctor, has certain responsibilities and duties toward a person who, by choice or emergency, comes under its care. No affirmative act of the patient is suggested as invading or threatening any right of the hospital. So we must decide whether an 'invasion' of legal right can be spelled out of a relationship between the patient's refusal to accept a standard medical treatment thought necessary to preserve life and the possible consequences to the hospital if, relying on her refusal of consent, it fails to give a transfusion and death or injury follows. The possible economic impact, apart from the moral implications inherent in its responsibilities, perhaps presented an arguable basis for the hospital's claim of protected economic right. It stood in an unenviable 'Good Samaritan' posture when the patient categorically refused to consent to a blood transfusion called for by a medical emergency. The choice between violating the patient's convictions of conscience and accepting her decision was hardly an easy one.

However, since it is not disputed that the patient and her husband volunteered to sign a waiver to relieve the hospital of any liability for the consequences of failure to effect the transfusion, any claim to a protected right in the economic damage sphere would appear unsupported.

Can a legally protected right arise out of some other duty-right of the hospital toward a patient, such as a moral obligation to preserve life at all costs?

For me it is difficult to construct an actionable or legally protected right out of this relationship. The affirmative enforcement of a right growing out of a possible moral duty of the hospital toward a patient does not seem to meet the standards of justiciability especially when the only remedy is judicial compulsion touching the sensitive area of conscience and religious belief . . .

Mr Justice Brandeis, whose views inspired much of the 'right to be let alone' philosophy, said in *Olmstead v United States*, 277 US 438, 478, 48 S Ct 564, 572, 72 L Ed 944, 956, 66 ALR 376 (1928), (dissenting opinion):

> The makers of our Constitution . . . sought to protect Americans in their beliefs, their thoughts, their emotions and their sensations. They conferred, as against the Government, the right to be let alone – the most comprehensive of rights and the right most valued by civilized man.

Nothing in this utterance suggests that Justice Brandeis thought an individual possessed these rights only as to *sensible* beliefs, *valid* thoughts, *reasonable* emotions, or *well-founded* sensations. I suggest he intended to include a great many foolish, unreasonable and even absurd ideas which do not conform, such as refusing medical treatment even at a great risk.

That judicial power is narrow and limited is a concept deeply embedded in our System. Thus the need for external restraints on the powers of Federal Judges was plainly an important corollary to their constitutionally secured tenure. It was quite as clear in the 1780s as it is today that men are not notorious for exercising self-restraint when they possess both permanent tenure *and* plenary power. Under our System no single Branch of Government has both, and no single Branch of Government could safely be entrusted with both.

Confronted by a unique episode such as this, it seems to me we must inquire where an assumption of jurisdiction over such matters could lead us. Physicians, surgeons and hospitals – and others as well – are often confronted with seemingly irreconcilable demands and conflicting pressures. Philosophers and theologians have pondered these problems and different religious groups have evolved different solutions; the solutions and doctrines of one group are sometimes not acceptable to other groups or sects. Various examples readily come to mind: a crisis in childbirth may require someone to decide whether the life of the mother or the child shall be sacrificed; absent a timely and decisive choice both may die. May the physician or hospital require the courts to decide? A patient may be in a critical condition requiring, in the minds of experts, a certain medical or surgical procedure. If the patient has objections to that treatment based on religious conviction, or if he rejects the medical opinion, are the courts empowered to decide for him?

Some of our greatest jurists have emphasized the need for judicial awareness of the limits on judicial power which is simply an acknowledgement of human fallibility. Cardozo, in The Nature of the Judicial Process, said:

> The judge, even when he is free, is still not wholly free. He is not to innovate at pleasure. He is not a knight-errant, roaming at will in pursuit of his own ideal of beauty or of goodness. He is to draw his inspiration from consecrated principles. He is not to yield to spasmodic sentiment, to vague and unregulated benevolence. He is to exercise a discretion informed by tradition, methodized by analogy, disciplined by system, and subordinated to 'the primordial necessity of order in the social life.' Wide enough in all conscience is the field of discretion that remains.

It is at the periphery of the boundaries of power where the guidelines are less clear that an appealing claim presents difficult choices, but this is precisely the area in which restraint is called for in light of the absolute nature of our powers and the finality which often, as here, attends our acts. But we should heed Cardozo's counsel of restraint and reconcile ourselves to the idea that there are myriads of problems and troubles which judges are powerless to solve; and this is as it should be. Some matters of essentially private concern and others of enormous public concern, are beyond the reach of judges. Cf. *Pauling v McNamara*, supra.

I am authorized to state that Wilbur K. Miller and Bastian, Circuit Judges, join in the above views.

The *Georgetown* case may be explicable on the basis that the judge regarded Mrs Jones as incompetent and, perhaps, in fact she was. To this extent, the case may not be of the greatest help to us here (see the explanation of the case in *Norwood Hospital v Munoz* (1991) 564 NE 2d 1017 at 1024, footnote 7, *per* Liacos CJ (Mass Sup Jud Ct) *infra*, p 376). If Mrs Jones were competent, however, the case can equally be explained (as indeed it was by the judge himself) as a case in which the court made an emergency order to maintain the 'status quo' pending a full review by the court. Either of these explanations is sufficient to warrant Judge Skelly Wright's decision. In the light of the other explanation, it would be wrong to consider the case as an authority justifying treatment on a competent adult patient simply because of the interests of that patient's existing children.

Subsequent cases in America have made this plain.

Norwood Hospital v Munoz (1991) 564 NE 2d 1017 (Mass Sup Jud Ct)

Liacos, Chief Justice: In this case, a competent adult, who is a Jehovah's Witness and a mother of a minor child, appeals from a judgment of the Probate and Family Court authorizing Norwood Hospital to administer blood or blood products without her consent.

We state the facts. Yolanda Munoz, a thirty-eight year old woman, lives in Dedham with her husband, Ernesto Munoz, and their minor son, Ernesto, Jr. Ernesto's father, who is over seventy-five years old, also lives in the same household.

Ms Munoz has a history of stomach ulcers. Approximately ten years ago, she underwent surgery for a bleeding ulcer. On April 11, 1989, Ms Munoz vomited blood and collapsed in her home. During the week before she collapsed, Ms Munoz had taken two aspirins every four hours to alleviate a pain in her arm. The aspirin apparently made her ulcer bleed. Ernesto took his wife to the Norwood Hospital emergency room. Physicians at Norwood Hospital gave Ms Munoz medication which stopped the bleeding. Ms Munoz was then admitted to the hospital as an inpatient. During the evening, her hematocrit (the percentage of red blood cells to whole blood) was 17%. A normal hematocrit level for an adult woman is approximately 42%. Ms Munoz was placed under the care of Dr Joseph L Perrotto. It was his medical opinion that the patient had a 50% probability of hemorrhaging again. If Ms Munoz started to bleed, Dr Perrotto believed that she would in all probability die unless she received a blood transfusion. Ms Munoz, however, refused to consent to a blood transfusion in the event of a new hemorrhage.

Ms Munoz and her husband were baptized as Jehovah's Witnesses over sixteen years ago. They are both members of the Jamaica Plain Kingdom Hall of Jehovah's Witnesses. Ms Munoz attends three religious meetings every week. A principal tenet of the Jehovah's Witnesses' religion is a belief, based on interpretations of the Bible, that the act of receiving blood or blood products precludes an individual resurrection and everlasting life after death.

Norwood Hospital has a written policy regarding patients who refuse to consent to the administration of blood or blood products. According to this policy, if the patient arrives at the hospital in need of emergency medical treatment and there is no time to investigate the patient's circumstances or competence to make decisions regarding treatment, the blood transfusion will be performed if necessary to save the patient's life. If the patient, in a non-emergency situation, refuses to consent to a blood transfusion, and the patient is a competent adult, not pregnant, and does not have minor children, the hospital will accede to the patient's refusal. If the patient, in a non-emergency situation, refuses to consent to a blood transfusion, and the patient is a minor, an incompetent adult, pregnant, or a competent adult with minor children, the hospital's policy is to seek judicial determination of the rights and responsibilities of the parties.

The patient in this case, while no longer in an emergency situation once her ulcer stopped bleeding, has a minor child. The hospital sought a court order; on April 12, the hospital filed a complaint for a declaratory judgment in the Norfolk Division of the Probate and Family Court pursuant to GL c 231A (1988 ed.) The hospital requested that Ms Munoz be required to accept blood transfusions which her attending physician believed to be reasonably necessary to save her life. On that same day, the judge granted a temporary restraining order authorizing the hospital to 'administer transfusions of blood or blood products in the event that [the patient] hemorrhages to the extent that her life is severely threatened by loss of blood in the opinion of her attending physicians.' The court also appointed Mr Jonathan Brant to serve as guardian ad litem for five year old Ernesto, Jr.

On April 13, the judge held a full evidentiary hearing. Dr Perrotto stated in an unchallenged affidavit that, if Ms Munoz were to begin bleeding again, she would have an excellent chance of recovering if she received a blood transfusion. If she started to bleed, however, and did not receive a blood transfusion, she would probably die. In addition, Dr Perrotto stated that there was no alternative course of medical treatment capable of saving the patient's life. Ernesto Munoz and James Joslin, Ms Munoz's brother-in-law, testified at the hearing in favor of allowing Ms Munoz to refuse the blood transfusion. The guardian ad litem's report, which recommended that the hospital's request for a declaratory judgment be denied, was admitted in evidence.

On April 14, the judge granted the declaratory judgment authorizing blood transfusions which were 'reasonably necessary to save [the patient's] life.' The judgment also absolved the hospital and its agents from any civil or criminal liability, except for negligence or malpractice, which might arise from a blood transfusion. On May 11, 1989, the judge issued a detailed opinion explaining his reasons for granting the declaratory judgment. The judge found the patient competent; she understood the nature of her illness, and the potential serious consequences of her decision, including the risk of imminent death if her bleeding resumed and blood transfusions were not administered. While recognizing that a competent adult may usually refuse medical treatment, the judge stated that the hospital could administer the blood transfusions because, if they did not and Ms Munoz subsequently died, Ernesto, Jr, would be 'abandoned.' The judge concluded that the State's interests in protecting the well-being of Ernesto, Jr, outweighed Ms Munoz's right to refuse the medical treatment.

In order further to understand the judge's reasoning, we need to discuss his factual finding in more detail. Ernesto works sixteen hours a day Monday through Friday and seven hours on Saturday driving his own commercial truck. Ms Munoz works at a beauty salon from 9 am to 3 pm three days a week. Ernesto, Jr, is enrolled in a day-care center Monday through Friday from 9 am until 4 pm. The judge found that Ms Munoz was the 'principal homemaker and principal caretaker of Ernesto, Jr.' The judge also found that, while Ernesto's father was available to assist in caring for Ernesto, Jr, his assistance would be inadequate because of his advanced age, his inability to speak English, his unemployment, his lack of a driver's license, and because he had not, in the past, played a significant role in caring for his grandson. In addition, the judge found, that while Sonia and James Joslin, Ernesto's sister and brother-in-law, expressed a willingness to help Ernesto take care of the child in the event that Ms Munoz died, the family had not formulated a concrete plan for the care and support of Ernesto, Jr. The judge concluded that Ms Munoz's death 'would be likely to cause an emotional abandonment of Ernesto, Jr, which would more probably than not be detrimental to his best interests.' The judge ruled that '[t]he State, as parens patriae, will not allow a parent to abandon a child, and so it should not allow this most ultimate of voluntary abandonments.'

Ms Munoz argues that the judge erred because she has a right, as a competent adult, to refuse life-saving medical treatment, and the State's interests do not override that right. We agree . . .

1. *The right to refuse treatment.* This court has recognized the right of a competent individual to refuse medical treatment. We have declared that individuals have a common law right to determine for themselves whether to allow a physical invasion of their bodies. See *Brophy v New England Sinai Hospital, supra* 398 Mass at 430, 497 NE 2d 626; *Harnish v Children's Hosp Medical Center*, 387 Mass. 152, 154, 439 NE 2d 240 (1982); *Saikewicz v Superintendent of Belchertown School* (1977) 373 Mass at 738-739, 370 NE 2d 417. See also GL c 214, s 1B (statutory right of privacy). We have stated that 'a person has a strong interest in being free from nonconsensual invasion of his bodily integrity.' *Saikewicz, supra* at 729, 370 NE 2d 417. Individuals also have a penumbral constitutional right of privacy to reject medical treatment. See *Roe v Wade*, 410 US 113, 93 S Ct 705, 35 L Ed 2d 147 (1973); *Griswold v Connecticut*, 381 US 85 S Ct 1678, 14 L Ed 2d 510 (1965); *Brophy, supra*; *Saikewicz, supra* 373 Mass at 739, 370 NE 2d 417.

The right to bodily integrity has been developed further through the doctrine of informed consent, which this court recognized in *Harnish v Children's Hosp. Medical Center, supra*. Under the doctrine, a physician has the duty to disclose to a competent adult 'sufficient information to enable the patient to make an informed judgment whether to give or withhold consent to a medical or surgical procedure.' *Id* 387 Mass at 154-155, 439 NE 2d 240. It is for the individual to decide whether a particular medical treatment is in the individual's best interests. As a result, '[t]he law protects [a person's] right to make her own decision to accept or reject treatment, whether that decision is wise or unwise.' *Lane v Candura*, 6 Mass App Ct 377, 383, 376 NE 2d 1232 (1978). See *Brophy, supra* 398 Mass at 430-431, 497 NE 2d 626.

There is no doubt, therefore, that Ms Munoz has a right to refuse the blood transfusion. Initially, it is for her to decide, after having been informed by the medical personnel of the risks involved in not accepting the blood transfusion, whether to consent to the medical treatment. The fact that the treatment involves life-saving procedures does not undermine Ms Munoz's rights to bodily integrity and privacy, except to the extent that the right must then be balanced against the State's interests. See *Brophy, supra*; *Saikewicz, supra*; *Matter of Conroy*, 98 NJ 321, 348, 486 A 2d 1209 (1985).

Ms Munoz argues that, in addition to her rights to bodily integrity and privacy, she has a right secured by the free exercise clause of the First Amendment to the United States Constitution to object to the administration of blood or blood products because to consent to the blood transfusions would violate one of the principal tenets of her Jehovah's Witnesses faith. Some courts have recognized a free exercise right on the part of Jehovah's Witnesses to refuse blood transfusions. See *In Re Estate of Brooks*, 32 Ill 2d 361, 205 NE 2d 435 (1965); *In Re Brown*, 478 So 2d 1033 (Miss 1985). We do not think it is necessary, however, to decide whether Ms Munoz has a free exercise right to refuse the administration of blood or blood products, since we have already held that she has a common law and constitutional privacy right to refuse a blood transfusion. Also, we need not decide whether a patient's right is strengthened because the objection to the medical treatment is based on religious principles.

2. *The State's interests.* The right to refuse medical treatment in life-threatening situations is not absolute. *Brophy, supra* 398 Mass at 432, 497 NE 2d 626. *Commissioner of Correction v Myers*, 379 Mass 255, 261-262, 399 NE 2d 452 (1979). We have recognized four countervailing interests: (1) the preservation of life; (2) the prevention of suicide; (3) the maintenance of the ethical integrity of the medical profession; and (4) the protection of innocent third parties. *Brophy, supra, Saikewicz, supra* 373 Mass at 741, 370 NE 2d 417 . . .

[The court having rejected the relevance of the first three interests moved on to consider the fourth.]

Protection of third parties. The final, and in this case the most compelling, State interest is the protection of the patient's minor child. The State as parens patriae has an interest in protecting the well-being of children. See *Prince v Massachusetts*, 321 US 158, 166-167, 64 S Ct 438, 442-443, 88 L Ed 645 (1944). The issue is whether a competent adult can be prevented from exercising her right to refuse life-saving medical treatment because of the individual's duties to her child.

The Florida State courts recently have addressed this issue. See *Wons v Public Health Trust of Dade County*, 500 So 2d 679 (Fla Dist Ct App 1987), aff'd, 541 So 2d 96 (Fla 1989). The patient in *Wons* was a thirty-eight year old woman, mother of two minor children, who suffered from dysfunctional uterine bleeding. The patient's physicians informed her that she required treatment in the form of blood transfusions. The patient, however, refused to consent to the transfusion because of her beliefs as a Jehovah's Witness. It was the physicians' medical opinion that, if the patient did not consent to the blood transfusions, she would probably die. The trial judge granted an order authorizing the transfusion, but a Florida District Court of Appeals reversed, holding that the State's interest in protecting the patient's children did not override the patient's right to refuse the medical treatment because the patient's possible death would not result in the abandonment of her two children. *Wons v Public Health Trust of Dade County*, 500 So 2d at 688. As the court pointed out, the testimony showed that the patient came from a tightly knit family, all practicing Jehovah's Witnesses, and all of whom supported her decision to refuse the blood transfusion. *Id.* The court also pointed out that the patient's husband and mother were willing to take care of the children in the event that the patient died. *Id.* The court concluded that 'there is no showing of an abandonment of minor children, and, consequently, [the patient's] constitutional right to refuse a blood transfusion is not overridden under the circumstances of this case.' *Id.*

In *Fosmire v Nicoleau*, 75 NY 2d 218, 551 NYS 2d 876, 551 NE 2d 77 (1990), the New York Court of Appeals apparently has held that the State's interest in protecting minor children will never be allowed to override the right of a competent individual to refuse medical treatment. The court explained that 'at common law the patient's right to decide the course of his or her own medical treatment was not conditioned on the patient['s] being without minor children or dependents.' *Id.* at 229-230, 551 NYS 2d 876, 551 NE 2d 77.

We need only state that we agree with the reasoning of the Florida court, and hold that, in the absence of any compelling evidence that the child will be abandoned, the State's interest in protecting the well-being of children does not outweigh the right of a fully competent adult to refuse medical treatment. Our review of the record in this case reveals no such compelling evidence.[7] The evidence shows that Ernesto Munoz supported his wife's decision not to consent to the blood transfusion. There is no evidence in the record that Ernesto was unwilling to take care of the child in the event that Ms Munoz died.[8] We note that the father has the financial resources to take care of the child and to make sure that the child's material needs are satisfied. We also note that Ernesto's sister and brother-in-law supported Ms Munoz's decision, and were willing to assist Ernesto in taking care of the child.

There can also be no doubt that, if Ms Munoz had died, the entire family, including the young child, would have suffered a great loss. However, the State does not have an interest in maintaining a two-parent household in the absence of compelling evidence that the child will be abandoned if he is left under the care of a one-parent household. 'The parens patriae doctrine invoked herein cannot, we think, measure increments of love; it cannot mandate a two-parent, rather than a one-parent, family; it is solely concerned with seeing that minor children are cared for and are not abandoned.' *Wons v Public Health Trust of Dade County*, 500 So 2d at 688. In these circumstances the State's interest in protecting the welfare of the patient's child does not outweigh her right to refuse the blood transfusions.

3. *Conclusion*. The patient had the right to refuse to consent to the blood transfusion even though she would have in all probability died if she had started to hemorrhage. The State's interests in preserving the patient's life, in maintaining the ethical integrity of the profession, and in protecting the well-being of the patient's child, did not override the patient's right to refuse life-saving medical treatment. Accordingly, the judgment is reversed and a new judgment declaring the rights of the parties, consistent with this opinion, is to be entered in the Probate Court.

Footnotes to extract

7.   The case most often cited in support of the proposition that the State's interest in protecting the well-being of the patient's children outweighs the patient's right to refuse life-saving treatment is *Application of the President & Directors of Georgetown College, Inc*, 331 F 2d 1000 (DC Cir), cert denied, 377 US 978, 84 S Ct 1883, 12 LE 2d 746 (1964). In that case, however, unlike the case before us, the patient was not competent to decide for herself whether to consent to the blood transfusion. The court stated that the patient was as 'little able competently to decide for herself as any child would be. Under the circumstances, it may well be the duty of a court . . . to assume the responsibility of guardianship for her, as for a child, at least to the extent of authorizing treatment to save her life' (footnote omitted). *Id* at 1008.

8.   A commentator's criticism of *Application of the President & Directors of Georgetown College, Inc, supra*, is relevant: '[T]he refusal of [the patient's] husband to authorize the transfusion indicates that he acceded to her wishes even though they might result in leaving the child motherless. It would not seem that one parent should be found guilty of child abandonment in a situation where the other parent has agreed to her leaving and, presumably, to provide for the child alone.' Case Comment. Constitutional Law – Transfusions Ordered for Dying Woman over Religious Objections, 113 U Pa L Rev 290, 294 (1964). See *Matter of Farrell*, 108 NJ 335, 352-353, 529 A 2d 404 (1987) (mother's right to refuse treatment upheld where 'father's capacity to care for [the children] in her absence is unquestioned').

Wilkins, Abrams and Greaney JJ agreed. O'Connor, Nolan and Lynch JJ concurred on the more limited ground that Mrs Munoz's decision to refuse treatment based upon her *religious* beliefs could not be overridden.

Thus, the majority of the Massachusetts' Supreme Judicial Court recognised that a competent patient's refusal of life-sustaining treatment could not be overridden by the interests of any existing children. Of course, on the facts, the Munoz children would not be abandoned because their father and the extended family would take of them. Would the result be the same if this were not so? The court left this open, as had the Florida Supreme Court in *Public Health Trust of Dade County v Wons* (1989) 541 So 2d 96. By contrast, the New York Court of Appeals in *Fosmire v Nicoleau* (1990) 551 NE 2d 770 (another case concerning a Jehovah's Witness who refused a blood transfusion) did not limit the patient's right to refuse life-sustaining treatment. In that case Wachtler CJ (speaking for the majority of the court) stated that:

On this appeal the hospital argues that a patient's right to decline lifesaving treatment should be limited to cases where the patient has a terminal or degenerative disease. When the patient is otherwise healthy the State has a stronger interest in preserving life, which should be held to outweigh the patient's choice. The State's interest is even stronger, the hospital contends, when the patient is a parent, and that the appellate Division erred in adopting a 'one-parent rule.' The argument here is that it is always in the child's best interest to have two parents and that the State will intervene to protect the child's welfare . . .

In the absence of any statute or decision from this court limiting the rights of patients who happen to be parents, the hospital turns to the law of domestic relations, and seeks to equate a parent who declines essential medical care with a parent who intentionally abandons a child. It is argued that since the State, as *parens patriae*, will not allow a parent to abandon a child, it will not permit 'this most ultimate of voluntary abandonments' (*Application of President & Directors of Georgetown Coll*, 331 F 2d 1000, 1008). This argument extends the concept of abandonment far beyond the boundaries recognized in this State, and into areas where it would conflict with other substantial interests.

Although the State will not permit a parent to abandon a child, the State has never gone so far as to intervene in every personal decision a parent makes which may jeopardize the family unit or the parental relationship. The laws of adoption and divorce show that the State recognizes competing interests and, in some instances, accords them priority. Indeed the State's need to punish those who violate its laws has never been held to be subordinate to the needs of the prisoner's family (*see, eg Ferrin v New York State Dept of Correctional Servs*, 71 NY 2d 42, 523 NYS 2d 485, 517 NE 2d 1370). Thus the State's concern with maintaining family unity and parental ties is not an interest which it enforces at the expense of all personal rights or conflicting interests.

The State's interest in promoting the freedom of its citizens generally applies to parents. The State does not prohibit parents from engaging in dangerous activities because there is a risk that their children will be left orphans. There are instances, as the hospital notes, where the State has prohibited the public from engaging in an especially hazardous activity or required that special safety precautions be taken by participants. But we know of no law in this State prohibiting individuals from participating in inherently dangerous activities or requiring them to take special safety precautions simply because they have minor children.

3. Concluding remarks

Before we leave the law relating to refusals of treatment by competent adult patients we should make a few brief final remarks.

The analysis so far has been concerned with adults who are competent at the time of their refusal of treatment. There are, of course, cases in which the adult, though now incompetent, has previously expressed his refusal of treatment. Such 'anticipatory refusals' may be oral or more formally stated in a written document often called an 'advanced directive' (see, for example, *Malette v Shulman* (1990) 67 DLR (4th) 321; *Re T (adult: refusal of medical treatment)* [1992] 4 All ER 649). We shall consider the law relating to 'anticipatory refusals' in detail later (see *infra*, ch 17). In principle, of course, whether a refusal be anticipatory or contemporaneous should not affect its validity (see *Airedale NHS Trust v Bland* [1993] 1 All ER 821 at 860 per Lord Keith; at 866 per Lord Goff; at 892 per Lord Mustill).

It follows also that once a refusal has clearly been given no appeal to 'necessity' can justify the doctor's intervention notwithstanding the good intentions of the doctor.

Mulloy v Hop Sang [1935] 1 WWR 714 (Alberta CA)

Jackson, DCJ: The plaintiff's claim is for professional fees for an operation involving the amputation of the defendant's hand which was badly injured in a motor-car accident. The accident took place near the town of Cardston and the defendant was taken to hospital there. The plaintiff, a physician and surgeon duly qualified to practice, was called to the hospital and the defendant, being a stranger and unacquainted with the plaintiff, asked him to fix up his hand but not to cut if off as he wanted to have it looked after in Lethbridge, his home city. Later on in the operating room the defendant repeated his request that he did not want his hand cut off. The doctor, being more concerned in relieving the suffering of the patient, replied that he would be governed by the conditions found when the anesthetic had been administered. The defendant said nothing. As the hand was covered by an old piece of cloth and it was necessary to administer an anesthetic before doing anything, the doctor was not in a position to advise what should be done. On examination he decided an operation was necessary and the hand was amputated. Dr Mulloy said the wounds indicated an operation as the condition of the hand was such that delay would mean blood poisoning with no possibility of saving it. In this he was supported by the two other attending physicians. I am, however, not satisfied that the defendant could not have been rushed to Lethbridge where he evidently wished to consult with a physician whom he knew and relied on. Dr Mulloy took it for granted when the defendant, a Chinaman without much education in English and probably not of any more than average mentality, did not reply or make any objection to his statement that he would be governed by conditions as he found them, that he had full power to go ahead and perform an operation if found necessary. On the other hand, the defendant did not, in my opinion, understand what the doctor meant, and he would most likely have refused to allow the operation if he did. Further, he did not consider it necessary to reply as he had already given explicit instructions.

Under these circumstances I think the plaintiff should have made full explanation and should have endeavored to get the defendant to consent to an operation, if necessary. It might have been different if the defendant had submitted himself generally to the doctor and had pleaded with him not to perform an operation and the doctor found it necessary to do so afterwards. The defendant's instructions were precedent and went to the root of the employment. The plaintiff did not do the work he was hired to do and must, in my opinion, fail in his action.

C. THE COMMON LAW: CHILDREN

To what extent may a competent child refuse medical treatment? To talk of a competent child is to rely upon the watershed decision of the House of Lords in *Gillick v West Norfolk Wisbech AHA* [1986] AC 112, [1985] 3 All ER 402. In that case, you will recall, the House of Lords recognised that a child was in law competent to make his own decisions providing he has 'a sufficient understanding and intelligence to enable him or her to understand fully what is proposed' (*per* Lord Scarman [1986] AC 112 at 188). It was widely believed that *Gillick* decided that a competent child could not only consent to medical treatment (which is what the case was actually concerned with) but by necessary logical extension could also refuse treatment regardless of the views of others. The Court of Appeal, led by Lord Donaldson MR, decided to set its face against this view of *Gillick*. In two cases – *Re R (a minor) (wardship: medical treatment)* (1991) 7 BMLR 147, [1992] Fam 11; *Re W (a minor) (medical treatment)* [1992] 4 All ER 627: concerned respectively with a competent child patient under 16 and one over 16 – the Court of Appeal accepted that the *Gillick* decision meant that a competent child could *consent* to treatment and that such consent could not be countermanded at least by the parents (or others with 'parental responsibility'). But the Court of Appeal took the view that the *refusal* of a competent child did not have the same force and could be countermanded by others, whether the parents or the courts.

Re R (a minor) (wardship: medical treatment) [1991] 4 All ER 177, [1992] Fam 11 (CA)

A 15-year old girl who had a history of family problems and who had been on the local authority's at-risk register was received into voluntary care after a fight with her father and was placed in a children's home. While in care her mental health deteriorated and she experienced visual and auditory hallucinations and her behaviour became increasingly disturbed. On one occasion she left the children's home and was found on a bridge threatening to commit suicide, while on another occasion she returned to her parent's home where she ran amok causing serious damage and attacked her father with a hammer. The local authority obtained place of safety and interim care orders and placed her in an adolescent psychiatric unit where she was sedated from time to time with her consent. The unit sought permission from the local authority to administer anti-psychotic drugs to her because she was behaving in a paranoid, argumentative and hostile manner. Although she had clear intervals when her mental illness was in recession the prognosis was that if the medication was not administered she would return to her psychotic state. However, in rational and lucid periods, when she had sufficient understanding to make the decision, she objected to taking the drugs. In those circumstances the local authority refused to authorise the administration of drugs against her will, while the unit was not prepared to continue to care for her unless it had authority to administer appropriate medication to control her. The local authority commenced wardship proceedings and applied for leave for the unit to administer medication, including anti-psychotic drugs, whether or not the ward consented. The questions arose (i) whether the judge had power to override the decision of a ward who was a minor to refuse medication and treatment irrespective of whether the minor was competent to give her consent and (ii) whether the ward had the requisite capacity to accept or refuse such medication or treatment. The judge granted the application, holding that although a wardship judge could not override the decision of a ward who had the requisite capacity on the facts the ward did not have that capacity. The Official Solicitor as guardian ad litem of the ward appealed, contending that if a child had the right to give consent to medical treatment the parents', and a fortiori the wardship court's, right to give or refuse consent was terminated. [In this extract we consider only the issue of the courts powers: for a discussion of competence see *supra*, ch 3, and the scope of the parents' powers see *infra*, p 393 et seq.

Lord Donaldson MR: This appeal from an order of Waite J on 9 July 1991 involves a consideration of the power of the court to override a refusal by its ward, a 15-year-old girl, to undergo medical treatment involving the taking of medication. So far as is known, such a question has arisen on only one previous occasion, namely in *Re E (a minor)* (1990) 9 BMLR 1, decided by Ward J, a 15-year-old boy who had religious objections, supported by his parents, to being given a life-saving blood transfusion. Possibly in that case, and certainly in this, the judge accepted that the effect of *Gillick v West Norfolk and Wisbech Area Health Authority* [1985] 3 All ER 402, [1986] AC 112 was that, if a child had achieved a sufficient understanding and intelligence to enable him or her to understand fully what was proposed and to be capable of making up his own mind on the matter, the parental right (and the court's right) to give or refuse consent yielded to the child's right to make his own decisions (see [1985] 3 All ER 402 at 422, 424, [1986] AC 112 at 186 and 189 per Lord Scarman and that this applied as much to a situation in which the child was refusing consent (this case and *Re E*) as to the case in which the child was consenting (the assumed position in *Gillick*'s case). However, in *Re E*, as in this case, the judge held that the child had not achieved the required degree of understanding . . .

The wardship jurisdiction
In considering the wardship jurisdiction of the court, no assistance is to be derived from *Gillick*'s case, where this simply was not in issue. Nor, I think, is any assistance to be derived from considering whether it is theoretically limitless if the exercise of such a jurisdiction in a particular way and in particular circumstances would be contrary to established practice. It is, however, clear that the practical jurisdiction of the court is wider than that of parents. The court can, for example, forbid the publication of information about the ward or the ward's family circumstances. It is also clear that this jurisdiction is not derivative from the parents' rights and responsibilities, but derives from, or is, the delegated performance of the duties of the Crown to protect its subjects, and particularly children, who are the generations of the future (see *Re C (a minor) (wardship: medical treatment) (No 2)* [1989] 2 All ER 791 at 793, [1990] Fam 39 a 46).

Whilst it is no doubt true to say, as Lord Upjohn did say in *J v C* [1970] AC 668 at 723, [1969] 1 All ER 788 at 831, that the function of the court is to 'act as the judicial reasonable parent', all that, in context, he was saying was that the court should exercise its jurisdiction in the interests of the children, 'reflecting and adopting the changing views, as the years go by, of reasonable men and women, the parents of children, on the proper treatment and methods of bringing up children'. This is very far from saying that the wardship jurisdiction is derived from, or in any way limited by, that of the parents. In many cases of wardship, the parents or other guardians will be left to make decisions for the child, subject only to standing instructions to refer reserved matters to the court, eg the taking of a serious step in the upbringing or medical treatment of a child, and to the court's right and, in appropriate cases, duty to override the decision of the parents or other guardians. If it can override such consents, as it undoubtedly can, I see no reason whatsoever why it would not be able, and in an appropriate case willing, to override decisions by 'Gillick competent' children who are its wards or in respect of whom applications are made for, for example, s 8 orders under the Children Act 1989.

Staughton LJ: I agree with the conclusion of Waite J that, on those facts, the court can authorise medication, consistently with the decision of the House of Lords in *Gillick v West Norfolk and Wisbech Area Health Authority* [1986] AC 112, [1985] 3 All ER 402, even if it has no greater powers than a parent.

The alternative solution to this appeal, which gave rise to the bulk of the argument and perhaps to the appeal itself, depends on two questions of law: (1) Does the parent of a competent minor have power to override the minor's decision, either by granting consent when the minor has refused it or vice versa? (2) Does the court have power to override the decision of a competent minor who is a ward? In both questions, I use the word 'competent' in the *Gillick* sense.

As to the first question, we were referred to the speech of Lord Scarman in *Gillick*'s case [1986] AC 112 at 188, [1985] 3 All ER 402 at 423:

> . . . I would hold that as a matter of law the parental right to determine whether or not their minor child below the age of 16 will have medical treatment terminates if and when the child achieves a sufficient understanding and intelligence to enable him or her to understand fully what is proposed.

The hypothetical situation under consideration in *Gillick*'s case was where a competent child did consent to medical treatment, but the parent either was not asked or expressly did not consent. The House of Lords decided, as it seems to me, that a doctor could lawfully administer treatment in such a case, although he would naturally take into account that the parent had not been asked or had expressly not consented.

Whether the doctor could lawfully administer treatment when the parent did consent, but the competent child either did not consent or had not been asked – save in the case of emergency – was not a question for decision in *Gillick*'s case. As Lord Donaldson MR points out, it may be putting a heavy burden on doctors if, having obtained the consent of the parent of a child under 16, they still have to consider whether the child is competent to give or refuse consent. Nevertheless the passage that I have quoted from Lord Scarman's speech, and particularly the words 'whether or not', suggests that the parent's consent is not sufficient in such a case. This is an important question. But it is not essential to the decision in this case, in my opinion, because I consider (as will shortly appear) that a wardship judge can validly consent to medical treatment even if the ward refuses her consent. In those circumstances, I do not suppose that any opinion of mine as to the effect of consent by a natural parent would be of much assistance in resolving the difference between what appears to have been Lord Scarman's view and that of Lord Donaldson MR; so I express none.

The second question is whether the court has power to override the decision of a competent minor who is a ward. Again it can arise in two forms: the court may be minded to consent when the ward does not (which would be the situation here, if I had found on the evidence that the ward is competent to take the decision); or the court may be minded not to consent when the ward does (as in the *Gillick* hypothetical case). I say at once that in my judgment *Gillick*'s case did not touch on this question.

It can be argued that a wardship judge, exercising the authority of the Crown as notional parent, should have no greater powers than a natural parent. I have a good deal of sympathy with that argument, for I accept as a general principle that good reason must be shown before the State exercises any power to control the decisions of a competent person, whether adult or minor, which only concern his own well-being.

There is, however, a group of decisions, mainly of Family Division judges, which supports the opposite conclusion. Thus in *BRB v JB* [1968] P 466 at 473, [1968] 2 All ER 1023 at 1025 Lord Denning MR said: '. . . the child's views are never decisive'. That, of course, was before *Gillick*'s case. In *Re P (a minor)* [1986] 1 FLR 272 at 279 Butler-Sloss J said that the child's wishes should not be given 'such paramount importance' as to be conclusive. In *Re G-U (a minor) (wardship)* [1984] FLR 811 at 812 Balcombe J said that an abortion required the leave of the court – although presumably the ward consented, as it had already happened. In *Re B (a minor)(wardship: abortion)* [1991] 2 FLR 426 Hollis J said in an abortion case that the ward's wishes were not decisive. And in *Re E (a minor)* (1990) 9

BMLR 1, which concerned a blood transfusion for a boy of 15, Ward J directly addressed the issue. He said:

> Whether or not he is of sufficient understanding to have given consent or to withhold consent is not the issue for me.

For my part, I do not read the judge as deciding that in wardship there is no power to override the decision of a competent minor. It seems to me that, while accepting that a competent minor can override the parent's choice, he held that the situation was different in wardship. Against that, there is the ruling of Waite J in the present case that the wardship judge could not override the decision of a competent minor.

Faced with such a substantial consensus of opinion among judges who have to deal with this problem from day to day, I conclude that the powers of a wardship judge do indeed include power to consent to medical treatment when the ward has not been asked or has declined. If that means that the wardship judge has wider powers than a natural parent (on the extent of which I have declined to express an opinion), it seems to me to be warranted by the authorities to which I have referred.

Farquharson LJ: Counsel for the Official Solicitor, Mr Munby QC, submitted that the court should determine the application on the *Gillick* principle (see *Gillick v West Norfolk and Wisbech Area Health Authority* [1986] AC 112, [1985] 3 All ER 402). Counsel argued on that authority that the parental right to determine whether a child should have medical treatment terminates if and when the child achieves a sufficient understanding and intelligence to enable him or her to understand fully what is proposed. If the child has the capacity to give a consent valid in law, it is not for the court to substitute its own different view. On the other hand, if the child is shown not to have that capacity, then the court has the power and duty to substitute its own decision if it is different from that of the child. . . .

It is to be emphasised that *Gillick*'s case was not a wardship case and was concerned with mentally normal children . . . The authority of a High Court judge exercising his jurisdiction in wardship is not constrained in this way. The judge's well-established task in deciding any question concerning the upbringing of the ward is to have regard to the welfare of the ward as the first and paramount consideration. In some cases, the decision might well be different if the *Gillick* test were applied. That the two approaches are distinct is vividly illustrated in the dramatic case of *Re E (a minor)* (1990) 9 BMLR 1 by the decision of Ward J.

It is clear in the present appeal that, whether R's capacity to withhold consent to medication was tested on the *Gillick* criteria or whether the court approached the issue on the basis of her welfare being paramount, the result would have been the same.

I would dismiss the appeal.

As we saw earlier (*supra*, ch 3), the Court of Appeal in fact held that R was incompetent to make the relevant medical decision because of her fluctuating mental condition. Thus, at one level the case need tell us nothing since all that was subsequently said about the law relating to competent children was unnecessary. But perhaps such a view could be said to be churlish.

Certainly, all three judges accept that *the court* has power to override the refusal of a competent child. As regards any conflict between the views of a competent child and those of the parents only Lord Donaldson MR expressed a concluded view.

Lord Donaldson MR: In the instant appeal Mr James Munby QC, appearing for the Official Solicitor, submits that (a) if the child has the right to give consent to medical treatment, the parents' right to give or refuse consent is terminated and (b) the court in the exercise of its wardship jurisdiction is only entitled to step into the shoes of the parents and thus itself has no right to give or refuse consent. Whilst it is true that he seeks to modify the effect of this rather startling submission by suggesting that, if the child's consent or refusal of consent is irrational or misguided, the court will readily infer that in the particular context that individual child is not competent to give or withhold consent, it is necessary to look very carefully at the *Gillick* decision to see whether it supports his argument and, if it does, whether it is binding upon this court.

The key passages upon which Mr Munby relies are to be found in the speech of Lord Scarman ([1985] 3 All ER 402 at 423-424, [1986] AC 112 at 188-189):

... as a matter of law the parental right to determine whether or not their minor child below the age of 16 will have medical treatment terminates if and when the child achieves a sufficient understanding and intelligence to enable him or her to understand fully what is proposed. It will be a question of fact whether a child seeking advice has sufficient understanding of what is involved to give a consent valid in law. Until the child achieves the capacity to consent, the parental right to make the decision continues save only in exceptional circumstances. Emergency, parental neglect, abandonment of the child or inability to find the parent are examples of exceptional situations justifying the doctor proceeding to treat the child without parental knowledge and consent; but there will arise, no doubt, other exceptional situations in which it will be reasonable for the doctor to proceed without the parent's consent.

And ([1985] 3 All ER 402 at 421-422, [1986] AC 112 at 186):

The underlying principle of the law was exposed by Blackstone (1 Bl Com (17th edn, 1830) chs 16 and 17) and can be seen to have been acknowledged in the case law. It is that parental right yields to the child's right to make his own decisions when he reaches a sufficient understanding and intelligence to be capable of making up his own mind on the matter requiring decision.

What Mr Munby's argument overlooks is that Lord Scarman was discussing the parents' right '*to determine* whether or not their minor child below the age of 16 will have medical treatment' (my emphasis) and this is the 'parental right' to which he was referring in the latter passage. A right of determination is wider than a right to consent. The parents can only have a right of determination if *either* the child has no right to consent, ie is not a keyholder, *or* the parents hold a master key which could nullify the child's consent. I do not understand Lord Scarman to be saying that, if a child was 'Gillick competent', to adopt the convenient phrase used in argument, the parents ceased to have an independent right of consent as contrasted with ceasing to have a right of determination, ie a veto. In a case in which the 'Gillick competent' child refuses treatment, but the parents consent, that consent *enables* treatment to be undertaken lawfully, but in no way determines that the child shall be so treated. In a case in which the positions are reversed, it is the child's consent which is the enabling factor and again the parents' refusal of consent is not determinative. If Lord Scarman intended to go further than this and to say that in the case of a 'Gillick competent' child, a parent has no right either to consent or to refuse consent, his remarks were obiter, because the only question in issue was Mrs Gillick's alleged right of veto. Furthermore I consider that they would have been wrong.

One glance at the consequences suffices to show that Lord Scarman cannot have been intending to say that the parental right to consent terminates with the achievement by the child of 'Gillick competence'. It is fundamental to the speeches of the majority that the capacity to consent will vary from child to child and according to the treatment under consideration, depending upon the sufficiency of his or her intelligence and understanding of that treatment. If the position in law is that upon the achievement of 'Gillick competence' there is a transfer of the right of consent from parents to child and there can never be a concurrent right in both, doctors would be faced with an intolerable dilemma, particularly when the child was nearing the age of 16, if the parents consented, but the child did not. On pain, if they got it wrong, of being sued for trespass to the person or possibly being charged with a criminal assault, they would have to determine as a matter of law in whom the right of consent resided at the particular time in relation to the particular treatment. I do not believe that that is the law.

I referred to a child who is nearing the age of 16, because at that age a new dimension is added by s 8 of the Family Law Reform Act 1969 to which Lord Fraser referred (see [1985] 3 All ER 402 at 407-408, [1986] AC 112 at 167). This is in the following terms:

(1) The consent of a minor who has attained the age of sixteen years to any surgical, medical or dental treatment which, in the absence of consent, would constitute a trespass to his person, shall be as effective as it would be if he were of full age; and where a minor has by virtue of this section given an effective consent to any treatment it shall not be necessary to obtain any consent for it from his parent or guardian . . .

(3) Nothing in this section shall be construed as making ineffective any consent which would have been effective if this section had not been enacted.

Mr Munby submits, rightly as I think, that consent by a child between the ages of 16 and 18 is no more effective than that of an adult if, due to mental disability, the child is incapable of consenting. That is, however, immaterial for present purposes. What is material is that the section is inconsistent with Mr Munby's argument. If Mr Munby's interpretation of Lord Scarman's speech was correct, where a child over the age of 16 gave effective consent to treatment, not only would it 'not be necessary' to obtain the consent of the parent or guardian, it would be legally impossible because the parent or guardian would have no power to give consent and the section would, or at least should, have so provided. Furthermore sub-s (3) would create problems since, if the section had not been enacted, a parent's consent would undoubtedly have been effective *as a consent*.

Both in this case and in *Re E* the judges treated *Gillick*'s case as deciding that a 'Gillick competent' child has a right to refuse treatment. In this I consider that they were in error. Such a child can consent, but if he or she declines to do so or refuses, consent can be given by someone else who has parental rights or responsibilities. The failure or refusal of the 'Gillick competent' child is a very important factor in the doctor's decision whether or not to treat, but does not prevent the necessary consent being obtained from another competent source.

As you will have seen above, Staughton LJ left this matter open although he seemed to suggest that there would be considerable difficulties with Lord Donaldson's approach.

Three issues remained unresolved by *Re R*. First, does the power to override a competent child's wishes extend to those children who are over 16, remembering that R was under 16, such that s 8 of the Family Law Reform Act 1969 did not apply? Secondly, what limits (if any) exist to restrict the court in exercising its power to override the refusal of the child? Thirdly, do parents also have the power to override their child's refusal to consent? These three issues were subsequently addressed by the Court of Appeal in *Re W (a minor) (medical treatment)* [1992] 4 All ER 627.

Re W (a minor)(medical treatment) [1992] 4 All ER 627, (1992) 9 BMLR 22 (CA)

W, a girl aged 16, was suffering from anorexia nervosa which first manifested itself in June 1990. By August 1991 her condition had deteriorated to the point at which for a short time and with her consent she was fed by nasogastric tube and had her arms encased in plaster. On 24 January 1992 Cazalet J granted the local authority leave, under the Children Act 1989, s 100(3), to make an application for the exercise by the court of the inherent jurisdiction of the High Court. The authority applied for (1) leave to move the minor to a named treatment unit or such other establishment as the Official Solicitor might approve, without the minor's consent and (2) leave to give the minor medical treatment without her consent.

Thorpe J held that he had the necessary jurisdiction and authorised the removal of W to and her treatment at a specialist London unit, subject to arrangements first being made for the approval of new foster parents.

On 29 June 1992, W's condition was stable or deteriorating slowly, although there had been some further loss of weight. On 30 June, she had not taken solid food since 21 June, her weight had dropped from 39 kg on 16 June, to 35.1 kg on 30 June with a final weight of 5 stone 7 lb for a girl 5 ft 7 in tall. Medical opinion agreed that should she continue in that way, within a week her capacity to have children in later life would be seriously at risk and a little later her life itself might be in danger.

On 30 June the Court of Appeal made an emergency order enabling her to be taken to and treated at a specialist hospital in London notwithstanding the lack of consent on her part.

Lord Donaldson MR:

Section 8 of the Family Law Reform Act 1969

I turn . . . to s 8 and to the common law against the background of which the section was enacted. The common law was authoritatively considered and defined in *Gillick v West Norfolk and Wisbech Area Health Authority* [1985] 3 All ER 402, [1986] AC 112 and there is no suggestion that it had altered significantly since 1969. Section 8 is in these terms.

Consent by persons over 16 to surgical, medical and dental treatment. – (1) The consent of a minor who has attained the age of sixteen years to any surgical, medical or dental treatment which in the absence of consent would constitute a trespass to his person shall be as effective as it would be if he were of full age; and where a minor has by virtue of this section given an effective consent to any treatment it shall not be necessary to obtain any consent for it from his parent or guardian.

(2) In this section surgical, medical or dental treatment includes any procedure undertaken for the purposes of diagnosis, and this section applies to any procedure (including in particular the administration of an anaesthetic) which is ancillary to any treatment as it applies to that treatment.

(3) Nothing in this section shall be construed as making ineffective any consent which would have been effective if this section had not been enacted.

In *Re R (a minor) (wardship: medical treatment)* [1991] 4 All ER 177, [1992] Fam 11 this court was concerned with a 15-year-old girl and accordingly the meaning and effect of s 8 was not directly in issue. I did, however, express my views on the construction and effect of the section, which, it now appears, were at variance with the views of academic and other writers (see Bainham 'The judge and the competent minor' (1992) 108 LQR 194 at 198, Thornton 'Multiple keyholders – wardship and consent to medical treatment' (1992) CLJ 34 at 36, Kennedy 'Consent to treatment; the capable person', Gostin 'Consent to treatment; the incapable person' and Dodds-Smith 'Clinical Research' in Dyer (ed) *Doctors, Patients and the Law* (1992) pp 60-61, 156-157 and Brazier *Medicine, Patients and the Law* (2nd edn 1992) p 346). Essentially what all are saying is that a right to consent to medical treatment, whether required under the common law (*Gillick*) or under statute (s 8), must and does carry with it a right not only to refuse consent to treatment, but to refuse the treatment itself. As it is put by the Department of Health *Guidelines for Ethics Committee* (August 1991):

> The giving of consent by a parent or guardian cannot override a refusal of consent by a child who is competent to make that decision.

Since my remarks were unnecessary for the decision, R not having yet attained the age of 16, I am free to reconsider the matter and to reach an opposite conclusion. Let me therefore start afresh by looking at the common law.

Gillick's case

In *Gillick*'s case the central issue was *not* whether a child patient under the age of 16 could refuse medical treatment if the parents or the court consented, but whether the parents could effectively impose a veto on treatment by failing or refusing to consent to treatment to which the child might consent. Mrs Gillick accepted that the court had such a power of veto and contended that the parents had a similar power (see [1985] 3 All ER 402 at 406, 412, 418, [1986] AC 112 at 165, 173, 181 per Lord Fraser of Tullybelton and Lord Scarman). Section 8 only came into the argument because it was contended on behalf of Mrs Gillick that, but for s 8, no minor could ever consent to medical treatment and that s 8 was designed only to lower the age of consent to such treatment from 18 to 16 ([1985] 1 All ER 533 at 539, [1986] AC 112 at 123, 144 per Parker LJ and Fox LJ). The area health authority and Department of Health and Social Security on the other hand contended that under the common law a minor of sufficient intelligence and understanding could always consent to treatment and that the effect of s 8 was to produce an irrebuttable presumption that a child of 16 or 17 had such intelligence and understanding.

The House of Lords decisively rejected Mrs Gillick's contentions and held that at common law a child of sufficient intelligence and understanding (the 'Gillick competent' child) could consent to treatment, notwithstanding the absence of the parents' consent and even an express prohibition by the parents. Only Lord Scarman's speech is couched in terms which might suggest that the refusal of a child below the age of 16 to accept medical treatment was determinative (see [1985] 3 All ER 402 at 423, [1986] AC 112 at 188-189) because there could never be concurrent rights to consent:

> . . . the parental right to determine whether or not their minor child below the age of 16 will have medical treatment terminates if and when the child achieves a sufficient understanding and intelligence to enable him or her to understand fully what is proposed.

If the parental right terminates, it would follow that, apart from the court, the only person competent to consent would be the child and a refusal of consent to treatment would indirectly constitute an effective veto on the treatment itself. I say 'indirectly' because the veto would be imposed by the civil and criminal laws, rather than by the refusal of consent.

In the light of the quite different issue which was before the House in *Gillick*'s case, I venture to doubt whether Lord Scarman meant more than that the *exclusive* right of the parents to consent to treatment terminated, but I may well be wrong. Thorpe J having held that 'There is no doubt at all that [W] is a child of sufficient understanding to make an informed decision', I shall assume that, so far as the common law is concerned, Lord Scarman would have decided that neither the local authority nor W's aunt, both of whom had parental responsibilities, could give consent to treatment which would be effective in the face of W's refusal of consent. This is of considerable persuasive authority, but even that is not the issue before this court. That is whether *the court* has such a power. That never arose in *Gillick*'s case, the nearest approach to it being the proposition, accepted by all parties, that the court had power to override any minor's consent (*not* refusal) to accept treatment.

The purpose of consent to treatment

There seems to be some confusion in the minds of some as to the purpose of seeking consent from a patient (whether adult or child) or from someone with authority to give that consent on behalf of the patient. It has two purposes, the one clinical and the other legal. The clinical purpose stems from the fact that in many instances the co-operation of the patient and the patient's faith or at least confidence in the efficiency of the treatment is a major factor contributing to the treatment's success. Failure to obtain such consent will not only deprive the patient and the medical staff of this advantage, but will usually make it much more difficult to administer the treatment. I appreciate that this purpose may not be served if consent is given on behalf of, rather than by, the patient. However, in the case of young children knowledge of the fact that the parent has consented may help. The legal purpose is quite different. It is to provide those concerned in the treatment with a defence to a criminal charge of assault or battery or a civil claim for damages for trespass to the person. It does not, however, provide them with any defence to a claim that they negligently advised a particular treatment or negligently carried it out.

Is s 8 ambiguous?

The wording of sub-s (1) shows quite clearly that it is addressed to the legal purpose and legal effect of consent to treatment, namely to prevent such treatment constituting in law a trespass to the person, and that it does so by making the consent of a 16- or 17-year-old as effective as if he were 'of full age'. No question of 'Gillick competence' in common law terms arises. The 16- or 17-year-old is conclusively presumed to be 'Gillick competent' or alternatively, the test of 'Gillick competence' is bypassed and has no relevance. The argument that W, or any other 16- or 17-year-old, can by refusing to consent to treatment veto the treatment notwithstanding that the doctor has the consent of someone who has parental responsibilities, involves the proposition that s 8 has the further effect of depriving such a person of the power to consent. It certainly does not say so. Indeed if this were its intended effect, it is difficult to see why the subsection goes on to say that it is not *necessary* to obtain the parents' consent, rather than providing that such consent, if obtained, should be ineffective. Furthermore, such a construction does not sit easily with sub-s (3), which preserves the common law as it existed immediately before the 1969 Act, which undoubtedly gave parents an effective power of consent for all children up to the age of 21, the then existing age of consent (see *Gillick*'s case [1985] 3 All ER 402 at 408, 419, [1986] AC 112 at 167, 182 per Lord Fraser of Tullybelton and Lord Scarman).

The most promising argument in favour of W having an exclusive right to consent to treatment and thus, by refusing consent to attract the protection of the law on trespass to the person lies in concentrating upon the words 'as effective as it would be if he were of full age'. If she were of full age her ability to consent would have two separate effects. First, her consent would be fully effective as such. Second, a failure or refusal to give consent would be fully effective as a veto, but only *because no one else would be in a position to consent*. If it is a possible view that s 8 is intended to put a 16- or 17-year-old in exactly the same position as an adult and there is thus some ambiguity, although I do not think that there is, it is a permissible aid to construction to seek to ascertain the mischief at which the section is directed.

The Latey Committee report

It is common ground that the Family Law Reform Act 1969 was Parliament's response to the *Report on the Age of Majority* (Cmnd 3342 (1967)). The relevant part is contained in paras 474-484. These show that the mischief aimed at was twofold. First, cases were occurring in which young people between 16 and 21 (the then age of majority) were living away from home and wished and needed urgent medical treatment which had not yet reached the emergency state. Doctors were unable to treat them unless and until their parents had been traced and this could cause unnecessary suffering. Second, difficulties were arising concerning –

> operations whose implications bring up the question of a girl's right to privacy about her sexual life. A particularly difficult situation arises in the case of a girl who is sent to hospital in need of a therapeutic abortion and refuses point blank to enter the hospital unless a guarantee is given that her parents shall not be told about it. (See para 478.)

The Committee had recommended that the age of majority be reduced to 18 generally. The report records that all the professional bodies which gave evidence recommended that patients aged between 16 and 18 should be able to give an effective consent to treatment and all but the Medical Protection Society recommended that they should also be able to give an effective refusal (see para 480). The point with which we are concerned was therefore well in the mind of the Committee. It did not so recommend. It recommended that –

> *without prejudice to any consent that may otherwise be lawful,* the consent of young persons aged 16 and over to medical or dental treatment shall be as valid as the consent of a person of full age. (My emphasis.)

Conclusion on s 8

I am quite unable to accept that Parliament in adopting somewhat more prolix language was intending to achieve a result which differed from that recommended by the Committee.

On reflection I regret my use in *Re R (a minor) (wardship: medical treatment)* [1991] 4 All ER 177 at 184, [1992] Fam 11 at 22 of the keyholder analogy, because keys can lock as well as unlock. I now prefer the analogy of the legal 'flak jacket' which protects the doctor from claims by the litigious whether he acquires it from his patient who may be a minor over the age of 16, or a 'Gillick competent' child under that age, or from another person having parental responsibilities which include a right to consent to treatment of the minor. Anyone who gives him a flak jacket (ie consent) may take it back, but the doctor only needs one and so long as he continues to have one he has the legal right to proceed.

The section extends not only to treatment, but also to diagnostic procedures (see sub-s (2)). It does not, however, extend to the donation of organs or blood since, so far as the donor is concerned, these do not constitute either treatment or diagnosis. I cannot remember to what extent organ donation was common in 1967, but the Latey Committee expressly recommended that only 18-year-olds and older should be authorised by statute to consent to *giving* blood (see paras 485–489). It seems that Parliament accepted this recommendation, although I doubt whether blood donation will create any problem as a 'Gillick competent' minor of any age would be able to give consent under the common law.

Organ transplants are quite different and, as a matter of law, doctors would have to secure the consent of someone with the right to consent on behalf of a donor under the age of 18 or, if they relied upon the consent of the minor himself or herself, be satisfied that the minor was 'Gillick competent' in the context of so serious a procedure which could not benefit the minor. This would be a highly improbable conclusion. But this is only to look at the question as a matter of law. Medical ethics also enter into the question. The doctor has a professional duty to act in the best interests of his patient and to advise accordingly. It is inconceivable that he should proceed in reliance solely upon the consent of an under-age patient, however 'Gillick competent', in the absence of supporting parental consent and equally inconceivable that he should proceed in the absence of the patient's consent. In any event he will need to seek the opinions of other doctors and may be well advised to apply to the court for guidance, as recommended by Lord Templeman in a different context in *Re B (a minor) (wardship: sterilisation)* [1987] 2 All ER 206 at 214–215, [1988] AC 199 at 205–206.

Hair-raising possibilities were canvassed of abortions being carried out by doctors in reliance upon the consent of parents and despite the refusal of consent by 16- or 17-year-olds. Whilst this may be possible as a matter of law, I do not see any likelihood, taking account of medical ethics, unless the abortion was truly in the basic interest of the child. This is not to say that it could not happen. This is clear from the facts of *Re D (a minor) (wardship: sterilisation)* [1976] 1 All ER 326, [1976] Fam 185, where the child concerned had neither the intelligence nor understanding either to consent or refuse. There medical ethics did not prove an obstacle, there being divided medical opinions, but the wardship jurisdiction of the court was invoked by a local authority educational psychologist who had been involved with the case. Despite the passing of the Children Act 1989, the inherent jurisdiction of the court could still be invoked in such a case to prevent an abortion which was contrary to the interests of the minor.

Thus far I have, in the main, been looking at the problem in the context of a conflict between parents and the minor, either the minor consenting and the parents refusing consent or the minor refusing consent and the parents giving it. Although that is not this case, I have done so both because we were told that it would be helpful to all those concerned with the treatment of minors and also perhaps the minors themselves and because it seems to be a logical base from which to proceed to consider the powers of the court and how they should be exercised.

W's case

. . . I have no doubt that the wishes of a 16- or 17-year-old child or indeed of a younger child who is 'Gillick competent' are of the greatest importance both legally and clinically, but I do doubt whether Thorpe J was right to conclude that W was of sufficient understanding to make an informed decision. I do not say this on the basis that I consider her approach irrational. I personally consider that religious beliefs which bar any medical treatment or treatment of particular kinds are irrational, but that does not make minors who hold those beliefs any the less 'Gillick competent'. They may well have sufficient intelligence and understanding fully to appreciate the treatment proposed and the consequences of their refusal to accept that treatment. What distinguishes W from them, and what with all respect I do not think that Thorpe J took sufficiently into account (perhaps because the point did not emerge as clearly before him as it did before us), is that it is a feature of anorexia nervosa that it is capable of destroying the ability to make an informed choice. It creates a compulsion to refuse treatment or only to accept treatment which is likely to be ineffective. This attitude is part and parcel of the disease and the more advanced the illness, the more compelling it may become. Where the wishes of the minor are themselves something which the doctors reasonably consider need to be treated in the minor's own best interests, those wishes clearly have a much reduced significance.

There is ample authority for the proposition that the inherent powers of the court under its parens patriae jurisdiction are theoretically limitless and that they certainly extend beyond the powers of a natural parent (see eg *Re R (a minor) (wardship: medical treatment)* [1991] 4 All ER 177 at 186, 189, [1992] Fam 11 at 25, 28). There can therefore be no doubt that it has power to override the refusal of a minor, whether over the age of 16 or under that age but 'Gillick competent'. It does not do so by ordering the doctors to treat which, even if within the court's powers, would be an abuse of them, or by ordering the minor to accept treatment, but by authorising the doctors to treat the minor in accordance with their clinical judgment, subject to any restrictions which the court may impose.

The remaining issue is how this power should be exercised in the context of a case in which a minor is refusing treatment or, whilst consenting to one form of treatment, is refusing to consent to another. Mr James Munby QC, appearing as amicus curiae, in his most helpful skeleton argument approached the matter as if 16- and 17-year-olds were in a special category. In a sense, of course, they are because s 8 applies to them. But Mr Munby so treated them because, in his submission, s 8 conferred complete autonomy on such minors, thus enabling them effectively to refuse medical treatment irrespective of how parental responsibilities might be sought to be exercised. That submission I have already rejected. This is not, however, to say that the wishes of 16- and 17-year-olds are to be treated as no different from those of 14- and 15-year-olds. Far from it. Adolescence is a period of progressive transition from childhood to adulthood and as experience of life is acquired and intelligence and understanding grow, so will the scope of the decision-making which should be left to the minor, for it is only by making decisions and experiencing the consequences that decision-making skills will be acquired. As I put it in the course of the argument, and as I sincerely believe, 'good parenting involves giving minors as much rope as they can handle without an unacceptable risk, that they will hang themselves'. As Lord Hailsham of St Marylebone LC put it in *Re B (a minor) (wardship: sterilisation)* [1987] 2 All ER 206 at 212, [1988] AC 199 at 202, the 'first paramount consideration [of the court] is the well-being, welfare or interests [of the minor]' and I regard it as self-evident that this involves giving them the maximum degree of decision-making which is prudent. Prudence does not involve avoiding all risk, but it does involve avoiding taking risks which, if they eventuate, may have irreparable consequences or which are disproportionate to the benefits which could accrue from taking them. I regard this approach as wholly consistent with the philosophy of s 1 of the Children Act 1989, and, in particular, sub-s(3)(*a*). It was submitted that whilst this might be correct, such an approach is inconsistent with ss 38(6), 43(8) and 44(7) of that Act and with paras 4 and 5 of the Sch 3. Here I disagree. These provisions all concern interim or supervision orders and do not impinge upon the jurisdiction of the court to make prohibited steps or specific issue orders under s 8 of the 1989 Act in the context of which the minor has no right of veto, unless it is to be found in s 8 of the 1969 Act.

Thorpe J was faced with having to choose between accepting one or other of two courses of action – leaving W where she was or transferring her to London – each of which was supported by responsible medical opinion. One of these doctors had consulted a Dr D, who was the pre-eminent expert in the treatment of anorexic cases. Initially Dr D was in favour of leaving W where she was, but he changed his mind when he came to give evidence. If ever there was a case for respecting the discretionary decision of the judge who had heard the witnesses, including W, this was it.

In seeking to escape from this conclusion it was submitted in argument that the reasoning of the judgment did not show, or show sufficiently, that Thorpe J had given due weight to W's wishes and that accordingly he had misdirected himself. I regard this criticism as wholly misconceived. Although much of the argument before him and much of his judgment were devoted to the legal rights of a 16-year-old, the only reason for exploring this was that W was resisting a change of regime. W's wishes could therefore never have been out of his mind. Furthermore, in explaining that discretionary decision he said:

> The past year has not been a year of successful treatment or progress. There are a number of indications of this lack of success. There are the coercive measures of the gastro-nasal tubes and the plastering of the arms to which I have referred. There is the fact that her therapy was interrupted by fortuitous circumstances. There is the fact that consistent care by her consultant was interrupted by his illness. There is the fact that more recently the unit has promulgated stark rules including a drastic sanction in the event of breach. [W] has breached the rules, the sanction has not been applied, [W] is manifestly in control and the unit is reduced to proposing that they should move away from psychological coercion to offering reward for good behaviour. That announcement to [W] could, in my judgment, only serve to underline to her the extent to which she is in control. The management options for the immediate future have been considerably constricted by recent developments. Although I have great respect for [W's] consultant and for the dedication of the staff, it seems to me that they have been manoeuvred into a position from which a change is necessary, even if it is a change that carries the risk of interpretation by [W] as 'yet another adult rejection and failure'. Obviously there are pros for the solution urged by her consultant. As well as [W's] views and her vulnerability there is the fact that there is a quasi-family bonding where she is. There is also the consideration that she seems to be flirting with the possibility of committing herself to re-entering mainstream education locally. There is also the proximity of the proposed foster parents and her own siblings.

In this passage Thorpe J was quite clearly not only bearing W's wishes in mind, but looking behind them to see why W wished to remain where she was. Not only would I have refrained from interfering with Thorpe J's decision on the footing that he had properly directed himself and that it was for him to decide, but because, even on the facts as they then were, I consider that his decision was plainly right.

Balcombe LJ: The first issue before us, as it was before Thorpe J, was whether Parliament had, by s 8 of the Family Law Reform Act 1969, conferred on a minor over the age of 16 years an absolute right to refuse medical treatment, in which case the limitation of the court's inherent jurisdiction exemplified by *A v Liverpool City Council* [[1981] 2 All ER 385, [1982] AC 363] would have operated so as to preclude any intervention by the court.

[Having set out s 8 of the 1969 Act, Balcombe LJ continued:]

It will be readily apparent that the section is silent on the question which arises in the present case, namely whether a minor who has attained the age of 16 years has an absolute right to refuse medical treatment. I am quite unable to see how, on any normal reading of the words of the section, it can be construed to confer such a right. The purpose of the section is clear: it is to enable a 16-year-old to consent to medical treatment which, in the absence of consent by the child or its parents, would constitute a trespass to the person. In other words, for this purpose, and for this purpose only, a minor was to be treated as if it were an adult. That the section did not operate to prevent parental consent remaining effective as well in the case of a child over 16 as in the case of a child under that age, is apparent from the words of sub-s (3).

If there were any ambiguity as to the meaning of the section – and in my judgment there is not – it would be resolved by a glance at the *Report of the Committee on the Age of Majority*

(Cmnd 3342 (1967)) (the Latey Report) to see what was the mischief which the section was intended to remedy. Paragraphs 471 to 489 of the Latey Report make it clear that doctors felt difficulty in accepting the consent of someone under 21 (the then age of majority) to medical treatment, even though parental consent might be unobtainable or, for reasons of the minor's privacy, undesirable. The nature of the problem is made apparent in para 479 of the Latey Report:

> The legal position is in itself obscure. A cause of action to which a hospital authority or a member of its medical staff (or both) may be liable as the result of the performance of an operation is trespass to the person, and treatment administered without the patient's express or implied consent constitutes an assault which may lead to an action for damages. Until recent years the general rule has been to require the consent of a parent or guardian for an operation or an anaesthetic on a person of under 21, but increasingly at the present time it is becoming customary to accept the consent of minors aged 16 and over. There is no rigid rule of English law which renders a minor incapable of giving his consent to an operation but there seems to be no direct judicial authority establishing that the consent of such a person is valid.

It was not until some 18 years after the publication of the Latey Report that the common law position on this topic was resolved by the decision of the House of Lords in *Gillick v West Norfolk and Wisbech Area Health Authority* [1985] 3 All ER 402, [1986] AC 112.

This interpretation of s 8 was given, obiter, by Lord Donaldson MR in *Re R* [1991] 4 All ER 177 at 185-186, [1992] Fam 11 at 24. His judgment attracted a considerable degree of academic criticism. I have to say that I find this criticism surprising since, as I have already said, the section is in my judgment clear, unambiguous and limited in its scope. One writer went so far as to say that this construction 'flies in the face of the settled interpretation of this provision'. Counsel were unable to suggest any case which may have settled the interpretation of the section other than *Gillick*'s case and to that I now turn.

The issue in *Gillick*'s case [1985] 3 All ER 402 at 406, [1986] AC 112 at 165 was stated by Lord Fraser of Tullybelton in the following terms:

> The central issue in the appeal is whether a doctor can ever, in any circumstances, lawfully give contraceptive advice or treatment to a girl under the age of 16 without her parents' consent.

To the like effect was Lord Scarman (see [1985] 3 All ER 402 at 418, [1986] AC 112 at 181). To that issue the construction of s 8 was at best peripheral.

The section was mentioned by both Parker and Fox LJJ in the Court of Appeal (see [1985] 3 All ER 402 at 418, [1986] AC 112 at 181), but neither attempted to give any definitive construction. In the House of Lords Lord Fraser of Tullybelton mentioned the section, but also did not attempt to define its meaning. Lord Bridge of Harwich, Lord Brandon of Oakbrook and Lord Templeman did not even mention the section. Lord Scarman did, however, mention the section at several points in the course of his speech, and after a consideration of its provisions and other matters said ([1985] 3 All ER 402 at 423, [1986] AC 112 at 188-189):

> In the light of the foregoing I would hold that as a matter of law the parental right to determine whether or not their minor child below the age of 16 will have medical treatment terminates if and when the child achieves a sufficient understanding and intelligence to enable him or her to understand fully what is proposed.

I accept that the words 'or not' in this passage suggest that Lord Scarman considered that the right to refuse treatment was co-existent with the right to consent to treatment. I also accept that if a 'Gillick competent' child under 16 has a right to refuse treatment, so too has a child over the age of 16. Nevertheless I share the doubts of the Master of the Rolls whether Lord Scarman was intending to mean that the parents of a 'Gillick competent' child had no right at all to consent to medical treatment of the child as opposed to no exclusive right to such consent. If he did so intend then, in the case of a child over the age of 16, his interpretation of the law was inconsistent with the express words of s 8(3) of the 1969 Act. It is also clear that Lord Scarman was only considering the position of the child vis-à-vis its parents: he was not considering the position of the child vis-à-vis the court whose powers, as I have already said, are wider than the parents'.

I am therefore satisfied that there is no interpretation of s 8 of the 1969 Act – and certainly no 'settled' interpretation – which persuades me that my view of the clear meaning of the section is wrong. I express no view on the question whether a young person, whether over the age of 16 or under that age if 'Gillick competent', should have complete autonomy in the field of medical treatment. That is a matter of social policy with which Parliament can deal by appropriate legislation if it wishes to do so. What I am clear about is that Parliament has not conferred such autonomy on a 16- to 18-year-old child by virtue of s 8 of the 1969 Act, and that the common law as interpreted by the House of Lords in *Gillick*'s case does not do so either.

Since Parliament has not conferred complete autonomy on a 16-year-old in the field of medical treatment, there is no overriding limitation to preclude the exercise by the court of its inherent jurisdiction and the matter becomes one for the exercise by the court of its discretion. Nevertheless the discretion is not to be exercised in a moral vacuum. Undoubtedly the philosophy behind s 8 of the 1969 Act, as well as being the decision of the House of Lords in *Gillick*'s case is that, as children approach the age of majority, they are increasingly able to take their own decisions concerning their medical treatment. In logic there can be no difference between an ability to consent to treatment and an ability to refuse treatment. This philosophy is also reflected by some provisions of the Children Act 1989 which give a child, of sufficient understanding to make an informed decision, the right to refuse 'medical or psychiatric examination or other assessment' or 'psychiatric and medical treatment' in certain defined circumstances – see ss 38(6), 43(8) and 44(7) and paras 4(4)(*a*) and 5(5)(*a*) of sch 3. Accordingly the older the child concerned the greater the weight the court should give to its wishes, certainly in the field of medical treatment. In a sense this is merely one aspect of the application of the test that the welfare of the child is the paramount consideration. It will normally be in the best interests of a child of sufficient age and understanding to make an informed decision that the court should respect its integrity as a human being and not lightly override its decision on such a personal matter as medical treatment, all the more so if that treatment is invasive. In my judgment, therefore, the court exercising the inherent jurisdiction in relation to a 16- or 17-year-old child who is not mentally incompetent will, as a matter of course, ascertain the wishes of the child and will approach its decision with a strong predilection to give effect to the child's wishes. (The case of a mentally incompetent child will present different considerations, although even there the child's wishes, if known, must be a very material factor.) Nevertheless, if the court's powers are to be meaningful, there must come a point at which the court, while not disregarding the child's wishes, can override them in the child's own best interests, objectively considered. Clearly such a point will have come if the child is seeking to refuse treatment in circumstances which will in all probability lead to the death of the child or to severe permanent injury. An example of such a case was *Re E (a minor)* [1992] 2 FCR 219, which came before Ward J. There a 15-year-old Jehovah's Witness, and his parents of the same faith, were refusing to allow doctors to give the boy a blood transfusion without which there was a strong risk (on the medical evidence) that the boy would die. Ward J authorised the blood transfusion. In my judgment he was right to do so. In the course of his judgment he said:

> There is compelling and overwhelming force in the submission of the Official Solicitor that this court, exercising its prerogative of protection, should be very slow to allow an infant to martyr himself.

I agree.

At the end of the first day's hearing before us we were told that W's condition had deteriorated rapidly since the hearing at first instance. Her weight had dropped from 41.7 kg at the beginning of May to 36.75 kg on 28 June. She had for ten days refused all solid food. If this pattern continued she would probably die: if it were not shortly reversed she would be likely to suffer permanent damage to her brain and reproductive organs. In those circumstances, the point had clearly been reached when the court should be prepared, in W's own interests, to overrule her refusal to consent to treatment, and we therefore ordered that she should be treated at the appropriate London unit.

I do not think it would be helpful to try to define the point at which the court should be prepared to disregard the 16- or 17-year-old child's wishes to refuse medical treatment. Every case must depend on its own facts. What I do stress is that the judge should approach the exercise of the discretion with a predilection to give effect to the child's wishes on the basis that prima facie that will be in his or her best interests.

If that is, as I believe to be, the correct approach, then it does not appear to have been adopted by Thorpe J in the present case. That is not said by way of criticism, because the case does not appear primarily to have been argued before him on that basis. It would appear from his judgment that the main argument before him on behalf of W was on the basis of s 8 giving W an absolute right to refuse treatment. Once he had (rightly) rejected that argument, he treated the matter as one for the unfettered exercise of his discretion, in which W's views were merely a relatively unimportant factor, and expressed the view that his real choice was between the conflicting medical views of Dr M, the consultant psychiatrist in whose care W had been for over a year, and Dr G, supported in the event by Dr D, another consultant psychiatrist with specialist experience in the field of anorexia nervosa. However, not merely was there a conflict of medical evidence, but even Dr D, upon whose opinion Thorpe J eventually based his decision, described W as having 'a mild case of anorexia nervosa' and that although he (Dr D) had eventually come round to the view that W should be treated at the specialist London unit, the decision was quite finely balanced. It must be remembered that W was not refusing all medical treatment – she was merely expressing her view that she wished to remain at Dr M's clinic. Even though her motive may have been a desire to manipulate the situation, her wish was supported by Dr M and, initially at least, by Dr D. In those circumstances I entertain grave doubts that if Thorpe J had directed himself in the way I have suggested, that W's wishes should be respected unless there were very strong reasons for rejecting them, he would have reached the decision which he did. However, as I have said, by the time the case was before us W's condition had changed so drastically that, whatever may have been the previous position, the court would have been in dereliction of its duty had it not overridden W's wishes and effectively confirmed the order made by Thorpe J that W should be treated at the specialist London unit.

In the course of the arguments before us it was suggested that a construction of s 8 of the 1969 Act which denies a 16- or 17-year-old girl an absolute right to refuse medical treatment, but leaves it open to her parents to consent to such treatment, could in theory lead to a case where a pregnant 16-year-old refuses an abortion, but her parents consent to her pregnancy being terminated. So it could in theory, but I cannot conceive of a case where a doctor, faced with the refusal of a mentally competent 16-year-old to having an abortion, would terminate the pregnancy merely upon the consent of the girl's parents. Leaving aside all questions of medical ethics, it seems to me inevitable that in such highly unlikely circumstances the matter would have to come before the court. I find it equally difficult to conceive a case where the court faced with this problem and applying the approach I have indicated above, would authorise an abortion against the wishes of a mentally competent 16-year-old. The dilemma is therefore more apparent than real.

Nolan LJ: I agree with Lord Donaldson MR that the effect of s 8 is to make it clear that a child of 16 or 17 years of age has the same capacity as an adult to consent to surgical, medical or dental treatment which would otherwise constitute a trespass. The phrase 'surgical, medical or dental treatment' is evidently used in a fairly narrow sense: otherwise it would not have been necessary for Parliament to provide, by s 8(2), that the expression includes diagnostic procedures, and ancillary procedures such as the administration of an anaesthetic. The section does not cover, for example, the giving of blood, it does not even include the taking of a blood sample. Separate provision for that is made by s 21 of the Act. In these circumstances it is impossible to my mind to regard s 8 as supporting the general proposition that in the exercise of its inherent jurisdiction the court should allow the child's decision to determine the matter, whether or not the court thinks that this is in the child's best interests. If the court took this view, it would be abdicating its responsibility.

Nor, to my mind, is the significance of s 8 enhanced by the decision in *Gillick*'s case. *Gillick*'s case was, of course, concerned with children under the age of 16. There were passing references to s 8 in the printed cases submitted to the House of Lords by the parties, but the section does not appear to have been mentioned in the course of oral argument. Lord Fraser described s 8(1) as having been enacted 'merely for the avoidance of doubt' (see [1985] 3 All ER 402 at 408, [1986] AC 150 at 167).

The general approach adopted by the House of Lords to the weight which should be attached to the views of a child who has sufficient understanding to make an informed decision is clearly of great importance, but it is essential to bear in mind that their Lordships were concerned with the extent of parental rights over the welfare of the child. They were not concerned with the jurisdiction of the court. It is of the essence of that jurisdiction that the court has the power and the responsibility in appropriate cases to override the views of both the child and the parent in determining what is in the child's best interests. Authoritative and instructive as they are, the speeches in *Gillick*'s case do not deal with the principles which should govern the exercise of this court's jurisdiction in the present case. In my judgment, those principles are to be found in s 1 of the Children Act 1989. The child's welfare is to be the paramount consideration: see s 1(1). In giving effect to that consideration, the court is to have particular regard to the factors set out in s 1(3). That subsection is expressed to apply only in certain defined circumstances, but it is, I think, common ground that it may be treated as having general application. It requires the court to have regard in particular to: (a) the ascertainable wishes and feelings of the child concerned (considered in the light of his age and understanding); (b) his physical, emotional and educational needs; (c) the likely effect on him of any change in his circumstances; (d) his age, sex, background and any characteristics of his which the court considers relevant; (e) any harm which he has suffered or is at risk of suffering; (f) how capable each of his parents, and any other person in relation to whom the court considers the question to be relevant, is of meeting his needs; and (g) the range of powers available to the court.

In other words, in the circumstances of the present case the wishes and feelings of W considered in the light of her age and understanding, are the first of the factors to which the court must have regard, but the court must have regard also to such of the other factors as may be relevant when discharging its overall responsibility for W's welfare.

I would emphasise that the only aspect of W's welfare with which we are concerned in the present case is her refusal to undergo a particular form of treatment for anorexia. So far in this judgment I have been principally concerned to explain why, as it seems to me, the court has not only the power but the inescapable responsibility of deciding, in that specific context, what is to be done in the interests of her welfare. I am very far from asserting any general rule that the court should prefer its own view as to what is in the best interests of the child to those of the child itself. In considering the welfare of the child, the court must not only recognise but if necessary defend the right of the child, having sufficient understanding to take an informed decision, to make his or her own choice. In most areas of life it would be not only wrong in principle but also futile and counter-productive for the court to adopt any different approach. In the area of medical treatment, however, the court can and sometimes must intervene.

It will, I think, be apparent from what I have said that even in the case of normal medical treatment, I cannot accept Mr Munby's proposition that the child's decision should determine the matter. The determination must always be that of the court. If one is then to try and specify the grounds upon which it would be right for the court to intervene I do not for my part find it particularly helpful to speak in terms of special or extraordinary cases as distinct from normal cases. . . . One must, I think, start from the general premise that the protection of the child's welfare implies at least the protection of the child's life. I state this only as a general and not as an invariable premise because of the possibility of cases in which the court would not authorise treatment of a distressing nature which offered only a small hope of preserving life. In general terms, however, the present state of the law is that an individual who has reached the age of 18 is free to do with his life what he wishes, but it is the duty of the court to ensure so far as it can that children survive to attain that age.

To take it a stage further, if the child's welfare is threatened by a serious and imminent risk that the child will suffer grave and irreversible mental or physical harm, then once again the court when called upon has a duty to intervene. It makes no difference whether the risk arises from the action or inaction of others, or from the action or inaction of the child. Due weight must be given to the child's wishes, but the court is not bound by them. In the present case, Thorpe J was apparently satisfied on the evidence before him that such a risk existed. In my judgment, he was fully entitled to take this view. By the time the matter came to this court, it was impossible to take any other view. For these reasons, I would dismiss the appeal save to the extent of making the necessary variation of the order of Thorpe J.

We are not directly concerned with cases in which the jurisdiction of the court has not been invoked, and in which accordingly the decision on treatment may depend upon the consent of the child or of the parent. I for my part would think it axiomatic, however, in order to avoid the risk of grave breaches of the law that in any case where time permitted, where major surgical or other procedures (such as an abortion) were proposed, and whereby the parents or those in loco parentis were prepared to give consent but the child (having sufficient understanding to make an informed decision) was not, the jurisdiction of the court should always be invoked. I would say the same of a case in which a child of any age consented to donate an organ; such a case is not, of course, covered by s 8 of the Family Law Reform Act 1969 on any view of the matter.

Undoubtedly, *Re W* is a controversial case. A number of arguments can be deployed to show that the court made a wrong turn in taking to itself and giving parents decision-making powers over their competent children. Let us first consider the arguments concerning the power of the court. In *Re R* and *Re W* the court was exercising its *parens patriae* power (in wardship or under the inherent jurisdiction of the court). While it is undeniable that the court's jurisdiction is unlimited, this is only true once it has been determined what falls within the jurisdiction in the first place. For instance, it is clear now that it does not cover adults. It is also arguably the case that it does not cover the competent, whether adult or not. Historically, the jurisdiction was concerned with children and 'idiots, lunatics and others of unsound mind' (*Re Eve* [1986] 2 SCR 388). It is also clear that the jurisdiction was 'founded on the obvious necessity that the law should place somewhere the care of individuals who cannot take care of themselves' (*Wellesley v Duke of Beaufort* (1827) 2 Russ 1 at 20). Competent adults would not have been subject to the *parens patriae* jurisdiction before 1960 when it ceased to exist in respect of adults (see *supra*, p 276 et seq). Only incompetent adults would have been the proper subjects of the court's jurisdiction. *Mutatis mutandis* the legal position should be the same for children. The courts in *Re R* and *Re W* overlook this and falsely move straight to the position that the court's *parens patriae* power is always limitless in its scope.

Even if this were not the case, the theoretically limitless jurisdiction of the court is subject to practical and policy-based limitations. There is a strong argument that just as courts stay their hand where enforcement would be impossible or where they are asked to review the exercise of a power conferred by statute on, for example, a local authority, so too they should stay their hand where the decision-maker subject to review is a *competent* child. This argument does not turn upon the rather arid point that s 8 of the 1969 Act ousts the court's jurisdiction. Rather it is founded upon the underlying ethos represented by s 8 and the *Gillick* decision. Whether or not s 8 and *Gillick* only relate expressly to consent, they both look to a more fundamental value, namely that of respecting the autonomy of the competent person (whether or not falling within the arbitrarily defined category of 'children'). State paternalism has no place simply on the basis that the 'state knows best'.

As regards a conflict between the parents and the child, a majority of the court (Nolan LJ *dubitante*) adopted the approach of Lord Donaldson MR in *Re R* that a child's refusal could be countermanded by the parents. Hence, while a child may validly consent to medical treatment and this consent may not be overriden by the parents (*Gillick*), a child's refusal will be valid subject to being overriden by the parents. This conclusion is open to a number of objections. First, it relies upon a literal interpretation of s 8 of the Family Law Reform Act 1969. While it is true that s 8 only speaks of a child over 16 having capacity to consent to medical treatment, the section could (and perhaps should) be interpreted as encompassing the right to refuse. Despite what the judges say in *Re W*, the Latey Committee (whose report led to s 8) is ambiguous and leaves open the point which the court claims that it concludes. More importantly, the common law, as developed in the *Gillick* case, takes a wholly different view of the law than the gloss placed upon it by Lord Donaldson MR. The House of Lords undoubtedly approached the *Gillick* case from the point of view of seeking to identify what *rights* a young person may have in the context of medical treatment. In particular, the majority of the House were concerned with the right of self-determination. From this starting point no distinction may properly be drawn between *agreeing to* and *refusing* treatment. They are merely two ways of exercising the same right. Thus, if the right to consent exists so does the right to refuse. Lord Donaldson's approach is to reject a rights-based analysis. He idiosyncratically believes that the only role of consent in the common law is not to give effect to a right of self-determination, but rather to serve as a piece of legal armour protecting a doctor who might otherwise be sued in battery. Approached in this way, consent is merely a formal device. It has no substance, least of all the substance of rights. Furthermore, it can readily be detached from any consideration of a refusal. But this is to deny the right to decide which is at the heart of the law of consent as was made clear, *inter alia*, by the House of Lords in *Sidaway v Board of Governors of Bethlem Royal Hospital* [1985] AC 871. After all, making *decisions* includes saying 'no' as well as saying 'yes' (see *Airedale NHS Trust v Bland* [1993] 1 All ER 821 at 865-866 *per* Lord Goff).

What these arguments, and indeed the Children Act 1989, demonstrate is that whatever the position when the Family Law Reform Act 1969 was passed, the law now does not recognise parental rights but rather parental duties. The latter exist only for the benefit and welfare of a child who has not yet achieved a level of understanding to be judged competent in a particular matter (see *Gillick* and *F v Wirral Metropolitan Borough Council* [1991] Fam 69, [1991] 2 All ER 648, CA). The argument of the judges, therefore, that s 8(3) preserves the parental right to consent is simply misplaced since all it tells us is that we must look to the general law to see who (if anyone) may consent when the child refuses. The overwhelming trend has been to say that no one may do so until *Re R* and *Re W*. Further, it may not be enough for the court to dismiss the 'hair-raising possibilities' (*per* Lord Donaldson MR) of abortions or sterilisations carried out on competent and unwilling, perhaps even protesting, young women with the consent of the court (or parents) as 'a dilemma . . . more apparent than real' (*per* Balcombe LJ). It is surely not appropriate for the court to wash its hands of these real and hard cases by simply asserting that they will not happen. Certainly if *the court* were to authorise such a procedure, some doctor would probably be prepared to carry it out, even if he would not do so merely on the basis of the parents' consent. It would be hard to imagine a legal development more designed to destroy trust in both the law and the medical profession.

A final point which serves to demonstrate how much of a departure from orthodoxy *Re W* constitutes, involves noticing its impact upon the law of confidentiality. Given that *competent* children are entitled to have their confidences respected, how may a parent consent to treatment if a child refuses and insists on the doctor observing confidentiality by not discussing the case with the parents? The only solution would be if the law recognised some sort of public interest exception, here based upon the best interests of the child. The difficulty with such a view is that it undermines the very nature of competence, ie that a person knows his own best interests and must be free to make his own mistakes (for a discussion see *infra*, ch 3).

Despite these major criticisms of *Re R* and *Re W*, and on the assumption that they currently represent the law, it is necessary to examine how the court views its power to override a child's refusal. In *Re R* little or no guidance was offered as to *when* the court would do so and what weight (if any) it would give to the child's refusal. In *Re W*, on the other hand, the judges did address this issue in the context of the *court's* powers. Presumably, *a fortiori* the court's views would define the scope of the parents' power. Balcombe LJ limited the court's power to cases where the refusal 'will in all probability lead to the death of the child or to severe permanent injury'. Similarly, Nolan LJ contemplated cases where 'the child's welfare is threatened by a serious and imminent risk that the child will suffer grave and irreversible mental or physical harm'. At this point, the court had a 'duty to intervene' (*per* Nolan LJ). Before that point is reached, however, the court should 'approach its decision with a strong predilection to give effect to the child's wishes' (*per* Balcombe LJ).

Given this approach, Balcombe LJ thought that the trial judge had wrongly overridden W's refusal since *at that time* her life was not threatened. By the time the case came before the Court of Appeal her condition had deteriorated. Nolan LJ was only prepared to accept Thorpe J's decision on the basis that he had found on the evidence that there was a 'serious and imminent risk' of 'grave and irreversible' harm to her mental or physical health.

As ever, Lord Donaldson MR appeared to give the court a wider power. The limit explicitly stated by the other judges is not readily apparent in his judgment and he entirely accepted the trial judge's decision that W's refusal should be overridden.

The case contemplated in *Re W* is that of the child who refuses and whose refusal is overridden – what of the child who wishes to consent but her parents or the court consider this not to be in her 'best interests'? We know, as regards the parents, that after *Gillick* they have no power to veto treatment by seeking to override the child's consent. In Lord Donaldson's picturesque language the child's consent unlocks the door for the doctor (*Re R*) or gives him a 'flak-jacket' (*Re W*). But, what of the court? Is the court's power similarly limited? Only Staughton LJ gave any consideration to this in *Re R* where he said:

> Then there is the converse case in wardship, where the ward consents but the court is minded either not to consent or positively to forbid treatment. Does the judge in such a case have an overriding power, which the natural parent of a competent child under the age of 16 does not have by reason of the *Gillick* decision? If so, there would again be a problem for doctors, who may have to ask if the child is a ward. But the trend of the cases seems to show that, if the treatment would constitute an important step in the child's life, the court does have that power.

Certainly, Staughton LJ's view is consistent with the reasoning in *Re R* and *Re W* if the child is a ward of court for the reason he gave (see also Lord Donaldson MR in *Re W* at 633, asserting that the court's power to override a child's consent was accepted by all parties in the *Gillick* case). If the child is not a ward, however, the answer is more difficult. When the court exercises its inherent jurisdiction or makes an order under s 8 of the Children Act 1989, it could grant an injunction in the former case or a 'prohibited steps' order in the latter case which would have the same effect as if the child were a ward. In practical terms, a court minded to refuse treatment fearing that it could be carried out by a doctor always has this option to prohibit treatment.

In conclusion, on any account the decisions in *Re R* and *Re W* are provocative. They threaten to undermine the landmark decision of the House of Lords in *Gillick* and render teenagers insecure of their rights just at the time when they are being encouraged to take responsibility for themselves. It is our view that these cases do not properly represent an ordered development in the law and should be reconsidered by the House of Lords when the opportunity arises. At this time, thought may be given to the following. There is no doubt that cases such as *Re R* and *Re W* are poignant, difficult and attract enormous popular interest. It is not surprising furthermore that the courts should have arrived at the decision that treatment should be given whatever the patient's wishes in the light of the harm that would otherwise ensue. Sadly, in reaching this decision the Court of Appeal has done violence to the development of the law begun by *Gillick*. There was another course open to the court. Ever since *Gillick* and, indeed, before, there had been speculation about the proper course to take in the following three classes of case. The *first* is the patient with fluctuating lucidity, for example the manic depressive who while lucid denies that he has been ill, refuses medication and plunges headlong back into illness. The *second* is the anorexic who is entirely competent in every regard save that she has an utterly distorted view of her body image and therefore embarks on a pattern of behaviour which might ultimately result in death. The *third* is the person addicted to drugs who may lead a perfectly ordered life provided he satisfies his craving for drugs. All of these three types of person could be regarded in law as incompetent as regards their need for treatment. Their incompetence lies in their inability or refusal to comprehend the true nature of their predicament (see *State of Tennessee v Northern* 563 SW 2d 197 (1978)). Such a view would leave intact the framework of the law of competence and the rights that flaw from it without in any way artificially manipulating the concept of competence (see *supra*, ch 3).

Chapter 5

Medical malpractice

Introduction

The background to actions for medical malpractice is explained by Margaret Brazier in *Medicine, Patients and the Law* (2nd edn 1992) (pp 21-2).

> [The patient] . . . may feel that he has not been fully consulted or properly counselled about the nature and risks of the treatment. He may have agreed to treatment and ended up worse, not better. Consequently a patient may seek compensation from the courts. Or he may simply want an investigation of what went wrong, and to ensure that his experience is not suffered by others.
>
> The law relating to medical errors, commonly described as medical malpractice, operates on two basic principles. (1) The patient must agree to treatment. (2) Treatment must be carried out with proper skill and care on the part of all members of the medical profession involved. Any doctor who operated on or injected, or even touched an adult patient against his will, might commit a battery, a trespass against the patient's person. [We dealt with this in detail in Chapter 3.] A doctor who was shown to have exercised inadequate care of his patient, to have fallen below the required standard of competence, would be liable to compensate the patient for any harm he caused him in the tort of negligence.
>
> In short, to obtain compensation the patient must show that the doctor was at fault. And if he sues for negligence he must show that the doctor's 'fault' caused him injury. Three overwhelming problems are inherent in these two simple statements.
>
> First, how do courts staffed by lawyer-judges determine when a doctor is at fault? . . . The judges in England defer in the most part to the views of the doctors. Unlike their American brethren, English judges will rarely challenge the accepted views of the medical profession. Establishing what that view is may cause the court some difficulty though. Each side is free to call its own experts and a clash of eminent medical opinion is not unusual.
>
> Second, as liability, and the patient's right to compensation, is dependent on a finding of fault, doctors naturally feel that a judgment against them is a body blow to their career and their reputation. Yet a moment's reflection will remind the reader of all the mistakes he has made in his own job. A solicitor overlooking a vital piece of advice in a conference with a client can telephone the client and put things right when he has a chance to check what he has done. A carpenter can have a second go at fixing a door or a cupboard. An overworked, overstrained doctor may commit a momentary error which is irreversible. He is still a good doctor despite one mistake.
>
> Finally, the doctor's fault must be shown to have caused the patient harm. In general, whether a patient is treated within the NHS or privately, the doctor only undertakes to do his best. He does not guarantee a cure. The patient will have a legal remedy if he can show that the doctor's carelessness or lack of skill caused him injury that he would not otherwise have suffered. So if I contract an infection and am prescribed antibiotics that a competent doctor would have appreciated were inappropriate for me or my condition, I will be able to sue the doctor only if I can show either (1) that the antibiotic prescribed caused me harm unrelated to my original sickness, for example brought me out in a violent allergy, or (2) that the absence of appropriate treatment significantly delayed my recovery. And in both cases I must prove that had the doctor acted properly the harm to me would have been avoided.

To maintain an action in negligence the plaintiff must establish (i) that the doctor owed him a duty of care, (ii) that the duty was breached, (iii) that he suffered harm caused by that breach. Let us remind ourselves of the basic elements of a case in medical negligence by looking at a decision which acquired some notoriety.

Whitehouse v Jordan [1981] 1 All ER 267, (1981) 1 BMLR 14 (HL)

Lord Wilberforce: My Lords, Stuart Whitehouse is a boy now aged ten; he was born on 7th January 1970, with severe brain damage. In these circumstances, tragic for him and for his mother, this action has been brought, by his mother as next friend, in which he claims that the damage to his brain was caused by the professional negligence of Mr J A Jordan who was senior registrar at the hospital at Birmingham where the birth took place. There were originally also claims against Professor McLaren, the consultant in charge of the maternity unit to which Mr Jordan belonged, and also against the hospital on its own account. But these have disappeared and the hospital, more exactly the West Midlands Regional Health Authority, remains in the case only as vicariously responsible for any liability which may be established against Mr Jordan.

A large number of claims have been made since the event, most of which have now been eliminated or withdrawn. The negligence ultimately charged against Mr Jordan is that in the course of carrying out a 'trial of forceps delivery', he pulled too long and too strongly on the child's head, thereby causing the brain damage. The trial judge, after a trial of 11 days in which eminent medical experts were called on each side, and numerous issues were canvassed, reached the conclusion which he expressed in a most careful judgment, that the plaintiff had made good his case: he awarded £100,000 damages. His decision was reversed by a majority of the Court of Appeal (Lord Denning MR and Lawton LJ, Donaldson LJ dissenting) ([1980] 1 All ER 650) which refused leave to appeal to this House. Leave was, however, granted by an Appeal Committee. The essential and very difficult question therefore has to be faced whether, on a pure question of fact, the Court of Appeal was justified in reversing the decision of the trial judge.

Mr Jordan was at the time a senior registrar, of near consultant status, esteemed by his professional colleagues. There is no question but that he brought the utmost care to bear on Mrs Whitehouse's labour and delivery. If he was negligent at all, this consisted in a departure, in an anxious situation, from a standard accepted by the profession at the time. Put very briefly, it was said to lie in continuing traction with the forceps after an obstruction had been encountered so that the baby's head 'impacted'. I shall not explain this word at this stage. It is obvious that the error, if error there was, lay centrally in the area of the exercise of expert judgment and experienced operation. Mr Jordan was a member of the obstetrical unit at the hospital headed by Professor McLaren, which had a high reputation; Professor McLaren himself was a distinguished obstetrician, unfortunately ill at the time of the birth.

Mrs Whitehouse was accepted as 30 years of age; this was her first baby. She was small, only 4ft 10½ inches in height. She was a difficult, nervous and at times aggressive patient. She was unable, or refused, to agree to vaginal examination during her pregnancy, or to have a lateral X-ray, though urged to do so by Professor McLaren. These processes would have helped to discover the exact shape of the pelvis. It is fair to say that when Mr Jordan came on the scene he was not greatly handicapped by this, because Mrs Whitehouse was at that time under epidural anaesthetic, and he was able to examine her vaginally. However, he had not the advantage of accurate measurement of the pelvis or of the ischial spines. . . . The mother was seen by a number of doctors in the course of her pregnancy including Professor McLaren and Mr Jordan. I do not think that any criticism can be made of what they did. She was identified clearly as likely to be a difficult case; on 31st December 1969 Professor McLaren recorded that he thought the outlet was tight and that a trial of labour would be needed. This means that labour would be permitted to start and to proceed under close supervision in order to see whether the head could, with safety, proceed down the birth canal.

Mrs Whitehouse was admitted to the hospital at 0200 hrs on 6th January 1970, her membranes having ruptured shortly before. The vertex was recorded as engaged at 0230, and this was confirmed by Mr Kelly, of consultant status, at 1000 hrs. He noted 'fair sized baby'.

So at this point we have a small woman, anxious and distressed, awaiting a baby, for her on the large side, with the head in a favourable position and engaged in the pelvis; noted as being probably a case for 'trial of labour'. At 1130 she was given an epidural anaesthetic which would prevent her from feeling pain and probably from sensation below the waist.

At 1830 she was seen by Dr Skinner. He examined her vaginally and abdominally. He reported 'vertex engaged, fetal heart satisfactory . . . pelvis seems adequate'.

Now comes the period critical for this case. At 2330 Mr Jordan, who was not on duty, came to talk to Dr Skinner. On his radio communicator the latter was told that Mrs Whitehouse was fully dilated. Dr Skinner thought that this was the case for a more senior man than he, and Mr Jordan agreed to go; he saw her at 2330 and examined her abdominally and vaginally. He read the notes on the case, which, as the above summary shows, informed him precisely of what he had to deal with: a difficult case calling for great care.

He made a detailed note which I need not copy in full. It gave all the necessary medical details. Against 'pelvis' he wrote 'small gynaecoid' (ie of appropriate female shape) and then 'Normal delivery out of the question'.

He decided to embark on a trial of forceps and did so at 2345. The full expression for this is 'trial of forceps delivery' which, as the evidence showed beyond doubt, means the operator tries to see whether with the use of forceps a delivery per vaginam is possible. This involves two things, first tentative and delicate handling at least at the start; second the necessity of continuously reviewing progress with the obligation to stop traction if it appears that the delivery per vaginam cannot be proceeded without risk. Then delivery will take place by Caesarian section.

Two things must be said at this stage. First, though for the plaintiff it was at one time otherwise contended, the decision to try for vaginal delivery rather than go at once to a Caesarian section was unquestionably the right and correct procedure, in order to avoid if possible the risk to the mother inevitably involved in section. Secondly, for the plaintiff an attempt was made to draw a line between trial of forceps, on the one hand, and delivery by forceps on the other hand, and to make a case that Mr Jordan was, unjustifiably, proceeding to the latter. This, to my mind, completely failed. There is no such clear-cut distinction. A trial of forceps (delivery) is what it says: it is an attempt at delivery accompanied by the two special conditions I have mentioned. There can be no doubt that this is what Mr Jordan was attempting. I take what happened from his notes. Under 'summary of reasons for operation' he wrote: 'Trial of forceps under epidural anaesthetic. Lower segment Caesarian section under GA'. Then:

> (1) Forceps begun at 23 45, 6 1 70. Head rotated to OA [occiput anterior] with Kiellands – no problem. [Kiellands is a kind of forceps used by some operators to rotate the head. This procedure was correct.] A very tight fit. No episiotomy [cutting of the perineum]. After pulling with 5 or 6 contractions, it was obvious that vaginal delivery would be too traumatic – so Caesarian section.

He then recorded the Caesarian which everyone agrees was impeccably performed in two minutes. He notes 'no apparent (vaginal) trauma'. To complete the history the baby, extracted apparently unharmed, was handed over to the paediatricians, found apnoeic, and made to breathe after 35 minutes, by which time irretrievable brain damage had occurred.

Here, with one possible exception, is a record of a birth carried out with all correct procedures, with, as unhappily occurs in the best managed hospitals and the best medical care, tragic results. The possible exception lies in the reference in Mr Jordan's own report to 'pulling with 5 or 6 contractions'. Did Mr Jordan pass the limits of professional competence either in continuing traction too long, or in pulling too hard? That is the whole issue.

Lord Edmund-Davies in his speech identified the issues.

The principal question calling for decision are: (a) in what manner did Mr Jordan use the forceps? and (b) was that manner consistent with the degree of skill which a member of his profession is required by law to exercise? Surprising though it is at this late stage in the development of the law of negligence, counsel for Mr Jordan persisted in submitting that his client should be completely exculpated were the answer to question (b), 'Well, at the worst he was guilty of an error of clinical judgment.'

We will return to this case later. In the result, the House of Lords unanimously dismissed the plaintiff's appeal. We can learn many things from *Whitehouse*; not least is that cases of medical negligence exemplify, *par excellence*, the proposition that cases turn on facts as well as law. Indeed, proving the facts alleged is often the greatest hurdle faced by any plaintiff, whatever the law may be. *Whitehouse* also illustrates two further issues which continue to challenge lawyers and courts: the wholly legal problem of defining what a doctor's duty consists of and the question, which mixes law and fact, of how to establish whether a doctor was in breach of his duty in any particular set of circumstances. *Whitehouse* does not illustrate what we shall identify as a further major hurdle in establishing the liability of a doctor – the proof of causation, ie that the conduct of the doctor caused the harm complained of. We shall return to these two issues shortly. For the present, let us turn to the first element of an action in medical negligence – the existence of a duty to take care.

An action for medical negligence

A. DUTY OF CARE

1. A doctor

Margaret Brazier observes: '[a] patient claiming against his doctor . . . usually has little difficulty in establishing that the defendant owes him a duty of care' (*Medicine, Patients and the Law* (2nd edn 1992) at pp 117-8). The precise point at which a duty to take care comes into being may not be as easy as Professor Brazier suggests, as our discussion in Chapter 2 illustrates.

Nevertheless, in general terms the essence of the duty is an undertaking by the doctor towards his patient. As Lord Hewart CJ said in *R v Bateman* (1925) 94 LJKB 791 (CCA) (a case of manslaughter brought against a doctor):

> If a person holds himself out as possessing special skill and knowledge, and he is consulted, as possessing such skill and knowledge, by or on behalf of a patient, he owes a duty to the patient to use due caution in undertaking the treatment. If he accepts the responsibility and undertakes the treatment and the patient submits to his discretion and treatment accordingly, he owes a duty to the patient to use diligence, care, knowledge, skill and caution in administering the treatment. No contractual relation is necessary, nor is it necessary that the service be rendered for reward.

This, of course, assumes something which already exists, namely that the individual has already become the doctor's patient (see Chapter 2 above).

As regards the NHS, the relationship of doctor and patient in the case of a GP is dealt with in the National Health Service (General Medical Services) Regulations 1992 (SI 1992 No 635) (as amended). Doctors who work within NHS hospitals do not come within these Regulations. Consequently, the creation of the doctor-patient relationship is wholly a matter for the common law, ie the existence or otherwise of an undertaking to take care. The common law position is illustrated by the following case.

Barnett v Chelsea and Kensington Hospital Management Committee [1969] 1 QB 428, [1968] 1 All ER 1068 (QBD)

> **Nield J:** At about 5 am on Jan 1, 1966, three night watchmen drank some tea. Soon afterwards all three men started vomiting. At about 8 am the men walked to the casualty

department of the defendants' hospital, which was open. One of them, the deceased, when he was in the room in the hospital, lay on some armless chairs. He appeared ill. Another of the men told the nurse that they had been vomiting after drinking tea. The nurse telephoned the casualty officer, a doctor, to tell him of the men's complaint. The casualty officer, who was himself unwell, did not see them, but said that they should go home and call in their own doctors. The men went away, and the deceased died some hours later from what was found to be arsenical poisoning. Cases of arsenical poisoning were rare, and, even if the deceased had been examined and admitted to the hospital and treated, there was little or no chance that the only effective antidote would have been administered to him before the time at which he died.

I turn to consider the nature of the duty which the law imposes on persons in the position of the defendants and their servants and agents. The authorities deal in the main with the duties of doctors, surgeons, consultants, nurses and staff when a person is treated either by a doctor at his surgery or the patient's home or when the patient is treated in or at hospital. In *Cassidy v Ministry of Health* [[1951] 2 KB 343], Denning LJ dealt with the duties of hospital authorities and said:

> In my opinion, authorities who run a hospital, be they local authorities, government boards, or any other corporation, are in law under the self-same duty as the humblest doctor. Whenever they accept a patient for treatment, they must use reasonable care and skill to cure him of his ailment. The hospital authorities cannot, of course, do it by themselves. They have no ears to listen through the stethoscope, and no hands to hold the knife. They must do it by the staff which they employ, and, if their staff are negligent in giving the treatment, they are just as liable for that negligence as is anyone else who employs others to do his duties for him. Is there any possible difference in law, I ask, can there be, between hospital authorities who accept a patient for treatment and railway or shipping authorities who accept a passenger for carriage? None whatever. Once they undertake the task, they come under a duty to use care in the doing of it, and that is so whether they do it for reward or not.

Here the problem is different and no authority bearing directly on it has been cited to me. It is to determine the duty of those who provide and run a casualty department when a person presents himself at that department complaining of illness or injury and before he is treated and received into the hospital wards. This is not a case of a casualty department which closes its doors and says that no patients can be received. The three watchmen entered the defendants' hospital without hindrance, they made complaints to the nurse who received them and she in turn passed those complaints on to the medical casualty officer, and he sent a message through the nurse purporting to advise the three men. Is there, on these facts, shown to be created a relationship between the three watchmen and the hospital staff such as gives rise to a duty of care in the defendants which they owe to the three men?

. . . In my judgment, there was here such a close direct relationship between the hospital and the watchmen that there was imposed on the hospital a duty of care which they owed to the watchmen. Thus I have no doubt that Nurse Corbett and Dr Banerjee were under a duty to the deceased . . .

You will recall that we have dealt in some detail with the creation of a doctor-patient relationship. Here, Nield J found that there was the necessary undertaking on the part of the doctor (Dr Banerjee) such that he had thereafter to behave reasonably. An alternative reading of the case can be that it turns on the hospital's primary duty since Nield J found 'that there was imposed upon the hospital a duty of care which they owed to the watchmen'. (See below.) In any event, the judge went on to find the doctor in breach of his duty in failing to examine and treat the deceased. His widow, nevertheless, lost her action because she could not show that this breach *caused* his death (see *infra*, p 469).

2. The institution

We are concerned here principally with the liability of hospitals within the NHS. In practice, of course, this means the liability of the relevant health authority responsible for the hospital, usually the District Health Authority. We also have to take account of other institutions: these include the NHS Trust (which are increasingly dominating the provision of hospital services), the private clinic and, exceptionally, the Secretary of State in the context of the provisions of services which he has not delegated to any other NHS body.

Since the introduction of the 'internal market' in the NHS (see above, ch 2) there is a further instance in which an institution may face liability. Not only the 'provider' of the services may face a negligence action but so may the 'purchaser' of the services, ie the relevant DHA or GP fund-holder for having, for example, negligently failed to make adequate provision in an NHS contract for health services for which it is responsible.

(a) Primary liability

Picard 'The Liability of Hospitals in Common Law Canada' (1981) 26 McGill LJ 997

> The earliest hospitals were charitable institutions and protected as such by the courts. They were sustained by endowments and voluntary contributions, which were encouraged in England by the creation of the charitable trust. In order to function hospitals had to purchase supplies of food and equipment, and hire persons to care for the patient and operate the physical plant. Provision was eventually made for some patients to pay for their accommodation. Thus, of necessity, hospitals entered into legal relationships and became accountable under contracts, and by 1907 it was clear that a hospital was liable for the negligence of its employees [*Hillyer v The Governors of St Bartholomew's Hospital* [1909] 2 KB 820]. But it was also held that a hospital could not be liable for the negligence of employees such as nurses or doctors in the execution of their professional duties, as opposed to administrative functions. The rationale for this limitation was that the hospital neither directed nor controlled the exercise of professional judgment.
>
> In the *Hillyer* case the English Court of Appeal concluded that a hospital undertook certain duties toward a patient:
>
>> The governors of a public hospital, by their admission of the patient to enjoy in the hospital the gratuitous benefit of its care, do, I think, undertake that the patient whilst there shall be treated only by experts, whether surgeons, physicians or nurses, of whose professional competence the governors have taken reasonable care to assure themselves; and, further, that those experts shall have at their disposal, for the care and treatment of the patient, fit and proper apparatus and appliances.
>
> Thus, approximately seventy-five years ago, a patient had some recourse against a hospital: in contract, depending on the terms thereof, or in tort, if the hospital had breached its duty to select competent staff and to supply proper equipment, or by vicarious liability, subject to the restriction in the *Hillyer* case. . . .
>
> The first hospital patients were the cast-offs of society. The middle and upper classes were treated in their own homes by doctors who called on them there and they were cared for by servants and family. It was only the indigent who went to the hospitals, and the hospital and doctor provided their services gratuitously to such patients. A patient injured by either would have had an extremely difficult time pursuing any compensation through legal action. An action in contract might well have failed for lack of intention, uncertainty of terms or lack of consideration. An action in tort might have been brought in trespass to the person but consent could have been implied rather easily. It was the negligence action of the mid-nineteenth century which first brought an opportunity for a patient to demand, in a court of law, that a hospital be held accountable for its actions. But the scope of such an action was quickly restricted by the courts, as outlined earlier. The two main bases for the liability of a hospital, namely a direct duty of care and vicarious liability, were carefully controlled so as to afford hospitals maximum immunity to the suits of patients.
>
> The situation of the modern patient is very different. Today the hospital is the primary institution for health care [in Canada]. It is in the modern hospital that a patient can receive the best health care available because that is where the skill, knowledge and judgment of health-care professionals may be combined with modern medical equipment and technology. Today a patient comes to hospital not seeking charity, but highly skilled

medical treatment and he might well have had his name on a waiting-list before being admitted!

. . . the greatest contrast between patients of the earlier hospitals and of the modern hospital lies in the legal relationships formed with the hospital. Any legal relationship the early patient had with a hospital was tenuous and if it gave rise to legal obligations the courts interpreted them restrictively. The modern patient has strong, well-defined legal relationships with his hospital.

. . . His relationship, in fact, with a hospital is that of being a patient *of the hospital* and it gives rise to certain duties owed to him by the institution. The hospital must not violate his right to be free from unauthorised touching, nor injure him by carrying out its duties in a sub-standard manner. The doctor-patient relationship likewise gives rise to certain duties but it is crucial to any analysis of the patient's position to remember that, while these duties of hospital and doctor may be concomitant, each set of duties is based on a separate and distinct relationship. . . .

The earliest duty of care held to be owed by a hospital to a patient was to select competent staff in order that patients would be attended by skilled persons. At first this duty was very narrowly interpreted. A hospital had only to ascertain that its professionals were qualified and competent. This seemed to be the scope of its direct or personal or corporate duty of care. . . .

The scope of the direct duty was expanded, first to include the instruction and supervision of personnel employed by the hospital and then to the provision of the systems and organisation to co-ordinate these activities so that the patient received reasonable care. Since a patient is treated in a physical plant with equipment and medical tools, it is not surprising that hospitals were also given a direct duty to provide and maintain proper facilities and equipment.

There is some authority for the existence of other duties but often it is not clear whether the court was basing the hospital's accountability on grounds of direct liability or vicarious liability. These include a duty to establish procedures to prevent patients from harming themselves or being injured by other patients. There are some older cases from which it might be concluded that a hospital has a duty to set up aseptic procedures and to protect patients and even visitors from infection.

Though in theory it is possible for further duties to be created, a review of the cases reveals that the courts have been most cautious when contrasted with their attitude respecting negligence law in general.

In summary, the precedents support these possible direct duties of a hospital to a patient:
(a) to select competent and qualified employees
(b) to instruct and supervise them
(c) to provide proper facilities and equipment
(d) to establish systems necessary to the safe operation of the hospital.

Since the other components of tort law apply, the hospital has to carry out these duties as competently as the reasonable hospital in the circumstances and, even if found sub-standard, would have to be found to have caused the patient's injuries before liability would result. All of the protection of tort law normally available to defendants is available to the hospital.

The quality of the duties owed by a hospital has led to their sometimes being referred to as 'non-delegable'. This has the significant effect of making the employer of an independent contractor strictly liable for any negligence of the contractor in carrying out the duty of care which was the employer's but which he had contracted or delegated to the independent contractor. This is an exception to the general rule that an employer is not liable for the negligence of an independent contractor employed by him.

. . . Fleming [*The Law of Torts* (5th edn) 1977] discusses the kinds of cases where non-delegable duties have been found and notes that the list is 'long and diverse', extending from dangerous situations, hazardous substances, fire, lateral support for land, maintenance of premises abutting a highway to instances where the duty would normally be to use reasonable care but where the designation of the duty as non-delegable assures that care will be taken (provision of a safe system of work, compliance with statutory safety standards, responsibilities of occupiers of land to certain others and of hospitals to care for their patients).

(See for a specific example of an 'unsafe system' argument, the discussion of a hospital's duty to prevent a disturbed patient from harming himself, first edition, pp 145-148.)

In establishing that an institution is liable *qua* institution (ie is in breach of its duty), it is important to realise that the *Bolam* test has no place. Instead, the normal rule of negligence liability will apply, *viz* that the institution will be judged by reference to the norm of practice, that norm being prescriptive rather than descriptive. There will, therefore, be a minimum standard of capability to which the institution will be held. Equally, where an institution claims to be a centre of excellence it will be held to the standard it claims or professes, by analogy to the specialist doctor (see *infra*, p 444).

(i) TWO STRANDS OF LIABILITY

Here we are concerned with the liability of NHS hospitals (ie health authorities) and NHS Trusts. We shall deal shortly with the liability, if any, of the Secretary of State.

You will see that Ellen Picard identifies the emergence of two strands of primary liability. The *first*, and probably more conventional, reflects the duty, in effect, to provide a reasonable regime of care, through its staff, facilities and the exercise of supervision. A useful analogy, here, would be with the well-known case of *Wilsons' & Clyde Co v English* [1938] AC 57 and the duty recognised there which an employer owes to an employee in respect of 'the provision of a competent staff, adequate material, and a proper system and effective supervision' (per Lord Wright at p 78). For the analogy to work here, 'employer' and 'employee' translate into 'hospital' and 'patient'.

The *second* strand of primary liability is both more conjectural and contentious although it may have a respectable history in judgments of Lord Denning and Morris LJ in the celebrated cases in the 1950s of *Cassidy v Ministry of Health* [1951] 1 All ER 574 and *Roe v Minister of Health* [1954] 2 All ER 131. The choice of which of these strands of liability (if either) is adopted as the law governing 'institutions' liability will have significant implications as we shall see. The New South Wales Court of Appeal found itself confronted by the need to choose in the following case and, perhaps not surprisingly, the judges differed as to the merits of both approaches.

Ellis v Wallsend District Hospital (1989) 17 NSWLR 553 (NSW CA)

In 1975 the plaintiff, Mrs Marie Ellis, consulted Dr A W Chambers, a neurosurgeon who had treated her on several occasions in the previous years, at his consulting room. Mrs Ellis, who had a background of intractable and very severe neck pain, drug dependence, drug overdoses, and failure of other treatment, was interested in having five-nerve separation microsurgery which Dr Chambers had already mentioned to her. Dr Chambers advised that the only concern that she need have was the risk of slight numbness in her right hand. Mrs Ellis agreed to have the operation. Dr Chambers arranged to have Mrs Ellis admitted to the defendant hospital, Wallsend District Hospital, where he was an 'honorary medical officer'. Under the by-laws and rules Dr Chambers was appointed to the 'honorary medical staff' of the hospital. Honorary medical officers received no payment from the hospital for services performed there. They were allowed to use the operating theatres for their own patients on a roster basis. When the patient was admitted to the hospital on an admission request form the hospital would book the patient in for surgery at a time when the doctor concerned was rostered to use the theatres. The doctor's fee was a matter for the doctor and his patient.

There was evidence that the operation carried a remote risk of paralysis and a more substantial risk of failure to relieve pain. Mrs Ellis gave evidence that if she had been warned of those risks she would not have undergone the operation. On June 18, 1975, Dr Chambers performed a laminectomy and a cervical posterior rhizotomy of the nerve roots at the cervical vertebrae 2 to 6. During the operation there was haemorrhage which was controlled; numerous adhesions surrounding the spinal cord were noted; Dr Chambers did not use magnification available. Six days after the operation Mrs Ellis developed quadriplegia.

Mrs Ellis commenced proceedings against Dr Chambers alleging that Dr Chambers had been negligent in (1) advising her to have the operation; (2) failing to warn her of the risks involved; (3) failing to obtain her consent to the operation; (4) in the performance of the operation. Dr Chambers died in 1986. On June 6, 1988, Mrs Ellis settled her claim against his estate for A$500,000. She then claimed against the hospital on the grounds that (1) the hospital was vicariously liable for Dr Chambers' negligence; (2) that the hospital was in breach of its independent and non-delegable duty to her as its patient to ensure that she received proper medical treatment and was warned of all material risks involved in the surgery. She failed in her claim that the hospital was vicariously liable (Kirby P dissenting). Thus the issue of the primary liability of the hospital became central if she was to recover more than the $500,000 she had recovered from Dr Chambers' insurers.

Samuels JA: There is another possible basis of liability which does not arise out of the hospital's relationship with Dr Chambers, but has its source in its relationship with the patient. Hence I must finally consider whether the hospital, to use the words of Reynolds JA in *Albrighton* [*v Royal Prince Albert Hospital* [1980] 2 NSWLR 542 (NSW CA)] (at 561):

> . . . was in breach of a duty which it owed directly to the plaintiff of which it could not divest itself by delegation.

Whether, in other words, the hospital owed the appellant an independent and non-delegable duty. The court in *Albrighton* thought that in that case there was evidence capable of establishing that the hospital did. Reynolds JA (at 561-562) put it thus:

> . . . The hospital, by admitting the appellant, could be regarded as undertaking that it would take reasonable care to provide for all her medical needs; and, whatever legal duties were imposed upon those who treated, diagnosed or cared for her needs from time to time, there was an overriding and continuing duty upon the hospital as an organization. It was not a mere custodial institution designed to provide a place where medical personnel could meet and treat persons lodged there, as it might have been regarded in years long since gone by.

That view his Honour regarded as being in conformity with the majority view in *Roe* [*v Minister of Health* [1954] 2 QB 66 (CA)] to which I have already referred. No doubt his Honour had in mind the judgments of Denning and Morris LJJ since Somervell LJ, in a passage which I have earlier set out, viewed the case as one of unvarnished vicarious liability. Certainly, as Blair JA observed in his dissenting judgment in *Yepremian v Scarborough General Hospital* (1980) 110 DLR (3d) 513 at 574, there is 'a clear line linking the views' of Lord Greene in *Gold* [*v Essex CC* [1942] 2 KB 293 (CA)] and those of Denning LJ in *Cassidy* [*v Ministry of Health* [1951] 2 KB 343 (CA)] and of Denning and Morris LJ in *Roe*; and it tends to lead to the proposition stated by Reynolds JA in the first part of the statement which I have just quoted. This line of reasoning is regarded by Professor Fleming, The Law of Torts, 7th edn (1987) at 346, as authorizing a view 'which has gained increasing support' and which tends to render irrelevant the distinction between servants and independent contractors

> . . . whenever a hospital offers a complete range of medical treatment to the patient and thereby assumes a non-delegable, personal duty to ensure that he receives careful treatment at the hands of such staff as it provides, including visiting specialists and other independent consultants.

It must be emphasized, however, and is of critical importance in the present case, that in that trilogy of authorities, *Gold*, *Cassidy* and *Roe*, the judges who were inclined to impose upon the hospital an independent duty to care for those patients whom it received, nonetheless excepted from this prescription the situation of consultants or independent specialists who had not been assigned by the hospital but had undertaken to provide care and treatment by direct arrangement with the patient. In *Gold*, Lord Greene MR (at 302), said, for example:

> . . . So far as consulting physicians and surgeons are concerned, clearly the nature of their work and the relationship in which they stand to the defendants precludes the drawing of an inference that the defendants undertake responsibility for their negligent acts.

But this statement is material to the question of vicarious liability rather than to any restrictions upon breach of the hospital's own independent duty. In *Cassidy*, however, Denning LJ having developed the notion of the hospital's independent liability, added (at 362):

. . . I think it depends on this: Who employs the doctor or surgeon – is it the patient or the hospital authorities? If the patient himself selects and employs the doctor or surgeon, as in *Hillyer's* case [1909] 2 KB 820, the hospital authorities are of course not liable for his negligence, because he is not employed by them. But where the doctor or surgeon, be he a consultant or not, is employed and paid, not by the patient but by the hospital authorities, I am of opinion that the hospital authorities are liable for his negligence in treating the patient. It does not depend on whether the contract under which he was employed was a contract of service or a contract for services.

In *Roe*, Denning LJ adhered to what he had said in *Cassidy*, but, it may be, took the matter a step further by minimizing the importance of the payment of the doctor (whether consultant or not) by the hospital; and he repeated the same exception. He said (at 82):

. . . It does not matter whether they are permanent or temporary, resident or visiting, whole-time or part-time. The hospital authorities are responsible for all of them. The reason is because, even if they are not servants, they are agents of the hospital to give the treatment. The only exception is the case of consultants or anaesthetists selected by the patient himself.

I am not wholly confident that Morris LJ in *Roe* did approach the matter as an example of the hospital's independent liability (see at 90-91) but he stressed that the nature of the obligation which a hospital may have assumed

. . . becomes, as it seems to me, ultimately a question of fact to be decided having regard to the particular circumstances of each particular case . . . [at 89]

This observation was taken up by Lord Nathan in Medical Negligence (1957) (at 132) where the learned author observes, having discussed the three cases:

In these circumstances it can be stated with some confidence that the weight of modern authority favours the view that a hospital authority by receiving a patient undertakes a personal obligation or duty towards that patient, for the breach of which it cannot escape liability by saying that it employed competent persons, to discharge the obligation or duty on its behalf; but that the exact extent of the duty is a question of fact in each particular case.

Leaving aside for the moment the recent development in Australia of the doctrine of independent or non-delegable duty, it seems to me that, so far as the responsibility of hospitals to their patients is concerned, the matter has been well stated, if I may say so, by Houlden JA in the second dissenting judgment in *Yepremian*. His Lordship said (at 581):

First, a general hospital may function as a place where medical care facilities are provided for the use of a physician and his patient. The patient comes to the hospital because his physician has decided that the hospital's facilities are needed for the proper care and treatment of the patient. This use of the hospital is made possible by an arrangement between the hospital and the physician by which the physician is granted hospital privileges. Where a hospital functions as merely the provider of medical care facilities, then, as the trial Judge pointed out, a hospital is not responsible for the negligence of the physician. The present case does not, of course, come with this classification.

Second, a general hospital may function as a place where a person in need of treatment goes to obtain treatment. Here the role of the hospital is that of an institution where medical treatment is made available to those who require it. The present case falls in this second classification. Tony Yepremian was brought to the Scarborough General Hospital because he was in need of treatment. Does a hospital in these circumstances have the duty to provide proper medical care to a patient? In my judgment, it does.

I need only observe that the second of these situations is exactly that which obtained in *Albrighton* and that the first of them is the one which applies in the instant case.

However, before arriving at any final conclusion I must consider whether, and to what extent, the decision of the High Court in *Kondis v State Transport Authority* (1984) 154 CLR 672 compels a particular solution of the problem. This case, if I may respectfully say so, authoritatively determines for this court the nature and scope of non-delegable duties in tort. Mason J, with whom Deane J and Dawson J agreed, notes (at 684 and 686) the criticisms that the notion of a non-delegable duty not only lacks any coherent conceptual foundation, but departs from

. . . the basic principles of liability in negligence by substituting for the duty to take reasonable care a more stringent duty, a duty to ensure that reasonable care is taken.

The justification for this special duty is found in a special relationship between the parties. His Honour said (at 687):

> The element in the relationship between the parties which generates a special responsibility or duty to see that care is taken may be found in one or more of several circumstances. The hospital undertakes the care, supervision and control of patients who are in special need of care. The school authority undertakes like special responsibilities in relation to the children whom it accepts into its care.

He goes on to instance the case of the occupier who invites persons to enter his premises, and that of the landlord who undertakes repairs. And then he continues:

> . . . In these situations a special duty arises because the person on whom it is imposed has undertaken the care, supervision or control of the person or property of another or is so placed in relation to that person or his property as to assume a particular responsibility for his or its safety, in circumstances where the person affected might reasonably expect that due care will be exercised.

I should add that, prior to the reference to the responsibility of hospitals, his Honour had referred to *Gold, Cassidy* and *Roe* as instances of the application of the concept of a personal duty arising in those cases out of the hospital's

> . . . undertaking an obligation to treat its patient, an obligation which carries with it a duty to use reasonable care in treatment, so that the hospital was liable, if a person engaged to perform the obligation on its behalf acts without due care [at 686].

The exemplification of the relationships between a hospital and the patients whose care it undertakes, and between the school authority and the children whom it accepts into its care, makes clear that the element which, as Mason J says (at 687)

> . . . generates a special responsibility or duty to see that care is taken . . .

involves a particular relationship of dependency, or what Fleming calls (op cit at 362)

> . . . a special protective relationship.

Hence the special duty arises only in particular circumstances upon which must depend the decision whether or not to assign the relationship they reveal to the special category. *Kondis* is not a direct authority upon the liability of hospitals, but its examples are highly persuasive. Accordingly it may be that once the relationship of hospital and patient is established it follows, as a matter of law, that the hospital owes the patient a non-delegable duty of care. In *Kondis* (at 686) Mason J put the proposition in this way:

> . . . The liability of a hospital arises out of its undertaking an obligation to treat its patient, an obligation which carries with it a duty to use reasonable care in treatment, so that the hospital is liable, if a person engaged to perform the obligation on its behalf acts without due care: *Gold* [1942] 2 KB at 304. Accordingly, the duty is one the performance of which cannot be delegated, not even to a properly qualified doctor or surgeon under a contract for services: *Cassidy* [1951] 2 KB at 364.

It can scarcely be supposed that Mason J was unaware of the limitations upon a hospital's duty of care expressed in *Gold* and *Cassidy*, and in *Roe* as well to which he earlier refers (at 685). It is necessary therefore to read his judgment subject to those statements, so that a hospital is bound to ensure that reasonable care is used in providing the treatment which it undertakes to carry out; but that duty does not extend to treatment which it undertakes to carry out; but that duty does not extend to treatment which is performed by a doctor pursuant to a direct engagement with the patient, and not on behalf of the hospital.

In my opinion therefore while proof of the relationship of hospital and 'patient' will generate a special duty of some kind, closer scrutiny of the facts (cf the analysis proposed by Mason J in *Stevens v Brodribb Sawmilling*) is necessary in order to establish its scope. It is a question of what medical services the hospital has undertaken to supply. In a case such as *Albrighton* where the patient went directly to the hospital for advice and treatment a special duty will arise and may well embrace the provision of the 'complete medical services' which Reynolds JA (at 561) thought it open to conclude that the hospital had undertaken to render, and that duty arose as soon as the plaintiff resorted to the hospital's out-patients' clinic; it did not wait upon admission. In such a case the hospital, by accepting the patient, undertakes to make available all the therapeutic skill and devices which it is reasonably able to deploy. The patients choice is determined by his or her decision to knock at the door of the defendant's hospital, as Lord Greene put it in *Gold* (at 302). If the hospital's response is to open the door and admit the patient to the benefits of the medical and surgical cornucopia within it remains responsible to ensure that whatever treatment or advice the horn disgorges is given with proper care; its duty cannot be divested by delegation.

But the evidence in a particular case may establish that the hospital's undertaking was of a more limited kind. As Morris LJ pointed out in *Roe* (at 89) and (at 91) the nature of the obligation which a hospital has assumed becomes ultimately a question of fact, a proposition which the Court of Appeal adopted in *Albrighton*. In the present case, however, it is quite clear that the appellant did not knock at the hospital's door in the sense contemplated by Lord Greene. It was not the hospital's door but the door of the late Dr Chambers' consulting rooms upon which she knocked, and it was that door which was opened to her and which admitted her to the treatment and advice upon which she thereafter principally relied. I do not think it can be doubted but that it was Dr Chambers and not the hospital to whom the appellant looked for medical care. The hospital, for reasons which I have already discussed and will not repeat, was merely the place in which surgical procedures which he had recommended and which the appellant had agreed to undergo were performed by Dr Chambers. The hospital in the present case was exactly what the hospital was not in *Albrighton*. To reverse Reynolds JA's words in that case (at 562) the hospital here was 'a mere custodial institution designed to provide a place where medical personnel could . . . treat persons lodged there . . .'. Of course the appellant stood in a 'special protective relationship' to both the hospital and Dr Chambers, but in respect of different kinds of care. The appellant looked to Dr Chambers for surgical intervention, and to the hospital for nursing care and perhaps the provision of other medical treatment. In rendering that care and treatment the hospital was no doubt under a non-delegable duty which might have been of relevant in certain circumstances. But in the event no question arises concerning matters of that sort.

My conclusion does not impose differential duties on a hospital. Following *Kondis* a hospital owes an independent non-delegable duty to ensure that the treatment it undertakes to provide is performed with reasonable care. The question in every case is the nature of that undertaking.

Meagher JA agreed with Samuels JA.

Contrast the approach of the President of the Court of Appeal.

Kirby P: [T]here is now a new and settled basis for the liability of the hospital. It is its direct responsibility pursuant to a non-delegable duty in tort which it owes the patient. The existence of this alternative and additional basis of responsibility in the hospital for the suggested negligence of Dr Chambers may be traced to the judgment of Lord Greene MR in *Gold v Essex County Council*. In *Cassidy*, Lord Denning was later to take pains to acknowledge his error in basing his arguments as counsel in *Gold* upon the grounds of vicarious liability. Lord Greene had not countenanced the error but looked instead to direct liability of the hospital authorities. In *Cassidy*, Lord Denning explained this liability thus (at p 365):

> . . . the hospital authorities accepted the plaintiff as a patient for treatment, and it was their duty to treat him with reasonable care . . . If those surgeons and nurses did not treat him with proper care and skill, then the hospital authorities must answer for it, for it means that they themselves did not perform their duty to him.

Although Somervell LJ confined his opinion to vicarious liability, Singleton LJ appears to have supported the Denning view that *Gold* established a direct duty on the part of the hospital.

This notion of direct liability soon acquired supporters in Canada. In *Yepremian*, Blair and Houlden JJA, in their dissenting opinions, upheld the plaintiff's claim on the basis of the hospital's primary liability. Blair JA (at 579) gave a social reason for adopting this approach:

> The recognition of a direct duty of hospitals to provide non-negligent medical treatment' reflects the reality of the relationship between hospitals and the public in contemporary society. This direct duty arises from profound changes in social structures and public attitudes relating to medical services and the concomitant

changes in the function of hospitals in providing them. It is obvious that as a result of these changes the role of hospitals in the delivery of medical services has expanded. The public increasingly relies on hospitals to provide medical treatment and, in particular, on emergency services. Hospitals to a growing extent hold out to the public that they provide such treatment and such services.

Yepremian was appealed to the Supreme Court of Canada: see (1980) 31 OR (2d) 383 (n). However, the case was settled on the payment of a substantial sum to the injured patient (as a report of the approval of the settlement shows). Accordingly the controversy posed by the conflicting opinions in that case has not yet been settled by the Supreme Court: see discussion G H L Fridman 'Hospital Liability for Professional Negligence' (1980) 4 Legal Med Q (Canada) 80 at 88; E Picard, Legal Liability of Doctors and Hospitals in Canada, 2nd edn (1984) at 322; see also note (1986) 64 Canadian Bar Rev 422 at 423. *Yepremian* was applied in *Van Ginkel v Hollenberg* (1985) 36 Man R 2d 291. The opinion of Blair JA was criticised in J E Magnet 'Corporate Negligence as a Basis for Hospital Liability – A Comment on Yepremian' 6 CCLT 121 at 127.

The theory of the direct non-delegable duty of the hospital has now gained acceptance in England: see *Wilsher v Essex Area Health Authority* [1987] QB 730. Although the case was conducted solely on the basis of the vicarious liability of the health authority, both Sir Nicholas Browne-Wilkinson VC and Glidewell LJ expressed the opinion, obiter, that in some circumstances, an action would lie against the hospital in respect of its own direct and non-delegable duty to the patient in respect of negligent conduct occurring in its operations.

In Australia, this additional basis for the liability of the hospital was accepted in this court in *Albrighton v Royal Prince Alfred Hospital* [1980] 2 NSWLR 542 at 561. Four years later, the High Court of Australia in *Kondis v State Transport Authority* (1984) 154 CLR 672 accepted that, in some relationships, a 'special duty' arises. The relationship of a hospital to patients is one such relationship, as is that of a school authority to children accepted into its care. In the case of the hospital it has a personal non-delegable duty arising out of its (at 686)

> . . . undertaking an obligation to treat its patient, an obligation which carries with it a duty to use reasonable care in treatment, so that the hospital is liable, if a person engaged to perform the obligation on its behalf acts without due care. . . . Accordingly, the duty is one the performance of which cannot be delegated, not even to a properly qualified doctor or surgeon under a contract for services.

I see no reason to read down these remarks. Nor do I see any justification for superimposing upon them a residual *Hillyer*-type distinction between the liability of the hospital for the negligence of staff surgeons and honorary staff surgeons. Again, I agree with the comment of Professor Giesen [*International Medical Malpractice Law* (1988)] (at 60-61):

> On this basis [direct liability], of course, it makes no difference whether an independent contractor (a specialist, a visiting consultant or a concessionaire) can be brought under the traditional head of 'servant' or not. Even if not, the hospital will still be liable if it has breached its own primary and non-delegable duty of care to the patient.
>
> Courts in Civil Law jurisdictions have arrived at similar results by extending the hospital's primary and non-delegable duty to organize and ensure what can be called a safe hospital system.
>
> Generally speaking, the raison d'etre of direct (corporate) hospital liability is to prevent substandard care in the health care system as a whole. The mere occurrence of a mishap will not necessarily give rise to an inference of substandard care under fault-oriented systems or to a compensable medical injury under no-fault systems. Nevertheless, a patient in a modern and well-staffed hospital is entitled to expect and rely upon the skill, circumspection and experience of hospital physicians and nurses to detect and treat negative occurrences such as sudden and unexpected cardiac arrest during surgery, or a disconnection of life-support equipment . . . or an infection, before crippling injury results. This goal can only be achieved where reasonable care is taken in securing competent personnel and an organization capable of providing and maintaining a safe hospital system.

It is true that some academic opinion is critical of the development of 'non-delegable duty' in the case of hospitals: see, eg, W P Whippy, 'A Hospital's Personal and Non-delegable Duty to Care for Its Patients – Novel Doctrine or Vicarious Liability Disguised?' (1989) 63 ALJ 182 at 201. However, the doctrine also has its academic supporters: see eg J Bettle,

'Suing Hospitals Direct: Whose Tort was it Anyhow?' (1987) 137 NLJ 573. More to the point, it was adopted by the High Court in *Kondis* in full knowledge (as Mason J indicated (at 686)) of the criticism which had been expressed of the conceptual foundation of the doctrine. It draws strength from the earlier statement of principle by the High Court in *Commonwealth v Introvigne* (1982) 150 CLR 258 – a case concerning the direct liability of the school authority for children in its care.

The authority of the High Court of Australia is binding on this Court. We are not bound by English, Canadian or other opinions to the contrary. As Giesen's text demonstrates, the High Court's principle in *Kondis* is not only in line with developments in other jurisdictions of the common law and civil law. It is supported by reasons of policy and practicality in the modern circumstances of Australian hospitals. It is wrong, in my opinion, to present the respondent hospital as the mere venue for the performance by Dr Chambers of his private surgical procedures. Such a conclusion flies in the face of the consent form, the by-laws and the mutually beneficial arrangement under which Dr Chambers operated at the hospital.

Accordingly, if there was negligence on the part of Dr Chambers, it was negligence for which the hospital was liable. It was so liable either because it was vicariously liable for his negligence as a member of its honorary medical staff, or it was liable directly to the patient which it could not fulfil merely by delegating its operation to a member of the honorary medical staff. As Reynolds JA said in *Albrighton* (at 562), the hospital was not a

> . . . mere custodial institution designed to provide a place where medical personnel could meet and treat persons lodged there, as it might have been regarded in years long since gone by.

It was, to the contrary, an integrated institution. And Dr Chambers was part of it.

Both Samuels JA and Kirby P refer to the Ontario case of *Yepremian v Scarborough General Hospital* (1980) 110 DLR (3d) 513. In that case also, the judges differed on the question of primary liability. It may be worthwhile to consider the case more closely.

Yepremian v Scarborough General Hospital (1980) 110 DLR (3d) 513 (Ont CA)

The plaintiff [Tony Yepremian] suffered a cardiac arrest with resultant brain damage at defendant hospital following the commencement of treatment for a diagnosed diabetic condition. The plaintiff had come home from work on a week-end feeling unwell. He was vomiting and had increased frequency of urination and increased frequency of drinking. The family doctor being away, his family took the plaintiff to see G, a physician, who had obtained his degree in medicine a year earlier, and was working in research, but who filled in on some week-ends as a doctor's replacement. G diagnosed tonsillitis, gave a prescription, and said it was unnecessary to take the plaintiff to a hospital. Later that night at home, the plaintiff began to hyperventilate and his family took him to the emergency department of the defendant hospital, where C, a general practitioner with hospital privileges, was on duty. C did not order a urinalysis and made no diagnosis, other than noting plaintiff's hyperventilation on the emergency record. Following two telephone calls to R, the internist on call and an endocrinologist, the plaintiff was admitted to the intensive care unit of the hospital. Eleven hours later, as a result of a nurse's observations, a diagnosis of diabetes was made. The plaintiff was immediately started on insulin. He continued to hyperventilate and remained unconscious or semi-conscious until he suffered the cardiac arrest about 12 hours later.

Arrup JA: Beyond doubt a patient admitted to a hospital expects to receive not only accommodation, food and competent nursing care but also competent medical care. The question still remains: does the hospital undertake to provide that medical care, or does it undertake to select competent doctors who will provide it? . . .

The trial Judge has founded liability upon a breach of the hospital's *own* duty – not that of any employed doctor, or of a doctor chosen by it to be on its staff, but an independent duty of its own, which is breached if there is a failure by a specialist on its staff to use reasonable skill and competence in the treatment of a patient in the hospital under his care. I agree that unless there exists in law a 'non-delegable duty of care' owed by the hospital to the patient, the hospital is not liable in this case.

No Court in Canada has ever found before that such a duty exists, and with great respect to the trial Judge, I am not persuaded by his reasons that there is such a duty. I am not dismissing those reasons perfunctorily, nor intending to denigrate them, when I say that he seems to me to be saying, in substance, 'In all the circumstances, the hospital *ought* to be liable.' In my view, if the criterion is to be what is fair and reasonable, it would be fair and reasonable that the highly skilled doctor whose negligence caused the damage should be called upon to pay for it. As the trial Judge did, I must put out of my mind that the plaintiff's chose not to sue him.

I agree with the trial Judge (and have said this earlier in my reasons) that the Yepremians had every right to expect that a large public hospital like Scarborough General would provide whatever was required to treat seriously ill or injured people but I do not think it follows that the public is entitled to add the further expectation: 'and if any doctor on the medical staff makes a negligent mistake, the hospital will pay for it'.

Rather, I think, a member of the public who knows the facts is entitled to expect that the hospital has picked its medical staff with great care, has checked out the credentials of every applicant, has caused the existing staff to make a recommendation in every individual case, makes no appointment for longer than one year at a time, and reviews the performance of its staff at regular intervals.

The minority view was expressed by Blair and Houlden JJA.

Blair JA: It is . . . well established that the hospital is liable to a patient directly for failure to provide what, in other areas of tort liability, would be called a 'safe system. . . . In some cases, the line is blurred between injury caused by the failure of the hospital to provide proper equipment or organisation and injury caused by the negligence of employees: none the less, the principle of direct liability is well established by the authorities. It is particularly demonstrated by the common law principle, accepted in *Hillyer's* case and elaborated by statute, that a hospital is responsible for the proper selection of qualified doctors to serve on its staff.

. . . [The hospital] contends that its responsibility to the patient is simply to ensure the provision of medical services by properly-qualified doctors without accepting any responsibility to the patient for the manner in which doctors perform those services . . .

The recognition of a direct duty of hospitals to provide non-negligent medical treatment reflects the reality of the relationship between hospitals and the public in contemporary society. This direct duty arises from profound changes in social structures and public attitudes relating to medical services and the concomitant changes in the function of hospitals in providing them. It is obvious that as a result of these changes the role of hospitals in the delivery of medical services has expanded. The public increasingly relies on hospitals to provide medical treatment and, in particular, on emergency services. Hospitals to a growing extent hold out to the public that they provide such treatment and such services.

At the outset of my review of the hospital's duty in tort I asked whether the Hospital *could* have undertaken a direct duty to provide medical treatment, and whether in the circumstances of this case it *did*. From the foregoing I conclude that the common law does recognise that hospitals *can* in certain circumstances be directly liable to patients for the negligent performance of medical services, as held by Holland J. As Lords Greene, Morris and Nathan have observed, whether and to what extent a hospital assumes a direct duty depends upon the circumstances of the particular case. I am of the opinion that in the circumstances of this case the Hospital *is* liable. It is unnecessary to refer again to the facts which I have quoted from the judgment of Holland J. In the emergency, the Hospital provided, as it held itself out to do, the only means of obtaining medical care for Tony. His life was placed completely in the Hospital's hands. He and his family relied entirely on the Hospital to use its resources of equipment and skilled, but anonymous, personnel to restore his health. With the greatest of respect for those who hold the contrary view, I believe that, in the circumstances of this case, the Hospital's obligation to Tony could not be limited merely to placing a qualified doctor at his disposal. The hospital assumed and would be expected to assume complete responsibility for Tony's treatment.

MacKinnon ACJO and Morden JA agreed with Arrup JA. Houlden JA dissented and agreed with Blair JA.

Kirby P referred in *Ellis* to the case of *Wilsher v Essex AHA* [1986] 3 All ER 801. Although that case eventually went to the House of Lords, for our purposes it is the judgments of the Court of Appeal which are important.

Wilsher v Essex Area Health Authority [1987] QB 730, [1986] 3 All ER 801 (CA)

The plaintiff was an infant child who was born prematurely suffering from various illnesses, including oxygen deficiency. His prospects of survival were considered to be poor and he was placed in the 24-hour special care baby unit at the hospital where he was born. The unit was staffed by a medical team, consisting of two consultants, a senior registrar, several junior doctors and trained nurses. While the plaintiff was in the unit a junior and inexperienced doctor monitoring the oxygen in the plaintiff's bloodstream mistakenly inserted a catheter into a vein rather than an artery but then asked the senior registrar to check what he had done. The registrar failed to see the mistake and some hours later, when replacing the catheter, did exactly the same thing himself. In both instances the catheter monitor failed to register correctly the amount of oxygen in the plaintiff's blood, with the result that the plaintiff was given excess oxygen. The plaintiff subsequently brought an action against the health authority claiming damages and alleging that the excess oxygen in his bloodstream had caused an incurable condition of the retina resulting in near blindness. At the trial of the action the judge awarded the plaintiff £116,199. In dismissing the appeal, the judge in the Court of Appeal had the following to say on the issue of a health authority's primary duty of care.

Mustill LJ: There is, however, a quite different proposition which might have been advanced, namely that the defendants are directly liable for any adverse consequences of the episode. For example, it might have been said that the defendants owed a duty to ensure that the special baby care unit functioned according to the standard reasonably to be expected of such a unit. This approach would not require any consideration of the extent to which the individual doctors measured up to the standards demanded of them as individuals, but would focus attention on the performance of the unit as a whole. A rather different form of the argument might have been advanced on the following lines. Although the catheter, with its monitor and sampling facility, is a valuable instrument, it will yield misleading and potentially dangerous results if the head is in the wrong place. The defendants therefore owed a duty, if they were to use the catheter on patients entrusted to their care, to ensure that those who were to operate the device knew how to detect when it was wrongly placed, and on their own evidence the junior doctors did not know this. Finally, it might have been said that, if the junior doctors did not have sufficient skill or experience to provide the special care demanded by such a premature baby, the defendants were at fault in appointing them to the posts which they held.

If the nature of the plaintiff's cause of action had been a live issue on this appeal, it would have been necessary to look with care at the developing line of authority on liability for medical negligence. For counsel for the defendants asserted roundly that no health authority ever had been, or in principle ever could be, under any such direct liability as suggested, except perhaps in the case of a person being appointed to a post for which he is not qualified. In the event, however, counsel for the plaintiff explicitly disclaimed on the plaintiff's behalf any intention to put forward a case of direct liability. The trial had been conducted throughout, he made clear, exclusively on the basis of vicarious liability. It is therefore unnecessary to express any opinion of the validity in law of a claim on the alternative basis.

While Mustill LJ thought it was unnecessary to decide the question, as you will see, Sir Nicolas Browne-Wilkinson V-C took the view that the case could not be properly analysed without deciding this point.

Browne-Wilkinson V-C: . . . I agree with the comments of Mustill LJ as to the confusion which has been caused in this case both by the pleading and by the argument below which blurred the distinction between the vicarious liability of the health authority for the negligence of its doctors and the direct liability of the health authority for negligently failing to provide skilled treatment of the kind that it was offering to the public. In my judgment, a health authority which so conducts its hospital that it fails to provide doctors of sufficient skill and experience to give the treatment offered at the hospital may be directly liable in negligence to the patient. Although we were told in argument that no case has ever been decided on this ground and that it is not the practice to formulate claims in this way, I can see no reason why, in principle, the health authority should not be so liable if its organisation is at fault: see *McDermid v Nash Dredging and Reclamation Co Ltd* [1986] 2 All ER 676 esp at 684-685, [1986] QB 965 esp at 978-979 (reported since the conclusion of the argument).

Glidewell LJ agreed with the Vice-Chancellor.

Glidewell LJ: I agree with Sir Nicolas Browne-Wilkinson V-C that there seems to be no reason in principle why, in a suitable case different on its facts from this, a hospital management committee [sic] should not be held directly liable in negligence for failing to provide sufficient qualified and competent medical staff.

Perhaps it is surprising that the court was so tentative in accepting the notion of primary or direct liability (and in accepting counsel's assertion that no English cases dealt with the issue) given the background we have already seen. What is important to notice, however, is that the court was not asked to consider, nor did it address, the possibility that the second strand of primary liability represented the law in England ie that the hospital had a non-delegable duty to *ensure* that reasonable care is taken in the provision of health care.

Earlier, we posed the question which, if either, strand of primary liability was recognised in English law. Although the Court of Appeal in *Wilsher* was somewhat tentative there seems little doubt that the first strand of primary liability (ie to provide a safe system etc) is part of English law. Indeed, it was accepted as such without demur subsequently by the Court of Appeal in *Bull v Devon AHA* in 1989.

Bull v Devon AHA [1993] 4 Med LR 117 (CA)

Mrs Bull sued the defendant Health Authority on behalf of herself and her disabled son. He was born at the maternity unit of the Exeter City Hospital for which the defendant and its predecessors were responsible. Mrs Bull claimed that her son was disabled due to asphyxia at birth which was attributable to the negligence of the Health Authority and the staff employed by it. As regards the direct claim against the Health Authority, she alleged that the asphyxia was due to the fact that the delivery of her son was delayed because a doctor was not available to attend her. This, in turn, she alleged, was due to the fact that the hospital had maintained its services on two sites and the system for summoning doctors had broken down.

In the course of holding the Health Authority liable in negligence, the Court of Appeal accepted that the Health Authority owed Mrs Bull and her son a duty of care directly. Slade LJ observed that it was 'indisputable' that the Authority owed a duty of care to Mrs Bull's son. He accepted the plaintiff's submission of the scope of that duty in the following terms (necessarily tailored to the facts of case).

Slade LJ: The duty of a hospital is to provide a woman admitted in labour with a reasonable standard of skilled obstetric and paediatric care, in order to ensure as far as reasonably practicable the safe delivery of the baby or babies and the health of the mother and offspring thereafter.

Applying this to the alleged unsafe system of summoning an obstetrician to look after Mrs Bull, Slade LJ went on to state:

Slade LJ: It is possible to imagine hypothetical contingencies which would have accounted for a failure, without any avoidable fault in the hospital's system or any negligence in its working, to secure for Mrs Bull attendance by any obstetrician qualified to deliver the . . . [plaintiff's son] . . . In my judgment, however, all the most likely explanations for this failure point strongly either (i) to inefficiency in the system for summoning the assistance of the registrar or consultant, in operation at the hospital in 1970, or (ii) to negligence by some individual or individuals in the working of that system.

Dillon LJ also held the Health Authority liable for breach of its primary duty.

Dillon LJ: In my judgment, the plaintiff has succeeded in proving, by the ordinary civil standards of proof, that the failure to provide for Mrs Bull the prompt attendance she needed was attributable to the negligence of the defendants in implementing an unreliable and essentially unsatisfactory system for calling the registrar.

Mustill LJ cast off his earlier reticence in *Wilsher*. Having examined the evidence relevant to the finding of carelessness against the Health Authority, he concluded that 'the judge had no choice but to decide [that the Authority was in breach of duty]'.

So much, then, for the first strand of primary liability and its acceptance as part of English law. What of the second strand of primary liability – the duty to *ensure* that care is taken in the provision of health services? Is this any part of English law? Properly understood this strand of primary liability amounts to the imposition on a health authority of vicarious liability for the negligent acts of anyone working in the institution whether as an employee *or independent contractor*. However attractive Kirby P's analysis in *Ellis* may be that, by analogy, an NHS hospital holds itself out, and thereby undertakes a duty, to ensure that a patient receives reasonable care in the hospital, an English court is most unlikely to accept it. Were it to do so it would impose upon a health authority the duty of a guarantor that care be taken, which is a duty rarely imposed upon anyone, as regards the conduct of independent contractors, in English law (see *Tarry v Ashton* (1876) 1 QBD 314; and *Honeywill and Stein Ltd v Larkin Brothers Ltd* [1934] 1 KB 191). In other contexts, both the Court of Appeal and House of Lords have set their faces against the expansion of this exceptional group of cases (see *Salsbury v Woodland* [1970] 1 QB 324; *D & F Estates v Church Comrs for England* [1989] AC 177).

Of course, in the context of the NHS the absence of this second strand of primary liability is of little practical significance. Rarely (if ever) will a situation arise where the negligent actor is not an employee of the health authority for whom, as we shall see, the health authority is vicariously liable. The appearance of NHS Trusts, however, may create something of a problem. A doctor may be 'lent' by one trust to another. In such circumstances, who would be liable for the doctor's negligence? Arguably, the trust hospital which 'lent' him would remain his employer and, hence, vicariously liable (*Mersey Docks and Harbour Board v Coggins and Griffiths (Liverpool) Ltd* [1947] AC 1). Additionally, however, the trust hospital that has 'borrowed' him could only be liable if this second strand of primary liability is the law (without prejudice to any liability that might incur under the first strands of primary liability) unless, of course, an additional contract of service is entered into between the doctor and the 'borrowing' hospital.

This second strand of liability is, however, important when deciding the liability of a hospital or clinic outside the NHS. The private clinic or hospital could, of course, be liable under the first strand if the facts show that it negligently failed to set up a 'safe system'. If, however, there is no such negligence (as may well be the case), given that the doctor will ordinarily be an independent contractor using the facilities and staff of the clinic or hospital, the only form of liability the clinic or hospital could face in tort would be under the second strand. Short of the very unlikely existence of an express term in the contract (if any) between the clinic and the patient accepting responsibility for the negligent acts of the doctor, the law of contract would only impose upon the clinic an implied term to exercise reasonable care; in effect the first strand of primary liability in tort. In tort, there is little doubt that in the usual situation in which the patient selects the doctor who then arranges facilities at a private clinic, the law regards the private clinic as being in precisely the same position as an NHS hospital, ie only the first strand of primary liability applies. It may conceivably be otherwise where the private clinic is judged, by the way in which it holds itself out, to have undertaken to provide a level of service amounting to a guarantee of reasonable care. This could arise where the patient has chosen the clinic on the basis of its reputation in the 'market place'.

(ii) LIABILITY OF THE SECRETARY OF STATE

In addition to the institutions or bodies, which we have just discussed, which may incur primary liability, we must also consider the possible primary liability of the Secretary of State. She may be liable for negligence or, possibly, for breach of statutory duty.

I. Negligence. As regards an action in negligence against the Secretary of State, the courts would have to consider whether, as a matter of law, the Secretary of State owed an individual patient a duty of care. Given that most of the functions which she has not delegated will involve policy decisions at the highest level within the NHS, the patient will face considerable difficulties in bringing a claim. The litigation against the Secretary of State brought by haemophiliacs who claimed to have contracted HIV from infected blood products illustrates this. You will recall that the supply of blood within the NHS is a responsibility retained by the Secretary of State.

Re HIV Haemophiliac Litigation **[1990] NLJR 1349 (CA)**

The plaintiffs were 962 haemophiliacs and their wives or children who had developed AIDS or would do so as the result of the haemophiliacs being treated under the NHS with blood made out of Factor VIII concentrate imported from the USA which was infected with the HIV virus. They brought an action against, inter alia, the Department of Health, the licensing authority under the Medicines Act 1968, the committee on the safety of medicines ('the central defendants'), all regional and district health authorities in England and Wales, and the central blood laboratories authority. As against the Department of Health the plaintiffs alleged that the department was in breach of its statutory duty under ss 1 and 3(1) of the National Health Service Act 1977 to promote a comprehensive health service in England and Wales designed to secure improvement (a) in the physical and mental health of the people and (b) in the prevention, diagnosis and treatment of illness, and to provide throughout England and Wales facilities for the prevention of illness and the care of persons suffering from illness, and was negligent in failing to ensure that the country was self-sufficient in blood supplies thereby causing haemophiliacs to be treated with infected blood from the USA. The plaintiffs applied for discovery of documents but the department claimed public interest immunity in respect of certain documents on the ground that they related to the formulation of policy by ministers or were briefings for ministers regarding whether a policy of self-sufficiency in blood products should be established, what resources should be allocated to implement such a policy, future planning on the role of the Blood Products Laboratory and whether and how to re-organise the National Blood Transfusion Service. The plaintiffs applied to the court for an order requiring the department to produce the documents in respect of which immunity was claimed. The department contended that production ought not to be ordered because the plaintiffs did not have a good cause of action either for breach of statutory duty or in negligence against the department. Rougier J held that the plaintiffs had no cause of action for breach of statutory duty and no cause of action in negligence for any alleged failure by the department for failure to perform duties imposed by statute but they did have a good cause of action for 'performance related negligence', ie negligence on the part of the department in performing its statutory duties.

The judge ordered production of policy documents and exchanges between officials except documents, such as those relating to whether to adopt a policy of self-sufficiency in blood products, which could not be relevant to 'performance' as opposed to 'breach' related negligence. The plaintiffs appealed on the ground that the excluded documents should be made available while the department cross-appealed on the ground that none of the documents in respect of which immunity was sought should be produced.

Ralph Gibson LJ: The main points advanced by Mr Jackson [for the plaintiffs] were:
(i)   There is no authority to support the proposition that a decision upon the construction of a statute, to the effect that there is no civil remedy available for breach of any duty imposed by it, necessarily means that there can be no claim in negligence in respect of the discharge of carrying out of these duties insofar as any breach of duty consists of a failure to act. Reference was made to *Bux v Slough Metals Ltd* [1973] 1 WLR 1358, 1369-1370; and to *Dorset Yacht Co v Home Office* [1970] AC 1004.
(ii)   If, as the judge found, the plaintiffs have sufficiently demonstrated an arguable case on the policy contentions as to proximity, etc, then it was wrong to draw the distinction between 'breach related' and 'performance related' matters as excluding or limiting the duty of care. The distinction between acts and omissions is relevant to the question whether breach of the duty has been shown.
(iii)   The distinction between acts and omissions is of significance in cases against public authorities, where the decision within the authority's discretion and policy making function may be impossible to attack as negligent. But the fact that the decision attacked is made as a matter of discretion or policy making does not make the decision immune in law. If it is ultra vires or wholly unreasonable the authority will be liable in negligence if the decision is shown to be negligent by reference to proximity and foreseeability. Reference was made to the *Dorset Yacht* case at pages 1031A-1032A per Lord Reid, 1036F-1037G per Lord Morris, and 1067F-1068C per Lord Diplock; and to *Meade v London Borough of Haringey* [1979] 1 WLR 637 at 647 per Lord Denning MR.
For the Department, Mr Collins did not support the proposition that rejection of the claim for breach of statutory duty must of itself negative any 'coterminous' claim in negligence, but submitted that the same result is achieved by reference to similar aspects of this case by proper application of the requirement that it be just and reasonable to impose the duty of care. The nature of the relationship between the plaintiffs and the Central Defendants, based upon the 1977 Act, is such that it is not just or reasonable to impose a duty of care directly enforceable by any member of the public. His protection should be by an action for negligence, if there is breach of duty, against those who directly provide care and treatment to him; and the remedy for imperfections in the performance of the duties imposed by the 1977 Act should be within Parliament or through the ballot box. All the alleged duties upon which the plaintiffs rely contain the elements of discretion.
        Further, as part of the concept of 'just and reasonable' Mr Collins argued that the nature of the discretion, and of the matters relevant to the decision made in discharge of the duties imposed by the 1977 Act, is such that a decision upon alleged negligence in the exercise of those functions should be held to be non-justiciable as unsuitable for judicial decisions: reference was made to *Rowling v Takaro Properties Ltd* [1988] AC 473, 501D-503H. Also it would be against public policy to impose liability in respect of those functions: see *Hill v Chief Constable for West Yorkshire* [1989] AC 53.
        For my part, as to those policy contentions I agree with Rougier J that the plaintiffs have made out at least an arguable case. It is obvious that it would be rare for a case on negligence to be proved having regard to the nature of the duties under the 1977 Act, and to the fact that, in the law of negligence, it is difficult to prove a negligent breach of duty when the party charged with negligence is required to exercise discretion and to form judgments upon the allocation of public resources. That, however, is not sufficient, in my judgment, to make it clear for the purposes of these proceedings, that there can in law be no claim in negligence. Nor, on the allegations of fact, can it be said that the plaintiffs have not alleged a case which could be upheld if in law the claim is viable.
        I have reached that conclusion on grounds which include the following . . .
        In *Rowling v Takaro Properties* at p 501E the question whether, having regard to all the relevant considerations, it is appropriate that a duty of care should be imposed is a question of

        an intensely pragmatic character, well suited for gradual development but requiring most careful analysis . . .

        . . . in *Murphy's* [*Murphy v Brentwood DC* [1991] 1 AC 398 (HL)] case the claim was for economic loss. These plaintiffs have suffered personal injury. It is possible, in my judgment, that the court, after full consideration, may in this case be driven to hold that in the circumstances of these claims, and notwithstanding the difficulties of proof of negligence for the reasons stated above, yet a duty of care is imposed by the law upon the Central Defendants in the discharge of their functions under the 1977 Act. Those difficulties of proof will, of course, include the matter of exercise of discretion, policy making, allocation of resources and the distinction between failing to confer a benefit as contrasted with the infliction of harm.

Bingham LJ: Mr Andrew Collins QC, for the Department . . . pointed out, relying on recent authority, that there is no close precedent for such a claim as the present, which differs in nature and scale from the negligence claims with which the courts customarily deal. Furthermore, he argued, the plaintiffs' complaints relate to matters within areas of political and administrative discretion which the courts are incompetent to evaluate (save, where *vires* are in issue, on applications for judicial review). There were, he said, by analogy with *Hill v Chief Constable of West Yorkshire* [1989] AC 53, strong reasons of public policy (or justice and reasonableness) for not holding a minister and a department exercising public functions for the benefit of the community as a whole to owe a duty of care towards individual members of the public.

These are points properly and responsibly argued and they may ultimately prevail, but on the necessarily brief argument which we have heard at this stage I am not at present satisfied that they must do so. Since I agree with the reasons of Ralph Gibson LJ on this point also I shall indicate very briefly the matters which particularly weigh with me:

(1)   While there may be no very close precedent for the present claim, there has not perhaps, at least in this country, been any comparable calamity. Of the plaintiffs still living, the great majority have throughout their lives suffered the grave affliction of haemophilia. To this there has now been added the even graver affliction of AIDS, now or in the future. The tragedy was avoidable in the sense that, had different measures been taken in the 1970s and early 1980s, it could, at least in large measure, have been prevented. The law cannot of course redress all ills, however grave, which afflict the human condition and the occurrence of a tragedy, however great, does not compel the conclusion that someone somewhere must be legally answerable. If, however, the plaintiffs can make good their factual allegations against the Department, as one must for present purposes assume in their favour, the law might arguably be thought defective if it did not afford redress.

(2)   . . . where as here foreseeability by a defendant of severe personal injury to a person such as the plaintiff is shown and the existence of a proximate relationship between plaintiff and defendant is accepted, the plaintiff is well on his way to establishing the existence of a duty of care. He may still fail to do so if it held that imposition of such a duty on the defendant would not in all the circumstances be just and reasonable, but it is by no means clear to me at this preliminary stage that the Department's submissions on that aspect must prevail.

(3)   Mr Rupert Jackson QC for the plaintiffs argued that his complaints relate not to any policy decision taken by the Secretary of State but to the Department's failure to implement the policy decision taken, that is, to the implementation not the formulation of policy. I am not persuaded that that contention is wrong, although detailed examination of the facts may well show the line between the two to be blurred.

(4)   While the court cannot review the merits of a decision taken by a public authority if it fell within the areas of a discretion conferred by Parliament, it may do so even in a common law action for damages for negligence if satisfied that the decision in question for any of the recognised reasons fell outside the area of such discretion. Whether the plaintiffs can discharge that considerable burden on the facts here I cannot at present determine.

Sir John Megaw agreed.

It could be said that the Court of Appeal is rejecting the too simplistic dichotomy drawn by Stuart-Smith J in *DHSS v Kinnear* (1984) 134 NLJ 886 between the Secretary of State making 'policy' decisions (no liability) and making 'operational' decisions (possible liability). In *Kinnear* Stuart-Smith J held that the decision of the Secretary of State to make the pertussis vaccine available was not amenable to examination in a negligence action despite contradictory views as to its safety. On the other hand, the notice of advice issued by the Secretary of State detailing the circumstances under which the vaccine should be administered could give rise to a cause of action if it was negligently prepared.

II. Breach of statutory duty. Turning now to breach of statutory duty, the question for consideration is whether the Secretary of State (or her delegate) may attract primary liability for breach of statutory duty. The National Health Service Act 1977, s 3(1) provides:

> 3. (1) It is the Secretary of State's duty to provide throughout England and Wales, to such extent as he considers necessary to meet all reasonable requirements -
> (a)   hospital accommodation;
> (b)   other accommodation for the purpose of any service provide under this Act;
> (c)   medical, dental, nursing and ambulance services;
> (d)   such other facilities for the care of expectant and nursing mothers and young children as he considers are appropriate as part of the health service;
> (e)   such facilities for the prevention of illness, the care of persons suffering from illness and the after-care of persons who have suffered from illness as he considers are appropriate as part of the health service;
> (f)   such other services as are required for the diagnosis and treatment of illness.

In turn, this duty is delegated to the health authorities created by the legislation. Paragraph 15(1) of Schedule 5 to the Act makes it quite clear that for failure to perform the duty under s 3 it is they and not the Secretary of State who must be sued.

> 15. (1) An authority shall, notwithstanding that it is exercising any function on behalf of the Secretary of State or another authority, be entitled to enforce any rights acquired in the exercise of that function, and be liable in respect of any liabilities incurred (including liabilities in tort) in the exercise of that function, in all respects as if it were acting as a principal.

Proceedings for the enforcement of such rights and liabilities shall be brought, and brought only, by or, as the case may be, against the authority in question in its own name.

Some judges have suggested that an action for breach of statutory duty would lie (*Yepremian v Scarborough General Hospital* (1980) 110 DLR (3d) 513 at 564 per Blair JA; Nathan, *Medical Negligence* (1957) p 144 et seq).

The issue arose directly, as we have seen, in the *HIV Litigation* case (*supra*).

Ralph Gibson LJ: The plaintiffs rely upon section 1 and section 3(1) of the National Health Service Act 1977. . . .

Next, by section 13, the Secretary of State may direct certain Health Authorities to exercise on his behalf such of his functions relating to the Health Service as are specified in the direction and (subject to section 14) it then becomes the duty of the body in question to comply with the directions.

The Minister has by statutory instrument delegated many of his functions including that under section 3(1)(e) of the 1977 Act with respect to the provision of facilities for the prevention of illness, the care of persons suffering from illness and the after care of persons who have suffered from illness. It is common ground that the definition of illness under the Act of 1977 includes the condition haemophilia. The Minister has also delegated his function under section 5(2)(d) of the 1977 Act. . . .

In *Cutler v Wandsworth Stadium Ltd* [1949] AC 398, Lord Simonds, on the question whether a statute is to be held to provide a cause of action for a breach of duty imposed by it, said at page 407:

> I do not propose to try to formulate any rules by reference to which such a question can infallibly be answered. The only rule which in all circumstances is valid is that the

answer must depend on a consideration of the whole Act and the circumstances, including pre-existing law, in which it was enacted. But that there are indications which point with more or less force to the one answer or the other is clear from authorities which . . . will have great weight with the House. For instance, if a statutory duty is prescribed but no remedy by way of penalty or otherwise for its breach is imposed, it can be assumed that a right of civil action accrues to the person who is demnified by the breach. For, if it were not so, the statute would be but a pious aspiration.

Under the 1977 Act no remedy by way of penalty or otherwise is prescribed for breach of the duties imposed upon the Secretary of State. Neither side has placed reliance on any aspect of the previously existing law or upon the terms of the statutes which preceded the 1977 Act.

Mr Jackson submitted that because the 1977 Act imposes a duty but provides no remedy for its breach, there is a presumption that Parliament intended that there be such a remedy, and he submitted that no reason is to be found in the provisions of the statute as a whole to justify a different conclusion. He acknowledged that the duties imposed upon the Secretary of State by the Act are of a general nature, and involve the exercise by him of discretion, but Mr Jackson contended that that was no sufficient reason to deny a cause of action for breach of them. Claims for such breach would be rare both because of the difficulty of proving breach of such duties and because the Secretary of State has delegated the performance of most of his functions to Health Authorities. Further, Mr Jackson submitted that paragraph 15 of Schedule 5 supported his argument. That paragraph provides that, upon delegation of a particular function to a Health Authority, it is the Health Authority and not the Secretary of State who is to be used. The proper inference is, it was said, that, with reference to a particular function which has not been delegated, if it is performed negligently, or if it is negligently not performed, the proper defendant is the Department of Health.

Mr Jackson relied upon the decision of Forbes J in *Booth and Co v NEB* [1978] 3 All ER 624 upon the provisions of the Industry Act 1975. A claim for breach of duty imposed by that Act, passed for the benefit of the United Kingdom economy, was held to be arguably good in law. The 1977 Act was passed to protect and to promote the health of the individual citizens of this country and breach of the duties imposed by it should be held to be actionable.

Mr Jackson acknowledged that no duty is imposed by the Act in absolute terms such as are found in statutes such as the Factories Act or in the Road Traffic Acts with reference to insurance. He further acknowledged that, if a claim for negligence is held to be available against the Central Defendants for breach of the common law duty of care in the performance of the functions performed by them under the 1977 Act, it is not possible to think of a claim which could succeed for breach of statutory duty which would fail if put forward as negligence. That concession was, as I understood the argument, not intended to be made if the court should hold the cause of action to be limited as Rougier J held it to be. Mr Jackson argued, however, that the existence of a cause of action in negligence was irrelevant to the process of the court's determination of the intention of Parliament by construction of the statute as a whole.

In answer to these submissions, Mr Collins relied upon the reasons for his decision given by Rougier J. He also relied upon the unreported decision of Wien J in January 1979 in *R v Secretary of State for Social Services and West Midlands R H A, ex Hincks*, in which at page 29 of the transcript he held that the 1977 Act does not give rise to a right to damages for a breach. The applicants appealed to the Court of Appeal on 18th March 1980 where the decisions and reasons of Wien J were approved. The question of a right of action for damages for breach of statutory duty was not considered in the Court of Appeal. As Mr Jackson submitted the decision of the question by Wien J was obiter.

For my part, I share the judge's view of the apparent nature of the duties imposed by the 1977 Act. They do not clearly demonstrate the intention of Parliament to impose a duty which is to be enforced by individual civil action.

Bingham LJ and Sir John Megaw agreed.

Arguable in the light of the views expressed by the court in the *HIV Litigation* case, the better view is that the 1977 Act only imposes a duty amenable to control in *public law* through the judicial review procedure under RSC Order 53.

(iii) QUESTIONS OF RESOURCE ALLOCATION

As is plain from the *HIV Litigation* case, many decisions involving the provision of health care turn upon the proper allocation of resources. This is so whether the Secretary of State has reserved the responsibility to herself (which is rare in practice) or has delegated her responsibility to the relevant health authority. The crucial question here is what weight, if any, should the law give to the argument, whether advanced by central government or by the health authority, that the service provided was all that could be done given the available resources? Before going further, it would be noticed that this argument could just as readily be adduced where the claim is in negligence as in an action for breach of statutory duty.

The question of the availability or otherwise of sufficient resources is a troubling one for courts (see the remarks of Lord Donaldson MR in *Re J (A Minor) (Wardship Medical Treatment)* [1992] 4 All ER 614 at 623-4). While their obligation is to determine the legal standard which defendants must meet, they cannot close their eyes to the fact that these standards must be set in a real world where resources are finite and where there is never enough to go around. If the courts allow themselves to be drawn too far into such questions they will enter territory which traditionally they have regarded the exclusive preserve of government. If, on the other hand, the courts wash their hands of the question they could face the charge that they were denying compensation to patients and drawing back from their duty to hold government accountable when asked to do so.

I. A proposed analysis. Faced with this dilemma, how should the law respond so that that which is properly for the courts (English-style) is done by the courts, and that which is for government is left to the Government? The law may develop as follows.

The 'benchmark' situation – The court could ask whether the complaint before it arises out of inadequacies in the delivery of a system of care which has been created by the health authority, for example, a maternity service with insufficient staff and equipment to meet a level of care which is clearly called for. If, indeed, the complaint does take this form then the court can take refuge in the traditional approach of negligence and avoid the charge of trespassing on foreign territory. The court can ask by reference to expert evidence what can reasonably be expected of a service of the type purportedly created by the health authority. This would set the benchmark against which to judge the level of service actually provided (of course, setting the benchmark is itself no easy matter). If the level of care did not reach the benchmark, *prima facie* there would be a breach of duty. Then, but not until then, would the question of resources fall for consideration. The health authority would then argue that, admittedly, the level of service fell below the legal standard, but the court should modify the legal standard to reflect the available resources in the light of the fact that the authority had done all that it could.

If the court accepts this argument then it is, in effect, agreeing to endorse the policy decision of the health authority. Some would say that this is the only proper course for a court since it cannot consider all the matters which go to make up a comprehensive health care policy. If the court rejects the argument it, in effect, is saying that the policy adopted is wrong or, at least, that if the authority does not change it, the court will make it pay for its failings (thereby further reducing the available resources).

Of these alternatives, arguably the former (ie accepting the health authority's argument) will be hard for a court to resist, although there will be factual circumstances which might tempt a court to reject the health authority's argument.

Non-provision – Next, the court may not be faced with a complaint about an existing system but with the *absence of any provision* of service in circumstances where it is said the service should be provided. For example, a health authority may choose not to make available kidney-dialysis whereby a patient with renal failure is harmed. In a claim based in negligence the court would have to ask whether the health authority had breached its duty to this particular patient by deciding not to provide the service. Traditional reasoning in negligence would require the court to ask what a reasonable health authority would do in these circumstances. It is difficult for a court to establish a standard. The issues involved in any such decision are so obviously matters of policy and judgment. Thus, a court would almost certainly refuse to entertain the action on the grounds that the patient's claim was non-justiciable, ie not for *them*.

Curtailed provision – Finally, the complaint before the court may be that a service previously involving a particular amount of resources is now being offered in a curtailed form with a reduced amount of resources. The claim in negligence would be that a patient was harmed not by reason of inadequate provision of care actually delivered, but rather by the absence of that particular care in his case. For example, a health authority may decide to close emergency services for one weekend in four. In such a case, the court may avoid being drawn into the policy of resource allocation by adopting the traditional legal approach of asking the question 'What did the health authority undertake to provide?' and 'Did it do so?' If the authority undertook only to provide a curtailed service, it would follow that a claim in negligence based upon the lack of provision of that care which would have been available had the service not been curtailed, would fail.

II. The case law. Do the English cases, such as they are, bear out this analysis?

The benchmark – A number of cases touch on what we have called the 'benchmark' situation. The first is inconclusive. In *Wilsher v Essex AHA* [1986] 3 All ER 801, the Vice-Chancellor, Sir Nicolas Browne-Wilkinson, at least raised the question of the extent to which a court should take account of resource allocation. Not surprisingly given the novelty of the argument, he chose to take refuge in the judicial incantation that '[t]hese are questions for Parliament . . . ' (at 834).

> **Browne-Wilkinson V-C:** Claims against a health authority that it has itself been directly negligent, as opposed to vicariously liable for the negligence of its doctors, will, of course, raise awkward questions. To what extent should the authority be held liable if (eg in the use of junior housemen) it is only adopting a practice hallowed by tradition? Should the authority be liable if it demonstrates that, due to the financial stringency under which it operates, it cannot afford to fill the posts with those possessing the necessary experience? But, in my judgment, the law should not be distorted by making findings of personal fault against individual doctors who are, in truth, not at fault in order to avoid such questions. To do so would be to cloud the real issues which arise. In the modern world with its technological refinements, is it sensible to persist in making compensation for those who

suffer from shortcomings in technologically advanced treatment depend on proof of fault, a process which the present case illustrates can consume years in time and huge sums of money in costs? Given limited resources, what balance is to be struck in the allocation of such resources between compensating those whose treatment is not wholly successful and the provision of required treatment for the world at large? These are questions for Parliament, not the courts. But I do not think the courts will do society a favour by distorting the existing law so as to conceal the real social questions which arise.

In *Bull v Devon AHA* [1993] 4 Med LR 117 (CA) (the facts of which we saw above) Mustill LJ was less inclined to judicial abstention. Mustill LJ referred to the hospital's expert evidence that the system operated by the defendant hospital was 'par for the course'.

Mustill LJ: . . . it seems to have been assumed by the experts that if this was so, the patient would have nothing to complain about.

Whatever the apparent appeal of this opinion to practical commonsense, I find its implications to be rather disturbing. Is there not a contradiction in asserting at the same time that the system put the foetus at risk and that it was good enough? . . .

The second suggested answer was on these lines: that hospitals such as the Devon and Exeter were in the dilemma of having to supply a maternity service, and yet not disposing of sufficient manpower to provide immediate cover, the more so since the small number of consultants and registrars had to deal with three different sites. They could not be expected to do more than their best, allocating their limited resources as favourably as possible.

Again, I have some reservations about this contention, which are not allayed by the submission that hospital medicine is a public service. So it is, but there are other public services in respect of which it is not necessarily an answer to allegations of unsafety that there were insufficient resources to enable the administrators to do everything which they would like to do. I do not for a moment suggest that public medicine is precisely analogous to other public services, but there is perhaps a danger in assuming that it is completely sui generis, and that it is necessarily a complete answer to say that even if the system in any hospital was unsatisfactory, it was no more unsatisfactory than those in force elsewhere.

It is however unnecessary to go further into these matters, which raise important issues of social policy, which the courts may one day have to address.

I mention the problem only because it underlies the apparent contradiction in the expert evidence, which caused me difficulty in finding the right starting point for a decision on this particular allegation of negligence.

Having considered the observation of Browne-Wilkinson V-C and Mustill LJ, Pill J in *Knight v Home Office* [1990] 3 All ER 237 addressed the same question.

Knight v Home Office [1990] 3 All ER 237, (1989) 4 BMLR 85 (QBD)

The widow of a suicidal prisoner, detained in Brixton Prison hospital wing, alleged that the Home Office was in breach of duty in failing to provide adequate supervision which would probably have prevented him from killing himself. Inter alia she sought to rely on the level of care which would be provided in a specialist psychiatric institution ie that set the benchmark. Pill J disagreed and held that the benchmark was not the optimum level of care provided in a leading specialist hospital and that there had been adequate care on the facts of the case. But he went on to remark as follows.

Pill J: Counsel for the plaintiffs submits that it is not a defence to establish that the standard of care was as good as that in other prisons or that it accorded with government circulars or standing orders in force at the time. While general practice in the prison service is a factor to be taken into account, I accept that the plaintiffs could succeed even if the current practice approved in the prison service had been followed in every respect. As Asquith LJ put it in *Daborn v Bath Tramways Motor co Ltd* [1946] 2 All ER 333 at 336:

In determining whether a party is negligent, the standard of reasonable care is that which is reasonably to be demanded in the circumstances.

It is for the court to consider what standard of care is appropriate to the particular relationship and in the particular situation. It is not a complete defence for a government department any more than it would be for a private individual or organisation to say that no funds are available for additional safety measures.

I cannot accept what was at one time submitted by counsel for the defendants that the plaintiffs' only remedy would be a political one. To take an extreme example, if the evidence was that no funds were available to provide any medical facilities in a large prison there would be a failure to achieve the standard of care appropriate for prisoners. In a different context, lack of funds would not excuse a public body which operated its vehicles on the public roads without any system of maintenance for the vehicle if an accident occurred because of lack of maintenance. The law would require a higher standard of care towards other road users.

Non-provision – As for the '*non-provision*' situation, the leading case is the following.

R v Secretary of State for Social Services ex p Hincks (1980) 1 BMLR 93 (CA)

Lord Denning MR: Four people living in Staffordshire have come to the court, urging that the health services are insufficient in their area. They desire a declaration of the court saying that the Secretary of State has not fulfilled his duty to provide a comprehensive health service. They are two elderly ladies, an elderly man, and a girl. They have been on a waiting list for surgery in the orthopaedic line for some years. Their complaint is supported by distinguished consultants and surgeons in that area, particularly by Mr John Cozens-Hardy, a Fellow of the Royal College of Surgeons, who was one of the first consultants to the Good Hope Hospital in Sutton Coldfield in Birmingham. As long ago as 1965, his duties were to organise a comprehensive orthopaedic and accident service for the area.

The area is an expanding area, with a large population. The position was that in 1971 plans were made for a section of the Good Hope Hospital to be expanded. Wards were to be opened in replacement of some old huts. That was to be done reasonably quickly. On 25 February 1971 the Department of Health and Social Security approved the reasonable hospital plan in the sum of nearly £2m for what was called 'Phase 3 of the Good Hope Hospital'. Although that plan was approved at that time, a question arose as to it being implemented because costs increased. So much so that by 1973 the estimated cost was just over £3m – but the lowest tender received was £4m. Then, in 1975, the estimated cost was nearly £4 million – but the lowest tender was nearly £7m. So, although the project had been approved for the extensions of the Good Hope Hospital (Phase 3), it could not be done within the cost which had been provided for in the estimate. The tenders were far too high.

This was very distressing for all those concerned with the hospital, as well as the consultants and the patients. Mr Cozens-Hardy speaks of the frustration and the upset which was caused to the medical staff because of these delays and the improbability of the plan going forward.

The matter was put before the Department of Health and Social Security in 1975: and a question was raised in Parliament. On 28 February 1975 the minister, Dr David Owen, wrote to the member of Parliament for the area. After explaining the necessity to cut expenditure, he said:

> It does, however, mean that only those hospitals with the very highest degree of priority will be able to start, and that many desirable hospital building schemes in the country as a whole will have to be postponed. The Good Hope scheme is one of the schemes which will now have to be postponed . . . I am sorry I cannot give you a more encouraging reply, but in the light of the very difficult economic circumstances we face plans are having to be revised all over the country and many painful decisions are having to be taken.

Then in February 1978 a letter was written to another member of Parliament by Mr Roland Moyle in which he said:

> . . . it is unfortunately true that there is a national problem of unsatisfactorily long waiting lists for traumatic and orthopaedic surgery because in an increasingly ageing population there are more patients with fractured necks and heads of femur and degenerative joint disease, which can nowadays in many cases best be treated by joint replacements.

As we all know, underlying that statement is the fact that modern surgery is such that many arthritic, rheumatic and other illnesses from which old people suffer can be treated, with very much improved methods. But that means, of course, that hospitals, operating theatres, and the surgeons who treat these people have to be paid for. At the end of the letter, Mr Moyle said:

> Whilst not denying the need for improving and extending facilities in Birmingham the (Regional Health Authority) have had to consider the needs of the other ten areas in the region. Their assessment, in the light of the resources likely to be available for capital developments, is that the Good Hope scheme does not command sufficient regional priority to start within the next ten years.

So in 1978 the scheme was put off for ten years and virtually abandoned – the scheme which had received approval as far back as 1971.

One can imagine, and sympathise with, the feelings of all those concerned in the health service in that area and with the frustration they feel. So, in the last resort, they brought an action to the courts. We are told that these patients received legal aid to bring the proceedings against the department to see if it was really its duty, and to see whether there could be some recourse to the courts.

Mr Blom-Cooper has urged before us all that can be said. He has referred us to the fact that there are no provisions in the statute which limit the expenditure of the Department. Section 3(1) of the National Health Service Act 1977 provides:

> It is the Secretary of State's duty to provide throughout England and Wales to such extent as he considers necessary to meet all reasonable requirements – (a) hospital accommodation . . . (c) medical, dental, nursing and ambulance services . . . (f) such other services as are required for the diagnosis and treatment of illness.

So that is his duty. It is a short point, and an important point that Mr Blom-Cooper raises. He says that that duty must be fulfilled. If the Secretary of State needs money to do it, then he must see that Parliament gives it to him. Alternatively if Parliament does not give it to him, then a provision should be put in the statute to excuse him from his duty. Mr Blom-Cooper says that that duty is plain and imperative, and it ought to be fulfilled by the Secretary of State.

That is an attractive argument, because there is no express limitation on the duty of the Secretary of State in the statute. But, in the course of the argument, many illustrations have been taken showing how necessary it is for a Secretary of State to have regard to forward planning (as it is called), to estimate changes in the population, for instance – or maybe the ageing population. He has to estimate for the future. For instance, when in 1971 the Good Hope Hospital scheme was approved, it was necessarily contemplated that it would be possible within the resources available. Indeed, as the discussion proceeded, it seemed to me inevitable that this provision had to be implied into s 3, 'to such extent as he considers necessary to meet all reasonable requirements such as can be provided within the resources available'. That seems to me to be a very necessary implication to put on that section, in accordance with the general legislative purpose. It cannot be supposed that the Secretary of State has to provide all the latest equipment. As Oliver LJ said in the course of argument, it cannot be supposed that the Secretary of State has to provide all the kidney machines which are asked for, or for all the new developments such as heart transplants in every case where people would benefit from them. It cannot be that the Secretary of State has a duty to provide everything that is asked for in the changed circumstances which have come about. That includes the numerous pills that people take nowadays: it cannot be said that he has to provide all these free for everybody.

I would like to read a few words from the judgment of Wien J, who gave a very comprehensive and good judgment in this matter. He said:

> The question remains: has there been a breach of duty? Counsel for the [Secretary of State] submits that s 3 does not impose an absolute duty. I agree. He further submits it does, by virtue of the discretion given, include an evaluation of financial resources or the lack of them is at the root of the whole problem in this case. If funds were unlimited, then of course regions and areas could go ahead and provide all sorts of services. But funds are not unlimited. The funds are voted by Parliament, and the health service has to do the best it can with the total allocation of financial resources.

I agree with that approach of the judge in this case. But there is a further aspect which he dealt with. He said, instead of looking at the health service as a whole, could you pinpoint a particular hospital or a particular area like the Good Hope Hospital in Birmingham, and say, 'That does require an extension, and it is a breach of duty for the Secretary of State not to provide for that hospital and that area'? It seems to me – as, indeed, Mr Roland Moyle said in the course of his letter – that you cannot pinpoint any particular hospital or any particular area. The Secretary of State has to do his best having regard to his wide responsibilities. For instance, there are 12 hospitals in this particular area. The service has to be provided over the whole country. Upon that point, the judge said:

> I have come to the conclusion that it is impossible to pinpoint any breach of statutory duty on the part of the Secretary of State. If he is entitled to take into account financial resources, as in my judgment he is, then it follows that every thing that can be done within the limit of the financial resources available has been done in the region and in the area. I doubt very much whether under s 3(1) it is permissible to put the spotlight, as it were, upon one particular department of one particular hospital and to say that conditions there are unsatisfactory.

It seems to me that those two paragraphs in the judge's judgment express the position very accurately. It is an interesting point, and it is important from the public point of view because of the grievances which many people feel nowadays about the long waiting list to get into hospital. So be it. The Secretary of State says that he is doing the best he can with the financial resources available to him: and I do not think that he can be faulted in the matter.

I think that the judge was quite right, and I would dismiss the appeal.

Bridge LJ: I agree. The evidence in this case puts a spotlight on the particular difficulties arising from the lack of resources at the Good Hope Hospital in Sutton Coldfield in particular, and more generally in the area of the Birmingham Area Health Authority's districts. But the situations here revealed are not unique. As the evidence shows and as we all know as a matter of common knowledge, the health service currently falls far short of what everyone would regard as the optimum desirable standard. That is very largely a situation which is brought about by lack of resources, lack of suitable equipment, lack of suitably qualified personnel, and above all lack of adequate finance.

The point on which this appeal turns is in the end a very short one which is whether, in performing his duty of considering to what extent it is necessary to meet reasonable requirements by the provisions of accommodation, facilities and services under s 3 of the National Health Service Act 1977, the Secretary of State can in regard to forward planning for the National Health Service, have regard to government economic policy. Mr Blom-Cooper accepts that in relation to current expenditure the Secretary of State can and must have regard to the amount which for any particular year has already been voted by Parliament for the financing of the National Health Service. He accepts that in relation to major projects involving large capital expenditure the Secretary of State and the staff of his department and the regional area health authorities exercising delegated powers and duties under the Secretary of State must all plan forward certainly very much further than one year ahead; but he says nevertheless that, in regard to that forward planning, no regard can be had whatsoever to what government policy may indicate as the likely prospect of future economic stringency limiting the amount of money which is going to be available to the service.

If he is right, then the rather startling conclusion clearly emerges that for the last ten years each successive holder of the office of Secretary of State for Social Services has been in flagrant breach of his duty under the statute and that has gone rather surprisingly unnoticed by Parliament. But, in my judgment, he is not right; and the dilemma in which he finds himself is this. He must either say that, in relation to future planning, the Secretary of State should assume that there will be unlimited resources available for the National Health Service – and, not unnaturally, Mr Blom-Cooper resiles from that extreme and manifestly untenable position – or, alternatively, he must say, as he does say, that the Secretary of State must plan to provide a service within the ambit of some limitation upon the resources which are going to be available to finance the service to be provided.

If there is to be some limitation, I ask myself the question: How is the nature and extent of that limitation to be determined? And the only sensible answer that I find it possible to give to that question is that the limitation must be determined in the light of current government economic policy. I think that is quite clearly an implication which must read into s 3(1) of the National Health Service Act 1977 if it is to be operated realistically. I feel extremely sorry for the particular applicants in this case who have to wait a long time, not being emergency cases, for necessary surgery. They share that misfortune with thousands up and down the country. I only hope that they have not been encouraged to think that these proceedings offered any real prospects that this court could enhance the standards of the National Health Service, because any such encouragement would be based upon manifest illusion.

I too would dismiss this appeal.

Oliver LJ agreed.

The facts of this case demonstrate clearly that when the courts can only avoid being drawn into policy questions in the distribution of resources within the health service by declaring the issue 'non-justiciable', they will have no hesitation in so deciding.

Curtailed provision – As for the '*curtailed provision*' situation, this has been considered in two cases concerned with cut-backs by a health authority in the provision of neonatal intensive care.

R v Central Birmingham HA ex p Walker (1987) 3 BMLR 32 (MacPherson J and CA)

MacPherson J: In this case Mr De Mello applies for leave to apply for judicial review of a decision of the Central Birmingham Health Authority, communicated on or about 20 October 1987, that the health authority were satisfied that a baby required an operation but that they were unable to conduct it at this time.

The relief sought is the quashing of that decision and an order that the authority carry out the operation and – I quote from the notice of application – 'provide proper care'. Furthermore, a declaration is sought that the decision not to conduct the operation was unlawful.

The facts of this matter are short and are set out in the affidavit of Mrs Diane Walker. Her baby was born on 9 October 1987. His name is David Barber Walker. He was premature, and he has been cared for in hospital since birth. He is under the care of two consultants. He is not in intensive care, nor is he in an incubator, but he is permanently monitored by hospital equipment and staff in a general ward. He has been treated obviously and, as Mrs Walker unreservedly accepts, with all possible skill. Unfortunately he needs an operation to repair his heart, which has been found to require surgery in order to repair a hole. That is a shorthand, layman's description of the procedure necessary, but I believe that it is all that need be said by way of description of what is required.

On a number of occasions the operation which will have to be performed on this baby has been arranged, or at least forecast to be about to take place, and so far the procedures have been cancelled.

I read now from the affidavit. Paragraph 10 reads:

> Apparently the problem is a shortage of specially trained nurses for the intensive care unit that my baby would have to go in after the operation. There are six beds in this unit but currently four trained nurses. There has to be a trained nurse for each bed in use. The four beds are occupied by other babies and, in the period that my baby has been at the hospital, whenever a bed has come free, which has been rare, Mr Giovanni and Mr Sethi have told me that, unfortunately, more urgent cases then [*sic*] my baby's have had to be admitted to the free beds.

Paragraph 11 reads:

> Mr Giovanni and Mr Sethi tell me that they are more than willing to carry out my baby's operation but simply cannot do so without the essential after-care available. They have of course said that if my baby's case becomes an 'emergency' then they will have to operate in any event, but there may be no aftercare.

I leave out Mrs Walker's belief as to the question of whether there is at present an emergency and pass to para 12:

> I should say at this point that I have absolutely no complaint against Mr Giovanni and Mr Sethi or the other doctors and nurses who are looking after my baby. They

have all been wonderful to me and my relatives, and of course my baby. Many have told me privately that they are just as distressed as I am by the whole situation.

Later the affidavit contains this, at para 15:

I ask this Honourable Court to order that the operation take place at once.

The position, then, is that at present the operation has not been done because of a shortage of specially trained nurses and accompanying facilities which do not allow the expansion of the intensive care unit, and this baby's operation has had to be postponed in order that more immediately urgent procedures should be carried out on other babies.

It must be firmly stressed that at present the evidence establishes that there is no danger to the baby. He is being treated and cared for with the fullest possible attention. To move him to another hospital could be risky but to wait will not be – unless of course an emergency develops, in which case, as the doctors have told the applicant, the operation will be done.

I say again that the reason for the postponement is because other more urgent cases have had to be dealt with, and there is a shortage of the human and perhaps also the physical facilities necessary to add this baby at once to the operating list. It need hardly be said that everybody sympathises with all those involved, both mother, baby, doctors and staff. But I have to consider whether this court could conceivably give the relief which is asked, which is in terms to order that the operation be carried out, and to say that the decision to postpone has been reached unlawfully and unreasonably to a point of irrationality.

I say at once that I find it quite impossible to say that there is in the decision made by the health authority, or by the surgeons who act on their behalf, any illegality, nor any procedural defect, nor any such unreasonableness. The fact that the decision is unfortunate, disturbing and in human terms distressing, simply cannot lead to a conclusion that the court should interfere in a case of this kind.

If the suggestion is, as it must be, that additional facilities should be provided, then the argument must be that the Secretary of State has failed, together with the health authority, to provide the necessary facilities, either because of lack of funds or because of the need to balance all the available factors which govern the staffing and running of the National Health Service.

It seems to me that this case is not truly an attack upon the actual decision made (although that is the matter set out in the application itself) and I detect a general criticism of the decisions as to the staffing and financing of the National Health Service and of those who provide its funds and facilities. It has been said before, and I say it again, that this court can no more investigate that on the facts of this case than it could do so in any other case where the balance of available money and its distribution and use are concerned. Those, of course, are questions which are of enormous public interest and concern – but they are questions to be raised, answered and dealt with outside the court.

I am wholly convinced that this decision of the health authority is not justiciable, that is to say that it is not a matter in which the court should intervene. If it were so, then any question of priority or clinical judgment of which case came first could be subject to review where it may depend on the location of available facilities.

I pause to say that there is no possible basis for suggesting that there could be any 'policy' of the health authority to deprive the hospital of staff other than for financial and general reasons which are well-known.

In my judgment the court would do a great disservice to those who have to work in difficult and straitened circumstances if it were to contemplate making an order in this case. No surgeon should be ordered to perform an operation by the court in the circumstances which this case reveals. I deprecate any suggestion that patients should be encouraged to think that the court has a role in a case of this kind.

Mr Demello has to satisfy me that he has an arguable case, upon the facts set out in this application and in the light of the principles which govern judicial review. He has wholly failed so to persuade me. Of course everybody hopes that this matter will be resolved as soon as is humanly possible. But in my judgment I would simply raise false hopes by giving leave. I am convinced that there are no prospects of success in this court in this application – and it must be dismissed.

The Court of Appeal dismissed the applicants' appeal.

Sir John Donaldson MR: This is a renewed application by Mrs Walker for judicial review in the context of facts which are very well known to everybody, namely the inability thus far of the Central Birmingham Health Authority to treat her child, the treatment taking the form of a heart operation.

It is accepted by Mr Bailey, who has appeared for the health authority, that the National Health Service authorities, and indeed the Secretary of State (although no doubt Mr Bailey has no authority to speak on behalf of the Secretary of State), are amenable to judicial review in circumstances in which there is reason to believe that the respondent or potential respondent is in breach of duties laid on him by public law. It is important that that should be known.

But equally, Mr Bailey says – and there is very substantial force in what he says – that in an organisation such as the National Health Service there will always be occasions when patients – with good reason, from their point of view – think that they are not being treated as quickly as they ought to be treated. That stems from the fact that, whatever is the proper level of funding, resources are, and perhaps always will be, finite.

It is not for this court, or indeed any court, to substitute its own judgment for the judgment of those who are responsible for the allocation of resources. This court could only intervene where it was satisfied that there was a prima facie case, not only of failing to allocate resources in the way in which others would think that resources should be allocated, but of a failure to allocate resources to an extent which was *Wednesbury* unreasonable, if one likes to use the lawyers' jargon, or, in simpler words, which involves a breach of a public law duty (see *Associated Provincial Picture Houses v Wednesbury Corpn* [1947] 2 All ER 680, [1948] 1 KB 223). Even then, of course, the court has to exercise a judicial discretion. It has to take account of all the circumstances of the particular case with which it is concerned.

Taking account of the evidence which has been put before us and all the circumstances, it seems to me that this would be an inappropriate case in which to give leave. If other circumstances arose in this case or another case it might be different, because the jurisdiction does exist. But we have to remember, as I think I have already indicated, that if the court is prepared to grant leave in all or even most cases where patients are, from their points of view, very reasonably disturbed at what is going on, we should ourselves be using up National Health Service resources by requiring the authority to stop doing the work for which they were appointed and to meet the complaints of their patients. It is a very delicate balance. As I have made clear and as Mr Bailey made clear, the jurisdiction does exist. But it has to be used extremely sparingly.

In all the circumstances I would not give leave in this case.

Nicholls LJ and Caulfield J agreed.

Consider the factually similar case of *R v Central Birmingham Health Authority, ex p Collier* (6 January 1988, unreported).

Stephen Brown LJ: Mr Demello [counsel for the applicant] has sought to distinguish the factual situation in this case by submitting that here, on the evidence of Mr Collier's affidavit, there is an immediate danger to health. I am not sure that I can accept that the affidavit establishes that fact. We have no medical evidence before us, but, even assuming that it does establish that there is immediate danger to health, it seems to me that the legal principles to be applied do not differ from the case of *Re Walker*. This court is in no position to judge the allocation of resources by this particular health authority. Mr Demello recognises that there is no hint of criticism, let alone of complaint, of any action on the part of the surgeon, or any other doctor at the hospital. There is no complaint of bad faith by the health authority. It is not suggested that they are in any way dragging their feet. Mr Demello asserts that, on the basis of what he would say is 'general knowledge', there is a lack of sufficient resources to enable every bed to be in use at the hospital; but there is no suggestion here that the hospital authority has behaved in a way which is deserving of condemnation or criticism. What is suggested is that somehow more resources should be made available to enable the hospital authorities to ensure that the treatment is immediately given.

Of course this is a hearing before a court. This is not the forum in which a court can properly express opinions upon the way in which national resources are allocated or distributed. [There] may be very good reasons why the resources in this case do not allow all the beds in the hospital to be used at this particular time. We have no evidence of that, and indeed, as the Master of the Rolls has said [in the *Walker* case], it is not for this court, or any court, to substitute its own judgment for the judgment of those who are responsible for the allocation of resources.

From the legal point of view, in the absence of any evidence which could begin to show that there was a failure to allocate resources in this instance in circumstances which would make it unreasonable in the Wednesbury sense to make those resources available, there can be no arguable case. I am bound to say that, whilst I have for my part every sympathy with the position of Mr Collier and his family and can understand their pressing anxiety in the case of their little boy, it does seem to me unfortunate that this procedure has been adopted. It is wholly misconceived in my view. The courts of this country cannot arrange the lists in the hospital, and, if [there] is [no] evidence that they are not being arranged properly due to some unreasonableness in the Wednesbury sense on the part of the authority, the courts cannot, and should not, be asked to intervene.

Having regard to the very recent decision of *Re Walker* it seems to me unfortunate that the step has been taken of bringing the matter before a court again. It may be that it is hoped that the publicity will assist in bringing pressure to bear upon the hospital; I do not know. This court cannot be concerned with matters of that kind. But simply upon the basis – which is a purely legal basis – that the matter comes before this court I can see no ground upon which the application can be granted.

Neill and Ralph Gibson LJJ agreed.

The language of the judges, at first blush, suggests that the courts do not distinguish the situation of 'curtailed provision' from that of 'non-provision'. A better analysis would be as we have seen, to consider the nature of the health authority's undertaking as regards the curtailed service. If on the facts the service provided does not comply with the undertaking, the authority will have failed to reach its own 'benchmark'. It could also be liable for a complete failure to comply with its duty as is made clear (albeit in the context of judicial review) by Lord Donaldson MR in *Walker*.

Thus, in both *Walker* and *Collier*, the health authorities arguably had not undertaken to provide neonatal intensive care services to all comers. There was, therefore, no failure to reach their own benchmark. It would have been otherwise if they had continued to run the service but with untrained nurses (at times) or cut-price and inadequate facilities by their own standards.

Clearly, in addition, the health authority offering the curtailed service could also face liability if the service was so curtailed as to amount effectively to a non-provision of it. This allows us to notice that, even as regards the non-provision of services although we have said that the courts would regard it as non-justiciable, in an extreme case reference must always be made to the statutory duty imposed on the Secretary of State or his delegates to provide a 'comprehensive health service' (s 1(1) of the National Health Service Act 1977). The complete failure of a health authority to provide, for example, any maternity services in an area with an average rate of childbirth could well be justiciable as a breach of this primary duty. Interestingly, as it happens the health authority's response to a finding of liability in a case like *Bull* could well be to limit its financial risk by closing down the maternity unit if it could not operate it safely.

(iv) THE 'INTERNAL MARKET' OF THE NHS

Before leaving the question of institutional liability, we should notice an issue which arises as a consequence of the 'internal market'. As we have seen, 'NHS contracts' may exist between a health authority (as purchaser) and an NHS Trust (as provider). The question arises whether the purchaser may incur primary liability if it agrees to an 'NHS contract' which results in the inadequate provision of services to a particular patient who is harmed. Additionally, could primary liability arise if the purchaser failed properly to monitor either the performance of the contract or the adequacy of the services provided under it, ie failed to meet the reasonable requirements of the community as is its delegated statutory duty under section 3 of the National Health Service Act 1977? In principle, there can be no doubt that such liability could arise if the service provided failed to meet that standard which expert evidence showed was the minimum reasonably necessary. This conclusion is fortified by the fact that the NHS Management Executive has issued guidelines to health authorities which, *inter alia*, stipulate the need for minimum standards of quality and for the need for regular monitoring of performance (see *Working for Patients, Contracts for Health Service: Operating Contracts* (HMSO, 1990). For a further discussion see, C Newdick, 'Rights to NHS Resources After the 1990 Act' (1993) 1 Med L Rev 53).

A final issue which arises from the 'internal market' concerns the extent to which an NHS Trust or doctor may argue that the best was done given the available resources under the NHS contract. In principle, the analysis here would reflect that set out earlier in relation to the NHS more generally albeit that the source of funds (and their limitation) is different. This means that the NHS Trust and the doctor would not be able to avoid liability based upon such arrangement when the care provided fell below the minimum standard. This approach was adopted in an analogous situation by the California Court of Appeal in *Wickline v California*.

Wickline v California (1986) 228 Cal Rptr 661 (Cal CA)

Mrs Wickline, a patient whose care was paid for by Medicaid, was hospitalized for surgery to treat vascular problems in her legs. On July 17, 1977, the date she was to be discharged, her doctors, realizing that she was having a difficult recovery, requested from Medicaid an eight day extension. The Medicaid utilization review nurse, after consulting with a consultant physician, authorized only four days. After four days Mrs Wickline was released. She subsequently suffered from complications that resulted in amputation of her leg. She sued the State, claiming that the complications were the result of the premature discharge, and recovered a jury verdict. The Court of Appeal reversed. Its opinion was based on the following reasoning.

Rowen JA: As to the principal issue before this court, ie, who bears responsibility for allowing a patient to be discharged from the hospital, her treating physicians or the health care payor, each side's medical expert witnesses agreed that, in accordance with the standards of medical practice as it existed in January 1977, it was for the patient's treating physician to decide the course of treatment that was medically necessary to treat the ailment.
. . .

The patient who requires treatment and who is harmed when care which should have been provided is not provided should recover for the injuries suffered from all those responsible for the deprivation of such care, including, when appropriate, health care payors. Third party payors of health care services can be held legally accountable when medically inappropriate decisions result from defects in the design or implementation of cost containment mechanisms as, for example, when appeals made on a patient's behalf for medical or hospital care are arbitrarily ignored or unreasonably disregarded or overridden. However, the physician who complies without protest with the limitations imposed by a third party payor, when his medical judgment dictates otherwise, cannot avoid his ultimate responsibility for his patient's care. He cannot point to the health care payor as the liability scapegoat when the consequences of his own determinative medical decisions go sour.

There is little doubt that Dr Polonsky [Mrs Wickline's doctor] was intimidated by the Medi-Cal program but he was not paralyzed by Dr Glassman's [the consultant's] response nor rendered powerless to act appropriately if other action was required under the circumstances. If, in his medical judgment, it was in his patient's best interest that she remain in the acute care hospital setting for an additional four days beyond the extended time period originally authorized by Medi-Cal, Dr Polonsky should have made some effort to keep Wickline there. He himself acknowledged that responsibility to his patient. It was his medical judgment, however, that Wickline could be discharged when she was. All the plaintiff's treating physicians concurred and all the doctors who testified at trial, for either plaintiff or defendant, agreed that Dr Polonsky's medical decision to discharge Wickline met the standard of care applicable at the time. Medi-Cal was not a party to that medical decision and therefore cannot be held to share in the harm resulting if such decision was negligently made.

In addition thereto, while Medi-Cal played a part in the scenario before us in that it was the resource for the funds to pay for the treatment sought, and its input regarding the nature and length of hospital care to be provided was of paramount importance, Medi-Cal did not override the medical judgment of Wickline's treating physicians at the time of her discharge. It was given no opportunity to do so. Therefore, there can be no viable cause of action against it for the consequence of that discharge decision. . . .

This court appreciates that what is at issue here is the effect of cost containment programs upon the professional judgment of physicians to prescribe hospital treatment for patients requiring the same. While we recognize, realistically, that cost consciousness has become a permanent feature of the health care system, it is essential that cost limitation programs not be permitted to corrupt medical judgment. We have concluded, from the facts in issue here, that in this case it did not.

(But see the subsequent case, *Wilson v Blue Cross of Southern California* (1990) 271 Cal Rptr 876, Turner JA *dubitante*.)

(b) Vicarious liability

Ellen Picard in 'The Liability of Hospitals in Common Law Canada' (1981) 26 McGill LJ 997, 1016-17, explains the background to vicarious liability in the context of a hospital.

An alternative basis for the liability of a hospital is based on the doctrine of *respondent superior*. It is an older and more settled area of law in regard to hospitals than that of direct, or personal or corporate duty. All of the principles of the law of vicarious liability as applied to hospitals, but therein lies the problem. Those principles, set up for masters and servants, shop keepers and clerks, do not fit the hospital and its professional staff. But most courts doggedly try to stretch the old garments to fit the new flesh. The concept that was the material measurement of vicarious liability, the control test, no longer covers modern hospital-doctor relationships. . . .

But control of that type is most uncommon today. Indeed almost from the moment the control test went into service its deficiencies were obvious. There is a strong consensus among authorities that it is in respect of its application to professional persons that the control test has broken down. An employer of a professional such as a doctor may know nothing about the practice of medicine. He is not only not in a position to control the doctor but if he attempts to do so will find that the employee has exercised his own form of control over the situation and quit.

. . . It seems the control test is not providing a credible, reliable measure of when there should be a shift in bearing the loss from the professional who has caused the negligence to the institution responsible for entering into a relationship with him in order to carry out its functions. Put succinctly, the hospital (X) is achieving many of its ends through professionals (Y). In terms of the 'rough justice' sought to be achieved through the concept of vicarious liability, when should X, (a hospital and in law a reasonable person) be held accountable for the negligence of Y (a professional)? Surely the answer is when Y is an integral part of X and is making it possible for X to fulfill its duties and obligations. The theory for determining whether liability should be borne by X has been given a name: the organization test. Fleming has described the organization test as asking whether Y's work was subject to coordinated control as to the *when* and the *where* rather than the *how*.

How has the case law accommodated these views? Picard describes the development of the law in her book, *Legal Liability of Doctors and Hospitals in Canada* (2nd edn 1984), pp 313-314:

In 1906 an English court [*Evans v Liverpool Corpn* [1906] 1 KB 160] held that a hospital was not vicariously liable for the negligence of a doctor who was an employee because it did not have control over him in his professional activities. Similarly, in a famous English case, *Hillyer v St Bartholomew's Hospital* [[1909] 2 KB 820] the court held that a hospital's responsibilities were to ensure that the persons giving medical care were competent and had proper apparatus and appliances. It would be vicariously liable for negligent acts of professionals while exercising their 'ministerial or administrative duties' but not while they were carrying out professional duties, the reason for the distinction being the perceived absence of control of the employer over those professional activities. It is worth noting that it was also held that in any case at the critical time the nurses were under control of the operator surgeon. This *obiter* comment lives on, seemingly full of potential never realized.

Thus, a hospital was for many years not liable for doctor-employees or for any negligence nurse-employees committed in carrying out their professional duties. Its main responsibility was to select personnel carefully. Eventually, however, in 1942 in *Gold v Essex County Council* [[1942] 2 KB 293], this strange split in responsibility was discarded as being 'unworkable and contrary to common sense'. The negligence involved was that of a radiology technician but the position was held to be the same as that of the nurse. Whatever confusion remained was removed in *Cassidy v Minister of Health* [[1951] 1 All ER 574], where the hospital was held liable for the negligence of a house surgeon employed as part of the permanent staff. The *Hillyer* decision was reviewed and restricted to its facts. Denning LJ said [at 586]:

> Relieved thus of *Hillyer's* case, this court is free to consider the question on principle, and this leads inexorably to the result that, when hospital authorities undertake to treat a patient and themselves select and appoint and employ the professional men and women who are to give the treatment, they are responsible for the negligence of those persons in failing to give proper treatment, no matter whether they are doctors, surgeons, nurses, or anyone else. Once hospital authorities are held responsible for the nurses and radiographers, as they have been in *Gold's* case, I can see no possible reason why they should not also be responsible for the house surgeons and resident medical officers on their permanent staff.

Denning LJ pointed out that it is employers who choose and can dismiss employees and this power is the reason that they should be held vicariously liable even where they cannot for various reasons control the employee. Furthermore, the old control test had become somewhat of an anachronism and it was apparent that one of the policy reasons for restricting the liability of hospitals, that of protecting the privately supported or charity hospital, was no longer present as state-supported hospitals became more common. Thus the questions became whether the person's work was an integral part of the hospital organisation and whether the patient employed him. As will be seen, the last question may have come to be paramount. In the last English case in the chain, *Roe v Minister of Health* [[1954] 2 QB 66], the English Court of Appeal went a step further by holding that a hospital would be liable for a part-time anaesthetist employed and paid by the hospital as a member of the permanent staff but who also carried on a private practice.

There appears to be no doubt that anyone who is a member of the medical staff of a hospital, whether part-time or full-time, will be judged to be an employee so as to render the health authority (whether district or regional) or NHS Trust vicariously liable for their torts. Some uncertainty was initially expressed after the creation of the NHS of the consultant's position. *Razzel v Snowball* [1954] 3 All ER 429, [1954] 1 WLR 1382 is often cited as putting the matter beyond doubt. In that case Denning LJ observed:

> Counsel for the plaintiff pressed us with some observations in the cases concerning consultants. He said that the defendant was a part time consultant, and that a consultant was in a different position from the staff of the hospital. I think that counsel for the defendant gave the correct answer when he said that, whatever may have been the position of a consultant in former times, nowadays, since the National Health Service Act, 1946, the term 'consultant' does not denote a particular relationship between a doctor and a hospital. It is simply a title denoting his place in the hierarchy of the hospital staff. He is a senior member of the staff, and is just as much a member of the staff as the house surgeon is. Whether he is called specialist or consultant makes no difference.

In fact, the case turned on whether a consultant in carrying out treatment was the agent of the Minister, fulfilling the Minister's statutory duty under what was then section 3 of the National Health Service Act 1946. Despite this rather unusual feature, the *dictum* of Denning LJ remains helpful.

Outside the NHS, the steady growth of the private sector will inevitably mean that the courts will be faced with issues of *respondent superior*. The decision of the New South Wales Court of Appeal in *Ellis v Wallsend DH* (1989) 17 NSWLR 553 is instructive.

Ellis v Wallsend District Hospital (1989) 17 NSWLR 553 (NSW CA)

Samuels JA: I consider first the appellant's submission that the hospital is vicariously liable for Dr Chambers' failure to warn her of the possible dangers and limited benefits of the proposed procedure.

In its conventional formulation the issue is whether Dr Chambers was an employee of the hospital under a contract of service or an independent contractor under a contract for services; in other words whether the relationship between them was one of employer and employee or of principal and independent contractor. Although an employer can be vicariously liable for the wrongs committed by his employees during the course of their employment, it has long been established that the principal of an independent contractor is not, as a general rule, vicariously liable for the wrongs committed by the contractor during the course of the engagement: *Laugher v Pointer* (1826) 5 B & C 547; 108 ER 204; *Quarman v Burnett* (1840) 6 M & W 499; 151 ER 509. Courts have traditionally applied a 'control test' to distinguish servants from independent contractors. An oft-cited formulation of the test is that of Bramwell LJ in *Yewens v Noakes* (1880) 6 QBD 530 at 532-533:

> . . . A servant is a person subject to the command of his master as to the manner in which he shall do his work.

Thus, it has been said that an employee, unlike an independent contractor, can be told by his employer not only what work to do, but also how to do it: *Collins v Hertfordshire County Council* [1947] KB 598 at 615 per Hilbery J. Although the quoted formulation of the test suggests the need for actual control over how the work is done, it is now well-established that 'what matters is lawful authority to command so far as there is scope for it': *Zuijs v Wirth Brothers Pty Ltd* (1955) 93 CLR 561 at 571; see also *Humberstone v Northern Timber Mills* (1949) 79 CLR 389 at 404 per Dixon J; *Stevens v Brodribb Sawmilling Co Pty Ltd* (1986) 160 CLR 16 at 24, 29 per Mason J. It is sufficient if this lawful authority to control be 'only in incidental or collateral matters': *Zuijs* (ibid).

Control in the sense discussed, however, is not the only indicium of a master and servant relationship to which a court may or should have regard. The 'modern approach' is to look to factors additional to control. In *Stevens v Brodribb Sawmilling* (at 24) Mason J, with whom Brennan and Deane JJ agreed, placed the control test in its proper context:

> . . . But the existence of control, whilst significant, is not the sole criterion by which to gauge whether a relationship is one of employment. The approach of this Court has been to regard it merely as one of a number of indicia which must be considered in the determination of that question [. . .] Other relevant matters include, but are not limited to, the mode of remuneration, the provision and maintenance of equipment, the obligation to work, the hours of work and provision of holidays, the deduction of income tax and the delegations of work by the putative employee.

Accordingly, the approach of Australian courts is to look at 'the totality of the relationship between the parties' (at 29), although control remains a significant and therefore relevant indicium of an employer and employee relationship.

This flexible and eclectic approach to the determination of whether a relationship of employer and employee exists seems inconsistent with the view that an alternative and exclusive manner of ascertaining the existence of the relationship is by the application of the so-called 'organisation test'. This test requires the court to look at the role of a putative employee in the employer's organisation. In *Stevenson Jordan and Harrison Ltd v Macdonald and Evans* [1952] 1 TLR 101 at 111, Denning LJ, a proponent of the test, put it thus:

> . . . One feature which seems to run through the instances is that, under a contract of service, a man is employed as part of the business, and his work is done as an integral part of the business; whereas, under a contract for services, his work, although done for the business, is not integrated into it but is only accessory to it.

See also *Bank voor Handel en Scheepwaart NV v Slatford* [1953] 1 QB 248 at 295 and *Roe v Minister of Health* [1954] 2 QB 66 at 91 per Morris LJ. As a matter of Australian law, the application of the organisation test is, at best, one relevant element in discerning the nature of the relationship between the parties. It is not a conclusive factor. As Mason J said in *Stevens v Brodribb Sawmilling* (at 27-28):

> . . . For my part I am unable to accept that the organisation test could result in an affirmative finding that the contract is one of service when the control test either on its own or with other indicia yields the conclusion that it is a contract for services. Of the two concepts, legal authority to control is the more relevant and the more cogent in determining the nature of the relationship. This comment applies with equal, if not greater, force to the competing view, expressed by Denning LJ in *Bank voor Handel* [1953] 1 QB at 295, that the test is an independent method of determining who is an employee and who is an independent contractor, and in this way seeks to replace the traditional approach of balancing all the incidents of the relationship between the parties.

It is not in dispute that Dr Chambers was an 'honorary medical officer' of the hospital during the relevant period. However, this appellation should not be given an unwarranted significance. The question whether a person is the employee of another is a question of fact: *Zuijs* (at 568-569) and *Albrighton v Royal Prince Alfred Hospital* [1980] 2 NSWLR 542 at 560. (*Davies v Presbyterian Church of Wales* [1986] 1 WLR 323; [1986] 1 All ER 705, in which the House of Lords held that whether a pastor of the Presbyterian Church of Wales is employed under a contract of service is a question of law concerning the true construction of the church's book of rules, is a rather special case and distinguishable.) Accordingly, as the preceding discussion of general principle indicates, one needs to look at all the incidents of the relationship disclosed by the evidence in the instant case, rather than examine in the abstract relationships of the type involved. In *Albrighton*, Reynolds JA (at 559) succinctly states the approach that this court should take in determining whether Dr Chambers, being an honorary medical officer, was a servant of the hospital:

> . . . The submissions based on English dicta made to us that honorary medical officers are not servants of a hospital afford no assistance whatever. The problem is to be solved by looking at the evidence in this case to ascertain what it is capable of showing as to the relationship between the hospital and the doctors, however they may be described. That evidence consists in the account of their activities within the hospital, their use of, and compliance with, hospital forms and routines, and the operation of the by-laws which were admitted in evidence.

. . . evidence was given by Mr Aitchison, the hospital's accountant between 1966 and 1979, about the practical operation of the by-laws and rules at the hospital during the period in question. This testimony was not generally objected to and is not now disputed.

Mr Aitchison was responsible for all the clerical functions relating to the payment of wages and creditors, for admission processes and for the collection of hospital fees. He testified that honorary medical officers received no payment from the hospital for services performed there. They were allowed to use the hospital's operating theatres for their own patients on a roster basis. In consideration for this right, they were obliged to be on call for emergency admissions and to care for the hospital's public ward patients free of charge. An honorary would admit patients from his private practice by either telephoning the hospital or giving the patient an admissions request form, as Dr Chambers did in this case, to take to the hospital. The hospital would then book the patient in for surgery at a time which coincided with a period during which the doctor was rostered to use the operating theatres. The doctor's fees in respect of services performed for these patients were regarded by the hospital as a private matter between the doctor and his patient; the hospital made no charge to private or intermediate patients (of which the appellant was one) for services rendered by doctors.

At the cost of some repetition, the evidence discloses the following. Dr Chambers, being an honorary medical officer, was subject to the by-laws and rules of the hospital. Public patients could be assigned to his care: he was obliged to treat them free of charge. But the honorary medical staff made the assignment, reporting their decision to the Board of Directors (rule 78). And the honorary medical staff prepared the 'roster of times during which [they] shall be available for duty' – presumably on call for emergency admissions – forwarding it to the board for consideration (by-law 44). His use of operating theatres for patients he admitted from his private practice was restricted to specified periods; but again this roster was prepared by the honorary medical staff (by-law 44). Visits to his patients in the wards had to be, wherever possible, at times that would not inconvenience the hospital routine. Grievances in respect of treatment of his patients in the hospital had to be reported. He was required, if necessary, to perform medical examinations of hospital personnel and be available for consultation by other members of staff at any time in respect of all cases. If he summarily discharged a patient on any of the grounds included in by-law 83 he had to report the fact to the chief executive officer.

There are other relevant indicia. Dr Chambers was selected and appointed by the board. Appointment was for a fixed three year term and renewable. At the trial it was conceded that his appointment had been successively renewed since the 1950s. The board had power to dismiss him 'after adequate inquiry' and to suspend him until that inquiry took place. He could not absent himself from his duties at the hospital without first obtaining the leave of the board and recommending a replacement. In addition, he was required under the by-laws to give 28 days' notice of his intention to resign.

It follows that the hospital, through the board and, in respect of other than professional matters (an amorphous category to say the least, but see rule 11), through the chief executive officer, possessed a measure of control over the work Dr Chambers did in the hospital. Rules 6 and 11 appear to me to assume, and thus suggest an admission, that the honorary medical officers are employees, although that term is not defined in the rules or by-laws; and although there is no evidence of any written conditions attached to Dr Chambers' original appointment or subsequent renewals (rule 2(b)), or of any acknowledgement under rule 3. But the degree of control revealed by the by-laws and rules was slight. It goes without saying that the hospital could control neither the treatment he prescribed nor the manner in which he performed surgery in its theatres. It is true that members of the honorary medical staff were bound to treat public patients and to be on hand for emergencies, but they themselves distributed the patients and drafted the rosters, and although the board may well have had some implied power of veto or revision it is probable that it was rarely exercised. The authority of the board appears to me to be confined to the formal minimum necessary to be reserved in order to ensure the administrative cohesion and integrity of the organisation in the hospital, but that might be sufficient to satisfy the modified control test enunciated in *Zuijs* (at 571); and see *Cassidy v Ministry of Health* [1951] 2 KB 343 at 354-355 and Atiyah, Vicarious Liability in the Law of Torts (1967) at 46-47.

As I have indicated, the majority judgments in *Stevens v Brodribb Sawmilling* reduce the potency of the control test below the diluted influence conceded to it in *Zuijs*. It is 'a prominent factor', or 'significant', but it is not the sole criterion: cf *Oceanic Crest Shipping Co v Pilbara Harbour Services Pty Ltd* (1986) 160 CLR 626 at 682, where Dawson J held that absence of control was not 'a decisive indication' that no relationship of employer and employee existed. It is merely one of a number of indicia which must be considered in determining whether a relationship is one of employment. 'Other relevant matters' – the list is not exclusive – are set out in the passage from Mason J's judgment in *Stevens v Brodribb Sawmilling* (at 24) which I quoted above.

In the same judgment (at 27) his Honour rejects both the capacity of the organisation test (to which I have previously referred) viewed as one of the relevant indicia, to override a conclusion reached by application of the control test, and its claim to be an independent method of determining the character of the relationship in question. It may be that the organisation test was partially rehabilitated by Wilson J in *Oceanic Crest* (at 646); but probably its apparent endorsement there was an accidental consequence of the special circumstances of the case. Hence *Stevens v Brodribb Sawmilling* authorises and entails consideration of 'the totality of the relationship between the parties' (at 29), a methodology presumably synonymous with 'the traditional approach of balancing all the incidents of the relationship between the parties' (at 28).

With all respect, this prescription seems likely to generate a problem. A balancing exercise assumes conflict, or at least incompatibility, between competing elements. Here I take these to be factors which are compatible with a contract of employment and those which are not. On this view a balance is struck awarding the net advantage of persuasion to one of the contending groups of indicators; and by this means the totality of the relationship is considered and a conclusion reached as to its character.

The problem is that this approach, tending as it does to define the relationship only in terms of its elements, does not provide any external test or requirement by which the materiality of the elements may be assessed. The assertion that a working relationship between A and B will constitute one of employment, provided that it manifests the elements of such a relationship, may be unhelpful unless those elements are certain in number, character, quality and importance, in which case their presence in the prescribed measure will establish the character of the relationship. For example, it was once possible to say that if A enjoyed the right to control B, so far as there was scope for it, in the performance of B's work, the relationship of employer and employee existed between them. When that test was in vogue, it was possible to say that the relationship of employer and employee existed whenever that element of control was present; so that the presence of that element of control manifested the relationship of employer and employee.

However, as Wilson and Dawson JJ observed in *Stevens v Brodribb Sawmilling* (at 35):

. . . The modern approach is, however, to have regard to a variety of criteria.

And then they pose much the same problem as that which I have endeavoured to raise:

. . . The approach is not without its difficulties because not all of the accepted criteria provide a relevant test in all circumstances and none is conclusive. Moreover, the relationship itself remains largely undefined as a legal concept except in terms of the various criteria, the relevance of which may vary according to the circumstances.

Then, their Honours observe that Windeyer J's remarks in *Marshall v Whittaker's Building Supply Co* (1963) 109 CLR 210 at 217 and Denning LJ's formulations of the organisation test really pose 'the ultimate question' in a different way rather than offer a definition capable of providing an answer. But they themselves close this discussion of the concepts involved by stating (at 37) that

. . . The ultimate question will always be whether a person is acting as the servant of another or on his behalf.

With this proposition may be compared the distinction drawn by Dixon J in *Queensland Stations Pty Ltd v Federal Commissioner of Taxation* (1945) 70 CLR 539 at 552 between a contract of service and 'what in essence is an independent contract', in a passage referred to by Mason J in *Stevens v Brodribb Sawmilling* (at 24) and quoted with approval by Wilson and Dawson JJ in the same case (at 36).

I venture to suggest that, as Wilson and Dawson JJ appear to have concluded in *Stevens v Brodribb Sawmilling*, an accurate formulation of the ultimate question constructively determines the means of answering it. It will at least set the limits of relevance for the indicia to be identified and analysed. It will, so far as this can be done, establish parameters; that is the quantities whose variable values, as they differ from case to case, will favour one answer or another to the ultimate question posed. Such quantities, identical to Mason J's 'indicia', will include the factors which he exemplified and their 'value' will be constituted by their factual content, varying, in the case of mode of remuneration, from fixed salary or wages to amounts determined by reference, for example, to the volume of timber delivered to a mill.

More importantly, the ultimate question will give shape and meaning to the raw facts which examination of the totality of the relationship will reveal. It will constitute the external pattern to which the facts will or will not conform. I would therefore approach the matter by seeking an answer to the question: 'In treating the appellant was Dr Chambers acting as the employee of the hospital (that is to say, on the hospital's behalf) or on his own behalf?'; cf *Oceanic Crest* (at 662) per Brennand J. In seeking the answer I must examine all relevant indicia; that is to say all facts capable of elucidating the question, and thus consider the whole of the relationship between the parties. And in order to point up my external pattern I would reduce my question to more fustian terms by asking whether: 'In treating the appellant was Dr Chambers engaged in his own business or the hospital's': cf *Federal Commissioner of Taxation v Barrett* (1973) 129 CLR 395 at 402 per Stephen J.

I must deal with the evidence again, but I can do so this time in a rather more sophisticated way. Dr Chambers at all material times carried on his own business, that is to say, his own specialist medical practice. The performance of surgery was a vital incident of that practice, and required the use of facilities which could be obtained only in an hospital which provided operating theatres with their standard fixtures and fittings (I interpolate that Dr Chambers provided other items of the surgeon's kit), together with wards, recovery rooms and trained nursing staff. The list is not exclusive. Without these resources Dr Chambers could not have carried on his practice as a surgeon.

For its part, the hospital needed senior physicians and surgeons in order to fulfil the objects prescribed by by-law 5, that is, 'to establish and maintain hospital facilities and afford relief to sick persons' in accordance with the provisions of the Public Hospitals Act 1929, section 3 of which defined 'relief' to include treatment of disease or injury and the provision of medical and surgical attention: cf *Razzel v Snowball* [1954] 1 WLR 1382 at 1385; [1954] 3 All ER 429 at 432. Hence Dr Chambers (and other specialist physicians and surgeons) and the hospital entered into an agreement (often renewed) which in 1975 at least represented the standard means of providing a range of surgical services to the community. I have already covered this ground; but at the risk of tedium I repeat its principal incidents. Dr Chambers undertook to treat free of charge those patients who had applied directly to the hospital for relief, in return for operating privileges, nursing care and accommodation in respect of those of his own patients whom he would book into the hospital. By 'his own patients' I mean those who had consulted Dr Chambers directly, or had been referred to him by other doctors, and who had agreed to pay him a fee for his services. They would pay the hospital for nursing and other care for accommodation as private or intermediate patients.

Dr Chambers received no remuneration from the hospital. The hospital through its board and the chief executive officer (save in respect of 'professional matters', that is, matters pertaining to the exercise of medical and surgical art and skill) retained that slight degree of control over the activities of the honorary medical staff (who were generally permitted themselves to manage the discharge of their obligations) necessary, as I said, to maintain administrative efficiency and integrity.

Most of the other indicia mentioned by Mason J do not apply. Considering the totality of the relationship between the parties I conclude that it points convincingly to the conclusion that in treating the appellant Dr Chambers was engaged in his own business and not the hospital's. He was conducting his independent practice as a neuro-surgeon and his relationship with the hospital was not one of employer and employee.

I have so far endeavoured to confine my examination of the relationship between Dr Chambers and the hospital to the manner in which it related to the treatment of the appellant; that is to say, whether he treated her as an employee of the hospital and on its behalf, or whether he treated her on his own account in the furtherance of his independent surgical practice. But I think that I am bound to go further and express a view as to whether there is any basis for the conclusion that he might have fulfilled two roles, being an independent specialist working on his own account in the treatment of those whom I have defined as his own patients, and working as an employee on the hospital's behalf when treating the hospital's patients, that is those who had gone directly to the hospital for relief as the plaintiff did in *Albrighton*. An affirmative answer to this last proposition placing the hospital and Dr Chambers in the relationship of employer and employee would mean that the relationship between them differed without the intervention of any new circumstances save those relating to the manner in which the patient came to the hospital. The degree of control exerted by the hospital over Dr Chambers would be the same whether he was treating a patient of the hospital or one of his own patients as I have defined those terms. The only difference between these two situations would arise from the character of the patient and not from anything in the relationship between Dr Chambers and the hospital. It would be curious, I think, in any case, if while conducting a full-time private practice he combined that undertaking with parallel employment (in the strict sense) by the hospital; and it is no more plausible to postulate that the truth of the situation was that he was an employee of the hospital with a right of private practice such as a member of an university's academic staff might enjoy. It seems to me that, for the reasons which I have already offered, Dr Chambers was never at any time an employee of the hospital, but was at all times an independent specialist who had an agreement with the hospital pursuant to which he provided certain services, and accepted a degree of management, in return for the provision of facilities and resources necessary to enable him to carry on his own practice as a surgeon.

Meagher JA agreed. Kirby P dissented.

Kirby P: The theory of the liability of hospitals for the acts of persons working within them has changed during the course of the present century. At first, it was held that hospitals were not liable for negligence arising in the course of the exercise of professional skill. The only duty of the hospital towards the patient treated there was to use due care and skill in selecting its medical staff. The relationship of master and servant did not exist between the hospital and the physicians and surgeons who gave their services at the hospital nor between the hospital and the nurses and other attendants assisting in the operation. Because the hospital could not control the way in which those persons performed their tasks, it was not to be held vicariously liable for mistakes which they made. An action brought against the hospital for the damage resulting from negligence alleged to have been caused during an operation was held by the English Court of Appeal to be not maintainable: see *Hillyer v Governors of St Bartholomew's Hospital* [1909] 2 KB 820. The decision called upon an earlier line of United States authority: see discussion S S Bobbe, 'Tort Liability of Hospitals in New York' (1951-52) 37 Cornell LQ 419. It was clearly influenced by 'the gratuitous benefit of its care' which hospitals, at that time, commonly provided to public patients (see ibid at 829).

For several decades, in England and elsewhere, but with waning enthusiasm as time wore on, the holding in *Hillyer* protected hospitals from suits in negligence based on the acts or omissions of professional staff.

The turnaround came in Canada in *Sisters of St Joseph of the Diocese of London in Ontario v Fleming* [1938] SCR 172; [1938] 2 DLR 417: discussed A M Linden, 'Changing Patterns of Hospital Liability in Canada' (1966) 5 Alberta L Rev 212 at 215. Gradually a new doctrine emerged. It reached Australia in *Henson v Board of Management of the Perth Hospital* (1939) 41 WALR 15 and England in *Gold v Essex County Council* [1942] 2 KB 293. It reached South Africa in 1957 in *Esterhuzen v Administrator, Transvaal* 1957 (3) SA 710 (T). Now, almost all common-law countries have rejected the *Hillyer* principle. Ireland did so belatedly: see *O'Donovan v Cork County Council* [1967] IR 173. Despite some early renunciations of hospital immunity (see, eg, *Bing v Thunig* 1653 NYS 2d 3 (1957) (NYCA)), the United States of America was an even more tardy convert; see, eg *Alden v Providence Hospital* 382 F 2d 163 (1967) (DC Circ). The developments are usefully discussed in J D Cunningham, 'The Hospital-Physician Relationship: Hospital Responsibility for Malpractice of Physicians' (1975) 50 Washington L Rev 385.

These changes in the particular context of the relation of professional staff to a hospital paralleled wider changes which were occurring in the law in the definition of the duty of employers to employees generally. The simple 'control' test was no longer considered adequate to determine the relationship of an employer and employee given advances in education, technology, the role of the modern corporation and social changes which necessarily enhance individual autonomy. These changes led to various attempts by the courts to state a new criterion by which the relationship would be defined and by which vicarious liability might be assigned to one body in respect of the acts or omissions of a highly qualified individual performing tasks relevant to its interests. The existence of control over the subordinate (to use a neutral expression) was no longer the principal, still less the sole, criterion accepted by the Australian courts. In place of this test the High Court of Australia suggested the need to look to a number of indicia from which the nature of the relationship and the responsibilities deriving from it would be defined: see *Stevens v Brodribb Sawmilling Co Pty Ltd* (1986) 160 CLR 16 at 24. In England, Lord Denning had earlier suggested a simple test of whether it could be said that the 'subordinate' was working within the 'organisation' of the 'superior'. However, in Australia, although not rejected as irrelevant, the 'organisation test' is not accepted as sufficient or as an independent method for determining that vicarious liability arises: see *Stevens* (at 27).

There are particular reasons why it was necessary for the common law to move away from *Hillyer* in the special context of modern hospitals. One of them, of general application, was explained by Lord Denning (then Denning LJ) in *Cassidy v Ministry of Health* [1951] 2 KB 343 at 359-362:

> If a man goes to a doctor because he is ill, no one doubts that the doctor must exercise reasonable care and skill in his treatment of him: and that is so whether the doctor is paid for his services or not. But if the doctor is unable to treat the man himself and sends him to hospital, are not the hospital authorities then under a duty of care in their treatment of him? I think they are. Clearly, if he is a paying patient, paying them directly for their treatment of him, they must take reasonable care of him; and why should it make any difference if he does not pay them directly, but only indirectly through the rates which he pays to the local authority or through insurance contributions which he makes in order to get the treatment; I see no difference at all. Even if he is so poor that he can pay nothing, and the hospital treats him out of charity, still the hospital authorities are under a duty to take reasonable care of him just as the doctor is who treats him without asking a fee. In my opinion authorities who run a hospital, be they local authorities, government boards, or any other corporation, are in law under the selfsame duty as the humblest doctor; whenever they accept a patient for treatment, they must use reasonable care and skill to cure him of his ailment. The hospital authorities cannot, of course, do it by themselves: they have no ears to listen through the stethoscope, *and no hands to hold the surgeon's knife*. They must do it by the staff which they employ; and if their staff are negligent in giving the treatment, they are just as liable for that negligence as is anyone else who employs others to do his duties for him . . .
>
> It is no answer to them to say that their staff are professional men and women who do not tolerate any interference by their lay masters in the way they do their work . . . The reason why the employers are liable in such cases is not because they can control the way in which the work is done – they often have not sufficient knowledge to do so

– but because they employ the staff and have chosen them for the task and have in their hands *the ultimate sanction for good conduct, the power of dismissal.* . . .

[The result then is that] when hospital authorities undertake to treat a patient, and themselves select and appoint and employ the professional men and women who are to give the treatment, then they are responsible for the negligence of those persons in failing to give proper treatment, no matter whether they are doctors, surgeons, nurses, or anyone else. [Emphasis added.]

These remarks concerned the negligence of a junior medical practitioner who was on the staff of the hospital. They are therefore limited, in their terms, to staff professionals actually employed by the hospital. But the reasoning is, in my opinion, applicable to other persons associated with the hospital, over whom the hospital has 'the ultimate sanction for good conduct, the power of dismissal'.

In *Yepremian v Scarborough General Hospital* (1980) 110 DLR (3d) 513 (Ont CA), Blair JA (at 558), in an influential dissenting judgment, traced the

. . . oft-told tale of how the Courts in a period of less than 50 years eliminated the anomaly which exempted hospitals from the ordinary rules of liability for negligence of doctors, nurses and other professionals acting within the scope of their employment.

The very nature of hospitals, the growth in the number of publicly funded hospitals, their importance as centres of assistance in times of personal crisis, their emergency wards with a burgeoning accretion of sophisticated equipment all suggested how inapposite was the old 'control' approach to determining the liability of the hospital for the acts of those working 'within it'. But once 'control' was overthrown and attention was paid to a range of considerations governing the relationship of the 'subordinate' to the hospital, the ambit of those for whom the hospital became vicariously liable was pushed ever further.

With copious reference to authority in many common-law countries, Giesen, International Medical Malpractice Law (1988) (at 52-54) concludes:

Hospitals and health care authorities in general are now held liable for negligence of all sorts of staff, including nurses, house pharmacists, laboratory technicians, audiologists, physiotherapists, psychiatrists, radiologists and radiographers, anaesthetists, (house) surgeons, orthopaedic surgeons and neurosurgeons, pathologists, gynaecologists and other specialists, whole-time (or resident) assistant medical officers, part-time medical officers, senior registrars, and consultants.

The same trend prevails in varying degrees in other Commonwealth countries. The same is true of Ireland, South Africa, and, in particular, the United States where, as in England, or in Canada, the immunity of charitable hospitals from negligence liability in tort for the negligence of their employees has in recent decades almost entirely disappeared. Only vestiges of this doctrine remain, primarily in the form of legislatively imposed restrictions, such as ceilings on the total of recoverable damages or restrictions on those who may bring an action. Absolute immunities, however, are becoming a thing of the past, and increasingly courts are narrowing the areas in which they apply.

This appeal is not the occasion to examine the theoretical bases for vicarious liability. Professor Atiyah has described as many as nine theories to explain why a superior should be liable, in law, for the acts and omissions of a subordinate: PS Atiyah, Vicarious Liability in Law of Torts (1967) at 12ff. Once 'control' is abandoned as the test and a range of considerations are taken into account to determine whether vicarious liability arises, it is difficult to see why 'honorary consultants' should, as such, be excluded from the list of those for whom the hospital can be held, in law, to be accountable. The range of specialities and skills already covered in the case of employed staff is clearly established. The hospital has its own reasons for including the 'honorary' amongst its officers. Such persons add to the prestige and community utility of the hospital. They become inseparably connected with the activities of the employed staff. Their activities, in an operation, may be inextricably mixed with those of employed staff. It is in the hospital's financial and professional interest to ensure that its facilities are used to the utmost, including by such 'honoraries'. Upon this basis, I agree with Giesen (op cit at 58) that hospitals should not be allowed to escape responsibility for injury to patients happening on their premises as a result of the activities of health professionals, including honorary surgeons. Other common-law appellate courts have so held: see eg, discussion Cunningham [(1975) 50 Wah L Rev 385] (at 413); the decision of the Illinois Supreme Court in *Darling v Charleston Community Memorial Hospital* 211 NE (2d) 253 (1965); cert denied 386 US 946 (1966). So should we.

Take the present case as an example. The relationship between Dr Chambers and the hospital was defined by the Model By-laws and Rules for Public Hospitals which were admitted into evidence without objection. The relevant provisions are contained in the judgment of Samuels JA. I do not repeat them. It is enough to record that an honorary medical officer (such as Dr Chambers) was appointed to the 'honorary medical staff' of the hospital. He made up, with others in the same category, the 'Honorary Medical Board' of the hospital. That board prepared a roster during which time Dr Chambers was required to be 'available for duty'. He held 'office' for three years from the date of his 'appointment'. He was required to give 28 days' notice of intention to resign. He was not permitted to 'absent himself' from his 'duties' without first obtaining leave of absence from the board and nominating a substitute during such absence. The board retained the ultimate power referred to by Denning LJ in *Cassidy* (at 360) namely, 'the power of dismissal': see by-law 80A. His duty, in association with the hospital, was not confined to public patients. It extended to all patients, including intermediate patients such as Mrs Ellis. It was:

> To render professional services to patients according to their need, give such systematic instruction and training as required by the Board . . . and conduct such medical examinations and arrange for such tests . . . as are required.

Dr Chambers was required to consult when requested by a colleague. He had the power to discharge summarily any patient refusing to obey a medical direction. Together with other 'officers and employees', he was 'under the control of' the hospital's chief executive officer. The only exception, in the case of 'medical officers (honorary and resident) [was] in respect of professional matters'.

In my opinion, these by-laws, for mutual benefit, tied Dr Chambers inextricably into the organisation of the hospital. True, he could not be directed on how to 'hold the knife' (*Cassidy*). But neither could the other professional staff be so directed. He was integrated into the discipline and direction of the hospital. What he did in his rooms was his affair. But when he came into the hospital, he was part of the hospital. When working on its premises, he was part of its integrated medical team. Nothing could demonstrate this more clearly than the consent form which patients (including Mrs Ellis) were required to sign upon their admission to the hospital. It is set out in full in the judgment of Samuels JA. It includes the statement:

> I understand that an assurance has not been given that the operation will be performed by a particular surgeon.

This showed that, although a patient would have every expectation that her own doctor would perform the operation, once she came into the hospital her relationship with Dr Chambers changes. She was thereafter (as was he) under the discipline, and subject to the requirements, of the hospital. This should not be surprising. More surprising would be the notion, in the necessarily interactive circumstances of a modern hospital conducting advanced microsurgery, that people could be performing health care activities within the hospital but entirely independent of it. This would envisage that in the one operation, if the nursing sister and the honorary surgeon both missed the removal of a swab, though the mistake was common to each and performed in the course of the mutually inter-dependent activity, the hospital would be responsible for one (the nurse) but not for the other (the surgeon). Such artificialities in the law should be avoided. They represent a relic of *Hillyer* thinking. They are especially inappropriate in the facts of the present case, where the integration of Dr Chambers into the activities of the hospital is so clearly shown.

B. STANDARD OF CARE

1. Generally

Bolam v Friern Hospital Management Committee **[1957] 2 All ER 118, [1957] 1 WLR 582 (McNair J)**

The plaintiff contended that the defendants were vicariously liable for the carelessness of a doctor who administered electro-convulsive therapy to the plaintiff without administering a relaxant drug or without restraining the convulsive movements of the plaintiff by manual control (save for his lower jaw). The plaintiff suffered a fractured hip as a consequence. He brought an action against the defendants in negligence. McNair J directed the jury as follows.

McNair J: I must explain what in law we mean by 'negligence'. In the ordinary case which does not involve any special skill, negligence in law means this: Some failure to do some act which a reasonable man in the circumstances would do, or doing some act which a reasonable man in the circumstances would not do; and if that failure or doing of that act results in injury, then there is a cause of action. How do you test whether this act or failure is negligent? In an ordinary case it is generally said, that you judge that by the action of the man in the street. He is the ordinary man. In one case it has been said that you judge it by the conduct of the man on the top of a Clapham omnibus. He is the ordinary man. But where you get a situation which involves the use of some special skill or competence, then the test whether there has been negligence or not is not the test of the man on the top of a Clapham omnibus, because he has not got this special skill. The test is the standard of the ordinary skilled man exercising and professing to have that special skill. A man need not possess the highest expert skill at the risk of being found negligent. It is well-established law that it is sufficient if he exercises the ordinary skill of an ordinary competent man exercising that particular art. I do not think that I quarrel much with any of the submissions in law which have been put before you by counsel. Counsel for the plaintiff put it in this way, that in the case of a medical man negligence means failure to act in accordance with the standards of reasonably competent medical men at the time. That is a perfectly accurate statement, as long as it is remembered that there may be one or more perfectly proper standards; and if a medical man conforms with one of those proper standards then he is not negligent. Counsel for the plaintiff was also right, in my judgment, in saying that a mere personal belief that a particular technique is best is no defence unless that belief is based on reasonable grounds. That again is unexceptionable. But the emphasis which is laid by counsel for the defendants is on this aspect of negligence: He submitted to you that the real question on which you have to make up your mind on each of the three major points to be considered is whether the defendants, in acting in the way in which they did, were acting in accordance with a practice of competent respected professional opinion. Counsel for the defendants submitted that if you are satisfied that they were acting in accordance with a practice of a competent body of professional opinion, then it would be wrong for you to hold that negligence was established. I referred, before I started these observations, to a statement which is contained in a recent Scottish case, *Hunter v Hanley* (1955 SLT 213 at p 217), which dealt with medical matters, where the Lord President (Lord Clyde) said this:

> In the realm of diagnosis and treatment there is ample scope for genuine difference of opinion, and one man clearly is not negligent merely because his conclusion differs from that of other professional men, nor because he has displayed less skill or knowledge than others would have shown. The true test for establishing negligence in diagnosis or treatment on the part of a doctor is whether he has been proved to be guilty of such failure as no doctor of ordinary skill would be guilty of if acting with ordinary care.

If that statement of the true test is qualified by the words 'in all the circumstances', counsel for the plaintiff would not seek to say that that expression of opinion does not accord with English law. It is just a question of expression. I myself would prefer to put it this way: A doctor is not guilty of negligence if he has acted in accordance with a practice accepted as proper by a responsible body of medical men skilled in that particular art. I do not think there is much difference in sense. It is just a different way of expressing the same thought. Putting it the other way round, a doctor is not negligent, if he is acting in accordance with such a practice, merely because there is a body of opinion that takes a contrary view. At the same time, that does not mean that a medical man can obstinately and pig-headedly carry on with some old techniques if it has been proved to be contrary to what is really substantially the whole of informed medical opinion. Otherwise you might get men today saying: 'I don't believe in anaesthetics. I don't believe in antiseptics. I am going to continue to do my surgery in the way it was done in the eighteenth century.' That clearly would be wrong.

The jury returned a verdict for the defendants.

Bolam was applied in *Whitehouse v Jordan* [1981] 1 All ER 267, [1981] 1 WLR 246, the case we saw at the outset of this chapter. Lord Edmund-Davies stated (pp 276-7):

Lord Edmund-Davies: The principal questions calling for decision are: (a) in what manner did Mr Jordan use the forceps? and (b) was that manner consistent with the degree of skill which a member of his profession is required by law to exercise? Surprising though it is at this late stage in the development of the law of negligence, counsel for Mr Jordan persisted in submitting that his client should be completely exculpated were the answer to question (b), 'Well, at the worst he was guilty of an error of clinical judgment'. My Lords, it is high time that the unacceptability of such an answer be finally exposed. To say that a surgeon committed an error of clinical judgment is wholly ambiguous, for, while some such errors may be completely consistent with the due exercise of professional skill, other acts or omissions in the course of exercising 'clinical judgment' may be so glaringly below proper standards as to make a finding of negligence inevitable. Indeed, I should have regarded this as a truism were it not that, despite the exposure of the 'false antitheses' by Donaldson LJ in his dissenting judgment in the Court of Appeal, counsel for the defendants adhered to it before your Lordships.

But doctors and surgeons fall into no special category, and, to avoid any future disputation of a similar kind, I would have it accepted that the true doctrine was enunciated, and by no means for the first time, by McNair J in *Bolam v Friern Hospital Management Committee* [1957] 2 All ER 118 at 121, [1957] 1 WLR 582 at 586 in the following words, which were applied by the Privy Council in *Chin Keow v Government of Malaysia* [1967] 1 WLR 813:

> . . . where you get a situation which involves the use of some special skill or competence, then the test as to whether there has been negligence or not is not the test of the man on the top of Clapham omnibus because he has not got this special skill. The test is the standard of the ordinary skilled man exercising and professing to have that special skill.

If a surgeon fails to measure up to that standard in *any* respect ('clinical judgment' or otherwise), he has been negligent and should be so adjudged.

The House of Lords returned again to the topic and reiterated the *Bolam* view in *Sidaway*. We referred to this *in extenso* in Chapter 3 and here we only need to refer again to Lord Bridge's speech.

Lord Bridge: Broadly, a doctor's professional functions may be divided into three phases: diagnosis, advice and treatment. In performing his functions of diagnosis and treatment, the standard by which English law measures the doctor's duty of care to his patient is not open to doubt. 'The test is the standard of the ordinary skilled man exercising and professing to have that special skill.' These are the words of McNair J in *Bolam v Friern Hospital Management Committee* [1957] 2 All ER 118 at 121, [1957] 1 WLR 582 at 586, approved by this House in *Whitehouse v Jordan* [1981] 1 All ER 267 at 277, [1981] 1 WLR 246 at 258 per Lord Edmund-Davies and in *Maynard v West Midlands Regional Health Authority* [1985] 1 All ER 635 per Lord Scarman. The test is conveniently referred to as the *Bolam* test. In *Maynard's* case Lord Scarman, with whose speech the other four members of the Appellate Committee agreed, further cited with approval the words of the Lord President (Clyde) in *Hunter v Hanley* 1955 SLT 213 at 217:

> In the realm of diagnosis and treatment there is ample scope for genuine difference of opinion and one man clearly is not negligent merely because his conclusion differs from that of other professional men . . . The true test for establishing negligence in diagnosis or treatment on the part of a doctor is whether he has been proved to be guilty of such failure as no doctor of ordinary skill would be guilty of if acting with ordinary care . . .

The language of the *Bolam* test clearly requires a different degree of skill from a specialist in his own special field than from a general practitioner. In the field of neuro-surgery it would be necessary to substitute for the Lord President's phrase 'no doctor of ordinary skill', the phrase 'no neuro-surgeon of ordinary skill'. All this is elementary and, in the light of the two recent decisions of this House referred to, firmly established law.

Who then sets the standard? Notice Lord Scarman's comment in *Sidaway*:

> The *Bolam* principle may be formulated as a rule that a doctor is not negligent if he acts in accordance with a practice accepted at the time as proper by a responsible body of medical

opinion even though other doctors adopt a different practice. In short, the law imposes the duty of care; but the standard of care is a matter of medical judgment.

We should note in passing the brief life-span of the 'false antithesis' between an error of judgment and an error amounting to a failure to exercise due care and skill. This was conceived by Lord Denning and given a brief moment in the light as Sheila Maclean writes in 'Negligence – A Dagger at the Doctor's Back?' in *Justice, Lord Denning and the Constitution* (ed P Robson and P Watchman), at p 104:

> In the case of *Roe v Minister of Health* [[1954] 2 QB 66] he said:
>
> . . . we should be doing a disservice to the community at large if we were to impose liability on hospitals and doctors for everything that happens to go wrong.
> . . . We must insist on due care for the patient at every point, but we must not condemn as negligent that which is only misadventure.
>
> Again in the case of *Hatcher v Black* [(1954) Times, 2 July] he pointed out the risks of holding doctors liable in these circumstances and suggested that to do so would mean that:
>
> . . . a doctor examining a patient, or a surgeon operating at a table, instead of getting on with his work, would be forever looking over his shoulder to see if someone was coming up with a dagger – for an action for negligence against a doctor is for him like unto a dagger.
>
> The interests of the community then are seen by Lord Denning not as being the facilitation of compensation in the event of damage as a result of medical intervention, but rather as being that medical practice should be interfered with as little as possible.

Lord Denning returned to his creation in *Whitehouse v Jordan* [1980] 1 All ER 650.

> **Lord Denning LJ:** We must say, and say firmly, that, in a professional man, an error of judgment is not negligent. To test it, I would suggest that you ask the average competent and careful practitioner: 'Is this the sort of mistake that you yourself might have made?' If he says: 'Yes, even doing the best I could, it might have happened to me', then it is not negligent. In saying this, I am only reaffirming what I said in *Hatcher v Black* (a case I tried myself), *Roe v Ministry of Health and Hucks v Cole* [(1968) 112 Sol Jo 483, CA].

Donaldson LJ (as he then was) disagreed:

> **Donaldson LJ:** It is said that the judge lost sight of the fact that the plaintiff had to establish negligence. The basis of this submission was in part that he nowhere referred to 'errors of clinical judgment' and contrasted such errors with negligence. I can understand the omission, because it is a false antithesis. If a doctor fails to exercise the skill which he has or claims to have, he is in breach of his duty of care. He is negligent. But if he exercised that skill to the full, but nevertheless takes what, with hindsight, can be shown to be the wrong course, he is not negligent and is liable to no one, much though he may regret having done so. Both are errors of clinical judgment. The judge was solely concerned with whether or not the defendant's actions were negligent. If they were not, it was irrelevant whether or not they constituted an error of clinical judgment. The question which Bush J [the trial judge] asked himself was whether there had been any failure by the defendant 'to exercise the standard of skill expected from the ordinary competent specialist having regard to the experience and expertise which that specialist holds himself out as possessing', and added the proviso that 'the skill and expertise which we are considering is that applying in 1969-70'. In my judgment, that was not only the correct question, it was the only relevant question.

Lord Fraser delivered the death-blow in the House of Lords ([1981] 1 All ER 267).

> **Lord Fraser:** Referring to medical men, Lord Denning MR said ([1980] 1 All ER 650 at 658):
> 'If they are to be found liable [*sc* for negligence] whenever they do not effect a cure, or

whenever anything untoward happens, it would do a great disservice to the profession itself.' That is undoubtedly correct, but he went on to say this: 'We must say, and say firmly, that, in a professional man, an error of judgment is not negligent.' Having regard to the context, I think that Lord Denning MR must have meant to say that an error of judgment 'is not *necessarily* negligent'. But in my respectful opinion, the statement as it stands is not an accurate statement of the law. Merely to describe something as an error of judgment tells us nothing about whether it is negligent or not. The true position is that an error of judgment may, or may not, be negligent; it depends on the nature of the error. If it is one that would not have been made by a reasonably competent professional man professing to have the standard and type of skill that the defendant held himself out as having, and acting with ordinary care, then it is negligent. If, on the other hand, it is an error that a man, acting with ordinary care, might have made, then it is not negligence.

What if the doctor is a specialist? When a doctor holds himself out as being a specialist the standard of care expected by the law was set out by Lord Scarman in *Maynard v West Midlands Regional Health Authority* [1985] 1 All ER 635 at 638: 'I would only add that a doctor who professes to exercise a special skill must exercise the ordinary skill of his speciality.'

What if the doctor is a novice? The well-known Canadian tort scholar, Allan Linden discusses this issue.

A Linden *Canadian Tort Law* (3rd edn) (1991)

Although it has toughened its general standard for specialists, tort law has not diluted it for inexperienced doctors. Hence, a 'novice surgeon' who had not performed a particular operation before was made liable when he severed a nerve. Nor are interns given any special dispensation if they present themselves as being fully qualified. In *Vancouver General Hospital v Fraser* [[1952] 2 SCR 36] two interns licensed to practice within the confines of a hospital wrongly read some X-rays of a car accident victim who came to their hospital, talked to his family doctor and then sent him away. The patient later died as a result of complications from a broken neck, which their examination had failed to detect. Their employer, the hospital, was held vicariously liable for their blunder. Mr Justice Rand based his decision on the fact that the interns' conduct was cloaked with 'all the ritual and paraphernalia of medical science'. An intern had to be 'more than a mere untutored communicant between [the family doctor] and the patient'. He must exercise the 'undertaken degree of skill and that cannot be less than the ordinary skill of a junior doctor'. One of the most vital things he must have is an 'appreciation of his own limitations'. By failing to notify a radiologist who was on call at the hospital and by relying on their own imperfect knowledge, they acted negligently.

Has Rand J in the case referred to answered the question posed? What does 'the ordinary skill of a junior doctor mean'? Does it mean the skill (*sic*) of a novice or some minimum standard of competence which even a junior doctor must have for the particular job involved?

Perhaps, the appropriate rule of English law can be derived from the case of *Nettleship v Weston* [1971] 2 QB 691, [1971] 3 All ER 591, CA. The case concerned a learner-driver who mounted the kerb in a car and damaged a lamp-post. Her instructor also suffered injuries.

Nettleship v Weston [1971] 2 QB 691 (CA)

Lord Denning MR: Mrs Weston is clearly liable for the damage to the lamp-post. In the civil law if a driver goes off the road on to the pavement and injures a pedestrian, or damages property, he is *prima facie* liable. Likewise if he goes on to the wrong side of the road. It is no answer for him to say: 'I was a learner-driver under instruction. I was doing my best and could not help it.' The civil law permits no such excuse. It requires of him the same standard of care as any other driver. 'It eliminates the personal equation and is independent of the idiosyncrasies of the particular person whose conduct is in question': see *Glasgow Corpn v Muir* [[1943] AC 448] *per* Lord Macmillan. The learner-driver may be doing his best, but his incompetent best is not good enough. He must drive in as good a manner as a driver of skill, experience and care, who is sound in wind and limb, who makes no errors of judgment, has good eyesight and hearing, and is free from any infirmity: see *Richley v Faull* [[1965] 1 WLR 1454] and *Watson v Thomas S Witney & Co Ltd* [[1966] 1 WLR 57].

Salmon LJ: I also agree that a learner-driver is responsible and owes a duty in civil laws towards persons on or near the highway to drive with the same degree of skill and care as that of the reasonably competent and experience driver. The duty in civil law springs from the relationship which the driver, by driving on the highway, has created between himself and persons likely to suffer damage by his bad driving . . .

Any driver normally owes exactly the same duty to a passenger in his car as he does to the general public, namely to drive with reasonable care and skill in all the relevant circumstances. As a rule, the driver's personal idiosyncrasy is not a relevant circumstance. In the absence of a special relationship what is reasonable care and skill is measured by the standard of competence usually achieved by the ordinary driver.

Megaw LJ agreed.

The Court of Appeal is saying, in essence, that as a matter of public policy the law must set a standard for the benefit of all below which everyone engaging in risk-creating behaviour may not fall. Thus, a junior doctor would be held to that minimum level of competence necessary for the safety and proper treatment of a patient regardless of his actual level of competence or experience.

The Court of Appeal has settled the question as regards English law in *Wilsher v Essex Health Authority* [1987] QB 730, [1986] 3 All ER 801. We have already seen the facts of this case set out *supra* at p 412.

Wilsher v Essex AHA [1987] QB 730, [1986] 3 All ER 801 (CA)

Mustill LJ: I now turn to the real content of the standard of care. Three propositions were advanced, the first by junior counsel for the plaintiff. It may, I think, be fairly described as setting a 'team' standard of care, whereby each of the persons who formed the staff of the unit held themselves out as capable of undertaking the specialised procedures which that unit set out to perform.

I acknowledge the force of this submission, so far as it calls for recognition of the position which the person said to be negligent held within this specialised unit. But, in so far as the proposition differs from the last of those referred to below, I must dissent, for it is faced with a dilemma. If he seeks to attribute to each individual member of the team a duty to live up to the standards demanded of the unit as a whole, it cannot be right, for it would expose a student nurse to an action in negligence for a failure to possess the skill and experience of a consultant. If, on the other hand, it seeks to fix a standard for the performance of the unit as a whole, this is simply a reformulation of the direct theory of liability which leading counsel for the plaintiff has explicitly disclaimed.

The second proposition (advanced on behalf of the defendants) directs attention to the personal position of the individual member of the staff about whom the complaint is made. What is expected of him is as much as, but no more than, can reasonably be required of a person having his formal qualifications and practical experience. If correct, this proposition entails that the standard of care which the patient is entitled to demand will vary according to the chance of recruitment and rostering. The patient's right to complain of faulty treatment will be more limited if he has been entrusted to the care of a doctor who is a complete novice in the particular field (unless perhaps he can point to some fault of supervision in a person further up the hierarchy) than if he has been in the hands of a doctor who has already spent months on the same ward, and his prospects of holding the health authority vicariously liable for the consequences of any mistreatment will be correspondingly reduced.

To my mind, this notion of a duty tailored to the actor, rather than to the act which he elects to perform, has no place in the law of tort. Indeed, the defendants did not contend that it could be justified by any reported authority on the general law of tort. Instead, it was suggested that the medical profession is a special case. Public hospital medicine has always been organised so that young doctors and nurses learn on the job. If the hospitals abstained from using inexperienced people, they could not staff their wards and theatres, and the junior staff could never learn. The longer-term interests of patients as a whole are best served by maintaining the present system, even if this may diminish the legal rights of the individual patient, for, after all, medicine is about curing, not litigation.

I acknowledge the appeal of this argument, and recognise that a young hospital doctor who must get onto the wards in order to qualify without necessarily being able to decide what kind of patient he is going to meet is not in the same position as another professional man who has a real choice whether or not to practise in a particular field. Nevertheless, I cannot accept that there be a special rule for doctors in public hospitals; I emphasise *public*, since presumably those employed in private hospitals would be in a different category. Doctors are not the only people who gain their experience, not only from lectures or from watching others perform, but from tackling live clients or customers, and no case was cited to us which suggested that any such variable duty of care was imposed on others in a similar position. To my mind, it would be a false step to subordinate the legitimate expectation of the patient that he will receive from each person concerned with his care a degree of skill appropriate to the task which he undertakes to an understandable wish to minimise the psychological and financial pressures on hard-pressed young doctors.

For my part, I prefer the third of the propositions which have been canvassed. This relates the duty of care, not to the individual, but to the post which he occupies. I would differentiate 'post' from 'rank' or 'status'. In a case such as the present, the standard is not just that of the averagely competent and well-informed junior houseman (or whatever the position of the doctor) but of such a person who fills a post in a unit offering a highly specialised service. But, even so, it must be recognised that different posts make different demands. If it is borne in mind that the structure of hospital medicine envisages that the lower ranks will be occupied by those of whom it would be wrong to expect too much, the risk of abuse by litigious patients can be mitigated, if not entirely eliminated.

Glidewell LJ agreed.

Glidewell LJ: In my view, the law requires the trainee or learner to be judged by the same standard as his more experienced colleagues. If it did not, inexperience would frequently be urged as a defence to an action for professional negligence.

If this test appears unduly harsh in relation to the inexperienced, I should add that, in my view, the inexperienced doctor called on to exercise a specialist skill will, as part of that skill, seek the advice and help of his superiors when he does or may need it. If he does seek such help, he will often have satisfied the test, even though he may himself have made a mistake.

Sir Nicolas Browne-Wilkinson V-C dissented.

Browne-Wilkinson V-C: In English law, liability for personal injury requires a finding of personal fault (eg negligence) against someone. In cases of vicarious liability such as this, there must have been personal fault by the employee or agent of the defendant for whom the defendant is held vicariously liable. Therefore, even though no claim is made against the individual doctor, the liability of the defendant health authority is dependent on a finding of personal fault by one or more of the individual doctors. The general standard of care required of a doctor is that he would exercise the skill of a skilled doctor in the treatment which he has taken on himself to offer.

Such being the general standard of care required of a doctor, it is normally no answer for him to say the treatment he gave was of a specialist or technical nature in which he was inexperienced. In such a case, the fault of the doctor lies in embarking on giving treatment which he could not skilfully offer: he should not have undertaken the treatment but should have referred the patient to someone possessing the necessary skills.

But the position of the houseman in his first year after qualifying or of someone (like Dr Wiles in this case) who has just started in a specialist field in order to gain the necessary skill in that field is not capable of such analysis. The houseman has to take up his post in order to gain full professional qualification; anyone who, like Dr Wiles, wishes to obtain specialist skills has to learn those skills by taking a post in a specialist unit. In my judgment, such doctors cannot in fairness be said to be at fault if, at the start of their time, they lack the very skills which they are seeking to acquire.

In my judgment, if the standard of care required of such a doctor is that he should have the skill required of the post he occupies, the young houseman or the doctor seeking to obtain specialist skills in a special unit would be held liable for shortcomings in the treatment without any personal fault on his part at all. Of course, such a doctor would be negligent if he undertook treatment for which he knows he lacks the necessary experience and skill. But one of the chief hazards of inexperience is that one does not always know the risks which exist. In my judgment, so long as the English law rests liability on personal fault, a doctor who has properly accepted a post in a hospital in order to gain necessary experience should only be held liable for acts or omissions which a careful doctor with his qualifications and experience would not have done or omitted. It follows that, in my view, the health authority could not be held vicariously liable (and I stress the word *vicariously*) for the acts of such a learner who has come up to those standards, notwithstanding that the post he held required greater experience than he in fact possessed.

Does the mere reference to the 'post' help? Is not Mustill LJ, with respect, confused by not really talking about a doctor with minimum competence for the task? Arguably Mustill LJ could have decided the case on the basis that the doctor should never have carried out the procedure complained of because he lacked a minimum competence.

Given the law is as the majority have stated it, how can the law accommodate the needs of public policy that a doctor learns at least part of the job through work experience? The answer must lie in the notion of supervision. If a doctor lacks a minimum competence to carry out a particular procedure but it is proper for him to be present, eg as a learner, then whatever he does must be done under the supervision of the experienced doctor. The negligence, if any, will now be that of the experienced doctor for failure adequately to supervise (this is what Glidewell LJ decided in *Wilsher*, as we have seen).

What of the situation, however, where the inexperienced doctor does not realise his own incompetence and so does not seek supervision? You will recall the words of the Vice-Chancellor in *Wilsher* '. . . one of the chief hazards of inexperience is that one does not always know the risks which exist'. Does *reasonable* supervision contemplate *constant* supervision or something else? If it be the former will the experienced doctor *necessarily* be liable? This cannot, in our view, be the law. As a matter of public policy it is recognised that the medical profession, like any other profession, can only acquire some knowledge and skill by taking independent responsibility albeit within the context of overall supervision by the more experienced.

This does leave unanswered the point raised by the Vice-Chancellor: 'the rights of a patient entering hospital will depend on the experience of the doctor who treats him'. This may somewhat overstate the case but certainly there is a problem here. One answer is the Vice-Chancellor's recourse to the primary liability of the hospital. Another answer is to recall the law relating to consent and consider what information the patient ought to be told so as to make any consent valid.

Linden (*op cit*) in discussing the Canadian law asks the question 'Whether a lower standard of care would be acceptable if an intern junior doctor identified himself as such to the patient?' In effect, Linden is asking whether a patient may by agreement lower the standard of care otherwise imposed by law. In *Nettleship v Weston* there was a difference of opinion.

Lord Denning MR: Mrs Weston took her son with her in the car. We do not know his age. He may have been 21 and have known that his mother was learning to drive. He was not injured. But if he had been injured, would he have had a cause of action? I take it to be clear that, if a driver has a passenger in the car, he owes a duty of care to him. But what is the standard of care required of the driver? Is it a lower standard than he or she owes towards a pedestrian on the pavement? I should have thought not. But suppose that the driver has never driven a car before, or has taken too much to drink, or has poor eyesight or hearing; and, furthermore, that the passenger *knows* it and yet accepts a lift from him. Does that make any difference? Dixon J thought it did. In *Insurance Comr v Joyce* [(1948) 77 CLR 39] he said:

> If a man accepts a lift from a car-driven whom he *knows* to have lost a limb or an eye or to be deaf, he cannot complain if he does not exhibit the skill and competence of a driver who suffers from no defect. . . If he knowingly accepts the voluntary services of a driver affected by drink, he cannot complain of improper driving caused by his condition, because it involves no breach of duty.

That view of Dixon J seems to have been followed in South Australia, see *Walker v Turton-Sainsbury*, but in the Supreme Court of Canada Rand J did not agree with it: see *Carr and General Insurance Corpn Ltd v Seymour and Maloney*.

We have all the greatest respect for Sir Owen Dixon, but for once I cannot agree with him. The driver owes a duty of care to every passenger in the car, just as he does to every pedestrian on the road; and he must attain the same standard of care in respect of each.

Megaw LJ agreed on this point. Salmon LJ, however, disagreed.

> **Salmon LJ:** . . . [T]here may be special facts creating a special relationship which displaces this standard or even negatives any duty, although the onus would certainly be on the driver to establish such facts. With minor reservations I respectfully agree with and adopt the reasoning and conclusions of Sir Owen Dixon in his judgment in *Insurance Comr v Joyce*. I do not however agree that the mere fact that the driver has, to the knowledge of his passenger, lost a limb or an eye or is deaf can affect the duty which he owes the passenger to drive safely. It is well known that many drivers suffering from such disabilities drive with no less skill and competence than the ordinary man. The position, however, is totally different when, to the knowledge of the passenger, the driver is so drunk as to be incapable of driving safely. Quite apart from being negligent, a passenger who accepts a lift in such circumstances clearly cannot expect the driver to drive other than dangerously.
>
> The duty of care springs from relationship. The special relationship which the passenger has created by accepting a lift in the circumstances postulated surely cannot entitle him to expect the driver to discharge a duty of care or skill which ex hypothesi the passenger knows the driver is incapable of discharging. Accordingly in such circumstances, no duty is owed by the driver to the passenger to drive safely . . .

In the context of medical treatment the law will probably reflect a court's unwillingness to accept that any agreement by the patient is really *voluntary* rather than reached under the duress of the circumstances. Two further questions also ought to be asked: What standard of care would the law expect of a doctor (a) who, unknown to the patient, had particular expertise beyond that normally found? and (b) who professed greater expertise to the patient than in fact he had?

The answers to these questions should take as a starting point the proposition that a professional will be held to the standard of care he possesses or professes in excess of the minimum standard required by law if this is what he claims to have.

Wimpey Construction UK Ltd v Poole [1984] 2 Lloyd's Rep 499 (Webster J)

> The plaintiffs constructed a quay wall. Cracks occurred in the structure and repairs were effected. The plaintiffs claimed the costs under a professional indemnity insurance policy held with the defendant in respect of 'any omission, error or negligent act in respect of design or specification of work'. The issue which arose was whether the plaintiffs were in breach of their duty.
>
> **Webster J:** [Counsel] on behalf of Wimpeys sought to put two glosses on the [*Bolam*] test for the purposes of this case. The first is that, as he submits, the test is not 'the standard of the ordinary skilled man exercising and professing to have that special skill' if the client deliberately obtains and pays for someone with specially high skills.

Mr Justice Megarry, as he then was, considered but did not decide the question in the *Duchess of Argyll v Beuselinck* [1972] 2 Lloyd's Rep 172, a claim of negligence against a solicitor. At pp 183-184 he said:

> ... One question that arose during the argument was that of the standard of care required of a solicitor; and although Counsel did their best to assist me, the question remained obscure. It was common ground that, at any rate in normal cases, an action for negligence by a solicitor is an action in contract: see *Groom v Crocker* [1939] 1 KB 194. At one stage, Mr Arnold asserted that this was of importance only in regard to limitation; but I think that later he accepted that this was too restricted a view. I can see that in actions in tort, the standard of care to be applied will normally be that of the reasonable man: those lacking in care and skill fail to observe the standards of the reasonable man at their peril, and the unusually careful and highly skilled are not held liable for falling below their own high standards if they nevertheless do all that a reasonable man would have done. But to say that in tort the standard of care is uniform does not necessarily carry the point in circumstances where the action is for breach of an implied duty of care in a contract whereby a client retains a solicitor. No doubt the inexperienced solicitor is liable if he fails to attain the standard of a reasonably competent solicitor. But if the client employs a solicitor of high standard and great experience, will an action for negligence fail if it appears that the solicitor did not exercise the care and skill to be expected of him though he did not fall below the standard of a reasonably competent solicitor? If the client engages an expert, and doubtless expects to pay commensurate fees, is he not entitled to expect something more than the standard of the reasonably competent? I am speaking not merely of those expert in a particular branch of the law, as contrasted with a general practitioner, but also of those of long experience and great skill as contrasted with those practising in the same field of the law but being of a more ordinary calibre and having less experience. The essence of the contract of retainer, it may be said, is that the client is retaining the particular solicitor or firm in question, and he is therefore entitled to expect from that solicitor or firm a standard of care and skill commensurate with the skill and experience which that solicitor or firm has. The uniform standard of care postulated for the world at large in tort hardly seems appropriate when the duty is not one imposed by the law of tort but arises from a contractual obligation existing between the client and the particular solicitor or firm in question. If, as is usual, the retainer contains no express term as to the solicitor's duty of care, and the matter rests upon an implied term, what is that term in the case of a solicitor of long experience or specialist skill? Is it that he will put at his client's disposal the care and skill of an average solicitor, or the care and skill that he has? I may say that Mr Arnold advanced no contention that it was the latter standard that was to be applied; but I wish to make it clear that I have not overlooked the point, which one day may require further consideration.

According to the researchers of Council that question has not yet received further consideration. Mr Justice Oliver, as he then was, referred to the *Duchess of Argyll's* case in *Midland Bank Trust Co Ltd v Hett, Stubbs and Kemp* [1979] Ch 384 at 403, but without, apparently, modifying the conventional test and for my part, if the question be material, I feel constrained by the clear words of the test as expressed by Mr Justice McNair, and by the approval of that test without qualification by the Privy Council and the House of Lords, to treat it as unqualified. Since the hearing ended I have considered the judgment of Mr Justice Kilner Brown in *Greaves & Co (Contractors) Ltd v Baynham Meikle & Partners* [1975] 1 Lloyd's Rep 31, [1974] 1 WLR 1261 where a similar point was considered. The decision in that case, however, rested on 'special circumstances' (see pp 35 and 1269 C-D) and is not, in my view, inconsistent with the conclusion I have reached.

2. Compliance with approved practice

The central question can be shortly stated: who sets the legal standard of care with which doctors must comply? Is it, as you would ordinarily expect, the law; or is it the medical profession? If it be the latter, this would mean that the medical profession would not only be offering evidence of good practice (a factual matter) but also determining what doctors ought to do (a legal matter).

The prevailing view, certainly in the medical profession and perhaps in the courts, is that it is indeed the medical profession which sets the legal standard. Let us now see how this has come about. We must first set out the state of the existing law.

(a) The case law

(i) CASES IN WHICH THERE IS ONLY ONE PROFESSIONAL PRACTICE

Marshall v Lindsey County Council [1935] 1 KB 516 (CA)

Maugham LJ: The practice of the Home in not refusing fresh patients after a single case of puerperal sepsis had occurred, taking, however, the recognised sterilisation precautions, is in accordance with the universal practice of maternity homes and hospitals throughout England. The Ministry of Health is in constant communication with the authorities in charge of maternity homes and hospitals. It has held many inquiries and has issued a number of reports and leaflets in connection with the problem of reducing maternal mortality. It is not suggested that the Ministry has ever proposed the drastic step which the jury appear to favour. In these circumstances I am of opinion that the defendant Council, assuming their responsibility for the acts of the medical officers and nursing staff, have acted in accordance with the recognised practice and are therefore free from liability on the ground of negligence. This is a matter of great importance in relation to the powers of juries. An act cannot, in my opinion, be held to be due to a want of reasonable care if it is in accordance with the general practice of mankind. What is reasonable in a world not wholly composed of wise men and women must depend on what people presumed to be reasonable constantly do. Many illustrations might be given and I will take one from the evidence given in this action. A jury could not, in my opinion, properly hold it to be negligent in a doctor or a midwife to perform his or her duties in a confinement without mask and gloves, even though some experts gave evidence that in their opinion that was a wise precaution. Such an omission may become negligent if, and only if, at some future date it becomes the general custom to take such a precaution among skilled practitioners.
    ... I do not doubt the general truth ... that a defendant charged with negligence can clear himself if he shows that he has acted in accord with general and approved practice.

Did it enter the mind of the court that the fact that there is unanimity in the profession may not entail the conclusion that this unanimously approved practice is legally appropriate as being *reasonable*? In other words why cannot a judgment of reasonableness be made by anyone other than a doctor?

Maugham LJ referred to the earlier case in the Privy Council of *Vancouver General Hospital v McDaniel* (1934) 152 LT 56. The plaintiff contracted smallpox while being treated in hospital for diphtheria. The Privy Council held that the defendants were not negligent because the expert evidence showed that the hospital's procedures for treating smallpox and preventing other patients catching it were in accordance with the general practice in Canada and the USA. Lord Alness said it was: 'difficult to affirm that negligence on the part of the [defendants] is proved. A defendant charged with negligence can clear his feet if he shows that he has acted in accordance with general and approved practice.'

Maugham LJ's *dictum* was approved by the House of Lords in *Whiteford v Hunter* [1950] WN 553 (*per* Lord Porter).

(ii) CASES IN WHICH THERE ARE TWO SCHOOLS OF THOUGHT

Maynard v West Midlands Regional Health Authority [1985] 1 All ER 635 (HL)

Lord Scarman: My Lords, the question in this appeal is whether a physician and a surgeon, working together in the treatment of their patient, were guilty of an error of professional judgment of such a character as to constitute a breach of their duty of care towards her. The negligence alleged against each, or one or other, of them is that contrary to the strong medical indications which should have led them to diagnose tuberculosis they held back from a firm diagnosis and decided that she should undergo the diagnostic operation, mediastinoscopy. It was an operation which carried certain risks, even when correctly performed, as it is admitted that it was in this case. One of the risks, namely damage to the left laryngeal recurrent nerve, did, as the judge has found and the respondent authority now accepts, unfortunately materialise with resulting paralysis of the left vocal cord. Comyn J, the trial judge, held that the two doctors were negligent. The Court of Appeal (Cumming-Bruce LJ and Sir Stanley Rees, Dunn LJ dissenting) held that they were not. The only issue for the House is whether the two medical men, Dr Ross who was the consultant physician and Mr Stephenson the surgeon, were guilty of an error of judgment amounting to a breach of their duty of care to their patient. Both accept that the refusal to make a firm diagnosis until they had available the findings of the diagnostic operation was one for which they were jointly responsible.

The issue is essentially one of fact; but there remains the possibility, which it will be necessary to examine closely, that the judge, although directing himself correctly as to the law, failed to apply it correctly when he came to draw the inferences on which his conclusion of negligence was based. Should this possibility be established as the true interpretation to be put on his judgment, he would, of course, be guilty of an error of law. . . .

The only . . . question of law in the appeal is as to the nature of the duty owed by a doctor to his patient. . . .

The present case may be classified as one of clinical judgment. Two distinguished consultants, a physician and a surgeon experienced in the treatment of chest diseases, formed a judgment as to what was, in their opinion, in the best interests of their patient. They recommended that tuberculosis was the most likely diagnosis. But in their opinion, there was an unusual factor, viz swollen glands in the mediastinum unaccompanied by any evidence of lesion in the lungs. Hodgkin's disease, carcinoma, and sarcoidosis were, therefore, possibilities. The danger they thought was Hodgkin's disease; though unlikely, it was, if present, a killer (as treatment was understood in 1970) unless remedial steps were taken in its early stage. They therefore decided on mediastinoscopy, an operative procedure which would provide them with a biopsy from the swollen gland which could be subjected to immediate microscopic examination. It is said that the evidence of tuberculosis was so strong that it was unreasonable and wrong to defer diagnosis and to put their patient to the risks of the operation. The case against them is not mistake or carelessness in performing the operation, which it is admitted was properly carried out, but an error of judgment in requiring the operation to be undertaken.

A case which is based on an allegation that a fully considered decision of two consultants in the field of their special skill was negligent clearly presents certain difficulties of proof. It is not enough to show that there is a body of competent professional opinion which considers that theirs was a wrong decision, if there also exists a body of professional opinion, equally competent, which supports the decision as reasonable in the circumstances. It is not enough to show that subsequent events show that the operation need never have been performed, if at the time the decision to operate was taken it was reasonable in the sense that a responsible body of medical opinion would have accepted it as proper. I do not think that the words of the Lord President (Clyde) in *Hunter v Hanley* 1955 SLT 213 at 217 can be bettered:

> In the realm of diagnosis and treatment there is ample scope for genuine difference of opinion and one man clearly is not negligent merely because his conclusion differs from that of other professional men . . . The true test for establishing negligence in diagnosis or treatment on the part of a doctor is whether he has been proved to be guilty of such failure as no doctor of ordinary skill would be guilty of if acting with ordinary care . . .

. . . The judge accepted not only the expertise of all the medical witnesses called before him but also their truthfulness and honesty. But he found Dr Hugh-Jones 'an outstanding witness; clear, definite, logical and persuasive'. The judge continued:

> I have weighed his evidence against that of the distinguished contrary experts. I do not intend or wish to take away from their distinction by holding that in the particular circumstances of this particular case I prefer his opinions and his evidence to theirs.

My Lords . . . I have to say that a judge's 'preference' for one body of distinguished professional opinion to another also professionally distinguished is not sufficient to establish negligence in a practitioner whose actions have received the seal of approval of those whose opinions, truthfully expressed, honestly held, were not preferred. If this was the real reason for the judge's finding, he erred in law even though elsewhere in his judgment he stated the law correctly. For in the realm of diagnosis and treatment negligence is not established by preferring one respectable body of professional opinion to another. Failure to exercise the ordinary skill of a doctor (in the appropriate speciality, if he be a specialist) is necessary.

This case merely reflects the approach of McNair J in *Bolam* (which we have already seen) where he said:

> A doctor is not guilty of negligence if he has acted in accordance with a practice accepted as proper by a responsible body of medical men skilled in that particular art.
> . . . Putting it the other way round, a doctor is not negligent, if he is acting in accordance with such a practice, merely there is a body of opinion that takes a contrary view.

A little later, however, McNair J said something you might find rather curious:

> Before I deal with the details of the case, it is right to say this, that it is not essential for you to decide which of two practices is the better practice, as long as you accept that what Dr Allfrey did was in accordance with a practice accepted by responsible persons; but if the result of the evidence is that you are satisfied that this practice is better than the practice spoken of on the other side, then it is a stronger case.

Does this not suggest that it is ultimately for the law to decide (and not for the medical profession) whether the doctor's conduct is reasonable?

(b) Comment on the case law

What seems to have happened is that the House of Lords in *Maynard* and also, as we will see, in *Sidaway* have elevated to the status of an unquestionable proposition of law derived from *Bolam* that professional practice *will not* be reviewed by the courts.

In the *Sidaway* case Lord Scarman made this quite clear: 'The *Bolam* principle may be formulated as a rule that a doctor is not negligent if he acts in accordance with a practice accepted at the time as proper by a responsible body of medical opinion even though other doctors adopt a different practice. In short, the law imposes the duty of care: but the standard of care is a matter of medical judgment.' This widely accepted interpretation of *Bolam* was followed by the Court of Appeal in *Hughes v Waltham Forest HA* [1991] 2 Med LR 155.

> **Beldam LJ:** In this case the allegations of fault with which the learned judge had to deal called in question the fully considered decision of two surgeons in a specialist field of surgery in which they were skilled and experienced. Their decision was endorsed as being in accordance with a practice accepted as proper within the profession by an eminent surgeon practising in the same field. There was evidence that the specialist unit which would have conducted the ERCP examination also considered the decision a proper one. The fact that two other distinguished surgeons were critical of the decision, or that the decision ultimately turned out to be mistaken, does not prove that Mr Wellwood and Mr Bursle fell short of the standard of care to be expected of competent surgeons.
>
> This was made abundantly clear by the decision in *Maynard v West Midlands Regional Health Authority* [1984] 1 WLR 634. . . .
>
> For the reasons I have given, the learned judge misdirected himself when deciding that Mr Wellwood and Mr Bursle were at fault in not referring the deceased for the ERCP examination. If he had applied the correct test, I consider that he could only have arrived at the conclusion that no fault had been proved against them in that respect.

Two questions arise:

(i)   Is this good law?
(ii) Is this law good?

(i) IS THIS GOOD LAW?

Consider the non-medical cases first.

Cavanagh v Ulster Weaving Co Ltd [1960] AC 145, [1959] 2 All ER 745 (HL)

The appellant, a labourer employed by the respondents, was carrying a bucket of cement weighing some three stones down a roof ladder laid flat against the slated aspect of a slanting roof. He put the bucket down on a plank before starting to descend the ladder facing forwards. Having placed his feet in a position on the second or third rung of the ladder from the top, he had to turn to pick up the bucket and in so doing slipped and fell some six feet against a sloping glass roof opposite him and injured himself. There was no handrail with which he could support himself with one hand as he descended the ladder with the bucket in the other hand, nor was there any protection to save him from the glass in the opposite roof if he should slip. He was wearing rubber boots which had been provided by the respondent in view of an accumulation of water in the gully between the slanting roofs along which he had to proceed after descending the ladder. In an action by the appellant against the respondents for damages for personal injuries, there was evidence that the rubber boots were two sizes larger than they should have been for a man with feet the size of the appellant's. An expert witness for the respondents was asked in relation to the system adopted for the carrying of cement on the roof, how far 'this set up' was in accord with good practice, and he testified it was perfectly in accord with good practice. His evidence was uncontradicted. A submission on behalf of the respondents that there was no evidence of negligence to go to the jury was disallowed. The jury found that the respondents had been negligent. The Court of Appeal allowed an appeal by the respondents. The House of Lords unanimously allowed the appellant's further appeal.

Viscount Simonds: The evidence given by the expert called for the defence in regard to what was called 'the set up', which was not seriously or perhaps at all challenged, was of very great weight, but I cannot say that it was so conclusive as to require the learned trial judge to withdraw the case from the jury. There were other matters also which they were entitled to take into consideration, and it was for them to determine whether, in all the circumstances, the respondents had taken reasonable care. I do not think that the learned judges of the Court of Appeal were justified in concluding that reasonable men might not find the verdict which this jury found. If I may respectfully say so, I think that the error of the majority of the court lay in treating as conclusive evidence which is not conclusive however great its weight, particularly where it has to be weighed against other evidence.

As to the evidence of practice, Lord Tucker said:

Lord Tucker: My Lords, I have already expressed my views on the value of this kind of evidence in *Morris v West Hartlepool Steam Navigation Co Ltd* ([1956] 1 All ER 385 at 400) which I need not repeat, but it was not necessary for me in that case to refer to the language of Lord Dunedin in *Morton v William Dixon, Ltd*. I would, however, desire to express my agreement with what was said by my noble and learned friend, Lord Cohen, in *Morris's* case where, after reviewing what had been said on this subject in *Paris v Stepney Borough Council* ([1951] 1 All ER 42), and considering the language used by Parker LJ, in the case under consideration, he said ([1956] 1 All ER at 402):

> I think that the effect of their Lordships' observations is that, when the court finds a clearly established practice 'in like circumstances', the practice weighs heavily in the scale on the side of the defendant and the burden of establishing negligence, which the plaintiff has to discharge, is a heavy one. . . .

Mr Lords, I would respectfully accept the statement of the law on this subject in the present case by the Lord Chief Justice (Lord MacDermott) . . .
He said that, where positive evidence is adduced for the defendant that an employer has not omitted to do anything that is commonly done by other persons in like circumstances,

Such a fact is clearly relevant, and once it is established, it is my opinion that a finding by the jury that it was folly in the [respondents] to neglect to provide something else, cannot be justified.

In *Thompson v Smiths Shiprepairers (North Shields) Ltd* [1984] QB 405, [1984] 1 All ER 881, the plaintiffs worked in shipbuilding yards for many years. They were exposed to excessive noise which, they alleged, affected their hearing. In an action for negligence brought against their employers, the trial judge, Mustill J (as he then was) considered the relevance of industrial practice in determining whether the employers were in breach of their duty to the plaintiffs.

Thompson v Smiths Shiprepairers (North Shields) [1984] QB 405 (QBD)

Mustill J: The plaintiffs allege that the defendants were negligent in the following respects: (i) in failing to recognise the existence of high levels of noise in their shipyards, and the fact that such noise created a risk of irreversible damage to hearing; (ii) in failing to provide any or sufficient ear protection devices, or to give the necessary advice and encouragement for the wearing of such devices as were provided; (iii) in failing to investigate and take advice on the noise levels in their yards; (iv) in failing to reduce the noise created by work in their yards; (v) in failing to organise the layout and timing of the work so as to minimise the effect of noise. In the first instance I will concentrate on items (i) and (ii), since these are by far the most substantial.

There was general agreement that the principles to be applied when weighing up allegations of this kind are correctly set out in the following passage from the judgment of Swanwick J in *Stokes v GKN (Bolts and Nuts) Ltd* [1968] 1 WLR 1776 at 1783:

> From these authorities I deduce the principles, that the overall test is still the conduct of the reasonable and prudent employer, taking positive thought for the safety of his workers in the light of what he knows or ought to know; where there is a recognised and general practice which has been followed for a substantial period in similar circumstances without mishap, he is entitled to follow it, unless in the light of common sense or newer knowledge, it is clearly bad; but, where there is developing knowledge, he must keep reasonably abreast of it and not be too slow to apply it; and where he has in fact greater than average knowledge of the risk, he may be thereby obliged to take more than the average or standard precautions. He must weigh up the risk in terms of the likelihood of injury occurring and the potential consequences if it does; and he must balance against this the probable effectiveness of the precautions that can be taken to meet it and the expense and inconvenience they involve. If he is found to have fallen below the standard to be properly expected of a reasonable and prudent employer in these respects, he is negligent.

I shall direct myself in accordance with this succinct and helpful statement of the law, and will make only one additional comment. In the passage just cited, Swanwick J drew a distinction between a recognised practice followed without mishap, and one which in the light of common sense or increased knowledge is clearly bad. The distinction is indeed valid and sufficient for many cases. The two categories are not, however, exhaustive, as the present actions demonstrate. The practice of leaving employees unprotected against excessive noise had never been followed 'without mishap'. Yet even the plaintiffs have not suggested that it was 'clearly bad', in the sense of creating a potential liability in negligence, at any time before the mid 1930s. Between the two extremes is a type of risk which is regarded at any given time (although not necessarily later) as an inescapable feature of the industry. The employer is not liable for the consequences of such risks, although subsequent changes in social awareness, or improvements in knowledge and technology, may transfer the risk into the category of those against which the employer can and should take care. It is unnecessary, and perhaps impossible, to give a comprehensive formula for identifying the line between the acceptable and the unacceptable. Nevertheless, the line does exist, and was clearly recognised in *Morris v West Hartlepool Steam Navigation Co Ltd* [1956] 1 All ER 385, [1956] AC 552. The speeches in that case show, not that one employer is exonerated simply by proving that other employers are just as negligent, but that the standard of what is negligent is influenced, although not decisively, by the practice in the industry as a whole. In my judgment, this principle applies not only where the breach of duty is said to consist of a failure to take precautions known to be available as a means of combating a known danger, but also where the omission involves an absence of initiative in seeking out knowledge of facts which are not in themselves obvious. The employer must keep up to date, but the court must be slow to blame him for not ploughing a lone furrow.

(The judge held that, on the facts, the defendants were not careless in respect of exposure to noise before 1963 but were thereafter.)

Even in professional negligence cases, compliance with approved practice has not been considered conclusive in determining whether a breach of duty has occurred. In *Edward Wong Finance Co Ltd v Johnson, Stokes and Master* [1984] AC 296, the Privy Council held that the defendant solicitors were careless even though they had complied with the 'normal customary conveyancing practice in Hong Kong'. The Privy Council approved the dissenting judgment of Li JA in the Hong Kong Court of Appeal.

Li JA: The test for negligence or otherwise in this case means whether a reasonable, diligent and competent solicitor could foresee in January 1976 that damage could result by adopting the Hong Kong practice of completion. . . . Applying this test to the present case I find Miss Leung, as a solicitor when adopting the Hong Kong practice for completion in January 1976 complied with the general practice which had been practised for years without ill result of the form of damage as in this case flowing from it. That goes a long way to show that she was not negligent. However, that is not conclusive. The further question to be asked is: could she foresee the risk of ill result at the material time as an ordinary, reasonably prudent person? I am afraid the answer must be in the affirmative. As a solicitor, even in January 1976, she should know that her client, the plaintiff, would not obtain what it lent its money for unless and until the vendor had executed the assignment and delivered the title deeds. If she parted with the money without such delivery she did not receive what her client had paid for apart from an undertaking or a promise by a fellow member of her profession. As a reasonable person of ordinary prudence she should or ought to have foreseen the risk of parting with the money before obtaining the property one bought in any ordinary transaction. It was not her skill that was put to test. It was her common sense, her prudence of any ordinary person that is put to test. The so called Hong Kong practice has an inherent risk in the ordinary sense. The fact that practically all her fellow solicitors adopted this practice is not conclusive evidence that it is prudent . . . acting in accordance with the general practice she took a foreseeable risk for her client while there was no necessity to do so. The fact that other solicitors did the same did not make the risk less apparent or unreal.

Why should the court approach a medical case any differently? What appears to have happened is that because technical matters are involved, on which expert evidence is needed, courts have regarded the issue of the standard of care as itself a technical matter for the profession. This is, of course, to fail to distinguish between what *is* ordinarily done and what *should* be done. As regards the latter, the court may in certain circumstances have something to say as the guardian of the interests of society, as the cases above show.

Consider now cases involving medical practice.

F v R (1983) 33 SASR 189 (Supreme Court of South Australia)

A married woman was advised to have a tubal ligation operation to sterilise her when she desired to have no further children. Although the operation was competently performed, the procedure naturally reversed itself sometime later and the plaintiff became pregnant. She brought an action in negligence against the doctor who had advised her for failing to warn her of the less than 1% failure rate. Evidence was given that this was in conformity with a responsible body of medical opinion. The Supreme Court held that the defendant had not been careless.

King CJ: In answering that question [whether the doctor is in breach of his duty] much assistance will be derived from evidence as to the practice obtaining in the medical profession. I am unable to accept, however, that such evidence can be decisive in all circumstances . . . There is great force in the following passage from the judgment of the Supreme Court of Canada in *Reibl v Hughes* (1980) 114 DLR (3d) 1:

> To allow expert medical evidence to determine what risks are material and, hence, should be disclosed and, correlatively, what risks are not material is to hand over to the medical profession the entire question of the scope of the duty of disclosure, including the question whether there has been a breach of that duty. Expert medical evidence is, of course, relevant to findings as to the risks that reside in or are a result of recommended surgery or other treatment. It will also have a bearing on their materiality but this is not a question that is to be concluded on the basis of the expert medical evidence alone. The issue under consideration is a different issue from that involved where the question is whether the doctor carried out his professional activities by applicable professional standards. What is under consideration here is the patient's right to know what risks are involved in undergoing or foregoing certain surgery or other treatment.

In many cases an approved professional practice as to disclosure will be decisive. But professions may adopt unreasonable practices. Practices may develop in professions, particularly as to disclosure, not because they serve the interests of the clients, but because they protect the interests or convenience of members of the profession. The court has an obligation to scrutinize professional practices to ensure that they accord with the standard of reasonableness imposed by the law. A practice as to disclosure approved and adopted by a profession or a section of it may be in many cases the determining consideration as to what is reasonable. On the facts of a particular case the answer to the question whether the defendant's conduct conformed to approved professional practice may decide the issue of negligence, and the test has been posed in such terms in a number of cases. The ultimate question, however, is not whether the defendant's conduct accords with the practices of his profession or some part of it, but whether it conforms to the standard of reasonable care demanded by the law. That is a question for the Court and the duty of deciding it cannot be delegated to any profession or group in the community.

. . . It is for the Court to decide what a careful and responsible doctor would explain to the patient in the circumstances, and I do not regard as decisive the opinions of the medical witnesses on the point or the existence of a practice of non-disclosure in a section of the profession. If the Court thought that that practice involved a failure to exercise reasonable care towards the patient, I would regard it as its duty to give effect to that view. Indeed I am of opinion that the better practice, and that which accords best with the rights and interests of the patient, is that adopted by those doctors who do warn of the possibility, however slight, of subsequent pregnancy. But this is not to say that in following the non-disclosure practice, the appellant was in breach of her duty of care to the patient. In the totality of the circumstances which I have discussed, and bearing in mind that the appellant was acting in pursuance of a considered judgment as to what was in the best interests of her patient and of a practice followed by a substantial part, probably the greater part, of those medical practitioners practising in this area of medical practice, I consider that her failure to volunteer the information as to the possibility of future pregnancy was not in breach of the legal duty of care.

Bollen J added the following remarks.

Bollen J: Mr Perry's [counsel for the doctor] answer was that the responsible body of medical opinion should prevail over the view of the Court. That would mean that there was no room for the opinion of the Court on vital issues. The Court's function would be limited to ascertaining that there was a responsible body of medical opinion and deciding whether the surgeon had followed it.

Many cases require the calling of expert evidence. These experts frequently express opinions on matters within their field. Sometimes they speak of what is usually done in any activity within that field. Why is the evidence received? It is received to guide or help the court. A court cannot be expected to know the correct procedure for performing a surgical operation. The Court cannot be expected to know why a manufacturer should guard against metal fatigue. A court cannot be expected to know how to mix chemicals. And so on. Expert evidence will assist the Court. But in the end it is the Court which must say whether there was a duty owed and a breach of it. The Court will have been guided and assisted by the expert evidence. It will not produce an answer merely at the dictation of the expert evidence. It will afford great weight to the expert evidence. Sometimes its decision will be the same as it would have been had it accepted dictation. But the Court does not merely follow expert evidence slavishly to a decision. The Court considers and weighs up all admissible evidence which it has received. If the Court did merely follow the path apparently pointed by expert evidence with no critical consideration of it and the other evidence, it would abdicate its duty to decide, on the evidence, whether in law a duty existed and had not been discharged. Acceptance of Mr Perry's first submission could amount to abdication here.

. . . I can find nothing in *Bolam v Friern Hospital Management Committee* which justifies any suggestion that evidence of the practice obtaining in the medical profession is automatically decisive of any issue in an action against a surgeon for damages in negligence. Sometimes that evidence will be decisive, sometimes not. It is least likely to be decisive when the allegation is of a failure to warn or to heed complaints of pain ie where no information about the method of procedure or basis of diagnosis is required.

. . . I respectfully think that some of the cases in England have concentrated rather too heavily on the practice of the medical profession.

Admittedly, this was a case on disclosure of risks inherent in a medical procedure. You will recall the difference of opinion about the relevance of professional practice in cases of disclosure of information exemplified in the *Sidaway* case.

We saw that the majority of the House of Lords in *Sidaway* were not wholly content to import the *Bolam* principle into this area of law. In the Court of Appeal in *Sidaway*, Sir John Donaldson MR seemed anxious to point out that *Bolam* had been misunderstood. To him, what doctors do is only to be regarded as lawful provided the law considers what they do to be *right*.

Sidaway v Board of Governors of Bethlem Royal Hospital [1984] 1 All ER 1018 (CA)

Sir John Donaldson MR: I accept the view expressed by Laskin CJC [in *Reibl v Hughes*] that the definition of the duty of care is not to be handed over to the medical or any other profession. The definition of the duty of care is a matter for the law and the courts. They cannot stand idly by if the profession, by an excess of paternalism, denies its patients a real choice. In a word, the law will not permit the medical profession to play God.

Thus, while I accept the *Bolam* test as the primary test of liability for failing to disclose sufficient information to the patient to enable that patient to exercise his right of choice whether or not to accept the advice proffered by his doctor, I do so subject to an important caveat. This is that the profession, or that section of it which is relied on by the defendant doctor as setting the requisite standard of care, is discharging the duty of disclosure as I have defined it. This, incidentally, accords with the approach of Parliament, which, in s 1(5) of the Congenital Disabilities (Civil Liability) Act 1976, enacted that –

> The defendant is not answerable . . . if he took reasonable care having *due regard* to then received professional opinion applicable . . . but this does not mean that he is answerable only because he departed from received opinion.

'Due regard' involves an exercise of judgment, *inter alia*, whether 'received professional opinion' is engaged in the same exercise as the law. This qualification is analogous to that which has been asserted in the context of treating a trade practice as evidencing the proper standard of care in *Cavanagh v Ulster Weaving Co Ltd* [1959] 2 All ER 745, [1960] AC 145 and in *Morris v West Hartlepool Steam Navigation Co Ltd* [1956] 1 All ER 385, [1956] AC 552 and would be equally infrequently relevant.

. . . I think that, in an appropriate case, a judge would be entitled to reject a unanimous medical view if he were satisfied that it was manifestly wrong and that the doctors must have been misdirecting themselves as to their duty in law.

Another way of expressing my view of the test is to add just one qualifying word (which I have emphasised) to the law as Skinner J summarised it, so that it would read:

> The duty is fulfilled if the doctor acts in accordance with a practice *rightly* accepted as proper by a body of skilled and experienced medical men.

But even in circumstances of diagnosis and treatment (rather than disclosure) in which it has been assumed that *Bolam* applies, a number of cases reject this view. (See also the decision of the Court of Appeal of Manitoba, *Anderson v Chasney* (1949) 4 DLR 71 and cases referred to therein.)

Hucks v Cole (1968) [1993] 4 Med LR 393 (CA)

A doctor failed to treat a patient with penicillin and injury resulted when septicaemia occurred. The trial judge held the doctor liable in negligence. His appeal was dismissed by the Court of Appeal.

Sachs LJ: In the present case Dr Cole knew on the 15th October that the septic places from which the plaintiff was suffering had been infected by streptococcus pyogenes; that for this streptococcus in this patient penicillin was bacteriocidal whereas tetracycline, which was being administered, was not; and that penicillin could easily and inexpensively be administered before the onset occurred. It was not administered and the onset occurred: if it had been administered the onset would not have occurred. Thus (unless there was some good cause for not administering it) the onset was due to a lacuna between what could easily have been done and what was in fact done. According to the defence, that lacuna was consistent with and indeed accorded with the reasonable practice of other responsible doctors with obstetric experience.

When the evidence shows that a lacuna in professional practice exists by which risks of grave danger are knowingly taken, then, however small the risks, the Courts must anxiously examine that lacuna – particularly if the risks can be easily and inexpensively avoided. If the Court finds, on an analysis of the reasons given for not taking those precautions that, in the light of current professional knowledge, there is no proper basis for the lacuna, and that it is definitely not reasonable that those risks should have been taken, its function is to state that fact and where necessary to state that it constitutes negligence. In such a case the practice will no doubt thereafter be altered to the benefit of patients.

On such occasions the fact that other practitioners would have done the same thing as the defendant practitioner is a very weighty matter to be put in the scales on his behalf; but it is not, as Mr Webster readily conceded, conclusive. The Court must be vigilant to see whether the reasons given for putting a patient at risk are valid in the light of any well-known advance in medical knowledge, or whether they stem from a residual adherence to out-of-date ideas – a tendency which in the present case may well have affected the views of at any rate one of the defendant's witnesses, who, at a considerable age, seemed not to have any particular respect for laboratory results. . . .

Despite the fact that the risk could have been avoided by adopting a course that was easy, efficient, and inexpensive, and which would have entailed only minimal chances of disadvantages to the patient, the evidence of the four defence experts to the effect that they and other responsible members of the medical profession would have taken the same risk in the same circumstances has naturally caused me to hesitate considerably on two points. Firstly, whether the failure of the defendant to turn over to penicillin treatment during the relevant period was unreasonable. On this, however, I was in the end fully satisfied that in the light of the admissions made by the defendant himself and by his witnesses – quite apart from Dr May's very cogent evidence – that failure to do this was not merely wrong but clearly unreasonable. The reasons given by the four experts do not to my mind stand up to analysis.

It is in this connection perhaps as well at this stage to mention one other point. The fact that great discoveries have been made which by their unremitting use so far eliminate dangers that the modern practitioner is unlikely ever to see the effects of these dangers is no reason for failing to be unremitting in their use even when the risks have become very small. It is not to my mind in point for a practitioner to say, as Dr Cole said (Day 5, page 20) and as Dr June Smith appeared to say (Day 6, page 32) that if he had previously actually seen how dire the effects were of not taking the relevant precaution he would have taken it, but his experience had not up till then led him to see such results. (The potential irrelevance of the rarity of remoteness of the risk, when the maturing of the risk may be disastrous, is incidentally illustrated in *Chin Keow's* case [1967] 1 WLR 813, PC.)

Secondly, as to whether, in the light of such evidence as to what other responsible medical practitioners would have done, it can be said that even if the defendant's error was unreasonable, it was [not] negligence in relation to the position as regards practice at that particular date. On this second point it is to be noted that this is not apparently a case of 'two schools of thought' (see the speech of Lord Goddard in *Chapman v Rix*, on the 21st December, 1960, at page 11): it appears more to be a case of doctors who said in one form or another that they would have acted or might have acted in the same way as the defendant did, for reasons which on examination do not really stand up to analysis.

Dr Cole knowingly took an easily avoidable risk which elementary teaching had instructed him to avoid; and the fact that others say they would have done the same neither ought to nor can in the present case excuse him in an action for negligence however sympathetic one may be to him. Moreover, in so far as the evidence shows the existence of a lacuna of the type to which reference was made earlier in this judgment, that lacuna was, in view of the magnitude of the dangers involved, so unreasonable that as between doctor and patient it cannot be relied upon to excuse the former in an action for negligence.

Lord Denning MR and Diplock LJ agreed that the defendant was in breach of his duty to the plaintiff. (See also *Clarke v Adams* (1950) 94 Sol Jo 599.)

Professor Fleming recognises the role of the court when he writes in his book *The Law of Torts* (8th edn) (1992), p 121:

> Common practice plays a conspicuous role in medical negligence actions. Conscious at once of the layman's ignorance of medical science and apprehensive of the impact of jury bias on a peculiarly vulnerable profession, courts have resorted to the safeguard of insisting that negligence in diagnosis and treatment (including disclosure of risks) cannot ordinarily be established without the aid of expert testimony or in the teeth of conformity with accepted medical practice. However there is no categorical rule. Thus an accepted practice is open to censure by a jury (no expert testimony required) at any rate in matters not involving diagnostic or clinical skills, on which an ordinary person may presume to pass judgment sensibly, like failure to remove a sponge, an explosion set-off by an admixture of ether vapour and oxygen or injury to a patient's body outside the area of treatment.

There is some indication that the courts will, at least in principle, assert their role. In *Bolitho v City & Hackney HA* (1992) 13 BMLR 111, the Court of Appeal considered the relationship between *Bolam* and *Hucks v Cole*. The case concerned a claim that a doctor's failure to attend a patient in hospital amounted to a breach of duty and caused asphyxia and consequent brain damage. The defendant admitted a breach of duty. Curiously, a majority of the court (Farquaharson and Dillon LJJ) considered *Bolam* to be relevant in determining causation ie whether the doctor probably would have intubated the plaintiff had he attended him. Simon Brown LJ dissented on this point. The importance of the case for us here is, assuming *Bolam* to be relevant, the judges' explanation of its relationship to *Hucks v Cole*.

Bolitho v City & Hackney HA (1993) 13 BMLR 111 (CA)

Farquaharson LJ: There is, of course, no inconsistency between the decisions in *Hucks v Cole* and *Maynard's* case. It is not enough for a defendant to call a number of doctors to say that what he had done or not done was in accord with accepted clinical practice. It is necessary for the judge to consider that evidence and decide whether that clinical practice puts the patient unnecessarily at risk.

Dillon LJ: In my judgment, the court could only adopt the approach of Sachs LJ and reject medical opinion on the ground that the reasons of one group of doctors do not really stand up to analysis, if the court, fully conscious of its own lack of medical knowledge and clinical experience, was nonetheless clearly satisfied that the views of that group of doctors were *Wednesbury* unreasonable, ie views such as no reasonable body of doctors could have held.

Simon Brown LJ expressed no view on the meaning of *Bolam*. While this is a somewhat radical departure by the Court of Appeal from previous thinking in

England, it is fair to say that what the court gives with one hand it takes away with the other. Both judges made it clear that the burden on the plaintiff of demonstrating the unreasonableness of accepted practice is very (perhaps impossibly) onerous. The attraction, however, of the judges' view is that, at least in principle the English Courts could recognise the role they should play (albeit at the margins in cases of treatment and diagnosis) in setting the legal standard of care. This is precisely the residuary role recognised by the leading Commonwealth cases which we have already seen. It was also an approach which appealed to the Irish Supreme Court in reviewing their own line of *Bolam*-type authority in *Dunne v National Maternity Hospital* [1988] IR 91 (Irish Supreme Court).

(ii) IS THIS LAW GOOD?

Is there not a fundamental problem underlying the approach of McNair J in *Bolam* and which has been followed thereafter? Is not the standard of care a *prescriptive* question rather than merely descriptive? Being prescriptive, is it not unusual for the court to allow a particular group (in this case the medical profession) to prescribe what the law is?

Professor Montrose with characteristic acumen saw the difficulties raised by *Bolam* immediately, as can be seen from the following article.

A Montrose 'Is Negligence an Ethical or a Sociological Concept?' (1958) 21 MLR 259

Ever since *Blyth v Birmingham Waterworks* [(1856) 11 Exch 781] it has been usual to state the standard for negligence by reference to the 'reasonable man', or the 'prudent and reasonable man', the terms used by Baron Alderson in his judgment. Sometimes mention is made of the 'ordinary' man, the 'man on the Clapham omnibus', but hitherto conduct has not been exonerated from being considered negligent merely because it is of the kind ordinarily done by ordinary people. A motorist is not excused because he shows that he acted in accordance with the common practice of motorists. The question of negligence is one of what *ought* to be done in the circumstances, not what *is* done in similar circumstances by most people or even by all people. In so far as negligence is concerned with what ought to be done, it may be called an ethical concept: in so far as it is concerned with what is done, with practice, it may be said to be a sociological concept.

. . . [The view of McNair J in *Bolam*] that conformity with practice cannot be negligent stems from a failure to heed the warning of Stallybrass that the 'imagery' of the 'man in the street' may be misleading. McNair J explained the law of negligence to the jury in these terms. 'In the ordinary case which does not involve any special skill negligence in law means this: Some failure to do some act which a reasonable man in the street would do, or doing some act which a reasonable man in the circumstances would not do: and if that failure or the doing of that act results in injury, then there is a cause of action. How do you test whether this failure or cause of action is negligent? In an ordinary case it is generally said that you judge that by the action of the man in the street. He is the ordinary man. In one case it has been said that you judge it by the conduct of the man on the top of a Clapham omnibus. He is the ordinary man.' But the suggested test, though useful as a guide in many cases, is not a universal test: it omits the important qualification stressed by Stallybrass: 'The "man in the street" does not always show the care of a reasonably prudent man in the circumstances.' From the premises of McNair J it does indeed follow that in 'a situation which involves the use of some special skill or competence', and where there are diverse practices followed by those possessed of that skill, then conformity with one of those practices cannot be negligence. But the qualification which has to be added to the premises has to be added also to the conclusion. It is for the court to say whether the ordinary behaviour of the man in the street, or the ordinary practice of those possessed of 'special skill or competence', is reasonable and prudent.

It is, perhaps, going too far to say the McNair J has entirely omitted the possibility of consideration of a recognised practice as negligence. In the passages already quoted there do occur the epithets 'proper' and 'reasonable', which may refer to objective qualifications and not to subjective beliefs of those following the practice. This attitude appears more clearly in another passage: 'I do not think that I quarrel much with any of the submissions in law which have been put before you by counsel. Counsel for the plaintiff put it this way, that in the case of a medical man negligence means failure to act in accordance with the standards of reasonably competent medical men at the time. That is a perfectly accurate statement, as long as it is remembered that there may be one or more perfectly proper standards; and if a medical man conforms with one of those proper standards then he is not negligent.' Moreover, in his survey of the evidence McNair J referred throughout to the objective reasons for holding that the practice of the defendant was reasonable. He discussed the evidence which had been given of the mortality risk from the use of relaxant drugs, and of the danger of fracture from the use of manual control.

Though it is submitted that the doctrine that mere conformity with practice is legally well established, analysis is required in order that its limits and value may be ascertained. In the first place is it important to distinguish between average practices and average standards, between what the ordinary man does and what the ordinary man thinks ought to be done. His practice is not a necessary determinant of his ethics. *Video meliora proboque, deteriora sequor* applies to peasants and poets. Chorley contends for the view that negligence in motoring cases should be determined by 'that which is regarded as reasonable by motorists generally': this is very different from a statistical average of the conduct of motorists. In the next place, we should consider a distinction suggested by the dictum of Lord Wright in *Lloyds Banks v E B Savory & Co* [[1933] AC 201]. It will be recalled that he considered a banking practice [to be negligent] for failure to provide against a risk. The distinction now to be examined is that between failure to provide against a risk, a fault of omission, and inefficiency in the technique employed to deal with a risk. The failure may be in connection with a known risk, or a risk which ought to have been known. It is true that Lord Wright referred only to risks 'fully known to those experienced in the business of banking', but that limitation arises from the facts of the case. It is surely negligent not to provide against risks which ought to have been known. The fact that it was not appreciated by men experienced in the particular province is, of course, strong evidence that it could not reasonably be expected to have been known and guarded against, but not conclusive evidence. Experts may blind themselves by expertise. The courts should protect the citizen against risks which professional men and others may ignore. A doctor in his enthusiasm for a new cure may not properly appreciate the dangers of his treatment; a trade unionist in his concern for less exhausting labour by his colleagues may not properly appreciate the dangers to others from his easier practice. It is sound ethics and good law for a court, judge or jury to condemn a professional practice which does not provide precautions against risks known to the profession or which the court says ought to have been known. But when the question arises of whether precautions in fact taken are adequate then different considerations may arise. If the practice adopted is one which is designed by those with skill and competence in the particular province to deal with a risk, is it then good law for the court to bring its own judgment to bear on the matter? Frankfurter J, in a case concerned with 'matters of geography and geology and physics and engineering', pointed out that the court had no expertise in these matters. Chorley likewise points out that in motoring cases, where the question is one of precautions to be taken against the well-known risks of collisions, a court does not as such possess expertise in driving, even though 'the learned trial judge is an experienced motorist' [(1938) 2 MLR 69]. Perhaps the attitude of McNair J in *Bolam's* case may be 'explained' as being concerned with the adequacy of precautions designed by those with skill and competence to safeguard against a realised risk. The case for the defence was that free movement of the limbs was the best precaution against injury. It is uniformity with a practice consisting in a technique of precautions against risks which eliminates negligence. We are, however, far from judicial recognition of a distinction between failure to provide against a risk, and adequacy of precautions. The most that can be said is at *Bolam's* case is consistent with the distinction.

Why do you think the courts have adopted the *Bolam* approach? One answer might be in the fact that the court is so often presented with an issue of apparent technical complexity. Finding it difficult to determine what is done and hearing evidence of what *is* done tends to depend upon particular facts of each case, the court has tended to elide the distinct issue of what *ought* to be done with its decision of what *is* done.

Take a simple case. Dr X testifies, supported by his witnesses, that he would never carry out a particular procedure when presented with facts 'P'. The plaintiff, supported by his witnesses, says the procedure should have been carried out when facts 'P' were present. The issue for the court, in essence, is to untangle the reasons offered by the differing medical experts, rather than to be concerned superficially with the description of their practice. The reasons offered may relate to, for example, the consequences of carrying (or not carrying) out the procedure, the risks and benefits associated with it, the quality of information to be gained as against any risk or benefit, the cost in terms of manpower or other expenditure of scarce resources. All of these questions, you will see, are questions of values and not technical medical issues at all. Being questions of value, in all other circumstances they would be properly regarded as for the court.

Another reason for the existing state of the law may be the expressed concern of the courts to avoid what has been called the American disease of malpractice litigation resulting in 'defensive medicine'. In *Whitehouse v Jordan (supra)*, Lord Denning MR described 'defensive medicine' thus (at p 658):

> Take heed of what has happened in the United States. 'Medical malpractice' cases there are very worrying, especially as they are tried by juries who have sympathy for the patient and none for the doctor, who is insured. The damages are colossal. The doctors insure but the premiums become very high: and these have to be passed on in fees to the patients. Experienced practitioners are known to have refused to treat patients for fear of being accused of negligence. Young men are even deterred from entering the profession because of the risks involved. In the interests of all, we must avoid such consequences in England.

See also Lawton LJ at p 659.

In the *Sidaway* case (*supra*), Lord Scarman offered the following description (at p 653):

> The proliferation of medical malpractice suits in the United States of America has led some courts and some legislatures to curtail or even to reject the operation of the doctrine in an endeavour to restrict the liability of the doctor and so discourage the practice of 'defensive medicine', by which is meant the practice of doctors advising and undertaking the treatment which they think is legally safe even though they may believe that it is not the best for their patient.
>
> The danger of defensive medicine developing in this country clearly exists, though the absence of the lawyer's 'contingency fee' (a percentage of the damages for him as his fee if he wins the case but nothing if he loses) may make it more remote. However that may be, in matters of civil wrong or tort courts are concerned with legal principle; if policy problems emerge, they are best left to the legislature: see *McLoughlin v O'Brian* [1982] 2 All ER 298, [1983] 1 AC 410.

(See also, when *Sidaway* was before the Court of Appeal [1984] 1 All ER 1018, Dunn LJ at 1031; Browne-Wilkinson LJ at 1035.)

We shall examine in greater detail the notion of defensive medicine shortly. It will suffice here to remind ourselves that what is meant by the notion is that the state of the law and the consequent fear for litigation cause (or may cause) doctors to carry out procedures which are not called for as a matter of good medical practice but are done to avoid legal liability. Whatever the validity of this as a theory (and you will see that not all judges would give it credence), there is little doubt that it is widely perceived to be a real risk. We shall notice that it may be theoretically incoherent. If the law requires doctors to do only *that which other doctors deem reasonable*, where is the need for defensive medicine? But the notion persists (for a fuller discussion, see *infra*, ch 6).

3. Departure from approved practice

Is this necessarily a breach of duty?

Hunter v Hanley 1955 SC 200 (Court of Session (Inner House))

In an action of damages against a doctor, the pursuer, who had suffered injury as a result of the breaking of a hypodermic needle while she was receiving an injection, alleged that the accident had been caused by the fault and negligence of the defender in failing to exercise the standard of care and competence which it was his duty to display in giving the injection. At the trial the presiding Judge directed the jury in the course of his charge that the test to be applied was whether there had been such a departure from the normal and usual practice of general practitioners as could reasonably be described as gross negligence. The jury having returned a verdict for the defender, the pursuer enrolled a motion for a new trial on the ground of misdirection.

The Court of Session (Inner House) ordered a new trial.

Lord President (Clyde): It follows from what I have said that in regard to allegations of deviation from ordinary professional practice – and this is the matter with which the present note is concerned – such a deviation is not necessarily evidence of negligence. Indeed it would be disastrous if this were so, for all inducement to progress in medical science would then be destroyed. Even a substantial deviation from normal practice may be warranted by the particular circumstances. To establish liability by a doctor where deviation from normal practice is alleged, three facts require to be established. First of all it must be proved that there is a usual and normal practice; secondly it must be proved that the defender has not adopted that practice; and thirdly, (and this is of crucial importance) it must be established that the course the doctor adopted is one which no professional man of ordinary skill would have taken if he had been acting with ordinary care. There is clearly a heavy onus on a pursuer to establish these facts, and without all three his case will fail. If this is the test, then it matters nothing how far or how little he deviates from the ordinary practice. For the extent of deviation is not the test. The deviation must be of a kind which satisfies the third of the requirements just stated.

Notice Lord Clyde's third requirement and his use of the word 'established'. It is by no means clear whether Lord Clyde intends it to be for the *court* to determine whether the deviation was justified, or to be a matter on which *doctors'* evidence is conclusive. Note the comment in support of the former view by Sellers LJ in *Landau v Werner* (1961) 105 Sol Jo 1008, (CA), that: 'a doctor might not be negligent if he tried a new technique but that if he did he must justify it before the court . . . Success was the best justification for unusual and unestablished treatment.' Consider in this context the early heart transplant operations: Were they a 'success' even though the patients died, and if not, was the doctor in breach of his duty to his patient? (See also *Holland v Devitt and Moore Nautical College Ltd* (1960) Times, 4 March, *per* Streatfield J.)

What, then, is the legal effect of deviating from approved practice?

Clark v MacLennan [1983] 1 All ER 416 (QBD)

The plaintiff, who was about to give birth to her first child, was admitted to a hospital administered by the second defendants, a health authority. The baby was delivered on 11 June 1975. Soon after birth the plaintiff began to suffer from stress incontinence, a not uncommon post-natal condition whereby normal bladder control was lost when the sufferer was subjected to mild physical stress. The plaintiff's disability was particularly acute and after conventional treatment failed to bring about an improvement the first defendant, a gynaecologist, performed an anterior colporrhaphy operation on 10 July 1975. It was normal practice among gynaecologists not to perform such an operation until at least three months after birth so as to ensure its success and to prevent the risk of haemorrhage. The operation was not successful and after it was performed haemorrhage occurred causing the repair to break down. Two further anterior colporrhaphy operations were necessary, and they were carried out on 16 January 1976 and in October 1979. Neither was successful with the result that the stress incontinence from which the plaintiff suffered became a permanent disability. She brought an action for damages claiming that the defendants had been negligent in the care and treatment administered to her.

Peter Pain J: Where however there is but one orthodox course of treatment and [the doctor] chooses to depart from that, his position is different. It is not enough for him to say as to his decision simply that it was based on his clinical judgment. One has to inquire whether he took all proper factors into account which he knew or should have known, and whether his departure from the orthodox course can be justified on the basis of these factors. . .

The burden of proof lies on the plaintiff. To succeed she must show, first, that there was a breach of duty and, second, that her damages flowed from that breach. It is against the second defendants that her attack is principally directed. . .

On the basis of . . . [*McGhee v National Coal Board* [1972] 3 All ER 1008, [1973] 1 WLR 1, HL], counsel for the plaintiff contended that, if the plaintiff could show (1) that there was a general practice not to perform an anterior colporrhaphy until at least three months after birth, (2) that one of the reasons for this practice was to protect the patient from the risk of haemorrhage and a breakdown of the repair, (3) that an operation was performed within four weeks and (4) that haemorrhage occurred and the repair broke down, then the burden of showing that he was not in breach of duty shifted to the defendants.

It must be correct on the basis of *McGhee* to say that the burden shifts so far as damages are concerned. But does the burden shift so far as the duty is concerned? Must the medical practitioner justify his departure from the usual practice?

It is very difficult to draw a distinction between the damage and the duty where the duty arises only because of a need to guard against the damage. In *McGhee's* case it was accepted that there was a breach of duty. In the present case the question of whether there was a breach remains in issue.

It seems to me that it follows from *McGhee* that where there is a situation in which a general duty of care arises and there is a failure to take a precaution, and that very damage occurs against which the precaution is designed to be a protection, then the burden lies on the defendant to show that he was not in breach of duty as well as to show that the damage did not result from his breach of duty.

Applying this, the judge found that the defendants had not discharged this burden and he entered judgment for the plaintiff.

Mustill LJ in the Court of Appeal in *Wilsher v Essex Area Health Authority* [1986] 3 All ER 801 at 815, has cast doubt on the validity of Peter Pain J's analysis.

Mustill LJ: If I may say so, the summary of the evidence contained in the judgment in *Clark v MacLennan* has certainly persuaded me that, as a decision on the facts, the case is unimpeachable. Moreover, although the judge indicated that he proposed to decide the case on burden of proof (at 425), this could be understood as an example of the forensic commonplace that, where one party has, in the course of the trial, hit the ball into the other's court, it is for that other to return it. But the prominence given in the judgment to *McGhee* and the citation from *Clark* in the present case suggest that the judge may have set out to assert a wider proposition, to the effect that in certain kinds of case of which *Clark* and the present action form examples, there is a general burden of proof on the defendant. If this is so, then I must respectfully say that I find nothing in . . . general principle to support it.

When the *Wilsher* case reached the House of Lords [1988] 1 All ER 871, it was emphatically affirmed that *McGhee* did not have the effect of shifting the burden of proof (per Lord Bridge at p 879, *infra*, pp 000-000).

What, however, is Mustill LJ deciding here? Undoubtedly the legal burden of proof does not shift, but is Mustill LJ conceding that the burden of adducing evidence has shifted in that once the plaintiff has established an approved practice and deviation therefrom he *may*, but not necessarily *must*, win unless the defendant brings evidence in reply.

C. PROOF

As we have seen, the *Bolam* test looks to the standards of the medical profession in setting the legal standard of care required of a doctor. It would seem to follow therefore, that to prove his care the plaintiff must adduce medical evidence sufficient to satisfy the burden of proof. Is this always the case? Would, for example, a plaintiff be non-suited if he demonstrated that his doctor had removed the wrong leg, but did not bring forward medical evidence to suggest that this was not accepted medical practice?

An exception, at least in theory, is *res ipsa loquitur*. Professor Picard in *Legal Liability of Doctors and Hospitals in Canada* (1984), pp 260-1, sets the scene:

> There has been judicial recognition in negligence cases of the hardship on the plaintiff who is attempting to prove negligence when he knows only that an accident has happened and that he was injured. In many instances the details of the accident are known only to the defendant, but sometimes the mere fact that an accident happened will itself give rise to a presumption of negligence on the part of the defendant because the event is such that it would be unlikely to occur unless there has been negligence. The accident 'speaks of negligence'; hence the term used for this circumstances: *res ipsa loquitur*, 'the thing speaks for itself'.
>
> Variously described as a rule, principle, doctrine and maxim, *res ipsa loquitur* is applied in Canada as part of the law of circumstantial evidence and has been called 'one of the great mysteries of tort law'.
>
> As with much of the law, the essentials of *res ipsa loquitur* are easy to state, but its application is complicated. The doctrine will only apply when:
> 1) there is no evidence as to how or why the accident occurred;
> 2) the accident is such that it would not occur without negligence; and
> 3) the defendant is proven to have been in control of or linked to the situation either personally or vicariously.

The courts within the common law system have been largely reluctant to accept that *res ipsa loquitur* has much, if any, place in medical law.

Girard v Royal Columbian Hospital (1976) 66 DLR (3d) 676 (British Columbia Supreme Court)

> **Andrews J:** . . . [T]he plaintiff underwent an operation at the Royal Columbian Hospital in New Westminster, British Columbia, which is described as being a left femoral popliteal saphenous vein by-pass graft. Shortly after the operation he noticed a weakness in both legs – more on the left than the right. Although there was no further surgical intervention he was in and out of rehabilitative centres for about a year until his condition stabilised to its present one, which consists of a permanent paralysis of the lower limbs accompanied by partial bladder and bowel deficiency and complete impotence. He is ambulatory by using two canes and is constantly uncomfortable from either sitting or standing for an extended period of time and from the loss of some control of both his bladder and bowel. . . .

As to the doctrine of *res ipsa loquitur* which had been relied upon by the plaintiff, he said:

> The human body is not a container filled with a material whose performance can be predictably charted and analysed. It cannot be equated with a box of chewing tobacco or a soft drink. Thus, while permissible inferences may be drawn as to the normal behaviour of

these types of commodities the same kind of reasoning does not necessarily apply to a human being. Because of this medical science has not yet reached the stage where the law ought to presume that a patient must come out of an operation as well or better than he went into it. From my interpretation of the medical evidence the kind of injury suffered by the plaintiff could have occurred without negligence on anyone's part. Since I cannot infer there was negligence on the part of the defendant doctors the maxim of *res ipsa loquitur* does not apply.

Lord Denning reflected this view in his judgment in *Whitehouse v Jordan* [1980] 1 All ER 650:

Lord Denning MR: The key sentence of the judge was this:

In getting it wedged or stuck, or unwedged or unstuck, Mr Jordan caused asphyxia which in turn caused the cerebral palsy. In this respect Mr Jordan fell below the very high standard of professional competence that the law requires of him.

The first sentence suggests that, *because* the baby suffered damage, *therefore* Mr Jordan was at fault. In other words *res ipsa loquitur*. That would be an error. In a high-risk case, damage during birth is quite possible, even though all care is used. No inference of negligence should be drawn from it.

(Note also Denning LJ's remarks in *Roe v Minister of Health* [1954] 2 QB 66 at 80.)

This is not to say that *res ipsa* will never be applied in medical cases, but merely to say that it will be exceptional. Curiously, it is Lord Denning's judgment in *Cassidy v Ministry of Health* [1951] 2 KB 343, [1951] 1 All ER 574, which is regarded as the *locus classicus* on the application of *res ipsa loquitur* in medical law.

Denning LJ: If the plaintiff had to prove that some particular doctor or nurse was negligent, he would not be able to do it. But he was not put to that impossible task: he says, 'I went into the hospital to be cured of two stiff fingers. I have come out with four stiff fingers, and my hand is useless. That should not have happened if due care had been used. Explain it, if you can.' I am quite clearly of opinion that that raises a *prima facie* case against the hospital authorities: see *per* Goddard LJ, in *Mahon v Osborne*. They have nowhere explained how it could happen without negligence. They have busied themselves in saying that this or that member of their staff was not negligent. But they have called not a single person to say that the injuries were consistent with due care on the part of all the members of their staff. They called some of the people who actually treated the man, namely Dr Fahrni, Dr Ronaldson, and Sister Hall, each of whom protested that he was careful in his part; but they did not call any expert at all, to say that this might happen despite all care. They have not therefore displaced the *prima facie* case against them and are liable in damages to the plaintiff.

The other well-known case, referred to by Denning LJ in *Cassidy* (and the fact that there are so few cases tells its own story) is *Mahon v Osborne*.

Mahon v Osborne [1939] 2 KB 14, [1939] 1 All ER 535 (CA)

The appellant, the resident surgeon, performed an abdominal operation with the help of an anaesthetist, a theatre sister and two nurses. The operation was admittedly a difficult one, and, at its conclusion, the usual count of the swabs which had been used was made, when the surgeon was informed that the count was correct. It was found, as a result of a further operation about 2 months later, that one swab had been left under the part of the liver which is close to the stomach. The patient died, and it was common ground that his death was due to the leaving of the swab in the abdomen. The system in use at the hospital of checking the count of the swabs was fully described in evidence, and was held to be satisfactory. In an action brought by the mother of the deceased against the surgeon for damages for negligence in the performance of the operation, the plaintiff contended that the doctrine of *res ipsa loquitur* was applicable to the circumstances. The Court of Appeal allowed the doctor's appeal against the trial judge's award of damages.

Scott LJ: It is difficult to see how the principle of *res ipsa loquitur* can apply generally to actions for negligence against a surgeon for leaving a swab in a patient, even if in certain circumstances the presumption may arise. If it applied generally, plaintiff's counsel, having, by a couple of answers to interrogatories, proved that the defendant performed the operation and that a swab was left in, would be entitled to ask for judgment, unless evidence describing the operation was given by the defendant. Some positive evidence of neglect of duty is surely needed. It may be that a full description of the actual operation will disclose facts sufficiently indicative of want of skill or care to entitle a jury to find a neglect of duty to the patient. It may be that expert evidence in addition will be requisite. To treat the maxim as applying in every case where a swab is left in the patient seems to me an error of law. The very essence of the rule, when applied to an action for negligence, is that, upon the mere fact of the event happening, for example, an injury to the plaintiff, there arise two presumptions of fact, (i) that the event was caused by a breach by somebody of the duty of care towards the plaintiff, and (ii) that the defendant was that somebody. The presumption of fact arises only because it is an inference which the reasonable man, knowing the facts, would naturally draw, and that is, in most cases, for two reasons (i) that the control over the happening of such an event rested solely with the defendant, and (ii) that in the ordinary experience of mankind such an event does not happen unless the person in control has failed to exercise due care.

In effect there are two reasons why *res ipsa loquitur* will not ordinarily be available to a plaintiff in a medical case. The first, as we have seen, turns upon the undoubted uncertainties of medical treatment. The second, which does not emerge from the cases we have seen so far, reflects the significant changes in procedure which occurred since the doctrine first developed. Nowadays, it is unlikely that a plaintiff will be at such a disadvantage in terms of knowing what went on that recourse to *res ipsa* will be warranted. The modern developments in the practice of discovery and exchange of evidence coupled with the more careful practice of recording and maintaining medical records has meant that the plaintiff is usually able to know what went on. Mustill LJ makes this point in commenting on the applicability of *res ipsa* in *Bull v Devon AHA* (see also, *Delaney v Southmead HA* (CA, 9 June 1992) *per* Stuart-Smith LJ).

Bull v Devon AHA [1993] 4 Med LR 117 (CA)

Mustill LJ: There still remains on the facts the question whether this interval was so long that negligence should be presumed. For my part, I am not sure that recourse to the maxim *res ipsa loquitur* really advances the matter. In *Byrne v Boadle* (1863) 2 H&C 722 and similar cases, there was an untoward event which the plaintiff put in evidence as constituting the whole of his case. What happened in the warehouse was unknown to the plaintiff, but he was able to say that barrels should not roll out of first storey openings on to passers-by. No further evidence was needed to establish the plaintiff's case, if the defendant chose to call none for himself. Here, the position seems to me different. The plaintiff's advisers were able to put in evidence from the records as part of their case the outlines of what actually happened. They called expert testimony to establish what should have happened, and could point to a disconformity between what the witnesses said should have happened and what actually happened. The defendants themselves also gave some evidence, meagre as it was because of the lapse of time, which added a few more facts about the course of events. I do not see that the present situation calls for recourse to an evidentiary presumption applicable in cases where the defendant does, and the plaintiff does not, have within his grasp the means of knowing how the accident took place. Here, all the facts that are ever going to be known are before the court. The judge held that they pointed to liability, and I agree.

Beyond issues of proof which arise in all litigation there are two additional points which are worth noting in the context of allegations of negligence in medical law.

The first point is made in R Jackson and J L Powell *Professional Negligence* (3rd edn 1992) para 6.43:

> Very often there is no 'general and approved practice' or specific school of thought by reference to which the defendant's conduct can either be justified or condemned as negligent. The question is simply whether, in all the circumstances of the particular case, the mistake made by the defendant was negligent. In this situation the obvious way that an expert witness can assist the court on the issue of negligence (ie the second of the two stages discussed above) is by saying what he would have done in the particular circumstances and/ or what he believes other medical practitioners would have done. In *Midland Bank v Hett Stubbs and Kemp* [[1979] Ch 384] (a claim for solicitors' negligence) Oliver J has expressed the view that such evidence is inadmissible. However, in solicitors' negligence cases the court is able to form its own independent opinion as to the reasonableness or skilfulness of the defendant's conduct on the basis of counsel's submissions alone – a task which is usually impossible in medical negligence cases. It is therefore submitted that the *dictum* of Oliver J referred to above is inapplicable in medical negligence cases. Certainly, in practice, evidence from expert witnesses as to what they would have done, or what they believe other medical practitioners would have done, in the particular circumstances is received and acted upon by the court.

The authors may accurately state what the courts do as a matter of practice but is Oliver J not right as a matter of law?

The second point is one of concern to many doctors. They feel they may well run the risk of being judged in their conduct by reference to the evidence of the most eminent practitioner in the particular field in question. This they feel is unfair. The standards of the centre of excellence or of the teaching hospital should not, they argue, be the standards against which those who do not have the benefit of working in such a centre should be judged (note the remarks of Mustill LJ in *Bull v Devon AHA* [1993] 4 Med LR 117 at 141; Pill J in *Knight v Home Office* [1990] 3 All ER 237 at 243; and Donnelly J in the High Court of Ontario in the case of *Malette v Shulman* (1988) 47 DLR (4th) 18. (In a different context see *Luxmoore-May v Messenger May Baverstock (a firm)* [1990] 1 All ER 1067 (CA).)

D. CAUSATION

It is one thing to show that the defendant doctor owed the plaintiff a duty which was breached and that the plaintiff has been harmed, it is quite another thing to establish that the breach *caused* the harm. But this is what the law requires.

1. Factual

This is not the place to rehearse the principles of the law of tort concerning factual causation. There are, however, problems particularly relevant in medical law which it is important to notice. They relate *first*, to the need to show that the doctors' or others' conduct *could* cause the plaintiff harm as a medical fact and *secondly*, whether in the particular case the harm *did* arise from the doctors' or others' conduct.

The first type of problem is illustrated by the well-known cases relating to the whooping cough vaccine – *Loveday v Renton* [1990] 1 Med LR 117. In *Loveday* the plaintiff alleged that the permanent brain-damage she suffered was caused by the administration of the petussis (whooping cough) vaccine. The court

(Stuart-Smith LJ) held that the scientific evidence did not establish a link between brain-damage in young children and the administration of the vaccine. (See also *Kay v Ayrshire and Arran Health Board* [1987] 2 All ER 417 (HL) where the House of Lords relied on the fact that there was no evidence that an overdose of penicillin caused deafness to reach the conclusion that it could not have done so in the case before them.) The second type of case is illustrated by the *Barnett* decision. The facts of this case are set out *supra*, p 400-401. You will recall that the deceased died from arsenic poisoning which was undetected by the hospital he attended because he was not examined.

Barnett v Chelsea and Kensington Hospital Management Committee [1969] 1 QB 428, [1968] 1 All ER 1068 (QBD)

Nield J: It remains to consider whether it is shown that the deceased's death was caused by this negligence or whether, as the defendants have said, the deceased must have died in any event. In his concluding submission counsel for the plaintiff submitted that Dr Banerjee should have examined the deceased and, had he done so, he would have caused tests to be made which would have indicated the treatment required and that, since the defendants were at fault in these respects, therefore the onus of proof passed to the defendants to show that the appropriate treatment would have failed, and authorities were cited to me. I find myself unable to accept this argument and I am of the view that the onus of proof remains on the plaintiff, and I have in mind (without quoting it) the decision quoted by counsel for the defendants in *Bonnington Castings Ltd v Wardlaw* [[1956] AC 613]. However, were it otherwise and the onus did pass to the defendants, then I would find that they have discharged it, as I would proceed to show.

There has been put before me a timetable which, I think, is of much importance. The deceased attended at the casualty department at 8.05 or 8.10 am. If Dr Banerjee had got up and dressed and come to see the three men and examined them and decided to admit them, the deceased (and Dr Lockett agreed with this) could not have been in bed in a ward before 11 am. I accept Dr Goulding's evidence that an intravenous drip would not have been set up before 12 noon, and if potassium loss was suspected it could not have been discovered until 12.30. Dr Lockett, dealing with this said 'If [the deceased] had not been treated until after 12 noon the chances of survival were not good.'

Without going in detail into the considerable volume of technical evidence which has been put before me, it seems to me to be the case that when death results from arsenical poisoning it is brought about by two conditions: on the one hand dehydration and on the other disturbance of the enzyme processes. If the principal condition is one of enzyme disturbance – as I am of the view that it was here – then the only method of treatment which is likely to succeed is the use of the specific antidote which is commonly called BAL. Dr Goulding said this in the course of his evidence:

> The only way to deal with this is to use the specific BAL. I see no reasonable prospect of the deceased being given BAL before the time at which he died,

and at a later point in his evidence:

> I feel that even if fluid loss had been discovered death would have been caused by the enzyme disturbance. Death might have occurred later.

I regard that evidence as very moderate, and that it might be a true assessment of the situation to say that there was no chance of BAL being administered before the death of the deceased.

For these reasons, I find that the plaintiff has failed to establish, on the grounds of probability, that the defendants' negligence caused the death of the deceased.

Barnett was a case where the evidence was clear that the breach of duty *did not* cause the deceased's death. In most cases of medical negligence the evidence of the cause of the plaintiff's harm will be, at best, unclear – either intrinsically so or because of the preparedness of experts so to testify. In such circumstances is it any part of the role of the court to assist the plaintiff to establish causation by, for example, adopting a less stringent definition of causation than is ordinarily employed? The House of Lords had the opportunity to develop the law in this way in *Wilsher v Essex Area Health Authority* [1988] 1 All ER 871 but, as you will see, chose not to do so.

Wilsher v Essex AHA [1988] 1 All ER 871 [1988] AC 1074 (HL)

Lord Bridge of Harwich: My Lords, the infant plaintiff was born nearly three months prematurely on 15 December 1978. He weighed only 1,200g. In the first few weeks of life he suffered from most of the afflictions which beset premature babies. He passed through a series of crises and very nearly died. The greatest danger which faces the very premature baby, on account of the imperfect function of incompletely developed lungs, is death or brain damage from failure of the oxygen supply to the brain. That Martin not only survived but also now retains unimpaired brain function is due both to the remarkable advances of medical science and technology in this field in comparatively recent years and to the treatment he received in the special baby care unit of the Princess Alexandra Hospital, Harlow.

Tragically, however, he succumbed to another well-known hazard of prematurity. He suffers from retrolental fibroplasia (RLF), an incurable condition of the retina which, in his case, has caused total blindness in one eye and severely impaired vision in the other. He sued the Essex Area Health Authority (the authority), who are responsible for the Princess Alexandra Hospital, Harlow, on the ground that his RLF was caused by an excess of oxygen tension in his bloodstream in the early weeks attributable to a want of proper skill and care in the management of his oxygen supply. The action was heard by Peter Pain J and the trial lasted 20 days. In addition to the evidence of the medical and nursing staff at the hospital, the judge heard expert evidence from two paediatricians and two ophthalmologists called for the plaintiff and from three paediatricians and one ophthalmologist called for the authority. All were highly qualified and distinguished experts in their respective fields. In addition, no less than 24 articles from medical journals about RLF covering 129 foolscap pages of print were put in evidence.

The allegations of negligence against the authority related to two quite distinct phases of Martin's treatment. The first concerned the first 38 hours after his birth. In order to monitor the partial pressure of oxygen (PO_2) in the arterial blood of a premature baby, it is standard practice to pass a catheter through the umbilical artery into the aorta. This enables the PO_2 to be measured in two ways. At the tip of the catheter is an electronic sensor connected to a monitor outside the body which, if correctly calibrated, should give an accurate reading of the PO_2. In addition, an aperture in the catheter close to the sensor enables samples of blood to be taken for conventional blood analysis at regular intervals to check and, if necessary, adjust the monitor's calibration. Again it is standard practice to check the location of the sensor by X-ray after the catheter has been inserted. In Martin's case the catheter was inserted by mistake into a vein instead of an artery so that the sensor and the sampling aperture were wrongly located in the heart instead of the aorta. This meant that they would sample a mixture of arterial and venous blood instead of pure arterial blood, which would consequently give a false reading of the level of PO_2 in the arterial blood. The house officer and the registrar who were on duty at the material time and who saw the X-ray which was taken both failed to notice the mistake. The judge held this failure to amount to negligence for which the authority were liable. The plaintiff's case in relation to this first allegation of negligence was that the misplaced catheter gave readings of PO_2 well below the true level of PO_2 in the arterial blood which led to excessive administration of oxygen in an attempt to raise the PO_2 level and that in consequence the true PO_2 level was excessively high for a substantial period until the mislocation of the catheter was realised at 8 o'clock on the morning of 17 December 1978.

A second phase of Martin's treatment alleged to have been negligent was between 20 December 1978 and 23 January 1979. Between these dates it was alleged that there were five distinct periods of differing duration when the medical and nursing staff responsible for Martin's care were in breach of duty in allowing the level of PO_2 in his arterial blood to remain above the accepted level of safety. The judge found that four of these five periods of exposure to an unduly high level of PO_2 were due to the authority's negligence.

In making his finding of negligence in relation to each of the periods of raised PO_2 levels except the first attributable to the misplaced catheter, the judge relied on a principle of law which he thought was laid down by this House in *McGhee v National Coal Board* [1972] 3 All ER 1008, [1973] 1 WLR 1 and which he had stated in his own earlier decision in *Clark v MacLennan* [1983] 1 All ER 416 at 427 in the following terms:

> It seems to me that it follows from *McGhee* that where there is a situation in which a general duty of care arises and there is a failure to take a precaution, and that very damage occurs against which the precaution is designed to be a protection, then the burden lies on the defendant to show that he was not in breach of duty as well as to show that the damage did not result from his breach of duty.

The judge thought that this proposition of law derived support from the decision at first instance of Mustill J in *Thompson v Smiths Shiprepairers (North Shields) Ltd* [1984] 1 All ER 881, [1984] QB 405. He held that the authority failed to prove on a balance of probabilities either that they were not negligent or that their negligence did not cause or materially contribute to Martin's RLF. He therefore held them liable in damages and gave judgment for the plaintiff for £116,119.14.

The Court of Appeal (Sir Nicolas Browne-Wilkinson V-C, Mustill and Glidewell LJJ) affirmed this judgment by a majority, the Vice-Chancellor dissenting (see [1986] 3 All ER 801, [1987] 1 QB 730). It gave leave on terms to the authority to appeal to this House. A number of issues were argued in the Court of Appeal. It unanimously affirmed the finding of negligence against the authority, though by marginally different processes of reasoning, on the ground of the authority's vicarious liability for the registrar's failure to observe from the X-ray that the first catheter inserted into Martin's umbilicus was located in a vein not in an artery. It unanimously reversed the judge's finding of negligence in relation to the later periods when the level of PO_2 in Martin's blood was raised on the ground that he had misdirected himself in holding that the burden of proof was reversed so that it lay on the authority to show that they were not negligent. On examination of the evidence the Court of Appeal found that no negligence was established in relation to these later periods. No issue arises in the present appeal to your Lordships' House in respect of either of these conclusions on liability and nothing more need be said about them. The crucial issue which now arises and on which the Court of Appeal was divided is whether the judgment can be affirmed on the ground that any raised level of PO_2 in Martin's arterial blood before 8 o'clock on the morning of 17 December 1978 consequent on misplacement of the catheter caused or materially contributed to Martin's RLF.

My Lords, I understand that all your Lordships agree that this appeal has to be allowed and that the inevitable consequence of this is that the outstanding issue of causation must, unless the parties can reach agreement, be retried by another judge. In these circumstances, for obvious reasons, it is undesirable that I should go into the highly complex and technical evidence on which the issue depends any further than is strictly necessary to explain why, in common with all your Lordships, I feel ineluctably driven to the unpalatable conclusion that it is not open to the House to resolve the issue one way or the other, so that a question depending on the consequence of an event occurring in the first two days of Martin's life will now have to be investigated all over again when Martin is nearly ten years old. On the other hand, the appeal raises a question of law as to the proper approach to issues of causation which is of great importance and of particular concern in medical negligence cases. This must be fully considered.

There was in the voluminous expert evidence given at the trial an irreconcilable conflict of opinion as to the cause of Martin's RLF. It was common ground that a sufficiently high level of PO_2 in the arterial blood of a very premature baby, if maintained for a sufficiently long period of time, can have a toxic effect on the immature blood vessels in the retina leading to a condition which may either regress or develop into RLF. It was equally common ground, however, that RLF may occur in premature babies who have survived without any artificial administration of oxygen and that there is evidence to indicate a correlation between RLF and a number of other conditions from which premature babies commonly suffer (eg apnoea, hypercarbia, intraventricular haemorrhage, patent ductus arteriosus, all conditions which afflicted Martin) although no causal mechanisms linking these conditions with the development of RLF have been identified. However, what, if any, part artificial administration of oxygen causing an unduly high level of PO_2 in Martin's arterial blood played in the causation of Martin's RLF was radically in dispute between the experts. There was certainly evidence led in support of the plaintiff's case that high levels of PO_2 in general and, more particularly, the level of PO_2 maintained when the misplaced catheter was giving misleadingly low readings of the level in the arterial blood were probably at least a contributory cause of Martin's RLF. If the judge had directed himself that it was for the plaintiff to discharge the onus of proving causation on a balance of probabilities and had indicated his acceptance of this evidence in preference to the contrary evidence led for the authority, a finding in favour of the plaintiff would have been unassailable. That is why it is conceded by counsel for the authority that the most he can ask for, if his appeal succeeds, is an order for retrial of the causation issue. However, the burden of the relevant expert evidence led for the authority, to summarise it in very general terms, was to the effect that any excessive administration of oxygen which resulted from the misplacement of the catheter did not result in the PO_2 in the arterial blood being raised to a sufficiently high level for a sufficient length of time to have been capable of playing any part in the causation of Martin's RLF. One of the difficulties is that, underlying this conflict of medical opinion, there was not only a profound difference of view about the aetiology and causation of RLF in general but also a substantial difference as to the inferences which were to be drawn from the primary facts, as ascertained from the clinical notes about Martin's condition and treatment at the medical time and amplified by the oral evidence of Dr Wiles, the senior house officer in charge, as to what the actual levels of PO_2 in Martin's arterial blood were likely to have been during a critical period between 10 pm on 16 December when Martin was first being administered pure oxygen through a ventilator and 8 am the next morning when, after discovery of the mistake about the catheter, the level of oxygen administration was immediately reduced.

Having found the authority negligent in relation to the five periods when the PO_2 level was unduly high, the judge added: 'There is no dispute that this materially increased the risk of RLF.' This statement, it is now accepted, was a misunderstanding of the evidence. Whilst it was common ground that one of the objects of monitoring and controlling the PO_2 level in the arterial blood of a premature baby in 1978 was to avoid or reduce the risk of RLF, it was certainly not accepted by the defence that any of the levels to which Martin was subjected were sufficient in degree or duration to have involved any material increase in that risk. This misunderstanding was one of the factors which led the judge to the conclusion that Martin had established a prima facie case on the issues of causation. He then said:

> But it is open to the defendants on the facts of this case to show that they are not liable for this negligence because on the balance of probability this exposure did not cause Martin's RLF.

It was on this premise that the judge examined the issue of causation. In judgment which runs to 68 pages of transcript, only 2½ pages are devoted to this issue. The judge repeatedly emphasised that the onus was on the authority, saying at one point:

> For the purpose of this action I need go no further than to consider whether the breaches have probably made no substantial contribution to the plaintiff's condition.

And, again, a little later on: 'So I have to consider whether the exposure that occurred probably did no harm.'

After a brief reference to the evidence of one of the plaintiff's witnesses and one of the authority's witnesses whose answers were based on an assumption of fact which he was invited to make, the judge expressed his conclusion in the following passage:

> On the basis of this evidence I find that the defendants fail to show that the first and third periods of exposure did not do any damage; *indeed, the probability is that they did.* As to the second, fourth and fifth periods the position is more doubtful. The trouble is the lack of data. The blood gas readings were not sufficiently frequent to enable us to assess whether the excessively high readings were a peak or whether they indicated a longer period; indeed, it is possible that the true figure went higher. The defendants, in my view, have failed to show that these periods did not cause or materially contribute to Martin's RLF. (My emphasis.)

Counsel for the plaintiff, seeking to uphold the judgment in Martin's favour, naturally relied heavily on the words I have emphasised in this passage and pointed to the contrast between the judge's view, thereby expressed, of the causative effect of what is now the only relevant period of exposure calling for consideration and his doubts about the effect of three of the four later periods. He urged your Lordships to read this as an indication by the judge that, if he had held the onus to lie on the plaintiff he would have found it discharged on a balance of probabilities. The Court of Appeal did not feel able to accede to a similar submission and I agree with it. As Mustill LJ pointed out ([1986] 3 All ER 801 at 823, [1987] QB 730 at 763), the judge expressed no preference for the plaintiff's experts on this point. Moreover, it is inconceivable that this very careful judge, if he had directed himself that the burden of proof lay on the plaintiff, would not have subjected the complex and conflicting evidence to a thorough scrutiny and analysis before committing himself to an orthodox finding of causation in the plaintiff's favour.

Both parties accepted that the conflict of evidence was of such a nature that it could not properly be resolved by your Lordships simply reading the transcript. Indeed, we were not asked to examine the totality of the voluminous medical evidence. Just as counsel for the authority accepted that it was not open to the House to dismiss the plaintiff's claim, so counsel for the plaintiff accepted that, if he failed in the submission which I have examined and rejected in the foregoing paragraphs, he could not invite the House to make an independent finding in the plaintiff's favour on the simple basis that the expert evidence on a balance of probabilities affirmatively established causation.

The Court of Appeal, although it felt unable to resolve the primary conflict in the expert evidence as to the causation of Martin's RLF, did make a finding that the levels of PO_2 which Martin experienced in consequence of the misplacement of the catheter were of a kind capable of causing RLF. Mustill LJ expressed his anxiety whether 'by making a further finding on an issue where there was a sharp conflict between the expert witnesses, we are not going too far in the effort to avoid a retrial' (see [1986] 3 All ER 801 at 825, [1987] QB 730 at 766). But he concluded that it was 'legitimate, after reading and rereading the evidence', to make this finding based on 'the weight of the expert evidence'. This finding by the Court of Appeal is challenged by counsel for the authority as one which it was not open to it to make. I must return to this later. But assuming, as I do for the present, that the finding was properly made, it carried the plaintiff's case no further than to establish that oxygen administered to Martin as a consequence of the negligent failure to detect the misplacement of the catheter was one of a number of possible causes of Martin's RLF.

Mustill LJ subjected the speeches in *McGhee v National Coal Board* [1972] 3 All ER 1008, [1973] 1 WLR 1 to a careful scrutiny and analysis and concluded that they established a principle of law which he expressed in the following terms ([1986] 3 All ER 801 at 829, [1987] QB 730 at 771-772):

> If it is an established fact that conduct of a particular kind creates a risk that injury will be caused to another or increases an existing risk that injury will ensue, and if the two parties stand in such a relationship that the one party owes a duty not to conduct himself in that way, and if the first party does conduct himself in that way, and if the other party does suffer injury of the kind to which the risk related, then the first party is taken to have caused the injury by his breach of duty, even though the existence and extent of the contribution made by the breach cannot be ascertained.

Applying this principle to the finding that the authority's negligence was one of the possible causes of Martin's RLF, he held that this was sufficient to enable the court to conclude that the negligence was 'taken to have caused the injury'. Glidewell LJ reached the same conclusion by substantially the same process of reasoning. Sir Nicholas Browne-Wilkinson V-C took the opposite view.

The starting point for any consideration of the relevant law of causation is the decision of this House in *Bonnington Castings Ltd v Wardlaw* [1956] 1 All ER 615, [1956] AC 613. This was the case of a pursuer who, in the course of his employment by the defenders, contracted pneumoconiosis over a period of years by the inhalation of invisible particles of silica dust from two sources. One of these (pneumatic hammers) was an 'innocent' source, in the sense that the pursuer could not complain that his exposure to it involved any breach of duty on the part of his employers. The other source (swing grinders), however, arose from a breach of statutory duty by the employer. Delivering the leading speech in the House of Lords, Lord Reid said ([1956] 1 All ER 615 at 617-618, [1956] AC 613 at 619-620):

> The Lord Ordinary and the majority of the First Division have dealt with this case on the footing that there was an onus on the defenders, the appellants, to prove that the dust from the swing grinders did not cause the respondent's disease. This view was based on a passage in the judgment of the Court of Appeal in *Vyner v Waldenberg Bros Ltd* ([1945] 2 All ER 547 at 549, [1946] KB 50 at 55) *per* Scott LJ: 'If there is a definite breach of a safety provision imposed on the occupier of a factory, and a workman is injured in a way which could result from the breach, the onus of proof shifts on to the employer to show that the breach was not the cause. We think that that principle lies at the very basis of statutory rules of absolute duty.' . . . Of course the onus was on the defendants to prove delegation (if that was an answer) and to prove contributory negligence, and it may be that that is what the Court of Appeal had in mind. But the passage which I have cited appears to go beyond that and, in so far as it does so, I am of opinion that it is erroneous. It would seem obvious in

principle that a pursuer or plaintiff must prove not only negligence or breach of duty but also that such fault caused, or materially contributed to, his injury, and there is ample authority for that proposition both in Scotland and in England. I can find neither reason nor authority for the rule being different where there is breach of a statutory duty. The fact that Parliament imposes a duty for the protection of employees has been held to entitle an employee to sue if he is injured as a result of a breach of that duty, but it would be going a great deal further to hold that it can be inferred from the enactment of a duty that Parliament intended that any employee suffering injury can sue his employer merely because there was a breach of duty and it is shown to be possible that his injury may have been caused by it. In my judgment, the employee must, in all cases, prove his case by the ordinary standard of proof in civil actions; he must make it appear at least that, on a balance of probabilities, the breach of duty caused, or materially contributed to, his injury.

Lord Tucker said of Scott LJ's dictum in *Vyner v Waldenberg Bros Ltd*:

> . . . I think it is desirable that your Lordships should take this opportunity to state in plain terms that no such onus exists unless the statute or statutory regulation expressly or impliedly so provides, as in several instances it does. No distinction can be drawn between actions for common law negligence and actions for breach of statutory duty in this respect. In both, the plaintiff or pursuer must prove (a) breach of duty, and (b) that such breach caused the injury complained of (see *Wakelin v London & South Western Rly Co* (1886) 12 App Cas 41, and *Caswell v Powell Duffryn Associated Collieries, Ltd* [1939] 3 All ER 722, [1940] AC 152). In each case, it will depend on the particular facts proved, and the proper inferences to be drawn therefrom, whether the respondent has sufficiently discharged the onus that lies on him.

(See [1956] 1 All ER 615 at 621, [1956] AC 613 at 624-625.)

Lord Keith said ([1956] 1 All ER 615 at 621, [1956] AC 613 at 625):

> The onus is on the respondent [the pursuer] to prove his case, and I see no reason to depart from this elementary principle by invoking certain rules of onus said to be based on a correspondence between the injury suffered and the evil guarded against by some statutory regulation. I think most, if not all, of the cases which professed to lay down or to recognise some such rule could have been decided as they were on simple rules of evidence, and I agree that *Vyner v Waldenberg Bros Ltd* ([1945] 2 All ER 547, [1946] KB 50), in so far as it professed to enunciate a principle of law inverting the onus of proof, cannot be supported.

Viscount Simonds and Lord Somervell agreed.

Their Lordships concluded, however, from the evidence that the inhalation of dust to which the pursuer was exposed by the defender's breach of statutory duty had made a material contribution to his pneumoconiosis which was sufficient to discharge the onus on the pursuer of proving that his damage was caused by the defenders' tort.

A year later the decision in *Nicholson v Atlas Steel Foundry and Engineering Co Ltd* [1957] 1 All ER 776, [1957] 1 WLR 613 followed the decision in *Bonnington Castings Ltd v Wardlaw* and held, in another case of pneumoconiosis, that the employers were liable for the employee's disease arising from the inhalation of dust from two sources, one 'innocent' the other 'guilty', on facts virtually indistinguishable from those in *Bonnington Castings Ltd v Wardlaw*.

In *McGhee v National Coal Board* [1972] 3 All ER 1008, [1973] 1 WLR 1 the pursuer worked in a brick kiln in hot and dusty conditions in which brick dust adhered to his sweaty skin. No breach of duty by his employers, the defenders, was established in respect of his working conditions. However, the employers were held to be at fault in failing to provide adequate washing facilities which resulted in the pursuer having to bicycle home after work with his body still caked in brick dust. The pursuer contracted dermatitis and the evidence that this was caused by the brick dust was accepted. Brick dust adhering to the skin was a recognised cause of industrial dermatitis and the provision of showers to remove it after work was a usual precaution to minimise the risk of the disease. The precise mechanism of causation of the disease, however, was not known and the furthest the doctors called for the pursuer were able to go was to say that the provision of showers would have materially reduced the risk of dermatitis. They were unable to say that it would probably have prevented the disease.

The pursuer failed before the Lord Ordinary and the First Division of the Court of Session on the ground that he had not discharged the burden of proof of causation. He succeeded on appeal to the House of Lords. Much of the academic discussion to which this decision has given rise had focused on the speech of Lord Wilberforce, particularly on two paragraphs. He said ([1972] 3 All ER 1008 at 1012, [1973] 1 WLR 1 at 6):

> But the question remains whether a pursuer must necessarily fail if, after he has shown a breach of duty, involving an increase of risk of disease, he cannot positively prove that this increase of risk caused or materially contributed to the disease while his employers cannot positively prove the contrary. In this intermediate case there is an appearance of logic in the view that the pursuer, on whom the onus lies, should fail – a logic which dictated the judgments below. The question is whether we should be satisfied in factual situations like the present, with the logical approach. In my opinion, there are further considerations of importance. First, it is a sound principle that where a person has, by breach of duty of care, created a risk, and injury occurs within the area of that risk, the loss should be borne by him *unless he shows that it had some other cause.* Secondly, from the evidential point of view, one may ask, why should a man who is able to show that his employer should have taken certain precautions, because without them there is a risk, or an added risk, of injury or disease, and who in fact sustains exactly that injury or disease, have to assume the burden of proving more: namely that it was the addition to the risk, caused by the breach of duty, which caused or materially contributed to the injury? In many cases of which the present is typical, this is impossible to prove, just because honest medical opinion cannot segregate the causes of an illness between compound causes. And if one asks which of the parties, the workman or the employers, should suffer from this inherent evidential difficulty, the answer as a matter of policy or justice should be that it is the creator of the risk who, ex hypothesi, must be taken to have foreseen the possibility of damage, who should bear its consequences. (My emphasis.)

He then referred to *Bonnington Castings Ltd v Wardlaw* and *Nicholson v Atlas Steel Foundry and Engineering Co Ltd* and added ([1972] 3 All ER 1008 at 1013, [1973] 1 WLR 1 at 7):

> The present factual situation has its differences: the default here consisted not in adding a material quantity to the accumulation of injurious particles but by failure to take a step which materially increased the risk that the dust already present would cause injury. And I must say that, at least in the present case, to bridge the evidential gap by inference seems to me something of a fiction, since it was precisely this inference which the medical expert declined to make. But I find in the cases quoted an analogy which suggests the conclusion that, *in the absence of proof that the culpable condition had, in the result, no effect,* the employers should be liable for an injury, squarely within the risk which they created and that they, not the pursuer, should suffer the consequence of the impossibility, foreseeably inherent in the nature of his injury, of segregating the precise consequence of their default. (My emphasis.)

My Lords, it seems to me that both these paragraphs, particularly in the words I have emphasised, amount to saying that, in the circumstances, the burden of proof of causation is reversed and thereby to run counter to the unanimous and emphatic opinions expressed in *Bonnington Castings Ltd v Wardlaw* [1956] 1 All ER 615, [1956] AC 613 to the contrary effect. I find no support in any of the other speeches for the view that the burden of proof is reversed and, in this respect, I think Lord Wilberforce's reasoning must be regarded as expressing a minority opinion.

A distinction is, of course, apparent between the facts of *Bonnington Castings Ltd v Wardlaw,* where the 'innocent' and 'guilty' silica dust particles which together caused the pursuer's lung disease were inhaled concurrently and the facts of *McGhee v National Coal Board* where the 'innocent' and 'guilty' brick dust was present on the pursuer's body for consecutive periods. In the one case the concurrent inhalation of 'innocent' and 'guilty' dust must both have contributed to the cause of the disease. In the other case the consecutive periods when 'innocent' and 'guilty' brick dust was present on the pursuer's body may both have contributed to the cause of the disease or, theoretically at least, one or other may have been the sole cause. But where the layman is told by the doctors that the longer the brick dust remains on the body, the greater the risk of dermatitis, although the doctors cannot identify the process of causation scientifically, there seems to be nothing irrational in drawing the inference, as a matter of common sense, that the consecutive periods when brick dust remained on the body probably contributed cumulatively to the causation of the dermatitis. I believe that a process of inferential reasoning on these general lines underlies the decision of the majority in *McGhee's* case.

In support of their view, I refer to the following passages. Lord Reid said ([1972] 3 All ER 1008 at 1010, [1973] 1 WLR 1 at 3-4):

> The medical witnesses are in substantial agreement. Dermatitis can be caused, and this dermatitis was caused, by repeated minute abrasion of the outer horny layer of the skin followed by some injury to or change in the underlying cells, the precise nature of which has not yet been discovered by medical science. If a man sweats profusely for a considerable time the outer layer of his skin is softened and easily injured. If he is then working in a cloud of abrasive brick dust, as this man was, the particles of dust will adhere to his skin in considerable quantity and exertion will cause them to injure the horny layer and expose to injury or infection the tender cells below. Then in some way not yet understood dermatitis may result. If the skin is not thoroughly washed as soon as the man ceases to work that process can continue at least for some considerable time. This man had to continue exerting himself after work by bicycling home while still caked with sweat and grime, so he would be liable to further injury until he could wash himself thoroughly. Washing is the only practicable method of removing the danger of further injury. The effect of such abrasion of the skin is cumulative in the sense that the longer a subject is exposed to injury the greater the chance of his developing dermatitis: it is for that reason that immediate washing is well recognised as a proper precaution.

He concluded ([1972] 3 All ER 1008 at 1011, [1973] 1 WLR 1 at 4-5):

> The medical evidence is to the effect that the fact that the man had to cycle home caked with grime and sweat added materially to the risk that this disease might develop. It does not and could not explain just why that is so. But experience shows that it is so. Plainly that must be because what happens while the man remains unwashed can have a causative effect, although just how the cause operates is uncertain. I cannot accept the view expressed in the Inner House that once the man left the brick kiln he left behind the causes which made him liable to develop dermatitis. That seems to me quite inconsistent with a proper interpretation of the medical evidence. Nor can I accept the distinction drawn by the Lord Ordinary between materially increasing risk that the disease will occur and making a material contribution to its occurrence. There may be some logical ground for such a distinction where our knowledge of all the material factors is complete. But it has often been said that the legal concept of causation is not based on logic or philosophy. It is based on the practical way in which the ordinary man's mind works in the everyday affairs of life. From a broad and practical viewpoint I can see no substantial difference between saying that what the respondents did materially increased the risk of injury to the appellant and saying that what the respondents did made a material contribution in his injury.

Lord Simon said ([1972] 3 All ER 1008 at 1014, [1973] 1 WLR 1 at 8):

> But *Bonnington Castings Ltd v Wardlaw* and *Nicholson v Atlas Steel Foundry & Engineering Co Ltd* establish, in my view, that where an injury is caused by two (or more) factors operating cumulatively, one (or more) of which factors is a breach of duty and one (or more) is not so, in such a way that it is impossible to ascertain the proportion in which the factors were effective in producing the injury or which factor was decisive, the law does not require a pursuer or plaintiff to prove the impossible, but holds that he is entitled to damages for the injury if he proves on a balance of probabilities that the breach or breaches of duty contributed substantially to causing the injury. If such factors do operate cumulatively, it is, in my judgment, immaterial whether they do so concurrently or successively.

Lord Kilbrandon said ([1972] 3 All ER 1008 at 1016, [1973] 1 WLR 1 at 10):

> In the present case, the appellant's body was vulnerable, while he was bicycling home, to the dirt which had been deposited on it during his working hours. It would not have been if he had had a shower. If showers had been provided he would have used them. It is admittedly more probable that disease will be contracted if a shower is not taken. In these circumstances I cannot accept the argument that nevertheless it is not more probable than not that, if the duty to provide a shower had been neglected, he would not have contracted the disease. The appellant has, after all, only to satisfy the court of a probability, not to demonstrate an irrefragable chain of causation, which in a case of dermatitis, in the present state of medical knowledge, he could probably never do.

Lord Salmon said ([1972] 3 All ER 1008 at 1017, [1973] 1 WLR 1 at 11-12):

> I, of course, accept that the burden rests on the appellant, to prove, on a balance of
> probabilities, a causal connection between his injury and the respondents' negligence.
> It is not necessary, however, to prove that the respondents' negligence was the only
> cause of injury. A factor, by itself, may not be sufficient to cause injury but if, with
> other factors, it materially contributes to causing injury, it is clearly a cause of injury.
> Everything in the present case depends on what constitutes a cause. I venture to
> repeat what I said in *Alphacell Ltd v Woodward* [1972] 2 All ER 475 at 489-490, [1972]
> AC 824 at 846: 'The nature of causation has been discussed by many eminent
> philosophers and also by a number of learned judges in the past. I consider, however,
> that what or who has caused a certain event to occur is essentially a practical
> question of fact which can best be answered by ordinary common sense rather than
> abstract metaphysical theory.' In the circumstances of the present case it seems to me
> unrealistic and contrary to ordinary common sense to hold that the negligence which
> materially increased the risk of injury did not materially contribute to causing the
> injury.

Then, after referring to *Bonnington Castings Ltd v Wardlaw* and *Nicholson v Atlas Steel
Foundry and Engineering Co Ltd* he added ([1972] 3 All ER 1008 at 1018, [1973] 1 WLR 1 at
12-13):

> I do not find the attempts to distinguish those authorities from the present case at all
> convincing. In the circumstances of the present case, the possibility of a distinction
> existing between (a) having materially increased the risk of contracting the disease,
> and (b) having materially contributed to causing the disease may no doubt be a
> fruitful source of interesting academic discussions between students of philosophy.
> Such a distinction is, however, far too unreal to be recognised by the common law.

The conclusion I draw from these passages is that *McGhee v National Coal Board* laid down
no new principle of law whatever. On the contrary, it affirmed the principle that the onus of
proving causation lies on the pursuer or plaintiff. Adopting a robust and pragmatic
approach to the undisputed primary facts of the case, the majority concluded that it was a
legitimate inference of fact that the defenders' negligence had materially contributed to the
pursuer's injury. The decision, in my opinion, is of no greater significance than that and the
attempt to extract from it some esoteric principle which in some way modifies, as a matter of
law, the nature of the burden of proof of causation which a plaintiff or pursuer must
discharge once he has established a relevant breach of duty is a fruitless one.

In the Court of Appeal in the instant case Sir Nicolas Browne-Wilkinson V-C, being in a
minority, expressed his view on causation with understandable caution. But I am quite
unable to find any fault with the following passage in his dissenting judgment ([1986] 3 All
ER 801 at 834-835, [1987] QB 730 at 779):

> To apply the principle in *McGhee v National Coal Board* [1972] 3 All ER 1008, [1973]
> 1 WLR 1 to the present case would constitute an extension of that principle. In
> *McGhee* there was no doubt that the pursuer's dermatitis was physically caused by
> brick dust; the only question was whether the continued presence of such dust on the
> pursuer's skin after the time when he should have been provided with a shower
> caused or materially contributed to the dermatitis which he contracted. There was
> only one possible agent which could have caused the dermatitis, viz brick dust, and
> there was no doubt that the dermatitis from which he suffered was caused by that
> brick dust. In the present case the question is different. There are a number of
> different agents which could have caused the RLF. Excess oxygen was one of them.
> The defendants failed to take reasonable precautions to prevent one of the possible
> causative agents (eg excess oxygen) from causing RLF. But no one can tell in this
> case whether excess oxygen did or did not cause or contribute to the RLF suffered by
> the plaintiff. The plaintiff's RLF may have been caused by some completely different
> agent or agents, eg hypercarbia, intraventricular haemorrhage, apnoea or patent
> ductus arteriosus. In addition to oxygen, each of those conditions has been
> implicated as a possible cause of RLF. This baby suffered from each of those
> conditions at various times in the first two months of his life. There is no satisfactory
> evidence that excess oxygen is more likely than any of those other four candidates to
> have caused RLF in this baby. To my mind, the occurrence of RLF following a
> failure to take a necessary precaution to prevent excess oxygen causing RLF provides
> no evidence and raises no presumption that it was excess oxygen rather than one or

more of the four other possible agents which caused or contributed to RLF in this case. The position, to my mind, is wholly different from that in *McGhee*, where there was only one candidate (brick dust) which could have caused the dermatitis, and the failure to take a precaution against brick dust causing dermatitis was followed by dermatitis caused by brick dust. In such a case, I can see the common sense, if not the logic, of holding that, in the absence of any other evidence, the failure to take the precautions caused or contributed to the dermatitis. To the extent that certain members of the House of Lords decided the question on inferences from evidence or presumptions, I do not consider that the present case falls within their reasoning. A failure to take preventative measures against one out of five possible causes is no evidence as to which of those five caused the injury.

Since, on this view, the appeal must, in any event, be allowed, it is not strictly necessary to decide whether it was open to the Court of Appeal to resolve one of the conflicts between the experts which the judge left unresolved and to find that the oxygen administered to Martin in consequence of the misleading PO_2 levels derived from the misplaced catheter was capable of having caused or materially contributed to his RLF. I very well understand the anxiety of the majority to avoid the necessity for ordering a retrial if that was at all possible. But, having accepted, as your Lordships and counsel have had to accept, that the primary conflict of opinion between the experts whether excessive oxygen in the first two days of life probably did cause or materially contribute to Martin's RLF cannot be resolved by reading the transcript, I doubt, with all respect, if the Court of Appeal was entitled to try to resolve the secondary conflict whether it could have done so. Where expert witnesses are radically at issue about complex technical questions within their own field and are examined and cross-examined at length about their conflicting theories, I believe that the judge's advantage in seeing them and hearing them is scarcely less important than when he has to resolve some conflict of primary fact between lay witnesses in purely mundane matters. So here, in the absence of relevant findings of fact by the judge, there was really no alternative to a retrial. At all events, the judge who retries the issue of causation should approach it with an entirely open mind uninfluenced by any view of the facts bearing on causation expressed in the Court of Appeal.

To have to order a retrial is a highly unsatisfactory result and one cannot help feeling the profoundest sympathy for Martin and his family that the outcome is once again in doubt and that this litigation may have to drag on. Many may feel that such a result serves only to highlight the shortcomings of a system in which the victim of some grievous misfortune will recover substantial compensation or none at all according to the unpredictable hazards of the forensic process. But, whether we like it or not, the law, which only Parliament can change, requires proof of fault causing damage as the basis of liability in tort. We should do society nothing but disservice if we made the forensic process still more unpredictable and hazardous by distorting the law to accommodate the exigencies of what may seem hard cases.

Leave to appeal was given by the Court of Appeal on terms that the authority should not seek an order for costs in this House or for variation of the orders for costs in the courts below. For the reasons I have indicated I would allow the appeal, set aside the order of the Court of Appeal save as to costs and order retrial of the issue whether the negligence of the authority, as found by the Court of Appeal, caused or materially contributed to the plaintiff's RLF.

Lords Fraser, Lowry, Griffiths and Ackner agreed.

In fact, the *Wilsher* case was settled before re-trial. It could be said that the House of Lords has adopted a restrictive view of the decision in *McGhee* thereby arguably making the position of the plaintiff in medical negligence cases even more difficult. But this is not the only view of *Wilsher* which could be taken.

Snell v Farrell (1990) 72 DLR (4th) 289 (Supreme Court of Canada)

The plaintiff lost the sight of an eye following an operation on it performed by the defendant surgeon. The trial judge found that the defendant had acted negligently in continuing the operation after noticing a haemorrhage in the plaintiff's eye. The medical evidence was that the operation was a possible cause of the loss of sight, but the medical witnesses could not say positively that it was the cause. The trial judge held that the burden had shifted to the defendant to disprove causation, that the burden had not been discharged, and accordingly that the defendant was liable.

Sopinka J: Both the trial judge and the Court of Appeal relied on *McGhee*, which (subject to its reinterpretation in the House of Lords in *Wilsher*) purports to depart from traditional principles in the law of torts that the plaintiff must prove on a balance of probabilities that, but for the tortious conduct of the defendant, the plaintiff would not have sustained the injury complained of. . . .

Proof of causation in medical malpractice cases is often difficult for the patient. The physician is usually in a better position to know the cause of the injury than the patient. . . . [T]here is an argument that the burden of proof should be allocated to the defendant. In some jurisdictions, this has occurred to an extent by operation of the principle of *res ipsa loquitur*: *Cross on Evidence,* 6th edn (1985), at p 138. In Canada, the rule has been generally regarded as a piece of circumstantial evidence which does not shift the burden of proof: see *Interlake Tissue Mills Co v Salmon* [1949] 1 DLR 207, [1948] OR 950 (CA); *Cudney v Clements Motor Sales Ltd* (1969) 5 DLR (3d) 3, [1969] 2 OR 209 (CA); *Kirk v McLaughlin Coal & Supplies Ltd* (1967) 66 DLR (2d) 321, [1968] 1 OR 311 (CA); *Jackson v Millar* (1972) 31 DLR (3d) 263, [1973] 1 OR 399 (CA). As the rule was properly held not to be applicable in this case and no argument was directed to this issue, I will refrain from commenting further upon it.

This brings me to the *McGhee* case and its influence on subsequent cases, particularly in the medical malpractice field. The appellant contracted dermatitis while employed as a labourer emptying pipe kilns. This work exposed him to clouds of abrasive dust. His employer provided no washing facilities with the result that the appellant would ride home on his bicycle caked with grime and sweat. He sued his employer, the respondent, for negligence. The medical evidence showed that the dermatitis was caused by the working conditions and that the longer the exposure to dust, the greater the chance of developing dermatitis. The medical evidence could not attribute the dermatitis to the additional exposure after work. The appellant's expert could not say that if washing facilities had been provided, the appellant would not have contracted the disease. A breach of duty was found with respect to the failure to provide washing facilities, but not with respect to the conditions under which the kilns were operated. The Lord Ordinary dismissed the action on the ground that it had not been shown that the breach of duty caused or contributed to the injury. An appeal to the First Division of the Court of Session failed, but an appeal was allowed by the House of Lords.

Of the five speeches in the House of Lords, only Lord Wilberforce advocated a reversal of the burden of proof. He did so in the following passage which has been the basis of decisions in a number of cases both in Canada and in Britain. He states (at pp. 6-7):

> First, it is a sound principle that where a person has, by breach of a duty of care, created a risk, and injury occurs within the area of that risk, the loss should be borne by him unless he shows that it had some other cause.

He added:

> And I must say that, at least in the present case, to bridge the evidential gap by inference seems to me something of a fiction, since it was precisely this inference which the medical expert declined to make.

Two theories of causation emerge from an analysis of the speeches of the Lords in this case. The first, firmly espoused by Lord Wilberforce, is that the plaintiff need only prove that the defendant created a risk of harm and that the injury occurred within the area of the risk. The second is that in these circumstances, an inference of causation was warranted in that there is no practical difference between materially contributing to the risk of harm and materially contributing to the harm itself.

The speeches were subjected to a careful examination and interpretation in *Wilsher v Essex Area Health Authority* [1988] 2 WLR 557, by Lord Bridge when some 15 years later, the House of Lords revisited the issue. The plaintiff claimed damages from the defendant health authority for negligence in medical treatment which resulted in a condition of the eyes leading to blindness. A likely cause of the condition, but not a definite one, in the opinion of medical experts, was too much oxygen. The plaintiff proved that for a period of time he was supersaturated with oxygen. A number of different factors other than excessive oxygen could have caused or contributed to the injury. The expert evidence was conflicting. The trial judge applied *McGhee* and held the defendant liable since it had failed to prove that the plaintiff's condition had not resulted from its negligence. The Court of Appeal dismissed the appeal by a majority judgment with the Vice-Chancellor dissenting. The House of Lords allowed the appeal and directed a new trial. Lord Bridge, delivering the unanimous judgment of the Court, reaffirmed the principle that the burden of proving causation rested on the plaintiff. Since the trial judge had not made the relevant finding of fact to sort out the conflicting evidence, a new trial was directed on this basis. Lord Bridge interpreted *McGhee* as espousing no new principle. Instead, *McGhee* was explained as promoting a robust and pragmatic approach to the facts to enable an inference of negligence to be drawn even though medical or scientific expertise cannot arrive at a definitive conclusion. . . .

Canadian cases decided after *McGhee*, but before *Wilsher*, tended to follow *McGhee* by adopting either the reversal of onus or the inference interpretation. Which interpretation was adopted made no practical difference, because even when the latter approach was applied, the creation of the risk by the defendant's breach of duty was deemed to have established a *prima facie* case, thus shifting the onus to the defendant: *Powell v Guttman* (1978) 89 DLR (3d) 180, [1978] 5 WWR 228, 6 CCLT 183 (Man CA) and *Letnick v Metropolitan Toronto (Municipality)* (1988) 49 DLR (4th) 707, [1988] 2 FC 399, 82 NR (CA), applied the reversal of proof theory. In *Dalpe v City of Edmundston* (1979) 25 NBR (2d) 102, the New Brunswick Court of Appeal, in a flooding case in which negligence was alleged against a municipal authority, held that in circumstances in which a risk of the type of harm which in fact occurred had been created, causation *should* be inferred in the absence of evidence to the contrary on the part of the defendant. In *Nowsco Well Service Ltd v Canadian Propane Gas & Oil Ltd* (1981) 122 DLR (3d) 228, 7 Sask R 291, 16 CCLT 23, the Saskatchewan Court of Appeal applied *McGhee* on the basis that proof that the breach of duty which gave rise to the risk 'is *prima facie* proof that the fire was caused by the escape of propane gas' (p 248).

Decisions in Canada after *Wilsher* accept its interpretation of *McGhee*. In the circumstances in which *McGhee* had been previously interpreted to support a reversal of the burden of proof, an inference was now permissible to find causation, notwithstanding that causation was not proved by positive evidence: See *Rendall v Ewart* (1989) 60 DLR (4th) 513, [1989] 6 WWR 97, 38 BCLR (2d) 1 (CA); *Kitchen v McMullen* (1989), 62 DLR (4th) 481, 100 NBR (2d) 91, 50 CCLT 213, [1989] NBJ No 815 (CA); *Westco Storage Ltd v Inter-City Gas Utilities Ltd* [1989] 4 WWR 289, 59 Man R (2d) 37, (CA) and *Haag v Marshall* (1989), 61 DLR (4th) 371, [1990] 1 WWR 361, 39 BCLR (2d) 205 (CA).

The question that this court must decide is whether the traditional approach to causation is no longer satisfactory in that plaintiffs in malpractice cases are being deprived of compensation because they cannot prove causation where it in fact exists.

Causation is an expression of the relationship that must be found to exist between the tortious act of the wrongdoer and the injury to the victim in order to justify compensation of the latter out of the pocket of the former. Is the requirement that the plaintiff prove that the defendant's tortious conduct caused or contributed to the plaintiff's injury too onerous? Is some lesser relationship sufficient to justify compensation? I have examined the alternatives arising out of the *McGhee* case. They were that the plaintiff simply prove that the defendant created a risk that the injury which occurred would occur. Or, what amounts to the same thing, that the defendant has the burden of disproving causation. If I were convinced that defendants who have a substantial connection to the injury were escaping liability because plaintiffs cannot prove causation under currently applied principles, I would not hesitate to adopt one of these alternatives. In my opinion, however, properly applied, the principles relating to causation are adequate to the task. Adoption of either of the proposed alternatives would have the effect of compensating plaintiffs where a substantial connection between the injury and the defendant's conduct is absent. Reversing the burden of proof may be justified where two defendants negligently fire in the direction of the plaintiff and then by their tortious conduct destroy the means of proof at his disposal. In such a case it is clear that the injury was not caused by neutral conduct. It is quite a different matter to compensate a plaintiff by reversing the burden of proof for an injury that may very well be due to factors unconnected to the defendant and not the fault of anyone. . . .

In Britain, proposals to reverse the burden of proof in malpractice cases which gained momentum by virtue of the *McGhee* case were not adopted. In 1978, the Royal Commission on Civil Liability and Compensation for Personal Injury (Pearson Report, vol I, London: HM Stationery Off, 1978), reported as follows (at p 285):

> Some witnesses suggested that, if the burden of proof were reversed, the patient's difficulties in obtaining and presenting his evidence would be largely overcome. It was said that doctors were in a better position to prove absence of negligence than patients to establish liability. At the Council of Europe colloquy, however, although

it was agreed that the patient was at a disadvantage when he sought to establish a claim, serious doubts were expressed on the desirability of making a radical change in the burden of proof. We share these doubts. We think that there might well be a large increase in claims, and although many would be groundless, each one would have to be investigated and answered. The result would almost certainly be an increase in defensive medicine.

The *Wilsher* decision in the House of Lords which followed ensured that the common law did not undermine this recommendation.

I am of the opinion that the dissatisfaction with the traditional approach to causation stems to a large extent from its too rigid application by the courts in many cases. Causation need not be determined by scientific precision. It is, as stated by Lord Salmon in *Alphacell Ltd v Woodward* [1972] 2 All ER 475 (HL), at p 490, ' . . . essentially a practical question of fact which can best be answered by ordinary common sense rather than abstract metaphysical theory'. Furthermore, as I observed earlier, the allocation of the burden of proof is not immutable. Both the burden and the standard of proof are flexible concepts. In *Blatch v Archer* (1774) 1 Cowp 63 at 65, 98 ER 969 at p 970, Lord Mansfield stated: 'It is certainly a maxim that all evidence is to be weighed according to the proof which it was in the power of one side to have produced, and in the power of the other to have contradicted.'

In many malpractice cases, the facts lie particularly within the knowledge of the defendant. In these circumstances, very little affirmative evidence on the part of the plaintiff will justify the drawing of an inference of causation in the absence of evidence to the contrary. This has been expressed in terms of shifting the burden of proof. In *Cummings v City of Vancouver* (1911) 1 WWR 31 at p 34, 16 BCR 494 (CA), Irving JA stated:

> Stephens in his Digest (*Evidence Act*, 1896) says: 'In considering the amount of evidence necessary to shift the burden of proof, the Court has regard to the opportunities of knowledge with respect to the fact to be proved, which may be possessed by the parties respectively.'
> *Hollis v Young* (1909) 1 KB 629, illustrates the rule that very little affirmative evidence will be sufficient where the facts lie almost entirely within the knowledge of the other side.

In *Dunlop Holdings Ltd's Application* [1979] RPC 523 (CA) at p 544, Buckley LJ affirmed this principle in the following terms:

> Where the relevant facts are peculiarly within the knowledge of one party, it is perhaps relevant to have in mind the rule as stated in Stephens' Digest, which is cited at page 86 of Cross on Evidence [3rd edn]:
> 'In considering the amount of evidence necessary to shift the burden of proof, the court has regard to the opportunities of knowledge with respect to the facts to be proved which may be possessed by the parties respectively.
> '*This does not mean,*' Sir Rupert continues, '*that the peculiar means of knowledge of one of the parties relieves the other of the burden of adducing some evidence with regard to the facts in question, although very slight evidence will often suffice.*' (Emphasis added.)

See also *Diamond v BC Thoroughbred Breeders' Society* (1965) 52 DLR (2d) 146 at p 158, 52 WWR 385 (BCSC); *Pleet v Canadian Northern Quebec R Co* (1921) 64 DLR 316 at pp 319-20, 50 OLR 223, 26 CRC 227 (CA), and *Guaranty Trust Co of Canada v Mall Medical Group* (1969) 4 DLR (3d) 1 at p 7, [1969] SCR 541.

These references speak of the shifting of the secondary or evidential burden of proof or the burden of adducing evidence. I find it preferable to explain the process without using the term secondary or evidential burden. It is not strictly accurate to speak of the burden shifting to the defendant when what is meant is that evidence adduced by the plaintiff may result in an inference being drawn adverse to the defendant. Whether an inference is or is not drawn is a matter of weighing evidence. The defendant runs the risk of an adverse inference in the absence of evidence to the contrary. This is sometimes referred to as imposing on the defendant a provisional or tactical burden: see Cross, *op cit*, at p 129. In my opinion, this is not a true burden of proof, and use of an additional label to describe what is an ordinary step in the fact-finding process is unwarranted.

The legal or ultimate burden remains with the plaintiff, but in the absence of evidence to the contrary adduced by the defendant, an inference of causation may be drawn, although positive or scientific proof of causation has not been adduced. If some evidence to the contrary is adduced by the defendant, the trial judge is entitled to take account of Lord

Mansfield's famous precept. This is, I believe, what Lord Bridge had in mind in *Wilsher* when he referred to a 'robust and pragmatic approach to the . . . facts' (p 569).

It is not, therefore, essential that the medical experts provide a firm opinion supporting the plaintiff's theory of causation. Medical experts ordinarily determine causation in terms of certainties whereas a lesser standard is demanded by the law. As pointed out in D W Louisell, *Medical Malpractice*, vol 3 (by Charles Kramer, New York: Matthew Bender, 1977-90), at pp 25-27, the phrase 'in your opinion with a reasonable degree of medical certainty', which is the standard form of question to a medical expert, is often misunderstood. The author explains that:

> Many doctors do not understand the phrase . . . as they usually deal in 'certainties' that are 100% sure, whereas 'reasonable' certainties which the law requires need only be more probably so, *ie*, 51%. . . .

The issue, then, in this case is whether the trial judge drew an inference that the appellant's negligence caused or contributed to the respondent's injury, or whether, applying the above principles, he would or ought to have drawn such an inference. . . .

The appellant [in this case] was present during the operation and was in a better position to observe what occurred. Furthermore, he was able to interpret from a medical standpoint what he saw. In addition, by continuing the operation which has been found to constitute negligence, he made it impossible for the respondent or anyone else to detect the bleeding which is alleged to have caused the injury. In these circumstances, it was open to the trial judge to draw the inference that the injury was caused by the retro-bulbar bleeding. There was no evidence to rebut this inference. The fact that testing the eye for hardness did not disclose bleeding is insufficient for this purpose. If there was any rebutting evidence, it was weak, and it was open to the trial judge to find causation, applying the principles to which I have referred.

I am confident that had the trial judge not stated that 'I cannot go beyond this since neither doctor did and I should not speculate,' he would have drawn the necessary inference. In stating the above, he failed to appreciate that it is not essential to have a positive medical opinion to support a finding of causation. Furthermore, it is not speculation but the application of common sense to draw such an inference where, as here, the circumstances, other than a positive medical opinion, permit.

(For an application of Lord Bridge's 'robust and pragmatic approach to the . . . facts' see *Bolitho v City and Hackney HA* (1992) 13 BMLR 111 per Simon Brown LJ (dissenting).)

The House of Lords had another opportunity to develop the law in a way more favourable to the plaintiff in *Hotson v East Berkshire AHA* [1987] AC 750, [1987] 2 All ER 909. In that case the plaintiff was unable to establish, on a balance of probabilities, that the defendants' failure to treat him promptly in breach of duty would have alleviated the injuries he suffered from as a result of falling out of a tree. The trial judge, Simon Brown J, found that there had always been a 75% chance that the injuries would have resulted in his disabilities in any event, but that due to the defendants' carelessness, this had become a 100% certainty. Therefore, even though the plaintiff could not show that 'but for' the defendants' carelessness he would be injury-free, he could establish that he had lost a 25% chance of avoiding his eventually permanent injuries. The issue in *Hotson* was whether this could found a claim for damages in the tort of negligence. The trial judge ([1985] 3 All ER 167) and the Court of Appeal ([1987] 1 All ER 210) held that it could.

Hotson v East Berkshire Area Health Authority **[1987] AC 750, [1987] 2 All ER 909 (HL)**

Lord Bridge of Harwich: My Lords, the respondent plaintiff is now 23 years of age. On 26 April 1977, as a schoolboy of 13, whilst playing in the school lunch hour he climbed a tree to which a rope was attached, lost his hold on the rope and fell some 12 feet to the ground. He sustained an acute traumatic fracture of the left femoral epiphysis. Within hours he was taken to St Luke's Hospital, Maidenhead, for which the appellant health authority (the authority) was responsible. Members of the hospital staff examined him, but failed to diagnose the injury and he was sent home. For five days he was in severe pain. On 1 May 1977 he was taken to the hospital once more and this time X-rays of his hip yielded the correct diagnosis. He was put on immediate traction, treated as an emergency case and transferred to the Heatherwood Hospital where, on the following day, he was operated on by manipulation and reduction of the fracture and pinning of the joint. In the event the plaintiff suffered an avascular necrosis of the epiphysis. The femoral epiphysis is a layer of cartilage separating the bony head from the bony neck of the femur in a growing body. Avascular necrosis results from a failure of the blood supply to the epiphysis and causes deformity in the maturing head of the femur. This in turn involves a greater or lesser degree of disability of the hip joint with a virtual certainty that it will in due course be aggravated by osteoarthritis developing within the joint.

The plaintiff sued the authority, who admitted negligence in failing to diagnose the injury on 26 April 1977. Simon Brown J, in a judgment delivered on 15 March 1985, sub nom *Hotson v Fitzgerald* [1985] 3 All ER 167, [1985] 1 WLR 1036, awarded £150 damages for the pain suffered by the plaintiff from 26 April to 1 May 1977 which he would have been spared by prompt diagnosis and treatment. This element of the damages is not in dispute. The authority denied liability for any other element of damages. The judge expressed his findings of fact as follows ([1985] 3 All ER 167 at 171, [1985] 1 WLR 1036 at 1040-1041):

> 1. Even had the defendants correctly diagnosed and treated the plaintiff on 26 April there is a high probability, which I assess as a 75% risk, that the plaintiff's injury would have followed the same course as it in fact has, ie he would have developed avascular necrosis of the whole femoral head with all the same adverse consequences as have already ensued and with all the same adverse future prospects. 2. That 75% risk was translated by the defendants' admitted breach of duty into inevitability. Putting it the other way, the defendants' delay in diagnosis denied the plaintiff the 25% chance that, given immediate treatment, avascular necrosis would not have developed. 3. Had avascular necrosis not developed, the plaintiff would have made a very full recovery. 4. The reason why the delay sealed the plaintiff's fate was because it followed the pressure caused by haemarthrosis (the bleeding of ruptured blood vessels into the joint) to compress and thus block the intact but distorted remaining vessels with the result that even had the fall left sufficient vessels to keep the epiphysis alive (which, as finding no 1 makes plain, I think possible but improbable) such vessels would have become occluded and ineffective for this purpose.

On the basis of these findings he held, as a matter of law, that the plaintiff was entitled to damages for the loss of 25% chance that, if the injury had been promptly diagnosed and treated, it would not have resulted in avascular necrosis of the epiphysis and the plaintiff would have made a very nearly full recovery. He proceeded to assess the damages attributable to the consequences of the avascular necrosis at £46,000. Discounting this by 75%, he awarded the plaintiff £11,500 for the lost chance of recovery. The authority's appeal against this element in the award of damages was dismissed by the Court of Appeal (Sir John Donaldson MR, Dillon and Croom-Johnson LJJ) ([1987] 1 All ER 210, [1987] 2 WLR 287). The authority now appeal by leave of your Lordships' House. . . .

In analysing the issue of law arising from his findings the judge said ([1985] 3 All ER 167 at 175, [1985] 1 WLR 1036 at 1043-1044):

> In the end the problem comes down to one of classification. Is this on true analysis a case where the plaintiff is concerned to establish causative negligence or is it rather a case where the real question is the proper quantum of damage? Clearly the case hovers near the border. Its proper solution in my judgment depends on categorising it correctly between the two. If the issue is one of causation then the defendants succeed since the plaintiff will have failed to prove his claim on the balance of probabilities. He will be lacking an essential ingredient of his cause of action. If, however, the issue is one of quantification then the plaintiff succeeds because it is trite law that the quantum of a recognised head of damage must be evaluated according to the chances of the loss occurring.

He reached the conclusion that the question was one of quantification and thus arrived at his award to the plaintiff of one quarter of the damages appropriate to compensate him for the consequence of the avascular necrosis.

It is here, with respect, that I part company with the judge. The plaintiff's claim was for damages for physical injury and consequential loss alleged to have been caused by the authority's breach of their duty of care. In some cases, perhaps particularly medical negligence cases, causation may be so shrouded in mystery that the court can only measure statistical chances. But that was not so here. On the evidence there was a clear conflict as to what had caused the avascular necrosis. The authority's evidence was that the sole cause was the original traumatic injury to the hip. The plaintiff's evidence, at its highest, was that the delay in treatment was a material contributory cause. This was a conflict, like any other about some relevant past event, which the judge could not avoid resolving on a balance of probabilities. Unless the plaintiff proved on a balance of probabilities that the delayed treatment was at least a material contributory cause of the avascular necrosis he failed on the issue of causation and no question of quantification could arise. But the judge's findings of fact, as stated in the numbered paragraphs (1) and (4) which I have set out earlier in this opinion, are unmistakably to the effect that on a balance of probabilities the injury caused by the plaintiff's fall left insufficient blood vessels intact to keep the epiphysis alive. This amounts to a finding of fact that the fall was the sole cause of the avascular necrosis.

The upshot is that the appeal must be allowed on the narrow ground that the plaintiff failed to establish a cause of action in respect of the avascular necrosis and its consequences. Your Lordships were invited to approach the appeal more broadly and to decide whether, in a claim for damages for personal injury, it can ever be appropriate, where the cause of the injury is unascertainable and all the plaintiff can show is a statistical chance which is less than even that, but for the defendant's breach of duty, he would not have suffered the injury, to award him a proportionate fraction of the full damages appropriate to compensate for the injury as the measure of damages for the lost chance.

There is a superficially attractive analogy between the principle applied in such cases as *Chaplin v Hicks* [1911] 2 KB 786, [1911-13] All ER Rep 224 (award of damages for breach of contract assessed by reference to the lost chance of securing valuable employment if the contract had been performed) and *Kitchen v Royal Air Forces Association* [1958] 2 All ER 241, [1958] 1 WLR 563 (damages for solicitors' negligence assessed by reference to the lost chance of prosecuting a successful civil action) and the principle of awarding damages for the lost chance of avoiding personal injury or, in medical negligence cases, for the lost chance of a better medical result which might have been achieved by prompt diagnosis and correct treatment. I think there are formidable difficulties in the way of accepting the analogy. But I do not see this appeal as a suitable occasion for reaching a settled conclusion as to whether the analogy can ever be applied.

As I have said, there was in this case an inescapable issue of causation first to be resolved. But if the plaintiff had proved on a balance of probabilities that the authority's negligent failure to diagnose and treat his injury promptly had materially contributed to the development of avascular necrosis, I know of no principle of English law which would have entitled the authority to a discount from the full measure of damage to reflect the chance that, even given prompt treatment, avascular necrosis might well still have developed. The decisions of this House in *Bonnington Castings Ltd v Wardlaw* [1956] 1 All ER 615, [1956] AC 613 and *McGhee v National Coal Board* [1972] 3 All ER 1008, [1973] 1 WLR 1 give no support to such a view.

I would allow the appeal.

As you will see, Lord Bridge allowed the appeal on a 'narrow ground'. Lords Brandon, Mackay, Ackner and Goff agreed with this conclusion.

Lord Bridge left open the issue of whether the plaintiff could have recovered had he established a lost chance of recovery. Lord Mackay in his speech examined this issue in some depth though, again, without reaching any conclusion.

Lord Mackay: I consider that it would be unwise in the present case to lay it down as a rule that a plaintiff could never succeed by proving loss of a chance in a medical negligence case. In *McGhee v National Coal Board* [1972] 3 All ER 1008, [1973] 1 WLR 1 this House held that where it was proved that the failure to provide washing facilities for the pursuer at the end of his shift had materially increased the risk that he would contract dermatitis it was proper to hold that the failure to provide such facilities was a cause to a material extent of his contracting dermatitis and thus entitled him to damages from his employers for their negligent failure measured by his loss resulting from dermatitis. Material increase of the risk of contraction of dermatitis is equivalent to material decrease in the chance of escaping dermatitis. Although no precise figures could be given in that case for the purpose of illustration and comparison with this case one might, for example, say that it was established that of 100 people working under the same conditions as the pursuer and without facilities for washing at the end of their shift 70 contracted dermatitis: of 100 people working in the same conditions as the pursuer when washing facilities were provided for them at the end of the shift 30 contracted dermatitis. Assuming nothing more were known about the matter than that, the decision of this House may be taken as holding that in the circumstances of that case it was reasonable to infer that there was a relationship between contraction of dermatitis in these conditions and the absence of washing facilities and therefore it was reasonable to hold that absence of washing facilities was likely to have made a material contribution to the causation of the dermatitis. Although neither party in the present appeal placed particular reliance on the decision in *McGhee* since it was recognised that *McGhee* is far removed on its facts from the circumstances of the present appeal your Lordships were also informed that cases are likely soon to come before the House in which the decision in *McGhee* will be subjected to close analysis [see now the *Wilsher* case]. Obviously in approaching the matter on the basis adopted in *McGhee* much will depend on what is known of the reasons for the difference in the figures which I have used to illustrate the position. In the circumstances I think it unwise to do more than say that unless this House departs from the decision in *McGhee* your Lordships cannot affirm the proposition that in no circumstances can evidence of loss of a chance resulting from the breach of a duty of care found a successful claim of damages, although there was no suggestion that the House regarded such a chance as an asset in any sense.

By agreement of the parties we were supplied with a list of American authorities relevant to the question arising in this appeal, although they were not examined in detail. Of the cases referred to, the one that I have found most interesting and instructive is *Herskovits v Group Health Cooperative of Puget Sound* 664 P 2d 474 (1983), a decision of the Supreme Court of Washington en banc. In this case the claim arose in respect of Mr Herskovits's death. He was seen at Group Health Hospital at a time when he was suffering from a tumour but this was not diagnosed on first examination. The medical evidence available suggested that at that stage, assuming the tumour was a stage 1 tumour, the chance of survival for more than five years was 30%. When he was treated later the tumour was a stage 2 tumour and the chance of surviving more than five years was 25%. The defendant moved for summary judgment on the basis that, taking the most favourable view of the evidence that was possible, the case could not succeed. The Superior Court of King County granted the motion. This decision was reversed by a majority on appeal to the Supreme Court. The first judgment for the majority in the Supreme Court was delivered by Dore J. Early in his judgment he read from the American Law Institute's Restatement of the Law, Second, Torts 2d (1965) vol 2, s 323, which is in these terms:

> One who undertakes, gratuitously or for consideration, to render services to another which he should recognize as necessary for the protection of the other's person or things, is subject to liability to the other for physical harm resulting from his failure to exercise reasonable care to perform his undertaking, if (a) his failure to exercise such care increases the risk of such harm . . .

After noting that the Supreme Court of Washington had not faced the issue of whether, under this paragraph, proof that the defendant's conduct had increased the risk of death by decreasing the chances of survival was sufficient to take the issue of proximate cause to the jury he said (664 2d 474 at 476):

> Some courts in other jurisdictions have allowed the proximate cause issue to go to the jury on this type of proof . . . These courts emphasized the fact that defendants' conduct deprived the decedent of a 'significant' chance to survive or recover, rather than requiring proof that with absolute certainty the defendants' conduct caused the physical injury. The underlying reason is that it is not for the wrongdoer, who put the possibility of recovery beyond realization, to say afterward that the result was inevitable . . . Other jurisdictions have rejected this approach, generally holding that unless the plaintiff is able to show that it was *more likely than not* that the harm was caused by the defendants' negligence, proof of a decreased chance of survival is not enough to take the proximate cause question to the jury . . . These courts have concluded that the defendant should not be liable where the decedent more than likely would have died anyway. (Dore J's emphasis.)

To the question whether the plaintiff should be allowed, in the case before him, to proceed to a jury he returned an affirmative answer, and gave as the reason (at 477):

> To decide otherwise would be a blanket release from liability for doctors and hospitals any time there was less than a 50 percent chance of survival, regardless of how flagrant the negligence.

In support of this reasoning he referred to *Hamil v Bashline* 481 Pa 256 (1978), a decision of the Pennsylvania Supreme Court, and said:

> The *Hamil* court distinguished the facts of that case from the general tort case in which a plaintiff alleges that a defendant's act or omission set in motion a force which resulted in harm. In the typical tort case, the 'but for' test, requiring proof that damages or death probably would not have occurred 'but for' the negligent conduct of the defendant, is appropriate. In *Hamil* and the instant case, however, the defendant's act or omission failed in a *duty* to protect against harm from *another source*. Thus, as the *Hamil* court noted, the fact finder is put in the position of having to consider not only what *did* occur, but also what *might* have occurred. (Dore J's emphasis.)

He goes on to quote from *Hamil's* case 481 Pa 256 at 271:

> Such cases by their very nature elude the degree of certainty one would prefer and upon which the law normally insists before a person may be held liable. Nevertheless, in order that an actor is not completely insulated because of uncertainties as to the consequence of his negligent conduct, Section 323(a) [of the Restatement of the Law, Second, Torts 2d] tacitly acknowledges that difficulty and permits the issue to go to the jury upon a less than normal threshold of proof.

He goes on to refer to another decision, namely *Hicks v US* 368 F 2d 626 at 632 (1966), as containing a succinct statement of the relevant doctrine, which he quotes (664 P 2d 474 at 478):

> Rarely is it possible to demonstrate to an absolute certainty what would have happened in circumstances that the wrongdoer did not allow to come to pass. The law does not in the existing circumstances require the plaintiff to show to a *certainty* that the patient would have lived had she been hospitalized and operated on promptly. (Judge Sobeloff's emphasis.)

He refers also to a general observation in the Supreme Court of the United States dealing with a contention similar to that argued before him by the doctors and the hospital. In *Lavender v Kurn* 327 US at 653 (1946) the Supreme Court said:

> It is no answer to say that the jury's verdict involved speculation and conjecture. Whenever facts are in dispute or the evidence is such that fair-minded men may draw different inferences, a measure of speculation and conjecture is required on the part of those whose duty it is to settle the dispute by choosing what seems to them to be the most reasonable inference.

He therefore concluded that the evidence available which showed at maximum a reduction in the 39% chance of five years' survival to a 25% chance of five years' survival was sufficient to allow the case to go to the jury on the basis that the jury would be entitled to infer from that evidence that the delay in treatment was a proximate cause of the decedent's death (see 664 P 2d 474 at 479). He pointed out, however, that causing reduction of the opportunity to recover (also described as a loss of chance) by one's negligence did not necessitate a total recovery against the negligent party for all damages caused by the victim's death. He held that damages should be awarded to the injured party and his family based only on damages caused directly by premature death, such as lost earnings and additional medical expenses and the like.

The approach of Dore J bears some resemblance to the approach taken by some members of this House in *McGhee v National Coal Board* [1972] 3 All ER 1008, [1973] 1 WLR 1 and by Lord Guthrie in *Kenyon v Bell* 1953 SC 125. Brachtenbach J dissented. He warned against the danger of using statistics as a basis on which to prove proximate cause and indicated that it was necessary at the minimum to produce evidence connecting the statistics to the facts of the case. He gave an interesting illustration of a town in which there were only two cab companies, one with three blue cabs and the other with one yellow cab. If a person was knocked down by a cab whose colour had not been observed it would be wrong to suggest that there was a 75% chance that the victim was run down by a blue cab and that accordingly it was more probable than not that the cab that ran him down was blue and therefore that the company running the blue cabs would be responsible for negligence in the running down. He pointed out that before any inference that it was a blue cab would be appropriate further facts would be required as, for example, that a blue cab had been seen in the immediate vicinity at the time of the accident or that a blue cab had been found with a large dent in the very part of the cab which had struck the victim. He concluded that the evidence available was not sufficient to justify the case going to the jury and noted (664 P 2d 474 at 491):

> The apparent harshness of this conclusion cannot be overlooked. The combination of the loss of a loved one to cancer and a doctor's negligence in diagnosis seems to compel a finding of liability. Nonetheless, justice must be dealt with an even hand. To hold a defendant liable without proof that his actions *caused* plaintiff harm would open up untold abuses of the litigation system. (Brachtenbach J's emphasis.)

Pearson J agreed that the appeal should be allowed but did not agree with the reasoning by which that result was supported by Dore J. Pearson J, after examining the authorities and an academic article, stated that he was persuaded that a middle course between the reasoning of Dore and Brachtenbach JJ was correct and concluded 'that the best resolution of the issue before us is to recognise the loss of a less than even chance as an actionable injury' (at 487).

He recognised that this also required that the damage payable be determined by the application of that chance expressed as a percentage to the damages that would be payable on establishing full liability.

I have selected references to the view expressed by the judges who took part in this decision to illustrate the variety of views open in this difficult area of the law. These confirm me in the view that it would not be right in the present case to affirm the general proposition for which counsel for the authority contended. On the other hand, none of the views canvassed in *Herskovits's* case would lead to the plaintiff succeeding in the present case since the judge's findings in fact mean that the sole cause of the plaintiff's avascular necrosis was the injury he sustained in the original fall, and that implies, as I have said, that when he arrived at the authority's hospital for the first time he had no chance of avoiding it. Accordingly, the subsequent negligence of the authority did not cause him the loss of such a chance.

Lord Mackay referred to the relevance of the *McGhee* case to the issue in *Hotson*. One of his reasons for not rejecting outright the plaintiff's argument concerning the recovery of damages for 'loss of a chance' was that the *McGhee* decision in recognising that damages could be recovered, where the plaintiff was able to show that the defendant had 'materially increased the risk' of injuring him, might imply that 'loss of a chance' of avoiding an injury could give rise to compensation in the tort of negligence. But, of course, *Hotson* was decided before *Wilsher* in which the House of Lords, as we have seen, gave *McGhee* a restrictive interpretation.

If *Wilsher* makes plain that a defendant cannot be liable merely if it is proved that he materially increased the risk of injuring the plaintiff, neither should he be liable if he merely deprived the plaintiff of a chance of recovery. The reasons for this are as follows. First, these are two sides of the same coin. Materially to increase the risk of injury to a plaintiff is, at the same time, to decrease the chance of the plaintiff remaining healthy or recovering. We tend to use the language of 'materially increasing the risk' in a *McGhee*- or *Wilsher*-type case where the plaintiff begins healthy and the claim is that the defendant injured him. We tend to use the language of 'loss of a chance' in a *Hotson*-type of case where the plaintiff begins injured and the claim is that the defendant failed to make him better or produce a complete recovery. But these different uses are merely a matter of convenience.

In both situations, therefore, the House of Lords' approach in *Wilsher* is applicable. The 'increased risk' or 'loss of chance' has a merely evidential function from which the court can (though not must) infer that the defendant's negligence (by act or omission) made *the* difference to the plaintiff's condition.

Secondly, the 'loss of a chance' language is often used in a statistical sense: 1 in 4 recover, 3 in 4 do not. In other words, the statistical evidence is not related to the plaintiff as such but refers to that abstract group of similar individuals familiar to statisticians. Only (as Lord MacKay remarks) if the statistics can be *personalised* to the plaintiff can the inference be made. Equally, if the statistics are so overwhelming, the court may feel compelled to take the view that 'how else did the plaintiff get like he is'. This would be the case in *McGhee* itself but not in *Hotson* or *Wilsher* (see Simon Brown LJ's application of *Wilsher* in his dissent in *Bolitho v City and Hackney HA* (1992) 13 BMLR 111 (CA)). Croom-Johnson LJ in the Court of Appeal in *Hotson* puts it as follows (p 223).

> **Croom-Johnson LJ:** In his closing speech, the plaintiff's counsel said:
>
> > It is our submission, first of all, that the loss of a chance, even a less than 50% chance, is enough to fund a claim for damages in tort . . . damage is proved by proving on the balance of probabilities the loss of a 25% chance.
>
> Put simply that way, the proposition is unsustainable. If it is proved statistically that 25% of the population have a chance of recovery from a certain injury and 75% do not, it does not mean that someone who suffers that injury and who does not recover from it has lost a 25% chance. He may have lost nothing at all. What he has to do is prove that he was one of the 25% and that his loss was caused by the defendant's negligence. To be a figure in a statistic does not by itself give him a cause of action. If the plaintiff succeeds in proving that he was one of the 25% and that the defendant took away that chance, the logical result would be to award him 100% of his damages and not only a quarter, but that might be left for consideration if and when it arises. In this case the plaintiff was only asking for a quarter.
>
> Even the judge at one point in his judgment said ([1985] 3 All ER 167 at 178, [1985] 1 WLR 1086 at 1047):
>
> > The defendants' breach of duty here (a) denied the plaintiff the 25% chance of escaping, and thus (b) *may have caused* the very disability which occurred. (My emphasis.)
>
> In the end he decided that the 25/75% split in the chances was something which went to quantification of damages and not to causation.
>
> The role of the 25/75% split as no more than part of the evidentiary material going to proof of liability seems to have been largely lost sight of.

Once the court resolves whether the plaintiff was one of the 75 who do not recover or one of the 25 who do, it resolves whether the plaintiff has established, on a balance of probabilities, whether the defendant caused the injuries. It is not tenable to talk of lost chances other than at the statistical level. Thus, the 'loss of a chance' argument was a 'red herring' in the *Hotson* case emerging from the unusual finding of fact by the trial judge which confused statistical chances with the actual effects of the defendants' breach of duty on the plaintiff.

It could be said that a discussion of 'loss of a chance' is a resort to labelling rather than analysis. Is not the real question how difficult or easy the courts are prepared to make the plaintiff's task in proving causation? A court could, of course, allow a plaintiff to succeed merely by pointing to statistical probability without more. By demanding more, as in *Hotson*, the plaintiff is forced to fulfil a burden of proof which involves demonstrating precisely that which he cannot, namely particular facts. Lord Mackay's observations in *Hotson* are instructive. Referring to the judgment of Brachtenbach J in the Washington Supreme Court decision of *Herskovits*, Lord Mackay said:

He gave an interesting illustration of a town in which there were only two cab companies, one with three blue cabs and the other with one yellow cab. If a person was knocked down by a cab whose colour had not been observed it would be wrong to suggest that there was a 75% chance that the victim was run down by a blue cab and that accordingly it was more probable than not that the cab that ran him down was blue and therefore that the company running the blue cabs would be responsible for negligence in the running down. He pointed out that before any inference that it was a blue cab would be appropriate further facts would be required as, for example, that a blue cab had been seen in the immediate vicinity at the time of the accident or that a blue cab had been found with a large dent in the very part of the cab which had struck the victim.

Lord Mackay may be right that 'it would be wrong . . . therefore that the company . . . would be responsible for negligence'. But are the other two propositions wrong in the sentence beginning 'If a person . . . '? Arguably, Lord Mackay's use of the word 'therefore' indicates that he is moving into the realm of the policy maker. (For a further view see T Hill, 'A Lost Chance for Compensation in the Tort of Negligence by the House of Lords' (1991) 54 MLR 511 and J Stapelton, 'The Gist of Negligence – II' (1988) 104 LQR 389.)

The Canadian Supreme Court, albeit in an appeal from the Civil Law courts of Quebec, went further than the House of Lords in *Hotson* and specifically rejected an argument based upon recovery for 'loss of a chance'. In effect, they approved the reasoning advanced earlier and the view of Croom-Johnson LJ.

Lawson v Laferrière (1991) 78 DLR (4th) 609 (Supreme Court of Canada)

In 1971 the defendant physician diagnosed cancer in a patient and removed a lump from her breast, but failed to inform her that the lump was cancerous. Further symptoms appeared, and in 1975 the patient was informed of the earlier diagnosis. She died in 1978 of cancer. An action was commenced by the patient and continued by the plaintiff on the patient's behalf. The trial judge found that the defendant was in breach of a duty to inform the patient, but the medical opinion being divided in 1971 on the proper method of treating breast cancer, the plaintiff's chances of survival would not have been greater if she had been informed. Consequently, he dismissed the action. The majority of the Quebec Court of Appeal held that the defendant's failure to inform the patient of the diagnosis had deprived her of a chance or opportunity of obtaining proper treatment, and that she was entitled to compensation for loss of this chance and for the distress she suffered on hearing of the defendant's failure to inform her of the diagnosis.

On further appeal to the Supreme Court of Canada, held, La Forest J dissenting, allowing the appeal in part, the plaintiff had failed to prove on the balance of probabilities that the defendant had caused the patient's death and, accordingly, the defendant was not, by the civil law of Quebec, liable for the death.

Gonthier J: It is only in exceptional loss of chance cases that a judge is presented with a situation where the damage can only be understood in probabilistic or statistical terms and where it is impossible to evaluate sensibly whether or how the chance would have been realized in that particular case. The purest example of such a lost chance is that of the lottery ticket which is not placed in the draw due to the negligence of the seller of the ticket. The judge has no factual context in which to evaluate the likely result other than the realm of pure statistical chance. Effectively, the pool of factual evidence regarding the various eventualities in the particular case is dry in such cases, and the plaintiff has nothing other than statistics to elaborate the claim in damages. Where the fault of the defendant has already been established and where no other identifiable competing causal factors have been identified, it may be open to the judge to evaluate the damage according to the chance alone. To transform this exceptional case into the theoretical basis for recovery in all loss of chance situations would be unnecessarily abstract, and, more importantly for the case before us, would give the mistaken impression that the court is more interested in the certainty of statistical chances than in the probable results which those chances represent.

With these considerations in mind, I turn to the role of loss of chance in the medical context.

Loss of chance becomes critically difficult, in France, Belgium and Quebec, as elsewhere, when it is employed as a method of analysis in the complex cases of medical responsibility. In the most difficult cases, such as the one which concerns us, the defendant doctor's fault cannot be easily attached even to any initial actual damage suffered by the plaintiff patient. Accordingly, it is analysis of the lost chance itself which will determine whether the doctor is at all responsible. The lost chance can be analysed in two ways.

In France and Belgium . . . it is the chance itself which is considered, usually described as a chance of recovery or survival. The chance must be 'real and serious', and this is said to include chances which are likely or probable . . . or chances where recovery or improvement is more likely than death or illness . . . The damages likely are, of course, awarded in relation to the chance itself, and therefore such damages are only partial. According to a recent commentator, loss of a chance analysis is said to be appropriate in cases involving faults of omission; faults of commission must be analyzed according to a method which connects the fault to the actual death or sickness: . . . It is acknowledged even by supporters of the full loss of chance analysis in the medical context that by focusing on the lost chance rather than the actual damage which that chance represents the judge is effectively permitted to translate his or her doubts as to the causal link between the fault and the final damage into a reduced award for the patient: . . .

In Quebec, courts are more inclined to examine the damage which has already occurred, and to consider whether that damage was caused by the doctor's fault or by other identifiable factors. If the fault was causal, then full damages are awarded. Faults of commission are treated in the same manner as faults of omission and, clearly, in more complicated cases both types of fault may be present . . . The judge attempts, in effect, to determine whether and to what extent the doctor's acts and omissions are responsible for the situation in which the patient now finds himself or herself. A positive result which should have been produced and a negative result which should have been avoided are considered on the same terms, whether they correspond with acts or omissions.

As I have stated earlier, I am inclined to favour an approach which focuses on the actual damage which the doctor can be said to have caused to the patient by his or her fault, and to compensate accordingly. First, as I have said, I can see no basis for treating acts and omissions differently. Accordingly, there is no theoretical imperative directing courts to abandon traditional causal analysis and to adopt instead an essentially artificial loss of chance analysis. Secondly, while I concede that loss of chance analysis is less objectionable when used to evaluate damages in cases where the defendant's responsibility is otherwise clearly established or, perhaps, where no other causal factors can be identified, this type of analysis must be viewed with extreme caution in cases where there are serious doubts as to the defendant's causal role in the face of other identifiable causal factors. Even though our understanding of medical matters is often limited, I am not prepared to conclude that particular medical conditions should be treated for purposes of causation as the equivalent of diffuse elements of pure chance, analogous to the non-specific factors of fate or fortune which influence the outcome of a lottery. Thirdly, as has been pointed out frequently, in the medical context the damage has usually occurred, manifesting itself in sickness or death . . . the chance is not suspended or crystallized as is the case in the classical loss of chance examples; it has been realized, and the morbid scenario has necessarily played itself out. It can and should be analyzed by means of the generally applicable rules regarding causation.

Overall, then, not only do I question the independent recognition of a lost chance in all but the exceptional classical cases (such as the case of the lottery ticket), but I can certainly see no reason to extend such an artificial form of analysis to the medical context where faults of omission or commission must be considered alongside other identifiable causal factors in determining that which has produced the particular result in the form of sickness or death. As far as possible, the court must consider the question of responsibility with the particular facts of the case in mind, as they relate concretely to the fault, causation and actual damage alleged in the case. While probabilities are unquestionably a part of the assessment of these elements in the finding of responsibility, I am very reluctant to remove the analysis from the concrete to the probabilistic plane.

It is important to recognize that, in cases where the proof indicates that a particular procedure or treatment would probably (though not certainly) have produced a positive result, the patient will usually be able to recover damages under both of the methods described above. If the chance itself is compensated, however, damages will only be measured according to the level of probability. If the actual damage which has been caused is compensated, then the full value of the actual damage will be accorded. . . .

Cases in which the evidence is scarce or seemingly inconclusive present the greatest difficulty. It is perhaps worthwhile to repeat that a judge will be influenced by expert scientific opinions which are expressed in terms of statistical probabilities or test samplings, but he or she is not bound by such evidence. Scientific findings are not identical to legal findings. Recently, in *Snell v Farrell* (1990) 72 DLR (4th) 289 at p 300, [1990] 2 SCR 311, 4 CCLT (2d) 229, this court made clear that '[c]ausation need not be determined by scientific precision' and that '[i]t is not . . . essential that the medical experts provide a firm opinion supporting the plaintiff's theory of causation' (p 301). Both this court and the Quebec Court of Appeal have frequently stated that proof as to the causal link must be established on the balance of probabilities taking into account *all* the evidence which is before it, factual, statistical and that which the judge is entitled to presume: see, *eg, Shawinigan v Naud* [1929] 4 DLR 57 at pp 59-61, [1929] SCR 341; *Morin v Blais* [1977] 1 SCR 570 at p 580, 10 NR 489; *Laurentide Motels Ltd v Beauport (City)* [1989] 1 SCR 705 at p 808; *J E Construction Inc v General Motors du Canada Ltee* [1985] Que CA 275 at p 278; *Dodds v Schierz* [1986] RJQ 2623 at pp 2635-6, 40 CCLT 167 (CA).

If one takes, for example, a case in which a doctor neglects to employ a recommended procedure which is said to have a 50% chance of complete cure, a judge would not necessarily be bound by expert opinion which declined to conclude that application of the procedure to the patient would have avoided the patient's present worsened condition. The judge might well be justified in finding that the procedure in question would probably have benefited the patient, if other factors particular to that plaintiff support that conclusion. The judge's duty is to assess the damage suffered by a particular patient, not to remain paralyzed by statistical abstraction.

If one moves then to a procedure which is recommended despite a mere 25% chance of success according to expert evidence, it is still not a foregone conclusion that the doctor's fault in not using this procedure must be said to have had no causal role in the patient's death or sickness. If the experts are examined properly, a judge might well find that he or she is justified in concluding that the omission of that procedure did not cause the death or sickness, but that it caused other lesser but clearly negative results (*eg* slightly shorter life, greater pain). The doctor's fault could then be judged causal to the extent of the aggravation of what was otherwise an inevitably terminal or morbid condition.

The plaintiff is aided in establishing his or her case by presumptions (as provided by art 1205 *CCLC*) and by such factual and statistical evidence as will aid the judge in appreciating what Moisan J described properly as (translation) 'reasonable and prudent behaviour', 'the natural order of things', 'the sequence of cause and effect' and, generally, 'the normal and ordinary course of events'. The judge will want to pay especially close attention to the various causal properties of the doctor's fault as well as the particular character of the damage which has manifested itself. In some cases, where a fault presents clear danger for the health and security of the patient and where such a danger materializes, it may be reasonable for a judge to presume the causal link between the fault and such damage, 'unless there is a demonstration or a strong indication to the contrary': *Morin v Blais* [[1977] 1 SCR 570] at p 580, per Beetz J. If, after all has been considered, the judge is not satisfied that the fault has, on his or her assessment of the balance of probabilities, caused any actual damage to the patient, recovery should be denied. To do otherwise would be to subject doctors to an exceptional regime of civil responsibility.

In conclusion, then, and with all due deference to those who have expressed other opinions, I do not feel that the theory of loss of chance, at least as it is understood in France and Belgium, should be introduced into the civil law of Quebec in matters of medical responsibility. In the Court of Appeal, Jacques JA states without elaboration that loss of chance is recognized in the common law. I have taken note of the vigorous debate which is taking place in the United States and can find no dominant jurisprudential position favouring loss of chance in that country. In the United Kingdom, the House of Lords has expressed reservations about loss of chance analysis, but has not, as yet, reached a settled conclusion about its possible application: *Hotson v East Berkshire Area Health Authority* [1987] AC 750 (HL). I have also made note of this court's recent decision in *Snell v Farrell, supra*, which I take to endorse traditional principles of causation, properly applied. . . .

In my view, the evidence amply supports the trial judge's finding that the appellant's fault could not be said to have caused Mrs Dupuis' death seven years after the first diagnosis of cancer of the breast. Unfortunately, I must agree with the trial judge that all the evidence clearly confirms the stubborn and virulent nature of this disease.

One final point we should note arises out of the case of *Bolitho v City and Hackney HA* (1992) 13 BMLR 111. There, a majority of the Court of Appeal applied the *Bolam* test to the issue of causation. In determining whether a doctor *would* have intubated a child patient who subsequently suffered brain damage after respiratory and cardiac arrest, the majority looked to whether that was something that all doctors would do. Since the evidence suggested some would but others would not, the majority held that it had not been shown that the doctor would have intubated and hence avoided the injury to the patient. Simon Brown LJ strongly dissented. The majority's decision confuses the issue of what *should* have been done (a breach of duty question) with what *would* have probably been done (a causation question). The medical evidence may well be relevant in determining the latter. It cannot, as the majority would have it, conclude the issue of causation.

2. Legal

Medical negligence cases are no different in attracting the traditional analysis adumbrated by the Privy Council in the *Wagon Mound* [1961] AC 388, [1961] 1 All ER 404. Clearly, issues of foreseeability or remoteness (or whatever term of policy is used) *can* arise. An example is *Emeh v Kensington and Chelsea and Westminster Area Health Authority* [1985] QB 1012, [1984] 3 All ER 1044, where the court had to make a policy decision as to whether a woman can properly be expected by the court to undergo an abortion after a failed sterilisation negligently performed rather than bear an 'unwanted child'. (See discussion *infra*, ch 13.)

E. DEFENCES

Largely *this* is a matter falling within the general law of torts. We notice here only a few points which are of interest to the medical lawyer.

1. Contributory negligence

Ellen Picard discusses this topic in her book *Legal Liability of Doctors and Hospitals in Canada* (1984) (2nd edn).

> A patient has certain duties toward the doctor and to himself. In carrying out these duties he is expected to meet the standard of care of a reasonable patient. If he does not and the breach of this standard is the factual and proximate cause of his injuries he is contributorily negligent, and his compensation will be reduced accordingly. Of course, if his injury is due exclusively to his own negligence his action will be dismissed. . . .
>
> A simple example of how apportionment legislation works follows. Assume a doctor is found to be negligent in his treatment of the patient, who is found to be contributorily negligent for failing to follow the doctor's instructions. If the judge assessed the patient's damages at $10,000 and apportioned liability as 60 per cent to the doctor and 40 per cent to the plaintiff, the result would be that the patient would recover $6,000.
>
> While contributory negligence has been discussed in a handful of Canadian cases, there are only two British Columbian and one from Quebec where it seems to have been applied. Theoretically the law and practice in a medical negligence case should be the same as in any other negligence case and the decision to find contributory negligence has been 'quite frequent' in the ordinary negligence action. One explanation for its rare application in medical negligence cases might be that the seemingly unequal position of the parties, in that the plaintiff patient may have been ill, submissive, or incapable of acting in his own best interests, has led the courts to set the standard of care that patients must meet for their own care at *an unreasonably low level* [our emphasis]. As patients strive for a more equal role in their medical care and for taking aggressive steps in their own treatment, it is predictable

and just that there will be more patients found to be contributorily negligent with a consequential reduction in the compensation that they will receive.

In the . . . British Columbia case [*Crossman v Stewart* (1977) 5 CCLT 45 (BCSC)] a patient was held to be two-thirds to blame for the blindness she suffered and her doctor, a dermatologist, one-third to blame. (Thus she would get $26,666 of the $80,000 assessed as damages.) She had consulted the dermatologist for a facial skin disorder and he prescribed a drug known as chloroquine or Aralen which she took for approximately six months under prescription. Because she was a medical receptionist she was able to obtain the drug from the drug salesman at one-half the price and without a prescription and for seven months she took the drug on this basis. At that time the dermatologist who had been alerted to the possible serious side effects of the drug to vision had all patients whom he had treated with it see an ophthalmologist. Unfortunately, he did not read carefully enough the resulting report on the plaintiff because it would have alerted him to the patient's unorthodox practice. Thereafter for two more years the patient obtained the drug from the salesman and when this man retired she went back to the defendant and was prescribed the drug for at least a further eight months. The trial judge found that at no time was the patient warned of the danger of the prolonged use of the drug but also that the defendant did not have actual knowledge of her continuous use of it either. The evidence indicated that her eyes would not have been damaged had her consumption been limited to the prescriptions.

The patient's negligence was found to lie in obtaining prescription drugs from an unorthodox source, using them on a prolonged basis, and not consulting her doctor. She had failed to meet the standard expected of a reasonable patient and was the major cause of her own injury. The doctor's negligence was based on his failure to carefully pursue the ophthalmologist's report and his failure to discern from 'corneal changes' in that report the probability of recent consumption of the drug. This was obviously a clear case for the application of the contributory negligence rules. In fact, it is even arguable that, like the dental patient who nearly bled to death before obtaining medical assistance, this patient was the sole cause of her injury. The standard of care expected of the reasonable patient is tied to the degree of knowledge with respect to medical matters possessed by the layman. Just as the reasonable person is taken to know that loss of a large volume of blood will seriously endanger his health, he ought also to be attributed with the knowledge that obtaining and consuming prescription drugs without medical supervision is risky. However, the fact remains that the plaintiff in this case was given no warning as to the danger of this particular drug and, in fact, after what she would believe was a satisfactory ophthalmological examination, may have had reason to believe that the drug was safe.

In the Quebec case [*Hôpital Notre-Dame de L'Esperance v Laurent* [1978] 1 SCR 605], the evidence of the doctor and patient was in substantial conflict, but the higher courts were not prepared to disturb the trial judge's holding that the patient was contributorily negligent. The doctor was held negligent for failing to diagnose a fracture of the head of the femur, but the patient did not get further medical treatment for over three months and her claim was reduced by one quarter. Unlike the patient in the British Columbia case who was active in her own treatment, this patient was passive: she failed to seek treatment. The difference in conduct is reflected in the amount by which each patient's compensation was reduced.

There is an unusual case from British Columbia [*Robitaille v Vancouver Hockey Club Ltd* (1979) 19 BCLR 158 (SC)] where the employer of the doctors, a hockey club, was successful in reducing its liability by 20 per cent because of the contributory negligence of a hockey player who failed to seek further medical care from the team doctor or consult his own doctor when serious symptoms persisted.

But, as Picard goes on to point out, it may not be easy to show that a patient was contributorily negligent.

The defence was pursued without success in three other Canadian cases. In *Foote v Royal Columbia Hospital* [(1982) 38 BCLR 222 (SC)] a doctor was found liable for failing to alert hospital staff to the risk that an epileptic patient whose medication he had changed might have a seizure at any time. During an unsupervised bath the 15-year-old did have a seizure and suffered injuries. The doctor alleged that she should be found contributorily negligent. The trial judge disagreed but said, *obiter*, that had he been convinced that the patient had understood instructions not to bath unsupervised, he would have held her contributorily negligent to the extent of 50 per cent. A man playing touch football broke a lens in his glasses and injured his eye. The optometrist and lens manufacturer whom he sued pleaded contributorily negligence, but the trial judge held that this had not been proven by the defendants. In *Bernier v Sisters of Service* [[1948] 1 WWR 113 (Alta SC)] the patient was admitted to hospital for an appendectomy. While recovering from the anaesthetic she received second and third degree burns to her feet from hot water bottles placed in her bed. The hospital was found liable for the negligence of the nurses who did not test the temperature and placed them without orders. It was argued that the patient was contributorily negligent in failing to call for help, in failing to disclose an earlier bout of frostbite to her feet and in leaving the hospital early against medical advice. All were rejected by the trial judge. He was of the opinion that the injury occurred to the patient while she was still anaesthetized and that it was not unreasonable to fail to disclose having frozen her feet upon entering hospital for an appendectomy. Furthermore, her leaving hospital had not aggravated her injuries. All in all this patient had acted as a reasonable patient. It is possible to see, however, that a patient who fails to disclose a material fact to a hospital or doctor might be found contributorily negligent, as might a patient who leaves hospital without notice or against medical advice and as a consequence suffers greater injuries.

Other conduct by a patient that might bring a finding of contributory negligence would include failure to return for treatment, to seek treatment, to co-operate during treatment, or to follow instructions. However, to date, in support there are primarily only *obiter* comments in case law from both inside and outside Canada. It remains to be seen whether the new vitality of the patient's role in his own health care will result in the law requiring a higher standard of him.

One issue which preoccupies some doctors is, what is called in medical journals, 'patient non-compliance'. This is intended to refer to situations in which a patient may not follow the instructions given by his doctor, eg as regards taking a prescribed medicine. Would a court regard this as contributory negligence? Would there be any scope here for the application of the doctrine in American products liability of 'foreseeable misuse' of a product when it is known that patients frequently depart from the instructions in prescriptions?

Consider the following two American cases.

Martineau v Nelson (1976) 247 NW 2d 409 (Sup Ct Minn)

Kelly J: A single issue is dispositive of the appeal: Was the jury's finding of 50% contributory negligence supported by the evidence?

Plaintiffs argue that the issue of contributory negligence was improperly submitted to the jury and that its finding on that issue is not supported by the evidence. This is a case of first impression on the issue of contributory negligence in a sterilisation case. While there have been several reported decisions dealing with actions for malpractice in performing sterilisation operations, including an early Minnesota case sustaining a demurrer to a complaint on a deceit theory, the bulk of the sterilisation cases deal with the burden of proof under theories of negligence and breach of warranty and the problem of provable damages.

Contributory negligence has been recognised as a defence in a number of malpractice cases in other jurisdictions. The defence has been recognised in cases in which the patient has (1) failed to follow the doctor's or nurse's instructions; or (2) refused suggested treatment; or (3) given the doctor false, incomplete, or misleading information concerning symptoms. This court expressly recognised the defence in 1970 in upholding a general verdict for defendant doctor following the submission of his negligence and plaintiff's contributory negligence. In that case, plaintiff had submitted misleading and inaccurate information about her employment status to the doctor and had no telephone, making it difficult for him to contact her regarding the positive result of her Pap smear test. *Ray v Wagner* 286 Minn 354, 176 NW 2d 101 (1970).

Both courts and text writers have emphasised, however, that the availability of a contributory negligence defence in a malpractice case is limited because of the disparity in medical knowledge between the patient and his doctor and because of the patient's right to rely on the doctor's knowledge and skill in the course of medical treatment. Thus, it has been held that it is not contributory negligence to follow the doctor's instructions or to fail to consult another physician when the patient has no reason to believe his pain is caused by the doctor's negligence. It has also been suggested that the patient's neglect of his own health after negligent treatment may be a factor in reducing damages, but should not bar all recovery . . .

The relevant issue in this case, which must be considered in light of the record and the authorities just discussed, is whether and to what extent plaintiffs may be charged with acting unreasonably in the face of certain statements and advice of defendant doctors. Confronted with the results of a pathological test showing the removal of a segment of an artery [instead of the intended Fallopian tube], and with equivocation on the part of her doctors as to the success of the operation and the necessity of further procedures, plaintiff wife might have acted unreasonably in failing to at least attempt to persuade her husband to have a vasectomy or, in the absence of vasectomy, in failing to continue a regimen of birth control. The record, however, provides only the barest minimum support for these inferences of negligence. The record does not clearly reveal what plaintiff wife did or did not tell her husband about her conference with the doctors. Furthermore, there is no clear evidence of what birth control methods plaintiff did or did not use after the conference and up to the time the child David was conceived.

The evidence of plaintiff husband's contributory fault is plainly insufficient. The only evidence as to his conduct is that he concluded that his wife could not become pregnant and he elected not to have a vasectomy. There is no evidence that he received any advice directly from the doctors nor any evidence that he acted unreasonably in arriving at his conclusion. Moreover, we think that the law of contributory fault should not compel a 32-year-old husband, who might possibly remarry and later change his mind regarding more children, to undergo sterilisation because of a surgeon's negligence. From our evaluation of the evidence, we have concluded that there must be a new trial for two reasons. First, since we have concluded that plaintiff husband could not have been guilty of any negligence, and since the jury was asked to apportion negligence to husband and wife together, we cannot be certain to what extent the jury relied on erroneous theories as to the husband's negligence in making its apportionment. Second, while there may be some evidence of negligence on the part of plaintiff wife and while the apportionment of such negligence is normally within the province of the jury, we think the 50-50 apportionment in this case is plainly contrary to the weight of the evidence.

We are confronted in this case with the initial failure of the surgeon to properly perform a tubal ligation, coupled with the equivocal statements of the doctors to plaintiff wife regarding the result (ie, both doctors say her tubes are blocked, one encourages vasectomy, the other encourages further procedure if plaintiff would feel uneasy about marital relations), and plaintiffs' reaction in electing not to pursue further procedures. Neither doctor apparently discussed with plaintiff wife the risks of pregnancy notwithstanding the operation or directly informed her that she could become pregnant again. Under these circumstances, plaintiffs cannot be held equally negligent with the surgeon because the subject matter of their negligence is the interpretation of medical matters about which the doctors owed a greater duty to them than plaintiffs owed to themselves. The superior knowledge and skill of the physicians in this case should have been reflected in straightforward, complete, and accurate information and advice to their patient. That patient should not be denied recovery because she could not sift from their equivocation this kind of information and advice.

For the reasons stated above, we have concluded that there must be a new trial against both defendants on the issues of their negligence, of the contributory negligence of plaintiff wife, and of damages.

Schliesman v Fisher (1979) 158 Cal Rptr 527 (Cal CA)

Stephens JA: Robert Fisher, MD and Leonard Lewis, MD (hereinafter appellants) had treated George Schliesman (hereinafter respondent) since 1969 for various medical problems, including diabetes mellitus, arterio-sclerotic heart disease, peripheral vascular disease, gout, hypertension and distal extremity ulcerations. The diabetes was generally controlled with the administration of Orinase in spite of the fact that respondent was approximately 100 pounds overweight and did not adhere to his prescribed diet. The recurrent ulcerations on his feet were treated with antibiotics, hot soaks, and elevation of the affected extremity.

From November 19 to 22 1972, respondent was hospitalised for congestive heart failure. At this time, Dr Fisher discontinued the Orinase, instituted a diabetic diet and recounselled respondent regarding the importance of diet as the preferred means of controlling his diabetes. Dr Fisher's decision to discontinue the Orinase was based upon a recent medical study linking Orinase to increased incidences of heart disease in diabetics. When respondent was seen for follow-up care on December 5, 1972, Dr Fisher felt that the cardiac risks associated with Orinase were sufficiently severe to justify keeping respondent off the medication in spite of elevated blood sugars. Further, Dr Fisher's experience with respondent had been such that he felt the respondent was not responsible enough to be given insulin. Respondent's failure to follow medical advice regarding adherence to his diabetic diet and the need for his discontinuance of beer drinking, together with his tendency to periodically stop taking his medication, led Dr Fisher to believe that respondent was sufficiently unreliable to be prescribed insulin for control of his diabetes, since misuse of that drug could cause rather immediate and life-threatening consequences.

Dr Fisher next saw respondent on December 18, 1972, regarding pain and inflammation of his left foot. The evidence is in conflict as to whether the foot was merely inflamed or had already ulcerated at the time of this examination. The usual antibiotic treatment, hot soaks and elevation were prescribed. Two days later, December 20, 1972, respondent presented at the Santa Monica Emergency Room with a draining ulcer on his left foot. Since the emergency room attending physician could reach neither Dr Fisher nor Dr Lewis by phone, respondent was given a tetanus shot and sent home. When respondent reached Dr Lewis a few hours later, immediate arrangements were made for hospitalisation. Once hospitalised, respondent was treated with a broad-spectrum antibiotic, Erythromycin. Orinase was reinstituted, culture and sensitivity tests were ordered to determine the organism that was causing the infection, and a general surgical consultation requested.

It was subsequently discovered that the plaintiff's foot was dead. The plaintiff's leg was amputated below the knee.

Appellants' first contention on appeal is that the trial court erred when it refused to give a proffered instruction for the defence on contributory negligence. For the reasons stated below, we are in agreement with appellants. Here, while the great bulk of testimony was aimed at establishing or refuting that the appellants' care of respondent fell below the applicable standard for medical care, there was still substantial evidence from which the jury could have found that respondent was himself negligent in failing to follow the orders of his physicians regarding diet, weigh reduction and medications and that such negligence proximately contributed to the ultimate loss of his leg.

Robert Uller, MD, testified for appellants. He is a physician who specialises primarily in endocrinology, with approximately 40% or more of his practice dealing with diabetic patients. Dr Uller testified that patients like respondents, who are 'adult-onset diabetics', are generally obese individuals whose pancreas manufactures a relatively normal amount of insulin, but because of the increased body weight, the amount is insufficient for that individual and the individual's blood sugar is correspondingly high. Further, he testified that a reduction in weight is the best treatment for such patients, as it results in a drop in the level of blood sugar, which can then be further controlled by diet. Speaking of respondent specifically, he said: 'In this particular problem the patient is his own worst enemy because you can only tell him what diet to follow, and the big problem here to date with the blood sugars by and large has been obesity. 290 pounds and six-foot-two, 280 pounds in a six-foot-two individual, that's about 100 pounds above ideal body weight for man of, say, large boned structures, six-foot-two individual, so if the individual would follow the diet, you know, the blood sugars would be no problem'. Further, Dr Uller testified that the fact that respondent responded extremely well to insulin therapy while hospitalized was an indication that his diabetes would respond well if he were to follow the recommended diabetic diet. In fact, the hospital records revealed that respondent had to be taken off of insulin after three days because of a suspected insulin reaction. Dr Uller attributed this response to the fact that while hospitalized, respondent was forced to adhere to the diet prescribed by his physicians, which brought his blood sugars close to the normal range. Administering insulin, then, had the effect, of producing an overabundance of insulin in respondent's system. This effect, Dr Uller testified, pointed to the fact that respondent's diabetes would have responded adequately to diet if respondent would have followed his doctors' orders in this regard.

Respondent contends that there is nothing in the record to indicate that there is a direct relationship between the control of diabetes or lack thereof, and the incidence of infection leading ultimately to gangrene and amputation. The testimony of his own experts, however, contradicts this assertion. Gerard F Smith, MD, testified on behalf of respondent. In the course of that testimony he stated: 'Diabetics are more prone to ulcerations, and develop infection because of their high blood sugar. High blood sugar is a media for bacteria to grow. Therefore, if the sugar is out of control and the area to this leg is impaired, we have two factors working: One, we got a good culture media of the existing blood that is there for the bacteria to grow on; Two, we have sugar that is markedly out of control, both of which will cause increased infection.' Also testifying for respondents, Saul Lieb, MD, testified: 'Infection in the presence of diabetes will spread if the treatment of diabetes is not undertaken.'

We note that the foregoing testimony was aimed primarily at the notion that Dr Lewis should not have taken respondent off the Orinase. However, such testimony also provides a foundation from which the jury could have inferred, when coupled with the prior testimony of Dr Uller, that an out-of-control diabetic whose blood sugars are elevated is more likely to get an infection such as the one that invaded respondent's foot and that such an infection will be much more difficult to treat and cure as a result of the out-of-control diabetes. That respondent's diabetes could have been controlled by weight reduction and proper diet is a significant fact. While respondent sought to place the blame for his diabetes being out of control on Dr Lewis for discontinuing the Orinase, it was a fact of some significance to be weighed by the jury that respondent could himself have brought his diabetes under control with diet and weight reduction and was, in fact, counselled by his doctors repeatedly to do so. The failure of the trial court to allow an instruction of contributory negligence took this consideration from the jury and denied appellants jury trial on an essential defence.

(See also *Brushnett v Cowan* (1990) 69 DLR (4th) 743 (Newfd CA) – contributory negligence when patient did not use crutches after leg operation.)

2. Voluntary assumption of risk

In the general law of torts this, in effect, means that the plaintiff has agreed to waive the duty owed by the defendant to observe the required standard of care. It need not be an express agreement although the courts are very reluctant to imply such an agreement, particularly since the Law Reform (Contributory Negligence) Act 1945.

You will recall Ellen Picard's reference to the lack of equality of power between the parties in a doctor-patient relationship in her discussion of contributory negligence. Does not this point apply with even greater force here, so as to suggest that a court would not find a patient had voluntarily waived the doctor's duty save in the most exceptional circumstances? Indeed, do you think a court would find that, as a matter of public policy, a patient should *never* be held to have waived a doctor's duty in the context of medical treatment?

3. Other defences

We do not rehearse here other defences to actions for medical negligence. Perhaps, the most important would be the defence of limitation of action to be found in the Limitation Act 1980. You are referred to the standard books on the law of torts. We content ourselves with the following summary offered by Margaret Brazier in *Medicine, Patients and the Law* (2nd edn 1992) at p 146:

A patient contemplating an action for medical negligence must act relatively promptly. The general rule is that all actions for personal injuries must be brought within three years of the infliction of the relevant injury. This is known as the limitation period and is laid down in the Limitation Act 1980. A writ must be served [*semble* issued] on the doctor or hospital authority no later than three years from the date of the alleged negligence. But sections 11 and 14 of the 1980 Act provide that where the patient originally either (1) was unaware that he had suffered significant injury, or (2) did not know about the negligence which could have caused his injury, the three-year period begins to run only from the time when he did discover, or reasonably should have discovered, the relevant facts. Where the patient knew all the relevant facts, but was ignorant of his legal remedy, the three-year limitation period runs from the time when he was or should have been aware of the facts.

All is not quite lost for the patient who delays beyond three years or who is ignorant of the law. A judge may still allow him to start an action later. Section 33 of the 1980 Act gives to the court a discretion to override the three-year limitation period where in all the circumstances it is fair to all parties to do so. The courts will examine the effect of allowing the action to go forward on both parties, taking into account, among other things, the effect of delay on the cogency of the evidence, the conduct of the parties, and the advice sought by and given to the patient by his lawyers and medical advisers. The three-year (or longer) limitation period applies only to *starting* legal proceedings. Once started, an action may drag on for years before it is settled or finally decided.

It is fair to say that this matter is not wholly free of difficulty. Judges have shown themselves to be in disagreement as to what it is that the plaintiff must know or should have known about the injury complained of for the limitation period to begin to run. By and large the courts required that the plaintiff know with a high degree of specificity what is wrong with him. Such knowledge often only arises once the plaintiff has consulted a medical expert. (See for example, *Bentley v Bristol & Weston HA* [1991] 2 Med LR 359; *Driscoll-Varley v Parkside HA* [1991] 2 Med LR 346. Contrast *Hendy v Milton Keyes HA* [1992] 3 Med LR 114.) The question has been considered by the Court of Appeal in *Nash v Eli Lilly* [1992] 3 Med LR 353 (CA) where Purchas LJ (with whom Ralph Gibson and Mann LJJ agreed) stated: 'It was not, in our judgment, the intention of Parliament to require for the purposes of section 11 and section 14 of the Act proof of knowledge of the terms in which it will be alleged that the act or omission of the defendants constituted negligence or breach of duty. What is required is knowledge of the essence of the act or omission to which the injury is attributable.' (See now *Broadley v Guy Clapham & Co* [1993] 4 Med LR 328 (CA) overruling *Bentley* and approving *Hendy*.)

F. WHO PAYS THE BILL?

Until 1 January 1990 a patient who succeeded in an action in negligence (or battery) or successfully settled such an action looked to the health authority or the doctor to meet the bill. It was a matter of no concern to the patient who paid providing one of them did. Obviously, it was a matter of concern to the doctor. A doctor practising in an NHS hospital was contractually obliged to belong to a 'defence organisation' – Medical Defence Union, Medical Protection Society, Medical and Dental Defence Union of Scotland. A general practitioner would customarily also become a member but was not obliged to do so. The functions of such organisations included the provision of legal advice and representation when claims were made against the doctor, and the indemnification of the doctor against any award of damages.

During the 1980s as medical litigation increased so also did the costs of membership of defence organisations. Furthermore, one organisation introduced differential rates which reflected the risks of practising in different specialities. Given that within the NHS doctors were largely unable to pass on the cost of these increases to patients, pressure mounted to replace the system. This was notwithstanding the fact that in the hospital sector where most litigation occurs, two-thirds of the cost of a doctor's membership of a defence organisation was borne by the health authority.

Health authorities were equally concerned since they faced an increasing financial burden in meeting the cost of their employees' membership. Additionally, since the health authority might itself be liable to contribute to the damages because of its own wrongdoing, it faced a growing charge on its funds as damage claims become more onerous during the 1980s. This was at a time when funds were already barely keeping pace with demands placed upon the service.

The basis for arranging the payment of damages was a circular agreed between government and the defence organisations in 1954 (HM(54)32). It sought to distribute the financial burden of litigation between health authority and defence organisation, save in so far as one was entirely to blame. The circular contemplated that the health authorities and defence organisation should agree the proportion of responsibility which they were prepared to accept without recourse to contribution proceedings. In the absence of such agreement, each would bear 50% of the burden of litigation.

Since the conduct of most litigation was in the hands of the defence organisations, the health authorities increasingly realised that they were being held financially responsible without being able to control the litigation and its financial consequences. Faced with this situation, the Government sought a scheme which would be in their view less expensive since it is they who fund the health authorities. On 1 January 1990 there was introduced what has become known as the NHS Indemnity Scheme with the coming into force of circular HC(89)34 'Claims of Medical Negligence Against NHS Hospitals and Community Doctors and Dentists'.

As will be seen, by this scheme health authorities assumed direct financial responsibility for claims in negligence brought against doctors in their employment. This responsibility extends not only to all new claims but retrospectively to existing claims arising before 1 January 1990.

'Claims of Medical Negligence Against Hospitals and Community Doctors and Dentists' (HC(89)34).

Summary

This circular describes the arrangements to apply from 1 January 1990 to the handling of claims of negligence against medical and dental staff employed in the hospital and community health services. General practitioners are not directly affected by these new arrangements, unless they have a contract of employment (for example, as a hospital practitioner) with a health authority.

Action required

Health authorities are asked, with effect from 1 January 1990, to:
(i) assume responsibility for new and existing claims of medical negligence;
(ii) ensure a named officer has sufficient authority to make decisions on the conduct of cases on the authority's behalf;
(iii) cease to require their medical and dental staff to subscribe to a reorganised professional defence organisation and cease to reimburse two-thirds of medical defence subscriptions;
(iv) encourage their medical and dental staff to ensure they have adequate defence cover as appropriate;
(v) distribute urgently to all their medical and dental staff, including those with honorary NHS contracts, copies of a leaflet explaining the new arrangements (which will be sent separately).

Handling claims of medical negligence

Claims lodged on or after 1 January 1990

1. Health authorities, as corporate bodies, are legally liable for the negligent acts of their employees in the course of their NHS employment. From 1 January 1990 health authorities will also be formally responsible for the handling and financing of claims of negligence against their medical and dental staff. With regard to claims lodged on or after 1 January

1990, it is for each health authority to determine how it wishes claims against its medical or dental staff to be handled. Health authorities may wish to make use of the services of the medical defence organisations (at rates to be agreed), but they may also put the word out to other advisers or deal with it in-house, provided they have the necessary expertise.

Claims notified to an MDO before 1 January 1990

2. Subject to final agreement with the medical defence organisations (MDOs) on the detailed financial arrangements, health authorities will take over financial responsibility for cases outstanding at 1 January 1990. The medical defence organisations have been asked to inform health authorities of the cases in which they may have a substantial liability.

3. Health authorities are entitled to take over the management of any cases outstanding, since they will become liable for the costs and damages arising. However, they are strongly advised to employ the MDOs to continue to handle such claims, in consultation with them and on their behalf, until completion. This is essential not only because of the amount of work in progress, but mainly because the re-insurance cover of the MDOs for claims initiated before 1990 would remain valid only if the MDO currently handling the case continued to do so. If required, health authorities should co-operate with an MDO's re-insurers in the conduct of a claim. Since some of the cover is on an aggregate basis the advice in this paragraph applies to both large and small claims. Health authorities are asked to give prior notice to the Department (finance contact point at paragraph 17) where they wish to adopt a different approach in the handling of claims notified before 1 January 1990.

General handling principles

4. Health authorities should take the essential decisions on the handling of claims of medical negligence against their staff, using MDOs or other bodies as their agents and advisers. Authorities should particularly ensure that authority is appropriately delegated to enable decisions to be made promptly, especially where representatives are negotiating a settlement, and are asked to give such authority to a named officer.

5. In deciding how a case should be handled, and in particular whether to resist a claim or seek an out-of-court settlement, health authorities and those advising them should pay particular attention to any view expressed by the practitioner(s) concerned and to any potentially damaging effect on the professional reputation of the practitioner(s) concerned. They should also have clear regard to:
(i)   any point of principle or of wider application raised by the case; and
(ii)   the costs involved.

6. Where a case involves both a health authority and a general medical practitioner (or any other medical or dental practitioner in relation to work for which a health authority is not responsible), the health authority should consult with the practitioners(s) cited or their representative to seek agreement on how the claim should be handled. Where a health authority (or its employees) alone is cited, but there is reason to believe that the action or inaction of a practitioner outside the health authority's responsibility was a material factor in the negligence concerned, the health authority should similarly consult with a view to obtaining a contribution to the eventual costs and damages. Conversely, in cases where such a practitioner alone is cited, there may be circumstances in which the MDO asks the health authority to make a similar contribution, as if it were a defendant. In any such circumstances, health authorities should co-operate fully in the formulation of the defence and should seek to reach agreement out of court on the proportion in which any costs and damages awarded to the plaintiff should be borne.

7. It is open to the practitioner concerned to employ at his or her expense an expert adviser, but the practitioner can be represented separately in court only with the agreement of the court. The plaintiff and the health authority may agree to separate representation for the practitioner, but under normal circumstances the health authority should not do so if it considers that this would lead to additional costs or damages falling on the health authority.

Coverage of the scheme and practical arrangements

8. The Health Departments' views on some of the questions that have arisen about the coverage and practical operation of the new arrangements are at Annex A. The indemnity scheme applies to all staff in the course of their HCHS employment, including those engaged

through private agencies. The Annex is to be reproduced as a leaflet, which the Health Departments will shortly be making available to health authorities who should distribute them to all their medical and dental staff, including those with honorary NHS contracts.

9. Since authorities will be taking financial responsibility in cases of medical negligence it will no longer be necessary for them to require employed staff to subscribe to a recognised professional defence organisation, for example, as in the recommended form of consultant contract at Annex D of PM(79)11. Authorities should inform their medical and dental staff that the provision no longer applies, but they should encourage such staff to ensure that they have adequate defence cover as appropriate.

Financial arrangements

Pooling arrangements for major settlements

10. Where they have not already done so RHAs are strongly recommended to introduce arrangements (for both medical and non-medical negligence) so as to share with Districts the legal costs and damages of individual large settlements or awards, whose incidence can be quite random. The Department will be making arrangements for Authorities without an RHA, for example the London SHAs, to limit the financial effects on them of substantial settlements.

Finding of claims

11. Subject to final agreement with the MDOs, the public sector will have access to a share of the MDOs' reserves in respect of the hospital and community health services. It is expected that the MDOs will each establish a fund to be drawn on according to criteria set by the Health Departments. The Health Departments will be introducing a transitional scheme under which these reserves will be made available to assist health authorities to meet the costs of particularly large settlements. These will usually, but not necessarily, be cases which arose from incidents before 1 January 1990. The Departments propose to set a threshold, initially £300,000 in England and Wales; 80 per cent of the costs of a settlement above this threshold, including the legal costs, would be met from this source, until the identified funds are exhausted. Detailed information on the means of access to the funds will be given in the December 1989 edition of 'Financial Matters'.

NHS Trusts

12. NHS Trusts will be responsible for claims of negligence against their medical and dental staff. The Departments are considering what arrangements will apply to NHS Trusts and further guidance will be issued in due course.

Monitoring resource consequences

13. To enable the Departments of Health to assess the resource consequences of these changes, health authorities will be required to submit a return (in the form set out at Annex B) shortly after the end of each financial year, starting with the period 1 January–31 March 1990 in order to obtain an early indication of the costs of the scheme.

Review

14. The Health Departments plan to review the operation of these arrangements in 1992, including the effects on individual practitioners.

Cancellation of existing guidance

15. Circulars HM(54)32 and HM(54)43 will be cancelled from 1 January 1990. Paragraph 4(iii) of Annex 1 of EL(89)P/148 (Hospital medical and dental staff: Locum tenens engaged through private agencies) will be cancelled from 1 January 1990.

16. Paragraph 310 of the Terms and Conditions of Service for Hospital Medical and Dental Staff, and paragraph 289 of the Terms and Conditions of Service for Doctors in Community Medicine and the Community Health Service, (the two-thirds reimbursement scheme) shall not have effect after 31 December 1989.

ANNEX A
MEDICAL NEGLIGENCE:
NEW NHS ARRANGEMENTS

Introduction

1. New arrangements for dealing with medical negligence claims in the hospital and community health service are being introduced from 1 January 1990. Subject to final agreement with the medical defence organisations on the financial arrangements, health authorities will take direct financial responsibility for cases initiated before that date, as well as for new claims. In future, medical and dental staff employed by health authorities (health boards in Scotland and Northern Ireland) will no longer be required under the terms of their contracts to subscribe to a medical defence organisation. However, the health authority indemnity will cover only health authority responsibilities. The Health Departments advise practitioners to maintain their defence body membership in order to ensure they are covered for any work which does not fall within the scope of the indemnity scheme.

Set out below are the Health Departments' replies to some of the questions most commonly asked about the operation of the new arrangement.

2. *Why is this change necessary?*

Medical defence subscriptions rose rapidly in the 1980s, because of growth both in the number of medical negligence cases and in the size of the awards made by the courts. Subscriptions tripled between 1986 and 1988, and the Doctors' and Dentists' Review Body concluded that to take account of the increase in subscription through practitioners' pay would lead to distortions in pay and pensions. The pressure to relate subscription rates to the practitioner's specialty underlined the difficulty of maintaining the system. The Health Departments issued in March 1989 a proposal for a health authority indemnity. The new arrangements follow discussions with the medical defence organisations, the medical profession, health authority management and other interested bodies.

Coverage

3. *Who is covered by the health authority indemnity scheme?*
Health authorities are liable at law for the negligence (acts or omissions) of their staff in the course of their NHS employment. The legal position is the same for medical and dental staff as for other NHS employees, but for many years doctors and dentists have themselves taken out medical defence cover through the three medical defence organisations (MDOs). Under the indemnity scheme, health authorities will take direct responsibility for costs and damages arising from medical negligence where they (as employees) are vicariously liable for the acts and omissions of their medical and dental staff.

4. *Does this include clinical academics and research workers?*

Health authorities are vicariously liable for the work done by university medical staff and other research workers under their honorary contracts in the course of their NHS duties, but not for pre-clinical or other work in the university.

5. *Is private work in NHS hospitals covered by the indemnity scheme?*

Health authorities will not be responsible for a consultant's private practice, even in an NHS hospital. However, where junior medical staff are involved in the care of private patients in NHS hospitals, they would normally be doing so as part of their contract with the health authority. It remains advisable that any junior doctor who might be involved in any work outside the scope of his or her employment should have medical defence (or insurance) cover.

6. *Is Category 2 work covered?*

Category 2 work (*eg* reports for insurance companies) is by definition not undertaken for the employing health authority, and will therefore not be covered by the indemnity scheme; medical defence cover would be appropriate.

7. Are GMC disciplinary proceedings covered?

Health authorities should not be financially responsible for the defence of medical staff involved in GMC disciplinary proceedings. It is the responsibility of the practitioner concerned to take out medical defence cover against such an eventuality.

8. Is a hospital doctor doing a GP locum covered?

This would not be the responsibility of the health authority, since it would be general practice. The hospital doctor and the general practitioners concerned should ensure that there is appropriate medical defence cover.

9. Is a GP seeing his own patient in hospital covered?

A GP providing medical care to patients in hospital under a contractual arrangement, *eg* where the GP was employed as a clinical assistant, will be covered by the health authority indemnity. On the other hand, if the health authority is essentially providing only hotel services and the patient(s) remain in the care of the GP, the GP would be responsible and medical defence cover would be appropriate.

10. Are GP trainees working in general practice covered?

In general practice the responsibility for training and for paying the salary of a GP trainee rests with the trainer (with funds from the FPC). Where the trainee's medical defence subscription is higher than the subscription of an SHO in the hospital service, he or she may apply through the trainer for the difference in subscription to be reimbursed. While the trainee is receiving a salary in general practice it is advisable that both the trainee and the trainer, and indeed other members of the practice, should have medical defence cover.

11. Are clinical trials covered?

The new arrangements do not alter the current legal position. If the health authority was responsible for a clinical trial authorised under the Medicines Act 1968 or its subordinate legislation and that trial was carried out by or on behalf of a doctor involving NHS patients of his, such a doctor would be covered by the indemnity scheme. Similarly, for a trial not involving medicines, the health authority would take financial responsibility unless the trial were covered by such other indemnity as may have been agreed between the health authority and those responsible for the trial. In any case, health authorities should take steps to make sure that they are informed of clinical trials in which their staff are taking part in their NHS employment and that these trials have the required Research Ethics Committee approval.

12. Would a doctor be covered if he was working other than in accordance with the duties of his post?

Such a doctor would be covered by the health authority indemnity for actions in the course of NHS employment, and this should be interpreted liberally. For work not covered in this way the doctor may have a civil, or even in extreme circumstances criminal, liability for his actions.

13. Are doctors attending accident victims ('Good Samaritan' acts) covered?

By definition, 'Good Samaritan' acts are not part of the doctor's work for the employing authority. Medical defence organisations are willing to provide low-cost cover against the (unusual) event of a doctor performing such an act being sued for negligence.

14. Are doctors in public health medicine or in community health services doing work for local authorities covered? Are occupational physicians covered?

Doctors in public health medicine, or clinical medical officers, carrying out local authority functions under their health authority contract would be acting in the course of their NHS employment. They will therefore be covered by the health authority indemnity. The same principle applies to occupational physicians employed by health authorities.

15. *Will NHS hospital doctors working for other agencies, eg the Prison Service, be covered?*

In general, health authorities will not be financially responsible for the acts of NHS staff when they are working on a contractual basis for other agencies. (Conversely, they will be responsible where, for example, a Ministry of Defence doctor works in an NHS hospital.) Either the agency commissioning the work would be responsible, or the doctor should have medical defence cover. However, health authorities' indemnity should cover work for which they pay a fee, such as domiciliary visits and family planning services.

16. *Are retired doctors covered?*

The health authority indemnity will apply to acts or omissions in the course of NHS employment, regardless of when the claim was notified. Health authorities will thus cover doctors who have subsequently left the Service, but they may seek their co-operation in statements in the defence of a case.

17. *Are doctors offering services to voluntary bodies such as the Red Cross or hospices covered?*

The health authority would be responsible for the doctor's actions only if the health authority were responsible for the medical staffing of the voluntary body. If not, the doctors concerned may wish to ensure that they have medical defence cover, as they do at present.

18. *Will a health authority provide cover for a locum hospital doctor?*

A health authority will take financial responsibility for the acts and omissions of a locum doctor, whether 'internal' or provided by an external agency.

19. *Are private sector rotations for hospital staff covered?*

The medical staff of independent hospitals are responsible for their own medical defence cover, subject to the requirements of the hospital managers. If NHS staff in the training grades work in independent hospitals as part of their NHS training, they would be covered by the health authority indemnity, provided that such work was covered by an NHS contract.

20. *Will academic general practice be covered?*

The Health Departments have no plans to extend the health authority indemnity to academic departments of general practice. In respect of general medical services FPCs will be making payments by fees and allowances which include an element for expenses, of which medical defence subscriptions are a part.

Practical arrangements

21. *On what basis will medical defence organisations handle claims for health authorities?*

MDOs, in advising on claims for health authorities, will act as their agent; the charging arrangements for such services are for agreement between the MDO and the authority concerned.

22. *Will doctors be reimbursed by MDOs for the 'unexpired' portion of their subscriptions?*

This is a matter between each MDO and its members.

23. *Will membership of a medical defence organisation continue to be a contractual obligation?*

On an individual basis doctors and dentists may wish to continue their membership in order to receive the cover referred to in paragraphs 5-20 above, as well as the other legal and advisory services provided by the MDOs. The Health Departments are advising health authorities that they should no longer require their medical and dental staff to subscribe to an MDO, but a health authority could require a doctor to be a member of an MDO if the doctor were to be carrying out private work on NHS premises. The two-thirds reimbursement of subscriptions will cease at the end of 1989.

24. *Will medical defence subscriptions be tax-allowable in future?*

The Health Departments understand that medical defence subscriptions will continue to be allowable under income tax rules.

25. *What happens if a doctor wishes to contest a claim which the health authority would prefer to settle out of court, eg where a point of principle or a doctor's reputation is at stake?*

While the final decision in a case rests with the health authority since it will bear the financial consequences, it should take careful note of the practitioner's view. Health authorities may seek the advice of the relevant MDO on whether a case should be contested, and they should not settle cases without good cause.

26. *If a doctor wishes to have separate representation in a case, what would be the extent of his liability?*

Since it is the health authority which is sued for the medical negligence of its staff and which will in future be solely financially liable, then it must have the ultimate right to decide how the defence of a case is to be handled. Subject to this, a health authority may welcome a practitioner being separately advised in a case without cost to the health authority. However, if a practitioner claims that his interests in any case are distinct from those of the health authority and wishes to be separately represented in the proceedings, he will need the agreement of the plaintiff, the health authority and the court. If liability is established, he would have to pay not only his own legal expenses but also any further costs incurred as a result of his being separately represented. The health authority would remain liable for the full award of damages to the plaintiff.

27. *Will the authorities put restrictions on the clinical autonomy of doctors?*

Health authorities have a responsibility to organise services in a manner which is in the best interests of patients. In the past, medical defence organisations have advised doctors and dentists on patterns of practice carrying unacceptable dangers to patients. However, there is no question of health authorities barring certain services which carry risks but are a high priority for patients.

28. *Will health authorities be able to secure statements from doctors for the defence of a case of medical negligence?*

Health authorities will need co-operation from medical and dental staff if they are to defend cases. As part of this, practitioners should supply such statements or documents as the health authority or its solicitors may reasonably require in investigating or defending any claim. A doctor's refusal without good reason to provide a statement could result in the health authority being unable to defend itself properly and so incurring additional costs.

29. *Will health authorities be able to trace doctors who formerly worked for them?*

It is accepted that health authorities may have difficulty in tracing the doctors responsible, especially if they were junior medical staff at the time, and in securing statements from them; they may find the MDOs helpful in this respect. Often, however, good medical records kept at the time will be of more value than statements made some years after the event.

30. *Will the new arrangements apply to NHS Trust hospitals (self-governing units)?*

As employers, NHS Trusts will be vicariously liable for the acts of their employed medical and dental staff, and will take the financial responsibility for negligence. Further guidance will be issued in due course.

Financial effects

31. *How can District Health Authorities meet damages which could be as much as £1m for a single case?*

RHAs have been asked to make arrangements under which they will provide an element of cost-sharing with Districts for medical negligence costs above a certain level, as most RHAs do for non-medical negligence actions at present. And for a transitional period health authorities will have access (under certain criteria) to some of the reserves of the MDOs.

32. *The incidence of medical negligence damages may be uneven as between Regions; how will that be met?*

It is quite likely that some Regions will have to pay out more under the new arrangement than they would in reimbursing two-thirds of medical defence subscriptions. The funds from the MDOs will be of some help in the short term, but in the longer run the incidence of medical negligence costs and damages will fall on the Regions where they arise.

UK Health Departments
December 1989

ANNEX B
INFORMATION TO BE RETURNED ANNUALLY, NO LATER THAN 31 MAY (STARTING 31/5/90)

1. Following information should be supplied for the previous financial year:
   i.   The number of claims of medical negligence against the health authority and/or its employees, including the number of cases brought forward from an earlier period;
   ii. the number of such cases settled during the period with the health authority's costs, including damages payable, in the following cost bands:

	Number of cases	£	£
(a)			0–100,000
(b)			100,000–200,000
(c)			200,000–300,000
(d)			over £300,000

   iii. The total cost of the settlements reached or awards made; distinguishing
        (a) the Authority's costs from the payment of the plaintiff's costs and damages; and
        (b) an estimate of costs and damages attributable to medical negligence, as distinct from negligence of other staff.

The first point that we should note is that the scheme does not extend to general practitioners. They must still make their own arrangements with a defence organisation. Where a patient sues a GP and a hospital doctor jointly, the circular envisages (paragraph 6) that the defence organisation and the health authority should seek to reach an agreement in meeting any claim.

Subsequent to HC(89)34 the Department of Health through the National Health Service Management Executive issued two Executive Letters which have the effect of modifying the scheme from 1 April 1991 (EL(90) 195 and EL(91) 19). *Firstly*, the underlying rationale of the Scheme is extended to NHS Trusts created on or after 1 April 1991 such that they are required to meet any claims arising out of the negligence of their employees. NHS Trusts do not, however, inherit any *existing* claims. These remain the responsibility of the health authority of which the Trust previously formed part.

Secondly, up until 1 April 1991 the arrangements for meeting claims had two specific features: (a) health authorities met any claim up to the value of £300,000 but 80% of any excess over £300,000 would ordinarily be met from a fund created from monies provided by the defence organisations (particularly if the claim arose before 1 January 1990) (see Paragraph 11); (b) a pooling arrangement existed within each Region whereby DHAs contributed to a centralised pool from which damages were paid so that in effect, the burden of financial loss was distributed across the Region (Paragraph 10).

Since 1 April 1991, the pooling arrangements seem to have been abandoned for NHS managed units so that like NHS Trusts they must pay awards of damages against them. This is subject to one proviso, namely that in the case of NHS Trusts, the Secretary of State and in the case of NHS Managed Units, the Regional Health Authority, will make a loan to the defendant institution to cover any liability in excess of a 'specified amount' in any particular claims (Paragraph 5, EL(90)195). Access to the defence organisations' reserve fund is limited to pre-1 April 1991 claims.

Thirdly, EL(91)19 makes it abundantly clear that the scheme is limited to claims arising in negligence since it defines the scope of the scheme as applying only to claims arising out of a 'breach of duty of care'. Since *Stubbings v Webb* [1993] 1 All ER 322 (HL), it is clear that this phrase does not extend to claims framed as intentional torts, primarily here, the tort of battery.

It is important to notice that the provisions of the scheme will be reviewed during 1993 since the scheme ceases to exist by its own terms on 1 December 1993. It may be that at that time the Secretary of State will take advantage of the powers conferred upon him by section 21 of the National Health Service and Community Care Act 1990 to create by regulation a statutory scheme for both NHS Managed Units and NHS Trusts.

Before leaving consideration of these financial arrangements we should not overlook their potential effect on the provision of health care. It is clear from EL(90) 195 that 'no additional funding will be available to regions' to meet the costs which they are required to bear through the 'loan provisions' introduced on 1 April 1991. While this may encourage Regions to develop appropriate risk management strategies, it may also have as a consequence the effect of limiting the available resources for health care. However, a development which may ease their financial position in the short term is the emerging practice of structured settlements (see, R Lewis *Structured Settlements: The Law and Practice* (1993)). By these a defendant pays an initial lump sum to meet already incurred costs and to cover the plaintiff's immediate needs. In addition, the defendant purchases an annuity which pays the plaintiff an annual sum to cover future needs. Although the total sum paid when a settlement is structured is often less (from the defendant's point of view) than would be the case if the plaintiff were paid a 'one-off' lump sum, the defendant nevertheless has to make a substantial capital outlay. The further development which health authorities may in the future take advantage of is to 'self-fund' the structured settlement, ie pay the annuity directly from their own funds each year (see, R Lewis 'Health Authorities and the Payment of Damages by Means of a Pension' (1993) 56 MLR 844). The effect of this practice would be to avoid paying the large capital outlay involved in purchasing the annuity from a private insurance company (for a discussion see Law Commission Consultation Paper No 125, *Structures Settlements and Interim and Provisional Damages* (1992) especially paras 3.65-3.66 and R Lewis *ibid*, at 851-853). In this way, health authorities may have the means to avoid the otherwise grave financial implications of the modified scheme introduced in April 1991.

Chapter 6

Reforming the law of malpractice

Litigation between patients and doctors has long been recognised as a less than satisfactory means of regulating the doctor/patient relationship and dealing with patients' unhappiness over treatment. Despite this the system of tort litigation continues with no significant change. Can, and should this system be reformed?

The starting point for this enquiry should be the Pearson Report: Royal Commission of *Civil Liability and Compensation for Personal Injury* in 1978 (Cmnd 7054), which made a number of somewhat modest (and some would say disappointing) recommendations about negligence in the context of medical practice.

Criticisms of the present compensation provisions
1325 Criticisms of the present compensation provisions fall into two parts. First, there are those which relate to the difficulty of making claims following negligent treatment. Secondly, there are those concerning the lack of provision for medical accidents.

Proving negligence
1326 The proportion of successful claims for damages in tort is much lower for medical negligence than for all negligence cases. Some payment is made in 30-40 per cent of claims compared with 86 per cent of all personal injury claims.
1327 We received a good deal of evidence about the difficulty of proving negligence. It was said that it was not always possible to obtain the necessary information on which to base a claim. The patient might not know what had happened and he might have difficulty in obtaining the services of a medical expert to assist him. When a doctor was accused of negligence, his colleagues might naturally be reluctant to give evidence. The medical records might not contain all the details of the case, leaving ample scope for different interpretations by witnesses for and against.
1328 One of our number, who attended a Council of Europe colloquy on the civil liability of physicians, held in Lyons in June 1975, reported that most of the doctors and lawyers there agreed that information should be more readily available to the patient's advisers.
1329 In England and Wales, on an order for discovery, the court may direct disclosure to the applicant or his solicitors. The courts have taken the line that, normally, disclosure would be only to a nominated medical adviser of the applicant. In Northern Ireland, the courts have decided that disclosure may be made to the applicant. This is also the position in Scotland.
1330 Any patient may approach the Health Service Commissioners for investigation of his complaint, but the Commissioners are expressly prevented from investigating a claim in respect of which the person aggrieved has or had a remedy in law (unless it would not be reasonable to expect him to resort to it) or in respect of any action taken solely in consequence of the exercise of clinical judgment.

Medical accidents
1331 We have so far discussed the evidence we received about negligence. But there are many more cases where individuals suffer injury which was not due to negligence. We received a good deal of evidence that the position here was unsatisfactory.
1332 The Royal College of Physicians instanced, 'the possible sequelae of coronary arteriograms, kidney biopsies or amniocentesis'. Injury or death might be associated with, 'the development of hypersensitivity to a drug or antibacterial substance that was properly

prescribed'. Dr White Franklin pointed out that a patient who stopped breathing under properly administered and controlled anaesthesia might die or recover with faculties grossly impaired.

1333 Some of these patients (or their dependents) would receive social security benefit, but many would receive no cash benefit of any kind.

What should be done?

1334 Our evidence showed that there was considerable dissatisfaction with the present position and some unease about the future.

1335 We considered various ways of compensating medical accidents with or without negligence. We look first at tort, where liability at present is based on negligence, and consider the possibility either of reversing the burden of proof or of imposing strict liability. Then we go on to examine the possibility of a no-fault scheme which would cover medical accidents irrespective of negligence.

Tort compensation

Reversed burden of proof

1336 Some witnesses suggested that, if the burden of proof were reversed, the patient's difficulties in obtaining and presenting his evidence would be largely overcome. It was said that doctors were in a better position to prove absence of negligence than patients were to establish liability. At the Council of Europe colloquy, however, although it was agreed that the patient was at a disadvantage when he sought to establish a claim, serious doubts were expressed on the desirability of making a radical change in the burden of proof. We share these doubts. We think that there might well be a large increase in claims, and although many would be groundless, each one would have to be investigated and answered. The result would almost certainly be an increase in defensive medicine.

Strict liability

1337 We also considered whether strict liability should be introduced. Whilst this would avoid the difficulties of proving or disproving negligence, there would remain the difficulty of proving that the injury was a medical accident, that is to say that it would not have occurred in any event. It would be necessary to define the area to be covered. For example, the foreseeable result of medical treatment such as amputation of a limb in a case of gangrene would not be included. The problems in defining the scope of medical injuries to be included would be the same as those we consider later in connection with the possibility of introducing a no-fault scheme.

1338 Even if it were possible to limit the scope satisfactorily, the imposition of strict liability, as with reversing the burden of proof, might well lead to an increase in defensive medicine. It would tend to imply rigid standards of professional skill beyond those which the present law requires to be exhibited, and beyond those which (in our view) can fairly be expected. We decided not to recommend that strict liability should be introduced. . . .

The negligence action

1342 In most of the evidence from the medical profession it was urged that tort should be retained. It was argued that, even if some other system were introduced, the tort action based on negligence should continue alongside. Liability was one of the means whereby doctors could show their sense of responsibility and, therefore, justly claim professional freedom. If tortious liability were abolished, there could be some attempt to control doctors' clinical practice to prevent mistakes for which compensation would have to be paid by some central agency. It was said that this could lead to a bureaucratic restriction of medicine and a brake on progress. It was further argued that the traditions of the profession were not sufficient in themselves to prevent all lapses which, although small in number, might have disastrous effects. Some penalty helped to preserve the patient's opportunity to express disapproval and obtain redress.

1343 We record these views as put to us, although some of us feel that they are unsound and at the least overstated. We also feel bound to ask whether the growth of insurance cover does not mitigate the effect claimed for the value of the tort action. On this point, the Medical Defence Union said that, although they paid the compensation, their investigation into the circumstances brought home to the doctor the part he had played and encouraged a sense of personal responsibility. We add the comment that the cases that come to court must often be those in which the Union advises the doctor to contest the claim because he has a good defence, whereas the much smaller number of cases of gross negligence must usually be settled out of court. The system, therefore, would appear to expose to publicity those doctors whose behaviour is on the face of it the least reprehensible.

1344 Nevertheless, in spite of the doubts we express about the particular arguments put to us by the medical profession for the retention of the tort action, it is clear that there would have to be a good case for exempting any profession from legal liabilities which apply to others, and we do not regard the special circumstances of medical injury as constituting such a case.

1345 We were impressed by the difficulties facing a patient who wishes to establish a case, but we doubt if the confidentiality of medical records adds significantly to the plaintiff's difficulties in view of the powers of the courts to order disclosure.

1346 Although the powers of the Health Service Commissioners are restricted to some extent, we note with interest the possibility of change following a report published in November 1977 by the Select Committee on the Parliamentary Commissioner for Administration (HC45) about an independent review of hospital complaints in the National Health Service. The Committee considers that there should be a simple straightforward system for handling complaints in every hospital with emphasis on listening carefully to the patient's or relative's concern and dealing with it promptly. When the complainant is not satisfied he should be able to pursue the matter with the district Administrator. For the most serious cases the Secretaries of State should continue to set up inquiries under the relevant Acts. All other cases not resolved by this procedure should be referable to the Health Service Commissioner, including complaints concerning clinical judgment.

1347 We recommend that, subject to our recommendation on volunteers for medical research or clinical trials, the basis of liability in tort for medical injuries should continue to be negligence.

No-fault compensation

1348 Changes made to improve the prospects of getting compensation in the cases of negligence could have no effect on the very much greater number of medical accidents where nobody is at fault.

1349 The employment of new techniques and the development of medical science have increased the ability of the doctor to attempt the treatment of severe diseases and to effect a cure, but at the same time have widened the area in which medical accidents may occur. This trend of greater risks for greater gain is likely to continue.

1350 An operation may have unexpected consequences. Blood products may be used which contain viruses the presence of which could not be foreseen. There are now 3,000 drugs in common use and 10,000 listed drug interactions, both detrimental and beneficial. More will doubtless be discovered.

1351 Many of our witnesses urged us to recommend the introduction of a scheme of no-fault compensation for medical accidents. Dr White Franklin said that negligence should not be the key to any form of monetary compensation. A circuit judge suggested that subsistence level compensation would be appropriate for a medical injury which did not involve negligence. The Royal College of Psychiatrists suggested that over the whole field of personal injury, compensation should not be tied to fault or negligence and should be based on the need of the individual and his family.

1352 Most of our witnesses saw a no-fault scheme as an addition to tort. It was put to us that such a scheme would often overcome the difficulties of proving negligence; and that a special scheme for medical injuries would be justified because of the reliance of the patient on the doctor to preserve his health and perhaps his life.

Overseas experience

1353 No-fault schemes which cover medical accidents have recently been introduced in New Zealand and Sweden. In Volume Three . . . we give a detailed description of the provisions; in this chapter we touch only on some relevant features.

1354 New Zealand's accident compensation scheme covers medical, surgical, dental and first aid misadventure. In an appraisal of the first two years' operation of the scheme, Professor Geoffrey Palmer refers to the Accident Compensation Commission's 'restrictive interpretation' of 'medical misadventure' which 'seems concerned to avoid sliding down the slippery slope and compensating illness or death every time medical treatment fails'. This means that in many cases the claimant is left only with recourse to the common law. The view that the Accident Compensation Commission is treading carefully in this difficult area is supported by reported decisions of the Commission.

1355 The Patient Insurance Scheme in Sweden provides no-fault compensation which is based on the rules for the assessment of tort damages. This includes provision for loss of earnings, necessary medical expenses not covered by social insurance, and non-pecuniary loss. The scheme is financed by the Government and by the county councils who are responsible for the hospitals and for public health facilities. Liability is limited to 20 million kronor (about £3 million) for each incident involving injury and there is an overall limitation of 60 million kronor (about £8½ million) for such injuries in the whole country in one year. This is about £1 a head of the population.

1356 Payments under the scheme are relatively modest because they supplement existing social insurance payments which cover virtually all the adult population, including housewives. Social insurance sickness benefit is 90 per cent of earnings with an earnings ceiling of over £10,000 a year. The Patient Insurance Scheme makes up the payments to 100 per cent. Under industrial agreements, benefit for work accidents is made up to 100 per cent and this further reduces the scope for the payments under the Patient Insurance Scheme. Of the compensation paid during the first year only 12½ per cent was for loss of income.

1357 The scheme covers injury or illness which has occurred as a direct consequence of examination, medication, treatment or any other similar procedure, and does not constitute a natural or probable consequence of an act justified from a medical point of view. Mental illness is not covered unless it results from bodily injury. Injuries resulting from risks which are justified in order to avoid a threat to life or of permanent disability or would have occurred regardless of the treatment are also excluded.

1358 The Swedish scheme is administered by the main insurance companies. The amount of compensation is settled in the same way as tort awards. Disputed claims and questions of principle are referred to a panel consisting of a chairman and one member appointed by the government, two members appointed by county councils and two by insurance companies. Specialist medical advice is available. Only 50 cases have been referred to the panel in the first 23 months of the scheme. The advice of the panel has been accepted in every case. There has been no need to use the arbitration machinery under the Swedish Arbitration Act.

1359 The Swedish and New Zealand schemes cater for relatively small populations, so that it is possible to ensure consistency in decisions by dealing with all difficult or borderline cases centrally. Both schemes have been in operation for a short time and claims will take some time to build up. It will be a few years yet before a useful appraisal can be made.

A no-fault scheme for the United Kingdom?

1360 In considering the possibility of a no-fault scheme for this country we looked first at the question of cost. There are two aspects: the overall cost of any scheme; and the machinery for financing it.

1361 It is difficult to be precise about cost. Minor injuries and complications of treatment could reasonably be excluded as in Sweden, where there has to be some incapacity for work for more than 14 days. If there were as many as 10,000 cases a year, and benefits were provided on the same lines as in our suggested work and road schemes, the total additional cost of compensation over the existing form of compensation would be about £6 million a year. Some addition would have to be made for the cost of administration. This could well be substantial. Judging by the Swedish experience there would be at least two claims for every one that was successful.

1362 We think that it would be appropriate to finance any such scheme through the National Health Service. But the question of what to do about medical accidents in private practice would raise difficulties. Although it might be argued that many doctors have both National Health Service and private patients, that private doctors use National Health Service facilities and that all taxpayers contribute to the National Health Service, nevertheless we think that it is out of the question that a no-fault scheme provided by public funds should cover injuries received in the course of private treatment. There might be other ways of solving the problem. For example, such injuries could be covered by private no-fault insurance, or it might be possible to provide no-fault compensation through a levy on the subscription to medical defence societies. But in view of the decision we come to, as explained below, not to recommend a no-fault scheme because of other even more compelling considerations, we have not worked out in any detail possible ways of meeting this particular difficulty over finance.

1363 Any attempt to devise a no-fault scheme would also run into the problem of whether, and if so, how, treatment given by the 'paramedical' professions should be covered. Most of those in such professions, for example, nurses and physiotherapists, work with or mainly under the direction of doctors or dentists; but there would remain the problem of treatment not given by a medical team, for example chiropody. Outside the National Health Service, there would be the further problem whether other practices, such as osteopathy, should be covered.

Establishing causation

1364 The main difficulty in the way of a no-fault scheme is how to establish causation, since the cause of many injuries cannot be identified. The Medical Research Council said that while future research was likely to establish more causal relationships it would also reveal increasingly complex interactions which would heighten the problems of proving causation in the individual case.

1365 Even with our definition of medical injury we were forced to conclude that in practice there would be difficulty in distinguishing medical accident from the natural progression of a disease or injury, and from a foreseeable side effect of treatment. It is quite normal for a patient not to recover completely for several weeks or months after a major operation; for complications to ensue after operations; and for a patient to find that the drugs prescribed cause serious side effects.

1366 How should words like 'expected' or 'foreseeable' be interpreted? Even rare side effects such as vaccine damage not caused by negligence are often foreseeable in the sense that they are well known to medical science. If such injuries were to be included in a no-fault scheme, where would the line be drawn between them and the accepted risks of treatment? If they were to be excluded, the scheme would do little more than convert the negligence test of tort into a statutory formula, thereby making it easier for the victims of negligence to obtain compensation, but doing nothing for those suffering medical injury from other causes.

1367 In establishing causation, who should take the decision? We envisage that a no-fault scheme would be the responsibility of the DHSS. The use of its adjudication procedure, however, would either place more burdens on the medical manpower available, or would put the onus of making the initial decision on the shoulders of junior officials who have neither the experience nor the training to determine those issues.

1368 To establish causation would involve deciding whether the condition was the result of the treatment and, if so, whether it was a result that might have been expected. This would have to be disentangled from the conditions resulting from the progress of the disease or advancing age or from some other purely fortuitous circumstances.

1369 It is easy to distinguish the completely unexpected result from that which was expected. The grey areas in between pose serious difficulties in knowing where to draw the line.

Conclusions on no-fault compensation

1370 We concluded that we could not recommend the introduction of a no-fault scheme for medical accidents in the United Kingdom. Some of us found this was a difficult decision and thought the arguments were finely balanced. All of us appreciate that circumstances may change, and that our conclusions may have to be reviewed in the future.

1371 We recommend that a no-fault scheme for medical accidents should not be introduced at present; but that the progress of no-fault compensation for medical accidents in New Zealand and Sweden should be studied and assessed, so that the experience can be drawn upon, if, because of changing circumstances, a decision is taken to introduce a no-fault scheme for medical accidents in this country.

'No fault', here, does not mean strict liability (as technically it should) but a system in which compensation is awarded not only without the need to prove fault (though there may be other threshold requirements) but, *more importantly*, without the need to have recourse to litigation to claim compensation.

Ten years on Ham, Dingwall *et al* in their magisterial short paper brought a fresh look to the problems.

C Ham, R Dingwall, P Fenn, D Harris *Medical Negligence: Compensation and Accountability* (1988)

The position today

In the decade that has passed since the Pearson Commission reported, the position in relation to medical negligence has changed significantly. The number of successful claims has risen (see below) and there have been increases in the damages awarded by the courts. These developments have given rise to fears that the UK might be following the example of the USA and may be about to experience a malpractice crisis.

In response, the defence societies have increased their subscription rates substantially. As Table 3 shows, subscription rates rose from £40 in 1978 to £1,080 in 1988. The increase in subscription rates was 71 per cent in 1987 and 87 per cent in 1988. This has created particular difficulties for junior doctors. Although concessionary rates are available to newly qualified doctors (see Table 4) and those on limited incomes, a junior doctor is required to pay the full rate seven years after qualifying. Until the introduction of new arrangements following the 1988 pay award (see below), this meant that subscription rates could amount to the equivalent of a month's salary. As a result of these pressures, the medical profession has reconsidered its position and has called for a review of existing arrangements.

Table 3. Defence Society Subscription Rates 1978-88

Year	Rate £	Annual Increase %
1988	1,080	87
1987	576	71
1986	336	17
1985	288	17
1984	264	35
1983	195	44
1982	135	13
1981	120	26
1980	95	36
1979	70	75
1978	40	—

Table 4. 1988 Defence Society Subscription Rates

	£
Full rate	1,080
Concessionary rates available to members who join within three months of qualification	
1st year	180
2nd year	240
3rd year	396
4th year	492
5th year	600
6th year	744
Non-clinical membership	132
Limited income concessionary rates	
Income ceiling of £6,230	360
Income between £6,231 and £12,460	720

Subscription rates from January 1 1988 for the Medical Protection Society and the Medical Defence Union

At the same time, health authorities have expressed their concern at the impact of increasing awards on cash limited budgets. As well as the cost of awards themselves, health authorities are worried that the threat of legal action will lead to more defensive medicine. By increasing the use of diagnostic tests and procedures, and by producing greater caution on the part of doctors, it is feared that defensive medicine will add to the pressure on health authority spending, particularly in the acute hospital services.

In parallel with the concern of health authorities and the medical profession, organisations representing patients and their relatives have drawn attention to the shortcomings of the tort system . . .

First, there is the lengthy and expensive procedure involved in pursuing a claim for damages. This means that cases are often brought only by the rich or those able to obtain legal aid. Cases take a considerable time to work their way through the courts: the average time for settling a claim is four years.

Second, the legal process is by definition adversarial. As such, it may cause doctors and health authorities to close ranks and not offer an adequate explanation to patients and their relatives when things go wrong. In addition, the legal process may itself be distressing in providing a constant reminder of painful or unhappy events.

Third, the emphasis on establishing fault and cause and effect in injury cases turns the tort system into a lottery. Compensation is based not on need but on the ability to prove that somebody was at fault. The rules of the legal process which put the burden of proof on those bringing a claim may create significant difficulties for plaintiffs. As a consequence, similar cases of injury may be compensated quite differently. For example, a child suffering brain damage after contracting encephalitis will receive no compensation, a child suffering brain damage as a result of vaccine damage will receive £20,000, and a child suffering brain damage following traumatic birth delivery may receive hundreds of thousands of pounds compensation. . . .

Fourth, only a small proportion of people suffering medical injuries are compensated through the tort system. This may mean that the losses incurred as a result of injury are inadequately compensated, although other sources of compensation are available.

Underlying these criticisms is a concern that the arrangements for maintaining high standards of medical practice and holding doctors to account for unacceptable standards of practice are inadequate. Action for the Victims of Medical Accidents (AVMA), established in 1982, has highlighted these issues, and has argued for much greater openness and accountability on the part of the medical profession in dealing with the consequences of accidents. One of the points emphasised by AVMA is that most people who suffer medical injuries are not seeking compensation but want an explanation of what went wrong. An adequate system for dealing with injuries needs to provide for this as well as to offer financial compensation.

Before considering these points more fully, it is worth noting a number of other criticisms levelled at the tort system as it applies to medical injury cases. These are:

- those making a claim may find it difficult to obtain the services of a solicitor with relevant expertise
- there may be difficulty in obtaining the services of doctors willing to act as expert witnesses for patients
- the legal process causes distress and expense to doctors and health authorities as well as to patients
- the availability of legal aid may result in legal action being initiated in inappropriate cases, that is cases where those making a claim have little chance of success. . . .

It is against this background that alternatives to existing arrangements have again come under scrutiny. One widely canvassed option is a no-fault compensation scheme. This has found favour with the British Medical Association (BMA) and the Association of CHCs in England and Wales (ACHCEW). Other possibilities include the introduction of differential premiums for doctors to reflect the risks involved in their work; shifting the cost of providing compensation to the NHS . . . reforming the tort law to overcome some of the shortcomings identified; providing more support to medical injury cases through the social security system; and extending first party insurance cover.

The view of AVMA is that a change in the existing arrangements is required but it is not clear what that change should be. The view of the Government is that the case for change remains not proven . . .

To shed more light on this debate, we now consider in more detail the available evidence on the present system and assess whether there is indeed a case for reform. . . .

Before accepting too readily the claim that the UK is experiencing a malpractice crisis, it is important to review the available evidence to establish whether this claim is justified. Ideally, this evidence would include:

- trends in the number of medical accidents occurring expressed as a proportion of patients treated
- trends in the number of medical accidents which result from negligence
- trends in the number of claims made expressed as a proportion of patients treated
- trends in the number of successful claims made expressed as a proportion of patients treated
- trends in damages awarded, including total damages awarded each year, the size of the biggest award and the size of the mean award

In practice, only some of this information is available. It is not possible to identify either the number of accidents occurring or the number of accidents which result from negligence because this information is not collected routinely. Information is available on claims and damages through the defence societies. The Medical Protection Society (MPS) has published some information on trends in awards (Figures 1 and 2) and has informed us that the number of claims received by the Society increased from around 1,000 in 1983 to over 2,000 in 1987 (personal communication). Similar trends are reported by the Medical Defence Union (MDU): the frequency of claims paid more than doubled between 1984 and 1987, and the average value of damages awarded also doubled in the same period (personal communication). The MDU has published a graph (Figure 3) showing changes in the highest sum awarded in medical negligence cases. More detailed data are not made public because the societies consider that this information is commercially sensitive and might be used by insurance companies seeking to enter the medical insurance market.

Figure 1
Maximum awards paid by the Medical Protection Society for failed sterilisation

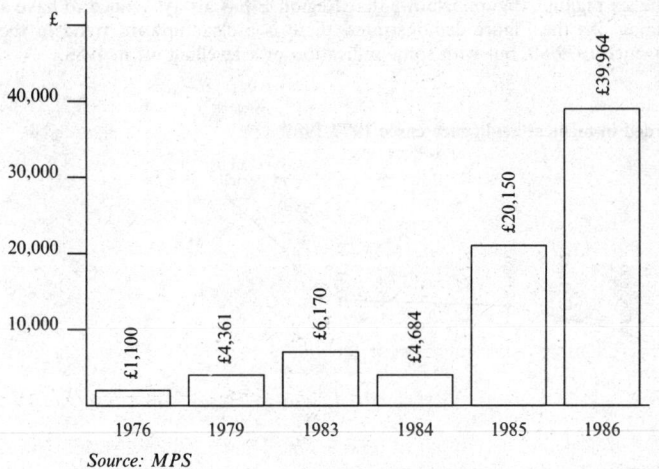

Source: MPS

Figure 2
Average costs of settlements. Percentage increase from January 1976

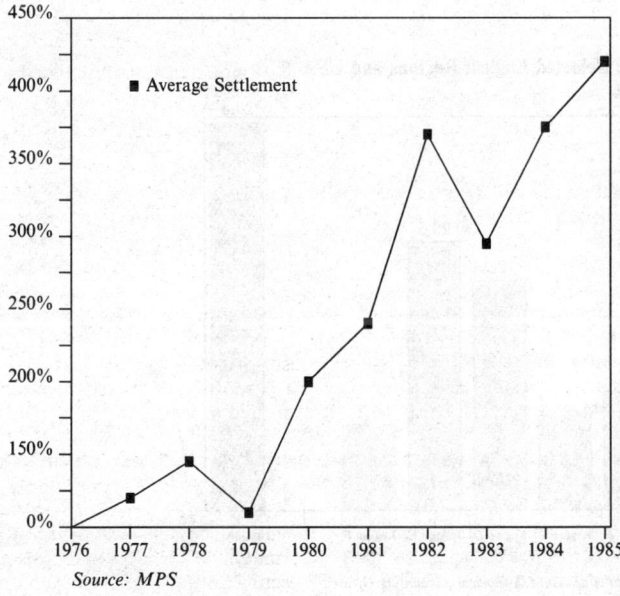

Source: MPS

Health authorities also collect information on claims and damages but again this has not been fully analysed and published. The DHSS only receives information from health authorities on awards over £100,000 and the Department is currently seeking to improve the quality of this information. The DHSS also collates information on the total payments for losses and compensation made by health authorities. In 1986-7 a total of £9.3 million was paid out by health authorities (Hansard, 24 November, 1987, col. 162) but this covers a range of cases including compensation for unfair dismissals and losses due to theft. There is no information held centrally on the proportion of these payments spent on compensation for medical negligence (DHSS, personal communication).

In view of the limited information held by the DHSS, we approached RHA legal advisers for assistance and received detailed replies from six regions. The experience of claims opened in these regions in the most recent available year is shown in Figure 4, together with the US rate for 1984. The variation with the UK is striking: most regions had an annual rate of around 8 claims per 100,000 population between 1986 and 1987, but two adjacent regions had annual rates which were more than double this. Time-series data were readily available for only two of the six regions. Figure 5 shows that Region E has always tended to have a high rate of claiming. As the Figure demonstrates, there is a clear upward trend in the number of claims since 1979/80, but with some indication of a levelling off in 1988.

Figure 3
Highest sum awarded in medical negligence cases 1977-1987

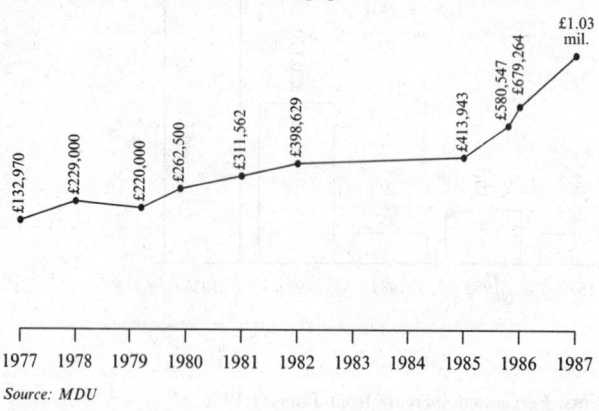

Source: MDU

Figure 4
Annual Claim Rates: Selected English Regions and USA

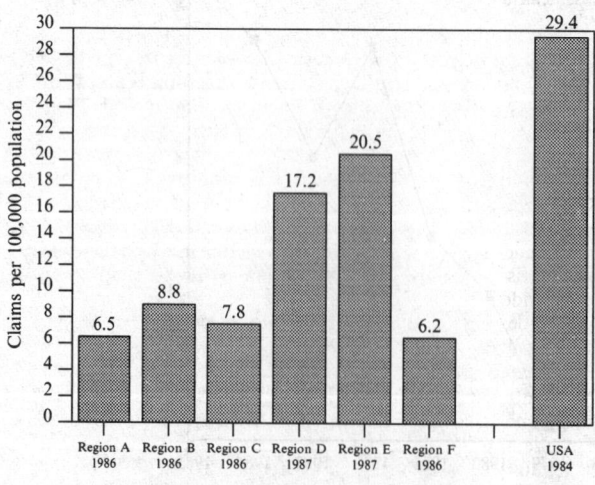

Sources: RHA solicitors and US General Accounting Office

It is difficult to go beyond these global figures to examine the experience of authorities in managing claims and to identify their specific origins. The most useful published data can be found in a study of 100 cases taken at random from the files of the West Midlands RHA . . . An audit of these cases found that at the end of three years, 73 actions had been withdrawn, 12 settled out of court and 1 lost in court. Fourteen cases were pending and the authors estimated that nine of these fourteen cases were likely to reach court.

In the context of the Pearson Commission's data, these figures do not suggest that the proportion of claims which are successful is increasing. Indeed the rate at which claims are abandoned would appear to have increased. On the other hand, it would appear that the proportion of claims going to court or likely to go to court is increasing.

Figure 5
Claim Rates for two English Regions 1977-87

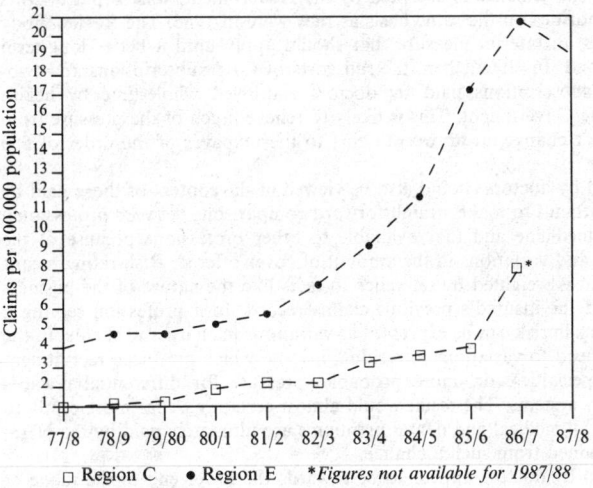

□ Region C   • Region E   *Figures not available for 1987/88*

Evidence we have obtained from another health authority confirms that the rate at which claims are abandoned has increased. In this authority, 75 per cent of claims were abandoned in the 1980s compared with around 50 per cent in the 1970s. There is no evidence from this authority that the severity of the claimants' injuries has reduced over time. However, the higher proportion of claims which are abandoned may mean that some claims are being pursued on weaker grounds than they were previously.

The claims experience of this health authority also revealed some interesting patterns in relation to the nature and sources of medical negligence claims. Most claims resulted from temporary injuries, with conditions like iatrogenic infections, fractures caused by mishandling or lack of supervision, and missed diagnosis of fractures being typical. There is some evidence that claim-provoking incidents in hospitals are most likely to occur on the wards rather than in the operating theatre. Moreover, claims arising from events in operating theatres seem rather more likely to be abandoned. All specialties attract claims, although some attract more claims that others. High risk specialties appear to be obstetrics and gynaecology, anaesthetics, accident and emergency, orthopaedics and neurosurgery.

The evidence from the West Midlands and elsewhere points to a picture in which there is a diversity of claims, many of which arise from relatively minor injuries, with little indication of any systematic variation in the incidence of claim-provoking occurrences. This diversity is reflected in a wide distribution of settlement amounts around a fairly modest average figure. In 1986 prices, the average settlement over the years 1981-86 would appear to be in the region of £15,000 with a standard deviation of £27,000. In addition, health authorities incur legal costs, even where cases are eventually abandoned. Again in 1986 prices, the legal costs of one authority varied between a mean of £210 for abandoned cases, through £1,200 in cases where some payment was made, to £3,000 in cases which were successfully defended in court. Where the authority was required to pay the plaintiff's costs as part of a settlement or award, the mean payment was £2,000.

The impact of subscriptions on the medical profession
As we have noted, a major cause of current concern with compensation arrangements is the impact of increases in defence society subscription rates on the medical profession. In considering this issue, it is worth noting that general practitioners' subscriptions are fully reimbursed by the Government as expenses. As far as hospital doctors are concerned, the increase in defence society subscriptions was taken into account by the Review Body on Doctors' and Dentists' Remuneration in making recommendations on salary levels in 1987.

The Review Body went a stage further in its 1988 report, proposing that two-thirds of the medical rate of subscriptions should be reimbursed as an expense to all whole-time employed practitioners or part-time employed practitioners working wholly for the NHS, with effect from 1 January 1988 (Review Body on Doctors' and Dentists' Remuneration, 1988). The Review Body argued that doctors should continue to bear part of the cost of subscriptions in order to maintain involvement in the handling of claims.

The aim of this proposal, which was accepted by the Government, was to put doctors employed by health authorities on the same basis as they were in 1986. The Review Body emphasised that this was an interim measure that should apply until a better long-term solution had been achieved. In effect, then, the full costs of GPs' subscriptions and two-thirds of the costs of subscriptions paid by doctors employed whole-time by health authorities are met by the Government. This is likely to relieve much of the pressure from the medical profession for change, at an overall cost to the taxpayer of the order of £50 million in England alone.

The subscriptions paid by doctors should also be viewed in the context of those paid by other professions. It is difficult to make straightforward comparisons between professional indemnity insurance in medicine and that available to other professions because of the prevalence of risk-rating and variations in the amount of cover offered. Risk-rating means that the premium charged is weighted by reference to facts like the nature of the business handled, its location and the insured's previous claims record. In a profession serving a private clientele, variations in risk can be expressed as variations in charges to clients. In the NHS, they would either lead to variations in residual income which produced recruitment problems in high-risk specialties, or, more probably, pressure for differential rewards through the Review Body systems. The result would almost certainly be far more costly to administer. Since almost all medical and dental premiums are ultimately paid by the NHS, there seems little to be gained from such a change.

The rates actually paid by doctors appear to be towards the lower end of the range of professional liability premiums. A telephone survey of insurers revealed the following:

Lawyers
Solicitors are required to pay into a mutual fund administered by the Law Society according to a complex scale varying from a minimum of 3.3 per cent of gross fee income below £30,000 in total for a practice to 0.1 per cent of gross fee income above £220,000 per partner, weighted to reflect the ratio between partners and assistant or unqualified staff and the nature of the work being undertaken. This buys £500,000 of cover for each and every claim. Larger practices dealing with high value commercial work obtain top-up cover on the commercial market.

The Bar set up its own mutual fund from 1 April 1988. This groups barristers into four categories depending upon the mix between civil and criminal work in their practice. The fund's directors expect to develop more sophisticated risk-rating in future years. The lowest contribution, for a barrister mainly engaged in criminal work, is 0.3 per cent of gross fee income with a minimum of £20 and a maximum of £390. The highest contributions, from barristers engaged mainly in civil work, are 0.7 per cent of gross fee income up to a maximum of £910 per annum. Coverage is offered in five bands, depending upon the premium paid, from £250,000 up to £2 million for each and every claim. £1 million of cover on this basis would cost between £300 and £499. Practitioners may raise their cover by voluntarily increasing their premium. Leading counsel handling tax cases would need to top up their cover in the insurance market to as much as £10 million but it is unlikely that anyone would pay more than one per cent of their gross fee income.

Financial services
Chartered accountants do not as yet have compulsory insurance although this is under active discussion within their institute. About 60 per cent of them, mostly in small firms, with an average of 3 partners, are covered under the institute's policy with a commercial insurer. The minimum coverage allowed is 3 times annual gross fees or 30 times the gross income from the largest single source, whichever is greater. The lower limit is fixed at

£50,000 for a 1986/7 premium of £385. The maximum currently available under the scheme is £1 million. All coverage is on an aggregate basis. Premiums paid vary between 1 and 3 per cent of a practice's gross fee income depending upon size and claims history. The 'Big Eight' international firms have set up their own mutual fund. In this sector, the highest premiums appear to be paid by insurance brokers where they can go up to 20 per cent of gross income.

Construction
About 40 per cent of architects are not insured at all, either by deliberate choice or as a result of falling behind with premiums during the recent recession in their industry. There is also a particular uncertainty about the position of architects employed in the public sector who do not normally carry their own insurance but whose employers, mostly local authorities, have not accepted liability on their behalf. Those who are insured are mostly covered by a scheme administered by the RIBA.

Current premium rates vary between 4 and 15 per cent of a practice's gross fee income with a minimum of £1,000 per partner. The average is about 7 per cent or around £14,300 per annum at 1987 prices. Rates are influenced by the nature of the business, claims experience and the amount of cover required. Most insured practices carry between £150,000 and £250,000 for each and every claim. Cover of £1 million would cost a typical practice about £80,000 per annum at current rates. Again, the largest firms have formed their own mutual scheme to cover their high-value work.

Chartered engineers pay upwards of £1,000 per head for £250,000 aggregate cover in the commercial market. Much depends on the nature and location of their work, so that anything involving a risky material like water or high value like oil rig design might lead to premiums of up to 8 or 9 per cent of a partner's gross income.

Other health professions
Veterinary surgeons are covered by a defence fund very similar in its operation to the medical defence societies, except that premiums are related to cover, with each practitioner determining his or her own needs. The minimum cover is £50,000 for each and every claim which costs £102 per annum. Practitioners involved in high value work such as racehorses or major intensive husbandry may seek up to £4 million worth of cover at a cost of £2,500 per annum. The package includes £750,000 for incidental injury to humans irrespective of the indemnity selected for liability in respect of animals.

Most independent retail pharmacists are covered by the Chemists' Defence Association which provides up to £3 million in respect of each and every claim. The premium forms part of their annual subscription to the National Pharmaceutical Association, currently £225 plus VAT, and it is not possible to disaggregate this component. The larger chains, such as Boots and some Co-operative societies, make their own arrangements for employed pharmacists. NHS-employed pharmacists are covered by a policy arranged at Lloyd's by the Pharmaceutical Society which covers them for £500,000 aggregate at an annual premium of £32.50.

The great variation in the nature of the cover provided and the methods of calculating premiums make it difficult to translate these figures into direct comparisons with the rates paid by doctors. If, however, we were to attempt an estimate of what a typical professional would pay for £1 million cover on each and every claim, which is broadly the benefit offered by the defence societies, then we would come up with a figure in the range of £1,500 to £5,000, with at least some paying a good deal more and a few paying rather less. This compares with the 1988 subscription of £1,080 for defence society membership and makes the new arrangements with two-thirds reimbursement to doctors working exclusively for the NHS appear a positive bargain.

As a proportion of income a registrar will pay about 2.75 per cent of gross salary once the concessionary rate for junior doctors expires after six years in practice and a senior consultant with an A plus award will pay about 0.5 per cent of gross NHS salary. Again, both seem to be at the lower end of the range for professionals. Insofar as there is a continuing problem, it would seem to be one of equity between practitioners at different stages in their careers with different earning capacities. There are ways of dealing with this short of a fundamental reform of the tort system. A BMA Working Party, for example, has suggested that the concessionary rate might be available for twelve years after qualification with a consequent increase in the full rate subscription to increase the element of cross-subsidy.

[Since this was written the authors' concerns have been met by the Government's introduction of the NHS Indemnity Scheme in HC(89) 34 with effect from 1 January 1990 (see ch 5 *supra*).]

Defensive medicine

A further cause of concern is that the increased likelihood of litigation will result in more defensive medicine. This claim is made regularly by the BMA and the defence societies. The argument more frequently articulated is that rather than risk legal action doctors will err on the side of caution by requesting additional diagnostic tests which may be clinically unnecessary. Lord Pitt recently summarised this argument:

> If doctors are to face these awards of severe damages they have to make sure of their defence. You are always better off in the witness box if you can say that you have done all the tests that are considered necessary . . . That means that one is wasting resources. We must therefore face the fact that if we are going to pursue the course that we are now pursuing we shall find an increase in defensive medicine with an alarming waste of resources (*Hansard*, House of Lords, 10 November 1987, cols 1350-51).

In fact, there is little hard evidence that defensive medicine is on the increase. A comprehensive American review of medical malpractice questioned the claim that doctors in the United States were becoming more defensive and noted that if more tests were carried out there could well be benefits for patients. . . . It is also worth reiterating that in the eyes of the law standards of reasonable care in practice are defined by doctors. There is therefore no obligation on doctors to carry out tests and procedures other than those considered reasonable by the profession.

Against this, Harvey and Roberts [(1987) 1 *Lancet* 145] have questioned whether doctors will see this as providing them with sufficient protection. These authors maintain that even where clinical guidelines exist doctors may still judge that tests are needed as a defence against possible litigation. However, Kennedy [*The Unmasking of Medicine* (1983)] argues that what is required is for doctors to be better informed of the legal position and to not feel constrained to practise in a way that is inappropriate. Similarly, Carson [(1982) XCII *Health and Social Service Journal* 1346] has maintained that changes in clinical practice involving reductions in the use of tests need not increase legal liability if the changes are discussed within the profession and receive the support of a responsible body of doctors. These arguments apply not only to tests but also to other areas of clinical practice, such as obstetrics, where it has been suggested that defensive medicine is also on the increase.

One of the most widely cited examples of defensive practice is the rise in caesarean section rates. This is, however, a phenomenon experienced by many countries with very different patterns of litigation (see Figure 6). The trend seems to be much better explained by other factors. These include changes in the perceived risk/benefit ratio following improvements in anaesthetic technology; changing clinical indications; the preference for conducting further deliveries by repeat caesarean; time management benefits for doctors and patients; and, for a time in the US, greater reimbursement for caesarean sections. Many of these factors are reflected in the rising British rates, independently of any concern over the risk of litigation . . .

Explanations

Various explanations have been proposed for the growth over the last decade in litigation arising from medical accidents. . . . [W]e do not think it is plausible simply to attribute the increase in litigation to a direct copying of American experience. Three other types of explanation have been put forward: a real increase in negligence; easier access to legal repres-entation; and a change in the propensity of patients to sue following an adverse outcome.

It is really quite impossible to determine whether rates of medical error have changed in the last ten years. Litigation rates are affected by so many factors that they cannot be treated as a reliable proxy for actual medical behaviour. However, the timing of the increase and the lag between events and claims tend to discount the suggestion that the recent squeeze on the real resources available to the NHS has put excessive pressure on staff and caused higher rates of error. The rates began to rise in relation to incidents occurring in the mid 1970s which predate the most acute stringency in health service resources, although it is not impossible that this is a factor in the recent acceleration of the trend.

A more important observation, though, is that this phenomenon is not unique to the medical profession. Almost without exception, other professions' liability insurers report a similar trend over a similar time scale. In the case of architects, for example, there was one claim for every 7 policies in 1979 and 7 for every 10 in 1987. Claims against veterinary surgeons doubled between 1981 and 1987. The real value of paid and reserved claims against accountants increased by 82 per cent between 1979 and 1984. It seems highly improbable that all professionals have simultaneously become more prone to error.

There have certainly been important changes in the market for legal services since 1979. A number of medical commentators, as well as insurers for retail pharmacists and veterinary surgeons, have argued that legal aid has become more freely available and that this has encouraged a proliferation of trivial claims. The statistical basis for this latter statement is uncertain. In the case of medicine, it is certainly not substantiated by any of the figures currently available to us.

Figure 6
Caesarean rates for selected countries 1970-84

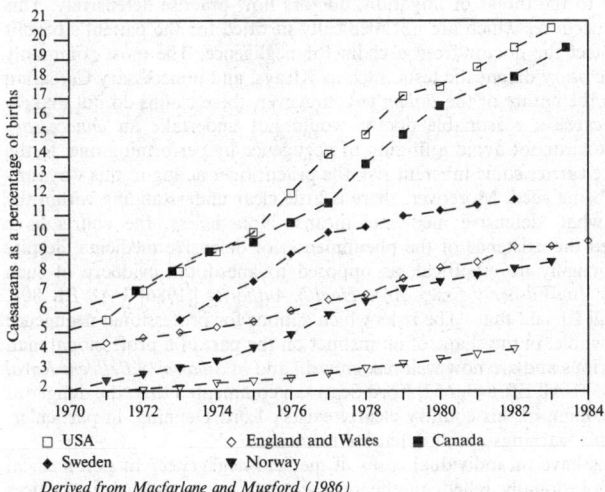

Derived from Macfarlane and Mugford (1986)

What is clear is that the capital and income limits for civil legal aid have consistently lagged behind inflation in the last ten years and the proportion of the population eligible for assistance has decreased. It is possible that the changing nature of the market for legal services, especially the growth of specialisation among solicitors, has improved the presentation of applications so that more are likely to be granted. It is also likely that the liberalisation of access to clinical records in recent years has increased the willingness of Legal Aid Committees to support the initial stages of an action because they know that information will be available at a reasonable cost. They can then take a considered decision on whether the action is worth supporting further.

Both of these developments would tend to facilitate more claims from a smaller pool of eligible claimants. This might be experienced by defendants as a growth in 'trivial' claims because many of them will inevitably prove insubstantial once the documents have been studied. Again, though, these developments must be put in the context of the general increase in litigation over the supply of professional services, which is as marked among those serving corporate customers as among those serving individuals. In architecture, the highest risk of litigation arises from work for housing associations. Accountancy cases almost invariably involve company liability.

The most likely explanation, then, relates to claims consciousness, the awareness among victims of the possibility of legal redress and their readiness to pursue this route. The more active marketing of legal services and the efforts of a number of statutory and voluntary bodies like CHCs, Citizens' Advice Bureaux and AVMA may well have had some impact, both in terms of public education and of practical support. If, however, we are dealing here with a particular case of a general phenomenon, more general explanations would be needed.

One possibility is that there may have been a cultural change towards a greater insistence on the right to be compensated for life's misfortunes and an increased distrust of the assumed skill and honour of professionals. Clients may be less ready to accept that adverse outcomes are intrinsic to the uncertainties of professional work and to insist that some dereliction of duty must underlie any failure. In this limited sense, there may be something to be said for the 'Americanisation' thesis.

The reference by the authors to 'defensive medicine' warrants further comment given the importance it occupies in the minds of the medical profession and, it seems, judges.

Michael Jones, *Medical Negligence* (1991) (paras 3.91-3.93)

The increase in medical malpractice litigation in recent years has been accompanied by claims that, in response to the threat of litigation, doctors now practise defensively. This involves undertaking procedures which are not medically justified for the patient's benefit but are designed to protect the doctor from a claim for negligence. The most commonly cited examples are unnecessary diagnostic tests, such as X-rays, and unnecessary Caesarian section deliveries. Given the nature of the *Bolam* test, however, these claims do not make a great deal of sense, because a reasonable doctor would not undertake an *unnecessary* procedure and so a doctor cannot avoid a finding of negligence by performing one; to the extent that the procedure carries some inherent risk the practitioner acting in this way may increase the chances of being sued. Moreover, there is little clear understanding within the medical profession of what 'defensive medicine' means. Nonetheless, the courts have apparently acknowledged the existence of the phenomenon of defensive medicine, despite the fact that there is virtually no empirical, as opposed to anecdotal, evidence of such practices in this country. In *Wilsher v Essex Area Health Authority* [[1986] 3 All ER 801, 810], for example, Mustill LJ said that: 'The risks which actions for professional negligence bring to the public as a whole, in the shape of an instinct on the part of a professional man to play for safety, are serious and are now well recognised,' and in *Sidaway v Bethlem Royal Hospital Governors* [[1985] 1 All ER 643, 653] Lord Scarman commented that 'the danger of defensive medicine developing in this country clearly exists'. Lord Denning, in particular, has been most vocal in his warnings about defensive medicine.

What impact does this have on individual cases of medical negligence? In non-medical cases the courts have occasionally relied on the prospect of unduly defensive practices developing in response to a potential liability in order to deny the existence of a duty of care. Clearly, this option is not available in the vast majority of medical negligence cases, since the doctor undoubtedly owes a duty of care to his patient. In *Barker v Nugent* [(1987) unreported QBD] counsel for the defendant doctor argued that as a matter of public policy, to avoid an escalation of defensive medicine, the courts should be slower to impute negligence to the medical profession than to others. Rougier J rejected the argument, pointing out that comparisons with the position in the United States of America are not entirely sound. Moreover, his Lordship added:

> I can think of only one thing more disastrous than the escalation of defensive medicine and that is the engendering of a belief in the medical profession that certain acts or omissions which would otherwise be classed as negligence can, in a sense, be exonerated.

Similarly, in *Wilsher v Essex Area Health Authority* Mustill LJ responded to his own acknowledgement of the risks of defensive practice with the comment that 'the proper response cannot be to temper the wind to the professional man. If he assumes to perform a task, he must bring to it the appropriate care and skill.' This was immediately followed, however, by the statement that the courts must constantly bear in mind that the fact that in retrospect the choice actually made can be shown to have turned out badly is not in itself a proof of negligence, and that the duty of care is not a warranty of a perfect result. Whilst this is perfectly accurate as a statement of the law, the linking of comments about defensive medicine, however vague and imprecise that notion may be, to the frequent reminders that the courts feel constrained to give themselves about the inherent risks of medical treatment suggests that 'defensive medicine' does sometimes play a role in medical litigation, as part of the judicial 'mind set' which creates an additional, though unquantifiable, hurdle that plaintiffs have to overcome. This may be reflected in the standard of proof that plaintiffs have to achieve in practice, although the formal standard of proof remains the same. But as Kilner Brown J observed in *Ashcroft v Mersey Regional Health Authority* [[1983] 2 All ER 245, 247]: 'the medical and social consequences of medical men being found guilty of negligence on insufficient evidence may be appropriate as a statement of probable consequences, but beg the question which has to be decided'. In other words, the question remains as to what constitutes 'sufficient' evidence.

Professor Nicholas Terry offers the following striking and illuminating comment from an American perspective on 'defensive medicine'.

N Terry 'The Malpractice Crisis in the United States: A Dispatch from the Trenches' (1986) 2 Professional Negligence 145

The crisis drama – an exposition of the characters

The health care industry. The principal characters in our cast here are, unsurprisingly, the doctors and the hospitals. The former point to massive increases in their malpractice insurance rates and their inability to see as many patients as they would like because of legal rules, enthusiastically embraced by flocks of vulture-like lawyers, making them order batteries of unnecessary tests; forcing them to practise what they refer to as 'defensive medicine'.

The hospitals, on the other hand, see themselves viewed as the ultimate 'deep pocket', liable not only for their employees' negligence but as the victims of the rule of joint and several liability. They argue that, almost invariably, they will be joined as co-defendants in a suit brought against, for example, a non-employee doctor and subsequently will be faced with a disproportionate share of the award when the doctor proves to be underinsured. Bearing the brunt of the malpractice crises, the hospitals feel they have no choice but to pass the costs along to the public in the form of rapidly escalating health care cost.

In short, not only are the health care providers faced with massive increases in insurance premiums but also difficulty in finding coverage. Primary coverage frequently is written by the providers' 'captive' insurers (for example, physician-owned non-profit companies). Health care providers are still dependent, however, on the traditional industry for much of the excess and reinsurance coverage they require.

Much of the available statistical information supports the argument and accusations emanating from the health industry. The number of claims per doctor has increased. Malpractice premiums are multiplying. There are increasing reports of multimillion awards; so called 'jumbo' awards. Newspaper reports continually highlight seemingly bizarre verdicts.

Overall the health industry has been able to paint a very credible 'crisis' picture. Avaricious lawyers are filing more and more law suits. Some of these are frivolous, unmeritorious claims which the doctors and their insurers have to settle because of high defence costs and the income the defendant-doctor would lose if he became embroiled in the lengthy pre-trial and trial processes. Other claims filed may have more merit but plaintiffs' attorneys, apparently unchecked by the Judges, are persuading juries to return massive, unrealistic awards.

As a result, medical care becomes more expensive because of the resulting costs of high insurance, defensive medicine and of physicians abandoning high-risk areas of practice. These higher costs are being passed onto the consumer; a consumer who finds an already expensive health care delivery system becoming less and less accessible. It is this scenario, expertly conveyed to legislatures by health industry lobbying efforts, that has led to the increasing diminution of the malpractice victim's legal rights through statutory 'reforms' of malpractice law.

The health industry scenario, however, is not without its critics. First, all the talk of 'crisis' tends to ignore one possible reason for the rise in malpractice claims – that there may be an increase in the amount of substandard medical care being foisted upon the American public. This argument may be considered from two perspectives: first, from the patient's point of view; second, from the doctor's. The former we can place under a general heading of consumer expectations. The last two decades have shown a declining public respect for the medical (and, for that matter) legal profession. Arrogance, flagrant pandering to self-interest and (at least in the United States) high salaries have tended to change the public's perception of the role of the professional. In brief one who attempts to perpetuate the idea that he can cure the ills of the world should not be surprised by a consumer complaint when a cure not only is not forthcoming but the consumer ends up worse than before. If the consumer perceives the medical (or legal) professional as being no better than a corporate raider or an executive hanging from a golden parachute, is he not more likely to complain about disappointing service?

What of the doctor's perspective? Ask one about his negligent colleagues and you will get a two part retort. First, most doctors are not negligent in the eyes of their peers; rather they are labelled 'negligent' by a legal system that permits judgments to be rendered in unmeritorious suits brought by greedy, ungrateful patients. Second, there may be a few 'bad apples' in the medical profession; they are usually physicians, however, whose incompetence results from drug or alcohol abuse. The doctor will say, 'Trust us and our self-regulatory peer review system and we will root them out.'

Let us leave the impaired physicians, however, and look to the incompetent one. Let us examine those occasions of incompetence that the AMA tells us the law is being too hard on – those doctors that make the 'honest mistakes' (or, as Lord Denning, MR, put it in *Whitehouse v Jordan* [1980] 1 All ER 650 at 658, those 'errors of judgment') – how do those honest mistakes occur?

Consider, just for the sake of argument, that a doctor, like any good rational maximiser, will attempt to capitalise on his education and opportunities by stressing volume in his practice. Maybe he will decide to see, say, 25 patients in a day rather than 20. It is possible that seeing those five extra patients a day opens up the possibility of an 'honest mistake'. How does the doctor react to his decision to see those extra patients a day? He (possibly) knows that by doing so he will be externalising the 'honest mistake' risks to his patients. He (probably) knows that his externalised risk could boomerang back onto him by way of a malpractice judgment. So parallel to externalising his 'mistake' risk to his patients, he needs to externalise his own financial (or liability) risk.

His solution is to externalise that malpractice liability risk to an insurance company. If the insurance company cannot externalise its own risks, it will turn back on its insured with higher premiums. These the doctor cannot or will not externalise to his patients in the form of higher fees. One alternative would be to reduce the number of patients he sees per day, thereby reducing the number of 'honest mistakes' for which he will be responsible. This, however, he is not prepared to do. Therefore he seeks to substitute his externalisation of financial risk of 'malpractice' with a modified externalisation of the malpractice liability risk itself; by persuading legislatures to roll back patient rights to recover for his negligence.

The second part of our alternate 'world view' and the second flaw in the health care providers' position concern their continual reference to jumbo jury awards. A figure often cited in newspaper reports is that the average US malpractice award is now $962,258. It has been pointed out that this statement is misleading for several reasons. First, when this number has been compared to previous years' figures, it has not been adjusted to reflect increases in the consumer price index. Second the data used to arrive at this figure has concerned jury *awards*. It has not taken into account either (usually lower) settlements or the fact that some of these awards may have been later reduced by the trial Judge or successfully appealed. Third the data used has not included cases where the jury had found for the defendant, ie, awarded $0.00 to the plaintiff; yet less than one half of jury cases result in a plaintiff verdict. Finally, it should be noted that, of the $1 million awards made, about 70 per cent are in cases involving permanent paralysis, permanent brain damage, death or multiple amputations.

The third major criticism that may be levelled at the health care provider crisis scenario concerns the industry's complaints with regard to spiralling malpractice insurance premiums. It seems clear that within the past decade, the average malpractice premium has doubled. Yet what is the real level of increase when these figures have been adjusted for inflation? An even more telling statistic concerns the relationship of malpractice premiums to the income of doctors. One report has asserted that, in the same 1976-84 period in which average premiums almost doubled ($4,700 in 1976 to $8,000 in 1984) as a percentage of doctors' gross incomes, the premiums actually *declined*, from 4.4 per cent to 4.2 per cent (*Time* 24 February 1986 at p 60).

The fourth set of doubts that has risen with regard to the health care providers' position concerns the relationship between rising insurance premiums and increases in health care costs generally. This issue should not be underestimated, because it has created for the health industry lobbyists one of their most potent arguments. For the sake of discussion let us accept that jury awards are increasing at a massive rate; further let us accept that those increases are reflected in increased malpractice insurance premiums. What effect do those increases have on the cost of health care?

One analysis of that relationship has concluded that, 'not only do malpractice insurance costs form a trifling percentage of medical costs, but historically medical costs have risen irrespective of malpractice legislation and a decline in insurance premiums'. That same report has suggested that since health care in the United States is such big business – in fact the nation's third largest industry – with large profits there for the taking, that this has attracted the large corporations into the health care industry leading to over-complex care, over-spending and overcharging.

Certainly, those reports as to the size of the industry are supportable. For example, last year the nation's largest hospital management chain (The Hospital Corporation of America) and the largest distributor of hospital supplies (The American Hospital Supply Corporation) merged to form a combine valued at $6.6 billion, one of the largest non-oil industry mergers in history. Indeed, profit-making chains now own 10 per cent of all US hospitals.

At the same time as the profit motive has become established in the United States medical system, so such profits are being jeopardised by outside forces. Both the federal government with its 'Medicare' plan (about 30 million disabled or elderly Americans qualify for Medicare) and private health insurers such as Blue Cross and Blue Shield are shifting to what is known as the 'prospective payment' system. Under this system, health care providers will no longer be reimbursed for the actual cost of a patient's care. Rather, set fees will be paid on a per-patient basis or on a per-patient, per-general type of medical problem basis. The health care industry will be faced with an interesting option: 'if a hospital spends less on a patient than the fixed amount, it makes money. If it spends more, it must absorb the loss . . . The incentive is to get the patient in and out of the hospital as quickly as possible' (*US News & World Report*, 14 April 1986 at p 60).

The Bar. A visitor to the United States quickly will become familiar with an incessant barrage of advertising in both print and broadcast media. That first reaction to the sheer volume of advertising will be followed, almost immediately, by dismay at its prevailing blandness. For the medical or legal professional, a third reaction will not be long delayed. How can there be all these hideously distasteful commercials for doctors and lawyers? The simple answer is that the Supreme Court has dismantled most of the legal controls on truthful, non-misleading professional advertising. According to the Supreme Court, 'Truthful advertising related to lawful activities is entitled to the protections of the First Amendment' *Re RMJ* 455 US 191, 203 (1982). As such, State Bar Associations and State Supreme Courts are now powerless to regulate lawyer advertising. Certainly many members of the plaintiffs' malpractice bar have not been slow to grasp this opportunity. Such rank commercialism may also be serving to lower the esteem that the medical profession and the public once held for the bar.

Because the malpractice liability system in the United States is financed by the contingency fees system, the lawyer's personal, financial interest in the size of the award leaves him particularly open to criticism. Before the contingency fee system is dismissed as an award-inflating disaster designed to encourage 'ambulance-chasing' consider the alternatives. In general, the United States has no (civil) legal aid system. Does the English legal aid system offer an improvement? Or may it too be criticised? First, for effectively restricting representation to the very poor. Second, for filtering out all but the 'safest' claims through local legal aid screening committees?

When the president of the plaintiffs' bar in the United States says, 'We represent the people that are the injured victims of society', is that merely an expression of avaricious self-interest or an honest evaluation of the lawyer's unique role in defending the rights of an otherwise unrepresented constituency?

The insurance industry. Of course, at the heart of the malpractice system-insurance industry interface is risk-externalisation. You don't need a PhD in economics to understand externalisation of risks – you merely have to understand gambling on an American football game.

The bettor (or mug) goes to the bookie. The bookie takes his bet and gives odds designed so that whoever wins he will pay out the same amount of cash. In other words, the bookie – in an ideal situation – does not gamble; he goes for an even play. How, therefore, do bookies get rich? Through the 'juice' – this is their percentage that they levy on the winning bet. Now if a bookie finds that one side of his equation, despite his odds-making, is getting too heavy he needs to externalise his loss – he will 'lay it off' to another bookie.

Insurance companies operate in much the same way. They take a bet (a premium) on a game (a liability risk) and if the bettor's number comes up (if he is found liable) they pay off the winnings (the claim). Like bookies, (wise) insurers do not try to make their profit on any win-loss (premium-claim) differential. Indeed just like bookies, they will lay-off (reinsure) any worrisome differential. Rather they make their profit on the 'juice'. For the insurance industry the 'juice' is not any percentage of winning bets, but rather the use of the premium money from the time it is paid to the time a claim (if any) is paid. In other words, the insurer's 'juice' is his investment income from collected premiums.

What has led to the insurers increasing their premiums by such large amounts? March 1986 saw the insurance industry launch a $6.5 million advertising campaign to persuade the public that those premium increases were the result of a 'lawsuit' crisis – the fault of the tort system. One of the catchphrases incorporated into such advertisements is 'The Lawsuit Crisis. We All Pay The Price'. Perhaps one explanation for this new insurance industry campaign is that some commentators have begun to speculate that the malpractice 'crisis' is not the fault of plaintiffs, or even lawyers or doctors: – but a 'non-crisis' manufactured by the insurance industry to protect its excessive profits.

Three reasons may be put forward to explain this insurance 'non-crisis'. First, insurance companies say that they have increased their premiums because of their losses. But insurers have a somewhat novel concept of 'loss'. When they cite 'losses', insurers cite their 'underwriting losses'. The property-casualty insurance industry has quoted a $21.4 billion underwriting loss for 1984 and estimated a $25.2 billion loss for 1985. But these are not actual losses. Rather they show the gap between premium dollars received in a given year when compared to the claim dollars predicted to be paid out in future years.

The second problem with 'underwriting losses' is that they do not take into account the insurer's future investment profits on the collected premiums prior to the payment of predicted claims. Take for example that estimated underwriting loss for 1985 of $25.2 billion when contrasted with the income of the property-casualty industry for 1985 (including investment income) of $32.8 billion, and there is an increase of $13 billion in net worth for the same period.

Such an analysis of the current crisis poses an important question leading to a third contradiction to the insurers' cry of 'torts crisis'. If this explanation of the insurance industry's practices is accurate, why do these insurance crises occur only occasionally? As Davies has pointed out (PN 1 (1985) p 169), the answer lies in low interest rates. During the late 1970s interest rates were high. Therefore, the insurance industry was able to record very high investment returns on its premiums prior to paying out any claims. High profits generated increased interest in writing policies by insurers to acquire investment income, and hence increased competition between insurers. As has been noted, 'These underwriting losses appear to be largely a result of coverage written in the late 1970s and early 1980s which may have been underpriced due to the industry's desire to obtain premium income to invest at the then prevailing high interest rates.' As the market went 'soft', so panic-stricken insurers either pulled out of markets or looked for areas where they could recoup their previous discounts quickly. The result – insurers increased medical malpractice premiums and orchestrated a 'crisis' scenario designed to focus the public's, the health industry's and the legislatures' anger upon the lawyers.

The judiciary. At the root of health care and insurance industry complaints about substantive malpractice doctrine has been the law's doctrinal growth through the last two decades and its potential for further, pro-plaintiff development. Concerns have been voiced that malpractice will follow in the footsteps of products liability. Whereas English products law became comatose in 1932 (although resuscitation is imminent courtesy of DIR 85/374/ EEC, [1985] OJ L210/29), American law had not forgotten the lessons of doctrinal growth learned in the nineteenth century. Both systems had started with rules of non-liability for negligent manufacturers, *Winterbottom v Wright* (1842) 152 ER 402; *Loop v Litchfield* 42 NY 2d 251 (1842); and had progressed by way of an exponential growth of exceptional cases to the imposition of a negligence-based risk-shifting system. *Donoghue v Stevenson* [1932] AC 562; *Macpherson v Buick* 111 NE 1050 (NY 1916). American law alone was to repeat that cycle in the twentieth century; its culmination being the adoption of a strict products liability system, *Greenman v Yuba Power Products Inc* 377 P 2d 897 (Cal 1963), Restatement (Second) of Torts 402A (1965).

Any products liability/malpractice parallel at first sight seems somewhat strained. After all, the basic principles of health care provider liability under the Anglo-American malpractice law were established as early as the latter part of the eighteenth century. *Slater v Baker and Stapleton* (1767) 95 ER 860, concerned allegations of negligence in the treatment of a broken leg. Specifically that the defendants, an apothecary and the then chief surgeon at St Bartholomew's Hospital, had rebroken the leg and, utilising some experimental *deus ex machina*, had attempted to straighten it through extension rather than by compression. In affirming the jury's verdict for the plaintiff, the Court stated:

> For anything that appears to the Court, this was the first experiment made with this new instrument; and if it was, it was a rash action, and he who acts rashly acts ignorantly: and although the defendants in general may be as skilful in their respective professions as any two gentlemen in England, yet the Court cannot help saying, that in this particular case they have acted ignorantly and unskilfully, contrary to the known rule and usage of surgeons (at 863).

From 1767, therefore, it has been clear, first, that the general principles of our judicial negligence-based regulatory system will apply to the medical malpractice claim. Second, neither the *bona fides* nor impeccable reputation of the defendant will immunise him from liability. Third, medical malpractice falls into a subset of negligence cases which make use of a custom standard requiring expert testimony to be considered by the trier of fact.

Twenty-seven years later, in the first reported American malpractice case, *Cross v Guthery* 2 Root 90 (Conn 1794), the Supreme Court of Connecticut apparently reached a similar conclusion. Therein a plaintiff prevailed with his allegation that his wife had died following a mastectomy 'performed . . . in the most unskilful ignorant and cruel manner, contrary to all the well-known rules and principles of practice in such cases . . . ' (at 91)

That professional standard of care-expert testimony nexus may have been established what seems to the modern torts lawyer eons ago. Nevertheless, in the United States, striking doctrinal changes have occurred since then. First, many jurisdictions have dismembered the odd locality rule by which the custom prevailing in the profession had been established by reference to the standard of care existing in the defendant's locality or in a similar locality. See *Small v Howard* 128 Mass 131 (188). The purpose of this rule was to encourage the 'small town practitioner' by immunising him from the (presumed) higher standards expected of the 'large city practitioner'. The locality rule effectively limited the number of treatment risks that would be reallocated by denying the plaintiff access to a large number of potential, non-local, expert witnesses. The first step taken to ameliorate the harshness of the locality rule was achieved by recharacterising the function of 'locality' as limited to an inquiry into 'available medical resources' to just one of the 'circumstances' to be taken into account by the trier of fact. See, eg, *Brune v Belinkoff* 235 NE 2d 793 at 798 (Mass 1968). Final dismemberment has occurred in those jurisdictions that have replaced such a 'local' test with an explicit 'national' standard of care. See, eg, *Hall v Hilbun* 466 So 2d 856 (Miss 1985). Obviously, in increasing the pool of experts available for the plaintiff, such a national standard leads to a higher proportion of medical treatment risks being reallocated.

If the growth of medical malpractice doctrine relating to the standard of care was to parallel, albeit in its own conservative way, that of products liability so also would malpractice law mirror products liability's reallocation of the traditional burden of proof. Through increasingly imaginative use of the *res ipsa loquitur* doctrine, plaintiffs have been able to get more marginal claims to the jury. See, eg, *Quintal v Laurel Grove Hosp* 397 P 2d 161 (Cal 1964). Specifically, cases involving patient-incurred risks which resulted in claims which were marginal due to evidentiary problems relating to either standard of care or causation issues. Furthermore, some Courts began to flirt with non-custom based standards of care. See, eg, *Darling v Charleston Community Mem Hosp* 211 NE 2d 253 (Ill 1965).

In addition to modifications to the standard of care came an increase in the breadth of the duty of care owed by health care providers. Many of these broader duties have concerned the supply of information to patients. Examples that come to mind are the informed consent and the so-called 'wrongful life' disclosure duties. Of course, one could analyse these doctrinal changes as being a function of increased judicial interest in the concept of patient autonomy in medical decision-making. An alternative view, however, could be that the Courts were attempting to provide compensation for medical risks which had occurred despite the absence of any active provider malpractice. Still further expansions of the duty of care have occurred; involving, for example, a duty to warn non-patients of the vicious propensities of patients. See, eg, *Tarasoff v Regents of the University of California* 551 P 2d 334 (Cal 1976) or a failure to report to the authorities a case of suspected child abuse, *Landeros v Flood* 551 P 2d 389 (Cal 1976). In passing, one might note that these last two expansive duties appear to have the worrisome effect of redistributing *non-medical* risks (for example, non-health care provider violence) through the *medical* malpractice insurance system.

It was hardly surprising, with these developments creating apparent exceptions to the traditional malpractice rule of custom-based negligence liability – exceptions almost as numerous as had appeared in the products liability context – that some Judges began to show enthusiasm for the introduction of a strict liability regime for malpractice. See, eg, *Johnson v Sears, Roebuck & Co* 355 F Supp 1065 at 1067 (ED. Wis 1973); *Clark v Gibbons* 426 P 2d 525 at 535 (Cal 1967) (Tobriner J, concurring); *Helling v Carey* 519 P 2d 981 at 984 (Wash 1974) (Utter J, concurring).

At this point, however, the products-malpractice parallel breaks down. In malpractice law there was to be no breakthrough case replacing a rule of negligence (non-strict) liability and its attendant exceptions and extensions with a strict liability regime. At least two reasons may be advanced to explain this absence of judicial climax. First, it is conceptually and practically difficult to fashion a strict liability doctrine for medical care risks. In products liability the Judges solved this problem, first, by constructively presuming foresight of the risk of harm, and second, by (conceptually) shifting their judgment focus from the conduct of the manufacturer to the condition of the product. The condition of the product was (practically) judged by setting up tests for 'defectiveness' which depend either upon an examination of objective 'consumer expectations' as to the safety of the product (see, eg, *Vincer v Esther Williams All Aluminium Swimming Pool Co* 230 NW 2d 794 (Wis 1975)) or upon the subjection of the product to a risk-benefit analysis in the light of (usually expert) testimony as to feasible economic alternatives (see, eg, *Barker v Lull Engineering Co* 573 P 2d 443 at 457-58 (Cal 1978)).

Second, as the American Judges were poised to make the breakthrough in the mid-1970s they were faced with the first cries of 'crisis! crisis!' This was to be the time for judicial conservation so as not to incur the wrath of state legislators. . . .

Conclusion

It would be convenient to conclude that the malpractice crisis in the United States is a minor skirmish which will leave no lasting impression on our tort system. Yet, from that day in 1770 when Shepherd threw his squib into the market square at Milborne Port and watched it bounce around until it exploded near Scott, *Scott v Shepherd* (1773) 96 ER 525, perhaps we have been moving inextricably towards a general torts crisis.

Following closely behind the malpractice crisis are reports of a products liability crisis, a local government liability crisis, a school liability crisis and a toxic waste crisis. Again the stated reason is spiralling insurance premiums. Legislators who give in to the medical malpractice doomsayers no doubt will follow by dismantling most of the other legal protections that we have developed for injured plaintiffs.

With specific regard to medical malpractice reform, the current American buzzword is 'compromise'. A belief that if the lawyers and doctors can get together they can work out a solution. Occasionally this can work. Generally, however, such compromises ignore victims' rights and eschew the tighter regulation of insurance companies. Also, their proponents underestimate the staunch individualism and jealously guarded independence of the legal and medical professions. At this time the battle, if anything, is intensifying.

Against this background, Ham, Dingwall *et al, op cit,* consider the case for reform (pp 26-34).

[O]ur analysis has demonstrated that tort law is deficient in a number of respects. In relation to the two main objectives of the law – compensating people injured as a result of negligence, and deterring doctors from acting negligently – the following shortcomings have been identified:

- the procedures involved in pursuing a claim for damages are lengthy and expensive for patients, doctors and health authorities
- only a small proportion of people suffering medically-related injuries obtain compensation
- the emphasis on establishing fault and cause and effect turns the tort system into a lottery: similar cases of injury giving rise to similar needs are compensated totally differently according to the circumstances surrounding their cause and the completeness of the evidence
- those making a claim may find it difficult to obtain the services of a solicitor with relevant expertise and of doctors willing to act as expert witnesses
- the legal process is adversarial and causes those involved to close ranks. Consequently, patients and their relatives are often not given adequate explanations or apologies when things do go wrong and doctors may be distressed by the apparent hostility and ingratitude of their patients
- the deterrent effect of the law is weakened by the availability of insurance coverage.

We have also emphasised the weakness of other arrangements for maintaining high standards of medical practice. These include the variable interest shown by doctors in medical audit and peer review, and the limitations of complaints and disciplinary procedures as mechanisms for ensuring professional accountability. Our analysis has demonstrated that the tort system is one element in a package of measures by which the medical profession is held accountable to the public. Any proposals for reform must consider the law's role in ensuring accountability and promoting high standards while recognising its shortcomings as a means of providing compensation.

Against this background, we now consider the range of policy instruments which are, in theory, available to those contemplating reform. Some of these instruments are concerned primarily to deter negligence, while others aim to provide compensation. The instruments may be used singly or in combination. We begin by outlining options for deterring doctors from acting negligently, and then consider methods of providing compensation. In the first part of the chapter, the menu of options is described briefly, and this is followed by more detailed analysis of those options which in our view merit most serious discussion.

Deterrence
There are three main options for deterring doctors from acting negligently. These are legal liability, regulation backed by statute and self-regulation.

Legal liability
Legal liability for medical accidents can take a number of forms. Doctors can be held strictly liable for all the adverse consequences resulting from medical treatment, or only for the adverse consequences resulting from negligence. Those held liable can be either individual practitioners or groups of individuals acting collectively. Figure 7 sets out the possibilities.

Figure 7
Deterrence through liability rules

		Who is liable	
		Individual doctor	Doctors as a group
What is the basis of liability?	Cause	STRICT LIABILITY	NO-FAULT LIABILITY
	Fault	NEGLIGENCE LIABILITY	VICARIOUS LIABILITY

Strict liability exists when individual doctors are held responsible to patients for all the adverse outcomes of medical treatment. *No-fault liability* imposes liability on doctors as a group. The group might be the whole profession or only those doctors involved in the treatment which gave rise to the adverse outcome. *Negligence liability* is the current rule. Under this rule, only those doctors whose standard of care is deemed inadequate by the courts are held liable for the adverse consequences of their actions. The NHS already assumes *vicarious liability* for most of its employees. Under this liability rule the fault of an individual employee renders the employer liable for the adverse consequences resulting from the employee's actions.

All these possibilities can in theory create appropriate incentives for doctors to avoid injuring patients, although in practice the incentives may not operate effectively. Moreover, it is, in principle, possible for patients to contract with individual doctors, hospitals or health authorities in order to agree on a different set of incentives to take care, although again the practical problems of this option may be considerable.

One other possibility should be mentioned, namely that there should be *no liability*. This would shift the entire responsibility to the patient to take his or her own measures to ensure the safety of the care received.

Regulation backed by statute

A second approach to deterrence is to give a regulatory body the power to monitor the adverse consequences of medical intervention. Such a body would receive reports of medical accidents, which would be required by law, and would determine appropriate action to be taken. This would include the power to levy a fine or injury tax. A body of this kind might develop out of the General Medical Council and would combine its regulatory role with oversight of registration and medical education. If this option were to be pursued, there would be a need to ensure that the regulatory body were genuinely independent and accountable to Parliament. This approach relies on a structure of incentives similar to those generated by the various liability rule options discussed above. Figure 8 illustrates the possibilities.

Figure 8
Deferrence through regulation

		Who is regulated	
		Individual doctor	Doctors as a group
What is the basis of the regulation?	Cause	INJURY TAX ON INDIVIDUAL	INJURY TAX ON GROUP
	Fault	DISCIPLINARY PROCEDURES	REGULATION OF PROFESSIONAL STANDARDS

The first option identified in figure 8 is the payment of an *injury tax by individual doctors*. This would not imply any direct payment by a doctor to a patient. Patients could seek compensation elsewhere, but each doctor would be subject to a regular audit and the payment of a levy corresponding to the estimated social costs of adverse outcomes from his or her interventions.

An alternative would be for the *injury tax to be levied on groups of doctors* or the profession as a whole. Estimates of harm could be based on sampling and aggregate analysis of injuries. A third option is to deter negligence through *disciplinary procedures*, as happens at present. This requires an agreed procedure for investigating complaints and imposing penalties on individual doctors. Penalties might be either professional or financial but need not be linked to the losses of individual patients.

Finally, the option of *group regulation* might be considered. Rather than having an independent regulatory agency involved with the review of individual doctors, the profession as a whole might be set specific standards of safety and effectiveness and left to develop its own systems of control. The effective sanction here is the risk of losing the privileges of the occupation's protected position in the delivery of health care. The incentive is the concern of colleagues to protect the profession's reputation and maintain public confidence.

Self-regulation
A third approach to deterrence avoids using either the civil or criminal law to impose financial incentives on doctors and instead relies on market-based incentives. Even where no one is held liable, there may be powerful incentives in a market situation for providers to maintain standards, simply as a way of ensuring commercial viability. In the NHS the incentives operate differently, relying more on the concern of the professions and health authorities to protect and improve their reputations. This is again an important element of the present system, although it does not always operate effectively.

Compensation
There are three main options for compensating those injured in medical accidents. These are liability insurance, first-party insurance and social security.

Liability insurance
Any system of legal liability could provide compensation for patients selected by the liability rules as long as those held responsible have the means to pay the damages awarded. Effectively this implies that arrangements must exist for the pooling of liabilities through

insurance. Of course, under a system of group liability, it is possible that some groups will be large enough to bear their own liability losses without insuring. For smaller groups and individuals, third-party liability insurance is a necessary adjunct to civil liability if the latter is to be an effective means of providing compensation.

First-party insurance
If doctors are not held legally responsible for the adverse consequences resulting from medical treatment, either because it is held that no one should be liable, or because only those accidents caused by negligence are compensated, then the burden of loss arising outside the liability system falls directly on the injured patients. Those at risk may therefore choose to insure against the prospective losses, either directly, by means of an income replacement or medical expenses policy with an insurance company, or indirectly, by means of a negotiated sick pay scheme through which employers meet such losses up to a maximum as part of a wages and conditions package. The payments under such schemes are made without necessary reference to the fault or causation of any other party.

Social security
Each of the above insurance options for spreading losses could be made compulsory by a government which was concerned about the possibility of uncompensated losses. Alternatively, government could itself provide social insurance financed out of employee contributions, general taxation, and/or specific levies on goods and services. Entitlement to benefits under such a scheme could be based on the fact of a disability, and not on its cause. In addition, injured patients may be treated and cared for through the further provision of public health care and social services. Effectively, this would be a system of compensation in kind.

Whatever form of compensation is provided, there always remains, in principle, the opportunity for individuals or groups of individuals to contract with each other in order to arrive at an alternative arrangement. For example, patients could agree to waive their rights to compensation through the courts in return for lower cost treatment. Equally, individuals covered by a social insurance fund may be permitted to contract-out in order to obtain preferable cover under a private insurance policy. In practice, however, people may be barred from restricting their coverage beyond a certain point or from completely opting out of compulsory contributions to a common insurance pool because of possible adverse selection problems.

The agenda for reform
Given the range of options available, it is possible to pursue the objectives of compensation and deterrence separately. As an illustration, doctors could be deterred from acting negligently through regulation by an independent agency with the power to levy an injury tax, while compensation could be provided by first-party or social insurance. However, separating the objectives in this way may be inefficient, in that it undervalues the role of the patient in providing information about negligence. This option may also deprive the patient of the satisfaction of securing an improvement in the circumstances which led to his or her injury and it reduces the opportunities available to victims to obtain psychological redress. Although the effectiveness of the tort system in serving these purposes should not be exaggerated, this element of the system may well be significant in some cases in helping to resolve events through the public attribution or exoneration of responsibility for harm.

The medical litigation system in the UK combines negligence liability and disciplinary procedures initiated by complaints with third-party liability insurance for doctors and self-insurance for health authorities. This system gives the individual patient a key role in the process of deterring negligence and obtaining compensation. However, as we have emphasised, the system has a number of shortcomings.

Many of the other options we have identified also have shortcomings. To give some examples, an injury tax levied on individual doctors would be cumbersome and costly to administer; disciplinary procedures may be ineffective as a form of deterrence if they are invoked only in the most serious cases; and self-regulation depends for its effectiveness on a strong commitment by health authorities and doctors to promote high standards through medical audit and quality assurance programmes. This commitment may not always be present.

Market-oriented solutions such as no liability and voluntary first-party insurance place an unreasonable burden on the patient in terms of assessing the quality of the services available. In extreme cases, the patient may be dead before the inadequacy of the care becomes apparent. This may deter others, but it is little consolation to the victim. The marked imbalance in information between patients and doctors is thus a major weakness of market-oriented options.

What then are the policy options which deserve serious consideration in reviewing how the shortcomings of existing arrangements might be overcome? In our view three options merit further analysis. These are:

- the modification of the tort law system and the strengthening of professional accountability
- the introduction of a no-fault compensation scheme, and
- the abandonment of the tort system in favour of providing compensation through social security

We have selected these options for analysis as they represent different points on the agenda of change facing policy makers. Modifying the existing system and strengthening professional accountability involve incremental reforms, many of which could be introduced at little or no cost. There are obvious attractions in this option to a government committed to tight control of public expenditure. Furthermore, in view of the government's stated position that the case for major reform remains not proven, it may be through a series of minor changes that the best prospects for improvement lie.

No-fault compensation, as we have noted, is an option favoured by a number of organisations active in the field of medical negligence, including the BMA and ACHCEW. There is also relevant overseas experience on which to draw and from which to learn . . . If there should be a further increase in the number of legal claims against doctors and in the size of court awards, the feasibility of this option may come under close scrutiny. There is therefore merit in assessing the costs of introducing such a scheme in the UK and the measures that would need to be taken to strengthen professional accountability in the context of no-fault compensation.

Abolishing the tort system in favour of providing compensation through social security – our third option – is a fundamental change which is best viewed as a long-term possibility. Nevertheless, it is an option that deserves analysis, if only to highlight the important part played by social security in supporting those suffering injuries. The issue of income support for disabled people is a major area of analysis in its own right, and in this chapter we are able only to illustrate its potential role in the case of medical negligence.

Changing the existing system

Changes to the existing system fall into three categories. These are increasing access to the courts, transferring negligence liability from individual doctors to health authorities while at the same time strengthening the accountability of doctors, and introducing differential insurance premiums for doctors. We now consider each in turn.

Increasing access to the courts

One set of reforms would seek to increase access to the legal system so that patients could more easily obtain compensation and more cases would result. Specific proposals have recently been put forward by the Citizens Action Compensation Campaign and by the report of the Review Body on Civil Justice to the Lord Chancellor. Both express sympathy for the development of contingency fees in Britain and the Civil Justice Review also discusses at length methods by which legal proceedings could be accelerated.

[Subsequently, the Courts and Legal Services Act 1990, section 58 conferred on the Lord Chancellor the power to provide by regulation for the provision of legal services by 'conditional fee arrangements' (ie contingency fees). See draft Conditional Fee Regulations 1993 and Conditional Fees Order 1993.]

Our view is that contingency fees and the acceleration of legal proceedings are of limited relevance to medical negligence cases. While it is understandable that both litigants and legal personnel are frustrated by delay in establishing liability and determining compensation, its causes are poorly understood. The pace of litigation towards trial or settlement is determined largely by the plaintiff's solicitor. It may be slowed down in order to establish exactly how serious someone's injuries are so as to calculate what would be an appropriate level of compensation. It may be necessary to wait until a victim can be examined by one of the relatively small number of doctors who are skilled in the preparation of expert evidence for civil cases. If the findings are uncertain or the clinical evaluation is contentious, further time may elapse before other specialists can accommodate the patient. Once a case is prepared, a solicitor may wish to have it presented by a specialist barrister who is fully aware of the complexities of the area. In short, there may be good reasons for delay.

Contingency fees have attracted attention as a possible private alternative to legal aid. In fact, their main virtue is that they substitute the judgment of individual solicitors for the monopoly of the local legal aid committee. The American evidence shows that contingency fees are far from representing a poor person's route to justice. Lawyers will not take on cases unless the certainty of winning and the likely profits are sufficient to justify the risk. Thus, they will take relatively low-value cases arising from road traffic accidents, which are cheap to run and have a highly predictable outcome: they are reluctant to take low-value cases in other areas, including medical malpractice, because the return is insufficient to cover their costs. Moreover, medical malpractice is seen as a particularly risky area, because of the intrinsic uncertainty of causation, so that the lawyer has a strong incentive to reject all but those cases on which his own medical advisers give him strong support. The comparative irrelevance of contingency fees in the British context can be seen from the limited use of speculative actions in Scotland. These are not pure contingency, in that lawyers are only allowed to charge on the basis of the work they have done rather than taking a percentage of the eventual recovery, but they are conditional on the outcome of the case.

A more important consideration is that cases should be handled by solicitors skilled in medical negligence work. Plaintiffs are particularly vulnerable because medical litigation is classically conducted by local law firms with limited knowledge and experience in complex personal injury work. They are opposed by a small group of highly specialised firms with great experience of representing defendants. The real requirement is for a means of identifying and certifying solicitors who are competent to handle such cases on behalf of plaintiffs. AVMA and a number of community health councils have developed panels of solicitors to whom they steer cases and whose effectiveness they attempt to monitor. AVMA has devoted particular effort to the development of a monitoring system in an attempt to improve the effectiveness of their panel members. It would be open to the Law Society to build on these initiatives, as they have done with practitioners in child care and mental health law.

If this change were to be fully effective, it would have to be accompanied by a number of other modifications to the present system. One would be greater publicity for legal services in general, either by encouraging solicitors' own marketing of their services or through the development of schemes like the Law Society's Accident Legal Advice Service (ALAS) initiative which has tried to heighten public awareness of the possibility of claiming for damages. These initiatives might be accompanied by a liberalisation of the rules governing the advertising of legal services to enable members of the public to identify more easily solicitors accredited in medical negligence work and to be better informed about the benefits of approaching a specialist.

It would also be desirable to modify the present rules on fee-splitting, so that generalist, High Street firms had a greater incentive to pass complex cases on to practices with a more appropriate level of skills in return for an introduction fee or a proportion of the eventual profit on a successful case. Some attention would have to be given too to the access barriers represented by the current means testing on civil legal aid. At present, the rewards are too low to encourage specialist firms to develop medical negligence work and the eligibility levels are so restricted as to prevent a considerable section of the population from obtaining redress.

If access to legal aid were made easier, an increase in the rate at which claims are made and pursued would be likely to occur. This might accentuate some of the problems of predicting the financial burden for health authorities. One way of responding would be to pool the risks on a national or regional basis, creating in effect an internal insurance scheme as already happens in some places.

Transferring liability to health authorities and strengthening accountability
A second possible change to the existing system would be to transfer negligence liability from individual doctors to health authorities and [Family Health Service Authorities]. This would put doctors on the same basis as most other NHS staff, with their employer assuming vicarious liability [see now NHS Indemnity Scheme, *supra*, ch 5]. Such a change would certainly imply a more active role for health authorities and [FHSAs] in promoting high standards of clinical practice and reducing mistakes . . . Interest in medical audit in the NHS has been uneven, and there are grounds for arguing that a more systematic and rigorous approach is needed.

Health authorities could give a lead by requiring doctors at the appropriate level (firm, department, group practice) to demonstrate that they routinely review the quality of their work. The recent report of the Confidential Enquiry into Perioperative Deaths . . . recommended that clinicians should assess themselves regularly and that surgeons and anaesthetists should actively audit their results. This recommendation applies with equal force to other branches of medicine.

There is increasing evidence that doctors themselves recognise the importance of audit, both as a form of continuing education and as a means of avoiding mistakes. Thus, several of the royal colleges have taken the initiative recently to encourage doctors systematically to assess their work and to discuss their results with colleagues. Equally, at the local level, a number of enthusiastic individuals have demonstrated what can be achieved when doctors set aside time to gather information about their practice and analyse differences in approach. It should be possible to build on this experience in the future to ensure that audit develops with the support of the profession.

There may also be lessons to learn from developments in the United States in risk management, in particular in encouraging reports of adverse events. Drug reactions, for example, are already monitored by the Yellow Card scheme. Hospitals might introduce similar arrangements for the reporting of surgical or other incidents on a confidential basis, rather in the same way as airline pilots are encouraged to report near misses. One incentive for this might be to impose a collective responsibility on the medical and nursing team for the care of a patient.

Modern health care depends so much on the contribution of a number of specialists in different aspects of any particular case that it is questionable whether the concept of individual liability remains entirely appropriate. If one person makes a mistake which others ignore or cover up, then, at least morally, they would seem to be just as responsible for the adverse outcome. An example might be of a surgeon who commits an error during a common procedure. It is argued by risk managers in the United States that anaesthetists and the theatre nurses should feel an obligation to challenge the surgeon as he makes the mistake and to record their dissent if he persists. If they do not, they should be equally vulnerable at law and to professional sanctions. The medical profession, however, sees this as a recipe for clinical anarchy. Individual liability, it is claimed, is the proper corollary of clinical autonomy.

As well as strengthening arrangements for medical audit in these and other ways, changes could be made to both disciplinary procedures and complaints procedures to ensure that doctors are held accountable for their clinical competence. In the case of disciplinary procedures, the GMC currently investigates cases of serious professional misconduct but other cases do not fall within its remit. Furthermore, as we have noted, the GMC's procedures are professionally dominated. Proposals are currently under discussion designed to enable the Council to consider less serious examples of misconduct, and this would mean that a wider range of cases could be investigated. But more radical change, involving the setting up of procedures similar to those that exist in Sweden . . . may be needed if the public is to be reassured that disciplinary procedures are adequate for their purpose.

At the local level, disciplinary procedures against hospital doctors concerning matters of professional competence are set out in circular HM(61) 112 and involve an investigation by a panel under a legally qualified chairman. These procedures have been criticised as complex, expensive and lengthy, and their operation is under review by the DHSS and the medical profession [now see HC(90) 9 replacing HM(61) 112]. This review provides a timely opportunity for change to be introduced to ensure that adequate arrangements are in place for handling all cases where concern about professional conduct and competence arises, not just those involving the most serious consequences.

Turning to complaints procedures . . . the existing complaints machinery is complex, fragmented and slow. A case can be made for improving this machinery independently of concern about medical negligence. A starting point would be to implement the proposals of the Davies Committee on hospital complaints. It is in this area that complaints procedures are most open to criticism, particularly as far as complaints about clinical judgment are concerned. If the Committee's proposals for independent investigating panels were implemented it would become easier for patients and their relatives to pursue complaints about clinical matters and to have confidence that these complaints would be thoroughly and rapidly investigated. This in turn might reduce the number of legal claims brought by patients seeking an explanation of what went wrong rather than financial compensation.

In the longer term, the aim should be to simplify the complaints procedures to establish one point of contact whatever the nature of the complaint (clinical or non-clinical; hospital, community health services or family practitioner services) and to guarantee that those hearing complaints are genuinely independent.

Differential premiums for doctors
A third way of reforming the existing system, and an alternative to the transfer of negligence liability to health authorities, would be to change the incentive structure facing doctors by

introducing differential insurance premiums . . . Such risk-rating is common in professional liability insurance and is applied to doctors in the United States. Where professional services are privately provided, there may be some merit in this arrangement. Differential risks can be reflected in differential fees so that there is no direct impact on recruitment to specialties. Doctors can be left with comparable post-premium incomes, or at least, incomes which vary only sufficiently to adjust for the non-pecuniary penalties of a high risk of litigation. Both patients and doctors are given appropriate indications of the hazards associated with different areas of medicine and an incentive either to safe practice or careful selection of doctor.

In the NHS, however, doctors are paid on a uniform scale. Individual effort and initiative are rewarded to an extent by merit awards or list sizes but there are no systematic differences between specialties in terms of the basic income available from NHS practice. In the absence of any variation, it is hard to imagine that recruitment to high-risk specialties would remain unaffected by differential premiums. Moreover, for practitioners working full time for the NHS, the introduction of such premiums would involve little more than an accounting exercise as the government would bear the major share of the cost through its policy of reimbursing two-thirds of the cost of defence society subscriptions.

The one exception to this argument concerns those doctors combining NHS work with private practice. The potential awards to a victim of negligent private treatment are larger than those to NHS patients because private patients would be able to obtain damages based on the assumption of future private care, whereas this might be disputable for NHS patients. It is debatable whether the NHS should in effect cross-subsidise private practice, although whether this happens in practice is difficult to estimate. In global terms, any subsidy is unlikely to be large, and is in any case roughly corrected by the recently announced arrangements which confine reimbursement of the major portion of defence society subscriptions to those doctors working exclusively for the NHS. It is also possible that the risks of private practice are less because of the different case-mix in that sector. Nevertheless, it remains possible that the public payments may be slightly larger than they would be if private medical practice formed a separate pool for insurance purposes.

Moving to no-fault
The term no-fault compensation refers, strictly, to all schemes which abandon the rule than an injured patient has to show that someone was negligent in order to obtain redress. However, there is an important distinction between those schemes which still require patients to identify an individual responsible for their condition and those which do not. The former, of which Sweden and New Zealand are examples, share with the negligence system the advantage of being able to make constructive use of the desire of injured patients to obtain redress. Adverse outcomes can be attributed to individual doctors and, at least potentially, used as a basis for promoting high standards. Those schemes which sever the link between victims and the agents of their injuries must find alternative ways of achieving this objective.

The extent to which this is a serious problem depends on the ability of individual doctors to avoid accidents. If it is believed that accidents are better understood as a result of organisational failures, rather than personal mistakes, then the attribution of responsibility to individuals is unnecessary. All that is needed is sufficient information to demonstrate that the patient's injury arose from medical treatment together with a means of referring that information to the appropriate manager or health authorities. Information on claims for compensation might be fed back to those responsible for service delivery at the local level and be used in national reviews to alert all care providers to common problems.

Whether a no-fault scheme is based on proof of individualised causation or not, there is likely to be a need for some form of risk-spreading. Health authorities are large enough to self-insure, although the predictable impact of awards at a time of scarce resources suggests that this may not be the most efficient means of managing their budgets. There may therefore be a case for pooling risks on a regional or national basis, as happens in Sweden. If causation is placed on an individual basis, then doctors would need to continue to obtain some form of insurance and this could be provided by a consortium of the defence societies.

The potential cost of a no-fault scheme varies greatly according to the assumptions that are made about the rate of claiming and the size of awards. At present, there are roughly ten claims relating to hospital treatment per 100,000 population in England each year. Approximately three of these claims are compensated and the average award is around £15,000. The total cost of the system, including both damages payments and legal expenses, is estimated to be £75 million, of which £65 million is attributed to the NHS, either directly or through the cost of subscriptions to the defence societies out of NHS employees' income.

The Swedish scheme generates about 60 claims per 100,000 population from all health care contacts, although, in practice, almost all of these seem to relate to hospital treatment. Fifty per cent of these claims receive compensation, averaging £3,200 at current exchange rates. If we assume that a Swedish-style system were introduced in the UK, at the same rates of claiming and payment, the estimated cost for England alone would be of the order of £50 million per year (see Table 8). This would appear to represent a substantial saving.

Table 8
Estimated costs of a no-fault compensation scheme

A. CURRENT SYSTEM (ENGLAND 1988)	£ mill	B. SWEDISH-STYLE NO-FAULT SYSTEM	£ mill
Estimated health authority cost:	15	Estimated cost if Swedish system replicated:	50

Assumptions:		**Assumptions:**
Claim rate = 10 per 100,000 population		claim rate = 60 per 100,000 population
abandonment rate = 70%		abandonment rate = 50%
average settlement = £15,000		average settlement = £3,200
administrative costs = 30%		administrative costs = 15%
defence society contribution = 50%		

Estimate defence society costs*: 60		Estimated cost with average settlement £15,000 235
		Estimated cost with average settlement £7,500 117

Assumptions:
income generated from doctors practising in England based on a) subscription rates for 1988 as in MPS/MDU annual reports b) breakdown of medical manpower in England as published by DHSS.

Total   75

* *This includes a sum for legal and administrative costs other than those related to negligence cases.*

However, given the more limited nature of the British social security system compared with Sweden, it would also represent a substantial degree of under-compensation. As we noted earlier, the Swedish scheme is designed to top-up other payments in recognition of the pain and suffering involved, and is the sole source of income replacement or service purchase. If a similarly accessible scheme were introduced in England, the lower barriers to access might allow the rate of claims to rise to Swedish levels. If these claims were compensated at current English rates, the overall cost would rise to £235 million per year. On the other hand, one might expect that the average payment per claim would fall, since an increase in the number of claimants is likely to be associated with a reduction in the average severity of claims. In this case, £235 million should be treated as an upper limit. If the average payment per claim were halved, the cost would be around £117 million per year. While this is certainly well above the present cost of tort litigation, it might be thought that the price were justifiable if the shortcomings of the tort system we have identified were overcome.

For this to happen, it would be important to learn from the experience of New Zealand and Sweden. In particular, careful consideration would need to be given to:
• the definition of accidents to be included in the scheme
• the procedures to be used to prevent accidents, to monitor standards of care, and to encourage rehabilitation
• the importance of ensuring equity in the treatment of accident victims and the sick and disabled

- the means by which doctors would be held accountable and patients would receive an explanation of why an accident happened

In relation to the last of these points, our proposals for reforming the existing system by extending medical audit and strengthening complaints and disciplinary procedures (see above) would have equal relevance under a no-fault scheme.

The issue of equity of treatment for accident victims and the sick and disabled is more complex. As recent developments in New Zealand have demonstrated, the establishment of special schemes for accident compensation can create distinctions which are difficult to defend. It is for this reason that proposals are now under discussion to reduce the benefits available to accident victims in New Zealand. One of the aims of the proposals is to enable the sick and disabled to be eligible for the same benefits as people injured during accidents. In Sweden, this issue is handled through the social security system which provides a generous level of benefits on the basis of need, with accident compensation supplementing these benefits. This suggests that a further radical option for reform is to introduce a general disability income. We now consider this in more detail.

A general disability income

The replacement of tort by social security is both radical and potentially expensive. As such, it is probably best viewed as a long-term possibility. The advantage of a general disability income is that individuals would receive support on the basis of the fact of their injury and its consequences, and would have to establish neither fault nor cause. The payment of benefits periodically rather than as a lump-sum would also remove much of the present uncertainty about whether a sum of money would be adequate to meet future expenses, and would also permit a continuing review of the victim's circumstances.

The principal advantages of social security as a means of providing compensation lie in its relative accessibility and simplicity. As a result, a large number of beneficiaries can be compensated at a low level of administrative expense. However, these advantages are the product of a generalised, rule-based approach to deciding the appropriate amount of compensation. Benefits may be payable in relation to a schedule of impairments and/or proof of incapacity for work, without any specific tailoring of payments to the individual's circumstances, as happens under tort law.

The generosity of the social security system is constrained by the extent to which the payment of benefits affects the recipients' recovery, and, when relevant, their return to work. This is a particular concern when disability benefits are payable to those who are permanently, but partially disabled, and who therefore retain some capacity to work. Designing a set of rules governing the determination of benefits without penalising the decision to return to work for this group of claimants is a task of considerable difficulty. . . .

Two possible solutions are to make awards conditional upon the severity of impairment alone, or to make the assessments irreversible or lump-sum. Either way, this would ensure that subsequent decisions to return to work would not result in a withdrawal of benefit. However, this kind of solution would exaggerate still further the inequities between different types of claimants noted above. The New Zealand approach to this problem has been to limit income replacement to 80 per cent of previous earnings, and to give the Accident Compensation Corporation additional responsibilities for rehabilitation. It is difficult to ascertain the extent to which this has been successful. . . . Clearly, the adoption of a general disability income scheme would not avoid difficult choices between equity and efficiency of the kind which bedevil the tort system.

Moreover, if this option were pursued, a considerable weight would be thrown on the adequacy of other arrangements for monitoring medical standards. Again, this brings into play our proposals . . . for extending medical audit, and strengthening complaints and disciplinary procedures. As the New Zealand experience has demonstrated, agreement must be reached on how to deter malpractice before radical changes are introduced.

Conclusion

Faced with these options, how should policy makers proceed? In our view there is a good case for reform, because of the considerable shortcomings of the existing arrangements. On the other hand, it is hard to argue strongly for any particular policy option on the basis of present information. Nevertheless, we can broadly summarise the policy choices in relation to both compensation and deterrence.

It is far from clear that the possibilities have been exhausted for improving the tort system as a means of obtaining compensation. As we have noted earlier . . . there are a number of ways in which the system could be changed. In summary, the key measures worth pursuing are:

- providing potential claimants with a means of identifying solicitors with appropriate skills in medical negligence cases
- giving greater publicity to legal services through advertising and other means in order to increase public awareness of the general possibilities of claiming for damages
- modifying fee-splitting arrangements among lawyers to create greater incentives for solicitors to pass on cases to specialists
- making access to legal aid easier, and
- developing a system to enable health authorities to pool their risks in order to cope with a larger number of successful claims

While these changes would overcome some of the weaknesses of the present system there would still be a basic inequality between defendants, represented by a small group of experienced and specialised lawyers, and plaintiffs, represented by a dispersed, heterogeneous group of lawyers with infrequent involvement in medical negligence cases. It would also remain difficult to prove fault given the intrinsic uncertainties of human biology and medical technology. In the longer term, then, the inadequacies of the tort system as a method of compensation seem likely to encourage its replacement by a more equitable alternative. If a general disability income is ruled out on grounds of expense, serious consideration could be given to the development of a no-fault scheme.

A no-fault scheme would overcome many of the shortcomings we have identified in the present system: the expense and time involved in pursuing a tort claim; the strong element of lottery; the small proportion of injured patients who receive compensation; and the adversarial nature of the legal process. But . . . neither the Swedish nor the New Zealand schemes offer a model which could be imported directly into the United Kingdom. Each has developed under a particular set of institutional conditions which are not reproduced here. Both also illustrate some of the inherent problems of no-fault schemes, such as the question of equity between people disabled as a result of different sorts of mishap and the means by which claims can be mobilised and screened.

The New Zealand experience also demonstrates the greatest weakness of no-fault schemes, namely the reduction in whatever deterrent effect the tort system may exert. The tort system has the unique feature of presenting the victim of negligence with a financial incentive to pursue a claim against the person believed to be responsible. But, given the difficulties of pursuing claims and the intervening effect of insurance, this is inadequate by itself as a method of preventing accidents.

For this reason, consideration needs to be given to a range of other policy options designed to encourage high quality medical care. In the short term, the most promising options worth pursuing are those which aim to strengthen professional accountability. As we have emphasised throughout this Paper, regardless of whether or not a system of no-fault compensation is introduced, a strong case can be made for improving complaints procedures, reforming the procedures used to discipline doctors, and encouraging the extension of medical audit. To summarise the discussion earlier in this chapter, this would involve:

- developing arrangements for medical audit by requiring doctors to demonstrate that they routinely review the quality of their work and by introducing procedures for the reporting of surgical and other incidents on a confidential basis
- extending and simplifying disciplinary procedures against doctors. This applies both to the GMC's procedures and to the procedures followed by health authorities. The aim should be to ensure that adequate arrangements are in place for handling cases where concern about professional conduct and competence arise, not just those involving the most serious consequences
- implementing the recommendations of the Davies Committee on hospital complaints in order to establish independent investigating panels to examine complaints about clinical matters

At the same time, careful consideration should be given to two further changes for implementation in the longer term. These are:

- the introduction of procedures for disciplining doctors based on Sweden's Medical Responsibility Board and involving significant lay participation, and
- the reform of complaints procedures to establish one point of contact whatever the nature of the complaint and to guarantee that those hearing complaints are genuinely independent

If implemented, these measures would help to deter doctors from acting negligently and would assist patients and their relatives to obtain an adequate explanation when things go wrong.

In conclusion, further research would help to clarify the policy choices we have mapped, but even more important is a political commitment to consider carefully ways in which improvements can be brought about to the benefit of all those involved with medical negligence. Above all, what is now required is an informed debate of the issues and the options, a debate which recognises the need both to provide compensation and to promote deterrence.

(You will notice that Ham, Dingwall *et al* refer to the Swedish system. For a detailed account of this system, see the paper by Carl Oldertz in *Compensation for Personal Injury in Sweden and Other Countries* (1988), pp 51-78.)

For a description of the New Zealand scheme now consolidated in the Accident Compensation Act 1982, see the Pearson Commission (*op cit*) Volume 3 (pp 191-200) and see the discussion of the scheme by McLean 'The Implications of No-Fault Liability for the Medical Profession', in *Medicine, Ethics and the Law* (1988) ed M D A Freeman, pp 151-158. Subsequently, a change of government and of economic policy in New Zealand has led to a narrowing of the scope of the application of the scheme in the Accident Compensation (Amendment) Act 1992. Significantly, the 1992 Act *restricts* recovery of compensation under the scheme for 'medical misadventure'. For a discussion of the amended law see Mahoney, 'New Zealand's Accident Compensation Scheme: A Reassessment' (1992) 40 American Journal of Comparative Law 159.

Finally, it is worthwhile to notice the parallel developments in the United States, which reflect the same concerns. The reforms have concentrated on changes within (some would say tinkering with) the existing tort system. They have been designed to strike at the heart of the problems associated with the perceived medical malpractice crisis in America. Consider the following extract.

Furrow, Johnson, Jost and Schwartz, *Health Law* (1991) (2nd edn)

ALTERING THE LITIGATION PROCESS
Starting in the 1970s, states enacted tort reform legislation. The preamble to the California Medical Injury Compensation Reform Act is typical of the legislative perceptions of the malpractice crisis:

> The Legislature finds and declares that there is a major health care crisis in the State of California attributable to skyrocketing malpractice premium costs and resulting in a potential breakdown of the health care delivery system, severe hardships for the medically indigent, a denial of access for the economically marginal, and depletion of physicians such as to substantially worsen the quality of health care available to citizens of this state.

Tort reform measures were intended by their proponents to reduce either the frequency of malpractice litigation or the size of the settlement or judgment. These measures can be subdivided into four groups:
– those affecting the filing of malpractice claims;
– those limiting the award recoverable by the plaintiff;
– those altering the plaintiff's burden of proof through changes in evidence rules and legal doctrine;
– those changing the role of the courts, usually in the direction of substitution of an alternative forum.

This section will outline the nature of these reforms, consider briefly some of the judicial responses to challenges brought against these reforms, and review several comprehensive reform proposals.

1. Common Tort Reforms
a. Reducing the filing of claims
If the frequency of litigation is lowered, it is reasonable to assume that insurance companies will have to pay out at a lower rate, which in turn should lower premiums. Several reforms

are intended to either bar certain claims that could previously have been brought, or create disincentives for the bringing of suits.

(1) Shortened statutes of limitations. Over forty states have now modified their statutes of limitations, in response to the criticism that long statutes of repose complicate insurance prediction of claims and result in uncertainty in portfolio management. Historically, the time period for a medical injury was tolled, or began to run, when the injury was discovered. This created the 'long tail' problem. States reduced the time period, typically by requiring that claims be brought within a short time, for example within two years of the injury or one year of the time that the injury should have been discovered with due diligence. . . .

(2) Controlling legal fees. More than twenty states have regulated attorney fees in a variety of ways, including establishing rigid contingency fee structures or requiring judicial review of the 'reasonableness' of the fees. The intended effect of these statutes was to make lawyers more selective in screening out nonmeritorious claims, thus eliminating excessive litigation. Danzon found that contingent fees tend to result in equalising plaintiff attorney compensation to that of the defence bar (whose income is not controlled), and that controls reduce not only lawyers' income, but also plaintiff compensation. Danzon [*Medical Malpractice: Theory, Practice and Public Policy* (1985)] at 198.

(3) Payment of costs for frivolous claims. Under such a statute or court rule, when the malpractice claimant is found to have acted frivolously in suing, he must reimburse the provider for reasonable legal fees, witness fees, and court costs. . . .

b. Limiting the plaintiff's award
If the previous reforms hoped to cut down on the number of cases in court, the next category hoped to reduce the overall size of the award.

(1) Elimination of the ad damnum clause. This clause, as part of the initial pleading, states the total monetary claim requested by the plaintiff, an amount presumably inflated beyond the level of actual damages suffered. It is feared that such claims expose the defendant to harmful pretrial publicity, damage his reputation, and induce juries to make larger awards than the evidence supports. Thirty-two states have legislated to eliminate the ad damnum clause.

(2) Periodic payments. Provisions, now in effect in 18 states, allow or require a court to convert awards for future losses from a single lump sum payment to periodic payments over the period of the patient's disability or life. Such a mode of payment is intended to eliminate a windfall payment to heirs if the injured party dies.

(3) Collateral source rule modifications. The collateral source rule has operated to prevent the trier of fact from learning about other sources of compensation (such as medical insurance) which the plaintiff might possess. The rule arguably permits double recovery. The modifications have either required the court to inform juries about payments from other sources to the patient, or to offset against the award some or all of the amount of payment from other sources. Seventeen states have modified this rule.

(4) Limits on liability. The most powerful reform in actually reducing the size of malpractice awards has been a dollar limit, or cap, on awards. Caps may take the form of a limit on the amount of recovery of general damages, typically pain and suffering; or a maximum recoverable per case, including all damages.

Indiana has a $500,000 limit per claim, Nebraska $1 million, South Dakota a limit of $500,000 for general damages, California $250,000 on recovery for noneconomic damages, including pain and suffering.

One interesting reform proposal has been to 'schedule' pain and suffering awards rather than capping them, to narrow the range of variability in jury awards . . .

c. Altering the plaintiff's burden of proof
Several reforms have altered evidentiary rules or legal doctrine in the direction of increasing the plaintiff's burden of proof.

(1) Res ipsa loquitur. Res ipsa loquitur was judicially expanded during the 1970's by a number of state courts, creating an inference of negligence (or in three states a presumption) even where expert testimony was needed to establish the 'obviousness' of the defendant's negligence. . . . Doctors objected that they were forced to shoulder a defence burden for some patient harms that were not the result of their negligence. Ten states now have barred the use of the doctrine or limited its operation.

(2) Expert witness rules . . . the plaintiff is normally required to present expert medical testimony as to the standard of care, the defendant's deviation from it, causation, and damages. Some states have now adopted specific requirements that plaintiff experts be qualified in the particular specialty at issue, or devote a large per cent of their practice to the specialty. The intent of these reforms is to reduce the ability of the plaintiff to use a so-called

'hired-gun', a forensic doctor who has never practised, or no longer practises, in the area of the defendant physician.

(3) Standards of care. The standard of care has evolved from a locality rule to a national standard in most states, not only as to specialists, but also as to general practitioners. Some states have refined the standard by statute to specify the particular locality (local, similar, state) which governs the litigation. The purpose of these changes has been fairness to rural practitioners and again to limit the use of forensic experts from other states.

d. Changing the judicial role

The role of the jury as trier of fact has been perceived by critics of the tort system as introducing bias against defendants and causing delay in compensating plaintiffs. Some argue that development of either screening or alternative dispute resolution devices (ADRs) will speed resolution of cases and screen out frivolous claims more effectively than common law litigation. These reforms are important, because they set up a complicated parallel track for disputes which reduces the judicial role.

(1) Pretrial screening devices. Twenty-five states have now put screening panels into place. These panels are intended to rule on the merits of the case before it can proceed to trial and to speed settlement of cases by pricing them in advance of trial. Screening panel laws vary significantly from state to state, but usually require that all cases be heard by the panel before the plaintiff is entitled to trial. A plaintiff is not prevented from filing suit after a panel's negative finding, but the panel's decision is admissible as evidence at trial. The panels range in size from three to seven members, and often have a judge or a lay person, at least one lawyer, and one or more health care providers from the defendant's specialty or type of institution. The panel conducts an informal hearing in which it hears testimony and reviews evidence. The findings of the panel may cover both liability and the size of the award. . . .

Proponents have contended that such panels are less formal and less time consuming, and therefore less expensive as a way of resolving claims. Better informed panel members, including health care professionals, may also lead to more accurate decisions than a lay jury would achieve. . . .

The concerns as to the panels are that they will delay dispute resolution, will favor the provider, and will be ignored unless their use is mandatory.

(2) Arbitration. While screening panels supplement jury trials, arbitration is intended to replace them. Thirteen states have laws promoting arbitration of malpractice disputes. The expected advantages of arbitration include reduced complexity in fact-finding, lower cost, fairer results, greater access for smaller claims, and a reduced burden on the courts. . . . None of the state statutes requires compulsory arbitration. Like screening panels, the arbitration process uses a panel to resolve the dispute after an informal presentation of evidence. The panel typically consists of a doctor, a lawyer and a lay person or retired judge. The arbitration panel, however, uses members trained in dispute resolution and has the authority to make a final ruling as to both provider liability and damages. The process is initiated only when there is an agreement between the patient and the health care provider to arbitrate any claims.

The authors later set out an imaginary example of legislative intervention in this area.

THE COLUMBIA MEDICAL MALPRACTICE JUSTICE ACT
Section 1.
No health care liability claim may be commenced unless the action is filed within two years from the occurrence of the breach or tort or from the date the health care treatment that is the subject of the claim is completed; provided that minors under the age of 12 shall have until their 14th birthday in which to file or have filed on their behalf, the claim.

Section 2.
(1) In an action for damages alleging medical malpractice against a person or party, damages for noneconomic loss which exceeds $500,000.00 shall not be awarded.
(2) In awarding damages in an action alleging medical malpractice, the trier of the fact shall itemise damages into economic and noneconomic damages.
(3) 'Noneconomic loss' means damages or loss due to pain, suffering, inconvenience, physical impairment, physical disfigurement, or other noneconomic loss.
(4) Subsection (1) of this section does not apply to the amount of damages awarded on a health care liability claim for the expenses of necessary medical, hospital, and custodial care received before judgment or required in the future for treatment of the injury.

(5) In any action on a health care liability claim that is tried by a jury in any court in this state, the following shall be included in the court's written instructions to the jurors: Do not consider, discuss, nor speculate whether or not liability, if any, on the part of any party is or is not subject to any limit under applicable law.

Section 3.
In any malpractice action in which the plaintiff seeks to recover for the cost of medical care, custodial care or rehabilitation services, loss of earnings or other economic loss, evidence shall be admissible for consideration by the court to establish that any such past or future cost or expense was or will, with reasonable certainty, be replaced or indemnified, in whole or in part, from any collateral source such as insurance, social security, workers' compensation or employee benefit programs. If the court finds that any such cost of expense was or will, with reasonable certainty, be replaced or indemnified from any collateral source, it shall reduce the amount of the award by such finding, minus an amount equal to the premiums paid by the plaintiff for such benefits for the two-year period immediately preceding the accrual of such action and minus an amount equal to the projected future cost to the plaintiff of maintaining such benefits.

Section 4.
(1) An action alleging medical malpractice shall be mediated pursuant to subsection (4).
(2) The judge to whom an action alleging medical malpractice is assigned or the chief judge shall refer the action to mediation by written order not less than 91 days after the filing of the answer or answers.
(3) An action referred to mediation pursuant to subsection (1) shall be heard by a mediation panel selected pursuant to subsection (4).
(4) A mediation panel shall be composed of 5 voting members, 3 of whom shall be licensed attorneys, one of whom shall be a licensed or registered health care provider selected by the defendant or defendants and one of whom shall be a licensed or registered health care provider selected by the plaintiff or plaintiffs. If a defendant is a specialist, the health care provider members of the panel shall specialise in the same or a related, relevant area of health care as the defendant.
(5) Except as otherwise provided in subsection (1), the procedure for selecting mediation panel members and their qualifications shall be as prescribed by the court rules or local court rules.
(6) A judge may be selected as a member of a mediation panel, but may not preside at the trial of any action in which he or she served as a mediator.
(7) In the case of multiple injuries to members of a single family, the plaintiffs may elect to treat the action as involving one claim, with the payment of one fee and rendering of one lump sum award to be accepted or rejected. If such an election is not made, a separate fee shall be paid for each plaintiff, and the mediation panel shall then make separate awards for each claim, which may be individually accepted or rejected.
(8) At least 7 days before the mediation hearing date, each party shall submit to the mediation clerk five copies of the documents pertaining to the issues to be mediated and give copies of a concise brief or summary setting forth that party's factual or legal position on issues presented by the action. In addition, one copy of each shall be served on each attorney of record.
(9) A party has the right, but is not required, to attend a mediation hearing. If scars, disfigurement, or other unusual conditions exist, they may be demonstrated to the mediation panel by a personal appearance; however, testimony shall not be taken or permitted of any party.
(10) The rules of evidence shall not apply before the mediation panel. Factual information having a bearing on damages or liability shall be supported by documentary evidence, if possible.
(11) Oral presentation shall be limited to 15 minutes per side unless multiple parties or unusual circumstances warrant additional time. The mediation panel may request information on applicable insurance policy limits and may inquire about settlement negotiations, unless a party objects. Following deliberation, the mediation panel shall render an evaluation, to which a majority of the panel must agree.
(12) Statements by the attorney and the briefs or summaries are not admissible in any subsequent court or evidentiary proceeding.
(13) If a party has rejected an evaluation and the action proceeds to trial, that party shall pay the opposing party's actual costs unless the verdict is more favorable to the rejecting party than the mediation evaluation. However, if the opposing party has also rejected the

evaluation, that party is entitled to costs only if the verdict is more favorable to that party than the mediation evaluation.

(14) For the purpose of subsection (13), a verdict shall be adjusted by adding to it assessable costs and interest on the amount of the verdict from the filing of the complaint to the date of the mediation evaluation. After this adjustment, the verdict is considered more favorable to a defendant if it is more than 10% below the evaluation, and is considered more favorable to the plaintiff if it is more than 10% above the evaluation.

(15) For the purpose of this section, actual costs include those costs taxable in any civil action and a reasonable attorney fee as determined by the trial judge for services necessitated by the rejection of the mediation evaluation.

(16) Costs shall not be awarded if the mediation award was not unanimous.

Section 5.

In an action alleging medical malpractice, if the defendant is a specialist, a person shall not give expert testimony on the appropriate standard of care unless the person is or was a physician licensed to practice medicine or osteopathic medicine and surgery or a dentist licensed to practice dentistry in this or another state and meets both of the following criteria:

(1) Specializes, or specialized at the time of the occurrence which is the basis for the action, in the same specialty or a related, relevant area of medicine or osteopathic medicine and surgery or dentistry as the specialist who is the defendant in the medical malpractice action.

(2) Devotes, or devoted at the time of the occurrence which is the basis for the action, a substantial portion of his or her professional time to the active clinical practice of medicine or osteopathic medicine and surgery or the active clinical practice of dentistry, or to the instruction of students in an accredited medical school, osteopathic medical school, or dental school in the same specialty or a related, relevant area of health care as the specialist who is the defendant in the medical malpractice action.

Section 6.

In order to determine what judgment is to be entered on a verdict in an action to recover damages for dental or medical malpractice under this article, the court shall proceed as follows:

(1) The court shall apply to the findings of past and future damages any applicable rules of law, including set-offs, credits, comparative negligence, additurs, and remittiturs, in calculating the respective amounts of past and future damages claimants are entitled to recover and defendants are obligated to pay.

(2) The court shall enter judgment in lump sum for past damages, for future damages not in excess of two hundred fifty thousand dollars, and for any damages, fees or costs payable in lump sum or otherwise under subsection (3). For the purposes of this section, any lump sum payment of a portion of future damages shall be deemed to include the elements of future damages in the same proportion as such elements comprise of the total award for future damages as determined by the trier of fact.

(3) With respect to awards of future damages in excess of two hundred fifty thousand dollars in an action to recover damages for dental or medical malpractice, the court shall enter judgment as follows:

After making any adjustments prescribed by this subsection and subsection (2), the court shall enter a judgment for the amount of the present value of an annuity contract that will provide for the payment of the remaining amounts of future damages in periodic instalments.

Section 7.

(1) Notwithstanding any inconsistent judicial rule, a contingent fee in a medical malpractice action shall not exceed the amount of compensation provided for in the following schedule:

30 per cent of the first $250,000 of the sum recovered;
25 per cent of the next $250,000 of the sum recovered;
20 per cent of the next $500,000 of the sum recovered;
15 per cent of the next $250,000 of the sum recovered;
10 per cent of any amount over $1,250,000 of the sum recovered.

(2) In the event that claimant's or plaintiff's attorney believes in good faith that the fee schedule set forth in subsection (1) of this section, because of extraordinary circumstances, will not give him adequate compensation, application for greater compensation may be made upon affidavit with written notice and an opportunity to be heard to the claimant or plaintiff and other person holding liens or assignments on the recovery.

The authors subsequently turn to consider the effects of the reforms in the USA:

THE EFFECTS OF REFORM: A PRELIMINARY ASSESSMENT
The Robert Wood Johnson Foundation, the federal government, and others have funded several major studies to determine the effects of reform. The results of these studies are solidifying our understanding of the benefits and the limits of reform.

A. CAPS ON AWARDS AND STATUTES OF LIMITATIONS
Caps on damage awards and reductions in the amount of time the plaintiff has to file suit have proved effective in lowering the amount paid to plaintiffs, by almost 40% according to one study of closed insurance company claims. See Sloan, Mergenhagen & Bovbjerg, Effects of Tort Reforms on the Value of Closed Medical Malpractice Claims: A Microanalysis, 14 J Health Pol, Pol, & Law 663 (1989).

Limits on payments produce savings per claim, which insurers are passing on to physicians through lower premiums. Shortening statutes of limitations also lowers premiums by reducing the number of claims against physicians, although severity of claims is not affected. See Zukerman, Bovbjerg, and Sloan, Effects of Tort Reforms and Other Factors on Medical Malpractice Insurance Premiums, 27 Inquiry 167, 180 (1990).

B. PRE-TRIAL SCREENING PANELS
The use of screening panels reduced obstetrics/gynecology premiums by about 7% the year after they were introduced and about 20% in the long run. Zukerman et al write:

> The results suggest that panels may be more effective in screening nonmeritorious cases or encouraging out-of-court settlements in claims involving OBGs. Since OBGs are among those incurring the highest insurance expenses and are often a driving force behind reform initiatives, legislators may view this somewhat limited finding of effectiveness as adequate reason for establishing panels. Id at 176.

The study by Zukerman et al followed up on an earlier study by Sloan, which had evaluated the effect of several reforms on the levels and rates of change in insurance premiums paid from 1974 through 1978 by general practitioners, ophthalmologists, and orthopedic surgeons. Sloan, State Responses to the Malpractice Insurance 'Crisis' of the 1970s: An Empirical Assessment, 9 J Health Pol, Pol, & Law 629 (1985). Sloan had studied caps on liability, limits on provider payments to plaintiffs, patient compensation funds, limits on res ipsa loquitur, shortened statutes of limitations, informed consent modifications, contingency fee restrictions, collateral source modifications, ad damnum elimination, imposition of a locality rule, screening panels, arbitration, joint underwriting associations, and health care mutual insurance companies. The reforms therefore included both tort system modification and insurance modification. He concluded that only screening panels displayed a statistically significant connection to lower malpractice insurance premiums.

A 1988 study of Maryland arbitration panels concluded that the panel system had reduced the number of claims requiring formal adjudication in the courts and decreased the average length of time for resolution. They also were more likely to find in favor of claimants. See Morlock and Malitz, Nonbinding Arbitration of Medical Malpractice Claims: A Decade of Experience with Pretrial Screening Panels in Maryland (1988); Thurston, Medical Malpractice Dispute Resolution in Maryland, 1 Courts, Health Science & The Law 81 (1990).

Several earlier studies had looked at panels or arbitration. A 1980 study of screening panels concluded that the panels were effective in disposing of claims before trial, resulting in a significant percentage of claims being dropped or settled after a panel hearing, from a high of 88% of claims disposed of after a panel decision in New Jersey to a low of 38% disposed of in Virginia. Carlin, Medical Malpractice Pre-Trial Screening Panels: A Review of the Evidence, 29, 31 (1980). The very threat of a panel hearing seemed to promote early disposition of claims in some states. The panels in some states also processed claims more quickly than conventional litigation. However, some states were having problems that impaired panel operation. In particular, panels were rarely used where their use was voluntary. Carlin at 32, 37, 39.

A study by the Florida Medical Association in 1985 found that the results of panels were mixed, with some states using panels effectively and others experiencing case backlogs and administrative problems. The authors concluded that panel effectiveness was unproven, and that other court efforts such as a special malpractice court, or other procedural reforms, might be more effective. Florida Medical Association, Medical Malpractice Policy Guidebook 188 (1985). Studies by several states of the performance of their panels have not been encouraging. New Jersey and New York both recommended that a mandatory screening approach be dropped in favor of some form of voluntary system, such as optional mediation. See Perna v Pirozzi, 92 NJ 446, 457-59, 457 A2d 431, 437 (1983) (presenting findings of a committee appointed by the New Jersey Supreme Court to evaluate New Jersey's panel system); see also Ad Hoc Committee on Medical Malpractice Panels, described in Bower, Malpractice Panels and Questions of Fact, 14 Trial L.Q. 4 (1982). An Arizona study found several problems with the Arizona panels, concluding that (1) settlements increased and claims filed decreased between 1976 and 1978 (the good news); but (the bad news) (2) neither the frequency or level of recovery by claimants was affected; (3) the time to process the malpractice case was lengthened by the panel system; (4) the panel system aggravated problems of difficulty and expense in handling cases, from the lawyers' and panel members' perspectives; (5) the panel hearings took longer than expected. See National Center for State Courts, Medical Liability Review Panels in Arizona: An Evaluation (1980); Spece, The Case Against (Arizona) Medical Malpractice Panels, 63 U Det L Rev 7 (1985).

C. OTHER REFORM MEASURES

Earlier studies had evaluated the effects of the reforms of the mid-1970s and 80s. One study looked at the effect of post-1975 reforms on the frequency of claims per capita, the amount per claim paid, and the claim cost per capita, using data from closed claims from 1975 to 1978 by all insurers writing malpractice premiums of a million dollars or more in any year since 1970. Danzon, The Frequency and Severity of Medical Malpractice Claims (1982). Its conclusions were:

- states with caps on awards had awards 19% lower two years after the effective date of the statutes;
- states with contingency fee limits had a somewhat lower amount paid per claim and total claim cost;
- states eliminating the ad damnum had lower total claim costs; there was otherwise no effect on the frequency or amount paid per claim;
- states requiring collateral source offset had 50% lower awards two years after the statute's effective date, but states admitting evidence of collateral sources without required offset displayed no significant effect;
- several reforms displayed no significant effects, including pre-trial screening panels, arbitration, res ipsa loquitur or informed consent limitations, and periodic payments.

Another study by Patricia Danzon updated her earlier studies, based upon analysis of claims nationally over the decade 1975 to 1984, for 49 states in some years, based on data from insurance companies that insured approximately 100,000 physicians. Danzon, The Frequency and Severity of Medical Malpractice Claims: New Evidence, 49 Law & Contemp Probs 57 (1986). Her conclusions are:

- the severity of claims rose twice as fast as the Consumer Price Index, a fact related to the fact that health care prices rose faster than consumer prices generally;
- claim severity continues to be higher in urbanized states, consistent with earlier studies, and is also higher in states 'with a high ratio of surgical specialists relative to medical specialists', id at 76;
- severity is less in states with larger elderly populations, a fact related to the low wage loss of the elderly and the low potential for damages in a tort suit;
- no correlation was found between the number of lawyers per capita and claim severity;
- the newer data was consistent with earlier findings as to the impact of tort reforms. Statutory caps reduced average severity by 23%. Collateral source offsets appeared to reduce awards by a range of 11 to 18%. Arbitration reduced claim severity by 20%, compared to states without such statutory arbitration. Screening panels did not have a consistent effect in reducing claims severity.

What do these widely varying, and often conflicting, results mean for the future of reform of the tort system? The results reflect to some extent the limits of the studies and the relative novelty of the reforms such as panels or arbitration at the time studied. Time will tell whether procedural reforms, requiring an elaborate administrative structure, will mature and prove effective. But any ultimate conclusions as to the merits and nature of reform still depend upon the goals sought for the system. Some of the reforms, such as caps and collateral source offset, appear to have slowed the growth of awards in some states. Some reforms, such as statutes of repose, reduce claims filings over the longer term. The claims-made insurance policy and mutual insurance companies may also be a more efficient way of allocating risk and protecting insurance availability.

The reforms of the tort system were enacted with the expectation that liability insurance premiums could be lowered, or at least stabilized, by a reduction in the frequency of malpractice suits and the severity of awards in such suits. It has proved difficult to assess the impact of the reforms. The GAO Report of 1985 surveyed six interest groups as to the effect of existing reforms. No consensus was found in their results, although a majority of providers felt that caps had a major impact on the severity of judgments, and a majority of consumers felt that screening panels had a major impact on decreasing the time to close claims. GAO Malpractice Reports, supra.

An assessment of reforms of the tort system and the insurance mechanism leaves the same question: is the conventional, fault-based litigation system worth keeping for medical accidents?

The impact, if any, of these reforms is hard to measure. The scale of the problems they were in part designed to address, and which some of them seem singularly to have failed to do, can be seen from the seminal Report of the Harvard Medical Practice Study to the State of New York in 1990: *Patients, Doctors and Lawyers: Medical Injury, Malpractice Litigation and Patient Compensation in New York*. The authors summarised the study in three papers published in the *New England Journal of Medicine* in 1991: (1991) 324 NEJM 370 and 377 and (1991) 325 NEJM 245.

'Incidence of Adverse Events and Negligence in Hospitalized Patients' (1991) N Engl J Med 370

Over the past decade there has been a steady increase in the number of malpractice claims brought against health care providers and in the monetary damages awarded to plaintiffs. This increase has precipitated numerous state programs designed to moderate the number of claims and encourage providers to develop quality-of-care initiatives. Advocates of tort reform argue that the existing system of malpractice litigation is inefficient in compensating patients injured by medical practice and in deterring the performance of poor-quality care that is sometimes responsible for the injuries. Others defend the role of tort litigation. These debates will probably continue even as claims rates begin to decrease.

Controversy over the virtues of common-law malpractice litigation occurs without much empirical information regarding the epidemiology of poor-quality care and iatrogenic injury. The most widely quoted estimates of the incidence of iatrogenic injury and substandard care were developed over 10 years ago. Other reviews by physicians to identify poor-quality care or adverse events have been restricted to non-random samples of much smaller numbers of records.

To address the need for empirical information, we undertook the Harvard Medical Practice Study. A primary goal was to develop more current and more reliable estimates of the incidence of adverse events and negligence in hospitalized patients. We defined an adverse event as an injury that was caused by medical management (rather than the underlying disease) and that prolonged the hospitalization, produced a disability at the time of discharge, or both. We defined negligence as care that fell below the standard expected of physicians in their community. To estimate the incidence of these critical events, we reviewed a random sample of more than 31,000 hospital records using techniques we have previously described.

Using our methods, we estimated that 3.7 percent of the patients hospitalized in 1981 suffered adverse events, whereas the rate of adverse events due to negligence was 1.0 percent. These results may be compared with those of the only other large-scale effort to estimate the incidence of iatrogenic injury and substandard care, the California Medical Association's Medical Insurance Feasibility Study. Investigators there found 870 potentially compensable events (a category comparable to our adverse events) in a convenience sample of 20,864 records, for an overall rate of 4.6 percent. This rate was 26 percent higher than our estimate of 3.7 percent. The California study revealed a negligence rate of 0.8 percent, 20 percent lower than the result of our review.

Because our sample of hospital records was random, we could provide for the first time population estimates of adverse events and adverse events due to negligence. Among the 2,671,863 discharges from New York hospitals in 1984, we estimate that there were 98,609 adverse events. Although 56,042 of them (56.8 percent) led to minimal disability with complete recovery in one month and another 13,521 (13.7 percent) to moderate disability with complete recovery in six months, 2550 (2.6 percent) produced permanent total disability, and 13,451 (13.6 percent) led to death. The burden of iatrogenic injury was thus large.

Even more disturbing was the number of adverse events caused by negligence. We estimated that 27,179 injuries, including 6895 deaths and 877 cases of permanent and total disability, resulted from negligent care in New York in 1984. Under the tort system, all of these could have led to successful litigation. We could not measure all negligent acts, and made no attempt to, but measured only those that led to injury. Medical records are probably a poor source of information on negligence that does not cause injury. Thus, our figures reflect not the amount of negligence, but only its consequences.

The analyses of rates of adverse events and the percentage of adverse events due to negligence according to characteristics of the patient are of special interest. Identifying risk factors for adverse events, whether negligent or not, constitutes a crucial first step toward their prevention, an important goal of quality assurance. In this study, we focused on patient age and sex and on clinical-speciality groups . . .

We found that both crude and standardized rates of adverse events increased with age. This suggests that elderly people are at higher risk of an adverse event, and it may reflect in part the fact that older people are likely to have more complicated illnesses and often require more complicated intervention. It may also be ascribable in part to their greater fragility. Such differences highlight the importance of controlling for age when comparing population groups. People over the age of 64 were at higher risk of an adverse event associated with negligence, a finding not readily explained by difference in the severity of illness. Presumably, this means that care for the elderly less frequently meets the standard expected of reasonable medical practitioners. Sex did not appear to represent a risk factor for adverse events or negligence.

Table 2.
*Population Distribution of Adverse Events According to Category of Disability.**

CATEGORY OF DISABILITY	ADVERSE EVENTS	ADVERSE EVENTS DUE TO NEGLIGENCE	PERCENTAGE DUE TO NEGLIGENCE
	NUMBER (PERCENT)		
Minimal impairment recovery 1 mo	56,042 (56.8 ± 1.6)	12,428 (45 ± 3.7)	22.2 ± 2.8
Moderate impairment, recovery > 1 to 6 mo	13,521 (13.7 ± 1.1)	3,302 (12.1 ± 2.2)	24.4 ± 4.8
Moderate impairment, recovery > 6 mo	2,762 (2.8 ± 0.5)	817 (3.0 ± 1.0)	29.6 ± 8.6
Permanent impairment, ≤ 50% disability	3,807 (3.9 ± 0.6)	869 (3.2 ± 1.1)	22.8 ± 6.8
Permanent impairment,	2,550 (2.6 ± 0.4)	877 (3.2 ± 0.8)	34.4 ± 8.1
Death	13,451 (13.5 ± 1.7)	6,895 (25. ± 44.2)	51.3 ± 6.9
Could not reasonably judge disability	6,477 (6.6 ± 0.7)	1,989 (7.3 ± 1.3)	30.7 ± 5.9
Total†	98,610	27,177	27.6 ± 2.4

* Plus-minus values are means ± SE.
† Values differ from the sums of those reported above because of rounding.

There is great variation among specialties with regard to the riskiness of the procedures employed and the severity of illness in the patients for whom care is provided. The finding that patients in certain specialty groups, as defined by DRGs [Diagnostic Related Groups], were at higher risk of adverse events was therefore not surprising. The percentage of adverse events due to negligence did not, however, vary according to specialty. The momentary lapse on the part of an internist who forgets to ask about sensitivity to an antibiotic until the end of an interview (but before writing a prescription) may have far different consequences than the neurosurgeon's momentary lapse during an operation on the brain or spinal cord. One goal of our study was to examine such issues, for the nature of medical injury and of medical injury due to negligence will help guide investigators who seek to reduce the occurrence of such injuries.

The observations concerning rates of adverse events and negligence among specialties have implications relevant to today's system of malpractice insurance. Practitioners of certain specialties are sued more frequently and thus pay much higher premiums than others. We found that these specialties (neurosurgery, cardiac and thoracic surgery, and vascular surgery) had higher rates of adverse events, but not higher rates of negligence. Our data suggest that variations among specialties in rates of litigation do not reflect differing levels of competence, but rather differences in the kinds of patients and diseases for which the specialist cares.

There were a number of potential sources of error in our estimates. One was missing records, but we were reassured by the fact that the rates of adverse events and negligence in the follow-up study were lower overall than in the initial survey. Another possible source of error was our use of hospital records for information on adverse events and negligence. We had, however, previously demonstrated the integrity of hospital records in this capacity.

Table 3.
Rates of Adverse Events and Negligence According to Age.*

AGE OF PATIENT	CASES REVIEWED	RATE OF ADVERSE EVENTS		RATE OF NEGLIGENCE
		CRUDE	STANDARDIZED	
	no.	mean ($\pm$SE) percent		
Newborn	3,595	0.6 ± 0.1	1.4 ± 0.3	20.8 ± 7.1
$\leqslant$15 yr	3,066	2.1 ± 0.4	2.7 ± 0.6	21.9 ± 6.0
16-44 yr	11,101	2.6 ± 0.2	2.6 ± 0.2	26.7 ± 2.8
45-64 yr	7,379	4.7 ± 0.4	4.4 ± 0.4	20.6 ± 2.4
$\geqslant$65 yr	4,980	5.9 ± 0.5	5.7 ± 0.6	33.1 ± 4.2
P value†			<0.0001	<0.01

* According to DRG class.
† For the distribution of rates of events.

Table 4.
Rates of Adverse Events and Negligence among Clinical-Specialty Groups.*

SPECIALTY	RATE OF ADVERSE EVENTS		RATE OF NEGLIGENCE	
	PERCENT	POPULATION ESTIMATE	PERCENT	POPULATION ESTIMATE
Orthopedics	4.1 ± 0.6	6,746	22.4 ± 4.7	1,514
Urology	4.9 ± 0.8	4,819	19.4 ± 6.5	933
Neurosurgery	9.9 ± 2.1	2,987	35.6 ± 8.6	1,063
Thoracic and cardiac surgery	10.8 ± 2.4	3,588	23.0 ± 9.3	826

SPECIALTY		RATE OF ADVERSE EVENTS		RATE OF NEGLIGENCE	
	PERCENT	POPULATION ESTIMATE	PERCENT	POPULATION ESTIMATE	
Vascular surgery	16.1±3.0	3,187	18.0±8.1	575	
Obstetrics	1.5±0.2	5,013	38.3±7.0	1,920	
Neonatology	0.6±0.1	1,713	25.8±6.9	442	
General surgery	7.0±0.5	22,324	28.0±3.4	6,247	
General medicine	3.6±0.3	37,135	30.9±4.4	11,475	
Other	3.0±0.4	11,097	19.7±4.9	2,183	
P Value†	<0.0001		0.64		

* Plus-minus values are means ± SE. Values differ from the sums of those reported above because of rounding.
† For the distribution of rates of events.

'The Nature of Adverse Events in Hospitalized Patients' (1991) 324 N Engl J Med 377

[A]n important objective for those concerned with both medical malpractice and quality of care is the prevention of iatrogenic injury. A first step in prevention is to develop a better understanding of the types of such injuries and their causes.

In our investigation of accidental injury in patients hospitalized in 1984 in the state of New York, we found that 3.7 percent of patients had injuries and that negligent care was responsible for 28 percent of them. In this report we analyze these injuries, including the types of adverse events, the types most likely to result in serious disability, the types most likely to be caused by negligence, the effects of various risk factors, and the management errors that were responsible. Finally, we develop a conceptual framework encompassing notions of negligence, error, and preventability in an effort to understand iatrogenic injury better. . .

RESULTS
Adverse Events

As reported elsewhere, we identified 1133 adverse events in our sample of records for 30,195 patients hospitalized in New York in 1984. Table 1 lists the distribution of the kinds of adverse events and negligence-related adverse events we discovered. Nearly half the adverse events (48 percent) resulted from operations. Wound infections were the most common surgical adverse event, accounting for 29 percent of surgical complications and nearly one seventh of all adverse events identified in the study.

Drug complications were the most common single type of adverse event (19 percent). Table 2 lists the classes of drugs responsible for adverse events in the order of their frequency, and Table 3 shows the various types of adverse events caused by drugs. These events covered a broad spectrum, from those that were unpredictable and unpreventable, such as allergic reactions to drugs to which the patient had had no known previous exposure, to those that might have been unavoidable, such as marrow depression from antitumor drugs, to those that resulted from errors in administration or monitoring, such as bleeding associated with the use of anticoagulant agents.

Negligence
Overall, 28 percent of the adverse events were judged to have resulted from negligent care, but there was wide variation among categories (Table 1).

Table 1.
Types of Adverse Events and Proportion of Events Involving Negligence.

TYPE OF EVENT	NO. OF EVENTS IN SAMPLE	WEIGHTED PROPORTION OF EVENTS*		
		IN POPUL-ATION	DUE TO NEGLIGENCE	WITH SERIOUS DISABILITY
		PERCENT		
Operative				
Wound infection	160	13.6	12.5†	17.9
Technical complication	157	12.9	17.6	12.0†
Late complication	137	10.6	13.6	35.7
Nontechnical complication	87	7.0	20.1	43.8
Surgical failure	58	3.6	36.4	17.5
All	599	47.7	17.0	24.0
Nonoperative				
Drug-related	178	19.4	17.7‡	14.1‡
Diagnostic mishap	79	8.1	75.2†	47.0‡
Therapeutic mishap	62	7.5	76.8†	35.4
Procedure-related	88	7.0	15.1	28.8
Fall	20	2.7	–	–
Fractures§	18	1.2	–	–
Postpartum¶	18	1.1	–	–
Anesthesia-related	13	1.1	–	–
Neonatal	29	0.9	–	–
System and other	29	3.3	35.9	36.0
All	534	52.3	37.2	25.3
Total	1133	100.0	27.6	24.7

* Dashes denote categories for which there were too few observations to determine a percentage.
† P < 0.001 for the difference between this rate and all others in the same column.
‡ P < 0.01 for the difference between this rate and all others in the same column.
§ Includes nonoperative fractures only.
¶ Includes noncesarean deliveries only.

Seventeen percent of the adverse events related to operations were due to negligence, ranging from 13 percent of the wound infections to 36 percent of the surgical failures (e.g., persistent back pain that responded to a second operation to remove a disk that had been treated inadequately in a previous laminectomy). Of the adverse events due to drug treatment, 18 percent resulted from negligence. By contrast, negligent care was identified as causing 75 percent of the adverse events due to problems in diagnosis (such as failure to diagnose an ectopic pregnancy) and 77 percent of those due to a therapeutic mishap (resulting from non-drug related, noninvasive treatment).

Disability
The large majority of the adverse events did not result in serious disability. More than half the patients had minimal impairment, recovering completely in a month or less. Seventy percent recovered completely in less than six months. Rates of serious disability were significantly lower than average for technical complications of surgery (12 percent) and drug-related adverse events (14 percent), and significantly higher than average for diagnostic mishaps (47 percent) (Table 1).

Effects of Age
We noted previously that patients over the age of 64 had adverse events and negligence-related adverse events at rates more than double the rate of patients under 45, and although only 27 percent of the hospitalized population in New York in 1984 was over 64, those patients accounted for 43 percent of all the adverse events.

Table 2.
Drug-Related Adverse Events, According to Class of Drug Involved.

DRUG CLASS	NO. OF EVENTS	WEIGHTED PERCENTAGE
Antibiotic	29	16.2
Antitumor	31	15.5
Anticoagulant	20	11.2
Cardiovascular	13	8.5
Antiseizure	15	8.1
Diabetes	8	5.5
Antihypertensive	10	5.0
Analgesic	6	3.5
Antiasthmatic	5	2.8
Sedative or hypnotic	4	2.3
Antidepressant	1	0.9
Antipsychotic	2	0.7
Peptic ulcer	1	0.5
Other	33	19.3
Total	178	100.0

Table 4 shows the frequency of each type of adverse event per 1000 discharges from the hospital in each of four age categories, based on the weighted number of patients in each age group in the sample. Drug-related complications were the most common type of adverse event for patients in all age groups, except those 16 to 44 years old, among whom drug complications ranked second to wound infections. Elderly patients were next most likely to have adverse events from noninvasive therapeutic mishaps and late surgical complications. Wound infections were the most frequent type of adverse event in young adults. Children had the lowest rates in every category.

Surgical failures constituted a much higher fraction of the total number of adverse events in young adults than in the other age groups. The operations most commonly associated with such failures were tubal ligation, procedures for back problems, tendon repair, meniscus repair, excision of pilonidal cysts, nasal reconstruction, cervical cerclage, and repair of tibial fractures – operations that are seldom performed in elderly patients or children.

Most other types of adverse events were more common among elderly patients. In the elderly, four classes of events occurred two or more times as often as was observed in younger patients: nontechnical postoperative complications, noninvasive treatment mishaps, fractures, and falls. The increased rates may reflect more frequent use of interventions, as well as increased risk of an adverse event with a given condition or treatment. For example, the elderly may have more noninvasive treatments per hospitalization than younger people.

Site of Adverse Events
The largest number of adverse events (41 percent) resulted from treatment provided in the operating room (Table 5). The next most frequent (27 percent) were those that occurred in the patient's hospital room. The emergency room, intensive care units, and labor and delivery rooms were each the site of approximately 3 percent of the adverse events. The number of events occurring in all other locations in the hospital added up to 5 percent of the total. Most adverse events occurring outside the hospital were attributed to interventions in the physician's office. (The only out-of-hospital adverse events measured in our study were those that resulted in hospitalization.)

Table 5 also shows the percentage of adverse events at each site that were caused by negligent care – an overall proportion of 28 percent. In the operating room the proportion was 14 percent, in the patient's hospital room it was 41 percent, and in the emergency room it was 70 percent. The differences at other sites were not significant. Rates of disability also varied according to site. The percentage of patients with serious disabilities was significantly lower than average in the case of adverse events occurring at home (8 percent) or in the labor and delivery room (10 percent). Other differences were not significant.

Physicians' Errors
The classification of errors is shown in Table 6, which includes the first choices of each reviewer. Because two physicians reviewed almost every case, the total number of observations shown is nearly double the number of cases for which there was a question of error. The physician-reviewers used their own criteria to identify errors in management, and they were asked to list the errors whether or not negligence was involved. They identified one or more management errors corresponding to 58 percent of all the adverse events, but only 28 percent of the events ultimately met our requirements for a judgment of negligence. For each class of error, the percentage of cases that were ultimately attributed to negligence is shown in Table 6.

Table 3.
Types of Drug-Related Complications.

TYPE OF COMPLICATION	NO.	WEIGHTED PERCENTAGE
Marrow suppression	29	16.3
Bleeding	26	14.6
Central nervous system	26	14.6
Allergic/cutaneous	25	14.0
Metabolic	18	10.1
Cardiac	17	9.6
Gastrointestinal	14	7.9
Renal	12	6.7
Respiratory	5	2.8
Miscellaneous	6	3.4
Total	178	100.0

The most common class of error, accounting for 35 percent of all the errors in this series, involved the performance of a procedure or operation. Errors in prevention (i.e., failure to take preventive measures) were the next most common (22 percent), followed by diagnostic errors (14 percent). Errors in diagnosis and prevention were the most likely to be considered negligent (75 percent and 60 percent involved negligence, respectively). Thus, errors in performance were the most common but the least likely to be attributed to negligence. In contrast, diagnostic errors, though much less common, were likely to be attributed to negligence.

Types of Error
Because the reviewers were asked to list all the types of error they found, the numbers shown in Table 7 for each class are higher than those in Table 6. In addition, since the reviewers were not limited to assigning a single category to each error, the percentages exceed 100.

Although technical errors were the most common class of error observed, the sum of the various types of 'errors of omission' composed a higher percentage of the total in several classes. These included failure to take precautions to prevent accidental injury, avoidable delays in treatment, failure to use indicated tests or to act on the results of such tests, and the entire gamut of diagnostic errors.

Disability as a Function of the Gravity of Negligence
Adverse events resulting from negligence were more likely than other adverse events to lead to serious disability, defined as a disability with a score greater than 2 (Table 8). Only 20 percent of the patients who had adverse events not attributed to negligence had serious

disabilities, whereas 38 percent of those who had adverse events due to negligence had such disabilities.

Table 4.
Rates of Adverse Events According to Age.

TYPE OF EVENT	AGE (YR)*			
	0-15	16-44	45-64	≥65
	EVENTS PER 1000 DISCHARGES			
Operative				
Wound infection	1.77	4.93	6.59	6.15
Technical complication	1.70	3.77	8.25	5.34
Late complication	1.01	2.40	5.17	6.77
Nontechnical complication	0.20	1.33	2.97	5.46
Surgical failure	0.39	2.22	0.84	1.22
All	5.07	14.65	23.82	24.94
Nonoperative				
Drug-related	2.36	3.87	11.18	11.46
Diagnostic mishap	1.71	1.78	3.56	5.08
Therapeutic mishap	0.38	0.81	2.54	7.04
Procedure-related	0.76	1.58	4.16	3.85
Fall	–	0.19	0.30	3.19
Fracture	0.22	0.31	0.24	0.84
Postpartum	0.05	0.18	–	–
Anesthesia-related	0.07	0.89	0.30	0.09
Neonatal	1.88	0.54	1.57	2.34
System and other	7.84	11.15	23.85	33.89
All	7.84	11.15	23.85	33.89
Both operative and nonoperative	12.91	25.84	47.43	58.85

* Dashes denote categories for which there were too few observations to determine a rate.

Table 5.
Sites of Care That Resulted in Adverse Events.

SITE	NO. OF EVENTS*	WEIGHTED PROPORTION OF EVENTS†		
		IN SAMPLE	DUE TO NEGLIGENCE	WITH SERIOUS DISABILITY
		PERCENT		
In hospital				
Operating room	1019	41.0	13.7‡	22.0
Patient's room	495	26.5	41.1‡	30.4
Emergency room	71	2.9	70.4‡	24.8
Labor and delivery room	123	2.8	27.7	9.8§
Intensive care unit	53	2.7	30.2	50.4
Radiology	32	2.0	36.9	35.8
Cardiac catherization laboratory	28	0.9	–	–
Ambulatory care unit	19	0.8	–	–
Other	47	1.7	–	–
All	1887	81.2	26.4	25.9
Outside hospital				
Physician's office	153	7.7	31.2	21.0
Home	48	2.7	11.4	8.2
Ambulatory care unit	32	1.4	53.6	13.7
Nursing home	11	0.9	–	–
Other	26	1.1	–	–

SITE	NO. OF EVENTS*	WEIGHTED PROPORTION OF EVENTS†		
		IN SAMPLE	DUE TO NEGLIGENCE	WITH SERIOUS DISABILITY
		PERCENT		
All	270	13.8	30.2	17.0
Unknown	61	5.1	38.6	25.6
Total	2218	100.0	27.6	24.7

* Numbers shown are based on the total number of reviews, not the number of cases.
† Dashes denote categories for which there were too few observations to determine a percentage.
‡ $P < 0.001$ for the difference between this rate and all others in the same column.
§ $P < 0.01$ for the difference between this rate and all others in the same column.

The percentage of adverse events resulting in serious disability increased progressively with the gravity (severity) of the negligence. Nearly three fourths of the patients who had adverse events attributed to grave negligence (grade 3) had serious disabilities. Two thirds of these patients died, as compared with 10 percent of the patients with adverse events not resulting from negligence.

DISCUSSION
Preventability, Error, and Negligence

Many of the adverse events we identified were neither preventable nor predictable, given the current state of medical knowledge – for example, idiosyncratic drug reactions in patients who had not taken the drugs previously, postoperative myocardial infarctions in young patients without previous evidence of heart disease, and adhesive intestinal obstructions. Other unpreventable adverse events occurred with predictable frequency, but patients accepted the risk of treatment because of the potential benefits. Examples of these include radiation injury and bone marrow suppression from chemotherapy. Preventing these 'unpreventable' adverse events will require advances in biomedical knowledge.

Most adverse events are preventable, however, particularly those due to error or negligence. Our findings confirm the observations of others – that errors in medical practice are common. Studies in other areas of human endeavor, such as the generation of nuclear power, shipping, and the airline industry, confirm that some degree of error is inherent in all human activity. In highly technical, complicated systems, even minor errors may have disastrous consequences. Medicine is no exception; errors in the performance of highly technical procedures, such as brain or open-heart surgery, can also have catastrophic results.

Table 6.
Types of Errors Leading to Adverse Events, as Classified by the
Reviewers in a Weighted Sample.

TYPE OF ERRORS	NO. OF REVIEWS	ERRORS OBSERVED	
		IN ENTIRE SAMPLE	ULTIMATELY JUDGED NEGLIGENT
		PERCENT	
Performance	537	35.2	28.2
Prevention	232	21.9	59.6
Diagnosis	168	13.8	74.7
Drug treatment	87	8.9	52.8
System and other	32	2.4	66.0
Unclassified	220	17.9	43.4
All	1276	100.0	47.3

Our physician-reviewers identified management errors in more than half the adverse events we studied. Technical errors were by far the most common class of error, but relatively few of these were judged to result from negligence. In contrast, errors of omission – failure or delay in making a diagnosis or instituting treatment, and failure to use indicated tests or take precautions to prevent injury – were often classed as negligent. When the errors of omission were combined, they were more common than the errors of commission.

Error is not the same as negligence. In tort law, medical negligence is defined as failure to meet the standard of practice of an average qualified physician practicing in the specialty in question. Negligence occurs not merely when there is error, but when the degree of error exceeds an accepted norm. The presence of error is a necessary but not significant condition for the determination of negligence.

Sometimes the evidence of negligence appears clear-cut, as when a physician fails to evaluate a patient with rectal bleedings. Other cases are less obvious. For example, depending on the circumstances, each of the following could be considered either negligent or not: a mistaken diagnosis of acute appendicitis, misinterpretation of a chest film of pneumonia as instead showing congestive heart failure, puncture of the pleura during the insertion of a central venous catheter, and perforation of the bowel during an operation to remove adhesive intestinal obstruction.

In the case of the mistaken diagnosis of acute appendicitis, the patient may have had a classic history, typical findings on physical examination, and laboratory-test results supportive of the diagnosis. If the physician then failed to make the diagnosis, it would be both an error in diagnosis and a case of negligence. If, however, the diagnosis was made but no appendicitis was found, there would also have been an error in diagnosis, but not one involving negligence, because the surgeon would have followed the generally accepted standard of practice. With the present state of medical knowledge, such errors are unavoidable and therefore not negligent.

Furthermore, the standards of practice that form the basis for such judgments are often not well defined, and thus they may be susceptible to considerable variation in interpretation. Perfection can never be the standard of practice, since the vagaries of biology and human behavior make perfection unattainable, in either execution or outcome, for any form of treatment. Accordingly, standards of practice must always include an acceptance of some degree of error.

Table 7.
*Incidence of Specific Types of Errors in a Weighted Sample.**

TYPE OF ERROR	NO.	PERCENT†
Performance (697)		
Inadequate preparation of patient before procedure	59	9
Technical error	559	76
Inadequate monitoring of patient after procedure	61	10
Use of inappropriate or outmoded form of therapy	24	3
Avoidable delay in treatment	41	7
Physician or other professional practicing	13	2
outside area of expertise		
Other	75	14
Prevention (397)		
Failure to take precautions to prevent accidental injury	178	45
Failure to use indicated tests	79	23
Failure to act on results of tests or findings	80	21
Use of inappropriate or outmoded diagnostic tests	6	1
Avoidable delay in treatment	120	31
Physician or other professional practicing	16	4
outside area of expertise		
Other	77	19
Diagnostic (265)		
Failure to use indicated tests	134	50
Failure to act on results of tests or findings	83	32
Use of inappropriate or outmoded diagnostic tests	3	1
Avoidable delay in diagnosis	149	55

TYPE OF ERROR	NO.	PERCENT†
Physician or other professional practicing outside area of expertise	17	6
Other	24	10
Reason not apparent	16	5
Drug treatment (153)		
Error in dose or method of use	67	42
Failure to recognize possible antagonistic or complementary drug-drug interactions	10	8
Inadequate follow-up of therapy	65	45
Use of inappropriate drug	38	22
Avoidable delay in treatment	21	14
Physician or other professional practicing outside area of expertise	8	5
Other	18	9
System (68)		
Defective equipment or supplies	8	8
Equipment or supplies not available	8	5
Inadequate monitoring system	8	10
Inadequate reporting or communications	11	26
Inadequate training or supervisions of physician or other personnel	15	31
Delay in provision or scheduling of service	10	14
Inadequate staffing	5	6
Inadequate functioning of hospital service	7	8
Other	12	20

* Numbers in parentheses after each category of error are the number of errors found by the reviewers for that category. Because the reviewers were asked to list as many errors as they found, the numbers in each class are larger than those in Table 6. In addition, since the reviewers were not limited to identifying a single reason for each error, the percentages exceed 100.

† Percentages are of the total number of errors in each category.

Table 8.
Disability and Gravity of Negligence.*

TYPE OF ADVERSE EVENT (GRADE)	NO. OF EVENTS	% OF TOTAL	SEVERITY OF DISABILITY					
			CLASS 1	CLASS 2	CLASS 3	CLASS 4	CLASS 5	CLASS 6
			PERCENT					
With negligence								
Slight (1-1.5)	76	7.2	77.4	16.2	4.1	0.5	1.9	1.8
Moderate (2-2.5)	141	13.3	47.0	17.2	4.3	7.8	0.5	21.7
Grave (3)	63	7.1	19.8	5.9	0.5	7.8	1.1	65.6
Without negligence	853	72.4	64.5	16.0	2.7	5.3	1.8	9.7
All	1133	100	59.9	15.4	2.9	5.5	1.6	14.7

* Negligence was graded by case, as the average of the scores from the two reviews or the score from the single review when there was only one. Percentages do not correspond directly to numbers of events because of weighting.

Programs of quality assurance should strive to reduce rates of error to an optimal level. Because the cost of preventing adverse events entirely would be prohibitive, defining an optimal level requires a realistic assessment of the effectiveness of efforts to reduce their occurrence. In industry, an error rate that exceeds defined norms is deemed unacceptable. We believe that similar considerations should apply in medicine. For example, in the absence of evidence of negligence, a rate of wound infection of 1 percent in the primary repair of hernias may be acceptable, since it is well recognized that infections occasionally develop even with carefully executed operations, and trying to reduce their occurrence further would not be cost effective. However, even without evidence of negligence, if the infection rate for such operations exceeds 5 or 10 percent, it is reasonable to conclude that the aseptic precautions followed during the operation need review and improvement. Norms for acceptable levels of various adverse events need to be established. Hospitals can then target their quality-assurance activities to the areas most likely to respond to such efforts.

Risk Factors
An important step in reducing the incidence of adverse events is to identify the patients at highest risk. The number and variety of adverse events described in this study testify clearly to the diversity of hazards in modern medical care. In a typical hospitalization, a patient may have hundreds of encounters with doctors, nurses, hospital staff, and equipment. Unexpected results or errors can occur with each encounter, perhaps causing an adverse event.

Many factors increase the risk that a patient will have an adverse event during hospitalization. Our findings suggest that one major determinant is the complexity of the disease or treatment. If, as seems likely, every intervention carries some level of risk, patients with complicated disease are more likely to have adverse events, if only because their care requires more interventions. Thus, it is not surprising that nearly half the adverse events we identified resulted from operations. In even a simple operation there are dozens, even hundreds, of maneuvers, from skin preparation to wound closure, as well as many interventions in the postoperative care. Each presents an opportunity for an adverse event. Our findings are very similar to those of a California study in which half the potentially compensable events (comparable to what we have called adverse events) were found to result from treatment in the operating room.

The high number of drug-related adverse events in our study may also be related in part to the quantity and variety of medications administered to hospitalized patients. Characteristics of patients also increase the risk of an adverse event. Elderly patients, for example, are far more likely not only to have more complicated disease, but also to have underlying degenerative conditions that increase the risk of such nontechnical postoperative complications as myocardial infarction, pulmonary embolism, and pneumonia. Insults or errors that are tolerated well by children or young healthy adults can be lethal in patients who are weakened by disease or who have impaired vital organs. In addition, elderly patients are at increased risk of falling and therefore of hip fractures.

Another factor that may account for the increased rate of adverse events in the elderly is the presence of coexisting conditions. Greenfield has shown that such conditions are a strong predictor of serious hospital complications (such as pulmonary embolism, septicemia, or stroke after hip surgery). Patients with severe coexisting conditions on admission are more than seven times as likely to have a complication as those without such conditions (Greenfield S, Apolone G, McNeil BJ, Cleary PD: personal communication).

Yet another risk factor is the location where care is provided. The high rate of negligence in adverse events resulting from treatment in the emergency room could be caused by several factors. Because no operations and only a few procedures are performed in the emergency room, the adverse events we identified that occurred there were more likely to involve diagnostic errors or mishaps of noninvasive treatment, which the reviewers frequently judged as negligent. Emergency rooms are sometimes staffed with part-time physicians who are not well trained in emergency care. Because they are frequently very busy, these physicians have less time to spend with each patient. Finally, some of the sickest patients enter the hospital through the emergency room.

Our experience is not unique. Dearden and Rutherford found that for 58 percent of patients with severe trauma treated in the emergency room there had been serious errors in treatment [(1985) T6 Injury 249]. Although many of these errors involved mistakes or delays in diagnosis, most were errors in treatment. The risk of error was increased with certain characteristics of the patient, such as alcoholism and the presence of multiple injuries, but the investigators concluded that the treating physician's inexperience was the chief cause of the high rate of error.

Finally, we believe that the risk of injury, particularly serious injury, is closely related to the medical nature of the intervention. A momentary lapse that delays the diagnosis of a skin rash is usually of little consequence, for example, whereas a similar lapse during a brain operation can have disastrous effects. It is unlikely that neurosurgeons are more prone to error than dermatologists, but the conditions under which they work are far less forgiving. As we have seen, certain specialties, such as thoracic surgery, obstetrics, and neurosurgery, had more adverse events than other specialties, but the events were not more likely to have been caused by negligence.

Limitations of the Study
Our observations and conclusions must be interpreted within the limitations of a retrospective review of records. Several features of the study could have biased the results. First, we relied exclusively on data from hospital records. Although we have shown that adverse events can be identified accurately from information in hospital records, such records may not provide evidence or insight into the specific causes of an adverse event. For example, in some of our study patients, the adverse event was caused by failure to diagnose an ectopic pregnancy. From the information in most hospital records, it would not be possible to tell whether such failures occurred because the physician (1) did not think of the diagnosis, (2) considered the diagnosis unlikely and therefore did no further follow-up examinations or testing, or (3) considered the diagnosis possible and recommended further testing, but the patient did not come for the test (in which case the outcome would not have been considered an adverse event). Nor can we tell whether (4) both the physician and the patient sought the test, but the equipment was broken (or overbooked, unavailable on weekends, or the like), (5) the examination was performed but the results were not reported, or (6) any one of many other possible problems arose that can be imagined.

Second, we relied on implicit, not explicit, review. Because we studied the entire range of medical services, it was not possible to set up explicit criteria for every conceivable type of adverse event. Accordingly, we relied on the judgments of physicians. To minimize variability therein, we structured the record-review process by means of an Adverse Event Analysis Form, which required the reviewers to conduct their analysis in a standardized way and to address specific questions about causation.

Third, we used general internists and surgeons as physician-reviewers, not specialists. For a study of this scope and magnitude, it would have been both difficult and expensive to do otherwise, since the reviewers were required to identify adverse events of all types. In our pilot study, we found that internists and surgeons could identify adverse events with a high degree of accuracy. As they had been instructed to do, the reviewers consulted with a panel of specialists when they needed to determine whether the care that had resulted in a possible adverse event met accepted standards.

Finally, our information on the follow-up of the patients was limited to data about care in the hospital (including the outpatient department). Although the reviewers had available the record of care provided at the same hospital after the index hospitalization, they had no access to the information in physicians' private offices. However, except for those that are rapidly fatal, adverse events not requiring hospital care are unlikely to result in serious disability.

Prevention of Adverse Events
As knowledge increases, in theory more adverse events will become preventable. Indeed, the safety and effectiveness of many current medical treatments result from the earlier reduction or elimination of complications similar or identical to those we have identified as adverse events here: high rates of heart block, bleeding, and mortality in the early years of heart surgery, problems associated with the initial attempts at organ transplantation, side effects of many drugs, and so forth. These were the adverse events of an earlier day, and they were greatly reduced in frequency after research led to an understanding of their causes.

Future reductions in the occurrence of adverse events also depend in part on research into causes. In the case of adverse events that are currently unpreventable, progress will come from scientific advances, such as the development of less hazardous chemotherapeutic agents. In the case of events due to error, control will require scientific advances in some instances, but we believe that progress will also depend heavily on systems analysis education, and the development and dissemination of guidelines and standards for practice. Automatic 'fail-safe' systems – such as a computerized system that makes it impossible to order or dispense a drug to a patient with a known sensitivity – are likely to have an increasing role.

The reduction of adverse events involving negligence will also require an increased emphasis on education. To the extent that failure to meet the standard of practice is due to ignorance, improved dissemination and enforcement of practice guidelines might be effective. The development of better mechanisms of identifying negligent behavior and instituting appropriate corrective or disciplinary action is equally important.

Preventing medical injury will require attention to the systemic causes and consequences of errors, an effort that goes well beyond identifying culpable persons. Such approaches have paid off handsomely in other highly technical and complicated enterprises, such as aviation. A similar strategy may work in medicine as well.

In this context, our description of adverse events represents an agenda for research on quality of care. Adverse events result from the interaction of the patient, the patient's disease, and a complicated, highly technical system of medical care provided not only by a diverse group of doctors, other care givers, and support personnel, but also by a medical-industrial system that supplies drugs and equipment. Reducing the risk of adverse events requires an examination of all these factors as well as of their relation with each other.

'Relation Between Malpractice Claims and Adverse Events Due to Negligence' (1991) 325 N Eng J Med 45

The frequency of malpractice claims among patients injured by medical negligence has been the subject of much speculation and little empirical investigation. Two fundamental questions about malpractice litigation have been how well it compensates patients who are actually harmed by medical negligence, and whether it promotes quality and penalizes substandard care. If negligent medical care infrequently leads to professional censure or a malpractice claim, then the deterrence of substandard care may be suboptimal and the civil justice system will compensate few patients for their medical injuries. If, as some allege, sizable numbers of malpractice claims are filed for medical care that is not negligence, then the costs of claims may be excessive, and the credibility and legitimacy of malpractice litigation as a means of obtaining civil justice may be reduced. . . .

Discussion

Other studies have examined the frequency of negligence in relation to the total number of claims. Our study has taken the next step by matching individual clinical records with individual claims records to determine what fraction of instances of negligence leads to claims. Our data suggest that the number of patients in New York State who have serious, disabling injuries each year as a result of clearly negligent medical care but who do not file claims (5400) exceeds the number of patients making malpractice claims (3570). Perhaps half the claimants will eventually receive compensation.

Why so few injured patients file claims has not been widely researched. Many may receive adequate health or disability insurance benefits and may not wish to spoil longstanding physician-patient relationships. Others may regard their injuries as minor, consider the small chance of success not worth the cost, or find attorneys repugnant. Trial lawyers usually accept only the relatively few cases that have a high probability of resulting in a judgment of negligence with an award large enough to defray the high costs of litigation. A final possible explanation is that many patients may fail to recognize negligent care.

Our results also raise questions about whether malpractice litigation promotes high quality in medical care. Historically, there has been scant empirical analysis of this issue. Our data reflect a tenuous relation between proscribed activity and penalty and thus are consistent with the view that malpractice claims provide only a crude means of identifying and remedying specific problems in the provision of health care. Our findings also support recent comments about the limited usefulness of the rate of claims as an indicator of the quality of care. Unless there is a strong association between the frequency of claims and that of negligence, the rate of claims alone will be a poor indicator of quality because rates can easily vary widely at the same underlying frequency of negligence or adverse events. The filing of a claim could, however, signal a need for further investigation because of the likelihood that an actual adverse event or actual negligence prompted the complaint.

Our study differs from previous work in that it goes beyond statements about the rate of negligence in relation to the rate of malpractice claims. The relative frequency 7.6 to 1 does not mean, as is commonly assumed, that 13 to 14 percent of injuries due to negligence lead to claims. As the linking of the medical-record reviews to the OPMC [Office of Professional Medical Conduct, New York Department of Health] claims files has shown, the fraction of medical negligence that leads to claims is probably under 2 percent. The difference is accounted for by injuries not caused by negligence, as defined by our protocol, that give rise to claims.

This finding does not mean that the 39 cases of claims in which our physician-reviewers did not find evidence of an adverse event due to negligence are groundless under prevailing malpractice law. Our study was not designed to evaluate the merits of individual claims. Patients sometimes file claims regarding medical outcomes that do not qualify as adverse events by our definitions; without access to the full insurance records, we cannot assess the prospects of individual cases.

More generally, the process of and criteria for making decisions about causation and negligence differ in a scientific study and in civil litigation. In this study, majority rule determined whether there had been an adverse event or an adverse event due to negligence. Our reviewers sometimes disagreed about causation and negligence; when only one found negligence, the case did not qualify as an adverse event due to negligence (except in the rare case when there was only a single reviewer). In a lawsuit, a single expert opinion might be sufficient to support a finding of negligence; under our protocol it would not. When experts differ, the final judgment is especially sensitive to the process of decision making. Thus, our findings are not directly comparable to the results of civil litigation.

Although this lack of strict comparability should warn us against drawing conclusions about the merits of individual malpractice claims, it does not undermine our findings about the small probability (under 2 percent) that a claim would be filed when medical negligence caused injury to the patient. . . .

The results of this study, in which malpractice claims were matched to inpatient medical records, demonstrate that the civil-justice system only infrequently compensates injured patients and rarely identifies and holds health care providers accountable for substandard medical care. Although malpractice litigation may fulfill its social objectives crudely, support for its preservation persists in part because of the perception that other methods of ensuring a high quality of care and redressing patients' grievances have proved to be inadequate. The abandonment of malpractice litigation is unlikely unless credible systems and procedures, supported by the public, are instituted to guarantee professional accountability to patients.

What we have seen in the United States is the appearance of a significant body of data which for the first time allows conclusions to be drawn about the medical malpractice system. Secondly, a wide range of possible responses have been put in place, none of which could be described as radical, and few of which do anything other than tinker with the existing systems (but note the Virginia Birth-Related Neurological Injury Compensation Act creating a no-fault system for obstetric mishaps: discussed by Duff (1990) 27 Harvard Journal of Legislation 391).

Turning now to Britain, the first point to notice is the absence of data of the range and depth collected by the Harvard Study which is so essential for any analysis and future proposals for change. Arguably, however, there has at least been a change of attitude, as pointed out by Arnold Simanowitz in 'Medical Accidents: The Problem and the Challenge' in *Medicine in Contemporary Society: King's College Studies 1986-7* (ed P Byrne).

. . . I do not believe that the number of accidents taking place proportionate to the number of patients treated, has increased (although the truth of the matter is that there are no statistics available which could demonstrate this or the contrary). It is simply that, thanks in part to the activity of AVMA [Action for the Victims of Medical Accidents], the public has become more aware of its right to complain about inferior medical attention and to seek compensation for negligence from health carers in the same way as it does from any other body or person that is guilty of negligence. As a result, doctors, to quote Dr Maurice Burroughs, the Chairman of the BMA working party, 'are increasingly worried about the rising number of complaints and negligence claims against them' and we often hear how anxious they are about the steep rise in their insurance premiums which in 1986 were increased to £576 a year. In other words, to the cynic it may seem that the impetus for the scheme [of no fault compensation] on the part of the BMA comes primarily not because of concern for the patient but because of concern for the position of their members. This is hardly the best basis for the introduction of 'no fault' compensation.

It is more surprising that the community health councils should have become involved in this aspect of the problem of medical accidents. They, as much as AVMA, will be aware that the vast majority of the victims of medical accidents do not initially seek financial compensation but want an explanation for what went wrong, sympathetic treatment and, if appropriate, an apology. They, as much as AVMA, will be aware how much the attitude of the health carers, when an accident takes place, is the cause of the distress to victims and their families; they as much as AVMA will be aware of the lack of accountability of doctors insofar as accidents are concerned. These major problems will not be solved by a 'no fault' compensation system. Indeed, the last mentioned will be exacerbated, not cured, by the introduction of such a system. It seems that they have made the same mistake as doctors, if for different reasons. They have assumed that the urgent problems which beset the issue of medical accidents can only be overcome by a 'no fault' system and without further investigation have decided to push for it.

There are, in my view, a number of major reasons why the BMA and patients' organisations such as ACHCEW are putting all their energies into pressing for a 'no fault' compensation scheme. One is the lack of information about the problem of medical accidents itself. It is quite extraordinary that two responsible bodies should be proposing a complex and expensive solution to a problem when they do not have the faintest idea what the size and nature of that problem is. Nobody knows how many medical accidents occur in Britain each year, what their distribution is, or what the nature of the accidents are. The DHSS refuses to keep statistics of medical accidents separately from ordinary accidents (see the reply from the Solicitor General to John Tilley MP, 7th May 1981: 'I regret that this information is not collected and could not be made available except at unacceptable expense'). There is no obligation on health authorities to keep or pool statistics. Even the doctors' defence organisations, the Medical Defence Union, the Medical and Dental Defence Union of Scotland and the Medical Protection Society, who do at least have statistics of doctors who consult them when they believe that they may have been involved in an accident, refuse to publish even that only partly helpful figure. The *British Medical Journal* in a recent editorial recognised that there is a need in Britain for a formal study of how many people are injured by medical treatment.

As regards the collection of data a study led by Professor Hazel Genn may, when completed, meet this need.

Notwithstanding the absence of data some minor initiatives have been taken. In 1991 the Department of Health published a discussion paper, *Arbitration for Medical Negligence in the National Health Service*. Not surprisingly, given its content it commanded little support. Michael Jones offers the following discussion and critique of it.

M Jones 'Arbitration for Medical Claims in the NHS' (1992) 8 Professional Negligence 142

During the second reading of the NHS (Compensation) Bill on 1 February 1991 the Secretary of State announced that the Department of Health would look into the possibility of introducing a system of arbitration for civil claims for medical negligence in the NHS. A consultation document was subsequently issued setting out the bare bones of a proposed scheme. The document did not invite proposals for changes to the present system. It was concerned with establishing the feasibility and desirability of a voluntary system of arbitration for medical negligence actions in the NHS, which would supplement, not replace, the tort system. . . .

The proposals
Any reference to arbitration would be voluntary. It would depend on the agreement of both parties. There would be a panel of three, comprising two doctors, one nominated by each party, and a lawyer skilled in medical negligence work and agreed to by both parties, to provide arbitration within the general framework of the Arbitration Acts. The panel would work on paper, having access to case notes, hospital records and any statements, medical reports and written submissions that the parties chose to submit. Oral evidence would not normally be taken.

The arbitration panel would apply the same test of negligence as the courts, namely the *Bolam* test, and the measure of damages would be determined in accordance with ordinary common law principles. There would be no artificial limit on the size of awards, which if both parties agreed could take the form of a structured settlement. Causation, which can be extremely difficult to establish in a medical negligence action, would also be determined applying common law principles. If the arbitrators were not unanimous the majority view would prevail, although 'on points of law the legal member's view would carry greater weight'. There would be no appeal, except on a point of law.

The consultation document asserts, rather blithely, that since arbitration would be based on paper 'legal representation would not be necessary, but legal assistance in the preparation of a case would be desirable'. On this approach advice and assistance under the Green Form scheme would be available (to those who qualify) for plaintiffs resorting to arbitration, but full Legal Aid would not be available. The consultation paper assumes that the normal rules for an arbitration would apply; in particular that the costs of administering the arbitration would fall on the parties, and the arbitrator would have the power to order the unsuccessful party to reimburse the winner for his share of the costs of arbitration.

The scheme would allow for reference to arbitration early in the litigation process, i.e. as soon as an allegation of negligence is made, or later in the proceedings after full medical and legal advice had been obtained and witness statements exchanged, but prior to commencement of full trial.

The crucial question, on which comments were invited, was whether, for a substantial number of cases that might otherwise be litigated, arbitration would be a more attractive alternative in terms of resolving disputes more quickly at lower cost. Moreover, given that cases of medical negligence can be complex on the issues of both breach and causation, would there be significant numbers of cases that could be dealt with by experts looking at the papers without taking oral evidence or cross-examining witnesses?

Would arbitration work?

The question of whether an arbitration scheme would 'work' turns on what advantages the scheme would have over the present tort system. The disadvantages of the current arrangements for bringing claims through the courts can be considered under at least five heads: delay; expense; access; entitlement; and damages.

Delay

Delay appears to be endemic in the adversarial system. The most recent estimate put the average time from accident to trial at over five years in the High Court and almost three years in the County Court. Delay in medical negligence cases tends to be greater, on average, than in other types of personal injuries action, and individual cases of over ten years' duration are not unknown. Although there have been a number of procedural reforms in recent years, following the Civil Justice Review, designed to speed up the process of litigation, it remains to be seen how effective these changes have been.

In theory, an arbitration scheme should reduce the time required to deal with a claim since 'administrative' dispute resolution mechanisms tend to be quicker than the judicial system. Much would depend upon the detail of the scheme and the approach taken by the arbitration panels. On the other hand, the parties would still have to prepare a detailed written case for submission to the panel, and it is the preparation of the case that takes most of the time involved in litigation. The only obvious point at which time would be saved is the hearing itself, where oral evidence and argument would not normally be permitted.

Expense

The cost of bringing an action for negligence is notoriously high, at least in relation to the sums recovered in damages. . . . The Pearson Commission put the administrative costs of the tort system at 85 per cent of the amounts paid in damages, whereas the cost of running the social security system came to 11 per cent of the total paid out. The *Civil Justice Review* estimated that legal costs alone amounted to up to 75 per cent of the sums recovered in the High Court and up to 175 per cent of the sums recovered in the County Court. By any measure this is not an efficient method of securing compensation for accident victims.

Arbitration would probably be cheaper, but the crucial question is by how much? The costs of a trial would be saved by cutting out an oral hearing, saving the expense of paying lawyers and witnesses for the hearing itself, but if a comparable effort goes into preparing the case for arbitration as for a trial the costs of preparation would not be reduced. Moreover, if, as the consultation document states, over 95 per cent of medical negligence cases are settled out of court, the savings in the cost of a trial will apply only to a comparatively small number of cases.

A crucial question under the arbitration proposals is who would pay for the costs of preparing for the arbitration, since the scheme contemplates that Legal Aid would not be available for plaintiffs, though Green Form advice and assistance would be available for plaintiffs who are financially eligible. This would be a serious drawback, since there would be no financial advantage to a plaintiff who currently qualifies for Legal Aid to opt for arbitration. Indeed, there would be a disadvantage because not only would financial assistance be limited to the Green Form scheme, but more importantly the plaintiff would be at risk on costs should the claim be rejected by the arbitration panel. A Legally Aided plaintiff whose action fails is not at risk of having to pay the defendant's costs, since costs are not normally awarded against a party who is Legally Aided, and even if, exceptionally, an order for costs against the Legal Aid fund is made, the plaintiff's risk is limited to the extent of his contribution.

Access

The cost of bringing an action excludes large numbers of people from pursuing otherwise legitimate claims for negligence, because financial restrictions on eligibility for civil Legal Aid mean that in practice only the poorest individuals qualify for assistance, and only the rich or the foolhardy are willing to accept the financial risk which bringing an action entails. This severely curtails access to the legal system by injured patients who may have perfectly valid claims for compensation but are simply financially unwilling to put all their personal assets at risk if, ultimately, they are unable to prove fault or causation.

It is doubtful whether arbitration would improve access. It may help those who presently do not qualify for Legal Aid but who might be willing to risk the lower cost of arbitration, though they are unwilling to risk the high costs of going to court. Even this, however, is questionable, since the substantial costs of preparing the case would still have to be met, and the plaintiff whose claim is unsuccessful would still face the risk of having to pay the defendant's costs.

Entitlement

Success in the tort of negligence depends upon proof of both fault and causation, which are particularly difficult to establish in cases of medical negligence. . . .

There is nothing in the arbitration proposals that would deal with this problem. The same rules of law requiring proof of fault and causation would apply. Arbitration does not attempt to solve the substantive problems facing injured patients; it is concerned almost exclusively with the procedural issues of cost and delay.

Damages

The fact that damages are awarded as a lump sum, notwithstanding the possibility of claims for provisional damages, means that if the plaintiff's circumstances change it is not possible to adjust the award. This can result in either over-compensation or under-compensation. Critics of the system point to cases where plaintiffs who have been awarded large sums have died earlier than expected, with a resultant windfall to the plaintiff's estate. But this can also work the other way, with damages 'running out' before the plaintiff dies. Further problems arise from the difficulty that plaintiffs experience in establishing liability, in that they will settle claims for considerably less than they would recover in court, because of the risk of losing the action at trial. Again, since the arbitration panels would assess damages on the same basis as the courts these problems would not be touched by the proposed scheme.

Unanswered questions

In addition to the substantive question of whether such an arbitration scheme could reduce both costs and delay in a significant number of cases, the consultation document identified a number of further issues that would have to be resolved.

1. *Should there be lists of suitably qualified people to which the parties could refer in selecting members of the tribunal?*

Well, why not?

2. *Who would provide the administrative support for the arbitration panel? There would be a need for accommodation and secretarial support, for example. Could this be done on health authority premises when plaintiffs are in dispute with the health authority?*

There is an obvious danger that patients may not see an arbitration panel which receives administrative support from a health authority as being a sufficiently independent body.

3. *What information should be provided to plaintiffs to protect their interests, and how could plaintiffs get help in the preparation and submission of evidence?*

This is a lawyer's job. An analogy could be drawn here with industrial tribunals which were originally intended to provide a cheap, informal system for dealing with employment disputes. They are now highly technical, applying a substantial body of law, and success rates for employees who are not legally represented are much lower than when an employee does have legal representation.

4. How should the arbitration panel be financed? Members of panels (doctors and lawyers) would require payment. The normal rule in arbitrations is that the parties bear the costs, with the arbitrator having power to order the unsuccessful party to bear all the costs. Possibly 'plaintiffs should be required to pay a deposit towards the costs of arbitration pending a decision by the panel on the allocation of costs?'

This is a vital issue. Most plaintiffs who bring actions for medical negligence are probably financed by Legal Aid. There is virtually no financial advantage to a plaintiff who qualifies for Legal Aid agreeing to submit a claim to arbitration. Making the parties pay the costs of the arbitration in addition to the costs of preparing the case would be a further disincentive. Requiring plaintiffs to pay a deposit towards the costs at the outset seems positively designed to discourage plaintiffs from resorting to this form of dispute resolution.

5. Should panels have to give reasons for the decision? Under current legislation arbitrators are not obliged to give the basis for their decisions unless required to do so at the outset by the parties or required by the courts. Should a majority decision be identified as such? Should decisions be published?

Without reasons the parties can never know whether they have grounds for an appeal.

6. There would be no appeal to the courts except on a point of law, otherwise some of the benefits of arbitration would be removed if disputed decisions had to be referred for a subsequent hearing in the courts. This leaves the question of whether there should be an appeals mechanism within the arbitration scheme itself.

A restriction on appeals to the courts is probably sensible, given the objectives of the proposed scheme, but this makes it more desirable that there should be an appeals mechanism within the scheme. Patients who suffer a medical accident often feel that they have been badly let down by the medical profession, and a sense of grievance could be exacerbated without some method of reviewing the decisions of arbitration panels, which would not necessarily be infallible.

7. At what stage should a plaintiff be required to elect for arbitration? At the outset or after litigation has commenced, but before trial?

If a plaintiff was able to elect for arbitration at any stage this might reduce the problem of the Legally Aided plaintiff who has no financial incentive to opt for arbitration. The case could at least be fully prepared before opting for arbitration as a quicker mechanism for resolving the dispute. The problem of the allocation of costs would remain, however, with the plaintiff being at risk of losing the arbitration and then being required to pay the defendant's costs.

8. The courts pay special regard to the interests of children, requiring the approval of settlements, for example. Should arbitration be restricted to adult plaintiffs?

Awards of damages could be subject to the approval of the court, following the present practice in the case of settlements.

9. Should there be a power to compel the production of evidence? How much control over proceedings should a panel have?

The parties should have the same powers of discovery and production as in the courts, with full exchange of witness statements and reports. There is no advantage in a return to a system of 'forensic blind-man's-buff' which would only serve to lengthen proceedings and ultimately produce injustice.

10. Should there be a time limit for resorting to arbitration? What if a plaintiff fails to prosecute a claim or a defendant fails to defend? Should the panel have the power to strike out claims or make summary awards?

If one object of arbitration is to reduce delay, the panel must have the power to require the parties to act expeditiously, though recognising that sometimes there are perfectly legitimate reasons for delay. Presumably the provisions of the Limitation Act 1980 would apply to any delay by the plaintiff before the action is started.

Conclusions

It is not entirely clear what type of medical negligence claim the arbitration proposal is aimed at. Given that most medical negligence cases are currently funded by Legal Aid, it is not apparent why anyone who is eligible for Legal Aid would opt for arbitration, when they may then have to meet the costs of the arbitration themselves, and would be at risk on the defendant's costs. If the parties (both defendants and plaintiffs) are to bear the costs of the arbitration, the savings on legal representation at the hearing may not be particularly great. Under the present arrangements the administrative costs of the court system, judges and other officials, are met by the Lord Chancellor's Department, and are to a large extent free to litigants. In a difficult case Green Form advice may be insufficient to enable the patient to assemble a case: to collect the documentary evidence; set out the basis of the claim; instruct experts, etc. The assistance to claimants is potentially insufficient. In addition, the parties would lose the ability to cross-examine and test the evidence.

On the other hand, patients who are not eligible for Legal Aid may find some advantage in arbitration. It should theoretically be quicker and cheaper than using the courts; but plaintiffs will have to prepare the case up to the arbitration, and to the extent that they are unable to rely on legal advice the claim may be poorly prepared, and therefore less likely to succeed. If plaintiffs do use lawyers, the costs saved will, in practice, be the costs of a trial. Not all cases of medical negligence are complex, however, and not all involve large sums of money. Possibly arbitration does have a role to play here. But if the case is clear-cut, it would normally settle in any event; indeed 95 per cent of claims do settle. Arbitration might take some cases out of the courts system, it would possibly reduce defendants' costs, and it might, incidentally, reduce the overall Legal Aid bill if plaintiffs who are eligible for Legal Aid could be persuaded to opt for arbitration. It is easy to see why such a scheme would be attractive to a government looking to reduce the cost of medical malpractice litigation; it is more difficult to find the benefit to injured patients of a scheme which merely tinkers with the real problems of compensating the victims of medical accidents.

A second initiative which has bearing on medical malpractice was taken by the Lord Chancellor in 1992. He referred to the Law Commission the issue of the award of damages in personal injury claims. Inter alia his concern was to examine the possibility of legislation providing for structured settlements whereby damages are awarded by paying an initial lump sum to the plaintiff for past and immediate losses followed by periodic payments to cover future financial loss (see discussion in Allen (1988) 194 LQR 448; Lewis (1988) 15 Journal of Law and Society 392 and (1993) 56 MLR 844). Subsequently, the Law Commission published a paper setting out possible options for the future: see *supra*.

A third initiative, which ultimately failed, would have been the most far-reaching. Mrs Rosie Barnes MP introduced in January 1991 her National Health Service (Compensation) Bill which would have created a no-fault compensation scheme, somewhat similar to the New Zealand scheme but limited to medical injuries within the NHS. The Bill failed to get a second reading.

Chapter 7

Complaints and discipline

Introduction

In this chapter we are concerned with means, other than recourse to law, whereby doctors may be held accountable and the public interest served. Ham, Dingwall *et al* discuss other means of achieving professional accountability in their 1988 paper.

C Ham, R Dingwall, P Fenn and D Harris *Medical Negligence: Compensation and Accountability* (1988) (pp 16-17)

The issue of accountability lies at the heart of the criticisms voiced against tort law by organisations representing patients and their relatives. The argument advanced by these organisations is that doctors are accountable to patients only in a weak sense and that changes are needed to ensure that adequate explanations are given when things go wrong and that appropriate action is taken against the doctors concerned.

There are various ways of ensuring accountability apart from through the courts. The two most important are professional self-regulation and procedures for holding doctors to account to the public or the public's representatives. The UK has traditionally relied most heavily on self-regulation. Like all professional groups, doctors have argued that responsibility for setting and maintaining standards should lie with the profession. We have noted already that what is defined as reasonable care in a legal context is determined by doctors, and more generally doctors take it upon themselves to ensure that the quality of care provided is satisfactory. The medical defence societies contribute to this through their educational activities. These activities take a number of forms: published reports warning doctors of the risks associated with different aspects of clinical practice; films and tape/slide programmes; and seminars and lectures given by staff of the societies. The aim of these activities is to warn doctors of well-known pitfalls and to improve standards of care.

Medical audit
To the extent that the profession actively monitors standards it does so on an informal basis by means of medical audit and peer review. This involves doctors regularly assessing their practice in discussion with colleagues. In the main, initiatives for audit in the UK have been organised locally by the doctors in a hospital department or the general practitioners in a group practice. In addition, there are examples of more formal mechanisms which are part of a national interest in audit. These include the Health Advisory Service, the National Development Team for Mentally Handicapped People, the Confidential Enquiry into Maternal Deaths, and the Confidential Enquiry into Peri-operative Deaths. All of these mechanisms involve an element of independent professional assessment of standards.

Despite the interest shown in audit both locally and nationally, Sir Raymond Hoffenberg has argued that the medical profession has shown considerable resistance to the concept of audit [R Hoffenberg *Clinical Freedom* (1987)]. Hoffenberg contends that the profession should welcome greater scrutiny of clinical competence, for only in this way will public confidence be maintained and the threat of external regulation avoided.

The General Medical Council
The accountability of doctors to the public is discharged principally through the various procedures that exist for handling complaints. Doctors are closely involved in these

procedures, most obviously in the case of the GMC. The GMC is an independent statutory body charged with maintaining a register of doctors, overseeing medical education, and handling disciplinary matters. The GMC is made up mainly of doctors and it investigates allegations of serious professional misconduct. Approximately 1,000 complaints are handled each year and these arise from criminal convictions as well as from the public and the professions. The complaints considered by the GMC include matters of professional etiquette such as advertising and the abuse of personal relationships with patients (for example, entering into a sexual relationship) as well as the neglect by doctors of their professional responsibilities to patients. It is that last category of complaints that includes examples of medical negligence.

Complaints are carefully screened and in the vast majority of cases the Council decides that no question of serious professional misconduct arises and hence no action is taken. Investigation of the remaining cases may result in a letter of advice or admonition to the doctor concerned, or reference to the professional conduct committee. This committee considers approximately five per cent of all cases received by the Council. Approximately one-third of these cases concern the professional responsibilities and clinical competence of doctors. The committee operates like a court and can impose a range of penalties, including in extreme cases striking a doctor off the register. A recent analysis of the work of the GMC concluded that, in comparison with Sweden and the United States, the Council's disciplinary procedures exhibited 'an extraordinary degree of control' by doctors themselves of professional conduct [M Rosenthal *Dealing with Medicine* (1987)].

Complaints

Apart from the GMC, separate arrangements exist for handling complaints in the hospital and community health services and the family practitioner services. The detail of these arrangements is complex but the basic principles are as follows. In the case of family practitioner services, complaints about breach of contract are heard by service committees of family practitioner committees. These usually comprise three lay members, three medical members and a lay chairman. A complaint normally has to be made within eight weeks of the event which gave rise to it (soon to be extended to 13 weeks). The remit of service committees is limited to breach of terms of service and excludes criticism of a doctor's manner or matters such as the efficiency of appointments systems.

In a study conducted in the early 1970s, Klein found that the most common types of complaint concerned failure to treat a patient in an emergency, failure to provide a proper surgery, failure of deputising services, and improper demands for fees [R E Klein *Complaints Against Doctors* (1973)]. Complaints involving the clinical judgment of GPs were also considered by service committees but these were in a minority. In the case of complaints about clinical judgment, Klein found that service committees relied heavily on the assessment of their medical members in determining whether doctors were in breach of their duty to provide proper and necessary treatment.

It is worth noting that the number of formal complaints against family practitioners, including GPs, is small: in 1983, 1,313 complaints were investigated in England and practitioners were found to be in breach of their contracts in 341 cases (26 per cent). In the same year, there were around 190 million consultations with family doctors and 30 million courses of dental treatment. . . .

Complaints concerning hospital and community health services are investigated by health authorities following procedures set out in circular HC(88) 37. Again, the number of written complaints received is small: 25,336 in relation to hospital services in 1985 in England, or around 3.5 complaints for every 1,000 in-patient and day cases. In the same year, 3,649 written complaints were received concerning community services (DHSS, personal communication).

Complaints about clinical judgment

Special procedures exist for handling hospital complaints in which issues of clinical judgment arise. These procedures involve the consultant in charge of the case initially investigating the complaint and seeking to satisfy the complainant. If this fails, the complaint is referred to the regional medical officer who may ask for an independent professional review to be conducted by two senior doctors. This is invoked in the case of serious complaints only and is intended as an alternative to legal action. A review conducted by regional medical officers early in 1984 . . . indicated that the officers involved believed they were providing a useful service to complainants but various proposals were made for speeding up and improving the procedures.

The procedures for handling complaints concerning clinical judgment are particularly relevant to our interests. This is because a major concern of the committees and organisations that have analysed these procedures in recent years has been to create a system which satisfies complainants who have the option of taking a case to court but who choose not to do so. It can be argued that if an adequate system can be devised for handling complaints concerning clinical judgments then patients and their relatives will be less likely to pursue a legal remedy. Against this, organisations representing the medical profession have argued that the option of taking a case to court should preclude other methods of independent review.

In addressing this question, the Davies Committee [Davies Committee *Report of the Committee on Hospital Complaints* (1973)] proposed the establishment of investigating panels of professional and lay members to conduct investigations into hospital complaints concerning clinical judgment. This proposal was not acceptable to the profession and was not implemented. A different stance was taken by the Select Committee on the Parliamentary Commissioner for Administration [Select Committee on the Parliamentary Commissioner for Administration (1977), Independent Review of Hospital Complaints in the NHS] which argued that the Health Service Commissioner or Ombudsman should be empowered to look into clinical complaints as well as other complaints incapable of being resolved by a health authority. This too was unacceptable to the profession.

Following lengthy neogotiations, the government secured the agreement of doctors to introduce in 1981 the procedures described above. These procedures place responsibility for investigating complaints about clinical judgment firmly in the hands of the profession and do not provide for the sort of lay and independent involvement envisaged by the Davies Committee and the Select Committee. The reason for this is the reluctance of the profession to relinquish control over the handling of complaints. This reluctance stems from the perceived threat to clinical freedom and the risk of double jeopardy if patients decide to go to court after using the independent review process. In fact, the evidence suggests that few complainants do initiate legal action following independent professional reviews. An analysis of complaints dealt with in this way between 1981 and 1983 found that in only 3 out of 94 completed inquiries was a civil action for damages started . . .

The Health Service Commissioner
The only other source of redress available to patients is the Health Service Commissioner. However, the Commissioner's remit is limited to complaints concerning injustice or hardship suffered by members of the public as a result of a failure in a service provided by a health authority or a failure of an authority to provide a service which it was its duty to provide. Cases outside the Commissioner's jurisdiction include those involving clinical judgment and cases where legal action is proposed. As Table 5 shows, there has been a steady increase in the number of complaints received by the Commissioner but many of these complaints are either rejected or referred back. The largest category of rejected cases (30 per cent in 1986-7) are those involving clinical judgment.

Table 5.
Health Service Commissioner Analysis of Activity 1977-1986. England

Year	Complaints Received	Rejected or Discontinued	Referred Back	Results Reports Issued
1977/78	494	267	59	94
1978/79	590	426	67	101
1979/80	484	334	58	90
1980/81	556	398	83	98
1981/82	586	419	95	89
1982/83	658	460	96	101
1983/84	770	520	145	96
1984/85	711	387	195	104
1985/86	807	407	238	116

Source: DHSS 1986

[See also M Stacey 'Medical Accountability: A Background Paper' in *Challenges in Medical Care* A Grubb (ed) (1992) 109-121.]

Let us now turn to examine some of these mechanisms referred to by Ham, Dingwall *et al* in greater detail.

The General Medical Council

First we must concern ourselves with what is perhaps the most important mechanism dealing with complaints and discipline that exists. The General Medical Council has, as we have seen, disciplinary powers over all registered medical practitioners.

The General Medical Council's powers are set out in section 36 of the Medical Act 1983.

> **36.**– (1) where a fully registered person–
> (a) is found by the Professional Conduct Committee to have been convicted in the British Islands of a criminal offence, whether while so registered or not; or
> (b) is judged by the Professional Conduct Committee to have been guilty of serious professional misconduct, whether while so registered or not;
> the Committee may, if they think fit, direct–
> (i) that his name shall be erased from the register;
> (ii) that his registration in the register shall be suspended (that is to say, shall not have effect) during such period not exceeding twelve months as may be specified in the direction; or
> (iii) that his registration shall be conditional on his compliance, during such period not exceeding three years as may be specified in the direction, with such requirements so specified as the Committee thinks fit to impose for the protection of members of the public or in his interests.

It will be seen that the GMC's powers in this regard are performed by the Professional Conduct Committee (PCC). In the so-called 'Blue Book' (*Professional Conduct and Discipline: Fitness to Practise* (January 1993)), the GMC explains the position of the PCC and the procedure at hearings before it (paragraphs 9-30):

> 9. The Professional Conduct Committee is elected anually by the Council and consists of 32 members, of whom only 11 sit on any case. Of the 32 members, 18 are elected members of the Council and six are lay members. The Committee normally sits in public and its procedure is closely akin to that of a court of law. Witnesses may be subpoenaed and evidence is given on oath. Doctors who appear before the Committee may be, and usually are, legally represented.
> 10. The Preliminary Proceedings Committee consists of 11 members, and is also elected annually. It sits in private and on the basis of written evidence and submissions determines which cases should be referred for inquiry by the Professional Conduct Committee. It may also refer cases to the Health Committee. . . . [A procedure for dealing with 'doctors impaired by physical or mental illness'.]
> 11. The Professional Conduct and Preliminary Proceedings Committees are advised on questions of law by a Legal Assessor, who is usually a Queen's Counsel and must be a barrister, advocate or solicitor of not less than ten years' standing.
>
> *Rules of procedure*
> 12. The proceedings of the Professional Conduct and Preliminary Proceedings Committees are governed by rules of procedure made by the Council after consultation with both representative medical organisations and bodies representing patients, and approved by the Privy Council. The current rules were made in 1988 and are printed by HM Stationery Office as Statutory Instrument 1988 No. 2255. Other rules govern the functions of the Legal Assessor and the procedure for appeals to the Judicial Committee of the Privy Council.
>
> *Proceedings: the preliminary stages*
> 13. Cases giving rise to proceedings by the Preliminary Proceedings Committee or the Professional Conduct Committee are of two kinds – those arising from a conviction of a doctor in the courts and those where a doctor is alleged to have done something which

amounts to serious professional misconduct. In either kind of case the Council acts only when relevant matters have been brought to its notice.

14. Convictions of doctors are normally reported to the Council by the police. Unless the conviction is of a minor motoring or other trivial offence it is normally referred to the Preliminary Proceedings Committee.

15. Information or complaints concerning behaviour which may be regarded as serious professional misconduct reach the Council from a number of sources. Frequently they concern matters which have already been investigated through some other procedure – for example a Medical Service Committee, or a Committee of Inquiry in the hospital service. Information or complaints received from individual doctors or members of the public, as distinct from public authorities, must be supported by evidence of the facts alleged in the form of one or more affidavits or statutory declarations made in a prescribed form before a Commissioner for Oaths or a Justice of the Peace.

16. Every complaint or item of information received is scrutinised meticulously. Only a very small proportion are both found to relate to matters which could be regarded as raising a question of serious professional misconduct and also supported, or capable of being supported, by adequate evidence. Where it appears from the allegations made that a question of serious professional misconduct may arise but the evidence initially received is insufficient or does not comply with the Rules, the Council's Solicitor may be asked to make inquiries to establish the facts. A decision whether action shall be taken on an allegation of serious professional misconduct is then taken by the President or by another member of the Council appointed for the purpose. A decision not to proceed, for example, because the matter does not raise a question of serious professional misconduct, is taken only after consultation between the President (or the Medical member of the Council) and a lay member appointed to assist in the screening of cases. In a case where it is decided to proceed the doctor is informed of the allegations and is invited to submit a written explanation which may include evidence in answer to the allegations. Any such explanation is placed before the Preliminary Proceedings Committee when it considers the case.

Powers of the Preliminary Proceedings Committee: warning letters and letters of advice
17. After considering a case of conviction or of alleged serious professional misconduct the Preliminary Proceedings Committee may decide either:
(a)   to refer the case to the Professional Conduct Committee for inquiry; or
(b)   to send the doctor a letter; or
(c)   to take no further action.

18. Many cases considered by the Preliminary Proceedings Committee are disposed of by a warning letter or a letter of advice – for example cases where a doctor has been convicted for the first time of driving a motor car when under the influence of drink, or of shoplifting, or cases where a doctor's professional conduct appears to have fallen below the proper standard but not to have been so serious as to necessitate a public inquiry.

19. If on considering a conviction, or allegations of serious professional misconduct, it appears to the Preliminary Proceedings Committee that the doctor's fitness to practise may be seriously impaired by a physical or mental condition, the Committee may refer the case to the Health Committee instead of the Professional Conduct Committee.

20. If the Preliminary Proceedings Committee decides to refer a case either to the Professional Conduct Committee or to the Health Committee, it may make an order for the interim suspension of the doctor's registration or for interim conditional registration if it is satisfied that this is necessary for the protection of members of the public or is in the doctor's own interests. Such orders may be made for a period not exceeding two months and are intended to be effective only until the case has been considered by the Professional Conduct Committee or by the Health Committee. No such order can be made unless the doctor has been offered an opportunity of appearing before the Preliminary Proceedings Committee and being heard on the question whether such an order should be made. For this purpose the doctor may be legally represented.

Inquiries before the Professional Conduct Committee
21. As already mentioned, the Professional Conduct Committee is bound to accept the fact that a doctor has been convicted as conclusive evidence that he was guilty of the offence of which he was convicted. Provided therefore that a doctor admits a conviction, proceedings in cases of conviction are concerned only to establish the gravity of the offence and to take due account of any mitigating circumstances. In cases of conduct however the allegations, unless admitted by the doctor, must be *strictly proved by evidence*, and the doctor is free to dispute and rebut the evidence called. If facts alleged in a conduct charge are found by the

Committee to have been proved, the Committee must subsequently determine whether, in relation to those facts, the doctor has been guilty of serious professional misconduct. Before taking a final decision the Committee invites the doctor or the doctor's legal representative to call attention to any mitigating circumstances and to produce testimonials or other evidence as to character. The Committee takes account of the previous history of the doctor. 22. The primary concerns of the Professional Conduct Committee are to protect the public and to uphold the reputation of the medical profession. Subject to these overriding considerations, the Committee will consider what is in the best interests of the doctor. If in the course of an inquiry it appears to the Committee that a doctor's fitness to practise may be seriously impaired by reason of a physical or mental condition, the Committee may refer that question to the Health Committee for determination. If the Health Committee finds that it is so impaired, the Professional Conduct Committee will then take no further action in the case.

Powers of the Professional Conduct Committee at the conclusion of an inquiry
23. At the conclusion of an inquiry in which a doctor has been proved to have been convicted of a criminal offence, or judged to have been guilty of serious professional misconduct, the Professional Conduct Committee must decide on one of the following courses:
(a) to conclude the case;
(b) to postpone its determination;
(c) to direct that the doctor's registration be conditional on compliance, for a period not exceeding three years, with such requirements as the Committee may think fit to impose for the protection of members of the public or in the doctor's interests;
(d) to direct that the doctor's registration shall be suspended for a period not exceeding 12 months; or
(e) to direct the erasure of the doctor's name from the Register.

Postponement of determination
24. In any case where the Committee's determination is postponed, the doctor's name remains on the Register during the period of postponement. When postponing its determination to a later meeting the Committee normally indicates that the doctor will be expected before the resumed hearing to provide the names of professional colleagues and other persons of standing to whom the Council may apply for information, to be given in confidence, concerning the doctor's conduct since the previous hearing. The replies received from these referees, together with any other evidence as to the doctor's conduct, are then taken into account when the Committee resumes consideration of the case. If the information is satisfactory, the case will then normally be concluded. If however the evidence is not satisfactory, the determination may be postponed for a further period, or the Committee may direct suspension or erasure or may impose conditions on the doctor's registration.

Conditional registration
25. Examples of conditions which may be imposed are that the doctor should not engage in specified branches of medical practice, or should practise only in a particular appointment or under supervision or should not prescribe or possess controlled drugs or should take specified steps to remedy evident deficiencies in knowledge, clinical skills, professional attitudes, or of management or communication skills.
26. When a doctor's registration has for a period been subject to conditions the Committee may, on resuming consideration of the case, revoke the direction for conditional registration, or revoke or vary any of the conditions, or it may extend the original period of conditional registration. If a doctor is judged by the Professional Conduct Committee to have failed to comply with any of the conditions, the Committee may direct either suspension of the doctor's registration or erasure.

Suspension of registration
27. If a doctor's registration is suspended, the doctor ceases to be entitled to practise as a registered medical practitioner during that period. When a doctor's registration has been suspended the Committee may, after notifying the doctor, resume consideration of the case before the end of the period of suspension. At that time, if the Committee thinks fit, it may extend the original period of suspension or order erasure or impose conditional registration. Before resuming consideration of the case in such circumstances the Committee may, as

when postponing its determination, ask the doctor to give the names of referees from whom information may be sought as to his or her conduct in the interval. This information will be taken into account when the Committee resumes consideration of the case.

Erasure
28. Whereas suspension can be ordered only for a specified period, a direction to erase remains effective unless and until the doctor makes a successful application for restoration to the Register. Such an application cannot be made until at least ten months have elapsed since the original order took effect.

Appeal procedure and immediate suspension
29. When the Committee has directed erasure from the Register, or that a doctor's registration shall be suspended or shall be subject to conditions, the doctor has 28 days in which to give notice of appeal against the direction to the Judicial Committee of the Privy Council. During that period and, if there is an appeal, until the appeal is heard, the doctor's registration is not affected unless the Professional Conduct Committee has made a separate order that the doctor's registration shall be suspended forthwith. The Committee may make such an order if it is satisfied that to do so is necessary for the protection of members of the public or would be in the best interests of the doctor. There is a right of appeal against an order for immediate suspension to the High Court (in Scotland, the Court of Session), but such an appeal, whether successful or not, does not affect the right of appeal to the Judicial Committee of the Privy Council referred to above.

Restoration to the Register after disciplinary erasure
30. Applications for restoration may legally be made at any time after ten months from the date of erasure. If such an application is unsuccessful, a further period of at least ten months must elapse before another application may be made. The names of many doctors which have been erased have subsequently been restored to the Register, after an interval. An applicant may, and normally does, appear in person before the Professional Conduct Committee, and may be legally represented. The Committee determines every application on its merits, having regard among other considerations to the nature and gravity of the original offence, the length of time since erasure, and the conduct of the applicant in the interval.

The detail of the procedure before the PCC is complex and the reader is referred to the appropriate statutory instrument – the General Medical Council Preliminary Proceedings Committee and Professional Conduct Committee (Procedure) Rules Order of Council 1988 (SI 1988 No 2255).

The GMC acts upon complaints or information from a variety of sources. These are helpfully set out by Adrian Whitfield QC in his paper 'The General Medical Council' in *Medical Malpractice* (1980, ed J Leahy Taylor).

1. The police are under instruction to report to the Registrar of the GMC convictions of doctors, 'particularly those involving violence, indecency, dishonesty, drink or drugs' (statement by Secretary of State for Home Department, 14 June 1973).
2. A general practitioner who, following NHS statutory proceedings, is prevented from acting as a principal GP anywhere within the NHS will also be reported by the DHSS.
3. The GMC may be informed of breaches of general practitioners' terms of service within the NHS in a limited number of serious cases.
4. In relation to hospital doctors, the Hospital Memorandum HM(61)37 provides that:

> In order that the statutory bodies responsible for professional discipline may be aware of convictions in the Courts leading to the dismissal or resignation of members of the professions concerned, the Minister asks that in every case the Hospital Authority should send a factual report of the charges and sentence to the Disciplinary Body. . . . A Hospital Authority is of course still free to report to the appropriate body the facts of any other dismissal or resignation where, in the Authority's view, these facts should be made known to the body even though there has been no conviction in the Courts. It is for the professional body concerned itself to decide what action, if any, to take on a report.

In practice, few cases reach the GMC from Hospital Authorities.

5. Complaints may be received from the Home Office or other Official Body, eg in relation to the issue of prescriptions for drugs otherwise than in the course of bona fide treatment.

6. Other doctors may complain, eg of advertisement or canvassing.

7. Patients may complain, eg of sexual misconduct.

8. Newspaper reports – 'investigative journalism' included – are also noted by the GMC.

In past years the GMC was unwilling to act save upon a conviction or a complaint supported by all necessary evidence. It is still the case that evidence in support of a private complaint is often prepared for presentation by the complainant's private solicitor. But nowadays the GMC frequently goes to trouble and expense in trying to amass evidence itself.

The central requirements under section 36 before action may be taken against a doctor are that, either (i) he has been convicted of a criminal offence, or (ii) that he has been found guilty of 'serious professional misconduct'.

We examine (ii) in detail shortly. Little need be said about (i) except that the offence need not be directly connected with the doctor's profession. In paragraph 49 of the 'Blue Book', the GMC states:

49. The public reputation of the medical profession requires that every member should observe proper standards of personal behaviour, not only in professional activities but at all times. This is the reason why a doctor's conviction of a criminal offence may lead to disciplinary proceedings even if the offence is not directly connected with the doctor's profession. In particular, three areas of personal behaviour can be identified which may occasion disciplinary proceedings:

– Personal misuse or abuse of alcohol or other drugs
– Dishonest behaviour
– Indecent or violent behaviour.

A. 'SERIOUS PROFESSIONAL MISCONDUCT'

The more difficult part of the GMC's disciplinary powers is that relating to 'serious professional misconduct'. This phrase was first introduced by the Medical Act 1969. Prior to that, the phrase used was 'infamous conduct in a professional respect'. The change in phraseology was not intended, however, to alter the GMC's jurisdiction. Instead, it was intended to explain the jurisdiction in modern terminology, by reference to the way in which 'infamous conduct in a professional respect' had been interpreted by the courts.

Allinson v General Council of Medical Education [1894] 1 QB 750 (CA)

Lord Esher MR: If it be shown that a medical man, in the pursuit of his profession, has done something with respect to it which would be reasonably regarded as disgraceful or dishonourable by his professional brethren of good repute and competency, then it is open to the General Medical Council to say that he has been guilty of 'infamous conduct in a professional respect'. The question is not merely whether what a medical man has done would be an infamous thing for anybody else to do, but whether it is infamous for a medical man to do it. An act done by a medical man may be infamous though it would not be infamous if done by anybody else, but to bring such an act within s 29 of the Medical Act 1858, it must also be shown to have been infamous if done by any other person, yet, if done by a medical man in relation to his profession, that is, with regard either to his patients or to his professional brethren, may be fairly considered as 'infamous conduct in a professional respect'. Such acts would, I think, come within s 29.

Lopes and Davey LJJ agreed.

Adopting terminology similar to that of s 36 of the 1983 Act, Scrutton LJ, in *R v General Council of Medical Education and Registration of the United Kingdom* [1930] 1 KB 562 at 569, stated that the GMC's jurisdiction extended to 'serious misconduct judged according to the rules, written or unwritten, governing the profession'. As we have seen, the GMC takes the view that this may arise in relation to a doctor's conduct other than in relation to conduct connected with his professional duties. This seems to be borne out by the case of *Marten v Royal College of Veterinary Surgeons' Disciplinary Committee* [1966] 1 QB 1, [1965] 1 All ER 949. This case concerned a practising veterinary surgeon who owned a farm. During the winter months a number of cattle died on his farm from husk. He was charged before the Disciplinary Committee of the Council of the Royal College of Veterinary Surgeons with, *inter alia*, conduct disgraceful to a man in a professional respect, in that he failed to provide adequate nursing for sick animals in his care and that he allowed conditions to exist on his farm which were likely to bring disgrace on the veterinary profession. He was found guilty and he appealed to the court.

Marten v Royal College of Veterinary Surgeons' Disciplinary Committee [1966] 1 QB 1, [1965] 1 All ER 949 (QBD Div Ct)

> **Lord Parker CJ:** The second way, however, in which counsel puts the case is this: that conduct, however disgraceful, cannot be conduct disgraceful to a man in a professional respect unless at the time he is actively practising in that profession or acting in pursuit of his profession. To return to the facts of this case, he says that in all these matters the appellant was not acting as a veterinary surgeon, he was acting merely as a farmer, and that what he did in effect had nothing to do with his profession.

Lord Parker CJ then cited Lord Esher MR's judgment in the *Allinson* case and continued:

> Counsel for the appellant says that as a matter of law a professional man's conduct cannot be said to be disgraceful to him in a professional respect unless it was done 'in pursuit of his profession', and he would add that 'in pursuit of his profession' meant 'in the course of the practice of the profession'. For my part I see no valid ground for limiting the words in the manner suggested. If, of course, the conduct complained of is equally reprehensible in any one, whether a professional man or not, as for example, conduct constituting some traffic offence, that conduct would not come within the expression. If the conduct, however, though reprehensible in anyone is in the case of the professional man so much more reprehensible as to be defined as disgraceful, it seems to me that it may, depending on the circumstances, amount to conduct disgraceful to him in a professional respect in the sense that it tends to bring disgrace on the profession which he practises. It seems to me, though I do not put this forward in any sense as a definition, that the conception of conduct which is disgraceful to a man in his professional capacity is conduct disgraceful to him as reflecting on his profession, or, in the present case, conduct disgraceful to him as a practising veterinary surgeon. Looked at in that way, which I think is the correct way, there was here abundant evidence on which the Disciplinary Committee could come to the conclusion that the conduct was disgraceful to the appellant in a professional capacity. At any rate, bearing in mind that this court, as has been said many times, is loath to interfere with the findings of a Disciplinary Committee on such a matter as this, I could not myself possibly interfere.

However, in a case concerned with 'serious professional misconduct' alleged against a dentist (see s 27 of the Dentists Act 1984) the Privy Council, in 1987, doubted the relevance of the pre-1969 case law in interpreting the modern statutory provisions.

Doughty v General Dental Council [1988] AC 164, [1987] 3 All ER 843 (PC)

Lord Mackay: This is an appeal from a decision of the Professional Conduct Committee of the General Dental Council on 12 March 1987 that the appellant had been guilty of serious professional misconduct in relation to three charges and that his name should be erased from the Dentists Register. The three charges in question were:

That being a registered dentist: (1) Between 10th January and 26th October 1984 you accepted 19 patients, whose names and addresses are shown on List 'A' [which is attached to the charge] for dental treatment as National Health Service patients, and thereafter provided them with dental treatment in the course of which, having obtained radiographs of these patients, you: (a) Failed to retain those radiographs for a reasonable period of time after completion of the treatment; (b) Failed to submit those radiographs to the Dental Estimates Board when required to do so by a letter from the Board dated 27th November, 1984. (2) Between 5th June and 16th November, 1984, you accepted 6 patients, whose names and addresses are shown on List 'B' [which is attached to the charge] for dental treatment as National Health Service patients and thereafter provided them with dental treatment in the course of which you failed to exercise a proper degree of skill and attention. (3) Between 21st August and 5th October, 1984, you accepted 4 patients, whose names and addresses are shown on List 'C' [which is attached to the charge] for dental treatment as National Health Service patients, and thereafter provided them with dental treatment in the course of which you failed satisfactorily to complete the treatment required by the patients . . . And that in relation to the facts alleged in each of the above charges you have been guilty of serious professional misconduct.

. . . The committee announced their decision in the following terms:

In relation to the facts alleged in head 1 of the charge which have been admitted, the Committee finds that you have been guilty of serious professional misconduct. In relation to the facts alleged against you in charge 2 in respect of the five remaining patients and in charge 3 in respect of the three remaining patients, the Committee finds that you have been guilty of serious professional misconduct.

The committee directed that the appellant's name be erased from the Dentists Register. . . .
[It was argued] by counsel for the appellant . . . that in order to prove charges 2 and 3 it was necessary to show that the opinion held by the appellant in relation to the treatment was not honestly held by him and could not honestly be held by a dentist. This submission was founded principally on the observations of Lord Jenkins when giving the judgment of this Board in *Felix v General Dental Council* [1960] 2 All ER 391 at 400, [1960] AC 704 at 721:

With respect to the treatment alleged to have been unnecessary, the evidence (as their Lordships have already observed) showed that, according to the appellant, he honestly believed it to be necessary (or likely to be found necessary) while the dentists who disagreed with him did not claim that the opinion expressed by the appellant was one which no dentist could honestly hold. In this state of the evidence, their Lordships think it would be wrong to impute to the Disciplinary Committee an implied finding to the effect that the appellant did not honestly hold that opinion. An honestly held opinion, even if wrong, in their Lordships' view plainly cannot amount to infamous or disgraceful conduct.

Counsel for the council submitted that the evidence was sufficient to entitle the committee both to hold the facts alleged in charges 2 and 3 proved so far as they had done so and also to hold that those facts constituted serious professional misconduct.
In considering the applicability of Lord Jenkins' observations to the circumstances of the present appeal, it has to be noted that Lord Jenkins was speaking of a case in which dishonesty was very much the issue and in the context of the statutory provision which was the basis of the proceedings in *Felix v General Dental Council*, namely s 25 of the Dentists Act 1957. So far as relevant it was in these terms:

(1) A registered dentist who either before or after registration . . . *(b)* has been guilty of any infamous or disgraceful conduct in a professional respect, shall be liable to have his name erased from the register . . .

At that time this was the only penalty available in respect of such conduct. The Dentists Act 1983, s 15(1), provided:

For section 25(1) of the [1957] Act (erasure from register for crime or infamous conduct) there shall be substituted – '(1) A registered dentist who (whether before or after registration) . . . (*b*) has been guilty of serious professional misconduct, shall be liable to have his name erased from the register, or to have his registration in it suspended, in accordance with section 26(3) of this Act . . . '

The suspension referred to is suspension for such period not exceeding 12 months as may be specified in the committee's determination. Counsel for the appellant suggests that this change in language was not intended to effect a change in substance. In *R v General Council of Medical Education and Registration of the UK* [1930] 1 KB 562 at 569, referring to the statutory provision there applicable, namely 'infamous conduct in a professional respect', Scrutton LJ said:

It is a great pity that the word 'infamous' is used to describe the conduct of a medical practitioner who advertises. As in the case of the Bar so in the medical profession advertising is serious misconduct in a professional respect and that is all that is meant by the phrase 'infamous conduct'; it means no more than serious misconduct judged according to the rules written or unwritten governing the profession.

In the General Medical Council's booklet entitled *Professional Conduct and Discipline: Fitness to Practise* (1985) the council stated: 'In proposing the substitution of the expression "serious professional misconduct" for the phrase "infamous conduct in a professional respect" the Council intended that the phrases should have the same significance.'

Their Lordships readily accept that what was infamous or disgraceful conduct in a professional respect would also constitute serious professional misconduct but they consider that it would not be right to require the council to establish now that the conduct complained of was infamous or disgraceful and therefore not right to apply the criteria which Lord Jenkins derived from the dictionary definitions of these words which he quoted in *Felix v General Dental Council.* Their Lordships consider it relevant, in reaching a conclusion on whether Parliament intended by the change of wording to make a change of substance, to notice that in addition to this change and in close conjunction with it the additional and much less severe penalty of suspension for a period not exceeding 12 months was provided. Further, in terms of s 1(2) of the Dentists Act 1984, which is the statute presently applicable, 'It shall be the general concern of the Council to promote high standards of dental education at all its stages and high standards of professional conduct among dentists . . . ' In the light of these considerations, in their Lordships' view what is now required is that the council should establish conduct connected with his profession in which the dentist concerned has fallen short, by omission or commission, of the standards of conduct expected among dentists and that such falling short as is established should be serious. On an appeal to this Board, the Board has the responsibility of deciding whether the committee were entitled to take the view that the evidence established that there had been a falling short of these standards and were also entitled to take the view that such falling short as was established was serious.

In the present case the three charges of serious professional misconduct of which the appellant has been found guilty do not impute any dishonesty on his part. It was not suggested that he was carrying out unnecessary treatments for the purpose of enhancing his remuneration. What was suggested was that, judged by proper professional standards in the light of the objective facts about the individual patients that were presented in evidence to the committee, the dental treatments criticised as unnecessary would be treatments that no dentists of reasonable skill exercising reasonable care would carry out. It was for the committee with their expertise in this matter to judge as between the witnesses called by the council and the appellant, who had every opportunity to give his own reasons and explanations for what he did, and to judge whether the allegation was made out subject to the matter already dealt with in relation to charge 3. The point taken by counsel for the appellant at this stage of his submission was pressed primarily in relation to the criticisms of the appellant's treatment as unnecessary. With regard to the other criticisms it appears to their Lordships that the failures admitted in relation to charge 1 and admitted in part and proved to a further extent in relation to charge 2 and proved in relation to charge 3 amounted to professional misconduct. Whether the misconduct was serious depended on a number of factors, for example in relation to charge 1 on the number of patients in respect of whom the failure occurred and the importance of preserving the record for the well being of the patient and as a basis for decision on future treatment of the patient. In relation to charges 2 and 3 the seriousness of the conduct depended on the appreciation of such factors as the number of patients involved, the number of treatments criticised in relation to each patient and particularly in relation to unsatisfactory treatments, and the nature and extent of the failure to complete the treatment properly. On all of these matters the committee were particularly well qualified to reach a view and their Lordships see no reason to disagree with their findings.

Lord Mackay proposes a two-stage test, requiring the PCC to ask itself two questions:

1. Did the doctor's conduct fall short, by act or omission, of the standard of conduct expected among doctors? If yes, then:
2. Was this falling short 'serious'?

The first question relates to a finding of 'professional misconduct' and the second question relates to a finding that it is 'serious'. How does Lord Mackay's approach differ from that adopted by a court in an action for medical negligence? This is a very important question because the GMC could well be urged in the future to consider cases of medical negligence as being within its jurisdiction. The GMC itself takes the following view in paragraph 38 of its 'Blue Book':

> 38. The Council is concerned with errors in diagnosis or treatment, and with the kind of matters which give rise to action in the civil courts for negligence, only when the doctor's conduct in the case has involved such a disregard of professional responsibility to patients or such a neglect of professional duties as to raise a question or serious professional misconduct . . .

The GMC thus distinguishes between misconduct which is merely negligent (and not within its jurisdiction) and misconduct which is both negligent and serious (which is within its jurisdiction). This appears to be reflected in Lord Mackay's approach.

Clearly, there must be cases of negligence which do amount to 'serious professional misconduct'. The GMC, also in paragraph 38 of its 'Blue Book', gives an illustration.

> . . . A question of serious professional misconduct may also arise from a complaint or information about the conduct of a doctor which suggests that the welfare of patients has been endangered by a doctor persisting in unsupervised practice of a branch of medicine without having the appropriate knowledge and skill or having acquired the experience which is necessary.

However, do paragraph 38 and the opinion of Lord Mackay in *Doughty* support the view that medical negligence can in itself ever be enough to amount to 'serious professional misconduct'? The distinction between negligence and serious professional misconduct was emphasised in an earlier decision of the Privy Council not mentioned by Lord Mackay in *Doughty*.

McEniff v General Dental Council [1980] 1 All ER 461, [1980] 1 WLR 328 (PC)

> The defendant, a dentist, was found guilty of 'infamous or disgraceful conduct in a professional respect' (s 25 of the Dentists Act 1957) and his name was erased from the register. He had allowed unqualified members of his staff to insert fillings after he had drilled his patients' teeth. He appealed, arguing that the legal assessor had wrongly advised the Disciplinary Committee to the GDC in law. The legal assessor had said:
>
> > As far as what constitutes infamous or disgraceful conduct is concerned, to which both advocates have referred, for me the words of Scrutton LJ of *serious* misconduct

in a professional respect mean quite plainly that it is for the committee, applying their own knowledge and experience, to decide what is the appropriate standard each practitioner should adhere to, not a special standard greater than is ordinarily to be expected, but the ordinary standard of the profession. I think I have said very little that is in any way new to any member of the committee, but having regard to the submissions made to you I thought I ought at least to say what I have said.

Lord Edmund-Davies: These observations have been criticised as wrong in law in that they failed to draw a distinction between mere negligent conduct and infamous or disgraceful conduct. The submission is that there was a misdirection, in that, although in his opening remarks counsel for the General Dental Council had made passing reference to *Felix v General Dental Council* [1960] AC 704, the legal assessor failed to remind the disciplinary committee of an important passage in the speech of Lord Jenkins, who, in delivering the judgment of this Board in that case, said:

> Granted that . . . the full derogatory force of the adjectives 'infamous' and 'disgraceful' in s 25 of the Act of 1957 must be qualified by the consideration that what is being judged is the conduct of a dentist in a professional respect, which falls to be judged in relation to the accepted ethical standards of his profession, it appears to their Lordships that these two adjectives nevertheless remain as terms denoting *conduct deserving of the strongest reprobation*, and, indeed, so heinous as to merit, when proved, the extreme professional penalty of striking-off. (Emphasis mine.)

Although the facts in *Felix v General Dental Council* were quite unlike those of the present case, these observations are of compelling significance. For it has respectfully to be said that although prolonged veneration of the oft-quoted words of Lopes LJ has clothed them with an authority approaching that of a statute, they are not particularly illuminating. It is for this reason that their Lordships regard Lord Jenkins' exposition as so valuable that, without going so far as to say that his words should invariably be cited in every disciplinary case, they think that to do so would be a commendable course. But having said that, it has to be added that the committee in the instant case were duly reminded of decisions which have long been approved of by this Board as accurately stating the relevant law. And their Lordships have in mind in this context the following observations of Lord Guest in *Sivarajah v General Medical Council* [[1964] 1 All ER 504]:

> The committee are masters both of the law and of the facts. Thus what might amount to a misdirection in law by a judge to a jury at a criminal trial does not necessarily invalidate the committee's decision. The question is whether it can 'fairly be thought to have been of sufficient significance to the result to invalidate the Committee's decision'.

In their Lordships' judgment, it cannot be said that the advice tendered by the legal assessor in this case contained such a defect, and the first ground of criticism must therefore be rejected.

Notice that, in *McEniff*, which was a case concerned with the statute which predated the Dentists Act 1984, the Privy Council expressly approved Lord Jenkins' approach in *Felix* (contrast Lord Mackay in *Doughty*). It may be that Lord Mackay overemphasised the 'dishonesty' requirement in Lord Jenkins' speech. (See, for example, the view of Lord Parker CJ in *Marten v Royal College of Veterinary Surgeons' Disciplinary Committee* [1965] 1 All ER 949 at 951.)

Mr David Bolt, a surgeon (and a frequent chairman of the PCC) offered an explanation in a lecture to the Medico-Legal Society in 1986.

D Bolt 'Dealing with Errors of Clinical Judgment' (1986) 54 Medico-Legal J 220

If you go back to the 1979 Blue Book you will find that it says:

> The General Medical Council is not concerned with errors of diagnosis or treatment.

That was a very clear position. However, if you take the 1985 Book, you will find that it is now saying something slightly different. It is saying:

The Council is concerned with errors in diagnosis or treatment and with the kind of matters which give rise to action in the Civil Courts for negligence, only when the doctor's conduct in the case has involved such a disregard of his professional responsibility to patients or such a neglect of his professional duties as to raise a question of serious professional misconduct.

I do not want to labour it too much, but from the same page perhaps I could just read you the little list of the things that the General Medical Council reminds doctors that the public now are entitled to expect from registered medical practitioners. They include 'Conscientious assessment of the history, symptoms and signs of a patient's condition. Sufficiently thorough professional attention, examination and, where necessary, diagnostic investigation. Competent and considerate professional management. Appropriate and prompt action upon evidence suggesting the existence of a condition requiring urgent medical intervention and readiness, where circumstances so warrant, to consult appropriate professional colleagues.'

That, taken altogether, is a fairly strong statement of what the General Medical Council expects of doctors in this context. It is fair, I think, to say that it is a field which is only just developing, because the terms that I have read to you have not been in the Blue Book for more than a short time. The difficulty that we have in looking at cases is that if what you are looking at is an isolated event in the career of an otherwise estimable doctor, it would seem to me very wrong and stupid that the profession should be seeking to take major action on that account. If, on the other hand, what you are looking at seems to you to be just a particular event in, shall we say, a pattern of practice which is casual and unconcerned and careless and generally inferior and shabby, then the Professional Conduct Committee may feel that this merits more substantial action.

It is always very difficult to know what form such action should take. Obviously, if you think that all you are looking at is a failure of understanding of a limited field of medicine, then imposing some kind of condition which would lead to a better understanding of that field upon the doctor's freedom to practise may be justified. But if you are looking at, shall we say, a general standard of practice, it is really terribly difficult. You do not necessarily improve the standard of a doctor's practice by taking him out of the practice altogether. This is why very often, let us say, it is seen by the public that the Professional Conduct Committee acts less strongly than might be justified.

[See *infra*, p 583 for the GMC's Consultation Document, *Proposals for New Performance Procedures* (May 1992) which responds to some of the points made by Mr Bolt.]

B. TYPES OF CONDUCT AMOUNTING TO SERIOUS PROFESSIONAL MISCONDUCT

What types of conduct are capable of being 'serious professional misconduct'? The GMC's 'Blue Book' (Part II) provides some guidance. The following are listed:

(i) Neglect or disregard of personal responsibilities to patients for their care and treatment.
This seems to include the 'serious' cases of medical negligence and improper delegations of duties to others to which we have referred.
(ii) Abuse of professional privileges or skills.
This includes unlawfully prescribing controlled drugs, issuing medical certificates and performing abortions. It also includes breaches of medical confidentiality, the exercise of undue influence on patients and sexual relationships with patients.
(iii) Personal behaviour which is derogatory to the reputation of the medical profession.
This includes personal misuse or abuse of alcohol or drugs, dishonest behaviour and indecent or violent behaviour.

(iv) Self-promotion, advertising and canvassing.
These, of course, are only illustrations because as paragraph 65 of the 'Blue Book' reminds us:

> [I]t must be emphasised that the categories of misconduct described in Part II cannot be regarded as exhaustive. Any abuse by doctors of any of the privileges and the opportunities afforded to them, or any grave dereliction of professional duty or serious breach of medical ethics, may give rise to a charge of serious professional misconduct.

What role should the Privy Council (on appeal from the PCC) play in setting *legal* limits to the conduct which is capable of being 'serious professional misconduct'? In considering this question, notice the following observations made by the Privy Council.

In *McCoan v General Medical Council* [1964] 3 All ER 143, [1964] 1 WLR 1107 the Privy Council was concerned with the case of a doctor who had been erased from the register by the PCC following a finding of 'infamous or disgraceful conduct in a professional respect' after he had carried on a sexual relationship with one of his patients.

> **Lord Upjohn:** One of the most fundamental duties of a medical adviser, recognised for as long as the profession has been in existence, is that a doctor must never permit his professional relationship with a patient to deteriorate into an association which would be described by responsible medical opinion as improper. It is for this reason that the Medical Acts have always entrusted the supervision of the medical advisers' conduct to a committee of the profession, for they know and appreciate better than anyone else the standards which responsible medical opinion demands of its own profession. Sexual intercourse with a patient has always been regarded as a most serious breach of the proper relationship between doctor and patient and their lordships do not see how the finding of the committee, on the facts of this case, that the appellant was guilty of infamous conduct in a professional respect can be successfully challenged before their lordships.

Similarly, in *Tamesby v General Medical Council* (20 July 1970, unreported) the Privy Council was concerned with the case of a doctor who was found guilty and whose name was erased from the register by the PCC because he had advertised abortion services. Lord Pearson said: '[i]n a matter of this kind the decision of the Disciplinary Committee, composed of members of the same profession, must carry weight'.

It seems clear, therefore, that the Privy Council is reluctant to interfere with a finding of 'serious professional misconduct' by the PCC. Only if it can be shown that something has clearly gone wrong at the hearing, whether in the legal principles adopted (or as applied to the facts) or in the procedure itself, will the Privy Council intervene.

C. THE ADEQUACY OF THE GMC'S PROCEDURES

In the light of the GMC's interpretation of its statutory remit and of the reluctance of the Privy Council to become involved, the question must be asked whether the GMC is adequately holding doctors to account so as to further the public interest.

Professor Brazier in *Medicine, Patients and the Law* (2nd edn 1992) observes that 'there is a widespread suspicion that doctors who fail their patients are let off lightly' (at 13) and calls for a re-evaluation of the GMC's procedures. At the heart of the problem is whether the GMC should concern itself only with misconduct which is 'serious' or whether it should cast its net more widely.

Some argue that a doctor who is ordinarily competent, but behaves in an incompetent manner in an isolated incident, should not be exposed to a procedure which could result in his being prevented from practising medicine. On the other hand to leave an aggrieved patient only with an action in negligence may not be sufficient to meet his needs or protect the public interest, both in holding the doctor to account and in seeking to ensure that mistakes are not made again, particularly bearing in mind the observations made earlier about actions in negligence.

In view of the doubts these questions raise, it has been proposed that the GMC's powers should not be restricted to 'serious professional misconduct'. In 1983, Nigel Spearing MP introduced the Medical Act 1983 (Amendment) Bill to widen the powers of the GMC. It provided:

> **1.** Section 36 of the Medical Act 1983 shall have effect with the addition of the following new subsection–
>
> > '(10) Where a fully registered person is judged by the Professional Conduct Committee to have behaved in a manner which cannot be regarded as acceptable professional conduct the Committee may, if they think fit, direct that the registration shall be made conditional in accordance with the foregoing subsection of this section.'

The Bill would have removed one barrier which some argue makes it undesirable for the GMC to consider merely negligent conduct, namely that, under the current legislation, the doctor faces (potentially at least) the severe sanction of having his name erased from the register. The argument behind the Bill was that if the GMC had only the lesser sanction available to it, that of making the doctor's registration 'conditional', it could then take jurisdiction over conduct that was itself less serious without the inappropriate threat of erasure being present.

The Bill never became law. The GMC resisted its enactment and set up a Working Party in 1984 under the chairmanship of Sir Douglas Black. The Working Party set out the GMC's objections in paragraph 6 of its report.

> (a) The amendment could result in confusion and injustice because it would allow the lesser offence of unacceptable conduct to carry a more severe penalty than may be imposed in cases of the greater offence of serious professional misconduct.
> (b) Enactment of the Bill would create judicial difficulty. It would be impracticable for the PCC to maintain a consistent and fair distinction between the lesser and greater offences. The single criterion of serious professional misconduct is well understood as conduct which a doctor's colleagues would regard as disgraceful or dishonourable.
> (c) The formal creation of a new, lesser offence would inevitably encourage defence lawyers to urge the PCC to find that the proven facts amounted to unacceptable rather than serious professional misconduct. Experience has shown that the arguments of defence lawyers can be cogent and persuasive. As case law accrued, the standards maintained by the GMC could be eroded, to the detriment of the public interest.
> (d) The Bill is unnecessary. Mr Spearing suggested the use of conditional registration to require a doctor to reappear at a later date citing referees from whom the Committee can obtain confidential reports on the doctor's conduct in the interval. The PCC already has the power to achieve that end by postponing its findings whether a doctor is guilty of serious professional misconduct until a resumed hearing when further evidence about the doctor's conduct in the interim is heard, although this power is rarely used.
> Enactment of the Bill would therefore be detrimental to the disciplinary procedure of the Council and it would inevitably result in a much greater proportion of cases being referred for formal inquiry.

The pressure for change remained strong. Professor Margot Stacey in her paper 'Medical Accountability – A Background Paper' in A Grubb (ed) *Challenges in Medical Care* (1992) 109 at 124 was able to conclude as follows:

> The GMC can justly claim that it has changed a great deal in the last 10 years. The mode of dealing with sick doctors is generally agreed to be a great advance on the situation before the 1978 Medical Act. The proportion, as well as the number, of lay members has been increased during the 1980s. A lay person is now involved in initial disciplinary screening; for some time there has even been a lay person on the Finance Committee; there are now two lay members on the disciplinary hearings, not just one as formerly. Furthermore, it was the GMC . . . which suggested the introduction of lay persons into the proposed intermediate disciplinary procedures. . . .
>
> Council's ethical guidelines (the blue pamphlet) have made it much plainer that bad practice as well as bad behaviour may constitute serious professional misconduct. In the past 10 years more cases involving clinical practice have been passed through to the Professional Conduct Committee, but seem still to be dealt with more leniently than other conduct offences. 'There but for the grace of God . . .' tempers judgments.
>
> It has been my belief that really bad practice could always have been construed as serious professional misconduct (and indeed was in gross cases). That more cases were not brought forward was more a matter of will on the part of the members than the powers of the GMC. There is now no doubt about their powers since the judgment about a dentist. Council is in a position to join those who are setting the tone for the profession that self-regulation does include monitoring outcome. Routinely to treat serious clinical errors as serious professional misconduct would constitute a major change in the way professional self-regulation has hitherto been understood, as would setting up any competence procedures under the heading of professional self-regulation.

Notwithstanding these changes, the central question identified by Spearing – what to do about misconduct which was not 'serious' as defined – remained. In 1989 a further GMC Working Party (set up in 1987) issued its report. The terms of reference of the Working Party were to:

> examine the issue of the establishment of competence procedures, under its jurisdiction, to help it respond to complaints about standards of care provided by doctors which appear to arise from failure of competence.

Professor Stacey (*supra*) summarised and commented upon the 16 recommendations as follows (at 114-116):

> This working party reported in May 1989. It made some 16 recommendations in all; in what follows I have grouped them somewhat differently from the way the working party did.
>
> The most innovatory proposal is that there should be new procedures established to deal with doctors alleged to be incompetent, not all within the Council; some should take place at local level. The Council will formulate such proposals and invite the profession to discuss them; the suggested procedures will take account of arrangements for medical audit in the NHS and bear in mind doctors not covered by these procedures.
>
> The working party reiterated the distinction which has in the past been made between 'serious professional misconduct' and incompetence. It rejected the idea that the definition of serious professional misconduct should be widened to include unacceptable or inappropriate conduct of a kind which would not call a doctor's continued registration into question. It also rejected any lowering of the threshold for formal disciplinary proceedings by substituting 'professional misconduct' for 'serious professional misconduct'. Nor did the working party recommend amendment of the 1983 Medical Act along the lines proposed by Nigel Spearing MP to introduce a second, lower tier of 'unacceptable professional conduct'. NHS issues in the category of 'unacceptable conduct' should continue to be dealt with under local NHS disciplinary procedures.
>
> Other recommendations were as follows:
> –   Initiatives to provide information to patients, both NHS and other, should be taken by local and NHS authorities, Health Councils and consumer and patients' associations. The Council itself should prepare a leaflet about the nature of its own disciplinary

jurisdiction and the procedures under which complaints are considered to supplement the individual advice which is already given to complainants.

– No change in the standing instructions whereby NHS patients who complain to the Council are immediately advised by the office to go through NHS procedures in the first instance.

– The GMC should initiate discussions about the improvement of procedures for licensing private clinics, for the appointment of GP locums and for checking the qualifications of doctors employed in the deputising service.

– Lay persons should be involved in the Council's initial screening of disciplinary cases to go forward for committee consideration and matters associated with the formal changes in procedure rules that this would involve.

– Council should convey its view to the Department of Health that lay persons be included in the 'intermediate procedures' proposed for the disciplining of NHS hospital consultants . . .

– The Department of Health should extend those procedures to junior grades.

– The drafting of charges in conduct cases should be kept under review.

After 18 months of discussion with organisations representing doctors and patients, the NHS and private hospitals, a Consultation Paper, *Proposals for New Performance Procedures* (May 1992) was produced. The GMC at its Council Meeting in November 1992 adopted the proposals. They must now be translated into law by way of legislation amending the Medical Act 1983. In essence it is proposed to establish a 'third fitness to practise procedure to investigate serious cases of poor performance' by a doctor. In its introduction, the Consultation Paper puts the new scheme in context.

1 The GMC currently has two 'fitness to practise' procedures – the conduct and the health procedures. It is proposed to add a new, third jurisdiction – performance procedures.

2 What performance procedures are designed for
2.1 The performance procedures are designed for those situations where a doctor's pattern of professional performance appears to be 'seriously deficient' – in other words, so blatantly poor that patients are potentially at risk, and action needs to be taken to resolve the deficiency and/or to restrict the doctor's freedom to practise.
2.2 The procedures are designed
–   to protect the public
–   to be remedial
–   to be wide-ranging in scope
–   to be based on a local assessment which is thorough and fair
–   to cover doctors in all types of practice
and they will be statutorily based.

2.3 The performance procedures will protect the public
2.3.1 The primary aim of the performance procedures is to protect patients by preventing potential risk from a doctor's poor standard of performance of professional duties.

2.4 They will be remedial
2.4.1 It is a feature in a significant number of complaints to the GMC that complainants stress that they do not wish the doctor to be 'struck off', but they ask that steps be taken to prevent recurrence of the matters which led to their complaint. It is in the public interest for the nature of the performance procedures to be supportive and remedial for the doctor, so as to raise the doctor's standard of performance by means of:
–   assessment by peers to identify areas of serious deficiency
–   remedial education and training in those areas
–   reassessment after training.
2.4.2 Doctors who cooperate with assessment and retraining, and successfully undergo reassessment, will not be required to appear before the GMC Professional Performance Committee. There has, however, to be such a Committee to consider cases of non-compliance and problems where deficiencies appear incapable of resolution by retraining alone.

2.5 They will be wide-ranging
2.5.1 Some reports of the GMC's proposals have called them 'competence procedures', but consideration of a doctor's professional performance goes wider than that. It encompasses all aspects which contribute to a doctor's standard of medical practice, including:
- standard of professional knowledge
- standards of professional skills
- professional attitudes towards patients and colleagues.

2.6 They will be based on a local assessment
2.6.1 Cases calling for investigation of performance will be carefully identified by experienced members of the GMC who will 'screen' the letters and referrals received by the GMC about individual doctors. These members will include a lay (ie non-medical) screener. It will not always be easy to decide at the outset whether a doctor's allegedly poor performance is the consequence of ill health, misconduct or serious deficiency of knowledge, skills or attitudes, and therefore transfer of a case between the three GMC fitness to practise procedures will be possible during the early stages of each procedure.
2.6.2 However, once it is decided that performance assessment is appropriate, the medical GMC screener will make the necessary arrangements. At least part of the assessment would in most cases have to be conducted at the doctor's place of work, but the remainder could be conducted elsewhere, if the doctor preferred. The assessment would be undertaken by a team including peers from the same branch of practice as the doctor. For example, a general practitioner would be assessed by a small team including two general practitioners, and part of the assessment would be carried out at the doctor's practice premises. Where the assessors identified areas of deficiency in which the doctor required advice or further training, this would normally be arranged locally, but might occasionally be arranged elsewhere, if the doctor concerned requested this, or if it was necessary for other reasons.

2.7 They will be thorough and fair
2.7.1 Assessors will follow guidelines for assessments, to be prepared by the GMC in consultation with those who have specialised knowledge and expertise in such matters. Measures will be built in to ensure consistency of assessment, standards and fairness. Doctors' performance would be judged against predetermined and well-publicised standards (see paragraph 8.2.1). . . .

3 What performance procedures are NOT designed for
3.1 They will not supersede existing conduct procedures
3.1.1 Concern has been expressed by some organisations that the performance procedures will provide a 'refuge' for doctors seeking to evade the conduct procedures. This is not so. The established procedures for dealing with serious professional misconduct will not be affected and the criteria for referring cases to the conduct procedures will not alter. For example, it has been established in law that one isolated act of gross incompetence may amount to serious professional misconduct and allegations about isolated acts of this kind will continue to be treated as conduct matters.

3.2 They will not deal with a 'lower tier' of professional misconduct or with all complaints about doctors' performance
3.2.1 It has been alleged in some reports of the proposals that the performance procedures will be an expansion of the conduct procedures. This is not correct; they will not represent a 'lower' or 'lesser' tier in relation to any of the GMC's present procedures: they will be different, because they will not deal with misconduct or ill health. Nor will the procedures provide a means of investigating every case in which there might be room for criticism of a doctor's professional performance: they will deal only with serious failures to achieve proper professional standards. This point is discussed further in paragraphs 4.8 and 4.11. . . .

3.5 The procedures will not be confrontational
3.5.1 The performance procedures will take the form of a general investigation, professionally based, but with lay input. It is expected that the majority of performance cases would be resolved without any committee hearing by the GMC, by means of a private, constructive, local assessment, and retraining designed to meet the doctor's needs, in the interests of his or her patients. This contrasts with the conduct procedures, which may lead to formal charges against the doctor at a public hearing of the GMC's Professional Conduct Committee. The performance procedures would be more akin to the GMC's health

procedures, which are both remedial in nature and designed to protect the public, and where the great majority of cases are concluded without the doctor ever appearing before the GMC's Health Committee.

3.6 They will not deal with contractual matters

3.6.1 Alleged failures by doctors to comply with the requirements of their contracts are not of themselves matters of concern to the GMC, but are issues to be considered in the first instance by the relevant health authority in each case.

4 Doctors' accountability and the limitations of existing non-GMC procedures for dealing with complaints*about doctors' performance.

4.1 Doctors are already accountable in a number of ways to various persons or authorities for their professional conduct and performance. For example, they are accountable

- to their patients, and may be liable to civil proceedings if a patient alleges that medical negligence has occurred;
- to the health authority or trust or other organisation which employs them or with which they are in contract;
- to their professional colleagues and peers;
- to their professional regulatory body, the GMC;
- under the criminal law.

* Throughout this paper the word 'complain' has been used merely for convenience to indicate letters, reports, referrals and other information which the GMC has received about a particular doctor's professional performance, and the term should be taken to include not only complaints from members of the public or the profession, or from other health care professionals, but also information referred to the GMC by health or other public authorities. Similarly the word 'complainant' is used to indicate any private individual or public authority referring complaints or information on such matters to the GMC.

4.2 There are various different complaints, disciplinary or other regulatory procedures which may be invoked, under the jurisdiction of various authorities, depending on the nature of the personal or professional misconduct or poor performance which is alleged.

4.3 Some medical organisations have suggested either:
(a) that there are sufficient procedures already for NHS doctors, with no need for another; or
(b) that the GMC could refer to the NHS procedures any complaint made direct to the GMC about an NHS doctor's professional performance.

4.4 . . . it has been generally accepted by those whom the GMC has consulted informally about this matter that the various NHS procedures do not satisfactorily cover doctors working as locums, doctors who resign their posts before NHS proceedings are completed, deputising doctors in general practice and doctors in private practice. The last group in particular are subject only to civil litigation (which is prohibitively expensive for most patients) and to the GMC. . . .

Furthermore, there is no NHS procedure currently in existence which can prevent an incompetent doctor from continuing in professional practice, in another area of the country, either in the NHS or in private practice, without retraining or monitoring.

4.5 The second suggestion in paragraph 4.3, above, has been discussed with representatives of NHS authorities, who firmly rejected it. It was pointed out that NHS procedures, like those of the GMC, serve specific statutory functions. They could not be used effectively for other purposes, and are not designed to be sub-contracted, as it were, to act for other agencies, such as the GMC. . . .

4.8 In developing the performance proposals the GMC has received advice from organisations representing patients about complainants' needs for redress and recompense in various circumstances. It appears that there is dissatisfaction with some of the existing complaints procedures, and that patients can feel daunted by the prospect of civil litigation. However, the GMC's power to respond to complaints can only be related to its jurisdiction and sanctions. Its jurisdiction derives from its duty to keep a Register of doctors who have achieved relevant standards of training and remain fit to practise. The only sanction available is to affect the individual doctor's registration. Thus the GMC cannot, for example, award compensation to claimants who have allegedly suffered from acts of medical negligence, or provide redress for complainants by way of requiring hospitals to review admissions or discharge procedures or other policies which may have led to the complaint.

4.9 It would not be practicable for the GMC to become a central agency for the investigation of each and every type of complaint in which a doctor might be involved. The introduction of performance procedures will not affect this position.

4.10 It is important to stress, therefore, that there are, and will continue to be, complaints about doctors which the GMC will not be able to investigate, including matters which are not serious enough to call the doctor's registration into question.

4.11 It will be apparent from Part B of this paper that the performance procedures are designed to protect patients not by holding a public inquiry into a particular complaint, but by investigating and, where necessary, attempting to improve, the general standard of medical care provided by the doctor concerned. Although complainants will be informed and involved in the procedures, the satisfaction which they will receive will be that the doctor's standards are being improved, rather than that their individual complaints have been tested in a public hearing and either upheld or not.

The Consultation Paper provides a Summary of principal recommendations.

Preliminary Screening of Complaints

19.8 The procedures would be initiated on the basis of complaints from individuals or referrals of cases by public authorities (paragraphs 7.11 – 7.12).

19.9 Complaints of alleged misconduct and complaints about performance issues would be considered under a common procedure initially (paragraph 7.1.4).

19.10 The preliminary screeners for conduct would also undertake the initial screening of complaints raising performance issues (paragraph 7.2.1).

19.11 The medical preliminary screener would continue to receive advice, as now, from lay screeners on any case which appeared not to justify GMC action (paragraph 7.2.3).

19.12 The preliminary screeners would be authorised to seek specialist advice in confidence as necessary on individual cases, either from another Council member or from an independent specialist appointed ad hoc by the relevant Royal College (paragraph 7.3.1).

19.13 The GMC would not usually institute performance procedures whilst another investigation into similar matters was already being conducted locally by another authority (paragraph 7.3.2).

19.14 There would be a screener with special responsibility for performance cases, (the performance screener) who would take the final decision to pursue formal action under the performance procedures in individual cases and would then assume responsibility for such cases (paragraph 7.4.1).

19.15 The performance screener would report regularly on his or her work to the full Council (paragraph 7.5.1).

19.16 Complainants would be kept informed of decisions and action taken in response to their complaints (paragraph 7.5.2 and section 14.2).

Referral of a Doctor for Performance Assessment

19.17 A doctor who was identified by the performance screener as requiring assessment under the procedures would first be invited to undergo assessment locally by independent assessors, usually three in number, comprising two medically-qualified experts practising in the same specialty as the doctor concerned, and one lay assessor (paragraphs 8.11 – 8.15).

19.18 The medically-qualified assessors for each case would be chosen by the performance screener not from local doctors but from panels nominated by the Royal Colleges and Faculties, appropriate BMA Committees and Local or Area Medical Committees (paragraphs 8.1.6 and 8.1.11).

19.19 The assessment team in the case of a doctor in a training grade would itself include a doctor who was, or was recently, in a training grade (paragraph 8.1.8).

19.20 Where appropriate, the performance screener would ensure that assessment teams included at least one person of the same gender as the doctor whose performance is to be assessed, and one doctor who qualified outside the United Kingdom (paragraph 8.1.9).

19.21 The lay assessor for each case would be chosen from nominations submitted to the GMC. Views are invited on suggested sources of nominations (paragraphs 8.1.9 – 8.1.14).

19.22 The GMC would publish new advice on the standards of professional performance expected of doctors (paragraph 8.2.1).

19.23 A doctor invited to undergo assessment would be sent information and evidence, indicating why his or her performance was considered to warrant review, and would be invited to comment (paragraph 8.3.1).

19.24 The nature and scale of the assessment would be tailored to the needs of each individual case (paragraph 8.4.1).

19.25 However, every assessment would include
(a) an extended interview with the doctor;
(b) an examination of the doctor's records, or records of cases in which he or she had been involved;
(c) obtaining evidence from third parties (paragraph 8.4.2).
19.26 In most cases at least part of the assessment would be carried out at the doctor's place of work; the remainder could be conducted at another reasonable and acceptable location (paragraph 8.4.3).
19.27 The assessors would be asked to prepare a joint report on
(a) the doctor's fitness to continue in unrestricted practice;
(b) any significant deficiencies in the doctor's performance which had been identified by the assessors;
(c) any remedial action which the assessors might recommend (paragraph 8.5.1).
19.28 Before submitting their report, the assessors would be asked to discuss their findings and proposed recommendations with the doctor (paragraph 8.5.2).
19.29 It would be open to the doctor to submit his or her own evidence regarding his or her performance (paragraph 8.5.3).
19.30 The assessors' report would be sent to the doctor, who would, where applicable, be invited to agree to the assessors' recommendations for retraining or counselling (paragraphs 8.5.4–8.5.6).
19.31 If the assessors found no evidence of any significant deficiency in the doctor's performance, the case would be concluded (paragraph 8.5.6).
19.32 If a doctor were to fail to agree to follow the assessors' recommendations, it would then be open to the preliminary screener to refer the case to the Professional Performance Committee (paragraph 8.5.5).

Refusal by a Doctor to Undergo Performance Assessment
19.33 If a doctor were without good reason to refuse to undergo assessment, his or her case would be referred by the screener to an Assessment Referral Panel (ARP), which would decide whether the refusal was justified (paragraphs 8.6.1 and 8.6.2).
19.34 If the refusal was not considered justified, the ARP would have power to impose on the doctor's registration, for a period of up to six months, the condition that the doctor should undergo assessment within a specified period (paragraph 8.6.3).
19.35 A doctor would be invited to attend the ARP's meeting in order to address the Panel, and would be entitled to legal representation (paragraphs 8.6.3 and 8.6.4).
19.36 ARPs would comprise three persons (two medical and one lay) drawn from the membership of the Professional Performance Committee (paragraph 8.6.5).
19.37 A doctor complying with assessment by direction of the ARP would return to the jurisdiction of the performance screener, but any doctor breaching a condition imposed by the ARP would be referred by the performance screener to the Professional Performance Committee (paragraph 8.6.6).
19.38 The performance screener's reports to Council would include reports of the work of ARPs (paragraph 8.6.7).

Counselling, Retraining and Reassessment
19.39 The GMC would initiate arrangements for doctors to receive any counselling or retraining recommended by the assessors in individual cases. The GMC would usually do this by putting the doctor in touch with the appropriate Regional Postgraduate Dean or Regional Adviser in General Practice or the Regional Adviser of the relevant Royal College (paragraph 9.1.1), or occasionally with an officer of some other professional body (paragraph 9.2.4).
19.40 The performance screener would monitor the doctor's progress at intervals, and in due course would commission a reassessment of the doctor's performance in the light of the counselling and retraining received by the doctor (paragraphs 9.1.2 and 9.2.1).
19.41 If the doctor's retraining had been completed satisfactorily, the performance screener would then either conclude the case, or arrange further retraining followed by a further assessment (paragraph 9.2.2).
19.42 Alternatively, if the doctor's performance had not significantly improved or actually deteriorated since the original assessment, the performance screener would have discretion to refer the case to the Professional Performance Committee (paragraph 9.3.1).
19.43 The performance screener would be obliged to consult two members of a panel of GMC members appointed for this purpose, before a case could be referred, at any stage of the procedure, to the Committee (paragraph 9.3.1).

The Professional Performance Committee

19.44 Doctors referred to the Committee would be invited to attend the Committee's hearing of their case, and would be entitled to legal representation (paragraph 10.1.2).

19.45 The constitution of the Committee would be: a medically-qualified Chairman and Deputy Chairman, nine elected members, three appointed members and four lay members (paragraph 10.2.1).

19.46 The Committee would, however, meet in panels to consider individual cases. Each panel would comprise the Chairman or Deputy Chairman, four elected members, one appointed member and two lay members (paragraph 10.2.1).

19.47 Cases of overseas-qualified doctors would be considered by a panel of the Committee which included an overseas-qualified GMC member or overseas-qualified expert adviser (paragraph 10.2.1).

19.48 Cases of female doctors would be considered by a panel of the Committee which included a female GMC member or a female expert adviser (paragraph 10.2.1).

19.49 At least one medical adviser, expert in the doctor's field of practice, would be appointed to advise the Committee on each case considered. Expert advisers would be selected from panels of specialists nominated by the Royal Colleges and Faculties, by Committees of the BMA, and by Local or Area Medical Committees (paragraph 10.2.4).

19.50 The function of the Professional Performance Committee would be to decide whether the doctor's professional performance was seriously deficient and, if so, to take appropriate action (paragraph 10.3.1).

19.51 The evidence considered at hearings would be primarily documentary, supplemented as necessary by oral evidence called on behalf of the GMC or the doctor concerned (paragraphs 10.3.1 – 10.3.2).

19.52 If the Professional Performance Committee judged that the doctor's performance was seriously deficient, it would be open to the Committee

(a)   to direct that conditions be imposed upon the doctor's registration for a period of up to three years; or

(b)   to direct that the doctor's registration be suspended for a finite period of up to twelve months, or for an indefinite period; or

(c)   exceptionally, to adjourn, or take no further action, for example because the Committee had also received evidence that the problem had now been resolved through recent counselling or retraining arranged locally (paragraph 10.4.2).

19.53 The doctor would have a right of appeal to the Judicial Committee of the Privy Council on points of law (paragraph 10.4.3).

19.54 The Professional Performance Committee would also be able to impose immediate suspension in certain cases (paragraph 10.4.3).

19.55 The Committee would resume consideration of any case in which conditions or suspension for a finite period had been imposed, in order to monitor the doctor's progress, and could then impose restrictions on registration for a further period (paragraph 10.4.4).

19.56 It should be open to a doctor whose registration had been suspended indefinitely to apply for the suspension to be lifted, when and if the doctor was able to produce evidence to show that he or she had now successfully completed appropriate retraining. Such an application could be made only after a period of at least two years' suspension had elapsed (paragraph 10.4.5).

19.57 It would not be appropriate for the Professional Performance Committee to have a power of erasure (paragraph 10.4.6).

19.58 For a trial period of three to five years the Professional Performance Committee should meet in private, subsequently publishing its decisions (section 10.5); the question of private or public hearings would then be reviewed in the light of experience.

19.59 Reports of the work of the Professional Performance Committee would be published regularly (paragraph 10.6.1).

Transfer of Cases Between the Performance, Conduct and Health Procedures

19.60 The legislation would permit transfer of cases between the respective conduct, health and performance procedures (section 11).

Commenting on the Report of the Working Party which formed the basis of the Consultation Paper, Professor Stacey writes as follows (*supra* at 125-6):

Changes yet to come: Council accepted the report of the working party on disciplinary procedure in May 1989. As noted . . . [the] procedures modelled on the GMC's Health

Committee (used to handle complaints against sick doctors) are being developed with the intention of assessing the performance of doctors against whom allegations of incompetence have been made.

. . . [I]n looking at performance, rather than outcome or competence in any one incident, the Council may have found a formula upon which doctors' leaders can agree. From the professional perspective the GMC has moved a great deal. From the lay point of view, until details are known, the suggested local aspects of the procedures raise doubts as to how fair and open they may be.

There is still a long road to travel if professional regulation is to catch up with the conditions of late 20th century medicine, of the modern state and the market place. In this light the changes the GMC has made seem less impressive. . . . The working party report, after two years of hard work, was disappointing in that it appeared defensive, dealing piecemeal with particular criticisms, recommending the Council wait for others before it acted, passing as much as possible to other authorities and making no strong proposals about how to deal with problems which arise in private medicine. It now seems possible that the performance formula may be a way of, yet again, ducking outcome. Let us hope not. But why the slowness and the timidity?

Arguably, Professor Stacey's misgivings remain justified now that the details of the scheme are known. It remains to be seen how the scheme will operate in practice, but the continued emphasis on the need for 'seriousness' and the implications of seeking to deal with matters at a local level may give some cause for concern as to whether the scheme is an adequate blueprint for the accountability of doctors in the next century. (For a full discussion of the work of the GMC, see M Stacey *Regulating British Medicine* (1992), John Wiley.)

Conscious of the strictures of Professor Stacey and others, the GMC embarked in 1990 upon a wide-ranging review of its constitution and functions.

The NHS complaints procedures

A. GENERAL PRACTITIONERS

General practitioners are, of course, subject to the disciplinary jurisdiction of the GMC. However, most complaints brought against a GP are not made to the GMC. Instead, they are investigated within the framework of procedures currently set out in the National Health Service (Service Committees and Tribunal) Regulations 1992 (SI 1992 No 664). Under these procedures, complaints are investigated and dealt with by the Family Health Services Authorities (FHSAs). In fact the FHSAs' functions are performed by a committee known as the Medical Service Committee (MSC).

A complaint must relate to a breach by the GP of his terms of service as laid down in the National Health Service (General Medical Services) Regulations 1992 (SI 1992 No 635) in Schedule 2. We have already seen some of these statutory provisions earlier. A complaint may relate to a breach of any of the paragraphs. In practice, complaints commonly centre around breaches of paragraphs 3 and 13.

These paragraphs embody a duty competently to treat and diagnose patients (ie in accordance with the *Bolam* test) and a duty in relation to visiting them. A breach of this latter duty is a common type of complaint (for the terms of these provisions, see *supra*, ch 2).

Professor Brazier in *Medicine, Patients and Law* (1992 2nd edn) pp 366-9 summarises the main features of the complaints procedure (current provisions

are referred to rather than previous regulations consolidated in the 1992
Regulations).

The FHSA, which administers general practice and with whom the GP contracts to offer his
services, also investigates any failure by the GP to comply with those terms of service. An
aggrieved patient makes his complaint to the FHSA. On receiving a complaint, the FHSA
may attempt to solve the difficulty by informal means. A 'negotiator' is appointed to
mediate between doctor and patient. He will usually be a lay member of the full FHSA, but
may ask that one of the doctors on the medical service committee advise him on the
complaint. The 'negotiator' has no power to impose any sanctions on the doctor. If informal
conciliation is not resorted to or fails, the full complaints procedure comes into play. The
FHSA is required to set up service committees for the various services they administer, for
example, a medical service committee for GPs, a dental service committee for dentists, and a
pharmaceutical service committee for pharmacists. It is the medical service committee with
which we are concerned. The service committee is obliged to investigate any complaint made
against a doctor. Complaints must normally be made within thirteen weeks of the event
giving rise to the complaint. The committee can hear complaints outside this thirteen-week
period if good cause for the delay is shown, as long as the doctor consents. If he disagrees,
the committee can seek approval from the Department of Health to go ahead.

Once the service committee has notice of the complaint, the chairman will make a
preliminary decision as to whether it discloses any evidence of failure by the doctor. If after a
further opportunity for the complainant to substantiate his complaint nothing further is
disclosed, the matter will go forward to the committee without a formal hearing being
required. Where a formal hearing takes place, the patient may ask someone else to assist him
to present his case. There is no legal aid in such cases. Even where the patient pays for advice
from a lawyer, the lawyer is not entitled to act as an advocate or to speak at all at the
hearing. The patient himself may speak and put questions to the doctor. The hearing is
private and the press are therefore excluded from such hearings.

The procedure before service committees has aroused much disquiet. The patient is
dependent to a large extent on his own articulacy in presenting a case. So is the doctor. He
too is denied an advocate. The likelihood is, though, that the doctor will be better educated
than the patient and will be advised throughout by lawyers and other experts from his
defence organization.

Once a hearing is complete, the service committee reports to the main FHSA. The FHSA
must decide what action to take if breach of the terms of service is shown. The have no
power to award compensation as such to the patient. The FHSA may (*inter alia*) limit the
number of patients for whom the doctor may provide treatment, recommend to the
Department of Health withholding of remuneration, or recommend to the Department of
Health that the doctor be warned to comply with his terms of service more closely in future.
Finally, the ultimate sanction available to the FHSA is to recommend to a special tribunal
specially established for the purpose that the doctor be removed from the medical list.

From any decision of the FHSA, either party may appeal if the decision is adverse to him.
The appeal lies to the Health Minister [delegated to the Yorkshire Regional Health
Authority under the National Health Service (Appellate and Other Functions) Regulations
1992 (SI 1992 No 660)]. No oral hearing is required to be held. Where an oral hearing is held
proceedings again take place in private. Where a recommendation to exclude a doctor from
the medical list is made, that recommendation is only the first step in a lengthy process. The
tribunal of three members must be chaired by a lawyer of no less than ten years' standing,
appointed by the Lord Chancellor. At least one of the other two members will be a doctor.
Proceedings are yet again in private, and the doctor is entitled to legal representation. If the
decision goes against the doctor he may appeal to the Secretary of State, or if he challenges a
point of law in the tribunal's decision he may go to the High Court.

Reforms of the system for complaints in 1990 have gone a little way to meet disquiet
about its operation. The time-limit for submitting complaints was extended from eight to
thirteen weeks. Equal numbers of lay and professional members must be present at service
committee hearings. It is made clear that patients are entitled to be represented by a trade-
union official or representative of the local community health council. The Council on
Tribunals, which supervises the operation of all tribunals in England and Wales, is still
unhappy about service committee procedures. The Council believes that patients should be
entitled to legal representation and that service committees need greater powers to compel
the attendance of witnesses and production of documents. Delays in the system remain too
great. The Health Service Ombudsman who has jurisdiction over FHSAs has equal concerns

over the informal conciliation procedures. He considers the informal procedures are too often used inappropriately when a formal investigation is called for.

The detailed procedure of these hearings under the 1992 Regulations is beyond the scope of our book. Reference should be made to the Regulations themselves (which are complex) and to the Medical Protection Society's book, *General Practice Complaints Procedure* (1992).

As Professor Brazier points out there are a number of general points of interest that arise under the Regulations. One that deserves a little more elaboration concerns judicial review of the decision of an FHSA or the Secretary of State on appeal.

Both the FHSA and the Secretary of State in exercising their functions under the 1992 Regulations are performing functions amenable to control by public law. Consequently, if a patient (or indeed a doctor) can establish that they have misconstrued the Regulations (ie acted illegally), failed to act fairly (ie procedural impropriety), or acted unreasonably (ie irrationally) then a successful application for judicial review may be made to the High Court. This is so even though the decision of the Secretary of State is stated to be 'final and conclusive' (regulation 12(9); *R v Medical Appeal Tribunal, ex p Gilmore* [1957] 1 QB 574). It is, however, likely that a court would require an individual who was aggrieved by a decision of the FHSA to exercise his right of appeal to the Secretary of State before the court would countenance judicial review proceedings. There are two reasons for this. First, the court may take the view that the appeal to the Secretary of State 'cures' any procedural defect before the FHSA (MSC). Secondly, in any event, the court generally requires an applicant for judicial review, as a matter of discretion, to exhaust his remedies under any statutory appeal procedure. (For a discussion of both of these points see *Johnson v Secretary of State for Health* (26 February 1992, unreported) CA.) As with all such applications, the court is concerned only with the lawfulness of the FHSA's or Secretary of State's conduct or decision. It is not entitled to consider the merits of their decisions.

B. HOSPITAL DOCTORS

The 1992 Regulations and the procedures they lay down do not apply to hospital doctors. They are subject to different procedures dealing separately with complaints and discipline.

1. Complaints procedure

The Hospital Complaints Procedure Act 1985 contemplates that health authorities must introduce and publicise complaints procedures.
    Section 1(1) provides:

1.– (1) It shall be the duty of the Secretary of State to give to each health authority in England and Wales and to each Health Board in Scotland such directions under section 17 of the National Health Service Act 1977 or section 2(5) of the National Health Service (Scotland) Act 1978 (directions as to exercise of functions) as appear to him necessary for the purpose of securing that, as respects each hospital for the management of which that authority or Board is responsible –
(a) such arrangements are made for dealing with complaints made by or on behalf of persons who are or have been patients at that hospital; and

(b)   such steps are taken for publicising the arrangements so made, as (in each case) are specified or described in the directions.

Pursuant to this statutory power the Secretary of State issued a circular, *Health Service Management Hospital Complaints Procedure Act 1985* in June 1988 (HC (88) 37) mandating health authorities to introduce by 29 July 1988 a procedure for hospital complaints. (In June 1993 the Government set up the NHS Complaints Review Committee chaired by Professor Alan Wilson to review the existing NHS complaints procedures. It is due to report in 1994.)

The current system for dealing with hospital complaints may be considered under two headings: (a) those not relating to the exercise of clinical judgment by a doctor; (b) those which do relate to clinical judgment.

(a) Complaints not relating to clinical judgment

(i) GOVERNMENT CIRCULARS

HM(66) 15 issued by the DHSS in 1966 laid down a procedure for investigating such complaints. This procedure was amplified (but not replaced) in 1981 by HC(81)5 as a result of the recommendations of a Committee, set up by the DHSS and chaired by Sir Michael Davies, on Hospital Complaints Procedures which reported in 1973.

The current procedure is contained in HC(88)37. Appendix A of the Circular contains a Direction from the Secretary of State pursuant to section 17 of the NHS Act 1977 and provides as follows:

1. In these Directions:–

'authority' means any district health authority or special health authority to whom these directions are given;
'complainant' means a person who is or who has been a patient at a hospital or the person acting on behalf of any such patient in making a complaint in relation to such hospital;
'designated officer' means a person who has been designated by a health authority as having responsibility for dealing with complaints made in relation to that hospital or group of hospitals.

2. (1) For each hospital or group of hospitals for which an authority has responsibility, there must be an officer designated by the authority as having responsibility for dealing with complaints made in relation to that hospital or group of hospitals.

(2) The duties of a designated officer must include responsibility for receiving, and seeing that action is taken upon, any formal complaint made at the hospital or hospitals for which he is given responsibility, and, where the complainant had indicated a wish for him so to do, assisting in dealing with a complaint that is likely to be able to be dealt with informally.

(3) Except to the extent that the subject matter of a complaint falls within any of the categories specified in the next sub-paragraph of these directions the duties of the designated officer must include responsibility for investigating and reporting on the investigation of any formal complaint to the complainant, to any person involved in the complaint, and to such other persons as the authority may require.

(4) To the extent that the subject matter of the complaint made at a hospital or group of hospitals for which a designated officer is responsible:-

(a)   concerns the exercise of clinical judgment by a hospital doctor or dentist and cannot be resolved by discussion with the consultant concerned [ie Annex B reproducing HC(81)15 *infra*, p 600]; or

(b)   relates to what the authority is satisfied constitutes a serious untoward incident involving harm to a patient [ie HM(66)15]; or

(c)   relates to the conduct of hospital medical or dental staff which the authority considers ought to be the subject of disciplinary proceedings [ie HC(90)9]; or

(d)   gives reasonable grounds for inviting a police investigation as to whether a criminal offence may have been committed;

the duties of the designated officer in accordance with arrangements made pursuant to these directions shall not involve responsibility for investigating the complaint but the designated officer shall be required to bring the matter to the attention of his authority who shall, in the case of a matter specified in (a), (b) or (c) of this sub-paragraph, secure that the matter is promptly dealt with in accordance with the appropriate procedure laid down in guidance issued to authorities by the Department of Health and Social Security [currently Department of Health] in respect of England and by the Welsh Office in respect of Wales.

(5) Arrangements made may include provision for a designated officer to have the assistance of other officers of the authority in carrying out his duties under those arrangements and, with the agreement of the designated officer, such other officers may act on his behalf in the performance of those duties.

3. Each authority shall secure that arrangements are made for staff at any hospital for which that authority is responsible to seek to deal informally to the satisfaction of the complainant with any complaint made at that hospital and to advise any complainant, whose complaint cannot be so dealt with to his satisfaction, to make a formal complaint to the designated officer for that hospital.

4. Arrangements for making formal complaints should secure that such complaints are made or recorded in writing. Such complaints should normally be made within three months of the matter complained of arising although the designated officer ought to have a discretion to allow a longer period if satisfied that the complainant had good cause for not having made the complaint earlier. Arrangements made should secure that formal complaints are investigated promptly and that both the complainant and any hospital staff involved are afforded an opportunity to bring to the attention of the designated officer any information or comments they wish to make that are relevant to his investigation of the complaint.

5. Each authority must monitor arrangements made for dealing with complaints at hospitals for which it is responsible. Arrangements must be made for reports to be prepared at quarterly intervals for use by the authority in monitoring progress on the procedure for dealing with complaints, for considering trends in complaints and for taking remedial action on complaints as appropriate.

6. Each authority shall take such steps as are necessary to ensure that any patients at, or visitors to, any hospital for which the authority is responsible, as well as the staff working at the hospital, and any Community Health Council covering an area served by that hospital, are fully informed of the arrangements for dealing with complaints made at the hospital and are informed of the identity and location of the designated officer for such hospital.

In the body of the Circular, the Secretary of State (at paragraph 5) restates the need for a complaints procedure and elaborates on what is required of health authorities.

THE NEED FOR A COMPLAINTS PROCEDURE

5. Patients are entitled to bring to the attention of health authorities aspects of their care and treatment about which they are unhappy. The Department recognises that suggestions, constructive criticism and complaints can be valuable aids to management in maintaining and developing better standards of health care. It is important that no one (staff or patients) should be inhibited from making valid complaints and that there is full confidence that these will be given full, proper and speedy consideration. Many matters that trouble patients can be dealt with as they arise. Staff should be encouraged to be aware of and to deal with these in a way which reassures the patient and to bring the complaint to the attention of management when this is appropriate.

PROCEDURAL REQUIREMENTS

6. The basis of any complaints procedure is good communication. Problems of communication between patients and staff can generate misunderstanding which can result in complaints. Good communications may help defuse awkward situations. However, not all complaints can be dealt with on the spot and in this informal way. Some complaints will be of such concern to the patient that they warrant consideration and a formal response by a senior officer of the authority or it may be that the complaint is comparatively trivial but the patient feels unwilling or unable to discuss the matter with the staff who are directly involved. Again, good communications will be necessary to ensure that the complainant can give full expression to his concerns and that the full facts about the complaint are obtained.

7. The directions outline the mandatory requirements which health authorities must adopt in establishing complaints procedures. They involve

i. *A designated officer.* Each Health Authority must designate a senior officer for each hospital or group of hospitals for which it is responsible. The designated officer should be located in the hospital for which he is responsible and his whereabouts made known to facilitate contact by patients or those acting on a patient's behalf. The Unit General Manager might be the appropriate person for this task. The designated officer will be the recipient of formal complaints made by or on behalf of patients and will be accountable for the investigation of complaints other than those involving clinical judgment, serious untoward incidents, disciplinary proceedings, physical abuse of patients or criminal offences. Where the designated officer is also the Unit General Manager he may well be directly involved in these particular complaints. But investigation of these may also involve other senior officers, eg the Regional Medical Officer (RMO) or the equivalent or the District General Manager (DGM), or members of the authority (see sub-paragraph iv below). The designated officer should not be denied access to relevant records which are essential for the investigation of a complaint. The designated officer should normally be available to assist in cases of minor grievances which the patient feels unable to discuss with eg ward staff.

ii. *Who may complain.* Any person who is or has been a patient at the hospital (either as an inpatient or outpatient) is eligible to make a complaint. If the person concerned has died or is otherwise unable to act for himself the complaint should be accepted from a close relative, or friend, or a body or individual suitable to represent him. The designated officer must be satisfied that where the patient is capable, the complaint is being made with his knowledge and consent.

iii. *Investigating the complaint.* In investigating the complaint, the designated officer must ensure that he has a full picture from the complainant of the events complained about. This may involve a preliminary interview to clarify the nature of the complaint or to obtain further information. It may be possible at this stage to resolve the issue to the complainant's satisfaction without taking the matter further. Care must be taken not to prejudice the outcome of any further investigation.

The designated officer, in liaison with other appropriate senior officers, should circulate details of the complaint to the staff concerned for their comments and seek to agree a reply. General complaints about, for example, the hotel services would be sent to the Head of the Department concerned for advice on a reply. Care must be taken not to introduce delays into the system by allowing excessive periods for comment. The aim should be to process the complaint speedily and thoroughly at all stages. The complainant must be kept informed of progress and where appropriate interim replies or holding letters must be sent. Where the designated officer considers that a complaint carries a threat of litigation he should seek legal advice on whether and in what form an investigation might proceed to minimise the risk of prejudicing any civil proceedings. The possibility of legal proceedings should not prevent the officer undertaking the investigations necessary to uncover faults in procedures and/or prevent a recurrence.

iv. *Further action to certain complaints.* Where the complaint concerns:

a.   the exercise of *clinical judgment* which cannot be resolved by discussion with the consultant concerned;

b.   what the authority is satisfied constitutes *a serious untoward incident* involving harm to a patient;

c.   the conduct of hospital medical or dental staff which the authority considers ought to be the subject of *disciplinary proceedings*;

d.   the alleged *physical abuse of patients*;

e.   a possible *criminal offence*;

the designated officer should bring the matter to his senior officers' attention (or if appropriate the RMO) without delay so that the appropriate action can be taken to ensure that the complaint is dealt with promptly in accordance with the Department's guidelines and local procedures.

v. *Conclusion of an investigation.* When an investigation into a complaint has been completed the designated officer must complete a report and send a letter detailing the results of the investigation to the person who made the complaint, to any person who is involved in the complaint and where appropriate to the manager of any Department or service concerned. The letter should be informative both as to the reasons for any failure in service and any steps taken to prevent a recurrence and should contain an apology where appropriate. If the complainant remains dissatisfied he should be advised to refer the matter to the Health Service Commissioner unless the complaint is clearly outside the Health Service Commissioner's jurisdiction or the complainant proposes to take further action through the courts.

vi. *Monitoring complaints.* Health authorities must monitor the arrangements. The purpose of this requirement is to ensure that health authorities monitor trends in complaints and can direct that appropriate action is taken. The designated officer should therefore provide summaries of complaints for the health authority. These summaries should be anonymised to preserve confidentiality of patients. The monitoring role must be undertaken by the authority itself, a committee of the authority or specified authority members. Progress in dealing with complaints should be kept under review by the District General Manager who should report to the authority at quarterly intervals about any cases outstanding.

vii. *Publicity*. Publicity must be given to the procedure. This is an essential part of improving the public perception of the complaints procedure. Health authorities should consider giving publicity to the procedures using:

a.   *Admission booklets*. Information about making a complaint should be given in the hospital booklet issued to patients on or prior to admission to hospital and [be] available in hospital outpatient departments. It is essential for the location of the designated officer to be included.

b.   *Leaflets*. A leaflet explaining the complaints procedure and including a reference to the Health Service Commissioner's role in investigating complaints should be available for all patients. In addition to explaining the procedure in straightforward terms, the leaflet should give the location of the designated officer. Authorities should consider the need to make leaflets available in ethnic minority languages.

c.   *Notices*. These should be displayed in health authority premises including reception areas. Notices should give the location of the designated officer to whom appropriate comments, suggestions and complaints should be addressed.

d.   *CHCs*. Publicity material should be available to CHCs for information and issue to the public.

e.   *Staff training*. All staff will need to be made aware of the complaints procedure and to know the name and location of the designated officer to enable them to refer patients. Training will be needed to ensure that staff attitudes are positive and do not deter legitimate complaints.

ADDITIONAL PROCEDURES

8. In considering their procedures health authorities are asked to take the following elements, which are not requirements under the directions, into account.

i. *Form of complaint*. It is not a requirement that a complaint should be in writing. But it is important that a note be made in cases where the complaint is not readily settled and where a dispute as to the precise nature of the complaint might arise. This is particularly so when a formal investigation is likely. Where the complainant is unable to put the formal complaint in writing the designated officer should ensure that a record of the complaint is made and ask the complainant to sign it. A refusal to sign by the complainant should not delay investigation of the complaint.

ii. *Time limits*. Complaints should be made and dealt with as quickly as possible. The longer the delay the more memories fade and the less fruitful the investigation of the complaint. It is reasonable to expect that complaints should be made within three months of the incident giving rise to the complaint and publicity should encourage this. However there may be circumstances in which this recommended time limit may not be appropriate and the directions provide the designated officer with the discretion to extend the period if it is considered that the complainant has good reason for delay.

iii. *Complaints about the Community Health Services*. Complaints about the Community Health Services do not come within the scope of the procedures to be laid down in the directions under the Hospital Complaints Procedure Act 1985. Health authorities are asked to consider that the procedure directed for the handling of general complaints about hospital services should also be adopted in respect of the community health services.

As a result of s 1A of the Hospital Complaints Procedure Act (introduced by the NHS and Community Care Act 1990, Sch 9, para 29), NHS trusts are required to comply with any directions under s 1 of the Act, ie to apply the complaints procedure within NHS trusts.

(ii) THE HEALTH SERVICE COMMISSIONER

We have already seen references to the Health Service Commissioner (HSC). This office was created by Part V of the National Health Service Act 1977. From

5 February 1994 these provisions are replaced by the Health Service Commissioners Act 1993. The HSC's functions are contained in s 3(1):

> 3. (1) On a complaint duly made to a Commissioner by or on behalf of a person that he has sustained injustice or hardship in consequence of
> (a)   a failure in a service provided by a health service body,
> (b)   a failure of such a body to provide a service which it was a function of the body to provide, or
> (c)   maladministration connected with any other action taken by or on behalf of such a body,
> the Commissioner many, subject to the provisions of this Act, investigate the alleged failure or other action.

(A 'health service body' is defined in s 2 so as to include regional or district health authorities, family health services authorities, NHS trusts and special hospital authorities.

Certain matters are beyond the jurisdiction of the HSC:

> 4. (1) A Commissioner shall not conduct an investigation in respect of action in relation to which the person aggrieved has or had
> (a)   a right of appeal, reference or review to or before a tribunal constituted by or under any enactment or by virtue of Her Majestys prerogative, or
> (b)   a remedy by way of proceedings in any court of law,
> unless the Commissioner is satisfied that in the particular circumstances it is not reasonable to expect that person to resort or have resorted to it.
> (2) A Commissioner shall not conduct an investigation in respect of action which has been, or is, the subject of an inquiry under section 84 of the National Health Service Act 1977 or section 76 of the National Health Service (Scotland) Act 1978 (general powers to hold inquiries).
> 5. (1) A Commissioner shall not conduct an investigation in respect of action taken in connection with
> (a)   the diagnosis of illness, or
> (b)   the care or treatment of a patient,
> which, in the opinion of the Commissioner, was taken solely in consequence of the exercise of clinical judgment, whether formed by the person taking the action or any other person.
> (2) In subsection (1), 'illness' includes a mental disorder within the meaning of the Mental Health Act 1983 or the Mental Health (Scotland) Act 1984 and any injury or disability requiring medical or dental treatment or nursing.
> 6. (1) A Commissioner shall not conduct an investigation in respect of action taken in connection with any general medical services, general dental services, general ophthalmic services or pharmaceutical services under the National Health Service Act 1977 by a person providing those services. . . .
> (3) A Commissioner shall not conduct an investigation in respect of action taken by a Family Health Services Authority in the exercise of its functions under the National Health Service (Service Committees and Tribunal) Regulations 1992, or any instrument amending or replacing those regulations.
> 7. (1) A Commissioner shall not conduct an investigation in respect of action taken in respect of appointments or removals, pay, discipline, superannuation or other personnel matters in relation to service under the National Health Service Act 1977 or the National Health Service (Scotland) Act 1978.
> (2) A Commissioner shall not conduct an investigation in respect of action taken in matters relating to contractual or other commercial transactions, except for
> (a)   matters relating to NHS contracts (as defined by section 4 of the National Health Service and Community Care Act 1990 and, in relation to Scotland, by section 17A of the National Health Service (Scotland) Act 1978, and
> (b)   matters arising from arrangements between a health service body and a body which is not a health service body for the provision of services for patients by that body.

So, you can see that there are several important exclusions. They include cases in which the patient has a remedy in a court of law (unless it would not be reasonable to expect the patient to pursue this remedy), GPs' dealings with their patients, any action concerned with the diagnosis of illness or the care or treatment of a patient which involved the exercise of clinical judgment and the performance of an FHSA's functions under the 1992 Service Regulations.

Further, s 3(2) and (3) provides:

> 3. (2) In determining whether to initiate, continue or discontinue an investigation under this Act, a Commissioner shall act in accordance with his own discretion.
>
> (3) Any question whether a complaint is duly made to a Commissioner shall be determined by him.

It is doubtful whether this provision would exclude judicial review proceedings if the HSC misconstrued any part of the statutory provisions setting up his jurisdiction to investigate complaints. But, s 3(2) and (3) does suggest that the courts might regard certain issues, for example whether it is reasonable to expect a patient to sue, as a discretionary matter for the HSC, with the consequential effect of greatly curtailing the court's power of review.

I. Who may complain? Sections 8(1) and 9(3) provide:

> 8. (1) A complaint under this Act may be made by an individual or a body of persons, whether incorporated or not, other than a public authority.
>
> 9. (3) The complaint shall not be entertained unless it is made
> (a) by the person aggrieved, or
> (b) where the person by whom a complaint might have been made has died or is for any reason unable to act for himself, by
>   (i) his personal representative,
>   (ii) a member of his family, or
>   (iii) some body or individual suitable to represent him.

The health authority may also refer a complaint to the Commissioner if received by it from a person who alleges maladministration (section 10).

II. How is a complaint made? Section 9 provides:

> 9. (1) The following requirements apply in relation to a complaint made to a Commissioner.
> (2) A complaint must be made in writing.
> (3) The complaint shall not be entertained unless it is made
> (a) by the person aggrieved, or
> (b) where the person by whom a complaint might have been made has died or is for any reason unable to act for himself, by
>   (i) his personal representative,
>   (ii) a member of his family, or
>   (iii) some body or individual suitable to represent him.
> (4) The Commissioner shall not entertain the complaint if it is made more than a year after the day on which the person aggrieved first had notice of the matters alleged in the complaint, unless he considers it reasonable to do so.
> (5) Before proceeding to investigate the complaint, the Commissioner shall satisfy himself that
> (a) the complaint has been brought to the notice of the health service body concerned by or on behalf of the person aggrieved, and
> (b) that body has been afforded a reasonable opportunity to investigate and reply to the complaint.
> (6) The Commissioner shall disregard the provisions of subsection (5) if the complaint is made under subsection (3)(b) on behalf of the person aggrieved by an officer of the health service body in question and the Commissioner is satisfied that in the particular circumstances those provisions ought to be disregarded.

The procedure to be followed in any investigation is set out in sections 11-18 of the Act. Professor Brazier, *op cit*, describes the investigation process (pp 195-6).

> His powers of inquiry are extensive. He and his staff investigate in private. They will contact all hospital staff involved with a complaint and seek their comments. The Commissioner has complete control of the investigation. If co-operation from hospital staff or administrators is not forthcoming, the production of records and documents may be ordered and staff may be compelled to testify to the Commissioner. Exceptionally evidence can be taken on oath, but this has happened only once so far to my knowledge. In that case the preliminary evidence from the parties had been totally irreconcilable. The Commissioner regretted this occasion. Successive Commissioners pride themselves on good relations with health service staff, rendering resort to powers of compulsion unnecessary.
>
> On completion of an investigation the Commissioner reports to the complainant, the health authority, and any individual against whom allegations were made. The report will contain a decision as to whether the complaint was justified and recommend a remedy. In 1989-90 42.7 per cent of complaints investigated were found to be justified. The most common remedy is an apology from the authority and the staff member involved. Increasingly he recommends too that the DHSS and health authorities make changes in practice to avoid a recurrence of similar complaints. For example, in 1984-5 on the initiative of the Commissioner steps were taken to review procedures for writing to GPs on the patient's discharge, to improve communication with relatives and to improve monitoring of complaints procedures. Very occasionally the Commissioner may additionally recommend the making of an *ex gratia* cash payment to a patient by way of compensation. These are usually small sums, arising from cases where maladministration has resulted in loss of patients' property or unnecessary expenses. The Commissioner does not regard it as his function to grant monetary compensation for pain and hardship suffered by patients.

Two points arise for comment. First, what is the staple diet of the HSC? Secondly, since many instances of maladministration might result in litigation, how does the HSC interpret his power to investigate a complaint notwithstanding this possibility?

As to the first, Professor Brazier, *op cit*, describes his work (pp 196-9).

> The reports of the Commissioner from 1974 onwards make interesting, if somewhat depressing, reading. Certain sorts of complaints recur. Waiting lists, lack of communication by medical staff, inadequate liaison with GPs, delay in attendance by doctors, and unsatisfactory supervision of the elderly and vulnerable appear again and again. Maternity and geriatric care seem to generate a disproportionate number of complaints. Rudeness, lack of sympathy and even in extreme cases allegations of assault by staff cause the Commissioner much concern.
>
> The Annual Report for 1984-5 identifies six topics which have caused the Commissioner particular concern. They are (1) care and supervision of the elderly and handicapped, (2) contents and use of medical records, (3) delay in doctors attending patients, (4) arrangements made for discharge from hospital, (5) recording and investigation of alleged assaults, and (6) the initial handling of complaints by hospitals. Five years later, in 1989-90, the main topics of concern were listed as (1) observation and management of patients, especially elderly or handicapped patients, (2) arrangements for discharge, (3) procedures and management, in particular delayed operations, (4) patients being led to believe they would have to opt for private treatment, as they were unlikely to receive NHS treatment promptly, (5) the handling of complaints by hospitals, (6) the procedures for independent professional review, and (7) the operation of Family Practitioner Committees. It is a profoundly depressing list. It is depressing because three of the main concerns expressed in 1984-5 recur again five years later. There seems no evidence of improvements in these areas. Two of the 'new' causes for concern, delayed operations and patients being misled into thinking that they must resort to the private sector, indicate a deep malaise in our public health service.
>
> What can the Commission do to allay such disquiets? Often his role can be no more than to advise and admonish. In cases relating to care and management of vulnerable patients, he has made it clear that rudeness and dictatorial behaviour are unacceptable. . . .

Failures relating to discharge arrangements require revised procedures and better communications between hospitals and patients and hospitals and community medical services. In one sadly typical case in 1984-5 an elderly woman was discharged from hospital after nine weeks' hospitalization for chest trouble. Earlier that week she had scalded herself and on the day of discharge she fell in the ward. The Commissioner found that inadequate arrangements were made to inform the GP of her condition and that her husband was given insufficient information to care for her at home. Successive Commissioners have been highly critical of poor communications within the NHS, alas to little avail.

The depressing theme of mishandled complaints generating further complaints to the Commissioners goes on and on. In his Annual Report for 1989-90 the new Commissioner, W K Reid, commented sadly:

> Sometimes an indifferent or careless local investigation or even the lack of an apology for an obvious mistake are all that is needed to send the complainant along a stressful – and perhaps increasingly exasperating – path to my door. Fear of litigation may at times lie behind defensiveness on the part of the person complained against, but that is quite possibly the last thing that the complainant had in mind when looking for an explanation.

Five years earlier his predecessor had lamented, '. . . a very large number of complaints would never reach me if they were dealt with more thoroughly, accurately, promptly and sympathetically in the first instance'. . . .

No one would deny that a number of complaints are trivial and that distressing allegations are sometimes made against doctors and nurses with absolutely no basis. But complainants do not go away if they are ignored or even threatened. Very often a simple explanation is all that is called for. If that is not forthcoming, the complainant will simply progress to the next stage of the procedure. Investigation by the Health Service Commissioner wastes more valuable medical time, causes more anxiety and is more likely to damage the doctor's or nurse's reputation than a thorough prompt internal inquiry. For this reason it is to be hoped that the Hospital Complaints Procedures Act leads, as was intended, to an effective and uniform scheme based on the individual hospital Ombudsman.

The concerns of the Commissioner in 1989-90 echo familiar themes from the previous fourteen years. Other areas which have generated complaints of particular importance include failing to tell patients of their right to object to the presence of medical students, inadequate explanations when obtaining consent to surgery, failing to listen to the patient, and many others in a catalogue illustrating the importance of the patient being treated as an intelligent individual. Other complaints arise from sheer mismanagement. Dentures get lost. Special diets are ignored and so on. A number of disquiets arise from the lack of resources. Waiting lists for hip replacements, and delays in surgery generally, have been investigated by the Commissioner several times. He cannot wave a magic wand and end the waiting. He can ensure that maladministration does not extend the waiting time, that the lists are properly organized, and once again that patients are kept fully informed.

As to the second point, the possibility of litigation, the HSC has taken a relatively relaxed view. He has investigated cases in which lack of consent or negligence have been the issue. Sometimes, he has agreed to investigate if the patient has undertaken not to pursue any legal action. But, since this is not legally binding, the patient may still pursue a claim in law. If he does so, of course, the patient will have the benefit of the investigatory process of the HSC and his findings. Professor Brazier (*op cit*) remarks (p 201):

> Apparently this has happened only twice. Of course, if it was a regular occurrence the Commissioner might feel bound to reject all cases where there was any possibility, however remote, of court action.
>
> Is the restriction on dual access to the Commissioner and the courts justifiable? The Commissioner seems to think so. In 1980 he expressed his concern that he might be used to provide a free investigation service to enable potential litigants to decide whether or not to sue. Is there anything wrong with that? We have seen the tremendous difficulties faced by patients in litigation. If negligence has resulted in injury, and investigation as opposed to adversary litigation discovers that negligence, the patient ought to get compensation. His only crime is that he has not played the game by the old English rules. The rules are wrong.

(b) Complaints relating to clinical judgment

Until 1981, there was no DHSS Circular which dealt with a complaints procedure in cases in which *clinical judgment* was an issue. HC(81)15 set up such a procedure which has three stages. Stage 1 involves an informal process to be conducted by the consultant in charge of the patient's case. Stage 2 involves a more formal process, if the patient remains dissatisfied. Again, the consultant is involved but so also is the Regional Medical Officer. Stage 3 sets up a review procedure whereby 'second opinions' are obtained from two independent consultants in active practice in the relevant specialty, nominated by the Joint Consultants Committee. The current procedure, reproducing HC(81)15, is set out in HC(88)37. It provides as follows.

First stage
18. As explained in Paragraph 5 of Part I, a complaint may initially be made, and dealt with, orally or in writing. Complaints concerning clinical matters may be made direct to the consultant concerned, or to a health authority or one of its officers. In either case it is the responsibility of the consultant in charge of the patient to look into the clinical aspects of the complaint. This must be the first step in handling the complaint at the *first stage*.
19. If another member of the medical staff is involved, the consultant should discuss the complaint with the doctor concerned, at the outset and at all later stages in this procedure. It may be helpful to discuss the complaint with the patient's general practitioner. The consultant should try to resolve the complaint within a few days preferably by offering to see the complainant to discuss the matter and seek to resolve his anxieties. If there is any delay, he should get in touch with the complainant and explain the reason. When the consultant sees the complainant, he should make a brief, strictly factual, record in the hospital notes.
20. Where a complaint is made which involves hospital medical staff other than consultants, the consultant in charge of the patient and the doctor concerned should both be involved in the handling of the complaint at all stages.
21. If the consultant feels the risk of legal action is significant, he should at once bring the matter to the notice of the district administrator. Where there are non-clinical aspects to a complaint made direct to a consultant, the consultant should inform the district administrator, who will arrange for these aspects of the complaint to be considered by an appropriate member of staff.
22. Where a complaint which has a clinical element is made to the authority or one of its officers, the district administrator should show the complaint to the consultant concerned and refer the clinical aspects to him.
23. The normal practice will be for the district administrator to send a written reply to the complainant on behalf of the authority. Any reference to clinical matters in the reply, whether interim or final, should be agreed by the consultant concerned. Sometimes it may be appropriate to confine this to mentioning that the clinical aspects had been discussed between the consultant and the complainant. On occasion, the consultant may wish to send the complainant a written reply direct covering the clinical aspects.

Second stage
24. Where a complainant is dissatisfied with the reply he has received at the first stage, he may renew his complaint either to the authority, one of its administrators or to the consultant. In any case, if he has not so far put his complaint in writing, he should now be asked to do so before his complaint is considered further. The next step, *in this second stage*, is for the Regional Medical Officer (RMO) to be at once informed; this should be done by the consultant, informing the district administrator that he has done so. The RMO will discuss the matter with the consultant.
25. At this point, the consultant may indicate to the RMO that he also wishes to discuss the matter with his professional colleagues. After these discussions, he may consider that a further talk with the complainant might resolve the complaint. If this fails, or if the consultant feels that such a meeting would serve no useful purpose, the RMO should discuss with the consultant the value of offering to the complainant the procedure – outlined more fully below – whereby the RMO would arrange for two independent consultants to see the complainant jointly to discuss the problem. If in the light of his discussion with the consultant and – where necessary – the complainant, the RMO considers it appropriate, the procedure of the *third stage* should be set in motion.

Third stage – independent professional review

26. The procedure at the third stage is intended to deal with complaints which are of a substantial nature, but which are not prima facie (and in the light of legal advice where appropriate) likely to be the subject of more formal action either by the health authority or through the courts. The procedure is intended for use in suitable instances as an alternative to the inquiry procedures provided in HM(66)15, though these will remain available for use when necessary. It would not be appropriate if legal powers such as subpoena seem likely to be required. Nor is it intended that the new procedure should be invoked for complaints of a trivial nature.

27. Arrangements should be made by the RMO for all aspects of the case to be considered by two independent consultants in active practice in the appropriate specialty or specialties. They should be nominated by the Joint Consultants Committee. At least one should be a doctor working in a comparable hospital in another Region. These 'second opinions' should have the opportunity to read all the clinical records. They should discuss the case with the consultant concerned and any other members of the medical staff involved as well as with the complainant. The meeting between the two independent consultants and the complainant should be in the nature of a medical consultation. The consultant who had been in charge of the patient at the time of the event giving rise to the complaint should not be present at the meeting, but should be available if required. The complainant should if he wishes, be accompanied by a relative or personal friend and might wish to ask the general practitioner to be present.

28. 'Second opinions' should discuss the clinical aspects of the problem fully with the complainant. In cases in which it is their view that the clinical judgment of the medical staff concerned has been exercised responsibly, they should endeavour to resolve the complainant's anxieties. The view they have reached and the outcome of the discussion with the complainant should be reported to the RMO on a confidential basis.

29. In other cases the 'second opinions' might feel that discussion with the medical staff concerned would avoid similar problems arising in the future. When they had held such a discussion they would inform the complainant and would explain to him, as far as appropriate, how it was hoped to overcome the problems which had been identified. They should not provide a detailed report for the complainant but they should report the action they had taken to the RMO. The 'second opinions' would also consider whether there were any other circumstances which had contributed to the problems in the case and on which they could usefully make recommendations, which they would include in their report to the RMO. These might include matters requiring action by the health authority, for example the workload carried by the medical or nursing staff.

30. In exceptional cases it may appear to the 'second opinions', at any stage of an investigation, that the particular case is not appropriate to the second opinions procedure and that the complaint would be best pursued by alternative means. In this event they should report to the RMO accordingly.

Concluding action by the health authority

31. The district administrator will, on completion of the review by the 'second opinions', write formally to the complainant on behalf of the authority, with a copy to the consultant. The district administrator will, where appropriate, explain any action the authority has taken as a result of the complaint but, where clinical matters are concerned, he will follow the RMO's advice regarding the comment which would be appropriate. So far as the authority is concerned the matter will remain confidential unless previous or subsequent publicity makes it essential for the authority to reply publicly, in which case comment on clinical matters will be confined to the terms of the district administrator's letter.

Beyond this procedure, there is no other way outside recourse to the courts in which the patient may pursue his complaint. The HSC's jurisdiction, as we have seen, specifically excludes any case involving a complaint about 'clinical judgment' (Health Service Commissioners Act 1993, s 5(1)).

It has been said that the 'second opinions' procedure does not provide a satisfactory remedy to an aggrieved patient. Mr David Bolt in his lecture to the Medico-Legal Society, *op cit*, said (at p 224): 'How well it works, I really do not know, I hear very conflicting reports from various sources as to what its success rate is.'

In the light of what some see as significant weaknesses in the procedure for dealing with complaints relating to clinical judgment, should the HSC's jurisdiction be extended to cover cases involving 'clinical judgment'? In his 1979-80 Annual Report (HC 650) the Commissioner wrote as follows:

> I am particularly concerned about the difficulties which appear to me to be inherent in a parallel jurisdiction between my office and the courts with respect to medical negligence. There is an obvious danger that if my jurisdiction were to be extended to include clinical judgment then a person dissatisfied with some aspect of the medical treatment he has received might take advantage of my office to obtain a 'free' investigation into the merits of a possible case against a Health Authority. If I issue a report in his favour, this report might then be used as the basis for obtaining legal aid for a subsequent action and generally as a means of bringing pressure to bear. While I would see this, in itself, as an abuse, unintended by Parliament, of the service I provide, there is the further – and, in my view, more fundamental – danger that if such an action were subsequently decided against the plaintiff, perhaps on different evidence, the standing of my reports, and hence of my office as a whole, might be diminished. Conversely, if the courts decided for the plaintiff, there might be the equally undesirable suspicion that my report had somehow prejudiced the trial against the Health Service and its employees. And, last, but not least, the co-operation and frankness which I enjoy in my investigations might be seriously lessened if NHS staff thought that my reports might somehow be used to found legal actions against them.
>
> The solution, which has been considerably canvassed elsewhere, might be to offer aggrieved persons a statutory choice: to complain to me, or to take legal action – but not both. I believe this would be acceptable to the great majority of people, since in many of the cases I see the aggrieved person is genuinely not wanting money but a simple, factual explanation of some unexpected death or complication and an assurance that an attempt will be made to prevent a recurrence.
>
> Even if the other serious problems associated with the proposal to extend my jurisdiction to include actions stemming solely from clinical judgment were to be solved, I would regard it as essential to provide also for the matters raised in the preceding paragraphs. And I would still wish to retain, in matters of clinical judgment, my discretion not to investigate a case if, in all the circumstances, I did not think it desirable or useful to do so.

The current HSC has not expressed a view. Professor Brazier explores the unsatisfactory distinction drawn between cases that involve 'clinical judgment' and those that do not (*op cit*, at pp 201-3).

> Narrowly and literally interpreted, this limitation could have put senior doctors at least beyond the Commissioner's reach. Successive Commissioners have declined to follow that path. In the case . . . of the woman with epilepsy sterilised without her consent, the consultant first raised the 'defence' of clinical judgment. The Commissioner's finding that the consultant's decision was not founded on any decision that sterilisation was necessary for her health enabled him to continue his investigation. In 1979-80 a complaint by a woman who had undergone mastectomy and was refused a breast prosthetic on the NHS was investigated. The consultant argued that he never authorised prosthetics, that they were unnecessary and purely cosmetic. The Commissioner rejected his claim that the decision was arrived at in the exercise of clinical judgment. It had nothing to do with treating the complainant's illness; it was not a medical decision. The Commissioner condemned the refusal. One final example: a consultant genuinely concerned with the accessibility of records and X-rays refused to honour an appointment with a patient when the X-rays and records failed to be delivered. He would not even remove the plaster on his leg. The Commissioner found the doctor at fault. His concern for proper access to records was commendable. He may have been in the right in his dispute with the administration but he did not treat that patient properly. Nor could he claim that he acted in the exercise of clinical judgment. His course of action was not related to the care of the patient before him.
>
> Despite the Commissioner's activism in restricting clinical judgment to its proper sphere, strictly medical decisions on the treatment of the individual patient, the exemption of clinical judgment still causes concern. Drawing the line is very difficult. The Commissioner is, as we have seen, unhappy about arrangements for discharge. He cannot, however, question the original medical decision that the patient is fit for discharge. The case of the elderly lady discharged after having been scalded and after a fall exemplifies his problem.

The essence of that complaint would seem to be whether she should have been discharged at all.

The Select Committee on the Health Service Commission has urged since 1978 that the Commissioner's jurisdiction be extended to cover clinical judgment. Commissioners have seemed less keen. The introduction of review of clinical judgment is seen as bringing radical change to the office. More senior medical staff would need to be attracted to the Commissioner's staff. And the Commissioner has expressed fears of complainants using the investigation as a pre-litigation service. The Commissioner felt that investigation should only be allowed if a choice between the Commissioner and the courts could be made binding. If you went to the Commissioner, you would be barred from court. At present the debate on clinical judgment and the Commissioner is at stalemate.

2. Disciplinary procedures

As regards general practitioners, the disciplinary procedure is the complaints procedure which we have already seen in the National Health Service (Service Committees and Tribunal) Regulations 1992 (SI 1992 No 664).

For doctors working within hospitals the position is explained by the late Brian Raymond in the following.

B Raymond 'The Employment Rights of the NHS Hospital Doctor' in (C Dyer ed) *Doctors, Patients and the Law* (1992) (pp 197-205)

The rights provided by the NHS contract

Each health authority has its own standard form of employment contract, but each NHS doctor or dentist has 'written in' to his or her contract certain disciplinary and appeal procedures which provide limited safeguards for practitioners and guidance for health authorities who want to discipline or dismiss doctors in their employment. These may be summarised as:
(a) The disciplinary procedure for cases of *personal conduct* (section 40 of the 'Blue Book').
(b) The procedure for dealing with allegations of *professional conduct* or *professional competence* (Department of Health Circular HC(90)9)
(c) The procedure for appeals to the Secretary of State in all but personal misconduct cases (paragraph 190 of the 'Red Book')
The voluminous labyrinth of national terms and conditions contained in the 'Red' and 'Blue' Books is part and parcel of the hospital doctor's contractual rights and thus section 40 and paragraph 190 will apply to everyone. The position of the HC(90)9 procedure for dealing with allegations of professional misconduct and incompetence – the basis of the Wendy Savage inquiry in 1986 – is slightly less clear. The circular, like its predecessor, HM(61)112, states itself to be *guidance* to health authorities, and in the High Court case brought by Dr Marietta Higgs against the Northern Regional Health Authority, the authority argued that the circular was not mandatory and that authorities were free to ignore it if they wished. In that case, the authority had imposed substantial disciplinary sanctions on Dr Higgs following the publication of Lord Justice Butler-Sloss' report on the Cleveland child abuse crisis of 1987, but without having any kind of disciplinary hearing and specifically avoiding using the procedure set out in the circular. In the High Court, the judge upheld this proposition, but Dr Higgs appealed to the Court of Appeal against that decision. In the Court of Appeal, the case was eventually settled on agreed terms and no formal decision was ever made on this point. In the course of argument, however, the Master of the Rolls, Lord Donaldson, expressed the view that the circular obviously represented custom and practice within the Health Service and that large employers within a national public service were therefore bound to observe the procedures laid down by the appropriate Government minister. The net result is that while this issue is tinged with grey, it is sensible to proceed on the basis that every practitioner employed by a health authority can insist that the procedure in the circular is used.

Somewhat less clear is the position of practitioners employed within the NHS trusts. Section 6 of the NHS and Community Care Act 1990 makes it clear that on day one of their existence the trusts take over all the employment duties and liabilities of the health authority, which must therefore include the disciplinary apparatus set out above. On the other hand, it has been stated repeatedly that trusts have the power to determine their own terms and conditions of service for staff and it is therefore open to a trust to introduce different systems by following the appropriate procedures for variation of contracts of employment. The net position for doctors employed by trusts is therefore that they are covered by the mainstream NHS procedures unless their own trust has introduced different procedures, in which case the latter are applicable.

Personal misconduct – section 40
Personal conduct is defined as:

> performance or behaviour of practitioners due to factors other than those associated with the exercise of medical or dental skills.

The NHS procedure for dealing with allegations of this nature is set out in section 40 of the 'Blue Book' which comprises the entirety of the system for this category of complaint: there is no right to an HC(90)9 type of inquiry, nor is there any right to a paragraph 190 appeal to the Secretary of State against dismissal.

The section 40 procedure applies to all NHS employees accused of personal misconduct, from hospital porters to consultants, and consists mainly of a procedure for appealing to a committee of the employing authority against disciplinary action (including dismissal) taken at a lower level. The appeal is to a committee of three health authority members, at least one of whom should have a special knowledge of the work of the employee. Where this is not possible, and the appeal is against dismissal, the doctor's representative can ask for the appointment of a specialist assessor who will advise the appeal committee on matters of professional conduct and/or competence. Section 40 then sets out the standard procedure for the appeal hearing, including the usual provisions for the calling and cross-examination of witnesses, final addresses and mitigation.

The significance of section 40 is that since the removal, in March 1990, of the right to a paragraph 190 appeal to the Secretary of State in cases of personal misconduct, this procedure provides health authorities with a 'fast-track' method of dismissing doctors that they wish to be rid of. If your district general manager accuses you of illicit private use of the photocopier, for example, and his recommendation for dismissal is confirmed by the full authority, then only the section 40 appeal committee stands between you and the cold comfort of the industrial tribunal. . . . If your contract is held at district level, there is a discretionary right of appeal to the region, but the discretion is theirs, not yours, and they cannot be compelled to hear your appeal at all.

Practitioners would be well advised, therefore, to contact their defence society as soon as any allegation of personal misconduct is raised, even if the subject matter appears to be trivial.

Intermediate procedure
In addition to updating the procedure for inquiries into allegations of professional misconduct and incompetence, Circular HC(90)9 introduced a wholly new procedure for dealing with allegations which were within those categories, but which fell short of the seriousness required for a full-blown inquiry procedure. Faced with such a case (which can include a 'clash of professional views') the Director of Public Health (DPH) of the employing authority may implement the new intermediate procedure.

His first step is to write to the Joint Consultative Committee (JCC) with brief details of the case, asking them to nominate assessors to conduct an investigation, while informing the practitioner at the same time. The assessors (normally two) will come from a different region and at least one will be of the same specialty as the consultant concerned. Once appointed, the assessors receive a written 'statement of the case' from the DPH which is also copied to the doctor concerned. The assessors can then decline to act on the basis that the case is either too serious or too trivial for them or because the case falls within the 'three wise men' procedure of Circular HC(82)13. . . but if they decide to proceed within the intermediate procedure, their next task is to visit the district where the problem has arisen and 'undertake the necessary investigations'.

They then draw up a list of people they would like to see and copy this to the practitioner who may suggest additional names. Anyone who agrees to be interviewed (the assessors have no power of compulsion) will be asked to provide a written statement or to sign an agreed record of the interview. The practitioner will also meet the assessors either alone or in the company of a representative or friend, if he wishes.

Having completed their investigations, the assessors depart to write their report which will comprise a first part containing findings of fact and a second part containing details of which doctors (if any) are at fault and recommendations concerning organisational matters or advice to be given to the consultant. The DPH then receives the report (again copied to the practitioner) and then decides what action to take in accordance with section 40 if appropriate.

It is too early to say how this new procedure will work out in practice and certainly no aspect of its operation has been taken before the courts for review. The welcome aspect of the procedure is the way in which the procedure cannot be implemented behind the practitioner's back, as he must be informed from the very start. What is unwelcome, however, is the apparent inability of the practitioner to have any influence over the choice of assessors. There is nothing to stop the JCC appointing assessors who are either known to favour policies and clinical practices at the opposite end of the spectrum from the practitioner under scrutiny or individuals who are known informal associates of the practitioner's accusers or antagonists in the dispute under review.

Similarly, the inquisitorial method by which evidence is taken in private and in the absence of the practitioner provides abundant opportunity for unfairness, bias and malice. The procedure should provide for the practitioner to be seen twice, once at the outset to respond to the DPH's written statement of case and then again after all the other witnesses have been seen, to respond to any points or allegations which may have been made against him, which the assessors should be bound to disclose. It is a cardinal principle of natural justice, as enforced by the courts, that no information should be used against an individual in these circumstances unless that individual is given the information and an opportunity to rebut or comment. Practitioners who find themselves being made the subject of intermediate procedure should demand that the assessors adopt this method.

The full-blown HC(90)9 – preliminary steps

Where an allegation of professional misconduct or incompetence is too serious to be dealt with via the intermediate procedure – where the practitioner is in jeopardy of serious disciplinary action including (but not confined to) dismissal – the full-blown HC(90)9 procedure must be used. The key figure in the early stages of this system is the health authority chairman, whose first task is to ascertain whether or not there is a *prima facie* case against the doctor concerned. Any preliminary inquiries must be conducted by the DPH who may also invoke the assistance of the authority's legal adviser. At this stage, the chairman is required to inform the practitioner immediately of the nature of the complaint made and that an inquiry, which could lead to dismissal, is under consideration. The practitioner is then given the opportunity to make representations to the chairman.

These 'early warning' provisions are less valuable than they seem. In the Wendy Savage case, which is the best documented example of the system in operation, the first 'complaints' were made over a year before Mrs Savage was notified in accordance with the above provisions. The first she knew that anything was afoot was when she was summoned out of a clinic to see the district medical officer . . .

The significance of the Savage case is not just that so much of what is normally conducted behind closed doors was done openly and in the public spotlight, but that it also resulted in her complete exoneration from any suggestion of incompetence. In other words, it was a case that should never have been started at all and having started should have been stopped at the earliest opportunity. Nevertheless, it ran its full course, costing Mrs Savage a 14-month suspension with all the associated personal distress and Tower Hamlets Health Authority £250,000 which could otherwise have been spent on improving patient care. It is nothing less than a tragedy that the new HC(90)9 procedure which replaced the old HM(61)112 should embody none of the lessons which should have been learned as a result of that case. The opening paragraphs of the new procedure are an almost *verbatim* replica of the old procedure and still allow charges to be accumulated without the practitioner's knowledge.

Suspension from duty

The most immediate, humiliating and professionally damaging consequence of an allegation of serious incompetence or misconduct is suspension from duty. Mrs Savage was suspended on 25 April 1985, the day she was notified that the inquiry procedure was under way, and not reinstated until 24 July 1986, after the inquiry had taken place and the report had been produced. By the standards of other doctors in that position, however, she was fortunate: suspensions of three and four years are far from uncommon. The longest is believed to be that of Dr Bridget O'Connell, a consultant paediatrician working in East London who was suspended in December 1982 and remains so at the time of writing.

Despite the devastating impact of suspension, you will search in vain in the HC(90)9 procedure for any discussion of it. The only reference is a sentence which simply states that the inquiry procedure does not 'prejudice the right of the authority to take immediate action (eg suspension from duty) where this is required in cases of a very serious nature' [see now *Lyndon v Yorkshire RHA* (1991) 10 BMLR 49 (CA)].

The unpalatable reality is that employers generally have a very wide freedom to suspend employees from duty and the courts have shown a notable reluctance to intervene. The reason is that the law regards employment as a kind of commercial contract between the employer and employee – the employee provides services and the employer pays money in return. Suspension on full pay therefore is in the blinkered eyes of the law no more than the employer fulfilling his side of the bargain without requiring the employee to put in his or her side of it, rather like a shop giving away goods for nothing. Thus the law regards the suspended doctor not as someone who is undergoing the most professionally damaging experience it is possible to have short of outright dismissal, but as an unusually fortunate individual who is being paid without being required to work. As the law stands at present, therefore, the courts will intervene only if a doctor has been suspended in breach of an established local procedure, as there are none which bind health authorities on a national basis.

Suspension without due cause, or for an unreasonable length of time could constitute constructive dismissal, but where does that leave the practitioner? Once again the industrial tribunal with its inadequate remedies is the only recourse. Sooner or later, the courts are going to have to acknowledge that for highly skilled and dedicated professionals, suspension from duty is not a bonus but a devastating body-blow for which employers should be held fully accountable. For the moment, however, unjustified suspension is a wrong for which English law provides no meaningful or adequate remedy.

HC(90)9 – the inquiry

After hearing from the practitioner, the authority chairman decides whether a *prima facie* case still exists, and if he thinks that it does, he must proceed to the next stage in the inquiry. Note that he is not required to take any expert advice before taking this step and a distinguished consultant may find himself suspended and subjected to an inquiry on the grounds of incompetence without any expert medical opinion other than that of the Director of Public Health. Even if expert advice is taken, there is nothing to prevent its being obtained from a known opponent or antagonist of the practitioner or someone known for holding opposing clinical views. And even under the new procedure, the health authority chairman can suspend and proceed against any consultant without taking any outside opinion at all.

Once a decision has been made that there is a *prima facie* case, the chairman must proceed to hold a full inquiry unless the facts are undisputed, in which case the section 40 procedure is used. This is also to be used when the facts have been established by an official inquiry or a criminal case. If there is a dispute over whether an official inquiry has dealt with precisely the same issues as in the HC(90)9 allegation, an inquiry panel may be convened to decide whether a full hearing is necessary.

These stipulations about official inquiries are additions introduced by the new procedure and should serve as a warning bell to any practitioners who find themselves involved in such an inquiry. In the Cleveland inquiry, Lord Justice Butler-Sloss was at pains to reassure all concerned that her purpose was not to attribute blame and the normal procedure for warning individuals that they might be subject to criticism in inquiries was not used. Nevertheless, had the health authority decided to use the new procedure against Dr Higgs, they would have been able to attempt to by-pass the HC(90)9 inquiry altogether by invoking this clause. Any doctor involved in an official inquiry, therefore, should regard himself as effectively on trial, regardless of what is said to the contrary.

The inquiry panel specified by HC(90)9 consists of a legally qualified chairman, chosen from a list kept by the Lord Chancellor's Department, together with two side members – a doctor and a lay person in cases of professional misconduct, but two doctors in cases of alleged incompetence, at least one from the same specialty as the doctor accused of incompetence. The circular requires that terms of reference should be drawn up and that these together with copies of correspondence and any written statements made should be provided to the practitioner. He should also be supplied with a list of witnesses to be called for the 'prosecution' together with a note of the main points on which they can give evidence. This again is inadequate. For these proceedings to be conducted fairly, the allegations against the practitioner must be specified in as much detail as possible (there were 55 separate charges in the Savage case) and witnesses should be compelled to provide full statements so that the practitioner knows precisely the case he has to meet.

The proceedings follow the familiar adversarial pattern, save that the circular contains an exhortation to both sides to 'reduce the formality of the proceedings'. In my view, this encouragement should be resisted. Formality of the merely ceremonial or ritualistic kind is of course out of place in a hearing of this nature, but formality in the sense of orderliness of procedure and disciplined attitudes to matters of fact and opinion is essential if the practitioner is to obtain a fair hearing. As far as possible, allegations should be narrowed down, and evidence subjected to sensible but strict tests of relevance and admissibility. When a career is at stake (as it must be in these proceedings) it is not unreasonable for considerable care to be taken to guard against unfairness of any kind and experience shows that a casual, undisciplined approach to these matters is the enemy of justice and fair play.

At the end of the inquiry, the panel produce a two-part report to the authority on the same lines as that described for the intermediate procedure. The panel have no disciplinary powers themselves and the practitioner must be given a chance to make further representations to the authority before sentence is passed. One of the most welcome innovations of the new system is the introduction of a model time scale which envisages a complete HC(90)9 inquiry, from the time of the first decision that a *prima facie* case exists to the final report to the authority, taking no more than 32 weeks. As the Savage inquiry, then one of the fastest on record, took 14 months to make the same progress, there must be a degree of scepticism as to whether this time scale is realistic, but it nevertheless represents a major step forward.

The appeal to the Secretary of State – paragraph 190
A consultant or associate specialist dismissed for any reason other than personal misconduct has an automatic right to appeal to the Secretary of State for Health. This covers, for example, someone made redundant or dismissed after a full HC(90)9 inquiry, or after a section 40 hearing on professional conduct or competence. Notice of appeal must be lodged before the date the dismissal takes effect, but the full statement of case should be provided within four months of the date upon which notice was given, unless an extension is allowed by the Secretary of State. Thus a doctor who received three months' notice of redundancy on 1 January must give notice of appeal before 1 April, and get his statement of case in before 1 May.

On receipt of notice of appeal, the Secretary of State must ask the authority for its written views which must be provided within two months, subject to similar extensions if granted. The Secretary of State must also set up a professional committee to advise him on the case. This is chaired by the Chief Medical Officer of the Department of Health or his deputy and includes a representative of the Secretary of State and a representative of the practitioner's profession. It is assisted by a qualified solicitor or barrister and may, if it thinks fit, interview the practitioner and representatives of the authority, but is under no obligation to do so. The professional committee usually holds some kind of hearing, but can, if it wishes, conduct the entire procedure on the basis of the written statements and see no one in person.

Having conducted its investigation and deliberations, the committee reports to the Secretary of State, advising termination or continuance of employment or a third course, which is or might be acceptable to both the practitioner and the authority. Within three months of receiving the Committee's report, the Secretary of State must either confirm the termination or direct that the practitioner's employment continue or arrange some other solution acceptable to the practitioner and the authority. Thus the authority has a veto over any solution other than straightforward reinstatement.

3. Formal inquiries

(a) Inquiries by health authorities

Circular HM(66)15 contains a further procedure in paragraph 7(iii)(b) which allows for the appointment of an independent person or committee in very serious cases. Paragraph 7(iii)(b) provides:

. . . [I]n the small number of cases which are so serious that they cannot be dealt with satisfactorily in this way . . . the investigation should be referred for independent enquiry. Action to refer such cases should be taken by the Board of Governors or the Regional Hospital Board concerned on a reference from the Hospital Management Committee. The general rule should be that an independent lawyer or other competent person from outside the hospital service should conduct the enquiry, or preside over a small committee set up for the purpose, whose membership should be independent of the authority concerned and should include a person or persons competent to advise on any professional or technical matters. The complainant and any other persons who are the subject of the complaint should have an opportunity of being present throughout the hearing, and of cross-examining witnesses, and should be allowed to make their own arrangements to be legally represented if they so wish.

Professor Brazier (*op cit*) comments on the HM(66)15 procedure (at 205-6).

Where at any stage in an investigation of a complaint further action is found to be necessary, the matter may be referred on to the regional health authority. The authority may appoint one or more of its own members to look into the complaint, or in serious cases may set up an independent inquiry. The inquiry will be conducted by a small committee consisting usually of a legally qualified chairman and two medical practitioners, one from the same specialty as the person whose competence is in issue. All inquiring members will be unconnected with the hospital where the complaint originated. Copies of all documents are circulated to all parties. The complainant and the subjects of the complaint may be legally represented, and cross-examination of witnesses is allowed. Legal aid is not available, and no one can be compelled to attend the inquiry. The committee's findings of fact are then submitted to the staff concerned for further comment. Finally the committee reports its findings and recommendations to the authority.

The inquiry procedure can be effective. . . . It can also be cumbersome and unfair. And if hospital staff refuse co-operation the procedure may break down altogether. In 1976 Elizabeth Shewin entered hospital for a gall-bladder operation. In the course of the operation she suffered irreversible brain damage. On the advice of their medical defence organization, all ten doctors involved with Miss Shewin refused to give evidence to the inquiry. They finally agreed to appear on condition that the authority met any costs and award that might result if court action were later taken. The inquiry discovered that Miss Shewin's injury resulted from her being given nitrous oxide instead of oxygen because of an improvised and inadequate repair to anaesthetic equipment in the operating theatre. Miss Shewin's relatives sued the authority for negligence and won damages of £262,500. The authority in turn sued the manufacturers of the anaesthetic equipment. The doctors were virtually exonerated.

In a second example, a 26-year-old man, David Woodhouse, entered hospital in 1981 for an appendectomy. He never regained consciousness and ten months later still lay in a coma. Pressure from MPs led the health authority to set up an inquiry. Again, on the advice of their defence organization the doctors refused to testify. The inquiry was abandoned. The authority then asked three independent experts to examine the case. They reported on a series of disasters. For example, the anaesthetist's command of English was poor, he could not spell the names of basic drugs, and neither he nor the duty registrar knew how to use the ventilator. Mr Woodhouse was left without oxygen for twenty minutes. The health authority promised to tighten up procedures. An out-of-court settlement was reached to pay compensation to David Woodhouse and his family.

(b) Inquiries by the Secretary of State

The National Health Service Act 1977, Section 84(1) provides that 'The Secretary of State may cause an inquiry to be held in any case where he deems it advisable to do so in connection with any matter arising under this Act or Part I of the National Health Service and Community Care Act 1990.'

Professor Brazier (*op cit*) comments on the section 84 procedure as follows (at pp 206-7):

At such an inquiry all those involved may be compelled to attend and to produce documents, and if the person appointed to hold the inquiry sees fit all evidence may have to be given on oath. The [Secretary of State] rarely uses his coercive power. MPs pressed him to do so in the David Woodhouse case. He refused. Inquiries by the Health Minister are at present limited to cases of national scandal, such as ill-treatment of mental patients or the conditions at Stanley Royde Hospital which led to an outbreak of salmonella food poisoning. Successive [Secretaries of State] have argued that their power to order an inquiry was not intended for use in cases of individual error or even gross incompetence. His powers are to be invoked only to protect the public at large. Yet serious cases of accidents involving individuals may reveal dangers to the public. The [Secretary of State] refused to order an inquiry in the Woodhouse case despite tremendous pressure in Parliament. The authority's own endeavours revealed grave risks to anyone accepting anaesthesia in the area. Was it not in the public interest that this be revealed? Are prospective patients not entitled to know that their health authority may be employing doctors whose knowledge of English and resuscitation procedures may be lamentably and dangerously inadequate?

C. COMPLAINTS AGAINST DOCTORS IN PRIVATE PRACTICE

All registered medical practitioners, whether in private practice or within the NHS, are subject to the disciplinary jurisdiction of the GMC. Apart from this, however, there is no other formal mechanism other than through the common law whereby doctors in private practice may be held accountable.

Chapter 8

Medical records

A doctor needs to maintain medical records as part of the care of his patient. This is expressly set out in the terms of service of a general practitioner as a duty owned to his employing FHSA (see the National Health Service (General Medical Services) Regulations 1992 (SI 1992 No 635), Schedule 2, paragraph 36). It is undoubtedly also a legal obligation owed to his patient in the case both of GPs and hospital doctors.

Records may be either written down or electronically stored, but increasingly the latter. A patient may wish to have *access* to his records in order to discover what is said about him or to verify its accuracy. Also the patient may wish to *control* disclosure of the record to others given the sensitive nature of the information. It is these twin issues of access and control that we are concerned with in this chapter and the subsequent chapter on confidence.

Access

A. THE COMMON LAW

Prior to the passage of a series of Acts in the last ten years or so, the question of a patient's right of access to his medical records was by no means easy to resolve. The position at common law is as follows.

1. Access based upon ownership

If it could be said that the medical record containing the information belonged in law to the patient, then clearly the patient would be entitled to call for the medical record whenever he wished. In whom, therefore, is the ownership of a medical record vested? In our view, this *prima facie* turns on who owns the paper being used.

(a) Private patient

If the patient's contract is with the doctor then the question who owns the document depends initially on the contract (if any) made, not between the patient and the doctor but between the doctor and the clinic or institution. For in the absence of any agreement between them whereby ownership of the document is given up by the clinic or institution to the doctor (such that the doctor could then transfer it to himself), the ownership must remain vested in the clinic or institution. If the doctor is made the owner (or as agent may transfer ownership) then whether he does this or not depends upon the relationship between the doctor and the patient (see below).

If, on the other hand, the patient's contract is with the clinic or institution, then ultimate ownership will turn on the terms of the agreement between the parties. Ordinarily, of course, there will be no express term. So, what, if any, term will be implied? There is no clear law on this. It is likely that a court would imply a term to the effect that ownership remained in the clinic or institution, save that the patient should be entitled to possession where this is necessary for his continued health care, eg on a change of doctor or when he seeks a second opinion (see, eg, *McInerney v McDonald* [1991] 2 Med LR 267 (NB CA)).

What, however, if the doctor uses his own paper? Where the contract is made between the patient and the clinic or institution, subject to any agreement between the doctor and the clinic or institution, the paper probably belongs to the doctor.

Where the contract is made between the patient and the doctor, ownership depends upon the express or implied terms of that contract. Ordinarily, again, there will be no express term, in which case what term would a court imply? Ordinarily it must be that the court would imply the one seen above, namely that ownership vests, this time, in the doctor subject to a right of possession by the patient in certain circumstances, such as those described above.

(b) NHS patient

(i) THE GENERAL PRACTITIONER

The medical records of GPs are made on forms 'supplied . . . for the purpose by the FHSA' and thus remain the FHSA's property (The National Health Service (General Medical Services) Regulations 1992 (SI 1992 No 635), Schedule 2, paragraph 36).

(ii) THE HOSPITAL DOCTOR

In *Rights and Responsibilities* (1992) the BMA observes that 'medical records written by hospital doctors are made on NHS property' (para 4.1). Thus, they belong to the relevant health authority. In any event, if a hospital doctor did not use NHS paper but rather his own, then 'as hospital doctors are employed by a health authority, any records made by them in the course of their employment are kept by the relevant health authority, and are ultimately the property of the Secretary of State' (*ibid*).

2. Access beyond ownership

If the patient does not own the document itself and so has no right to call for it, what of his right to access, if any, to the information in the record?

Generally, the common law has not recognised a right in the patient to have access to the information in medical records about himself. What this means is that the common law has not recognised a cause of action. This may be because, to do so, ie to order the owner of a medical record to surrender that record to the extent of allowing others to see what is in that record, would represent a curtailment of the right of ownership previously recognised. For, if ownership in this context means a right to property good against everyone, it might contradict this right to allow another to call for the record so as to be able to examine it.

The courts have, however, carved out some exceptions to this general principle. There seem to be three exceptions, but they would appear to be of limited application to doctors and their patients.

The first is illustrated by the decision of the House of Lords in *Secretary of State for Defence v Guardian Newspaper* [1985] AC 339, [1984] 3 All ER 601, but is restricted to obtaining access to documents or copies thereof *by the owner* and, therefore, is irrelevant here. The second derives from the case of *Norwich Pharmacal v Customs and Excise Comrs* [1974] AC 133, [1973] 2 All ER 943. This case permits someone to discover the identity of a wrongdoer by requiring a third party who has information relevant to the wrongdoer, to disgorge it. Conceivably, this could be of use in a medical context where, for example, a patient wishes to obtain the identity of an attending doctor whom the patient wishes to sue and whose name is recorded in notes, but who is otherwise unknown to the patient. The third, based on *C v C* [1946] 1 All ER 562, actually concerned a doctor and his patient.

C v C [1946] 1 All ER 562 (Birmingham Assizes)

Lewis J: The circumstances which gave rise to this application are as follows: The respondent, a short time after marriage, exhibited symptoms which caused her to go to a venereal disease clinic where, on Feb 28, 1945, it was found she was suffering from a venereal disease in a communicable state. On this being discovered the petitioner went to the clinic and was examined, observed and treated by the same doctor who had examined and was treating the respondent. After some time it was found that there was no evidence whatever that the petitioner was suffering from this disease in any form. The respondent was not told that the disease from which she was in fact suffering was in a communicable form or, if it was, on Feb 28, in a communicable form, how long it had been in that form. On Aug 3, 1945, divorce proceedings having been instituted, the doctor was asked, *inter alia*, by the respondent to state particulars of her illness and if it was possible to say the approximate date of the commencement of that illness. Except to say that secondary syphilis was the disease, the doctor did not answer the respondent's request for the further information, which was vital to her and her advisers for the purpose of the defence of the proceedings. On or about Feb 27, 1946, a questionnaire consisting of six questions was sent to the doctor signed personally by the petitioner and the respondent, with the approval of the solicitors for both parties, asking for information as to the condition of the respondent, information which was vital to the parties to have for the proposed presentation of their respective cases. If those questions had been answered in one way the petitioner would have failed in proving what it was necessary to prove, if he was to succeed, and the respondent would have been able successfully to defend the case. To put it another way, the petitioner would have been unable to prove his case and the success of the respondent would have been a foregone conclusion. The doctor refused to give the information, stating that he would, if subpoenaed, give his evidence in court. He appeared in court and gave evidence and answered all questions put to him, and no sort of suggestion was made or could be made as to his good faith.

The question which arises out of these circumstances is: Is a doctor, when asked by his patient to give him or her particulars of his or her condition and illness to be used in a court of law, when those particulars are vital to the success or failure of the case, entitled to refuse and in effect to say: 'Go on with your case in the dark and I will tell you in court when I am subpoenaed what my conclusions are'? In the present case the patient asked the doctor to give her this information and asked him also to give the petitioner that same information, with the object of their being placed in a position which would enable them to know whether or not the petitioner had a case against the respondent: in other words, to assist the course of justice. It is, of course, of the greatest importance from every point of view that proper secrecy should be observed in connection with venereal disease clinics, and that nothing should be done to diminish their efficiency or to infringe the confidential relationship existing between doctor and patient. But, in my opinion, those considerations do not justify a doctor in refusing to divulge confidential information to a patient or to any named person or persons when asked by the patient so to do. In the circumstances of this case the information should have been given, and in all cases where the circumstances are similar the doctor is not guilty of any breach of confidence in giving the information asked for.

As we shall see, it was thought that the only means of responding to the legitimate claim of the patient was by way of legislation. The Canadian Supreme Court has shown, however, that the common law is sufficiently flexible to provide an answer.

McInerney v MacDonald (1992) 93 DLR (4th) 415 (Canadian Sup Ct)

La Forest J: The central issue in this case is whether in the absence of legislation a patient is entitled to inspect and obtain copies of his or her medical records upon request.

Facts
The facts are simple. The appellant, Dr Elizabeth McInerney, is a medical doctor who is licensed to practice in New Brunswick. The respondent, Mrs Margaret MacDonald, was her patient. Before her consultations with Dr McInerney, Mrs MacDonald was treated by various physicians over a period of years. On Dr McInerney's advice, Mrs MacDonald ceased taking thyroid pills previously prescribed by other physicians. She then became concerned about her medical care before consulting Dr McInerney, and wrote the latter requesting copies of the contents of her complete medical file. The doctor delivered copies of all notes, memoranda and reports she had prepared herself but refused to produce copies of consultants' reports and records she had received from other physicians, stating that they were the property of those physicians and that it would be unethical for her to release them. She suggested that Mrs MacDonald contact the other physicians for release of their records.
. . .

Issues
The appellant raises two issues in this appeal:
1. Are a patient's medical records prepared by a physician the property of that physician or are they the property of the patient?
2. If a patient's medical records are the property of the physician who prepares them, does a patient nevertheless have the right to examine and obtain copies of all documents in the physician's medical record, including records that the physician may have received which were prepared by other physicians?

Analysis
. . . I am prepared to accept that the physician, institution or clinic compiling the medical records owns the physical records. This leaves the remaining issue of whether the patient nevertheless has a right to examine and obtain copies of all documents in the physician's medical records. The majority of the Court of Appeal based the patient's right of access on an implied contractual term. While it may be possible to pursue the contractual route in the civil law system, I do not find it particularly helpful in the common law context. Accordingly, I am not entirely comfortable with the approach taken by the Court of Appeal. However, I do agree that a patient has a vital interest in the information contained in his or her medical records.

Medical records continue to grow in importance as the health care field becomes more and more specialized. As L E Rozovsky and F A Rozovsky put it in **The Canadian Law of Patient Records** (1984), at pp 73-74:

> The twentieth century has seen a vast expansion of the health care services. Rather than relying on one individual, a physician, the patient now looks directly and indirectly to dozens and sometimes hundreds of individuals to provide him with the services he requires. He is cared for not simply by his own physician but by a veritable army of nurses, numerous consulting physicians, technologists and technicians, other allied health personnel and administrative personnel.

While a patient may, in the past, have relied primarily upon one personal physician, the trend now tends to favour referrals to a number of professionals. Each of the pieces of information provided by this 'army' of health care workers joins with the other pieces to form the complete picture. As the number and use of specialists increase, the more difficult it is for the patient to gain access to that picture. If the patient is only entitled to obtain particular information from each health care provider, the number of contacts he or she may be required to make may become enormous. The problem is intensified when one considers the mobility of patients in modern society.

Medical records are also used for an increasing number of purposes. This point is well made by A F Westin, **Computers, Health Records and Citizen Rights** (1976), at p 27:

> As to medical records, when these were in fact used only by the physician or the hospital, it may have been only curiosity when patients asked to know their contents. But now that medical records are widely shared with health insurance companies, government payers, law enforcement agencies, welfare departments, schools, researchers, credit grantors, and employers, it is often crucial for the patient to know what is being recorded, and to correct inaccuracies that may affect education, career advancement or government benefits.

This then is the general context in which medical records are compiled and the broad purposes they serve in our day. The nature of the information contained in medical records must now be examined.

When a patient approaches a physician for health care, he or she discloses sensitive information concerning personal aspects of his or her life. The patient may also bring into the relationship information relating to work done by other medical professionals. The policy statement of the Canadian Medical Association . . . indicates that a physician cannot obtain access to this information without the patient's consent or a court order. Thus, at least in part, medical records contain information about the patient revealed by the patient, and information that is acquired and recorded on behalf of the patient. Of primary significance is the fact that the records consist of information that is highly private and personal to the individual. It is information that goes to the personal integrity and autonomy of the patient. As counsel for the respondent put it in oral argument: '[The respondent] wanted access to information on her body, the body of Mrs. MacDonald.' In *R v Dyment* [1988] 2 SCR 417, 89 NR 249, 73 Nfld & PEIR 13, 229 APR 13, 45 CCC (3d) 244, at p 429, I noted that such information remains in a fundamental sense one's own, for the individual to communicate or retain as he or she sees fit. Support for this view can be found in *Halls v Mitchell* [1928] SCR 125, at p 136. There Duff J held that professional secrets acquired from a patient by a physician in the course of his or her practice are the patient's secrets and, normally, are under the patient's control. In sum, an individual may decide to make personal information available to others to obtain certain benefits such as medical advice and treatment. Nevertheless, as stated in the **Report of the Task Force on Privacy and Computers** (1972), at p 14, he or she has a 'basic and continuing interest in what happens to this information, and in controlling access to it'.

A physician begins compiling a medical file when a patient chooses to share intimate details about his or her life in the course of medical consultation. The patient 'entrusts' this personal information to the physician for medical purposes. It is important to keep in mind the nature of the physician-patient relationship within which the information is confided. In *Kenny v Lockwood* [1932] OR 141 (CA), Hodgins JA, stated, at p 155, that the relationship between physician and patient is one in which 'trust and confidence' must be placed in the physician. This statement was referred to with approval by LeBel J in *Henderson v Johnston* [1956] OR 789, who himself characterized the physician-patient relationship as 'fiduciary and confidential', and went on to say, 'It is the same relationship as that which exists in equity between a parent and his child, a man and his wife, an attorney and his client, a confessor and his penitent, and a guardian and his ward' (p 799). Several academic writers have similarly defined the physician-patient relationship as a fiduciary or trust relationship: see for example, E I Picard, **Legal Liability of Doctors and Hospitals in Canada** (2nd edn 1984), at p 3; A Hopper, **The Medical Man's Fiduciary Duty** (1973), 7 Law Teacher 73; A J Meagher, P J Marr and R A Meagher, **Doctors and Hospitals: Legal Duties** (1991), at p 2; M V Ellis, **Fiduciary Duties in Canada** (1988), at pp 10-11. I agree with this characterization.

In characterizing the physician-patient relationship as 'fiduciary', I would not wish it to be thought that a fixed set of rules and principles apply in all circumstances or to all obligations arising out of the doctor-patient relationship. As I noted in *Canson Enterprises Ltd et al v Boughton & Co* [1991] 3 SCR 534, 131 NR 321, not all fiduciary relationships and not all fiduciary obligations are the same; these are shaped by the demand of the situation. A relationship may properly be described as 'fiduciary' for some purposes, but not for others. That being said, certain duties do arise from the special relationship of trust and confidence between doctor and patient. Among these are the duty of the doctor to act with utmost good faith and loyalty, and to hold information received from or about a patient in confidence. (Picard, supra, at pp 3 and 8; Ellis, supra, at pp 10-11 and 10-12, and Hopper, supra at pp 73-74.) When a patient releases personal information in the context of the doctor-patient relationship, he or she does so with the legitimate expectation that these duties will be respected. . . .

The fiduciary duty to provide access to medical records is ultimately grounded in the nature of the patient's interest in his or her records. As discussed earlier, information about oneself revealed to a doctor acting in a professional capacity remains, in a fundamental sense, one's own. The doctor's position is one of trust and confidence. The information conveyed is held in a fashion somewhat akin to a trust. While the doctor is the owner of the actual record, the information is to be used by the physician for the benefit of the patient. The confiding of the purposes gives rise to an expectation that the patient's interest in and control of the information will continue.

Certain textbooks and case law go further and assert that the patient has a 'proprietary' or 'property' interest in the medical records. For example, Meagher et al supra, write, at p 289:

> In the absence of an agreement, a doctor or hospital owns the records of the patient, but the patient is considered to have a property interest in the medical information contained in the record, with a right of access to it, but not to its possession.

Judicial support for the 'proprietary interest' of the patient can be found in *Re Mitchell and St Michael's Hospital* (1980) 112 DLR (3d) 360 (Ont HC). Although Maloney J there held that he did not have jurisdiction to order the release of hospital records on an originating notice of motion, he had this to say, at 364:

> By virtue of s 11 of the [Public Hospitals Act, RSO 1970, c 378], medical records are 'the property of the hospital and shall be kept in the custody of the administrator', but it seems to me that a patient, or the personal representative of a deceased patient, has something akin to a proprietary interest in the contents of those records and s 11 should in no way operate to prevent appropriate inspection or provision of copies.

A similar sentiment is expressed in the American text by R D Miller, **Problems in Hospital Law** (4th edn 1983). The author has this to say, at pp 276-277:

> The medical record is an unusual type of property because physically it belongs to the hospital and the hospital must exercise considerable control over access, but the patient and others have an interest in the information in the record. One way of viewing this is that the hospital owns the paper or other material on which the information is recorded, but it is just a custodian of the information. Thus, as stated in *Cannell v Medical and Surgical Clinic*, 21 Ill App 3d 383, 315 NE 2d 278 (1974), the patient and others have a right of access to the information in many circumstances, but they do not have a right to possession of the original records.

I find it unnecessary to reify the patient's interest in his or her medical records and, in particular, I am not inclined to go so far as to say that a doctor is merely a 'custodian' of medical information. The fiduciary duty I have described is sufficient to protect the interest of the patient. The trust-like 'beneficial interest' of the patient in the information indicates that, as a general rule, he or she should have a right of access to the information and that the physician should have a corresponding obligation to provide it. The patient's interest being in the information, it follows that the interest continues when that information is conveyed to another doctor who then becomes subject to the duty to afford the patient access to that information.

There is a further matter that militates in favour of disclosure of patient records. As mentioned earlier, one of the duties arising from the doctor-patient relationship is the duty of the doctor to act with utmost good faith and loyalty. If the patient is denied access to his or her records, it may not be possible for the patient to establish that this duty has been fulfilled. As I see it, it is important that the patient have access to the records for the very purposes for which it is sought to withhold the documents, namely, to ensure the proper functioning of the doctor-patient relationship and to protect the well-being of the patient. If there has been improper conduct in the doctor's dealing with his or her patient, it ought to be revealed. The purpose of keeping the documents secret is to promote the proper functioning of the relationship, not to facilitate improper conduct.

Disclosure is all the more important in our day when individuals are seeking more information about themselves. It serves to reinforce the faith of the individual in his or her treatment. The ability of a doctor to provide effective treatment is closely related to the level of trust in the relationship. A doctor is in a better position to diagnose a medical problem if the patient freely imparts personal information. The duty of confidentiality that arises from the doctor-patient relationship is meant to encourage disclosure of information and communication between doctor and patient. In my view, the trust reposed in the physician by the patient mandates that the flow of information operate both ways. As B Knoppers puts it in **Confidentiality and Accessibility of Medical Information: A Comparative Analysis** (1982), 12 RDUS 395, at p 431:

> In a relationship often characterized as fiduciary, that is, based on mutual trust and confidence, reciprocity implies an exchange. The personal privacy of the patient which he entrusts to a certain extent to the physician must be met with a corresponding openness and full disclosure. . . . Personal privacy and access to medical information are not incompatible partners but interchangeable rights.

Robinson J, in *Emmett*, supra, at p 935, note 19, also notes the link between disclosure of medical records and doctor-patient trust: 'The duty of disclosure is a concomitant of the patient's inescapable reliance upon the unadulterated good faith as well as the professional skill of those to whom he has entrusted his treatment.' Rather than undermining the trust inherent in the doctor-patient relationship, access to medical records should enhance it. Indeed, H E Emson observes that the practice of giving patients their own records 'has been said to improve patient understanding, cooperation and compliance'; see **The Doctor and the Law: A Practical Guide for the Canadian Physician** (2nd edn 1989), at p 214. In this sense, reciprocity of information between the patient and physician is prima facie in the patient's best interests. It strengthens the bond of trust between physician and patient which, in turn, promotes the well-being of the patient.

While patients should, as a general rule, have access to their medical records, this policy need not and, in my mind, should not be pursued blindly. The related duty of confidentiality is not absolute. In *Halls v Mitchell*, supra, at p 136, Duff J stated that, prima facie, the patient has a right to require that professional secrets acquired by the practitioner shall not be divulged. This right is absolute *unless* there is some paramount reason that overrides it. For example, 'there may be cases in which reasons connected with the safety of individuals or the public, physical or moral, would be sufficiently cogent to supersede or qualify the obligations prima facie imposed by the confidential relation'. Similarly, the patient's general right of access to his or her records is not absolute. The patient's interest in his or her records is an equitable interest arising from the physician's fiduciary obligation to disclose the records upon request. As part of the relationship of trust and confidence, the physician must act in the best interest of the patient. If the physician reasonably believes it is not in the patient's best interest to inspect his or her medical records, the physician may consider it necessary to deny access to the information. But the patient is not left at the mercy of this discretion. When called upon, equity will intervene to protect the patient from an improper exercise of the physician's discretion. In other words, the physician has a discretion to deny access, but it is circumscribed. It must be exercised on proper principles and not in an arbitrary fashion. Where a person, in this case a doctor, is under a fiduciary duty to inform another, equity acts in personam to prevent that person from acting in a manner inconsistent with the interests of the person to whom the duty is owed. As stated by Dickson, J (as he then was), in *Guerin v Canada* [1984] 2 SCR 335, 55 NR 161, at p 384:

> . . . where by statute, agreement, or perhaps by unilateral understanding, one party has an obligation to act for the benefit of another, and that obligation carries with it a discretionary power, the party thus empowered becomes a fiduciary. Equity will then supervise the relationship by holding him to the fiduciary's strict standard of conduct.

I hasten to add that, just as a relationship may be fiduciary for some purposes and not for others, this characterization of the doctor's obligation as 'fiduciary' and the patient's interest in the records as an 'equitable interest' does not imply a particular remedy. Equity works *in the circumstances* to enforce the duty. This foundation in equity gives the court considerable discretion to refuse access to the records where nondisclosure is appropriate.

In my view, the onus properly lies on the doctor to justify an exception to the general rule of access. Not only is the information in some fundamental sense that of the patient; the doctor has primary access to it. In comparison, the records are unavailable to the patient. To some extent, what the documents contain is a matter of speculation for the patient. Consequently, there is a marked disparity in the ability of each party to prove its case. The burden of proof should fall on the party who is in the best position to obtain the facts.

If a physician objects to the patient's general right of access, he or she must have reasonable grounds for doing so. Although I do not intend to provide an exhaustive analysis of the circumstances in which access to medical records may be denied, some general observations may be useful. I shall make these in a response to a number of arguments that have been advanced by the appellant and in the literature for denying a patient access to medical records. These include: (1) disclosure may facilitate the initiation of unfounded law suits; (2) the medical records maybe meaningless; (3) the medical records maybe misinterpreted; (4) doctors may respond by keeping less thorough notes; and (5) disclosure of the contents of the records may be harmful to the patient or a third party.

The argument that patients' may commence unfounded litigation if they are permitted to examine their medical records is not a sufficient ground for withholding them. The comments of Eberle J in *Strazdins v Orthopaedic & Arthritic Hospital Toronto* (1978) 7 CCLT 117 (Ont HC), at pp 119-120, are helpful in this regard. He states:

> . . . I believe that it is part of our system of government and of the administration of justice that persons are entitled to start law suits against persons whom they feel have wronged them. The persons who start such actions do so at the risk of costs, the risk of having the action dismissed at some stage if it turns out that it is groundless or even if not groundless turns out to be unsuccessful, and that right of any person to start a law suit does carry with it a correlative obligation on the part of every person in our society; that is, that any one of us may be subject to groundless law suits and it may be that our only weapon to fight them is the penalty in costs. . . . I am not forgetting that if any particular person makes a habit of starting groundless law suits or repetitive lawsuits against a particular person or persons, there are controls which may be exercised to prevent such matters from occurring.

Denial of access may actually *encourage* unfounded law suits. If a law suit is started, a patient can generally obtain access to his or her records under rules of civil procedure relating to discovery of documents. Thus, if a patient strongly wishes to see his or her records, one way of achieving this result is to commence an action *before* ascertaining whether or not there is a valid basis for the action.

The arguments that the records may be meaningless or that they may be misinterpreted do not justify nondisclosure in the ordinary case. If the records are, in fact, meaningless, they will not help the patient but neither will they cause harm. It is always open to the patient to obtain assistance in understanding the file. In the **Report of the Commission of Inquiry into the Confidentiality of Health Information** (Ontario, 1980) (the '**Krever Report**'), vol 2, at p 469, Krever J expressed the opinion that habitual use of jargon or technical terminology is not a sufficiently sound reason for denying a patient access to health records. He did note, however, that a re-evaluation of record keeping methodology may be necessary if a general rule of access is established. If it is possible that the patient will misconstrue the information in the record (for example, misinterpret the relevance of a particular laboratory test), the doctor may wish to advise the patient that the medical record should be explained and interpreted by a competent health-care professional.

The concern that disclosure will lead to a decrease in the completeness, candour and frankness of medical records, can be answered by reference to the obligation of a physician to keep accurate records. A failure to do so may expose the physician to liability for professional misconduct or negligence. It is also easy to exaggerate the importance of this argument. Certainly physicians may become more cautious in what they record, but it cannot be assumed as a natural consequence that this will detrimentally affect the standard of care given to the patient. Generally I doubt that the quality of medical records will be measurably affected by a general rule allowing access to the patient. As Krever J put it in the '**Krever Report**', supra, at p 487: 'I say, at once, that I do not believe that any responsible and ethical physician would omit from a medical record any information that, in the interests of proper medical care, belongs in it because of the possibility that the patient may ask to inspect it.'

Nondisclosure may be warranted if there is a real potential for harm either to the patient or to a third party. This is the most persuasive ground for refusing access to medical records. However, even here, the discretion to withhold information would not be exercised readily. Particularly in situations that do not involve the interests of third parties, the court should demand compelling grounds before confirming a decision to deny access. As H Beatty observes in **The Consumer's Right of Access to Health Care Records** (1986) 3:4 Just Cause 3, at p 3, paternalistic assumptions such as the 'best interests of the patient' may have carried more weight in an area where patients had little education or information with respect to health care and relied upon the trusted family doctor. However, these assumptions 'do not apply today, where consumers typically have brief contacts with many health care providers and institutions, none of which knows the person well enough to determine his or her "best interests"'. Assessing the 'best interests of the patient' is a complex task. Nondisclosure can itself affect the patient's well-being. If access is denied, the patient may speculate as to what is in the records and imagine difficulties greater than those that actually exist. In addition, the physical well-being of the patient must be balanced with the patient's right to self-determination. Both are worthy of protection. In short, patients should have access to their medical records in all but a small number of circumstances. In the ordinary case, these records should be disclosed upon the request of the patient unless there is a significant likelihood of a substantial adverse effect on the physical, mental or emotional health of the patient or harm to a third party.

If a physician refuses a request for access to a patient's medical records, the patient may apply to the court for a remedy. The court will then exercise its superintending jurisdiction and may order access to the records in whole or in part notwithstanding the physician's refusal. Even though the court may ultimately disagree with the physician's view that access should be denied, I have no doubt that in many cases it will be satisfied that the physician acted in good faith in the performance of his or her fiduciary duties. However, if the court is not satisfied that the physician acted in good faith, it should not hesitate to exercise its discretion to grant appropriate relief by way of costs. The general rule of access should not be frustrated by the patient's fear of incurring costs in the pursuit of what is fundamentally his or her right.

Since I have held that the tangible records belong to the physician, the patient is not entitled to the records themselves. Medical records play an important role in helping the physician to remember details about the patient's medical history. The physician must have continued access to the records to provide proper diagnosis and treatment. Such access will be disrupted if the patient is able to remove the records from the premises. Accordingly, the patient is entitled to reasonable access to examine and copy the records, provided the patient pays a legitimate fee for the preparation and reproduction of the information. Access is limited to the information the physician obtained in providing treatment. It does not extend to information arising outside the doctor-patient relationship.

Conclusion

In the absence of regulatory legislation, the patient is entitled, upon request, to inspect and copy all information in the patient's medical file which the physician considered in administering advice or treatment. Considering the equitable base of the patient's entitlement, this general rule of access is subject to the superintending jurisdiction of the court. The onus is on the physician to justify a denial of access. The majority of the Court of Appeal came to essentially the same conclusion, although, as is evident from the above discussion, for different reasons.

In this case, there is no evidence that access to the records would cause harm to the patient or a third party; nor does the appellant offer other compelling reasons for nondisclosure. Accordingly, in my opinion, the lower courts quite properly held that the respondent was entitled to copies of the documentation in her medical chart.

This case is of interest not simply in its own right but because claims could still arise in England in which patients seek access to medical records compiled before 1 November 1991 (when the Access to Health Records Act 1990 came into force). In responding to such a claim would an English court adopt the Canadian Supreme Court's mode of analysis? In our view there is much to commend La Forest J's judgment. An English court would, however, have to take a significant step in developing the law relating to doctors and patients which would go beyond the mere question of access to records. The court would have to redefine the doctor-patient relationship as being a fiduciary relationship. Though this approach has considerable merit (see *Norberg v Wynrib* (1992) 92 DLR (4th) 449 per McLachlin and L'Heureux-Dubé JJ) it may be that an English court would regard it as too radical a step (see *Sidaway v Governors of Bethlem Royal Hospital* [1984] 1 All ER 1018 (CA) at 1031-2 per Browne-Wilkinson LJ and [1985] 1 All ER 643 (HL) at 650-1 per Lord Scarman). If the court were able to take this step the Canadian Supreme Court offers two important insights which might serve to reassure the doubters. *First*, La Forest J specifically retains the notion of the 'therapeutic privilege', thereby allowing for the situation in which it would not be in the patient's medical interests to allow access. It will be seen that this is an important feature of the statutory schemes which have been established. *Secondly*, La Forest J examines and demolishes the *in terrorem* arguments advanced by those who would prefer secrecy and thereby exclude the patient's right of access.

Having said this, the approach of the Canadian Supreme Court received short shrift in *R v Mid-Glamorgan FHSA, ex p Martin*, where Poppelwell J reviewed the relevant English case law and statutes together with the *McInerney* case.

R v Mid-Glamorgan FHSA, ex p Martin (1993) Times, 2 June

Popplewell J: The question which arises in this case is whether a patient has an unconditional right of access at common law to his medical records . . . The Applicant is now 45 years old. He had an unhappy and loveless childhood. He suffered depression and/or psychological problems over a period of years since at least 1966. In 1969 he was diagnosed as suffering from catatonic schizophrenia, psychopathy and accelerated intellectual maturity. In 1966 he received psychotherapy from a consultant psychiatrist and a social worker whom I propose to identify merely as Miss B. He fell in love with Miss B but during the course of treatment she was withdrawn as an act of clinical judgment prompted by his relationship with her. Ever since 1966 the Applicant has continued to request sight of records of his diagnosis and of the decision to withdraw Miss B. On 25 August 1969 the Applicant was detained at Whitchurch Hospital under the Mental Health Act 1959 . . .

The Law
The claim is a public law claim and does not depend on any contractual rights. It is conceded indeed that there are no contractual rights. While a number of statutory provisions are relied on as assisting the court as to whether the Applicant does have a right of access the application is based firstly on a common law right under English law and a breach of Article 8 of the European Convention for the Protection of Human Rights and Fundamental Freedoms 1950. Additionally it is contended that there has been irrationality and a fettering of discretion and that the imposition of preconditions was irrational and improper. Further that inconsistent reasons have been given for the decision and in the light of Department guidelines there was a legitimate expectation that these documents would be disclosed.

It is the Respondents' contention that they have an absolute right to refuse access at common law and that a wide variety of statutory provisions which do give a right of access (though not in the instant case) make it clear that there is no common law right of access. Alternatively and very much a secondary argument they say, that having offered voluntarily to show the records to the Applicant's medical adviser which has been refused, the Court in its discretion should not grant relief because there is plainly a risk that the release of these records to the Applicant is likely to cause a detriment to his health leaving aside any problem of the confidentiality of the documents.

I turn therefore to the relevant statutory provisions to which my attention has been drawn. The first and most important is the Access to Health Records Act 1990. It is described 'as an Act to establish a right of access to health records by the individuals to whom they relate and the other persons'. The Respondents rely very much on the word 'establish' . . .

It seems clear that this Act came into existence as a result of the decision of the European Court of Human Rights in *Gaskin v United Kingdom* (1990) 12 EHRR 36. In that case the Applicant who had been taken into the care of Liverpool's City Council contended he was ill treated in care and he had tried to obtain details of the information on the records. He was refused access to all the records and he claimed that that was in breach of his right to respect for his private and family life under Article 8 of the Convention and the Court so held.

The Respondents argue with some force that as Parliament specifically excluded access to records which had come into existence before the commencement of the Act (1 November 1991) it is the clearest possible indication that there was no such right pre-existing the Act.

The Department put out guidelines for the assistance of those in the Health Service dated 23 August 1991. The material parts to which my attention has been draw contain these phrases:

> NHS Authorities should note that health professionals already have the discretion to open records to their patients and the principles underlying the Act encourage these arrangements and do not cut across . . .
>
> The Department of Health *policy* (my emphasis) has long been that as a matter of principle patients should be allowed to see what has been written about them . . .
>
> The access to health records gives patients a *new right* (my emphasis) of access to their health records.

Both parties rely on that document. The Applicant relies on it as showing that prior to the Act there was a policy of disclosure, while the Respondents observe that it is creating a new right.

The judge then referred to sections 33 to 35 of the Supreme Court Act 1981 and the Data Protection Act 1984 and continued:

> It is pertinent to observe that the [Data Protection] Act and orders have no limitation as to the time when the records were made. Thus if the records with which we are concerned in this case had been put on to computer subject to the question of serious harm and identity, the Applicant would have had a right of access. It may be thought somewhat illogical that a hospital which chooses to put all its written records on to a computer to bring it into the modern world should then be subject to a claim for access by a patient but the hospital which chooses to keep all its records in an old fashioned file can maintain, so it is argued, its right to refuse access.
>
> The Respondents make the point again that this Act would have been unnecessary if there were a common law right . . .

Having referred to the Access to Medical Reports Act 1988 and the Access to Health Records Act 1990, the judge continued:

> Those Acts of Parliament seem to me to be an almost insuperable obstacle to the submission made on the Applicant's behalf that there is a common law right. However, Mr Allan has submitted that there is what he describes as an 'access principle'. This is an aspect of the basic public interest in any modern democratic society to ensure respect for private and family life. In support of this he cited to me a number of authorities . . .

The judge then referred to *C v C* [1946] 1 All ER 562, *Sidaway* [1984] 1 All ER 1018, *Lee v South West Thames RHA* [1985] 2 All ER 385 (CA) and *Naylor v Preston AHA* [1987] 2 All ER 353 (CA) and continued:

> While it is true that [*Lee* and *Naylor*] were concerned with litigation and the observations of the Master of the Rolls were obiter the logic behind the observations can scarcely be doubted. There may of course be a difference between the doctor generally explaining what has happened and the patient being provided with the detailed written records which it was never intended for his eyes to see. Thus a doctor may be perfectly willing to give factual information but be disinclined to allow the patient to see opinions for instance expressed about the reliability or otherwise or the sanity or otherwise of that patient.
>
> There is an argument which was accepted in Canada and the United States that as the information which the doctor receives is the information which comes from the patient and it relates to the patient's own person that is material which is not the property of the receiver but the property of the giver. In *McInerney v MacDonald* (1992) 93 DLR (4th) 415 the Supreme Court of Canada was concerned with a patient who was treated by various physicians over a period of years before being treated by the Appellant physician. She sought the contents of her complete medical file from the Appellant physician. The Appellant physician delivered copies of all notes and reports that she had prepared herself but refused to produce copies of the reports and records that she had received from other physicians. The Supreme Court held that she was entitled to see all the reports. . .
>
> It is appropriate to point out that in *Sidaway*, which is not referred to in this decision, a notion of fiduciary relationship was expressly disavowed. In my judgment there is a

distinction to be made between the information conveyed by a patient for the benefit of the doctor's consideration and the conclusion to which the doctor comes based on that information. The opinion of the doctor is wholly the property of the doctor. It does not seem to me that the fact that the patient provides the original information entitles him, subject to exception, to see the conclusions of the doctor based on that information, any more than a litigant who provides a proof of evidence has any right of access to the opinion written by his Counsel the copyright of which no doubt rests in Counsel. No distinction was drawn in *McInerney* between those two circumstances. The case proceeded upon the basis that once a patient had put himself in the hands of the doctor any record thereafter was open to him, and the onus lay on the doctor to justify an exception to the general rule of access.

I do not with great respect accept the basis on which the decision was based. It is not in accordance with the decision of *Sidaway* [1984] 1 QB 498 either in the House of Lords or in the Court of Appeal. See per Lord Justice Browne-Wilkinson as he then was at page 518.

It is pertinent to observe that even the fertile mind of the Master of the Rolls did not suggest that Judicial Review of a Health Authority's decision was an appropriate remedy. However based on these authorities it is submitted on behalf of the Applicant that the refusal of access involves a denial of the respect for a person's private life and that a patient of sound mind has a right to receive on request all relevant information which he seeks. Mr Allan did not shrink from the submission that subject only to an exception protecting the names of informants the holder of the records is bound to disclose them even if there is a serious risk of harm to the patient's health provided only that the patient is so informed. The Applicant has taken a consistent line namely that if he is entitled quite irrationally not to accept treatment which will protect his life he is equally entitled rationally or not to require information whatever damage it may do to his health. Thus contends [counsel for the Applicant] the common law rule is and has been that the confidential relationship between a doctor and patient requires subject only to the exception of protecting informants access as of right to ensure respect for private and family life.

There seems to me to be a number of insuperable difficulties in that submission. They are:

(1)   None of the English authorities so suggest.
(2)   All the English authorities to which my attention were drawn implicitly acknowledge that so far as medical records are concerned there is no access principle.
(3)   In so far as the Courts have ruled on what a doctor should tell a patient it seems to me that there is an important distinction albeit difficult to define between a record prepared in the absence of the patient and an explanation to that patient which is likely to be or may be more guarded.
(4)   The Access to Health Records Act 1990 specifically excludes these records. It can scarcely be the position that a common law right of unlimited access subject only to the informant exemption could continue to exist in addition to the statutory right or
(5)   That the Statutory Provision should be more restrictive than the Courts of Law.
(6)   The various statutes to which I have been referred could only have come into existence in order to give a right of access to records which otherwise the patient did not have.
(7)   Whatever may be the proper approach in 1993 as to what the law ought to be given that the 'candour' reasoning has been somewhat discredited see *Conway v Rimmer* [1968] AC 920 it does not impose upon the Court a duty to legislate which function is expressly reserved to Parliament. This they have done by the introduction of the Access to Health Records Act 1990.

[Counsel for the Applicant] has presented a formidable argument that there ought to be a right of access by a patient to his records. What I have to decide is not whether there should be but whether there is. For the reasons which I have given I have come to the clearest possible conclusion that there is no right at common law in this patient to access to any records which pre-existed the Access to Health Records Act 1990 . . .

Exceptions

I have already stated my view that there is no right of access to the records at common law. However, a secondary argument has been put forward by [counsel for the Respondent] which is this. If there is a right to see the records it is subject to exceptions. Those exceptions are (1) protection of informants, (2) detriment to the patient. I use both those phrases as legal shorthand. The common law rights and exceptions must coincide with the statutory position.

Doctor Williams has been criticised because he has only examined the patient's medical records. He has not met with the patient or spoken to him, has no knowledge of why he wants their production and the records relate to events twenty years ago.

It is quite obvious from the attitude taken by the Applicant (which he was entitled to take) that he is not prepared to co-operate with the Respondents and therefore any suggestion that Doctor Williams might have been able to examine him seems to me to be without foundation. What is clear is that although the Respondents have taken their stand that they have a right to withhold the documents, their letter of 24 March 1993 to which I have referred proposes disclosure to the Applicant's own medical advisers:

> . . . in all the circumstances it appears to the Respondents disclosure to a nominated medical expert could be a reasonable and acceptable resolution to this dispute and I shall be most grateful if you would take your client's instructions and let me have the name of your medical expert if we can proceed along these lines.

The Applicant has taken the view that he is entitled as of right to the records, that he is entitled to have access unconditionally and that if he chooses irrationally to be provided with information which may adversely affect him that is his right.

I do not accept that contention. It seems to me that the Applicant's position at best must be governed by an exception where there is a risk of injury to his own health or that of others. All the statutory provisions to which reference has been made contain that sort of exception including the 1990 Act.

Accordingly if I were to take the view (which I do not), that the Applicants did have some right of access to his records I would be bound to hold that it was conditional. The Respondents have offered sight of the records to an independent person namely the Applicant's medical adviser for them to consider whether the information was likely to cause harm to him or anyone else.

In those circumstances even if I were to hold that there was such a right of access I would hold that it was subject to that condition. Accordingly in the exercise of my discretion I would not grant the Applicant relief because it seems to me that the Respondents have offered all that is necessary to comply with what is said to be their duty to the Applicant.

The judge also rejected the patient's reliance on Article 8 of the European Convention of Human Rights, stating that 'the common law is quite clear and needs no assistance from Europe'.

You may well think that the judge's rejection of the reasoning in *McInerney* was, to say the least, perfunctory. Further, his argument that the 1990 Act would not have been necessary if a common law right of access already existed should not have taken the argument very far since Parliament often legislates where the common law position has not been established by a court, and is, therefore, uncertain. Applying Popplewell J's reasoning, no action at common law would lie for injuries caused prior to 1976 to a child whilst *in utero* because Parliament has legislated in the form of the Congenital Disabilities (Civil Liability) Act 1976. Yet, the Court of Appeal took just the opposite view of the common law in *Burton v Islington HA* [1992] 3 All ER 833 (CA). Popplewell J's approach is, therefore, difficult to sustain.

More interesting is the distinction the judge draws between *information* obtained from the patient and *the opinion* of the doctor set out in the patient's medical records. Of course, it is a distinction without any valid difference since the patient is not, as Popplewell J would have us believe, asserting a 'property' claim to his information. Instead, the patient is asserting a right of access to information *about* him obtained or created during the course of the professional relationship of doctor and patient. It is, of course, the doctor's views which are often most of interest to the patient in understanding his medical condition and treatment. After all, information 'conveyed by a patient' will, by definition, be within the knowledge of the patient anyway. In *McInerney*, therefore, the Canadian Supreme Court was right to grant access to all material once the doctor-patient relationship was characterised as fiduciary. A fiduciary must divulge all material relating to the person to whom he owes his fiduciary duty. In truth, Popplewell J's reference to the doctor's copyright in his medical opinion is a 'red herring'. Even if the doctor has such a right (which is extremely doubtful), the patient's *access* is not a breach of copyright – he is not seeking to *unlawfully reproduce* the medical records, after all.

The common law could, therefore, as we have suggested above, accommodate a patient's right of access to medical information. The *Martin* case is unlikely to be the last word on the issue.

B. STATUTORY PROVISIONS

1. In the course of litigation

Quite apart from the developments of the last decade referred to in the *Martin* case, we should notice first the right of access granted to a patient originally in 1970 as a preliminary to, or in the course of, personal injury litigation.

Margaret Brazier *Medicine, Patients and the Law* (2nd edn) (1992)

When considering whether he has a claim in respect of negligence and whom he should sue, the patient and his legal advisers will clearly benefit by gaining access to the patient's notes, reports and X-ray and other test records. Disclosure of records benefits the public interest too. A claim may be seen to be fruitless or a particular individual exonerated. Money and effort will be saved. Before 1970 the patient usually had to go ahead in the dark and ask at the trial for a subpoena ordering the health authority and the doctor to produce their records. Legislation in 1970 introduced a right to pre-trial access to records. [Administration of Justice Act 1970, ss 32-5 (the legislation was based on recommendations of the Winn Committee, Cmnd 3691 (1968))] That original legislation has now been replaced by the Supreme Court Act 1981.

The effect of section 33 of the 1981 Act is this. A patient may apply for a court order requiring the doctor or the authority whom he plans to sue to disclose any records or notes likely to be relevant in forthcoming proceedings. Section 34 goes further. The court may order a person *not* a party to proceedings to produce relevant documents. So if the patient has started proceedings against the doctor but believes that the hospital authority or clinic holds notes of value to his claim, the authority or clinic can be made to hand over the notes. This will help the private patient in a dilemma as to whether he should properly proceed against doctor or hospital. And it may of course lead to the hospital being brought into the proceedings.

Once legislation compelling disclosure of documents was enacted, hospitals and medical defence organizations reluctantly became prepared to hand over documents voluntarily. They feared a spate of fishing expeditions by aggrieved patients. But they preferred to disclose records to the patient's medical adviser alone, and not to the patient or his lawyers. Indeed, they sought to argue that this was the limit of their obligation. The House of Lords disagreed. [*McIvor v Southern Health and Social Services Board, Northern Ireland* [1978] 2 All ER 625] Under the 1970 statute, they said, the patient himself was entitled to see the documents produced. Pleas that patients would be unduly distressed and fail to understand medical data cut little ice with their Lordships. The 1981 Act is less favourable to patients. A court may limit disclosure to (a) the patient's legal advisers, or (b) the patient's legal and medical advisers, or (c) if the patient has no legal adviser, to his 'medical or other professional adviser'. It is up to the court to decide whether the patient sees the records. But as long as he has retained a lawyer, his lawyer must be permitted to examine the documents. Hospitals and medical protection societies offering voluntary disclosure often still try to keep records even from the patient's lawyers. Lawyers in the medico-legal field advise against accepting such an offer: a lawyer may spot relevant material in support of a claim which even the most experienced medical advisers could miss.

Three important matters on disclosure need a mention. First, the intention to bring proceedings and the likelihood that they will go ahead must be real before the court will order disclosure. The patient must have some solid ground for thinking he has a claim. He cannot use an application for disclosure as a 'fishing expedition' on the off-chance that some evidence of negligence will come to light. [*Dunning v United Liverpool Hospitals' Board of*

Governors [1973] 2 All ER 454] Medical defence organizations used to advise doctors to say nothing and disclose no records without first consulting them. The Medical Defence Union and the Medical Protection Society always refuted allegations that they then attempted to obstruct disclosure of records in all cases. And indeed, if a claim by a patient on its face suggested obvious negligence the defence organization representing the doctor's interests had good reason to co-operate with the patient's lawyers and settle quickly and quietly. Whatever the truth of allegations that the defence organizations sought to prevent disclosure of records, in many cases now their views are marginal. Where the claim arises out of alleged mistreatment in an NHS hospital, NHS indemnity means that the health authority or NHS trust controls defence of the action and *their* lawyers decide whether to disclose records voluntarily or force the patient to seek a court order. Problems with health authorities in the past have tended to relate not to any deliberately obstructive attitude but to difficulties in locating the right records. How far regional health authority legal departments have the resources to cope with claims may determine how efficiently those claims are dealt with. It remains to be seen too how far if at all the enactment of the Access to Health Records Act 1990 will change the atmosphere for disclosure of records. That Act gives patients a qualified right to see their records even where no litigation is contemplated. It would be odd if patients with a legal grievance were offered less generous disclosure. And may it be that a knowledgeable patient, believing he has a grievance, might resort first to the 1990 Act?

Second, will the patient be able to see notes of any inquiry ordered by the health authority into his misadventure? The position is complex. If the inquiry was held mainly to provide the basis of information on which legal advice as to the authority's legal liability is based, then the records are protected by legal professional privilege. But if the dominant purpose of the inquiry was otherwise, for example to improve hospital procedures or to provide the basis of disciplinary proceedings against staff, then the patient may be allowed access to the notes of the inquiry. [*Waugh v BRB* [1980] AC 521; and see Diana M Kloss (1984) 289 BMJ 66] That is the legal position. The Court of Appeal has expressed its disquiet about the effect such claims of legal professional privilege may have on the patient's claim. Claims of privilege can be and are used to frustrate the patient's attempt to find out what happened, what went wrong. In *Lee v South West Thames RHA* [[1985] 2 All ER 385] a little boy, Marlon Lee, suffered a severe scald at home but he should have recovered completely. He was taken to a hospital run by health authority A and then transferred to a burns unit controlled by health authority B. The next day he developed breathing problems, was put on a respirator, and still on the respirator was sent back to A in an ambulance provided by health authority C, the South West Thames RHA. When three days later the boy was taken off the respirator he was found to have suffered severe brain damage, probably due to lack of oxygen. In her attempts to find out what went wrong, the child's mother sought disclosure of records and notes on her son prepared by staff of all three authorities. Health authority A asked South West Thames RHA to obtain a report from their ambulance crew. South West Thames RHA complied and forwarded the report to A. It was this report which the plaintiffs went to court to obtain access to. South West Thames RHA had revealed its existence but refused to hand it over to the family. They claimed it had been prepared in contemplation of litigation and to enable legal advice to be given in connection with that litigation. So it had, but it had been prepared on the request of health authority A to obtain advice as to A's liability to the child. Reluctantly the Court of Appeal held that the privilege attaching to the document was enjoyed by health authority A. South West Thames could not be ordered to disclose the report. Even had they been prepared to do so they could not have handed over the report without A's agreement. The principle was that defendants or potential defendants should be '. . . free to seek evidence without being obliged to disclose the result of his researches to his opponent'.

So a child was damaged for life in circumstances pointing to negligence on someone's part, and the law was powerless to help his mother find out what exactly caused his brain damage. The Court of Appeal expressed their disquiet and called for reform of the law. Within the doctor/patient relationship Sir John Donaldson MR said there was a duty to answer questions put before treatment was agreed to. [See *Sidaway v Board of Governors of the Bethlem Royal and the Maudsley Hospital* [1985] 2 WLR 480] Why should the duty to be frank with the patient be different once treatment was completed? And in 1987 [*Naylor v Preston AHA* [1987] 2 All ER 353] he again emphasized the importance he placed on what he termed a duty of candour. How such a duty should be enforced is less clear. In *Lee* the president of the Court of Appeal had suggested that some new remedy based on breach of a duty to inform might evolve. Such a remedy came too late for Marlon Lee. What seems to have happened since though is that judges now recognize that patients have a right to see their records. Access to records is not a concession kindly granted or withheld at the discretion of the health authority. Health authorities or other defendants who drag their feet may ultimately be punished by an order of costs against them.

Third, the court retains the power to refuse to order disclosure where to do so would be injurious to the public interest. [Supreme Court Act 1981, s 35] This is unlikely to be the case where what is asked for is the plaintiff's own medical notes. An attempt by the Secretary of State for Health to plead public interest immunity to avoid disclosure of records in the actions brought by several haemophiliac patients who had contracted HIV and AIDS from contaminated blood products failed. [*HIV: Haemophiliac Litigation, Guardian*, 28 September 1990, CA]

[See *Supply of Information about Hospital Patients in the Context of Civil Legal Proceedings* (HC (82) 16) explaining the application of the legislation.]

2. Data Protection Act 1984

Under the Data Protection Act 1984, any person (the 'data subject') who has reason to believe that personal data about him is held by another (the 'data user') in circumstances where the information is electronically stored, for example on a computer disc or tape, may apply to the data user to discover whether information is held and, if so, to obtain access to it (s 21(1)). [For a discussion of access to information relating to infertility treatment, see *infra*, ch 11.] The information must be intelligible to the data subject and the Act imposes an obligation on the data user to provide an explanation of any unintelligible terms (s 21).

21. (1) Subject to the provisions of this section, an individual shall be entitled –
(a) to be informed by any data user whether the data held by him include personal data of which that individual is the data subject; and
(b) to be supplied by any data user with a copy of the information constituting any such personal data held by him;
and where any of the information referred to in paragraph (b) above is expressed in terms which are not intelligible without explanation the information shall be accompanied by an explanation of those terms.

(2) A data user shall not be obliged to supply any information under subsection (1) above except in response to a request in writing and on payment of such fee (not exceeding the prescribed maximum) as he may require; but a request for information under both paragraphs of that subsection shall be treated as a single request and a request for information under paragraph (a) shall, in the absence of any indication to the contrary, be treated as extending also to information under paragraph (b).

(3) In the case of a data user having entries in the register in respect of data held for different purposes a separate request must be made and a separate fee paid under this section in respect of the data to which each entry relates.

(4) A data user shall not be obliged to comply with a request under this section –
(a) unless he is supplied with such information as he may reasonably require in order to satisfy himself as to the identity of the person making the request and to locate the information which he seeks . . .

By virtue of section 29(1) the Secretary of State promulgated in 1987 the Data Protection (Subject Access Modification) (Health) Order 1987 (SI 1987 No 1903), to modify as section 29(1) puts it, 'the subject access provisions, in relation to, personal data consisting of information as to the physical or mental health of the data subject'. In short, a separate regime was established in the case of health professionals (as widely defined in the Schedule to the Order). Articles 3 and 4 of the Order provide as follows:

3. (1) This Order applies to personal data consisting of information as to the physical or mental health of the data subject if –
(a) the data are held by a health professional; or

(b)   the data are held by a person other than a health professional but the information constituting the data was first recorded by or on behalf of a health professional.

(2) This Order is without prejudice to any exemption from the subject access provisions contained in any provision of the Act or of any Order made under the Act.

4. (1) The subject access provisions shall not have effect in relation to any personal data to which this Order applies in any case where either of the requirements specified in paragraph (2) below is satisfied with respect to the information constituting the data and the obligations contained in paragraph (5) below are complied with by the data user.

(2) The requirements referred to in paragraph (1) above are that the application of the subject access provisions –

(a)   would be likely to cause serious harm to the physical or mental health of the data subject; or

(b)   would be likely to disclose to the data subject the identity of another individual (who has not consented to the disclosure of the information) either as a person to whom the information or part of it relates or as the source of the information or enable that identity to be deduced by the data subject either from the information itself or from a combination of that information and other information which the data subject has or is likely to have.

(3) Paragraph (2) above shall not be construed as excusing a data user –

(a)   from supplying the information sought by the request for subject access where the only individual whose identity is likely to be disclosed or deduced as mentioned in sub-paragraph (b) thereof is a health professional who has been involved in the care of the data subject and the information relates to him or he supplied the information in his capacity as a health professional; or

(b)   from supplying so much of the information sought by the request as can be supplied without causing serious harm as mentioned in sub-paragraph (a) thereof or enabling the identity of another individual to be disclosed or deduced as mentioned in sub-paragraph (b) thereof, whether by the omission of names or other particulars or otherwise.

(4) . . .

(5) A data user who is not a health professional shall not supply information constituting data to which this Order applies in response to a request under section 21 and shall not withhold any such information on the ground that one of the requirements specified in paragraph (2) above is satisfied with respect to the information unless the data user has first consulted the person who appears to the data user to be the appropriate health professional on the question whether either or both of those requirements is or are so satisfied.

(6) In paragraph (5) above 'the appropriate health professional' means –

(a)   the medical practitioner or dental practitioner who is currently or was most recently responsible for the clinical care of the data subject in connection with the matters to which the information which is the subject of the request relates; or

(b)   where there is more than one such practitioner, the practitioner who is the most suitable to advise on the matters to which the information which is the subject of the request relates; or

(c)   where there is no practitioner available falling within sub-paragraph (a) or (b) above, a health professional who has the necessary experience and qualifications to advise on the matters to which the information which is the subject of the request relates.

The Explanatory Note to the Order indicates its intent:

This Order provides for the partial exemption from the provisions of the Data Protection Act 1984 which confer rights on data subjects to gain access to data held about them ('the subject access provisions') of data relating to the physical or mental health of the data subject held by any data user where the data are held by a health professional or the information constituting the data was first recorded by or on behalf of a health professional. Schedule 1 to the Order lists the persons who are health professionals for the purposes of the Order.

The subject access provisions are disapplied only where to supply the data subject with particulars of the information constituting the data would be likely to cause serious harm to his physical or mental health or lead to the identification of another person (other than a health professional who has been involved in the care of the data subject). Before deciding whether either of those criteria is met (and, accordingly, whether to grant or withhold subject access) a data user who is not a health professional is obliged by the Order to consult the medical practitioner or dental practitioner responsible for the clinical care of the data subject or, if there is more than one, the most suitable available medical or dental practitioner or if there is none available a health professional who has the necessary experience and qualifications to advise on the matters to which the information which is requested relates.

It is important to notice that the Act confers a right to compensation for any distress or damage caused by inaccurate data (ss 22(1) and (4)), but curiously not for unauthorised disclosure (cf section 23 and data bureaux).

How may a patient challenge the propriety of withholding information where the doctor alleges that the terms of this Order apply? The patient has two hurdles to overcome. First, he must know and demonstrate that there is additional information to that which has been revealed. Secondly, he must show that the doctor has acted unlawfully in exercising the statutory discretion. The second is really what the patient is interested in, but he may have the gravest difficulty in reaching this stage because of his need to overcome the first hurdle. In the absence of obvious deletions, how will he know? Would the mere threat of litigation persuade the court to order discovery? If so, would this not defeat the purpose of the exemption in the first place? If not, what effective safeguard does a patient have? Perhaps the court would adopt the approach it uses when examining claims of public interest immunity and examine the documents itself without disclosing them to the other side.

Would the court entertain proceedings if faced with a bare assertion of 'I think information has been withheld'? Unfortunately neither the Act nor the Order gives any clue as to what burden of evidence the patient bears.

Are there any limits on those data subjects who can request access? Two specific categories are worthy of note. *First* there is the 'mentally disordered' who, presumably, though the subject of data, may be unable through mental impairment to comply with the formal procedure to obtain access. Section 21(9) specifically addresses this problem. It provides:

21. (9) The Secretary of State may by order provide for enabling a request under this section to be made on behalf of any individual who is incapable by reason of mental disorder of managing his own affairs.

Presumably the request for access may only be made by a person who otherwise has authority in law to manage the affairs of the person in question under the Mental Health Act 1983. Consequently, s 29(1) seems not to contemplate that the Secretary of State may authorise by Order *anyone* to apply for access. Any such order might be amenable to challenge by judicial review on the ground that it is *ultra vires.* Given our view below, that legal competence to make a request for access under s 21 is simple, ie the 'data subject' must merely be able to complete the request form and appreciate what the making of a request entails, the phrase management of 'affairs' in s 21(9), therefore, must be understood as referring only to an incapacity to do this. (For a similar approach in the context of the Enduring Powers of Attorney Act 1985, see *Re K* [1988] Ch 310, [1988] 1 All ER 358.) The powers of comprehension of a mentally disordered individual will, therefore, have to be very considerably affected before s 21(9) (and any Regulations made under it) will be applicable to him.

Secondly, let us consider the case of the child who is a patient. In the absence of any specific statutory provision, as is found in s 21(9), the right of access to data is regulated by the general provisions of section 21.

These provisions make it clear that it is only the 'data subject' who is entitled to be informed (on request) whether personal data concerning him is held by a 'data user', and only he who can subsequently be supplied with this data. Furthermore, it would appear that the formalities necessary to exercise the right of access consist only of making the relevant request in writing and paying the appropriate fee (s 21(2)). Therefore, it would follow that when the 'data subject' is a child, providing he is capable of making a request in writing accompanied by the fee, the 'data user' is obliged to respond to that request and provide the information.

The question may be raised whether a parent has a right of access to information relating to his or her child? In the light of the above analysis there would be no such right if the 'data subject' is the child and the child is *competent* in his own right to make a request. It would be otherwise if the child had authorised a parent to make a relevant request. The parent would then be acting as the agent of the 'data subject'.

On the other hand, if the child is *incompetent* to make the relevant request in writing, would a parent then have a right of access to any information? It would appear that under section 21 no such right exists since the parent is not the 'data subject'. If this were the end of the matter the legal position would be unfortunate since in those very cases in which a parent may legitimately need to obtain information about his child so as to carry out his parental obligations, the Act would prevent him from doing so. The situation is saved, however, by realising that the Act sharply distinguishes between the right of access by the 'data subject' and the power of the 'data user' to disclose. Nothing in the right of access provisions prevents the 'data user' from disclosing information to others provided that the 'data user' has named those others in the classes of potential recipients of information at the time he registered under the Act as a 'data user' (see ss 4(3)(d) and 5(2)(d)). Thus, if the 'data user' has included 'parents' among those to whom he may wish to disclose information, he may be at liberty to disclose to a parent the information (see *infra*, ch 9 on the power to disclose and confidentiality). However, notice that when the discretion to disclose to a parent is contemplated by the 'data user', it is probably the case that the 'data user' must divulge all necessary and relevant information to enable the parent to make a considered decision. The fear that the information could harm the 'data subject', were it to be disclosed to him, would not of itself serve as a reason for refusing to disclose to the parent.

3. Access to Health Records Act 1990

The Access to Health Records Act 1990 complements for manually stored records the right of a patient which already exists under the Data Protection Act 1984 to obtain access to electronically stored health records.

The general scheme of the Act is as follows. Section 3 provides:

3. (1) An application for access to a health record, or to any part of a health record, may be made to the holder of the record by any of the following, namely –
(a) the patient;
(b) a person authorised in writing to make the application on the patient's behalf;
(c) where the record is held in England and Wales and the patient is a child, a person having parental responsibility for the patient;
(d) where the record is held in Scotland and the patient is a pupil, a parent or guardian of the patient;

(e)   where the patient is incapable of managing his own affairs, any person appointed by a court to manage those affairs; and

(f)   where the patient has died, the patient's personal representative and any person who may have a claim arising out of the patient's death.

(2) Subject to section 4 below, where an application is made under subsection (1) above the holder shall, within the requisite period, give access to the record, or the part of a record, to which the application relates –

(a)   in the case of a record, by allowing the applicant to inspect the record or, where section 5 below applies, an extract setting out so much of the record as is not excluded by that section;

(b)   in the case of a part of a record, by allowing the applicant to inspect an extract setting out that part or, where that section applies, so much of that part as is not so excluded; or

(c)   in either case, if the applicant so requires, by supplying him with a copy of the record or extract.

(3) Where any information contained in a record or extract which is so allowed to be inspected, or a copy of which is so supplied, is expressed in terms which are not intelligible without explanation, an explanation of those terms shall be provided with the record or extract, or supplied with the copy . . .

(5) For the purposes of subsection (2) above the requisite period is –

(a)   where the application relates to a record, or part of a record, none of which was made before the beginning of the period of 40 days immediately preceding the date of the application, the period of 21 days beginning with that date;

(b)   in any other case, the period of 40 days beginning with that date.

(6) Where –

(a)   an application under subsection (1) above does not contain sufficient information to enable the holder of the record to identify the patient or, in the case of an application made otherwise than by the patient, to satisfy himself that the applicant is entitled to make the application; and

(b)   within the period of 14 days beginning with the date of the application, the holder of the record requests the applicant to furnish him with such further information as he may reasonably require for that purpose,

subsection (5) above shall have effect as if for any reference to that date there were substituted a reference to the date on which that further information is so furnished.

The Act allows a patient to make an application in writing for access to his health records. This means *any record* which (1) consists of information, including expressions of opinion; (2) relates to the patient's 'physical or mental health'; (3) identifies the patient or when the patient may be identified from other information held by the record holder; and (4) was made, including compiled by or on behalf of a health professional with the care of the patient. The 'record holder' is required to allow the patient to inspect the record or part sought and obtain a copy if requested along with an explanation of any of the terms which are 'not intelligible without explanation'.

By virtue of section 5(1)(b) the right of access generally applies only to records created after 1 November 1991. However, by virtue of section 5(2) access must be given to records created before that date if '*in the opinion of the holder of the record,* the giving of access is *necessary in order to make intelligible*' the records created after 1 November 1991 (our emphasis).

Subject to some exceptions (see below), access must be granted within 40 days of the application or, if any part of the record was made within the last 40 days, within 21 days of the application. No fee may be charged except, in the case of records more than 40 days old, up to a maximum permitted under the Data Protection Act 1984 (currently £10) and, where a copy is supplied, the cost of copying and posting it to the patient (s 3(4)).

A patient who had been granted access to his health record may apply to have it corrected if he believes it is inaccurate, ie incorrect, misleading or incomplete (s 6(1) and (3)). The record holder may comply if he agrees (s 6(2)(a)). If he does not, he must add a note recording the patient's views (s 6(2)(b)). In both cases, he must provide the patient with a copy of the correction or of the note (s 6(2)(c)).

Finally, under section 8(3) of the Act the Secretary of State may promulgate regulations creating a complaints procedure for patients who believe that the Act has not been complied with. Providing a patient has followed such a complaints procedure, he may, thereafter, appeal to the courts for an order requiring compliance with the Act (ss 8(1) and (2)).

At the time of writing no regulations exist. It is, however, anticipated that complaints within the NHS will eventually be dealt with under the complaints procedure established pursuant to the Hospital Complaints Procedure Act 1985 (see HSC(91)6).

Three important aspects of the Act should be noted.

(a) Who may apply for access?

The adult patient or his agent may apply in writing (ss 3(1)(a) and (b)).
But what of the child patient? Section 4 provides as follows:

> **4.** (1) Where an application is made under subsection (1)(a) or (b) of section 3 above and –
> (a)   in the case of a record held in England and Wales, the patient is a child; or
> (b)   in the case of a record held in Scotland, the patient is a pupil,
> access shall not be given under subsection (2) of that section unless the holder of the record is satisfied that the patient is capable of understanding the nature of the application.
>
> (2) Where an application is made under subsection (1)(c) or (d) of section 3 above, access shall not be given under subsection (2) of that section unless the holder of the record is satisfied either –
> (a)   that the patient has consented to the making of the application; or
> (b)   that the patient is incapable of understanding the nature of the application and the giving of access would be in his best interests.

As we can see, the Act specifically recognises that a child under the age of 16 may apply for access providing he is 'capable of understanding the nature of the application' (s 4(1)). The Act does not, as such, deal with the child who has reached the age of 16 but is not yet 18 (see definition of 'child' in s 11 as being someone under 16). Presumably, since such a child is treated as an adult for the purposes of consenting to treatment (Family Law Reform Act 1969, s 8(1)), he is also considered to be an adult 'patient' under the Act (s 3(1)(a)).

Also, in the case of a child patient, a parent or other with parental responsibility may apply for access (s 3(1)(c)). However, access may not be granted to the *parent* unless the *child* consents or, if he is incapable of understanding the nature of the application, giving access to the parent would be in the child's best interests (s 4(2)). Since the level of understanding required will be relatively low (see, for example *Re K* [1988] 1 All ER 358) a child under 16 will often be able to prevent a doctor disclosing to his parents his medical records. Section 5(3) arguably goes further.

> 5. (3) Where an application is made under subsection (1)(c), (d), (e) or (f) of section 3 above, access shall not be given under subsection (2) of that section to any part of the record which in the opinion of the holder of the record, would disclose –
> (a)   information provided by the patient in the expectation that it would not be disclosed to the applicant; or
> (b)   information obtained as a result of any examination or investigation to which the patient consented in the expectation that the information would not be so disclosed.

This prohibits a doctor from disclosing information when 'the patient' (here surely referring to the child) expects that it will not be disclosed to the applicant. This would seem to cover the case where a child discloses information to his doctor on the understanding that he should not tell the parents even if the child is so young that he is incapable of understanding the nature of an access application. This may create a conflict between the parents, who have consented to the treatment on behalf of the child, and the doctor who cannot be required to grant them access to the medical records relating to that treatment.

Section 5(3) also prohibits a parent gaining access where a competent child has previously requested that the parent not be given access even though the child has subsequently become incompetent, for example through an accident, and the parent would normally have a right of access under section 3(1)(c). This, of course, is quite apart from *disclosure* of information which the doctor may think it proper to make within the law of confidentiality (see *infra*, ch 9).

In the case of a person who is subject to the Court of Protection's jurisdiction because he is 'incapable of managing his own affairs', a person appointed by the court may apply (s 3(1)(e)). In the case of a patient who has died, his personal representatives may apply (s 3(1)(f)) providing the information is relevant to a claim arising out of his death (s 5(4)) and the deceased has not requested that they should not have access on his death (s 4(3)). In both cases, as with the case of the child we saw above, an expectation that the records would not be disclosed also prohibits access being granted (s 5(3)).

(b) Against whom may access be sought?

The Act applies to all 'health records' made by a 'health professional'. 'Health record' is defined in section 1(1) as follows:

> **1.** (1) In this Act 'health record' means a record which –
> (a)   consists of information relating to the physical or mental health of an individual who can be identified from that information, or from that and other information in the possession of the holder of the record; and
> (b)   has been made by or on behalf of a health professional in connection with the care of that individual;
> but does not include any record which consists of information of which the individual is, or but for any exemption would be, entitled to be supplied with a copy under section 21 of the Data Protection Act 1984 (right of access to personal data).

'Health professional' is widely defined in section 2(1) as follows:

> **2.** (1) In this Act 'health professional' means any of the following, namely –
> (a)   a registered medical practitioner;
> (b)   a registered dentist;
> (c)   a registered optician;
> (d)   a registered pharmaceutical chemist;
> (e)   a registered nurse, midwife or health visitor;
> (f)   a registered chiropodist, dietician, occupational therapist, orthoptist or physiotherapist;
> (g)   a clinical psychologist, child psychotherapist or speech therapist;
> (h)   an art or music therapist employed by a health service body; and
> (i)   a scientist employed by such a body as head of a department.

The application must be directed to the 'record holder' which will be the patient's GP or the FHSA of his last GP or, in the case of a 'health professional' employed within the NHS or NHS Trust, the responsible Health Authority or Trust and in all other cases the 'health professional' personally (s 1(2)).

(c) Access excluded

As might be expected there are a number of situations in which a patient (or other) may be denied access. These are set out in section 5 of the Act.

5. (1) Access shall not be given under section 3(2) above to any part of a health record –
(a) which, in the opinion of the holder of the record, would disclose –
  (i)   information likely to cause serious harm to the physical or mental health of the patient or of any other individual; or
  (ii) information relating to or provided by an individual, other than the patient, who could be identified from that information; or
(b) which was made before the commencement of this Act.
  (2) Subsection (1)(a)(ii) above shall not apply –
(a) where the individual concerned has consented to the application; or
(b) where that individual is a health professional who has been involved in the care of the patient;
and subsection (1)(b) above shall not apply where and to the extent that, in the opinion of the holder of the record, the giving of access is necessary in order to make intelligible any part of the record to which access is required to be given under section 3(2) above.
  (3) Where an application is made under subsection (1)(c), (d), (e) or (f) of section 3 above, access shall not be given under subsection (2) of that section to any part of the record which, in the opinion of the holder of the record, would disclose –
(a) information provided by the patient in the expectation that it would not be disclosed to the applicant; or
(b) information obtained as a result of any examination or investigation to which the patient consented in the expectation that the information would not be so disclosed.

We have already seen a number of these situations where access may be excluded. In addition access may be excluded where in the *opinion of the record holder*, either disclosure of the information would be 'likely to cause serious harm to the physical or mental health of the patient or of any other individual' or it relates to, or was provided by, another person who could be identified from that information (s 5(1)(a)). In the latter case access may be granted if the provider consents or was a health professional who has been involved in the care of the patient (s 5(2)).

You will notice that the 1990 Act confers upon the holder of the record the right to make a judgment as to whether, for example, the record is inaccurate or that its disclosure is 'likely to cause serious harm' to the patient. It could be said that by adopting this language Parliament seriously weakens its purported commitment to patients' access to health information. It is instructive to compare the wording of the Data Protection (Subject Access Modification) (Health) Order 1987 (SI 1987 No 1903) (*supra*, p 626). There, the balance seems more favourable to the patient's right of access since the criteria for excluding access are expressed in more objective language in that no reference is made to the formula 'in the opinion of the holder of the record'.

Finally, where the medical record relates to infertility treatment, access may be restricted (see Access to Health Records (Control of Access) Regulations 1993 (SI 1993 No 746), discussed *infra*, ch 11).

4. Access to Medical Reports Act 1988

This Act came into force on 1 January 1989. The Act established a right of access to *medical reports* prepared by a doctor for employment or insurance purposes. When an employer (or potential employer) or an insurance company seeks a medical report on an individual, it must obtain that individual's consent (s 3(1)). As a condition for granting consent, an individual may require that he be given access to the medical report prior to its supply to the employer or insurance company.

Section 1 sets out the general principle.

1. It shall be the right of an individual to have access, in accordance with the provisions of this Act, to any medical report relating to the individual which is to be, or has been, supplied by a medical practitioner for employment purposes or insurance purposes.

Section 4 provides that:

4. (1) An individual who gives his consent under section 3 above to the making of an application shall be entitled, when giving his consent, to state that he wishes to have access to the report to be supplied in response to the application before it is so supplied; and, if he does so, the applicant shall
(a) notify the medical practitioner of that fact at the time when the application is made, and
(b) at the same time notify the individual of the making of the application; and each such notification shall contain a statement of the effect of subsection (2) below.
    (2) Where a medical practitioner is notified by the applicant under subsection (1) above that the individual in question wishes to have access to the report before it is supplied, the practitioner shall not supply the report unless –
(a) he has given the individual access to it and any requirements of section 5 below have been complied with, or
(b) the period of 21 days beginning with the date of the making of the application has elapsed without his having received any communication from the individual concerning arrangements for the individual to have access to it.

Even if the individual does not stipulate that he be given access as a condition for granting consent, he may none the less by section 4(3) request access prior to the doctor's supplying it by giving notice to the doctor. If it has already been supplied, the individual is entitled to access for up to six months thereafter (s 6). Access is defined in section 6(3) as meaning inspection of a copy of the medical report or obtaining such a copy.

An individual's right of access is not absolute. Section 7 of the Act provides for *three* situations where a doctor will be justified in not granting access to the whole or part of the report.

7. (1) A medical practitioner shall not be obliged to give an individual access, in accordance with the provisions of section 4(4) or 6(3) above, to any part of a medical report whose disclosure would in the opinion of the practitioner be likely to cause serious harm to the physical or mental health of the individual or others or would indicate the intentions of the practitioner in respect of the individual.
    (2) A medical practitioner shall not be obliged to give an individual access, in accordance with those provisions, to any part of a medical report whose disclosure would be likely to reveal information about another person, or to reveal the identity of another person who has supplied information to the practitioner about the individual, unless –
(a) that person has consented; or
(b) that person is a health professional who has been involved in the care of the individual and the information relates to or has been provided by the professional in that capacity.

In essence the three situations are (1) where in the doctor's opinion, disclosure would be 'likely to cause serious harm to the physical or mental health of the individual or others'; (2) where in the doctor's opinion, it could indicate his intentions in respect of that individual (*semble*: where the doctor intends to suggest further investigations in the light of the examination); (3) where disclosure would be likely to reveal information about another or identify another who had supplied information to the doctor unless that other had consented or had been the individual's doctor.

You will notice the subjective language of the first two exceptions: 'in the opinion of the practitioner' and the objective language of the third exception. Parliament in 1987 (the Data Protection Order) voted for an objective approach. In 1988, it hedged its bets. By 1990 (Access to Health Records Act) it had voted with equal conviction for the subjective approach.

If an individual believes that he has wrongly been refused access he may by virtue of section 8 make an application to the county court alleging failure to comply with the Act. If persuaded the court may order compliance.

Finally, it is important to notice that the provisions of the Act only apply where the doctor making the report is a doctor 'who is or has been responsible for the clinical care of the individual' (s 2(1)). Arguably, the employer or insurance company can quite easily circumvent the provisions of the Act and thereby deny the individual any right of access by stipulating that the individual present himself to a doctor who has not previously treated him. The report that follows will not be prepared by a doctor 'responsible for the clinical care of the individual' and thus there will be no right of access. The converse situation in which the doctor is someone who is caring for the individual whether GP or hospital doctor is clearly within the Act.

There then remains a third situation: where the doctor is an occupational health physician (OHP) within the employer's organisation. If the OHP has undertaken the clinical care of the employee in the past, the Act will apply. This means that the Act may not be avoided where an employer seeks to obtain a report from an OHP (based on his existing knowledge of the employee) even where the employer chooses to categorise the report as an internal memorandum rather than a medical report.

Control

Turning now from the question of access by a patient, we must consider the extent to which the patient may control information about him contained in his medical records so as to prevent others learning of it without his authority. We should look first to the common law and then statute.

A. THE COMMON LAW

We have seen that arguments based upon ownership of the medical record are futile. Except in the rarest of cases, the ownership of the record will not be vested in the patient. Thus the patient can have no right of control based upon ownership.

The alternative, and much more significant, common law device whereby a patient may control if not the record then the disclosure of the information which it contains, is the law of confidentiality. In essence, a doctor breaches his obligation of confidence to his patient if he discloses medical information without the patient's consent save in exceptional circumstances. We examine the law of confidence in the next chapter.

B. STATUTE

1. Data Protection Act 1984

Section 5(2)(d) of the 1984 Act provides that a 'data user' within the Act shall not 'disclose [data held by him] to any person' who is not listed as a potential recipient under section 4(3) at the time of the date user's registration under the Act. Unauthorised disclosure whether knowingly or recklessly is a criminal offence (s 5(5)). Hence, on the one hand the Act creates a principle of 'non-disclosure'. On the other hand, however, it permits disclosure to any person or body named in the register as potential recipients. The effect, therefore, is that there is a statutory regime of control which vests a power of control in the patient coupled with a power to disclose under the Act which the patient cannot influence. It should be noticed that the Act does not give an individual a claim for compensation for any 'damage' or 'distress' caused by unauthorised disclosure (cf s 23 in relation to computer bureaux). In addition, the 'non-disclosure' principle does not apply in a number of situations set out in section 34.

34. (5) Personal data are exempt from the non-disclosure provisions in any case in which the disclosure is –
(a) required by or under any enactment, by any rule of law or by the order of a court; or
(b) made for the purpose of obtaining legal advice or for the purposes of, or in the course of, legal proceedings in which the person making the disclosure is a party or a witness.
(6) Personal data are exempt from the non-disclosure provisions in any case in which –
(a) the disclosure is to the data subject or a person acting on his behalf; or
(b) the data subject or any such person has requested or consented to the particular disclosure in question; or
(c) the disclosure is by a data user or a person carrying on a computer bureau to his servant or agent for the purpose of enabling the servant or agent to perform his functions as such; or
(d) the person making the disclosure has reasonable grounds for believing that the disclosure falls within any of the foregoing paragraphs of this subsection . . .
(8) Personal data are exempt from the non-disclosure provisions in any case in which the disclosure is urgently required for preventing injury or other damage to the health of any person or persons; and in proceedings against any person for contravening [the non-disclosure provisions] above it shall be a defence to prove that he had reasonable ground for believing that the disclosure in question was urgently required for that purpose.

A similar set of exemptions was judged to be necessary in relation to information relating to infertility treatment. Some appeared in the original Act – the Human Fertilisation and Embryology Act 1990, s 33 – others, previously omitted, were added in amending legislation – the Human Fertilisation and Embryology (Disclosure of Information) Act 1992 amending section 33 (see discussion *infra*, ch 11). The language used in the two statutory regimes is different. As a consequence the scope of the exemptions from non-disclosure differs whether intentionally or otherwise (eg compare s 34(5) and (6) of the 1984 Act with s 33(6)(f) of the 1990 Act). Of course, disclosure of such information would only be permissible if *both* sets of provisions are complied with.

Whatever the position as regards authorised disclosure under the 1984 Act, it does not follow that the patient will not have a right to control the information through the civil law of confidence. Complying with the statute provides a defence to prosecution, but may not be conclusive that the disclosure is a lawful breach of confidence. Suffice it to say here that the law of confidence recognises that a breach may be justified as being in the public interest. It may be argued that the statutory exemptions would be regarded by the common law as reflecting the public interest. That issue is a distinct one which we return to in the next chapter.

2. Access to Medical Reports Act 1988

We have already considered the access provisions of the Access to Medical Reports Act 1988. The Act also gives an individual a limited right to control a medical report created for employment or insurance purposes. An employer, or insurance company must obtain an individual's consent prior to seeking a medical report upon the individual (s 3(1)). The Act seems to confer an absolute right upon an individual to refuse his consent to this.

The more usual case will be, however, that the individual does consent to the application for the report if he realistically wants the job, promotion or insurance policy that he seeks. Then, the Act contemplates two situations: *conditional* and *unconditional* consent.

Firstly, the individual (as we saw earlier in this chapter), may consent to the making of the application *on condition* that he is granted access to the report. If access has to be granted under the Act (ie the report or the relevant part of it does not fall within the exemption provisions of s 7) then the medical report cannot be supplied to the employer or insurance company without the individual's consent once the individual has obtained access to the report (s 5(1)). Again, the individual's right to refuse consent seems absolute.

However, instead of refusing consent to the supply of the report the individual is entitled, as a condition of his consent, to request that the doctor 'amend any part of the report which the individual considers to be incorrect or misleading' (s 5(2)). Thereafter, the doctor may only supply the report to the employer or insurance company if (i) he accedes to this request (s 5(2)(a)) or (ii) he attaches to the report a statement by the individual concerning the part of the report which the doctor has refused to amend (s 5(2)(b)).

Secondly, the individual may give his consent to the making of the application for the report *unconditionally*. As we saw earlier, he may still, prior to its supply, notify the doctor that he wishes to have access to the report (s 4(3)). Supply of the report is then subject to the same restrictions as if the consent had been initially conditional.

If, however, the individual's unconditional consent remains unchanged, the Act confers upon him no right to control the supply or content of the medical report. In other words, requiring (and obtaining) access to a report is, under the Act, a necessary condition to exercising any control over the supply or content of the report.

Chapter 9

Confidentiality

The obligation of confidence

A. GENERALLY

One of the most fundamental *ethical* obligations owed by a doctor to his patient is to respect the confidences of his patient. That this has long been a central premise in our approach to medicine can be seen from the fact that the Hippocratic Oath states:

> Whatsoever things I see or hear concerning the life of men, in my attendance on the sick or even apart therefrom, which ought not to be noised abroad, I will keep silence thereon, counting such things to be as sacred secrets.

But is there a concomitant *legal* obligation? Francis Gurry in *Breach of Confidence* (1985) examines the law relating to breach of confidence (pp 58-60):

> While the jurisdictional basis is fundamental to the breach of confidence action, considerable uncertainty still surrounds it. For this reason, any conclusions drawn about it must necessarily be tentative and devoid of dogmatism. The view offered here is that the courts have relied on principles freely drawn from the fields of contract, equity, and property, and that the liberal use of these principles points to the existence of a *sui generis* action which has, in terms of conventional categories, a composite jurisdictional basis.
>
> The approach adopted by the courts seems to have two dominant characteristics. First, the courts' attitude to jurisdiction has been a *pragmatic* one. What has mattered, it seems, is the existence of *a* jurisdiction on which to act in the case immediately in hand. Considerations of conceptual neatness have been secondary to this pragmatic question:
>
> > The true question is whether, *under the circumstances of this case*, the Court ought to interpose by injunction, upon the ground of breach of faith or of contract.
> >
> > That the Court has exercised jurisdiction in cases of this nature does not, I think, admit of any question. Different grounds have indeed been assigned for the exercise of that jurisdiction . . . but, upon whatever grounds the jurisdiction is founded, the authorities leave no doubt as to the exercise of it [*Morison v Moat* (1851) 9 Hare 241 at 255, 68 ER 492 at 498 per Turner VC].
>
> Secondly, the courts' approach to the question of jurisdiction has been a *flexible* one. This flexibility is nowhere better illustrated than in the relationship between contract and equity. Here the courts have been prepared to introduce an obligation of confidence based on implied contract when the independent jurisdiction in equity has cast doubt on their ability to award damages as well as an injunction [*The Nichrotherm* case (1957) RPC 207]. Similar flexibility is demonstrated within the scope of contract alone, where the courts have supplemented a limited express term of confidence with a broader obligation based on the implied terms of the contract [*Thomas Marshall (Exporters) Ltd v Guinle* [1979] Ch 227].
>
> This flexibility indicates that something more basic than jurisdictional source lies at the foundation of the breach of confidence action. This can be found, it is submitted, in the policy which underlies the circumstances in which relief has been granted – the policy of

holding confidences sacrosanct. Thus, the broad notion of a confidence existing between two parties has provided, in the language of the American realists, 'a sort of doctrinal bridge' [*L Fuller 'American Legal Realism'* (1934) 82 University of Pennsylvania L Rev 492-62, 441] between contract, equity, and property. The confidence arises out of both the circumstances in which information has been disclosed and the nature of the information itself. The circumstances of a disclosure may be such that the confider is placing the confidant in a position of trust. If so, either equity or contract will provide a means by which the trust can be honoured. But a disclosure will not betray a confidence if what has been disclosed is common knowledge. It is only when the information is private or 'confidential', when its general publication would reveal something which the confider wishes to keep secret, that the confidence can be regarded as having been reposed by one person in another. Here, the notion of confidence links contract and equity with property, for the courts have recognised that the publication or misuse of confidential information may injure a person either emotionally [*Prince Albert v Strange* (1849) 2 De G and Sm 652, 64 ER 293; (on appeal) 1 Mac & G 25, 41 ER 1171] or materially [*Exchange Telegraph Co v Howard* (1906) 22 TLR 375] even though no *immediate* relationship of trust has been broken. By acknowledging a right of property in information of this kind, the courts have been able to grant relief where the defendant has acquired the information by reprehensible means. But, it may be said, how can the acquisition of confidential information by reprehensible means, rather than the abuse of a relationship of confidence created by a limited disclosure, involve a breach of a *confidence*? The answer may lie in the combination of two factors. First, the person who has the confidential information and who guards its secret places a trust in the rest of society by demonstrating that he wishes to preserve an element of himself or his business free from general publicity. Secondly, the acquirer, as a member of society, can be said to breach that confidence or trust because of the means which he has used to gain the information. These means force an unwanted communication of the information on the possessor of the information. The act of resorting to such means on the part of the acquirer indicates that he is aware of the other's desire to preserve the confidentiality of the information in respect of which his means have forced a disclosure.

In *A-G v Guardian Newspapers (No 2)* [1988] 3 All ER 545 at 658, Lord Goff summarised the law:

> I start with the broad general principle . . . that a duty of confidence arises when confidential information comes to the knowledge of a person (the confidant) in circumstances where he has notice, or is held to have agreed, that the information is confidential, with the effect that it would be just in all the circumstances that he should be precluded from disclosing the information to others. I have used the word 'notice' advisedly, in order to avoid the . . . question of the extent to which actual knowledge is necessary, though I of course understand knowledge to include circumstances where the confidant has deliberately closed his eyes to the obvious. The existence of this broad general principle reflects the fact that there is such a public interest in the maintenance of confidences, that the law will provide remedies for their protection.
>
> I realise that, in the vast majority of cases, in particular those concerned with trade secrets, the duty of confidence will arise from a transaction or relationship between the parties, often a contract, in which event the duty may arise by reason of either an express or an implied term of that contract. It is in such cases as these that the expressions 'confider' and 'confidant' are perhaps most aptly employed. But it is well-settled that a duty of confidence may arise in equity independently of such cases.

Although there had been little doubt that a legal obligation of confidence is owed in law by a doctor to his patient, curiously there was little authority directly on the point (see *Hunter v Mann* [1974] QB 767 at 772 per Boreham J; *Goddard v Nationwide Building Society* [1986] 3 All ER 264 at 271 per Nourse LJ; *A-G v Guardian Newspapers (No 2)* [1988] 3 All ER 545 at 639 per Lord Keith). The cases of *X v Y* [1988] 2 All ER 648 and *W v Egdell* [1990] 1 All ER 835, (1989) 4 BMLR 96 (CA) put the matter beyond doubt. In both cases the court moved to a consideration of allegations of breach of confidence assuming, without feeling the need to establish, the existence of the duty of confidence in general terms. For example, in *Egdell*, Bingham LJ states:

It has never been doubted that the circumstances here were such as to impose on Dr Egdell a duty of confidence owed to W. He could not lawfully sell the contents of his report to a newspaper, as the judge held. Nor could he, without a breach of the law as well as professional etiquette, discuss the case in a learned article or in his memoirs or in gossiping with friends, unless he took appropriate steps to conceal the identity of W. It is not in issue here that a duty of confidence existed. . . .

We were referred, as the judge was, to the current advice given by the General Medical Council to the medical profession pursuant to s 35 of the Medical Act 1983. Rule 80 provides:

> It is a doctor's duty, except in the cases mentioned below, strictly to observe the rule of professional secrecy by refraining from disclosing voluntarily to any third party information about a patient which he has learnt directly or indirectly in his professional capacity as a registered medical practitioner . . .

I do not doubt that this accurately states the general rule as the law now stands, and the contrary was not suggested.

Indeed the obligation of confidence is not only recognised by the common law. There are specific instances where Parliament has chosen to put the obligation into a statutory form because of the particular circumstances, for example, National Health Service (Venereal Diseases) Regulations 1974 (SI 1974 No 29); Abortion Regulations 1991 (SI 1991 No 499); Human Fertilisation and Embryology Act 1990, section 33. (But notice that the law does not recognise a 'privilege' against disclosure of medical confidences in court proceedings: *Duchess of Kingston's Case* (1776) 20 State Trials 355 and *Cross on Evidence* (ed Tapper) (7th edn 1990) at pp 448-449.)

Granted the law does recognise a duty of confidence between a doctor and his patient, the next question to be considered is the precise scope of the duty. Gurry, in his book *Breach of Confidence* (1985) (at 148-9), writes:

> A doctor is under a legal obligation not to disclose confidential information concerning a patient which he learns in the course of his professional practice:
>
> > [I]n common with other professional men, for instance a priest . . . the doctor is under a duty not to disclose [voluntarily], without the consent of his patient, information which he, the doctor, has gained in his professional capacity [*Hunter v Mann* [1974] QB 767 at 772 per Boreham J].
>
> By analogy with the banker's obligation, it would seem that the doctor's duty of non-disclosure applies not only to information acquired directly from the patient, but also to information concerning the patient which the doctor learns from other sources *in his character as the patient's doctor*. Thus, the obligation of secrecy would extend to reports received by a doctor about a patient from medical specialists or from para-medical services.

You will notice that Gurry considers that the obligation would extend to all information received by the doctor 'in his character as the patient's doctor'. Perhaps, this needs further elaboration.

Where the doctor acquires information directly from the patient or by his own examination or observation of the patient, there can be no doubt that the obligation of confidence attaches to this information.

Where the doctor acquires this information from a third party in circumstances in which the third party knows of the doctor-patient relationship, there would seem to be no reason to distinguish this from the usual case already mentioned. It may be asserted, however, that there should be some distinction between the doctor acquiring information from another health care professional as distinct from a lay person. We do not subscribe to this view since, in both situations, the doctor receives the information *qua* professional vis-à-vis the third party (see, eg, *Confidentiality, Use and Disclosure of NHS Information*, HSG (92), para 2.3).

Where the doctor acquires the information from a third party in circumstances in which the third party is unaware that he is speaking to the patient's doctor, the answer is not so clear. On one view, since the doctor does not receive the information *qua* professional vis-à-vis the third party, he has no professional obligation of confidence. The better view, perhaps, is that a court would recognise a duty to respect confidentiality since what lies at the root of the doctor-patient relationship is the patient's trust that the doctor will not reveal any *clinical* information to another without permission and this would extend to all such information however received.

B. SPECIAL CASES

1. Children

Obviously the responsibility a parent has for a child means that the parent will be anxious to know all about the child's life and what the child is involved in. As it grows to maturity so the child will want to have its own secrets even from its parents. How this process is managed is, of course, the key to successful parenting. Complications arise when a third party, for example a doctor, knows something about a child. The child may not wish the parents to be told. The example most often referred to is that of a young girl who seeks contraceptive advice or treatment but asks the doctor to keep the consultation and any treatment secret. There is a danger, however, that this example is so overladen with moral controversy that if it is used as the paradigm for legal analysis it may distort our approach to the law. A principled analysis would proceed as follows. Under what circumstances does a legal duty of confidence arise between a child and a doctor?

(a) A status approach

On one view, when a child is taken to a doctor for treatment by its parent (and thus becomes the doctor's patient), there arises out of that status relationship a duty of confidence. The implication of this view is that *prima facie* the doctor has a duty to observe the child's confidences. Should the doctor choose to tell the parent he will need to demonstrate that his breach of confidence falls within one of the recognised exceptions justifying disclosure of confidential information. But a doctor must usually inform the parents of a young child what he discovers in order to obtain consent to further treatment and so enable the parents to carry out their duty to care for the child. Thus, this view, based as it is upon status, seems out of consonance with the legal and actual reality flowing from the parents' responsibilities to their child. It must be open to doubt, therefore, that the law begins with the premise that the doctor should tell no one and then allows the doctor (or others later if the doctor's decision is called into question) to judge whether in the particular circumstances of the case disclosure to a parent is justified. Such a view leaves too much discretion to the doctor and strikes an improper balance between disclosure and non-disclosure particularly as regards young children.

(b) A capacity approach

Another (and preferable) view would have it that the obligation of confidence arises between a child and a doctor when, but only when, the child is competent to form a relationship of confidence, ie to understand what secrecy entails. Analytically, an approach based upon competence is more in keeping with the general law as regards children since generally the courts, and Parliament, have moved away from a status approach towards a concern for a child's capacity (eg Children Act 1989; Access to Health Records Act 1990 and *Gillick v West Norfolk and Wisbech AHA* [1986] AC 112).

The implication of this approach is significant. It is that *prima facie* when the child is *incompetent* to form a relationship of confidentiality the doctor is obliged to disclose information which he has learned to the parents. Only if the doctor can provide good reasons can he be justified in not doing so. The balance is struck in favour of disclosure. This is entirely in keeping with the fundamental principle that the law's paramount concern is with the welfare of the child and *prima facie* that welfare is best served by others coming to know what the doctor has learnt. Ordinarily, it will be the parents who need to know so as to care for their child. On occasions, it will be others, for example, the social services department when the doctor discovers evidence of parental abuse.

Adopting this latter approach, ie of capacity, there are three distinct sets of circumstances which fall to be examined.

(i) THE CHILD WITH COMPLETE INCAPACITY

Here we consider the child who lacks the capacity to consent to treatment and also lacks the capacity to enter into a confidential relationship. In such a case, the child would ordinarily be very young. By contrast to the status approach, no obligation of confidence will arise between the child and the doctor. Ordinarily, therefore, as we have seen, the doctor will be entitled to disclose to the parent what he has learned so as to advance the care of the child.

To test the validity of this approach we can imagine a situation in which the doctor learns from the child information, unassociated with the reasons for the parent's bringing the child to the doctor. Assume further that it is information which causes the doctor to suspect that the child is at risk of harm. The general law requires that the doctor must act in the child's 'best interests'. The law of confidence reflects this by requiring that in such a case the doctor should tell those who can protect the child from the risk. There cannot be any doubt that the balance, in law, is struck in favour of disclosure. The doctor would need very strong reasons for not disclosing what he has learnt. Does this mean that a doctor has a *duty* to disclose this information to parents (or exceptionally to others)? Or, does it mean that he has a *discretion* to do so? In our view, his obligation to act in the 'best interests' of the child will create a very strong presumption in favour of disclosure. Normally, this would be reflected by the law imposing a duty upon the doctor the breach of which would give rise to a claim in negligence for damages if harm resulted. It does not follow, of course, that it should always be the parents who should be informed. The doctor in acting in the 'best interests' of the child must determine whether the information should more properly be disclosed to others if the child is at risk from a parent.

To deduce that no obligation of confidence is owed to a child who lacks capacity to understand the nature of a confidential relationship provokes its own difficulties. What if, for example, a doctor decided to disclose information learned about the child to a newspaper for no good reason? If the doctor's intention was discovered before publication, the newspaper could be enjoined, but on what basis? Arguably, an interested party would have to invoke the court's inherent jurisdiction to act in the 'best interests' of the child. What if, however, the newspaper had already published the information? What legal action, if any, could be brought against the doctor? If the status approach were adopted, the doctor would be liable for breach of confidence but we have rejected this approach. In our view no civil action will lie at the suit of the child or the parents unless the disclosure causes harm, in which case a negligence action could be brought on behalf of the child. Absent any action for the infringement of parental rights, no claim could be brought by the parents (see *F v Wirral MBC* [1991] Fam 69).

It is fair to notice that the law, as we see it, may differ from the doctor's ethical responsibility as set out in the GMC's 'Blue Book' (January 1993). There, the notion of an obligation of confidence is cast more widely to reflect ethical principles (see paragraphs 76 and 84).

(ii) THE CHILD WITH CAPACITY

Here we consider the child who has the capacity both to consent to treatment and to enter into a confidential relationship. In such a case, an obligation of confidence arises and in principle the law is no different from that applicable to adults. As with adults the obligation is not absolute. A breach of confidence may be justified if, for example, it is made in the public interest. This justification (which we shall consider later) suggests in this context that if a doctor can show that disclosure is in the 'best interests' of his child patient he will act lawfully (*Re C (A Minor) (Evidence: Confidential Information)* (1991) 7 BMLR 138, CA) in appropriately compelling circumstances such as cases of physical or sexual abuse.

It is important to state that this should not be interpreted as giving the doctor *carte blanche* to inform others just because he disagrees with his child patient's views and wishes to ignore the prohibition against disclosure. In our view, appropriately compelling circumstances should be limited to cases where the child's life is threatened or the child is exposed to a demonstrable risk of serious harm (see *Re W (A Minor) (Medical Treatment)* [1992] 4 All ER 627).

Some support for the position argued here can be found in the Access to Health Records Act 1990. This recognises that a parent may only claim a right of access to the health records of a child if *either* the child is incompetent to make an application for access and access by the parent is in that child's best interests *or* the child is competent and consents (section 4(2)).

(iii) THE CHILD WITH INCOMPLETE CAPACITY

Here we refer to the child who has the capacity to enter into a confidential relationship but lacks the capacity to consent to treatment. On the basis that competence to enter into a confidential relationship is the guiding principle in establishing whether there is a duty of confidence, the law in this situation is the same as that set out in (ii) above.

2. The incompetent adult

In the case of an adult patient who has always been incompetent, the approach which we have adopted leads to the conclusion that no duty of confidence is owed to the patient since the patient is incompetent to enter into a relationship of confidence. This surprising conclusion could have been avoided, of course, if we had adopted the status approach: the incompetent adult merely by being a patient would be owed a duty of confidence and could sue through his best friend if any breach occurred. We rejected the status approach on the ground that we thought the balance of law in the case of the incompetent child was in favour of there being a presumption in favour of disclosure so as best to serve the incompetent's interests. This conclusion is driven by a concern for situations in which it is desirable for the doctor to disclose information and that the law should be seen to endorse this, eg where the doctor learns that a child may have been abused. Indeed, the law would recognise a duty in negligence to prevent the child from suffering avoidable harm.

You will recall that we accepted that our view is problematic in some situations. If no obligation of confidence is owed by the doctor, absent a legal right to restrain him, what then is to stop the doctor, for example, from disclosing information about his incompetent adult patient to a newspaper? In the case of a child patient, as we have seen, a parent or other may invoke the inherent jurisdiction of the court. But, as regards an incompetent adult, you will recall that the court has no *parens patriae* jurisdiction. Thus a court cannot, *prima facie*, restrain the doctor from disclosing information simply because it is not in the patient's interest to have it disclosed.

There are two solutions to this unsatisfactory state of affairs. Either the court should be given back the *parens patriae* power over adults that it lost in 1960, or the court more radically could recognise that the relationship between a doctor and a patient is a fiduciary relationship from which would flow, of course, an obligation not to disclose information when it is not in the patient's interests to do so (see on 'fiduciary relationship' *supra*, p 613 *et seq*).

3. The dead

What effect does the death of a patient have on the obligation of confidence? The traditional ethical principle is stated by the GMC in the 'Blue Book' in paragraph 91: 'The fact of a patient's death does not of itself release a doctor from the obligation to maintain confidentiality.' Is this the legal position? We are not considering here the separate and equally difficult question of whether an action for a breach of confidence which occurred during the life of a patient survives his death. Instead, we are concerned with an action by a patient's estate for disclosures after the death of the patient. Such a claim could only be brought if the estate had itself suffered a legal wrong. Arguably, the estate can only be legally wronged in this context if it inherits a right of the deceased which is unlawfully interfered with after death. So, for example, the right to sue on a contract passes to the estate. Similarly, where property passes to the estate on death any unlawful dealing with it by others will give the estate a right of action. Thus the crucial question is whether the right to have confidences observed is a right which passes as a chose in action to the estate. There is no clear answer. It could be argued that since what is at stake is the deceased's feelings and reputation the analogy with the law of defamation is persuasive (ie the cause of action does not survive death). Of course, in relation to defamation, the position is governed by statute. In our view the courts would reflect this policy in the case of breach of medical confidence. Even if this view were wrong, the law may require the estate to show detriment as a condition of the claim. This would, of course, be difficult.

Modification of the obligation

In *W v Egdell* [1990] 1 All ER 835 the Court of Appeal accepted that the obligation of confidence was not absolute (see Bingham LJ at 848). This is well recognised, as Gurry (*op cit*) points out in his book (at 148-9):

> As is the case with all obligations of confidence, the doctor's duty is not absolute but is subject to the requirement of disclosure under compulsion of law and in the public interest. Furthermore, his obligation can be released with the express or implied consent of the patient.

A. CONSENT TO DISCLOSURE

The GMC's *Professional Conduct and Discipline: Fitness to Practise* (January 1993) para 77 states:

> 77. Where a patient, or a person properly authorised to act on a patient's behalf, consents to disclosure, information to which the consent refers may be disclosed in accordance with that consent.

Although consent is often regarded as an exception to the obligation of confidence, in fact it is not. It is merely a recognition by the patient that the doctor is no longer under an obligation to keep the confidence – it defeats the *existence* of the obligation. (See eg Hirst J in *Fraser v Thames Television Ltd* [1983] 2 All ER 101 at 122: 'Counsel for the plaintiffs accepts that . . . the communication . . . in the spring or summer of 1974 was legitimate, since it was done with the plaintiff's consent.')

Consent to disclose is usually *express* but it may also be *implied*. A common example of the latter is when the patient is in the care of more than one person. In such a case the patient may be assumed to consent to all medical and nursing members of the team being informed so as properly to carry out their respective obligations. The members of the 'team' who receive the information receive it in confidence.

The GMC's view, as expressed in its *Professional Conduct and Discipline: Fitness to Practise* (1993) para 79, is as follows:

> 79. Most doctors in hospital and general practice are working in health care teams, some of whose members may need access to information, given or obtained in confidence about individuals, in order to perform their duties. It is for doctors who lead such teams to judge when it is appropriate for information to be disclosed for that purpose. They must leave those whom they authorise to receive such information in no doubt that it is given to them in professional confidence. The doctor also has a responsibility to ensure that arrangements exist to inform patients of the circumstances in which information about them is likely to be shared and to give patients the opportunity to state any objection to this.

The ethical principle embraced by the GMC appears to be one of express consent whenever that is possible. The law may not go so far and it may be content with implied consent whenever the circumstances justify it.

It is a continually vexing question whether information should be imparted to those members of the team who do not belong to a profession with a strictly enforced professional code and who may not preserve records under the same circumstances of confidentiality and yet may have a legitimate interest. It may be that the practical needs involved in the management of a patient would lead a court to say that a doctor has a discretion to disclose to all those professionals who also 'need to know' so as properly to serve the medical needs of the patient. Such a discretion must necessarily be exercised with caution. (For a discussion see *Rights and Responsibilities of Doctors* (2nd edn 1992) BMA para 3.6 and *Confidentiality, Use and Disclosure of NHS Information* (HSG (92)) paras 4.9-4.10, 5.3 and 5.6.)

B. STATUTORY

There are a number of statutory provisions which create exceptions to or modifications of the obligation of confidence including for example the following.

The Abortion Regulations 1991 (SI 1991 No 499)

5. A notice given or any information furnished to a Chief Medical Officer in pursuance of these Regulations shall not be disclosed except that disclosure may be made –
  (a) for the purposes of carrying out their duties.
      (i)   to an officer of the Department of Health authorised by the Chief Medical Officer of that Department, or to an officer of the Welsh Office authorised by the Chief Medical Officer of that Office, as the case may be, or
      (ii) to the Registrar General or a member of his staff authorised by him; or
  (b) for the purposes of carrying out his duties in relation to offences under the Act or the law relating to abortion, to the Director of Public Prosecutions or a member of his staff authorised by him; or
  (c) for the purposes of investigating whether an offence has been committed under the Act or the law relating to abortion, to a police officer not below the rank of superintendent or a person authorised by him; or
  (d) pursuant to a court order, for the purposes of criminal proceedings which have begun; or
  (e) for the purposes of bona fide scientific research; or
  (f) to the practitioner who terminated the pregnancy; or
  (g) to a practitioner, with the consent in writing of the woman whose pregnancy was terminated; or
  (h) when requested by the President of the General Medical Council for the purpose of investigating whether there has been serious professional misconduct by a registered medical practitioner, to the President of the General Medical Council or a member of its staff authorised by him.

Public Health (Control of Disease) Act 1984

Notifiable diseases
10. In this Act, 'notifiable disease' means any of the following diseases –
  (a) cholera;
  (b) plague;
  (c) relapsing fever;
  (d) smallpox; and
  (e) typhus.

Cases of notifiable disease and food poisoning to be reported
11. (1) If a registered medical practitioner becomes aware, or suspects, that a patient whom he is attending within the district of a local authority is suffering from a notifiable disease or from food poisoning, he shall, unless he believes, and has reasonable grounds for believing, that some other registered medical practitioner has complied with this subsection with respect to the patient, forthwith send to the proper officer of the local authority for that district a certificate stating –

(a)   the name, age and sex of the patient and the address of the premises where the patient is,
(b)   the disease or, as the case may be, particulars of the poisoning from which the patient
        is, or is suspected to be, suffering and the date, or approximate date, of its onset, and
(c)   if the premises are a hospital, the day on which the patient was admitted, the address of
        the premises from which he came there and whether or not, in the opinion of the
        person giving the certificate, the disease or poisoning from which the patient is, or is
        suspected to be, suffering was contracted in the hospital. . . .
    (4) A person who fails to comply with an obligation imposed on him by subsection (1)
above shall be liable on summary conviction to a fine not exceeding level 1 on the standard
scale.

These provisions are supplemented by the Public Health (Infectious Diseases)
Regulations 1988 (SI No 1546) which refer to a wide range of further infectious
conditions which must be reported by doctors.

National Health Service (Venereal Diseases) Regulations 1974 (SI 1974 No 29)

2. Every Regional Health Authority and every District Health Authority shall take all
necessary steps to secure that any information capable of identifying an individual obtained
by officers of the Authority with respect to persons examined or treated for any sexually
transmitted disease shall not be disclosed except –
(a)   for the purpose of communicating that information to a medical practitioner, or to a
        person employed under the direction of a medical practitioner in connection with the
        treatment of persons suffering from such disease or the prevention of the spread
        thereof, and
(b)   for the purpose of such treatment or prevention.

This regulation was introduced so as to give statutory emphasis to the
obligation of confidence in this area of medical practice. The reasons are
obvious: thus, the circumstances under which disclosure can be made are
carefully circumscribed. Curiously, the Regulations have not been amended to
apply to NHS trusts (but see NHS Trust (Venereal Disease) Directions 1991). It
could be argued that the wording of the provision is such as to allow a patient's
GP to be informed by those working in a Genito-Urinary Clinic without the
consent of, and even in the face of the refusal of, the patient. This has particular
significance in the context of HIV infection where some have argued for the
right of the GP to be informed of a patient's HIV status, allegedly in the
interests of the patient so as to ensure any future care is medically optimal but,
in the case of some doctors at least, in their own perceived interests.

A careful reading of the words of the regulation suggests that it is only information relating to treatment for venereal disease *and* only when the GP himself
is also treating for the disease that the exception comes into play. In essence it is
merely an example of sharing information in the context of team care.

Even if this is wrong, a further point can be made. The notion of *treatment*
entails the need for the patient's consent which itself entails agreement to share
information about his condition. Arguably regulation 2(b) can have no
application in the absence of the patient's agreement to the transfer of the
information to his GP.

A small, but important, point to notice is that the obligation of confidence
under the Regulations applies to any disease which is 'sexually transmitted'. If
this is so, a patient who is HIV positive may need to look to the common law
for protection of his confidence if he became infected by some other means as,
for example, if he is a haemophiliac or has otherwise become HIV positive as a
result of an infected blood donation. Alternatively a 'sexually transmitted
disease' within the regulations could be said to be one usually transmitted

through sexual contact but which may be transmitted by other means. Blood, for example, may be infected with syphilis and transfused into someone who then develops the disease. The disease remains a 'sexually transmitted disease'. On this analysis HIV infection would be within the regulations regardless of the means of infection. (See *X v Y* [1988] 2 All ER 648 in which Rose J assumes the latter to be the case.)

Police and Criminal Evidence Act 1984

Special provisions as to access
9. (1) A constable may obtain access to excluded material . . . for the purposes of a criminal investigation by making an application under Schedule 1 below and in accordance with that Schedule [ie, to a circuit judge]. . . .

Meaning of 'excluded material'
11. (1) Subject to the following provisions of this section, in this Act 'excluded material' means –
(a)   personal records which a person has acquired or created in the course of any trade, business, profession or other occupation or for the purposes of any paid or unpaid office and which he holds in confidence;
(b)   human tissue or tissue fluid which has been taken for the purposes of diagnosis or medical treatment and which a person holds in confidence . . .
   (2) A person holds material other than journalistic material in confidence for the purposes of this section if he holds it subject –
(a)   to an express or implied undertaking to hold it in confidence or
(b)   to a restriction on disclosure or an obligation of secrecy contained in any enactment, including an enactment contained in an Act passed after this Act.

Meaning of 'personal records'
12. In this Part of this Act 'personal records' means documentary and other records concerning an individual (whether living or dead) who can be identified from them, and relating –
(a)   to his physical or mental health;
(b)   to spiritual counselling or assistance given or to be given to him;
(c)   to counselling or assistance given or to be given to him, for the purposes of his personal welfare, by any voluntary organisation or by any individual who –
   (i)   by reason of his office or occupation has responsibilities for his personal welfare; or
   (ii)   by reason of an order of a court, has responsibilities for his supervision.

These provisions apply to medical records, human tissue or tissue fluid, taken for the purposes of diagnostic or medical treatment.

In addition, there are a number of other statutory modifications where a duty to disclose will displace the obligation of confidence: National Health Service (Notification of Births and Deaths) Regulations 1982 (SI 1982 No 286); Misuse of Drugs (Notification of, and Supply to Addicts) Regulations 1973 (SI 1973 No 799); see further, *Rights and Responsibilities of Doctors* (1992) Ch 3. We discuss earlier the provisions of the Data Protection Act 1984 and its relevance to breach of confidence (*supra*, pp 625-628 and 635-663).

C. PUBLIC INTEREST

Lion Laboratories v Evans [1984] 2 All ER 417 (CA)

Griffiths LJ: The first question to be determined is whether there exists a defence of public interest to actions for breach of confidentiality and copyright, and, if so, whether it is limited to situations in which there has been serious wrongdoing by the plaintiffs, the so-called 'iniquity' rule.

I am quite satisfied that the defence of public interest is now well established in actions for breach of confidence and, although there is less authority on the point, that it also extends to breach of copyright: see by way of example *Fraser v Evans* [1969] 1 All ER 8, [1969 1 QB 349; *Hubbard v Vosper* [1972] 1 All ER 1023, [1972] 2 QB 84; *Woodward v Hutchins* [1977] 2 All ER 751, [1977] 1 WLR 760 and *British Steel Corpn v Granada Television Ltd* [1981] 1 All ER 417, [1981] AC 1096.

I can see no sensible reason why this defence should be limited to cases in which there has been wrongdoing on the part of the plaintiffs. I believe that the so-called iniquity rule evolved because in most cases where the facts justified a publication in breach of confidence the plaintiff had behaved so disgracefully or criminally that it was judged in the public interest that his behaviour should be exposed. No doubt it is in such circumstances that the defence will usually arise, but it is not difficult to think of instances where, although there has been no wrongdoing on the part of the plaintiff, it may be vital in the public interest to publish a part of his confidential information.

Clearly this is potentially a very widely drawn modification to the obligation of confidence. If interpreted too widely, it might swallow up the obligation. What guidance do the cases give to the doctor as to when it is in the public interest to disclose confidential information? Lord Wilberforce was anxious to make clear that: 'there is a wide difference between what is interesting to the public and what it is in the public interest to make known' (*British Steel Corpn v Granada Television Ltd* [1981] 1 All ER 417 at 455). You may think that this does not take us much further. The GMC's 'Blue Book', paragraph 86, takes us a little further:

86. Rarely, cases may arise in which disclosure in the public interest may be justified, for example, a situation in which the failure to disclose appropriate information would expose the patient, or someone else, to a risk of death or serious harm.

The extent to which concern for the public interest may serve as a justification for breach of medical confidences has been considered in two leading cases.

X v Y [1988] 2 All ER 648, (1987) 3 BMLR 1 (QBD)

In February 1987 one or more employees of the plaintiffs, a health authority, supplied the first defendant, a reporter on a national newspaper owned and published by the second defendants, with information obtained from hospital records which identified two doctors who were carrying on general practice despite having contracted the disease AIDS. The second defendants made one or more payments of £100 for the information. On 28 February the plaintiffs obtained an order restraining the defendants from 'publishing . . . or making any use whatsoever of any confidential information' which was the property of the plaintiffs and contained in their hospital records. On 15 March the second defendants published an article written by the first defendant, under the headline 'Scandal of Docs with AIDS', which implied that there were doctors in Britain who were continuing to practise despite having contracted AIDS and that the Department of Health and Social Security wished to suppress that fact. The defendants intended to publish a further article identifying the doctors. The plaintiffs sought (i) an injunction restraining the defendants from publishing the identify of the two doctors, (ii) disclosure by the defendants of their sources. . . . The question arose whether the second defendants were justified in the public interest in publishing and using the information disclosed to the first defendant.

Rose J: Under the National Health Service (Venereal Diseases) Regulations 1974 the plaintiffs and their servants have a statutory duty to take all necessary steps to secure that any information capable of identifying patients examined or treated for AIDS shall not be disclosed except to a medical practitioner, or a person under his direction, in connection with and for the purpose of treatment, or prevention of the spread, of the disease. Confidentiality is of paramount importance to such patients, including doctors. The plaintiffs take care to ensure it. Their servants are contractually bound to respect it. If it is breached, or if the patients have grounds for believing that it may be or has been breached they will be reluctant to come forward for and to continue with treatment and, in particular, counselling. If the actual or apprehended breach is to the press that reluctance is likely to be very great. If treatment is not provided or continued the individual will be deprived of its benefit and the public are likely to suffer from an increase in the rate of spread of the disease. The preservation of confidentiality is therefore in the public interest . . .

I keep in the forefront of my mind the very important public interest in freedom of the press. And I accept that there is some public interest in knowing that which the defendants seek to publish (in whichever version). But in my judgment those public interests are substantially outweighed when measured against the public interests in relation to loyalty and confidentiality both generally and with particular reference to AIDS patients' hospital records. There has been no misconduct by the plaintiffs. The records of hospital patients, particularly those suffering from this appalling condition should, in my judgment, be as confidential as the courts can properly keep them in order that the plaintiffs may 'be free from suspicion that they are harbouring disloyal employees'. The plaintiffs have 'suffered a grievous wrong in which the defendants became involved . . . with active participation'. The deprivation of the public of the information sought to be published will be of minimal significance if the injunction is granted; for, without it, all the evidence before me shows that a wide-ranging public debate about AIDS generally and about its effect on doctors is taking place among doctors of widely differing views, within and without the BMA, in medical journals and in many newspapers, including the Observer, the Sunday Times and the Daily Express. Indeed, the sterility of the defendants' argument is demonstrated by the edition of the second defendants' own newspaper dated 22 March 1987. It is there expressly stated, purportedly quoting a Mr Milligan, that three general practitioners two of whom are practising (impliedly in Britain) have AIDS. Paraphrasing Templeman LJ in the *Schering* case, the facts, in the most limited version now sought to be published, have already been made available and may again be made available if they are known otherwise than through the medium of the informer. The risk of identification is only one factor in assessing whether to permit the use of confidential information. In my judgment to allow publication in the recently suggested restricted form, would be to enable both defendants to procure breaches of confidence and then to make their own selection for publication. This would make a mockery of the law's protection of confidentiality when no justifying public interest has been shown. These are the considerations which guide me, whether my task is properly described as a balancing exercise, or an exercise in judicial judgment, or both.

No one has suggested that damages would be an adequate remedy in this case.

It follows that the answer to the first question is No. The plaintiffs are entitled to a permanent injunction in the form of para 1(i) of the interlocutory order made by Ian Kennedy J.

You will notice that Rose J rightly characterises the law's concern with the protection of confidences as being a public interest. Some have characterised the right to confidence as a private interest. The danger of doing so is that private interests tend to give way to the public interest when they are weighed against each other. Interests are far more fairly balanced when public interest is set against public interest and private interest against private interest. The leading case of *W v Egdell* [1990] 1 All ER 835 (CA) illustrates this balancing process between competing *public* interests.

W v Egdell [1990] 1 All ER 835, (1989) 4 BMLR 96 (CA)

W was detained as a patient in a secure hospital without limit of time as a potential threat to public safety after he shot and killed five people and wounded two others. Ten years after he had been first detained he applied to a mental health review tribunal to be discharged or transferred to a regional secure unit with a view to his eventual discharge. His responsible medical officer, who had diagnosed him as suffering from schizophrenia which could be treated by drugs, supported the application but it was opposed by the Secretary of State. His solicitors instructed a consultant psychiatrist, E, to examine W and report on his mental condition with a view to using the report to support W's application to the tribunal. In his report E strongly opposed W's transfer and recommended that further tests and treatment of W would be advisable, and drew attention to W's long-standing interest in firearms and explosives. E sent the report to W's solicitors in the belief that it would be placed before the tribunal, but, in view of the contents of the report, W through his solicitors withdrew his application. When E learnt that the application had been withdrawn and that neither the tribunal nor the hospital charged with W's clinical management had received a copy of his report he contacted the medical director of the hospital, who, having discussed W's case with E, agreed that the hospital should receive a copy of the report in the interests of W's further treatment. At E's prompting the hospital sent a copy of his report to the Secretary of State, who, in turn, forwarded the report to the tribunal when referring W's case to them for consideration.

When W discovered that the report had been disclosed he issued a writ against E and the recipients of the report seeking (i) an injunction to restrain them from using or disclosing the report, (ii) delivery up of all copies of the report and (iii) damages for breach of the duty of confidence. Scott J held that the duty of confidentiality owed by E to W as his patient was subordinate to E's public duty to disclose the results of his examination to the authorities responsible for W because such disclosure was necessary to ensure that the authorities were fully informed about W's mental condition when making decisions concerning his future. The judge accordingly dismissed W's claim against E and the recipients of the report. W appealed against the dismissal of his action against E, contending that the public interest in the duty of confidentiality owed by E to W should override any public interest considerations in disclosing the report to the authorities responsible for W.

Stephen Brown P: In the course of his judgment Scott J said ([1980] 1 All ER 1089 at 1101-1102, [1989] 2 WLR at 709-710):

> The basis of W's case is that his interview with Dr Egdell on 23 July 1987 and the report written by Dr Egdell on the basis of that interview is, or ought to have been, protected from disclosure by the duty of confidence resting on Dr Egdell as W's doctor. It is claimed that Dr Egdell was in breach of his duty of confidence in telling Dr Hunter about the report, in sending a copy of the report to Dr Hunter and in urging the despatch of a copy to the Home Office . . . It is convenient for me first to ask myself what duty of confidence a court of equity ought to regard as imposed on Dr Egdell by the circumstances in which he obtained information from and about W and prepared his report. It is in my judgment plain, and the contrary has not been suggested, that the circumstances did impose on Dr Egdell a duty of confidence. If, for instance Dr Egdell had sold the contents of his report to a newspaper, I do not think any court of equity would hesitate for a moment before concluding that his conduct had been a breach of his duty of confidence. The question in the present case is not whether Dr Egdell was under a duty of confidence; he plainly was. The question is as to the breadth of that duty. Did the duty extend so as to bar disclosure of the report to the medical director of the hospital? Did it bar disclosure to the Home Office? In the *Spycatcher* case [*A-G v Guardian Newspapers Ltd (No 2)*] [1988] 3 All ER 545 at 658-659, [1988] 3 WLR 776 at 805, 807 in the House of Lords Lord Goff, after accepting 'the broad general principle . . . that a duty of confidence arises when confidential information comes to the knowledge of a person (the confidant) in circumstances where he has notice, or is held to have agreed, that the information is confidential, with the effect that it would be just in all the circumstances that he should be precluded from disclosing the information to others', formulated three limiting principles. He said: 'The third limiting principle is of far greater importance. It is that, although the basis of the law's protection of confidence is that, there is a public interest that confidences should be preserved and protected by the law, nevertheless that public interest may be outweighed by some other countervailing public interest which favours disclosure. This limitation may apply, as the learned judge pointed out, to all types of confidential information. It is this limiting principle which may require a court to carry out a balancing operation weighing the public interest in maintaining confidence against a countervailing public interest favouring disclosure.' In *X v Y* [1988] 2 All ER 648 at 653, a case which concerned doctors who were believed to be continuing to practise despite having contracted AIDS, Rose J said: 'In the long run, preservation of confidentiality is the only way of securing public health; otherwise doctors will be discredited as a source of education, for future individual patients "will not come forward if doctors are going to squeal on them". Consequently, confidentiality is vital to secure public as well as private health, for unless those infected come forward they cannot be counselled and self-treatment

does not provide the best care . . .' The question in a particular case whether a duty of confidentiality extends to bar particular disclosures that the confidant has made or wants to make requires the court to balance the interest to be served by non-disclosure against the interest served by disclosure. Rose J struck that balance. It came down, he held, in favour of non-disclosure. In the *Spycatcher* case that balance too was struck. In that case the balance did not come down in favour of non-disclosure. I must endeavour to strike the balance in the present case.

Counsel for W agreed that the judge was required to carry out a balancing exercise. He said that it is a question of degree.

As a starting point Scott J turned to 'Advice on Standards of Professional Conduct and of Medical Ethics' contained in the General Medical Council's 'Blue Book' on professional conduct and discipline. The judge said ([1989] 1 All ER 1089 at 1103, [1989] 2 WLR 689 at 711-712):

> These rules do not provide a definitive answer to the question raised in the present case as to the breadth of the duty of confidence owed by Dr Egdell. They seem to me valuable, however, in showing the approach of the General Medical Council to the breadth of the doctor/patient duty of confidence.

These rules do not themselves have statutory authority. Nevertheless, the General Medical Council in exercising its disciplinary jurisdiction does so in pursuance of the provisions of the Medical Act 1983. Under the heading 'Professional Confidence', rr [80] to 82 provide as follows:

> 80. It is a doctor's duty, except in the cases mentioned below, strictly to observe the rule of professional secrecy by refraining from disclosing voluntarily to any third party information about a patient which he has learnt directly or indirectly in his professional capacity as a registered medical practitioner.
> 81. The circumstances where exceptions to the rule may be permitted are as follows
> . . .
> (b) Confidential information may be shared with other registered medical practitioners who participate in or assume responsibility for clinical management of the patient. To the extent that the doctor deems it necessary for the performance of their particular duties, confidential information may also be shared with other persons (nurses and other health care professionals) who are assisting and collaborating with the doctor in his professional relationship with the patient. It is the doctor's responsibility to ensure that such individuals appreciate that the information is being imparted in strict professional confidence . . .
> (g) Rarely, disclosure may be justified on the ground that it is in the public interest which, in certain circumstances such as, for example, investigation by the police of a grave or very serious crime, might override the doctor's duty to maintain his patient's confidence . . .
> 82. Whatever the circumstances, a doctor must always be prepared to justify his action if he has disclosed confidential information. If a doctor is in doubt whether any of the exceptions mentioned above would justify him in disclosing information in a particular situation he will be wise to seek advice from a medical defence society or professional association. . . .

The judge said that paras (b) and (g) of r 81 seemed to him to be particularly relevant. He then rehearsed the circumstances of the disclosure by Dr Egdell of his report and asked the question ([1989] 1 All ER 1089 at 1104, [1989] 2 WLR 689 at 713):

> Did these circumstances impose on Dr Egdell a duty not to disclose his opinions and his report to Dr Hunter, the medical director at the hospital? In my judgment they did not. Dr Egdell was expressing opinions which were relevant to the nature of the treatment and care to be accorded to W at the hospital. Dr Egdell was, in effect, recommending a change from the approach to treatment and care that Dr Ghosh was following. He was expressing reservations about Dr Ghosh's diagnosis. The case seems to me to fall squarely within para (b) of r 81. But I would base my conclusion on broader considerations than that. I decline to overlook the background to Dr Egdell's examination of W. True it is that Dr Egdell was engaged by W. He was the doctor of W's choice. None the less, in my opinion, the duty he owed to W was not his only duty. W was not an ordinary member of the public. He was, consequent on the killings he had perpetrated, held in a secure hospital subject to a regime whereby

decisions concerning his future were to be taken by public authorities, the Home Secretary or the tribunal. W's own interests would not be the only nor the main criterion in the taking of those decisions. The safety of the public would be the main criterion. In my view, a doctor called on, as Dr Egdell was, to examine a patient such as W owes a duty not only to his patient but also a duty to the public. His duty to the public would require him, in my opinion, to place before the proper authorities the result of his examination if, in his opinion, the public interest so required. This would be so, in my opinion, whether or not the patient instructed him not to do so.

The judge then referred to the submission of counsel for W that the dominant public interest in the case was the public interest in patients being able to make full and frank disclosure to their doctors, and in particular to their psychiatrist, without fear that the doctor would disclose the information to others. The judge said ([1989] 1 All ER 1089 at 1104-1105, [1989] 2 WLR 689 at 713-714):

> I accept the general importance in the public interest that this should be so. It justifies the General Medical Council's r 80 . . . In truth, as it seems to me, the interest to be served by the duty of confidence for which counsel for W contends is the private interest of W and not any broader public interest. If I set the private interest of W in the balance against the public interest served by disclosure of the report to Dr Hunter and the Home Office, I find the weight of the public interest prevails . . . In my judgment, therefore, the circumstances of this case did not impose on Dr Egdell an obligation of conscience, an equitable obligation, to refrain from disclosing his report to Dr Hunter, or to refrain from encouraging its disclosure to the Home Office.

In this court counsel for W acknowledges that, in addition to the duty of confidence admittedly owed by Dr Egdell to W, it was necessary for the judge to consider the public interest in the disclosure by Dr Egdell of his report to the authorities. There are two competing public interest considerations. However, he submitted that the dominant public interest was the duty of confidence owed by Dr Egdell to W. The burden of proving that that duty was overridden by public interest considerations in disclosing his opinion to the public authorities rested fairly and squarely on Dr Egdell. He contended that, where the public interest relied on to justify a breach of confidence is alleged to be the reduction or elimination of a risk to public safety, it must be shown (a) that such a risk is real, immediate and serious, (b) that it will be substantially reduced by disclosure, (c) that the disclosure is no greater than is reasonably necessary to minimise the risk and (d) that the consequent damage to the public interest protected by the duty of confidentiality is outweighed by the public interest in minimising the risk. He relied on the decision of Rose J in *X v Y* [1988] 2 All ER 648. He also cited a passage from the judgment of Boreham J in *Hunter v Mann* [1974] 2 All ER 414 at 417-418, [1974] QB 767 AT 772:

> The second proposition is this: that in common with other professional men, for instance a priest and there are of course others, the doctor is under a duty not to disclose, without the consent of his patient, information which he, the doctor, has gained in his professional capacity, save, says counsel for the appellant, in very exceptional circumstances. He quoted the example of the murderer still manic, who would be a menace to society. But, says counsel, save in exceptional circumstances, the general rule applies. He adds that the law will enforce that duty.

He referred to the American case of *Tarasoff v Regents of the University of California* (1976) 17 Cal 3d 358 as an example of extreme circumstances and submitted that only in the most extreme circumstances could a doctor be relieved from observing the strict duty of confidence imposed on him by reason of his relationship with his patient. In this instance, said counsel for W, there was no immediate prospect of W being released or of being detained other than under secure conditions and furthermore any change in his circumstances would be conditional on further expert analysis and recommendation.

The two interests which had to be balanced in this case were both public interests. The judge was wrong to refer to W's 'private' interest. The judge was also in error, said counsel for W, in saying: 'The case seems to me to fall squarely within para *(b)* of r 81' (of the General Medical Council's rules). Dr Egdell did not have any clinical responsibility for W and accordingly that particular rule could not be relied on by Dr Egdell in the present circumstances . . .

Counsel for Dr Egdell argued that Dr Egdell is acknowledged to be a responsible and experienced consultant psychiatrist having particular knowledge of the procedures relating to the management and treatment of restricted patients detained in secure conditions under the provisions of the Mental Health Act 1983. His evidence on matters of fact was not challenged. It must be accepted that he was genuinely seriously concerned by the revelation of what seemed to him to be entirely new facts relating to W's long-standing interest in guns and explosives. It is not challenged he said, that he acted in good faith in disclosing his report to Dr Hunter and in urging its disclosure to the Home Secretary. He plainly believed that he was acting in the public interest.

The balance of public interest clearly lay in the restricted disclosure of vital information to the director of the hospital and to the Secretary of State who had the onerous duty of safeguarding public safety.

In this case the number and nature of the killings by W must inevitably give rise to the gravest concern for the safety of the public. The authorities responsible for W's treatment and management must be entitled to the fullest relevant information concerning his condition. It is clear that Dr Egdell did have highly relevant information about W's condition which reflected on his dangerousness. In my judgment the position came within the terms of r 81*(g)* of the General Medical Council's rules. Furthermore, Dr Egdell amply justified his action within the terms of r 82. The suppression of the material contained in his report would have deprived both the hospital and the Secretary of State of vital information, directly relevant to questions of public safety. Although it may be said that Dr Egdell's action in disclosing his report to Dr Hunter fell within the letter of r 81*(b)*, the judge in fact based his conclusion on what he termed 'broader considerations', that is to say the safety of the public. I agree with him.

In so far as the judge referred to the 'private interest' of W, I do not consider that the passage in his judgment (see [1989] 1 All ER 1089 at 1105, [1989] 2 WLR 689 at 714) accurately stated the position. There are two competing public interests and it is clear that by his reference to *X v Y* [1989] 2 All ER 648 the judge was fully seised of this point. Of course W has a private interest but the duty of confidence owed to him is based on the broader ground of public interest described by Rose J in *X v Y*.

Accordingly I agree with the judge's decision to dismiss W's claim. Dr Egdell was clearly justified in taking the course that he did.

Bingham LJ: The breadth of [a duty of confidence] in any case is . . . dependent on circumstances. Where a prison doctor examines a remand prisoner to determine his fitness to plead or a proposer for life insurance is examined by a doctor nominated by the insurance company or a personal injury plaintiff attends on the defendant's medical adviser or a prospective bidder instructs accountants to investigate (with its consent) the books of a target company, the professional man's duty of confidence towards the subject of his examination plainly does not bar disclosure of his findings to the party at whose instance he was appointed to make his examination. Here, however, Dr Egdell was engaged by W, not by the tribunal or the hospital authorities. He assumed at first that his report would be communicated to the tribunal and thus become known to the authorities but he must, I think, have appreciated that W and his legal advisers could decide not to adduce his report in evidence before the tribunal.

The decided cases very clearly establish (1) that the law recognises an important public interest in maintaining professional duties of confidence but (2) that the law treats such duties not as absolute but as liable to be overridden where there is held to be a stronger public interest in disclosure. Thus the public interest in the administration of justice may require a clergyman, a banker, a medical man, a journalist or an accountant to breach his professional duty of confidence (*A-G v Mulholland* [1963] 1 All ER 767 at 771, [1963] 2 QB 477 at 489-490, *Chantrey Martin & Co v Martin* [1953] 2 All ER 691, [1953] 2 QB 286). In *Parry-Jones v Law Society* [1968] 1 All ER 177, [1969] 1 Ch 1 a solicitor's duty of confidence towards his clients was held to be overridden by his duty to comply with the law of the land, which required him to produce documents for inspection under the Solicitors' Accounts Rules. A doctor's duty of confidence to his patient may be overridden by clear statutory language (as in *Hunter v Mann* [1974] 2 All ER 414, [1974] QB 767). A banker owes his customer an undoubted duty of confidence, but he may become subject to a duty to the public to disclose, as where danger to the state or public duty supersede the duty of agent to principal (*Tournier v National Provincial and Union Bank of England* [1924] 1 KB 461 at 473, 486, [1923] All ER Rep 550 at 554, 561). An employee may justify breach of a duty of confidence towards his employer otherwise binding on him when there is a public interest in the subject matter of his disclosure (*Initial Services Ltd v Putterill* [1967] 3 All ER 145, [1968] 1 QB 396, *Lion Laboratories v Evans* [1984] 2 All ER 417, [1985] QB 526). These qualifications of the duty of confidence arise not because that duty is not accorded legal recognition but for the reason clearly given by Lord Goff in his speech in (*A-G v Guardian*

Newspapers Ltd (No 2) [1988] 3 All ER 545 at 659, [1988] 3 WLR 776 at 807, *the Spycatcher* case), quoted by Scott J ([1989] 1 All ER 1089 at 1102, [1989] 2 WLR 689 at 710):

> The third limiting principle is of far greater importance. It is that, although the basis of the law's protection of confidence is that there is a public interest that confidences should be preserved and protected by the law, nevertheless that public interest may be outweighed by some other countervailing public interest which favours disclosure. This limitation may apply, as the judge pointed out, to all types of confidential information. It is this limiting principle which may require a court to carry out a balancing operation, weighing the public interest in maintaining confidence against a countervailing public interest favouring disclosure.

These principles were not in issue between the parties to this appeal. Counsel for W accepted that W's right to confidence was qualified and not absolute. But it is important to insist on the public interest in preserving W's right to confidence because the judge in his judgment concluded that while W had a strong private interest in barring disclosure of Dr Egdell's report he could not rest his case on any broader public interest (see [1989] 1 All ER 1089 1104-1105, [1989] 2 WLR 689 at 713-714). Here, as I think, the judge fell into error. W of course had a strong personal interest in regaining his freedom and no doubt regarded Dr Egdell's report as an obstacle to that end. So he had a personal interest in restricting the report's circulation. But these private considerations should not be allowed to obscure the public interest in maintaining professional confidences. The fact that Dr Egdell as an independent psychiatrist examined and reported on W as a restricted mental patient under s 76 of the Mental Health Act 1983 does not deprive W of his ordinary right to confidence, underpinned, as such rights are, by the public interest. But it does mean that the balancing operation of which Lord Goff spoke falls to be carried out in circumstances of unusual difficulty and importance . . .

. . . [T]he judge regarded r 81*(b)* as accurately stating the law and held that Dr Egdell's disclosure in the present case fell squarely within it. I have some reservations about this conclusion. It is true that the disclosure here may be said to fall within the letter of the first sentence of para *(b)*. But I think the paragraph is directed towards the familiar situation in which consultants or other specialised experts report to the doctor with clinical responsibility for treating or advising the patient, and the second sentence shows that the doctor whose duty is in question is regarded as having a continuing professional relationship with the patient. I rather doubt if the draftsman of para *(b)* had in mind a consultant psychiatrist consulted on a single occasion –

> 'for the purpose of advising whether an application to a Mental Health Review Tribunal should be made by or in respect of a patient who is liable to be detained or subject to guardianship under Part II of this Act or of furnishing information as to the condition of a patient for the purposes of such an application . . .' (See s 76(1) of the Mental Health Act 1983). Nor do I think that Dr Egdell, in making disclosure, was primarily motivated by the ordinary concern of any doctor that a patient should receive the most efficacious treatment. Had that been his primary object, I think he would, consistently with the spirit of para *(d)*, have tried to reason with W to obtain his consent to disclosure in W's own interest. I need not, however, reach a final view. The judge preferred to rest his conclusion on a broader ground, which was in effect the exception set out in r 81 *(g)* of the General Medical Council advice, and I think that if the disclosure cannot be justified under that exception it would be unsafe to justify it under any other.

Rule 81*(g)* provides:

> Rarely, disclosure may be justified on the ground that it is in the public interest which, in certain circumstances such as, for example, investigation by the police of a grave or very serious crime, might override the doctor's duty to maintain his patient's confidence.

It was this exception which, as I understand, the judge upheld and applied when he held, in what is perhaps the crucial passage in this judgment ([1989] 1 All ER 1089 at 1104, [1989] 2 WLR 689 at 713):

> In my view, a doctor called on, as Dr Egdell was, to examine a patient such as W owes a duty not only to his patient but also a duty to the public. His duty to the public would require him, in my opinion, to place before the proper authorities the result of is examination if, in his opinion, the public interest so required. This would be so, in my opinion, whether or not the patient instructed him not to do so.

Counsel for W criticised this passage as wrongly leaving the question whether disclosure was justified or not to the subjective decision of the doctor. He made the same criticism of a passage where Scott J said ([1989] 1 All ER 1089 at 1105, [1989] 2 WLR 689 at 714):

> If a patient in the position of W commissions an independent psychiatrist's report, the duty of confidence that undoubtedly lies on the doctor who makes the report does not, in my judgment, bar the doctor from disclosing the report to the hospital that is charged with the care of the patient if the doctor judges the report to be relevant to the care and treatment of the patient, nor from disclosing the report to the Home Secretary if the doctor judges the report to be relevant to the exercise of the Home Secretary's discretionary powers in relation to that patient.

In my opinion these criticisms are just. Where, as here, the relationship between doctor and patient is contractual, the question is whether the doctor's disclosure is or is not a breach of contract. The answer to that question must turn not on what the doctor thinks but on what the court rules. But it does not follow that the doctor's conclusion is irrelevant. In making its ruling the court will give such weight to the considered judgment of a professional man as seems in all the circumstances to be appropriate.

The parties were agreed, as I think rightly, that the crucial question in the present case was how, on the special facts of the case, the balance should be struck between the public interest in maintaining professional confidences and the public interest in protecting the public against possible violence. Counsel for W submitted that on the facts here the public interest in maintaining confidences was shown to be clearly preponderant. In support of that submission he drew our attention to a number of features of the case, of which the most weighty were perhaps these.

(1) Section 76 of the Mental Health Act 1983 shows a clear parliamentary intention that a restricted patient should be free to seek advice and evidence for the specified purposes from a medical source outside the prison and secure hospital system. Section 129 ensures that the independent doctor may make a full examination and see all relevant documents. The examination may be in private, so that the authorities do not learn what passes between doctor and patient.

(2) The proper functioning of s 76 requires that a patient should feel free to bare his soul and open his mind without reserve to the independent doctor he has retained. This he will not do, if a doctor is free, on forming an adverse opinion, to communicate it to those empowered to prevent the patient's release from hospital.

(3) Although the present situation is not one in which W can assert legal professional privilege, and although tribunal proceedings are not strictly adversarial, the considerations which have given rise to legal professional privilege underpin the public interest in preserving confidence in a situation such as the present. A party to a forthcoming application to a tribunal should be free to unburden himself to an adviser he has retained without fearing that any material damaging to his application will find its way without his consent into the hands of a party with interests adverse to his.

(4) Preservation of confidence would be conducive to the public safety; patients would be candid, so that problems such as those highlighted by Dr Egdell would become known, and steps could be taken to explore and if necessary treat the problems without disclosing the report.

(5) It is contrary to the public interest that patients such as W should enjoy rights less extensive than those enjoyed by other members of the public, a result of his judgment which the judge expressly accepted (see [1989] 1 All ER 1089 at 1105, [1989] 2 WLR 689 at 714).

Of these considerations, I accept (1) as a powerful consideration in W's favour. A restricted patient who believes himself unnecessarily confined has, of all members of society, perhaps the greatest need for a professional adviser who is truly independent and reliably discreet. (2) also I, in some measure, accept, subject to the comment that if the patient is unforthcoming the doctor is bound to be guarded in his opinion. If the patient wishes to enlist the doctor's wholehearted support for his application, he has little choice but to be (or at least convince an expert interviewer that he is being) frank. I see great force in (3). Only the most compelling circumstances could justify a doctor in acting in a way which would injure the immediate interests of his patient, as the patient perceived them, without obtaining his consent. Point (4), if I correctly understand it, did not impress me. Counsel's submissions appeared to suggest that the problems highlighted by Dr Egdell could be explored and if necessary treated without the hospital authorities being told what the problems were thought to be. I do not think this would be very satisfactory. As to (5), I agree that restricted patients should not enjoy rights of confidence less valuable than those enjoyed by other patients save in so far as any breach of confidence can be justified under the stringent terms of r 81*(g)*.

Counsel for Dr Egdell justified his client's disclosure of his report by relying on the risk to the safety of the public if the report were not disclosed. The steps of his argument, briefly summarised, were these.

(1) As a result of his examination Dr Egdell believed that W had a long-standing and abnormal interest in dangerous explosives dating from well before his period of acute illness.

(2) Dr Egdell believed that this interest had been overlooked or insufficiently appreciated by those with clinical responsibility for W.

(3) Dr Egdell believed that this interest could throw additional light on W's interest, also long-standing and in this instance well documented, in guns and shooting.

(4) Dr Egdell believed that exploration of W's interest in explosives and further exploration of W's interest in guns and shooting might lead to a different and more sinister diagnosis of W's mental condition.

(5) Dr Egdell believed that these explorations could best be conducted in the secure hospital where W was.

(6) Dr Egdell believed that W might possibly be a future danger to members of the public if his interest in firearms and explosives continued after his discharge.

(7) Dr Egdell believed that these matters should be brought to the attention of those responsible for W's care and treatment and for making decisions concerning his transfer and release.

Dr Egdell's good faith was not in issue. Nor were his professional standing and competence. His opinions summarised in (1), (2), (3) and (4) (although not accepted) were not criticised as ill-founded or irrational. Dr Egdell deferred to the greater knowledge of another medical expert relied on by W concerning the regime in a regional secure unit but did not (as I understood) modify his view that the explorations he favoured should take place before transfer.

Counsel for W contended that Dr Egdell's belief summarised in (6) did not in all the circumstances justify disclosure of the report. There was, he said, no question of W's release, whether absolutely or conditionally, in the then foreseeable future. The Home Office had made plain that it would not sanction transfer to a regional secure unit for about 18 months. Even if he were transferred he would remain a patient of the special hospital for the first 6 months and the high staff ratio in such units would ensure a very high level of security thereafter. Much further testing would in any event be done before W was again at large. Disclosure of the report would do nothing to protect the public.

I do not find these points persuasive. When Dr Egdell made his decision to disclose, one tribunal had already recommended W's transfer to a regional secure unit and the hospital authorities had urged that course. The Home Office had resisted transfer in a qualified manner but on a basis of inadequate information. It appeared to be only a matter of time, and probably not a very long time, before W was transferred. The regional secure unit was to act as a staging post on W's journey back into the community. While W would no doubt be further tested, such tests would not be focused on the source of Dr Egdell's concern, which he quite rightly considered to have received inadequate attention up to then. Dr Egdell had to act when he did or not at all.

There is one consideration which in my judgment, as in that of the judge, weighs the balance of public interest decisively in favour of disclosure. It may be shortly put. Where a man has committed multiple killings under the disability of serious mental illness, decisions which may lead directly or indirectly to his release from hospital should not be made unless a responsible authority is properly able to make an informed judgment that the risk of repetition is so small as to be acceptable. A consultant psychiatrist who becomes aware, even in the course of a confidential relationship, of information which leads him, in the exercise of what the court considers a sound professional judgment, to fear that such decisions may be made on the basis of inadequate information and with a real risk of consequent danger to the public is entitled to take such steps as are reasonable in all the circumstances to communicate the grounds of his concern to the responsible authorities. I have no doubt that the judge's decision in favour of Dr Egdell was right on the facts of this case.

Counsel for W argued that even if Dr Egdell was entitled to make some disclosure he should have disclosed only the crucial paragraph of his report and his opinion. I do not agree. An opinion, even from an eminent source, cannot be evaluated unless its factual premise is known, and a detailed 10-page report cannot be reliably assessed by perusing a brief extract.

No reference was made in argument before us (or, so far as I know, before the judge) to the European Convention on Human Rights (Convention for the Protection of Human

Rights and Fundamental Freedoms (Rome, 4 November 1950; TS 71 (1953); Cmd 8969)), but I believe this decision to be in accordance with it. I would accept that art 8(1) of the convention may protect an individual against the disclosure of information protected by the duty of professional secrecy. But art 8(2) envisages that circumstances may arise in which a public authority may legitimately interfere with the exercise of that right in accordance with the law and where necessary in a democratic society in the interests of public safety or the prevention of crime. Here there was no interference by a public authority. Dr Egdell did, as I conclude, act in accordance with the law. And his conduct was in my judgment necessary in the interests of public safety and the prevention of crime.

I would dismiss the appeal. Having reached that conclusion I do not think it necessary to consider whether, had W succeeded, he could have recovered damages in contract for shock and distress.

Sir John May agreed.

Given the court's acceptance of the fact that confidence may be breached in the public interest, are there any factors which limit the extent to which information may be disclosed? *Egdell* suggests that there may be several. *First*, as Bingham LJ makes clear the disclosure may be made only to those whom it is necessary to tell so as to protect the public interest.

Bingham LJ: He could not lawfully sell the contents of his report to a newspaper, as the judge held. Nor could he, without a breach of the law as well as professional etiquette, discuss the case in a learned article or in his memoirs or in gossiping with friends, unless he took appropriate steps to conceal the identity of W. It is not in issue here that a duty of confidence existed.

Of course, it may be necessary in a particular circumstance to disclose the confidence more widely in order, for example, to protect the public from a danger. An analogy which may assist here is the law of defamation and the defence of qualified privilege (see, for example, *Blackshaw v Lord* [1983] 2 All ER 311 per Stephenson LJ).

Secondly, to justify disclosure the risk must be 'real' rather than fanciful (see Bingham LJ at 853). *Thirdly*, the risk in *Egdell* was to physical safety of members of the public (per Stephen Brown P at 846 and Bingham LJ at 853). It can be argued that only a risk involving the *danger of physical harm* warrants disclosure, given the emphasis placed on this aspect of the case by all the judges.

There is a further point in *Egdell* which does not appear to have been acknowledged by the court. It is not clear whether Dr Egdell in his examination of W discovered new facts about W's propensity to be a danger or whether he merely disagreed with other doctors' interpretation of the same facts. If the former is the case, then clearly there is fresh evidence, which on the court's view of public interest, Dr Egdell was justified in bringing to the attention of the proper authorities. If, however, the latter is the case, the decision becomes more problematic. All we have is a difference of opinion among experts, one of whom claims that his opinion is right where the consequences of holding that view will undoubtedly lead to the continued detention of W. Arguably, the fact that the evidence was merely a difference of opinion should be a relevant factor in determining whether the public interest justifies disclosure. Of course, if the medical evidence is the *only* evidence in the case relevant to the patient's dangerous conduct the argument against disclosure has less validity since *ex hypothesi* this medical opinion is adding something new (*R v Crozier* (1990) 8 BMLR 128 (CA)). At the very least the doctor would be entitled to press that further medical opinion be obtained and, perhaps, as a last resort if he judges the situation to be sufficiently serious to disclose his views to the proper authorities.

A case which considers the point unacknowledged by the court in *Egdell* and the other factors involved in determining where the balance of the public interest lies is the New Zealand case of *Duncan v Medical Practitioners' Disciplinary Committee* [1986] 1 NZLR 513.

Duncan v Medical Practitioners' Disciplinary Committee [1986] 1 NZLR 513 (NZ HCt)

Jeffries J: Ian Alfred Duncan (referred to as the applicant) is a registered medical practitioner at present living in Fielding. By these proceedings he has applied to the High Court for declarations and orders pursuant to the Judicature Amendment Act 1972 and its amendments. In the proceedings the applicant seeks judicial review of separate decisions made pursuant to statutory powers under the Medical Practitioners Act 1968 (referred to as the Act).

By letter dated 3 June 1983 Mr Henry laid a complaint with the Chairman of the Disciplinary Committee. The substance of his complaint was in the following terms. He is by occupation a bus driver having owned and operated a passenger service business in Whangamata for 30 years. As a passenger service driver he is required to furnish a medical certificate annually for the renewal of his licence. In February 1982 he suffered a heart attack and was admitted to Cook Hospital, Gisborne. Later in the year he suffered a second heart attack, a pulmonary embolism and a cardiac arrest. On these occasions he was attended by the applicant as his general practitioner. During this period he had been admitted to Thames Hospital under the care of Dr S A Maar, a physician. On 1 December 1982 Mr Henry was admitted to Greenlane Hospital and underwent a triple coronary artery bypass operation performed by Mr David Hill. He was discharged on 11 December 1982 following a successful operation. In February 1983 during a routine check by Dr Maar as an outpatient at Thames Hospital, he asked if she would issue a medical certificate for him to drive passenger service vehicles. According to Mr Henry she replied that in her opinion he should not have one, but as she was not a heart specialist she advised him to go to the doctor most qualified to know of his condition and medical history, namely Mr Hill of Greenlane Hospital, who had performed the bypass operation. He was examined later by Mr Hill who issued him with the necessary certificate enabling him to obtain a licence to drive passenger service vehicles.

Now follows the essence of the complaints made by Mr Henry against the applicant. On 27 April 1983 Mr Henry intended to take his bus to Auckland on a charter trip. The night before at 6 pm he received a telephone call from the applicant informing him that he had no licence, or medical clearance, and could not drive. Mr Henry corrected the applicant's understanding about the licence and he says Dr Duncan inferred that he had obtained the licence under false pretences and therefore it was not valid. The applicant, according to Mr Henry, trenchantly criticised the doctor who had issued the certificate. At this particular phone call Dr Duncan did not realise it was the surgeon who had performed the bypass operation who had issued the certificate but he learned that later in the evening. Even before communicating with Mr Henry Dr Duncan had already spoken to a Mrs Ada Verney, a passenger for the trip, informing her that Mr Henry was not fit to drive and could have a heart attack at any time. After speaking with Mr Henry Dr Duncan sought assistance from the local police constable to have Mr Henry's licence revoked. Apparently the constable informed him that it was impossible and Dr Duncan rang Mr Henry again on which occasion he acknowledged Mr Henry could drive but made threats, according to Mr Henry, but Dr Duncan later denied making threats. He said in his letter of complaint he was outraged at Dr Duncan's actions but decided to leave the matter in abeyance for a time. Apparently what decided him to act by way of laying a complaint was to discover on 23 May that a friend of his, Mr D Knight, had been asked by Dr Duncan at his surgery to help organise a petition to have Mr Henry barred from driving passenger service vehicles. Mr Knight refused to do this.

Mr Henry's letter of complaint concluded with the following:

The basis of my complaint is that –
1.   I am being unjustly victimised by a doctor with very limited experience.
2.   There has been a breach of patient confidentiality.

The letter of complaint was forwarded to the applicant for his comments. He replied on 20 September 1983 not disputing the primary facts of Mr Henry's allegations but denying he had conducted himself in any reprehensible way, or that he was victimising Mr Henry. In substance he sought to justify his actions.

The Chairman of the Disciplinary Committee resolved, pursuant to s 42A of the Act, that the letter dated 3 June 1983 from Mr Henry was a charge of professional misconduct against Dr Duncan, and he was notified that the charge of professional misconduct would be inquired into by the Medical Practitioners Disciplinary Committee on 14 December 1983. On that day the Committee assembled and heard evidence of the complaint. Mr Henry appeared and was represented by Mr P Keane, as counsel. Dr Duncan appeared and was represented by Mr P F Boshier, as counsel. Notes were taken of proceedings and the full record was placed before this Court. In due course in dealing with the allegations made by the applicant it will be necessary to refer to the conduct of those proceedings. The Committee comprised four members, three of whom are doctors, namely Dr D L Richwhite, Chairman, Sir Randal Elliott and Dr H K Way. The fourth was Sir Leonard Thornton who fulfilled the role of a lay member. The Disciplinary Committee reserved its decision and gave it in writing on 17 February 1984. The Committee surveyed the primary facts which as found by them differed little from those contained in Mr Henry's original letter of complaint dated 3 June 1983. Throughout the hearing Dr Duncan did not deny he had breached medical confidence and advanced the defence of justification. I mention here there are inconsequential inconsistencies raised by the evidence at the inquiry about the exact order of events on the night of 26 April. The decision itself did not embark upon an analysis of the evidence enabling resolution of the inconsistencies as that was not necessary. The last three paragraphs of the decision are now reproduced which contain the reasons for the orders made.

7. The Committee accepts that Dr Duncan was motivated by concern for the welfare of his community but considers that his actions and intervention were both unwise and unwarranted and amounted to professional misconduct.

8. The Committee finds Dr Duncan guilty of professional misconduct in that he breached professional confidence in informing lay people of his patient's personal medical history. The Committee takes the view that professional confidence can only be breached in most exceptional circumstances and then only if the public interest is paramount. In such a case a junior doctor should only proceed after seeking and accepting advice from a senior colleague, and communication should be made only to the responsible authority. In this case, Dr Duncan spoke to Dr Maar concerning her view of Mr Henry's fitness to drive, and she advised him to proceed with caution.

9. His breach of confidence on the 26th April was serious; however the Committee took an even more serious view of his breach of confidentiality one month after the first instance to an individual who, in no circumstances, could have been a responsible authority.

The Disciplinary Committee censured Dr Duncan as a result of finding him guilty of professional misconduct and ordered him to pay costs and a penalty to the New Zealand Medical Association. There was a further order concerning publication in the New Zealand Medical Journal.

The first observation is that pursuant to s 53 of the Act the applicant was entitled to appeal the decision of the Disciplinary Committee to the Medical Council of New Zealand. He chose not to avail himself of that right but instead rejected the Disciplinary Committee findings by going to the national media and making statements about the second respondent's fitness to drive and thereby impliedly refused to accept the judgment of the Disciplinary Committee as contained in their decision. I examine further this aspect for it arises again under Part B of the judgment.

Notwithstanding he did not appeal the applicant now seeks judicial review of the Disciplinary Committee's findings and a declaration that the decision was ultra vires, unauthorised and invalid. The applicant advances three alternative grounds for review and I deal with each in turn [the second and third grounds are omitted here].

The essence of the first ground is that the Disciplinary Committee misdirected itself, or erred in law, as to the nature or basis of professional misconduct and/or medical professional privilege. For reasons set out hereafter I think it is incorrect to equate the words 'medical privilege' with 'medical confidence' as was done in the pleadings. The following particulars were pleaded in para 8 of the statement of claim . . .

    (b) In applying a too narrow and inflexible view of medical professional confidence, and in particular in holding: (i) that a communication to a lay person was per se a breach of medical professional confidence; (ii) that medical professional confidence could only be breached in the most exceptional circumstances and then only if the public interest was paramount; and (iii) that

communication of confidential information, if warranted, should only be made
to 'the responsible authority', and (in the case of a 'junior doctor') only after
seeking and accepting advice from a 'senior colleague'; . . .

In argument the applicant's counsel chose to argue (b) above before (a), and as the decision
on what constituted professional misconduct was breach of medical professional confidence,
I think that a convenient course.

The letter of complaint nominated as the basis of the charge against Dr Duncan 'breach
of confidentiality'. By his decision to inquire the Chairman of the Disciplinary Committee
pursuant to s 42A(2) decided there was sufficient ground to face Dr Duncan with a charge of
professional misconduct, the particular of which was 'breach of patient confidentiality'. The
disciplinary offence of breach of patient confidentiality is nowhere defined as we understand
criminal offences are statutorily defined in New Zealand. What is required, therefore, is an
examination of patient confidentiality, which will hereon be referred to mostly as 'medical
confidence', to decide whether the conduct amounted to professional misconduct.

The Court now addresses directly what is medical confidence? It is not difficult to grasp
the broad concept of professional confidence for it is fundamental to the relationship of a
professional man with a lay person. On a strict analysis of legal relationships, it is probably
contractually based, as several cases have suggested. It is primarily an ethical issue and must
be distinguished from say medical privilege which is an evidentiary rule whereby a patient
has the right to exclude from evidence protected communications made by him to a doctor.
See ss 32 and 33 of the Evidence Amendment Act (No 2) 1980. It is acknowledged privilege
and confidentiality have much in common, but privilege is more limited than confidentiality
which is an ethical obligation of a professional man to preserve the confidence and secrets of
a lay person. The source of information and the fact that others might share the knowledge
do not affect the ethical precept. Overall, confidentiality has recently become more
prominent as an issue. Society's response has been articulate in that it seeks to break down
unnecessary official secrecy but to strengthen protection of personal confidences and secrets.

That there is such an identifiable concept as medical confidence was accepted by the
Disciplinary Committee without it attempting to provide a description, or to examine where
the boundaries lay. Counsel in argument in this Court did not suggest a test. It is the basis of
the Disciplinary Committee's decision and a principal ground upon which that decision is
now attacked. As will become clear, the nature of the attack on the Disciplinary
Committee's decision was that its view of medical confidence was generally too narrow and
inflexible. Unless some attempt is made to formulate a verbal description which has at least
some precision, how could it be said the approach of the Disciplinary Committee was wide
or narrow, supple or inflexible? Without a description the challenge would be ungraspable.

The platform support of a description of medical confidence is to identify the doctor/
patient relationship as a fiduciary one. Without trust it would not function properly so as to
allow freedom for the patient to disclose all manner of confidences and secrets in the
practical certainty they would repose with the doctor. There rests with a doctor a strong
ethical obligation to observe strict confidentiality by holding inviolate the confidences and
secrets he receives in the course of his professional ministerings. If he adheres to that ethical
principle then the full scope of his ability to administer medical assistance to his patient will
develop.

The foregoing embodies the principle of medical confidence, but it cannot be left there
without identifying the existence of qualifications and modifications for I have described,
not defined exhaustively the concept. Confidentiality is not breached by private discussions
with colleagues in pursuance of treatment, but this may require full disclosure and consent.
The confidentiality may be waived by the patient. The doctor may be required by law to
disclose. A doctor may be in a group practice where common filing systems are used. Staff
who have access to information must be impressed with the requirement of confidence.
Limited information to some outside agencies may be made available by a doctor from his
files for statistical, accounting, data processing or other legitimate purposes. A doctor may
be treating more than one person that requires, or mandates, exchange of information, but
here caution and prudence must be carefully observed and consents obtained. As this very
case demonstrates a doctor may reveal confidences and secrets if he is required to defend
himself, or others, against accusations of wrongful conduct. There may be occasions, they
are fortunately rare, when a doctor receives information involving a patient that another's
life is immediately endangered and urgent action is required. The doctor must then exercise
his professional judgment based upon the circumstances, and if he fairly and reasonably
believes such a danger exists then he must act unhesitatingly to prevent injury or loss of life
even if there is to be a breach of confidentiality. If his actions later are to be scrutinised as to

their correctness, he can be confident any official inquiry will be by people sympathetic about the predicament he faced. However, that qualification cannot be advanced so as to attenuate, or undermine, the immeasurably valuable concept of medical confidence. If it were applied in that way it would be misapplied, in my view, because it would be extravagant with what is essentially a qualification to the principle. Some might say that is line-drawing and if they do then so be it. The line-drawing is not arbitrary but based upon reason and experience, and is the exercise of professional judgment which is part of daily practice for a doctor. The foregoing, either in the description or the qualifications, is not advanced as anything but an outline.

I turn then to the precise attack of the first ground and deal with (b). Notwithstanding the Disciplinary Committee did not isolate and describe medical confidence as has been done in this judgment, I am satisfied that by their decision they acted in no way contrary to these statements on medical confidence, and the decision is in accord with them.

Subgrounds (b)(i) and (ii) are in conflict for (b)(ii) gives the lie to (b)(i). The Disciplinary Committee did not mandate communications to a lay person per se but correctly, and properly in my view, confined such communication to exceptional circumstances, and then only if the public interest was paramount. As an application to the principle enunciated above, those words could hardly be improved upon. I can detect no cause for substantial complaint about (b)(iii). It is meant to be advisory and helpful. I think a doctor who has decided to communicate should discriminate and ensure the recipient is a responsible authority.

[For an appeal in respect of other aspects of the case see [1986] 1 NZLR 513 at 537.]

Having set out the general principle of the public interest modifications, there are a number of circumstances which merit particular attention: teaching, research, management and problems arising from infectious diseases particularly infection with HIV.

1. Teaching and research

In paragraph 89 of its 'Blue Book', the GMC identifies the guiding principle in relation to teaching:

> 89. Medical teaching . . . necessarily involves the disclosure of information about individuals, often in the form of medical records, for purposes other than their own health care. Where such information is used in a form which does not enable individuals to be identified, no question of breach of confidentiality will usually arise. Where the disclosure would enable one or more individuals to be identified, the patients concerned, or those who may properly give permission on their behalf, must wherever possible be made aware of that possibility and be advised that it is open to them, at any stage, to withhold their consent to disclosure.

In essence by insisting on consent the GMC is stating that disclosure of information in these circumstances cannot be said to fall within the public interest exception. Notice, however, that the Government has taken a different view in its guidance contained in HSG (92). It stated that for teaching purposes disclosure may be justified on the basis of the patient's implied consent or in the public interest (paras 5.25 and 5.26). Arguably the law should (and would) reflect the GMC's view (see the weight attached by the Court of Appeal to the Blue Book's advice concerning confidentiality in *W v Egdell*).

As regards research, the government has provided guidance in its document, *Local Research Ethics Committee* (HSG (91)5).

> 3.11 Researchers should be asked to confirm that personal health information will be kept confidential, that data will be secured against unauthorised access and that no individual will be identifiable from published results, without his or her explicit consent. All data from which an individual is identifiable should be destroyed when no longer required for the purposes of the original research. If, exceptionally, the researcher wishes to retain confidential information beyond the completion of the research, the LREC, the relevant

NHS body and the research subject must first be made aware of the reasons for retaining the information and the circumstances in which this might be disclosed. The subject's consent to these arrangements must be recorded.

3.12 Epidemiological research through studies of medical records can be extremely valuable. Patients are however entitled to regard their medical records as confidential to the NHS and should in principle be asked if they consent to their own records being released to research workers. However there will be occasions when a researcher would find it difficult or impossible to obtain such consent from every individual and the LREC will need to be satisfied that the value of such a project outweighs, in the public interest, the principle that individual consent should be obtained. Where a patient has previously indicated that he or she would *not* want their records released then this request should be respected.

3.13 The LREC will need to be assured that this kind of research will be conducted in accordance with current codes of practice and data protection legislation. Wherever possible consent should also be sought from the health professional responsible for the relevant aspect of the subject's care. Once information has been obtained from the records no approach should be made to the patient concerned without the agreement of the health professional currently responsible for their care.

3.14 Certain enquiries and surveys, involving only access to patient records, such as the national morbidity surveys and post-marketing surveillance of drugs, which are in the public interest, do not need prior approval of an LREC. Appendix A gives a list of these.

Clearly these Guidelines begin from a premise requiring the research subjects' consent to disclosure. They do, however, address the issue of the public interest where consent may be 'difficult or impossible to obtain'. Arguably, this single example of the public interest in research outweighing the public interest in confidence is limited to the conduct of epidemiological research. In our view, again, the Guidelines properly reflect the law (but notice the apparently less stringent terms of HSG (92)).

2. Management

As regards management, the BMA in its book *Rights and Responsibilities of Doctors* (1992) offers the following observation in paragraph 3.8.

With the development of an 'internal market' in the NHS concerns have arisen about safeguarding the confidentiality of patient data which might appear on bills for extra-contractual referrals, etc. The Department of Health booklet *NHS Review Information Systems: Action for Managers* stated that 'very strict, tightly controlled administrative and computer security arrangements will be necessary to safeguard confidentiality and to deal with subject access requests'. This emphasis on such a breach of confidentiality as a very serious matter has been reinforced in NHS management executive letter EL(91)49.

All grades of NHS staff, including clerical officers who might handle confidential bills relating to individual patients, are reminded in this letter that breach of confidence is a disciplinary offence, and arrangements for handling data containing patients' details must be agreed with an appropriate senior medical officer. Despite these guidelines pressure is mounting for a coding system on NHS bills and contracts which would ensure complete confidentiality.

The difficulty with the view expressed by the BMA is that it proceeds from a misunderstanding of what confidentiality is about. A patient confides in his doctor. He does not confide in the staff in general, eg accountants, managers and office staff (or, indeed, other doctors not concerned with his care). To purport to justify disclosure to these on the grounds that they will keep the patient's secret misses the point. The patient may not want (or expect) them to know in the first place. This is what confidentiality is about.

Of course, a patient's information has always been available to lots of eyes. But this has been regarded as something that is wrong and to be avoided though almost a fact of life. It is another thing to institutionalise the practice and thereby legitimise it (see *Confidentiality, Use and Disclosure of NHS Information* (HSG (92)) – justifying disclosure, *inter alia*, for management purposes within the 'NHS family' on the basis of the implied consent of the patient (paras 4.9-4.10 and 5.3-5.5)). No one can doubt the need of management in the current NHS to have access to patients' information. Equally, no one can doubt that routinising such access drives a coach and horses through confidentiality. Whether the public interest is served by this development is by no means clear.

3. HIV and AIDS

Special difficulties as regards confidentiality have always attended infectious diseases, in particular those that are sexually transmitted. The information is particularly sensitive given its potential for stigmatising those infected. HIV infection and AIDS are at the same time merely another example of this and *sui generis*, given the extraordinary potential for discrimination against those infected. It is not surprising, therefore, that HIV infection (in particular) and sexually transmitted diseases (in general) have attracted considerable concern in the context of confidentiality.

We have already seen the National Health Service (Venereal Diseases) Regulations 1974 (SI 1974 No 29) which represent the long-standing recognition by Parliament of the need to safeguard confidence in this sensitive area. Building on this general approach, the GMC issued specific guidance concerning HIV infection in August 1988 (amended in June 1993). What is clear from the guidance is the recognition by the GMC of the need to balance the importance of observing confidence in this situation against a legitimate concern for the interests of others who may be affected by the person infected with HIV. There are a number of categories of person who could be affected: for example, other health care workers charged with the care of the patient; the patient's spouse or other sexual partner (including previous sexual partners); those who may be treated by an infected health care worker; and the employer of an infected person.

The GMC Guidance addresses some of these issues:

CONFIDENTIALITY
15. Doctors are familiar with the need to make judgements about whether to disclose confidential information in particular circumstances, and the need to justify their action where such a disclosure is made. The Council believes that, where HIV infection or AIDS has been diagnosed, any difficulties concerning confidentiality which arise will usually be overcome if doctors are prepared to discuss openly and honestly with patients the implications of their condition, the need to secure the safety of others, and the importance for continuing medical care of ensuring that those who will be involved in their care know the nature of their condition and the particular needs which they will have. The Council takes the view that any doctor who discovers that a patient is HIV positive or suffering from AIDS has a duty to discuss these matters fully with the patient.

Informing other health care professionals
16. When a patient is seen by a specialist who diagnoses HIV infection or AIDS, and a general practitioner is or may become involved in that patient's care, then the specialist should explain to the patient that the general practitioner cannot be expected to provide adequate clinical management and care without full knowledge of the patient's condition. The Council believes that the majority of such patients will readily be persuaded of the need for their general practitioners to be informed of the diagnosis.
17. If the patient refuses consent for the general practitioner to be told, then the doctor has two sets of obligations to consider: obligations to the patient to maintain confidence, and obligations to other carers whose own health may be put unnecessarily at risk. In such circumstances the patient should be counselled about the difficulties which his or her condition is likely to pose for the team responsible for providing continuing health care and about the likely consequences for the standard of care which can be provided in the future.

If, having considered the matter carefully in the light of such counselling, the patient still refuses to allow the general practitioner to be informed then the patient's request for privacy should be respected. The only exception to that general principle arises where the doctor judges that the failure to disclose would put the health of any of the health care team at serious risk. The Council believes that, in such a situation, it would not be improper to disclose such information as that person needs to know. The need for such a decision is, in present circumstances, likely to arise only rarely, but if it is made the doctor must be able to justify his or her action.

18. Similar principles apply to the sharing of confidential information between specialists or with other health care professionals such as nurses, laboratory technicians and dentists. All persons receiving such information must of course consider themselves under the same general obligation of confidentiality as the doctor principally responsible for the patient's care.

Informing the patient's spouse or other sexual partner
19. Questions of conflicting obligations also arise when a doctor is faced with the decision whether the fact that a patient is HIV positive or suffering from AIDS should be disclosed to a third party, other than another health care professional, without the consent of the patient. The Council has reached the view that there are grounds for such a disclosure only where there is a serious and identifiable risk to a specific individual who, if not so informed, would be exposed to infection. Therefore, when a person is found to be infected in this way, the doctor must discuss with the patient the question of informing a spouse or other sexual partner. The Council believes that most such patients will agree to disclosure in these circumstances, but where such consent is withheld the doctor may consider it a duty to seek to ensure that any sexual partner is informed, in order to safeguard such persons from a possibly fatal infection.

As regards infected health care workers, the Department of Health's Guidance: *AIDS – HIV Infected Health Care Workers* (December 1991) states:

6. RESPONSIBILITIES OF EMPLOYERS AND RIGHTS OF HEALTH CARE WORKERS
6.1 Patient safety is dependent on the voluntary self declaration of the health care worker and employers must promote a climate which encourages such disclosure.
6.2 It is thus extremely important that HIV infected health care workers receive the same rights of confidentiality as any patient seeking or receiving medical care. Occupational physicians, who work within strict guidelines with respect to confidentiality, have a key role in this process, since they are able to act as advocate for the health care worker and advisor to the employing authority. The close involvement of occupational health departments in developing local procedures for managing HIV infected health care workers is strongly recommended.

In its amended Statement in June 1993 the GMC advised that:

It is unethical for doctors who know or believe themselves to be infected with HIV to put patients at risk by failing to seek appropriate counselling or by failing to act upon it when given. Such behaviour may result in proceedings by the Council which could lead to the restriction or removal of a doctor's registration if this were necessary to protect patients or the doctor's own health. The Council has already given guidance, in paragraph 63 of the booklet 'Professional Conduct and Discipline: Fitness to Practise' on doctors' duty to inform an appropriate person or authority about a colleague whose professional conduct or fitness to practise may be called into question. A doctor who knows that a health care worker is infected with HIV and is aware that the person has not sought or followed advice to modify his or her professional practice, has a duty to inform the appropriate regulatory body and an appropriate person in the health care worker's employing authority, who will usually be the most senior doctor.

The final sentence is clearly significant. The current review of the Department of Health's Guidance is expected to incorporate a similar approach. The effect is to fix a doctor with at least an *ethical* obligation to inform on colleagues (as well as patients), all else having failed.

As regards partner notification, the Department of Health's Guidance of December 1992 (PLICO (92) 5) provides as follows:

GUIDANCE ON PARTNER NOTIFICATION FOR HIV INFECTION
Development of Partner Notification
2. Partner notification (contact tracing) for sexually transmitted disease (STD) has been a central activity in the control of STDs in the UK for more than 40 years. In the early years of the HIV epidemic, when many of those infected had multiple partners over many years, it was the view of some experts that it was impractical and unproductive as a method of limiting the spread of the infection. Nevertheless, the majority of physicians have always counselled those infected with HIV about the need to inform their sexual or drug injecting partners.
3. Because of the advent of therapies which delay the progression of HIV disease and also because of changes in the nature of the epidemic (ie spread to heterosexuals in low prevalence areas where those infected might not perceive themselves at risk) there has been increasing discussion about, and research into, the importance of partner notification, including notification by clinic staff.
4. While most physicians actively encourage partner notification by or with the consent of the infected person, practice varies, most partner notification being undertaken by the infected person with the support of the clinic.

The Benefits of Partner Notification
–   identification of contacts who are given the opportunity to consider whether they wish to be tested,
–   those who have unknowingly been infected may wish to know that they are to enable them to take steps to prevent transmission to others,
–   women who may have been infected may wish to be tested to help them decide whether to take steps to prevent conception and to help them make decisions about the management of a pregnancy and about breast feeding,
–   access of infected contacts (including children of infected mothers) to treatment and support programmes so that they may benefit from long term monitoring of their clinical condition and from appropriate therapies (ie prophylaxis against pneumocystis pneumonia and possibly anti-retroviral therapy) and from appropriate psychological support,
–   identification of uninfected contacts who could also, where appropriate, be counselled about avoiding risky behaviour in the future. . . .

Issues to Consider and Potential Disadvantages
Informed consent to testing and to partner notification . . .
7. Partner notification by the provider should be undertaken only with the infected individual's explicit consent obtained without undue pressure. The General Medical Council has issued guidance on the exceptional instances when partner notification without consent might be considered.
8. The infected person should understand the consequences for himself or herself of notifying partners and the consequences for those partners. For example:
–   for the infected person
    •   when the index case informs partner(s) (or where information implicitly identifies the index case) there will be automatic loss of confidentiality about his or her HIV status to those partners who may then inform others and
    •   consequent risk of discrimination and of harassment.
–   for the person notified
    •   anxieties about possibly having a potentially lethal illness;
    •   the need to decide whether to seek a test;
    •   possible future difficulty obtaining insurance for those not infected.

Confidentiality
9. All health professionals owe patients a common law duty of confidentiality and additionally within Health Authorities and Trusts are bound by the duty of confidentiality imposed under the NHS (Venereal Disease) Regulations 1974 and the National Health Service Trust (Venereal Disease) Directions 1991 which apply to all Health Authority and Trust clinics.
10. That patients have a right, albeit not an absolute right, to medical confidentiality is well recognised by health care workers.

11. Equally there is the need to recognise that confidentiality helps to protect the public health. Without it patients with sexually transmitted diseases, including HIV infection, may be unwilling to come forward for diagnosis, treatment and counselling.

Undue pressure
12. Clinic attenders have a right to expect to be treated sensitively and not to be put under undue pressure to notify partners or to agree to provider referral. There is also the danger that if there is a perception that patients are put under pressure to reveal names of partners then those at risk might be deterred from coming forward.

None of these official statements, of course, has legal force. They all, however, represent significant statements of public policy.

To what extent do they also represent the law? In particular, does the public interest justification in the context of HIV infection or indeed any other context place a *duty* on a doctor to breach confidence in certain circumstances? One way that this can be determined is to ask whether someone infected with HIV by a patient would have a claim in negligence against the patient's doctor. In beginning to answer this question we should bear in mind that the law would undoubtedly limit those to whom a doctor owes any duty. You will recall that the GMC's Guidance talks of the need for a 'serious identifiable risk to a specific individual'.

There are no English cases directly in point. The starting point for analysis must be the following well-known Californian case.

Tarasoff v Regents of the University of California (1976) 131 Cal Rptr 14 (Cal Sup Ct)

Tobriner Justice: On October 27, 1969, Prosenjit Poddar killed Tatiana Tarasoff. Plaintiffs, Tatiana's parents, allege that two months earlier Poddar confided his intention to kill Tatiana to Dr Lawrence Moore, a psychologist employed by the Cowell Memorial Hospital at the University of California at Berkeley. They allege that on Moore's request, the campus police briefly detained Poddar, but released him when he appeared rational. They further claim that Dr Harvey Powelson, Moore's superior, then directed that no further action be taken to detain Poddar. No one warned plaintiffs of Tatiana's peril . . .

Plaintiffs' complaints predicate liability on two grounds: defendants' failure to warn plaintiffs of the impending danger and their failure to bring about Poddar's confinement . . . Defendants, in turn, assert that they owed no duty of reasonable care to Tatiana . . . We shall explain that defendant therapists cannot escape liability merely because Tatiana herself was not their patient. When a therapist determines, or pursuant to the standards of his profession should determine, that his patient presents a serious danger of violence to another, he incurs an obligation to use reasonable care to protect the intended victim against such danger. The discharge of this duty may require the therapist to take one or more of various steps, depending upon the nature of the case. Thus it may call for him to warn the intended victim or others likely to apprise the victim of the danger, to notify the police, or to take whatever other steps are reasonably necessary under the circumstances.

In the case at bar, plaintiffs admit that defendant therapists notified the police, but argue on appeal that the therapists failed to exercise reasonable care to protect Tatiana in that they did not confine Poddar and did not warn Tatiana or others likely to apprise her of the danger . . .

Plaintiffs can state a cause of action against defendant therapists for negligent failure to protect Tatiana.

The second cause of action can be amended to allege that Tatiana's death proximately resulted from defendants' negligent failure to warn Tatiana or others likely to apprise her of her danger. Plaintiffs contend that as amended, such allegations of negligence and proximate causation, with resulting damages, establish a cause of action. Defendants, however, contend that in the circumstances of the present case they owed no duty of care to Tatiana or her parents and that, in the absence of such duty, they were free to act in careless disregard of Tatiana's life and safety.

In analysing this issue, we bear in mind that legal duties are not discoverable facts of nature, but merely conclusory expressions that, in cases of a particular type, liability should be imposed for damage done. As stated in *Dillon v Legg* 68 Cal 2d 728, 734, 69 Cal Rptr 72, 76, 441 P 2d 912, 916 (1968): 'The assertion that liability must . . . be denied because defendant bears no "duty" to plaintiff "begs the essential question – whether the plaintiff's interests are entitled to legal protection against the defendant's conduct . . . [Duty] is not sacrosanct in itself, but only an expression of the sum total of those considerations of policy which lead the law to say that the particular plaintiff is entitled to protection." (Prosser, Law of Torts [3rd edn 1964] at pp 332-333.)'

In the landmark case of *Rowland v Christian* 69 Cal 2d 108, 70 Cal Rptr 97, 443 P 2d 561 (1968), Justice Peters recognised that liability should be imposed 'for an injury occasioned to another by his want of ordinary care or skill' as expressed in section 1714 of the Civil Code. Thus, Justice Peters, quoting from *Heaven v Pender* (1883) 11 QBD 503 at 509 stated: '"whenever one person is by circumstances placed in such a position with regard to another . . . that if he did not use ordinary care and skill in his own conduct . . . he would cause danger of injury to the person or property of the other, a duty arises to use ordinary care and skill to avoid such danger."'

We depart from 'this fundamental principle' only upon the 'balancing of a number of considerations'; major ones 'are the foreseeability of harm to the plaintiff, the degree of certainty that the plaintiff suffered injury, the closeness of the connection between the defendant's conduct and the injury suffered, the moral blame attached to the defendant's conduct, the policy of preventing future harm, the extent of the burden to the defendant and consequences to the community of imposing a duty to exercise care with resulting liability for breach, and the availability, cost and prevalence of insurance for the risk involved'.

The most important of these considerations in establishing duty is foreseeability. As a general principle, a 'defendant owes a duty of care to all persons who are foreseeably endangered by his conduct, with respect to all risks which make the conduct unreasonably dangerous'. (*Rodriguez v Bethlehem Steel Corpn* 12 Cal 3d 382, 399, 115 Cal Rptr 765, 776, 525 P 2d 669, 680 (1974); *Dillon v Legg, supra*, 68 Cal 2d 728, 739, 69 Cal Rptr 72, 441 P 2d 912; *Weirum v RKO General, Inc* 15 Cal 3d 40, 123 Cal Rptr 468, 539 P 2d 36 (1975); see Civ Code, 1714.) As we shall explain, however, when the avoidance of foreseeable harm requires a defendant to control the conduct of another person, or to warn of such conduct, the common law has traditionally imposed liability only if the defendant bears some special relationship to the dangerous person or to the potential victim. Since the relationship between a therapist and his patient satisfies this requirement, we need not here decide whether foreseeability alone is sufficient to create a duty to exercise reasonable care to protect a potential victim of another's conduct.

Although, as we have stated above, under the common law, as a general rule, one person owes no duty to control the conduct of another (*Richards v Stanley* 43 Cal 2d 60, 65, 271 P 2d 23 (1954); *Wright v Arcade School Dist* 230 Cal App 2d 272, 277, 40 Cal Rptr 812 (1964); Rest 2d Torts (1965) 315), nor to warn those endangered by such conduct (Rest 2d Torts, *supra*, 314, com c; Prosser, Law of Torts (4th ed 1971) 56, p 341), the courts have carved out an exception to this rule in cases in which the defendant stands in some special relationship to either the person whose conduct needs to be controlled or in a relationship to the foreseeable victim of that conduct (see Rest 2d Torts, *supra* 315-320). Applying this exception to the present case, we note that a relationship of defendant therapists to either Tatiana or Poddar will suffice to establish a duty of care; as explained in section 315 of the Restatement Second of Torts, a duty of care may arise from either '(a) a special relation . . . between the actor and the third person which imposes a duty upon the actor to control the third person's conduct, or (b) a special relation . . . between the actor and the other which gives to the other a right of protection'.

Although plaintiffs' pleadings assert no special relation between Tatiana and defendant therapists, they establish as between Poddar and defendant therapists the special relation that arises between a patient and his doctor or psychotherapist. Such a relationship may support affirmative duties for the benefit of third persons. Thus, for example, a hospital must exercise reasonable care to control the behaviour of a patient which may endanger other persons. A doctor must also warn a patient if the patient's condition or medication renders certain conduct, such as driving a car, dangerous to others.

Although the Californian decisions that recognise this duty have involved cases in which the defendant stood in a special relationship *both* to the victim and to the person whose conduct created the danger, we do not think that the duty should logically be constricted to such situations. Decisions of other jurisdictions hold that the single relationship of a doctor to his patient is sufficient to support the duty to exercise reasonable care to protect others against dangers emanating from the patient's illness. The courts hold that a doctor is liable to persons infected by his patient if he negligently fails to diagnose a contagious disease (*Hofmann v Blackmon* 241 So 2d 752 (Fla App, 1970)), or, having diagnosed the illness, fails to warn members of the patient's family (*Wojcik v Aluminum Co of America* 18 Misc 2d 740, 183 NYS 2d 351, 357-358 (1959); *Davis v Rodman* 147 Ark 385, 227 SW 612 (1921); *Skillings v Allen* 143 Minn 323, 173 NW 663 (1919); see also *Jones v Stanko*, 118 Ohio St 147, 160 NE 456 (1928).

Since it involved a dangerous mental patient, the decision in *Merchants National Bank & Trust Co of Fargo v United States* 272 F Supp 409 (DND, 1967) comes closer to the issue. The Veterans Administration arranged for a patient to work on a local farm, but did not inform the farmer of the man's background. The farmer consequently permitted the patient to come and go freely during nonworking hours; the patient borrowed a car, drove to his wife's residence and killed her. Notwithstanding the lack of any 'special relationship' between the Veterans Administration and the wife, the court found the Veterans Administration liable for the wrongful death of the wife.

In their summary of the relevant rulings Fleming and Maximov conclude that the 'case law should dispel any notion that to impose on the therapists a duty to take precautions for the safety of persons threatened by a patient, where due care so requires, is in any way opposed to contemporary ground rules on the duty relationship. On the contrary, there now seems to be sufficient authority to support the conclusion that by entering into a doctor-patient relationship the therapist becomes sufficiently involved to assume some responsibility for the safety, not only of the patient himself, but also of any third person whom the doctor knows to be threatened by the patient.' (Fleming & Maximov, *The Patient or His Victim: The Therapist's Dilemma* (1974) 62 Cal L Rev 1025, 1030.) . . .

We recognise the public interest in supporting effective treatment of mental illness and in protecting the rights of patients to privacy (see *Re Liftschutz, supra,* 2 Cal 3d at 432, 85 Cal Rptr 829, 467 P 2d 557), and the consequent public importance of safeguarding the confidential character of psychotherapeutic communication. Against this interest, however, we must weigh the public interest in safety from violent assault. The Legislature has undertaken the difficult task of balancing the countervailing concerns. In Evidence Code section 1014, it established a broad rule of privilege to protect confidential communications between patient and psychotherapist. In Evidence Code section 1024, the Legislature created a specific and limited exception to the psychotherapist-patient privilege: 'There is no privilege . . . if the psychotherapist has reasonable cause to believe that the patient is in such mental or emotional condition as to be dangerous to himself or to the person or property of another and that disclosure of the communication is necessary to prevent the threatened danger.'

We realise that the open and confidential character of psychotherapeutic dialogue encourages patients to express threats of violence, few of which are ever executed. Certainly a therapist should not be encouraged routinely to reveal such threats; such disclosures could seriously disrupt the patient's relationship with his therapist and with the persons threatened. To the contrary, the therapist's obligations to his patient require that he not disclose a confidence unless such disclosure is necessary to avert danger to others, and even then that he do so discreetly, and in a fashion that would preserve the privacy of his patient to the fullest extent compatible with the prevention of the threatened danger. (See Fleming & Maximov, *The Patient or His Victim: The Therapist's Dilemma* (1974) 62 Cal L Rev 1025, 1065-1066).

The revelation of a communication under the above circumstances is not a breach of trust or a violation of professional ethics; as stated in the Principles of Medical Ethics of the American Medical Association (1957), section 9: 'A physician may not reveal the confidence entrusted to him in the course of medical attendance . . . *unless he is required to do so by law or unless it becomes necessary in order to protect the welfare of the individual or of the community.*' (Emphasis added.) We conclude that the public policy favoring protection of the confidential character of patient-psychotherapist communications must yield to the extent to which disclosure is essential to avert danger to others. The protective privilege ends where the public peril begins.

Our current crowded and computerised society compels the interdependence of its members. In this risk-infected society we can hardly tolerate the further exposure to danger that would result from a concealed knowledge of the therapist that his patient was lethal. If the exercise of reasonable care to protect the threatened victim requires the therapist to warn the endangered party or those who can reasonably be expected to notify him, we see no sufficient societal interest that would protect and justify concealment. The containment of such risks lies in the public interest. For the foregoing reasons, we find that plaintiffs' complaints can be amended to state a cause of action against defendants Moore, Powelson, Gold and Yandell and against the Regents as their employer, for breach of duty to exercise reasonable care to protect Tatiana.

Subsequent cases involving dangerous patients as in *Tarasoff* have interpreted that decision widely so as to impose a duty to warn whenever it is foreseeable that persons will be endangered by the patient (eg *Davis v Lhim* (1983) 335 NW 2d 481 (Mich Sup Ct)). Other courts, on the other hand, have limited the application of *Tarasoff*, requiring not only that a victim be foreseeable, but also that the particular victim be readily identifiable (*Thompson v County Alameda* (1980) 614 P 2d 728 (Cal Sup Ct), despite a strong dissent by Tobriner J). In a few jurisdictions the courts have refused to apply the *Tarasoff* reasoning at all (*Hasenai v United States* (1982) 541 F Supp 999 (D Md)). For a discussion of developments since *Tarasoff* see: Franklin and Rabin, *Cases and Materials on Tort Law and Alternatives* (4th edn 1987) pp 141-51.

The cases and discussion above are concerned with situations similar to that which arose in *Tarasoff*, ie the dangerous psychiatric patient. In the following case the court was concerned with a duty to warn where the patient suffered from an infectious disease.

Gammill v United States (1984) 727 F 2d 950 (10th Cir)

Barrett, Circuit Judge: Plaintiffs Lawrence A Gammill and Cynthia A Gammill (the Gammills) appeal from an adverse judgment of the district court. . . .

On April 20, 1978, Lauralee Johnson was diagnosed as having infectious hepatitis and gastroenteritis. This diagnosis was made at Fort Carson, Colorado, a United States military installation, by Dr James Hamilton (Hamilton), a civilian physician employed by the United States.

The next day, Ladonna Gammill, wife of plaintiff Lawrence Gammill, and mother of plaintiff Cynthia Gammill, was told by a member of her church that Mrs Johnson was ill with hepatitis and there was a need for someone to take care of her two small children, Christie and Stephanie. Mrs Gammill agreed to baby-sit the children and they were consequently brought to her home for the day. Neither child showed symptoms of serious illness, although Stephanie had diarrhea which required Mrs Gammill and Cynthia Gammill to change her diapers. When Mr Gammill came home after work, Mrs Gammill informed him that Mrs Johnson had hepatitis. At dinner that evening Mr Gammill sat next to Stephanie and assisted in feeding her. The children were returned to the Johnson home later that evening. Mr Gammill was cautious in not entering their home because he knew hepatitis was contagious.

Seven days later, on April 28, 1978, Mrs Johnson was informed by the staff at Fort Carson that her daughter, Stephanie, also had hepatitis. Dr Hamilton had also examined Stephanie, and he recommended that the whole family receive gamma globulin inoculations. Neither Dr Hamilton, nor the staff at Fort Carson notified the public health authorities of the hepatitis in the Johnson household; such notification is required by Colorado law, CRS 25-1-649 (1973), Department of the Army Regulation 40-418, and regulations regarding communicable diseases at Fort Carson.

On May 16, 1978, Mr Gammill was brought home from work because of illness. Some time after May 21st, Dr Pollard, the Gammills' family physician, tested Mr Gammill for hepatitis and reported a suspected case of hepatitis to the county health authorities. Mr Gammill's hepatitis tests were later confirmed and it was also determined that Cynthia Gammill had contracted the disease. As a result of Dr Pollard's report to the health authorities, five other cases of hepatitis were identified by epidemiological techniques. Mr Gammill was hospitalized for a time and was ill at home for about five months.

At trial, the Gammills presented testimony that tended to establish that Stephanie Johnson was the source of infection in the Gammill family (Tr 39), that the Gammills would likely have been contacted by the county health department within twenty-four to seventy-two hours if the department had been properly notified by Dr Hamilton (Tr 43), and that if the Gammills had been contacted within that time period they would have had several days to receive effective gamma globulin inoculations (Tr 43). [Such inoculations are effective if received within two weeks of exposure to hepatitis. (Tr 157).]

FINDINGS AND CONCLUSIONS OF THE DISTRICT COURT
The district court concluded that the Gammills could not recover against the United States pursuant to the Federal Tort Claims Act. *Gammill v United States*, No 80-A-1518, (D Colo Oct 27, 1981). First, the court found no common-law duty running from the United States to the Gammills that would require the United States to notify the county health department of the hepatitis in the Johnson home. *Id*, slip op at 11. To create such a duty would allow liability for nonfeasance on the part of the United States. The court noted that liability for 'nonfeasance' was limited to situations where there was a 'special relationship' between the parties, and that there was no such relationship in this case. *Id*. . . .

COMMON LAW CLAIM: The Gammills also contend that the United States breached a duty owed to them deriving from common law. In support of this, they cite various cases suggesting that the spread of hepatitis to the Gammill family was a foreseeable risk, and that the United States had a duty to disclose this risk to the public via the county health department. After reviewing the cases, however, we are convinced that these arguments are without merit.

Colorado courts have never directly addressed the issue of a physician's duty to prevent harm to a third person who is not a patient. Generally, however, a person does not have a duty to protect another from harm except when a special relationship exists between the parties, or when the first person placed the other in peril. See Restatement (Second) of Torts 314-314(A) (1965). Clearly, there is no 'special relationship' between Dr Hamilton and the Gammills; they were not even acquainted. Neither could it be said that Dr Hamilton placed the Gammills in peril.

The Gammills contend, however, that Dr Hamilton's duty to them arises from his *professional position* and relation to people who contract disease. They argue that, as a physician, Dr Hamilton owed the public the duty of ordinary care to protect them from the disease of his patients. In support thereof they cite *Davis v Rodman*, 147 Ark 385, 227 SW 612 (1921); *Wojcik v Aluminum Co of America*, 18 Misc 2d 740, 183 NYS 2d 351 (1959); 61 Am Jur 2d *Physicians and Surgeons* 245; 41 Am Jur *Physicians and Surgeons* 101; and 70 CJS *Physicians and Surgeons* 48. We understand these authorities, however, as expressing a much more limited duty than that urged by the Gammills. A physician may be found liable for failing to warn a patient's *family, treating attendants,* or other *persons* likely to be exposed to the patient, of the nature of the disease and the danger of exposure. 61 Am Jur 2d *Physicians and Surgeons, supra; Davis v Rodman, supra*. We note the limited persons to whom such a duty is owed, again suggesting the necessity of some special relationship between the physician and those to be warned. It would appear that at the bare minimum the physician must be aware of the specific risks to specific persons before a duty to warn exists. Here, Dr Hamilton did not know the Gammills; clearly he was unaware of their risk of exposure. Under these circumstances, we agree with the district court that to impose a duty upon Dr Hamilton to warn the Gammills would constitute an 'unreasonable burden' upon physicians.

We hold that the Gammills' claim has no basis in law.

[The American case law is discussed in Hermann and Gagliano, 'AIDS, Therapeutic Confidentiality, and Warning Third Parties' (1989) Maryland Law Review 55.]

Having examined the American law, the first question for us is whether the rule in *Tarasoff* would ever be regarded as English law. Michael Jones in his book, *Medical Negligence* (1992) discusses the current position in English law (paras 2.62 – 2.66 and 2.68).

It is debatable whether *Tarasoff* would be followed in this country. In the one case which comes closest to it, *Holgate v Lancashire Mental Hospitals Board* [1937] 4 All ER 19] a hospital was held liable for negligently releasing on licence a dangerous patient who had been compulsorily detained following convictions for violent offences. The patient entered the plaintiff's home and assaulted her. The trial judge seemed to assume that a duty of care existed and the report deals largely with the question whether there had been negligence. The case may be justified on the basis of the degree of control exercised by the defendants over the dangerous patient, a control analogous to the relationship between gaoler and prisoner which may give rise to a duty of care. This is the basis upon which a hospital authority may be held liable for injuries to a patient inflicted by a fellow patient as a result of negligent supervision, and there is no obvious reason why this duty should be owed only to patients, and not, for example, to visitors to the hospital. However, in *Home Office v Dorset Yacht Co Ltd* [[1970] AC 1004, 1002-63] Lord Diplock specifically reserved his opinion on *Holgate v Lancashire Mental Hospitals Board*, and it has been suggested that the case is of doubtful authority today on the basis that the discretion to admit or release a patient under the Mental Health legislation constitutes the exercise of a statutory power for which there can be civil liability only where the exercise of power is *ultra vires*.

An independent psychiatrist does not exercise this degree of control over the patient, and thus some alternative basis for a duty of care would have to be established. It has been argued that this is to be found in the doctor's unique capacity to influence the patient's behaviour, whether through treatment or advice. This is questionable, however, given that the doctor's ability to influence the patient may be limited, and in some circumstances it may be virtually non-existent.

The basis of any potential duty of care must be the foreseeability of harm to the victim. Foreseeability alone is not, however, sufficient to impose a duty of care. There must also be a proximate relationship between plaintiff and defendant, and it must be just and reasonable in the circumstances to impose a duty. The more foreseeable the harm the more likely it is that a court will find the relationship between the parties to be proximate. Thus, if a patient made genuine threats of serious injury to an identified third person and there was a real risk that the threats would be carried out, it is arguable that a doctor would come under a duty of care to the potential victim. The duty, if any, arises from the defendant's knowledge of the foreseeable danger of serious physical harm to the third party.

There are difficulties, however, with imposing such a duty. There is no general obligation in the tort of negligence to take positive steps to confer a benefit on others by preventing harm befalling them, and there is no obligation to rescue someone in danger, even if rescue would involve little or no effort and involves no danger to the rescuer. In the absence of a special relationship giving the defendant some degree of control over the patient, there is nothing upon which to base a duty to intervene, other than the mere foreseeability of the harm, which in the case of damage caused by a third party (here the patient) is not normally sufficient to impose a duty of care.

A second objection might be that imposing a duty of care could create a conflict of duties for the doctor, between the duty of confidence owed to the patient and the duty of care owed to a third party. It is true that where the imposition of a duty of care might lead to a defendant being subject to conflicting duties the courts may be reluctant to find a duty of care but where the public interest defence to an action for breach of confidence applies there is no duty to maintain confidentiality and so no conflict with a possible duty of care. The public interest defence recognises that in some circumstances other, more valued, social considerations outweigh the confidentiality of the doctor/patient relationship, and it is arguable that the public interest in safety from individuals known to be lethal falls into this category. It was this point which the court considered to be persuasive in *Tarasoff* . . .

If a duty does arise the question would be: in what circumstances? If the doctor considered the patient to be 'dangerous' but the patient had made no threats against specific individuals, the courts would probably not impose a duty of care, on the basis that the victim was merely a member of a large unascertained class. This would be consistent with the approach of the American courts. [*Thompson v County of Alameda* 614 P 2d 728 (1980); see also *Brady v Hopper* 751 F 2d 329 (1984).] This is linked to a further problem, namely what would be required of the doctor in order to satisfy the duty of care. Although a duty to give a warning is not a particularly onerous duty for the 'reluctant rescuer' to comply with, the assumption, of course, is that it is possible to give an effective warning about a dangerous psychiatric patient, either to a hospital, the potential victim or the police. But where the patient is not compulsorily detained or has not made threats against specific individuals this may be difficult.

Given the difficulties of introducing the general principle of *Tarasoff* into English law it could be said that a *duty to warn* in the context of HIV infection will equally be problematic. A counter-argument, however, is that the factual circumstances, ie infection of a spouse by a patient in circumstances which the doctor could eminently have foreseen, could persuade the court to create an *exception* to the general rule of no liability for the acts of third parties.

D. REMEDIES

It goes without saying that a patient may obtain an injunction if he acts in time to restrain an unlawful breach of confidence. But, can he seek damages after the event for the fact of disclosure and any distress, harm or loss it may have caused him? By analogy with the cases related to commercial confidence, it seems clear that the patient may recover any foreseeable economic loss arising from the breach, for example, if he loses his job (*Seager v Copydex Ltd* [1967] 1 WLR 923). As regards physical harm, the patient may be able to establish a claim in negligence.

Furniss v Fitchett **[1958] NZLR 396 (NZ HCt)**

> The defendant doctor, at the invitation of the plaintiff's husband, wrote the following letter, which he then gave to the husband. The plaintiff (and, indeed, the husband) were patients of the defendant.

> Mrs Phyllis C L Furniss   21.5.56
> 32 Mornington Road
> The above has been attending me for some time and during this period I have observed several things:
> (1)   Deluded that her husband is doping her.
> (2)   Accuses her husband of cruelty and even occasional violence.
> (3)   Considers her husband to be insane and states that it is a family failing.
> On the basis of the above I consider she exhibits symptoms of paranoia and should be given treatment for same if possible. An examination by a Psychiatrist would be needed to fully diagnose her case and its requirements.
> Yours faithfully
> A J Fitchett

> The husband later used the letter in separation proceedings brought by the plaintiff. This was the first that she knew of its existence. She sued the defendant for breach of confidence.

Barrowclough CJ: The relationship between the plaintiff and the defendant was that of doctor and patient. The doctor knew – he admitted that he knew – that the disclosure to his patient of his opinion as to her mental condition would be harmful to her. He was careful not to tell her directly what that opinion was. Nevertheless, he wrote out and gave to Mrs Furniss's husband a certificate, expressing that opinion. If he ought reasonably to have had in contemplation that Mrs Furniss might be injured physically, though not financially, as the result of his giving that certificate – and that on the evidence is beyond dispute – then it seems clear that he should have regarded her as 'his neighbour' in Lord Atkin's phrase. If she was his neighbour in that sense, he was under a duty to take care to avoid an act which he could reasonably foresee would be likely to injure her – again physically though not financially . . .

On the facts, it is clear that if Mrs Furniss were to be confronted by this certificate, it was likely to do her harm. The certificate was handed to Mr Furniss, who was then living with his wife. Their relations were extremely strained. She regarded him as mentally unsound and as intent on doping or poisoning her. She had not hesitated to make these accusations against him, and it was because of her accusations that he had been brought to the distraught condition in which he found himself when he begged the doctor to give him a certificate. In these circumstances, it seems to me not only likely, but extremely likely, that when the husband was charged by his wife with mental instability, he would be goaded into a 'tu quoque' retort, and that he would disclose to her either the certificate or at all events its contents. That he apparently did not disclose it, and that the certificate remained hidden from Mrs Furniss for a whole year, speaks volumes for the husband's restraint. It is also to be noted that, in giving the certificate to Mr Furniss, the doctor placed no restrictions on its use. It was not even marked 'confidential'. On that evidence I can only conclude that Dr Fitchett ought reasonably to have foreseen that the contents of his certificate were likely to come to his patient's knowledge, and he knew that if they did, they would be likely to injure her in her health.

I do not hold that the doctor ought to have foreseen the precise manner in which the contents of his certificate did in fact come to Mrs Furniss's knowledge; though, I think, that, in the circumstances disclosed by the evidence, he ought to have foreseen that the certificate could be expected to be used in some legal proceedings, in which his patient would be concerned and thus come to her knowledge. It is sufficient to say that, in my view, on the evidence in the special circumstances of this case, Dr Fitchett should have foreseen that his patient would be likely to be injured as the result of his action in giving her husband such a certificate as he did give, and in giving it to him without placing any restriction on its use. In these circumstances, I am of opinion that, on the principle of *Donoghue v Stevenson* [1932] AC 562, there arose a duty of care on his part. I have not forgotten that the certificate was true and accurate, but I see no reason for limiting the duty to one of care in seeing that it is accurate. The duty must extend also to the exercise of care in deciding whether it should be put in circulation in such a way that it is likely to cause harm to another.

However, the patient's claim may not be limited to damages merely for distress caused by the disclosure. The law was examined by Scott J in *W v Egdell* [1989] 1 All ER 1089 (not discussed on appeal: [1990] 1 All ER 835). W's action, it will be recalled, was based upon a contractual obligation of confidence though, as we shall see, the judge did not regard this as necessarily significant.

W v Egdell [1989] 1 All ER 1089 (QBD)

Scott J: I think [it] open to question whether shock and distress caused by the unauthorised disclosure of confidential information can, in any event, properly be reflected in an award of damages.

In *Bliss v South East Thames Regional Health Authority* [1987] ICR 700 at 717-718 Dillon LJ said:

> The general rule laid down by the House of Lords in *Addis v Gramophone Co Ltd.* ([1909] AC 488, [1908-10] All ER Rep 1) is that where damages fall to be assessed for breach of contract rather than in tort it is not permissible to award general damages for frustration, mental distress, injured feelings or annoyance occasioned by the breach. Modern thinking tends to be that the amount of damages recoverable for a wrong should be the same whether the cause of action is laid in contract or in tort. But in the *Addis* case Lord Loreburn regarded the rule that damages for injured feelings cannot be recovered in contract for wrongful dismissal as too inveterate to be altered, and Lord James of Hereford supported his concurrence in the speech of Lord Loreburn by reference to his own experience at the Bar. There are exceptions now recognised where the contract which has been broken was itself a contract to provide peace of mind or freedom from distress: see *Jarvis v Swans Tours Ltd* ([1973] 1 All ER 71, [1973] QB 233) and *Heywood v Wellers* ([1976] 1 All ER 300, [1976] QB 446). Those decisions, do not however cover this present case. In *Cox v Philips Industries Ltd* [1976] 3 All ER 161, [1976] 1 WLR 638) Lawson J took the view that damages for distress, vexation and frustration, including consequent ill-health, could be recovered for breach of contract of employment if it could be said to have been in the contemplation of the parties that the breach would cause such distress etc. For my part, I do not think that that general approach is open to this court unless and until the House of Lords has reconsidered its decision in the *Addis* case.

This Court of Appeal authority seems to me to preclude W from recovering damages (save nominal damages) to the extent that his claim is based on breach of an implied contractual term. I do not see any reason, on this point, why equity should not follow the law.

Accordingly, in my judgment, W would not, even if I had found Dr Egdell to be liable, have been entitled to damages. He would have had to be content with a declaration and an injunction.

By contrast, the Law Commission in its Report No 110, entitled *Breach of Confidence* (Cmnd 838, 1981) recommended that damages for mental stress caused by a breach of confidence should be available (see paras 6.5 and 6.114), but the recommendation has not been enacted into law.

Part III

Medical law in action

A: The beginning of life

Chapter 10

Contraception

Non-surgical methods

A. LEGALITY OF CONTRACEPTION

The forms of contraception considered here are the condom, the intra-uterine device (IUD), long-acting injectable contraceptives (Depo-provera), and the female contraceptive pill (the pill). Apart from the condom, these require the involvement of doctors to prescribe or fit them. A threshold question is whether these amount to medical treatment.

Lord Scarman, in *Gillick* [1985] 3 All ER 402 at 418, said:

> ... as is clear in the light of s 5 of the National Health Service Act 1977 (re-enacting earlier legislation) and s 41 of the National Health Service (Scotland) Act 1978, contraceptive medical treatment is recognised as a legitimate and beneficial treatment in cases in which it is medically indicated. ...

Section 5(1)(b) of the National Health Service Act 1977 imposes a duty upon the Secretary of State:

> to arrange, to such extent as he considers necessary to meet all reasonable requirements in England and Wales, for the giving of advice on contraception, the medical examination of persons seeking advice on contraception, the treatment of such persons and the supply of contraceptive substances and appliances.

Lord Fraser, in *Gillick, op cit* at 407, pointed out:

> These, and other, provisions show that Parliament regarded 'advice' and 'treatment' on contraception and the supply of appliances for contraception as essentially medical matters. So they are, but they may also raise moral and social questions on which many people feel deeply, and in that respect they differ from ordinary medical advice and treatment.

1. Contraception and children

Non-surgical forms of contraception in the context of the young are typically identified with prescribing contraceptive pills for a girl. This is the medical example we analyse here.

The law identifies three areas of difficulty. They are: first, problems of *consent*; secondly, problems of confidentiality; and thirdly, problems of *public policy* and the criminal law. We have already examined in detail the circumstances under which a child may give consent to medical treatment (*supra*, ch 3). Of course, the leading case of *Gillick* specifically concerns the legal capacity of a child to give consent to contraceptive advice and treatment. As we saw, the House of Lords, by a majority, found that providing the child has sufficient maturity and understanding of what is involved, her consent is legally valid.

Further, we have also examined the law relating to confidence and how it applies to children (*supra*, ch 9). The only question which remains, therefore, is the extent to which, if at all, public policy or the criminal law constrains doctors from providing contraceptive treatment to children who have the capacity to consent.

Gillick v West Norfolk & Wisbech AHA [1986] AC 112, [1985] 3 All ER 402 (HL)

The Department of Health and Social Security, in the exercise of its statutory functions, issued a circular to area health authorities containing, inter alia, advice to the effect that a doctor consulted at a family planning clinic by a girl under 16 would not be acting unlawfully if he prescribed contraceptives for the girl, so long as in doing so he was acting in good faith to protect her against the harmful effects of sexual intercourse. The circular further stated that, although a doctor should proceed on the assumption that advice and treatment on contraception should not be given to a girl under 16 without parental consent and that he should try to persuade the girl to involve her parents in the matter, nevertheless the principle of confidentiality between doctor and patient applied to a girl under 16 seeking contraceptives and therefore in exceptional cases the doctor could prescribe contraceptives without consulting the girl's parents or obtaining their consent if in the doctor's clinical judgment it was desirable to prescribe contraceptives. The plaintiff, who had five daughters under the age of 16, sought an assurance from her local area health authority that her daughters would not be given advice and treatment on contraception without the plaintiff's prior knowledge and consent while they were under 16. When the authority refused to give such an assurance the plaintiff brought an action against the authority and the department seeking (i) as against both defendants a declaration that the advice contained in the circular was unlawful, because it amounted to advice to doctors to commit the offence of causing or encouraging unlawful sexual intercourse with a girl under 16, contrary to s 28(1) of the Sexual Offences Act 1956, or the offence of being an accessory to unlawful sexual intercourse with a girl under 16, contrary to s 6(1) of that Act, and (ii) as against the area health authority a declaration that a doctor or other professional person employed by it in its family planning service could not give advice and treatment on contraception to any child of the plaintiff below the age of 16 without the plaintiff's consent, because to do so would be unlawful as being inconsistent with the plaintiff's parental rights. The plaintiff conceded that, in order to be entitled to the first declaration sought, she was required to show that a doctor who followed the advice contained in the circular would necessarily be committing a criminal offence or acting unlawfully.

Lord Fraser: Three strands of argument are raised by the appeal. These are: (1) whether a girl under the age of 16 has the legal capacity to give valid consent to contraceptive advice and treatment including medical examination; (2) whether giving such advice and treatment to a girl under 16 without her parents' consent infringes the parents' rights; and (3) whether a doctor who gives such advice or treatment to a girl under 16 without her parents' consent incurs criminal liability. I shall consider these strands in order.

[Having considered the first two strands of argument, Lord Fraser continued:]

3. Is a doctor who gives contraceptive advice or treatment to a girl under 16 without her parents' consent likely to incur criminal liability?

The submission was made to Woolf J on behalf of Mrs Gillick that a doctor who provided contraceptive advice and treatment to a girl under 16 without her parents' authority would be committing an offence under s 28 of the Sexual Offences Act 1956 by aiding and abetting the commission of unlawful sexual intercourse. When the case reached the Court of Appeal counsel on both sides conceded that whether a doctor who followed the guidelines would be committing an offence or not would depend on the circumstances. It would depend on the doctor's intentions; this appeal is concerned with doctors who honestly intend to act in the best interests of the girl, and I think it is unlikely that a doctor who gives contraceptive advice or treatment with that intention would commit an offence under s 28. It must be remembered that a girl under 16 who has sexual intercourse does not thereby commit an offence herself, although her partner does: see the Sexual Offences Act 1956, ss 5 and 6. In any event, even if the doctor would be committing an offence, the fact that he had acted with the parents' consent would not exculpate him as Woolf J pointed out ([1984] QB 581 at 595, [1984] 1 All ER 365 at 373). Accordingly, I regard this contention as irrelevant to the question that we have to answer in this appeal. Parker LJ in the Court of Appeal dealt at some length with the provisions of criminal law intended to protect girls under the age of 16 from being seduced, and perhaps also to protect them from their own weakness. Parker LJ expressed his conclusion on this part of the case as follows ([1985] 2 WLR 413 at 435, [1985] 1 All ER 533 at 550):

> It appears to me that it is wholly incongruous, when the act of intercourse is criminal, when permitting it to take place on one's premises is criminal and when, if the girl were under 13, failing to report an act of intercourse to the police would up to 1967 have been criminal, that either the department or the area health authority should provide facilities which would enable girls under 16 the more readily to commit such acts. It seems to me equally incongruous to assert that doctors have the right to accept the young, down, apparently, to any age, as patients, and to provide them with contraceptive advice and treatment without reference to their parents and even against their known wishes.

My Lords, the first of those two sentences is directed to the question, which is not in issue in this appeal, of whether contraceptive facilities should be available at all under the NHS for girls under 16. I have already explained my reasons for thinking that the legislation does not limit the duty of providing such facilities to women of 16 or more. The second sentence, which does bear directly on the question in the appeal, does not appear to me to follow necessarily from the first and with respect I cannot agree with it. If the doctor complies with the first of the conditions which I have specified, that is to say if he satisfies himself that the girl can understand his advice, there will be no question of his giving contraceptive advice to very young girls.

For those reasons I do not consider that the guidance interferes with the parents' rights.

Lord Scarman also rejected Mrs Gillick's argument based on the criminal law. Like Lord Fraser he adopted the views of Woolf J at first instance.

> **Woolf J:** So far as the offence against section 6 of the Sexual Offences Act 1956 is concerned, I accept that a doctor who is misguided enough to provide a girl who is under the age of 16, or a man, with advice and assistance with regard to contraceptive measures with the intention thereby of encouraging them to have sexual intercourse, is an accessory before the fact to an offence contrary to section 6. I stress the words 'with the intention thereby of encouraging them to have sexual intercourse'. However, this, I assume, will not usually be the attitude of a doctor.
>
> There will certainly be some cases, and I hope the majority of cases, where the doctor decides to give the advice and prescribe contraceptives despite the fact he was firmly against unlawful sexual intercourse taking place but felt, nevertheless, that he had to prescribe the contraceptives because, whether or not he did so, intercourse would in fact take place, and the provision of contraceptives would, in his view, be in the best interests of the girl in protecting her from an unwanted pregnancy and the risk of a sexually transmitted disease. It is as to whether or not in such a situation the doctor is to be treated as being as accessory, that I have found the greatest difficulty in applying the law.

The judge then referred to the well-known cases of *National Coal Board v Gamble* [1959] 1 QB 11 and *DPP for Northern Ireland v Lynch* [1975] AC 653 and continued:

> . . . three matters have to be borne in mind. First of all, contraceptives do not in themselves directly assist in the commission of the crime of unlawful sexual intercourse. The analogy of providing the motor car for a burglary or providing poison to the murderer, relied on in argument, are not true comparisons. While if the man wears a sheath, there may be said to be a physical difference as to the quality of intercourse, the distinction that I am seeking to draw is clearer where the woman takes the pill or is fitted with an internal device, when the unlawful act will not be affected in any way. The only effect of the provision of the means of contraception is that in some cases it is likely to increase the likelihood of a crime being

committed by reducing the inhibitions of the persons concerned to having sexual intercourse because of their fear of conception or the contraction of disease. I therefore see a distinction between the assistance or aiding . . . and the act of the doctor in prescribing contraceptives. I would regard the pill prescribed to the woman as not so much 'the instrument for a crime or anything essential to its commission' but a palliative against the consequences of the crime.

The second factor that has to be borne in mind is that the girl herself commits no offence under section 6 since the section is designed to protect her from herself: see *R v Tyrrell* [1894] 1 QB 710. This creates problems with regard to relying upon any encouragement by the doctor as making him the accessory to the offence where the girl alone attends the clinic. The well-known case, *R v Bourne* (1952) 36 Cr App Rep 125, has to be distinguished because there, the woman can be said to have committed the offence although she was not criminally responsible because of duress. The doctor, if he is to be an accessory where the woman alone consults him, will only be an accessory if it can be shown that he acted through the innocent agency of the woman, the situation dealt with in *R v Cooper* (1833) 5 C & P 535.

The final point that has to be borne in mind, is that there will be situations where long-term contraceptive measures are taken to protect girls who, sadly, will strike up promiscuous relationships whatever the supervision of those who are responsible for their well-being, the sort of situation that Butler-Sloss J had to deal with in *Re P (a minor)* (1982) 80 LGR 301. In such a situation the doctor will prescribe the measures to be taken purely as a safeguard against the risk that at some time in the future, the girl will form a casual relationship with a man when sexual intercourse will take place. In order to be an accessory, you normally have to know the material circumstances. In such a situation the doctor would know no more than that there was a risk of sexual intercourse taking place at an unidentified place with an unidentified man on an unidentified date – hardly the state of knowledge which is normally associated with an accessory before the fact.

Under this limb of the argument, the conclusion which I have therefore come to is, that while a doctor could, in following the guidance, so encourage unlawful sexual intercourse as to render this conduct criminal, in the majority of situations the probabilities are that a doctor will be able to follow the advice without rendering himself liable to criminal proceedings. Before leaving this limb of the argument, I should make it absolutely clear that the absence of consent of the parents makes no difference to the criminal responsibility of the doctor. If his conduct would be criminal without the parents' consent, it would be equally criminal with their consent.

Lord Bridge agreed on the impact of the criminal law on the outcome of the case.

By contrast, Lord Brandon in his vigorous dissent saw the case *wholly* in terms of criminal law and the public policy underlying it. Questions of consent for him were irrelevant.

Lord Brandon: In my opinion the formulation of the question whether such activities can be lawfully carried on without the prior knowledge and consent of the parents of any girl of the age concerned . . . involves the rolling up in one composite question of two separate and distinct points of law. The first point of law is whether the three activities to which I have referred [giving advice, examining and prescribing] can be carried on lawfully in any circumstances whatever. If, on the one hand, the right answer to the first point of law is No, then no second point of law arises for decision. If, on the other hand, the answer to the first question is Yes, then a second point of law arises, namely whether the three activities referred to can only be lawfully carried on with the prior knowledge and consent of the parents of the girl concerned.

The first point of law appears to me to be one of public policy, the answer to which is to be gathered from an examination of the statutory provisions which Parliament has enacted from time to time in relation to men having sexual intercourse with girls either under the age of 13 or between the ages of 13 and 16.

It is, I think, sufficient to begin with the Criminal Law Amendment Act 1885 and then to go on to the Sexual Offences Act 1956, by which the former Act was repealed and largely replaced.

Part 1 of the 1885 Act, which contained ss 2 to 12, had the cross-heading 'Protection of Women and Girls'. Sections 4 and 5 provided, so far as material:

4. Any person who unlawfully and carnally knows any girl under the age of thirteen years shall be guilty of felony, and being convicted thereof shall be liable at the

discretion of the court to be kept in penal servitude for life, or for any term not less than five years, or to be imprisoned for any term not exceeding two years, with or without hard labour . . .

5. Any person who – (1) Unlawfully and carnally knows or attempts to have unlawfully carnal knowledge of any girl being of or above the age of thirteen years and under the age of sixteen years . . . shall be guilty of misdemeanour, and being convicted thereof shall be liable at the discretion of the court to be imprisoned for any term not exceeding two years, with or without hard labour . . .

In *R v Tyrrell* [1894] 1 QB 710, [1891-4] All ER Rep 1215 it was held by the Court for Crown Cases Reserved that it was not a criminal offence for a girl between the ages of 13 and 16 to aid and abet a man in committing, or to incite him to commit the misdemeanour of having carnal knowledge of her contrary to s 5 of the Criminal Law Amendment Act 1885 set out above. The ground of this decision was that the 1885 Act had been passed for the purpose of protecting women and girls against themselves: see the judgment of Lord Coleridge CJ [1894] 1 QB 710 at 712, [1891-4] All ER Rep 1215 at 1215-1216:

The Sexual Offences Act 1956 represents the latest pronouncement of Parliament on these matters. Sections 5 and 6 provide, so far as material:

5. It is a felony for a man to have unlawful sexual intercourse with a girl under the age of thirteen.
6. (1) It is an offence . . . for a man to have unlawful sexual intercourse with a girl under the age of sixteen . . .

Further, by s 37 and Sch 2, the maximum punishment for an offence under s 5 is imprisonment for life, and that for an offence under s 6 imprisonment for two years. Since the passing of the 1956 Act the distinction between felonies and misdemeanours has been abolished. For the purposes of this case, however, nothing turns on this change of terminology.

My Lords, the inescapable inference from the statutory provisions of the 1885 and 1956 Acts to which I have referred is that Parliament has for the past century regarded, and still regards today, sexual intercourse between a man and a girl under 16 as a serious criminal offence so far as the man who has such intercourse is concerned. So far as the girl is concerned, she does not commit any criminal offence, even if she aids, abets or incites the having of such intercourse. The reason for this, as explained earlier, is that the relevant statutory provisions have been enacted by Parliament for the purpose of protecting the girl from herself. The having of such intercourse is, however, unlawful, and the circumstances that the man is guilty of such a criminal offence, while the girl is not, cannot alter that situation.

On the footing that the having of sexual intercourse by a man with a girl under 16 is an unlawful act, it follows necessarily that for any person to promote, encourage or facilitate the commission of such an act may itself be a criminal offence, and must, in any event, be contrary to public policy. Nor can it make any difference that the person who promotes, encourages or facilitates the commission of such an act is a parent or a doctor or a social worker.

The question then arises whether the three activities to which I referred earlier should properly be regarded as, directly or indirectly, promoting, encouraging or facilitating the having, contrary to public policy, of sexual intercourse between a man and a girl under 16. In my opinion there can be only one answer to this question, namely that to give such a girl advice about contraception, to examine her with a view to her using one or more forms of protection and finally to prescribe contraceptive treatment for her, necessarily involves promoting, encouraging or facilitating the having of sexual intercourse, contrary to public policy, by that girl with a man.

The inhibitions against the having of sexual intercourse between a man and a girl under 16 are primarily twofold. So far as the man is concerned there is the inhibition of the criminal law as contained in ss 5 and 6 of the 1956 Act. So far as both are concerned there is the inhibition arising from the risk of an unwanted pregnancy. To give the girl contraceptive treatment, following appropriate advice and examination, is to remove largely the second of these two inhibitions. Such removal must involve promoting, encouraging or facilitating the having of sexual intercourse between the girl and the man.

It has been argued that some girls under 16 will have intercourse with a man whether contraceptive treatment is made available to them or not, and that the provision of such treatment does not, therefore, promote, encourage or facilitate the having of such intercourse. In my opinion this argument should be rejected for two quite separate reasons. The first reason is that the mere fact that a girl under 16 seeks contraceptive advice and treatment, whether of her own accord or at the suggestion of others, itself indicates that she, and probably also the man with whom she is having, or contemplating having, sexual intercourse, are conscious of the inhibition arising from the risk of an unwanted pregnancy. They are conscious of it and are more likely to indulge their desire if it can be removed. The second reason is that, if all a girl under 16 needs to do in order to obtain contraceptive treatment is to threaten that she will go ahead with, or continue, unlawful sexual intercourse with a man unless she is given such treatment, a situation tantamount to blackmail will arise which no legal system ought to tolerate. The only answer which the law should give to such a threat is, 'Wait till you are 16.'

The DHSS has contended that s 5(1) of the National Health Service Act 1977 imposes on it a statutory duty to carry out, in relation to girls under 16 as well as to older girls or women, the three activities to which I referred earlier. That provision reads:

> It is the Secretary of State's duty . . . (b) to arrange, to such extent as he considers necessary to meet all reasonable requirements in England and Wales, for the giving of advice on contraception, the medical examination of persons seeking advice on contraception, the treatment of such persons and the supply of contraceptive substances and appliances.

This provision does not define the 'persons' who are the subject matter of it, nor is there any definition of that expression anywhere else in the Act. In these circumstances it seems to me that a court, in interpreting the provision, must do so in a way which conforms with considerations of public policy rather than in a way which conflicts with them. For the reasons which I have given earlier, I am of the opinion that, in the case of girls under 16, the giving of advice about contraception, medical examination with a view to the use of one or other form of contraception, and the prescribing of contraceptive treatment are all contrary to public policy. It follows that I would interpret the expression 'persons' in s 5(1)(b) above as not including girls under 16. Alternatively, I would say that the expression 'all reasonable requirements', which occurs earlier in the provisions, cannot be interpreted as including the requirements of a girl under 16 which, if satisfied, will promote, encourage or facilitate unlawful acts of sexual intercourse between a man and her.

My Lords, reference was made in the course of the argument before you to a decision of Butler-Sloss J in *Re P (a minor)* (1982) 80 LGR 301. In that case the judge, in wardship proceedings, ordered that a girl of 15, who had been pregnant for the second time and was in the care of a local authority, should be fitted with a contraceptive appliance because it appeared that it was impossible for the local authority, in whose care she was, to control her sexual conduct. It was contended that this decision was authority for the proposition that, in wardship proceedings at any rate, an order could lawfully be made for the supply and fitting of a contraceptive appliance to a girl under 16.

I do not know what arguments were or were not addressed to Butler-Sloss J in that case, and it is, in any event, unnecessary for your Lordships to decide in these proceedings the limits of the powers of a court exercising wardship jurisdiction. As at present advised, however, I am of opinion, with great respect to Butler-Sloss J, that the order which she made was not one which she could lawfully make.

My Lords, great play was made in the argument before you of the disastrous consequences for a girl under 16 of becoming pregnant as a result of her willingly having unlawful sexual intercourse with a man. I am fully conscious of these considerations, but I do not consider that, if the views which I have so far expressed are right in law, those considerations can alter the position.

It is sometimes said that the age of consent for girls is presently 16. This is, however, an inaccurate way of putting the matter, since, if a man has sexual intercourse with a girl under 16 without her consent, the crime which he thereby commits is that of rape. The right way to put the matter is that 16 is the age of a girl below which a man cannot lawfully have sexual intercourse with her. It was open to Parliament in 1956, when the Sexual Offences Act of that year was passed, and it has remained open to Parliament throughout the 29 years which have since elapsed, to pass legislation providing for some lower age than 16, if it thought fit to do so. Parliament has not thought fit to do so, and I do not consider that it would be right for your Lordships' House, by holding that girls under 16 can lawfully be provided with contraceptive facilities, to undermine or circumvent the criminal law which Parliament has enacted. The criminal law and the civil law should, as it seems to me, march hand in hand on all issues, including that raised in this case, and to allow inconsistency or contradiction between them would, in my view, serve only to discredit the rule of law as a whole.

Since I am of opinion that the first question which I posed earlier, namely whether the provision of contraceptive facilities to girls under 16 was lawful in any circumstances at all, should be answered in the negative, the second question which I posed, relating to the need for prior parental knowledge and consent, does not arise. This is because, on the view which I take of the law, making contraception available to girls under 16 is unlawful, whether their parents know of and consent to it or not.

Lord Templeman in his dissenting speech similarly concentrated on public policy. For him, however, public policy was relevant not in determining the ambit of the criminal law, but, in the context of medical care, whether a child could consent to *contraceptive* as distinct from other forms of medical treatment.

Lord Templeman: I accept also that a doctor may lawfully carry out some forms of treatment with the consent of an infant patient and against the opposition of a parent based on religious or any other grounds. The effect of the consent of the infant depends on the nature of the treatment and the age and understanding of the infant. For example, a doctor with the consent of an intelligent boy or girl of 15 could in my opinion safely remove tonsils or a troublesome appendix. But any decision on my part of a girl to practise sex and contraception requires not only knowledge of the facts of life and of the dangers of pregnancy and disease but also an understanding of the emotional and other consequences to her family, her male partner and to herself. I doubt whether a girl under the age of 16 is capable of a balanced judgment to embark on frequent, regular or casual sexual intercourse fortified by the illusion that medical science can protect her in mind and body and ignoring the danger of leaping from childhood to adulthood without the difficult formative transitional experiences of adolescence. There are many things which a girl under 16 needs to practise but sex is not one of them. Parliament could declare this view to be out of date. But in my opinion the statutory provisions discussed in the speech of my noble and learned friend Lord Fraser and the provisions of s 6 of the Sexual Offences Act 1956 indicate that as the law now stands an unmarried girl under 16 is not competent to decide to practise sex and contraception . . .

In the present case it is submitted that a doctor may lawfully make a decision on behalf of the girl and in so doing may overrule or ignore the parent who has custody of the girl. It is submitted that a doctor may at the request of a girl under 16 provide contraceptive facilities against the known or assumed wishes of the parent and on terms that the parent shall be kept in ignorance of the treatment. The justification is advanced that, if the girl's request is not met, the girl may persist in sexual intercourse and run the risk of pregnancy. It is not in the interests of a girl under 16 to become pregnant and therefore the doctor may, in her interests, confidentially provide contraceptive facilities unless the doctor can persuade the girl to abstain from sexual intercourse or can persuade her to ensure that precautions are taken by the male participant. The doctor is not bound to provide contraceptive facilities but, it is said, is entitled to do so in the best interests of the girl. The girl must be assured that the doctor will be pledged to secrecy otherwise the girl may not seek advice or treatment but will run all the risks of disease and pregnancy involved in sexual activities without adequate knowledge or mature consideration and preparation. The Department of Health and Social Security (DHSS) memorandum instructs a doctor to seek to persuade the girl to involve the parent but concludes that 'the decision whether or not to prescribe contraception must be for the clinical judgment of a doctor'.

There are several objections to this approach. The first objection is that a doctor, acting without the views of the parent, cannot form a 'clinical' or any other reliable judgment that the best interests of the girl require the provision of contraceptive facilities. The doctor at the family planning clinic only knows that which the girl chooses to tell him. The family doctor may know some of the circumstances of some of the families who form his registered patients but his information may be incomplete or misleading. The doctor who provides contraceptive facilities without the knowledge of the parent deprives the parent of the opportunity to protect the girl from sexual intercourse by persuading and helping her to avoid sexual intercourse or by the exercise of parental power which may prevent sexual intercourse. The parent might be able to bring pressure on a male participant to desist from the commission of the offence of sexual intercourse with a girl under 16. The parent might be able and willing to exercise parental power by removing the family or the girl to a different neighbourhood and environment and away from the danger of sexual intercourse.

The second objection is that a parent will sooner or later find out the truth, probably sooner, and may do so in circumstances which bring about a complete rupture of good relations between members of the family and between the family and the doctor. It is inevitable that, when the parent discovers that the girl is practising sexual intercourse, the girl will in self-justification and in an attempt to reassure the parent reveal that she is relying on contraceptive facilities provided by the doctor in order to avoid pregnancy. The girl and the doctor will be the losers by this revelation.

The third and main objection advanced on behalf of the respondent parent, Mrs Gillick, in this appeal, is that the secret provision of contraceptive facilities for a girl under 16 will, it is said, encourage participation by the girl in sexual intercourse and this practice offends basic principles of morality and religion which ought not to be sabotaged in stealth by kind permission of the National Health Service. The interests of a girl under 16 require her to be protected against sexual intercourse. Such a girl is not sufficiently mature to be allowed to decide to flout the accepted rules of society. The pornographic press and the lascivious film may falsely pretend that sexual intercourse is a form of entertainment available to females on request and to males on demand but the regular, frequent or casual practice of sexual intercourse by a girl or a boy under the age of 16 cannot be beneficial to anybody and may cause harm to character and personality. Before a girl under 16 is supplied with contraceptive facilities, the parent who knows most about the girl and ought to have the most influence with the girl is entitled to exercise parental rights of control, supervision, guidance and advice in order that the girl may, if possible, avoid sexual intercourse until she is older. Contraception should only be considered if and when the combined efforts of parent and doctor fail to prevent the girl from participating in sexual intercourse and there remains only the possibility of protecting the girl against pregnancy resulting from sexual intercourse.

These arguments have provoked great controversy which is not legal in character. Some doctors approve and some doctors disapprove of the idea that a doctor may decide to provide contraception for a girl under 16 without the knowledge of the parents. Some parents agree and some parents disagree with the proposition that the decision must depend on the judgment of the doctor. Those who favour doctor power assert that the failure to provide confidential contraceptive treatment will lead to an increase in pregnancies amongst girls under 16. As a general proposition, this assertion is not supported by evidence in this case, is not susceptible to proof and in my opinion is of doubtful validity. Availability of confidential contraceptive treatment may increase the demand for such treatment. Contraceptive treatment for females usually requires daily discipline in order to be effective and girls under 16 frequently lack that discipline. The total number of pregnancies amongst girls of under 16 may, therefore, be increased and not decreased by the availability of contraceptive treatment. But there is no doubt that an individual girl who is denied the opportunity of confidential contraceptive treatment may invite or succumb to sexual intercourse and thereby become pregnant. Those who favour parental power assert that the availability of confidential contraceptive treatment will increase sexual activity by girls under 16. This argument is also not supported by evidence in the present case and is not susceptible to proof. But it is clear that contraception removes or gives an illusion of removing the possibility of pregnancy and therefore removes restraint on sexual intercourse. Some girls would come under pressure if contraceptive facilities were known to be available and some girls under 16 are susceptible to male domination.

Parliament could decide whether it is better to have more contraception with the possibility of fewer pregnancies and less disease or whether it is better to have less contraception with the possibility of reduced sexual activity by girls under 16. Parliament could ensure that the doctor prevailed over the parent by reducing the age of consent or by expressly authorising a doctor to provide contraceptive facilities for any girl without informing the parent, provided the doctor considered that his actions were for the benefit of the girl. Parliament could, on the other hand, ensure that the parent prevailed over the doctor by forbidding contraceptive treatment for a girl under 16 save by or on the recommendation of the girl's general medical practitioner and with the consent of the parent who has registered the girl as a patient of that general practitioner. Some girls, it is said, might pretend to be over 16 but a doctor in doubt could always require confirmation from the girl's registered medical practitioner.

In sum, therefore, the House of Lords in *Gillick* has decided that a doctor need not fear the criminal law in the form of the crime of aiding and abetting an offence under s 6 of the Sexual Offences Act 1956 if he gives contraceptive advice or treatment to a young girl under the age of 16. This is clear from the judgment of Woolf J adopted by both Lords Fraser and Scarman (with whom Lord Bridge concurred).

Lord Brandon's dissenting speech is not, as you will have seen, exclusively concerned with the niceties of the criminal law but with larger questions of social policy. Lord Templeman is also concerned with the wider question of the relationship between the criminal law and public policy. Both Lord Brandon and Lord Templeman interpret social policy as requiring that contraception be treated separately by the law and not be made available to young persons.

The majority, however, saw public policy as pointing in the opposite direction.

Lord Fraser: Once the rule of the parents' absolute authority over minor children is abandoned, the solution to the problem in this appeal can no longer be found by referring to rigid parental rights at any particular age. The solution depends on a judgment of what is best for the welfare of the particular child. Nobody doubts, certainly I do not doubt, that in the overwhelming majority of cases the best judges of a child's welfare are his or her parents. Nor do I doubt that any important medical treatment of a child under 16 would normally only be carried out with the parents' approval. That is why it would and should be 'most unusual' for a doctor to advise a child without the knowledge and consent of the parents on contraceptive matters. But, as I have already pointed out, Mrs Gillick has to go further if she is to obtain the first declaration that she seeks. She has to justify the absolute right of veto in a parent. But there may be circumstances in which a doctor is a better judge of the medical advice and treatment which will conduce to a girl's welfare than her parents. It is notorious that children of both sexes are often reluctant to confide in their parents about sexual matters, and the DHSS guidance under consideration shows that to abandon the principle of confidentiality for contraceptive advice to girls under 16 might cause some of them not to seek professional advice at all, with the consequence of exposing them to 'the immediate risks of pregnancy and of sexually-transmitted diseases'. No doubt the risk could be avoided if the patient were to abstain from sexual intercourse, and one of the doctor's responsibilities will be to decide whether a particular patient can reasonably be expected to act on advice and abstain. We were told that in a significant number of cases such abstinence could not reasonably be expected. An example is *Re P (a minor)* (1981) 80 LGR 301, in which Butler-Sloss J ordered that a girl aged 15 who had been pregnant for the second time and who was in the care of a local authority should be fitted with a contraceptive appliance because, as the judge is reported to have said (at 312):

> I assume that it is impossible for this local authority to monitor her sexual activities, and, therefore, contraception appears to be the only alternative.

There may well be other cases where the doctor feels that because the girl is under the influence of her sexual partner or for some other reason there is no realistic prospect of her abstaining from intercourse. If that is right it points strongly to the desirability of the doctor being entitled in some cases, in the girl's best interests, to give her contraceptive advice and treatment if necessary without the consent or even the knowledge of her parents. The only practicable course is, in my opinion, to entrust the doctor with a discretion to act in accordance with his view of what is best in the interests of the girl who is his patient. He should, of course, always seek to persuade her to tell her parents that she is seeking contraceptive advice, and the nature of the advice that she receives. At least he should seek to persuade her to agree to the doctor's informing the parents. But there may well be cases, and I think there will be some cases, where the girl refuses either to tell the parents herself or to permit the doctor to do so and in such cases the doctor will, in my opinion, be justified in proceeding without the parents' consent or even knowledge provided he is satisfied on the following matters: (1) that the girl (although under 16 years of age) will understand his advice; (2) that he cannot persuade her to inform her parents or to allow him to inform the parents that she is seeking contraceptive advice; (3) that she is very likely to begin or to continue having sexual intercourse with or without contraceptive treatment; (4) that unless she receives contraceptive advice or treatment her physical or mental health or both are likely to suffer; (5) that her best interests require him to give her contraceptive advice, treatment or both without the parental consent.

That result ought not to be regarded as a licence for doctors to disregard the wishes of parents on this matter whenever they find it convenient to do so. Any doctor who behaves in such a way would, in my opinion, be failing to discharge his professional responsibilities, and I would expect him to be disciplined by his own professional body accordingly. The medical profession have in modern times come to be entrusted with very wide discretionary powers going beyond the strict limits of clinical judgment and, in my opinion, there is nothing strange about entrusting them with this further responsibility which they alone are in a position to discharge satisfactorily.

As is clear, speaking for the majority Lord Fraser sees public policy as concerned to protect young girls from the harmful consequences of engaging in sexual intercourse without contraception. Furthermore, Lord Fraser sees the true purpose of the criminal law as being to protect young girls since they are under the Sexual Offences Act 1956 'victims' of others' crimes. Why victimise them further by denying them contraception is a question implicit in both his speech and that of Lord Bridge. This is not to say that Lord Fraser contemplated that contraception should be made available to young girls without any legal constraint beyond the consent of the child. Conscious of the gravity of such decisions he is anxious to establish guiding criteria which condition the circumstances under which doctors may prescribe contraception. In effect, what Lord Fraser is doing is vesting in the doctor the authority to determine what it is in the girl's 'best interests' while defining in general terms the criteria which must inform the doctor's decision.

Lord Fraser's approach may be distinguished from that of Lord Scarman. For Lord Fraser the young girl's consent is a necessary but not sufficient condition for treating her. There must be a further enquiry conducted by the doctor as to whether it would be in her 'best interests' to treat her. This enquiry invites the doctor to go beyond concern for 'medical' or even 'health interests' to consider the wider social and moral factors. Lord Scarman, on the other hand, appears to regard consent alone as the key, always assuming, as we must, that the doctor is prepared on medical grounds to treat the patient. He does not invite the doctor to engage in any enquiry about wider interests. He does, however, insist that in determining whether the child *is* consenting the doctor must consider a range of factors far greater than those normally associated with the issue of capacity (see *supra*, ch 3). This is clearly Lord Scarman's attempt to recognise the special nature of contraceptive treatment by setting a higher threshold for capacity while at the same time ensuring that young girls are not completely denied access to treatment.

Lord Bridge pithily addresses the issue of public policy in agreeing with Lords Fraser and Scarman as follows:

Lord Bridge: On the issue of public policy, it seems to me that the policy consideration underlying the criminal sanction imposed by statute on men who have intercourse with girls under 16 is the protection of young girls from the untoward consequences of intercourse. Foremost among these must surely be the risk of pregnancy leading either to abortion or the birth of a child to an immature and irresponsible mother. In circumstances where it is apparent that the criminal sanction will not, or is unlikely to, afford the necessary protection it cannot, in my opinion, be contrary to public policy to prescribe contraception as the only effective means of avoiding a wholly undesirable pregnancy.

We should permit Professor Sir John Smith to have the last word. In his commentary ([1986] Crim LR 114) on *Gillick*, he proposes an alternative mechanism within the criminal law in order to give effect to the public policy conclusions reached by the majority.

The case decides no more than that such conduct [ie, contraceptive treatment] is sometimes lawful and it leaves open the possibility that the doctor will on other occasions be acting unlawfully and even criminally by aiding and abetting the offence under the Sexual Offences Act 1956, s.6. It is with this aspect of the case that this commentary is concerned.

Lord Brandon's dissenting speech is based mainly on his interpretation of the relevant principles of the criminal law. He drew from the Criminal Law Amendment Act 1885 and the Sexual Offences Act 1956 (which replaced it) the 'inescapable inference' that Parliament has for the past century regarded, and still regards, sexual intercourse by a man with a girl under 16 as a serious criminal offence by the man though not by the girl, even though she may have incited, aided, abetted, counselled and procured the man to do the act. Such intercourse is 'unlawful' and 'it follows necessarily that for any person to promote, encourage or facilitate the commission of any such act may itself be a criminal offence and must, in any event, be contrary to public policy'. The commission of the act is, of course, a criminal offence, so anyone who promotes, encourages or facilitates it would seem to be, prima facie, guilty of the crime as a secondary party. Lord Brandon's caution in saying that it *may be* a criminal offence is probably due to his regard for the fact that it would be necessary to prove *mens rea* in the case of any alleged abettor. In his Lordship's opinion the giving of contraceptive advice to the girl *necessarily* involves promoting, encouraging or facilitating the having of sexual intercourse by the girl with the man. For both parties, contraceptive advice to the girl largely removes the inhibition of the risk of an unwanted pregnancy and thus *necessarily* promotes, encourages or facilitates the sexual intercourse. Since these consequences, in Lord Brandon's opinion, necessarily follow, such advice is always unlawful – and this is so whether the parent concurs in it or not. If this reasoning is correct, the doctor giving the advice might find it hard to raise any doubt whether he was aware of consequences which would necessarily follow from his advice; and so would appear to be liable as a secondary party when these consequences did follow.

Lord Brandon was dissenting, but one of the majority, Lord Bridge, acknowledged the 'logical cogency' of this reasoning and it is indeed difficult to see any flaw in it. Yet the decision of the majority is that, sometimes at least, the doctor may prescribe contraception to the girl under 16 without committing an offence. According to Lord Fraser, he acts lawfully if he is satisfied:

(1) that the girl (although under 16 years of age) will understand his advice; (2) that he cannot persuade her to inform her parents or to allow him to inform the parents that she is seeking contraceptive advice; (3) that she is very likely to begin or to continue having sexual intercourse with or without contraceptive treatment; (4) that unless she receives contraceptive advice or treatment her physical or mental health or both are likely to suffer; (5) that her best interests require him to give her contraceptive advice, treatment or both without the parental consent.

The question now to be considered is how such considerations exclude the application of the doctrine of secondary liability. None of their Lordships gave detailed consideration to this question, Lord Scarman and Lord Bridge being content to adopt the relevant passage of the judgment of Woolf J. [1984] Q.B. 581, 593-595. In the light of this and the other observations of the House, why is the doctor who gives advice in accordance with the conditions stated not guilty of aiding and abetting?

1. Is it because he lacks the necessary intent? There is considerable support for this view in the judgment and speeches but it deserves closer examination. Woolf J recognised that a doctor who provided contraceptive advice to the girl or to the man 'with the intention thereby of encouraging them to have sexual intercourse' would be guilty of an offence; so he was of the opinion that the innocent doctor has no such intent. Unfortunately, as in other contexts, the meaning of 'intention' is obscure. Woolf J recognised that, where a person has such an intention, an 'unimpeachable motive' is not an answer, following Devlin J in *National Coal Board v Gamble* [1959] 1 Q.B. 11, 20 and Lord Simon's consideration of that judgment in *Lynch v DPP for Northern Ireland* [1975] AC 653, 698-699. Where all the conditions specified by Lord Fraser are satisfied, the doctor may well be aware that the provision of contraception will make it more likely that the girl will begin or continue having sexual intercourse – indeed, accepting Lord Brandon's realistic approach, he can hardly fail to be aware of it. If he knows that this will be the result, does he not intend it? Of course, it is not the result he desires, but Devlin J. in the passage cited by Woolf J expressly rules out any necessity to prove that the aider and abettor desires the proscribed result – 'If one man deliberately sells to another a gun to be used for murdering a third, he may be indifferent whether the third man lives or dies and interested only in the cash profit to be made out of the sale, but he can still be an aider and abettor.' It is true that Devlin J also said, 'I would agree that proof that the article was knowingly supplied is not conclusive evidence of intent to aid,' citing *Fretwell* (1862) 9 Cox C.C. 152 and *Steane* [1947] KB 997. These, however, were both cases which depended on the fact that the court required desire to produce a result in order to constitute the particular intent; and in *A-G v Able* [1984] 1 All ER 277, 287 (the

'Exit' case) Woolf J himself held that *Fretwell* was inconsistent with *National Coal Board v Gamble* and was to be 'confined to its own facts'. What is this further mental element called 'intent to aid' of which the defendant's knowledge, that the act he is doing will aid, is evidence, but not conclusive evidence? Hard thought by many students has produced nothing but the desire to aid – and that has been expressly ruled out. There is only one proper way to deal with a proposition to which no meaning can be given and that is to ignore it. It follows then, that a person who *knows that his acts will* aid or encourage an act by another *intends* to aid or encourage that act. If that is right, the doctor who is aware of the obvious fact that his advice will encourage the commission of the crime intends to encourage it and cannot be exempted from liability on the ground that he lacks the intent ordinarily required for an aider and abettor.

2. Having quoted *Gamble's* and *Lynch's* cases, Woolf J took account of three matters. (i) Contraception does not directly assist sexual intercourse, as the provision of a motor car may assist a burglary, or poison a murderer. (ii) The girl commits no offence so the doctor can be accessory to the man's offence only through the innocent agency of the girl. (iii) In some cases the doctor will know no more than that there is a risk of sexual intercourse taking place 'at an unidentified place with an unidentified man on an unidentified date'. With respect, however, it is by no means clear that the presence of any or all of these considerations will negative the principles of secondary liability. Consider the matter in the context of burglary. Suppose (i) D sends a message to E: 'If you must commit burglary (I hope you won't) I will be prepared to swear that you were elsewhere at the relevant time'; (ii) he sends this message by a nine year old child; and (iii) he has no idea where and when the contemplated burglary might take place. The encouragement is indirect, it is given through an innocent agent, and the time, place and victim are all unascertained. But if E is encouraged to commit a burglary (whether or not he would have committed that burglary without that encouragement) D would surely be liable to conviction as a secondary party.

3. Is the doctor not liable because the unlawful sexual intercourse will (or probably will) take place anyway, whether he prescribes contraceptives or not? Again it is submitted that in principle this is not an answer to the charge. In *A-G v Able* [1984] 1 All ER 277 Woolf J had to consider whether the publishers of a booklet containing advice on how to commit suicide were guilty of aiding and abetting suicide. He held that there had to be a connection between the suicide and the supply of the booklet to make the supplier responsible but added: 'This does not mean that the suicide or attempted suicide would not have occurred but for the booklet'; [1984] 1 All ER 287. A charge of procuring requires proof of causation but 'the same close causal connection is not required when what is being done is the provision of assistance'. *Cf. Calhaem* [1985] 2 All ER 266. One out of 20 spectators at an unlawful prize-fight who shouts encouragement to the contestants is clearly guilty of aiding and abetting, although it is perfectly clear that the fight would have begun and continued in exactly the same way if he had not been there. The doctor's case is no different in principle.

4. Is the answer that the doctor is not liable because the man may well not know that the girl has been supplied with contraceptive advice and so will not be encouraged thereby? Again, it is submitted that the answer is in the negative – at least if the commission of the offence has in fact been facilitated. If assistance is in fact given, it should not be necessary to prove that the principal offender knew it had been given. If P's butler, D, leaves P's door unlocked with the intention and effect of facilitating the entry of a burglar, E, it is submitted that D is guilty of aiding and abetting the burglary even though the assistance was given without the burglar's knowledge or consent. To take a closer analogy, D would surely be guilty of aiding and abetting an offence under section 6 if he gave a 15 year old girl an aphrodisiac or other drug with the intention and effect of causing her more readily to submit to sexual intercourse with E, even if E was quite unaware of D's conduct.

A concealed defence of necessity

The conclusion is that a doctor who satisfies all the conditions for accessory liability will yet not be liable to conviction in the limited circumstances by the majority of the House of Lords. Lord Scarman, like Lord Fraser (above), suggested specific restrictions on the doctor's right to prescribe:

> He may prescribe only if she has the capacity to consent or if exceptional circumstances exist which justify him in exercising his clinical judgment without parental consent. The adjective 'clinical' emphasises that it must be a medical judgment based on what he honestly believes to be necessary for the physical, mental and emotional health of his patient. The bona fide exercise by a doctor of his clinical judgment must be a complete negation of the guilty mind which is an essential

ingredient of the criminal offence of aiding and abetting the commission of unlawful sexual intercourse.

Where the conditions specified by Lords Fraser and Scarman are satisfied, it is clear that the doctor does not commit an offence. Yet he may be well aware that the provision of contraception will encourage both the girl and the man to have intercourse and that what is likely will become more likely. Their Lordships make no condition that he should not be so aware.

The assistance or encouragement given to the man may be exactly the same whether these conditions exist or not. So, if the doctor may be sometimes liable and sometimes not, the difference depends on his motive in prescribing contraception. Yet it is recognised that 'an unimpeachable motive' is generally no answer. The answer to this conundrum, it is suggested, is that we have here encountered a concealed defence of necessity. The doctor is acting lawfully if he is doing what he honestly believes to be necessary. All the normal conditions for liability as an aider and abettor may be satisfied; yet the doctor is to be excused. The commission of the offence may be, as Lord Brandon asserts it is, promoted, encouraged or facilitated; but the evil of the encouragement, etc, of the offence is outweighed by the good which flows from the provision of the advice.

The second dissenting judge, Lord Templeman, also seems, in effect, to have recognised a defence of necessity but of a more limited nature than that propounded by Lords Fraser and Scarman. The additional condition is that the parents must concur in giving the contraceptive advice.

Section 6 of the Sexual Offences Act 1956 does not, however, in my view, prevent parent and doctor from deciding that contraceptive facilities shall be made available to an unmarried girl under the age of 16 whose sexual activities are recognised to be uncontrolled and uncontrollable. Section 6 is designed to protect the girl from sexual intercourse. But if the girl cannot be deterred then contraceptive facilities may be provided, not for the purpose of aiding and abetting an offence under s.6 but for the purpose of avoiding the consequences, principally pregnancy, which the girl may suffer from illegal sexual intercourse where sexual intercourse cannot be prevented.

The American Model Penal Code propounds a general defence of necessity:

Conduct which the actor believes to be necessary to avoid a harm or evil to himself or to another is justifiable, provided that:
(a) the harm or evil sought to be avoided by such conduct is greater than that sought to be prevented by the law defining the offence charged.

Our law clearly does not recognise any such general defence but the courts, while reluctant to admit it, do from time to time allow the application of something very like it in exceptional circumstances. The most obvious example is *Bourne* [1939] 1 KB 687 where it was held that it was a defence to the statutory felony of procuring an abortion to show that the act was done in good faith for the purpose only of preserving the life of the mother although there was no provision for any such defence in any statute.

It is submitted that it would be better to recognise that the same has been done in the present case than to attempt to justify the result by straining the accepted principles of secondary liability, with possibly harmful results in later cases.

2. Contraception and the mentally ill or disabled

The other apparently special case apart from children involves contraceptive treatment for the mentally ill and disabled. In our view, this only raises the issue of capacity to consent and is not, as a matter of law, special in any other way. It may be otherwise, of course, if, for example, the pill or long-acting injectable contraception were actually being given for reasons of managing personal hygiene rather than contraception. This would raise questions as to the propriety of the action and whether it amounted to treatment. It cannot be treatment, of course, if it is done for the interests of others.

As the Panel of Persons appointed by the Licensing Authority to Hear the Application for a Product Licence to Market the Drug Depo-Provera as a long-term contraceptive stated in their Report (1983, paragraphs 5.4, 5.6):

There was considerable discussion before us on the issue of consent. We believe that the use of a drug that is long acting and with common and often unpleasant side effects is only acceptable if informed consent is obtained from the recipient. Some potential recipients would, of course, be able to understand and weigh the issues involved and give valid consent to treatment. A number of witnesses told us that these would include some of the mentally ill and mentally handicapped in institutional care, and the socially disadvantaged or socially maladapted in the community, provided that proper counselling was given to them. We believe, however, that for a number of reasons it will be difficult for many potential recipients to give informed consent. This is due to such factors as the lack of time available for explanation and counselling by medical and nursing staff, the lack of training and skills in such counselling among doctors not specialising in family planning, patients not being given information on which to make a decision, the inability of patients to understand and weigh the issues, whether through lack of intelligence, general inadequacy, mental handicap, psychiatric illness or through language difficulties, or because they are unable or unwilling to question or challenge the doctor's guidance.

It would only be in very exceptional circumstances that patients who were unable to give real consent would be given the drug. The type of situation that we have in mind is that mentioned by Dr Rona McClean in her written evidence, where the patient is mentally handicapped to such a degree that she cannot give consent to any type of medical treatment. In such circumstances the doctor concerned should apply the same criteria to treatment with Depo-Provera as would be applied when considering any form of medical treatment.

3. Contraception or contragestation?

One form of non-surgical contraception which poses special legal problems is that form known as post-coital birth control. This is more properly called contragestation rather than contraception. Section 58 of the Offences Against the Person Act 1861 provides:

> **58.** – Every woman, being with child, who, with intent to procure her own *miscarriage*, shall unlawfully administer to herself any poison or other noxious thing, or shall unlawfully use any instrument or other means whatsoever with the like intent and whosoever, with intent to procure the *miscarriage* of any woman, whether she be or not with child, shall unlawfully administer to her or cause to be taken by her any poison or other noxious thing, or shall unlawfully use any instrument or other means whatsoever with the like intent, shall be guilty of an offence and being convicted thereof shall be liable to imprisonment [our emphasis].

(Note also s 59 dealing with the 'supply' and procurement of poison and instruments 'with intent to procure a miscarriage'.) The Abortion Act 1967 (as amended) provides a defence to a charge under s 58 or 59 provided one of the grounds set out in s 1 is satisfied (see *infra*, ch 12).

Is a doctor who prescribes post-coital birth control, sometimes known as the 'morning after' pill, guilty of an offence under s 58 unless he complies with the terms of the 1967 Act? The central question is when, as a matter of law, can a person be said to act 'with intent to procure a miscarriage'? In turn this requires us to understand the meaning of the word 'miscarriage' in s 58 and 59. Needless to say, there is no definition offered in English law either in statute or in case law.

One view advanced is that a 'miscarriage' is procured whenever a fertilised egg is destroyed or expelled from the body whether or not it had been implanted in the uterus. If this view were correct, it would mean that any intervention after conception done with the intention of 'procuring a miscarriage' as so defined, would amount to an offence under the Offences Against the Person Act 1861. It may be interesting, however, to notice the authority and arguments on which this view is based.

John Keown 'Miscarriage: A Medico-Legal Analysis' [1984] Criminal Law Review 608

Judicial authority

In addition to the guidance afforded by the actual wording of the abortion provisions, the construction of 'miscarriage' has arisen in several reported cases. These cases, drawn from India, Victoria and the United States, are of persuasive value on account of the similarity between section 58 and the statutory provisions with which they deal. They point unanimously to an unrestricted construction of 'miscarriage'.

The leading Indian case on the question is *Ademma* [[1886] ILR IX Mad 369], decided by the Court of Appeal at Madras. The defendant was charged under section 312 of the Indian Penal Code 1860 with procuring her own miscarriage. The evidence showed that she had only been pregnant for about a month and that all that came away was a mass of blood. The Sessions Judge ruled that she had not been 'with child' within the meaning of the section. He observed: 'There was nothing which could be called even a rudimentary foetus or child' [*ibid* 370]. Accordingly, Ademma was acquitted. The Court of Appeal, however, consisting of Muttusami Ayyar and Brandt JJ, ordered a re-trial, holding that the offence could be committed from conception onward:

> The term 'miscarriage' is not defined in the Penal Code. In its popular sense it is synonymous with abortion, and consists in the expulsion of the embryo or foetus, ie the immature product of conception. The stage to which pregnancy has advanced and the form which the ovum or embryo may have assumed are immaterial [*ibid* 370].

The court continued:

> Section 312 requires proof that the woman is 'with child', but it is enough if the fact of pregnancy and the intended expulsion of the immature contents of the uterus are established. The words 'with child' mean pregnant, and it is not necessary to show that 'quickening', ie perception by the mother of the movements of the foetus, has taken place, or that the embryo has assumed a foetal form [*ibid*].

Although the defendant had been pregnant for one month and implantation had, therefore, already occurred somewhere, the broad basis of the court's decision affords sound authority for the legal irrelevance of implantation.

The meaning of 'miscarriage' was also considered by an Australian court in *Trim* [[1943] VLR 109]. There, the defendant was charged with the murder of one Edna Freeman. The Crown alleged that death had resulted from the defendant's use of a syringe with intent to procure Freeman's miscarriage, and secured a conviction for manslaughter. Trim appealed, contending *inter alia* that the judge had been guilty of a misdirection by ruling that the use of the syringe with intent to evacuate the uterus was an offence under section 62 of the Crimes Act 1928 (the section corresponding to section 58) even if the foetus was believed to be dead. By a majority, the Full Court of the Supreme Court of Victoria dismissed the appeal. Martin J delivered the majority judgment. He observed that, as section 62 did not require proof of pregnancy, 'one, and perhaps the chief, evil which the Legislature wished to prevent was the possibility of harm being done to the woman' [*ibid* at 115]. In construing 'miscarriage' broadly enough to prohibit the attempt to expel even a dead foetus, he remarked; 'In popular use the word "abortion" frequently is used as synonymous with "miscarriage", and the presence of the heading, "Attempts to procure abortion", to sections 62 and 63 suggests that the Legislature intended the word "miscarriage" in those sections to cover "abortion"' [*ibid*]. He continued: 'In *Webster's Dictionary* appears the following comprehensive definition of "Abortion": "Act of giving premature birth; specifically, the expulsion of the human fetus prematurely, particularly at any time before it is viable, or capable of sustaining life; miscarriage"' [*ibid*]. Martin J then adverted to the restricted definition of 'miscarriage' as abortion between the 'quickening' of the foetus – around the fourth month of pregnancy – and the point of its viability. However, he concluded that just as the word 'birth' in section 64 of the Crimes Act had been broadly interpreted to include even stillbirth, 'The word "miscarriage" should be given no restricted meaning in sections 61 and 62, as one reason for all three sections is the safeguarding of the health of a woman who is or may be with child' [*ibid* at 116]. In support of this unrestricted construction, Martin J cited the sixth edition of *Taylor's Principles and Practice of Medical Jurisprudence* [6th edn, 1910, (ed F Smith), Vol II, page 142], which declared in relation to section 58:

> the statute only uses the word 'miscarriage', including in that term comprehensively the emptying of a pregnant uterus at any time of conception, ignoring altogether the

technical terms abortion, miscarriage, premature confinement, which are merely convenient descriptive words for medical men.

By using such a popular term, it added, the law 'intends, thereby, to mean the contents of a gravid uterus, whether such contents be well or ill-formed, living or dead, moles or any other result of conception . . .' [*ibid* at 178]. Martin J did not regard this definition as authoritative in relation to section 62, but conceded:

it does convey the sense in which that word is there used, as, by reason of the heading in the material section, and the apparent purpose of the legislation, I consider it is wide enough to include abortion which, in the same work (vol II, p 141) is defined as 'an untimely emptying of a uterus which contains the products of a conception' [*supra* at 116].

A further source of judicial authority supporting an unrestricted interpretation of 'miscarriage' takes the form of a long and substantial line of case law from the United States, which establishes that 'miscarriage' and 'abortion' are legally synonymous and refer to the expulsion of the products of conception at any period of pregnancy. As early as 1850, the Supreme Court of Pennsylvania stated: 'Miscarriage, both in law and philology, means the bringing forth the foetus before it is perfectly formed and capable of living . . . The word abortion is synonymous and equivalent to miscarriage, in its primary meaning' [*Mills v Commonwealth* (1850) 13 Pa (1 Harris) 630 at 632]. The court's statement of the law has been consistently supported by the courts of other states. [See, eg, *Wells v New Eng Mutual Life Insurance Co of Boston, Mass* 43 A 126 (SC Penn) (1899); *People v Rankin* 74 P 2d 71 (1937) (SC *Calif*); *Hall v People* 201 P 2d 382 (1948) (SC Col); *Scott v State* 117 A 2d 831 (1955) (SC Del).]

Victor Tunkel in [1974] Criminal Law Review 461 seeks to provide a further basis for this position by relying on a sentence in Professor Williams's *Sanctity of Life and the Criminal Law*, published in 1958.

At present both English law and the law of the great majority of the United States regard any interference with the pregnancy, however early it may take place, as criminal, unless for therapeutic reasons. The foetus is a human life to be protected by the criminal law from the moment when the ovum is fertilised.

Relying on this, Tunkel argues (at p 465):

. . . [T]he use of the word 'miscarriage' has always been understood to include any fatal interference with the fertilised ovum: . . . To hold otherwise would, in effect, give a sort of free-for-all moratorium of a week or more after intercourse during which every sort of abortionist could ply his craft with impunity. The law may permit the douching of the vagina soon after intercourse, but that seems the limit of allowable post-coital prevention.

These arguments do not appear to be relevant to the discussion concerning the difference between pre-implantation and implantation. They appear to be more concerned with the difference between 'conception' and 'quickening', particularly in the light of the fact that the nineteenth-century authorities were unaware of the detail of the physiological processes involved between conception and birth, save in the most general terms. Furthermore, it should be added that Professor Williams, when he gave his mind to this particular point, wrote as follows (*Textbook of Criminal Law* (2nd edn, 1983) p 294):

Where exactly is the line drawn between contraception and abortion?
Formerly it was thought that the vital point of time was fertilisation, the fusion of spermatozoon and ovum, but it is now realised (although the point has not come before the courts) that this position is not maintainable, and that conception for legal purposes must be dated at earliest from implantation.
    The legislation is unspecific. The abortion section does not expressly refer to conception; it speaks merely of a 'miscarriage'. There is, therefore, nothing to prevent the courts interpreting the word 'miscarriage' in a way that takes account of customary and approved birth control practices.

As Professor Williams goes on to point out, to hold the view advanced by Keown *et al* carries the further consequence that the fitting of an intra-uterine device, sometimes known as the 'coil' (IUD) would also be governed by the Abortion Act and be unlawful. It cannot be doubted that a doctor who fits an IUD does so with knowledge that intercourse may take place and, in those circumstances, his intention will be to prevent the intercourse resulting in the implantation of a fertilised egg in the uterus. (There is also evidence that an IUD when fitted may prevent fertilisation, but clearly if done with this intention such a practice could never be unlawful under the 1861 Act. It is, however, questionable whether the two intentions could be separable.)

Surely Professor Williams is correct in writing (*op cit*, pp 294-5) that:

> . . . [N]o one who uses or fits IUDs supposes that they are illegal or are governed by the Abortion Act. The only way to uphold the legality of present medical practice, to make IUDs contraceptives and not abortifacients, is to say that for legal purposes conception is not complete until implantation.

He goes on to reach the same view concerning post-coital birth control by use of the 'morning after' pill when he concludes that 'the legal argument (concerning IUDs and "morning after" pills) is that the word "miscarriage" in s 58 means the miscarriage of an implanted blastocyst'.

The view reflected in Professor Williams's conclusion was the one accepted by the (then) Attorney-General in a written answer to the House of Commons in May 1983 (42 Parl Deb HC 238 at 239).

> The sole question for resolution therefore is whether the prevention of implantation constitutes the procuring of a miscarriage within the meaning of sections 58 to 59 of the Offences against the Person Act 1861. The principles relating to interpretation of statutes require that the words of a statute be given the meaning which they bore at the time the statute was passed. Further, since the words were used in a general statute, they are *prima facie* presumed to be used in their popular, ordinary or natural sense.
>
> In this context it is important to bear in mind that a failure to implant is something which may occur in the manner described above or quite spontaneously. Indeed in a significant proportion of cases the fertilised ovum is lost either prior to implantation or at the next menstruation. It is clear that, used in its ordinary sense, the word 'miscarriage' is not apt to describe a failure to implant – whether spontaneous or not. Likewise, the phrase 'procure a miscarriage' cannot be construed to include the prevention of implantation. Whatever the state of medical knowledge in the 19th century, the ordinary use of the word 'miscarriage' related to interference at a stage of pre-natal development later than implantation.
>
> In the light of the above I have come to the conclusion that this form of post-coital treatment does not constitute a criminal offence within either sections 58 or 59 of the Offences Against the Person Act 1861.

Besides removing doubts about the legality of fitting IUDs, this view of the 'morning after' pill also can be said to conform with a common-sense understanding of the word 'miscarriage'. To 'miscarry' clearly entails that something has been 'carried'. It would be unusual to say that a woman is carrying anything when all that has transpired is that an egg has been fertilised and is travelling through her body. It would accord with common sense and be quite natural to describe her as carrying something once a fertilised egg is implanted in her uterus. Indeed, the Human Fertilisation and Embryology Act 1990 takes such a view in s 2(3) that '[F]or the purposes of the Act, a woman is not to be treated as carrying a child until the embryo has become implanted.'

It follows, therefore, on this interpretation that the 'morning after' pill may be prescribed up to the point at which medical evidence establishes that implantation is likely to occur, which seems to be anywhere between five and ten days after intercourse has taken place.

An example of this common-sense view being adopted by legislation can be found in the 1977 amendment to the Crimes Act 1961 of New Zealand. Section 182A provides:

> **182A.** For the purposes of sections 183 to 187 of this Act the term 'miscarriage' means -
> (a) The destruction or death of an embryo or fetus after implantation; or
> (b) The premature expulsion or removal of an embryo or fetus after implantation, otherwise than for the purpose of inducing the birth of a fetus believed to be viable or removing a fetus that has died.

B. PRODUCTS LIABILITY AND CONTRACEPTION

The area of products liability is large and specialised. (The reader is referred to Miller and Lovell *Products Liability and Safety Encyclopedia* (1979); Dias and Markesinis *Tort Law* (2nd edn) ch 6; Fleming *The Law of Torts* (8th edn (1992) ch 23.) We discuss it here, albeit briefly, since as far as patients are concerned it is of considerable importance. It provides the basis on which patients may recover compensation for injury suffered as a consequence of defective drugs. Products liability, of course, is not limited to contraceptive drugs (as will be seen from some of the cases) but this context serves as a convenient occasion to sketch out the framework of the law.

1. The common law

Under the English common law any allegation that an English contraceptive drug or appliance was defective would sound in negligence. There are three ways in which a contraceptive drug or appliance could be defective, namely: (i) that it was carelessly manufactured so as to expose the user to an unreasonable risk of harm; (ii) that it was badly designed so as to expose the user to an unreasonable risk of harm; (iii) and that it was unaccompanied by appropriate warnings or directions so as to make it not reasonably safe for the user.

(a) Manufacture

There would appear to be no special problems of law relating to contraceptives. They are treated as any other product in that liability depends upon proof that the manufacturer has failed to exercise reasonable care and skill. He must take reasonable steps to ensure that his manufacturing process is such that the product would meet the appropriate standard of safety, quality and efficacy.

In the case of contraceptives, it is likely that the law also requires the manufacturer to demonstrate that he has taken all reasonable steps to establish an adequate system of post-market surveillance and recall (by, for example recording batch numbers and being able to locate to whom batches were supplied).

(b) Design

Similarly, contraceptives are regarded in law in the same way as other products as regards the reasonableness of their design. Manufacturers, as a consequence, will be expected to have carried out all reasonable research, eg on animals and through clinical trials, and to have taken account of all scientific knowledge available through reasonable endeavour at the time of deciding upon their design. This entails keeping abreast of what is often called the 'state of the art' (see *infra* under the Consumer Protection Act 1987). It follows that what was said in (i) above about recall and surveillance applies here.

(c) Warnings and directions

A product may be adequately manufactured and designed but still be defective if, in the circumstances, a court would decide that it should be accompanied by appropriate warnings and directions for use.

(i) WARNINGS

The common law is as stated by the Ontario Court of Appeal in the following case:

Buchan v Ortho Pharmaceuticals (Canada) Ltd (1986) 54 OR (2d) 92

Robins JA: As a matter of common law, it is well settled that a manufacturer of a product has a duty to warn consumers of dangers inherent in the use of its product of which it knows or has reason to know . . .

In determining whether a drug manufacturer's warnings satisfy the duty to make adequate and timely warning to the medical profession of any dangerous side-effects produced by its drug of which it knows, or has reason to know, certain factors must be borne in mind. A manufacturer of prescription drugs occupies the position of an expert in the field; this requires that it be under a continuing duty to keep abreast of scientific developments pertaining to its product through research, adverse reaction reports, scientific literature and other available methods. When additional dangerous or potentially dangerous side-effects from the drug's use are discovered, the manufacturer must make all reasonable efforts to communicate the information to prescribing physicians. Unless doctors have current, accurate and complete information about a drug's risks, their ability to exercise the fully informed medical judgment necessary for the proper performance of their vital role in prescribing drugs for patients may be reduced or impaired.

Whether a particular warning is adequate will depend on what is reasonable in the circumstances. But the fact that a drug is ordinarily safe and effective and the danger may be rare or involve only a small percentage or users does not necessarily relieve the manufacturer of the duty to warn. While a low probability of injury or a small class of endangered users are factors to be taken into account in determining what is reasonable, these factors must be balanced against such considerations as the nature of the drug, the necessity for taking it, and the magnitude of the increased danger to the individual consumer. Similarly, where medical evidence exists which tends to show a serious danger inherent in the use of a drug, the manufacturer is not entitled to ignore or discount that information in its warning solely because it finds it to be unconvincing; the manufacturer is obliged to be forthright and to tell the whole story. The extent of the warning and the steps to be taken to bring the warning home to physicians should be commensurate with the potential danger – the graver the danger, the higher the duty.

A reading of Ortho US's warning to physicians makes it manifest that Ortho was aware or should have been aware of the association between oral contraceptive use and stroke. Moreover, the expert testimony and the exhibits in this case disclose an abundance of published information in medical and scientific journals prior to and at the time the plaintiff was prescribed Ortho-Novum which linked the use of oral contraceptives with stroke. Ortho US provided American physicians with data from and the conclusions of the studies in Britain and the United States, and warned of the risk of cerebral damage posed by the pill. Yet, in Canada, Ortho chose not to provide physicians with any similar warning. Why the medical profession in this country, and, through it, consumers in this country, should be given a less explicit and meaningful warning by the Canadian manufacturer of the same drug is a question that has not been answered. Be that as it may, I think it evident that Ortho failed to give the medical profession warnings commensurate with its knowledge of the dangers inherent in the use of Ortho-Novum; more specifically, it breached its duty to warn of the risk of stroke associated with the use of Ortho-Novum.

Earlier he had said:

> The guiding principle of liability underlying the present law of products liability in this country was formulated by Lord Atkin in his classic statement in *M'Alister (or Donoghue) v Stevenson* [1932] AC 562 at 599, HL:
>
> > . . . a manufacturer of products, which he sells in such a form as to show that he intends them to reach the ultimate consumer in the form which they left him with no reasonable possibility of intermediate examination, and with the knowledge that the absence of reasonable care in the preparation or putting up of the products will result in an injury to the consumer's life or property, owes a duty to the consumer to take that reasonable care.
>
> This statement has been the source of subsequent developments in products liability law based on negligence. The *rationale* is that one who brings himself into a relation with others through an activity which foreseeably exposes them to danger if proper care is not observed must exercise reasonable care to safeguard them from that danger. It can now be taken as a legal truism that the duty of reasonable care which lies at the foundation of the law of negligence commonly comprehends a duty to warn of danger, the breach of which will, when it is the cause of injury, give rise to liability: see, generally, Fleming, *The Law of Torts*, 6th edn (1983), at p 459 ff, and Linden *Canadian Tort Law*, 3rd edn (1982), at p 563 ff.
>
> Once a duty to warn is recognised, it is manifest that the warning must be adequate. It should be communicated clearly and understandably in a manner calculated to inform the user of the nature of the risk and the extent of the danger; it should be in terms commensurate with the gravity of the potential hazard, and it should not be neutralised or negated by collateral efforts on the part of the manufacturer. The nature and extent of any given warning will depend on what is reasonable having regard to all the facts and circumstances relevant to the product in question.
>
> The general principle to be applied in determining the degree of explicitness required in a warning was enunciated by the Supreme Court of Canada, speaking through Laskin J, in *Lambert v Lastoplex Chemicals Co Ltd* [1972] SCR 569 at 574-5, 25 DLR (3d) 121 at 125, as follows:
>
> > Where manufactured products are put on the market for ultimate purchase and use by the general public and carry danger (in this case, by reason of high inflammability), although put to the use for which they are intended, *the manufacturer, knowing of their hazardous nature, has a duty to specify the attendant dangers, which it must be taken to appreciate in a detail not known to the ordinary consumer or user.* A general warning, as for example, that the product is inflammable, will not suffice where the likelihood of fire may be increased according to the surroundings in which it may reasonably be expected that the product will be used. *The required explicitness of the warning will, of course, vary with the danger likely to be encountered in the ordinary use of the product.* (Emphasis added.)
>
> The duty is a continuous one requiring that the manufacturer warn, not only of dangers known at the time of sale, but also of dangers discovered after the product has been sold and delivered. In the words of Ritchie J., speaking for the majority of the Supreme Court of Canada in *Rivtow Marine Ltd v Washington Iron Works* [1974] SCR 1189 at 1200, 40 DLR (3d) 530 at 536, [1973] 6 WWR 692:
>
> > . . . the knowledge of the danger involved in the continued use of these cranes for the purpose for which they were designed carried with it a duty to warn those to whom the cranes had been supplied, and this duty arose at the moment when the respondents or either of them became seized with the knowledge.
>
> Ordinarily, the warnings must be addressed directly to the person likely to be injured. It is not, however, necessary that that be done in every case. Where, for example, the product is a highly technical one that is intended or expected to be used only under the supervision of experts, a warning to the experts will suffice; *Murphy v St Catharines General Hospital* [1964] 1 OR 239, 41 DLR (2d) (HCJ). Similarly, a warning to the ultimate user may not be necessary where intermediate examination is anticipated or the intervention of a learned intermediary is understood. As the English Court of Appeal pointed out in *Homes v Ashford* [1950] 2 All ER 76 at 80:

In the present case . . . it must have been in the contemplation of the manufacturers supplying these goods to hairdressers that hairdressers may be expected to interpose their judgment and reason whether they are going to use a hair dye or not. In my view, if they give a warning which, if read by a hairdresser, is sufficient to intimate to him the potential dangers of the substance with which he is going to deal, that is all that can be expected of them. I think it would be unreasonable and impossible to expect that they should give warning in such form that it must come to the knowledge of the particular customer who is going to be treated. Counsel for the plaintiff says they must take reasonable steps to see that it will come to the notice of any customer. I cannot contemplate any steps which could be calculated to bring a matter of this kind to the knowledge of any person who is treated with the preparation. The most that can be expected of the manufacturer of goods of this kind is to see that the hairdresser is sufficiently warned.

There are surprisingly few reported decisions in Canada or in the United Kingdom involving a drug manufacturer's duty to warn with respect to either over-the-counter or prescription drugs. On the other hand there is a considerable body of case-law in the United States in which the subject is exhaustively and authoritatively discussed. Counsel, in their very thorough presentation, made reference to many of these decisions in support of their respective positions. In my view, they are pertinent to the issues in this appeal and instructive. American jurisprudence dealing with products liability based on negligence, it may be remembered, is rooted in the same fundamental philosophy and is based on the same general principles of negligence as our law since *M'Alister (or Donoghue) v Stevenson*: see *Prosser and Keeton on Torts*, 5th edn (1984), at p 677 ff. I might add that the plaintiff as an alternative ground for relief, sought recovery on a theory of strict liability. However, on the view I take of the case, I consider it unnecessary to discuss the imposition of liability on that basis.

In the present state of human knowledge, many drugs are clearly incapable of being made totally safe for their intended or ordinary use even though they have been properly manufactured and are not impure or defective. Notwithstanding a medically recognisable risk, their marketing may be justified by their utility. Apart from any regulatory scheme under the *Food and Drugs Act*, the general rule at common law is that the manufacturer of such drugs, like the manufacturer of other products, has a duty to provide consumers with adequate warning of the potentially harmful side-effects that the manufacturer knows or has reason to know may be produced by the drug. There is, however, an important exception to that general rule. In the case of prescription drugs, the duty of manufacturers to warn consumers is discharged if the manufacturer provides prescribing physicians, rather than consumers, with adequate warning of the potential danger.

This exception, which has come to be known in the United States as the 'learned intermediary' rule, adopts an approach similar to that taken in cases involving intermediate inspection or intervening cause under the rule in *M'Alister (or Donoghue) v Stevenson*. The *rationale* for the exception is that prescription drugs are more likely to be complex medicines, esoteric in formula and varied in effect and, by definition, are available only by prescription. The prescribing physician is in a position to take into account the propensities of the drug and the susceptibilities of his patient. He has the duty of informing himself of the benefits and potential dangers of any medication he prescribes, and of exercising his independent judgment as a medical expert based on his knowledge of the patient and the product. In taking the drug, the patient is expected to, and it can be presumed does, place primary reliance on his doctor's judgment. In this relationship, the prescribing physician is said to act as a learned intermediary between the manufacturer and the ultimate consumer. Thus, while the general rule is that manufacturers of drugs have a duty to warn users of known dangers in the use of their products, manufacturers of prescription drugs, because of the intervention of the learned intermediary, have a duty to warn only prescribing physicians; *Reyes v Wyeth Laboratories* 498 F 2d 1264 (1974); *cert den* 419 US 1096; *Terhune v A H Robins Co* 577 P 2d 975 (1978) (Wash); *Sterling Drug Inc v Cornish* 370 F 2d 82 (1966); *McEwen v Ortho Pharmaceutical Corpn* 528 P 2d 522 (1974) (Or).

There are no decisions dealing specifically with oral contraceptives in this country or in England. In most of the jurisdictions in the United States in which the question has been considered, the learned intermediary rule has been adhered to, and manufacturers of oral contraceptives have accordingly been held under a duty to warn only prescribing physicians of the risks associated with their product. Very recently, however, several state courts have concluded that oral contraceptives bear characteristics which render them vastly different from other prescription drugs and which demand that manufacturers be required to warn users directly of risks associated with their use. The reasoning which prompted these courts to hold the learned intermediary rule inapplicable to birth control pills is clearly articulated in the decision of the Supreme Judicial Court of Massachusetts in *MacDonald v Ortho Pharmaceutical Corpn* 475 NE 2d 65 (1985) (Mass); *cert den* 106 S Ct 250.

In that case, which, like this one, involved a stroke found to have been caused by the ingestion of Ortho-Novum, the majority (4:1) of the court, *per* Abrams J, said at 70:

> The oral contraceptive thus stands apart from other prescription drugs in light of the heightened participation of patients in decisions relating to use of 'the pill'; the substantial risks associated with the product's use; the feasibility of direct warnings by the manufacturers to the user; the limited participation of the physician (annual prescriptions); and the possibility that oral communications between physicians and consumers may be insufficient or too scanty standing alone fully to apprise consumers of the product's dangers at the time the initial selection of a contraceptive method is made as well as at subsequent points when alternative methods may be considered. *We conclude that the manufacturer of oral contraceptives is not justified in relying on warnings to the medical profession to satisfy its common law duty to warn, and that the manufacturer's obligation encompasses a duty to warn the ultimate user.* Thus, the manufacturer's duty is to provide to the consumer written warnings conveying reasonable notice of the nature, gravity, and likelihood of known or knowable side effects, and advising the consumer to seek fuller explanation from the prescribing physician or other doctor of any such information of concern to the consumer. [Emphasis added.]

See also: *Re Certified Questions* 358 NW 2d 873 (Mich) (1984); *Odgers v Ortho Pharmaceutical Corpn* 609 F Supp 867 (Mich)(1985); *Stephens v G D Searle & Co* 602 F Supp 379 (Mich)(1985); *Lukaszewicz v Ortho Pharmaceutical Corpn* 510 F Supp 961 (Wis)(1981).

Later Robins JA said:

> I think it axiomatic that a drug manufacturer who seeks to rely on the intervention of prescribing physicians under the learned intermediary doctrine to except itself from the general common law duty to warn consumers directly must actually warn prescribing physicians. The duty, in my opinion, is one that cannot be delegated. I shall consider the warning as it relates specifically to the plaintiff's physician later, but as a general proposition, a manufacturer cannot justify a failure to warn by claiming that physicians were in a position to learn of the risks inherent in its products through other sources. The manufacturer's duty to warn continues notwithstanding that the information may be otherwise available. In this regard, I respectfully agree with the apt observation of Linden J in *Davidson v Connaught Laboratories* (1980) 14 CCLT 251 (Ont HCJ) at 276:
>
> > A drug company cannot rely upon doctors to read all the scientific literature outlining the specific dangers involved in the many drugs they have to administer each day. They are busy people, administering to the needs of the injured and the sick. They have little time for deep research into the medical literature. They rely on the drug companies to supply them with the necessary data. With very little effort the defendant company could have included in the material that it gave to the doctors, who were administering the injections, all the necessary facts. They did not. Even though these severe reactions were 'extremely rare', I think it would have been advisable for the company to have presented the figures that were available, or at least to have referred the doctors to publications where those figures could be learned. Once they have the figures, then the doctors can properly assess the situation and decide whether they will recommend the vaccine or not, and how much information about the risks they should give to their patients. The doctors, however, should have as full information as is reasonable in the circumstances.
>
> See also *Mahr v G D Searle & Co* 390 NE 2d 1214 (1979) (Ill); *Brochu v Ortho Pharmaceutical Corpn* 642 F 2d 652 (1981). . . .

Before leaving this case, I would return to the question of whether a manufacturer of oral contraceptives is under a duty at common law to warn consumers directly. In doing so, I am not unmindful of the fact that anything I may say at this stage is not necessary to my decision. In deference, however, to the thorough arguments presented on the issue, I make these brief comments.

I do not quarrel with the general proposition advanced by the defendant that where prescription drugs are concerned, the manufacturer's duty to warn is limited to an obligation to warn prescribing physicians of potential dangers that may result from the drug's use. This special standard represents an understandable and sensible exception to the well-recognised common law principle of tort liability that the manufacturer of a product has a duty to warn users of dangers inherent in the use of the product. The question here comes down to whether the *rationale* which is relied on to support this exception with respect to prescription drugs generally can be justified in the case of oral contraceptives.

There can be little doubt that oral contraceptives have presented society with problems unique in the history of human therapeutics. At no time have so many people taken such potent drugs voluntarily over such a protracted time for an objective other than the control of disease. This has introduced a novel element in the doctor-patient relationship. As the advisory committee pointed out, 'in prescribing these drugs, the doctor is usually acting neither to treat nor to prevent a disease. He is prescribing for socioeconomic reasons.' Furthermore, unlike the selection of an appropriate drug for the treatment of illness or injury where patient involvement is typically minimal or non-existent, consumer demand for oral contraceptives prompts their use more often than doctors' advice. The decision to use the pill is one in which consumers are actively involved; more frequently than not, they have made the decision before visiting a doctor to obtain a prescription.

For these reasons, as well as those stated in *MacDonald v Ortho Pharmaceutical Corpn* 475 NE 2d 65 (1985), which I quoted earlier, I am of the view that oral contraceptives bear characteristics distinguishing them from most therapeutic, diagnostic and curative prescription drugs. The *rationale* underlying the learned intermediary rule, in my opinion, does not hold up in the case of oral contraceptives. Manufacturers of this drug should be obliged to satisfy the general common law duty to warn the ultimate consumer as well as prescribing physicians. To require this would not be to impose any real burden on drug manufacturers or to unduly interfere with the doctor-patient relationship as it exists with regard to the prescription of this drug. What is more, appropriate warnings conveying reasonable notice of the nature, gravity and likelihood of known or knowable side-effects and advising the consumer to seek further explanation from her doctor of any information of concern to her, would promote the desired objective of ensuring that women are fully apprised of the information needed to balance the benefits and risks of this form of birth control and to make informed and intelligent decisions in consultation with their doctors on whether to use or continue to use oral contraceptives.

(ii) DIRECTIONS

It is often overlooked that in addition to a duty to warn, a manufacturer may also be under a duty to give adequate directions on how properly to use a product. This is particularly important in the case of contraceptives (eg frequency, dosage etc). Furthermore, that which has been said about the 'learned intermediary' in the context of warnings, applies equally in the case of directions.

Thus, in conclusion, to be reasonably safe, a contraceptive drug or appliance must be competently manufactured and designed and accompanied by such warnings and directions so as to make foreseeable users reasonably safe. As Fleming points out in his book, *The Law of Torts* (8th edn), at p 49:

A warning would not be sufficient unless it is given to a competent person and is adequate to acquaint him fully with the dangerous properties of the substance so that he can himself adopt suitable precautions to prevent it from becoming a source of injury to himself and others.

2. Consumer Protection Act 1987

The 1987 Act imposes strict liability upon a producer (as defined) of a contraceptive drug or appliance if it is defective (as defined). Section 3(1) states:

3. (1) Subject to the following provisions of this section, there is a defect in a product for the purposes of this Part if the safety of the product is not such as persons generally are entitled to expect; and for those purposes 'safety', in relation to a product, shall include safety with respect to products comprised in that product and safety in the context of risks of damage to property, as well as in the context of risks of death or personal injury.

This is elaborated in s 3(2):

3. (2) In determining for the purposes of subsection (1) above what persons generally are entitled to expect in relation to a product all the circumstances shall be taken into account, including –

(a)   the manner in which, and purposes for which, the product has been marketed, its get-up, the use of any mark in relation to the product and any instructions for, or warnings with respect to, doing or refraining from doing anything with or in relation to the product;

(b)   what might reasonably be expected to be done with or in relation to the product; and

(c)   the time when the product was supplied by its producer to another;

and nothing in this section shall require a defect to be inferred from the fact alone that the safety of a product which is supplied after that time is greater than the safety of the product in question.

Following the pattern previously adopted, the product can be said to be defective in respect of its manufacture or design, or because it is not safe having regard to any instructions or warnings (or the absence thereof). To what extent, if at all, can it be said that the Act introduces a form of liability other than negligence as regards contraceptive and other drugs? It is important to notice that in many pharmaceutical products cases the manufacturers' defence is that they did not know nor ought they to have known of the danger posed by their product. This, it is clear, is a *fault*-based argument.

The question is what place does such an argument have in products liability law. We have seen s 3 and should now notice s 4(1)(e). It provides that:

4. (1) In any civil proceedings by virtue of this Part against any person ('the person proceeded against') in respect of a defect in a product it shall be a defence for him to show – . . .

(e)   that the state of scientific and technical knowledge at the relevant time was not such that a producer of products of the same description as the product in question might be expected to have discovered the defect if it had existed in his products while they were under his control . . .

Sections 3 and 4(1)(e) are the key provisions as regards products liability in the context of pharmaceutical products. Currently, there are no English cases which consider their application. It is clear, however, that s 4(1)(e) introduces a fault-based approach where the manufacturer claims not to have known of the risk that eventually injures the patient. This would provide the manufacturer with a defence where the dangerous design of the product or a failure to warn was the issue (see generally, C Newdick 'The Development Risk Defence of the Consumer Protection Act 1987' [1988] CLJ 455). While this may be a questionable position in product liability generally, it has, as the following American case shows, proved attractive to courts in pharmaceutical product cases in the United States.

Brown v Superior Court (Abbott Laboratories) **(1988) 751 P 2d 470 (Cal Sup Ct)**

Mosk J: In current litigation several significant issues have arisen relating to the liability of manufacturers of prescription drugs for injuries caused by their products. Our first and broadest inquiry is whether such a manufacturer may be held strictly liable for a product that is defective in design . . .

I. Strict Liability in General
A. STRICT LIABILITY IN GENERAL

The doctrine of strict liability had its genesis in a concurring opinion by Justice Roger Traynor in *Escola v Coca Cola Bottling Co* (1944) 24 Cal 2d 453, 461, 150 P 2d 436. He suggested that a manufacturer should be absolutely liable if, in placing a product on the market, it knew the product was to be used without inspection, and it proved to have a defect that caused injury. The policy considerations underlying this suggestion were that the manufacturer, unlike the public, can anticipate or guard against the recurrence of hazards, that the cost of injury may be an overwhelming misfortune to the person injured whereas the manufacturer can insure against the risk and distribute the cost among the consuming public, and that it is in the public interest to discourage the marketing of defective products. This court unanimously adopted Justice Traynor's concept in *Greenman v Yuba Power Products, Inc* (1963) 59 Cal 2d 57, 62, holding a manufacturer strictly liable in tort and using the formulation of the doctrine set forth in *Escola*.

Strict liability differs from negligence in that it eliminates the necessity for the injured party to prove that the manufacturer of the product which caused injury was negligent. It focuses not on the conduct of the manufacturer but on the product itself, and holds the manufacturer liable if the product was defective . . .

This court refined and explained the application of the principle in *Cronin v JBE Olson Corpn* (1972) 8 Cal 3d 121, and *Barker v Lull Engineering Co* (1978), 20 Cal 3d 413 (hereinafter *Barker*). In *Cronin*, we rejected the requirement of section 402A that the defect in a product must be 'unreasonably dangerous' to the consumer in order to invoke strict liability, holding that the requirement 'rings of negligence' (8 Cal 3d at p 132) and that the showing of a defect which proximately caused injury is sufficient to justify application of the doctrine.

Barker defined the term 'design defect' in the context of strict liability. In that case the plaintiff was injured while operating a piece of heavy construction equipment, and claimed that a safety device called an 'outrigger' would have prevented the accident. We held that the defendant could be held liable for a defect in design.

Barker identified three types of product defects. (20 Cal 3d at p 428.) First, there may be a flaw in the manufacturing process, resulting in a product that differs from the manufacturer's intended result. The archetypal example of such a defect was involved in *Escola*, supra, 24 Cal 2d 453, where a Coca Cola bottle exploded. Such a manufacturing defect did not exist in the heavy equipment that caused the injury in *Barker*, and is not alleged in the present case.

Second, there are products which are 'perfectly' manufactured but are unsafe because of the absence of a safety device, ie, a defect in design. This was the defect alleged in *Barker*. It held that a product is defectively designed if it failed to perform as safely as an ordinary consumer would expect when used as intended or in a manner reasonably foreseeable, or if, on balance, the risk of danger inherent in the challenged design outweighs the benefits of the design. (20 Cal 3d at p 430.) Plaintiff asserts this test should be applied in the present case because DES contained a design defect.

The third type of defect identified in *Barker* is a product that is dangerous because it lacks adequate warnings or instructions. According to plaintiff, defendants here failed to warn of the dangers inherent in the use of DES. We are concerned, therefore, with the second and third types of defects described in *Barker*.

B. STRICT LIABILITY AND PRESCRIPTION DRUGS

Even before *Greenman* was decided, the members of the American Law Institute, in considering whether to adopt a rule of strict liability, pondered whether the manufacturer of a prescription drug should be subject to the doctrine. (38 ALI Proc 19, 90-92, 98 (1961).) During a rather confusing discussion of a draft of what was to become section 402A, a member of the Institute proposed that drugs should be exempted from strict liability on the ground that it would be 'against the public interest' to apply the doctrine to such products because of 'the very serious tendency to stifle medical research and testing.' Dean Prosser, who was the reporter for the Restatement Second of Torts, responded that the problem was a real one, and that he had it in mind in drafting section 402A. A motion to exempt prescription drugs from the section was defeated on the suggestion of Dean Prosser that the problem could be dealt with in the comments to the section. However, a motion to state the exemption in a comment was also defeated. (39 ALI Proc 19, 90-98, supra.) At the next meeting of the institute in 1962, section 402A was approved together with comment *k* thereto. (41 ALI Proc 227, 244 (1962).)

The comment provides that the producer of a properly manufactured prescription drug may be held liable for injuries caused by the product only if it was not accompanied by a warning of dangers that the manufacturer knew or should have known about . . .

Comment *k* has been analyzed and criticized by numerous commentators. While there is some disagreement as to its scope and meaning, there is a general consensus that, although it purports to explain the strict liability doctrine, in fact the principle it states is based on negligence. (Eg, Schwartz, Unavoidably Unsafe Products (1985) 42 Wash & Lee L Rev 1139, 1141; McClellan, Drug Induced Injury (1978) 25 Wayne L Rev 1,2.) That is, comment *k* would impose liability on a drug manufacturer only if it failed to warn of a defect of which it either knew or should have known. This concept focuses not on a deficiency in the product – the hallmark of strict liability – but on the fault of the producer in failing to warn of the dangers inherent in the use of its product that were either known or knowable – an idea which 'rings of negligence,' in the words of *Cronin*, supra, 8 Cal 3d 121, 132.

Comment *k* has been adopted in the overwhelming majority of jurisdictions that have considered the matter . . . [citations omitted].

We are aware of only one decision that has applied the doctrine of strict liability to prescription drugs. (*Brochu v Ortho Pharmaceutical Corpn* (1st Circ 1981) 642 F 2d 652, 654-657.) Most cases have embraced the rule of comment *k* without detailed analysis of its language. A few, notably *Kearl v Lederle Laboratories* (1985) 172 Cal App 3d 812 (hereinafter *Kearl*), have conditioned application of the exemption stated therein on a finding that the drug involved is in fact 'unavoidably dangerous,' reasoning that the comment was intended to exempt only such drugs from strict liability . . .

We appear, then, to have three distinct choices:

(1)   to hold that the manufacturer of a prescription drug is strictly liable for a defect in its product because it was defectively designed, as that term is defined in *Barker*, or because of a failure to warn of its dangerous propensities even though such dangers were neither known nor scientifically knowable at the time of distribution;

(2)   to determine that liability attaches only if a manufacturer fails to warn of dangerous propensities of which it was or should have been aware, in conformity with comment *k*; or

(3)   to decide, like *Kearl and Toner v Lederle Laboratories* . . . 732 P 2d 297, 303-309, that strict liability for design defects should apply to prescription drugs unless the particular drug which caused the injury is found to be 'unavoidably dangerous'.

We shall conclude that

(1)   a drug manufacturer's liability for a defectively designed drug should not be measured by the standards of strict liability;

(2)   because of the public interest in the development, availability, and reasonable price of drugs, the appropriate test for determining responsibility is the test stated in comment *k*; and

(3)   for these same reasons of policy, we disapprove of the holding of *Kearl* that only those prescription drugs found to be 'unavoidably dangerous' should be measured by the comment *k* standard and that strict liability should apply to drugs that do not meet the description.

1. Design defect

Barker, as we have seen, set forth two alternative tests to measure a design defect: first, whether the product performed as safely as the ordinary consumer would expect when used in an intended and reasonably foreseeable manner, and second, whether, on balance, the benefits of the challenged design outweighed the risk of danger inherent in the design. In making the latter determination, the jury may consider these factors: 'the gravity of the danger posed by the challenged design, the likelihood that such danger would occur, the mechanical feasibility of a safer alternative design, the financial cost of an improved design, and the adverse consequences to the product and to the consumer that would result from an alternative design.' (20 Cal 3d at p 431.)

Defendants assert that neither of these tests is applicable to a prescription drug like DES. As to the 'consumer expectation' standard, they claim, the 'consumer' is not the plaintiff but the physician who prescribes the drug, and it is to him that the manufacturer's warnings are directed. A physician appreciates the fact that all prescription drugs involve inherent risks, known and unknown, and he does not expect that the drug is without such risks. We agree that the 'consumer expectation' aspect of the *Barker* test is inappropriate to prescription drugs. While the 'ordinary consumer' may have a reasonable expectation that a product such as a machine he purchases will operate safely when used as intended, a patient's expectations regarding the effects of such a drug are those related to him by his physician, to whom the manufacturer directs the warnings regarding the drug's properties. The manufacturer cannot be held liable if it has provided appropriate warnings and the doctor fails in his duty to transmit these warnings to the patient or if the patient relies on inaccurate information from others regarding side effects of the drug.

The second test, which calls for the balancing of risks and benefits, is inapposite to prescription drugs, according to defendants, because it contemplates that a safer alternative design is feasible. While the defective equipment in *Barker* and other cases involving mechanical devices might be 'redesigned' by the addition of safety devices, there is no possibility for an alternative design of a drug like DES, which is a scientific constant compounded in accordance with a required formula. (See *Sindell* [v *Abbott Laboratories*, 1980] 26 Cal 3d 588 at p 605.)

We agree with defendants that *Barker* contemplates a safer alternative design if possible, but we seriously doubt their claim that a drug like DES cannot be 'redesigned' to make it safer. For example, plaintiff might be able to demonstrate at trial that a particular component of DES rendered it unsafe as a miscarriage preventative and that removal of that component would not have affected the efficacy of the drug. Even if the resulting product, without the damaging component, would bear a name other than DES, it would do no violence to semantics to view it as a 'redesign' of DES.

Or plaintiff might be able to prove that other, less harmful drugs were available to prevent miscarriage; the benefit of such alternate drugs could be weighed against the advantages of DES in making the risk benefit analysis of *Barker*. As the Court of Appeal observed, defendants' attempt to confine the issue to whether there is an 'alternative design' for DES poses the problem in an 'unreasonably narrow' fashion. (See Comment, The Failure to Warn Defect (1983), 17 USFL Rev 743, 755-762.) . . .

. . . It is indisputable, as plaintiff contends, that the risk of injury from such drugs is unavoidable, that a consumer may be helpless to protect himself from serious harm caused by them, and that, like other products, the cost of insuring against strict liability can be passed on by the producer to the consumer who buys the item. Moreover, as we observe below, in some cases additional testing of drugs before they are marketed might reveal dangerous side effects, resulting in a safer product.

But there is an important distinction between prescription drugs and other products such as construction machinery . . . the producers of which were held strictly liable. In the latter cases, the product is used to make work easier or to provide pleasure, while in the former it may be necessary to alleviate pain and suffering or to sustain life. Moreover, unlike other important medical products (wheelchairs, for example), harm to some users from prescription drugs is unavoidable. Because of these distinctions, the broader public interest in the availability of drugs at an affordable price must be considered in deciding the appropriate standard of liability for injuries resulting from their use.

Perhaps a drug might be made safer if it was withheld from the market until scientific skill and knowledge advanced to the point at which additional dangerous side effects would be revealed. But in most cases such a delay in marketing new drugs – added to the delay required to obtain approval for release of the product from the Food and Drug Administration – would not serve the public welfare. Public policy favors the development and marketing of beneficial new drugs, even though some risks, perhaps serious ones, might accompany their introduction, because drugs can save lives and reduce pain and suffering.

If drug manufacturers were subject to strict liability, they might be reluctant to undertake research programs to develop some pharmaceuticals that would prove beneficial or to distribute others that are available to be marketed, because of the fear of large adverse monetary judgments. Further, the additional expense of insuring against such liability – assuming insurance would be available – and of research programs to reveal possible dangers not detectable by available scientific methods, could place the cost of medication beyond the reach of those who need it most . . .

The possibility that the cost of insurance and of defending against lawsuits will diminish the availability and increase the price of pharmaceuticals is far from theoretical. Defendants cite a host of examples of products which have greatly increased in price or have been withdrawn or withheld from the market because of the fear that their products would be held liable for large judgments.

For example, according to defendant ER Squibb & Sons, Inc, Bendectin, the only antinauseant drug available for pregnant women, was withdrawn from sale in 1983 because the cost of insurance almost equaled the entire income from sale of the drug. Before it was withdrawn, the price of Bendectin increased by over 300%. (132 Chemical Week (June 12, 1983) p 14.)

Drug manufacturers refused to supply a newly discovered vaccine for influenza on the ground that mass inoculation would subject them to enormous liability. The government therefore assumed the risk of lawsuits resulting from injuries caused by the vaccine. (Franklin & Mais, Mass Immunization Programs (1977) 65 Cal L Rev 754, 769 et seq; *Feldman v Lederle Laboratories* (1983) 460 A 2d 203, 209.) One producer of diphtheria-tetanus-pertussis vaccine withdrew from the market, giving as its reason 'extreme liability exposure, cost of litigation and difficulty of continuing to obtain adequate insurance.' (Hearing Before Subcom. on Health and the Environment of House Com. on Energy and Commerce on Vaccine Injury Compensation, 98th Cong, 2nd Sess (Sept 10, 1984) p 295.) There are only two manufacturers of the vaccine remaining in the market, and the cost of each dose rose a hundredfold from 11 cents in 1982 to $11.40 in 1986, $8 of which was for insurance reserve. The price increase roughly paralleled an increase in the number of lawsuits from one in 1978 to 219 in 1985. (232 Science (June 13, 1986) p 1,339.) Finally, a manufacturer was unable to market a new drug for the treatment of vision problems because it could not obtain adequate liability insurance at a reasonable cost. (NY Times (Oct 14, 1986) p 10.)

There is no doubt that, from the public's standpoint, these are unfortunate consequences. And they occurred even though almost all jurisdictions follow the negligence standard of comment *k*. It is not unreasonable to conclude in these circumstances that the imposition of a harsher test for liability would not further the public interest in the development and availability of these important products.

We decline to hold, therefore, that a drug manufacturer's liability for injuries caused by the defective design of a prescription drug should be measured by the standard set forth in *Barker*.

2. Failure to warn

For these same reasons of policy, we reject the plaintiff's assertion that a drug manufacturer should be held strictly liable for failure to warn of risks inherent in a drug even though it neither knew nor could have known by the application of scientific knowledge available at the time of distribution that the drug could product the undesirable side effects suffered by the plaintiff . . .

3. *The* Kearl *test*

One further question remains in this aspect of the case. Comment *k*, as we have seen, provides that the maker of an 'unavoidably safe' product is not liable for injuries resulting from its use if the product is 'properly prepared, and accompanied by proper directions and warning.' With the few exceptions noted above, the courts which have adopted comment *k* have viewed all prescription drugs as coming within its scope.

Kearl suggested that not all drugs are 'unavoidably dangerous' so as to merit the protection of the negligence standard of comment *k*, and it devised a test to separate those which meet that description from those which do not. It held that the question whether a drug should be exempt from strict liability as 'unavoidably dangerous' presents a mixed question of law and fact which should be decided on the basis of evidence to be taken by the trial judge out of the presence of the jury. The judge should determine, after hearing the evidence:

(1)   whether, when distributed, the product was intended to confer an exceptionally important benefit that made its availability highly desirable;

(2)   whether the then-existing risk posed by the product was both 'substantial' and 'unavoidable'; and

(3)   whether the interest in availability (again measured as of the time of distribution) outweighs the interest in promoting enhanced accountability through strict liability design defect review . . .

If these questions are answered in the affirmative the liability of the manufacturer is tested by the standard of comment *k*; otherwise, strict liability is the applicable test.

The Court of Appeal in the present case refused to adopt this approach on the ground that it required the trial judge to decide questions of fact which were ordinarily left to the jury, and that it presented the specter of inconsistent verdicts in various trial courts: in one case the question of liability for injuries caused by a specific drug would be tested by a negligence standard, while in another, involving the same drug, the judge might conclude that strict liability was the appropriate test.

We acknowledge that there is some appeal in the basic premise of *Kearl*. It seems unjust to grant the same protection from liability to those who gave us thalidomide as to the producers of penicillin. If some method could be devised to confine the benefit of the comment *k* negligence standard to those drugs that have proved useful to mankind while denying the privilege to those that are clearly harmful, it would deserve serious consideration. But we know of no means by which this can be accomplished without substantially impairing the public interest in the development and marketing of new drugs, because the harm to this interest arises in the very process of attempting to make the distinction . . .

Kearl gives the manufacturer a chance to avoid strict liability. But the eligibility of each drug for favorable treatment must be tested at a trial, with its attendant litigation costs, and the drug must survive two risk/benefit challenges, first by the judge and then by the jury. In order to vindicate the public's interest in the availability and affordability of prescription drugs, a manufacturer must have a greater assurance that his products will not be measured by a strict liability standard than is provided by the test stated in *Kearl*. Therefore, we disapprove the portion of *Kearl* which holds that comment *k* should not be applied to a prescription drug unless the trial court first determines that the drug is 'unavoidably dangerous.'

In conclusion, and in accord with almost all our sister states that have considered the issue, we hold that a manufacturer is not strictly liable for injuries caused by a prescription drug so long as the drug was properly prepared and accompanied by warning of its dangerous propensities that were either known or reasonably scientifically knowable at the time of distribution . . .

The judgment of the Court of Appeal is affirmed.

If negligence theory requires a manufacturer to use technology that was available at the time of manufacture or to warn of risks which were known (or should have been) at that time, a theory of *strict* products liability should require more. Complying with the state of the art at the time of manufacture ought not to suffice to excuse him in design defect cases. Warning only about risks that were known (or capable of being known) also should not be sufficient. Strict liability should on one view require, for example, that a manufacturer warn about even *un*knowable risks (an impossibility but required by the logic of strict liability) and perhaps (though less likely) that he be liable even though he complied with the state of the art. As Lord Scarman stated in the course of the debate in the House of Lords: '[i]f you introduce the "state of the art" defence, you are really introducing negligence or fault by the back door' (414 HL Deb col 1427). While the 1987 Act will be interpreted in the spirit of *Brown* in this particular area of products liability (ie re-importing negligence), section 4 does at least shift the burden of establishing that the risk was not known nor capable of being known on to the manufacturer. An example of this compromise position being created at common law is found in the following case:

Feldman v Lederle Laboratories (1984) 479 2d 374 (NJ Sup Ct)

Schreiber J: When the strict liability defect consists of an improper design or warning, reasonableness of the defendant's conduct is a factor in determining liability. See *Suter* [v *San Angelo Foundary and Machine Co* (1979)] 81 NJ at 171, 406 A 2d 140; *Cepeda* [v *Cumberland Engineering Co*] 76 NJ at 171-72, 386 A 2d 816; *Torsiello v Whitehall Laboratories*, 165 NJ *Super* 311, 320 n, 2, 398 A 2d 132 (App Div), *cert den*, 81 NJ 50, 404 A 2d 1150 (1979). The question in strict liability design defect and warning cases is whether, assuming that the manufacturer knew of the defect in the product, he acted in a reasonably prudent manner in marketing the product or in providing the warnings given. Thus, once the defendant's knowledge of the defect is imputed, strict liability analysis becomes almost identical to negligence analysis in its focus on the reasonableness of the defendant's conduct. In *Cepeda*, *supra*, 76 NJ at 172, 386 A 2d 816, and *Suter*, *supra*, 81 NJ at 171, 406 A 2d 140, we quoted approvingly Prosser's treatise on torts: 'Since proper design is a matter of reasonable fitness, the strict liability adds little or nothing to negligence on the part of the manufacturer . . .' *W Prosser, Law of Torts* 659 n 72 (4th edn 1971).

Generally, the state of the art in design defect cases and available knowledge in defect warning situations are relevant factors in measuring reasonableness of conduct. Thus in *Suter, supra,* we explained that other than assuming that the manufacturer knew of the harmful propensity of the product, the jury could consider "the technological feasibility of manufacturing a product whose design would have prevented or avoided the accident, given the known state of the art." *Id* at 172, 406 A 2d 140. We observed that 'the state of the art refers not only to the common practice and standards in the industry but also to the other design alternatives within practical and technological limits at the time of distribution.' *Id.* Moreover, in *O-Brien* [*v Muskin Corpn* (1983)], we again referred to the state of the art as an appropriate factor to be considered by the jury to determine whether feasible alternatives existed when the product was marketed. 94 NJ at 183-84, 463 A 2d 298.

Similarly, as to warnings, generally conduct should be measured by knowledge at the time the manufacturer distributed the product. Did the defendant know, or should he have known, of the danger, given the scientific, technological, and other information available when the product was distributed; or, in other words, did he have actual or constructive knowledge of the danger? The *Restatement* . . . has adopted this test in comment j to section 402A, which reads in pertinent part as follows:

> *Directions or warning.* In order to prevent the product from being unreasonably dangerous, the seller may be required to give directions or warnings, on the container, as to its use. . . . Where the product contains an ingredient . . . whose danger is not generally known, or if known is one which the consumer would reasonably not expect to find in the product the seller is required to give warning against it, *if he has knowledge, or by the application of reasonable, developed human skill and foresight should have knowledge,* of the presence of the ingredient and the danger. [Emphasis added.]

Under this standard negligence and strict liability in warning cases may be deemed to be functional equivalents. See *Sterling Drug Inc v Yarrow,* 408 F 2d 978, 992 (8th Circ 1979); *Chambers v G D Searle & Co,* 441 F Supp 377, 380 (D Md 1975), aff'd *per curiam,* 567 F 2d 269 (4th Circ 1977); *Incollingo v Ewing,* 444 Pa 263, 285 n 8, 282 A 2d 206, 220 n 8 (1971); *2 Interagency Task Force on Product Liability, US Dep't of Commerce, Product Liability: Legal Study* 67-68 (1977). Constructive knowledge embraces knowledge that should have been known based on information that was reasonably available or obtainable and should have alerted a reasonably prudent person to act. Put another way, would a person of reasonable intelligence or of the superior expertise of the defendant charged with such knowledge conclude that defendants should have alerted the consuming public? See *Restatement, supra* para 12(2).

Further, a manufacturer is held to the standard of an expert in the field. *Karjala v Johns-Manville Prods Corpn,* 523 F 2d 155, 159 (8th Circ 1975); see *Garst v General Motors Corpn,* 207 *Kan* 2, 20, 484 P 2d 47, 61 (1971); *Micallef v Miehle Co.* 39 NY 2d 376,386, 358 NE 2d 571, 578, 384 NYS 2d 115, 121 (1976). A manufacturer should keep abreast of scientific advances. Harper and James, in their treatise on torts, explained that a manufacturer is held to the skill of an expert in that particular business and to an expert's knowledge of the arts, materials and processes. Thus he must keep reasonably abreast of scientific knowledge and discoveries touching his product and of techniques and devices used by practical men in his field. He may also be required to make tests to determine the propensities and dangers of his product. [2 *F. Harper & F. James, The Law of Torts* para 28.4 (1956) (footnotes omitted).] See 2 *R Hursch & H Bailey, American Law of Products Liability* 153-54 (2nd edn 1974). Were the available scientific data or other pertinent information such as to 'give rise to a reasonable inference that the danger is likely to exist'?; Wade (1983), NYUL Rev 734 at 749. Implicit in the requirement that such a manufacturer is held to the standard applicable to experts in the field is the notion that at least in some fields, such as those impacting on public health, a manufacturer may be expected to be informed and affirmatively to seek out information concerning the public's use of its own product.

Furthermore, a reasonably prudent manufacturer will be deemed to know of reliable information generally available or reasonably obtainable in the industry or in the particular field involved. Such information need not be limited to that furnished by experts in the field, but may also include material provided by others. Thus, for example, if a substantial number of doctors or consumers had complained to a drug manufacturer of an untoward effect of a drug, that would have constituted sufficient information requiring an appropriate warning. See *Hoffman v Sterling Drug Inc,* 485 F 2d 132, 146 (3d Circ 1973) (in judgment for plaintiff alleging negligence and strict products liability in failure-to-warn case against prescription drug manufacturer of Aralen, court found jury question whether defendants used foresight appropriate to their enterprise in view of the number of letters from physicians reporting visual injury in patients using Aralen and subsequent medical literature); *Skill v Martinez*, 91 FRD 498, 514 (DNJ 1981), affd on other grounds, 677 F 2d 368 (3d Circ 1982) (jury finding in products liability action for plaintiff upheld because 'sufficient knowledge' existed, in the form of articles on preliminary findings by two leading researchers in the field, of danger inherent in taking birth-control pill while smoking to warrant drug manufacturer's giving proper warning); *Hamilton v Hardy*, 37 Colo App 375, 385, 549, P 2d 1099, 1108 (1976) (under strict liability theory, manufacturer of prescription drugs must warn of dangers and risks whether or not a causal relationship between use of product and various attendant injuries has been definitely established at the time of the warning); *McKee v Moore*, 648 P 2d 21, 24 (Okla 1982) (duty to warn requires prescription drug manufacturer to maintain current information 'gleaned from research, adverse reaction reports, scientific literature and other available methods') (footnote omitted); 39 Fed Reg 33,230-31 (1974)(FDA requires warnings on drug labels 'when there is significant medical evidence of a possible health hazard, without waiting for a causal relationship to be established by definitive studies which, in some instances, may not be feasible or would take many years').

This test does not conflict with the assumption made in strict liability design defect and warning cases that the defendant knew of the dangerous propensity of the product, if the knowledge that is assumed is reasonably knowable in the sense of actual or constructive knowledge. A warning that a product may have an unknowable danger warns one of nothing. Neither *Cepeda* nor *Suter* stated that the manufacturer would be deemed to know of the dangerous propensity of the chattel when the danger was unknowable. See *Ferrigno v Eli Lilly and Co*, 175 NJ Super 551, 576, 420 A2d 1305 (Law Div. 1980). In our opinion *Beshada* [*v Johns Manville Products Corpn* 447 A 2d 539 (1982)] would not demand a contrary conclusion in the typical design defect or warning case. If *Beshada* were deemed to hold generally or in all cases, particularly with respect to a situation like the present one involving drugs vital to health, that in a warning context knowledge of the unknowable is irrelevant in determining the applicability of strict liability, we would not agree. Many commentators have criticized this aspect of the *Beshada* reasoning and the public policies on which it is based. See eg, Page, 'Generic Product Risks: The Case Against Comment K and for Strict Tort Liability.' 58 NYUL *Rev* 853, 877-82 (1983); Schwartz, 'The Post-Sale Duty to Warn: Two Unfortunate Forks in the Road to a Reasonable Doctrine', 58 NYUL *Rev* 892, 901-05 (1983); Wade (1983), *supra*, at 754-56; Comment, 'Requiring Omniscience: The Duty to Warn of Scientifically Undiscoverable Product Defects', 71 *Geo LJ* 1635 (1983); Comment, '*Beshada v Johns Manville Products Corpn*: Adding Uncertainty to Injury', 35 *Rutgers L Rev* 982, 1008-15 (1983): Note, 'Products Liability – Strict Liability in Tort – State-of-the-Art Defence Inapplicable in Design Defect Cases', 13 *Seton Hall L Rev* 625 (1983). But see *Hayes v Ariens Co*, 391 *Mass* 407, 413, 462 NE 2d 273, 277-78 (1984) (citing *Beshada* with approval for the proposition that in strict liability the seller 'is presumed to have been informed at the time of sale of all risks whether or not he actually knew or reasonably should have known of them'). The rationale of *Beshada* is not applicable to this case. We do not overrule *Beshada*, but restrict *Beshada* to the circumstances giving rise to its holding. See eg, *Friedman v Podell*, 21 NJ 100, 105, 121 A 2d 17 (1956); *Konrad v Anheuser-Busch, Inc*, 48 NJ Super 386, 388, 137 A 2d 633 (Law Div 1958) ('Cases state principles but decide facts, and it is only the decision on the facts that is binding precedent'). We note, in passing, that, although not argued and determined in *Beshada*, there were or may have been data and other information generally available, aside from scientific knowledge, that arguably could have alerted the manufacturer at an early stage in the distribution of its product to the dangers associated with its use.

In strict liability warning cases, unlike negligence cases, however, the defendant should properly bear the burden of proving that the information was not reasonably available or obtainable and that it therefore lacked actual or constructive knowledge of the defect. Wade (1983), *supra*, at 760-61; see Pollock, 'Liability of a Blood Bank or Hospital for a Hepatitis Associated Blood Transfusion in New Jersey', 2 *Seton Hall L Rev* 47, 60 (1970) ('burden of proof that hepatitis is not detectable and unremovable should rest on the defendants' blood bank or hospital'). The defendant is in a superior position to know the technological material or data in the particular field or specialty. The defendant is the expert, often performing self-testing. It is the defendant that injected the product in the stream of commerce for its economic gain. As a matter of policy the burden of proving the status of knowledge in the field at the time of distribution is properly placed on the defendant. See *State v Toscano*, 74 NJ 421, 443, 378 A 2d 755 (1977) (shifting burden to criminal defendant of proving duress); *Anderson v Somberg*, 67 NJ 291, 300-02, 388 A 2d 1 (*per* Pashman J, burden of persuasion on multiple defendants in malpractice action where plaintiff was not in a position to identify the responsible party), *cert den*, 423 US 929, 96 S Ct 279, 46 L Ed 2d 258 (1975); *cf Griggs v Bertram* 88 NJ 347, 365-68, 443 A 2d 163 (1982) (in insurance case, shifting to settlor insured burden of going forward, but not of persuasion, on question of whether a settlement was made in good faith); NOPCO *Chem Div v Blau-Knox Co*, 59 NJ 274, 284-85, 281 A 2d 793 (1971) (shifting burden of production to defendants where machine damage in transit but buyer did not know which carrier or bailee had damaged it).

One other aspect with respect to warnings based on subsequently obtained knowledge should be considered. Communication of the new warning should unquestionably be given to prescribing physicians as soon as reasonably feasible. Although a manufacturer may not have actual or constructive knowledge of a danger so as to impose upon it a duty to warn, subsequently acquired knowledge, both actual and constructive, also may obligate the manufacturer to take reasonable steps to notify purchasers and consumers of the newly-discovered danger. Compare *Bacardi v Holzman*, 182 NJ Super 422, 425, 442 A 2d 617 (App Div 1981) (holding that '[t]he manufacturer has no duty to prepare a warning for the consumer when, under all circumstances, the product only comes into the consumer's hands after it is prescribed by the physician'), with *Lukaszewicz v Ortho Pharmaceutical Corp*, 510 F Supp 961 (ED Wis 1981) (manufacturer of oral contraceptive had duty under strict liability to warn patients directly of possible side effects where FDA regulation mandated such warning and Wisconsin law made a violation of such a regulation negligence *per se*) and *Pharmaceutical Mfrs Association v Food and Drug Administration*, 484 F Supp 1179, 1182 (D Del), aff'd *per curiam*, 634 F 2d 106 (3d Circ 1980) (upholding FDA regulation requiring direct warning to consumers of prescription drugs containing estrogens because Congress, in enacting the Food, Drug and Cosmetic Act, 'intended patients using prescription drugs, as well as those using over-the-counter drugs, to receive' material facts directly).

The timeliness of the warning issue is obliquely present in this case. It is possible that Dr Feldman already had Declomycin on hand when defendant became aware of Declomycin's side effect. If that state of affairs existed, defendant would have had an obligation to warn doctors and others promptly. This most assuredly would include those to whom defendant had already furnished the product. See *Schenebeck v Sterling Drug, Inc* 423 F 2d 919, 922 (8th Cir 1970); *Basko [v Sterling Drug Inc]* 416 F 2d at 426. See generally Note 'The Manufacturer's Duty to Notify of Subsequent Safety Improvements', 33 *Stan L Rev* 1087 (1981). The extent and nature of post-distribution warnings may vary depending on the circumstances but in the context of this case, the defendant at a minimum would have had a duty of advising physicians, including plaintiff's father, whom it had directly solicited to use Declomycin.

The trial court charged the jury that the manufacturer of a drug has the obligation to warn if he knew or should have known of the need to issue such a warning. In determining whether defendant should have known of the danger, it referred the jury to the circumstances, relating particularly to the state of knowledge, as evidenced by the literature, in the scientific community. However, upon the retrial the charge should also include the principle expressed herein that a reasonably prudent drug manufacturer should be deemed to know of reasonably obtainable and available reliable information. In addition, we now place the burden of proving the lack of knowledge on the defendant.

Surgical methods

A. WITH CONSENT

1. Legality

Can an individual give a valid consent to a surgical operation for sterilisation?

Bravery v Bravery [1954] 1 WLR 1169 (CA)

Denning LJ: An ordinary surgical operation, which is done for the sake of a man's health, with his consent, is, of course, perfectly lawful because there is just cause for it. But when there is no just cause or excuse for an operation, it is unlawful, even though the man consents to it.

... Likewise with a sterilisation operation. When it is done with a man's consent for a just cause, it is quite lawful; as, for instance, when it is done to prevent the transmission of an hereditary disease. But when it is done without just cause or excuse, it is unlawful, even though the man consents to it. Take a case where a sterilisation operation is done so as to enable a man to have the pleasure of sexual intercourse, without shouldering the responsibilities attaching to it. The operation then is plainly injurious to the public interest. It is degrading to the man himself. It is injurious to his wife and to any woman whom he may marry, to say nothing of the way it opens to licentiousness; and, unlike contraceptives, it allows no room for a change of mind on either side.

This view, however, probably did not represent the law even in 1954 as Hodson LJ indicated in *Bravery* itself.

Hodson LJ: In our view these observations are wholly inapplicable to operations for sterilisation as such, and we are not prepared to hold in the present case that such operations must be regarded as injurious to the public interest.

In the circumstances of the present case and for the reasons we have given, we are unable to accept the conclusion of Denning LJ at the end of his judgment.

Sir Raymond Evershed MR agreed with Hodson LJ.

Today, there can be no doubt that such operations are lawful and cannot be said to be contrary to public policy since sterilisation for contraceptive purposes is recognised as 'just cause'. If confirmation be needed, Parliament has provided for vasectomy operations to be carried out within the NHS, see the NHS Act 1977, s 5(1)(b):

It is the Secretary of State's duty . . .
(b)   to arrange, to such extent as he considers necessary to meet all reasonable requirements in England and Wales, for the giving of advice on contraception, the medical examination of persons seeking advice on contraception, the treatment of such persons and the supply of contraceptive substances and appliances.

Other jurisdictions have reached a similar view, eg Canada (*Cataford v Moreau* (1978) 114 DLR (3d) 585), and New Zealand where 61A of the Crimes Act 1961 provides that:

61A. Further provisions relating to surgical operations – (1) Every one is protected from criminal responsibility for performing with reasonable care and skill any surgical operation upon any person if the operation is performed with the consent of that person, or of any person lawfully entitled to consent on his behalf to the operation, and for a lawful purpose.

(2) Without limiting the term 'lawful purpose' in subsection (1) of this section, a surgical operation that is performed for the purpose of rendering the patient sterile is performed for a lawful purpose.

2. Involvement of others

Are there circumstances in which the law requires not only the consent of the person to be sterilised, but also of some other person, such as a spouse or, in the case of a child, a parent?

(a) Spouse

At one time, it was common for consent forms to require the 'agreement' of a spouse to a sterilisation operation. The general consent form recommended by the Medical Protection Society for all surgical procedures, including sterilisations, until 1988 contained the following clause:

> I, husband/wife,* of the above-named patient, hereby confirm my consent to the above.†
> Date... Signature of spouse............................
>
> * Delete whichever inapplicable.
>
> † It is recommended that if the patient be married and the procedure likely to affect sexual or reproductive functions, the signature of the spouse should also, when reasonably possible, be obtained.

(The MPS's current suggested consent form does not require a doctor to obtain a spouse's consent.) Arguably, the pre-1988 clause was aimed more at maintaining good domestic relations rather that meeting any legal requirement. If it were a valid legal limitation on a spouse's capacity to be sterilised, it would mean uniquely that in this area of medical treatment an adult competent person would not have the right to self-determination nor be entitled to confidentiality. Furthermore, it would suggest that a spouse who opposed the sterilisation could apply for an injunction if it were thought that the procedure would be carried out without his consent. If a person may not obtain an injunction to prevent a spouse from having an abortion (*Paton v British Pregnancy Advisory Service* [1979] QB 276, [1978] 2 All ER 987), it must be the case that *a fortiori* no action could lie to prevent sterilisation. Thus, it cannot be the case that a requirement of spousal consent has any force in law. It is, of course, another matter whether a sterilisation carried out without the knowledge or consent of a spouse could serve as evidence of 'irretrievable breakdown' for the purpose of divorce. On the other hand, there would seem to be no legal remedy available to a person whom a doctor refuses to sterilise unless the spouse consents; short, perhaps of complaining to the General Medical Council.

Support for the proposition that this analysis reflects the common law can be found in the Oklahoma case of *Murray v Vandevander* 552 P 2d 302, which unlike the well-known case of *Planned Parenthood of Missouri v Danforth* 428 US 52 (1976) and its progeny does not rely on constitutional law arguments.

Murray v Vandevander (1974) 522 P 2d 302 (Oklahoma CA)

> **Box J:** The question presented on appeal is whether a husband can recover from a physician and hospital for damage to a marital relationship resulting from an operation on the wife, consented to by her. It is the opinion of this court that such recovery was rightfully denied by the trial court.
> ... The natural right of a married woman to her health is not qualified by requiring that she have the consent of her husband in order to receive surgical care from a physician ...
> We have found no authority and plaintiff has cited none which hold that the husband has a right to a childbearing wife as an incident to their marriage. We are neither prepared to create a right in a husband to have a fertile wife nor to allow recovery for damage to such a right. We find that the right of a person who is capable of competent consent to control his own body is paramount.
> There is no allegation in the petition that plaintiff's wife was of diminished capacity or otherwise incapable of consent. There was no necessity for the physician in the instant case to obtain the consent of the plaintiff. No duty was breached by performance of the operation without consent of the husband of the patient.

The current consent form recommended by the Department of Health in its *A Guide to Consent for Examination or Treatment* (HC (90) 22) is set out in Appendix A(2) as follows:

CONSENT FORM

For sterilisation or vasectomy

Health Authority .... Patient's Surname ....
Hospital .... Other Names...................................
Unit Number .... Date of Birth...............................
Sex: (please tick) Male   Female

DOCTORS *(This part to be completed by doctor. See notes on the reverse)*
Type of operation: Sterilisation or Vasectomy

Complete this part of the form
I confirm that I have explained the procedure and any anaesthetic (general/regional)
required, to the patient in terms which in my judgment are suited to his/her understanding.

Signature .... Date..

Name of doctor..

PATIENT

1. Please read this form very carefully.
2. If there is anything that you don't understand about the explanation, or if you want
   more information, you should ask the doctor.
3. Please check that all the information on the form is correct. If it is, and you understand
   the explanation, then sign the form.

I am the patient

I agree
- ■ to have this operation, which has been explained to me by the doctor named on this form.
- ■ to have the type of anaesthetic that I have been told about.

I understand
- ■ that the operation may not be done by the doctor who has been treating me so far.
- ■ that the aim of the operation is to stop me having any children and it might not be possible to reverse the effects of the operation.
- ■ that sterilisation/vasectomy can sometimes fail, and that there is a very small chance that I may become fertile again after some time.
- ■ that any procedure in addition to the investigation or treatment described on this form will only be carried out if it is necessary and in my best interests and can be justified for medical reasons.

I have told
- ■ the doctor about the procedures listed below I would #not# wish to be carried out straightaway without my having the opportunity to consider them first.
  ....
  ....

For vasectomy

I understand
- ■ that I may remain fertile or become fertile again after some time.
- ■ that I will have to use some other contraceptive method until 2 tests in a row show that I am not producing sperm, if I do not want to father any children.

Signature   ....

You will notice that there is no longer any clause concerning spousal
agreement.

(b) Parent

In the case of sterilisation the same considerations apply concerning the role of parents and doctors and the capacity of children to consent as were discussed in our analysis of *Gillick* in chapter 3 and its particular application to contraception earlier in this chapter.

B. WITHOUT CONSENT

We are concerned here with issues of substantive law: the circumstances in which it may be lawful to sterilise an incompetent person. This enquiry does not require us to distinguish between adults and children. We have already seen that the inherent jurisdiction of the court to authorise medical treatment extends to children but not to adults. As a consequence, a court may not authorise the sterilisation of an adult incompetent. But, as the House of Lords made clear in *Re F (mental patient: sterilisation)* [1990] 2 AC 1, any case in which sterilisation is proposed should be brought before the court and a declaration of its legality sought (see *supra*, ch 4).

As regards the *principles* to be applied in determining the legality of the sterilisation, it is largely irrelevant whether the incompetent person is an adult or a child. We propose first to set out the judgments in the leading cases in England and Canada. They represent two polar points on a spectrum of approaches to sterilising the intellectually disabled. Thereafter, we shall rely upon a subsequent decision of the Australian High Court to explore and comment critically upon the English and Canadian approaches.

1. Canada: 'Best interests' and therapy/non-therapy

Re Eve (1986) 2 SCR 388: (1981) 115 DLR (3d) 283 (Sup Ct Can)

La Forest J:

Background
When Eve was a child, she lived with her mother and attended various local schools. When she became twenty-one, her mother sent her to a school for retarded adults in another community. There she stayed with relatives during the week, returning to her mother's home on weekends. At this school, Eve struck up a close friendship with a male student: in fact, they talked of marriage. He too is retarded, though somewhat less so than Eve. However, the situation was identified by the school authorities who talked to the male student and brought the matter to an end.

The situation naturally troubled Mrs E. Eve was usually under her supervision or that of someone else, but this was not always the case. She was attracted and attractive to men and Mrs E feared she might quite possibly and innocently become pregnant. Mrs E was concerned about the emotional effect that a pregnancy and subsequent birth might have on her daughter. Eve, she felt, could not adequately cope with the duties of a mother and the responsibility would fall on Mrs E. This would understandably cause her great difficulty; she is a widow and was then approaching sixty. That is why she decided Eve should be sterilised. Eve's condition is more fully described by McQuaid J as follows:

> The evidence established that Eve is 24 years of age, and suffers from what is described as extreme expressive aphasia. She is unquestionably at least mildly to moderately retarded. She has some learning skills, but only to a limited level. She is described as being capable of being attracted to, as well as attractive to, the opposite sex. While she might be able to carry out the mechanical duties of a mother, under supervision, she is incapable of being a mother in any other sense. Apart from being able to recognise the fact of a family unit, as consisting of a father, a mother, and

children residing in the same home, she would have no concept of the idea of marriage, or indeed, the consequential relationship between, intercourse, pregnancy, and birth.

Expressive aphasia was described as a condition in which the patient is unable to communicate outwardly thoughts or concepts which she might have perceived. Particularly in the case of a person suffering from any degree of retardation, the result is that even an expert such as a psychiatrist is unable to determine with any degree of certainty if, in fact, those thoughts or concepts have actually been perceived, or whether understanding of them does exist. Little appears to be known of the cause of this condition, and even less of its remedy. In the case of Eve, this condition has been diagnosed as extreme.

From the evidence, he further concluded:

[t]hat Eve is not capable of informed consent, that her moderate retardation is generally stable, that her condition is probably non-inheritable, that she is incapable of effective alternative means of contraception, that the psychological or emotional effect of the proposed operation would probably be minimal, and that the probable incidence of pregnancy is impossible to predict.

General considerations

Before entering into a consideration of the specific issues before this Court, it may be useful to restate the general issue briefly. The Court is asked to consent, on behalf of Eve, to sterilisation since she, though an adult, it unable to do so herself. Sterilisation by means of a tubal ligation is usually irreversible. And hysterectomy, the operation authorised by the Appeal Division, is not only irreversible; it is major surgery. Eve's sterilisation is not being sought to treat any medical condition. Its purposes are admittedly non-therapeutic. One such purpose is to deprive Eve of the capacity to become pregnant so as to save her from the possible trauma of giving birth and from the resultant obligations of a parent, a task the evidence indicates she is not capable of fulfilling. As to this, it should be noted that there is no evidence that giving birth would be more difficult for Eve than for any other woman. A second purpose of the sterilisation is to relieve Mrs E of anxiety about the possibility of Eve's becoming pregnant and of having to care for any child Eve might bear.

The *parens patriae* jurisdiction is, as I have said, founded on necessity, namely the need to act for the protection of those who cannot care for themselves. The courts have frequently stated that it is to be exercised in the 'best interest' of the protected person, or again, for his or her 'benefit' or 'welfare'.

The situations under which it can be exercised are legion; the jurisdiction cannot be defined in that sense. As Lord MacDermott put it in *J v C* [1970] AC 668, at 703, the authorities are not consistent and there are many twists and turns, but they have inexorably 'moved towards a broader discretion, under the impact of changing social conditions and the weight of opinion . . .'. In other words, the categories under which the jurisdiction can be exercised are never closed. Thus I agree with Latey J in *Re X* ([1975] 1 All ER 697), at 699, that the jurisdiction is of a very broad nature, and that it can be invoked in such matters as custody, protection of property, health problems, religious upbringing and protection against harmful associations. This list, as he notes, is not exhaustive.

What is more, as the passage from *Chambers* cited by Latey J underlines, a court may act not only on the ground that injury to person or property has occurred, but also on the ground that such injury is apprehended. I might add that the jurisdiction is a carefully guarded one. The courts will not readily assume that it has been removed by legislation where a necessity arises to protect a person who cannot protect himself.

I have no doubt that the jurisdiction may be used to authorise the performance of a surgical operation that is necessary to the health of a person, as indeed it already has been in Great Britain and this country. And by health, I mean mental as well as physical health. In the United States, the courts have used the *parens patriae* jurisdiction on behalf of a mentally incompetent to authorise chemotherapy and amputation, and I have little doubt that in a proper case our courts should do the same. Many of these instances are related in *Strunk v Strunk* 445 SW 2d 145 (Ky 1969), where the court went to the length of permitting a kidney transplant between brothers. Whether the courts in this country should go that far, or as in *Quinlan*, permit the removal of life-sustaining equipment, I leave to later disposition.

Though the scope or sphere of operation of the *parens patriae* jurisdiction may be unlimited, it by no means follows that the discretion to exercise it is unlimited. It must be exercised in accordance with its underlying principle. Simply put, the discretion is to do what is necessary for the protection of the person for whose benefit it is exercised; see the passages from the reasons of Sir John Pennycuick in *Re X* at 706-07, and Heilbron J in *Re D* [(*a minor*) (*wardship: sterilisation*) [1976] 1 All ER 326] at 332, cited earlier. The discretion is to be exercised for the benefit of that person, not for that of others. It is a discretion, too, that must at all times be exercised with great caution, a caution that must be redoubled as the seriousness of the matter increases. This is particularly so in cases where a court might be tempted to act because failure to do so would risk imposing an obviously heavy burden on some other individual.

There are other reasons for approaching an application for sterilisation of a mentally incompetent person with the utmost caution. To begin with, the decision involves values in an area where our social history clouds our vision and encourages many to perceive the mentally handicapped as somewhat less than human. This attitude has been aided and abetted by now discredited eugenic theories whose influence was felt in this country as well as the United States. Two provinces, Alberta and British Columbia, once had statutes providing for the sterilisation of mental defectives; *The Sexual Sterilization Act*, RSA 1970, c 341, repealed by SA 1972, c 87; *Sexual Sterilization Act*, RSBC 1960, c 353, s 5(1), repealed by SBC 1973, c 79.

Moreover, the implications of sterilisation are always serious. As we have been reminded, it removes from a person the great privilege of giving birth, and is for practical purposes irreversible. If achieved by means of a hysterectomy, the procedure approved by the Appeal Division, it is not only irreversible; it is major surgery. Here, it is well to recall Lord Eldon's admonition in *Wellesley's* case, [*Wellesley v Duke of Beaufort*] *supra*, at 2 Russ p 18, 38 ER p 242, that 'it has always been the principle of this Court, not to risk the incurring of damage to children which it cannot repair, but rather to prevent the damage being done'. Though this comment was addressed to children, who were the subject matter of the application, it aptly describes the attitude that should always be present in exercising a right on behalf of a person who is unable to do so.

Another factor merits attention. Unlike most surgical procedures, sterilisation is not one that is ordinarily performed for the purpose of medical treatment. The Law Reform Commission of Canada tells us this in *Sterilisation*, Working Paper 24 (1979), a publication to which I shall frequently refer as providing a convenient summary of much of the work in the field. It says at p 3:

> Sterilisation as a medical procedure is distinct, because except in rare cases, if the operation is not performed, the *physical* health of the person involved is not in danger, necessity or emergency not normally being factors in the decision to undertake the procedure. In addition to its being elective it is for all intents and purposes irreversible.

As well, there is considerable evidence that nonconsensual sterilisation has a significant negative psychological impact on the mentally handicapped; see *Sterilisation*, *supra*, at pp 49-52. The Commission has this to say at p 50:

> It has been found that, like anyone else, the mentally handicapped have individually varying reactions to sterilisation. Sex and parenthood hold the same significance for them as for other people and their misconceptions and misunderstandings are also similar. Rosen maintains that the removal of an individual's procreative powers is a matter of major importance and that no amount of *reforming zeal* can remove the significance of sterilisation and its effect on the individual psyche.
>
> In a study by Sabagh and Edgerton, it was found that sterilised mentally retarded persons tend to perceive sterilisation as a symbol of *reduced* or *degraded* status. Their attempts to *pass for normal* were hindered by negative self perceptions and resulted in withdrawal and isolation rather than striving to conform . . .

The psychological impact of sterilisation is likely to be particularly damaging in cases where it is a result of coercion and when the mentally handicapped have had no children.

In the present case, there is no evidence to indicate that failure to perform the operation would have any detrimental effect on Eve's physical or mental health. The purposes of the operation, as far as Eve's welfare is concerned, are to protect her from possible trauma in giving birth and from the assumed difficulties she would have in fulfilling her duties as a parent. As well, one must assume from the fact that hysterectomy was ordered, that the operation was intended to relieve her of the hygienic tasks associated with menstruation. Another purpose is to relieve Mrs E of the anxiety that Eve might become pregnant, and give birth to a child, the responsibility for whom would probably fall on Mrs E.

I shall dispose of the latter purpose first. One may sympathise with Mrs E. To use Heilbron J's phrase, it is easy to understand the natural feelings of a parent's heart. But the *parens patriae* jurisdiction cannot be used for her benefit. Its exercise is confined to doing what is necessary for the benefit and protection of persons under disability like Eve. And a court, as I previously mentioned, must exercise great caution to avoid being misled by this all too human mixture of emotions and motives. So we are left to consider whether the purposes underlying the operation are necessarily for Eve's benefit and protection.

The justifications advanced are the ones commonly proposed in support of non-therapeutic sterilisation (see *Sterilisation, passim*). Many are demonstrably weak. The Commission dismisses the argument about the trauma of birth by observing at p 60:

> For this argument to be held valid would require that it could be demonstrated that the stress of delivery was greater in the case of mentally handicapped persons than it is for others. Considering the generally known wide range of post-partum response would likely render this a difficult cause to prove.

The argument relating to fitness as a parent involves many value-loaded questions. Studies conclude that mentally incompetent parents show as much fondness and concern for their children as other people; see *Sterilisation, supra*, p 33 et seq, 63-64. Many, it is true may have difficulty in coping, particularly with the financial burdens involved. But this issue does not relate to the benefit of the incompetent; it is a social problem, and one, moreover, that is not limited to incompetents. Above all it is not an issue that comes within the limited powers of the courts, under the *parens patriae* jurisdiction, to do what is necessary for the benefit of persons who are unable to care for themselves. Indeed, there are human rights considerations that should make a court extremely hesitant about attempting to solve a social problem like this by this means. It is worth noting that in dealing with such issues, provincial sterilisation boards have revealed serious differences in their attitudes as between men and women, the poor and the rich, and people of different ethnic backgrounds; see *Sterilisation, supra*, at p 44.

As far as the hygienic problems are concerned, the following view of the Law Reform Commission (at p 34) is obviously sound:

> . . . if a person requires a great deal of assistance in managing their own menstruation, they are also likely to require assistance with urinary and fecal control, problems which are much more troublesome in terms of personal hygiene.

Apart from this, the drastic measure of subjecting a person to a hysterectomy for this purpose is clearly excessive.

The grave intrusion on a person's rights and the certain physical damage that ensues from non-therapeutic sterilisation without consent, when compared to the highly questionable advantages that can result from it, have persuaded me that it can never safely be determined that such a procedure is for the benefit of that person. Accordingly, the procedure should never be authorised for non-therapeutic purposes under the *parens patriae* jurisdiction.

To begin with, it is difficult to imagine a case in which non-therapeutic sterilisation could possibly be of benefit to the person on behalf of whom a court purports to act, let alone one in which that procedure is necessary in his or her best interest. And how are we to weigh the best interests of a person in this troublesome area, keeping in mind that an error is irreversible? Unlike other cases involving the use of the *parens patriae* jurisdiction, an error cannot be corrected by the subsequent exercise of judicial discretion. That being so, one need only recall Lord Eldon's remark, *supra*, that 'it has always been the principle of this Court, not to risk damage to children which it cannot repair' to conclude that non-therapeutic sterilisation may not be authorised in the exercise of the *parens patriae* jurisdiction. McQuaid J was, therefore, right in concluding that he had no authority or jurisdiction to grant the application.

Nature or the advances of science may, at least in a measure, free Eve of the incapacity from which she suffers. Such a possibility should give the courts pause in extending their power to care for individuals to such irreversible action as we are called upon to take here. The irreversible and serious intrusion on the basic rights of the individual is simply too great to allow a court to act on the basis of possible advantages which, from the standpoint of the individual, are highly debatable. Judges are generally ill-informed about many of the factors relevant to a wise decision in this difficult area. They generally know little of mental illness, of techniques of contraception or their efficiency. And, however well presented a case may be, it can only partially inform. If sterilisation of the mentally incompetent is to be adopted as desirable for general social purposes, the legislature is the appropriate body to do so. It is in a position to inform itself and it is attuned to the feelings of the public in making policy in this sensitive area. The actions of the legislature will then, of course, be subject to the scrutiny of the courts under the *Canadian Charter of Rights and Freedoms* and otherwise.

Many of the factors I have referred to as showing that the best interests test is simply not a sufficiently precise or workable tool to permit the *parens patriae* power to be used in situations like the present are referred to in *Re Eberhardy's Guardianship*, [307 NW 2d 881 (1981)]. Speaking for the court in that case, Heffernan J had this to say, at p 894:

> Under the present state of the law, the only guideline available to circuit courts faced with this problem appears to be the 'best interests' of the person to be sterilised. This is a test that has been used for a number of years in this jurisdiction and elsewhere in the determination of the custody of children and their placement – in some circumstances placement in a controlled environment . . .
>
> No one who has dealt with this standard has expressed complete satisfaction with it. It is not an objective test, and it is not intended to be. The substantial workability of the test rests upon the informed fact-finding and the wise exercise of discretion by trial courts engendered by long experience with the standard. Importantly, however, most determinations made in the best interests of a child or of an incompetent person are not irreversible; and although a wrong decision may be damaging indeed, there is an opportunity for a certain amount of empiricism in the correction of errors of discretion. Errors of judgment or revisions of decisions by courts and social workers can, in part at least, be rectified when new facts or second thoughts prevail. And, of course, alleged errors of discretion in exercising the 'best interest' standard are subject to appellate review. Sterilisation as it is now understood by medical science is, however, substantially irreversible.

Heffernan J also alluded to the limited capacity of judges to deal adequately with a problem that has such general social overtones in the following passage, at p 895:

> What these facts demonstrate is that courts, even by taking judicial notice of medical treatises, know very little of the techniques or efficacy of contraceptive methods or of thwarting the ability to procreate by methods short of sterilisation. While courts are always dependent upon the opinions of expert witnesses, it would appear that the exercise of judicial discretion unguided by well thought-out policy determination reflecting the interests of society, as well as of the person to be sterilised, are hazardous indeed. Moreover, all seriously mentally retarded persons may not *ipso facto* be incapable of giving birth without serious trauma, and some may be good parents. Also, there has been a discernible and laudable tendency to 'mainstream' the developmentally disabled and retarded. A properly thought-out public policy on sterilisation or alternative contraceptive methods could well facilitate the entry of these persons into a more nearly normal relationship with society. But again this is a problem that ought to be addressed by the legislature on the basis of fact-finding and the opinions of experts.

The foregoing, of course, leaves out of consideration therapeutic sterilisation and where the line is to be drawn between therapeutic and non-therapeutic sterilisation. On this issue, I simply repeat that the utmost caution must be exercised commensurate with the seriousness of the procedure. Marginal justifications must be weighed against what is in every case a grave intrusion on the physical and mental integrity of the person.

It will be apparent that my views closely conform to those expressed by Heilbron J in *Re D*, *supra*. She was speaking of an infant, but her remarks are equally applicable to an adult. The importance of maintaining the physical integrity of a human being ranks high in our scale of values, particularly as it affects the privilege of giving life. I cannot agree that a court can deprive a woman of that privilege for purely social or other non-therapeutic purposes without her consent. The fact that others may suffer inconvenience or hardship from failure to do so cannot be taken into account. The Crown's *parens patriae* jurisdiction exists for the benefit of those who cannot help themselves, not to relieve those who may have the burden of caring for them.

I should perhaps add, as Heilbron J does, that sterilisation may, on occasion, be necessary as an adjunct to treatment of a serious malady, but I would underline that this, of course, does not allow for subterfuge or for treatment of some marginal medical problem. Heilbron J was referring, as I am, to cases where such treatment is necessary in dealing with a serious condition. The recent British Columbia case of *Re K*, [(1985) 19 DLR (4th) 255], is at best dangerously close to the limits of the permissible.

. . . However, [counsel] also argued that there is what he called a fundamental right to free procreative choice. Not only, he asserted, is there a fundamental right to bear children; there is as well a fundamental right to choose not to have children and to implement that choice by means of contraception. Starting from the American courts' approach to the due process clause in the United States Constitution, he appears to base this argument on s 7 of the *Charter*. But assuming for the moment that liberty as used in s 7 protects rights of this kind (a matter I refrain from entering into), counsel's contention seems to me to go beyond the kind of protection s 7 was intended to afford. All s 7 does is to give a remedy to protect individuals against laws or other state action that deprive them of liberty. It has no application here.

Another *Charter*-related argument must be considered. In response to the appellant's argument that a court-ordered sterilisation of a mentally incompetent person, by depriving that person of the right to procreate, would constitute an infringement of that person's rights to liberty and security of the person under s 7 of the *Canadian Charter of Rights and Freedoms*, counsel for the respondent countered by relying on that person's right to equality under s 15(1) of the *Charter*, saying 'that the most appropriate method of ensuring the mentally incompetent their right to equal protection under s 15(1) is to provide the mentally incompetent with a means to obtain non-therapeutic sterilisations, which adequately protects their interests through appropriate judicial safeguards'. A somewhat more explicit argument along the same lines was made by counsel for the Public Trustee of Manitoba. His position was stated as follows:

> It is submitted that in the case of a mentally incompetent adult, denial of the right to have his or her case presented by a guardian *ad litem* to a Court possessing jurisdiction to give or refuse substituted consent to a non-therapeutic procedure such as sterilisation, would be tantamount to a denial to that person of equal protection and equal benefit of the law. Such a denial would constitute discrimination on the basis of mental disability, which discrimination is prohibited by Section 15 of *The Canadian Charter of Rights and Freedoms*.

Section 15 of the *Charter* was not in force when these proceedings commenced but, this aside, these arguments appear flawed. They raise in different form an issue already dealt with, ie, that the decision made by a court on an application to consent to the sterilisation of an incompetent is somehow that of the incompetent. More troubling is that the issue is, of course, not raised by the incompetent, but by a third party.

The court undoubtedly has the right and duty to protect those who are unable to take care of themselves, and in doing so it has a wide discretion to do what it considers to be in their best interests. But this function must not, in my view, be transformed so as to create a duty obliging the court, at the behest of a third party, to make a choice between the two alleged constitutional rights – the right to procreate or not to procreate – simply because the individual is unable to make that choice. All the more so since, in the case of non-therapeutic sterilisation as we saw, the choice is one the courts cannot safely exercise.

Other issues
In light of the conclusions I have reached, it is unnecessary for me to deal with the *Charter* issues raised by the appellant and some of the interveners. It is equally unnecessary to comment at length on some of the subsidiary issues such as the burden of proof required to warrant an order of sterilisation and the precautions that judges should, in the interests of justice, take in dealing with applications for such orders. These do not arise because of the view I have taken of the approach the courts should adopt in dealing with applications for non-therapeutic sterilisation. Since these issues may arise in cases involving applications for sterilisation for therapeutic purposes, however, I will venture a few words about them. Since, barring emergency situations, a surgical procedure without consent ordinarily constitutes battery, it will be obvious that the onus of proving the need for the procedure is on those who seek to have it performed. And that burden, though a civil one, must be commensurate with the seriousness of the measure proposed. In conducting these procedures, it is obvious that a court must proceed with extreme caution; otherwise as MacDonald J noted, it would open the way for abuse of the mentally incompetent. In particular, in any such proceedings, it is essential that the mentally incompetent have independent representation.

Even though Eve was not a minor, but an incompetent adult, the Supreme Court held that it had jurisdiction akin to wardship derived from the Crown's *parens patriae* prerogative power. We have already seen that this is not so in England (see *supra*, ch 4).

You will have noticed the reference to the earlier decision of the Court of Appeal of British Columbia in *Re K and Public Trustee* (1985) 19 DLR (4th) 255 in La Forest J's judgment. The Supreme Court regarded this case as illustrating the difference between a therapeutic sterilisation and the non-therapeutic sterilisation in *Re Eve*.

> More germane for the present purposes is the recent case of *Re K and Public Trustee* (1985) 19 DLR (4th) 255, where the Court of Appeal of British Columbia ordered that a hysterectomy be performed on a seriously retarded child on the ground that the operation was therapeutic. The most serious factor considered by the court was the child's alleged aversion to blood, which it was feared would seriously affect her when her menstrual period began. It should be observed, and the fact was underscored by the judges in that case, that *Re K and Public Trustee* raised a quite different issue from that in the present case. As Anderson JA put it at p 275: 'I say now, as forcefully as I can, this case cannot and must not be regarded as a precedent to be followed in cases involving sterilisation of mentally disabled persons for contraceptive purposes'.

2. England: 'best interests' without more

Re B (A Minor) (Wardship: Sterilisation) [1988] AC 199, [1987] 2 All ER 206 (HL)

> A local authority had the care of a mentally handicapped and epileptic 17-year-old girl who had a mental age of five or six. Expert advice was that she had no understanding of the connection between sexual intercourse and pregnancy and birth, and would not be able to cope with birth nor care for a child of her own. She was not capable of consenting to marriage. She was, however, exhibiting the normal sexual drive and inclinations for someone of her physical age. There was expert evidence that it was vital that she should not be permitted to become pregnant and that certain contraceptive drugs would react with drugs administered to control her mental instability and epilepsy. There was further evidence that it would be difficult, if not impossible, to place her on a course of oral contraceptive pills. The local authority, which had no wish to institutionalise her, applied to the court for her to be made a ward of court and for leave to be given for her to undergo a sterilisation operation. The application was supported by the minor's mother. The Official Solicitor, acting as the minor's guardian *ad litem*, did not support the application. The judge granted the application, and an appeal by the Official Solicitor was dismissed by the Court of Appeal. The Official Solicitor appealed to the House of Lords.

Lord Hailsham of St Marylebone LC: There is no doubt that, in the exercise of its wardship jurisdiction, the first and paramount consideration is the well-being, welfare or interests (each expression occasionally used, but each, for this purpose, synonymous) of the human being concerned, that is the ward herself or himself. In this case I believe it to be the only consideration involved. In particular there is no issue of public policy other than application of the above principle which can conceivably be taken into account, least of all (since the opposite appears to have been considered in some quarters) any question of eugenics. The ward has never conceived and is not pregnant. No question therefore arises as to the morality or legality of an abortion.

The ward in the present case is of the mental age of five or six. She speaks only in sentences limited to one or two words. Although her condition is controlled by a drug, she is epileptic. She does not understand and cannot learn the causal connection between intercourse and pregnancy and the birth of children. She would be incapable of giving a valid consent to contracting a marriage. She would not understand, or be capable of easily supporting, the inconveniences and pains of pregnancy. As she menstruates irregularly, pregnancy would be difficult to detect or diagnose in time to terminate it easily. Were she to carry a child to full term she would not understand what was happening to her, she would be likely to panic, and would probably have to be delivered by Caesarian section, but, owing to her emotional state, and the fact that she has a high pain threshold she would be quite likely to pick at the operational wound and tear it open. In any event, she would be 'terrified, distressed and extremely violent' during normal labour. She has no maternal instincts and is not likely to develop any. She does not desire children, and, if she bore a child, would be unable to care for it.

In these circumstances her mother, and the local authority under whose care she is by virtue of a care order, advised by the social worker who knows her, a gynaecologist, and a paediatrician, consider it vital that she should not become pregnant, and in any case she would not be able to give informed consent to any act of sexual intercourse and would thus be a danger to others. Notwithstanding this, she has all the physical sexual drive and inclinations of a physically mature young woman of 17, which is in fact what she is. In addition, she has already shown that she is vulnerable to sexual approaches, she has already once been found in a compromising situation in a bathroom, and there is significant danger of pregnancy resulting from casual sexual intercourse. To incarcerate her or reduce such liberty as she is able to enjoy would be gravely detrimental to the amenity and quality of her life, and the only alternative to sterilisation seriously canvassed before the court is an oral contraceptive to be taken daily for the rest of her life whilst fertile, which has only a 40% chance of establishing an acceptable regime, and has serious potential side effects. In addition, according to the evidence, it would not be possible in the light of her swings of mood and considerable physical strength to ensure the administration of the necessary daily dose. As her social worker put it, 'if she [the ward] is . . . in one of her moods . . . there is no way' she would try to give her a pill.

In these circumstances, Bush J and the Court of Appeal both decided that the only viable option was sterilisation by occlusion of the Fallopian tubes (not hysterectomy). Apart from its probably irreversible nature, the detrimental effects are likely to be minimal. For my part, I do not myself see how either Bush J or the Court of Appeal could sensibly have come to any other possible conclusion applying as they did as their first and paramount consideration the correct criterion of the welfare of the ward.

The ward becomes of age (18) on 20 May next. There seems some doubt whether some residual *parens patriae* jurisdiction remains in the High Court after majority (cf Hoggett *Mental Health Law* (2nd edn, 1984) p 203 and 8 Halsburys Laws (4th edn) para 901, note 6). I do not take this into account. It is clearly to the interest of the ward that this matter be decided now and without further delay. We should be no wiser in 12 months' time than we are now and it would be doubtful then what legal courses would be open in the circumstances.

We were invited to consider the decision of Heilbron J in *D (a minor) (wardship: sterilisation)* [1976] 1 All ER 326, [1976] Fam 185 at 193, when the judge rightly referred to the irreversible nature of such an operation and the deprivation, which it involves, of a basic human right, namely the right of a woman to reproduce. But this right is only such when reproduction is the result of informed choice of which this ward is incapable. I have no doubt whatsoever that that case was correctly decided, but I venture to suggest that no one would be more astonished than that wise, experienced and learned judge herself if we were to apply these proper considerations to the extreme and quite different facts of the present case.

We were also properly referred to the Canadian case of *Re Eve* (1986) 31 DLR (4th) 1. But whilst I find La Forest J's history of the *parens patriae* jurisdiction of the Crown (at 14-21) extremely helpful, I find, with great respect, his conclusions (at 32) that the procedure of sterilisation 'should *never* be authorised for non-therapeutic purposes' (my emphasis) totally unconvincing and in startling contradiction to the welfare principle which should be the first and paramount consideration in wardship cases. Moreover, for the purposes of the present appeal I find the distinction he purports to draw between 'therapeutic' and 'non-therapeutic' purposes of this operation in relation to the facts of the present case above as totally meaningless, and, if meaningful, quite irrelevant to the correct application of the welfare principle. To talk of the 'basic' right' to reproduce of an individual who is not capable of knowing the causal connection between intercourse and childbirth, the nature of pregnancy, what is involved in delivery, unable to form maternal instincts or to care for a child appears to me wholly to part company with reality.

In the event, I am quite sure that the courts below had jurisdiction, and applied the right criterion for the right reasons, after careful consideration of all the evidential material before them.

Lord Bridge: It is unfortunate that so much of the public comment on the decision should have been based on erroneous or, at best, incomplete appreciation of the facts and on mistaken assumptions as to the grounds on which the decision proceeded. I can only join with others of your Lordships in emphasising that this case has nothing whatever to do with eugenic theory or with any attempt to lighten the burden which must fall on those who have the care of the ward. It is concerned, and concerned only, with the question of what will promote the welfare and serve the best interests of the ward.

There is no reason to doubt that the Canadian decision in *Re Eve* was correct on its own facts. La Forest J, delivering the judgment of the Supreme Court, emphasised (at 9) that 'there is no evidence that giving birth would be more difficult for Eve than for any other woman'. The supposed conflict between the views of the Supreme Court in Canada and of the Court of Appeal in England arises from the passage where it is said (31 DLR (4th) 1 at 32):

> The grave intrusion on a person's rights and the certain physical damage that ensues from non-therapeutic sterilisation without consent, when compared to the highly questionable advantages that can result from it, have persuaded me that it can never safely be determined that such a procedure is for the benefit of that person. Accordingly, the procedure should never be authorised for non-therapeutic purposes under the *parens patriae* jurisdiction.

This sweeping generalisation seems to me, with respect, to be entirely unhelpful. To say that the court can never authorise sterilisation of a ward as being in her best interests would be patently wrong. To say that it can only do so if the operation is 'therapeutic' as opposed to 'non-therapeutic' is to divert attention from the true issue, which is whether the operation is in the ward's best interests, and remove it to an area of arid semantic debate as to where the line is to be drawn between 'therapeutic' and 'non-therapeutic' treatment.

In *Re D (a minor) (wardship: sterilisation)* [1976] 1 All ER 326 at 332, [1976] Fam 185 at 193 Heilbron J correctly described the right of a woman to reproduce as a basic human right. The Supreme Court of Canada in *Re Eve* (1986) 31 DLR (4th) 1 at 5 refer, equally aptly, to 'the great privilege of giving birth'. The sad fact in the instant case is that the mental and physical handicaps under which the ward suffers effectively render her incapable of exercising that right or enjoying that privilege. It is clear beyond argument that for her pregnancy would be an unmitigated disaster. The only question is how she may best be protected against it. The evidence proved overwhelmingly that the right answer is by a simple operation for occlusion of the Fallopian tubes and that, quite apart from the question whether the court would have power to authorise such an operation after her eighteenth birthday, the operation should now be performed without further delay. I find it difficult to understand how anybody examining the facts humanely, compassionately and objectively could reach any other conclusion.

Lord Oliver: My Lords, none of us is likely to forget that we live in a century which, as a matter of relatively recent history, has witnessed experiments carried out in the name of eugenics or for the purpose of population control, so that the very word 'sterilisation' has come to carry emotive overtones. It is important at the very outset, therefore, to emphasise as strongly as it is possible to do so, that this appeal has nothing whatever to do with eugenics. It is concerned with one primary consideration and one alone, namely the welfare and best interest of this young woman, an interest which is conditioned by the imperative necessity of ensuring, for her own safety and welfare, that she does not become pregnant. . . .

What prompted the application to the court was the consciousness on the part of her mother and officers of the council responsible for her care that she was beginning to show recognisable signs of sexual awareness and sexual drive exemplified by provocative approaches to male members of the staff and other residents and by touching herself in the genital area. There was thus brought to their attention the obvious risk of pregnancy and the desirability of taking urgent and effective contraceptive measures. Although at present she is subject to effective supervision, her degree of incapacity is not such that it would be thought right that she should, effectively, be institutionalised all her life. The current approach to persons of her degree of incapacity is to allow them as much freedom as is consistent with their own safety and that of other people and although the likelihood is that she will, for the foreseeable future, continue to live at the residential institution, she visits her mother and her siblings at weekends and will, inevitably, be much less susceptible to supervision when she goes to an adult training centre. At the same time the risks involved in her becoming pregnant are formidable. The evidence of Dr Berney is that there is no prospect of her being capable of forming a long-term adult relationship such as marriage, which is within the capacity of some less mentally handicapped persons. She has displayed no maternal feelings and indeed has an antipathy to small children. Such skills as she has been able to develop are limited to those necessary for caring for herself at the simplest level and there is no prospect of her being capable of raising or caring for a child of her own. If she did give birth to a child it would be essential that it be taken from her for fostering or adoption although her attitude towards children is such that this would not cause her distress. So far as her awareness of her sexuality is concerned, she has, as has already been mentioned, been taught to manage for herself the necessary hygienic mechanics of menstruation, but it has not been possible to teach her about sexuality in any abstract form. She understands the link between pregnancy and a baby but is unaware of sexual intercourse and its relationship to pregnancy. It is not feasible to discuss contraception with her and even if there should come a time when she becomes capable of understanding the need for contraception, there is no likelihood of her being able to develop the capacity to weigh up the merits of different types of contraception or to make an informed choice in the matter. Should she become pregnant, it would be desirable that the pregnancy should be terminated, but because of her obesity and the irregularity of her periods there is an obvious danger that her condition might not be noticed until it was too late for an abortion to take place safely. On the other hand, the risks if she were permitted to go to full term are serious, for although it is Dr Berney's opinion that she would tolerate the condition of pregnancy without undue distress, the process of delivery would be likely to be traumatic and would cause her to panic. Normal delivery would be likely to require heavy sedation, which would be injurious to the child, so that it might be more appropriate to deliver her by Caesarean section. If this course were adopted, however, past experience of her reaction to injuries suggests that it would be very difficult to prevent her from repeatedly opening up the wound and thus preventing the healing of the post-operative scar. It was against this background and in the light of the increasing freedom which must be allowed her as she grows older and the consequent difficulty of maintaining effective supervision that those having the care of the minor concluded that it was essential in her interests that effective contraceptive measures be taken. Almost all drugs appear to have a bad effect on her and the view was formed, in which her mother concurred, that the only appropriate course offering complete protection was for her to undergo sterilisation by occluding the Fallopian tubes, a relatively minor operation carrying a very small degree of risk to the patient, a very high degree of protection and minimal side effects. There is, however, no possibility that the minor, even if of full age, would herself have the mental capacity to consent to such an operation. Hence the application to the court.

The necessity for the course proposed has been exhaustively considered by the Official Solicitor on the minor's behalf and there have been obtained two very careful and detailed reports from Dr Berney who is a consultant in child and adolescent psychiatry, and Mr Barron, a consultant of obstetrics and gynaecology to the Newcastle Health Authority. Both agree on the absolute necessity of taking effective contraceptive measures and the report of Mr Barron, in particular, contains a detailed consideration of the various options. It is unnecessary for present purposes to dilate on the numerous possible courses which have been considered. Her limited intelligence effectively rules out mechanical methods while at the same time the way in which certain contraceptive drugs are likely to react with anti-convulsant drugs administered for her epileptic condition severely limits the available choices. In the end it emerges as common ground that the only alternative to sterilisation which even merits consideration is the administration daily in pill form of the drug progesteron supplemented for the present, at any rate, by the danazol which she is presently taking. This involves a number of disadvantages and uncertainties. In the first place, it involves a regular and uninterrupted course which must be pursued over the whole of the minor's reproductive life of some 30 years or so. Secondly, it involves a *daily* dosage, a matter which has given great concern to those having the care of the minor. Miss Ford, the social worker most closely connected with her, was of the opinion that if the minor was in one of her violent moods there was no possible way in which the pill could be administered. Thirdly, the side effects of the drug over a long term are not yet known. Possibilities canvassed in the course of the evidence of Dr Lowry, the consultant paediatrician at Sunderland District General Hospital, were weight-gain, nausea, headaches and depression. But fourthly, and perhaps even more importantly, the effectiveness of this course is entirely speculative. The matter can perhaps best be summed up on the answer given by Mr Barron when he was asked in examination-in-chief for an assessment of the prospect of achieving a satisfactory contraceptive regime by way of pill. He said:

> It would be very speculative because you have a problem here of a girl who is obese, who is still quite young, who has all kinds of problems like, for example, taking anti-convulsant therapy for epilepsy, which affect the manner of working certainly of oestrogens, all of which make her a particularly difficult person in whom to perform a normal judgment. Therefore, I think that we might find a successful modus vivendi, but it is difficult to be certain. I think it is perhaps – if you want a kind of guess, I would say that we have a 30 to 40% chance of getting some formulation that would be successful. But of course it would have to be taken for a very long time.

In answer to a further question he surmised that an experimental period of 12 to 18 months might be required.

Here then is the dilemma. The vulnerability of this young woman, her need for protection, and the potentially frightening consequences of her becoming pregnant are not in doubt. Of the two possible courses, the one proposed is safe, but irreversible, the other speculative, possibly damaging and requiring discipline over a period of many years from one of the most limited intellectual capacity. Equally it is not in doubt that this young woman is not capable and never will be capable herself of consenting to undergo a sterilisation operation. Can the court and should the court, in the exercise of its wardship jurisdiction, give on her behalf that consent which she is incapable of giving and which, objectively considered, it is clearly in her interests to give?

My Lords, I have thought it right to set out in some detail the background of fact in which this appeal has come before your Lordships' House because it is, in my judgment, essential to appreciate, in considering the welfare of this young woman which it is the duty of the court to protect, the degree of her vulnerability, the urgency of the need for protective measures and the impossibility of her ever being able at this age or any later age either to consent to any form of operative treatment or to exercise for herself the right of making any informed decision in matters which, in the case of a person less heavily handicapped, would rightly be thought to be matters purely of personal and subjective choice.

My Lords, the arguments advanced against the adoption of the expedient of a sterilisation operation are based almost entirely (and, indeed, understandably so) on its irreversible nature. It was observed by Dillon LJ in the Court of Appeal that the jurisdiction in wardship proceedings to authorise such an operation is one which should be exercised only in the last resort and with that I respectfully agree. What is submitted is that, in concluding as it did that the instant case was one in which, as the last resort, that jurisdiction ought to be exercised, the Court of Appeal was in error and had not given sufficient weight to the alternative course of experimentation with the progesteron pill. That submission has been reinforced before your Lordships by a further submission not made in either court below that there lies in the court an inherent jurisdiction in the case of a mentally handicapped subject of any age to sanction, as *parens patriae*, an operation such as that proposed whenever it should be considered necessary. Thus, it is argued, some of the urgency is taken out of the case, for further application can be mounted at any time should alternative methods of contraception prove ineffective. My Lords, speaking for myself, I should be reluctant to express any view regarding the correctness of this submission without very much fuller argument than it has been possible for counsel in the time available to present to your Lordships. But in fact I do not consider that in the instant case the point is of more than of academic interest for I am, for my part, prepared to assume for present purposes that the *parens patriae* jurisdiction continues into full age. Making that assumption, I remain wholly unpersuaded that the Court of Appeal failed to give full weight to the alternative proposed or that it erred in any way in the conclusion to which it came. It was faced, as your Lordships are faced, with the necessity of deciding here and now what is the right course in the best interests of the ward. The danger to which she is exposed and the speculative nature of the alternative proposed are such that, on any footing, the risk is not one which should properly be taken by the court. For my part I have not been left in any doubt that Bush J and the Court of Appeal rightly concluded that there was no practicable alternative to sterilisation and that the authority sought by the council should be given without further delay.

Your Lordships' attention has, quite properly, been directed to the decision of Heilbron J in *Re D (a minor) (wardship: sterilisation)* [1976] 1 All ER 326, [1976] Fam 185, a case very different from the instant case, where the evidence indicated that the ward was of an intellectual capacity to marry and would in the future be able to make her own choice. In those circumstances Heilbron J declined to sanction an operation which involved depriving her of her right to reproduce. That, if I may say so respectfully, was plainly a right decision. But the right to reproduce is of value only if accompanied by the ability to make a choice and in the instant case there is no question of the minor ever being able to make such a choice or indeed to appreciate the need to make one. All the evidence indicates that she will never desire a child and that reproduction would in fact be positively harmful to her. Something was sought to be made of the description of the operation for which authority was sought in *Re D* as 'non-therapeutic', using the word 'therapeutic' as connoting the treatment of some malfunction or disease. The description was, no doubt, apt enough in that case, but I do not, for my part, find the distinction between 'therapeutic' and 'non-therapeutic' measures helpful in the context of the instant case, for it seems to me entirely immaterial whether measures undertaken for the protection against future and foreseeable injury are properly described as 'therapeutic'. The primary and paramount question is only whether they are for the welfare and benefit of this particular young woman situate as she is situate in this case.

Your Lordships have also been referred to *Re Eve* (1986) 31 DLR (4th) 1, a decision of the Supreme Court of Canada which contains an extremely instructive judgment of La Forest J in which he considered the extent of the *parens patriae* jurisdiction over mentally handicapped persons. His conclusion was that sterilisation should never be authorised for non-therapeutic purposes under the *parens patriae* jurisdiction. If in that conclusion the expression 'non-therapeutic' was intended to exclude measures taken for the necessary protection from future harm of the person over whom the jurisdiction is exercisable, then I respectfully dissent from it for it seems to me to contradict what is the sole and paramount criterion for the exercise of the jurisdiction, viz the welfare and benefit of the ward. La Forest J observed (at 32-33):

> If sterilisation of the mentally incompetent is to be adopted as desirable for general social purposes, the legislature is the appropriate body to do so.

With that I respectfully agree but I desire to emphasise once again that this case is not about sterilisation for social purposes; it is not about eugenics, it is not about the convenience of those whose task it is to care for the ward or the anxieties of her family; and it involves no general principle of public policy. It is about what is in the best interests of this unfortunate young woman and how best she can be given the protection which is essential to her future well-being so that she may lead as full a life as her intellectual capacity allows. That is and must be the paramount consideration as was rightly appreciated by Bush J and by the Court of Appeal. They came to what, in my judgment, was the only possible conclusion in the interests of the minor. I would accordingly dismiss the appeal.

The test which the English court adopts is the same as that in *Eve*, namely that of 'best interests'. Of course, they reach diametrically opposed conclusions in applying the test. We must, therefore, consider the fundamental issue: what is the meaning of 'best interests' here? There are, in fact, two distinct ways of determining 'best interests'. The *first*, and narrower, approach may be that ordinarily adopted by the English family law which tends to invite a court to form a judgment based upon the particular case before it. This approach tends to eschew regard for any general principle governing all children or incompetent adults. Furthermore, and this may be a jurisprudential flaw, it tends to treat normative issues as if they were issues of fact. Facts do not suggest what *ought* to be done; it is the values and policies by reference to which these facts are evaluated which perform this function. The *second*, and wider approach, neglected (or rejected) by the English courts, is that which would import into 'best interests' issues related to human rights – in this case the rights of the child. This was the approach, as we saw earlier, adopted by the Canadian Supreme Court in *Re Eve*, curiously without reliance upon the Canadian Charter of Rights and Freedoms.

Given the approach adopted by the House of Lords in *Re B*, there is, of course, a most significant issue which is left untouched by the Law Lords. Should not the court articulate guidelines both for itself and others who have to determine whether a sterilisation operation is in an incompetent individual's best interests? We know from *Re B* that a sterilisation performed for eugenic reasons does not fall within the 'best interests' test, but this is all we know. In the next case the House of Lords had an opportunity to take the development of the law further.

Re F (a mental patient: sterilisation) [1990] 2 AC 1, [1989] 2 All ER 545 (HL)

Lord Brandon: My Lords, this appeal concerns the proposed sterilisation of an adult woman, F, who is disabled by mental incapacity from consenting to the operation. . . .

The material facts relating to F, which are not in dispute, are these. She was born on 13 January 1953, so that she is now 36. She suffers from serious mental disability, probably as a consequence of an acute infection of the respiratory tract which she had when she was about nine months old. She has been a voluntary in-patient at Borocourt Hospital (a mental hospital under the control of the health authority) since 1967, when she was 14. Her mental disability takes the form of an arrested or incomplete development of the mind. She has the verbal capacity of a child of two and the general mental capacity of a child of four to five. She is unable to express her views in words but can indicate what she likes or dislikes, for example people, food, clothes and matters of routine. She experiences emotions such as enjoyment, sadness and fear, but is prone to express them differently from others. She is liable to become aggressive. Her mother is her only relative and visits her regularly. There is a strong bond of affection between them. As a result of the treatment which F has received during her time in hospital she has made significant progress. She has become less aggressive and is allowed considerable freedom of movement about the hospital grounds, which are large. There is, however, no prospect of any development in her mental capacity.

The question of F being sterilised has arisen because of a relationship which she has formed with a male patient at the same hospital, P. This relationship is of a sexual nature and probably involves sexual intercourse or something close to it, about twice a month. The relationship is entirely voluntary on F's part and it is likely that she obtains pleasure from it. There is no reason to believe that F has other than the ordinary fertility of a woman of her age. Because of her mental disability, however, she could not cope at all with pregnancy, labour or delivery, the meaning of which she would not understand. Nor could she care for a baby if she ever had one. In these circumstances it would, from a psychiatric point of view, be disastrous for her to conceive a child. There is a serious objection to each of the ordinary methods of contraception. So far as varieties of the pill are concerned she would not be able to use them effectively and there is a risk of their causing damage to her physical health. So far as an interuterine device is concerned, there would be danger of infection arising, the symptoms of which she would not be able to describe so that remedial measures could not be taken in time.

In the light of the facts set out above Scott Baker J concluded that it would be in the best interests of F to have an operation for sterilisation by ligation of her fallopian tubes. The Court of Appeal unanimously affirmed that conclusion, and no challenge to its correctness was made on behalf of any party at the hearing of the appeal before your Lordships . . .

In my opinion . . . a doctor can lawfully operate on, or give other treatment to, adult patients who are incapable, for one reason or another, of consenting to his doing so, provided that the operation or other treatment concerned is in the best interests of such patients. The operation or other treatment will be in their best interests if, but only if, it is carried out in order either to save their lives or to ensure improvement or prevent deterioration in their physical or mental health . . .

There is one further matter with which I think that it is necessary to deal. That is the standard which the court should apply in deciding whether a proposed operation is or is not in the best interests of the patient. With regard to this Scott Baker J said:

> I do not think they [the doctors] are liable in battery where they are acting in good faith and reasonably in the best interests of their patients. I doubt whether the test is very different from that for negligence.

This was a reference to the test laid down in *Bolam v Friern Hospital Management Committee* [1957] 2 All ER 118, [1957] 1 WLR 582, namely that a doctor will not be negligent if he establishes that he acted in accordance with a practice accepted at the time by a responsible body of medical opinion skilled in the particular form of treatment in question.

All three members of the Court of Appeal considered that the *Bolam* test was insufficiently stringent for deciding whether an operation or other medical treatment was in a patient's best interests. Lord Donaldson MR said:

> Just as the law and the courts rightly pay great, but not decisive, regard to accepted professional wisdom in relation to the duty of care in the law of medical negligence (the *Bolam* test), so they equally would have regard to such wisdom in relation to decisions whether or not and how to treat incompetent patients in the context of the law of trespass to the person. However, both the medical profession and the courts have to keep the special status of such a patient in the forefront of their minds. The ability of the ordinary adult patient to exercise a free choice in deciding whether to accept or to refuse medical treatment and to choose between treatments is not to be dismissed as desirable but inessential. It is a crucial factor in relation to all medical treatment. If it is necessarily absent, whether temporarily in a emergency situation or permanently in a case of mental disability, other things being equal there must be greater caution in deciding whether to treat and, if so, how to treat, although I do not agree that this extends to limiting doctors to treatment on the necessity for which are 'no two views' (per Wood J in *T v T* [1988] 1 All ER 613 at 621, [1988] Fam 52 at 62).

There will always or usually be a minority view and this approach, if strictly applied, would often rule out all treatment. On the other hand, the existence of a significant minority view would constitute a serious contra-indication.

Neil LJ said:

I have therefore come to the conclusion that, if the operation is necessary and the proper safeguards are observed, the performance of a serious operation, including an operation of sterilisation, on a person who by reason of a lack of mental capacity is unable to give his or her consent is not a trespass to the person or otherwise unlawful. It therefore becomes necessary to consider what is meant by 'a necessary operation'. In seeking to define the circumstances in which an operation can properly be carried out Scott Baker J said: 'I do not think they are liable in battery where they are acting in good faith and reasonably in the best interests of their patients. I doubt whether the test is very different from that for negligence.' With respect, I do not consider that this test is sufficiently stringent. A doctor may defeat a claim in negligence if he establishes that he acted in accordance with a practice accepted at the time as proper by a responsible body of medical opinion skilled in the particular form of treatment in question. This is the test laid down in *Bolam v Friern Hospital Management Committee*. But to say that it is not negligent to carry out a particular form of treatment does not mean that that treatment is necessary. I would define necessary in this context as that which the general body of medical opinion in the particular specialty would consider to be in the best interests of the patient in order to maintain the health and to secure the well-being of the patient. One cannot expect unanimity but it should be possible to say of an operation which is necessary in the relevant sense that it would be unreasonable in the opinion of most experts in the field not to make the operation available to the patient. One must consider the alternatives to an operation and the dangers or disadvantages to which the patient may be exposed if no action is taken. The question becomes: what action does the patient's health and welfare require?

Butler-Sloss LJ agreed with Neill LJ.

With respect to the Court of Appeal, I do not agree that the *Bolam* test is inapplicable to cases of performing operations on, or giving other treatment to, adults incompetent to give consent. In order that the performance of such operations on, and the giving of such other treatment to, such adults should be lawful, they must be in their best interests. If doctors were to be required, in deciding whether an operation or other treatment was in the best interests of adults incompetent to give consent, to apply some test more stringent than the *Bolam* test, the result would be that such adults would, in some circumstances at least, be deprived of the benefit of medical treatment which adults competent to give consent would enjoy. In my opinion it would be wrong for the law, in its concern to protect such adults, to produce such a result.

Lord Griffiths: My Lords, the argument in this appeal has ranged far and wide in search of a measure to protect those who cannot protect themselves from the insult of an unnecessary sterilisation. Every judge who has considered the problem has recognised that there should be some control mechanism imposed on those who have the care of infants or mentally incompetent women of child bearing age to prevent or at least inhibit them from sterilising the women without approval of the High Court. I am, I should make it clear, speaking now and hereafter of an operation for sterilisation which is proposed not for the treatment of diseased organs but an operation on a woman with healthy reproductive organs in order to avoid the risk of pregnancy. The reasons for the anxiety about sterilisation which it is proposed should be carried out for other than purely medical reasons, such as the removal of the ovaries to prevent the spread of cancer, are readily understandable and are shared throughout the common law world . . .

In the United States and Australia the solution has been to declare that, in the case of a woman who either because of infancy or mental incompetence cannot give her consent, the operation may not be performed without the consent of the court [see now, *Dept of Health and Community Services v JWB* (1992) 66 ALJR 300 (Aust High Ct)]. In Canada the Supreme Court has taken an even more extreme stance and declared that sterilisation is unlawful unless performed for therapeutic reasons, which I understand to be as a life-saving measure or for the prevention of the spread of disease: see *Re Eve* (1986) 31 DLR (4th) 1. This extreme position was rejected by this House in *Re B (a minor) (wardship: sterilisation)* [1987] 2 All ER 206, [1988] AC 199, which recognised that an operation might be in the best interests of a woman even though carried out in order to protect her from the trauma of pregnancy which she could not understand and with which she could not cope. Nevertheless Lord Templeman stressed that such an operation should not be undertaken without the approval of a High Court judge of the Family Division. In this country *Re D (a minor) (wardship: sterilisation)* [1976] Fam 185 stands as a stark warning of the danger of leaving the decision to sterilise in the hands of those having the immediate care of the woman, even when they genuinely believe that they are acting in her best interests.

I have had the advantage of reading the speeches of my noble and learned friends Lord Brandon and Lord Goff and there is much therein with which I agree. I agree that those charged with the care of the mentally incompetent are protected from any criminal or tortious action based on lack of consent. Whether one arrives at this conclusion by applying a principle of 'necessity' as do Lord Brandon and Lord Goff or by saying that it is in the public interest as did Neill LJ in the Court of Appeal, appear to me to be inextricably interrelated conceptual justifications for the humane development of the common law. Why is it necessary that the mentally incompetent should be given treatment to which they lack the capacity to consent? The answer must surely be because it is in the public interest that it should be so.

In a civilised society the mentally incompetent must be provided with medical and nursing care and those who look after them must do their best for them. Stated in legal terms the doctor who undertakes responsibility for the treatment of a mental patient who is incapable of giving consent to treatment must give the treatment that he considers to be in the best interests of his patient, and the standard of care required of the doctor will be that laid down in *Bolam v Friern Hospital Management Committee* [1957] 2 All ER 118, [1957] 1 WLR 582. The doctor will however be subject to the specific statutory constraints on treatment for mental disorder provided by Pt IV of the Mental Health Act 1983. Certain radical treatments such as surgical destruction of brain tissue cannot be performed without the consent of the patient and if the patient is incapable of giving consent the operation cannot be performed, however necessary it may be considered by the doctors. Other less radical treatment can only be given with the consent of the patient or, if the patient will not or cannot consent, on the authority of a second medical opinion. There are however no statutory provisions that deal with sterilisation . . .

I cannot agree that it is satisfactory to leave this grave decision with all its social implications in the hands of those having the care of the patient with only the expectation that they will have the wisdom to obtain a declaration of lawfulness before the operation is performed. In my view the law ought to be that they must obtain the approval of the court before they sterilise a woman incapable of giving consent and that it is unlawful to sterilise without that consent. I believe that it is open to your Lordships to develop a common law rule to this effect. Although the general rule is that the individual is the master of his own fate the judges through the common law have, in the public interest, imposed certain constraints on the harm that people may consent to being inflicted on their own bodies. Thus, although boxing is a legal sport, a bare knuckle prize fight in which more grievous injury may be inflicted is unlawful (see *R v Coney* (1882) 8 QBD 534), and so is fighting which may result in actual bodily harm (see *Re A-G's Reference (No 6 of 1980)* [1981] 2 All ER 1057, [1981] QB 715). So also is it unlawful to consent to the infliction of serious injury on the body in the course of the practice of sexual perversion (see *R v Donovan* [1934] 2 KB 498, [1934] All ER Rep 207). Suicide was unlawful at common law until Parliament intervened by the Suicide Act 1961.

The common law has, in the public interest, been developed to forbid the infliction of injury on those who are fully capable of consenting to it. The time has now come for a further development to forbid, again in the public interest, the sterilisation of a woman with healthy reproductive organs who, either through mental incompetence or youth, is incapable of giving her fully informed consent unless such an operation has been inquired into and sanctioned by the High Court. Such a common law rule would provide a more effective protection than the exercise of parens patriae jurisdiction which is dependent on some interested party coming forward to invoke the jurisdiction of the court. The parens patriae jurisdiction is in any event now only available in the case of minors through their being made wards of court. I would myself declare that on grounds of public interest an operation to sterilise a woman incapable of giving consent on grounds of either age or mental incapacity is unlawful if performed without the consent of the High Court. I fully recognise that in so doing, I would be making new law. However, the need for such a development has been identified in a number of recent cases and in the absence of any parliamentary response to the problem it is my view that the judges can and should accept responsibility to recognise the need and to adapt the common law to meet it. If such a development did not meet with public approval it would always be open to Parliament to reverse it or to alter it by perhaps substituting for the opinion of the High Court judge the second opinion of another doctor as urged by counsel for the Mental Health Act Commission.

As I know that your Lordships consider that it is not open to you to follow the course I would take I must content myself by accepting, but as second best, the procedure by way of declaration proposed by Lord Brandon and agree to the dismissal of this appeal.

Lord Goff: We are searching for a principle on which, in limited circumstances, recognition may be given to a need, in the interests of the patient, that treatment should be given to him in circumstances where he is (temporarily or permanently) disabled from consenting to it. It is this criterion of a need which points to the principle of necessity as providing justification.

That there exists in the common law a principle of necessity which may justify action which would otherwise be unlawful is not in doubt . . .

We are concerned here with action taken to preserve the life, health or well-being of another who is unable to consent to it. Such action is sometimes said to be justified as arising from an emergency; in Prosser and Keeton *Torts* (5th edn, 1984) p 117 the action is said to be privileged by the emergency. Doubtless, in the case of a person of sound mind, there will ordinarily have to be an emergency before such action taken without consent can be lawful; for otherwise there would be an opportunity to communicate with the assisted person and to seek his consent. But this is not always so; and indeed the historical origins of the principle of necessity do not point to emergency as such as providing the criterion of lawful intervention without consent . . . when a person is rendered incapable of communication either permanently or over a considerable period of time (through illness or accident or mental disorder), it would be an unusual use of language to describe the case as one of 'permanent emergency', if indeed such a state of affairs can properly be said to exist. In truth, the relevance of an emergency is that it may give rise to a necessity to act in the interests of the assisted person without first obtaining his consent. Emergency is however not the criterion or even a prerequisite; it is simply a frequent origin of the necessity which impels intervention. The principle is one of necessity, not of emergency . . . the [legal] principle, [is that] not only (1) must there be a necessity to act when it is not practicable to communicate with the assisted person, but also (2) the action taken must be such as a reasonable person would in all the circumstances take, acting in the best interests of the assisted person.

Take the example of an elderly person who suffers a stroke which renders him incapable of speech or movement. It is by virtue of this principle that the doctor who treats him, the nurse who cares for him, even the relative or friend or neighbour who comes in to look after him will commit no wrong when he or she touches his body.

[This is an example of] a permanent or semi-permanent state of affairs. Another example of the latter kind is that of a mentally disordered person who is disabled from giving consent. I can see no good reason why the principle of necessity should not be applicable in his case as it is in the case of the victim of a stroke. Furthermore, in the case of a mentally disordered person, as in the case of a stroke victim, the permanent state of affairs calls for a wider range of care than may be requisite in an emergency which arises from accidental injury. When the state of affairs is permanent, or semi-permanent, action properly taken to preserve the life, health or well-being of the assisted person may well transcend such measures as surgical operation or substantial medical treatment and may extend to include such humdrum matters as routine medical or dental treatment, even simple care such as dressing and undressing and putting to bed . . .

I have said that the doctor has to act in the best interests of the assisted person. In the case of routine treatment of mentally disordered persons, there should be little difficulty in applying this principle. In the case of more serious treatment, I recognise that its application may create problems for the medical profession; however, in making decisions about treatment, the doctor must act in accordance with a responsible and competent body of relevant professional opinion, on the principles set down in *Bolam v Friern Hospital Management Committee* [1957] 2 All ER 118, [1957] 1 WLR 582. No doubt, in practice, a decision may involve others besides the doctor. It must surely be good practice to consult relatives and others who are concerned with the care of the patient. Sometimes, of course, consultation with a specialist or specialists will be required; and in others, especially where the decision involves more than a purely medical opinion, an inter-disciplinary team will in practice participate in the decision. It is very difficult, and would be unwise, for a court to do more than to stress that, for those who are involved in these important and sometimes difficult decisions, the overriding consideration is that they should act in the best interests of the person who suffers from the misfortune of being prevented by incapacity from deciding for himself what should be done to his own body in his own best interests.

In the present case, your Lordships have to consider whether the foregoing principles apply in the case of a proposed operation of sterilisation on an adult woman of unsound mind, or whether sterilisation is (perhaps with one or two other cases) to be placed in a separate category to which special principles apply. Again, counsel for the Official Solicitor assisted your Lordships by deploying the argument that, in the absence of any parens patriae jurisdiction, sterilisation of an adult woman of unsound mind, who by reason of her mental incapacity is unable to consent, can never be lawful. He founded his submission on a right of reproductive autonomy or right to control one's own reproduction, which necessarily involves the right not to be sterilised involuntarily, on the fact that sterilisation involves irreversible interference with the patient's most important organs, on the fact that it involves interference with organs which are functioning normally, on the fact that sterilisation is a topic on which medical views are often not unanimous and on the undesirability, in the case of a mentally disordered patient, of imposing a 'rational' solution on an incompetent patient. Having considered these submissions with care, I am of the opinion that neither singly nor as a whole do they justify the conclusion for which counsel for the Official Solicitor contended. Even so, while accepting that the principles which I have stated are applicable in the case of sterilisation, the matters relied on by counsel provide powerful support for the conclusion that the application of those principles in such a case calls for special care.

It was urged before your Lordships by counsel for the Mental Health Act Commission (the Commission having been given leave to intervene in the proceedings) that a court vested with the responsibility of making a decision in such a case, having first ensured that an independent second opinion has been obtained from an appropriate consultant of the appropriate specialty, should not, if that second opinion supports the proposal that sterilisation should take place, exercise any independent judgment but should simply follow the opinion so expressed. For my part, I do not think that it is possible or desirable for a court so to exercise its jurisdiction. In all proceedings where expert opinions are expressed, those opinions are listened to with great respect; but in the end, the validity of the opinion has to be weighed and judged by the court. This applies as much in cases where the opinion involves a question of judgment as it does in those where it is expressed on a purely scientific matter. For a court automatically to accept an expert opinion, simply because it is concurred in by another appropriate expert, would be a denial of the function of the court . . . I do not feel that the Commission need fear that the opinions of the experts will in any way be discounted. On the contrary, they will be heard with the greatest respect; and, as the present case shows, there is a high degree of likelihood that they will be accepted.

Lord Bridge and Lord Jauncey agreed with the speeches of Lord Brandon and Lord Goff.

When comparing the approaches of the House of Lords and the Supreme Court of Canada two particular strands of analysis warrant careful attention. These are: the distinction between 'therapeutic' and 'non-therapeutic' interventions and the 'best interests' criterion. Unlike the court in *Eve*, the House of Lords in *Re B* flatly rejects the distinction between 'therapeutic' and 'non-therapeutic' interventions as unhelpful and meaningless. In *Re F* the House of Lords simply ignores the point. Instead, the Law Lords rely wholly on the criterion of 'best interests'. Again, however, unlike the Canadian Supreme Court they give barely any substantive content to it. And, what content they do supply cannot be said to offer precise guidance in what is a controversial area of medical decision-making. Lord Brandon, you will recall, speaks of an intervention as being in a patient's 'best interest' if carried out 'in order either to save [the individual's life], or to ensure improvement or prevent deterioration in [his] physical or mental health'. Lord Goff talks of action taken by a doctor 'to preserve the life, health or well-being of another'. It could be thought that Lord Goff's reference to 'well-being' offers the decision-maker a virtual carte blanche. Somewhat revealing is the comment of Lord Keith (himself not a party to the decisions in *Re B* and *Re F*) in *Airedale NHS Trust v Bland* [1993] 1 All ER 821 at 860) that:

In *In Re F (Mental patient: sterilisation)* [1990] 2 A.C. 1 this House held that it would be lawful to sterilise a female mental patient who was incapable of giving consent to the procedure. The ground of the decision was that sterilisation would be in the patient's best interests because her life would be fuller and more agreeable if she were sterilised than if she were not.

The approach to 'best interests' epitomised by Lord Goff's language is in stark contrast to that employed in *Re Eve* where La Forest J recognised that what is at stake is a consideration of fundamental human rights. Concern for human rights is a far cry from someone making a judgment about an incompetent person's 'well-being'. The difference between the courts is even more sharply drawn when it is realised that the House of Lords in *Re F* held that it will be doctors who determine the patient's 'best interests', ie, her 'well-being'. This is because the Law Lords in *Re F* import into their decision the *Bolam* test. *Bolam*, of course, embodies a test used to establish breach of duty in a negligence action. It is questionable whether the *Bolam* test has any place in determining what is clearly not a matter of medical fact such as diagnosis, prognosis or treatment *(Airedale NHS Trust v Bland* [1993] 1 All ER 821 at 895 per Lord Mustill). It is beyond doubt that what is involved are questions of value and social policy which are not the unique domain of doctors. The more one moves from an obviously therapeutic (ie medically indicated) sterilisation towards a sterilisation carried out for social management, the less weight need be given to the views of doctors. As we saw, even Lord Goff at the end of the speech in *Re F* appeared to doubt the wisdom of relying on *Bolam*.

3. Australia: 'best interests' analysed

In *Re Eve* the Canadian Supreme Court addressed society's values and reached a conclusion on what social policy called for. The House of Lords, by contrast, it could be said, did not make explicit the values which they considered and the weight they ascribed to them. Subsequently, the High Court of Australia undertook an altogether more systematic review of the issues involved in sterilising incompetent patients in *Dept of Health and Community Services v JWB and SMB* (1992) 66 ALJR 300. As you will see, the majority of the court adopted as a means of analysing the law the distinction between 'therapeutic' and 'non-therapeutic' procedures, while recognising the inherent uncertainty in these terms. For the majority, only therapeutic sterilisation could be lawfully carried out on the basis of parental consent alone. But, unlike the Canadian Supreme Court in *Re Eve*, the majority held that some sterilisations albeit non-therapeutic in nature could be carried out with the court's permission. For the majority, only if the sterilisation was 'a by-product of surgery appropriately carried out to treat some malfunction or disease' would it be therapeutic. For these judges, therefore, all procedures performed or carried out for the benefit of an intellectually disabled girl but solely intended to result in sterilisation required the approval of the court. The court would not, however, approve a sterilisation where the intention was eugenic or entirely for the convenience of others, such as those caring for her. Therefore, a sterilisation performed solely for contraceptive purposes could be lawful if it were demonstrated to be necessary for the girl's general welfare. The court recognised the need to develop guidelines so as to give content to the criterion of 'best interests' in the context.

Deane J, in essence, agreed with the majority that a sterilisation for purely contraceptive purposes could be lawful with the court's approval. McHugh J in large part also accepted the legality of such procedures where 'the child has no real understanding of sexual relationships or pregnancy . . . if no [other] method of contraception is reasonably feasible'. But, in any event, as we shall see, for him these procedures could be consented to by the parents.

Brennan J, however, considered that all non-therapeutic procedures intended to sterilise the girl were unlawful. Hence, for him, purely contraceptive sterilisations would never be lawful. His view of what amounted to a non-therapeutic sterilisation was, however, somewhat narrower than that of the majority of the court. Like Deane J, he considered that where the procedure was carried out to avoid demonstrable future physical or mental harm to the girl, the procedure could be lawful and could be consented to by the parents. Hence, the Canadian case of *Re K and Public Trustee* (1985) 19 DLR (4th) 255 (BCCA) (where the girl has a 'phobic aversion' to blood) and the New Zealand case of *Re X* [1991] 2 NZLR 365 (where menstruation would have had disastrous psychological consequences) were cases in which the performance of a hysterectomy was justified on therapeutic grounds.

Department of Health & Community Services (NT) v JWB and SMB (1992) 66 ALJR 300 (High Court of Australia)

Mason CJ, Dawson, Toohey and Gaudron JJ: Marion, the pseudonym of the teenager who is the subject of this appeal, is now 14 years old. She suffers from mental retardation ('mental retardation' is the language of the application to the Family Court. Throughout this judgment different expressions are used to reflect the terminology of argument and of decisions under consideration. Current usage prefers the term 'intellectual disability'), severe deafness and epilepsy, has an ataxic gait and 'behavioural problems'. She cannot care for herself. Her parents, who were married in 1976 and who, with their children, are residents of the Northern Territory, applied to the Family Court of Australia for an order authorising performance of a hysterectomy and an ovariectomy (referred to in the application as ovarienectomy) on Marion; alternatively, a declaration that it is lawful for them to consent to the performance of those procedures. A hysterectomy is proposed for the purpose of preventing pregnancy and menstruation with its psychological and behavioural consequences; an ovariectomy is proposed in order to stabilise hormonal fluxes with the aim of helping to eliminate consequential stress and behavioural responses. While the term 'sterilisation' is used throughout this judgment, it must be understood that what the Court is concerned with are the two procedures proposed for Marion. The term is used as a shorthand for these procedures in the particular circumstances unless the context indicates that sterilisation in a different sense or in different circumstances is intended.

The issue specifically before the court was procedural: Who, if anyone, could authorise the proposed sterilisation? The court necessarily, however, had also to address the question of the legality of the sterilisation itself.

In arguing that there are kinds of intervention which are excluded from the scope of parental power, the Commonwealth submitted that the power does not extend to, for example, the right to have a child's foot cut off so that he or she could earn money begging, and it is clear that a parent has no right to take the life of a child. But these examples may be met with the proposition that such things are forbidden because it is inconceivable that they are in the best interests of the child. Even if, theoretically, begging could constitute a financially regarding occupation, there is a presumption that other interests of the child must prevail. Thus, the overriding criterion of the child's best interests is itself a limit on parental power. None of the parties argued, however, that sterilisation could never be said to be in the best interests of a child with the result that it could never be authorised. On the contrary, the question whether parental power is limited only arises because the procedure may be authorised. But, the question whether it is in the best interests of the child and, thus, should be authorised is not susceptible of easy answer as in the case of an amputation on other than medical grounds. And the circumstances in which it arises may result from or involve an imperfect understanding of the issues or an incorrect assessment of the situation. (See, for example, *In Re D (A minor)* [1976] 2 WLR 279 at 288; [1976] 1 All ER 326 at 334; *Re Jane* (1988) 94 FLR 1 at 26, 27. See also *In Re F* [1990] 2 AC, per Lord Griffiths, at 69 and per Lord Goff, at 79.)

It is useful, at this point, to look at how sterilisation has been treated in this regard in relevant cases. That is to say whether, and on what bases, sterilisation has been treated as a special case, outside the ordinary scope of parental power to consent to medical treatment.

Australia

There are four relevant Australian decisions concerning sterilisation, apart from the Family Court's decision in the present case. They are: *Re a Teenager* (1988) 94 FLR 181; *Re Jane*; *Re Elizabeth* (1989) 13 Fam LR 47; [1989] FLC 92-023; and *Attorney-General (Qld) v Parents ('In Re S')* (1989) 98 FLR 41. All were first instance decisions, all involved minors, and the result of each decision was to permit the sterilisation of the girl or young woman involved. With respect to the question of mandatory court involvement, however, authority is evenly divided. *Re a Teenager* and *In Re S* held that it was unnecessary for parents, as guardians, to seek approval from a court to authorise sterilisation; further, that parental consent was sufficient. *Re Jane* and *Re Elizabeth* held that a court's consent was required.

In *Re a Teenager* an application was made by an intellectually disabled 14 year old girl, through her next friend, to restrain her parents from permitting a planned hysterectomy on her to proceed. She was assessed as having the mental ability of a child of about two and a half years. A member of staff of a government centre, on hearing about the operation, contacted a solicitor. The solicitor, acting bona fide, informed the doctor who intended to carry out the operation that the procedure was unlawful without a court order. In dismissing the application, Cook J held that it is within the scope of the powers of parents to authorise the sterilisation of their child. He said (*Re a Teenager* (1988) 94 FLR, at 220-221):

> So far as the *Family Law Act* is concerned, prima facie thoughtful, caring and loving parents, acting in concert, aided by appropriate medical advice, have a right and indeed a duty to make decisions as to medical treatment including major operations in respect of the children of their marriage, whether such children are normal or are mentally handicapped. There must be some clear and obvious factors, over and above those usually attendant on such operative treatment, before any form of interference by the Court at the behest of the child or any other person, is justified.

Sterilisation in itself, in his Honour's opinion, involved no such 'clear and obvious factors'.

His Honour's conclusion appears to have been based on the principle that in the 'intimate environment' of family life 'parents are given a unique opportunity to become aware of the special needs' (at 196) of their child and that, as against this experience and proximity, a court has no special expertise. Moreover, taking such a decision 'out of the hands of thoughtful, caring and loving parents' (at 197) would risk the denial of the protection granted families by s 43(b) of the *Family Law Act* which provides that the Court shall have regard to 'the need to give the widest possible protection and assistance to the family as the natural and fundamental group unit of society, particularly while it is responsible for the care and education of dependent children'.

In *Re Jane*, the Acting Public Advocate of Victoria applied to the Family Court to be appointed the next friend of Jane and, on Jane's behalf, sought an injunction restraining her parents from permitting a hysterectomy to be performed on her without the approval of the Family Court. The Human Rights Commission intervened. Jane was 17 years old and was assessed to have the mental ability of a child of two. The purpose of the proposed operation was to prevent menstruation and the risk of pregnancy. In deciding that only a court, as distinct from the guardians of a child, can give lawful consent to a hysterectomy, Nicholson CJ appears to have considered the fundamental, independent rights of a child involved in a sterilisation decision to be at too great a risk without the safeguard of a court's participation. His conclusion also rested on the characterisation of the sterilisation as 'non-therapeutic' (*Re Jane* (1988) 94 FLR, at 30-31). The Chief Justice identified two rights recognised by the common law and which might be said to be affected by such a decision: the fundamental principle that every person's body is 'inviolate' (at 8) and the right, or liberty, to reproduce or to choose not to do so (at 9-11). It was argued before his Honour that if the Family Court has the power to consent to this kind of operation under its parens patriae jurisdiction, then parents have such power also because in the exercise of its parens patriae jurisdiction the Court simply stands in the place of the parents. Nicholson CJ relied on the judgment of Sachs LJ in *Hewer v Bryant* [1969] 3 WLR 425 at 433; [1969] 3 All ER 578 at 584-585 to conclude that the powers of the Crown as the historic parens patriae were more extensive than those of a parent. He then went on to consider the consequences of the Court's consent being held to be unnecessary (*Re Jane* (1988) 94 FLR, at 26):

> The consequences of a finding that the court's consent is unnecessary are far reaching both for parents and for children. For example, such a principle might be used to justify parental consent to the surgical removal of a girl's clitoris for religious or quasi cultural reasons, or the sterilisation of a perfectly healthy girl for misguided, albeit sincere, reasons. Other possibilities might include parental consent to the donation of healthy organs such as a kidney from one sibling to another.

And his Honour did not accept that unqualified trust in the medical profession expressed by Cook J in *Re a Teenager* (1988) 94 FLR, at 223, saying (*Re Jane* (1988) 94 FLR, at 26):

> Like all professions, the medical profession has members who are not prepared to live up to its professional standards of ethics . . . Further, it is also possible that members of that profession may form sincere but misguided views about the appropriate steps to be taken.

In defining the circumstances in which a court's consent is required for an operative procedure to be performed on a minor or an intellectually retarded person, Nicholson CJ employed, though somewhat tentatively, the distinction between 'therapeutic' and 'non-therapeutic' operations (at 30-31), where the term 'therapeutic' means treatment of some malfunction or disease. This criterion was used as a test in the Canadian case of *E(Mrs) v Eve ('Re Eve')* [1986] 2 SCR 388; (1986) 31 DLR (4th) 1, but was criticised in *In Re B (A Minor)* [1988] AC 199 at 203-204, 205, 211-212 by the House of Lords as a test for determining the scope of the parens patriae jurisdiction. In the end Nicholson CJ found both the distinction between therapeutic and non-therapeutic treatment and the idea of a basic human right to be determinative. He concluded that consent to a medical procedure which involves 'interference with a basic human right such as a person's right to procreate' and which has as 'the principal or a major aim' a non-therapeutic purpose was outside the scope of parental power (*Re Jane* (1988) 94 FLR, at 31).

Ross-Jones J in *Re Elizabeth* agreed with Nicholson CJ, and for the same reasons, that the approval of the Family Court is required. His Honour also relied on the judgment of Lord Donaldson MR in the Court of Appeal's decision In *In Re F* saying (*Re Elizabeth* (1989) 13 Fam LR, at 62; [1989] FLC, at 77,376) that a sterilisation operation is 'irreversible and is of an emotive, sensitive and potentially controversial character'. But his Honour found it unnecessary to examine these factors any further or explain why they should mean that court involvement was necessary.

In *In Re S*, Simpson J relied on the conclusion of the House of Lords in *In Re F*, that there is no necessity for the consent of a court to be obtained for medical procedures to be performed on an adult person under a disability, to come to the same conclusion with respect to a minor.

In the case now before the Court Nicholson CJ adhered to the conclusion he had reached in *Re Jane,* saying (*Re Marion* (1990) 14 Fam LR, at 558; [1991] FLC, at 78,301):

> I think it can be said of sterilisation that it does stand in the category of procedures that require the authorisation of a court for all the reasons contained in the various passages from the speeches of the House of Lords in *Re B* and *Re F*, which I have cited, to which further support is given by the American and Canadian authorities.

He drew further support from the *Human Rights and Equal Opportunity Commission Act*. It is necessary to turn now to some of the decisions upon which Nicholson CJ relied and later to the *Family Law Act*.

New Zealand

In *Re X* [1991] 2 NZLR 365 Hillyer J, in the exercise of the parens patriae jurisdiction, made an order consenting to a child of 15 years, with a mental age of three months, undergoing a hysterectomy operation to prevent menstruation, which, according to the evidence, would have had extremely harmful consequences for the child who, by virtue of the relevant New Zealand legislation, had authority to consent to such an operation. Hillyer J considered that doctors undertaking an operation which would result in sterilisation were obliged to satisfy themselves that the parental consent was an informed one and that the operation would be in the best interests of the child. His Honour held that, although this would in many cases call for an exercise of the court's jurisdiction, there would be obvious cases in which the existence of a consensus of opinion would make it unnecessary to approach the courts and for the parents to incur the expense, inconvenience and anxiety which such an approach would entail.

England

In *In Re B*, a case concerning the sterilisation of a 17 year old girl assessed to have the understanding of a normal six year old, the House of Lords endorsed ([1988] AC, per Lord Bridge of Harwich, at 205; see also Lord Templeman, at 206 and Lord Oliver of Aylmerton, at 211) the reasoning of Heilbron J in *In Re D*, a case decided some 12 years earlier. In the earlier case Heilbron J said ([1976] 2 WLR, at 286; [1976] 1 All ER, at 332):

> The type of operation proposed is one which involves the deprivation of a basic human right, namely, the right of a woman to reproduce, and, therefore, it would be, if performed on a woman for non-therapeutic reasons and without her consent, a violation of such right.

Much of the discussion by the House of Lords in *In Re B* about this 'basic human right' was, however, in the context of the main question before the Court – whether or not sterilisation of a mentally disabled person could be authorised by the Court in *any* circumstances – and was in response to the issues raised by the decision of the Canadian Supreme Court in *Re Eve* that such a procedure 'should never be authorised for non-therapeutic purposes under the parens patriae jurisdiction'. ([1986] 2 SCR, at 431; (1986) 31 DLR (4th), at 32. See *In Re B* [1988] AC, at 203-204, 204-205.) The House of Lords found that the basic human right to reproduce did not preclude a sterilisation of a minor in appropriate circumstances but only Lord Templeman commented on the issue of mandatory court authorisation. He concluded ([1988] AC at 205) that consent to sterilisation of a minor was outside the scope of parental power and 'should only be carried out with the leave of a High Court judge'. Again, since the major issue before the House of Lords was the question whether *any* person or body could consent to sterilisation on behalf of a disabled minor, his Lordship did not elaborate his view that court authorisation is necessary. He said (at 206) that '[n]o-one has suggested a more satisfactory . . . method [than proceedings before a judicial tribunal] of reaching a decision which vitally concerns an individual but also involves principles of law, ethics and medical practice', and he referred again to 'the fundamental right of a girl to bear a child'.

Between publication of the judgments in *Re Elizabeth* and *In Re S* in Australia, the judgment of the House of Lords in *In Re F* was delivered. The House of Lords there held that a court's consent to the sterilisation of a 36 : ar old woman was unnecessary ([1990] 2 AC, per Lord Bridge, at 51-52; per Lord Brandon of Oakbrook, at 56; per Lord Goff, at 79; per Lord Jauncey of Tullichettle, at 83-84), and that the procedure was lawful if it was in the best interests of the woman (per Lord Bridge, at 51-52; per Lord Brandon, at 83-84). However, as Nicholson CJ said in the present case (*Re Marion* (1990) 14 Fam LR, at 437; [1991] FLC, at 78,291), the decision of the House of Lords is consistent with the proposition that, in the case of a minor, a court's consent is required. Furthermore, the House of Lords' decision was influenced by the particular jurisdictional framework involved. A lacuna in jurisdiction resulted from the revocation by Royal Warrant in 1960 of the parens patriae jurisdiction of the High Court with respect to adults with mental disability. Therefore, in the circumstances, the Court had no jurisdiction to authorise sterilisation. Even so, Lord Griffiths held (*In Re F* [1990] 2 AC, at 70-71) that it should, on the grounds of 'public interest', be the law that the consent of the High Court is necessary. Furthermore, each of their Lordships urged the wisdom of making an application to the Court (per Lord Bridge, at 51; per Lord Brandon (with whom Lord Jauncey agreed), at 57; per Lord Goff, at 79), though such an application was not mandatory. In this regard Lord Brandon elaborated the special features of the procedure which make it 'highly desirable' that the Court be involved (at 56):

> These features are: first, the operation will in most cases be irreversible; secondly, by reason of the general irreversibility of the operation, the almost certain result of it will be to deprive the woman concerned of what is widely, and as I think rightly, regarded as one of the fundamental rights of a woman, namely, the right to bear children; thirdly, the deprivation of that right gives rise to moral and emotional considerations to which many people attach great importance; fourthly, if the question whether the operation is in the best interests of the woman is left to be decided without the involvement of the court, there may be a greater risk of it being

decided wrongly, or at least of it being thought to have been decided wrongly; fifthly, if there is no involvement of the court, there is a risk of the operation being carried out for improper reasons or with improper motives; and, sixthly, involvement of the court in the decision to operate, if that is the decision reached, should serve to protect the doctor or doctors who perform the operation, and any others who may be concerned in it, from subsequent adverse criticisms or claims.

United States

The constitutional bases mentioned at times in the United States cases differ from our own, as does the social and legal history of that country, particularly with regard to the widespread acceptance in North America during the early part of this century of the theory of eugenics. (See the statement of Holmes J in *Buck v Bell* (1927) 274 US 200 at 207, that '[t]hree generations of imbeciles are enough'; Law Reform Commission of Canada (Working Paper No 24, 1979), *Sterilization: Implications for Mentally Retarded and Mentally Ill Persons,* (hereafter 'the Canadian Report'), pp 24-29; see also Goldhar, 'The Sterilization of Women with an Intellectual Disability' (1991) 10 *University of Tasmania Law Review* 157.) Nevertheless, much of what is said in those cases derives from and discusses common law principles; given the number of cases concerning sterilisation in those jurisdictions, some reference to them is warranted.

The case of *AL v GRH* (1975) 325 NE 2d 501 is directly in point. AL filed a complaint seeking a declaration of her right under the common law attributes of the parent-child relationship to have her son, GRH, sterilised. The boy, aged 15, had suffered brain damage as the result of a car accident during his childhood. The Court of Appeals of Indiana said (at 502):

> [T]he facts do not bring the case within the framework of those decisions holding . . . that the parents may consent on behalf of the child to medical services necessary for the child . . .
>
> [T]he common law does not invest parents with such power over their children even though they sincerely believe the child's adulthood would benefit therefrom.

In *Stump v Sparkman* (1978) 435 US 349 the Supreme Court of the United States held that a judge who had authorised, after an ex parte hearing, a sterilisation of a minor on the application of the minor's mother, had jurisdiction to do so under an Indiana statute conferring general jurisdiction on the Court. There, a 'somewhat retarded' 15 year old girl was sterilised, having been told she was to have her appendix removed. Two years later, when she was married and unable to become pregnant, she was told that she had been sterilised. The Supreme Court referred without disapproval to the opinion of the court below with respect to parental powers of consent, which was in accordance with the decision in *AL v GRH* just mentioned (at 358-359).

One of the leading United States cases in this context is that of *In Re Grady* (1981) NJ 426 A 2d 467 in which the Supreme Court of New Jersey held that the Court could, within its parens patriae jurisdiction, decide whether to authorise sterilisation of a legally incompetent person and that the decision should, ultimately, be made by a court, not by the guardian of the person concerned. The Court began with the idea of a fundamental right to procreate. It said (at 471-472).

> Sterilisation may be said to destroy an important part of a person's social and biological identity – the ability to reproduce. It affects not only the health and welfare of the individual but the well-being of all society. Any legal discussion of sterilisation must begin with an acknowledgement that the right to procreate is 'fundamental to the very existence and survival of the race' (*Skinner v Oklahoma* (1942) 316 US 535 at 541) . . . This right is 'a basic liberty' of which the individual is 'forever deprived' through unwanted sterilisation.

The Court then examined the constitutional right of privacy which involved the right to choose among procreation, sterilisation and other methods of contraception. This was based on United States constitutional provisions but, as Nicholson CJ said in the present case (*Re Marion* (1990) 14 Fam LR, at 443; [1991] FLC, at 78,296), that basic right has been held to be allied with, or to have been derived from, the common law principle of bodily inviolability as well as from written constitutional guarantees.

According to the Supreme Court of New Jersey, the right to procreate and the right to privacy could only be protected adequately if the decision to sterilise was the subject of independent, judicial decision-making (*In Re Grady* (1981) NJ 426 A 2d at 475):

We need not determine here the full range of persons who may assert such a right on behalf of the incompetent. The parents are unquestionably eligible to do so. The question of who besides the parents has standing to represent the purported interests of the incompetent can await future determination. Nevertheless, we believe that an appropriate court must make the final determination whether consent to sterilisation should be given on behalf of an incompetent individual. It must be the court's judgment, and not just the parents' good faith decision, that substitutes for the incompetent's consent.

Thus, the two fundamental rights involved in the decision to sterilise required, in the Court's opinion, reference to the court to ensure sufficient protection against their abuse. That is to say, the nature of the rights themselves distinguished this decision from others made by parents in the ordinary course of caring for their children.

Other United States cases which have held that the court's consent is required on the basis that the operation interferes with the fundamental right to procreate include *Ruby v Massey* (1978) 452 F Supp 361, *Matter of Guardianship of Hayes* (1980) Wash 608 P 2d 635 and *Matter of Moe* (1982) Mass 432 NE 2d 712.

Summary of earlier decisions

In summary, Australian authority prior to the present case is evenly divided on the question whether court authorisation is a mandatory requirement. The New Zealand decision in *Re X* depended partly on legislation which enabled parents of an intellectually handicapped child to consent to an operation resulting in sterilisation. Neither of the English cases is directly in point, but in *In Re B* Lord Templeman expressed the opinion that court authorisation was required. *In Re F* concerned an adult, not a minor. It held that court authorisation was not required though this was in the context of the court having no jurisdiction to order a sterilisation. In *Re Eve* the Canadian Supreme Court held that non-therapeutic sterilisation can never safely be said to be in the best interests of a person and so can never be authorised by a court under the parens patriae jurisdiction. There is, on the other hand, strong United States authority to the effect that sterilisation for contraceptive purposes is outside the scope of parental power but comes within the scope of the court's parens patriae jurisdiction.

In the cases reviewed, the bases which emerge for isolating the decision to sterilise a child as a special case requiring authorisation from a source other than the child's parents appear to be: first, the concept of a fundamental right to procreate; secondly, in some cases, a similarly fundamental right to bodily inviolability or its equivalent; thirdly, the gravity of the procedure and its ethical, social and personal consequences, though these consequences are not examined in any detail.

Can parents, as guardians, consent to sterilisation? Conclusion

There are, in our opinion, features of a sterilisation procedure or, more accurately, factors involved in a decision to authorise sterilisation of another person which indicate that, in order to ensure the best protection of the interests of a child, such a decision should not come within the ordinary scope of parental power to consent to medical treatment. Court authorisation is necessary and is, in essence, a procedural safeguard. Our reasons for arriving at this conclusion, however, do not correspond precisely with any of the judgments considered. We shall, therefore, give our reasons. But first it is necessary to make clear that, in speaking of sterilisation in this context, we are not referring to sterilisation which is a by-product of surgery appropriately carried out to treat some malfunction or disease. We hesitate to use the expressions 'therapeutic' and 'non-therapeutic', because of their uncertainty. But it is necessary to make the distinction, however unclear the dividing line may be.

As a starting point, sterilisation requires invasive, irreversible and major surgery. But so do, for example, an appendectomy and some cosmetic surgery, both of which, in our opinion, come within the ordinary scope of a parent to consent to. However, other factors exist which have the combined effect of marking out the decision to authorise sterilisation as a special case. Court authorisation is required, first, because of the significant risk of making the wrong decision, either as to a child's present or future capacity to consent or about what are the best interests of a child who cannot consent, and secondly, because the consequences of a wrong decision are particularly grave.

The factors which contribute to the significant risk of a wrong decision being made are:

(i) The complexity of the question of consent. Although there are some cases, of which the facts in *Re X* are an example, in which the parents can give an informed consent to an operation of sterilisation on an intellectually disabled child and in which that operation is clearly for the benefit of the child, there is no unproblematic view of what constitutes informed consent . . . And, even given a settled psychological or legal rule, its application in many cases is fraught with difficulty. The fact that a child is disabled does not of itself mean that he or she cannot give informed consent or, indeed, make a meaningful refusal. And there is no reason to assume that those attempting to determine the capacity of an intellectually disabled child, including doctors, may not be affected by commonly held misconceptions about the abilities of those with intellectual disabilities. . . . the Canadian Report, pp 50, 60-70; and note the striking results of unconscious race, class and gender bias on decisions to sterilise which are recorded at pp 42-44.) There is no doubt that some sterilisation operations have been performed too readily and that the capacity of a child to give consent (and, later, to care for a child) has been wrongly assessed both here and overseas, historically and at the present time. (Strahan (ed) *On the Record: A Report on the 1990 STAR conference on sterilisation* (Vic), pp 6-7; the Canadian Report, pp 36-49; Goldhar, op cit, at p 157 (reference to recent government reports). See also *In Re D and Stump v Sparkman*. In the latter case there was court involvement but the application for sterilisation was heard ex parte.)

(ii)   The medical profession very often plays a central role in the decision to sterilise as well as in the procedure itself. Indeed the question has been 'medicalised' to a great degree. (See, for example, *Re a Teenager* (1988) 94 FLR, at 221-222, 223-224; *In Re F* [1990] 2 AC, per Lord Goff, at 78; *Re Eve* [1986] 2 SCR, at 399; (1986) 31 DLR (4th), at 7-8, citing from the judgment of the provincial Supreme Court in that case.) Two concerns emerge from this. It is hard to share the view of Cook J in *Re a Teenager* (1988) 94 FLR, at 223 that absolute faith in the integrity of all medical practitioners is warranted. We agree with Nicholson CJ in *Re Jane* (1988) 94 FLR, at 26 that, as with all professions, there are those who act with impropriety as well as those who act bona fide but within a limited frame of reference. And the situation with which they are concerned is one in which incorrect assessment may be made. (See, for example, *In Re D (A Minor)* [1976] 2 WLR 279; [1976] 1 All ER 326; *Re Jane* (1988) 94 FLR 1; *In Re F* [1990] 2 AC 1.) The second concern is that the decision to sterilise, at least where it is to be carried out for contraceptive purposes, and especially now when technology and expertise make the procedure relatively safe, is not merely a *medical* issue. This is also reflected in the concern raised in several of the cases reviewed, that the consequences of sterilisation are not merely biological but also social and psychological. The requirement of a court authorisation ensures a hearing from those experienced in different ways in the care of those with intellectual disability and from those with experience of the long term social and psychological effects of sterilisation.

(iii)   The decision by a parent that an intellectually disabled child be sterilised may involve not only the interests of the child, but also the independent and possibly conflicting (though legitimate) interests of the parents and other family members. (See, for example, *Re Jane* (1988) 94 FLR, at 27, 30; *Re K and Public Trustee* [1985] 3 WWR 204, per Wood J, at 224, at first instance and (1985) 19 DLR (4th) 255, per Anderson JA, at 279, cited with approval by Cook J in *Re a Teenager* (1988) 94 FLR, at 208.) There is no doubt that caring for a seriously handicapped child adds a significant burden to the ordinarily demanding task of caring for children. (See Yura, 'Family Subsystem Functions and Disabled Children: Some Conceptual Issues' in Ferrari and Sussman (eds), 'Childhood Disability and Family Systems' (1987) 11 *Marriage and Family Review*, 1/2, 135; Kazak, 'Professional Helpers and Families with Disabled Children: A Social Network Perspective' in Ferrari and Sussman (eds), op cit, 177.) Subject to the overriding criterion of the child's welfare, the interests of other family members, particularly primary care-givers, are relevant to a court's decision whether to authorise sterilisation. However, court involvement ensures, in the case of conflict, that the child's interests prevail.

The gravity of the consequences of wrongly authorising a sterilisation flows both from the resulting inability to reproduce and from the fact of being acted upon contrary to one's wishes or best interests. The fact of violation is likely to have social and psychological implications concerning the person's sense of identity, social place and self-esteem. As the Court said in *In Re Grady* (1981) NJ 426 A 2d at 471-472, a decision to sterilise involves serious questions of a person's 'social and biological identity'. As with anyone, reactions to sterilisation vary among those with intellectual disabilities but it has been said (The Canadian Report, p 50, reporting on Sabagh and Edgerton, 'Sterilized Mental Defectives Look at Eugenic Sterilization' (1962) 9 *Eugenics Quarterly* 213.) that 'sterilised mentally retarded persons tend to perceive sterilisation as a symbol of *reduced* or *degraded* status'.

Another study found (Roos, 'Psychological Impact of Sterilization on the Individual' (1975) 1 *Law and Psychology Review* 45 at 54, in the Canadian Report, pp 50-51 and see generally pp 49-52) that:

> Existential anxieties commonly associated with mental retardation are likely to be seriously reinforced by coercive sterilisation of those who have had no children. Common sources of these anxieties include low self-esteem, feelings of helplessness, and need to avoid failure, loneliness, concern over body integrity and the threat of death.

The far-reaching consequences of a general rule of law allowing guardians to consent to all kinds of medical treatment, as well as the consequences of a wrong decision in any particular case, are also relevant. As Nicholson CJ pointed out in *Re Jane* in the passage quoted earlier ((1988) 94 FLR, at 26), such a rule may be used to justify other procedures such as a clitoridectomy or the removal of a healthy organ for transplant to another child.

For the above reasons, which look to the risks involved in the decision, particularly in relation to the threshold question of competence and in relation to the consequences of a wrong assessment, our conclusion is that the decision to sterilise a minor in circumstances such as the present falls outside the ordinary scope of the powers, rights and duties of a guardian under s 63E(1) of the *Family Law Act*. This is not a case where sterilisation is an incidental result of surgery performed to cure a disease or correct some malfunction. Court authorisation in the present case is required. Where profound permanent incapacity is indisputable, where all psychological and social implications have in fact been canvassed by a variety of care-givers and where the child's guardians are, in fact, only considering the interests of the child or where their own interests do not conflict with those of the child, court authorisation will ordinarily reproduce the wishes of the guardian. But it is not possible to formulate a rule which distinguishes these cases. Given the widely varying circumstances, it is impossible to apply a single rule to determine what are, in the respondents' words, the 'clear cases'.

Children with intellectual disabilities are particularly vulnerable, both because of their minority and their disability, and we agree with Nicholson CJ (at 27) that there is less likelihood of (intentional or unintentional) abuse of the rights of children if an application to a court is mandatory, than if the decision in all cases could be made by a guardian alone. In saying this we acknowledge that it is too costly for most parents to fund court proceedings, that delay is likely to cause painful inconvenience and that the strictly adversarial process of the court is very often unsuitable for arriving at this kind of decision. These are clear indications of the need for legislative reform, since a more appropriate process for decision-making can only be introduced in that way. The burden of the cost of proceedings for parents would in the meantime, of course, be alleviated by the application being made by a relevant public body pursuant to s 63C(1) of the *Family Law Act*. (See generally Blackwood, 'Sterilisation of the Intellectually Disabled: The Need for Legislative Reform' (1991) 5 *Australian Journal of Family Law* 138.)

One more thing should be said about the basis upon which we have concluded that sterilisation is a special case with respect to parental powers. As we have indicated, the conclusion relies on a fundamental right to personal inviolability existing in the common law, a right which underscores the principles of assault, both criminal and civil, as well as on the practical exigencies accompanying this kind of decision which have been discussed. Our conclusion does not, however, rely on a finding which underpins many of the judgments discussed; namely, that there exists in the common law a fundamental right to reproduce which is independent of the right to personal inviolability. We leave that question open. It is debatable whether the former is a useful concept, when couched in terms of a basic right, and how fundamental such a right can be said to be. (See Kingdom, 'The Right to Reproduce' in Ockelton (ed), *Medicine, Ethics and Law* (1986), 55; cf Freeman, 'Sterilising the Mentally Handicapped' in Freeman (ed), *Medicine, Ethics and the Law* (1988), 55.) For example, there cannot be said to be an absolute right in a man to reproduce (except where a woman consents to bear a child), unless it can be contended that the right to bodily integrity yields to the former right, and that cannot be so. That is to say, if there is an absolute right to reproduce, is there a duty to bear children? But if the so-called right to reproduce comprises a right not to be prevented from being biologically capable of reproducing, that is a right to bodily integrity. The same applies, though in a different way, to a woman's 'right to reproduce'. Again, if the right is, in fact, a right to do with one's person what one chooses, it is saying no more than that there is a right to bodily and personal integrity. Furthermore, it is quite impossible to spell out all the implications which may flow from saying that there is a right to reproduce, expressed in absolute terms and independent from a right to personal

inviolability. We think it is important, in the terms of this judgment, to make it quite clear
that it is inviolability that is protected, not more.

Brennan J: The social and legal context

The questions raised by this case starkly demonstrate the quandary of the law when it is
invoked to settle an issue which is a subject of ethical controversy and there are no
applicable or analogous cases of binding authority. Although the issues in this case relate to
the law's protection of the physical integrity of a person suffering from an intellectual
disability, there is no clear community consensus on these issues which the courts or the
legislature can translate into law. Nevertheless, concrete and poignant cases – Marion's
among them – arise for decision. In such a case, a court must try to identify the basic
principles of our legal system and to decide the issues in conformity with those principles.

The appeal to this Court does not require the ultimate merits of the application to be
decided, but the questions of authority and jurisdiction raised by the amended stated case
cannot be answered except by reference to the principles which define and govern the law's
protection of physical integrity. The questions of authority and jurisdiction are adjectival
and it is not possible to answer them without determining the substantive law which the
respective repositories of authority and jurisdiction are to apply. To determine the
repository of a power to grant a valid authority for sterilisation without reference to the
governing principles is simply to leave the repository to decide for or against sterilisation
according to an unguided discretion. Conversely, to ascertain the governing principles
without determining the repository of the power is to state a rule without providing for its
application.

The questions in the amended stated case are directed to ascertaining the repository of a
power to grant a valid authority for the removal of Marion's organs without her consent but
those questions do not in terms refer to the scope of the power. The questions, though stated
with specific reference to Marion, were posed before the facts have been ascertained and the
only fact which can therefore be assumed is Marion's incapacity to consent or to refuse
consent to surgery. If the questions be understood as inquiring whether a parent, a guardian
or a court has power validly to authorise the sterilisation of any child who is intellectually
incapable of giving or refusing consent to his or her sterilisation, the answer is that there is
no such broad power: neither parents nor other guardians nor courts have power to
authorise sterilisation simply because a child is intellectually disabled . . .

I turn to examine the circumstances in which a repository of a power to authorise
sterilisation can be justified in exercising it. An obvious justification exists when the
proposed treatment is therapeutic.

Therapeutic medical treatment

It is necessary to define what is meant by therapeutic medical treatment. I would define
treatment (including surgery) as therapeutic when it is administered for the chief purpose of
preventing, removing or ameliorating a cosmetic deformity, a pathological condition or a
psychiatric disorder, provided the treatment is appropriate for and proportionate to the
purpose for which it is administered. 'Non-therapeutic' medical treatment is descriptive of
treatment which is inappropriate or disproportionate having regard to the cosmetic
deformity, pathological condition or psychiatric disorder for which the treatment is
administered and of treatment which is administered chiefly for other purposes.

The distinction between therapeutic and non-therapeutic medical treatment was adopted
by the Supreme Court of Canada in *Re Eve (E(Mrs) v Eve (Re Eve)* (1986) 2 SCR 388;
(1986) 31 DLR (4th) 1) as the criterion for distinguishing permissible from impermissible
sterilisation of an intellectually disabled child, though the definitions which I have attempted
were implied rather than expressed in the judgment of the Court delivered by La Forest J.
Notwithstanding the unanimous judgment of that Court, in *In Re B (A Minor)* [1988] AC
199 at 204, Lord Hailsham of St Marylebone LC dismissed the distinction in relation to the
facts in that case as 'totally meaningless, and, if meaningful, quite irrelevant to the correct
application of the welfare principle' which his Lordship stated in these terms (at 202; see, to
the same effect, the speech of Lord Oliver of Aylmerton, at 211):

> in the exercise of its wardship jurisdiction the first and paramount consideration is
> the well being, welfare, or interests (each expression occasionally used, but each, for
> this purpose, synonymous) of the human being concerned, that is the ward herself or
> himself.

Similarly, Lord Bridge of Harwich (at 205) thought that the drawing of a distinction between therapeutic and non-therapeutic operations would 'divert attention from the true issue, which is whether the operation is in the ward's best interest'.

The welfare principle is, in England and elsewhere, statutorily binding on courts exercising jurisdiction over the guardianship and custody of infants. The effect of a statute which declares the welfare of an infant to be 'the first and paramount consideration' was explained by Dixon J in *Storie v Storie* (1945) 80 CLR 597 at 611-612:

> The word 'first' as well as the word 'paramount' shows that other considerations are not entirely excluded and are only subordinated. The provision proceeds, however, to deny superiority to the claim of one parent over the other 'from any other point of view' scil other than the welfare of the child. Section 145, which comes from the earlier *Guardianship of Infants Act* 1886 s 5, gives the Court power to make such order as it thinks fit 'having regard to the welfare of the infant and to the conduct of the parents and to the wishes as well of the mother as of the father'.
>
> In administering these provisions the courts do not assume the functions of a children's welfare board seeking to discover, independently of parental and family relationship, the most eligible custodian, locality and environment for the upbringing of the infant: cf per Lord *Clyde* and Lord *Sands, Hume v Hume* 1926 SC 1008 at 1014 and 1015 respectively.
>
> The traditional view is still followed in the courts that prima facie it is for the welfare of a child that it should enjoy the affection and care of parents and be brought up under their guidance and influence.

In ascertaining where the welfare of a child lies, the courts have sought to discover what is in the child's 'best interests'. The 'best interests' approach focuses attention on the child whose interests are in question. By asserting that the *child's* 'best interests' are 'the first and paramount consideration', the law is freed from the degrading doctrines of earlier times which gave priority to parental or, more particularly, paternal rights to which the interests of the child were subordinated. (As in *In Re Agar-Ellis. Agar-Ellis v Lascelles* (1878) 10 Ch D 49.) But, that said, the best interests approach does no more than identify the person whose interests are in question: it does not assist in identifying the factors which are relevant to the best interests of the child. (As Grubb and Pearl point out in 'Sterilization and the Courts' (1987) 46 *Cambridge Law Journal* 439 at 442.) The summary rejection by the House of Lords of the criterion offered by *Re Eve* left their Lordships without any guidelines by which to decide *In Re B* – or, at least, without guidelines that could be articulated for general application.

That is because the best interests approach offers no hierarchy of values which might guide the exercise of a discretionary power to authorise sterilisation, much less any general legal principle which might direct the difficult decisions to be made in this area by parents, guardians, the medical profession and courts. It is arguable that, in a field where the law has not developed, where ethical principles remain controversial and where each case turns on its own facts, the law should not pretend to too great a precision. Better, it might be said, that authority and power conferred on a suitable repository – whether it be parents or guardians, doctors or the court – to decide these difficult questions according to the repository's view as to the best interests of the child in the particular circumstances of the case. In that way, it can be said, the blunt instrument of legal power will be sharpened according to the exigencies of the occasion. The absence of a community consensus on ethical principles may be thought to support this approach. But it must be remembered that, in the absence of legal rules or a hierarchy of values, the best interests approach depends upon the value system of the decision-maker. Absent any rule or guideline, that approach simply creates an unexaminable discretion in the repository of the power. Who could then say that the repository of the power is right or wrong in deciding where the best interests of an intellectually disabled child might lie when there is no clear ethical consensus adopted by the community? An authorisation to sterilise might be reviewable by a tribunal, but what guidance would the best interests approach give the tribunal? The problem was identified by Professor Ian Kennedy (in his paper 'Patients, Doctors and Human Rights', in Blackburn and Taylor (eds), *Human Rights for the 1990s* (1991), pp 90-91):

> To decide any case by reference to the formula of the best interests of the child must be suspect. To decide *Re B* this way is profoundly to be regretted. The best interests formula may be beloved of family lawyers but a moment's reflection will indicate that although it is said to be a test, indeed *the* legal test for deciding matters relating to children, it is not really a test at all. Instead, it is a somewhat crude conclusion of

social policy. It allows lawyers and courts to persuade themselves and others that theirs is a principled approach to law. Meanwhile, they engage in what to others is clearly a form of '*ad hocery*'. The best interests approach of family law allows the courts to atomise the law, to claim that each case depends on its own facts. The court can then respond intuitively to each case while seeking to legitimate its conclusion by asserting that it is derived from the general principle contained in the best interests formula. In fact, of course, there is no general principle other than the empty rhetoric of best interests; or rather, there is some principle (or principles) but the court is not telling. Obviously the court must be following *some* principles, otherwise a toss of the coin could decide cases. But these principles, which serve as pointers to what amounts to the best interests, are not articulated by the court. Only the conclusion is set out. The opportunity for reasoned analysis and scrutiny is lost.

Of course the variable circumstances of each case require evaluation and judicial evaluations of circumstances vary, but the power to authorise sterilisation is so awesome, its exercise is so open to abuse, and the consequences of its exercise are generally so irreversible, that guidelines if not rules should be prescribed to govern it. The courts must attempt the task in the course of, and as a necessary incident in, the exercise of their jurisdiction. That is not to say that the courts should arrogate to themselves the power to authorise sterilisations of intellectually disabled children, but it is to say that it has become the duty of the courts – and, in the present case, specifically the duty of this Court – to define the scope of the power to authorise sterilisations of intellectually disabled children and the conditions of exercise of the power, and to determine the repository of the power. The power cannot be left in a state so amorphous that it can be exercised according to the idiosyncratic views of the repository as to the 'best interests' of the child. That approach provides an insubstantial protection of the human dignity of children; it wraps no cloak of protective principle around the intellectually disabled child. And yet, as Professor Kennedy points out, that is the very purpose of involving the legal process – a purpose which the best interests approach defeats so that 'the law fails the woman-about-to-be-sterilised' (Kennedy, ibid, at p 91).

The anxious goodwill of the repository of the power – whether parents, guardians or courts – can generally be assumed, but there are too many factors which tend to distort a dispassionate and accurate assessment of the true interests of the child. There are some powerful if unarticulated influences affecting, albeit in good faith, the presentation of information on which a decision as to the best interests of the child is to be made and the making of that decision. I mention some of those influences: the interests of those who bear the burden of caring for the child, the interests of those who will be involved in the sterilisation if it proceeds, the scarcity of public resources, the widespread tendency to dismiss intellectually disabled people as not deserving of full human dignity (especially if their powers of communication are defective) and common misconceptions (see the factors referred to by Professor F J Bates, 'Sterilising the Apparently Incapable: Further Thoughts and Developments' (1987) 12 *Australian Child and Family Welfare* 4 at 5) (for example, that there is a substantial risk that any intellectually disabled female will bear defective children). Again, Professor Kennedy points out that, by transforming a 'complex moral and social question' into a question of fact, the best interests approach leaves the court in the hands of 'experts' who assemble a dossier of fact and opinion on matters which they deem relevant 'without reference to any check-list of *legal requirements*' (Kennedy, op cit, at pp 91-92). It is not possible for the law to neutralise those influences, but it is possible for the law to define the issues with sufficient objectivity to minimise the prospect that those influences will undermine the law's protection of the human dignity of the intellectually disabled child.

If the pragmatism of the best interests approach were to be embraced for want of principle to govern the exercise of the power, the choice of the repository of power would be extremely difficult. On the one hand, parents and guardians, who bear the immediate responsibility for a child's welfare and frequently bear the burden of her care, would have a strong claim to be the repository of the power. On the other, the courts, whose judges are removed from the burdens of and pressures upon parents and guardians and who would bear no personal responsibility for any decision they might make, could offer some check upon abuses of the power. A third choice would be to require the concurrence both of parents or guardians and of the court as a condition of the exercise of the power. If no principle other than the best interests approach is to govern the exercise of the power, it would be necessary to adopt the third choice to secure for the child the protection which neither of the first two choices could offer, making provision for a special procedure (as was proposed in *In Re F (Mental Patient: Sterilization)* [1990] 2 AC 1 at 65; and cf *In Re Grady* (1981) NJ 426 A 2d 467 at 481-483; *Matter of Guardianship of Hayes* (1980) Wash 608 P 2d 635 at 639-641, 643) in an attempt to safeguard the interests of the child. That would be a cumbersome and costly expedient which, if the approach in *Re Eve* is followed, need not be adopted.

With the greatest respect for the views expressed by their Lordships in *Re B*, I find the decision of their Lordships in *Re Eve* more conducive to the maintenance of the human dignity of the intellectually disabled and more in accord with legal principle. The test of therapeutic medical treatment recognises the importance of personal integrity and of the maintenance and enhancement of natural attributes to the welfare of the child. By comparison, the best interests approach is useful only to the extent of ensuring that the first and paramount consideration is the interests of the child, not the interests of others. That approach furnishes no general guidance as to the factors which are relevant to the welfare of the child.

Of course, factual difficulties are unavoidable in deciding whether medical treatment is therapeutic or non-therapeutic but, in principle, the distinction is clear and, in particular, the purpose of therapeutic medical treatment can be clearly distinguished from other purposes. Therapeutic medical treatment is calculated to enhance or maintain as far as practicable the physical or mental attributes which the patient naturally possesses; it is not calculated to impair or destroy those attributes and the capacities they afford. Thus, there is a rationale which justifies the administration of therapeutic medical treatment without the patient's consent when the patient is incapable of consenting or refusing consent. It needs no argument to show that a malignant tumour of the uterus justifies the performance of an hysterectomy or that multiple cysts on an ovary may dictate its surgical removal. However, where menstruation produces or is likely to produce a psychiatric disorder of such severity as to require its suppression – as occurred in *Re X* [1991] 2 NZLR 365 – consideration must be given to the different treatments reasonably available and appropriate to suppress menstruation and to their medical advantages and disadvantages in order to ensure that the least invasive of the treatments is selected. Proportionality and purpose are the legal factors which determine the therapeutic nature of medical treatment. Proportionality is determined as a question of medical fact. Purpose is ascertained by reference to all the circumstances but especially to the physical or mental condition which the treatment is appropriate to affect.

The propriety of authorising sterilisation for therapeutic purposes is not reasonably open to doubt. Therapeutic medical treatment falls clearly within the exception of 'medical treatment . . . reasonably needed' in s 187(c) of the Code. When the purpose of a proposed sterilisation is therapeutic, the invasion of the child's physical integrity, the disquieting of her mind and any change in her self-perception are justified by the need to maintain to the maximum extent or to enhance the child's natural physical and mental attributes. The invasion of the child's personal integrity is then the means of maintaining or enhancing the attributes and functions which, so far as they may, contribute to her human dignity. The propriety of authorising sterilisation for non-therapeutic purposes is more problematic.

Non-therapeutic sterilisation

If sterilisation is contemplated to secure a non-therapeutic purpose, the invasion of the child's personal integrity can be justified only if it can be shown that the non-therapeutic purpose possesses some higher value than the preservation of her physical integrity. Clearly, sterilisation could not be justified in order to secure some base purpose – for example, to prevent the birth of a child who would disappoint the testamentary expectations of a residuary beneficiary. Another base purpose which would now be commonly recognised as such, though it was given a higher value in earlier days (see per Holmes J in *Buck v Bell* (1927) 274 US 200 at 207) before the uncivilised practices of Nazism revealed its hideous implications, is the purpose of eugenic selection. Economic arguments can be mounted in support of a policy of preventing the birth of defective children and those arguments can be supported by a desire to alleviate the emotional and physical burden of caring for them but, even in a case where an intellectual disability is transmissible, the involuntary sterilisation of a girl is too high a price to pay to avoid the risk. A law which sacrifices the human dignity of individuals in order to avoid reasonable calls by the disabled upon public resources and to avoid the need for compassionate assistance to the disabled inverts the civilised priority of values and depletes the humanity of society. Financial security and comfort, though legitimate objectives in themselves, are not to be preferred over the equal protection by the law of the human rights of every member of the community. The sterilisation of a human being simply in order to prevent him or her from becoming a parent is an extreme denial of that person's human rights.

However, between therapeutic purposes on the one hand and manifestly base purposes on the other, a variety of different purposes may appear which many would regard as of significant value in assessing the 'best interests' of an intellectually disabled child. The purposes which fall into this category can be gathered under the broad description of 'preventative': to prevent the risk of a pregnancy which the child could not properly understand and the concomitant risk of parenthood with responsibilities beyond the capacity of the child to discharge. These risks are an understandable source of anxiety to parents, guardians and others who have a genuine concern for the welfare of an intellectually disabled child. These are risks which create an understandable anxiety in many parents, guardians and others who have a genuine concern for the welfare of a normal child. In the case of a normal female child, it would be wholly unacceptable to permit sterilisation in order to prevent pregnancy or parenthood, though those events might be thought to be tragedies in particular circumstances by reasonable persons concerned with the welfare of the child. Depending on the circumstances, the use – or, a fortiori, the exploitation – of the sexual attributes of a female child may entail tragic consequences, yet the risk of even the likelihood of tragic consequences affords no justification for her sterilisation. What difference does it make that the risk is occasioned by an intellectual disability? The answer to this question depends on the view taken of the proposition earlier set out in the Declaration on the Rights of Mentally Retarded Persons: they are entitled to the *same* rights as other humans to the maximum degree of feasibility. To accord in full measure the human dignity that is the due of every intellectually disabled girl, her right to retain her capacity to bear a child cannot be made contingent on her imposing no further burdens, causing no more anxiety or creating no further demands. If the law were to adopt a policy of permitting sterilisation in order to avoid the imposition of burdens, the causing of anxiety and the creating of demands, the human rights which foster and protect human dignity in the powerless would lie in the gift of those who are empowered and the law would fail in its function of protecting the weak.

Where it is desirable to avoid the risk of pregnancy, the risk may be avoidable by means which involve no invasion of the girl's personal integrity. Those who are charged with responsibility for the care and control of an intellectually disabled girl (by which I mean a female child who is sexually mature) – whether parents, guardians or the staff of institutions – have a duty to ensure that the girl is not sexually exploited or abused. If her disability inclines her to sexual promiscuity, they have a duty to restrain her from exposing herself to exploitation. It is unacceptable that an authority be given for the girl's sterilisation in order to lighten the burden of that duty, much less to allow for its neglect. In any event, though pregnancy be a possibility, sterilisation, once performed, is a certainty. If a non-therapeutic sterilisation could be justified at all, it could be justified only by the need to avoid a tragedy that is imminent and certain. Such a situation bespeaks a failure of care, and sterilisation is not the remedy for the failure. Nor should it be forgotten that pregnancy and motherhood may have a significance for some intellectually disabled girls quite different from the significance attributed by other people. Though others may see her pregnancy and motherhood as a tragedy, she, in her world, may find in those events an enrichment of her life.

Because non-therapeutic purposes are, by definition, related to social values or values other than the maintenance and enhancement of the natural attributes and functions of the intellectually disabled female child, I am unable to postulate a case where it would be justifiable to authorise her sterilisation. I am conscious that courts which have adopted the best interests approach have been accustomed to balance the risks of what may appear to be likely social tragedies against the physical invasion, incapacitation and mental and emotional impact of sterilisation. In my respectful opinion, a balancing exercise is impossible to perform. On one side is the immediate and serious invasion of physical integrity with the resulting grave impairment of human dignity. On the other, there is a risk of what is adjudged to be a future tragedy involving dependence on others, inability to cope, social incompetence or some other matter apparently diminishing the quality of the child's life. The values on either side of the balance are not comparable. If there is to be a rule – as, in my view, there must be – the rule must give priority to the right to physical integrity and the human dignity it protects, even though such a rule imposes burdens on parents, guardians and those having the care of the intellectually disabled child who are entitled to the active support of the State which must bear the ultimate burden.

Such a rule, it may be said, is too idealistic and is out of touch with contemporary community standards. There is much force in that criticism but this is an area of the law in which it is necessary to guard against the tyranny which majority opinion may impose on a weak and voiceless minority. The history of intellectually disabled people contains a surfeit of examples of degrading treatment administered under laws which reflected the standards of the time – standards which were a reproach to the civilisation then enjoyed. If equality under the law, human rights and the protection of minorities are more than the incantations of legal rhetoric, it is in this area of the law that they have real work to do.

I would hold that the power to authorise sterilisation of an intellectually disabled child extends to therapeutic sterilisations but no further . . . the power to authorise non-therapeutic sterilisation of an intellectually disabled child is a novel power which some courts have, by their own decision, assumed to themselves. (In the United States, judicial opinion as to the existence of the power has fluctuated: see the cases collected in *In Re Grady* (1981) NJ 426 A 2d at 480.) It is not only the assumption of a novel power which is significant but the assertion that it is assumed in exercise of the wardship or parens patriae jurisdiction. If that be so, the power is exercisable over the objection of parents or guardians and simply on the footing that the court deems its exercise to be in the 'best interests' of the child. Of course the parents or guardians will be heard on any application to the court, but the idiosyncratic views of the judge are given, by this theory, overwhelming effect.

In the United States, the assumption by courts of a power to authorise sterilisation of intellectually disabled people has been accompanied by judicial prescription of protective procedures and criteria for determining whether sterilisation is in the patient's best interests: see *In Re Grady* (at 481-483) and *Matter of Guardianship of Hayes* (1980) Wash 608 P 2d at 639-641, 643. Though the desirability of protective procedures and criteria is manifest, their prescription gave the Courts' decisions a legislative character in the eyes of Rosselini J who, speaking for the minority in *Matter of Guardianship of Hayes*, expressed his concern that the courts not become 'an imperial judiciary' (at 646). I share his concern. The hypothesis that a court is empowered to authorise the non-therapeutic sterilisation of intellectually disabled children is asserted in order to satisfy what the court perceives to be a lacuna in the powers which ought to be available to satisfy the exigencies of the situation of some disabled children. But the court is an instrument of State power, and the powers of the State to authorise interference with the personal integrity of any of its subjects otherwise than for therapeutic purposes is not self-evident. If such a power can be exercised to secure what the court may deem to be the welfare of an intellectually disabled child, may not a like power be exercised to secure what the court may deem to be the welfare of any child? It is a power which would be exercised not by an anxious and anguishing parent or guardian who can be called to account, but by a judge to whom the case is assigned in a court's list and who, having exercised his or her discretion, is discharged from all responsibility for the consequences. The case of *Stamp v Sparkman* (1978) 435 US 349, which left the sterilised woman and her husband without remedy, despite a demonstrably erroneous exercise of judicial power to authorise her sterilisation, is a distressing reminder that courts, for all their independence and wisdom, are not appropriate repositories of so awesome a power.

Moreover, the assumption of a power to authorise non-therapeutic sterilisations without legislative authority is tantamount to the assumption of a power to dispense from compliance with the criminal laws which otherwise protect personal integrity. Justification by court order for what is otherwise an offence is neither an orthodox doctrine of the common law nor consistent with the proper function of a court. Though some statutes create offences exempting instances in which a court is satisfied that particular circumstances exist, the proposition that a court can assume a power to dispense from the criminal laws which protect personal dignity when the judge believes the dispensation is for the welfare of a child is truly judicial imperialism. If that proposition were valid, the laws which presently bear on organ and tissue donations, medical experimentation, abortion or other surgical procedures could be overriden if an application were made to a judge vested with the parens patriae jurisdiction who took the view that the application of the law in the particular circumstances of the case would not be in the child's best interests. It is one thing for a court to exercise the power possessed by parents and guardians to authorise surgical procedures on a child and for the criminal law to accept that authorisation, as it accepts an authorisation by the parents or guardians, to be the equivalent of consent to what would otherwise be an unlawful application of force. It is another thing for a court to exercise an exclusively curial power to authorise a surgical procedure and to require that authorisation to be treated both as an effective consent and as conclusively determining the lawfulness of the procedure. In the former case, the criminal law is simply construed to take account of the parental power which has always been recognised; in the latter case, protection which the criminal law has been fashioned to provide is undone by the exercise of a novel power, created by declaration of the instrument of government claiming to exercise it.

Deane J: Irreversible sterilisation involves the destruction of a natural human attribute and the removal of an integral part of complete human personality. Its eventual psychological consequences will commonly be unforeseeable. They may include emotional devastation, destruction of self-esteem and perceived deprivation of an essential element and purpose of life itself. Nonetheless, circumstances can arise in which surgery involving irreversible sterilisation is, according to general community standards, clearly conducive to the welfare of an incapable child. The most obvious example of such circumstances is where such surgery is necessary to preserve the life of the child: eg, excision or other treatment to avert death by reason of cancer of the ovaries or testicles. Where that is so, it is, as a matter of general principle, within the authority of parents to authorise the surgery in the same way as it is within the authority of parents of an incapable child to authorise the amputation of an incurably gangrenous limb. Similarly, the parents of an incapable child have authority to authorise surgery involving irreversible sterilisation in a case where such surgery is, according to competent medical advice, necessary for the conventional purpose of treating or preventing grave physical illness. In such cases, the common law requirement of due inquiry and adequate consideration is satisfied by competent medical advice, including or supplemented by appropriate multi-specialist and inter-disciplinary input (eg, psychological or vocational).

In the present case, the reasons for the suggested surgery are not purely medical. In some judgments in the decided cases, and in argument in the present case, the phrases 'therapeutic surgery' and 'non-therapeutic surgery' have been used to distinguish between surgery for the traditional medical purpose of preserving life or directly treating or preventing physical illness and surgery for other or wider purposes, such as the enhancement or preservation of the quality of life. The use of those phrases in a context such as the present must, however, be accompanied by two important caveats. The first is that the borderline between 'therapeutic' and 'non-therapeutic' surgery is far from precise and, particularly where psychiatric illness is involved, may be all but meaningless. In particular, surgery involving the sterilisation of a young intellectually disabled female to avoid the special and aggravated problems of menstruation would not appear to me to be for conventional medical purposes but is often described as being for 'therapeutic purposes'. (See, eg, *Re E (A Minor) (Medical Treatment)* [1991] 2 FLR 585 at 586; *Re GF (A Patient)* [1991] FCR 786 at 787-788.) The second is that the common law does not, as a matter of principle, draw a general distinction between 'therapeutic' and 'non-therapeutic' surgery for the purposes of parental authority. (See, eg, per Lord Hailsham of St Marylebone LC, *In Re B (A Minor)* [1988] AC, at 203-204.) . . .

. . . [T]here are circumstances in which it is plain that, according to the general standards of our society, surgery involving sterilisation of an incapable child for reasons other than the conventional medical ones of preventing death or treating or preventing physical illness is or is not clearly in the interests of the welfare of the child. The New Zealand case of *Re X* [1991] 2 NZLR 365 provides a convenient example of circumstances in which such surgery is plainly in the interests of the welfare of an incapable child.

The judgment in *Re X* was delivered on X's 15th birthday. She was a profoundly multi-handicapped girl with the intellectual capacity (other than as regards gross motor skills such as walking) of a three to eight-month-old infant. She could not speak, was not toilet-trained despite intensive efforts by both her family and the staff of the special school which she attended, had no 'control whatever over her bodily functions' (at 367) and was, and would obviously remain, quite incapable of understanding human relations, sex or human procreation. This lack of understanding and her inability to express herself meant that the only indications that she gave when sustaining pain were non-specific reactions which included fits of irritability capable of lasting for an entire day and involved threatening conduct and violence towards others and a degree of self-mutilation.

The onset of menstruation was imminent and the overall evidence, both lay and medical, led inevitably to the conclusion that the child's reaction to menstrual pain would be uncomprehending irritability involving likely violence and some self-mutilation. X's parents, who were unusually knowledgeable about retarded children and heroically devoted to X and her interests, were convinced that she could not cope either with menstrual periods or with the associated hygienic problems. The trial judge, Hillyer J, summarised (at 368) their approach, with which he agreed, as follows:

> X's parents believe there is very little point in her having monthly periods for the next 30 years. She has a very strong heart and is likely to live that long. She will never be able to have children, and that function in her life is quite unnecessary. They believe X goes through enough pain and agony without having to deal with monthly periods as well. She has had to have operations to cure club feet and to straighten her back. She came through these well, and in hospital was given pain relief mainly by suppositories because of the difficulty in getting her to swallow anything, let alone giving her injections. The mother says X is hopeless with medicines. She will not let other people touch her or put anything in her mouth except food.

In circumstances where there was no prospect of any significant improvement in X's condition as she grew older it was obvious – as Hillyer J found (at 367) – that it was 'absolutely vital' that 'she should not become pregnant' since she 'most certainly could not cope with motherhood, pregnancy or labour' and the 'only way she could become pregnant would be by being raped, because she is unable under any circumstances to consent'. The application by X's parents for an order consenting to a hysterectomy operation upon X was supported by medical evidence that the surgery was desirable and that there was no less drastic treatment which would, in the circumstances, be appropriate. Hillyer J held that the High Court of New Zealand had jurisdiction to make such an order under its residual parens patriae jurisdiction (see, generally, per Cooke J, *Pallin v Department of Social Welfare* [1983] NZLR 266 at 272), and that, in the circumstances of the case, such an order should be made. His Honour made clear ([1991] 2 NZLR, at 369) that he saw the purpose of the operation as not sterilisation but the prevention of menstruation. That being so, the importance of his Honour's conclusion that it was 'absolutely vital' that X should never become pregnant was that it turned what would, in the case of a normal child, have probably been a decisive countervailing consideration into a supporting factor.

As I have indicated, the reason for my referring at length to the facts of *Re X* is that the case provides an example of circumstances in which it is quite clear that surgery involving irreversible sterilisation for other than conventional medical purposes is necessary for the welfare of an incapable child. Once it is recognised that parental authority to authorise medical treatment extends, in some circumstances, to the authorisation of surgery involving irreversible sterilisation (eg for the treatment of serious illness), there is no basis in legal principle for excluding from the scope of that parental authority circumstances such as those involved in *Re X*. Certainly it cannot be said that such surgery for the treatment of a serious illness, in a case where it involves the sterilisation of a mentally normal child, is more obviously for the overall welfare of the child than surgery involving irreversible sterilisation in a case such as *Re X* where there are, from the point of view of the child's interests and welfare, compelling physical and social reasons for such surgery and where there is no significant countervailing detriment. It is true that there is a passage in the judgment of La Forest J in *Re Eve* (see (1986) 31 DLR (4th) at 32) which, if read in isolation, suggests that the Supreme Court of Canada accepted the proposition that it can never be safely concluded that 'non-therapeutic sterilisation' is for the benefit of a person incapable of consenting to it. *Re Eve* was, however, a case involving the suggested sterilisation for contraceptive purposes of an intellectually disabled woman of whom it was said (at 9) that 'there is no evidence that giving birth would be more difficult for Eve than for any other woman'. The circumstances of the case were simply not comparable to a case such as *Re X* and it seems to me to be quite clear that the references to 'non-therapeutic sterilisation' in the judgment of La Forest J should not be understood as intended to cover a case where what is involved is surgery upon a profoundly mentally disabled girl to prevent extraordinary difficulty, discomfort and pain which would accompany menstruation. (See, in particular, La Forest J's comments (ibid, at 22) about *Re K and Public Trustee* (1985) 19 DLR (4th) 255; and see, also, the use of the phrases 'therapeutic reasons' and 'therapeutic purposes' in *Re E (A Minor) (Medical Treatment)* [1991] 2 FLR, at 586 and *Re GF (A Patient)* [1991] FCR, at 787.) Be that as it may, I respectfully agree with Lord Bridge of Harwich (*In Re B (A Minor)* [1988] AC, at 205) that:

> To say that the court can never authorise sterilisation of a ward as being in her best interests would be patently wrong. To say that it can only do so if the operation is 'therapeutic' as opposed to 'non-therapeutic' is to divert attention from the true issue, which is whether the operation is in the ward's best interests, and remove it to an area of arid semantic debate as to where the line is to be drawn between 'therapeutic' and 'non-therapeutic' treatment.

Nor can such a confinement of the authority of parents be justified by reason of the gravity of irreversible sterilisation since, as has also been seen, it is plainly within the authority of parents to authorise surgery involving irreversible sterilisation in at least some circumstances. Indeed, the consequences of surgery involving irreversible sterilisation are immeasurably less grave in a case, such as *Re X*, where it is meaningless to speak of the fundamental right to procreate than they are in the case of such surgery upon an intellectually normal child for conventional medical purposes.

On the other hand, the requirement that parental authority to authorise surgery be exercised for the purpose, and only for the purpose, of advancing the welfare of the child necessarily excludes from the scope of that authority some categories of case involving the surgical sterilisation of an incapable child for other than conventional medical purposes.

The most obvious example of such a category of case is surgery for so-called 'eugenic' purposes. Whatever may have been the approach accepted in other times and in other places, surgery upon a retarded person cannot, within the limits imposed by general community standards in this country, be justified by eugenic or 'public welfare' reasons such as those advanced by Holmes J in *Buck v Bell* (1927) 274 US 200 at 207. Nor can such surgery upon a mentally retarded child be justified as necessary for the welfare of the child *merely* because it will make easier the task of those responsible for the child's protection and care. That is not, of course, to deny that the easing of the burden of protecting and caring for an incapable child may, in most cases, be also at least indirectly in the interests of the welfare of the child.

Between the extreme categories of cases, where surgery involving irreversible sterilisation plainly can and plainly cannot be justified as necessary for the welfare of an incapable child are other cases in which there may be room for legitimate differences of opinion about what promotes the welfare of an incapable child in the circumstances of a particular case. Within that area, the welfare principle embodied in the common law propositions stated earlier operates at two levels to define the extent of parental authority. If the circumstances of a particular case are such that surgery involving irreversible sterilisation can reasonably be seen, according to general community standards, as being necessary for the welfare of the particular child, it will lie within the scope of parental authority to authorise it. That parental authority is, however, confined to the authorisation of what the parents, after due inquiry and adequate consideration, consider to be in the interests of the welfare of the child.

In what has been written above, I have already identified the two principal categories of case in which surgery involving irreversible sterilisation of an incapable child is, according to general community standards, obviously necessary for the welfare of the child. The first is where such surgery is immediately necessary for conventional medical purposes, that is to say, the preservation of life or the treatment or prevention of grave physical illness.

The second category is that of which *Re X* constitutes an example. (See, also, *Re E (A Minor) (Medical Treatment)* [1991] 2 FLR 585; *Re GF (A Patient)* [1991] FCR 786.) A case will fall into this category if, but only if, it involves surgery upon a girl and the following conditions are all clearly and convincingly satisfied. (See the discussion of standard of proof in *Re K and Public Trustee* (1985) 19 DLR (4th), at 268-272; and the implicit approval of the 'clear and convincing' standard in *Re Jane* (1988) 94 FLR, at 20-21.) First the child is so profoundly intellectually disabled that she is not and never will be capable of being a party to a mature human relationship involving informed sexual intercourse, of responsible procreation or of caring for an infant. Second, the surgery must be necessary to avoid grave and unusual problems and suffering which are or would be involved in menstruation which has either commenced or which is virtually certain to commence in the near future. These problems could arise from inability to comprehend or cope with pain; a phobic aversion to blood; a complete inability to cope with problems of hygiene with psychiatric or psychological consequences; or any of a variety of other possible complications. The problems or suffering which would result from menstruation must be such that it is plain that, according to general community standards, it would be quite unfair for the child and ultimate adult to be required to bear the additional burden of them. Third, the surgery must be a treatment of last resort in the sense that no alternative and less drastic treatment would be appropriate and effective. I would expect that the second and third requirements could not be satisfied in many cases until menstruation had actually commenced. Fourth, there must be competent medical advice from a multidisciplinary team, acting on the basis of appropriate paediatric, social and domestic reports, that the above conditions are all satisfied. When parents have received such multidisciplinary advice, they will have discharged the obligation of due inquiry and adequate consideration and will be justified in authorising the particular surgery.

The question arises whether there are any other categories of case in which surgery involving irreversible sterilisation of an incapable child can be said to be obviously necessary for the welfare of the child. On balance, it seems to me that there are not. Like Hillyer J in *Re X* [1991] 2 NZLR, at 369-370, Anderson JA in *Re K and Public Trustee* (1985) 19 DLR (4th), at 274-275 and Brown P in *Re E (A Minor) (Medical Treatment)* [1991] 2 FLR, at 586, I would draw a distinction between the category of case (see above) in which the primary purpose of the surgery is to prevent pain and extraordinary behavioural and personal problems which are, in the circumstances of a particular case, involved in menstruation and the case where the purpose of the operation is sterilisation for contraceptive purposes. Notwithstanding the views expressed by the Supreme Court of Canada in *Re Eve* (1986) 31 DLR (4th), esp at 32, it appears to me that there may well be circumstances in which surgery involving sterilisation of a profoundly intellectually disabled child for contraceptive purposes may, in the circumstances of a particular case, be necessary for the welfare of the child. I am not, however, persuaded that sterilisation for contraceptive purposes could ever be said to be so obviously necessary for the welfare of an incapable child that parents would be justified in dispensing with the impartial and independent advice of a court or other statutory tribunal which has the capacity to deliver an authoritative and binding opinion on the question.

The judges of the Family Court have, in earlier cases and in the present case, made evident their appreciation of the multiplicity of factors which may be relevant to the question whether parents would be justified in authorising surgery involving irreversible sterilisation in the circumstances of a particular case. A list of a number of those factors is set out near the end of the thoughtful and helpful judgment of Hillyer J in *Re X* [1991] 2 NZLR, at 376-378. His Honour, in my view correctly, places at the forefront of those factors the need to identify the child's level of functioning and development and to consider whether there is any real likelihood of a significant increase in the child's capabilities in the future. The importance of those two aspects cannot be over-emphasised. In dealing with them, a court must be vigilant against the danger of making false and adverse assumptions about the ability of an intellectually disabled person to become a party to a mature human relationship involving informed sexual relations, to engage in responsible procreation and to care for an infant. A court must also be vigilant against the danger of discounting the possibility of significant future improvement in the capabilities of an intellectually disabled person with regard to those matters. Indeed, unless the case is one in which there is no real likelihood that the child in question will ever be able to make a responsible decision for herself or himself about surgery involving irreversible sterilisation, it is difficult to envisage circumstances in which a court would be justified in pre-empting that decision in a case where such surgery was not at that time necessary for compelling medical or quasi-medical (eg the near certainty of trauma or psychological damage) reasons.

The material before the Court in the present case does not establish that the case falls within either of the categories of case (conventional medical reasons or the *Re X* type of case) in which it can be said that surgery involving sterilisation of an incapable girl is obviously justified in the interests of the child's welfare. On the other hand, the material before the Court does not seem to me to preclude the possibility that the present case does fall within the second of those categories.

McHugh J: [A] parent has authority to consent to the sterilisation of a child in his or her custody if it will advance or protect the welfare of the child. What is in the best interests of the child is conventionally seen as being synonymous with the welfare of the child. To say that a medical or surgical procedure is in the best interests of a child, however, is merely to record a result. Before the best interests of the child can be determined, some principle, rule or standard must be applied to the facts and circumstances of the case (cf Kennedy, 'Patients, Doctors, and Human Rights', Blackburn and Taylor (eds), *Human Rights for the 1990s* (1991), pp 90-91).

Since sterilisation has grave consequences for a person's adult life, it cannot be in the best interests of a child to pre-empt a choice about that procedure which the child would otherwise have as an adult person. If there is any real possibility that, at some future time, the child will acquire the capacity and maturity to choose whether he or she should be sterilised, the carrying out of that procedure cannot be in the best interests of the child unless, of course, protection of the child's health urgently requires that the procedure be carried out during incompetency. Moreover, it must not be assumed that, simply because the child is intellectually disabled, he or she does not have or cannot acquire the capacity to consent to sterilisation. Intellectually disabled persons will frequently have the capacity to make the choice as to whether they should be sterilised (Committee on Rights of Persons with Handicaps (SA), *The Law and Persons with Handicaps*, vol 2: *Intellectual Handicaps* (1981), p 125). Furthermore, sterilisation involves invasive procedures resulting in the permanent deprivation of a person's right or liberty to reproduce, with the potentiality for psychological harm including the lowering – perhaps the destruction – of self-esteem and, in the case of the intellectually disabled, the reinforcement of anxieties which are commonly the result of intellectual disability. (See Law Reform Commission of Canada (Working Paper No 24 1979), *Sterilization: Implications for Mentally Retarded and Mentally Ill Persons*, pp 49-52.)

So grave are the certain and potential effects of sterilisation that that procedure can only be for the welfare of the child if the circumstances are so compelling and so likely to endure that they justify the invasive surgery or procedure involved in sterilisation. The circumstances may be compelling if the failure to carry out the procedure is likely to result in the child's physical or mental health being seriously jeopardised or if it is likely to result in the suffering of pain, fear or discomfort of such severity and duration or regularity that it is not reasonable to expect the child to suffer that pain, fear or discomfort. In these cases, the right of the incompetent person to have his or her body protected against invasive procedures resulting in removal or destruction of reproductive organs is outweighed by the necessity for appropriate 'treatment'. The circumstances may also be compelling if the failure to carry out the procedure is likely to result in a real risk that an intellectually disabled child will become pregnant and she does not, and never will, have any real understanding of sexual relationships or pregnancy. In such a case, to speak of a fundamental right of reproduction is meaningless. The human dignity of an intellectually disabled child is not advanced, and indeed is denied, by allowing her (by, what is in point of law, rape) to become pregnant and to give birth in circumstances which she cannot understand and which may result in a frightening ordeal for her not only at the time of birth, but for many months prior thereto.

What constitutes sufficiently compelling circumstances to justify sterilisation will have to be worked out on a case by case basis. But, unless the case falls within one of the above categories or a category analogous thereto, it should be held that the sterilisation of a child is not for his or her welfare. In particular, it is not for the welfare of an intellectually disabled child to sterilise that child merely to avoid pregnancy or to give effect to eugenic policies. Nor is it for the welfare of the child to sterilise her merely because of the hygiene problems associated with menstruation. At the Law Reform Commission of Canada has pointed out, intellectually disabled females who require a great deal of assistance in managing their menstruation are already likely to require assistance with urinary and faecal control, problems which are much more troublesome in terms of personal hygiene (at 34). Moreover, even if the case falls within one of the three categories which I have mentioned or an analogous category, it is not in the best interests of a child to sterilise him or her if the harm can reasonably be avoided by means less drastic than sterilisation.

Furthermore, as I have indicated, sterilisation is one area where the potential for conflict between the parent's interests and the child's interest exists. As Justice Horowitz pointed out in *Matter of Guardianship of Hayes* (1980) Wash 608 P 2d 635 at 640:

> unlike the situation of a normal and necessary medical procedure, in the question of sterilisation the interests of the parent of a retarded person cannot be presumed to be identical to those of the child.

Thus, parents may see sterilisation as relieving them of the worry and distress of the child becoming pregnant or of the burden of caring for a grandchild whom the child would not be able or fully able to care for. If a decision to consent is actuated by interests such as these, a conflict of interest arises. In such a case, the parents have no authority to consent to the sterilisation of their child. However, since parents have authority to consent to a sterilisation procedure only in cases where the grounds for the procedure are compelling it is unlikely that, in practice, conflict will arise. If it does, a court of general jurisdiction invested with the parens patriae jurisdiction or the Family Court may give consent in substitution for the parents.

The principles which apply to the sterilisation of children, as I have adumbrated them, fall somewhere between the approach of the Supreme Court of Canada in *Re Eve (E(Mrs) v Eve ('Re Eve')* [1986] 2 SCR 388; 31 DLR (4th) 1) and the approach of the House of Lords in *In Re F*. *In Re Eve*, the Supreme Court held that, in the exercise of the parens patriae jurisdiction, a court should not give consent to a non-therapeutic sterilisation. The distinction between therapeutic and non-therapeutic treatment was strongly criticised by members of the House of Lords in *In Re B (A Minor)* [1988] AC 199 at 203-294, 205. I agree with Professor Kennedy, in the article to which I have earlier referred, where he said (Kennedy, op cit, p 102) that, although 'there are problems at the edges' of the two concepts, '[a]n intervention is therapeutic if treatment (therapy) is intended thereby'. This definition would include the first two categories of justification to which I have referred but exclude the third category. However, for the reasons that I have already given, I think that, where the child has no real understanding of sexual relationships or pregnancy, sterilisation may be justified if no method of contraception is reasonably feasible. In that respect, I would go beyond the approach of the Supreme Court in *Re Eve*. Moreover, it would be inconsistent with the historical development of common law principles to close the categories to which they apply. Consequently, unlike the Supreme Court of Canada, I would hold that sterilisation may also be carried out for purposes which are analogous to the three categories to which I have referred. Such an approach allows the law to develop incrementally, guided by the overarching principle that the circumstances must be so compelling that they justify such an invasive procedure as sterilisation.

In *In Re F*, the House of Lords held that sterilisation of an incompetent child was justified if it was necessary or in the public interest and that it would be in the public interest if the procedure was in the best interests of the child. Their Lordships held that it will be in the best interests of the patient if a doctor has formed the opinion that sterilisation should be carried out provided that that opinion corresponds with a respectable body of medical opinion among those experienced in the field. Their Lordships (Lord Griffith dissenting on this point) held that the involvement of a court was highly desirable as a matter of good practice although it was not necessary as a matter of law. The approach of their Lordships goes well beyond what I consider is the proper view of the common law, even when the decision to sterilise is ultimately made by a court.

In effect, the approach of their Lordships transfers the issue to the medical profession for determination. As Professor Kennedy points out (at pp 89-90, 91, 98), once the doctors approve the procedure, the court gives its consent to the procedure on the basis of what the doctors and social workers 'regard as important or significant'. In substance, as Professor Kennedy asserts (at p 90):

> The courts will be presented with a fait accompli. Those who wish to challenge it will have what amounts to a near impossible task. They will have to persuade the court to reject, wholly or in part, the evidence of the 'experts', evidence that is often unanimous and which has all the trappings of expertise. It will be too late to argue that the answers may be wrong because the questions were wrong.

Whatever may be the position in England, the approach of their Lordships is not consistent with the common law of Australia.

The decision of the Australian High Court is instructive for two reasons. *First*, whatever the merits of the position adopted by the majority or by the other judges, at least the court shows its hand. The majority state expressly what factors and values they regard as important, as do the judges in the minority. If it does nothing else this provides the basis for an informed debate on what is clearly an issue which, it may be thought, has been resolved for the present in the UK but which may attract Parliamentary attention in the future. *Secondly*, the variety of judgments and the significant differences in the analyses adopted illustrate how complex and troubling is the question of sterilising incompetent patients. This also prompts the enquiry whether a court is the proper arbiter of the issue or whether it should be a matter for Parliament.

4. England: the cases post *Re F*

In the meantime, given that the English courts must follow the law as established by the House of Lords, this will involve (as we have seen) the application of a less than precise criterion of 'best interests' interpreted by reference to the *Bolam* test. The consequences of this approach can already be seen from a series of first instance cases. Professor Margaret Brazier discusses two early decisions: *Re M (A Minor)(Wardship: Sterilisation)* [1988] 2 FLR 497 (Bush J) (tubal ligation) and *Re P (A Minor)(Wardship: Sterilisation)* [1989] 1 FLR 182 (Eastham J) (tubal ligation).

Margaret Brazier 'Sterilisation: Down the Slippery Slope?' (1990) 6 Professional Negligence 25

The judgments in *Re M* and *Re P* [requiring the authorisation of a judge] cast doubt on how effective the judicial safeguard has turned out to be. M was another seventeen-year-old girl with a mental age of five or six. Like Jeannette [in *Re B*], she appeared to have no maternal feelings. Two features of her case are pertinent. First, the gynaecologist who was intending to carry out the operation testified, and the judge placed great emphasis on his testimony, that with the improvements in tubal surgery there was a 50 to 75 per cent chance of successfully reversing sterilisation should M's condition ever improve. Second, there was said to be a 50 per cent chance any child born to M might suffer from some degree of mental retardation. Bush J stated very firmly that eugenic considerations were in themselves irrelevant but then did appear to take into account evidence that if M should become pregnant an abortion on the ground of foetal handicap might be recommended. And he was clearly influenced in his decision to authorise sterilisation by the evidence advanced of the operation's reversibility.

Perhaps, apart from a slight inference that eugenics banned from the front door is being let in at the back, the decision in *Re M* is little different from *Re B*. But *Re M* laid the foundation for the next and truly disturbing judgment of Eastham J in *Re P*. P was a seventeen-year-old of normal and attractive appearance who was said to have a mental age of six. In contrast to Jeannette, her communication skills were good, at least at the level of the average six-year-old. Her intellectual development would, it was thought, not improve although her social skills were advancing with care and training. She appeared to be vulnerable to seduction and seemed to have some maternal feelings. Her mother feared that if she became pregnant and understood what was happening she would refuse to agree to an abortion. Taking her child away from her at birth would be traumatic. It would be a disaster for her to have a child.

Eastham J authorised the sterilisation of P. He found that she might eventually attain the level of understanding needed for capacity to marry. He agreed that, as at present P regarded sexual intercourse as painful, there was no current risk of pregnancy. She was quite clearly a young woman with greater understanding of human relationships and maternity than B. The 'right' to reproduce, to bear a child and give birth appeared to be something P might well value. So what persuaded Eastham J to authorise an operation said just two years earlier to be a measure of 'last resort'? Three factors stand out as crucial to his decision: (1) He agreed with arguments advanced that P was vulnerable to exploitation by unscrupulous males; (2) He was concerned by evidence that if P gave birth and her child was taken from her that event would be traumatic and damaging for her; (3) And most importantly, the judge was impressed by the evidence of Professor Robert Winston that reversal of female sterilisation carried out by clips on the Fallopian tubes now has a 95 per cent success rate. On the basis of this evidence, his Lordship concluded that in 1989 sterilisation should no longer be regarded as the 'last resort'. The House of Lords in *Re B* in 1987 had perceived female sterilisation as irreversible:

> The situation today is that the operation is not irreversible, although it is still current ethical practice to tell patients that it is an irreversible operation as part of the information to be given to them when they are giving consent for the operation to be carried out, although if such a patient changes her mind, no doubt it would be explained to her that the more serious reversal operation could be contemplated.

The judgment in *Re P* must cast doubt on the validity of criteria applied to the question of sterilising mentally handicapped girls. It is no doubt the case that Professor Winston, a world-renowned expert in tubal surgery, achieves a 95 per cent rate in sterilisation reversals. However, 50 to 75 per cent would be considered a good success rate by most competent gynaecologists. Can the possibility, even probability, of successful reversal justify no longer treating sterilisation as the 'last resort' but rather as a convenient method of contraception? Resources for non-urgent gynaecological surgery are scarce. Waiting lists in many districts are long. How easy would it be for M or P to find a surgeon willing to reverse their sterilisation if their mental conditions improved? They are never likely to be of high or even average intelligence. It is doubtful whether a gynaecologist would be willing to reverse the sterilisation of even a relatively mildly mentally impaired woman. And as Eastham J acknowledged, reversal is more complex and serious surgery that the original sterilisation operation. He is in effect saying to P that because there is available the technology to reverse her sterilisation, the initial decision to sterilise may be taken more lightly, albeit the actual chances of her obtaining a reversal operation are minimal and that the operation, if undertaken, would be attended by greater risk and discomfort to her than the original surgery.

What of the other reasons for sterilising P? Clearly she is vulnerable to seduction and must be protected from exploitation, particularly as her current perception of sexual intercourse is of something unpleasant and painful. Sterilisation will do nothing to safeguard her from unscrupulous men. It protects her only against one possible consequence of seduction, pregnancy. She remains exposed to venereal desease, trauma, and perversion. And indeed, in the knowledge that she cannot now conceive, her carers may understandably be less stringent in their efforts to protect P from unwanted or damaging sexual experience.

Pregnancy, the judge found, would be a disaster for P. No doubt that is true. But of itself that finding is manifestly insufficient to justify non-consensual sterilisation. Pregnancy is a disaster for all too many women. Yet no one suggests that all women likely to be incapable of coping with childbirth and/or child care should be forcibly sterilised. P was to be sterilised because she is labelled as 'mentally handicapped'. That label appeared to enable the judge to address the question of whether sterilisation was in P's best interests with only a cursory analysis of the girl's competence or potential competence to decide for herself or whether to agree to sterilisation.

The incompetence of the several young women now sterilised by order of the court in England has tended to be assumed rather than explained; much is made of the girl's mental age. P, like Jeannette, was said to have a mental age of six. Such a statement conjures up an image of a little girl whose chronological age and mental age coincide and the idea of allowing a child who is actually six to decide whether or not to be sterilised seems ludicrous. However, P is in reality a girl of 17 who understands to some extent the workings of her body and copes with its needs. Her social skills are good and, unlike Jeannette, she communicates with others quite well. Presumably, it is her reasoning capacity which is to be equated with a six-year-old's. What does a patient have to understand to be competent to give a valid consent to medical treatment? For a competent patient's consent to be valid, he must have been informed in broad terms of the nature and purpose of the treatment proposed. His consent will not be vitiated by a failure to explain the risks, implications and side effects of treatment. It must therefore follow that to be competent to give a valid consent, the patient need only be able to understand in broad terms the nature and purpose of treatment. In the context of sterilisation that means that she should understand that she will be put to sleep while a doctor operates on her tummy to ensure that she is never able to have babies. Most six-year-olds who have learned something of how babies are born would comprehend that information. And P, of course, adds to the reasoning capacity of the child of six the appearance of puberty and an understanding of menstruation.

The judge expressly conceded that with further development and training P might attain the necessary capacity to marry. Her mother testified that she was naturally concerned that if P became pregnant she would refuse an abortion. Neither of those factors suggest that P's handicap was such that she would *never* be capable of making a choice for herself of whether or not to bear a child, or that she could not comprehend pregnancy and birth. Childbirth for P might well be an unwise choice, but if she had or may have developed the ability to make a choice at all then the decision on her interests should have remained hers and hers alone.

It was suggested at one stage at the hearing in *Re P* that, as it is now clear that adult women may be lawfully sterilised where a woman herself is and always will be incapable of giving her own consent to sterilisation, the decision on whether or not to sterilise P should be delayed. Those caring for P should 'wait and see' how she developed. The judge felt delay was unnecessary, a finding heavily influenced by his fallacious emphasis on the potential reversibility of sterilisation. *Re P* has, however, disturbing implications for the practice of sterilising adult handicapped women. The House of Lords held in *F v West Berkshire Health Authority* that the court had no jurisdiction to give or withhold consent to sterilisation of a woman over 18. Such surgery was, however, lawful where the woman is incapable of giving consent for herself, and the operation is in the existing circumstances in her best interests, and is carried out in conformity with good medical practice. Good medical practice is to be judged by the *Bolam* test and not by any more stringent measure. While as a matter of law application to a court to authorise sterilisation was not required, their Lordships laid down a procedure whereby an application might be made for a declaration that the proposed operation was not unlawful. Lord Goff commented at the end of his judgment:

> If, however, it became the invariable practice of the medical profession not to sterilise an adult woman who is incapacitated from giving her consent unless a declaration that the proposed course of action is lawful is first sought from the court, I can see little, if any, practical difference between seeking the court's approval under the *parens patriae* jurisdiction and seeking a declaration as to the lawfulness of the operation.

Adult women, like girls under 18, thus enjoy *de facto* if not *de jure*, the safeguard of judicial protection from over-hasty or ill-considered sterilisation. But what is that safeguard worth? The *Bolam* test defines the question of whether sterilisation of the woman is 'good practice'. The *Bolam* test lays down that a practitioner is not negligent if he conforms with a responsible body of medical opinion even though another equally responsible body of opinion dissents. Confronted by evidence from gynaecologist A that he and gynaecologists

B-L now regard sterilisation as a reversible operation, a sort of surgical **Depo-Provera**, must a judge ignore gynaecologists M-Z who doubt the success or even the relevance of reversibility?

A declaration that a proposed sterilisation is not unlawful is a valuable safeguard but a safeguard for the doctor not the patient. A surgeon sterilising a young woman having first obtained a declaration that the operation is not unlawful eliminates the risk that she might later sue him for negligence. For the woman, if the *Bolam* test and the *Bolam* test alone establishes the lawfulness of surgery, then judicial intervention does little more than protect her from the complete maverick whom none of his colleagues would back in his decision to sterilise her. Of course, judicial intervention *ought* to serve one other function too, to ascertain that the woman is in fact incapable of consenting to or refusing treatment on her own behalf. The judgments in *Re M* and *Re P* do not inspire confidence in the judiciary's readiness to develop and apply clear guidelines defining competence.

Again and again in the judgments on sterilisation lipservice is paid to the serious import of a decision to sterilise a woman. Reference is made to 'a right to reproduce' or to 'reproductive autonomy'. How is it then that a decision of such import may appear to be taken, as in *Re P*, without proper analysis of what should be the *primary* question, is the woman capable of consenting to, or refusing, sterilisation herself? For what may be in her best interests cannot be relevant unless and until it is established that she is and will continue to be incapable of understanding what is entailed in sterilisation, that she is incapable of determining what her own interests. The likelihood that she may make an unwise choice cannot justify depriving her of choice. Perhaps the reality is that doctors and judges do not, maybe cannot, assess the woman's interests alone divorced from the circumstances of her life. Sterilising P may be justifiable in her mother's interests, relieving her of anxiety and enabling her to give P more freedom and a better quality of care. The burden on those charged with the institutional care of handicapped girls may be eased by sterilising those girls, and certainly community care becomes a more viable option where there is no risk of pregnancy. Ensuring P does not have a baby who may either be cared for inadequately by his mother or condemned to a series of foster homes is certainly in the baby's interest. Yet in *Re B* an assurance was given that non-consensual sterilisation was lawful only in the girl herself's interests and as a measure of last resort. Experience must cause us to wonder whether, in the event, the Canadian Supreme Court was right in proclaiming in *Re Eve* that non-therapeutic involuntary sterilisation should never be lawful. In England we have slithered down the slippery slope at a frightening speed.

(See the further cases of *Re W (Mental Patient)(Sterilisation)* [1993] 1 FLR (Hollis J) (tubal ligation); *Re HG (Specific Issue Order: Sterilisation)* [1993] 1 FLR 587 (Peter Singer QC) (tubal ligation); *Re E (A Minor)(Mental Treatment)* [1991] 2 FLR 585 (Stephen Brown P) (hysterectomy); *Re GF (A Patient)* [1992] 1 FLR 293 (Stephen Brown P) (hysterectomy).)

Interestingly, the Official Solicitor, once the House of Lords had handed down its decision in *Re F*, sought extra-judicially to do the very thing which the House of Lords had been reluctant to do, ie make explicit the factors relevant to deciding whether an incompetent person should be sterilised. The Official Solicitor chose to do this in what he described as a 'Practice Note' and which is now reported at [1993] 3 All ER 222. Paragraph 8 provides:

8. The Official Solicitor anticipates that the judge will expect to receive comprehensive medical, psychological and social evaluations of the patient from appropriately qualified experts. Without in any way attempting either to define or to limit the factors which may require to be taken into account in any particular case the Official Solicitor anticipates that the judge will normally require evidence clearly establishing:

(1) That (a) the patient is incapable of making his or her own decision about sterilisation and (b) the patient is unlikely to develop sufficiently to make an informed judgment about sterilisation in the foreseeable future. (In this connection it must be borne in mind (i) that the fact that a person is legally incompetent for some purposes does not mean that he or she necessarily lacks the capacity to make a decision about sterilisation and (ii) that in the case of a minor his or her youth and potential for development may make it difficult or impossible to make the relevant finding of capacity.)

(2) That the condition which it is sought to avoid will in fact occur, e.g. in the case of a contraceptive sterilisation that there is a need for contraception because (a) the patient is physically capable of procreation and (b) the patient is likely to engage in sexual activity, at the present or in the near future, under circumstances where there is a real danger as opposed to mere chance that pregnancy is likely to result.

(3) That the patient will experience substantial trauma or psychological damage if the condition which it is sought to avoid should arise, e.g. in the case of a contraceptive sterilisation that (a) the patient (if a woman) is likely if she becomes pregnant or gives birth to experience substantial trauma or psychological damage greater than that resulting from the sterilisation itself and (b) the patient is permanently incapable of caring for a child even with reasonable assistance, e.g. from a future spouse in a case where the patient has or may have the capacity to marry.

(4) That there is no practicable less intrusive alternative means of solving the anticipated problem than immediate sterilisation, in other words that: (a) sterilisation is advisable at the time of the application rather than in the future; (b) the proposed method of sterilisation entails the least invasion of the patient's body; (c) sterilisation will not itself cause physical or psychological damage greater than the intended beneficial effects; (d) the current state of scientific and medical knowledge does not suggest either (i) that a reversible sterilisation procedure or other less drastic solutions to the problem sought to be avoided, e.g., some other contraceptive method, will shortly be available or (ii) that science is on the threshold of an advance in the treatment of the patient's disability; and (e) in the case of a contraceptive sterilisation all less drastic contraceptive methods, including supervision, education and training, have proved unworkable or inapplicable.

Had this been recognised as the law, it would have been a significant development. But, of course, such a Note has no legal force. This was pointedly made clear in *J v C* (1990) 5 BMLR 100, albeit on a question of procedure. It is fair to say that the decisions in *Re P*, *Re M*, and *Re W* and *Re HG* may be difficult to reconcile with para 8 of the Note (particularly para 8(3)(a)).

5. Starting again

What is required given the limitations of judicial law-making and the controversial subject matter, is a thoroughgoing review of the whole subject: the medical and psychiatric realities, the social implications, the ethical concerns and the appropriate legal framework. The following example of such a review can be found in the work of the Institute of Law Research and Reform, in Alberta, Canada: *Competence and Human Reproduction* (Report No 52, February 1989).

Factors for Judge to Consider
(1) The Factors

Before making an order authorizing a sterilization the judge would be required to consider the factors enumerated in a statutory list – factors of the sort that a person who is competent would ordinarily weigh in coming to a personal decision. All of the factors would be weighed from the perspective of their impact on the best interests of the person for whom sterilization is being considered, and not from the perspective of their impact on the interests of others.

The factors are simply listed in this section and will be discussed in paragraphs (2) to (4) below.

(a) Elective Sterilization

For an elective sterilization, the foremost factor would be:
- the wishes and concerns expressed by the person for whom sterilization is being sought, to the extent they can be ascertained.

   (These wishes and concerns would be ascertained and introduced in evidence after steps have been taken to inform the person of the factors affecting the decision, and to assist the person, to the full extent her intellectual capacity allows, to participate in making a decision.)

There would be fifteen other specific factors:

- the age of the person,
- the likelihood that the person will become competent to consent to the proposed sterilization,
- the physical capacity of the person to reproduce,
- the likelihood that the person will engage in sexual activity,
- the risks to the physical health of the person if the sterilization is or is not performed,
- the risks to the mental health of the person if the sterilization is or is not performed,
- the availability and medical advisability of alternative means of medical treatment or contraception,
- the previous experience, if any, of the person with alternative means of medical treatment or contraception,
- the likelihood that any child of the person would be born with a physical or mental disability and the likely effect of that disability on the ability of the person to cope,
- the ability of the person to care for a child at the time of the application and any likely changes in that ability,
- the likelihood that a child of the person could be cared for by some other person,
- the likely effect of foregoing the proposed sterilization on the life of the person as it limits or otherwise affects the ability of those who care for the person to provide required care (it is the consequential effect on the person for whom sterilization is being considered that would be weighed in considering this factor),
- the likely effect of the proposed sterilization on the opportunities the person will have for satisfying human interaction,
- the religious beliefs, cultural and other values of the person, and
- the wishes, concerns, religious beliefs, cultural and other values of the family or other person providing personal care insofar as they affect the interests of the person.

(We emphasize that the decision must be made in the best interests of the person whose sterilization is in issue. The views of family members or other personal caregivers are relevant only to the extent that they affect the best interests of the person. We have kept the category narrow because we think that a real and substantial connection with the person ought to be shown before the views of any other person are taken into consideration.)

To these would be added as a residual factor:

- any other matter that the judge considers relevant.

(b) Hysterectomy for Menstrual Management

For a hysterectomy for menstrual management, the following would be added to the above list of factors:

- the availability and medical advisability of alternative means of menstrual management, and
- the previous experience, if any, of the person with alternative means of menstrual management.

As well, the proposed legislation would permit the judge to make the order authorizing the performance of a hysterectomy only where no less drastic alternative method of menstrual management is reasonably available.

(c) In General

In a situation where evidence on a factor is not available or not readily available, the judge would be able to make an order in the absence of evidence only if he is satisfied that evidence cannot reasonably be obtained.

As one respondent observed, the requirement that the factors *must* be considered is a strength of our proposal in that it goes a long way toward ensuring that a decision would be based on the fullest possible information and consideration.

(2) Factors Raising Risk of Confusion with Interests of Others

The choice of the 'best interests' test confirms our guiding principle that a sterilization should be authorized only where it would be for the benefit of the person to be sterilized. Benefit to others – be it the family, caregivers, a future spouse, or a child who may be conceived and born – is not a consideration.

In consultation, a number of respondents expressed the concern that some of the factors listed in the proposed legislation would permit the interests of others to be brought in through the back door. They pointed to factors such as:

- the ability of the person to care for a child at the time of the application and any likely changes in that ability,
- the likelihood that any child of the person would be born with a physical or mental disability and the likely effect of that disability on the ability of the person to cope,
- the likelihood that a child of the person could be cared for by some other person,
- the likely effect of foregoing the proposed sterilization on the ability of those who care for the person to provide required care, and
- the wishes, concerns, religious beliefs, cultural and other values of the family or other person providing personal care insofar as they affect the interests of the person.

We hasten to dispel any such misapprehension. Under our proposal, these factors are to be considered only insofar as they have an impact on the best interests of the person for whom sterilization is sought. We emphatically do not intend that the consideration of these factors should derogate from our overriding principle of benefit to the person herself. They are *not* to be considered from the point of view of the interests or welfare of any other person.

At the same time, we think it would be a mistake to pretend that persons who are not competent to make sterilization decisions live in a social vacuum when in fact they depend on a network of family, friends and others to assist them in living as normal a life as possible. As we see it, the nature and extent to which a person can count on others is relevant to the determination of her present and likely future circumstances and this, in turn, is relevant to the consideration of her best interests.

Admittedly, the distinction between the interests of others insofar as they affect the interests of the person whose sterilization is sought and the interests of others in their own right carries with it the risk of misapplication. However, we think the risk is minimized, if not eliminated, by the choice of a superior court judge as decision maker and by the provision of a broad range of substantive and procedural safeguards for the judge to observe. We have revised the proposed legislation in an effort to make it irrefutably clear that these factors are to be considered only insofar as they relate to and impact on the best interests of the person for whom sterilization is sought.

Finally, in our tentative recommendations, the last factor set out above was phrased to include the wishes, concerns, religious beliefs and other values of the family 'or other interested person' insofar as they affect the interests of the person. The definition we propose for an 'interested person' would be an adult who, because of his relationship to the person in respect of whom an order is sought, is concerned for the welfare of the person. The judge would have the authority to decide whether a person is or is not an interested person for a purpose named in the legislation.

Some respondents felt that the definition of 'interested person' would require consideration of the wishes, concerns, religious beliefs and other values of primary caregivers including medical professionals and persons who are employed in an institution where the person is resident. We do not think a judge would interpret the words this widely. However, we do agree that the definition of 'an interested person' is overly broad for this section. In our final proposal we have substituted the words 'or other person providing personal care' for the words 'an interested person' in this factor. Where the judge considers the views of an individual who is not a family member to be relevant, he would be obliged to consider them under the residual factor in any event.

(3) Other Factors Attracting Specific Comment

(a) Wishes of the Person for Whom Sterilization is Sought

As already stated, the factor to receive the foremost attention of the judge would be:

- the wishes and concerns expressed by the person for whom sterilization is being sought.

These would be ascertained after the person has been informed of the factors affecting the decision and assisted, to the full extent of her intellectual capacity, to participate in making a sterilization decision.

Embodied in this factor is the recognition that a person who is not competent to consent may nevertheless indicate preferences or wishes that should be considered. A minor would be able to do so more and more expressly as she approaches adulthood when the presumption of competence would apply.

Some respondents felt that the objection to sterilization by a normally developing minor should be decisive of the issue. While we are of the view that a case in which the decision of the judge would prevail over the wishes of a normally developing minor would be highly unusual, we have stopped short of this position for two reasons. First, a minor is, by our definition, a person who is not competent to make a decision about an elective sterilization or a hysterectomy for menstrual management. Second, it should not be overlooked that sterilization for optional medical treatment and for the protection of mental health comes within the statutory regime. Bearing these points in mind, we think it best to entrust the decision to the judge after hearing all the facts of an individual case.

(b) Religious Beliefs, Cultural and Other Values

In Report for Discussion No. 6, we listed the religious beliefs and other values of the person for whom sterilization is being sought along with the wishes and concerns of the person. In the final proposals we have added *cultural* values to this factor in response to a suggestion received during consultation. *Cultural* values have also been added to the parallel factor which now requires the judge to consider the wishes, concerns, religious beliefs, *cultural* and other values of the family or other person providing personal care to the person for whom sterilization is sought.

(c) Likelihood of Future Competence

Another factor the judge would be required to consider is:
• the likelihood that the person will become competent to consent to the proposed sterilization.
The discussion of the wishes and concerns of the person to be sterilized underscores the significance of the likelihood of future competence as a factor in the case of a normally developing minor. The latter factor is also significant for a person whose lack of competence stems from a mental disability that is transient in nature and unlikely to persist for the whole of the person's reproductive life.

One respondent submitted that if there is evidence of past competence and evidence making it reasonable to conclude that the person may be competent again in the future, such evidence should be conclusive and no non-therapeutic sterilization decision ought to follow. We take the point, but can imagine a case in which the likelihood of return to competence is remote and the reasons for sterilization lie at the medical treatment end of the spectrum of sterilization purposes under the new regime. Again, we think it preferable to trust to the discretion of the judge who is in a position to weigh this evidence along with all the other circumstances in an individual case.

(d) Age

Discussion on the issue of the likelihood of future competence has prompted us to add as a specific factor:
• the age of the person.
One reason for specifying age is that its inclusion in the list helps to draw attention to the fact that maturation can be expected of minors for whom sterilization is being considered. Another reason for enumerating age is that reproductive choices tend to vary with age. For example, in the general population persons nearing the end of their reproductive years are more likely to choose sterilization than persons in younger age groups. Recognizing such tendencies would facilitate normalcy in decision making on behalf of persons who are not competent to consent personally.

(e) Physical Capacity to Reproduce

A further factor the judge would be required to consider is:
• the physical capacity of the person to reproduce.
In the Report for discussion, we tentatively recommended that a presumption of fertility should be raised if the medical evidence indicates normal development of sexual organs and the evidence does not otherwise raise doubts about fertility. We made our recommendation because fertility is difficult to prove. Nevertheless, it would obviously be pointless and wrong to perform a sterilization on a person who is physically unable to reproduce.

Some respondents observed that the presumption has the effect of placing the onus on the person under a disability to prove there is some existing physical dysfunction that has rendered her sterile. They suggested that the more appropriate and reasonable evidentiary requirement would be to place the onus on the applicant to prove that the person is capable of reproduction. This point was made by respondents who are opposed in principle to sterilization for birth control or menstrual management. The onus they suggest would be virtually impossible to meet in cases where no prior offspring have been conceived.

We are satisfied that the proposed presumption reflects the more reasonable likelihood of normal reproductive functioning.

(f) Alternative Means of Birth Control or Menstrual Management

Two further factors the judge would be required to consider are:
- the availability and medical advisability of alternative means of medical treatment or contraception, or of menstrual management, and
- the previous experience, if any, of the person with alternative means of medical treatment or contraception, or of menstrual management.

The tentative recommendations in the Report for Discussion referred only to the 'availability and medical advisability' of alternatives. The factor referring to 'the previous experience, if any, of the person' has been added for both elective sterilization and hysterectomy for menstrual management as a result of a suggestion made in consultation on our tentative recommendations. Although information about previous experience is likely to form part of the foundation for an expert opinion on medical advisability, we agree that it would be helpful to specify it for consideration by the judge.

(4) Factors Attracting Little or No Comment

Most of the remaining factors received little or no specific comment one way or the other. We have omitted from our final proposals one factor that was included in our tentative recommendations. It is the likelihood that the person might in the future be able to marry. We are now persuaded that flagging this factor would be misconceived. Because we are living in an era when reproduction decisions are being made independently of marriage, marriage is not of direct relevance to the sterilization issue. The reference to the likelihood of marriage in the future could unduly arouse the traditional view that having children is fundamental to marriage and unacceptable outside of marriage, thereby tipping the balance against the weight of other factors in an individual case. That is to say, it could lead to the undue approval of sterilization in cases where marriage is unlikely and the undue refusal of sterilization where marriage is a possibility.

Where there is a chance that a future spouse would be able to provide help with the care of a child, our proposals cover the possibility in the factor relating to any other care that might be available for a child if born.

(g) Method of Sterilization

The choice of surgical operation or other medical procedure to be used for sterilization would, in most instances, be a matter for medical decision. Our proposals do, however, contain two provisions relating to the method of sterilization. In the case of an *elective sterilization*, the proposed legislation would prohibit the sterilization from being performed by hysterectomy unless the judge, by order, expressly authorizes it on the basis of persuasive medical evidence. In the case of a *hysterectomy for menstrual management*, the proposed legislation would permit the judge to make an order authorizing the performance of a hysterectomy only where no less drastic alternative method of menstrual management is reasonably available.

In both cases, our proposals reflect the principle that the least injurious or least intrusive means of accomplishing the intended purpose should be used.

You will notice, from the terms of the report, that it recommended that a sterilisation procedure may only be carried out if approved by a judge. This issue has been central to many of the cases, for example the *JWB* case in Australia. The extent to which in England a court must be involved is discussed earlier in ch 4.

Chapter 11

Medically assisted reproduction

Introduction

Medicine has made extraordinary advances in responding to the desire of
women (and their partners) to have a child. These advances, as it may be
imagined, have not been free from moral and legal difficulties. In this chapter
we explore how the law has responded to these developments. The medical
background to the problem of infertility is well described by the Canadian Law
Reform Commission.

Medically Assisted Procreation (Working Paper 65) (1992)

Infertility
Infertility is the involuntary, significant reduction of reproductive capacity. In North
America, the generally recognized threshold of infertility is an inability to become pregnant
after one year of unprotected intercourse. The World Health Organization's standard is two
years.

Although Canadian studies of infertility prevalence are scarce, it has been reported that
15 percent of couples seek medical advice for infertility. In the United States the prevalence
of infertility has not changed significantly from 13.3 percent in 1965 to about 13.9 percent in
1982, excluding surgically induced sterility.

Some of the factors influencing the prevalence of infertility are: (1) trends toward
childbearing later in life; (2) environmental factors, such as infection from sexually
transmitted diseases, and occupational exposure; (3) medical treatments such as those used
for high blood pressure, stomach ulcer and cancer, as well as non-therapeutic drugs such as
narcotics, alcohol and tobacco.

A. Evaluation of the Infertile Couple
The infertile couple seeking medical help undergoes a series of procedures to determine the
nature and severity of the problem. First a medical history is taken and, if necessary,
counselling about timing effective intercourse is given.

The woman is tested to detect hormonal dysfunction. There may be a biopsy of the
uterine lining, and a hysterosalpingogram, which is an X-ray that reveals blockages of the
fallopian tubes. Laparoscopy, which is the introduction of an endoscope into the abdomen,
may be used to inspect the outer surfaces of the uterus, fallopian tubes and surrounding
structures for any abnormalities. These procedures are often painful, include slight risks of
infection, and may result in the puncture of the uterus, although this last is rare. Medical
precautions, such as the administration of antibiotics, are therefore taken to minimize risks.

The man must undergo a semen analysis to evaluate the number and quality of sperm. If
the semen is abnormal, blood tests may be performed to detect hormonal abnormalities. A
post-coital test may also be used to determine if there is incompatibility between the semen
and female reproductive factors. This test requires the couple to have sexual intercourse
timed to coincide with ovulation; within a few hours, post-coital tests of cervical mucus are
performed.

B. Causes of and Treatments for Infertility
Infertility may be traced to one partner, both partners, or to biochemical or immunological
incompatibility between partners. Most female infertility is due to: ovulation disorders,

usually because of hormonal abnormality; tubal blockage as a result of infection and other disease processes; endometriosis; and other causes, including abnormalities of the vagina or cervix, and mucous incompatibilities with sperm.

Treatments for female infertility include hormone or drug therapy, surgery, and medically assisted procreation technologies such as IVF and GIFT.

Infertility due to an ovulation disorder is treated with ovulatory stimulants, which are very successful if infertility is due only to an ovulation disorder. Other medical treatments include drugs to treat endometriosis, infection, and immune incompatibilities. For fallopian tube blockage, surgery may be used. When other infertility treatments are unsuccessful, artificially assisted procreation may be employed, but as a last resort.

Male infertility typically results from decreased numbers or an absence of sperm in the semen, abnormal motility and structural abnormalities, all of which prevent normal fertilization of the egg. Precise causes of male infertility are often undetectable, but varicocele (varicose veins of the testes) or infection may play a role. The absence of sperm (azoospermia) may be caused by impaired production of sperm or blockage of passageways. Although greatly reduced numbers of sperm (oligospermia) reduce fertility, there is still controversy as to the number of sperm necessary for normal reproductive functioning.

When sperm counts fall below five million, fertility is significantly reduced. Therefore, couples unwilling to wait the several years often necessary to achieve 'natural' pregnancy may seek treatment for male factor infertility. These treatments include hormonal therapy and such laboratory techniques as the 'swim up' procedure that aim to improve the concentration of normal sperm available for fertilization. However, the success of these procedures in conjunction with the use of artificial insemination is less than 20 percent.

In theory, one might expect that IVF could be useful in the treatment of male factor infertility. Once the egg is placed directly in a container with the partner's sperm, the normal sperm, even if there are relatively few, should be able to fertilize the egg. This would provide the couple with a child genetically related to both parents. But the ability of the sperm to fertilize the egg appears to be only half as successful as in cases of IVF with non-male factors. Nevertheless, there are reports that find IVF for male factor infertility as successful as IVF for other reasons. In any event, artificial insemination by donor (AID) is considered a leading remedy for both the infertile and sterile male because it is less costly, less invasive, and statistically much more successful than IVF.

The various developments in treating the infertile include, principally, artificial insemination using donated sperm (AI); *in vitro* fertilisation techniques (IVF), and surrogacy. While AI and surrogacy have been with us for a long time and may, in some cases, be accomplished without any medical involvement, IVF was developed in the 1970s and requires medical intervention. Of course, AI and surrogacy will usually be carried out under medical supervision.

Medically assisted reproduction sometimes involves treating infertile couples using their own genetic material. In other cases, the treatment will involve the use of donated material, whether sperm, eggs or even embryos. It was the development of IVF procedures which raised concerns about the practices of medically assisted reproduction and led to a call for regulation. In response, the government set up a Committee of Inquiry into Human Fertilisation and Embryology chaired by Baroness Warnock (as she became) which reported in 1984 (Cmnd 9314). The 'Warnock Committee', as it became known, identified the range of concerns which arose from the rapid development in medically assisted reproduction.

Report of the Committee of Inquiry into Human Fertilisation and Embryology (Cmnd 9314) (1984), paras 2.1-2.4

2.1 In the past, there was considerable public ignorance of the causes and extent of infertility, as well as ignorance of possible remedies. At one time, if a couple were childless, there was very little they could do about it. Generally the cause of infertility was thought to be something in the woman which made her childless; only occasionally was it thought that there might be something wrong with the man. Even today, there is very little factual information about the prevalence of infertility. A commonly quoted figure is that one couple in ten is childless, but accurate statistics are not available, nor is it known what proportion of this figure relates to couples who choose not to have children. In certain religious and cultural traditions, infertility was, and still is, considered sufficient grounds for divorce. In our own society childless couples used to be advised to adopt a child. Now, as a result of improved contraception, the wider availability of legal abortion and changed attitudes towards the single mother, far fewer babies are placed for adoption.

2.2 Childlessness can be a source of stress even to those who have deliberately chosen it. Family and friends often expect a couple to start a family, and express their expectations, either openly or by implication. The family is a valued institution within our present society: within it the human infant receives nurture and protection during its prolonged period of dependence. It is also the place where social behaviour is learnt and where the child develops its own identity and feeling of self-value. Parents likewise feel their identity in society enhanced and confirmed by their role in the family unit. For those who long for children, the realisation that they are unable to found a family can be shattering. It can disrupt their picture of the whole of their future lives. They may feel that they will be unable to fulfil their own and other people's expectations. They may feel themselves excluded from a whole range of human activity and particularly the activities of their child-rearing contemporaries. In addition to social pressures to have children there is, for many, a powerful urge to perpetuate their genes through a new generation. This desire cannot be assuaged by adoption.

2.3 Arguments have been put to us both for and against the treatment of infertility. First, we have encountered the view that in an over-populated world it is wrong to take active steps to create more human beings who will consume finite resources. However strongly a couple may wish to have children, such a wish is ultimately selfish. It has been said that if they cannot have children without intervention, they should not be helped to do so. Secondly, there is a body of opinion which holds that it is wrong to interfere with nature, or with what is perceived to be the will of God. Thirdly, it has been argued that the desire to have children is no more than a wish; it cannot be said to constitute a need. Other people have genuine needs which must be satisfied if they are to survive. Thus services designed to meet these needs must have priority for scarce resources.

2.4 In answer to the first point, it is never easy to counter an argument based on the situation of the world as a whole with an argument relying on the desires of individuals. We saw it as our function to concentrate on individuals rather than on the world at large. Questions about the distribution of resources within the world as a whole lie far outside our terms of reference. In any event, the number of children born as a result of techniques to assist in the treatment of infertility will always be insignificant in comparison with the naturally increasing world population. On the second point, the argument that to offer treatment to the infertile is contrary to nature fails to convince in view of the ambiguity of the concepts 'natural' and 'unnatural'. We took the view that actions taken with the intention of overcoming infertility can, as a rule, be regarded as acceptable substitutes for natural fertilisation. Thirdly, the argument that the desire to have children is only a wish, not a need, and therefore should not be satisfied at the expense of other more urgent demands on resources can be answered in several ways. There are many other treatments not designed to satisfy absolute needs (in the sense that the patient would die without them) which are readily available within the NHS. Medicine is no longer exclusively concerned with the preservation of life, but with remedying the malfunctions of the human body. On this analysis, an inability to have children is a malfunction and should be considered in exactly the same way as any other. Furthermore infertility may be the result of some disorder which in itself needs treatment for the benefit of the patient's health. Infertility is not something mysterious, nor a cause of shame, nor necessarily something that has to be endured without attempted cure. In addition, the psychological distress that may be caused by infertility in those who want children may precipitate a mental disorder warranting treatment. It is, in our view, better to treat the primary cause of such distress than to alleviate the symptoms. In summary, we conclude that infertility is a condition meriting treatment.

In the light of its analysis, the committee recommended statutory regulation of medically assisted reproduction. In the immediate aftermath of the Warnock Report, the Medical Research Council and the Royal College of Obstetricians and Gynaecologists set up the Voluntary (later Interim) Licensing Authority. This body served to provide a self-regulatory mechanism for licensing infertility treatment and research on human embryos and gametes. It ceased to exist on 1 August 1991 when the Act establishing the Human Fertilisation and Embryology Authority came into force. It is the framework of the Human Fertilisation and Embryology Act 1990 which resulted from the recommendations of the Warnock Committee that we are concerned with here. However, by way of introduction, before we turn to a detailed account of the 1990 Act, it will be helpful to consider one or two preliminary matters.

First, the complexities of the issues to be considered are well illustrated by the following table set out in Professor Bernard Dickens's article, 'Reproduction Law and Medical Consent' (1985) 35 Toronto Law Journal 255 at 280:

Table of reproductive options

Sperm	Ovum	Uterus	Means of conception	Intended child custody	Explanation
H	W	W	natural	H and W	normal conception
H	W	W	AI	H and W	AI by husband
H	W	W	IVF	H and W	IVF
D	W	W	AI/IVF	H and W	conception by sperm donor
H	D	W	IVF or IV + F and ET	H and W	conception by ovum donor
H	D1	D1	AI	H and W	'SM' and SPA by W
H	W	D	any and ET	H and W	SM and SPA by W
H	D1	D2	any and ET	H and W	ovum donation, SM and SPA by W
D	W	D	any and ET	H and W	SM of W's ovum and adoption
D	D	W	any and ET	H and W	W bears (unrelated) child and SPA by H
D	D1	D1	any	H and W	adoption
D	D1	D2	any and ET	H and W	adoption
F	M	M	any	F and M	child of the union
F	D1	D1	any	F	father has child
D	M	M	any	M	mother has child
F	D1	D2	any and ET	F	father has true surrogate child
D	M	D	any and ET	M	mother has true surrogate child
D	D1	D2	any and ET	D2	true surrogate has child
D	D1	D1	any	third party	adoption
D	D1	D2	any and ET	third party	adoption
H	W	W	posthumous AI/IVF	W	widow has child
H	W	D	posthumous IVF/IV + F and ET	W	widow has true surrogate child
H	W	D	posthumous IVF and ET	H	widower has true surrogate child

H	= husband (legal or common law)	F	= single father
W	= wife (legal or common law)	M	= single genetic mother
D	= donor of sperm, ovum, or uterine service	SPA	= step-parent adoption
AI	= artificial insemination	IVF	= *in vitro* fertilisation
ET	= embryo transplantation	IV + F	= *in vivo* fertilisation (by AI) and flushing
'SM'	= so-called surrogate motherhood		
SM	= surrogate motherhood	any	= natural conception, AI, IVF, or IV + F

A slightly different scheme is offered by Professor Alexander Capron in 'Alternative Birth Technologies: Legal Challenges' (1987) 20 UC Davis Law Review:

Reproductive possibilities

No	Name of Method	Genetic Source	Fertilization	Gestation	Social Parent
1	Traditional Reproduction	$X_M\&Y_M$	Natural	M	M & M
2	Artificial Insemination, Husband	$X_M\&Y_M$	AI	M	M & M
3	Test Tube Baby	$X_M\&Y_M$	IVF	M	M & M
4	Artificial Insemination, Donor	$X_M\&Y_D$	AI	M	M & M
5A	Donated Egg	$X_D\&Y_M$	IVF	M	M & M
5B	Transferred Egg	$X_D\&Y_m$	AI with embryo flushing	M	M & M
6	Surrogate Motherhood	$X_D\&Y_M$	AI	D	M & M
7A	Test Tube Baby in Rented Womb	$X_M\&Y_M$	IVF	D	M & M
7B	Transfer to Rented Womb	$X_M\&Y_M$	Natural or AI w/embryo flushing	D	M & M
8	Postnatal Adoption	$X_D\&Y_D$	Natural, AI, or IVF	D	M & M
9	Substitute Father	$X_M\&Y_D$	IVF	M	M & M
10	Brave New World	$X_1\&Y_2$	IVF or Natural/AI/ w/embryo flushing	3	4 & 5

Abbreviations: X = female, Y = male, AI = artificial insemination,
IVF = *in vitro* fertilization, D = donor, M = member or married couple

Secondly, as we saw earlier, the Warnock Committee recommended legislation as the mechanism for regulation. We should pause to consider other ways in which society may respond to the issues raised by medically assisted reproduction. It should be noticed that, in general, particular aspects of medical practice are rarely regulated by statute in England. The 1990 Act is a significant exception to this, perhaps reflecting the fine balance between assisting the infertile and the fears of what could flow from the technologies as they are developed.

In an important report, the Ontario Law Reform Commission examined in detail the arguments for and against regulation and the options for regulation if appropriate.

Human Artificial Reproduction and Related Matters (1985)

In this chapter, the Commission has set forth the extent to which the common law, existing statutory and regulatory provisions, and professional rules of conduct may bear on the use and consequences of the new reproductive technologies in Ontario. At the outset, we cautioned that the 'law' in this area is, in a sense, astigmatic – in the main, ignoring or inadvertently applying to the various legal issues arising from the growth of artificial conception services. While the relatively recent advent of these services goes some distance to explain the present state of affairs, the novelty of at least some of the procedures is rapidly diminishing. As a consequence, hitherto reasonable explanations for the dearth of law in the area of artificial conception are beginning to wear thin.

The Commission is quite aware . . . that the fact that legislation does not speak directly to a certain matter is not, in itself, a damning criticism necessitating immediate remedial action. Silence may well reflect continuing, deep-seated controversy, so that there may be a justifiable wish to permit the law to develop without legislative fetters. Even inadvertent solutions may be equitable responses – a manifestation of the capacity of the legal regime, created to deal with one set of circumstances, to grow and flourish in a new milieu.

On the other hand, the Commission is acutely conscious of the pervasive notion in many circles that the dictates of medical science, when followed to their logical extremes, will lead inexorably to horrors hitherto characterised as fantasy or science fiction. The spectre of cloning, wholly 'test tube' babies, genetic engineering and manipulation – these and other fears frequently feed the view that the only proper response of the law in this area is prohibition and criminalisation.

While, like others, we are seriously concerned about the nature and implications of certain types of medical and other related research and experimentation, we do not subscribe to this rather cataclysmic, certainly pessimistic view. The automatic invocation of 'logical extremes' and 'worst case scenarios' is not, of course, unique to the present context. But, as a precept for action, these arguments must be viewed with extreme caution; they ought not to animate the proper reaction of the law to all developments in the field of medicine. Keeping pace with new and beneficial scientific advances does not thereby make the law an accomplice with regard to those facets of science unacceptable to the community. The law need not meekly trim its sails to accommodate such unwanted developments. Law and law reform comprehend more than merely wholesale endorsement or outright prohibition; as a manifestation of the perceived needs and wishes of the community, they can also, for example, limit or actively facilitate, encourage, or discourage certain kinds of activity to one degree or another. The Commission's reaction to, and perception of, the present law and its adequacy, insofar as it relates to the new reproductive technologies, largely mirrors this more flexible approach to what we believe to be the proper role of the law in this area.

Some issues are of such fundamental importance to parents, children, and third parties that they no longer ought to be left to the uncertainties and vicissitudes of evolutionary legal development. Perhaps the most obvious example concerns the status of an artificially conceived child. Leaving aside the contentious issue of surrogate motherhood, should the law expressly acknowledge the social reality of a child conceived with the use of donor gametes, so that the social parents are recognised in law as the only parents? Or should the gamete donor, the biological parent, who is almost invariably, but not always, anonymous, be treated in law as a parent, with all the rights and responsibilities attendant upon such a role? Should the rules respecting birth registration further acknowledge the social realities and reflect the intentions and expectations of all the parties? Is society well served by legislation that basically ignores artificial conception in this context and even, occasionally, encourages subterfuge and prompts individuals to evade strictures of the law, for example, by registering children to suit their own predilections? . . .

In relation to these technologies, the vision of the present law is uncomfortably out of focus; indeed, it simply has been overtaken by events. To a significant degree, the existing legal regime cannot escape the confines of the natural reproduction mould. And the search for doctrine that is even remotely relevant to the many serious, complex questions raised in the context of artificial conception involves arduous and generally fruitless legal circumnavigation around frequently foreign principles. It is this uncertainty in the legal implications of various activities – particularly, but not exclusively, in relation to status, parentage, and surrogate motherhood – that pervades the law and practice relating to the use of the new reproductive technologies. A broad cross-section of society, from lawyers to doctors, social workers, ethicists, and others, has decried the absence of clear legal rules to guide the actions of all persons participating, or wishing to participate, in artificial conception programmes. Accordingly, we believe that the law must be re-examined and refashioned. It must reflect the benefits of the new technologies and the reasonable hopes of infertile men and women, while at the same time guarding against those excesses perceived to be injurious to the fabric of society. . . . we are constrained to caution against any wholesale abandonment of the view that the law may, and should, act as a progressive, normative guide, not simply a reflection of present community standards. When we consider state intervention in the case of the new reproductive technologies, we may view the issue, at least in part, as a privacy matter. And when the law deals with matters of personal privacy, it frequently swings its pendulum in favour of individual interests. This issue of personal privacy is critical to our study, and any wish on the part of a segment of society to constrict or limit the ability of individuals to choose whatever method they wish to bring a child into a family, and to regularise their relationship with that child, must be balanced against the human costs attending such intervention. The law may reflect the community's level of tolerance; but it may also stretch or fashion it in the interests of a worthy goal.

For the purpose of our conceptual analysis in this chapter, we shall differentiate between two fundamental approaches to reform, representing the two extreme points on what is clearly a continuum. One basic approach we shall term the 'private ordering' approach, where the legal regime is designed to give effect to the intentions of the parties. The other basic approach we shall call the 'state regulation' approach, where the free choice of the parties does not determine what they may do or the consequences of their actions, but where the state actively intervenes to set mandatory normative standards of conduct. With the latter approach, there are certain ancillary matters that must be addressed. For example, how should the state attempt to persuade people to comply with the rules of behaviour to which adherence is deemed essential?

It bears mentioning here that the so-called private ordering model – exemplified, for example, in the case of one's choice to conceive children by natural reproduction – does not necessarily eschew legislative initiatives. Statutory provisions may indeed be required to give effect to, or preclude interference with, the wishes of individuals. This type of legislation differs from that contemplated by the state intervention approach in its essentially facultative animus: it does not, in effect, tell people what to do or not to do, but serves to facilitate their activities where necessary.

We also wish to note that the two basic approaches set forth in this chapter represent conceptual paradigms of how the law might deal with reproductive choices and their consequences. Accordingly, they each provide a theoretical model against which we may measure the kind of legal regime that ought to govern our conduct. However, a consideration of these general approaches is but one stage in the development of our proposals for reform: it is necessary to determine whether this macroscopic approach to law reform – where all aspects of the subject matter are governed by the same broad conceptual approach – is appropriate in the context of artificial conception. Indeed, it may become clear that the special characteristics of the various artificial reproduction technologies, or certain facets of these technologies, must be dealt with differently. In other words, the legal regime governing such matters need not necessarily be uniform and all-embracing; rather, a more flexible approach, sensitive to the requirements of different aspects of the problem in different ways, may be desirable. Such a hybrid approach may, then, marry aspects of the private ordering and state regulation approaches, and then leave room for common law evolution and for the development of normative guidelines outside the Legislature . . .

. . . the Commission came to the conclusion that the law must take special cognisance of the new artificial conception technologies. In the present chapter, we have examined two main conceptual approaches to law reform in this area, the state regulation approach and the private ordering approach.

When attempting to assess which of the two approaches ought to be adopted in the case of artificial reproduction – or indeed, whether some hybrid approach is preferable – the models of natural reproduction and adoption immediately spring to mind. More specifically, we inevitably come face to face with a general, fundamental question: should the law treat artificial reproduction differently than the manner in which it treats natural reproduction, at least insofar as the decision to conceive a child is concerned? If the private ordering approach is eschewed in favour of the state regulation approach in the case of artificial reproduction, on what basis is such a determination to be made? . . .

. . . while no one can legitimately assume to speak for all segments of the community on so controversial a topic as artificial reproduction, the Commission can attempt to give serious consideration to the conflicting views presented to us directly or gleaned from the increasingly voluminous literature. Our proposals for reform, then, are based on our perception of prevailing community standards, however amorphous they may appear to be, and our view of what members of the community appear to want or be willing to tolerate. Without slavishly and uncritically adopting such standards, they do serve to indicate how members of society believe we ought to be governed. We cannot simply ignore prevailing views, in a sense placing ourselves above the community, enlightening it concerning the 'best' ordering of society. In the area of human conception, whether natural or artificial, it would be presumptuous to take such licence.

Having regard to the considerations just described, we have come to the conclusion that the law must impose a degree of intervention in the case of artificial conception that is neither desirable nor possible in the case of natural reproduction. The wishes of the parties – particularly, the desire of the prospective social parents to have a child – are, in fact, only one of many considerations that should affect the determination of the nature of the new legal regime. Given the implications of artificial conception for persons other than the prospective parents, we strongly believe that 'private ordering' cannot be the sole governing factor. In our view, there are sound philosophical and practical reasons for embracing, at least in some areas, an approach that does not give free rein to the wishes of the parties . . .

Having concluded that, under certain circumstances, the state ought to intervene in respect of artificial conception in the interest of broader societal values, several subsidiary, but no less critical, questions arise. For example, to what extent and in respect of what activities, if any, should such intervention take the form of either outright prohibition or regulation? If regulation is desirable in respect of any or all of the activities in question, how should the guiding norms be set, and who should set and apply them?

(a) Prohibition or regulation?

We turn first to consider the two forms by which limits may be placed on an individual's private activities, namely, prohibition and regulation. It should first be made clear that the law need not necessarily adopt only one of these two interventionist means. While clearly a wholesale prohibition respecting the use of artificial conception services would leave nothing to regulate, it is entirely reasonable to envisage a legal regime in which some aspects of the new technologies are prohibited, some are strictly controlled, and some are the subject of minimal regulation.

For example, one might wish to prohibit minors from donating ova for use in IVF programmes because extraction of ova may involve surgical intrusion and because a woman's complement of ova is finite. One might believe it essential to prohibit all forms of what may be termed 'genetic engineering', but countenance research at approved or licensed research centres that have ethical review committees to oversee such activities. Or some latitude might be tolerated in respect of payment of semen donors of their reasonable expenses.

The list of possible permutations and combinations involving prohibition and regulation could easily be expanded. But the essential point is that our perception of the different facets of the subject matter should not be static or rigid; we must be open to the suggestion that a hybrid regime, in which a spectrum of responses, from total prohibition to slight regulation, may be both desirable and possible.

The determination of where specific activities ought to be placed on this spectrum – and not left to the unfettered discretion of individuals – is influenced by several more or less obvious factors. As we indicated in the Introduction to this chapter, matters of logic almost inevitably mix with basic human fears and emotions to produce in each of us a sense of what we may be willing or able to tolerate. The spectre of cloning or experimental genetic manipulation may well be anathema to almost everyone in the community, so that a doctrinaire stance – outright prohibition – may be palatable. But, in other areas, consensus may be difficult, even impossible, to achieve. For example, there has been a continuing debate concerning whether adopted children ought to be entitled to have access to information respecting their natural parents, a debate that arises as well in the context of artificial conception where 'anonymous' donor gametes are used. Rational reasons favouring disclosure vie with concerns respecting the possible emotional reactions of the various parties. And so, insofar as adoption law in Ontario is concerned, we have moved slowly away from an extreme posture of secrecy to a regulated access regime.

Aside from assessing the necessity for, or desirability of, either prohibition or some type of regulation based on the particular attributes of each activity, it must be borne in mind that complete prohibition or strict regulation, however justifiable in the abstract, may produce evasion, especially by the desperate or more affluent who may seek to obtain services in more accommodating jurisdictions. And such violation of the law may well be seen as legitimate in the eyes of the majority or a substantial minority of the population.

But the danger of evasion as such is not the only problem respecting strict punitive measures directed at certain activities. For example, given the relative simplicity of the artificial insemination procedure, its prohibition or strict control may encourage laypersons to perform the insemination on themselves and others, without medical supervision. In other words, this type of artificial reproduction may be driven underground, away from physicians who have the requisite skills and knowledge to prevent or remedy any medical complications that may arise in the recipient or child.

In the case of surrogate motherhood, it is clear that key medical, legal, and other services are available – and have been delivered, to our knowledge, on at least one occasion – outside Ontario to Ontario residents, largely because of the perceived, and correct, view that surrogate motherhood agreements are not enforceable in this Province. Again, attempted suppression does not necessarily result in the elimination of the activity, but may create more perils than anticipated. Indeed, one of the dangers of any prohibition of artificial conceptions is that it may prejudicially affect children conceived in this fashion. We have already seen that the present law deals only inadvertently with such critical issues as the legal status of an artificially conceived child.

There are, then, important human and other costs of prohibition that must be weighed in the balance before seeking to render a particular practice illegal, even though it may be deemed not to be worthy of any active protection. As in the case of our choice between the state regulation and private ordering as a general approach to law reform in this area, these factors have led us to the conclusion that a hybrid regime is both necessary and desirable. Such a regime most adequately reflects the complexity of the subject and the differing norms that, we believe, ought to govern different aspects of each of the new technologies.

(b) The instruments of regulation

Assuming the adoption of a regulatory approach, at least for some purposes, a second set of issues concerns the particular instruments of regulation. Who should set the requisite standards, how should they be set, and who should apply them? Again there are several alternative approaches to the resolution of these questions.

The establishment of norms governing conduct may be left to the Legislature, by means of legislation, to the courts, through the development of common law principles, to governmental or other tribunals, to professional bodies, such as the College of Physicians and Surgeons of Ontario, or to a combination of such institutions. In some cases, a statute or regulation may set a standard to be applied by the medical profession itself. In other cases, legislation may be monitored and interpreted by an administrative body or by the courts. Again, there is no universal rule; the particular combination selected in respect of the establishment and application of normative guides depends on several factors, including the type of the particular activity in question and the nature and extent of the control sought.

Regulation need not, of course, take the form of formal, written norms emanating from some body specifically charged with developing applicable guidelines, for example, the Legislature or even the College of Physicians and Surgeons of Ontario (by means of rules of professional conduct). Regulation of conduct may take place incrementally, through the medium of the courts. The courts, utilising existing common law or developing new rules, may either interpret or add glosses on legislation or written guidelines from some other source, or may deal with controversial issues in respect of which there is no universal social policy or consensus and, hence, no 'legislated' philosophy.

Courts may, for example, exercise a valuable role in determining such issues as the standard of care that is to be applied by practitioners of artificial conception, and whether institutions such as clinics and hospitals, through their infertility units, bear responsibility for their practitioners' negligence. The advantage of leaving such matters to judicial development is that such development will occur within a generalised jurisprudence, and not be, without justification, distinctive or anomalous to artificial conception.

Further, regarding the establishment of the requisite standard of care, court decisions in some cases may reflect developments in the state of the reproductive art as they occur, unfettered by a legislated or regulated framework that may become based upon outmoded techniques or discredited practices. This may be particularly important, since artificial conception technologies are still evolving and many variations in clinical practice exist, the relative advantages of which have yet to be determined by properly conducted studies. A legislated scheme that embodies any particular practice may give undue preference to a procedure that proves to be no better than others and possibly worse, and may inhibit development of superior alternatives. Courts may well compel the raising of standards by finding that the existing practice – for example, on screening gamete donors for adverse genetic traits or venereal infection – does not satisfy legal requirements respecting the standard of care.

It has been observed that '[t]he most ethically and politically controversial aspect of IVF is the status of the embryo'. A legislated solution to this controversy would be of far-reaching effect, and would have implications for many areas of the law. A judicial approach would define the fact situations in which a particular judicial decision is to apply, and the purposes for which a given solution is designed. Judicial explanation, which itself may undergo several reinterpretations, may be preferable to the structured and traditional language of legislation to say within what limits a particular resolution is to operate.

However, a difficulty with entrusting matters to the courts is that, in some cases, they may adhere to precedents that are not related to advances in artificial conception technologies. Judgments may continue to embody public policy perceptions conditioned by the supposition that conception results only from sexual intercourse, or, perhaps at some future time, that artificial conception results only from artificial insemination or IVF, or a particular mode of artificial conception. The early disposition to equate AID with adultery shows how judicial attitudes, while perhaps understandable in one era, may become and remain part of the problem in another era, which legislation may be required to resolve. Courts may take strict and limiting views, for instance, regarding the inheritance rights of a child not genealogically related to a testator, such as the parent of a husband whose wife had the child by AID, when the testator made a bequest to the husband and the 'heirs of his body'.

There is, however, a dynamic interaction between legislation and judicial attitudes, since courts tend to note the thrust of legislative initiatives, and often take leads from them. If legislation were enacted specifically to accommodate all or certain types of artificial conception, for instance, it might be unlikely that the courts would regard agreements made in furtherance of such particular conceptions as void as against public policy. Courts may, of course, decline to admit a new kind of claim, on the ground that the matter raises a significant issue of public policy that should be tackled by the Legislature before a solution is incorporated into the law by the courts; and they may similarly feel that private arrangements regarding sensitive areas, such as surrogate motherhood agreements, should be approved by an Act of the Legislature rather than by a court. Once generally accommodating legislation has been passed, however, the courts may find such legislation to be an expression of public acceptance or tolerance in which they may find inspiration and direction.

It is never certain, on the other hand, that courts will follow the lead of legislation, or interpret, apply, or extend its provisions in a collaborative way. Judges may hesitate to go further than recent legislation, reasoning that, had the Legislature intended its scheme to embrace an additional step, it would have so provided, and that its failure so to provide is evidence of a contrary intention. For avoidance of doubt, legislation may have to be drafted comprehensively in order to address foreseeable areas of possible application. Oversights and issues beyond anticipation may then have to be left to the courts, but the legislative design may, in principle, aim to be all-embracing, as a self-contained and definitive code.

Alternatively, it may not be necessary to resolve every detail in order to achieve legislation that is sufficiently comprehensive to address a given issue. Depending on the particular issue, minimal legislation may be enacted, fashioning the critical skeleton of a new policy, but leaving the developed form to be supplied by an emerging jurisprudence. Legislation also may properly be structured in order to anticipate and accommodate further developments in related case law, without seeking to affect its direction. If the case law fails to develop, or follows an unsatisfactory direction the Legislature always retains its residual power to supplement or supersede judgments.

In the same way that certain matters may be left to be resolved by the courts, other matters may best be resolved according to medical professional ethics, bearing in mind that the practice of medicine may include artificial conception and, accordingly, that such a practice may be undertaken only by doctors or persons under their supervision or direction.

We have seen that the Legislature has granted the College of Physicians and Surgeons of Ontario wide powers of self-government. Among other things, the College may regulate the practice of medicine and establish standards of knowledge, skill, qualification, and practice among members. In addition, the College may set ethical standards for doctors.

Having regard to the fact that the statutory mandate of the College is exercised 'in order that the public interest may be served and protected', it is not surprising that persons who are authorised to practise medicine by the College are subject to compulsory discipline for professional misconduct. 'Professional misconduct' is defined in regulations made under the *Health Disciplines Act*, primarily in collaboration with the provincial Ministry of Health. The list of activities constituting professional misconduct tends to be specific, but a residual category exists for 'conduct or an act relevant to the practice of medicine that, having regard to all the circumstances, would reasonably be regarded by members as disgraceful, dishonourable or unprofessional'.

The College of Physicians and Surgeons of Ontario conscientiously consults with those whom it regulates and with the wider community beyond, in the process of formulating its ethical position on various matters, and it is open to public and media comment and ministerial influence. It may strike committees to address particular issues and may involve non-professionals in its deliberations and recommendations. Accordingly, it may reflect an ethical consensus with considerable credibility, although it may be expected that the opinions of the professionals it regulates, who are also strongly represented on the governing council, will be heard with special clarity.

The College periodically updates its principles of ethical practice, and contributes to public education and discussion concerning such principles. It attempts to respond to past events and to anticipate future possibilities, so that practitioners generally are offered guidance when they contemplate innovative practices. Further, unlike courts of law, the College will accommodate requests from doctors for *ad hoc* ethical rulings based upon hypotheses and anticipated scenarios. Its familiarity with the realities of practice and its access to scientific and technical data may afford its judgments a conviction that more abstract theorising may lack.

Contributions to the debate of the ethics of professional practice may come through initiatives of many organisations other than the provincial College. The views of responsible bodies, such as the Medical Research Council, may be of significance regarding, for example, research concerning the use of gametes and embryos. Moreover, the reports of governmental agencies or professional bodies in Canada and around the world can be expected to be seriously considered. Professional ethical principles may, therefore, be informed by a variety of national and international considerations that may influence perceptions of what provincial ethical practice requires. Inasmuch as the ethical assessments of the College of Physicians and Surgeons of Ontario may draw from the same body of knowledge that would be relevant to the design of statutes or regulations, such assessments may serve equally to control conduct within the medical profession, and may even enjoy the greater confidence and sympathetic compliance of individual physicians.

Accordingly, it is possible to leave some matters unaddressed by statute, to be determined by authorised practitioners acting under professional guidance. Practitioners are accountable both through the courts, for the injuries they wrongfully cause to individuals they have a legal duty to protect, and through their professional disciplinary councils, for breach of ethical rules, professional misconduct, or falling below the established standards of their profession. Further, while legislation may be introduced to govern such activities as research, it may be equally appropriate, and perhaps preferable, to confine sensitive research, such as research on embryos, to special centres that maintain credible ethical screening of research proposals through institutional review boards, and that undertake departmental and other monitoring of clinical and research practices.

An advantage of this approach to the control of individual practice is that it would utilise existing personnel, institutions, and established mechanisms, whereas new regulatory legislation might require a policing and enforcement service that might be less than comprehensive, costly, and poorly received among professionals conscious of their responsibilities. By the same token, some may argue that professionals are generally too socially conservative, health professionals in particular having been suspected of undue paternalism in pursuing patients' perceived interests rather than patients' expressed wishes. These and other advantages and disadvantages that attach to the control of artificial conception through medical and related professional guidelines must be balanced against the advantages and disadvantages of seeking control through express legislation.

In light of the Commission's philosophy and previous conclusions respecting the appropriate approach to law reform in the case of the new reproductive technologies and respecting the nature of the limits that should be placed on an individual's private actions, it should come as no surprise that, in the present context, we once again eschew a dogmatic approach that would require uniform treatment to be provided in all cases. We believe that some matters – clearly those that involve outright prohibition of certain activities – necessitate statutory control. Other matters, setting out procedural details or licensure requirements, may be left to the regulations. And yet further matters, involving essentially medical judgment or involving ethical issues relating to the conduct of physicians, may be determined by the medical profession, either formally or informally. In all, or most, of these cases, recourse may well be had to the courts to interpret legislation or relevant codes of ethics or professional conduct.

As we saw, the government in the UK has regulated through the Human Fertilisation and Embryology Act 1990 (hereafter the 1990 Act). The regulatory framework took effect on 1 August 1991.

Infertility treatment

The infertility treatments regulated by the 1990 Act are those that involve the use of donated genetic material (whether sperm, eggs or embryos) or those which involve the creation of an embryo outside the human body. In addition, the 1990 Act regulates the storage of all genetic material. What is not directly regulated by the 1990 Act is the practice of surrogacy. Only in so far as a surrogate birth is achieved through the use, in part or whole, of donated genetic material or using IVF techniques is the framework of the 1990 Act applicable. Otherwise, the practice of surrogacy is regulated, in part, by the Surrogacy Arrangements Act 1985 (which we will consider later in this chapter).

At the heart of the 1990 Act is the establishment of an authority charged generally with the implementation of the statute. This is the Human Fertilisation and Embryology Authority (HFEA) (s 5). The membership of HFEA is prescribed in Schedule 1 to the 1990 Act. It consists of a chairman and deputy chairman and such other members as the Secretary of State appoints. In appointing such members the Secretary of State must ensure that there is a majority of members who are neither doctors nor research scientists. Similarly, the chairman and deputy chairman must not be drawn from these professional groups.

The principal functions of the HFEA are as follows:

(i)   to license treatment services, the storage of gametes and embryos and research on embryos (s 11);
(ii) to monitor and inspect premises and activities carried out under statutory licence (s 9);
(iii) to submit an annual report to the Secretary of State on its activities (s 7); and
(iv) to maintain a code of practice as guidance for the proper conduct of activities carried out under a licence (s 25).

By section 8 of the 1990 Act, HFEA has the following additional 'general' functions:

8. General functions of the Authority
The Authority shall –
(a)   keep under review information about embryos and any subsequent development of embryos and about the provision of treatment services and activities governed by this Act, and advise the Secretary of State, if he asks it to do so, about those matters,
(b)   publicise the services provided to the public by the Authority or provided in pursuance of licences,
(c)   provide, to such extent as it considers appropriate, advice and information for persons to whom licences apply or who are receiving treatment services or providing gametes or embryos for use for the purposes of activities governed by this Act, or may wish to do so, and
(d)   perform such other functions as may be specified in regulations.

A. LICENSING

The 1990 Act divides activities involving human gametes and embryos into three categories. First, there are those activities, for example, cloning, which are illegal (ie criminal) and cannot be licensed. Secondly, there are those activities which are illegal (ie criminal) unless carried out pursuant to a licence granted by HFEA, for example, the creation of an embryo *ex utero* or the storage of gametes or embryos. Thirdly, there are those activities which are not covered by the Act and so are lawful even without a licence, for example, the treatment of a couple using the sperm of the male partner (ie artificial insemination by the husband).

1. The general scheme

The basic framework for regulation can be found in sections 1-4 of the Human Fertilisation and Embryology Act 1990:

Principal terms used

1. Meaning of 'embryo', 'gamete' and associated expressions
    (1) In this Act, except where otherwise stated –
(a)   embryo means a live human embryo where fertilisation is complete, and
(b)   references to an embryo include an egg in the process of fertilisation,
and, for this purpose, fertilisation is not complete until the appearance of a two cell zygote.
    (2) This Act, so far as it governs bringing about the creation of an embryo, applies only to bringing about the creation of an embryo outside the human body; and in this Act –
(a)   references to embryos the creation of which was brought about *in vitro* (in their application to those where fertilisation is complete) are to those where fertilisation began outside the human body whether or not it was completed there, and
(b)   references to embryos taken from a woman do not include embryos whose creation was brought about *in vitro*.
    (3) This Act, so far as it governs the keeping or use of an embryo, applies only to keeping or using an embryo outside the human body.
    (4) References in this Act to gametes, eggs or sperms, except where otherwise stated, are to live human gametes, eggs or sperms but references below in this Act to gametes or eggs do not include eggs in the process of fertilisation.

2. Other terms
    (1) In this Act –

    'the Authority' means the Human Fertilisation and Embryology Authority established under section 5 of this Act, . . .
    'Licence' means a licence under Schedule 2 to this Act and, . . .
    'treatment services' means medical, surgical or obstetric services provided to the public or a section of the public for the purpose of assisting women to carry children.

    (2) References in this Act to keeping, in relation to embryos or gametes, include keeping while preserved, whether preserved by cryopreservation or in any other way; and embryos or gametes so kept are referred to in this Act as 'stored' (and 'store' and 'storage' are to be interpreted accordingly).
    (3) For the purposes of this Act, a woman is not to be treated as carrying a child until the embryo has become implanted.

Activities governed by the Act

3. Prohibitions in connection with embryos
    (1) No person shall –
(a)   bring about the creation of an embryo, or
(b)   keep or use an embryo,
except in pursuance of a licence.
    (2) No person shall place in a woman –
(a)   a live embryo other than a human embryo, or
(b)   any live gametes other than human gametes.
    (3) A licence cannot authorise –
(a)   keeping or using an embryo after the appearance of the primitive streak,
(b)   placing an embryo in any animal,
(c)   keeping or using an embryo in any circumstances in which regulations prohibit its keeping or use, or
(d)   replacing a nucleus of a cell of an embryo with a nucleus taken from a cell of any person, embryo or subsequent development of an embryo.
    (4) For the purposes of subsection (3)(a) above, the primitive streak is to be taken to have appeared in an embryo not later than the end of the period of 14 days beginning with the day when the gametes are mixed, not counting any time during which the embryo is stored.

4. Prohibitions in connection with gametes
    (1) No person shall –
(a)   store any gametes, or
(b)   in the course of providing treatment services for any woman, use the sperm of any man unless the services are being provided for the woman and the man together or use the eggs of any other woman, or

(c)   mix gametes with the live gametes of any animal,
except in pursuance of a licence.

(2) A licence cannot authorise storing or using gametes in any circumstances in which regulations prohibit their storage or use.

(3) No person shall place sperm and eggs in a woman in any circumstances specified in regulations except in pursuance of a licence.

(4) Regulations made by virtue of subsection (3) above may provide that, in relation to licences only to place sperm and eggs in a woman in such circumstances, sections 12 to 22 of this Act shall have effect with such modifications as may be specified in the regulations.

(5) Activities regulated by this section or section 3 of this Act are referred to in this Act as 'activities governed by this Act'.

A number of points should be noted arising from these sections establishing the basic framework.

First, the Act wholly regulates the creation, use and storage of human embryos *ex utero*, whether for treatment or research purposes. By contrast, the Act only partially regulates dealing with human gametes. Storage of sperm or eggs does require a licence. However, the use of human gametes is only regulated in the case of use for treatment if donated gametes are involved and, in the case of research, if the gametes are to be mixed with gametes of an animal. In general, therefore, other use of gametes for research (not involving storage) is unregulated. Similarly, infertility procedures involving the patients' own gametes and not involving the creation of embryos are also unregulated. The best known example of this is the procedure know as GIFT (Gamete Intra-Fallopian Transfer). At the time the legislation was passing through Parliament a move was made to include GIFT within the regulatory framework. In the event this failed but, as you will see, s 4(3) and 4(4) permit the making of regulations which could bring procedures such as GIFT within the Act: there are none at present.

Secondly, the Act permits research on human embryos providing HFEA has licensed the research project. However, s 3(3)(a) and 3(4) when read together limit the power to grant a licence for such research to embryos which have not developed a primitive streak. Section 3(4) irrebuttably presumes that this takes place 'not later than the end of the period of 14 days beginning with the day when the gametes are mixed, not counting any time during which the embryo is stored'. (For a discussion of the arguments surrounding the use of human embryos for research, see 1st edition at pp 660-682.)

Thirdly, it is important to notice the statutory definition given to the word 'embryo' by s 1(1) given that any activity which results in the creation of an embryo *ex utero* triggers the need for the activity to be licensed. The wording of s 1(1) is curious. It contemplates an embryo being the product of the 'complete' fertilisation of an egg by a sperm. Further, in order to bring within the Act research at an early stage of fertilisation, s 1(1)(b) broadens that definition so as to include 'an egg in the *process* of fertilisation'. So far so good. However, s 1(1)(b) goes on to state that 'fertilisation is not complete until the appearance of a two cell zygote'. The definition of 'embryo' now contradicts itself. An embryo is both 'complete' in the process of fertilisation and not 'complete' until that process is over. Parliament's intention is clear; the wording of the Act is, however, unfortunate.

Fourthly, artificial insemination which does not involve donated gametes is outside the Act. This is clear from the wording of s 4(1)(b). As can be seen from s 4(1)(b), the Act is concerned, on the whole, with the provision of 'treatment services'. The Act makes it clear that it is only concerned with infertility treatments provided 'to the public or a section of the public', arguably, by the appropriate medical personnel (s 2(1)). Thus, the do-it-yourself artificial insemination, even using sperm donated by someone else, does not fall within the Act (unless the sperm has been stored).

Finally, we should notice the definition of 'store' or 'storage' in s 2(2) of the Act. This provision defines the relevant terms widely. Of course, the most obvious form of storage is cryopreservation (ie freezing). But under the Act, any form of 'keeping while preserved' gametes or embryo amounts to storage. The definition is, however, limited in this respect. It would not cover the 'keeping' of gametes or embryos in the laboratory or clinic while fresh before use *unless* preservative measures have been taken. Mere 'keeping' is not storage although what mounts to 'preservation' is not entirely clear.

2. Licensed activities

HFEA has statutory power to grant licences for the following activities: infertility treatment, research and storage. While storage licences may be combined with licences for treatment or research, licences may not be granted combining research and treatment. The detail of the licensing procedure is set out in ss 9, 10 and 16-22 of the 1990 Act (and see HFEA, *Manual for Centres* (June 1991)). The essence of the scheme is described in HFEA's *Second Annual Report* in 1993:

> Once an application has been received, the process is as follows:
>
> i.   a site visit by a team of inspectors;
> ii. consideration of the application and inspection report by a licence committee;
> iii. notification of the outcome to the applicant.
>
> If the applicant is not content with the decision, representations may be made to the committee before the decision takes effect. This may be followed by an appeal to the full Authority and finally, on a point of law, an applicant may appeal to the High Court.
>
> One of the most important aspects of the whole inspection and licensing process is to promote and sustain good practice and, in doing so, to ensure a consistent approach. At the beginning, the Authority established a number of procedures to ensure that these objectives are met and regularly reviewed. . . .
>
> After an inspection, a report is submitted to a licence committee. The committee's decision to issue or refuse a licence takes account of the recommendations of the inspection teams.
>
> . . . **Licence Committees**
>
> Licence committees consist of five members of the Authority, with a quorum of three. . . .
>
> In considering licence applications and the standards to be met, licence committees must be guided by the Act and the Code of Practice. Where new or major issues arise, such as home insemination, licence committees have taken policy advice from the Authority. Guidance has then been given as an addition to the Code of Practice which, following consultation, has been revised accordingly.
>
> To ensure that the Authority maintained a consistent approach to licensing, a strategy was developed for assessing and monitoring standards in centres based on the following:
>
> (i) As well as the standard conditions attached to all licences, additional conditions are attached to licences on occasions where the inspection team or the licence committee discovers a breach (or breaches) of the Act or of the Code of Practice. Centres may be given a certain amount of time to comply with conditions of licence or, alternatively, compliance may be assessed at the next full inspection. Licence conditions have been used, when appropriate, as a means of applying pressure on centres to conform quickly in areas where there have been observed deficiencies in their practice. In this first year, it has been only those centres where this approach was not thought to be sufficient to achieve the required result which have been refused treatment licences. Monitoring of conditions is also carried out by the inspector coordinators who act as the point of contact between the Authority and the centre.

(ii) Licences are issued for a specific period of time with twelve months being the standard duration. A number of fifteen month licences were issued in the first year in order to spread the expiry dates more evenly throughout the year. Centres which have particularly stringent (or numerous) conditions attached to their licence have normally been given short-term licences so that the concerns of a licence committee can be reassessed at further inspections. The licence committee judges what is a reasonable length of time within which the centre should be expected to meet the conditions before a decision is made on the duration of the licence.

The following table shows the length of time for which treatment licences were issued in the first year of licensing.

Length of licence issued (months)

	Three	Six	Twelve	Fifteen
No. of Centres	4	3	81	19

(iii) Licence committees may ask that a letter be sent to a centre which includes specific recommendations. Generally a recommendation is practical advice, based on the Authority's experience of good practice.

The Authority has reviewed all of the conditions and recommendations attached to licences issued in the first year. Not only has this demonstrated a good degree of consistency in the decision-making process, but it has also led to standardisation in the wording of some of the more common conditions and recommendations.

(iv) Centres are commended for particularly high standards of practice and their procedures and methods may be used by the Authority to help other centres obtain equally high standards. Communication between centres is encouraged.

. . . Licences Issued and Refused

The Authority currently licenses 107 treatment centres of which 65 are for IVF and 37 for donor insemination only. A total of 32 research and 8 storage only licences have been issued. Lists of currently licensed centres and research projects are set out at Annexes 3 and 4. Five licence applications have been refused, including 2 research applications.

Where treatment licences have been refused the reasons for the refusal have been given to the applicants. Generally these have been cases where the centres failed in significant ways to meet the standards required by the Act and Code of Practice, and where it appeared to the licence committee that the centre would be unable to meet the required standard within a reasonable period of time.

Licence conditions have related to aspects of the Code of Practice. However, given the emphasis placed on certain issues in the Act and the Code of Practice, it is not surprising that many of the conditions relate to counselling, confidentiality and security, the welfare of the child and information for patients. These are all new statutory obligations which some centres are considering for the first time. It is reasonable therefore for the Authority to recognise that in some centres it may take a little time to develop adequate procedures.

. . . Appeals

Appeals against licence committee decisions may be made to the full Authority. If the appellant is unhappy with the outcome of an appeal and believes there are grounds, on a point of law, a further appeal may be lodged with the High Court. The Authority has, so far, heard one appeal against a licence committee's decision to refuse a treatment licence application. This was an application for an IVF licence in a centre which offered GIFT as a treatment and the centre wished to use IVF as a diagnostic means of establishing the likelihood of fertilisation in vivo. The Authority took the view that the quality of embryology support needed to make this procedure worthwhile in these circumstances was as great as that demanded in an IVF treatment centre and that it should therefore only be used in centres which had the expertise to offer IVF treatment. In this particular case the centre was unable to meet that standard and the resulting appeal did not succeed. The principle that emerged from this has subsequently been included in the Authority's revised Code of Practice.

Breaches of the Code of Practice

Licence committees have also considered cases where centres are in breach of Code of Practice guidelines. Most notably there have been some cases where centres have transferred to a woman four embryos during a single treatment cycle. The limit stated in the Code of Practice is three. In each case the centres concerned had done this on only a single occasion which was shortly after the Code of Practice took effect on 1 August 1991. Each of the centres concerned provided the licence committee with a report of how the breach had occurred. They also gave assurances that this was the only occasion on which four embryos had been transferred, and that their policies were to limit the number to three in all cases. Having seen the centres' reports, the licence committees asked the Chief Executive to write to the centres concerned informing them of the seriousness with which the Authority viewed the breach and warning them of the possible consequences of any further breach of this limit. This might include suspension or revocation of licences.

. . . Review Procedures

While much of the licensing procedure is set out in statute, the corresponding administrative arrangements are entirely at the discretion of the Authority. The Authority is aware that it is important to ensure that the right information is available to centres, to inspectors and to licence committees.

The Licensing and Fees Committee has therefore examined the inspection and licensing procedures in the light of experience from the first year. The views of centres and of inspectors have been taken into account in this review process.

The Authority's first year of licensing has been very successful. In order to maintain consistency, licence conditions will, in future, be standardised as far as possible to show how they relate to particular parts of the Code of Practice. Information gained from experience of licensing will continue to be used to develop and improve the licensing process.

The manual for centres is being updated to take account of recent amendments to the Code of Practice, and to other procedures and guidance.

The Inspection Process

For some centres the inspection process was an entirely new experience and was somewhat daunting. Over the last year inspections lasted between two hours and a full day depending on the size of the centre, the applications made and the services offered. The aim has been to ensure that the centre is adhering to the Act and the Code of Practice, that the staff are properly qualified and that the facilities are of an appropriately high standard.

During the inspection the team meets the 'Person Responsible', whose duty it is to ensure that the centre complies with the requirements of the Act and the Code of Practice. The team also meets the medical and scientific staff, nurses, counsellors and staff in charge of record-keeping. Each is questioned about the procedures at the clinic and about their particular role. In addition questions are asked and investigations made in the following areas:

Staff

The inspectors ensure that all staff have appropriate qualifications and experience.

Facilities

The visiting team inspects the facilities used during treatment and research. Particular consideration is given to ensuring that the facilities and laboratory conditions are of a sufficiently high standard and that attention has been given to overall security as well as to monitoring clinical, counselling and laboratory practice.

Assessing Clients

Centres are required, by law, to take account of the welfare of any child who may be born or affected by the treatment. Questions are asked about what medical and social investigations are performed before treatment begins and the criteria used in deciding whether to treat and which treatment is most appropriate.

Donors

Centres using donated eggs, sperm or embryos are asked about their procedures for the recruitment and counselling of donors and the screening performed before donated material is used. The team also ensures that there are suitable procedures for limiting the number of children born from a single donor.

Information and Consent

Centres are required, by law, to provide information to those considering treatment. Any written information given to patients before, during or after treatment is assessed by the inspection team to ensure that it is accurate, comprehensive and easily understood. In particular, it should not be misleading, any success rates quoted should be accurate for that particular centre and all charges should be clearly set out with no hidden costs. The consent forms are also reviewed.

Counselling

All centres are required, by law, to offer counselling to those considering or undergoing treatment and to potential donors. On inspection visits consideration is given to when, where and how the offer of counselling is made.

Handling, Use, Storage and Disposal of Gametes and Embryos

By speaking to staff and inspecting the facilities, a judgement is made on the standard of service offered and the centre's adherence to the guidelines on good practice set out in the Code of Practice.

Records

Particular attention is given to the precautions taken for the security of patient and donor records and the system of record-keeping.

Research

In those centres undertaking licensed research, the inspection team meets the chairman or a member of the local research ethics committee and the staff involved in the research. The reasons for undertaking the research, its aims, the justification for the use of human embryos and the ethics committee's deliberations are all discussed.

Other

Centres are required to have a formal complaints procedure and questions about the number, nature and outcome of any complaints are asked during the inspection visit. Enquiries are also made about any other issues which may be of interest to the HFEA.

As we have seen, the regulatory framework is a creature of statute. The Act is complex. Here is not the place to engage in a detailed exegesis of all the statutory provisions. Instead, we will set out for completeness the essential provisions governing the terms under which licences will be granted in Sch 2 and ss 12-15. Then, we will take up and examine a number of important issues concerning access to treatment, consent to use and control of genetic material, access to and control of information and the status of children born after infertility treatment.

Schedule 2 to the 1990 Act lays out HFEA's powers concerning the granting and scope of licences under the Act (see also s 11).

SCHEDULE 2
ACTIVITIES FOR WHICH LICENCES MAY BE GRANTED

Licences for treatment

1.—(1) A licence under this paragraph may authorise any of the following in the course of providing treatment services –
(a) bringing about the creation of embryos *in vitro*,
(b) keeping embryos,
(c) using gametes,
(d) practices designed to secure that embryos are in a suitable condition to be placed in a woman or to determine whether embryos are suitable for that purpose,

(e)   placing any embryo in a woman,

(f)   mixing sperm with the egg of a hamster, or other animal specified in directions, for the purpose of testing the fertility or normality of the sperm, but only where anything which forms is destroyed when the test is completed and, in any event, not later than the two cell stage, and

(g)   such other practices as may be specified in, or determined in accordance with, regulations.

(2) Subject to the provisions of this Act, a licence under this paragraph may be granted subject to such conditions as may be specified in the licence and may authorise the performance of any of the activities referred to in sub-paragraph (1) above in such manner as may be so specified.

(3) A licence under this paragraph cannot authorise any activity unless it appears to the Authority to be necessary or desirable for the purpose of providing treatment services.

(4) A licence under this paragraph cannot authorise altering the genetic structure of any cell while it forms part of an embryo.

(5) A licence under this paragraph shall be granted for such period not exceeding five years as may be specified in the licence.

Licences for storage

2.—(1) A licence under this paragraph or paragraph 1 or 3 of this Schedule may authorise the storage of gametes or embryos or both.

(2) Subject to the provisions of this Act, a licence authorising such storage may be granted subject to such conditions as may be specified in the licence and may authorise storage in such manner as may be so specified.

(3) A licence under this paragraph shall be granted for such period not exceeding five years as may be specified in the licence.

Licences for research

3.—(1) A licence under this paragraph may authorise any of the following –

(a)   bringing about the creation of embryos *in vitro*, and

(b)   keeping or using embryos,

for the purposes of a project of research specified in the licence.

(2) A licence under this paragraph cannot authorise any activity unless it appears to the Authority to be necessary or desirable for the purpose of –

(a)   promoting advances in the treatment of infertility,

(b)   increasing knowledge about the causes of congenital disease,

(c)   increasing knowledge about the causes of miscarriages,

(d)   developing more effective techniques of contraception, or

(e)   developing methods for detecting the presence of gene or chromosome abnormalities in embryos before implantation,

or for such other purposes as may be specified in regulations.

(3) Purposes may only be so specified with a view to the authorisation of projects of research which increase knowledge about the creation and development of embryos, or about disease, or enable such knowledge to be applied.

(4) A licence under this paragraph cannot authorise altering the genetic structure of any cell while it forms part of an embryo, except in such circumstances (if any) as may be specified in or determined in pursuance of regulations.

(5) A licence under this paragraph may authorise mixing sperm with the egg of a hamster, or other animal specified in directions, for the purpose of developing more effective techniques for determining the fertility or normality of sperm, but only where anything which forms is destroyed when the research is complete and, in any event, not later than the two cell stage.

(6) No licence under this paragraph shall be granted unless the Authority is satisfied that any proposed use of embryos is necessary for the purposes of the research.

(7) Subject to the provisions of this Act, a licence under this paragraph may be granted subject to such conditions as may be specified in the licence.

(8) A licence under this paragraph may authorise the performance of any of the activities referred to in sub-paragraph (1) or (5) above in such manner as may be so specified.

(9) A licence under this paragraph shall be granted for such period not exceeding three years as may be specified in the licence.

General

4.—(1) A licence under this Schedule can only authorise activities to be carried on on premises specified in the licence and under the supervision of an individual designated in the licence.

(2) A licence cannot –
(a) authorise activities falling within both paragraph 1 and paragraph 3 above,
(b) apply to more than one project of research,
(c) authorise activities to be carried on under the supervision of more than one individual, or
(d) apply to premises in different places.

Three general points need to be made briefly. First, a licence (of whatever kind) is granted to an individual known in the Act as the 'person responsible' (see ss 16 and 17). This individual remains responsible for complying with the terms and conditions of the licence. Secondly, treatment licences authorise particular classes of treatments to be carried out under the control of the 'person responsible' at the designated premises (similarly in the case of a storage licence). By contrast, licences for research are granted for a specific project of research for one or more of the purposes set out in paragraph 3 of Schedule 2. Thirdly, licences for all activities are subject to a maximum time-limit: five years in the case of licences for treatment and storage and three years for research.

As you will notice from the terms of Schedule 2, licences are subject to conditions. The Act spells out a number of standard conditions for all licences (s 12) and for the particular activities contemplated by the Act (s 13 (treatment); s 14 (storage); s 15 (research)).

Licence conditions

12. General conditions
The following shall be conditions of every licence granted under this Act –
(a) that the activities authorised by the licence shall be carried on only on the premises to which the licence relates and under the supervision of the person responsible,
(b) that any member or employee of the Authority, on production, if so required, of a document identifying the person as such, shall at all reasonable times be permitted to enter those premises and inspect them (which includes inspecting any equipment or records and observing any activity),
(c) that the provisions of Schedule 3 to this Act shall be complied with,
(d) that proper records shall be maintained in such form as the Authority may specify in directions,
(e) that no money or other benefit shall be given or received in respect of any supply of gametes or embryos unless authorised by directions,
(f) that, where gametes or embryos are supplied to a person to whom another licence applies, that person shall also be provided with such information as the Authority may specify in directions, and
(g) that the Authority shall be provided, in such form and at such intervals as it may specify in directions, with such copies of or extracts from the records, or such other information, as the directions may specify.

13. Conditions of licences for treatment
(1) The following shall be conditions of every licence under paragraph 1 of Schedule 2 to this Act.
(2) Such information shall be recorded as the Authority may specify in directions about the following –
(a) the persons for whom services are provided in pursuance of the licence,
(b) the services provided for them,
(c) the persons whose gametes are kept or used for the purposes of services provided in pursuance of the licence or whose gametes have been used in bringing about the creation of embryos so kept or used,
(d) any child appearing to the person responsible to have been born as a result of treatment in pursuance of the licence,

(e) any mixing of egg and sperm and any taking of an embryo from a woman or other acquisition of an embryo, and

(f) such other matters as the Authority may specify in directions.

(3) The records maintained in pursuance of the licence shall include any information recorded in pursuance of subsection (2) above and any consent of a person whose consent is required under Schedule 3 to this Act.

(4) No information shall be removed from any records maintained in pursuance of the licence before the expiry of such period as may be specified in directions for records of the class in question.

(5) A woman shall not be provided with treatment services unless account has been taken of the welfare of any child who may be born as a result of the treatment (including the need of that child for a father), and of any other child who may be affected by the birth.

(6) A woman shall not be provided with any treatment services involving –

(a) the use of any gametes of any person, if that person's consent is required under paragraph 5 of Schedule 3 to this Act for the use in question,

(b) the use of any embryo the creation of which was brought about *in vitro*, or

(c) the use of any embryo taken from a woman, if the consent of the woman from whom it was taken is required under paragraph 7 of that Schedule for the use in question,

unless the woman being treated and, where she is being treated together with a man, the man have been given a suitable opportunity to receive proper counselling about the implications of taking the proposed steps, and have been provided with such relevant information as is proper.

(7) Suitable procedures shall be maintained –

(a) for determining the persons providing gametes or from whom embryos are taken for use in pursuance of the licence, and

(b) for the purpose of securing that consideration is given to the use of practices not requiring the authority of a licence as well as those requiring such authority.

14. Conditions of storage licences

(1) The following shall be conditions of every licence authorising the storage of gametes or embryos –

(a) that gametes of a person or an embryo taken from a woman shall be placed in storage only if received from that person or woman or acquired from a person to whom a licence applies and that an embryo the creation of which has been brought about *in vitro* otherwise than in pursuance of that licence shall be placed in storage only if acquired from a person to whom a licence applies,

(b) that gametes or embryos which are or have been stored shall not be supplied to a person otherwise than in the course of providing treatment services unless that person is a person to whom a licence applies,

(c) that no gametes or embryos shall be kept in storage for longer than the statutory storage period and, if stored at the end of the period, shall be allowed to perish, and

(d) that such information as the Authority may specify in directions as to the persons whose consent is required under Schedule 3 to this Act, the terms of their consent and the circumstances of the storage and as to such other matters as the Authority may specify in directions shall be included in the records maintained in pursuance of the licence.

(2) No information shall be removed from any record maintained in pursuance of such a licence before the expiry of such period as may be specified in directions for records of the class in question.

(3) The statutory storage period in respect of gametes is such period not exceeding ten years as the licence may specify.

(4) The statutory storage period in respect of embryos is such period not exceeding five years as the licence may specify.

(5) Regulations may provide that subsection (3) or (4) above shall have effect as if for ten years or, as the case may be, five years there were substituted –

(a) such shorter period, or

(b) in such circumstances as may be specified in the regulations, such longer period, as may be specified in the regulations.

15. Conditions of research licences

(1) The following shall be conditions of every licence under paragraph 3 of Schedule 2 to this Act.

(2) The records maintained in pursuance of the licence shall include such information as the Authority may specify in directions about such matters as the Authority may so specify.

(3) No information shall be removed from any records maintained in pursuance of the licence before the expiry of such period as may be specified in directions for records of the class in question.

(4) No embryo appropriated for the purposes of any project of research shall be kept or used otherwise than for the purposes of such a project.

Of course, the HFEA can, and does, impose further conditions in particular cases where circumstances make it appropriate. As we saw in its Annual Report for 1993, the HFEA often imposes conditions relating to matters in the *Code of Practice* maintained pursuant to the statutory duty in s 25 of the Act.

Breach of a condition in a licence may lead HFEA to revoke a licence. We will return to consider particular aspects of the *Code of Practice* later, and here we should note that breach of its provisions *may* also lead to revocation or variation of a licence. Section 25(6) provides:

25. (6) A failure on the part of any person to observe any provision of the code shall not of itself render the person liable to any proceedings, but –

(a)   a licence committee shall, in considering whether there has been any failure to comply with any condition of a licence and, in particular, conditions requiring anything to be 'proper' or 'suitable', take account of any relevant provision of the code, and

(b)   a licence committee may, in considering, where it has power to do so, whether or not to vary or revoke a licence, take into account any observations of or failure to observe the provisions of the code.

B. ACCESS TO TREATMENT

The 1990 Act does not specifically address the entitlement of a person to gain access to treatment services. The issue was recognised as important by the Warnock Committee (op cit). The conclusions arrived at may be regarded as conventionally satisfactory but somewhat under-argued.

Report of the Committee of Inquiry into Human Fertilisation and Embryology (1984) (Cm 9314)

2.5 It is sometimes suggested that infertility treatment should be available only to married couples, in the interests of any child that may be born as a result. While we are vitally aware of the need to protect these interests, we are not prepared to recommend that access to treatment should be based exclusively on the legal status of marriage.

2.6 In discussing treatment for infertility, this report takes the term *couple* to mean a heterosexual couple living together in a stable relationship, whether married or not. We use the words *husband* and *wife* to denote a relationship, not a legal status (except where the context makes differentiation necessary, for example in relation to legitimacy).

2.7 In the evidence, concern was expressed that infertility treatment may be provided for couples without due regard for the interests of any child that may be born as a result. For example the couple may have a previous conviction for child abuse. It has been argued that the greater the degree of intervention in the creation of a child, the more responsibility must be taken for that child. However, the evidence also drew attention to the absence of any restrictions of procreation by fertile couples, whatever their circumstances. Indeed, some of the evidence referred to the fact that Articles 8 and 12 of the European Convention on Human Rights guarantee a respect for family life and the right to found a family. It has been argued that these provisions create a right to take full advantage of the techniques which are available to alleviate infertility.

2.8 There are other considerations which many believe should be taken into account. For example, a woman may seek treatment when she has herself, at an earlier stage, been sterilised at her own request. Perhaps because of a new marriage, she now very much wants children. The question may be raised whether, if she has children, albeit from another marriage, she should be eligible for infertility treatment. Again, a woman who has had a child may subsequently become infertile. Opinions may be divided about whether she should be eligible for treatment.

2.9 Furthermore, the various techniques for assisted reproduction offer not only a remedy for infertility, but also offer the fertile single woman or lesbian couple the chance of parenthood without the direct involvement of a male partner. To judge from the evidence, many believe that the interests of the child dictate that it should be born into a home where there is a loving, stable, heterosexual relationship and that, therefore, the *deliberate* creation of a child for a woman who is not a partner in such a relationship is morally wrong. On the other side some expressed the view that a single woman or lesbian couple have a right under the European Convention to have children even though those children may have no legal father. It is further argued that it is already accepted that a single person, whether man or woman, can in certain circumstances provide a suitable environment for a child, since the existence of single adoptive parents is specifically provided for in the Children Act 1975 [now repealed].

2.10 In the same way that a single woman may believe she has a right to motherhood, so a single man may feel he has a right to fatherhood. Though the feminist position is perhaps more frequently publicised, we were told of a group of single, mainly homosexual, men who were campaigning for the right to bring up a child. Their primary aim at present is to obtain in practice equal rights in the adoption field, but they are also well aware of the potential of surrogacy for providing a single man with a child that is genetically his. There have been cases in other countries of surrogacy in such circumstances. It can be argued that as a matter of sex equality if single women are not totally barred from parenthood, then neither should single men be so barred.

2.11 We have considered these arguments, but, nevertheless, we believe that as a general rule it is better for children to be born into a two-parent family, with both father and mother, although we recognise that it is impossible to predict with any certainty how lasting such a relationship will be.

2.12 We have considered very carefully whether there are circumstances where it is inappropriate for treatment which is solely for the alleviation of infertility to be provided. In general we hold that everyone should be entitled to seek expert advice and appropriate investigation. This will usually involve referral to a consultant. However, at the present time services for the treatment of infertility are in short supply, both for initial referral and investigation and for the more specialised treatments considered in this report. In this situation of scarcity some individuals will have a more compelling case for treatment than others. In the circumstances medical practitioners will, clearly, use their clinical judgment as to the priority of the individual case bearing in mind such considerations as the patient's age, the duration of infertility and the likelihood that treatment will be successful. So far this is not contentious. However, notwithstanding our view that every patient is entitled to advice and investigation of his or her infertility, we can foresee occasions where the consultant may, after discussion with professional health and social work colleagues, consider that there are valid reasons why infertility treatment would not be in the best interests of the patient, the child that may be born following treatment, or the patient's immediate family.

2.13 This question of eligibility for treatment is a very difficult one, and we believe that hard and fast rules are not applicable to its solution. We recognise that this will place a heavy burden of responsibility on the individual consultant who must make social judgments that go beyond the purely medical, in the types of case we have discussed. We considered whether it was possible for us to set out the wider social criteria that consultants, together with their professional colleagues, should use in deciding whether infertility treatment should be provided for a particular patient. We decided it was not possible to draw up comprehensive criteria that would be sensitive to the circumstances of every case. We recognise however that individual practitioners are on occasions going to decline to treat a particular patient and **we recommend that in cases where consultants decline to provide treatment they should always give the patient a full explanation of the reasons**. This would at least ensure that patients were not kept in ignorance of the reason for refusal, and would be able to exercise their right to seek a second opinion.

During the course of the legislation passing through Parliament, an attempt was made to restrict access to infertility treatment to married couples or, at least, to heterosexual couples in a stable relationship. The Bill was not amended to take account of this. However, s 13(5) was introduced so as to provide some limits upon access to treatment. It provides:

13. (5) A woman shall not be provided with treatment services unless account has been taken of the welfare of any child who may be born as a result of the treatment (including the need of that child for a father), and of any other child who may be affected by the birth.

The important principle of the welfare of the child which runs through legislation concerned with children is, therefore, made part of the doctor's obligation in determining whether to make infertility treatment available to any given person(s). It is, of course, the requirement that the doctor should take account of 'the need of [the] child for a father' and 'of any other child who may be affected by the birth' that is significant. In these words, Parliament has required that the clinical judgment of the doctor must be exercised having regard to others and not just in the 'best interests' of his patient. In this respect, the 1990 Act departs from what would be the normal understanding of a doctor's duty to his patient.

We are concerned with what are, in fact, two distinct but related issues: first, the general question of the suitability of *anyone* to be a parent; and secondly, the suitability of an applicant who is not married. These two issues, together with the possibility of a judicial remedy for denying access to treatment, are discussed by Gillian Douglas.

Gillian Douglas *Law, Fertility and Reproduction* (1991) pp 119-122

Fitness to parent

This arises in two ways. First, suppose a couple present for treatment, but the doctor considers them as unsuitable to act as parents because of their life-style or previous history. Those with a record of child abuse, or drug-taking, might fall into this category. The doctor could argue that it is preferable to deny them treatment rather than have to take emergency measures to protect any resulting child from harm at their hands. A refusal to treat by a private clinic could not be legally challengeable unless it infringed the Sex Discrimination Act 1975 or the Race Relations Act 1976. But it is hard to see how the first could be prayed in aid, and it will be very difficult to prove racial discrimination in order to rely upon the second.

It is also debatable whether a refusal in the NHS could be challenged on other grounds, although an action for judicial review was brought in *R v Ethical Committee of St Mary's Hospital (Manchester) ex parte H* ([1988] 1 FLR 512). There, the applicant had been turned down as a suitable foster or adoptive parent, because she had a criminal record involving prostitution offences, and a 'poor understanding' of fostering. She accordingly sought IVF treatment, but was removed from the waiting list after the hospital became aware of her background. At St Mary's, the criteria for offering treatment were that couples

> must, in the ordinary course of events, satisfy the general criteria established by adoption societies in assessing suitability for adoption . . . [and there] must be no medical, psychiatric or psychosexual problems which would indicate an increased probability of a couple not being able to provide satisfactory parenting to the offspring or endanger the mother's life or health if she became pregnant.

She sought judicial review of the refusal to treat her, but failed on the basis that she had been given an opportunity to make representations against the refusal, so that there was no procedural unfairness. Schiemann J. was prepared to accept, *obiter*, that a blanket policy to refuse treatment to 'anyone who was a Jew or coloured' might be illegal. But here, the hospital's criteria were apparently regarded as acceptable. . . .

Centres offering IVF treatment were required by the ILA guidelines to have an ethical committee to scrutinise their treatment and research programmes, and their objectives included the protection of the interests of patients and of any children resulting from the use of assisted reproduction. No guidance was given on how this was to be done. It is therefore unsurprising that the St Mary's Hospital committee might have had regard to the adoption criteria, which were the only semi-official tests of fitness to parent available. Under section 13(5) of the 1990 Act, treatment licences must contain a condition that

> A woman shall not be provided with treatment services unless account has been taken of the welfare of any child who may be born as a result of the treatment (including the need of that child for a father), and of any other child who may be affected by the birth.

Under section 25(2) the code of practice must also contain guidance on this for those providing treatment services [*Code of Practice* (1993) paras 3.12-3.30]. Such a provision is undesirable. The concept of welfare is hard enough to apply in cases concerning children who are in existence, let alone those who are only a twinkle in the doctor's eye. It is also open to many different assessments, depending on the values of the person making the judgment.

This becomes particularly important in relation to the second type of situation which raises the question of fitness to parent. This is where a woman (or, perhaps less likely, a man) does not have, or seek a partner of the opposite sex, but wants a child. Here, the question is whether children should always ideally be brought up in a household containing a mother and a father. The matter was considered by the Warnock Committee, whose view was that 'as a general rule it is better for children to be born into a two-parent family, with both father and mother', although they did not make a recommendation to limit treatment to members of a couple.

Attempts during the passage of the Act through Parliament to limit treatment to the married, or at least to members of a heterosexual cohabiting couple, were unsuccessful, but section 13(5) does require consideration to be given to the child's need for a father – presumably meaning a man who will fulfil the *social* role of father. This requirement was put in as an amendment expressly to prevent the creation of one-parent families through assisted reproduction (and implicitly to prevent lesbian woman from receiving treatment). Yet there is no evidence for the supposition that the children of such families suffer *because* they are cared for by only one parent, homosexual or otherwise. Children from one-parent families might experience poverty, or the emotional trauma of their parents' relationship breaking up, but children who are born after assisted reproduction are arguably less likely to experience such problems, since their birth was planned when the parent was already settled into her life-style.

In addition to the welfare test operating as a means of excluding those regarded as unfit to parent from the benefits of treatment, it has been suggested that section 38, which provides that a person who has a conscientious objection to participating in any activity governed by the Act is under no duty to do so, will be relied upon by those who oppose not only the principle of donation, or creation of embryos in vitro, but also, for example, by those who do not wish to treat lesbians. Such as approach would mirror that found in relation to abortion, where doctors may help or hinder women seeking terminations, depending upon their own views of the 'rightness' of the woman's case. . . .

Although there were almost 60 clinics (both NHS and private) offering insemination in 1990, only about six were prepared to treat single or lesbian women. The requirement in section 13 is likely to deter any more clinics from offering treatment to these women, and may force them to resort to unlicensed treatment.

Gillian Douglas talks of how hard it is to apply the concept of welfare concerning children 'who are only a twinkle in the doctor's eye'. Arguably, we can go further and suggest that s 13(5) is, in fact, incoherent. If there is an option to bring about the birth of a child, it can never (or almost never) be in its welfare or interests not to be born. Existence for the child is preferable to non-existence. Thus, the reference in s 13(5) to the child's 'welfare' cannot have its ordinary family law meaning. Instead, s 13(5) must be directing us elsewhere and this can only be to the suitability of the proposed parent(s). Given that those who become parents by conventional means do not need to pass any suitability test, the dangers of prejudice and discrimination are obvious. For example, if suitability to be a parent means the ability to meet the needs of the child, it is arguable that the more affluent the applicant for treatment, the more likely a child's *material* needs would be met. Assuming that the capacity to meet the child's spiritual needs does not vary according to social class and status, it would follow that treatment should primarily be offered to the affluent (as those who can afford to pay for this treatment often are). Only by arguing that s 13(5) imports some element of equality of opportunity could this approach, distasteful as it is, be rebutted. The dangers of discrimination and the need to pursue equality as a principle are emphasised by the Canadian Law Reform Commission when considering the issue of access to infertility treatment.

Medically Assisted Procreation (Working Paper No 65) (1992)

In a number of countries, discussion papers have proposed limiting, or legislation has limited, access to medically assisted procreation to stable heterosexual couples who are sterile or infertile or carry a transmissible genetic disorder. The interest of the child (often expressed as the child's right to have a father, a mother and a stable family) and society's interest in protecting the family unit, which is fundamental in our society, are the two arguments most commonly advanced to support such restrictions.

Before it can be determined whether it is necessary and appropriate to entrench such limits in legislation, the above-mentioned criteria must be analysed in terms of the individuals likely to request such medical assistance, and the other values, principles and interests that come into play. For the purposes of this analysis, we considered infertile or sterile persons (physiological infertility), persons who are unable or do not wish to procreate through sexual relations with the opposite sex (social infertility) and persons likely to transmit a genetic disorder (genetic infertility).

Most of those who turn to medically assisted procreation are physiologically infertile. As a rule, the access criteria proposed for these individuals are that they be living as a heterosexual couple and that they be stable. The appropriateness of these criteria is not entirely clear. The criteria of heterosexuality and family status will be discussed later in connection with social infertility; our focus here will be on *stability*.

The criterion of stability, desirable though it may be, raises a number of questions. First, would it be fair to apply this criterion in cases of artificial insemination and in vitro fertilization when the stability of the couple or individual is not a factor in natural procreation, hormone treatment or surgery to correct infertility problems (other forms of medically assisted procreation)? While it is true that the use of gametes from a third person can cause special problems (disclosure of the child's origins and so on), we believe that the objective of using the stability criterion, that is, the welfare of the child, would be more easily attained by ensuring proper support before, during and after the child is conceived. Second, this type of criterion is arbitrary and difficult to evaluate, and because it involves the application of non-medical criteria by health professionals it creates the risk of discrimination. We therefore feel it would be inappropriate to include in legislation stability – or, for that matter, any other criterion based on parental aptitude – as one of the criteria for determining access to medically assisted procreation.

The situation of people who are physiologically and genetically capable of procreating but for personal reasons cannot or do not wish to do so in the context of a heterosexual union poses a more difficult problem. These people fall into two categories: single people and homosexual people. Access to medically assisted procreation for these people raises the whole question of equality rights as compared to protection of the child and the traditional family. It would be difficult for the state to consider any legislative limit on access to the various technologies used in medically assisted procreation without taking into account the spirit and letter of the *Canadian Charter of Rights and Freedoms*. However, we need only consult various legislative provisions and recommendations made in other countries to see that the special situation of these individuals is rarely accepted as grounds for using medically assisted procreation. In fact many jurisdictions make access to medically assisted procreation conditional on physiological infertility, sterility or the existence of transmissible genetic disorders, or simply limit access to heterosexual couples.

Making access to medically assisted procreation conditional on the existence of pathological conditions (sterility, physiological and genetic infertility) may seem normal, since the technologies were developed to circumvent these problems. However, we cannot ignore the fact that establishing such a condition with respect to artificial insemination would deny access to single people and to homosexual people.

Such limitations therefore raise the question of non-discriminatory access to available medical technologies. This means weighing a number of different interests: on the one hand, the interest of single people and homosexual people who express a desire to have children and to use the available technologies, as would infertile or sterile persons living as part of a heterosexual couple, to overcome the obstacles they face; and on the other, the interest of the child and society's interest in protecting the traditional family with two heterosexual parents.

The conflict between respect for the rights guaranteed by the *Charter* and protection of the traditional family unit leads to a number of fundamental questions. How far do we wish to go in protecting rights and freedoms, especially the right to equality? How far do we wish to extend the definition of the family? Do we wish to include homosexual families and single-parent families in that definition?

For some, the interest of the child and society's interest in preserving families with two heterosexual parents must take precedence over the fundamental rights of single people and homosexual people. According to this position, having the freedom to choose one's sexual orientation is one thing, but depriving a child of a father and a mother is something else entirely. The technologies used in medically assisted procreation must be used to overcome sterility and infertility (physiological and genetic), not as an easy way out of the consequences of a social choice.

For others, who make the analogy with the criteria used in adoption, these objections are an expression of old prejudices. Furthermore, through the years the state has not intervened to protect the traditional family, the structure of which has been greatly eroded.

Resolving the issue of access to medically assisted procreation technologies thus requires a thorough examination of the family unit at the dawn of the twenty-first century. Are we prepared not only to accept single-parent families and families with two homosexual parents, but also to place them on an equal footing, in terms of our social values, with families with two heterosexual parents? If so, should we not, in the interest of consistency, change our family laws in order to incorporate these new definitions? Or do we wish instead to make protection of the traditional family a public interest that would take precedence over the rights and freedoms guaranteed by the *Charter* and thus limit the right to procreate as we limit the right to marry in our society?

In considering these questions, we could draw on similar situations in the area of 'natural' procreation, where single-parent families and families with two homosexual parents are a reality.

For the moment, taking current social conditions into account, the Commission is of the opinion that with regard to artificial insemination, protection for the traditional family should not be incorporated in legislation at the expense of the right to equality. Moreover, given the nature of artificial insemination, we believe that state intervention in this area should be kept to a minimum. With respect to in vitro fertilization, the issue of the right to equality creates few problems. However, since these technologies raise the question of the allocation of scarce and costly resources, a legislative limit on access could prove necessary. In any event, caution dictates that such action be taken in accordance with the principles of fundamental justice.

Finally, the use of medically assisted procreation by persons who are physiologically capable of procreating but are carriers of a genetic disorder leads to the question of choosing which genetic disorders justify access to medically assisted procreation, and of which gametes and embryos should be considered 'acceptable.' There is a risk, in making such choices, of opening the door to eugenic practices. This concern also raises another issue, namely, the selection of donors or donor characteristics.

Using medically assisted procreation technologies to avoid transmitting a genetic predisposition or a characteristic trait that is deemed undesirable or to choose the sex or select the desired qualities of the unborn child is unacceptable. In more general terms, such practices lead the way to the development of a traffic in gametes and embryos with particular qualities, breed intolerance of human imperfection and disrupt the demographic and social balance between the sexes for future generations, and could have a tremendous impact on these 'made-to-measure' children. It therefore seems appropriate to generally limit individual freedoms in the name of respect for human dignity.

What genetic disorders justify the use of medically assisted procreation? This question can be answered indirectly by permitting the selection of gametes and embryos for specific qualities only in situations where the goal is to prevent the transmission of a serious genetic disease. . . .

RECOMMENDATIONS

1. Legislation governing access to medically assisted procreation technologies should respect the right to equality. Access should be limited only in terms of the cost and scarcity of resources. Where limitation is necessary, selection should not be based on unlawful grounds

for discrimination within the meaning of federal and provincial legislation (family status, marital status, sexual orientation, and so on).

You will notice the Canadian Law Reform Commission's reference to the Canadian *Charter*. Earlier (at pp 96-98) in their Working Party Report they discuss the impact of the *Charter* on the issue of access:

> . . . there is little doubt that any legislative limitations placed on access to reproductive technologies will have to be tailored to avoid discrimination on the basis of family status, marital status and sexual orientation. On the other hand, legislation requiring applicants to be assessed on the basis of their merits and capacities as potential parents would not violate section 15 [creating the right to equality]. Such an approach would also be in line with current Canadian adoption law and the recommendations contained in several provincial reports concerning reproductive technologies. For example, Ontario adoption law has recently been changed to allow for equal consideration of single applicants, as is the case in all other Canadian jurisdictions. Similarly, three recent provincial reports on reproductive technology recognized that limiting access to married couples would violate human rights laws. The Ontario Law Reform Commission [*Report on Human Artificial and Related Matters* (1985)] concluded that restricting access to reproductive technologies to couples
>
>> would appear to contravene human rights legislation applicable in this Province. Moreover, any *a priori* exclusions based simply on membership in a particular group (such as married persons) would automatically eliminate from consideration single persons or unmarried couples who, by any standard, would make suitable parents.
>
> The Ontario Law Reform Commission accordingly recommended that eligibility to participate in a medically assisted procreation program 'should be limited to stable single women and to stable men and stable women in stable marital or nonmarital unions.' Similarly, the British Columbia Royal Commission [*Ninth Report on Family and Children's Law: Artificial Insemination* (1985)] proposed that the guiding standard should be an applicant's 'ability to nurture':
>
>> [A]n attempt to judge the recipient in terms of her conformity to prevailing mores about marriage and lifestyle should be made in the context of their current state of flux and, more importantly, should concentrate on the conduct of the individual which can be shown to relate directly to her ability to nurture. As suggested above, the central concern in evaluating the prospective AID recipient should focus directly (and singularly) on her ability to be a successful parent. It is the potential child's interest which must be paramount in this situation.
>
> If a limit on access is considered necessary, such an approach, similar to the criteria applied in Canadian adoption law, would be needed to satisfy the requirements of section 15 of the *Charter*. . . .
> For example, let us consider infertility as a potential criterion for access to a reproductive technology. In the case of IVF, legislation making demonstrated infertility a precondition for access would be constitutionally unimpeachable. IVF is a procedure that will mainly be sought by women who are infertile; fertile women can bear children without the assistance of IVF. However, making infertility a precondition for access to surrogate motherhood and AI would give rise to section 15 objections. Such a requirement would impose a disproportionate burden on fertile men and women who wish to exercise their right to procreate non-coitally. These people are defined by their lack of a heterosexual partner, which is to say, by their marital status or their sexual orientation. Legislation imposing infertility as a requirement for access to AI and surrogacy arrangements would effectively deny these men and women the right to procreate. This disproportionate burden suffered by individuals as a result of their marital status or sexual orientation would constitute discrimination for the purposes of section 15.
> In addition, care will have to be taken to ensure that criteria neutral on their face in terms of their impact on groups protected by section 15 or analogous groups, such as 'ability to parent,' are not in practice applied in such a way as to impose an unequal burden on unmarried, single, gay or lesbian applicants for access to reproductive technologies.

The Canadian Law Commission's reference to the Canadian Charter should remind us of the relevance of the European Convention on Human Rights, in particular Articles 8 and 12 (respectively the right to private and family life and to marry and found a family). The current approach taken by the Commission and European Court of Human Rights, however, makes it doubtful whether such limiting access to infertility treatment in the ways described by the Canadian Law Reform Commission would violate the Convention.

HFEA's *Code of Practice* (1993) accepts 'the right of people who are or may be infertile to the proper consideration of their request for treatment' (page 1). This, on its face, seems to endorse (or come close to endorsing) the principle of equality of access. It seeks to give substance to the basic principle in the detailed provisions of the *Code of Practice* dealing with access to treatment.

HFEA, Code of Practice (1993)

Factors to be Considered

3.14 Centres should take all reasonable steps to ascertain who would be the legal parents (or parent) of any child born as a result of the procedure and who it is intended will be bringing him or her up. When clients come from abroad, centres should not assume that the law of that country relating to the parentage of a child born as a result of donated gametes is the same as that of the United Kingdom.

3.15 People seeking treatment are entitled to a fair and unprejudiced assessment of their situation and needs, which should be conducted with the skill and sensitivity appropriate to the delicacy of the case and the wishes and feelings of those involved.

3.16 Where people seek licensed treatment, centres should bear in mind the following factors:

a.   their commitment and that of their husband or partner (if any) to having and bringing up a child or children;

b.   their ages and medical histories and the medical histories of their families;

c.   the needs of any child or children who may be born as a result of treatment, including the implications of any possible multiple births and the ability of the prospective parents (or parent) to meet those needs;

d.   any risk of harm to the child or children who may be born, including the risk of inherited disorders, problems during pregnancy and of neglect or abuse; and

e.   the effect of a new baby or babies upon any existing child of the family.

3.17 Where people seek treatment using donated gametes, centres should also take the following factors into account:

a.   a child's potential need to know about his or her origins and whether or not the prospective parents are prepared for the question which may arise while the child is growing up;

b.   the possible attitudes of other members of the family towards the child, and towards his or her status in the family;

c.   the implications for the welfare of the child if the donor is personally known within the child's family and social circle; and

d.   any possibility known to the centre of a dispute about the legal fatherhood of the child
. . .

3.18 Further factors will require consideration in the following cases:

a.   where the child will have no legal father. Centres are required to have regard to the child's need for a father and should pay particular attention to the prospective mother's ability to meet the child's needs throughout his or her childhood. Where appropriate, centres should consider particularly whether there is anyone else within the prospective mother's family and social circle willing and able to share the responsibility for meeting those needs, and for bringing up, maintaining and caring for the child. . . .

Enquiries to be Made

3.21 Centres should take a medical and social history from each prospective parent. They should be seen together and separately. This should include all the information relevant to paragraphs 3.12 to 3.18 above.

3.22 Centres should seek to satisfy themselves that the client's GP knows of no reason why the client might not be suitable to be offered treatment, including anything which might adversely affect the welfare of any resulting child.

3.23 Centres should obtain the client's consent before approaching the GP. However, failure to give consent should be taken into account in considering whether or not to offer treatment.
3.24 If any of these particulars or inquiries give cause for concern, eg, evidence that prospective parents have had children removed from their care, or evidence of a previous relevant conviction, the centre should make further inquiries of any relevant individual, authority or agency as it can.
3.25 Centres should obtain the client's consent before approaching any individual authority or agency for information. However, failure to give consent should be taken into account in deciding whether or not to offer treatment.

Multidisciplinary Assessment

3.26 The views of all those at the centre who have been involved with the prospective parents should be taken into account when deciding whether or not to offer treatment. Prospective parents should be given a fair opportunity to state their views before any decision is made and to meet any objections raised to providing them with treatment.
3.27 If a member of the team has a cause for concern as a result of information given to him or her in confidence, he or she should obtain the consent of the person concerned before discussing it with the rest of the team. If a member of the team receives information which is of such gravity that confidentiality *cannot* be maintained, he or she should use his or her own discretion, based on good professional practice, in deciding in what circumstances it should be discussed with the rest of the team.
3.28 The decision to provide treatment should be taken in the light of all the available information. Treatment may be refused on clinical grounds. Treatment should also be refused if the centre believes that it would not be in the interests of any resulting child, or any child already existing, to provide treatment, or is unable to obtain sufficient information or advice to reach a proper conclusion.
3.29 If treatment is refused for any reason, the centre should explain to the woman and, where appropriate, her husband or partner, the reasons for this and the factors, if any, which might persuade the centre to reverse its decision. It should also explain the options which remain open and tell clients where they can obtain counselling.
3.30 Centres should record in detail the information which has been taken into account when considering the welfare of the child or children. The record should reflect the views of all those who were consulted in reaching the decision, including those of potential parents.

On its face the *Code of Practice* does not exclude anyone *in limine* from treatment, leaving the decision to turn upon the suitability of the particular applicant(s). Whether this is a satisfactory means of ensuring equality is, at best, debatable. It may be that judicial review, as cases such as *Harriot* (referred to by Gillian Douglas above), will operate to provide guidance and ensure that patent discrimination of whatever kind does not occur. In particular, the courts are likely to achieve this by requiring (as does the *Code of Practice*) that reasons for refusal of access be given by the responsible clinician.

C. CONSCIENTIOUS OBJECTION

Like the Abortion Act 1967, the 1990 Act contains a 'conscientious objection' provision designed to permit individuals to opt out of participating in any of the activities covered by the Act. Section 38 provides as follows:

38. (1) No person who has a conscientious objection to participating in any activity governed by this Act shall be under a duty, however arising, to do so.
   (2) In any legal proceedings the burden of conscientious objection shall rest on the person claiming to rely on it.

This provision is closely modelled upon that which appears in s 4 of the Abortion Act 1967 (discussed *infra*, ch 12). Unlike s 4 of the Abortion Act 1967, however, s 38 does not contain an exception to the right to object where action is necessary to save the patient's life or to prevent grave permanent injury (see Abortion Act 1967, s 4(2)). This omission from the 1990 Act probably reflects the fact that such a situation is very unlikely to arise in the context of infertility treatment (*a fortiori* research on embryos) and hence is unnecessary.

Under s 38 the objection must, of course, be a matter of conscience and the burden is on the individual to establish it (s 38(2)). But a matter of conscience is widely understood to cover, for example, religious, moral or other principled beliefs which lead the individual to conclude that the activity is wrong. Section 38 allows a doctor, nurse or other individual to refuse to 'participate' in a licensed activity to which they have such a conscientious objection.

There may be difficulties in some cases of determining when an individual is being asked to 'participate' (see, *Janaway v Salford HA* [1989] AC 537, discussed *infra*, pp 893 *et seq*). However, there is no doubt that a doctor or nurse who objected to IVF treatment because it involved the creation of an embryo outside the body could not be required to 'participate' in infertility treatment using IVF. Similarly, a research scientist or laboratory technician could not be required to work in a research project involving human embryos if he objected to this.

The right of 'conscientious objection' applies to *any* activity governed by the 1990 Act. It follows that an individual may object to some but not all the activities, for example, to IVF treatment but not artificial insemination. A difficult question is whether the individual must object to participating in a whole class of activity, as in the examples so far, or whether he may also object (a) to participating in particular instances or (b) parts of a licensed activity. Two examples will illustrate the point.

Could, for example, a doctor refuse to treat a lesbian woman by artificial insemination because he 'objected' to her life style and sexual orientation even though he has no objection to artificial insemination in principle? In our view, he could not (contrast, G Douglas, *supra*, at p 782). There are two reasons. First, it could be argued that the doctor's objection is not conscientious as usually understood since it appears to be the product of prejudice rather than principle. Secondly, and more importantly, his objection is not to participating in *an activity* governed by the 1990 Act but rather to treating *this patient*.

By way of further example, could an individual object to participating in part of a licensed activity? Would an individual's objection to being involved in embryo biopsy (to detect a genetic defect) or to allowing a surplus embryo to perish after successful IVF treatment, fall within s 38 even if that individual had no objection to IVF in principle? The answer is not clear from the statute. But, again it could be argued that s 38 only permits an individual to have a conscientious objection to a class of activity licensed under the Act ie, IVF treatment, artificial insemination, storage or research and so on. Beyond this, the Act does not allow the individual to pick and choose which parts of licensed activities that he is prepared to be involved in (contrast, Mrs Virginia Bottomley, *Hansard* (Standing Committee B) 15 May 1990, col 203).

D. CONSENT TO USE AND CONTROL OF GENETIC MATERIAL

As we saw in Chapter 3, consent is a (if not *the*) central legal issue in determining the legality of medical treatment. It is no less so in the case of medically assisted reproduction. Here, however, the 1990 Act has given further prominence to the consent of those involved in the medical procedures. Consent is relevant in two distinct ways. *First*, there is the need for those who are donating genetic material and those being treated for infertility to consent to the medical procedure. As we shall see, the need for, and content of the consents is a matter of common law supplemented by the statute (and *Code of Practice*). *Secondly*, consent is relevant (as a result of the statute) to the future use or storage of an individual's genetic material. Schedule 3 to the 1990 Act requires that a donor of genetic material should give written consent to its future use. Similarly, the Act requires that those who wish their genetic material to be stored should consent to that storage. We shall return to consider the relevant provisions relating to use and storage shortly. For the present, however, it can be seen that the consent of the provider of the genetic material will often determine the fate of that material subject to certain limitations imposed by the statute.

When the 1990 Act came into force on 1 August 1991, there already existed in storage quantities of sperm and embryos, since infertility treatment had been part of medical practice for some years. This caused a number of problems because to continue to store or to use the genetic material required compliance with the detailed consent and information provisions of the Act. Many (if not most) of the donors were untraceable and, therefore, their consents to storage or future use under the Act could not be obtained. In order to obviate the need to destroy the sperm or embryos, the Human Fertilisation and Embryology Act 1990 (Commencement No 3 and Transitional Provisions) Order 1991 (SI 1991 No 1400) permitted their storage (without consent) until such time as consent might be obtained for use in the future. Of course, contacting some donors has proved impossible and hence the stored material may not be used. Once the statutory maximum storage period has expired it will have to be destroyed.

1. Consent to the procedure

A donor of genetic material (for example, of eggs) or a patient undergoing infertility treatment must consent to the medical interventions involved. This is no more than to state the position at common law. In the *Code of Practice* Annex C, HFEA sets out two standard consent forms for use by patients receiving infertility treatment. Only one point of particular interest is worth noting. The forms, which are examples only, contain a section for the husband or male partner of the patient to complete whereby he agrees to the treatment. The purpose of this is not, as the form itself makes clear, because the partner's consent is necessary 'to make the treatment lawful'. Rather, it is designed to avoid any evidential difficulty that might arise when establishing the parentage of any child born after treatment (see *infra*, pp 815–819 discussion of ss 27 and 28 of the 1990 Act).

The 1990 Act acknowledges the common law position and provides in s 13(6) in the case of those receiving treatment services as follows:

13. (6) A woman shall not be provided with any treatment services involving –
(a)   the use of any gametes of any person, if that person's consent is required under paragraph 5 of Schedule 3 to this Act for the use in question,
(b)   the use of any embryo the creation of which was brought about *in vitro*, or
(c)   the use of any embryo taken from a woman, if the consent of the woman from whom it was taken is required under paragraph 7 of that Schedule for the use in question,

unless the woman being treated and, where she is being treated together with a man, the man have been given a suitable opportunity to receive proper counselling about the implications of taking the proposed steps, and have been provided with such relevant information as is proper.

There are two requirements before consent can be given, therefore: an *opportunity for counselling* and the *provision of relevant information.* Similarly, donors and those storing genetic material must also be given the opportunity of counselling and be provided with relevant information prior to donation or storage (see Sch 3, para 3). It is important to notice that the obligations are different as regards counselling and information: namely *a duty to give the opportunity* of counselling but *a duty to provide* information.

HFEA's *Code of Practice* (July 1993) seeks to provide guidance as to the meaning of the statutory provisions. As regards counselling, the *Code of Practice* provides as follows:

General

6.1 People seeking licensed treatment (ie, *in vitro* fertilisation or treatment using donated gametes) or consenting to the use or storage of embryos, or to the donation or storage of gametes, **must** be given 'a suitable opportunity to receive proper counselling about the implications of taking the proposed steps', before they consent.

6.2 Counselling should be clearly distinguished from:

a.   the information which is to be given to everyone, in accordance with the guidance in Part 4 [see below];

b.   the normal relationship between the clinician and the person offering donation or seeking storage or treatment, which includes giving professional advice; and

c.   the process of assessing people in order to decide whether to accept them as a client or donor, or to accept their gametes and embryos for storage, in accordance with the guidance given in Part 3.

6.3 No-one is obliged to accept counselling. However, it is generally recognised as beneficial.

6.4 Three distinct types of counselling should be made available in appropriate cases:

a.   *implications counselling*: this aims to enable the person concerned to understand the implications of the proposed course of action for himself or herself, for his or her family, and for any children born as a result;

b.   *support counselling*: this aims to give emotional support at times of particular stress, eg when there is a failure to achieve a pregnancy.

c.   *therapeutic counselling*: this aims to help people to cope with the consequences of infertility and treatment, and to help them to resolve the problems which these may cause. It includes helping people to adjust their expectations and to accept their situation.

Centres **must** make implications counselling available to everyone. They should also provide support or therapeutic counselling in appropriate cases or refer people to sources of more specialist counselling outside the centre.

6.5 Centres should present the offer of counselling as part of normal routine, without implying either that the person concerned is in any way deficient or abnormal, or that there is any pressure to accept. Centres should allow him or her sufficient time to consider the offer.

6.6 Centres should allow sufficient time for counselling to be conducted sensitively, in an atmosphere which is conducive to discussion. The length and content of counselling, and the pace at which it is conducted, should be determined by the needs of the individual concerned.

6.7 Centres should offer people the opportunity to be counselled by someone other than the clinician responsible for their treatment, donation or storage.

6.8 Centres should offer people the opportunity to be counselled individually and with their partner if they have one. Group counselling sessions may also be offered, but it is not acceptable for a centre to offer only group sessions.

6.9 People should be able to seek counselling at any stage of their investigation or treatment. However, counselling should normally be made available after the person seeking treatment or providing the gametes or embryos has received the oral and written explanations described in paragraph 4.4 and 4.5 [see below]. Discussion may then focus on the meaning and consequences of the decision, rather than on its practical aspects.

Implications Counselling

6.10 Counsellors should invite potential clients or providers of gametes and embryos to consider the following issues:
a. the social responsibilities which centres and providers of genetic material bear to ensure the best possible outcome for all concerned, including the child;
b. the implications of the procedure for themselves, their family and social circle, and for any resulting children;
c. their feelings about the use and possible disposal of any embryos derived from their gametes;
d. the possibility that these implications and feelings may change over time, as personal circumstances change;
e. the advantages and disadvantages of openness about the procedures envisaged, and how they might be explained to relatives and friends.

6.11 Counsellors should invite *clients* to consider in particular:
a. the client's attitude to his or her own, or partner's infertility;
b. the possibility that treatment will fail.

6.12 Where treatment using donated gametes or embryos is contemplated, clients should also be invited to consider:
a. their feelings about not being the genetic parents of the child;
b. their perceptions of the needs of the child throughout his or her childhood and adolescence.

6.13 If a woman is already undergoing infertility treatment when the question of treatment with donated gametes or embryos derived from them arises, counselling about the implications of receiving donated material should be offered separately from counselling about the other implications of treatment. Treatment with donated material should not proceed unless the woman and, where appropriate, her partner have been given a suitable opportunity to receive counselling about it.

6.14 If a woman is undergoing infertility treatment and the possibility of her or her partner's becoming a donor also arises, counselling about the implications of donation should be undertaken separately from counselling about the implications of treatment in the first instance. If the possibility of donation arises at a later stage in the treatment, donation should not proceed unless the woman and, where appropriate, her partner have been given a suitable opportunity to receive counselling about it.

6.15 Counselling about the implications of donation may be combined with counselling about the other implications of treatment at a later stage, if this is advisable in the light of the initial counselling sessions and the client's or potential donor's wishes.

6.16 Counsellors should invite potential *donors* of gametes and embryos to consider in particular:
a. their reasons for wanting to become a donor;
b. their attitudes to any resulting children, and their willingness to forego knowledge of and responsibility for such children in the future;
c. the possibility of their own childlessness;
d. their perception of the needs of any children born as a result of their donation;
e. their attitudes to the prospective legal parents of their genetic offspring;
f. their attitudes to allowing embryos which have been produced from their gametes to be used for research.

6.17 If a person seeking to donate or store genetic material is married or has a long-term partner, the centre should counsel them together if they so wish. If a partner wishes to be counselled separately about the implications of donation or storage, centres should take all practicable steps to offer counselling at the centre, or to assist him or her in contacting an external counselling organisation.

Later Counselling

6.18 Centres should take all practicable steps to provide further opportunities for counselling about the implications of treatment, donation or storage after consent has been given, and throughout the period in which the person is providing gametes, or receiving treatment, if this is requested. If someone who has previously been a donor or client returns to the centre asking for further counselling, the centre should take all practicable steps to help him or her obtain it.

Support Counselling

6.19 Centres should also take all practicable steps to offer support to people who are not suitable for treatment, whose treatment has failed, prospective donors who are found to be unsuitable and people who have previously unsuspected defects, to help them come to terms with their situation.
6.20 These steps should include, wherever practicable, reasonable assistance in contacting or establishing a support group.
6.21 Centres should ensure that, as part of their training, all staff are prepared to offer appropriate emotional support at all stages of their investigation, counselling and treatment to clients who are suffering distress.

Therapeutic Counselling

6.22 Procedures should be in place to identify people who suffer particular distress and to offer them, as far as is practicable, therapeutic counselling, with the aim of helping them to come to terms with their situation.
6.23 If a client experiences mental ill-health or a severe psychological problem which may or may not be related to infertility, for which it would be more appropriate to seek help and advice outside the centre, the centre should take all practicable steps to help him or her to obtain it.

Records

6.24 A record should be kept of all counselling offered and whether or not the offer is accepted.
6.25 All information obtained in the course of counselling should be kept confidential, subject to paragraph 3.27, above.

As regards the duty to give information, the *Code of Practice* provides as follows:

General Obligation

4.1 Before anyone is given licensed treatment (ie, in vitro fertilisation or treatment using donated gametes) or consents to the use or storage of embryos, or to the donation or storage of gametes, he or she **must** be given 'such relevant information as is proper'. This should be distinguished from the requirement to offer counselling, which clients and donors need not accept.
4.2 Clients and donors should be given oral explanations supported by relevant written material. They should be encouraged to ask for further information and their questions should be answered in a straightforward, comprehensive and open way.
4.3 Centres should devise a system to ensure that:
a.   the right information is given;
b.   the person who is to give the information is clearly identified, and has been given sufficient training and guidance to enable him or her to do so; and
c.   a record is kept of the information given.

Information to be Given to Clients

4.4 Information should be given to people seeking treatment on the following points:
a.   the limitations and possible outcomes of the treatment proposed, and variations of effectiveness over time;
b.   the possible side effects and risks of the treatment to the woman and any resulting child, including (where relevant) the risks associated with multiple pregnancy;
c.   the possible disruption of the client's domestic life which treatment will cause, and the length of time he or she will have to wait for treatment;
d.   the techniques involved, including (where relevant) the possible deterioration of gametes or embryos associated with storage, and the possible pain and discomfort;
e.   any other infertility treatments which are available, including those for which a licence is not necessary;
f.   that counselling is available;
g.   the cost to the client of the treatment proposed and of any alternative treatments;
h.   the importance of telling the treatment centre about any resulting birth;

i. who will be the child's parent or parents under the Act. Clients who are nationals or residents of other countries, or who have been treated with gametes obtained from a foreign donor should understand that the law in other countries may be different from that of the United Kingdom . . . ;

j. the child's right to seek information about his or her origins on reaching 18 or on contemplating earlier marriage;

k. the information which centres must collect and register with the Authority and the extent to which that information may be disclosed to people born as a result of the donation;

l. a child's potential need to know about his or her origins;

m. the centre's statutory duty to take account of the welfare of any resulting or affected child; and

n. (where relevant) the advantages and disadvantages of continued treatment after a certain number of attempts.

Information to be Given to People Providing Gametes and Embryos

4.5 Information should be given to people consenting to the use or storage of embryos, or to the donation or storage of gametes, on the following points:

a. the procedures involved in collecting gametes, the degree of pain and discomfort and any risks to that person, eg, from the use of superovulatory drugs;

b. the screening which will be carried out, and the practical implications of having an HIV antibody test, even if it proves negative;

c. the purposes for which their gametes might be used;

d. whether or not they will be regarded under the Act as the parents of any child born as a result;

e. that the Act generally permits donors to preserve their anonymity;

f. the information which centres must collect and register with the Authority and the extent to which that information may be disclosed to people born as a result of the donation;

g. that they are free to withdraw or vary the terms of their consent at any time, unless the gametes or embryos have already been used;

h. the possibility that a child born disabled as a result of a donor's failure to disclose defects, about which he or she knew or ought reasonably to have known, may be able to sue the donor for damages;

i. in the case of egg donation, that the woman will not incur any financial or other penalty if she withdraws her consent after preparation for egg recovery has begun;

j. that donated gametes and embryos created from them will not normally be used for treatment once the number of children believed to have been born from them has reached 10, or any lower figure specified by the donor; and

k. that counselling is available.

It is undoubtedly the case that the level of detail required to be disclosed under the *Code of Practice* goes beyond that which the common law would otherwise require (see supra, ch 3). What would the consequence be if a doctor failed to comply with the code? You will have noticed that s 25(6) begins, 'A failure on the part of any person to observe any provision of the code shall not of itself render the person liable to any proceedings . . . ' A literal meaning may suggest that the code is not intended to set any standard for the purposes of civil liability in negligence (though it may be relevant in proceedings concerning revocation of a licence). On the other hand, a good argument could be made that the code establishes what a reasonable doctor should do, ie the *Bolam* test, such that failure to comply with the code would constitute a breach of duty. The prominence the code has in this area of treatment suggests that the latter view will prevail.

2. Control of gametes and embryos

We are concerned with the issue of the extent to which the providers of gametes and embryos may exercise legal control over their genetic material. For example, who may decide the fate of spare embryos stored after infertility treatment is completed or abandoned? Do the gamete providers have any proprietary claims over their genetic material?

The 1990 Act seeks, in essence, to vest control of gametes and embryos in the providers of the genetic material. It does so through an elaborate scheme of consents. Schedule 3 to the Act requires that a gamete provider must, at the time that the gametes are procured, indicate in a written consent what use(s) those gametes may be put to. The gametes (or any resulting embryos) may only be used in accordance with the consents or, as we shall see, in accordance with those consents as subsequently varied under the Human Fertilisation and Embryology Act 1990 (s 12(c) and Sch 3). Schedule 3 provides as follows:

CONSENTS TO USE OF GAMETES OR EMBRYOS

Consent

1. A consent under this Schedule must be given in writing and, in this Schedule, 'effective consent' means a consent under this Schedule which has not been withdrawn.

2.—(1) A consent to the use of any embryo must specify one or more of the following purposes –
(a)   use in providing treatment services to the person giving consent, or that person and another specified person together,
(b)   use in providing treatment services to persons not including the person giving consent, or
(c)   use for the purposes of any project of research,
and may specify conditions subject to which the embryo may be so used.

(2) A consent to the storage of any gametes or any embryos must –
(a)   specify the maximum period of storage (if less than the statutory storage period), and
(b)   state what is to be done with the gametes or embryo if the person who gave the consent dies or is unable because of incapacity to vary the terms of the consent or to revoke it,
and may specify conditions subject to which the gametes or embryo may remain in storage.

(3) A consent under this Schedule must provide for such other matters as the Authority may specify in directions.

(4) A consent under this Schedule may apply –
(a)   to the use or storage of a particular embryo, or
(b)   in the case of a person providing gametes, to the use or storage of any embryo whose creation may be brought about using those gametes,
and in the paragraph (b) case the terms of the consent may be varied, or the consent may be withdrawn, in accordance with this Schedule either generally or in relation to a particular embryo or particular embryos.

Procedure for giving consent

3.—(1) Before a person gives consent under this Schedule –
(a)   he must be given a suitable opportunity to receive proper counselling about the implications of taking the proposed steps, and
(b)   he must be provided with such relevant information as is proper.

(2) Before a person gives consent under this Schedule he must be informed of the effect of paragraph 4 below.

Variation and withdrawal of consent

4.—(1) The terms of any consent under this Schedule may from time to time be varied, and the consent may be withdrawn, by notice given by the person who gave the consent to the person keeping the gametes or embryo to which the consent is relevant.

(2) The terms of any consent to the use of any embryo cannot be varied, and such consent cannot be withdrawn, once the embryo has been used –
(a)   in providing treatment services, or
(b)   for the purposes of any project of research.

Use of gametes for treatment of others

5.—(1) A person's gametes must not be used for the purposes of treatment services unless there is an effective consent by that person to their being so used and they are used in accordance with the terms of the consent.

(2) A person's gametes must not be received for use for those purposes unless there is an effective consent by that person to their being so used.

(3) This paragraph does not apply to the use of a person's gametes for the purpose of that person, or that person and another together, receiving treatment services.

In vitro fertilisation and subsequent use of embryo

6.—(1) A person's gametes must not be used to bring about the creation of any embryo *in vitro* unless there is an effective consent by that person to any embryo the creation of which may be brought about with the use of those gametes being used for one or more of the purposes mentioned in paragraph 2(1) above.

(2) An embryo the creation of which was brought about *in vitro* must not be received by any person unless there is an effective consent by each person whose gametes were used to bring about the creation of the embryo to the use for one or more of the purposes mentioned in paragraph 2(1) above of the embryo.

(3) An embryo the creation of which was brought about *in vitro* must not be used for any purpose unless there is an effective consent by each person whose gametes were used to bring about the creation of the embryo to the use for that purpose of the embryo and the embryo is used in accordance with those consents.

(4) Any consent required by this paragraph is in addition to any consent that may be required by paragraph 5 above.

Embryos obtained by lavage, etc.

7.—(1) An embryo taken from a woman must not be used for any purpose unless there is an effective consent by her to the use of the embryo for that purpose and it is used in accordance with the consent.

(2) An embryo taken from a woman must not be received by any person for use for any purpose unless there is an effective consent by her to the use of the embryo for that purpose.

(3) This paragraph does not apply to the use, for the purpose of providing a woman with treatment services, of an embryo taken from her.

Storage of gametes and embryos

8.—(1) A person's gametes must not be kept in storage unless there is an effective consent by that person to their storage and they are stored in accordance with the consent.

(2) An embryo the creation of which was brought about *in vitro* must not be kept in storage unless there is an effective consent, by each person whose gametes were used to bring about the creation of the embryo, to the storage of the embryo and the embryo is stored in accordance with those consents.

(3) An embryo taken from a woman must not be kept in storage unless there is an effective consent by her to its storage and it is stored in accordance with the consent.

(a) The consents

Schedule 3 makes clear that a gamete provider must specify the purpose to which the gametes may be put, ie, whether they may be used for treatment (and, if so, for whose treatment) (para 5(1)); may be stored (para 8(1)) or used to created embryos (para 6(1)). In the last of these, the gametes providers must *both* consent to the future use (ie for treatment, and if so, whose treatment and/or for research) and/or storage of the embryos (paras 2(1), 6(3) and 8(2)).

In addition, a consent to storage of gametes and embryos must address *three* specific issues: the maximum period of storage (if less than the statutory maximum); what is to be done if the gamete provider(s) dies; and what is to happen if the gamete provider(s) becomes incapable of varying or revoking consent.

In essence, therefore, the statutory scheme confers a power of veto upon each (of the) gamete provider(s) over what use the gametes may be put to. This power of veto must be seen in the light of certain statutory limits. First, s 14(1)(b) makes it a condition of every storage licence:

(b)   that gametes or embryos which are or have been stored shall not be supplied to a
person otherwise than in the course of providing treatment services unless that person
is a person to whom a licence applies.

Thus, the gamete provider(s) may not indicate someone other than a person
who is being provided with licensed treatment or is another licence-holder.

Secondly, the Act sets a maximum storage period for gametes and embryos
and requires that at the end of the period if stored they 'shall be allowed to
perish' (s 14(1)(c)) regardless of the wishes of the gamete providers. The
maximum storage period in respect of gametes is ten years (s 14(3)) and in
respect of embryos is five years (s 14(4)). Section 14(5) permits these periods to
be varied by regulation. The Human Fertilisation and Embryology (Statutory
Storage Period) Regulations 1991 (SI 1991 No 1540) extend the storage period
for gametes where in the terms of regulation 2(2):

... the gametes were provided by a person –
(a)   whose fertility since providing them has or is likely to become, in the written opinion of
a registered medical practitioner, significantly impaired,
(b)   who was aged under 45 on the date on which the gametes were provided, and
(c)   who does not consent to the gametes' being used for the purpose of providing
treatment services to persons other than that person, or that person and another
together, and never has so consented while the gametes were ones to which this
regulation applied.

The Regulations extend the period from ten years by the difference between the
patient's current age and the age of 45 (ie the storage period for a 30-year-old
would be (45 minus 30) + 10 = 25 years). The justification for this extended
period is to permit, for example, patients undergoing radiotherapy for cancer
to store gametes for an extended period.

Thirdly, you will have noticed that Sch 3, para 2(1) and 2(2) permit gamete
providers to specify conditions subject to which an embryo may be used or
gametes or embryos may be stored. Are there limits to conditions which may be
specified? For example, could a gamete provider validly stipulate that his
gametes may not be used for the treatment of individuals from a particular
ethnic or religious group? The Act does not provide an answer to this question.
We must look, therefore, to the general law. There is little doubt that a court
would regard as invalid a condition which discriminated for no good reason
against certain members of society (see, by analogy *Re Dominion Students' Hall
Trust* [1947] Ch 183 (gift for the benefit of students of European origin only);
and *Re Lysaght* [1966] Ch 191 (gift for the creation of medical studentships
excluding students of the Jewish or Roman Catholic faiths)).

The question then arises whether such a condition if found to be unlawful
would invalidate the 'effective consent' of the gamete provider *in toto* or could
the invalid condition be severed if that were possible? English law offers two
analogies. The first – the charitable trust analogy – would suggest that if the
consent could be valid with the condition excised, then it should be regarded as
valid so as to serve the public interest in having gametes and embryos available.
This, of course, could not happen if to excise the condition would leave a gap in
the gamete provider's consent which the statute did not permit, for example, as
to what is to happen on the death of the gamete provider. The second – the
testamentary analogy – would suggest that the consent would only be valid if
what remained once the condition was excised still gave effect to the gametes
provider's underlying intention. In our view, the latter analogy would probably
be followed by a court.

Fourthly, we should notice s 12(e), which provides:

> (e) that no money or other benefit shall be given or received in respect of any supply of gametes or embryos unless authorised by directions.

The directions made by HFEA provide that individual donors of gametes may be paid up to a maximum of £15 for each donation plus any reasonable expenses incurred. Other benefits may also be given to the donor but are limited to 'treatment services and sterilisation'. Licence-holders who supply other licence-holders with gametes or embryos may only be paid reimbursement of reasonable expenses which may include all the supplier's costs and not just out-of-pocket expenses (HFEA, Directions 1991/92). It is a summary offence under section 41(8) of the 1990 Act if the condition in section 12(e) is not complied with. The effect of these provisions is to prohibit trade in human gametes and embryos (see also Human Organ Transplants Act 1989, s 1(3) discussed *infra*, ch 15).

The final matter to notice in relation to consents is that of variation and withdrawal. Paragraph 4 of Sch 3 provides:

> *Variation and withdrawal of consent*
>
> 4.—(1) The terms of any consent under this Schedule may from time to time be varied, and the consent may be withdrawn, by notice given by the person who gave the consent to the person keeping the gametes or embryo to which the consent is relevant.
>
>   (2) The terms of any consent to the use of any embryo cannot be varied, and such consent cannot be withdrawn, once the embryo has been used –
>
> (a) in providing treatment services, or
> (b) for the purposes of any project of research.

You will recall that, by paragraph 1, consent by a gamete provider must be in writing for it to be an 'effective consent'. Paragraph 4 refers to 'notice' – it does not specify that this must be in writing. However, the definition of 'notice' in s 46 implies that 'notice' should be in writing and this would be consistent with the need for the gamete providers' intentions as to the use of their gametes (or embryos) to be certain and provided in recorded form to HFEA. Paragraph 4(2) limits the gamete providers' capacity to vary or withdraw their consents. If an embryo has not been used it follows that consent to its use can be withdrawn. Thus, para 4(2) seeks to avoid the problems created by disputes over the fate of frozen embryos which may arise when the gamete providers disagree, for example, in the case of marital breakdown (see discussion of *Davis v Davis* (1992) 842 SW 2d 588, *infra*, pp 799 *et seq*).

Once consent to storage is validly withdrawn by at least one gamete provider, para 8 of Sch 3 (see above) applies such that any gametes or embryos may no longer be lawfully stored. They must, thereafter, either be used in accordance with any remaining consents to their use or, if no such consent exists, the gametes and embryos must be 'allowed to perish'. Although the Act does not spell out this latter consequence, it is the only conclusion that the statute allows. (The procedure for disposal should be 'sensitively devised' because of the special status of the human embryo (see, *Code of Practice* (1993) paras 7.19-7.21).)

(b) Remedies

As we have seen, the 1990 Act determines what must happen to gametes or embryos in any given circumstance. Either the gamete providers' consents must be acted upon or, where statutory provisions dictate an outcome, they must be 'allowed to perish'. But what happens if the licence-holder fails to comply with the consents or fails to allow the gametes or embryos to perish? Obviously, the HFEA could review the relevant licence given that this would amount to a breach of a condition of the licence. This would not, of course, necessarily assist the providers of the gametes. Would they have any remedy in law? On its face, the 1990 Act does not provide a remedy. However, there may be four possible avenues of redress.

(i) JUDICIAL REVIEW

The gamete providers might seek a remedy, whether a declaration or, perhaps, an order of mandamus, by way of an application for judicial review under RSC Ord 53, against the licence-holder. The crucial question in such a case would be: is the licence-holder exercising a *public* function? The courts have given a broad meaning to this (see *R v Take-Over and Mergers Panel, ex p Datafin* [1987] QB 815, CA). It is possible that the court would conclude that a licence-holder was exercising a public function. However, it is unlikely. The licence-holder is, in reality, operating or carrying out a *private* activity, heavily regulated by statute but nevertheless no different in principle from any provider of services whether doctor or company. The fact that the licence-holder may be a public employee within the health service is irrelevant if the functions he is performing are *private* in nature (*R v East Berkshire HA, ex p Walsh* [1985] QB 152, CA).

(ii) CONTRACT

Where infertility treatment (or storage) is provided outside the NHS, there will be a contract between the licence-holder and the relevant parties. Of course, express provision may be made in the contract which, providing it is not inconsistent with the 1990 Act, would give the contracting parties a remedy for breach of contract if the licence-holder did not act in relation to the gametes or embryos as required. This, however, would be unusual. More likely is that the terms of Sch 3 (ie the relevant consents of the parties) could be said to be implied into the contract such that a claim for breach of contract could be brought against the licence-holder. The terms are clear; the parties will have known of their existence and will appreciate that they are intended to apply to regulate the relationship between them. On this basis, remedies would include injunction or specific performance as well as damages (perhaps even for any distress caused given the personal nature of the contract: *Bliss v South East Thames RHA* [1987] ICR 700, CA and *Hayes v Dodd* [1990] 2 All ER 815, CA).

Even if the treatment or storage occurs within the NHS, payment may be made by the patients. Hence, the above argument would also apply in that context.

(iii) BREACH OF STATUTORY DUTY

Section 17 of the 1990 Act imposes a statutory duty upon the licence-holder, *viz* that 'the conditions of the licence are complied with'. Failure to comply with the provisions of Sch 3 or the duty to allow the embryos or gametes to perish under s 14(1)(c) would constitute a breach of that duty. Would such a breach give rise to a private right of action? The Act is silent on whether civil liability should arise for breach of the Act (but note s 25(6) as regards breach of the

Code of Practice, supra, p 779). In our view, the 1990 Act is so emphatic in its commitment to the wishes of gamete providers that a court might well take the view that a private right of action should arise. The provisions of Sch 3 clearly contemplate gamete providers as the beneficiaries of the obligations imposed upon licence-holders. The argument gains force from the fact that otherwise an aggrieved party might not have a remedy in law for breach of the terms of the Act.

(iv) THE 'PROPERTY' CLAIM

Could any gamete provider alleging non-compliance with the Act by the licence-holder claim that the non-compliance interferes with a property right he has in the gametes or embryos? A 'property' claim was considered in the following case.

Davis v Davis (1992) 842 SW 2d 588 (Tenn Sup Ct)

Daughtrey Justice: This appeal presents a question of first impression, involving the disposition of the cryogenically-preserved product of *in vitro* fertilization (IVF), commonly referred to in the popular press and the legal journals as 'frozen embryos.' The case began as a divorce action, filed by the appellee, Junior Lewis Davis, against his then wife, appellant Mary Sue Davis. The parties were able to agree upon all terms of dissolution, except one: who was to have 'custody' of the seven 'frozen embryos' stored in a Knoxville fertility clinic that had attempted to assist the Davises in achieving a much-wanted pregnancy during a happier period in their relationship.

. . . Introduction

Mary Sue Davis originally asked for control of the 'frozen embryos' with the intent to have them transferred to her own uterus, in a post-divorce effort to become pregnant. Junior Davis objected, saying that he preferred to leave the embryos in their frozen state until he decided whether or not he wanted to become a parent outside the bounds of marriage.

Based on its determination, that the embryos were 'human beings' from the moment of fertilization, the trial court awarded 'custody' to Mary Sue Davis and directed that she 'be permitted the opportunity to bring these children to term through implantation.' The Court of Appeals reversed, finding that Junior Davis has a 'constitutionally protected right not to beget a child where no pregnancy has taken place' and holding that 'there is no compelling state interest to justify ordering implantation against the will of either party.' The Court of Appeals further held that 'the parties share an interest in the seven fertilized ova' and remanded the case to the trial court for entry of an order vesting them with 'joint control . . . and equal voice over their disposition.'

Mary Sue Davis then sought review in this Court, contesting the validity of the constitutional basis for the Court of Appeals decision. We granted review, not because we disagree with the basic legal analysis utilized by the intermediate court, but because of the obvious importance of the case in terms of the development of law regarding the new reproductive technologies, and because the decision of the Court of Appeals does not give adequate guidance to the trial court in the event the parties cannot agree.

We note, in this latter regard, that their positions have already shifted: both have remarried and Mary Sue Davis (now Mary Sue Stowe) has moved out of the state. She no longer wishes to utilize the 'frozen embryos' herself, but wants authority to donate them to a childless couple. Junior Davis is adamantly opposed to such donation and would prefer to see the 'frozen embryos' discarded. The result is, once again, an impasse, but the parties' current legal position does have an effect on the probable outcome of the case, as discussed below.

At the outset, it is important to note the absence of two critical factors that might otherwise influence or control the result of this litigation: When the Davises signed up for the IVF program at the Knoxville clinic, they did not execute a written agreement specifying what disposition should be made of any unused embryos that might result from the cryopreservation process. Moreover, there was at that time no Tennessee statute governing such disposition nor has one been enacted in the meantime. . . .

. . . we have no statutory authority or common law precedents to guide us, we do have the benefit of extensive comment and analysis in the legal journals. In those articles, medical-legal scholars and ethicists have proposed various models for the disposition of 'frozen embryos' when unanticipated contingencies arise, such as divorce, death of one or both of the parties, financial reversals, or simple disenchantment with the IVF process. Those models range from a rule requiring, at one extreme, that all embryos be used by the gamete-providers or donated for uterine transfer, and, at the other extreme, that any unused embryos be automatically discarded. Other formulations would vest control in the female gamete-provider – in every case, because of her greater physical and emotional contribution to the IVF process, or perhaps only in the event that she wishes to use them herself. There are also two 'implied contract' models: one would infer from enrolment in an IVF program that the IVF clinic has authority to decide in the event of an impasse whether to donate, discard, or use the 'frozen embryos' for research; the other would infer from the parties' participation in the creation of the embryos that they had made an irrevocable commitment to reproduction and would require transfer either to the female provider or to a donee. There are also the so-called 'equity models': one would avoid the conflict altogether by dividing the 'frozen embryos' equally between the parties, to do with as they wish; the other would award veto power to the party wishing to avoid parenthood, whether it be the female or the male progenitor.

Each of these possible models has the virtue of ease of application. Adoption of any of them would establish a bright-line test that would dispose of disputes like the one we have before us in a clear and predictable manner. As appealing as that possibility might seem, we conclude that given the relevant principles of constitutional law, the existing public policy of Tennessee with regard to unborn life, the current state of scientific knowledge giving rise to the emerging reproductive technologies, and the ethical considerations that have developed in response to that scientific knowledge, there can be no easy answer to the question we now face. We conclude, instead, that we must weigh the interest of each party to the dispute, in terms of the facts and analysis set out below, in order to resolve that dispute in a fair and responsible manner. . . .

. . . The 'Person' vs 'Property' Dichotomy

One of the fundamental issues the inquiry poses is whether the preembryos in this case should be considered 'persons' or 'property' in the contemplation of the law. The Court of Appeals held, correctly, that they cannot be considered 'persons' under Tennessee law:

> The policy of the state on the subject matter before us may be gleaned from the state's treatment of fetuses in the womb. . . . The state's Wrongful Death Statute, Tenn. Code Ann. S 20-5-106 does not allow a wrongful death for a viable fetus that is not first born alive. Without live birth, the Supreme Court has said, a fetus is not a 'person' within the meaning of the statute. *See eg, Hamby v McDaniel*, 559 SW 2d 774 (Tenn 1977); *Durrett v Owens*, 212 Tenn 614, 371 SW 2d 433 (1963); *Shousha v Matthews Drivurself Service*, 210 Tenn, 384, 358 SW 2d 471 (1962); *Hogan v McDaniel*, 204 Tenn 235, 319 SW 2d 221 (1958). Other enactments by the legislature demonstrate even more explicitly that viable fetuses in the womb are not entitled to the same protection as 'persons'. Tenn Code Ann S 39-15-201 incorporates the trimester approach to abortion outlined in *Roe v Wade*, 410 US 113 [93 S Ct 705, 35 L Ed 2d 147] (1973). A woman and her doctor may decide on abortion within the first three months of pregnancy but after three months, and before viability, abortion may occur at a properly regulated facility. Moreover, after viability, abortion may be chosen to save the life of the mother. This statutory scheme indicates that as embryos develop, they are accorded more respect than mere human cells because of their burgeoning potential for life. But, even after viability, they are not given legal status equivalent to that of a person already born. This concept is echoed in Tennessee's murder and assault statutes, which provide that an attack or homicide of a viable fetus may be a crime but abortion is not. *See* Tenn. Code Ann. SS 39-13-107 and 39-13-210.

Junior Lewis Davis v. Mary Sue Davis, Tennessee Court of Appeals at Knoxville, No.190, slip op at 5-6, 1990 WL 130807 (Sept. 13, 1990).

Nor do preembryos enjoy protection as 'persons' under federal law. . . .

Left undisturbed, the trial court's ruling would have afforded preembryos the legal status of 'persons' and vested them with legally cognizable interests separate from those of their progenitors. Such a decision would doubtless have had the effect of outlawing IVF programs in the state of Tennessee. But in setting aside the trial court's judgment, the Court of Appeals, at least by implication, may have swung too far in the opposite direction.

The intermediate court, without explicitly holding that the preembryos in this case were 'property,' nevertheless awarded 'joint custody' of them to Mary Sue Davis and Junior Davis, citing TCA SS 68-30-101 and 30-15-208, and *York v Jones*, 717 F Supp 421 (ED Va 1989), for the proposition that 'the parties share an interest in the seven fertilized ova.' The intermediate court did not otherwise define this interest. . . .

The intermediate court's reliance on *York v Jones*, is troublesome. That case involved a dispute between a married couple undergoing IVF procedures at the Hones Institute for Reproductive Medicine in Virginia. When the Yorks decided to move to California, they asked the Institute to transfer the one remaining 'frozen embryo' that they had produced to a fertility clinic in San Diego for later implantation. The Institute refused and the Yorks sued. The federal court assumed without deciding that the subject matter of the dispute was 'property.' The *York* court held that the 'cryopreservation agreement' between the Yorks and the Institute created a bailment relationship, obligating the Institute to return the subject of the bailment to the Yorks once the purpose of the bailment had terminated. 717 F Supp at 424-425.

In this case, by citing to *York v Jones* but failing to define precisely the 'interest' that Mary Sue Davis and Junior Davis have in the preembryos, the Court of Appeals has left the implication that it is in the nature of a property interest. For purposes of clarity in future cases, we conclude that this point must be further addressed.

To our way of thinking, the most helpful discussion on this point is found not in the minuscule number of legal opinions that have involved 'frozen embryos,' but in the ethical standards set by The American Fertility Society, as follows:

> Three major ethical positions have been articulated in the debate over preembryo status. At one extreme is the view of the preembryo as a human subject after fertilization, which requires that it be accorded the rights of a person. This position entails an obligation to provide an opportunity for implantation to occur and tends to ban any action before transfer that might harm the preembryo or that is not immediately therapeutic, such as freezing and some preembryo research.
>
> At the opposite extreme is the view that the preembryo has a status no different from any other human tissue. With the consent of those who have decision-making authority over the preembryo, no limits should be imposed on actions taken with preembryos.
>
> A third view – one that is most widely held – takes an intermediate position between the other two. It holds that the preembryo deserves respect greater than that accorded to human tissue but not the respect accorded to actual persons. The preembryo is due greater respect than other human tissue because of its potential to become a person and because of its symbolic meaning for many people. Yet, it should not be treated as a person, because it has not yet developed the features of personhood, is not yet established as developmentally individual, and may never realize its biologic potential.

Report of the Ethics Committee of The American Fertility Society, *supra*, at 34S-35S.

Although the report alludes to the role of 'special respect' in the context of research on preembryos not intended for transfer, it is clear that the Ethics Committee's principal concern was with the treatment accorded the transferred embryo. Thus, the Ethics Committee concludes that 'special respect is necessary to protect the welfare of potential offspring . . . [and] creates obligations not to hurt or injure the offspring who might be born after transfer [by research or intervention with a preembryo].' *Id* at 35S.

In its report, the Ethics Committee then calls upon those in charge of IVF programs to establish policies in keeping with the 'special respect' due preembryos and suggests:

> Within the limits set by institutional policies, decision-making authority regarding preembryos should reside with the persons who have provided the gametes. . . . As a matter of law, it is reasonable to assume that the gamete providers have primary decision-making authority regarding preembryos in the absence of specific legislation on the subject. A person's liberty to procreate or to avoid procreation is directly involved in most decisions involving preembryos.

Id at 36S.

We conclude that preembryos are not, strictly speaking, either 'persons' or 'property,' but occupy an interim category that entitles them to special respect because of their potential for human life. It follows that any interest that Mary Sue Davis and Junior Davis have in the preembryos in this case is not a true property interest. However, they do have an interest in the nature of ownership, to the extent that they have decision-making authority concerning disposition of the preembryos, within the scope of policy set by law.

. . . The Enforceability of Contract

Establishing the locus of the decision-making authority in this context is crucial to deciding whether the parties could have made a valid contingency agreement prior to undergoing the IVF procedures and whether such an agreement would now be enforceable on the question of disposition. Under the trial court's analysis, obviously, an agreement of this kind would be unenforceable in the event of a later disagreement, because the trial court would have to make an ad hoc 'best interest of the child' determination in every case. In its opinion, the Court of Appeals did not address the question of the enforceability of prior agreements, undoubtedly because that issue was not directly raised on appeal. Despite our reluctance to treat a question not strictly necessary to the result in the case, we conclude that discussion is warranted in order to provide the necessary guidance to all those involved with IVF procedures in Tennessee in the future – the health care professionals who administer IVF programs and the scientists who engage in infertility research, as well as prospective parents seeking to achieve pregnancy by means of IVF, their physicians, and their counsellors.

We believe, as a starting point, that an agreement regarding disposition of any untransferred preembryos in the event of contingencies (such as the death of one or more of the parties, divorce, financial reversals, or abandonment of the program) should be presumed valid and should be enforced as between the progenitors. This conclusion is in keeping with the proposition that the progenitors, having provided the gametic material giving rise to the preembryos, retain decision-making authority as to their disposition.

At the same time, we recognize that life is not static, and that human emotions run particularly high when a married couple is attempting to overcome infertility problems. It follows that the parties' initial 'informed consent' to IVF procedures will often not be truly informed because of the near impossibility of anticipating, emotionally and psychologically, all the turns that events may take as the IVF process unfolds. Providing that the initial agreements may later be modified *by agreement* will, we think, protect the parties against some of the risks they face in this regard. But, in the absence of such agreed modification, we conclude that their prior agreements should be considered binding.

It might be argued in this case that the parties had an implied contract to reproduce using *in vitro* fertilization, that Mary Sue Davis relied on that agreement in undergoing IVF procedures, and that the court should enforce an implied contract against Junior Davis, allowing Mary Sue to dispose of the preembryos in a manner calculated to result in reproduction. The problem with such an analysis is that there is no indication in the record that disposition in the event of contingencies other than Mary Sue Davis's pregnancy was ever considered by the parties, or that Junior Davis intended to pursue reproduction outside the confines of a continuing marital relationship with Mary Sue. We therefore decline to decide this case on the basis of implied contract or the reliance doctrine.

We are therefore left with this situation: there was initially no agreement between the parties concerning disposition of the preembryos under the circumstances of this case; there has been no agreement since; and there is no formula in the Court of Appeals opinion for determining the outcome if the parties cannot reach an agreement in the future.

In granting joint custody to the parties, the Court of Appeals must have anticipated that, in the absence of agreement, the preembryos would continue to be stored, as they now are, in the Knoxville fertility clinic. One problem with maintaining the status quo is that the viability of the preembryos cannot be guaranteed indefinitely. Experts in cryopreservation who testified in this case estimated the maximum length of preembryonic viability at two years. Thus, the true effect of the intermediate court's opinion is to confer on Junior Davis the inherent power to veto any transfer of the preembryos in this case and thus to insure their eventual discard or self-destruction.

As noted [above], the recognition of such a veto power, as long as it applies equally to both parties, is theoretically one of the routes available to resolution of the dispute in this case. Moreover, because of the current state of law regarding the right of procreation, such a rule would probably be upheld as constitutional. Nevertheless, for the reasons set out [below] we conclude that it is not the best route to take, under all the circumstances.

. . . The Right of Procreational Autonomy

Although an understanding of the legal status of preembryos is necessary in order to determine the enforceability of agreements about their disposition, asking whether or not they constitute 'property' is not an altogether helpful question. As the appellee points out in his brief, '[as] two or eight cell tiny lumps of complex protein, the embryos have no [intrinsic] value to either party.' Their value lies in the 'potential to become, after implantation, growth and birth *children*.' Thus, the essential dispute here is not where or how or how long to store the preembryos, but whether the parties will become parents. The Court of Appeals held in effect that they will become parents if they both agree to become parents. The Court did not say what will happen if they fail to agree. We conclude that the answer to this dilemma turns on the parties' exercise of their constitutional right to privacy . . . the right of procreational autonomy is composed of two rights of equal significance – the right to procreate and the right to avoid procreation. . . .

The equivalence of and inherent tension between these two interests are nowhere more evident than in the context of *in vitro* fertilization. None of the concerns about a woman's bodily integrity that have previously precluded men from controlling abortion decisions is applicable here. We are not unmindful of the fact that the trauma (including both emotional stress and physical discomfort) to which women are subjected in the IVF process is more severe than is the impact of the procedure on men. In this sense, it is fair to say that women contribute more to the IVF process than men. Their experience, however, must be viewed in light of the joys of parenthood that is desired or the relative anguish of a lifetime of unwanted parenthood. As they stand on the brink of potential parenthood, Mary Sue Davis and Junior Lewis Davis must be seen as entirely equivalent gamete-providers.

It is further evident that, however far the protection of procreational autonomy extends, the existence of the right itself dictates that decisional authority rests in the gamete-providers alone, at least to the extent that their decisions have an impact upon their individual reproductive status. As discussed . . . above, no other person or entity has an interest sufficient to permit interference with the gamete-providers' decision to continue or terminate the IVF process, because no one else bears the consequences of these decisions in the way that the gamete-providers do.

Further, at least with respect to Tennessee's public policy and its constitutional right of privacy, the state's interest in potential human life is insufficient to justify an infringement on the gamete-providers' procreational autonomy. . . .

. . . the state's interest in the potential life embodied by these four to eight-cell preembryos (which may or may not be able to achieve implantation in a uterine wall and which, if implanted, may or may not begin to develop into fetuses, subject to possible miscarriage) is at best slight. When weighed against the interests of the individuals and the burdens inherent in parenthood, the state's interest in the potential life of these preembryos is not sufficient to justify any infringement upon the freedom of these individuals to make their own decisions as to whether to allow a process to continue that may result in such a dramatic change in their lives as becoming parents.

The unique nature of this case requires us to note that the interests of these parties in parenthood are different in scope than the parental interest considered in other cases. Previously, courts have dealt with the child-bearing and child-rearing aspects of parenthood. Abortion cases have dealt with gestational parenthood. In this case, the Court must deal with the question of genetic parenthood. We conclude, moreover, that an interest in avoiding genetic parenthood can be significant enough to trigger the protections afforded to all other aspects of parenthood. The technological fact that someone unknown to these parties could gestate these preembryos does not alter the fact that these parties, the gamete-providers, would become parents in that event, at least in the genetic sense. The profound impact this would have on them supports their right to solo decisional authority as to whether the process of attempting to gestate these preembryos should continue. This brings us directly to the question of how to resolve the dispute that arises when one party wishes to continue the IVF process and the other does not.

. . . Balancing the Parties' Interests

Resolving disputes over conflicting interests of constitutional import is a task familiar to the courts. One way of resolving these disputes is to consider the positions of the parties, the significance of their interests, and the relative burdens that will be imposed by differing resolutions. In this case, the issue centres on the two aspects of procreational autonomy – the right to procreate and the right to avoid procreation. We start by considering the burdens imposed on the parties by solutions that would have the effect of disallowing the exercise of individual procreational autonomy with respect to these particular preembryos.

Beginning with the burden imposed on Junior Davis, we note that the consequences are obvious. Any disposition which results in the gestation of the preembryos would impose unwanted parenthood on him, with all of its possible financial and psychological consequences. The impact that this unwanted parenthood would have on Junior Davis can only be understood by considering his particular circumstances, as revealed in the record.

Junior Davis testified that he was the fifth youngest of six children. When he was five years old, his parents divorced, his mother had a nervous break-down, and he and three of his brothers went to live at a home for boys run by the Lutheran Church. Another brother was taken in by an aunt, and his sister stayed with their mother. From that day forward, he had monthly visits with his mother but saw his father only three more times before he died in 1976. Junior Davis testified that, as a boy, he had severe problems caused by separation from his parents. He said that it was especially hard to leave his mother after each monthly visit. He clearly feels that he has suffered because of his lack of opportunity to establish a relationship with his parents and particularly because of the absence of his father.

In light of his boyhood experiences, Junior Davis is vehemently opposed to fathering a child that would not live with both parents. Regardless of whether he or Mary Sue had custody, he feels that the child's bond with the non-custodial parent would not be satisfactory. He testified very clearly that his concern was for the psychological obstacles a child in such a situation would face, as well as the burdens it would impose on him. Likewise, he is opposed to donation because the recipient couple might divorce, leaving the child (which he definitely would consider his own) in a single-parent setting.

Balanced against Junior Davis's interest in avoiding parenthood is Mary Sue Davis's interest in donating the preembryos to another couple for implantation. Refusal to permit donation of the preembryos would impose on her the burden of knowing that the lengthy IVF procedures she underwent were futile, and that the preembryos to which she contributed genetic material would never become children. While this is not an insubstantial emotional burden, we can only conclude that Mary Sue Davis's interest in donation is not as significant as the interest of Junior Davis has in avoiding parenthood. If she were allowed to donate these preembryos, he would face a lifetime of either wondering about his parental status or knowing about his paternal status but having no control over it. He testified quite clearly that if these preembryos were brought to term he would fight for custody of his child or children. Donation, if a child came of it, would rob him twice – his procreational autonomy would be defeated and his relationship with his offspring would be prohibited.

The case would be closer if Mary Sue Davis were seeking to use the preembryos herself, but only if she could not achieve parenthood by any other reasonable means. We recognize the trauma that Mary Sue has already experienced and the additional discomfort to which she would be subjected if she opts to attempt IVF again. Still, she would have a reasonable opportunity, through IVF, to try once again to achieve parenthood in all its aspects – genetic, gestational, bearing and rearing.

Further, we note that if Mary Sue Davis were unable to undergo another round of IVF, or opted not to try, she could still achieve the child-rearing aspects of parenthood through adoption. The fact that she and Junior Davis pursued adoption indicates that, at least at one time, she was willing to forego genetic parenthood and would have been satisfied by the child-rearing aspects of parenthood alone.

. . . Conclusion

In summary, we hold that disputes involving the disposition of preembryos produced by *in vitro* fertilization should be resolved, first, by looking to the preferences of the progenitors. If their wishes cannot be ascertained, or if there is dispute, then their prior agreement concerning disposition should be carried out. If no prior agreement exists, then the relative interests of the parties in using or not using the preembryos must be weighed. Ordinarily, the party wishing to avoid procreation should prevail, assuming that the other party has a reasonable possibility of achieving parenthood by means other than use of the preembryos in question. If no other reasonable alternatives exist, then the argument in favor of using the preembryos to achieve pregnancy should be considered. However, if the party seeking control of the preembryos intends merely to donate them to another couple, the objecting party obviously has the greater interest and should prevail.

But the rule does not contemplate the creation of an automatic veto, and in affirming the judgment of the Court of Appeals, we would not wish to be interpreted as so holding.

For the reasons set out above, the judgment of the Court of Appeals is affirmed, in the appellee's favor. This ruling means that the Knoxville Fertility Clinic is free to follow its normal procedure in dealing with unused preembryos, as long as that procedure is not in conflict with this opinion.

Reid CJ and Drowota, O'Brien and Anderson JJ concurred.

We are not concerned here with the detailed analysis of the Tennessee court in determining what should be done with any particular frozen embryo. Rather, we are concerned to notice what the court called the 'person v property dichotomy'. Having decided that an embryo is not a 'person', the court also decided that the embryo is not 'property' either. It occupies, therefore, some special category *sui generis* (see our discussion of the 'dead body' *infra*, ch 15). The court, however, concluded that gamete providers have dispositional control over embryos produced from their gametes. This conclusion echoes the position under the 1990 Act (although in England, unlike Tennessee, each gamete provider has, as we have seen, a power of veto over what may be done).

Davis v Davis, therefore, provides no support for the gamete providers' claim to exercise a 'property' right over their embryos in the case of non-compliance with the 1990 Act. It may be otherwise as regards sperm or eggs in that it could be argued that they are property in the same way as it could be said that blood and other body tissue is property once separated from the individual (see *infra*). The California case of *Hecht v Superior Court* (1993) 20 Cal Rptr 2d 275 (Cal CA) rejected this view, preferring the middle ground marked out in *Davis*. Whatever is right, whether as regards embryos or sperm, the framework established by the 1990 Act makes such enquiries pointless. This is because wherever the 'property' approach may lead us, it cannot take us further than the 1990 Act already allows.

There are, however, two examples where a court could be drawn into determining whether the 'property' claim exists. The first is where a gamete provider requests that the gametes or embryo be transferred to another licence-holder and the licence-holder who currently has the gametes or embryos refuses (eg *York v Jones* (1989) 717 F Supp 421 (ED Va)). In such a case, (assuming the gamete providers withdraw their consent to storage) the court could avoid the need to be drawn into a property analysis by deciding that the appropriate remedy lay in an action for breach of statutory duty.

The second is where the gametes or embryos are lost, damaged or destroyed. Of course, even here a claim might be brought in negligence for any psychiatric damage caused to the gamete providers by the loss (see, eg. *Del Zio v Columbia Presbyterian Medical Centre* (SDNY, 12 April 1976) see 1st edn, pp 656-660). Could they, however, also succeed in a claim for conversion? Here, the Act will not provide a way out. Given that there is no reasoned solution of what is essentially a question of metaphysical proportions it would be idle to predict the outcome of such a case should these very limited circumstances, which are the only ones that pose the problem, arise.

E. ACCESS TO AND CONTROL OF INFORMATION

Section 31 of the 1990 Act imposes upon the HFEA a statutory obligation to keep a register of information which relates to the following information specified in s 31(2):

(a) the provision of treatment services for any identifiable individual, or
(b) the keeping or use of the gametes of any identifiable individual or of an embryo taken from any identifiable woman,
or if it shows that any identifiable individual was, or may have been, born in consequence of treatment services.

In essence, this information consists of that relating to gamete donors, patients receiving infertility treatment and any children born as a consequence (hereafter 'the statutory information'). The Act requires licence-holders to collect this information and provide it to HFEA (see ss 12-15). Two issues arise: (a) who, if anyone, may gain access to this statutory information? and (b) beyond these circumstances when may the statutory information be disclosed by HFEA or a licence-holder?

1. Access

(a) Information held by HFEA

First, let us consider access to the statutory information held by HFEA.

(i) SECTION 31(3)-(5)

The following provisions of s 31 require that the authority give access to certain statutory information in the case of a person who has reached the age of 18.

> **31.** (3) A person who has attained the age of eighteen ('the applicant') may by notice to the Authority require the Authority to comply with a request under subsection (4) below, and the Authority shall do so if –
> (a)   the information contained in a register shows that the applicant was, or may have been, born in consequence of treatment services, and
> (b)   the applicant has been given a suitable opportunity to receive proper counselling about the implications of compliance with the request.
>   (4) The applicant may request the Authority to give the applicant notice stating whether or not the information contained in the register shows that a person other than a parent of the applicant would or might, but for sections 27 to 29 of this Act, be a parent of the applicant and, if it does show that –
> (a)   giving the applicant so much of that information as relates to the person concerned as the Authority is required by regulations to give (but no other information), or
> (b)   stating whether or not that information shows that, but for sections 27 to 29 of this Act, the applicant, and a person specified in the request as a person whom the applicant proposes to marry, would or might be related.
>   (5) Regulations cannot require the Authority to give any information as to the identity of a person whose gametes have been used or from whom an embryo has been taken if a person to whom a licence applied was provided with the information at a time when the Authority could not have been required to give information of the kind in question.

Notice that as regards information relating to the genetic origins of the child, only that information permitted by regulations must be disclosed (s 31(4)(a)). The effect of 31(5) is to ensure that, at any given time, a donor of gametes (or embryos) will know what information may subsequently (ie, 18 years later) be divulged to any child. The donor looks to the terms of the regulations in force at the time of the donation. The regulations cannot retrospectively affect what HFEA has to disclose. To illustrate this point, imagine two children are born on a certain day, one as a result of sperm donated at a time when the regulations specified only certain information (eg, ethnic and social background of the donor) while the other child was conceived using sperm donated under a different regime of regulations which did not permit such disclosure. The effect would be that, although they would both become 18 on the same day, what they may learn about their genetic background would be significantly different. Currently, there are no regulations and hence any children conceived using donated material will not be able to obtain *any* information about their genetic background. A contrast, therefore, has been made between children who are adopted – who at 18 have a legal right to discover their natural parents (see

Adoption Act 1976, s 51) – and children born through medically assisted reproduction. The Warnock Committee recommended that certain 'basic information', though not identifying information, should be made available.

Report of the Committee of Inquiry into Human Fertilisation and Embryology (Cm 9314) (1984)

4.19 It is the practice of some clinics in the USA to provide detailed descriptions of donors, and to permit couples to exercise choice as to the donor they would prefer. In the evidence there was some support for the use of such descriptions. It is argued that they would provide information and reassurance for the parents and, at a later date, for the child. They might also be of benefit to the donor, as an indication that he is valued for his own sake. A detailed description also offers some choice to the woman who is to have the child, and lack of such choice can be said to diminish the importance of the woman's right to choose the father of her child.

4.20 The contrary view, also expressed in the evidence, is that detailed donor profiles would introduce the donor as a person in his own right. It is also argued that the use of profiles devalues the child who may seem to be wanted only if certain specifications are met, and this may become a source of disappointment to the parents if their expectations are unfulfilled.

4.21 As a matter of principle we do not wish to encourage the possibility of prospective parents seeking donors with specific characteristics by the use of whose semen they hope to give birth to a particular type of child. We do not therefore want detailed descriptions of donors to be used as a basis for choice, but we believe that the couple should be given sufficient relevant information for their reassurance. This should include some basic facts about the donor, such as his ethnic group and his genetic health. A small minority of the Inquiry, while supporting the principle set out above, and without compromising the principle of anonymity, consider that a gradual move towards making more detailed descriptions of the donor available to prospective parents, if requested, could be beneficial to the practice of AID, provided this was accompanied by appropriate counselling. **We recommend that on reaching the age of eighteen the child should have access to the basic information about the donor's ethnic origin and genetic health and that legislation be enacted to provide the right of access to this.** This legislation should not be retrospective.

The arguments for and against semen donors remaining anonymous are made by Jonathan Glover in the following extract from his Report to the European Commission on Reproductive Technologies.

Glover Report, *Fertility and the Family* (1989)

Most semen donors express a preference for anonymity. This is partly to avoid paternity suits. (In most countries, the legal position is unclear.) But it is also to avoid unwanted later contact with their 'offspring'.

Swedish law has given the child the right to know the identity of the semen donor, on reaching maturity at the age of eighteen. Paternity suits are eliminated by assigning paternity to the married woman's husband, who gives his irrevocable written consent. The donor remains anonymous as far as the social parents are concerned. The law equates AID with adoption, so the donor has a socially recognised position, though one without rights. Is this alternative model preferable to anonymity?

Let us look first at the family in which the child will grow up. Social parenthood often out-ranks biological parenthood, Being a social father is much more important in life than being a semen donor. And the emotional bond with the social father is usually far more important to children than the genetic links with the donor.

The social parents may want their family to be a closed unit, as much like other families as possible, unencumbered by ambiguous half-relationships with donors. A social father may feel rejected if he sees the donor as a rival.

Parents often prefer anonymous donors who will disappear afterwards. But some opponents of anonymity favour the Swedish model, where the potential identification of the donor would only take place eighteen years after the child's birth. This seems to give plenty of time for the development of family bonds which will survive. And parents themselves sometimes prefer a known or related donor. This can be because they think they have some idea of the likely genetic characteristics of the child. And, in the case of related donors, they may value the extra genetic link with the child this gives, as well as their more intimate knowledge of the kind of person the donor is. It is possible to have a known or related donor whose identity is kept from the child; but this involves the drawbacks of family secrets. The desire for a genetic or other link may lead some social parents to prefer a system without anonymity.

What about the position of donors? As in the Swedish system, the donor can be given complete legal protection, so that the child has no rights against the donor other than knowledge of his identity.

The effect of abolishing anonymity in Sweden seems to have been an initial decline in numbers of donors. This may suggest that many donors prefer to be anonymous, quite apart from fear of paternity suits. But this must be linked to two other effects of the new law. There was a decline in demand: couples felt less comfortable at the thought that the child might eventually wish to contact the donor. And physicians in some AID centres refused to continue offering AID under the new law. In the centres still continuing with AID, the numbers of donors have returned to normal, although they are now more often older and more often married . . .

Policies on anonymity represent a social choice about the meaning of donation. Do we accept and recognise the donor's contribution as an act of altruism, perhaps as part of a system in which a husband donates with the full agreement of his wife? Or do we prefer the anonymous student as a source, treating the contribution as an embarrassment, to be accepted but swept under the carpet? There may be more dignity for the donor in a system of openness rather than anonymity. In the case of donors, there seems something to be said for eliminating anonymity, but against this must be set what appears to be their own widespread preference for retaining it.

What about the children? The child's concern with his or her origin was the main motive for the Swedish policy.

Some adopted children find they come to care very much who their biological parents are, and may go to great lengths to find out. Our sense of who we are is bound up with the story we tell about ourselves. A life where the biological parents are unknown is like a novel with the first chapter missing. Also there are the marked similarities between children and their biological parents. The child may wonder who is the person, perhaps among those passed in the street, who has that degree of closeness.

On the other hand, for young children who know who the semen donor was, there may be problems about their identity. They may see neither person as being unambiguously their father. This suggests that it may not be in the children's best interest to be told who the donor is at an early age, but is not a point against a system of the Swedish type, setting the right to know at the age of eighteen. And, since the legal right to know need not be exercised, no child loses anything by it. Since some people care so much about their origins, seeing them as an important part of their identity, the interests of the children count strongly in favour of the right to know.

What relative weight should be given to the different interests of the various people involved? This is the kind of problem where no absolute general rule is likely to give best results in all cases. So much depends on the individual case: who the particular people are, their relationships and what they care about. As a committee we unsurprisingly found ourselves differing in the weight we gave to the different interests.

Some of us felt that it can be very hard on the parents to have the donor intrude on the family. But most of us were inclined to think that, by the time the child is eighteen, the family should usually be strong enough to weather this.

Some of us were inclined to see knowledge of one's origins as so central to identity as to be a right. We all accept that ignorance of it can be a severe psychological disadvantage, and we give this great weight in thinking about policy. But the claim that this knowledge is an absolute right suggests, for instance, that it should always outweigh any degree of unwillingness by donors to discard the protection of anonymity. Is this plausible?

In a system without anonymity, donors need not themselves be hugely disadvantaged. As in Sweden, their legal position can be protected. There may be some disadvantages in later contact by their offspring. But no-one need become a donor if they think this possibility is a terrible one. Perhaps the interests of the children count for more than the possible disadvantages to the donors.

But the case for anonymity does not here simply rest on a direct appeal to the interests of the donors. The fear is that, through putting off potential donors, abolition of anonymity will damage the whole programme. The losers will be infertile couples who will no longer be able to have this help in having children because potential donors have voted with their feet.

The extreme views are, on the one hand, that knowledge of the donor is an inviolable right, and, on the other hand, that anonymity should always be guaranteed. Perhaps a reasonable middle course can be found.

We suggest that the child's interests create a strong *presumption* in favour of openness, but with protection for the various parties involved. As in the Swedish model, the social parents should be protected from intrusion when the 'child' still *is* a child, and the donor should be protected from paternity claims. But, although we favour openness, this is a presumption rather than an absolute right. There is a case for adopting a Swedish-type law for an experimental period, and seeing what happens to donor recruitment. If it slumps disastrously, public appeals could be tried to counteract the effects of the new system. If none of this worked, there would then be a case for abandoning the experiment.

To put the point briefly: it can be better for a child to be born without the right to know the biological father than for that child not to be born at all. But, if the donor programmes can be kept up, best of all might be to be born with the right to know.

In addition to the information which an 18 year old may gain access to, there is a special category of information which may be made available to someone between the ages of 16 and 18 where the person is concerned that someone whom he or she proposed to marry may be genetically related to them (s 31(6)-(7)):

31. (6) A person who has not attained the age of eighteen ("the minor") may by notice to the Authority specifying another person ("the intended spouse") as a person whom the minor proposes to marry require the Authority to comply with a request under subsection (7) below, and the Authority shall do so if –

(a) the information contained in the register shows that the minor was, or may have been, born in consequence of treatment services, and

(b) the minor has been given a suitable opportunity to receive proper counselling about the implications of compliance with the request.

(7) The minor may request the Authority to give the minor notice stating whether or not the information contained in the register shows that, but for sections 27 to 29 of this Act, the minor and the intended spouse would or might be related.

A similar provision exists, as we saw, for the person over 18 (see s 31(4)(b) above) although, interestingly, the statutory requirement for counselling only applies to the minor (contrast the positions for adoption under s 51 of the Adoption Act 1976).

(ii) SECTION 32

The Registrar General may request information from the HFEA in fulfilling his statutory functions:

Information to be provided to Registrar General
32. (1) This section applies where a claim is made before the Registrar General that a man is or is not the father of a child and it is necessary or desirable for the purpose of any function of the Registrar General to determine whether the claim is or may be well-founded.

(2) The authority shall comply with any request made by the Registrar General by notice to the Authority to disclose whether any information on the register kept in pursuance of section 31 of this Act tends to show that the man may be the father of the child by virtue of section 28 of this Act and, if it does, disclose that information.

(iii) SECTION 34

A court may require the HFEA to disclose information (excluding that relating to any donor) where a dispute over parentage arises:

Disclosure in interests of justice
34. (1) Where in any proceedings before a court the question of whether a person is or is not the parent of a child by virtue of sections 27 to 29 of this Act falls to be determined, the court may on the application of any party to the proceedings make an order requiring the Authority –

(a)   to disclose whether or not any information relevant to that question is contained in the register kept in pursuance of section 31 of this Act, and

(b)   if it is, to disclose so much of it as is specified in the order, but such an order may not require the Authority to disclose any information falling within section 31(2)(b) of this Act.

(2) The court must not make an order under subsection (1) above unless it is satisfied that the interests of justice require it to do so, taking into account –

(a)   any representations made by any individual who may be affected by the disclosure, and

(b)   the welfare of the child, if under 18 years old, and of any other person under that age who may be affected by the disclosure.

(3) If the proceedings before the court are civil proceedings, it –

(a)   may direct that the whole or any part of the proceedings on the application for an order under subsection (2) above shall be heard in camera, and

(b)   if it makes such an order, may then or later direct that the whole or any part of any later stage of the proceedings shall be heard in camera.

(4) An application for a direction under subsection (3) above shall be heard in camera unless the court otherwise directs.

(iv) SECTION 35

A court may require HFEA to disclose the identity of a donor when a child wishes to bring a claim for injury caused before the birth under s 1 of the Congenital Disabilities (Civil Liability) Act 1976. The section seems to contemplate the situation where, for example, the proposed action will be against the donor for *his* negligence:

Disclosure in interests of justice: congenital disabilities, etc.
35. (1) Where for the purposes of instituting proceedings under section 1 of the Congenital Disabilities (Civil Liability) Act 1976 (civil liability to child born disabled) it is necessary to identify a person who would or might be the parent of a child but for sections 27 to 29 of this Act, the court may, on the application of the child, make an order requiring the Authority to disclose any information contained in the register kept in pursuance of section 31 of this Act identifying that person. . . .
(3) Subsections (2) to (4) of Section 34 of this Act apply for the purposes of this section as they apply for the purposes of that.

(v) DATA PROTECTION ACT 1984

We have already discussed the application of the Data Protection Act 1984 (see *supra*, ch 8). It applies to the computerised records of HFEA, subject to s 35A of the 1984 Act which prevents access by a child to information concerning their origins unless that information may be obtained under the 1990 Act, s 31.

Information about human embryos, etc.
35A. Personal data consisting of information showing that an identifiable individual was, or may have been, born in consequence of treatment services (within the meaning of the Human Fertilisation and Embryology Act 1990) are exempt from the subject access provisions except so far as their disclosure under those provisions is made in accordance with section 31 of that Act (the Authority's register of information).

If, however, any of HFEA's records were manually stored, it is important to notice that the provisions of the Access to Health Records Act 1990 would not apply since HFEA is not a 'holder' within s 1(2) of the Act from whom access may be sought.

(b) Information held by the licence-holder

The licence-holder would, in principle, have to comply with a request for access under the Data Protection Act 1984 or the Access to Health Records Act 1990 (if he is a health professional). We discussed these statutory provisions in Chapter 8.

As regards the DPA 1984, we have already seen the limitation imposed in s 35A when the applicant is a child born as a consequence of infertility treatment. The Access to Health Records Act 1990 curiously imposed no such limitation. However, the Access to Health Records (Control of Access) Regulations 1993 (SI 1993 No 746) closes the gap by providing, in reg 2:

> 2. Access shall not be given under section 3(2) of the [Access to Health Records] Act to any part of a health record which would disclose information showing that an identifiable individual was, or may have been, born in consequence of treatment services within the meaning of the Human Fertilisation and Embryology Act 1990.

2. Disclosure of information

Section 33 of the 1990 Act imposes a strict secrecy requirement for statutory information held by HFEA of a licence-holder. As regards HFEA, s 33(1) and (2) provide:

> **33.** (1) No person who is or has been a member or employee of the Authority shall disclose any information mentioned in subsection (2) below which he holds or has held as such a member or employee.
>   (2) The information referred to in subsection (1) above is –
> (a)   any information contained or required to be contained in the register kept in pursuance of section 31 of this Act, and
> (b)   any other information obtained by any member or employee of the Authority on terms or in circumstances requiring it to be held in confidence.

As regards a licence-holder, s 33(5) provides:

> **33.** (5) No person who is or has been a person to whom a licence applies and no person to whom directions have been given shall disclose any information falling within section 31(2) of this Act which he holds or has held as such a person.

The strict limits (and limited exceptions) of the 1990 Act as originally drafted proved problematic and led to the passage of the Human Fertilisation and Embryology (Disclosure of Information) Act 1992 which amended s 33 considerably so as to permit a greater degree of disclosure by licence-holders.

(a) By HFEA

As regards statutory information, disclosure by HFEA is permitted in the following circumstances:

> **33.** (3) Subsection (1) above [ie the non-disclosure rule] does not apply to any disclosure of information mentioned in subsection (2)(a) above made –
> (a)   to a person as a member or employee of the Authority,
> (b)   to a person to whom a licence applies for the purposes of his functions as such,
> (c)   so that no individual to whom the information relates can be identified,
> (d)   in pursuance of an order of a court under section 34 or 35 of this Act,
> (e)   to the Registrar General in pursuance of a request under section 32 of this Act, or
> (f)   in accordance with section 31 of this Act.

Section 33(7) also permits HFEA to disclose information to patients or donors which relates exclusively to themselves. It provides:

33. (7) [section 33(1) and (5)] does not apply to the disclosure to any individual of information which –
(a) falls within section 31(2) of this Act by virtue of paragraph (a) or (b) of that subsection, and
(b) relates only to that individual or, in the case of an individual treated together with another, only to that individual and that other.

As regards confidential information held by HFEA which is not 'statutory information', the Act in s 33(2)(b) imposes a statutory obligation of confidence. Section 33(4) permits disclosure in the following circumstances.

33. (4) Subsection (1) [ie the non-disclosure rule] above does not apply to any disclosure of information mentioned in subsection (2)(b) above –
(a) made to a person as a member or employee of the Authority,
(b) made with the consent of the person or persons whose confidence would otherwise be protected, or
(c) which has been lawfully made available to the public before the disclosure is made.

(b) By the licence-holder

It must always be remembered that the general law relating to confidentiality applies to the licence-holder. What s 33 is concerned with is the statutory information held by the licence-holder and its provisions may go further than the general law in limiting disclosure. It is also a criminal offence to breach the provisions of s 33 (see s 41(8)).

Section 33(6), (6A), (6B), (6C), (6D), (6E), (6F), (6G), (7) and (9) set out the *only* circumstances in which disclosure of statutory information is permitted.

33. (6) Subsection (5) [ie the non-disclosure rule] above does not apply to any disclosure of information made –
(a) to a person as a member or employee of the Authority,
(b) to a person to whom a licence applies for the purposes of his functions as such,
(c) so far as it identifies a person who, but for sections 27 to 29 of this Act, would or might be a parent of a person who instituted proceedings under section 1A of the Congenital Disabilities (Civil Liability) Act 1976, but only for the purpose of defending such proceedings, or instituting connected proceedings for compensation against that parent.
(d) so that no individual to whom the information relates can be identified,
(e) in pursuance of directions given by virtue of section 24(5) or (6) of this Act.
(f) necessarily –
    (i) for any purpose preliminary to proceedings, or
    (ii) for the purposes of, or in connection with, any proceedings,
(g) for the purpose of establishing, in any proceedings relating to an application for an order under subsection (1) of section 30 of this Act, whether the condition specified in paragraph (a) or (b) of that subsection is met, or –
(h) under section 3 of the Access to Health Records Act 1990 (right of access to health records).
    (6A) Paragraph (f) of subsection (6) above, so far as relating to disclosure for the purpose of, or in connection with, any proceedings, does not apply –
(a) to disclosure of information enabling a person to be identified as a person whose gametes were used, in accordance with consent given under paragraph 5 of Schedule 3 to this Act, for the purposes of treatment services in consequence of which an identifiable individual was, or may have been, born, or
(b) to disclosure, in circumstances in which subsection (1) of section 34 of this Act applies, of information relevant to the determination of the question mentioned in that subsection.
    (6B) In the case of information relating to the provision of treatment services for any identifiable individual –
(a) where one individual is identifiable, subsection (5) above does not apply to disclosure with the consent of that individual;

(b) where both a woman and a man treated together with her are identifiable, subsection (5) above does not apply –
   (i) to disclosure with the consent of them both, or
   (ii) if disclosure is made for the purpose of disclosing information about the provision of treatment services for one of them, to disclosure with the consent of that individual.

(6C) For the purposes of subsection (6B) above, consent must be to disclosure to a specific person, except where disclosure is to a person who needs to know –
(a) in connection with the provision of treatment services, or any other description of medical, surgical or obstetric services, for the individual giving the consent,
(b) in connection with the carrying out of an audit of clinical practice, or
(c) in connection with the auditing of accounts.

(6D) For the purposes of subsection (6B) above, consent to disclosure given at the request shall be disregarded unless, before it is given, the person requesting it takes reasonable steps to explain to the individual from whom it is requested the implications of compliance with the request.

(6E) In the case of information which relates to the provision of treatment services for any identifiable individual, subsection (5) above does not apply to disclosure in an emergency, that is to say, to disclosure made –
(a) by a person who is satisfied that it is necessary to make the disclosure to avert an imminent danger to the health of an individual with whose consent the information could be disclosed under subsection (6B) above, and
(b) in circumstances where it is not reasonably practicable to obtain that individual's consent.

(6F) In the case of information which shows that any identifiable individual was, or may have been, born in consequence of treatment services, subsection (5) above does not apply to any disclosure which is necessarily incidental to disclosure under subsection (6B) or (6E) above.

(6G) Regulations may provide for additional exceptions from subsection (5) above, but no exception may be made under this subsection –
(a) for disclosure of a kind mentioned in paragraph (a) or (b) of subsection (6A) above, or
(b) for disclosure, in circumstances in which section 32 of this Act applies, of information having the tendency mentioned in subsection (2) of that section.

(7) This section does not apply to the disclosure to any individual of information which –
(a) falls within section 31(2) of this Act by virtue of paragraph (a) or (b) of that subsection, and
(b) relates only to that individual or, in the case of an individual treated together with another, only to that individual and that other.

(9) In subsection (6)(f) above, references to proceedings include any formal procedure for dealing with a complaint.

Until the amendments to s 33 in 1992, the range of disclosure was limited to the circumstances set out in s 33(6)(a) to (e) and 33(7). As regards these, only that in s 33(6)(c) calls for comment. It permits disclosure of the identity of a donor by a licence-holder who is sued by a disabled child for negligence arising from the infertility treatment in order to defend himself (see *infra*, ch 13 for a discussion of these actions and s 1A of the Congenital Disabilities (Civil Liability) Act 1976).

As regards the amended provisions, there are *six* important areas to consider:

(i) LEGAL PROCEEDINGS

The Act permits disclosure where it is *necessary* for the purpose of, or in connection with, 'proceedings' or as a preliminary to such proceedings (s 33(6)(f)). This provision is, on its face, both wide and general in its application. It is important to notice, however, that disclosure must be *objectively* necessary. It would not suffice, in itself, for the doctor to believe that disclosure was necessary or otherwise to act in good faith since these subjective terms are conspicuous by their absence from s 33(6)(f). The provision applies to 'any proceedings' and this term is not defined other than to state that it includes 'any formal procedure for dealing with a complaint' (s 33(9)). Clearly, however, it would include: any legal proceedings brought against a licensed doctor; a complaint brought against a general practitioner (where, perhaps, she is licensed to provide artificial insemination) under the National Health Service (Service Committee and Tribunal) Regulations 1992 (SI 1992 No 664); and a complaint against an NHS hospital doctor under the complaints procedure set out in HC (88) 37. Given the generality of the wording of s 33(6)(f), disclosure might also be permitted in, or as a preliminary to, legal proceedings to which the doctor is not a party. Subject to this disclosure would still have to be required by law or otherwise not be a breach of confidence by the doctor. Importantly, under this new provision disclosure is restricted to information which relates to *the patient or any children born*: information that identifies a donor (at least where a child has subsequently been born) is not permitted (s 33(6A)(a)). The latter information may be important where the medical negligence claim is based upon inadequate screening of the donor(s) or testing of the donated material. Here what passed between the doctor and the donor may well be important to the doctor's defence and yet he cannot disclose any identifying information to his legal advisers. Only the court has power to order disclosure of information which identifies a donor (eg s 35) and then only for the purpose of instituting proceedings against the donor. Presumably, such proceedings would be under the Congenital Disabilities (Civil Liability) Act 1976, brought by a disabled child who alleges that the donor negligently failed to disclose his medical or genetic history which subsequently affected the child. Is it really necessary to protect a donor's identity and related information at all costs? Surely, at the very least, the court should have power to order disclosure here also?

(ii) CONSENT OF PATIENT

Disclosure of information relating to a patient's infertility treatment is now permitted with the consent of the patient or both parents if they are being treated together (s 33(6B)-(6D)). A patient's consent will not be valid unless reasonable steps have been taken to explain to the patient the implications of disclosure (s 33(6D)). Where disclosure is to be to another concerned with the medical care of the patient or for audit or account-ing purposes, the consent to disclosure may be general; but where it is to others the patient must consent to disclosure to a *specific person*. This amendment overcomes one of the major perceived problems with the 1990 Act as originally drafted. It obviates the need to use the circumlocutory procedure advised by the Authority whereby the patient would be given a sealed envelope to deliver to the patient's general practitioner (see *Code of Practice* (1991) at paragraph 3.6).

(iii) ACCESS TO HEALTH RECORDS

Disclosure is permitted to comply with a request under the Access to Health Records Act 1990 (s 33(6)(h)). This must have been originally an oversight in the drafting of the 1990 Act. Of course, in so far as the patient seeks access for herself disclosure has always been permitted under s 33(7). In so far as another (such as a parent or personal representative) may apply on behalf of a patient who is, for example, incompetent to make a request, this new provision now also allows the doctor to disclose the patient's medical records relating to her infertility treatment. The Access to Health Records Act 1990 already exempts from the access provisions any part of the record which contains information relating to another (s 5(1)(a)(ii)). This exemption would therefore prevent a patient gaining access to information relating to the donor(s). The Access to Health Records (Control of Access) Regulations 1993 (SI 1993 No 746) prohibit a child from obtaining disclosure of information relating to their birth (see *supra*, p 811).

(iv) EMERGENCIES

The Act permits disclosure in an emergency where the doctor is '*satisfied that it is necessary* to avert an imminent danger to the health' of the patient and 'it is not reasonably practicable to obtain that patient's consent' (s 33(6E), emphasis added). Although, as in the provision relating to legal proceedings (discussed above), disclosure must be necessary, this provision is more subjectively worded and so may be more easily satisfied. It should however be noted that the doctor must be satisfied that the danger to the patient is *imminent*; foreseeable danger will not of itself suffice. In other words, the danger must be faced there and then before it can properly be said to be 'imminent'. It should also be noted that the patient's consent must be sought if that is reasonably practicable.

(v) DECLARATION OF PARENTAGE

Disclosure is permitted for the purpose of establishing the genetic parenthood of a child who is the subject of an application for a parental order in a surrogacy case under s 30 of the 1990 Act (s 33(6)(g)).

(vi) BY REGULATIONS

Disclosure of 'statutory information' is permitted in such circumstances as may be specified in Regulations promulgated by the Secretary of State (s 33(6G)). The Act therefore avoids the dilemma faced up until its passing, namely that unforeseen problem situations required primary legislation to make disclosure lawful.

F. STATUS OF CHILDREN

You will recall that early in this chapter we set out tables devised by Professors Dickens and Capron demonstrating the potential complexities of the relationship between donors of gametes and offspring. For the law the question is quite simple. In the case of any child who, in law, is the mother and who, in law, is the father?

At common law, parenthood was almost certainly defined by genetic make-up. In other words, where sperm was donated, the donor was the legal father of the child albeit that presumptively if the child were born within a marriage the husband would be rebuttably deemed the father. As regards egg or embryo donation, the common law's unfamiliarity with these practices (which separate the gestational from the genetic) would probably have led it to prefer the claims of the gestational mother. The inconsistency between the two positions could, however, have persuaded a court to opt for the genetic determination of parenthood both as regards the mother and father (see, eg, *Johnson v Calvert* (1993) 851 P 2d 776 (Cal Sup Ct)).

As regards sperm donation, Parliament acted in s 27 of the Family Law Reform Act 1987 to reverse the common law rule and make the husband of a patient who was artificially inseminated, the father of any child unless it was proved that he did not consent to the procedure.

In the 1990 Act, Parliament acted to resolve questions of parenthood (whether it be mother or father) whenever a child was born as a consequence of infertility treatment.

1. The mother

Sections 27 and 29 of the 1990 Act provide as follows:

Meaning of 'mother'

27. (1) The woman who is carrying or has carried a child as a result of the placing in her of an embryo or of sperm and eggs, and no other woman, is to be treated as the mother of the child.

(2) Subsection (1) above does not apply to any child to the extent that the child is treated by virtue of adoption as not being the child of any person other than the adopter or adopters.

(3) Subsection (1) above applies whether the woman was in the United Kingdom or elsewhere at the time of the placing in her of the embryo or the sperm and eggs.

Effect of sections 27 and 28

29. (1) Where by virtue of section 27 or 28 of this Act a person is to be treated as the mother or father of a child, that person is to be treated in law as the mother or, as the case may be, father of the child for all purposes.

(2) Where by virtue of section 27 or 28 of this Act a person is not to be treated as the mother or father of a child, that person is to be treated in law as not being the mother or, as the case may be, father of the child for any purpose.

(3) Where subsection (1) or (2) above has effect, references to any relationship between two people in any enactment, deed or other instrument or document (whenever passed or made) are to be read accordingly.

These provisions make clear that the gestational woman (and no one else) is, in law, the mother of any child born as a result of IVF procedures or, for example, GIFT. A potential omission would arise where egg donation occurs but does not involve IVF or GIFT, ie where the egg is directly implanted in the woman for natural fertilisation. Here the common law would apply.

2. The father

Section 28 of the 1990 Act provides as follows:

Meaning of 'father'

28. (1) This section applies in the case of a child who is being or has been carried by a woman as the result of the placing in her of an embryo or of sperm and eggs or her artificial insemination.

(2) If –

(a) at the time of the placing in her of the embryo or the sperm and eggs or of her insemination, the woman was a party to a marriage, and

(b) the creation of the embryo carried by her was not brought about with the sperm of the other party to the marriage,

then, subject to subsection (5) below, the other party to the marriage shall be treated as the father of the child unless it is shown that he did not consent to the placing in her of the embryo or the sperm and eggs or to her insemination (as the case may be).

(3) If no man is treated, by virtue of subsection (2) above, as the father of the child but –

(a)   the embryo or the sperm and eggs were placed in the woman, or she was artificially inseminated, in the course of treatment services provided for her and a man together by a person to whom a licence applies, and

(b)   the creation of the embryo carried by her was not brought about with the sperm of that man,

then, subject to subsection (5) below, that man shall be treated as the father of the child.

(4) Where a person is treated as the father of the child by virtue of subsection (2) or (3) above, no other person is to be treated as the father of the child.

(5) Subsections (2) and (3) above do not apply –

(a)   in relation to England and Wales and Northern Ireland, to any child who, by virtue of the rules of common law, is treated as the legitimate child of the parties to a marriage,

(b)   in relation to Scotland, to any child who, by virtue of an enactment or other rule of law, is treated as the child of the parties to a marriage, or

(c)   to any child to the extent that the child is treated by virtue of adoption as not being the child of any person other than the adopter or adopters.

(6) Where –

(a)   the sperm of a man who had given such consent as is required by paragraph 5 of Schedule 3 to this Act was used for a purpose for which such consent was required, or

(b)   the sperm of a man, or any embryo the creation of which was brought about with his sperm, was used after his death,

he is not to be treated as the father of the child.

(7) The references in subsection (2) above to the parties to a marriage at the time there referred to –

(a)   are to the parties to a marriage subsisting at that time, unless a judicial separation was then in force, but

(b)   include the parties to a void marriage if either or both of them reasonably believed at that time that the marriage was valid; and for the purposes of this subsection it shall be presumed, unless the contrary is shown, that one of them reasonably believed at the time that the marriage was valid.

(8) This section applies whether the woman was in the United Kingdom or elsewhere at the time of the placing in her of the embryo or the sperm and eggs or her artificial insemination.

(9) In subsection (7)(a) above, 'judicial separation' includes a legal separation obtained in a country outside the British Islands and recognised in the United Kingdom.

The effect of this provision, in essence, is fivefold. First, if the woman who is being treated (and gives birth) is married, her husband is, as always, presumed to be the father of the child because of the presumption of legitimacy (s 28(5)(a)). Of course, a husband may seek to rebut this presumption through, for example, DNA profiling. If successful, he will still be deemed in law to be the father under s 28(2) unless he proves that he did not consent to the infertility treatment. As we saw earlier, HFEA's *Code of Practice* includes, in the relevant standard consent form, a requirement that the husband acknowledge his consent to the infertility procedure. Although, of course, this is only evidence of his consent, it will be difficult to show that it does not truly represent his state of mind.

Secondly, if the woman is not married and she receives 'treatment services provided for her and a man *together*' (s 28(3), our emphasis) her partner is deemed to be the father even though donated sperm or an embryo is used. Where his own sperm is used the section does not apply (s 28(3)(b)) but it is, of course, unnecessary since he remains the father under the common law. Unlike the case of the husband, it would appear that the unmarried partner cannot displace his deemed parenthood under s 28(3) even if he is subsequently able to show that he did not really consent to what was done. Perhaps to avoid any arguments, again the relevant consent form in the *Code of Practice* should be used to record his consent. At the very least this will put him on notice if he continues to agree to be treated together with the woman.

Section 28(3) was intended to cover the unmarried couple who live in what is sometimes called a *de facto* or common law marriage. The Act seeks to put them in the same position as the married couple. The statutory phrase, that the 'treatment services' should be 'provided for her and a man together', is not, however, defined in the Act. Could it be construed to go further and include, for example, the case of an unmarried woman who brings along to the infertility clinic a male friend for support? In one sense, they are being treated 'together'. However, it would be absurd to regard the male friend as the child's father. On the other hand, if he is not the father, the child will be legally fatherless if donated sperm is used in accordance with the provisions of the Act (s 28(6)(a) below) and the court might be tempted to strive to avoid such a conclusion.

The better view is, however, that s 28(3) should be given a more narrow and limited interpretation. Parliament was probably only contemplating treatment by unmarried 'couples' in situations closely analogous to that of married couples (see, Hansard, HL Vol 517, cols 210-11). Thus, s 28(3) only applies when the couple are seeking treatment with a view to having a child to bring up together. On this basis, the male friend who accompanies the woman to the clinic would not be the father of the child under s 28(3).

This interpretation of s 28(3) is bolstered by the wording of s 4(1) of the Act which is very similar to that of s 28(3). As we saw earlier, s 4(1)(a) seeks to bring within the regulatory framework infertility treatment using donor sperm but not treatment where the sperm of the male partner being treated is used. Hence, a licence is required where sperm is used 'in the course of providing treatment services for any woman, us[ing] the sperm of any man *unless the services are being provided for the woman and the man together*' (s 4(1)(b), our emphasis). These words closely mirror those in s 28(3). Suppose a woman brought a friend who was to act as the sperm provider to the clinic with her. The Act's regulatory provisions would only apply if the treatment services were not being provided for them 'together' since *his sperm* is being used. Can this situation really be distinguished from the situation where an anonymous sperm donor is used? We would suggest not. Where artificial insemination is carried out, the regulatory framework should apply unless the couple are seeking a child which is genetically theirs and intended to be brought up as their child. This is, of course, the interpretation offered above of the same words in s 28(3).

Thirdly, in all circumstances the Act ensures, in s 28(6)(a), that the donor of sperm used in accordance with the Act is not, in law, the father of the child. Unlike the position at common law, therefore, being a sperm donor carries no risk of being exposed to the responsibilities of a father. Thus, the public policy of facilitating sperm donation is furthered.

What, however, is the position if the donor's sperm is used not in accordance with his consent? For example, suppose he has agreed to its use only for research but it is mistakenly used for treatment services. Section 28(6)(a) does not apply. Nevertheless, he may still not be the father of any children. If the woman being treated is married and s 28(2) applies or she is unmarried and s 28(3) applies, her partner is the legal father, then the donor will not be the child's father (s 28(4)). Consequently, the donor will only remain the father in the unlikely event that his sperm is misused *and* either the woman's husband establishes that he did not consent to her treatment or the woman is unmarried and is treated alone. These possibilities are, of course, extremely unlikely in practice.

Fourthly, the position if an infertile couple do not resort to licensed treatment should be noted, ie if 'DIY' insemination is used. The provisions in s 28(2) – where the woman is married – apply to *all* cases of artificial insemination including those not carried out pursuant to a licence under the Act (the presumption of legitimacy will also apply). Consequently, her husband, and not the donor, is, as we have seen, the father of the child. However, s 28(3) – which applies where the woman is not married – does not apply to 'DIY' insemination since it is restricted to situations where she, together with a man, receives *treatment services* under the Act, ie at a licensed clinic. Therefore, cases of 'DIY' insemination, where the woman is unmarried, continue to be governed by the common law. The donor remains legally the father of any child born.

Fifthly, there are a number of circumstances in which the provisions of the Act serve to bring about the result that a child will not have a father in law. Where the woman has received treatment using donated gametes or embryos in circumstances where, under the Act, her male partner is not the father of the child, the child will be fatherless. An example would be where a husband was able to show that he had not consented to her treatment under s 28(2)(b) or if she was treated alone. The final situation in which a child will be fatherless arises because of s 28(6)(b), where 'the sperm of a man, or any embryo the creation of which was brought about with his sperm, was used after his death'. Hence, although the Act does not prohibit posthumous use of stored sperm or embryos, the Act ensures that any child born will not, for example, have a claim on the estate of the dead man.

Surrogacy

A. INTRODUCTION

In this section we examine the law as it pertains to surrogate motherhood, a modern practice which as Peter Singer and Deane Wells in *New Ways of Making Babies: The Reproduction Revolution* (1984) (pp 107-108) point out, has historical precedents:

> . . . there is nothing new about the basic idea of surrogate motherhood. It is even in the Bible. The sixteenth chapter of Genesis tells the following story about Abraham and his wife Sarah (who have, at this stage, not yet been given the new names they received from God after he makes his covenant with Abraham, and hence are referred to by their original names of Abram and Sarai):
>
> > Abram's wife Sarai had borne him no children. Now she had an Egyptian slave-girl whose name was Hagar, and she said to Abram, 'You see that the Lord has not allowed me to bear a child. Take my slave-girl; perhaps I shall found a family through her.' Abram agreed to what his wife said, so Sarai, Abram's wife, brought her slave-girl, Hagar the Egyptian, and gave her to her husband Abram as a wife . . . He lay with Hagar and she conceived . . .

The Warnock Committee in its 1984 Report offered an answer to the question 'What is surrogacy?'

> **8.1** Surrogacy is the practice whereby one woman carries a child for another with the intention that the child should be handed over after birth. The use of artificial insemination and the recent development of *in vitro* fertilisation have eliminated the necessity for sexual intercourse in order to establish a surrogate pregnancy. Surrogacy can take a number of

forms. The commissioning mother may be the genetic mother, in that she provides the egg, or she may make no contribution to the establishment of the pregnancy. The genetic father may be the husband of the commissioning mother, or of the carrying mother; or he may be an anonymous donor. There are thus many possible combinations of persons who are relevant to the child's conception, birth and early environment. Of these various forms perhaps the most likely are surrogacy involving artificial insemination, where the carrying mother is the genetic mother inseminated with semen from the male partner of the commissioning couple, and surrogacy using *in vitro* fertilisation where both egg and semen come from the commissioning couple, and the resultant embryo is transferred to and implants in the carrying mother.

8.2 There are certain circumstances in which surrogacy would be an option for the alleviation of infertility. Examples are where a woman has a severe pelvic disease which cannot be remedied surgically, or has no uterus. The practice might also be used to help women who have suffered repeated miscarriages. There are also perhaps circumstances where the genetic mother, although not infertile, could benefit from the pregnancy being carried by another woman. An example is where the genetic mother is fit to care for a child after it is born, but suffers from a condition making the pregnancy medically undesirable.

8.3 If surrogacy takes place it generally involves some payment to the carrying mother. Payment may vary between reimbursement of expenses, and a substantial fee. There may, however, be some instances where no money is involved, for example, where one sister carries the pregnancy for another.

B. THE ISSUES

The modern practice of surrogacy is thought to raise the following problems. The Warnock Committee summarised the arguments as follows:

8.10 There are strongly held objections to the concept of surrogacy, and it seems from the evidence submitted to us that the weight of public opinion is against the practice. The objections turn essentially on the view that to introduce a third party into the process of procreation which should be confined to the loving partnership between two people, is an attack on the value of the marital relationship . . . Further, the intrusion is worse than in the case of AID, since the contribution of the carrying mother is greater, more intimate and personal, than the contribution of a semen donor. It is also argued that it is inconsistent with human dignity that a woman should use her uterus for financial profit and treat it as an incubator for someone else's child. The objection is not diminished, indeed it is strengthened, where the woman entered an agreement to conceive a child, with the sole purpose of handing the child over to the commissioning couple after birth.

8.11 Again, it is argued that the relationship between mother and child is itself distorted by surrogacy. For in such an arrangement a woman deliberately allows herself to become pregnant with the intention of giving up the child to which she will give birth, and this is the wrong way to approach pregnancy. It is also potentially damaging to the child, whose bonds with the carrying mother, regardless of genetic connections, are held to be strong, and whose welfare must be considered to be of paramount importance. Further, it is felt that a surrogacy agreement is degrading to the child who is to be the outcome of it, since, for all practical purposes, the child will have been bought for money.

8.12 It is also argued that since there are some risks attached to pregnancy, no woman ought to be asked to undertake pregnancy for another, in order to earn money. Nor, it is argued, should a woman be forced by legal sanctions to part with a child, to which she has recently given birth, against her will.

More fully, the arguments are put by Peter Singer and Deane Wells in *New Ways of Making Babies: The Reproduction Revolution*, (1984) (pp 114-120).

Objections to surrogacy

Surrogate motherhood is one of the few applications of IVF of which the general public disapproves. That, at least, is the finding of the 1982 Morgan Gallup Poll in Australia and in Britain. After people had answered questions about more straightforward use of IVF, they were told the following:

The fertilised egg from one married couple could be put into *another* woman, who would then become pregnant. She would *give the baby back* to the couple after it was born.

More than 70 per cent of the sample in each country said they had heard about this procedure. They were then asked:

Do you think this sort of test-tube baby treatment for married couples to have a child by *another* woman should be *allowed*, or *not*?

In Australia, 32 per cent thought it should be allowed, but 44 per cent thought it should not be. In Britain only 20 per cent thought it should be allowed, with a solid majority of 55 per cent against allowing it. In both countries around a quarter of respondents either had no opinion, or said that they needed to know more, or that the answer depended on other factors.

The poll data do not tell us why so many people thought that full surrogate motherhood should not be allowed. The response is a contrast to the more approving reaction we noted in the previous chapter to the question about the donation of fertilised eggs – or 'pre-natal adoption'. One reason for this different response might be that people do not like the idea of a woman having to 'give back' a baby to whom she has given birth. We shall see in a moment that there is some reason for concern about this aspect of surrogate motherhood. But there is also a crucial difference in the way the two questions were put, which makes the answers not strictly comparable. When people were asked about the donation of fertilised eggs, they were told that the eggs were to be given to another married couple 'so that they can have a child'. The clear implication is that the married couple to whom the eggs are given could not have a child by any other method. In the question asked about surrogate motherhood there was no such implication. Respondents therefore may not have had the plight of the childless couple in mind when they answered. It was open to them to interpret the question as one about a married couple who could have children by the normal method but find it more convenient to use a surrogate. If some respondents did interpret the question in this way, the negative response is easily explained.

No doubt a significant number of people do oppose surrogate motherhood even for couples who cannot otherwise have children. Some may think of it as unnatural, and for that reason wrong . . . We will simply repeat our conclusion that the naturalness or unnaturalness of a new procedure is not the real issue; the crucial question is whether the procedure is likely to do more good than harm.

Here opponents of surrogacy will point to the horrendous legal tangles that could arise with full surrogacy. Some of these tangles have already arisen among the relatively small number of partial surrogacy arrangements made so far. Although partial surrogacy differs in some respects from full surrogacy, the problems that have arisen with partial surrogacy are at present the best guide to the likely problems of full surrogacy.

Noel Keane, the American lawyer who helped Stefan and Nadia arrange their partial surrogacy contract, has written a book, *The Surrogate Mother*, describing his work in this new field. Keane credits himself with the path-breaking legal work that has made partial surrogacy a reality for many infertile couples. There is no doubt about his enthusiasm for surrogacy. 'Surrogate parenting', he tells us, 'is an idea whose time is coming . . . I think it will replace adoption.' The book itself, Keane says, 'is my legal brief on behalf of a controversial cause to make surrogate motherhood a common reality in the years ahead'.

Given Keane's advocacy of the cause, some sections of *The Surrogate Mother* are alarming. Perhaps most dramatic is the story of Bill and Bridget. In fairness to Keane, it has to be said that the case was one of his early ones. It began in 1977, before he quite knew what he was getting into; nevertheless it illustrates some possible pitfalls of surrogacy.

Bill and Bridget were an infertile couple. Keane put them in touch with Diane. Diane had seen a television talk show in which Keane appeared with another infertile couple and their pregnant partial surrogate. After the show, Diane had phoned offering to help a couple to have a child. She was a thirty-one-year-old divorcee, living in Tennessee with a two-year-old son: when interviewed she seemed a good mother and responsible parent. At that time Keane had not discovered that Kentucky State law allowed the payment of a fee to surrogate mothers, so Diane was told that nothing could be paid except expenses. She signed an agreement to that effect.

Diane soon became pregnant with Bill's child. Then things began to go wrong. She asked Bill and Bridget for money to travel to Boston to visit her mother. They sent her the money. She said she had been robbed of expense money they had sent her. They sent her another cheque. Then her car needed repairs, she had extra medical expenses . . . and so on. Often when she phoned asking for money, she sounded drunk or stoned on drugs. Sometimes she threatened to kill herself unless she got more money. Bill and Bridget did not dare call her bluff. Shortly before the baby was due, Diane demanded $3,000 to pay for a computer course she planned to take. Bill and Bridget paid. In all, they calculated that they sent Diane more than $12,000.

Finally, two weeks before the due date, Diane phoned to say that she was in jail on a drunk-driving charge, and needed bail money. Bill and Bridget flew to Tennessee to stay with Diane and try to prevent anything else going wrong before she had the baby. That is when they found that Diane's 'roommate', Vicky, was really her lover. In despair Bridget turned on her husband. 'Bill', she screamed, 'do you realise that the woman you got pregnant is not only an alcoholic and drug addict but also a lesbian!'

Amazingly, the story has a happy ending. Diane gave birth to a boy, below normal weight and suffering from drug withdrawal symptoms; but after five days in hospital Bill, Jr was healthy enough to go home with his father and his new mother. Diane tried for some time to extract more money by threatening to hold up the adoption proceeding; but when this threat failed to have any effect, she moved interstate without leaving any forwarding address. At the time of writing Keane described the child as 'in legal limbo', but Bill and Bridget were so happy with 'their' child that they told Keane: 'He has made it all worthwhile.'

Two other bizarre Keane stories ended less happily. The first, related in *The Surrogate Mother*, concerns John and Lorelei, a married Connecticut couple unable to have children: Lorelei was a transsexual. Until the age of twenty-one, she had been male. For Keane, this was no obstacle. He took the couple on as his clients. They found Rita, a divorced Californian mother of three who said she was interested in being a surrogate mother 'for humanitarian reasons'. Rita became pregnant, and then asked for $7,500. Keane advised John and Lorelei that they would be breaking the law if they paid; in any case they could not afford to pay. They refused. Rita wrote back: 'I have decided to keep my baby, and the deal is off.'

The baby, a boy, was born in April 1981. Keane brought a custody suit on behalf of John. Blood tests showed with 99 per cent probability that he was the father. Before the case came to court, however, it became apparent that Lorelei's transsexualism would come out into the open and probably damage their already slim chances of success. In a vain attempt to avoid publicity, John and Lorelei decided to give up the legal battle for custody.

Our final Keane disaster is not taken from the pages of his book. It was, however, anticipated by a prescient quotation in the book, taken from an editorial in the *Detroit News*. Writing of the possible legal dilemmas of the new method of motherhood, the editorial asked:

> What happens if the proxy mother gives birth to a defective child and the couple refuses to adopt it? Can the surrogate mother sue the father for damages arising from pregnancy? How can the husband be sure he is indeed the father of his 'investment', short of isolating the surrogate from other male contacts?

Keane did not answer these questions in *The Surrogate Mother*. Soon after the book appeared, however, he found himself unable to avoid them.

Late in 1981 Judy Stiver, a Michigan housewife, noticed an advertisement in a local paper. It was one placed regularly by Keane, and it sought women willing to become surrogate mothers for a fee. Judy and her husband, Ray, had a two-year-old daughter, and going through a pregnancy again seemed a good way to earn some extra cash. 'We wanted the money to pay some bills and take a vacation', she explained later to a reporter.

Through Keane, Judy Stiver met Alexander and Nadia Malahoff, of New York. She agreed to be impregnated with Alexander Malahoff's sperm and to abstain from sexual intercourse until the baby was conceived. In return, Malahoff agreed to take the baby and pay Mrs Stiver $10,000. All went well until the baby was born, when it was discovered that he suffered from microcephaly, a condition in which the head is abnormally small, and the child often turns out to be mentally retarded.

At first the child was not expected to live: when it became apparent that he would, Malahoff claimed that the baby's blood tests showed that he could not have been the father. Accordingly he refused to accept the baby, and to pay Judy Stiver the agreed fee. At first the Stivers also refused to take the baby, saying that they had come to accept that the baby would be taken from Mrs Stiver, and they did not want another child. When further court-ordered blood tests confirmed that Alexander Malahoff was not the father, however, the Stivers finally agreed to keep the baby.

Many people would consider these episodes provide sufficient grounds for prohibiting surrogacy, whether partial or full. Once we mess around with conventional arrangements for bearing and rearing children, there is no end to the complications that can arise. The result is distress for all concerned.

To those who argue that couples and would-be surrogates have the right to make their own private contractual arrangements in matters that concern no one else, the opponents of surrogacy could reply that in surrogacy contracts someone else is always affected. Society has a right, they would claim, to prohibit such arrangements in order to prevent children being born in undesirable circumstances. They might add that the childless couple are usually too desperate to take proper steps to ensure that a woman offering to act as a surrogate really is a fit and proper person for that purpose. The story of Bill and Bridget suggests this; and Lorelei told Keane that when Rita offered to act as surrogate, 'we were so excited we would have taken someone with purple skin from Mozambique'.

Discussion

We have seen that when A and B have a surrogate motherhood contract with C, at least four things are liable to go wrong:

(1) C might have contracted to refrain from taking alcohol or drugs, but might do it anyway.
(2) C might, during pregnancy, attempt to extort payment, or additional payment beyond any agreed fees, from A and B. To do this she might threaten to have an abortion, or to keep the baby.
(3) C might decide, once the baby is born, that she wishes to keep it, in spite of her contract to give it to A and B.
(4) A and B might decide, once the baby is born, that they do not wish to accept it, perhaps because it is born with a handicap, perhaps because they do not believe it is their genetic child.

No doubt there are many other complications that could arise, but these instances are enough to indicate where surrogacy can lead.

No one denies that surrogacy can cause problems – least of all Keane, who has to be given credit for having openly displayed the troubles some of his clients found themselves in. Keane does not, of course, believe that the problems are a reason for prohibiting surrogacy. He would point to the cases like that of Stefan and Nadia, in which a surrogacy agreement went smoothly, leaving a couple ecstatic over the fulfilment of their otherwise impossible dream of having a child, and a surrogate mother happy with her fee, or perhaps even simply happy with the knowledge that she has helped to bring to others the joy of parenthood. Stefan and Nadia are, Keane could add, more typical that Bill and Bridget, John and Lorelei or the Malahoffs.

In *The Surrogate Mother* Keane gave an account of his first nine cases. If we take that as a sample, then the cases of Bill and Bridget and of John and Lorelei were the two most tangled of these nine. Even so, one of these two had a happy ending. So would it have been right to prevent eight couples having the child they wanted, just in order to save John and Lorelei's disappointment?

Shelley Roberts summarises her detailed consideration of the issue in 'Warnock and Surrogate Motherhood: Sentiment or Argument', in *Rights and Wrongs in Medicine* (1986, ed P Byrne) as follows:

Arguments against surrogacy: a review

Having explored some of the objections to surrogacy raised in the Warnock committee's report, several points emerge as particularly problematic. Specifically, these are:

1. that paid surrogacy may be exploitative of the women concerned in that the amount of money offered may overcome the normal, expected refusal to submit to such an onerous invasion of their private lives;
2. that it may be against public policy to permit the transfer of money in respect of the use of the woman's body, in particular her womb;
3. that surrogacy violates the principles of maternal responsibility;
4. that it entails the use of children as means rather than regarding them as ends in themselves;
5. that it may potentially cause distress to children who are witnesses of the process.

Taken together, these points certainly appear to provide sufficient justification for imposing restrictions on at least some sorts of surrogacy. Thus, it is suggested that, in general terms, the Warnock committee's negative response to surrogacy was quite appropriate. The difficulty, however, with the proposals outlined in the report is that they do not seem to meet the specific problems identified as arising in surrogacy. If we consider, for example, that, as has been suggested, the exchange of money for the use of a bodily organ is contrary to public policy, then the appropriate solution would seem to be a ban on all paid surrogacy. If we also believe that it is impermissible for a woman to conceive a child for the purpose of giving it away, this suggests that all surrogacy, paid or voluntary, should be prohibited. And, if another major area of concern is the welfare of children born to surrogate mothers, then, if the practice is to continue in any fashion, it must be regulated so as to ensure that welfare. None of these conclusions was reached by the Warnock committee.

The recommendations proposed in the report and adopted in the Government's bill introduced in 1985 [see, Surrogacy Arrangements Act 1985] attack, instead, only that which is superficially distasteful about surrogate motherhood. The effect of the provisions would be to reduce the volume of surrogacy transactions but sweep the remainder out of sight, where the real problems would be beyond society's ability to respond to or to remedy.

(For a sympathetic view of surrogacy see, L Andrews *Between Strangers* (1989) and for a discussion of the arguments for and against surrogacy see, M Field *Surrogate Motherhood: The Legal and Human Issues* (1988).)

C. POSSIBLE RESPONSES

The Warnock Committee's view, which Shelley Roberts refers to in the above extract, was as follows:

8.17 The question of surrogacy presented us with some of the most difficult problems we encountered. The evidence submitted to us contained a range of strongly held views and this was reflected in our own views. The moral and social objections to surrogacy have weighed heavily with us. In the first place we are all agreed that surrogacy for convenience alone, that is, where a woman is physically capable of bearing a child but does wish to undergo pregnancy, is totally ethically unacceptable. Even in compelling medical circumstances the danger of exploitation of one human being by another appears to the majority of us far to outweigh the potential benefits, in almost every case. That people should treat others as a means to their own ends, however desirable the consequences, must always be liable to moral objection. Such treatment of one person by another becomes positively exploitative when financial interests are involved. It is therefore with the commercial exploitation of surrogacy that we have been primarily, but by no means exclusively, concerned.
8.18 We have considered whether the criminal law should have any part to play in the control of surrogacy and have concluded that it should. We recognise that there is a serious risk of commercial exploitation of surrogacy and that this would be difficult to prevent without the assistance of the criminal law. We have considered whether a limited, non-profit making surrogacy service, subject to licensing and inspection, could have any useful part to play but the majority agreed that the existence of such a service would in itself encourage the growth of surrogacy. **We recommend that legislation be introduced to render criminal the creation or the operation in the United Kingdom of agencies whose purposes include the recruitment of women for surrogate pregnancy or making arrangements for individuals or couples who wish to utilise the services of a carrying mother; such legislation should be wide enough to include both profit and non-profit making organisations. We further recommend that the legislation be sufficiently wide to render criminally liable the actions of professionals and others who knowingly assist in the establishment of a surrogate pregnancy.**
8.19 We do not envisage that this legislation would render private persons entering into surrogacy arrangements liable to criminal prosecution, as we are anxious to avoid children being born to mothers subject to the taint of criminality. We nonetheless recognise that there will continue to be privately arranged surrogacy agreements. While we consider that most, if not all, surrogacy arrangements would be legally unenforceable in any of their terms, we feel that the positions should be put beyond any possible doubt in law. **We recommend that it be provided by statute that all surrogacy agreements are illegal contracts and therefore unenforceable in the courts.**
8.20 We are conscious that surrogacy like egg and embryo donation may raise the question as to whether the genetic or the carrying mother is the true mother. Our recommendations in 6.8 and 7.6 cover cases where eggs or embryos have been donated. There remains however

the possible case where the egg or embryo has not been donated but has been provided by the commissioning mother or parents with the intention that they should bring up the resultant child. If our recommendation in 8.18 is accepted, such cases are unlikely to occur because of the probability that the practitioner administering the treatment would be committing an offence. However, for the avoidance of doubt, we consider that the legislation proposed in 6.8 and 7.6 [ie making the gestational mother the legal mother] should be sufficiently widely drawn to cover any such case. If experience shows that this gives rise to an injustice for children who live with their genetic mother rather than the mother who bore them then in our view the remedy is to make the adoption laws more flexible so as to enable the genetic mother to adopt.

In the introduction to her book *A Question of Life*, Baroness Warnock writes (at p xii):

> Similarly, in the controversial matter of surrogate mothers, the Inquiry agreed unanimously that they disapproved of the practice (largely because of possible consequences for the child); but they also agreed that it could not be prevented by law, because of the intrusiveness of any law that would be enforceable. The Inquiry therefore concentrated on how surrogacy for commercial purposes might be checked, leaving on one side the question whether surrogacy was intrinsically morally right or wrong. We might all of us have answered the primary moral question in a way which made surrogacy wrong. This did not pre-empt the answer to the second-order moral question, Should the law be invoked to stop surrogacy? We all agreed that it would be morally wrong to envisage a law which would intrusively curtail human freedom, and which would in addition be impossible to enforce (how could the law tell whether the child whom Abraham claimed as his own was born to Sara, or to a servant girl who happened to be more fertile?) The Inquiry then, while unanimously answering the first-order question negatively, holding that surrogacy was wrong, nevertheless held that legislation should not be invoked to prevent it. We did however by a majority recommend that the commercial use of surrogacy arrangements, as a way of making money for an agency, could and should be made a criminal offence. For not only was the wrongness of surrogacy compounded by its being exploited for money, but also a law against agencies would not be intrusive into the private lives of those who were actually engaged in setting up a family.

We find helpful the distinction that Baroness Warnock draws between what is morally permissible and the extent to which the law should respond to the immoral. (We are puzzled by the apparent misunderstanding of the Committee's conclusions which, as we have seen, would outlaw *all* agencies whether profit-making or not.)

Several possible responses of the law are set out by Shelley Roberts in her paper already referred to (*op cit*), at pp 104-109:

A. Total prohibition

How, then, *ought* the issue of surrogacy to be settled? If we are convinced by the argument that no one should be permitted deliberately to avoid her maternal responsibilities, either for love or money, then the obvious solution is to attempt to devise a method of preventing all surrogacy transactions.

This, of course, raises tremendous practical difficulties. First, it is quite possible that couples may be sufficiently determined to have children by surrogacy that they will opt for the practice regardless of whether or not it is prohibited. Secondly, if the law were to make all surrogacy criminally unlawful, it could find itself hindered in the detection and regulation of possible harms and abuses that might result from 'underground' surrogacy. In addition, secrecy in and outside the family about the nature of a child's provenance could well undermine the stability of the families concerned, and consequently, of society.

Finally, the enforcement of laws against surrogacy, given the intimate nature of the arrangements, would be both difficult and possibly counter-productive. What sanctions could be imposed on transgressors? Fines would be unlikely to deter those intent upon paying huge sums of money for a child. If we imprison his parents for conceiving him, it will be the child who will suffer most. Similarly, his position will be jeopardised if we insist he stays with a mother who does not want him, or publicly declare him illegitimate, or refuse to allow the only family that claims him as theirs to have legal recognition as his parents. Thus, it seems that the most obvious response to the problems of surrogate motherhood may be impractical.

B. Licensing and regulation

If indeed it would not be plausible to seek to outlaw surrogacy, then thought must be given to practical methods by which surrogacy could be regulated. How could the most detrimental features of the practice be avoided? One method might be to regulate surrogate transactions by imposing a licensing scheme for agencies, requiring various forms of mandatory screening and counselling for participants.

There are serious problems with this approach. The most obvious is that government interference in, or control of, surrogacy would imply a legitimisation of the practice and perhaps act to encourage participants. If surrogacy clinics were established and licensed, it seems likely that the publicity would increase the popularity of surrogacy as a means of overcoming childlessness. If, however, it is accepted that there are serious problems inherent in surrogacy *per se*, then it is arguable that government ought to discourage rather than encourage the practice. The most serious objections to surrogacy will not be removed even if the process as a whole is subject to close scrutiny, and it would seem wrong to spend sums of public money on the licensing of an activity that has been judged to be contrary to public policy. Thus, it appears that the only legitimate form of regulation would be one which sought to eliminate aspects of surrogacy found to be particularly problematical.

C. Prohibition of commercial surrogacy

1. The role of intermediaries

The solution adopted by the Warnock committee and incorporated into the government's bill is to curtail surrogacy by imposing restrictions on the participation of intermediaries. No person or organisation is to initiate, take part in negotiations or compile information for use in surrogacy arrangements if such is done 'on a commercial basis' (that is, in return for payment to the intermediary).

The prohibition of commercial agencies would certainly limit the growth in the number of surrogate transactions. It would also specifically overcome the sort of abuse seen in the 'stud farms' previously described. One suspects, however, that the measure is designed more to cover up what the public finds distasteful about surrogacy (profit-hungry agencies) than to counteract any ill effects the practice may have upon its participants and on society at large. The more sensational possibilities for exploitation aside, there seems little difference, as regards most of surrogacy's problems, between a commercial agency and a volunteer agency and a volunteer one, between a transaction mediated by an agency and one conducted privately.

One of the distinctly counterproductive features of the move to curtail intermediaries recommended by the Warnock committee and found in the bill is the effective exclusion of professionals such as doctors and solicitors from surrogacy arrangements. If no person is permitted, in exchange for payment, to compile information in respect of a surrogate arrangement, then couples and prospective surrogates would not, for example, be able to consult their physicians for genetic testing. If no one may take part in the negotiations, then solicitors would not be allowed to assist in facilitating the legal adoption of children born to surrogates.

A prohibition on professional assistance adds to, rather than detracts from, the difficulties associated with surrogacy. It prevents couples from seeking advice that may either lead them to decide against surrogacy or help them to proceed in the way least prejudicial to the interests of all concerned, especially the child. Without in any way encouraging surrogacy, the availability of professional assistance could point towards an informal screening process and allow the resulting child to be properly incorporated into the family that will be caring for him.

On both sides of the Atlantic, professional bodies have already begun to prohibit their members from any form of active recruiting of surrogates. This might be the most sensible way in which to regulate the participation of doctors, solicitors, psychologists and others in the surrogacy process and would be preferable to excluding them completely.

2. The role of surrogates

Both the Warnock committee and the drafters of the Government's bill recognised that one of the principal problems involved in surrogacy was its commercial aspect. It is suggested, however, that they approached the problem in the wrong way. Instead of seeking to prohibit payment to those assisting in surrogacy arrangements, they should have concentrated on the prohibition of payment to surrogates themselves. Although this solution would not resolve all the fundamental objections to surrogacy, it may be the practical alternative best suited to the protection of those concerned and of society in general.

The result of such a prohibition would probably be to limit the participants in surrogacy arrangements to friends or relatives of the couple seeking a child. Few women would voluntarily bear a child for a stranger. If there were to be an additional ban on advertising, as proposed in section 3 of the bill, then strangers could not ordinarily become involved.

Such a limitation of surrogacy to voluntary arrangements may resolve beneficially a number of the problems associated with surrogacy. First, volunteers would be much less likely to be victims of financial coercion. Equally, they would be unlikely to exploit the couples involved. It is of course arguable that the emotional pressure exerted by a relative or friend could be considerable. However, emotional pressure to perform voluntarily a lawful act is not the sort of duress that is sufficiently severe as to involve sanctions of law.

Secondly, if we refer back to the criteria for organ donations, voluntary womb-leasing ought to fit within the 'approved' category, in that it is the sort of disposition that was thought to be permissible if offered as a donation, but probably contrary to public policy if done in exchange for money. Paid surrogacy, of course, would have been against public policy, according to this test.

A third issue was the disruption of the marriage of the commissioning couple by the surrogate. There is no doubt that the presence of a friend or relative as a 'third party' to the marriage may present a considerable amount of tension. Morally, however, it may be less problematical than a similar intrusion by a stranger. If ties of blood or affection bind the commissioning parents and surrogate, they suggest that the second woman already has a link with the marriage. If anyone could be deemed appropriate as a substitute for the wife, then perhaps it is someone closely related or connected to her and to the family.

The final and perhaps most serious difficulty with surrogacy was the effect of the process upon the children concerned and upon our notions of childhood. At an individual level, the insistence that surrogate transactions be unpaid might well reduce the likelihood of the agreement dissolving into a dispute detrimental to the child. The involvement of friends would result in an arrangement where participants would be inclined to understand and care about each other's interests in the process. An additional benefit is a sort of built-in screening mechanism. A woman who is acting out of love rather than money and who deals directly with the commissioning father is much more likely to ask herself whether or not he is a suitable parent and similarly to consider the prospective mother.

It has been argued, of course, that it is not fair to ask a woman to go through the hardship of a surrogate pregnancy without compensating her for the pain, inconvenience and time. Surely, the better question is whether it is fair to *ask* a woman to undergo a pregnancy for someone else *at all*, and the answer is clearly 'no'. Only if a friend, out of love or compassion, *offers* herself in such a way can the offer be tolerated as a gift of self. The surest way to limit surrogacy to the cases most likely to proceed smoothly is to require an exceptional altruism in the surrogate mother.

However, by allowing even voluntary surrogacy, it is hard to avoid the allegations that surrogacy is equivalent to constructive abandonment and entails the use of a child as the means to an end. The elimination of paid surrogacy would, of course, improve the situation somewhat. The absence of a formal contract and exchange of 'goods' for money would eliminate some of the factors leading to a child-as-product mentality. Although problems could arise either as the result of over-solicitous interference from a surrogate who was a close relative or friend, or confusion for the child as to which woman was his real mother, children might still find it easier to comprehend the idea of 'auntie helping mummy' than of a business transaction between strangers. And it is arguable that a woman who knows the family well into which her child will be adopted, or is herself a member of that family, is committing a less reprehensible act than one who gives her infant to strangers. Nevertheless, the basic philosophical objections remain and nothing short of total prohibition, dismissed as impractical, could remove them. The continuing existence of such problems must serve as a reminder that the scheme proposed here is simply a way in which some forms of surrogacy may be tolerated and not an endorsement of a process which remains fundamentally at odds with public policy.

Given the complexities of the issues arising and the nature of the interests involved, it is inevitable that the law will be involved in some shape or form and to some or other extent. The question then becomes what form that law should take.

One option could be to leave matters to *ad hoc* resolution by the courts as they arise. Alternatively some regulatory scheme could be devised which aims to deal comprehensively with the subject. The latter approach appears to have near universal support. This does not, of course, determine the content of the legal regulation. Professor Alexander Capron, however, adopts an interesting stance urging a minimalist approach through legislation, thereafter relying on traditional family law to achieve the necessary regulation.

A Capron, 'Alternative Birth Technologies: Legal Challenges' (1987) 20 UC Davis LR 697

Is legislation desirable?

Should we remedy this problem by legislating a framework for surrogate contracts? On the one hand, to do so may well increase the frequency of such arrangements – not a salutary development in my view. On the other hand, the primary interest in protection of the offspring is not well-served by the absence of a statutorily established system. What ought such a statute encompass? At a minimum, I would suggest the following.

First, careful medical screening should be performed for all participants in 'surrogacy' to prevent avoidable illness. Granted, this does not exist for ordinary reproduction – but, then, surrogacy is not ordinary. The result may well be achieved through the threat of sanctions on the professionals (physicians, social workers, lawyers, etc) who superintend the arrangements; their failure to screen could be a basis for liability. The risk of eugenic controls being exercised by the state places this aspect of a statute into a difficult balancing act, but the interest in protecting the child is strong enough to compel a hard effort to find a solution that stops short of state control of reproduction.

Second, surrogacy should be regarded as a form of prenatal adoption of the child of one parent by the other parent and provisions for state supervision, including confidential recordkeeping, should parallel those applicable to postnatal adoption. The harder question is whether standards of 'fitness' ought to be applied to the couples; it may be enough to achieve this indirectly through medical supervision. There may, of course, be some issues that cannot be well resolved by the law but must be left to the development of social norms. For example, should the procedure be limited to infertile couples and those with medical reason (genetic or gestational risks) for not reproducing themselves? Rather than trying to develop clear rules on what qualifies as sufficient 'infertility' or 'medical contraindication,' it may be sufficient to leave the question to physicians and potential surrogates: 'Is this couple's problem serious enough to warrant surrogacy?'

Third, and perhaps most important, the parties to the contract should each be bound by their normal parental obligations of care and support, regardless of the breach or alleged breach of contract by the party. The Malahoff case [referred to *supra*, p 822] indicates the potential for abandonment of the child if the parties are free to regard the situation as one of a contract for delivery of a product.

All of these suggestions made thus far aim to protect the interest of the child, which I view as the primary aim of public policy in this field. Other provisions in a statute would expand on this goal, while also attempting to promote additional values.

Fourth, the law should provide that the child is the legal child of the surrogate mother. This was the position of the Warnock Committee in England in 1984. Such a legal rule would do three things. First, it would reinforce the child's interest in having a legally responsible mother at birth. Second, it would place the surrogate in the same position as other women who decide to allow a child to be adopted, which includes having the right to change her mind within a specified time period. Third, it would also discourage surrogacy by exposing the biological father to the risk that he might end up with a financial obligation to the child but without any guarantee of other parental rights (which would lodge instead with the surrogate's husband).

The rule I suggest regarding maternity raises the more difficult issues of the presumption of paternity. Under the law in the thirty or so states with AID statutes, a child born after AID is presumed to be the legal offspring of her husband if he has consented to the insemination. Applying that rule to surrogacy would make the child the legal offspring of the surrogate's husband if he consents, or would open the physician (and others) to suit if the husband 'non-consented' and later became dissatisfied with the situation. A Michigan decision declining to allow the paternity act to be used to declare prenatally the paternal status of a contracting father was revised on appeal, [*Sykowski v Appleyard* (1985) 362 NW 211] while a Kentucky court declined to allow a 'mere affidavit' to rebut the presumption of the paternity of the surrogate's husband [*Re Baby Girl* No 83 AD (Jefferson Circ Ct, March 8, 1983)].

A fifth control that a statute might exercise would be to regulate the amount of payment made. Obviously, such agreements are notoriously difficult to supervise. The major risk that a person runs in going outside the terms permitted in the regulation is the same risk as already exists – namely, holding an unenforceable contract – and that has not deterred hundreds of people so far. Moreover, besides difficulties of enforcement, the question arises, which way should the regulation tend – to hold down payments to the level of actual out-of-pocket expenses (including life and health insurance premiums), which would lead to surrogacy only by true altruists, or to push the price up to a level commensurate with the values of the service and the time and effort involved? The latter would doubtlessly lead to a flood of eager surrogates, but without at least some control, more cases are likely to arise like the one now being litigated in San Diego, in which a Mexican woman is trying to retain custody of the child she bore under a surrogate contract for $1500.

Suppose that the legal regulations adopted are seen as disadvantaging surrogacy compared to AID. Is this unfair discrimination because it treats couples differently based on male versus female infertility? I do not believe that the claimed objection based on 'procreative freedom' is persuasive, for several reasons. First, there is a substantial difference between the role of the 'donor' in AID (merely contributing the germinal material, which is obtained in a risk-free procedure) and the 'donor' in a surrogate contract (who not only contributes the germinal material but carries the child for nine months and gives birth to it). These differences – in time, in risk, in attachment, and in effects on fetal development – implicate the values of well-being and of exploitation set forth earlier. Second, the legal rule in question – that a child born to a woman is legally hers until she gives the child up for adoption – is facially neutral between the situations of AID and surrogacy. In both instances, it vests parental rights and obligations in the woman who is inseminated and her husband. Third, the analogy between AID and surrogate motherhood is inexact; the correct analogue to AID is egg donation... In that case, the 'adoptive mother,' who gestates the donated egg (fertilised by the sperm of her husband or another donor) would be the legal mother.

The development of alternative birth technologies is seemingly pushing back the limits of human biology, and in the process sorely testing the limits of human law. The *Baby M* case in New Jersey reminds us of these limits, since it involves at its core the interest of a child who is not a party to the contract. My sense is that, in the absence of a statute that clearly establishes the rules I have recommended in this essay, the *Baby M* court should rule on grounds of the child's 'best interests' in a custodial sense, not on the basis of the contract. Moreover, in so ruling there must be no presumption that wealth or social class is determinative. As the California Supreme Court recently ruled, in a custody dispute over an out-of-wedlock child whose father was seeking custody based on the greater financial means and better home environment he and his new wife could offer compared with the child's working (and still unwed) mother, 'the purpose of child support awards is to ensure that the [parent] otherwise best fit for custody receives adequate funds,' and not to use the poorer parent's position as a ground for denying custody. [*Burchard v Garay* (1986) 724 P 2d 486] At the heart of best interests – or 'beyond' it – is stability and continuity for the child. In the *Baby M* case, that consideration could lead custody to be awarded to Dr Stern and his wife (who have had primary custody of most of the child's first year), even if the physician who performed the insemination were now to announce that he had used semen from a man other than Dr Stern.

Given the controversial nature of the issues raised by surrogate arrangements, it is, therefore, perhaps no surprise that legislation in countries around the world has adopted different policy options. The Canadian Law Reform Commission summarised the position as follows.

Medically Assisted Procreation (1992) (Working Paper 65) (pp 180-182)

The countries that have taken a position on surrogacy have chosen to ban, discourage or, in very rare cases, regulate the practice.

A complete prohibition of all forms of surrogacy is relatively rare [eg Surrogate Parenthood Act 1988 (Qd)]. Instead, countries try to discourage surrogate motherhood and to tackle the commercial aspect of the practice. Thus, they prohibit even non-commercial activity by agencies or other intermediaries [eg, Infertility (Medical Procedures) Act 1984, s 30 (Vic)]; the use of any advertising related to surrogate mother [eg Surrogate Parenthood Act 1981 (Qd) and Infertility (Medical Procedures) Act 1984 s 30 (Vic)]; and paying or accepting any financial or other compensation in connection with a surrogacy contract [eg Queensland and Victoria, *ibid*].

Other countries do not prohibit surrogacy, permit gratuitous contracts, or have refrained from passing legislation to counter private agreements. Accordingly, intermediaries working free of charge or on a not-for-profit basis are not prohibited [eg, Victoria, *ibid*]. Reimbursement to expenses is possible. In certain cases the parties themselves cannot be prosecuted. Finally, the most frequently recommended measure is to make surrogacy contracts unenforceable in a court of law or declare them null and void [eg Victoria and Queensland, *ibid*].

The American Fertility Society allows surrogate motherhood for strictly medical reasons and views it as a clinical experiment that has to be studied in detail. The parties would be informed of the psychological risks surrogacy may entail.

The report of the Ontario Law Reform Commission recommends the legalization of regulated agreements. A major role is assigned to the courts, which would have to approve agreements before conception but after evaluating the parenting abilities of the future parents, their stability as individuals and as a couple, and the medical reasons for using the procedure. The judge would also have to consider the prospective surrogate: physical and mental health, marital situation and partner's opinion, and the impact on any other children. He or she would have to ensure that blood tests are performed in order to prevent any subsequent challenge respecting the child's parentage, approve any possible payment and ensure that the parties agree on the following matters: insurance, death or separation of the applicants, behaviour and diet before and during the pregnancy, diagnostic examinations, terms and conditions for transferring the child, and future relations between the surrogate and the child.

In England, in response to the highly publicised birth of 'Baby Cotton' to a surrogate mother in January 1985 (see *Re C (a minor)* [1985] FLR 846), Parliament enacted the Surrogacy Arrangements Act 1985. We shall discuss this in detail later. It takes a middle ground. While not prohibiting surrogacy, it seeks to discourage it as a practice by, for example, making it illegal to facilitate *commercial* surrogacy arrangements.

Following the Warnock Report, the government returned to the issue of legislation in respect of surrogate arrangements in a 1987 White Paper.

Human Fertilisation and Embryology: A Framework for Legislation (1987, Cmnd 259)

66. The consultation document [*Legislation on Human Infertility Services and Embryo Research* (Cm 83), 1986] invited views on whether a non-commercial surrogacy service should be permitted to develop, under strict controls, or whether it should be prohibited by law as a majority of the Warnock Committee recommended. Some respondents considered that there was a role for such a service (as had two members of the Warnock Committee). It argued that in a very few cases surrogacy may be an acceptable solution to a couple's childlessness; and that, since surrogacy will always continue to be practised, whatever the rights or wrongs, it is in the best interests of all concerned – particularly the unborn child – that there should be proper counselling and assessment of the arrangements proposed.

67. Those who supported the majority view of the Warnock Committee, on the other hand, argue that the existence of a non-commercial service would encourage the growth of surrogacy and would sanction a situation in which the interests of the child can never be guaranteed. A further consideration is that if surrogacy were permitted under licence on a non-commercial basis it might be difficult to avoid criminalising individuals who made their arrangements outside this structure. Such criminalisation is felt by many to be against the child's best interests.

68. The Warnock Report recommended that, in addition to the operation of commercial or non-commercial surrogacy agencies, the actions of professionals and others who knowingly assist in the establishment of a surrogate pregnancy should also be rendered criminally liable. The Report did not envisage that legislation would make individuals entering into private surrogacy arrangements with each other liable to criminal prosecution, and the

Committee was anxious that children born as a result of such arrangement should not be subject to the taint of criminality.

69. In response to the consultation document, there was a marked division of opinion on whether legislation should prohibit private surrogacy arrangements of this kind especially if they involved payment of a fee and/or expenses to the surrogate mother. It would, in practice, be virtually impossible to enforce such legislation, although of course any surrogate pregnancy which was brought about as a result of one of the methods of treatment regulated by the [Statutory Licensing Authority] (eg AID) would be subject to the controls outlined elsewhere in the White Paper.

70. There was also a division of opinion about how far liability in respect of unlawful surrogacy arrangements should extend. Under the 1985 Act only third parties are liable. The surrogate mother and commissioning parents remain free from prosecution even when the arrangement is on a commercial basis. This situation is supported by those who argue that, in the best interests of the child, those immediately involved should not be criminalised. Some feel, however, that liability should extend to anyone making financial gain from the arrangement, while others consider that all parties, including the commissioning parents and surrogate mother, should be criminally liable if they take part in an unlawful arrangement at all.

71. No clear view emerged, either, on whether it should be a criminal offence for a doctor, lawyer or other professional knowingly to assist in establishing a surrogate pregnancy. There is, however, a strong body of opinion opposed to any measures which might prevent the surrogate mother from obtaining proper professional care and advice during her pregnancy. (It should be noted, too, that any professional person who took part in negotiations for a commercial surrogacy arrangement would already be guilty of an offence under existing law.)

72. While there is widespread agreement about the problems surrogacy poses, there is no consensus about the most constructive role legislation might play in dealing with it. It is widely accepted that the interests of the child are paramount, but there is no agreement about whether these are best served by prohibiting surrogacy altogether or allowing it to take place in strictly controlled circumstances.

73. The Government has concluded that legislation should not give any encouragement to the parties of surrogacy arranged privately or on a non-commercial basis. The Bill will contain no provision for licensing non-commercial surrogacy services and will make it clear that any contract drawn up as part of a surrogacy arrangement will be unenforceable, in all its aspects, in the UK Courts. The Government does not however consider that it is appropriate, nor necessarily in the child's best interests, to bring the practice of surrogacy – other than the operation of commercial agencies – within the scope of the criminal law and the Bill will not add to the criminal sanctions contained in the 1985 Act.

74. A clearer view on these complex issues may emerge in the light of developments and the Government believes it is important that the position should be kept under review. This is a task for which the SLA, as an independent body with a balance of lay and specialist views, is well suited. The Government therefore proposes to ask the SLA to look at the position as regards the practice of surrogacy in this country and report to Ministers as requested. It is hoped that this will enable Parliament to review the situation from time to time on the basis of informed and considered advice.

75. As far as future action is concerned, the Bill will contain a provision empowering the Secretary of State to lay regulations extending the scope of activities controlled by the SLA [see now s 8(d) Human Fertilisation and Embryology Act 1990]. This could be used if, in the light of future developments, it were concluded that, for example, non-commercial surrogacy services should be brought within the framework of the law.

As we shall see, apart from legislation declaring surrogate contracts to be unenforceable (Surrogacy Arrangements Act 1985, s 1A), there has been no legislation in England directly regulating surrogate arrangements.

D. ENGLISH LAW

1. The validity of the agreement

The typical terms of a surrogacy contract can be seen in the New Jersey case of *In the Matter of Baby M* (1988) 537 A 2d 1227. The contract referred to, and set out below, is that used by the Infertility Center of New York (ICNY), the senior executive of which is the attorney, Noel Keane, regarded as the leading exponent of surrogacy arrangements in the United States.

SURROGATE PARENTING AGREEMENT

THIS AGREEMENT is made this   day of   , 19   by and between MARY BETH WHITEHEAD, a married woman (herein referred to as 'Surrogate'), RICHARD WHITEHEAD, her husband (herein referred to as 'Husband'), and WILLIAM STERN (herein referred to as 'Natural Father').

Recitals

THIS AGREEMENT is made with reference to the following facts:
(1) WILLIAM STERN, Natural Father, is an individual over the age of eighteen (18) years who is desirous of entering into this Agreement.
(2) The sole purpose of this Agreement is to enable WILLIAM STERN and his infertile wife to have a child which is biologically related to WILLIAM STERN.
(3) MARY BETH WHITEHEAD, Surrogate, and RICHARD WHITEHEAD, her husband, are over the age of eighteen (18) years and desirous of entering into this Agreement in consideration of the following:
NOW THEREFORE, in consideration of the mutual promises contained herein and the intentions of being legally bound hereby, the parties agree as follows:
    1. MARY BETH WHITEHEAD, Surrogate, represents that she is capable of conceiving children. MARY BETH WHITEHEAD understands and agrees that in the best interest of the child, she will not form or attempt to form a parent-child relationship with any child or children she may conceive, carry to term and give birth to pursuant to the provisions of this Agreement, and shall freely surrender custody to WILLIAM STERN, Natural Father, immediately upon birth of the child; and terminate all parental rights to said child pursuant to this Agreement.
    2. MARY BETH WHITEHEAD, Surrogate, and RICHARD WHITEHEAD, her husband, have been married since 12/2/73, and RICHARD WHITEHEAD is in agreement with the purposes, intents and provisions of this Agreement and acknowledges that his wife, MARY BETH WHITEHEAD, Surrogate, shall be artificially inseminated pursuant to the provisions of this Agreement. RICHARD WHITEHEAD agrees that in the best interest of the child, he will not form or attempt to form a parent-child relationship with any child or children MARY BETH WHITEHEAD, Surrogate, may conceive by artificial insemination as described herein, and agrees freely and readily to surrender immediate custody of the child to WILLIAM STERN, Natural Father; and terminate his parental rights;
RICHARD WHITEHEAD further acknowledges he will do all acts necessary to rebut the presumption of paternity of any offspring conceived and born pursuant to aforementioned agreement as provided by law, including blood testing and/or HLA testing.
    3. WILLIAM STERN, Natural Father, does hereby enter into this written contractual Agreement with MARY BETH WHITEHEAD, Surrogate, where MARY BETH WHITEHEAD shall be artificially inseminated with the semen of WILLIAM STERN by a physician. MARY BETH WHITEHEAD, Surrogate, upon becoming pregnant, acknowledges that she will carry said embryo/fetus(s) until delivery. MARY BETH WHITEHEAD, Surrogate, and RICHARD WHITEHEAD, her husband, agree that they will cooperate with any background investigation into the Surrogate's medical, family and personal history and warrant the information to be accurate to the best of their knowledge. MARY BETH WHITEHEAD, Surrogate, and RICHARD WHITEHEAD, her husband, agree to surrender custody of the child to WILLIAM STERN, Natural Father, immediately upon birth, acknowledging that it is the intent of this Agreement in the best interests of the child to do so; as well as institute and cooperate in proceedings to terminate their respective parental rights to said child, and sign any and all necessary affidavits, documents, and the like, in order to further the intent and purposes of this Agreement. It is understood by MARY BETH WHITEHEAD, and RICHARD WHITEHEAD, that the child to be conceived is being done so for the sole purpose of giving said child to WILLIAM STERN, its natural and biological father. MARY BETH WHITEHEAD and RICHARD WHITEHEAD agree to sign all necessary affidavits prior to and after the birth of the child and voluntarily participate in any paternity proceedings necessary to have WILLIAM STERN'S name entered on said child's birth certificate as the natural or biological father.

4. That the consideration for this Agreement, which is compensation for services and expenses, and in no way is to be construed as a fee for termination of parental rights or a payment in exchange for a consent to surrender the child for adoption, in addition to other provisions contained herein, shall be as follows:

(A) $10,000 shall be paid to MARY BETH WHITEHEAD, Surrogate, upon surrender of custody to WILLIAM STERN, the natural and biological father of the child born pursuant to the provisions of this Agreement for surrogate services and expenses in carrying out her obligations under this Agreement;

(B) The consideration to be paid to MARY BETH WHITEHEAD, Surrogate, shall be deposited with the Infertility Center of New York (hereinafter ICNY), by the representative of WILLIAM STERN, at the time of the signing of this Agreement, and held in escrow until completion of the duties and obligations of MARY BETH WHITEHEAD, Surrogate, (see Exhibit 'A' for a copy of the Escrow Agreement), as herein described.

(C) WILLIAM STERN, Natural Father, shall pay the expenses incurred by MARY BETH WHITEHEAD, Surrogate, pursuant to her pregnancy, more specifically defined as follows:

(1) All medical, hospitalization, and pharmaceutical, laboratory and therapy expenses incurred as a result of MARY BETH WHITEHEAD'S pregnancy, not covered or allowed by her present health and major medical insurance, including all extraordinary medical expenses and all reasonable expenses for treatment of any emotional or mental conditions or problems related to said pregnancy, but in no case shall any such expenses be paid or reimbursed after a period of six (6) months have elapsed since the date of the termination of the pregnancy, and this Agreement specifically excludes any expenses for lost wages or other non-itemized incidentals (see Exhibit 'B') related to said pregnancy.

(2) WILLIAM STERN, Natural Father, shall not be responsible for any latent medical ex78penses occurring six (6) weeks subsequent to the birth of the child, unless the medical problem or abnormality incident thereto was known and treated by a physician prior to the expiration of said six (6) week period and in written notice of the same sent to ICNY, as representative of WILLIAM STERN by certified mail, return receipt requested, advising of this treatment.

(3) WILLIAM STERN, Natural Father, shall be responsible for the total costs of all paternity testing. Such paternity testing may, at the option of WILLIAM STERN, Natural Father, be required prior to release of the surrogate fee from escrow. In the event WILLIAM STERN, Natural Father, is conclusively determined not to be the biological father of the child as a result of an HLA test, this Agreement will be deemed breached and MARY BETH WHITEHEAD, Surrogate, shall not be entitled to any fee. WILLIAM STERN, Natural Father, shall be entitled to reimbursement of all medical and related expenses from MARY BETH WHITEHEAD, Surrogate, and RICHARD WHITEHEAD, her husband.

(4) MARY BETH WHITEHEAD'S reasonable travel expenses incurred at the request of WILLIAM STERN pursuant to this Agreement.

5. MARY BETH WHITEHEAD, Surrogate, and RICHARD WHITEHEAD, her husband, understand and agree to assume all risks, including the risk of death, which are incidental to conception, pregnancy, childbirth, including but not limited to, postpartum complications. A copy of said possible risks and/or complications is attached hereto and made a part hereof (see Exhibit 'C').

6. MARY BETH WHITEHEAD, Surrogate, and RICHARD WHITEHEAD, her husband, hereby agree to undergo psychiatric evaluation by JOAN EINWOHNER, a psychiatrist as designated by WILLIAM STERN or an agent thereof. WILLIAM STERN shall pay for the cost of said psychiatric evaluation. MARY BETH WHITEHEAD and RICHARD WHITEHEAD shall sign, prior to their evaluations, a medical release permitting dissemination of the report prepared as a result of said psychiatric evaluations to ICNY or WILLIAM STERN and his wife.

7. MARY BETH WHITEHEAD, Surrogate, and RICHARD WHITEHEAD, her husband, hereby agree that it is the exclusive and sole right of WILLIAM STERN, Natural Father, to name said child.

8. 'Child' as referred to in this Agreement shall include all children born simultaneously pursuant to the inseminations contemplated herein.

9. In the event of the death of WILLIAM STERN, prior or subsequent to the birth of said child, it is hereby understood and agreed by MARY BETH WHITEHEAD, Surrogate, and RICHARD WHITEHEAD, her husband, that the child will be placed in the custody of WILLIAM STERN'S wife.

10. In the event that the child is miscarried prior to the fifth (5th) month of pregnancy, no compensation, as enumerated in paragraph 4(A), shall be paid to MARY BETH

WHITEHEAD, Surrogate. However, the expenses enumerated in paragraph 4(C) shall be paid or reimbursed to MARY BETH WHITEHEAD, Surrogate. In the event the child is miscarried, dies or is stillborn subsequent to the fourth (4th) month of pregnancy and said child does not survive, the Surrogate shall receive $1,000.00 in lieu of the compensation enumerated in paragraph 4(A). In the event of a miscarriage or stillbirth as described above, this Agreement shall terminate and neither MARY BETH WHITEHEAD, Surrogate, nor WILLIAM STERN, Natural Father, shall be under any further obligation under this Agreement.

11. MARY BETH WHITEHEAD, Surrogate, and WILLIAM STERN, Natural Father, shall have undergone complete physical and genetic evaluation, under the direction and supervision of a licensed physician, to determine whether the physical health and well-being of each is satisfactory. Said physical examination shall include testing for venereal diseases, specifically including but not limited to, syphilis, herpes and gonorrhea. Said venereal diseases testing shall be done prior to, but not limited to, each series of inseminations.

12. In the event that pregnancy has not occurred within a reasonable time, in the opinion of WILLIAM STERN, Natural Father, this Agreement shall terminate by written notice to MARY BETH WHITEHEAD, Surrogate, at the residence provided to the ICNY by the Surrogate, from ICNY, as representative of WILLIAM STERN, Natural Father.

13. MARY BETH WHITEHEAD, Surrogate, agrees that she will not abort the child once conceived except, if in the professional medical opinion of the inseminating physician, such action is necessary for the physical health of MARY BETH WHITEHEAD or the child has been determined by said physician to be physiologically abnormal. MARY BETH WHITEHEAD further agrees, upon the request of said physician to undergo amniocentesis (see Exhibit 'D') or similar tests to detect genetic and congenital defects. In the event said test reveals that the fetus is genetically or congenitally abnormal, MARY BETH WHITEHEAD, Surrogate, agrees to abort the fetus upon demand of WILLIAM STERN, Natural Father, in which event, the fee paid to the Surrogate will be in accordance to Paragraph 10. If MARY BETH WHITEHEAD refuses to abort the fetus upon demand of WILLIAM STERN, his obligations as stated in this Agreement shall cease forthwith, except as to obligations of paternity imposed by statute.

14. Despite the provisions of Paragraph 13, WILLIAM STERN, Natural Father, recognizes that some genetic and congenital abnormalities may not be detected by amniocentesis or other tests, and therefore, if proven to be the biological father of the child, assumes the legal responsibility for any child who may possess genetic or congenital abnormalities. (See Exhibits 'E' and 'F'.)

15. MARY BETH WHITEHEAD, Surrogate, further agrees to adhere to all medical instructions given to her by the inseminating physician as well as her independent obstetrician. MARY BETH WHITEHEAD also agrees not to smoke cigarettes, drink alcoholic beverages, use illegal drugs, or take non-prescription medication or prescribed medications without written consent from her physician. MARY BETH WHITEHEAD agrees to follow a prenatal medical examination schedule to consist of no fewer visits than: one visit per month during the first seven (7) months of pregnancy, two visits (each to occur at two-week intervals) during the eighth and ninth month of pregnancy.

16. MARY BETH WHITEHEAD, Surrogate, agrees to cause RICHARD WHITE-HEAD, her husband, to execute a refusal of consent form as annexed hereto as Exhibit 'G'.

17. Each party acknowledges that he or she fully understands this Agreement and its legal effect, and that they are signing the name freely and voluntarily and that neither party has any reason to believe that the other(s) did not freely and voluntarily execute said Agreement.

18. In the event any of the provisions of this Agreement are deemed to be invalid or unenforceable, the same shall be deemed severable from the remainder of this Agreement and shall not cause the invalidity or unenforceability of the remainder of this Agreement. If such provision shall be deemed invalid due to its scope or breadth, then said provision shall be deemed valid to the extent of the scope or breadth permitted by law.

19. The original of this Agreement, upon execution, shall be retained by the Infertility Center of New York, with photocopies being distributed to MARY BETH WHITEHEAD, Surrogate and WILLIAM STERN, Natural Father, having the same legal effect as the original.

WILLIAM STERN   DATE
Natural Father

STATE OF:
COUNTY OF

On the   day of   , 19   , before me personally came WILLIAM
STERN, known to me, and to me known, to be the individual described in the foregoing
instrument and he acknowledged to me that he executed the same as his free and voluntary
act.

NOTARY PUBLIC

A central question in English law is to what extent is such a contract
enforceable. There are two principal ways in which the parties might seek to
enforce the contract. First, the parties might wish to enforce one of the terms
during the course of the surrogate's pregnancy, for example, that the surrogate
mother undergo certain medical tests or refrains from particular conduct which
might be harmful to the unborn child. Secondly, the parties might wish to
enforce the terms of the contract requiring the surrogate mother to hand over
the baby to the commissioning couple after its birth. We shall return to the
latter issue shortly. It was the one that arose in the *Baby M* case. The problems
that would be faced if the law were to permit enforcement of the detailed terms
of surrogate arrangements are discussed in the following extracts.

C Sappideen 'The Surrogate Mother – A Growing Problem' (1983) University of New South Wales Law Review 79

. . . [I]f those contracts were enforceable, difficult problems would arise on breach of
contract. Independently of the issue of public policy, a court of equity will not specifically
enforce contracts for personal services. Two reasons may be given for this rule; the first is
that contracts which require constant supervision will not be enforced and secondly, that a
court will not order performance of contracts requiring special confidence and trust. A court
of law can, however, enforce the contract by awarding damages for breach of contract.
Examples will be given to illustrate inherent difficulties.

(a) Breach by the surrogate

The surrogate may breach the contract (depending on its terms) in a variety of ways, for
example smoking, drinking during pregnancy, terminating the pregnancy by abortion, or
refusal to hand over custody of the baby. Taking the first examples, smoking and drinking
during pregnancy – would this breach allow the couple to treat the contract as at an end?
Should the contract provide that the breach of any of its terms renders the contract voidable
by the innocent party? Would a fraudulent misrepresentation that the surrogate did not
smoke or drink allow the innocent party to rescind? If the innocent party reaffirmed the
contract and sued for damages, what would be the damages? For example, how could
damage be measured and proved if all that could be shown was that the surrogate had had
one cigarette, or one drink? If the surrogate terminated the pregnancy what damages could
be recovered by the couple? Presumably all that could be obtained here would be damages
for emotional distress suffered as flowing naturally from the breach.

(b) Breach by the couple

Depending on the terms of the contract, breaches could include failure to pay, failure to take
custody of the child, or failure to provide health insurance or to adopt the child. If the
couple refused to take custody of the child, would the surrogate be able to recover the cost
of upkeep for the child until aged eighteen, or would the surrogate be obliged to mitigate her
loss by placing the child for adoption?

Specific questions which arise from contracts such as these are addressed in
Theresa Mady's article. Although some of the discussion concerns uniquely
American law, the analysis (and suggested approach) remains of great interest.

In this article the following abbreviations are adopted: S = surrogate mother; H = commissioning male; W = commissioning female.

T Mady 'Surrogate Mothers: The Legal Issues' (1981) American Journal of Law and Medicine 324

Given that the surrogate mother arrangement is legal, parties still must determine what terms they can include that will be judicially enforced in a written contract. Although the parties' written agreement may be persuasive to a court in establishing their intent, courts are not bound to enforce provisions which are contrary to public policy. Clearly, public policy concerns permeate the surrogate mother arrangement, especially where the interests of an unborn child are at stake. In addition, attempts to contract to specifically enforce personal services are not necessarily binding, for parties cannot divest a court of law of its power to grant relief.

1. Rights and liabilities of S

The rights and liabilities of the surrogate mother stem from two basic promises that she makes to H and W. First, S promises to be inseminated with H's semen and carry the child to term. This includes the assurance that she will seek the necessary medical attention to maintain and ensure the health and safety of the fetus. Second, S promises to surrender to H and W all rights in the child. If S is married, this second promise may become complicated if her husband wishes to retain custody of the child.

The law presumes that a child born to a married woman is the child of the woman and her husband. Since this presumption is rebuttable, S and her husband should state explicitly that they will make no claim to the child; without this statement the intention of the parties may be undercut. Such a provision would help eliminate emotional strain and probably litigation, and would avoid harming the child by involving it in custody proceedings.

If S breaches by not adhering to one or both of these promises, courts will have difficulty devising appropriate remedies. The proper remedy will depend on the type of breach. Three major possibilities for breach arise: S may wish to abort the child, S may negligently cause harm to the fetus, or S may refuse to give up the child after birth.

If S desires to abort for any reason, within certain constitutional limits, it is unclear whether she can be legally prevented from so doing. The United States Supreme Court has held that the right to decide to abort is one of constitutional dimension which cannot be limited by the exercise of state law unless pursuant to a compelling state interest. The Court has also held that a woman may decide to abort irrespective of her husband's consent. If a husband cannot veto his wife's decision to abort, it is unclear whether H and W, who are merely in a contractual relationship with S, can impose their will. However, some constitutional rights can be waived prior to their exercise. It is unclear whether all constitutional rights can be irrevocably waived. It has never been decided which category encompasses the right to choose to abort. If S cannot irrevocably waive her right to choose to have an abortion, she will retain this right. If S aborts the fetus, however, she breaches by destroying the essence of the contract. Classical contract remedies do not allow recovery for the emotional upset which H and W would inevitably suffer. Restitution for expenses already paid may be the only viable recourse. Although a tort action for infliction of emotional distress might more appropriately compensate H and W, few jurisdictions have accepted this cause of action. In addition, wrongful death actions may not presently extend to abortion of a fetus.

The second type of breach can occur if S negligently causes harm to the fetus, abrogating the promise to provide proper care during pregnancy. In this event, H and W have two possible avenues of recovery: an action for breach of the terms of the contract, or a tort action based on negligence. Both actions would require H and W to prove essentially the same elements, although the likelihood of equitable relief rather than damages increases when predicated on the contract action. In either case, H and W would have to demonstrate that the contract imposed a duty on S, whether explicit or implied, to maintain an adequate level of care during pregnancy. If the contract makes explicit the level of care S will undertake, including the activities she must forego, then the extent of her duty will be clear. In the absence of specific terms in the contract, the standard of necessary medical attention that S must observe would be the same that a reasonable pregnant woman in the circumstances would receive. The range of activities undertaken by reasonable women during pregnancy is expansive, and proving that any given activity falls outside this range would be difficult. Since this duty is not easily defined in the abstract, parties would be well advised to include an explicit statement in the contract, in order to eliminate ambiguities and needless legal complications.

After establishing a duty and breach of that duty, *H* and *W* must prove that the breach proximately caused or will cause the alleged specific injury in order to succeed under either a tort or contract theory. Proof of proximate cause, however, may be difficult because tracing the origin of a congenital defect in a particular child back to a particular source may be impossible. For example, alcohol or caffeine consumption may cause birth defects, but demonstrating that any specific birth defect resulted from such consumption is difficult. Thus, any suit for breach of that duty to provide adequate care will have to overcome this serious obstacle.

Once *H* and *W* establish the elements of a cause of action, two forms of relief are available. In most legal actions, courts assess the inquiry to the plaintiff and direct the defendant to pay the plaintiff money damages. When payment of money damages is inadequate, because either the harm is not clearly quantifiable, or the underlying basis of the suit depends upon something that money cannot replace or compensate the plaintiff, courts are willing to prescribe equitable relief: to enjoin the defendant from doing an act or to do an act. Injunction, however, is considered an extraordinary remedy and will not ensue absent a showing that the legal remedy is inadequate.

Obtaining either equitable or legal relief will be difficult, since the real purpose of the promise to receive proper care is to protect the welfare of the unborn child. Retrospective legal relief, obtained after a child is born deformed, for instance, clearly is inadequate since money damages will not cure the deformity. Perhaps *H* and *W* can include a liquidated damages clause in the contract, which would provide a specific measure of damages in the event of a specific breach. Yet, courts often strike down liquidated damages as penalties. Thus the damage remedy contains inherent weaknesses that make resort to it unsatisfactory. Given the uncertainties of the equitable remedy, however, the damage remedy may be the only viable means of enforcing this agreement. If *S*'s negligence results in a miscarriage, money damages will be the only possible remedy. Damages are as difficult to determine as if *S* had aborted the fetus, leaving restitution for expenses paid as the only quantifiable measure. Of course, if *H* and *W* are unable to prove negligence on the part of *S*, they would be obligated to pay for the services rendered up to this point. The clearer the contract is concerning the measure of damages, the more likely courts will be to award them.

In the event that *H* and *W* discover, during the term of *S*'s pregnancy, that she has been remiss in obtaining the appropriate level of medical attention, they can request a court to order her compliance. Showing the inadequacy of the legal remedy should not be difficult. Certainly the health and well-being of a child is so unique that a court, if possible, will employ its equity powers to further that end. The problem with injunctions, however, lies in administering orders that direct a woman to receive medical care or to refrain from a certain diet. Courts historically have been reluctant to enjoin parties where the resultant order demands close personal supervision or personal services. Thus, even though the remedy at law would be inadequate, courts may require that alternative, due to the problems inherent in administering equitable orders.

In sum neither remedy for breach of this promise seems satisfactory. Although injunctive relief is more desirable, it may be judicially unacceptable. In that event only the damage remedy would remain. Damages, however, would be difficult to quantify. In addition, the difficulty in proving proximate cause increases when *H* and *W* must demonstrate that a particular activity caused a particular defect. This additional burden will not exist in the case of prospective relief, for *H* and *W* will only have to show either that it was prohibited in the terms of the contract, or that it may cause birth defects and that a reasonably prudent pregnant woman would not take the risk. In light of these burdens on *H* and *W*, the possibility exists that this promise to obtain adequate medical care, although important to the purpose of the contract, may be wholly unenforceable.

The third way that *S* can breach the contract is by refusing to give up the child after birth. Monetary damages for *H* and *W* in this event do not suffice since the whole purpose of the agreement was to provide them with what they could not otherwise obtain, a child of their own. Since in many cases they are willing to pay money to obtain that child, giving them money as damages would be wholly inadequate. In addition there is no ethically acceptable standard by which a jury can measure the worth of the child. Specific performance, that is, forcing *S* to surrender the child to *H* and *W*, is an equally tenuous alternative. Courts have manifested an extreme reluctance to intervene in domestic relationships. Although *S* is not a part of the family consisting of *H* and *W*, and therefore *S*, *H* and *W* do not comprise a domestic relationship, it seems unlikely that a court would force a woman to give up a child she carried merely on the basis of a contract. Therefore *H* and *W* would have to obtain relief in a custody suit where a court would determine the best interests of the child. If the custody suit did not prove favorable for *H* and *W*, there would be little recourse. Restitution for expenses incurred by *H* and *W* provides the only clear-cut compensable contractual damage.

2. Rights and liabilities of H and W

As consideration for the promise of *S*, *H* and *W* promise to pay to *S* the financial costs of pregnancy and medical care, and to accept the child after birth. Sometimes they also agree to pay *S* an additional fee for her services. Since *H* and *W* have a keen interest in providing good care during pregnancy, presumably they will pay these expenses. However, if *H* and *W* breach their promises to pay the costs of pregnancy or to pay the fee to *S*, recovery would be fairly straightforward, since these expenses either will be delineated in the contract, or easily ascertained by assessing the costs of medical care. If *H* and *W* refuse to accept the child after birth, problems will occur in determining the appropriate remedy, similar to those that occur when *S* refuses to give up the child. Specific performance is unlikely since a court would not force *H* and *W* to accept an unwanted child, thereby jeopardizing the child's best interests.

In this instance, *S* could sue for child support payments. Just as an unwed mother may sue the father of the child for support, *S* should be able to sue *H* in the event that he refuses custody. Since *S* reasonably relied on *H* and *W*'s promise, she should not have to incur the expenses of bringing up a child that she believed would not be in her custody after its birth. On the other hand, if *S* wishes to retain custody of the child, she should not be coerced into putting up the child for adoption, despite the rationale of mitigating damages or because she cannot afford to provide adequately for the child. In either case, the father, *H*, should be estopped from denying responsibility. It should be noted, however, that in the typical artificial insemination case a donor of semen usually does not incur liability for child support unless the donor was the donee's husband. However, regarding the surrogate mother arrangement, *H* not only recognizes that he is the genetic father but also contracts to accept the child and become the father in all respects. The same policy considerations, therefore, which demand insulating the donor from liability in artificial insemination cases do not apply in the surrogate mother cases. In order to make resolution of this issue easier, the contract should include a provision for payment of child support in the event that this sort of breach occurs.

If neither family wants to retain custody of the child, *S* is free to offer the child for adoption. Perhaps *H* and *W* must bear the costs of adoption, but this amount is likely to be small, given the high demand for adoptable babies. The likelihood that either *S* or *H* and *W* will refuse to accept the child increases if the child is born with a deformity or a handicap. Screening procedures should minimize this possibility, and exclude those couples not willing to accept a deformed or handicapped child. Attempting to eliminate these couples at the outset decreases the likelihood of such a problem subsequently arising. In the event, however, that the child is unadoptable, the legal responsibility for care of the child should rest with *H* and *W*.

(For a full discussion of the arguments concerning the enforcement of surrogate arrangements, see M Field *Surrogate Motherhood: The Legal and Human Issues* (1988), arguing that the surrogate mother should have a right to renounce the contract up to the time of the birth of the child.)

So, what is the position in English law: is a surrogate contract valid, unenforceable or void on grounds of public policy?

(a) The criminal law

Is the agreement unlawful *in limine* as constituting a crime? There are at least three possibilities. First, the parties' agreement may constitute a conspiracy to corrupt public morals or outrage public decency. No English case has addressed this question. Arguably, the fact that a number of surrogacy arrangements have been widely publicised and been the object of litigation without prompting any intervention by the DPP is, at least, *prima facie* evidence that the agreement would not amount to a criminal conspiracy in

England. Further, it has sometimes been urged that the fulfilment of a surrogacy arrangement amounts to the crime of 'baby selling'. However, it seems clear that no such crime is known to the common law. 'Baby selling' (the handing over of a child for money) is merely treated at common law as conduct *contra bonos mores*. It is a separate question whether the agreement should be so regarded. We would suggest that it should not.

Secondly, an offence may be committed under s 57 of the Adoption Act 1976 if the commissioning couple intend to adopt the child once born:

57. (1) Subject to the provisions of this section, it shall not be lawful to make or give to any person any payment or reward for or in consideration of –
(*a*) the adoption by that person of a child;
(*b*) the grant by that person of any agreement or consent required in connection with the adoption of a child;
(*c*) the handing over of a child by that person with a view to the adoption of the child; or
(*d*) the making by that person of any arrangements for the adoption of a child.

The forerunner of this section, s 50 of the Adoption Act 1958, was interpreted in the following case.

Re an Adoption Application (Surrogacy) [1987] Fam 81, [1987] 2 All ER 826

Latey J: Mr and Mrs A apply to adopt a little child, now aged 2 years and 4 months. The child's mother (whom I shall call 'the mother') is Mrs B. The child was conceived as a result of a surrogacy arrangement, as it is described, between Mr and Mrs A and Mrs B and her husband, Mr B. As a result of that arrangement Mr A and Mrs B had sexual intercourse on a few occasions and in due course the child was conceived. It was in no sense a love affair. It was physical congress with the sole purpose of procreating a child. As soon as there was conception intercourse ceased.

What led up to this arrangement was this: Mr and Mrs A are a devoted couple. To complete and fulfil their union they dearly wanted a child. For medical reasons Mrs A was and is unable to have a baby. They did everything they could with medical help and advice, including surgery, to overcome this but to no avail. They then tried to adopt a child both in this country and abroad, again to no avail. As to this country, the principal reason given was their ages. This is surprising. At that time Mr A was barely 40, and Mrs A in her mid-30s, well within the normal age of parenthood, I would have thought. Another and subsidiary reason may have been that it was their second marriage, each having been divorced. But there is no doubt that their marriage is solid and stable, especially now that they have the baby, or toddler as it now is.

Then they heard a radio programme, and Mrs A saw a television programme, about surrogacy. They saw it as their last chance.

In the meanwhile, Mr and Mrs B had two children of their own. They decided at that time to have no more (though recently they have had a third child). Mrs B is one who enjoys pregnancy despite sickness and backache. She too heard, saw and read about surrogacy. She was deeply and genuinely moved about the plight of childless couples. There is no question about her sincerity about this. After much thought she decided to embark on this path. She discussed it with her husband, who was not, at first, enthusiastic but acquiesced and later supported her.

She put an advertisement in a magazine. Mr and Mrs A saw it and answered it. They met and the arrangement was made. Finance entered into it and this aspect of it is at the heart of whether an adoption order can be made in this case and, if it can be, whether it should be made. This is because of the terms of certain statutory enactments which I will come to shortly.

The mother, Mrs B, was in full-time employment. She and her husband's joint income enabled them and their children to live in comfort. If she became pregnant it would mean giving up her job and earnings. It would mean incurring other expenses. She had responses from other couples – one couple in particular who offered a very large sum of money. This was not what she wanted.

She agreed with Mr and Mrs A to act as a surrogate because as she says:

I wanted to help a childless couple. My own children are very precious to me and I sympathised greatly with any couple who were unable to have children of their own, so much so that I was willing to have another pregnancy in order to give someone else that joy.

She wanted a couple with whom she could be friendly, empathise, have a rapport. She and Mr and Mrs A found each other and she declined the others, including the couple offering the very large sum.

The two couples agreed a global sum of £10,000. The mother says:

The money represented only my loss of earnings, expenses in connection with the pregnancy, and emotional and physical factors. I emphasise that I did not go into the arrangements for commercial reasons, nor did I accept the money to hand [the child] over. I would have done that in any event. In fact, overall, I was marginally worse off. This does not bother me since my motive was not financial.

In his report the child's guardian ad litem says:

The mother does *not* appear to have been primarily motivated in entering into the arrangements by financial considerations. She appears to have felt strongly that through a surrogacy arrangement she could offer an important service to a childless couple and to have regarded the money mainly as the equivalent of compensation for loss of earnings while pregnant. . . . Her interest in surrogacy the mother attributes to a particular pleasure she has in having babies and a great sympathy for women who are unable to experience the joy of having and caring for a baby. The public discussions and debates she heard about this subject struck a special chord for her, thus her initiative in advertising herself.

I have heard the mother speak about this in her evidence. I am left in no doubt that it is the plain, unvarnished truth.

Mr and Mrs A paid £1,000 when she was some months pregnant, and £4,000 shortly after the baby was born. The balance of £5,000 was due some months later, but the mother refused to accept it. This was because she and a professional writer as co-author wrote a book: 'Surrogate Mother. One Woman's Story', from which she made money. That book has been put in as part of the material in this case. It was written pseudonymously and with care to conceal the identity of the child and those connected with the child. I have tried to do the same in this judgment. In the interest of the child nothing must be published which might point to the child's identity with serious consequences to the child later in life, if it were publicly known. Mr and Mrs A's close circle know the facts. They accept and love the child. Mr and Mrs A are very intelligent people who adore the child. They have already worked out what and when they are going to tell the child, and done so admirably, as it seems to me. But for any public publicity to happen about this child as it grows up would certainly damage its emotional development and might be disastrous.

If the word 'commercial' has any bearing on what has to be decided in this case and if it connoted a profit or financial reward element there was nothing commercial in what happened. There was no written contract or agreement; no lawyers were consulted until after the baby was born. The arrangement was one of trust which was fully honoured on both sides.

The rest of the history can be told briefly. The child was born in hospital with Mrs A present at the birth and Mr A joining them almost immediately. Two days later the mother and child went to Mr and Mrs A's home. The four of them spent a week together. The mother went back to her own home. Mr and Mrs A and the child have been together since. The child thrived. The three of them have been and are supremely happy. The mother and Mr and Mrs A have kept in contact. The mother and Mr B have a third child. They are closer than they ever have been.

The first question, therefore, is whether in the present case there has been 'any payment or reward' within the meaning of section 50 of the Adoption Act 1958 – 'for adoption', to put it conveniently albeit imprecisely. This is a question of fact to be decided on the evidence. Mr and Mrs A and Mrs B have all given evidence. All are transparently honest. They did not make notes. They did not take legal advice. Not surprisingly, their recollection of the precise sequence of events and what was discussed and when is not clear. What does come out strongly is that what was wanted was a baby and that Mr and Mrs A should have it from birth to care for and bring up. And that it was upon this that they were all concentrating. It was only after the payments had been made and the baby was born that any of them began to turn their minds in any real sense to adoption and the legalities.

In my judgment there was no payment or reward within the meaning of section 50(1) of the Adoption Act 1958.

It may be that in his desire to arrive at a conclusion which he thought served the best interests of all the parties, Latey J was somewhat relaxed in his application of s 50 to the facts. Contrast the view of the New Jersey Supreme Court on hearing the appeal in the case of *In the Matter of Baby M* (1988) 537 A 2d 1227 (discussed at first instance by Capron, *supra*, p 828).

In the Matter of Baby M (1988) 537 A 2d 1227 (NJ Sup Ct)

Wilentz CJ: Our law prohibits paying or accepting money in connection with any placement of a child for adoption. . . . Excepted are fees of an approved agency (which must be a non-profit entity) and certain expenses in connection with childbirth.

Considerable care was taken in this case to structure the surrogacy arrangement so as not to violate this prohibition. The arrangement was structured as follows: the adopting parent, Mrs Stern, was not a party to the surrogacy contract; the money paid to Mrs Whitehead was stated to be for her services – not for the adoption; the sole purpose of the contract was stated as being that 'of giving a child to William Stern, its natural and biological father'; the money was purported to be 'compensation for services and expenses and in no way . . . a fee for termination of parental rights or a payment in exchange for consent to surrender a child for adoption'; the fee to the Infertility Center ($7,500) was stated to be for legal representation, advice, administrative work, and other 'services'. Nevertheless, it seems clear that the money was paid and accepted in connection with an adoption.

The Infertility Center's major role was first as a 'finder' of the surrogate mother whose child was to be adopted, and second as the arranger of all proceedings that led to the adoption. Its role as adoption finder is demonstrated by the provision requiring Mr Stern to pay another $7,500 if he uses Mary Beth Whitehead again as a surrogate, and by ICNY's agreement to 'coordinate arrangements for the adoption of the child by the wife'. The surrogacy agreement requires Mrs Whitehead to surrender Baby M for the purposes of adoption. The agreement notes that Mr *and* Mrs Stern wanted to have a child, and provides that the child be 'placed' with Mrs Stern in the event Mr Stern dies before the child is born. They payment of the $10,000 occurs only on surrender of custody of the child and 'completion of the duties and obligations' of Mrs Whitehead, including termination of her parental rights to facilitate adoption by Mrs Stern. As for the contention that the Sterns are paying only for services and not for an adoption, we need note only that they would pay nothing in the event the child died before the fourth month of pregnancy, and only $1,000 if the child were stillborn, even though the 'services' had been fully rendered. Additionally, one of Mrs Whitehead's estimated costs, to be assumed by Mr Stern, was an 'Adoption Fee', presumably for Mrs Whitehead's incidental costs in connection with the adoption.

Mr Stern knew he was paying for the adoption of a child; Mrs Whitehead knew she was accepting money so that a child might be adopted; the Infertility Center knew that it was being paid for assisting in the adoption of a child. The actions of all three worked to frustrate the goals of the statute. It strains credulity to claim that these arrangements, touted by those in the surrogacy business as an attractive alternative to the usual route leading to an adoption, really amount to something other than a private placement adoption for money.

Arguably, the New Jersey court's approach is more persuasive than that of Latey J in *Re An Adoption Application*.

It should be noted that s 57(3) of the Adoption Act 1976 provides: 'This section does not apply . . . to any payment or reward authorised by the court to which an application for an adoption order in respect of a child is made.' In *Re An Adoption Application*, Latey J held that 'authorised by the court' in s 50(3) of the 1958 Act (s 57(3)'s forerunner) covered not only authorisation in advance of making a payment but could also cover retrospective authorisation after it had been made. Latey J (at p 36) acknowledged that otherwise:

. . . It would mean, for example, that any payment, however modest and however innocently made, would bar an adoption and do so however much the welfare of the child cried aloud for adoption with all the security and legal rights and status it carried with it: and that, be it said, within the framework of legislation whose first concern is promoting the welfare of the children concerned.

I do not believe that Parliament ever intended to produce such a result (not, anticipating, has it done so in my judgment). The result it intended to produce is wise and humane. It produced a balance by setting its face against trafficking in children, on the one hand, but recognising that there may be transactions which are venial and should not prohibit adoption, on the other hand.

In applying s 50(3) and making the adoption order in favour of the commissioning parents, the judge said:

It follows that in each case the court has a discretion whether or not to authorise any payment or reward which has already been made or may be contemplated in the future. In exercising that discretion the court would no doubt balance all the circumstances of the case with the welfare of the child as first consideration against what [Counsel for the guardian *ad litem*] well described as the degree of taint of the transaction for which authorisation is asked.

It is at best arguable whether 'authorisation' was intended to include subsequent ratification by a court. If Latey J is right, he should, perhaps, have made clear the grounds for doing so. But, if he had done so, they would in fact probably have been contrary to the spirit of the adoption legislation.

Finally, there is the Surrogacy Arrangements Act 1985. We shall return to consider its terms in detail shortly. For the present it is sufficient to note that it creates a number of criminal offences for those involved in *commercial* surrogate arrangements. But it specifically excludes the surrogate mother or commissioning couple from liability under the Act (see s 2(2), discussed *infra*, pp 847-849).

(b) The civil law

In the New Jersey case of *In the Matter of Baby M* (1988) 537 A 2d 1227 the New Jersey Supreme Court examined the validity of a surrogacy contract.

In the Matter of Baby M (1988) 537 A 2d 1227 (NJ Sup Ct)

Wilentz CJ: In this matter the Court is asked to determine the validity of a contract that purports to provide a new way of bringing children into a family. For a fee of $10,000, a woman agrees to be artificially inseminated with the semen of another woman's husband; she is to conceive a child, carry it to term, and after its birth surrender it to the natural father and his wife. The intent of the contract is that the child's natural mother will thereafter be forever separated from her child. The wife is to adopt the child, and she and the natural father are to be regarded as its parents for all purposes. The contract providing for this is called a 'surrogacy contract', the natural mother inappropriately called the 'surrogate mother'.

. . . In February 1985, William Stern and Mary Beth Whitehead entered into a surrogacy contract. It recited that Stern's wife, Elizabeth, was infertile, that they wanted a child, and that Mrs Whitehead was willing to provide that child as the mother with Mr Stern as the father.

The contract provided that through artificial insemination using Mr Stern's sperm, Mrs Whitehead would become pregnant, carry the child to term, bear it, deliver it to the Sterns, and thereafter do whatever was necessary to terminate her maternal rights so that Mrs Stern could thereafter adopt the child. Mrs Whitehead's husband, Richard, was also a party to the contract; Mrs Stern was not. Mr Whitehead promised to do all acts necessary to rebut the presumption of paternity under the Parentage Act. *NJSA* 9:17-43a(1), -44a. Although Mrs Stern was not a party to the surrogacy agreement, the contract gave her sole custody of the child in the event of Mr Stern's death. Mrs Stern's status as a nonparty to the surrogate parenting agreement presumably was to avoid the application of the baby-selling statute to this arrangement. *NJSA* 9:3-54.

Mr Stern, on his part, agreed to attempt the artificial insemination and to pay Mrs Whitehead $10,000 after the child's birth, on its delivery to him. In a separate contract, Mr Stern agreed to pay $7,500 to the Infertility Center of New York ('ICNY'). The Center's advertising campaigns solicit surrogate mothers and encourage infertile couples to consider surrogacy. ICNY arranged for the surrogacy contract by bringing the parties together, explaining the process to them, furnishing the contractual form, and providing legal counsel.

. . . After several artificial inseminations over a period of months, Mrs Whitehead became pregnant. The pregnancy was uneventful and on March 28, 1986, Baby M was born.

[The court then examined the legislation of New Jersey in relation to (1) the prohibition of adoption for money; (2) the termination of parental rights; and (3) the surrender of custody and consent to adopt. The court concluded that the surrogate agreement was in direct conflict with the legislation and hence was invalid and unenforceable. The court then went on to consider public policy considerations:]

. . . The contract's basic premise, that the natural parents can decide in advance of birth which is to have custody of the child, bears no relationship to the settled law that the child's best interests shall determine custody. . . .

The surrogacy contract guarantees permanent separation of the child from one of its natural parents. Our policy, however, has long been that to the extent possible, children should remain with and be brought up by both of their natural parents. . . . This is not simply some theoretical ideal that in practice has no meaning. The impact of failure to follow that policy is nowhere better shown than in the results of this surrogacy contract. A child, instead of starting off its life with as much peace and security as possible, finds itself immediately in a tug-of-war between contending mother and father.

The surrogacy contract violates the policy of this State that the rights of natural parents are equal concerning their child, the father's right no greater than the mother's. . . . The whole purpose and effect of the surrogacy contract was to give the father the exclusive right to the child by destroying the rights of the mother.

The policies expressed in our comprehensive laws governing consent to the surrender of a child . . . stand in stark contrast to the surrogacy contract and what it implies. Here there is no counseling, independent or otherwise, of the natural mother, no evaluation, no warning.

The only legal advice Mary Beth Whitehead received regarding the surrogacy contract was provided in connection with the contract that she previously entered into with another couple. Mrs Whitehead's lawyer was referred to her by the Infertility Center, with which he had an agreement to act as counsel for surrogate candidates. His services consisted of spending one hour going through the contract with the Whiteheads, section by section, and answering their questions. Mrs Whitehead received no further legal advice prior to signing the contract with the Sterns.

Mrs Whitehead was examined and psychologically evaluated, but if it was for her benefit, the record does not disclose that fact. The Sterns regarded the evaluation as important, particularly in connection with the question of whether she would change her mind. Yet they never asked to see it, and were content with the assumption that the Infertility Center had made an evaluation and had concluded that there was no danger that the surrogate mother would change her mind. From Mrs Whitehead's point of view, all that she learned from the evaluation was that 'she had passed.' It is apparent that the profit motive got the better of the Infertility Center. Although the evaluation was made, it was not put to any use, and understandably so, for the psychologist warned that Mrs Whitehead demonstrated certain traits that might make surrender of the child difficult and that there should be further inquiry into this issue in connection with her surrogacy. To inquire further, however, might have jeopardised the Infertility Center's fee. The record indicates that neither Mrs Whitehead nor the Sterns were ever told of this fact, a fact that might have ended their surrogacy arrangement.

Under the contract, the natural mother is irrevocably committed before she knows the strength of her bond with her child. She never makes a totally voluntary, informed decision, for quite clearly any decision prior to the baby's birth is, in the most important sense, uninformed, and any decision after that, compelled by a pre-existing contractual commitment, the threat of a lawsuit, and the inducement of a $10,000 payment, is less than totally voluntary. Her interests are of little concern to those who controlled this transaction.

Although the interest of the natural father and adoptive mother is certainly the predominant interest, realistically the *only* interest served, even they are left with less than what public policy requires. They know little about the natural mother, her genetic makeup, and her psychological and medical history. Moreover, not even a superficial attempt is made to determine their awareness of their responsibilities as parents.

Worst of all, however, is the contract's total disregard of the best interests of the child. There is not the slightest suggestion that an inquiry will be made at any time to determine the fitness of the Sterns as custodial parents, of Mrs Stern as an adoptive parent, their superiority to Mrs Whitehead, or the effect on the child of not living with her natural mother.

This is the sale of a child, or, at the very least, the sale of a mother's right to her child, the only mitigating factor being that one of the purchasers is the father. Almost every evil that prompted the prohibition on the payment of money in connection with adoptions exists here.

The differences between an adoption and a surrogacy contract should be noted, since it is asserted that the use of money in connection with surrogacy does not pose the risks found where money buys an adoption. Katz 'Surrogate Motherhood and the Baby-Selling Laws', 20 *Colum JL & Soc Probs* 1 (1986).

First, and perhaps most important, all parties concede that it is unlikely that surrogacy will survive without money. Despite the alleged selfless motivation of surrogate mothers, if there is no payment, there will be no surrogates, or very few. That conclusion contrasts with adoption; for obvious reasons, there remains a steady supply, albeit insufficient, despite the prohibitions against payment. The adoption itself, relieving the natural mother of the financial burden of supporting an infant, is in some sense the equivalent of payment.

Second, the use of money in adoptions does not *produce* the problem – conception occurs, and usually the birth itself, before illicit funds are offered. With surrogacy, the 'problem', if one views it as such, consisting of the purchase of a woman's procreative capacity, at the risk of her life, is caused by and originates with the offer of money.

Third, with the law prohibiting the use of money in connection with adoptions, the built-in financial pressure of the unwanted pregnancy and the consequent support obligation do not lead the mother to the highest paying, ill-suited, adoptive parents. She is just as well-off surrendering the child to an approved agency. In surrogacy, the highest bidders will presumably become the adoptive parents regardless of suitability, so long as payment of money is permitted.

Fourth, the mother's consent to surrender her child in adoptions is revocable, even after surrender of the child, unless it be to an approved agency, where by regulation there are protections against an ill-advised surrender. In surrogacy, consent occurs so early that no amount of advice would satisfy the potential mother's need, yet the consent is irrevocable.

The main difference, that the unwanted pregnancy is unintended while the situation of the surrogate mother is voluntary and intended, is really not significant. Initially, it produces stronger reactions of sympathy for the mother whose pregnancy was unwanted than for the surrogate mother, who 'went into this with her eyes wide open'. On reflection, however, it appears that the essential evil is the same, taking advantage of a woman's circumstances (the unwanted pregnancy or the need for money) in order to take away her child, the difference being one of degree.

In the scheme contemplated by the surrogacy contract in this case, a middleman, propelled by profit, promotes the sale. Whatever idealism may have motivated any of the participants, the profit motive predominates, and ultimately governs the transaction. The demand for children is great and the supply small. The availability of contraception, abortion, and the greater willingness of single mothers to bring up their children has led to a shortage of babies offered for adoption . . . The situation is ripe for the entry of the middleman who will bring some equilibrium into the market by increasing the supply through the use of money.

Intimated, but disputed, is the assertion that surrogacy will be used for the benefit of the rich at the expense of the poor. See eg Radin 'Market Inalienability', 100 *Harv L Rev* 1849, 1930 (1987). In response it is noted that the Sterns are not rich and the Whiteheads not poor. Nevertheless, it is clear to us that it is unlikely that surrogate mothers will be as proportionately numerous among those women in the top twenty percent income bracket as among those in the bottom twenty percent. *Ibid*. Put differently, we doubt that infertile couples in the low-income bracket will find upper-income surrogates.

In any event, even in this case one would not pretend that disparate wealth does not play a part simply because the contrast is not the dramatic 'rich versus poor'. At the time of the trial, the Whiteheads' net assets were probably negative – Mrs Whitehead's own sister was foreclosing on a second mortgage. Their income derived from Mr Whitehead's labors. Mrs Whitehead is a homemaker, having previously held part-time jobs. The Sterns are both professionals, she a medical doctor, he a biochemist. Their combined income when both were working was about $89,500 a year and their assets sufficient to pay for the surrogacy contract arrangements.

The point is made that Mrs Whitehead *agreed* to the surrogacy arrangement, supposedly fully understanding the consequences. Putting aside the issue of how compelling her need for money may have been, and how significant her understanding of the consequences, we suggest that her consent is irrelevant. There are, in a civilized society, some things that money cannot buy. In America, we decided long ago that merely because conduct purchased by money was 'voluntary' did not mean that it was good or beyond regulation and prohibition. *West Coast Hotel Co v Parrish, 300 US 379, 57 SCt 578, 81 L Ed 703* (1937). Employers can no longer buy labor at the lowest price they can bargain for, even though that labor is 'voluntary', 29 *USC* § 206 (1982), or buy women's labor for less money than paid to men for the same job, 29 *USC* § 206(d), or purchase the agreement of children to perform oppressive labor, 29 *USC* § 212, or purchase the agreement of workers to subject themselves to unsafe or unhealthful working conditions, 29 *USC* §§ 651 t 678. (Occupational Safety and Health Act of 1970.) There are, in short, values that society deems more important than granting to wealth whatever it can buy, be it labor, love or life. Whether this principle recommends prohibition of surrogacy, which presumably sometimes results in great satisfaction to all of the parties, is not for us to say. We note here only that, under existing law, the fact that Mrs Whitehead 'agreed' to the arrangement is not dispositive.

The long-term effects of surrogacy contracts are not known, but feared – the impact on the child who learns her life was bought, that she is the offspring of someone who gave birth to her only to obtain money; the impact on the natural mother as the full weight of her isolation is felt along with the full reality of the sale of her body and her child; the impact on the natural father and adoptive mother once they realize the consequences of their conduct. Literature in related areas suggests these are substantial considerations, although, given the newness of surrogacy, there is little information.

The surrogacy contract is based on principles that are directly contrary to the objectives of our laws. It guarantees the separation of a child from its mother; it looks to adoption regardless of suitability; it totally ignores the child; it takes the child from the mother regardless of her wishes and her maternal fitness; and it does all of this, it accomplishes all of its goals, through the use of money.

Beyond that is the potential degradation of some women that may result from this arrangement. In many cases, of course, surrogacy may bring satisfaction, not only to the infertile couple, but to the surrogate mother herself. The fact, however, that many women may not perceive surrogacy negatively but rather see it as an opportunity does not diminish its potential for devastation to other women.

In sum, the harmful consequences of this surrogacy arrangement appear to us all too palpable. In New Jersey the surrogate mother's agreement to sell her child is void. Its irrevocability infects the entire contract, as does the money that purports to buy it.

In England, is the agreement void on grounds of public policy or, if not, unenforceable? In two cases (*A v C* [1985] FLR 445 and 543 and *Re P (Minors) (Wardship: Surrogacy)* [1987] 2 FLR 421) the court offered its view on the validity of surrogacy agreements. In *Re P*, Sir John Arnold P said:

. . . One possible view about that matter is that there is, or may in certain circumstances be, an element concerning the surrogacy agreement which is repellent to proper ideas about the procreation of children, so as to make any such agreement one which should be rejected by law as being contrary to public policy. It is not necessary in this case, for the reasons which I have indicated, to come to any conclusion upon that point. The existence of the agreement is relevant to this extent, that plainly one of the factors which has to be taken into account in determining where the welfare of the children lies, is the factor of the character of the rival custodians who were put forward for consideration and it might be that the willingness of those persons to enter into a surrogacy agreement would reflect upon their moral outlook so adversely as to disqualify them as potential custodians at all, but I do not think that that factor enters into the present case.

In *A v C*, at first instance, ([1985] FLR 445), Comyn J stated:

. . . The agreement between the parties I hold as being against public policy. None of them can rely upon it in any way or enforce the agreement in any way. I need only give one of many grounds for saying this, namely that this was a purported contract for the sale and purchase of a child.

In the Court of Appeal ([1985] FLR 543), Ormrod LJ described the arrangement as 'most extraordinary and irresponsible, bizarre and unnatural' and 'a sordid commercial bargain'. He concluded that the arrangement was a 'wholly artificial situation from the very beginning which should never have happened and which no responsible adult should ever have allowed to happen'. Cumming-Bruce LJ described the arrangement in similar terms, '. . . a kind of baby-farming operation of a wholly distasteful and lamentable kind'; and 'a guilty bargain which should never have been made'; and a 'lamentable commercial transaction'. Stamp LJ confined his judgment to one sentence but could not resist describing the arrangement as 'this ugly little drama'.

In these cases the courts were not specifically considering the validity of the surrogacy agreements and the remarks were, therefore, no more than judicial comment. How would a court approach this issue if it had to face it squarely? It is likely that the court would in such a situation have endorsed the view of Comyn J at first instance in *A v C* that 'the agreement . . . I hold as being against public policy. None of them can rely upon it any way or enforce the agreement in any way.' Comyn J gives as 'one of the many grounds for saying this . . . that this was a purported contract for the sale and purchase of a child'. As we said earlier, the government in its 1987 White Paper indicated that legislation should put beyond the fact that surrogate arrangements were unenforceable in the English courts (see para 65). Subsequently, the Human Fertilisation and Embryology Act 1990 inserted a new s 1A into the Surrogacy Arrangements Act 1985 to give effect to this:

> **1A.** No surrogacy arrangement is enforceable by or against any of the persons making it.

The section applies to 'surrogate arrangements' as defined in the 1985 Act. We shall see shortly that the Act defines 'surrogate arrangements' widely but that it does not include agreements reached *after* the child is conceived and which are intended to result in the child being handed over by the surrogate mother. Such arrangements would remain governed by the common law.

2. Regulation of surrogate arrangements

English law only partially regulates surrogate arrangements. While it does not prohibit them, it does not seek to encourage them either. Unlike the regulatory framework created for medically assisted reproduction, surrogate arrangements are left largely alone by the law. As we have already seen, they are, of course, unenforceable in the courts. However, there is regulation in two ways.

A surrogate pregnancy using the genetic material of the commissioning couple will often require the involvement of medical personnel. The use of IVF or AI techniques to achieve the pregnancy will be licensed activities under the Human Fertilisation and Embryology Act 1990. As such, the HFEA may regulate the *use* of the techniques to achieve a surrogate pregnancy. HFEA's *Code of Practice* (1993) provides, in paragraph 3.19, as follows:

> 3.19 The application of assisted conception techniques to initiate a surrogate pregnancy should only be considered where it is physically impossible or highly undesirable for medical reasons for the commissioning mother to carry the child.

It follows from paragraph 3.19 that a licence-holder may be subject to sanction through variation or withdrawal of his licence if he assists in a surrogate pregnancy which is sought by the commissioning couple merely as a convenient (rather than a medically desirable) way of having a child.

Further, the Surrogacy Arrangements Act 1985 prohibits, through criminal sanction, certain activities carried out 'on a commercial basis'. The Surrogacy Arrangements Act 1985, ss 1-2 provide:

Meaning of 'surrogate mother', 'surrogacy arrangement' and other terms

1. (1) The following provisions shall have effect for the interpretation of this Act.

(2) 'Surrogate mother' means a woman who carries a child in pursuance of an arrangement –
(a) made before she began to carry the child, and
(b) made with a view to any child carried in pursuance of it being handed over to, and parental responsibility being met (so far as practicable) by, another person or other persons.

(3) An arrangement is a surrogacy arrangement if, were a woman to whom the arrangement relates to carry a child in pursuance of it, she would be a surrogate mother.

(4) In determining whether an arrangement is made with such a view as is mentioned in subsection (2) above regard may be had to the circumstances as a whole (and, in particular, where there is a promise or understanding that any payment will or may be made to the woman or for her benefit in respect of the carrying of any child in pursuance of the arrangement, to that promise or understanding).

(5) An arrangement may be regarded as made with such a view though subject to conditions relating to the handing over of any child.

(6) A woman who carries a child is to be treated for the purposes of subsection (2)(a) above as beginning to carry it at the time of the insemination or of the placing in her of an embryo, of an egg in the process of fertilisation or of sperm and eggs, as the case may be, that results in her carrying the child.

(7) 'Body of persons' means a body of persons corporate or unincorporate.

(8) 'Payment' means payment in money or money's worth.

(9) This Act applies to arrangements whether or not they are lawful.

Negotiating surrogacy arrangements on a commercial basis, etc.

2. (1) No person shall on a commercial basis do any of the following acts in the United Kingdom, that is –
(a) initiate or take part in any negotiations with a view to the making of a surrogacy arrangement,
(b) offer or agree to negotiate the making of a surrogacy arrangement, or
(c) compile any information with a view to its use in making, or negotiating the making of, surrogacy arrangements;
and no person shall in the United Kingdom knowingly cause another to do any of those acts on a commercial basis.

(2) A person who contravenes subsection (1) above is guilty of an offence; but it is not a contravention of that subsection –
(a) for a woman, with a view to becoming a surrogate mother herself, to do any act mentioned in that subsection or to cause such an act to be done, or
(b) for any person, with a view to a surrogate mother carrying a child for him, to do such an act or to cause such an act to be done.

(3) For the purposes of this section, a person does an act on a commercial basis (subject to subsection (4) below) if –
(a) any payment is at any time received by himself or another in respect of it, or
(b) he does it with a view to any payment being received by himself or another in respect of making, or negotiating or facilitating the making of, any surrogacy arrangement.
In this subsection 'payment' does not include payment to or for the benefit of a surrogate mother or prospective surrogate mother.

(4) In proceedings against a person for an offence under subsection (1) above, he is not to be treated as doing an act on a commercial basis by reason of any payment received by another in respect of the act if it is proved that –
(a) in a case where payment was received before he did the act, he did not do the act knowing or having reasonable cause to suspect that any payment had been received in respect of the act; and
(b) in any other case, he did not do the act with a view to any payment being received in respect of it.

In essence these provisions seek to outlaw commercial surrogacy agencies. A number of points arise.

First, the terms of s 2(1) are widely drafted so as to include any activity leading up to, and concluding with, a surrogate arrangement. Also, s 1 defines the terms 'surrogate mother' and 'surrogate arrangement' broadly, although, as noted earlier, the Act would not cover an arrangement reached *after* conception (s 1(2)(a) and 1(6)). Contrast the Infertility (Medical Procedures) Act 1984 (Vic), s 30(1)). Importantly, however, the legislation does not cover non-profit making agencies which the Warnock Committee had recommended should also be outlawed (see para 8.18 *supra*). The Act appears, therefore, to endorse the view that it is only the *exploitive* nature of commercial agencies which merits prohibition. The 1985 Act, therefore, stands in stark contrast to legislation in other countries which prohibits even non-profit-making agencies (see, for example, Infertility (Medical Procedures) Act 1984 (Vic), s 30).

Secondly, the Act does not prohibit the *making* of surrogate arrangements whether or not payment is made to the surrogate. Section 2(2) of the Act specifically excludes the surrogate mother and the commissioning couple from the provisions of the legislation and any payment to the surrogate mother is ignored in determining whether the arrangement was made 'on a commercial basis' (s 2(3)). Again, there is a contrast to be made here with legislation in other countries where (exceptionally) surrogacy itself is illegal (Surrogate Parenthood Act 1988, (Qd) ss 2 and 3), or surrogacy for reward is illegal (Infertility (Medical Procedures) Act 1984 (Vic), s 30). Indeed, the position under the 1985 Act stands in stark contrast to the provisions in England dealing with organ donation in the Human Organ Transplants Act 1989. That Act prohibits, and makes criminal, the giving or receiving of money in return for the donation of an organ for transplantation (see *infra*, ch 15). The difference must be based, if anything, on the avoidance of tainting any child born to a surrogate by the criminal conduct of the surrogate or commissioning parents (see Warnock Report, para 8.19). This danger is, of course, not present in situations covered by the Human Organ Transplants Act 1989.

Finally, the 1985 Act does not prevent medically assisted surrogacy arrangements unless the doctors engage in any of the activities (such as initiating or negotiating the arrangement) prohibited by s 2(1). Merely to provide medical assistance by, for example, providing IVF treatment does not fall within the Act's provisions even where the treatment is provided privately (and so the doctor is paid) or where the parties to the surrogacy arrangement have *themselves* negotiated a payment to the surrogate. The British Medical Association in its *Surrogacy Report* (1990) has issued guidelines for practitioners. In particular, the BMA anticipates that doctors will exercise 'extreme caution' before helping to achieve a surrogate pregnancy, and will only do so as a 'last resort' (*op cit* at p 6).

In addition to the provisions concerned with commercial agencies, the 1985 Act goes further in prohibiting advertising by, or for, a surrogate mother. Section 3 provides:

Advertisements about surrogacy

3. (1) This section applies to any advertisement containing an indication (however expressed) –
(a)   that any person is or may be willing to enter into a surrogacy arrangement or to negotiate or facilitate the making of a surrogacy arrangement, or
(b)   that any person is looking for a woman willing to become a surrogate mother or for persons wanting a woman to carry a child as a surrogate.
(2) Where a newspaper or periodical containing an advertisement to which this section applies is published in the United Kingdom, the proprietor, editor or publisher of the newspaper or periodical is guilty of an offence.
(3) Where an advertisement to which this section applies is conveyed by means of a

telecommunication system so as to be seen or heard (or both) in the United Kingdom, any person who in the United Kingdom causes it to be so conveyed knowing it to contain such an indication as is mentioned in subsection (1) above is guilty of an offence.

(4) A person who publishes or causes to be published in the United Kingdom an advertisement to which this section applies (not being an advertisement contained in a newspaper or periodical or conveyed by means of a telecommunication system) is guilty of an offence.

(5) A person who distributes or causes to be distributed in the United Kingdom an advertisement to which this section applies (not being an advertisement contained in a newspaper or periodical published outside the United Kingdom or an advertisement conveyed by means of a telecommunication system) knowing it to contain such an indication as is mentioned in subsection (1) above is guilty of an offence.

(6) In this section 'telecommunication system' has the same meaning as in the Telecommunications Act 1984.

This section has two effects. First, it makes it a criminal offence to publish an advertisement seeking a surrogate mother or offering to act as a surrogate mother in a newspaper or periodical (s 3(2)). The offence is committed by the proprietor, editor or publisher. An offence is also committed by the 'conveyor' of an advertisement through radio or television (s 3(3)) or otherwise, for example, where a shopkeeper places a notice in his window (s 3(5)).

Secondly, s 3 *may* also cover advertising by a potential surrogate mother or a commissioning couple. (You will recall that this occurred in *Re An Adoption Application* before the 1985 Act was passed.) Section 3 (unlike s 2) does not specifically exempt them from liability. They may, therefore, be accessories to the crimes of others committed under s 3. Also, the wording of s 3(3), 3(4) and 3(5) are sufficiently wide to cover their acts. It could well be said that they 'cause' an advertisement to be conveyed or to be published or to be distributed by *placing* the advertisement with the publisher. (Since these phrases do not appear in s 3(2) dealing with publication in a newspaper, the only liability in such a case would be as an accessory.)

3. Parental responsibility for the child

Here we are primarily concerned with the question of with whom the child born as a consequence of a surrogacy arrangement should live. Of course, the purpose of a surrogate arrangement is that the child should be handed over to the commissioning couple and live with them. If all the parties are in agreement, as we shall see, this is the most likely outcome. Sometimes, however, there may be disagreement: the surrogate mother may wish to keep the child or, though less likely, none of the parties may want the child where, for example, it is born disabled. In the language of the Children Act 1989 we are concerned here with who will have 'parental responsibility' for the child.

(a) Who are the child's parents?

We have already seen (*supra*, pp 815-819) how ss 27 to 29 of the Human Fertilisation and Embryology Act 1990 allocate parenthood when medically assisted reproduction occurs. Those provisions are equally applicable to surrogate pregnancies when IVF or AI is used.

(i) THE MOTHER

As a consequence, the surrogate mother will, in law, be the mother of any child born whether or not she is genetically related to the child. The woman of the commissioning couple will not be the mother even if her eggs were used during an IVF procedure.

(ii) THE FATHER: WHERE THE SURROGATE IS MARRIED

In all cases the surrogate mother's husband will be the father of the child unless he can prove he did not consent to the procedure. Again, the man of the commissioning couple will not be the father of the child even if his sperm is used for AI or IVF (s 28(4)).

(iii) THE FATHER: WHERE THE SURROGATE IS UNMARRIED

What, however, if the surrogate is unmarried? At common law, if the commissioning father's sperm is used he will be the father of the child. Hence, if the child is born after 'DIY' insemination or sexual intercourse, he will be the father since the 1990 Act does not affect the position.

However, if a doctor is involved the question arises whether s 28 alters the position. It will do so, as we saw earlier, if the surrogate and the commissioning male are receiving licensed treatment. This in turn depends upon whether the woman is being treated using the sperm of a man who is being treated *together* with her (s 4(1)). Clearly, we are concerned with the situation where the commissioning male's sperm is being used. But, can it be said that he and the surrogate are being treated *together*? It was argued above that to be treated *together* a couple must be seeking treatment with a view to bringing up the child together. Clearly, this is not the case with a surrogacy arrangement. Consequently, the provision of treatment must be licensed. The commissioning male's consent to the use of his sperm is required under Sch 3 of the 1990 Act and, by virtue of s 28(6)(a), when it is used in accordance with his consent he ceases in law to be the father. He is in effect considered to be, and dealt with under the Act, as a sperm donor. The common law position is, thus, reversed. (Section 28(3) does not rescue the situation by deeming him to be the father because (a) he is not being treated *together* with the surrogate and (b) his sperm is being used. Both are requirements for s 28(3) to apply (see *supra*, pp 818-819). It should be noted also that if the surrogate has a partner he also cannot be the child's father unless s 28(3) applies to him. It does not as he too is not being treated together with the surrogate since there is no intention for them to bring up the child together.) For a full discussion of the problems of parentage in surrogacy arrangements see, K Stern, 'The Regulation of Assisted Conception in England' (1994) 1 *European Journal of Health Law* (forthcoming).

(b) Allocating parental responsibility

Of course, to be in law the parents of the child at birth is not necessarily to determine with whom the child should live thereafter. (Contrast *Johnson v Calvert* (1993) 851 P 2d 776 (Cal Sup Ct) where the California Supreme Court equated 'parenthood' with who should have custody of a child born to a surrogate mother using the commissioning couple's embryo.) The English courts are required to act on the basis that 'the child's welfare [is] the court's paramount consideration' (Children Act 1989, s 1(1)). It may be that a child's 'best interests' dictate that 'parental responsibility' should be allocated elsewhere, for example, in the commissioning couple. It is to this issue that we now turn.

(i) WHERE THE PARTIES ARE AGREED

Where both the surrogate mother (and her husband or partner) and the commissioning couple are agreed that the child be handed over to be brought up by the commissioning couple, there are a number of legal mechanisms through which this may be achieved. First, the couple may seek to *adopt* the child; secondly, the couple may seek a 'parental order' under s 30 of the Human Fertilisation and Embryology Act 1990; and thirdly, the couple may invoke the court's *inherent jurisdiction* (probably through wardship in this type of case).

As regards adoption, the procedure and technicalities are discussed by Gillian Douglas in *Law, Fertility and Reproduction* (1991), pp 161-162:

> Where the surrogate mother is unmarried, or the pregnancy was achieved after sexual intercourse, or her husband did not consent to the artificial fertilisation procedure, so that the commissioning father is the putative father, he ranks as a relative of the child under section 72(1) of the Adoption Act 1976 and an adoption order could be made provided the child is at least 19 weeks old and at all times during the preceding 13 weeks has lived with the commissioning parents. A joint adoption order can only be made in favour of a married couple under section 14, so that cohabiting commissioning parents could not both be made legal parents. A single applicant can adopt a child under section 15, so that where the surrogacy had been undertaken for a single man, for example, that would not of itself prevent the order being made.
>
> Where the surrogate is married and the child resulted from artificial fertilisation techniques, with her husband's consent, the commissioning father would not be the legal father, but a stranger to the child in law. The child would accordingly have to have lived with the commissioning parents for at least 12 months, [s 13(1) and (2) Adoption Act 1976] but the situation is complicated by section 11(1) of the Adoption Act, which prohibits the placement of a child for adoption other than by a relative, unless arranged by an adoption agency or authorised by an order of the High Court. Contravention of the section is a criminal offence, but it has been held that private placements can be sanctioned after the event by the High Court. Where a child has not been placed by an adoption agency, the applicant for adoption must notify the local authority, and they must report to the court on the suitability of the applicant and whether there has been a contravention of section 11. In all adoption applications, a reporting officer must be appointed to ensure proper parental agreement to the making of the order (including investigating the circumstances relevant to the agreement), and where the child's welfare seems to require it, a guardian *ad litem* must be appointed to safeguard the child's interests. It is likely that a guardian would be appointed when a surrogacy arrangement is revealed during an adoption application.

As Gillian Douglas points out, the effect of ss 27 to 29 of the Human Fertilisation and Embryology Act 1990 makes the adoption procedure a cumbersome one.

A second procedure is available under s 30 of the Human Fertilisation and Embryology Act 1990:

Parental orders in favour of gamete donors

30. (1) The court may make an order providing for a child to be treated in law as the child of the parties to a marriage (referred to in this section as "the husband" and "the wife") if –

(a) the child has been carried by a woman other than the wife as the result of the placing in her of an embryo or sperm and eggs or her artificial insemination,

(b) the gametes of the husband or the wife, or both, were used to bring about the creation of the embryo, and

(c) the conditions in subsection (2) to (7) below are satisfied.

(2) The husband and the wife must apply for the order within six months of the birth of the child or, in the case of a child born before the coming into force of this Act, within six months of such coming into force.

(3) At the time of the application and of the making of the order –

(a) the child's home must be with the husband and the wife, and

(b) the husband or the wife, or both of them, must be domiciled in a part of the United Kingdom or in the Channel Islands or the Isle of Man.

(4) At the time of the making of the order both the husband and the wife must have attained the age of eighteen.

(5) The court must be satisfied that both the father of the child (including a person who is the father by virtue of section 28 of this Act), where he is not the husband, and the woman who carried the child have freely, and with full understanding of what is involved, agreed unconditionally to the making of the order.

(6) Subsection (5) above does not require the agreement of a person who cannot be found or is incapable of giving agreement and the agreement of the woman who carried the child is ineffective for the purposes of that subsection if given by her less than six weeks after the child's birth.

(7) The court must be satisfied that no money or other benefit (other than for expenses reasonably incurred) has been given or received by the husband or the wife for or in consideration of –

(a)   the making of the order,

(b)   any agreement required by subsection (5) above,

(c)   the handing over of the child to the husband and the wife, or

(d)   the making of any arrangements with a view to the making of the order,

unless authorised by the court. . . .

(11) Subsection (1)(a) above applies whether the woman was in the United Kingdom or elsewhere at the time of the placing in her of the embryo or the sperm and eggs or her artificial insemination.

This provision was introduced during the course of the Bill through Parliament in 1990. It is designed to allow a commissioning couple to obtain a 'parental order' where they are wholly or partially genetically related to a child born to a surrogate mother. Six conditions must be fulfilled before an order may be made.

1.   The child must be genetically related to at least one of the commissioning couple;

2.   The surrogate mother (and her husband or partner) must consent to the parental order (unless they cannot be found) and their consents must be given no earlier than six weeks after the birth;

3.   The commissioning couple must be married to each other and both must be at least 18;

4.   The application must be made within six months of the birth of the child or for births before the Act came into force within six months of that;

5.   No money or other benefit other than expenses must have been given or received by the commissioning couple unless authorised by the court;

6.   The child must be living with the commissioning couple at the time of the application and when the court makes the order;

7.   The commissioning couple must not be domiciled abroad.

Section 30 will undoubtedly be used in the future when all the parties are agreed. It should be noticed, however, that its scope is limited. The commissioning couple must be *married*. Other legal mechanisms will need to be used where the commissioning couple are not married or where one person acts alone to make the surrogate arrangement. The condition that the child be living with the commissioning couple at the time of the application and the making of the order may also be problematic.

It is clear that an order under s 30 will, for all intents and purposes, have the same effect as an adoption order in favour of the commissioning couple. The Parental Orders for Gamete Donors Regulations 1993 (draft) apply with appropriate modifications many of the provisions in the Adoption Act 1976 to s 30 applications and orders. For example, the proceedings for a s 30 order will be in private, a guardian ad litem will be appointed for the child and the court will have a duty to safeguard and promote the welfare of the child. Further, a parental order will confer on the commissioning couple parental rights and duties relating to the child and will extinguish those of the surrogate mother and her husband or partner.

Significantly, the regulations do not apply s 51 of the Adoption Act 1976 to children the subject of a 'parental order'. Hence, these children will not have the right at 18 to discover the identity of their surrogate mother. Perhaps this is no surprise, since the child's right under the Adoption Act is the right to discover her *genetic* origins. Children subject to a 'parental order' under s 30 will have been brought up by one (if not both) of their genetic parents.

How, then, will a court acting in the child's 'best interests' determine with whom a child should live? As we have seen, the determination of who should bring up the child is not a matter for the parties to agree amongst themselves. As Sir John Arnold P put it in *Re P (minors)(wardship: surrogacy)* [1987] 2 FLR 421:

> ... [T]he court's duty is to decide the case, taking into account as the first and paramount consideration, the welfare of the child or children concerned and if that consideration leads the court to override any agreement that there may be in the matter, then that court is fully entitled to do.

Even though the parties are agreed that the commissioning parents should bring up the child, the court may choose to disregard the terms of the agreement and place the child with another.

The following case concerned what was said to be the first commercial surrogacy agreement in England. It illustrates that even where all the parties to the agreement are content with who should have custody, the court in the exercise of its wardship jurisdiction must make the ultimate decision, based on its perception of the child's 'best interests'. The case also illustrates the judiciary's uneasiness with the publication of the names of the parties involved – in this case at least the surrogate mother was already well-known – and as we shall see, the judge made an order restraining the press from discovering or publishing the names of the parties.

Re C (A Minor) [1985] FLR 846 (Fam Div)

Latey J: The baby's father is Mr A, as I will describe him. He and his wife, Mrs A, are in their 30s and have been married for several years. Mr A is fertile. Mrs A has a congenital defect which prevents her from ever having children. Both dearly wanted a baby. In their home country adoption is slow and a child is usually aged 4 to 5 at adoption. They wanted a baby to bring up from birth. They made inquiries.

In 1983 the father contacted an agency in America and entered into a contract whereby he paid a sum of money and the agency undertook to find a surrogate mother to bear his child. She also would be paid. In England there is a similar agency. A surrogate mother was found.

In 1984 the father came to England, by arrangement, for the sole purpose of providing seminal fluid for insemination of the surrogate mother. It was so arranged that he provided his semen to a qualified nurse and it was introduced into the mother. The father and the mother did not meet and have not met. The insemination was successful, resulting in conception.

The agreement was that the baby on birth was to be handed over to the father and his wife, Mr and Mrs A, to be theirs to care for and bring up.

The father and his wife came to this country in anticipation of the birth and on Friday, 4 January, the baby was born. On the same day the local authority, the London Borough of Barnet, obtained a place of safety order. The baby remained at the hospital, cared for by the nurses.

On Tuesday, 8 January 1985 the father issued a wardship summons. On the same evening there was a hearing before me, when the father was represented by counsel and solicitors, and the London Borough of Barnet was represented by counsel and its legal department. The father and his wife were present.

At that time the social services department had already carried out a good deal of its inquiries, but still had some to complete. It was a fairly lengthy hearing and I made interim orders and directions.

The social services department thought that they could conclude their inquiries by Friday last and I directed that the matter be restored for hearing on that day. They did complete their inquiries and the matter was heard on Friday last.

The inquiries which were deposed to in evidence, were very full and covered every relevant matter. They established that the father, Mr A, is the natural father of the baby; that the natural mother has voluntarily relinquished all parental rights in the child; and that she in fact left the baby in hospital some hours after birth and has not seen her since. The evidence deals in the fullest details with Mr and Mrs A and their health, living and family circumstances and their suitability as parents, about which I will say a little more in a moment.

In the result, the local authority supports to the full the application that the baby be given into the care and upbringing of Mr and Mrs A.

First and foremost, and at the heart of the prerogative jurisdiction in wardship, is what is best for the child or children concerned. That and nothing else. Plainly, the methods used to produce a child as this baby has been, and the commercial aspects of it, raise difficult and delicate problems of ethics, morality and social desirability. These problems are under active consideration elsewhere.

Are they relevant in arriving at a decision on what now and, so far as one can tell, in the future is best for this child? If they are relevant, it is incumbent on the court to do its best to evaluate and balance them.

In my judgment, however, they are not relevant. The baby is here. All that matters is what is best for her now that she is here and not how she arrived. If it be said (though it has not been said during these hearings) that because the father and his wife entered into these arrangements it is some indication of their unsuitability as parents, I should reject any such suggestion. If what they did was wrong (and I am not saying that it was), they did it in total innocence.

It follows that the moral, ethical and social considerations are for others and not for this court in its wardship jurisdiction.

So, what is best for this baby? Her natural mother does not ask for her. Should she go into Mr and Mrs A's care and be brought up by them? Or should some other arrangement be made for her, such as long-term fostering with or without adoption as an end?

The factors can be briefly stated. Mr A is the baby's father and he wants her, as does his wife. The baby's mother does not want her. Mr and Mrs A are a couple in their 30s. They are devoted to each other. They are both professional people, highly qualified. They have a very nice home in the country and another in a town. Materially they can give the baby a very good upbringing. But, far more importantly, they are both excellently equipped to meet the baby's emotional needs. They are most warm, caring, sensible people, as well as highly intelligent. When the time comes to answer the child's questions, they will be able to do so with professional advice if they feel they need it. Looking at this child's well-being, physical and emotional, who better to have her care? No one.

Accordingly, the orders which I made on Friday evening are that the wardship will continue until further notice; the care and control of the baby is committed to Mr and Mrs A until further order; on their undertaking to return the child to the jurisdiction if the court should so order (an unlikely contingency in this case) there is leave for them to take her to live outside the jurisdiction. There are further orders that RSC Ord 63, r 4 shall not apply, and that no one may search for, inspect or take a copy of any of the documents filed in these proceedings without leave of the court; and an order to similar effect regarding the documents in the possession of the social services department, again without leave of the court.

I also approved arrangements for the immediate handover of the baby to Mr and Mrs A. These were worked out with the object, amongst others, of avoiding the identification of Mr and Mrs A. . . .

Finally, I issued a specific order that there must be no disclosure or publicity which *might* (and I stress that word) lead to the identification of Mr and Mrs A. The reasons for this are or should be self-evident. Is this baby to grow into childhood, adolescence and adulthood with the finger pointed at her as 'This is the girl who . . . ' It is unthinkable that it should be so. Were it otherwise the injury to her mental and emotional heath might be grave indeed. The wardship continues and with it that specific order. Any breach of it would be a very serious contempt.

It is inconceivable that leave ever will be given to publish the identities of Mr and Mrs A. That being so, it would be kind and compassionate to discontinue any inquiries which may be on foot and leave this couple to bring up their child in peace and quietness of mind.

(ii) WHERE THE PARTIES ARE NOT AGREED

Difficulties may arise, where the surrogate mother refuses to surrender the custody of the child to the commissioning couple, as in the following cases: *A v*

C (custody to surrogate); *Baby M* (custody to commissioning parents); *Re P (Minors)* (custody to surrogate). Here, of course, the s 30 procedure is not available because the surrogate mother is refusing to consent. While adoption is possible if the court takes the view that she is unreasonably withholding her consent, these types of dispute are most likely to be raised under the court's inherent jurisdiction.

This situation looks the most difficult to resolve since there is a 'tug of war' between the parties to the agreement for the child. A judicial determination of what are the child's best interests will not necessarily result in any particular party to the agreement obtaining parental responsibility. The attitude of Comyn J and the Court of Appeal in *A v C* – which can only be described as open antagonism towards the commissioning father – might not be so likely now.

The American case of *Baby M*, the facts of which we have already seen, illustrates how the court can perceive the child's best interests as lying with the commissioning parents and not with the surrogate who is the natural mother of the child.

In the Matter of Baby M (1988) 537 A 2d 1227 (NJ Sup Ct)

Wilentz CJ: Having decided that the surrogacy contract is illegal and unenforceable, we now must decide the custody question without regard to the provisions of the surrogacy contract that would give Mr Stern sole and permanent custody. (That does not mean the existence of the contract and the circumstances under which it was entered may not be considered to the extent deemed relevant to the child's best interests.) With the surrogacy contract disposed of, the legal framework becomes a dispute between two couples over the custody of a child produced by the artificial insemination of one couple's wife by the other's husband. . . . The applicable rule given these circumstances is clear: the child's best interests determine custody.

We note again that the trial court's reasons for determining what were the child's best interests were somewhat different from ours. It concluded that the surrogacy contract was valid, but that it could not grant specific performance unless to do so was in the child's best interests. The approach was that of a Chancery judge, unwilling to give extraordinary remedies unless they well served the most important interests, in this case, the interests of the child. While substantively indistinguishable from our approach to the question of best interests, the purpose of the inquiry was not the usual purpose of determining custody, but of determining a contractual remedy.

. . . The question of custody in this case, as in practically all cases, assumes the fitness of both parents, and no serious contention is made in this case that either is unfit. The issue here is which life would be better for Baby M, one with primary custody in the Whiteheads or one with primary custody in the Sterns.

The circumstances of this custody dispute are unusual and they have provoked some unusual contentions. The Whiteheads claim that even if the child's best interests would be served by our awarding custody to the Sterns, we should not do so, since that will encourage surrogacy contracts – contracts claimed by the Whiteheads, and we agree, to be violative of important legislatively-stated public policies. Their position is that in order that surrogacy contracts be deterred, custody should remain in the surrogate mother unless she is unfit, regardless of the best interests of the child. We disagree. Our declaration that this surrogacy contract is unenforceable and illegal is sufficient to deter similar agreements. We need not sacrifice the child's best interests in order to make that point sharper . . . Some of Mrs Whitehead's alleged character failings, as testified to by experts and concurred in by the trial court, were demonstrated by her actions brought on by the custody crisis. For instance, in order to demonstrate her impulsiveness, those experts stressed the Whiteheads' flight to Florida with Baby M; to show her willingness to use her children for her own aims, they noted the telephone threats to kill Baby M and to accuse Mr Stern of sexual abuse of her daughter; in order to show Mrs Whitehead's manipulativeness, they pointed to her threat to kill herself; and in order to show her unsettled family life, they noted the innumerable moves from one hotel or motel to another in Florida. Furthermore, the argument continues, one of the most important factors, whether mentioned or not, in favor of custody in the Sterns is their continuing custody during the litigation, now having lasted for one-and-a-half years. The Whiteheads' conclusion is that had the trial court not given initial custody to the Sterns during the litigations, Mrs Whitehead not only would have demonstrated her perfectly acceptable personality – the general tenor of the opinion of experts was that her personality problems surfaced primarily in crises – but would also have been able to prove better her parental skills along with an even stronger bond than may now exist between her and Baby M. Had she not been limited to custody for four months, she could have proved all of these things much more persuasively through almost two years of custody.

The argument has considerable force. It is of course possible that the trial court was wrong in its initial award of custody. It is also possible that such error, if that is what it was, may have affected the outcome. We disagree with the premise, however, that in determining custody a court should decide what the child's best interests *would be* if some hypothetical state of facts had existed. Rather, we must look to what those best interests *are, today,* even if some of the facts may have resulted in part from legal error. The child's interests come first . . . The custody decision must be based on all circumstances, on everything that *actually* has occurred, on everything that is relevant to the child's best interests. Those circumstances include the trip to Florida, the telephone calls and threats, the substantial period of successful custody with the Sterns, and all other relevant circumstances. . . .

There were eleven experts who testified concerning the child's best interests, either directly or in connection with matters related to that issue. Our reading of the record persuades us that the trial court's decision awarding custody to the Sterns (technically to Mr Stern) should be affirmed . . .

Our custody conclusion is based on strongly persuasive testimony contrasting both the family life of the Whiteheads and the Sterns and the personalities and characters of the individuals. The stability of the Whitehead family life was doubtful at the time of the trial. Their finances were in serious trouble (foreclosure by Mrs Whitehead's sister on a second mortgage was in process). Mr Whitehead's employment, though relatively steady, was always at risk because of his alcoholism, a condition that he seems not to have been able to confront effectively. Mrs Whitehead had not worked for quite some time, her last two employments having been part-time. One of the Whiteheads' positive attributes was their ability to bring up two children, and apparently well, even in so vulnerable a household. Yet substantial question was raised even about that aspect of their home life. The expert testimony contained criticism of Mrs Whitehead's handling of her son's educational difficulties. Certain of the experts noted that Mrs Whitehead perceived herself as omnipotent and omniscient concerning her children. She knew what they were thinking, what they wanted, and she spoke for them. As to Melissa, Mrs Whitehead expressed the view that she alone knew what that child's cries and sounds meant. Her inconsistent stories about various things engendered grave doubts about her ability to explain honestly and sensitively to Baby M – and at the right time – the nature of her origin. Although faith in professional counseling is not a *sine qua non* of parenting, several experts believed that Mrs Whitehead's contempt for professional help, especially professional psychological help, coincided with her feelings of omnipotence in a way that could be devastating to a child who most likely will need such help. In short, while love and affection there would be, Baby M's life with the Whiteheads promised to be too closely controlled by Mrs Whitehead. The prospects for wholesome, independent psychological growth and development would be at serious risk.

The Sterns have no other children, but all indications are that their household and their personalities promise a much more likely foundation for Melissa to grow and thrive. There *is* a track record of sorts – during the one-and-a-half years of custody Baby M has done very well, and the relationship between both Mr and Mrs Stern and the baby has become very strong. The household is stable, and likely to remain so. Their finances are more than adequate, their circle of friends supportive, and their marriage happy. Most important, they are loving, giving, nurturing, and openminded people. They have demonstrated the wish and ability to nurture and protect Melissa, yet at the same time to encourage her independence. Their lack of experience is more than made up for by a willingness to learn and to listen, a willingness that is enhanced by their professional training, especially Mrs Stern's experience as a pediatrician. They are honest; they can recognize error, deal with it, and learn from it. They will try to determine rationally the best way to cope with problems in their relationship with Melissa. When the time comes to tell her about her origins, they will probably have found a means of doing so that accords with the best interests of Baby M. All in all, Melissa's future appears solid, happy, and promising with them.

Based on all of this we have concluded, independent of the trial court's identical conclusion, that Melissa's best interests call for custody in the Sterns . . .

It seems to us that given her predicament, Mrs Whitehead was rather harshly judged – both by the trial court and by some of the experts. She was guilty of a breach of contract, and indeed, she did break a very important promise, but we think it is expecting something well beyond normal human capabilities to suggest that this mother should have parted with her newly born infant without a struggle. Other than survival, what stronger force is there? We do not know of, and cannot conceive of, any other case where a perfectly fit mother was expected to surrender her newly born infant, perhaps forever, and was then told she was a bad mother because she did not. We know of no authority suggesting that the moral quality of her act in those circumstances should be judged by referring to a contract made before she became pregnant. We do not countenance, and would never countenance, violating a court order as Mrs Whitehead did, even a court order that is wrong; but her resistance to an order that she surrender her infant, possibly forever, merits a measure of understanding. We do not find it so clear that her efforts to keep her infant, when measured against the Sterns' efforts to take her away, make one, rather than the other, the wrongdoer. The Sterns suffered, but so did she. And if we go beyond suffering to an evaluation of the human stakes involved in the struggle, how much weight should be given to her nine months of pregnancy, the labor of childbirth, the risk to her life, compared to the payment of money, the anticipation of a child and the donation of sperm?

There has emerged a portrait of Mrs Whitehead, exposing her children to the media, engaging in negotiations to sell a book, granting interviews that seemed helpful to her, whether hurtful to Baby M or not, which suggests a selfish, grasping woman ready to sacrifice the interests of Baby M and her other children for fame and wealth. That portrait is a half-truth, for while it may accurately reflect what ultimately occurred, its implication, that this is what Mary Beth Whitehead wanted, is totally inaccurate, at least insofar as the record before us is concerned. There is not one word in that record to support a claim that had she been allowed to continue her possession of her newly born infant, Mrs Whitehead would have ever been heard of again; not one word in the record suggests that her change of mind and her subsequent fight for her child was motivated by anything other than love – whatever complex underlying psychological motivations may have existed.

We have a further concern regarding the trial court's emphasis on the Sterns' interest in Melissa's education as compared to the Whiteheads'. That this difference is a legitimate factor to be considered we have no doubt. But it should not be overlooked that a best-interest test is designed to create not a new member of the intelligentsia but rather a well-integrated person who might reasonably be expected to be happy with life. 'Best interests' does not contain within it any idealized lifestyle; the question boils down to a judgment, consisting of many factors, about the likely future happiness of a human being, *Fantony v Fantony* 21 *NJ* at 536, 122 *A* 2d 593. Stability, love, family happiness, tolerance, and, ultimately support of independence – all rank much higher in predicting future happiness than the likelihood of a college education. We do not mean to suggest that the trial court would disagree. We simply want to dispel any possible misunderstanding on the issue.

Even allowing for these differences, the facts, the experts' opinions, and the trial court's analysis of both argue strongly in favor of custody of the Sterns. Mary Beth Whitehead's family life, into which Baby M would be placed, was anything but secure – the quality Melissa needs most. And today it may be even less so. Furthermore, the evidence and expert opinion based on it reveal personality characteristics, mentioned above, that might threaten the child's best development. The Sterns promise a secure home, with an understanding relationship that allows nurturing and independent growth to develop together.

The court awarded custody to Mr and Mrs Stern.

The result reached in the *Baby M* case will not always be the court's solution. All will depend upon the court's view of the child's 'best interests'.

Re P (Minors) (Wardship: Surrogacy) [1987] 2 FLR 421 (Fam Div)

A woman offered her services as a surrogate mother to a married professional man who donated sperm by artificial insemination and agreed to pay a lump sum to adopt the child. During the pregnancy she began to have misgivings about giving up the child and when she had given birth to twins in October 1986 her disinclination hardened increasingly. After a period of indecision, and despite her concern and regret about disappointing the father and his wife, she decided to keep the children. She and the father independently approached the local authority who applied to the court to make the children wards of court and to deal with the matter. By the date of the hearing the twins had been cared for by their mother for 5 months.

Sir John Arnold P: What then are the factors the court should take into account? I have already mentioned on the side of Mrs P the matters which weigh heavily in the balance are the fact of her maternity, that she bore the children and carried them for the term of their gestation and that ever since she has conferred upon them the maternal care which they have enjoyed and has done so successfully. The key social worker in the case who has given evidence testifies to the satisfactory nature of the care which Mrs P has conferred upon the children and this assessment is specifically accepted by Mr B as being an accurate one. I start, therefore, from the position that these babies have bonded with their mother in a state of domestic care by her of a satisfactory nature and I now turn to the factors which are said to outweigh those advantages, so as to guide the court upon the proper exercise of the balancing function to the conclusion that the children ought to be taken away from Mrs P, and passed over, under suitable arrangements, to Mr and Mrs B. They are principally as follows. It is said, and said quite correctly, that the shape of the B family is the better shape of a family in which these children might be brought up, because it contains a father as well as a mother and that is undoubtedly true. Next, it is said that the material circumstances of the B family are such that they exhibit a far larger degree of affluence than can be demonstrated by Mrs P. That, also, is undoubtedly true.

Then it is said that the intellectual quality of the environment of the Bs' home and the stimulus which would be afforded to these babies, if they were to grow up in that home, would be greater than the corresponding features in the home of Mrs P. That is not a matter which has been extensively investigated, but I suspect that that is probably true. Certainly, the combined effect of the lack of affluence on the part of Mrs P and some lack of resilience to the disadvantages which that implies has been testified in the correspondence to the extent that I find Mrs P saying that shortage of resources leads to her sitting at home with little E and overeating, because she has no ability from a financial point of view to undertake anything more resourceful than that. Then it is said that the religious comfort and support which the Bs derive from their Church is greater than anything of that sort available to Mrs P. How far that is true, I simply do not know. I do know that the Bs are practising Christians and do derive advantages from that circumstance, but nobody asked Mrs P about that and I am not disposed to assume that she lacks that sort of comfort and support in the absence of any investigation by way of cross-examination to lay the foundations for such a conclusion. Then it is said, and there is something in this, that the problems which might arise from the circumstance that these children who are, of course, congenitally derived from the semen of Mr B and bear traces of Mr B's Asiatic origin would be more easily understood and discussed and reconciled in the household of Mr and Mrs B, a household with an Asiatic ethnic background, than they would be if they arose in relation to these children while they were situated in the home of Mrs P, which is in an English village and which has no non-English connections. Obviously that is expressed contingently as a factor, although there is no means by which the court can measure the likelihood or otherwise of the contingency which has regard to racial discrimination. The situation in which Mrs P lives is not, as it seems to me, likely to breed that sort of intolerance. She lives in a smallish country community, large in terms of a village but small in terms of a town, where there is very little penetration by any immigrant citizens, which does not seem to me to be a community in which racial discrimination is very likely, but it is a factor which contingently at least may have some importance.

Those are the particular matters which are put forward as counterweights to the advantages to which Mrs P can point, and additionally there is the matter to which I have already referred, that it is said that in the letter of mid-November 1986, Mrs P was, herself, recognising that the balance of advantage, which the court is required to consider for the reason I have indicated, operated in favour of the solution of placing the children with the Bs and taking them away from Mrs P, but I do not think that that last factor is of substantial importance. At the time when that letter was written there was, as independent evidence testifies, a prevalent state of things in which Mrs P was suffering from post-natal depression, or at least post-natal stress, so that her expressions of opinion were not likely to have been very reliable at that time. Secondly, any such opinion was expressed at a stage when the children were 1 month old and might not be valid in the circumstances such as now prevail. They are 5 months old and have consistently been looked after by their mother during that 5 months' period and, thirdly, the court is not only not bound, although it might be influenced, by such an expression of opinion, but is required in the due exercise of the jurisdiction to come to its own conclusion upon that topic.

As regards the other factors, they are, in the aggregate, weighty, but I do not think, having given my very best effort to the evaluation of the case dispassionately on both sides, that they ought to be taken to outweigh the advantages to these children of preserving the link with the mother to whom they are bonded and who has, as is amply testified, exercised over them a satisfactory level of maternal care, and accordingly it is, I think, the duty of the court to award the care and control of these babies to their mother.

One final point requires notice. Although *A v C* began as a dispute about custody of a child, eventually the commissioning father's claim was for access (what today would be a 'contact order' under the Children Act 1989) alone. This the Court of Appeal rejected. Ormrod LJ said (at 458):

> I can see absolutely no advantage to this child in continuing to be in contact with the father, except possibly a financial advantage to which I attach no significance whatever, in this case. If the father is to continue to turn up in the mother's house or to keep meeting her somewhere to take over this child, or to meet some member of her family to take over the child and return the child, the whole of this sordid story will be revived weekly or monthly as the case may be. The mother's position will be handicapped, and the handicapping of her position handicaps the child.

Cumming-Bruce LJ said (at 460-1):

> In my view, the effect of the access ordered by the judge must, inevitably, be to introduce such a disruptive factor into the mother's emotional life that it is bound to have an adverse effect upon the boy. The boy's interest in this case is identified with the mother's interest, and the boy must be given a mother free from the threat of repeated confrontation with a man with whom she has never had any sort of relationship at all, save one of sordid pecuniary advantage. In my view, any advantage that the father could confer on the child is wholly outbalanced and obviously outbalanced by the disadvantage to the child of being brought up by the mother, who is subject to such a dangerous and persistent reminder of an episode in her life which, though she will never forget it, must be kept as completely in the background as possible.

It is interesting to note that in the *Baby M* case where, by contrast, custody was awarded to the commissioning parents, the Supreme Court of New Jersey remitted the issue of access by the surrogate mother, Mary Beth Whitehead, to the trial court. The court observed:

> We have decided that Mrs Whitehead is entitled to visitation at some point, and that question is not open to the trial court on this remand. The trial court will determine what kind of visitation shall be granted to her, with or without conditions, and when and under what circumstances it should commence. . . .
> While probably unlikely, we do not deem it unthinkable that, the major issues having been resolved, the parties' undoubted love for this child might result in a good faith attempt to work out the visitation themselves, in the best interests of their child.

It seems most unlikely that a court would make a 'contact order' in favour of a surrogate mother if it were minded to grant the commissioning parents parental responsibility.

(iii) WHERE NONE OF THE PARTIES WANTS THE CHILD

Difficulties are also posed where the parties are agreed that, because it has transpired that the child has been born disabled, neither party should be obliged to have custody. This problem is not resolved merely by saying 'parental responsibility' is inalienable, even though this is true (Children Act 1989 s 2(9)). This begs the question who the parents should be? The court will determine who should have parental responsibility and a 'residence order' on the 'best interests' approach. In doing so, the court will clearly have regard to the fact that the child is unwanted by the parties to the agreement. It may well be in such a case that the child's best interests lie elsewhere than living with any of the parties to the agreement. Adoption or long-term fostering to third parties may be the most likely outcome in this sort of case.

Chapter 12

Abortion

Historical background

Professor Bernard Dickens in his book *Abortion and the Law* (1966), pp 20-28 sets the scene.

The position at common law

. . . [B]ecause the offence was of ecclesiastical cognisance . . . the writings of authorities on English criminal law have few references to abortion. The protection the Common Law afforded to human life certainly extended to the unborn child but whether abortion (ie after quickening) amounted to homicide or a lesser offence is not clear beyond doubt from the authorities, and possibly altered at different periods. Bracton, writing in the early part of the thirteenth century said that abortion after animation was homicide. Furthermore, George Crabbe alleges this to have been the position long before; 'If, in Bracton's time, anyone struck a pregnant woman so as to cause abortion, it was homicide, after the foetus was formed. This appears to have been the law in the time of the Saxons.'

An epitome of Bracton, written near the end of the thirteenth century by Fleta is more explicit. His chapter 'De Homocidio' asserts 'He, too, in strictness is a homicide who has pressed upon a pregnant woman or has given her poison or has struck her in order to procure an abortion or to prevent conception, if the foetus was already formed and quickened, and similarly he who has given or accepted poison with the intention of preventing procreation or conception. A woman also commits homicide if, by a potion or the like, she destroys a quickened child in her womb.'

Later authorities, however, do not follow this view, and Coke while quoting Bracton and mentioning Fleta, nevertheless denies homicide. 'If a woman be quick with childe (sic), and by a Potion or otherwise Killeth it in her wombe; or if a man beat her whereby the child (sic) dieth in her body, and she is delivered of a dead childe, this is a great misprision, and no murder; but if the childe be borne alive, and dieth of the Potion, battery or other cause, this is murder; for in law it is accounted a reasonable creature, in *rerum natura*, when it is born alive..

Coke then demonstrates that a man is accessory to murder who counsels a pregnant woman to kill the child when it is born and continues, 'and yet at the time of the commandment, or counsel, no murder could be committed of the childe in *utero matris.*'

The consequence of this 'great misprision' is not described, but Hawkins wrote in 1716 that the procuring of the abortion of a quick child amounts to a Common Law misdemeanour and is murder if the child is born alive but dies in consequence of its premature birth, or of the means employed.

Blackstone, in his *Commentaries on the Laws of England* (1765) suggests that manslaughter was a possible interpretation of Bracton's characterisation of abortion. He wrote 'Life . . . begins in contemplation of law as soon as an infant is able to stir in the mother's womb. For if a woman is quick with child, and by a potion or otherwise, killeth it in her womb; or if any one beat her, whereby the child dieth in her body, and she is delivered of a dead child; this, though not murder, was by the antient (sic) law homicide or manslaughter (Bracton). But Sir Edward Coke doth not look upon this offence in quite so atrocious a light, but merely as a heinous misdemenor.'

That Blackstone should translate as 'a heinous misdemenor' what Coke earlier called 'a great misprision' may suggest the contemporary evaluation of the crime of abortion, as the law of misprision was well known to Blackstone. In his *Commentaries* he wrote 'Misprisions . . . are, in the acceptance of our law, generally understood to be all such high offences as are under the degree of capital, but nearly bordering thereon.' His rejection of this word to describe Coke's view suggests that while the ancient law regarded abortion as homicide or manslaughter, the contemporary view was that it was not a capital offence, nor even close thereto. After classifying misprisions into negative and positive, the latter consisting in the commission of something which ought not to be done, he continued 'Misprisions, which are merely positive, are generally denominated contempts, or high misdemeanors' and are usually punishable with fines and imprisonment.

Blackstone does not adopt the modern division of crimes into felonies and misdemeanours, but draws the distinction 'A crime or misdemeanour, is an act committed, or omitted, in violation of a public law, either foi bidding or commanding it. The general definition comprehends both crimes and misdemeanors; which, properly speaking, are mere synonymous terms; though, in common usage, the word "crimes" is made to denote such offences as are of a deeper and more atrocious dye; while smaller faults, and omissions of less consequence, are comprised under the gentler name of "misdemeanors" only.'

The *Commentaries on the Laws of England* were written by Blackstone for the lay public, and one may suppose that they were intended to be read according to the common usage, by which misdemeanours were 'smaller fruits, and omissions of less consequence'.

Nevertheless, even accepting that in Coke's period (1552-1634) abortion was an offence bordering on the capital, it would probably not have been prosecuted in the Common Law courts, as the ecclesiastical courts retained a criminal jurisdiction, and abortion was generally regarded as their province. However, the Reformation in the mid-sixteenth century challenged this jurisdiction, and in 1641, during the political turmoil immediately before the Civil War, Parliament abolished the senior ecclesiastical courts, the Court of High Commission and the Court of Delegates and these took into abolition with them the whole system of ecclesiastical courts. In these new circumstances, the Common Law courts would have dealt with the crime of abortion, giving the Common Law an impetus to develop its own principles, but at the Restoration in 1661 the ordinary ecclesiastical courts were re-established, and much of their old criminal jurisdiction revived, in theory. However, in fact, this was becoming increasingly diminished by the growing practice of making ecclesiastical offences statutory felonies, which took them into the Common Law courts. Moreover even where offences were not so removed from the ecclesiastical courts, the Common Law was generating its own concurrent growth, and it was not until 1803 that procuring abortion was made a statutory felony.

Blackstone in 1765 treated it as a Common Law misdemeanour, and support for this is provided in Chitty's *Criminal Law* (1816) which provides precedents from an indictment both under the 1803 Act and under the Common Law, where drawing on a case of 1802 EF is charged in the third count of the indictment with 'unlawfully . . . giving and administering to AE, . . . pregnant with child divers other . . . dangerous pills . . . with a wicked intent to cause and procure the said AE to miscarry . . .' However, references to the procuring of abortion as a crime at Common Law before it became a statutory offence in 1803 are not numerous, and are fairly late in date.

Statutory provisions

It appears that before 1803 the crime of abortion was a Common Law misdemeanour capable of commission by the pregnant woman herself and by other persons on her, but in either case only provided that the stage of 'quickening' had been reached. There are scanty records of the crime, because it was mainly regarded as a matter for the ecclesiastical courts and even where prosecuted in the Common Law courts it would be a rare case, as most abortion is committed before the stage of quickening has been reached (a widely accepted time being fourteen weeks after conception).

Lord Ellenborough's Act, receiving the Royal assent on June 24th 1803, for the first time placed the offence of criminal abortion on a statutory basis. Explaining that 'certain . . . heinous Offences, committed with Intent to destroy the Lives of his Majesty's Subjects by Poison, or with Intent to procure the miscarriage of Woman . . . have been of late also frequently committed; but no adequate Means have been hitherto provided for the Prevention and Punishment of such Offences', it provides in section 1 'That if any Person or Persons . . . shall wilfully, maliciously, and unlawfully administer to, or cause to be administered to or taken by any of his Majesty's Subjects, any deadly Poison, or other noxious and destructive Substance or Things, with Intent . . . thereby to cause and procure the Miscarriage of any Woman then being quick with child . . . then and in every such case the Person or Persons so offending, their Counsellors, Aiders, and Abettors, knowing of and privy to such Offence, shall be and are hereby declared to be Felons, and shall suffer Death.'

Although this section created a capital offence, introducing a more severe penalty than was available for the Common Law misdemeanour, it did not substantially alter the legal definition. Indeed it may have been more restricted, as it dealt only with the abortion of women quick with child, procured by use of 'poison, or other noxious and destructive substance or thing'. By the *ejusdem generis* rule of construction, 'thing' may have excluded instruments of manipulations or exercises.

There was no specific reference to a woman procuring her own abortion, but the words of the section probably included such a case, and the statute was directed to the punishment of such an offence, which was consistent with the position at Common Law. Nevertheless the infrequent prosecution of offenders prevented the matter from being clarified beyond doubt, and it may have been that where a woman procured her own abortion by another, she would be charged as an aider and abettor to that other's offence, or still be liable for the Common Law misdemeanour.

The great innovation of the 1803 Act was in section 2; abortion before quickening became a crime for the first time, and was a felony, although not punished as severely as abortion after quickening. The practical significance of this provision was widespread, as nearly all woman who procure their own abortion do so in the early months of pregnancy, before quickening.

Section 2 provides 'And whereas it may sometimes happen that Poison or some other noxious and destructive Substance or Thing may be given, or other means used, with Intent to procure Miscarriage or Abortion where the Woman may not be quick with Child at the Time, or it may not be proved that the Woman was quick with Child, be it therefore further enacted, that if any Person or Persons . . . shall wilfully and maliciously administer to, or cause to be administered to, or taken by any Woman, any Medicines, Drug, or other Substance or Thing whatsoever, or shall use or employ, or cause or procure to be used or employed, any Instrument or other Means whatsoever, with Intent thereby to cause or procure the Miscarriage of any Woman not being, or not being proved to be, quick with Child at the time of administering such Things or using such Means', that this shall be felonious, and punishable with fine, imprisonment, whipping or transportation for up to fourteen years.

This section is of interest for two main reasons. First, it adopts the ecclesiastical distinction between the *embryo formatus* and the *embryo informatus*, capital punishment being reserved only for the abortion of the former. Second, this is the only occasion upon which a statute has actually used the word 'abortion'. Other references here and in future statutes, are to 'miscarriage', and one may conclude from the fact that this section is the only one to contain the word, and also the first to deal with the termination of pregnancy before quickening, that the legislature assumed that termination before quickening was probably called 'abortion', and termination after quickening was described as 'procuring a miscarriage'. This linguistic distinction does not appear in Lord Lansdowne's Act of 1828.

This Act, repealing the 1803 Act, preserved the ecclesiastical distinction, and provided in section 8 'That if any Person, with Intent to procure the Miscarriage of any Woman then being quick with Child, unlawfully and maliciously shall administer to her, or cause to be taken by her, any Poison or other noxious Thing, or shall use any Instrument or other Means whatever with the Intent, every such Offender, and every Person counselling, aiding or abetting such Offender, shall be guilty of Felony, and being convicted thereof, shall suffer Death as a Felon; and if any person, with Intent to procure the Miscarriage of any Woman not being or not being proved to be, then quick with Child, unlawfully and maliciously shall administer to her, or cause to be taken by her, any Medicine or other Thing, or shall use any Instrument or other Means whatever with the like Intent, every such Offender, and every Person counselling, aiding or abetting such Offender, shall be guilty of Felony.' The punishment was imprisonment, transportation or whipping.

The 1828 Act is more explicit than the 1803 Act on the question of whether an unaided woman procuring, or attempting to procure her own abortion, is covered by the Act, but the same presumption of inclusion may be made, although the uncertainty must be recognised. No authority has suggested her exclusion, and apart from introducing slightly more lenient punishments for abortion before quickening, the 1828 Act made little change to the statutory position. In any event a woman could be indicted as an accessory before the fact to an abortion committed upon herself, and to an operation performed upon her with like intent before quickening.

The words 'any woman not being, or not being proved to be, then quick with Child' in the Acts of 1803 and 1828, probably relate to the method of determining the state of pregnancy, ie to see if the embryo was *formatus* or *informatus*. The same method was adopted where a woman liable to sentence of death for any offence pleaded her pregnancy as a reason why sentence should not be passed upon her in accordance with law. A Jury of Matrons was sworn in, composed of twelve married women then present in court, and these examined the woman to see if she was 'quick with Child'. Medical aid could be sought to ensure a true verdict, but it appears that women were reluctant to sit; before the court announced that a Jury of Matrons was to be empanelled the doors of the court were locked, to prevent them from leaving. Their reluctance may have been justified in that it may not have been clear at the time just what they were deciding.

If a woman has quickened, the position and the consequences are clear; but if she has been found not to be quick with child, this may be because her pregnancy is not sufficiently advanced, or because she is not pregnant. This latter condition could have affected the position.

In *R v Scudder* [(1828) 1 Mood CC 216], a case under section 2 of the 1803 Act, but equally applicable to section 13 of the 1828 Act, which used identical words, ie 'any woman not being, or not being proved to be, quick with child', it was held a complete answer to an indictment for abortion before quickening, to show that the woman was not pregnant. This judgment was, however, at variance with *R v Phillips* [(1811) 3 Camp 76], where Lawrence J said 'It is immaterial whether . . . or not it (savin) was capable of procuring abortion, or even whether the woman was actually with child; if the prisoner believed at the time that it would procure abortion, and administered it with that intent, the case is within the Statute.' This judgment is consistent with the words of the Acts of 1803 and 1828, but interprets simply a division between women who have quickened and those who have not, without distinguishing whether the latter are pregnant or not. This lack of distinction assimilates the *embryo informatus* to the absence of any embryo at all, which is inconsistent with the theological conditioning of the law.

The Offences Against the Person Act, 1837 did not adopt the distinction between women quick or not quick with child, and therefore the case of *R v Wycherley* [(1838) 8 C & P 262] can reveal an issue of exclusively academic interest. In this case, where a surgeon was aiding a Jury of Matrons after a verdict of guilty of murder Guerney B distinguished for him "Quick with Child" as having conceived. "With quick Child" is when the child has quickened.' Applying this definition to the Acts of 1803 and 1828, it could be said that the capital offence was committed in the case of a pregnant woman, the less serious offence relating to a woman who was not pregnant. In terms of medical knowledge the critical distinction is between pregnancy and non-pregnancy, and this legal division might therefore have been rational. 'Quickening' is merely a change in the position of the uterus, and is not evidence of animate life coming to the foetus, which might justify the greater protection provided by the greater punishment.

The Offences Against the Person Act, 1837 not only abandoned the distinction between the *embryo formatus* and the *embryo informatus* in applying its sanction, but did not distinguish a pregnant woman from one who was not. It provided in section 6 'That whosoever, with Intent to procure the Miscarriage of any Woman, shall unlawfully administer to her or cause to be taken by her any Poison or other noxious Thing, or shall unlawfully use any Instrument or other Means whatsoever with the like Intent, shall be guilty of Felony.' The punishment was transportation or imprisonment, this being one of Lord John Russell's reform measures abolishing the death sentence.

There was still no express reference to a woman who procured her own abortion, but there was no doubt that the Act was intended and understood to include her within its ambit. An early draft of the section had distinguished the position of such a woman from that of another person charged with procuring her abortion, in whose case there was a requirement of proof of pregnancy. Lord Lyndhurst's criticisms of this requirement prevailed to omit this from the final draft.

One may consider the use of the word 'unlawfully' at this stage in the development of the law relating to abortion. The 1803 Act used the expression 'wilfully, maliciously, and unlawfully' to characterise acts of abortion performed after quickening, and 'wilfully and maliciously' for the offence committed before quickening. The 1828 Act used 'unlawfully and maliciously' for both cases. Neither of these Acts suggests when abortion could be lawful, and the 1837 Act is equally silent (as indeed is the current statute, passed in 1861). However, although one may dismiss the use of the formulae in early statutes as being part of the prolix style of draftsmanship then favoured, in 1837 the word may have had some distinctive purpose, however elusive. The Criminal Law Commissioners, commenting in 1846 that other countries' codes have this proviso, suggested the expediency of adding to the then existing law 'Provided that no act specified in the last preceding Article shall be punishable when such act is done in good faith with the intention of saving the life of the mother whose miscarriage is intended to be procured.' This proviso was later incorporated into the Infant Life (Preservation) Act, 1929 as a defence in child destruction prosecutions, but regarding abortion, no guidance was given on the meaning of the word 'unlawfully' until nearly a century after this recommended proviso, in the leading case of *R v Bourne* in 1938.

The present law

A. THE CRIME

The following statutory provisions create the criminal offences relating to abortion.

OFFENCES AGAINST THE PERSON ACT 1861

58. – Every woman, being with child, who, with intent to procure her own miscarriage, shall unlawfully administer to herself any poison or other noxious thing, or shall unlawfully use any instrument or other means whatsoever with the like intent and whosoever, with intent to procure the miscarriage of any woman, whether she be or not with child, shall unlawfully administer to her or cause to be taken by her any poison or other noxious thing, or shall unlawfully use any instrument or other means whatsoever with the like intent, shall be guilty of an offence, and being convicted thereof shall be liable to imprisonment.

59. – Whosoever shall unlawfully supply or procure any poison or other noxious thing, or any instrument or thing whatsoever, knowing that the same is intended to be unlawfully used or employed with intent to procure the miscarriage of any woman, whether she be or not be with child, shall be guilty of an offence, and being convicted thereof shall be liable to imprisonment for a term not exceeding five years.

B. THE LAWFUL ABORTION: THE ABORTION ACT 1967

1. Introduction

At Common Law there was thought to be no defence to conduct amounting to a crime under sections 58 and 59. Then, in 1938, Mr Bourne, a well-known surgeon, challenged this view.

R v Bourne [1939] 1 KB 687, [1938] 3 All ER 615 (CCC)

Macnaughten J: The evidence called on behalf of the Crown proved that on June 14, 1938, the defendant performed an operation on the girl in question at St Mary's Hospital, and thereby procured her miscarriage. The following facts were also proved: On April 27, 1938, the girl, who was then under the age of fifteen, had been raped with great violence in circumstances which would have been most terrifying to any woman, let alone a child of fourteen, by a man who was in due course convicted of the crime. In consequence of the rape the girl became pregnant. Her case was brought to the attention of the defendant, who, after examination of the girl, performed the operation with the consent of her parents.

The defence put forward was that, in the circumstances of the case, the operation was not unlawful. The defendant was called as a witness on his own behalf and stated that, after he had made careful examination of the girl and had informed himself of all the relevant facts of the case, he had come to the conclusion that it was his duty to perform the operation. He had satisfied himself that the girl was in fact pregnant in consequence of the rape committed on her. He had also satisfied himself that she had not been infected with venereal disease; if he had found that she was so infected, he would not have performed the operation, since in that case there would have been a risk that the operation would cause a spread of the disease. Nor would he have performed the operation if he had found that the girl was either feeble-minded or had what he called a 'prostitute mind', since in such cases pregnancy and child-birth would not be likely to affect a girl injuriously. He satisfied himself that she was a normal girl in every respect, though she was somewhat more mature than most girls of her age. In his opinion the continuance of the pregnancy would probably cause serious injury to the girl, injury so serious as to justify the removal of the pregnancy at a time when the operation could be performed without any risk to the girl and under favourable conditions.

The evidence of the defendant was supported and confirmed by Lord Horder, and also by Dr JR Rees, a specialist in medical psychology. Dr Rees expressed the view that, if the girl gave birth to a child, the consequence was likely to be that she would become a mental wreck. . . .

The charge against Mr Bourne is made under s 58 of the Offences Against the Person Act 1861, that he unlawfully procured the miscarriage of the girl who was the first witness in the case. It is a very grave crime, and judging by the cases that come before the Court it is a crime by no means uncommon. This is the second case at the present session of this Court where a charge has been preferred of an offence against this section, and I only mention the other case to show you how different the case now before you is from the type of case which usually comes before a criminal court. In that other case a woman without any medical skill or medical qualifications did what is alleged against Mr Bourne here; she unlawfully used an instrument for the purpose of procuring the miscarriage of a pregnant girl; she did it for money; *2l 5s* was her fee; a pound was paid on making the appointment, and she came from a distance to a place in London to perform the operation. She used her instrument, and, within an interval of time measured not by minutes but by seconds, the victim of her malpractice was dead on the floor. That is the class of case which usually comes before the Court.

The case here is very different. A man of the highest skill, openly, in one of our great hospittals, performs the operation. Whether it was legal or illegal you will have to determine, but he performs the operation as an act of charity, without fee or reward, and unquestionably believing that he was doing the right thing, and that he ought, in the performance of his duty as a member of a profession devoted to the alleviation of human suffering, to do it. That is the case that you have to try to-day. . . .

Nine years ago Parliament passed an Act called the Infant Life (Preservation) Act 1929 (19 & 20 Geo 5, c 34). Sect 1, sub-s 1, of that Act provides that 'any person who, with intent to destroy the life of a child capable of being born alive, by any wilful act causes a child to die before it has an existence independent of its mother, shall be guilty of felony, to wit, of child destruction, and shall be liable on conviction thereof on indictment to penal servitude for life: Provided that no person shall be found guilty of an offence under this section unless it is proved that the act which caused the death of the child was not done in good faith for the purposes only of preserving the life of the mother.' It is true, as Mr Oliver has said, that [the 1929 Act] provides for the case where a child is killed by a wilful act at the time when it is being delivered in the ordinary course of nature; but in my view the proviso that it is necessary for the Crown to prove that the act was not done in good faith for the purpose only of preserving the life of the mother is in accordance with what has always been the common law of England with regard to the killing of an unborn child. No such proviso is in fact set out in s 58 of the Offences Against the Person Act 1861; but the words of that section are that any person who 'unlawfully' uses an instrument with intent to procure miscarriage shall be guilty of felony. In my opinion the word 'unlawfully' is not, in that section, a meaningless word. I think it imports the meaning expressed by the proviso in s 1, sub-s 1, of the Infant Life (Preservation) Act 1929, and that s 58 of the Offences Against the Person Act 1861, must be read as if the words making it an offence to use an instrument with intent to procure a miscarriage were qualified by a similar proviso.

In this case, therefore, my direction to you in law is this – that the burden rests on the Crown to satisfy you beyond reasonable doubt that the defendant did not procure the miscarriage of the girl in good faith for the purpose only of preserving her life. If the Crown fails to satisfy you of that, the defendant is entitled by the law of this land to a verdict of acquittal. If, on the other hand, you are satisfied that what the defendant did was not done by him in good faith for the purpose only of preserving the life of the girl, it is your duty to find him guilty. It is said, and I think said rightly, that this is a case of great importance to the public and, more especially, to the medical profession; but you will observe that it has nothing to do with the ordinary case of procuring abortion to which I have already referred. In those cases the operation is performed by a person of no skill, with no medical qualifications, and there is no pretence that it is done for the preservation of the mother's life. Cases of that sort are in no way affected by the consideration of the question which is put before you to-day.

What then is the meaning to be given to the words 'for the purpose of preserving the life of the mother'? There has been much discussion in this case as to the difference between danger to life and danger to health. It may be that you are more fortunate than I am, but I confess that I have found it difficult to understand what the discussion really meant, since life depends upon health, and it may be that health is so gravely impaired that death results. A question was asked by the learned Attorney-General in the course of his cross-examination of Mr Bourne. 'I suggest to you, Mr Bourne', said the Attorney-General, 'that there is a perfectly clear line – there may be border-line cases – there is a clear line distinction between danger to health and danger to life.' The answer of Mr Bourne was: 'I cannot agree without qualifying it; I cannot say just yes or no. I can say there is a large group whose health may be damaged, but whose life almost certainly will not be sacrificed. There is another group at the other end whose life will be definitely in very great danger.' And then he adds: 'There is a large body of material between those two extremes in which it is not really possible to say how far life will be in danger, but we find, of course, that the health is depressed to such an extent that life is shortened, such as in cardiac cases, so that you may say that their life is in danger, because death might occur within measurable distance of the time of their labour.' If that view commends itself to you, you will not accept the suggestion that there is a clear line of distinction between danger to health and danger to life. Mr Oliver wanted you to give what he called a wide and liberal meaning to the words 'for the purpose of preserving the life of the mother'. I should prefer the word 'reasonable' to the words 'wide and liberal'. I think you should take a reasonable view of those words.

It is not contended that those words mean merely for the purpose of saving the mother from instant death. There are cases, we are told, where it is reasonably certain that a pregnant woman will not be able to deliver the child which is in her womb and survive. In such a case where the doctor anticipates, basing his opinion upon the experience of the profession, that the child cannot be delivered without the death of the mother, it is obvious that the sooner the operation is performed the better. The law does not require the doctor to wait until the unfortunate woman is in peril of immediate death. In such a case he is not only entitled, but it is his duty to perform the operation with a view to saving her life. . . .

As I have said, I think those words ought to be construed in a reasonable sense, and, if the doctor is of opinion, on reasonable grounds and with adequate knowledge, that the probable consequence of the continuance of the pregnancy will be to make the woman a physical or mental wreck, the jury are quite entitled to take the view that the doctor who, under those circumstances and in that honest belief, operates, is operating for the purpose of preserving the life of the mother.

The jury acquitted the defendant.

If the effect of *Bourne* is to make lawful a 'therapeutic' abortion, the question arises as to the limits at common law of this notion. As Glanville Williams wrote in his paper, 'The Law of Abortion' (1952) Current Legal Problems 128 at p 136:

The decision in *Bourne* has ameliorated the law but has not yet taken full practical effect. The medical practitioner is said to be still chary to act, except in the clearest cases, partly because he fears that public opinion may not be in favour and partly because he is not certain how far the *Bourne* decision protects him.

There were some further English cases which were considered in a leading New Zealand case. The court was asked to interpret section 183 of the Crimes Act 1961 (NZ) which adopts, in essence, the language of section 58 of the English statute.

R v Woolnough [1977] 2 NZLR 508 (NZ CA)

Richmond P: Since *Bourne* there have been two further cases spaced at intervals of 10 years in England to which we were referred by counsel. The first was *R v Bergmann* (unreported, UK, 1948, Morris J). In *Smith and Hogan's Criminal Law* (3rd edn) 273-274 the learned authors state that Morris J (as he then was) ' . . . is reported to have said that the court will not look too narrowly into the question of danger to life where danger to health is anticipated'. The later case is *R v Newton* . . . In that case Ashworth J is reported as directing the jury in the following way:

The law about the use of instruments to procure miscarriage is this: 'Such use of an instrument is unlawful unless the use is made in good faith for the purpose of preserving the life or health of the woman.' When I say health I mean not only the physical health but also her mental health. But although I have said that 'it is unlawful unless', I must emphasise and add that the burden of proving that it was not used in good faith is on the Crown ([1958] Crim L Rev 469).

In New Zealand there is no real authority on the point. In *R v Anderson* [1951] NZLR 439 at 443, it appears to have been assumed that *Bourne's* case applied in New Zealand but the point was not really in issue. When the question arose for consideration at the first trial of Dr Woolnough, and again at the second trial, Speight J and Chilwell J accordingly had no New Zealand authority on which to found an opinion. In effect what they have done is to expand the *Bourne* test, in words at least, if not so greatly as a matter of substance, by accepting the preservation of the *health* of the mother as an alternative justification to preserving the *life* of the mother. This is the way the matter was put by Ashworth J in *R v Newton*, but Speight J and Chilwell J have in another respect qualified the test by stressing the need for an honest belief that the abortion was necessary to preserve the woman from *serious* danger to her life or physical or mental health, not being merely the normal dangers of pregnancy and childbirth. As earlier mentioned, the most fundamental criticism made by the Solicitor-General is to the effect that Speight J and Chilwell J went too far when they accepted that serious danger to the *health* of the mother could be a justification for an abortion irrespective of whether or not such danger to health carried with it a real threat to the mother's *life* . . .
In the present case the court is concerned only with the concept of the welfare of the mother as a justification for an abortion in the early stages of pregnancy. In that field we have the assistance of s 182(2), which at least shows that the legislature itself was positively of the view that a bona fide intention to preserve the *life* of the mother in the late stages of pregnancy would justify the procurement of her miscarriage. The narrow question, then, is whether the courts ought not, in the case of early pregnancy at least, to extend that concept to include a bona fide intention to preserve the *health* of the mother from serious harm.
I can see no sufficient reason why this should not be done. In the first place it seems to me that the 'reasonable' interpretation of preservation of the *life* of the mother which was accepted in *Bourne* is likely to be an artificial and perhaps difficult one in practice. That this is the view of some English judges appears from the gradual shift away in emphasis disclosed in the directions given to the jury by Morris J and Ashworth J in the two cases to which I have earlier referred. The textbooks favour the open acknowledgement of preservation of health as well as preservation of life as preventing an abortion from being unlawful. Reference may be made to *Glanville Williams* (op cit) 153-154 and to *Smith and Hogan* (op cit) 274. Moreover, it is important to remember that the function impliedly entrusted to the courts by s 183 is not to say who is right and who is wrong as between the extreme views held by different sections of the community as regards this highly controversial subject. Rather the courts have to do their best to draw a line at a point where the procuring of a miscarriage ceases to be merely a matter of debate, from a religious, moral or ethical point of view, and becomes activity of a kind which warrants its designation as criminal. Finally I remind myself that as at the time when the Crimes Act 1961 was enacted, after lengthy preliminary consideration by a committee and then by the late Sir George Finlay, Ashworth J's direction in *R v Newton* had not only been reported in the *Criminal Law Review* but had also been the subject of an extensive article in that same journal. All this affords some indication that our legislature was content to accept the developing views of the English judges as applicable in this country.
Woodhouse J agreed. Wild CJ dissented.

[New Zealand law is now governed by section 187A of the Crimes Act 1961 (as amended in 1977) which defines 'unlawfully'. See DB Collins, *Medical Law in New Zealand* (1992) paras 7.13.9 *et seq*.]

2. The Act

Even after these cases, what was lawful still remained uncertain. The consequences, which served as the springboard for the 1967 Abortion Act, are described in the following extract.

Glanville Williams, *Textbook of Criminal Law* **(2nd edn 1983)**

Bourne's acquittal did not at once produce a large increase in medical abortions. The attitude of the medical profession in general was hostile, and tragic cases continued to occur. A girl of 12, pregnant by her father, was refused an abortion. Special boarding schools were opened for expectant mothers aged from 12 upwards, in order that they might continue with their lessons while looking after their babies. Woman who had been raped, woman deserted by their husbands, and overburdened mothers living in poverty with large families, also failed to get a medical abortion. One 'liberal' hospital in London and one in Newcastle performed the operation comparatively freely, and abortions could be readily bought in Harley Street; but in general the mass of woman could only go to a 'back-street abortionist', wielding a knitting needle, syringe or stick of slippery elm, or to a skilled operator acting illegally for large fees. Some unwilling mothers-to-be used dangerous methods on themselves, or occasionally committed suicide. Although illegal abortions ran into thousands each year, convictions were comparatively few (less than a hundred a year), largely because women who had sought help of an abortionist were unwilling to give him away, but partly also because the police themselves tended not to look upon abortions as a real crime. The only people who were effectively deterred by the law were the doctors, who alone could operate safely. The problem was common to all Christian countries that started with an unqualified prohibition of abortion.

At the same time as these evils were beginning to be acknowledged, the opinion arose that a woman had the right to control her own fertility. But against the pro-abortionists was arrayed a powerful religious lobby basing itself upon the 'sanctity of life'.

The Abortion Act 1967 was a compromise measure which, while not satisfying all demands, substantially liberalised the law. In England and Scotland it superseded the case law, including *Bourne*.

The report of a committee chaired by Mrs Justice Lane described the situation before the 1967 Act.

Committee on the Working of the Abortion Act **(Cmnd 5579), 1974**

The Acts of 1861 and 1929, with the new and liberal interpretation given to them by Mr Justice Macnaughten remained the law of England and Wales until the passing of the Abortion Act 1967. The number of abortions performed in reliance upon that interpretation (as distinct from those which were certainly illegal) rose; eg in 1966 in NHS hospitals alone there were 6,100 recorded abortions. Nevertheless, it was felt by many, though by no means all, concerned with the problems that there was insufficient precision in the law and that doctors and patients alike ought to have a clearer indication of when abortion was permissible. This, quite apart from the views of those who advocated a more liberal view, was why a new Act was considered to be necessary.

In 1937, a year or so before the Bourne case was tried, a Home Office and Ministry of Health Inter-Department Committee, under the chairmanship of Mr Norman Birkett, KC (later Lord Birkett) was set up to 'enquire into the prevalence of abortion, and the law relating thereto, and to consider what steps might be taken by more effective enforcement of the law or otherwise to secure a reduction of the maternal mortality and morbidity arising therefrom'. The Committee of course considered the effect of the Bourne case before recommending, in 1939, that: -

> the law should . . . be amended to make unmistakably clear that a medical practitioner is acting legally, when in good faith he procures the abortion of a pregnant woman in circumstances which satisfy him that continuance of the pregnancy is likely to endanger her life or seriously to impair her health.

Neither the government of the day, nor any succeeding government, introduced any legislation to implement the recommendation. Various private members introduced Bills to amend the abortion law, including Mr Joseph Reeves in 1952, Mr Kenneth Robinson in 1961 and Lord Silkin in the House of Lords in 1965. Lord Silkin's measure was superseded in 1966 by Mr David Steel's 'Medical Termination Bill' which, after considerable amendment, was passed as the Abortion Act 1967, coming into force on the 27 April 1968.

The Abortion Act 1967 provided a defence to the crimes under sections 58 and 59 of the Offences Against the Person Act 1861 providing certain conditions were satisfied. The most significant was that by section 1(1):

1(1) . . . two registered medical practitioners are of the opinion, formed in good faith –
(a) that the continuance of the pregnancy would involve risk to the life of the pregnant woman, or of injury to the physical or mental health of the pregnant woman or any existing children of her family, greater than if the pregnancy were terminated; or
(b) that there is a substantial risk that if the child were born it would suffer from such physical or mental abnormalities as to be seriously handicapped.

However, the 1967 Act did not affect liability for the crime of child destruction under the Infant Life (Preservation) Act 1929 when an abortion involved the destruction before birth of a child 'capable of being born alive' (section 1(1)).

Under section 1(2) of the 1929 Act evidence that a woman had been pregnant for 28 weeks or more raised a presumption that her child was 'capable of being born alive'. Dissatisfaction felt by some that this limit of 28 weeks carried the necessary implication that a child of less than 28 weeks' gestation was not 'capable of being born alive' (even though the courts interpreted the Act to apply to less mature foetuses), led to calls for the introduction of a shorter period of time. A number of Private Members' Bills were introduced in both Houses of Parliament. The best-known were introduced by John Corrie MP in 1979 and by David Alton MP in 1987 and on a number of occasions thereafter. Corrie proposed an upper time limit of 20 weeks except in the case where the foetus would be 'seriously handicapped' when the upper limit would be 28 weeks. David Alton proposed an even more restricted upper limit of 18 weeks with certain exceptions (for the texts and comment thereon see 1st Edition, p 799-806A).

During the passage of the Human Fertilisation and Embryology Bill in 1990 with all its attendant controversy the government conceded that reform of the Abortion Act 1967 should be considered. A series of complex and alternative amendments to the 1967 Act were tabled proposing changes in both the time limits and the grounds for abortion. After a flurry of late-night voting in the House of Commons on 21 June 1990, section 37, amending section 1 of the 1967 Act, emerged. Both the House of Lords and the House of Commons subsequently confirmed what had been decided that night. Ironically, although the pressure for reform was from those who wished to see limitations introduced into the 1967 Act, section 37, in fact, has the effect of significantly liberalising the law.

1 (1) Subject to the provisions of this section, a person shall not be guilty of an offence under the law relating to abortion when a pregnancy is terminated by a registered medical practitioner if two registered medical practitioners are of the opinion, formed in good faith –
(a) that the pregnancy has not exceeded its twenty-fourth week and that the continuance of the pregnancy would involve risk, greater than if the pregnancy were terminated, of injury to the physical or mental health of the pregnant woman or any existing children of her family; or
(b) that the termination is necessary to prevent grave permanent injury to the physical or mental health of the pregnant woman; or
(c) that the continuance of the pregnancy would involve risk to the life of the pregnant woman, greater than if the pregnancy were terminated; or
(d) that there is a substantial risk that if the child were born it would suffer from physical or mental abnormalities as to be seriously handicapped.
(2) In determining whether the continuance of a pregnancy would involve such risk of injury to health as is mentioned in paragraph (a) or (b) of subsection (1) of this section, account may be taken of the pregnant woman's actual or reasonably foreseeable environment. . . .

(4) Subsection (3) of this section, and so much of subsection (1) as relates to the opinion of two registered medical practitioners, shall not apply to the termination of a pregnancy by a registered medical practitioner in a case where he is of the opinion, formed in good faith, that the termination is immediately necessary to save the life or to prevent grave permanent injury to the physical or mental health of the pregnant woman.

3. The grounds

Under the amended Act there are four subsections spelling out the grounds for a lawful abortion, in contrast to the two grounds under the old law. What changes have taken place?

(a) 'Risk of physical or mental injury' – s 1(1)(a)

The ground contained in this subsection in part repeats the ground most commonly relied upon for abortions under the old law. There are four features of the subsection which call for comment. First, the pregnant woman's doctors must be satisfied that the risk to her physical or mental health would be greater if the pregnancy were to continue than if it were to be terminated. What is being contrasted here in this *comparative* exercise are the risks inherent in terminating the pregnancy *now* and the relevant risks to the mother in going to full term. The risks to her need not, therefore, be greater at the time of the termination itself.

Prior to the amendment, what had to be contrasted was the risk of injury to the pregnant woman's physical or mental health or *her life*. This latter risk is now dealt with separately in subsection 1(1)(c) which is dealt with below. What is important to notice for the moment is that the old ground could as a matter of logic always be satisfied at least during the first trimester. This is because of the so-called 'statistical argument', namely that it is always of less risk to the mother to terminate rather than to continue the pregnancy if what is being considered is the risk to her *life*. Although the risk to her life in being pregnant is low, the modern procedures used to terminate pregnancy during the first trimester pose an even lower risk. Now that *risk to life* is no longer relevant under this subsection, does the 'statistical argument' still apply when considering only the risk to the pregnant woman's health? If not, the net effect is that a doctor must rely upon the ground under subsection 1(1)(c) if she wishes to justify the termination solely on the basis of the 'statistical' argument.

A second point to notice is what is meant by a risk to the pregnant woman's health? The subsection refers to 'physical or mental health'. The former is self-evident; the latter, however, requires further consideration.

Glanville Williams, *Textbook of Criminal Law* (2nd edn) 1983

What is meant by 'the mental health of the pregnant woman'?
. . . Narrowly interpreted, it may require the doctor to fear that the patient will suffer from what is commonly called a mental illness, whether a psychosis or severe neurosis. This may include a depressive psychosis, and the British Medical Association recognises that termination may properly be advised on account of a 'reactive depression', which is a pathological state of hopeless despair resulting from circumstances. If the question is one of mental illness, the natural course would be to call in a psychiatrist, a specialist in mental disorder.

But 'mental health' is susceptible of a wider meaning. The definition of health advanced by the World Health Organisation is that it is 'the state of complete mental, physical and social well-being, and not merely an absence of disease or infirmity'. Gynaecologists who take this broad view do not insist upon a psychiatric opinion, but are ready to act on their own opinion of the case, backed by the family doctor.

Thirdly, so far we have concentrated upon the risk to a pregnant woman's health. Subsection 1(1)(a) also permits abortion if there is a risk of 'injury to the physical or mental health of . . . any existing children of her family' which is 'greater than if the pregnancy were terminated'.

Professor Glanville Williams in his *Textbook of Criminal Law (op cit)* poses the question 'How can existing children be affected in health by having another brother or sister?'

> Sometimes it may be reasonable to make this judgment. Consider the mother of a 'problem family'. She is living in poverty, with a large brood of children. Her husband has been in prison and has now been arrested again. Her existing children are badly cared for and play truant. Now she is pregnant once more. It may confidently be predicted that if the pregnancy is allowed to go to term, matters will be worsened for the existing children to the extent that their health may be affected. In practice, doctors who terminate on this ground generally tick it as an extra to the health of the woman.
>
> *Can the doctor take the poverty of the family into account?*
> Not directly, but he can if the woman's poverty, aggravated by the addition to her family, is likely to affect her health or that of her other children.

Even if this is so, the question arises as to who are 'children of the pregnant woman's family'? As in other legal contexts, the notion of 'family' can be given a variety of meanings, some broader than others. So, for example, 'children of her family' could be restricted to children born in wedlock and particularly limited to children of her current marriage. At its widest, it could extend to all children whom she has treated as part of her family. Also, the notion of a 'child' could, and perhaps should, be said to include an adult who remains dependent upon the woman and within her immediate family by reason of disability. In the case of such a disabled child, perhaps the risk of injury is easier to envisage. The arguments are examined in the following article.

AJC Hoggett, 'The Abortion Act 1967' [1968] Crim LR 247

> It is submitted that, for the purposes of this Act, 'family' means the sociological and not the legal unit. It thus includes not only the mother's illegitimate children living with her but also the illegitimate children of her husband by a previous mistress. Clearly the words cover adopted children but there seems no reason why they should not cover children living in the family who are adopted in all but law. 'Children of her family', it is submitted, also includes the case of the daughter of a widower when [the pregnant woman is] acting *in loco matris*. This wide interpretation of the Act seems sanctioned by the fact that reference may be made to the pregnant woman's actual environment which includes the children mentioned above. The courts have shown a tendency to interpret the words 'child of the family' in a generous fashion.

A wide interpretation is consistent with Parliament's having given an extended meaning to 'child of the family' in, for example, the Children Act 1989 (s 105). This legislation is concerned with the 'child of a family' in marriage. Of course, the Abortion Act is concerned with a child of *her* family and, therefore, an even wider view is justified.

Fourthly, section 1(2) provides that in assessing the relative risk of injury to health 'account may be taken of the pregnant woman's actual or reasonably foreseeable environment'. Does this allow a doctor to have regard to a risk of injury to health arising after she has given birth? Professor Glanville Williams in his *Textbook of Criminal Law (op cit)* suggests a wide interpretation of s 1(2).

> The Act refers to 'risk of injury to the health of the *pregnant* woman', and one may argue that when the child has been born the woman is no longer pregnant. Moreover, it must be 'the continuance of the pregnancy' that produces this risk, and it is perhaps slightly strange, though not impossible, to say that the burden on a mother of having to rear a child was a result of 'the continuance of the pregnancy'.
>
> On the other hand there are two clues in the Act making it reasonably clear that the wider meaning was intended by Parliament.
>
> 1   The words just quoted are used with regard to both the health of the woman and the health of existing children of her family. If one pays regard to the health of existing children, as the Act allows, it would be illogical to do this only during the time of gestation of the new addition to the family. What was evidently intended was that existing children might be adversely affected by the extra child being born and having to be brought up by an already overburdened mother.
>
> 2   Subsection (2) provides that 'account may be taken of the pregnant woman's actual or reasonably foreseeable environment'. This is not, as has sometimes been thought, a purely 'social' ground for termination, since it is related to the question of health. It does not allow the operation merely because the patient will otherwise lose her job or her husband. Still, the statutory words make it clear that the question of health is to be considered broadly. There is not much point in directing the doctor to look ahead to the woman's future environment if he is to consider only the time of pregnancy. So it is really quite clear that the Act is intended to provide for the case of the overburdened mother.

If Professor Williams is correct, and it would appear that he is, such that account may be taken of the environment in which she or the existing children will find themselves, would a termination under s 1(1)(a) be justified on the basis that a child of the other sex is desired? This, of course, is a serious problem in some ethnic communities. The birth of a boy may be more desirable. A pregnant woman may be under pressure to terminate her pregnancy once it is discovered she is carrying a girl. Alternatively, existing girl children may have their future interest including their health affected by the birth of a brother who may be treated preferentially. Leaving aside a termination based solely upon the 'statistical argument', the legality of such a termination would depend on a doctor forming the view that the pregnant woman's health or that of her female children would be put at greater risk than if she terminated the pregnancy. Given that the Act confers a wide discretion to the doctors, such a case could well fall within s 1(1)(a) providing the doctors act in good faith.

Fifthly, and perhaps most importantly, s 1(1)(a) introduces a time-limit of 24 weeks for terminations under this ground alone. The crucial issue here, therefore, is the meaning of the words 'the pregnancy has not exceeded its twenty-fourth week', ie at what point in time can it first be said that woman is 'pregnant'? Undoubtedly, the meaning of the word 'pregnant' is a matter of law for the court (see, for example, *C v S* [1987] 1 All ER 1230 at 1242 per Sir John Donaldson MR on the meaning of the phrase 'capable of being born alive' in the Infant Life (Preservation) Act 1929).

There are at least four possible points in time at which the clock could start running in calculating the 24 weeks: (A) the first day of the woman's last period; (B) the date of conception (up to 14 days later); (C) the date of implantation (up to 10 days later) and (D) the first day of the woman's first missed period (about four weeks after (A)).

In England the medical profession calculates the length of gestation of a baby on the basis of (A) because it is the most certain date of any of these alternatives. Options (B) and (C), namely the date of conception and the date the fertilised egg implants into the woman, by contrast, cannot be known for certain. But there are difficulties with option (D), because although the first day of the woman's first missed period is certain, it may be quite misleading to indicate length of pregnancy where, for example, following conception during the last week of a cycle the woman does not miss the next period but only the one that follows. The date calculated on the basis of (D) could be about five weeks after conception has actually occurred.

So, when does time start to run? The law might accept the medical profession's approach in option (A) because of the certainty it would achieve. More importantly, however, it might be accepted because it is the basis upon which Parliament introduced the 24 week time-limit in section 1(1)(a). The 24 week limit (as calculated by the medical profession) represents Parliament's view of the stage of development when a foetus is capable of surviving. At this point the legislative intent is that the foetus should not be aborted except under the more restrictive grounds set out in the remainder of section 1(1). If any of the other options for starting time to run were accepted, this premise would be nullified. On that basis, in order to conform to the underlying premise that a foetus which is capable of surviving should not be aborted on the ground in section 1(1)(a), the time-limit should actually be 22 weeks or even less.

On the other hand, there are a number of arguments which suggest that options (B) or (C) are more appropriate interpretations of section 1(1)(a). First, it is wrong to adopt an interpretation which leads to the absurd conclusion that a woman is pregnant in the 14 days (approximately) between the first day of her last period and the time of conception when this is patently not the case. Secondly, the medical profession's approach exemplified in option (A) could act to the detriment of a defendant since it results in the shortest possible time for the 24-week period to run. After all, the medical profession's view is only as to when pregnancy begins and was not formulated with an eye to setting the upper time-limit for abortion. A pregnancy calculated on the basis of (A) at 25 weeks is likely, in fact, to be a case where conception and implantation will have occurred less than 24 weeks before the abortion. Ambiguities in criminal statutes should be construed in a defendant's favour and not against him, particularly when interpreting a section providing a defence to a criminal offence.

This would support one of the other alternatives: but which one? It is suggested that (C) is legally the more justifiable. It is widely recognised that the offence of procuring a miscarriage under section 58 of the Offences Against the Person Act 1861 only applies after an embryo has implanted. There is even indirect Parliamentary support for this interpretation in section 2(3) of HUFEA which states that '[f]or the purposes of [HUFEA], a woman is not to be treated as carrying a child until the embryo has become implanted'. Hence, the use of contragestive birth control measures such as post-coital birth control pills and IUDs are not illegal under section 58 if they are intended to act on the woman by preventing implantation. Surely, there is some attraction to the symmetry of interpreting the Abortion Act so that the defence to the offence in section 58 operates from the point in time when that crime could first be committed, ie at implantation?

(b) 'Necessary to prevent grave permanent injury to physical or mental health' – s 1(1)(b)

This is a new ground introduced by the amendments. Its genesis is probably s 1(4) of the 1967 Act which, as we shall see, creates a justification for performing an abortion in certain situations of emergency where a doctor ' . . . is of the opinion, formed in good faith, that the termination is immediately necessary to save the life or to prevent grave permanent injury to the physical or mental health of the pregnant woman'.

Section 1(4) does not create a *ground* for performing an abortion but merely removes the need to satisfy the conditions under the Act relating to the place where the abortion is to be performed and the need for two medical opinions when a ground otherwise exists. Such abortions would have been justified under the ground in the unamended s 1(1)(a). With the amendment to s 1(1)(a) introducing a time-limit of 24 weeks, Parliament considered that where the risk to the mother was more serious than injury to her physical or mental health, abortions should not be restricted to 24 weeks. Hence, the new s 1(1)(b) (and s 1(1)(c) on 'risk to life', see below) was introduced to achieve this aim.

There are two points to notice in relation to s 1(1)(b). First, unlike s 1(1)(a) (and s 1(1)(c)) this ground for abortion does not appear to require the certifying doctors to engage in a comparison of risks between the continuation and termination of the pregnancy. What the doctors have to be satisfied of is 'that the termination is necessary'. What is involved in a determination by the doctors that the termination is 'necessary'? You will recall that the Act only requires the doctors to be satisfied of a ground 'in good faith'. Hence, they need not show that it was necessary but merely that they formed that view in good faith at the time. A termination will only be necessary, however, and the doctors could only be so satisfied, if termination was the only course available 'to prevent grave permanent injury to the physical or mental health of the pregnant woman'. Consequently, it may be insufficient for the doctors merely to be satisfied that there was such a risk to the woman or even that continuing the pregnancy involved a greater risk than termination of the pregnancy. This is because an alternative course of action may be available to deal with the danger to the pregnant woman. Only if there are no alternative courses of action which a reasonable doctor would contemplate, could it be said that a termination is 'necessary'.

The second point to notice concerns the meaning of the phrase 'grave permanent injury'. The words should be given their ordinary meaning. A court would, therefore, not interpret the phrase so as to cover transitory conditions affecting the mother's health but would not require, necessarily, that the mother's life be at risk. In a debate in the House of Lords, Lord Mackay LC provided some guidance:

Hansard, HL vol 522, Col 1039 (18 October 1990)

An additional category already specified in the 1967 Act as a ground for emergency abortion on the opinion of one doctor is that of preventing grave permanent injury to the physical or mental health of the woman. The use of the words 'grave' and 'permanent' suggest that there is a stiff legal test to cover special situations where termination might be contemplated primarily in the interest of the pregnant woman. An example of this might be where she has severe hypertension and continuation of the pregnancy might result in permanent kidney, brain or possibly heart damage. In those circumstances the method of termination used would be selected in the best interests of the woman, but the intention would be to deliver a living baby where possible.

(c) 'Risk to life' – s 1(1)(c)

As under s 1(1)(a), this ground requires the doctors to balance the risk in continuing the pregnancy against the risk of termination. Here, the risk involved is the 'risk to the life of the pregnant woman'. On the face of it, this is restricted to circumstances where the pregnant woman's condition threatens to end her life. However, the ground only requires that the termination *reduces* the risk to her life. In other words, the doctors are not required to be satisfied that the termination will *eliminate* the risk to her life – there may exist a continuing, though lesser, risk to her life. (The termination will be justified, however, if the woman though still at risk stands a better chance of surviving than if she remains pregnant.)

A further point to notice concerns the meaning of the phrase 'risk to the *life* of the pregnant woman' (our emphasis). In *Bourne* we saw Macnaughten J gave a broad interpretation to section 1(1) of the Infant Life (Preservation) Act 1929. This provides a defence to the crime of child destruction where the unborn child is killed 'for the purpose only of preserving the life of the mother'.

> **Macnaughten J:** As I have said, I think those words ought to be construed in a reasonable sense, and, if the doctor is of opinion, on reasonable grounds and with adequate knowledge, that the probable consequence of the continuance of the pregnancy will be to make the woman a physical or mental wreck, the jury are quite entitled to take the view that the doctor who, under those circumstances and in that honest belief, operates, is operating for the purpose of preserving the life of the mother.

This broad interpretation of 'risk to life' cannot be appropriately applied to section 1(1)(c) since it is inconsistent with the existence of the grounds in sections 1(1)(a) and (b). That is to say that if the decision is made during the first 24 weeks of pregnancy that the woman would become a 'mental wreck', section 1(1)(a) would apply. If this determination is made after 24 weeks providing her condition amounts to a 'grave permanent injury to [her] mental health' then the abortion can be performed under section 1(1)(b), but not otherwise.

(d) 'Substantial risk' (so as to be) 'seriously handicapped' – s 1(1)(d)

The final ground under the amended 1967 Act is contained in s 1(1)(d). This permits an abortion to be performed in cases where:

> there is a substantial risk that if the child were born it would suffer from such physical and mental abnormalities as to be seriously handicapped.

Professor Williams in his *Textbook of Criminal Law* (*op cit*) explains the basis of this ground.

> It is sometimes justified for eugenic reasons, but in fact the contribution that abortion is likely to make to the betterment of man's genetic inheritance is slight. No: the argument for abortion on the fetal indication relates to the welfare of the parents, whose lives may well be blighted by having to rear a grossly defective child, and perhaps secondarily by consideration for the public purse. That this is the philosophy of the Act is borne out by the fact that it allows termination only where the child if born would be seriously handicapped, not where it is merely carrying undesirable genes.
>
> Whereas the health grounds recognised in the Act merely enlarge on the attitude of the judge in *Bourne*, that the health of full human beings is to be preferred to the interests of the fetus in being born where the two interests conflict, the fetal ground marks a new departure. The fetus is destroyed not necessarily in its own interest (the physician need make no judgment that life will be a burden for it), but in the interest either of the parents or of society at large, though of course only upon the request of the mother.
>
> Although argument still rages on whether abortion should be permitted merely as a matter of convenience to the woman, the fetal ground is almost universally accepted. But it

is of some interest to note that anyone who does accept the fetal ground for abortion commits himself to the view that the moral status of the fetus is not the same as that of a child. For we do not permit children to be killed because they are seriously handicapped.

Professor Williams was discussing this ground as it first appeared in the Abortion Act in 1967. His point about its almost universal acceptance as a ground for abortion is supported by the fact that the wording was unchanged by the amendments in 1990. There is, however, one important point to notice. Abortion on this ground, as it *now* appears, is not subject to any time-limit, in contrast to the previous state of the law affected as it was by the Infant Life (Preservation) Act 1929 as we shall shortly see. Whether this change in the law will have impact on practice will primarily depend upon two matters: first, the extent to which some foetal abnormalities, not currently detectable early in pregnancy, in fact become detectable but only at a much later stage; and secondly, even in these cases, the extent to which doctors are prepared to perform abortions under this ground late in pregnancy.

We should now turn our attention to the meaning of the two crucial phrases – 'substantial risk' and 'seriously handicapped'. Professor Glanville Williams in his *Textbook of Criminal Law (op cit)* writes:

> The physician must decide whether there is a 'substantial' risk that the child if born would be 'seriously' handicapped. Advances in knowledge and medical skills make it more and more possible to attach a precise mathematical weight to the chance of the fetus being affected by genetic defects or by what happens to it in the womb. But the doctor still has to decide whether the case is sufficiently grave to justify termination. He may, of course, take the view that a relatively low risk justifies termination if the risk is of a relatively serious handicap: in common sense, the two factors are inversely related. Even when the doctor thinks that the 'fetal indication' is not itself sufficiently present, the fact that the patient is extremely depressed by worry that the child may be affected can itself be a reason for termination on the health ground.

Arguably when Professor Williams asserts that 'a relatively low risk justifies termination if the risk is of a relatively serious handicap', he adopts an interpretation which is difficult to sustain. A risk is either 'substantial' or it is not irrespective of what degree of handicap it relates to.

AJC Hoggett, 'The Abortion Act 1967' [1968] Crim LR 247

> ... it seems to have been assumed that 'substantial risk' was one where it was more probable than not that the child would suffer from an abnormality. This quasi-mathematical interpretation is not satisfactory since it could lead to the view that it is possible only to take into account those cases where it is known that an abnormality has at least a one in two chance of appearing. It may be possible to diagnose the presence of the abnormality with absolute certainty as in certain cases of mongolism. In other cases, there may be an equal chance that a child will suffer from an abnormality. Such is the case, for example, where a male haemophiliac is married to a haemophilia-carrier or where blood group incompatibilities exist between parents. Other examples exist. It seems wrong, in principle, to exclude cases where the risk is less than one in two. Thus the chance of a haemophilia-carrying woman having a haemophiliac son is one in four and if parents have already produced one child with phenylketonuria, the chances that a subsequent child will have the disease are again one in four.
>
> Moreover, there are cases where for genetical or other reasons it is not possible to calculate the risk with mathematical precision. A child, born to a woman who contracts german measles during early pregnancy, has roughly a two in three chance of being affected if the disease was present in the first weeks, a one in two chance if present during weeks four to eight and a one in three chance if present in weeks eight to twelve. Again, although the genetics of such abnormalities as anencephaly, hydrocephaly and spina bifida is not fully understood,

the involvement of hereditary factors is sufficiently established to have the result that many doctors would recommend an abortion where the woman had already given birth to a child so affected even though the risk is quite small. It is surely proper for a doctor to accept higher odds against an abnormality manifesting itself if its effects would be very severe.

Judgment is also complicated by the fact that there must not only be a substantial risk of abnormality but also of resultant serious handicap. It is often impossible to tell how serious the handicap will be. In the case of german measles, the child may only be suffering from cataracts amenable to treatment. There are also differing degrees of spina bifida. It has been suggested that 'seriously handicapped' means 'incapable of carrying out any normal activity'. This seems dangerously strict since a haemophiliac, for instance, is capable of many normal activities although his disease may severely limit their range.

Despite its restrictive wording, section 1(1)(*b*) [now s 1(1)(d)] should be liberally interpreted so as to protect the doctor who has made a difficult decision in good faith. Should it ever be necessary to interpret the words 'substantial risk' or 'seriously handicapped', for example where the risk is exactly known, then it is submitted that the test to be applied should be – could any reasonable doctor consider this a substantial risk or a serious handicap. In such cases, it may also be possible to pray in aid section 1(1)(*a*). For example, a woman who knows that she has had german measles may suffer six months of anxiety before birth and it may be months after the birth before it can be determined whether the child has been affected.

There is a further question concerning the meaning of 'seriously handicapped'. Notice that section 1(1)(d) requires that '*if born*, the child would suffer from such physical and mental abnormalities as to be seriously handicapped' (our emphasis). Does this mean that the abnormalities must constitute or amount to a handicap *at birth* or will it suffice that a latent condition exists at birth which will, *or may*, manifest itself later in life? And, if the latter, must it manifest itself during *childhood* since section 1(1)(d) refers to the 'child' suffering the serious handicap?

On one view the section requires that the handicap must exist at birth. As a consequence, on this view, an abortion could not be performed if the physical or mental symptoms of handicap will only manifest themselves at some later point in time.

Another view, however, can be taken of the meaning of the section. This would permit an abortion providing the handicap will manifest itself at some point in the future during the baby's childhood, for example, Tay Sachs disease. However, there are two further points that require consideration. First, even if this view is correct some conditions will not manifest themselves until adulthood, for example, Huntington's disease. Although it is more difficult to interpret the section as covering this situation, once it is accepted that the handicap need not manifest itself at birth, it would seem to undermine the purpose of the provision narrowly to restrict it to childhood.

Finally, what if there is no certainty that there will be a handicap but merely a chance of inheriting the condition which will lead to handicap? This does not give rise to any new problem. It is a matter of interpreting the statutory phrase 'substantial risk' which we considered earlier. What, however, this last point does illustrate is that whenever there is a chance of inheriting a condition there is also a chance of inheriting a gene which merely makes the individual a carrier who will not develop the condition itself. Assuming there is a 'substantial risk' of the individual becoming a carrier, will this fall within section 1(1)(d)? In other words, can it be said that a carrier of a genetic abnormality suffers from a 'serious handicap'?

Whilst the section should be given a wide meaning to cover physical or mental handicaps which manifest themselves at any time after a child's birth, there is no justification for including carrier status alone. This is because the legislative purpose behind this ground would not be furthered. If Professor Williams is correct that the ground 'relates to the welfare of the parents whose lives may well be blighted by having to rear a grossly defective child' (see *supra*) a child who is merely a carrier would not produce this hardship. There is, of course, another purpose underlying this ground, namely to avoid the birth of children whose quality of life would be intolerable because of their handicap. Again, a carrier could not be said to be bearing an intolerable burden merely by being a carrier even if he may face some social stigma or some hard choices about reproduction may be forced upon him later in life.

4. Time limits

Prior to the amendments of the Abortion Act which came into effect on 1 April 1991, the legality of any abortion had to be considered not only in the light of the Abortion Act 1967 but also taking account of the Infant Life (Preservation) Act 1929.

Infant Life (Preservation) Act 1929

1 (1) Subject as hereinafter in this subsection provided, any person who, with intent to destroy the life of a child *capable of being born alive*, by any wilful act causes a child to die before it has an existence independent of its mother, shall be guilty of felony, to wit, of child destruction, and shall be liable on conviction thereof on indictment to penal servitude for life:

Provided that no person shall be found guilty of an offence under this section unless it is proved that the act which caused the death of the child was not done in good faith for the purpose only of preserving the life of the mother.

(2) For the purpose of this Act, evidence that a woman had at any material time been pregnant for a period of twenty-eight weeks or more shall be *prima facie* proof that she was at that time pregnant of a child capable of being born alive.

(*Our emphasis*)

It would appear that the provisions of the 1929 Act are now irrelevant because by amendment to the 1967 Act it is now provided that:

5 (1) No offence under the Infant Life (Preservation) Act 1929 shall be committed by a registered medical practitioner who terminates a pregnancy in accordance with the provisions of this Act [ie, the Abortion Act 1967].

Hence, it could be said that the only relevant question in determining the legality of an abortion is whether the terms of the 1967 Act as amended have been complied with. It will be recalled that only section 1(1)(a) imposes a time-limit (of 24 weeks). While in general, therefore, the provisions of the 1929 Act may no longer be relevant in the context of a lawful abortion, there is one important point to bear in mind. Consider a civil action brought by a mother whose pregnancy pre-dated the 1991 amendments and who has given birth to a disabled child. She claims that she was negligently not given the opportunity to choose an abortion. In such a case, a defendant might argue that the disability was only discovered (or discoverable) at a time when an abortion would have been illegal under the 1929 Act. Cases of this kind, raising questions of the legality of pre-1991 abortions, may well arise for some years to come.

In these cases, the crucial legal question is the meaning of the statutory phrase 'capable of being born alive'. What the Act provides is that a foetus will *prima facie* be so regarded if it has reached 28 weeks of gestational age. The Act does not, therefore, preclude the possibility that a child may be *capable of being born alive* at an earlier gestational age. Thus, the issue is what is the precise meaning of the phrase 'capable of being born alive' and does this equate with a particular period of time? This critically important question fell to be considered in the case of *C v S* [1988] QB 135, [1987] 1 All ER 1230. The case concerned an application by C, the father of a child carried by S, his former girlfriend, for an injunction to prevent her seeking or obtaining an abortion. At first instance, Heilbron J set out the facts, the medical testimony and the legal background.

C v S [1988] QB 135, [1987] 1 All ER 1230 (Heilbron J and CA)

Heilbron J: [Counsel for the applicant] . . . submits that . . . the doctor would be contravening the provisions of [the 1929 Act] and would be guilty, because he would be aborting a foetus of 18 weeks. Indeed, he further submitted that any doctor who has since 1967, or who proposed to, abort a foetus of that duration must be guilty of the offence.

Counsel did not resile from the implications of that assertion, relying for it on the terms of the 1929 Act and the statements of Mr Norris in his affidavits, particularly in that which stated that 'an unborn child of eighteen weeks gestation were it to be delivered by hysterotomy *would be* live born' (my emphasis).

The affidavits are important. They indicate very clearly the wide difference in thinking and interpretation between medical men, all of high reputation and great experience, in regard to the language used in the 1929 Act. I will now read the affidavits, so as to incorporate their explanation of certain phrases and terms into this judgment. I begin, because it was the first, with that of Mr Norris, emeritus consultant gynaecologist at St Peter's Hospital, Chertsey. He stated in para 2 of his first affidavit that 'an unborn child of eighteen weeks gestation were it to be delivered by hysterotomy would be live born'. He then went on to refer to a definition of this expression or condition by the World Health Assembly under art 23 of the Constitution of the World Health Organisation in 1976 (subsequent to both the Acts in this matter) as being –

> the complete expulsion or extraction from its mother of a product of conception irrespective of the duration of pregnancy, which after such separation breathes or [and I emphasise the 'or' in his affidavit] shows any other evidence of life such as beating of the heart, pulsation of the umbilical cord or definite movement of voluntary muscle whether or not the umbilical cord has been cut or the placenta is attached.

To that affidavit Professor John Richard Newton replied. He did so, in his first affirmation, on 16 February. He said:

> I am the Layson Tait Professor of Obstetrics and Gynaecology and Head of Department at the Birmingham University Medical School Queen Elizabeth Hospital Edgbaston Birmingham. I have been a Gynaecologist for twenty years and held my present position since 1979.

He had been shown a copy of Mr Norris's affidavit and asked to comment on it and in regard to para 2 he said:

> I believe it confusing in the circumstances to use the words 'live born' for a foetus of 18 weeks gestation. As Mr Norris says the term has been defined by Article 23 of the World Health Assembly in 1976. There is now produced . . . a copy of a report known as 'Report on Foetal Viability and Clinical Practice' which was prepared in August 1985 by a representative committee on behalf of the Royal College of Obstetricians and Gynaecologists, the British Paediatric Association, Royal College of General Practitioners, Royal College of Midwives, British Medical Association and the Department of Health and Social Security . . . I refer in particular to the twelfth page of that report in which reference is made to the recommendation of the World Health Organisation concerning perinatal statistics. The committee to which I have referred above was charged with the task of considering foetal viability and

comparison is made between the World Health Organisation definition and the concept of foetal viability. As will be seen from the report the purpose behind the World Health Organisation definition was to standardise the perinatal statistics for member countries of births. The purpose behind the definition was specifically not to define independent foetal viability and the committee go on to consider that concept and I believe that to be the important concept in these circumstances. Foetal viability means that the foetus is capable of independent human existence separate from the mother.

He then refers to the contents of this report of the various prestigious colleges and associations of doctors and says:

It will be seen that in the survey of 29 neo-natal intensive care units in the United Kingdom during 1982 no foetus of less than 23 weeks survived after delivery. It is my conclusion therefore that a foetus of anything below 23 weeks cannot survive independent of its mother and has therefore no viability.

A few days later Mr Norris swore a second affidavit, in order to amplify the first. He then suggested that the period of gestation was 2, or possibly 3, weeks more than the 18 weeks which had been mentioned. He went on to explain the expression 'live born' which had been used in his first affidavit:

4 . . . In case there is any ambiguity I wish to assert that in so stating I mean that in my opinion any foetus of eighteen weeks or longer gestation is capable of being born alive and that by 'alive' I mean showing real and discernible signs of life within the meaning of the World Health Organisation definition set out in my original Affidavit and of the Births and Deaths Registration Act 1926 current when the Infant Life (Preservation) Act 1929 was passed and also of the Births and Deaths Registration Act 1953 now current. Under the provisions of both these statutes such a child shall be registered as a live birth.

5. A child of eighteen or even twenty-one weeks gestational age although capable of being born alive and capable of surviving for some time outside the womb is not generally regarded by the medical profession as being viable because present paediatric skills are insufficient to assist it to remain alive for more than a limited time.

On the same day, 19 February, Professor Newton, having read the second affidavit of Mr Norris, stated in a further affidavit:

1 . . . Although he uses the expression 'live born' in [his first] affidavit he does not mention, nor did I understand that he was specifically referring to the words actually appearing in an Act of Parliament namely the words 'born alive' in Section 1 Infant Life (Preservation) Act 1929. This has now been drawn to my attention and I give my comments.

2. The expression 'born alive' used in the Infant Life (Preservation) Act 1929 raises difficulties before the expiration of 28 weeks of gestation.

3. Although it is difficult to generalise, for reasons which I will refer to in paragraph 4 after 8 weeks of gestation some fetuses will exhibit some primitive fetal movement, have a primitive heart tube which contracts and the circulation has started to develop but these fetuses will be quite incapable of life separate from the mother.

4. Each individual fetus in each individual mother develops differently and at different rates.

He then refers to the difficulty of the medical assessment of the gestational period in any particular case, which must be approximate and which may be complicated, as indeed in this case, by irregular menstruation. However, there are some firm generalisations on development which could be made.

In a foetus of 18-21 weeks gestation the cardiac muscle is contracting and a primitive circulation is developing, but in my opinion lung development does not occur until after 24 weeks gestation; before this time the major air passages have been formed and there is gradual development of the bronchioles but these terminate in a blind sac incapable of gas exchange prior to 24 weeks.

He says that a foetus of 18 to 21 weeks gestation could be delivered by hysterotomy but that would not be routinely used on such a fetus, and he describes the type of operation:

Once placental separation occurs whether the delivery has been by hysterotomy or vaginally it will not be able to respirate . . . What constitutes 'born alive' is controversial among the medical profession and often turns not only on medical knowledge but on the moral views of the person giving his opinion. I would mention that the development of each particular foetus in each particular mother is an individual process, the progress of which [at] any stage before 28 weeks can best be ascertained by an examination of the particular mother in question or at the very least detailed knowledge of that individual person.

With that I must entirely agree, and counsel for Mr C conceded that that must be so. It is an important aspect of this case, to which I will later refer. Professor Newton continued:

Whether or not a foetus up to 24 weeks of gestation is delivered by hysterotomy or vaginal delivery it will not be capable of surviving once the placental separation occurs. Up to 24 weeks in my opinion the lungs are incapable of sustaining life because they are not adequately developed. The development of other organs within the foetus is at an equally primitive stage incapable of sustaining life. I do not consider the indicia referred to in paragraph 3 hereof to equate with being 'alive'. I equate 'alive' with being able to sustain a separate independent existence and in my opinion this a foetus is clearly not capable of being able to do until after 24 weeks of gestation.

. . . Counsel's case that Mr C was entitled to an injunction because a crime was threatened depended, it appears, partly, as counsel for Miss S submitted, on the extraordinary and dogmatic assertion with regard to the ability to be born alive of *every* 18-week foetus, without any personal knowledge or examination of any of these countless unborn children, partly on his interpretation of 'being born alive' and partly on the view adumbrated by counsel for Mr C that, if any doctor was intending to perform an abortion on an 18-week foetus, it would be perverse of him or her to assert other than that the foetus was capable of being born alive. Counsel, though not Mr Norris, submitted that no other interpretation of 'live born' than that of Mr Norris is within the words of the Act.

I disagree. Counsel for Mrs S pointed out that Mr Norris did not disagree with Professor Newton that an 18-week foetus cannot breathe and cannot even be mechanically ventilated. I would have thought that to say, as he has, that a child is live born or alive, even though it cannot breathe, would surprise not only doctors but many ordinary people.

The word 'viable' is, I believe from what I have heard in this case, sometimes used interchangeably and in a number of cases where others might use the words 'born alive'. In the United States of America, in the Supreme Court, in *Roe v Wade* 410 US 113 at 163 (1973) it was said:

With respect to the State's important and legitimate interest in potential life, the 'compelling' point is at *viability*. This is so because the fetus then presumably has the capability of meaningful life outside the mother's womb. State regulation protective of fetal life after viability thus has both logical and biological justifications. (My emphasis.)

As far as the phrase in the 1929 Act is concerned, counsel for Mr C submits, it either contains an ambiguity or the phrase is a technical one. In my view, one or both of those submissions is or are correct. That expression, in my judgment, does not have a clear and plain meaning. It *is* ambiguous. It is a phrase which is capable of different interpretations, and probably for the reason that it is also a medical concept and, as with the example of earlier days, the expertise of doctors may well be required and gratefully received to assist the court.

Even distinguished medical men have found considerable difficulties but have discovered that it is more helpful to equate that phrase with viability, possibly with the example from the parliamentary draftsman in mind.

I cannot accept counsel for the plaintiff's submission that this is not, at any rate in this court, even partly a matter of expert opinion as to the meaning of 'alive', for I have to point out that the first expert, namely Mr Norris, who produced an affidavit on that very topic was introduced by him. Professor Newton replied later.

Counsel on behalf of the Official Solicitor, acting as amicus curiae, submitted that the alleged threatened criminality raised a difficult question of interpretation and pointed out that s 5(1) of the 1967 Act itself incorporates the word 'viable' in the phrase which refers to 'protecting the life of the viable foetus', a section to which I have already referred. By that date, he argued, Parliament would no doubt be aware of the controversies over the law on abortion and it is possible that the use of that word is some indication that Parliament thought it necessary to use that particular qualifying word. I think that that is possible too, though I would not attach too much weight to the parenthesis containing that word as an aid to construction.

Perhaps it is more significant that, though the reference to a foetus of 28 weeks or more being deemed 'capable of being born alive' is referable to the burden of proof, it is probably dealing with a foetus of an age that would be known or expected to be viable in 1929.

Mr Norris, of course, does not limit his statement to a question of presumption. He goes much further and in effect makes his 18 weeks an irrebuttable presumption, thus at a stroke as it were, reducing the 28 weeks to 18.

Counsel for the Official Solicitor submitted that the court should reject Mr Norris's interpretation of 'born alive' as the minimum indicia, without breathing, possibly with circulation and minus a number of indications referred to by Professor Newton.

In considering this submission, I find Mr Norris's statements as to the inevitability of every 18-week foetus being born alive unacceptable. It is not necessary for me, nor would I want, to try to decide on affidavit evidence in a somewhat limited sphere the answer, which baffles men and women with great scientific expertise, to a very profound question. I would, however, say that I am not greatly attracted to the very limited definition relied on by Mr Norris and I do not accept it as a realistic one.

Heilbron J, however, does not seem to reach a final view on this issue since she dismissed the plaintiff's application on other grounds. On appeal, the Court of Appeal dealt squarely with the point.

Sir John Donaldson MR: We have received affidavit evidence from three doctors, none of whom has examined Miss S. Their evidence is thus necessarily directed at the stage in the development of a foetus which can normally be expected to have been reached by the 18th to 21st week. On this, as one would expect, they are in substantial agreement. At that stage the cardiac muscle is contracting and a primitive circulation is developing. Thus the foetus could be said to demonstrate real and discernible signs of life. On the other hand, the foetus, even if then delivered by hysterotomy, would be incapable ever of breathing either naturally or with the aid of a ventilator. It is not a case of the foetus requiring a stimulus or assistance. It cannot and will never be able to breathe. Where the doctors disagree is as to whether a foetus, at this stage of development, can properly be described as 'a child capable of being born alive' within the meaning of the 1929 Act. That essentially depends on the interpretation of the statute and is a matter for the courts.

We have no evidence of the state of the foetus being carried by Miss S but, if it has reached the normal stage of development and so is incapable ever of breathing, it is not in our judgment 'a child capable of being born alive' within the meaning of the 1929 Act and accordingly the termination of this pregnancy would not constitute an offence under that Act.

Stephen Brown and Russell LJJ agreed.

Is it not the case that the Court of Appeal has interpreted the 1929 Act as protecting the 'viable foetus'? Even if this is so, it still leaves the question of what 'viable' means? Does it mean 'capable of surviving'? If it does, even this needs further clarification. For how long must a foetus be capable of surviving to come within this definition? The rule in homicide cases is that it is immaterial how long the person (including the newborn child) would have lived. As Glanville Williams tells us: ' . . . every instance of killing is an instance of accelerating death; and even if death is hastened by as little as five minutes it is still a criminal homicide.' (*Textbook of Criminal Law*, *supra*, at p 378.)

Support for this wide view of 'the capacity to survive' is to be found in Heilbron J's tentative observation that 'viability . . . embraces not only being born alive but surviving, for however short a time . . .' (at p 1238). Would a court adopt this view when considering a foetus *in utero*? Or would a court determine that a crime was committed only where it could be shown that a foetus would have been capable of being born alive or surviving for a reasonable period of time?

The issue arose directly in *Rance v Mid-Downs HA*.

Rance v Mid-Downs HA [1991] 1 QB 587, [1991] 1 All ER 801 (Brooke J)

The plaintiffs were a married couple. In late 1982 or early 1983 the first plaintiff became pregnant. On 9 June 1983 when the first plaintiff was about 26 weeks pregnant she had an ultrasound scan at a hospital administered by the defendant health authority. The radiographer taking the scan thought that the scan showed a possible abnormality in the foetus and marked on her notes '??F. Spine'. Later that day she discussed her suspicions of abnormality with the consultant radiologist at the hospital, who decided that no further action should be taken because there was 'no firm evidence of abnormality'. On 13 September the baby was born and was found to be suffering from spina bifida. The plaintiffs subsequently discovered that the spina bifida may have shown up on one of the scans taken of the first plaintiff and they brought an action against the health authority and the consultant radiologist claiming that the defendants had been negligent in not ascertaining whether the foetus was abnormal when that possibility was raised by the radiographer and had thereby deprived the plaintiffs of the possibility of having the pregnancy terminated. The defendants denied negligence and contended that in any event if the abnormality had been discovered at 26 weeks it would have been an offence under s 1 of the Infant Life (Preservation) Act 1929 to have terminated the first plaintiff's pregnancy then because the termination would have taken place when the foetus was 27 weeks old and by that time the foetus was 'a child capable of being born alive' whose destruction before it had an existence independent of its mother was unlawful except where it was necessary to preserve the mother's life.

Brooke J: To interpret the intention of Parliament when it enacted the 1929 Act, I must put myself in the draftsman's chair in 1929. I must identify the historical background and the mischief which the Act was enacted to remedy and I must construe the words in dispute in the context of the Act as a whole. If the natural and ordinary meaning of the words is clear, I must give effect to them, even if I find their effect goes beyond what was needed to deal with the mischief. If that meaning is ambiguous, then I must call in aid other appropriate canons of construction to help me to identify Parliament's intention. I must also consider the effect, if any, on the construction of the 1929 Act, of s 5(1) of the 1967 Act. . . .

English law has always made a distinction between the status of a foetus or child in its mother's womb and the status of a child born alive. It is manslaughter unlawfully to kill a child born alive and murder if the requisite intent is proved. Four nineteenth century cases illustrate the approach of English judges when the termination of life occurred at or near the moment of birth. In *R v Poulton* (1832) 5 C & P 329, 172 ER 997 there was evidence that the baby had breathed but insufficient evidence that the child had ever been fully born. The jury was told by a medical expert that it frequently happened that a child was born as far as the head was concerned but that death took place before the whole delivery was complete. Littledale J directed the jury that they must be satisfied that the child had been born alive before they could convict and added (5 C & P 329 at 330, 172 ER 997 at 998):

> With respect to the birth, the being born must mean that the whole body is brought into the world; it is not sufficient that the child respires in the progress of the birth.

In *R v Enoch* (1833) 5 C & P 539, 172 ER 1089 Parke J adopted this ruling when he directed the jury that the child might breathe before it was born but its having breathed was not sufficiently life to make the killing of the child murder and that there must have been an independent circulation of the child.

In *R v Brain* (1834) 6 C & P 349, 172 ER 1272 Parke J directed a jury that if a child had been wholly born, and was alive, it was not essential that it should have breathed at the time it was killed, since many children were born alive, yet did not breathe for some time after birth.

Finally, in *R v Handley* (1874) 13 Cox CC 79 Brett J was concerned with a case in which a newly born child was found dead. The umbilical cord was separated, the internal viscera were healthy and the bowels had acted soon after birth. The bladder and stomach were empty. The general effect of the medical evidence was that the child was full born, was born alive and from the inflated condition of the lungs had lived for an hour or more. Brett J directed the jury that a child was considered to have been born alive, ie whether it existed as a live child, that is to say, breathing and living by reason of its breathing through its own lungs alone, without deriving any of its living or power of living by or through any connection with the mother.

Parliament showed that it was aware of the common law approach to the concept of being alive in its legislation relating to the registration of births and deaths. For example, the statutory definition of the expression 'still-born', in s 12 of the Births and Deaths Registration Act 1926, is that it:

> . . . shall apply to any child what has issued forth from its mother after the twenty-eighth week of pregnancy and which did not at any time after being completely expelled from its mother, breathe or show any other signs of life.

In 1929, therefore, the law protected the foetus in utero when it prohibited acts done unlawfully to procure a miscarriage. It protected the child which was born as a live child, breathing and living without any connection with its mother. It provided no protection, however, to the child while it was in the process of being born and before it had been completely separated from its mother, and the extinction of the child's potential life at this intermediate stage was not an offence. This lacuna in the law was identified by Talbot J when charging the grand jury at the Liverpool Assizes in June 1928 in these words:

> The law upon the matter is unsatisfactory and it is right that every appropriate opportunity should be taken to call public attention to it. It is a felony to procure abortion and it is murder to take the life of a child when it is fully born, but to take the life of a child while it is being born and before it is fully born is no offence whatever.

(Cited in the *Report of the Select Committee on the Infant Life (Preservation) Bill* (HL Paper (1987-88) no 50) para 8.)

I am satisfied that this was the mischief which Parliament intended to remedy when it enacted the 1929 Act. In remedying the mischief, it adopted the concept of 'born alive', which was now well understood following the direction of Brett J in *R v Handley*, and it extended the protection of the law to the child who was capable of being born alive up to the moment when it was in fact born alive and therefore qualified to receive the protection of the law of homicide. It was agreed between counsel that in the event the words used by Parliament in 1929 extended to cover not only the actual period of birth but also the period when the child capable of being born alive was still in its mother's womb.

Parliament gave effect to its new determination to protect the existence of the child capable of being born alive in s 1(1) of the 1929 Act. In contrast, s 1(2) of the Act was concerned with practical ways and means of giving effect to Parliament's intentions. Parliament could have chosen to resolve the difficult problem of proving in a criminal court that the child whose existence was terminated was capable of being born alive, by enacting a cut-off date, say at 28 weeks, before which there was a conclusive presumption that a child was incapable of being born alive and after which there was a rebuttable presumption that it was so capable. However, this course was not adopted. Parliament created the rebuttable presumption that a child of over 28 weeks' gestation was capable of being born alive, but it was otherwise silent on matters of evidential proof. Therefore, if the Crown succeeded in proving, to a criminal standard of proof, that a particular child of under 28 weeks' gestation had been capable of being born alive, the defendant would be convicted of an offence under the new Act if the other ingredients of the offence were proved. The difficulty was not with the concept 'capable of being born alive', but with proving to a jury's satisfaction without the help of a statutory presumption or information derived from modern technological know-how, that the child in question had had those attributes.

In my judgment the meaning of the words 'born alive' are clear, and the meaning of the words 'capable of being born alive' are also clear. The anencephalic child (who lacks all or most of the cerebral hemispheres but is capable of using its lungs) and the spina bifida child (who possesses one or more of the adverse criteria identified by Professor Lorber) is each born alive if, after birth, it exists as a live child, that is to say breathing and living by reason of its breathing through its own lungs alone, without deriving any of its living or power of living by or through any connection with its mother. For the purposes of this judgment I do not have to consider the case of life before breathing, which was referred to in *R v Brain*. Once the foetus has reached a state of development in the womb that it is capable, if born, of possessing those attributes, it is capable of being born alive within the meaning of the 1929 Act. My confidence in this conclusion is strengthened by reference to *C v S* [1987] 1 All ER 1230 at 1242, [1988] QB 135 at 151. In giving the judgment of the Court of Appeal Sir John Donaldson MR rejected the proposition that a foetus between 18 and 21 weeks of age was, or might be, a child 'capable of being born alive', in these words:

> . . . the fetus, even if then delivered by hysterotomy, would be incapable ever of . . . requiring a stimulus or assistance. It cannot and will never be able to breathe . . . if [this fetus] has reached the normal stage of development and so is incapable ever of

breathing, it is not in our judgment 'a child capable of being born alive' within the meaning of the 1929 Act . . .

I have taken into account the view of Heilbron J in the same case that the phrase 'capable of being born alive' does not have a clear and plain meaning and is ambiguous (see [1987] 1 All ER 1230 at 1239-1240, [1988] QB 135 at 147). However, in my judgment, the words are for all practical purposes clear and on ordinary principles of statutory construction the intention of Parliament in 1929 is clear and I must give effect to it.

I do not consider that the enactment of s 5(1) of the 1967 Act ('Nothing in this Act shall affect the provisions of the Infant Life (Preservation) Act 1929 (protecting the life of the viable foetus)') changes or modifies the meaning of the 1929 Act in any way. The primary dictionary meaning of the word 'viable', which is derived from the French word 'vie', is 'capable of living'. I was also referred to *Larousse*, which shows that the primary meaning of the French word 'viable' is 'qui peut vivre'. I have allowed for the fact that the 1967 Act was derived from a private member's Bill, of which Lord Diplock commented in *Royal College of Nursing of the UK v Dept of Health and Social Security* [1981] 1 All ER 545 at 567, [1981] AC 800 at 824:

> . . . maybe for that reason, it lacks that style and consistency of draftsmanship both internal to the Act itself and in relation to other statutes which one would expect to find in legislation that had its origin in the office of parliamentary counsel.

However, even if I was persuaded that Parliament could alter the clear meaning of an earlier Act by this rather elliptic means – and there is certainly nothing in the excerpt from *Craies on Statute Law* (7th edn, 1971) pp 146-149 to which I was referred, to suggest that this method of 'legislative declaration' or 'parliamentary exposition' has any precedent – I do not consider that in 1967 Parliament intended to do so. In my judgment the word 'viable' was simply being used as a convenient shorthand for the words 'capable of being born alive' and I cannot discern any Parliamentary intention in 1967 to change the effect of the 1929 Act.

Counsel for the plaintiffs submitted at the beginning of his closing speech that the words 'capable of being born alive' meant 'viable', in the sense of 'capable of being born alive and surviving into old age in the normal way without intensive care or surgical intervention'. He submitted that in 1929 Parliament can only have had in mind the natural capacity given to a child to survive without artificial aids and interventions unthought of in 1929. He pointed out that any other interpretation, given the wider meaning for which he contended, introduced considerably more uncertainty. If not into old age, then what length of survival should be postulated? Why stop at 7 or 28 days? If intensive care, what degree of intensive care? The care of a specialist referral centre or a peripheral hospital? Is operative intervention to be postulated or not?

When I tested this submission in argument, he appeared to be willing to withdraw from it, and his fall-back submission was that the words entailed the concept of being alive and surviving for a reasonable period. He said that it would be for a jury to decide how long was reasonable, but he suggested that 28 days, or possibly seven days, would have been the sort of period which Parliament would have had in mind.

The posing of all these questions, and the shifting stances adopted by counsel in argument, strengthen me in my conviction that my preferred construction of the disputed words is correct. I do not believe for one moment that Parliament intended the protection it was affording to children in the course of being born to be limited to the class of healthy children originally identified by counsel and to be denied to those children whose expectation of long life was not so assured at the moment of birth. Nor do I consider, particularly in the light of the historical background to the Act, that Parliament intended the concept of 'capable of being born alive' to be left to be decided by different juries' views of what period of survival after birth should be regarded as reasonable in order to qualify the child for the protection of the Act. . . .

[In conclusion] I am satisfied to a very high standard of proof that [the baby] would have been capable of being born alive at the time any hypothetical abortion had taken place and that abortion would therefore have been unlawful.

5. Places

Section 1(3) of the 1967 Act provides:

> Except as provided by subsection (4) of this section, any treatment for the termination of pregnancy must be carried out in a hospital vested in the Secretary of State for the purposes

of his functions under the National Health Services Act 1977 or the National Health Service (Scotland) Act 1978 or in a hospital vested in a National Health Service trust or in a place approved for the purposes of this section by the Secretary of State.

Ordinarily, no difficulty arises over this provision since the 'treatment for the termination' either has or has not been carried out in an institution covered by subsection 3. The development of the drug RU-486 (Mifepristone) creates problems with this provision.

Mifepristone blocks the action of the female hormone, progesterone, and causes the surface of the endometrium to be shed. In doing this, Mifepristone can have two distinct effects. First, if taken a short time after sexual intercourse it can prevent the implantation of a fertilised egg. As such, it does not have a contraceptive effect but rather it acts as a contragestive. Importantly, by acting to prevent implantation, it is not an abortifacient (*R v Dhingra* (1991) *Times* 25 January).

Secondly, however, Mifepristone can also act to dislodge a fertilised egg which has implanted at the time the drug is taken. As such it is an abortifacient. In July 1991 Mifepristone was granted a product licence in the UK for use as an abortifacient and is marketed by its developers, Roussel, under the brand name *'Mifegyne'* (Product Licence No: PL 0109/0232).

The use of Mifepristone is regulated by the conditions of its product licence granted under the Medicines Act 1968. These, in turn, are reflected in the approved Data Sheet for *'Mifegyne'* (08 DSF 91 UK) as follows. Medicinal abortion using Mifepristone does not require that the woman be admitted to hospital as an in-patient. Instead, it may be prescribed within the first seven weeks of pregnancy (or nine weeks after the first day of the last monthly period); the woman should be under 35 and a fit non-smoker; 600mg of the drug should be taken (in divided doses of 200mg); the woman will be observed for at least 2 hours; following which she will be discharged home to return 36-48 hours later for the insertion of a prostaglandin vaginal pessary which ensures the termination is successful in 95% of cases. For the remaining 5% of cases surgical intervention will be necessary. While it is essential that the woman should remain under the care of a doctor, she does not have to remain in a clinic or hospital except for the initial administration and subsequent insertion of the prostaglandin pessary.

Two difficulties of interpretation of the Abortion Act arise here out of the use of Mifepristone: (1) does the 'treatment for the termination of pregnancy' take place at an NHS hospital, NHS Trust or other place approved by the Secretary of State as is required by section 1(3) of the Act? (2) in determining this, what is the 'treatment' which must be carried out at one of these places?

Until the development of Mifepristone, legal terminations of pregnancy were, and were always intended to be, carried out in an NHS hospital or an approved clinic. The procedures involving surgery, dilatation and curettage (D & C) or by medical induction require that they are carried out in such institutions because of the need for their facilities and staff. As we have seen Mifepristone does not require that the patient be hospitalised and it was certainly contemplated that Mifepristone might be administered in a GP's surgery (see *Hansard* HC vol 174, col 1199, Kenneth Clarke). If Mifepristone were prescribed by a general practitioner in a surgery, the surgery would need to be individually approved by the Secretary of State under section 1(3) as an approved place. This would have presented a practical difficulty given the number of GP surgeries that exist. To meet this, section 1(3A) was added to the

1967 Act (by section 37 of the Human Fertilisation and Embryology Act 1990) specifically to cover the use of Mifepristone and its prescription by GPs.
Section 1(3A) provides:

1 (3A) The power under subsection (3) of this section to approve a place includes power, in relation to treatment consisting primarily in the use of such medicines as may be specified in the approval and carried out in such manner as may be so specified, to approve a class of places.

As a result, the Secretary of State may approve, as a class, such places as GPs' surgeries although she does not appear to have done so to date.

Another problem still remains if Mifepristone is prescribed in an NHS hospital or approved place. What sections 1(3) and 1(3A) require is that the '*treatment* for the termination of pregnancy' must be carried out at an NHS (or Trust) hospital or approved place. If the word 'treatment' is limited in meaning to the prescription, the initial administration of the drug and the follow-up use of the prostaglandin pessary, it is clear from the conditions of the product licence that these must occur in an NHS hospital or approved place.

However, this assumes a somewhat narrow view of the meaning of 'treatment'. As we have seen, when Mifepristone is prescribed the woman will take three 200mg pills at the hospital. If, after two hours, she displays no effects she will be discharged home to return 36 to 48 hours later for the prostaglandin pessary to be inserted unless she has already aborted. Consequently, Mifepristone will affect her throughout this period. Arguably, her 'treatment' relates to the whole of this period of time during which the drug is acting on her. Such a view is entirely consistent with the case, *Royal College of Nursing of the UK v DHSS* [1981] AC 800 (see *infra*, p 914) where it is clear that the House of Lords viewed 'termination of pregnancy . . . as being a process of treatment' (*per* Lord Keith at 834).

If this wider view is right, there are two options. First, the Secretary of State could seek to approve every place under the sun where the woman might go. But this would be impracticable and, in any event, almost certainly beyond the powers conferred by section 1(3) and 1(3A). On one view, the power to approve a class of place appears to be unfettered and, therefore, approval of any class of place would seem to be within the powers given the Secretary of State under section 1(3). However, statutory powers are rarely considered by the courts to be beyond review. Certainly, the exercise of this power would be subject to judicial review and the court would require the Secretary of State to act for a purpose implicitly contemplated by the Act. If he does not, the exercise of his power under s 1(3A) will be *ultra vires*. It could be argued that the purpose of the statute is to require that any terminations that are to be performed be performed in a medical environment.

Secondly, once the treatment has begun, she will have to stay in the NHS hospital or approved place until the pregnancy is terminated. This latter consequence was clearly not intended and would defeat the purpose underlying the development of Mifepristone. It would, however, appear to be the correct interpretation of section 1(3) and 1(3A), notwithstanding the assumption embodied in Schedule 2 of the Abortion Regulations 1991 (SI 1991 No 499). There, the doctor performing the termination is required to notify the Chief Medical Officer, *inter alia*, of the 'date of treatment' and the 'address of place of treatment'. Both of these clearly do not contemplate that 'treatment' should be a continuing process over several days.

6. The operation of the 1967 Act

(a) The regulations

By section 2 of the Abortion Act 1967, the Secretary of State is empowered to make regulations.

> 2 – (1) The Secretary of State in respect of England and Wales, and the Secretary of State in respect of Scotland, shall by statutory instrument make regulations to provide –
> (a) for requiring any such opinion as is referred to in section 1 of this Act to be certified by the practitioners or practitioner concerned in such form and at such time as may be prescribed by the regulations, and for requiring the preservation and disposal of certificates made for the purposes of the regulations;
> (b) for requiring any registered medical practitioner who terminates a pregnancy to give notice of the termination and such other information relating to the termination as may be so prescribed;
> (c) for prohibiting the disclosure, except to such persons or for such purposes as may be so prescribed, of notices given or information furnished pursuant to the regulations.

Contravention of these Regulations is, by virtue of s 2(3), a summary criminal offence. The Abortion Regulations 1991 (SI 1991 No 490), which came into effect on 1 April 1991, deal with two main areas.

(i) CERTIFICATION OF THE NECESSARY MEDICAL OPINIONS UNDER THE ACT

The Abortion Regulations 1991 in regulation 3, provide as follows:

Certificate of opinion
3 (1) Any opinion to which section 1 of the Act refers shall be certified –
(a) in the case of a pregnancy terminated in accordance with section 1(1) of the Act, in the form set out in Part I of Schedule 1 to these Regulations, and
(b) in the case of a pregnancy terminated in accordance with section 1(4) of the Act, in the form set out in Part II of that Schedule.
(2) Any certificate of an opinion referred to in section 1(1) of the Act shall be given before the commencement of the treatment for the termination of the pregnancy to which it relates.
    (3) Any certificate of an opinion referred to in section 1(4) of the Act shall be given before the commencement of the treatment for the termination of the pregnancy to which it relates or, if that is not reasonably practicable, not later than 24 hours after such termination.
    (4) Any such certificate as is referred to in paragraphs (2) and (3) of this regulation shall be preserved by the practitioner who terminated the pregnancy to which it relates for a period of not less than three years beginning with the date of the termination.
    (5) A certificate which is no longer to be preserved shall be destroyed by the person in whose custody it then is.

Schedule 1 provides two standard certificates contemplated in regulation 3(1). We set out here Certificate A which deals with the usual case of termination of pregnancy. Certificate B, which deals with situations of emergency, is set out *infra*, p 891.

SCHEDULE 1

PART I

IN CONFIDENCE   **CERTIFICATE A**
ABORTION ACT 1967

Not to be destroyed within three years of the date of operation
Certificate to be completed before an abortion is
performed under Section 1(1) of the Act

I, ...

(Name and qualifications of practitioner in block capitals)

of...

....

(Full address of practitioner)

Have/have not* seen/and examined* the pregnant woman to whom this certificate relates at

....

....

(full address of place at which patient was seen or examined)

on ....

and I...

(Name and qualifications of practitioner in block capitals)

of...

....

(Full address of practitioner)

Have/have not* seen/and examined* the pregnant woman to whom this certificate relates at

....

....

(Full address of place at which the patient was seen or examined)

on ....

We hereby certify that we are of the opinion, formed in good faith, that in the case

of...

(Full name of pregnant woman in block capitals)

of...

....

(Usual place of residence of pregnant woman in block capitals)

(Ring appropriate letter(s))

A the continuance of the pregnancy would involve risk to the life of the pregnant woman greater than if the pregnancy were terminated;

B the termination is necessary to prevent grave permanent injury to the physical or mental health of the pregnant woman;

C the pregnancy has NOT exceeded its 24th week and that the continuance of the pregnancy would involve risk, greater than if the pregnancy were terminated, of injury to the physical or mental health of the pregnant woman;

D the pregnancy has NOT exceeded its 24th week and that the continuance of the pregnancy would involve risk, greater than if the pregnancy were terminated, of injury to the physical or mental health of any existing child(ren) of the family of the pregnant woman;

E there is a substantial risk that if the child were born it would suffer from such physical or mental abnormalities as to be seriously handicapped.

This certificate of opinion is given before the commencement of the treatment for the termination of pregnancy to which it refers and relates to the circumstances of the pregnant woman's individual case.

Signed... Date...

Signed... Date...

*Delete as appropriate   Form HSA 1 (revised 1991)

The only case dealing with the issue of certification is *R v Smith* [1974] 1 All ER 376, CA.

R v Smith [1974] 1 All ER 376, [1973] 1 WLR 1510 (CA)

Scarman LJ: The Act, though it renders lawful abortions that before its enactment would have been unlawful, does not depart from the basic principle of the common law as declared in *R v Bourne*, namely that the legality of an abortion depends on the opinion of the doctor. It has introduced the safeguard of two opinions: but, if they are formed in good faith by the time the operation is undertaken, the abortion is lawful. Thus a great social responsibility is firmly placed by the law on the shoulders of the medical profession.

On 28th April 1970 at the Hayward Nursing Home a Miss Rodgers underwent an operation performed by the appellant, the initial purpose of which was to terminate her pregnancy. The prosecution's case was that when he operated, the appellant was not acting in good faith; he had not formed a bona fide opinion as to the balance of risk between termination and continuation of her pregnancy, that is to say, that its continuance would involve risk to her physical or mental health greater than if it were terminated. The appellant's defence was twofold: he said that he formed an honest opinion as to the need for an abortion, but that when he had the girl on the operating table, he found she was starting an inevitable abortion. Thus, according to him, his operation became not a termination but a facilitating and tidying up of an inevitable abortion – a natural process which had already begun. If this be the truth, the prosecution concedes that the operation would be lawful without the need of recourse to the Abortion Act 1967.

. . . If the jury rejected, as they did, the tale of an inevitable abortion, the sequence of events was such as to call for very careful consideration whether it was possible to believe that the appellant had formed in good faith, or at all, the opinion necessary to give him the protection of the 1967 Act. Had he, or had he not, abused the trust reposed in him by the Act of Parliament? The burden was on the prosecution to prove beyond reasonable doubt that he had. All this was faithfully explained to the jury by the recorder. We quote only one passage towards the end of the summing-up:

'[The appellant] took the view that if any girl wanted her pregnancy terminated, that of itself was, if not entirely sufficient, a very powerful indication of the risk of injury to her mental health if the pregnancy continued being greater than if the pregnancy was terminated. He told you that all his actions were within the Act, so he was telling you that, though he took the view that really with every girl or woman who wanted her pregnancy terminated that was a very powerful reason for terminating it, because it may involve risk to her mental health, he still acted within the Act and balanced the risks of termination against the risks of continuation. If two doctors genuinely form an opinion in each case that they deal with that the risk of continuance is more than the risk of termination, it does not matter whether they are right or wrong in that view. If they form that opinion genuinely and in good faith, that in fact comes within the Act, and there is no guilt attached to it. You have to wonder in the case of [the appellant] whether such a view could genuinely be held by a medical man, whether it was held in the case of Miss Rodgers in particular. The only indication on the case notes about any danger to her mental or physical health was the word 'depressed', 'not willing to marry and depressed'. Those are the only words about it on the case notes. You have to ask yourselves, was there any balancing of the risks involved in allowing the pregnancy to continue and allowing the pregnancy to be terminated, or was this a mere routine abortion for cash? That is what you have to consider. Was a second opinion even contemplated as a necessity in this case of Miss Rodgers? If, on the very first interview when the girl was seen by [the appellant], the very first interview he had with her, he offered to operate on her the next morning, was there any real contemplation or thought that a second opinion was necessary?'

These were the questions for the jury; and they have been answered adversely to the appellant. The view the jury took was one fully open to them on the evidence; and we can see no reason for the suggestion that their view was wrong or unsafe or unsatisfactory . . .

(See also, *Wall v Livingston* [1982] 1 NZLR 734 (NZCA).)

(ii) COLLECTION OF DATA

The 1991 Regulations require 'any practitioner' who terminates a pregnancy to notify the appropriate Chief Medical Officer (regulation 4(1)). Significantly, the Regulations, while requiring such notification, impose careful restrictions upon further dissemination of the notice or information by the appropriate Chief Medical Officer. These are set out in regulation 5 reproduced in Chapter 9.

(b) Emergencies

So far we have considered the operation of the Act in what might be described as usual circumstances. The Act, however, makes specific provisions for emergencies in section 1(4).

> 1 (4) Subsection (3) of this section, and so much of subsection (1) as relates to the opinion of two registered medical practitioners, shall not apply to the termination of a pregnancy by a registered medical practitioner in a case where he is of the opinion, formed in good faith, that the termination is immediately necessary to save the life or to prevent grave permanent injury to the physical or mental health of the pregnant woman.

As a consequence of this provision, where a termination is (a) immediately necessary (b) to save the life of the mother or prevent grave permanent injury to her physical or mental health, the decision to carry out the termination can be made by one doctor alone and need not be carried out in an NHS hospital, NHS Trust hospital or other approved place. Subsection 4 does not remove the need for the single doctor to form the view in good faith that there are grounds for termination under section 1(1), specifically those set out in section 1(1)(b) or (c). This poses no problem since there is (now) virtual symmetry between the grounds in section 1(1)(b) and (c) and the wording of subsection 4.

As regards certification in the case of an emergency, regulation 3(1)(b) of the Abortion Regulations 1991 states that:

> 3(1) Any opinions to which section 1 of the Act refers shall be certified . . .
> (b)   in the case of a pregnancy terminated in accordance with section 1(4) of the Act, in the form set out in Part II of [Schedule 1].

Certificate B in Schedule 1 is as follows:

PART II

SCHEDULE 1

IN CONFIDENCE   **Certificate B**

Not to be destroyed within three years of the date of operation

ABORTION ACT 1967
CERTIFICATE TO BE COMPLETED IN RELATION TO ABORTION PERFORMED IN EMERGENCY UNDER SECTION 1(4) OF THE ACT

I, ...

(Name and qualifications of practitioner in block capitals)

of...

....

(Full address of practitioner)

hereby certify that I *am/was of the opinion formed in good faith that it *is/was necessary immediately to terminate the pregnancy of

....

(Full name of pregnant woman in block capitals)

of...

....

(Usual place of residence of pregnant woman in block capitals)

	in order
(Ring appro-priate number)	1. to save the life of the pregnant woman; or
	2. to prevent grave permanent injury to the physical or mental health of the pregnant woman.
	This certificate of opinion is given—
(Ring appro-priate number)	A. before the commencement of the treatment for the termination of the pregnancy to which it relates; or, if that is not reasonably practicable, then
	B. not later than 24 hours after such termination.

Signed...

Date...

*Delete as appropriate

Notice from the wording of the certificate, which reflects regulation 3(3), that in the case of an emergency where it is not reasonably practical to complete the certification before the termination, it must be completed no later than 24 hours afterwards.

(c) Conscientious objection

The Abortion Act 1967, s 4 reads as follows:

4 – (1) Subject to subsection (2) of this section, no person shall be under any duty, whether by contract or by any statutory or other legal requirement, to participate in any treatment authorised by this Act to which he has a conscientious objection:
    Provided that in any legal proceedings the burden of proof of conscientious objection shall rest on the person claiming to rely on it.
    (2) Nothing in subsection (1) of this section shall affect any duty to participate in treatment which is necessary to save the life or to prevent grave permanent injury to the physical or mental health of a pregnant woman.

The effect of this provision is discussed in the following.

Mason and McCall Smith, *Law and Medical Ethics* (3rd edn 1991)

[An] important and unfortunate result of the 1967 Act is that some discrimination takes place against doctors, and especially those seeking to become gynaecologists, who are unable to accept its wide terms. It is, however, to be noted that while a doctor may, in general, refuse to take part in the abortion procedure, he remains under an obligation to advise. Such advice is subject to the normal rules of medical negligence and the conscientious objector's only recourse is, therefore, to refer his patient to another practitioner, a practice which is only marginally compatible with a strong conscience and which must damage the essential bond of trust between doctor and patient . . . The doctor's conscience does not absolve him from treating a woman when the continuation of the pregnancy is life-threatening and there is of course, no right to conscience in treating the *results* of a legal abortion; these considerations apply equally to the nursing staff.

The scope of section 4 has only been considered by the courts on one occasion in *Janaway v Salford Area Health Authority* [1989] AC 537, [1988] 3 All ER

1079. The central question of difficulty raised in section 4 relates to the meaning of the words 'participate in any treatment' under the Abortion Act. The situation contemplated by section 4 is one in which a person *but for* the subsection would be under a legal duty to participate in treatment under the Act. The effect of section 4 is to absolve that person of any such duty whether it be a duty owed to his employer because of the terms of his contract of employment or to his patient. While it will be perfectly obvious in most cases whether a person is being asked to participate in a termination of pregnancy and thus may rely upon section 4, some problems arise the less closely involved the person may be.

Janaway v Salford Health Authority [1989] AC 537, [1988] 3 All ER 1079 (HL)

Lord Keith: My Lords, the appellant, Mrs Janaway (the applicant), took up employment with the respondent health authority on 25 June 1984. She was engaged as a secretary/receptionist at Irlam Health Centre, working for a Dr Barooah. On 11 September 1984 she was asked by Dr Barooah to type a letter which had to do with referring a pregnant patient for an appointment with a consultant with a view to the latter forming an opinion as to whether the pregnancy should be terminated under the Abortion Act 1967. The applicant, a Roman Catholic holding the belief that abortion is morally wrong, refused to type the letter, which was eventually written by hand by another doctor at the health centre. On 31 October 1984 the applicant was interviewed by a personnel officer from the authority and told him that she felt entitled to refuse to type the letter, and any others concerned with termination of pregnancy, by virtue of the conscientious objection provision contained in s 4(1) of the 1967 Act, to which I shall refer later. On 7 November 1984 the personnel officer wrote to the applicant stating that her refusal to type correspondence of the kind in question amounted to a breach of the authority's disciplinary rules as being 'unjustified refusal of a lawful and reasonable instruction' and asking for a firm assurance that she would in future carry out such instructions. The applicant sent in reply a letter dated 12 November 1984 which concluded:

> '. . . except insofar as I stand by the protection afforded by S 4(1) of the Abortion Act [1967] I confirm that I will continue, as I have done in the past, to carry out my contractual duties as detailed in my job description.'

On 27 November 1984 the applicant had a meeting, at which she reaffirmed her position, with the personnel officer and the community services administrator. On 30 November the latter wrote to her saying that legal advice had been obtained to the effect that s 4(1) of the 1967 Act did not apply to her refusal, and that her employment had been terminated from 27 November on grounds of misconduct. The applicant appealed against her dismissal to the authority's appeal tribunal, but her appeal was dismissed, and the authority formally ratified the decision on 6 February 1985.

On 17 June the applicant, with leave, applied for judicial review in the shape of an order of certiorari to quash the authority's decision of 6 February 1985 and a declaration that, by reason of her conscientious objection to typing correspondence of the kind in question, she was not under any duty to carry out such work.

The application was dismissed by Nolan J on 12 February 1985, and his decision was affirmed by the Court of Appeal (Slade, Balcombe and Stocker LJJ) ([1988] 2 WLR 442) on 18 December 1987. The applicant now appeals, with leave granted by the Court of Appeal, to your Lordships' House. . . .

The applicant claims the protection of s 4(1). The issue in the case turns on the true construction of the words in that subsection 'participate in any treatment authorised by this Act'. For the applicant it is maintained that the words cover taking part in any arrangement preliminary to and intended to bring about medical or surgical measures aimed at terminating a pregnancy, including the typing of letters referring a patient to a consultant. The health authority argues that the meaning of the words is limited to taking part in the actual procedures undertaken at the hospital or other approved place with a view to the termination of a pregnancy.

The argument for the applicant proceeds on the lines that the acts attracting the protection afforded by s 4(1) are intended to be coextensive with those which are authorised by s 1(1) and which in the absence of that provision would be criminal. The criminal law about accessories treats one who aids and abets, counsels or procures a criminal act as liable to the same extent as a principal actor. In the absence of s 1(1) the applicant by typing a letter of referral would be counselling or procuring an abortion, or at least helping to do so, and subject to a possible defence on the principle of *R v Bourne* [1938] 3 All ER 615, [1939] 1 KB 687 would be criminally liable. Therefore any requirement to type such a letter is relieved, in the face of a conscientious objection, by s 4(1).

The majority of the Court of Appeal (Slade and Stocker LJJ) accepted the main thrust of the applicant's argument, to the effect that ss 1(1) and 4(1) are coextensive, but decided against her on the ground that her intention in typing a letter of referral would not be to assist in procuring an abortion but merely to carry out the obligations of her employment. In their view the typing of such a letter by the applicant would not be a criminal offence in the absence of s 1(1).

Nolan J, however, and Balcombe LJ in the Court of Appeal rejected the applicant's main argument. They accepted the argument for the health authority that on a proper construction the word 'participate' in s 4(1) did not import the whole concept of principal and accessory residing in the criminal law, but in its ordinary and natural meaning referred to actually taking part in treatment administered in a hospital or other approved place in accordance with s 1(3), for the purpose of terminating a pregnancy.

In my opinion Nolan J and Balcombe LJ were right to reach the conclusion they did. I agree entirely with their view about the natural meaning of the word 'participate' in this context. Although the word is commonly used to describe the activities of accessories in the criminal law field, it is not a term of art there. It is in any event not being used in a criminal context in s 4(1). Ex hypothesi treatment for termination of a pregnancy under s 1 is not criminal. I do not consider that Parliament can reasonably have intended by its use to import all the technicalities of the criminal law about principal and accessory, which can on occasion raise very nice questions about whether someone is guilty as an accessory. Such niceties would be very difficult of solution for an ordinary health authority. If Parliament had intended the result contended for by the applicant, it could have procured it very clearly and easily by referring to participation 'in anything authorised by this Act' instead of 'in any treatment [so] authorised'. It is to be observed that s 4 appears to represent something of a compromise in relation to conscientious objection. One who believes all abortion to be morally wrong would conscientiously object even to such treatment as is mentioned in sub-s (2), yet the subsection would not allow the objection to receive effect.

The applicant's argument placed some reliance on a passage in the speech of Lord Roskill in *Royal College of Nursing of the United Kingdom v Department of Health and Social Security* [1981] 1 All ER 545 at 577, [1981] AC 800 at 837-838:

> My Lords, I read and reread the 1967 Act to see if I can discern in its provisions any consistent pattern in the use of the phrase 'a pregnancy is terminated' or 'termination of a pregnancy' on the one hand and 'treatment for the termination of a pregnancy' on the other hand. One finds the former phrase in s 1(1) and (1) (*a*), the latter in s 1(3), the former in ss 1(4) and 2(1)(*b*) and the latter in s 3(1)(*a*) and (*c*). Most important to my mind is s 4, which is the conscientious objection section. This section in two places refers to 'participate in treatment' in the context of conscientious objection. If one construes s 4 in conjunction with s 1(1), as surely one should do in order to determine to what it is that conscientious objection is permitted, it seems to me that s 4 strongly supports the wider construction of s 1(1). It was suggested that acceptance of the department's submission involved rewriting that subsection so as to add words which are not to be found in the language of the subsection. My Lords, with great respect to that submission, I do not agree. If one construes the words 'when a pregnancy is terminated by a registered medical practitioner' in s 1(1) as embracing the case where the 'treatment for the termination of a pregnancy is carried out under the control of a doctor in accordance with ordinary current medical practice' I think one is reading 'termination of pregnancy' and 'treatment for termination of pregnancy' as virtually synonymous and as I think Parliament must have intended they should be read. Such a construction avoids a number of anomalies as, for example, where there is no pregnancy or where the extra-amniotic process fails to achieve its objective within the normal limits of time set for its operation.

That case was concerned with a particular process of treatment for the termination of pregnancy carried out in hospital, important parts of which were performed not by a registered medical practitioner but by a nurse acting under his instructions.

The issue was whether the actions of the nurse were unlawful, and it was held that they were not, on the ground that what was authorised by the Act was the whole medical process resulting in termination of pregnancy and that the process was carried out by a registered medical practitioner when that was done under his supervision and in accordance with his instructions, notwithstanding that certain parts of the process were carried out by others. The House was not concerned with the meaning of the word 'participate' in s 4(1) in relation to anything other than the actual medical process carried out in the hospital, and then only indirectly. So Lord Roskill's words cannot be read as having any bearing on the decision of the present case.

The question could also arise in the case of a GP. A woman may present herself seeking a termination of pregnancy. Assuming he has a conscientious objection, what is the extent of his legal duty to her, or, putting it another way, at what point can he rely upon section 4(1)?

In the Court of Appeal, in *Janaway* Stocker LJ raised this question in the context of a doctor's refusal to certify that a ground for termination existed:

In my view, apart from section 4(1), a doctor would be under a duty in the performance of his professional duties to certify on the green form [ie the certificate] and to take such other steps as he might consider advisable in any case in which his medical and clinical opinion was that an abortion should be performed for any of the reasons set out in the Act, or in the green form itself. Apart from section 4(1) he would be in breach of his professional duty to his patient and [where relevant] of his duty to the employing authority if he refused to do so . . .

In the House of Lords, Lord Keith left the point open:

A certain amount of argument was addressed to the Abortion Regulations 1968, SI 1968/ 390 [see now Abortion Regulations 1991] which, inter alia, set out the form of certificate, known as 'the green form', to be signed by two registered medical practitioners in pursuance of s 1(1)(a) of the 1967 Act, and to the position in relation to s 4(1) of practitioners who might be required to sign such a certificate. The regulations do not appear to contemplate that the signing of the certificate would form part of treatment for the termination of pregnancy, since reg 3(2) provides:

Any certificate of an opinion referred to in section 1(1) of the Act shall be given before the commencement of the treatment for the termination of the pregnancy to which it relates.

It does not appear whether or not there are any circumstances under which a doctor might be under any legal duty to sign a green form, so as to place in difficulties one who had a conscientious objection to doing so. The fact that during the 20 years that the 1967 Act has been in force no problem seems to have surfaced in this connection may indicate that in practice none exists. So I do not think it appropriate to express any opinion on the matter.

Lord Keith clearly disagreed with Stocker LJ that 'participating in any treatment' extends to cover certification (ie signing the statutory form). On the face of it, the regulation referred to by Lord Keith justifies his conclusion. If this is correct that section 4(1) does not apply, it is crucial to determine this scope of the doctor's duty to his patient, ie at what point can the doctor say that he is not prepared to go further. Stocker LJ took the view that a doctor is under a legal duty to certify when he considers it medically justified. Lord Keith chose not to express a concluded view. Certainly, the doctor has a legal duty to exercise the usual due care and skill which would involve ascertaining the relevant medical facts. The woman may, after all, be in danger from the pregnancy.

In the case of an emergency, the conscientious objection provision does not apply.

4 (2) Nothing in subsection (1) of this section shall effect any duty to participate in treatment which is necessary to save the life or to prevent grave permanent injury to the physical or mental health of a pregnant woman.

Assuming, however, that there is no emergency, two questions arise. First, does the GP have a duty under his terms of service (and, therefore, implicitly to the patient) to sign the green form and *refer* the woman to a consultant? Secondly, even if no such duty arises, does the GP have a duty again under his terms of service (and, therefore, implicitly to the patient) at least to refer his patient to another GP who, he knows, is prepared to contemplate signing a certificate?

The answer to both questions turns upon the provisions of his terms of service under Schedule 2 of the NHS (General Medical Services) Regulations 1992 (SI 1992 No 635).

Paragraph 12 provides, *inter alia*, as follows:

12 (1) Subject to paragraphs 3, 13 and 44 a doctor shall render to his patients all necessary and appropriate personal medical services of the type usually provided by general medical practitioners.

(2) The services which a doctor is required by sub-paragraph (1) to render shall include the following

. . .

(d) arranging for the referral of patients, as appropriate, for the provision of any other services under the Act. . . .

The provision of services involving the termination of pregnancy is one of the 'other services' under the 1977 Act (ss 1 and 3). Consequently, it is beyond argument that in answer to our second question the GP must refer in the sense of 'pass on' his patient to another doctor who he knows is prepared to refer her (including signing the appropriate form) to a consultant obstetrician with a view to performing a termination. Notice this latter use of the word 'refer'. Herein lies the answer to the first question we posed. We regard the natural meaning of 'refer' and 'referral' in paragraph 12 as covering the situation where a GP sends his patient to a consultant for further consultation. This necessarily involves signing the appropriate form. Thus, it follows that the GP's duty under his terms of service, in our view, requires that, whatever his conscientious objection, he should sign the appropriate form. It follows that a GP is unable in this context to rely upon s 4(1) of the Abortion Act 1967.

7. The claims of others

(a) To prevent an abortion

(i) THE FATHER QUA FATHER

Paton v Trustees of British Pregnancy Advisory Services [1979] QB 276, [1978] 2 All ER 987 (QBD)

Sir George Baker P: . . . the plaintiff, who is the husband of the second defendant, seeks an injunction in effect to restrain the first defendants, a charitable organisation, and particularly his wife, the second defendant, from causing or permitting an abortion to be carried out on his wife without his consent . . .

So this plaintiff must, in my opinion, bring his case, if he can, squarely within the framework of the fact that he is a husband. It is, of course, very common for spouses to seek injunctions for personal protection in the matrimonial courts during the pendency of or, indeed, after divorce actions, but the basic reason for the non-molestation injunction often granted in the family courts is to protect the other spouse or the living children, and to ensure that no undue pressure is put on one or other of the spouses during the pendency of the case and during the breaking-up of the marriage.

There was, of course, the action of restitution of conjugal rights, a proceeding which always belied its name and was abolished in 1970. It arose because in ecclesiastical law the parties could not end the consortium by agreement. In a sense the action for restitution was something of a fiction. The court ordered the spouse to return to cohabitation. If the spouse did not return then that spouse was held to be in desertion. No more could happen. The court could not compel matrimonial intercourse: *Forster v Forster* [(1790) 161 ER 504]. So matrimonial courts have never attempted the enforcement of matrimonial obligations by injunction.

The law is that the court cannot and would not seek to enforce or restrain by injunction matrimonial obligations, if they be obligations such as sexual intercourse or contraception (a non-molestation injunction given during the pendency of divorce proceedings could, of course, cover attempted intercourse). No court would even grant an injunction to stop sterilisation or vasectomy. Personal family relationships in marriage cannot be enforced by the order of a court. An injunction in such circumstances was described by Judge Mager in *Jones v Smith* [(1973) 278 So 2d 339] in the District Court of Appeal of Florida as 'ludicrous'.

I ask the question 'If an injunction were ordered, what could be the remedy?' and I do not think I need say any more than that no judge could even consider sending a husband or wife to prison for breaking such an order. That, of itself, seems to me to cover the application here; this husband cannot by law by injunctions stop his wife having what is now accepted to be a lawful abortion within the terms of the Abortion Act 1967.

The case which was first put forward to me a week ago, and indeed is to be found in the writ, is that the wife had no proper legal grounds for seeking a termination of her pregnancy and that, not to mince words, she was being spiteful, vindictive and utterly unreasonable in seeking so to do. It now appears I need not go into the evidence in the affidavits because it is accepted and common ground that the provisions of the 1967 Act have been complied with, the necessary certificate has been given by two doctors and everything is lawfully set for the abortion.

. . . The two doctors have given a certificate. It is not and cannot be suggested that that certificate was given in other than good faith and it seems to me that there is the end of the matter in English law. The 1967 Act gives no right to a father to be consulted in respect of the termination of a pregnancy. True, it gives no right to the mother either, but obviously the mother is going to be right at the heart of the matter consulting with the doctors if they are to arrive at a decision in good faith, unless, of course, she is mentally incapacitated or physically incapacitated (unable to make any decision or give any help) as, for example, in consequence of an accident. The husband, therefore, in my view, has no legal right enforceable at law or in equity to stop his wife having this abortion or to stop the doctors from carrying out the abortion. . . .

Very helpfully I have been referred to American authorities. The Supreme Court of the United States has reached the same conclusion, that a husband, or an illegitimate father, has no right to stop his wife, or the woman who is pregnant by him, from having a legal abortion. In *Planned Parenthood of Central Missouri v Danforth, Attorney-General of Missouri* [(1976) 428 US 52] the Supreme Court by a majority held that the State of Missouri

> may not constitutionally require the consent of the spouse, as is specified under s 3(3) of the Missouri Act, as a condition for abortion during the first 12 weeks of pregnancy . . . clearly since the State cannot regulate or proscribe abortion during the first stage when the physician and his patient make that decision, the State cannot delegate authority to any particular person, even the spouse, to prevent abortion during that same period.

It is interesting to note that the Missouri spousal consent provision would have required the husband's consent even if he was not the father.

A spousal consent provision in an English Act could not of course be challenged as unconstitutional but there is no such provision in the 1967 Act or in the Abortion Regulations 1968 to which a challenge of ultra vires could be made. There is no provision even for consultation with the spouse and reg 5 prohibits disclosure except in specified instances of which disclosure to the spouse is not one.

Counsel have been unable to discover any extant decision in those countries whose laws derive from the common law that the consent of the husband is required before an otherwise legal abortion can be performed on the wife. Counsel for the husband's researches show that in Roman law, centuries ago, the father's consent was required or otherwise abortion was a crime, but today the only way he can put the case is that the husband has a right to have a say in the destiny of the child he has conceived. The law of England gives him no such right; the 1967 Act contains no such provision. It follows, therefore, that in my opinion this claim for an injunction is completely misconceived and must be dismissed.

In *C v S (op cit)*, the *Paton* case was applied where the father was not married to the mother. At first instance, the judge said:

> **Heilbron J:** Counsel's case on behalf of Mr C is that he has the locus standi to bring these proceedings, based on his personal interest, which he does not put as high as a legal right, and because the proposed termination encompasses, he submits, a threatened crime concerning the life of his child.
>
> If it were to be decided that there was no such threat, he concedes that he has no standing qua father, for he does not contend that as a father he has any special rights. He concedes too that a husband has no special rights qua husband, and he accepts the correctness of the decision in *Paton v Trustees of BPAS* [1978] 2 All ER 987, [1979] QB 276 in that regard.

In the Court of Appeal the Master of the Rolls said the following:

> **Sir John Donaldson MR:**. . . Technically, and now in substance in the light of what counsel for Mr C has said, the questions whether a putative father has any right to be heard on an application of this nature and whether a fetus is a legal person in law capable of suing do not arise, and of course we do not rule on them. But I have also to say that, if we had been in favour of Mr C on all other points, we should have had to have given very considerable thought to the words of Baker P in *Paton v Trustees of BPAS* [1978] 2 All ER 987 at 992, [1979] QB 276 at 282 where he said:
>
> > . . . not only would it be a bold and brave judge . . . who would seek to interfere with the discretion of doctors acting under the [Abortion Act 1967], but I think he would really be a foolish judge who would try to do any such thing, unless possibly, there is clear bad faith and an obvious attempt to perpetrate a criminal offence.
>
> Even then, of course, the question is whether that is a matter which should be left to the Director of Public Prosecutions and the Attorney-General.
>
> So, with that addendum on behalf of the court, we dismiss the appeal.

Mr Paton took his case to the European Commission of Human Rights claiming that Article 8 of the European Convention on Human Rights guaranteeing to everyone the right to 'respect for family life' gave him the right *qua* father to the injunction he sought. The Commission rejected his argument.

Paton v United Kingdom (1980) 3 EHRR 408 (EComHR)

> 25. In its examination of the applicant's complaints concerning the Abortion Act 1967 and its application in this case, the Commission has next had regard to Article 8 of the Convention which, in paragraph (1), guarantees to everyone the right to respect for his family life. The Commission here notes, apart from his principal complaint concerning the permission of the abortion, the applicant's ancillary complaint concerning the permission of the abortion, the applicant's ancillary submission that the 1967 Act denies the father of the foetus a right to be consulted, and to make applications, about the proposed abortion.
>
> The Commission also observes that the applicant, who under Article 2 claims to be the victim of a violation of the right to life of the foetus of which he was the potential father, under Article 8 invokes a right of his own.
>
> 26. As regards the principal complaint concerning the permission of the abortion, the Commission recalls that the pregnancy of the applicant's wife was terminated in accordance with her wish and in order to avert the risk to her physical or mental health. The Commission therefore finds that this decision, in so far as it interfered in itself with the applicant's right to respect for his family life, was justified under paragraph (2) of Article 8 as being necessary for the protection of the rights of another person. It follows that this complaint is also manifestly ill-founded within the meaning of Article 27(2).

In 1989 the Canadian Supreme Court reached the same view in an appeal from the Court of Appeal for Quebec. The case concerned an application for an injunction by a former boyfriend Monsieur Tremblay to restrain his former girlfriend, Mlle Daigle, from terminating her pregnancy, then in its 21st week.

Tremblay v *Daigle* (1989) 62 DLR (4th) 634 (Can Sup Ct)

The argument based upon 'father's rights' (more accurately referred to as 'potential father's' rights) is the third and final basis on which the substantive rights necessary to support the impugned injunction might be founded. This argument would appear to be based on the proposition that the potential father's contribution to the act of conception gives him an equal say in what happens to the foetus. Little emphasis was put on this argument in the appeal. It was alluded to by several of the parties in an indirect fashion, although it does appear to have been accepted by both Viens J in the Superior Court and LeBel JA in the Court of Appeal.

There does not appear to be any jurisprudential basis for this argument. No court in Quebec or elsewhere has ever accepted the argument that a father's interest in a foetus which he helped create could support a right to veto a woman's decisions in respect of the foetus she is carrying. A number of cases in various jurisdictions outside of Quebec have considered this argument and explicitly rejected it: *Paton v British Pregnancy Advisory Service Trustees*, supra; *Medhurst v Medhurst*, supra; *Whalley v Whalley* (1981) 122 DLR (3d) 717 (BCSC); *Mock v Brandanburg* (1988), 61 Alta, LR (2d) 235 (QB); *Doe v Doe* 314 NE 2d 128 (Mass 1974); *Jones v Smith* 278 So 2d 339 (Fla Dist Ct App 1973). We have been unable to find a single decision in Quebec or elsewhere which would support the allegation of 'father's rights' necessary to support this injunction. There is nothing in the Civil Code or any legislation in Quebec which could be used to support the argument. This lack of a legal basis is fatal to the argument about 'father's rights'.

(ii) THE FATHER QUA NEXT FRIEND OF THE UNBORN CHILD

Even if the father cannot rely upon any right of his own to seek an injunction, can he act on behalf of the unborn child to enforce *its* rights? The following cases answer that question in the negative.

Paton v *Trustees of BPAS* [1979] QB 276, [1978] 2 All ER 987 (QBD)

Sir George Baker P: The foetus cannot, in English law, in my view, have any right of its own at least until it is born and has a separate existence from the mother. That permeates the whole of the civil law of this country (I except the criminal law, which is now irrelevant), and is, indeed, the basis of the decisions in those countries where law is founded on the common law, that is to say, in America, Canada, Australia and, I have no doubt in others.

For a long time there was great controversy whether after birth a child could have a right of action in respect of pre-natal injury. The Law Commission considered that and produced a working paper in 1973, followed by a final report, but it was universally accepted, and has since been accepted, that in order to have a right the foetus must be born and be a child. There was only one known possible exception which is referred to in the working paper, an American case, *White v Yup* [(1969) 458 P 2d 617], where the wrongful death of an eight months viable foetus, stillborn as a consequence of injury, led an American court to allow a cause of action, but there can be no doubt, in my view, that in England and Wales, the foetus has no right of action, no right at all, until birth. The succession cases have been mentioned. There is no difference. From conception the child may have succession rights by what has been called a 'fictional construction' but the child must be subsequently born alive. See per Lord Russell of Killowen in *Elliot v Joicey* [[1935] AC 209].

The point was further elaborated by Heilbron J in *C v S*:

Heilbron J: As to the position of the second plaintiff and his claim that the unborn child has the locus standi to make this application, counsel produced a wealth of authorities from far and wide, some of which he cited. His research and that of his junior was extensive, but it would serve no useful purpose, nor do I propose, to refer to most of them, for they did appear to be somewhat remote from the issue whether or not the unborn child could be a party to this motion. Counsel indeed referred me to *Mullick v Mullick* (1925) LR 52 Ind App 245, a Privy Council case relating to the right of an Indian idol to participate in legal proceedings. The facts of that case were so exceptional and so far removed from anything I have to decide as to be of little assistance.

The authorities, it seems to me, show that a child, after it has been born, and only then in certain circumstances based on his or her having a legal right, may be a party to an action brought with regard to such matters as the right to take, on a will or intestacy, or for damages for injuries suffered before birth. In other words, the claim crystallises on the birth, at which date, but not before, the child attains the status of a legal persona, and thereupon can then exercise that legal right.

This also appears to be the law in a number of Commonwealth countries. In *Medhurst v Medhurst* (1984) 46 OR (2d) 263 Reid J held in the Ontario High Court that an unborn child was not a person and that any rights accorded to the fetus are held contingent on a legal personality being acquired by the fetus on its subsequent birth alive. Nor could its father, the husband in that case, act as the fetus's next friend.

A similar decision was taken in *Dehler v Ottawa Civil Hospital* (1979) 25 OR (2d) 748, quoted with approval by Reid J, and affirmed by the Ontario Court of Appeal (see (1980) 29 OR (2d) 677n).

Having cited *Paton*, the judge continued:

I agree entirely.

In his reply, counsel's final position was summarised in this way: (1) he no longer relied on the numerous succession cases but he wished to retain some reliance on the position of the unborn child in *Thellusson v Woodford* (1799) 4 Ves 227, 31 ER 117; (2) he did not claim that a child had either a right to be born or a right to life in view of the terms of the 1967 Act; but (3) he maintained that the unborn child had a right to be a party because it was the subject of a threatened crime, that is to say that of child destruction. If there was no such threat, then this claim too failed.

In my judgment, there is no basis for the claim that the fetus can be a party, whether or not there is any foundation for the contention with regard to the alleged threatened crime, and I would dismiss the second plaintiff from this suit and the first plaintiff in his capacity as next friend.

The legal status of the foetus arose in a different context in the case of *Re F (in utero)* [1988] Fam 122, [1988] 2 All ER 193 CA. In this case, a local authority applied to the court to make an unborn child a ward of court to protect it from what the local authority considered to be dangerous behaviour by the mother. The Court of Appeal rejected the local authority's application on two grounds.

Re F (In Utero) [1988] Fam 122, [1988] 2 All ER 193 (CA)

May LJ: in the absence of authority I am driven to the conclusion that the court does not have the jurisdiction contended for. I respectfully agree with the dictum from the judgment of Baker P in *Paton v Trustees of BPAS*. I also agree with the comments made by Heilbron J in her judgment in *C v S*.

Secondly, I respectfully agree with the judge below in this case that to accept such jurisdiction and yet to apply the principle that it is the interest of the child which is to be predominant is bound to create conflict between the existing legal interests of the mother and those of the unborn child and that it is most undesirable that this should occur.

Next, I think that there would be insuperable difficulties if one sought to enforce any order in respect of an unborn child against its mother, if that mother failed to comply with the order. I cannot contemplate the court ordering that this should be done by force, nor indeed is it possible to consider with any equanimity that the court should seek to enforce an order by committal. . . .

I have considerable sympathy with the local authority in their position on the facts of the instant case, but I am driven to the conclusion that the judge was right and that the court has no jurisdiction to ward an unborn child. If the courts are to have this jurisdiction in a sensitive situation such as the present, I think that this is a matter for Parliament and not for the courts themselves. I do not think that even if the courts were minded to extend the jurisdiction in this type of case, they could in law or in practice limit this, as counsel suggested, to children having a gestation period of not less than 28 weeks.

Balcombe LJ, having cited Baker P's judgment in *Paton* and Heilbron J's judgment in *C v S*, took the view that: 'these decisions only relate directly to the legal rights of the foetus: they are not decisive of the question before us, namely, has the court power to protect a foetus by making it a ward of court?'

Balcombe LJ: Approaching the question as one of principle, in my judgment there is no jurisdiction to make an unborn child a ward of court. Since an unborn child has, ex hypothesi, no existence independent of its mother, the only purpose of extending the jurisdiction to include a foetus is to enable the mother's actions to be controlled. Indeed, that is the purpose of the present application. . . . Lowe gives examples of how this might operate in practice (96 LQR 29 at 30):

It would mean, for example, that the mother would be unable to leave the jurisdiction without the court's consent. The court being charged to protect the foetus' welfare would surely have to order the mother to stop smoking, imbibing alcohol and indeed any activity which might be hazardous to the child. Taking it to the extreme were the court to be faced with saving the baby's life or the mother's it would surely have to protect the baby's.

Another possibility is that the court might be asked to order that the baby be delivered by Caesarian section: in this connection see Fortin 'Legal Protection for the Unborn Child' (1988) 51 MLR 54 at 81 and the US cases cited in note 16, in particular *Jefferson v Griffin Spalding County Hospital Authority* 274 SE 2d 457 (1981). Whilst I do not accept that the priorities mentioned in the last sentence of the passage cited above are necessarily correct, it would be intolerable to place a judge in the position of having to make such a decision without any guidance as to the principles on which his decision should be based. If the law is to be extended in this manner, so as to impose control over the mother of an unborn child, where such control may be necessary for the benefit of that child, then under our system of parliamentary democracy it is for Parliament to decide whether such controls can be imposed and, if so, subject to what limitations or conditions. Thus, under the Mental Health Act 1983, to which we were also referred, there are elaborate provisions to ensure that persons suffering from mental disorder or other similar conditions are not compulsorily admitted to hospital for assessment or treatment without proper safeguards: see ss 2, 3 and 4 of that Act. If Parliament were to think it appropriate that a pregnant woman should be subject to controls for the benefit of her unborn child, then doubtless it will stipulate the circumstances in which such controls may be applied and the safeguards appropriate for the mother's protection. In such a sensitive field, affecting as it does the liberty of the individual, it is not for the judiciary to extend the law.

Staughton LJ in a short judgment relied on reasoning similar to that of Balcombe LJ. Although only May LJ expressly approved the reasoning in *Paton* and *C v S*, Balcombe LJ did not doubt these cases. He chose instead to base his decision upon grounds of policy. Of course, the policy he identifies is equally valid in cases where a father seeks to prohibit a woman from seeking and obtaining a termination of pregnancy.

The position reached in English law has been reflected in other common law jurisdictions such as Australia (*A-G of Queensland (ex re Kerr) v T* (1983) 46 ALR 275 (High Ct)) and Canada (*Borowski v AG of Canada* [1987] 4 WWR 385 (Sask CA)). In North America by recourse also to written constitutions, courts have arrived at the same result by holding that an unborn child is not protected by the constitution, for example, the United States of America (*Roe v Wade* 410 US 113 (1973)); Quebec (*Tremblay v Daigle* (1989) 62 DLR (4th) 634 (Can Sup Ct): *dubitante* on the Charter of Rights and Freedom in Canada).

Of more importance to us is the *Paton* case in which the European Commission considered the status of the unborn child under the European Convention on Human Rights.

Paton v United Kingdom (1980) 3 EHRR 408, (EComHR)

4. The Commission, therefore, has to examine whether this application discloses any appearance of a violation of the provisions of the Convention invoked by the applicant, in particular Articles 2 and 8. It here recalls that the abortion law of High Contracting Parties to the Convention has so far been the subject of several applications under Article 25. The applicants either alleged that the legislation concerned violated the (unborn child's) right to life (Article 2) or they claimed that it constituted an unjustified interference with the (parents') right to respect for private life (Article 8). Two applications invoking Article 2 were declared inadmissible by the Commission on the ground that the applicants – in the absence of any measure of abortion directly affecting them by reason of a close link with the foetus – could not claim to be 'victims' of the abortion laws complained of. One application, invoking Article 8, was declared admissible by the Commission, in so far as it had been brought by two women. The Commission, and subsequently the Committee of Ministers, concluded that there was no breach of Article 8. That conclusion was based on an interpretation of Article 8 which, *inter alia*, took into account the High Contracting Parties' law on abortion as applied at the time when the Convention entered into force.

5. The question whether the unborn child is covered by Article 2 was expressly left open in Application No 6959/75 and has not yet been considered by the Commission in any other case. It has, however, been the subject of proceedings before the Constitutional Court of Austria, a High Contracting State in which the Convention has the rank of constitutional law. In those proceedings the Austrian Constitutional Court, noting the different view expressed on this question in legal writings, found that Article 2(1), first sentence, interpreted in the context of Article 2, paras (1) and (2), does not cover the unborn life.

6. Article 2(1), first sentence, provides: 'Everyone's right to life shall be protected by law' (in the French text: '*Le droit de toute personne à la vie est protegé par la loi*'). The Commission, in its interpretation of this clause and, in particular, of the terms 'everyone' and 'life', has examined the ordinary meaning of the provision in the context both of Article 2 and the Convention as a whole, taking into account the object and purpose of the Convention.

7. The Commission first notes that the term 'everyone' ('toute personne') is not defined in the Convention. It appears in Article 1 and in Section 1, apart from Article 2(1), in Articles 5, 6, 8 to 11 and 13. In nearly all these instances the use of the word is such that it can apply only postnatally. None indicates clearly that it has any possible prenatal application, although such application in a rare case – eg under Article 6(1) – cannot be entirely excluded.

8. As regards, more particularly, Article 2, it contains the following limitations of 'everyone's' right to life enounced in the first sentence of paragraph (1):

–   a clause permitting the death penalty in paragraph (1), second sentence: 'No one shall be deprived of his life intentionally save in the execution of a sentence of a court following his conviction of a crime for which this penalty is provided by law'; and

–   the provision, in paragraph (2), that deprivation of life shall not be regarded as inflicted in contravention of Article 2 when it results from 'the use of force which is no more than absolutely necessary' in the following three cases: 'In defence of any person from unlawful violence'; 'in order to effect a lawful arrest or to prevent the escape of a person lawfully detained'; 'in action lawfully taken for the purpose of quelling a riot or insurrection'.

All the above limitations, by their nature, concern persons already born and cannot be applied to the foetus.

9. Thus both the general usage of the term 'everyone' ('toute personne') of the Convention (para 7 above) and the context in which this term is employed in article 2 (para 8 above) tend to support the view that it does not include the unborn.

10. The Commission has next examined, in the light of the above considerations, whether the term 'life' in Article 2(1), first sentence, is to be interpreted as covering only the life of persons already born or also the 'unborn life' of the foetus. The Commission notes that the term 'life', too, is not defined in the Convention.

11. It further observes that another, more recent international instrument for the protection of human rights, the American Convention on Human Rights of 1969, contains in Article

4(1), first and second sentences, the following provisions expressly extending the right to life to the unborn:

> Every person has the right to have his life respected. This right shall be protected by law and, in general, from the moment of conception.

12. The Commission is aware of the wide divergence of thinking on the question of where life begins. While some believe that it starts already with conception others tend to focus upon the moment of nidation, upon the point that the foetus becomes 'viable', or upon live birth.

13. The German Federal Constitutional Court, when interpreting the provision 'everyone has a right to life' in Article 2(2) of the Basic Law, stated as follows:

> Life in the sense of the historical existence of a human individual exists according to established biological and physiological knowledge at least from the 14th day after conception (Nidation, Individuation) . . . The process of development beginning from this point is a continuous one so that no sharp divisions or exact distinction between the various stages of development of human life can be made. It does not end at birth: for example, the particular type of consciousness peculiar to the human personality only appears a considerable time after the birth. The protection conferred by Article 2(2) first sentence of the Basic Law can therefore be limited neither to the 'complete' person after birth nor to the foetus capable of independent existence prior to birth. The right to life is guaranteed to everyone who 'lives'; in this context no distinction can be made between the various stages of developing life before or between born and unborn children. 'Everyone' in the meaning of Article 2(2) of the Basic Law is 'every living human being', in other words; every human individual possessing life; 'everyone' therefore includes unborn human beings.

14. The Commission also notes that, in a case arising under the Constitution of the United States, the State of Texas argued before the Supreme Court that, in general, life begins at conception and is present throughout pregnancy. The Court, while not resolving the difficult question where life begins, found that, 'with respect to the State's important and legitimate interest in potential life, the "compelling" point is at viability'.

15. The Commission finally recalls the decision of the Austrian Constitutional Court mentioned in paragraph 6 above which, while also given in the framework of constitutional litigation, had to apply, like the Commission in the present case, Article 2 of the European Convention on Human Rights.

16. The Commission considers with the Austrian Constitutional Court that, in interpreting the scope of the term 'life' in Article 2(1), first sentence, of the Convention, particular regard must be had to the context of the Article as a whole. It also observes that the term 'life' may be subject to different interpretations in different legal instruments, depending on the context in which it is used in the instrument concerned.

17. The Commission has already noted, when discussing the meaning of the term 'everyone' in Article 2 (para 8 above), that the limitations, in paragraphs (1) and (2) of the Article, of 'everyone's' right to 'life', by their nature, concern persons already born and cannot be applied to the foetus. The Commission must therefore examine whether Article 2, in the absence of any express limitation concerning the foetus, is to be interpreted:

- as not covering the foetus at all;
- as recognising a 'right to life' of the foetus with certain implied limitations; or
- recognising an absolute 'right to life' of the foetus.

18. The Commission has first considered whether Article 2 is to be construed as recognising an absolute 'right to life' of the foetus and has excluded such an interpretation on the following grounds.

19. The 'life' of the foetus is intimately connected with, and cannot be regarded in isolation from, the life of the pregnant woman. If Article 2 were held to cover the foetus and its protection under this Article were, in the absence of any express limitation, seen as absolute, an abortion would have to be considered as prohibited even where the continuance of the pregnancy would involve a serious risk to the life of the pregnant woman. This would mean that the 'unborn life' of the foetus would be regarded as being of a higher value than the life of the pregnant woman. The 'right to life' of a person already born would thus be considered as subject not only to the express limitations mentioned in paragraph 8 above but also to a further, implied limitation.

20. The Commission finds that such an interpretation would be contrary to the object and purpose of the Convention. It notes that, already at the time of the signature of the Convention (4 November 1950), all High Contracting Parties, with one possible exception,

permitted abortion when necessary to save the life of the mother and that, in the meanwhile, the natural law on termination of pregnancy has shown a tendency towards further liberalisation.

21. Having thus excluded, as being incompatible with the object and purpose of the Convention, one of the three different constructions of Article 2 mentioned in paragraph 17 above, the Commission has next considered which of the two remaining interpretations is to be regarded as the correct one – ie whether Article 2 does not cover the foetus at all or whether it recognises a 'right to life' of the foetus with certain implied limitations.

22. The Commission here notes that the abortion complained of was carried out at the initial stage of the pregnancy – the applicant's wife was ten weeks pregnant – under section 1(1)(*a*) of the Abortion Act 1967 in order to avert the risk of injury to the physical or mental health of the pregnant woman. It follows that, as regards the second of the two remaining interpretations, the Commission is in the present case not concerned with the broad question whether Article 2 recognises a 'right to life' of the foetus during the whole period of the pregnancy but only with the narrower issue whether such a right is to be assumed for the initial stage of the pregnancy. Moreover, as regards implied limitations of a 'right to life' of the foetus at the initial stage, only the limitation protecting the life and health of the pregnant woman, the so-called 'medical indication', is relevant for the determination of the present case and the question of other possible limitations (ethnic indication, eugenic indication, social indication, time limitation) does not arise.

23. The Commission considers that it is not in these circumstances called upon to decide whether Article 2 does not cover the foetus at all or whether it recognises a 'right to life' of the foetus with implied limitations. It finds that the authorisation, by the United Kingdom authorities, of the abortion complained of is compatible with Article 2(1), first sentence because, if one assumes that this provision applies at this initial stage of the pregnancy, the abortion is covered by an implied limitation, protecting the life and health of the woman at that stage, of the 'right to life' of the foetus.

24. The Commission concludes that the applicant's complaint under Article 2 is inadmissible as being manifestly ill-founded within the meaning of Article 27(2).

Currently, then, the applicability of Article 2 of the Convention to the unborn child has yet to be determined. (Note, however, *Open Door Counselling Ltd and Dublin Well Woman Centre Ltd v Ireland* (Case 64/1991) 316/387-88) (1992) Times, 5 November, (ECtHR) where the dissenting judges argue for a recognition of the unborn child's right to life under the Convention.) If in a subsequent case the European Court of Human Rights were to decide that the unborn child is, in fact, protected by Article 2, this could have a variety of effects on English law. Any effect would first depend upon the point at which the court found the right to life accrued to the unborn child, for example, at conception or at the point of viability. It would also depend (even if the right had accrued) on what weight the court was prepared to give to the conflicting right to life of the pregnant woman. In our view, the court could only adopt one approach. In any apparent clash between the rights of the mother and of the unborn child, it must necessarily prefer one of these two (there is simply no room for compromise). It would undoubtedly give precedence to the right to life of the pregnant woman. The woman would, however, have to show that a compelling circumstance existed to justify her right gaining precedence. We would adopt the language of Beetz J (with whom Estey J agreed) in *Morgentaler v R* (1988) 44 DLR (4th) 385 (Can Sup Ct) at 420-1, that 'the interest in the life or health of the pregnant woman takes precedence over the interest in prohibiting abortions, including the interest of the state in the protection of the foetus, when the continuance of the pregnancy of each female person would or would be likely to endanger her life or health . . .'. On this view, most of section 1 of the Abortion Act would survive a challenge based upon the rights of the unborn child. On the other hand, terminations of pregnancy justified on the basis of the risk to the health of existing children of the pregnant woman's family would not satisfy this standard of review under the Convention. Similarly, terminations performed under section 1(1)(d) because of foetal handicap would infringe the Convention. A doctor who sought to justify termination in these circumstances would have to show that it fell within section 1(1)(a) on the basis of risk to the pregnant woman's health.

(iii) THE FATHER QUA PROTECTOR OF THE PUBLIC INTEREST

If it be correct that in law no rights vest in the father or the unborn child, can a father claim to prevent an abortion as protector of the public interest? The problem is one of *locus standi*. The question can only arise if the father's claim is that the abortion, if carried out, would be a criminal offence.

League for Life in Manitoba Inc v Morgentaler [1985] 4 WWR 633 (Manitoba Queen's Bench)

Kroft J: The plaintiffs, the League for Life in Manitoba Inc and Patricia Frances Soenen, are proponents of the pro-life position. I do not question that their concern is honest and deeply felt. They have, through the civil process, sued Dr Morgentaler as well as the owners and lessees of the clinic from which he operates in the city of Winnipeg, seeking first a temporary and ultimately a permanent injunction restraining them from procuring or allowing the procuring of the miscarriage of female persons in contravention of s 251 of the Criminal Code.

The right of an attorney general as chief law officer of the Crown to bring proceedings for enforcement of the criminal law, either on his own initiative or ex relatione at the initiative of others, is of course not at issue (although, as will be indicated, the use of the civil injunction, even by an attorney-general, is open to some question). The position of a citizen or group whose interests and status are no different than any other member of the general public is much different and much more difficult. The motion to strike out the statement of claim is first and foremost an attack on the status of the plaintiffs. Simply put, the defendants say that on the face of the material filed the plaintiffs as private citizens have no standing, and that without standing they have no right to seek injunctive or any other relief.

The question of standing in the present proceedings has two components. Firstly, it must be determined whether the nature of the interest claimed by these particular plaintiffs gives them any right to be parties to these proceedings. Secondly, it must be decided if the statement of claim reveals a justiciable or triable issue. Unless there is an interest which the court recognises, and an issue to be tried, then the defendants are correct in saying that the statement of claim and the entire proceedings should be struck out. . . .

There is no difficulty in defining the rules that have been traditionally applied to determine whether a citizen, on his own, has sufficient standing and sufficient cause of action to permit him, through a private action, to enforce the public criminal law. Those rules were acknowledged even by counsel for the plaintiff to be quite stringent. There has, however, in recent years, been a trend toward relaxation of liberalisation. Notwithstanding the efforts of Lord Denning, the trend is less marked in Britain than in Canada, probably because we are a federal state, and now because we have the Charter of Rights.

The argument advanced on behalf of the plaintiffs was that the rules in Canada have been, by court decisions, sufficiently changed to justify a conclusion that they have standing and have a good cause of action.

When I speak of traditional rules I do not imply that they are outmoded. They have received recognition by courts of the highest level in Britain, in Canada, and elsewhere. For convenience I will list what I think to be an accurate statement of the criteria to be considered when a member of the public claims that there is a justiciable issue to be tried, and that he is entitled to a restraining order to prevent an anticipated breach of the criminal law.

1. The criminal law creates public not private rights.
2. Public rights can, in appropriate circumstances, be asserted in a civil action by the Attorney General, as the Crown officer who represents the public; or alternatively, by an individual acting with the consent of the Attorney General in a relator action.
3. A private individual may sue in his own name in respect of public rights if he can show that he faces the infringement of some personal right, or that he will suffer special and personal damages.

These principles were recognised in 1977 by the House of Lords in the *Gouriet* case [*Gouriet v Union of Post Office Workers* [1978] AC 435] . . .

The *Gouriet* decision was one in which the British Postal Union threatened to break the law to impose an embargo on mail to South Africa. The Attorney General refused to take action and Mr Gouriet proceeded on his own. At the Appeal Court level all three judges would have granted an interim injunction while the justiciable issue was being determined; that is, while a declaration with respect to the role of the Attorney General was under consideration. Lord Denning, in a far more forceful way than his colleagues, was prepared to say that when an attorney-general refuses to take action, or delays in respect to a request for a relator action, the court, in an appropriate case, can in effect overrule him, thereby giving the right to any citizen to come directly to court and ask that the criminal law be enforced. That view was explicitly overruled by the House of Lords; and it is the House of Lords which has been followed in the Canadian cases which I mentioned.

It should be noted as well that there are important distinctions between *Gouriet* and the case before us now, so that even the Court of Appeal decisions might not necessarily be applicable here. To begin with, the Attorney General of England had refused to lay charges. In our case two sets of criminal charges have already been laid. Secondly, the majority of the English Court of Appeal, although allowing the interim injunction, did so because there was a separate issue to be tried. There is no such issue here.

Procuring an abortion contrary to s 251 of the Code is a crime in Canada. It has been declared to be such by Parliament and does not require my declaration to confirm it.

It is interesting to note that when the *Island Records* case [[1978] Ch 122] . . . came before the court in England, one year after *Gouriet*, the same Lord Denning acknowledged the general law to be as I have stated it. He held that a private citizen can enforce the criminal law only where the criminal act is both an offence against the public at large, and also where, at the same time, it causes or threatens to cause special damage to a private individual. No such allegation appears in the statement of claim of the League and Ms Soenen. . . .

I have given serious consideration and weight to the arguments advanced on behalf of the plaintiffs. Nonetheless, I have reached the conclusion that they do not have the status or standing to maintain their action.

. In *Paton* (*op cit*), Sir George Baker P referred to this point:

The law relating to injunctions has been considered recently in the House of Lords, in *Gouriet v Union of Post Office Workers*. Many passages from their Lordships' speeches have been cited. I do not propose to go through them because it is now as clear as possible that there must be, first, a legal right in an individual to found an injunction and, second, that the enforcement of the criminal law is a matter for the authorities and for the Attorney-General. As counsel for the husband concedes, any process for the enforcement of the criminal law in a civil suit must be used with great caution, if at all. The private individual may have the right only if his right is greater than the public right, that is to say, that he would suffer personally and more than the general public unless he could restrain this offence. That proposition is not accepted by counsel for the first defendants or by counsel for the wife, and in any event it is not now suggested that the proposed abortion on the wife will be other than lawful. So, it is not necessary for me to decide that question or to consider *Gouriet v Union of Post Office Workers* further.

(See also *Wall v Livingston* [1982] 1 NZLR 734 (NZCA), where it was held that a doctor who was not treating the pregnant woman lacked *locus standi* to challenge the decision of two consultants to authorise an abortion on a teenage girl.)

Given that the whole force of the argument in *C v S* (*op cit*) was the alleged illegality of the proposed abortion, how was it that the court was prepared to hear the plaintiff's argument? All Heilbron J had to say on the matter was:

. . . I have not thought it necessary to add to this already long judgment by considering another hurdle that counsel might have encountered by reason of the decisions with regard to a private individual seeking to prevent the commission of an offence by way of an injunction, following the *Gouriet* line of cases.

It is intriguing that the Court of Appeal felt inclined to hear argument (and dispose of the case) on the assumption that the father had *locus standi* with not a single reference being made to *Gouriet*. Perhaps it was one of those occasions when the Court of Appeal was tempted to issue a declaratory judgment without wishing to appear to do so?

(b) To be consulted

There is no English law which precisely covers the question of whether a woman can be obliged in law to consult another, for example, her husband or the father of the child before undergoing an abortion.

In the United States the issue came before the Supreme Court in 1992. Necessarily the context was one of the constitutionality of legislation in Pennsylvania which imposed a duty upon a woman to provide evidence that she had consulted her husband. While the constitutional framework is obviously inapplicable in England, the judges rehearse arguments which would be relevant in determining whether English law *should* impose a duty to consult.

Planned Parenthood of SE Pennsylvania v Casey (1992) 112 S Ct 2791 (US Sup Ct)

At issue were five provisions of the Pennsylvania Abortion Control Act of 1982: s 3205, which required that a woman seeking an abortion give her informed consent prior to the procedure, and specified that she be provided with certain information at least 24 hours before the abortion is performed; s 3206, which mandated the informed consent of one parent for a minor to obtain an abortion, but provided a judicial bypass procedure; s 3209, which commanded that, unless certain exceptions apply, a married woman seeking an abortion must sign a statement indicating that she has notified her husband; s 3203, which defined a 'medical emergency' that will excuse compliance with the foregoing requirements; and ss 3207(b), 3214(a), and 3214(f), which imposed certain reporting requirements on facilities providing abortion services. Before any of the provisions took effect, the petitioners, five abortion clinics and a physician representing himself and a class of doctors who provide abortion services, brought this suit seeking a declaratory judgment that each of the provisions was unconstitutional on its face, as well as injunctive relief. The District Court held all the provisions unconstitutional and permanently enjoined their enforcement. The Court of Appeals affirmed in part and reversed in part, striking down the husband notification provision but upholding the others.

O'Connor, Kennedy and Souter JJ: Some guiding principles should emerge. What is at stake is the woman's right to make the ultimate decision, not a right to be insulated from all others in doing so. Regulations which do no more than create a structural mechanism by which the State, or the parent or guardian of a minor, may express profound respect for the life of the unborn are permitted, if they are not a substantial obstacle to the woman's exercise of the right to choose. See infra . . . (addressing Pennsylvania's parental consent requirement). Unless it has that effect on her right of choice, a state measure designed to persuade her to choose childbirth over abortion will be upheld if reasonably related to that goal. Regulations designed to foster the health of a woman seeking an abortion are valid if they do not constitute an undue burden.

Even when jurists reason from shared premises, some disagreement is inevitable. Compare *Hodgson*, 497 US . . . (opinion of Kennedy J) with id . . . (O'Connor J, concurring in part and concurring in judgment in part). That is to be expected in the application of any legal standard which must accommodate life's complexity. We do not expect it to be otherwise with respect to the undue burden standard. We give this summary:

(a) To protect the central right recognized by *Roe v Wade* [(1973) 410 US 113] while at the same time accommodating the State's profound interest in potential life, we will employ the undue burden analysis as explained in this opinion. An undue burden exists, and therefore a provision of law is invalid, if its purpose or effect is to place a substantial obstacle in the path of a woman seeking an abortion before the fetus attains viability.

(b) We reject the rigid trimester framework of *Roe v Wade*. To promote the State's profound interest in potential life, throughout pregnancy the State may take measures to ensure that the woman's choice is informed, and measures designed to advance this interest will not be invalidated as long as their purpose is to persuade the woman to choose childbirth over abortion. These measures must not be an undue burden on the right.

(c) As with any medical procedure, the State may enact regulations to further the health or safety of a woman seeking an abortion. Unnecessary health regulations that have the purpose or effect of presenting a substantial obstacle to a woman seeking an abortion impose an undue burden on the right.

(d) Our adoption of the undue burden analysis does not disturb the central holding of *Roe v Wade*, and we reaffirm that holding. Regardless of whether exceptions are made for particular circumstances, a State may not prohibit any woman from making the ultimate decision to terminate her pregnancy before viability.

(e) We also reaffirm Roe's holding that 'subsequent to viability, the State in promoting its interest in the potentiality of human life may, if it chooses, regulate, and even proscribe, abortion except where it is necessary, in appropriate medical judgment, for the preservation of the life or health of the mother' *Roe v Wade* 410 US, at 164-165.

These principles control our assessment of the Pennsylvania statute, and we now turn to the issue of the validity of its challenged provisions. . . .

Section 3209 of Pennsylvania's abortion law provides, except in cases of medical emergency, that no physician shall perform an abortion on a married woman without receiving a signed statement from the woman that she has notified her spouse that she is about to undergo an abortion. The woman has the option of providing an alternative signed statement certifying that her husband is not the man who impregnated her; that her husband could not be located; that the pregnancy is the result of spousal sexual assault which she has reported; or that the woman believes that notifying her husband will cause him or someone else to inflict bodily injury upon her. A physician who performs an abortion on a married woman without receiving the appropriate signed statement will have his or her license revoked, and is liable to the husband for damages.

The District Court heard the testimony of numerous expert witnesses, and made detailed findings of fact regarding the effect of this statute:

273. The vast majority of women consult their husbands prior to deciding to terminate their pregnancy. . . .

279. The 'bodily injury' exception could not be invoked by a married woman whose husband, if notified, would, in her reasonable belief, threaten to (a) publicize her intent to have an abortion to family, friends or acquaintances; (b) retaliate against her in future child custody or divorce proceedings; (c) inflict psychological intimidation or emotional harm upon her, her children or other persons; (d) inflict bodily harm on other persons such as children, family members or other loved ones; or (e) use his control over finances to deprive of necessary monies for herself or her children . . .

281. Studies reveal that family violence occurs in two million families in the United States. This figure, however, is a conservative one that substantially understates (because battering is usually not reported until it reaches life-threatening proportions) the actual number of families affected by domestic violence. In fact, researchers estimate that one of every two women will be battered at some time in their life. . . .

282. A wife may not elect to notify her husband of her intention to have an abortion for variety of reasons, including the husband's illness, concern about her own health, the imminent failure of the marriage, or the husband's absolute opposition to the abortion. . . .

283. The required filing of the spousal consent form would require plaintiff-clinics to change their counseling procedures and force women to reveal their most intimate decision-making on pain of criminal sanctions. The confidentiality of these revelations could not be guaranteed, since the woman's records are not immune from subpoena. . . .

284. Women of all class levels, educational backgrounds, and racial, ethnic and religious groups are battered. . . .

285. Wife-battering or abuse can take on many physical and psychological forms. The nature and scope of the battering can cover a broad range of actions and be gruesome and torturous. . . .

286. Married women, victims of battering, have been killed in Pennsylvania and throughout the United States. . . .

287. Battering can often involve a substantial amount of sexual abuse, including marital rape and sexual mutilation. . . .

288. In a domestic abuse situation, it is common for the battering husband to also abuse the children in an attempt to coerce the wife. . . .

289. Mere notification of pregnancy is frequently a flashpoint for battering and violence within the family. The number of battering incidents is high during the pregnancy and often the worst abuse can be associated with pregnancy. . . . The battering husband may deny parentage and use the pregnancy as an excuse for abuse.
. . .

290. Secrecy typically shrouds abusive families. Family members are instructed not to tell anyone, especially police or doctors, about the abuse and violence. Battering husbands often threaten their wives or her children with further abuse if she tells an outsider of the violence and tells her that nobody will believe her. A battered woman, therefore, is highly unlikely to disclose the violence against her for fear of retaliation by the abuser. . . .

291. Even when confronted directly by medical personnel or other helping professionals, battered women often will not admit to the battering because they have not admitted to themselves that they are battered. . . .

294. A woman in a shelter or a safe house unknown to her husband is not 'reasonably likely' to have bodily harm inflicted upon her by her batterer, however her attempt to notify her husband pursuant to section 3209 could accidentally disclose her whereabouts to her husband. Her fear of future ramifications would be realistic under the circumstances.

295. Marital rape is rarely discussed with others or reported to law enforcement authorities, and of those reported only few are prosecuted. . . .

296. It is common for battered women to have sexual intercourse with their husbands to avoid being battered. While this type of coercive sexual activity would be spousal sexual assault as defined by the Act, many women may not consider it to be so and others would fear disbelief. . . .

297. The marital rape exception to section 3209 cannot be claimed by women who are victims of coercive sexual behavior other than penetration. The 90-day reporting requirement of the spousal sexual assault statute, 18 Pa Con Stat Ann s 3218(c), further narrows the class of sexually abused wives who can claim the exception, since many of these women may be psychologically unable to discuss or report the rape for several years after the incident. . . .

298. Because of the nature of the battering relationship, battered women are unlikely to avail themselves of the exceptions to section 3209 of the Act, regardless of whether the section applies to them. (744 F Supp, at 1360-1362.)

These findings are supported by studies of domestic violence. The American Medical Association (AMA) has published a summary of the recent research in this field, which indicates that in an average 12-month period in this country, approximately two million women are the victims of severe assaults by their male partners. In a 1985 survey, women reported that nearly one of every eight husbands had assaulted their wives during the past year. The AMA views these figures as 'marked underestimates', because the nature of these incidents discourages women from reporting them, and because surveys typically exclude the very poor, those who do not speak English well, and women who are homeless or in institutions or hospitals when the survey is conducted. According to the AMA, '[r]esearchers on family violence agree that the true incidence of partner violence is probably double the above estimates; or four million severely assaulted women per year. Studies suggest that from one-fifth to one-third of all women will be physically assaulted by a partner or ex-partner during their lifetime.' AMA Council on Scientific Affairs, Violence Against Women 7 (1991) (emphasis in original). Thus on an average day in the United States, nearly 11,000 women are severely assaulted by their male partners. Many of these incidents involve sexual assault. Id, at 3-4; Shields & Hanneke, Battered Wives' Reactions to Marital Rape, in The Dark Side of Families: Current Family Violence Research 131, 144 (D Finkelhor, R Gelles, G Hataling, & M Straus eds 1983). In families where wife-beating takes place, moreover, child abuse is often present as well (Violence Against Women, supra, at 12).

Other studies fill in the rest of this troubling picture. Physical violence is only the most visible form of abuse. Psychological abuse, particularly forced social and economic isolation of women, is also common (L Walker, The Battered Women Syndrome 27-28 (1984)). Many victims of domestic violence remain with their abusers, perhaps because they perceive no superior alternative (Herbert, Silver, & Ellard, Coping with an Abusive Relationship: I. How and Why do Women Stay? 53 J Marriage & the Family 311 (1991)). Many abused women who find temporary refuge in shelters return to their husbands, in large part because they have no other source of income (Aguirre, Why Do They Return? Abused Wives in Shelters, 30 J Nat Assn of Social Workers 350, 352 (1985)). Returning to one's abuser can be dangerous. Recent Federal Bureau of Investigation statistics disclose that 8.8% of all homicide victims in the United States are killed by their spouse (Mercy & Saltzman, Fatal Violence Among Spouses in the United States, 1976-86, 79 Am J Public Health 595 (1989)). Thirty percent of female homicide victims are killed by their male partners (Domestic Violence: Terrorism in the Home, Hearing before the Subcommittee on Children, Family, Drugs and Alcoholism of the Senate Committee on Labor and Human Resources, 101st Cong, 2d Sess, 3 (1990)).

The limited research that has been conducted with respect to notifying one's husband about an abortion, although involving samples too small to be representative, also supports the District Court's findings of fact. The vast majority of women notify their male partners of their decision to obtain an abortion. In many cases in which married women do not notify their husbands, the pregnancy is the result of an extramarital affair. Where the husband is the father, the primary reason women do not notify their husbands is that the husband and wife are experiencing marital difficulties, often accompanied by incidents of violence (Ryan & Plutzer, When Married Women Have Abortions: Spousal Notification and Marital Interaction, 51 J Marriage & the Family 41, 44 (1989)).

This information and the District Court's findings reinforce what common sense would suggest. In well-functioning marriages, spouses discuss important intimate decisions such as whether to bear a child. But there are millions of women in this country who are the victims of regular physical and psychological abuse at the hands of their husbands. Should these women become pregnant, they may have very good reasons for not wishing to inform their husbands of their decision to obtain an abortion. Many may have justifiable fears of physical abuse, but may be no less fearful of the consequences of reporting prior abuse to the Commonwealth of Pennsylvania. Many may have a reasonable fear that notifying their husbands will provoke further instances of child abuse; these women are not exempt from s 3209's notification requirement. Many may fear devastating forms of psychological abuse from their husbands, including verbal harassment, threats of future violence, the destruction of possessions, physical confinement to the home, the withdrawal of financial support and friends. These methods of psychological abuse may act as even more of a deterrent to notification than the possibility of physical violence, but women who are the victims of the abuse are not exempt from s 3209's notification requirement. And many women who are pregnant as a result of sexual assaults by their husbands will be unable to avail themselves of the exception for spousal sexual assault, s 3209(b)(3), because the exception requires that the woman have notified law enforcement authorities within 90 days of the assault, and her husband will be notified of her report once an investigation begins, s 3128(c). If anything in this field is certain, it is that victims of spousal sexual assault are extremely reluctant to report the abuse to the government; hence, a great many spousal rape victims will not be exempt from the notification requirement imposed by s 3209.

The spousal notification requirement is thus likely to prevent a significant number of women from obtaining an abortion. It does not merely make abortions a little more difficult or expensive to obtain; for many women, it will impose a substantial obstacle. We must not blind ourselves to the fact that the significant number of women who fear for their safety and the safety of their children are likely to be deterred from procuring an abortion as surely as if the Commonwealth had outlawed abortion in all cases.

Respondents attempt to avoid the conclusion that s 3209 is invalid by pointing out that it imposes almost no burden at all for the vast majority of women seeking abortions. They begin by noting that only about 20 percent of the women who obtain abortions are married. They then note that of these women about 95 percent notify their husbands of their own violation. Thus, respondents argue, the effects of s 3209 are felt by only one percent of the women who obtain abortions. Respondents argue that since some of these women will be able to notify their husbands without adverse consequences or will qualify for one of the exceptions, the statute affects fewer then one percent of women seeking abortions. For this reason, it is asserted, the statute cannot be invalid on its face. See Brief for Respondents 83-86. We disagree with respondents' basic method of analysis.

The analysis does not end with the one percent of women upon whom the statute operates; it begins there. Legislation is measured for consistency with the Constitution by its impact on those whose conduct it affects. For example, we would not say that a law which requires a newspaper to print a candidate's reply to an unfavorable editorial is valid on its face because most newspapers would adopt the policy even absent the law. See *Miami Herald Publishing Co v Tornillo* 418 US 241 (1974). The proper focus of constitutional inquiry is the group for whom the law is a restriction, not the group for whom the law is irrelevant.

Respondents' argument itself gives implicit recognition to this principle, at one of its critical points. Respondents speak of the one percent of women seeking abortions who are married and would choose not to notify their husbands of their plans. By selecting as the controlling class women who wish to obtain abortions, rather than all women or all pregnant women, respondents in effect concede that s 3209 must be judged by reference to those for whom it is an actual rather than irrelevant restriction. Of course, as we have said, s 3209's real target is narrower even than the class of women seeking abortions identified by the State: it is married women seeking abortions who do not wish to notify husbands of their intentions and who do not qualify for one of the statutory exceptions to the notice requirement. The unfortunate yet persisting conditions we document above will mean that in a large fraction of the cases in which s 3209 is relevant, it will operate as a substantial obstacle to a woman's choice to undergo an abortion. It is an undue burden, and therefore invalid . . . We recognize that a husband has a 'deep and proper concern and interest . . . in his wife's pregnancy and in the growth and development of the fetus she is carrying.' *Danforth,* supra, at 69. With regard to the children he has fathered and raised, the Court has recognized his 'cognizable and substantial' interest in their custody. *Stanley v Illinois* 405 US 645, 651-652 (1972); see also *Quilloin v Walcott* 434 US 246 (1978); *Caban v Mohammed* 441 US 380 (1979); *Lehr v Robertson* 463 US 248 (1983). If this case concerned a State's ability to require the mother to notify the father before taking some action with respect to a living child raised by both, therefore, it would be reasonable to conclude as a general matter that the father's interest in the welfare of the child and the mother's interest are equal.

Before birth, however, the issue takes on a very difficult cast. It is an inescapable biological fact that state regulation with respect to the child a woman is carrying will have a far greater impact on the mother's liberty than on the father's. The effect of state regulation on a woman's protected liberty is doubly deserving of scrutiny in such a case, as the State has touched not only upon the private sphere of the family but upon the very bodily integrity of the pregnant woman. Cf *Cruzan v Director, Missouri Dept of Health* 497 US, at 281. The Court has held that 'when the wife and the husband disagree on this decision, the view of only one of the two marriage partners can prevail. Inasmuch as it is the woman who physically bears the child and who is the more directly and immediately affected by the pregnancy, as between the two, the balance weighs in her favor.' *Danforth,* supra, at 71. This conclusion rests upon the basic nature of marriage and the nature of our Constitution: '[T]he marital couple is not an independent entity with a mind and heart of its own, but an association of two individuals each with a separate intellectual and emotional makeup. If the right of privacy means anything, it is the right of the *individual*, married or single, to be free from unwarranted governmental intrusion into matters so fundamentally affecting a person as the decision whether to bear or beget a child.' *Eisenstadt v Baird* 405 US, at 453 (emphasis in original). The Constitution protects individuals, men and women alike, from unjustified state interference, even when that interference is enacted into law for the benefit of their spouses.

There was a time, not so long ago, when a different understanding of the family and of the Constitution prevailed. In *Bradwell v Illinois* 16 Wall 130 (1873), three Members of this Court reaffirmed the common-law principle that 'a woman had no legal existence separate from her husband, who was regarded as her head and representative in the social state; and, notwithstanding some recent modifications of this civil status, many of the special rules of law flowing from and dependent upon this cardinal principle still exist in full force in most States.' Id, at 141 (Bradley J, joined by Swayne and Field JJ, concurring in judgment). Only one generation has passed since this Court observed that 'woman is still regarded as the center of home and family life' with attendant 'special responsibilities' that precluded full and independent legal status under the Constitution. *Hoyt v Florida* 368 US 57, 62 (1961). These views, of course, are no longer consistent with our understanding of the family, the individual, or the Constitution.

In keeping with our rejection of the common-law understanding of a woman's role within the family, the Court held in *Danforth* that the Constitution does not permit a State to require a married woman to obtain her husband's consent before undergoing an abortion. 428 US at 69. The principles that guided the Court in *Danforth* should be our guides today. For the great many women who are victims of abuse inflicted by their husbands, or whose children are the victims of such abuse, a spousal notice requirement enables the husband to wield an effective veto over his wife's decision. Whether the prospect of notification itself deters such women from seeking abortions, or whether the husband, through physical force or psychological pressure or economic coercion, prevents his wife from obtaining an abortion until it is too late, the notice requirement will often be tantamount to the veto found unconstitutional in *Danforth*. The women most affected by this law – those who most reasonably fear the consequences of notifying their husbands that they are pregnant – are in the gravest danger.

The husband's interest in the life of the child his wife is carrying does not permit the State to empower him with this troubling degree of authority over his wife. The contrary view leads to consequences reminiscent of the common law. A husband has no enforceable right to require a wife to advise him before she exercises her personal choices. If a husband's interest in the potential life of the child outweighs a wife's liberty, the State could require a married woman to notify her husband before she uses a postfertilization contraceptive. Perhaps next in line would be a statute requiring pregnant married women to notify their husbands before engaging in conduct causing risks to the fetus. After all, if the husband's interest in the fetus' safety is a sufficient predicate for state regulation, the State could reasonably conclude that pregnant wives should notify their husbands before drinking alcohol or smoking. Perhaps married women should notify their husbands before using contraceptives or before undergoing any type of surgery that may have complications affecting the husband's interest in his wife's reproductive organs. And if a husband's interest justifies notice in any of these cases, one might reasonably argue that it justifies exactly what the *Danforth* Court held it did not justify – a requirement of the husband's consent as well. A State may not give to a man the kind of dominion over his wife that parents exercise over their children.

Section 3209 embodies a view of marriage consonant with the common-law status of married women but repugnant to our present understanding of marriage and of the nature of the rights secured by the Constitution. Women do not lose their constitutionally protected liberty when they marry. The Constitution protects all individuals, male or female, married or unmarried, from the abuse of governmental power, even where that power is employed for the supposed benefit of a member of the individual's family. These considerations confirm our conclusion that s 3209 is invalid.

Stevens and Blackman JJ joined in the opinion of O'Connor, Kennedy and Souter JJ as regards the spousal notification provision. Four Justices, however, dissented.

Rehnquist CJ, White, Scalia and Thomas JJ: The question before us is therefore whether the spousal notification requirement rationally furthers any legitimate state interests. We conclude that it does. First, a husband's interests in procreation within marriage and in the potential life of his unborn child are certainly substantial ones. See *Planned Parenthood of Central Mo v Danforth* 428 US at 69 ('We are not unaware of the deep and proper concern and interest that a devoted and protective husband has in his wife's pregnancy and in the growth and development of the fetus she is carrying'); id, at 93 (White J, concurring in part and dissenting in part); *Skinner v Oklahoma ex rel Williamson* 316 US at 541. The State itself has legitimate interests both in protecting these interests of the father and in protecting the potential life of the fetus, and the spousal notification requirement is reasonably related to advancing those state interests. By providing that a husband will usually know of his spouse's intent to have an abortion, the provision makes it more likely that the husband will participate in deciding the fate of his unborn child, a possibility that might otherwise have been denied him. This participation might in some cases result in a decision to proceed with the pregnancy. As Judge Alito observed in his dissent below, '[t]he Pennsylvania legislature could have rationally believed that some married women are initially inclined to obtain an abortion without their husband's knowledge because of perceived problems – such as economic constraints, future plans, or the husband's previously expressed opposition – that may be obviated by discussion prior to the abortion.' 947 F 2d, at 726 (Alito, J, concurring in part and dissenting in part).

The State also has a legitimate interest in promoting 'the integrity of the marital relationship.' 18 Pa Cons Stat s 3209(a) (1990). This Court has previously recognized 'the importance of the marital relationship in our society.' *Planned Parenthood of Central Mo v Danforth* supra, at 69. In our view, the spousal notice requirement is a rational attempt by the State to improve truthful communication between spouses and encourage collaborative decisionmaking, and, thereby fosters marital integrity. See *Labine v Vincent* 401 US 532, 538 (1971) ('[T]he power to make rules to establish, protect, and strengthen family life' is committed to the state legislatures). Petitioners argue that the notification requirement does not further any such interest; they assert that the majority of wives already notify their husbands of their abortion decision, and the remainder have excellent reasons for keeping their decisions a secret. In the first case, they argue, the law is unnecessary, and in the second case it will only serve to foster marital discord and threats of harm. Thus, petitioners see the law as a totally irrational means of furthering whatever legitimate interest the State might have. But, in our view, it is unrealistic to assume that every husband-wife relationship is either (1) so perfect that this type of truthful and important communication will take place as a matter of course, or (2) so imperfect that, upon notice, the husband will react selfishly, violently, or contrary to the best interests of his wife. See *Planned Parenthood of Central Mo v Danforth* supra, at 103-104 (Stevens J concurring in part and dissenting in part) (making a similar point in the context of a parental consent statute). The spousal notice provision will admittedly be unnecessary in some circumstances, and possibly harmful in others, but 'the existence of particular cases in which a feature of a statute performs no function (or is even counterproductive) ordinarily does not render the statute unconstitutional or even constitutionally suspect.' *Thornburgh v American College of Obstetricians and Gynecologists* 476 US at 800 (White J dissenting). The Pennsylvania Legislature was in a position to weigh the likely benefits of the provision against its likely adverse effects, and presumably concluded, on balance, that the provision would be beneficial. Whether this was a wise decision or not, we cannot say that it was irrational. We therefore conclude that the spousal notice provision comports with the Constitution. See *Harris v McRae* 448 US at 325-326 ('It is not the mission of this Court or any other to decide whether the balance of competing interests . . . is wise social policy').

In a footnote the dissenting Justices challenge the majority's view on the impact of a spousal notification provision.

In most instances the notification requirement operates without difficulty. As the District Court found, the vast majority of wives seeking abortions notify and consult with their husbands, and thus suffer no burden as a result of the provision. 744 F Supp 1323, 1360 (ED Pa 1990). In other instances where a woman does not want to notify her husband, the Act provides exceptions. For example, notification is not required if the husband is not the father, if the pregnancy is the result of a reported spousal sexual assault, or if the woman fears bodily injury as a result of notifying her husband. Thus, in these instances as well, the notification provision imposes no obstacle to the abortion decision. The joint opinion puts to one side these situations where the regulation imposes no obstacle at all, and instead focuses on the group of married women who would not otherwise notify their husbands and who do not qualify for one of the exceptions. Having narrowed the focus, the joint opinion concludes that in a 'large fraction' of those cases, the notification provision operates as a substantial obstacle . . . and that the provision is therefore invalid. There are certainly instances where a woman would prefer not to notify her husband, and yet does not qualify for an exception. For example, there are the situations of battered women who fear psychological abuse or injury to their children as a result of notification; because in these situations the women do not fear bodily injury, they do not qualify for an exception. And there are situations where a woman has become pregnant as a result of an unreported spousal sexual assault; when such an assault is unreported, no exception is available. But, as the District Court found, there are also instances where the woman prefers not to notify her husband for a variety of other reasons. See 744 F Supp, at 1360. For example, a woman might desire to obtain an abortion without her husband's knowledge because of perceived economic constraints or her husband's expressed opposition to abortion. The joint opinion concentrates on the situations involving battered women and unreported spousal assault, and assumes, without any support in the record, that these instances constitute a 'large fraction' of those cases in which women prefer not to notify their husbands (and do not qualify for an exception). . . . This assumption is not based on any hard evidence, however. And were it helpful to an attempt to reach a desired result, one could just as easily assume that the battered women situations form 100 percent of the cases where women desire not to notify, or that they constitute only 20 percent of those cases. But reliance on such speculation is the necessary result of adopting the undue burden standard.

In England, the courts would undoubtedly consider that Parliament had pre-empted any common law development by virtue of enacting a 'code' in the form of the Abortion Act 1967. The arguments, therefore, addressed by the judges in the US Supreme Court are, in fact, ones more pertinent in England to legislators should it be proposed that the 1967 Act be amended to require spousal notification. In the unlikely event that legislation were passed it would be open to an affected individual to petition the European Court of Human Rights alleging a breach of the European Convention on Human Rights.

In *Paton* (*supra*) the European Commission of Human Rights dealt with an application under Article 8 of the Convention in such a case.

27. The Commission has next considered the applicant's ancillary complaint that the Abortion Act 1967 denies the father of the foetus a right to be consulted, and to make applications, about the proposed abortion. It observes that any interpretation of the husband's and potential father's right, under Article 8 of the Convention, to respect for his private and family life, as regards an abortion which his wife intends to have performed on her, must first of all take into account the right of the pregnant woman, being the person primarily concerned in the pregnancy and its continuation or termination, to respect for her private life. The pregnant woman's right to respect for her private life, as affected by the developing foetus, has been examined by the Commission in its Report in the *Bruggemann and Scheuten* case. In the present case the Commission, having regard to the right of the pregnant woman, does not find that the husband's and potential father's right to respect for his private and family life can be interpreted so widely as to embrace such procedural rights as claimed by the applicant, ie a right to be consulted, or a right to make applications, about an abortion which his wife intends to have performed on her. The Commission concludes that this complaint is incompatible *ratione materiae* with the provisions of the Convention within the meaning of Article 27(2).

8. Involvement of others in the medical procedure

The Abortion Act 1967 only applies 'when a pregnancy is terminated by a registered medical practitioner . . .' (section 1(1)). In *Royal College of Nursing of United Kingdom v Department of Health and Social Security* [1981] 1 All ER 545, [1981] AC 800, the House of Lords interpreted this provision. Although dissenting, Lord Wilberforce sets out the medical background to the case.

Royal Colleges of Nursing of UK v DHSS [1981] AC 800, [1981] 1 All ER 545 (HL)

Lord Wilberforce: There is an agreed statement as to the nature of this treatment and the part in it played by the doctors and the nurses or midwives. Naturally this may vary somewhat from hospital to hospital, but, for the purpose of the present proceedings, the assumption has to be made of maximum nurse participation, ie that the nurse does everything which the doctor is not required to do. If that is not illegal, participation of a lesser degree must be permissible.

1. The first step is for a thin catheter to be inserted via the cervix into the womb so as to arrive, or create, a space between the wall of the womb and the amniotic sac containing the fetus. This is necessarily done by a doctor. It may, sometimes, of itself bring on an abortion, in which case no problem arises: the pregnancy will have been terminated by the doctor. If it does not, all subsequent steps except no 4 may be carried out by a nurse or midwife. The significant steps are as follows (I am indebted to Brightman LJ for their presentation):

2. The catheter (ie the end emerging from the vagina) is attached, probably via another tube, to a pump or to a gravity feed apparatus. The function of the pump or apparatus is to propel or feed the prostaglandin through the catheter into the womb. The necessary prostaglandin is provided and put into the apparatus.

*3. The pump is switched on, or the drip valve is turned, thus causing the prostaglandin to enter the womb.

4. The doctor inserts a cannula into a vein.

*5. An oxytocin drip feed is linked up with the cannula. The necessary oxytocin (a drug designed to help the contractions) is supplied for the feed.

6. The patient's vital signs are monitored; so is the rate of drip or flow.

*7. The flow rates of both infusions are, as necessary, adjusted.

*8. Fresh supplies of both infusions are added as necessary.

9. The treatment is discontinued after discharge of the fetus, or expiry of a fixed period (normally 30 hours) after which the operation is considered to have failed.

The only steps in this process which can be considered to have a direct effect leading to abortion (abortifacient steps) are those asterisked. They are all carried out by the nurse or midwife. As the agreed statement records 'the causative factor in inducing . . . the termination of pregnancy is the effect of the administration of prostaglandin and/or oxytocin and not any mechanical effect from the insertion of the catheter or cannula'.

All the above steps 2 to 9 are carried out in accordance with the doctor's instructions, which should, as regards important matters, be in writing. The doctors will moreover be on call, but may in fact never be called.

On these facts the question has to be answered: has the pregnancy been terminated by the doctor; or has it been terminated by the nurse; or has it been terminated by doctor and nurse? I am not surprised that the nurses feel anxiety as to this.

The majority's view is stated in the speeches of Lords Diplock and Roskill.

Lord Diplock: My Lords, the wording and structure of [section 1 of the Abortion Act 1967] are far from elegant, but the policy of the Act, it seems to me, is clear. There are two aspects to it: the first is to broaden the grounds on which abortions may be lawfully obtained; the second is to ensure that the abortion is carried out with all proper skill and in hygienic conditions. Subsection (1) which deals with the termination of pregnancies other than in cases of dire emergency consists of a conditional sentence of which a protasis, which is a condition precedent to be satisfied in order to make the abortion lawful at all, is stated last: 'if two registered medical practitioners are of the opinion etc'. It is this part of the subsection which defines the circumstances which qualify a woman to have pregnancy terminated lawfully. . . .

The requirement of the Act as to the way in which the treatment be carried out, which in my view throws most light on the second aspect of its policy and the true construction of the phrase in sub-s (1) of s 1 which lies at the root of the dispute between the parties to this appeal, is the requirement in sub-s (3) that, except in cases of dire emergency, the treatment must be carried out in a national health service hospital (or private clinic specifically approved for that purpose by the minister). It is in my view evident that, in providing that treatment for termination of pregnancies should take place in ordinary hospitals Parliament contemplated that (conscientious objections apart) like other hospital treatment, it would be undertaken as a team effort in which, acting on the instructions of the doctor in charge of the treatment, junior doctors, nurses, paramedical and other members of the hospital staff would each do those things forming part of the whole treatment which it would be in accordance with accepted medical practice to entrust to a member of the staff possessed of their respective qualifications and experience.

Subsection (1) although it is expressed to apply only 'when a pregnancy is terminated by a registered medical practitioner' (the subordinate clause that although introduced by 'when' is another protasis and has caused the differences of judicial opinion in the instant case) also appears to contemplate treatment that is in the nature of a team effort and to extend its protection to all those who play a part in it. The exoneration from guilt is not confined to the registered medical practitioner by whom a pregnancy is terminated, it extends to any person who takes part in the treatment for its termination.

What limitation on this exoneration is imposed by the qualifying phrase, 'when a pregnancy is terminated by a registered medical practitioner'? In my opinion, in the context of the Act, what it requires is that a registered medical practitioner, whom I will refer to as a doctor, should accept responsibility for all stages of the treatment for the termination of the pregnancy. The particular method to be used should be decided by the doctor in charge of the treatment for termination of the pregnancy; he should carry out any physical acts, forming part of the treatment, that in accordance with accepted medical practice are done only by qualified medical practitioners, and should give specific instructions as to the carrying out of such parts of the treatment as in accordance with accepted medical practice are carried out by nurses or other members of the hospital staff without medical qualifications. To each of them, the doctor, or his substitute, should be available to be consulted or called on for assistance from beginning to end of the treatment, In other words, the doctor need not do everything with his own hands; the requirements of the subsection are satisfied when the treatment for termination of a pregnancy is one prescribed by a registered medical practitioner carried out in accordance with his directions and of which a registered medical practitioner remains in charge throughout.

My noble and learned friend Lord Wilberforce has described the successive steps taken in the treatment for termination of pregnancies in the third trimester by medical induction; and the parts played by registered medical practitioners and nurses respectively in the carrying out of the treatment. This treatment satisfies the interpretation that I have placed on the requirement of s 1 of the Act. I would accordingly allow the appeal and restore the declarations made by Woolf J.

Lord Roskill: . . . the crucial issue is whether 'a pregnancy is terminated by a registered medical practitioner' assuming, as of course I do for present purposes, that the other prerequisites of s 1(1) of the 1967 Act are also satisfied. If a narrow meaning is given to the phrase I have just quoted, then it is the nurse and not the doctor who terminates the pregnancy. If that be right the doctor and the nurse are each guilty of a separate offence against the 1861 Act, the nurse because she is carrying out an abortion when she is not a doctor and the doctor because he is attempting to carry out an abortion when he engages in the first step which is not authorised by the 1967 Act. In addition, he is aiding and abetting the nurse's offence and both, and maybe others as well, are guilty of conspiracy to infringe the 1861 Act. This is the position which the Royal College of Nursing feared might arise and which led them to institute the present proceedings on behalf of the nursing profession in order that the question whether or not their profession are, in these circumstances, entitled to the protection of the 1967 Act might be finally determined. . . .

My Lords, I read and reread the 1967 Act to see if I can discern in its provisions any consistent pattern in the use of the phrase 'a pregnancy is terminated' or 'termination of a pregnancy' on the one hand and 'treatment for the termination of a pregnancy' on the other hand. One finds the former phrase in s 1(1) and (1)(*a*), the latter in s 1(3), the former in ss 1(4) and 2(1)(*b*) and the latter in s 3(1)(*a*) and (*c*). Most important to my mind is s 4, which is the conscientious objection section. This section in two places refers to 'participate in treatment' in the context of conscientious objection. If one construes s 4 in conjunction with s 1(1), as surely one should do in order to determine to what it is that conscientious objection is permitted, it seems to me that s 4 strongly supports the wider construction of s 1(1). It was suggested that acceptance of the department's submission involved rewriting that subsection so as to add words which are not to be found in the language of the subsection. My Lords, with great respect to that submission, I do not agree. If one construes the words 'when a pregnancy is terminated by a registered medical practitioner' in s 1(1) as embracing the case where the 'treatment for the termination of a pregnancy is carried out under the control of a doctor in accordance with ordinary current medical practice' I think one is reading 'termination of pregnancy' and 'treatment for termination of pregnancy' as virtually synonymous and as I think Parliament must have intended they should read. Such a construction avoids a number of anomalies as, for example, where there is no pregnancy or where the extra-amniotic process fails to achieve its objective within the normal limits of time set for its operation. . . . I think that the successive steps taken by a nurse in carrying out the extra-amniotic process are fully protected provided that the entirety of the treatment for the termination of the pregnancy and her participation in it is at all times under the control of the doctor even though the doctor is not present throughout the entirety of the treatment.

Lord Keith agreed. Lords Wilberforce and Edmund-Davies dissented.

This case effectively settles questions concerning the involvement of members of a team in a hospital or clinic who are not registered medical practitioners. There remains, however, one outstanding problem which has so far attracted no attention. We referred earlier to the drug RU-486 or Mifepristone. This drug is prescribed by a doctor, dispensed by a pharmacist, but administered to herself by the pregnant woman. In this situation who *terminates* the pregnancy?

There are two possible situations which might arise. First, the termination is only completed after the woman has returned to the hospital some 36 to 48 hours later after the prostaglandin pessary has been inserted. Here, undoubtedly the termination would be *by* the doctor even if the prostaglandin were given by a nurse under his supervision (*Royal College of Nursing* case). This is not problematic for the law. However, the alternative situation that might arise is.

Suppose, instead, the effects of Mifepristone occur before the woman returns to the hospital for the prostaglandin pessary. In 55% of cases bleeding (and, therefore, the potential for a 'miscarriage') occur within 48 hours of administering Mifepristone. In a proportion of cases (about 3%) termination will occur before readmission. In our view, in this situation it must be the pregnant woman and not the doctor who terminates the pregnancy. It is she who does the last voluntary act necessary to effect the termination. Legally, the situation is analogous to a case where a doctor provides the means (eg pills) for a patient to kill himself. It is the patient who commits suicide. The doctor is guilty of assisting suicide, if anything. It cannot be said that he is guilty of murder since the law regards the patient's actions as the cause of death. *Mutatis mutandis*, here the woman causes her own termination. The provisions of the Abortion Act 1967 would not be complied with. Clearly, Parliament overlooked this fundamental point when it sought to bring Mifepristone within the framework of the Abortion Act.

However, an argument which would challenge this view could be mounted on the basis of the *Royal College of Nursing* case. There, the House of Lords (by a majority of 3-2) extended 'medical practitioner' to include all acts performed by the medical team for whom the doctor is responsible. Lord Diplock stated that 'the requirements of [the Act] are satisfied when the treatment for the termination . . . is one prescribed by a registered medical practitioner carried out in accordance with his directions and of which a registered medical practitioner remains in charge throughout' (at 828-9). Hence, termination by induced labour using prostaglandin was held to be a 'termination by a registered medical practitioner', and so within the 1967 Act, even though others, such as nurses, and not a doctor, carried out many of the acts.

Could this wider notion of 'termination by a registered medical practitioner' covering all action for which the doctor takes responsibility (or 'charge') help in the case of Mifepristone? In one sense, a doctor does have responsibility for the patient throughout the treatment. However, it is a different kind of responsibility from that contemplated in the *Royal College of Nursing* case. In that case the responsibility denoted the right to control those who acted on his behalf in a professional capacity. In the case of Mifepristone, the responsibility relates to the doctor's ethical and legal duty to his patient. The relationship is neither one of control nor one where the patient (in administering the drug to herself) can be said to act on the doctor's behalf or be in his charge. It is unlikely that a future court would further expand the meaning of the 1967 Act to cover the use of Mifepristone.

9. Abortion procedures raising special problems

As we saw earlier, post-coital birth control by recourse to the 'morning after pill' or an IUD (an intra-uterine device) can only be regarded in law as birth control rather than abortion provided that the procedure is carried out before a fertilised egg is implanted in the uterus and not done with the intent to procure a miscarriage. (See the discussion *ante*, ch 10.)

(a) Early abortions?

More problematical for our purposes is the procedure known as menstrual extraction or aspiration. This is considered in the following article.

V Tunkel 'Abortion: how early, how late and how legal?' (1979) BMJ 253

... In view of the legal uncertainties, a doctor who regularly performed menstrual extraction (a convenient but question-begging euphemism) might until recently have thought it best to play safe by complying hypothetically with the Abortion Act; although the girl's pregnancy, if any, cannot at such an early stage be diagnosed, it would be prudent to certify as for a termination, and certainly to notify if the pregnancy was subsequently confirmed histologically.

The DPP and Mr Goldthorp

One such practitioner was Mr W O Goldthorp, the Manchester consultant gynaecologist, who in an article in the *BMJ* described how he performed menstrual extractions from 10 to 18 days after a missed period. The Chief Constable of Manchester referred the matter to the Director of Public Prosecutions. Early in 1978 the DPP expressed the opinion that menstrual extraction in these circumstances was illegal, and that purported compliance with the Abortion Act made no difference. Mr Goldthorp thereupon ceased these extractions.

The DPP's opinion was based on his understanding of the Abortion Act, which gives protection to doctors 'when a pregnancy is terminated'. This was understood by the Lane Committee to exclude 'speculative' operations, done before the existence of a pregnancy could be known. To fill this gap the committee proposed that the Act be amended by adding a new subsection: 'In this Act references to termination of pregnancy include acts done with intent to terminate a pregnancy if such exists', but there has been no legislation to implement this. And since the Act in s 5(2) states categorically that 'anything done with intent to procure the miscarriage of a woman is unlawfully done unless authorised by section 1 of this Act', it seems to be a simple either/or choice. The DPP gave a further reason for his opinion: no doctor could hold the opinion in good faith, as required by the Act, that there was a risk to the woman or the child in the continuance of the pregnancy if he did not know that she was in fact pregnant.

If to some medical readers there seems an excessive literalism in these reasons it would be as well for them to realise that this is for better or worse part of our legal tradition in the interpretation of statutes. It serves to emphasise the importance of focusing on the actual words used by Parliament and not accepting some widely repeated paraphrase or believed meaning. We return to this point below. But on the question of menstrual extraction there is now further news: the DPP subsequently had his mind changed by his superiors, the Law Officers (the Attorney-General and Solicitor-General). In March 1979 they expressed the opinion (giving no reasons) that what Mr Goldthorp described in his article was protected by the Abortion Act; and that the Act's references to termination of pregnancy should be understood as including steps taken to terminate a pregnancy which two practitioners in good faith believe to exist.

In this unsatisfactory state of affairs it is difficult to say with confidence what the law is. If Mr Goldthorp or others have resumed these extractions there could be a test case, as the Lane Committee suggested. For the present we have the reasoned opinion of the DPP that the operations are illegal in all circumstances and the later bald statement of the Law Officers that words may be read into the Abortion Act which would make them legal. (It is perhaps worth adding that the words suggested by the Law Officers might in any event still do not confer protection, since the two practitioners do not positively 'believe a pregnancy to exist' if they merely think that there is a chance it might. The Lane Committee's amendment is much clearer; but it would take a bold judge to read that into the unamended Act.)

Would a criminal court today adopt the DPP's opinion or the Law Officers' second thoughts? The answer – or rather the question – is complicated by the fact that, although anyone may bring a prosecution for abortion, the police have to inform the DPP. He is thus given an opportunity to intervene, but he is subject to the control of the Law Officers. And, while the DPP who gave the anti-Goldthorp opinion is still in the saddle, the Law Officers who overrode him changed with the Government in May. Here, then, is rich material – medical, legal, and political – for those who enjoy speculating on current affairs. But it would be well to keep in mind what we are pondering: the prospect of prosecuting highly respected medical men. Their crime (maximum penalty, life imprisonment) is their open and ethical performance, with skill and success, of routine procedures at just the time when these are medically most desirable. Should there be even a shadow of criminality over this situation?

This is not all. Even given that the Law Officers were right and there is no longer any question of these early postcoital extractions being regarded as criminal, this exemption is achieved only by complying with the Abortion Act. The effect of this is to declare all non-statutory extraction criminal where the operator thinks, even erroneously, that the woman might be pregnant. However satisfied he may be with his diagnosis of, say, amenorrhoea, would not an honest practitioner admit that there is almost always a chance that he may be mistaken, may perhaps have been misled by his patient, and that possibly she has a very early pregnancy? If he thinks that this is a possibility then even though he does not believe it to be so, he extracts intending to remove the contents of the uterus, including any conception that may be present. It would seem odd (and perhaps even insulting to the patient) to insist on certifying under the Abortion Act in such a case. But if he does not, s 58 is inescapable: '. . . whosoever, with intent to procure the miscarriage of any woman, whether she be or be not with child, shall lawfully use any instrument . . . shall be guilty . . .'. Perhaps the ultimate irony is that it is immaterial that she was never in fact pregnant at all. The crime is committed because of his conditional intent.

To summarise: if this account of the present law is correct, it follows that in all cases where very early, undiagnosable, pregnancy is a possibility, (1) no doctor is safe to perform a menstrual extraction, for whatever reason, without complying with the Abortion Act; and possibly also – (2) even with such compliance there may still be an offence.

Since Tunkel wrote his paper, the House of Lords in the *Royal College of Nursing* case *(supra)* has given its mind to the central question which is the meaning of the words in the Abortion Act, 'when a pregnancy is terminated'. Lord Wilberforce (who dissented in the final decision) stated that:

> The argument for the department is carried even further than this, for it is said that, the words 'when a pregnancy is terminated by a registered medical practitioner' mean 'when treatment for the termination of pregnancy is carried out by a registered medical practitioner'. This is said to be necessary in order to cover the supposed cases where the treatment is unsuccessful, or where there is no pregnancy at all. The latter hypothesis I regard as fanciful; the former, if it was Parliament's contemplation at all in 1967 (for failures under post-1967 methods are not in point), cannot be covered by any reasonable reading of the words. Termination is one thing; attempted and unsuccessful termination wholly another. I cannot be persuaded to embark on a radical reconstruction of the Act by reference to a fanciful hypothesis or an improbable casus omissus.

Lord Diplock, on the other hand, took a different view:

> . . . [I]f 'termination' or 'terminated' meant only the event of miscarriage and not the whole treatment undertaken with that object in kind, lack of success, which apparently occurs in 1% to 2% of cases, would make all who had taken part in the unsuccessful treatment guilty of an offence under s 58 or s 59 of the Offences against the Person Act 1861. This cannot have been the intention of Parliament.

Lord Edmund-Davies, while agreeing with Lord Diplock in his conclusion, took a somewhat different line:

> In the foreground was the submission that, were a termination of pregnancy embarked on when (as it turned out) the woman was not pregnant, the Act would afford no defence to a doctor prosecuted under the 1861 Act. And it was secondly urged that he would be equally defenceless even where he personally treated a pregnant woman throughout if, for some reason, the procedure was interrupted and the pregnancy not terminated. I have respectfully to say that in my judgment it is these objections which are themselves absurd. Lawful termination under the Act predicates the personal services of a doctor operating in s 1(3) premises and armed with the opinion of two medical practitioners. But where termination is nevertheless not achieved the appellants invite this House to contemplate the doctor and his nursing staff being prosecuted under s 58 of the 1861 Act, the charge being, of course, not the unlawful termination of pregnancy (for *ex hypothesi* there was *no* termination) but one of unlawfully administering a noxious thing or unlawfully using an instrument with intent to procure miscarriage. And on *that* charge unlawfulness has still to be established and the prosecution would assuredly fail. For the circumstances predicated themselves establish the absence of any mens rea in instituting the abortive treatment, and its initial lawfulness could

not be rendered unlawful either by the discovery that the woman was not in fact pregnant or by non-completion of the abortive treatment. Were it otherwise, the unavoidable conclusion is that doctors and nurses could in such cases be convicted of what in essence would be the extraordinary crime of attempting to do a *lawful* act.

My Lords, it was after drafting the foregoing that I happened on the following passage in Smith and Hogan's Criminal Law (4th Edn, 1978, p 346) which I now gratefully adopt, for it could not be more apposite:

> . . . the legalisation of an abortion must include the steps which are taken towards it. Are we really to say that these are criminal until the operation is complete, when they are retrospectively authorised, or alternatively that they are lawful until the operation is discontinued or the woman is discovered not to be pregnant when, retrospectively, they become unlawful? When the conditions of the Act are otherwise satisfied, it is submitted that [the doctor] is not unlawfully administering, etc., and that this is so whether the pregnancy be actually terminated or not.

(b) Selective reduction

Another procedure, which may arguably be an abortion, has caused controversy. This is the procedure known as 'selective reduction'. This, to quote the description of the Voluntary Licensing Authority in its 3rd Report (April 1988), in Annex 5:

> . . . is the term used to describe the procedure whereby one or more embryos in a multiple pregnancy are selectively killed to allow others to develop. In multiple pregnancies resulting from infertility treatment the procedure is used to avoid large multiple births though the technique was originated to stop the development of abnormal embryos in a multiple pregnancy where the remainder were normal.

The potentially crucial factual distinction between this procedure and other abortions is that when selective reduction is performed the destroyed foetus may be absorbed into the mother's body and is not expelled. Is selective reduction lawful? This requires us to consider two questions: (1) does the procedure come within the offence under s 58 of the Offences Against the Person Act 1861 of acting 'with intent to procure a miscarriage'?; and, if it does, (2) would compliance with the terms of the Abortion Act 1967 render it lawful?

(i) THE SECTION 58 ARGUMENT

Two inter-related arguments are put here to determine whether the procedure falls within s 58. First, is the medical practitioner acting with intent to procure *a miscarriage*, and secondly, is he terminating a pregnancy?

In the following article, Keown examines the arguments and considers that the procedure may come within s 58.

I J Keown 'Selective Reduction of Multiple Pregnancy (1987) NLJ 1165

The first argument is that there is no need to invoke the protection of the Abortion Act since selective reduction is not prohibited by s 58. The argument runs that s 58 prohibits acts done with intent to procure miscarriage; that the word 'miscarriage' presupposes the expulsion of the fetus from the uterus, and that since selective reduction, which is performed in early pregnancy, results not in the expulsion of the fetus but in its absorption by the uterus, the procedure is not caught by the section. In support of this line of argument could be cited the many definitions of 'miscarriage', both medical and legal, which refer to the expulsion of the fetus from the uterus or to the emptying of the uterus. Against this, it may be argued that such definitions are sufficiently broad to include cases of termination of pregnancy followed by fetal absorption. In any event there is no evidence (either from medical practice or from the conduct of prosecutions for criminal abortion) that these definitions exclude such cases, nor is there any reason why they should do so. On the contrary, it has long been accepted by both medical and legal authorities that 'miscarriage' pertains not to the destination of the fetal remains but to the failure of gestation.

Defining miscarriage
In 1882, for example, a leading medical dictionary defined 'miscarriage' as the 'Interruption of gestation before the fetus has become viable'. More significantly, legal authorities have defined the word sufficiently broadly to include the failure of gestation without subsequent fetal expulsion. In the Australian case of *R v Trim* ([1943] VLR 109) a case on s 62 of the Crimes Act 1928 – the equivalent of s 58 – decided by the Full Court of the Supreme Court of Victoria, Marfarlan J stated that s 62 merely required 'an intent to cause in the case of the woman in question the event of birth, carriage or bearing which would take place in the ordinary course of nature to go amiss – go wrong or fail'.

Again, Professor Glanville Williams defines the offence of abortion as follows:

'Abortion (or miscarriage) . . . may be deliberately induced when it is a serious crime. For legal purposes, abortion means feticide: the *intentional* destruction of the fetus in the womb, or any untimely delivery brought about with intent to cause the death of the fetus.

In addition to these broad definitions of miscarriage, which indicate that s 58 prohibits the termination of pregnancy even if the fetus is not thereafter expelled, it is relevant to point to the mischief against which the section is directed, namely, the destruction of the unborn child. As Professor Williams wrote in 1958:

both English law and the law of the great majority of the United States regard any interference with pregnancy, however early it may take place, as criminal, unless for therapeutic reasons. The fetus is a human life to be protected by the criminal law from the moment when the ovum is fertilised.

Is it also possible that a subsidiary purpose of s 58 was to protect women from the dangers of attempted abortion? Clearly, both purposes would be frustrated by an interpretation of 'miscarriage' which would allow anyone to attempt abortion provided the intention was to cause the fetus to be absorbed and not expelled.

A second argument against the need to comply with the Abortion Act 1967 is that in aborting a fetus in a multiple pregnancy the intention of the operator is not to cause the miscarriage of the woman but to ensure the better carriage of the remaining fetuses. With respect, this argument too founders on the established meaning of 'miscarriage' and on the mischief against which s 58 is directed. The section is infringed whether the woman miscarries of all the fetuses or only of one.

Another argument is explained (only to be rejected) in the following extract.

DPT Price 'Selective Reduction and Feticide: The Parameters of Abortion' [1988] Crim LR 199

The other argument put forward by fertility specialists in favour of the legality of selective reduction *per se* is that they have not by their action terminated the pregnancy. It still continues by virtue of the fact that one or more foetuses still survive. Admittedly on one interpretation of that phrase this does appear to be true, although it might be countered that the expressions multiple pregnancy and multipregnancy themselves admit the existence of more than one pregnancy. However, one should bear in mind that the words 'termination of pregnancy' do not in fact appear in the 1861 Act but in the Abortion Act 1967, ie not in the statute creating the offence but only in the statute containing an exclusion of liability. It cannot be supposed that it was the intention of Parliament when passing either Act that it should be lawful to terminate the development of a foetus or foetuses forming part of a multiple pregnancy, especially as techniques for selective termination of pregnancy are of such recent origin. Such foetuses not 'capable of being born alive' would then be denied any protection whatsoever under the criminal law. Whether the purpose of the law is seen as the protection of the mother, the protection of the foetus, or both, there can be no justification for drawing a distinction between single pregnancies and multipregnancies. The potential for life has equally been taken away, and there has additionally been a physical intrusion upon the mother.

(ii) THE ABORTION ACT 1967 ARGUMENT

The arguments of Keown and Price are compelling. However, Price's argument has further implications. If selective reduction falls within s 58 then it may only be carried out lawfully if done in compliance with the terms of the Abortion Act 1967. Until the 1990 amendments to the 1967 Act, Price's argument would have led to the conclusion that the 1967 Act did not apply. If this had been so, then the procedure could never have been performed, since 'anything done with intent to procure the miscarriage of a woman is unlawfully done unless authorised by' the 1967 Act (section 5(2)).

In an opinion appended to the Voluntary Licensing Authority's 3rd Report, John Keown puts this point as follows:

> As the better view is therefore that selective reduction is caught by section 58, the doctor would be well advised to comply with the requirements of the Abortion Act 1967 to render the procedure lawful. Compliance with the Abortion Act may, however, be ineffective. This is because the Act only affords protection when, in the words of section 1(1) 'a pregnancy is terminated'. As selective reduction results in the destruction of one or more but not all the fetuses, a court might rule that it does not terminate a pregnancy, and that compliance with the Abortion Act is ineffective.

Parliament has now put the matter beyond doubt. Section 5(2) was amended by the Human Fertilisation and Embryology Act 1990 (s 37) to provide as follows:

> 5(2) For the purposes of the law relating to abortion, anything done with intent to procure a woman's miscarriage (or, in the case of a woman carrying more than one foetus, her miscarriage of any foetus) is unlawfully done unless authorised by section 1 of this Act and, in the case of a woman carrying more than one foetus, anything done with intent to procure her miscarriage of any foetus is authorised by that section if –
> (a) the ground for termination of the pregnancy specified in subsection (1)(d) of that section applies in relation to any foetus and the thing is done for the purpose of procuring the miscarriage of that foetus, or
> (b) any of the other grounds for termination of the pregnancy specified in that section applies.

Consequently, selective reduction is lawful in two situations. First, in a case where the foetus (or foetuses) fall(s) within the foetal abnormality ground under s 1(1)(d) and the foetus(es) is/are terminated. Secondly, in a case where a multiple pregnancy exists so as to give rise to the required degree of risk of injury to the mother under s 1(1)(a), (b) or (c) and any number of the foetus(es) are terminated to reduce that risk to the mother. Notice in this situation the doctor can, in effect, randomly select any (or all) the foetuses since no foetus in particular gives rise to the risk to the mother.

What section 5(2) does not allow is the selective reduction of a pregnancy solely on the ground that the fact of its being a multiple pregnancy increases the *risk to the foetuses* the mother carries. This is not a ground under section 1 of the Abortion Act.

As a footnote, it is perhaps interesting to note that section 5(2) only tackles 'the Abortion Act 1967 argument' we discussed above. It simply assumes that selective reduction constitutes a 'miscarriage' and so accepts (perhaps conclusively) the argument above in respect of s 58 of the Offences Against the Person Act 1861.

(c) Later abortions

You will recall that under the Abortion Act as amended, terminations of pregnancy are not subject to any time-limit except when reliance is placed upon section 1(1)(a). Thus, the possibility exists that termination may be performed at a point when the foetus might survive if delivered alive. So, termination of the pregnancy need not in practice entail the death of the foetus. What, therefore, is the doctor's duty in this situation?

There are a number of ways of analysing the problem, some of which produce awkward conclusions. Consider four different situations, remembering always that the foetus has the capacity to survive:

(1) both the pregnant woman and doctor agree that the foetus should die in the process;
(2) both the pregnant woman and doctor agree that the foetus should be delivered alive, all things being equal;
(3) the pregnant woman wishes the foetus to be delivered alive but the doctor decides to cause its death in the process;
(4) the pregnant woman wishes the foetus to die in the process but the doctor decides to deliver the child alive.

The *first* situation poses no new difficulties. Providing the doctor complies with the provisions of the Abortion Act 1967, the termination will be lawful. This situation is most likely to arise if the termination is performed under section 1(1)(d) because of 'foetal abnormality'.

The *second* situation could arise where the termination is justified under section 1(1)(b) or (1)(c) where the pregnant woman's life is at risk or in order to avoid grave permanent injury to her. Again, providing the doctor complies with the provisions of the Abortion Act 1967, the termination will be lawful.

In the *third*, albeit highly improbable situation, again, providing the Abortion Act is complied with, the termination is lawful. It is a separate question, given the different understanding of the doctor and woman as to the outcome of the procedure, whether the pregnant woman has given a valid consent in law. Arguably, knowledge that the death of the foetus will result is an essential ingredient of consent to avoid an action in battery.

The *fourth* situation could arise where the pregnant woman seeks a termination under section 1(1)(d) but the doctor, perhaps because of his beliefs, delivers the baby alive. Here, *mutatis mutandis* the same arguments in respect of battery apply. However, providing the doctor complies with the Abortion Act, there can be no question of the termination being unlawful.

It is a further question, in this fourth situation, whether as a matter of law the doctor is under a *duty* to deliver a live child, if at all possible. (The same question arises in relation to the first situation.) When the amendments to the Abortion Act were before the House of Lords, an attempt was made to introduce a provision which would have placed a *duty* on a doctor to take all reasonable steps to secure that a child is born alive when a termination is performed under section 1(1)(b), 1(1)(c) or 1(1)(d). However, the attempt failed. Certainly, as regards a termination under section 1(1)(d) such a duty would not sit easily with the underlying premise of the ground that the pregnant woman is carrying an *unwanted child*. Both the pregnancy and the child are undesired because of its physical or mental disability. So, it would be inconsistent for the law to recognise that a doctor had the duty to deliver the child alive. Of course, this reasoning does not necessarily apply to terminations under section 1(1)(b) and (c) where only the *pregnancy* is unwanted but not necessarily the child. However, in both cases a doctor's duty must be conditioned by the mother's consent. Consequently, he could not, in law, be under a duty to deliver the child alive if the pregnant woman did not agree.

The above analysis of late terminations assumes that all terminations of pregnancy must be brought within the Abortion Act and that, if they are not, they would constitute the offence of 'procuring a *miscarriage*' under section 58 of the Offences Against the Person Act 1861.

This assumption may require reconsideration, not least because, if it is correct, a doctor who, for example, induces labour in a pregnant woman whose pregnancy has gone to term, and thereby terminates her pregnancy, would have to justify this conduct under the 1967 Act (as amended). For, on the face of it, the induction of labour is a termination of pregnancy and, hence, falls within the Abortion Act. However, compliance with the Abortion Act is only necessary so as to avoid liability under section 58 of the Offences Against the Person Act, *viz*, the crime of 'procuring a miscarriage'. The crucial question, therefore, is what does it mean to procure a *miscarriage*? If miscarriage means 'to be delivered prematurely of a child' (*Oxford English Dictionary*), which is the traditional view, then compliance with the Abortion Act is essential. However, if miscarriage also entails the destruction (ie death) of the foetus, then induced labour, or any termination intended to produce a live birth, need not mean that the doctor has to comply with the Abortion Act because no offence would be committed under section 58 of the Offences Against the Person Act 1861 because it would not be a *miscarriage*.

This somewhat orthodox conclusion clearly flies in the face of Parliament's intention when reforming the Abortion Act 1967. While limiting terminations under s 1(1)(a) to a time-limit of 24 weeks, Parliament considered it necessary to provide for later terminations where the pregnant woman's health needs made it essential. Hence, sections 1(1)(b) and (c) do not contain time-limits. In practice, in these cases there will be a live birth because only the *pregnancy* will be *unwanted* rather than the child itself. Only very exceptionally would the health needs of the pregnant woman demand that the child die in the process of terminating the pregnancy.

10. Abortion and homicide

What is the relationship between homicide and the law of abortion?

Glanville Williams, *Textbook of Criminal Law* (2nd edn 1983)

> The law protecting neonates and the unborn is not ordinarily met with in legal practice; but it is of importance for obstetric surgeons and is a matter of philosophical and human interest. It is also the subject of strongly-felt differences of moral opinion.
>
> The definition of homicide . . . requires the victim to be in *rerum natura* or 'in being', which means that he must be 'completely born alive'.
>
> Although injuries to a fetus causing its death do not generally amount to homicide, there is a curious rule by which they can do so. If a fetus is injured in the womb and is subsequently born alive but dies as a result of the prenatal injury, this is murder or manslaughter according to the mental element. So whether the offender is guilty of the crime will sometimes depend upon whether a doctor is able to remove the fetus from the womb while it is still alive, even though it is so premature that it is doomed to die almost immediately.

In a New Jersey case, D shot a pregnant woman whose twin sons were then delivered by caesarean section (hysterotomy) but died a short time later. He was convicted of murder of the infants. Had they died in the womb it would not have been murder.

The rule also applies to illegal abortionists. In this it seems to be over-severe, for it makes what may be a purely accidental fact turn the abortionist into a murderer.

The Supreme Court of California examined the question when interpreting the provisions of the California Penal Code in the following case.

Keeler v Superior Court of Amador County (1970) 470 P 2d 617 (Cal Sup Ct)

Mosk J: On February 23, 1969, Mrs Keeler was driving on a narrow mountain road in Amador County after delivering the girls to their home. She met petitioner driving in the opposite direction; he blocked the road with his car, and she pulled over to the side. He walked to her vehicle and began speaking to her. He seemed calm, and she rolled down her window to hear him. He said, 'I hear you're pregnant. If you are you had better stay away from the girls and from here.' She did not reply, and he opened the car door; as she later testified. 'He assisted me out of the car . . . [I]t wasn't roughly at this time.' Petitioner then looked at her abdomen and became 'extremely upset.' He said, 'You sure are, I'm going to stomp it out of you.' He pushed her against the car, shoved his knee in her abdomen, and struck her in the face with several blows. She fainted, and when she regained consciousness petitioner had departed.

Mrs Keeler drove back to Stockton, and the police and medical assistance were summoned. She had suffered substantial facial injuries, as well as extensive bruising of the abdominal wall. A Caesarian section was performed and the fetus was examined *in utero*. Its head was found to be severely fractured, and it was delivered stillborn. The pathologist gave as his opinion that the cause of death was skull fracture with consequent cerebral hemorrhaging, that death would have been immediate, and that the injury could have been the result of force applied to the mother's abdomen. There was no air in the fetus' lungs, and the umbilical cord was intact.

Upon delivery the foetus weighed five pounds and was 18 inches in length. Both Mrs Keeler and her obstetrician testified that fetal movements had been observed prior to February 23, 1969. The evidence was in conflict as to the estimated age of the fetus; the expert testimony on the point, however, concluded 'with reasonable medical certainty' that the fetus had developed to the stage of viability, ie, that in the event of premature birth on the date in question it would have had a 75 percent to 96 percent chance of survival.

An information was filed charging petitioner, in Court I, with committing the crime of murder (Pen Code, s 187) in that he did 'unlawfully kill a human being, to wit Baby Girl VOGT, with malice aforethought'. . . :

Penal Code section 187 provides: 'Murder is the unlawful killing of a human being, with malice aforethought'. The dispositive question is whether the foetus which petitioner is accused of killing was, on February 23, 1969, a 'human being' within the meaning of this statute. If it was not, petitioner cannot be charged with its 'murder' and prohibition will lie.

Section 187 was enacted as part of the Penal Code of 1872. Inasmuch as the provision has not been amended since that date, we must determine the intent of the Legislature at the time of its enactment. But section 187 was, in turn, taken verbatim from the first California statute defining murder, part of the Crimes and Punishment Act of 1850. (Stats 1850, ch 99, s 19, 0 231.) Penal Code section 5 (also enacted in 1872) declares: 'The provisions of this Code, so far as they are substantially the same as existing statutes, must be construed as continuations thereof, and not as new enactments'. We begin, accordingly, by inquiring into the intent of the Legislature in 1850 when it first defined murder as the unlawful and malicious killing of a 'human being'.

It will be presumed, of course, that in enacting a statute the Legislature was familiar with the relevant rules of the common law, and, when it couches its enactment in common law language, that its intent was to continue those rules in statutory form. (*Baker v Baker* 13 Cal 87, 95-96 (1859); *Morris v Oney* 217 Cal App 2d 864 at 870, 32 Cal Rptr 88 (1963).) This is particularly appropriate in considering the work of the first session of our Legislature: its precedents were necessarily drawn from the common law, as modified in certain respects by the Constitution and by legislation of our sister states.

We therefore undertake a brief review of the origins and development of the common law of abortional homicide. (For a more detailed treatment, see Means, The Law of New York concerning Abortion and the Status of the Foetus, 1664-1968: A Case of Cessation of Constitutionality (1968) 14 NYLF 411 [hereinafter cited as Means]: Stern, Abortion: Reform and the Law (1968) 59 J Crim L, C & PS 84; Quay, Justifiable Abortion – Medical and Legal Foundations II (1961) 49 Geo LJ 395.) From that inquiry it appears that by the year 1850 – the date with which we are concerned – an infant could not be the subject of homicide at common law *unless it had been born alive.* Perhaps the must influential statement of the 'born alive' rule is that of Coke, in Mid-17th century: '[If a woman be quick with childe, and by a potion or otherwise killeth it in her wombe, or if a man beat her, whereby the childe dyeth in her body, and she is delivered of a dead childe, this is a great misprision [ie, misdemeanor], and no murder; but if the childe be borne alive and dyeth of the potion, battery, or other cause, this is murder; for in law it is accounted a reasonable creature, *in rerum natura,* when it is born alive.]' (3 Coke, Institutes *58 (1648).) In short 'By Coke's time, the common law regarded abortion as murder only if the foetus is (1) quickened, (2) born alive, (3) lives for a brief interval, and (4) then dies'. (Means, at p 420.) Whatever intrinsic defects there may have been in Coke's work (see 3 Stephen, A History of the Criminal Law of England (1883) pp 52-60), the common law accepted his views as authoritative. In the 18th century, for example, Coke's requirement that an infant be born alive in order to be the subject of homicide was reiterated and expanded by both Blackstone and Hale. . . .

We conclude that in declaring murder to be the unlawful and malicious killing of a 'human being' the Legislature of 1850 intended that term to have the settled common law meaning of a person who had been born alive, and did not intend the act of feticide – as distinguished from abortion – to be an offense under the laws of California. . . .

Notes to extract
Aftermath Cal Pen Code s 187. 'Murder is the unlawful killing of a human being, *or a fetus,* with malice aforethought. . . .' The words in italics were added by amendment in 1970, 'triggered' by *Keeler.*

The word 'fetus' in section 187 is interpreted to mean 'a viable unborn child'. *People v Smith* 129 Cal Rptr 498 (1976).

By contrast, the Supreme Judicial Court of Massachusetts held in 1989 that the intentional killing of a *viable* foetus *in utero* could be murder at common law, reflecting the change made to the California Penal Code noted above after *Keeler: Commonwealth v Lawrence* (1989) 404 Mass 378. English law would, undoubtedly, continue to reflect the view of Professor Williams.

Chapter 13

Actions by children and parents arising from occurrences before birth

In this chapter we explore the way in which the general principles of medical negligence apply to the various factual situations where the alleged negligent occurrence takes place before the birth of a child.

We can usefully consider the factual situations under two headings, each divided into two subheadings:

Actions by the child:
A. pre-natal injury
B. wrongful life

Actions by the parents:
A. wrongful conception
B. wrongful birth

We use these labels as convenient devices conscious of the fact that they need explanation. In short, they are terms of art, each of which describe a group of particular situations that call for the application of common principles.

Actions by the child

A. PRE-NATAL INJURY

A claim for pre-natal injury arises when a child is born injured and alleges that *his injury was caused* by the negligence of another prior to his birth. The occurrence may occur prior to his conception, while *ex utero* as an embryo (ie during IVF treatment) or *in utero* (including during the process of birth).

1. The common law

(a) The background

P J Pace, 'Civil Liability for Pre-Natal Injuries' (1977) 40 MLR 141

Although Blackstone was able to assert confidently that in criminal law 'Life is the immediate gift of God, a right inherent by nature in every individual, and it begins in contemplation of the law as soon as an infant is able to stir in the mother's womb' [*Commentaries* (15th edn), Vol 1, p 129], subsequent legal development in relation to the unborn child in a civil context does not wholly endorse this view. The rights of such a child are recognised at law for certain limited purposes only, eg in connection with succession to property, the Fatal Accidents Acts and certain crimes, and there was an apparent hiatus in the law which was highlighted by the national tragedy caused by the devastating effects of the drug thalidomide. This apparent gap, which the Law Commission, in August 1974, [*Report on Injuries to Unborn Children* (No 60, Cmnd 5709)] proposed should be filled by the Congenital Disabilities (Civil Liability) Bill, was suggested by the absence of any English decision on whether a tortious action would subsist at the suit of a plaintiff in respect of post-natal damage suffered as a result of pre-natal fault.

In considering whether a right of action is to be granted in such circumstances, there are at least four possible approaches which can be, and in other jurisdictions have been, adopted. The first, a fiction applied in Civil Law jurisdictions and based upon Roman Law, is that a child *in utero*, if subsequently born alive, is deemed as already born if that would be to its advantage. The second involves attributing to the child *in utero* legal personality which, in the absence of a live birth, would have important implications for both opponents and proponents of abortion law reform. The third, and biologically unsound, view is that the unborn child is merely a part of his mother and, therefore, there can be no action on his behalf, but only on behalf of his mother if she, while pregnant, sustained injuries though another's negligence. The fourth approach takes the view that, since the tort of negligence is incomplete unless and until damage is suffered by the plaintiff, that tort is in fact completed on the live birth of the injured infant, at which time the infant has legal personality and is able to sue through his next friend, albeit that injuries were inflicted on the infant while he was *in utero*. . . .

If the point had fallen to be decided [an English] court would doubtless have been swayed by the words of Lamont J spoken . . . in the Canadian case of *Montreal Tramways v Leveille* [[1933] 4 DLR 337 at 340]: 'the great weight of judicial opinion in the common law courts denies the right of a child when born to maintain an action for pre-natal injuries'. This was a reflection of various American authorities and of the Irish case of *Walker v Great Northern Rly Co of Ireland* [(1890) 28 LR Ir 69] . . . In *Montreal Tramways*, a post-*Donoghue v Stevenson* case, the court had concluded in favour of liability but this would have been of little help to an English court. There the Supreme Court of Canada had to decide whether the defendant company was liable in respect of its negligence which, the majority of the court accepted, caused a pregnant woman passenger to give birth to a child with club-feet. The action was brought under a provision of the Quebec Civil Code whereby 'Every person . . . is responsible for the damage caused by his fault to another. . . .' . . . This case was not . . . directly in point on the question of whether a duty of care was owed in the situation under consideration; it merely decided that in the circumstances of that case an unborn child, through the application of a fiction, was deemed to exist and so was 'another' for the purposes of the Quebec Civil Code.

An inherent and perennial difficulty in claims for pre-natal injuries, and one which was largely the reason for the one-time refusal of a right of recovery by the American courts, is the ascertainment of a causal *nexus* between the pre-natal negligence of the defendant and the post-natal harm to the child. Though Smith J's first reason for his dissent in *Montreal Tramways* was his view that the civil law fiction favoured by the majority was restricted to property questions, his second was that he doubted whether the medical evidence adduced would allow the reasonable inference that the plaintiff's club-feet resulted from the injury to the mother. Furthermore, in *Walker* a subsidiary ground advanced by O'Brien J for denying the claim was that it would be difficult to 'trace a hare lip to nervous shock, or a bunch of grapes on the face to the fright' [(1890) 28 Lr Ir 69 at 81]. Obviously the difficulty of establishing a connection between the defendant's conduct and the plaintiff's injury is not a sufficient reason for denying a right of action, though, on the state of medical knowledge at the time of *Walker*, difficulties in establishing a connection would in many cases have proved insurmountable. Advances in medical science will more often show the required connection without resort to mere speculation and conjecture, although the difficulty of establishing such a connection will increase the more removed in time is the wrongful act from the accrual of the cause of action. . . .

In *Watt v Rama* [[1972] VR 353] the Full Court of the Supreme Court of Victoria had to decide certain preliminary points of law which arose out of a car crash in which a pregnant woman had been injured by the faulty driving of the defendant. The woman driver had subsequently given birth to the plaintiff who suffered from brain damage, epilepsy and paralysis from the neck downwards. The questions which fell to be determined were whether (1) the defendant owed a duty of care not to cause injury to the unborn plaintiff; (2) he owed a duty of care to the infant plaintiff not to injure her mother; and (3) whether the damage complained of was in law too remote. For the purposes only of the determination of those questions it was *assumed* in the plaintiff's favour that the injuries sustained by her were caused by the defendant's faulty driving. Thus, at the subsequent trial of the action the ascertainment of a connection might well produce difficulties.

All three members of the court, after a comprehensive investigation of judicial and academic authorities, resorted to basic tort principles, in particular the statement of the 'neighbour principle' by Lord Atkin in *Donoghue v Stevenson*. Winneke CJ and Pape J held that it was reasonably foreseeable at the time of the collision that the defendant's conduct might cause injury to a pregnant woman in the car with which he collided. Therefore, the possibility of injury on birth to the child she was carrying must also be reasonably foreseeable. This gave rise to a potential relationship capable of imposing a duty on the defendant *vis-à-vis* the child if, and when, born alive. On such birth this relationship crystallised, since it was then that the child suffered injuries as a living person and there arose a duty on the defendant to take reasonable care in relation to the child. They concluded that the answers to the questions posed by the preliminary determination they were called upon to make were: (1) yes; (2) an answer was unnecessary; and (3) no.

The third member of the court, Gillard J, reached the same conclusions but by a somewhat different route. The application of the 'neighbour principle' resulted in the finding that, on the assumed facts, the plaintiff was a member of a class which might reasonably and probably be affected by the defendant's carelessness:

> The unborn child should be included in the class of persons likely to be affected by [the driver's] carelessness since the regeneration of the human species implies the presence on the highway of many pregnant women. [*Ibid* at p 374]

Furthermore, the defendant as a reasonable driver should have foreseen the presence of such a woman and the risk to her child, if his failure to reach the standard of a reasonably careful driver caused him to collide with and injure the mother.

All three judges emphasised that there was nothing unusual in there being a time-lag between the defendant's careless driving and the consequential damage suffered by the plaintiff, since, particularly in cases under *Donoghue v Stevenson*, the duty of care was not dependent on the existence, at the time of the defendant's fault, of a person with the right correlative to the defendant's duty to take care. This lapse of time was relevant only in relation to the child's capacity to sue.

In *Duval v Seguin* [(1972) 26 DLR (3d) 418] the High Court of Ontario recognised that there were no authorities binding upon it and, as above, Fraser J had recourse to fundamental principles of tort. . . . He took the view that, applying *Donoghue v Stevenson*, an unborn child was:

> within the foreseeable risk incurred by a negligent motorist. When the unborn child becomes a living person and suffers damages [sic] as a result of pre-natal injuries caused by the negligent motorist the cause of action is completed. A tortfeasor is as liable to a child who has suffered pre-natal injury as to the victim with a thin skull or other physical defect. [*Ibid* at p 434.]

It is to be noted that, save for Gillard J who was prepared to deem an unborn child a person in being at the time of the defendant's negligence, the judges in these cases avoided the question of whether legal status should be accorded to a foetus. The approach adopted was basically that, since damage is essential to the tort of negligence, that tort is not completed until the damage is suffered. As the damage was not suffered in both cases until the birth of the plaintiff the tort was completed at birth, at which time there was no difficulty in attributing legal personality to the live plaintiff. On this view, according to *Watt v Rama*, pre-natal damage to the foetus is merely an evidentiary fact in relation to the issue of the causation of damage at birth.

This solution requires the establishment of a causal *nexus* between the defendant's wrongful act and the plaintiff's defective condition on birth. It is a *sine qua non* of this view that there is a birth and that that birth is a live one. The factual situation in these Commonwealth cases was such that it did not require the courts to discuss the problem of the point in time at which there is a live birth and consequent legal personality.

The absence of case law in England had, as Pace points out, led the Law Commission in 1974 in its Report on 'Injuries to Unborn Children' (No 60, Cmnd 5709) to recommend legislation creating a claim for pre-natal injury. We will deal later with the Congenital Disabilities (Civil Liability) Act 1976 which applies to births after 21 July 1976. It may be asked why it is important to consider the position at common law given the existence of the 1976 Act. The answer lies in the fact that claims arising from births before the Act came into force continue to be brought before the courts. There are two principal reasons. First, the limitation period for such claims only begins to run (if at all) when the child bringing the claim reaches the age of 18. Secondly, since April 1992, legal aid is (at least until they reach majority) more widely available to children who wish to bring such a claim since they are no longer assessed on the basis of their parents' income.

For ease of exposition, it is helpful to consider the legal issues by reference to the factual groupings we identified earlier: pre-conception occurrences; *ex utero* but post-conception occurrences and *in utero* occurrences. Here we will not consider the middle of these situations since IVF treatment was not available until sometime after the common law was replaced by the 1976 Act. Since most of the case law involves occurrences *in utero* we begin with that situation.

(b) Occurrences in utero

It was assumed or conceded by the parties in a number of cases that a *common law* claim for pre-natal injury could be brought (*Williams v Luff* (1978) 122 Sol Jo 164; *McKay v Essex AHA* [1982] QB 1166. Cf *S v Distillers Co* [1970] 1 WLR 114.) One of the most important cases in medical negligence, *Whitehouse v Jordan* [1981] 1 WLR 246 (HL) involved allegations of negligence *in utero* and during the process of birth while the plaintiff child was as yet unborn. The legal difficulties for the plaintiff raised by such an allegation went unnoticed and unremarked upon throughout the litigation. It was not until the cases of *Burton v Islington HA* and *de Martell v Merton and Sutton HA* that the issue directly arose for decision by an English court.

(i) WHERE THE CHILD IS BORN ALIVE

Burton v Islington HA and *de Martell v Merton and Sutton HA* [1992] 3 All ER 833, (1992) 10 BMLR 63 (CA)

Dillon LJ: The court has before it two appeals which raise the same point of law, that is to say can a child who is born alive, but suffering from disabilities occasioned by negligence on the part of the proposed defendant at a time when the child was en ventre and unborn, maintain an action for damages for negligence against the defendant.

In both these cases the alleged negligence was that of the medical staff at a hospital, but, as the decided cases show, it could have arisen from a range of other contexts, for instance from negligent driving of a motor-vehicle or negligence on the part of a railway company or tramway company in respect of a train or tram in which the mother of the child was travelling as a passenger while pregnant.

The two decisions appealed from are, firstly, that of Potts J in *Burton v Islington Health Authority* (1990) 6 BMLR 13, [1991] 1 QB 638 and, secondly, that of Phillips J in *de Martell v Merton and Sutton Health Authority* [1992] 3 All ER 820 . . .

Since we are only concerned with a point of law, the precise facts do not matter but I should indicate them briefly to show the limited scope of this decision.

In *de Martell* the plaintiff's complaint is of negligence by medical staff when the plaintiff's mother was in labour at the time of her delivery and his birth.

In *Burton* the plaintiff's complaint is of negligence by medical staff at a much earlier period – they carried out a dilation and curettage procedure at a time when the plaintiff's mother was about five weeks pregnant with the plaintiff but did not know it, and they failed to carry out any pregnancy test before the D and C procedure. It is said that they should have done so, especially as there were circumstances which might have put and should, it is said, have put experienced medical staff on inquiry. Neither case is concerned at all with the position where a child has been stillborn as a result of a third party's negligence or has, as a result of such negligence, survived birth for only a minimal period.

. . . [T]he appellants say that the damage in the present case was suffered by the plaintiff whilst still en ventre and therefore while not a person in the eyes of the English law. Therefore, it is said, each plaintiff, though subsequently born alive and still now surviving, cannot sue.

There are cases not in any way in doubt on this appeal which establish the general proposition that a foetus enjoys, while still a foetus, no independent legal personality – a foetus cannot, while a foetus, sue and cannot be made a ward of court: see *Paton v Trustees of BPAS* [1978] 2 All ER 987, [1979] QB 276, *Re F (in utero)* [1988] 2 All ER 193, [1988] Fam 122 and *C v S* (1987) 2 BMLR 143 [1987] 1 All ER 1230, [1988] QB 135.

There are other contexts, however, to which I shall come, in which the English courts have adopted as part of English law the maxim of the civil law that an unborn child shall be deemed to be born whenever its interests require it – or as put by Lord Westbury LC quoting from *Justinian's Digest* (D1,5, 7) 'De Statu Hominum' in *Blasson v Blasson* (1864) 2 De GJ & SM 665 at 670, 46 ER 534 at 536:

> Qui in utero est, perinde ac si in rebus humanis esset, custoditur, *quoties de commodis ipsius partus quaertitur*. . . [Lord Westbury LC's emphasis].

On that basis of the civil law, the majority of the Supreme Court of Canada held in *Montreal Tramways v Leveille* [1933] 4 DLR 337 that when a child not actually born at the time of an accident was subsequently born alive and viable it was clothed with all the rights of action which it would have had if actually in existence at the date of the accident to the mother. That was a case of an accident when, by reason of the negligence of the tramway company's motor man, the infant's mother fell from a tram to the street and was injured. Two months later she gave birth to a female child who was born with club feet.

The leading judgment, expressing the majority view, was given by Lamont J. The maxim, which I have already quoted, led to the conclusion that as the child en ventre was born alive it was to be treated as having been alive while en ventre and so could claim damages for an injury at that time. The civil law applied because the case was a Quebec case and the Civil Code of Quebec is founded on the civil law. Cannon J, who delivered his judgment in French, seems to have taken a wider view since he reached the same conclusion without reliance on the maxims of the civil law or the Quebec Civil Code: 'On peut dire que son droit est né en même temps qu'elle' (see [1933] 4 DLR 337 at 367). Certain comments in relation to the problem in the judgment of Lamont J (at 345) are cited by Phillips J in his judgment in *de Martell* [1992] 3 All ER 820 at 825-826 and have been cited in other common law jurisdiction decisions since 1933.

> If a child after birth has no right of action for pre-natal injuries, we have a wrong inflicted for which there is no remedy, for, although the father may be entitled to compensation for the loss he has incurred and the mother for what she has suffered, yet there is a residuum of injury for which compensation cannot be had save at the suit of the child. If a right of action be denied to the child it will be compelled, without any fault on its part, to go through life carrying the seal of another's fault and bearing a very heavy burden of infirmity and inconvenience without any compensation therefore. To my mind it is but natural justice that a child, if born alive and viable, should be allowed to maintain an action in the Courts for injuries wrongfully committed upon its person while in the womb of its mother.

The main contexts in which the maxim of the civil law above quoted has been adopted as part of English law are set out in the speech of Lord Atkinson in *Villar v Gilbey* [1907] AC 139 at 149-150. [1904-7] All ER Rep 779 at 783-784. The best known is that, where there is a gift to a class of children living at a particular date, a child en ventre sa mère at that date but later born alive will be treated as having been living at the date and thus included in the class. A child in its mother's womb is considered as absolutely born to all intents and purposes for the child's benefit. Incidentally, and irrelevantly for present purposes, that reasoning has led to the well-established conclusion that a child en ventre at a testator's death but later born alive may rank as a life in being for the purposes of the rule against perpetuities, which is a rule of public policy under English law: see *Long v Blackall* (1799) 3 Ves 486, 30 ER 1119.

More significantly the same civil law principle led Sir Robert Phillimore in the Admiralty Court in *The George and Richard* (1871) LR 3 A & E 466 at 480 to hold that a posthumous child, later born alive, ranks as a child of its father – in that case a ship's carpenter, who lost his life when his ship was blown on to the rocks and wrecked following disablement in a collision – for the purposes of Lord Campbell's Act, the Fatal Accidents Act 1846.

For my part, I think it would be open to the English courts to apply the civil law maxim directly to the situations we have in these two appeals, and treat the two plaintiffs as lives in being at the times of the events which injured them as they were later born alive, but it is not necessary to do so directly in view of the effect which the *Montreal Tramways* case has already had in the development of the common law in this field in other common law jurisdictions.

Mr Ashworth helpfully referred us to a substantial number of United States decisions. His general thesis was that the decisions from 1884 to 1945, which held that the child when born cannot recover damages for pre-natal injury, represent the pure doctrine of the common law, while all the decisions from 1946 onwards, which all took the opposite view, are to be rejected as heretical and wrong. The effect of the post-1945 decisions is that the courts of every American state have now held, as a development of the common law and despite previous decisions to the contrary, that a child can recover damages for a pre-natal injury, and even that damages can be recovered by the estate of a stillborn child.

It is wholly unnecessary to go that far in the present case and I would not for a moment suggest that the common law of England is bound or even likely to follow every twist of the development of the common law in the United States. None the less, I would be most reluctant to hold that the common law, though capable of development in this field in every other jurisdiction, has crystallised in England at a date long past – 1891 was Mr Ashworth's preferred date. It may be added that the *Montreal Tramways* case was cited and relied on in the earliest United States case of 1946, *Bonbrest v Kotz* (1946) 65 F Supp 138, where the changed view, that a child could sue, was adopted.

The main Commonwealth case from a country with a common law jurisdiction is *Watt v Rama* [1972] VR 353, a decision of the Supreme Court of Victoria in an appellate capacity which has since been accepted by other appellate courts in Australia as a correct statement of the law, that is to say the common law of Australia. That was a case which arose out of injuries in a motor accident. The leading judgment is that of Winneke CJ and Pape J. It is founded on an analysis – in my judgment, correct – of the tort of negligence by reference to decisions of the House of Lords and the Privy Council and certain Australian decisions, and it is founded also on the *Montreal Tramways* decision. The judgment says (at 358-359):

> The real question posed for our decision is not whether an action lies in respect of pre-natal injuries but whether a plaintiff born with injuries caused by the pre-natal neglect of the defendant has a cause of action in negligence against him in respect of such injuries. To this question the defendant answers 'No', because at the time of his neglect the plaintiff was not in existence as a living person, had no separate existence apart from her mother, was not capable of suing to assert a legal right, and was not a legal person to whom he could be under a duty.

There is then reference to well-known authorities like *Donoghue v Stevenson* [1932] AC 562, [1932] All ER Rep 1, *Home Office v Dorset Yacht Co Ltd* [1970] 2 All ER 294, [1970] AC 1004, *Bourhill (or Hay) v Young* [1942] 2 All ER 396, [1943] AC 92, *Watson v Fram Reinforced Concrete Co (Scotland) Ltd* 1960 SC 92 and *Grant v Australian Knitting Mills Ltd* [1936] AC 85, [1935] All ER Rep 209, and then to a South African decision which followed the *Montreal Tramways* case, *Pinchin v Santam Insurance Co Ltd* 1963 2 SA 254, and to the *Montreal Tramways* case itself. After the citations the judgment continues (at 360-361):

> Those circumstances, accordingly, constituted a potential relationship capable of imposing a duty on the defendant in relation to the child if and when born. On the birth the relationship crystallized and out of it arose a duty on the defendant in relation to the child. On the facts which for present purposes must be assumed, the child was born with injuries caused by the act or neglect of the defendant in the driving of his car. But as the child could not in the very nature of things acquire rights correlative to a duty until it became by birth a living person, and as it was not until then that it could sustain injuries as a living person, it was, we think, at that stage that the duty arising out of the relationship was attached to the defendant, and it was at that stage that the defendant was, on the assumption that his act or omission in the driving of the car constituted a failure to take reasonable care, in breach of the duty to take reasonable care to avoid injury to the child . . . Whether, as a matter of expression, you say, as was said in the case of *Watson v Fram Reinforced Concrete Co Ltd*, that this is to be explained by postulating a continuing duty, or merely projecting the relationship of duty into the future, or whether you regard it as possible to establish a breach of duty as at birth by reference to an act antecedent to the accrual of the cause of action, may be open to debate, but it has no bearing on the precise question we are called upon to answer, namely, whether the defendant owed a duty of care to the infant plaintiff.

The other judgment in the court is that of Gillard J, who reached the same conclusion. His reasoning is lengthy and perhaps not quite the same as that of the leading judgment. He has again referred to the principal English authorities and also to *Overseas Tankship (UK) Ltd v Morts Dock and Engineering Co Ltd, The Wagon Mound (No 1)* [1961] 1 All ER 404, [1961] AC 388. He says ([1972] VR 353 at 363, 374-375):

> Having emphasised these three points, it would appear that the vital matter for determination is whether at the time that the infant plaintiff avers that she suffered the *damnum*, i.e. at the date of her birth, had the defendant committed a breach of any and what duty to the infant plaintiff causing such *damnum*? In seeking an answer to this question one cannot but be influenced by a thought expressed by Lamont J, speaking for the majority of the Supreme Court of Canada in *Montreal Tramways v Leveille* [1933] 4 DLR 337 at 345 where, for the first time, it was accepted in a superior court that an infant plaintiff should be able after birth to recover damages for pre-natal injuries. [Then he refers to the passage which I have already read. I can pass on over very thorough further citations.] I now return to consider the arguments of the defendant. Each of them really turns around the theory that prior to birth the unborn child is not a *persona juridica* and, therefore, no duty of care can be or is owed to it. . . .
> In my view, there are two answers to this assertion. The first depends on the views I have already expressed. The cause of action for negligence only comes into existence when the damage is suffered. The infant plaintiff at that period on the facts assumed is, I repeat, a *persona juridica*, with capacity to institute proceedings and to whom a duty might be owed. The injury whilst *ventre sa mère* was but an evidentiary incident in the causation of damage suffered at birth by the fault of the defendant. If, in *Grant v Australian Knitting Mills Ltd* [1936] AC 85, [1935] All ER Rep 209, the plaintiff had been a babe in arms less than 12 months old, who had worn the defective singlet instead of Dr Grant, could the action had been defeated by the knitting mills proving that the mills negligently manufactured the goods before the infant plaintiff was born? It becomes clear from the expressions used by Lord Wright speaking for the Privy Council to describe the duty and its breach, the important and significant date in relation thereto was not the date of manufacture but when the damage occurred: see also *Watson v Fram Reinforced Concrete Co Ltd*. . . .

Then a bit further on he refers to *Villar v Gilbey*, which I have mentioned, and other English or Scottish authorities in that field, including a statement of Lord Hardwicke LC in *Wallis v Hodson* (1740) 2 Atk 114 at 117, 26 ER 472 at 473:

> . . . the plaintiff was *en ventre sa mère* at the time of her brother's death, and consequently a person *in rerum natura*, so that both by the rules of the common and civil law, she was, to all intents and purposes, a child . . .

That is of course a child for the purposes of claiming a benefit. So he comes to the conclusion at the end of further citation from the *Montreal Tramways* case that the plaintiff was entitled to maintain the action.

Phillips J in *de Martell* [1992] 3 All ER 820 at 829 was inclined to prefer the approach of Gillard J to the approach of Winneke CJ and Pape J. But both, to my mind, lead to the same conclusion and the differences between them are not, in my judgment, significant in the context of the present appeal.

The next significant decision is the decision of Fraser J at first instance in the High Court of Ontario in *Duval v Seguin* (1972) 26 DLR (3d) 418. That case also arose out of a motor accident at the time when the infant's mother was carrying the unborn child. Fraser J had the advantage of the citation of *Watt v Rama* [1972] VR 353 even though it had not then been reported. The infant was called Ann. The judge said, after referring in passing to *S v Distillers Co (Biochemicals) Ltd* [1969] 3 All ER 1412, [1970] 1 WLR 114:

> Ann's mother was plainly one of a class within the area of foreseeable risk and one to whom the defendants therefore owed a duty. Was Ann any the less so? I think not. Procreation is normal and necessary for the preservation of the race. If a driver drives on a highway without due care for other users it is foreseeable that some of the other users of the highway will be pregnant women and that a child *en ventre sa mère* may be injured. Such a child therefore falls well within the area of potential danger which the driver is required to foresee and take reasonable care to avoid. In my opinion it is not necessary in the present case to consider whether the unborn child was a person in law or at which stage she became a person. For negligence to be a tort there must be damages [sic]. While it was the foetus or child *en ventre sa mère* who was injured,

the damages sued for are the damages suffered by the plaintiff Ann since birth and which she will continue to suffer as a result of that injury. [The judge then referred to *Watt v Rama* and continued] The reasons given in this case contain a comprehensive analysis of all the relevant cases and literature. The members of the Court held that the cause of action was not complete until after the birth of the plaintiff when the damages were suffered. Some of the older cases suggest that there should be no recovery by a person who has suffered prenatal injuries because of the difficulties of proof and of the opening it gives for perjury and speculation. Since those cases were decided there have been many scientific advances and it would seem that chances of establishing whether or not there are causal relationships between the act alleged to be negligent and the damage alleged to have been suffered as a consequence are better now than formerly. In any event the Courts now have to consider many similar problems and plaintiffs should not be denied relief in proper cases because of possible difficulties of proof. To refuse to recognize such a right would be manifestly unjust and unreasonable. In my opinion, and for the reasons I have tried to formulate, such a refusal would not be consonant with relevant legal principles as they have developed and have been applied in the last 50 years. Under the doctrine of *M'Allister (or Donoghue) v Stevenson*, and the cases cited, an unborn child is within the foreseeable risk incurred by a negligent motorist. When the unborn child becomes a living person and suffers damages as a result of prenatal injuries caused by the fault of the negligent motorist the cause of action is completed.

(See 26 DLR (3d) 418 at 435-434).

Mr Ashworth and Mr McGregor none the less submit that, so far as the common law of England is concerned, the position crystallised with the latest actual decision in the United Kingdom before the enactment of the 1976 Act, that is the decision in 1891 of the Divisional Court of the Queen's Bench Division in Ireland in *Walker v Great Northern Rly Co of Ireland* (1890) 28 LR Ir 69.

That was a case in which the mother of the infant, then pregnant with the infant, was being carried as a passenger in a train of the railway company in Co Down when she fell by the negligence, it was said, of the railway company and the infant was thereby permanently injured and born crippled and deformed. The court held on demurrer that the statement of claim disclosed no cause of action. The decision is however profoundly unsatisfactory, not least in that two, if not three, of the members of the court attached weight to the fact that the railway company as a common carrier had sold the pregnant mother one ticket and not two – a conclusion which, if valid today, would carry the consequence that a child under three who can travel without a ticket on British Railways would have no remedy against British Railways if injured by the negligence of the British Rail employees.

Potts J in *Burton's* case (1990) 6 BMLR 13 at 23, [1991] 1 QB 638 at 650 said that he derived no assistance from *Walker v Great Northern Rly Co of Ireland*. Phillips J in *de Martell* [1992] 3 All ER 820 at 825, having read the judgments in *Walker's* case, said he was not surprised at the view of Potts J. I agree with Potts J that the case is of no assistance today. Had a case of a claim by a child for damages for pre-natal injury come before the English courts in the period from 1972 to the enactment of the 1976 Act, and had it been as well argued as the present cases have been in this court, I have no doubt that the English court would have been referred to *Watt v Rama* and *Duval v Seguin* and would have preferred the views there expressed to *Walker's* case.

Mr Ashworth and Mr McGregor none the less submit either that, so far as the English common law is concerned *Walker's* case is to be preferred to any inconsistent later decision in any other jurisdiction, or that, as an action by a child for damages for pre-natal injuries had not been recognised as valid in the English courts before 1976 – the enactment of the 1976 Act – such an action could not now be allowed to develop and the English common law should be taken as being what the latest United Kingdom cases available might have indicated before 1976. It is further submitted that, as Parliament has intervened by the 1976 Act in the matter of prenatal injuries to unborn children, it should be left to Parliament to effect any further change in the law that may be thought necessary or to develop the law from where it was left by the Divisional Court in Ireland in *Walker's* case.

I do not agree. Parliament, by the 1976 Act, deliberately left these cases where the children were born before the enactment of the 1976 Act to be decided by the law in force before the passing of that Act, that is to say the common law. But that does not simply mean *Walker's* case but the law, whatever it might be, that the English court would apply in the absence of the 1976 Act in the light of all relevant authorities including decisions, so far as helpful, of other Commonwealth jurisdictions. Moreover, the fact that Parliament by the

1976 Act deliberately refrained from legislating for cases such as these, where the child was born before the enactment of the 1976 Act, does not in any way support the view that these cases should be left for future legislation. They were left to the existing law whatever it might be held to be.

Mr Ashworth and Mr McGregor point also to the extravagant lengths, as they would put it, to which some of the United States decisions have gone and to the dangers of conflict between the mother and her child, with the child suing for damages for injuries allegedly caused by the negligence of the mother before the child's birth. If the floodgates prove to be open too wide no doubt Parliament can intervene. But I doubt very much whether there are any claims now outstanding which are not statute-barred, in respect of children stillborn before 22 July 1976 or any children born before that date, who are locked in litigation with their mothers over whether the mother tasted alcohol or followed a diet other than that recommended by the current phase of medical opinion during pregnancy.

For the reasons mentioned I would dismiss these appeals.

Balcombe and Leggatt LJJ agreed.

Claims for pre-natal injury, of course, are negligence actions. Therefore, issues of breach of duty, causation and quantum of damages can arise. There is nothing especially problematic about these issues in this context for medical law. Thus, as *Burton* and *de Martell* show, our concern here is with the threshold question of whether a duty is owed. The Court of Appeal was satisfied that a duty is owed, but without determining the precise analytical route to reach that conclusion.

The judgments of both Winneke CJ and Gillard J in *Watt v Rama* were relied upon by Dillon LJ. Phillips J in *de Martell* had preferred the approach of Gillard J, while Potts J in *B v Islington Health Authority* had preferred that of the Chief Justice. To Dillon LJ, however, 'they both . . . lead to the same conclusion and the differences between them are not . . . significant'.

With respect to Dillon LJ the theoretical basis on which the cause of action rests is not dealt with entirely satisfactorily. To Winneke CJ a duty attached to the defendant at the birth of the plaintiff and it was then that the defendant breached his duty. Aware of the difficulties of this approach, Winneke CJ went on to suggest that there were in fact a number of theoretical approaches available, each of which produced the result that the defendant owed a duty to the infant plaintiff, viz there was a continuing duty; the duty could be projected into the future; or a duty was breached by an act antecedent to the accrual of the cause of action. It may be interjected that each of these poses considerable theoretical difficulties. Gillard J adopted a different route. For him, the cause of action in negligence only came into existence when the damage complained of was suffered. At that time the infant plaintiff had legal personality and could be owed a duty. The antecedent inquiry is merely evidence of the causation of the damage at birth. Aware, however, of the equally problematic theoretical objections to this line of reasoning, Gillard J also relied on such cases as *Villar v Gilbey* [1907] AC 139. This case reflects a long line of English authorities which have, largely in the context of property law, incorporated the civil law principle of *nasciturus* into English law.

Arguably, the civil law approach adopted in *Montreal Tramways* is the only sound basis on which to ground a cause of action for injuries sustained while *in utero*. All attempts to manoeuvre the common law's building blocks of duty, breach and damage seem at best contrived and at worst flawed. Leggatt LJ, for example, giving the third judgment in the Court of Appeal, concluded that the basis of the plaintiff's claim was that 'each was injured when at birth he or she became a legal person damaged by the prior act of the respective defendants, and that when such act was done it was reasonably foreseeable that it might result in the plaintiff being born damaged'. In deciding thus he appeared to rely on the decision of the High Court of Ontario in *Duval v Seguin* (1972) 26 DLR (3rd) 418. There, Fraser J made foreseeability that the injured woman may be pregnant the key, such that if the pregnancy was foreseeable, the plaintiff could sue for the damage suffered since birth. The difficult question of the basis on which the defendant could owe the unborn child, foreseeable or not, a duty was avoided.

Since the Court of Appeal assumed that the child suffered 'physical injury', the Court of Appeal was able to recognise that the unborn child was owed a duty and their reasoning proceeded on that basis. In fact the judges failed to analyse the real nature of the harm suffered by the child. It did not appear to cross their minds that the harm could be of any other kind. In *Burton* [(1990) 6 BMLR 13] Potts J went so far as to reject the argument that the plaintiff suffered economic loss.

Potts J: [counsel] made a submission concerning economic loss. As I understood it it was that at the time the plaintiff acquired legal status on birth in April 1967 the only damages recoverable by her could be for economic loss and that since a cause of action for such loss in such circumstances is not recognised by English law her statement of claim must be struck out. However, the statement of claim specifically alleges that the plaintiff was born with numerous abnormalities. On proof that such was the case the plaintiff would be entitled to be compensated for such abnormalities and their consequences, they having become manifest on birth. Thus the plaintiff's claim is essentially for damages for injury to the person and consequential loss. It is not a claim for economic loss, however that concept is defined, and I reject this submission.

A more careful analysis might cause us to consider whether this is correct. Arguably, the child's harm is purely economic, ie the loss incurred arising out of the child's disability. The disability itself is not an injury caused by the doctor unless the child was a legal person (or possibly deemed to be so) at the time of the pre-natal occurrence. Thus, any action the child may have is for economic loss. Given the English courts' reluctance to allow such claims save where there is *reliance*, ie in the *Hedley Byrne* type of case, does this mean that the court should have reached a different conclusion? Perhaps not: it could be said that a doctor who treats a pregnant woman assumes responsibility to both her *and* the unborn child. In turn, the woman relies upon the doctor both for her own care and that of the unborn child. In a sense, there is reliance by the child through the agency of the mother. Certainly, there seems no good reason for not permitting a claim by a child against a doctor in such circumstances, irrespective of the classification of the child's harm. Not to allow the claim would be a triumph of form over content. We shall deal shortly with the Australian case of *X and Y v Pal* (1991) 23 NSWLR 26, [1992] 3 Med LR 195 (NSW CA). Here it suffices to notice the way in which Clarke JA approaches the issue of duty in a claim by a child for injuries as a result of a pre-natal occurrence:

Once it is accepted that Dr Pal owed a duty of care to his patient and that it was foreseeable that if he did not exercise due care in treating her he may cause damage to children later born to her it is difficult to see why those children should not be within the category of persons to whom the doctor was in a relevant relationship of proximity. The fundamental elements underlying his proximity relationship with his patient were assumption of responsibility and reliance. The doctor assumed the responsibility of exercising due care in the treatment of his patient and the patient relied upon him to administer that treatment with due care. Furthermore, the doctor was working in an area in which he could, if he were not careful, so damage his patient and the child she was carrying that either that child or children later born to the patient might suffer damage.

Given our argument that the pregnant woman acts as the agent of her unborn child in establishing reliance, can it also be said that she acts as an agent so as to affect the child's claim when her conduct is wholly or partly deleterious to the child's interests? For example, would contributory negligence by the mother affect the child's claim? More significantly for us, would the refusal of a mother to agree to treatment necessary for the health of her unborn child mean that no claim would lie against the doctor by the child subsequently born suffering harm? (We do not consider the possibility of the mother's liability. See the comment of Dillon LJ in *Burton* and *Lynch v Lynch* [1992] 3 Med LR 62 (NSW CA) (mother liable for injury to her unborn child whilst driving negligently)).

You will recall the cases we discussed in Chapter 4 such as *Re S (Adult: Refusal of Treatment)* [1992] 4 All ER 671, (1992) 9 BMLR 69 where the court authorised a doctor to carry out a Caesarean section *against the wishes of a mother* to prevent the death of her unborn child. We have already doubted that these cases are correctly decided. However, even if they are, they are only of assistance here *if* they establish that a doctor has a *duty* to intervene (even against the mother's wishes) to protect the unborn child. Since they do not go this far and merely *permit* a doctor to intervene, the cases take us no further on the question which we are concerned with here.

Returning then to the question of whether a mother as agent of the child may affect the child's claim, the conclusion based upon principle must be that it cannot. We reach this view because we would argue that the mother as agent may only act for the benefit and not to the detriment of the unborn child: an echo of the civil law doctrine of the *nasciturus*. The Law Commission, however, in its Report, *Injuries to Unborn Children (op cit)* recommended that the conduct of the mother should be attributed to the child and consequently affect any claim of the child.

The mother's contributory negligence
65. Our provisional conclusion as to a mother's liability to her own child led us, almost inevitably, to the opinion that a mother's own contributory negligence ought not to effect any reduction in her child's damages. On consultation many have expressed the opinion that such a rule would be grossly unfair to tortfeasors and their insurers in a fault based tort system, and that the physical fact of identification between mother and foetus during pregnancy ought to mean that the mother's own negligence should reduce the damages payable by a tortfeasor. The medical treatment and medication of a pregnant woman depends so much upon her co-operation and care for herself that the possibility of joint liability (perhaps with the mother herself most to blame) is one which cannot be ignored. In such circumstances we think it would be wrong if, perhaps for very slight carelessness in comparison with the mother's own negligence, a doctor, chemist or drug manufacturer had to compensate the child in full for his disability.

Conclusion as to the mother's contributory negligence
66. These arguments and our own change of mind as to the mother's liability to her own child lead us now to advise that a mother's negligence should be available as a partial defence to a tortfeasor where her fault has also contributed to her child's pre-natal injury.

Contractual exemption or limitation of liability: Volenti non fit injuria
67. Strict adherence to legal principle led us in our working paper to the provisional conclusion that neither an exception clause in a mother's contract nor a mother's own voluntary assumption of risk should negative or reduce a defendant's liability. On consultation the majority of those who commented upon this provisional conclusion disagreed with it. The Bar Council's memorandum most clearly expressed the contrary view to that at which provisionally we had arrived:–

Paragraph 25 of the Working Paper raises the cognate questions of contractual exclusion or limitation of liability and *volenti non fit injuria* . . . In either instance, we find it difficult to evade the effects of physical identification between mother and foetus. If two women engage in a wrestling match for the entertainment of television viewers, is the child of one who was pregnant at the time entitled to sue the other for damage for assault if he is born with an incapacity traceable to the fight? And are women to be perhaps denied transport by air or sea or employment in a particular industry on the ground that it is impossible to limit liability in contract with a foetus? Moreover we think that identification of mother with foetus in contractual relations with other members of the community is socially both acceptable and desirable.

68. Added emphasis to one of these points was given by Dr OM Stone, a member of the Family Law Sub-Committee of the Society of Public Teachers of Law, who wrote: 'I think there is a real danger that what may be a remote possibility of liability to an unborn child may be seized upon as justifying refusal to enter into a wide variety of contracts or social relationships with women of any age or status'.

69. We are convinced by these arguments that our provisional conclusion was wrong. Contractual exemptions from liability are often objectionable, but we believe that the proper way to control them is to deal with them as exemption clauses, and not as a consequence of the fact that a particular claim is being brought by a child in respect of pre-natal injuries. We are at present engaged in a full study of exemption clauses, including exemptions from or limitations of liability for negligence in respect of personal injury. In our working paper on that subject we expressed the provisional view that certain exemption clauses should be made void and that others might be subjected to a judicial test of reasonableness. Our consultation on that complex subject has confirmed our provisional view that in some circumstances it may be reasonable to rely on an exemption clause. If in a particular case it would be reasonable for a defendant to rely on a contractual exemption in a claim brought by the mother with whom he contracted, we see no reason why he should not seek to rely on the same exemption in a claim brought by the child in respect of pre-natal injury. Again, if the contract with the mother purports specifically to exclude or limit liability to her unborn child we see no reason why the defendant should not be entitled to rely upon it in an action brought by the child. Clearly, if an exemption clause is void (such as a contractual exemption from liability in respect of the death of or bodily injury to a passenger in a public service vehicle) or subject to judicial control in relation to the mother it should be similarly void or subject to control in relation to the child she is bearing.

70. There is one problem with respect to contractual exemptions: that the child, unborn when the contract with the mother is made, can never be a party to the contract so that the doctrine of privity of contract will prevent the clause from binding him. If our policy that the child should be identified with the mother in relation to such provisions is right, this must constitute a new exception to the doctrine of privity of contract.

Conclusion as to contractual exemption or limitation of liability and volenti non fit injuria
71. We are convinced by the arguments of the Bar Council that our provisional conclusion was wrong and that we ought now to advise that a defendant should be able to rely upon a contractual term binding upon the mother which exempts him from or limits his liability either towards her or towards her unborn child and upon a mother's voluntary assumption of risk. While contractual exemptions from liability are often objectionable, we believe that the proper way to control them is to deal with them generally. Our present conclusion has been arrived at in the knowledge that we are at present engaged on a full study of exemption clauses and we envisage that any recommendations which we ultimately make on this subject should become applicable in cases where pre-natal injury has been caused.

(We will see later the provisions of the Congenital Disabilities (Civil Liability) Act 1976 which reflect these recommendations below. It should be noticed here, however, that as regards contractual exemption the child's claim is now only affected to the extent that the law allows for contractual exemption by virtue of the Unfair Contract Terms Act 1977.)

(ii) WHERE THE CHILD IS BORN DEAD

It would seem that no claim could be brought in English law on behalf of a child born dead. The law is discussed in the following paper.

A Whitfield 'Common Law Duties to Unborn Children' (1993) 1 Med L Rev 28

In a number of American states, recovery by a child who dies *in utero* as a result of the defendant's negligent conduct has been permitted under Wrongful Death Acts. [See, for example, *White v Yup* 456 P 2d 617 (1969) (Nev Sup Ct) and *Mone v Greyhound Lines* 331 NE 2d 916 (1975) (Mass Sup Jud Ct). Contrast, *Justus v Atchison* 565 P 2d (1977) (Cal Sup Ct).] The Second Restatement of the Law of Torts, however, states: 'if the child is not born alive, there is no liability unless the applicable wrongful death statute so provides' [at para 869].

The English position, it is submitted, is that in the case of stillbirth there is no liability under statute to anyone for the following reasons . . . [N]o right, either of dependency or for bereavement, can arise out of the Fatal Accidents Act 1976 because death is a precondition of such rights. The courts will inevitably conclude that one who, in the eyes of the law, has never become a 'person', cannot be said to have attained life, and therefore cannot be said to have suffered death. . . For the same reasons there will be no claim under the Law Reform (Miscellaneous Provisions) Act 1934 which applies only 'on the death of any person' [s 1(1)].

When considering the common law position in *Burton* and *de Martell*, Dillon LJ seemed to contemplate, obiter, that a still birth may give rise to some sort of claim by the child. He stated:

> I doubt very much whether there are any claims now outstanding which are not statute-barred, in respect of children still-born before 22 July 1976 or any children born before that date who are locked in litigation with their mothers over whether the mother tasted alcohol or followed a diet other than that recommended by the current phase of medical opinion during pregnancy.

This is surprising. There can be no actionable breach of duty to those born dead: before they are born they are not 'persons' and after they are born they have no legal rights. Therefore, they cannot sue.

The only claim likely to exist, therefore, is a straightforward claim for personal injuries by a parent, usually a mother, based on circumstances giving rise to a stillbirth and quantified by reference to its consequences. That was the position in *Bagley v North Hertfordshire Health Authority* [[1986] NLJ Rep 1014]. Simon Brown J accepted that a statutory bereavement claim could not arise where a child was born dead, but only where a live child was tortiously killed. However, he awarded damages to the mother not only for her physical illness but also for her loss of the satisfaction of bringing her pregnancy, confinement and labour to a successful and joyous conclusion, and for the frustration of her plans to enlarge her family. By this sensible route the common law thus provides direct compensation based on the experiences and sufferings and loss of the surviving parent(s) alone.

(c) Occurrence before conception

A child may be born harmed as a result of an occurrence which took place before conception rather than *in utero*. Our concern here is only with situations where an analogy may be drawn with the cases already discussed, ie where the defendant's conduct *causes* the disability or harm which the child suffers. We discuss later pre-conception occurrences which do not cause harm to the child but which, when the child is conceived, mean that the child will be born with disabilities which result from a cause independent of the defendant, ie negligent genetic counselling (see 'wrongful life' *infra*).

A Whitfield 'Common Law Duties to Unborn Children' (1993) 1 Med L Rev 28

At common law the central issue is whether there is an act or omission leading to an injury to a child as yet to be conceived which will amount to a breach of *duty to the child later born*. There are no English authorities on the point. Dicta in the judgment of Clarke JA in *X and Y v Pal* [(1991) 23 NSWLR 26 at 37; 40; 41; and 42], imply that no distinction should be drawn between children injured by pre-conception wrongs and those injured by wrongs occurring during pregnancy . . .

The Law Commission, while not distinguishing between types of pre-conception occurrence, gave several examples of injury which in fact fall within this category. One is where physical injury is caused to a woman's pelvis as a result of which injury is caused to her child *in utero* when it is subsequently conceived and born. Such an occurrence could be the responsibility of almost anybody whether a car driver, an employer or an assailant. A doctor too might be responsible for such an occurrence, though a better example in practice might be where an abortion is negligently performed which so weakens the uterus that it ruptures at the end of a subsequent pregnancy and injures the child during labour. Another example would be that of pre-conception exposure through chemicals or radiation which causes gene mutation and consequent disability.

In such cases, it may well be possible to show that 'but for' the occurrence complained of the children concerned would have been born in any event and would (absent the pre-conception occurrence) have been healthy. These claims are, in fact, indistinguishable legally from *Burton* and *de Martell*. The accident of timing in the negligent conduct of the defendant ought to be irrelevant. Take, for example, the case of the negligent manufacturer of a toxic nappy. On the *Burton* and *de Martell* analysis, he will be liable to a baby whose buttocks are scorched even though the baby is *in utero* at the time of manufacture [See *Grant v Australian Knitting Mills Ltd* [1936] AC 85]. It is difficult to see any justice in the defence that a similarly injured baby who was not in fact conceived at the time of manufacture should have no claim.

It should not matter, therefore, when the negligent conduct occurs, but rather liability should turn upon the nature of the plaintiff's injury. Consequently, children born disabled as a result of pre-conception occurrences would, therefore, have claims in England, subject to questions of proof and remoteness.

As you will have noticed, Adrian Whitfield refers to the New South Wales case of *X and Y v Pal* where the occurrences which were alleged to have caused the child plaintiff's harm took place both before she was conceived as well as while she was *in utero*.

X and Y v Pal (1991) 23 NSWLR 26, [1992] Med LR 195 (NSW CA)

Clarke JA: This judgment concerns two appeals by X and her daughter Y each of whom unsuccessfully sued the three respondents, who were medical practitioners, for negligence. The reason why the appellants are named in the papers as X and Y is that Allen J made an order that they should be so known in order to conceal their true identity. During the trial the parties agreed that X should be referred to as 'AA' and Y as 'CA' and for the sake of convenience I will describe them in that way.

In about January 1973, AA became pregnant. She was at that time suffering from syphilis although she was unaware of that fact. On 2 March 1973, she consulted Dr Pal, the first respondent (I shall refer to him as Dr Pal), who was an obstetrician and gynaecologist and whose patient she remained throughout her pregnancy. Prior to her confinement Dr Pal submitted her for a number of tests. However, he failed to have her screened for syphilis. On 23 October 1973, she gave birth to a child by caesarean section. At birth the child had gross hydrocephaly and other physical deformities from which he died on 22 November 1973.

Prior to the birth of her first child, AA had been referred to the third respondent, a specialist paediatrician Dr Grunseit, by Dr Pal and she saw him on 23 October prior to the caesarean section. Dr Grunseit was also present at the delivery of the child.

On 3 July 1974, AA, who had decided that she would like to change gynaecologists, saw Dr Harris, the second respondent, with a view to determining whether she was likely to encounter problems with a further pregnancy. Following this consultation she saw Dr Grunseit again. He told her that her first baby had died from toxoplasmosis and that there was no reason why she should not proceed to become pregnant again. There was some suggestion in the evidence that AA was in fact pregnant at the time she first saw Dr Harris but if she was there is no doubt that neither she nor Dr Harris knew that fact. She was first diagnosed as being pregnant on 4 September 1974 and remained under the care of Dr Harris until after the birth of CA on 27 March 1975. She was submitted for various tests by Dr Harris but at no stage was she screened for syphilis.

CA was born dysmorphic and mentally retarded. As a result of a number of tests which were carried out on CA shortly after her birth it was discovered that both CA and AA were suffering from syphilis. This discovery shocked AA who had not been aware until that time that she was suffering from syphilis. CA has continued to suffer from a number of abnormalities, the principal of which are mental retardation and disfigurement. In her action it was claimed that all her abnormalities resulted from the negligent failure of each of the three respondents to submit her mother AA for syphilis testing.

For her part AA claimed that she suffered from nervous and emotional shock and depression as a consequence of having given birth to a deformed child who was suffering from syphilis. She also claimed that her syphilis predated her first pregnancy and that the failure of each of the doctors to ensure that testing for syphilis was carried out was negligent.

Both actions were heard by Sully J who found that each of the doctors had been negligent, in the sense that they had failed to take reasonable care, in failing to have AA screened for syphilis.

On the appeal it was common ground between the parties that if AA had been screened for syphilis before her pregnancy with CA, or within the first trimester (twelve weeks) of that pregnancy, steps could have been taken which would have ensured that CA was not affected by the disease; that CA was born with congenital syphilis and that, but for the negligence of each of the respondents, CA would not have contracted congenital syphilis . . .

The primary submission of senior counsel for the respondents took the following course. A cause of action in negligence is dependent upon proof of damage consequential upon the breach of a duty to take care; it follows that proof of a duty to take care is essential to the claim of negligence; further the duty must be owed to the person claiming against the allegedly careless person – except in particular cases, of which this is not one, the fact that a duty may be owed to a person other than the one claiming damages is irrelevant; importantly, the relevant duty must be in existence when the conduct said to constitute a breach of that duty occurred; at the time Dr Pal was careless C had not been conceived; it followed that Dr Pal did not owe her a duty of care. Summarised, the submission was that the law does not recognise a duty to take care to a person conceived subsequent to the conduct said to constitute a breach of that duty.

Fleming, *The Law of Torts* 7th edn (1987) at 152, saw two problems in a claim brought by a child deformed as a consequence of negligent conduct occurring before her birth. First, the lack of legal personality and, secondly, the absence of foreseeability.

The latter is a problem to be resolved on the facts of the case just as in the more usual cases which come before the courts. In some instances it may not be possible for a plaintiff to establish this element but in others the pre-natal injury leading to a child being born deformed may be just the kind of thing which a doctor would recognise may occur if he did not use due care. Fleming postulated two ways of overcoming the problem of the absence of legal personality. One was to deem the child 'to be a person entitled on birth to compensation for injury . . .' The other was to consider the position upon the birth of the child (when the damage occurred and the cause of action arose) and resting liability solely on foreseeability.

If one postulates the duty in terms of the class or category of persons to whom it is owed, as I believe one should, and accepts that there may be within that class persons who are not born when the careless conduct occurs there is no need to resort to artificial concepts, such as deeming, or to be unduly troubled about the child's lack of legal personality at the time of that conduct.

While in particular cases the relevant question may simply be whether it can be said that A owed a duty to B there will be other cases in which the question, more accurately phrased, is whether A owes a duty to a category of persons so that if he breaches that duty any of the persons within that category, subject to particular defences which may arise in relation to the claim being pursued, may sue. Of course, proof that a duty is owed by A to B which duty is breached by A will not, without more, give rise to a cause of action in B. That will only arise if B suffers damage as a result of the breach. In a case such as the present that damage will be suffered, or at least the law will only recognise that it has been suffered, upon the birth of the child. The fact that damage was suffered many years after the breach of duty has never been regarded as an impediment to the cause of action. Nor should, in my view, the fact that a particular plaintiff acquired legal personality (and suffered damage) years after the breach . . .

For my part I would . . . say that if the injured person falls within the class to whom the duty was owed it matters not that he was not identified, or not in existence, at the time when those acts occurred which constituted the breach of the duty to take care . . .

In principle therefore it should be accepted that a person may be subjected to a duty of care to a child who was neither born nor conceived at the time of his careless acts or omissions such that he may be found liable in damages to that child. Whether or not that duty will arise depends upon whether there is a relevant relationship between the careless person and the class of persons of whom the child is one . . .

Accordingly while it must be accepted that the fact that a person who was injured by the careless acts or omissions of another, was neither born nor conceived at the time of those careless acts or omissions may be relevant to a determination whether a relationship of proximity existed it is certainly not the only relevant consideration.

The conclusion that a child, when born, may be able to sue in respect of careless conduct occurring before the child's birth, or even conception, leads inevitably to the next question whether Dr Pal owed a duty of care to CA. Given the undemanding nature of the test of foreseeability it is not difficult to conclude that it was foreseeable that if Dr Pal was careless in his treatment of AA damage might be suffered by children later born to her: see *Wyong Shire Council v Shirt* (1980) 146 CLR 40. But, as has been made clear by a recent series of cases in the High Court (*Jaensch v Coffey* (1984) 155 CLR 549; *San Sebastian Pty Ltd v Minister Administering the Environmental Planning and Assessment Act 1979* (1986) 68 ALR 161; *Sutherland Shire Council v Heyman* and *Hawkins v Clayton*) a relevant duty of care would arise only if there existed a relationship of proximity between CA and Dr Pal. In *Cook v Cook* (1986) 162 CLR 376 at 382, it was said that a relationship of proximity operates as:

> . . . an overriding control of the test of reasonable foreseeability . . . It constitutes the general determinant of the categories of case in which the common law of negligence recognizes the existence of a duty to take reasonable care to avoid a reasonably foreseeable and real risk of injury to another.

Although CA complains of physical injury this is not a case in which it can be said, as it can in settled areas of the law involving direct physical injury or damage caused by negligent act, that the reasonable foreseeability of injury to CA provides an adequate indication that the relationship between CA and Dr Pal bore the requisite degree of proximity.

Where a doctor gives careless advice, or carelessly fails to ensure that specific tests are administered to a patient it is foreseeable that damage may be caused to the patient as a consequence of that carelessness. In those circumstances it is beyond dispute that there is a relevant relationship of proximity between the doctor and the patient. But it may be difficult to determine whether the doctor in question owes a duty to take care to any other persons. For instance, to take an example raised during the hearing of the appeal, if a doctor negligently failed to diagnose a child's illness as German measles so that the child continued attending school, transferred the disease to another child whose mother was then pregnant and who, as a consequence, gave birth to a child suffering from abnormalities, could that last-mentioned child sue the doctor? Given the undemanding nature of the test of foreseeability it may well be that that chain of events was foreseeable. On the other hand it is clear that there was no element of reliance by either the pregnant mother or her child on the doctor and it would be difficult to suppose that he would have had such persons in contemplation when tending to his own patient . . . [I]t is therefore necessary to inquire whether Dr Pal as a specialist gynaecologist and obstetrician undertaking the care of AA in her confinement was placed in such a position vis-à-vis a particular category of persons that he owed to persons within that category a duty of care. More specifically the question is whether the doctor could have reasonably foreseen that if he did not exercise due care in carrying out his functions harm might be caused to persons other than AA and, if so, whether those persons fell within a category the members of which were within a relationship of proximity with the doctor.

It seems clear to me that if Dr Pal had applied his mind to the problem he would have recognized that unless he exercised due care he could cause harm to persons intimately related to his patient and in particular the child which was then en ventre sa mère and also children who may later be born. Reference to two American cases sufficiently makes good the point that the possibility that a doctor placed in the position of Dr Pal could, if careless, do or omit to do something which caused later children of his patient to be born with defects was, while unlikely, not a remote possibility. In *Renslow v Mennonite Hospital* 367 NE 2d 1250 (1977), a blood transfusion was carelessly administered to a woman causing sensitisation of her blood which led, years later, to her first child suffering a pre-natal insult and being born with brain damage. Again in *Bergstreser v Mitchell* 577 F 2d 22 (1978) two doctors performed a caesarean section on a woman and in doing so carelessly ruptured her uterus and failed to inform her that this had occurred. As a consequence of her damaged uterus she was forced to undergo another caesarean section on her next confinement during which the baby suffered hypoxia or anoxia causing him to be born with brain damage.

Once it is accepted that Dr Pal owed a duty of care to his patient and that it was foreseeable that if he did not exercise due care in treating her he may cause damage to children later born to her it is difficult to see why those children should not be within the category of persons to whom the doctor was in relevant relationship of proximity. The fundamental elements underlying his proximity relationship with his patient were assumption of responsibility and reliance. The doctor assumed the responsibility of exercising due care in the treatment of his patient and the patient relied upon him to administer that treatment with due care. Furthermore, the doctor was working in an area in which he could, if he were not careful, so damage his patient and the child she was carrying that either that child or children later born to the patient might suffer damage.

In this context it is not difficult, in the light of my earlier conclusions, to include the child then en ventre sa mère within the category of persons to whom the duty was owed. That child would clearly be a person that Dr Pal ought to have had in contemplation and it would not accord with notions of fairness and justice or considerations of policy to exclude that child from the category. If it be necessary to assign a specific reason for including the child within the category then it is to be found in the fact that the patient was relying on the doctor to exercise reasonable care to ensure, so far as was possible, that the child was born safe and healthy. But the patient's reliance was not limited to that aspect of the treatment but extended generally to her well being and the doctor assumed the responsibility of exercising the appropriate care to ensure that, putting it generally, she was not affected in such a manner as to lead her later to give birth to deformed children. Upon this view the relevant category would include CA. . .

Although factors, such as the passage of time or the intervention of other medical practitioners, might serve to deny the existence of a causal connection between any breach of the duty to which an obstetrician placed in the position of Dr Pal would owe to his patient and any children later born to her and injury suffered by one or other of them, I see no reason why ordinarily the doctor should not be regarded as having been in a relationship of proximity with a category of persons including the patient and children later born to her. For thee reasons I would conclude that there was a relevant relationship in this case and that Dr Pal owed a duty of care to CA which, in his failure to submit AA to syphilis testing, he breached.

Mahoney and Meagher JJA concurred.

As the court makes clear, in principle there is no distinction between pre-conception occurrences and those *in utero* which cause harm to the unborn child.

American cases have, on a number of occasions, considered liability for pre-conception occurrences: *Bergstreser v Mitchell* (1978) 577 F 2d 22 (8th Circ) (negligent rupture of uterus damaged child *in utero* subsequently conceived); *Renslow v Mennonite Hospital* (1977) 367 NE 2d 1250 and *Yeager v Bloomington Obstetrics and Gynaecology Inc* (1982) 585 NE 2d 696 (Ind CA) (negligent failure to deal with mother's sensitisation to Rh-positive, baby damaged *in utero* subsequently conceived child). Cf, *Hegyes v Unjican Enterprises Inc* (1991) 286 Cal Rptr 85 (Cal CA) (no action against negligent driver who injured woman such that her subsequently conceived child sustained injuries *in utero*: no 'special relationship' existed between driver and woman). See also the observations of Clarke JA in *X and Y v Pal* above.

One further unresolved issue under the common law is where the occurrence causes harm not to the unborn child of the patient but rather to the *grandchild*. In principle, the common law should treat this situation no differently. Of course, in fact it may be more difficult to establish a causal link between the occurrence and the subsequent harm. However, there are powerful policy considerations which may persuade a court to reject the claim, not least of which is the indeterminate nature of the potential liability to future generations, as the following case illustrates.

Enright v Eli Lilly & Co (1991) 570 NE 2d 198 (NYCA)

Wachtler, Chief Judge: The question in this case is whether the liability of manufacturers of the drug diethylstilbestrol (DES) should extend to a so-called 'third generation' plaintiff, the granddaughter of a woman who ingested the drug. According to the allegations of the complaint, the infant plaintiff's injuries were caused by her premature birth, which in turn resulted from damage to her mother's reproductive system caused by the mother's in utero exposure to DES. We hold, in accord with our decision in *Albala v City of New York*, 54 NY 2d 269, 445 NYS 2d 108, 429 NE 2d 786, that in these circumstances no cause of action accrues in favour of the infant plaintiff against the drug manufacturers.

I.

The plaintiffs in this case are Karen Enright, born August 8, 1981, and her parents, Patricia and Earl Enright. According to their complaint, the events underlying this action began more than 30 years ago, when Karen Enright's maternal grandmother ingested DES during a pregnancy which resulted in the birth of plaintiff Patricia Enright on January 29, 1960. Plaintiffs allege that because of her in utero exposure to DES, Patricia Enright developed a variety of abnormalities and deformities in her reproductive system. As a result, several of her pregnancies terminated in spontaneous abortions and another resulted in the premature birth of Karen Enright. Karen suffers from cerebral palsy and other disabilities that plaintiffs attribute to her premature birth and, ultimately, to her grandmother's ingestion of DES.

This action was commenced by Patricia and Earl Enright individually and on behalf of their daughter against several manufacturers of DES. After issue was joined, the defendants sought summary judgment dismissing the complaint. Defendants contended that the actions were barred by the Statute of Limitations and by plaintiffs' inability to identify the manufacturer of the drug ingested by Karen's grandmother. In addition, defendants argue that Karen's claims of a preconception tort presented no cognizable cause of action . . .

II.

The tragic DES tale is well documented in this Court's decisions and need not be recounted here (*see eg Hymowitz v Lily & Co* [(1989) 539 NE 2d 1069; 73 NY 2d 487], *Bichler v Lilly & Co* 55 NY 2d 571, 450 NYS 2d 776, 436 NE 2d 182). It is sufficient to note that between 1947 and 1971, the drug, a synthetic estrogen-like substance produced by approximately 300 manufacturers, was prescribed for use and ingested by millions of pregnant women to prevent miscarriages. In 1971, the Food and Drug Administration banned the drug's use for the treatment of problems of pregnancy after studies established a link between in utero exposure to DES and the occurrence in teen-age women of a rare form of vaginal and cervical cancer. Plaintiffs allege that in utero exposure to DES has since been linked to other genital tract aberrations in DES daughters, including malformations or immaturity of the uterus, cervical abnormalities, misshapen Fallopian tubes and abnormal cell and tissue growth, all of which has caused in this population a marked increase in the incidence of infertility, miscarriages, premature births and ectopic pregnancies.

The Legislature and this Court have both expressed concern for the victims of this tragedy by removing legal barriers to their tort recovery – barriers which may have had their place in other contexts, but which in DES litigation worked a peculiar injustice because of the ways in which DES was developed, marketed and sold and because of the insidious nature of its harm.

For example, prior to 1986, the longstanding rule in this State was that a cause of action for personal injuries caused by a toxic substance accrued and the limitations period began to run upon exposure to the substance (*see Fleishman v Lilly & Co* 62 NY 2d 888, 478 NYS 2d 853, 467 NE 2d 517, *cert, denied* 469 US 1192, 105 S Ct 967, 83 L Ed 2d 972). The Legislature, recognizing that under this rule claims for injuries caused by exposure to DES and other toxic substances were often time barred before the harmful effects of the exposure could be discovered, changed the law to provide that the limitations period in exposure cases begins to run upon discovery of the injury (*see* CPLR 214-c; L 1986 ch 682 s 2). At the same time, the Legislature revived for one year previously time-barred causes of action based on exposure to DES and four other toxic substances (L 1986 ch 682 s 4).

More recently, this Court responded to the fact that – for a variety of reasons unique to the DES litigation context – a DES plaintiff generally finds it impossible to identify the manufacturer of the drug that caused her injuries. We held that liability could be imposed upon DES manufacturers in accordance with their share of the national DES market, notwithstanding the plaintiff's inability to identify the manufacturer particularly at fault for her injuries (*see Hymowitz v Lilly & Co supra*).

III.

In the present case, we are asked to do something significantly different. We are asked, not to remove some barrier to recovery that presents unique problems in DES cases, but to recognize a cause of action not available in other contexts simply (or at least largely) because this is a DES case.

In *Albala v City of New York* 54 NY 2d 269, 271, 445 NYS 2d 108, 429 NE 2d 786, *supra*, we were presented with the question 'whether a cause of action lies in favour of a child for injuries suffered as a result of a preconception tort committed against the mother'. There, the mother suffered a perforated uterus during the course of an abortion. Four years later, she gave birth to a brain-damaged child, whose injuries were allegedly attributable to the defendants' negligence in perforating the mother's uterus. We declined, as a matter of policy, to recognize a cause of action on behalf of the child, believing that to do so would 'require the extension of traditional tort concepts beyond manageable bounds' (*id* at 271-272, 445 NYS 2d 108, 429 NE 2d 786). Among other things, we were concerned with 'the staggering implications of any proposition which would honour claims assuming the breach of an identifiable duty for less than a perfect birth' and the difficulty, if such a cause of action were recognized, of confining liability by other than artificial and arbitrary boundaries (*id* at 273, 445 NYS 2d 108, 429 NE 2d 786, citing *Park v Chessin* 46 NY 2d 401, 413 NYS 2d 895, 386 NE 2d 807; *Howard v Lecher*, 42 NY 2d 109, 397 NYS 2d 363, 366 NE 2d 64).

The case now before us differs from *Albala* only in that the mother's injuries in this cause were caused by exposure to DES instead of by medical malpractice. A different rule is justified, therefore, only if that distinction alters the policy balance we struck in *Albala*.

The primary thrust of plaintiffs' argument and the Appellate Division's decision is that DES itself alters that balance. From the Legislature's actions in modifying the applicable Statute of Limitations and reviving time-barred DES cases and from our adoption of a market-share liability theory in *Hymowitz*, plaintiffs perceive a public policy favouring a remedy for DES-caused injuries sufficient to overcome the countervailing policy considerations we identified in *Albala*. The implication, of course, is that the public interest in providing a remedy for those injured by DES is stronger than the public interest in providing a remedy for those injured by other means – medical malpractice, for example. We do not believe that such a preference has been established.

To be sure, recent developments demonstrate legislative and judicial solicitude for the victims of DES, but they do not establish DES plaintiffs as a favoured class for whose benefit all traditional limitations on tort liability must give way. To the extent that special rules have been fashioned, they are a response to unique procedural barriers and problems of proof peculiar to DES litigation.

In the present case, however, neither plaintiffs, the Appellate Division, nor the dissent has identified any unique feature of DES litigation that justifies the novel proposition they advance – recognition of a multigenerational cause of action that we have refused to recognize in any other context. The fact that this is a DES case does not by itself justify a departure from the *Albala* rule.

Closer to the mark, though still falling short, is plaintiffs' second argument. They note that *Albala* was a negligence case and that we left open the question whether a different result might obtain under a strict products liability theory because of the potentially different policy considerations in such a case (*see Albala v City of New York supra* 54 NY 2d at 274 n, 445 NYS 2d 108, 429 NE 2d 786). Having now examined the question in the context of this particular strict products liability claim, we find no basis for reaching a different conclusion than we did in *Albala*.

. . . the concerns we identified in *Albala* are present in equal measure here. The nature of the plaintiffs' injuries in both cases – birth defects – and their cause – harm to the mothers' reproductive systems before the children were conceived – are indistinguishable for these purposes. They raise the same vexing questions with the same 'staggering implications' (*Albala v City of New York supra* 54 NY 2d at 273, 445 NYS 2d 108, 429 NE 2d 786). As in *Albala*, the cause of action plaintiffs ask us to recognize here could not be confined without the drawing of artificial and arbitrary boundaries. For all we know, the rippling effects of DES exposure may extend for generations. It is our duty to confine liability within manageable limits (*see Tobin v Grossman* 24 NY 2d 609, 619, 301 NYS 2d 554, 249, NE 2d 419; Prosser, *Palsgraf Revisited* 52 Mich L Rev 1, 27). Limiting liability to those who ingested the drug or were exposed to it *in utero* serves this purpose.

At the same time, limiting liability in this fashion does not unduly impair the deterrent purposes of tort liability. The manufacturers remain amenable to suit by all those injured by exposure to their product, a class whose size is commensurate with the risk created . . .

That the product involved here is a prescription drug raises other considerations as well. First, as in most prescription drug cases (*see* Vinson & Slaughter, Products Liability: Pharmaceutical Drug Cases, at 123-140), liability here is predicated on a failure to warn of dangers of which the manufacturers knew or with adequate testing should have known.

Such a claim, though it may be couched in terms of strict liability, is indistinguishable from a negligence claim (*see Wolfgruber v Upjohn Co* 72 AD 2d 59, 423 NYS 2d 95 *aff'd on opn, below* 52 NY 2d 768, 436 NYS 2d 614, 417 NE 2d 1002). Concepts of reasonable care and foreseeability are not divorced from this theory of liability, as they may be under other strict products liability predicates. Thus, the effort to distinguish this case from *Albala* is strained . . .

The dissent would have us believe that this case involved nothing but application of straightforward strict products liability doctrine. But this case is fundamentally different in the same way that *Albala* was fundamentally different from other negligence cases. In neither this case nor *Albala* was the infant plaintiff exposed to the defendants' dangerous product or negligent conduct; rather, both were injured as a consequence of injuries to the reproductive systems of their mothers.

We agree with the dissenter that 'like cases should be treated alike' (Dissenting opn at 397 p 561 of 568 NYS 2d p 209 of 570 NE 2d). This is not only a fundamental principle of justice, it is also the underpinning of the doctrine of stare decisis. It is, indeed, precisely why we are bound to apply the rule of *Albala* here, in the absence of some difference between the two cases upon which a principled distinction can be drawn.

The dissent, however, discounts the precedential value of *Albala* because it was based on '*policy grounds*' and therefore – in the dissenter's view – 'poses no *legal bar* to recovery' (dissenting opn at 394, p 560 of 568 NYS 2d, p 208 of 570 NE 2d). That the *Albala* rule is based on policy grounds, however, should not diminish its status as a rule of law. All legal rules, including those the dissent relies upon, are policy-based.

By adhering to *Albala*, therefore, our decision today follows established law. The dissenter, on the other hand, would expand liability beyond traditional bounds in the face of precedent from this court to the contrary, and accuses the majority of unsurping the legislative function by failing to do so (dissenting opn at 397, p 561 of 568 NYS 2d, 209 of 570 NE 2d). It strikes us as a unique view of the judicial role that would allow the court to expand liability at will, but require legislative action before adhering to established limits.

In sum, the distinctions between this case and *Albala* provide no basis for a departure from the rule that an injury to a mother which results in injuries to a later conceived child does not establish a cause of action in favor of the child against the original tort-feasor. For this reason, we decline to recognize a cause of action on behalf of plaintiff Karen Enright

Judge Hancock (dissenting): What, then, are the policy reasons seen by the majority as compelling today's decision? There appear to be three. None is availing.

First, the majority cites defendants' arguments concerning the 'staggering implications' and 'rippling effects' (majority opn at 386, 387, pp 554, 555 of 568 NYS 2d, pp 202, 203 of 570 NE 2d) that a decision upholding Karen Enright's claim might have. But this sort of 'floodgates of litigation' alarum seems singularly unpersuasive in view of our Court's repeated admonitions that it is not 'a ground for denying a cause of action that there will be a proliferation of claims' and '*if a cognizable wrong has been committed that there must be a remedy, whatever the burden of the courts*' (*Tobin v Grossman* 24 NY 2d 609, 615, 301 NYS 2d 554, 249 NE 2d 419 (emphasis added); *see, Bovsun v Sanperi* 61 NY 2d 219, 231, 473 NYS 2d 357, 461 NE 2d 843; *Battalla v State of New York* 10 NY 2d 237, 240-242, 219 NYS 2d 34, 176 NE 2d 729). Beyond that, however, when defendants' arguments are applied here to urge that although claims of DES daughters should be allowed the claims of granddaughters should not be their forebodings strike a peculiarly ironic note: ie the very fact of the 'insidious nature' of DES which may make the defendants liable for injuries to a future generation is advanced as the reason why they should not be liable for injuries to that generation. Should we be saying to these defendants and other companies which manufacture drugs 'you must be careful to produce reasonably 'safe' drugs and to warn of the risks of taking such drugs but in deciding whether a drug is 'safe' you may completely ignore the havoc a particular drug may wreck on a future generation?' I think not.

Second, the majority suggests that permitting a cause of action for Karen Enright could result in 'overdeterrence – the possibility that research will be discouraged or beneficial drugs withheld from the market' (Majority opn at 388, p 556 of 568 NYS 2d, p 204 of 570 NE 2d). But in deciding whether a particular claim for injuries from DES should be sustained, the deterrence factor is inconsequential. The wrongful conduct of the drug companies in producing and marketing DES and similarly harmful products for use by pregnant women stopped more than a generation ago when the enormity of the damage from DES became known. The sole question now involves the remedy for this past wrong, not deterrence: ie whether the remedy for DES victims made possible by the Legislature in CPLR 214-c and given effect by our Court in *Hymowitz* should be withheld from a granddaughter who suffers injuries from this wrong. But even if deterrence is assumed to be a relevant issue, should we be any less concerned with deterring the development of unsafe drugs which may cause latent damage to the third generation than in the second? Again, I think not.

Finally, in what has the ring of an economic cost-benefit analysis, the majority suggests that its generational line-drawing is proper because the manufacturers' exposure to liability is 'commensurate with the risk created' (Majority opn at 387, p 555 of 568 NYS 2d, p 203 of 570 NE 2d). The argument is seen at once to be at odds with the rule that on this motion to dismiss Karen Enright's complaint (CPLR 3211[a][7]) the court must accept as true her allegations that she is a member of the class of persons to whom the risk of injury was foreseeable (*see Becker v Schwartz, supra* 46 NY 2d at 408, 413 NYS 2d 895, 386 NE 2d 807). But, in any event, the statement that liability should stop at Karen's mother's generation because it 'is commensurate with the risk' is not a statement of an argument or of a legal or policy reason for a particular result. Rather, it is simply a statement of the Court's own policy determination as to where the risk – and, hence, the liability – stops. If, as the majority apparently believes, there are economic and social considerations which require that there be some arbitrary cutoff point in cases of this kind, such a statute of repose could easily be engrafted on the Toxic Torts legislation which revived the long-outlawed dormant injury claims for DES and other substances (*see* CPLR 2140-c; *see generally*, Comment, *Preconception Torts: Foreseeing the Unconceived*, 48 U Colo L Rev 621; Phillips, *An Analysis of Proposed Reform of Products Liability Statutes of Limitations*, 56 NCL Rev 663; Note, *Statutes of Limitations and the Discovery Rule in Latent Injury Claims*; *An Exception or the Law?* 43 U Pitt L Rev 501, 520-523). Suffice it to say, our Legislature has not chosen to cut off the claims of injured persons in Karen Enright's generation.

Simons, Kaye, Alexander and Titone JJ concurred with Wachtler CJ.

The New York Court of Appeals' decision rests upon policy factors which would be likely to influence an English court. Of course, it should be noticed that the court's earlier decision in *Albala* denied a claim for a pre-conception occurrence affecting the plaintiff's mother. English law would probably recognise such an action. The *Enright* court refused (perhaps not unnaturally) to go even further in recognising liability to a second generation plaintiff.

2. Statute: Congenital Disabilities (Civil Liability) Act 1976

The 1976 Act replaces the common law for births after July 21, 1976. For our purposes, the relevant provisions of the Act are as follows:

1. – (1) If a child is born as the result of such an occurrence before its birth as is mentioned in subsection (2) below, and a person (other than the child's own mother) is under this section answerable to the child in respect of the occurrence, the child's disabilities are to be regarded as damage resulting from the wrongful act of that person and actionable accordingly at the suit of the child.

(2) An occurrence to which this section applies is one which –

(a) affected either parent of the child in his or her ability to have a normal, healthy child; or

(b) affected the mother during her pregnancy, or affected her or the child in the course of its birth, so that the child is born with disabilities which would not otherwise have been present.

(3) Subject to the following subsections, a person (here referred to as 'the defendant') is answerable to the child if he was liable in tort to the parent or would, if sued in due time, have been so; and it is no answer that there could not have been such liability because the parent suffered no actionable injury, if there was a breach of legal duty which, accompanied by injury, would have given rise to the liability.

(4) In the case of an occurrence preceding the time of conception, the defendant is not answerable to the child if at that time either or both of the parents knew the risk of their child being born disabled (that is to say, the particular risk created by the occurrence); but should it be the child's father who is the defendant, this subsection does not apply if he knew of the risk and the mother did not.

(5) The defendant is not answerable to the child, for anything he did or omitted to do when responsible in a professional capacity for treating or advising the parent, if he took reasonable care having due regard to then received professional opinion applicable to the particular class of case; but this does not mean that he is answerable only because he departed from received opinion.

(6) Liability to the child under this section may be treated as having been excluded or limited by contract made with the parent affected, to the same extent and subject to the same restrictions as liability in the parent's own case; and a contract term which could have been set up by the defendant in an action by the parent, so as to exclude or limit his liability to him or her, operates in the defendant's favour to the same, but no greater, extent in an action under this section by the child.

(7) If in the child's action under this section it is shown that the parent affected shared the responsibility for the child being born disabled, the damages are to be reduced to such extent as the court thinks are equitable having regard to the extent of the parent's responsibility. . . .

4. – (1) Reference in this Act to a child being born disabled or with disabilities are to its being born with any deformity, disease or abnormality, including predisposition (whether or not susceptible of immediate prognosis) to physical or mental defect in the future.

(2) In this Act –

(a) 'born' means born alive (the moment of a child's birth being when it first has a life separate from its mother), and 'birth' has a corresponding meaning; . . .

(3) Liability to a child under section 1, 1A or 2 of this Act is to be regarded –

(a) as respects all its incidents and any matters arising or to arise out of it; and

(b) subject to any contrary context or intention, for the purpose of construing references in enactments and documents to personal or bodily injuries and cognate matters,

as liability for personal injuries sustained by the child immediately after its birth. . . .

(5) This Act applies in respect of births after (but not before) its passing, and in respect of any such birth it replaces any law in force before its passing, whereby a person could be liable to a child in respect of disabilities with which it might be born; but in section 1(3) of this Act the expression 'liable in tort' does not include any reference to liability by virtue of this Act, or to liability by virtue of any such law.

This Act is of general application but in the context of medical law it is important to develop three issues: the first concerns negligent conduct before conception producing harm to a child conceived thereafter; the second concerns a child who is negligently harmed *en ventre sa mère*; the third concerns a child harmed whilst an embryo *ex utero*.

(a) Occurrences before conception

Having seen the position under the common law, it is helpful to see how the Law Commission approached the question in recommending legislation.

Report on 'Injuries to Unborn Children' Law Commission (Report No 60, 1974)

76. As we have pointed out in paragraph 33 above, one of the differences between pre-natal injury and other personal injury is that the event of occurrence resulting from a negligent act or omission happens, in the case of pre-natal injury, at a time when the plaintiff is not in existence and to someone other than himself, namely his mother, or, exceptionally and, of course, only prior to conception, his father. So far as the negligent act or omission itself is concerned, it is of no consequence that it may happen before the plaintiff exists; the present common law rules easily comprehend this possibility. If a manufacturer negligently manufactures and markets a pram it is no answer to the claim of the child under whom it collapses that he was not alive at the date of its manufacture. In the case of pre-natal injuries, however, the equivalent of the pram's 'collapse' necessarily also occurs before the plaintiff is in existence and may occur even before the plaintiff is conceived. It is this latter possibility which has caused great concern amongst those whom we have consulted.

77. We have been given examples of cases where something happening to a child's parents before its conception can lead to its being born with disabilities. An obvious example is physical injury to a woman's pelvis causing injury to a child subsequently conceived and born. It is known that radiation of the reproductive organs of animals causes gene mutations and it can almost certainly do so also in man. The exposure of mother or father to radiation could cause gene mutations which might not become manifest for several generations. A claim has succeeded before the German Supreme Court for damages for pre-natal injury in the form of congenital syphilis caused by a blood transfusion given negligently to the mother before conception, the blood donor having suffered from the illness. The negligent supply of male sperm for artificial insemination would seem to be another possible source of pre-natal injury. The possibility that a contraceptive pill might prove both ineffective and damaging to the child born because of its ineffectiveness was not ruled out by our consultation with the medical profession. There are, no doubt, a number of other possible fact situations where pre-natal injury could be caused by an event happening before conception.

The 1976 Act, which seeks to implement the Law Commission's views, is discussed by Pace.

P J Pace, 'Civil Liability For Pre-Natal Injuries' (*op cit*)

[T]he Act provides that pre-conception occurrences may found a cause of action. This situation could arise when negligent X-ray treatment or defective birth-control substances affected a parent's reproductive system to such an extent that the child subsequently conceived was born disabled [s 1(2)(a)]. The child has no right of action if at the time of the occurrence either parent knew of the risk of the child being born disabled, though this does not apply if the father is the defendant or where the occurrence is coincident with or *post* conception [s 1(4)]. This poses problems since 'new embryological data . . . purport to indicate that conception is a "process" over time, rather than an event'. Apart from this difficulty, the point has been made that to allow recovery for pre-conception negligence would be to recognise a legal interest in *not* being conceived. If this analysis is correct then English law will recognise the validity of 'wrongful life' actions and, indeed, Tedeschi [[1966] Israel LR 513, 531] would argue that pre-conception negligence does give rise to a 'wrongful life' action:

> When a person fathers a child and infects it with a disease by one and the same act, then either the semen was already infected when it came into contact with the ovum, so that the new entity created is diseased from its conception (and this is the true meaning of congenital disease), or the single act results in paternity and in the infection of the mother, which will be transmitted from her to the infant. In the first case it is obvious that there was only one alternative to the new being, either not to exist or to exist with the disease. But in the second case as well no separation can be made between the act of the parent causing paternity and that causing the infection, as we are faced with a single act.

The Law Commission, favouring an action in such circumstances, approached the situation on the basis that, if a child has a legal right to begin life with a sound mind and body, and this is the effect of the proposed legislation, there is a correlative duty on its parents and others to avoid producing conception where the circumstances are likely to result in the birth of a disabled child. In other words, the remedy is sought not for being born but 'for compensation for the disability resulting from the sexual intercourse'. It should also be noted that in pre-conception cases compensation would not, without the help of the fiction provided by the Act, fulfil the function, as in other areas of tort, of restoring, as far as money can, the *status quo*. The fiction is contained in section 4(3) which states that 'Liability under this Act is to be regarded . . . as liability for personal injuries sustained by the child immediately after its birth.'

The argument by Pace needs to be examined carefully. He suggests that in the circumstances contemplated the Act creates a claim by the child for 'wrongful life'. We will deal with this claim later in this chapter. There are, as we shall see, a number of theoretical problems in establishing such a claim. For the present, it is sufficient to notice that at the heart of such a claim is the allegation by the child that 'but for' the negligence of the defendant it would not have been born at all. Here, on the other hand, the child is complaining that the pre-conception occurrence deprived it of a normal healthy life, ie the defendant's negligence *caused* its disabilities.

This leads to a consideration of the application of section 1(2) of the Act. On its face section 1(2)(a) appears to be concerned with pre-conception occurrences while section 1(2)(b) is concerned with post-conception occurrences. However, while in general this is true, it is not accurate to interpret them as mutually exclusive. For example, the facts of a case such as *Bergstreser* – where the mother's uterus is damaged prior to conception – fall within section 1(2)(a) since the mother's 'ability' in the sense of physical capacity to have a 'normal, healthy child' is affected. Equally, the facts could fall within section 1(2)(b) since the pre-conception occurrence is a continuing one which 'affected [her] during pregnancy' such that the child is born with disabilities that it would otherwise not have.

We saw a number of unresolved problems under the common law. Does the Act provide solutions? As regards the question of whether the conduct of the mother affects the child's claim, notice the terms of section 1(4). This makes it clear that where the basis of an action is a pre-conception occurrence the child has no claim if the mother or father of the child had knowledge of the *particular risk* of the child being born disabled (unless the father is the defendant when the mother must have knowledge).

Further, for all claims (not limited only to pre-conception occurrences), the contributory negligence of a parent or a valid restriction or exclusion of liability affects the child's claim (section 1(7) and (6)).

We considered earlier the nature of the harm caused to the child and suggested it should be categorised as economic loss arising out of its disabilities. The Act, however, deems the child's harm to be a personal injury. Section 4(3) explicitly provides that an action brought under the Act shall be regarded as an action for 'personal injury sustained by the child immediately after its birth'.

Finally, we considered whether a defendant's liability could extend beyond one generation. Whatever the position at common law, a combination of sections 1(3) and 4(5) makes it clear that no such claim may be brought under the Act. Liability only arises where the defendant is 'liable in tort to the parent' of the plaintiff. However, in a second-generation claim the defendant could only be liable to the plaintiff's parent under the Act and section 4(5) excludes from the definition of 'liable in tort' any 'liability by virtue of this Act'.

(b) Occurrences in utero

Section 1(2)(b) makes it clear that an occurrence *in utero* which *causes* disabilities in the unborn child will give rise to an action. Equally, the occurrence may take place during the course of birth, for example, as in *Whitehouse v Jordan* [1981] 1 WLR 246. The Act only applies, however, if it is established that the child would not have suffered the disabilities if there had not been negligence, ie, it would have been born healthy (this will be important later when we consider the 'wrongful life' action).

As we saw before, however, section 1(2)(a) and (b) are not mutually exclusive and an *in utero* occurrence will fall within section 1(2)(a) also if it affects the mother's 'ability to have a normal, healthy child'.

A claim under the Act only arises if the child is 'born alive' as defined in section 4(2)(a). Hence, no claim will arise on behalf of the child when it is still-born. The position is the same as at common law.

One situation creates a problem given the wording of section 1(2)(b). You will notice that that section requires that the occurrence be one which 'affected *the mother* during her pregnancy' (our emphasis). Unlike the situation when the occurrence arises in the course of birth, no liability appears to exist if the occurrence merely affects *the child*. Although this will not usually be problematic, because the mother will be affected, this may not always be true. For example, if a pregnant woman is exposed to x-rays which damage the child, can it be said that the mother is 'affected'? If 'affected' means 'has a detrimental consequence upon' her, then the exposure to the x-rays does not affect her at all, only the child is affected. Even if she *were* 'affected', what she would suffer would be some form of emotional distress on learning what may have happened to the child. But this will not do. This statute requires a causal connection between her being affected and the disability in the child.

Two further points, applicable to pre- and post-conception occurrences, are of interest to the medical lawyer.

The child's cause of action is a deprivative one, dependent upon a breach of the duty owed to the parent although no injury need be suffered by the parent. Being derivative it also follows, as we have seen, that defences may be mounted based upon the conduct of the parent. John Eekelaar and Robert Dingwell raise, as yet, unanswered questions for medical law arising from the derivative nature of the action.

J Eekelaar and R Dingwell 'Some Legal Issues in Obstetric Practice' [1984] JSWL 258

. . . If a child is to recover compensation, it is now necessary to show that the defendant was 'liable in tort' to a parent of the child, although this requirement has the modification that the parent does not have to have suffered some 'actionable injury' [s 1(3)]. Nevertheless, there must still have been some breach of legal duty towards the parent.

What difference does this make to the position of a child who has been injured by negligent delivery procedures? The answer would seem to be that unless the culpable acts or omissions can also be construed as breaching a legal duty to the mother, the child has lost its remedy. It is by no means clear that all such failure can be so construed. Inexpert manipulation of forceps, inadequate use of available monitoring equipment or a failure to make a Caesarean incision at an appropriate time all appear to be wrongs which primarily affect the child's well-being rather than the mother's and outside the scope of any duty to her. It is possible that the child's position could be saved by treating any default as a breach of duty towards the mother on the grounds that injury to the child is foreseeably likely to cause her consequential emotional distress. The child's action would then be parasitic upon her actual or potential claim.

This circuitous reasoning breaks down, however, if the attendant's default is the result of undue consideration for the mother or, particularly, if it was at her insistence by rejecting available and offered treatments. It is hard to see how the attendant could be in breach of a legal duty towards the mother when he is doing what she demands. Indeed, the Act itself compels a child's claim to be reduced by the extent to which the parent had contributed to the disability and, even, to be totally excluded if this has been done in respect to the parents' own case [s 1(6)]. If a woman, for example, refuses a Caesarean section when indicated on sound professional grounds, or rejects the application of foetal monitoring, and the child subsequently goes into distress and sustains brain damage as a result of protracted labour, the child has no claim, either against the attendant (who will have committed no tort against the mother) or against the woman herself (since the 1976 Act disallows any claim by the child against its mother for ante-natal injuries unless they were incurred while she was driving) [ss 1(1) and 2].

Moreover, the abolition of an independent duty of care towards the child makes it harder for an attendant to resist a possible claim in assault if, in the child's interests, he disregards the mother's wishes in respect of procedures involving her person. The presence of such a duty would fortify any defence to such a claim founded on the principle of necessity or of using reasonable force to prevent a crime, viz negligent manslaughter of the child [Criminal Law Act 1967, s 3(1)]. Its absence may call into question the application of the law of manslaughter for grossly negligent delivery procedures.

Women's groups have shown an increasing interest in adopting the tactic of legal action as a way of enforcing demands for alternative childbirth. With the weakening of the common law defence, obstetric attendants now find themselves caught between their long-established child protection duties and a statute which appears to give greater weight to the wishes of mothers. This unenviable position for obstetric attendants does not seem to have been created intentionally. There is no indication that the Law Commission recognised the possible consequences when they recommended the reforms represented by the 1976 Act. With the agreement of the medical bodies which they consulted, the Commission accepted the proposition that 'a child born fully alive should have a right of action, accruing at birth, in respect of injury either sustained by it after conception and before birth, or resulting from injury sustained by its mother during pregnancy due to the fault of a third party' [paras 31 and 32]. The technique which they adopted for translating this right into a legal form was, however, determined largely by 'the fact of physical identification of mother and foetus'. It was thought that this could give rise to special legal problems.

The first of these was to do with the ascertainment of prospective liability. Lawyers have long considered it desirable that people entering into contractual or other relationships should be able to be reasonably confident of the possible extent of their duties. Pregnancy complicates that. Over a wide range of legal relationships, it was thought that, if potential defendants could not regulate their liability by contract with the mother, they would simply refuse to deal with women [para 68]. By making the child's action derivative from the mother's, third parties could be assured of the extent of their liability. This point does not, however, have any bearing on the problem under discussion. . . . Until the passage of the Congenital Disabilities (Civil Liability) Act 1976 . . . it seems that the combination of their statutory monopoly and the common law rules allowed obstetric attendants to balance the interests of mothers and children . . . gave them protection if they felt it necessary to defer to the latter. The monopoly shared by obstetricians and midwives was granted as a licence to represent the state as the ultimate guardian of the nation's children. Thus, while the wishes of mothers could never be lightly disregarded, they could not have the power of veto. Under the [Nurses, Midwives and Health Visitors Act 1979], this duty began with the commencement of professional attendance at any particular labour. The Congenital Disabilities (Civil Liability) Act 1976 only recognises a separate duty to the child after the moment of birth, defined as the point when the child has a life 'separate from its mother' [s 4(2)(a)]. Both medically and legally this is not a clear-cut concept, but obviously relates to a point later than the onset of labour. Before that, the attendant's first duty appears to be the care of the mother in which, clearly, deference to her wishes will be a significant feature. If, in deferring to her and giving her correct professional attention, the child is injured, the law appears to hold that this is just too bad. On the other hand, if the attendant overrides the mother's wishes in attending to the child, he would seem to be at risk of litigation. . . .

Such arguments lead us towards concluding that the balance of policy was more or less properly struck before 1976. At the end of the day, parents should not ultimately be free to dictate the terms under which their children are born. An obstetric attendant would be well advised to listen carefully to their requests and to consider how far they could be followed consistently with sound professional practice and the child's well-being. The child is entitled to the benefits of available technological resources and professional expertise to minimise the risks of being severely prejudiced at the outset of his life. The risks of obstetric dictatorship are partially reduced by the freedom of parents to shop around licensed attendants and influence obstetric practice. The interests of the child are protected by the basic standards represented by the monopoly.

The attenuation of the attendant's duty of care by the Congenital Disabilities (Civil Liability) Act 1976 seems to run contrary to the spirit of legislative developments in the twentieth century. No convincing arguments have been produced for abrogating the common law rights of children . . . We believe that this aspect of the statute should be reviewed as a matter of some urgency. In the process, however, we would also draw attention to the emerging problem of the point at which child protection duties should properly begin. The new technologies of pre-natal intervention raise issues which could not have been foreseen by the drafters of the present statutes. It is important not to confound these with the perennial disputes about abortion or the relative priority of preserving the life of mother or child in extreme cases. We do not think that these have much to contribute to the circumstances we are addressing here, of routine childbirth and regularly available pre-natal intervention.

Secondly, the reference in section 1 to a 'parent' does not take account of developments having to do with infertility treatment. With these developments there appeared the phenomena of the 'gestational parent' and the 'biological parent'. As we saw in Chapter 11, sections 27-29 of the Human Fertilisation and Embryology Act 1990 defined a parent under these circumstances.

To square the circle, the 1990 Act inserted a new section 4(4A) into the 1976 Act which provides as follows:

> 4 (4A) In any cases where a child carried by a woman as the result of the placing in her of an embryo or of sperm and eggs or her artificial insemination is born disabled, any reference in section 1 of this Act to a parent includes a reference to a person who would be a parent but for sections 27 to 29 of the Human Fertilisation and Embryology Act 1990.

Hence, a donor of gametes who has been negligently exposed to radiation such that the gametes are damaged is a 'parent' for the purposes of the child's claim under section 1.

(c) Occurrences ex utero

If an embryo is damaged prior to its being placed in a woman as part of infertility treatment (whether during its storage or use), may a child subsequently born with disability have an action under the Act?

Under section 1(2) a claim could only arise if the doctor's negligence 'affected either parent of the child in his or her ability to have a normal, healthy child' (s 1(2)(a)). Everything turns on the meaning of the word 'ability'. If 'ability' means 'physical capacity', then a claim could not be brought. If, however, 'ability' includes also the 'opportunity' to have a normal, healthy child, then a claim could be brought.

In order to resolve this problem, Parliament introduced a new section 1A into the Act when passing the Human Fertilisation and Embryology Act 1990. Section 1A provides as follows:

Extension of section 1 to cover infertility treatments

1A. (1) In any case where –
(a) a child carried by a woman as the result of the placing in her of an embryo or of sperm and eggs or her artificial insemination is born disabled,
(b) the disability results from an act or omission in the course of the selection, or the keeping or use outside the body, of the embryo carried by her or of the gametes used to bring about the creation of the embryo, and
(c) a person is under this section answerable to the child in respect of the act or omission
the child's disabilities are to be regarded as damage resulting from the wrongful act of that person and actionable accordingly at the suit of the child.

(2) Subject to subsection (3) below and the applied provisions of section 1 of this Act, a person (here referred to as 'the defendant') is answerable to the child if he was liable in tort to one or both of the parents (here referred to as 'the parent or parents concerned') or would, if sued in due time, have been so; and it is no answer that there could not have been such liability because the parent or parents concerned suffered no actionable injury, if there was a breach of legal duty which, accompanied by injury, would have given rise to the liability.

(3) The defendant is not under this section answerable to the child if at the time the embryo, or the sperm and eggs, are placed in the woman or the time of her insemination (as the case may be) either or both of the parents knew the risk of their child being born disabled (that is to say, the particular risk created by the act or omission).

(4) Subsections (5) to (7) of section 1 of this Act apply for the purposes of this section as they apply for the purposes of that section but as if references to the parent or the parent affected were references to the parent or parents concerned.

In reading this provision it is important to notice that Section 4(2) of the 1976 Act provides that:

reference to embryos shall be construed in accordance with section 1 of the Human Fertilisation and Embryology Act 1990.

Section 1A attempts to create a scheme of liability identical to that under section 1. You will notice the provisions in section 1A(3) relating to *volenti* by either of the child's parents, ie, in this context the couple receiving the infertility treatment (see, ss 27-29 of HUFEA 1990).

As we can see from its terms, section 1A gives a disabled child a claim when the negligence during fertility treatment arises from 'an act or omission' related to 'selection', 'keeping' or 'use' outside the body of the genetic material. On its face, it was intended to cover all the conventional forms of treatment, ie IVF, GIFT and artificial insemination. Arguably, however, it fails to achieve this comprehensive coverage. It appears that it may be limited to IVF procedures. Notwithstanding the generality of section 1A(1)(a), section 1A(1)(b) is limited to acts or omissions in respect of embryos or gametes that result in the creation of an embryo *ex utero* which is placed in the patient. If, therefore, the negligence concerns 'selection', 'keeping' or 'use' of the gametes with which the woman is artificially inseminated, the section will not apply. This apparent oversight is curious; it is probably not intended and is certainly not justified. Unfortunately, short of amending legislation the section is so clear that a court could not avoid the conclusion we have advanced here.

There is one final point we should notice. Negligence in relation to the 'keeping' or the 'use' of embryos (or gametes used to produce the embryo) will cause harm to the eventual child which would otherwise not have been present. On this analysis the child's claim is analogous to the pre-natal injury situations we have considered so far. By contrast, negligence in the 'selection' of embryos (or gametes used to produce the embryo) will not cause harm in this sense. Instead, the essence of the child's claim is that its genetic material should not have been selected and it should not, therefore, have been born at all. This, as we shall see later, is the so-called 'wrongful life' action which presents distinct problems for the law. It is to that action that we now turn our attention.

B. WRONGFUL LIFE

A 'wrongful life' action is one brought by a child complaining of negligent conduct prior to birth which results in its birth when had there been no negligence it would not have been born. In short, the essence of the claim is that the child would have been better off not born at all. It is important to notice that the defendant in these actions does not *cause* the child's disability. Instead, the defendant fails to avert it. This may arise in three ways. *Firstly*, the defendant may negligently advise the parents prior to conception of the risk of any child inheriting a genetic disability. *Secondly*, the negligence could arise *ex utero* in, for example, the selection of a damaged embryo for implantation during infertility treatment. *Thirdly*, the negligence may arise after conception, for example, where the doctor fails to advise the mother that she is carrying a disabled child.

1. The common law

(a) The disabled child

Can a child who has been disabled from the moment of conception bring a claim? The English common law was examined by the Court of Appeal in *McKay v Essex Area Health Authority* [1982] QB 1166, [1982] 2 All ER 771.

McKay v Essex AHA [1982] QB 1166, [1982] 2 All ER 771 (CA)

Ackner LJ: Mary McKay was born on 15 August 1975 and is therefore 6 1/2 years old. Whilst in her mother's womb she was infected with rubella (German measles) and as a result she is partly blind and deaf and is apparently disabled in other respects, the details of which have not been provided to us. She alleges in her statement of claim that Dr Gower-Davies, the second defendant, owed her a duty of care when she was *in utero*. She claims that he was negligent in that he failed to treat the rubella infection, after being told that it was suspected by her mother, the second plaintiff. She contends that this can be arrested by the injection of globulins into the mother which, although it cannot reverse or ameliorate damage already done to the unborn child, can reduce the likelihood of further damage . . . in addition to the claims referred to above, Mary seeks to add an additional claim against the doctor. Quite apart from his alleged failure to arrest the progress of the rubella infection by a process of injections, she claims that the duty of care which the doctor owed her when she was *in utero* involved advising her mother of the desirability of an abortion, which advice, as previously stated, the mother alleges she would have accepted. She accordingly claims that she has suffered damage by 'entry into a life in which her injuries are highly debilitating, and distress, loss and damage'. She makes a similar claim, *mutatis mutandis*, against the Essex Area Health Authority by reason of their alleged negligence in relation to their handling and testing of the samples and their failure to advise the doctor of the results of any such tests as they may have performed. . . .

(1) *The duty.* I can consider this in relation to the claim against the doctor, since what can be said in relation to the claim made against him applies, *mutatis mutandis*, to the claim against the area health authority.

The duty alleged is the duty to take care in relation to the unborn child. Hence the first claim for failing to treat the suspected rubella by injection, so as to reduce the likelihood of further damage. Thus, the selfsame duty is relied on for prenatal injuries as would be relied on postnatally, if there was a failure to give proper treatment after the child had been born. The embryo, or fetus, is in a comparable position to the child and adult which it may ultimately become. However, in stark contrast to the plea that the doctor should have advanced the prospect of a healthy birth of the child, the additional plea, which is still based on the same duty of care to the unborn child, relies on a negligent failure to prevent its birth. The basis of this additional claim is that, had the doctor properly discharged his obligation of care *toward the unborn child*, he would have advised the mother 'of the desirability of an abortion' (para 13), which advice the mother would have accepted (para 9). Accordingly, the fetus's existence *in utero* would have been terminated. Thus, the duty of care is said to involve a duty *to the fetus*, albeit indirectly, by advice to the mother to cause its death.

I cannot accept that the common law duty of care to a person can involve, without specific legislation to achieve this end, the legal obligation to that person, whether or not *in utero*, to terminate his existence. Such a proposition runs wholly contrary to the concept of the sanctity of human life.

Counsel for the plaintiffs contends that, where it can be established that a child's disabilities are so severe that it can be properly stated that she would be better off dead, the duty of care involves the duty to terminate its life. He seeks to support this proposition by reference to *Re B (a minor) (wardship: medical treatment)* [1981] 1 WLR 1421. As Griffiths LJ has pointed out, this was an urgent application made to the Court of Appeal in vacation and the two judgments were extempore. I am quite satisfied that Templeman LJ was saying no more than that, conceding for the purpose of argument that where the life of a child is so bound to be full of pain and suffering that it could be contended that the court could, in the exercise of its wardship jurisdiction, refuse to sanction an operation to prolong its life, the case before it clearly was not such a case. I do not consider that *Re B* provides any support to counsel for the plaintiffs' contention.

Counsel for the plaintiffs was constrained to concede that, if his submission was correct, then a child born with a very minor disability, such as a squint, would be entitled to sue the doctor for not advising an abortion, which advice would have been accepted, given that the risk (which fortunately did not eventuate) of serious disabilities was due to some infection which the doctor should have diagnosed. This would indeed be an odd position. Moreover, he accepted that, if the duty of care to the fetus involved a duty on the doctor, albeit indirectly, to prevent its birth, the child would have a cause of action against its mother who had unreasonably refused to have an abortion. Apart from the complicated religious and philosophical points that such an action would raise, the social implications in the potential disruption of family life and bitterness which it would cause between parent and child led the Royal Commission to conclude that such a right of action would be against public policy (see Cmnd 7054-I, para 1465).

Of course, the doctor, in accordance with his duty of care *to the mother*, owes her a duty to advise her of the rubella infection and its potential serious and irreversible effects and on the advisability of an abortion, such an operation having in such circumstances been legalised by the Abortion Act 1967. This is, however, *nihil ad rem*.

(2) *The injury and the damages.* The disabilities were caused by the rubella and not by the doctor (I ignore whether their extent could have been reduced through injections, because that is the subject of the infant's first claim). What then are her injuries, which the doctor's negligence has caused? The answer must be that there are none in any accepted sense. Her complaint is that she was allowed to be born at all, given the existence of her prenatal injuries. How then are her damages to be assessed? Not by awarding compensation for her pain, suffering and loss of amenities attributable to the disabilities, since these were already in existence before the doctor was consulted. She cannot say that, but for his negligence, she would have been born without her disabilities. What the doctor is blamed for is causing or permitting her to be born at all. Thus, the compensation must be based on a comparison between the value of non-existence (the doctor's alleged negligence having deprived her of this) and the value of her existence in a disabled state.

But how can a court begin to evaluate non-existence, 'The undiscover'd country from whose bourn No traveller returns'? No comparison is possible and therefore no damage can be established which a court could recognise. This goes to the root of the whole cause of action.

Counsel for the plaintiffs has provided no answer to the damage problem. His suggestion that you assess the compensation on the basis that the doctor had caused the disabilities and then you make some discount on a basis which he could not particularise because the doctor did not cause the disabilities does not, in my judgment, advance the matter, except to tend to confirm the impossibility of making such an assessment. . . .

Stephenson LJ: The importance of this cause of action to this child is somewhat reduced by the existence of her other claim and the mother's claims, which, if successful, will give her some compensation in money or in care.

However, this is the first occasion on which the courts of this country or the Commonwealth have had to consider this cause of action, and I shall give my reasons for holding that it should be struck out.

If, as is conceded, any duty is owed to an unborn child, the authority's hospital laboratory and the doctor looking after the mother during her pregnancy undoubtedly owed the child a duty not to injure it, and, if she had been injured as a result of lack of reasonable care and skill on their part after birth, she could have sued them (as she is suing the doctor) for damages to compensate her for the injury they had caused her in the womb. (Cf the thalidomide cases, where it was assumed that such an action might lie: eg *Distillers Co (Biochemicals) Ltd v Thompson* [1971] 1 All ER 694, [1971] AC 458.) But this child has not been injured by either defendant, but by the rubella which has infected the mother without fault on anybody's part. Her right not to be injured before birth by the carelessness of others has not been infringed by either defendant, any more than it would have been if she had been disabled by disease after birth. Neither defendant has broken any duty to take reasonable care not to injure her. The only right on which she can rely as having been infringed is a right not to be born deformed or disabled, which means, for a child deformed or disabled before birth by nature or disease, a right to be aborted or killed; or, if that last plain word is thought dangerously emotive, deprived of the opportunity to live after being delivered from the body of her mother. The only duty which either defendant can owe to the unborn child infected with disabling rubella is a duty to abort or kill her or deprive her of that opportunity.

It is said that the duty does not go as far as that, but only as far as a duty to give the mother an opportunity to choose her abortion and death. That is true as far as it goes. The doctor's alleged negligence is in misleading the mother as to the advisability of an abortion, failing to inform or advise her of its advisability or desirability; the laboratory's alleged negligence is not so pleaded in terms but the negligence pleaded against them in failing to make or interpret the tests of the mother's blood samples or to inform the doctor of their results must, like the doctor's negligence, be a breach of their duty to give the doctor an opportunity to advise the mother of the risks in continuing to let the fetus live in the womb and be born alive. But the complaint of the child, as of the mother, against the health authority, as against the doctor, is that their negligence burdened her (and her mother) with her injuries. That is another way of saying that the defendants' breaches of their duties resulted not just in the child's being born but in her being born injured or, as the judge put it, with deformities. But, as the injuries or deformities were not the result of any act or omission of the defendants, the only result for which they were responsible was her being born. For that they were responsible because if they had exercised due care the mother would have known that the child might be born injured or deformed, and the plaintiffs' pleaded case is that, if the mother had known that, she would have been willing to undergo an abortion, which must mean she would have undergone one or she could not claim that the defendants were responsible for burdening her with an injured child. If she would not have undergone an abortion had she known the risk of the child being born injured, any negligence on the defendants' part could not give either plaintiff a cause of action in respect of the child being born injured.

I am accordingly of opinion that, though the judge was right in saying that the child's complaint is that she was born with deformities without which she would have suffered no damage and have no complaint, her claim against the defendants is a claim that they were negligent in allowing her, injured as she was in the womb, to be born at all, a claim for 'wrongful entry into life' or 'wrongful life'.

This analysis leads inexorably on to the question: how can there be a duty to take away life? How indeed can it be lawful? It is still the law that it is unlawful to take away the life of a born child or of any living person after birth. But the Abortion Act 1967 has given mothers a right to terminate the lives of their unborn children and made it lawful for doctors to help to abort them.

That statute (on which counsel for the plaintiffs relies) permits abortion in specified cases of risks to the mother and the child. I need not read those provisions which are enacted in the mother's interest, but there is one provision relevant to the interests of the child. Section 1(1) provides:

> Subject to the provisions of this section, a person shall not be guilty of an offence under the law relating to abortion when a pregnancy is terminated by a registered medical practitioner if two registered medical practitioners are of the opinion, formed in good faith . . . (*b*) that there is a substantial risk that if the child were born it would suffer from such physical or mental abnormalities as to be seriously handicapped.

That paragraph may have been passed in the interests of the mother, the family and the general public, but I would prefer to believe that its main purpose, if not its sole purpose, was to benefit the unborn child; and, if and in so far as that was the intention of the legislature, the legislature did make a notable inroad on the sanctity of human life by recognising that it would be better for a child, born to suffer from such abnormalities as to be seriously handicapped, not to have been born at all.

The inroad, however, seems to stop short of a child capable of being born alive, because the sanctity of the life of a viable fetus is preserved by the enactment of s 5(1) that 'Nothing in this Act shall affect the provisions of the Infant Life (Preservation) Act 1929 (protecting the life of the viable foetus)'.

Another notable feature of the 1967 Act is that it does not directly impose any duty on a medical practitioner or anyone else to terminate a pregnancy, though it relieves conscientious objectors of a duty to participate in any treatment authorised by the Act in all cases with one exception: see s 4 of the Act. It is, however, conceded in this case that a medical practitioner is under a duty to the mother to advise her of her right under the Act to have her pregnancy terminated in cases such as the present. There was, on the pleaded facts of this case, a substantial risk that if the child were born it would suffer such physical or mental abnormalities as to be seriously handicapped. And, from what we have been told without objection of her present mental and physical condition, that risk has become tragically actual.

There is no doubt that this child could legally have been deprived of life by the mother's undergoing an abortion with the doctor's advice and help. So the law recognises a difference between the life of a fetus and the life of those who have been born. But, because a doctor can lawfully by statute do to a fetus what he cannot lawfully do to a person who has been born, it does not follow that he is under a legal obligation to a fetus to do it and terminate its life, or that the fetus has a legal right to die.

Like this court when it had to consider the interests of a child born with Down's syndrome in *Re B (a minor) (wardship: medical treatment)* [1981] 1 WLR 1421, I would not answer until it is necessary to do so the question whether the life of a child could be so certainly 'awful' and 'intolerable' that it would be in its best interests to end it and it might be considered that it had a right to be put to death. But that is not this case. We have no exact information about the extent of this child's serious and highly debilitating congenital injuries; the judge was told that she is partly blind and deaf, but it is not and could not be suggested that the quality of her life is such that she is certainly better dead, or would herself wish that she had not been born or should now die.

I am therefore compelled to hold that neither defendant was under any duty to the child to give the child's mother an opportunity to terminate the child's life. That duty may be owed to the mother, but it cannot be owed to the child.

To impose such a duty towards the child would, in my opinion, make a further inroad on the sanctity of human life which would be contrary to public policy. It would mean regarding the life of a handicapped child as not only less valuable than the life of a normal child, but so much less valuable that it was not worth preserving, and it would even mean that a doctor would be obliged to pay damages to a child infected with rubella before birth who was in fact born with some mercifully trivial abnormality. These are the consequences of the necessary basic assumption that a child has a right to be born whole or not at all, not to be born unless it can be born perfect or 'normal', whatever that may mean.

Added to that objection must be the opening of the courts to claims by children born handicapped against their mothers for not having an abortion. For the reasons given by the Royal Commission on Civil Liability and Compensation for Personal Injury (report, vol 1; Cmnd 7054-I), cited by Ackner LJ, that is, to my mind, a graver objection than the extra burden on doctors already open to actions for negligent treatment of a fetus, which weighed with the Law Commission.

Finally, there is the nature of the injury and damage which the court is being asked to ascertain and evaluate.

The only duty of care which courts of law can recognise and enforce are duties owed to those who can be compensated for loss by those who owe the duties, in most cases, including cases of personal injury, by money damages which will as far as possible put the injured party in the condition in which he or she was before being injured. The only way in which a child injured in the womb can be compensated in damages is by measuring what it has lost, which is the difference between the value of its life as a whole and healthy normal child and the value of its life as an injured child. But to make those who have not injured the child pay for that difference is to treat them as if they injured the child, when all they have done is not taken steps to prevent its being born injured by another cause.

The only loss for which those who have not injured the child can be held liable to compensate the child is the difference between its condition as a result of their allowing it to be born alive and injured and its condition if its embryonic life had been ended before its life in the world had begun. But how can a court of law evaluate that second condition and so measure the loss to the child? Even if a court were competent to decide between the conflicting views of theologians and philosophers and to assume an 'afterlife' or non-existence as the basis for the comparison, how can a judge put a value on the one or the other, compare either alternative with the injured child's life in this world and determine that the child has lost anything, without the means of knowing what, if anything, it has gained?

Judges have to pluck figures from the air in putting many imponderables into pounds and pence. Loss of expectation of life, for instance, has been held so difficult that the courts have been driven to fix for it a constant and arbitrary figure. Counsel for the plaintiffs referred us to what judges have said on that topic in *Rose v Ford* [1937] 3 All ER 359, [1937] AC 826 and *Benham v Gambling* [1941] 1 All ER 7, [1941] AC 157. But, in measuring the loss caused by shortened life, courts are dealing with a thing, human life, of which they have some experience; here the court is being asked to deal with the consequences of death for the dead, a thing of which it has none. And the statements of judges on the necessity for juries to assess damages and their ability to do so in cases of extreme difficulty do not touch the problem presented by the assessment of the claims we are considering. To measure loss of expectation of death would require a value judgment where a crucial factor lies altogether outside the range of human knowledge and could only be achieved, if at all, by resorting to the personal beliefs of the judge who has the misfortune to attempt the task. If difficulty in assessing damages is a bad reason for refusing the task, impossibility of assessing them is a good one. A court must have a starting point for giving damages for a breach of duty. The only means of giving a starting point to a court asked to hold that there is the duty on a doctor or a hospital which this child alleges is to require the court to measure injured life against uninjured life, and that is to treat the doctor and the hospital as responsible not for the child's birth but for its injuries. That is what in effect counsel for the plaintiffs suggests that the court should do, tempering the injustice to the defendants by some unspecified discount. This seems almost as desparate an expedient as an American judge's suggestion that the measure of damages should be the 'diminished childhood' resulting from the substantial diminution of the parents' capacity to give the child special care: see the dissenting judgment of Handler J in *Berman v Allan* 404A 2d 8 at 15, 19, 21 (1979). If there is no measure of damage which is not unjustified and indeed unjust, courts of law cannot entertain claims by a child affected with parental damage against those who fail to provide its mother with the opportunity to end its damaged life, however careless and unskilful they may have been and however liable they may be to the mother for that negligent failure.

If a court had to decide whether it were better to enter into life maimed or halt than not to enter it at all, it would, I think, be bound to say it was better in all cases of mental and physical disability, except possibly those extreme cases already mentioned, of which perhaps the recent case of *Croke v Wiseman* [1981] 3 All ER 852, [1982] 1 WLR 71 is an example, but certainly not excepting such a case as the present. However that may be, it is not for the courts to take such a decision by weighing life against death or to take cognisance of a claim like this child's. I would regard it on principle as disclosing no reasonable cause of action and would accordingly prefer the master's decision to the judge's.

I am happy to find support for this view of the matter in the Law Commission's Report and the Congenital Disabilities (Civil Liability) Act 1976, to which I have already referred, and in the strong current of American authority, to which we have been referred. Direct decisions of courts in the United States of America on the same topic are of no more than persuasive authority but contain valuable material and with one exception would rule out the infant plaintiff's claims in our case. . . .

Judicial opinion expressed in the American decisions can, I think, be summarised in the following propositions: (1) though what gives rise to the cause of action is not just life but life with defects, the real cause of action is negligence in causing life; (2) negligent advice or failure to advise is the proximate cause of the child's life (though not of its defects); (3) a child has no right to be born as a whole, functional being (without defects); (4) it is contrary to public policy, which is to preserve human life, to give a child a right not to be born except as a whole, functional being, and to impose on another a corresponding duty to prevent a child being born except without defects, that is, a duty to cause the death of an unborn child with defects; (5) it is impossible to measure the damages for being born with defects because it is impossible to compare the life of a child born with defects and non-existence as a human being; (6) accordingly, by being born with defects a child has suffered no injury cognisable by law and if it is to have a claim for being so born the law must be reformed by legislation.

The current of opinion has run in favour of the fourth consideration and against the fifth consideration even to the point of dismissing it altogether. Authority for that, and for the consideration which I have formulated, is to be found in particular in the judgment of the Supreme Court of New Jersey given by Pashman J in *Berman v Allan* 404 A 2d 8 at 11-13 (1979), in the judgments of Presiding Judge Cercone and Judge Spaeth in *Speck v Finegold* 408 A 2d 496 at 508, 51 (1979) and in the judgment of District Judge Blatt in *Phillips v USA* 508 F Supp 537 at 543 (1980) . . .

There are indications, to which counsel for the plaintiff called our attention, that some of the judges' opinions on the sanctity of human life were influenced by the illegality of abortion in some states; but those indications do not, in my opinion, play a decisive part in their decisions or weaken their persuasive force in considering the right answer to the same question in a jurisdiction where abortion has some statutory sanction.

I do not think it matters whether the injury is not an injury recognised by the law or the damages are not damages which the law can award. Whichever way it is put, the objection means that the cause of action is not cognisable or justiciable or 'reasonable', and I can draw no distinction between the first two terms and the third as it is rather artificially used in RSC Ord 18, r 19.

The defendants must be assumed to have been careless. The child suffers from serious disabilities. If the defendants had not been careless, the child could not be suffering now because it would not be alive. Why should the defendants not pay the child for its suffering?

The answer lies in the implications and consequences of holding that they should. If public policy favoured the introduction of this novel cause of action, I would not let the strict application of logic or the absence of precedent defeat it. But, as it would be, in my judgment, against public policy for the courts to entertain claims like those which are the subject of this appeal, I would for this reason, and for the other reasons which I have given, allow the appeal . . .

Griffiths LJ: The child's claim for 'wrongful life' is put against the hospital by the following steps. (1) The hospital when analysing the mother's blood owed a duty of care to the fetus in her womb. This point is conceded by the hospital for the purposes of this appeal. (2) The hospital discharges that duty of care by correctly advising whether the analysis shows that the mother has been infected. (3) In breach of that duty the hospital negligently advised that the analysis showed that the mother was not infected. (4) That breach of duty caused the birth of the child because, if the hospital had correctly advised that the mother was infected, she would have decided to have an abortion. (5) As a result of being born the child has to bear the afflictions of deafness, partial blindness and some degree of mental retardation, which society and the law should concur in treating as something that should not have happened to the child and for which she would be compensated by the negligent hospital.

It can thus be seen that the child's allegation is that but for the negligence of the hospital she would not have been born; it is a result of their wrong that she has been born; hence the term 'wrongful life'. The claim is put in a similar manner against the doctor.

Whether the law should give a remedy in such circumstances has been considered by the Law Commission. They concluded that there should be no liability for wrongful life and deliberately drafted cl 1 of the Congenital Disabilities (Civil Liability) Bill to exclude any such liability. Parliament accepted that advice and enacted the material part of the Congenital Disabilities (Civil Liability) Act 1976 in precisely the same language as the Law Commission's Bill. I am unable to accept the submission of counsel for the plaintiffs that the language of s 1 does not exclude the action for wrongful life; I have no doubt that it achieves its objective.

We have referred to seven decisions of courts in the United States of America; all save one of those courts have denied a remedy for wrongful life.

The remedy has been denied on a variety of different grounds. The Law Commission were of the opinion that it would impose an intolerable burden on the medical profession because of a subconscious pressure to advise abortions in doubtful cases for fear of actions for damages. I do not myself find this a convincing reason for denying the action if it would otherwise lie. The decision whether or not to have an abortion must always be the mother's; the duty of the medical profession can be no more than to advise her of her right to have an abortion and of the pros and cons of doing so. If there is a risk that the child will be born deformed, that risk must be explained to the mother, but it surely cannot be asserted that the doctor owes a duty to the fetus to urge its destruction. Provided the doctor gives a balanced explanation of the risks involved in continuing the pregnancy, including the risk of injury to the fetus, he cannot be expected to do more, and need have no fear of an action being brought against him.

To my mind, the most compelling reason to reject this cause of action is the intolerable and insoluble problem it would create in the assessment of damage. The basis of damages for personal injury is the comparison between the state of the plaintiff before he was injured and his condition after he was injured. This is often a hard enough task in all conscience and it has an element of artificiality about it, for who can say that there is any sensible correlation between pain and money? Nevertheless, the courts have been able to produce a broad tariff that appears at the moment to be acceptable to society as doing rough justice. But the whole exercise, difficult as it is, is anchored in the first place to the condition of the plaintiff before the injury which the court can comprehend and evaluate. In a claim for wrongful life how does the court begin to make an assessment? The plaintiff does not say, 'But for your negligence I would have been born uninjured'; the plaintiff says, 'But for your negligence I would never have been born.' The court then has to compare the state of the plaintiff with non-existence, of which the court can know nothing; this I regard as an impossible task. Counsel for the plaintiffs suggested that the court should assess the damages on the assumption that the plaintiff's injury had been caused by the hospital, and then discount the damages because it had not been so caused. But he was quite unable, and I do not blame him, to suggest any principle on which the discount should be calculated.

Again, suppose by some happy chance the child is born with only a slight deformity, can it bring an action on the basis that it would have been killed in the womb if the mother had been told of the risk of greater deformity? Such a claim seems utterly offensive; there should be rejoicing that the hospital's mistake bestowed the gift of life on a child. If such claims are rejected, on what basis could a claim be brought for a more serious injury? Only, it would seem, on the basis that the state of the child is such that it were better dead than alive. But, knowing nothing of death, who is to answer this question, and what two minds will approach the answer by the same route? I regard the question as wholly outside the competence of judicial determination.

I would reject this novel cause of action because I see no way of determining which plaintiffs can claim, that is, how gravely deformed must the child be before a claim will lie? and secondly because of the impossibility of assessing the damage it has suffered.

The common law does not have the tools to fashion a remedy in these cases. If society feels that such cases are deserving of compensation, some entirely novel and arbitrary measure of damage is called for, which I agree with the American judge would be better introduced by legislation than by judges striving to solve the insoluble.

There are a number of strands of argument relied upon by the Court of Appeal in rejecting the child's claim. *Firstly*, no duty could be owed by the doctor to the child, in particular, because it would be contrary to public policy for the doctor to owe a 'duty to the foetus to urge its destruction'. *Secondly*, the child had not suffered any damage known to the law by being born. *Thirdly*, the assessment of a child's damages would be impossible given that it would require the court 'to compare the state of the plaintiff with non-existence, of which the court can know nothing'.

The position at common law is by no means as straightforward or as clear as these judgments would have it. Initially, courts in the United States adopted a similar view of the law as that set out in *McKay*. However, during the 1980s a number of jurisdictions sought to fashion a means of giving the child *some* remedy and so adopted an alternative analysis. The breakthrough occurred in the California Court of Appeal in 1980 which reviewed, only to reject, the existing body of case law.

Curlender v Bio-Science Laboratories (1980) 165 Cal Rptr 477 (Cal CA)

Jefferson J: The appeal presents an issue of first impression in California: What remedy, if any, is available in this state to a severely impaired child – generally defective – born as the result of defendants' negligence in conducting certain genetic tests of the child's parents – tests which, if properly done, would have disclosed the high probability that the actual, catastrophic result would occur?

In the first cause of action against the named defendants, plaintiff Shauna alleged that on January 15, 1977, her parents, Phillis and Hyam Curlender, retained defendant laboratories to administer certain tests designed to reveal whether either of the parents were carriers of genes which would result in the conception and birth of a child with Tay-Sachs disease, medically defined as 'amaurotic familial idiocy'. The tests on plaintiff's parents were performed on January 21, 1977, and, it was alleged, due to defendants' negligence, 'incorrect and inaccurate' information was disseminated to plaintiff's parents concerning their status as carriers.

The complaint did not allege the date of plaintiff's birth, so we do not know whether the parents relied upon the test results in conceiving plaintiff, or, as parents-to-be when the tests were made, relied upon the results in failing to avail themselves of amniocentesis and an abortion. In any event, on May 10, 1978, plaintiff's parents were informed that plaintiff had Tay-Sachs disease.

As the result of the disease, plaintiff Shauna suffers from 'mental retardation, susceptibility to other diseases, convulsions, sluggishness, apathy, failure to fix objects with her eyes, inability to take an interest in her surroundings, loss of motor reactions, inability to sit up or hold her head up, loss of weight, muscle atrophy, blindness, pseudobulper palsy, inability to feed orally, decerebrate rigidity and gross physical deformity'. It was alleged that Shauna's life expectancy is estimated to be four years. The complaint also contained allegations that plaintiff suffers 'pain, physical and emotional distress, fear, anxiety, despair, loss of enjoyment of life, and frustration. . . .'

The complaint sought costs of plaintiff's care as damages and also damages for emotional distress and the deprivation of '72.6 years of her life'. In addition, punitive damages of three million dollars were sought, on the ground that '[a]t the time that Defendants . . . [tested the parents] Defendants, and each of them, had been expressly informed by the nation's leading authority on Tay-Sachs disease that said test procedures were substantially inaccurate and would likely result in disastrous [sic] and catastrophic consequences to the patients, and Defendants knew that said procedures were improper, inadequate and with insufficient controls and that the results of such a testing were likely to be inaccurate and that a false negative result would have disastrous [sic] and catastrophic consequences to the Plaintiff, all in conscious disregard of the health, safety and well-being of Plaintiff. . . .'

A major (and much cited) opinion considering a claim for damages by an impaired infant plaintiff and his parents is *Gleitman v Cosgrove* 49 NJ 22, 227 A 2d (1967) from the New Jersey Supreme Court. The Gleitmans brought a malpractice action against Mrs Gleitman's physician for damages because the Gleitman child, Jeffrey, had been born with serious impairments of sight, speech, and hearing. Mrs Gleitman had contracted rubella (measles) during the first trimester of pregnancy (the first three months). Defendant was made aware of this fact, but failed to inform the mother-to-be of any potentially harmful consequences to her child; Mrs Gleitman was assured by him that such consequences would not occur, although it was common medical knowledge that rubella, contracted during early pregnancy, often causes the type of defects suffered by Jeffrey, who was also mentally retarded.

The majority of the *Gleitman* court barred recovery by *either* the parents or the child on two grounds: (1) the perceived impossibility of computing damages and (2) public policy. With respect to the computation of damages, the court explained that '[t]he normal measure of damages in tort actions is compensatory. Damages are measured by comparing the condition plaintiff would have been in, had the defendants not been negligent, with plaintiff's impaired condition as a result of the negligence. The infant plaintiff would have us measure the difference between his life with defects against the utter void of nonexistence, but it is impossible to make such a determination. This Court cannot weigh the value of life with impairments against the nonexistence of life itself. By asserting that he should not have been born, the infant plaintiff makes it logically impossible for a court to measure his alleged damages because of the impossibility of making the comparison required by compensatory remedies' (*Gleitman, supra* 227 A 2d 689, 692).

Any decision negating the value of life directly or by implication was seen by the majority in *Gleitman* as an impermissible expression of public policy. There was considerable discussion of the legality of any abortion which would have been undertaken to prevent Jeffrey's birth. The majority referred with approval to the analysis presented in Israel Law Review 513 (1966) by Tedeschi, entitled 'On Tort Liability for "Wrongful Life"'.

A vastly different view was expressed by a dissenting opinion in *Gleitman*. It was there declared that the majority 'permits a wrong with serious consequential injury to go wholly unredressed. That provides no deterrent to professional irresponsibility and is neither just nor compatible with expanding principles of liability in the field of torts' (*Gleitman, supra*, 227 A 2d 689, 703 (dis opn)). As to the impossibility of computing damages, reference was made to a statement by the United States Supreme Court in *Story Parchment Co v Paterson Co* 282 US 555, 563, 51 S Ct 248, 250, 75 L Ed 544 (1931), that difficulties encountered in computing damages cannot be permitted to justify a denial of liability. However, the reasoning and result in *Gleitman's* majority opinion have been, in the main, followed (albeit blindly in our opinion) in other jurisdictions. (See *Steward v Long Island College Hospital* 58 Misc 2d 432, 296 NYS 2d 41 (1968) and *Dumer v St Michael's Hospital* 69 Wis 2d 766, 233 NW 2d 372 (1975).) It has also been analysed and criticised. (See Note, 55 Minn L Rev 58 (1971).)

Of some significance with respect to this question is the fact that in 1973, *Roe v Wade*, 410 US 113, 93 S Ct 705, 35 L Ed 2d 147, was decided by the United States Supreme Court. The nation's high court determined that parents have a *constitutionally protected right* to obtain an abortion during the first trimester of pregnancy, free of state interference. We deem this decision to be of considerable importance in defining the parameters of 'wrongful-life' litigation.

The *Roe v Wade* case played a rather substantial part in the partial retreat from the *Gleitman* holding by the New Jersey Supreme Court majority in *Berman v Allan* 80 NJ 421, 404 A 2d 8 (1979). The Bermans, parents and child, brought suit for medical malpractice. Mrs Berman had become pregnant in her late thirties, a circumstance involving a substantial risk that the child would be born with Down's syndrome (mongolism), one of the major characteristics of which is mental retardation. Sharon Berman, the child, was so afflicted.

Amniocentesis – by that time a well established technique for discerning birth defects *in utero* – had not been suggested to the Bermans. The majority in the *Berman* court held that the *parents* had stated a cause of action, and that they could recover damages for emotional distress, but that lifetime support for Sharon could not be awarded.

But the *Berman* court rejected the concept that the infant Sharon possessed an independent cause of action. Referring to the difficulty of measuring damages in such a case, the court declared that '[n]onetheless, were the *measure* of damages our sole concern, it is possible that some judicial remedy could be fashioned which would redress plaintiff, if only in part, for injuries suffered'. Here, the majority chose to rely on public policy considerations. The *Berman* court considered that Sharon had not suffered any damage cognisable at law by being brought into existence. It was explained that '[o]ne of the most deeply held beliefs of our society is that life – whether experienced with or without a major physical handicap – is more precious than nonlife. . . . Sharon, by virtue of her birth, will be able to love and be loved and to experience happiness and pleasure – emotions which are truly the essence of life and which are far more valuable than the suffering she may endure. To rule otherwise would require us to disavow the basic assumption upon which our society is based. This we cannot do.' (*Berman, supra*, 404 A 2d 8, 12-13.)

The dissenting opinion in *Berman*, noting that the majority had in effect partially overruled *Gleitman*, urged complete rejection of the majority view on the ground that '[t]he child . . . was owed directly, during its gestation, a duty of reasonable care from the same physicians who undertook to care for its mother – then expectant – and that duty, to render complete and competent medical advice, was seriously breached'. (*Berman, supra*, 404 A 2d 8, 15 (dis opn).) Taking cognisance of the present legality of abortions in the first trimester, the dissent perceived a duty on the part of medical practitioners to ensure that, under certain circumstances, parents-to-be had the opportunity to decide the future of their child – its existence or nonexistence. 'To be denied the opportunity – indeed, the right – to apply one's own moral values in reaching that decision [concerning the child's future], is a serious, irreversible wrong.' (*Id* 404 A 2d at p 18.)

The dissenting opinion in *Berman* expressed the cogent observation that, as for the child, '[a]n adequate comprehension of the infant's claims under these circumstances *starts with the realisation that the infant has come into this world and is here*, encumbered by an injury attributable to the malpractice of the doctors'. (*Berman, supra*, 404 A 2d 8, 19.) (Emphasis added.)

In New York . . . there have been a series of decisions wrestling with 'wrongful-life' problems with the quite predictable divergent expressions by the judiciary. In only one case, however (overruled by a higher court) did the court grant recognition to a cause of action by a child so born.

In *Park v Chessin* 60 AD 80, 400 NYS 2d 110 (1977), an intermediate New York appellate court considered the following facts. The Parks had had one child born with polycystic kidney disease, a fatal hereditary ailment. The baby died. The parents consulted defendant doctors and informed them of this; assured that the condition would not reoccur, the Parks had a second child, who also had the disease but survived for a short life span of 2 and 1/2 years. The court held that these facts gave both the parents and child causes of action, that 'decisional law must keep pace with explaining technological, economic and social change. Inherent in the abolition of the statutory ban on abortion . . . is a public policy consideration which gives potential parents the right, within certain statutory and case law limitations, *not* to have a child. This right extends to instances in which it can be determined with reasonable medical certainty that the child would be born deformed. The *breach of this right may also be said to be tortious to the fundamental right of a child to be born as a whole, functional human being*.' (*Park, supra*, 400 NYS 2d 110, 114.) (Emphasis added.)

But this view of the law also had a short life span. This decision was reviewed in *Becker v Schwartz* 46 NY 2d 401, 413 NYS 2d 895, 386 NE 2d 807 (1978) (as a companion case) and overruled. The Beckers and their mongoloid infant sought damages from medical doctors who had not, despite the mother's age when she became pregnant, warned of the danger or informed the Beckers of amniocentesis. The parents, declared *Becker*, had stated a cause of action and could recover their pecuniary loss but *not* damages for emotional distress, as the latter recovery would offend public policy. The infant plaintiffs in both *Becker* and *Park* were held to be barred from recovery because of the inability of the law to make a comparison between human existence with handicaps and no life at all. The court particularly rejected the idea that a child may expect life without deformity: 'There is no precedent for recognition at the Appellant Division of a "fundamental right of a child to be born as a whole, functional human being". . . .' (*Becker, supra*, 413 NYS 2d 895 at 900, 386 NE 2d 807 at 812.)

The high court in Pennsylvania issued an exhaustive opinion in 1979 concerning the various aspects of the 'wrongful-life' problem. The case was *Speck v Finegold*, – Pa Super – , 408 A 2d 496, a malpractice suit by parents and child occasioned by the birth of the child with neurofibromatosis, a seriously crippling condition already evidenced in the child's siblings. Overruling the trial court, *Speck* recognised the parents' cause of action but not that of the infant plaintiff.

We quote at length from the *Speck* court's opinion:

> In the instant case, we deny Francine's [infant plaintiff] claim to be made whole. When we examine Francine's claim, we find regardless of whether her claim is based on 'wrongful life' or otherwise, there is a failure to state a legally cognisable cause of action even though, admittedly, the defendants' actions of negligence were the proximate cause of her defective birth. Her claims to be whole have two fatal weaknesses. First, there is no precedent in appellate judicial pronouncements that holds a child has a fundamental right to be born as a whole, functional human being. Whether it is better to have never been born at all rather than to have been born with serious mental defects is a mystery more properly left to the philosophers and theologians, a mystery which would lead us into the field of metaphysics, beyond the realm of our understanding or ability to solve. . . . [This] cause of action . . . demands a calculation of damages dependent on a comparison between Hobson's choice of life in an impaired state and nonexistence. This the law is incapable of doing. [Fn omitted.] . . . unfortunately . . . this is not an action cognisable in law. Thus, the recognised principle, not peculiar to traditional tort law alone, that it would be a denial of justice to deny all relief where a wrong is of such a nature as to preclude certain ascertained damages, is inapposite and inapplicable here.

(*Speck, supra*, 408 A 2d 496, 508.)

Other jurisdictions, following the lead of the New Jersey and New York cases, have rejected the concept of an infant's cause of action for 'wrongful life'. (See *Elliott v Brown* 361 So 2d 546 (Ala 1978), rejecting the 'wrongful life' cause of action in that jurisdiction; see also *Jacobs v Theimer* 519 SW 2d 846 (Tex 1975), holding that the mother of a defective child had stated a cause of action for failure of the defendant physician to diagnose rubella during early pregnancy and counsel accordingly; also, recovery was allowed for those costs reasonably related to caring for the child's physical defects. The court declared that '[n]o public policy obstacle should be interposed to that recovery' (519 SW 2d 846, 849).)

Two decisions of note have involved Tay-Sachs impairment – the condition involved in the case before us. In *Howard v Lecher* 42 NY 2d 109, 397 NYS 2d 363, 366 NE 2d 64 (1977), an intermediate appellate court in New York considered an action brought by the parents to recover damages for emotional distress from the consulting physicians. In *Howard*, the child died. Denying recovery, the *Howard* majority reasoned that recognition of the parents' cause of action 'would require the extension of traditional tort concepts beyond manageable bounds'. (397 NYS 2d at 364, 366 NE 2d at 65.)

A dissenting judge in *Howard* expostulated that the issue was simply whether a patient and parent-to-be, the mother, may recover damages from her physician for the latter's negligence. He found it not unreasonable, given the present state of medical knowledge concerning genetically caused birth deformities and the procedures available for avoiding such deformities, for the law to require an attending physician to take a genealogical history of the parents, to perform any available appropriate tests indicated by such history, and inform the parents of any potential dangers so that they would be able to make an informed decision concerning continuation of pregnancy.

In *Gildiner v Thomas Jefferson Univ Hospital* 451 F Supp 692 (ED Pa 1978), the parents had been tested for Tay-Sachs; the tests indicated that amniocentesis should be performed; it was performed, but negligently; the parents were both carriers, and the infant born to them suffered from Tay-Sachs. Relying on *Gleitman v Cosgrove, supra*, 49 NJ 22, 227 A 2d 689, the federal district court held that the parents could recover damages, but the child could not. A strong public policy was perceived in allowing parental recovery: 'Tay-Sachs disease can be prevented only by accurate genetic testing combined with the right of parents to abort afflicted fetuses within appropriate time limitations. *Society has an interest in insuring that genetic testing is properly performed and interpreted.*' (*Gildiner, supra*, 451 F Supp 692,696.) (Emphasis added.) . . .

From our analysis and study, we conclude that certain general observations are appropriate concerning the decisional law in this country to date with respect to the 'wrongful life' problem.

First. For clear analysis it is important to recognise certain distinctions among the cases purportedly dealing with the 'wrongful-life' concept. One such distinction is that concerning the condition of the child involved. Surely there is a world of difference between an unwanted healthy child who is illegitimate (*Stills v Gratton* [127 Cal Rptr 652 (Cal CA)]), the unwanted tenth child of a marriage (*Custodio v Bauer* 251 Cal App 2d 303, 59 Cal Rptr 463 (1967)) and the severely deformed infant plaintiff, Shauna, in the case at bench. Illegitimacy is a status which may or may not prove to be a hindrance to one so born, depending on a multitude of other facts; it cannot be disputed that in present society such a circumstance, both socially and legally, no longer need present an overwhelming obstacle. The same is true for the simply unwanted child. We agree with the reasoning of *Zepeda* [*v Zepeda* (1963) 190 NE 2d 849 (Ill CA)] and *Stills* that a cause of action based upon impairment of status – illegitimacy contrasted with legitimacy – should not be recognisable at law *because* a necessary element for the establishment of any cause of action in tort is missing, *injury* and damages consequential to that injury. A child born with severe impairment, however, presents an entirely different situation because the necessary element of *injury* is present.

Second. The decisional law of other jurisdictions, while not dispositive of Shauna's claim pursuant to California law, is of considerable significance in defining the basic issues underlying the true 'wrongful-life' action – one brought by the infant whose painful existence is a direct and proximate result of negligence by others. That decisional law demonstrates some measure of progression in our law. Confronted with the fact that the births of these infants may be directly traced to the negligent conduct of others, and that the result of that negligence is palpable injury, involving not only pecuniary loss but untold anguish on the part of all concerned, the courts in our sister states have progressed from a stance of barring all recovery to a recognition that, at least, the parents of such a child may state a cause of action founded on negligence.

We note that there has been a gradual retreat from the position of accepting 'impossibility of measuring damages' as the sole ground for barring the infant's right of recovery, although the courts continue to express divergent views on how the parents' damages should be measured, in terms of allowing recovery for both pecuniary loss and damages for emotional distress, or, in recognising one element of recovery only, but not the other.

The concept of public policy has played an important role in this developing field of law. Public policy, as perceived by most courts, has been utilised as the basis for denying recovery; in some fashion, a deeply held belief in the sanctity of life has compelled some courts to deny recovery to those among us who have been born with serious impairment. But the dissents, written along the way, demonstrate that there is not universal acceptance of the notion that 'metaphysics' or 'religious beliefs', rather than law, should govern the situation; the dissents have emphasised that considerations of public policy should include regard for social welfare as affected by careful genetic counselling and medical procedures.

We have alluded to the monumental implications of *Roe v Wade, supra,* 410 US 113, 93 S Ct 705, 35 L Ed 2d 147, one of which is the present legality of, and availability of, eugenic abortion in the proper case. Another factor of substantial proportions in 'wrongful-life' litigation is the dramatic increase, in the last few decades, of the medical knowledge and skill needed to avoid genetic disaster. As the author of the article in the Yale Law Journal points out (see fn, 8): 'Genetic defects represent an increasingly large part of the overall national health care burden.' (87 Yale Law Journal 1496.) The writer concluded that the law indeed has an appropriate function in encouraging adequate and careful medical practice in the field of genetic counselling, observing that '[t]ort law, a well-recognised means of regulating the practice of medicine, can be used both to establish and to limit the duty of physicians to fulfil this [genetic counselling] function'. (87 Yale Law Journal 1499.)

Third. Despite the cool reception accorded such 'wrongful-life' litigation, both parents and their children have continued to seek redress for the wrongs committed, presumably for a number of reasons: (1) the serious nature of the wrong; (2) increasing sophistication as to the causes, which may not with present knowledge be attributed to the fine hand of providence but rather to lack of care; and (3) the understanding that the law reflects, perhaps later than sooner, basic changes in the way society views such matters.

. . . We have no difficulty in ascertaining and finding the existence of a duty owed by medical laboratories engaged in genetic testing to parents and their as yet unborn children to use ordinary care in administration of available tests for the purpose of providing information concerning potential genetic defects in the unborn. The public policy considerations with respect to the individuals involved and to society as a whole dictate recognition of such a duty, and it is of significance that in no decision that has come to our attention which has dealt with the 'wrongful-life' concept has it been suggested that public policy considerations negate the existence of such a duty. Nor have other jurisdictions had any difficulty in finding a breach of duty under appropriate circumstances or in finding the existence of the requisite proximate causal link between the breach and the claimed injury;

we find no bar to a holding that the defendants owed a duty to the child plaintiff before us and breached that duty.

The real crux of the problem is whether the breach of duty was the proximate cause of *an injury cognisable at law*. The injury, of course, is not the particular defect with which a plaintiff is afflicted – considered in the abstract – but it is the birth of plaintiff with such defect.

The circumstance that the birth and injury have come hand in hand has caused other courts to deal with the problem by barring recovery. The reality of the 'wrongful-life' concept is that such a plaintiff both *exists* and *suffers*, due to the negligence of others. It is neither necessary nor just to retreat into meditation on the mysteries of life. We need not be concerned with the fact that had defendants not been negligent, the plaintiff might not have come into existence at all. The certainty of genetic impairment is no longer a mystery. In addition, a reverent appreciation of life compels recognition that plaintiff, however impaired she may be, has come into existence as a living person with certain rights.

One of the fears expressed in the decisional law is that, once it is determined that such infants have rights cognisable at law, nothing would prevent such a plaintiff from bringing suit against its own parents for allowing plaintiff to be born. In our view, the fear is groundless. The 'wrongful-life' cause of action with which we are concerned is based upon negligently caused failure by someone under a duty to do so to inform the prospective parents of facts needed by them to make a conscious choice *not* to become parents. If a case arose where, despite due care by the medical profession in transmitting the necessary warnings, parents made a conscious choice to proceed with a pregnancy, with full knowledge that a seriously impaired infant would be born, that conscious choice would provide an intervening act of proximate cause to preclude liability insofar as defendants other than the parents were concerned. Under such circumstances, we see no sound public policy which should protect those parents from being answerable for the pain, suffering and misery which they have wrought upon their offspring.

In our consideration of whether the child plaintiff has stated a cause of action, we find it instructive to look first to the statutory law of this state. Our Civil Code section 3281 provides that '*[e]very person* who suffers detriment from the unlawful act or omission of another, may recover from the person in fault a compensation therefor in money, which is called damages'. Civil Code section 3282 defines detriment as 'a loss or harm suffered in person or property'. Civil Code section 3333 provides: 'For the breach of an obligation not arising from contract, the measure of damages, except where otherwise expressly provided by this Code, is the amount which will compensate for all the detriment proximately caused thereby, whether it could have been anticipated or not'.

In addition, we have long adhered to the principle that there should be a remedy for every wrong committed. 'Fundamental in our jurisprudence is the principle that for every wrong there is a remedy and that an injured party should be compensated for all damage proximately caused by the wrongdoer. Although we recognise exceptions from these fundamental principles, no departure should be sanctioned unless there is a strong necessity therefor. The general rule of damages in tort is that the injured party may recover for all detriment caused whether it could have been anticipated or not.' (*Crisci v Security Ins Co* 66 Cal 2d 425 at 433, 58 Cal Rptr 13 at 18, 426 P 2d 173 at 178 (1967).)

We have concluded that it is clearly consistent with the applicable principles of the statutory and decisional tort law in this state to recognise a cause of action stated by plaintiff against the defendants . . . the extent of recovery, however, is subject to certain limitations due to the nature of the tort involved. While ordinarily a defendant is liable for all consequences flowing from the injury (*Custodio v Bauer, supra*), it is appropriate in the case before us to tailor the elements of recovery, taking into account particular circumstances involved (as was done in *Stills v Gratton, supra*).

The complaint seeks damages based upon an actuarial life expectancy of plaintiff of more than 70 years – the life expectancy if plaintiff had been born without the Tay-Sachs disease. The complaint sets forth that plaintiff's actual life expectancy, because of the disease, is only four years. We reject as untenable the claim that plaintiff is entitled to damages as if plaintiff had been born without defects and would have had a normal life expectancy. Plaintiff's right to damages must be considered on the basis of plaintiff's mental and physical condition at birth and her expected condition during the short life span (four years according to the complaint) anticipated for one with her impaired condition. In similar fashion, we reject the notion that a 'wrongful-life' cause of action involves an attempted evaluation of a claimed right *not* to be born. In essence, we construe the 'wrongful-life' cause of action by the defective child as the right of such child to recover damages for the pain and suffering to be endured during the limited life span available to such a child and any special pecuniary loss resulting from the impaired condition.

The approach in *Curlender* was subsequently modified by the Supreme Court of California in the following case.

Turpin v Sortini (1982) 643 P 2d 954 (Sup Ct Cal)

Kaus J: This case presents the question of whether a child born with an hereditary affliction may maintain a tort action against a medical care provider who – before the child's conception – negligently failed to advise the child's parents of the possibility of the hereditary condition, depriving them of the opportunity to choose not to conceive the child. Although the overwhelming majority of decisions in other jurisdictions recognise the right of *the parents* to maintain an action under these circumstances, the out-of-state cases have uniformly denied *the child's* right to bring what has been commonly termed a 'wrongful life' action. In *Curlender v Bio-Science Laboratories* (1980) 106 Cal App 3d 811, 165 Cal Rptr 477, however, the Court of Appeal, 119 Cal App 3d 690, 174 Cal Rptr 128, concluded that under California common law tort principles, an afflicted child could maintain such an action and could 'recover damages for the pain and suffering to be endured during the limited life span available to such a child and any special pecuniary loss resulting from the impaired condition' (*id*, at p 831, 165 Cal Rptr 477), including the costs of medical care to the extent such costs were not recovered by the child's parents. In the case at bar, a different panel of the Court of Appeal disagreed with the conclusion in *Curlender* and affirmed a trial court judgment dismissing the child's cause of action on demurrer. We granted a hearing to resolve the conflict. . . .

The allegations of the complaint disclose the following facts. On September 24, 1976, James and Donna Turpin, acting on the advice of their paediatrician, brought their first – and at that time their only – daughter, Hope, to the Leon S Peters Rehabilitation Center at the Fresno Community Hospital for evaluation of a possible hearing defect. Hope was examined and tested by Adam J Sortini, a licensed professional specialising in the diagnosis and treatment of speech and hearing defects.

The complaint alleges that Sortini and other persons at the hospital negligently examined, tested and evaluated Hope and incorrectly advised her paediatrician that her hearing was within normal limits when, in reality, she was 'stone deaf' as a result of an hereditary ailment. Hope's parents did not learn of her condition until October 15, 1977 when it was diagnosed by other specialists. According to the complaint, the nature of the condition is such that there is a 'reasonable degree of medical probability' that the hearing defect would be inherited by any offspring of James and Donna.

The complaint further alleges that in December 1976, before learning of Hope's true condition and relying on defendant's diagnosis, James and Donna conceived a second child, Joy. The complaint avers that had the Turpins known of Hope's hereditary deafness they would not have conceived Joy. Joy was born August 23, 1977, and suffers from the same total deafness as Hope.

On the basis of these facts, James, Donna, Hope and Joy filed a complaint setting forth four causes of action against defendants Sortini, the hospital, the rehabilitation center and various Does. The first cause of action, brought on behalf of Hope, seeks damages for the harm Hope has allegedly suffered as a result of the delay in the diagnosis of her condition. The second cause of action – the only cause before us on this appeal – was brought on behalf of Joy and seeks (1) general damages for being 'deprived of the fundamental right of a child to be born as a whole, functional human being without total deafness' and (2) special damages for the 'extraordinary expenses for specialised teaching, training and hearing equipment' which she will incur during her lifetime as a result of her hearing impairment. The third and fourth causes of action, brought on behalf of James and Donna, seek, respectively, special damages relating to the support and medical care of Joy to the age of majority, and general damages for emotional distress sustained by James and Donna 'attendant to the raising and caring of a totally deaf child'. . . .

The explanation for the divergent results [in other jurisdictions] is that while courts have been willing to permit parents to recover for medical costs or – in some cases – other harms which the parents would not have incurred 'but for' the defendants' negligence, they have been reluctant to permit the child to complain when, but for the defendants' negligence, he or she would not have been born at all.

In this context the recent decisions have either concluded that the child has sustained no 'legally cognisable injury' or that appropriate damages are impossible to ascertain. . . . Defendants' basic position – supported by the numerous out-of-state authorities – is that

Joy has suffered no legally cognisable injury or rationally ascertainable damages as a result of their alleged negligence. Although the issues of 'legally cognisable injury' and 'damages' are intimately related and in some sense inseparable, past cases have generally treated the two as distinct matters and, for purposes of analysis, it seems useful to follow that approach.

With respect to the issue of legally cognisable injury, the parties agree that the difficult question here does not stem from the fact that defendants' allegedly negligent act and plaintiff's asserted injury occurred before plaintiff's birth. Although at one time the common law denied recovery for injuries inflicted before birth, California – in tune with other American jurisdictions – has long abandoned that arbitrary limitation. (See Civ Code, s 29; *Scott v McPheeters* 33 Cal App 2d 629, 92 P 2d 678 (1939). See generally Robertson, *Toward Rational Boundaries of Tort Liability for Injury to the Unborn: Prenatal Injuries, Preconception Injuries and Wrongful Life*, 1978 Duke LJ 1401, 1402-1413.) Thus, if Joy's deafness was caused by negligent treatment of her mother during pregnancy, or if it resulted from a tort committed upon her mother before conception (see, eg. *Renslowe v Mennonite Hospital* (1977) 67 Ill 2d 348 [10 Ill Dec 484, 367 NE 2d 1250]; *Bergstreser v Mitchell* (8th Circ 1978) 577 F 2d 22; Annot (1979) 91 ALR 3d 316), it is clear that she would be entitled to recover against the negligent party.

Joy's complaint attempts, in effect, to bring her action within the scope of the foregoing line of cases, asserting that as a result of defendants' negligence she was 'deprived of the fundamental right of a child to be born as a whole, functional human being without total deafness. . . .' While the *Curlender* decision did not embrace this approach to 'injury' completely – refusing to permit the plaintiff to recover for a reduced lifespan – it too maintained that the proper point of reference for measuring defendants' liability was simply plaintiff's condition after birth, insisting that '[w]e need not be concerned with the fact that had defendants not been negligent, the plaintiff might not have come into existence at all' (106 Cal App 3d at 829), and rejecting 'the notion that a "wrongful life" cause of action involves any attempted evaluation of a claimed right *not* to be born'. (Original italics.) (*Id*, at pp 830-831, 165 Cal Rptr 477.)

The basic fallacy of the *Curlender* analysis is that it ignores the essential nature of the defendants' alleged wrong and obscures a critical difference between wrongful life actions and the ordinary prenatal injury cases noted above. In an ordinary prenatal injury case, if the defendant had not been negligent, the child would have been born healthy; thus, as in a typical personal injury case, the defendant in such a case has interfered with the child's basic right to be free from physical injury caused by the negligence of others. In this case, by contrast, the obvious tragic fact is that plaintiff never had a chance 'to be born as a whole, functional human being without total deafness'; if defendants had performed their jobs properly, she would not have been born with hearing intact, but – according to the complaint – would not have been born at all.

A plaintiff's remedy in tort is compensatory in nature and damages are generally intended not to punish a negligent defendant but to restore an injured person as nearly as possible to the position he or she would have been in had the wrong not been done. (See generally Rest 2d Torts, s 901, com a; *Stills v Gratton, supra*, 55 Cal App 3d at 706, 127 Cal Rptr 652; 4 Witkin, Summary of Cal Law (8th ed 1974) Torts, s 842, p 3137 and cases cited.) Because nothing defendants could have done would have given plaintiff an unimpaired life, it appears inconsistent with basic tort principles to view the injury for which defendants are legally responsible solely by reference to plaintiff's present condition without taking into consideration the fact that if defendants had not been negligent she would not have been born at all. (See Capron, *Tort Liability and Genetic Counseling* (1979) 79 Colum L Rev 619, 654-657; Comment *'Wrongful Life': The Right Not to be Born* (1980) 54 Tulane L Rev 480, 494-497.)

If the relevant injury in this case is the change in the plaintiff's position attributable to the tortfeasor's actions, then the injury which plaintiff has suffered is that, as a result of defendants' negligence, she has been born with an hereditary ailment rather than not being born at all. Although plaintiff has not phrased her claim for general damages in these terms, most courts and commentators have recognised that the basic claim of 'injury' in wrongful life cases is '[i]n essence . . . that [defendants], through their negligence, [have] forced upon [the child] the worse of . . . two alternatives[,] . . . that nonexistence – never being born – would have been preferable to existence in [the] diseased state'. (*Speck v Finegold* 268 Pa Super 342, 408 A 2d 496, 511-512 (1979) (conc & dis opn by Spaeth J), affd (1981) 439 A 2d 110.)

Given this view of the relevant injury which the plaintiff has sustained at the defendants' hands, some courts have concluded that the plaintiff has suffered no legally cognisable injury on the ground that considerations of public policy dictate a conclusion that life – even with the most severe of impairments – is, as a matter of law, always preferable to nonlife. The decisions frequently suggest that a contrary conclusion would 'disavow' the sanctity and value of less-than-perfect human life. (See, eg, *Berman v Allan, supra*, 404 A 2d at 12-13; *Phillips v United States, supra*, 508 F Supp at 543.)

Although it is easy to understand and to endorse these decisions' desire to affirm the worth and sanctity of less-than-perfect life, we question whether these considerations alone provide a sound basis for rejecting the child's tort action. To begin with, it is hard to see how an award of damages to a severely handicapped or suffering child would 'disavow' the value of life or in any way suggest that the child is not entitled to the full measure of legal and nonlegal rights and privileges according to all members of society.

Moreover, while our society and our legal system unquestionably place the highest value on all human life, we do not think that it is accurate to suggest that this state's public policy establishes – as a matter of law – that under all circumstances 'impaired life' is 'preferable' to 'nonlife'. For example, Health and Safety Code section 7186, enacted in 1976, provides in part: 'The Legislature finds that adult persons have the fundamental right to control the decisions relating to the rendering of their own medical care, including the decision to have life-sustaining procedures withheld or withdrawn in instances of terminal condition. . . . The Legislature further finds that, in the interest of protecting individual autonomy, such prolongation of life for persons with a terminal condition may cause loss of patient dignity and unnecessary pain and suffering, while providing nothing medically necessary or beneficial to the patient.' This statute recognises that – at least in some situations – public policy supports the right of each individual to make his or her own determination as to the relative value of life and death. (Cf *Matter of Quinlan* (1976) 70 NJ 10 [355 A 2d 647, 662-664]; *Superintendent of Belchertown v Saikewicz* (1977) 373 Mass 728 [370 NE 2d 417, 423-427].)

Of course, in the wrongful life context, the unborn child cannot personally make any choice as to the relative value of life or death. At that stage, however, just as in the case of an infant after birth, the law generally accords the parents the right to act to protect the child's interests. As the wrongful birth decisions recognise, when a doctor or other medical care provider negligently fails to diagnose an hereditary problem, parents are deprived of the opportunity to make an informed and meaningful decision whether to conceive and bear a handicapped child. (See, eg, *Robak v United States, supra* 658 F 2d 471 at 476; *Berman v Allan, supra*, 404 A 2d 8 at 1; *Jacobs v Theimer, supra*, 519 SW 2d 846 at 849; cf *Cobbs v Grant* (1972) 8 Cal 3d 229 at 242-243, 104 Cal Rptr 505, 502 P 2d 1.) Although in deciding whether or not to bear such a child parents may properly, and undoubtedly do, take into account their own interests, parents also presumptively consider the interests of their future child. Thus, when a defendant negligently fails to diagnose an hereditary ailment, he harms the potential child as well as the parents by depriving the parents of information which may be necessary to determine whether it is in the child's own interest to be born with defects or not to be born at all.

In this case, in which the plaintiff's only affliction is deafness, it seems quite unlikely that a jury would ever conclude that life with such a condition is worse than not being born at all. Other wrongful life cases, however, have involved children with much more serious, debilitating and painful conditions, and the academic literature refers to still other, extremely severe hereditary diseases. Considering the short life span of many of these children and their frequently very limited ability to perceive or enjoy the benefits of life, we cannot assert with confidence that in every situation there would be a societal consensus that life is preferable to never having been born at all.

While it thus seems doubtful that a child's claim for general damages should properly be denied on the rationale that the value of impaired life, as a matter of law, always exceeds the value of nonlife, we believe that the out-of-state decisions are on sounder grounds in holding that – with respect to the child's claim for pain and suffering or other general damages – recovery should be denied because (1) it is simply impossible to determine in any rational or reasoned fashion whether the plaintiff has in fact suffered an injury in being born impaired rather than not being born, (2) even if it were possible to overcome the first hurdle, it would be impossible to assess general damages in any fair, nonspeculative manner.

. . . We believe . . . however, that there is a profound qualitative difference between the difficulties faced by a jury in assessing general damages in a normal personal injury or wrongful death action, and the task before a jury in assessing general damages in a wrongful life case. In the first place, the problem is not . . . simply the fixing of damages for a conceded injury, but the threshold question of determining whether the plaintiff has in fact suffered an injury by being born with an ailment as opposed to not being born at all. As one judge explained: 'When a jury considers the claim of a once-healthy plaintiff that a defendant's negligence harmed him – for example, by breaking his arm – the jury's ability to say that the plaintiff has been "injured" is manifest, for the value of a healthy existence over an impaired existence is within the experience [or] imagination of most people. The value of nonexistence – its very nature – however, is not.' (*Speck v Finegold, supra*, 408 A 2d at p 512 (Spaeth J, conc & dis), affd 439 A 2d 110.)

Furthermore, the practical problems are exacerbated when it comes to the matter of arriving at an appropriate award of damages. As already discussed, in fixing damages in a tort case the jury generally compares the condition plaintiff would have been in but for the tort, with the position the plaintiff is in now, compensating the plaintiff for what has been lost as a result of the wrong. Although the valuation of pain and suffering or emotional distress in terms of dollars and cents is unquestionably difficult in an ordinary personal injury action, jurors at least have some frame of reference in their own general experience to appreciate what the plaintiff has lost – normal life without pain and suffering. In a wrongful life action, that simply is not the case, for what the plaintiff has 'lost' is not life without pain and suffering but rather the unknowable status of never having been born. In this context, a rational, nonspeculative determination of a specific monetary award in accordance with normal tort principles appears to be outside the realm of human competence.

The difficulty in ascertaining or measuring an appropriate award of general damages in this type of case is also reflected in the application of what is sometimes referred to as the 'benefit' doctrine in tort damages. Section 920 of the Restatement Second of Torts – which embodies the general California rule on the subject (see, eg *Maben v Rankin* (1961) 55 Cal 2d 139, 144, 10 Cal Rptr 353, 358 P.2d 681) – provides that '[w]hen the defendant's tortious conduct has caused harm to the plaintiff . . . and in so doing has conferred a special benefit to the interest of the plaintiff that was harmed, the value of the benefit conferred is considered in mitigation of damages, to the extent that this is equitable'.

In requesting general damages in a wrongful life case, the plaintiff seeks monetary compensation for the pain and suffering he or she will endure because of his or her hereditary affliction. Under section 920's benefit doctrine, however, such damages must be offset by the benefits incidentally conferred by the defendant's conduct 'to the interest of the plaintiff that was harmed'. With respect to general damages, the harmed interest is the child's general physical, emotional and psychological well-being, and in considering the benefit to this interest which defendants' negligence has conferred, it must be recognised that as an incident of defendants' negligence the plaintiff has in fact obtained a physical existence with the capacity both to receive and give love and pleasure as well as to experience pain and suffering. Because of the incalculable nature of both elements of this harm-benefit equation, we believe that a reasoned, nonarbitrary award of general damage is simply not obtainable. . . .

Although we have determined that the trial court properly rejected plaintiff's claim for general damages, we conclude that her claim for the 'extraordinary expenses for specialised teaching, training and hearing equipment' that she will incur during her lifetime because of her deafness stands on a different footing.

Although the parents and child cannot, of course, both recover for the same medical expenses, we believe it would be illogical and anomalous to permit only parents, and not the child, to recover for the cost of the child's own medical care. If such a distinction were established, the afflicted child's receipt of necessary medical expenses might well depend on the wholly fortuitous circumstances of whether the parents are available to sue and recover such damages or whether the medical expenses are incurred at a time when the parents remain legally responsible for providing such care.

Realistically, a defendant's negligence in failing to diagnose an hereditary ailment places a significant medical and financial burden on the whole family unit. Unlike the child's claim for general damages, the damage here is both certain and readily measurable. Furthermore, in many instances these expenses will be vital not only to the child's well-being but to his or her very survival. (See *Schroeder v Perkel, supra*, 432 A 2d 834 at 841.) If, as alleged, defendants' negligence was in fact a proximate cause of the child's present and continuing need for such special, extraordinary medical care and training, we believe that it is consistent with the basic liability principles of Civil Code section 1714 to hold defendants liable for the cost of such care, whether the expense is to be borne by the parents or by the child. As Justice Jacobs of the New Jersey Supreme Court observed in his dissenting opinion in *Gleitman v Cosgrove, supra*, 227 A 2d at 703: 'While the law cannot remove the heartache or undo the harm, it can afford some reasonable measure of compensation toward alleviating the financial burdens.'

Moreover, permitting plaintiff to recover the extraordinary, additional medical expenses that are occasioned by the hereditary ailment is also consistent with the established parameters of the general tort 'benefit' doctrine discussed above. As we have seen, under that doctrine an offset is appropriate only insofar as the defendants' conduct has conferred a special benefit 'to the interest of the plaintiff that was harmed'. Here, the harm for which plaintiff seeks recompense is an economic loss, the extraordinary, out-of-pocket expenses that she will have to bear because of her hereditary ailment. Unlike the claim for general damages, defendants' negligence has conferred no incidental, offsetting benefit to this interest of plaintiff. (Cf *Schroeder v Perkel, supra*, 432 A 2d at 842.) Accordingly, assessment of these special damages should pose no unusual or insoluble problems.

In sum, we conclude that while a plaintiff-child in a wrongful life action may not recover general damages for being born impaired as opposed to not being born at all, the child – like his or her parents – may recover special damages for the extraordinary expenses necessary to treat the hereditary ailment.

Mosk J: I dissent.

An order is internally inconsistent which permits a child to recover special damages for a so-called wrongful life action, but denies all general damages for the very same tort. While the modest compassion of the majority may be commendable, they suggest no principle of law that justifies so neatly circumscribing the nature of damages suffered as a result of a defendant's negligence.

As recently as 1980, the Court of Appeal unanimously decided in *Curlender v Bio-Science Laboratories* 106 Cal App 3d 811, 165 Cal Rptr 477 (1980) that a cause of action exists for a wrongful-life tort. This court subsequently denied a petition for hearing. Thus *Curlender* was, and remains, the prevailing law of California. I see no persuasive reason to either abandon its doctrine, or to dilute its effectiveness by limiting recovery to special damages.

The revised approach in *Turpin* has been taken up in two other jurisdictions (*Harbeson v Parke-Davis Inc* (1983) 656 P 2d 483 (Wash Sup Ct) and *Procanik v Cillo* (1984) 478 A 2d 755 (NJ Sup Ct)). Most notably in the latter case, the distinguished New Jersey Supreme Court, like the California Supreme Court before it, modified its earlier view, though on this occasion it expanded liability by departing from its decisions in *Berman v Allan* (1979) 404 A 2d 8 and *Gleitman v Cosgrove* (1967) 227 A 2d 689 (1967) which we have already seen in the extracts above have been relied upon consistently by other courts to deny recovery (see Teff, 'The Action for "Wrongful Life" in England and the United States' (1985) 34 ICLQ 423).

Which common law analysis is more consistent with principle and policy? In our view, English law could adopt the approach which has found favour in *Turpin, Procanik* and *Harbeson*. To do so, the English courts could embrace the following analysis. Three issues have to be considered: what is the doctor's duty to the child? what harm known to the law does the child suffer? and what damages should be recoverable?

As regards *duty*, surely the doctor's duty is to inform of the risk of disability? This is a duty owed to the unborn child. But, of course, a doctor cannot inform an unborn child (or one not yet conceived). It must, therefore, be a duty to inform the mother on behalf of the child. The Court of Appeal in *McKay* was, consequently, wrong to see the doctor's duty as one owed *only* to the mother such that the child could not sue. Thus, the duty would not be that contemplated by the Court of Appeal in *McKay*, namely to counsel with a view to persuading the mother to agree to an abortion. Even if that were the duty in a case like *McKay*, it could not be so in a case like *Turpin v Sortini*. There, of course, the doctor's duty arises *before* conception of the child. His duty properly to provide genetic counselling cannot possibly be seen as a duty to seek to persuade a mother to have an abortion. Thus, this situation most clearly establishes that the doctor's duty is merely to provide information.

A related strand of argument can be seen in the *McKay* case. This is that public policy dictates that the law should not, or should not be seen to, encourage abortions. On this reasoning, even if the doctor's duty is to inform the mother of the risk of disability in her unborn child, to impose a duty to provide the information is tantamount to encouraging an abortion. This strand of argument does not stand up to close analysis. *Firstly*, the premise that public policy points in the direction identified by *McKay* need not be accepted. This is demonstrated by the New Jersey case of *Procanik v Cillo*.

Procanik v Cillo (1984) 478 A 2d 755 (NJ Sup Ct)

Pollock J: The infant plaintiff, Peter Procanik, alleges that the defendant doctors, Joseph Cillo, Herbert Langer, and Ernest P Greenberg, negligently failed to diagnose that his mother, Rosemary Procanik, had contracted German measles in the first trimester of the pregnancy. As a result, Peter was born with congenital rubella syndrome. Alleging that the doctors negligently deprived his parents of the choice of terminating the pregnancy, he seeks general damages for 'his pain and suffering and for 'his parents' impaired capacity to cope with his problems.' He also seeks special damages attributable to the extraordinary expenses he will incur for medical, nursing, and other health care. . . .

The Court [in *Gleitman v Cosgrove* (1967) 227 A 2d 689] denied the parents' claim for emotional distress and the costs of caring for the infant, because of the impossibility of weighing the intangible benefits of parenthood against the emotional and monetary injuries sustained by them. Prevailing policy considerations, which *included a reluctance to acknowledge the availability of abortions and the mother's right to choose to terminate her pregnancy*, prevented the Court from awarding damages to a woman for not having an abortion. Another consideration was the Court's belief that '[i]t is basic to the human condition to seek life and hold on to it however heavily burdened.' 49 *NJ* at 30, 227 *A* 2d 689.

In the seventeen years that have elapsed since the *Gleitman* decision, both this Court and the United States Supreme Court have reappraised, albeit in different contexts, the rights of pregnant women and their children. The United States Supreme Court has recognized that women have a constitutional right to choose to terminate a pregnancy. *Roe v Wade*, 410 *US* 113, 93 *S Ct* 705, 35 *L Ed* 2d 147 (1973). Recognition of that right by the high court subsequently influenced this Court in *Berman v Allan*, *supra*, 80 *NJ* 421, 404 *A* 2d 8.

In *Berman*, the parents sought to recover for their emotional distress and for the expenses of raising a child born with Down's Syndrome. Relying on *Roe v Wade*, *supra*, 410 *US* 113, 93 *S Ct* 705, 35 *L Ed*.2d 147, the Court found that public policy now supports the right of a woman to choose to terminate a pregnancy. *Berman v Allan*, *supra*, 80 *NJ* at 431-32, 404 *A*.2d 8. That finding eliminated one of the supports for the *Gleitman* decision – *i.e.* that public policy prohibited an award for depriving a woman of the right to choose whether to have an abortion [our emphasis].

Here, the New Jersey court follows the reasoning we have seen in *Turpin* even though the doctor's negligence concerned his failure to provide the plaintiff's mother with information that might lead to her choose to *abort* the plaintiff.

Secondly, if public policy were as the Court of Appeal would lead us to believe in *McKay*, it would suggest that the parents' related action for 'wrongful birth' (on which see below) should not be allowed as it too would be contrary to public policy. The parents' claim *also* turns upon the doctor's failure to inform the mother and thereby deprive her of the choice of whether or not to have an abortion (see *Rance v Mid-Downs HA* [1991] 1 All ER 801).

Thirdly, it is surely difficult to sustain the public policy argument given the existence of the Abortion Act 1967. The fact that Parliament has made available in a given case the opportunity of an abortion, in itself destroys the public policy argument: a point made by the New Jersey court in the context of the American constitutional 'right to choose to terminate a pregnancy'.

Fourthly, of course, the *McKay* argument could have no application in a case like *Turpin* where the doctor's negligence occurs before the plaintiff's conception. In such a case the negligent genetic counselling deprives the parents of the choice of whether or not to *conceive* the plaintiff.

As regards the second question, namely that of what harm the child has suffered, there are two possibilities. They are that the child is *born disabled* or that it suffers *economic loss* arising out of its disability. The Court of Appeal in *McKay* chose the first option and held that it was not a harm recognised in law. The better view is that the child's loss is financial. Of course, this would bring into play the restrictive rules relating to the recovery of damages for economic loss currently imposed by the House of Lords. Even on these restrictive rules, however, there is a perfectly respectable argument that the relationship between the doctor and mother acting on behalf of the child is sufficiently close (and indeed is quintessentially one of reliance) that the nature of the child's harm is no impediment to the claim (see by analogy the reasoning of Clarke JA in *X and Y v Pal, supra*, pp 942-943).

As regards the final question, namely that of damages, the Court of Appeal's insistence that damages for pain and suffering and for being disabled are incalculable is no reason for denying recovery of the child's past or future financial loss, as the American cases make clear.

(b) Disadvantaged life

So far we have been concerned with cases about children born disabled. Would the common law allow any action if the complaint is that the child has been born into circumstances that are alleged to be disadvantaged but the child is otherwise whole and healthy? Early in the development of this area of tort law, the American courts rejected claims of this kind.

Williams v State of New York (1966) 223 NE 2d 343 (NY CA)

Chief Judge, Desmond: We are to decide whether the infant claimant Christine Williams (the claim of her mother Lorene Williams is not before us now) has alleged a sufficient cause of action against the State of New York. The claim asserts negligence of the State in the care and custody of the infant's mother while the latter was a patient at a State hospital for the mentally ill 'and more particularly in failing to provide adequate, sufficient and proper care and supervision over her while she was in the custody of the State and in negligently failing to protect and safeguard her health and physical body from attack and harm from others, which negligence resulted in the infant Christine Williams being conceived, being born and being born out of wedlock to a mentally deficient mother'. The theory of suit becomes clearer when we examine the paragraph where the particulars of claimant's damage are set out thus: as a result of this neglect of the State, the child has been 'deprived of property rights; deprived of a normal childhood and home life; deprived of proper parental care, support and rearing; caused to bear the stigma of illegitimacy'.

No such theory of suit has ever before, it seems, been put forward in any court anywhere (the closest being *Zepeda v Zepeda*, 41 Ill App 2d 240, 190 NE 2d 849, cert den 379 US 945, 85 S Ct 444, 13 L Ed 2d 545, of which more will be said hereafter). The Court of Claims Judge who heard the motion thought that this lack of precedent was not fatal, and that recovery of damages was possible since there had been a wrong by the State with resulting and reasonably to be anticipated harm to the child. The Appellate Division, reversing the Court of Claims and dismissing the claim, rejected the idea that there could be an obligation of the State to a person not yet conceived and, secondly, the Appellate Division held that the 'damages' are not susceptible of ascertainment, resting as they do 'upon the very fact of conception'.

Impossibility of entertaining this suit comes not so much from difficulty in measuring the alleged 'damages' as from the absence from our legal concepts of any such idea as a 'wrong' to a later-born child caused by permitting a woman to be violated and to bear an out-of-wedlock infant. If the pleaded facts are true, the State was grievously neglectful as to the mother, and as a result the child may have to bear unfair burdens as have many other sons and daughters of shame and sorrow. But the law knows no cure of compensation for it, and the policy and social reasons against providing such compensation are at least as strong as those which might be thought to favor it. Being born under one set of circumstances rather than another or to one pair of parents rather than another is not a suable wrong that is cognisable in court. The furthest reach of our law is to paternity proceedings (see Family Ct Act) and that was accomplished by statute.

In *Williams* the court relied on the following case.

Zepeda v Zepeda (1963) 190 NE 2d 849 (App Ct Ill)

Presiding Justice, Dempsey: The plaintiff is the infant son of the defendant. He seeks damages from his father because he is an illegitimate child . . . the defendant is the plaintiff's father; the defendant induced the plaintiff's mother to have sexual relations by promising to marry her; this promise was not kept and could not be kept because, unbeknown to the mother, the defendant was already married. The complaint charges that the promise was fraudulent, that the acts of the defendant were wilful and that the defendant injured the plaintiff in his person, property and reputation by causing him to be born an adulterine bastard. The plaintiff seeks damages for the deprivation of his right to be a legitimate child, to have a normal home, to have a legal father, to inherit from his father, to inherit from his parental ancestors and for being stigmatised as a bastard.

. . . An illegitimate's very birth places him under a disability. It is of this that the plaintiff complains. His adulterine birth has placed him under a permanent disability. He protests not only the act which caused him to be born but birth itself. Love of life being what it is, one may conjecture whether, if he were older, he would feel the same way. As he grows from infancy to maturity the natural instinct to preserve life may cause him to cherish his existence as much as, through his next friend, he now deplores it. But be that as it may, the quintessence of his complaint is that he was born and that he is. Herein lies the intrinsic difficulty of this case, a difficulty which gives rise to this question: are there overriding legal, social, judicial or other considerations which should preclude recognition of a cause of action?

Bearing in mind that an action for damages is implicit in any wrong that is called a tort (Prosser, Law of Torts, 2d edn, sec 1, pp 2-4) it may be inconsistent to say, as we do, that the plaintiff has been injured by a tortious act and then to question, as we do, his right to maintain an action to recover for this act. This is done deliberately, however, because on the one hand, we believe that the elements of a wilful tort are presented by the allegations of the complaint and, on the other hand, we approach with restraint the creation, by judicial sanction, of the new action required by the complaint.

Recognition of the plaintiff's claim means creation of a new tort: a cause of action for wrongful life. The legal implications of such a tort are vast, the social impact could be staggering. If the new litigation were confined just to illegitimates it would be formidable. In 1960 there were 224,330 illegitimate births in the United States, 14,262 in Illinois and 10,182 in Chicago. Vital Statistics of the United States 1960, Vol 1, secs 1, 2 (1962). Not only are there more such births year after year (in Illinois and Chicago the number in 1960 was twice that of 1950) but the ratio between illegitimate and legitimate births is increasing. This increase is attested by a report of the Illinois Department of Public Health, released in July 1962. This report revealed that in Chicago in 1961, of the 87,989 live births 11,021 were illegitimate, a ratio of eight to one. In 1951 out of 81,801 births, 5,212 were illegitimate, a ratio of fifteen to one. The present Chicago ratio is twice that of the State and more than three times that of the Nation. The number of children who remain illegitimate is also of importance in estimating possible litigation. Accurate figures are not available, but a report made in October 1962 by the Illinois Public Aid Commission disclosed that in Cook County as of December 1961 there were 54,984 illegitimate children participating in the Aid to Department Children program. How many of these were born under circumstances making legitimation impossible, the report does not reveal.

That the doors of litigation would be opened wider might make us proceed cautiously in approving a new action, but it would not deter us. The plaintiff's claim cannot be rejected because there may be others of equal merit. It is not the suits of illegitimates which give us concern, great in numbers as these may be. What does disturb us is the nature of the new action and the related suits which would be encouraged. Encouragement would extend to all others born into the world under conditions they might regard as adverse. One might seek damages for being born of a certain color, another because of race; one for being born with a hereditary disease, another for inheriting unfortunate family characteristics; one for being born into a large and destitute family, another because a parent has an unsavory reputation.

The English courts did not consider this issue before the enactment of the Congenital Disabilities (Civil Liability) Act 1976. Given the approach of the court in *McKay*, there is no doubt the English common law would adopt the same course as that taken in the American cases (see also, *Cowe v Forum Group Inc* (1991) 575 NE 2d 630 (Ind Sup Ct)).

2. The Congenital Disabilities (Civil Liability) Act 1976

(a) The conventional view

The 1976 Act resulted from the recommendations of the Law Commission contained in its Report No 60, *Report on Injuries to Unborn Children* (1974). In paragraph 89 the Law Commission concluded as follows:

> **89.** We do not think that, in the strict sense of the term, an action for 'wrongful life' should lie. In the cases referred to of negligent treatment of a woman during pregnancy and the hypothetical drug preventing spontaneous abortion, had it not been for the negligence, the child would not have been born at all. To justify an action in logic, therefore, it is necessary to argue that the child would have been better off had he never existed. Nor would it be easy to assess his damages on any logical basis for it would be difficult to establish a norm with which the plaintiff in his disabled state could be compared. He never had a chance of being born other than disabled. We have given this problem the most careful consideration and have not, we think, been unduly influenced by these considerations of logic. Law is an artefact and, if social justice requires that there should be a remedy given for a wrong, then logic should not stand in the way. A measure of damages could be artificially constructed. We react in different ways to the various situations we have postulated, but the one which is much the most likely to give rise to claims is that which arises out of medical advice. In this situation we are clear in our opinion that no cause of action should lie. Such a cause of action, if it existed, would place an almost intolerable burden on medical advisers in their socially and morally exacting role. The danger that doctors would be under subconscious pressures to advise abortions in doubtful cases through fear of an action for damages is, we think, a real one. It must not be forgotten that in certain circumstances, the parents themselves might have a claim in negligence. Similar considerations lead us to the same conclusion in respect of the negligent performance of a therapeutic abortion.

As a consequence, in *McKay* the Court of Appeal interpreted the 1976 Act as reflecting the Law Commission's conclusion. You will recall the wording of section 1(2)(b).
Section 1(2)(b) provides:

> (2) An occurrence to which this section applies is one which –
>
> . . .
> (b) affected the mother during her pregnancy, or affected her or the child in the course of its birth, so that the child is born with disabilities which would not otherwise have been present.

Ackner LJ in *McKay* stated that:

> Subsection (2)(*b*) is so worded as to import the assumption that, but for the occurrence giving rise to a disabled birth, the child would have been born normal and healthy, not that it would not have been born at all. Thus, the object of the Law Commission that the child should have no right of action for 'wrongful life' is achieved. In para 89 of the report the commission stated that they were clear in their opinion that no cause of action should lie:
>
> > Such a cause of action, if it existed, would place an almost intolerable burden on medical advisers in their socially and morally exacting role. The danger that doctors would be under subconscious pressures to advise abortions in doubtful cases through fear of an action of damages is, we think, a real one.

This view was adopted by the Royal Commission on Civil Liability and Compensation for Personal Injury (report vol 1; Cmnd 7054-I, para 1485). . . .

Thus, there can be no question of such a cause of action arising in respect of births after 22 July 1976.

Stephenson and Griffiths LJJ agreed.

(b) A challenge to this view

It may be that the wording of section 1(2)(b) is such that a 'wrongful life' action cannot be brought *under the Act* in a situation like *McKay* where during the pregnancy the doctor negligently fails to advise the mother of the risk of the child being disabled. Is it the case, however, that the common law claim, which we have argued for above, could survive the enactment of the 1976 Act? Section 4(5) provides that:

4(5) – This Act applies in respect of births after (but not before) its passing, and in respect of any such birth it replaces any law in force before its passing, whereby a person could be liable to a child in respect of disabilities with which it might be born . . .

In *McKay*, Ackner LJ infers from this that any claim at common law (if it were to exist) has been abolished. There is, however, an alternative view.

Jane Fortin 'Is the "Wrongful Life" Action Really Dead?' [1987] JSWL 306

It is submitted that in reaching [the] conclusion [that the common law was abolished] on the interpretation of the 1976 Act, the Court of Appeal in *McKay* was unduly influenced by the Law Commission's expressed intentions and that there are alternative approaches which were not considered. It is indeed clear that neither section 1, nor indeed any part of the 1976 Act itself, refers to liability which might arise in situations where the disability itself was neither caused by nor could have been prevented by medical interventions. Nevertheless, the common law supplements this statutory omission, if as argued above, there is indeed a common law duty on the doctor to advise the foetus through its mother, of the risks of disabilities resulting, for example from infection. There is, however, a further obstacle to the acceptance of such an approach, in the form of section 4(5) of the 1976 Act which was, *inter alia*, clearly intended to counter such an argument by stating that it 'replaces any law in force before its passing, whereby a person could be liable to a child in respect of disabilities with which it might be born'. Although the Court of Appeal in *McKay* was convinced that these words precluded any wrongful life action being brought on the basis of common law principles after the operation of the Act, an alternative interpretation is possible. The provisions of section 4(5) can be avoided quite simply because, in such cases, the doctor's liability does not arise '*in respect of disabilities*' themselves, since he had no part in their cause or effect. His liability arises solely due to his failure to advise on the unborn child's potential quality of life, *in the light of those disabilities*. This approach avoids the provisions of section 4(5) of the 1976 Act and consequently, a claim for wrongful life would be sustainable under the existing common law.

Of course, this argument if correct merely preserves the common law claim for 'wrongful life' in so far as it exists. A more far-reaching argument which was not addressed by the Court of Appeal in *McKay* is that the Act itself creates a 'wrongful life' claim in situations such as arose in *Turpin v Sortini*.

Section 1(2)(a) provides that:

An occurrence to which this section applies is one which –
(a)   affected either parent of the child in his or her ability to have a normal, healthy child.

In a case of negligent genetic counselling it could be argued that the doctor's failure to advise the mother of the risk of her conceiving a disabled child 'affected . . . her *ability* to have a normal, healthy child' (our emphasis). Normally, section 1(2)(a) (as we saw earlier) is interpreted to apply to pre-conception occurrences which *cause* harm to what would be an otherwise healthy child. The doctor's negligence in that context 'affects' the parent's 'ability' in the sense of her physical capacity to have a normal, healthy child. Here, the doctor's negligence only 'affects' the parent's 'ability' in the sense of her *opportunity* to have a normal, healthy child. The word 'ability' in section 1(2)(a) could certainly be interpreted as including 'opportunity'.

On that basis, providing the negligent advice leads to the parents conceiving a disabled child which they would not otherwise have done, the child could bring a claim under section 1(2)(a). Its claim, of course, would be a 'wrongful life' action since the normal, healthy child who would otherwise have been born would have been someone else.

This interpretation of section 1(2)(a) would only go so far in that it would be limited to pre-conception occurrences. Although it could be argued that the facts of *McKay* fell within section 1(2)(a), this would be so counter to the Law Commission's (and Parliament's) intent that the court would not adopt it. Perhaps this is because post-conception cases like *McKay* necessarily raise the 'spectre' of abortions (see the Law Commission's view in paragraph 89 above).

Further support for the argument that section 1(2)(a) of the 1976 Act should be interpreted to cover claims by a child alleging negligent genetic counselling is provided by section 1A of the 1976 Act. This provision, as we have seen, was introduced in 1990 to allow a child, born disabled as a result of negligence during its parents' infertility treatment, to bring a claim. In addition to covering situations where the child is caused harm by the infertility treatment, it also covers negligence in the 'selection' of the embryo that becomes the child. Here, of course, the child's claim is one for 'wrongful life' since had the selection process not been conducted negligently, the embryo would not have been selected and thus the child would not have been born. Parliament by enacting section 1A has clearly recognised a 'wrongful life' claim. Whether it appreciated this is another matter. Of course, the Act deems the child's disabilities to be 'personal . . . injuries' (s 4(3)(b)). This does not, however, alter the reality that the policy of the law appears to have shifted from that stated in *McKay*. Further, although the court's task in assessing damages is no easier in principle, this did not, apparently, deter Parliament. If, therefore, the courts are required to face up to the child's action when it arises from negligence *ex utero*, should they not equally do so when it arises from negligence before conception?

Actions by the parents

We have up to this point been concerned with the circumstances in which a disabled or disadvantaged child may bring a claim arising out of negligence occurring before its birth. We now turn to consider the claim a *parent* may have in respect of the birth of either a healthy child following, for example, a failed sterilisation ('wrongful conception') or a disabled child ('wrongful birth').

A. WRONGFUL CONCEPTION

We consider here the question whether parents may bring an action following the negligence which has led to the birth of a *healthy child*. The claim may arise typically in two situations – where the negligence relates to contraceptive advice or treatment (eg a failed sterilisation); or where the negligence involves a failed abortion carried out to prevent the birth of a child who would be healthy (eg under section 1(1)(a) of the Abortion Act 1967).

1. An action in contract

Most doctors ordinarily treat patients within the NHS and in that case no contract arises between them. Sterilisation, being elective surgery, is quite commonly practised outside the NHS in circumstances where a contract *will* arise. As in any action in contract, the ability of a party to recover in any action depends upon the terms of the contract.

Those advising doctors will undoubtedly take their lead from the two cases and so draft their terms that it would be most unlikely that an action could sound in contract if it could not sound in tort. The two cases are *Thake v Maurice* and *Eyre v Measday*. Both raise the issue of what the doctor contracts to do: in particular, whether there is a guarantee of sterility.

Eyre v Measday [1986] 1 All ER 488 (CA)

In 1978 when the plaintiff and her husband decided that they did not wish to have any more children the plaintiff consulted the defendant gynaecologist with a view to undergoing a sterilisation operation. The defendant explained to the couple the nature of the particular operation he intended to perform, emphasising that it was irreversible. He stated that the operation 'must be regarded as a permanent procedure' but he did not inform the plaintiff that there was a small risk (less than 1%) of pregnancy occurring following the operation. Consequently, both the plaintiff and her husband believed that the result of the operation would be to render her absolutely sterile and incapable of bearing further children. In 1979 the plaintiff became pregnant and gave birth to a child. The plaintiff brought an action against the defendant for damages for, inter alia, breach of contract, contending that his representation that the operation was irreversible and his failure to warn her of the minute risk of the procedure being unsuccessful amounted to a breach of the contractual term, or express or implied collateral warranty, to render her irreversibly sterile. The judge dismissed her claim and the plaintiff appealed to the Court of Appeal.

Slade LJ: It is, I think, common ground that the relevant contract between the parties in the present case was embodied as to part in the oral conversations which took place between the plaintiff and her husband and the defendant at the defendant's consulting rooms, and as to the other part in the written form of consent signed by the plaintiff, which referred to the explanation of the operation which had been given in that conversation. It is also common ground, I think, that, in order to ascertain what was the nature and what were the terms of that contract, this court has to apply an objective rather than a subjective test. The test thus does not depend on what either the plaintiff or the defendant *thought* were the terms of the contract in her or his own mind. It depends on what the court objectively considers that the words used by the respective parties must be reasonably taken to have meant. It would, therefore, be of no assistance to the defendant to say that he did not intend to enter into a contract which absolutely guaranteed the plaintiff's future sterility. It would likewise be of no assistance to the plaintiff to say that she firmly believed that she was being offered a contract of this nature.

I now turn to the first of the two principal issues which I have indicated. At the start of his argument for the plaintiff counsel indicated that his primary ground of appeal would be that the effect of the contract between the plaintiff and the defendant was one by which the defendant contracted to render the plaintiff absolutely sterile. That, of course, was the effect of Peter Pain J's decision on the particular facts of *Thake v Maurice* [1984] 2 All ER 513 [reversed on appeal, [1986] 1 All ER 497, see below]. Nevertheless, on the facts of this case, I, for my part, find this contention quite impossible to sustain. It seems to me quite clear from the evidence which we have as to the conversation which took place between the plaintiff and her husband and the defendant at the defendant's consulting rooms that he explained to them that the operation which he would propose to perform on the plaintiff was an operation by way of *laparoscopic sterilisation* and that that was the method he intended to adopt and no other. Equally, that was the nature of the operation to which the plaintiff herself agreed, as is shown by the form of consent which she signed. The contract was, to my mind, plainly a contract by the defendant to perform that particular operation.

The matter may be tested in this way. Suppose that when the plaintiff had been under anaesthetic the defendant had formed the view that an even more effective way of sterilising her would be to perform a hysterectomy and had carried out that operation, the plaintiff would, of course, have had the strongest grounds for complaint. She could have said:

> I did not give you a general discretion to perform such operation as you saw fit for the purpose of sterilising me. I gave my consent to one particular form of operation. That was the operation I asked you to do and that was the operation you agreed to do.

In the end, as I understood him, counsel for the plaintiff did not feel able to press his argument on the first issue very strongly. The nature of the contract was, in my view, indubitably one to perform a laparoscopic sterilisation.

That, however, is by no means the end of the matter. The question still arises: did the defendant give either an express warranty or an implied warranty to the effect that the result of the operation when performed would be to leave the plaintiff absolutely sterile? In response to our inquiry counsel for the plaintiff helpfully listed the two particular passages in the evidence on which he relied for the purpose of asserting that there was an *express* warranty. The first was a passage where, in the course of examination by her counsel, the plaintiff said:

> We went to the consulting rooms and we saw Mr Measday and we discussed sterilisation. He told us the method that he used for sterilising was the clip. He told us once I had had it done it was irreversible.

Counsel for the plaintiff also relied on a passage in which the plaintiff was asked in chief:

> *Q.* Did he show you a clip? *A.* He showed us a clip and he also showed us the diagram and told us where the clips go on the tubes. He said once I had the operation done there was no turning back, I could not have it reversed.

Counsel for the plaintiff referred us to para 2 of the defence in the action which read as follows:

> On the 30th October 1978 the Plaintiff consulted the Defendant about an operation of sterilisation. The Defendant examined her and agreed to carry out the operation and advised her that it must be regarded as a permanent procedure. He did not warn the Plaintiff of the slight risk of failure, nor did he guarantee success.

There was thus a specific admission in the defence that the defendant advised the plaintiff that it must be 'regarded as a permanent procedure'.

In the light of these various representations or statements by the defendant, counsel for the plaintiff submitted that it was being expressly represented to the plaintiff that the effect of the operation would be to render her sterile absolutely and for ever. I, for my part, cannot accept that submission. There has been some discussion in the course of argument on the meaning of the phrase 'irreversible' and as to the relevance of the statement, undoubtedly made by the defendant to the plaintiff, that the proposed operation must be regarded as being irreversible. However, I take the reference to irreversibility as simply meaning that the operative procedure in question is incapable of being reversed, that what is about to be done cannot be undone. I do not think it can reasonably be construed as a representation that the operation is bound to achieve its acknowledged object, which is a different matter altogether. For my part, I cannot spell out any such express warranty as is asserted from the particular passages in the evidence and in the pleadings relied on by counsel for the plaintiff to support it, or from any other parts of the evidence. . . .

The test to be applied by the court in considering whether a term can or cannot properly be implied in a contract is that embodied in what is frequently called the doctrine of *The*

Moorcock (1889) 14 PD 64, [1886-90] All ER Rep 530. It is conveniently set out in 9 Halsbury's Laws (4th edn) para 355:

> A term can only be implied if it is necessary in the business sense to give efficacy to the contract; that is if it is such a term that it can confidently be said that if at the time the contract was being negotiated someone had said to the parties, 'What will happen in such a case', they would both have replied, 'Of course, so and so will happen; we did not trouble to say that; it is too clear.'

Counsel for the plaintiff, in the light of the passage in cross-examination which I have just read and in the light of all the other background of the case to which I have referred, submitted that if someone had said to the parties, 'Is it intended that the defendant should warrant that the operation will render the plaintiff absolutely sterile?', the answer of both parties must have been, 'Yes.' This, he submitted, is really the only possible inference from what had been said on both sides in the defendant's consulting rooms. He particularly drew attention to the question that he had put to the defendant, 'Would it have been reasonable for her to have gone away from your consulting rooms thinking that she would be sterilised and that would be the end of the matter?', to which the defendant had replied, 'Yes, it would.' Counsel for the plaintiff submitted that the defendant himself was thus acknowledging that the reasonable inference would have been as he suggested.

Applying *The Moorcock* principles, I think there is no doubt that the plaintiff would have been entitled reasonably to assume that the defendant was warranting that the operation would be performed with reasonable care and skill. That, I think, would have been the inevitable inference to be drawn, from an objective standpoint, from the relevant discussion between the parties. The contract did, in my opinion, include an implied warranty of that nature. However, that inference on its own does not enable the plaintiff to succeed in the present case. She has to go further. She has to suggest, and it is suggested on her behalf, that the defendant, by necessary implication, committed himself to an unqualified guarantee as to the success of the particular operation proposed, in achieving its purpose of sterilising her, even though he were to exercise all due care and skill in performing it. The suggestion is that the guarantee went beyond due care and skill and extended to an unqualified warranty that the plaintiff would be absolutely sterile.

On the facts of the present case, I do not think that any intelligent lay bystander (let alone another medical man), on hearing the discussion which took place between the defendant and the other two parties, could have reasonably drawn the inference that the defendant was intending to give any warranty of this nature. It is true that in cross-examination he admitted that it would have been reasonable for the plaintiff to have gone away from his consulting rooms thinking that she would be sterilised. He did not, however, admit that it would have been reasonable for her to have left his consulting rooms thinking that he had given her a *guarantee* that after the operation she would be absolutely sterile; this, I think, is the really relevant point. She has to say that this would have been the reasonable inference from what she said to her and from what she and her husband said to him. But, in my opinion, in the absence of any express warranty, the court should be slow to imply against a medical man an unqualified warranty as to the results of an intended operation, for the very simple reason that, objectively speaking, it is most unlikely that a responsible medical man would intend to give a warranty of this nature. Of course, objectively speaking, it is likely that he would give a guarantee that he would do what he had undertaken to do with reasonable care and skill; but it is quite another matter to say that he has committed himself to the extent suggested in the present case.

Purchas LJ and Sir Roualeyn Cumming-Bruce agreed.

You may think that Slade LJ's discussion of the word 'irreversible' and his application of the *Moorcock* principle has an element of the unreal about it. The contract arguments were further explored in the next case, concerned, this time, with a vasectomy.

Thake v Maurice [1986] QB 644, [1986] 1 All ER 497 (CA)

The plaintiffs, a married couple, did not wish to have any more children and consulted the defendant to see whether the first plaintiff could be sterilised by vasectomy. The first plaintiff signed a form stating that he consented to undergo the vasectomy operation, which was carried out by the defendant in October 1975. In 1977 the second plaintiff became pregnant but failed to recognise the symptoms until it was too late for an abortion. In 1978 she gave birth to a baby girl. The plaintiffs brought an action against the defendant claiming that their contract with the defendant was a contract to sterilise the first plaintiff and that that contract had been broken when he became fertile again, alternatively that they were induced to enter into the contract by a false warranty or innocent misrepresentation that the operation would render the first plaintiff permanently sterile, or in the further alternative that the defendant had failed to warn them that there was a small risk that the first plaintiff might become fertile again. There was no suggestion that the defendant had not performed the operation properly, and at the time of the operation it was known in medical circles that in rare cases the effect of the operation could be reversed naturally. The judge held, inter alia, that the defendant was in breach of a contract to make the first plaintiff irreversibly sterile. The defendant appealed to the Court of Appeal.

Neill LJ: It is common ground that the defendant contracted to perform a vasectomy operation on Mr Thake and that in the performance of that contract he was subject to the duty implied by law to carry out the operation with reasonable skill and care. The question for consideration is whether in the circumstances of the instant case the defendant further undertook that he would render Mr Thake permanently sterile by means of this operation.

On behalf of the plaintiffs it is conceded that the defendant never used the word 'guarantee' in relation to the outcome of the operation, but is submitted that what the defendant said and did at the consultation on or about 25 September 1975 would have led a reasonable person in the position of the plaintiffs to the conclusion that the defendant was giving a firm promise that the operation would lead to permanent sterility.

It is not in dispute that the task of the court is to seek to determine objectively what conclusion a reasonable person would have reached having regard to (a) the words used by the defendant, (b) the demonstration which he gave and (c) the form which Mr and Mrs Thake were asked to sign.

Counsel for the plaintiffs placed particular reliance on the following matters: (1) that on more than one occasion the defendant explained to the plaintiffs that the effect of the operation was 'irreversible', subject to the remote possibility of later surgical intervention, and counsel pointed out that this explanation was reinforced by the statement in the form: 'I understand that the effect of the operation is irreversible'; (2) that the defendant agreed in evidence that the word 'irreversible' would have been understood by the plaintiffs as meaning 'irreversible by God or man'; (3) that the demonstration which the defendant gave with his hands and arms and the sketch which he drew have led the plaintiffs to believe that, because a piece of the vas was to be severed and the severed ends were to be turned back, there was no possibility whatever of the channels being reunited unless some further surgery took place; (4) that the defendant stated that two sperm tests were required to ensure that the operation was successful; this statement would have strengthened the impression given to his listeners that the operation when completed would render the patient sterile.

. . . For my part, however, I remain unpersuaded. It seems to me that it is essential to consider the events of 25 September 1975 and the words which the defendant used against the background of a surgeon's consulting room. It is the common experience of mankind that the results of medical treatment are to some extent unpredictable and that any treatment may be affected by the special characteristics of the particular patient. It has been well said that 'the dynamics of the human body of each individual are themselves individual'.

I accept that there may be cases where, because of the claims made by a surgeon or physician for his method of treatment, the court is driven to the conclusion that the result of the treatment is guaranteed or warranted. But in the present case I do not regard the statements made by the defendant as to the effect of his treatment as passing beyond the realm of expectation and assumption. It seems to me that what he said was spoken partly by way of warning and partly by way of what is sometimes called 'therapeutic reassurance'.

Both the plaintiffs and the defendant expected that sterility would be the result of the operation and the defendant appreciated that that was the plaintiffs' expectation. This does not mean, however, that a reasonable person would have understood the defendant to be giving a binding promise that the operation would achieve its purpose or that the defendant was going further than to give an assurance that he expected and believed that it would have the desired result. Furthermore, I do not consider that a reasonable person would have expected a responsible medical man to be intending to give a guarantee. Medicine, though a highly skilled profession, is not, and is not generally regarded as being, an exact science. The reasonable man would have expected the defendant to exercise all the proper skill and care of a surgeon in that speciality; he would not in my view have expected the defendant to give a guarantee of 100% success.

Accordingly, though I am satisfied that a reasonable person would have left the consulting room thinking that Mr Thake would be sterilised by the vasectomy operation, such a person would not have left thinking that the defendant had given a *guarantee* that Mr Thake would be absolutely sterile.

Nourse LJ: The function of the court in ascertaining, objectively, the meaning of words used by contracting parties is one of everyday occurrence. But it is often exceedingly difficult to discharge it where the subjective understandings and intentions of the parties are clear and opposed. Here the plaintiffs understood that Mr Thake would be permanently sterile. The defendant himself recognised that they would have been left with that impression. On the other hand, he did not intend, and on the state of his knowledge he could not have intended, to guarantee that that would be the case. Both the understanding and the intention appear to them, as individuals, to have been entirely reasonable, but an objective interpretation must choose between them. In the end the question seems to be reduced to one of determining the extent of the knowledge which is to be attributed to the reasonable person standing in the position of the plaintiffs. Would he have known that the success of the operation, either because it depended on the healing of human tissue, or because in medical science all things, or nearly all things, are uncertain, could not be guaranteed? If he would, the defendant's words could only have been reasonably understood as forecasts of an almost certain, but nevertheless uncertain, outcome and his visual demonstrations as no more than explanations of how the operation would be done. He could not be taken to have given a guarantee of its success.

I do not suppose that a reasonable person standing in the position of the plaintiffs would have known that a vasectomy is an operation whose success depends on a healing of human tissue which cannot be guaranteed. To suppose that would be to credit him with an omniscience beyond all reason. But it does seem to me to be reasonable to credit him with the more general knowledge that in medical science all things, or nearly all things, are uncertain. That knowledge is part of the general experience of mankind, and in my view it makes no difference whether what has to be considered is some form of medical or surgical treatment or the excision, apparently final, of a section of the vas. Doubtless the general experience of mankind will acknowledge the certainty that a limb, once amputated, has gone forever. Such has been the observation from time immemorial of a species to whom the spectacle of war and suffering is commonplace. But where an operation is of modern origin, its effects untried over several generations, would a reasonable person, confronted even with the words and demonstrations of the defendant in this case, believe that there was not one chance in ten thousand that the object would not be achieved? I do not think that he would.

Nourse LJ's reasoning echoes that of Slade LJ in *Eyre* but equally seems to depart from the approach to contract law ordinarily adopted by the courts. The dissenting view of Kerr LJ more closely reflects the orthodox approach.

Kerr LJ: On this appeal it was common ground that the court's task was to determine objectively the terms of the contract whereby the defendant offered and agreed to operate on the male plaintiff. What would a reasonable person in the position of Mr and Mrs Thake have concluded in that regard? Was it merely that the defendant would perform a vasectomy operation subject to the duty implied by law that he would do so with reasonable skill and care? Or was it that the defendant would perform this operation so as to render Mr Thake permanently sterile? Counsel for the defendant submitted that, even if the latter was the correct objective construction of the terms of the offer made by the defendant, it was nevertheless not so understood by Mr and Mrs Thake. He said that this was merely what they believed would be the result of the operation, not what they believed the defendant had undertaken to do, and he relied on the decision of this court in *Allied Marine Transport Ltd v Vale do Rio Doce Navegacao SA, The Leonidas D* [1985] 2 All ER 796 at 804-805, [1985] 1 WLR 925 at 935-986. But in my view no such further question arises here, since it is plain on the evidence that Mr and Mrs Thake intended that Mr Thake should be rendered permanently sterile and believed that this is what the defendant had agreed to do. No submission on these lines was made below, and it would clearly have been rejected by the judge. The only issue is as to the objective interpretation of the offer made by the defendant once he had agreed to perform the operation.

On this issue I have reached the same conclusion as the judge. Having regard to everything that passed between the defendant and the plaintiffs at the meeting, coupled with the absence of any warning that Mr Thake might somehow again become fertile after two successful sperm tests, it seems to me that the plaintiffs could not reasonably have concluded anything other than that his agreement to perform the operation meant that, subject to two successful sperm tests, he had undertaken to render Mr Thake permanently sterile. In my view this follows from an objective analysis of the undisputed evidence of what passed between the parties, and it was also what the plaintiffs understood and intended to be the effect of the contract with the defendant.

The considerations which lead me to this conclusion can be summarised as follows. First, we are here dealing with something in the nature of an amputation, not treatment of an injury or disease with inevitably uncertain results. The nature of the operation was the removal of parts of the channels through which sperm had to pass to the outside in such a way that the channels could not reunite. This was vividly demonstrated to the plaintiffs by the defendant's pulling apart his arms and fists and turning back his wrists, as well as by a sketch. The defendant repeatedly and carefully explained that the effect of the operation was final, as the plaintiffs said again in their evidence, subject only to a remote possibility of surgical reversal, and that was the only warning which the defendant impressed on them. Subject to this and the two sperm tests of which the plaintiffs were told, designed to make sure that the operation had in fact been successful, I cannot see that one can place any interpretation on what the defendant said and did other than that he undertook to render Mr Thake permanently sterile by means of the operation. Nor can I see anything in the transcripts of the evidence which leads to any other conclusion, and the defendant himself agreed that in the context of the discussion as a whole, the word 'irreversible' would have been understood by the plaintiffs as meaning 'irreversible by God or man'. On the evidence in this case the position is quite different, in my view, from what was in the mind of Lord Denning MR in *Greaves & Co (Contractors) Ltd v Baynham Meikle & Partners* [1975] 3 All ER 99 at 103-104, [1975] 1 WLR 1095 at 1100 when he said: 'The surgeon does not warrant that he will cure the patient.' That was said in the context of treatment or an operation designed to cure, not in the context of anything in the nature of an amputation. The facts of the present case are obviously extremely unusual, but I do not see why the judge's and my conclusion on these unusual facts should be viewed by surgeons with alarm, as mentioned by the judge. If the defendant had given his usual warning, the objective analysis of what he conveyed would have been quite different.

The spate of claims arising out of failed sterilisation led to a redrafting of the standard consent forms by the government which were adopted by the defence organisations for use in private practice. The terms of the relevant consent form now fully explain the risks of failure.

> I understand
>
> that the aim of the operation is to stop me having any children and it might not be possible to reverse the effects of the operation.
>
> that sterilisation/vasectomy can sometimes fail, and that there is a very small chance that I may become fertile again after some time.
>
> For vasectomy I understand
>
> that I will have to use some other contraceptive method until 2 tests in a row show that I am not producing sperm, if I do not want to father any children.
>
> that I may remain fertile or become fertile again after some time.

(*A Guide to Consent for Examination or Treatment* (1991) National Health Service Management Executive; Appendix A(2).)

Hence, claims of the sort in *Eyre* and *Thake* are unlikely to arise in the future.

2. Negligence

We do not consider here the substantive law concerned with establishing a breach of duty arising out of a failed sterilisation (or abortion) or negligent advice. These we have dealt with earlier as a matter of general principle in Chapters 3 and 5.

(a) Duty

Having said this, we are, however, interested in the question of to whom the duty is owed. It is obvious that the doctor would owe a duty to the person whom he advised or treated. This question only becomes significant when the action is brought by someone other than the person who is treated or advised. The range of possible plaintiffs extends from the patient's husband or wife, to the casual sexual partner, to existing offspring of the patient. In England the only case where such a *plaintiff* has brought a claim was *Thake v Maurice* [1986] QB 644. Here, both the patient and his wife sued. In holding the defendant liable in tort, the court did not question the existence of a duty to the wife.

Of course, it is obvious that such a duty would be owed in a case like *Thake* where the couple are treated and advised together. The same result would probably follow if the partner was known to the doctor even though not involved in the consultation. The following case from New York illustrates the approach an English court is likely to take.

Miller v Rivard (1992) 585 NYS 2d 523 (Sup Ct NY, App Div)

Levine J: In this action, plaintiffs, John Miller and Sharon Miller, have sued defendant Capital Area Community Health Plan Inc. (hereinafter CHP) and its physician, employee, defendant Donald Rivard, for various damages arising out of the conception and subsequent birth of a normal, healthy child in January 1989. The gravamen of their suit is what courts and commentators have come to call 'wrongful conception' or 'wrongful pregnancy', ie, the negligent performance of a sterilization or abortion procedure by a physician, or the negligent filling of a contraceptive prescription by a pharmacist, as a result of which the plaintiffs conceived and became the parents of a healthy but unwanted child (see, *Weintraub v Brown*, 98 AD 2d 339, 342; see also, *Phillips v United States*, 508 F Supp 544, 545 n 1; Prosser and Keeton *Torts* s 55, at 370-372 (5th edn).

As set forth in the allegations of the complaint and in plaintiffs' submissions to Supreme Court on the cross motions for summary judgment herein, after having had three children in a period of only 2 1/2 years, plaintiffs consulted their physicians at CHP regarding sterilization to prevent a fourth pregnancy and Mr Miller was then referred to Rivard, a urologist on the staff at CHP, regarding a vasectomy. Rivard was told that a prime motivating factor was the couple's concern for Mrs Miller's physical well-being 'and the need to protect her from the ardures [sic] of another pregnancy'.

Rivard performed a vasectomy on Mr Miller on April 30, 1987. Pursuant to Rivard's instructions and as a regular part of the vasectomy procedure fertility tests were performed at CHP on Mr Miller's semen on June 30, 1987 and August 5, 1987. Also pursuant to Rivard's instructions, Mr Miller called Rivard's office two days after the second test and was advised by his nurse that the vasectomy was successful, that his sperm count was at an infertile level and that he and Mrs Miller could resume sexual relations without any other contraceptive measures. However, the following spring, Mrs Miller discovered that she was pregnant and a further fertility test revealed that Mr Miller was still fertile. Mrs Miller experienced severe medical complications during her pregnancy and delivery of the child, ultimately resulting in further surgery and the performance of a hysterectomy under emergency conditions.

Plaintiffs' suit was commenced by service of a summons and complaint on February 6, 1990. The complaint alleged defendants' negligence and malpractice with respect to the performance of the vasectomy, the fertility testing of Mr Miller and the reporting to him of the results of such testing. Causes of action were set forth for (1) Mr Miller's personal physical and emotional injuries and pecuniary losses, (2) Mrs Miller's loss of consortium while her husband was recovering from the vasectomy, (3) Mrs Miller's personal physical and emotional injuries and pecuniary losses as a result of the unwanted pregnancy and delivery of the child, (4) Mr Miller's derivative claim for loss of consortium as a result of his wife's physical injuries, and (5) both plaintiffs' claim for the expenses of rearing their fourth child until the age of majority. . . .

. . . defendants argue that the absence of a doctor-patient relationship between Rivard and Mrs Miller precludes the existence of any duty directly to her which may have been breached by malpractice committed upon her husband. Therefore, according to defendants, to permit her to recover against her husband's doctors for her own personal injuries and pecuniary losses arising from this wrongful conception, no matter how foreseeable, would be an unwarranted, unmanageable extension of traditional tort principles. We disagree. First, recognition of an independent right of recovery for Mrs Miller's own injuries from wrongful conception due to an unsuccessful vasectomy performed on her husband is fully supported by precedent. In this State, two other Departments have explicitly recognized a cause of action on behalf of the wife of a vasectomy patient against the physician who performed the procedure, for her pain and suffering and emotional distress resulting from the pregnancy and delivery of the child (see, *Weintraub v Brown* 98 AD 2d 339 [2d Dept]; *Sorkin v Lee* 78 AD 2d 180 [4th Dept], appeal dismissed 53 NY2d 797). To deny recovery to Mrs Miller on the theory that defendants' duty only extended to her husband, as their patient, also appears to be inconsistent with the holding in *Becker v Schwartz* (46 NY 2d 501). In the companion cases in *Becker*, the Court of Appeals upheld an award of damages to the plaintiff husbands as well as wives, for their respective pecuniary losses for wrongful birth, as against the wives' obstetricians, finding a breach of duty to each plaintiff spouse in the defendants' failure to give genetic advice (id., at 412-413). Moreover, affording Mrs Miller a primary cause of action on her own behalf for her physical injuries accords with the overwhelming majority position in other jurisdictions, under which each spouse is entitled to recover as damages his or her own physical, emotional and pecuniary loss from a wrongful conception, irrespective of which spouse was the actual recipient of the negligently performed sterilization, fertility testing or test result reporting (see, Prosser and Keeton, Torts s 55, at 372 [5th edn]; Annot, 83 ALR 3d 15; Annot, 27 ALR 3d 906).

Nor can we accept defendants' claim that recognizing a cause of action on Mrs Miller's behalf for her own injuries incurred from the wrongful conception caused by the vasectomy unsuccessfully performed on her husband would extend traditional tort liability beyond manageable bounds. . . .

. . . the basic parameters of the damages sought here are the same as would admittedly have been recoverable had the unsuccessful form of sterilization chosen by plaintiffs been a tubal ligation of Mrs Miller, rather than Mr Miller's vasectomy. . . . There is no sound reason in policy, fairness or in the fulfillment of the role of tort law as a deterrent to negligent conduct for there to be any distinction in exposure to liability as between medical practitioners depending upon the type of sterilization performed.

In our view, imposing liability on Mr Miller's physicians for Mrs Miller's claim, despite the lack of a doctor-patient relationship between them, also falls well within traditional tort principles. According to plaintiffs' submissions, it was not merely foreseeable that Mrs Miller might suffer serious injuries in the event of becoming pregnant as a result of any negligent performance of her husband's vasectomy or fertility testing. As Rivard was made aware, avoidance of a potentially injurious fourth pregnancy for Mrs Miller was the essential purpose of Mr Miller's undergoing the entire sterilization procedure. Such awareness is sufficient, under long-standing tort doctrine, to subject Rivard to liability for Mrs Miller's injuries resulting from his negligent performance of the procedures she relied upon, despite the lack of any direct doctor-patient relationship between them. Thus, in *Glanzer v Sheppard* (23 NY 236), the public weighers hired by the seller of beans were held liable to the buyers for negligent weighing, despite the lack of any direct relationship between them, because the buyers' reliance on the accuracy of the defendants' weight certificate 'was not an indirect or collateral consequence of the action of the weighers. It was a consequence which, to the weighers' knowledge, was the end and aim of the transaction' (id, at 230-239 [emphasis supplied]). More recently, the Court of Appeals has specifically recognized that a physician preparing a report of a medical examination may owe a duty of care to a limited class of persons other than the patient examined. 'In completing this particular report, the physician plainly owed a duty of care to his patient and to persons he knew or reasonably should have known were relying on him for this service to his patient' (*Eiseman v State of New York*, 70 NY 2d 175, 188 [emphasis supplied]).

Nor can we accept defendants' contention that granting a cause of action to Mrs Miller for her pain and suffering from wrongful conception results in unmanageable liability against physicians because it creates an arbitrary distinction between wives and other women who may incur wrongful conception as a result of an unsuccessful vasectomy performed upon their mates. Restricting recovery of tort claimants to the legal spouse or family of the person directly acted upon is not an uncommon method of limiting the scope of liability to a manageable, predictable class, as applied, for example, to derivative claims (see, *Briggs v Butterfield Mem Hosp* 104 AD 2d 626; *Rademacher v Torbensen* 257 App Div 91), and to claims for injuries from shock or fright caused by observation of the serious injury or death of another person in the plaintiff's presence (see, *Boysun v Sanperi*, 61 NY 2d 219, 231-232). For all the foregoing reasons, we uphold Supreme Court's denial of defendants' motion to dismiss the third cause of action for legal insufficiency.

Weiss PJ, Mikoll and Mercure JJ concurred.

What this case shows us is that a clear line can be drawn between the *known* (even if unidentified) sexual partner, on the one hand, and the casual sexual partner on the other. *Miller* makes this clear, referring to 'the legal spouse or family' of the patient. English law, likewise, can, for reasons of policy (ie to limit liability) restrict claims to a manageable class of known plaintiffs (see *Alcock v Chief Constable of West Yorkshire* [1992] 1 AC 310 and *Caparo Industries plc v Dickman* [1990] 2 AC 605). The word 'family' used by the court in *Miller*, however, raises a further problem. Does it mean that a sibling may bring an action for loss of a portion of the family's wealth and parental attention? In so far as this is a claim for the *loss of society of the parent*, the English common law never recognised such a claim. Loss of society by one spouse of another was actionable (*Best v Samuel Fox & Co Ltd* [1952] AC 716). Also, a parent had a claim for loss of his child's services (*Lough v Ward* [1945] 2 All ER 338). No other claims, however, were recognised (see *F v Wirral MBC* [1991] 2 All ER 648 (CA)). In any event, the policy of English law today is to reject all such actions (see, for example, the Law Reform (Miscellaneous Provisions) Act 1970 s 5, Administration of Justice Act 1982, s 2). In so far as it represents a claim for economic loss, there seems no reason in principle why a sibling's claim should not be upheld, always provided that the doctor was aware of the siblings and their material circumstances, eg if the sterilisation was sought for economic reasons. In practice, however, the siblings' loss will be part of the claim by the parents for their own economic loss, such that only rarely would they have a claim of their own of any substance.

(b) Nature of the harm

In any action the plaintiff must show that the harm he complains of is of a type which the law recognises as remediable. Here, it is critically important to identify precisely the harm complained of. What is the plaintiff in the context of failed sterilisation complaining of: becoming pregnant, giving birth, having a child to support, or having the economic burden of a child to support? If the plaintiff is the father alone, only some are, of course, relevant.

The exact nature of the harm conditions the response a court might make to the claim – ie is it physical injury or economic loss – since different legal consequences (such as limitation periods and the nature of the duty owed to the plaintiff in law) may apply.

Although this is central to a proper analytical understanding of the cause of action, the courts seem to have preferred to ignore the analytical point and assumed that some remedy ought to be available without being troubled too greatly about the precise basis of the cause of action. By so doing, it may well be that the courts have merely avoided, for the moment, the inevitable task of analysis. Brooke J grasped the nettle in *Allen v Bloomsbury HA* [1993] 1 All ER 651, (1992) 13 BMLR 47, a case involving a claim arising out of the birth of a healthy child following a failed abortion. He said:

I am content to assume that the Court of Appeal has recognised that in the unique circumstances surrounding the breach of a doctor's duty to a pregnant woman (or a woman who may become pregnant against her wishes) she should be entitled to recover damages for the two quite distinct foreseeable heads of loss which I identified when I was analysing the principles which should guide me in this case. The first, a claim for damages for personal injuries during the period leading up to the delivery of the child, is a claim which is comparable to, though different from, a claim for damages for personal injuries resulting from the infliction of a traumatic injury to a plaintiff by a negligent defendant. The second, a claim for the economic loss involved in the expense of losing paid employment and the obligation of having to pay for the upkeep and care of an unwanted child, is a totally different type of claim, although it may in turn be associated with a different type of claim for damages for the loss of amenity associated with bringing up a handicapped child.

I realise that if Parliament does not intervene this is likely to mean that different limitation periods may apply to the two types of claim, since it is hard to see how s11 of the Limitation Act 1980 would apply to a claim limited to the financial costs associated with the upbringing of the unwanted child since this would be, on the facts of a case like the present, a straightforward *Hedley Byrne* (see *Hedley Byrne & Co Ltd v Heller & Partners Ltd* [1963] 2 All ER 575, [1964] AC 465) type of claim for foreseeable economic loss caused by negligent advice or misstatement. However, this is not a matter I have to decide in this case.

Brooke J's analysis that the essence of the claim for the costs of rearing the child and for any lost income of the parents is one of economic loss seems right. A convincing demonstration of this can be found in the following decision of the New Mexico Supreme Court.

Lovelace Medical Center v Mendez (1991) 803 P 2d 603 (NM Sup Ct)

Montgomery J: Joseph Mendez was conceived after his mother, Maria Mendez, underwent a tubal ligation, which allegedly was negligently performed by a physician employee of the defendant, Lovelace Medical Center. The physician found and ligated only one of Maria's two fallopian tubes and then failed to inform her of the unsuccessful outcome of the operation. She thus remained fertile, took no birth-control precautions, and conceived Joseph in due course. He was born as a normal, healthy baby.

. . . The district court in Mr and Mrs Mendez's medical malpractice action against Lovelace granted its motion for partial summary judgment, holding as a matter of law that the costs of raising Joseph to majority were not recoverable . . .

We believe the couple suffered at least two forms of harm. First, as indicated previously, Mrs Mendez remained fertile despite her desire to be infertile. From the standpoint of the couple, their desire to limit the size of their family – to procreate no further – was frustrated. Within the *Restatement's* [*Tort* (2d)] definition of harm, this was a loss of detriment to them.

Second, their interest in financial security – in the economic stability of their family – was impaired. The undesired costs of raising another child to adulthood – costs which they had striven to avoid and had engaged Lovelace to help them avert – were suddenly thrust upon them. This was a detriment to their pecuniary advantage – ie, harm . . .

In holding that Mr and Mrs Mendez could not recover the costs of rearing Joseph to majority, the district court was declaring, in effect, that their interests in financial security and in limiting the size of their family were not worthy of legal protection.

We agree with the court of appeals that the district court was mistaken in so holding. The interest in one's economic stability is clearly an example of an interest that receives legal protection in a wide variety of contexts . . .

In the context of a negligently performed, unsuccessful sterilization operation, the Supreme Court of Wisconsin has very recently held that the costs of raising the child to majority may be recovered because, among other things:

> Individuals often seek sterilization precisely because the burdens of raising a child are substantial and they are not in a position to incur them. . . .
> . . . [T]he love, affection, and emotional support they [the parents] are prepared to give do not bring with them the economic means that are also necessary to feed, clothe, educate and otherwise raise the child. That is what this suit is about. . . . Relieving the family of the economic costs of raising the child may well add to the emotional well-being of the entire family, including this child, rather than bring damage to it.

Marciniak v Lundborg 153 Wis 2d 59, 67, 450 NW 2d 243, 246 (1990).

Other courts have allowed recovery of child-rearing costs based at least in part on the recognition that an interest to be protected in this setting is the parents' desire to safeguard the financial security of their family. *See, eg, Burke v Rivo* 406 Mass 764, 551 NE 2d 1 (1990) (but allowing off-set for emotional benefits); *University of Ariz Health Sciences Center v Superior Court* 136 Ariz 579, 667 P 2d 1294 (1983) (en banc) (allowing offset for benefits); *Ochs v Borrelli*, 187 Conn 253, 259, 445 A 2d 883, 885-86 (1982) ('raising a child from birth to maturity is a costly enterprise, and *hence injurious,* . . . parental pleasure softens but does not eradicate economic reality') (emphasis added).

In some of these cases, the courts have required that concern for economic factors must have motivated the decision to seek sterilization in order for recovery of a child-rearing expenses to be awarded. *See, eg, Burke*, 406 Mass at 773, NE 2d at 6; *University of Ariz Health Sciences Center*, 136 Ariz at 585, 667 P 2d at 1300; *Jones v Malinowski* 299 Md 257, 270, 473 A 2d 429, 436 (1984). These cases rely on *Hartke v McKelway* 707 F 2d 1544 (DC Cir 1983), in which the mother's reason for sterilization was therapeutic – *ie* to avoid the danger to herself from pregnancy – and the court held that, the danger not having materialized and a healthy baby having been born, 'the jury could of not rationally have found that the birth of this child was an injury to this plaintiff. Awarding child-rearing expenses would only give Hartke a windfall.' 707 F 2d at 1557.

The reasoning in *Jones* has much to commend it:

[T]he assessment of damages associated with the healthy child's birth, if any, should focus upon the specific interests of the parents that were *actually* impaired by the physician's negligence, *ie,* was the sterilization sought for reasons that were (a) genetic – to prevent the birth of defective child, or (b) therapeutic – to prevent harm to the mother's health or (c) economic – to avoid the additional expense of raising a child. [Emphasis in original.]

299 Md at 270-71, 473 A 2d at 436. However, we are reluctant to hold that child-rearing expenses are recoverable only when the parents' sole, or even primary, motivation is economic. A person's original reasons for seeking sterilization should not be conclusive as to whether an economic interest has been injured. A professional woman, for example, might seek sterilization for a reason unrelated to financial hardship. However, if a negligently performed sterilization results in an unexpected birth, her financial situation and even long-term prospects may abruptly change. On a practical note, the motivation rule entails difficult tasks for the jury in sorting out the parents' differing motivations and encourages after-the-fact reformulations of the parents' actual intentions. In any event, in *this* case we need not struggle with these difficulties, because the record before the district court on Lovelace's motion for summary judgment established that a powerful, if not the only, motive for Maria Mendez's seeking sterilization was to conserve family resources.

We hold, therefore, that the Mendezes' interest in the financial security of their family was a legally protected interest which was invaded by Lovelace's negligent failure properly to perform Maria's sterilization operation (if proved at trial), and that this invasion was an injury entitling them to recover damages in the form of the reasonable expenses to raise Joseph to majority.

Sosa CJ and Ransom J agreed.

Given this analysis, would the English courts accept the claim once it is realised that it is a claim for economic loss? In *Allen* Brooke J, as we have seen, had no doubt that the claim fell within the *Hedley Byrne* principle. As we saw when considering the child's claim for 'wrongful life', we too would agree with that view. It requires, however, acceptance that the principle in *Hedley Byrne* goes beyond situations of reliance upon the defendant's statement to include those where the plaintiff relies in a wider sense on the defendant's conduct to the knowledge of the defendant.

(c) Causation

As regards factual causation, no special problems arise distinct from those already identified earlier when discussing liability for a breach of duty to inform a patient (see ch 3). Hence, a plaintiff will have to show, on a balance of probabilities, that if she had been given adequate information, she would have acted in such a way as to avoid the conception of the child.

There are, however, difficulties in relation to legal causation. In particular, can a defendant argue that the birth of the child which gives rise to the claim could have been avoided by the mother's undergoing an abortion? Of course, this argument is only possible if an abortion would legally have been available (see *Rance v Mid-Downs HA* [1991] 1 All ER 801 (a 'wrongful birth' case)). If available, however, must a mother undergo an abortion?

Emeh v Kensington and Chelsea and Westminster Area Health Authority [1985] QB 1012, [1984] 3 All ER 1044 (CA)

The plaintiff, the mother of three normal children, had an abortion to terminate a fourth pregnancy and at the same time a sterilisation operation to prevent further pregnancies. The operation was performed negligently by two doctors employed by the defendant health authority and some months later the plaintiff again became pregnant, although she did not discover the fact until she was some 20 weeks' pregnant. She then decided that because she did not want any more operations she would not have another abortion but would continue with the pregnancy. She later gave birth to a child which was congenitally abnormal. She brought an action against the health authority claiming damages for, in particular, her own loss of future earnings, maintenance of the child, and pain, suffering and loss of amenity, including the extra care which the child would require. The trial judge held that the plaintiff's refusal to have an abortion was so unreasonable as to amount to a novus actus interveniens or a failure to mitigate damage and eclipse the negligence for which the health authority was responsible. The judge accordingly limited the award of damages to compensation for the plaintiff's pain and suffering up to the time she discovered the pregnancy and the pain and inconvenience of undergoing a second sterilisation operation. The plaintiff appealed.

Slade LJ: The judge, in saying that her failure to obtain an abortion was so unreasonable as to eclipse the defendants' wrongdoing, was, I think, really saying that the defendants had the right to expect that, if they had not performed the operation properly, she would procure an abortion even if she did not become aware of its existence until nearly 20 weeks of her pregnancy had elapsed.

I do not, for my part, think that the defendants had the right to expect any such thing. By their own negligence, they faced her with the very dilemma which she had sought to avoid by having herself sterilised.

For the reasons which I have attempted to give, I think that they could, and should, have reasonably foreseen that if, as a consequence of the negligent performance of the operation, she would find herself pregnant again, particularly after some months of pregnancy, she might well decide to keep the child. Indeed, for my part I would go even a little further. Save in the most exceptional circumstances, I cannot think it right that the court should ever declare it unreasonable for a woman to decline to have an abortion, in a case where there is no evidence that there were any medical or psychiatric grounds for terminating the particular pregnancy. And no such evidence has been drawn to our attention relating to this particular pregnancy of the plaintiff in the present case.

Waller LJ: Can it be said that the plaintiff's conduct was so unreasonable as to eclipse the defendants' wrongdoing? In *McKew v Holland & Hannen & Cubitts (Scotland) Ltd* [1969] 3 All ER 1621 at 1624 Lord Reid, dealing with rather different facts but in considering an argument concerning the chain of causation, said:

> But I think it right to say a word about the argument that the fact that the appellant made to jump when he felt himself falling is conclusive against him. When his leg gave way the appellant was in a very difficult situation. He had to decide what to do in a fraction of a second. He may have come to a wrong decision; he probably did. But if the chain of causation had not been broken before this by his putting himself in a position where he might be confronted with an emergency, I do not think that he would put himself out of court by acting wrongly in the emergency unless his action

was so utterly unreasonable that even on the spur of the moment no ordinary man would have been so foolish as to do what he did.

That speech of Lord Reid was concurred in by Lord Guest and Lord Upjohn.

So the degree of unreasonable conduct which is required is, on Lord Reid's view, very high. In my opinion, on the findings of the judge, even as they were, I would be disposed to say that this conduct on the part of the plaintiff was not so unreasonable as to eclipse the defendants' wrongdoing. But when there is taken into account, first of all, the judge's misunderstanding of the earlier part of the plaintiff's evidence concerning dates, when she was in fact entirely truthful, and, secondly, when one sees no reference was paid by the judge to the difference between a 20-week pregnancy and an 8-week pregnancy, it would seem that, when the plaintiff decided to have the baby and, having made that decision, she then decided to sue the defendants, her conduct could not be described as utterly unreasonable. Especially when one bears in mind that she had an argument with her husband about it, he apparently wanted her to have an abortion (and the judge accepted that evidence) that makes her decision all the more understandable.

I would therefore come to the conclusion that that finding of the judge, namely her failure to undergo an abortion was so unreasonable as to eclipse the defendants' wrongdoing, is incorrect, and that the plea of *novus actus*, or the failure to take steps to minimise the damage (in whatever way the matter is put), fails.

Purchas LJ: For my part, however, I would respectfully agree with what has fallen from Slade LJ, that it would be intolerable if a defendant, admittedly by his own admission standing charged with negligence of a professional character and having, through that negligence, placed the plaintiff in a position in which a choice or decision had to be made, was able closely to analyse that decision so as to show that it might not have been the right choice, and could thereby escape his liability.

I find it unacceptable that the court should be invited to consider critically in the context of a defence of *novus actus interveniens* the decision of a mother to terminate or not her pregnancy which has been caused by the defendants' negligence. I am satisfied that taking the features of this case as highly as one can against the plaintiff, namely that on 19 January she knew or had reason to suspect she was pregnant, her decision cannot be questioned. Although the judge put her term of pregnancy at as short a period as 16 1/2 weeks, it must be recalled that from the notes of her general practitioner he recorded and communicated to her a pregnancy period of 18 to 20 weeks. The judge, in coming to his conclusion on a break in the chain of causation, studies the professional evidence of Sir John Dewhurst, and considered the risks and inconvenience and discomfort of a further operation, matters which would not have been in the mind of the plaintiff at all in fact, and discounted her evidence, which he quoted in his judgment and then found not to be established because of his view of the motive of the plaintiff. Those were matters which, in my judgment, were not relevant to the decision within the objective test which the judge had taken from the textbook. They are decisions whether or not the plaintiff might have acted reasonably or not, in mitigation of damage, but in my judgment they certainly have no relevance to the more formal decision whether or not the chain of causation has been broken or at all.

What are the judges saying here? Firstly, Slade LJ's statement beginning 'save in the most exceptional circumstances . . .' is difficult to fathom. He appears to mean that *even if* there were evidence of (rather than 'no evidence' of) medical or psychiatric grounds for an abortion, the woman's refusal will not be deemed to be unreasonable. He qualifies this by reference to 'exceptional circumstances'. It is difficult to understand when these words would apply given that the child is healthy and even if the mother's decision is not based upon her religious beliefs or her moral views. Secondly, both Waller and Purchas LJJ leave open the possibility of the mother's decision being deemed unreasonable; since they decide the case on the basis that the plaintiff's pregnancy was well advanced at the relevant time.

(American courts have similarly rejected the defendant's plea that the woman should have had an abortion: *Burke v Rivo* (1990) 551 NE 2d 1 (Mass Sup Jud Ct) and cases cited at 4 *per* Wilkins J.)

(d) Damages

In his judgment in *Allen v Bloomsbury HA* [1993] 1 All ER 651, (1992) 13 BMLR 47, Brooke J summarised the legal principles relevant in assessing damages in claims alleging 'wrongful conception'.

Brooke J: Although a claim of this type has not yet been considered by the House of Lords, the principles on which damages are to be awarded have been considered a number of times by the Court of Appeal and I was referred to all the leading cases which have been decided in the last seven years. I derive from these cases the following principles which should guide me when I consider Mrs Allen's claim.

(1) If a doctor fails to act towards his patient with the standard of care reasonably to be expected of him, and as a foreseeable result of the doctor's breach of duty a child is born whose potential for life would have been lawfully terminated but for the doctor's negligence, the law entitles the mother to recover damages for the foreseeable loss and damage she suffers in consequence of the doctor's negligence (see *Emeh v Kensington and Chelsea and Westminster Area Health Authority* [1984] 3 All ER 1044, [1985] QB 1012).

(2) A plaintiff mother is entitled to recover general damages (and any associated financial special damage) for the discomfort and pain associated with the continuation of her pregnancy and the delivery of her child, although she must set off against this claim a sum in respect of the benefit of avoiding the pain and suffering and associated financial loss which have resulted from the termination of her pregnancy under general anaesthetic, since in the events which have happened she has not had to undergo that operation (see *Emeh's* case [1984] 3 All ER 1044 at 1056, [1985] QB 1012 at 1028 per Purchas LJ, *Thake v Maurice* [1986] 1 All ER 497 at 508, [1986] QB 644 at 682 per Kerr LJ, *Gardiner v Mounfield* (1989) 5 BMLR 1 at 5-6 per Scott Baker J).

(3) She is also entitled to damages for economic loss quite unassociated with her own physical injury which falls into two main categories: (i) the financial loss she suffers because when the unwanted baby is born she has a growing child to feed, clothe, house, educate and care for until the child becomes an adult; (ii) the financial loss she suffers because she has lost or may lose earnings or incur other expense because of her obligations towards her child which she would have sought to avoid (see *Emeh's* case [1984] 3 All ER 1044 at 1053, 1056, [1985] QB 1012 at 1025, 1028 per Slade and Purchas LJJ respectively; adopted and applied by the Court of Appeal in *Thake v Maurice* [1986] 1 All ER 497, [1986] QB 644).

(4) Although the law recognises that it is foreseeable that if an unwanted child is born following a doctor's negligence a mother may suffer wear and tear and tiredness in bringing up a healthy child, the claim for general damages she might otherwise have had on this account is generally set off against and extinguished by the benefit of bringing a healthy child into the world and seeing one's child grow up to maturity (see *Thake v Maurice* [1986] 1 All ER 497 at 508, [1986] QB 644 at 682 per Kerr LJ).

(5) However, the law is willing to recognise a claim for general damages in respect of the foreseeable additional anxiety, stress and burden involved in bringing up a handicapped child, which is not treated as being extinguished by any countervailing benefit although this head of damages is different in kind from the typical claim for anxiety and stress associated with and flowing from an injured plaintiff's own personal injuries (see *Emeh's* case [1984] 3 All ER 1044 at 1052, [1985] QB 1012 at 1022 per Waller LJ). . . .

In my judgment in this type of case defendants are liable to pay for all such expenses as may be reasonably incurred for the education and upkeep for the unplanned child, having regard to all the circumstances of the case and, in particular, to his condition in life and his reasonable requirements at the time the expenditure is incurred. . . .

If an unplanned child is born after a failure by a hospital doctor to exercise the standard of care reasonably to be expected of him and the child's parents have sent all their other children to expensive private boarding schools for the whole of their education then it appears to me that as the law now stands a very substantial claim for the cost of private education of a healthy child of a reasonably wealthy family might have to be met from the funds of the health authority responsible for the doctor's negligence. However, if this is regarded as inappropriate on policy grounds it is, as Waller LJ pointed out in *Emeh's* case, for Parliament, not the courts to determine policy questions: judges at first instance, at any rate, can do no more than try to identify and apply principles approved by the higher courts unless and until Parliament intervenes.

Our principal interest lies in the question whether the parents should be able to recover the costs associated with raising a *healthy* child. As we saw earlier, such a claim, if it is for anything, is for pure economic loss. The issue here is one of policy: whether some overriding policy considerations dictate that it should not be recovered even though ordinarily it would be.

In the cases where the costs of rearing have been claimed the courts have reached different conclusions. In *Udale v Bloomsbury Area Health Authority*, The plaintiff brought an action arising out of the negligent performance of a sterilisation. She sought compensation, *inter alia*, for the cost of rearing the fifth and unexpected child who was born healthy and normal.

Udale v Bloomsbury Area Health Authority [1983] 2 All ER 522, [1983] 1 WLR 1098 (QBD)

Jupp J: Counsel for the defendants . . . submits that as a matter of public policy damages should not be awarded for the birth of a normal, happy, healthy and, as it happens to be in this case, a much loved child. Whilst damages might be claimed if the child was handicapped or deformed, a normal child, says counsel, should as a matter of public policy be regarded as loved and wanted. I pause to emphasise that any decision of mine is not intended to deal one way or the other with an abnormal child. It would be intolerable, he says, if a child ever learned that a court had publicly declared him so unwanted that medical men were paying for his upbringing because their negligence brought him into the world. Our society, the argument runs, is founded on the basic unit of the family and assumes that children are the natural and desirable consequence of marriage and that the child's subsistence is a benefit alike to the child, the parents, the family and to society as a whole. In short, the law must assume that children are a blessing. It is pointed out that to allow claims against doctors to include the cost of bringing up a child would affect medical decisions which they might have to make whilst the child is being carried in the mother's womb. He refers to the judgment of Ackner LJ in *McKay v Essex Area Health Authority* [1982] 2 All ER 771 at 786, [1982] QB 1166 at 1187, where the Lord Justice cites the Law Commission's Report on Injuries to Unborn Children (Law Com No 60, August 1974; Cmnd 5709) para 89:

> Such a cause of action, if it existed, would place an almost intolerable burden on medical advisers in their socially and morally exacting role. The danger that doctors would be under subconscious pressures to advise abortions in doubtful cases through fear of an action of damages, is, we think, a real one.

Counsel for the defendants also submits that it would be invidious to weigh up the benefit of having a child against the cost of bringing it up, and that to give, in effect, a free child to some parents would be invidious. If this kind of damage is recoverable, a court would have to quantify in money the blessings and benefit of having a child and set that sum against the capital cost of the child's upbringing and award the difference if the latter exceeded the former. Plaintiff mothers might be tempted to pretend to a lack of affection of their offspring which ought not to be encouraged.

Finally, counsel for the defendants points to the material advantages that are on the side of having a child. Financial support or assistance, especially perhaps from a son, can be a considerable help to parents in their old age. Daughters often give help with housework, shopping, laundry and the like to their ageing parents. Parents can make a claim in suitable cases under the Fatal Accidents Act 1976 in the event of the child being killed and their losing that support.

In so far as these submissions are based on the *difficulty* of assessing the benefits of parenthood, I do not think they can be right. There is ample authority that courts must, as best they can, assess imponderables of all sorts and value them in money terms. Courts often have to find a figure to represent possible financial and other material benefit, however remote, and also immaterial matters of gain and loss, including emotional matters. But, in so far as it is said it is far more satisfactory for reasons of public policy that such damages should be irrecoverable, the submission has to be examined carefully. There is ample authority, in my judgment, showing that the courts have approached damages in this way: see 12 Halsbury's Laws (4th edn) para 1133. In particular I was referred to passages in *Spartan Steel and Alloys Ltd v Martin & Co (Contractors) Ltd* [1972] 3 All ER 557 at 562, [1973] 1 QB 27 at 37 per Lord Denning MR, *McLoughlin v O'Brian* [1982] 2 All ER 298 at

303, 308-309, [1983] AC 410 at 420, 427 per Lord Wilberforce and Lord Edmund-Davies. It is not necessary to quote these passages. They make it clear that considerations of public policy may have to be applied. The question is only whether there are such considerations, and whether they are so powerful that they should be applied in this particular case. Only last year, the Court of Appeal in *McKay v Essex Area Health Authority* [1982] 2 All ER 771, [1982] QB 1166 rejected a claim based on the birth of a child as being contrary to public policy. It was a case akin, to some extent at least, to the present case . . .

. . . [S]ome considerations mentioned in *McKay's* case may be relevant here. (1) The objection that the courts would be open to claims for maintenance by children against doctors who negligently allowed them to be born. (2) The extra burden this would impose on the medical profession and the danger that doctors would be under subconscious pressure to advise abortions for fear of actions for damages. (3) The social implications in the potential disruption of family life and the bitterness it would cause between parent and child. (4) The sanctity of human life which the law must regard as such that failure to prevent it should not be recognised as a cause of action. In other words, the law will not allow an action based on negligence which caused, or at least allowed, a human life to come into being. (5) There should be rejoicing, not dismay, that the surgeon's mistake bestowed the gift of life on the child.

Mrs Udale's claim does not match the claim which the Court of Appeal disallowed in that case. However, the considerations of public policy there put forward are impressive and are relevant to this case. Together with some of the submissions made by counsel for the defendants, they persuade me to the view that on the grounds of public policy the plaintiff's claims in this case, in so far as they are based on negligence which allowed David Udale to come into this world alive, should not be allowed.

The considerations that particularly impress me are the following. (1) It is highly undesirable that any child should learn that a court has publicly declared his life or birth to be a mistake, a disaster even, and that he or she is unwanted or rejected. Such pronouncements would disrupt families and weaken the structure of society. (2) A plaintiff such as Mrs Udale would get little or no damages because her love and care for her child and her joy, ultimately, at his birth would be set off against and might cancel out the inconvenience and financial disadvantages which naturally accompany parenthood. By contrast, a plaintiff who nurtures bitterness in her heart and refused to let her maternal instinct take over would be entitled to large damages. In short virtue would go unrewarded; unnatural rejection of womanhood and motherhood would be generously compensated. This, in my judgment, cannot be just. (3) Medical men would be under subconscious pressure to encourage abortions in order to avoid claims for medical negligence which would arise if the child were allowed to be born. (4) It has been the assumption of our culture for time immemorial that a child coming into the world, even if, as some say, 'the world is a vale of tears', is a blessing and an occasion for rejoicing.

I am reinforced in the second of these considerations by the fact that, if I had to award damages to Mrs Udale under the disputed heads, I would have to regard the financial disadvantages as offset by her gratitude for the gift of a boy after four girls. Accordingly, in my judgment, the last three heads of damage are irrecoverable. In that event, counsel for the defendants submits that the plaintiff's damages cease at the birth. I do not accept that submission altogether. It seems to me that it is legitimate, without detracting from the above principles of public policy, to have some regard to the disturbance to the family finances which the unexpected pregnancy causes. One may look at the cost of the layette and the sudden necessity of having to find more ample accommodation in assessing the damages for the unwanted pregnancy, without regarding the child as unwanted. One has to bear in mind here that the child has, up until the age of 4 years 2 months, in fact lived in that house without the extension. It has not of course been built. Accordingly, in my view, it is proper to increase the award of damages with this in mind when awarding general damages for the pain, suffering, inconvenience, anxiety and the like, mentioned at the beginning of this judgment. I do so by awarding the sum of £8,000 for these matters together.

Contrast the view of Peter Pain J in the following case.

Thake v Maurice [1984] 2 All ER 513, [1986] QB 644 (QBD)

Peter Pain J: In approaching this problem I firmly put sentiment on one side. A healthy baby is so lovely a creature that I can well understand the reaction of one who asks: how could its birth possibly give rise to an action for damages? But every baby has a belly to be filled and a body to be clothed. The law relating to damages is concerned with reparation in money terms and this is what is needed for the maintenance of a baby.

I have to have regard to the policy of the state as it expresses itself in legislation and in social provision. I must consider this in the light of modern developments. By 1975 family planning was generally practised. Abortion had been legalised over a wide field. Vasectomy was one of the methods of family planning which was not legal but was available under the national health service. It seems to me to follow from this that it was generally recognised that the birth of a healthy baby is not always a blessing. It is a blessing when the baby is to be born to the happy family life which we would all like a baby to have. Many people hold that that end can be best achieved by restricting natural fertility.

The policy of the state, as I see it, is to provide the widest freedom of choice. It makes available to the public the means of planning their families or planning to have no family. If plans go awry, it provides for the possibility of abortion. But there is no pressure on couples either to have children or not to have children or to have only a limited number of children. Even the one-parent family, whether that exists through choice or through misfortune, is given substantial assistance.

Against that background I ask myself whether the reasons advanced by Jupp J are so compelling that I ought to follow his decision. I do not think they are and, in deference to his careful reasoning, I will consider them one by one.

I do not think that if I award damages here it will lead little Samantha to feel rejection. She is surrounded by a happy, albeit somewhat poverty-stricken, family life. It is this that must make her feel wanted and not rejected. She may learn in years to come that her conception was unwanted. But there is nothing exceptional about this. What matters to a child is how it is received when it enters life. It so often happens that parents reconcile themselves to an unwelcome conception and accept the child with joy. If Samantha is as bright as her father thinks, by the time she comes to consider this judgment (if she ever does) she will, I think, welcome it as a means of having made life easier for her family.

Next I have to consider the difficulty in setting off the joy of Samantha against the financial disadvantages that her parents would undergo. If I adopt the public policy which Jupp J favours then virtue will indeed go unrewarded. Every credit is due to the plaintiffs for the way in which they have welcomed Samantha into the family. The method of set-off presents difficulties but, once again, I think it can be solved by looking at the hard cash flow and ignoring the intangibles. Both plaintiffs suffered great distress on learning of Mrs Thake's pregnancy. Mrs Thake underwent pain and discomfort in the course of her labour, although it was not particularly difficult. As a result of these sufferings they had a healthy child. But the fact that she has been such a joy to them is largely of their own making. If they had been reluctant to accept her and grudging in the sacrifices they had to make for her support, then they might have had little joy. As I see it, the birth of a healthy child should be set off against their disappointment and the labour pains so that they cancel each other out. The joy they have for Samantha is largely of their own making in the way they have met their difficulties. The claim for Samantha's support and for the costs of the birth remain.

If the principle of public policy applies it should apply throughout and there should be no award in respect of the birth. The injustice of this course was apparent to Jupp J who said ([1983] 2 All ER 522 at 531-532. [1983] 1 WLR 1098 at 1109-1110):

> It seems to me that it is legitimate, without detracting from the above principles of public policy, to have some regard to the disturbance to the family finances which the unexpected pregnancy causes. One may look at the cost of the layette and the sudden necessity of having to find more ample accommodation in assessing the damages for the unwanted pregnancy, without regarding the child as unwanted. One has to bear in mind here that the child has, up until the age of 4 years 2 months, in fact lived in that house without the extension. It has not of course been built. Accordingly, in my view, it is proper to increase the award of damages with this in mind when awarding general damages for the pain, suffering, inconvenience, anxiety and the like, mentioned at the beginning of this judgment.

I do not see the logical basis of this approach.

The third reason advanced hardly applies here since there was no possibility of an abortion. But, in view of the divisions within the medical profession, I think it has little force. The decision whether to abort or not will usually rest with an obstetrician, who may well be quite independent of the medical man who faces a possible charge of negligence.

As to the fourth ground, for the reasons I have already given I do not accept that it is part of our culture that the birth of a healthy child is always a blessing. It may have been the assumption in the past. I feel quite satisfied it is not the assumption today.

I entirely accept that the reasons put forward by Jupp J may be valid considerations in the assessment of damages in a particular case. But I feel that to erect them into a rule of public policy applicable to all cases would work great injustice, as it would here. I therefore prefer to follow Watkins J in [*Sciuriaga v Powell* (1979) 123 Sol Jo 406].

The Court of Appeal subsequently in *Emeh* preferred the view of Peter Pain J in *Thake* to that of Jupp J in *Udale*.

Emeh v Kensington, Chelsea and Westminster Area Health Authority [1985] QB 1012 (CA)

Waller LJ: [W]e were referred [to] *Udale v Bloomsbury Area Health Authority* [1983] 2 All ER 522, [1983] 1 WLR 1098, a decision of Jupp J in a case where the plaintiff had had a sterilisation operation but had thereafter become pregnant and the sterilisation operation had failed by reason of the negligence of the surgeon. So the question was one of damage. Jupp J gave very careful consideration to the question of public policy. I do not propose to quote his reasons; it is sufficient to say that he came to the conclusion that there were policy objections to the award of damages in relation to the upkeep of the child concerned after birth. He thought there were social implications; he thought that the sanctity of human life had to be considered, and the risk of the child becoming aware that he was so unwanted that damages were being paid by doctors for his maintenance, and so on.

The next case to which we were referred was *Thake v Maurice* [1984] 2 All ER 513, a decision of Peter Pain J. That case concerned an operation of vasectomy on a railway worker who had five children. He and his wife had decided that they should have no more, so the operation was performed on him but then his wife became pregnant again. However, I should say at this stage that in this case, as in the *Udale* case, when the child arrived, the parents were absolutely delighted and were very happy with it. However, in the *Thake* case the reason for the vasectomy operation was because there were five children of the family already, and from the point of view of cost it would be difficult if they had another child. Peter Pain J considered very carefully the matters referred to by Jupp J in the *Udale* case, and he came to the conclusion that he was not prepared to lay down any public policy objections to the claim which was being made.

I do not find the arguments in favour of the public policy objection convincing. If public policy prevents a recovery of damages, then there might be an incentive on the part of some to have late abortions. On the other hand, damages can be awarded which may in some cases be an encouragement and help to bring up an unplanned child. I see unfortunate comparisons which can be made between the case of a child where the mother receives damages, and a case of another child whose mother does not, as being something which is unfortunate, but which is something which cannot be helped.

Lastly, our attention was drawn to *McLoughlin v O'Brian* [1982] 2 All ER 298, [1983] 1 AC 410, and to the words of Lord Scarman and also Lord Edmund Davies, which seem to be apposite to the decision which we have to make in this case. In that case the House of Lords was concerned with the possibility of a claim for damages for nervous shock by a plaintiff whose family had been injured in a motor accident. She was told of the accident some two hours after it had happened by a neighbour, and she alleged that the impact of what she heard and saw caused her severe shock. The argument was raised that she was out of the range of foreseeability. Lord Scarman said ([1982] 2 All ER 298 at 310, [1983] 1 AC 410 at 430):

> The distinguishing feature of the common law is this judicial development and formulation of principle. Policy considerations will have to be weighed; but the objective of the judges is the formulation of principle. And, if principle inexorably requires a decision which entails a degree of policy risk, the court's function is to adjudicate according to principle, leaving policy curtailment to the judgment of Parliament. Here lies the true role of the two law-making institutions in our constitution. By concentrating on principle the judges can keep the common law alive, flexible and consistent, and can keep the legal system clear of policy problems which neither they, nor the forensic process which it is their duty to operate, are equipped to resolve. If principle leads to results which are thought to be socially unacceptable, Parliament can legislate to draw a line or map out a new path.

In my judgment the court should not be too ready to lay down lines of public policy: and I would reject the argument in this case that public policy requires that damages should be confined in the way in which it has been submitted.

Slade LJ: As to public policy, counsel for the defendants naturally referred us to, and relied strongly on, the decision of Jupp J in *Udale v Bloomsbury Area Health Authority* [1983] 2 All ER 522, [1983] 1 WLR 1098. In that case Jupp J held that it was contrary to public policy that damages should be recoverable arising from the cost of the coming into the world of a healthy, normal child. Counsel for the defendants did not feel able to go so far to submit that there was any principle of public policy which prevented damages from being recoverable for the cost of the birth of a child who was not normal. Nevertheless, in reliance on the *Udale* principle, he submitted that, if we were to reject his principal argument, then, in assessing the measure of damages, the cost of raising a normal child should be deducted from the cost of raising the little girl in the present case.

I do not think that this submission is well founded. Following *mutatis mutandis* the same reasoning as Watkins J at first instance in *Sciuriaga v Powell* (1979) 123 Sol Jo 406, the operation performed on the plaintiff in this case was in accordance with the law; not everyone may approve of that law, but it is the law. So if a woman wishes to be sterilised, and in a legal way causes herself to be operated on for that purpose, I can, for my part, see no reason why, under public policy, she should not recover such financial damage as she can prove she has sustained by the surgeon's negligent failure to perform the operation properly, whether or not the child is healthy.

Jupp J, in his very careful judgment in the *Udale* case, gave a number of reasons for reaching a contrary conclusion, in the case of a normal healthy child, but Peter Pain J, in an equally careful judgment, gave his answers to all of Jupp J's points in the later case of *Thake v Maurice* [1984] 2 All ER 513. In this context I think I need only say that, with great respect to both these judges, I, for my part, prefer the reasoning of Peter Pain J on these particular points; I respectfully agree with what Waller LJ has said in this context.

Purchas LJ: I see no reason for the courts to introduce into the perfectly ordinary, straightforward rules of recovery of damages, whether they are damages flowing from a breach of contract or from tort, some qualification to reflect special social positions. If something has to be done in that respect, as Waller LJ cited from the speech of Lord Scarman in *McLoughlin v O'Brian* [1982] 2 All ER 298 at 310, [1983] 1 AC 410 at 430, then that is a matter which falls more properly within the purview of Parliament. The ordinary rules of remoteness of damage, once the question of a break in the causation has been disposed of, can apply equally well to cases of this sort. Where the arrival of the child has mitigating features, such as those referred to in the judgment to which I have just referred, then, in the ordinary assessment of damages, there will be an appropriate diminution in the damages awarded.

In *Gold v Haringey Health Authority* [1987] 2 All ER 888, [1988] QB 481, Lloyd LJ chose to refer to the observation of Ognall J in the unreported case of *Jones v Berkshire Area Health Authority*.

Before relating the history of the matter, I wish to make one point clear. We are not in this case called on to decide whether it is desirable or not that a plaintiff should be able to claim damages for the birth of a healthy child, and a child which, in this particular case, the plaintiff and her husband are now delighted to have. In *Jones v Berkshire Area Health Authority* (2 July 1986, unreported), another unwanted pregnancy case, Ognall J said:

I pause to observe that, speaking purely personally, it remains a matter of surprise to me that the law acknowledges an entitlement in a mother to claim damages for the blessing of a healthy child. Certain it is that those who are afflicted with a handicapped child or who long desperately to have a child at all and are denied that good fortune would regard an award for this sort of contingency with a measure of astonishment. But there it is: that is the law.

Many would no doubt agree with the observation. But the desirability of permitting such a claim does not concern us here. At one time there was a conflict of decisions at first instance whether it was against public policy to allow a plaintiff to recover damages for the birth of a healthy child. But that conflict has been resolved, so far as this court is concerned, by the unanimous decision of this court in *Emeh v Kensington and Chelsea and Westminster Area Health Authority* [1984] 3 All ER 1044, [1985] QB 1012. So in the present appeal we are concerned solely with the question whether the plaintiff has established negligence against the defendants by reason of their failure to warn the plaintiff that the operation might not succeed.

As Lloyd LJ points out in *Gold*, the issue is now settled as far as the Court of Appeal is concerned. It is, however, still open to the House of Lords to consider it afresh, although it is worth noting that leave to appeal was denied in *Thake v Maurice* by the House of Lords. When the House of Lords considers the issue it may be instructive to take account of the weight of judicial opinion in the United States which is against allowing recovery of the costs associated with rearing a healthy child. The following case, although itself reflecting the English position, helpfully reviews the US cases.

Burke v Rivo (1990) 551 NE 2d 1 (Mass Sup Jud Ct)

Wilkins, Justice: A judge in the Superior Court reported to the Appeals Court pursuant to Mass R Civ P 64, 365 Mass 831 (1974), the question of the proper measure of damages recoverable by the parents of a normal, healthy child who was conceived and born (1) following the defendant physician's alleged negligent performance of a sterilization procedure on the mother, and (2) following the physician's alleged guarantee that the sterilization procedure would prevent any future pregnancy . . .

In December, 1983, the plaintiff Carole Burke met with the defendant physician to discuss her desire not to have more children. The Burke family was experiencing financial difficulties. She wanted to return to work to support her family and to fulfil her career goals. The Burkes assert that the defendant recommended that Carole undergo a bipolar cauterization procedure and that he guaranteed that she would not again become pregnant if she did so. In February, 1984, the defendant performed a laparoscopic bilateral tubal ligation by bipolar cauterization.

On June 25, 1985, a pregnancy test confirmed that Carole was pregnant. On February 12, 1986, she gave birth to a fourth child, and the next day she underwent a second sterilization procedure, known as bilateral salpingectomy. A pathology report showed that there had been a recanalization of the left fallopian tube. The Burkes assert that, if the defendant had told Carole of the risk of recanalization, however small, she would initially have selected a different sterilization procedure . . .

We reject [the] arguments that in Massachusetts there should be no liability for negligently performing a sterilization procedure when the result is the conception of a child; no liability for negligently failing to advise a patient of the risks of conceiving a child following a particular sterilization operation (where the patient, properly informed, would have selected a different and more certain sterilization operation); and no liability for breach of a guarantee that following a sterilization procedure there would be no further pregnancy.

The great weight of authority permits the parents of a normal child born as a result of a physician's negligence to recover damages directly associated with the birth (sometimes including damage for the parents' emotional distress), but courts are divided on whether the parents may recover the economic expense of rearing the child. See *Boone v Mullendore* 416 So 2d 718, 721 (Ala 1982) (damages include physical pain and suffering and mental anguish of mother, husband's loss of consortium, and medical expenses of pregnancy, but not child-rearing expenses); *Wilbur v Kerr* 275 Ark 239, 244, 628 SW 2d 568 (1982) (all 'proper damages' connected with failed vasectomy and unwanted pregnancy recoverable, but for reasons of public policy not expenses of rearing child); *Coleman v Garrison* 349 A 2d 8, 11 n 5, 13-14 (Del 1975) (pregnancy-related damage allowed below and not challenged on appeal; no liability for rearing and educating child); *Flowers v District of Columbia*, 478 A 2d 1073, 1074,1077-1078 (DC 1984) (recovery of medical expenses, pain and suffering, and lost wages during pregnancy; wages lost after birth until mother returned to work; and cost of a properly performed tubal ligation, allowed below and not challenged on appeal; child-rearing costs not recoverable); *Public Health Trust v Brown*, 388 So 2d 1084, 1085 (Fla Dist Ct App 1980) (damages for medical expenses, lost wages, and pain and suffering caused by unwanted pregnancy not appealed; reasonable cost of rearing child offset by the value of child's companionship not recognized); *Cockrum v Baumgartner*, 95 Ill 2d 193, 200-201, 69 Ill Dec 168, 447 NE 2d 385, cert denied, 464 US 846, 104 S Ct 149, 78 L Ed 2d 139 (1983) (child-rearing expenses not recoverable); *Nanke v Napier*, 346 NW 2d 520, 522 (Iowa 1984) (same); *Schork v Huber*, 648 SW 2d 861, 863 (Ky 1983) (same); *Macomber v Dillman*, 505 A 2d 810, 813 (Me 1986) (medical expenses of pregnancy and sterilization, mother's pain and suffering, mother's lost earnings, husband's loss of consortium, recoverable, but child-rearing costs not recoverable); *Kingsbury v Smith* 122 NH 237, 242-243, 442 A 2d 1003

(1982) (recovery limited to medical expenses, cost of sterilization, pain and suffering of the pregnancy, mother's lost wages, husband's loss of consortium); *Mason v Western Pa. Hosp* 499 Pa 484, 486-487, 453 A 2d 974 (1982) (tort and contract recovery for medical expenses and lost wages related to prenatal care, delivery, and postnatal care, and associated pain and suffering; no recovery for financial and emotional costs of child-rearing); *Smith v Gore* 728 SW 2d 738, 751 (Tenn 1987) (allowing recovery for medical expenses, recovery, delivery, pain and suffering, and emotional distress during pregnancy but not child-rearing costs); *McKernan v Aasheim* 102 Wash 2d 411, 419-421, 687 P 2d 850 (1984) (pain and suffering, loss of consortium, expenses of failed sterilization procedure and child-birth, but not child-rearing expenses, recoverable); *James G v Caserta* 332 SE 2d 872, 876-878 (W Va 1985) (medical expenses of unsuccessful sterilization, child-birth, subsequent sterilization operation; wife's pain and suffering; loss of consortium recoverable, but not child-rearing expenses); *Rieck v Medical Protective Co* 64 Wis 2d 514, 518-519, 219 NW 2d 242 (1974) (no recovery for child-rearing costs); *Beardsley v Wierdsma,* 650 P 2d 288, 292 (Wyo 1982) (various pregnancy and sterilization related expenses, but not child-rearing expenses, recoverable). Contrast *Szekeres v Robinson* 102 Nev 93, 95, 715 P 2d 1076 (1986) (no tort liability for any expenses incurred as result of allegedly negligent sterilization operation; contract liability for, at least, cost of failed surgery, recognized).

The judge below recognized that damages properly would include the cost of the unsuccessful sterilization procedure and costs directly flowing from the pregnancy: the wife's lost earning capacity; medical expenses of the delivery and care following the birth; the cost of care for the other children while the wife was incapacitated; the cost of the second sterilization procedure and any expenses flowing from that operation; and the husband's loss of consortium. We would add the wife's pain and suffering in connection with the pregnancy and birth and with the second sterilization procedure. We also see no reason why the plaintiffs should not recover for emotional distress they sustained as a result of the unwanted pregnancy. Emotional distress could be the probable consequence of a breach of the duty the defendant owed directly to the plaintiffs. See *Gallagher v Duke Univ,* 852 F 2d 773, 778-779 (4th Circ 1988); *Fassoulas v Ramey,* 450 So 2d 822, 823 (Fla 1984); *Smith v Gore,* 728 SW 2d 738, 751-752 (Tenn 1987); *Naccash v Burger,* 223 Va 406, 290 SE 2d 825, 831 (1982).

The principal issue is whether the plaintiffs are entitled, if they establish liability, to the cost of raising their child. Under normal tort and contract principles, that cost is both a reasonably foreseeable and natural and probable consequence of the wrongs that the plaintiffs allege. The question is whether there is any public policy consideration to which we should give effect to limit traditional tort and contract damages. We conclude that there is none as to parents who have elected sterilization for economic reasons.

Many justifications often relied on for declining to allow recovery of the cost of rearing a healthy child born as a result of a physician's negligence are outstandingly unimpressive. See Note, Judicial Limitations on Damages Recoverable for the Wrongful Birth of a Healthy Infant, 68 Va L Rev 1311, 1315-1323 (1982). The judicial declaration that the joy and pride in raising a child always outweigh any economic loss the parents may suffer, thus precluding recovery for the cost of raising the child (see, eg *Boone v Mullendore,* 416 So 2d 718, 722 [Ala 1982]), simply lacks verisimilitude. The very fact that a person has sought medical intervention to prevent him or her from having a child demonstrates that, for that person, the benefits of parenthood did not outweigh the burdens, economic and otherwise, of having a child. The extensive use of contraception and sterilization and the performance of numerous abortions each year show that, in some instances, large numbers of people do not accept parenthood as a net positive circumstance. We agree with those courts that have rejected the theory that the birth of a child is for all parents at all times a net benefit. See *Hartke v McKelway,* 707 F 2d 1544, 1551-1552 (DC Circ), cert. denied, 464 US 983, 104 S Ct 425, 78 L Ed 2d 360 (1983) (construing District of Columbia law before *Flowers v District of Columbia,* 478 A 2d 1073 [DC 1984]); *University of Ariz Health Sciences Center v Superior Court,* 136 Ariz 579, 583-584, 667 P 2d 1294 (1983); *Ochs v Borrelli,* 187 Conn 253, 259-260, 445 A 2d 883 (1982); *Sherlock v Stillwater Clinic,* 260 NW 2d 169, 175 (Minn 1977); *McKernan v Aasheim,* 102 Wash 2d 411, 418, 687 P 2d 850 (1984). . .

We are also unimpressed with the reasoning that child-rearing expenses should not be allowed because some day the child could be adversely affected by learning that he or she was unwanted and that someone else had paid for the expense of rearing the child. See *Hartke v McKelway, supra* at 1552 n. Courts expressing concern about the effect on the child nevertheless allow the parents to recover certain direct expenses from the negligent physician without expressing concern about harm to the child when the child learns that he or she was unwanted. See, eg, *Boone v Mullendore,* 416 So 2d 718, 721-722 (Ala 1982); *Wilbur v Kerr,* 275 Ark 239, 244, 628 SW 2d 568 (1982); *McKernan v Aasheim,* 102 Wash 2d 411, 421, 687 P

2d 850 (1984). The once unwanted child's knowledge that someone other than the parents had been obliged to pay for the cost of rearing him or her may in fact alleviate the child's distress at the knowledge of having been once unwanted. See *Custodio v Bauer*, 251 (Cal App 2d 303, 325, 59 Cal Rptr 463 (1967). In any event, it is for the parents, not the courts, to decide whether a lawsuit would adversely affect the child and should not be maintained. See *University of Ariz Health Sciences Center v Superior Court*, 136 Ariz 579, 585, 667 P 2d 1924 (1983), and cases cited.

We see no validity to the arguments, sometimes made, that the costs of child-rearing are too speculative or are unreasonably disproportionate to the doctor's negligence. See, eg, *Schork v Huber*, 648 SW 2d 861, 863 (Ky 1983); *James G v Caserta*, 332 SE 2d 872, 878 (W Va 1985); *Rieck v Medical Protective Co*, 64 Wis 2d 514, 519, 219 NW 2d 242 (1974). The determination of the anticipated costs of child-rearing is no more complicated or fanciful than many calculations of future losses made every day in tort cases. If a physician is negligent in caring for a newborn child, damage calculations would be made concerning the newborn's earning capacity and expected medical expenses over an entire lifetime. The expenses of rearing a child are far more easily determined. If there is any justification for denying recovery of normal tort damages in a case of this character, it is not that the cost of rearing a child is incapable of reasonable calculation or is too great to impose on a negligent physician.

A substantial number of jurisdictions have allowed recovery of the cost of rearing a normal child to adulthood, offset, however, by the benefits that the parents receive in having a normal, healthy child. See *University of Ariz Health Sciences Center v Superior Court*, 136 Ariz 579, 584-585, 667 P 2d 1294 (1983); *Ochs v Borrelli*, 187 Conn 253, 259-260, 445 A 2d 883 (1982); *Jones v Malinowski*, 299 Md 257, 270-271, 473 A 2d 429 (1984); *Sherlock v Stillwater Clinic*, 260 NW 2d 169, 175-176 (Minn 1977). See also *Hartke v McKelway*, 707 F 2d 1544, 1552 (D.C.Cir.1983) ('allowing the plaintiff to prove that raising a child constitutes damage is the course of greater justice'). Such a balancing by the trier of fact requires a comparison of the economic loss of child-rearing with the emotional gains of having a normal, healthy child (converted into a dollar value). These courts have thought that comparison expressed in Restatement (Second) of Torts s 920 (1979). A few courts have thought that, because the benefit conferred did not affect the economic interest that was harmed, no mitigation of the cost of child-rearing should be recognized. See discussion in *Hartke v McKelway*, *supra* at 1557-1558 n, 16.

If the parents' desire to avoid the birth of a child was founded on eugenic reasons (avoidance of a feared genetic defect) or was founded on therapeutic reasons (concern for the mother's health) and if a healthy normal baby is born, the justification for allowing recovery of the costs of rearing a normal child to maturity is far less than when, to conserve family resources, the parents sought unsuccessfully to avoid conceiving another child. See *University of Ariz Health Sciences Center v Superior Court*, 136 Ariz 579, 585, 667 P 2d 1294 (1983) ('For example, where the parent sought sterilization in order to avoid the danger of genetic defect, the jury could easily find that the uneventful birth of a healthy, nondefective child was a blessing rather than a "damage"'); *Jones v Malinowski*, 299 Md 257, 270-271, 473 A 2d 429 (1984) ('the assessment of damages associated with the healthy child's birth, if any, should focus upon the specific interests of the parents that were *actually* impaired by the physician's negligence, ie, was the sterilization sought for reasons that were (a) genetic – to prevent birth of a defective child, or (b) therapeutic – to prevent harm to the mother's health or (c) economic – to avoid the additional expense of raising a child') (emphasis in original). See also *Hartke v McKelway*, *supra* at 1553-1555, and authorities cited (no recovery of expenses of raising normal child where sterilization was sought solely because of fear of childbirth).

We conclude that, in addition to the recoverable damages described earlier in this opinion, parents may recover the cost of rearing a normal, healthy but (at least initially) unwanted child if their reason for seeking sterilization was founded on economic or financial considerations. In such a situation, the trier of fact should offset against the cost of rearing the child the benefit, if any, the parents received and will receive from having their child. We discern no reason founded on sound public policy to immunize a physician from having to pay for a reasonably foreseeable consequence of his negligence or from a natural and probable consequence of a breach of his guarantee, namely, the parents' expenses in rearing the child to adulthood.

Liacos CJ, Abrams and Greaney JJ agreed. O'Connor, Nolan and Lynch JJ dissented.

(See *Lovelace Medical Center v Mendez* (1991) 805 P 2d 603 (NM Sup Ct), Appendix note 1 (judgment of Judge Alarid in which he states that 29 of the

US jurisdictions denied recovery of rearing costs and only a handful allowed recovery).)

These are two final points we should notice. The first was raised by Purchas LJ in *Emeh*. He stated that:

> We have been referred to a series of authorities in the American courts, and I only refer to one passage to identify the problem, not to solve it, from *Sherlock v Stillwater Clinic* (1977) 260 NW 2d 169, a decision of the Supreme Court of Minnesota in banc, with two dissenting judgments, where the problem is summarised in this way:
>
> > We hold that in cases such as this an action for 'wrongful conception' may be maintained, and that compensatory damages may be recovered by the parents of the unplanned child. These damages may include all prenatal and postnatal medical expenses, the mother's pain and suffering during pregnancy and delivery, and loss of consortium. Additionally, the parents may recover the reasonable costs of rearing the unplanned child subject to offsetting the value of the child's aid, comfort and society during the parents' life expectancy.
>
> > . . . The ordinary rules of remoteness of damage, once the question of a break in the causation has been disposed of, can apply equally well to cases of this sort. Where the arrival of the child has mitigating features, such as those referred to in the judgment to which I have just referred, then, in the ordinary assessment of damages, there will be an appropriate diminution in the damages awarded.

While the application of the principle of set-off must be correct, the issue remains: against which part of the plaintiff's claim should any set-off be made?

In *Thake*, Peter Pain J cancelled out the plaintiff's damages for pain and suffering during pregnancy because of the corresponding joy as a consequence of the birth of the baby. The Court of Appeal disagreed.

Thake v Maurice [1986] QB 644 (CA)

Kerr LJ: The judge awarded damages to the plaintiffs under certain heads in agreed amounts, but he declined to make any award for the plaintiffs' distress when they knew that Mrs Thake would have to have another child, nor for the discomfort, pain and suffering which she had to undergo, though fortunately it was not a difficult pregnancy or delivery. He awarded agreed damages for the cost of the layette and of Samantha's upkeep to the age of 17 in a total of £6,667 and an agreed sum of £2,000 to Mrs Thake for loss of earnings during this period, plus agreed interest in the sum of £1,000, making a total of £9,677. The plaintiffs now cross-appeal against his refusal to make any award for what I can refer to in short as pain and suffering. He gave his reasons for this conclusion as follows ([1984] 2 All ER 513 at 526-527, [1985] 2 WLR 215 at 231):

> Next I have to consider the difficulty in setting off the joy of Samantha against the financial disadvantages that her parents would undergo . . . Every credit is due to the plaintiffs for the way in which they have welcomed Samantha into the family. The method of set-off presents difficulties but, once again, I think it can be solved by looking at the cash involved and ignoring the intangibles. Both plaintiffs suffered great distress on learning of Mrs Thake's pregnancy. Mrs Thake underwent pain and discomfort in the course of her labour, although it was not particularly difficult. As a result of these sufferings they had a healthy child. But the fact that she has been such a joy to them is largely of their own making. If they had been reluctant to accept her and grudging in the sacrifices they had to make for her support, then they might have had little joy. As I see it, the birth of a healthy child should be set off against their disappointment and the labour pains so that they cancel each other out. The joy they have for Samantha is largely of their own making in the way they have met their difficulties.

On behalf of the plaintiffs it was accepted that credit would have to be given, in effect by way of a set-off, for the happiness which the plaintiffs ultimately derived from having Samantha as a healthy child. Their counsel accepted that neither of the plaintiffs, in particular Mrs Thake, could therefore claim anything for the time and trouble which would have to be devoted to her care and upbringing, and he pointed out that no such claim had been made. But he contested that the relief and joy which they felt after Samantha has been born should set off so as to extinguish any claim for their earlier distress, and the pain and suffering of Mrs Thake before and during the birth. I would uphold this submission. The joy of having Samantha should in my view be set off against the time, trouble and care which is inevitably involved in her upbringing. The plaintiffs have rightly made no claim for this. But the pre-natal distress, pain and suffering in my view stand on a separate footing, and I think that it would be wrong to apply this set-off to this head of claim as well, in effect twice over, bearing in mind that the claim for pain and suffering was otherwise unchallenged. One can perhaps take the analogy of a defendant who sustains some injury and suffers distress because of the risk that he may become paralysed. If he then fortunately and happily makes a full recovery, his ultimate well-being will of course be reflected in a low award of damages. But his relief and joy at the outcome cannot properly be used as a basis for reducing, let alone extinguishing, an appropriate award for his initial pain and suffering. This conclusion also appears to me to be in line with such authority as there is on this point. In his judgment in *Emeh v Kensington and Chelsea and Westminster Area Health Authority* [1984] 3 All ER 1044 at 1056, [1985] QB 1012 at 1028 Purchas LJ approved the following passage from a decision of the Supreme Court of Minnesota in *Sherlock v Stillwater Clinic* (1977) 260 NW 2d 169 at 170-171:

> We hold that in cases such as this an action for 'wrongful conception' may be maintained, and that compensatory damages may be recovered by the parents of the unplanned child. These damages may include all prenatal and postnatal medical expenses; the mother's pain and suffering during pregnancy and delivery, and loss of consortium. Additionally, the parents may recover the reasonable costs of rearing the unplanned child subject to offsetting the value of the child's aid, comfort and society during the parents' life expectancy.

> It was submitted on behalf of the defendant that, once it is accepted that a set-off must be made, it does not matter against which head of claim it is applied, and I recognise that the passage quoted above is by no means conclusive in the plaintiffs' favour of this aspect. Nevertheless, for the reasons already given, I respectfully differ from the judge that the claim for ante-natal pain and suffering should be extinguished by the happiness of the post-natal events. The joy of parents at the birth of a healthy child, though with the consequent time and trouble which need to be devoted to its upbringing, are both virtually impossible to assess in terms of money. It is therefore right that in law they should be treated as cancelling each other out. But awards of damages for pain and suffering are an everyday feature of our law, and it was not suggested on behalf of the defendant that such damages are irrecoverable in principle for the discomfort and pain of pregnancy and delivery when these occur normally and without adverse incidents. Accordingly, I would uphold the plaintiffs' claim under this head and allow the cross-appeal.

As a consequence, as Brooke J made clear in *Allen* (*supra*), general damages for harm caused during pregnancy are recoverable without set-off as are the costs of raising the healthy child. The only circumstance in which set-off could occur against the latter award would be if the birth were to produce some economic gain for the parents, for example, some form of inheritance. Secondly, once the courts allowed actions for failed sterilisations then the damages claims were bound to increase in size. The most obvious example of this is the possible expenditure on the child's upbringing and education. You will recall Brooke J's reluctant conclusion in *Allen* that 'heavy future awards of damages for the cost of maintaining children' cannot be avoided.

B. WRONGFUL BIRTH

The term 'wrongful birth' refers to a claim brought by the parents of a child *born disabled* as a consequence of negligence before its birth. As you will see, this action arises out of the same circumstances as the 'wrongful life' claim of a child which we discussed earlier. As with the 'wrongful life' claim, therefore, the breach of duty may occur before conception (eg negligent genetic counselling), *ex utero* (eg negligence during infertility treatment) or *in utero* (eg negligent failure to diagnose the child's disabilities).

In England no cases directly analyse the basis for the parents' 'wrongful birth' claim. However, a number of decisions have recognised the claim without raising any doubts as to its validity (eg *Rance v Mid-Downs HA* [1991] 1 All ER 801 (Brooke J); *Salih v Enfield HA* [1991] 3 All ER 400 (CA)).

A model for analysis which an English court might well adopt is provided by the following decision of the Washington Supreme Court.

Harbeson v Parke-Davis (1983) 656 P 2d 483 (Wash Sup Ct)

Pearson J: Plaintiff Leonard Harbeson has at all material times been a member of the United States Air Force. In 1970, while Mr Harbeson was stationed at Malstrom Air Force Base, his wife Jean conceived their first child. In December 1970, Mrs Harbeson learned, after suffering a grand mal seizure, that she was an epileptic. To control Mrs Harbeson's seizures, physicians at the Air Force Base prescribed Dilantin, an anticonvulsant drug, which was the first choice of doctors in the treatment of epilepsy. Mrs Harbeson took Dilantin during the remainder of her pregnancy and in March 1971 gave birth to Michael, a healthy and intelligent child.

After Michael's birth, Mr Harbeson was transferred to McChord Air Force Base, near Tacoma. The medical facility serving the base was Madigan Army Medical Center. In May 1972, Mrs Harbeson went to Madigan for evaluation and treatment of her epilepsy. A neurologist at Madigan prescribed Dilantin to control her seizures. Between November 1972 and July 1973, the Harbesons informed three doctors at Madigan that they were considering having other children, and inquired about the risks of Mrs Harbeson's taking Dilantin during pregnancy. Each of the three doctors responded that Dilantin could cause cleft palate and temporary hirsutism. None of the doctors conducted literature searches or consulted other sources for specific information regarding the correlation between Dilantin and birth defects. The Harbesons relied on the assurances of the Madigan doctors and thereafter Mrs Harbeson became pregnant twice giving birth to Elizabeth in April 1974, and Christine in May 1975. Throughout these pregnancies, Mrs Harbeson continued to take Dilantin as prescribed by the Madigan doctors. . . . Elizabeth and Christine have been diagnosed as suffering from 'fetal hydantoin syndrome'. They suffer from mild to moderate growth deficiencies, mild to moderate developmental retardation, wide-set eyes, lateral ptosis (drooping eyelids), hypoplasia of the fingers, small nails, low-set hairline, broad nasal ridge, and other physical and developmental defects. Had Mr and Mrs Harbeson been informed of the potential birth defects associated with the use of Dilantin during pregnancy, they would not have had any other children. . . .

Wrongful birth

The epithet wrongful birth has been used to describe several fundamentally different types of action. See Annot, *Tort Liability for Wrongfully Causing One to Be Born*, 83 ALR 3d 15 (1978). Many of the actions once entitled wrongful birth are now referred to as wrongful conception and wrongful pregnancy actions. *Phillips v United States*, 508 F Supp 544, 545 n1 (DSC 1981); Rogers, *Wrongful Life and Wrongful Birth: Medical Malpractice In Genetic Counseling and Prenatal Testing*, 33 SCL Rev 713, 739-41 (1982). A recent definition of a wrongful birth action is an action brought by the parents against

> a physician [who] failed to inform [them] of the increased possibility that the mother would give birth to a child suffering from birth defects . . . [thereby precluding] an informed decision about whether to have the child.

(Footnotes omitted.) Comment, *Berman v Allan*, 8 Hofstra L Rev 257, 258 (1979), cited in *Phillips*, at 545 n 1.

Such an action was recognised by the New Jersey Supreme Court in *Schroeder v Perkel*, 87 NJ 53, 432 A 2d 834 (1981). Mr and Mrs Schroeder had two children, both of whom suffered from cystic fibrosis, a fatal genetic disorder. It was not until Mrs Schroeder was 8 months pregnant with their second child that the Schroeders learned they were carriers of the recessive gene which causes the disorder. They claimed that defendant paediatricians were negligent in failing to make an earlier diagnosis of cystic fibrosis in their first child. Had they known earlier of the condition, the Schroeders would either avoided the conception of their second child, or terminated the pregnancy. The basis of their claim, therefore, was that 'they were deprived of an informed choice of whether to assume the risk of a second child'. 87 NJ at 57, 432 A 2d 834. The New Jersey Supreme Court recognised the cause of action and held that the parents could recover the extraordinary medical expenses of raising the second child.

Schroeder is a paradigm wrongful birth case. The parents brought an action for the birth of a defective child. They claimed that defendant physicians had breached a duty to inform them of the risk of the child's being born defective. They claimed that had they known of this risk they would have prevented the birth of the child by contraception or abortion. They claimed that defendants' failure to inform was a proximate cause of the birth of the claim and that the birth was an injury compensable in damages.

Although the definition we refer to above comprehends the *Schroeder* action, it excludes the cause of action recognised in a similar case, *Speck v Finegold*, 497 Pa 77, 439 A 2d 110 (1981). Mr Speck suffered from neurofibromatosis, a disorder caused by a genetic defect. After having two children who suffered from the disorder, Mr Speck decided to undergo a vasectomy. The vasectomy was unsuccessful, and Mrs Speck became pregnant. Mr and Mrs Speck decided to terminate the pregnancy. The abortion was unsuccessful, and Mrs Speck gave birth to a daughter who suffered from neurofibromatosis.

The court allowed the parents a cause of action to recover expenses attributable to the birth and rearing of their daughter. There appears to be no reason to exclude the action in *Speck* from the definition of wrongful birth. Like *Schroeder*, it is founded upon the birth of a defective child. The parents of the child alleged defendants breached a duty of care in performing the vasectomy and abortion procedures. Had these procedures been successful, they would have prevented conception or birth of the child. The parents alleged defendants' breach was a proximate cause of the birth, and that birth was an injury to the parents, compensable in damages.

Both *Schroeder* and *Speck* recognise the right of parents to prevent the conception or birth of children suffering defects. They recognise that physicians owe a duty to parents to preserve that right. Physicians may breach this duty either by failure to impart material information or by negligent performance of a procedure to prevent the birth of a defective child. The parents' right to prevent a defective child and the correlative duty flowing from that right is the heart of the wrongful birth action.

For the purposes of the analysis which follows, therefore, wrongful birth will refer to an action based on an alleged breach of the duty of a health care provider to impart information or perform medical procedures with due care, where the breach is a proximate cause of the birth of a defective child. We do not in this opinion address issues which may arise where the birth of a healthy child is allegedly caused by a breach of duty owed to the parents. Such actions are referred to as wrongful conception or wrongful pregnancy, rather than wrongful birth. See generally, *Phillips*, at 545 n 1. Other jurisdictions have consistently treated such actions as different from, although related to, wrongful birth. We do likewise.

Having defined the scope of our inquiry, we now consider whether the wrongful birth action should be allowed in this state.

First, we measure the proposed wrongful birth action against the traditional concepts of duty, breach, injury, and proximate cause. The critical concept is duty. The core of our decision is whether we should impose upon health care providers a duty correlative to parents' right to prevent the birth of defective children.

Until recently, medical science was unable to provide parents with the means of predicting the birth of a defective child. Now, however, the ability to predict the occurrence and recurrence of defects attributable to genetic disorders has improved significantly. Parents can determine before conceiving a child whether their genetic traits increase the risk of that child's suffering from a genetic disorder such as Tay-Sachs disease or cystic fibrosis. After conception, new diagnostic techniques such as amniocentesis and ultrasonography can reveal defects in the unborn fetus. See generally, Peters and Peters, *Wrongful Life: Recognising the Defective Child's Right to a Cause of Action*, 18 Duq L Rev 857, 873-75 (1980). Parents may avoid the birth of the defective child by aborting the fetus. The difficult moral choice is theirs. *Roe v Wade* 410 US 113, 93 S Ct 705, 35 L Ed 2d 147 (1973). We must decide, therefore, whether these developments confer upon potential parents the right to prevent, either before or after conception, the birth of a defective child. Are these developments the first steps towards a 'Fascist-Orwellian societal attitude of genetic purity', *Gildiner v Thomas Jefferson Univ Hosp* 451 F Supp 692, 695 (EDPa 1978), or Huxley's Brave

New World? Or do they provide positive benefits to individual families and to all society by avoiding the vast emotional and economic cost of defective children?

We believe we must recognise the benefits of these medical developments and therefore we hold that parents have a right to prevent the birth of a defective child and health care providers a duty correlative to that right. This duty requires health care providers to impart to their patients material information as to the likelihood of future children being born defective, to enable the potential parents to decide whether to avoid the conception or birth of such children. If medical procedures are undertaken to avoid the conception or birth of defective children, the duty also requires that these procedures be performed with due care. This duty includes, therefore, the requirement that a health care provider who undertakes to perform an abortion use reasonable care in doing so. The duty does not, however, affect in any way the right of a physician to refuse on moral or religious grounds to perform an abortion. Recognition of the duty will 'promote societal interests in genetic counseling and prenatal testing, deter medical malpractice, and at least partially redress a clear and undeniable wrong'. (Footnotes omitted.) Rogers, *Wrongful Life and Wrongful Birth: Medical Malpractice in Genetic Counseling and Prenatal Testing*, 33 SCL Rev 713, 757 (1982) (hereinafter cited as Rogers).

We find persuasive the fact that all other jurisdictions to have considered this issue have recognised such a duty. These decisions are conveniently collected in Rogers, at 739-52, and we need not list them here.

Having recognised that a duty exists, we have taken the major step toward recognising the wrongful birth action. The second element of the traditional tort analysis is more straightforward. Breach will be measured by failure to conform to the appropriate standard of skill, care, or learning. RCW 4 24 290; RCW 7 70 040. *Gates v Jensen* 92 Wash 2d 246, 595 P 2d 919 (1979).

More problematical is the question of whether the birth of a defective child represents an injury to the parents. The only case to touch on this question in this state did not resolve it. *Ball v Mudge* 64 Wash 2d 247, 250, 391 P 2d 201 (1964). However, it is an inevitable consequence of recognising the parents' right to avoid the birth of a defective child that we recognise that the birth of such a child is an actionable injury. The real question as to injury, therefore, is not the existence of the injury, but the extent of that injury. In other words, having recognised that the birth of the child represents an injury, how do we measure damages? Other courts to have considered the issue have found this question troublesome. In particular, the New Jersey Supreme Court has taken a different approach to the question on each of the three occasions it has confronted it. In *Gleitman v Cosgrove* 49 NJ 22, 227 A 2d 689 (1967), the court rejected the wrongful birth action altogether. One of the reasons for the rejection was the difficulty of measuring damages. When the court next considered the issue in *Berman v Allan* 80 NJ 421, 404 A 2d 8 (1979), it upheld an action for wrongful birth and permitted damages for mental anguish. However, the court refused to allow damages to compensate for the medical and other costs incurred in raising, educating, and supervising the child. The court retreated from this position in the third case, *Schroeder v Perkel* 87 NJ 53, 432 A 2d 834 (1981), and allowed the parents damages for certain medical expenses related to the child's affliction.

Other courts to have considered the issue exhibit widely divergent approaches. Comment, *Wrongful Birth Damages, Mandate and Mishandling by Judicial Fiat* 13 Val U L Rev 127 (1978); Rogers, at 750-51.

More certain guidance than that provided by decisions of other jurisdictions on the issue of damages is provided by the Legislature in RCW 4 24 010. This statute provides that, in an action by parents for injury to a child, compensation may be recovered for four types of damages: medical, hospital, and medication expenses, loss of the child's services and support, loss of the child's love and companionship, and injury to the parent-child relationship. Recovery of damages for loss of companionship of the child, or injury or destruction of the parent-child relationship is not limited to the period of the child's minority. *Balmer v Dilley* 81 Wash 2d 367, 502 P 2d 456 (1972). We have held that this section allows recovery for parental grief, mental anguish and suffering. *Hinzman v Palmanteer* 81 Wash 2d 327, 501 P 2d 1228 (1972). The statute is not directly in point because a wrongful birth claim does not allege injury to the child as the cause of the parents' injury; rather it alleges the birth of the child is the cause of the injury. Nevertheless, the statute reflects a policy to compensate parents not only for pecuniary loss but also for emotional injury. There appears to be no compelling reason that policy should not apply in wrongful birth actions. Accordingly, we hold that recovery may include the medical, hospital, and medication expenses attributable to the child's birth and to its defective condition, and in addition damages for the parents' emotional injury caused by the birth of the defective child. In considering damages for emotional injury, the jury should be entitled to consider the countervailing emotional benefits attributable to the birth of the child. Restatement (Second) of Torts s 920 (1977). Rogers, at 751-52; *Eisbrenner v Stanley*, 106 Mich App 357, 308 NW 2d 209 (1981); *Kingsbury v Smith*, 442 A 2d 1003 (1982).

The final element to be considered is whether a breach of duty can be a proximate cause of the birth of the child. Proximate cause must be established by, first, a showing that the breach of duty was a cause in fact of the injury, and, second, a showing that as a matter of law liability should attach. *King v Seattle*, 84 Wash 2d 239, 249, 525 P 2d 228 (1974). Cause in fact can be established by proving that but for the breach of duty, the injury would not have occurred. *King v Seattle, supra*, The legal question whether liability should attach is essentially another aspect of the policy decisions which we confronted in deciding whether the duty exists. We therefore hold that, as a matter of law in wrongful birth cases, if cause in fact is established, the proximate cause element is satisfied. This conclusion is consistent with the decisions of those other jurisdictions which have accepted wrongful birth actions, eg, *Robak v United States* 658 F 2d 471 (7th Circ 1981).

The action for wrongful birth, therefore, fits within the conceptual framework of our law of negligence. An action in negligence claiming damages for the birth of a child suffering congenital defects may be brought in this state.

The parents may therefore recover damages for the wrongful births of Elizabeth and Christine. These damages may include pecuniary damages for extraordinary medical, educational, and similar expenses attributable to the defective condition of the children. In other words, the parents should recover those expenses in excess of the cost of the birth and rearing of two normal children. In addition, the damages may compensate for mental anguish and emotional stress suffered by the parents during each child's life as a proximate result of the physicians' negligence. Any emotional benefits to the parents resulting from the birth of the child should be considered in setting the damages.

The court's analysis in *Harbeson* raises the traditional issues found in any negligence action: duty, breach, causation, harm and damages. As we saw, each of these requires special consideration where what is complained of is the birth of a child. Much of the analysis required in respect of the action for 'wrongful birth' is the same as that for actions for 'wrongful conception', which we saw earlier: in particular, arguments concerning 'duty', 'the nature of the harm' suffered and 'causation'. Here, of course, we are concerned with the birth of a *disabled* child and, therefore, the public policy arguments raised in cases such as *Udale*, *Thake* and *Emeh*, pose no obstacle to the recovery of damages.

There are, however, three points that we should advert to. *Firstly*, you will notice that the court in *Harbeson* did not allow the parents to recover the costs of raising a normal healthy child but only those associated with its disability, ie the extraordinary financial costs and the parents' 'mental anguish and emotional stress'. In England, the courts would allow *all* the reasonable foreseeable costs of raising the child. The reason for the difference lies in the fact that, as we have seen, the vast majority of US jurisdictions (including Washington) do not award the costs of rearing when what is complained of is the birth of a *healthy* child.

Secondly, albeit in unusual circumstances, an English court would refuse to allow a claim for the ordinary costs of rearing the disabled child which would be incurred by any parent if it could be established that the parents would, in any event, have gone on to have a further healthy child (see *Salih v Enfield HA* [1991] 3 All ER 400 (CA)).

Thirdly, we have already seen when considering claims arising from 'wrongful conception', that the Court of Appeal in *Emeh* was asked to consider the argument that the mother faced with the knowledge of her pregnancy ought to have had an abortion. We saw that the court gave this argument short shrift. In a 'wrongful birth' claim where the negligence occurs before conception (eg during genetic counselling) the argument could be made that if the child's disability is subsequently discovered during the mother's pregnancy she ought to have an abortion. The argument has more force to it here. If there is a 'substantial risk that if the child were born it would suffer from such physical or mental abnormalities as to be seriously handicapped', then an abortion would be available under section 1(1)(d) of the Abortion Act 1967 throughout the duration of the pregnancy. It is unlikely, however, that the court even in these circumstances would impose, what is in effect, an obligation to undergo an abortion. To do so would impose upon the mother the unenviable 'choice' of bearing the burden of paying for the child's upkeep or undergoing an abortion.

Part III

Medical law in action

B: During life

Chapter 14

Research

Introduction

It is a truism that for medical practice to develop and improve in any systematic and ordered way research must be carried out. It is equally a truism that such research must include research on human beings whether they are patients or are healthy.

When we speak of research we adopt the analysis set out in Nicholson (ed), *Medical Research with Children* (1986) (at pp 24-26):

> *Research* may be defined as in the *Shorter Oxford English Dictionary*: 'An investigation directed to the discovery of some fact by careful study of a subject; a course of critical or scientific inquiry'. The second part of that definition is more useful when considering medical research because of the potential confusion, caused by the use of the word 'investigation' in the first part. 'Investigation' tends to be used more specifically in medical practice to denote the ascertainment of a particular anatomical, biochemical, or physiological value in a patient. Examples of such 'investigations' are a chest X-ray, the measurement of the haemoglobin level in blood, or lung function tests. In our discussions, however, 'research' was seldom used by itself, without some other word attached. Phrases such as 'research project', 'research procedure', or 'therapeutic research' were used more frequently.
>
> A *research project* is a systematic enquiry designed to contribute to generalisable knowledge. It is important to emphasise that it is systematic in design and execution, and requires honest and accurate recording of all information obtained. A speculative or haphazard attempt at a new therapy, for instance, cannot be regarded as a research project.
>
> A *research intervention* is a specific act performed on a research subject during the course of a research project. Such an intervention may involve the performance of an investigation, used in the medical sense noted above, such as the taking of a blood sample or the measurement of lung function tests, or even simply weighing the subject. Alternatively, an intervention might be manipulation of the subject's diet, or the giving of a substance.
>
> Research interventions may be either *invasive* or *non-invasive*. Essentially, any activity, part or all of which involves an entrance of any sort into a subject's body, is invasive. For instance, urine may be collected by both invasive and non-invasive techniques. If a urine bag is attached to an infant to collect urine voided normally, that is a non-invasive intervention, even though it may cause the infant some discomfort. If on the other hand the urine is collected by supra-pubic aspiration – that is, by passing a needle through the abdominal wall into the bladder and withdrawing some urine – the intervention is invasive. The borderline between invasive and non-invasive may sometimes be difficult to ascertain. Swabbing the skin so as to obtain a sample of bacteria growing thereon is a non-invasive intervention; swabbing the throat for similar purposes, while not involving the breaking of any skin or tegument, should be regarded as an invasive intervention.
>
> Some research projects do not involve any interventions and consist only in *observation*. The *Concise Oxford Dictionary* defines an observation as 'accurate watching and noting of phenomena as they occur in nature with regard to cause and effect or mutual relations', and it is in that sense that 'observation' has been used in this report. In medical research such 'accurate watching' might just be of the colour of a subject's skin, or the size of the pupils of his eyes. Were the pulse to be measured by feeling it at the wrist, that would constitute an intervention rather than an observation. Pure observation is an activity more commonly

found in psychological research, particularly that undertaken by human ethologists, when the behaviour of one or more subjects is observed and recorded.

Our concern here is with research interventions as defined. As the law stands, no legal complaint can arise from observational research as described.

Research on human beings has undoubtedly been carried out in one way or another as long as there has been medicine. As Carolyn Faulder, in her book *Whose Body Is It?* (1985), puts it (pp 64-65):

> Few people would seriously argue that doctors are wrong to want to increase their understanding of the human body and the ills to which it is prone. Doctors want to be able to do the best they can for their present patients and they would like to do even better for future patients. *We* want them to find the cure for cancer and other serious diseases and to help us to live longer and healthier lives. *We* expect them to give us the best available treatment. *We* want to feel safe in their hands, reassured that whatever they suggest to us is backed by sound scientific knowledge and that our welfare is their first consideration. We want it all, but medical advance is impossible without research and experimentation – and some of that experimentation must be done on human beings.
>
> In a sense all medical treatment is experimental. However well tried a particular therapy may be, the doctor can never be entirely sure how the individual patient will respond. Far more experimental is any treatment which is offered to patients simply because the doctor believes it works, even though it may never have been put to the test in a comparison with a control group of patients who either are not getting the treatment or are being offered an alternative.

By the end of the nineteenth century, as Faulder (*op cit*) writes (pp 62-64):

> New treatments were proliferating and it became increasingly apparent to the more scientifically minded members of the profession that clinical observation and judgment, although valuable, was too easily distorted by prejudice and personal bias to be reliable. What was needed was some more objective method of verification. The first trial by numbers was done in the early nineteenth century by a Frenchman, Professor Pierre-Charles-Alexandre Louis, who was able to demonstrate the uselessness of blood-letting by comparing the results of large numbers of cases.
>
> However, it was not until well into this century that controlled clinical trials began to be accepted as a method of scientific evaluation. And it was not until after the Second World War that the principle of randomisation was introduced into clinical research. This concept of random allocation was described by its innovator, the statistician Sir Ronald Fisher, who first used it in studies of agricultural crop production, as the primary principle of experimental design. It was another eminent statistician, Sir Austin Bradford Hill, who initiated its use in medical research with the historical trial in 1946 of the antibiotic Streptomycin for tuberculosis. Very simply, randomisation operates on the 'toss of a coin' principle: subjects suffering from a particular illness at the same stage are randomly allocated to different groups for different treatments and then carefully observed and followed up to compare the results. Its purpose is to eliminate any element of human or accidental bias in selecting patients for treatment which would distort the assessment of the results. Clinical trials using this principle of randomisation are called randomised controlled trials [RCT] . . .
>
> That RCTs have become so widely used is probably due as much as anything to the pithy monograph extolling their virtues written by Dr Archibald Cochrane in the early seventies. He advocated not merely that they were efficient for testing new treatments but that they provided a cost-effective method for testing traditional procedures, many of them outdated and illogical, which the NHS was finding difficulty in discarding. He urged that even simple measures, like when a patient should be got out of bed after surgery, should be put to the test by this rigorous method.
>
> Since then RCTs have been considerably developed and refined and they are now extensively used to test new drugs, surgical techniques, radiotherapy, screening procedures, alternative methods of delivering medical care and a host of other medical interventions.

Faulder asserts that (p 64):

This means that although only a relatively small percentage of patients actually receiving medical treatment are doing so in a trial (approximately 10 per cent), there are many more of us drawn from the so-called healthy population who may be involved in a trial, with or without our knowledge. For example, a trial testing different methods of counteracting hypertension or a new way of offering a screening service, say for cervical cancer, can be done on a regional basis throughout the community. Very often in such trials neither of the comparison groups taken out of a selected population will be aware that they are being monitored in a study.

Faulder goes on to identify types of research on humans as follows (pp 65-6):

. . . there is the non-therapeutic trial which is carried out on healthy volunteers who will get no personal benefit from the experiment but who offer their bodies, or their minds, to test a hypothesis, the effects of a drug or perhaps a psychological theory. The second form of human experimentation, or study, as doctors prefer to call it, is that done on patients with a particular illness or condition in clinical trials to compare the merits of different treatments. This type of clinical research combined with professional care enables doctors who are genuinely uncertain about which treatment they should be offering to their patients to feel secure that those who get the new treatment will be carefully monitored and that the final judgment of the results does not rely on their opinion alone.

Both forms of research contemplate the use of controls, that is, as Nicholson (ed) in *Medical Research with Children* (1986) (p 31) explains, 'controls are subjects who are used for the purposes of comparison. In a trial of a new drug, for instance, the subjects may . . . receive either the drug or an inert substance, a placebo. Those receiving the placebo act as controls, since they will come under all the same influences – whether pathological, environmental or psychological – as the subjects, except for the influence of the drug that is on trial'.

In the case of *clinical* trials, as Faulder adds (p 66): '[a] control group of patients in a clinical trial receives the "best standard therapy" and is used as a measure of comparison with another group of patients allotted to the new treatment under study.'

Finally, Carolyn Faulder identifies (p 66):

. . . three provisos [which] are fundamentally important in the ethical conduct of any trial using human subjects and [which] should be equally well understood by both categories of participants – patients/volunteers and doctors.

These are:

- Provided that the patients or volunteers who participate in all these types of experiments are fully informed and freely give their consent, they are not being used as guinea pigs.
- Provided that the trials are well designed and conform to the conditions prescribed in the Declaration of Helsinki, they are a reliable and ethical way of conducting medical research.
- Provided that the doctors who participate in a trial always put the welfare of their individual patients before the interests of science and society, they can be sure that they are caring for their patients according to the highest medical and ethical standards.

A. THE NUREMBERG TRIALS

Undoubtedly, the greatest incentive to regulate research on human beings was the awareness of, and revulsion at, what had been done in the name of medical research during World War II. Jay Katz in his book *Experimentation with Human Beings* (1972) sets out the major elements of the trial of Dr Karl Brandt and others before the Nuremberg Military Tribunals (pp 292-306).

1. Indictment

The United States of America, by the undersigned Telford Taylor, Chief of Counsel for War Crimes, duly appointed to represent said Government in the prosecution of war criminals, charges that the defendants herein participated in a common design or conspiracy to commit and did commit war crimes and crimes against humanity, as defined in Control Council Law No 10, duly enacted by the Allied Control Council on 20 December 1945 . . .

Count Two [and Three] – War Crimes [and Crimes against Humanity]
Between September 1939 and April 1945 all of the defendants herein unlawfully, wilfully, and knowingly committed war crimes [and crimes against humanity], as defined by Article II of Control Council Law No 10, in that they were principals in, accessories to, ordered, abetted, took a consenting part in, and were connected with plans and enterprises involving medical experiments without the subjects' consent, upon [German civilians and] civilians and members of the armed forces of nations then at war with the German Reich . . . in the course of which experiments the defendants committed murders, brutalities, cruelties, tortures, atrocities, and other inhuman acts. Such experiments included, but were not limited to the following:

High-altitude experiments. From about March 1942 to about August 1942 experiments were conducted at the Dachau concentration camp, for the benefit of the German Air Force, to investigate the limits of human endurance and existence at extremely high altitudes. The experiments were carried out in a low-pressure chamber in which the atmospheric conditions and pressures prevailing at high altitude (up to 68,000 feet) could be duplicated. The experimental subjects were placed in the low-pressure chamber and thereafter the simulated altitude therein was raised. Many victims died as a result of these experiments and others suffered grave injury, torture, and ill-treatment . . .

Freezing experiments. From about August 1942 to about May 1943 experiments were conducted at the Dachau concentration camp, primarily for the benefit of the German Air Force, to investigate the most effective means of treating persons who had been severely chilled or frozen. In one series of experiments the subjects were forced to remain in a tank of ice water for periods up to 3 hours. Extreme rigor developed in a short time. Numerous victims died in the course of these experiments. After the survivors were severely chilled, rewarming was attempted by various means. In another series of experiments, the subjects were kept naked outdoors for many hours at temperatures below freezing. The victims screamed with pain as parts of their bodies froze.

Malaria experiments. From about February 1942 to about April 1945 experiments were conducted at the Dachau concentration camp in order to investigate immunization for and treatment of malaria. Healthy concentration-camp inmates were infected by mosquitoes or by injections of extracts of the mucous glands of mosquitoes. After having contracted malaria the subjects were treated with various drugs to test their relative efficacy. Over 1,000 involuntary subjects were used in these experiments. Many of the victims died and others suffered severe pain and permanent disability.

Sulfanilamide experiments. From about July 1942 to about September 1943 experiments to investigate the effectiveness of sulfanilamide were conducted at the Ravensbrueck concentration camp for the benefit of the German Armed Forces. Wounds deliberately inflicted on the experimental subjects were infected with bacteria such as streptococcus, gas gangrene, and tetanus. Circulation of blood was interrupted by tying off blood vessels at both ends of the wound to create a condition similar to that of a battlefield wound. Infection was aggravated by forcing wood shavings and ground glass into the wounds. The infection was treated with sulfanilamide and other drugs to determine their effectiveness. Some subjects died as a result of these experiments and others suffered serious injury and intense agony . . .

Epidemic jaundice experiments. From about June 1943 to about January 1945 experiments were conducted at the Sachsenhausen and Natzweiler concentration camps, for the benefit of the German Armed Forces, to investigate the causes of, and inoculations against, epidemic jaundice. Experimental subjects were deliberately infected with epidemic jaundice, some of whom died as a result, and others were caused great pain and suffering . . .

Spotted fever [typhus] experiments. From about December 1941 to about February 1945 experiments were conducted at the Buchenwald and Natzweiler concentration camps, for the benefit of the German Armed Forces, to investigate the effectiveness of spotted fever and other vaccines. At Buchenwald numerous healthy inmates were deliberately infected with spotted fever virus in order to keep the virus alive; over 90 percent of the victims died as a result. Other healthy inmates were used to determine the effectiveness of different spotted fever vaccines and of various chemical substances. In the course of these experiments 75 percent of the selected number of inmates were vaccinated with one of the vaccines or nourished with one of the chemical substances and, after a period of 3 to 4 weeks, were infected with spotted fever germs. The remaining 25 percent were infected without any previous protection in order to compare the effectiveness of the vaccines and the chemical substances. As a result, hundreds of the persons experimented upon died . . .

Experiments with poison. In or about December 1943, and in or about October 1944, experiments were conducted at the Buchenwald concentration camp to investigate the effect of various poisons upon human beings. The poisons were secretly administered to experimental subjects in their food. The victims died as a result of the poison or were killed immediately in order to permit autopsies. In or about September 1944 experimental subjects were shot with poison bullets and suffered torture and death . . .

Between June 1943 and September 1944 the defendants Rudolf Brandt and Sievers . . . were principals in, accessories to, ordered, abetted, took a consenting part in, and were connected with plans and enterprises involving the murder of civilians and members of the armed forces of nations then at war with the German Reich and who were in the custody of the German Reich in exercise of belligerent control. One hundred [and] twelve Jews were selected for the purpose of completing a skeleton collection for the Reich University of Strasbourg. Their photographs and anthropological measurements were taken. Then they were killed. Thereafter, comparison tests, anatomical research, studies regarding race, pathological features of the body, form and size of the brain, and other tests, were made. The bodies were sent to Strasbourg and defleshed.

Opening statement of the prosecution by Brigadier General Telford Taylor
I turn now to the main part of the indictment and will outline at this point the prosecution's case relating to those crimes alleged to have been committed in the name of medical or scientific research . . . What I will cover now comprehends all of the experiments charged as war crimes . . and as crimes against humanity in . . . the indictment . . .

A sort of rough pattern is apparent on the face of the indictment. Experiments concerning high altitude, the effect of cold, and the potability of processed sea water have an obvious relation to aeronautical and naval combat and rescue problems. The mustard gas and phosphorous burn experiments, as well as those relating to the healing value of sulfanilamide for wounds, can be related to air-raid and battlefield medical problems. It is well known that malaria, epidemic jaundice, and typhus were among the principal diseases which had to be combated by the German Armed Forces and by German authorities in occupied territories.

To some degree, the therapeutic pattern outlined above is undoubtedly a valid one, and explains why the Wehrmacht, and especially the German Air Force, participated in these experiments. Fanatically bent upon conquest, utterly ruthless as to the means or instruments to be used in achieving victory, and callous to the sufferings of people whom they regarded as inferior, the German militarists were willing to gather whatever scientific fruit these experiments might yield.

But our proof will show that a quite different and even more sinister objective runs like a red thread through these hideous researches. We will show that in some instances the true object of these experiments was not how to rescue or to cure, but how to destroy and kill. The sterilization experiments were, it is clear, purely destructive in purpose. The prisoners at Buchenwald who were shot with poisoned bullets were not guinea pigs to test an antidote for the poison; their murderers really wanted to know how quickly the poison would kill. This destructive object is not superficially as apparent in other experiments, but we will show that it was often there.

Mankind has not heretofore felt the need of a word to denominate the science of how to kill prisoners most rapidly and subjugate people in large numbers. This case and these defendants have created this gruesome question for the lexicographer. For the moment we will christen this macabre science 'thanatology', the science of producing death. The thanatological knowledge, derived in part from these experiments, supplied the techniques for genocide, a policy of the Third Reich, exemplified in the 'euthanasia' program and in the widespread slaughter of Jews, gypsies, Poles, and Russians. This policy of mass extermination could not have been so effectively carried out without the active participation of German medical scientists . . .

The experiments known as 'high-altitude' or 'low-pressure' experiments were carried out at the Dachau concentration camp in 1942. According to the proof, the original proposal that such experiments be carried out on human beings originated in the spring of 1941 with a Dr Sigmund Rascher. Rascher was at that time a captain in the medical service of the German Air Force, and also held officer rank in the SS. He is believed now to be dead.

The origin of the idea is revealed in a letter which Rascher wrote to Himmler in May 1941 at which time Rascher was taking a course in aviation medicine at a German Air Force headquarters in Munich. According to the letter, this course included researches into high-altitude flying and

> considerable regret was expressed at the fact that no tests with human material had yet been possible for us, as such experiments are very dangerous and nobody volunteers for them. (1602-PS.)

Rascher, in this letter, went on to ask Himmler to put human subjects at his disposal and baldly stated that the experiments might result in death to the subjects but that the tests theretofore made with monkeys had not been satisfactory.

Rascher's letter was answered by Himmler's adjutant, the defendant, Rudolf Brandt, who informed Rascher that – '. . . Prisoners will, of course, gladly be made available for the high-flight researches.'

. . . The tests themselves were carried out in the spring and summer of 1942, using the pressure chamber which the German Air Force had provided. The victims were locked in the low-pressure chamber, which was an airtight ball-like compartment, and then the pressure in the chamber was altered to simulate the atmospheric conditions prevailing at extremely high altitudes. The pressure in the chamber could be varied with great rapidity, which permitted the defendants to duplicate the atmospheric conditions which an aviator might encounter in falling great distances through space without a parachute and without oxygen.

. . . The first report by Rascher was made in April 1942, and contains a description of the effect of the low-pressure chamber on a 37-year-old Jew. (1971-A-PS.) I quote:

> The third experiment of this type took such an extraordinary course that I called an SS physician of the camp as witness, since I had worked on these experiments all by myself. It was a continuous experiment without oxygen at a height of 12 kilometers conducted on a 37-year-old Jew in good general condition. Breathing continued up to 30 minutes. After 4 minutes the experimental subject began to perspire and wiggle his head, after 5 minutes cramps occurred, between 6 and 10 minutes breathing increased in speed and the experimental subject became unconscious; from 11 to 30 minutes breathing slowed down to three breaths per minute, finally stopping altogether.
> Severest cyanosis developed in between and foam appeared at the mouth.
> At 5 minute intervals electrocardiograms from three leads were written. After breathing had stopped Ekg (electrocardiogram) was continuously written until the action of the heart had come to a complete standstill. About ½ hour after breathing had stopped, dissection was started . . .

Another series of experiments carried out at the Dachau concentration camp concerned immunization for and treatment of malaria. Over 1,200 inmates of practically every nationality were experimented upon. Many persons who participated in these experiments have already been tried before a general military court held in Dachau, and the findings of that court will be laid before this Tribunal. The malaria experiments were carried out under the general supervision of a Dr Schilling, with whom the defendant Sievers and others in the box collaborated. The evidence will show that healthy persons were infected by mosquitoes or by injections from the glands of mosquitoes. Catholic priests were among the subjects. The defendant Gebhardt kept Himmler informed of the progress of these experiments. Rose furnished Schilling with fly eggs for them, and others of the defendants participated in various ways which the evidence will demonstrate.

After the victims had been infected they were variously treated with quinine, neosalvarsan, pyramidon, antipryrin, and several combinations of these drugs. Many deaths occurred from excessive doses of neosalvarsan and pyramidon. According to the findings of the Dachau court, malaria was the direct cause of 30 deaths and 300 to 400 others died as the result of subsequent complications . . .

From December 1941, until near the end of the war, a large program of medical experimentation was carried out upon concentration camp inmates at Buchenwald and Natzweiler to investigate the value of various vaccines. This research involved a variety of diseases – typhus, yellow fever, smallpox, paratyphoid A and B, cholera, and diphtheria . . .

The general pattern of these typhus experiments was as follows. A group of concentration camp inmates, selected from the healthier ones who had some resistance to disease, were injected with an anti-typhus vaccine, the efficacy of which was to be tested. Thereafter, all the persons in the group would be infected with typhus. At the same time, other inmates who had not been vaccinated were also infected for purposes of comparison – these unvaccinated victims were called the 'control' group. But perhaps the most wicked and murderous circumstance in this whole case is that still other inmates were deliberately infected with typhus with the sole purpose of keeping the typhus virus alive and generally available in the bloodstream of the inmates . . .

The 20 physicians in the dock range from leaders of German scientific medicine, with excellent international reputations, down to the dregs of the German medical profession. All of them have in common a callous lack of consideration and human regard for, and an unprincipled willingness to abuse their power over the poor, unfortunate, defenseless creatures who had been deprived of their rights by a ruthless and criminal government. All of them violated the Hippocratic commandments which they had solemnly sworn to uphold and abide by, including the fundamental principle never to do harm – *'primum non nocere'*.

Outstanding men of science, distinguished for their scientific ability in Germany and abroad, are the defendants Rostock and Rose. Both exemplify, in their training and practice alike, the highest traditions of German medicine. Rostock headed the Department of Surgery at the University of Berlin and served as dean of its medical school. Rose studied under the famous surgeon, Enderlen, at Heidelberg and then became a distinguished specialist in the fields of public health and tropical diseases. Handloser and Schroeder are outstanding medical administrators. Both of them made their careers in military medicine and reached the peak of their profession. Five more defendants are much younger men who are nevertheless already known as the possessors of considerable scientific ability, or capacity in medical administration. These include the defendants Karl Brandt, Ruff, Beiglboeck, Schaefer, and Becker-Freyseng.

A number of others such as Romberg and Fischer are well trained, and several of them attained high professional position. But among the remainder few were known as outstanding scientific men. Among them at the foot of the list is Blome who has published his autobiography entitled 'Embattled Doctor' in which he sets forth that he eventually decided to become a doctor because a medical career would enable him to become 'master over life and death' . . .

I intend to pass very briefly over matters of medical ethics, such as the conditions under which a physician may lawfully perform a medical experiment upon a person who has voluntarily subjected himself to it, or whether experiments may lawfully be performed upon criminals who have been condemned to death. This case does not present such problems. No refined questions confront us here.

None of the victims of the atrocities perpetrated by these defendants were volunteers, and this is true regardless of what these unfortunate people may have said or signed before their tortures began. Most of the victims had not been condemned to death, and those who had been were not criminals, unless it be a crime to be a Jew, or a Pole, or a gypsy, or a Russian prisoner of war.

Were it necessary, one could make a long list of the respects in which the experiments which these defendants performed departed from every known standard of medical ethics. But the gulf between these atrocities and serious research in the healing art is so patent that such a tabulation would be cynical.

These experiments revealed nothing which civilized medicine can use. It was, indeed, ascertained that phenol or gasoline injected intravenously will kill a man inexpensively and within 60 seconds. This and a few other 'advances' are all in the field of thanatology . . .

Apart from these deadly fruits, the experiments were not only criminal but a scientific failure. It is indeed as if a just deity had shrouded the solutions which they attempted to reach with murderous means. The moral shortcomings of the defendants and the precipitous ease with which they decided to commit murder in quest of 'scientific results', dulled also that scientific hesitancy, that thorough thinking-through, that responsible weighing of every single step which alone can insure scientifically valid results. Even if they had merely been forced to pay as little as two dollars for human experimental subjects, such as American investigators may have to pay for a cat, they might have thought twice before wasting unnecessary numbers, and thought of simpler and better ways to solve their problems. The fact that these investigators had free and unrestricted access to human beings to be experimented upon misled them to the dangerous and fallacious conclusion that the results would thus be better and more quickly obtainable than if they had gone through the labor of preparation, thinking, and meticulous preinvestigation.

A particularly striking example is the sea-water experiment. I believe that three of the accused . . . will today admit that this problem could have been solved simply and definitively within the space of one afternoon. On 20 May 1944 when these accused convened to discuss the problem, a thinking chemist could have solved it right in the presence of the assembly within the space of a few hours by the use of nothing more gruesome than a piece of jelly, a semipermeable membrane and a salt solution, and the German Armed Forces would have had the answer on 21 May 1944. But what happened instead? The vast armies of the disenfranchised slaves were at the beck and call of this sinister assembly; and instead of thinking, they simply relied on their power over human beings rendered rightless by a criminal state and government . . .

Who could German medicine look to to keep the profession true to its traditions and protect it from the ravaging inroads of Nazi pseudo-science? This was the supreme responsibility of the leaders of German medicine – men like Rostock and Rose and Schroeder and Handloser. That is why their guilt is greater than that of any of the defendants in the dock. They are the men who utterly failed their country and their profession, who showed neither courage nor wisdom nor the vestiges of moral character. . . .

3. Extracts from argumentation and evidence of prosecution and defense

a. Testimony of defense expert witness Dr Franz Vollhardt
Direct examination.

Dr Marx: Please, would you briefly tell the Tribunal what your scientific activities have been and in what special field you have taken a particularly great interest, and since when?

Witness Vollhardt: I am Professor of Internal Medicine at Frankfurt and predominantly I have dealt with the questions of circulation, metabolism, blood pressure, and kidney diseases. . . .

Q: Which foreign academies and foreign societies have you been a member of? . . .

A: I am Honorary Doctor of the Sorbonne, Paris, of Goettingen and Freiburg; and as far as societies are concerned, there are a lot of them, Medical Society of Edinburgh, at Geneva, at Luxembourg. I am an Honorary Member of the University at Santiago, and so on and so forth. . . .

Q: Now, Professor, have you sufficient insight into the planning and carrying out of the so-called sea-water experiments to give an expert opinion on that subject? . . .

A: I think that scientifically speaking the planning was excellent and I have no objection to the entire plan. It was good to add a hunger-and-thirst group because we know by experience that thirst can be borne less well than hunger, and if people are suffering from hunger and thirst too, they do not suffer from hunger, but do suffer from thirst; and that resembles what shipwrecked persons would be subjected to because they only suffer from thirst. It was excellent that Wofatit was to be introduced into the experiments too, although it was expected from the beginning that this wonderful discovery would show its value. . . .

Q: Could the aim of these experiments have been achieved with a semipermeable membrane?

A: I don't understand how one can imagine this. What we are concerned with is the question of how long the human body can survive without water and under the excess quantity of salt. Now, that is subject to the water content of the body and it depends first of all, upon whether water is only used by the intermediary tissues or whether the cell liquid too is being used up. In the latter case, there is a danger which becomes apparent through excess potassium quantities, and this was also continuously observed and checked during such experiments, and there were no excess potassium quantities such as can be expected after 6 days.

Q: Nor would it be right to say that these experiments were not planned scientifically and medically, is that correct?

A: Absolutely not.

Q: Could they have been planned differently?

A: I couldn't imagine how.

Q: Were these experiments in the interests of active warfare, or in the interests of the care of shipwrecked sailors or soldiers?

A: The latter.

Q: In other words, for aviators and sailors who were shipwrecked or might be shipwrecked?

A: Towards the end of the war there was an increase in the number of pilots shot down as well as of shipwrecked personnel, and it was, therefore, the duty of the hygiene department concerned to consider the question of how one could best deal with such cases of shipwrecked personnel . . .

Q: Now, Professor, the experiments we were talking about; did they have a practical valuable aim and did they show a corresponding result?

A: Yes, that is correct. For instance an important observation was made which Eppinger had expected; he wanted to see if the kidneys did concentrate salt under such extreme conditions to an even higher extent than one expected previously. One thought that it would be something like 2.0 percent but 2.6 or 2.7 percent and record figures of 3.0, 3.5, 3.6 and 4 percent are shown, so that the fortunate man who is in a position to concentrate 3.6 percent or 4 percent of salt would be able to live on sea water for quite a long period. . . .

Finally, one unsuspected fact was shown which may be connected with this, and that is that the drinking of small quantities of sea water up to 500 cc given over a lengthy period turned out to be better than unalleviated thirst. . . .

Q: So, you think that the result of these experiments is not only of importance in war-time, but is also of importance for the problems of seafaring nations?

A: Quite right, it is a wonderful thing for all seafaring nations.

b. Final plea for defendant Joachim Mrugowsky . . .

The case with the typhus experiments is different. No order was given to kill a man in order to obtain knowledge. But the typhus experiments were dangerous experiments. Out of 724 experimental persons, 154 died. But these 154 deaths from the typhus experiments have to be compared with the 15,000 who died of typhus every day in the camps for Soviet prisoners of war, and the innumerable deaths from typhus among the civilian population of the occupied eastern territories and the German troops. This enormous number of deaths led to the absolute necessity of having effective vaccines against typhus in sufficient quantity. The newly developed vaccines had been tested in the animal experiments as to their compatibility. . . .

The Tribunal will have to decide whether, in view of the enormous extent of epidemic typhus, in view of the 15,000 deaths it was causing daily in the camps for Russian prisoners of war alone, the order given by the government authorities to test the typhus vaccines was justified or not. If the answer is in the affirmative, then the typhus experiments at Buchenwald were not criminal, since the prosecution did not contest that they were carried out according to the rules of medical science. . . .

c. Testimony of defendant Gerhard Rose
Direct examination . . .

Dr Fritz: What do you know about the reasons for this protest (against experiments) being ignored and the typhus experiments being carried out in spite of it? . . .

Defendant Rose: The Buchenwald experiments (with typhus vaccine) had four main results. First of all, they showed that belief in the protective effect of Weigl vaccine was a mistake, although this belief seemed to be based on long observation. Secondly, they showed that the useful vaccines did not protect against infection, but almost certainly prevented death, under the conditions of the Buchenwald experiments. Thirdly, they showed that the objections of the biological experts to the vitelline membrane vaccines and to the lice vaccines were unjustified, and that vitelline membrane, rabbit lungs, and lice intestines were of equal value. We learned this only through the Buchenwald experiments. This left the way open to mass production of typhus vaccines.

The Buchenwald experiments showed in time that several vaccines were useless: First, the process according to Otto and Wohlrab, the process according to Cox, the process of Rickettsia Prowazeki murina, that is, vaccine from egg cultures; secondly, the vaccines of the Behring works which were produced according to the Otto process, but with other concentrations; finally the Ipsen vaccines from mouse liver. The vaccines of the Behring works were in actual use at that time in thousands of doses. They always represented a danger to health. Without these experiments the vaccines, which were recognized as useless, would have been produced in large quantities because they all had one thing in common: their technical production was much simpler and cheaper than that of the useful vaccines. In any case, one thing is certain, that the victims of this Buchenwald typhus test did not suffer in vain and did not die in vain. There was only one choice, the sacrifice of human lives, of persons determined for that purpose, or to let things run their course, to endanger the lives of innumerable human beings who would be selected not by the Reich Criminal Police Office but by blind fate. . . .

d. Testimony of prosecution expert witness Dr Andrew C Ivy
Direct examination . . .

Mr Hardy: It is your opinion, then, that the state cannot assume the moral responsibility of a physician to his patient or experimental subject?
  Witness Dr Ivy: That is my opinion.
  Q: On what do you base your opinion? What is the reason for that opinion?
  A: I base that opinion on the principles of ethics and morals contained in the oath of Hippocrates. I think it should be obvious that a state cannot follow a physician around in his daily administration to see that the moral responsibility inherent therein is properly carried out. This moral responsibility that controls or should control the conduct of a physician should be inculcated into the minds of physicians just as moral responsibility of other sorts, and those principles are clearly depicted or enunciated in the oath of Hippocrates with which every physician should be acquainted.
  Q: Is the oath of Hippocrates the Golden Rule in the United States and to your knowledge throughout the world?
  A: According to my knowledge it represents the Golden Rule of the medical profession. It states how one doctor would like to be treated by another doctor in case he were ill. And in that way how a doctor should treat his patients or experimental subjects. He should treat them as though he were serving as a subject.
  Q: Several of the defendants have pointed out in this case that the oath of Hippocrates is obsolete today. Do you follow that opinion?
  A: I do not. The moral imperative of the oath of Hippocrates I believe is necessary for the survival of the scientific and technical philosophy of medicine. . . .

e. Closing brief for defendant Siegfried Ruff . . .

Experiments which time and again have been described in international literature without meeting any opposition do not constitute a crime from the medical point of view. For nowhere did a plaintiff arise from the side of the responsible professional organization, or from that of the administration of justice, to denounce as criminal the experiments described in literature. On the contrary, the authors of those reports on their human experiments gained general recognition and fame; they were awarded the highest honors; they gained historical importance. And in spite of all this, are they supposed to have been criminals? No! In view of the complete lack of written legal norms, the physician, who generally knows only little about the law, has to rely on and refer to the admissibility of what is generally to be admissible all over the world.
  The defense is convinced that the Tribunal, when deciding this problem without prejudice, will first study the many experiments performed all over the world on healthy and sick persons, on prisoners and free people, on criminals and on the poor, even on children and mentally ill persons, in order to see how the medical profession in its international totality answers the question of the admissibility of human experiments, not only in theory but also in practice.
  It is psychologically understandable that German research workers today will, if possible, have nothing to do with human experiments and will try to avoid them, or would like to describe them as inadmissible even if before 1933 they were perhaps of the opposite opinion. However, experiments performed in 1905-1912 by a highly respected American in Asia for the fight against the plague, which made him famous all over the world, cannot and ought not to be labeled as criminal because a Blome is supposed to have performed the same experiments during the Hitler period (which, in fact, however, were not performed at all); and experiments for which, before 1933, a foreign research worker, the Englishman Ross,

was awarded the Nobel Prize for his malaria experiments, do not deserve to be condemned only because a German physician performed similar experiments during the Hitler regime . . .

f. Testimony of prosecution expert witness Dr Andrew C Ivy
Cross-examination . . .

Dr Sauter: Witness, you spoke yesterday of a number of experiments carried out in the United States and in other countries outside Germany. For example, pellagra, swamp fever, beri-beri, plague, etc. Now, I should like to have a very clear answer from you to the following question. In these experiments which you heard of partly from persons involved in them and partly from international literature, did deaths occur during the experiments and as a result of the experiments or not? Professor, I ask you this question because you said yesterday that you examined all international literature concerning this question, and, therefore, have a certain specialized knowledge on this question.

Witness Dr Ivy: I also said that when one reviews the literature, he cannot be sure that he has done a complete or perfect job.

So far as the reports I have read and presented yesterday are concerned, there were no deaths in trench fever. There were no deaths mentioned, to my knowledge, in the article on pellagra. There were no deaths mentioned, to my knowledge, in the article on beri-beri, and there were no deaths in the article, according to my knowledge, in Colonel Strong's article on plague. I would not testify that I have read all the articles in the medical literature involving the use of human beings as subjects in medical experiments.

Q: And, in the literature which you have read, Witness, there was not a single case where deaths occurred? Did I understand you correctly?

A: Yes, in the yellow fever experiments I indicated that Dr Carroll and Dr Lazare died.

Q: That is the only case you know of?

A: That's all that I know of. . . .

g. Testimony of defendant Gerhard Rose
Cross-examination . . .

Mr McHaney: Now, would the extreme necessity for the large-scale production of typhus vaccines and the resultant experiments on human beings in concentration camps have arisen had not Germany been engaged in a war?

Defendant Rose: That question cannot simply be answered with 'yes' or 'no'. It is, on the whole, not very probable that without the war typhus would have broken out in the German camps, but it is not altogether beyond the bounds of possibility because in times of peace too typhus has broken out in individual cases from time to time. The primary danger in the camps is the louse danger, and infection by lice also occurs in times of peace. If typhus breaks out in a camp that is infected with lice, a typhus epidemic can arise in peacetime too, of course.

Q: But Germany had never experienced any difficulty with typhus before the war. Isn't that right?

A: Not for many decades, no.

Q: You stated that nine hundred persons were used in Dr Strong's plague experiments?

A: Yes, I know that number from the literature on the subject.

Q: What is the usual mortality in plague?

A: That depends on whether it is bubonic plague or lung pest. In one, namely, bubonic plague, the mortality can be as high as sixty or seventy percent. It also can be lower. In lung pest, the mortality is just about one hundred.

Q: How many people died in Dr Strong's plague experiments?

A: According to what his report says, none of them died, but this result could not have been anticipated because this was the first time that anyone had attempted to inoculate living plague virus into human beings, and Strong said in his first publication in 1905 that he himself was surprised that no unpleasant incidents occurred and that there was only severe fever reaction. That despite this unexpectedly favorable outcome of Strong's experiments the specialists had considerable misgivings about this procedure can be seen first of all from publications where that is explicitly stated; for example, two Englishmen say that, contrary to expectations, these experiments went off well but nevertheless this process cannot be used for general vaccination because there is always the danger that, through some unexpected event, this strain again becomes virulent. Moreover, from other works that Strong later published it can be seen that guinea pigs and monkeys that he vaccinated with this vaccine died not of the plague, but of the toxic effects of the vaccine. All these difficulties are the reason why this enormously important discovery, which Koller and Otto made in 1903, and Strong in 1905, has only been generally applied, for all practical purposes, since 1926. That is an indication of the care and fear with which this whole matter was first approached, and Strong could not know ahead of time that his experiments would turn out well. I described here the enormous concern that Strong felt during all these months regarding the fact that that might happen which every specialist feared, viz, that the virus would become virulent again. That is an enormous responsibility.

Q: Be that as it may, nobody died. That is a fact, isn't it?

A: If anyone did die, the publications say nothing about it. There were deaths only among the monkeys and guinea pigs that are mentioned in the publication. If human beings died, there is no mention in the publication. It is generally known that if there are serious accidents in such experiments as this, they are only most reluctantly made public. . . .

NOTE

Leo Alexander, 'Medical Science under Dictatorship' 241 *New England Journal of Medicine* 39, 43 (1949). . . .

[A] series of experiments gave results that might have been an important medical contribution if an important lead had not been ignored. The efficacy of various vaccines and drugs against typhus was tested at the Buchenwald and Natzweiler concentration camps. Prevaccinated persons and non-vaccinated controls were injected with live typhus rickettsias, and the death rates of the two series compared. After a certain number of passages, the Matelska strain of typhus rickettsia proved to become avirulent for man. Instead of seizing upon this as a possibility to develop a live vaccine, the experimenters, including the chief consultant, Professor Gerhard Rose, who should have known better, were merely annoyed at the fact that the controls did not die either, discarded this strain and continued testing their relatively ineffective dead vaccines against a new virulent strain. This incident shows that the basic unconscious motivation and attitude has a great influence in determining the scientist's awareness of the phenomena that pass through his vision.

4. Final plea for defendant Karl Brandt by Dr Robert Servatius . . .

It is contended that the state finds its limits in the eternal basic elements of law, which are said to be so clear that anyone could discern their violation as a crime, and that loyalty to the state beyond these limits is therefore a crime. One forgets that eternal law, the law of nature, is but a guiding principle for the state and the legislator and not a counter-code of law which the subject might use as a support against the state. It is emphasized that no other state had made such decisions up to now. This is true only to a certain extent. It is no proof, however, that such decisions were not necessary and admissible now. There is no prohibition against daring to progress.

The progress of medical science opened up the problem of experiments on human beings already in the past century, and eventually made it ripe for decision. It is not the first time that a state has adopted a certain attitude with regard to euthanasia with a change of ideology.

Only the statesmen decide what is to be done in the interests of the community, and they have never hesitated to issue such a decision whenever they deemed it necessary in the interest of their people. Thereupon their rules and orders were carried through under the authority of the state, which is the basis of society.

Inquisition, witch trials, and revolutionary tribunals have existed in the name of the state and eternal justice, and the executive participants did not consider themselves criminals but servants of their community. They would have been killed if they had stood up against what was believed to be newly discovered eternal justice. What is the subject to do if the orders of the state exceed the customary limits which the individual himself took for inviolable according to tradition?

What did the airman think who dropped the first atomic bomb on Hiroshima? Did he consider himself a criminal? What did the statesmen think who ordered this atomic bomb to be used? We know from the history of this event that the motive was patriotism, based on the harsh necessity of sacrificing hundreds of thousands to save their own soldiers' lives. This motive was stronger than the prohibition of the Hague Convention, under which belligerents have no unlimited right in the choice of methods for inflicting damage on the enemy.

'My cause is just and my quarrel honorable', says the King. And Shakespeare's soldier answers him: 'That's more than we know.' Another soldier adds: 'Ay, or more than we should seek after; for we know enough if we know we are the king's subjects; if his cause be wrong, our obedience to the king wipes the crime out of us.'

It is the hard necessity of the state on which the defense for Karl Brandt is based against the charge of having performed criminal experiments on human beings.

Here also – in addition to the care for the population – the lives of soldiers were at stake, soldiers who had to be protected from death and epidemics. In Professor Bickenbach's experiment, the issue was the lives of women and children who without 45 million gas masks would have been as unprotected against the expected gas attack as the Japanese were against the atomic bomb. Biological warfare was imminent, even praised abroad as cheaper and more effective than the atomic bomb.

The prosecution opposes to this necessity the condition of absolute voluntariness.

It was a surprise to hear from the expert Professor Ivy that in the penitentiaries many hundreds of volunteers were pressing for admission to experiments, and that more volunteered than could be used. I do not want to dispose of this phenomenon with irony and sarcasm. There may be people who realize that the community has the right to ask them for a sacrifice. Their feelings of justice may tell them that insistence on humanity has its limits. If humanity means the appeal to the strong not to forget the weak in the abundance of might and wealth, the weak should also make their contribution when all are in need.

But what if in the emergency of war the convicts, and those declared to be unworthy to serve in the armed forces, refuse to accept such a sacrifice voluntarily, and only prove an asocial burden to state and community and bring about the downfall of the community? Is not compulsion by the state then admissible as an additional expiation?

The prosecution says 'No.' According to this, human rights demand the downfall of human beings.

But there is a mixture of voluntariness and compulsory expiation, 'purchased voluntariness'. Here the experimental subject does not make a sacrifice out of conviction for the good of the community but for his own good. The subject gives his consent because he is to receive money, cigarettes, a mitigation of punishment, etc. There may be isolated cases of this nature where the person is really a volunteer, but as a rule it is not so.

If one compares the actual risk with the advantage granted, one cannot admit the consent of these 'voluntary prisoners' as legal, in spite of all the protective forms they have to sign, for these can only have been obtained by taking the advantage of inexperience, imprudence, or distress.

Looking through medical literature, one cannot escape the growing conviction that the word 'volunteer', where it appears at all, is used only as a word of protection and camouflage; it is hardly ever missing since the struggle over this problem became acute.

I will touch only briefly on what I have explained in detail in my closing brief. No one will contend that human beings really allowed themselves to be infected voluntarily with venereal disease; this has nowhere been stated explicitly in literature. Cholera and plague are also not minor inconveniences one is likely to undergo voluntarily for a trifle in the interest of science. Above all, it is not customary to hand over children for experimental purposes, and I cannot believe that in the 13 experiments carried out on a total of 223 children, as stated in Document Karl Brandt 117 . . . the mothers gave their consent. Would not the mothers have deserved the praise of the scientist for the sacrifice they trustfully made in the interest of science, praise which is otherwise liberally granted to real volunteers in reports on experiments?

Is it not likely to have been similar to the experiments carried out by Professor McCance? The German authorities who condemn the defendants in a particularly violent form have no objection to raise here against the order to hand over weakling children to a research commission for experimental purposes. The questionnaires which the Tribunal approved for me in order to get further information about this matter have not been answered as the higher authorities did not give permission for such statements to be made. This silence says enough; it is proof of what is supposed to be legal today in the line of 'voluntariness'.

It is repeatedly shown that the experiments for which no consent was given were permitted with the full knowledge of the government authorities. It is further shown that these experiments were published in professional literature without meeting any objection, and that they were even accepted by the public without concern as a normal phenomenon when reports about them appeared in popular magazines.

This happens at a time when the same press is stigmatizing as crimes against humanity the German experiments which were necessary in the interests of the state. Voluntariness is a fiction; the emergency of the state hard reality.

In all countries experiments on human beings have been performed by doctors, certainly not because they took pleasure in killing or tormenting, but only at the instigation and

under the protection of their state, and in accordance with their own conviction of the
necessity for these experiments in the struggle for the existence of the people. . . .

5. Final statements of the defendants . . .

a. Final statement of defendant Siegfried Handloser . . .

More than 150 years ago, the motto and guiding principle created for German military
doctors and their successors was 'Scientiae, Humanitati, Patriae' (for Science, Humanity,
and Fatherland). Like the medical officers in their entirety I also have remained true to that
guiding principle in thought and in deed. Realizing the outcome of the events of these recent
times, may the joint endeavors of all the nations succeed in avoiding in future the
immeasurable misfortune of war, the dreadful side of which nobody knows better than the
military doctor.

b. Final statement of defendant Gerhard Rose

. . . Everyone who, as a scientist, has an insight into the history of dangerous medical
experiments, knows with certainty the following fact. Aside from the self-experiments of
doctors, which represent a very small minority of such experiments, the extent to which
subjects are volunteers is often deceptive. At the very best they amount to self-deceit on the
part of the physician who conducts the experiment, but very frequently to a deliberate
misleading of the public. In the majority of such cases, if we ethically examine facts, we find
an exploitation of the ignorance, the frivolity, the economic distress, or other emergency on
the part of the experimental subjects. I may only refer to the example which was presented
to the Tribunal by Dr Ivy when he presented the forms for the American malaria
experiments.

You yourselves, gentlemen of the Tribunal, are in a position to examine whether, on the
basis of the information contained in these forms, individuals of the average education of an
inmate of a prison can form a sufficiently clear opinion of the risks of an experiment made
with pernicious malaria. These facts will be confirmed by any sincere and decent scientist in
a personal conversation, though he would not like to make such a statement in public. . . .

6. Judgment
. . .

Beals, Sebring, Crawford, JJ: . . . Judged by any standard of proof the record clearly shows
the commission of war crimes and crimes against humanity substantially as alleged in counts
two and three of the indictment. Beginning with the outbreak of World War II criminal
medical experiments on non-German nationals, both prisoners of war and civilians,
including Jews and 'asocial' persons, were carried out on a large scale in Germany and the
occupied countries. These experiments were not the isolated and casual acts of individual
doctors and scientists working solely on their own responsibility, but were the product of
coordinated policy-making and planning at high governmental, military, and Nazi Party
levels, conducted as an integral part of the total war effort. They were ordered, sanctioned,
permitted, or approved by persons in positions of authority who under all principles of law
were under the duty to know about these things and to take steps to terminate or prevent
them.

The great weight of the evidence before us is to the effect that certain types of medical
experiments on human beings, when kept within reasonably well-defined bounds, conform
to the ethics of the medical profession generally. The protagonists of the practice of human
experimentation justify their views on the basis that such experiments yield results for the
good of society that are unprocurable by other methods or means of study. All agree,
however, that certain basic principles must be observed in order to satisfy moral, ethical,
and legal concepts:

1. The voluntary consent of the human subject is absolutely essential.

This means that the person involved should have legal capacity to give consent; should be
so situated as to be able to exercise free power of choice, without the intervention of any
element of force, fraud, deceit, duress, over-reaching, or other ulterior form of constraint or
coercion; and should have sufficient knowledge and comprehension of the element of the
subject matter involved as to enable him to make an understanding and enlightened
decision. This latter element requires that before the acceptance of an affirmative by the

experimental subject there should be made known to him the nature, duration, and purpose of the experiment; the method and means by which it is to be conducted; all inconveniences and hazards reasonably to be expected; and the effects upon his health or person which may possibly come from his participation in the experiment.

The duty and responsibility for ascertaining the quality of the consent rests upon each individual who initiates, directs, or engages in the experiment. It is a personal duty and responsibility which may not be delegated to another with impunity.

2. The experiment should be such as to yield fruitful results for the good of society, unprocurable by other methods or means of study, and not random and unnecessary in nature.

3. The experiment should be so designed and based on the results of animal experimentation and a knowledge of the natural history of the disease or other problem under study that the anticipated results will justify the performance of the experiment.

4. The experiment should be so conducted as to avoid all unnecessary physical and mental suffering and injury.

5. No experiment should be conducted where there is an *a priori* reason to believe that death or disabling injury will occur; except, perhaps, in those experiments where the experimental physicians also serve as subjects.

6. The degree of risk to be taken should never exceed that determined by the humanitarian importance of the problem to be solved by the experiment.

7. Proper preparations should be made and adequate facilities provided to protect the experimental subject against even remote possibilities of injury, disability, or death.

8. The experiment should be conducted only by scientifically qualified persons. The highest degree of skill and care should be required through all stages of the experiment of those who conduct or engage in the experiment.

9. During the course of the experiment the human subject should be at liberty to bring the experiment to an end if he has reached the physical or mental state where continuation of the experiment seems to him to be impossible.

10. During the course of the experiment the scientist in charge must be prepared to terminate the experiment at any stage, if he has probable cause to believe, in the exercise of the good faith, superior skill, and careful judgment required of him that a continuation of the experiment is likely to result in injury, disability, or death to the experimental subject.

Of the ten principles which have been enumerated our judicial concern, of course, is with those requirements which are purely legal in nature – or which at least are so clearly related to matters legal that they assist us in determining criminal culpability and punishment. To go beyond that point would lead us into a field that would be beyond our sphere of competence. However, the point need not be labored. We find from the evidence that in the medical experiments which have been proved, these ten principles were much more frequently honored in their breach than in their observance. Many of the concentration camp inmates who were the victims of these atrocities were citizens of countries other than the German Reich. They were non-German nationals, including Jews and 'asocial persons', both prisoners of war and civilians, who had been imprisoned and forced to submit to these tortures and barbarities without so much as a semblance of trial. In every single instance appearing in the record, subjects were used who did not consent to these experiments; indeed, as to some of the experiments, it is not even contended by the defendants that the subjects occupied the status of volunteers. In no case was the experimental subject at liberty of his own free choice to withdraw from any experiment. In many cases experiments were performed by unqualified persons; were conducted at random for no adequate scientific reason, and under revolting physical conditions. All of the experiments were conducted with unnecessary suffering and injury, and but very little, if any, precautions were taken to protect or safeguard the human subjects from the possibilities of injury, disability, or death. In every one of the experiments the subjects experienced extreme pain or torture, and in most of them they suffered permanent injury, mutilation, or death, either as a direct result of the experiments or because of lack of adequate follow-up care.

Obviously all of these experiments involving brutalities, tortures, disabling injury, and deaths were performed in complete disregard of international conventions, the laws and customs of war [and] the general principles of criminal law as derived from the criminal laws of all civilized nations . . . Manifestly human experiments under such conditions are contrary to 'the principles of the law of nations as they result from the usages established among civilized peoples, from the laws of humanity, and from the dictates of public conscience'. . . .

There is some evidence to the effect that the camp inmates used as subjects in the first series submitted to being used as experimental subjects after being told that the experiments were harmless and that additional food would be given to volunteers. But these victims were not informed that they would be artificially infected with a highly virulent virus nor that they might die as a result. Certainly no one would seriously suggest that under the circumstances these men gave their legal consent to act as subjects. One does not ordinarily consent to be the special object of a murder, and if one did, such consent would not absolve his slayer. . . .

[Sixteen of the twenty-three defendants were found guilty of war crimes and crimes against humanity. Seven, including Karl Brandt, Rudolf Brandt, and Joachim Mrugowsky, were sentenced to death by hanging; the other nine, including Siegfried Handloser and Gerhard Rose, to imprisonment varying from ten years to life.]

The ten principles set out in the above judgment have become known as the Nuremberg Code. It is sometimes thought that they constitute the first modern attempt to lay down the principles upon which research is to be conducted. Nicholson (ed), however, points out in *Medical Research with Children* (1986) that (p 154):

> The first modern guidelines for the conduct of clinical research were produced by the German Ministry of the Interior in 1931 . . . They were produced in response to frequent allegations, in both the German Press and Parliament, of unethical conduct by doctors during the previous decade. At that time Germany had a thriving chemical industry, collaboration with which had enabled researchers to develop the first chemotherapeutic agents for infections such as malaria, trypanosomiasis, and leishmaniasis, and led to animal trials of Prontosil, the first sulphonamide, in 1933. Howard-Jones suggests that doctors may well not have been 'sufficiently critical in exploiting the multiplicity of new remedies' placed at their disposal. In the midst of the public debate, the Berlin Medical Board suggested that there should be an official body to regulate all proposed experiments on humans: it seems likely that this was the first time that peer review of modern clinical research had been suggested. Little came of the suggestion, however.

Obviously, these earlier guidelines proved irrelevant once the Nazis embarked upon the kind of investigation mentioned in the *Brandt* trial.

B. THE HELSINKI DECLARATION

The Nuremberg Code represented the basis on which civilised society was expected to conduct itself until it was supplemented by the Declaration of Helsinki of the World Medical Association in 1964 (as amended).

> It is the mission of the medical doctor to safeguard the health of the people. His or her knowledge and conscience are dedicated to the fulfilment of this mission.
>
> The Declaration of Geneva of the World Medical Association binds the physician with the words, 'The health of my patient will be my first consideration', and the International Code of Medical Ethics declares that 'A physician shall act only in the patient's interest when providing medical care which might have the effect of weakening the physical and mental condition of the patient'.
>
> The purpose of biomedical research involving human subjects must be to improve diagnostic, therapeutic and prophylactic procedures and the understanding of the aetiology and pathogenesis of disease.
>
> In current medial practice most diagnostic, therapeutic or prophylactic procedures involve hazards. This applies especially to biomedical research.
>
> Medical progress is based on research which ultimately must rest in part on experimentation involving human subjects.
>
> In the field of biomedical research a fundamental distinction must be recognised between medical research in which the aim is essentially diagnostic or therapeutic for a patient, and medical research, the essential object of which is purely scientific and without implying direct diagnostic or therapeutic value to the person subjected to the research.

Special caution must be exercised in the conduct of research which may affect the environment, and the welfare of animals used for research must be respected.

Because it is essential that the results of laboratory experiments be applied to human beings to further scientific knowledge and to help suffering humanity, the World Medical Association has prepared the following recommendations as a guide to every physician in biomedical research involving human subjects. They should be kept under review in the future. It must be stressed that the standards as drafted are only a guide to physicians all over the world. Physicians are not relieved from criminal, civil and ethical responsibilities under the laws of their own countries.

I. Basic principles

(1) Biomedical research involving human subjects must conform to generally accepted scientific principles and should be based on adequately performed laboratory and animal experimentation and on a thorough knowledge of the scientific literature.

(2) The design and performance of each experimental procedure involving human subjects should be clearly formulated in an experimental protocol which should be transmitted for consideration, comment and guidance to a specially appointed committee independent of the investigator and the sponsor provided that this independent committee is in conformity with the laws and regulations of the country in which the research experiment is performed.

(3) Biomedical research involving human subjects should be conducted only by scientifically qualified persons and under the supervision of a clinically competent medical person. The responsibility for the human subject must always rest with the medically qualified person and never rest on the subject of the research, even though the subject has given his or her consent.

(4) Biomedical research involving human subjects cannot legitimately be carried out unless the importance of the objective is in proportion to the inherent risk to the subject.

(5) Every biomedical research project involving human subjects should be preceded by careful assessment of predictable risks in comparison with foreseeable benefits to the subject or to others. Concern for the interests of the subject must always prevail over the interests of science and society.

(6) The right of the research subject to safeguard his or her integrity must always be respected. Every precaution should be taken to respect the privacy of the subject and to minimise the impact of the study on the subject's physical and mental integrity and on the personality of the subject.

(7) Physicians should abstain from engaging in research projects involving human subjects unless they are satisfied that the hazards involved are believed to be predictable. Physicians should cease any investigation if the hazards are found to outweigh the potential benefits.

(8) In publication of the results of his or her research, the physician is obliged to preserve the accuracy of the results. Reports of experimentation not in accordance with the principles laid down in this Declaration should not be accepted for publication.

(9) In any research on human beings, each potential subject must be adequately informed of the aims, methods, anticipated benefits and potential hazards of the study and the discomfort it may entail. He or she should be informed that he or she is at liberty to abstain from participation in the study and that he or she is free to withdraw his or her consent to participation at any time. The physician should then obtain the subject's freely-given informed consent, preferably in writing.

(10) When obtaining informed consent for the research project the physician should be particularly cautious if the subject is in a dependent relationship to him or her or may consent under duress. In that case the informed consent should be obtained by a physician who is not engaged in the investigation and who is completely independent of this official relationship.

(11) In case of legal incompetence, informed consent should be obtained from the legal guardian in accordance with national legislation. Where physical or mental incapacity makes it impossible to obtain informed consent, or when the subject is a minor, permission from the responsible relative replaces that of the subject in accordance with national legislation.

Whenever the minor child is in fact able to give a consent, the minor's consent must be obtained in addition to the consent of the minor's legal guardian.

(12) The research protocol should always contain a statement of the ethical considerations involved and should indicate that the principles enunciated in the present Declaration are complied with.

II. Medical research combined with professional care
(Clinical research)

(1) In the treatment of the sick person, the physician must be free to use a new diagnostic and therapeutic measure, if in his or her judgment it offers hope of saving life, re-establishing health or alleviating suffering.

(2) The potential benefits, hazards and discomfort of a new method should be weighed against the advantages of the best current diagnostic and therapeutic methods.

(3) In any medical study, every patient – including those of a control group, if any – should be assured of the best proven diagnostic and therapeutic method.

(4) The refusal of the patient to participate in a study must never interfere with the physician-patient relationship.

(5) If the physician considers it essential not to obtain informed consent, the specific reasons for this proposal should be stated in the experimental protocol for transmission to the independent committee (I.2).

(6) The physician can combine medical research with professional care, the objective being the acquisition of new medical knowledge, only to the extent that medical research is justified by its potential diagnostic or therapeutic value for the patient.

III. Non-therapeutic biomedical research involving human subjects
(Non-clinical biomedical research)

(1) In the purely scientific application of medical research carried out on a human being, it is the duty of the physician to remain the protector of the life and health of that person on whom biomedical research is being carried out.

(2) The subjects should be volunteers – either healthy persons or patients for whom the experimental design is not related to the patient's illness.

(3) The investigator or the investigating team should discontinue the research if in his/her or their judgment it may, if continued, be harmful to the individual.

(4) In research on man, the interest of science and society should never take precedence over considerations related to the well-being of the subject.

C. THE IMPACT OF HELSINKI

Despite the Declaration of Helsinki in 1964, Beecher could still write his seminal paper in the *New England Journal of Medicine*:

H Beecher 'Ethics and Clinical Research' (1966) 274 New Eng J Med 1354

Nearly everyone agrees that ethical violations do occur. The practical question is, how often? A preliminary examination of the matter was based on 17 examples, which were easily increased to 50. These 50 studies contained references to 186 further likely examples, on the average 3.7 leads per study; they at times overlapped from paper to paper, but this figure indicates how conveniently one can proceed in a search for such material. The data are suggestive of widespread problems, but there is need for another kind of information, which was obtained by examination of 100 consecutive human studies published in 1964, in an excellent journal; 12 of these seemed to be unethical. If only one quarter of them is truly unethical, this still indicates the existence of a serious situation. Pappworth, in England, has collected, he says, more than 500 papers based upon unethical experimentation. It is evident from such observations that unethical or questionably ethical procedures are not uncommon. . . .

Known effective treatment withheld
Example 1. It is known that rheumatic fever can usually be prevented by adequate treatment of streptococcal respiratory infections by the parenteral administration of penicillin. Nevertheless, definitive treatment was withheld, and placebos were given to a group of 109 men in service, while benzathine penicillin G was given to others.

The therapy that each patient received was determined automatically by his military serial number arranged so that more men received penicillin than received placebo. In the small group of patients studied 2 cases of acute rheumatic fever and 1 of acute nephritis developed in the control patients, whereas these complications did not occur among those who received benzathine penicillin G.

Example 2. The sulfonamides were for many years the only antibacterial drugs effective in shortening the duration of acute streptococcal pharyngitis and in reducing its suppurative complications. The investigators in this study undertook to determine if the occurrence of the serious nonsuppurative complications, rheumatic fever and acute glomerulonephritis, would be reduced by this treatment. This study was made despite the general experience that certain antibiotics, including penicillin, will prevent the development of rheumatic fever.

The subjects were a large group of hospital patients; a control group of approximately the same size, also with exudative Group A streptococcus, was included. The latter group received only non-specific therapy (no sulfadiazine). The total group denied the effective penicillin comprised over 500 men.

Rheumatic fever was diagnosed in 5.4 percent of those treated with sulfadiazine. In the control group rheumatic fever developed in 4.2 percent.

In reference to this study a medical officer stated in writing that the subjects were not informed, did not consent and were not aware that they had been involved in an experiment, and yet admittedly 25 acquired rheumatic fever. According to this same medical officer *more than 70* who had had known definitive treatment withheld were on the wards with rheumatic fever when he was there.

Example 3. This involved a study of the relapse rate in typhoid fever treated in two ways. In an earlier study by the present investigators chloramphenicol had been recognized as an effective treatment for typhoid fever, being attended by half the mortality that was experienced when this agent was not used. Others had made the same observations, indicating that to withhold this effective remedy can be a life-or-death decision. The present study was carried out to determine the relapse rate under the two methods of treatment; of 408 charity patients 251 were treated with chloramphenicol, of whom 20, or 7.97 percent, died. Symptomatic treatment was given, but chloramphenicol was withheld in 157, of whom 36, or 22.9 per cent died. According to the data presented, 23 patients died in the course of this study who would not have been expected to succumb if they had received therapy. . . .

Physiologic studies

Example 5. In this controlled, double-blind study of the hematologic toxicity of chloramphenicol, it was recognized that chloramphenicol is 'well known as a cause of aplastic anemia' and that there is a 'prolonged morbidity and high mortality of aplastic anemia' and that 'chloramphenicol-induced aplastic anemia can be related to dose . . .' The aim of the study was 'further definition of the toxicology of the drug' . . .

Forty-one randomly chosen patients were given either 2 or 6 gm of chloramphenicol per day; 12 control patients were used. 'Toxic bone-marrow depression, predominantly affecting erythropoiesis, developed in 2 of 20 patients given 2.0 gm and in 18 of 21 given 6 gm of chloramphenicol daily.' The smaller dose is recommended for routine use.

Example 6. In a study of the effect of thymectomy on the survival of skin homografts 18 children, three and a half months to eighteen years of age, about to undergo surgery for congenital heart disease, were selected. Eleven were to have total thymectomy as part of the operation, and 7 were to serve as controls. As part of the experiment, full-thickness skin homografts from an unrelated adult donor were sutured to the chest wall in each case. (Total thymectomy is occasionally, although not usually part of the primary cardiovascular surgery involved, and whereas it may not greatly add to the hazards of the necessary operation, its eventual effects in children are not known.) This work was proposed as part of a long-range study of 'the growth and development of these children over the years'. No difference in the survival of the skin homograft was observed in the 2 groups. . . .

Example 8. Since the minimum blood-flow requirements of the cerebral circulation are not accurately known, this study was carried out to determine 'cerebral hemodynamic and metabolic changes . . . before and during acute reductions in arterial pressure induced by drug administration and/or postural adjustments'. Forty-four patients whose ages varied from the second to the tenth decade were involved. They included normotensive subjects, those with essential hypertension and finally a group with malignant hypertension. Fifteen had abnormal electrocardiograms. Few details about the reasons for hospitalization are given.

Signs of cerebral circulatory insufficiency, which were easily recognized, included confusion and in some cases a nonresponsive state. By alteration in the tilt of the patient 'the clinical state of the subject could be changed in a matter of seconds from one of alertness to confusion, and for the remainder of the flow, the subject was maintained in the latter state'. The femoral arteries were cannulated in all subjects, and the internal jugular veins in 14.

The mean arterial pressure fell in 37 subjects from 109 to 48 mm of mercury, with signs of cerebral ischemia. 'With the onset of collapse, cardiac output and right ventricular pressures decreased sharply.'

Since signs of cerebral insufficiency developed without evidence of coronary insufficiency the authors concluded that 'the brain may be more sensitive to acute hypotension than is the heart' . . .

Studies to improve the understanding of disease

Example 14. In this study of the syndrome of impending hepatic coma in patients with cirrhosis of the liver certain nitrogenous substances were administered to 9 patients with chronic alcoholism and advanced cirrhosis; ammonium chloride, diammonium citrate, urea or dietary protein. In all patients a reaction that included mental disturbance, a 'flapping tremor', and electroencephalographic changes developed. Similarly signs had occurred in only 1 of the patients before these substances were administered.

> The first sign noted was usually clouding of the consciousness. Three patients had a second or a third course of administration of a nitrogenous substance with the same results. It was concluded that marked resemblance between this reaction and impending hepatic coma implied that the administration of these [nitrogenous] substances to patients with cirrhosis may be hazardous . . .

Example 18. Melanoma was transplanted from a daughter to her volunteering and informed mother, 'in the hope of gaining a little better understanding of cancer immunity and in the hope that the production of tumor antibodies might be helpful in the treatment of the cancer patient'. Since the daughter died on the day after the transplantation of the tumor into her mother, the hope expressed seems to have been more theoretical than practical, and the daughter's condition was described as 'terminal' at the time the mother volunteered to be a recipient. The primary implant was widely excised on the twenty-fourth day after it had been placed in the mother. She died from metastatic melanoma on the four hundred and fifty-first day after transplantation. The evidence that this patient died of diffuse melanoma that metastasised from a small piece of transplanted tumor was considered conclusive.

Technical study of disease

Example 19. During bronchoscopy a special needle was inserted through a bronchus into the left atrium of the heart. This was done in an unspecified number of subjects both with cardiac disease and with normal hearts.

The technique was a new approach whose hazards were at the beginning quite unknown. The subjects with normal hearts were used, not for their possible benefit but for that of patients in general. . . .

Example 21. This was a study of the effect of exercise on cardiac output and pulmonary-artery pressure in 8 'normal' persons (that is, patients whose diseases were not related to the cardiovascular system), in 8 with congestive heart failure severe enough to have recently required complete bed rest, in 6 with hypertension, in 2 with aortic insufficiency, in 7 with mitral stenosis, and in 5 with pulmonary emphysema.

Intracardiac catheterization was carried out, and the catheter then inserted into the right or left main branch of the pulmonary artery. The brachial artery was usually catheterized; sometimes, the radial or femoral arteries were catheterized. The subjects exercised in a supine position by pushing their feet against weighted pedals. 'The ability of these patients to carry on sustained work was severely limited by weakness and dyspnea.' Several were in severe failure. This was not a therapeutic attempt but rather a physiologic study.

Bizarre study

Example 22. There is a question whether ureteral reflux can occur in the normal bladder. With this in mind, vesicourethrography was carried out on 26 normal babies less than forty-eight hours old. The infants were exposed to x-rays while the bladder was filling and during voiding. Multiple spot films were made to record the presence or absence of ureteral reflux. None was found in this group, and fortunately no infection followed the catheterization. What the results of the extensive x-ray exposure may be, no one can yet say.

Comment on death rates

In the foregoing examples a number of procedures, some with their own demonstrated death rates, were carried out. The following data were provided by 3 distinguished investigators in the field and represent widely held views.

Cardiac catheterization: right side of the heart, about 1 death per 1,000 cases; left side, 5 deaths per 1,000 cases. 'Probably considerably higher in some places, depending on the portal of entry.' (One investigator had 15 deaths in his first 150 cases.) It is possible that catheterization of a hepatic vein or the renal vein would have a lower death rate than that of catheterization of the right side of the heart, for if it is properly carried out, only the atrium is entered en route to the liver or the kidney, not the right ventricle, which can lead to serious cardiac irregularities. There is always the possibility, however, that the ventricle will be entered inadvertently. This occurs in at least half the cases, according to 1 expert – 'but if properly done is too transient to be of importance'.

Liver biopsy: the death rate here is estimated at 2 to 3 per 1,000, depending in considerable part on the condition of the subject.

Anesthesia: the anesthesia death rate can be placed in general at about 1 death per 2,000 cases. The hazard is doubtless higher when certain practices such as deliberate evocation of ventricular extrasystoles under cyclopropane are involved.

In England, as Nicholson (ed) points out in *Medical Research with Children* (p 4):

. . . 1967 saw the publication of the first report of the Royal College of Physicians 'Committee on the supervision of the ethics of clinical investigations in institutions', which also recommended that every hospital or institution in which clinical research was undertaken should have a group of doctors that 'should satisfy itself of the ethics of all proposed investigations'. In the same year, M H Pappworth published his book *Human Guinea Pigs*, which detailed several hundred reports of medical experiments that he considered unethical, most of which had been carried out either in the United Kingdom or in the United States of America. He proposed that 'research committees', each with at least one lay member, should be established in every region to review the ethics of proposed investigations, and that, by law, they should be responsible to the General Medical Council.

Over the next few years many hospitals in the United Kingdom did establish ethics committees to review proposed clinical research investigations. Even to this day, however, there is no statutory duty on health authorities, boards of governors, or other hospital managers to set up such research ethics committees and, indeed, some have not yet done so. At the request of the Chief Medical Officer of the Department of Health and Social Security (DHSS) in 1973, the Royal College of Physicians committee again made recommendations, [*Supervision of the Ethics of Clinical Research Investigations*] suggesting principally (1) that all proposals for clinical research investigations should be referred to the appropriate ethics committee for approval, and (2) that there should be a lay member on each research ethics committee. The DHSS finally published an advisory circular in 1975 [*Supervision of the Ethics of Clinical Research Investigations and Fetal Research* (1975) HSC (IS) 153] confirming the 1967 and 1973 recommendations of the Royal College of Physicians, but without giving them the force of statute.

The concern over the conduct of research remains; for example the judicial inquiry under Judge Cartwright into *Allegations Concerning the Treatment of Cervical Cancer at National Women's Hospital* (July 1988) in New Zealand (for a discussion see A V Campbell, 'A Report from New Zealand: An "Unfortunate Experiment"' (1989) 3 *Bioethics* 59).

D. TERMINOLOGY

Traditionally, any analysis of the law and ethics concerning research on human beings has drawn a distinction between therapeutic and non-therapeutic research. Unless carefully analysed these terms may lead to confusion. Thus, it is important at the outset to understand what is meant by them before embarking on any examination of the law.

The Institute of Medical Ethics in its Working Party Report, *Medical Research with Children* (1986) defines the distinction between these terms and illustrates it as follows (pp 33-36):

The central point is that since therapy is distinguished from research by the intention of the person doing it, research can never be, in itself, therapy.

Therefore the distinction has to be that *therapeutic research* is research consisting in an activity which has also a therapeutic intention, as well as a research intention, towards the subjects of the research, and *non-therapeutic research* is research activity which has not also a therapeutic intention.

A therapeutic intention is to have as one's purpose therapy . . .

This definition of the distinction between therapeutic and non-therapeutic research was approved by the working group because it makes clear the dual intent of therapeutic research. It was also argued, however, that such dual intent was unlikely or even impossible; a researcher would always have the primary intent of gaining new knowledge. Such a suggestion seems improbable, however: in reality, a researcher would be using his clinical and therapeutic acumen in the interests of the research element of his activity, at the same time as using his research skills for the clinical benefit of his research subject. If one invites friends round for dinner, one has the dual intent of feeding them and talking with them: it would indeed be a strange occasion if one fed them only without saying a word the whole evening: or vice versa!

One research proposal examined by the working group illustrates both the need in some circumstances to decide whether a project is therapeutic or non-therapeutic, and the difficulties that may be met in so deciding. The proposal had been submitted to the working group by the chairman of a research ethics committee which had been in difficulty when trying to decide whether or not to approve the proposal.

The purpose of the project was to study water fluxes in sick pre-term infants and to assess in particular the insensible water gain from humidifiers attached to artificial ventilators, and the insensible water loss from the lungs and skin. Ten infants requiring artificial ventilation for hyaline membrane disease would be studied. In such infants, water balance is very important in determining the development of several potentially fatal complications, but little is known about insensible water gain or loss from the expiratory tract in particular. In the study, deuterium oxide, heavy water or D_2O, would be added to the humidifier water in the artificial ventilator. Its accumulation in the neonate could then be followed by measuring the proportion of D_2O to ordinary water, H_2O, in blood samples taken sequentially. These blood samples would be very small, since only five microlitres (about one-twentieth of a drop) of blood would be required in order to measure D_2O by mass spectrometry; they would be taken – over a period of three days, and with no discomfort – from an umbilical arterial catheter, which is usually inserted when infants are artificially ventilated.

The problem that has arisen with this proposal concerned the obtaining of parental consent. The policy in the special baby care unit where the proposed project would be undertaken was not to obtain informed consent for this type of study. The researchers therefore proposed to dispense with informed consent, while the research ethics committee thought that it should be obtained.

One reason why it is necessary to establish whether such a project is therapeutic or non-therapeutic is a legal one. The removal of blood samples from the infants would be an assault unless consent had been given. Although there is no specific statement of the law in such circumstances, it is likely that the courts would always regard unconsented invasive non-therapeutic research as unlawful. They might take a somewhat more lenient view of unconsented therapeutic research, though not necessarily.

The basic difficulty in considering whether or not this project is therapeutic research is to decide whether there is a therapeutic intention towards the infant subjects. It is essential to provide humidified air to infants on artificial ventilators: one argument therefore states that the addition of D_2O to humidifier water merely alters slightly one therapeutic activity without in any way altering the therapeutic intention. It is a necessary part of medical practice to examine the results of therapies that are used in order that they may be improved: such assessment of a therapy is inevitably therapeutic research.

Another view would suggest that the addition of D_2O to humidifier water is not a necessary part of therapy, and is not intended, in itself, to be therapy. The taking of additional blood samples – even though they amount to a very small total quantity – is not a therapeutic activity; the researchers have not stated how soon the measurements of D_2O might be made, and nowhere in their protocol have they suggested that the measurements might be used to improve the control of water balance in the infant subjects. The project is therefore designed to gain physiological knowledge, and there is no therapeutic intention towards the infant subjects in the proposed activities that are additional to standard therapy.

The problem of deciding which argument is correct seems finally to be insoluble. In terms of the definitions adopted by the working group . . . it is possible, however, to conclude that this is a therapeutic research project since the researchers have both a therapeutic intention, in humidifying the air supplied by the ventilators, and a research intention. It is not suggested that the definitions adopted by the working group will solve all the problems with which research ethics committees are in practice faced. The researchers in the anorectal manometry project, for instance, had no therapeutic intention towards the controls that they used. To identify the controls as taking part in therapeutic research because there was a therapeutic intention towards the subjects of the research project seems invidious and inherently inequitable. In some circumstances it may then be important to abandon attempts to describe a whole research project as either therapeutic or non-therapeutic, and to consider instead the nature of the actual procedures undertaken. In this case, the subjects had therapeutic interventions performed on them, while the controls had non-therapeutic interventions performed.

The definitions adopted by the working group allow firm conclusions to be reached about some other projects mentioned earlier. When the Willowbrook experiments started, there was no therapeutic intention in them towards the handicapped subjects, although some benefits may have accrued to them incidentally. By the working group's definitions, they were therefore non-therapeutic research projects. On the other hand, the comparative trials of treatment regimes for leukaemia and other malignancies were and are therapeutic research, since there has always been a therapeutic intention towards each of the subjects, even when the major benefits would probably fall to later cohorts. The definitions also obviate the need for such complicating expressions as 'partly therapeutic', that have been suggested to describe an intervention such as the taking of an additional two millilitres of blood for a research purpose, when a blood specimen is to be taken anyway as part of therapy. Since the act of taking the blood sample has both a therapeutic and a research intention, the act is therapeutic – by definition.

Professor Richard Hare, a member of the Working Party, in his paper 'Little Human Guinea Pigs', in *Moral Dilemmas in Modern Medicine* (1985) (ed M Lockwood) states that: 'therapeutic research is thus an activity which has both aims [therapy and research]; non-therapeutic research is an activity which has only a research and not a therapeutic aim'. We would suggest some caution is necessary before adopting this approach. It is acceptable if therapeutic research is taken to mean that the intention to carry out therapy and research *relates to the same activity*. It is problematic if it seeks to suggest that once engaged on therapy, anything done thereafter by way of research, though unconnected with the therapy, qualifies as therapeutic research.

The Institute's Working Party drew attention to one further term which warrants consideration in any examination of the regulation of research, namely, *innovative therapy* (pp 36-7).

Innovative therapy consists in the performance of a new or non-standard intervention as all or part of a therapeutic activity and not as part of a formal research project.

Innovative therapy may therefore be quite haphazard, starting just when a doctor has a bright idea that he wants to try out. If the bright idea seems to be any good, then innovative therapy can become research as soon as the bright idea is examined in a systematic manner. Much innovative therapy is surgical in nature, since surgeons often try out modifications to existing surgical procedures and occasionally try out new operations. It is rare for these modifications or new operations to be undertaken as part of a formal research project and they have not in general been subject first to peer review or review by a research ethics committee. Another sort of innovative therapy would be the introduction of new instruments, if these were not formally compared with existing ones. Innovative therapy is comparatively rare in the use of medicines, but it can still occur. A doctor may decide that a drug that is already available for the treatment of one disease might be useful in the treatment of another, and he is at liberty within the limits of his professional expertise to go ahead and try it. One example a few years ago was the use of injectable phenothiazine drugs. These were introduced to help in the treatment of schizophrenia, their value being that a schizophrenic could have his illness controlled by a monthly injection. Doctors looking after mentally handicapped children with severe behaviour disturbances realized that these drugs might help: it was found that monthly injections of quite small doses produced considerable improvement in the behaviour of the few children in whom the drugs were tried. It was then decided to set up a controlled trial to discover whether the results were real: ie what started as innovative therapy became therapeutic research as the trial was set up, and the haphazard procedures became formalised.

(See also definition of 'innovative therapy' in *Research Involving Patients* (1990) Royal College of Physicians, paragraph 2-8.) In our view, the Working Party was right to draw attention to innovative therapy and highlight the fact that it may consist in doing the same things with the same intentions as researchers may do, but without any of the constraints associated with the proper conduct of research. To the extent that the intention is to acquire knowledge and not solely to care for the patient it is our view that innovative therapy should be subject to the same regime of control that attends research properly so-called.

The regulation of research

Research on animals has been regulated by law since the Cruelty to Animals Act 1876. (The current law is contained in the Animals (Scientific Procedures) Act 1986.) In contrast, there has never been any statute specifically regulating the conduct of research on human beings. You may think this is not atypical of the state of affairs in England. In 1991 the Department of Health issued Guidelines on *Local Research Ethics Committees*. The accompanying NHS Management Executive letter (HSG (91)5) set out the objectives of the guidelines and action required of NHS bodies.

Every health district should have a local research ethics committee (LREC) to advise NHS bodies on the ethical acceptability of research proposals involving human subjects. District Health Authorities are responsible for establishing and maintaining LRECs, in consultation with NHS bodies in their districts. The booklet 'Local Research Ethics Committees' gives detailed guidance on:
● the establishment and function of LRECs, and the administrative framework within which they work (Chapter 2);
● the ethical principles to which LRECs should have regard (Chapter 3);
● particular groups as research subjects (Chapter 4).
Responsibility for deciding whether a research proposal should proceed, within the NHS, lies with the NHS body under whose auspices the research would take place.

Action
NHS bodies should take into account the following specific requirements:
● As soon as possible and no later than 1 February 1992, each District Health Authority should establish an LREC (or, exceptionally, more than one) and provide it (or them) with adequate administrative support.
● Any NHS body asked to agree a research proposal falling within its sphere of responsibility should ensure that it has been submitted to the appropriate LREC for research ethics approval:
  – district health authorities, about research within their hospitals or community health services, or in private sector providers under contract to the DHA;
  – special health authorities, about research within their units;
  – family health services authorities, about research involving general medical, general dental, or other family health services;
  – NHS trusts, about research within the units they control;

and should take the LREC's advice into account before deciding whether the research project should go ahead. Projects which do not have LREC approval must not be agreed.

The guidelines contemplate as the principal regulatory mechanism the creation of what are called Local Research Ethics Committees (LRECs) whose task is to consider research protocols and advise the relevant NHS body. It will be realised, of course, that the guidelines relate only to research conducted within the NHS. LRECs may, by agreement, consider the proposals of researchers outside the NHS.

1.1. Medical research is important, and the NHS has a key role in enabling it. The approval of research projects is an important management responsibility involving the availability of resources, financial implications, and ethical issues. Such considerations are generally best left to the local management team, but on ethical issues they need to take into account independent advice. The purpose of a local research ethics committee is to consider the ethics of proposed research projects which will involve human subjects, and which will take place broadly within the NHS. The LREC's task is to advise the NHS body under the auspices of which the research is intended to take place. It is that NHS body which has the responsibility to decide whether or not the project should go ahead taking account of the ethical advice of the LREC. For convenience, local research ethics committees are normally organised on a health district basis, but they exist to advise any NHS body. They are not in any sense management arms of the District Health Authority.

1.2. The NHS bodies which will look to an LREC for advice on the ethics of proposed research projects are therefore:
– district health authorities (in respect of research taking place within their hospitals or community health services or in private sector providers under contract to the DHA)
– special health authorities (in respect of research taking place within their units)
– family health services authorities (in respect of research involving general medical, general dental, or other family health services)
– NHS trusts (in respect of research taking place within the units they control).

1.3. An LREC must be consulted about any research proposal involving:
– NHS patients (ie subjects recruited by virtue of their past or present treatment by the NHS) including those treated under contracts with private sector providers
– fetal material and IVF involving NHS patients
– the recently dead, in NHS premises
– access to the records of past or present NHS patients
– the use of, or potential access to, NHS premises or facilities.

1.4. No NHS body should agree to such a research proposal without the approval of the relevant LREC. No such proposal should proceed without the permission of the responsible NHS body. These requirements apply equally to researchers already working within the NHS and having clinical responsibility for the patients concerned, as they do to those who have no other association with the NHS and its patients, beyond the particular research project.

1.5. The relevant LREC in each case is normally that constituted in respect of the health district within the area of which the research is planned to take place. Special arrangements apply to multi-centre research, and these are referred to in Chapter 2 paragraph 18.

1.6. By agreement an LREC may also advise on the ethics of studies not involving NHS patients, records or premises, carried out for example by private sector companies, the Medical Research Council or universities.

ESTABLISHMENT
2.1 Although the LREC exists to provide independent advice to any NHS body within the geographical area of a health district, it is necessary for one of the NHS bodies to take the responsibility for establishing the LREC, and for providing its administrative support. This

task falls to the District Health Authority. However each DHA should consult all the NHS bodies which are likely to use the LREC before establishing it.

2.2 It does not follow, however, that the members of the LREC are in any way representative of, nor beholden to, any of the NHS bodies which collaborate in its establishment, nor that the LREC as a whole is an arm of the management of any of them. The object of consultation is to ensure that all the NHS bodies which will use the LREC should have confidence in its ability to provide sound research ethics advice.

2.3 In exceptional circumstances it may be appropriate to establish two LRECs in one District. An example of this might be where there is a particularly high burden of work, perhaps originating from two distinct research centres within the locality. In such a case the DHA should secure agreement from all the relevant NHS bodies concerning the respective responsibilities of the LRECs, and should ensure that the administrative arrangements enable both to work together effectively.

MEMBERSHIP
2.4 An LREC should have eight to twelve members. This should allow for a sufficiently broad range of experience and expertise, so that the scientific and medical aspects of a research proposal can be reconciled with the welfare of research subjects, and broader ethical implications.

2.5 Members should be drawn from both sexes and from a wide range of age groups. They should include:
- hospital medical staff
- nursing staff
- general practitioners
- two or more lay persons.

2.6 Despite being drawn from groups identified with particular interests or responsibilities in connection with health issues, LREC members are not in any way the representatives of those groups. They are appointed in their own right, to participate in the work of the LREC as individuals of sound judgement and relevant experience.

2.7 The health professionals should include those occupied chiefly in active clinical care as well as those experienced in clinical investigation and research. As well as consulting the relevant NHS bodies in connection with health professional appointments DHAs should consult local professional advisory committees and relevant health professional associations. Lay members should be appointed after consultation with the Community Health Council. At least one lay member should be unconnected professionally with health care and be neither an employee nor adviser of any NHS body.

CHAIRMAN AND VICE-CHAIRMAN
2.8 After consultation with the relevant NHS bodies the DHA should appoint a chairman and vice-chairman from amongst the members of the committee. At least one of these posts should be filled by a lay person.

PERIOD OF APPOINTMENT
2.9 Members should serve on LRECs for terms of three to five years. Terms of appointment may be renewed, but normally not more than two terms of office should be served consecutively.

CO-OPTION
2.10 The LREC should, on its own initiative, seek the advice of specialist referees, or co-opt members to the committee, so as to cover any aspect, professional, scientific or ethical, of a research proposal which lies beyond the expertise of the existing members.

LEGAL LIABILITY
2.11 Concern has been expressed by some LREC members that they may be legally liable for injury caused to patients participating in research projects. DHAs will wish to advise appointees on these matters. Legal advice available to the Department of Health is that there is little prospect of a successful claim against an LREC member for a mishap arising

from research approved as ethical by the LREC. Any such claim would lie principally against the researcher concerned, and against the NHS body under the auspices of which the research took place. The principal defendants should seek to have any claim against an LREC member struck out. Those members of an LREC who are employees of an NHS body are already covered by NHS indemnity arrangements. The DHA should also bear any costs in the case of other LREC members unless the member concerned is guilty of misconduct or gross lack of care in the performance of his or her duties and provided that, if any claim is threatened or made, the member notifies the DHA and assists it in all reasonable ways. If necessary, the DHA may give the following undertaking to this effect to LREC members who are not employees of an NHS body:

> We confirm that the DHA will take full responsibility for all your actions in the course of the performance of your duties as a member of the LREC other than those involving bad faith, wilful default or gross negligence; you should, however, notify the DHA if any action or claim is threatened or made, and in such an event be ready to assist the authority as required.

DHAs should keep a record of which LREC members are covered by virtue of their NHS employment and which are not.

WORKING PROCEDURES
2.12 The LREC should always be able to demonstrate that it has acted reasonably in reaching a particular decision. When research proposals are rejected by the LREC, the reasons for that decision should be made available to the applicant. Good standing orders and accurate record keeping are important. Standing orders should be drawn up by the DHA covering frequency of meetings and working methods. Conducting business by post or telephone should be discouraged and the situations in which chairman's action can be taken should be clearly described.

KEEPING A REGISTER
2.13 The LREC should keep a register of all the proposals which come before it. The register should include the name and address of the organisation carrying out the research; names and qualifications of the research team; details of the premises in which the research will be conducted; medical support and other facilities available; a brief description of what is required of the research subjects and confirmation of compliance with any other guidelines (such as RCP or ABPI). This register would not normally be available for public consultation but should be open to the relevant NHS bodies for management purposes.

FOLLOWING UP
2.14 Once the LREC has approved a proposal, the researcher should be required to notify the committee, in advance, of any significant proposed deviation from the original protocol. Reports to the committee should also be required once the research is underway if there are any unusual or unexpected results which raise questions about the safety of the research. Reports on success (or difficulties) in recruiting subjects may also provide the LREC with useful feedback on perceptions of the acceptability of the project among patients and volunteers.

CONFIDENTIALITY OF PROCEEDINGS
2.15 LREC members do not sit on the committee in any representative capacity and need to be able to discuss the proposals which come before them freely. For these reasons LREC meetings will normally be private and the minutes taken will be confidential to the committee.

PRODUCING AN ANNUAL REPORT
2.16 Each year the LREC should submit a report to the DHA, and copies should be sent to all the NHS bodies which the LREC exists to advise, and to the CHC. The names of committee members, the number of meetings held and a list of proposals considered (including whether they were approved, approved after amendment, rejected or withdrawn) should be included. This report should be available for public inspection.

ADVICE TO NON-NHS BODIES
2.17 Not all medical research involving human subjects takes place within the NHS. Even where there is *no* NHS involvement of any kind, the body conducting the research should be

encouraged to submit its proposals to the LREC for advice. In such cases, the LREC should report to the DHA the cost of its work so that the cost can be recovered from the outside body conducting the research. The LREC must also seek a full indemnity from the outside body against the possibility of future legal action.

MULTICENTRE RESEARCH

2.18 Each LREC is free to arrive at its own decision when considering a proposal which is planned to take place in more than one area. It would, however, obviously be sensible – in the interests of eliminating unnecessary delay and of ensuring that similar criteria are used to consider a proposal – that committees should arrive at a voluntary arrangement under which one LREC is nominated to consider the issue on behalf of them all. Health authorities should positively encourage networks for neighbouring LRECs so that such co-operation is more easily achieved.

It should be noted at the outset that in law there is no obligation on a Health Authority, a hospital, a pharmaceutical company or other such body to set up a Research Ethics Committee when involved in research on patients or healthy volunteers. The Department of Health's Circular requires District Health Authorities to set up Research Ethics Committees, but by virtue of its being in a Circular, rather than legislation, this is not a formal legal requirement.

Further, there is no obligation in law on a potential researcher to submit a protocol to an Ethics Committee for review and approval.

Thus, any authority which an Ethics Committee wields is informal and extra-legal. Such authority should not, however, be minimised. As regards the NHS in England, the Department of Health's Circular places a clear duty on DHAs to appoint them and thereby endows them with considerable status. Those who fund research ordinarily stipulate that research, to be funded, must be approved by an Ethics Committee. Researchers within the NHS will be denied access to patients without such approval according to the Circular. Finally, research results may not be published, at least in British journals.

Once a Research Ethics Committee constitutes itself and reviews research proposals, though it has no legal standing, it takes on legal duties. These duties derive from the central purposes of the Committee: to protect research subjects and maintain proper standards of practice in research, while ensuring that valid and worthwhile research is carried out. (For a discussion see *Discussion Paper on Legal Liability, Insurance and Indemnity Arrangements for Institutional Ethics Committees*, Australian National Health and Medical Research Council (November 1993).)

The single most important legal duty imposed on the Committee is to address those issues which are relevant to any decision about a research proposal before deciding whether or not to approve it. More accurately, this duty is imposed on Committee members, since the Committee as a Committee has no separate legal identity. We shall consider later the question of legal liability which members may incur for breach of this duty.

To comply with their duty, Committee members must satisfy themselves on a number of matters. These include, as reflected in the forms of application for approval of research projects now commonly used, consideration of the following:

(a) on examination of the question to be answered and the outline of the research, that the research project is scientifically sound;

(b) whether the research is, by reference to the intention of the researcher, therapeutic or non-therapeutic, since the law places greater limits on the pursuit of non-therapeutic research out of concern to protect the research subject. In this context and generally it may be advisable to seek assurance that the proposal complies with the law;

(c) that the duration of the project is stated and is reasonable given the aims;
(d) that in the context of therapeutic research the risks to the subject which may be involved in the research can be justified by reference to the intended aims, both as regards the care of the patient and the advancement of knowledge;
(e) that any discomfort suffered by a subject of research is not greater than necessary and commensurate with the intended benefit, and that where the research is non-therapeutic, the risk to the subject is no more than minimal;
(f) that the investigator is suitably qualified and experienced;
(g) that the premises on which the research is to be conducted are adequate and that medical supervision, if appropriate, is available;
(h) that consent is to be obtained (except in exceptional circumstances), that the method of obtaining consent is appropriate and that any money to be paid to a volunteer does not serve as an inducement to persuade an otherwise unwilling person to participate;
(i) that, where appropriate and with the consent of the subject, contact is to be established with the subject's GP, such that anyone who refuses contact with his GP should be rejected as a research subject;
(j) that proper procedures exist to ensure medical confidentiality;
(k) that, where a drug is to be used, the legal status of the drug is established;
(l) that arrangements for compensation in the case of mishap and injury exist;
(m) that appropriate procedures exist for monitoring the progress of the research;
(n) that particular care is taken, especially as regards consent, in the case of research subjects who may be particularly vulnerable, eg children, elderly, mentally ill, mentally handicapped, students, employees, and the unemployed;
(o) that in the case of multi-centre trials, each Committee must be entitled to make its own decision.

The legal duty of a member of an Ethics Committee is, at its most general, to behave as a reasonable member of such a Committee. In the absence of any legal guidance it is a matter for debate what the law would require of a reasonable Committee member. Arguably, the duties set out above could, with some variation depending on the circumstances, be held to define what is reasonable.

Thus, failure on the part of a Committee member to satisfy himself on any of these questions may render him liable to a legal claim in negligence at the suit of a research subject if the research subject suffers harm as a consequence. (Obviously, the Committee member will not be in breach of his duty if a subject is harmed through the carelessness of the researcher.) Notice, however, that the law does not require the Committee member to get things right. Rather, as has been said, the obligation is to behave reasonably. Clearly, the expertise of the member may limit what he can do, but the law is likely to require that any reasonable member finding a matter on which he is unsure, should seek advice, (subject to the constraints of confidentiality), and may not simply remain in a state of ignorance. Further attempts to particularise what is reasonable may not be helpful, since much will depend on the facts of any particular case, and the resources and backgrounds of the particular Committee (subject, of course, to the proviso that a certain basic minimum of resources must be available). For example, the obligation to satisfy themselves that proper arrangements exist for compensation in the event of injury may appear onerous to many members who would argue that they are not specialists in insurance and finance. The response may be that their duty is to make reasonable enquiry, to ascertain, in other words, that compensation has been raised with the subject and that some provision has been made. To expect more of members may be unreasonable.

As has been said, liability would be personal. Thus, each Committee member must, if he is to serve on a Committee, make all reasonable efforts to comply with these various duties. If unable to do so, despite his reasonable efforts, the wise course would be to resign so as to avoid incurring possible liability. Notice that members who serve on the Committee as nominees of a Health Authority, Company, or some such body, which employs them, may well be able to arrange to be indemnified by their employer if sued in negligence. This will not assist the member who serves in a personal capacity and has no employer to look to. Such members are well advised to seek some formal arrangement as to indemnity in the case of being sued, as a condition of agreeing to serve.

The views expressed here concerning legal liability are not supported unanimously (but see *Weiss v Solomon* (1989) 48 CCLT 280 (Qu Sup Ct) – hospital liable for negligence of research committee). The Department of Health's Circular, however, somewhat grudgingly supports the view expressed (see para 2.11, *supra*, pp 1034-1035).

Professor Margaret Brazier examines the legal problems surrounding any claim in negligence in this context.

M Brazier 'Liability of Ethics Committee and Their Members' (1990) PN 186

A patient injured by what he believes to be a wrongly authorised trial will sue in negligence. Against whom will he serve his writ? The ethics committee itself lacks the necessary legal personality to be a defendant in a civil action. . . .

Any action in respect of the committee's decisions . . . will lie against [the health] authority. The plaintiff, of course, is free to sue any or all of the members of the committee individually as well. But would it be worth his while? As he has a right of action against the authority, why bother to pursue probably impecunious committee members? And, as we shall see later, any action against an individual member would generate even more formidable problems of proving negligence than is the case in an action against the district health authority.

Patients suing non-NHS Committees may find it a little harder to identify a clearly solvent defendant and so may be more likely to resort to an action against individual committee members. The private hospital or drug company ethics committee itself has no corporate status. It has no legal personality enabling the committee as an entity to be sued. It is less clear than in the case of the NHS whether a 'private' ethics committee can be seen as simply an organ of the relevant institution, so that the hospital or company could be sued as responsible for a tortious act of its own, albeit made on its behalf by the committee. Consider, for example, a committee appointed by a company which exists solely to provide drug testing services for the pharmaceutical industry. It may well be argued that the company undertakes a duty of care to each and every volunteer recruited for trials and discharges that duty in part via the scrutiny of trials by its ethics committee. Similarly when a private hospital or clinic sets up an ethics committee to scrutinise either clinical trials or treatment, it may be argued that the hospital is in breach of the duty it undertakes to all patients admitted for treatment if 'its' ethics committee wrongfully approves a trial or treatment. But the case for direct liability on the part of the private sector institution is not as clearcut as the case for liability on the part of the health authority within the NHS. A patient might well be advised to join individual members of private sector ethics committees as defendants 'just in case'.

In no case, of course, is the health authority, private hospital or company vicariously liable for any tort committed by individual committee members. The public authority or corporate defendant will have to be found to be in breach of a direct and primary duty to the patient or volunteer. [Without such a primary duty obviously the health authority or private institution can thus not be sued by the patient or volunteer. For discussion of the potential to extend primary, non-delegable duties beyond the ambit of *Cassidy v Ministry of Health*, see *Street on Torts* (8th edn) 1988 at pp 543-59.] A local research ethics committee will include hospital medical staff and nursing staff who are employees of the authority. In their role as ethics committee members they are not acting in the course of their employment, and so the authority is no more vicariously liable for them than for their colleagues who are lay members or local general practitioners. Medical practitioners serving on ethics committees may well be covered against liability by their medical protection organisation. Other members should consider asking for an indemnity from the district health authority against any liability in tort arising from membership of an ethics committee . . .

A plaintiff suing any health authority or private sector institution on the grounds that its ethics committee wrongfully sanctioned a trial or treatment faces a series of difficulties proving breach of duty and causation . . .

[W]ould . . . the ethics committee also commit a tort if they had authorised the trial knowing that no valid consent would be obtained from a patient or volunteer? The first line of attack against the committee would be to argue that the committee, and its members, are joint tortfeasors with the clinician. By authorising a battery the committee shares responsibility for that battery. That argument has been pursued in the USA where Elizabeth Bouvia contended that the ethics committee which endorsed doctors' decisions to go on feeding her artificially against her will shared their liability for battery.

The alternative course is for the plaintiff to allege negligence against the committee. He would argue that to authorise a trial which entailed a battery by the clinician was negligent. The complexity of 'medical battery' and the application of *Chatterton v Gerson* and *Sidaway* confuses lawyers. Not many ethics committees of any type have lawyer members. How would a court decide whether a reasonable ethics committee would/should have noted the potential illegality in the trial? What would be the relevance, if any, of the Declaration of Helsinki, which states that in certain circumstances it is ethical not to obtain consent from patients in therapeutic research programmes? A plaintiff surmounting these hurdles in an action for negligence would finally have to prove that had the ethics committee acted properly and required a valid consent to participation in the trial, he would have refused his consent. Otherwise he fails to prove that 'but for' the committee's negligence, he would never have suffered the relevant injury.

When the patient's grievance is not that he did not agree to take part in the trial, but rather that the committee should never have authorised such a dangerous trial, proving breach of duty is even more problematic. Consider this (as far as I know) hypothetical trial. An obstetrician wishes to conduct a controlled trial to assess the need for Caesarian section in women with mild to moderate *placenta praevia*. Women are, with their consent, randomly allocated to caesarian and non-caesarian groups. Several women allowed to go into labour suffer devastating haemorrhages and lose their babies. Whether the obstetrician was negligent depends on expert evidence from obstetricians as to whether in embarking on the trial at all the defendant conformed to a responsible body of professional opinion. It does not follow that proving the obstetrician was negligent means the ethics committee was negligent too. Applying the *Bolam* test to ethics committees requires evidence from expert ethicists. Would a properly informed and conducted committee have discovered the dangers of, and/or lack of merit in the trial? The relevant experts may be chairpersons of other ethics committees.

Suing a health authority or private sector body for the negligence of its ethics committee creates enough problems of proving breach of duty; suing an individual member might be a nightmare. What is the relevant standard of care? Sued personally each member can only be responsible for his or her own negligence. . . .

Suppose the committee approves a trial any responsible medical practitioner should have recognised as unmeritorious and unacceptably dangerous. [Would a lay member be] exonerated because no reasonable lay member could have seen the danger while medical colleagues are held liable? By contrast, if the committee approves a trial [the lay member] should have realised entailed a battery, [is he] liable in negligence while they are exculpated? The 'reasonable member of the ethics committee' is a myth, unless some compromise figure knowing a bit of everything is constructed. Perhaps the test should be not was the decision reasonable, but was the procedure reasonable? Did each member assess the project conscientiously and seek to ensure the project was accurately and thoroughly reviewed? In that case maybe missing a meeting for no good reason might be negligent, as might reviewing the proposals at 1.00 a.m. after a lengthy dinner engagement!

Finally a plaintiff suing in respect of a drug trial faces again the bugbear of causation. If the drug is experimental, the lack of documentation as to its effects may make it difficult to prove the drug caused the injury complained of. So far, the House of Lords has been entirely unsympathetic to pleas to infer causation in medical negligence claims.

As we shall see shortly, in Ireland research is regulated by statute. In an amendment to the original statutory scheme (Control of Clinical Trials Act 1987) a provision was introduced in 1990 in the Control of Clinical Trials and Drugs Act 1990 to grant, *inter alia*, immunity from liability to ethics committees and their members. Section 5(1) provides:

> 5. (1) No action or other proceeding shall lie or be maintainable (except in the case of wilful neglect or default) against –
> (a) . . .
> (b) . . .
> (c)   an ethics committee or any member thereof.

Apart from possible liability in tort, is there any other system of legal accountability? There are a further cluster of duties imposed on Research Ethics Committees, the precise nature of which is unclear. They undoubtedly reflect ethical concerns. What legal standing, if any, they have is problematical. It may be that failure to observe them could result not in the personal liability of a member but in a court being asked to examine by way of judicial review a decision of the Committee with a view to declaring it invalid. The consequence would be that any authority for the research given by the Committee would be null.

Before we turn to consider these duties, we should examine whether it is correct that in principle an LREC is amenable to judicial review. As we have seen, LRECs are not creatures of statute. However, the courts have extended the scope of judicial review to include non-statutory bodies and functions providing the body is exercising a public function (*R v Take Overs and Mergers Panel, ex p Datafin plc* [1987] QB 815).

Subsequently, in one case it was assumed by a court that an LREC was amenable to judicial review (*R v Ethical Committee of St Mary's Hospital (Manchester), ex p H* [1988] 1 FLR 512). Given the fact that the Government has adopted LRECs as the institution to perform an important public role, there is little doubt that the court would entertain an application for judicial review.

Returning to consider the public law obligations of an LREC, the first duty is the duty of the Committee to act within the terms of reference and scope established by the formal mechanism by which it came into being.

The second duty is to be properly constituted. This does not refer to the vexed question of membership, ie whether particular constituencies should be represented or what is the proper balance between health-care professionals and others. Instead it refers to the need to have rules concerning, for instance, the nomination and selection of members, their period of office, the terms on which they serve, the selection of a chair, the minimum and maximum size of the Committee, what constitutes a quorum and the power to co-opt members from time to time.

Thirdly, the Committee has a duty to establish proper working procedures or Standing Orders, as they are sometimes called. These should include, *inter alia*, establishing rules concerning:

(i)   frequency of meetings;
(ii)   preparation of agenda and minutes;
(iii) development of a standard application form;
(iv)   distribution of papers prior to meetings;
(v)   the scope of Chairman's action;

(vi)   confidentiality;
(vii)   conflicts of interest in members as regards applicants or applications;
(viii) delegation of tasks to sub-committees, and the consequent relationship between the Committee and such sub-committees;
(ix)   the maintenance of a register of all research proposals and all action taken regarding them;
(x)   the basis of decision-making, ie bare majority, 2/3 majority, etc and any special rules on decisions concerning types of research projects, eg on the vulnerable;
(xi)   procedures for recording in writing the decisions of the Committee;
(xii)   procedures for reporting adverse occurrences;
(xiii) giving reasons for decisions.

There is very considerable uncertainty as to whether these are in fact *legal* duties. Furthermore, even if some are, others (the more trivial or detailed) may not be. The legal criterion which a court would apply is that of 'fairness', or 'natural justice', ie is the Committee acting in a way which meets these criteria?

Finally, the Committee, so as to demonstrate that it is acting properly and responsibly, has a duty to submit itself to public scrutiny by rendering an account periodically of its conduct. This is best achieved as regards the general public by producing and publishing an annual report with sufficient detail to allow scrutiny. As regards the research community, this is best achieved by providing, in addition to any annual report, reasoned responses to any inquiry or complaint it may receive.

This approach to the regulation of research is common to most European countries (though not America). There is, however, another approach.

C Hodges, 'Harmonisation of European Controls over Research: Ethics Committees, Consent, Compensation and Indemnity' in *Pharmaceutical Medicine and the Law* (ed A Goldberg and I Dodds-Smith)

> It is relevant to contrast the approach taken in the recent French, Irish and Spanish legislation on clinical research [France: Law on the Protection of Persons Undergoing Biomedical Research, 1988, 1990, 1991; Republic of Ireland: Control of Clinical Trials Act, 1987, 1990; Spain: Medicaments Law 1990], which all provide that permission to carry out research is under the control of the Minister of Health but that the opinion of an ethical committee must first be obtained. The French legislation is supplemented by detailed decrees and a fixed regional network of ethics committees. Under none of these systems is there a requirement for continued monitoring by the committees or for adverse reactions to be reported to them: their role appears to cease after initial approval has been given (subject to possible reconsideration of amendments to the protocol) and regulatory responsibility passes to the regulatory authorities. . . .
>
> [T]he French law specifies that each regional advisory committee shall consist of 12 permanent members, each of which is to have a specific specialisation. There are to be four researchers, one GP, two pharmacists, and one each of a nurse, a person qualified in ethical matters, a person active in the social field, a psychologist and a lawyer. Each member shall also have an alternate. At least six members must be present for a valid decision to be made, four of whom must be from particular categories of specialisation. Members are chosen at random from a list of candidates drawn up by the regional government on nominations from relevant bodies. The members receive no remuneration but their expenses are defrayed. The French law also specifies that all places where healthy volunteer research is to be carried out must be authorised by the regional government.
>
> The French legislation is therefore extremely detailed. This is not the case with the Irish legislation, since there is little call for permanent ethics committees to be established there on a regional basis. For each individual trial, the membership of a proposed committee has to be submitted to the minister, who will approve it if he considers that

the committee . . . is competent to consider the justification for conducting the proposed clinical trial and the circumstances under which it is to be conducted. [Control of Clinical Trials Act 1987, s 8(1)]

The composition of the committee may at any time be changed with the approval of the minister. [*ibid*, s 8(5)] Non-statutory guidelines encourage the selection of committees to include lay, legal and business representation as well as medical and paramedical expertise.

The Spanish law is a little more detailed, specifying that ethics committees

should be constituted, at least, by an interdisciplinary team made up of medical doctors, hospital pharmacists, clinical pharmacologists, nursing personnel and persons unrelated with health professionals of which, at least one, shall be a jurist. [Medicaments Law 25/1990, Title 3, Article 64.3] . . .

The French, Irish and Spanish legislation provides that the ultimate decision on an application rests with the minister. [Control of Clinical Trials Act, 1987, Section 4; Law on the protection of persons undergoing biomedical research, Article L.209-12; Medicaments Law 25/1990, Article 65] Curiously, neither the French nor Irish legislation specifies any criteria on which the minister may exercise his power – there is not even a reference to the Declaration of Helsinki. This is in contrast to the extensive criteria specified in that legislation for consideration by an ethics committee. The Spanish law, however, does specify that clinical trials must:

–   only be undertaken after sufficient scientific data are available which guarantee that the risks are reasonable;
–   be conducted in accordance with the Declaration of Helsinki;
–   only be commenced if there is reasonable doubt as to the efficacy and safety of the matter to be tested. [Medicaments Law 25/1990, Article 60] . . .

As far as procedure is concerned, positive ministerial approval is required in Ireland, within 12 weeks of the application and after consultation with the National Drugs Advisory Board. In France, there is a negative approval system on a similar basis to the UK CTX system: the sponsor forwards a letter of intent to the minister together with the opinion of the committee. Spain requires positive authorisation by the Ministry of Health and Consumption, but the law also establishes a negative approval system under which the ministry has 60 days to object in the case of further similar trials of a product for which one clinical trial has already been approved, and of trials for new dosages or indications of medicines already licensed. [*ibid*, Article 65]

Therapeutic research

There are at least three situations in which therapeutic research may be carried out:

(1)   a doctor tests the efficacy of a new treatment where none had previously been available and the patient would have received ordinary nursing care, symptomatic relief but nothing else;

(2)   a doctor tests the efficacy of a new treatment as against other established forms of treatment;

(3)   a doctor tests treatments A, B and C (all of which are established) because it has not been established which is the most efficacious.

All of these types of research can be generically described as 'clinical trials'. They can be carried out in a variety of ways which are the subject of considerable scientific dispute, for example the allocation of the patient to one treatment or another may, or may not, be *random*. As we shall see, the use of randomisation calls for particular examination.

Before considering in detail the law applicable to clinical trials, it is important to make a general point. Since clinical trials entail a doctor-patient relationship, the general law concerning the duty of the doctor to act in the best interests of his patient and not to harm him applies. This has certain consequences for the conduct of trials.

First, if the trial consists in testing a new treatment, the doctor must have reasonable grounds for believing that the new treatment may be efficacious. For example, all necessary and appropriate research on animals and other studies must have been carried out.

Secondly, patients not receiving any new treatment which is the subject of the trial (ie these in the 'control' group) must receive the best available established treatment.

Thirdly, the trial must contain an appropriate mechanism (a 'stopping rule') whereby it may be discontinued if (a) a new treatment proves less beneficial than established treatment; or (b) a new treatment proves more beneficial than existing therapies or the best available other; or (c) therapy A shows a marked benefit over therapies B and C or vice versa (see for a description, W A Silverman, *Human Experimentation* (1986), ch 9).

In addition to these general propositions derived from the doctor's general duty to his patient, the law relating to the conduct of clinical trials is, in effect, the law relating to consent.

A. THE COMPETENT PATIENT

1. Competence

We have already analysed the meaning of 'competence'. The only additional point which needs to be made here relates to the applicability of s 8(1) of the Family Law Reform Act 1969. This provision, you will recall, states that:

> the consent of a minor who has attained the age of 16 to any surgical, medical or dental treatment which, in the absence of consent, would constitute a trespass to his person, shall be as effective as it would be if he were of full age . . .

The question to be considered is whether therapeutic research is 'treatment' within the Act, so that a person over the age of 16 is *prima facie* competent. Arguably, therapeutic research, because it entails two intentions – to treat and to do research – is more than 'treatment' within the Act, such that the power to consent would remain with the proxy until the minor reaches majority, ie 18, unless found to be competent as explained in the *Gillick* decision. On this analysis, a minor between 16 and 18 years of age would not *prima facie* be competent to consent to therapeutic research. Furthermore in applying *Gillick*, a relatively high standard of comprehension by the minor would have to be shown since therapeutic research entails research on a *sick* minor. It could be said that the law would protect such a minor from consenting save when the illness and the research were trivial because a court might well find any given minor lacked the necessary maturity to consent. This analysis would apply, perhaps, with even greater force, to a minor under 16. [See, *Local Research Ethics Committees* (1991) HSE (91)5, paras 4.1-4.4 endorsing the view expressed above.]

The concern for the competence of the patient is not, of course, limited to the minor. Therapeutic research on adults equally contemplates research on a sick person. The law would insist that those contemplating research satisfy themselves that in assessing a patient's competence to volunteer they have taken account of the possible effect of such factors as pain, other medication and other therapies.

2. Voluntariness

We have already considered the law concerning voluntariness (*supra*, ch 3). It is easy to state that the law requires that a patient truly must volunteer his consent. It is quite another thing to ensure that this is so.

The point is well put by the President's Commission in its 1982 Report 'Making Health Care Decisions' (pp 66-68).

> ... Blatant coercion may be of so little concern in professional-patient relationships because, as physicians so often proclaim, it is so easy for health professionals to elicit a desired decision through more subtle means. Indeed, some physicians are critical of the legal requirement for informed consent on the grounds that it must be mere window dressing since 'patients will, if they trust their doctor, accede to almost any request he cares to make'. On some occasions, to be sure, this result can be achieved by rational persuasion, since the professional presumably has good reasons for preferring a recommended course of action. But the tone of such critics suggests they have something else in mind: an ability to package and present the facts in a way that leaves the patient with no real choice. Such conduct, capitalising on disparities in knowledge, position, and influence, is manipulative in character and impairs the voluntariness of the patient's choice.
>
> Manipulation has more and less extreme forms. At one end of the spectrum is behaviour amounting to misrepresentation or fraud. Of particular concern in health care contexts is the withholding or distortion of information in order to affect the patient's beliefs and decisions. The patient might not be told about alternatives to the recommended course of action, for example, or the risks or other negative characteristics of the recommended treatment might be minimised. Such behaviour is justly criticised on two grounds: first, that it interferes with the patient's voluntary choice (and thus negates consent) and, second, that it interferes with the patient's ability to make an informed decision. At the other end of the spectrum are far more subtle instances: a professional's careful choice of words or nuances of tone and emphasis might present the situation in a manner calculated to heighten the appeal of a particular course of action.
>
> It is well known that the way information is presented can powerfully affect the recipient's response to it. The tone of voice and other aspects of the practitioner's manner of presentation can indicate whether a risk of a particular kind with a particular incidence should be considered serious. Information can be emphasised or played down without altering the content. And it can be framed in a way that affects the listener – for example 'this procedure succeeds most of the time' versus 'this procedure has a 40 percent failure rate'. Health professionals who are aware of the effects of such minor variations can choose their language with care; if, during discussion with a patient, they sense any unintended or confused impressions being created, they can adjust their presentation of information accordingly.
>
> Because many patients are often fearful and unequal to their physicians in status, knowledge, and power, they may be particularly susceptible to manipulations of this type. Health care professionals should, therefore, present information in a form that fosters understanding. Patients should be helped to understand the prognosis for their situation and the implications of different courses of treatment. The difficult distinction, both in theory and in practice, is between acceptable forms of informing, discussion, and rational persuasion on the one hand, and objectionable forms of influence or manipulation on the other.
>
> Since voluntariness is one of the foundation stones of informed consent, professionals have a high ethical obligation to avoid coercion and manipulation of their patients. The law penalises those who ignore the requirements of consent or who directly coerce it. But it can do little about subtle manipulations without incurring severe disruptions of private relationships by intrusive policing, and so the duty is best thought of primarily in ethical terms.

An English court would approach the issue of whether any particular individual's consent was voluntarily given, as did the Court of Appeal in *Freeman v Home Office (No 2)* [1984] 1 All ER 1036 at 1044-5 (see *supra*, ch 3), as a matter of fact rather than a matter of law.

3. Information

The proposition that the patient must be adequately informed to make any consent to therapeutic research valid poses the question, what legal action would lie if the patient was not so informed? We have discussed already the relationship between the torts of battery and negligence and the adequacy of information given to patients (*supra*, ch 3). We will not rehearse the general points here. We must, however, ask whether in the specific context of therapeutic research any failure adequately to inform a patient would render the doctor liable to an action in battery or negligence.

(a) Battery

One view, and it is ours, is that where there is a dual intention on the part of the doctor, ie to treat *and* to conduct research, any failure to inform the patient concerning *both* of these intentions and their possible consequences would amount in law to a battery. This is because in the absence of such knowledge the patient will have assented to a procedure which is materially different in its nature from that which the doctor intends to carry out. To put it another way, research adds a further component to the quality of the consent that the law requires.

The law does not require people to volunteer and will provide a remedy to the patient against the doctor who conscripts him, the remedy being in battery to demonstrate the law's concern for the rights of the patient. Indeed, arguably the failure to disclose the intention to conduct research would amount to fraud sufficient to vitiate any consent which might otherwise be valid. If this is the law, that failure to inform is a battery, then what must the doctor do to act lawfully? In short, the answer must be that the doctor must make explicit his intention to carry out research. A court may insist on the patient being informed of three particular matters in addition to this generalised intention. Each of them is an aspect of those interests of the patient which the law of battery seeks to protect. The patient must be informed: (1) that he may refuse to take part in the research project or may at any time withdraw from the research and that in either case if he does so he will suffer no adverse consequences in terms of the treatment he will then receive; (2) that the nature of the research may be such that he may be a member of a control group in a trial which is intended to evaluate the efficacy of a new therapy; (3) that the trial is a randomised controlled trial (RCT) if it be such.

As regards (2), one consequence of being a member of a control group could be that the patient does not receive the form of treatment which subsequently proves to be the more efficacious. To meet this ethical difficulty researchers ordinarily would be expected to provide for periodic examination of the emerging data. It is our view that a patient's consent is not informed for the purpose of the tort of battery unless he is made aware of this periodic review.

As regards (3), randomisation means that a treatment regime is assigned to a patient randomly without regard to the particular circumstances of that patient, his needs, his preferences or the preferences of his doctor. Again, it is our view that a patient may volunteer for such a trial but his consent is only valid if he is given the opportunity of knowing it is randomised and he is aware of what this means.

(b) Negligence

Putting aside the question of whether a battery action would lie, what is the duty of the doctor, looking now to the tort of negligence? Is the doctor merely obliged to conform with what we have seen to be his duty of care as regards information in cases of treatment? Or are there additional obligations placed upon him by virtue of his dual intentions?

If the general duty were all that was required it would mean that in undertaking clinical trials a doctor would be held to the duty as explained in *Sidaway*. We have seen that this gives considerable weight to the views of the medical profession (*supra*, ch 3). Does *Sidaway* apply to clinical trials? One view is that *Sidaway* is limited to circumstances in which the doctor's only intention is to treat the patient and does not extend to cases of dual intention. This is because if we look to the majority views in *Sidaway*, the primary reliance on what doctors would do as a professional body has no relevance when what is being considered is research. Whether or not it is proper to engage in research is a matter of public policy and not professional opinion. That being so, what amounts to proper disclosure is a matter of law for the courts.

If we look at Lord Scarman's speech, as perhaps we would be entitled to in this context, we would say that ordinarily the doctor must advise the patient that he is involved in a clinical trial and what this entails. We would further say that Lord Scarman's recourse to the 'therapeutic privilege' as justifying non-disclosure of information does not apply to information relating to the fact that the patient is in a clinical trial and what that entails. To argue that a doctor need not tell a patient that he is in a clinical trial since this would mean that he had to be told of other things concerning his condition, would be to use one justifiable non-disclosure as support for an entirely distinct non-disclosure. Arguably this puts the cart before the horse! If the patient's interests require that he not be informed of certain matters concerning his condition for the purposes of his treatment, this is an argument against using him in a clinical trial rather than serving to justify his use and the subsequent non-disclosure of this to him.

If the above view, that *Sidaway* and its reliance upon professional opinion does not govern the conduct of clinical trials, is right, what does the law of negligence say is the doctor's duty as regards disclosing information? In our view, the law would demand disclosure of the following (bearing in mind that the term 'disclosure' refers not only to the volunteering of information but also to the truthful answering of any questions asked):

(1) The information which we earlier considered essential so as to avoid a claim in battery;
(2) The information which apprises the patient of the *material risks* associated with the research.

What does 'material' mean in this context? The meaning given to it in cases of informed consent to treatment in North America is that, a risk is material if it would be judged to be so by a *reasonable patient*. Here, where we are discussing an intention to carry out research, a good argument exists for saying that it should be those risks of which the *particular patient* volunteering for the research would wish to be informed.

In *Halushka v University of Saskatchewan* (1965) 52 WWR 608 at 616, Hall JA said:

> There can be no exceptions to the ordinary requirements of disclosure in the case of research as there may well be in ordinary medical practice. The researcher does not have to balance the probable effect of lack of treatment against the risk involved in the treatment itself. The example of risks being properly hidden from a patient when it is important that he should not worry can have no application in the field of research. The subject of medical experimentation is entitled to a full and frank disclosure of all the facts, probabilities and opinions which a reasonable man might be expected to consider before giving his consent.

Picard in *Legal Liability of Doctors and Hospitals in Canada* (2nd edn, 1984) comments; '[a] point of concern about the test he [Hall JA] used is its use of the objective reasonable patient test when the more pro-patient subjective test would be more appropriate to the research setting . . .' (p 118).

(3) The information, in addition to any risks, which is material to allow the patient to make an informed decision.

Here we have in mind such information as the fact that the patient may have to undergo additional (and perhaps discomforting) tests; may have to stay in hospital when otherwise he would be at home; may have to visit the hospital more frequently for tests and other such inconveniencing circumstances associated with the research.

Explicit recognition of the importance of the disclosure of information can be found in the *Guidelines on Good Clinical Practice for Trials on Medicinal Products in the European Community* – issued by the CPMP of the European Community in 1991.

1.8   The principles of informed consent in the current revision of the Helsinki Declaration should be implemented in each clinical trial.

1.9   Information should be given in both oral and written form whenever possible. No subject should be obliged to participate in the trial. Subjects, their relatives, guardians or, if necessary, legal representatives must be given ample opportunity to enquire about details of the trial. The information must make clear that refusal to participate or withdrawal from the trial at any stage is without any disadvantages for the subject's subsequent care. Subjects must be allowed sufficient time to decide whether or not they wish to participate.

1.10   The subject must be made aware and consent that personal information may be scrutinized during audit by competent authorities and properly authorized persons, but that personal information will be treated as strictly confidential and not be publicly available.

1.11   The subject must have access to information about the procedures for compensation and treatment should he/she be injured/disabled by participating in the trial.

1.12   If a subject consents to participate after a full and comprehensive explanation of the study (including its aims, expected benefits for the subjects and/or others, reference treatments/placebo, risks and inconveniences – eg invasive procedures – and, where appropriate, an explanation of alternative, recognized standard medical therapy), this consent should be appropriately recorded. Consent must be documented either by the subject's dated signature or by the signature of an independent witness who records the subject's assent. In either case the signature confirms that the consent is based on information which has been understood, and that the subject has freely chosen to participate without prejudice to legal and ethical rights while allowing the possibility of withdrawal from the study without having to give any reason unless adverse events have occurred . . .

1.15   Any information becoming available during the trial which may be of relevance for the trial subjects must be made known to them by the investigator.

The GCP Guidelines are not in themselves law, although they serve as the basis for the conduct of research by most major enterprises engaged in medical research, ie where medicinal products are involved. In July 1991 Directive 91/507/EEC (having to do with the harmonisation of the laws on the licensing and testing of medicinal products) required Member States to implement its provisions by 1 January 1992. This has been effected through the Medicines (Applications for Grant of Product Licences – Products for Human Use) Regulations 1993 (SI 1993 No 2538) which came into force on 29 November 1993. *Inter alia*, paragraph 1.1 of Part 4 of the Annex to the Directive provides that:

> All phases of clinical investigation, including bioavailability and bioequivalence studies, shall be designed, implemented and reported in accordance with *good clinical practice* (our emphasis).

It is a matter of conjecture whether the reference to 'good clinical practice', without this phrase being given any specific prominence or meaning, represents an incorporation by reference of the Guidelines on GCP. If the Guidelines are part of the Directive, then it may be thought that English law will have been extended even beyond what in our view represents the common law. One oddity of the Guidelines on GCP is the reference in paragraph 1.8 to the Helsinki Declaration. You will recall that the Helsinki Declaration, while requiring informed consent as a 'basic principle', in II.5 provides that in certain circumstances it may be dispensed with. The traditional interpretation of this exception is that it applies when the doctor does not wish to tell the patient what is wrong with him because such information, in the view of the doctor, would be deleterious to the patient's best interests. The logic is that if the doctor chooses not to tell the patient about his condition, *a fortiori* the doctor cannot ask for permission to involve that patient in research on his condition. We have already seen that this position is legally untenable in England. Furthermore, it sits ill with the remainder of the Guidelines on GCP and the importance they give to informed consent. Therein lies the oddity.

By contrast to the position in England, American law has gone much further in prescribing a framework for regulating research, not least as regards informed consent. By way of introduction, the history leading to regulation is described in the following.

Furrow, Johnson, Jost and Schwartz, *Health Law* (2nd edn, 1991)

> In the United States research has . . . been tainted by racially and politically motivated choices of subject for medical investigation. Indeed, one of the defenses raised at the Nazi war trials was that there was no relevant distinction between what the Nazi physicians did and the contemporaneous American practice of using conscientious objectors and prisoners (including 'political' prisoners, such as those convicted of treason) as subjects in research designed to improve America's military strength. The argument that the United States applied a double standard that condemned only Nazi research is bolstered by the fact that there was no effort to seek retribution against Japanese experimenters who were doing work with serious implications for biological warfare, but who cooperated with the United States after their capture.
>
> The most famous twentieth century American breach of research ethics was the Tuskegee Syphilis Study. In this study, hundreds of poor African American men in the South were studied so that the research agency, the United States Public Health Service, could develop an understanding of the natural history of syphilis. Poor rural African Americans were chosen as subjects because of the difficulty they might have in seeking treatment for syphilis and because it was thought that African Americans, who were considered naturally more sexually active and physically and mentally weaker than whites, would be more likely to benefit from the outcome of the study. The natural history of the disease could be discovered

only if any treatment provided to the subjects were ineffective. The United States Public Health Service continued this research for some forty years. Even when penicillin, the first truly effective treatment for syphilis, became available, the Public Health Service physicians failed to offer that treatment to most of their subjects, and many were regularly discouraged from getting other forms of treatment. The study came to public light in 1972 and was the topic of federal administrative and Congressional hearings in 1973. While participants in the study successfully sued the Public Health Service for compensation, no criminal actions arose out of the case. For a complete account of this tawdry episode in American medical history, see J Jones, Bad Blood (1981).

The Tuskegee Syphilis Study is not unique as an example of American medical research failing to respect individual subjects. Other publicized cases include the Jewish Chronic Disease Hospital case, in which live cancer cells were injected into patients without their knowledge, and the Willowbrook State Hospital hepatitis study, in which children admitted to a state hospital rife with hepatitis were given the disease as a condition of admission. In each of these cases, as in the Nazi experiments, the only authorities determining whether the subjects were properly selected were the medical investigators themselves.

The first formal federal policy requiring outside review of research involving human subjects was imposed in 1966 by the Public Health Service upon those seeking grants from it. The 1966 policy required prior consideration of 'the risks and potential medical benefits of the investigation' before a protocol could be submitted to the Public Health Service.

In 1974, one year after the public disclosure of the Tuskegee Syphilis Study, Congress enacted the National Research Act establishing the National Commission for Protection of Human Subjects of Biomedical and Behavioral Research, which was to 'conduct a comprehensive investigation and study to identify basic ethical principles' that should underlie the conduct of human subjects research. That Commission was also to develop procedures to assure that the research would be consistent with those ethical principles and to recommend guidelines that could apply to human subjects research supported by the Department of Health, Education and Welfare. In recognition of the interdisciplinary nature of the issue, the Act also required the establishment of institutional review boards (IRBs) at institutions under contract with the Department of Health, Education and Welfare.

By 1975, when the Department of Health, Education and Welfare issued its 'Policy for the Protection of Human Research Subjects', virtually every university, medical school, and research hospital had established IRBs which operated within the requirements of both federal and state regulations. The federal regulations were revised by what had become the Department of Health and Human Services (DHSS) in 1981 to remove the necessity of IRB reviews from some low-risk research and to provide for informal consent procedures in some cases. This year in the United States, hundreds of IRBs will review thousands of research protocols. No federally funded research will be carried out at an institution without that institution's IRB approval.

The current regulations on 'Protection of Human Subjects' (1990) 45 CFR provide in paragraphs 46.116 and 46.117:

§ 46.116 General requirements for informed consent

Except as provided elsewhere in this or other subparts, no investigator may involve a human being as a subject in research covered by these regulations unless the investigator has obtained the legally effective informed consent of the subject or the subject's legally authorized representative. An investigator shall seek such consent only under circumstances that provide the prospective subject or the representative sufficient opportunity to consider whether or not to participate and that minimize the possibility of coercion or undue influence. The information that is given to the subject or the representative shall be in language understandable to the subject or the representative. No informed consent, whether oral or written, may include any exculpatory language through which the subject or the representative is made to waive or appear to waive any of the subject's legal rights, or releases or appears to release the investigator, the sponsor, the institution or its agents from liability for negligence.

(a) Basic elements of informed consent. Except as provided in paragraph (c) or (d) of this section, in seeking informed consent the following information shall be provided to each subject:

(1)   A statement that the study involves research, an explanation of the purposes of the research and the expected duration of the subject's participation, a description of the procedures to be followed, and identification of any procedures which are experimental;

(2)   A description of any reasonably foreseeable risks or discomforts to the subject;

(3)   A description of any benefits to the subject or to others which may reasonably be expected from the research;

(4)   A disclosure of appropriate alternative procedures or courses of treatment, if any, that might be advantageous to the subject;

(5)   A statement describing the extent, if any, to which confidentiality of records identifying the subject will be maintained;

(6)   For research involving more than minimal risk, an explanation as to whether any compensation and an explanation as to whether any medical treatments are available if injury occurs and, if so, what they consist of, or where further information may be obtained;

(7)   An explanation of whom to contact for answers to pertinent questions about the research and research subjects' rights, and whom to contact in the event of a research-related injury to the subject; and

(8)   A statement that participation is voluntary, refusal to participate will involve no penalty or loss of benefits to which the subject is otherwise entitled, and the subject may discontinue participation at any time without penalty or loss of benefits to which the subject is otherwise entitled.

(b) Additional elements of informed consent. When appropriate, one or more of the following elements of information shall also be provided to each subject:

(1)   A statement that the particular treatment or procedure may involve risks to the subject (or to the embryo or fetus, if the subject is or may become pregnant) which are currently unforeseeable;

(2)   Anticipated circumstances under which the subject's participation may be terminated by the investigator without regard to the subject's consent;

(3)   Any additional costs to the subject that may result from participation in the research;

(4)   The consequences of a subject's decision to withdraw from the research and procedures for orderly termination of participation by the subject;

(5)   A statement that significant new findings developed during the course of the research which may relate to the subject's willingness to continue participation will be provided to the subject; and

(6)   The approximate number of subjects involved in the study. . . .

(d) An IRB may approve a consent procedure which does not include, or which alters, some or all of the elements of informed consent set forth above, or waive the requirements to obtain informed consent provided the IRB finds and documents that:

(1)   The research involves no more than minimal risk to the subjects;

(2)   The waiver or alteration will not adversely affect the rights and welfare of the subjects;

(3)   The research could not practicably be carried out without the waiver or alteration; and

(4)   Whenever appropriate, the subjects will be provided with additional pertinent information after participation.

(e) The informed consent requirements in these regulations are not intended to preempt any applicable federal, state, or local laws which require additional information to be disclosed in order for informed consent to be legally effective.

(f) Nothing in these regulations is intended to limit the authority of a physician to provide emergency medical care, to the extent the physician is permitted to do so under applicable federal, state, or local law.

§ 46.117 Documentation of informed consent

(a) Except as provided in paragraph (c) of this section, informed consent shall be documented by the use of a written consent form approved by the IRB and signed by the subject or the sub-ject's legally authorized representative. A copy shall be given to the person signing the form.

(b) Except as provided in paragraph (c) of this section, the consent form may be either of the following:

(1)   A written consent document that embodies the elements of informed consent required by § 46.116. This form may be read to the subject or the subject's legally authorized representative, but in any event, the investigator shall give either the subject or the representative adequate opportunity to read it before it is signed; or

(2)   A 'short form' written consent document stating that the elements of informed consent required by § 46.116 have been presented orally to the subject or the subject's legally authorized representative. When this method is used, there shall be a witness to the oral presentation. Also, the IRB shall approve a written summary of what is to be said to the subject or the representative. Only the short form itself is to be signed by the

subject or the representative. However, the witness shall sign both the short form and a copy of the summary, and the person actually obtaining consent shall sign a copy of the summary. A copy of the summary shall be given to the subject or the representative, in addition to a copy of the 'short form.'

(c) An IRB may waive the requirement for the investigator to obtain a signed consent form for some or all subjects if it finds either:

(1) That the only record linking the subject and the research would be the consent document and the principal risk would be potential harm resulting from a breach of confidentiality. Each subject will be asked whether the subject wants documentation linking the subject with the research, and the subject's wishes will govern; or

(2) That the research presents no more than minimal risk of harm to subjects and involves no procedures for which written consent is normally required outside of the research context.

4. Limits of research

As with treatment, the permissible limits of therapeutic research are measured in law by reference to a risk-benefit ratio. A patient may only be exposed in the course of treatment to risks which can be demonstrated to bring with them the likelihood of greater benefit. Clearly, the more severe the patient's illness the greater are the risks which can lawfully be taken in treating him if a real probability of benefiting him exists. Similarly, in the context of therapeutic research the risks which research might expose the patient to (even without his knowledge) must be demonstrably outweighed by the expected benefits.

Prima facie, however, concern for the relationship between risk and benefit is of greater importance in the regulation of research which is non-therapeutic or which involves those who are incompetent to consent. We will consider this in greater detail later. When the research is therapeutic and the patient is competent it will ordinarily be left to the patient to determine the risk-benefit ratio for himself – having, of course, been properly informed.

A further question needs to be examined. Is the doctor limited in the form of research to be employed in that he may not involve his patient in a randomised controlled trial? The question arises because randomisation, as we have seen, entails assigning a patient to a treatment category without reference to the patient's particular circumstances or preferences or, indeed, the doctor's preferences. For example, a patient may prefer fewer hospital visits or interventions but because he is in an RCT will not be able to have his preference respected. Being involved in an RCT requires that he waive his preferences. Provided he is informed of the implications of randomisation and agrees to be part of the trial this will not create a legal problem. Also, the doctor may prefer one form of treatment rather than another when two are being compared but may as a consequence of the trial have to offer what, to him, is less preferable. The apparent answer is that if the patient is apprised of all that is involved in being in a randomised controlled trial then his consent is properly informed. The law may not, however, be so simple. It will be clear from the brief description of randomisation that it may involve the patient in waiving the doctor's duty to act in his best medical interests. It is undoubtedly in the patient's best medical interests to have a doctor who is confident that the treatment he is offering is the best for the patient. If the doctor does not believe this (and *a fortiori* if the trial is 'double blind'), the patient may become aware of his doctor's lack of confidence and consequently lose confidence in his treatment himself. This is an illustration of what a number of commentators identify as an inevitable conflict of loyalties intrinsic, in particular, in RCTs. (See, eg, A Schafer 'The Ethics of the Randomised Clinical Trial', (1982) 307 New Eng J Med 719).

Even if such a conflict is not *inevitable* in RCTs, the possibility nevertheless exists. This being so, the argument is that in law a patient who is ill should as a matter of public policy be prevented from absolving the doctor from his duty to do his best for his patient.

B. THE INCOMPETENT PATIENT

1. Children

Can a proxy, who will usually be a parent, consent to therapeutic research on an incompetent child?

If we address the three issues which we have identified as significant, it goes without saying first of all that the consent of the proxy must be voluntarily given. A court would, of course, be vigilant to ensure that consent by, for example, a parent was not obtained by improper pressure. An example of this could be where a child would only receive otherwise available treatment *if* it was entered into a clinical trial. There may be circumstances where treatment is *only* available as part of a trial, ie when no accepted treatment currently exists. In such a case the offering of treatment only on these terms would not amount to unlawful pressure.

As regards the information which (now) the proxy and not the patient must be given, the doctor must make *at least* as full a disclosure as the law would require him to give to the competent patient. Arguably, the law would also require the doctor to disclose to the proxy that information which materially affects the proxy in his continued care of the child, for example the consequences for the proxy of the participation of the child in the trial or of the occurrence of a risk entailed in the trial *for the proxy*.

Finally, as regards the limits of the proxy's authority to consent, since we are considering *therapeutic* research these must fundamentally reflect the risk-benefit ratio of participation in the trial. The proxy must be satisfied that on a reasonable assessment of this ratio, it is in the best interests of the child to participate.

What about RCTs? Is there, however, a difference for participation in a trial which involves randomisation? *Prima facie* it would appear that randomisation would be legally acceptable because the proxy can be informed of what it involves. But, since randomisation entails a possible conflict of loyalties for the doctor it could be said that a proxy was not acting in the child's best interests in consenting to a child's participation in an RCT. Indeed, can it *ever* be in a child's best interests to waive the doctor's duty to do his best for his patient?

One further point is worth noting. Clearly as a matter of considerate decision-making by the proxy and good medical practice, the *assent* of the child should be sought and obtained when it can be meaningfully given. If the child refuses to assent, however, a court would not find that involvement of the child was unlawful providing the procedure was in the child's 'best interests'. (See *Guidelines for the Ethical Conduct of Medical Research Involving Children* (British Paediatric Association) 1992, Ch 6.)

2. Adults

Any valid consent in the case of an incompetent adult would have to come from someone other than the patient. We have seen, however, that even in the context of treatment, without specific statutory authority the law does not empower anyone to consent as a proxy. You will recall (in chapter 4) that the House of Lords in *Re F (a mental patient: sterilisation)* [1990] 2 AC 1 developed the doctrine of necessity so as to provide the legal basis for the treatment of incompetent adults. As a consequence, a doctor may treat such a patient provided that it is in the patient's best interests to do so. Does the approach in *Re F* apply to therapeutic research? The prevailing view, as the following commentator indicates, is that the analysis in *Re F* does apply to therapeutic research.

C Hodges 'Legal and Ethical Issues in Research in the United Kingdom: Children, the Elderly and the Mentally Incapacitated' (1992) 6 Pharmaceutical Medicine 309

> *Re F* concerned treatment, not research, so a definitive legal statement in relation to research is, therefore, not available. Since the case concerned the sterilization of a mentally handicapped woman, it will immediately be seen that by defining the 'best interests' of the patient as to save life, or to ensure improvement, or to prevent deterioration in physical or mental health, all non-therapeutic research and possibly even some therapeutic research, such as giving a placebo, might be illegal if the same interpretation of the phrase 'best interests' were to be applied in research. The decision established what is referred to as a 'doctrine of necessity' for treatment without consent. The necessity is, or course, that of the individual patient rather than society, or any other individual. However, both the RCP [*Research Involving Patients* (1990) para 7.34] and MCR [*The Ethical Conduct of Research on the Mentally Incapacitated* (1991) para 7.2.2] consider that the 'best interests' principle should equally apply when the treatment in question is still in the research phase.

You will notice that Christopher Hodges refers to the MRC's Working Party Report on *Research on the Mentally Incapacitated* (1991) chaired by Mrs Renee Short.

Paragraphs 7.2.2 and 7.2.4 offer the following analysis:

> 7.2.2 While the judgment in *Re F* concerned conventional medical treatment and not research, we agree with the conclusion of the RCP 1990 Report 'Research Involving Patients', that the principle enunciated should equally apply when the treatment in question is still in the research phase. An experimental medicinal procedure may be the only appropriate therapy and provided the relevant health professional acts with proper skill and care and in the best interests of the patient, neither liability for trespass nor negligence should arise . . .
>
> 7.2.4 We are clear that, provided the necessary safeguards are in place, the ethical grounds for including mentally incapacitated people in therapeutic research (and indeed for not denying them the opportunity to participate in research that offers the prospect of improving their health) are so great, that it would be contrary to accepted good practice to be deterred by the comparative lack of clarity surrounding the legal position. However, it may be prudent for doctors contemplating special categories of treatment of a serious and irreversible nature in a research context to consider whether it is appropriate to seek endorsement of their actions by the court, no doubt in consultation with the relevant ethics committee.

We agree in principle with the analysis suggested by Christopher Hodges and the MRC. We saw above that it is lawful for a proxy to consent to therapeutic research on a child. Obviously, the proxy must act in the best interests of the child and be satisfied that the risk-benefit ratio is in the child's favour. If it were unlawful to conduct therapeutic research on an incompetent adult, the adult would be in a worse position as a matter of law than a child. This is because any proposed therapeutic research though it carries risks, must, to be lawful, also carry an expected benefit. The adult would, consequently, be denied by law this chance of a benefit.

Therefore, in our view, a court would decide that the law is as follows: an incompetent adult may be the subject of therapeutic research where that research would be justified in the case of a competent adult (ie, in his 'best interests') provided that the researcher has satisfied an appropriately constituted LREC as to the scientific validity of the proposed research and the need for, and the ethical propriety of, such research.

You will notice that the MRC's Working Party Report suggests that it would be 'prudent' to obtain the court's approval where the intervention is of 'a serious and irreversible nature'. While such caution was understandable in the aftermath of *Re F*, subsequent decisions of the High Court have cast doubt on the need to involve the court where what is contemplated is therapeutic. Although the cases do not specifically concern therapeutic *research*, the import is clear, namely that where it is proposed to treat the patient in his 'best interests' recourse to the court is not essential (see, for example, *Re H (mental patient)* (1992) 9 BMLR 71).

Non-therapeutic research

You will recall that here we are concerned with research where the researcher has only one intention, ie to obtain information through systematic enquiry so as to contribute to generalisable knowledge. There is no intention to treat the person who is the subject of the research.

There are two categories of persons upon whom non-therapeutic research may be carried out: patients and the healthy.

A. PATIENTS

We can perhaps deal shortly with patients. Ordinarily, a doctor's duty to care for his patient would preclude his engaging in non-therapeutic research on such a person. This is because it would ordinarily be difficult to show that it was in the best medical interests of the patient to be exposed to additional interventions which carry risks and which are not designed to aid in his treatment.

There may be, of course, circumstances in which a patient with a minor illness may volunteer to take part in non-therapeutic research. If the proposed research carries no demonstrable risk of harm to the patient nor will it affect deleteriously the patient's condition, then it may be that the patient may lawfully be party to non-therapeutic research. In our view, however, the evidence of absence of risk would have to be clear and compelling. In such a (rare) case the legal position of the patient will be the same as that of the healthy volunteer which we now turn to consider.

B. HEALTHY VOLUNTEERS

We noticed in the context of therapeutic research that there are some basic conditions to be met in any clinical trial. Equally, this is so in the conduct of non-therapeutic research. In addition to those points made earlier (see *supra* at pp 1043) which are relevant here also, the following conditions must also be observed:

(1) the doctor must obtain an appropriate medical history from the volunteer so as to ensure that the proposed procedure carries no increased risk in the light of that history;
(2) the doctor must obtain the permission of the volunteer to inform his family doctor that he is participating in a trial and should obtain from that doctor any relevant medical details about the volunteer;
(3) the doctor must satisfy himself that the volunteer is not participating in any other trial contemporaneously nor engaging in other conduct, eg an intention to drive home in certain circumstances, whereby the volunteer's health may be put at risk;
(4) the doctor must have available all appropriate medical equipment to meet any foreseeable eventuality arising out of the trial, eg in appropriate circumstances resuscitation equipment;
(5) the doctor must ensure that the volunteer is prepared to keep him informed of any changes in the volunteer's circumstances.

A failure to fulfil any of these obligations could well expose the doctor to liability in negligence if any harm ensues. Beyond these general points, as with therapeutic research, the central legal issue warranting analysis is consent. If a valid consent is not obtained then liability in battery or negligence may arise.

1. The competent volunteer

(a) Competence

As we have seen before, the common law looks to the understanding and maturity of an individual in determining competence. Just as with therapy, an adult would *prima facie* be presumed competent to volunteer for non-therapeutic research.

In the case of children, we have seen that s 8(1) of the Family Law Reform Act 1969 deems children between the ages of 16 and 18 to be competent to consent to treatment to the same extent as an adult. The Act has no application to non-therapeutic research since its wording is limited to 'surgical, medical or dental *treatment*' (our emphasis) (see *Re W (a minor) (medical treatment)* [1992] 4 All ER 627, CA, at 635 per Lord Donaldson MR and at 649 per Nolan LJ). The capacity of a child under 18 to consent to non-therapeutic research is, therefore, governed by the common law.

As we saw earlier, it is our view that the approach of the House of Lords in *Gillick* is applicable to therapeutic research. In our view this is equally true of non-therapeutic research. A child (under the age of 18) who has the capacity to understand what is involved in the research may be able to give a valid consent. The capacity of a child will, therefore, depend upon his or her understanding and maturity.

As we saw in relation to therapeutic research, this is likely to be a relatively high standard of comprehension. Since non-therapeutic research lacks any potentially beneficial consequences for the child and may indeed carry a risk of harm, in our view the law would require an even greater level of comprehension for this type of research.

(b) Voluntariness

A court would analyse the voluntariness or otherwise of a healthy volunteer in accordance with the principles we have already seen in the context of thera-peutic research, relying principally on the dictum of Lord Donaldson MR in *F Rreeman v Home Office (No 2) (supra*, ch 3). In short, it will be a matter of fact in every case. The matter which may be of primary concern is the possibility of exploitation of persons who may 'volunteer' for research because of some felt pressure. Pressure can come in a number of forms. There is the obvious case of financial inducements and the effect they may have on the financially disad-vantaged (see *Local Research Ethics Committees* (HSG (91) 5) paras 3.15-3.16: 'payment in cash or kind to volunteers should only be for expense, time and inconvenience reasonably incurred'. See also Royal College of Physician's Report, *op cit* paras 17.1-17.3.) The less obvious case, perhaps, is what some have called 'contextual duress' when, for example, a student 'volunteers' to participate in research at the 'invitation' of his teacher, or an employee at the behest of his employer, or a junior colleague at the behest of the leader of the research team, or any person who is a junior or subordinate member of a hierarchically structured group. As Professor Gerald Dworkin points out in 'Law and Medical Experimentation' (1987) 13 Monash ULR 189, 204:

> It does not follow that financial inducements should destroy the voluntary nature of all responses, yet where students and out of work youths are offered significant sums of money to test new drugs, as happened in London recently, the nature of consents and inducements should be examined very carefully. In defining the use of such volunteers it was argued that there was nothing unethical in paying volunteers to test new drugs so long as they were fully informed of any possible risks; and a further justification was put forward that there was a non-fault compensation scheme in case anything went wrong. This does seem to miss the point: volunteers certainly can give informed consent to properly conducted research procedures, but even informed consent can be involuntary.

Particularly problematical is the position of prisoners who may have been told repeatedly that their sentence or conditions of imprisonment will not be affected but may none the less volunteer because (they think) their chances of parole, for example, may be improved.

In all such cases the law will begin with the premise that a competent adult is free to do what he wishes and must be assumed to have acted voluntarily if he participates. Thus, these particular examples and classes of person will not be treated any differently by the law. Professor Somerville weighs the arguments well concerning the use of prisoners in research in *Consent to Medical Care* (1980), pp 96-98:

> ... there is at least one commentator who believes that one is never, under any conditions, justified in using these persons as research subjects. Bronstein argues that the distinguishing and prohibitive element in the use of prisoners as subjects, is the involvement of the state and the necessary rights it has over the prisoners' bodies simply by virtue of the fact of imprisonment [AE Sabin, AJ Bronstein, WN Hubbard, 'The Military/The Prisoner', in 'Experiments and Research with Humans: Values in Conflict', National Academy of Sciences, Academy Forum, Washington, 1975, p 127, per Bronstein, at pp 130-5]. He makes the thought-provoking statement that '[i]t is not so much the actual, occasional abuse of captive human subjects, but the potential for abuse which concerns [him]'. Thus it is not necessary to show abuses to invalidate experimentation in prisons, because the 'potential for abuse' is sufficient to do this. It is important to consider these matters because it makes one realise that a discussion of 'informed' consent in relation to the use of prisoners as research subjects is not enough, as there may be a duty to not even request the prisoner's consent to participation in the experiment. Kilbrandon states this in a very effective way when he says

that to put a man in prison is to deprive him of a large number of consents, therefore it is distasteful to confer on him a consent which is not for his own benefit [Lord Kilbrandon, 'Final Discussion', in Wolstenholme and O'Connor (eds), CIBA Foundation symposium, 'Ethics in Medical Progress: with special reference to transplantation' p 202 at 205].

An argument contrary to the above views advocating prohibition of medical experiments on prisoners or only allowing it under much more restrictive conditions than apply to the unconfined population, is that prisoners should not be deprived of any more rights that accrue to other members of society, than absolutely necessary. One such right is that of personal inviolability of both mind and body, any exceptions normally depending on consent. And thus the corollary, the right to consent and the right not to consent. For reasons quite apart from medical experimentation, for instance to give a legal right of action against brutality in prisons it may be important to retain for prisoners these rights to inviolability, and to consent, and not to consent. Therefore, in the context of medical treatment or research, the right to consent should not be abrogated for fear that the rights associated with it, that of inviolability and the right not to consent, will also be affected. Rather its exercise must be safeguarded. This is expressed by Ramsey in the following words: 'I am one who happens to believe that prisoners have not been and should not be drummed out of the human race. They ought, therefore, not to be excluded in principle from the community of risk-filled human consent to good purposes, even if the needed practical protections for them are so formidable as to prohibit the general use of prisoners in medical research.' [P Ramsey, 'The Ethics of a Cottage Industry in an Age of Community and Research Medicine' NEJM 284(13) 700 (1971) at 705.]

It may be that if research participation is seen as a privilege, it should not be allowed because distribution of this privilege can become a coercive tool in the hands of wardens and prison authorities, thus affecting the voluntariness of prisoners' consent. This is related to another reason for not allowing research on prisoners. It is that the attitude of prison staff towards prisoners often leaves much to be desired and may amount to coercion to consent, or even ignores, in all but theory, the necessity for free and informed consent. For instance, with respect to prisoner experimentation, a warden at Montana State Prison stated: 'we want our prison to be a living laboratory for the people of Montana . . . There should be no conflict in offering *our* physical and human resources [prisoners] to other disciplines . . .'

Further, some arguments put forward in support of prison experimentation rely on the *control factor* inherent in imprisonment, as an advantage justifying research on prisoners taking place. But these arguments themselves provide further arguments *against* using prisoners, because they raise serious doubts about the validity of the consent given. Examples of such reasoning are that it is beneficial for experimental purposes to be able to totally control the subjects, and the experimentation and the rewards it offers may themselves augment the effective power of the prison authorities over prisoners. Newman found a reason given to justify the use of prisoner subjects was the doubtful altruism that wardens, as public officials, were interested in promoting science and, perhaps more realistically if still not acceptable, in promoting a research programme which helps the training and education of prisoners [RW Newman, 'The Participation of Prisoners in Clinical Research', in Ladimer and Newman eds 'Clinical Investigation in Medicine: Legal Ethical and Moral Aspects' at 467]. Both these words, training and education, may be used in their genuine sense, but may also be euphemisms for establishing and justifying a more effective system of control of prisoners, without corresponding educative benefit to them. Thus the very advantage of using prisoners – their availability, the convenience they offer as subjects, the ease with which they can be controlled – are precisely the factors throwing doubt on the validity of their consent and weighing against their participation in medical research.

(c) Information

We set out all the relevant legal points relating to the duty to disclose when we considered therapeutic research (*supra*, at pp 1045-1051): that research is being carried out; that the volunteer may withdraw at any time without adverse consequences; the form of the research, eg that it is an RCT; the need for the disclosure of material risks and information; answering any questions truthfully. We would only add one point. In the context of research on healthy volunteers we have no doubt that the courts would adopt a *subjective test* of materiality which would require disclosure of all information which the particular volunteer would want to know.

Contrast the following decision of the Saskatchewan Court of Appeal.

Halushka v University of Saskatchewan (1965) 52 WWR 608 (Sask CA)

Hall JA: The appellants, Wyant and Merriman, were medical practitioners employed by the appellant, University of Saskatchewan. . . .

The respondent, a student at the University of Saskatchewan, had attended summer school in 1961. On August 21, 1961, he went to the employment office to find a job. At the employment office he was advised that there were no jobs available but that he could earn $50 by being the subject of a test at the University Hospital. The respondent said that he was told the test would last a couple of hours and that it was a 'safe test and there was nothing to worry about'.

The respondent reported to the anaesthesia department at the University Hospital and there saw the appellant, Wyant. The conversation which ensued concerning the proposed test was related by the respondent as follows:

> Dr Wyant explained to me that a new drug was to be tried out on the Wednesday following. He told me that electrodes would be put in both my arms, legs and head and then he assured me that it was a perfectly safe test, it has been conducted many times before. He told me that I was not to eat anything on Wednesday morning that I was to report at approximately nine o'clock, then he said it would take about an hour to hook me up and the test itself would last approximately two hours, after the time I would be given fifty dollars, pardon me, I would be allowed to sleep first, fed and then given fifty dollars and driven home on the same day.

The appellant, Wyant, also told the respondent that an incision would be made in his left arm and that a catheter or tube would be inserted into the vein.

The respondent agreed to undergo the test and was asked by the appellant, Wyant, to sign a form of consent. This form, entered as Ex D1, reads as follows:

Intensive Care 460-57-2

Halushka, Walter
72756 Jan 2'40 MR.
Dr. Nanson

Consent for tests on volunteers

I, Walter Halushka, age 21 of 236 – 3rd Street Saskatoon hereby state that I have volunteered for tests upon my person for the purpose of study of

Heart & Blood Circulation Response under General Anaesthesia

The tests to be undertaken in connection with this study have been explained to me and I understand fully what is proposed to be done. I agree of my own free will to submit to these tests, and in consideration of the remuneration hereafter set forth, I do release the chief investigators, *Dr G M Wyant and J E Merriman* their associates, technicians, and each thereof, other personnel involved in these studies, the University Hospital Board, and the University of Saskatchewan from all responsibility and claims whatsoever, for any untoward effects or accidents due to or arising out of said tests, either directly or indirectly.

I understand that I shall receive a remuneration of $50.00 for each test . . .
Witness my hand and seal.

[Sgd.] WALTER HALUSHKA
[Sgd.] IRIS ZAECHTOWSKI (Witness)
Date: Aug 22/61

The respondent described the circumstances surrounding the signing of D1, saying:

> He then gave me a consent form, I skimmed through it and picked out the word 'accident' on the consent form and asked Doctor Wyant what accidents were referred to, and he gave me an example of me falling down the stairs at home after the test and

then trying to sue the University Hospital as a result. Being assured that any accident that would happen to me would be at home and not in the Hospital I signed the form.

The test contemplated was known as 'The Heart and Blood Circulation Response under General Anaesthesia', and was to be conducted jointly by the appellants, Wyant and Merriman, using a new anaesthetic agent known commercially as 'Fluoromar'. This agent had not been previously used or tested by the appellants in any way.

The respondent returned to the University Hospital on August 23, 1961, to undergo the test. The procedure followed was that which had been described to the respondent and expected by him, with the exception that the catheter, after being inserted in the vein in the respondent's arm, was advanced towards his heart. When the catheter reached the vicinity of the heart, the respondent felt some discomfort. The anaesthetic agent was then administered to him. The time was then 11:32 am. Eventually the catheter tip was advanced through the various heart chambers out into the pulmonary artery where it was positioned.

The appellants, Wyant and Merriman, intended to have the respondent reach medium depth of surgical anaesthesia. However, an endotracheal tube which had been inserted to assist the respondent in breathing caused some coughing. In the opinion of the appellant, Wyant, the coughing indicated that the respondent was in the upper half of a light anaesthesia – on the verge of waking up. At 12:16 pm, therefore, the concentration of the mixture of the anaesthetic was increased. The respondent then descended into deeper surgical anaesthesia.

At about 12:20 pm there were changes in the respondent's cardiac rhythm which suggested to the appellants, Wyant and Merriman, that the level of the anaesthetic was too deep. The amount of anaesthetic was then decreased, or lightened.

At 12:25 pm the respondent suffered a complete cardiac arrest.

The appellants, Wyant and Merriman, and their assistants took immediate steps to resuscitate the respondent's heart by manual massage. To reach the heart, an incision was made from the breastbone to the line of the arm-pit and two of the ribs were pulled apart. A vasopressor was administered as well as urea, a drug used to combat swelling of the brain. After one minute and 30 seconds the respondent's heart began to function again.

The respondent was unconscious for a period of four days. He remained in the University Hospital as a patient until discharged 10 days later. On the day before he was discharged, the respondent was given $50 by the appellant, Wyant. At that time the respondent asked the appellant, Wyant, if that was all he was going to get for all he went through. The appellant said that $50 was all that they had bargained for but that he could give a larger sum in return for a complete release executed by the respondent's mother or elder sister.

As a result of the experiment, the appellants concluded that as an anaesthetic agent 'Fluoromar' had too narrow a margin of safety and it was withdrawn from clinical use in the University Hospital.

The respondent brought action against the appellants, basing his claim for damages on two grounds, namely, trespass to the person and negligence. . . .

The main issue before the jury concerning the respondent's claim of trespass to the person was that of consent. . . .

It was on the basis of the ordinary physician-patient relationship that the learned trial judge charged the jury on the matter of consent. In dealing with this part of the case he said:

> In the circumstances of this case I will say that before signing such a document the plaintiff was entitled to a reasonably clear explanation of the proposed test and of the natural and expected results from it.

In my opinion, the duty imposed upon those engaged in medical research, as were the appellants, Wyant and Merriman, to those who offer themselves as subjects for experimentation, as the respondent did here, is at least as great as, if not greater than, the duty owed by the ordinary physician or surgeon to his patient. There can be no exceptions to the ordinary requirements of disclosure in the case of research as there may well be in ordinary medical practice. The researcher does not have to balance the probable effect of lack of treatment against the risk involved in the treatment itself. The example of risks being properly hidden from a patient when it is important that he should not worry can have no application in the field of research. The subject of medical experimentation is entitled to full and frank disclosure of all the facts, probabilities and opinions which *a reasonable man* (our emphasis) might be expected to consider before giving his consent. . . . The respondent was not informed that the catheter would be advanced to and through his heart but was admittedly given to understand that it would be merely inserted in the vein in his arm. While it may be correct to say that the advancement of the catheter to the heart was not in itself dangerous and did not cause or contribute to the cause of the cardiac arrest, it was a circumstance which, if known, might very well have prompted the respondent to withhold his consent. The undisclosed or misrepresented facts need not concern matters which directly cause the ultimate damage if they are of a nature which might influence the judgment upon which the consent is based.

The court dismissed the appeal.

In our view, Hall JA's reference to the 'reasonable man' standard does not go far enough. English law would insist upon a subjective standard (see the subsequent case in Canada of *Weiss v Solomon* (1989) 48 CCLT 280 (Qu Sup Ct) requiring the 'highest possible' standard of disclosure; discussed by B Freedman and K Glass (1990) 18 Law, Medicine and Health Care 395).

(d) Limits

We are considering here the limits imposed by law to that which a healthy volunteer may consent, such that any consent given thereafter is invalid.

A competent person may, of course, agree to expose himself to a variety of risks. Indeed, society approves of this, eg by encouraging sport. But the example of sport is informative, for boxing matches which are inevitably risky encounters may lawfully be engaged in; prize fights, however, are unlawful despite the apparent consent of the participants. So it is with non-therapeutic research. A person *can* lawfully take some risks with his body by volunteering for non-therapeutic research but the law would impose certain limits as a matter of public policy. Nicholson (ed) (*op cit*) sets out in table form risk equivalents, ie an 'attempt to find equivalence between different scales of risks and the statistical probabilities of certain adverse events' (p 119).

Table 5.6 Risk equivalents

British definition	Negligible	Minimal	More than minimal.
American definition	Minimal	Minor increase over minimal	Greater than minor increase over minimal.
Risk of death	less than 1 per million	1 to 100 per million	Greater than 100 per million.
Risk of major complication	less than 10 per million	10 to 100 million	Greater than 1000 per million.
Risk of minor complication	less than 1 per thousand	1 to 100 thousand	Greater than 100 per thousand.

Referring to this table he states that (p 120):

... the overall risks of non-therapeutic research ... would lie in the category 'minor increase over minimal' for both major and minor complications. It seems perfectly acceptable to subject adults, who have given informed consent, to such a level of risk.

The American term 'minimal risk' equivalent to the British term 'negligible risk' is defined in the HHS Regulations on the Protection of Human Research Subjects in 1990 as (para 46.102 (g)):

(g) 'Minimal risk' means that the risks of harm anticipated in the proposed research are not greater, considering probability and magnitude, than those ordinarily encountered in daily life or during the performance of routine physical or psychological examinations or tests.

We agree that the limit suggested by the relevant guidelines and Nicholson (ed) is probably that which a court would endorse. The implication of such a view is, of course, that any research on a healthy volunteer which on the basis of existing knowledge properly analysed poses a risk which is more than a 'minor increase over minimal' would in law amount to a battery and even, possibly, a crime in appropriate circumstances.

2. The incompetent volunteer

Here, we are considering the circumstances under which an incompetent individual may lawfully be volunteered for non-therapeutic research.

(a) Children

There are two issues which need to be considered: who, if anyone, can lawfully volunteer a child for non-therapeutic research and if anyone can, what are the limits to what the child can be volunteered for? We will consider these issues together.

In a seminal article in 1978, Professor Gerald Dworkin explained the background.

G Dworkin, 'Legality of Consent to Nontherapeutic Medical Research on Infants and Young Children' (1978) 53 Archives of Disease in Childhood 443

> For some years the view of lawyers advising the medical profession has been that such . . . research is unlawful. This is a view expressed, for example, by Speller, [Speller, S R (1971) *Law Relating to Hospitals and Kindred Institutions*, 5th ed, pp 144-145. H K Lewis, London.] the Medical Research Council, [Medical Research Council (1964). Responsibility in investigations on human subjects. *British Medical Journal*, **2**, 178-180.] the Medical Protection Society, [Leahy Taylor, J (1975). Ethical and legal aspects of non-therapeutic clinical investigation, *Medico-Legal Journal*, **43**, 53-68.] the Medical Defence Union, [Pratt, H (1977). Research on infants. *Lancet*, **1**, 699; 1052.] Sir Harvey Druitt (a former Treasury Solicitor), [Curran, W J, and Beecher, H K (1969). Experimentation in children; a reexamination of legal and ethical principles. *Journal of the American Medical Association*, **210**, 77-83.] Sir George Godber (a former Chief Medical Officer to the Department of Health and Social Security (DHSS)) [Godber, G (1974). Discussion. Symposium on Constraints on the Advance of Medicine. *Proceedings of the Royal Society of Medicine*, **67**, 1311.] and to the DHSS itself. The authority for this view rests on general legal principle rather than on any specific rule or ruling. Thus, the general philosophy of the law is that parents are under a duty to look after a child's interests and so any nontherapeutic procedures cannot be justified.

He ended his article with the following bold conclusion (at p 445):

> It is submitted that it is quite proper for those medical bodies which give guidance to the profession to change their present uncertain statements as to the law and replace them with a much clearer guide to the effect that 'although there is as yet no clear legal authority, it appears that it is lawful to conduct nontherapeutic research procedures on infants and young children provided the following requirements are strictly observed:
> (a) the design, details, and ethical criteria of the research are approved by the appropriate ethical committee;
> (b) there is voluntary, informed, parental consent; and
> (c) there is no, or a minimal, risk'.

By 1987 when Professor Dworkin wrote his paper 'Law and Medical Experimentation' (1987) 13 Monash ULR 189, there had grown up a considerable volume of scholarship which tended to support his previous view. For example, we have referred on several occasions to the Working Group set up by the Institute of Medical Ethics whose report was published in 1986 entitled *Medical Research with Children*. In Chapter 5 on 'Risks and Benefits in Research on Children', Nicholson (ed) writes (p 120):

> After a long debate, the working group agreed unanimously, however, that it was not acceptable to subject children, for whom only a proxy consent was available, to even a minor increase over minimal risk in non-therapeutic research. In other words, non-therapeutic research on children, regardless of possible benefits, can only be undertaken ethically if the risks of the procedures involved are in the 'minimal' category.

Furthermore, the climate of opinion and the popular understanding of what was involved had changed. Still Professor Dworkin (*op cit*) was cautious in analysing the law (pp 198-203):

> There is a widespread agreement that it is ethical, in some circumstances, to carry out non-therapeutic research with children. The fourth International Summit Conference on Bioethics, held in Canada in April 1987, summarised the generally accepted controlling conditions: 'The specific project must be approved by a research ethics committee; all needed knowledge must have been obtained through research with adults or animals; there must be no valid alternative to the use of children in the research; a valid proxy consent (by family, guardians, ombudsman, those with power of attorney or others) must have been obtained for each research subject; and to the extent possible, the child should have given assent.' Is this ethical statement, however, reflected in the law?

> *The 'best interests' of the child approach*
> For a long time, in England, the advice given to the medical profession was that non-therapeutic research upon young children was unlawful. The Medical Research Council stated that ' . . . in the strict view of the law parents and guardians of minors cannot give consent on their behalf to any procedures which are of no particular benefit to them and which may carry some risk of harm'. The authority for all this rested on general legal principle, rather than on any specific rule or ruling. Since the general philosophy of the law is that parents and guardians are under a duty to look after a child's interests, it seems to follow that non-therapeutic procedures cannot be justified.
> Thus, in the well known case of *Wellesley v Duke of Beaufort* [(1827) 2 Russ 1] Lord Eldon, when exercising the Crown's power as *parens patriae*, showed that: 'it has always been the principle of this Court not to risk the incurring of damage to children . . . which it cannot repair, but rather to prevent the damage being done'. The American Supreme Court, admittedly in a different context, expressed the view that:

>> parents may be free to become martyrs themselves. But it does not follow [that] they are free, in identical circumstances, to make martyrs of their children before they have reached the age of full and legal discretion when they can make that choice for themselves. [*Prince v Massachusetts* (1944) 321 US 158 at 170]

> Recent developments in the law relating to sterilisation emphasise the courts' concern to safeguard the 'best interests' of incompetent subjects, although the extent to which courts should go in giving effect to those interests has varied in different jurisdictions. Thus, the Supreme Court of Canada refused to sanction a 'non-therapeutic' sterilisation of a mentally retarded girl even though it was said to be in her best interests, because it felt that the legislature was better equipped to decide such an important policy matter [*Re Eve* (1986) 31 DLR (4th) 1] whereas the House of Lords, scorning the value of the therapeutic/non-therapeutic distinction in this context, took a more robust view of its role and authorised the sterilisation of a 17 year old girl 'in her best interests'. [*Re B (a minor)* [1987] 2 All ER 206] It would not have acted on a lower criterion than the best interests of the child; and other dicta also emphasise the parental duty to apply this standard. [*Gillick v West Norfolk and Wisbech AHA* [1985] 3 All ER 432, per Lord Templeman]
> Thus, there is at least an arguable case in favour of the view that proxy consent cannot be given for non-therapeutic research. But a total ban would be Draconian and certainly out of line with national and international ethical codes. Accordingly, it becomes necessary to look for an alternative view of the law.

Alternative views

(a) Distorting the concept of 'therapy'

Some of the views advanced have been unprepossessing. One extreme approach turned on the therapeutic/non-therapeutic distinction. If the concept of 'therapeutic' could be widened, then the scope for proxy consent would be increased. For example, the World Health Organisation defines 'health' as a state of complete physical, mental and *social* well-being and not merely the absence of disease or infirmity. Accordingly, it could be argued that carefully considered proxy consents for clinical research are exercises in social responsibility which could benefit the future well-being of the volunteered subject since one can reasonably expect a child in later life to identify with the objects of the research. This smacks very much of the 'ends justifying the means', and is not attractive as a legal argument. Yet similar semantic arguments have been upheld.

For example, the early kidney transplantations could only be effected between very close relatives and American courts were asked to consider the legality of such transplantations from infant donors to twin donees, in cases where the ages of the sets of twins ranged from 14 to 19. Evidence was advanced that each donor twin and the parents had been fully informed of the nature of the operation and had given voluntary informed consents and psychiatrists testified that if the operations were not performed and the sick twins were to die, the healthy potential donor twins could suffer 'grave emotional impact' for the remainder of their lives. The operations were accordingly adjudged 'therapeutic': they were necessary for the continued good health and future well-being of, and conferred benefits upon, the donors as well as upon the donees.

Understandably, there are many who view such artificial attempts to distort descriptive terminology with distaste. For example, one Canadian court which was looking for a 'therapeutic' reason for ordering a hysterectomy to be performed on a seriously retarded child, found that reason in the child's alleged phobic aversion to blood which, it was feared, would seriously affect her when her menstrual periods began. Accordingly, sterilisation was authorised. The Supreme Court of Canada stated that whilst sterilisation may, on occasion, be necessary as an adjunct to treatment of a serious malady, there was no room for subterfuge and [that] that decision was, at best, dangerously close to the limits of the permissible. [*Re Eve supra*, commenting on *Re K and Public Trustee* (1985) 19 DLR (4th) 255 (BC CA)]

(b) The concept of 'substituted judgment'

Another concept which is creeping into American case-law in contrast to the traditional 'best interests' approach to proxy consent is that of 'substituted judgment'. The proxy, or court, does not attempt to decide what is in the 'best interests' of the patient, but rather what decision would be made by the individual if he were competent. The court 'dons the mental mantle of the incompetent and substitutes itself as nearly as possible for the individual in the decision-making process'. [*Superintendent of Belchertown State School v Saikewicz* (1977) 370 NE 2d 417] It is one of those strange doctrines which was used in England in the early nineteenth century in connection with the administration of the estates of incompetent persons, [*Ex p Whitbread* (1816) 2 Mer 99] forgotten, and then rediscovered recently by American courts. It has been raised in cases involving incompetent persons to help establish whether, for example, to consent to the withdrawal of life support systems or to certain unusual or controversial types of medical treatment, such as shock therapy or psychosurgery.

It is a controversial concept, not the least because of the inherent difficulties of attempting to assess what an incompetent patient would have decided were he competent, whether that assessment should be subjective or objective and, if objective, how it can really differ from a 'best interests' approach. No court has yet been called upon to authorise its use in connection with clinical research, although it was raised in *Kaimowitz v Michigan Dept of Mental Health* [(1973) 42 USLW 2063] where it was held, understandably, that no proxy consent could be given for experimental psychosurgery. It is unlikely to be of much help in the current debate.

(c) The 'not against the interests of the child' approach

The most likely approach is to reconsider more carefully the emphasis which the legislature and the courts understandably place upon the need for proxies only to act in the best interests of the child or other incompetent person.

Most of these statements have been made in contexts quite different to those of non-therapeutic clinical research. Although much welfare legislature does stress that the welfare of a child is 'paramount', other provisions refer to the welfare of a child being the *first* consideration. 'First consideration', of course, suggests that there are other considerations which can be balanced by a parent against the best interests of the child, and indeed override it. And where a court has to carry out these tasks it usually has to act as a 'judicial reasonable parent'.

The balancing of various interests can best be seen in ward of court cases. For example, in *Re X (a Minor)* [[1975] 1 All ER 697] the defendants proposed to publish a book describing the depraved behaviour of the deceased father of a 14 year old girl. It was accepted that if she were to read the book or hear about it from others, it would be *psychologically* grossly damaging to her. The Court of Appeal, in exercising its wardship jurisdiction, was not prepared to allow the interests of the child to prevail over the wider interest of freedom of publication. It is not correct to say 'that in every case where a minor's interests are involved, those interests are always paramount and must prevail . . . The court is required to do a difficult balancing act'. Here the court found the scale tipped heavily in favour of publication and against the minor.

Perhaps the most relevant analogy, however, concerns the power to take blood tests from children in paternity actions. Here, the conflict is between the interests of the child and that of doing justice. In 1970 the House of Lords considered a case [*S v S* [1970] 3 All ER 107] where an official guardian had objected to a blood test on a child in paternity proceedings on the ground that this intrusive procedure was not for the child's benefit. This argument was not accepted by the court, and statements abound in the judgments that the benefit of the child is not always an adequate criterion. Lord Reid analysed the situation clearly: first, he proclaimed the principle of physical integrity as: 'There is no doubt that a person of full age and capacity cannot be ordered to undergo a blood test against his will. . . . The real reason is that English law goes to great lengths to protect a person of full age and capacity from interference with his personal liberty.' Secondly, he struck a blow against one modern theory of children's rights by denying them an absolute right to physical integrity as against their parents: 'But the position is very different with regard to young children. It is a legal wrong to use constraint on an adult beyond what is authorised by statute or ancient common law powers connected with crime and the like. But it is not and could not be a legal wrong for a parent or person authorised by him to use constraint to his young child provided it is not cruel or excessive.' Thirdly, such a power goes beyond simple domestic situations such as chastisement: 'It seems to me to be impossible to deny that a parent can lawfully require that his young child should submit to a blood test. And if a parent can require that, why not the court?' And fourthly, a move away from the 'best interests' approach:

> Surely a reasonable parent would have some regard to the general public interest and would not refuse a blood test unless he thought that would clearly be against the interests of the child? . . . I would hold that the court ought to permit a blood test of a young child to be taken unless satisfied that this would be against the child's interest.

Thus, there seems to be strong authority for saying that in some cases the 'best interests of the child' approach can give way to a rule that a parent should not do anything 'clearly against the interests' of the child. This certainly makes sense. In real life, reasonable parents cannot, and should not, always opt for that activity which presents the least physical risk to the child. Children must be allowed to run risks: climbing trees, riding bicycles, playing 'rough' sports, where the statistical risks may far outweigh anything involved in properly conducted clinical research. Medical procedures involving slight risks, for example vaccinations, occur daily where the benefit may be primarily for other children and the community. Thus, a reasonable and socially responsible parent might think that there was merit in taking the social interest into account and contributing to medical research, provided always that the risk to the child was 'minimal'.

This view of the law accords with the ethical codes and is now being acted upon by the medical profession. Unfortunately, however, the law is not clear beyond all reasonable doubt. A blind development of the 'best interests' approach could box the law into an inflexible position. This appears to have happened in South Australia. The *Consent to Medical and Dental Procedures Act* 1985, which was passed presumably to clarify the law relating to teenage girls receiving contraceptive help from doctors, follows the *Gillick* line providing that a minor under 16 has full capacity to consent to medical procedures if two practitioners are of the opinion first, that the minor is capable of understanding the nature and consequences of the procedure; and secondly, that 'the procedure is in the best interests of the health *and* well-being of the minor'. It also provides for parental proxy consent, which presumably must be exercised subject to similar restraints. This would seem to authorise a 'medical procedure', which is defined as 'any procedure carried out by, or pursuant to directions given by, a medical practitioner' [section 4] only if it complies with the best interests rule; in which case it would be difficult to argue that the scope for non-therapeutic research can be wider. Does that mean that, inadvertently, all clinical research on children under 16 has been ruled out?

There seems to be a strong case for general legislative consideration, and clarification, of the power to give proxy consent for the purposes of research on children.

You will notice that Professor Dworkin in the penultimate paragraph of his paper refers to the 'ethical codes' and the responses of the medical profession. In its 1992 *Guidelines for the Ethical Conduct of Medical Research Involving Children* the British Paediatric Association makes the case for non-therapeutic research on children but limits it to situations where the child is not exposed to more than a minimal risk.

> Medical research involving children is an important means of promoting child health and wellbeing. Such research includes systematic investigation into normal childhood development and the aetiology of disease, as well as careful scrutiny of the means of promoting health and of diagnosing, assessing and treating disease. It is also important to validate in children the beneficial results of research conducted in adults.
>   Research with children is worthwhile, if each project:
> - has an identifiable prospect of benefit to children;
> - is well designed and well conducted;
> - does not simply duplicate earlier work;
> - is not undertaken primarily for financial or professional advantage;
> - involves a statistically appropriate number of subjects;
> - and eventually is to be properly reported . . .
> It would be unethical to submit child subjects to more than minimal risk when the procedure offers no benefit to them, or only a slight or very uncertain one.

This view is reflected in the Guidelines published by the Royal College of Physicians (*Guidelines on the Practice of Ethics Committees in Medical Research Involving Human Subjects* (1990) paras 11.13 and 13.2) and the Medical Research Council (*The Ethical Conduct of Research on Children* (1991)).

(b) Adults

The first criterion which must be satisfied in law is that there is a real and justified need for research on *incompetent* adults, ie that the knowledge sought may not be discovered from research on competent consenting adults. This is only a particular illustration of the general legal principle that the law seeks to protect the vulnerable. Satisfying this criterion by no means implies that it is lawful thereafter to carry out non-therapeutic research. Indeed, it would appear that such research cannot lawfully be carried out. There is no one who, in law, can authorise it as a proxy. Even the court if it were to have a *parens patriae* power could not authorise such research since the power exists specifically for cases where 'some care should be thrown round [the ward]' (*Wellesley v Duke of Beaufort* (1827) 38 ER 236 at 243). Also, of course, the approach of the House of Lords in *Re F* would not assist since non-therapeutic research could not be said to be in the '*best* interests' of the incompetent adult. If, however, the law does not permit any non-therapeutic research on an incompetent adult, the curious situation would arise that such research may be permissible in the case of children but not in the case of adults. This apparent anomaly could be explained by noticing that in the case of children the parent can act as the protector of the child's interests whereas no such person exists in the case of the adult.

Whatever the legal position, it is undoubtedly the case that there has been a shift in thinking about the ethics of non-therapeutic research on the incompetent adult.

The Ethical Conduct of Research on the Mentally Incapacitated (MRC, 1991)

6.3 Non-therapeutic research
6.3.1 Because it might infringe the rights of a group which society should take particular care to protect, the participation of people who cannot consent in non-therapeutic research raises more complex ethical issues. We do not seek to argue that a mentally incapacitated person's participation in non-therapeutic research is directly in his interests. But we recognise that there are circumstances in which it is important to gain knowledge which may be of benefit to mentally incapacitated people in general and which can only be acquired as a result of research which involves those who are unable to consent.
6.3.2 We therefore believe that there is a strong case for including those unable to consent in such research, but it is essential that the safeguards listed at 6.1.3 are observed, and that those included are placed at no more than negligible risk of harm.
6.3.3 The degree of risk involved in a project should be given particularly careful scrutiny by the LREC when mentally incapacitated people are to be included. There have been various attempts to describe and define degrees of risk. We use the term negligible risk to mean that the risks of harm anticipated in the proposed research are not greater, considering the probability and magnitude of physiological or psychological harm or discomfort, than those ordinarily encountered in daily life or during the performance of routine physical or psychological examination or tests. Examples of procedures involving negligible risk would include the observation of behaviour, non-invasive physiological monitoring, physical examinations, changes in diet and obtaining blood and urine specimens . . .
6.3.4 We are clear that participation in such research of an individual unable to consent can only be ethical if a relative, friend or person acceptable to the LREC and not directly involved in the research agrees that participation would place that individual at no more than negligible risk of harm and is therefore not against that individual's interests.

Paragraph 6.3.2 refers back to paragraph 6.1.3. This states:

6.1.3 At the same time, there is agreement on the need for strict safeguards for such research. In particular:
– those unable to consent should take part in research only if it relates to their condition and if the relevant knowledge could not be gained by research in persons able to consent
– all projects must be approved by the appropriate LRECs
– the inclusion of an individual unable to consent should be subject to the agreement of an informed, independent person acceptable to the LREC that that individual's welfare and interests have been properly safeguarded
– those included in the research do not object or appear to object in either words or action.

(See also Royal College of Physicians *op cit* paragraph 13.11.)
The current law, however, is probably more restrictive in its approach, given the law's commitment to the criterion of 'best interests'. As a consequence, the Law Commission in its Consultation Paper No 129, *Mentally Incapacitated Adults and Decision-Making: Medical Treatment and Research* (April 1993) proposes that legislation be enacted. This would provide, in keeping with the scheme recommended by the Law Commission, that a 'medical treatment proxy' or 'attorney' (see *supra*, ch 4) could, in limited circumstances, also consent to non-therapeutic research as an extension of their powers.

5. Non-therapeutic research or experiments on an incapacitated subject should not be lawful unless:

(a)   the research is into the mental disorder, or other incapacitating condition, suffered by the subject;

(b)   the research entails only an insubstantial foreseeable risk to the subject's physical or mental health. Views are invited on what should constitute an insubstantial risk;

(c)   the research has been approved by the appropriate local research ethics committee;

(d)   the consent of a medical treatment proxy or attorney appointed with authority to give such consent has been obtained, or (if no such person has been appointed) the subject's nearest relative has agreed in writing;

(e)   before seeking such agreement or consent, the purpose of the research, the procedures to be used and the foreseeable risk to participants, have been explained;

(f)   the subject does not object to participating in the research, and has made no anticipatory decision refusing to participate.

We have already seen, however, that English law may not now be the sole determinant of the legality of conducting research, at least as regards clinical trials involving medicinal products. Notwithstanding the Law Commission's proposals it is important to notice the position adopted in the EC Guidelines on GCP referred to earlier. While paragraph 1.13 permits in limited circumstances *therapeutic* research on the incompetent if certain safeguards are observed, paragraph 1.14 provides:

> 1.14 Consent must always be given by the signature of the subject in a non-therapeutic study, ie when there is no direct clinical benefit to the subject.

It could not be clearer from this paragraph that the European Guidelines prohibit non-therapeutic research on incompetent adults. Should this already be, or become, English law the Law Commission's proposals could not be enacted. Many might regret the absolute nature of the prohibition. Given the history of Europe in the 1930s and 1940s which culminated in the Nuremberg Trials which we referred to at the outset, however, it is entirely understandable that some European countries would hold the view that an absolute prohibition was the only defensible one.

The same depth of concern arose in New Zealand after Judge Cartwright's Report into *Allegations Concerning the Treatment of Cervical Cancer at the National Women's Hospital* (1988). As a result section 10 of the New Zealand Bill of Rights Act 1990 provides that:

> **10. Right not to be subjected to medical or scientific experimentation.** – Every person has the right not to be subjected to medical or scientific experimentation without that person's consent.

The clear and intended effect of section 10 is to outlaw medical research on those not competent to consent for themselves.

Compensation

We are not concerned here with legal actions brought by participants in research who have been injured through some fault or misdeed on the part of the researcher. Instead, we are concerned with the question that has increasingly occupied the attention of medical researchers, commentators and the Government: if a participant in a trial, whether patient or healthy volunteer, suffers harm in some way related to the trial and has need for compensation, should there be some method of compensation available to him in circumstances where the existing forms of legal liability (eg negligence and under the Consumer Protection Act 1987) do not apply? The Government's involvement through the Department of Health in this question arose from the public concern following the deaths of two students (one in Cardiff and the other in Dublin) in 1985 who were healthy volunteers in drug trials.

The argument raised is that society gains through the willingness of some to participate in research and society should be prepared, therefore, to provide for any casualties of such research rather than leave them to the vagaries of litigation and the existing social security system. This argument was put by the Royal Commission on Civil Liability and Compensation for Personal Injury (Cmnd 7054) in 1978 and is reflected in their recommendation (paras 1339-1341).

Volunteers for medical research

1339 People may volunteer to take part in research or clinical trials of new forms of treatment or new drugs. Strict precautions are imposed, including the screening of experiments by medical ethical committees. Nevertheless the Medical Research Council stated in their evidence to us:

> despite the exercise of the highest degree of care and skill by the medical investigator concerned, death or a personal injury which was quite unforeseen and indeed quite unforeseeable might be suffered by a person who volunteers to participate in such an investigation. For example, a volunteer taking part in a recent trial of live attenuated influenza vaccine developed a neurological lesion shortly after the administration of the vaccine – the first known neurological sequela to any attenuated influenza virus despite the fact that many hundreds of thousands of such inoculations had been given during the preceeding ten years; a causal connection between the administration of the vaccine and the neurological lesion could neither be proved nor disproved. In such a situation, the Medical Research Council would seek authority to make an *ex gratia* payment from public funds to the volunteer or his dependants and such a payment has been approved for the volunteer who developed the lesion in question.

Patients undergoing clinical trials

1340 Patients as well as healthy volunteers may be asked if they will agree to accept a new form of treatment in the interests of research. If a patient is given such treatment, and through it suffers injury, or a worsening of his condition which would not have been expected with conventional treatment, he is in the same position as a healthy person volunteering to take part in research.

1341 We think that it is wrong that a person who exposes himself to some medical risk in the interests of the community should have to rely on *ex gratia* compensation in the event of injury. **We recommend** that any volunteer for medical research or clinical trials who suffers severe damage as a result should have a cause of action, on the basis of strict liability, against the authority to whom he has consented to make himself available.

In the 15 years since these recommendations, no progress has been made towards providing compensation for research subjects. What has emerged instead is a series of recommendations from bodies such as the Royal College of Physicians and the Association of the British Pharmaceutical Industry (ABPI). In addition, the Department of Health's Guidance on LRECs refers to arrangements for compensation. Despite their existence, these recommendations are no more than that. You will see that a feature of the approach adopted by the ABPI is to seek to endow their arrangements with some semblance of legal form through the device of a contract between the researcher and the research subject in the case of healthy volunteer studies. The ABPI scheme is described by Christopher Hodges in the following extract.

C Hodges, 'Harmonisation of European Controls over Research: Ethics Committees, Consent, Compensation and Indemnity' in *Pharmaceutical Medicine and the Law* **(1991) (ed A Goldberg and I Dodds-Smith)**

In the UK the provision of compensation for research injury is left to a non-statutory regime, dependent merely upon whether or not the sponsor and/or contract research house [ie, a company not a member of the ABPI] in fact abide by the ABPI guidelines. Curiously, the DoH Guidelines are entirely silent on the advisability of or any requirement for adherence to the ABPI guidelines. Different ABPI guidelines cover different types of research:

Non-patient human volunteers: 1983 ABPI guidelines
The relationship between the volunteer and the sponsor should be governed by the terms of a written contract included in the consent form which the volunteer signs to signify his agreement to take part in the study. The ABPI guidelines state:

11.7 The agreement should clearly record the obligation the pharmaceutical company or research establishment has accepted in terms of financial rewards for participation and compensation in the event of injury. In particular, the volunteer should be given a clear commitment that in the event of bodily injury he will receive appropriate compensation without having to prove either that such injury arose through negligence or that the product was defective in the sense that it did not fulfil a reasonable expectation of safety. The agreement should not seek to remove that right of the volunteer, as an alternative, to pursue a claim on the basis of either negligence or strict liability if he is so minded.

11.8 Where pharmaceutical companies sponsor studies to be performed in outside research establishments, the responsibility for paying compensation should be clarified and reflected in the contractual documentation with the volunteer. Where the sponsor company is to provide the undertaking regarding compensation, it is recommended that the sponsor company enters into an unqualified obligation to pay compensation to the volunteer on proof of causation, having previously protected its rights to recourse against the research establishment in its agreement with that establishment, to cover the position where the negligence of its contractor may have caused or contributed to the injury to the volunteer. A volunteer can reasonably expect that compensation will be paid quickly and that any dispute regarding who will finally bear the cost of the compensation paid to him will be resolved separately by the other parties to the research.

A model agreement is attached to the guidelines, in which the relevant clauses read:

8(iii) In the event of my suffering any significant deterioration in health or well-being caused directly by my participation in the study, compensation will be paid to me by the company.

(iv) The amount of such compensation shall be calculated by reference to the amount of damages commonly awarded for similar injuries by an English court if liability is admitted, provided that such compensation may be reduced to the extent that I, by reason of contributory fault, am partly responsible for the injury (or where I have received equivalent payment for such injury under any policy of insurance effected by the company for my benefit) . . .

Negligence by an investigator is therefore irrelevant as far as a claim by an injured party for compensation is concerned. He is to be paid forthwith by the sponsor, who may then have a claim against the investigator (and the contractual documentation between them should provide for this). There is also a provision for arbitration in the event of a dispute over payment of compensation.

In 1986, the RCP criticised the fact that compensation for injury suffered as a result of research conducted in and sponsored by universities, NHS hospitals, the Medical Research Council and other similar establishments is not covered by any guideline commitment but is dependent on an *ex gratia* payment.

We believe that universities and other institutions should make binding commitments to provide compensation, because we consider it unacceptable that a healthy volunteer should have to rely on an *ex gratia* payment.

Patient volunteers: 1991 ABPI guidelines

The 1983 guidelines were revised in 1991 in the light of developing considerations, especially the 1990 Report of the RCP's Working Party, *Research involving patients*. The relationship between the sponsor and subject is, in the case of [research on patients for whose condition the treatment is intended], not contractual and the guidelines state that the sponsor's assurance to abide by them is 'without legal commitment'.

1.2 Compensation should be paid when, on the balance of probabilities, the injury was attributable to the administration of a medicinal product under trial or any clinical intervention or procedure provided for by the protocol that would not have occurred but for the inclusion of the patient in the trial.

1.3 Compensation should be paid to a child injured *in utero* through the participation of the subject's mother in a clinical trial as if the child were a patient-volunteer with the full benefit of these guidelines.

1.4 Compensation should only be paid for the more serious injury of an enduring and disabling character (including exacerbation of an existing condition) and not for temporary pain or discomfort or less serious or curable complaints.

1.5 Where there is an adverse reaction to a medicinal product under trial and injury is caused by a procedure adopted to deal with that adverse reaction, compensation should be paid for such injury as if it were caused directly by the medicinal product under trial.

1.6 Neither the fact that the adverse reaction causing the injury was foreseeable or predictable, nor the fact that the patient has freely consented (whether in writing or otherwise) to participate in the trial should exclude a patient from consideration for compensation under these guidelines, although compensation may be abated or excluded in the light of the factors described in paragraph 4.2 below.

1.7 For the avoidance of doubt, compensation should be paid regardless of whether the patient is able to prove that the company has been negligent in relation to research or development of the medicinal product under trial or that the product is defective and therefore, as the producer, the company is subject to strict liability in respect of injuries caused by it. . . .

4.1 The amount of compensation paid should be appropriate to the nature, severity and persistence of the injury and should in general terms be consistent with the quantum of damages commonly awarded for similar injuries by an English court in cases where legal liability is admitted.

4.2 Compensation may be abated, or in certain circumstances excluded, in the light of the following factors (on which will depend the level of risk the patient can reasonably be expected to accept):

4.2.1 the seriousness of the disease being treated, the degree of probability that adverse reactions will occur and any warnings given;

4.2.2 the risks and benefits of established treatments relative to those known or suspected of the trial medicine.

This reflects the fact that flexibility is required given the particular patient's circumstances. As an extreme example, there may be a patient suffering from a serious or life-threatening disease who is warned of a certain defined risk of adverse reaction. Participation in the trial is then based on an expectation that the benefit/risk ratio associated with participation may be better than that associated with alternative treatment. It is, therefore, reasonable that the patient accepts the high risk and should not expect compensation for the occurrence of the adverse reaction of which he or she was told.

There is provision for arbitration by an independent expert in the event of any difference of opinion.

Compensation is excluded, however, where

1. The product failed to have its intended effect.
2. The injury was caused by another licensed medicinal product which was administered as a comparison with the product under trial.
3. A placebo has failed to provide a therapeutic benefit.

Compensation should not be paid, or should be abated, to the extent that the injury has arisen through:

1. A significant departure from the agreed protocol.
2. The wrongful act or default of a third party, including a doctor's failure to deal adequately with an adverse reaction.
3. Contributory negligence by the patient.

None of these exclusions represents a departure from the 1983 guidelines, except perhaps for the first, that 'the product failed to have its intended effect', which may have been implicit before.

The approach set out in these guidelines is a logical application of legal principles. The subject is given the considerable benefit of not having to prove negligence, but the guidelines do not constitute a 'no-fault' compensation scheme because of the applicability of rules on causation, most notably in the exclusions. The subject is also at a disadvantage because there is no legal commitment to pay by the sponsor. The RCP criticised the 1983 guidelines for this reason, and recommended that there should be a contractual commitment to compensate patient volunteers, perhaps with the investigator acting as the company's agent for this limited purpose. The ABPI did not adopt this view in its 1991 revision. The matter is certainly not susceptible to a simple answer, since the imposition of a contractual relationship on a treatment situation which is not normally contractual is not a simple matter, either for reasons of achieving universality or practicability, or from the point of view of effecting an alteration in the nature of the patient-doctor relationship, with the potential for conflict that exists here. The ABPI would point to the absence of any practical problem over compensation which needs to be resolved: research injuries are fortunately extremely rare and companies are generally well aware of the need to avoid adverse criticism. In practice, the guidelines might therefore be interpreted liberally in any given case.

It is interesting to note that although the RCP recommended that compensation should be paid for *involvement* in research and not confined to injury due to a treatment under test itself (which the ABPI has adopted) and also to injury due to withholding active treatment (which the ABPI has not adopted), it did *not* recommend that compensation should be paid for injury due to a standard medicine used for comparison or to failure of a treatment to have its hoped for or intended effect. A strong case could, however, be made that these exclusions and the exclusion of placebo-induced injury should all be compensated. Again, it is possible that in practice a company might be well advised to avoid any unduly restrictive stance.

In its report of 1990, the RCP criticised the fact that patients injured in publicly funded research have to rely on an *ex gratia* and *ad hoc* system:

> ... patients ... [should be] compensated on an agreed basis which should be made clear to them before they consent ... The absence of [a policy to compensate] should be treated as a material fact to be disclosed by the investigator to the patient.

The Department of Health's Guidelines refer to compensation somewhat shortly and inconclusively.

3.17 Arrangements for compensation in the event of a research subject being harmed, whether by negligence or not, will vary according to what type of body is sponsoring the research proposal. The LREC should ensure that those who agree to participate in research which may involve some risk, whether as patients or healthy volunteers, are told at the outset what arrangements will apply in their case. The LREC should seek evidence from the sponsor that these arrangements have adequate financial backing.
3.18 NHS bodies are not empowered to offer advance indemnity to participants in research projects. A person suffering injury as a result of having taken part in research would be able to pursue a claim for negligence through litigation. Each case would of course have to be considered on its merits.
3.19 Private sector companies sponsoring research are usually able to ensure that effective provision is made to compensate any research subject whose health may be affected. To this end LRECs should seek confirmation that any such company conducting or sponsoring a patient or healthy volunteer study accepts responsibility for compensation and provides details of the basis on which it will be provided i.e. causation, fault etc, plus evidence of their ability to fulfil it.
3.20 Volunteers must therefore be told in advance of all known risks and be made aware that there could also be unforeseen risks and of the possible difficulties in obtaining compensation.

The terms of paragraph 3.18 have been widely criticised since they offer no assurance that compensation will be available. The explanation lies in the established practice of the Treasury which does not permit Government bodies to act as insurers (but notice our reference to the development of structured settlements *supra*, ch 5).

The current position could be regarded as less than satisfactory, especially given the altruism of those who take part in research. Some other European countries regard the making of proper provision for compensation of such importance that legislation is demanded. The position is discussed by Christopher Hodges in his paper in *Pharmaceutical Medicine and the Law (op cit)*.

In Germany, drug manufacturers are subject to an insurance based compensation system with absolute liability. [German Federal Drug Law 1976 sections 1, 2, 84-94] . . .

The German Drug Law specifies that insurance must be held which must stand in appropriate relation to the risks involved in the clinical trial and in the case of death or permanent disability must total at least DM 500,000. [*ibid* section 40]

The recent legislation in Ireland, France and Spain also provides for consideration of insurance. Under a French decree a sponsor has to hold quite a high level of insurance: cover of at least FFr 5 million per victim, FFr 30 million per research protocol and FFr 50 million for all claims made in an insurance year must be held until 10 years after the end of the research. [French Decree No. 91-440 of 14 May 1991] The Irish Act is silent on the question of the basis of compensation. It provides merely that the sponsor and investigator must establish to the satisfaction of the minister in advance of each trial on a case by case basis that they have sufficient security to provide for payments of damages on their own behalf if they are personally negligent. [Control of Clinical Trials Act 1987, section 10 (as amended)] This does not give rise to an obligation to pay compensation as such, on any basis. 'Security' is defined as including a contract of insurance, a contract of indemnity, a guarantee, a surety, a warranty and a bond. [Control of Clinical Trials and Drugs Act 1990, section 3 amending section 10 of 1987 Act] Neither the Spanish law nor the Irish legislation and guidelines mention any financial sums or limits. However the Spanish law does include some interesting provisions. [Ley Del Medicamento 25/1990, Article 62] First, a trial can only be started if 'insurance covering the damages' is in place. This presumably refers to damages which might be awarded by a Spanish court, but up to what level? Compensation for many injuries might be awarded at a trivial level, but equally it might be the case that very high damages might be awarded in individual cases. Although regulations might be made under the Spanish law which set further guidelines, the approach seems to be to leave the risk with the promoter, chief researcher and owner of the hospital or centre in question, since the law specifically provides that these people shall be severally liable without proof of fault if the insurance does not cover the damages. It is, of course, inherent in this approach that the appropriate level of damages should be set by a court: there is no specific arbitration or mediation procedure under the law, unlike the approach under the UK ABPI guidelines. The Spanish law does, however, assist the injured research subject by reversing the burden of proof in his favour for injuries which occur during the trial or within one year after its termination.

Recurrent questions arise in relation to compensation for injury as to who should bear the responsibility for compensation in the event of the subject suffering injury which might not be attributable to the compound under research. The French statute and the various ABPI guidelines attempt to deal with this point, but are perhaps not entirely successful.

The provisions of the French law relating to compensation essentially place the responsibility for compensation on the sponsor, whether in non-therapeutic or therapeutic research, irrespective of the negligence of the investigator, although the wording in the latter case is ambiguous:

In the case of biomedical research with no direct benefit to the individual, the sponsor, even when not at fault, takes responsibility for the compensation of any harmful effects of the research on a person undergoing it, notwithstanding the possible action of a third party or the voluntary withdrawal of the person who initially consented to undergo the research.

In the case of biomedical research with direct benefit to the individual, the sponsor takes responsibility for the compensation of any harmful effects of the research on a person undergoing it, unless he proves that such adverse effects are not attributable to his or any participating party's action, notwithstanding the possible action of a third party or the voluntary withdrawal of the person who initially consented to undergo the research.

In all biomedical research, the sponsor shall take out insurance covering his and any other participating party's liability as it results from this article, irrespective of the relationship between the sponsor and the participating parties. The provisions of this article are binding on all parties. [Law on the Protection of Persons Undergoing Biomedical Research, Article L.209-7]

The essential burden of compensation is therefore firmly on the sponsor. In the case of research in healthy volunteers, the burden is absolute and negligence of an investigator is, at least as between sponsor and subject, irrelevant. However, the provisions of the second paragraph, dealing with research on patients, are somewhat ambiguous as to the extent to which proof of the action of a third party excuses the sponsor.

Innovative therapy

We have already commented upon the notion of 'innovative therapy' and its relationship with research. We reached the conclusion (*supra*, at pp 1031-1032) that where the doctor's intention is to acquire knowledge and not merely to care for his patient, the constraints normally associated with the conduct of research should apply. There is, of course, a scientific as well as a moral and legal basis for this view. The pursuit of knowledge is best conducted in a systematic fashion. Bad science is bad ethics. Innovative therapy should properly be regarded as one of two things: either *research*, with all that flows therefrom; or *therapy*, where the sole intention is to care for the particular patient involved. Consequently, the law does not inhibit development. It says, however, that any development must be defended as research or justified as appropriate albeit innovative therapy, against the background of a possible claim in negligence.

Pursuing the point concerning a claim in negligence relating to the performance of the procedure, we must take as our point of departure *Hunter v Hanley* 1955 SC 200. In that case, you will recall, Lord Clyde said:

It follows from what I have said that in regard to allegations of deviation from ordinary professional practice . . . such a deviation is not necessarily evidence of negligence. Indeed it would be disastrous if this were so, for all inducement to progress in medical science would then be destroyed. Even a substantial deviation from normal practice may be warranted by the particular circumstances. To establish liability by a doctor where deviation from normal practice is alleged, three facts require to be established. First of all it must be proved that there is a usual and normal practice; secondly it must be proved that the defender has not adopted that practice; and thirdly (and this is of crucial importance) it must be established that the course the doctor adopted is one which no professional man of ordinary skill would have taken if he had been acting with ordinary care.

In the later care of *Landau v Werner* (1961) 105 Sol Jo 1008 (CA) Sellers LJ stated that:

A doctor might not be negligent if he tried a new technique but if he did he must justify it before the Court. If his novel or exceptional treatment had failed disastrously he could not complain if it was held that he went beyond the bounds of due care and skill as recognised generally.

These cases illustrate the desire of the courts to allow doctors some discretion so as to develop medical practice while wishing to set proper limits to the extent to which they may go. Notice the following words of Hunter J in *Brook v St John's Hickey Memorial Hospital* 380 NE 2d 72 (1978) (Sup Ct Ind):

Too often courts have confused judgmental decisions and experimentation. Therapeutic innovation has long been recognised as permissible to avoid serious consequences. The everyday practice of medicine involves constant judgmental decisions by physicians as they move from one patient to another in the conscious institution of procedures, special tests, trials and observations recognised generally by their profession as effective in treating the patient or providing a diagnosis of a diseased condition. Each patient presents a slightly different problem to the doctor. A physician is presumed to have the knowledge and skill necessary to use some innovation to fit the peculiar circumstances of each case.

If doctors are to be given some leeway but not encouraged to leap too far into the dark there must be some criterion in law to which the doctor can refer. The notion of 'minimal risk' may be of assistance, or would such a criterion unnecessarily inhibit the doctor from trying new techniques outside the ambit of systematic research? Consider the following case which arose in the United States.

Karp v Cooley (1974) 493 F 2d 408 (US CA, 5th Cir)

Circuit Judge Bell: Medical history was made in 1969 when Dr Denton A Cooley, a thoracic surgeon, implanted the first totally mechanical heart in 47-year-old Haskell Karp. This threshold orthotopic cardiac prosthesis also spawned this medical malpractice suit by Mr Karp's wife, individually and as executrix of Mr Karp's estate, and his children, for the patient's wrongful death. . . .

There is no dispute that prior to entering St Luke's Episcopal Hospital in Houston on March 5, 1969, Haskell Karp had a long and difficult ten-year history of cardiac problems. He suffered a serious heart attack in 1959 and was hospitalised for approximately two months because of diffuse anterior myocardial infarction. He had incurred four heart attacks, thirteen cardiac hospitalisations and considerable medical care culminating in the insertion of an electronic demand pacemaker in May, 1968. Subsequent hospitalisation in September and October, 1969 occurred, and finally the decision was made to seek the assistance of Dr Cooley. . . . [Dr Cooley testified]:

> I told [Mr Karp] we had no heart donor available, had no prospect of one . . . I told him that there was a possibility that we had a device which would sustain his life in the event that he would die on the operating table. We had a device which would sustain his life, hopefully, until we could get a suitable donor. I had told him that I did not know whether it would take a matter of hours or days, weeks, or maybe not at all, but it would sustain his life and give us another possibility of salvaging him through heart transplantation.

Dr Cooley said he did not recall who was present when these discussions began. Dr Cooley described his discussion of this device:

> I told him that it was a heart pump similar to the one that we used in open-heart surgery; that it was a reciprocating-type pump with the membrane, in which the pumping element never became in contact with the bloodstream; that it was designed in such a manner that it would not damage the bloodstream or it would cause minimal damage to the bloodstream; that it would be placed in his body to take over the function of the dead heart and to propel blood throughout his body during this interim until he could have a heart transplant. . . . I told him this device had not been used in human beings; that it had been used in the laboratory; that we had been able to sustain the circulation in calves and that it had not been used in human beings. It had been used on the bench in what we call *in vitro* experiments, *in vitro* as opposed to *in vivo*. . . . I told him it had been tested in the laboratory, it had not been used in a human being, but I was confident that it would support his circulation. . . . I told him that we had been successful in keeping an animal alive for more than forty hours with the device, but that this was a calf. It was a 300-pound animal in which the demands on the pump were far greater than they would be in the human body, and that I was reasonably confident that this device would sustain his life until we could get a heart transplant. But no guarantees were made at all.

Dr Cooley admitted he and Mr Karp did not discuss the number of animals in which the device had been tested, nor whether the animals sustained damage to their bodies by the use of his pump.

Asked by appellants' counsel whether he described it as a heart-lung pump similar to that used in other open heart surgeries, Dr Cooley said, 'I told him it was a pump. I didn't tell him it was a lung. I told him it was an artificial heart, that it was a pump which would replace temporarily the heart.' . . .

According to the anaesthesia record, . . . Mr Karp was brought into the operating room at about 1:15 pm. When Dr Keats saw Mr Karp at that time he believed Mr Karp's death to be imminent. Dr Keats said Mr Karp was in great distress; he was having difficulty breathing, shortness of breath and he was pale and sweating. Dr Keats said he hurriedly got Mr Karp on the operating table, started giving him oxygen, and put him to sleep as rapidly as possible so that they could put a tube in his windpipe to assist his breathing. Dr Keats then sent word to Dr Cooley that they 'had better go ahead with the operation as expeditiously as possible, otherwise the patient may not last long enough to have the operation'. . . . Dr Cooley says Mr Karp was near death when he entered the operating room, 'mottled and blue'. He said he felt Mr Karp was 'virtually moribund' at that time.

The operation was then begun with Dr Cooley as chief surgeon, Dr Liotta as first assistant, Dr Grady Hallman as second assistant, and Dr Keats as anaesthesiologist. [Dr Cooley] said that he opened the pericardium and that as a result of a very feeble heart action the heart pump was started as quickly as possible. Dr Keats remembers that as Mr Karp's heart became visible 'it was a very large heart that filled the entire surgical field'. Dr Cooley said that the heart was functioning very feebly, was virtually noncontractile and could not support Mr Karp. After Mr Karp had been on the heart-lung or heart oxygenator a sufficient time to get his heart going again an incision was made in the left ventricle. Dr Cooley said that Mr Karp had scar tissue circumferentially around the inside of his left ventricle, that his entire interventricular septum was one solid piece of scar tissue, the anterior ventricle was almost completely displaced by scar tissue, and there was an aneurysm on the posterior aspect of the ventricle. . . .

Although Dr Cooley said the situation was then 'virtually hopeless', he began to do what he could with the resection procedure. He excised the most severely damaged part of the ventricular myocardium in his repair of the left ventricle. Because of the extensive scarring it was necessary to excise part of the right ventricle. In completing this complicated repair it was then necessary to sew the partition back to the right ventricle, and sew the left ventricle back to them. Dr Cooley said that Mr Karp did not have an anterior aneurysm but that the anterior myocardium was diffusely dilated. He added that it was very difficult to differentiate between a dilated scarred heart and an aneurysm. He described the nonfunctioning large area on the left ventricle as having a paradoxical motion and a ballooning out effect. He compared the size of the balloon to a cantaloupe. He said there was no threat of break or rupture in lesions like this; that he had never seen one rupture; and that he never told a patient a ventricular aneurysm would burst.

It is to be noted here that although Mrs Karp testified her husband had appeared normal on the day of the surgery, there is no lay or expert testimony other than that Mr Karp was near death at the time of the operation.

According to Dr Hallman, the repair described above was done in the manner that cardiovascular surgeons normally go about performing this operation. However, Dr Hallman said that due to the extensive scarring of the heart, there simply was not sufficient healthy heart muscle remaining to form an efficient pump to support Mr Karp's life. Dr Hallman, Dr Keats and Dr Cooley all testified that at this point, that is after the attempted resection, Mr Karp was again faced with imminent death.

Dr Cooley said that it took about 20 minutes to make the resection repair. He said that after the repair the clamp was taken off the ascending aorta to attempt to restart the myocardium. He stated that there was fibrillation and that he attempted an electrical countershock at least once. He stated that there was a sinus type or nodal rhythm at that point but that the rhythm contraction was too weak to support life due to the fact that there simply was too much scar tissue in the heart. Dr Hallman testified that some thirty minutes elapsed between the end of the repair and the decision to remove the heart. Mr Karp's heart was then removed and the mechanical device was inserted. Dr Cooley said that the mechanical heart functioned very well and Mr Karp responded to stimulation within 15 or 20 minutes after the incision was closed. His blood pressure was well sustained according to Dr Cooley and he showed signs of cerebral activity. Dr Keats said that Mr Karp was amazingly well following the operation, that the records reflect that he was responding reasonably to commands within 20 minutes post-operatively. Dr Keats testified that the endocracheal [sic] tube was removed about 1:20 am, and that he saw Mr Karp some time the next morning at which time he was responsive and could communicate.

After the mechanical heart had been inserted, Dr Cooley said he went to Mrs Karp and told her that the wedge procedure had been unsuccessful; that he had proceeded with the use of the mechanical device and that they were going to try to get a donor. The transplant operation was performed on the morning of April 7, 1969, approximately 64 hours after the mechanical device had been implanted in Mr Karp. He died the next day, April 8, 1969, some 32 hours after the transplant surgery. . . .

Suits charging failure by a physician adequately to disclose the risks and alternatives of proposed treatment are not innovations in American law. They date back a good half-century, and in the last decade have increased in number.

. . . Physicians and surgeons have a duty to make a reasonable disclosure to a patient of risks that are incident to medical diagnosis and treatment. True consent to what happens to one's self is the informed exercise of a choice, and that entails an opportunity to evaluate knowledgeably the options available and the risks attendant upon each. From these general principles, however, the focus in each individual case must necessarily relate back to what the physician said or failed to say and what the law requires him to say.

The Texas standard against which a physician's disclosure or lack of disclosure is tested is a medical one which must be proved by expert medical evidence of what a reasonable practitioner of the same school of practice and the same or similar locality would have advised a patient under similar circumstances. . . . As we understand appellants' contention, it is that Mr Karp was not told about the number of animals tested or the results of those tests; that he was not told there was a chance of permanent injury to his body by the mechanical heart, that complete renal shutdown could result from the use of the prosthesis, that the device was 'completely experimental'; and that Dr Cooley failed to tell Mr Karp that Dr Beazley had said Mr Karp was not a suitable candidate for surgery. Nine physicians testified, but none suggested a standard of disclosure required by Texas law under these circumstances. Appellants argue Dr Cooley himself set the standard requiring the disclosure of Dr Beazley's evaluation. Texas law does permit the defendant doctor to establish the standard of disclosure, but Dr Cooley's testimony says no more than that what is a reasonable medical practice is a question of medical judgment. Dr Cooley's admitted failure to tell Mr Karp of Dr Beazley's March 6 notation is of no import; Dr Leachman testified he did not think the notation made any difference. The March 6 notation, made during the course of an initial evaluation, was in Dr Beazley's view not a medical opinion but a reservation about the psychological or emotional acceptance of less than a perfect result.

What is missing from the evidence presented is the requisite expert testimony as to *what* risks under these circumstances a physician should disclose.

. . . What is significant then is what Mr Karp was told, and Mrs Karp's testimony is relevant only to the extent that it evidences what Mr Karp was told when she was present. Dr Cooley's undisputed testimony is that he began discussing with Mr Karp the proposed wedge excision and the alternative procedure of a mechanical heart as a stop-gap to a transplant about a week before the April 4 operation. He said he next talked with Mr Karp the evening of April 2. The consent form was prepared on April 3 and although there is a dispute as to *when* it was signed, there is no question it was signed by Mr Karp. Thus it was against the backdrop of at least two conversations with Dr Cooley, at which Mrs Karp was not present, that Mr Karp was presented and signed the consent document. The consent form is consistent with Dr Cooley's testimony of what he told Mr Karp. Although not necessarily conclusive, what Haskell Karp consented to and was told is best evidenced by this document. It is of considerable import that each step of the three-stage operation, objected to due to an alleged lack of informed consent, was specifically set out in the consent document signed by the patient. . . .

Appellants have not introduced evidence required by Texas law to show a lack of Karp's informed consent or of breach of Dr Cooley's duty to adequately apprise Karp of the nature and risks of the operation that warrant . . . submission of this issue to the jury. . . .

To meet the proper standard of medical care, the physician must possess a reasonable degree of skill and exercise this skill with ordinary care and diligence. A specialist like Dr Cooley is bound to exercise the degree of skill and knowledge that is ordinarily possessed by similar specialists. As with the doctrine of informed consent, supra, plaintiffs are obligated under Texas law to produce expert medical testimony to establish a medical standard of conduct, deviation from that standard and proximate cause. Appellants again assert Dr Cooley testified to the established standard and that he did not meet it. The apparent theory is that Dr Cooley was negligent in proceeding with the wedge resection when he said it could not be beneficial. This language, however, cannot be considered alone as a standard, even if it were construed to be one; rather, it must be read in the context of his total testimony, which in no wise establishes negligence. Appellants also failed to raise a fact issue on the proximate cause question. . . . Since the expert testimony failed to evidence that there were negligent acts or omissions by defendants or that any of their acts or omissions were a proximate cause of Mr Karp's death, a directed verdict for both defendants was proper. . . .

Appellants contend that the trial court erred in directing a verdict on the issue of experimentation. They acknowledge that no Texas case has expressly dealt with a cause of action based on experimentation, but assert that our court's decision in *Bender v Dingwerth* suggests that the decision as to what is actionable experimentation should be left to a jury. We do not agree.

A Texas court bound in traditional malpractice actions to expert medical testimony to determine how a reasonably careful and prudent physician would have acted under the same or similar circumstances would not likely vary that evidentiary requirement for an experimentation charge. This conclusion is also suggested by the few reported cases where experimentation has been recognised as a separate basis of liability. The record contains no evidence that Mr Karp's treatment was other than therapeutic and we agree that in this context an action for experimentation must be measured by traditional malpractice evidentiary standards. Whether there was informed consent is necessarily linked to the charge of experimentation, and Mr Karp's consent was expressly to all three stages of the operation actually performed – each an alternative in the event of a preceding failure. As previously discussed, appellants have not shown an absence of Mr Karp's informed consent. Causation and proximate cause are also requisite to an actionable claim of experimentation. Even if Dr DeBakey's testimony, as discussed subsequently, were admitted and did establish a standard and a departure from that standard in using this prosthetic device, substantial evidence . . . on causation and proximate cause simply is not reflected in the record. That alone would warrant the directed verdict on this issue. . . .

We cannot conclude that the trial court's decision to exclude Dr DeBakey's testimony was clearly erroneous. His testimony would have shown at most that, in his opinion, the pump tested under his supervision was not ready for use in humans and that he would not have recommended its use. He may have demonstrated that the animals tested with a prosthetic device at Baylor died of renal failure, but he refused to state that the prosthetic heart used in those experiments was the reasonable medical probable cause of the renal failure. He repeatedly declined to give an opinion regarding the pump used in Mr Karp stating only that the Karp pump was similar to the ones developed under his supervision. He declined to answer the only hypothetical question propounded, even though he had examined at the court's request Karp's medical records, since he had not personally examined Mr Karp. While it is conceivable that relevance *might* have been established between Dr DeBakey's experiments and conclusions regarding his mechanical heart and the Karp device and its use, the record does not supply the link. Further, because of the absence of evidence on proximate cause on the informed consent and experimentation issues, Dr DeBakey's testimony, even if admitted, would not change the requirement . . . to direct a verdict for defendants. We therefore do not disturb the trial court's determination.

As you can see, this case also points us to another aspect of liability in negligence which warrants analysis in the context of innovative therapy. What must the doctor disclose to the patient so as to comply with his legal duty and thereby obtain a valid consent?

In the case of *Zimmer v Ringrose* the Alberta Court of Appeal appears to draw a distinction between the information which must be disclosed on the one hand if the case is one of research and on the other, if it is a case of innovative therapy.

Zimmer v Ringrose (1981) 124 DLR (3d) 215 (Alb CA)

The plaintiff underwent an ineffective silver nitrate sterilisation operation. The defendant did not indicate to her that the procedure was not generally accepted in the medical community. The plaintiff subsequently became pregnant and underwent an abortion. The plaintiff sued the defendant, *inter alia*, in negligence for damages to compensate her for her injuries.

Prowse JA: I would not impose upon the appellant the duty of disclosure owed by a medical researcher to the subject of his experiment. The scope of this duty was described by Hall JA in *Halushka v University of Saskatchewan et al.* (1965) 53 DLR (2d) 436 at 443-4, 52 WWR 608 at 616:

> ... the duty imposed upon those engaged in medical research ... to those who offer themselves as subjects for experimentation ... is at least as great as, if not greater than, the duty owed by the ordinary physician or surgeon to his patient. .... The subject of medical experimentation is entitled to a full and frank disclosure of all the facts, probabilities and opinions which a reasonable man might be expected to consider before giving his consent.

In the case of a truly 'experimental' procedure, like the one conducted in *Halushka v University of Saskatchewan*, no therapeutic benefit is intended to accrue to the participant. The subject is simply part of a scientific investigation designed to enhance human knowledge. By contrast, the sterilisation procedure performed by the appellant in this case was directed towards achieving a therapeutic end. By means of a successful sterilisation, the respondent could avoid the occurrence of an unwanted pregnancy and the adverse health problems associated with it. In my opinion, the silver nitrate method was experimental only in the sense that it represented an innovation in sterilisation techniques which were relatively untried. According to the testimony of the respondent's expert witness, the procedure itself could not be dismissed out of hand as being medically untenable. Indeed, his primary criticism of the method appears to have been the absence of adequate clinical evaluation. To hold that every new development in medical methodology was 'experimental' in the sense outlined in *Halushka v University of Saskatchewan* would be to discourage advances in the field of medicine. In view of these considerations, the application of the standard of disclosure stated in the *Halushka* case would be inappropriate in this instance.

In the case at bar, the medical procedure performed was one to which the respondent had consented. Mrs Zimmer understood the nature of the silver nitrate technique and agreed to undergo that method of sterilisation. Consequently, the appellant is not liable for battery. However, the evidence does raise the question of negligence.

At trial, Macdonald J found that there was no comparison given by the appellant between his method and other methods of effecting sterilisation. As a result, the respondent had no opportunity to measure the risks involved in the silver nitrate method against those involved in other forms of sterilisation. Furthermore, the appellant failed to apprise Mrs Zimmer of the fact that the silver nitrate technique had not been approved by the medical profession. A reasonable practitioner would have made such a disclosure for he would have realised that this information would likely influence his patient's decision whether to undergo the procedure. In view of his failure to satisfy this duty of care, I must conclude that the appellant's conduct was indeed negligent.

It should be emphasised that the problem here was not that the doctor was utilising an innovative technique but rather that he breached the duty of care imposed upon him by the doctor-patient relationship. A physician is entitled to decide that the situation dictates the adoption of an innovative course of treatment. As long as he discharges his duty of disclosure, and is not otherwise in breach of his duties of skill and care, eg, has not negligently adopted the procedure given the circumstances, the doctor will not be held liable for implementing such a course of treatment.

There is currently no English case which has specifically addressed this issue. Of course, since *Reibl v Hughes* the *Halushka* standard is now the standard for treatment. In England a court would begin its analysis of the extent of the duty to disclose with the House of Lords decision in *Sidaway*. One case may be instructive. As it happens, *Sidaway* did not serve as the basis for the court's analysis in this case. This may be explicable, however, on the ground that the court considered a statutory provision which seems to contemplate an action in battery in the case of non-compliance with the Act.

R v Mental Health Commission, ex p X (1988) 9 BMLR 77 (Div Ct)

Stuart-Smith LJ: The applicant is a young man of 27. Unhappily he is a compulsive paedophile. This had led him into trouble with the courts, such that over the past ten years or so he has been convicted of 16 offences of indecency or indecent assault on young boys under the age of 16. On three occasions he has served custodial sentences. He was released from a two year sentence on 19th September 1986. His evidence is that while in prison he had determined to try and change his ways; but he realised that he needed medical help in doing so. Within days of his release he consulted Dr Silverman, who is consultant psychiatrist at Ealing Hospital and has had considerable experience in dealing with sexual deviation and sex offenders. Dr Silverman prescribed treatment by means of Cyproterone acetate which is an antiandrogen. Despite increasing doses the drug was not successful in suppressing the applicant's sexual urges.

. . . The applicant was afraid that he might re-offend again [sic] and also afraid about the high dosage he was receiving. He was therefore anxious to see if Dr Silverman could prescribe some more effective drug. Dr Silverman made enquiries both from a distinguished endocrinologist and ICI, the manufacturers of the drug, Goserelin, which they manufactured under the trade name Zoladex.

Goserelin is manufactured for the treatment of cancer of the prostate, but it operates by reducing the testosterone to castrate levels, which apparently allows a tumour to regress. As a result of his enquiries Dr Silverman concluded that Goserelin might be a suitable and safer treatment for the applicant. He explained to the applicant how it worked and gave him the ICI data sheet. The applicant was enthusiastic to receive it.

The treatment consists of a monthly subcutaneous injection of an implant into the abdomen. The implant is a small solid cylindrical depot 1 cm long and 1 mm in diameter. The cylinder is composed of polymer and degrades over the ensuing month, gradually releasing the drug. The applicant received the first injection on 8th July 1987. Within a short time the applicant found that he was no longer having sexual urges and was very pleased with the result. A second injection was given on about 8th August.

Meanwhile Dr Silverman had contacted the Mental Health Act Commissioners and told them that he was treating the applicant with Goserelin and that the applicant suffered from mental disorder within the meaning of the Mental Health Act 1983. He was unsure if the treatment came within the purview of section 57 of the Mental Health Act 1983.

On 18th August three Commissioners visited Ealing Hospital and interviewed the applicant. It is clear that the Commissioners concluded that the treatment was governed by section 57 of the Mental Health Act 1983 and the applicant was capable of understanding the nature, purpose and likely effects of it and had consented to it. . . .

A further injection was given on 8th September 1987, but it was made clear by the Commission that no further treatment could be given . . . The applicant consulted his solicitors who by letter of 30th September 1987 protested that the treatment did not fall within section 57 of the Mental Health Act 1983 and that therefore the Commission had no jurisdiction in the matter. . . .

Section 57(2)(a) of the Mental Health Act 1983 provides: 'a registered medical practitioner appointed for the purposes of this Part of this Act by the Secretary of State (not being the responsible medical officer) and two other persons appointed for the purposes of this paragraph by the Secretary of State (not being registered medical practitioners) have certified in writing that the patient is capable of understanding the nature, purpose and likely effects of the treatment in question and has consented to it'.

A number of points should be made. . . . The subsection is concerned both with capacity and consent, and the Commissioners have to be satisfied on both heads. . . . [T]he words are 'capable of understanding' and not 'understands'. Thus the question is capacity and not actual understanding. . . . [I]t is capacity to understand the likely effects of the treatment and not possible side effects, however remote.

But there is a dispute between the parties as to the concept of consent and the proper test to be applied. [Counsel for the applicant] submits that this part of the Mental Health Act 1983 was passed to deal with the difficult problem when a mental patient does not have the capacity to understand the nature and likely effects of treatment, which in some cases may be irreversible, and therefore may not be able to consent as a matter of law, so that such treatment, if given, would amount to an assault. He therefore submits that the provisions of Section 57(2)(a) of the Mental Health Act 1983 are designed to meet this problem and that accordingly the question of consent should be approached in the same way that the Court considers this problem when deciding if a normal patient has consented to medical treatment. The question therefore is whether, as a matter of fact, the patient has consented or agreed to the treatment. An apparent consent will not be a true consent if it has been obtained by fraud, misrepresentation, duress or fundamental mistake; but that is the extent of the enquiry.

In support of this proposition [counsel for the applicant] relies upon *Chatterton v Gerson* [1981] QB 432, [1981] 1 All ER 257, at 442 of the former report where Bristow J said:

In my judgment what the court has to do in each case is look at all the circumstances and say 'Was there a real consent?' I think justice requires that in order to vitiate the reality of consent there must be a greater failure of communication between doctor and patient than that involved in a breach of duty if the claim is based on negligence. When the claim is based on negligence the plaintiff must prove not only the breach of duty to inform, but that had the duty not been broken she would not have chosen to have the operation. Where the claim is based on trespass to the person, once it is shown that the consent is unreal, then what the plaintiff would have decided if she had been given the information which would have prevented vitiation of the reality of her consent is irrelevant. In my judgment once the patient is informed in broad terms of the nature of the procedure which is intended, and gives her consent, that consent is real, and the cause of action on which to base a claim for failure to go into risks and implications is negligence, not trespass. Of course if information is withheld in bad faith, the consent will be vitiated by fraud.

[Counsel for the Commission], on the other hand, submits that this test is not appropriate in a public law setting; I confess I do not follow this distinction. He submits that whether or not a patient consents is a matter for the subjective judgment of the Commissioners and they can apply any test which in their discretion they think fit. I cannot accept this. No doubt the consent has to be an informed consent in that he knows the nature and likely effect of the treatment. There can be no doubt that the applicant knew this. So too in this case, where the treatment was not routinely used for control of sexual urges and was not sold for this purpose, it was important that the applicant should realise that the use on him was a novel one and the full implications with use on young men had not been studied, since trials had only been involved with animals and older men.

The Court held that the Regulations made under section 57 of the Mental Health Act 1983 only applied to 'the surgical implantation of hormones for the purposes of reducing male sexual drive' and that the synthetic compound 'Goserelin' given to the applicant was neither a 'hormone' nor was it given by 'surgical implantation'. (On these issues see P Fennell, 'Sexual Suppressants and the Mental Health Act' [1988] Crim LR 660.) In a case which did not involve the Mental Health Act or some such statute, the court would be more likely to use an analysis based upon negligence.

Chapter 15

Donation and transplant of human tissue and fluids

The living donor

A. CONSENT: THE COMMON LAW

1. Adults

The first issue that we should consider is whether an adult may, as a matter of law, validly consent to the removal of an organ for transplantation.

Jesse Dukeminier 'Supplying Organs for Transplantation' (1970) 68 Michigan Law Review 811

Mayhem is the crime of intentionally and maliciously maiming or disfiguring a person. At common law, mayhem was limited only to deprivation of such of a man's organs 'as may render him the less able, in fighting, either to defend himself or to annoy his adversary'. Included were a man's hand, his finger, his foot, his testicle, or his eye. The significance of the organs in fighting is irrelevant today, and modern statutes have extended the crime of mayhem to disfigurings in general and to the disfiguring of women as well as of men. Under modern law, it is possible to contend that surgically removing an internal organ from a person constitutes mayhem.

Again the question arises whether, if removing a kidney for transplantation is mayhem, consent by the donor is a defense to the charge. Only two cases are even remotely relevant, and in both of those the victim's consent had no effect. In *Wright's Case*, recorded by Lord Coke in 1603, [1 *Coke on Littleton* para 194 at 126.6] 'a strong and lustie rogue' directed his companion to cut off the rogue's left hand so that he might get out of work and beg more effectively. Both the rogue and his companion were convicted of mayhem; consent was held to be no defense to the crime. In *State v Bass*, [(1961) 130 SE 2d 481] a man wanted his fingers cut off so that he could collect insurance money. With full knowledge of the purpose, a physician deadened four fingers of the man's left hand, which were then cut off by another man using an electric saw. The physician was convicted of being an accessory to mayhem. The court held that consent of the person was no defense to the charge. Although the opinion of the court in *State v Bass* was extremely vague, the court apparently thought that cutting off the fingers was no 'benefit' to the man and that the conduct was 'antisocial'. The court did not indicate what policy propositions it assumed in its determination that insurance proceeds provided no offsetting benefits for the loss of the fingers and that the conduct was antisocial.

The Law Reform Commission of Australia's Report No 7 (1977) on 'Human Tissue Transplants' (pp 22-24) states as follows:

The common law of . . . England, offers no rule or principle dealing with human tissue transplants as such, nor, for that matter, with surgery as such. There is a lack of case law, and in the rare decisions when judges have spoken on the common law principles applicable to surgery, the central issues have not involved the lawfulness of the surgery, but other legal questions such as divorce, or injury during a sporting event. This has caused resort to analogy and rationalisation by some legal writers, resulting in suggestions that common law principles applicable to transplantation may be derived from consideration of recondite legal rules such as the ancient common law offence of 'maim'. More accepted and authoritative (but in the opinion of some hardly less bizarre) has been the suggestion that surgery amounts in law to 'assault and battery' (hereafter called assault), thus falling under the law of trespass 'based on the inviolability of the person'. In extra-curial analyses of the common law both Lord Devlin [*Samples of Law Making* (1962) at 83-103] and Lord Justice Edmund Davies [(1969) 62 *Proc of Roy Soc of Med* 633] have taken this view of surgery. The opinions of such judges as these, and the lack of judicial precedent, expose the failure of the common law to provide acceptable answers to the modern medical practice of transplantation. There is little prospect of a constructive reply to the plea for reform made by Professor Daube in 1966 [*Ethics in Medical Progress* (1966) at 183]:

> An operation should be treated as a positive, beneficent, admirable action from the outset, not as a lawful infliction of harm. It is a cure, and only where essential elements are lacking in a situation does it become wrongful. After all, we do not construe marital . . . intercourse as rape licensed by virtue of consent . . .

Briefly, the common law principles of assault, in their application to the transplantation of human tissue (and to surgery generally) may be seen from the following summary. First, assault amounts to a tort, or civil wrong, giving rise to a private claim for damages enforceable in the courts. Assault is also a crime, punishable by criminal process. Secondly, the common law regards all surgery as a trespass to the person but one which can be justified or defended, in the case of the tort of assault, on the basis of consent given by the patient. Thus, it will be a defence to a claim for damages for assault if the surgeon proves that the patient consented to the operation. This defence, unfortunately, may not extend to the case of the emergency-unconscious patient, or the patient who lacks legal capacity (a small child or a mental patient). Worse, it may have no application at all in the case of a live donor of tissue, because, despite his consent, it cannot be said that the surgery on him is for his benefit. Thirdly, in the case of the crime of assault, at least, occasioning 'grievous bodily harm', consent of the patient or victim is no defence to a charge . . .

. . . However, the proposition that consent is no defence to a criminal charge is the general rule, and exceptions have been made to it. Presumably normal surgery would be an exception, but there is no decided case directly in point. The consent should be free and informed. The surgeon should advise the patient of all material facts relevant to the operation so that the patient may balance risk and benefit. Deception or even failure to make full disclosure may vitiate consent. The law and literature on 'consent' is extensive, requiring separate consideration of the adult patient, the child, the mentally incompetent, and the patient who is unconscious or an emergency case . . .

Consent to assault: What does the common law have to say to a 'normal' donor, that is to say an adult, with mental competence, properly advised, and anxious to give tissue for transplant, for example, one of two healthy kidneys? At first sight it may seem that removal of the tissue would not offend any legal principle. However, the criminal law is not entirely sympathetic to the defence of 'consent'. In addition, it cannot be said, in any normal sense, that the removal of the tissue is for the benefit of the donor. It follows that the surgeon's legal position is not easily determined.

Professor Gerald Dworkin, writing in 1970, states the following.

G Dworkin, 'The Law Relating to Organ Transplantation in England' (1970) 33 MLR 353

To determine the legality of live donor transplantations it is first necessary to examine the legal basis for surgical operations generally. Under medieval law, a person committed the crime of mayhem (maim) if he so injured another as to make him less able to fight or to defend himself or to annoy an adversary. To amputate a limb, even with the victim's consent was, on the face of it, an unlawful act, since it deprived the king of a fighting man. In early Victorian times when soldiers, as part of their training, had to bite cartridges, a soldier got a dentist to pull out his front teeth to enable him to avoid training and it was thought that both were guilty of a crime. The modern law is obscure but the crime, to some extent, turns on two interconnected factors. The first is the nature of the physical harm: one person does not have a licence to mutilate or cause bodily harm to another for any purpose merely because that person has consented. The degree of bodily harm is, of course, important: the test is no longer whether it impairs or may impair the victim's ability to fight for his country, but presumably the seriousness of the harm must be of that order. 'Bodily harm . . . includes any hurt or injury calculated to interfere with the health or comfort of the prosecutor. Such hurt or injury need not be permanent, but must, no doubt, be more than merely transient or trifling.' The second factor involves questions of public policy. The law may permit some kinds of assault and battery but not others: the dividing line between the permissible and the impermissible is not clear but the courts have accepted and still accept the burden of safeguarding individuals even against themselves.

The relevance of this aspect of the criminal law is that it provides a basis for saying that many surgical operations are *prima facie* unlawful. Without further justification not only would operations be criminal acts, but they would also be unlawful in the civil law and surgeons might be liable to pay compensation for the consequences of their acts, even though they had exercised all reasonable care. What are the criteria, then, which convert unlawful acts into lawful surgical operations? In some countries the criminal codes absolve from responsibility persons who perform in good faith and with reasonable care and skill a surgical operation upon another person, with his consent and for his benefit, if the performance of the operation is reasonable in the circumstances. No such provision appears in any United Kingdom legislation but it is clear, of course, that surgery, within limits, is a perfectly legal activity. Sir James Fitzjames Stephen formulated the general proposition that 'everyone has a right to consent to the infliction of any bodily injury in the nature of a surgical operation upon himself' and stated that although he knew of no authority for this, the existence of surgery as a profession assumed its truth . . .

Professor Dworkin then identified four conditions to be satisfied:

(i) *The patient must give a full, free and informed consent . . .*
(ii) *The operation must be therapeutic; it must be expressly for the patient's benefit.* The major distinguishing feature between surgical operations and unlawful mutilation is, of course, that all surgical operations are allegedly in the medical interests of the patient. Coke refers to a case in 1603 where 'a young and lustie rogue prevailed upon a friend to cut off his left hand, so that he might be better able to beg'. Both were found guilty of the crime of maim; today, they would also be criminally liable. In the criminal codes of some countries, the provisions concerning surgical operations expressly state that they must be for the patient's benefit; in other countries this, until recently, has been accepted as being obvious.
(iii) *There must be lawful justification.* This is a relatively unexplored and open-ended requirement. Ethical and social questions are more relevant here and the courts may occasionally use this rubric to extend the law to meet new circumstances. Most surgical operations are lawful. The most obvious example of an unlawful operation is that of abortion because, apart from those cases where abortion is permissible under the Abortion Act 1967, abortions are statutory criminal offences, whether performed by doctors or unqualified persons . . . It is unlikely that the courts would condemn circumcision as unlawful. No doubt the ritual circumcision of Jewish infants could be upheld on grounds of religious toleration, although circumcision for non-religious reasons would have to be accepted on wider public policy grounds.
(iv) *Generally, the operation must be performed by a person with appropriate medical skills.*

Professor Dworkin goes on to examine the legality of transplantation in the context of kidney transplants.

Is it lawful to remove a kidney from a live donor?
The legality of live donor transplants turns upon whether or not the first three conditions for lawful surgical operations are satisfied.
First, is the operation therapeutic? There is no doubt that the purpose of a kidney transplant is to benefit the donee. It seems equally clear that to take a kidney from a living donor can rarely be of any benefit to him. It is arguable that the donor who is left with one healthy kidney may be in no worse position than he is with two, since after a time the remaining kidney apparently does the work of two. Indeed, it may be that life insurance companies would accept an otherwise healthy donor as a normal risk. The difficulty, however, arises should anything happen to the solitary kidney: a kidney illness to a person

with only one kidney is generally far more serious than to a person with two. A kidney transplant, then, in most cases can be of no therapeutic value to the donor.

Secondly, is there lawful justification for the surgical procedure? It has been suggested that the removal of a kidney from a healthy donor is not a maiming in the accepted sense because it is no great disability in most cases to lose one kidney. One calculation suggests that the total risk involved to the donor is 0.12 per cent, divided into an immediate risk of 0.05 per cent as a post-operative accidental risk, and 0.07 per cent as the risk of any kind of accident occurring later to affect the remaining kidney. Whether or not this can be said to be a maiming, it is most certainly the infliction of bodily harm which is capable of being more than transient or trifling.

Arguments, of varying force, can be put forward to support the view that such transplants are lawfully justified. Thus, the courts have by implication recognised the legality of some kinds of homografts; for example, the practice of taking blood from donors for the purposes of blood transfusions is incapable, without more, of being legally challenged today. The position of a blood donor and a kidney donor, although in some ways similar in kind, is, however, clearly different in degree. It is difficult to categorise the blood transfusion procedure as the infliction of bodily harm of more than a trifling or transient nature.

Perhaps a closer, though by no means close, analogy is that of skin-grafting. In an American case, *Bonner v Moran* [(1941) 126 F 2d 121 (US CA DC)], a court held a surgeon liable for trespass when a fifteen-year-old boy consented to skin grafts being taken from his body for the benefit of his badly burned cousin. The basis of the decision was that the boy was not old enough to give his consent, and his parents should have done so for him. By implication, it can be argued that the court would have allowed a non-therapeutic skin-graft had the proper consent been obtained.

Another argument is that the courts should treat a volunteer in this situation in the same favourable way as rescuers. A volunteer who risks his life or exposes himself to injury, for example, in rescuing a person from a fire, is not condemned for his actions if he has acted reasonably, nor are they regarded as unlawful; instead, he may be entitled to recover damages for any injury he suffers from the person whose negligence created the dangerous situation. The courts treat rescuers favourably: 'danger invites rescue' is now an accepted phrase. If this is so, the law should look favourably on a volunteer donor so that the act would not be categorised as unlawful.

These are merely some arguments which a willing court might use if it was prepared to restate the existing law to meet new medical trends. Speaking extra-judicially, Edmund Davies LJ has said [(1969) 63 *Proc Roy Soc Med* 633 at 634] that he would

> be surprised if a surgeon were successfully sued for trespass to the person or convicted of causing bodily harm to one of full age and intelligence who freely consented to act as donor – always provided that the operation did not present unreasonable risk to the donor's life or health. That proviso is essential. A man may declare himself ready to die for another, but the surgeon must not take him at his word.

Until this issue is judicially or legislatively resolved, however, it is arguable in legal theory that the taking of a kidney from a healthy donor is normally an unlawful operation.

Thirdly, is there an informed voluntary consent? Even if the courts were to decide that live donor transplants were, within limits, lawfully justified, problems could arise in connection with the donor's consent to the removal of a kidney. In addition to all the strict requirements that the donor must be fully informed of all the relevant facts and risks, so that he can make up his own mind, difficulties may arise in those situations where the donor and donee are related. The relationship between donor and donee may be, for example, that of twins or parent and child: in these family situations the social and psychological pressures upon a person who knows that his failure to give consent will result in the death of the sick person must be very strong indeed. It may often be difficult to decide whether a consent in this situation is truly voluntary. It is true that where doctors are in doubt whether the donor's consent is in fact voluntary they may solve the problem (for the donor, at least, and his family, though not for the potential donee) by saying that the donor is medically unsuitable. Although the medical prospects are better where the blood relationship is closest, the chances of a truly voluntary consent are greater where the relationship is distant or non-existent.

Thus, our view is that *prima facie* an adult can give valid consent to the removal of an organ or other tissue for the purposes of transplantation.

However, in determining whether in any particular case a valid consent may have been given the law may take account of a number of factors.

First, the law will have regard to whether the tissue is regenerative (eg blood or bone marrow) or is non-regenerative (eg a kidney). (See Dukeminier and Sanders 'Medical Advances and Legal Lag: Haemodialysis and Kidney Transplantation' (1968) 15 UCLA Law Review 357.) The distinction is a factual one. Its relevance in law arguably lies in the fact that in the case of non-regenerative tissue the risks to the donor's health will ordinarily be greater (even in the case of the donor's consent of twinned organs such as kidneys) such that the law in determining the validity of the consent will scrutinise more carefully the benefit/burden ratio.

Secondly, if the tissue is not only non-regenerative but is also vital for life, eg a liver or heart, any consent would be invalid since the surgeon would commit murder.

Thirdly, it is doubtful that the donation is beneficial to the donor in that it is in his medical interests. It may be enough, however, that it does not harm him despite the normal notion that medical treatment to be lawful should be in the patient's interests, if not best interests.

As regards this third point, Peter Skegg comments, in *Law, Ethics and Medicine* (at p 36):

> . . . Indeed, sometimes a procedure is performed on a person in the knowledge that it will certainly be to that person's bodily detriment. This is the case when a kidney is removed from a healthy person, for transplantation into someone who is in need of it. The operation is a major one, and is not without risks. But it is not unreasonably dangerous, and the probable benefit to the recipient far outweighs the probable detriment to the donor. Hence, if called upon to deal with a case in which a kidney had been removed from a consenting adult, for transplantation into someone in need of it, the courts may confidently be expected to take the view that the operation did not amount to the offence of battery. Even though the operation causes serious bodily harm, there is clearly a good reason for it . . .

He continues (p 37):

> . . . A court is not likely to inquire closely into whether there are good reasons for a particular intervention. There is no danger of a court attempting to decide whether there were good reasons for removing a kidney from a living donor, instead of keeping the patient on dialysis in the hope that a suitable cadaver kidney would become available . . .

He concludes (p 43):

> To revert to the example of the removal of a kidney from a living person for transplantation to another: as there is a shortage of kidneys for transplantation, and as transplants from living donors are at least as successful as those from cadavers, the courts may be expected to accept that there is a 'just cause or excuse' or 'good reason', for such operations. Where consent is also present, such operations will not amount to the offence of causing grievous bodily harm.

2. Children

Can a child in his own right ever in law consent to donate an organ or tissue to another? In the absence of any statutory guidance, two views of the common law may be advanced. The first would mirror the analysis in *Gillick*; the second would suggest that there are some things to which a child may not in law consent and thereby equates competence with majority or some other particular cut-off point.

If we take the second view first, not only does this apparently fly in the face of *Gillick* but it also poses problems for a traditional common law approach which does not rely on particular cut-off points. Granted that there may be a distinction between the situation of transplantation and *Gillick* in that here the intervention may not be 'treatment' in the narrow sense of *obviously* benefiting the child; none the less there seems no reason to limit *Gillick* to that sort of procedure. Furthermore, it leaves unclear what the particular cut-off point would be. The age of 16 seems to have no particular relevance because s 8(1) of the Family Law Reform Act 1969 would only put the matter beyond doubt if every donation by a child was indisputably seen as 'treatment'.

In fact, very few donations can be seen as treatment even given a liberal interpretation of that term (see *Re W (A Minor) (Medical Treatment)* [1992] 4 All ER 627 at 647 per Nolan LJ). But yet, can it be said that a donation of blood by a 17-year-old highly intelligent person, which is unlikely to attract the description 'treatment', is unlawful in every case? If our legal instinct leads us to answer no, then we must look elsewhere for a guiding principle. What of the attainment of the age of 18, the only other candidate? Why should the attaining of majority be relevant? Can it be the case that, until majority, every donation is unlawful? Our example of the 17-year-old blood donor, which admittedly is proposed without authority, suggests otherwise.

This takes us back to our first view that the *Gillick* decision would also be relevant in this context, ie that the competence in law of a child must turn on the child's capacity to understand or comprehend the proposed procedure. This would produce the conclusion that the validity of the child's consent will turn on such factual questions as the seriousness of the intervention, the degree of risk intrinsic in the procedure, the long-term implications for the donor and so on. It may be, therefore, that it would be a rare child whom the law would find competent to consent to the donation of a kidney as against the donation of blood (see *Re W, supra, per* Lord Donaldson MR at 635). But the law has no hard and fast rule.

3. Parents, the court and others

The question here is the extent in law to which a proxy, usually a parent, can volunteer a child as the donor of an organ or other tissue. In analysing the legal regime regulating the proxy's authority, a significant factor must be the seriousness of the procedure involved and its consequences. Removal of a kidney calls for more careful deliberation than perhaps the removal of a small quantity of skin or blood. Removal of bone marrow, which may be a painful process carrying certain risks but which is less serious in its consequences than the removal of a kidney since it regenerates, falls somewhere between these.

We have already seen the general approach adopted by the law in analysing the authority of the proxy (*supra,* ch 4) in our discussion of the general law of consent, specifically in cases such as *Bonner v Moran* (1941) 126 F 2d 121; *Hart v Brown* (1972) 289 A 2d 386; *Strunk v Strunk* (1969) 445 SW 2d 145 and *Curran v Bosze* (1990) 566 NE 2d 1319 (Ill Sup Ct). The cases make two points. First, if the legal test is 'best interests' of the incompetent donor, then they appear to identify a doubtful notion of benefit, ie the psychological and emotional benefits derived from altruism. Secondly, if the courts are not adopting this approach then are they introducing another test, that the proxy may consent to that which is 'not against the interests' of the incompetent donor. This would allow the proxy to consent to a wider range of interventions, including some tissue donations. But, it is doubtful whether this would be so where the procedure involves other than minimal risk, ie kidney rather than blood donation.

Where an incompetent person is an adult, we have seen that the law does not empower anyone to consent to treatment regarding that adult. *A foriori,* this would apply to decisions regarding the removal of healthy tissue. Further, we have seen that the court has no power to consent as *parens patriae* to treatment; *a fortiori* to the removal of healthy tissue. Thus, the question is whether the removal of tissue for transplantation would fall within the approach of the House of Lords in *Re F*, ie as being in the person's 'best interests'.

There is little doubt that if this were the test applied, removal of tissue from an incompetent adult for transplantation would be unlawful. It is an open question, therefore, whether the analytical strategy referred to above as regards children, namely resort to a test of 'not against the interests' of the incompetent represents the law.

Given the nature and the context of organ or tissue donation from an incompetent adult or child, it is likely that the courts will either require (in the case of the child) or consider it desirable (in the case of an adult), that any case in which donation is contemplated should be brought before the court. We discussed this earlier (*supra*, ch 4) where it will be recalled that Neill LJ and Lord Bridge in *Re F* specifically mentioned 'live organ donation' as just such a situation (see also *Re W (A Minor) (Medical Treatment)* [1992] 4 All ER 627 at 648-669 *per* Nolan LJ).

B. CONSENT: STATUTORY LIMITATIONS

The Human Organ Transplants Act 1989 limits the scope of donation by living donors of organs for transplantation by setting restrictions on transplants between persons who are not 'genetically related'.

There are two matters of definition that we should address at the outset.

1. 'Organ'

The Act applies only to 'organs'. Section 7(2) of the Act states that:

7(2) . . . '[O]rgan' means any part of a human body consisting of a structured arrangement of tissues which, if wholly removed, cannot be replicated by the body.

It is clear that under the Act the statutory meaning of 'organ' is intended to be a term of art which may not be coterminous with the medical definition of organ. It would appear that the intention of the legislature was to distinguish between parts of the body which are capable of regeneration and those which are not. Blood, skin, semen, bone marrow and hair are examples of regenerative parts of the body. On the other hand, the heart, kidneys, liver, pancreas and lungs are examples of non-regenerative parts of the body.

The statutory definition is not, however, without its difficulties. First, an organ must consist of 'a structured arrangement of tissues' and must be a 'part of a human body'. While this causes no difficulties in obvious cases of a solid mass of tissue, such as the heart, it is not entirely clear whether bodily fluids come within the statutory (though not medical) definition of 'organ'. Generally, bodily 'tissue' is understood within the medical profession to relate to the epithelial (eg skin), connective (eg cartilage or muscle) or nervous (eg a nerve) tissues. These tissues are structured in the sense that they consist of an aggregation of cells in an interwoven fabric or network. Semen or ova would not fall within this meaning. Similarly, blood and bone marrow though consisting of an aggregation of cells are not structured in that way.

The second difficulty concerns that aspect of the definition of 'organ' which requires that the part of the body in issue 'if wholly removed, cannot be replicated by the body'. Clearly, these words were intended to capture the essence of the non-regenerative nature of the body part. To a large extent, s 7(2) succeeds. Where the part removed is the whole of the organ (used in the medical sense) and that part cannot be replicated (ie replaced) by the body, no difficulty arises; the part is 'an organ' within the Act. A problem arises, however, when the 'part' removed is a part of an organ (used in the medical sense). The best example would be the removal of a part (ie the lobe) of a liver. Is the removal of a part of an organ (used in the medical sense) covered by the Act? Clearly the phrase 'part of a human body' can include a part of an organ (used in the medical sense). The lobe of a liver is as much a 'part of a human body' as is the liver itself. The difficulty is that s 7(2) requires that the 'part', if 'wholly removed', will not regenerate. In the case of the lobe of a liver this will not be so if the 'part' which has to be visualised as not regenerating if wholly removed is the 'part' which is removed, *ie* the lobe, since the lobe can regenerate. If, however, the 'part' which has to be visualised as not regenerating if wholly removed is the liver itself, then it will be covered by the Act because if wholly removed the liver will not regenerate. This latter interpretation is difficult to sustain. Nevertheless, it has been assumed that removal of a liver lobe would be covered by the Act (see forms issued to comply with The Human Organ Transplants (Supply of Information) Regulations 1989 (SI 1989 No 2108)).

This view could only be justified if the word 'part' in s 7(2) is interpreted in this sort of case as referring to the organ (used in the medical sense) of which the removed portion is itself a part. Hence, to bring the removal of portions of an organ (used in the medical sense) within the Act, we are required first to consider that portion as a 'part of a human body' under s 7(2) and then give these words a different meaning as referring to the totality of the organ (used in the legal sense) as regards which regeneration cannot occur. This is an interpretation which defies common sense.

However, the better interpretation equally has its difficulties. If 'part of a human body' refers to the portion removed, the words 'if wholly removed' have no sense at all. This is because the intention will always be to remove the whole of the relevant portion. The Act, therefore, merely asks whether the part will regenerate 'if removed'. The word 'wholly' adds nothing. Thus, if the portion removed, as in the case of the lobe of the liver , will regenerate then the removal for transplantation of a portion, though it be a part of the body and therefore an organ, will not be within the Act because *it* will regenerate when it is removed.

Furthermore, if the Act were interpreted to capture cases such as a liver lobe transplant, that interpretation would have unexpected effects. For example, skin transplants will be covered because even if only some skin is removed and that will regenerate, looking at the totality of the skin, if 'wholly removed' *this* will not regenerate. Thus, skin and liver lobe transplants are either both covered by the Act, or neither is covered. Parliament, however, only intended to include the former.

During the progress of the Bill through the House of Commons the important question arose as to whether the Act would apply to human gametes, ie sperm and ova, or, indeed, human embryos. As we have already seen in Chapter 11, the Human Fertilisation and Embryology Act 1990 creates a regulatory framework in this area. In particular, it deals with payment for human gametes and embryos and the donation of them. If the 1989 Act applies also to them, there will be a clear conflict between the two statutory regimes which was not Parliament's intention (see Parl. Deb. (HC) (2nd Reading Ctte) 16 May 1989 at p 38). Although it has been suggested otherwise (Price and Mackay, 'The Trade in Human Organs' (1991) NLJ 1272 at 1273), it is plain that the 1989 Act does not apply for the following reasons. First, human gametes and embryos do not fall within the definition of 'organ' under s 7(2). As regards human gametes, they are not 'a structured arrangement of tissues', being unicellular. As regards embryos, even if they are this, they are not 'any part of a human body'. Secondly, it may be stretching the language of the 1989 Act too far to describe as a 'transplant' the removal and donation of human gametes and embryos by a process which is, in fact, an implant. A transplant involves replacement of that which existed.

2. 'Genetically related'

The second matter of definition we should note concerns the phrase 'genetically related'.

Section 2 provides:

2.—(1) Subject to subsection (3) below, a person is guilty of an offence if in Great Britain he –
(a) removes from a living person an organ intended to be transplanted into another person; or
(b) transplants an organ removed from a living person into another person,
unless the person into whom the organ is to be or, as the case may be, is transplanted is genetically related to the person from whom the organ is removed.
   (2) For the purposes of this section a person is genetically related to –
(a) his natural parents and children;
(b) his brothers and sisters of the whole or half blood;
(c) the brothers and sisters of the whole or half blood of either of his natural parents; and
(d) the natural children of his brothers and sisters of the whole or half blood or of the brothers and sisters of the whole or half blood of either of his natural parents;
but persons shall not in any particular case be treated as related in any of those ways unless the fact of the relationship has been established by such means as are specified by regulations made by the Secretary of State.

For the purposes of the Act, you will see that the phrase 'genetically related' is, under s 2(2), a term of art. Only certain relatives fall within the definition. Grandparents and grandchildren, for example, are excluded. Spouses equally are excluded. The following diagram reflects those who are 'genetically related' under the Act to 'X', the donor or recipient of the transplanted organ.

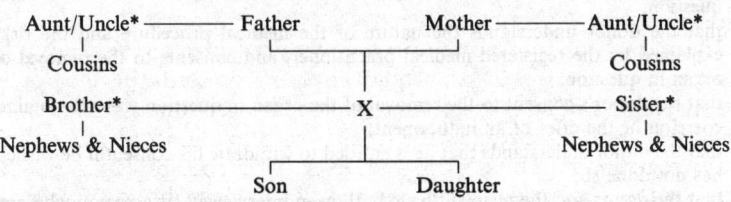

* include 'of the half-blood' (s 2(2)(c) and (d))

If s 2 imposes restrictions upon transplants between genetically unrelated persons, how is the genetic relationship to be established? Section 2(2) requires that 'the fact of the relationship has been established by such means as are specified by regulations made by the Secretary of State'. The Human Organ Transplants (Establishment of Relationship) Regulations 1989 (SI 1989 2107) provide for testing by approved testers using 'appropriate tests', ultimately including DNA profiling, as set out in detail in reg 2 of the Regulations. Unless the relationship has been so established an offence will be committed under s 2(1) by the doctors involved in the removal for transplant of an organ or the transplant itself.

3. ULTRA

Despite this, s 2(3) of the Human Organ Transplants Act 1989 provides as follows:

> 2. (3) The Secretary of State may by regulations provide that the prohibition in subsection (1) above shall not apply in cases where –
> (a) such authority as is specified in or constituted by the regulations is satisfied –
>   (i)   that no payment has been or is to be made in contravention of section 1 above; and
>   (ii) that such other conditions as are specified in the regulations are satisfied; and
> (b) such other requirements as may be specified in the regulations are complied with.

This provision allows the Secretary of State to provide a mechanism for allowing transplants between genetically unrelated persons. As can be seen, this mechanism can only come into play if the prior condition – which is a central feature of the Act – is satisfied, namely that there has been no commercial dealing in the organ (for a discussion of s 1 of the 1989 Act see *infra*, pp 1093-1095).

The Human Organ Transplants (Unrelated Persons) Regulations 1989 (SI No 2480) create an authority called the Unrelated Live Transplant Regulatory Authority (ULTRA).

Regulation 3 provides as follows:

> 3.—(1) The prohibition in section 2(1) of the Act (restriction of transplants between persons not genetically related) shall not apply in cases where a registered medical practitioner has caused the matter to be referred to the Authority and where the Authority is satisfied:–
> (a) that no payment has been, or is to be, made in contravention of section 1 of the Act;
> (b) that the registered medical practitioner who has caused the matter to be referred to the Authority has clinical responsibility for the donor; and
> (c) except in a case where the primary purpose of removal of an organ from a donor is the medical treatment of that donor, that the conditions specified in paragraph (2) of this regulation are satisfied.
> (2) The conditions referred to in paragraph (1)(c) of this regulation are:–
> (a) that a registered medical practitioner has given the donor an explanation of the nature of the medical procedure for, and the risk involved in, the removal of the organ in question;
> (b) that the donor understands the nature of the medical procedure and the risks, as explained by the registered medical practitioner, and consents to the removal of the organ in question;
> (c) that the donor's consent to the removal of the organ in question was not obtained by coercion or the offer of an inducement;
> (d) that the donor understands that he is entitled to withdraw his consent if he wishes, but has not done so;
> (e) that the donor and the recipient have both been interviewed by a person who appears to the Authority to have been suitably qualified to conduct such interviews and who

has reported to the Authority on the conditions contained in sub-paragraphs (a) to (d) above and has included in his report an account of any difficulties of communication with the donor or the recipient and an explanation of how those difficulties were overcome.

The following points should be noticed. The effect of the Regulations is to require the potential donor's doctor to refer the matter to ULTRA where the parties are not proved to be 'genetically related' under the Act. Further, ULTRA has to be satisfied on three questions, the first of which is that no payment has been made in contravention of s 1. The second is that (by reg 3(1)(b) the referring doctor is the doctor who 'has clinical responsibility for the donor'. What does this phrase mean? Clearly it is intended that it should refer to the surgeon who would be responsible for removing the organ. The form of words is odd since at the time of referral to ULTRA the surgeon may not yet have assumed any 'clinical responsibility' for the would-be donor.

The third question is that certain conditions set out in the Regulations are satisfied. This is subject to the exception where the 'primary purpose of removal of an organ from a donor is the medical treatment of that donor'. This recognises the medical fact that when a patient undergoes a lung transplant it is customary to remove his heart also. The heart, if healthy, is then available for transplant into another. The conditions specified in the Regulations, the object of which is to prevent a would-be donor from being exploited, has no relevance in this special situation (see HC(90) 7, para 10 referring to 'a domino transplant').

The conditions (set out in reg 3(2)) are relatively self-explanatory but call for some comment. The doctor referred to in reg 3(2)(a) and (b) may, in practice, not be the surgeon who has 'clinical responsibility for the donor'. This view that they need not be the same follows from the phrase '*a* registered medical practitioner' (our emphasis) in reg 3(2)(a). Proper recognition is thereby given to variations in practice as to which doctor in the team actually explains the procedure to, and obtains consent from, the donor. Secondly, reg 3(2)(a) to (d) when read together provide the code for obtaining a valid consent from an organ donor. Two important variations from the general law are worthy of note. Unlike the general law, reg 3(2)(a) imposes upon a doctor *the obligation* to advise the donor of 'the risk (sic) involved in, the removal of the organ'. There is no room here for an application of the *Bolam* test. Further, reg 3(2)(b) requires that the donor '*understands* the nature of the medical procedure and the risks' (our emphasis). The general law probably requires no more than that the doctor should have reasonable grounds to believe either that the patient has the capacity to understand what he is told (or knows) or, possibly, that he has in fact understood it. Whichever view is correct (and it is not clear), the general law certainly does not require that a patient *actually understand* the information. The difference here may be that we are not concerned with the treatment of a patient and therefore the law may require more from the doctor.

A very significant consequence of reg 3(2) of the Regulations is that the requirement of explicit consent based upon understanding by the donor means that an incompetent person (whether child or adult) who is not 'genetically related' to the intended recipient of the organ cannot be an organ donor.

Given the lack of clarity in the common law (as we have seen), as to whether an incompetent (who for these purposes would have to be genetically related) can legally be an organ donor, it may well be that a court would be guided by the prohibitions in the Regulations and apply them *mutatis mutandis* so as to have a further reason for holding that all incompetents cannot legally be organ donors.

Next, why did Parliament distinguish between donations between genetically related persons and those who are not?

The explanation offered by the then Parliamentary Under Secretary of State for Health, in the House of Commons (HC Deb, 6 July 1989) during the passage of the Bill was as follows:

> The Bill already excludes genetically related people from scrutiny by the authority. A reason for that is that the existence of a close genetic relationship can be verified with a high degree of accuracy by laboratory testing. In this country, the vast majority of live transplants would be covered by that exemption, as close family members are both more likely to come forward to offer themselves as donors and to prove compatible, in the medical sense.
>
> Under the Bill, the existence of a genetic relationship would be verified in each case in an objective way by such testing. Appropriate tests may have already been carried out in the process of trying to establish the compatibility of the donor and would-be recipient. In case of relatives 'in law' or people not related at all to the would-be recipient, the existence of some kind of relationship or personal tie is more difficult to establish. Unfortunately, we cannot rule out the possibility of non-genetic 'relationships' being formed solely for the purpose of the operation or of pressure – economic or otherwise – being brought to bear upon a donor to submit to a transplant operation.
>
> For those reasons, it is intended that the authority will consider the available evidence in each case where no genetic relationship has been established, before giving an independent decision on whether an offer of donation is altruistic. However, the fact that the authority will scrutinise all cases of live donation between non-related persons does not imply that unnecessary obstacles will be placed in the way of transplants between spouses or 'in law' relations.

As this makes plain, Parliament was concerned that the donation be entirely altruistic and presumes that this will be so in the case of those who are 'genetically related' whereas it may not be otherwise. It is fair to ask, however, if the key to altruism is close family ties, why should a spouse be treated as a stranger? Furthermore, grandparents and grandchildren *are* genetically related and may surely be presumed to act as altruistically as those included within the Act, yet they too are excluded as if they were strangers. It cannot be that a grandparent is necessarily too old to be a donor because someone may be a grandparent at 40!

By contrast, if altruism *is* the key, why should Parliament restrict unregulated donation to the genetically related? It could be said that intra-family donations may well be the product of severe social pressure ('coercion') rather than altruism (notice the wording of reg 3(2)(c) of the Regulations set out above). In some jurisdictions, consequently, legislation prohibits the removal of non-regenerative tissue from a minor for the purpose of transplantation, recognising the danger of pressure within the family (see, for example, the Human Tissue Act 1982 s 14 (1) in Victoria, Australia).

C. THE AGREEMENTS TO DONATE

An initial point that we should notice is that we are not concerned here with those arrangements which are covered by the Human Fertilisation and Embryology Act 1990, that is arrangements having to do with infertility and involving eggs, sperm or embryos.

As regards the arrangements we are concerned with in this chapter, there will, ordinarily, be two distinct agreements. The first will be between the donor and a doctor or other agency involved in the removal and storage of the tissue or organ or, possibly, directly between the donor and the intended recipient ('the donation agreement'). An example of the latter where there will not be a doctor or other agency involved may be the case of sperm donation.

The second agreement will be between the doctor or storage institution and the recipient ('the transfer agreement').

1. The Human Organ Transplants Act 1989

The validity of an agreement to donate or transfer any organ to a patient must now take account of the Human Organ Transplants Act 1989. By s 1 commercial dealings in human organs are prohibited. The government took swift action because of concerns about possible trafficking in human organs and, in particular, the so-called 'kidneys for sale' case. In that case, the General Medical Council found three doctors guilty of 'serious professional misconduct' for having been involved in arrangements to buy organs for transplantation.

Section 1 provides:

Prohibitions of commercial dealings in human organs
1. (1) A person is guilty of an offence if in Great Britain he –
(a) makes or receives any payment for the supply of, or for an offer to supply, an organ which has been or is to be removed from a dead or living person and is intended to be transplanted into another person whether in Great Britain or elsewhere;
(b) seeks to find a person willing to supply for payment such an organ as is mentioned in paragraph (a) above or offers to supply such an organ for payment;
(c) initiates or negotiates any arrangement involving the making of any payment for the supply of, or for an offer to supply, such an organ; or
(d) takes part in the management or control of a body of persons corporate or unincorporated whose activities consist of or include the initiation or negotiation of such arrangements.
   (2) Without prejudice to paragraph (b) of subsection (1) above, a person is guilty of an offence if he causes to be published or distributed, or knowingly publishes or distributes, in Great Britain an advertisement –
(a) inviting persons to supply for payment any such organs as are mentioned in paragraph (a) of that subsection or offering to supply any such organs for payment; or
(b) indicating that the advertiser is willing to initiate or negotiate any such arrangement as is mentioned in paragraph (c) of that subsection.

(a) The scope of section 1

There are three types of conduct which are made criminal by this provision. The offences are committed whether the organ is removed from a dead or living person provided that there is an intention that it be used for transplantation.

(i) 'PAYMENT' FOR 'SUPPLY'

The first offence relates to making or receiving payment for the supply of an organ (s 1(1)(a)) or offering to supply (s 1(1)(b)). Of particular importance here is the meaning of the words 'supply' and 'payment'. Clearly, the provision of an organ by a donor is covered. But what of the surgeon who removes the organ and the surgeon, if different, who transplants the organ into the patient? Do either of these 'supply' an organ within s 1(1)(a)? It could be argued that both 'supply' in the sense that they *provide* an organ by their conduct. A better view is, however, that only a donor supplies an organ within the Act. Support for this view is found in s 1(1)(b), which seems to limit the supplier to the donor because it is an offence directed at the donor. (It could be said that a supplier could also be someone (or an institution) who holds organs in a tissue bank.) If the surgeon who removes or transplants an organ were a 'supplier', the consequence would be *prima facie* that the surgeon in the private sector could not be paid for doing his job. As regards the removal of an organ, however, the surgeon would not commit an offence in that the word 'payment' is defined in s 1(3) so as to exclude 'payment for . . . the cost of removing'. No reference is made to payment for the cost of transplanting but the surgeon in private practice who transplants rather than removes ought not to be in any worse position. Consequently, 'supply' must be restricted to the action of the donor.

There are a number of implications that flow from this interpretation. What is the purpose behind the exclusion from the Act in s 1(3) of payments for 'defraying' or 'reimbursing': '(a) the cost of removing, transporting or preserving the organ to be supplied'?

Clearly, Parliament did not intend that payments received or made and relating to the removal of an organ should fall within the Act. The assumption seemed to be that they needed to be explicitly excluded. As we have seen, however, the limited meaning of 'supply' excludes anything to do with the removal in any event. Thus s 1(3)(a) is superfluous.

Given its existence, however, it raises the difficulty that Parliament was concerned to exclude only costs associated with removal, etc and not with transplanting. Does this mean that payment to the transplant surgeon for his services is a crime? The answer would be 'yes' unless the limited meaning of 'supply' is correct, ie that only the donor supplies. Once this limited meaning is accepted the fact that payment for transplant is not excluded from the meaning of 'payment' is irrelevant.

Finally, it is worth noting that s 1(3)(b) excludes certain payments to the donor from the Act. It provides as follows:

> (3) In this section 'payment' means payment in money or money's worth but does not include any payment for defraying or reimbursing – . . .
> (b)   any expenses or loss of earning incurred by a person so far as reasonably and directly attributable to his supplying an organ from his body.

(ii) 'BROKERING'

The second offence created by s 1 relates to what, in essence, could be described as 'brokering' (s 1(1)(b), (c) and (d)). The Act is very broadly drawn so as to catch a wide range of activities which would lead to commercial dealings in organs. Hence, those who seek a donor willing to supply his organ for payment or those who initiate or negotiate an arrangement involving the supply of such an organ, will all commit criminal offences. Curiously, the Act goes even further by making it a criminal offence to initiate or negotiate an arrangement for what can only be described as an option on such an organ. This is the only meaning that can be given to that part of s 1(1)(c) which makes it a crime to initiate or negotiate 'any arrangement involving the making of any payment . . . for an offer to supply, such an organ'.

(iii) 'ADVERTISING'

The third offence relates to advertising for, or to be, a donor in return for payment. Section 1(4) gives the word 'advertisement' a wide meaning such that it includes 'any form of advertising', whether permanent or not, and whether oral or in writing. Also, the Act includes advertisements directed to the public at large, a section of the public or, it seems, to selected individuals.

(iv) GENERALLY

Two general points relating to all the offences must be made. First, as regards s 1(1), the Act does not explicitly identify what state of mind (*mens rea*) is required for the offences. Undoubtedly, *mens rea* would be required notwithstanding that the offences are only triable summarily with a maximum sentence of three months' imprisonment. A court would probably require an 'intention' to do the prohibited conduct.

Secondly, an attempt or conspiracy to commit one of the offences under the Act would also be a crime under the Criminal Attempts Act 1981 and the Criminal Law Act 1977.

(b) A counter-view on commercial dealings

The UK Government's response in 1989 reflected a widespread antipathy towards the notion of commerce, eg the Guidelines of the British Transplantation Society (1985), the Resolution of the Council of Ministers of the European Community (art 9, Resolution (78) 29) (for the text of these see 1st edition, pp 1003-1007). The arguments concerning commercialisation were rehearsed as long ago as 1970.

J Dukeninier 'Supplying Organs for Transplantation' (1970) 68 Michigan Law Review 811

There are at least four basic positions from which one may approach the problem of organ sale. The first is founded upon an acceptance of the general ethical principle of preservation of life. That principle, simply stated, is that an individual should not endanger his life except for the love of another or in a case such that the danger is an indirect consequence of the activity. This position has deep roots in Judaeo-Christian, and even earlier, teachings that man should not seek his own destruction. Unlike the Eskimos, who encourage suicide by the elderly when they can no longer contribute to the family larder, most western societies have long condemned taking one's own life. In ancient Athens a man who unsuccessfully attempted suicide was punished by the cutting off of his hand. In mediaeval England a stake was driven through the heart of a man who committed suicide and all his property was forfeited to the crown; Christians who committed suicide could not be buried in consecrated ground. Remnants of this attitude can still be found in laws against abetting and, in some places, attempting suicide.

However, the principle of preserving life does permit some exceptions. Society condones, and even praises, some acts of heroism and self-sacrifice, such as that of the man who gives up his seat in the lifeboat, the passerby who enters a burning building to save the occupants, or the mother who jumps into the rapids to save her child. These are heroic acts motivated by the desire to help others. Under this view, the sole motivation for risking one's life by giving up an organ must be the love of one's fellow man, and a gift of a spare organ to a specific donee is permissible so long as such a motivation exists. Otherwise, allowing the removal of an organ for transplantation is condemned.

Yet if a charitable motive is so important in judging conduct in situations involving a risking of one's life, how can we permit men to risk their lives in driving racing cars, in entering boxing contests, and in pursuing all kinds of paid risky occupations and still object to the paid kidney donor? When confronted with this question many moral theologians draw a line between direct and indirect effects. For race car drivers and others in risky occupations, dying or being functionally impaired is an indirect consequence, which is foreseen as only possible. In the transplantation case, they argue, removal of the organ from the donor is a life-risking procedure which is the necessary means to the end. If, however, the direct-indirect distinction is accepted, the conclusion that it is unethical to pay a man for a kidney to save life, even though the risks to him are small, but ethical to pay a race car driver at the Indianapolis 500 for entertainment, even though the risks to him are great, can hardly be avoided. Such a principle is troubling indeed.

The second position from which the problem of organ sale can be approached may be characterised as one of 'free will'. This position is based upon the principle that a person should be able to do whatever he chooses, so long as he does not harm another. Particularly among the young, this position is now much in vogue. It underlies much of the current trend to liberate 'sins', such as private deviate sexual conduct and fornication by the unmarried, from criminal sanction. Undoubtedly this principle has also influenced the judicial decisions which have relaxed old proscriptions against obscenity, and it is the base of the recent decisions holding that statutes requiring motorcyclists to wear helmets are unconstitutional since the state may not require a citizen to protect his health alone. As applied to organ sales, the argument would be that an individual has the right to decide for himself whether to sell an organ.

A principal difficulty with this view is that in harming himself a person may harm society; a person who gives or sells a kidney might, if his other kidney fails, have to be maintained by the government on an artificial kidney machine. If he gives or sells other spare organs, the risk that he will disable himself is greater and the resulting harm to society may be substantial. To represent society's interest, a person other than the donor, such as a judge or a physician, must appraise the possible harm to society at large.

A variation of the free-will view is that free will, or informed consent as it is known in medico-legal terminology, should be the ethical criterion, but that a monetary payment for an organ would constitute economic coercion so that the consent would not really represent an act of free will. This is merely a conclusion, however, and is not a reason. What is really at issue is the determination of criteria by which to measure 'unfair inducement' or 'economic coercion' in situations involving the risking of life. Why is it unfair to induce a man to sell a kidney and not unfair to induce him into the boxing ring or into a coal mine?

The third way of evaluating the propriety of permitting organ sale is not to start from any general ethical rule of human conduct but to narrow the problem to the context of the physician-patient relationship. Professor Paul Freund [(1965) 273 New Eng J Med 687 at 689] has pointed out that '[t]he great traditional safeguard in the field of medical experimentation is the disciplined fidelity of the physician to his patient: *primum non nocere*. First of all, do not do injury.' From this viewpoint the basic question is not the donor's motivation or free will; the issue is whether buying this particular organ from this individual patient is for his welfare. If the principle of totality permits sacrificing a part of the body for the good of the whole – which includes spiritual gain and the avoidance of psychological trauma – it is not difficult to conceive of situations in which a physician could ethically conclude that the sale is for the patient's welfare. Suppose, for example, that a very rich man needs a kidney and the closest tissue match is his sister, who is poor. While the sister is thinking about offering a kidney, her brother lets her know that he will accept it only in exchange for 100,000 dollars – an exchange which may have income and estate tax advantages for him. If the sister decides to sell the kidney, her knowledge of forthcoming remuneration makes it impossible to conclude that she acts solely for spiritual gain, and yet it does not seem unethical to allow her to sell the kidney. Under the principle of totality, the surgeon must conclude that the donor benefits by removal of his kidney. To arrive at that conclusion the surgeon may have to inquire as to how the donor proposes to use any monetary payment and may then have to decide for himself whether the donor will benefit physically or mentally from that particular use.

Finally, the question of organ sale can be probed by disregarding ethical positions and analysing only the consequences of permitting such sales. Sales will have some impact both on the total amount of economic resources which are to be allocated to medicine and on the selection of recipients, but the precise nature of that impact is not clear. The nature of the impact will depend upon the manner in which two distinguishable problems are approached: (1) creating an adequate quantity of organs supplied and (2) selecting the persons to receive them. The quantity of organs supplied could be increased by buying them, and they could then be allocated among recipients by some method other than sale. For example, a third party, such as the government or a hospital, might absorb the cost. But the consequence of the government's purchase of organs for recipients might be that the government's economic resources which are committed to medicine would be used for the purchase of organs rather than for other medical needs. To achieve the best use of the resources available for medical purposes, other ways of securing a satisfactory quantity of organs should first be exhausted. If the cost of buying organs is passed on to the recipient, life-saving resources would be distributed on the basis of ability to pay. The use of wealth as a means of selecting who shall be saved among the dying raises immensely troublesome ethical and legal quandaries.

Under some approaches to the problem the procedure of buying organs may be thought to be impermissible in some or all circumstances. The sounder arguments however, appear to permit a surgeon to offer remuneration if, acting in accordance with contemporary ethical standards and with the permission of a hospital review committee, he concludes that in a particular case the operation will promote the physical or mental health of the donor. In arriving at that conclusion, the surgeon and the review committee must balance various interests, but the most important is the doctor's duty to his patient.

(For a detailed argument in favour of commercial dealings and against the position taken by the 1989 Act, see Lori Andrews, 'My Body, My Property' (1986) 16 Hastings Center Report (October 1986), 28. See also the thoughtful comments of Janet Radcliffe Richards in 'What Price Personal Choice?' *Daily Telegraph*, 8 February 1989.)

2. Agreements not affected by the 1989 Act

It is important to recognise that there are two distinct types of arrangement to consider. They are non-commercial arrangements to donate tissue or other bodily materials including that covered by the 1989 Act (ie 'organ' as defined in s 7(2)) and commercial arrangements to donate tissue or other bodily materials not falling within the definition of 'organ' under the 1989 Act.

(a) Non-commercial arrangements

Reminding ourselves that there are two distinct arrangements in play – 'the donation agreement' and 'the transfer agreement' – what we are concerned with here is whether these agreements are valid gifts. As regards the *donation agreement*, its validity will depend upon considerations of public policy involving such issues as consent which we explored earlier in Chapter 3. As regards the *transfer agreement*, there would seem to be no reason why such an agreement would not be valid as a gift if intended for the treatment of a patient.

In relation to both agreements if they be valid gifts, clearly any conditions in the gift (such as, that the tissue be transplanted into a particular person) have to be complied with. Of course, any legal redress in this situation which the donor may seek would depend on a civil action being available to him which, in turn, would appear to depend upon there being some form of proprietorial claim over the tissue (see *infra*).

If these arrangements can only be categorised as gifts, are there any ways in which they may be enforced by the intended *recipient*? As regards the donation agreement this very question arose in the case of *McFall v Shimp* (1978) 10 Pa D&C (3d) 90. Russell Scott describes the background to the case.

R Scott, *The Body as Property* (1981) (pp 127-9)

Robert McFall of Pittsburgh, Pennsylvania, was overwhelmed by the symptoms of aplastic anaemia in June 1978. A nightmare began for the thirty-nine-year-old bachelor when he began to develop bruises after bumping into objects during his work installing insulation materials in confined spaces in buildings. The bruises would not go away, and soon he began to have nose bleeds that continued for hours at a time. He went to a local hospital in suburban Pittsburgh, where the doctors diagnosed aplastic anaemia, a rare, almost certainly fatal disease of the bone marrow and blood. The prospects of death after contracting this disease have been put by some medical studies at 90 percent with an average survival period somewhere between three and four months. There is only one real source of cure, and that is a transplant of compatible bone marrow. This transplant gives a good expectation of complete recovery. Without it, the patient must expect to die.

The statistical likelihood of finding compatible bone marrow is almost one in sixty thousand. In practice, the prospect is hopeless, because no means exist for testing the community. There are as yet no computerised banks containing comprehensive national tissue information (though in some parts of the world, for example, at Westminster Hospital in London, computerised tissue banks are being built up and already contain information about thousands of prospective donors). On the other hand, the prospect of finding tissue compatibility inside a family is far higher, and increases with the closeness of the relationship.

Robert McFall had three brothers and three sisters. They had all gone their separate ways following their mother's death in 1949, and there had been little family communication after that time. By means of computer checks through driver's licence records, they were all traced, and agreed to submit to tissue-typing tests. None of them turned out to be a compatible donor. It was then decided to enquire whether a first cousin of McFall, David Shimp, a crane operator in a steel mill, would agree to be tested. Shimp was aged forty-three and married. When both men were younger they had gone to camps together and had shared many experiences.

Shimp agreed to undergo a preliminary test but did not bother to tell his wife. The test proved to be positive, suggesting that Shimp's bone marrow would be a perfect match for Robert McFall. A second test was arranged, but Shimp cancelled the appointment. He had changed his mind, and from that time onward refused to have anything more to do with the affair. According to reports, Shimp said his wife was angry that he had taken the test without discussing it with her, and wanted him to discontinue his participation. His mother had expressed the same wish. One report said that Shimp had been influenced by a dream that if he went into hospital for the bone marrow removal, he would never come out. Friends and other relatives put great pressure on him to proceed with the tests, but he would not budge. It was even said that he considered bringing legal proceedings to stop harassment, because the story had gotten into the hands of the media, which gave it considerable publicity. However, it was Robert McFall who first resorted to the courts.

In the last week of July, McFall sued David Shimp in Allegheny County Court, Pennsylvania, asking for an order that would compel Shimp to submit to further tests, and eventually to the removal of a quantity of his bone marrow for transplant to McFall. Time was now all-important for McFall, and the normal delays of court hearings too risky. His lawyers asked for an urgent preliminary injunction, which, if granted, would direct Shimp forthwith to undergo the further tests. In this atmosphere events moved rapidly, and *McFall v Shimp* was dealt with and disposed of on July 25 and 26 by the Civil Division of the Allegheny County Court, Judge John P Flaherty, Jr, presiding.

The plaintiff's brief was a document of originality and persuasion, skilfully prepared by his attorney, John W Murtagh, Jr. Its opening words went straight to the heart of the matter, posing for determination an issue as profound as any that could be put to a court of law. The judge was asked, in so many words, to determine whether society may overrule a citizen's claim to an absolute right to his bodily security in order to save the life of one of its members. The brief submitted, for reasons it set out in detail, that the answer 'is and must be "yes". It then tackled some of the medical questions, asserting that the removal procedure was medically safe, would at most result in minor and temporary discomfort, and would deprive the defendant of nothing but his time because bone marrow is a regenerative tissue that promptly replaces itself.

McFall's lawyers had found no precedent or comparable case that could directly assist the court, and the judge himself later commented that 'a diligent search has produced no authority'. Accordingly, the claim for legal relief was put in fundamental terms, based on morality, ethics, custom, scholarly legal pronouncements, and judicial opinion. . . .

McFall's case then cited some well-known circumstances in which bodily integrity is lawfully disregarded because of overriding social considerations: public health requirements for vaccination and quarantine; criminal law powers to take hair, blood, clothes, and semen; marriage law requirements of blood tests; defence law requirements of military service; and compulsory assistance to law enforcement officers in emergencies. To these McFall sought to add his own case as representing a new category. To demonstrate that the court could, by reference to principle and precedent, extend the law in this fashion if it wished, the plaintiff produced the fruits of some extremely original research.

Power to make an order of the kind requested was traced back some seven hundred years from the Allegheny County Court, through the Pennsylvanian and United States legal systems, to the ancient English Courts of Chancery and the powers to dispense justice granted to those courts in the reign of King Edward I. This English king ascended his throne in the year 1272, and in the thirteenth year of his reign, Parliament passed the statute now known as the second Statute of Westminster. It contained the following provision: 'Whensoever from thenceforth a writ shall be found in the Chancery, and in a like case falling under the same right and requiring a like remedy, no precedent of a writ can be produced, the Clerks in Chancery shall agree in forming a new one; lest it happen for the future that the Court of our lord the king be deficient in doing justice to the suitors'. . . .

The question was whether Robert McFall's claim should be recognised by the courts, and whether the law should regard David Shimp as having a duty towards him. 'Has the duty the Plaintiff seeks to impose upon the Defendant ever been recognised in law or equity?' asked the brief. In support of an affirmative answer, reliance was next placed upon the so-called Rescue Cases.

The legal principle of rescue recognises the social duty of a citizen to act positively to attempt to rescue another who is in personal danger. A yachtsman may be found to have a positive duty to try to save a drowning man. American and British laws have not favoured the rescue concept and have been reluctant to equate moral with legal obligation. Generally speaking, their approach has been to recognise that certain relationships should produce legal duties and obligations, for example, the relationship of doctor and patient. They have been slow to build specific legal duties on the foundation of general moral concepts, particularly when this might result in conflict with 'individualist' philosophy. In the words of one American judge, 'common law courts have been reluctant to impose affirmative duties on individuals even in situations in which most people would feel under a moral obligation to act' . . .

McFall's lawyer claimed that in recent years American and English lawmakers had undergone some change of heart. Examples were provided of the 'ebbing of the strongly individualist philosophy of the early common law', and of cases in which courts had countenanced exceptions to the general rule that refuses to impose a duty to rescue. On the subject of yachtsmen, he was able to point to a decision in which a court held that a yacht owner whose guest fell overboard was under a positive duty to rescue the guest. He put to the court that it was possible to detect a growing Anglo-American acceptance of the principle that legal consequences should attach to conduct that displays indifference to the peril of a stranger. On McFall's behalf, he also put forward and supported a model set of standards proposed in 1965 by a prominent advocate of the rescue principle. These standards, which did not reach the statute book, contained specific suggestions for the provision of medical aid by means of blood transfusion. The basic proposal was that a person should have a legal duty to attempt rescue whenever another was in imminent danger and the first person was the only practical source of help. The duty would apply only if the danger would lead to substantial harm to person or property, and the risk to the rescuer would be 'disproportionately' less than the prospective harm. On the subject of blood transfusion, no objection was seen to a general rule that citizens should be placed under a community duty to give blood. The drafter urged that, at the very least, any blood donor could logically be placed under a duty to continue to give blood, for by giving his tissue in the first place, he indicated that his bodily security was 'subordinated to some other interest'; it was accepted, however, that a person opposed to blood transfusion should not normally be held liable for failure to give blood even if it resulted in loss of life. When these standards were formulated in 1965, the safe removal of bone marrow had not appeared as a lifesaving procedure, but presumably the same philosophy of compulsory donation could be applied to bone marrow donation, and to any other body tissue or organ which, as medicine develops, may be removed without impairing a person's health or well-being. It should not be forgotten in considering this argument that right now a person with one healthy kidney is as acceptable to life insurance companies as a person with two.

The plaintiff's brief argued that Shimp's behaviour in undergoing the first test had placed him in the same position as the blood donor who has previously given blood. By permitting himself to be tissue-typed and by demonstrating a four-tissue match with his cousin, he had obligated himself to continue. The brief claimed that Shimp had 'cruelly abandoned the Plaintiff after the Plaintiff was allowed to hope for a successful end to his ordeal', and should be compelled to continue to offer aid because the plaintiff had thereby been exposed to the risk of greater harm: McFall's chances of cure had been diminished due to the delays caused by Shimp's initial embarkation on a programme of assistance and his later refusal to proceed.

The brief ended with the plea that the court, as the voice of society, should not in the name of the defendant's bodily security abandon Robert McFall to a short, medically dominated life and certain death. 'Our noblest tradition as a free people and our common sense of decency, society and morality all point to the proper result in this case. We respectfully suggest that it is time our law did likewise.'

On July 25, 1978, in a preliminary hearing, Judge Flaherty had to decide whether Robert McFall had disclosed any kind of legal case at all and whether David Shimp had an obligation even to offer a defence. He considered the matter and heard medical evidence of the plaintiff's low chance of survival, the 'minimal risks' in bone marrow removal, and the fact that the plaintiff would have at least a 50 percent chance of cure after a transplant from the defendant. The judge then directed that Shimp's attorney file a brief setting out the reasons why he should not be ordered to give the bone marrow. A hearing was fixed for the next day. McFall had negotiated his first legal hurdle.

The essence of Shimp's defence was contained in his attorney's argument that the law of Pennsylvania did not impose upon him any duty to help his cousin. Whatever had been said about 'minimal risks' of bone marrow donation, the fact remained that the risks existed, and it could be dangerous. Though it is regarded medically as safe, bone marrow removal involves general anaesthetic and extraction of the marrow from the pelvic bone by means of a specially designed needle, which may be inserted as many as two hundred times in order to obtain the required quantity. This process can have a strong psychological effect upon the donor, particularly if he has a fear of surgery, or a fear of losing part of his body, and can cause him to develop hostility towards the recipient. Even if no risk existed, his client was still under no legal obligation to come to anybody's aid, said Shimp's attorney. Finally, he said, McFall's claim was suspect because it rested upon a view of what the law ought to be, not upon the reality of the law as it then was.

McFall v Shimp (1978) 10 Pa D&C (3d) 90 (Ct Comm Pl, Pa)

Flaherty J: The plaintiff, Robert McFall, suffers from a rare bone marrow disease and the prognosis for his survival is very dim, unless he receives a bone marrow transplant from a compatible donor. Finding a compatible donor is a very difficult task, and limited to a selection among close relatives. After a search and certain tests, it has been determined that only the defendant is suitable as a donor. The defendant refuses to submit to the necessary transplant, and before the Court is a request for a preliminary injunction which seeks to compel the defendant to submit to further tests, and, eventually, the bone marrow transplant.

Although a diligent search has produced no authority, the plaintiff cites the ancient statute of King Edward I, *St Westminster* 2, 13 Ed 1, c 24, pointing out, as is the case, that this Court is a successor to the English Courts of Chancery and derives power from this statute, almost 700 years old. The question posed by the plaintiff is that, in order to save the life of one of its members by the only means available, may society infringe upon one's absolute right to his 'bodily security'?

The common law has consistently held to a rule which provides that one human being is under no legal compulsion to give aid or to take action to save that human being or to rescue. A great deal has been written regarding this rule which, on the surface, appears to be revolting in a moral sense. Introspection, however, will demonstrate that the rule is founded upon the very essence of our free society. It is noteworthy that counsel for the plaintiff has cited authority which has developed in other societies in support of the plaintiff's request in this instance. Our society, contrary to many others, has as its first principle, the respect for the individual, and that society and government exist to protect the individual from being invaded and hurt by another. Many societies adopt a contrary view which has the individual existing to serve the society as a whole. In preserving such a society as we have it is bound to happen that great moral conflicts will arise, and will appear harsh in a given instance. In this case, the Chancellor is being asked to force one member of society to undergo a medical procedure which would provide that part of that individual's body would be removed from him and given to another so that the other could live. Morally, this decision rests with the defendant, and, in the view of the Court, the refusal of the defendant is morally indefensible. For our law to *compel* the defendant to submit to an intrusion of his body would change every concept and principle upon which our society is founded. To do so would defeat the sanctity of the individual, and would impose a rule which would know no limits, and one could not imagine where the line would be drawn.

This request is not to be compared with an action at law for damages, but rather is an action in equity before a chancellor, which in the ultimate, if granted, would require the forcible submission to the medical procedure. For a society, which respects the rights of *one* individual, to sink its teeth into the jugular vein or neck of one of its members and suck from it sustenance for *another* member, is revolting to our hard-wrought concepts of jurisprudence. Forcible extraction of living body tissue causes revulsion to the judicial mind. Such would raise the spectre of the swastika and the Inquisition, reminiscent of the horrors this portends.

This Court makes no comment on the law regarding the plaintiff's right in an action at law for damages, but has no alternative but to deny the requested equitable relief. An Order will be entered denying the request for a preliminary injunction.

McFall concerns the enforcement of the *donation agreement.* As far as the *transfer agreement* is concerned, there can be no question of the law specifically enforcing an agreement to transplant tissue or an organ into a patient by analogy to the traditional ground that equity will not enforce a contract for personal services.

This disposes of one aspect of enforcing the transfer agreement: there is, however, another issue to consider. Could a donee seek through the law to enforce the transfer to him of the tissue of other bodily material *once removed* from the donor? The answer must be that this would be a case of an imperfect gift. Assuming the tissue is property, delivery actual or constructive would not have taken place and, therefore, the donee would have no cause of action.

(b) Commercial arrangements outside the 1989 Act

The existence of the 1989 Act does not preclude the possibility of commercial dealings in tissue and other body material not covered by the statutory definition of 'organ'. We have already discussed the threshold issue of public policy, *viz* whether commercial agreements are lawful. Here it is important to notice that a court might be influenced by the fact that Parliament appears to have deliberately refrained from legislating as regards certain material by adopting a limited definition of 'organ'. Therefore, the court should be slow to legislate judicially where Parliament has chosen not to. Further, the material we are concerned with here will be regenerative and usually will be bodily fluids such as blood. The public policy arguments against commercial dealings which we saw earlier, are less powerful in this context.

On the assumption that commercial dealings are not proscribed by law, the remaining question is what would be the terms of any such contracts. The terms may be implied by law as well as being expressly agreed between parties. Consideration of implied terms, of course, only becomes important as regards the *transfer agreement.*

Here it may be asked whether the provisions of the Sale of Goods Act 1979 and of the Supply of Goods and Services Act 1982 apply? Both the 1979 and the 1982 Acts apply only where the supplier of the goods or service acts 'in the course of a business'. It seems clear that the activities of a private hospital, blood bank or the like would constitute a 'business'. (So, too, would the activities of an NHS hospital or Trust were it to contract with the donee: see s 18(1) of the 1982 Act.) If so, should the transfer agreement be categorised as a contract for the supply of *goods* or *services*?

Paul Matthews, 'The Body as Property' (1983) 36 Current Legal Problems 193

More problematic is the potential application of the Sale of Goods Act 1979, with its terms regarding quality implied into contracts of sale. If a private hospital sells blood to a patient which turns out not to be fit for its purpose (eg because contaminated by hepatitis), is there a breach of section 14 of the Act? The American courts, as one might expect, have long had to grapple with this kind of question. Broadly, cases have fallen into two categories: first, where the court has held the supply of blood to constitute a *service* rather than a *sale of goods*, [eg *Perlmutter v Beth David Hospital* (1955) 123 NE 2d 792] and secondly, where the court has held the supply to be a sale of goods [eg *Belle Bonfils Memorial Blood Bank v Hansen* (1978) 579 P 2d 1158]. Which way the courts have decided has been influenced by a number of factors, such as whether the defendant was a hospital or a blood bank, whether either was profit-making or non profit-making, and so on. In any case, the American law of product liability and general negligence is now so highly developed there is no longer a substantial difference between supplying a service badly and selling faulty goods, but the American experience has (as always) proved instructive. On principle, it is submitted that blood ought to be 'goods' within the 1979 Act wherever it is dealt with commercially.

Since the 1982 Act, the point that Paul Matthews argues is more complex since identical terms will be implied into a contract for the supply of goods or goods linked to services (ss 2-5). Only if the contract is entirely one for services would the obligation under the contract be simply one to exercise reasonable care and skill (ss 5, 13). The better view is that the contracts under discussion here would fall within the 1982 Act as being a contract for the supply of goods *and* services.

D. CONTROL OVER TISSUE AND OTHER BODILY MATERIAL WHICH HAS BEEN REMOVED

At a number of points in our discussion so far, it has been assumed tacitly that tissue and other bodily materials when removed can legally be categorised as *property* amenable to ownership, or at least, the assertion of rights over it. If this assumption be correct, a new set of issues emerges for discussion. These have to do with the rights of the person from whom the tissue is removed and any other party dealing with it to exercise some control over its use and, perhaps, be entitled to a part (or the whole) of any financial gain made through its use.

We saw in Chapter 11 that dealing with human ova, sperm and embryos is regulated by the Human Fertilisation and Embryology Act 1990. Control of these turns upon the terms of the legislation and not (in all probability) upon questions of property. Here, we are concerned with other body parts or material. The sort of circumstances the law must address include the following: the use by a pathologist of a piece of tissue removed for histological analysis, the retention of excised material so as to develop an archive for teaching and research and the use of excised material as part of the process of producing a new therapeutic agent.

Bernard M Dickens 'The Control of Living Body Materials' (1977) 27 University of Toronto Law Journal 142

A. THE SOURCE'S INCHOATE TITLE

The positive functions of control of a live person's separated body materials are to serve his interests as a human being, paying due regard to his autonomy and confidentiality, and in part to apply the means of acquisition of body materials to the uses that can be made of them, consistent with communal approval or tolerance. Negatively, the function of control is to give the human source preventive or remedial power over detrimental use of his body materials. It may be proposed that the donor's autonomy is served by providing for his indicated wishes and preferences to prevail posthumously as to the disposition of his body materials, and the law should make comparable provision for disposition during his lifetime. The legal principles that may be applied to this cause require identification, however, and no single principle may necessarily be derived from the different means of acquisition of body materials, nor govern the variety of their uses.

A philosophical approach to the origination from a living body of independently tangible material or of fluids capable of isolation may be to consider them *res nullius*, that is, corporeal items in the legal ownership of nobody. They might be reduced into possession by the first person to obtain physical control who intends to exercise control over them, in accordance with the test of classical jurisprudence. This prescription of possession from which ownership may be inferred would by definition afford the human source no prior interest. In a sophisticated legal system where personal property rights are highly developed, the list of items constituting *res nullius* is short. The concepts of property and ownership have tended to be pragmatic, evolving in response to the economic or spiritual recognition of objects as having value; 'property' describes a valuable right or interest in a thing, moreover, rather than the thing itself. In pre-history, for instance, when humans could survive only where land, natural crops, wild animals, and game were available without the application of systematic labour to agriculture and hunting or trapping, they had no value, and were not considered ownable. Use may expose scarcity, however, scarcity begets value, and value is concretized in property. Value is both material (or economic) and superstitious (including sentimental and spiritual), but it is only in recent times that separated body materials have become capable of a use that gives them value, whether for sale or for philanthropic dedication. Even in the case of cadavers, their employment in medical education occurred on a significant scale only when medicine evolved the conceit of being scientific, which happened after the common law had largely exhausted its capacity for free growth, so that creative legal use of cadavers required the formulation of legislation, namely anatomy acts.

No theoretical limit can be set to how far the law may go in recognizing new property interests. Materials as abstract as gas can be possessed and stolen, as may electricity, and vibration has been treated as an 'object' in trespass and possibly nuisance law. In 1940 it was observed that 'Atmospheric or etheric vibrations, in the form of radiated waves, have become one of the most important forces in the world, and at any moment a legal question may arise whether they are capable of property or possession.' While 'Knowledge or ideas, as such, do not constitute property', the mode of expression of an idea can attract copyright protection. Thus, a person's interest in producing the electrochemical activity that can be monitored in his brain may in the future be analysed in terms of property, rather than of privacy, and as, for instance, a meditative or creative technique, may become comparable to intellectual, literary, and industrial property.

The characterization of separated body materials as *res nullius* may serve the interests of neither the human source nor others. To suggest that material immediately passes into the absolute ownership of the hospital or physician undertaking or supervising its removal and intending to appropriate it might defeat the source's justifiable interest in its use or disposition and the purpose of its specific donation, for instance for diagnosis, transplantation, or a particular research project. It may be inadequate regarding even body waste, of which a person will normally relieve himself as speedily and conveniently as possible compatibly with social delicacy, expecting and hoping never to hear of it again. Sanitary regulations and the general law on nuisance require one in charge of premises or land on which such waste is discharged adequately to dispose of it . . .

Recognizing waste materials as *res nullius*, capable of exclusive legal control by the person first possessing them, clearly will not serve the interests of the human source. Similarly, recognition as *res nullius* of material such as a limb or digit severed from the human source in an accident or an assault may be inconsistent with his interest in its preservation for prompt surgical rejoining to his body. His claim to it should not be impaired by the chance of the item falling upon another's land or being retrieved and retained by a stranger not implicated in causing the loss. A better approach, therefore, may be to consider the human source as having an inchoate right of property in materials issuing from his body, which right he may expressly or by implication abandon to another, or similarly make prevail over a contending claim.

This may well accord to the sentimental reaction to the origination of body material in its separate state. The right is better considered inchoate than fully constituted, since the material may never in fact come under the source's notional or physical control. He may be unconscious, for instance, when it is separated, and it may be deemed abandoned, perhaps to a hospital, very soon after it is first isolated. Traditional jurisprudential tests of, for instance, intention, possession, and control as affecting ownership may more easily be preserved by considering the initial interest of the source *prima facie* a superior right to that of any other person, but a right only in prospect.

B. REMOVED AND DISCHARGED MATERIALS

In the absence of an express claim to ownership by the source of materials removed or discharged from his body, or of a necessary assumption of his best right, as in the case of an unconscious or dazed victim's interest in a severed replaceable limb, he may be required continuously to act or otherwise to show an intention to maintain his control in better repair than that of any other person. The required degree of demonstration of continuing interest will depend, of course, upon the circumstances. The analogy may be invoked of rights in international law to newly discovered territory, where it has been observed that 'an inchoate title could not prevail over the continuous and peaceful display of authority by another'. A source of materials may, for instance, set conditions upon another's possession, as when blood is donated upon condition that a contract price be paid, urine is given for diagnosis, or an eye is given for the purpose of pathologic examination, or he may give directions as to disposition.

In *Browning v Norton Children's Hospital* [(1974) 504 SW 2d 713 (Ky CA)], for instance, the court observed that 'when one consents to and authorizes an operation while a patient in a hospital (*absent any specific reservation, demand, or objection* to some normal procedure), he then and thereby, in effect, accepts all the rules, regulations, and the modus operandi of that hospital' as to disposal of surgically removed tissue. The right to make specific reservation, demand, or objection that supersedes the hospital's normal practice is worthy of note. The court's additional opinion that 'Is it the duty of the surgeon to take a dismembered part of a human body into his care and custody – for the amputee? We think not,' may be discounted in favour of a later view that 'It could not be said that a person has no property rights in wastes or other materials which were once a part of or contained within his body, but which normally are discarded after their separation from the body.' Nevertheless both judgments require the patient to take the initiative to express any specific reservation, demand, or objection prior to surgery or other removal. When surgery or discharge is complete, or when a pathologist has completed inspection of the material, the assumption of abandonment may arise.

The legal inference of the source's silence and passivity is that his inchoate right to his separated body material is yielded to the hospital or other possessor, such as a hairdresser. The proposal favouring the hospital's right is based both on the policy that the hospital's potential for creative use should prevail over a presumption that the silent patient gives possession on an implied condition of destruction, and on observable practice. In *Venner v State of Maryland* [(1976) 354 A 2d 483 (Md CA)] for instance, the court noted that 'It is not unknown for a person to assert a continuing right of ownership, dominion, or control, for good reason or for no reason, over such things as excrement, fluid waste, secretions, hair, fingernails, toenails, blood, and organs or other parts of the body, whether their separation from the body is intentional, accidental or merely the result of normal body functions,' but that 'By the force of social custom, we hold that when a person does nothing and says nothing to indicate an intent to assert his right of ownership, possession, or control over such material, the only rational inference is that he intends to abandon the material.'

In practice, of course, the material usually is fit only for destruction, and nothing is gained from asking whether this reflects the prevailing intention of the patient or of the hospital . . .

Regarding discharged material bearing less symbolic or spiritual weight than an advanced fetus, it may accordingly be proposed that the passive human source be deemed in principle to have abandoned his legal interest in it. If it comprises 'tissue' to be used for transplantation, his consent may be required under human tissue gift laws, but use may be made for other therapy and for research and teaching without reference to him; his consent, and a fortiori his informed consent, is not required. Reference to such use in a hospital admission or consent to treatment form may be useful, however, since this might overcome problems of using material immediately upon its origination from the source, perhaps while he is still under anaesthetic or otherwise of impaired perception.

This legal position should meet at least in part the despairing complaint of Dr Hugh Fudenberg that 'In most university hospitals [in the United States] it is not possible to take excess urine that is discarded after urinalysis or the excess few drops of blood discarded after blood is drawn for a blood test and use them to work out some new tests that could then be standardized for a new diagnosis of disease without getting the written consent of the person involved.' Nevertheless, the ethical constraints upon a physician with a professional or other interest in a potential tissue recipient attending or certifying the death of a potential donor may have to be extended by analogy to cover the situation of a source's presumed abandonment of usable materials. If an attending physician is going to want such materials for a use affording the patient no therapeutic or diagnostic benefit, the patient's express consent may have to be independently sought beforehand, lest abandonment of his property may appear to have been effected by the exercise of undue influence. The rebuttable legal presumption of the physician's undue influence serves generally to redress the inequality of the doctor-patient relation, but in this case it also affords protection to both parties against the donor later suspecting that the material did not have to be removed at all, but was taken to serve the physician's research interests . . .

It has been seen that abandonment must be into the legal control of another, as opposed to constituting the property *res nullius*. Express abandonment to an identified volunteer may be tantamount to a gift, but both spoken or another abandonment, and in particular implied abandonment, may leave some question as to the identity of the legal recipient. Varieties of usable materials and the means of their separation differ too widely for a definitive answer, but, because of scarcity of materials and competition for their use between patients in need, and also between physicians, surgeons, and comparable health professionals, an assumption of an institutional rather than a private successor may be favoured; that is, a hospital, clinic, or laboratory rather than an individual such as a removal surgeon, inspecting pathologist, potential researcher, or, for instance, transplant surgeon. Apart from obviating problems of succession to title upon death of the individual, and reducing the effect of the legal presumption of undue influence, this will increase the likelihood that use of the scarce material will be debated in scientific and ethical terms, rather than allowing decisions to be taken according to the private or secret choice of any one person. Just how scarce resources are institutionally allocated in medicine to assist the living and to promote research is a matter of grave and occasionally vital concern, on which far more information should be made available to the public. Development of this theme lies beyond the present study, but it may be preferable in itself, and compatible with observable trends in other areas where novel property interests have become identified, that control should rest with public rather than with private agencies. Such a preference would also be compatible with anatomy acts, which tend to provide for distribution of corpses to teaching hospitals and similar institutions but not to purely private agencies.

C. SPECIFICALLY DONATED MATERIALS
Beyond consideration of control of materials in which the source has no further interest, except perhaps as to the choice between destruction or general use, lies the issue of the source identifying a specific use or user. This may concern material he would not otherwise release, such as a healthy kidney or his bone marrow, and those whose release is for his therapeutic, diagnostic, or cosmetic advantage, but which he does not abandon. Where he sells material such as blood, skin, or urine, he may be taken to give an absolute title in the normal way of commerce, including rights to such aspects of his confidentiality as the sale may require. This is not to say, of course, that confidentiality is necessarily sacrificed, since a sale of, for instance, semen for artificial insemination, may require confidentiality to be preserved, even to the extent of prohibiting the donor from revealing his identity. Where sale does not occur or is illegal, philanthropic dedication may similarly pass title to the appointed recipient, which may be an institution or, for instance, a named sick relative . . .

It is clear that donation of material for application to a specified person or purpose (such as the donor's diagnosis) would give the hospital and its personnel no proprietary interest in it, except the 'special property' or 'qualified ownership' of a bailee. The bailment relation may remain until termination by the donor's revocation or by execution in the form of prescribed application of the materials to the intended recipient or purpose. It may be, however, that property will pass when the donor totally divests himself of possession by delivering them to, or allowing acquisition by, appropriate hospital personnel, who then become bailees of the identified recipient. The labour that medical specialists may need to give to preservation of the materials, and the skills they must devote to achieving effecting transfer to the recipient, may render it unsuitable to consider that the hospital or individuals concerned hold the materials for transfer as mere servants or agents of the donors or the donees. Destruction of an organ after transplantation would appear to be a personal injury, the organ being in the category of *res quae usu consumuntur*, but legal action would be more easily conceivable in negligence than in trespass to the person; indeed, trespass in the sense of interference unjustified by consent or necessity might be hard to show.

A hospital that holds as bailee an organ or other material that has been dedicated to a specific recipient or given for diagnosis or, for instance, to assist genetic counselling, but that either uses it for another recipient or purpose, or simply destroys it, would seem in principle to be liable in conversion. Action would be at the instance of the human source or the recipient, depending on which of them had the immediate right to possession of the material. A slight conceptual problem with the tort of conversion concerns the traditional remedy of pecuniary damages, however, since 'the measure of damages for conversion is the full value of the chattel so that the action, in effect, forces an involuntary purchase on the convertor'. Human tissue legislation may make active promotion of a sale 'invalid as being contrary to public policy', but clearly public policy does not prevent such 'involuntary purchase'; the difficulty raised is establishing 'the full value' in terms of market criteria or the cost of replacement. This lack of apparent value may protect the hospital from a larceny charge, but liability in conversion may remain, since 'the plaintiff is also entitled to compensation for any special damage which the law does not regard as too remote'. A quantifiable loss may be shown regarding the lost opportunity for receiving satisfaction from giving benefit to the specified recipient or cause, or for obtaining a transplant or transfusion or the benefit of better diagnosis or counselling. Whether a potential plaintiff can show such special damage more easily by acting in conversion rather than in negligence is a matter of judgment in each particular case. The question of causation in negligence goes to liability itself, however, whereas in conversion it goes only to the quantum of damages recoverable, giving advantage to proceedings in conversion. Since a hospital's duty as bailee generally arises only upon the owner expressly intimating his interest in the separated materials, however, an intended recipient may have difficulty acting in conversion.

An uncertain issue arises when the source expressly directs a hospital to destroy material it appropriates instead. Such instruction, if a hospital is prepared to accept it, may amount to abandonment, but a patient's need for confidentiality may give him an interest in his body material being destroyed rather than simply left at large. In principle, destruction is a right of ownership, and frustration of its exercise may amount to such interference with the right of a person entitled to possession as constitutes conversion. A claim in conversion regarding anonymous material may offend against the public interest, but a court not wishing to dismiss a claim on policy grounds, and not wishing to find for a fractious plaintiff and require the defendant hospital to pay even nominal damages and perhaps costs, could exonerate the hospital under the principle *de minimis non curat lex*.

Principles of the reasoning above would be generally applicable to materials a subject dedicates to experimentation specified, by reference to institution, project, or principal investigator, in a consent form or as understood in a verbal consent. When a project proves abortive, for instance because its early results are too adverse to subjects, because its funds fail, or because a key investigator departs, and when a project has materials surplus to its needs for completion, materials already isolated may conscientiously be used in another project without renewed consent, rather than be wasted. If consent can conveniently be sought there may be a case in ethics and etiquette for requiring the subject-donor to be approached, but the donation may be seen preferably in legal principle as a gift rather than a bailment. Conditions may be imposed upon gifts, but not if they are contrary to public policy or too inconsistent with the nature of an absolute gift. In practice, details of the research given in a consent form contribute to the informed quality of the subject's consent, and are not a guarantee of specific use. Law and ethics may coincide, however, in proscribing the deceitful use of such information to induce the donation of materials intended *ab initio* for another use.

The condition for alternative use without express consent is, however, preservation of the subject's confidentiality. No legal problem may arise in conscientious use in one project of material given for another project where data accompanying the material are anonymous. Where the subject is identifiable from data already given, however, or where further information may be required from him in person or from his medical record, confidentiality requires that his prior consent be obtained. A research subject is frequently informed expressly of his rights to withdraw from the study at any time, but withdrawal is not retrospective so as to deny either use of body materials already contributed, or access to data already gathered for that project, so that material and data may be used for any subsequent project in which they may anonymously serve. It may seem that giving wider circulation than was initially agreed upon with an identifiable subject to information about, for instance, his body weight, allergies, eating habits, and blood pressure, can cause him so little detriment as to fall within the legal principle *de minimis non curat lex*, but neutral physiological data may in some cases be socially sensitive, as, for instance, results of phallometric testing disclosing a male's erotic preferences.

Professor Dickens identifies the two central questions:

(1) can the donor assert any *right to control* tissue once removed from him? and,

(2) if he can in principle, in what circumstances, if any, will he lose that right?

1. The right to control

It is important to notice the historical context in which these questions fall to be considered. In particular, it was assumed by the middle of the nineteenth century that it was a rule of English law that a corpse cannot be the subject of property. This 'non-property rule' may have influenced the law's attitude to the living body and parts of it.

Peter Skegg 'Human Corpses, Medical Specimens and the Law of Property' (1976) 4 Anglo-American Law Review 412

The no property rule appears to have been first mentioned in a court of law in the eighteenth century, in *Dr Handayside's* trover was there brought against the doctor, for the body of a pair of 'Siamese twins'. The case was not reported, nor was it mentioned in the legal works published later in the eighteenth century, where reference to it might have been expected. It was first noted early in the nineteenth century, by East, who could not have had any personal knowledge of the case. He simply recorded that in 'the case of Dr Handayside, where trover was brought against him for two children that grew together; Lord CJ Willes held the action would not lie, as no person had any property in corpses'. . . .

The one properly reported case in which an English judge has used the no property doctrine to support his decision is *Williams v Williams* [(1882) 20 Ch D 659] . . .

In delivering his judgment, Jay, J said that in English law there can be no property in the dead body of a human being. He quoted Erle, J's dictum in *R v Sharpe* to support that view. He then went on to discuss the executors' right to possession of the body prior to burial, and said that it followed from this that a man could not dispose of his body by will. Having reached this conclusion, he said that it also followed from there being no property in a corpse, that a man could not dispose of it by will. . .

It is remarkable how slight is the authority in favour of the no property rule. *Dr Handayside's* case and *Williams v Williams* are the only cases in which the no property rule appears to have constituted at least part of the *ratio decidendi*. Neither of these cases is binding on the higher English courts. But, granted that these courts are free to take a different view, are there cogent reasons for their doing so?

A change in the traditional view need not bring about very far-reaching changes in the law relating to corpses. It has already been suggested that treating the corpse as the subject of property need not of itself enable a person to bequeath his body, or to give binding directions as to what is done with it after his death. Ownership could vest in the executors, or whoever else is now under the duty to dispose of it and has a right to possession for that purpose. Then, as now, that person could have a considerable discretion as to the mode of disposal.

Treating the corpse as the subject of property would not necessarily affect the sale of bodies or parts of bodies. The property interest in the corpse could be treated as one which could not be divested. In any case, the fact that corpses have not been regarded as the subject of property has not prevented payments for whole corpses in the past, and does not prevent payments for parts of corpses at present . . .

It is undesirable that, for example, many anatomical specimens on the shelves of medical schools, and cadaveric organs and tissues awaiting transplantation, should be to a greater or lesser extent outside the range of the law. Quaint anomaly that the no property rule may be, there is little to be said for retaining it if it has this effect and could be jettisoned without undesirable consequences.

The higher courts could reverse the earlier line of authority, and hold that a corpse is the subject of property. However, they are more likely to avoid a direct challenge to the traditional view, and simply qualify it in a way which enables them to deal with the problem before them. There are several ways in which this could be done.

One possibility would be to retain the traditional view in relation to whole corpses, but to hold that, just as things severed from reality become personalty, so things severed from bodies become the subject of property. This approach, which is highly desirable with parts removed from living bodies, would provide adequate legal protection in respect of anatomical specimens and tissues and organs for transplantation. However, it would not improve the existing legal position in relation to whole corpses. Fortunately, there are more wide-ranging approaches which could be adopted by the courts.

There is no hint of a qualification to the no property rule in the decided English cases. However, Sir James Fitzjames Stephen mentioned one possible qualification in his extrajudicial writings. He wrote that the dead body of a human being 'cannot, so long at all events as it exists as such, become the property of any one', and explained this qualification with the observation: 'I suppose, however, that anatomical specimens and the like are personal property.' This presaged the decision of the High Court of Australia in *Doodeward v Spence* [(1908) 6 CLR 406]. The subject matter of this action for conversion and detinue was the corpse of a two-headed child. The child had died before birth in New Zealand, 40 years earlier, and its mother's doctor had taken the body away with him. He preserved it in a bottle of spirits, and kept it in his surgery as a curiosity. On his death the specimen was sold by auction. The successful bidder was Doodeward's father, from whom it passed to Doodeward. The bottle and its contents were seized under warrant, for use in criminal proceedings, in which Doodeward was prosecuted for publicly exhibiting the specimen for gain, 'to the manifest outrage of public decency'. At the conclusion of the prosecution, in which Doodeward had pleaded guilty, the judge refused to order that the corpse be handed back to him. Doodeward then commenced proceedings to recover it. He was non-suited in a District Court on the ground that there was no property in the subject matter of the action. He appealed, first to the Supreme Court of New South Wales, as the District Court of Appeal, and then to the High Court of Australia. By the time the case reached the High Court, the bottle and spirits had been returned to him. However, the corpse was retained at the University Museum, on behalf of the defendant, a Sub-Inspector of Police.

In the High Court, all three Judges accepted that immediately after death a corpse is not the subject of property. However, the judgment of Griffith, CJ, with which the other judge who made up the majority expressed his agreement, can be interpreted as laying down that a corpse can be so changed that it becomes the subject of property. Griffith, CJ, took the view that, at least in Australia, it was not necessarily unlawful to retain a corpse for a purpose other than immediate burial. He laid down a proposition which applied to those cases where a person had, by the lawful exercise of work or skill, so dealt with a corpse in his lawful possession that it had acquired some attributes differentiating it from a mere corpse awaiting burial. In these cases, he said, the person acquires a right to possession of the corpse or part thereof – at least as against anyone who is not entitled to have the object delivered up to him, for the purpose of burial. Griffith, CJ, said he did not know of any definition of property which was not wide enough to include such a right of permanent possession. He said that, so far as this right constitutes property, a corpse or part thereof is capable by law of becoming the subject of property. Applying his principle to the case before him, Griffith, CJ, said that the evidence showed that the body had come 'not unlawfully' into the doctor's possession, that 'some – perhaps not much – work and skill had been bestowed by him upon it', and that it had acquired an actual pecuniary value. He allowed the appeal.

One drawback of Griffith, CJ's principle is the difficulty of its application. If the principle were adopted in England, it would no doubt apply to Egyptian mummies in museum collections and probably also to shrunken heads, or heads which had been tattooed after death. But much more difficult would be the question of whether it would apply to anatomical specimens, and tissues and organs awaiting transplantation. If the English courts were prepared to apply the principle in the same way as the majority of the High Court of Australia in *Doodeward v Spence* these objects might very often be considered the subject of property. However, when dealing with an object on which no more labour or skill had been expended than was on the corpse in *Doodeward v Spence*, which had simply been placed in spirits, an English court might favour the approach of the dissenting Judge in *Doodeward v Spence*. He said that 'No skill or labour has been exercised on it; and there has been no change in its character.' It would be better to find a principle which applies more naturally to parts taken from corpses for medical purposes, and indeed, in some circumstances, to whole bodies. To find such a principle, it is desirable to look to Scots law.

Scots institutional writers, and *dicta* in the Court of Justiciary in *Dewar v HM Advocate* [1945 JC 5] support the view that in Scots law a corpse is the subject of property (and can therefore be stolen), until such time as it is buried or otherwise disposed of. This view appears to have resulted from a misunderstanding of an earlier case [*Mackenzie* (1733)]. However, it is more in keeping with the raison d'etre of the traditional English view than any of the other approaches, including the one hitherto adopted in the English courts. It was only after the corpse had been buried in consecrated ground that ecclesiastical law prevented interferences with it. Buried corpses are now perfectly adequately protected by the common law crime exemplified in *R v Sharpe,* which is the English equivalent of the Scots crime of violation of sepulchres. Where English law is inadequate is in the rather limited protection it extends to corpses or parts of corpses prior to burial or cremation. This inadequacy could be overcome by the courts taking the view that, until such time as a corpse or part thereof is buried, cremated, or otherwise disposed of, it is the subject of property. Unburied corpses, and anatomical specimens and transplant material removed from corpses, would then be protected by, amongst other things, the crime of theft and the tort of trespass to goods.

It would be desirable for the English courts to go further than Scots authority yet does, and take the view that it is only while corpses or the remains of corpses are buried, or dispersed following cremation, that they are not the subject of property. This would enable the courts to extend more effective legal control, not only over corpses awaiting burial and cremation, but also over ashes which had not been buried or dispersed, and human remains which had been disinterred.

For a further scholarly discussion of the 'no property' rule and its basis, see P Matthews 'Whose Body? People as Property' [1983] Current Legal Problems 193, especially 208-214. There are very few English cases to assist us in reaching a view. This may not be surprising historically, but given the current growth in medical and pharmaceutical research there is an increasingly urgent need to clarify the law. In *R v Welsh* [1974] RTR 478 and *R v Rothery* [1976] RTR 550, the matter for the court was whether, respectively, urine and blood were capable of being stolen, ie were property. In both cases the Court of Appeal assumed that they could be.

Apart from these cases, the English case law is of little help. Indeed, there are few cases in the common law world. In *Procurement and Transfer of Human Tissues and Organs* (Working Paper 66, 1992) the Canadian Law Reform Commission surveyed what little case law there is, including the most significant case, *Moore v Regents of University of California* (1990) 793 P 2d 479.

Canadian Law Reform Commission, Procurement and Transfer of Human Tissues and Organs (Paper No 66, 1992)

In the transplantation and biotechnological age of the late twentieth century, should the law affirm or abandon the seventeenth-century legal maxim that there is no property in a body? Modern medical practice and the evolution of the law have called into question the validity of that rule. Human bodies, bodily parts, tissues and substances are increasingly given, transferred, taken and preserved for years, for a variety of therapeutic uses and purposes. Some bodily substances are sold. If we cannot own our bodies or bodily parts, what may we do with them?

Our analysis suggests that the common law recognizes limited property interests in the human body for particular purposes. Seeking to avoid abhorrent ethical and commercial connotations, the common law reiterates the no-property rule. At the same time, it recognizes an executor's or a family's rights of possession to the body of a deceased potential donor. Such limited possessory interests protect familial, moral and religious sentiment. For living donors, the law has also been loath to recognize property concepts in the body. It tends to depend on important, but sometimes limited, principles of informed consent and emotional distress damages, to govern the control, transfer or non-consensual use of extracorporeal tissue. In the face of the new biomedical and biotechnological imperative, our legal concept and definition of property seem increasingly critical. New developments challenge the traditional legal ambivalence of the no-property rule. They invite society to rethink its choices for a tissue transfer regime that continues to advance human dignity, privacy and bodily integrity in this new age.

Does the no-property rule encompass living donors? In Canada, there appears to be no case that specifically addresses the issue. In cases in the United States, the courts have tended to apply the no-property rule to tissue disputes involving living donors, although there are recent trends to the contrary. Four general areas in which property concepts have been at issue involve the non-consensual discarding of donated tissue, the control and transfer of deposited bodily substances, the use of non-consensually extracted bodily tissues or substances and the commercial value of bodily substances and tissue.

Cases in the United States have arisen over the discarding of donated or deposited human tissue without the consent of the patient-depositor. In two cases, one involving lost eye tissue that was being examined for cancer and another involving the disposal without consent of reproductive matter in an infertility clinic, courts have avoided resolving patients' damage claims in terms of property. Instead, they have preferred to analyse them in terms of mental shock or distress to the patient. Those cases seem to suggest that some courts in the United States have extended the no-property-in-a-corpse rule to a no-property-in-bodily-parts rule.

Commentators have critiqued the no-property-in-bodily-parts tendency for living donors. Some jurisdictions significantly limit nervous shock claims. It is argued that even when nervous shock claims and damages are available, they do not address instances when the return of valuable human tissue or material is sought. The suggestion is that property concepts would better protect an individual's autonomy and person, in addition to clarifying legal rights and duties regarding the control of human tissue in particular circumstances. For example, when an institution destroys a valuable human tissue without consent in a jurisdiction that limits mental damages, common law property principles concerning the destruction or spoilage of materials rightfully in one's possession might prove helpful in defining legal rights, duties and grounds of recovery.

. . . Control and Transfer Cases

The issue of rights and duties regarding the control and transfer of human tissues has arisen most acutely in some recent cases involving human reproductive material. While there are no reported Canadian cases on this point, an American couple was recently successful in litigating the control of and right to transfer their frozen embryo from an east-coast infertility clinic to a west-coast clinic [*York v Jones* (1989) 717 F Supp 421 (ED Va)]. In France, the wife of a deceased sperm depositor argued that she had a right to her husband's frozen sperm, which he had deposited for preservation after learning that he would undergo cancer treatments that risked making him sterile [*Parpalaix v CECOS* (1984)]. The court expressly rejected the argument that frozen semen was property, on grounds that human reproductive material was neither inheritable nor an object of commerce. Nevertheless, it ruled that the sperm bank must return the frozen semen to the wife of the depositor, as a result of an understanding between the depositor and the sperm bank. That decision suggests that agreements between tissue banks and depositors, as reflected in well-drafted informed consent forms, might help minimize disputes over the control of deposited tissues, in the absence of legislation or professional standards that sufficiently address the issue.

Disputes over reproductive substances are helpful in identifying concerns and values at issue in potential disputes over other human tissues and substances. For example, the growth in tissue banking may make the rights and duties in controlling other deposited, valuable human tissue a more prominent medical-legal issue. Consent forms for autologous blood banking in Canada have referred to deposited blood in terms of property, as have professional protocols for the banking of reproductive and genetic materials in the United States.

. . . Non-consensual Invasion Cases

As the consent doctrine of medical malpractice law protects against the non-consensual invasion of a patient's body, so too might bodily-property principles help protect against the non-consensual use or disposition of bodily substances or tissues that have been removed from the body. The idea was recently broached by the Supreme Court of Canada [*R v Dyment* [1988] 2 SCR 417].

The court held a physician's non-consensual taking and use of a patient's blood to be an unreasonable seizure under the *Canadian Charter of Rights and Freedoms*. After taking a blood sample from an unconscious, hospitalized patient who had been injured in an automobile accident, the physician gave the sample to a police officer. The blood was analysed and later offered as evidence of drunken driving. The opinion may suggest a relationship between bodily property, patient autonomy, physical integrity and human dignity.

> As I have attempted to indicate earlier, *the use of a person's body without his consent to obtain information about him, invades an area of personal privacy essential to the maintenance of his human dignity*. . . . It was a perfectly reasonable thing for a doctor

who had been entrusted with the medical care of a patient to do. However, I would emphasize that the doctor's sole justification for taking the blood sample was that it was to be used for medical purposes. He had no right to take Mr. Dayment's blood for other purposes. *I do not wish to put the matter on the basis of property considerations, although it would not be too far-fetched to do so.* Some provinces expressly vest the property of blood samples in the hospital, a matter I consider wholly irrelevant . . . Specifically, I think the protection of the *Charter* extends to prevent a police officer, an agent of the state, from taking a substance as intimately personal as a person's blood from a person who holds it subject to a duty to respect the dignity and privacy of that person.

. . . Property and Personhood Cases

The concept of property as a protectorate of fundamental values of personhood has been debated in a recent American case of international significance. In *Moore v Regents of the University of California* [(1990) 793 P 2d 479] a leukemia patient claimed that, without his knowledge or consent, his university doctors used his cells and tissue to develop and patent a commercially valuable anticancer drug. The drug is based on a cell line derived from the patient's diseased spleen which had been surgically removed for treatment. The patient argued that he is owed a rightful share of money generated by the patent, owing to the misappropriation of his bodily tissues.

Important aspects of the case were recently decided by the California Supreme Court. A lower court had upheld the patient's right to sue on the basis of a property interest:

> We have approached this issue with caution. The evolution of civilization from slavery to freedom, from regarding people as chattels to recognition of the individual dignity of each person, necessitates prudence in attributing the qualities of property to human tissue. There is, however, a dramatic difference between having property rights in one's own body and being the property of another. . . .
>
> *The essence of a property interest – the ultimate right of control – therefore exists with regard to one's human body. . . .*
>
> *A patient must have the ultimate power to control what becomes of his or her tissues. To hold otherwise would open the door to a massive invasion of human privacy and dignity in the name of medical progress.*

In reviewing the lower court decision, the California Supreme Court agreed that the patient may sue for violations of bodily integrity and human dignity, but it limited the basis for doing so to more conventional medico-legal grounds.

The majority of the court held that the patient may sue for a breach of informed-consent duties and for a breach of the duties of loyalty to the patient. The majority reasoned that if the patient's claims were proven true, those claims would show that the doctor had an undisclosed commercial interest in the patient's tissue at the time he recommended the surgical removal of the spleen, that this non-therapeutic interest might influence the doctor's recommended course of treatment and that a reasonable patient in those circumstances would generally want to be informed of potentially conflicting interests before treatment.

> Accordingly, we hold that a physician who is seeking a patient's consent for a medical procedure must, in order to satisfy his fiduciary duty and to obtain the patient's informed consent, disclose personal interests unrelated to the patient's health, whether research or economic, that may affect his medical judgment.

A minority of the court agreed that the patient should be able to sue on informed-consent and fiduciary-duty grounds, but insisted that property grounds would best protect a patient's bodily integrity, privacy and dignity.

The divergent conclusions on the property claim flow, in part, from divergent views on existing law. The majority and minority views differed sharply over: (1) whether a state law that regulates the disposal of excised tissue extinguishes, or lets survive, patients' pre-excision proprietary rights to control post-excision use of the tissue; (2) whether the patented cell line and resulting drug were distinct proprietary products invented from raw materials; and (3) whether the protections of federal law affect a property-based claim for unauthorized use of excised tissue – especially for the six-year post-surgical, pre-patent era, when Moore's bodily substances were periodically extracted allegedly to supply the defendants' research and commercialization efforts.

The majority and minority opinions also sharply diverged on broader policy concerns, such as the role of the courts and legislature in judging whether novel patient bodily-property claims would create liability destructive of beneficial medical research. Without absolutely ruling out such claims, the majority found 'no pressing need' to recognize them, given the protection it perceived in the informed-consent and fiduciary-duty remedies. The minority rejected this view, arguing that the equities of preventing unjust enrichment and physical and moral exploitation of patients outweighed overstated liability concerns. It argued further that the commercial relations and ambiguities in the case – over whether informed consent or fiduciary duties extend to biotechnological and drug companies – meant that patients would be insufficiently protected without bodily property claims.

Clearly, it is important to examine the judgments in *Moore* in some detail.

Moore v Regents of the University of California (1990) 793 P 2d 479 (Cal Sup Ct)

Panelli J: Our only task in reviewing a ruling on a demurrer is to determine whether the complaint states a cause of action. Accordingly, we assume that the complaint's properly pleaded material allegations are true and give the complaint a reasonable interpretation by reading it as a whole and all its parts in their context. (*Phillips v Desert Hospital Dist* (1989) 49 Cal. 3d 699, 702; *Bland v Kirwan* (1985) 39 Cal 3d 311, 318; *Tameny v Atlantic Richfield Co* (1980) 27 Cal 3d 167, 170.) We do not, however, assume the truth of contentions, deductions, or conclusions of fact or law. (*Daar v Yellow Cab Co* (1967) 67 Cal 2d 695, 713.) For those purposes we briefly summarize the pertinent factual allegations of the 50-page complaint.

The plaintiff is John Moore (Moore), who underwent treatment for hairy-cell leukemia at the Medical Center of the University of California at Los Angeles (UCLA Medical Center). The five defendants are: (1) Dr. David W. Golde (Golde), a physician who attended Moore at UCLA Medical Center; (2) the Regents of University of California (Regents), who own and operate the university; (3) Shirley W. Quan, a researcher employed by the Regents; (4) Genetics Institute, Inc. (Genetics Institute); and (5) Sandoz Pharmaceuticals Corporation and related entities (collectively Sandoz).

Moore first visited UCLA Medical Center on October 5, 1976, shortly after he learned that he had hairy-cell leukemia. After hospitalizing Moore and 'withdr[awing] extensive amounts of blood, bone marrow aspirate, and other bodily substances,' Golde confirmed that diagnosis. At this time all defendants, including Golde, were aware that 'certain blood products and blood components were of great value in a number of commercial and scientific efforts' and that access to a patient whose blood contained these substances would provide 'competitive, commercial, and scientific advantages.'

On October 8, 1976, Golde recommended that Moore's spleen be removed. Golde informed Moore 'that he had reason to fear for his life, and that the proposed splenectomy operation . . . was necessary to slow down the progress of his disease.' Based on Golde's representations, Moore signed a written consent form authorizing the splenectomy.

Before the operation, Golde and Quan 'formed the intent and made arrangements to obtain portions of [Moore's] spleen following its removal' and to take them to a separate research unit. Golde gave written instructions to this effect on October 18 and 19, 1976. These research activities 'were not intended to have . . . any relation to [Moore's] medical . . . care.' However, neither Golde nor Quan informed Moore of their plans to conduct this research or requested his permission. Surgeons at UCLA Medical Center, whom the complaint does not name as defendants, removed Moore's spleen on October 20, 1976.

Moore returned to the UCLA Medical Center several times between November 1976 and September 1983. He did so at Golde's direction and based upon representations 'that such visits were necessary and required for his health and well-being, and based upon the trust inherent in and by virtue of the physician-patient relationship. . . .' On each of these visits Golde withdrew additional samples of 'blood, blood serum, skin, bone marrow aspirate, and sperm.' On each occasion Moore traveled to the UCLA Medical Center from his home in Seattle because he had been told that the procedures were to be performed only there and only under Golde's direction.

'In fact, [however] throughout the period of time that [Moore] was under [Golde's] care and treatment, . . . the defendants were actively involved in a number of activities which they concealed from [Moore]. . . .' Specifically, defendants were conducting research on Moore's cells and planned to 'benefit financially and competitively . . . [by exploiting the cells] and [their] exclusive access to [the cells] by virtue of [Golde's] on-going physician-patient relationship. . . .

Sometime before August 1979, Golde established a cell-line from Moore's T-lymphocytes. On January 30, 1981, the Regents applied for a patent on the cell-line, listing Golde and Quan as inventors. '[B]y virtue of an established policy . . . [the] Regents, Golde, and Quan would share in any royalties or profits . . . arising out of [the] patent.' The patent issued on March 20, 1984, naming Golde and Quan as the inventors of the cell-line and the Regents as the assignee of the patent. (U.S. Patent No. 4,438, 032 (Mar. 20, 1984).)

The Regent's patent also covers various methods for using the cell-line to produce lymphokines. Moore admits in his complaint that 'the true clinical potential of each of the lymphokines [is] difficult to predict, [but] . . . competing commercial firms in these relevant fields have published reports in biotechnology industry periodicals predicting a potential market of approximately $3.01 Billion Dollars by the year 1990 for a whole range of [such lymphokines] . . .'

With the Regent's assistance, Golde negotiated agreements for commercial development of the cell-line and products to be derived from it. Under an agreement with Genetics Institute, Golde 'became a paid consultant' and 'acquired the rights to 75,000 shares of common stock'. Genetics Institute also agreed to pay Golde and the Regents 'at least $330,000 over three years, including a pro-rata share of [Golde's] salary and fringe benefits, in exchange for . . . exclusive access to the materials and research performed' on the cell-line and products derived from it. On June 4, 1982, Sandoz 'was added to the agreement,' and compensation payable to Golde and the Regents was increased by $110,000. '[T]hroughout this period, . . . Quan spent as much as 70 [percent] of her time working for [the] Regents on research' related to the cell-line.

Based upon these allegations, Moore attempted to state 13 causes of action. Each defendant demurred to each purported cause of action. The superior court, however, expressly considered the validity of only the first cause of action, conversion. Reasoning that the remaining causes of action incorporated the earlier defective allegations, the superior court sustained a general demurrer to the entire complaint with leave to amend. In a subsequent proceeding, the superior court sustained Genetics Institute's and Sandoz's demurrers without leave to amend on the grounds that Moore had not stated a cause of action for conversion and that the complaint's allegations about the entities' secondary liability were too conclusory. In accordance with its earlier ruling that the defective allegations about conversion rendered the entire complaint insufficient, the superior court took the remaining demurrers off its calendar.

With one justice dissenting, the Court of Appeal reversed, holding that the complaint did state a cause of action for conversion. The Court of Appeal agreed with the superior court that the allegations against Genetics Institute and Sandoz were insufficient, but directed the superior court to give Moore leave to amend. The Court of Appeal also directed the superior court to decide 'the remaining causes of action, which [had] never been expressly ruled upon.' . . .

Moore also attempts to characterize the invasion of his rights as a conversion – a tort that protects against interference with possessory and ownership interests in personal property. He theorizes that he continued to own his cells following their removal from his body, at least for the purpose of directing their use, and that he never consented to their use in potentially lucrative medical research. Thus, to complete Moore's argument, defendants' unauthorized use of his cells constitutes a conversion. As a result of the alleged conversion, Moore claims a proprietary interest in each of the products that any of the defendants might ever create from his cells or the patented cell-line.

No court, however, has ever in a reported decision imposed conversion liability for the use of human cells in medical research. While that fact does not end our inquiry, it raises a flag of caution. In effect, what Moore is asking us to do is to impose a tort duty on scientists to investigate the consensual pedigree of each human cell sample used in research. To impose such a duty, which would affect medical research of importance to all of society, implicates policy concerns far removed from the traditional, two-party ownership disputes in which the law of conversion arose. Invoking a tort theory originally used to determine whether the loser or the finder of a horse had the better title, Moore claims ownership of the results of socially important medical research, including the genetic code for chemicals that regulate the functions of every human being's immune system.

Accordingly, we first consider whether the tort of conversion clearly gives Moore a cause of action under existing law. We do not believe it does. Because of the novelty of Moore's claim to own the biological materials at issue, to apply the theory of conversion in this context would frankly have to be recognized as an extension of the theory. Therefore, we consider next whether it is advisable to extend the tort to this context.

1. Moore's Claim Under Existing Law

'To establish a conversion, plaintiff must establish an actual interference with his ownership or right of possession. . . . Where plaintiff neither has title to the property alleged to have been converted, nor possession thereof, he cannot maintain an action for conversion.' (*Del E Webb Corpn v Structural Materials Co* (1981) 123 Cal App 3d 593, 610-611. See also *General Motors A Corpn v Dallas* (1926) 198 Cal, 365, 370.)

Since Moore clearly did not expect to retain possession of his cells following their removal, to sue for their conversion he must have retained an ownership interest in them. But there are several reasons to doubt that he did retain any such interest. First, no reported judicial decision supports Moore's claim, either directly or by close analogy. Second, California statutory law drastically limits any continuing interest of a patient in excised cells. Third, the subject matters of the Regents' patent – the patented cell-line and the products derived from it – cannot be Moore's property.

Neither the Court of Appeal's opinion, the parties' briefs, nor our research discloses a case holding that a person retains a sufficient interest in excised cells to support a cause of action for conversion. We do not find this surprising, since the laws governing such things as human tissues, transplantable organs, blood, fetuses, pituitary glands, corneal tissue, and dead bodies deal with human biological materials as objects sui generis, regulating their disposition to achieve policy goals rather than abandoning them to the general law of personal property. It is these specialized statutes, not the law of conversion, to which courts ordinarily should and do look for guidance on the disposition of human biological materials . . .

The next consideration that makes Moore's claim of ownership problematic is California statutory law, which drastically limits a patient's control over excised cells. Pursuant to Health and Safety Code section 7054.4, '[n]otwithstanding any other provision of law, recognizable anatomical parts, human tissues, anatomical human remains, or infectious waste following conclusion of scientific use shall be disposed of by interment, incineration, or any other method determined by the state department [of health services] to protect the public health and safety.' Clearly the Legislature did not specifically intend this statute to resolve the question of whether a patient is entitled to compensation for the nonconsensual use of excised cells. A primary object of the statute is to ensure the safe handling of potentially hazardous biological waste materials. Yet one cannot escape the conclusion that the statute's practical effect is to limit, dramatically, a patient's control over excised cells. By restricting how excised cells may be used and requiring their eventual destruction, the statute eliminates so many of the rights ordinarily attached to property that one cannot simply assume that what is left amounts to 'property' or 'ownership' for purposes of conversion law.

It may be that some limited right to control the use of excised cells does survive the operation of this statute. There is, for example, no need to read the statute to permit 'scientific use' contrary to the patient's expressed wish. A fully-informed patient may always withhold consent to treatment by a physician whose research plans the patient does not approve. That right, however, as already discussed, is protected by the fiduciary-duty and informed-consent theories.

Finally, the subject matter of the Regent's patent – the patented cell-line and the products derived from it – cannot be Moore's property. This is because the patented cell-line is both factually and legally distinct from the cells taken from Moore's body. Federal law permits the patenting of organisms that represent the product of 'human ingenuity,' but not naturally occurring organisms. (*Diamond v Chakrabarty, supra*, 447 US 303, 309-310.) Human cell-lines are patentable because '[l]ong term adaptation and growth of human tissues and cells in culture is difficult – often considered an art . . .' and the probability of success is low. (OTA Rep., *supra*, at p. 33.) It is this inventive effort that patent law rewards, not the discovery of naturally occurring raw materials. Thus, Moore's allegations that he owns the cell-line and the products derived from it are inconsistent with the patent, which constitutes an authoritative determination that the cell-line is the product of invention. Since such allegations are nothing more than arguments or conclusions of law, they of course do not bind us. (*Daar v Yellow Cab Co, supra*, 67 Cal, 2d at p 71.)

2. Should Conversion Liability Be Extended?

As we have discussed, Moore's novel claim to own the biological materials at issue in this case is problematic, at best. Accordingly, his attempt to apply the theory of conversion within this context must frankly be recognized as a request to extend that theory. While we do not purport to hold that excised cells can never be property for any purpose whatsoever, the novelty of Moore's claim demands express consideration of the policies to be served by extending liability (cf. *Nally v Grace Community Church, supra*, 47 Cal.3d at pp. 291-300; *Foley v Interactive Data, supra*, 47 Cal.3d at pp. 634-700; *Brown v Superior Court, supra*, 44 Cal 3d at pp 1061-1065) rather than blind deference to a complaint alleging as a legal conclusion the existence of a cause of action.

There are three reasons why it is inappropriate to impose liability for conversion based upon the allegations of Moore's complaint. First, a fair balancing of the relevant policy considerations counsels against extending the tort. Second, problems in this area are better suited to legislative resolution. Third, the tort of conversion is not necessary to protect patients' rights. For these reasons, we conclude that the use of excised human cells in medical research does not amount to a conversion . . .

The extension of conversion law into this area will hinder research by restricting access to the necessary raw materials. Thousands of human cell-lines already exist in tissue repositories, such as the American Type Culture Collection and those operated by the National Institutes of Health and the American Cancer Society. These repositories respond to tens of thousands of requests for samples annually. Since the patent office requires the holders of patents on cell-lines to make samples available to anyone, many patent holders place their cell-lines in repositories to avoid the administrative burden of responding to requests. (OTA Rep, *supra*, at p 53.) At present, human cell-lines are routinely copied and distributed to other researchers for experimental purposes, usually free of charge. This exchange of scientific materials, which still is relatively free and efficient, will surely be compromised if each cell sample becomes the potential subject matter of a lawsuit (OTA Rep, *supra*, at p 52).

To expand liability by extending conversion law into this area would have a broad impact. The House Committee on Science and Technology of the United States Congress found that '49 percent of the researchers at medical institutions surveyed used human tissues or cells in their research.' Many receive grants from the National Institute of Health for this work (OTA Rep, *supra*, at p 52). In addition, 'there are nearly 350 commercial biotechnology firms in the United States actively engaged in biotechnology research and commercial product developments and approximately 25 to 30 percent appear to be engaged in research to develop a human therapeutic or diagnostic reagent . . . Most, but not all, of the human therapeutic products are derived from human tissues and cells, or human cell-lines or cloned genes.' (*Id*, at p 56.) . . .

Lucas CJ, Eagelson, Kennard and Arabian JJ concurred.

The majority remanded the case for trial on the issue of whether Moore gave a valid consent for research to be undertaken on his tissue given that the doctors owed Moore a fiduciary duty to disclose their 'personal interests unrelated to the patient's health, whether research or economic, that may affect [the doctor's] medical judgment'. Mosk J filed a powerful dissent.

Mosk J: The majority first take the position that Moore has no cause of action for conversion under existing law because he retained no 'ownership interest' in his cells after they were removed from his body. To state a conversion cause of action a plaintiff must allege his 'ownership or right to possession of the property at the time of the conversion' (*Baldwin v Marina City Properties Inc* (1978) 79 Cal App 3d 393, 410). Here the complaint defines Moore's 'Blood and Bodily Substances' to include inter alia his blood, his bodily tissues, his cells, and the cell-lines derived therefrom. Moore thereafter alleges that 'he is the owner of his Blood and Bodily Substances and of the by-products produced therefrom. . . .' And he further alleges that such blood and bodily substances 'are his tangible personal property, and the activities of the defendants as set forth herein constitute a substantial interference with plaintiff's possession or right thereto, as well as defendants' wrongful exercise of dominion over plaintiff's personal property rights in his Blood and Bodily Substances.'

The majority impliedly hold these allegations insufficient as a matter of law, finding three 'reasons to doubt' that Moore retained a sufficient ownership interest in his cells, after their excision, to support a conversion cause of action. In my view the majority's three reasons, taken singly or together, are inadequate to the task.

The majority's first reason is that 'no reported judicial decision supports Moore's claim, either directly or by close analogy.' Neither, however, is there any reported decision rejecting such a claim. The issue is as new as its source – the recent explosive growth in the commercialization of biotechnology.

The majority next cite several statutes regulating aspects of the commerce in or disposition of certain parts of the human body, and conclude in effect that in the present case we should also 'look for guidance' to the Legislature rather than to the law of conversion. Surely this argument is out of place in an opinion of the highest court of this state. As the majority acknowledge, the law of conversion is a creature of the common law, 'The inherent capacity of the common law for growth and change is its most significant feature. Its development has been determined by the social needs of the community which it serves. It is constantly expanding and developing in keeping with advancing civilization and the new conditions and progress of society, and adapting itself to the gradual change of trade, commerce, arts, inventions, and the needs of the country'. In short, as the United States Supreme Court has aptly said, 'This flexibility and capacity for growth and adaptation is the peculiar boast and excellence of the common law.' . . . Although the Legislature may of course speak to the subject, in the common law system the primary instruments of this evolution are the courts, adjudicating on a regular basis the rich variety of individual cases brought before them (*Rodriguez v Bethlehem Steel Corpn* (1974) 12 Cal 3d 382, 394). . . .

The majority's second reason for doubting that Moore retained an ownership interest in his cells after their excision is that 'California statutory law . . . drastically limits a patient's control over excised cells.' For this proposition the majority rely on Health and Safety Code section 7054.4 (hereafter section 7054.4). The majority concede that the statute was not meant to directly resolve the question whether a person in Moore's position has a cause of action for conversion, but reason that it indirectly resolves the question by limiting the patient's control over the fate of his excised cells: 'By restricting how excised cells may be used and requiring their eventual destruction, the statute eliminates so many of the rights ordinarily attached to property that one cannot simply assume that what is left amounts to "property" or "ownership" for purposes of conversion law.' As will appear, I do not believe section 7054.4 supports the just quoted conclusion of the majority.

First, in my view the statute does not authorize the principal use that defendants claim the right to make of Moore's tissue, i.e., its commercial exploitation. In construing section 7054.4, of course, 'we look first to the words of the statute themselves' (*Long Beach Police Officers Assn v City of Long Beach* (1988) 46 Cal 3d 736, 741), and give those words their usual and ordinary meaning (*California Teachers Assn v San Diego Community College Dist* (1981) 28 Cal 3d 692, 698).

By its terms, section 7054.4 permits only 'scientific use' of excised body parts and tissue before they must be destroyed. We must therefore determine the usual and ordinary meaning of that phrase. I would agree that 'scientific use' at least includes routine postoperative examination of excised tissue conducted by a pathologist for diagnostic or prognostic reasons (e.g., to verify preoperative diagnosis or to assist in determining postoperative treatment). I might further agree that 'scientific use' could be extended to include purely scientific study of the tissue by a disinterested researcher for the purpose of advancing medical knowledge – provided of course that the patient gave timely and informed consent to that use. It would stretch the English language beyond recognition, however, to say that commercial exploitation of the kind and degree alleged here is also a usual and ordinary meaning of the phrases 'scientific use.'

The majority dismiss this difficulty by asserting that I read the statute to define 'scientific use' as 'not-for-profit scientific use,' and by finding 'no reason to believe that the Legislature intended to make such a distinction.' The objection misses my point. I do not stress the concept of profit, but the concept of science: the distinction I draw is not between nonprofit scientific use and scientific use that happens to lead to a marketable by-product; it is between a truly scientific use and the blatant commercial exploitation of Moore's tissue that the present complaint alleges. Under those allegations, defendants Dr David W Golde and Shirley G Quan were not only scientists, they were also full-fledged entrepreneurs; the complaint repeatedly declares that they appropriated Moore's tissue in order 'to further defendants' independent research and commercial activities and promote their economic, financial and competitive interests.' The complaint also alleges that defendant Regents of the University of California (hereafter Regents) actively assisted the individual defendants in applying for patent rights and in negotiating with bioengineering and pharmaceutical companies to exploit the commercial potential of Moore's tissue. Finally, the complaint alleges in detail the contractual arrangements between the foregoing defendants and defendants Genetics Institute, Inc, and Sandoz Pharmaceuticals Corporation, giving the latter companies exclusive rights to exploit that commercial potential while providing substantial financial benefits to the individual defendants in the form of cash, stock options, consulting fees, and fringe benefits. To exclude such traditionally commercial activities from the phrase 'scientific use,' as I do here, does not give it a restrictive definition; rather, it gives the phrase its usual and ordinary meaning settled law requires.

Secondly, even if section 7054.4 does permit defendants' commercial exploitation of Moore's tissue under the guise of 'scientific use,' it does not follow that – as the majority concluded – the statute 'eliminates so many of the rights ordinarily attached to property' that what remains does not amount to 'property' or 'ownership' for purposes of the law of conversion.

The concepts of property and ownership in our law are extremely broad. (See Civ. Code, §§ 654, 655.) A leading decision of this court approved the following definition: 'The term "property" is sufficiently comprehensive to include every species of estate, real and personal, and everything which one person can own and transfer to another. It extends to every species of right and interest capable of being enjoyed as such upon which it is practicable to place a money value.' (*Yuba River Power Co v Nevada Irr Dist* (1923) 207 Cal 521, 523.)

Being broad, the concept of property is also abstract: rather than referring directly to a material object such as a parcel of land or the tractor that cultivates it, the concept of property is often said to refer to a 'bundle of rights' that may be exercised with respect to that object – principally the rights to possess the property, to use the property, to exclude others from the property, and to dispose of the property by sale or by gift. 'Ownership is not a single concrete entity but a bundle of rights and privileges as well as of obligations.' (*Union Oil Co v State Bd of Equal.* (1963) Cal 2d 441, 447.) But the same bundle of rights does not attach to all forms of property. For a variety of policy reasons, the law limits or even forbids the exercise of certain rights over forms of property. For example, both law and contract may limit the right of an owner of real property to use his parcel as he sees fit. Owners of various forms of personal property may likewise be subject to restrictions on the time, place, and manner of their use. Limitations on the disposition of real property, while less common, may also be imposed. Finally, some types of personal property may be sold but not given away, while others may be given away but not sold, and still others may neither be given away nor sold.

In each of the foregoing instances, the limitation or prohibition diminishes the bundle of rights that would otherwise attach to the property, yet what remains is still deemed in law to be a protectible property interest. 'Since property or title is a complex bundle of rights, duties, powers and immunities, the pruning away of some or a great many of these elements does not entirely destroy the title. . . .' (*People v Walker* (1939) 33 Cal App 2d 18, 20 [even the possessor of contraband has certain property rights in it against anyone other than the state].) The same rule applies to Moore's interest in his own body tissue: even if we assume that section 7054.4 limited the use and disposition of his excised tissue in the manner claimed by the majority, Moore nevertheless retained valuable rights in that tissue. Above all, at the time of its excision he at least had the right to do with his own tissue whatever the defendants did with it: ie, he could have contracted with researchers and pharmaceutical companies to develop and exploit the vast commercial potential of his tissue and its products. Defendants certainly believe that their right to do the foregoing is not barred by section 7054.4 and is a significant property right, as they have demonstrated by their deliberate concealment from Moore of the true value of his tissue, their efforts to obtain a patent on the Mo cell-line, their contractual agreements to exploit this material, their exclusion of Moore from any participation in the profits, and their vigorous defense of this lawsuit. The Court of Appeal summed up the point by observing that 'Defendants' position that plaintiff cannot own his tissue, but that they can, is fraught with irony.' It is also legally untenable. As noted above, the majority cite no case holding that an individual's right to develop and exploit the commercial potential of his own tissue is not a right of sufficient worth or dignity to be deemed a protectible property interest. In the absence of such authority – or of legislation to the same effect – the right falls within the traditionally broad concept of property in our law.

The majority's third and last reason for their conclusion that Moore has no cause of action for conversion under existing law is that 'the subject matter of the Regents' patent – the patented cell-line and the products derived from it – cannot be Moore's property.' The majority then offer a dual explanation: 'This is because the patented cell-line is factually and legally distinct from the cells taken from Moore's body.' Neither branch of the explanation withstands analysis.

First, in support of their statement that the Mo cell-line is 'factually distinct' from Moore's cells, the majority assert that 'Cells change while being developed into a cell-line and continue to change over time,' and in particular may acquire an abnormal number of chromosomes. No one disputes these assertions but they are nonetheless irrelevant. For present purposes no distinction can be drawn between Moore's cells and the Mo cell-line. It appears that the principal reason for establishing a cell-line is not to 'improve' the quality of the parent cells but simply to extend their life indefinitely, in order to permit long-term study and/or exploitation of the qualities already present in such cells. The complaint alleges that Moore's cells naturally produced certain valuable proteins in larger than normal quantities; indeed, that was why defendants were eager to culture them in the first place. Defendants do not claim that the cells of the Mo cell-line are in any degree more productive of such proteins than were Moore's own cells. Even if the cells of the Mo cell-line in fact have an abnormal number of chromosomes, at the present stage of this case we do not know if that fact has any bearing whatever on their capacity to produce proteins; yet it is in the commercial exploitation of that capacity – not simply in their number of chromosomes – that Moore seeks to assert an interest. For all that appears, therefore, the emphasized fact is a distinction without a difference.

Second, the majority assert in effect that Moore cannot have a ownership interest in the Mo cell-line because defendants patented it. The majority's point wholly fails to meet Moore's claim that he is entitled to compensation for defendants' unauthorized use of his bodily tissues before defendants patented the Mo cell-line: defendants undertook such use immediately after the splenectomy on October 20, 1976, and continued to extract and use Moore's cells and tissue at least until September 20, 1983; the patent, however, did not issue until March 20, 1984, more than seven years after the unauthorized use began. Whatever the legal consequences of that event, it did not operate retroactively to immunize defendants from accountability for conduct occurring long before the patent was granted.

Nor did the issuance of the patent in 1984 necessarily have the drastic effect that the majority contend. To be sure, the patent granted defendants the exhaustive right to make, use, or sell the invention for a period of 17 years (35 U.S.C. § 154). But Moore does not assert any such right for himself. Rather, he seeks to show that he is entitled, in fairness and equity, to some share in the profits that defendants have made and will make from their commercial exploitation of the Mo cell-line. I do not question that the cell-line is primarily the product of defendants' inventive effort. Yet likewise no one can question Moore's crucial contribution to the invention – an invention named, ironically, after him: but for the cells of Moore's body taken by defendants, there would have been no Mo cell-line. Thus the complaint alleges that Moore's 'Blood and Bodily Substances were absolutely essential to defendants' research and commercial activities with regard to his cells, cell-lines, [and] the Mo cell-line . . . and that defendants could not have applied for and had issued to them the Mo cell-line patent and other patents described herein without obtaining and culturing specimens of plaintiff's Blood and Bodily Substances.' Defendants admit this allegation by their demurrers, as well they should: for all their expertise, defendants do not claim they could have extracted the Mo cell-line out of thin air.

Nevertheless the majority conclude that the patent somehow cut off all Moore's rights – past, present, and future – to share in the proceeds of defendants' commercial exploitation of the cell-line derived from his own body tissue. The majority cite no authority for this unfair result, and I cannot believe it is compelled by the general law of patents: a patent is not a license to defraud. Perhaps the answer lies in an analogy to the concept of 'joint inventor.' I am aware that 'patients and research subjects who contribute cells to research will not be considered inventors.' (OTA Rep., *supra*, at p. 71.) Nor is such a person strictly speaking a 'joint inventor' within the meaning of the term in federal law (35 U.S.C. § 116). But he does fall within the spirit of that law. 'The joint invention provision guarantees that all who contribute in a substantial way to a product's development benefit from the reward that the product brings. Thus, the protection of joint inventors encourages scientists to cooperate with each other and ensures that each contributor is rewarded fairly . . .

'Although a patient who donates cells does not fit squarely within the definition of a joint inventor, the policy reasons that inform joint inventor patents should also apply to cell donors. Neither John Moore nor any other patient whose cells become the basis for a patentable cell-line qualifies as a "joint inventor" because he or she did not further the development of the product in any intellectual or conceptual sense. Nor does the status of patients as sole owners of a component part make them deserving of joint inventorship status. What the patients did do, knowingly or unknowingly, is collaborate with the researchers by donating their body tissue. . . . By providing the researchers with unique raw materials, without which the resulting product could not exist, the donors become necessary contributors to the product. Concededly, the patent is not granted for the cell as it is found in nature, but for the modified biogenetic product. However, the uniqueness of the product that gives rise to its patentability stems from the uniqueness of the original cell. A patient's claim to share in the profits flowing from a patent would be analogous to that of an inventor whose collaboration was essential to the success of a resulting product. The patient was not a coequal, but was a necessary contributor to the cell-line.' (Danforth, Cells, Sales, & Royalties: The Patient's Right to a Portion of the Profits (1985) 6 Yale L & Pol'y Rev 179, 197, fns omitted, (hereafter Danforth).)

Under this reasoning, which I find persuasive, the law of patents would not be a bar to Moore's assertion of an ownership interest in his cells and their products sufficient to warrant his sharing in the proceeds of their commercial exploitation. . . .

Having concluded – mistakenly, in my view – that Moore has no cause of action for conversion under existing law, the majority next consider whether to 'extend' the conversion cause of action to this context. Again the majority find three reasons not to do so, and again I respectfully disagree with each.

The majority's first reason is that a balancing of the 'relevant policy considerations' counsels against recognizing a conversion cause of action in these circumstances. The memo identifies two such policies, but concedes that one of them – 'protection of a competent patient's right to make autonomous medical decisions' – would in fact be promoted, even though 'indirectly,' by recognizing a conversion cause of action.

The majority focus instead on a second policy consideration, i.e., their concern 'that we not threaten with disabling civil liability innocent parties who are engaged in socially useful activities, such as researchers who have no reason to believe that their use of a particular cell sample is, or may be, against a donor's wishes.' As will appear, in my view this concern is both overstated and outweighed by contrary considerations.

The majority begin their analysis by stressing the obvious facts that research on human cells plays an increasingly important role in the progress of medicine, and that the manipulation of those cells by the methods of biotechnology has resulted in numerous beneficial products and treatments. Yet it does not necessarily follow that, as the majority claim, application of the law of conversion in this area 'will hinder research by restricting access to the necessary raw materials,' ie, to cells, cell cultures, and cell-lines. The majority observe that many researchers obtain their tissue samples routinely and at little or no cost, from cell-culture repositories. The majority then speculate that 'This exchange of scientific materials which is still relatively free and efficient, will surely be compromised. Each cell sample becomes the potential subject matter of a lawsuit.' There are two grounds to doubt that this prophecy will be fulfilled.

To begin with, if the relevant exchange of scientific materials was ever 'free and efficient,' it is much less so today. Since biological products of genetic engineering became patentable in 1980 (*Diamond v Chakrabarty* (1980) 447 US 303), human cell-lines have been amenable to patent protection and, as the Court of Appeal observed in its opinion below, 'The rush to patent for exclusive use has been rampant.' Among those who have taken advantage of this development, of course, are the defendants herein: as we have seen, defendants Golde and Quan obtained a patent on the Mo cell-line in 1984 and assigned it to defendant Regents. With such patentability has come a drastic reduction in the formerly free access of researchers to new cell-lines and their products: the 'novelty' requirement for patentability prohibits public disclosure of the invention at all times up to one year before the filing of the patent application. (35 USC § 102(b).) Thus defendants herein recited in their patent specification, 'At no time has the Mo cell-line been available to other than the investigators involved with its initial discovery and only the conditioned medium from the cell-line has been made available to a limited number of investigators for collaborative work with the original discoverers of the Mo cell-line.'

An even greater force for restricting the free exchange of new cell-lines and their products has been the rise of the biotechnology industry and the increasing involvement of academic researchers in that industry. When scientists became entrepreneurs and negotiated with biotechnological and pharmaceutical companies to develop and exploit the commercial potential of their discoveries – as did defendants in the case at bar – layers of contractual restrictions were added to the protections of the patent law.

In their turn, the biotechnological and pharmaceutical companies demanded and received exclusive rights in the scientists' discoveries, and frequently placed those discoveries under trade secret protection. Trade secret protection is popular among biotechnology companies because, among other reasons, the invention need not meet the strict standards of patentability and the protection is both quickly acquired and unlimited in duration. (Note, Patent and Trade Secret Protection in University Industry Research Relationships in Biotechnology (1987) 24 Harv J of Legis, 191, 218-219.) Secrecy as a normal business practice is also taking hold in university research laboratories, often because of industry pressure (id., at pp. 204-208): 'One of the most serious fears associated with university-industry cooperative research concerns keeping work private and not disclosing it to the researcher's peers. . . . Economic arrangements between industry and universities inhibit open communication between researchers, especially for those who are financially tied to smaller biotechnology firms.' (Howard, *supra*, 44 Food Drug Cosm LJ at p 339, fn 72.)

Secondly, to the extent that cell cultures and cell-lines may still be 'freely exchanged,' e.g., for purely research purposes, it does not follow that the researcher who obtains such material must necessarily remain ignorant of any limitations on its use: by means of appropriate record keeping, the researcher can be assured that the source of the material has consented to his proposed use of it, and hence that such use is not a conversion. To achieve this end the originator of the tissue sample first determines the extent of the source's informed consent to its use – eg, for research only, or for public but academic use, or for specific or general commercial purposes; he then enters this information in the record of the tissue sample, and the record accompanies the sample into the hands of any researcher who thereafter undertakes to work with it. 'Record keeping would not be overly burdensome because researchers generally keep accurate records of tissue sources for other reasons: to trace anomalies to the medical history of the patient, to maintain title for other researchers and for themselves, and to insure reproducibility of the experiment.' (Toward the Right of Commerciality, *supra*, 34 UCLA L Rev, at p. 241.) As the Court of Appeal correctly observed, any claim to the contrary 'is dubious in light of the meticulous care and planning necessary in serious modern medical research.' . . .

. . . [I]n my view whatever merit the majority's single policy consideration may have is outweighed by two contrary considerations, i.e., policies that are promoted by recognizing that every individual has a legally protectible property interest in his own body and its products. First, our society acknowledges a profound ethical imperative to respect the human body as the physical and temporal expression of the unique human persona. One manifestation of that respect is our prohibition against direct abuse of the body by torture or other forms of cruel or unusual punishment. Another is our prohibition against indirect abuse of the body by its economic exploitation for the sole benefit of another person. The most abhorrent form of such exploitation, of course, was the institution of slavery. Lesser forms, such as indentured servitude or even debtor's prison, have also disappeared. Yet their specter haunts the laboratories and boardrooms of today's biotechnological research-industrial complex. It arises wherever scientists or industrialists claim, as defendants claim here, the right to appropriate and exploit a patient's tissue for their sole economic benefit – the right, in other words, to freely mine or harvest valuable physical properties of the patient's body: 'Research with human cells that results in significant economic gain for the researcher and no gain for the patient offends the traditional mores of our society in a manner impossible to quantify. Such research tends to treat the human body as a commodity – a means to a profitable end. The dignity and sanctity with which we regard the human whole, body as well as mind and soul, are absent when we allow researchers to further their own interests without the patient's participation by using a patient's cells as the basis for a marketable product.' (Danforth, *supra*, 6 Yale L & Pol'y Rev at p 190, fn omitted.)

A second policy consideration adds notions of equity to those of ethics. Our society values fundamental fairness in dealings between its members, and condemns the unjust enrichment of any member at the expense of another. This is particularly true when, as here, the parties are not in equal bargaining positions. We are repeatedly told that the commercial products of the biotechnological revolution 'hold the promise of tremendous profit.' (Toward the Right of Commerciality, *supra*, 34 UCLA L Rev at p 211.) In the case at bar, for example, the complaint alleges that the market for the kinds of proteins produced by the Mo cell-line was predicted to exceed $3 billion by 1990. These profits are currently shared exclusively between the biotechnology industry and the universities that support that industry. The profits are shared in a wide variety of ways, including 'direct entrepreneurial ties to genetic-engineering firms' and 'an equity interest in fledgling biotechnology firms' (Howard, *supra*, 44 Food Drug Cosm LJ at p 338). Thus the complaint alleges that because of his development of the Mo cell-line defendant Golde became a paid consultant of defendant Genetics Institute and acquired the rights to 75,000 shares of that firm's stock at a cost of 1 cent each; that Genetics Institute further contracted to pay Golde and the Regents at least $330,000 over 3 years, including a pro rata share of Golde's salary and fringe benefits; and that defendant Sandoz Pharmaceuticals Corporation subsequently contracted to increase that compensation by a further $110,000.

There is, however, a third party to the biotechnology enterprise – the patient who is the source of the blood or tissue from which all these profits are derived. While he may be a silent partner, his contribution to the venture is absolutely crucial: as pointed out above (pt 3, ante, but for the cells of Moore's body taken by defendants there would have been no Mo cell-line at all). Yet defendants deny that Moore is entitled to any share whatever in the proceeds of this cell-line. This is both inequitable and immoral. As Dr Thomas H. Murray, a respected professor of ethics and public policy, testified before Congress, 'the person [who furnishes the tissue] should be justly compensated. . . . If biotechnologists fail to make provision for a just sharing of profits with the person whose gift made it possible, the public's sense of justice will be offended and no one will be the winner.' (Murray, Who Owns the Body? On the Ethics of Using Human Tissue for Commercial Purposes (Jan-Feb 1986) IRB: A Review of Human Subjects Research, at p 5.)

There will be such equitable sharing if the courts recognize that the patient has a legally protected property interest in his own body and its products: 'property rights in one's own tissue would provide a morally acceptable result by giving effect to notions of fairness and preventing unjust enrichment. . . . Societal notions of equity and fairness demand recognition of property rights. There are bountiful benefits, monetary and otherwise, to be derived from human biologies. To deny the person contributing the raw material a fair share of these ample benefits is both unfair and morally wrong.' (Toward the Right of Commerciality, *supra*, 34 UCLA L Rev, at p 229.) 'Recognizing a donor's property rights would prevent unjust enrichment by giving monetary rewards to the donor and researcher proportionate to the value of their respective contributions. Biotechnology depends upon the contributions of both patients and researchers. If not for the patient's contribution of cells with unique attributes, the medical value of the bioengineered cells would be negligible. But for the physician's contribution of knowledge and skill in developing the cell product, the commercial value of the patient's cells would also be negligible. Failing to compensate the patient unjustly enriches the researcher because only the researcher's contribution is recognized.' (*Id* at p 230.) In short, as the Court of Appeal succinctly put it, 'if the science has become science for profit, then we fail to see any justification for excluding the patient from participation in these profits.'. . .

The majority's second reason for declining to extend the conversion cause of action to the present context is that 'the Legislature should make that decision,' I do not doubt that the Legislature is competent to act on this topic. The fact that the Legislature may intervene if and when it chooses, however, does not in the meanwhile relieve the courts of their duty of enforcing – or if need be, fashioning – an effective judicial remedy for the wrong here alleged. As I observed above (pt 1, *ante*), if a conversion cause of action is otherwise an appropriate remedy on these facts we should not refrain from recognizing it merely because the Legislature has not yet addressed the question. To do so would be to abdicate pro tanto our responsibility over a body of law – torts – that is particularly a creature of the common law. And such reluctance to act would be especially unfortunate at the present time, when the rapid expansion of biotechnological science and industry makes resolution of these issues an increasingly pressing need.

The inference I draw from the current statutory regulation of human biological materials, moreover, is the opposite of that drawn by the majority. By selective quotation of the statutes the majority seem to suggest that human organs and blood cannot legally be sold on the open market – thereby implying that if the Legislature were to act here it would impose a similar ban on monetary compensation for the use of human tissue in biotechnological research and development. But if that is the argument, the premise is unsound: contrary to popular misconception, it is not true that human organs and blood cannot legally be sold.

As to organs, the majority rely on the Uniform Anatomical Gift Act (Health & Saf Code, § 7150 et seq, hereafter the UAGA) for the proposition that a competent adult may make a post mortem gift of any part of his body but may not receive 'valuable consideration' for the transfer. But the prohibition of the UAGA against the sale of a body part is much more limited than the majority recognized: by its terms (Health & Saf Code, § 7155, subd (a)) the prohibition applies only to sales for 'transplantation' or 'therapy.' Yet a different section of the UAGA authorizes the transfer and receipt of body parts for such additional purposes as 'medical or dental education research, or advancement of medical or dental science.' (Health & Saf Code, § 7153, subd (a)(1).) No section of the UAGA prohibits anyone from selling body parts for any of those additional purposes; by clear implication, therefore, such sales are legal. Indeed, the fact that the UAGA prohibits no sales of organs other than sales for 'transportation' or 'therapy' raises a further implication that it is also legal for anyone to sell human tissue to a biotechnology company for research and development purposes.

With respect to the sale of human blood the matter is much simpler: there is in fact no prohibition against such sales. The majority rely on Health and Safety Code 1606, which provides in relevant part that the procurement and use of blood for transfusion 'shall be construed to be, and is declared to be the rendition of a service . . . and shall not be construed to be, and is declared not to be, a sale . . .' There is less here, however, than meets the eye; the statute does mean that a person cannot sell his blood or, by implication, that his blood is not his property. 'While many jurisdictions have classified the transfer of blood or other human tissue as a service rather than a sale, this position does not conflict with the notion that human tissue is property.' (Columbia Note, supra, 90 Colum.L.Rev. at p 544, fn 76.) The reason is plain: 'No State or Federal statute prohibits the sale of blood, plasma, semen, or other replenishing tissues if taken in nonvital amounts. Nevertheless, State laws usually characterize these paid transfers as the provision of services rather than the sale of a commodity. [Para] The primary legal reason for characterizing these transactions as involving services rather than goods is to avoid liability for contaminated blood products under either general product liability principles of the [Uniform Commercial Code's] implied warranty provisions.' (OTA Rep., at p. 76, fn. omitted.) The courts have repeatedly recognized that the foregoing is the real purpose of this harmless legal fiction. (See, eg *Hyland Therapeutics v Superior Court* (1985) 175 Cal App 3d 509; *Cramer v Queen of Angels Hosp.* (1976) 62 Cal App 3d 812; *Shepard v Alexian Brothers Hosp* (1973) 33 Cal App 3d 606.) Thus despite the statute relied on by the majority, it is perfectly legal in this state for a person to sell his blood for transfusion or for any other purpose – indeed, such sales are commonplace, particularly in the market for plasma. (See OTA Rep., *supra* at p. 121.)

It follows that the statutes regulating the transfers of human organs and blood do not support the majority's refusal to recognize a conversion cause of action for commercial exploitation of human blood cells without consent. On the contrary, because such statutes treat both organs and blood as property that can legally be sold in a variety of circumstances, they impliedly support Moore's contention that his blood cells are likewise property for which he can and should receive compensation, and hence are protected by the law of conversion . . .

The majority's final reason for refusing to recognize a conversion cause of action on these facts is that 'there is no pressing need' to do so because the complaint also states another cause of action that is assertedly adequate to the task; that cause of action is 'the breach of a fiduciary duty to disclose facts material to the patient's consent or, alternatively . . . the performance of medical procedures without first having obtained the patient's informed consent'). Although last, this reason is not the majority's least; in fact, it underlies much of the opinion's discussion of the conversion cause of action, recurring like a leitmotiv throughout that discussion.

The majority hold that a physician who intends to treat a patient in whom he has either a research interest or an economic interest is under a fiduciary duty to disclose such interest to the patient before treatment; that his failure to do so may give rise to a nondisclosure cause of action; and that the complaint herein states such a cause of action at least against defendant Golde. I agree with that holding as far as it goes.

I disagree, however, with the majority's further conclusion that in the present context a nondisclosure cause of action is an adequate – in fact, a superior – substitute for a conversion cause of action. In my view the nondisclosure cause of action falls short on at least three grounds.

First, the majority reason that 'enforcement of physicians' disclosure obligations' will ensure patients' freedom of choice. The majority do not spell out how those obligations will be 'enforced'; but because they arise from judicial decision (the majority opinion herein) rather than from legislative or administrative enactment, we may infer that the obligations will primarily be enforced by the traditional judicial remedy of an action for damages for their breach. Thus the majority's theory apparently is that the threat of such an action will have a prophylactic effect: it will give physician-researchers incentive to disclose any conflicts of interest before treatment, and will thereby protect their patients' right to make an informed decision about what may be done with their body parts.

The remedy is largely illusory. '[A]n action based on the physician's failure to disclose material information sounds in negligence. As a practical matter, however, it may be difficult to recover on this kind of negligence theory because the patient must prove a causal connection between his or her injury and the physician's failure to inform.' (Martin & Lagod, Biotechnology and the Commercial Use of Human Cells: Toward an Organic View of Life and Technology (1989) 5 Santa Clara Computer & High Tech LJ 211, 222, fn omitted.) There are two barriers to recovery. First, 'the patient must show that if he or she had been informed of all pertinent information, he or she would have declined to consent to the procedure in question.' (Ibid.) As we explained in the seminal case of *Cobbs v Grant* (1972) 8 Cal 3d 229, 245, 'There must be a causal relationship between the physician's failure to inform and the injury to the plaintiff. Such a causal connection arises only if it is established that had the revelation been made consent to treatment would not have been given.'

The second barrier to recovery is still higher, and is erected on the first: it is not even enough for the plaintiff to prove that he personally would have refused consent to the proposed treatment if he had been fully informed; he must also prove that in the same circumstances no reasonably prudent person would have given such consent. The purpose of this 'objective' standard is evident: 'Since at the time of trial the uncommunicated hazard has materialized, it would be surprising if the patient-plaintiff did not claim that had he been informed of the dangers he would have declined treatment. Subjectively he may believe so, with the 20/20 vision of hindsight, but we doubt that justice will be served by placing the physician in jeopardy of the patient's bitterness and disillusionment. Thus an objective test is preferable: i.e., what would a prudent person in the patient's position have decided if adequately informed of all significant perils.' (*Cobbs v Grant, supra,* 8 Cal.3d 229, 245.)

Even in an ordinary *Cobbs*-type action it may be difficult for a plaintiff to prove that no reasonably prudent person would have consented to the proposed treatment if the doctor had disclosed the particular risk of physical harm that ultimately caused the injury. (See, eg, *Morganroth v Pacific Medical Center Inc,* (1976) 54 Cal App 3d 521, 534 [affirming nonsuit in a *Cobbs*-type action on ground, inter alia, of lack of proof that plaintiff would have refused coronary arteriogram if he had been told of risk of stroke].) This is because in many cases the potential benefits of the treatment to the plaintiff clearly outweigh the undisclosed risk of harm. But that imbalance will be even greater in the kind of nondisclosure action that the majority now contemplate: here we deal not with a risk of physical injuries such as a stroke, but with the possibility that the doctor might later use some of the patient's cast-off tissue for scientific research or the development of commercial products. Few if any judges or juries are likely to believe that disclosure of such a possibility of research or development would dissuade a reasonably prudent person from consenting to the treatment. For example, in the case at bar no trier of fact is likely to believe that if defendants had disclosed their plans for using Moore's cells, no reasonably prudent person in Moore's position – i.e., a leukemia patient suffering from a grossly enlarged spleen – would have consented to the routine operation that saved or at least prolonged his life. Here, as in *Morganroth (ibid)* a motion for nonsuit for failure to prove proximate cause will end the matter. In this context, accordingly, the threat of suit on a nondisclosure cause of action is largely a paper tiger.

The second reason why the nondisclosure cause of action is inadequate for the task that the majority assign to it is that it fails to solve half the problem before us: it gives the patient only the right to refuse consent, i.e., the right to prohibit the commercialization of his tissue; it does not give him the right to grant consent to that commercialization on the condition that he share in its proceeds. 'Even though good reasons exist to support informed consent with tissue commercialization; a disclosure requirement is only the first step toward full recognition of a patient's right to participate fully. Informed consent to commercialization, absent a right to share in the profits from such commercial development, would only give patients a veto over their own exploitation. But recognition that the patient[s] [have] an ownership interest in their own tissues would give patients an affirmative right of participation. Then patients would be able to assume the role of equal partners with their physicians in commercial biotechnology research.' (Howard, *supra,* 44 Food Drug Cosm LJ at p 344.)

Reversing the words of the old song, the nondisclosure cause of action thus accentuates the negative and eliminates the positive: the patient can say no, but he cannot say yes and expect to share in the proceeds of his contribution. Yet as explained above . . . there are sound reasons of ethics and equity to recognize the patient's right to participate in such benefits. The nondisclosure cause of action does not protect that right; to that extent, it is therefore not an adequate substitute for the conversion remedy, which does protect the right.

Third, the nondisclosure cause of action fails to reach a major class of potential defendants: all those who are outside the strict physician-patient relationship with the plaintiff. Thus the majority concede that here only defendant Golde, the treating physician, can be directly liable to Moore on a nondisclosure cause of action: 'The Regents, Quan, Genetics Institute and Sandoz are not physicians. In contrast to Golde, none of these defendants stood in a fiduciary relationship with Moore or had the duty to obtain Moore's informed consent to medical procedures.' As to these defendants, the majority can offer Moore only a slim hope of recovery: if they are to be liable on a nondisclosure cause of action, say the majority, 'it can only be on account of Golde's acts and on the basis of a recognized theory of secondary liability, such as respondeat superior.' Although the majority decline to decide the question whether the secondary-liability allegations of the complaint are sufficient, they strongly imply disapproval of those allegations. And the majority further note that the trial court has already ruled insufficient the allegations of agency as to the corporate defendants.

To the extent that a plaintiff such as Moore is unable to plead or prove a satisfactory theory of secondary liability, the nondisclosure cause of action will thus be inadequate to reach a number of parties to the commercial exploitation of his tissue. Such parties include, for example, any physician-researcher who is not personally treating the patient, any other researcher who is not a physician, any employer of the foregoing (or even of the treating physician), and any person or corporation thereafter participating in the commercial exploitation of the tissue. Yet some or all of those parties may well have participated more in, and profited more from, such exploitation than the particular physician with whom the plaintiff happened to have a formal doctor-patient relationship at the time.

In sum, the nondisclosure cause of action (1) is unlikely to be successful in most cases, (2) fails to protect patients' rights to share in the proceeds of the commercial exploitation of their tissue, and (3) may allow the true exploiters to escape liability. It is thus not an adequate substitute, in my view, for the conversion cause of action.

Broussard J dissented on the conversion claim.

The Canadian Law Reform Commission (*op cit*), having taken account of *Moore*, offered the following conclusion:

The sharply contrasted opinions in *Moore* may help crystallize the issues for legislative or judicial deliberations in jurisdictions beyond California. For the case is not an isolated incident. A United States government report has documented other disputes over the patenting of human biological materials. More recently, a female patient claimed that her blood, placenta and umbilical cord were, without her knowledge or consent, transferred from a hospital to a California biotechnological company to develop an rDNA drug, Tissue Plasminogen Activator (TPA), which has been patented and is now licensed in Canada for use in dissolving blood clots after heart attacks. While disputes over the development and commercial use of human tissues and biologics are noteworthy in the United States, the cases may have import for other jurisdictions. . . .

Biotechnology is accelerating the rate at which medical science may convert formerly useless human tissue into therapeutic substances with a commercial value. The traditional legal maxim 'The law cares not for trifles' – *de minimis no curat lex* – may no longer apply to excised tissue and secreted substances long regarded as valueless and abandoned.

> Until recently, the physical human body, as distinguished from the mental and spiritual, was believed to have little value, other than as a source of labor. In recent history, we have seen the human body assume astonishing aspects of value. Taking the facts of this case, for instance, we are told that John Moore's mere cells could become the foundation of a multi-billion dollar industry from which patent holders could reap fortunes. *For better or worse, we have irretrievably entered an age that requires examination of our understanding of the legal rights and relationships in the human body and the human cell.*

Parallel legal developments have also emerged. Legal recognition of the patenting of life forms in the United States, which increased by 300 per cent the number of patent applications for inventions involving human biologics, has also proceeded in Canada, where human cell-lines have received patent protection since the early 1980s. Human genetic and cellular materials manipulated into therapeutic products thus appear to have been granted intellectual-property protection for exclusive commercial exploitation under Canadian law as well.

The confluence of these unprecedented legal and medical developments accentuates the potential for conflicts between the sources and the users or exploiters of human cells and tissues. Cultural and legal differences between the United States and Canada may help Canadian society avoid such disputes in transit through the biotechnological age. At the least, however, the parallel medical and legal developments challenge society to rethink its choices for a tissue-transfer legal regime consonant with this new age. *Moore*-like disputes are perhaps symptomatic of technico-legal revolutions which so jar pre-existing legal structure that society must endure a period of confusion and conflict before creating new, or recalibrating old, legal regimes. In this instance, biotechnology calls into question what the moral and legal integrity of the human body will continue to mean.

Taken together, *Moore*, *Parpalaix* and *Dyment* further suggest that these biotechnological developments should proceed in a manner consistent with human rights. Will the recognition of limited property interest protect against non-consensual commercial use or development in those presumably rare, compelling circumstances in which bodily resources have been commercially exploited without the express and specific authorization of the patient? While individual rights cannot be absolute in a pluralist society, what legal tools will help maintain the sovereignty of human rights? Will it help to reform patent law or to require doctors or researchers to disclose commercial or non-commercial potentials in research on excised human tissue? Will limited bodily-property interests help? Viewed from an eighteenth-century perspective, such thoughts may seem ethically and legally abhorrent. Both law and medicine are dynamic enterprises, however. A Canadian commentator has written that '[t]he meaning of property is not constant. The actual institution, and the way people see it, and hence the meaning they give to the word, all change over time.' Viewed from a late twentieth-century human rights perspective, society might ponder whether a legal notion of limited property interests in human tissue may best serve to protect physical integrity, individual autonomy and the fundamental values of personhood.

To minimize disputes between the sources and commercial users of human cells and tissues, fiduciary principles may provide initial guidance. Patients seek medical care with the expectation and trust that medical interventions on their bodies will be undertaken for their benefit. Some courts have deemed this patient expectation to be a right, which imposes a corresponding duty on physicians to act with utmost good faith and loyalty. The ethical and legal rights that attach to this patient-centred ethic have long been the hallmark of doctor-patient relations. When an interest arises that potentially conflicts with a doctor's duty to exercise independent professional judgment on behalf of the patient, the duty of loyalty requires a disclosure of the conflict and the informed consent of the patient to continued medical treatment. Applied here, the principles require a doctor to disclose a potential commercial interest in the patient's tissues or bodily substances. Full disclosure and the patient's informed consent would permit the patient [sc. doctor] to continue treatment. If the patient declines further involvement, or if it becomes reasonably clear to the doctor that his or her commercial interest compromises the exercise of independent professional judgment, the doctor would have an obligation to transfer care of the patient.

Yet, even a broad range of common law concepts – from fiduciary duties, to informed consent to property interests – may not provide sufficient clarity or certainty on the competing interests, rights and duties of patients, doctors, researchers, hospitals or biotechnology firms. The complexity of the issues and interests indicate that they merit further multi-disciplinary study to discover how society may best balance the need to encourage creative biotechnological therapeutic human tissue development with the need to protect basic human rights.

In the light of this discussion, in resolving the first question arising from Professor Dickens' analysis (can a donor control the use of excised tissue?), it seems that there are three issues which English lawyers need to address:

1. Is human tissue once excised 'property' under the existing law?
2. If it is not, should the courts expand the law to make it so, or is this a matter where Parliament should legislate?
3. If the courts were to develop the law, are there any indications in existing legislation or otherwise as to how as a matter of policy this should be done?

As regards the first of these issues, there is, at best, only weak authority that the law currently accepts what might be called the property approach (*Welsh* and *Rothery*). Before reaching an authoritative view a court will surely need, as did the Supreme Court of California in *Moore*, to take account of the policy implications of adopting the property approach. This takes us on to the next two issues. The obvious complexity of the circumstances in which the legal status of excised body material arises may persuade a court that the matter is really one for Parliament. You will recall that this was the approach endorsed by the majority in *Moore*. Although an English court may find it hard to resist this temptation, it would be unfortunate if, in this fast-moving area of medical development, the law remained in a state of uncertainty until such a time as Parliament took a view.

If courts decided to grasp the nettle, should the property approach be adopted? You will recall that the judges in *Moore* looked for guidance from existing legislation as to how the law as expressed by the legislature viewed human tissue. If the same search were undertaken by an English court, is there any English legislation or other sources of public policy to serve as a guide? There are four legislative sources to note: the Human Tissue Act 1961; s 25 of the National Health Service Act 1977; the Human Organ Transplants Act 1989 and the Human Fertilisation and Embryology Act 1990.

None of these Acts deals explicitly with the property approach. Our concern is whether there is any underlying assumption as to the legal status of human tissue in these Acts. The Human Tissue Act 1961 only deals with disposition of human tissue on death. Even in that context, the Act creates a special statutory scheme for post-mortem donation which is not based upon notions of property. The 1961 Act, therefore, takes us no further. By contrast, s 25 of the NHS Act and the Human Organ Transplants Act 1989 appear to be based upon an implicit adoption of the property approach. Section 25 of the 1977 Act provides that:

25. Where the Secretary of State has acquired –
(a) supplies of human blood for the purpose of any service under this Act, or
(b) any part of a human body for the purpose of or in the course of providing, any such service, or
(c) supplies of any other substances or preparations not readily obtainable,
he may arrange to make such supplies or that part available (on such terms, including terms as to charges, as he thinks fit) to any person. . . .

We have already analysed the provisions of the 1989 Act (*supra*, pp 1093-1095) which prohibit commercial dealings in human organs (s 1). Both of these statutory provisions assume that human tissue is amenable to transfer and disposal in that the tissue is treated as if it were a *res* albeit *extra commercium*. By far the strongest support for the property approach can be found in HUFEA. As we have seen (*supra*, ch 11), the control and disposal of human gametes and embryos rest with the donor(s) (see, principally, Sch 3). Placing control in the hands of the donor(s) reflects a reliance upon the property approach without explicitly stating it.

The combination of these statutory provisions strongly suggests a growing legislative acceptance of the property approach which a court may treat as a guide.

2. Loss of the right to control

To have resolved the question of the legal status of human tissue in favour of its being property, albeit subject to some public policy limitations as to its use and disposal, still leaves the need to address Dickens' second question: under what circumstances, if any, does the donor lose his right to control the tissue?

A donor will lose the right to control where the tissue is used with his express or implied consent. Alternatively, the donor may have expressly abandoned his tissue or be deemed to have impliedly done so. The doctrine of abandonment is well known to the law of personal property. Its application in this context was examined by a Maryland court in the following case.

Venner v State (1976) 354 A 2d 483 (Ct of Spec App Md)

Powers J: It could not be said that a person has no property right in wastes or other materials which were once a part of or contained within his body, but which normally are discarded after their separation from the body. It is not unknown for a person to assert a continuing right of ownership, dominion, or control, for good reason or for no reason, over such things as excrement, fluid waste, secretions, hair, fingernails, toenails, blood, and organs or other parts of the body, whether their separation from the body is intentional, accidental, or merely the result of normal body functions.

But it is all but universal custom and human experience that such things are discarded – in a legal sense, abandoned – by the person from whom they emanate, either 'on the spot', or, if social delicacy requires it, at a place or in a manner designed to cause the least offense to others.

By the force of social custom, we hold that when a person does nothing and says nothing to indicate an intent to assert his right of ownership, possession, or control over such material, the only rational inference is that he intends to abandon the material. When one places, or permits others to place waste material from his body into the stream of ultimate disposition as waste, he has abandoned whatever legal right he therefore had to protect it from prying eyes or acquisitive hands.

While Justice Powers recognises the general case, there are limits to the circumstances in which a court will find that tissue has been abandoned *impliedly*. This was explored in the intermediate appeal court in *Moore* when it adopted the property approach subsequently rejected by the Supreme Court.

Moore v Regents of University of California (1988) 249 Cal Rptr 494 (Cal CA)

Rothman JA: Defendants argue that even if plaintiff's spleen is personal property, its surgical removal was an abandonment by him of a diseased organ. They assert that he cannot, therefore, bring an action for conversion.

The essential element of abandonment is the intent to abandon. The owner of the property abandoned must be "entirely indifferent as to what may become of it or as to who may thereafter possess it." (*Martin v Cassidy* (1957) 149 Cal App 2d 106, 110, 307 P 2d 981, quoting 1 Cal Jur 2d, Abandonment, § 2, p 2.)

'It may be said that abandonment is made up of two elements, act and intent, and the intent must be gathered from all the facts and circumstances of the case. [Citations.]' (*Paul v Gulf Red Cedar Co* (1936) 15 Cal App 2d 196, 199, 59 P 2d 183.)

The question whether the plaintiff abandoned his spleen, or any of the other tissues taken by the defendants, is plainly a question of fact as to what his intent was at the time . . . A consent to removal of a diseased organ, or the taking of blood or other bodily tissues, does not necessarily imply an intent to abandon such organ, blood or tissue. The only fact alleged in the complaint on the subject is that the spleen was surgically removed, and that, had plaintiff known of defendants' intentions regarding the spleen, he would not have consented to its removal at UCLA. While it may be true that many people under such circumstances would be entirely indifferent to the disposition of removed tissue, we cannot assume plaintiff shared this state of mind. Nothing in the complaint indicates that plaintiff had an intent to abandon his spleen, and we do not find that, as a matter of law, anyone who consents to surgery abandons all removed tissue to the first person to claim it. Certainly, in the example of an unconscious patient, the concept of abandonment becomes ridiculous.

In California, absent evidence of a contrary intent or agreement, the reasonable expectation of a patient regarding tissue removed in the course of surgery would be that it may be examined by medical personnel for treatment purposes, and then promptly and permanently disposed of by interment or incineration in compliance with Health and Safety Code section 7054.4. Simply consenting to surgery under such circumstances hardly shows indifference to what may become of a removed organ or who may assert possession of it. Any use to which there was no consent, or which is not within the accepted understanding of the patient, is a conversion. It cannot be seriously asserted that a patient abandons a severed organ to the first person who takes it, nor can it be presumed that the patient is indifferent to whatever use might be made of it.

An inference of abandonment is particularly inappropriate when it comes to the use undertaken by defendants involving recombinant DNA technology. Almost from the beginning, this technology has incited intense moral, religious and ethical concerns. There are many patients whose religious beliefs would be deeply violated by use of their cells in recombinant DNA experiments without their consent, and who on being informed, would hardly be disinterested in the fate of their removed tissue. . . .

Rothman JA's thesis is that rarely (if ever) will a person be impliedly deemed to abandon his property for all purposes. Instead, he will abandon it 'on terms' to be determined in the light of the factual circumstances pertaining at the time (see also *Williams v Phillips* (1957) 121 JP 163).

3. Working out the property approach

We have seen that there is a plausible case for a court to adopt the property approach. The major test of nerve for the court minded to adopt the approach would come when a donor, sought in a property-based action, to link a claim for profits arising out of the use or exploitation of his tissue as, of course, occurred in *Moore*. An English court might resile from being drawn into what could be regarded as an unsavoury exercise as well as raising, as it would, complicated biotechnological issues and potential conflicts with the intellectual property rights which researchers may have.

Another reason why the court might be reluctant to adopt the property approach in circumstances in which the tissue has been exploited so as to generate financial gain (as in the *Moore* case) is as follows. Quite apart from specific restitution of the tissue (if that be possible or even desired!) what is the donor entitled to? Clearly, he would be entitled to the notional value of the tissue, but this is likely to be nominal. His real claim would be for the whole or a share of the financial gain from the exploitation of the tissue.

Paul Matthews examines the complexities of the law of conversion and improvements made to the thing allegedly converted. In reading the extract, it may help to substitute the phrase 'human tissue' for 'coal' in following his line of reasoning and applying it in the context with which we are concerned.

Paul Matthews 'Freedom, Unrequested Improvements, and Lord Denning' [1981] CLJ 340

The improver in possession

We shall first take the case of the improver B who acts without A's consent, and is a tortfeasor. Suppose that he digs a tunnel under A's land, hews coal from a seam, brings it to the surface, and grades and washes it so it is now ready for sale. It is worth many times more than it was underground. Suppose also that B is acting mala fide, perfectly aware that the chattels (for such they become once severed from the realty) belong to A, from under whose land they have been hewn. If A now comes along and demands the valuable coal, and B refuses, this refusal being held to amount to a conversion, what is the measure of damages?

As Lord Blackburn said in *Livingstone v Rawyards Coal Co* [(1880) 5 App Cas 25]:

> [I]n estimating the damages against a person who had carried away that chattel, it was considered and decided that the owner of the fee was to be paid the value of the chattel at the time when it was converted, and it would in fact have been improper, as qualifying his own wrong, to allow the wrongdoer anything for that mischief which he had done, or for what expense which he had incurred in converting the piece of rock into a chattel, which he had no business to do.

An actual decision of this kind is *Martin v Porter* [(1839) 5 M & W 351] where the defendant claimed to deduct the expenses of working the mine and bringing the coal to the surface from the damages in trespass. Lord Abinger C.B. said:

> If the plaintiff had demanded the coals from the defendant, no lien could have been set up in respect of the expense of getting them. How, then, can he now claim to deduct it? He cannot set up his own wrong. The plaintiff had a right to treat these coals as a chattel to which he was entitled. He did so, and the only question then was their value. That the jury have found. It may seem a hardship that the plaintiff should make this extra profit of the coal, but still the rule of law must prevail.

Thus our mala fide tortfeasor B is taken to have conferred a gratuitous benefit on A: A remains the owner of the coal despite its greatly enhanced value, and B has no claim either upon it (*ie*, such as a lien) or upon A personally. It should be noted, however, that A's damages are assessed as at the time of the conversion founding the action. If that conversion takes place at the moment of hewing, the value recovered by A is the value at the coalface, which is obviously less than the value at the mouth of the mine. If B sells at the surface and then pays damages to A he clearly retains the difference between coalface and surface values, *ie*, approximately the cost of raising. To this extent even a mala fide tortfeasor can be allowed something for his labour. But this 'allowance' depends on the act of conversion proved. If B converts the coal a second time, in selling it at the mouth of the mine, and A sues upon *that* conversion, then damages must be assessed by reference to surface value and B gets nothing for his trouble.

However, where B was bona fide and non-negligent, he was formerly entitled to deduct, as a matter of practice, if not law, any expenses which A would himself have had to incur in realising the value of the goods, such as the costs of raising, and even of severing the coal in the first place. As Lord Macnaghten explained in *Peruvian Guano v Dreyfus Bros* [(1892) AC 166]:

> [i]n cases of trover and in cases of trespass, where there were no circumstances of aggravation, juries were told that they might take into consideration, in mitigation of damages, payments which the plaintiff himself would have had to make if the defendants had not made them.

What the courts were doing was avoiding the 'inconvenient' consequences of the common law rule, as Lord Macnaghten put it, 'by the convenient instrumentality of a jury, more concerned to administer what they thought justice than to maintain the strict rules and rigorous maxims of the Common Law.'

Thus for example, in *Wood v, Morewood* [(1841) 3 QB 440] at Nisi Prius, Parke B (who had been at both Nisi Prius and in the Exchequer in the earlier case of *Martin v Porter*) told the jury:

> that, if there was fraud or negligence on the part of the defendant, they might give, as damages under the count in trover, the value of the coals at the time they first became chattels, on the principle laid down in *Martin v Porter*; but, if they thought that the defendant was not guilty of fraud or negligence, but acting fairly and honestly in the full belief that he had a right to do what he did, they might give the fair value of the coals as if the coal field had been purchased from the plaintiff.

It should be noted that Parke B.'s direction requires for the full allowance not merely bona fides from the defendant, but also *no negligence* in believing the goods to be his.

The 'fair value' of the property as if purchased in its unimproved state would depend on the circumstances of the particular case: it might be the open market value (less the necessary costs of hewing, raising, and selling), as in *Jegon v Vivian* [(1871) 6 Ch App 742] or it might be the value to a particular individual (less those costs), there being no open market, as happened in *Livingstone v Rawyards Coal Co*. In the former case the property owner would expect to retain the overall profit for himself: in the latter case much of this profit would go to the improver, and the property owner would have to be content with a royalty (as in *Livingstone's* case).

This practice, of distinguishing bona and mala fide defendants, was approved by the highest authority, the House of Lords, in both *Livingstone v Rawyards Coal Co*. and *Peruvian Guano v Dreyfus Bros*. Yet the courts have perhaps not always observed this distinction. *Munro v Wilmott* [[1949] 1 KB 295] is a case in point. Here the plaintiff was permitted to leave her motor car with the defendant 'temporarily,' but in fact the plaintiff moved away from the district, became untraceable, and the car remained there for several years. Eventually the defendant, finding the car an obstacle and being unable to communicate with the plaintiff, sold it for £100. To make the car saleable at all, given its poor condition after so long in the open, the defendant had spent £85 in repairs and renovations. The plaintiff sued the defendant in detinue and conversion, and the judge found the car's value at judgment to be £120, although without the defendant's work it would have been worth only £20. The question was, what was the plaintiff to recover, and was the defendant entitled to any allowance for his work? Lynskey J. said:

> It seems to me that, in assessing that value [*ie*, of the plaintiff's property in the car], I must have regard to what the defendant has spent in making the car saleable; otherwise I should be taking the saleable value of something which was partly the

plaintiff's property and partly that of somebody else, because of the cost of the defendant's work on and materials in the car. In my view, the statement of law in *Salmond on Torts* (10th edn, p 309), is correct: 'If, on the other hand, the property increases in value after the date of the conversion, a distinction has to be drawn. If the increase is due to the act of the defendant, the plaintiff has no title to it, and his claim is limited to the original value of the chattel.' *Reid v Fairbanks* [(1853) 13 CB 692] is referred to . . .

The learned judge awarded the plaintiff £35, as being the car's improved value (£120) less the cost of the improvements (£85). Prima facie, therefore, it seems that a defendant who well knew he had no title is being allowed to deduct what he spent, unnecessarily, in improving the plaintiff's property. But two points may be made. The first, and less important, is this: the materials and parts added by the defendant would continue to belong to him (as the judge recognised) and not to the plaintiff by some doctrine such as the Roman *accessio*, and so the plaintiff's property lost was less than the conglomerate whole. Some means had to be found to take this into account.

The second, and more substantial, point is this. We are not told what was the act of conversion relied on by the plaintiff in *Munro v Wilmott*. The most obvious one would be the purported sale, ie, *after* the improvements had been effected. But the extract from *Salmond on Torts*, and the case of *Reid v Fairbanks* on which it is based, are clearly dealing with situations where the act of conversion *precedes* the improvements. *Reid v Fairbanks* was a case where probably there were two acts of conversion: first procuring a registration certificate of the ship in question (then unfinished) in the names of persons not the true owners, and secondly (several months later) a demand by the true owners, and refusal by the defendants to deliver up possession. Between these two events the ship was completed by the defendants at some expense. The plaintiffs' case was conversion, based *entirely* on the procuring of the registration certificate, and *not* on the demand and refusal. Jarvis CJ said during the argument:

> If the conversion had taken place at Liverpool [*i.e.*, on the occasion of the demand and refusal], the point would have been presented more favourably for the plaintiffs. The demand and refusal, however, are only evidence of a conversion; and here there was proof of an actual conversion by the alteration of the registry at Nova Scotia.

Thus damages were awarded for the pre-completion conversion, which damages were ascertained by reference to the value of the ship *as at that date*.

If this is the principle approved as correct in *Munro v Wilmott*, it can easily be seen how such a small sum as £35 is arrived at: it represents (perhaps rather too generously) the value of the car before the improvements, assuming a pre-improvement conversion. If the conversion, however, took place on the purported sale by the defendant, it is very difficult to see how the principle cited from Salmond, or *Reid v Fairbanks*, can be of any assistance.

Further, it is even more difficult to see why damages for detinue 'must be similar, if not the same', since detinue used to be ascertained as at the date of judgment, not the date of any conversion. However, this is no longer a problem, as by the Torts (Interference with Goods) Act 1977, s 2 (1), 'Detinue is abolished.'

It must be said, then, that *Munro v Wilmott* is a slightly odd case. It does not sit quite squarely with existing principles even though in some way explicable on an orthodox basis, and must therefore be regarded with some suspicion. As we shall see, in any case, it may be that the most heterodox aspects of the case have been nullified by the 1977 Act.

On the whole, however, we see that the improver, though he could not claim any part of the ownership of the improved goods, could in practice claim an allowance for his improvement in proceedings against him for, say, conversion of the goods, an allowance increasing in value as the improver was honest and reasonable. This practice has now become a legal rule, by the Torts (Interference with Goods) Act 1977, s 6(1), which reads:

> If in proceedings for wrongful interference against a person (the 'improver') who has improved the goods, it is shown that the improver acted in the mistaken but honest belief that he had a good title to them, an allowance shall be made for the extent to which, at the time at which the goods fall to be valued in assessing damages, the value of the goods is attributable to the improvement.

It will be noted that section 6(1) set out above is wider than the previous 'law' in one respect: even a negligent improver will fall within its purview, provided only that he is honest.

The Act does not, however, deal with the case of the improver who is mala fide. Are we to infer from the fact that he is not mentioned that he is denied all allowance (thus effecting a change in the law)? Or may we say that since the statute does not expressly abolish his right to be allowed any expenses which he would previously have been allowed he must continue to be so allowed those expenses? The former view is espoused by McGregor [*McGregor on Damages* (14th edn) 1980] and Sacks, [41 MLR, 713] and the latter by Palmer [*Bailment* 1979]. However, it is submitted that a distinction is to be drawn between the accidental 'allowance' resulting in practice from the plaintiff's reliance on an act of conversion earlier than the sale realising the goods (by which time the defendant had made them more valuable), and the allowance arguably made as of right in *Munro v Wilmott* (if the purported sale were the occasion of the conversion founded upon). The latter allowance is clearly inconsistent with the enactment of section 6 of the 1977 Act: if this view of *Munro v Wilmott* were ever and remained good law the section would be a waste of time. On the other hand, the former 'allowance' might perfectly well remain available for mala fide defendants, so that only those bona fide could claim the full section 6 allowance. Since the 1977 Act does not claim to be a complete code, but only 'to amend the law concerning conversion and other torts affecting goods', it seems proper to infer that unless the Act expressly or by implication abolishes or replaces pre-existing rules those rules continue to have effect. It is therefore submitted that *Munro v Wilmott* is overruled, so far as it established the allowance as of right, but that the accidental 'allowance' resulting from the plaintiff's suing on an early conversion is still available to mala fide defendants.

You will notice that Matthews reaches the conclusion that whether under s 6(1) (the 'good faith improver') or under the common law (the 'bad faith improver') the law is that the donor gets all the financial gain made (if the act of conversion relied on is the ultimate realisation of the gain) or nothing, ie in our context the notional value of the tissue (if the act of conversion relied upon precedes the improvement).

A middle position which does not depend upon the technical matter of the date of conversion relied upon is proposed by Sir Eric Scowen commenting on the *Moore* case.

E Scowen, 'The Human Body – Whose Property and Whose Profit' (1990) 1 (1) *Dispatches* 1 at 2-3

Perhaps of greater interest in the *Moore* case is the Supreme Court's decision on the ability of a person to own and control after removal his tissues and body parts. Moore argued that he continued to own his cells and hence retained the right to direct their use in potentially lucrative research and, consequently, he was entitled to the profits generated. No court had previously decided this issue. To apply the notion of ownership (and hence the tort of conversion) in this context would have been novel, and an extension of the common law. The Supreme Court refused to take this step forward.

The court agreed that for Moore to establish an action for conversion, he would have to prove he owned the excised cells or, at least, had a right to possession of them. Moore did not expect to retain possession of his cells after removal, and thus he could only sue for conversion if he retained ownership in them. The Court was influenced by a number of factors in denying this part of Moore's claim. First, there were no judicial precedents. Second, the statutory law in California strongly suggested that a patient could at best have a very limited right to control research on excised cells. Thus, in the light of this, it would be inconsistent to view Moore's cells as property at common law entailing the consequent right to control their use. Thirdly, the Court drew a distinction between the cells removed from the body and the profitable cell-line. Even if Moore could own the former, the cell-line, which was subsequently produced by the defendants, was sufficiently distinct from the original cells that Moore could not claim he owned that. Fourthly, the Court took the view that enforcing a physician's obligations to disclose his research interests and any potential for commercial exploitation sufficiently protected patients from the type of harm which Moore alleged, without the need to recognise his proprietary claim.

The decision of the Supreme Court is something of a disappointment. The dismissal of the property claim rests on somewhat slender authority. The absence of judicial precedent is quoted, but as remarked by the two dissenting judges, no case law dictated the majority's view either. The statutory law in California exerted a strong influence on the Court, but in truth is ambiguous in the present context. Although the statute regulates scientific research, it makes no mention of bodily material for commercial exploitation. Hence, the statutory provisions do not necessarily deny Moore's conversion claim.

Finally, the Court took the view that any impediment to research on human cells was against the public interest. To recognise a patient's property rights over excised body material could adversely affect research and so the grant of such rights was a matter solely for the state legislature.

If the case depends upon the statutory context in California, the impact on English law might not be significant since there is no legislative indication that an individual has only limited rights over excised bodily tissue in England. Arguably in this country, public policy points in the opposite direction (for example, see the Polkinghorne Report on the use of fetal tissue) and hence, the English courts might find the dissenting judgment of Justice Mosk more persuasive. He held that at common law a patient retained proprietary rights over excised cells unless the patient had abandoned them. Mosk J strongly rejected all the arguments pressed by the majority of the court and concluded that it would be 'inequitable and immoral' not to allow Moore a share of the profits arising from an enterprise to which his 'contribution . . . [was] absolutely crucial'.

As this highlights, an important reason for accepting a proprietary claim in a situation like the *Moore* case, is the underlying belief that the provider of the raw 'materials' which are commercially exploited should receive at least some share of the profit. The majority of the Court argued that if Moore succeeded in establishing a breach of fiduciary duty or a lack of informed consent this would be achieved. But, as Justice Mosk pointed out, it is unlikely for two reasons: first, in a negligence action the measure of damages is the patient's loss due to harm and not loss of profits due to improper use of his cells; secondly, the major profits, if they arise, will not primarily accrue to the doctors against whom these two actions lie, but the commercial concerns at one remove from them. Whilst the doctrine of vicarious liability might reach the profit makers if the doctors were their employees, this will not be the case in many circumstances.

Only by recognising the patient's proprietary claim could a court ensure, as equity requires, that the provider of the cells should receive a reasonable share in the profits.

It is important to note a point not developed in *Moore's* case. A proprietary claim would only entitle the patient to a share, perhaps even a small share of the profits, because equity would recognise the elements of work and skill employed in the development of a cell-line, and compensate the medical researchers accordingly. Their share might be the greater. It is arguable that the majority of the Court may have been influenced by the belief that if Moore succeeded in his proprietary claim all profits would be his or at least he could decide on any distribution.

All the legal problems associated with the property approach might be made to go away if the practice of obtaining the donor's consent to subsequent use and exploitation were to be adopted. Of course, if the property approach is correct then the donor's consent is essential (subject to the doctrine of abandonment) if the user is to avoid liability in conversion. Alternatively, consent may be necessary to avoid a claim by the donor that his bodily integrity was invaded unlawfully. This, you will recall, was the approach of the majority in the *Moore* case. We have already discussed whether there is any basis for this approach in English law, involving as it does an extensive duty to disclose or an extension of the law of battery (*supra*, ch 3).

What the donor must consent to will, of course, depend upon the circumstances. If the use to which the tissue is to be put is of a general nature, eg archiving or teaching, then a general consent to those uses will be sufficient. This is so also if the tissue is to be used for research. The problematic point is where the research leads or may lead to financial gain. Under the property approach if there is no consent given for the *exploitation* of the tissue, even if such exploitation was not contemplated at the time of removal, the consent is exceeded. The donor has a claim. If, however, the need for consent derives from the laws concerned with the protection of bodily integrity, it is clear that exploitation not contemplated at the time of removal would not retrospectively affect the valid consent given at the time of removal and would not, therefore, give rise to a claim.

The position is less clear if there was an undisclosed intention to exploit the tissue removed. American law tends to regard the relationship between doctor and patient as a fiduciary one thus casting upon the doctor a duty not to create a situation of conflict of interests with the patient whereby the doctor benefits at the patient's expense, unless the patient consents to the conflict arising. English law, as we have seen in Chapters 3 and 9, does not see the relationship as a fiduciary one. Hence the argument of there being a duty to disclose, as we saw, is harder to make. Unfortunately, the tissue may not be used or exploited by the doctor who treated the patient. There will not be, on any view, a fiduciary relationship between the researcher or biotechnology company and the donor. Hence, as against them, only the property approach could assist the donor (see Mosk J's views in *Moore*). (An example of resort to a framework of consents so at to avoid the need to determine the legal status of extra-corporeal bodily material can be seen in Sch 3 of the Human Fertilisation and Embryology Act 1990 (discussed *supra*, ch 11).)

E. LIABILITY IN TORT

1. Negligence

(a) Action by donee

When, if ever, can the donor of tissue or an organ, or a doctor or procurement agency, be liable to the donee who suffers harm as a consequence of the donation?

The ordinary principles of negligence apply in any possible action brought by a donee of tissue or an organ. What may be helpful here is to notice the sorts of particular problems which arise in any possible negligence action (see generally, Kusanovich, 'Medical Malpractice Liability and the Organ Transplant' (1971) 5 USFL Rev 223).

(i) AN ACTION VERSUS THE DONOR

The donor's potential liability will most probably arise from allegations of non-disclosure of a known (or knowable?) genetic problem or other relevant history which could cause injury to the donee. The question is what is the donor's duty of disclosure in such circumstances?

There is a growing body of law in the United States which may help us to deal with this question. It concerns the liability of a sexual partner for a sexually transmitted disease. In the 1989 Supplement to *Law, Science and Medicine*, Areen, King, Goldberg and Capron write at pp 129-130:

> . . . A legal basis for such a suit can be found in earlier cases involving nondisclosure of venereal disease, such as *Kathleen K v Robert B* 150 Cal App 3d 992, 198 Cal Rptr 273 (1984), in which a woman sued her former boyfriend for infecting her with genital herpes. In reversing the trial court's summary judgment for defendant, a District Court of Appeal observed that the defendant's constitutional right of privacy is overcome both by the allegedly tortious nature of his conduct, and by the state's interest 'in the prevention and control of contagious and dangerous disease'. *Id* at 996, 198 Cal Rptr at 276. Noting that herpes is not listed among the venereal diseases in the California Health and Safety Code, the court stated:
>
> > [T]hat section was enacted in 1957, long before herpes achieved its present notoriety. We are not inclined to bar appellant's cause of action on the basis that genital herpes

is not a venereal disease. It is a disease that can be propagated by sexual contact. Like AIDS it is now known by the public to be a contagious and dreadful disease. At the core of this action is the misrepresentation of defendant that he did not have a contagious disease that could be passed to his partner. If a person knowingly has genital herpes, AIDS or some other contagious and serious disease, a limited representation that he or she does not have venereal disease is no defense to this type of action.

Id at 996-997, n 3, 198 Cal Rptr at 276, n 3. The court went on to say that consent to sexual intercourse was vitiated by one partner's concealment of the risk of infecting the other with a contagious disease. *Id* at 997, 198 Cal Rptr at 276. A Georgia court has allowed a man to use a negligence theory in suing his former girlfriend for infecting him with herpes. The court ruled that whether an infected person exercised due care is a jury question, and declined to impose a specific duty to warn in all herpes cases: *Long v Adams* 175 Ga App 538, 333 SE 2d 852 (1985). See also Note, Liability in Tort for the Sexual Transmission of Disease: Genital Herpes and the Law, 70 Cornell L Rev 101 (1984) (discussing recovery based on theories of negligence and battery).

The English courts could well reach a similar conclusion to the California decision. The duty of the donor might well turn on such factors as (i) knowledge that he suffers from some infection or is the carrier of a defective gene; (ii) knowledge that he has taken part in high risk activity (eg in the context of infection with HIV).

However, whether a donor of an organ or tissue owes a duty of care to a recipient is a novel question. It must be borne in mind that the recent approach to the tort of negligence suggests that the House of Lords would be reluctant to recognise liability here (eg *Caparo Industries plc v Dickman* [1990] 2 AC 605 and *Murphy v Brentwood DC* [1991] 1 AC 398).

Furthermore, even if a duty to disclose on the part of the donor were found to exist, it may still be said that the conduct of others, such as the doctors or those in a pathology laboratory, if careless, breaks the chain of causation. The better view is, however, that carelessness of this sort is reasonably foreseeable and should not therefore be held to constitute a *novus actus interveniens* (see Hart and Honoré *Causation in the Law* (2nd edn, 1985) at p 184).

This body of law, important as it is, does not entirely resolve questions of the liability of a donor to a donee in the context of the donation of body tissue or an organ. This is because what we are concerned with may differ in one significant respect from sexually transmitted disease: the tissue and organ donation may be between non-genetically related persons and thus would take place in circumstances of anonymity. In such a case, the donee cannot trace who the donor was. And, when a donee attempted to do so, the Florida court in the following case refused his application.

Rasmussen v South Florida Blood Service (1987) 500 So 2d 533 (Sup Ct Florida)

Barkett, Justice: We have for review *South Florida Blood Service, Inc v Rasmussen*, 467 So 2d 798 (Fla 3d DCA 1985). In that decision, the district court certified the following as a question of great public importance:

Do privacy interests of volunteer blood donors and a blood service's and society's interest in maintaining a strong volunteer blood donation system outweigh a plaintiff's interest in discovering the names and addresses of the blood donors in the hope that further discovery will provide some evidence that he contracted AIDS from transfusions necessitated by injuries which are the subject of his suit?

We answer the question in the affirmative.

On May 24, 1982, petitioner, Donald Rasmussen, was sitting on a park bench when he was struck by an automobile. He sued the driver and alleged owner of the automobile for personal injuries he sustained in the accident. While hospitalised as a result of his injuries, Rasmussen received fifty-one units of blood via transfusion. In July of 1983, he was diagnosed as having 'Acquired Immune Deficiency Syndrome' (AIDS) and died of that disease one year later. In an attempt to prove that the source of his AIDS was the necessary medical treatment he received because of injuries sustained in the accident, Rasmussen served respondent, South Florida Blood Service (Blood Service), with a *subpoena duces tecum* requesting 'any and all records, documents and other material indicating the names and addresses of the [51] blood donors'. (South Florida Blood Service is not a party to the underlying personal injury litigation, and there has been no allegation of negligence on the part of the Blood Service.)

The Blood Service moved the trial court to either quash the *subpoena* or issue a protective order barring disclosure. . . .

It is now known that AIDS is a major health problem with calamitous potential. At present, there is no known cure and the mortality rate is high. As noted by the court below, medical researchers have identified a number of groups which have a high incidence of the disease and are labelled 'high risk' groups . . .

As the district court recognised, petitioner needs more than just the names and addresses of the donors. His interest is in establishing that one or more of the donors has AIDS or is in a high risk group. Petitioner argues that his inquiry *may* never go beyond comparing the donors' names against a list of known AIDS victims, or against other public records (eg conviction records in order to determine whether any of the donors is a known drug user). He contends that because a limited inquiry *may* reveal the information he seeks, with no invasion of privacy, the donors' privacy rights are not yet at issue. We find this argument disingenuous. As we have already noted, the discovery rules allow a trial judge upon good cause shown to set conditions under which discovery will be given. Some method could be formulated to verify the Blood Service's report that none of the donors is a known AIDS victim while preserving the confidentiality of the donors' identities. However, the *subpoena* in question gives petitioner access to the names and addresses of the blood donors with no restrictions on their use. There is nothing to prohibit petitioner from conducting an investigation without the knowledge of the persons in question. We cannot ignore, therefore, the consequences of disclosure to nonparties, including the possibility that a donor's coworkers, friends, employers, and others may be queried as to the donor's sexual preferences, drug use, or general life-style.

The threat posed by the disclosure of the donors' identities goes far beyond the immediate discomfort occasioned by a third party probing into sensitive areas of the donors' lives. Disclosure of donor identities in any context involving AIDS could be extremely disruptive and even devastating to the individual donor. If the requested information is released, and petitioner queries the donors' friends and fellow employees, it will be functionally impossible to prevent occasional references to AIDS. As the district court recognised:

> AIDS is the modern day equivalent of leprosy. AIDS, or a suspicion of AIDS, can lead to discrimination in employment, education, housing and even medical treatment.

We wish to emphasise that although the importance of protecting the privacy of donor information does not depend on the special stigma associated with AIDS, public response to the disease does make this a more critical matter. By the very nature of this case, disclosure of donor identities is disclosure in a damaging context. We conclude, therefore, that the disclosure sought here implicates constitutionally protected privacy interests.

Our analysis of the interests to be served by denying discovery does not end with the effects of disclosure on the private lives of the fifty-one donors implicated in this case. Society has a vital interest in maintaining a strong volunteer blood supply, a task that has become more difficult with the emergence of AIDS. The donor population has been reduced by the necessary exclusion of potential blood donors through AIDS screening and testing procedures as well as by the unnecessary reduction in the donor population as a result of the widespread fear that donation itself can transmit the disease. In light of this, it is clearly 'in the public interest to discourage any serious disincentive to volunteer blood donation'. Because there is little doubt that the prospect of inquiry into one's private life and potential association with AIDS will deter blood donation, we conclude that society's interest in a strong and healthy blood supply will be furthered by the denial of discovery in this case.

In balancing the competing interests involved, we do not ignore Rasmussen's interest in obtaining the requested information in order to prove aggregation of his injuries and obtain full recovery. We recognise that petitioner's interest parallels the state's interest in ensuring full compensation for victims of negligence. However, we find that the discovery order requested here would do little to advance that interest. The probative value of the discovery sought by Rasmussen is dubious at best. The potential of significant harm to most, if not all, of the fifty-one unsuspecting donors in permitting such a fishing expedition is great and far outweighs the plaintiff's need under these circumstances. . . .

We think that this reflects what an English court would decide. The point arose directly in *AB v Scottish Blood Transfusion Service* (1990) SCLR 263 (Court of Session (Outer House)) where Lord Morrison held that public policy (as evidenced by the certificate of the Secretary of State) demanded that the anonymity of the blood donor be preserved in the interests of maintaining a national blood transfusion service. For an analogous example of the balancing of the factors of public policy in English law, see *D v National Society for the Prevention of Cruelty to Children* [1978] AC 171, [1977] 1 All ER 589.

By contrast, some courts in the United States have held otherwise, Even then, however, they have allowed discovery of the donor's identity but have prevented contact with him or have refused to identify the donor but allowed questions to be put to him through the court (eg *Tarrant County Hospital District v Hughes* (1987) 734 SW 2d 675 (Tx CA) and *Belle Bonfils Memorial Blood Center v District Court of Denver* (1988) 763 P 2d 1003 (Colo Sup Ct)).

(ii) AN ACTION VERSUS THE DOCTOR OR PROCUREMENT AGENCY

Here the donee will be alleging negligence in carrying out the particular procedure, a failure to discover relevant medical information from the donor or the donee, not carrying out proper tests or failing to inform a donee of the risks and alternatives, in breach of the doctor's legal duty.

Kenneth Norrie illustrates some of the situations in 'Human Tissue Transplants: Legal Liability in Different Jurisdictions', (1985) International and Comparative Law Quarterly 442 at pp 445-446

> . . . For example, to transfer blood taken from a hepatitis sufferer to a recipient would surely suggest liability in damages for the person responsible to ensure that the blood was uninfected. In *Ravenis v Detroit General Hospital* [234 NW 2d 411 (1975)], a claim was held competent where it was alleged that the hospital was negligent in the selection of cornea donors who were not fit within the medical standard of care of the community. Similarly, concern has lately been expressed about patients receiving blood transfusions from donors who suffer from acquired immunodeficiency syndrome (AIDS) [*semble* infected with HIV]. Since the person actually performing the operation is ultimately responsible for the recipient's health, it is with him that liability must eventually rest, though he may also share it with the physician responsible for the extraction of the donation if he is different. Giesen cites a French case in which a surgeon was held liable for transplanting a cornea into a recipient having taken it from a donor who had died from rabies. The recipient shortly afterwards also died from rabies. In this case it would appear that the transplanting surgeon was responsible not only for the transplantation, but also for the wrongful diagnosis of the donor's death as being from brain-fever. Difficulties as to who is liable to the recipient may arise if the person performing the transplant into the recipient is different from the person extracting the organ from the donor (as will generally be the case, for example, with blood transfusions). It is submitted that the determination of the person liable in such circumstances shall depend upon the extent to which the surgeon performing the transplant is entitled to rely on what he is told by the person extracting the donation. While the transplanting surgeon, being ultimately responsible for the patient's welfare, must in the general case be held liable for failing personally to ensure the suitability of the donation (just as a surgeon, being ultimately responsible for the procedure in any operation, is not entitled to rely on a swab count reported correct to him by a nurse), it is nevertheless possible to envisage circumstances in which he may escape liability. In, for example, the case of blood transfusions, it is suggested that the doctor performing the transfusion is entitled to rely on the information concerning the blood which he is given from the blood bank or persons

responsible for taking the donation, because it would be unreasonable to expect him to carry out his own (repeat) tests to determine the blood group etc of the donation.

For a discussion of the law in the United States, see Annotation 'Liability of hospital, physician, or other individual medical practitioner for injury or death resulting from blood transfusion' 20 ALR 4th 129.

As Norrie notes, the questions raised here have acquired particular importance because of the spread of HIV infection. There have been a number of cases in Australia (eg *H v The Royal Alexandra Hospital for Children* [1990] 1 Med LR 297 and *E v Australian Red Cross Society* [1992] 2 Med LR 303) and a large number in the US (eg *Kozup v Georgetown University* (1987) 663 F Supp 1048 (D DC) and (1988) 851 F 2d 437 (DC Cir)). For an account of developments in the law see *AIDS and the Law* (ed M Rhodes) 1991 Cumulative Supplement pp 9-18 in which the donee of blood or blood products has brought an action after becoming infected with HIV.

In the UK in *Re HIV Haemophiliac Litigation* 1990 NLJR 1349, 962 haemophiliacs sued the government in negligence and for breach of statutory duty under the National Health Service Act 1977. The plaintiffs were infected with the Human ImmunoDeficiency Virus (HIV), which causes AIDS, as a result of receiving infected Factor VIII (the clotting agent) imported from America during the early 1980s.

The plaintiffs made a wide range of allegations of negligence against the government including: (1) failure to achieve self sufficiency in UK blood products and continuing to import blood products from America; (2) failure to use heat treated blood products, a process which destroys HIV; (3) failure to screen out infected blood donors in the UK; (4) failure to use tests to detect infected donated blood; (5) failure to revoke or suspend the licences granted under the Medicines Act 1968 to commercially produced blood products from America. The action was not a trial of the plaintiff's claims against the government but was an application for discovery of a large number of government documents. The documents were, on the whole, internal government documents relating to the formulation of government policy on the activities of, and allocation of resources to, the Blood Transfusion Service and, in addition, the importation of American blood products. The government resisted their disclosure, claiming it was against the public interest. The main argument of the government was that the documents were irrelevant because the plaintiffs' allegations of negligence could not be legally sustained.

The Court of Appeal held that it was impossible to say that the haemophiliacs did not have an arguable legal case in negligence against the government. The court held that the government could owe a duty to the haemophiliacs to exercise reasonable care in the running of the NHS so as to protect them from receiving infected blood products even though many of the plaintiffs' allegations involved challenges to the government formulation of policy within the NHS. Where the formulation of government policy is challenged in a negligence action the courts have been reluctant to impose legal duties on government, regarding such issues as political and non-justiciable in the courts. The court emphasised that there would be difficulties at the trial because the claims involved 'the exercise of discretion, policy making, allocation of resources' but that at this preliminary stage of the case it could not be emphatically held that no legal action could be brought. However, the court emphasised that the trial court might, after a full consideration, decide there was no case in law.

In addition, the court also emphasised that at the trial the plaintiffs might still fail because the Court of Appeal was assuming the facts favourable to their claim at this preliminary stage. Establishing negligence might be difficult when the facts were fully investigated. As Ralph Gibson LJ said, '[i]t may be that, at the dates alleged, the nature and gravity of the risks to the plaintiffs were not as alleged or were not known to be such; and that the alleged steps for eliminating the risk were not available, or were reasonably judged to be of inadequate utility'.

As regards the plaintiffs' claims based upon a breach of statutory duty under the National Health Service Act 1977, the Court of Appeal was more circumspect about the potential success of the claim. The court took the view that the duties imposed upon the Secretary of State for Health under the Act were vague and general and not such as to 'clearly demonstrate the intention of Parliament to impose a duty which is to be enforced by individual civil action'. Ralph Gibson LJ described the plaintiffs' actions as being 'at best of uncertain validity in law'.

Nevertheless, since the plaintiffs' negligence claims were legally arguable, the court referred the case back to a judge who would decide, after inspecting the documents, whether they were 'very likely to assist' the plaintiffs and, if so, order their production. The Court of Appeal allowed the plaintiffs' claim to continue. In the words of Bingham LJ, '. . . the law might arguably be thought defective if it did not afford redress'.

In December 1990, the government agreed a settlement with the plaintiffs and so the liability of the defendants was never determined. In March 1992 the government settled the remaining claims of plaintiffs who had been infected through blood transfusions. Hence, the legal issues which were so clearly focused in this case remain unanswered in the UK.

As this case and the litigation abroad show, there are a variety of potential bases for liability. They include the adequacy of screening blood donors, the existence and adequacy of procedures for testing blood for HIV infection and failure to warn adequately (or at all) of the risks of transmissions. These potential bases for liability can apply, *mutatis mutandis*, to infection transmitted through other body fluids (eg semen) or tissue (eg kidneys). (For the UK Government's position on testing for HIV as regards tissue and body fluids (other than blood) see, CMO (87)5 and CMO(90)2. Routine testing of blood for HIV-1 was introduced in October 1985 and for HIV-2 in June 1990.)

(b) Action by donor

(i) AN ACTION VERSUS THE DOCTOR

Is the extent of the doctor's duty to disclose the same when the doctor is advising the donor as when he is advising the donee? As regards the genetically *unrelated* donor the matter is dealt with in the 1989 Regulations (see *supra*, pp 1090-1092). Failure to comply would give the donor a cause of action in negligence if he suffered harm because the court would regard the Regulation as setting the standard for disclosure. Where the donor is genetically *related* to the intended donee the court might similarly be guided by the Regulations. After all, the donor is a healthy person who is being subjected to procedures of varying degrees of risk. Here, there can be no justification for withholding relevant information on medical grounds.

This duty encompasses an obligation to explain the alternatives, consequences and risks and importantly may include a duty to advise about the possible psychological, as well as physical, reactions which the donor may develop after the donation.

In addition to actions based upon a failure to inform the donor, a doctor might, of course, be sued for the negligent performance of the procedure. We are here in the realm of medical malpractice law which we have already considered in Chapter 5.

(ii) AN ACTION VERSUS A THIRD PARTY

Urbanski v Patel (1978) 84 DLR (3d) 650 (Manitoba Queen's Bench)

Wilson J: These two suits for medical malpractice were consolidated for trial. Plaintiffs Shirley and Stanley Firman, husband and wife, claim damages caused by defendants' negligence in mistakenly removing Mrs Firman's one and only kidney, whereby both their lives have been seriously disrupted. Plaintiff Urbanski, Mrs Firman's father, donated one of his own kidneys (as what father would not?) for transplant, in a vain effort to ease the disaster, and claims his own costs and other expenses associated with that operation . . .

Patel admits negligence, and concedes liability to the Firmans, but denies any responsibility to Urbanski as a result of his negligent treatment of Mrs Firman . . .

. . . Shirley Firman and her doctor decided that, all things considered, it would be just as well if there were no more children. And so, it was arranged she would undergo a tubal ligation. And, because for some time she had felt occasional abdominal discomfort (nothing specific or disabling and perhaps caused, thought her doctor, by an ovarian cyst) her operation was to include exploration for and, if found, removal of that offender.

Otherwise in good health, on April 17th Mrs Firman submitted to this procedure when, by mistake, defendant incorrectly identified a body found in the lower left quadrant of her abdomen and excised this, believing it to be an ovarian cyst.

But, it was a kidney, out of place indeed (ectopic) but a kidney none the less. Indeed, her only kidney, this being a congenital accident hitherto unknown, or even suspected. And while seemingly one can get along quite well – as had this plaintiff – with only half the normal complement of two kidneys, the situation is altogether different if the patient has none at all.

Within two days of the operation Mrs Firman had been admitted to the emergency department of the Health Sciences Centre in Winnipeg. By that time, the material removed had been correctly identified, and the total absence of any renal function was confirmed. On the day following, April 20th, the significance of this irreversible disaster was explained to the plaintiff husband and wife, and Mrs Firman was put on peritoneal dialysis . . .

. . . [A] suitable candidate may be invited to surrender one of his two kidneys to someone else who has none at all, the risk to the donor, seemingly not that great in any event, being entirely overborne by the desperate condition of the other, and the expected improvement in life-style for the donee.

Search elsewhere was finally abandoned, and in the spring of 1976 Shirley's father, the plaintiff Urbanski, volunteered one of his kidneys, implanted on May 8th. Unhappily this was not a success, and it had to be removed three days later, when of course she went back to the machine. On May 31st a cadaveric transplant was attempted, with no more success, and this was removed on June 4, 1976.

. . . [As for] Victor Urbanski, in its simplest terms this plaintiff says that he did no more than would any other father, faced with the obvious distress of his daughter, namely, donated one of his own kidneys so that she – who had none – may have a better chance of survival.

Defendant's plea is that this act, and the expenses attendant thereon, may not be looked upon as a foreseeable consequence of the wrong done to Shirley Firman.

That argument prevailed in *Sirianni v Anna* 285 NYS 2d 709 (1967). In that case because of the acute infection which set in after a routine hernia repair, an exploratory operation was done to see if, perhaps, the patient's condition was caused by a wound abscess or by appendicitis. In the course of this surgery a kidney was removed. And, as with Mrs Firman, that was the patient's only kidney. Dialysis was not a full answer, and his mother donated one of her kidneys, and sued for her expenses and general damages.

Her action failed, Ward, J, considering (p 712) that:

The premeditated, knowledgeable and purposeful act of this plaintiff in donating one of her kidneys to preserve the life of her son did not extend or reactivate the consummated negligence of these defendants. The conduct of the plaintiff herein is a clearly defined, independent, intervening act with full knowledge of the consequences.

Mrs Sirianni's decision to give up one of her kidneys he thought was wilful, intentional, voluntary, free from accident, and could not be laid at defendant's door. The classical tests of foreseeability and proximate cause, thought the learned Judge, precluded recovery, because the plaintiff's conduct was a clearly defined, independent, intervening act. And, since that act was independent, as well as unforeseeable, it broke the causation, and superseded defendant's negligence in removing the kidney.

But in 1963, when Mrs Sirianni's son lost his kidney, indeed in 1967 when her case was decided, the notion of organ transplant was in its infancy. We all know that not until December, 1967, did Dr Christiaan Barnard accomplish the first heart transplant in man. So then, Ward, J, could well comment, as he did (p 713) that, 'The miracle of modern medical science seems not to be on the threshold of successfully transferring many organs from one human body to another.'

Sirianni, of course, is not binding on me. Apart from that, in studying that case one should read, too, the commentary thereon included in the very useful article 'Medical Malpractice Liability and the Organ Transplant', published with the April, 1971 issue, 5 USFL Rev 223, by Mark Kusanovich, who wrote, at pp 258-9:

Kidney transplantation is of recent origin. Thus, the date on which Sirianni's kidney was negligently removed is relevant to determine whether a contingency of transplant from a live donor was foreseeable. Apparently, the first successful human kidney transplant was performed in 1954. By 1963, 244 kidney transplants had involved live donors. But at that time the field was still very new with live donors coming from close members of the family and with some physicians discouraging donation except from identical twins. Thus, in 1963, the date of the Sirianni transplant, the question whether it was foreseeable that Sirianni, who had no twin, would receive a live organ donation was debatable. Since 1963, kidney transplantation has progressed rapidly. The statistics up to 1970 indicate that approximately 4,000 kidney transplants have been performed and registered. Therefore, it is arguable in the future that whenever disease or removal of kidneys is foreseeable, human donation will likewise be foreseeable.

In testifying before me, Dr Thomson spoke of 123 kidney transplants in Winnipeg alone; both he and Dr Fenton spoke of the many thousands performed in the United States and Europe. If not routine – because of the danger of rejection, and so worsening of the patient's chance for a successful operation by risking the build-up of antibodies – certainly I think it can fairly be said, in light of today's medicine, kidney transplant is an accepted remedy in renal failure. Certainly defendant here can hardly be heard to deny its 'foreseeability', in the dictionary sense of that word.

In other terms, the transplant, surely, must be viewed as an expected result, something to be anticipated, as a consequence of the loss of normal kidney function.

The world of medicine has progressed beyond the *ratio* in *Sirianni*, so that, given the disaster which befell Shirley Firman, it was entirely foreseeable that one of her family would be invited, and would agree, to donate a kidney for transplant, an act which accords, too, with the principle developed in the many 'rescue' cases.

American jurisprudence perhaps anticipated our own in this field, Mr Justice Cardozo's classic remarks in *Wagner v International Railway Co* 232 NY Rep 176 (1921), being penned in 1921. From that judgment, p 180:

Danger invites rescue. The cry of distress is the summons to relief. The law does not ignore these reactions of the mind in tracing conduct to its consequences. It recognises them as normal. It places their effects within the range of the natural and probable. The wrong that imperils life is a wrong to the imperilled victim; it is a wrong also to his rescuer . . . The risk of rescue, if only it be not wanton, is born of the occasion. The emergency begets the man. The wrongdoer may not have foreseen the coming of a deliverer. He is accountable as if he had . . .

In 1935, with *Hayes v Harwood* [1935] 1 KB 146 at 156-7, Greer, LJ, accepted the American rule as stated by Professor Goodhart in the Cambridge Law Journal, vol V (1935), p 132:

In accurately summing up the American authorities . . . the learned author says this (at p 196): 'The American rule is that the doctrine of the assumption of risk does not apply where the plaintiff has, under an exigency caused by the defendant's wrongful misconduct, consciously and deliberately faced a risk, even of death, to rescue another from imminent danger of personal injury or death, whether the person endangered is one to whom he owes a duty of protection, as a member of his family, or is a mere stranger to whom he owed no such special duty.' In my judgment that passage not only represents the law of the United States, but I think it also accurately represents the law of this country.

Both pronouncements were adopted by our own Supreme Court in *Corothers v Slobodian* (1974) 51 DLR (3d) 1, [1975] 2 SCR 633, [1975] 3 WWR 142, wherein Ritchie, J, disposed of the notion of *novus actus*, or 'independent' act by the rescuer, so long as the one imperilled continues in the situation which prompts rescue.

And so, defendant, I find, is answerable to Victor Urbanski.

Technical considerations behind the decision to invite him to undergo such an operation are adequately reviewed in Dr Thomson's letter of March 30, 1976, wherein the doctor presents the primacy of the woman's father as most likely source for the attempt, and the very significant advantages to Mrs Firman in the event of success. Given the situation so outlined, and the relationship between the proposed donor and donee, the man's response to the invitation is not surprising.

Following an extensive series of tests and examinations, for which he was obliged to attend the Health Sciences Centre, on May 5, 1976, Victor Urbanski was admitted to hospital, and his left kidney was removed the day following. Up and around within a day or so, he was discharged from hospital on May 14th. No involvement or abnormalities were noted on his post-operative examinations, May 31 and November 16, 1976, with the exception of some hernia problems, present before the event. Removal of the left kidney does not affect his life expectancy, and apart from the annual medical examination recommended in such cases, his life-style should not be changed by what he has undergone.

For all that, this plaintiff now has but one kidney, and stands in some prejudice, should his kidney function suffer distress by reason of illness or trauma.

For the operation itself, loss of his kidney and post-operative recovery (for which the doctors thought six weeks would suffice, although his discomfort, perhaps loss of confidence, persisted somewhat beyond that period) I would allow $5,000.

Although he operates a farm, Victor Urbanski's principal income is from his trade as a carpenter, seasonal work done in the local district. I am not persuaded there was any serious disruption of the farm; on the other hand, he lost the best part of the building season. For loss of income $3,500 is not unreasonable. Adding $150 for the cost of his several trips into Winnipeg for tests, etc, his claim is allowed at $8,650.

And finally, for Manitoba Hospital Services Commission as to medical and hospital services, drugs, etc, related to Victor Urbanski's operation, $1,906.26.

The approach of the court in *Urbanski* is not without its critics. G Robertson in 'A New Application of the Rescue Principle' (1980) 96 LQR 19, 20 writes:

[The] treatment of the foreseeability question is, however, open to criticism. In regarding the issue of foreseeability as being relevant only to the question of remoteness, the court failed to consider *whether or not the defendant owed the plaintiff a duty of care*. The defendant was unaware, until after the operation, that the patient had only one kidney, and thus he could not be expected to have foreseen, at the time of the operation, that removal of the patient's kidney would result in the need for transplantation. It follows, therefore, that since injury to the plaintiff was not reasonably foreseeable at the time of the negligent act, no duty of care was owed to him by the defendant. (Our emphasis.)

Perhaps, the most important aspect of *Urbanski* is the way in which the court treated the plaintiff's conduct as not amounting to a voluntary assumption of the risk of injury. Again, Robertson (*op cit*) explains.

The significance of *Urbanski* lies in the fact that it extends the basis for recovery in rescue cases to an entirely new type of situation. In previous cases, the rescue attempt has involved a *risk* of physical injury to the rescuer, which he has chosen, either consciously or instinctively, to ignore in going to the assistance of the person in danger. In the *Urbanski* situation, physical injury is inevitable, and it is the rescuer's conscious decision to submit to such injury that forms the basis of the rescue attempt.

Despite this distinction, the court regarded the plaintiff's claim as falling within the established 'rescue principle', and it is submitted that an English court would be likely to do the same. There is no reason why the plaintiff's claim should be prejudiced merely because the sustaining of physical injury is a necessary part, and not merely an incidental consequence, of the rescue attempt. Moreover, it is now clear . . . that the law affords as much protection to the rescuer who stops for reflection before making his attempt, as it does to the person who rescues on impulse: *Haynes v Harwood* [1935] 1 KB 146 at 159.

The court also concluded that the defence of *volenti* should be rejected . . . The plaintiff in *Urbanski* can scarcely be said to have *voluntarily* assumed the risk of injury, notwithstanding that he realised that such injury was inevitable, given the dilemma in which he had been placed by the defendant's negligent act. The plaintiff's parental feelings towards his daughter, coupled with an understandable sense of moral obligation, left him without any real choice in the matter.

The case has not been followed in the United States of America. In four decisions (*Sirianni v Anna* 285 NYS 2d 709 (1967); *Moore v Shah* 458 NYS 2d 33 (1982); *Ornelas v Fry* 727 P 2d 819 (1986) and *Petersen v Farberman* 736 SW 2d 441 (1987)), the courts have refused to apply the 'rescue doctrine' in this type of situation.

Moore v Shah (1982) 458 NYS 2d 33 (Sup Ct NY (App Div))

Weiss, Justice: In what appears to be a case of first impression for an appellate court, we are called upon today to determine whether the donor for a kidney transplant has a cause of action against a physician who was allegedly guilty of negligence in the diagnosis and prescribed treatment of his patient, the donee, in this case the donor's father. The complaint alleges that the negligent diagnosis and treatment caused the father's kidney failure, necessitating later transplantation. Plaintiffs would have this court extend the well-defined principles of the rescue doctrine to one whose decision to come to the aid of his father was deliberate and reflective, not made under the pressures and exigencies of an emergency situation, and significantly, at a time after defendant's alleged negligent acts. For the reasons stated, we decline to do so and affirm the order at Special Term which granted defendant's motion to dismiss the third cause of action asserted in the complaint by plaintiff Marvin Richard Moore.

The predicate for holding a defendant liable must be that a duty is owed the plaintiff, the breach of which duty is the proximate cause of plaintiff's injury (*Palsgraf v Long Is RR Co*, 248 NY 339, 162 NE 99). In order to establish the existence of such duty, a defendant must foresee that his negligence could cause injury, in this case not only to his patient, but to the patient's son as well. While questions concerning what is foreseeable are generally issues for resolution by the finder of fact, there are certain instances where only one conclusion may be drawn from the established facts and where the question of legal cause may be decided as a matter of law (*Derdiarin v Felix Contr Corpn*, 51 NY 2d 308 at 315, 434 NYS 2d 166, 414 NE 2d 666). Plaintiff contends, however, that the rescue doctrine serves to establish the requisite foreseeability between the doctor's negligence in treatment of his father and injury to himself as the rescuer (see Prosser, Torts [4th edn], § 44, p 277; see, also, *Gibney v State of New York*, 137 NY 1, 6, 33 NE 142; *Eckert v Long Is RR Co,* 43 NY 502), arguing that defendant knew or should have known plaintiff would logically be the first person to donate a kidney to his father. It is true that a wrong perpetrated upon a victim is also a wrong to his rescuer (*Wagner v International Ry Co*, 232 NY 176, 180, 133 NE 437), and that so long as the rescue is not a rash or wanton act, the rescue doctrine extends a defendant's liability to the rescuer (*Provenzo v Sam*, NY 2d 256, 296 NYS 2d 322, 244 NE 2d 26; *Wagner v International Ry Co*, 232 NY 176, 180-181, 133 NE 437, *supra; Lafferty v Manhasset Med Center Hosp*, 79 AD 2d 996, 1000, 435 2d 307; affd 54 NY 2d 277, 445 NYS 2d 111, 429 NE 2d 789). While plaintiff did not act compulsively or instinctively under pressures of emergency requiring the immediate action usually attendant upon rescues, there are authorities which have applied the doctrine in other than spontaneous reaction situations (see *Guarina v Mine Safety Appliance Co*, 25 NY 2d 460, 306 NYS 2d 942, 255 NE 2d 173;

Rucker v Andress, 38 AD 2d 684, 327 NYS 2d 848; *Keith v Payne*, 164 App Div 642, 150 NYS 37). However, we find that foreseeability alone is not enough to impose liability. Since plaintiff was never defendant's patient, no duty to him originally existed. Therefore, we are here involved with a question of whether foreseeability should be employed as the sole means to create a duty where none existed before (see 2 Harper & James, Torts, § 18.2, particularly p 1027; see generally, §§ 18.3-18.5). It is obvious that extension of liability of a physician to every person who conceivably might come forward as a kidney donor could create a group beyond manageable limits. Then Associate Judge Cooke, writing for the Court of Appeals in *Pulka v Edelman*, 40 NY 2d 781, 390 NYS 2d 393, 358 NE 2d 1019, said:

> If a rule of law were established so that liability would be imposed in an instance such as this, it is difficult to conceive of the bounds to which liability logically would flow. The liability potential would be all but limitless and the outside boundaries of that liability, both in respect to space and the extent of care to be exercised, particularly in the absence of control, would be difficult of definition. (*Id* at 786, 390 NYS 2d 393, 358 NE 2d 1019.)

We agree. In order to recover, a plaintiff must be one within the 'zone of danger' (*Tobin v Grossman*, 24 NY 2d 609, 616, 301 NYS 2d 554, 249 NE 2d 419; *Palsgraf v Long Is RR* Co, 248 NY 339, 162 NE 99, *supra*). It is difficult to charge a physician with the responsibility to foresee each and every person other than his patient who might conceivably be affected by his negligence.

> A duty arises when the relationship between individuals, the asserted plaintiff and defendant, is such as to impose upon the latter a legal obligation for the benefit of the former . . . 'While a court might impose a legal duty where none existed before . . . such an imposition must be exercised with extreme care . . .' In the absence of duty, there is no breach and therefore no liability . . . (*De Angelis v Lutheran Med Center*, 84 AD 2d 17, 22, 445 NYS 2d 188).

Our research has disclosed but one reported case in which the plaintiff was an actual organ donor. In *Sirianni v Anna* 55 Misc 2d 553, 285 NYS 2d 709, where a similar factual pattern to the instant case existed, Special Term granted defendant's motion to dismiss the complaint. While this court is not bound by *stare decisis* to follow that decision, we are persuaded by subsequent cases that it was correct. Only one year ago, the Court of Appeals held that where there is no allegation that the defendant was negligent with respect to the plaintiff as opposed to the patient, the case does not fall within recognised limits to the rescue doctrine and it declined to extend existing principles of law so as to include third parties who suffer (shock) as a result of direct injury to others. (*Lafferty v Manhasset Med Center Hosp* 54 NY 2d 277, 445 NYS 2d 111, 429 NF 2d 789, citing *Tobin v Grossman* 24 NY 2d 609, 301 NYS 2d 544, 249 NE 2d 419, *supra*; *Vaccaro v Squib Corpn* 52 NY 2d 809, 436 NYS 2d 871, 418 NE 2d 386; *Becker v Schwartz* 46 NY 2d 401, NYS 2d 895, 386 NE 2d 807; *Howard v Lecher* 42 NY 2d 109, 397 NYS 2d 363, 366 NE 2d 64.) We agree with the opinion of the Appellate Division, Second Department, 'that courts should not shirk their duty to overturn unsound precedent and should strive to continually develop the common law in accordance with our changing society . . . Yet, the mere potential ability to change the common law is not the same as the desirability of making a particular change . . .' (*De Angelis v Lutheran Med Center*, 84 AD 2d 17, 24, 445 NYS 2d 188, *supra*.) There are serious policy considerations which militate against the recovery sought here. Our decision may best be summarised in the words of then Associate Judge Breitel in *Tobin v Grossman*, 24 NY 2d 609, 301 NYS 2d 554, 249 NE 2d 419, *supra*: 'Every injury has ramifying consequences, like the ripplings of the waters, without end. The problem for the law is to limit the legal consequences of wrongs to a controllable degree' (*id* at 619, 301 NYS 2d 554, 249 NE 2d 419). We decline here to extend the common law to create a remedy for these plaintiffs.

John Spencer in 'Tissue Donors: Are They Rescuers, or Merely Volunteers?' [1979] CLJ 45, 46-7 justifies the decision in *Urbanski*, in the face of the considerable difficulties of principle involved, as follows:

> . . . what are the unspoken factors in cases such as these which influence judges to find that consequences are or are not reasonably foreseeable? To a large extent, they are how badly the defendant has behaved, and how meritoriously the plaintiff. It is hard to think of a more striking piece of medical negligence than removing a kidney in mistake for an ovarian cyst.

And it is hard to think of a more meritorious plaintiff than the altruistic Mr Urbanski who, in the face of pain, risk and personal inconvenience, volunteered his vital organs in an attempt to repair the mistake.

Urbanski was followed in a decision of the German Federal Supreme Court on 30 June 1987, JZ 1988, 150 (see B S Markesinis *The German Law of Torts* (2nd edn, 1990) at pp 461-468). If an English court did follow *Urbanski* there are certain implications which might follow. Robertson (*op cit*) considers a number of them:

> . . . [I]f the plaintiff in *Urbanski* had had only one kidney, would it have been 'reasonable' for him to offer this for transplantation? (a hypothetical situation, given that the medical profession would almost certainly refuse such an offer). There must come a point in such cases at which the extent of the proposed injury to the rescuer is so great as to make it unreasonable for him to decide to submit to such injury . . .
>
> The *Urbanski* decision also leaves other interesting questions unanswered. For example, as mentioned above, the transplant of the plaintiff's kidney proved to be unsuccessful. What if the patient's husband had then agreed to donate one of *his* kidneys, would he have been able to recover damages from the defendant as well? If there had been several unsuccessful transplants from members of the patient's family before success was finally achieved, would all the donors have had a cause of action against the defendant? Although one might instinctively answer this question in the negative, it is difficult to see the legal grounds on which such an answer could be substantiated. Surely it is reasonably foreseeable that a kidney transplant, even successive transplants, may be unsuccessful; and that suitable members of the patient's family will continue to come forward as donors until success is achieved. Moreover, the mere fact that previous transplants have been unsuccessful does not *necessarily* mean that transplants from other donors will also fail. Thus, it may be as reasonable for the last in the succession of donors, as it is for the first, to come to the assistance of the patient.
>
> Secondly, the court in *Urbanski* was obviously influenced by the father/daughter relationship that existed between rescuer and rescuee. Would the court's decision have been the same if the rescuer had been a complete stranger, inspired by altruistic rather than parental sentiment? Although such transplants are presently uncommon in most countries, the point is not without legal significance. It would seem unreasonable to make the outcome of the plaintiff's claim depend on the existence of a special relationship between himself and the rescuee. Whether the rescuer is a relation of the rescuee or a mere stranger, he should be entitled to compensation if he acts reasonably, out of a genuine desire to assist a person who has been placed in danger due to the defendant's negligence. Certainly, this has been the approach adopted in previous cases: see, for example, *Chadwick v British Railways Board* [1967] 2 All ER 945, [1967] 1 WLR 912. However, it is thought unlikely that courts would be willing to extend this approach to the *Urbanski* situation. One suspects that policy considerations, possibly couched in terms of the defence of *volenti*, would weigh heavily against the plaintiff. In a country which frowns upon payment even to blood donors, the possibility of a non-relative receiving compensation, albeit from a negligent defendant, for the voluntary act of donating a kidney is one which courts would be unlikely to encourage.

Spencer (*op cit*) does not accept Robertson's final point. He states:

> It is inconceivable that anyone not closely connected with Mrs Firman would have succeeded in a claim. Perhaps the decision can be seen as part of a general recognition by the courts that members of a family feel morally obliged to do more for each other than they are legally required to do, and a consequential willingness to compensate them, directly or indirectly, when they do it . . .

2. The Consumer Protection Act 1987

We have seen the Consumer Protection Act 1987 earlier (see ch 10). The issue for us here is whether the strict liability regime of that Act for 'defective products' could be applied to tissue or an organ which caused harm to the donee. Could the donor, the doctor or the procurement agency be liable for such harm? The Act concerns itself, you will recall, with defective products. Thus, we must ask two questions. First, and fundamentally, is tissue or an organ properly to be described as a 'product' within the meaning of the Act? B Werthmann in *Medical Malpractice Law* describes the approach of the American courts in relation to strict product liability in tort (pp 31-32):

> Whether blood used in a transfusion is such a 'product' has been the subject of considerable debate. In *Cunningham v MacNeil Memorial Hospital,* [266 WE 2d 897 (Ill 1970)] the Illinois Supreme Court held that whole blood used in a transfusion is a product for purposes of products liability. Subsequently, however, the Illinois legislature passed legislation providing that the furnishing of blood, blood products, and other human tissues is a service, not a product, for purposes of liability in tort or contract. Ultimately, all jurisdictions, either by decisional law or by legislative enactment, have decreed blood transfusions performed in a hospital to be a service incident to treatment and not a product.
>
> Some courts have, however, distinguished between blood furnished by a blood bank and blood furnished by a hospital. Reasoning that the sale of blood is incidental to the function of a hospital, whose primary purpose is to provide a service, whereas provision of blood is itself the primary function of a blood bank, the Supreme Court of Colorado ruled in *Belle Bonfils Memorial Blood Bank v Hansen* [597 P 2d 1158 (Colo 1978)] that a patient could maintain an action for strict liability and breach of warranty against a blood bank.

Werthmann is concerned only with blood but there cannot be any difference between blood and other tissue and organs in determining whether the 1987 Act applies. Would an English court draw the distinction referred to by Werthmann between a hospital and an agency involved in the supply of blood, ie the National Blood Authority for the purposes of determining what is a 'product' under the Act? The distinction Werthmann draws seems to be based upon commerce. However, in Britain commerce is unlawful when organs are involved, but not in the case of sperm or blood. Consequently, if commerce is the key, the supplier of an organ could not be liable under the 1987 Act since he would not be supplying a product but only providing a service, whereas a supplier of blood could be liable. An alternative explanation would be that in the case of a doctor or hospital, the supplying of the organ or blood is merely incidental to the medical service provided to the patient and therefore is properly analysed as being the provision of services. By contrast, in the case of a supplier such as the National Blood Authority which does not provide medical services to patients, the proper analysis is that they supply *a product* and therefore could be liable under the Act.

The second question we must consider is whether in the circumstances in which the tissue or organ is held to be a product within the Act, it is *defective* in any particular case. This is obviously a question of fact, ie whether the product meets the definition of 'defective' contained in s 3. Ordinarily, there will be no real issue here. The only significant circumstance in which a matter of legal argument will arise is when section 4(1)(e) is relied upon: 'that the state of scientific and technical knowledge at the relevant time was not such that a producer of products of the same description as the product in question might be expected to have discovered the defect if it had existed in his products while they were under his control'. This is the so-called 'state of the art' defence. An example in our context would be if at the time the tissue or organ was donated there was no test which would allow the discovery of what subsequently proved to be harmful (see, for example, *Dwan v Farquhar* 1 Qd R 234 (1988) (Sup Ct Qd) which makes the same point but in an action in negligence). (For further discussion of the 1987 Act see A Grubb and D Pearl, *Blood Testing, AIDS and DNA Profiling* (1990) ch 5.)

The dead donor

A. INTRODUCTION

Gerald Dworkin, in 'The Law Relating to Organ Transplantation in England' (1970) 33 MLR 353, 364-5 writes as follows:

> Because of the practical difficulties of obtaining organs from live donors, medical attention was directed to the possibility of obtaining organs from the bodies of dead donors. The practical advantages are obvious: the donor, once pronounced dead, is not exposed to any of the hazards which face the live donor; in some cases, such as heart or liver transplants, it is not possible to take organs from live donors; and the potential supply of organs from cadavers is much greater than from live volunteers. Practical difficulties also exist: until recently, although eyes could be 'kept' for several hours after death all other organs had to be taken and used with an hour of death; even with rapid medical progress it will be desirable for some time to come to perform the operation as soon as possible after the death of the donor.
>
> . . . **The existing law**
> (a) *Common law.* The common law position concerning corpses is curious but relatively well established. A corpse cannot ordinarily be the subject of ownership. Usually the executor or next-of-kin will have lawful possession of the body and there is a duty to arrange for burial at the earliest opportunity. It follows that, at common law, a man cannot by his will, or otherwise, legally determine what shall happen with his body after his death, although in most cases his wishes concerning the disposal of his body will be observed. That does not, of itself, authorise organs to be taken from corpses for the purpose of transplantation.
> (b) *Statute.* The need for human bodies for medical purposes is not new: bodies have always been required for anatomical teaching and research. But any attempt on the part of persons in possession of a body to sell it, even for the purpose of dissection, was unlawful; the bodies of persons convicted of murder were alone capable of being used for dissection. The scandals of body-snatching and the publicity of the murder trial of Burke and Hare led to the passing of the Anatomy Act 1832, which enabled bodies to be supplied legally to medical schools for the purpose of anatomical examination. The demand for corpses was then successfully met for over a century.
> It is only in recent times that the medical profession realised that the law relating to cadavers was far too restrictive. The successful development of the corneal graft operation focused attention on the lack of supply of eyes and the inability of potential donors to bequeath their eyes for such purposes. In a little debated, but carefully prepared, piece of legislation the Corneal Grafting Act 1952 (the wording of which to some extent followed the Anatomy Act 1832) was passed authorising the use of eyes of deceased persons for therapeutic purposes. This Act quickly proved to be too narrow, for it did not enable any other part of the body to be removed. However, once this kind of provision was on the statute book, it was much easier to extend it. The Human Tissue Act 1961 at present governs the English law relating to cadaver transplantation.

B. THE HUMAN TISSUE ACT 1961

The Human Tissue Act 1961, s 1 (as amended) provides:

> **1.** – (1) If any person, either in writing at any time or orally in the presence of two or more witnesses during his last illness, has expressed a request that his body or any specified part of his body be used after his death for therapeutic purposes or for purposes of medical education or research, the person lawfully in possession of his body after his death may, unless he has reason to believe that the request was subsequently withdrawn, authorise the removal from the body of any part or, as the case may be, the specified part, for use in accordance with the request.

(2) Without prejudice to the foregoing subsection, the person lawfully in possession of the body of a deceased person may authorise the removal of any part from the body for use for the said purposes if, having made such reasonable enquiry as may be practicable, he has no reason to believe –

(a) that the deceased had expressed an objection to his body being so dealt with after his death, and had not withdrawn it; or

(b) that the surviving spouse or any surviving relative of the deceased objects to the body being so dealt with.

(3) Subject to subsections (4) and (5) of this section, the removal and use of any part of a body in accordance with an authority given in pursuance of this section shall be lawful.

(4) No such removal shall be effected except by a fully registered medical practitioner, who must have satisfied himself by personal examination of the body that life is extinct.

(4A) No such removal of an eye or part of an eye shall be effected except by –

(a) a registered medical practitioner, who must have satisfied himself by personal examination of the body that life is extinct; or

(b) a person in the employment of a health authority or NHS trust acting on the instructions of a registered medical practitioner who must, before giving those instructions, be satisfied that the person in question is sufficiently qualified and trained to perform the removal competently and must also either –

(i)   have satisfied himself by personal examination of the body that life is extinct, or

(ii) be satisfied that life is extinct on the basis of a statement to that effect by a registered medical practitioner who has satisfied himself by personal examination of the body that life is extinct. [Inserted by Corneal Tissue Act 1986.]

(5) Where a person has reason to believe that an inquest may be required to be held on any body or that a post-mortem examination of any body may be required by the coroner, he shall not, except with the consent of the coroner, –

(a) give an authority under this section in respect of the body; or

(b) act on such an authority given by any other person.

(6) No authority shall be given under this section in respect of any body by a person entrusted with the body for the purpose only of its interment or cremation.

(7) In the case of a body lying in a hospital, nursing home or other institution, any authority under this section may be given on behalf of the person having the control and management thereof by any officer or person designated for that purpose by the first-mentioned person.

(8) Nothing in this section shall be construed as rendering unlawful any dealing with, or with any part of, the body of a deceased person which is lawful apart from the Act.

(9) In the application of this section to Scotland, for subsection (5) there shall be substituted the following subsection –

'(5) Nothing in this section shall authorise the removal of any part from a body in any case where the procurator fiscal has objected to such removal.'

1. Authorisation of removal

(a) Donation under section 1(1)

The requirements to be satisfied are as follows:

(i)   request by deceased prior to death;

(ii) in the appropriate form;

(iii) no withdrawal of request;

(iv) life is extinct;

(v)   an authorisation within s 1(1):
– by a person lawfully in possession;
– concerning the removal of that specified in s 1(1).

In considering these requirements it is important to notice that the drafting of the Act gives rise to a number of problems of interpretation but there are no cases to assist us.

(i) REQUEST BY DECEASED

To be valid the request must have been made by a competent person. The precise nature of competence is not specified in the Act. An analogy may be drawn with capacity to make a valid will.

Cockburn CJ put it as follows in *Banks v Goodfellow* (1870) LR 5 QB 549 at 567:

> ... [H]e ought to be capable of making his will with an understanding of the nature of the business in which he is engaged, a recollection of the property he means to dispose of, of the persons who are the objects of his bounty, and the manner in which it is to be distributed between them. It is not necessary that he should view his will with the eye of a lawyer, and comprehend its provisions in their legal form. It is sufficient if he has such a mind and memory as will enable him to understand the elements of which it is composed, and the disposition of his property in its simple forms.

An English court could insist upon this level of comprehension. Perhaps the better approach would be that which we suggested as regards making a valid request under the Data Protection Act 1984 (*supra*, ch 8). In *Re K* (1988) Ch 310, [1988] 1 All ER 358, Hoffman J asked the question whether a power of attorney created under the Enduring Powers of Attorney Act 1985 was 'valid if the donor understood the nature and effect of an enduring power of attorney notwithstanding that she was at the time of its execution incapable by reason of mental disorder of managing her property and affairs' (at 360-361). He concluded that: '[I]n principle . . . an understanding of the nature and effect of the power [ie the transaction] was sufficient for its validity' (at 361).

A related question is whether the provisions of the Wills Act 1831, s 7 requiring that the testator be 18 or over, would be applicable by analogy here? Lanham argues otherwise, and we agree.

David Lanham 'Transplants and the Human Tissue Act 1961' (1971) 11 Med Sci Law 16

> There is no mention in the Act of any age limit within which it is possible to make a request. At the committee stage in the House of Commons Mr Page raised the problem of the age of consent. He asked whether a request by a teenager would be sufficient under the section and suggested a provision that a request could be made on behalf of very young children by the guardian (HC Deb, Vol 643, col 839). The Ministry of Health in a brief reply (*ibid*, col 846) said that there was no age limit. No special provision was made to cover the position of very young children. The solution is probably that if a child is old enough to understand the position sufficiently to make the request, the request is valid for section 1(1). If the child is not old enough, section 1(1) will not be applicable and authorisation will have to be made under section 1(2).

(ii) APPROPRIATE FORM

Given that the request may be made in writing, some concern has been expressed as to whether a printed card (a donor card) comes within the terms of the Act. It may well be that Parliament had in mind that the request be written by hand. However, such a narrow view (excluding all cases of printed requests) would probably be rejected by a court as out of touch with modern society. The British Transplant Society took the view that in addition to amending s 1(2) of the Act (on which see *infra*), the following new subsection should be added:

> For the avoidance of doubt in the interpretation of this section it is hereby declared:

... that a printed but personally signed donor card or other document, is 'in writing' for the purpose of subsection 1 of this section.

A further question is whether the request in writing must be signed. Again the statute is silent on the matter. Arguably the purpose of the statute would be defeated if a court interpreted 'in writing' as demanding a signature.

Finally, if the request is made orally it must be made in the 'last illness'. Ordinarily this would pose problems of interpretation but since the request only falls to be considered after death, hindsight resolves the question.

(iii) WITHDRAWAL OF REQUEST

Lanham (*op cit*) at p 7, writes as follows:

> If the person who is lawfully in possession of the body has reason to believe that the request has been withdrawn, he is not permitted to authorise the removal and use of the body in accordance with the request. No form of withdrawal is specified, so that the request can be withdrawn orally even if it was given in writing. Nor if the withdrawal is oral need it be made in the presence of two witnesses. It will only operate, however, if it is communicated in some way to the person who becomes the person lawfully in possession of the body, since the original request is effective unless the person lawfully in possession does have reason to believe that the request has been withdrawn. If the patient changes his mind again after withdrawing the request, he must presumably renew his request in writing or in the presence of two or more witnesses. There appears, however, to be no duty upon the person lawfully in possession to make inquiries about whether a request once given had been withdrawn ... It is presumably for any person knowing of the withdrawal to acquaint the person lawfully in possession of the body with the fact of withdrawal.

(iv) LIFE IS EXTINCT

The obvious importance of this is reflected in the fact that there is a further specific provision in s 1(4) that death be established by personal examination by the transplant surgeon.

Prima facie this means that the death of the donor should first be established by those caring for the patient/donor using the established criteria and procedures for determining death (see *infra*, ch 18). Then, for a second time, death must be determined to have occurred by the transplant surgeon. Because of the development of ventilators and other means of life-support, the determination of death is not incompatible with the continued presence of heartbeat and respiration (see *infra*, ch 18). This gives rise to the so-called 'beating heart cadaver' whereby an organ can be removed from a corpse, the heart and respiration of which is artificially maintained after the declaration of death so as to preserve the organ's viability prior to transplant.

(v) AN AUTHORISATION WITHIN SECTION 1(1)

I. **'Lawfully in possession'.** The authorisation for the removal of an organ must be given by a person lawfully in possession of the corpse. The meaning of this phrase is explained by Lanham in his article, *op cit* (pp 18-20):

> It is almost commonplace knowledge that in general a dead body cannot be owned. This means that at common law a body cannot be stolen. The law does, however, recognise a right to possession of a dead body and is prepared to protect that possession. Possession is one of the most difficult concepts of the law and it is perhaps not surprising that there has been some doubt as to its meaning under the Human Tissue Act 1961.
>   The leading case of possession of a dead body is *Williams v Williams* (1882) 20 Ch D 659 where Kay J held that the deceased's executors were lawfully entitled to the possession of his

body. If the deceased has died intestate, his administrators will then be entitled to possession. In *R v Fox* (1841) 2 QB 246 the executors were able to enforce their right to possession against a gaoler who refused to deliver up the body of a deceased prisoner unless the executors first satisfied certain claims made by the gaoler against the deceased. But the fact that the executors or administrators have a better right than the person in whose custody the body is does not mean that the latter person is not lawfully in possession until the executors claim their right.

That persons other than the executors or administrators might lawfully be in possession of the body was recognised in *R v Feist* (1858) Dears & B 590 where it was held that the master of a workhouse was a person having lawful possession of the body of a deceased pauper for the purposes of permitting the body to undergo anatomical examination under the Anatomy Act 1832. The case has been criticised (see *Russell on Crime*, 12th edn, p 1419) on the ground that the master of the workhouse was merely the servant of the poor law authority and that possession of the workhouse was in the latter body. Even if the criticism is valid it does not affect the principle that a person other than the executor or administrator may be lawfully in possession of a dead body.

If it be accepted that a person other than the executor may be lawfully in possession of a dead body certain cases at common law indicate the persons who are in possession in different circumstances. In *Williams v Williams* (*supra*) the executors' right to possession of the body was linked with the responsibility for its burial. In the cases below responsibility for burial was established, and by parity of reasoning those under the duty to bury must have had the right to possession of the body.

In *Ambrose v Kerrison* (1851) 10 CB 776 it was held that a husband was under a duty to dispose of the body of his deceased wife even though he was separated from her. Jarvis CJ expressly likened the position of the husband to that of an executor. The case was followed in *Bradshaw v Beard* (1862) 12 CBNS 344. It was held in *R v Vann* (1851) 2 Den 325 that a father was under a duty to dispose of the body of his deceased child if he had the means to do so, and in *R v Stewart* (1840) 12 Ad & El 773 it was said that every householder in whose house a person died was bound to arrange for the burial of the body.

As might be expected, any statement of general principles is lacking in the cases referred to above. It is submitted, however, that the person who has actual physical custody of the body has lawful possession (and the duty of disposal) of it until someone with a higher right (eg an executor or parent) claims the body. Though in no way authoritative in court, the following statement in *Hansard*, HC Deb Vol 643, col 835, seems to represent the law: 'In the absence of executors there is a common law duty to see that the body is buried and the person lawfully in possession is normally the occupier of the premises where the body lies, or the person who has the body.'

One particular aspect of very great importance in the present context is the legal position when a person dies in hospital. When the Human Tissue Bill was passing through Parliament it was said that 50 per cent of the deaths in this country occur in hospital. It would appear on the general principles discussed above that where a person dies in hospital the hospital management committee or board of governors are legally in possession of the body until someone with a better title to possession (eg an executor) claims it. When the Bill was in committee in the House of Commons, an amendment was moved to make it clear beyond any doubt that where a body lay in a hospital the person having control of the management of the hospital was lawfully in possession. The Government resisted the amendment on the ground that it might be interpreted as giving the hospital authorities a right to possession enforceable against executors. (HC Deb, Vol 643, col 836.) Nonetheless it seems clear at common law that the hospital authorities are lawfully in possession of the body and this position is impliedly confirmed by section 1(7) of the 1961 Act – 'In the case of a body lying in a hospital, nursing home or other institution, any authority under this section may be given on behalf of the person having the control and management thereof by any officer or person designated for that purpose by the first-mentioned person.' This provision clearly assumes that the hospital authorities are normally in possession of a body lying in hospital and provides a convenient system whereby a designated person (eg the medical superintendent) may carry out the function of the person lawfully in possession. . . .

Despite the seemingly overwhelming case for arguing that the hospital authority is capable of being lawfully in possession of the deceased's body, Dr Addison, in his letter to the *British Medical Journal* [(1968) 1 Br Med J 516] says that the Medical Defence Union has been advised by leading counsel that, save in the exceptional case, the hospital where a patient dies is not lawfully in possession of the body for the purposes of the Act. It is respectfully suggested that, at least in the context of the road accident victim, counsel is wrong.

The strongest case is one in which the person who dies in hospital dies intestate and without a spouse or relatives. In such a case there is no one at the time of death with a better right to possession than the hospital and it cannot be doubted that the hospital is lawfully in possession of the body. But even if there is someone with a better right to possession than the hospital, it does not follow that he is in possession as soon as the patient dies. Suppose the patient has made a will naming executors. The executors will have a better right to possession than the hospital, but at the time of the patient's death they may not even know that there is a body over which they have a right to possession. Without knowledge they cannot have the intention to possess and so one of the elements normally required for the acquisition of possession is missing. The same holds true if the person leaves a widow or other surviving relatives. The cases where a person possesses objects of which he has no knowledge but which are contained in his property (eg *Elwes v Brigg Gas Co* (1886) 33 Ch D 562) are not in point and do not invalidate the general rule requiring *animus possidendi*. If Professor Woodruff's statement that many grafts are lost because next-of-kin cannot be contacted in time is right, cases in which the executors or relatives cannot be found in time can hardly be regarded as 'exceptional'. At the very least until the executors or relatives know about the death, the hospital must be regarded as lawfully in possession of the body.

In other cases there is more room for argument. Presumably the mere fact that the executors or relatives know about the death is not enough to vest possession in them. There must be an intention to possess. Furthermore that intention must presumably be communicated to the hospital, since intention by itself does not constitute possession: see *Salmond on Jurisprudence* (11th edn, p 322).

But once a person with a better right of possession communicates his intention to possess to the hospital, the hospital's authority under the 1961 Act ceases. If, as is almost certainly the case, the hospital recognises that person's right to possession, the latter becomes the possessor. While the body remains in the hospital, the hospital may also be in possession but since there will be another person lawfully in possession, his consent will be a necessary condition to the giving of authority under the Act. If on the other hand the hospital were to refuse to recognise the executor's or relative's rights (a situation which seems most unlikely), the hospital and not the executors or relatives would remain in possession, but the hospital would not then be lawfully in possession, and once again the hospital's powers under the Act would cease.

Finally, one class of person who might be regarded as lawfully in possession of the body is specifically denied the right of granting authority under the Act. Section 1(6) provides that: 'No authority shall be given under this section in respect of any body by a person entrusted with the body for the purpose only of its interment or cremation.' Accordingly, a funeral undertaker is not able to give authority as a person lawfully in possession of the body.

It will be noticed that the statute states that the person 'lawfully in possession' *may* authorise. It is clear, therefore, that the donor's expressed request need not necessarily be complied with, since the person lawfully in possession retains an absolute discretion. This must be right since there will be circumstances in which it would be undesirable to remove any tissue, whatever the donor's wishes.

II. Removal of that specified in section 1(1). It will be noted that there is a discrepancy in the wording of s 1(1) between what the donor may have requested and what the person 'lawfully in possession' may authorise. The Human Tissue Act 1961, s 1(1) states (our emphasis):

1. – (1) If any person, either in writing at any time or orally in the presence of two or more witnesses during his last illness has expressed a request that *his body or any specified part of his body* be used after his death for therapeutic purposes or for purposes of medical education or research, the person lawfully in possession of his body after his death may, unless he has reason to believe that the request was subsequently withdrawn, authorise the removal from the body of *any part or, as the case may be the specified part,* for use in accordance with the request.

The upshot would appear to be that, although no problems arise in relation to transplantation where by definition only 'parts' will be removed and used, the donor may, under s 1(1), purport to leave 'his body' for purposes of medical education and research but the person lawfully in possession may only authorise the removal and use of 'part' of his body.

(vi) CONSENT OF THE CORONER

Lanham, *op cit*, writes at pp 21-22:

> An inquest may be required where there is reasonable cause to suspect that the deceased died either a violent or unnatural death or a sudden death of which the cause is unknown or has died in prison or in such place or circumstances as to require an inquest in pursuance of any Act: [Coroners Act 1988, s 8(1)]. In the case of a sudden death of which the cause is unknown the coroner may, as an alternative, order a post mortem examination: [Coroners Act 1988, s 19] . . .
>
> The importance of these provisions in relation to organ transplants is that in practice the victims of motoring accidents may constitute an important category of potential donors and that this is the kind of case in which the coroner's consent is necessary. The attitude of coroners is therefore of great significance. In the nature of things there is no reported case giving guidance on how coroners ought to exercise their discretion.
>
> . . . First, the Act itself does not state any absolute bars to the coroner's granting consent. It may be that for practical reasons it will not be possible to obtain organs from a victim of homicide in time for transplantation because of the desirability of preserving the body so far as possible intact for the post mortem examination. But there may be cases where the investigation of the causation of the injuries would in no way be impeded by the removal of organs unconnected with the injuries (eg, where the kidneys are removed in the case of fatal head injuries) and in such circumstances a coroner might be prepared to give consent. Secondly, the meaning of 'consent' is not entirely clear. An express prior consent to the removal of organs from a specified dead body is obviously adequate. But can the coroner give a general consent in advance? Can he, for instance, notify the hospitals in his area that 'in the following circumstances . . . I consent to the removal of the following organs . . . from any dead body over which I have jurisdiction'? Alternatively, can he delegate to his pathologist the power to give consent in certain defined circumstances? Generally when a statute confers on a public officer or body a discretion to consent to a certain course of action the discretion must be exercised on a specific application for consent and a general statement of policy is not regarded as an exercise of the discretion. . . .
>
> . . . Again, a person or body given discretionary powers by Parliament is generally expected to exercise those powers himself and not to delegate their exercise. But neither of these rules is absolute. A body given a discretion may sometimes 'in the honest exercise of its discretion, adopt a policy and announce it to those concerned, so long as it is ready to listen to reasons why, in an exceptional case, that policy should not be applied'; see *Schmidt v Secretary of State* [1969] 2 Ch 149 at 169. Furthermore, in one of the leading cases on delegation, *Vine v National Dock Labour Board* [1957] AC 488, Lord Somervell, far from stating an absolute rule against delegation, said (at p 512) 'In deciding whether a "person" has power to delegate one has to consider the nature of the duty and the character of the person.' For a case which illustrates the fact that the rule against delegation is not absolute see *Osgood v Nelson* (1872) LR 5 HL 636. These cases are, like those in which the general rules about fettering discretion and non-delegation are discussed, far removed from the question of the coroner's jurisdiction but it is thought they may be used to support the very beneficial practice whereby coroners give general advance consent. Provided that the coroner's policy clearly achieves the purpose of section 1(5) – to preserve relevant evidence – there is every reason why the law should recognise the legality of the practice.

Margaret Brazier in her book, *Medicine, Patients and the Law* (2nd edn, 1992) at 405-406 argues that the obtaining of authority from the coroner:

> . . . could have the effect of delaying for an unacceptably long period the opportunity to remove organs. This may be the case particularly where a coroner regards his duty to act as coroner as being of greater importance than the secondary power which he has to authorise the use of organs before his coroner's duties are complete. In a controversial case in Leicester in 1980, the father of a girl who had died in a road accident had given surgeons permission to use any of her organs, including her heart, which had been removed by surgeons. At a subsequent inquest, the coroner complained that he had not given permission

for the heart to be removed since permission had been sought from him only for the removal of a kidney. He therefore directed that in future written permission would have to be obtained from him and countersigned by a pathologist. This incident highlighted the problem that coroners, acting in pursuance of what they regarded as their legal duties, could adversely restrict the use of organs even where parents or other relatives had consented. It was for such reasons that the Home Secretary circularised coroners, stressing that it was not part of a coroner's function to place obstacles in the way of the development of medical science or to take moral or ethical decisions in this matter, and that the coroners should assist rather than hinder the procedure for organ removal. A coroner should refuse his consent only where there might be later criminal proceedings in which the organ might be required as evidence, or if the organ itself might be the cause or partial cause of the death, or where its removal might impede further inquiries [HC (77) 28 August (1975)].

(See for further discussion, *Jervis on Coroners* (11th edn, 1993) paras 6.53-6.59.)

(b) Donation under section 1(2)

The Human Tissue Act 1961, s 1(2) provides:

> Without prejudice to the foregoing subsection, the person lawfully in possession of the body of a deceased person may authorise the removal of any part from the body for use for the said purposes if, having made such reasonable enquiry as may be practicable, he has no reason to believe –
> (a) that the deceased had expressed an objection to his body being so dealt with after his death, and had not withdrawn it; or
> (b) that the surviving spouse or any surviving relative of the deceased objects to the body being so dealt with.

The requirements to be satisfied under s 1(2) are largely those already considered, ie the requirements relating to (a) the persons lawfully in possession; (b) the need for a deceased person; (c) removal of only a part or parts of the body.

There are, in addition, other requirements which only arise in s 1(2). These relate to the following statutory words:

(i) 'having made such reasonable enquiry as may be practicable';
(ii) 'the person lawfully in possession has no reason to believe . . .';
(iii) 'that the deceased has (not) expressed an objection';
(iv) 'that the surviving spouse or any surviving relative . . .';
(v) 'that the surviving spouse or any surviving relative *"objects"'*.

These are considered separately below.

(i) 'HAVING MADE SUCH REASONABLE ENQUIRY AS MAY BE PRACTICABLE'

Professor Peter Skegg in 'Human Tissue Act 1961' (1976) 16 Med Sci Law 197, examines this requirement.

> Had it been so desired, s 1(2) could easily have specified that the person lawfully in possession of the body should never authorise the removal of parts of it unless the surviving spouse, and any relatives of the deceased, had agreed to this being done. But s 1(2) imposes no such requirement. Nor does it require the person lawfully in possession of the body to make all possible enquiries whether there is a relevant objection. He need only make 'such reasonable enquiry as may be practicable'.
> If the requirement of reasonable enquiries stood on its own, there could clearly be considerable discussion of the extent to which the impracticability of an enquiry should be given weight in determining whether that enquiry was 'reasonable'. However, as s 1(2) requires, not the making of all reasonable enquiries, but only 'such reasonable enquiry as may be practicable', that consideration need not be pursued at this stage. Putting aside the issue of practicability, what enquiries are reasonable?
> In determining whether the person lawfully in possession of the body has made reasonable enquiries, some weight must clearly be given to the resources – both in terms of

finance and manpower – available to him, and to the other claims on those resources. Where a hospital authority is the person lawfully in possession of a body, it is clearly not reasonable for all other administrative activities to cease for a day, while staff assist in an enquiry as to whether any one of the dozens of traceable relatives of the deceased has any objection to the removal of a pituitary gland for research purposes, or an eye for corneal transplantation. Where the newly bereft spouse or parent is the person lawfully in possession of the body, he or she can hardly be expected to spend many hours telephoning distant relatives, with whom they may have had no contact for years, enquiring whether they have any objection to the removal of a specimen from the body of the deceased spouse or child.

Another factor which should be taken into account in determining the reasonableness of an enquiry is its likely utility. An enquiry would not be unreasonable because every available colleague or friend of the deceased has not been contacted, to enquire whether the deceased ever expressed an objection to the use of his body for the envisaged purpose. Although it is possible that any one of them may recall some relevant statement of the deceased, the likelihood of the enquiry producing relevant information would normally be so slight that it would not be unreasonable to omit to make it.

A third consideration in determining whether it is reasonable to enquire of a particular person is that person's age and his physical and emotional condition. It would surely be unreasonable to enquire of young children, or of someone who was critically ill as a result of the accident in which the potential donor died. It would probably also be considered unreasonable to approach a severely distressed spouse or relative, whose health could be detrimentally affected in consequence of an enquiry.

In determining what amounts to a reasonable enquiry, a court would undoubtedly give considerable weight to accepted attitudes concerning what is a reasonable enquiry. In practice, it is widely accepted that a reasonable enquiry normally requires no more than enquiring of either the spouse or a close relative whether he or she has reason to believe that the deceased had expressed an objection, or whether some other person, whose objection is relevant, objects. Even where a more extensive enquiry is practicable, this enquiry is generally regarded as reasonable (see eg HSC (IS) 156, para 11). Given this consensus, it is unlikely that a court would take a different view.

As already stressed, s 1(2) does not require the making of all reasonable enquiries. It requires only 'such reasonable enquiry as may be practicable'. The crucial issue is whether, in determining the practicability of an enquiry, it is permissible to take account of the time within which the part must be removed if it is to be of use for the desired purpose. The Long Title of the Act indicates that the main purpose of s 1 was 'to make provision with respect to the use of parts of bodies of deceased persons for therapeutic purposes and purposes of medical education and research'. The purpose of s 1(2) is not simply to allow the relative to object if he so wishes . . . If it was, it would require that the person lawfully in possession of the body contact every relative and enquire whether he or she objects. As it stands, s 1(2) attempts a compromise between the interests of the parties specified and the interests of those who may benefit from the use of parts of the body. For this reason, it requires only 'such reasonable enquiry as may be practicable'. In determining the practicability of an enquiry, there is no warrant for excluding from consideration the time within which a part must be removed if it is to be of use for the intended and approved purpose. Indeed, this factor will sometimes be crucial. For example, when it is desired to remove a kidney for transplantation from a body which is not being maintained on a ventilator, it will not be practicable to make as extensive enquiries as when it is desired to remove a bone for the purpose of medical education. This is because a kidney which is left in a body for more than an hour after the cessation of respiration and circulation becomes irreversibly damaged.

The issue of whether it is permissible to take account of the time available in determining the practicability of an enquiry is closely related to, but distinct from, one other issue. This is whether the person lawfully in possession may ever give his authority without making any enquiry, on the grounds that no enquiry was both reasonable and practicable. On one view, s 1(2) requires that at least some enquiry always be made before the person lawfully in possession of the body may authorise the removal. But on another view, an enquiry need only be made if it is both reasonable and practicable to make one. On this interpretation, if no enquiry was both reasonable and practicable the person lawfully in possession of the body could still give his authority, if he had no reason to believe that there was a relevant objection. In such circumstances, s 1(2) would operate like its predecessor in the Corneal Grafting Act 1952, where there was no obligation to make an enquiry in any circumstances. If a choice must be made between these two approaches, the second seems preferable. But it may be questioned whether in practice any choice is necessary. It is difficult to envisage a situation where at least some enquiry is not both reasonable and practicable. Extensive enquiries are clearly impracticable in the case of an accident victim who is brought into hospital dead, and whose kidneys must be removed within a very short time if they are to be of use for transplantation. However, at the very least, it is always both reasonable and practicable to enquire whether the deceased is carrying on his person any indication that he expressed an objection to the proposed use of his body.

Notice the interpretation given to the important word 'practicable'. Professor Gerald Dworkin argues otherwise in his paper 'The Law Relating to Organ Transplantation in England' (*op cit*) pp 367-368:

> . . . The only guidance given to the hospital is that it may act provided it has made such reasonable inquiry as may be practicable . . . . [The argument that] it would not be practicable to spend too long trying to trace relatives since the body must be used within a short time after death would not be decisive. The practicability of the inquiry must relate to the steps taken to trace the relatives not to the practicability of using the body, since the basis of the provision is to allow the relative to object if he so wishes. Where a close relative is available and does not object then the medical authorities are on slightly safer ground in proceeding in spite of the possibility that other relatives who were within the range of immediate contact and who were not consulted might object and claim that the use of the body was unlawful. It is clear, however, that a hospital will rarely be in a position to guarantee that it has made all reasonable inquiries if the body is used within a few hours of death.

On balance, in our view Professor Dworkin's view of the likely interpretation of the word 'practicable' more closely reflects the intent behind, and the structure of, s 1(2).

(ii) 'THE PERSON LAWFULLY IN POSSESSION HAS NO REASON TO BELIEVE . . .'

These words may call for a somewhat different interpretation in subsection (2) than in subsection (1). As regards subsection (2), there can be no doubt that the person lawfully in possession is under a duty to enquire so as to enable him to conclude that there is no reason to believe that an objection has not been made. Subsection (1) makes no specific reference to an 'enquiry' such that it is less clear there that having 'a reason to believe' involves the obligation to seek out information. In contrast to s 1(2), therefore, it is our view that, under s 1(1), the person lawfully in possession of a body can act provided he does not have actual (or possibly, constructive) knowledge that a request has been withdrawn from the information already available to him.

(iii) 'THAT THE DECEASED HAS (NOT) EXPRESSED AN OBJECTION'

The short point here is that the statute is silent as to the form in which the objection must be expressed. It could be argued that a written objection is required for the sake of certainty. However, as we have seen, wherever writing was thought necessary by Parliament it was so stated, eg written request in s 1(1).

(iv) 'THAT THE SURVIVING SPOUSE OR ANY SURVIVING RELATIVE (HAS NOT OBJECTED)'

Peter Skegg in 'Human Tissue Act 1961' (1976) 16 Med Sci Law (*op cit*), writes:

> . . . The Act does not provide any definition of 'relative', but the separate reference to 'any surviving spouse' lends support to the view that in this context 'relative' does not include persons to whom the deceased was related only by marriage. The courts have given a restrictive interpretation to 'relative' or 'relation' when used by a testator in his will (see eg *Anon* (1716) 1 P Wms 327; *Eagles v Le Breton* (1873) 42 LJ Ch 362 at 363; *Re Bridgen, Chaytor v Edwin* [1938] Ch 205 at 208-210). However, this is because 'else it would be uncertain; for the relation may be infinite' (*Anon, supra*), and it would be unwise to assume

that 'relative' would be interpreted in a limited sense in this context. The original Memorandum on the Act advised hospital authorities of the Minister's opinion that the word should be interpreted in its widest sense, to include those who claim quite a distant relationship with the deceased (HM (61) 98, para 8). The recent Guidance Circular was more equivocal. It simply advised that there are 'some circumstances' in which 'relative' should be interpreted 'in the widest sense, eg to include those who although claiming only a distant relationship are nevertheless closely connected with the deceased' (HSC (IS) 156, para 11). In fact, there is no warrant for interpreting the word differently according to the circumstances. The Circular appears to confuse the issue of who is a relative with the issue of whether it is reasonable and practicable to enquire of a particular relative.

The precise words of the Health Service Circular to which Peter Skegg referred are: 'In most instances it will be sufficient to discuss the matter with any one relative who had been in close contact with the deceased, asking him his own views, the views of the deceased and also if he has any reason to believe that any other relative would be likely to object.' (DHSS Working Party Report (1983) 'Cadaveric Organs for Transplantation. Code of Practice'.)

(v) 'OBJECTS'

Peter Skegg (*op cit*) analyses this requirement:

> It has been said that, 'You cannot consent to a thing unless you have knowledge of it' (*Re Caughey, ex p Ford* (1876) 1 Ch D 521 at 528 per Jessel MR). Similarly, it could be said that a person cannot object to something being done unless he is aware of the proposal to do it (cf. *R v Feist, supra*). But it may also be argued that a person can have a sufficiently clear and consistent attitude to certain conduct for it to be said that he 'objects' to it, even though he is ignorant of a particular proposal to act. Even on this broader interpretation of 'objects', there would still be many people who could not be said to object, even though on being informed of a particular proposal they might well object. The problem in practice is that the person lawfully in possession of the body could not know into which category of actual or potential objector a spouse or relative came. At present, it would be wise to act as if s 1(2)(b) read 'objects *or* would object', rather than simply 'objects'.

This view that the section contemplates *potential* objectors is to be preferred, notwithstanding Professor Skegg's more narrow reading of the statute in other contexts.

2. Failure to comply with the Human Tissue Act 1961

All that has gone before in our analysis of the Human Tissue Act 1961 rests in part, at least, on the assumption that someone aggrieved at a failure properly to comply with the terms of the Act can in law do something about it. Curiously, this is at the same time the most important question and yet the most neglected. It is commonly assumed that if the Act is not complied with 'something can be done', but we must examine this premise closely.

(a) Criminal law

(i) THE COMMON LAW

Peter Skegg 'Liability for the Unauthorized Removal of Cadaveric Transplant Material' (1974) 14 Med Sci Law 53

> It has long been established that it is a common law crime to prevent the disposal of a corpse by detaining it for a claim upon a debt (*R v Scott* (1842) 2 QB 248) or by selling it when retained and employed to bury it (*R v Cundick* (1822) Dow & Ry NP 13). As it seems that

there is a more general offence of preventing the lawful disposal of the body (see *R v Young* (1784) 4 Wentworth's System of Pleading 219, which appears to be the case referred to in *R v Lynn*; *R v Hunter* [1974] QB 95) the question arises whether, by removing transplant material, a donor could be said to prevent the disposal of the body. If the removal involved the retention of the whole body, despite the request of the person entitled to possession that the body be delivered up to him, then the doctor would almost certainly incur liability. However, so long as that which was available for disposal was recognizable as the body of the deceased it is doubtful whether the unauthorized retention of internal parts of the body could be said to prevent the disposal of the body. Doctors often retain parts of bodies after post-mortem examinations – indeed, where sufficient material is retained after an official post-mortem examination, coroners sometimes permit the disposal of the corpse before inquiries into the death are completed. It does not appear to have been suggested that by retaining parts of a body a doctor prevents the disposal of the corpse. The unauthorized removal and retention of transplant material would, therefore, be unlikely to amount to a common law crime of preventing disposal of the body, much less to the narrower statutory crime of wilfully obstructing a burial (Burial Laws Amendment Act 1880, s 7).

There are *dicta* to the effect that the common law will not allow any indecent interference with the bodies of the dead (eg, *Foster v Dodd* (1866) LR 1 QB 475 at 485). The cases along these lines have all concerned interferences with bodies after burial, but the courts might well hold that certain interferences with dead bodies at any earlier stage also constitute a common law crime. Touchings of a sexual nature and pointless mutilation might be held to amount to such a crime. For the present purpose, the important question is whether unauthorized interferences with an unburied corpse for medical purposes would amount to a common law crime. Although the means by which bodies used to be acquired for the practice of anatomy were sometimes unlawful, there is reason to believe that the practice of anatomy was itself perfectly lawful at common law (Anatomy Act 1832, Preamble; *R v Price* (1884) 12 QBD 251 at 252, 253; *R v Feist* (1858) Dears & B 590 at 594-5, *in arguendo*). This being so, the very much more limited interference with a body involved in the removal of organs or tissues for transplantation, should not amount to any common law crime of indecent or improper interference with a corpse.

Arguably, the last suggestion of Professor Skegg can be dealt with by noticing that the transplant doctor will lack the necessary intention to act indecently.

(ii) UNDER THE ACT

The Act itself does not provide for any sanction for failure to comply with its terms. However, the suggestion has been put that the ancient crime of disobedience of a statute may be relevant, which is a common law crime.

R v Lennox-Wright [1973] Crim LR 529 (CCC)

HH Judge Lawson QC: The defendant, who had taken and failed two medical examinations abroad, gained admission to the ophthalmic department of an English hospital by means of false representations, and a forged document which purported to show that he had qualified as an MD of Louvain University in Belgium.

In the course of his work at the hospital, he removed the eyes from a dead body for their further use in a different hospital. He was charged *inter alia*, with (after amendment): 'Doing an act in disobedience of a statute by removing parts of a dead body, contrary to section 1(4) of the Human Tissue Act 1961'.

The Human Tissue Act 1961, makes provision for the use of parts of bodies of deceased persons for therapeutic purposes and purposes of medical education and research and with respect to the circumstances in which the removal of parts of a body may be carried out. Section 1(4) of the Act provides that: 'No such removal shall be effected except by a fully registered medical practitioner, who must have satisfied himself by personal examination of the body that life is extinct'.

On a motion to quash the count it was contended by the defence that the Act was merely regulatory and created no offence; and that the Act provided no punishment for contravening section 1(4).

Held, (1) The law was well settled that if a statute prohibits a matter of public grievance to the liberties and securities of the subject or commands a matter of public convenience (such as repairing of highways or the like) all acts or omissions contrary to the prohibitions or command of the statute are misdemeanours at common law punishable by indictment unless such method manifestly appears to be excluded by statute. (2 Hawkins, c 25, s 4; *R v Hall* [1891] 1 QB 747; *R v Wright* (1841) 9 C & P 754.) See paragraph 6 of *Archbold*.

(2) It followed that the punishment was governed by the common law and therefore an unlimited term of imprisonment or an unlimited fine could apply.

Professor Sir John Smith in his commentary in the *Criminal Law Review* wrote:

> According to Stephen, *Digest of the Criminal Law*, Art 152: 'Every one commits a misdemeanour who wilfully disobeys any statute of the realm by doing any act which it forbids, or by omitting to do any act which it requires to be done, and which concerns the public or any part of the public, unless it appears from the statute that it was the intention of the Legislature to provide some other penalty for such disobedience.'
>
> It is usual at the present day for Parliament, when it intends to create a criminal offence, expressly so to provide and to lay down a maximum punishment for the offence. So common is this practice that it might be thought that, when Parliament does not provide in express terms for a criminal sanction at the present day, none is intended. This is particularly so since the effect of applying the principle stated above is that the offence is a misdemeanour triable on indictment and punishable with fine and imprisonment at the discretion of the court.

Section 1(8) of the Human Tissue Act provides:

> Nothing in this section shall be construed as rendering unlawful any dealing with, or with any part of, the body of a deceased person which is lawful apart from this Act.

Is the effect of s 1(8) that even if *R v Lennox-Wright* is correct, *viz* that there is a common law crime of failing to obey a statute, it has no application to the Human Tissue Act? Now the matter seems beyond dispute, since the case of *R v Horseferry Road Justices, ex p Independent Broadcasting Authority* [1987] QB 54, [1986] 2 All ER 666 shows that the ancient crime does not have much life, if any, left in it and certainly does not apply in the case of the Human Tissue Act.

R v Horseferry Road Justices, ex p Independent Broadcasting Authority [1987] QB 54, [1986] 2 All ER 666 (Div Ct)

> **Lloyd LJ:** In 1976 the Law Commission in their Report on Conspiracy and Criminal Law Reform (HC Paper (1975-76) no 176) p 140 para 6.1 described the 'doctrine' of contempt of statute as obsolete, but not dead. They recommended that the doctrine be abolished (p 142, para 6.5):
>
> > In essence [they said] this is a matter of statutory construction; and the modern approach would, we think, be to ask whether, in the absence of an express provision making particular conduct an offence, there was any intent by Parliament to penalise that conduct. The answer today, we suggest, would always be in the negative . . .
>
> In *Maxwell on the Interpretation of Statutes* (12th edn, 1969) pp 334-335 it is said that the procedure by way of indictment for breach of a statutory duty is never used today.
>
> How then does the matter stand? The one thing which to my mind emerges clearly from all the authorities to which I have referred and in particular from the qualification in *Hawkins*, 'unless such method of proceeding do manifestly appear to be excluded', is that it is a question of construction in each case whether a breach of statutory duty for which Parliament has provided no remedy creates an offence or not. Among the factors which will have to be considered are: (i) whether the duty is mandatory or prohibitory; (ii) whether the statute is ancient or modern; for in ancient statutes it was far more common than it is today for no offence to be defined, but to leave enforcement, for example, to a common informer; and (iii) whether there are any other means of enforcing the duty. In the case of a mandatory duty imposed by a modern statute, enforceable by way of judicial review, the inference that

Parliament did *not* intend to create an offence in the absence of an express provision to that effect is, nowadays, almost irresistible.

Counsel for the IBA urged us to hold that *R v Price* (1840) 11 Ad & El 727, 113 ER 590, *Rathbone v Bundock* [1962] 2 All ER 257, [1962] 2 QB 260 and *R v Lennox-Wright* [1973] Crim LR 529 were wrongly decided, if they cannot be distinguished. He argued that the rule as stated in *Hawkins* has ceased to exist: cessante ratione legis, cessat lex ipsa. I do not find it necessary to go that far; for, as I have said, the 'rule' or 'doctrine' never was more than a rule of construction. It is not a substantive rule of law. The only difference between today and 1716, when *Hawkins* was first published, is that it is easier to infer in the case of a modern statute that Parliament does not intend to create an offence unless it says so. There is no longer any presumption, if indeed there ever were, that a breach of duty imposed by statute is indictable. Nowadays the presumption, if any, is the other way; although I would prefer to say that it requires clear language, or a very clear inference, to create a crime.

(b) Tort liability

Professor Skegg examines this in his article 'Liability for the Unauthorized Removal of Cadaveric Transplant Material' (1974) 14 Med Sci Law 53.

There do not appear to be any reported English cases in which a plaintiff has recovered damages for an unauthorized interference with a corpse. Nor are there any established torts which are obviously applicable to such conduct.

The English courts have not recognized any property interest in a corpse (*Dr Handayside's* case (C 18), 1 Hawk. PC 148, n 8, 2 East PC 652; *R v Sharpe* (1857) Dears & B 160 at 163; *Williams v Williams* (1882) 20 Ch D 659 662-3, 665; *R v Price* (1884) 12 QBD 247 at 252); so the unauthorized removal of cadaveric transplant material would not give rise to an action in trespass to goods, conversion, or detinue (see, eg, *Dr Handayside's* case, also *Hamps v Darby* [1948] 2 KB 311 at 319, 320, 322, 328). The tort of negligence would very rarely be applicable, for the doctor would not normally owe a duty of care to the person aggrieved by the unauthorized removal (see the comments on *Owens v Liverpool Corpn* [1939] 1 KB 394 in *Bourhill v Young* [1943] AC 92 at 100, 105, 110, 116). In the rare cases where the doctor did owe such a duty, knowledge of the unauthorized removal would be unlikely to cause nervous shock, or to harm health. The innominate tort of intentional acts calculated to cause bodily injury (see *Wilkinson v Downton* [1897] 2 QB 57; *Janvier v Sweeney* [1919] 2 KB 316) would rarely, if ever, apply.

Although the courts have not recognized any property interest in the corpse of a human being, they have recognized that the person under a duty to dispose of the body has a right to possession for that purpose (eg, *R v Fox* (1841) 2 QB 246). On the principle *ubi jus ibi remedium*, an intentional and unauthorized interference with this right should render the interferer liable, at the suit of the person entitled to possession. Recovery was permitted in one Canadian case (*Edmonds v Armstrong Funeral Home Ltd* [1931] 1 DLR 676), where a doctor had made an unauthorized post-mortem examination of the corpse. The unauthorized removal of transplant material would probably also be actionable. There would not be any need to prove actual damage, although the measure of damages would obviously be greater if the plaintiff could show that he suffered in consequence of the interference. Of course, in many cases the unauthorized interference would not come to the notice of the potential plaintiff and, even if it did, it might be difficult for him to establish that he was the person entitled to possession of the corpse. If the potential plaintiff had consented to the removal of the transplant material, and the doctor had complied with any conditions he expressly or impliedly laid down, it would not be open to him to recover damages on the ground of interference with his right to possession. The fact that the doctor did not comply with the provisions of the Human Tissue Act 1961 would be irrelevant.

Subsequently, Professor Skegg considered whether an action in negligence for nervous shock would lie. He concluded (in 'Liability for the Unauthorized Removal of Cadaveric Transplant Material: Some Further Comments' (1977) 17 Med Sci Law 123 at 124 that:

There is, at present [ie 1977] however, an important restriction on recovery for nervous shock . . . This is the principle in *Hambrook v Stokes Bros* ([1925] 1 KB 141 at 152, 159, 165), which could be held to preclude the recovery of damages for nervous shock where the potential plaintiff learnt of the unauthorized removal from others after the event, rather than witnessed the removal or its consequences for himself.

The 1991 decision of the House of Lords, on recovery of damages for psychiatric injury, supports Professor Skegg's view (see *Alcock v Chief Constable of South Yorkshire Police* [1991] 4 All ER 907 at 915, 917, 932).

Reform of the law

A. INTRODUCTION

The Report of the Working Party on the 'Supply of Donor Organs for Transplantation' (1987), chaired by Sir Raymond Hoffenberg, stated that:

Transplantation of the kidneys and other organs has been one of the great advances of the last quarter of a century. There is much public interest and support. Most people are prepared to give organs in appropriate circumstances, yet there is a shortfall in organ supply and a growing list for transplants. For kidneys this has risen from 2,500 to 3,500 in the last five years. The waiting lists for heart transplants, liver transplants and corneal grafts have doubled in the last two years. We, a working party from the Conference of Medical Royal Colleges and their Faculties in the UK, have been asked by the Department of Health and Social Security to find out why there is a shortfall and to make recommendations to remedy this. . . .

It has been estimated that about 4,000 brain stem deaths occur each year in the United Kingdom. In 1986, 800 donors provided 1,600 kidneys and in the same year there were 200 heart, 120 liver and about 1,500 corneal donations. In the first quarter of 1987 kidney donation fell by 19.1% in comparison with the same period in 1986. Heart donations increased by 37% and liver donations by 10%, showing that there were more multiple donations from a smaller number of donors.

There are insufficient kidneys to meet the needs of those waiting for renal transplantation and for those who will during succeeding years will develop renal failure. About 2,500 people start dialysis each year and this could rise to around 4,000. The projected need for kidneys, therefore, is at least 2,500 and might be as high as 4,000 each year. This could be achieved if a higher proportion of those with brain stem death were to become donors. The cost savings to the health service of a kidney transplant have recently been estimated at £30,000, this being the amount that would otherwise be spent on chronic dialysis. . . .

Reasons for the shortfall
1) Lack of medical experience and knowledge
Most doctors will have little experience of brain stem death and of requesting organ donation. Knowledge of the criteria for brain stem death, of the arrangements for transplantation and of the benefit of transplantation is not universal. Skill and sensitivity in the approach to bereaved relatives is variable. As a result there may be a reluctance to diagnose brain stem death and a failure to ask for organ donation. Some hospitals seldom provide organs for transplantation, yet when a sympathetic and experienced person talks with the relatives, permission is likely to be granted. Some hospitals have obtained 90% agreement to donation.

2) Doubts about the success of the transplant programme
This should no longer be entertained since the benefits of transplantation to the majority of recipients are proven. The three-year survival rate of kidney transplants is now commonly in excess of 75%, for hearts about 75% at one year and for livers 70% at one year. The actuarial patient survival statistics for kidney recipients show a better prognosis than is experienced by patients with gastrointestinal cancer, stage II carcinoma of the breast and carcinoma of the prostate, for example. Patients with kidney transplants have been recorded to survive in good health for 25 years, liver transplants for 16 years, heart transplants for 15 years and pancreas transplants for 8 years. Lung transplants have survived up to 3 years.

With improvements in tissue matching and immunosuppression in more recent years, more patients with organ transplants can be expected to survive with their transplant for long periods of time, if not for the term of their natural life. For the failing heart, liver and lung, transplantation may be the only option. For the failing kidney, transplantation provides a better quality of life at lower cost than dialysis. The public is well aware of the benefits of transplantation in adults and in children.

3) Doubts about the criteria for brain stem death
The BBC Panorama programme of 1980 which cast doubt on the criteria was followed by a fall in the number of organ donations, but this has since risen and an increase of about a third followed the BBC 'That's Life' programme in 1985. In the three months since the publication of articles on brain stem death in the Sunday Times at the end of 1986, there has been a 19.1% fall in the number of kidney donations.

We have taken evidence from a physician and from an anaesthetist who are opposed to the removal of organs from heart-beating donors. They accept that the fulfilment of the criteria for brain stem death does permit withdrawal of ventilation but they believe that death only occurs when circulation and respiration cease. Further refinement of tests of brain stem function would not satisfy them that death had occurred before the heart stops beating. The difference between our views and theirs is in the concept of when death occurs.

We are convinced that the criteria for brain stem death are adequate and believe that once the brain stem is dead, sentient existence is no longer possible and that the person is dead. We do not think that electro-encephalography, four-vessel arteriography, doppler or isotope studies of cerebral blood flow would give further useful information.

We accept that a small minority of doctors and some members of the public have reservations about that concept of brain stem death despite full explanation, and that patients and their relatives must always be free to decline consent to organ donation.

The Society of British Neurological Surgeons at its meeting in April 1987 unanimously supported the view that the clinical criteria for the diagnosis of brain stem death were entirely satisfactory. There is overwhelming informed professional opinion that ventilation after death does no more than allow the heart to beat, so maintaining circulation. This makes possible the donation in good condition of kidneys, heart, lung, liver and pancreas.

4) Demand for intensive care beds
It is not possible to transfer to intensive care units all those who might become brain stem dead. Transfer and treatment should be in the interest of the patient. A possible exception is when relatives have particularly requested organ donation. If there is an insufficient number of staffed intensive care beds for all those who require intensive care, organ donation will be reduced. Many clinicians in charge of intensive care units agree that given more beds, equipment and staff, more potential donors could be managed.

5) Constraints of time
It may take several hours to discuss matters with bereaved relatives and to make the arrangements for organ donation with a transplant team.

6) Limited theatre time
Because of pressure on operating theatres for other emergencies, there may be reluctance to embark upon organ removal, especially more lengthy multiple organ retrieval, which may occupy a theatre for several hours. The disruption to the donor hospitals' routine has been a significant disincentive to further referral of donors in some hospitals.

7) Cost
There is no rational basis for financial arguments against procurement. As clinical budgeting takes hold, there will be greater awareness both of the costs of removing organs and the cost savings to the health service of a successful transplant.

8) Medico-legal constraints
We have found general praise for the attitude and helpfulness of coroners. Seldom has the need for a coroner's post mortem examination prevented the donation of organs.

Arthur Caplan reviewed the situation in the US and Europe in a seminal article in 1984.

A Caplan, 'Organ Procurement: It's Not in the Cards' (1984) 14 Hastings Center Report 9 (number 5)

Not so long ago the distinguished Senator from Vermont, George Aitken, proposed a novel solution to the problem of ending the Vietnam War. He wryly observed that the fastest way to stop that conflict was simply to declare ourselves the winners and go home.

Defenders of the philosophy of voluntarism in the procurement of cadaver organs for transplantation seem to have taken to heart Aitken's proposal for resolving an apparently intractable problem. Alfred and Blair Sadler declare that they are unable to see 'any significant developments in transplantation [that] would justify discarding the principles of informed consent and encouraged voluntarism embodied in the Uniform Anatomical Gift Act'. They are not looking carefully enough. The facts about both the supply of and the demand of cadaver organs do not support their decision to solve the crisis in organ procurement by declaring the system a success. Our society's decision in the late 1960s to rely on a public policy of voluntarism as the primary means for assuring an adequate supply of organs for transplantation is no longer tenable. Perhaps such a system was appropriate when organ transplantation was in its infancy, but this is no longer the case.

The Center for Disease Control estimates that about 20,000 persons die each year under circumstances that would make them suitable for cadaver organ donation. This number should provide a maximum possible pool of 40,000 kidneys for transplant. Yet in 1982 only 3,691 cadaver kidney transplants were performed. The best estimates are that less than 15 percent of potential donors are utilized under the present policy.

Recent studies estimate that between 6,000 and 10,000 persons on hemodialysis are waiting for kidney transplants. Some believe the number of possible recipients in the United States would be as high as 22,500 per year if transplant surgeons were not forced by the severe inadequacy of the present supply of cadaver kidneys to be so conservative in formulating criteria for eligibility for renal transplantation. Similar statistics exist concerning the shortfall of tissues for corneal transplants, hearts, lungs and, as the media remind us every day, livers. And unless something is done to modify the present reliance on a voluntary system, the shortage in cadaver organs will continue to worsen. Rapid progress in the development of surgical techniques, tissue matching, and immunosuppressive drugs will lead to incessant demands for more cadaver organs in the years ahead.

Transplantation may be, as the Sadlers observe, a 'halfway' solution to the problem of organ failure. But for those suffering from renal failure, kidney transplants afford a better quality of life than dialysis, and they are far cheaper. Medicare's End-Stage Renal Disease Program has passed the $2 billion mark in reimbursing the costs of more than 70,000 dialysis patients. How can anyone possibly conclude that the present approach to procurement is adequate, acceptable, or working well?

Nor is it at all evident that donor cards have played a significant role in helping to produce even the small degree of procurement success that has been attained in the United States. Less than 15 percent of the population carry donor cards. Transplant coordinators estimate that less than 3 percent of donors have cards in their possession at the time of death. Where data are available on the number of drivers designated as donors in states where organ donation boxes are provided on licenses the compliance rate is not impressive.

Three possible alternatives

What then are the possible policy alternatives to the present system of voluntarism and donor cards? And more important, which of these alternatives is most consistent with the values of individual choice, altruism, and freedom?

One possible public policy alternative is to allow the creation of a market in cadaver organs. There are two variants of this approach. The 'strong market approach' would allow individuals or, after death, their next of kin to auction organs for sale to the highest bidder. The 'weak market approach', on the other hand, would discourage direct compensation of donors by recipients but would allow for the creation of various tax incentives or in-kind reimbursements (those who donate could guarantee their loved ones or friends priority for future transplants) to encourage donation.

A second approach – that of 'presumed consent' – would grant medical personnel the authority to remove organs from cadavers for transplantation whenever usable organs were available at the time of death. Again, there are two variants. In 'strong presumed consent' the state would grant physicians complete authority to remove usable tissues regardless of the wishes of the deceased or family members. In 'weak presumed consent' the law would presume that organ procurement can be undertaken in the absence of some form of objection from the deceased or family members. Weak consent places the burden of opting out of organ donation on those who have objections to this procedure rather than, as is the case under the present system of voluntarism, upon those who wish to opt for organ donation.

A third approach, which has not been widely discussed in the current debate about organ procurement policies, is what I have termed 'required request'. In the strong version, every citizen would be asked to indicate his or her willingness to participate in organ donation, perhaps by means of a mandatory check-off on applications for a driver's license, a social security card, or on tax returns.

In the weak version, current legislation pertaining to the definition of death might be modified to state that at the time death is declared a person who has no connection to the process of determining death would be required to ask family members about the possibility of organ donation.

What the public thinks

There has been a good deal of public debate about the moral acceptability of the strong market approach to procuring cadaver organs. Near unanimity of public opinion has emerged about the unacceptability of an open market in cadaver organs. At least one state, Virginia, banned the sale of organs for transplantation. Other states are considering such bans, as is the United States Congress [this subsequently occurred in the National Organ Transplant Act 1984]. Transplant surgeons have repeatedly stated their adamant opposition to market solutions. The moral revulsion that has characterized discussions in the popular press and in professional journals about the spectacle of the desperately ill furiously bidding against one another for a kidney or a liver has, at least for the present, rendered both versions of this policy academic.

Similarly, little public enthusiasm has emerged for a system of strong presumed consent. In a recent survey the Battelle National Heart Transplantation Study found that less than 8 percent of those interviewed felt that 'doctors should have the power to remove organs from people who died recently but have not signed an organ donor card without consulting the next-of-kin'.

Public opinion aside, the Sadlers argue that any form of presumed consent would have a corrosive effect on the trust that exists between the medical community and the public. They also note that presumed consent would not necessarily lead to an increase in the supply of cadaver organs for transplant. But those European nations that have adopted versions of presumed consent lack evidence to determine whether these concerns are justified.

The European experience

Various European nations, including Austria, Denmark, Poland, Switzerland, and France, have legislation mandating a policy of strong presumed consent. Other nations such as Finland, Greece, Italy, Norway, Spain, and Sweden have adopted versions of weak presumed consent. However, as the Sadlers correctly observe, the available empirical data do not show that these countries have dramatically increased their supply of cadaver organs.

The Swedes, for example, transplant nearly as many patients suffering from kidney failure as they maintain on hemodialysis. This compares quite favourably with the one-to-nine ratio that prevails in the United States. However, statistics on the rates of organ procurement in Sweden and other European countries are not readily available. Indeed, all these countries still have waiting lists for those needing kidney transplants.

In June 1984 I visited France to discuss organ procurement with a number of transplant surgeons and nurses. Organ transplantation in France has been confined almost exclusively to corneas and kidneys. French physicians and government officials estimated that approximately 800 kidney transplants were performed in 1982. This suggests a rate that is only slightly higher than the rate of kidney transplantation in the United States. There are indeed waiting lists for those on hemodialysis who hope for a transplant.

Why should this be so, given that France has a policy of strong presumed consent? French physicians offer two explanations. First, though the law has resulted in an increase in the number of cadaver organs available for transplant, this increase is not reflected in the overall rates because the additional organs have been utilized to decrease the numbers of live donors. Whereas live donors have provided about a third of the kidneys available for transplant in France in the late 1970s, today live donors make up less than 10 percent of the donor pool. (Live donors constitute nearly a third of the donor pool in the United States, Britain, and other nations with public policies of voluntarism based upon donor cards.)

Second, French physicians note that, despite a public policy allowing strong presumed consent, doctors are not willing to remove organs from cadavers without the consent of family members. Strong presumed consent exists only on paper in France. In practice French physicians find it psychologically intolerable to remove tissues from a body without obtaining the permission of next-of-kin.

In the view of both physicians and nurses, however, the French public strongly supports organ transplantation. The physicians I spoke with reported consent rates of between 90 and 95 percent when permission was sought to remove solid organs. In practice French physicians believe strongly in allowing family members to retain the right to object to organ removal. But few family members actually do object, indicating that a public policy of weak presumed consent is compatible with the moral values of both health professionals and the public in France.

Even if French physicians are only willing to participate in a system whose governing philosophy is one of weak presumed consent, why, given the low rate of refusal, are a larger number of organs not available for transplant? The answer is illuminating for its policy implications for the United States.

France, unlike the United States, does not have a cadre of highly trained personnel to handle the process of organ procurement. Health professionals, usually nurses, must bear the burdens of inquiring about objections to organ removal, locating a suitable recipient, and arranging the removal of organs. French hospital administrators, physicians, and nurses all reported that this process was both time-consuming and costly. Given the growing concern in France over the rising costs of health care there is reluctance to devote scarce medical resources to organ procurement. French transplant surgeons also noted that, at present, there were severe limits both in terms of personnel and hospital space on the number of transplants of all types that can now be performed. One surgeon noted that 'if we had your resources and facilities for transplantation we would be much more aggressive in pursuing organ donors'. Limits on the availability of transplant services in France seem to dampen the ardor with which organ procurement is undertaken.

Moreover, the French, like their American counterparts, find it psychologically difficult to approach grieving family members about the prospect of organ procurement even if to ascertain whether the family objects to what is usually described in the consent process as a routine, customary, and legally sanctioned practice. Busy emergency room personnel are loath to take the time necessary to fully discuss the subject of transplantation with distraught family members. In sum, despite the existence on paper of a strong version of presumed consent, health care professionals in France are only willing to operate within the boundaries of weak presumed consent. And while this approach has helped to increase the supply of available cadaver kidneys to the point where few live donations are utilized, economic, organizational, and psychological factors limit the willingness of French medical personnel to ask about objections to removing kidneys and other solid organs for transplantation.

The French experience with strong presumed consent legislation holds important lessons for those, such as myself, who believe that our system of organ procurement must be changed. The French physicians' unwillingness to act upon the authority granted them by the state to remove organs regardless of the wishes of family members parallels the unwillingness of American physicians to remove organs solely on the basis of the legal authority granted by donor cards. As organ procurement specialists know all too well, donor cards are almost never viewed by hospital administrators and physicians as adequate authorization for allowing organ retrieval. The permission of family members is always sought prior to organ removal whether or not a donor card or other legal document can be found.

On the other hand, the practical experience obtained by the French with a version of weak presumed consent does not support the sorts of concerns raised by the Sadlers about presumed consent. French physicians are impressed with the fact that objections have been raised by less than 10 percent of the families who have been given the opportunity to refuse consent. The French press has not reported any dissatisfaction on the part of the public with presumed consent. And French physicians were uniformly relieved to be able to decrease their earlier dependence on live donors. A policy of weak presumed consent appears to have produced a significant amount of social good while allowing for family choice and autonomy in an atmosphere of mutual respect.

The organizational, financial, and psychological factors at work in the French system of organ procurement are also present in the United States. Unlike the French, we have a large number of highly trained and proficient specialists available in the field of organ procurement, but constant pressure to reduce costs in combination with an increasingly litigious atmosphere in medicine make it unlikely that the modest reforms of the present voluntary system proposed by the Sadlers and others will lead to significant improvement in the supply of cadaver organs.

The existing legal arrangements for obtaining organs from cadavers have come to be known as a system of 'opting in', ie the donor or relative has to opt to donate. To the extent that the law may be responsible for the under-supply of organs (as mentioned above), apart from a programme of public education which seems to have produced little over the last decade or so, two proposals for reform have been advanced in England – a system of 'opting out' and the principle of 'required request'.

B. 'OPTING OUT'

Consider, first, the article by Jesse Dukeminier.

J Dukeminier, 'Supplying Organs for Transplantation', (1970) 68 Michigan Law Review 811

Routine salvaging of cadaver organs unless there is objection

A significant increase in the supply of organs for transplantation would result if usable organs were removed from cadavers routinely unless, before the time of removal, an objection had been entered, either by the decedent during his life or by his next of kin after the decedent's death. This approach is not as extreme as the proposal to salvage useful organs without regard to objection, since under this approach persons who do not wish to make their organs available may object and opt out. Nor is this approach as radical a departure from traditional humanist values as the Uniform Anatomical Gift Act, for, by making the basic presumption one which favors life, and by thus putting the burden of objecting upon persons who would deny life to another, the policy of saving human life is given first priority and the wishes of persons to preserve a corpse inviolate are also accommodated. This method would produce far more organs for transplantation than are produced by statutes permitting organ donation by the decedent.

Some time ago Dr David Sanders and the author proposed legislation to make removal of usable cadaver organs routine unless the decedent or his next of kin instructed otherwise. In light of the 1967 Gallup poll results, it appears that a carefully drawn statute embodying such an approach would be acceptable to a majority of people in this country. Indeed, in a recent questionnaire submitted to physicians, Dr Robert Williams found that the Dukeminier-Sanders proposal was favored by seventy-one percent of those responding. Similar figures from Britain indicate that two-thirds of the British people favor routine removal of cadaver kidneys. A leading kidney transplant surgeon from England, Professor Roy Calne, [Renal Transplantation 154 (1976)], writes that in his experience most relatives would prefer not to be asked for the kidneys but would rather that the kidneys be removed routinely.

Perhaps the simplest way to provide for routine salvaging of cadaver organs would be to enact a statute permitting prompt autopsies for organ removal on all persons who die in authorized hospitals, unless objection is first entered. In many countries the public already accepts routine autopsies. In France, for example, cadaver organs may be removed without permission of the family if the person dies in a hospital approved by the Minister of Public Health. In several European countries, autopsies are performed on all persons who die in hospitals unless some objection is made. In Israel the Anatomy and Pathology Act, passed in 1953, permits an autopsy without consent so long as three physicians formally attest in writing that the autopsy may help the lives of other existing patients; and ninety percent of all persons who die in hospitals in Israel are subjected to autopsies. In the United States, where consent for an autopsy must always be secured before such an operation may be performed, the autopsy rate in those hospitals approved for internships and residencies by the Council on Medical Education varies from twenty-five percent to one hundred per cent of the persons who die within the hospital. The average autopsy rate is approximately fifty per cent.

If a broad autopsy statute is unacceptable, the best substitute is a statute dealing solely with removal of organs for transplantation. The details of such a statute need to be carefully considered. There are at least four major problems. First, what organs may be routinely removed? The legislative draftsman might conclude that only those organs with a high degree of transplantation success could be removed – at the present time, corneas and kidneys. In England a Renal Transplantation Bill was introduced in Parliament on November 27, 1968; section 2 of the bill provided:

It shall be lawful to remove from the body of a human person, duly certified as dead, any kidney or kidneys required for the direct purpose of saving the life of another sick human being, unless there is reason to believe that the deceased during his lifetime had instructed otherwise.

The bill failed on second reading because, among other things, the Minister of Health objected to legislation for a single organ. Since each new successful development in transplantation would require an amendment to the statute, the legislature might appropriately conclude that the more useful statute would permit the removal of all organs usable in transplantation.

A middle position might be taken between permitting only specified organs to be removed and permitting all usable organs to be removed. For example, a medical board or the state director of public health could be empowered to promulgate administrative regulations specifying the organs that could be removed routinely; the statute could provide a general guideline, such as a provision that the list be limited to organs which can be transplanted with a good chance of success when transplantation is recognized by the medical profession as appropriate therapy. Such an approach, however, would prevent routine removal of organs for experimental purposes, including experiments to save life; and such a limitation on experimentation might be felt to be too restrictive.

The second problem to be solved in drafting an organ removal statute is the determination of which persons are to be authorized to remove organs routinely. This problem is probably best solved by administrative regulations that enumerate the capabilities and qualifications that are required of the medical staff, and the supporting equipment and facilities that must be available, before organs may be removed routinely. Again, these regulations could be drawn up by an authorized medical board or a state health official. In France, for example, the Minister of Public Health approves hospitals at which autopsies may be performed without permission of the family. The regulations could license hospitals, qualified surgeons, or both.

The third problem which must be faced in drafting an appropriate statute is whether any bodies should be excluded from routine removal of organs. Section 3 of the British Renal Transplantation Bill provided an exclusion for any person who, at the time of his death, was
(a)   mentally insane, or
(b)   mentally handicapped, or
(c)   below the age of 18, or
(d)   65 years old or more than that age, or
(e)   deprived of his liberty by the conviction and judgment of a court, or
(f)   a permanent resident of a hostel, home or institution for the aged, the disabled, or the handicapped.
The primary purpose of these exclusions was to ensure that only those who are free to object fall within the terms of the bill. A secondary purpose was to set at ease the minds of older persons, who might fear that doctors would hasten their demise in order to transplant their organs into a younger person.

The fourth drafting problem concerns the method of registering objections so that organs cannot be removed at death. There are various possible methods: a card could be carried by the person, a statement could be made to the hospital upon entering, a statement could be made to the physician, or a central computer registry could be established. One of the problems discussed previously in connection with organ donation statutes reappears in another form here. That problem was how to provide a means to aid the surgeon in finding out quickly and conclusively that he has a valid consent. The problem under the approach being examined here is determining how the surgeon can find out quickly and conclusively that there is no objection. Fortunately, the latter is more readily soluble than the former and does not contain within it any subsidiary problems. The presumption is that there is no objection which the surgeon knew or ought to have known from the next of kin. Hence the problem is narrowed to the determination of what inquiry the surgeon ought to be required to make. The statute could provide that a valid objection must be entered in a specific way, such as through registration with a national computer system. For instance, section 7 of the British Renal Transplantation Bill provided for a central renal registry in the Ministry of Health in which any person might register his objection to the transplantation of his kidneys. With such a provision, the only inquiry the surgeon would have to make would be to the computer, and it would be possible for surgeons to ascertain within minutes whether the donor had entered any objection. If a computer error occurs, the next of kin would have a cause of action against the organisation responsible for the computer, not against the surgeon. Alternatively, a statute might contain a provision for a compensation fund for the next of kin in cases involving a decedent who had filed an objection but whose objection had been ignored by a mistake. As a practical matter, few suits would probably be brought as a result of computer malfunction, because if organ removal becomes routine, the practice will become part of the expectations of the next of kin and the public, just as routine autopsies are part of the expectations of persons in some European countries. If a surgeon removes an organ, not knowing that a valid objection has been filed, the damages would be measured by the mental pain and suffering of the next of kin; if the public accepts routine organ removal, the damages awarded by a jury for unauthorized removal are not likely to be great. Hence there would be little incentive to sue either a computer organization or a surgeon in case of an error.

A final question which pertains to the filing of objections is whether the next of kin, as well as the decedent, should have the power to object and thereby to prevent removal of organs. The British bill permitted only the decedent to object, but the next of kin could bring the decedent's objection to the attention of the surgeons. In any event, the question is not very important, because if the next of kin objects, either on the ground that the decedent instructed otherwise or for his own personal reasons, it is unlikely that a surgeon will remove the organs. A tug of war for organs with the next of kin would be most unseemly. Nonetheless, a statute in the United States should expressly permit the next of kin to object, since such a provision would help to avoid first amendment difficulties.

No Bill advocating 'opting out' or any other major reform has reached the statute book in England. The latest dismissal of the idea of 'opting out' is contained in the Report of the Working Party on the Supply of Organs for Transplantation, chaired by Sir Raymond Hoffenberg, (*op cit*) p 6:

> We have been told that an *Opting Out* Scheme might increase donations by allowing organs to be removed after brain stem death from those who had not recorded an objection, but we do not recommend this. There would be a risk that organs might be removed when this had not been the wish of the person or their relatives. It does not in itself enlist the co-operation of doctors. We would prefer organ donation to be seen as a positive gift with the consent of relatives who in practice would always be approached.

The French law, which has developed since Jesse Dukeminier was writing in 1970, is discussed by Ruth Redmond-Cooper in 'Transplants Opting Out or In – the Implications' (1984) 134 New Law Journal 648:

> In France the contracting out system was introduced by a Law of December 22, 1976, article 2(i) of which provides that organs may be removed from a body for therapeutic or scientific ends where the deceased had not, during his lifetime, made known his objection to such a removal. The implementing *decret* of the Conseil d'Etat was passed on March 31, 1978, and prescribes the conditions under which removal of organs may be effected. Objections to removal may be general or limited to particular organs and can be expressed by any means. If a person is hospitalised immediately before death, any indication of objection, coming either from the victim himself or from statements made by his family (relating to the *deceased's* objection, not that of the relatives) and supported by necessary evidence, must be entered on a special register.
>
> In practice, however, French doctors prefer to obtain the consent of the next of kin (although in a recent decision the Conseil d'Etat held that the *decret* was correct in not providing a right of refusal for relatives), possibly since the majority of French people would seem to be unaware of the provisions of the Law of 1976. The result of this is that the number of transplants performed in France is lower than in the UK.
>
> Any opting out system introduced in the UK would therefore need to be different in both conception and implementation from the French Law of 1976. It is clear that if relatives are asked at the time of death whether they wish to exercise a veto over the removal of organs, a great many, through grief and shock, will refuse permission. By placing the onus of objection on the individual and removing all rights from the next of kin, the problem becomes an ethical one: who has the ultimate moral right to decide on the disposal of a dead body? A possible solution might be to permit next of kin to register a binding objection at the time of death, but not to require formal consultation by surgeons. In any event, an opting out system would need to be accompanied by adequate publicity in order to avoid the situation which has arisen in France and also to protect the rights and beliefs of individuals and their families.

In the event of a sudden death of a non-hospitalised person, it is standard medical procedure to perform a post mortem before removing body organs for transplantation. If an opting out system is introduced this practice should become mandatory. In France the Law of 1976 makes no provision for a post mortem examination, although the Law of 1949 relating to corneal grafts refers specifically to the necessity for such an examination. Without a post mortem there is a very real possibility that a latent disease in the deceased may be passed on to the recipient of an organ.

In October 1979 a woman died suddenly in France and her eyes were immediately used to provide a corneal transplant. The operation was successful and the recipient was allowed to return home, but he died soon after from rabies. At a subsequent enquiry the dead woman's family revealed that she had been in Egypt immediately before her death where she had been bitten by a dog. As a result of this incident the director of the eye bank involved was charged with manslaughter. The case is still pending before the French courts.

Difficulties of opting out

The difficulties raised by a system of opting out may therefore be summarised as follows: in order to avoid the risk of large numbers of people opting out through fear or misunderstanding, great care must be exercised in the installation of the system; there should be a statutory definition of what constitutes death and this should be in line with the popular notion of death; adequate publicity is essential in order to ensure that anyone who wishes to opt out may do so on the basis of an informed decision; a post mortem examination should be a statutory requirement.

However, it may not be necessary to take the radical step of introducing an opting out system. A better solution might consist in maintaining a revised form of opting in. This could be implemented, not through the use of cards as at present, but through a centralised computer. Consent could be given at the level of the local GP who would be available to advise potential donors and to ask all patients coming to the surgery whether they would be willing to donate their organs. The names of all those in agreement could then be placed by the GP on a national register, together with details of relevant illnesses and drug treatment, and possibly, consent of next of kin. The information contained in this register would be available only in the event of the death of the individual and the possibility of his body being used for a transplant.

The solution to the shortage of body organs available for transplant does not therefore necessarily reside in the introduction of a system of opting out: a similar result could be achieved through a revised form of opting in.

In 1986 Belgium enacted legislation adopting an 'opting out' system, the Law of 13 June 1986 on the removal and transplantation of organs (*Moniteur belge*, 14 February 1987, No 32, pp 2129-2132).

CHAPTER III
Removal after death

10.—(1) Organs and tissues for transplantation, and for the preparation of therapeutic substances in accordance with the conditions laid down in Section 2, may be removed from the body of any person recorded in the Register of the Population or any person recorded for more than six months in the Aliens Register, unless it is established that an objection to such a removal has been expressed.

It shall be a requirement, in the case of persons other than those mentioned above, that they have explicitly expressed their consent to the removal.

(2) Only a person who has attained 18 years of age and is capable of making known his wishes may express the objection provided for in subsection 1.

If a person has not attained 18 years of age but is capable of making known his wishes, the objection may be expressed either by him or, during his lifetime, by his close relatives living with him.

If a person has not attained 18 years of age and is incapable of making known his wishes, the objection may be expressed during his lifetime by his close relatives living with him.

If a person is incapable of making known his wishes by reason of his mental condition, the objection may be expressed during his lifetime by any legal representative or guardian for the time being he may have, failing which, by his closest relative.

(3) The Crown shall make provision for a method of expressing an objection to the removal for the donor or the persons referred to in subsection 2.

For this purpose, the Crown shall be empowered, under the conditions and in accordance with the rules laid down by it:

(a) at the request of the person concerned, to have the objection made known through the Services of the National Register;

(b) to regulate access to this information, so that the physicians carrying out the removal can be informed of the objection.

(4) A physician may not proceed to carry out the removal:

1. if an objection has been expressed in the manner provided for by the Crown;
2. if an objection has been expressed by the donor in another manner that has nevertheless been communicated to the physician; or
3. if a close relative has communicated his objection to the physician. This objection may not override the expressed wishes of the donor.

'Close relative' means a relative up to the first degree of, or the spouse residing with, the donor.

C. REQUIRED REQUEST

Arthur Caplan 'Organ Procurement: It's Not in the Cards' (*op cit*) writes:

One key factor emerges from both the French and the American experience: the major obstacle to organ procurement is the failure to ask family members about organ donation. French physicians are entitled by law to take tissues without asking anyone but are unwilling to do so. American physicians are entitled by the Uniform Anatomical Gift Act to take tissues from those who sign donor cards but they are unwilling to do so. Whether or not one believes that the wishes of the family should supersede either the wishes of the public, as in France, or the wishes of the individual, as in the United States, in fact both countries always treat the family as the final authority insofar as the disposition of the dead is concerned.

The respect accorded family members' wishes in these two large and medically sophisticated nations would seem to dictate the kind of public change that has the greatest chance of alleviating the shortage in cadaver donors. The French experience indicates that the only practical policy options are those that recognise and respect the role of family members in participating in decisions about cadaver donation. The weak version of required request acknowledges the role of family members, while at the same time ensuring that an optimal environment exists for eliciting organ donations.

Physicians, nurses, or other hospital personnel should be required to inquire whether available family members will give their consent to organ donation. This could be accomplished by modifying the current legal process for declaring death in all states to include a provision requiring that a request concerning organ donation be made to available family members by a party not connected with the determination of death. When family members are not available, organs would be removed only if a donor card or other legal document were present. Or, hospital accreditation requirements could be revised to include a provision mandating that at death the families of potential donors be approached about their willingness to consent.

. . . People must be asked to act if their altruistic motivations are to make a significant difference in helping those in need.

Cadaver organ donation is, whether we like it or not, a family matter. Families should be given every opportunity to act upon their desire to transform the tragedy of death into the gift of life. But they must be asked. If our society were to institute a policy of weak required request, those who are, according to the public opinion polls, willing to give would have a maximal opportunity to do so. We should not allow our concern for the rights and values of the individual to blind us to policy options that can accommodate both individual autonomy and community good.

An example of legislation in the United States can be seen in a 1985 amendment to the New York Public Health Law.

4351. 1. Where, based on accepted medical standards, a patient is a suitable candidate for organ or tissue donation, the person in charge of such hospital, or his designated representative, other than a person connected with the determination of death, shall at the time of death request any of the following persons, in the order of priority stated, when persons in prior classes are not available and in the absence of (1) actual notice of contrary intentions by the decedent, or (2) actual notice of opposition by a member of any of the classes specified in paragraph (*a*), (*b*), (*c*), (*d*), or (*e*) hereof or (3) other reason to believe that an anatomical gift is contrary to the decedent's religious beliefs, to consent to the gift of all or any part of the decedent's body for any purpose specified in article forty-three of this chapter.

(*a*)   the spouse;
(*b*)   a son or daughter twenty-one years of age or older;
(*c*)   either parent;
(*d*)   a brother or sister twenty-one years of age or older;
(*e*)   a guardian of the person of the decedent at the time of his death.

Where said hospital administrator or his designee shall have received actual notice of opposition from any of the persons named in the subdivision or where there is otherwise reason to believe that an anatomical gift is contrary to the decedent's religious beliefs, such gift of all or any part of the decedent's body shall not be requested. Where a donation is requested, consent or refusal need only be obtained from the person or persons in the highest priority class available.

2. Where a donation is requested, said person in charge of such hospital or his designated representative shall complete a certificate of request for an anatomical gift, on a form supplied by the commissioner [for Health]. Said certificate shall include a statement to the effect that a request for consent to an anatomical gift has been made, and shall further indicate thereupon whether or not consent was granted, the name of the person granting or refusing the consent, and his or her relationship to the decedent. Upon completion of the certificate, said person shall attach the certificate of request for an anatomical gift to the death certificate required by this chapter or, in the city of New York, to the death certificate required by the administrative code of the city of New York.

3. A gift made pursuant to the request required by this section shall be executed pursuant to applicable provisions of article forty-three of this chapter.

4. The commissioner shall establish regulations concerning the training of hospital employees who may be designated to perform the request, and the procedures to be employed in making it.

5. The commissioner shall establish such additional regulations as are necessary for the implementation of this section.

(See further on the position in the US, Daphne Sipes 'Requesting Organ Donations: A New State Approach to Organ Transplants' (1987) 8 Health Law in Canada 39).

In the UK, not only legislation but even the idea of a 'legally required request' was rejected by the Hoffenberg Working Party:

> We have considered *legally required request*. In the USA, 30 States have in the past two years enacted legislation requiring either than the hospital administrator or his designee should ask for the gift of organs, or that protocols are established for requesting the gift. In a smaller number of States there are penalties for non-compliance by fine or loss of licence. We agree with the Society of British Neurological Surgeons and with some others who have given evidence to us that the establishment of the above procedures for referral with an effective audit would be preferable to legally required request.

This seems a rather perfunctory rejection of the notion of a legally 'required request'. It could be said that the Working Party was more concerned with legal sanction against doctors who do not 'request' as a statute would require, rather than with the notion of required request *per se*.

D. OTHER REFORMS

1. Clarifying the 1961 Act

The most extensive review of the Human Tissue Act with a view to clarifying its provisions within the framework of a system of 'opting in' was attempted by the British Transplantation Society in its Report in 1975.

The Committee agreed that, in view of the unhelpful interpretations of the Human Tissue Act which persist in some quarters, statutory clarification of the Act was desirable.

The existing s.1(2) . . . should be repealed, and the following provision substituted:

'Without prejudice to the foregoing subsection, the person lawfully in possession of the body of a deceased person may authorise the removal of any part from the body for use for the said purpose if, *having made such inquiry as is both reasonable and practicable in the time available,* he has no reason to believe that the deceased had expressed an objection (which he was not known to have withdrawn) to his body being so dealt with after his death.

Provided that authorisation shall not be given under this subsection if the person lawfully in possession of the body has reason to believe that the surviving spouse or any surviving relative of the deceased objects to the body being so dealt with.'

In addition there should be a new subsection, providing that:

'For the avoidance of doubt in the interpretation of this section, it is hereby declared:

(a) That the hospital authority is the person in possession of the body of a deceased person lying in the hospital, and that this possession is lawful until such time as the hospital authority fails to comply with a request for possession of the body, made by the person who has the right to immediate possession of it.

(b) That a printed but personally signed "donor card", or other document, is "in writing" for the purpose of subsection 1 of this section.

(c) The "time available", for the purpose of an inquiry under subsection 2 of this section, extends only until the moment at which steps must be taken to remove the part of the body, if it is to be suitable for the therapeutic or other purpose in question.'

The effect of these provisions would be to overcome the unfortunate (and, it is thought, unjustified) doubts concerning the interpretation of 'such reasonable inquiry as may be practicable' and 'person lawfully in possession of the body' under the present law, and to prevent any doubts arising over the interpretation of 'in writing'.

Only in one respect does the suggested amendment seek to alter what the Committee understands to be the current legal position. Though authorisation could not be given under the proposed s 1 (2) if the person lawfully in possession of the body had reason to believe that the spouse or any relative of the deceased objected, he would no longer be under a duty to make enquiries as to whether they did object. He would, however, invariably approach the closest available relatives, in the course of making 'such inquiry as is both reasonable and practicable' to determine whether the deceased had expressed an objection. They would thus have the opportunity of making known their own (or others') objections. This change would represent a reversion to the legal position of the spouse and relatives under the Corneal Grafting Act, 1952, which was very much more satisfactory in this respect.

Some members of the Committee favoured a more radical amendment of the Human Tissue Act. But in view of the failure of more radical proposals to make progress through Parliament, and in view of the general consensus among surgeons that it would be undesirable to remove organs for transplantation in the face of objections from the spouse of relatives, it was decided to press for a limited amendment.

2. Without permission and ignoring objections

Jesse Dukeminier 'Supplying Organs for Transplantation', Michigan Law Review (*op cit*):

Removal of cadaver organs regardless of objection

A recent analysis of the problem of supplying organs resulted in the suggestion that legislation be enacted to authorise the removal, with or without consent, of cadaver organs useful for transplantation. The ethical basis for this solution to the problem of organ supply is that saving human life is paramount to all other policies and that no one has the right to deny another the chance to live.

Today, in disposing of the dead, the principle of protecting life requires that a coroner perform an autopsy on a body when homicidal behaviour is suspected, even though the next of kin objects. Courts have uniformly held that the rights of the decedent and next of kin are subordinate to the paramount public interest in apprehending killers. In these circumstances the autopsy may be held without the consent of the next of kin or even over his positive objection. Catching a murderer both prevents further homicidal behaviour by the man apprehended and deters homicidal behaviour by others. The overriding principle is protecting the lives of the survivors. . . .

If one accepts the view that saving human life requires the removal of useful cadaver organs regardless of the wishes of the decedent or next of kin the question arises whether a statute effectuating that policy would run foul of any constitutional provisions prohibiting the taking of property without compensation. One recent study concludes that such a statute would constitute a taking of the property of the next of kin, who would have to be paid compensation for the cadaver organs. That conclusion, however, is erroneous. Even accepting the highly questionable assumption that it is appropriate to classify the next of kin's interest in a cadaver as a property right, the next of kin's claim does not become an 'interest' in property until the death of the decedent. At any time prior to the occurrence of that event, the potential interest may be abolished without paying compensation, as may be seen by an analysis of the law relating to the closely analogous cases of a right of dower or an expectancy of an heir. While the decedent is alive, these rights are contingent upon surviving the decedent; in legal parlance, dower remains inchoate, and the expectancy of an heir is not recognised as an interest or right at all. Inchoate dower may be abolished without violating the Constitution. Indeed almost a hundred years ago the Supreme Court [*Rendall v Kreiger*] (1874) 90 US (23 Wall) 137, 148] declared:

> [Dower] is wholly given and the power that gave it may increase, diminish, or otherwise alter it, or wholly take it away. It is upon the same footing with the expectancy of heirs, apparent or presumptive, before the death of the ancestor. Until that event occurs the law of descent and distribution may be moulded according to the will of the legislature.

Thus, by analogy to inchoate dower or to the expectancy of an heir, it may be concluded that the rights of the next of kin to control the cadavers of persons living can be changed or abolished without paying any compensation.

It might also be thought that the decedent has an interest in what is done with his body, but the common-law rule is that there is no property in a dead body and that consequently a man cannot by will dispose of his body. If, however, cadaver organs are deemed to be property, compensation for their taking is not required, since succession to a man's property at death can be changed, and perhaps even abolished, by a legislature without violating the Constitution.

> Rights of succession to the property of a deceased, whether by will or by intestacy, are of statutory creation, and the dead hand rules succession only by sufferance. Nothing in the Federal Constitution forbids the legislature of a state to limit, condition, or even abolish the power of testamentary disposition over property within its jurisdiction. [*Irving Trust Co v Day* (1942) 314 US 556 562]

State supreme courts, with the exception of that of Wisconsin, agree that the power to dispose of property by will may be controlled by the legislature, subject only to the constitutional guarantees of equal protection and due process of law. These broad statements may not be wholly reliable, inasmuch as the power of the legislature to abolish testation has never been directly tested. Yet if the state can take by taxation a percentage of a man's property at death in order to raise revenue and to break up great fortunes, it is difficult to find any reason why the state cannot constitutionally take a specific item, such as a kidney, to save a human life.

Moreover, if organs are treated as property of the decedent, the decedent may have no power to order destruction of his organs by burial or cremation so long as the organs have value. It has been held in a number of cases that a direction to destroy one's own property at death is against public policy and is therefore void. Although these cases could provide the basis for an argument that permitting the destruction of valuable human organs to satisfy a decedent's wish is against public policy, courts today probably would not accept such an argument. Thinking of a cadaver as a valuable resource is still too startling; but as organ transplants become very successful courts may become more receptive to the argument.

It is, however, extremely troublesome to use property terms in the litany of justification for the taking of cadaver organs, for cadaver organs are not property in any conventional sense. Under modern law the next of kin is given a cause of action for unauthorised dissection, and courts have sometimes characterised this right in the next of kin as a property or a quasi-property right. But as Dean Prosser points out, 'it is in reality the personal feelings of the survivors which are being protected under a fiction likely to deceive no one but a lawyer' [*The Law of Torts* 51 (3d edn, 1964)]. Even if the fiction is accepted for purposes of unauthorised dissection cases, the answer to the question whether the rights are property rights for purposes of the Constitution should not turn upon a characterisation made by state courts in such an entirely different context. In determining the constitutionality of legislation authorising the removal of cadaver organs regardless of objection it is inappropriate to begin the analysis by accepting a characterisation of cadaver organs as property. As Justice Jackson said some years ago with reference to another claim of a constitutionally protected 'property right': 'We cannot start the process of decision by calling such a claim as we have here a "property right"; whether it is a property right is really the question to be answered.' [*United States v Willow River Power Co* (1945) 324 US 499 at 502]

In striking a balance between the interests of the public and the desires of the decedent and the survivors, legislatures have already subordinated the interests of the decedent and survivors to the public interest in saving human life, to interests of public health and convenience, and to the economic welfare of undertakers, employers, and insurers. In view of that background, it would surely be odd to find that the fourteenth amendment forbids subordinating the interest of the decedent and next of kin to the public interest in saving the life of a human being.

Use of fetal tissue

A. THE BACKGROUND

The following article by Raanan Gillon, from (1988) 296 *British Medical Journal* 1212, sets the scene:

Ethics of fetal brain cell transplants
In analysing the ethical issues provoked by the technique of transplanting fetal brain cells into the brains of patients with Parkinson's disease . . . it may be helpful to consider the various affected parties within the framework of four widely acceptable moral considerations: respect for people and their autonomy, beneficence (doing good), non-maleficence (avoiding doing harm), and justice (fairness in distribution of resources, in respect for rights, and in respect for morally acceptable laws). Such analysis is benefited by discussion on this subject at Britain's first multidisciplinary conference on philosophy and ethics in reproductive medicine, which was held [in April 1988] in Leeds.

Obligations to the recipients of the fetal brain cells seem well met. Thus, as the conference heard from Dr Richard West, chairman of the ethics committee that approved the research, the committee followed the standard research ethics committee guidelines of the Royal College of Physicians. Theoretical considerations, animal research, and preliminary results of clinical research abroad had shown a reasonable prospect of benefiting the severely affected patients (beneficence) with an acceptably low risk of harming them (non-maleficence). The requirement of adequately informed consent respected their autonomy, and no justice considerations were infringed either in terms of fair distribution of resources or infringement of the subject's rights; and the procedures were legally acceptable.

Moral qualms were expressed at the conference about the women whose aborted fetuses were used. Although such women signed consent forms disclaiming any views on the disposal of the fetus, some participants vigorously argued that the women concerned ought to be given more explicit information if the fetal tissues might be used for transplantation or other research and their specific unpressured consent obtained. On the other hand, a woman lawyer argued that not to be satisfied with an adult woman's signature disclaiming views on disposal of the fetus smacked of patronising sexism. In addition, such women might be benefited by being told the outcome, where successful, of any use made of fetal tissues, as proposed by the Conference of Medical Royal Colleges for transplantation.

The women's welfare might be adversely affected if special and more risky abortion techniques were used in order to preserve the fetal brains for transplantation. Furthermore, if such use became widespread women might be increasingly exploited by commercial or other pressures to become pregnant to provide aborted tissues. But given suitable controls to prevent such problems no insuperable moral objections seemed to arise from the perspective of the pregnant women. Their autonomy could be respected, they could be benefited with low probability of harm, their rights could be respected, and they could actually contribute to greater distributive justice by permitting their fetuses to be used to benefit others medically; and provided the abortions are carried out according to the requirements of the Abortion Act the procedures are lawful.

But is the Abortion Act a morally acceptable law? The main ethical objections offered at the conference concerned precisely that question in relation to the third affected party, the aborted fetuses. One of the main speakers, Miss Pamela Sims, a consultant obstetrician and gynaecologist and moral opponent of abortion, argued that, since abortion and the Abortion Act were morally unacceptable, using fetal parts for transplantation after abortion was also morally unacceptable – 'the end cannot justify the means'.

Clearly if the fetus is to be accorded full moral status destroying it for the benefit of others would be unacceptable: but, as the ethics committee reportedly reasoned, it was not for its members to deploy their personal moral reservations about abortions in coming to their decisions. It, like the Peel Committee, to whose advice it had scrupulously adhered, started from the presumption that abortions were to be carried out. The moral question then becomes: *given* that abortions have been carried out is it morally acceptable to use fetal tissues to benefit others? The relevant means here, as philosopher Jenifer Jackson pointed out, was the transplantation of tissues from already aborted fetuses, and those means could be morally acceptable even to those who believed the abortions themselves and the Abortion Act to be morally wrong. Dr Wendy Greengross, general practitioner and member of the Warnock Committee, illustrated the point succinctly – the fact that a brain dead man on a respirator had been murdered would not morally prohibit using his organs for transplantation.

Finally, are the interests of society threatened by this development? Some concern was expressed at the conference that ethics committees were able locally to make socially controversial decisions including decisions about 'human brain transplants' with only one lay member on the committee and without any of the members having had any formal training in ethical analysis. Ms Jean Robinson, a lay member of the General Medical Council, vigorously argued that there should be a minimum of two lay members on an ethics committee, which should always be prepared to justify its decisions to the public (as it had in this case). Several of the foreign visitors found it peculiar that no national bioethics committee had been established, at least to provide analysis and advice on particularly contentious or difficult medicomoral issues. Such a committee, if also charged to anticipate developments in bioethics, would provide a foothold on the 'slippery slope' about which Miss Sims warned the conference.

B. IS IT LAWFUL?

We are here concerned with the use of the tissue from a dead fetus.

Since the tissue is harvested only when the fetus is *ex utero* as a consequence of an abortion (or still birth), the legal problem only concerns the 'legality of the means' whereby the death was brought about. It would be otherwise if it were proposed to use tissues from a fetus which would be capable of surviving *ex utero*. In such a case, no tissue could be used until the fetus died naturally and clearly any attempts to bring about its death would be either child destruction (if it did not fall within s 1(1)(b)-(d) of the Abortion Act 1967) or homicide depending upon whether the fetus yet had an 'existence independent of its mother' (see ch 12 for a discussion). Some objections have been raised against the possibility of a woman becoming pregnant by her spouse or partner solely with the intention of aborting the fetus and thereby providing tissue for transplant into the spouse or partner. Apart from possible ethical objections, are there legal objections to this? There may be, of course; principally objections under the Abortion Act if it were properly applied. In addition, there may be an argument that their conduct so offends against public policy as to amount to a crime, ie conduct calculated to outrage public decency – if this be a crime in itself. If, however, as may be the case, the crime consists only in conspiracy to outrage public decency, a charge could only be brought if the couple were not married (see G Williams, *Textbook of Criminal Law* (2nd edn) at p 432).

On the assumption that the above legal conditions are satisfied, it was recommended by the Polkinghorne Committee (Cm 762, 1989) (discussed by Keown (1993) 19 Journal of Medical Ethics 114) that the consent of the mother be obtained before the fetal tissue may be used. Is this a legal requirement?

Consent can only be a *legal* requirement if the mother retains some proprietorial rights in or over the foetus, or, the use of the tissue constitutes an invasion of her bodily integrity (as we discussed earlier, see *supra*, pp 1102 *et seq*). (For an insightful discussion from an American perspective see J A Robertson 'Fetal Tissue Transplants' (1988) 66 Washington University Law Quarterly 443.)

Part III

Medical law in action

C: The end(ing) of life

Chapter 16

The end(ing) of life: the incompetent patient

In any analysis of the law relating to medical treatment at the end of life it would appear natural to start with a consideration of the position of the competent patient who may make his own decisions about treatment before considering the position of the incompetent patient. We will, however, for a number of reasons, begin with the incompetent patient. First, it will be clear that most of the issues which arise when the patient is competent involve a particular application of what we have already said about the law of consent in Chapter 3. Indeed, you will recall that we dealt with a number of cases concerned with decisions at the end of life in that chapter. Secondly, it is the law relating to the incompetent which is much more problematic and exposes the need to examine the fundamental principles underlying treatment decisions at the end of life.

An illustrative case

Although it is an American case, *In the Matter of Conroy* raises the issues that any common law courts would face.

In the Matter of Claire Conroy (1985) 486 A 2d 1209 (NJ Sup Ct)

Schrieber J: At issue here are the circumstances under which life-sustaining treatment may be withheld or withdrawn from incompetent, institutionalised, elderly patients with severe and permanent mental and physical impairments and a limited life expectancy . . .

At the time of trial, Ms Conroy was no longer ambulatory and was confined to bed unable to move from a semi-fetal position. She suffered from arteriosclerotic heart disease, hypertension, and diabetes mellitus; her left leg was gangrenous to her knee; she had several necrotic decubitus ulcers (bed sores) on her left foot, leg, and hip; an eye problem required irrigation; she had a urinary catheter in place and could not control her bowels; she could not speak; and her ability to swallow was very limited. On the other hand, she interacted with her environment in some limited ways: she could move her head, hands, and arms to a minor extent; she was able to scratch herself, and had pulled at her bandages, tube, and catheter; she moaned occasionally when moved or fed through the tube, or when her bandages were changed; her eyes sometimes followed individuals in the room; her facial expressions were different when she was awake from when she was asleep; and she smiled on occasions when her hair was combed, or when she received a comforting rub.

Dr Kazemi and Dr Davidoff, a specialist in internal medicine who observed Ms Conroy before testifying as an expert on behalf of the guardian, testified that Ms Conroy was not brain dead, comatose, or in a chronic vegetative state. They stated, however, that her intellectual capacity was very limited, and that her mental condition probably would never improve. Dr Davidoff characterised her as awake, but said that she was severely demented, was unable to respond to verbal stimuli, and, as far as he could tell, had no higher functioning or consciousness. Dr Kazemi, in contrast, said that although she was confused and unaware, 'she responds somehow' . . .

The starting point in analysing whether life-sustaining treatment may be withheld or withdrawn from an incompetent patient is to determine what rights a competent patient has to accept or reject medical care. It is therefore necessary at the outset of this discussion to identify the nature and extent of a patient's rights that are implicated by such decisions.

The right of a person to control his own body is a basic societal concept, long recognised in the common law:

> No right is held more sacred, or is more carefully guarded by the common law, than the right of every individual to the possession and control of his own person, free from all restraint or interference of others, unless by clear and unquestionable authority of law. As well said by Judge Cooley, 'The right to one's person may be said to be a right of complete immunity: to be let alone.' Cooley on Torts, 29. [*Union Pac Rly Co v Botsford* 141 US 250 at 251, 11 *S Ct* 1000 at 1001, 35 *L Ed* 734, 737 (1891) (refusing to compel personal injury plaintiff to undergo pretrial medical examination).]

Accord Perna v Pirozzi, 92 NJ 446 at 459-65, 457, *A* 2d 431 (1983). Judge Cardozo succinctly captured the essence of this theory as follows: 'Every human being of adult years and sound mind has a right to determine what shall be done with his own body; and a surgeon who performs an operation without his patient's consent commits an assault, for which he is liable in damages.' *Schloendorff v Society of New York Hosp* 211 *NY* 125 at 129-30, 105 *NE* 92 at 93 (1914).

The doctrine of informed consent is a primary means developed in the law to protect this personal interest in the integrity of one's body. 'Under this doctrine, no medical procedure may be performed without a patient's consent, obtained after explanation of the nature of the treatment, substantial risks, and alternative therapies.' Cantor, 'A Patient's Decision to Decline Life-Saving Medical Treatment: Bodily Integrity Versus the Preservation of Life', 26 *Rutgers L Rev* 288, 237 (1973) (footnote omitted); see also *Perna v Pirozzi, supra*, 92 *NJ* at 461, 457 *A 2d* 431 ('Absent an emergency, patients have the right to determine not only whether surgery is to be performed on them, but who shall perform it').

The doctrine of informed consent presupposes that the patient has the information necessary to evaluate the risks and benefits of all the available options and is competent to do so. Cf Wanzer, Adelstein, Cranford, Federman, Hook, Moertel, Safar, Stone, Taussig & Van Eys, 'The Physician's Responsibility Toward Hopelessly Ill Patients', 310 *New Eng J Med* 955, 957 (1984) ('There are three basic prerequisites for informed consent: the patient must have the capacity to reason and make judgments, the decision must be made voluntarily and without coercion, and the patient must have a clear understanding of the risks and benefits of the proposed treatment alternatives or nontreatment, along with a full understanding of the nature of the disease and the prognosis'). In general, it is the doctor's role to provide the necessary medical facts and the patient's role to make the subjective treatment decision based on his understanding of those facts. Cf Hilfiker, *supra* 308 *New Eng J Med* at 718 (acknowledging that 'our ability [as doctors] to phrase options, stress information, and present our own advice gives us tremendous power').

The patient's ability to control his bodily integrity through informed consent is significant only when one recognises that this right also encompasses a right to informed refusal. Note, 'Informed Consent and the Dying Patient', 83 *Yale LJ* 1632, 1648 (1974). Thus, a competent adult person generally has the right to decline to have any medical treatment initiated or continued. See *Superintendent of Belchertown State School v Saikewicz* 373 *Mass* 728 at 738, 370 *NE 2d* 417 at 424 (1977); In *Re Quackenbush*, 156 *NJ Super* 282 at 290, 383 *A 2d* 785 (Cty Ct 1978); cf *Bennan v Parsonnet, 83 NJL* 20 at 22-23, 26-27, 83 *A* 948 (Sup Ct 1912) (acknowledging common-law rule that patient is 'the final arbiter as to whether he shall take his chances with the operation or take his chances of living without it', but holding that surgeon had implied consent while patient was unconscious to perform necessary surgical operation).

The right to make certain decisions concerning one's body is also protected by the federal constitutional right of privacy. The Supreme Court first articulated the right of privacy in *Griswold v Connecticut*, 381 *US* 479, 85 *S Ct* 1678, 14 *L Ed 2d* 510 (1965), which held that married couples have a constitutional right to use contraceptives. The Court in *Roe v Wade*, 410 *US* 113, 93 *S Ct* 705, 35 *L Ed 2d* 147 (1973), further extended its recognition of the privacy right to protect a woman's decision to abort a pregnancy although the woman's right to choose abortion directly conflicted with the state's legitimate and important interest in preserving the potentiality of fetal life. Finally, in *Quinlan, supra* 70 *NJ* at 40, 355 *A 2d* 647, we indicated that the right of privacy enunciated by the Supreme Court 'is broad enough to encompass a patient's decision to decline medical treatment under certain circumstances', even if that decision might lead to the patient's death. *Accord Saikewicz, supra,* 373 *Mass* at 738, 370 *NE 2d* at 424; *Quackenbush, supra,* 156 *NJ Super* at 289-90, 383 *A 2d* 785. While this right of privacy might apply in a case such as this, we need not decide that issue since the right to decline medical treatment is, in any event, embraced within the common-law right to self-determination. *Accord In Re Storar* 52 *NY 2d* 363 at 376-77, 420 *NE 2d* 64 at 70, 438 *NYS* 2d 266 at 272-73; *cert* denied, 454 *US* 858, 102 *S Ct* 309, 70 *L Ed 2d* 153 (1981); Note, 'Live or Let Die; Who Decides an Incompetent's Fate? *In Re Storar and Eichner*', 1982 *BYUL Rev* 387, 390-92

. . . In view of the case law, we have no doubt that Ms Conroy, if competent to make the decision and if resolute in her determination, could have chosen to have her nasogastric tube withdrawn. Her interest in freedom from nonconsensual invasion of her bodily integrity would outweigh any state interest in preserving life or in safeguarding the integrity of the medical profession. In addition, rejecting her artificial means of feeding would not constitute attempted suicide, as the decision would probably be based on a wish to be free of medical intervention rather than a specific intent to die, and her death would result, if at all, from her underlying medical condition, which included her inability to swallow. Finally, removal of her feeding tube would not create a public health or safety hazard, nor would her death leave any minor dependents without care or support . . .

Whether based on common-law doctrines or on constitutional theory, the right to decline life-sustaining medical treatment is not absolute. In some cases, it may yield to countervailing societal interests in sustaining the person's life. Courts and commentators have commonly identified four state interests that may limit a person's right to refuse medical treatment: preserving life, preventing suicide, safeguarding the integrity of the medical profession, and protecting innocent third parties. *See, eg Satz v Perlmutter* 362 *So 2d* at 162; *Re Spring,* 380 *Mass* 629, 640, 405 *NE 2d* 115, 123 (1980); *Comr of Correction v Myers,* 379 *Mass* 255, 261, 399 *NE 2d* 452, 456 (1979); *Saikewicz, supra,* 373 *Mass* at 728, 370 *NE 2d* at 425; *Re Torres,* 357 *NW 2d* 332, 339 (Minn 1984); *Re Colyer,* 99 *Wash 2d* 114, 121, 660 *P 2d* 738, 743 (1983); *President's Commission Report, supra,* at 31-32; Note, '*Re Storar:* The Right to Die and Incompetent Patients', 43 *U Pitt L Rev* 1087, 1092 (1982).

The state's interest in preserving life is commonly considered the most significant of the four state interests. *See, eg, Spring, supra,* 380 *Mass* at 633, 405 *NE 2d* at 119; *Saikewicz, supra,* 373 *Mass* at 740, 370 *NE 2d* at 425; *President's Commission Report, supra,* at 32. It may be seen as embracing two separate but related concerns: an interest in preserving the life of the particular patient, and an interest in preserving the sanctity of all life. Cantor, '*Quinlan,* Privacy, and the Handling of Incompetent Dying Patients', 30 *Rutgers L Rev* 239, 249 (1977); *see* Annas, 'In re Quinlan: Legal Comfort for Doctors', '*Hastings Center Rep,* June 1976, at 29.

While both of these state interests in life are certainly strong, in themselves they will usually not foreclose a competent person from declining life-sustaining medical treatment for himself. This is because the life that the state is seeking to protect in such a situation is the life of the same person who has competently decided to forego the medical intervention; it is not some other actual or potential life that cannot adequately protect itself. *Cf Roe v Wade, supra,* 410 *US* 113, 93 *S Ct* 705, 35 *L Ed 2d* 147 (authorising state restrictions or proscriptions of woman's right to abortion in final trimester of pregnancy to protect viable fetal life); *State v Perricone,* 37 *NJ* 463, 181 *A 2d* 751, *cert* denied, 371 *US* 890, 83 *S Ct* 189, 9 *L Ed 2d* 124 (1962) (affirming trial court's appointment of guardian with authority to consent to blood transfusion for infant over parents' religious objections); *Muhlenberg Hosp v Patterson,* 128 *NJ Super* 498, 320 *A 2d* 518 (Law Div 1974) (authorising blood transfusion to save infant's life over parents' religious objections).

In cases that do not involve the protection of the actual or potential life of someone other than the decision maker, the state's indirect and abstract interest in preserving the life of the competent patient generally gives way to the patient's much stronger personal interest in directing the course of his own life. *See, eg, Quackenbush, supra,* 156 *NJ Super* at 290, 383 *A 2d* 785; Cantor, *supra,* 30 *Rutgers L Rev* at 249-50. Indeed, insofar as the 'sanctity of individual free choice and self-determination [are] fundamental constituents of life,' the value of life may be lessened rather than increased 'by the failure to allow a competent human being the right of choice'. *Saikewicz, supra,* 373 *Mass* at 742, *NE 2d* at 426; *see also* Cantor, *supra,* 30 *Rutgers L Rev*n at 250 ('Government tolerance of the choice to resist treatment reflects concern for individual self-determination, bodily integrity, and avoidance of suffering, rather than a depreciation of life's value.').

It may be contended that in conjunction with its general interest in preserving life, this state has a particular legislative policy of preventing suicide. *See NJSA* 30: 4-26.3a (subjecting any person who attempts suicide to temporary hospitalisation when the person's behaviour suggests the existence of mental illness and constitutes a peril to life, person, or property); see also NJSA 2C:11-6 ('A person who purposely aids another to commit suicide is guilty of a crime of the second degree if his conduct causes such suicide or an attempted suicide, and otherwise of a crime of the fourth degree.') This state interest in protecting people from direct and purposeful self-destruction is motivated by, if not encompassed within, the state's more basic interest in preserving life. Thus, it is questionable whether it is a distinct state interest worthy of independent consideration.

In any event, declining life-sustaining medical treatment may not properly be viewed as an attempt to commit suicide. Refusing medical intervention merely allows the disease to take its natural course; if death were eventually to occur, it would be the result, primarily, of the underlying disease, and not the result of a self-inflicted injury. See *Satz v Perlmutter, supra,* 362 *So 2d* at 162; *Saikewicz, supra,* 373 *Mass* at 743 n 11, 370 *NE* 2d at 426 n 11; *Colyer, supra* 99 *Wash* 2d at 121, 660 *P* 2d at 743; *see also President's Commission Report, supra,* at 38 (summarising case law on the subject). But cf *Caulk,* NH 480 *A* 2d 93, 96-97 (1984) (stating that attempt of an otherwise healthy prisoner to starve himself to death because he preferred death to life in prison was tantamount to attempted suicide, and that the state, to prevent such suicide, could force him to eat). In addition, people who refuse life-sustaining medical treatment may not harbour a specific intent to die, *Saikewicz, supra,* 373 *Mass* at 743, n 11, 370 *NE* 2d at 426 n 11; rather, they may fervently wish to live, but to do so free of unwanted medical technology, surgery, or drugs, and without protracted suffering, see *Satz v Perlmutter, supra* 362 *So* 2d at 162-63 ('The testimony of Mr Perlmutter . . . is that he really wants to live, but [to] do so God and Mother Nature willing, under his own power.').

Recognising the right of a terminally ill person to reject medical treatment respects that person's intent, not to die, but to suspend medical intervention at a point consonant with the 'individual's view respecting a personally preferred manner of concluding life'. 'Note, 'The Tragic Choice: Termination of Care for Patients in a Permanent Vegetative State', *51 NYUL Rev* 285, 310 (1976). The difference is between self-infliction or self-destruction and self-determination. See Byrn, 'Compulsory Lifesaving Treatment for the Competent Adult', 44 *Fordham L Rev* 1, 16-23 (1975). To the extent that our decision in *John F Kennedy Memorial Hosp v Heston,* 58 *NJ* 576, 581-82, 279 *A* 2d 670 (1971), implies the contrary, we now overrule it.

The third state interest that is frequently asserted as a limitation on a competent patient's right to refuse medical treatment is the interest in safeguarding the integrity of the medical profession. This interest, like the interest in preventing suicide, is not particularly threatened by permitting competent patients to refuse life-sustaining medical treatment. Medical ethics do not require medical intervention in disease at all costs. As long ago as 1624, Francis Bacon wrote, 'I esteem it the office of a physician not only to restore health, but to mitigate pain and dolours; and not only when such mitigation may conduce to recovery, but when it may serve to make a fair and easy passage.' *F Bacon, New Atlantis, quoted in* Mannes, 'Euthanasia vs The Right to Life', 27 *Baylor L Rev* 68, 69 (1975). More recently, we wrote in *Quinlan, supra,* 70 *NJ* at 47, 355 *A* 2d 647, that modern-day 'physicians distinguish between curing the ill and comforting and easing the dying; that they refuse to treat the curable as if they were dying or ought to die, and that they have sometimes refused to treat the hopeless and dying as if they were curable'. Indeed, recent surveys have suggested that a majority of practising doctors now approve of passive euthanasia and believe that it is being practised by members of the profession. See sources cited in *Storar, supra NY* 2d at 385-386 n 3, 420 *NE* 2d at 75-76 n 3, 438 *NYS* 2d at 277-78 n 3 (Jones J, dissenting), and in Collester, 'Death, Dying and the Law: A Prosecutorial View of the *Quinlan* Case', 30 *Rutgers L Rev* 304, n 3, 312 & n 27.

Moreover, even if doctors were exhorted to attempt to cure or sustain their patients under all circumstances, that moral and professional imperative, at least in cases of patients who were clearly competent, presumably would not require doctors to go beyond advising the patient of the risks of foregoing treatment and urging the patient to accept the medical intervention. *Storar, supra,* 52 *NY* 2d at 377, 420 *NE* 2d at 71, 438 *NYS* 2d at 273; see *Colyer, supra,* 99 *Wash* 2d at 121-23, 660 *P* 2d at 743-44, citing *Saikewicz, supra,* 373 *Mass* at 743-44, 370 *NE* 2d at 417. If the patient rejected the doctor's advice, the onus of that decision would rest on the patient, not the doctor. Indeed, if the patient's right to informed consent is to have any meaning at all, it must be accorded respect even when it conflicts with the advice of the doctor or the values of the medical profession as a whole.

The fourth asserted state interest in overriding a patient's decision about his medical treatment is the interest in protecting innocent third parties who may be harmed by the patient's treatment decision. When the patient's exercise of his free choice could adversely and directly affect the health, safety, or security of others, the patient's right of self-determination must frequently give way. Thus, for example, courts have required competent adults to undergo medical procedures against their will if necessary to protect the public health. *Jacobson v Massachusetts, 197 US 11, 25 S Ct 358, 49 L Ed* 643 (1905) (recognising enforceability of compulsory smallpox vaccination law); to prevent a serious risk to prison security, *Myers, supra, 379 Mass* at 263, 265, 399 *NE* 2d at 457, 458 (compelling prisoner with kidney disease to submit to dialysis over his protest rather than acquiescing in his demand to be transferred to a lower-security prison); *accord Caulk, supra,* 480 *A* 2d at 96; or to prevent the emotional and financial abandonment of the patient's minor children, *Application of President & Directors of Georgetown College, Inc, 331 F* 2d 1000, 1008 (DC Cir), *cert* denied, 377 *US* 978, 84 *S Ct* 1883, 12 *L Ed* 2d 746 (1964) (ordering mother of seven-month-old infant to submit to blood transfusion over her religious objections because of the mother's 'responsibility to the community to care for her infant'); *Holmes v Silver Cross Hosp, 340 F Supp* 125, 130 (ND Ill 1972) (indicating that patient's status as father of minor child might justify authorising blood transfusion to save his life despite his religious objections).

On balance, the right to self-determination ordinarily outweighs any countervailing state interests, and competent persons generally are permitted to refuse medical treatment, even at the risk of death. Most of the cases that have held otherwise, unless they involved the interest in protecting innocent parties, have concerned the patient's competency to make a rational and considered choice of treatment. See Annot, 93 *ALR* 3d 67, at 80-85 (1979) ('Patient's Right to Refuse Treatment Allegedly Necessary to Sustain Life'). For example, in *Heston, supra, 58 NJ* 576, 270 *A* 2d 670, this Court approved a blood transfusion to save the life of a twenty-two-year-old Jehovah's Witness who had been severely injured and was rushed to the hospital for treatment, despite the fact that a tenet of her faith forbade blood transfusions. The evidence indicated that she was in shock on admittance to the hospital and was then or soon became disoriented and incoherent. Part of the Court's rationale was that hospitals, upon which patients' care is thrust, 'exist to aid the sick and the injured', *id 58 NJ* at 582, 279 *A* 2d 670, and that it is difficult for them to assess a patient's intent in an emergency and to determine whether a desire to refuse treatment is firmly and competently held, *id 58 NJ* at 581, 582, 279 *A* 2d 670. Similarly, courts in other states have authorised blood transfusions over the objections of Jehovah's Witnesses when the patient's opposition to the treatment was expressed in equivocal terms. *Compare Georgetown College, supra,* 331 F 2d at 1006-07 (authorising transfusion to save life of patient who said that for religious reasons she would not consent to the transfusion, but who seemed to indicate that she would not oppose the transfusion if court ordered it since it would not then be her responsibility), *and United States v George, 239 F Supp* 752, 753 (D Conn 1965) (transfusion was authorised for patient who told court that he would not agree to the transfusion, but volunteered that if the court ordered it he would not resist in any way since it would be the court's will and not his), *with Re Osborne, 294 A* 2d 372, 374, 375 (DC 1972) (stating that guardian should not be appointed to consent to transfusion on behalf of man who told court that he would be deprived of 'everlasting life' if compelled by a court to submit to the transfusion, and who explained, 'it is between me and Jehovah; not the courts . . . I'm willing to take my chances. My faith is that strong.') . . .

. . . We are now faced with [the] situation: . . . of elderly, formerly competent nursing-home residents who . . . are awake and conscious and can interact with their environment to a limited extent, but whose mental and physical functioning is severely and permanently impaired and whose life expectancy, even with the treatment, is relatively short. The capacities of such people, while significantly diminished, are not as limited as those of irreversibly comatose persons, and their deaths, while no longer distant, may not be imminent. Large numbers of aged, chronically ill, institutionalised persons fall within this general category.

Such people (like newborns, mentally retarded persons, permanently comatose individuals, and members of other groups with which this case does not deal) are unable to speak for themselves on life-and-death issues concerning their medical care. This does not mean, however, that they lack a right to self-determination. The right of an adult who, like Claire Conroy, was once competent, to determine the course of her medical treatment remains intact even when she is no longer able to assert that right or to appreciate its effectuation. *John F Kennedy Memorial Hosp., Inc. v Bludworth, 452 So.*2d 921, 924 (Fla. 1984). As one commentator has noted:

> Even if the patient becomes too insensate to appreciate the honoring of his or her choice, self-determination is important. After all, law respects testamentary dispositions even if the testator never views his gift being bestowed. [Cantor, *supra, 30 Rutgers L. Rev.* at 259.]

. . . Any other view would permit obliteration of an incompetent's panoply of rights merely because the patient could no longer sense the violation of those rights. [*Id.* at 252.]

Since the condition of an incompetent patient makes it impossible to ascertain definitively his present desires, a third party acting on the patient's behalf often cannot say with confidence that his treatment decision for the patient will further rather than frustrate the patient's right to control his own body. Cf Smith, '*In Re Quinlan*: Defining the Basis for Terminating Life Support Under the Right of Privacy', 12 *Tulsa LJ* 150, 161 (1976) (arguing that permitting a guardian to make personal medical decisions for an incompetent patient actually interferes with the patient's right of privacy). Nevertheless, the goal of decision-making for incompetent patients should be to determine and effectuate, insofar as possible, the decision that the patient would have made if competent. Ideally, both aspects of the patient's right to bodily integrity – the right to consent to medical intervention and the right to refuse it – should be respected.

In light of these rights and concerns, we hold that life-sustaining treatment may be withheld or withdrawn from an incompetent patient when it is clear that the particular patient would have refused the treatment under the circumstances involved. The standard we are enunciating is a subjective one, consistent with the notion that the right that we are seeking to effectuate is a very personal right to control one's own life. The question is not what a reasonable or average person would have chosen to do under the circumstances but what the particular patient would have done if able to choose for himself.

The patient may have expressed, in one or more ways, an intent not to have life-sustaining medical intervention. Such an intent might be embodied in a written document, or 'living will', stating the person's desire not to have certain types of life-sustaining treatment administered under certain circumstances. It might also be evidenced in an oral directive that the patient gave to a family member or friend, or health care provider. It might consist of a durable power of attorney or appointment of a proxy authorising a particular person to make the decisions on the patient's behalf if he is no longer capable of making them for himself. See *NJSA* 46; 2B-8 (providing that principal may confer authority on agent that is to be exercisable 'notwithstanding later disability or incapacity of the principal at law or later uncertainty as to whether the principal is dead or alive'). It might take the form of reactions that the patient voiced regarding medical treatment administered to others. See, eg, *Storar, supra,* 52 *NY* 2d 363, 420 *NE* 2d 64, 438 *NYS* 2d 266 (withdrawal of respirator was justified as an effectuation of patient's stated wishes when patient, as member of Catholic religious order, had stated more than once in formal discussions concerning the moral implications of the *Quinlan* case, most recently two months before he suffered cardiac arrest that left him in an irreversible coma, that he would not want extraordinary means used to keep him alive under similar circumstances). It might also be deduced from a person's religious beliefs and the tenets of that religion, *id* at 378, 420 *NE* 2d at 72, 438 *NYS* 2d at 274, or from the patient's consistent pattern of conduct with respect to prior decisions about his own medical care. Of course, dealing with the matter in advance in some sort of thoughtful and explicit way is best for all concerned.

Any of the above types of evidence, and any other information bearing on the person's intent, may be appropriate aides in determining what course of treatment the patient would have wished to pursue. In this respect, we now believe that we were in error in *Quinlan, supra,* 70 *NJ* at 21, 41, 355 *A* 2d 647, to disregard evidence of statements that Ms Quinlan made to friends concerning artificial prolongation of the lives of others who were terminally ill. See criticism of this portion of *Quinlan* opinion in Collester, *supra,* 30 *Rutgers L Rev* at 318; Smith, *supra,* 12 *Tulsa LJ* at 163; and *D Meyers, supra,* at 282 n 65. Such evidence is certainly relevant to shed light on whether the patient would have consented to the treatment if competent to make the decision.

Although all evidence tending to demonstrate a person's intent with respect to medical treatment should properly be considered by surrogate decision-makers, or by a court in the event of any judicial proceedings, the probative value of such evidence may vary depending on the remoteness, consistency, and thoughtfulness of the prior statements or actions and the maturity of the person at the time of the statements or acts. *Colyer, supra,* 99 *Wash* 2d at 131, 660 *P* 2d at 748. Thus, for example, an offhand remark about not wanting to live under certain circumstances made by a person when young and in the peak of health would not in itself constitute clear proof twenty years later that he would want life-sustaining treatment withheld under those circumstances. In contrast, a carefully considered position, especially if written, that a person had maintained over a number of years or that he had acted upon in comparable circumstances might be clear evidence of his intent.

Another factor that would affect the probative value of a person's prior statements of intent would be their specificity. Of course, no one can predict with accuracy the precise circumstances with which he ultimately might be faced. Nevertheless, any details about the level of impaired functioning and the forms of medical treatment that one would find tolerable should be incorporated into advance directives to enhance their later usefulness as evidence.

Medical evidence bearing on the patient's condition, treatment and prognosis, like evidence of the patient's wishes, is an essential prerequisite to decision-making under the subjective test. The medical evidence must establish that the patient fits within the Claire Conroy pattern: an elderly, incompetent nursing-home resident with severe and permanent mental and physical impairments and a life expectancy of approximately one year or less. In addition, since the goal is to effectuate the patient's right of informed consent, the surrogate decision-maker must have at least as much medical information upon which to base his decision about what the patient would have chosen as one would expect a competent patient to have before consenting to or rejecting treatment. Such information might include evidence about the patient's present level of physical, sensory, emotional, and cognitive functioning; the degree of physical pain resulting from the medical condition, treatment, and termination of treatment, respectively; the degree of humiliation, dependence, and loss of dignity probably resulting from the condition and treatment; the life expectancy and prognosis for recovery with and without treatment; the various treatment options; and the risks, side effects, and benefits of each of those options. Particular care should be taken not to base a decision on a premature diagnosis or prognosis. See *Colyer, supra* 99 *Wash* 2d at 143-45, 660 *P* 2d at 754-55 (Dore J, dissenting).

We recognise that for some incompetent patients it might be impossible to be clearly satisfied as to the patient's intent either to accept or reject the life-sustaining treatment. Many people may have spoken of their desires in general or casual terms, or, indeed, never considered or resolved the issue at all. In such cases, a surrogate decision-maker cannot presume that treatment decisions made by a third party on the patient's behalf will further the patient's right to self-determination, since effectuating another person's right to self-determination presupposes that the substitute decision-maker knows what the person would have wanted. Thus, in the absence of adequate proof of the patient's wishes, it is naive to pretend that the right to self-determination serves as the basis for substituted decision-making. See *Storar, supra*, 52 *NY* 2d at 378-380, 420 *NE* 2d at 72-73, 438 *NYS* 2d at 274-75; Veatch, 'An Ethical Framework for Terminal Care Decisions: A New Classification of Patients', 32(9) *J Am Geriatrics Soc'y*, 666 (1984).

We hesitate, however, to foreclose the possibility of humane actions, which may involve termination of life-sustaining treatment, for persons who never clearly expressed their desires about life-sustaining treatment but who are now suffering a prolonged and painful death. An incompetent, like a minor child, is a ward of the state, and the state's *parens patriae* power supports the authority of its courts to allow decisions to be made for an incompetent that serve the incompetent's best interests, even if the person's wishes cannot be clearly established. This authority permits the state to authorise guardians to withhold or withdraw life-sustaining treatment from an incompetent patient if it is manifest that such action would further the patient's best interests in a narrow sense of the phrase, even though the subjective test that we articulated above may not be satisfied. We therefore hold that life-sustaining treatment may also be withheld or withdrawn from a patient in Claire Conroy's situation if either of two 'best interests' tests – a limited-objective or a pure-objective test – is satisfied.

Under the limited-objective test, life-sustaining treatment may be withheld or withdrawn from a patient in Claire Conroy's situation when there is some trustworthy evidence that the patient would have refused the treatment, and the decision-maker is satisfied that it is clear that the burdens of the patient's continued life with the treatment outweigh the benefits of that life for him. By this we mean that the patient is suffering, and will continue to suffer throughout the expected duration of his life, unavoidable pain, and that the net burdens of his prolonged life (the pain and suffering of his life with the treatment less the amount and duration of pain that the patient would likely experience if the treatment were withdrawn) markedly outweigh any physical pleasure, emotional enjoyment, or intellectual satisfaction that the patient may still be able to derive from life. This limited-objective standard permits the termination of treatment for a patient who had not unequivocally expressed his desires before becoming incompetent, when it is clear that the treatment in question would merely prolong the patient's suffering.

Medical evidence will be essential to establish that the burdens of the treatment to the patient in terms of pain and suffering outweigh the benefits that the patient is experiencing. The medical evidence should make it clear that the treatment would merely prolong the patient's suffering and not provide him with any net benefit. Information is particularly important with respect to the degree, expected duration, and constancy of pain with and without treatment, and the possibility that the pain could be reduced by drugs or other means short of terminating the life-sustaining treatment. The same types of medical evidence that are relevant to the subjective analysis, such as the patient's life expectancy, prognosis, level of functioning, degree of humiliation and dependency, and treatment options, should also be considered.

This limited-objective test also requires some trustworthy evidence that the patient would have wanted the treatment terminated. This evidence could take any one or more of the various forms appropriate to prove the patient's intent under the subjective test. Evidence that, taken as a whole, would be too vague, casual, or remote to constitute the clear proof of the patient's subjective intent that is necessary to satisfy the subjective test – for example, informally expressed reactions to other people's medical conditions and treatment – might be sufficient to satisfy this prong of the limited-objective test.

In the absence of trustworthy evidence, or indeed any evidence at all, that the patient would have declined the treatment, life-sustaining treatment may still be withheld or withdrawn from a formerly competent person like Claire Conroy if a third, pure-objective test is satisfied. Under that test, as under the limited-objective test, the net burdens of the patient's life with the treatment should clearly and markedly outweigh the benefits that the patient derives from life. Further, the recurring, unavoidable and severe pain of the patient's life with the treatment should be such that the effect of administering life-sustaining treatment would be inhumane. Subjective evidence that the patient would not have wanted the treatment is not necessary under this pure-objective standard. Nevertheless, even in the context of severe pain, life-sustaining treatment should not be withdrawn from an incompetent patient who had previously expressed a wish to be kept alive in spite of any pain that he might experience.

Although we are condoning a restricted evaluation of the nature of a patient's life in terms of pain, suffering, and possible enjoyment under the limited-objective and pure-objective tests, we expressly decline to authorise decision-making based on assessments of the personal worth or social utility of another's life, or the value of that life to others. We do not believe that it would be appropriate for a court to designate a person with the authority to determine that someone else's life is not worth living simply because, to that person, the patient's 'quality of life' or value to society seems negligible. The mere fact that a patient's functioning is limited or his prognosis dim does not mean that he is not enjoying what remains of his life or that it is in his best interests to die. But cf *In Re Dinnerstein*, 6 *Mass App Ct* 466 at 473, 380 *NE* 2d 134 at 138 (1978) (indicating, in reference to possible resuscitation of half-paralysed, elderly victim of Alzheimer's disease, that prolongation of life is not required if there is no hope to return to a 'normal, integrated, functioning, cognitive existence'); see also *President's Commission Report, supra*, at 135 (endorsing termination of treatment whenever surrogate decision-maker in his discretion believes it is in the patient's best interests, defined broadly to 'take into account such factors as the relief of suffering, the preservation or restoration of functioning, and the quality as well as the extent of life sustained'). More wide-ranging powers to make decisions about other people's lives, in our view, would create an intolerable risk for socially isolated and defenceless people suffering from physical or mental handicaps.

We are aware that it will frequently be difficult to conclude that the evidence is sufficient to justify termination of treatment under either of the 'best interests' tests that we have described. Often, it is unclear whether and to what extent a patient such as Claire Conroy is capable of, or is in fact, experiencing pain. Similarly, medical experts are often unable to determine with any degree of certainty the extent of a nonverbal person's intellectual functioning or the depth of his emotional life. When the evidence is insufficient to satisfy either the limited-objective or pure-objective standard, however, we cannot justify the termination of life-sustaining treatment as clearly furthering the best interests of a patient like Ms Conroy.

The surrogate decision-maker should exercise extreme caution in determining the patient's intent and in evaluating medical evidence of the patient's pain and possible enjoyment, and should not approve withholding or withdrawing life-sustaining treatment unless he is manifestly satisfied that one of the three tests that we have outlined has been met. Cf *In Re Grady*, 85 *NJ* 235 at 266, 426, *A* 2d 467 (1981) (requiring that evidence be clear and convincing before a court would approve sterilisation of an incompetent, mentally retarded adult). When evidence of a person's wishes or physical or mental condition is equivocal, it is best to err, if at all, in favour of preserving life. See *Osborne, supra*, 294 *A* 2d at 374 (stating in dictum that when a patient is 'suffering impairment of capacity for choice, it may be better to give weight to the known instinct for survival'); Dyck, 'Ethical Aspects of

Care for the Dying Incompetent', 32(9) *J Am Geriatrics Soc'y* 661, 663 (1984) ('[S]ituations in which [decision-makers] are uncertain about what is best should be resolved in favor of extending life where possible.'). Or, as one writer has said as a justification for requiring a high degree of safety and certainty of diagnosis in the determination of brain death; '[I]f there is a lot to lose by being wrong, it is generally better to stick to the safer, known way in the absence of the highest probability for proceeding otherwise.' D Walton, *Ethics of Withdrawal of Life-Support Systems: Case Studies on Decision Making in Intensive Care 82* (1983).

In the event, the court determined that the evidence did not satisfy any of the three tests laid down by the court. However, since Ms Conroy had subsequently died the case was not remanded to the trial court for further hearing. Examining the evidence Schrieber J concluded as follows:

The evidence that Claire Conroy would have refused the treatment, although sufficient to meet the lower showing of intent required under the limited-objective test, was certainly not the 'clear' showing of intent contemplated under the subjective test. More information should, if possible, have been obtained by the guardian with respect to Ms Conroy's intent. What were her ethical, moral, and religious beliefs? She did try to refuse initial hospitalisation, and indeed had 'scorned medicine.' 188 *NJ Super* at 525, 457 A 2d 1232. However, she allowed her nephew's wife, a registered nurse, to care for her during several illnesses. It was not clear whether Ms Conroy permitted the niece to administer any drugs or other forms of medical treatment to her during these illnesses. Although it may often prove difficult, and at times impossible, to ascertain a person's wishes, the Conroy case illustrates the sources to which the guardian might turn. For example, in more than eight decades of life in the same house, it is possible that she revealed to persons other than her nephew her feelings regarding medical treatments, other values, and her goals in life. Some promising avenues for such an inquiry about her personal values included her response to the illnesses and deaths of her sisters and others, and her statements with respect to not wanting to be in a nursing home.

Moreover, there was insufficient information concerning the benefits and burdens of Ms Conroy's life to satisfy either the limited-objective or pure-objective test. Although the treating doctor and the guardian's expert testified as to Claire Conroy's condition, neither testified conclusively as to whether she was in pain or was capable of experiencing pain or thirst. There was medical agreement that removal of the tube would have caused pain during the period of approximately one week that would have elapsed before her death, or at least until she were to lapse into a coma. On the other hand, there was little, if any, evidence of the discomfort, suffering, and pain she would endure if she continued to be fed and medicated through the tube during her remaining life – contemplated to be up to one year. Apparently her feedings sometimes occasioned moaning, but it remains unclear whether these were reflex responses or expressions of discomfort. Moreover, although she tried to remove the tube, it is not clear that this was intentional, and there was little evidence that she was in distress. Her treating physician also offered contradictory views as to whether the contractures of her legs caused pain or whether, indeed, they might be the result of pain, without offering any evidence on that issue. The trial court rejected as superfluous the offer to present as an expert witness a neurologist, who might have been able to explain what Ms Conroy's reaction to the environment indicated about her perception of pain.

The evidence was also unclear with respect to Ms Conroy's capacity to feel pleasure, another issue as to which the information supplied by a neurologist might have been helpful. What was known of her awareness of the world? Although Ms Conroy had some ability to smile and scratch, the relationship of these activities to external stimuli apparently was quite variable.

The trial transcript reveals no exploration of the discomfort and risks that attend nasogastric feedings. A casual mention by the nurse/administrator of the need to restrain the patient to prevent the removal of the tube was not followed by an assessment of the detrimental impact, if any, of those restraints. Alternative modalities, including gastrostomies, intravenous feeding, subcutaneous or intramuscular hydration, or some combination, were not investigated. Neither of the expert witnesses presented empirical evidence regarding the treatment options for such a patient.

It can be seen that the evidence at trial was inadequate to satisfy the subjective, the limited-objective, or the pure-objective standard that we have set forth.

You will see that the New Jersey Supreme Court established a procedural framework within which treatment decisions at the end of life should be made. We are not concerned with that framework here since it relates to the particular law of New Jersey and has little relevance in England. Subsequently, in a series of cases, the court expanded upon its framework and broadened its application: see *Re Peter* (1987) 529 A 2d 419; *Re Jobes* (1987) 529 A 2d 434; *Re Farrell* (1987) 529 A 2d 404 (a competent patient). (For a discussion by one of the Justices of the Court, see S Pollock 'Life and Death Decisions: Who Makes Them and by What Standards?' (1989) 41 Rutgers LR 505.)

However, a number of matters in *Conroy* are important for us here. First, there are the substantive principles identified by the court, in particular, its adoption of the three tests: '*the subjective*', the '*limited-objective*' and the '*pure-objective*' tests. We will see shortly how the English law resolves the same question and whether its approach is the same or similar to that adopted in *Conroy*.

Secondly, *Conroy* acknowledges that the law must strike a balance between its concern for a patient's right of self-determination and society's interests, which may conflict (see *supra*, ch 3).

Thirdly, the court exposes the fallacies in a number of arguments often marshalled in cases concerning treatment decisions at the end of life, for example, between ordinary and extraordinary treatment and withdrawing and withholding treatment.

The value of our setting out at some length the decision in *Conroy* is that it offers a *tour d'horizon* of this difficult area. This is not to say that *Conroy* is the last word on the subject. Indeed, later cases in New Jersey and elsewhere demonstrated the imperfections of *Conroy* and improved upon it. *Conroy* is nevertheless a significant decision because of the court's struggle to develop a comprehensive legal framework. As such it represented a considerable advance upon the earlier case law and, in particular, the much relied upon (yet much criticised) decision of the Massachusetts' Supreme Judicial Court in *Saikewicz*.

Superintendent of Belchertown v Saikewicz (1977) 370 NE 2d 417 (Mass Sup Jud Ct)

Liacos J: . . . Joseph Saikewicz, at the time the matter arose, was sixty-seven years old, with an IQ of ten and a mental age of approximately two years and eight months. He was profoundly mentally retarded. The record discloses that, apart from his leukemic condition, Saikewicz enjoyed generally good health. He was physically strong and well built, nutritionally nourished, and ambulatory. He was not, however, able to communicate verbally – resorting to gestures and grunts to make his wishes known to others and responding only to gestures or physical contacts. In the course of treatment for various medical conditions arising during Saikewicz's residency at the school, he had been unable to respond intelligibly to inquiries such as whether he was experiencing pain. It was the opinion of a consulting psychologist, not contested by the other experts relied on by the judge below, that Saikewicz was not aware of dangers and was disoriented outside his immediate environment. As a result of his condition Saikewicz had lived in State institutions since 1923 and had resided at the Belchertown State School since 1928. Two of his sisters, the only members of his family who could be located, were notified of his condition and of the hearing, but they preferred not to attend or otherwise become involved.

On April 19, 1976, Saikewicz was diagnosed as suffering from acute myeloblastic monocytic leukemia . . .

Chemotherapy, as was testified at the hearing in the Probate Court, involves the administration of drugs over several weeks, the purpose of which is to kill the leukemia cells. This treatment unfortunately affects normal cells as well . . . Estimates of the effectiveness of chemotherapy are complicated in cases, such as the one presented here, in which the patient's age becomes a factor. According to the medical testimony before the court below, persons over age sixty have more difficulty tolerating chemotherapy and the treatment is likely to be less successful than in younger patients. This prognosis may be compared with the doctor's estimates that, left untreated, a patient in Saikewicz's condition would live for a matter of weeks or, perhaps, several months. According to the testimony, a decision to allow the disease to run its natural course would not result in pain for the patient, and death would probably come without discomfort.

An important facet of the chemotherapy process, to which the judge below directed careful attention, is the problem of serious adverse side effects caused by the treating drugs. Among these side effects are severe nausea, bladder irritation, numbness and tingling of the extremities, and loss of hair. The bladder irritation can be avoided, however, if the patient drinks fluids, and the nausea can be treated by drugs. It was the opinion of the guardian *ad litem*, as well as the doctors who testified before the probate judge, that most people elect to suffer the side effects of chemotherapy rather than to allow their leukemia to run its natural course.

Drawing on the evidence before him, including the testimony of the medical experts, and the report of the guardian *ad litem*, the probate judge issued detailed findings, with regard to the costs and benefits of allowing Saikewicz to undergo chemotherapy. The judge's findings are reproduced in part here because of the importance of clearly delimiting the issues presented in this case. The judge below found:

> 5. That the majority of persons suffering from leukemia who are faced with a choice of receiving or foregoing such chemotherapy, and who are able to make an informed judgment thereon, choose to receive treatment in spite of its toxic side effects and risks of failure.
> 6. That such toxic side effects of chemotherapy include pain and discomfort, depressed bone marrow, pronounced anemia, increased chance of infection, possible bladder irritation, and possible loss of hair.
> 7. That administration of such chemotherapy requires cooperation from the patient over several weeks of time, which cooperation said Joseph Saikewicz is unable to give due to his profound retardation.
> 8. That, considering the age and general state of health of said Joseph Saikewicz, there is only a 30-40 percent chance that chemotherapy will produce a remission of said leukemia, which remission would probably be for a period of time of from 2 to 13 months, but that said chemotherapy will certainly not completely cure such leukemia.
> 9. That if such chemotherapy is to be administered at all it should be administered immediately, inasmuch as the risks involved will increase and the chances of successfully bringing about remission will decrease as time goes by.
> 10. That, at present, said Joseph Saikewicz's leukemia condition is stable and is not deteriorating.
> 11. That said Joseph Saikewicz is not now in pain and will probably die within a matter of weeks or months a relatively painless death due to the leukemia unless other factors should intervene to themselves cause death.
> 12. That it is impossible to predict how long said Joseph Saikewicz will probably live without chemotherapy or how long he will probably live with chemotherapy, but it is to a very high degree medically likely that he will die sooner, without treatment than with it.

Balancing these various factors, the judge concluded that the following considerations weighed *against* administering chemotherapy to Saikewicz: '(1) his age, (2) his inability to cooperate with the treatment, (3) probable adverse side effects of treatment, (4) low chance of producing remission, (5) the certainty that treatment will cause immediate suffering, and (6) the quality of life possible for him even if the treatment does bring about remission.'

The following considerations were determined to weigh in *favor* of chemotherapy: '(1) the chance that his life may be lengthened thereby; and (2) the fact that most people in his situation when given a chance to do so elect to take the gamble of treatment.'

Concluding that, in this case, the negative factors of treatment exceeded the benefits, the probate judge ordered on May 13, 1976, that no treatment be administered to Saikewicz for his condition of acute myeloblastic monocytic leukemia except by further order of the court. The judge further ordered that all reasonable and necessary supportive measures be taken, medical or otherwise, to safeguard the well-being of Saikewicz in all other respects and to reduce as far as possible any suffering or discomfort which he might experience.

. . . Saikewicz died on September 4, 1976, at the Belchertown State School hospital. Death was due to bronchial pneumonia, a complication of the leukemia. Saikewicz died without pain or discomfort.

. . . The question what legal standards govern the decision whether to administer potentially life-prolonging treatment to an incompetent person encompasses two distinct and important subissues. First, does a choice exist? That is, is it the unvarying responsibility of the State to order medical treatment in all circumstances involving the care of an incompetent person? Second, if a choice does exist under certain conditions, what considerations enter into the decision-making process?

We think that principles of equality and respect for all individuals require the conclusion that a choice exists . . . we recognize a general right in all persons to refuse medical treatment in appropriate circumstances. The recognition of that right must extend to the case of an incompetent, as well as a competent, patient because the value of human dignity extends to both.

This is not to deny that the State has a traditional power and responsibility, under the doctrine of *parens patriae*, to care for and protect the 'best interests' of the incompetent person. Indeed, the existence of this power and responsibility has impelled a number of courts to hold that the 'best interests' of such a person mandate an unvarying responsibility by the courts to order necessary medical treatment for an incompetent person facing an immediate and severe danger to life. *Application of the President & Directors of Georgetown College, Inc*, 118 US App DC 80, 331 F 2d 1000; cert denied 377 US 978, 84 S Ct 1883, 12 L Ed 2d 746 (1964). *Long Island Jewish-Hillside Medical Center v Levitt*, 73 Misc 2d 395, 342 NYS 2d 356 (NY Sup Ct 1973). Cf *In Re Weberlist*, 79 Misc 2d 753, 360 NYS 2d 783 (NY Sup Ct 1974). Whatever the merits of such a policy where life-saving treatment is available – a situation unfortunately not presented by this case – a more flexible view of the 'best interests' of the incompetent patient is not precluded under other conditions. For example, other courts have refused to take it on themselves to order certain forms of treatment or therapy which are not immediately required although concededly beneficial to the innocent person. *In Re CFB* 497 SW 2d 831 (Mo App 1973). *Green's Appeal*, 448 Pa 338, 292 A 2d 387 (1972). *In Re Frank*, 41 Wash 2d 294, 248 P 2d 553 (1952). Cf *In Re Rotkowitz*, 175 Misc 948, 25 NYS 2d 624 (NY Dom Rel Ct 1941); *Mitchell v Davis*, 205 SW 2d 812 (Tex App 1947). While some of these cases involved children who might eventually be competent to make the necessary decisions without judicial interference, it is also clear that the additional period of waiting might make the task of correction more difficult. See, eg, *In Re Frank, supra*. These cases stand for the proposition that, even in the exercise of the *parens patriae* power, there must be respect for the bodily integrity of the child or respect for the rational decision of those parties, usually the parents, who for one reason or another are seeking to protect the bodily integrity or other personal interest of the child. See *In Re Hudson*, 13 Wash 2d 673, 126 P 2d 765 (1942).

The 'best interests' of an incompetent person are not necessarily served by imposing on such persons results not mandated as to competent persons similarly situated. It does not advance the interest of the State or the ward to treat the ward as a person of lesser status or dignity than others. To protect the incompetent person within its power, the State must recognize the dignity and worth of such a person and afford to that person the same panoply of rights and choices it recognizes in competent persons. If a competent person faced with death may choose to decline treatment which not only will not cure the person but which substantially may increase suffering in exchange for a possible yet brief prolongation of life, then it cannot be said that it is always in the 'best interests' of the ward to require submission to such treatment. Nor do statistical factors indicating that a majority of competent persons similarly situated choose treatment resolve the issue. The significant decisions of life are more complex than statistical determinations. Individual choice is determined not by the vote of the majority but by the complexities of the singular situation viewed from the unique perspective of the person called on to make the decision. To presume that the incompetent person must always be subjected to what many rational and intelligent persons may decline is to downgrade the status of the incompetent person by placing a lesser value on his intrinsic human worth and vitality.

The trend in the law has been to give incompetent persons the same rights as other individuals. *Boyd v Registrars of Voters of Belchertown*, 334 NE 2d 629 (1975). Recognition of this principle of equality requires understanding that in certain circumstances it may be appropriate for a court to consent to the withholding of treatment from an incompetent individual. This leads us to the question of how the right of an incompetent person to decline treatment might best be exercised so as to give the fullest possible expression to the character and circumstances of that individual.

The problem of decision-making presented in this case is one of first impression before this court, and we know of no decision in other jurisdictions squarely on point. The well publicized decision of the New Jersey Supreme Court in *Re Quinlan* 70 NJ 10, 355 A 2d 647 (1976), provides a helpful starting point for analysis, however. [Karen Quinlan was diagnosed as being in a persistent vegetative state sustained by a ventilator. The case concerned an application by her father as guardian under New Jersey law to discontinue her treatment on the ventilator.]

The exposition by the New Jersey court of the principle of substituted judgment, and of the legal standards that were to be applied by the guardian in making this decision, bears repetition here.

> If a putative decision by Karen to permit this non-cognitive, vegetative existence to terminate by natural forces is regarded as a valuable incident of her right of privacy, as we believe it to be, then it should not be discarded solely on the basis that her condition prevents her conscious exercise of the choice. The only practical way to prevent destruction of the right is to *permit the guardian and family of Karen to render their best judgment*, subject to the qualifications [regarding consultation with attending physicians and hospital 'Ethics Committee'] hereinafter stated, *as to whether she would exercise it in these circumstances*. If their conclusion is in the affirmative this decision should be accepted by a society the overwhelming majority of whose members would, we think, in similar circumstances, exercise such a choice in the same way for themselves or for those closest to them. It is for this reason that we determine that Karen's right of privacy may be asserted in her behalf, in this respect, by her guardian and family under the particular circumstances presented by this record (emphasis supplied). *Id* at 41-42, 355 A 2d 647.

The court's observation that most people in like circumstances would choose a natural death does not, we believe, detract from or modify the central concern that the guardian's decision conform, to the extent possible, to the decision that would have been made by Karen Quinlan herself. Evidence that most people would or would not act in a certain way is certainly an important consideration in attempting to ascertain the predilections of any individual, but care must be taken, as in any analogy, to ensure that operative factors are similar or at least to take notice of the dissimilarities. With this in mind, it is profitable to compare the situations presented in the *Quinlan* case and the case presently before us. Karen Quinlan, subsequent to her accident, was totally incapable of knowing or appreciating life, was physically debilitated, and was pathetically reliant on sophisticated machinery to nourish and clean her body. Any other person suffering from similar massive brain damage would be in a similar state of total incapacity, and thus it is not unreasonable to give weight to a supposed general, and widespread, response to the situation.

Karen Quinlan's situation, however, must be distinguished from that of Joseph Saikewicz. Saikewicz was profoundly mentally retarded. His mental state was a cognitive one but limited in his capacity to comprehend and communicate. Evidence that most people choose to accept the rigors of chemotherapy has no direct bearing on the likely choice that Joseph Saikewicz would have made. Unlike most people, Saikewicz had no capacity to understand his present situation or his prognosis. The guardian *ad litem* gave expression to this important distinction in coming to grips with this 'most troubling aspect' of withholding treatment from Saikewicz. 'If he is treated with toxic drugs he will be involuntarily immersed in a state of painful suffering, the reason for which he will never understand. Patients who request treatment know the risks involved and can appreciate the painful side-effects when they arrive. They know the reason for the pain and their hope makes it tolerable.' To make a worthwhile comparison, one would have to ask whether a majority of people would choose chemotherapy if they were told merely that something outside of their previous experience was going to be done to them, that this something would cause them pain and discomfort, that they would be removed to strange surroundings and possibly restrained for extended periods of time, and that the advantages of this course of action were measured by concepts of time and mortality beyond their ability to comprehend.

To put the above discussion in proper perspective, we realize that an inquiry into what a majority of people would do in circumstances that truly were similar assumes an objective viewpoint not far removed from a 'reasonable person' inquiry. While we recognize the value of this kind of indirect evidence, we should make it plain that the primary test is subjective in nature – that is, the goal is to determine with as much accuracy as possible the wants and needs of the individual involved. This may or may not conform to what is thought wise or prudent by most people. The problems of arriving at an accurate substituted judgment in matters of life and death vary greatly in degree, if not in kind, in different circumstances. For example, the responsibility of Karen Quinlan's father to act as she would have wanted could be discharged by drawing on many years of what was apparently an affectionate and close relationship. In contrast, Joseph Saikewicz was profoundly retarded and noncommunicative his entire life, which was spent largely in the highly restrictive atmosphere of an institution. While it may thus be necessary to rely to a greater degree on objective criteria, such as the supposed inability of profoundly retarded persons to conceptualize or fear death, the effort to bring the substituted judgment into step with the values and desires of the affected individual must not, and need not be abandoned.

The 'substituted judgment' standard which we have described commends itself simply because of its straightforward respect for the integrity and autonomy of the individual . . . [W]e now reiterate the substituted judgment doctrine as we apply it in the instant case. We believe that both the guardian *ad litem* in his recommendation and the judge in his decision should have attempted (as they did) to ascertain the incompetent person's actual interests and preferences. In short, the decision in cases such as this should be that which would be made by the incompetent person, if that person were competent, but taking into account the present and future incompetency of the individual as one of the factors which would necessarily enter into the decision-making process of the competent person. Having recognized the right of a competent person to make for himself the same decision as the court made in this case, the question is, do the facts on the record support the proposition that Saikewicz himself would have made the decision under the standard set forth. We believe they do.

The two factors considered by the probate judge to weigh in favor of administering chemotherapy were: (1) the fact that most people elect chemotherapy and (2) the chance of a longer life. Both are appropriate indicators of what Saikewicz himself would have wanted, provided that due allowance is taken for this individual's present and future incompetency. We have already discussed the perspective this brings to the fact that most people choose to undergo chemotherapy. With regard to the second factor, the chance of a longer life carries the same weight for Saikewicz as for any other person, the value of life under the law having no relation to intelligence or social position. Intertwined with this consideration is the hope that a cure, temporary or permanent, will be discovered during the period of extra weeks or months potentially made available by chemotherapy. The guardian *ad litem* investigated this possibility and found no reason to hope for a dramatic breakthrough in the time frame relevant to the decision.

The probate judge identified six factors weighing against administration of chemotherapy. Four of these – Saikewicz's age, the probable side effects of treatment, the low chance of producing remission, and the certainty that treatment will cause immediate suffering – were clearly established by the medical testimony to be considerations that any individual would weigh carefully. A fifth factor – Saikewicz's inability to cooperate with the treatment – introduces those considerations that are unique to this individual and which therefore are essential to the proper exercise of substituted judgment. The judge heard testimony that Saikewicz would have no comprehension of the reasons for the severe disruption of his formerly secure and stable environment occasioned by chemotherapy. He therefore would experience fear without the understanding from which other patients draw strength. The inability to anticipate and prepare for the severe side effects of the drugs leaves room only for confusion and disorientation. The possibility that such a naturally uncooperative patient would have to be physically restrained to allow the slow intravenous administration of drugs could only compound his pain and fear, as well as possibly jeopardize the ability of his body to withstand the toxic effects of the drugs.

The sixth factor identified by the judge as weighing against chemotherapy was 'the quality of life possible for him even if the treatment does bring about remission.' To the extent that this formulation equates the value of life with any measure of the quality of life, we firmly reject it. A reading of the entire record clearly reveals, however, the judge's concern that special care be taken to respect the dignity and worth of Saikewicz's life precisely because of his vulnerable position. The judge, as well as all the parties, were keenly aware that the supposed ability of Saikewicz, by virtue of his mental retardation, to appreciate or experience life had no place in the decision before them. Rather than reading the judge's formulation in a manner that demeans the value of the life of one who is mentally retarded, the vague, and perhaps ill-chosen, term 'quality of life' should be understood as a reference to the continuing state of pain and disorientation precipitated by the chemotherapy treatment. Viewing the term in this manner, together with the other factors properly considered by the judge, we are satisfied that the decision to withhold treatment from Saikewicz was based on a regard for his actual interests and preferences and that the facts supported this decision . . .

In this case, a ward of a State institution was discovered to have an invariably fatal illness, the only effective – in the sense of life-prolonging – treatment for which involved serious and painful intrusions on the patient's body. While an emergency existed with regard to taking action to begin treatment, it was not a case in which immediate action was required. Nor was this a case in which life-saving, as distinguished from life-prolonging, procedures were available. Because the individual involved was thought to be incompetent to make the necessary decisions, the officials of the State institutions properly initiated proceedings in the Probate Court.

. . . We note here that many health care institutions have developed medical ethics committees or panels to consider many of the issues touched on here. Consideration of the findings and advice of such groups as well as the testimony of the attending physicians and other medical experts ordinarily would be of great assistance to a probate judge faced with such a difficult decision. We believe it desirable for a judge to consider such views wherever available and useful to the court. We do not believe, however, that this option should be transformed by us into a required procedure. We take a dim view of any attempt to shift the ultimate decision-making responsibility away from the duly established courts of proper jurisdiction to any committee, panel or group, ad hoc or permanent. Thus, we reject the approach adopted by the New Jersey Supreme Court in the *Quinlan* case of entrusting the decision whether to continue artificial life support to the patient's guardian, family, attending doctors, and hospital 'ethics committee'. 70 NJ at 55, 355 A 2d 647, 671. One rationale for such a delegation was expressed by the lower court judge in the *Quinlan* case, and quoted by the New Jersey Supreme Court: 'The nature, extent and duration of care by societal standards is the responsibility of a physician. The morality and conscience of our society places this responsibility in the hands of the physician. What justification is there to remove it from the control of the medical profession and place it in the hands of the courts?' *Id* at 44, 355 A 2d at 655. For its part, the New Jersey Supreme Court concluded that 'a practice of applying to a court to confirm such decisions would generally be inappropriate, not only because that would be a gratuitous encroachment upon the medical profession's field of competence, but because it would be impossibly cumbersome. Such a requirement is distinguishable from the judicial overview traditionally required in other matters such as the adjudication and commitment of mental incompetents. This is not to say that in the case of an otherwise justiciable controversy access to the courts would be foreclosed; we speak rather of a general practice and procedure.' *Id* at 50, 355 A 2d at 669.

We do not view the judicial resolution of this most difficult and awesome question – whether potentially life-prolonging treatment should be withheld from a person incapable of making his own decision – as constituting a 'gratuitous encroachment' on the domain of medical expertise. Rather, such questions of life and death seem to us to require the process of detached but passionate investigation and decision that forms the ideal on which the judicial branch of government was created. Achieving this ideal is our responsibility and that of the lower court, and is not to be entrusted to any other group purporting to represent the 'morality and conscience of our society', no matter how highly motivated or impressively constituted.

Conroy enlarges on the test suggested by *Saikewicz* by making clear, as we saw, that there are *three* tests. The first test in *Conroy* – the 'subjective test' – demands that the decision-maker must follow the treatment choice which the incompetent person made prior to the onset of incompetence. Thus, the law requires that the patient's earlier decision be complied with (see *infra*, ch 17 'anticipatory decisions'). (See *Re Peter* (1987) 529 A 2d 419 (NJ Sup Ct) permitting discontinuation of artificial hydration and nutrition on the basis of the 'subjective test'.)

The second test in *Conroy* – the 'limited-objective' test – was intended by the court to reflect to some extent the decision that the patient *would* have made, while providing for some element of objective evaluation of the patient's interests. As Handler J explained in the subsequent case of *Re Jobes* (1987) 529 A 2d 434 at 458, this test seeks out a 'middle-ground which combined elements of both self-determination and objective physical factors'. This test calls for careful examination. On the one hand it represents an improvement on the law as stated in *Saikewicz*, but on the other hand it too has its drawbacks. In

Saikewicz you will recall that Liacos J used the test of 'substituted judgment'. This, in truth, should be the second *Conroy* test. Liacos J misused it by applying it to a patient who never was competent to have views or express wishes on the treatment he would like to receive. Substituted judgment, properly understood, requires that the decision-maker should take account of the views and values of the now incompetent person as a guide in determining what the now incompetent person *would have chosen* for himself. The decision-maker acts as the substitute for the patient who can no longer speak for himself. He does *not* substitute his view for that of the patient. Clearly, if the patient has never had the capacity to have a view then the 'substituted judgment' test can have no application (see *supra*, pp 282-293). *Conroy* recognises this (and the error committed by Liacos J). But *Conroy* takes a wrong turning in that its second test is not pure substituted judgment (as it should be) but is what the court calls 'limited objective'. The addition of an objective element undermines the commitment of the court to give effect wherever possible to the views and values of the patient. The flaw in the *Conroy* approach was subsequently exposed by the same court in the case of *Re Jobes* (1987) 529 A 2d 434. This case concerned a patient in a persistent vegetative state. There was no evidence that Mrs Jobes had made a prior decision concerning her treatment. The New Jersey Supreme Court permitted her family members to decide what treatment she should receive on the basis of the substituted judgment test.

Garibaldi J explained the test as follows:

> **Garibaldi J:** [Substituted judgment] is intended to ensure that the surrogate decision-maker effectuates as much as possible the decision that the incompetent patient would make if he or she were competent. Under the substituted judgment doctrine, where an incompetent's wishes are not clearly expressed, a surrogate decisionmaker considers the patient's personal value system for guidance. The surrogate considers the patient's prior statements about and reactions to medical issues, and all the facets of the patient's personality that the surrogate is familiar with – with, of course, particular reference to his or her relevant philosophical, theological, and ethical values – in order to extrapolate what course of medical treatment the patient would choose.

She continued:

> Where an irreversibly vegetative patient like Mrs Jobes has not clearly expressed her intentions with respect to medical treatment, the *Quinlan* 'substituted judgment' approach best accomplishes the goal of having the patient make her own decision. In most cases in which the 'substituted judgment' doctrine is applied, the surrogate decisionmaker will be a family member or close friend of the patient. Generally it is the patient's family or other loved ones who support and care for the patient, and who best understand the patient's personal values and beliefs. Hence they will be best able to make a substituted medical judgment for the patient.

In a concurring judgment Handler J added:

> **Handler J:** Today this Court holds that though Mrs Jobes' intention to accept or refuse life-sustaining treatment has not been clearly established by clear and convincing evidence, the Court will uphold the decision of close family members who made the treatment determination based on what they believe Mrs Jobes would have decided. *Ante* at 446-447. The court is satisfied to effectuate the decision of the patient's family. It has in these circumstances adopted the individual right of self-determination reflected by the substituted judgment of a surrogate decisionmaker as the standard for resolving the fundamental issue of whether to terminate life-sustaining treatment.
>
> While this 'substituted judgment' standard fits well the facts of this case, the Court notes that in many cases this standard will not be workable, eg, in cases where the patient has always been incompetent or when there is no one sufficiently familiar with the patient to be

able to know how the patient would have decided. *Ante* at 449-450. The Court does not suggest standards for how treatment decisions should be made in such cases. *Id.* I would add that there will be difficult cases in which the relationship of family members or putative friends of the patient may not be close enough for them to be an appropriate source for the awesome decision of whether to discontinue life-perpetuating treatment.

In the cases now before the Court, the decision to discontinue or to refuse treatment was either made by the patient herself or made by the patient's guardian on the basis of trustworthy evidence of what the patient would have decided.

The third *Conroy* test – the 'pure objective test' – appears to be no different from the 'best interests' test familiar to English law. It can be argued, however, that *Conroy*, while developing the law, again muddied the waters. The majority of the court recognised that any decision about 'best interests' involves weighing burdens and benefits. Curiously, however, they restricted the relevant burdens to *pain and suffering*. This is clearly too narrow, not least because it either prejudges the answer which will be arrived at, or is of no assistance, where a patient can no longer feel pain – for example, when in a persistent vegetative state. This is because the absence of burden (ie no pain) suggests either that the benefit of treating mandates that treatment continue or, if it is recognised that treatment produces no benefit, in such a case there is neither burden nor benefit and so the test is meaningless. Any decision about treatment should, therefore, be based upon a test where burden is not limited to pain. Handler J in a concurring opinion in *Conroy* reflects the force of these arguments:

Handler J: In my opinion, the Court's objective tests too narrowly define the interests of people like Miss Conroy. While the basic standard purports to account for several concerns, it ultimately focuses on pain as the critical factor. The presence of significant pain in effect becomes the sole measure of such a person's best interests. 'Pain' thus eclipses a whole cluster of other human values that have a proper place in the subtle weighing that will ultimately determine how life should end.

The Court's concentration on pain as the exclusive criterion in reaching the life-or-death decision in reality transmutes the best-interests determination into an exercise of avoidance and nullification rather than confrontation and fulfilment. In most cases the pain criterion will dictate that the decision be one not to withdraw life-prolonging treatment and not to allow death to occur naturally. First, pain will not be an operative factor in a great many cases. '[P]resently available drugs and techniques allow pain to be reduced to a level acceptable to virtually every patient, usually without unacceptable sedation.' *President's Commission Report, supra*, at 50-51. See *id* at 19 n 19 *citing* Saunders, 'Current Views on Pain Relief and Terminal Care' in *The Therapy of Pain* 215 (Swerdlow, ed 1981) (a hospice reports complete control of pain in over 99% of its dying patients). See generally *id* at 277-95. See also generally *The Management of Terminal Disease* (Saunders, ed 1978); *The Experience of Dying* (Pattison, ed 1977); *Psychopharmacologic Agents for the Terminally Ill and Bereaved* (Goldberg *et al*, eds 1973). Further, as was true in Miss Conroy's case, health care providers frequently encounter difficulty in evaluating the degree of pain experienced by a patient. Finally, '[o]nly a minority of patients – fewer than half of those with malignancies, for example – have substantial problems with pain . . .' *President's Commission Report, supra* at 278 *citing* Twycross, 'Relief of Pain' in *The Management of Terminal Disease, supra*, at 66. Thus, in a great many cases, the pain test will become an absolute bar to the withdrawal of life-support therapy.

The pain requirement, as applied by the Court in its objective tests, effectively negates other highly relevant considerations that should appropriately bear on the decision to maintain or to withdraw life-prolonging treatment. The pain standard may dictate the decision to prolong life despite the presence of other factors that reasonably militate in favour of the termination of such procedures to allow a natural death. The exclusive pain criterion denies relief to that class of people who, at the very end of life, might strongly disapprove of an artificially extended existence in spite of the absence of pain. See *Re Torres*, 357 NW 332 at 340 (Minn 1984) (although a patient 'cannot feel pain', that patient may have a guardian petition to forego life-sustaining treatment). Thus, some people abhor dependence on others as much, or more, than they fear pain. Other individuals value personal privacy and dignity, and prize independence from others when their personal needs and bodily functions are involved. Finally, the ideal of bodily integrity may become more important than simply prolonging life at its most rudimentary level. Persons, like Miss Conroy, 'may well have wished to avoid . . . '[t]he ultimate horror [not of] death but the possibility of being maintained in limbo, in a sterile room, by machines controlled by strangers.' In *Re Torres, supra*, 357 NW 2d at 340, quoting Steel, 'The Right to Die: New Options in California', 93 *Christian Century* [July-Dec 1976].

Clearly, a decision to focus exclusively on pain as the single criterion ignores and devalues other important ideals regarding life and death. Consequently, a pain standard cannot serve as an indirect proxy for additional and significant concerns that bear on the decision to forego life-prolonging treatments . . .

I would therefore have the Court adopt a test that does not rely exclusively on pain as the ultimately determinative criterion. Rather, the standard should consist of an array of factors to be medically established and then evaluated by the decisionmaker both singly and collectively to reach a balance that will justify the determination whether to withdraw or to continue life-prolonging treatment. The withdrawal of life-prolonging treatment from an unconscious or comatose, terminally ill individual near death, whose personal views concerning life-ending treatment cannot be ascertained, should be governed by such a standard.

Several important criteria bear on this critical determination. The person should be terminally ill and facing imminent death. There should also be present the permanent loss of conscious thought processes in the form of a comatose state or profound unconsciousness. Further, there should be the irreparable failure of at least one major and essential bodily organ or system. See, eg, *Re Quinlan*, 70 NJ 10, 355 A 2d 647 (1976) (respiratory system); *Barber, supra* (same); *Re Dinnerstein*, 6 *Mass App* 466, 380 NE 2d 134 (1978) (heart); *Saikewicz, supra* (circulatory system); *Conroy, supra* (swallowing reflex); *Torres, supra* (cerebral cortex and brain-stem); *Re Hamlin*, 102 *Wash* 2d 810, 689 P 2d 1372 (1984) (cerebral cortex). Obviously the presence or absence of significant pain is highly relevant.

In addition, the person's general physical condition must be of great concern. The presence of progressive, irreversible, extensive and extreme physical deterioration, such as ulcers, lesions, gangrene, infection, incontinence and the like, which frequently afflict the bed-ridden, terminally ill, should be considered in the formulation of an appropriate standard. The medical and nursing treatment of individuals *in extremis* and suffering from these conditions entails the constant and extensive handling and manipulation of the body. At some point, such a course of treatment upon the insensate patient is bound to touch the sensibilities of even the most detached observer. Eventually, pervasive bodily intrusion, even for the best motives, will arouse feelings akin to humiliation and mortification for the helpless patient. When cherished values of human dignity and personal privacy, which belong to every person living or dying, are sufficiently transgressed by what is being done to the individual, we should be ready to say: enough.

Against this analytical background we now turn to the English law. The question is whether English law brings the same subtlety of analysis found in the judgments in New Jersey. The New Jersey cases reflect, of course, the very significant commitment of the courts in the United States to the patient's right to self-determination whenever this can safely be effected. English courts, by contrast, have historically been wary of the language of rights. Furthermore, as we have seen in Chapter 4, they are not slow, the moment there is the slightest doubt as to a patient's views, to fall back on the 'best interests' test with a dash of *Bolam* thrown in for good measure. This may reflect the tendency towards paternalism and 'doctor knows best' which is endemic in English medical law.

Decision-making in English law

A. WHO DECIDES?

It is as well to remember that although we have been considering cases concerning adult patients, the incompetent also include young children. We are concerned with both in this chapter. You will have noticed in the American cases that while the law relating to decision-making in the case of children is similar to English law, as regards adults there are significant differences. The differences lie not in the type of decision that may be made or the basis for making it, but in the decision-maker. Most American jurisdictions provide for family members to make decisions either as of right (under what are known as 'family consent statutes') or after application to a court to be appointed a guardian. In England neither of these possibilities exists. We have set out in detail in Chapter 4 the law which pertains in England as to who may be the decision-maker in the case of incompetent adults. In short, you will recall that in *Re F* the House of Lords vested decision-making in doctors.

B. BASIS FOR DECIDING

Whether the patient is a young child or an adult, the law which comes into play is the same. It is as well to remember the context: the possible end of a patient's life and the consequent responsibility of the doctor (and parent). In matters of life or death the criminal law, specifically the law of murder, comes to the fore and sets the agenda. Of course, as ever, the law of tort – specifically negligence and battery – and family law in the case of children remain central. Thus, an analysis of the criminal law will, for the most part, provide a means for resolving the issues which arise in tort and family law concerning the respective legal duties of doctors and parents. You will see that the crucial legal question is 'what is the legal duty of the doctor (or parent)?'

1. Unhelpful arguments

Before we can begin to answer this question we must recognise that there are a number of unhelpful arguments which bedevil this area of law and need to be addressed at the outset.

(a) Sanctity of life

Helga Kuhse and Peter Singer put (without accepting) the argument of those who would rely upon an absolutist view of the sanctity of human life, in their book, *Should the Baby Live?* (1985) (at pp 18-20).

> . . . [A]ll human life is of equal worth. According to this view, the life of a Down's syndrome baby is no less valuable than the life of a normal baby, or of any other patient. Since all human life is of equal worth, it is as wrong to let a Down's syndrome baby die, when it could be kept alive, as it would be to let any other patients die when they could be kept alive.
>
> **The sanctity of human life**
> The simple answer gains support from two quite distinct sources. One is the traditional doctrine of the sanctity of human life. Those who speak of 'the sanctity of life' hold a cluster of related ideas, rather than a single doctrine; nevertheless they agree in rejecting claims that one human life is more valuable than another . . . For the moment it is enough to note that it has had a dominant influence on both morality and law in Western civilisation. The central idea is well expressed by Sanford Kadish, writing on the view of human life taken by Anglo-American law:
>
> > all human lives must be regarded as having an equal claim to preservation simply because life is an irreducible value. Therefore, the value of a particular life, over and above the value of life itself, may not be taken into account.

Here the key claim is that life is an irreducible value – that is, the value of life cannot be reduced to anything else, such as the happiness, self-consciousness, rationality, autonomy, or even simple consciousness, that life makes possible. Life is not valuable because of the qualities it may possess; it is valuable in itself. It is easy to see how this claim leads to the conclusion that all human life is of equal value.

The traditional sanctity of life doctrine is also sometimes supported by the claim that human life is of *infinite* value. The Chief Rabbi of Great Britain, Rabbi Immanuel Jakobovits, has referred to this idea as the ground for opposition to euthanasia:

> The basic reasoning behind the firm opposition of Judaism to any form of euthanasia proper is the attribution of *infinite* value to every human life. Since infinity is, by definition, indivisible, it follows that every fraction of life, however small, remains equally infinite so that it makes morally no difference whether one shortens life by seventy years or by only a few hours, or whether the victim of murder was young and robust or aged and physically or mentally debilitated.

Dr Moshe Tendler, a professor of Talmudic law, confirms this position:

> human life is of infinite value. This in turn means that a piece of infinity is also infinity, and a person who has but a few moments to live is no less of value than a person who has 60 years to live . . . a handicapped individual is a perfect specimen when viewed in an ethical context. The value is an absolute value. It is not relative to life expectancy, to state of health, or to usefulness to society.

The Protestant theologian Paul Ramsey, Professor of Religion at Princeton University, takes a similar view:

> there is no reason for saying that [six months in the life of a baby born with the invariably fatal Tay Sachs disease] are a life span of lesser worth to God than living seventy years before the onset of irreversible degeneration. A genuine humanism would say the same thing in other language. It is only a reductive naturalism or social utilitarianism that would regard those months of infant life as worthless because they lead to nothing on a time line of earthly achievement. All our days and years are of equal worth whatever the consequence; death is no more a tragedy at one time than at another time.

A value might be irreducible without being infinite, and if human life is of irreducible rather than infinite value, there may not be great value in prolonging human existence by a few moments. On the other hand, if human life is of infinite value, every second of prolonged life would be as valuable as a lifetime. This is, on the face of it, implausible; most of us are indifferent to the prospect of our life being shortened by one second, but we are very far from indifferent to the thought that our life might be cut short by thirty years. As far as the treatment of John Pearson [in the *Arthur* case] and Baby Doe [a similar case in the USA] is concerned, however, the difference between irreducible value and infinite value does not matter. Both babies could, with appropriate care, have lived for many years, possibly a near-normal lifespan. (The life expectancy of people with Down's syndrome is less than normal, but some do live into their forties or even fifties.) So if human life is in itself a value, irrespective of the quality of the particular life, the presence of Down's syndrome is not relevant to the value a life has.

Gordon Dunstan in *The Dictionary of Medical Ethics* also gives a helpful explanation (pp 384-5):

> **Sanctity or sacredness of human life**. Phrases, having overtones taken from religious terminology, used to express the presumptive inviolability of the human person, his right to life, with its attendant right to protection in the enjoyment of his total integrity. The principle is implicit in the Hippocratic tradition . . . and was heavily reinforced by Jewish and Christian theology. It finds modern expression in the Geneva Declaration of the World Medical Association, 'I will maintain the utmost respect for human life from the time of conception, even under threat. I will not use my medical knowledge contrary to the laws of humanity.' In Judaism, every moment of life is infinitely precious, and has therefore an inviolable claim to protection. The words 'sanctity' and 'sacredness' imply – indeed, taken literally, they assert – a divine sanction for this inviolability as in itself divinely willed for man, proper to the created nature of man and the divine purpose of his existence. *Sanctity* (from the Latin *sanctus*) denotes 'holiness', a word which, in its historic evolution, denoted the numinous separateness

of God, then his ethical purity, then the ethical purity, or saintliness, of those 'separated' or dedicated to God; thence a claim to religious reverence and protection, inviolability. *Sacredness* (from the Latin *sacer*) has a similar meaning: set apart, dedicated to religious use; holy by association; and therefore to be respected, protected.

The words are sometimes used in controversy, eg about abortion . . . as though they self-evidently gave *absolute* protection, or imposed *absolute* prohibitions on the taking of life. The supposition cannot be supported from the moral tradition in which the concepts themselves have been preserved. The Jewish Law, for instance, which forbade murder in the Sixth (Fifth) Commandment (Exodus 20: 13), also enjoined capital punishment for a number of crimes. The principle, properly used, asserts a human right to enjoy protection in life and bodily integrity; that right may be violated only for just cause approved by the general moral sense and by public authority. It is for society itself to work out and maintain the second-order conventions and rules by means of which the principle can operate in professional practice as in the other activities of ordered human life.

The courts in England have been anxious to assert the law's commitment to the sanctity of life. As Lord Donaldson MR put it in *Re J (A Minor) (Wardship: Medical Treatment)* [1990] 3 All ER 930 at 938: 'We know that the instinct and desire for survival is very strong. We all believe in and assert the sanctity of human life.' The courts have gone on, however, to demonstrate that they do not see this 'principle' in absolute terms. While recognising its importance, it has not been endorsed as a form of slogan designed to prevent the court from considering competing principles. In *Re J*, Taylor LJ stated (at 943) that, 'the court's high respect for the sanctity of human life imposes a strong presumption in favour of taking all steps capable of preserving it, save in exceptional circumstances'.

The principle of the 'sanctity of life' received its most careful examination by an English court in the case of *Airedale NHS Trust v Bland* [1993] 1 All ER 821 by Lords Keith (at 861) Goff (at 865-866) and Mustill (at 891).

Lord Keith: The principle [of the sanctity of life] is not an absolute one. It does not compel a medical practitioner on pain of criminal sanctions to treat a patient, who will die if he does not, contrary to the express wishes of the patient. It does not authorise forcible feeding of prisoners on hunger strike. It does not compel the temporary keeping alive of patients who are terminally ill where to do so would merely prolong their suffering.

Lord Goff: The fundamental principle . . . of the sanctity of human life [is] . . . a principle long recognised not only in our own society but also in most, if not all, civilised societies throughout the modern world, as is indeed evidenced by its recognition both in art 2 of the European Convention on Human Rights (Convention for the Protection of Human Rights and Fundamental Freedoms, Rome 4 November 1950; TS 71 (1953); (Cmd 8969)) and in art 6 of the International Covenant on Civil and Political Rights (New York, 19 December 1966; TS6 (1977); Cmd 6702).

But this principle, fundamental though it is, is not an absolute. Indeed there are circumstances in which it is lawful to take another man's life, for example by a lawful act of self-defence, or (in the days when capital punishment was acceptable in our society) by lawful execution.

Lord Mustill: The interest of the state in preserving the lives of its citizens is very strong, but it is not absolute. There are contrary interests, and sometimes these prevail; as witness the over-mastering effect of the patient's refusal of treatment, even where this makes death inevitable.

(b) Ordinary/extraordinary treatment

The argument based on the distinction between ordinary and extraordinary treatment, accepting as it does the moral propriety of withholding treatment in some cases, can, of course, only be advanced once an absolutist view of the sanctity of life is rejected. An outstanding analysis, pinpointing the deficiencies of this argument, can be found in the President's Commission for the Study of Ethical Problems in Medical and Biomedical and Behaviorial Research, Report of 1983.

President's Commission, *Deciding to Forego Life-Sustaining Treatment* (pp 82-88)

Ordinary versus extraordinary treatment. In many discussions and decisions about life-sustaining treatment, the distinction between ordinary and extraordinary (also termed 'heroic' or 'artificial') treatment plays an important role. In its origins within moral theology, the distinction was used to mark the difference between obligatory and nonobligatory care – ordinary care being obligatory for the patient to accept and others to provide, and extraordinary care being optional. It has also played a role in professional policy statements and recent judicial decisions about life-sustaining treatment for incompetent patients. As with the other terms discussed, defining and applying a distinction between ordinary and extraordinary treatment is both difficult and controversial and can lead to inconsistent results, which makes the terms of questionable value in the formulation of public policy in this area.

The meaning of the distinction. 'Extraordinary' treatment has an unfortunate array of alternative meanings, as became obvious in an exchange that took place at a Commission hearing concerning a Florida case [*Satz v Perlmutter* 379 So 2d 358 (1980)] involving the cessation of life-sustaining treatment at the request of a 76-year-old man dying of amyotrophic lateral sclerosis. The attending physician testified:

> I deal with respirators every day of my life. To me, this is not heroic. This is standard procedure . . . I have other patients who have run large corporations who have been on portable respirators. Other people who have been on them and have done quite well for as long as possible.

By contrast, the trial judge who had decided that the respirator could be withdrawn told the Commission:

> Certainly there is no question legally that putting a hole in a man's trachea and inserting a mechanical respirator is extraordinary life-preserving means. I do not think that the doctor would in candor allow that that is not an extraordinary means of preserving life. I understand that he deals with them every day, but in the sense of ordinary as against extraordinary, I believe it to be extraordinary.
>   There was no question in this case, nobody ever raised the question that this mechanical respirator was not an extraordinary means of preserving life.

The most natural understanding of the ordinary/extraordinary distinction is as the difference between common and unusual care, with those terms understood as applying to a patient in a particular condition. This interprets the distinction in a literal, statistical sense and, no doubt, is what some of its users intend. Related, though different, is the idea that ordinary care is simple and that extraordinary care is complex, elaborate, or artificial, or that it employs elaborate technology and/or great efforts or expense. With either of these interpretations, for example, the use of antibiotics to fight a life-threatening infection would be considered ordinary treatment. On the statistical interpretation, a complex of resuscitation measures (including physical, chemical, and electrical means) might well be ordinary for a hospital patient, whereas on the technological interpretation, resuscitation would probably be considered extraordinary. Since both common/unusual and simple/complex exist on continuums with no precise dividing line, on either interpretation there will be borderline cases engendering disagreement about whether a particular treatment is ordinary or extraordinary.

A different understanding of the distinction, one that has its origins in moral theology, inquires into the usefulness and burdensomeness of a treatment. Here, too, disagreement persists about which outcomes are considered useful or burdensome. Without entering into the complexity of these debates, the Commission notes that any interpretation of the ordinary/extraordinary distinction in terms of usefulness and burdensomeness to an individual patient has an important advantage over the common/unusual or simple/complex interpretations in that judgments about usefulness and burdensomeness rest on morally important differences.

Despite the fact that the distinction between what is ordinary and what is extraordinary is hazy and variably defined, several courts have employed the terms in discussing cases involving the cessation of life-sustaining treatment of incompetent patients. In some cases, the courts used these terms because they were part of the patient's religious tradition. In other cases, the terms have been used to characterise treatments as being required or permissibly foregone. For example, the New Jersey Supreme Court in the *Quinlan* case [*Re Quinlan* (1976) 355 A 2d] recognised a distinction based on the possible benefit to the individual patient.

One would have to think that the use of the same respirator or life support could be considered 'ordinary' in the context of the possibly curable patient but 'extraordinary' in the context of the forced sustaining by cardio-respiratory processes of an irreversibly doomed patient.

Likewise, the Massachusetts Supreme Judicial Court [*Superintendent of Belchertown State School v Saikewicz* (1977) 370 NE 2d 417] quoted an article in a medical journal concerning the proposition that ordinary treatment could become extraordinary when applied in the context of a patient for whom there is no hope:

We should not use *extraordinary* means of prolonging life or its semblance when, after careful consideration, consultation and application of the most well conceived therapy it becomes apparent that there is no hope for the recovery of the patient. Recovery should not be defined simply as the ability to remain alive; it should mean life without intolerable suffering.

Even if the patient or a designated surrogate is held to be under no obligation to accept 'extraordinary' care, there still remains the perplexing issue about what constitutes the dividing line between the two. The courts have most often faced the question of what constitutes 'ordinary' care in cases when the respirator was the medical intervention at issue. Generally the courts have recognised, in the words of one judge, that 'the act of turning off the respirator is the termination of an optional, extraordinary medical procedure which will allow nature to take its course'.

For many, the harder questions lie in less dramatic interventions, including the use of artificial feeding and antibiotics. In one criminal case involving whether the defendant's robbery and assault killed his victim or whether she died because life-supporting treatments were later withdrawn after severe brain injury was confirmed, the court held that 'heroic' (and unnecessary) measures included 'infusion of drugs in order to reduce the pressure in the head when there was no obvious response to those measures of therapy'. In another case, in which a patient's refusal of an amputation to prevent death from gangrene was overridden, antibiotics were described by the physician 'as heroic measures meaning quantities in highly unusual amounts risking iatrogenic disease in treating gangrene'. Here the assessment, in addition to relying on 'benefits', also seems to rely to some degree upon the risk and invasiveness of the intervention. One court did begin to get at the scope of the questions underlying the ordinary/extraordinary distinction. Faced with the question of treatment withdrawal for a permanently unconscious automobile accident victim, the Delaware Supreme Court [*Severns v Wilmington Medical Center* (1980) 421 A 2d 1334] asked what might constitute life-sustaining measures for a person who has been comatose for many months:

Are 'medicines' a part of such life-sustaining systems? If so, which medicines? Is food or nourishment a part of such life-sustaining systems? If so, to what extent? What extraordinary measures (or equipment) are a part of such systems? What measures (or equipment) are regarded by the medical profession as not extraordinary under the circumstances? What ordinary equipment is used? How is a respirator regarded in this context?

The moral significance of the distinction. Because of the varied meanings of the distinction, whether or not it has moral significance depends upon the specific meaning assigned to it. The Commission believes there is no basis for holding that whether a treatment is common or unusual, or whether it is simple or complex, is in itself significant to a moral analysis of whether the treatment is warranted or obligatory. An unusual treatment may have a lower success rate than a common one; if so, it is the lower success rate rather than the unusualness of the procedure that is relevant to evaluating the therapy. Likewise, a complex, technological treatment may be costlier than a simple one, and this difference may be relevant to the desirability of the therapy. A patient may choose a complex therapy and shun a simple one, and the patient's choice is always relevant to the moral obligation to provide the therapy.

If the ordinary/extraordinary distinction is understood in terms of the usefulness and burdensomeness of a particular therapy, however, the distinction does have moral significance. When a treatment is deemed extraordinary because it is too burdensome for a particular patient, the individual (or a surrogate) may appropriately decide not to undertake it. The reasonableness of this is evident – a patient should not have to undergo life-prolonging treatment without consideration of the burdens that the treatment would impose. Of course, whether a treatment is warranted depends on its usefulness or benefits as well. Whether serious burdens of treatment (for example, the side effects of chemotherapy treatments for cancer) are worth enduring obviously depends on the expected benefits – how long the treatment will extend life, and under what conditions. Usefulness might be understood as mere extension of life, no matter what the conditions of that life. But so long as mere biological existence is not considered the *only* value, patients may want to take the nature of that additional life into account as well.

This line of reasoning suggests that extraordinary treatment is that which, in the patient's view, entails significantly greater burdens than benefits and is therefore undesirable and not obligatory, while ordinary treatment is that which, in the patient's view, produces greater benefits than burdens and is therefore reasonably desirable and undertaken. The claim, then, that the treatment is extraordinary is more of an expression of the conclusion than a justification for it.

Raanon Gillon, in an editorial in (1981) 7 Journal of Medical Ethics 56, supports the view of the President's Commission:

. . . [T]houghtful proponents of the use of the distinction between ordinary and extraordinary means agree with opponents that the moral assessment of any individual's case must properly come *before* it is decided whether any particular treatment is to be classified as ordinary or extraordinary; moreover not only the 'means' (ie the proposed means of treatment) but also the patient's particular circumstances and the anticipated harms and benefits to him in those circumstances of those means of treatment must be assessed before the means can be classified as being either ordinary or extraordinary. Thus there is no question of observing whether some proposed means of treatment X is, as a matter of non-evaluative fact, ordinary or extraordinary and then using this observation or 'fact' to decide whether or not patient Y in circumstances Z should be treated with X; rather it is a matter of first deciding whether or not it would be *right* to treat patient Y in context Z with treatment X and then, depending on that decision, classifying X as ordinary or extraordinary means of treatment.

Non-Catholics are often – perhaps always – surprised at this revelation when first they meet it, supposing reasonably enough that 'ordinary' means 'usual, common-place, not exceptional' (to quote the Oxford English Dictionary) and conversely that 'extraordinary' means 'unusual, uncommon, exceptional.' However, although these concepts may obliquely enter the analysis of specific cases it is clear that, as Strong explicitly states, the conflation of 'ordinary' with 'customary' and of 'extraordinary' with 'unusual' must be rejected; he indeed goes further and suggests that for the purpose of medical ethics 'perhaps we would avoid confusion if we used the terms 'ethically indicated,' and 'ethically non-indicated' in place of the terms 'ordinary' and 'extraordinary.' Of course once we accept such understanding of the distinction it remains open to ask what are the criteria upon which it should be made – what are the substantive moral principles upon which we can decide whether treatment X is or is not 'ethically indicated' (ie indicated by some process of ethical analysis) for patient Y in circumstances Z.

Roman Catholic authorities have proposed excessive expense, excessive pain, excessive difficulty or other inconvenience, and no reasonable or 'proportionate' hope of benefit as criteria for deciding that a treatment is 'extraordinary' in the context of a particular patient in particular circumstances. This approach is reflected by the Church of England. Thus the moral theologian Professor G R Dunstan in an article on this subject in the *Dictionary of Medical Ethics* suggests that the distinction has different connotations for moralists and for doctors but is used by both with the same intention, notably 'to insist that it is the patient's ultimate interest which should determine the treatment he receives, that interest being seen in relation to his unique being and his unique human and social environment'. Dunstan states that ordinary (and hence morally obligatory) procedures are for the moralist those which, when relativized to a particular patient in a particular context offer the patient 'a reasonable hope of benefit, without excessive expense, pain or other serious inconvenience'. Similarly in medical usage 'ordinary' would indicate 'what is normal, established, well-tried;

of known effectiveness, within the resources and skills available; of calculable and acceptable risk; of generally low mortality; involving pain, disturbance, inconvenience, all within predictable limits of acceptability and control; and all proportionate to an expected and lasting benefit to the patient'.

Conversely 'extraordinary' (and hence morally optional) means are for the moralist those means which, when relativized to a particular patient in a particular context, do not satisfy the criteria for being 'ordinary' and which would impose on the patient 'undue suffering or expense, or, it may be, an undue distortion of his personality or a barrier in his relationships with his kin, a lessening of his human capacity, and all without a reasonable hope of benefit'. In the medical connotation extraordinary procedures would be those which in relation to a particular patient in a particular context would fail to meet the criteria for being ordinary – they would include for instance 'investigatory and experimental procedures of uncertain efficacy, or even carrying a high mortality rate; those involving a heavy disproportion between the pain, mutilation, disfigurement or psychological disruption of the patient and any immediate or long-term benefit reasonably predictable; or of disproportionate cost.'

There can be few people involved in making medical-ethical decisions, whether in practice or merely in theory, who would disagree with the general principles of assessment proposed in either the Roman Catholic or Church of England positions as outlined above. Both, however, knowingly leave many important moral questions unanswered. What is to count as 'excessive' expense, pain, difficulty or other inconvenience; what is a 'reasonable' or 'proportionate' hope of benefit; what indeed is to count as a 'benefit'; and who should decide these weighty matters? No attempt is made to answer such questions here. Rather, the crucial point for health workers not versed in Christian theology to appreciate is that an appeal to the ordinary/extraordinary means distinction cannot help them to answer these questions, for the distinction itself can only be made *after* the questions have been answered.

The distinction between ordinary means and extraordinary means has a dangerously deceptive appearance of simplicity. It appears to be a distinction made by assessing means of treatment, whereas in fact, as Dunstan puts it 'the criteria for decision relate primarily to the patient not to the remedy'. It appears to be a distinction made by determining whether particular means of treatment are usual or unusual, and again this is not the case. It appears to give a single *criterion* for making a moral decision whereas in fact it is only a label for a decision-making process which uses a cluster of different moral criteria; above all it appears to be a distinction based upon a simple, uncontroversial, morally non-evaluative assessment, whereas in fact it is based upon complex potentially controversial and essentially moral assessments.

Those who are motivated by their religious orientations to use the distinction between ordinary and extraordinary means in the context of medical ethics may be expected to be aware of all this; those who are not so motivated need to appreciate these complexities before using the distinction at all. However all health workers will risk less confusion, if not for themselves then at least for their patients and for their patients' relatives, if they specify the moral criteria which they believe should be used when deciding whether or not to undertake particular treatments for particular patients in particular circumstances. Specifying the criteria, which may well relate to risks, costs, pain, likelihood of success, anticipated results and side effects, both physical and psychological, of a proposed treatment, will not only reduce confusion but will also provide an opportunity for discussion of the complex issues, both among staff involved and also with patients and/or their relatives. Moreover once the actual criteria of decision are specified the misleading labels 'ordinary means' and 'extraordinary means' become superfluous and may be safely allowed to 'drop out of the picture' by those who have no special reason to retain them.

In short, the distinction is unhelpful in that the words represent a conclusion reached in the light of the consideration of a number of factors. It is the identification and relevance of these factors which any proper analysis of the doctor's (or parent's) duty should concentrate upon.

(c) Acts and omissions

Traditionally, the criminal law has drawn a distinction between acts and omissions. Criminal liability has ordinarily depended upon there being *an act* done by the defendant. Given the difficulties involved in determining precisely what conduct amounts to an act or omission, it will come as no surprise that this distinction has bedevilled medical law just as it has created problems elsewhere. Before trying to find a way out of the problem, not least the question of what is an act as distinct from an omission, it is important to take note of what the traditional approach consists of.

(i) ACTS

Although positive conduct in the form of an act is ordinarily required for there to be criminal liability, it does not follow that every positive act when death results by a doctor in caring for an incompetent patient will be unlawful. Some obviously are unlawful; some may not be. Professor Skegg in his book *Law, Ethics and Medicine*, analyses this issue at pp 128-131.

P Skegg, *Law, Ethics and Medicine* (1984)

The fact that a patient would be severely handicapped if he were to live, or would find life a burden, does not affect the general principle that it is murder to kill a person by doing some positive act, with the intention of hastening death. There were several statements to this effect in Farquharson J's direction to the jury in *R v Arthur*. He said that it was an important principle in law that 'However serious the case may be; however much the disadvantage of a mongol or, indeed, any other handicapped child, no doctor has the right to kill it.' There was, he said, no special power, facility, or licence to kill children who are handicapped or seriously disadvantaged in any irreversible way. *R v Arthur* resulted from the death of a newly-born child, but what was said on this matter is equally applicable to other patients.

As the consent of the patient or others, or the patient's medical condition, will not provide a doctor with a defence if he administers a drug for the purpose of ending the patient's life, it is as well to consider whether the doctor's exemplary motive, medical qualifications, or compliance with medical ethics, would provide him with a defence . . . [I]t is clear that the motive of alleviating suffering will not provide a legal justification for a doctor who intentionally administers what he knows to be a lethal dose of a drug. In *R v Arthur* Farquharson J said that it was accepted that the doctor had acted from the highest of motives, but directed the jury that 'however noble his motives were . . . that is irrelevant to the question of your deciding what his intent was' . . . If a doctor acts with the intention of bringing about the death of a patient, the fact that he was acting to alleviate suffering, or for some other exemplary motive, would not at present provide him with a defence to a charge of murder.

In some circumstances the fact that a person has particular medical qualifications will affect that person's liability for murder or manslaughter. If a patient died in the course of a heart transplant operation, performed by a doctor with appropriate qualifications and experience, the doctor would not normally be liable. But if the operation were performed by a layman it would be very difficult to resist the conclusion that he exposed the patient to an unjustified risk, and that he was grossly negligent in attempting the operation. However, the fact that someone was medically qualified would make no difference if he administered a drug – or took any other action – for the purpose of hastening the death of a patient. In the few cases in which doctors have been prosecuted for murder or attempted murder in consequence of things done in the course of medical practice, trial judges have stressed that the law does not place doctors in any special position. In *R v Adams* Devlin J said that the law was the same for all: there was not any special defence for medical men. And in *R v Arthur* Farquharson J said there 'is no special law . . . that places doctors in a separate category and gives them extra protection over the rest of us'. They are, he said, 'given no special power . . . to commit an act which causes death'.

Even if a doctor acted in compliance with statements on medical ethics propounded by the British Medical Association, or any other organisation, this would not of itself provide a doctor with a defence if he administered a drug – or did any other act – for the purpose of hastening the death of a patient. In *R v Arthur* Farquharson J commented that it was customary for a profession to agree on rules of conduct for its members but instructed the jury that 'that does not mean that any profession can set out a code of ethics and say that the law must accept it and take notice of it. It may be that in any particular feature the ethic is wrong.' He said that 'whatever a profession may evolve as a system of standards of ethics, cannot stand on its own, and cannot survive if it is in conflict with the law'. It would therefore be open to a jury to find a doctor guilty of murder even though they believed that he acted in accordance with the ethical standards currently accepted by the medical profession.

The conclusion must be that neither the consent of the patient or anyone else, nor the condition of the patient, nor the doctor's exemplary motive, professional qualifications, or compliance with accepted standards of medical ethics, would provide any defence for a doctor who prescribed or administered a drug – or did any other act – for the purpose of hastening the death of the patient.

Some acts, however, are lawful even though they may hasten death:

R v Bodkin Adams [1957] CLR 365 (CCC)

Devlin J: But that does not mean that a doctor who is aiding the sick and the dying has to calculate in minutes, or even in hours, and perhaps not in days or weeks, the effect upon a patient's life of the medicines which he administers or else be in peril of a charge of murder. If the first purpose of medicine, the restoration of health, can no longer be achieved there is still much for a doctor to do, and he is entitled to do all that is proper and necessary to relieve pain and suffering, even if the measures he takes may incidentally shorten life. That is not because there is any special defence for medical men; it is not because doctors are put into any category different from other citizens for this purpose. The law is the same for all, and what I have said to you rests simply upon this: no act is murder which does not cause death. 'Cause' means nothing philosophical or technical or scientific. It means what you twelve men and women sitting as a jury in the jury box would regard in a common-sense way as the cause . . . If, for example, because a doctor has done something or has omitted to do something death occurs, it can be scientifically proved – if it could – at eleven o'clock instead of twelve o'clock, or even on Monday instead of Tuesday, no people of common sense would say, 'Oh, the doctor caused her death.' They would say the cause of her death was the illness or the injury, or whatever it was, which brought her into hospital, and the proper medical treatment that is administered and that has an incidental effect of determining the exact moment of death, or may have, is not the cause of death in any sensible use of the term. But it remains the fact, and it remains the law, that no doctor, nor any man, no more in the case of the dying man than of the healthy, has the right deliberately to cut the thread of life.

We must be very clear what Devlin J means, because it must be clear that we are on the edge of a discussion about euthanasia, voluntary or otherwise. The mere mention of the word 'euthanasia' is instantly a recipe for confused (and emotive) thinking. Devlin J may be resting his conclusion that 'no action is murder which does not cause death' on either of two legal grounds.

I. No intention. Devlin J may have been saying that although the doctor did an act which 'played some part in' the death of the patient, the doctor should not be liable, unless he intended to bring about the death. Devlin J must have meant that the doctor should not be held to have intended the death because of the theory of 'double effect', if the jury found that his primary intention was to relieve the pain of his patient.The theory of 'double effect' which Devlin J introduces into English criminal law purports to be a theory about intention. It seems to say that if an act may have two effects and the actor *desires* only one of them, which is considered a *good* effect, then he should be regarded as blameless even though his act also produces a bad effect. The words 'primary' and 'secondary' are used to describe the intention concerning the good and the bad effect.

For the lawyer, this theory is not without difficulties; see, for example, Glanville Williams *The Sanctity of Life and the Criminal Law* (1957) at p 286:

. . . When you know that your conduct will have two consequences, one in itself good and one in itself evil, you are compelled as a moral agent to choose between acting and not acting by making a judgment of value, that is to say by deciding whether the good is more to be desired than the evil is to be avoided. If this is what the principle of double effect means, well and good; but if it means that the necessity of making a choice of values can be avoided merely by keeping your mind off one of the consequences, it can only encourage a hypocritical attitude towards moral problems.

What is true of morals is true of the law. There is no legal difference between desiring or intending a consequence as following from your conduct, and persisting in your conduct with a knowledge that the consequence will inevitably follow from it, though not desiring that consequence. When a result is foreseen as certain, it is the same as if it were desired or intended. It would be an undue refinement to distinguish between the two.

Professor Williams must be right on the law when he makes clear that the consequence that is undesired may nevertheless be intended in law (*R v Moloney* [1985] AC 905 and *R v Nedrick* [1986] 3 All ER 1). Thus for the lawyer, if not for the moral philosopher, the judgment that an act is blameless cannot analytically rest on a theory of intention as expressed in the 'double-effect' theory. It must rest, if anywhere, on a judgment that acts (though intended) ought as a matter of moral judgment and public policy to be regarded as attracting no blame because of their social worth. This, of course, raises its own problems; what is the principle which underlies any specific determination that a particular course of conduct is blameless?

II. Absence of causation. Devlin J may, in the alternative, have meant to rely on causation: that a doctor's act in such circumstances would not be regarded in law as the cause of the patient's death.

Again, Glanville Williams addresses the issue as follows in his book (*op cit*), at pp 289-290:

> ... While I am reluctant to criticise a legal doctrine that gives a beneficial result, the use of the language of causation seems here to conceal rather than to reveal the valuation that is being made. To take an example, suppose that it were shown that the administration of morphine in regular medical practice caused a patient to die of respiratory failure or pneumonia. Medically speaking, this death would not be caused by the disease: it would be caused by the administration of morphine. There seems to be some difficulty in asserting that for legal purposes the causation is precisely the opposite.

Lord Devlin responded to this observation in a lecture in 1960 later published in *Samples of Law Making*. Having referred to his direction to the jury concerned with double effect, the judge went on, at p 95:

> This direction was not, however, given on the basis that the relief of pain justified an act that would otherwise be murder in law. Before a man can be convicted of murder, it must be proved that his act was the cause of the death. That does not invariably, or even frequently, mean the medical cause of death. Medicine is concerned with the immediate physical cause and the criminal law with the guilty cause. On a death certificate no one would put dangerous driving, for example, as a cause of death; but there is an offence known to the law as causing death by dangerous driving. If a man injured in a road crash by dangerous driving was taken to hospital and there died, the driver could not escape conviction unless he could show that there was improper treatment in the hospital of a man who would otherwise have lived. The law might regard negligent treatment as a new and supervening cause of death, but proper medical treatment consequent upon illness or injury plays no part in legal causation; and to relieve the pains of death is undoubtedly proper medical treatment.

Attractive as Lord Devlin's response may be, is it not somewhat question-begging to say that the criminal law is concerned with the 'guilty' cause? Surely our problem is to determine which cause *is* the guilty cause? Has not Lord Devlin in fact conceded Professor Williams' point and admitted that the doctor by his acts does cause the death of a patient but now seeks to rely on another ground? Is not this other ground the same as that which was hinted at in our discussion of intention?

It is suggested that the more appropriate analysis is as follows: the doctor by his act *intends* (on any proper understanding of the term) the death of his patient and by his act *causes* (on any proper understanding of the term) the death of his patient, but the intention is not culpable and the cause is not blameworthy because the law permits the doctor to do the act in question.

On what basis, as a matter of principle, does the law permit the doctor to *act* in this way? In the House of Lords decision in *Airedale NHS Trust v Bland* [1993] 1 All ER 821, Lord Goff (at 868) offered a way of resolving the question:

> **Lord Goff:** The established rule [is] that a doctor may, when caring for a patient who is, for example, dying of cancer, lawfully administer painkilling drugs despite the fact that he knows that an incidental effect of that application will be to abbreviate the patient's life. Such a decision may properly be made as part of the care of the living patient, in his best interests; and, on this basis, the treatment will be lawful. Moreover, where the doctor's treatment of his patient is lawful, the patient's death will be regarded in law as exclusively caused by the injury or disease to which his condition is attributable.

By contrast, Lord Mustill in *Bland* (at 892-893) was not prepared to follow the view of Lord Goff that lawful treatment could not be a cause of the patient's death.

> **Lord Mustill:** One argument in support of the conclusion that if the proposed conduct is carried out and Anthony Bland then dies the doctors will nevertheless be guilty of no offence depends upon a very special application of the doctrine of causation. This has powerful academic support: Skegg *Law, Ethics and Medicine* (1985) ch 6, where it represents the author's chosen solution, and also Glanville Williams *Textbook of Criminal Law* (2nd edn, 1983) pp 282-283 and Professor Ian Kennedy's paper *Treat Me Right, Essays in Medical Law and Ethics* (1988) pp 360-361, where it is offered by way of alternative. Nevertheless I find it hard to grasp. At several stages of his discussion Professor Skegg frankly accepts that some manipulation of the law of causation will be needed to produce the desired result. I am bound to say that the argument seems to me to require not manipulation of the law so much as its application in an entirely new and illogical way. In one form the argument presented to the House asserts that for the purpose of both civil and criminal liability the cause of Anthony Bland's death, if and when it takes place, will be the Hillsborough disaster. As a matter of the criminal law of causation, this may well be right, once it is assumed that the conduct is lawful: see *R v Blaue* [1975] 3 All ER 446 [1975] 1 WLR 1411, *R v Malcherek* [1981] 2 All ER 422, [1981] 1 WLR 690 and *Finlayson v HM Advocate* 1979 JC 33. It does not perhaps follow that the conduct of the doctors is not also causative, but this is of no interest since if the conduct is lawful the doctors have nothing to worry about. If on the other hand the proposed conduct is unlawful, then it is in the same case as active euthanasia or any other unlawful act by doctors or laymen. In common sense they must all be causative or none; and it must be all, for otherwise euthanasia would never be murder.
>
> A variant of the argument appears to put the ordinary law of causation into reverse. Normally, when faced with an act and a suggested consequence one begins by ascertaining the quality of the act and then, if it is found to be unlawful, one considers its connection to the consequence. This variant, by contrast, seems to begin the inquiry with the connection and then by applying a special rule of causation determine the character of the act. I confess that I cannot understand what mechanism enables this to be done. If the declarations are wrong and the proposed conduct is unlawful it is in my judgment perfectly obvious that the conduct will be, as it is intended to be, the cause of death, and nothing in the literature or the reported cases from other jurisdictions persuades me to any other conclusion.

(See generally on palliative care, D Casswell 'Rejecting Criminal Liability for Life-Shortening Palliative Care' (1990) 6 Journal of Contemporary Health Law and Policy 127.)

(ii) OMISSIONS

Let us now consider the other half of the traditional analysis – omissions. Professor Glanville Williams writes, in his *Textbook of Criminal Law* (2nd edn), at pp 148-149:

> A crime can be committed by omission, but there can be no omission in law in the absence of a duty to act. The reason is obvious. If there is an act, someone acts; but if there is an omission, everyone (in a sense) omits. We omit to do everything in the world that is not done. Only those of us omit in law who are under a duty to act.

Ordinarily there is no liability under the criminal law if a person omits to act to save life. An exception to this proposition exists where the law imposes an obligation to act. The problem arises as to what amounts to an omission and how it can be distinguished from an act.

The difficulty in defining what is an omission does not lie in saying what it is, that much is clear; it is a non-action or failure to act. Rather, the difficulty lies in saying whether in any particular set of circumstances there is, in a person's behaviour (the propriety of which is under scrutiny), something that can be called an act rather than omission since the former more readily attracts liability. If, for example, the facts are that 'X' has suffered harm and 'Y' appears responsible, a court may set out on a voyage of discovery to find some act by 'Y' on which to base liability. That the voyage may lead to the land of Humpty Dumpty can be seen in the following analysis by Professor Williams, of a doctor who turns off the respirator of a patient who is not dead. For Professor Williams, a traditionalist in his analysis here, the issue can be put as follows (*Textbook of Criminal Law* (1st edn) p 237):

> The question then arises whether stopping a respirator is an act of killing or a decision to let nature take its course. Common sense suggests it is the latter. Suppose that the respirator worked only as long as the doctor turned a handle. If he stopped turning, he would be regarded as merely commencing to omit to save the patient's life. Suppose, alternatively, that the respirator worked electrically but was made to shut itself off every 24 hours. Then the deliberate failure to restart it would be an omission. It can make no moral difference that the respirator is constructed to run continuously and has to be stopped. Stopping the respirator is not a positive act of killing the patient, but a decision not to strive any longer to save him.

Another commentator, Roger Leng, suggests the following in 'Death and the Criminal Law' (1982) 45 MLR 206:

> It is submitted that it is correct to characterise termination [of life support] as an omission. This entails recognition that the act/omission distinction does not rest upon what is done, or upon a concept of willed muscular contraction, but upon the impact of what is done on the victim. The *provision* of life support is in fact a series of acts (albeit accomplished mechanically): termination of support is an omission to continue such acts which has no positive effect on the patient but merely fails to avert the natural cessation of vital functions.
>
> If this characterisation and the general proposition that the doctor/patient relationship imports a duty recognised by the criminal law are accepted, a doctor deliberately discontinuing support to a patient who is not legally dead escapes liability only if it is further accepted that sometimes *it lies within a doctor's duty to allow a patient to die*.
>
> This proposition may not be as problematic as first appears. Whereas the jurisprudence of duty relationships is well developed there has been relatively little consideration of the scope of a duty once found. Where duty and breach have been established the act required has not been onerous: eg alerting a doctor or social worker, provision of food at no personal expense or performing one's contract of employment. The law clearly allows some balancing of the interests of the person under the duty as against those of the person to whom it is owed. Stated briefly the doctor's duty is to preserve life and health. This is an unreal oversimplification. The doctor (with the policeman and judge) implements the state's

broad duty to preserve the life and health of citizens. The state does not take every measure to preserve life but must balance competing calls upon its resources. The doctor gives practical effect to this balance. He must take decisions on allocation of skilled attention, drugs, blood and equipment, involving qualitative judgments of cost-effectiveness, likelihood of survival, and the value of the life involved. Some such decisions will adversely affect chances of survival. From this broad perspective, a responsible and procedurally correct decision to terminate life-support to a brain-dead patient may fall within a doctor's duty although it leads to immediate death as traditionally defined.

The distinction between acts and omissions, and its contribution to analysis, fell four-square to be addressed in the *Bland* case. The case involved a 21-year-old patient in a persistent vegetative state after being crushed in the infamous Hillsborough Football Stadium disaster in 1989. The question for the court was whether it would be lawful to discontinue artificial life-support in the form of hydration and nutrition given both the hopelessness of his condition and also that this would lead to his death. In determining that the doctors would behave lawfully the court was forced to indulge in the act/omission analysis.

Airedale NHS Trust v Bland [1993] 1 All ER 821, (1993) 12 BMLR 64 (HL)

Lord Browne-Wilkinson: Murder consists of causing the death of another with intent so to do. What is proposed in the present case is to adopt a course with the intention of bringing about Anthony Bland's death. As to the element of intention, or mens rea, in my judgment there can be no real doubt that it is present in this case: the whole purpose of stopping artificial feeding is to bring about the death of Anthony Bland.

As to the guilty act, or actus reus, the criminal law draws a distinction between the commission of a positive act which causes death and the omission to do an act which would have prevented death. In general an omission to prevent death is not an actus reus and cannot give rise to a conviction for murder. But where the accused was under a duty to the deceased to do the act which he omitted to do, such omission can constitute the actus reus of homicide, either murder (*R v Gibbins* (1918) 13 Cr App Rep 134) or manslaughter (*R v Stone* [1977] 2 All ER 341, [1977] QB 354) depending upon the mens rea of the accused. The Official Solicitor submits that the actus reus of murder is present on two alternative grounds, viz (1) the withdrawal of artificial feeding is a positive act of commission or (2) if what is proposed is only an omission, the hospital and the doctors have assumed a duty to care for Anthony Bland (including feeding him) and therefore the omission to feed him would constitute the actus reus of murder . . .

Mr Munby QC, in his powerful but balanced argument for the Official Solicitor, submits that the removal of the nasogastric tube necessary to provide artificial feeding and the discontinuance of the existing regime of artificial feeding constitute positive acts of commission. I do not accept this. Apart from the act of removing the nasogastric tube, the mere failure to continue to do what you have previously done is not, in any ordinary sense, to do anything positive: on the contrary it is by definition an omission to do what you have previously done.

The positive act of removing the nasogastric tube presents more difficulty. It is undoubtedly a positive act, similar to switching off a ventilator in the case of a patient whose life is being sustained by artificial ventilation. But in my judgment in neither case should the act be classified as positive, since to do so would be to introduce intolerably fine distinctions. If, instead of removing the nasogastric tube, it was left in place but no further nutrients were provided for the tube to convey to the patient's stomach, that would not be an act of commission. Again, as has been pointed out (Skegg, *Law, Ethics and Medicine* (1985) pp 169 ff), if the switching off of a ventilator were to be classified as a positive act, exactly the same result can be achieved by installing a time-clock which requires to be reset every 12 hours: the failure to reset the machine could not be classified as a positive act. In my judgment, essentially what is being done is to omit to feed or to ventilate: the removal of the nasogastric tube or the switching off of a ventilator are merely incidents of that omission: see Glanville Williams, *Textbook of Criminal Law* (2nd edn, 1983) p 282 and Skegg p 169.

In my judgment, there is a further reason why the removal of the nasogastric tube in the present case could not be regarded as a positive act causing the death. The tube itself, without the food being supplied through it, does nothing. The removal of the tube by itself does not cause the death since by itself it did not sustain life. Therefore even if, contrary to my view, the removal of the tube is to be classified as a positive act, it would not constitute the actus reus of murder since such positive act would not be the cause of death.

Lord Goff: At the heart of this distinction lies a theoretical question. Why is it that the doctor who gives his patient a lethal injection which kills him commits an unlawful act and indeed is guilty of murder, whereas a doctor who, by discontinuing life support, allows his patient to die may not act unlawfully and will not do so, if he commits no breach of duty to his patient? Professor Glanville Williams has suggested (see *Textbook of Criminal Law* (2nd edn, 1983) p 282) that the reason is that what the doctor does when he switches off a life support machine 'is in substance not an act but an omission to struggle' and that 'the omission is not a breach of duty by the doctor, because he is not obliged to continue in a hopeless case'.

I agree that the doctor's conduct in discontinuing life support can properly be categorised as an omission. It is true that it may be difficult to describe what the doctor actually does as an omission, for example where he takes some positive step to bring the life support to an end. But discontinuation of life support is, for present purposes, no different from not initiating life support in the first place. In each case, the doctor is simply allowing his patient to die in the sense that he is desisting from taking a step which might, in certain circumstances, prevent his patient from dying as a result of his pre-existing condition; and as a matter of general principle an omission such as this will not be unlawful unless it constitutes a breach of duty to the patient. I also agree that the doctor's conduct is to be differentiated from that of, for example, an interloper who maliciously switches off a life support machine because, although the interloper may perform exactly the same act as the doctor who discontinues life support, his doing so constitutes interference with the life-prolonging treatment then being administered by the doctor. Accordingly, whereas a doctor, in discontinuing life support, is simply allowing his patient to die of his pre-existing condition, the interloper is actively intervening to stop the doctor from prolonging the patient's life, and such conduct cannot possibly be categorised as an omission.

The distinction appears, therefore, to be useful in the present context in that it can be invoked to explain how discontinuance of life support can be differentiated from ending a patient's life by a lethal injection. But in the end the reason for that difference is that, whereas the law considers that discontinuance of life support may be consistent with the doctor's duty to care for his patient, it does not, for reasons of policy, consider that it forms any part of his duty to give his patient a lethal injection to put him out of his agony.

(ii) THE WAY OUT!

You may well feel that reliance on the acts/omissions distinction is unhelpful. Indeed, you may wonder whether such a complicated question of responsibility can be resolved by being encapsulated in one word. It is even more unhelpful when it is recalled that the act/omission distinction, whatever it is, ceases to be of legal significance where there is a duty to act. Doctors caring for patients are under a *duty* to care for their patients; any liability for their conduct will turn on whether they have breached this duty, *whether by act or omission.* Lord Mustill in *Bland* accepted the unhelpfulness of the act/omission distinction:

Lord Mustill: The English criminal law, and also it would appear from the cases cited, the law of transatlantic state jurisdictions, draws a sharp distinction between acts and omissions. If an act resulting in death is done without lawful excuse and with intent to kill it is murder. But an omission to act with the same result and with the same intent is in general no offence at all. So also with lesser crimes. To this general principle there are limited statutory exceptions, irrelevant here. There is also one important general exception at common law, namely that a person may be criminally liable for the consequences of an omission if he stands in such a relation to the victim that he is under a duty to act. Where the result is death the offence will usually be manslaughter, but if the necessary intent is proved it will be murder: see *R v Gibbins* (1918) 13 Cr App Rep 134.

Precisely in what circumstances such a duty should be held to exist is at present quite unclear. . . . For the time being all are agreed that the distinction between acts and omissions exists, and that we must give effect to it.

2. The duty to the patient

If *duty* is the basis for analysing the legality of treatment decisions at the end of life, as it clearly is, the only issue is what is the content of the duty. We saw in Chapter 4 that, in principle, the law requires a doctor or parent to act in the 'best interests' of the incompetent patient. This is the test which the courts have embraced notwithstanding the limitations and imperfections of resort to this intrinsically imprecise formula (see *supra*, ch 4). We also saw, when we considered the case of *In the Matter of Conroy* earlier, that two further tests could be relevant in this context. We defer until later the question of 'anticipatory decisions' by once competent patients. However, in the case of adults (or indeed children) who *have been competent*, the court could adopt the 'substituted judgment' test which we discussed in Chapter 4. We have also seen in Chapter 4 that the test to be applied by the doctor or parent is set by the law. In the case of children, the court may, under its inherent jurisdiction, review decisions made by others and act in the child's best interests. Such a jurisdiction does not exist in English law in the case of adults. Nevertheless, the court's function when deciding about treatment in the case of an incompetent adult should be no different in the sense that the court has to decide where the 'best interests' of the patient lie (for a not wholly convincing judicial attempt to distinguish the court's roles in the case of children and adults see, *Airedale NHS Trust v Bland* [1993] 1 All ER 821 at 882 per Lord Browne-Wilkinson). So the courts have decided that, in the case of incompetent patients, the test to be used by the decision-maker is that of the 'best interests' of the patient.

We now turn to consider how the courts have *applied* the test of 'best interests' in the case of an incompetent patient, whether child or adult, in making treatment decisions at the end of life. In doing so, it will be helpful to separate out a number of factual situations.

(a) The dying patient

We are concerned with the dying. We use this description conscious of its limitations, as expressed by the President's Commission *Deciding to Forego Life-Sustaining Treatment* (1983) (pp 24-26).

> Other phrases – though useful as general descriptions – are similarly unacceptable when an unambiguous definition is required. For example, attempts – such as those in several statutes – to make the obligations of patients and providers different when a patient is 'terminally ill' are dubious for several reasons. First, although a decision to undertake life-sustaining treatment will frequently depend on whether the patient believes the treatment is likely to extend life substantially enough to be worth its burdens, patients with similar prognoses evaluate relevant facts very differently. The closeness of death may be strongly felt by someone who has only a remote chance of dying soon, while for another person it may not seem imminent until his or her organs have nearly ceased to function. Moreover, prognostication near the end of life is notoriously uncertain. At best, confidence in predicting death is possible only in the final few hours. Patients with the same stage of a disease but with different family settings, personalities, and 'things to live for' actually do live for strikingly varied periods of time. It seems difficult to devise or to justify policies that restrict people's discretion to make appropriate decisions by allowing some choices only to 'terminally ill' patients or by denying them other choices.
>
> Although the Commission has attempted to avoid rhetorical slogans so as to escape the ambiguities and misunderstandings that often accompany them, it uses 'dying' and 'terminally ill' as descriptive terms for certain patients, not as ironclad categories. There seem to be no other terms to use for a patient whose illness is likely to cause death within

what is to that person a very short time. Of course, the word 'dying' is in some ways an unilluminating modifier for 'patient' – since life is always a 'terminal' condition – and further refinements, such as 'imminently', do little to clarify the situation. Therefore, words like 'dying' are used in the Report in their colloquial sense and with a caution against regarding them as a source of precision that is not theirs to bestow.

The dying patient is the patient for whom there is no prospect of cure nor of preventing the continued progress of the disease to imminent death. What is the scope and extent of the doctor's duty to care for his dying patient? A doctor faced with a dying patient should change his treatment from treatment for living to treatment for dying. The primary duty is to comfort the patient by symptomatic relief and other appropriate care (see M Somerville, 'Pain and Suffering at the Interfaces of Medicine and Law' (1986) 36 U of Toronto LJ 286). We have seen that it may include the administration of drugs which may hasten death if the primary intention is the relief of pain. In his summing up to the jury in *R v Bodkin Adams* [1957] CLR 365 (discussed *supra*), Devlin J said:

> If the first purpose of medicine, the restoration of health, can no longer be achieved there is still much for a doctor to do, and he is entitled to do all that is proper and necessary to relieve pain and suffering, even if the measures he takes may incidentally shorten life.

The obligation of the doctor is discussed by the President's Commission (*op cit*) in their 1983 Report (pp 78-81):

> . . . [A]lthough medication is commonly used to relieve the suffering of dying patients (even when it causes or risks causing death), physicians are not held to have violated the law. How can this failure to prosecute be explained, since it does not rest on an explicit waiver of the usual legal rule?
>
> The explanation lies in the importance of defining physicians' responsibilities regarding these choices and of developing an accepted and well-regulated social role that allows the choices to be made with due care. The search for medical treatments that will benefit a patient often involves risk, sometimes great risk, for the patient: for example, some surgery still carries a sizeable risk of mortality, as does much of cancer therapy. Furthermore, seeking to cure disease and to prolong life is only a part of the physician's traditional role in caring for patients; another important part is to comfort patients and relieve their suffering. Sometimes these goals conflict, and a physician and patient (or patient's surrogate) have the authority to decide which goal has priority. Medicine's role in relieving suffering is especially important when a patient is going to die soon, since the suffering of such a patient is not an unavoidable aspect of treatment that might restore health, as it might be for a patient with a curable condition.
>
> Consequently, the use of pain-relieving medications is distinguished from the use of poisons, though both may result in death, and society places the former into the category of acceptable treatment while continuing the traditional prohibition against the latter. Indeed, in the Commission's view it is not only possible but desirable to draw this distinction. If physicians (and other health professionals) became the dispensers of 'treatments' that could only be understood as deliberate killing of patients, patients' trust in them might be seriously undermined. And irreparable damage could be done to health care professionals' self-image and to their ability to devote themselves wholeheartedly to the often arduous task of treating gravely ill patients. Moreover, whether or not one believes there are some instances in which giving a poison might be morally permissible, the Commission considers that the obvious potential for abuse of a public, legal policy condoning such action argues strongly against it.
>
> For the use of morphine or other pain-relieving medication that can lead to death to be socially and legally acceptable, physicians must act within the socially defined bounds of their role. This means that they are not only proceeding with the necessary agreement of the patient (or surrogate) and in a professionally skilful fashion (for example, by not taking a step that is riskier than necessary), but that there are sufficiently weighty reasons to run the risk of the patient dying. For example, were a person experiencing great pain from a condition that will be cured in a few days, use of morphine at doses that would probably lead to death by inducing respiratory depression would usually be unacceptable. On the other hand, for a patient in great pain – especially from a condition that has proved to be

untreatable and that is expected to be rapidly fatal – morphine can be both morally and legally acceptable if pain relief cannot be achieved by less risky means.

This analysis rests on the special role of physicians and on particular professional norms of acceptability that have gained social sanction (such as the difference between morphine, which can relieve pain, and strychnine, which can only cause death). Part of acceptable behaviour – from the medical as well as the ethical and legal standpoints – is for the physician to take into account all the foreseeable effects, not just the intended goals, in making recommendations and in administering treatment. The degree of care and judgment exercised by the physician should therefore be guided not only by the technical question of whether pain can be relieved but also by the broader question of whether care providers are certain enough of the facts in this case, including the patient's priorities and subjective experience, to risk death in order to relieve suffering. If this can be answered affirmatively, there is no moral or legal objection to using the kinds and amounts of drugs necessary to relieve the patient's pain.

Re C (A Minor) (Wardship: Medical Treatment) [1989] 2 All ER 782, CA

Lord Donaldson MR: I have, most regretfully, to start with one fundamental and inescapable fact. Baby C is dying and nothing that the court can do, nothing that the doctors can do and nothing known to medical science can alter that fact.

The problem of how to treat the terminally ill is as old as life itself. Doctors and nurses have to confront it frequently, but it is never easy. Parents and relatives have to confront it less often and that makes it all the more difficult for them. Judges are occasionally faced with it when terminally ill children are wards of court. It is an awesome responsibility only made easier for them than for parents to the extent that judges are able to approach it with greater detachment and less emotional involvement.

The present case is one of the saddest which can be imagined. Not only are we concerned with a very young baby, but one who became terminally ill before she was even born, a fact which only became apparent at a later date.

C was born prematurely on 23 December 1988. She is now 16 weeks old. At birth she was found to be afflicted with a much more serious condition than the usual type of hydrocephalus. There was not merely a blockage of cerebral spinal fluid within the brain, but as a result the brain structure itself was poorly formed. Her progress since then and further examinations have revealed how exceptionally she has been affected. . . .

One of the first decisions which the court had to make was whether or not to agree to the child being operated on to relieve pressure on the brain. This is often done in cases of hydrocephalus with good results, but alas in the case of C all that could be hoped for was that it would prevent her head becoming so enlarged that nursing would become impossible. The damage to her brain had been done before birth and was irreparable.

Those who, understandably, have been moved by the story of C, but who have no personal involvement, have publicly commented that this operation should have been performed. I am bound to say that I think it might have been better if they had first made sure of the facts. In fact, the registrar of the court readily consented to its being undertaken and it was. The actual order was dated 11 January 1989 and it required that C 'who is suffering from congenital hydrocephalus, receive such treatment, including surgical treatment, as is considered medically appropriate' to her condition. It was pursuant to this order that the doctors operated on C and inserted a shunt to relieve pressure on her brain.

At all times since her birth C has received the finest and most caring medical and nursing attention which this country has to offer. However, the time came when a decision had to be made on what further treatment should be provided. In a critical situation such as this such decisions should not be, and are not, taken without wide consultation. And so it came about that the local authority's medical and social services departments became involved. The essential problem was what treatment should be given in the best interests of C if, as sooner or later was inevitable, she suffered some infection or illness over and above the handicaps from which she was already suffering. In the middle of last month a social worker expressed the view that in such a situation the court would expect the doctors to embark on 'treatment appropriate to a non handicapped child'. The legal department of the local authority, on the other hand, expressed the view that C should 'receive such treatment as is appropriate to her condition'.

For my part, I have no doubt that the legal department was right and the social worker was wrong. You do not treat a blind child as if she was sighted, or one with a diseased heart as if she was wholly fit. But this difference of opinion created a problem for Dr W, the physician in charge of C, for his paediatric colleague, Dr S, and for the nursing staff. Sooner or later he or the local authority would have been bound to seek instructions from the court because, as Heilbron J said in *Re D (a minor) (wardship: sterilisation)* [1976] 1 All ER 326 at 335, [1976] Fam 185 at 196:

> . . . once a child is a ward of court, no important step in the life of that child, can be taken without the consent of the court . . .

In the circumstances, and quite rightly, the local authority decided to consult the court sooner rather than later. In previous correspondence, which was of course made available to the judge, Dr W had raised the question of what he should do if the time came when it proved impossible to feed C through a syringe, in itself a procedure fraught with difficulty. In such circumstances should he resort to the use of a nasal-gastric tube? If C vomited, should he set up an intravenous drip? If C developed a terminal respiratory infection, should she be given antibiotics? All these were legitimate and difficult questions, given the sad but fundamental truth that C was dying and the only question was how soon this would happen.

Faced with these problems, the judge invited the intervention of the Official Solicitor, who asked one of the nation's foremost paediatricians to examine C and to make recommendations. I do not name him, simply because it might serve to identify where C is being treated; I refer simply to 'the professor'. The professor reported as follows and I read from his report:

> The records revealed that at birth she had a much more serious condition than the usual type of hydrocephalus. The detailed investigations which were done showed that there was not merely a blockage of cerebro-spinal fluid within the brain, but that the brain structure itself was poorly formed. Thus the operation that was done to relieve the pressure within the brain was no more than a palliative procedure to prevent her head from becoming so excessively large that nursing would be impossible. The operation could not be expected to restore brain function. [C's] appearance is of a tiny baby. Although she is 16 weeks old, she is the size of a 4 week baby apart from her head, which is unusually large by way of being tall and thin – squashed because of sleeping on her side. She lies quiet until handled and then she cries as if irritated. Her eyes move wildly in an uncoordinated way and she does not appear to see. (Her pupils do not respond to light so it is most unlikely that the mechanism for vision is present). She did not respond to very loud noises that I made, though the nurses said that she sometimes seems startled by their loud noises. However, my impression was that she did not hear, or had very poor hearing. She holds her limbs in a stiff flexed position. More detailed examination suggested that she had generalised spasticity of all her limbs as a result of the brain damage. The only social response she makes is the irritable crying when handled, though sometimes she can be pacified by stroking her face. She does not smile and does not respond in any other way. The only certain evidence of her feeling or appreciating events is the report of her quietening when her face is stroked. Thus she does not have the developmental skills and abilities of a normal new born baby. It is inconceivable that appreciable skills will develop, bearing in mind that there has been no progress during the past four months. She has severe brain damage. She is very thin and has not gained weight despite devoted nursing care at [the hospital]. She is receiving regular small doses of the sedative Chloral. If she does not receive that she cries 'as if in pain', though the carers are unsure where the pain originates. I do not believe that there is any treatment which will alter the ultimate prognosis, which appears to be hopeless. She has massive handicap as a result of a permanent brain lesion. Her handicap appears to be a mixture of severe mental handicap, blindness, probable deafness and spastic cerebral palsy of all four limbs. In addition, although given a normal amount of food, her body is not absorbing or using it in the normal way so that she is not growing. I do not believe that she can be said to be enjoying her life and I find it hard to know if she is experiencing very much, though the reports of irritable crying suggest that certain things upset her. She is receiving outstandingly devoted care . . . which could not be replicated in many children's units, or in many homes. The high standard of care makes it difficult to forecast how long she will live . . . In the event of her acquiring a serious infection, or being unable to take feeds normally by mouth I do not think it would be correct to give antibiotics, to set up intravenous fusions or nasal-gastric feeding regimes. Such action would be prolonging a life which has no future and which appears to be unhappy for her. However, the opinions of the local nurses and carers should be taken into account for they know her well, show great love to her, and have a feeling for her needs that an

outsider cannot have. Thus if they believed she was in pain or would suffer less by a particular course of action, it would be correct to consider that course of action, always bearing in mind the balance between short-term gain and needless prolongation of suffering.

It will be seen that the professor took the view that the goal should be to ease the suffering of C rather than to achieve a short prolongation of her life. But he did not rule out the giving of antibiotics, intravenous fusions or nasal-gastric feeding if this would achieve this result. Above all, he felt that, in reaching decisions as events unfolded, the opinions of local nurses and carers should be given the greatest possible weight.

In giving the reasons for his decision Ward J said:

> That poor baby has now been nursed and attended by the hospitals with a degree of devotion to duty which deserves the very highest commendation, and I pay tribute to those who have had part in the care of this ward, and I give my thanks to those for so looking after my ward on my behalf. I have had the advantage of a report by an eminent professor of paediatrics, instructed by the Official Solicitor, whom I caused to become involved in this matter to represent the interests of the baby. The professor observes in his report that the outstandingly devoted care she has received could not be replicated in many children's units or in many children's homes, and it is important that that should receive its proper tribute and its proper commendation. Sadly, notwithstanding that devotion this child has not prospered. I have had the benefit of reading the report and hearing the evidence of Dr W, who is the consultant physician at the hospital, a physician of 21 years' experience, and I give him my thanks for the assistance he has given me. He reports to me that this baby has made virtually no progress since her birth.

I omit some other matters and quote again from the judge's judgment, where he said: 'The damage which she has suffered is quite exceptionally severe.' Then he set out the evidence in support of that proposition and continued:

> The medical evidence satisfies me that the damage to the cortex of the brain is gross and abnormally severe. The cortex of the brain is that part of the brain which serves the higher functions; those functions of intellect which make human life distinguishable, perhaps, from other forms of life. That damage, moreover, is irreparable, and about that all the medical witnesses are wholly agreed. There is, therefore, no prospect of a happy life for this child, sadly; no prospect whatever. The prognosis, in the conclusion of [the professor], is that it is inconceivable that appreciable skills will ever develop, and that is, of course, confirmed by the total failure of progress in those few short weeks of her life. There is, in the united opinion of the medical experts, no treatment which will alter that prognosis, and the prognosis is therefore one of hopelessness. I am therefore dealing with a child massively handicapped by a mixture of severe or permanent brain lesions, blindness, probable deafness and generalised spastic cerebral palsy of all four limbs. . . .

[C] is, as I have already said, dying, and there is no medical or surgical treatment which can alter this fact. The judge continued in his judgment, saying:

> But here I am quite satisfied that the damage is severe and irreparable. In so far as I can assess the quality of life, which as a test in itself raises as many questions as it can answer, I adjudge that any quality to life has already been denied to this child because it cannot flow from a brain incapable of even limited intellectual function. Inasmuch as one judges, as I do, intellectual function to be a hallmark of our humanity, her functioning on that level is negligible if it exists at all. Coupled with her total physical handicap, the quality of her life will be demonstrably awful and intolerable . . . Asking myself what capacity she has to interact mentally, socially, physically, I answer none. This is her permanent condition.

It was shortly after this that the judge, in a brief passage in his judgment, failed to express himself with his usual felicity. He said:

> Putting the interests of this child first and putting them foremost so that they override all else, and in fulfilment of the awesome responsibility which Parliament has entrusted on me, I direct that leave be given to the hospital authorities to treat the ward to die, to die with the greatest dignity and the least of pain, suffering and distress.

No judge giving an extempore judgment has not, at one time or another, realised that he has not expressed himself as he intended. For this reason, and because the reasons for a decision in one case are published and are rightly taken into account in deciding others, it has long been the practice for judges in appropriate cases to make small revisions in the wording of their judgments when they receive a transcript from the shorthand writers. So it was in this case. The judge revised the first sentence of that passage to read:

> I direct that leave be given to the hospital authorities to treat the ward in such a way that she may end her life and die peacefully with the greatest dignity and the least of pain, suffering and distress.

Unfortunately, the formal order also contained the misleading phrase 'treat the minor to die'. Such orders are not seen by the judge unless he specifically asks to approve its wording, and the judge was at first unaware of its phraseology. When it was drawn to his attention, he at once exercised his powers under the slip rule to amend that part of the order to read: 'the hospital authority be at liberty to allow her life to come to an end peacefully and with dignity'.

The Official Solicitor in appealing to this court does not take issue on this part of the judge's order. Nor do the local authority or the mother, both of whom have been represented. All concerned accept that the judge correctly directed himself that the first and paramount consideration was the well-being, welfare and interests of C as required by the decision of this court in *Re B (a minor) (wardship: medical treatment)* and by the House of Lords in a later and different case with the same name, *Re B (a minor) (wardship: sterilisation)* [1987] 2 All ER 206 at 211, [1988] AC 199 at 202 per Lord Hailsham LC.

Counsel for the local authority nevertheless felt it his duty to direct our attention to a decision of the British Columbia Supreme Court in *Re SD* [1983] 3 WWR 618, while submitting that the facts were very different. In so doing he was fulfilling the fundamental duty of members of the legal profession to assist the courts in the administration of justice, regardless of the views or interests of their client. He was wholly right so to do. In the event, I am fully satisfied that it does nothing to cast doubts on the correctness of his clients', and the judge's, view that the advice of the professor should be accepted. It was another case in which a child suffered from hydrocephalus, but the child concerned was very much older. The child had twice been operated on to implant a shunt and the question was whether he should now undergo a third operation.

He was undoubtedly severely handicapped, but not as severely as some in his class at the hospital school. If a third operation were to be performed he would probably continue to live as he had done before and would do so for some years. The parents thought that there should be no operation and that he should be allowed to die at once. The higher court authorised the operation, saying it was too simplistic to say, as did the parents, that the child would be allowed to die in peace. There was a real possibility that, without the operation, the child would endure in a state of progressive disability and pain. That is a wholly different case.

The Official Solicitor in bringing this appeal had three objectives. The first was to question the propriety of an order expressed to be 'liberty to treat the minor to die'. As I hope I have made clear, neither Ward J nor anyone else would uphold such phraseology and he himself amended it. Second, the Official Solicitor wished to question that part of the order of the judge which appeared to provide that in no circumstances should certain treatment be undertaken. To that I will return in a moment. Third, the Official Solicitor wished to allay anxieties in some quarters that the hospital staff were treating C in a way designed to bring about her death. These anxieties, while no doubt sincerely felt, were wholly without foundation and, when expressed, were deeply wounding to the dedicated staff caring for C who, as the professor said, were providing C with devoted care which could not be replicated in many children's units.

Balcombe and Nicholls LJJ agreed.

The conclusion arrived at by the Master of the Rolls seems eminently the right one and puts the law beyond doubt. Parenthetically it may be objected that a close examination of the facts suggests that C was not in fact dying. You will notice that Ward J, the trial judge, refers to C's prognosis as being one of 'hopelessness', namely, C was very severely disabled and would not get better. This is not the same as saying she was dying, ie that she would die regardless of any care or treatment which she received. This view of the facts of the case does not, of course, affect its status as the leading authority on the doctor's duty to a dying patient. On the other hand, it could be said that by regarding C as dying the Court of Appeal was able to duck the far more difficult problem of the patient who is disabled but who is not dying – but not for long (see *Re J* (*infra*)).

Before we leave the law relating to the doctor's duty to the dying, one final point must be made. It is all very well for the courts to say that the doctor's duty is to comfort and 'ease the suffering' of the patient. We have already seen from our consideration of the acts/omissions distinction that the courts talk easily of the doctor having a duty to care but not to kill. How does this square with the facts of modern medicine? Morphine to relieve suffering is legally permissible but poison to kill is not. But what of increasing doses of morphine which will comfort *and* kill and which is known to do this? All we say here is that the rhetoric of the courts in dealing with the care of the dying obscures the fact that what happens in practice is lawful or unlawful depending entirely on how it is described rather than on what is done. We will return to this at some length (see *infra*, ch 17).

(b) The patient who is not dying but who will do so if not given life-sustaining treatment

We can divide this category of patient into two broad groups. First, there is the patient who is in a state which we may call a 'living death' (group 1). Perhaps the best known manifestation of this is the persistent vegetative state. Secondly, there are those patients for whom medical intervention may offer some benefit but the question arises whether the benefit to be gained by the patient justifies the intervention (group 2).

In analysing the law in respect of these two groups of patients you will notice that we will be concerned with two questions in particular. First, what test must the decision-maker use when deciding on treatment in any particular case. Secondly, are there circumstances in which a doctor or parent must refer the decision to the court and cannot make it himself? As we have suggested throughout this chapter, the crucial question for the law is to determine what is the *doctor's duty to his patient*. It is with this that we shall primarily be concerned in analysing the law as it applies to the two groups of patients described above.

(i) GROUP 1 PATIENTS

Until recently, the state of English law was uncertain although there had been numerous cases decided in the United States (see Kennedy & Grubb *Medical Law* (1st edn (1987) pp 1107-1116)). The House of Lords in the *Bland* case establishes the law in England. We will see, however, that the Law Lords differ in their approach and reasoning.

Airedale NHS Trust v Bland [1993] 1 All ER 821, (1993) 12 BMLR 64 (HL)

Lord Goff: My Lords, the facts of the present case are not in dispute . . .
They reveal a tragic state of affairs, which has evoked great sympathy, both for Anthony Bland himself and for his devoted family, and great respect for all those who have been responsible for his medical treatment and care since he was admitted to hospital following the terrible injuries which he suffered at Hillsborough in April 1989. For present purposes, I

propose simply to adopt the sympathetic and economical summary of Sir Thomas Bingham MR . . . which, for convenience of reference, I will now incorporate into this opinion.

Mr Anthony David Bland, then aged 17½, went to the Hillsborough ground on 15 April 1989 to support the Liverpool Football Club. In the course of the disaster which occurred on that day his lungs were crushed and punctured and the supply of oxygen to his brain was interrupted. As a result, he suffered catastrophic and irreversible damage to the higher centres of the brain. The condition from which he suffers, and has suffered since April 1989, is known as a persistent vegetative state (PVS). PVS is a recognised medical condition quite distinct from other conditions sometimes known as 'irreversible coma', 'the Guillain-Barre syndrome', the 'locked-in syndrome' and 'brain death'. Its distinguishing characteristics are that the brain stem remains alive and functioning while the cortex of the brain loses its function and activity. Thus the PVS patient continues to breathe unaided and his digestion continues to function. But, although his eyes are open, he cannot see. He cannot hear. Although capable of reflex movement, particularly in response to painful stimuli, the patient is incapable of voluntary movement and can feel no pain. He cannot taste or smell. He cannot speak or communicate in any way. He has no cognitive function and can thus feel no emotion, whether pleasure or distress. The absence of cerebral function is not a matter of surmise; it can be scientifically demonstrated. The space which the brain should occupy is full of watery fluid. The medical witnesses in this case include some of the outstanding authorities in the country on this condition. All are agreed on the diagnosis. All are agreed on the prognosis also: there is no hope of any improvement or recovery. One witness of great experience describes Mr Bland as the worst PVS case he had ever seen. Mr Bland lies in bed in the Airedale General Hospital, his eyes open, his mind vacant, his limbs crooked and taut. He cannot swallow, and so cannot be spoon-fed without a high risk that food will be inhaled into the lung. He is fed by means of a tube, threaded through the nose and down into the stomach, through which liquefied food is mechanically pumped. His bowels are evacuated by enema. His bladder is drained by catheter. He has been subject to repeated bouts of infection affecting his urinary tract and chest, which have been treated with antibiotics. Drugs have also been administered to reduce salivation, to reduce muscle tone and severe sweating and to encourage gastric emptying. A tracheostomy tube has been inserted and removed. Urino-genitary problems have required surgical intervention. A patient in this condition requires very skilled nursing and close medical attention if he is to survive. The Airedale National Health Service Trust have, it is agreed, provided both to Mr Bland. Introduction of the nasogastric tube is itself a task of some delicacy even in an insensate patient. Thereafter it must be monitored to ensure that it has not become dislodged and to control inflammation, irritation and infection to which it may give rise. The catheter must be monitored: it may cause infection (and has repeatedly done so); it has had to be resited, in an operation performed without anaesthetic. The mouth and other parts of the body must be constantly tended. The patient must be repeatedly moved to avoid pressure sores. Without skilled nursing and close medical attention a PVS patient will quickly succumb to infection. With such care, a young and otherwise healthy patient may live for many years. At no time before the disaster did Mr Bland give any indication of his wishes should he find himself in such a condition. It is not a topic most adolescents address. After careful thought his family agreed that the feeding tube should be removed and felt that this was what Mr Bland would have wanted. His father said of his son in evidence: 'He certainly wouldn't want to be left like that.' He could see no advantage at all in continuation of the current treatment. He was not cross-examined. It was accordingly with the concurrence of Mr Bland's family, as well as the consultant in charge of his case and the support of two independent doctors, that the Airedale NHS Trust as plaintiff in this action applied to the Family Division of the High Court for declarations that they might – '(1) . . . lawfully discontinue all life-sustaining treatment and medical support measures designed to keep AB [Mr Bland] alive in his existing persistent vegetative state including the termination of ventilation nutrition and hydration by artificial means; and (2) . . . lawfully discontinue and thereafter need not furnish medical treatment to AB except for the sole purpose of enabling AB to end his life and die peacefully with the greatest dignity and the least of pain suffering and distress.' After a hearing in which he was assisted by an amicus curiae instructed by the Attorney General, Sir Stephen Brown P made these declarations (subject to a minor change of wording) on 19 November 1992. He declined to make further declarations which were also sought.

The Official Solicitor, acting on behalf of Anthony Bland, appealed against that decision to the Court of Appeal, which dismissed the appeal. Now, with the leave of the Court of Appeal, the Official Solicitor has appealed to your Lordships' House . . .

The central issue in the present case has been aptly stated by Sir Thomas Bingham MR to be whether artificial feeding and antibiotic drugs may lawfully be withheld from an insensate patient with no hope of recovery when it is known that if that is done the patient will shortly thereafter die. The Court of Appeal, like Sir Stephen Brown P, answered this question generally in the affirmative, and (in the declarations made or approved by them) specifically also in the affirmative in relation to Anthony Bland. I find myself to be in agreement with the conclusions so reached by all the judges below, substantially for the reasons given by them. But the matter is of such importance that I propose to express my reasons in my own words.

I start with the simple fact that, in law, Anthony is still alive . . .

[I]n many cases not only may the patient be in no condition to be able to say whether or not he consents to the relevant treatment or care, but also he may have given no prior indication of his wishes with regard to it. In the case of a child who is a ward of court, the court itself will decide whether medical treatment should be provided in the child's best interests, taking into account medical opinion. But the court cannot give its consent on behalf of an adult patient who is incapable of himself deciding whether or not to consent to treatment. I am of the opinion that there is nevertheless no absolute obligation upon the doctor who has the patient in his care to prolong his life, regardless of the circumstances. Indeed, it would be most startling, and could lead to the most adverse and cruel effects upon the patient, if any such absolute rule were held to exist. It is scarcely consistent with the primacy given to the principle of self-determination in those cases in which the patient of sound mind has declined to give his consent that the law should provide no means of enabling treatment to be withheld in appropriate circumstances where the patient is in no condition to indicate, if that was his wish, that he did not consent to it. The point was put forcibly in the judgment of the Supreme Judicial Court of Massachusetts in *Belchertown State School Superintendent v Saikewicz* (1977) 373 Mass 728 747 as follows:

> To presume that the incompetent person must always be subjected to what many rational and intelligent persons may decline is to downgrade the status of the incompetent person by placing a lesser value on his intrinsic human worth and vitality. . . .

I return to the patient who, because for example he is of unsound mind or has been rendered unconscious by accident or illness, is incapable of stating whether or not he consents to treatment or care. In such circumstances, it is now established that a doctor may lawfully treat such a patient if he acts in his best interests, and indeed that, if the patient is already in his care, he is under a duty so to treat him: see *F v West Berkshire Health Authority* [1989] 2 All ER 545, [1990] 2 AC 1, in which the legal principles governing treatment in such circumstances were stated by this House. For my part I can see no reason why, as a matter of principle, a decision by a doctor whether or not to initiate, or to continue to provide, treatment or care which could or might have the effect of prolonging such a patient's life should not be governed by the same fundamental principle. Of course, in the great majority of cases, the best interests of the patient are likely to require that treatment of this kind, if available, should be given to a patient. But this may not always be so. To take a simple example given by Thomas J in the High Court of New Zealand in *Auckland Area Health Board v A-G* [1993] 1 NZLR 235 at 253, to whose judgment in that case I wish to pay tribute, it cannot be right that a doctor, who has under his care a patient suffering painfully from terminal cancer, should be under an absolute obligation to perform upon him major surgery to abate another condition which, if unabated, would or might shorten his life still further. The doctor who is caring for such a patient cannot, in my opinion, be under an absolute obligation to prolong his life by any means available to him, regardless of the quality of the patient's life. Common humanity requires otherwise, as do medical ethics and good medical practice accepted in this country and overseas. As I see it, the doctor's decision whether or not to take any such step must (subject to his patient's ability to give or withhold his consent) be made in the best interests of the patient . . .

It is of course the development of modern medical technology, and in particular the development of life support systems, which has rendered cases such as the present so much more relevant than in the past. Even so, where, for example, a patient is brought into hospital in such a condition that, without the benefit of a life support system, he will not continue to live, the decision has to be made whether or not to give him that benefit, if available. That decision can only be made in the best interests of the patient. No doubt, his best interests will ordinarily require that he should be placed on a life support system as soon as necessary, if only to make an accurate assessment of his condition and a prognosis for the future. But, if he neither recovers sufficiently to be taken off it nor dies, the question will ultimately arise whether he should be kept on it indefinitely. As I see it, that question (assuming the continued availability of the system) can only be answered by reference to the best interests of the patient himself, having regard to established medical practice. Indeed, if the justification for treating a patient who lacks the capacity to consent lies in the fact that the treatment is provided in his best interests, it must follow that the treatment may, and indeed ultimately should, be discontinued where it is no longer in his best interests to provide it. The question which lies at the heart of the present case is, as I see it, whether on that principle the doctors responsible for the treatment and care of Anthony Bland can justifiably discontinue the process of artificial feeding upon which the prolongation of his life depends.

It is crucial for the understanding of this question that the question itself should be correctly formulated. The question is not whether the doctor should take a course which will kill his patient, or even take a course which has the effect of accelerating his death. The question is whether the doctor should or should not continue to provide his patient with medical treatment or care which, if continued, will prolong his patient's life. The question is sometimes put in striking or emotional terms, which can be misleading. For example, in the case of a life support system, it is sometimes asked: should a doctor be entitled to switch it off, or to pull the plug? And then it is asked: can it be in the best interests of the patient that a doctor should be able to switch the life support system off, when this will inevitably result in the patient's death? Such an approach has rightly been criticised as misleading, for example by Professor Ian Kennedy (in his paper in *Treat Me Right, Essays in Medical Law and Ethics* (1988)), and by Thomas J in *Auckland Area Health Board v A-G* [1993] 1 NZLR 235 at 247. This is because the question is not whether it is in the best interests of the patient that he should die. The question is whether it is in the best interests of the patient that his life should be prolonged by the continuance of this form of medical treatment or care.

The correct formulation of the question is of particular importance in a case such as the present, where the patient is totally unconscious and where there is no hope whatsoever of any amelioration of his condition. In circumstances such as these, it may be difficult to say that it is in his best interests that the treatment should be ended. But, if the question is asked, as in my opinion it should be, whether it is in his best interests that treatment which has the effect of artificially prolonging his life should be continued, that question can sensibly be answered to the effect that it is not in his best interests to do so. . . .

[In PVS cases] there is in reality no weighing operation to be performed. Here the condition of the patient, who is totally unconscious and in whose condition there is no prospect of any improvement, is such that life-prolonging treatment is properly regarded as being, in medical terms, useless. As Sir Thomas Bingham MR pointed out in the present case, medical treatment or care may be provided for a number of different purposes. It may be provided, for example, as an aid to diagnosis, for the treatment of physical or mental injury or illness, to alleviate pain or distress, or to make the patient's condition more tolerable. Such purposes may include prolonging the patient's life, for example to enable him to survive during diagnosis and treatment. But for my part I cannot see that medical treatment is appropriate or requisite simply to prolong a patient's life when such treatment has no therapeutic purpose of any kind, as where it is futile because the patient is unconscious and there is no prospect of any improvement in his condition. It is reasonable also that account should be taken of the invasiveness of the treatment and of the indignity to which, as the present case shows, a person has to be subjected if his life is prolonged by artificial means, which must cause considerable distress to his family – a distress which reflects not only their own feelings but their perception of the situation of their relative who is being kept alive. But in the end, in a case such as the present, it is the futility of the treatment which justifies its termination. I do not consider that, in circumstances such as these, a doctor is required to initiate or to continue life-prolonging treatment or care in the best interests of his patient. It follows that no such duty rests upon the respondents, or upon Dr Howe, in the case of Anthony Bland, whose condition is in reality no more than a living death, and for whom such treatment or care would, in medical terms, be futile.

In the present case it is proposed that the doctors should be entitled to discontinue both the artificial feeding of Anthony and the use of antibiotics. It is plain from the evidence that Anthony, in his present condition, is very prone to infection and that, over some necessarily uncertain but not very long period of time, he will succumb to infection which, if unchecked, will spread and cause his death. But the effect of discontinuing the artificial feeding will be that he will inevitably die within one or two weeks.

Objection can be made to the latter course of action on the ground that Anthony will thereby be starved to death, and that this would constitute a breach of the duty to feed him which must form an essential part of the duty which every person owes to another in his care. But here again it is necessary to analyse precisely what this means in the case of Anthony. Anthony is not merely incapable of feeding himself. He is incapable of swallowing, and therefore of eating or drinking in the normal sense of those words. There is overwhelming evidence that, in the medical profession, artificial feeding is regarded as a form of medical treatment; and, even if it is not strictly medical treatment, it must form part of the medical care of the patient. Indeed, the function of artificial feeding in the case of Anthony, by means of a nasogastric tube, is to provide a form of life support analogous to that provided by a ventilator which artificially breathes air in and out of the lungs of a patient incapable of breathing normally, thereby enabling oxygen to reach the bloodstream. The same principles must apply in either case when the question is asked whether the doctor in charge may lawfully discontinue the life-sustaining treatment or care; and, if in either case the treatment is futile in the sense I have described, it can properly be concluded that it is no longer in the best interests of the patient to continue it. It is true that, in the case of discontinuance of artificial feeding, it can be said that the patient will as a result starve to death; and this may bring before our eyes the vision of an ordinary person slowly dying of hunger and suffering all the pain and distress associated with such a death. But here it is clear from the evidence that no such pain or distress will be suffered by Anthony, who can feel nothing at all. Furthermore, we are told that the outward symptoms of dying in such a way, which might otherwise cause distress to the nurses who care for him or to members of his family who visit him, can be suppressed by means of sedatives. In these circumstances, I can see no ground in the present case for refusing the declarations applied for simply because the course of action proposed involves the discontinuance of artificial feeding.

In *F v West Berkshire Health Authority* [1989] 2 All ER 545, [1990] 2 AC 1 it was stated that, where a doctor provides treatment for a person who is incapacitated from saying whether or not he consents to it, the doctor must, when deciding on the form of treatment, act in accordance with a responsible and competent body of relevant professional opinion, on the principles set down in *Bolam v Friern Hospital Management Committee* [1957] 2 All ER 118, [1957] 1 WLR 582. In my opinion, this principle must equally be applicable to decisions to initiate, or to discontinue, life support, as it is to other forms of treatment. However, in a matter of such importance and sensitivity as discontinuance of life support, it is to be expected that guidance will be provided for the profession; and, on the evidence in the present case, such guidance is for a case such as the present to be found in a discussion paper on *Treatment of Patients in Persistent Vegetative State*, issued in September 1992 by the medical ethics committee of the British Medical Association. Anybody reading this substantial paper will discover for himself the great care with which this topic is being considered by the profession. Mr Francis for the respondents drew to the attention of the Appellate Committee four safeguards in particular which, in the committee's opinion, should be observed before discontinuing life support for such patients. They are: (1) every effort should be made at rehabilitation for at least six months after the injury; (2) the diagnosis of irreversible PVS should not be considered confirmed until at least 12 months after the injury, with the effect that any decision to withhold life-prolonging treatment will be delayed for that period; (3) the diagnosis should be agreed by two other independent doctors; and (4) generally, the wishes of the patient's immediate family will be given great weight.

In fact, the views expressed by the committee on the subject of consultation with the relatives of PVS patients are consistent with the opinion expressed by your Lordships' House in *F v West Berkshire Health Authority* that it is good practice for the doctor to consult relatives. Indeed the committee recognises that, in the case of PVS patients, the relatives themselves will require a high degree of support and attention. But the committee is firmly of the opinion that the relatives' views cannot be determinative of the treatment. Indeed, if that were not so, the relatives would be able to dictate to the doctors what is in the best interests of the patient, which cannot be right. Even so, a decision to withhold life-prolonging treatment, such as artificial feeding, must require close co-operation with those close to the patient; and it is recognised that, in practice, their views and the opinions of doctors will coincide in many cases.

Study of this document left me in no doubt that if a doctor treating a PVS patient acts in accordance with the medical practice now being evolved by the medical ethics committee of the British Medical Association he will be acting with the benefit of guidance from a responsible and competent body of relevant professional opinion, as required by the *Bolam* test. I also feel that those who are concerned that a matter of life and death, such as is involved in a decision to withhold life support in a case of this kind, should be left to the doctors would do well to study this paper. The truth is that, in the course of their work, doctors frequently have to make decisions which may affect the continued survival of their patients, and are in reality far more experienced in matters of this kind than are the judges. It is nevertheless the function of the judges to state the legal principles upon which the lawfulness of the actions of doctors depend; but in the end the decisions to be made in individual cases must rest with the doctors themselves. In these circumstances, what is required is a sensitive understanding by both the judges and the doctors of each other's respective functions, and in particular a determination by the judges not merely to understand the problems facing the medical profession in cases of this kind, but also to regard their professional standards with respect. Mutual understanding between the doctors and the judges is the best way to ensure the evolution of a sensitive and sensible legal framework for the treatment and care of patients, with a sound ethical base, in the interests of the patients themselves. This is a topic to which I will return at the end of this opinion, when I come to consider the extent to which the view of the court should be sought, as a matter of practice, in cases such as the present. . . .

Certainly, in *F v West Berkshire Health Authority* your Lordships' House adopted a straightforward test based on the best interests of the patient; and I myself do not see why the same test should not be applied in the case of PVS patients, where the question is whether life-prolonging treatment should be withheld. This was also the opinion of Thomas J in *Auckland Area Health Board v A-G* [1933] 1 NZLR 235, a case concerned with the discontinuance of life support provided by ventilator to a patient suffering from the last stages of incurable Guillain-Barre syndrome. Of course, consistent with the best interests test, anything relevant to the application of the test may be taken into account; and, if the personality of the patient is relevant to the application of the test (as it may be in cases where the various relevant factors have to be weighed), it may be taken into account, as was done in *Re J (a minor) (wardship: medical treatment)* [1990] 3 All ER 930, [1991] Fam 33. But, where the question is whether life support should be withheld from a PVS patient, it is difficult to see how the personality of the patient can be relevant, though it may be of comfort to his relatives if they believe, as in the present case, and indeed may well be so in many other cases, that the patient would not have wished his life to be artificially prolonged if he was totally unconscious and there was no hope of improvement in his condition.

I wish to add however that, like the courts below, I have derived assistance and support from decisions in a number of American jurisdictions to the effect that it is lawful to discontinue life-prolonging treatment in the case of PVS patients where there is no prospect of improvement in their condition. Furthermore, I wish to refer to the section in Working Paper No 28 (1982) on *Euthanasia, Aiding Suicide and Cessation of Treatment* published by the Law Reform Commission of Canada concerned with cessation of treatment, to which I also wish to express my indebtedness. I believe the legal principles as I have stated them to be broadly consistent with the conclusions summarised in the Working Paper (at pp 65-66), which was substantially accepted in the Report of the Commission (1983) pp 32-35. Indeed, I entertain a strong sense that a community of view on the legal principles applicable in cases of discontinuing life support is in the course of development and acceptance throughout the common law world.

In setting out my understanding of the relevant principles, I have had very much in mind the submissions advanced by Mr Munby on behalf of the Official Solicitor, and I believe that I have answered, directly or indirectly, all his objections to the course now proposed. I do not, therefore, intend any disrespect to his argument if I do not answer each of his submissions seriatim. In summary, his two principal arguments were as follows. First, he submitted that the discontinuance of artificial feeding would constitute an act which would inevitably cause, and be intended to cause, Anthony's death; and as such, it would be unlawful, and indeed criminal. As will be plain from what I have already said, I cannot accept this proposition. In my opinion, for the reasons I have already given, there is no longer any duty upon the doctors to continue with this form of medical treatment or care in his case, and it follows that it cannot be unlawful to discontinue it. Second, he submitted that discontinuance of the artificial feeding of Anthony would be a breach of the doctor's duty to care for and feed him; and since it will (as it is intended to do) cause his death, it will necessarily be unlawful. I have considered this point earlier in this opinion, when I expressed my view that artificial feeding is, in a case such as the present, no different from life support by a ventilator, and as such can lawfully be discontinued when it no longer fulfils any therapeutic purpose. To me, the crucial point in which I found myself differing from Mr Munby was that I was unable to accept his treating the discontinuance of artificial feeding in the present case as equivalent to cutting a mountaineer's rope, or severing the air pipe of a deep sea diver. Once it is recognised, as I believe it must be, that the true question is not whether the doctor should take a course in which he will actively kill his patient, but rather whether he should continue to provide his patient with medical treatment or care which, if continued, will prolong his life, then, as I see it, the essential basis of Mr Munby's submission disappears. I wish to add that I was unable to accept his suggestion that recent decisions show that the law is proceeding down a 'slippery slope', in the sense that the courts are becoming more and more ready to allow doctors to take steps which will result in the ending of life. On the contrary, as I have attempted to demonstrate, the courts are acting within a structure of legal principle, under which in particular they continue to draw a clear distinction between the bounds of lawful treatment of a living patient and unlawful euthanasia.

I turn finally to the extent to which doctors should, as a matter of practice, seek the guidance of the court, by way of an application for declaratory relief, before withholding life-prolonging treatment from a PVS patient. Sir Stephen Brown P considered that the opinion of the court should be sought in all cases similar to the present. In the Court of Appeal Sir Thomas Bingham MR expressed his agreement with Sir Stephen Brown P in the following words (see p 842, ante):

> This was in my respectful view a wise ruling, directed to the protection of patients, the protection of doctors, the reassurance of patients' families and the reassurance of the public. The practice proposed seems to me desirable. It may well be that with the passage of time a body of experience and practice will build up which will obviate the need for application in every case but for the time being I am satisfied that the practice which Sir Stephen Brown P described should be followed.

Before the Appellate Committee this view was supported both by Mr Munby for the Official Solicitor and by Mr Lester as amicus curiae. For the respondents, Mr Francis suggested that an adequate safeguard would be provided if reference to the court was required in certain specific cases, ie (1) where there was known to be a medical disagreement as to the diagnosis or prognosis, and (2) problems had arisen with the patient's relatives – disagreement by the next of kin with the medical recommendation; actual or apparent conflict of interest between the next of kin and the patient; dispute between members of the patient's family; or absence of any next of kin to give their consent. There is, I consider, much to be said for the view that an application to the court will not be needed in every case, but only in particular circumstances, such as those suggested by Mr Francis. In this connection I was impressed not only by the care being taken by the medical ethics committee to provide guidance to the profession, but also by information given to the Appellate Committee about the substantial number of PVS patients in the country, and the very considerable cost of obtaining guidance from the court in cases such as the present. However, in my opinion this is a matter which would be better kept under review by the President of the Family Division than resolved now by your Lordships' House. I understand that a similar review is being undertaken in cases concerned with the sterilisation of adult women of unsound mind, with a consequent relaxation of the practice relating to applications to the court in such cases. For my part, I would therefore leave the matter as proposed by Sir Thomas Bingham MR; but I wish to express the hope that the President of the Family Division, who will no doubt be kept well informed about developments in this field, will soon feel able to relax the present requirement so as to limit applications for declarations to those cases in which there is a special need for the procedure to be invoked. . . .

For these reasons, I would dismiss the appeal.

Lord Keith and Lord Lowry, while delivering short concurring speeches, agreed with the reasons given by Lord Goff.

Lord Keith: The first point to make is that it is unlawful, so as to constitute both a tort and the crime of battery, to administer medical treatment to an adult, who is conscious and of sound mind, without his consent: see *F v West Berkshire Health Authority (Mental Health Act Commission intervening)*[1989] 2 All ER 545, [1990] 2 AC 1. Such a person is completely at liberty to decline to undergo treatment, even if the result of his doing so will be that he will die. This extends to the situation where the person, in anticipation of this, through one cause or another, entering into a condition such as PVS, gives clear instructions that in such event he is not to be given medical care, including artificial feeding, designed to keep him alive . . .

The object of medical treatment and care is to benefit the patient. It may do so by taking steps to prevent the occurrence of illness, or, if an illness does occur, by taking steps towards curing it. Where an illness or the effects of an injury cannot be cured, then efforts are directed towards preventing deterioration or relieving pain and suffering. In Anthony Bland's case the first imperative was to prevent him from dying, as he would certainly have done in the absence of the steps that were taken. If he had died, there can be no doubt that the cause of this would have been the injuries which he had suffered. As it was, the steps taken prevented him from dying, and there was instituted the course of treatment and care which still continues. For a time, no doubt, there was some hope that he might recover sufficiently for him to be able to live a life that had some meaning. Some patients who have suffered damage to the cerebral cortex have, indeed, made a complete recovery. It all depends on the degree of damage. But sound medical opinion takes the view that if a PVS patient shows no signs of recovery after six months, or at most a year, then there is no prospect of any recovery. There are techniques available which make it possible to ascertain the state of the cerebral cortex, and in Anthony Bland's case these indicate that, as mentioned above, it has degenerated into a mass of watery fluid. The fundamental question then comes to be whether continuance of the present regime of treatment and care, more than three years after the injuries that resulted in the PVS, would confer any benefit on Anthony Bland. . . .

In the case of a permanently insensate being, who if continuing to live would never experience the slightest actual discomfort, it is difficult, if not impossible, to make any relevant comparison between continued existence and the absence of it. It is, however, perhaps permissible to say that to an individual with no cognitive capacity whatever, and no prospect of ever recovering any such capacity in this world, it must be a matter of complete indifference whether he lives or dies.

Where one individual has assumed responsibility for the care of another who cannot look after himself or herself, whether as a medical practitioner or otherwise, that responsibility cannot lawfully be shed unless arrangements are made for the responsibility to be taken over by someone else. Thus a person having charge of a baby who fails to feed it, so that it dies, will be guilty at least of manslaughter. The same is true of one having charge of an adult who is frail and cannot look after herself: see *R v Stone* [1977] 2 All ER 341, [1977] QB 354. It was argued for the guardian ad litem, by analogy with that case, that here the doctors in charge of Anthony Bland had a continuing duty to feed him by means of the nasogastric tube and that if they failed to carry out that duty they were guilty of manslaughter, if not murder. This was coupled with the argument that feeding him by means of the nasogastric tube was not medical treatment at all, but simply feeding indistinguishable from feeding by normal means. As regards this latter argument, I am of opinion that regard should be had to the whole regime, including the artificial feeding, which at present keeps Anthony Bland alive. That regime amounts to medical treatment and care, and it is incorrect to direct attention exclusively to the fact that nourishment is being provided. In any event, the administration of nourishment by the means adopted involves the application of a medical technique. But it is, of course, true that in general it would not be lawful for a medical practitioner who assumed responsibility for the care of an unconscious patient simply to give up treatment in circumstances where continuance of it would confer some benefit on the patient. On the other hand a medical practitioner is under no duty to continue to treat such a patient where a large body of informed and responsible medical opinion is to the effect that no benefit at all would be conferred by continuance. Existence in a vegetative state with no prospect of recovery is by that opinion regarded as not being a benefit, and that, if not unarguably correct, at least forms a proper basis for the decision to discontinue treatment and care: see *Bolam v Friern Hospital Management Committee* [1957] 2 All ER 118, [1957] 1 WLR 582. . . .

The decision whether or not the continued treatment and care of a PVS patient confers any benefit on him is essentially one for the practitioners in charge of his case. The question is whether any decision that it does not and that the treatment and care should therefore be discontinued should as a matter of routine be brought before the Family Division for indorsement or the reverse. The view taken by Sir Stephen Brown P and the Court of Appeal was that it should, at least for the time being and until a body of experience and practice has been built up which might obviate the need for application in every case. As Sir Thomas Bingham MR said (at p 842, ante), this would be in the interests of the protection of patients, the protection of doctors, the reassurance of patients' families and the reassurance of the public. I respectfully agree that these considerations render desirable the practice of application.

Lord Lowry: In answer to the respondents' reliance on accepted medical opinion that feeding (nutrition and hydration), particularly by sophisticated artificial methods, is part of the life-supporting medical treatment, [the Official Solicitor] says that the duty to feed a helpless person, such as a baby or an unconscious patient, is something different – an elementary duty to keep the patient alive which exists independently of all questions of treatment and which the person in charge cannot omit to perform: to omit deliberately to perform this duty in the knowledge that the omission will lead to the death of the helpless one, and indeed with the intention, as in the present case, of conducing to that death, will render those in charge guilty of murder. One of the respondents' counter-arguments, albeit not conclusive, is based on the overwhelming verdict of informed medical opinion worldwide, with particular reference to the common law jurisdictions, where the relevant law generally corresponds closely with our own, that therapy and life-supporting care, including sophisticated methods of artificial feeding, are components of medical treatment and cannot be separated as the Official Solicitor contends. In this connection it may also be emphasised that an artificial feeding regime is inevitably associated with the continuous use of catheters and enemas and the sedulous avoidance and combating of potentially deadly infection. I consider that the court, when intent on reaching a decision according to law, ought to give weight to informed medical opinion both on the point now under discussion and also on the question of what is in the best interests of a patient. . . .

The real answer to the Official Solicitor, as your Lordships are already agreed, is that his argument starts from the fallacious premise, which can be taken as correct in ordinary doctor-patient relationships, namely that feeding in order to sustain life is *necessarily* for the benefit of the patient. But in the prevailing circumstances the opposite view is over-whelmingly held by the doctors and the validity of that view has been accepted by the courts below. The doctors consider that in the patient's best interests they ought not to feed him and the law, as applied by your Lordships, has gone further by saying that they are not entitled to feed him without his consent, which cannot be obtained. So the theory of the 'duty to feed' is founded on a misapprehension and the Official Solicitor's argument leads to a legally erroneous conclusion. Even though the intention to bring about the patient's death is there, there is no proposed guilty act because, if it is not in the interests of an insentient patient to continue the life-supporting care and treatment, the doctor would be acting unlawfully if he continued the care and treatment and would perform no guilty act by discontinuing.

Lord Browne-Wilkinson delivered speeches agreeing that the appeal should be dismissed.

I. Understanding *Bland*. *Nature of the duty* – The House of Lords confirmed that the relevant test to determine a doctor's duty was that of 'best interests'. The judges relied upon their earlier decision in *Re F*. The interesting question is how the judges explained the meaning of that test. All agreed that the correct question was whether it was in Anthony Bland's 'best interests' to continue to receive treatment and not whether it was in his 'best interests' to die. To some, this question involved the traditional concern whether there was any benefit accruing to the patient by the continuation of the treatment (per Lord Goff, Lord Lowry and Lord Browne-Wilkinson, *sed quaere* Lord Keith). They accepted that Tony Bland was permanently insensate. Thus, he could not possibly benefit, since his condition could not be improved. Lord Goff, you will recall, referred to the treatment as being in 'medical terms futile'. Further, it was burdensome to Tony Bland by reason of 'the invasiveness of the treatment and of [its] indignity . . .'

To others of their Lordships (Lord Mustill and, perhaps, Lord Keith), however, if 'best interests' means weighing the benefits of treatment against the burdens of treatment and non-treatment, this could have alarming implications when what is being weighed is, in effect, whether the patient lives or dies. Thus, for these judges, the task was to endorse 'best interests' as the test generally but then immediately to try to find a way to avoid what they saw as its implications in the case. The way they chose was to say that in a case of PVS the law need not proceed to weigh the various interests of the patient because the patient by being permanently insensate *has no interests*. In particular, the patient has no interest in treatment being continued.

Lord Keith: In the case of a permanently insensate being, who if continuing to live would never experience the slightest actual discomfort, it is difficult, if not impossible, to make any relevant comparison between continued existence and the absence of it. It is, however, perhaps permissible to say that to an individual with no cognitive capacity whatever, and no prospect of ever recovering any such capacity in this world, it must be a matter of complete indifference whether he lives or dies.

The argument is more elaborately put by Lord Mustill.

Lord Mustill: Just as in *F v West Berkshire Health Authority*, so the argument runs, the best interests of the patient demand a course of action which would normally be unlawful without the patient's consent. Just as in *F v West Berkshire Health Authority* the patient is unable to decide for himself. In practice, to make no decision is to decide that the care and treatment shall continue. So that the decision shall not thus be made by default it is necessary that someone other than Anthony Bland should consider whether in his own best interests his life should now be brought to an end, and if the answer is affirmative the proposed conduct can be put into effect without risk of criminal responsibility.

I cannot accept this argument, which, if sound, would serve to legitimate a termination by much more direct means than are now contemplated. I can accept that a doctor in charge of a patient suffering the mental torture of Guillain-Barre syndrome, rational but trapped and mute in an unresponsive body, could well feel it imperative that a decision on whether to terminate life could wait no longer and that the only possible decision in the interests of the patient, even leaving out all the other interests involved, would be to end it here and now by a speedy and painless injection. Such a conclusion would attract much sympathy, but no doctrine of best interests could bring it within the law.

Quite apart from this the case of Anthony Bland seems to me quite different. He feels no pain and suffers no mental anguish. Stress was laid in argument on the damage to his personal dignity by the continuation of the present medical regime, and on the progressive erosion of the family's happy recollections by month after month of distressing and hopeless care. Considerations of this kind will do doubt carry great weight when Parliament comes to consider the whole question in the round. But it seems to me to be stretching the concept of personal rights beyond breaking point to say that Anthony Bland has an interest in ending these sources of others' distress. Unlike the conscious patient he does not know what is happening to his body, and cannot be affronted by it; he does not know of his family's continuing sorrow. By ending his life the doctors will not relieve him of a burden become intolerable, for others carry the burden and he has none. What other considerations could make it better for him to die now rather than later? None that we can measure, for of death we know nothing. The distressing truth which must not be shirked is that the proposed conduct is not in the best interests of Anthony Bland, for he has no best interests of any kind. . . .

After much expression of negative opinions I turn to an argument which in my judgment is logically defensible and consistent with the existing law. In essence it turns the previous argument on its head by directing the inquiry to the interests of the patient, not in the termination of life but in the continuation of his treatment. It runs as follows. (i) The cessation of nourishment and hydration is an omission not an act. (ii) Accordingly, the cessation will not be a criminal act unless the doctors are under a present duty to continue the regime. (iii) At the time when Anthony Bland came into the care of the doctors decisions had to be made about his care which he was unable to make for himself. In accordance with *F v West Berkshire Health Authority* [1989] 2 All ER 545, [1990] 2 AC 1 these decisions were to be made in his best interests. Since the possibility that he might recover still existed his best interests required that he should be supported in the hope that this would happen. These best interests justified the application of the necessary regime without his consent. (iv) All hope of recovery has now been abandoned. Thus, although the termination of his life is not in the best interests of Anthony Bland, his best interests in being kept alive have also disappeared, taking with them the justification for the non-consensual regime and the correlative duty to keep it in being. (v) Since there is no longer a duty to provide nourishment and hydration a failure to do so cannot be a criminal offence. . . .

I therefore consider the argument to be soundly based. Now that the time has come when Anthony Bland has no further interest in being kept alive, the necessity to do so, created by his inability to make a choice, has gone; and the justification for the invasive care and treatment together with the duty to provide it have also gone. Absent a duty, the omission to perform what had previously been a duty will no longer be a breach of the criminal law.

Whose decision? – Their Lordships make it clear that it is the doctor, following *Re F*, who applies the 'best interests' test in any particular case (or, in the case of a child, the parents in consultation with the doctor). Just as we saw, however, in the cases on sterilisation of intellectually disabled women (see Chapter 10), the Law Lords were anxious that, at least for a time, the court should have a supervisory role (*per* Lord Keith, Lord Goff, Lord Lowry and Lord Browne-Wilkinson). The Law Lords approved the view of Sir Thomas Bingham MR expressed in the Court of Appeal:

> **Sir Thomas Bingham MR:** [In] cases of this kind application should be made to the court to obtain its sanction for the course proposed. This was in my respectful view a wise ruling, directed to the protection of patients, the protection of doctors, the reassurance of patients' families and the reassurance of the public. The practice proposed seems to me desirable. It may very well be that with the passage of time a body of experience and practice will build up which will obviate the need for application in every case, but for the time being I am satisfied that the practice . . . should be followed.

II. Questions which arise from *Bland*. *The relevance of Bolam* – Four of the Law Lords regarded the *Bolam* test as a central factor in determining the doctor's duty ie, in determining whether to continue treatment is in the patient's 'best interests'. For example, Lord Browne-Wilkinson put it as follows (at 882):

> [A] doctor's decision whether invasive care is in the best interests of the patient falls to be assessed by reference to the test laid down in *Bolam v Friern Hospital Management Committee* [1957] 2 All ER 118, [1957] 1 WLR 582, viz is the decision in accordance with a practice accepted at the time by a responsible body of medical opinion?

The difficulty of using *Bolam* to determine the *legality* of a doctor's conduct as opposed to its reasonableness, is made clear by Lord Mustill (at 895):

> I venture to feel some reservations about the application of the principle of civil liability in negligence laid down in *Bolam v Friern Hospital Management Committee* [1957] 2 All ER 118, [1957] 1 WLR 582 to decisions on 'best interests' in a field dominated by the criminal law. I accept without difficulty that this principle applies to the ascertainment of the medical raw materials such as diagnosis, prognosis and appraisal of the patient's cognitive functions. Beyond this point, however, it may be said that the decision is ethical, not medical, and that there is no reason in logic why on such a decision the opinions of doctors should be decisive. If there had been a possibility that this question might make a difference to the outcome of the appeal I would have wished to consider it further, but since it does not I prefer for the moment to express no opinion upon it.

As we saw in Chapter 4, the genesis of the approach in *Bland* is the House of Lords decision in *Re F*. In that case, the court (in our view, quite without justification) translated a test from an area in which it sits at best uncomfortably (medical negligence) to an area where it has no place at all, ie judgments as to the legality of future professional conduct. *Bolam* may have a place in facilitating the evaluation of conduct after a mishap has taken place. It is hard to argue that it has a place when the enquiry is not concerned with the responsibility for the mishap but how to respond to it. In our view, the latter question cannot be a matter of professional opinion and practice and in deciding that it is, the House of Lords has taken the law in the wrong direction.

In the Court of Appeal in *Bland*, Hoffman LJ (at 858) would have taken the law in a different direction.

> **Hoffman LJ:** Sir Stephen Brown P laid some emphasis upon the fact that according to professional medical opinion and the BMA's statement on ethics, ending artificial feeding would be

in accordance with good medical practice. Some have felt concern at the suggestion that questions of whether patients should live or die should be decided according to what was thought to be good practice by the medical profession. Once again, I sympathise with this concern.

I do not think that Sir Stephen Brown P was saying that the views of the medical profession should determine the legal and moral questions which I have discussed in this judgment. Nor do I think that the profession would be grateful to the court for leaving the full responsibility for such decisions in its hands. It seems to me that the medical profession can tell the court about the patient's condition and prognosis and about the probable consequences of giving or not giving certain kinds of treatment or care, including the provision of artificial feeding. But whether in those circumstances it would be lawful to provide or withhold the treatment or care is a matter for the law and must be decided with regard to the general moral considerations of which I have spoken. As to these matters, the medical profession will no doubt have views which are entitled to great respect, but I would expect medical ethics to be formed by the law rather than the reverse.

An irony of the approach adopted by the Law Lords is that it appears to have been unnecessary. If Lord Goff's speech is seen as representing the majority view, it is clear that by reference to the general principle of 'best interests' he had already reached the conclusion that Tony Bland need no longer be treated with artificial hydration and nutrition. The reliance on *Bolam* seems at best designed to bolster him in the conclusion he had already reached, rather than provide the critical legal justification for that conclusion.

Duty not to treat? – When the doctor arrives at the conclusion that it is not in the patient's 'best interests' to continue treatment any longer, what must he do? On one view, he may have a discretion to withdraw treatment. On another view, however, once the doctor decides that continuation is not in the patient's 'best interests' his legal licence to treat (following *Re F*) no longer exists and he *must cease* treatment. In *Bland* Lord Browne-Wilkinson and Lord Lowry clearly endorse this latter view.

Lord Browne-Wilkinson: [I]f there comes a stage where the responsible doctor comes to the reasonable conclusion (which accords with the views of a responsible body of medical opinion) that further continuance of an intrusive life support system is not in the best interests of the patient, he can no longer lawfully continue that life support system: to do so would constitute the crime of battery and the tort of trespass to the person. Therefore he cannot be in breach of any duty to maintain the patient's life . . . perpetuation of life can only be achieved if it is lawful to continue to invade the bodily integrity of the patient by invasive medical care. Unless the doctor has reached the affirmative conclusion that it is in the patient's best interest to continue the invasive care, such care must cease.

(See also Lord Lowry at 876-877, *supra*.)

Lord Browne-Wilkinson's categorical assertion that to continue to treat after a determination that it would not be in the best interests of the patient to do so, would be a tort and a crime, although entailed from his previous analysis, is not free from difficulty. Consider the case of a patient from whom it is hoped to remove a kidney to transplant into another. A number of hospitals have adopted the practice of managing the dying of a patient in such a way that vital organs intended for transplantation will not be damaged in the process of dying. If Lord Browne-Wilkinson's views were taken literally this practice, which is already of doubtful ethical and legal propriety, would most certainly be unlawful. In this context it is interesting to notice Lord Browne-Wilkinson's comment (at p 879):

. . . it is not legitimate in reaching a view as to what is for the benefit of one individual whose life is in issue to take into account the impact on third parties of altering the time at which death occurs.

A corollorary of Lord Browne-Wilkinson's approach is that just as the doctor is not entitled to continue treatment so the relatives may not insist on treatment being continued. Further, a doctor may not purport to justify a continuation of treatment simply by reference to requests by the relatives (see discussion of *Re J* [1992] 4 All ER 614 *supra*, p 273).

Hydration and nutrition: is it treatment? – The House of Lords refused to draw a distinction between the provision of food and fluids by artificial means (eg by naso-gastric tube) and medical treatment. It was argued by the Official Solicitor that artificial hydration and nutrition were of a different order from medical treatment since they represented the basic necessities of life. Thus, while medical treatment might be withheld or discontinued, food and water could not be, not least because the patient would then starve to death. As to this argument, as the speeches set out earlier make clear, Lord Keith and Lord Lowry describe hydration and nutrition as being included within the general term 'medical treatment'. Lord Goff, less helpfully, holds that if not 'medical treatment' they are 'part of the medical care' of the patient.

In deciding this issue in this way, the House of Lords avoids (at least as regards *artificial* hydration and nutrition), the controversy which dogged the American courts because of its emotive association with both euthanasia and suicide until the US Supreme Court's decision in *Cruzan v Director, Missouri Department of Health* (1990) 110 SCt 2841. While the plurality of the US Supreme Court did not specifically address the question, Justice O'Connor (in her concurrence) and Justice Brennan (in his dissent, with whom Marshall and Blackmun JJ agreed) both reached the same view as the House of Lords in *Bland*.

Cruzan v Director, Missouri Department of Health (1990) 110 S Ct 2841 (US Sup Ct)

Justice O'Connor: Artificial feeding cannot readily be distinguished from other forms of medical treatment. See, eg, Council on Ethical and Judicial Affairs, American Medical Association, AMA Ethical Opinion 2.20, Withholding or Withdrawing Life-Prolonging Medical Treatment. Current Opinions 13 (1989); The Hastings Center, Guidelines on the Termination of Life-Sustaining Treatment and the Care of the Dying 59 (1987). Whether or not the techniques used to pass food and water into the patient's alimentary tract are termed 'medical treatment' it is clear they all involve some degree of intrusion and restraint. Feeding a patient by means of a nasogastric tube requires a physician to pass a long flexible tube through the patient's nose, throat and esophagus and into the stomach. Because of the discomfort such a tube causes, '[m]any patients need to be restrained forcibly and their hands put into large mittens to prevent them from removing the tube.' Major, The Medical Procedures for Providing Food and Water: Indications and Side Effects, in By No Extraordinary Means: The Choice to Forgo Life-Sustaining Food and Water 25 (J Lynn ed 1986). A gastrostomy tube (as was used to provide food and water to Nancy Cruzan, see *ante*, at 2) or jejunostomy tube must be surgically implanted into the stomach or small intestine. Office of Technology Assessment Task Force, Life-Sustaining Technologies and the Elderly 282 (1988). Requiring a competent adult to endure such procedures against her will burdens the patient's liberty, dignity, and freedom to determine the course of her own treatment. Accordingly, the liberty guaranteed by the Due Process Clause must protect, if it protects anything, an individual's deeply personal decision to reject medical treatment, including the artificial delivery of food and water.

Justice Brennan: No material distinction can be drawn between the treatment to which Nancy Cruzan continues to be subject – artificial nutrition and hydration – and any other medical treatment. See *ante*, (O'Connor, J, concurring). The artificial delivery of nutrition and hydration is undoubtedly medical treatment. The technique to which Nancy Cruzan is subject – artificial feeding through a gastrostomy tube – involves a tube implanted surgically into her stomach through incisions in her abdominal wall. It may obstruct the intestinal tract, erode and pierce the stomach wall or cause leakage of the stomach's contents into the abdominal cavity. See Page, Andrassy, & Sandler, Techniques in Delivery of Liquid Diets, in Nutrition in Clinical Surgery 66-67 (M Deitel 2d edn 1985). The tube can cause pneumonia from redux of the stomach's contents into the lung. See Bernard & Forlaw, Complications and Their Prevention, in Enteral and Tube Feeding 553 (J Rombeau & M Caldwell eds 1984). Typically, and in this case (see Tr 377), commercially prepared formulas are used, rather than fresh food. See Matarese, Enteral Alimentation, in Surgical Nutrition 726 (J Fischer edn 1983). The type of formula and method of administration must be experimented with to avoid gastrointestinal problems. *Id*, at 748. The patient must be monitored daily by medical personnel as to weight, fluid intake and fluid output; blood tests must be done weekly. *Id*, at 749, 751.

Artificial delivery of food and water is regarded as medical treatment by the medical profession and the Federal Government. According to the American Academy of Neurology, '[t]he artificial provision of nutrition and hydration is a form of medical treatment . . . analogous to other forms of life-sustaining treatment, such as the use of the respirator. When a patient is unconscious, both a respirator and an artificial feeding device serve to support or replace normal bodily functions that are compromised as a result of the patient's illness.' Position of the American Academy of Neurology on Certain Aspects of the Care and Management of the Persistent Vegetative State Patient, 39 Neurology 125 (Jan 1989). See also Council on Ethical and Judicial Affairs of the American Medical Association, Current Opinions, Opinion 2.20 (1989) ('Life-prolonging medical treatment includes medication and artificially or technologically supplied respiration, nutrition or hydration'); President's Commission 88 (life-sustaining treatment includes respirators, kidney dialysis machines, special feeding procedures).

But where does that leave hydration and nutrition which is not artificially administered, eg where the patient can swallow and is spoon-fed? Is this a form of medical treatment and thus may be discontinued or withheld? Or, is it a separate regime of care which the doctor is obliged to continue even though the patient's condition is hopeless and further medical treatment is agreed to be futile? In our view, the solution to the problem does not lie in the process of labelling the intervention as 'treatment' or 'care' or indeed anything else. Instead, the solution lies in reminding ourselves that the doctor's obligation is to act in the 'best interests' of the patient which in the example we have given means that the patient be allowed to die. Continuing to spoon-feed the patient would frustrate this end and thus would not be in the patient's 'best interests'. Of course, the validity of this analysis must be set against the quite natural repugnance some might feel at the idea of denying a patient what look like the basic requirements of life. Indeed, this repugnance may persuade a court to accept that there is a difference between artificial feeding and spoon-feeding. In *Re Conroy*, the New Jersey Supreme Court did precisely this:

Schrieber J: Once one enters the realms of complex, high-technology medical care, it is hard to shed the 'emotional symbolism' of food. *See Barber, 147 Cal.App.3d* at 1016, 195 *Cal.Rptr.* at 490. However, artificial feedings such as nasogastric tubes, gastrostomies, and intravenous infusions are significantly different from bottle-feeding or spoonfeeding – they are medical procedures with inherent risks and possible side effects, instituted by skilled health-care providers to compensate for impaired physical functioning.

While understandable, we think this is wrong. This is not to say that we argue that the patient should suffer before he dies. Rather, we revert to the doctor's general duty to comfort which would entitle the doctor to administer whatever medicine necessary to alleviate any distress which may be caused to the patient.

Substituted judgment? – Tony Bland had never expressed any views on what should be done if he was ever rendered incompetent. As we saw in Chapter 4, in such a case the court (or indeed anyone else) cannot apply the 'substituted judgment' test, ie determine what the patient would have wished in the light of his previously expressed views and values. Therefore, any decision *must* be based upon the 'best interests' test. Nevertheless, both Lord Goff and Lord Mustill went out of their way to reject the 'substituted judgment' test as not being part of English law (see *supra,* pp 288-289). It may be said that both judges' rejection of it was based upon a misunderstanding of the true nature of the test (*supra,* p 289). (For a proper application of the 'substituted judgment' tests in a PVS case, see Garibaldi and Handler JJ in *Re Jobes* (1987) 529 A 2d 434 (NJ Sup Ct).) As Handler J put it in *Re Jobes*: 'the decision to discontinue or to refuse treatment was made by the patient's guardian on the basis of *trustworthy* evidence of what the patient would have decided' (our emphasis). (See also, *Brophy v New England Sinai Hospital* (1986) 497 NE 2d 626 (Mass Sup Jud Ct); *In Re Estate of Longeway* (1989) 549 NE 2d 292 (Ill Sup Ct) and see the cases discussed in *Cruzan, supra.*)

We have already examined the test of 'substituted judgment' in some detail. It is our view that properly understood and applied appropriately it could, and should, have a place in English law and the courts should adopt it. Having said this, the Law Commission's Consultation Paper No 129, *Mentally Incapacitated Adults and Decision-Making: Medical Treatment and Research* (April 1993) specifically rejects it in favour of a modified version of the best interests test:

> 12. In deciding whether a proposed medical treatment is in the best interests of an incapacitated person, consideration should be given to:
>   (1) the ascertainable past and present wishes and feelings (considered in the light of his or her understanding at the time) of the incapacitated person;
>   (2) whether there is an alternative to the proposed treatment, and in particular whether there is an alternative which is more conservative or which is less intrusive or restrictive;
>   (3) the factors which the incapacitated person might be expected to consider if able to do so, including the likely effect of the treatment on the person's life expectancy, health, happiness, freedom and dignity.

The difficulty with this proposal is that it appears to look simultaneously in two different directions. It both looks to the objective 'best interests' of the patient and urges that account be taken, in effect, of what the patient himself considered to be in his 'best interests'. No solution is offered for the situation in which these two do not coincide. In so far as the English courts seem always to fall back on the 'best interests' test, any such conflict would be decided by reference to what *others* consider to be in the patient's best interests, thereby weakening any purported concern to take account of the patient's views.

III. Applying *Bland* Beyond PVS. On one view the law as expressed by the Law Lords in *Bland* is applicable only to decisions regarding the treatment of patients in PVS. The judges appeared prepared to accept the lawfulness of withholding or withdrawing treatment because Tony Bland was permanently insensate, which they took to mean that he no longer had any interests which counted in any calculation of his best interests (see especially, *per* Lord Keith and Lord Mustill). The much more difficult question concerning medical decisions when the patient is *not* insensate clearly troubled the court. It is to this question that we must turn. First, however, we must notice that the borderline between patients who are insensate and those who are not is by no means well defined. The New Zealand case of *Auckland AHB v Attorney-General* [1993] 1 NZLR 235, cited with approval by Lords Goff and Mustill in *Bland*, offers an example.

Auckland AHB v Attorney General [1993] 1 NZLR 235 (NZ HCt)

Thomas J: At the present moment Mr L is lying in a hospital bed in the intensive care unit of the Auckland Hospital. He is suffering from an extreme case of Guillain-Barre syndrome. This terrible disease affects the nervous system. Although Mr L is not what is called 'brain dead', his brain is unable to communicate with his body or his body with his brain. The two are disconnected. In stark terms, Mr L has a living, but impaired, brain which is entirely disengaged from his body. So he cannot move a muscle or limb. He lies lifeless and motionless, unable to communicate by even elementary means. His condition is so severe that he has no prospect of recovery.

If nature were to have taken its course Mr L would long since be dead. None of his 'vital functions' would be active. But as part of his early treatment he was connected with a ventilatory-support system. By this mechanical means his breathing and heartbeat were maintained. Now, many months later, it is clear that his condition will never improve and that there is no therapeutic or medical benefit in continuing with the artificial ventilation. The unanimous view of eight specialists who have examined Mr L is that the support cannot be medically justified.

If and when the artificial ventilation is discontinued, Mr L will suffer an almost immediate cardiac arrest and quickly, but painlessly, die. Otherwise he will continue to exist in his current condition indefinitely.

In these tragic circumstances, the doctors who have been caring for Mr L decided to withdraw the ventilatory support. They have the full support of Mrs L, and they have adopted and meticulously followed a cautious procedure in reaching their decision . . .

The question in issue, therefore, is whether the doctors' action in withdrawing the artificial ventilatory-support system from Mr L would make them guilty of culpable homicide . . .

[T]he Auckland Area Health Board seek to establish . . . that the doctors would not, in withdrawing Mr L's ventilator in the circumstances of this case, be guilty of culpable homicide and that, for that purpose, ss 151(1) and 164 [of the Crimes Act 1961] have no application to this case. . . .

Mr L was born on 13 April 1933. He is now 59 years old. He was a truck driver, and he and his wife lived in Eltham. On about 14 March 1990 Mr L was involved in a motor vehicle accident. He was admitted to Taranaki Base Hospital suffering from facial and rib fractures. A left femoral fracture was fixed internally with a pin. Mr L was discharged from the hospital and readmitted on 17 July 1991 to have the pin removed. At this stage, he was apparently well. He was discharged again on 22 July 1991 but returned to the hospital the following day suffering from numbness in his right hand.

On 26 July Mr L was readmitted to the Taranaki Base Hospital suffering from numbness in his other hand. He was unable to raise his arms. Upon his readmission, doctors noted that Mr L suffered profound weakness in both arms, weakness in his hips and a complete loss of deep tendon reflexes. Arrangements were made for him to be transferred to the neurology ward at Auckland Hospital on 29 July. He was brought into the hospital in a wheelchair in a weak state and a diagnosis of Guillain-Barre syndrome was confirmed.

Mr L's condition continued to deteriorate. The Guillain-Barre syndrome started to adversely affect his ability to breathe. On 4 August Mr L was transferred to the department of critical care medicine to guard against the possibility that he might require artificial ventilation. Initially, he did not require this assistance and was transferred back to the neurological ward but, later in the same day, he was brought back and connected to an artificial ventilator. Since 4 August of last year Mr L has been completely dependent upon artificial ventilation. On 5 August a tracheostomy was performed to facilitate his care.

The deterioration continued. Mr L lost the ability to move his limbs altogether. He could not control any muscles governed by the brain stem, including the muscles in his face and eyes. For a while the doctors were able to establish limited communication with him, but by 11 August he could barely blink, either to communicate or to keep his corneas lubricated. By 15 August there was only a flicker of eyebrow movement and Mr L was totally paralysed. His eyeball muscles became inert and his pupils became fixed and dilated.

Extensive tests undertaken by the doctors revealed a complete absence of conduction along Mr L's nerves and the degeneration of the nerve axons. Beginning with marked demyelination, the syndrome had progressed to secondary axonal degeneration. The nerves involving hearing do not function and, although the visual pathways are seemingly intact when tested neurophysiologically, it is not known whether Mr L receives visual impressions or not. (The visual function is not wholly dependent on the peripheral nervous system.) As best as can be ascertained, Mr L's brain is in a drowsy semi-working state, but this is probably due to sensory deprivation rather than brain damage. Mr L has no responses and displays no awareness to anything happening in his room or to himself. His muscles have now degenerated and are transforming into useless fibrous tissue.

Mr L is not brain dead. However, in effect, his brain is not connected to any part of his body apart, possibly, from his visual faculties. He is denervated and unable to interact in any way with his environment. He is properly described as being in a 'locked in' and 'locked out' state. For that reason, he is incapable of an independent existence and is completely dependent on artificial ventilatory support.

Mr L's prognosis is now hopeless. It must be concluded that his condition is irreversible. Overseas opinions which were obtained 10 months ago may have held out some remote hope of improvement, but no evidence emerged to justify even that guarded optimism. Dr Trubuhovich reiterated in cross-examination that a current examination had confirmed that the degeneration is continuing and that there is no sign of improvement. Nor is there any prospect of improvement. . . .

[T]he proceeding is concerned with a [narrow] question; whether a doctor is obliged to continue treatment which has no therapeutic or medical benefit, notwithstanding that the discontinuance of the treatment may result in the clinical death of the patient.

The problem arises when life passes into death but obscurely. It is a problem made acute by the enormous advances made in technology and medical science in recent decades. With the use of sophisticated life-support systems, life may be perpetuated well beyond the reach of the natural disease. The process of living can become the process of dying so that it is unclear whether life is being sustained or death being deferred.

This is the plight of the irreversibly doomed patient. Maintained by mechanical means they exist suspended in a state of moribund inanimation. Whether a body devoid of a mind or, as in the case of Mr L, a brain destitute of a body, does not matter in any sensible way. In their chronic and persistent vegetative condition they lack self-awareness or awareness of their surroundings in any cognitive sense. They are the 'living dead'. Whether, in such circumstances, or in this particular case, it is fairer to say that the life-support system is being used to sustain life or being used to defer death is at the heart of the question I must resolve. . . .

Section 151(1) seeks to ensure that those who have the care of one who cannot care for him- or herself supply that person with the necessaries of life. The section reads:

> **151. Duty to provide the necessaries of life** – (1) Every one who has charge of any other person unable, by reason of detention, age, sickness, insanity, or any other cause, to withdraw himself from such charge, and unable to provide himself with the necessaries of life, is (whether such charge is undertaken by him under any contract or is imposed upon him by law or by reason of his unlawful act or otherwise howsoever) under a legal duty to supply that person with the necessaries of life, and is criminally responsible for omitting without lawful excuse to perform such duty if the death of that person is caused, or if his life is endangered or his health permanently injured, by such omission.

In his carefully prepared submission, Mr Collins advanced four arguments in support of the claim that, in withdrawing the ventilatory support from Mr L, the doctors would not be in breach of this section. First, he submitted that in his case ventilatory support is not a necessary of life; secondly, he argued that the withdrawing of the ventilatory support would not be the cause of death; thirdly, he contended that there is no legal duty to continue to maintain Mr L on a ventilator; and, finally, he urged that the doctors concerned have a 'lawful excuse' to turn off the ventilator.

During the course of argument it was accepted by Mr Collins that the third point had no validity independently of his other submissions and it was abandoned.

(i) Cause of death?

For reasons which will become clear, I propose to first address the question of whether the withdrawal of the ventilator would be the cause of Mr L's death.

The contention advanced is that artificial ventilation cannot prevent, cure or alleviate Mr L's extreme Guillain-Barre syndrome so as to enable him to survive the illness. If the artificial ventilator is disconnected, argued Mr Collins, Mr L will not die because he no longer has the benefits of the machine. He will have died because of the effects of extreme

Guillain-Barre syndrome. The point is expressed in this way by Dr Gillett: 'In my opinion it would be fair to conclude that in this case what caused his [Mr L's] death was the underlying disease process which prevented him from breathing on his own or sustaining his own vital functions.' This observation formed the basis of the acknowledgement proffered by Ms Goddard as part of the agreed facts. It reads: 'His [Mr L's] death will be caused by the underlying disease process of Guillain-Barre syndrome which prevents him from breathing on his own or sustaining his own vital functions.'

In the case of Mr L it is an argument which is easy to accept. But with due respect to counsel I am not certain that the point can be advanced in these relatively straightforward terms. There may be many circumstances in which a patient is kept alive by a life-support system where it would not be appropriate to discontinue that support. A polio victim unable to breathe or avoid cardiac arrest without mechanical assistance but who is nevertheless alive, and even perhaps desirous of remaining alive, is one example. No question of withdrawing the ventilator-support system would arise in such a case unless requested by the patient. But if the patient's doctor did in fact withdraw the support it is not acceptable that he or she should escape criminal responsibility on the ground that their action was not the cause of death. Yet, as a matter of logic, it is difficult to distinguish this example from a case such as Mr L's. The fact that in one case the application of ventilatory support is futile and has no real therapeutic or medical benefit is not a difference which could, at least on the face of it, go to the question of causation.

I suspect that the reason why this argument is pressed in a case such as Mr L's is that it accords with common sense. A doctor who withdraws a life-support system from a patient who is effectively lifeless should not be held responsible for the ensuing death when the support system is disconnected. Nor should he or she be obliged to regard their action as the cause of death. The difficulty is to perceive the rationale which would allow it to be said that the underlying disease was the cause of death when the doctors withdraw the life-support apparatus of one whose condition is irretrievably hopeless but not the cause of death when a doctor withdraws the support from one whose continued life is sustainable.

. . . The basic question must be whether the doctor was legally justified in doing what he did. Essentially, this is to ask whether the doctor was under a duty to continue the life-support system or had a 'lawful excuse' for withdrawing it. To my mind, these two questions are the critical questions. If the doctor is not under a legal duty to provide or continue with the life-support system, or he has a 'lawful excuse' for discontinuing it, it may then be said that he or she has not *legally* caused the death of the patient. This point may be re-examined later, but it is useful first to turn to these two critical questions.

(ii) The duty to provide the necessaries of life
There is no doubt that the section applies to a patient admitted to hospital care. Nor is there any doubt that the phrase 'necessaries of life' includes medical treatment. 'Medical aid', *R v Senior* [1899] 1 QB 283; *R v Burney* [1958] NZLR 745, 'medical care', *R v Books* (1902) 9 BCR 13, and 'medical attention', *R v Moore* [1954] NZLR 893, have been all held to be a necessary of life. I agree with Mr Collins that nothing hinges upon interchanging terminology. But in all these cases the medical intervention which was construed to be a necessary of life was medical intervention necessary to prevent, cure or alleviate a disease that threatened life or health; see also *R v Tutton* (1989) 48 CCC (3d) 129.

No cases are known – and I believe counsel's researches will have been exhaustive – in which the question of whether a ventilator is to be construed as a necessary of life has been in issue. So the question can be approached afresh. To my mind, however, there is no absolute answer; the answer in each case must depend on the facts. Thus, the provision of artificial respiration may be regarded as a necessary of life where it is required to prevent, cure or alleviate a disease that endangers the health or life of the patient. If, however, the patient is surviving only by virtue of the mechanical means which induces heartbeat and breathing and is beyond recovery, I do not consider that the provision of a ventilator can properly be construed as a necessary of life. It is repugnant that a doctor who has in good faith and with complete medical propriety undertaken treatment which has failed should be held responsible to continue that treatment on the basis that it is, or continues to be, a necessary of life. Nor is it possible to say at one and the same time that a life-support machine is serving no other purpose than deferring certain death and, on the other hand, regard the provision of the machine as a necessary of life in the sense that the term is used in the section. Such a patient has passed the point of 'life' and the obligation contemplated by the section is otiose.

However, as I have indicated, this would not be the case if a life-support system served the purpose of preventing, curing or alleviating a disease which threatened the life or health of the patient. Artificial ventilation may have this effect in many cases. In itself it does not prevent or cure the condition which threatens life or death. Rather, it has a therapeutic or medical advantage in that it may enable a patient to live long enough to recover from the illness. In such a case it alleviates the effects of the illness while nature or other medical intervention overcomes the condition. In that sense it has a therapeutic or medical function.

In Mr L's case there is no prospect of any improvement. Neither further medical treatment nor nature itself can intervene to repel the disease. Without the life-support system death is unavoidable. In these circumstances it serves no purpose and, for that reason, properly cannot be regarded as a necessary of life.

(iii) Lawful excuse

Even if it could be said, however, that the doctors are under a duty to provide the ventilator support to Mr L as a necessary of life, I am of the firm view that for the purpose of the section they are legally justified in withdrawing that support. They would not be acting without 'lawful excuse'.

The phrase 'lawful excuse' has no defined meaning. The Court of Appeal in *R v Burney* (at p 753) approved the dicta of the Privy Council in *Wong Pooh Yin v Public Prosecutor* [1955] AC 93 where it was said at p 100:

> Their Lordships doubt if it is possible to define the expression 'lawful excuse' in a comprehensive and satisfactory manner and they do not propose to make the attempt. They agree with the Court of Appeal that it would be undesirable to do so and that each case requires to be examined on its individual facts.

In my view, doctors have a lawful excuse to discontinue ventilation when there is no medical justification for continuing that form of medical assistance. To require the administration of a life-support system when such a system has no further medical function or purpose and serves only to defer the death of a patient is to confound the purpose of medicine. In such circumstances, the continuation of the artificial ventilation may be lawful, but that does not make it unlawful to discontinue it if the discontinuance accords with good medical practice.

A phrase such as 'good medical practice' may not have the precision of meaning that the medical profession or the public would desire. But that imprecision is inherent in the problem itself. There can be no single or fixed rule as to exactly when a doctor may withhold a life-support system which would cover the infinite variety of factual situations arising in practice. Consequently, the criterion can only be a general phrase such as 'good medical practice'.

Nor is it imperative that the phrase 'good medical practice' be accepted in any exclusive or dogmatic sense. It has been selected because it already enjoys some currency. But any description such as 'sound medical practice' or 'proper medical standards and procedures' would serve equally well. What is important is its perceived content. Clearly, it must begin with a bona fide decision on the part of the attending doctors as to what, in their judgment, is in the best interests of the patient. Equally, it must encompass the prevailing medical standards, practices, procedures and traditions which command general approval within the medical profession. All relevant tests would need to be carried out. In making vital decisions of the present kind specialist opinions and agreement will no doubt be required and extended consultation with other consultants is likely to be appropriate. Consultation with the medical profession's recognised ethical body is also critical. It must approve the doctor's decision. Finally, the patient's family or guardian must be fully informed and freely concur in what is proposed. It is knowledge of this practice, and the assurance that the procedures are conscientiously followed, which will provide the public with the confidence to accept the decisions which are then made.

I have already made the point that it is unacceptable to suggest that what constitutes good medical practice should not at the same time constitute a 'lawful excuse' for the purpose of s 151. Doctors who follow good medical practice should not, it is suggested, be liable to be held 'criminally responsible' in terms of s 151 or any related section. The strength of this contention was recognised by Ms Goddard for the Attorney-General. She acknowledged that:

> . . . if the Court were to comment that 'lawful excuse' in this medical context encompasses a collegiate decision made by doctors charged with the care of a patient, endorsed by the appropriate medical ethical committee and with the informed consent of family members concerned, then prima facie such a decision must be lawful. It could only be unlawful if, in a particular case, the decision itself had been

made on a wrong exercise of principle, or, if account had not been taken of differing opinion or practice accepted as proper by a responsible body of medical opinion.

I agree. In the present case, the decision that Mr L's life-support system should be discontinued has been made by a number of medical specialists and supported by others. Extensive tests have been carried out and repeated. Overseas consultants have been approached. The decision has been endorsed by the appropriate medical ethical body, and the informed consent of the family members has been obtained. There is, in this process, the assurance of good medical practice. . . .

[T]he determination of what is good medical practice in any particular situation can be best assisted by having regard to the essential nature of a doctor's duty in attending a patient whose life-support system has ceased to serve any therapeutic or medical function. Indeed, what is good practice probably cannot be determined without regard to the fundamental duty which arises from this doctor/patient relationship. This is because it needs to be recognised that a doctor is under no legal duty to prolong life – or to defer death – in circumstances such as exist in this case.

While they are not numerous, there are sufficient authorities which support this proposition for it to be accepted that it represents the law, certainly when combined with the dictates of common sense.

Questions of good medical practice, with some modification, form the basis of a number of decisions in the United Kingdom which enable doctors to perform sterilisation procedures upon adults unable to consent to such operations because of mental disability; see eg *T v T* [1988] 1 All ER 613; and *F v West Berkshire Health Authority* [1989] 2 All ER 545. . . .

As I perceive it, what is involved is not just medical treatment, but medical treatment in accordance with the doctor's best judgment as to what is in the best interests of his or her patient. They remain responsible for the kind and extent of the treatment administered and, ultimately, for its duration. In exercising their best judgment in this regard it is crucial for the patient and in the overall interests of society that they should not be inhibited by considerations pertinent to their own self-interest in avoiding criminal sanctions. Their judgment must be a genuinely independent judgment as to what will best serve the well-being of their dying patients.

Conscientious doctors will undoubtedly continue to strive with dedication to preserve and promote the life and health of their patients. That is their primary mission. But with a patient such as Mr L, where 'life' is being prolonged for no therapeutic or medical purpose or, in other words, death is merely being deferred, the doctor is not under a duty to avert that death at all costs. If, in his judgment, the proper medical practice would be to discontinue the life-support system, and that would be in the best interests of his patient, he may do so subject to adhering to a procedure which provides a safeguard against the possibility of individual error.

A doctor acting responsibly and in accordance with good medical practice recognised and approved as such in the medical profession would not therefore be liable, in my opinion, to any criminal sanction based upon the application of s 151(1). He or she will have acted with lawful excuse.

(iv) The question of the cause of death re-examined
Before leaving this section I will briefly revert to the question of causation. From what I have said it will be plain, I think, that it is not enough to hold that, where the doctor discontinues the life-support system, the resulting brain-stem death is caused by the patient's illness. Apart from this test being equally appropriate in the case of the polio victim which I have previously given, it would, without further qualification, exonerate a doctor who did not adhere to good medical practice or follow the accepted procedure for terminating the operation of a life-support system. To my mind, therefore, it can only be said that the withdrawal of the ventilatory system is not the cause of death as a *matter of law* if and when one or other of the two primary conditions have been met, that is, the doctor is not under a duty to provide the ventilator as part of the necessaries of life or has a lawful excuse for declining to do so. Both questions then turn on whether or not the doctor has followed good medical practice and the guidelines or procedures which have been laid down.

To leave the matter there, however, would be unfair to doctors. Finding that, in such circumstances, they are not *legally* the cause of death may suggest that they are morally or otherwise the cause of death. This is not so. Indeed, the opposite is the case. Most objective observers would accept that where a life-support system which has ceased to serve any medical purpose or benefit to the patient is withdrawn, the certain death which it had for a time arrested would be the outcome of the original disease and not the withdrawal of the support. Nature has been permitted to take its course. To hold, therefore, that where a doctor is under no legal duty to provide that support and has a lawful excuse for withholding it, the discontinuance of the life support is not *legally* the cause of death is simply to make the law coincide with the perception dictated by good sense. . . .

There will therefore be an order in the following terms:

If:

(i) the doctors responsible for the care of Mr L, taking into account a responsible body of medical opinion, conclude that there is no reasonable possibility of Mr L ever recovering from his present clinical condition;

(ii) there is no therapeutic or medical benefit to be gained by continuing to maintain Mr L on artificial ventilatory support, and to withdraw that support accords with good medical practice, as recognised and approved within the medical profession; and

(iii) Mrs L and the ethics committee of the Auckland Area Health Board concur with the decision to withdraw the artificial ventilatory support;

then, ss 151 and/or 164 of the Crimes Act 1961 will not apply, and the withdrawal of the artificial ventilatory support from Mr L will not constitute culpable homicide for the purposes of that Act.

If *Bland* is to be understood as limited to cases where the patient has no interests, how should we perceive Mr L in the above case? On one level he is *not* insensate in that his higher brain is functioning. On the other hand, given that he is 'locked in' and 'locked out', ie receiving no sensory input and incapable of responding to the environment around him, he could be described as insensate and, therefore, having no interests. In our view the idea of an individual having 'no interests', given that it is philosophically problematic, is best restricted (if indeed valid at all) to the patient in a persistent vegetative state.

The consequence is that even in the extreme case of Mr L, the court is required to engage in a different reasoning process from that which the judges in the House of Lords were able to avail themselves of in *Bland*. The court in using the 'best interests' test cannot avoid being drawn into weighing the burdens and benefits of continued medical intervention. This task which is crudely captured in the notion of making life or death decisions was thought at least by Lord Browne-Wilkinson and Lord Mustill to be possibly beyond the remit of the courts and, therefore, one for Parliament.

Lord Browne-Wilkinson: [B]ehind the questions of law lie moral, ethical, medical and practical issues of fundamental importance to society. As Hoffmann LJ in the Court of Appeal emphasised, the law regulating the termination of artificial life support being given to patients must, to be acceptable, reflect a moral attitude which society accepts. This has led judges into the consideration of the ethical and other non-legal problems raised by the ability to sustain life artificially which new medical technology has recently made possible. But in my judgment in giving the legal answer to these questions judges are faced with a dilemma. The ability to sustain life artificially is of relatively recent origin. Existing law may not provide an acceptable answer to the new legal questions which it raises. Should judges seek to develop new law to meet a wholly new situation? Or is this a matter which lies outside the area of legitimate development of the law by judges and requires society, through the democratic expression of its views in Parliament, to reach its decisions on the underlying moral and practical problems and then reflect those decisions in legislation?

I have no doubt that it is for Parliament, not the courts, to decide the broader issues which this case raises. . . .

I am very conscious that I have reached my conclusions on narrow, legalistic, grounds which provide no satisfactory basis for the decision of cases which will arise in the future where the facts are not identical. I must again emphasise that this is an extreme case where it can be overwhelmingly proved that the patient is and will remain insensate: he neither feels pain from treatment nor will feel pain in dying and has no prospect of any medical care improving his condition. Unless, as I very much hope, Parliament reviews the law, the courts will be faced with cases where the chances of improvement are slight, or the patient has very slight sensate awareness. I express no view on what should be the answer in such circumstances: my decision does not cover such a case.

Lord Mustill: The formulation of the necessary broad social and moral policy is an enterprise which the courts have neither the means nor in my opinion the right to perform. This can only be achieved by democratic process through the medium of Parliament. . . .

My Lords, I believe that I have said enough to explain why, from the outset, I have felt serious doubts about whether this question is justiciable, not in the technical sense, but in the sense of being a proper subject for legal adjudication. The whole matter cries out for exploration in depth by Parliament and then for the establishment by legislation not only of a new set of ethically and intellectually consistent rules, distinct from the general criminal law, but also of a sound procedural framework within which the rules can be applied to individual cases. The rapid advance of medical technology makes this an ever more urgent task, and I venture to hope that Parliament will soon take it in hand.

(ii) GROUP 2 PATIENTS

The patients in our group 2 may be babies, children or adults. They are ill and may be dying but are patients for whom there is some therapy available. The therapy offers either the possibility of benefit to the patient but is accompanied by very considerable risks of harm or does nothing to benefit the patient's *underlying* condition which is itself severely debilitating whether physically or mentally.

I. Best interests: 'quality of life'. We saw earlier an example of a case concerned with a patient in what we have called Group 2 – the important decision in *Saikewicz*. We saw there how the Massachusetts' Supreme Judicial Court sanctioned the withdrawal of treatment applying a 'substituted judgment' test. Of course, the case is problematic for English law because of the English courts' reluctance to embrace the 'substituted judgment' test (notwithstanding that it was inapplicable, if properly understood, to Joseph Saikewicz who had always been incompetent). However, a close reading of the case demonstrates that the court, in essence, balanced the burdens of treatment against any benefits that would accrue, ie the court applied a 'best interests' (in the sense of 'quality of life') test in reality though not in form.

The baby cases – How would English law approach a case which necessitates the court's having to balance burdens and benefits? The first case in which a court considered this question was in *Re B*.

Re B (A Minor) (Wardship: Medical Treatment) [1981] 1 WLR 1421 (CA)

Templeman LJ: This is a very poignantly sad case. Although we sit in public, for reasons which I think will be obvious to everybody in court, and if not will be obvious in the course of this judgment, it would be lamentable if the names of the parents of the child concerned were revealed in any way to the general public. The press and people who frequent these courts are usually very helpful in referring to names by initials, and this is a case where nothing ought to be leaked out to identify those concerned with the case.

It concerns a little girl who was born on July 28, 1981. She was born suffering from Down's syndrome, which means that she will be a mongol. She was also born with an intestinal blockage which will be fatal unless it is operated upon. When the parents were informed of the condition of the child they took the view that it would be unkind to this child to operate upon her, and that the best thing to do was for her not to have the operation, in which case she would die within a few days. During those few days she could be kept from pain and suffering by sedation. They took the view that would be the kindest thing in the interests of the child. They so informed the doctors at the hospital, and refused to consent to the operation taking place. It is agreed on all hands that the parents came to that decision with great sorrow. It was a firm decision: they genuinely believed that it was in the best interests of this child. At the same time, it is of course impossible for parents in the unfortunate position of these parents to be certain that their present view should prevail. The shock to caring parents finding that they have given birth to a child who is a mongol is very great indeed, and therefore while great weight ought to be given to the views of the parents they are not views which necessarily must prevail.

What happened then was that the doctors being informed that the parents would not consent to the operation contacted the local authority who very properly made the child a ward of court and asked the judge to give care and control to the local authority and to authorise them to direct that the operation be carried out, and the judge did so direct. But when the child was moved from the hospital where it was born to another hospital for the purposes of the operation a difference of medical opinion developed. The surgeon who was to perform the operation declined to do so when he was informed that the parents objected. In a statement he said that when the child was referred to him for the operation he decided he wished to speak to the parents of the child personally and he spoke to them on the telephone and they stated that in view of the fact that the child was mongoloid they did not wish to have the operation performed. He further stated:

> I decided therefore to respect the wishes of the parents and not to perform the operation, a decision which would, I believe (after about 20 years in the medical profession), be taken by the great majority of surgeons faced with a similar situation.

Therefore the local authority came back to the judge. The parents were served in due course and appeared and made their submissions to the judge, and in addition inquiries were made and it was discovered that the surgeon in the hospital where the child was born and another surgeon in a neighbouring hospital were prepared and advised that the operation should be carried out. So there is a difference of medical opinion.

This morning the judge was asked to decide whether to continue his order that the operation should be performed or whether to revoke that order, and the position now is stark. The evidence, as I have said, is that if this little girl does not have this operation she will die within a matter of days. If she has the operation there is a possibility that she will suffer heart trouble as a result and that she may die within two to three months. But if she has the operation and it is successful, she has Down's syndrome, she is mongoloid, and the present evidence is that her life expectancy is short, about 20 to 30 years.

The parents say that no one can tell what will be the life of a mongoloid child who survives during that 20 or 30 years, but one thing is certain. She will be very handicapped mentally and physically and no one can expect that she will have anything like a normal existence. They make that point not because of the difficulties which will be occasioned to them but in the child's interests. This is not a case in which the court is concerned with whether arrangements could or could not be made for the care of this child, if she lives, during the next 20 or 30 years; the local authority is confident that the parents having for good reason decided that it is in the child's best interests that the operation should not be performed, nevertheless good adoption arrangements could be made and that in so far as any mongol child can be provided with a happy life then such a happy life can be provided.

The question which this court has to determine is whether it is in the interests of this child to be allowed to die within the next week or to have the operation in which case if she lives she will be a mongoloid child, but no one can say to what extent her mental or physical defects will be apparent. No one can say whether she will suffer or whether she will be happy in part. On the one hand the probability is that she will not be a cabbage as it is called when people's faculties are entirely destroyed. On the other hand it is certain that she will be very severely mentally and physically handicapped.

On behalf of the parents, Mr Gray has submitted very movingly, if I may say so, that this is a case where nature has made its own arrangements to terminate a life which would not be fruitful and nature should not be interfered with. He has also submitted that in this kind of decision the views of responsible and caring parents, as these are, should be respected, and that their decision that it is better for the child to be allowed to die should be respected. Fortunately or unfortunately, in this particular case the decision no longer lies with the parents or with the doctors, but lies with the court. It is a decision which of course must be made in the light of the evidence and views expressed by the parents and the doctors, but at the end of the day it devolves on this court in this particular instance to decide whether the life of this child is demonstrably going to be so awful that in effect the child must be condemned to die, or whether the life of this child is still so imponderable that it would be wrong for her to be condemned to die. There may be cases, I know not, of severe proved damage where the future is so certain and where the life of the child is so bound to be full of pain and suffering that the court might be driven to a different conclusion, but in the present case the choice which lies before the court is this: whether to allow an operation to take place which may result in the child living for 20 to 30 years as a mongoloid or whether (and I think this must be brutally the result) to terminate the life of a mongoloid child because she also has an intestinal complaint. Faced with that choice I have no doubt that it is the duty of this court to decide that the child must live. The judge was much affected by the reasons given by the parents and came to the conclusion that their wishes ought to be respected. In my judgment he erred in that the duty of the court is to decide whether it is in the interests of the child that an operation should take place. The evidence in this case only goes to show that if the operation takes place and is successful then the child may live the normal span of a mongoloid child with the handicaps and defects and life of a mongol child, and it is not for this court to say that life of that description ought to be extinguished.

Accordingly the appeal must be allowed and the local authority must be authorised themselves to authorise and direct the operation to be carried out on the little girl.

Dunn LJ: I agree, and as we are differing from the view expressed by the judge I would say a few words of my own. I have great sympathy for the parents in the agonising decision to which they came. As they put it themselves, 'God or nature has given the child a way out.' But the child now being a ward of court, although due weight must be given to the decision of the parents which everybody accepts was an entirely responsible one, doing what they considered was the best, the fact of the matter is that this court now has to make the decision. It cannot hide behind the decision of the parents or the decision of the doctors; and in making the decision this court's first and paramount consideration is the welfare of this unhappy little baby.

One of the difficulties in the case is that there is no prognosis as to the child's future, except that as a mongol her expectation of life is confined to 20 or 30 years. We were told that no reliable prognosis can be made until probably she is about two years old. That in itself leads me to the route by which the court should make its decision, because there is no evidence that this child's short life is likely to be an intolerable one. There is no evidence at all as to the quality of life which the child may expect. As Mr Turcan on behalf of the Official Solicitor said, the child should be put into the same position as any other mongol child and must be given the chance to live an existence. I accept that way of putting it.

I agree with Templeman LJ that the court must step in to preserve this mongol baby's life.

The approach adopted by the Court of Appeal in *Re B* seems to mean that 'best interests', became for the court, 'quality of life', another general (and in itself, meaningless) test; but one which offers some hope for further analysis and articulation. Also, if 'quality of life' is the test this serves to highlight two further critical points. First, the test is not factual but *normative*. Secondly, being normative, it has to be *established* as a matter of principle by the courts (though it will ordinarily be *applied* in particular cases by those caring for the patient).

The vagueness and imprecision involved in recourse to the 'quality of life' test in the context of neonates is well put by Professor Gostin in his article 'A Moment in Human Development: Legal Protection, Ethical Standards and Social Policy on the Selective Non-Treatment of Handicapped Neonates', (1985) 11 American Journal of Law and Medicine 32:

The term 'quality of life' has been introduced into Anglo-American jurisprudence[24] and by commentators [see, eg, Goldstein, 'Medical Care for the Child at Risk: On State Supervention of Parental Autonomy' 86 Yale LJ 645 (1977) at 651-61; Williams, 'Down's Syndrome and the Duty to Preserve Life' 131 New LJ 1020 (1981) at 1020-21] to justify the withholding of medically indicated treatment for severely handicapped infants whose life would be so bereft of enjoyment as not to be worth living. As under social utilitarian thought, medically effective treatment, even if available and efficacious for an otherwise normal infant, could be withheld based upon broader consideration of the infant's handicaps. The relevant factors under a 'quality of life' assessment relate not to social worth or to economic cost, but to the infant's potential for human contentment.

It is difficult to argue with the premise underlying the 'quality of life' position, for there must come a point for most of us where life is so devoid of meaning and contentment that it is not worth living. As a philosophic position, its weakness is that the factors which would justify forsaking continued life are seldom, if ever, specified. If one accepts that continued life is not in the infant's interests, then those who make this decision must be clear about the criteria to be adopted. Yet the basis for identifying and measuring those interests under a 'quality of life' standard is unclear.

In practice, the term 'quality of life' often is not used as a coherent moral theory which defines with any certainty which handicapping conditions should or should not be treated. Rather, the term is employed as a signal by those who believe that selective non-treatment decisions are too delicate and complex to be governed by any coherent legal or ethical standard. Accordingly, most of those who advocate a 'quality of life' assessment seek to maintain the decision-making process within a confidential doctor/patient framework.

Footnote 24: Courts have been reluctant expressly to adopt a 'quality of life' criterion and have been careful not to demarcate a class of individuals, such as the mentally retarded or senile, as deserving a lower standard of legal protection. Yet several courts have made implicit assessments of personal quality of life and normalcy in coming to their decisions. It is helpful to distinguish between two groupings of cases to determine whether a court is actually employing a 'quality of life' standard. The first are cases which are decided principally by an assessment of medical benefits, risks and adverse effects of the treatment in question. (Is there a 'substantial chance for cure?' Are there 'medically effective alternative treatments?') Here, the court's decision follows directly from the medical assessment. The principal finding is factual, ie, whether a medical consensus exists that the treatment is indicated and that there are no medically recognised alternatives. Given this finding of fact courts will usually come to the same decision, irrespective of the legal standard applied. See, eg, *Custody of a Minor*, 375 Mass 733, 379 NE 2d 1053 (1978), *affd*, 378 Mass 732, 393 NE 2d 836 (1979) (order permitting chemotherapy for minor patient suffering from acute lymphocytic leukemia over parental objection; court found chemotherapy offered a 'substantial chance for cure' and the alternative treatment of metabolic therapy was medically ineffective and poisonous); *Hofbauer* Re, 65 AD 2d 108, 411 NYS 2d 416 (1978), affd, 47 NY 2d 648, 393 NE 2d 1109, 419 NYS 2d 936 (1979) (a child suffering from Hodgkins Disease whose parents failed to follow attending physician's recommendation for treatment by radiation and chemotherapy, but rather placed child under care of licensed physician advocating nutritional or metabolic therapy, was not a neglected child; court found parents had justifiable concerns about deleterious effects of radiation and chemotherapy, that alternative treatments were controlling the child's condition, and that conventional treatments would be administered if child's condition so warranted); *Ex rel Cicero*, 101 Misc 2d 699, 421 NYS 2d 965 (Sup Ct 1979) (guardian appointed to consent to corrective surgery for infant born with meningomyelocele. The court found child unlikely to live beyond 24 months without surgery and that surgery would permit the child to walk with leg braces and to have 'normal intellectual development' with little future risk of mental retardation).

The cases cited above should be distinguished from those where the court is influenced not only by its findings of fact as to the choices of treatment, but also by the person's wider characteristics, including his or her potential for intellectual and social functioning. See, eg, *Re Phillip B*, 92 Cal App 3d 796, 156 Cal Rptr 48 (1979), cert denied sub nom 445 US 949 (1980) (court declined to order life-prolonging heart surgery for minor suffering from congenital ventricular septal heart defect. The trial court found corrective surgery to be medically indicated with 5 to 10 per cent mortality rate but noted that the child had Down's syndrome; the judge commented that he personally could not handle it, 'if it happened to me'); *Infant Doe*, [*in re the Treatment and Care of Infant Doe*, No GU 8204-004A (Ind Cir Ct, April 12, 1982)] (court order barring doctors from providing nourishment or treatment for Down's Syndrome infant born with a deformity in the stomach wall which prevented food being digested; the condition could have been corrected by surgery which was serious but considered within the range of standard medical practice); *Re Spring*, 380 Mass 529, 405 NE 2d 115 (1980) (court approval for removal of 78 year old patient from kidney dialysis, probate court found patient to be senile and incapable of restoration to a 'normal, cognitive, integrated functioning existence'); *Superintendent of Belchertown State School v Saikewicz*, 373 Mass 728, 370 NE 2d 417 (1977) (authorisation for non-treatment of 67 year old mentally retarded ward suffering from acute myeloblastic monocytic leukemia; probate court found chemotherapy was life-prolonging and was treatment of choice, but patient's profound retardation was a significant issue in the case); *Re Conroy* 98 NJ 321, 486 A 2d 1209 (1985) (nursing home resident with severe and permanent mental and physical defects and limited life expectancy could have life-sustaining treatment withdrawn in certain circumstances).

If one were to remove the wider 'quality of life' element from the facts of these cases the results would appear anomalous and, in some instances, clearly erroneous. It is highly probable that the court in each of these cases would have opted to prolong a life it considered worth living. See Annas, *Quality of Life in the Courts: Early Spring in Fantasyland,* 10 Hast Cen Rpt 9 (Aug 1980). A further, albeit less apparent, instance of a quality of life assessment occurred in *Re Quinlan*, 70 NJ 10, 355 A 2d 647, cert denied, 429 US 922 (1976) and its progeny. . . . See also, Annas, *Reconciling Quinlan and Saikewicz: Decision-Making for the Terminally Ill Incompetent*, 4 Am JL & Med 367 (1979).

An analysis of 'best interests' in the context of neonates is helpfully set out in the President's Commission Report (*op cit*), *Deciding to Forego Life-Sustaining Treatment*, at pp 217-223:

Best interests of the infant. In most circumstances, people agree on whether a proposed course of therapy is in a patient's best interests. Even with seriously ill newborns, quite often there is no issue – either a particular therapy plainly offers net benefits or no effective therapy is available. Sometimes, however, the right outcome will be unclear because the child's 'best interests' are difficult to assess.

The Commission believes that decision-making will be improved if an attempt is made to decide which of three situations applies in a particular case – (1) a treatment is available that would clearly benefit the infant, (2) all treatment is expected to be futile, or (3) the probable benefits to an infant from different choices are quite uncertain (see Table 1 . . .). The three situations need to be considered separately, since they demand differing responses.

Clearly defined beneficial therapies. The Commission's inquiries indicate that treatments are rarely withheld when there is a medical consensus that they would provide a net benefit to a child. Parents naturally want to provide necessary medical care in most circumstances, and parents who are hesitant at first about having treatment administered usually come to recognise the desirability of providing treatment after discussions with physicians, nurses and others. Parents should be able to choose among alternative treatments with similarly beneficial results and among providers, but not to reject treatment that is reliably expected to benefit a seriously ill newborn substantially, as is usually true if life can be saved.

Table 1:
Treatment options for seriously ill newborns – physician's assessment in relation to parents' preference

Physician's Assessment of Treatment Options*	Parents Prefer to Accept Treatment**	Parents Prefer to Forego Treatment**
Clearly beneficial	Provide treatment	Provide treatment during review process
Ambiguous or uncertain	Provide treatment	Forego treatment
Futile	Provide treatment unless provider declines to do so	Forego treatment

*The assessment of the value to the infant of the treatments available will initially be by the attending physician. Both when this assessment is unclear and when the joint decision between parents and physician is to forego treatment, this assessment would be reviewed by intra-institutional mechanisms and possibly thereafter by court.
**The choice made by the infant's parents or other duly authorised surrogate who has adequate decision-making capacity and has been adequately informed, based on their assessment of the infant's best interests.

Many therapies undertaken to save the lives of seriously ill newborns will leave the survivors with permanent handicaps, either from the underlying defect (such as heart surgery not affecting the retardation of a Down's Syndrome infant) or from the therapy itself (as when mechanical ventilation for a premature baby results in blindness or a scarred trachea). One of the most troubling and persistent issues in this entire area is whether, or to what extent, the expectation of such handicaps should be considered in deciding to treat or not to treat a seriously ill newborn. The Commission has concluded that a very restrictive standard is appropriate: such permanent handicaps justify a decision not to provide life-sustaining treatment only when they are so severe that continued existence would not be a net benefit to the infant. Though inevitably somewhat subjective and imprecise in actual application, the concept of 'benefit' excludes honoring idiosyncratic views that might be allowed if a person were deciding about his or her own treatment. Rather, net benefit is absent only if the burdens imposed on the patient by the disability or its treatment would lead a competent decision-maker to choose to forego the treatment. As in all surrogate decision-making, the surrogate is obligated to try to evaluate benefits and burdens from the infant's own perspective. The Commission believes that the handicaps of Down's Syndrome, for example, are not in themselves of this magnitude and do not justify failing to provide medically proven treatment, such as surgical correction of a blocked intestinal tract.

This is a very strict standard in that it excludes consideration of the negative effects of an impaired child's life on other persons, including parents, siblings, and society. Although abiding by this standard may be difficult in specific cases, it is all too easy to undervalue the lives of handicapped infants; the Commission finds it imperative to counteract this by treating them no less vigorously than their healthy peers or than older children with similar handicaps would be treated.

Clearly futile therapies. When there is no therapy that can benefit an infant, as in anencephaly or certain severe cardiac deformities, a decision by surrogates and providers not to try predictably futile endeavors is ethically and legally justifiable. Such therapies do not help the child, are sometimes painful for the infant (and probably distressing to the parents), and offer no reasonable probability of saving life for a substantial period. The moment of death for these infants might be delayed for a short time – perhaps as long as a few weeks – by vigorous therapy. Of course, the prolongation of life – and hope against hope – may be enough to lead some parents to want to try a therapy believed by physicians to be futile. As long as this choice does not cause substantial suffering for the child, providers should accept it, although individual health care professionals who find it personally offensive to engage in futile treatment may arrange to withdraw from the case.

Just as with older patients, even when cure or saving of life are out of reach, obligations to comfort and respect a dying person remain. Thus infants whose lives are destined to be brief are owed whatever relief from suffering and enhancement of life can be provided, including feeding, medication for pain, and sedation, as appropriate. Moreover, it may be possible for parents to hold and comfort the child once the elaborate means of life-support are withdrawn, which can be very important to all concerned in symbolic and existential as well as physical terms.

Ambiguous cases. Although for most seriously ill infants there will be either a clearly beneficial option or no beneficial therapeutic options at all, hard questions are raised by the smaller number for whom it is very difficult to assess whether the treatments available offer prospects of benefit – for example, a child with a debilitating and painful disease who might live with therapy, but only for a year or so, or a respirator-dependent premature infant whose long-term prognosis becomes bleaker with each passing day.

Much of the difficulty in these cases arises from factual uncertainty. For the many infants born prematurely, and sometimes for those with serious congenital defects, the only certainty is that without intensive care they are unlikely to survive; very little is known about how each individual will fare with treatment. Neonatology is too new a field to allow accurate predictions of which babies will survive and of the complications, handicaps, and potentials that the survivors might have.

The longer some of these babies survive, the more reliable the prognosis for the infant becomes and the clearer parents and professionals can be on whether further treatment is warranted or futile. Frequently, however, the prospect of long-term survival and the quality of that survival remain unclear for days, weeks, and months, during which time the infants may have an unpredictable and fluctuating course of advances and setbacks.

One way to avoid confronting anew the difficulties involved in evaluating each case is to adopt objective criteria to distinguish newborns who will receive life-sustaining treatment from those who will not. Such criteria would be justified if there were evidence that their adoption would lead to decisions more often being made correctly.

Strict treatment criteria proposed in the 1970s by a British physician for deciding which newborns with spina bifida should receive treatment rested upon the location of the lesion (which influences degree of paralysis), the presence of hydrocephalus (fluid in the brain, which influences degree of retardation), and the likelihood of an infection. Some critics of this proposal argued with it on scientific grounds, such as objecting that long-term effects of spina bifida cannot be predicted with sufficient accuracy at birth. Other critics, however, claimed this whole approach to ambiguous cases exhibited the 'technical criteria fallacy'. They contended that an infant's future life – and hence the treatment decisions based on it – involves value considerations that are ignored when physicians focus solely on medical prognosis.

> The decision [to treat or not] must also include evaluation of the meaning of existence with varying impairments. Great variation exists about these essentially evaluative elements among parents, physicians, and policy makers. It must be an open question whether these variations in evaluation are among the relevant factors to consider in making a treatment decision. When Lorber uses the phrase 'contraindications to active therapy', he is medicalising what are really value choices.

The Commission agrees that such criteria necessarily include value considerations. Supposedly objective criteria such as birth weight limits or checklists for severity of spina bifida have not been shown to improve the quality of decision-making in ambiguous and complex cases. Instead, their use seems to remove the weight of responsibility too readily from those who should have to face the value questions – parents and health care providers.

Furthermore, any set of standards, when honestly applied, leaves some difficult or uncertain cases. When a child's best interests are ambiguous, a decision based upon them will require prudent and discerning judgment. Defining the category of cases in a way that appropriately protects and encourages the exercise of parental judgement will sometimes be difficult.

A study written for the Law Reform Commission of Canada by Edward Keyserlinck takes the analysis further.

E Keyserlinck 'Sanctity of Life or Quality of Life' (1979) (pp 50 *passim*)

The answer of course depends upon what is meant, or what meaning *we give* to 'quality of life'. What makes the question one of practical relevance and not just academic interest is that quality of life concerns are already and long have been influencing medical decisions. But what makes the question an urgent and somewhat worrisome one for society, medicine and law is that quality of life can and does mean many very different things, has no single, generally accepted meaning, and some of its connotations and the uses to which the concept is put are definitely opposed to and in conflict with the sanctity of life principle as outlined earlier.

It is probably its very elusiveness which makes the concept so attractive to media and public. It is so vague and glibly used in such quite different contexts (environmental and medical for instance) and in support of such quite different positions (for instance to improve the quality of air, or to cease medical treatment) that the concept seems to commit one to nothing specific, and is seldom given tangible content.

But its very elusiveness encourages as well the polarised, extreme and hostile views about its moral legitimacy and usefulness. There are those who think it answers all questions, and those who think it answers none. There are those who would welcome the replacement of the 'traditional' ethic of the absolute value of human life by an ethic of its relative value. There are others who see any recognition of quality of life factors as a danger to be resisted at all costs.

But it is also possible, and in my view legitimate and preferable, to see no need to choose between an old ethic and a new one. Instead, to recognise an urgent need to on the one hand articulate and refine the 'old' ethic, and on the other hand to propose a carefully delineated and restricted meaning and purpose for quality of life. The purpose of such an exercise would be to encourage both medical decision-making and (perhaps) law-making to more formally recognise an interest in considering and protecting *both* the intrinsic value of each human life, *and* the quality of those lives, even when this involves a decision to cease or not initiate treatment or life support.

But to make this case successfully depends first of all of course on the meaning we intend for quality of life. . . .

Quality is a comparative property, an evaluative property. And it is true that quality of life used in environmental/social contexts does essentially involve a comparison with other things – a ranking of the conditions which maximise optimal human life or general happiness requirements of a region. Implicit in the comparison is a readiness to discard or improve certain conditions because of where they rank on the scale.

But in the medical/health context, quality of life *need* not involve a comparison of *different human lives* as the basis for decisions to treat some and not others. Ideally, at the heart of quality of life concerns in this context should be only a comparison of the qualities *this patient* now has with the qualities deemed by *this patient* (or if incompetent or irreversibly comatose, by the patient's agents) to be normative and desirable, and either still or no longer present actually or potentially.

The real comparison in question is in a sense one between what the patient is and was, is and can or cannot be in the future. The quality of life comparison or evaluation in the medical context need not be a comparison *with others* or a relativising of persons' lives. And the quality of life norm and decision need not be arbitrary or based upon how treatment or non-treatment will relieve or burden others or society. The norm can and must include whatever the value sciences, medicine and public policy agree upon concerning the essential quality or qualities of a human person; and the decision can and must be in the first instance by, and for the benefit of the patient and no one else.

To include quality of life considerations in life saving or life support decision-making by no means must imply *harm* rather than improvement or benefit to the patients. If quality of life is limited only to what is intended here, then quite the contrary is the case and must be the case if the concept is to have any justifiably normative value.

In the first place, investigations, prognoses and conclusions arrived at concerning a patient's actual or potential level of function or degree of suffering, need not inevitably and exclusively lead to decisions *to cease* or *not to initiate* life supporting treatment. Given that the sanctity of life principle imposes the burden of proof on those who would cease to support life, the consideration of quality of life factors should more often lead to the opposite decision – to initiate or continue that treatment if there is any realistic hope of minimal human function and controllable pain and suffering.

Secondly, even when quality of life factors do contribute to a decision to cease or not initiate life saving or supporting treatment, there remains the continuing obligation to seek to improve the newborn's or the patient's *care and comfort*. Neither physician nor patient are usually faced with only two options – to continue or discontinue life support treatment. The third option and continuing responsibility of health care professionals and families, no matter how damaged the patient's condition, is to seek to improve the level of care and comfort of the dying, including being physically present to them. The sanctity of life surely calls for at least the same respect and consideration for dying life as for healthy life. And if greater needs call for greater care and concern, then the dying deserve more, not less of it, than the healthy.

Thirdly, even decisions to cease or not initiate life saving treatments, based partly on quality of life considerations, can and must offer a reasonable hope of *benefit* to the patient. In other words, death should not always be resisted at any cost in terms of present and future suffering and damage, as if anything is an improvement over death. It is an integral part of my thesis that this is not so, that some conditions of human life are so damaged, and will likely remain so or become worse if treatment is continued or initiated, that death can reasonably be seen as beneficial, as an improvement for that patient.

The final weighing and balancing of reasons and criteria normally belongs to the patient, and within morally acceptable parameters different patients may and will weigh the criteria differently and come to different decisions. For the incompetent, the determination of benefit to patient or newborn must be made by proxies. While it remains enormously difficult to make such decisions in the interests and for the benefit of others, it is my contention that they must sometimes be made, and that reasonable and morally justifiable decisions for the benefit of others, based partially at least on quality of life matters, are possible. There will be occasion to come back to the 'who decides' question and the other points in more detail as the argument unfolds.

In the light of the above, quality of life in the medical context need not come out the loser when compared to quality of life in the environmental/social context. As noted, there are of course great differences in the contexts and the functions within them of quality of life criteria. But in both contexts the ultimate aim of these criteria is objective improvement and benefit, even if in the medical context that will often be limited to reducing rather than eliminating the patient's discomfort and indignity. In claiming this, the medical cases envisioned are primarily those in which the quality of life criteria are used in decisions made *by others* for the incompetent patient. In such cases the use of these criteria for the patient's objective improvement or reduction of discomfort or some other benefit is a realistic aim. Obviously it may be otherwise for patients able to *themselves* accept or refuse treatment. Since, as I shall argue below, competent patients have the right to refuse treatment on any grounds at all, whether they seem reasonable or foolish to others, there can be no guarantee at all of objective improvement and benefit in the decisions made and criteria used by competent patients for themselves.

Just before attempting to put flesh on the dry bones, to offer more argument for the claims made, the thesis of this quality of life section of the paper should be summarised.

Quality of life need not mean the 'relativising of lives'. Excluded here in this paper from that concept and its criteria are considerations such as social worth, social utility, social status or relative worth. The sanctity of life principle rightly insists on the intrinsic worth and equal value of every life. In excluding these elements from the meaning intended for quality of life, one need not of course deny that they can be ingredients of quality of life in wider contexts than our own. At least some of them are factors which a 'general' quality of life theory must consider and weigh in other contexts. I am only excluding these factors from this particular context of medical decision-making in life and death matters, and primarily when such decisions are made by proxies or patients' agents for patients or newborns unable to make these decisions themselves. Whatever the merits and realities of characteristics such as social status in other areas of concern, here I do not believe they should have determinative weight.

New circumstances such as increasingly sophisticated life support systems and treatment have challenged us to recognise in human life a distinction between mere existence and quality with more clarity than previously needed. But that does not mean that in our context the shifting sands of new medical technology, evolving social realities or subjective preferences comprise an adequate source for the meaning and criteria of a quality of life concept, or in themselves validly answer our questions. What is involved here, or should be, is a search for and a weighing of the *inherent features* of human life. That is an objective meaning of 'quality' light years away from mere considerations of relative and changing circumstances, facts and values. It does not make the task easier, or ensure an immediate consensus but at least the task is defensible.

In this sense, meaning and criteria for quality of life in life or death decision-making, should focus not on features or conditions which permit patients to act comfortably, well and without burdening others or society, but rather on features and conditions which allow them to act *at all*, even to a minimal extent. The real question and issue raised by considerations of quality of life is not about the value of this patient's *life* – it is about the value of this patient's *treatment*.

The meaning and criteria of quality of life should focus on *benefit to the patient*, and in some circumstances to initiate treatment or prolong or postpone death can reasonably be seen as non-beneficial to the patient. One such circumstance is *excruciating, intractable and prolonged pain and suffering*. Another is the lack of capacity for what can be considered an inherent feature of human life, namely a *minimal capacity to experience, to relate with other human beings*. In such instances to preserve life could in some cases be a dishonouring of the sanctity of life itself, and allowing even death could be a demonstration of respect for the individual and for human life in general. . . .

In particular there are two such quality of life criteria, relevant to decisions to treat, or to continue treatment or to stop treatment. The first considers the capacity to experience, to relate. The second considers the intensity and susceptibility to control of the patient's pain and suffering. If despite treatment there is not and cannot be even a minimal capacity to experience, and to relate, or if the level of pain and suffering will be prolonged, excruciating and intractable, then a decision to cease or not initiate treatment (of for instance a comatose patient) can be preferable to treatment.

The word 'life' can mean two things in this context. It can mean vital or metabolic processes alone, a life incapable of experiencing or communicating and one which therefore could be called 'human biological life'. Or it could mean a level or quality of life which includes *both* metabolic functions and at least a minimal capacity to experience or communicate, which together could be called 'human personal life'. . . .

Given that the sanctity of life principle imposes the burden of proof on those who would cease to support the lives of others, the consideration of quality of life criteria should not inevitably and exclusively lead to decisions to cease or not initiate life supporting or saving treatment. Quite the opposite should just as often or more often be the case.

While a degree of 'indignity' is an inescapable element of death and dying, and while not every instance of a patient's life being externally supported is thereby undignified, there are cases in which the refusal to consider and weigh the patient's quality of life can result in a prolongation of treatment to the point that a real and further indignity is being done.

Both medical decision-making and law should continue to protect the intrinsic sanctity and value of each human life. But medicine (and perhaps law as well) should formally acknowledge that in some cases the quality or conditions of a patient's life can be so damaged and minimal that treatment or further treatment could be a violation precisely of that life's sanctity and value.

Even in those cases for which it is decided to cease or not initiate external life supporting *treatment*, there always remains a continuing obligation no matter how damaged the patient's condition, to provide whatever amount of *care and comfort* is needed and possible.

The elusiveness of the concept of 'quality of life' leading, perhaps, to confusion, is well illustrated by the judgment of Liacos J in *Superintendent of Belchertown v Saikewicz* (1976) 370 NE 2d 417. Liacos J appeared to want to take advantage of the concept and yet not be seen to be engaging in the calculation that the concept necessarily entails. When discussing whether a mentally retarded person suffering from acute myeloblastic monocytic leukaemia, who was adult but incompetent to consent, should have chemotherapy, he said:

Liacos J: The sixth factor identified by the judge as weighing against chemotherapy was 'the quality of life possible for him even if the treatment does bring about remission'. To the extent that this formulation equates the value of life with any measure of the quality of life, we firmly reject it. A reading of the entire record clearly reveals, however, the judge's concern that special care be taken to respect the dignity and worth of Saikewicz's life precisely because of his vulnerable position. The judge, as well as all the parties, were keenly aware that the supposed ability of Saikewicz, by virtue of his mental retardation, to appreciate or experience life had no place in the decision before them. Rather than reading the judge's formulation in a manner that demeans the value of the life of one who is mentally retarded, the vague, and perhaps ill-chosen term 'quality of life' should be understood as a reference to the continuing state of pain and disorientation precipitated by the chemotherapy treatment.

Clearly, the Court of Appeal in *Re B* was feeling its way towards what we can call a 'quality of life' approach. The court's judgment was, however, *ex tempore*, delivered within an hour of argument, given the urgency of the case. It is no surprise, therefore, that later cases would return to the issue.

The landmark decision in English law which sought to do so was *Re J (a minor) (wardship: medical treatment)* [1990] 3 All ER 930, CA. We must consider this case carefully. Before doing so, however, we need to notice what was at the time a case of considerable notoriety but which from the point of view of legal analysis must be regarded as aberrant.

In *R v Arthur* (1981) 12 BMLR 1, a baby was born with Down's syndrome. His mother told the consultant paediatrician, Dr Leonard Arthur, that 'she did not wish the baby to survive' as recorded in the medical notes. Thereafter, Dr Arthur prescribed dihydrocodeine, a powerful analgesic, and 'nursing care only'. Shortly afterwards, the baby died. Dr Arthur was charged with murder but after medical evidence showed that the prosecution could not prove the cause of death, the charge was reduced to one of attempted murder. In his summing up to the jury, Farquharson J set out the law as he saw it.

R v Arthur (1981) 12 BMLR 1 (Leicester CC)

Farquharson J: In this case the act, or acts, upon which the prosecution rely to say this was an attempt to kill on the part of Dr Arthur, is the preparation of those two documents: the case notes and the treatment chart. It was his endorsement on the case notes to the effect that the child should receive nursing care only, coupled with the prescription he wrote into the treatment chart, that the child should have 5 mg of dihydrocodeine not less than every four hours and at the discretion of the nurse in charge of the child; that is to say, it was under the general heading 'as required'. The prosecution contend before you that those acts set in train the course of events which could only have resulted in the child's death and therefore, they say, that the preparation and endorsement of those treatment charts and case notes must have amounted to an attempt to kill. Whether it does or not is one of the important and vital questions that you have got to decide.

The defence, of course, contend that this does not amount to an act that could properly be described as an attempt. They point out the act was revocable; it could have been stopped, halted and reversed because at any time the mother could have changed the opinion which, in the agony of giving birth, she had already expressed. The fact that the treatment prescribed by Dr Arthur can be recalled, or revoked, does not in itself mean that it could not be an attempt, but it is something that you should take very carefully into account.

. . . the defence do not rest their case there. They go further and say that Dr Arthur was not committing an act, a positive act, at all; he was simply prescribing a treatment which involved the creation of a set of circumstances whereby the child would peacefully die, and that there is all the difference in the world between the one and the other. . . . The nurses were acting as the doctor's agents, in carrying out that task, contend the prosecution.

. . . However serious the case may be; however much the disadvantage of a mongol or, indeed, any other handicapped child, no doctor has the right to kill it.

There is no special law in this country that places doctors in a separate category and gives them extra protection over the rest of us. Neither, in law, is there any special power, facility or licence to kill children who are handicapped or seriously disadvantaged in an irreversible way.

But, perhaps the most agonising part of this case, is that it has become very clear that it is a very difficult area to decide precisely where a doctor is doing an act, a positive act, or allowing a course of events, or a set of circumstances to ensue. It is because no doctor has a special exemption, or a special right in this way, that this case comes before you.

We have heard a good deal about medical ethics and it is a fact that in virtually every profession, or any trade where there is a guild or association of any kind, rules of conduct are set out, and when those rules are broken, the professional body or guild would take action to punish the offender.

But that does not mean that any profession can set out a code of ethics and say that the law must accept it. In this case it has been suggested that what Dr Arthur did here, whatever may be the medical ethics of the matter, has gone beyond what any doctor is entitled to do and has committed a crime. If a child is born with a serious handicap – for example, where a mongol has an ill-formed intestine whereby that child will die of the ailment if he is not operated on – a surgeon may say: 'as this child is a mongol I do not propose to operate; I shall allow nature to take its course'. No one could say that that surgeon was committing an act or murder by declining to take a course which would save the child.

Equally, if a child not otherwise going to die, who is severely handicapped, is given a drug in such an excessive amount by the doctor that the drug itself will cause his death and the doctor does that intentionally it would be open to the jury to say: 'Yes, he was killing; he was murdering that child.' It is very easy to draw the line between those two examples. They are opposite ends of the spectrum. It is very much more difficult to say where the line should be drawn in relation to this case.

Where, perhaps, somebody is suffering from the agonies of terminal cancer and the doctor is obliged to give increasing dosages of an analgesic to relieve the pain, there comes a point where the amounts of those doses are such that in themselves they will kill off the patient, but he is driven to it on medical grounds. There again, you will, undoubtedly, say that that could never be murder. That would be a proper practice of medicine.

Where a child gets pneumonia and is a child with an irreversible handicap whose mother has rejected him, if the doctor said: 'I am not going to give it antibiotics', and by a merciful dispensation of providence he dies, once again it would be very unlikely, I would suggest, that you (or any other jury) would say that that doctor was committing murder. But what is the position here? Was what Dr Arthur did, in setting out that course of management, prescribing that drug in the way of a holding operation – in the nature of setting conditions where the child could, if it contracted pneumonia, die peacefully? Or, if it revealed any other organic defect, die peacefully? Or, was it a positive act on the part of Dr Arthur which was likely to kill the child and represented an attempt (within the definition I have given you), accompanied by an intent on his part that it should, as a result of the treatment that he prescribed, die?

If the prosecution have proved the latter, members of the jury, and you draw the line, so to speak, at that point, well, then he would be guilty of attempted murder. If, on the other hand, they have not been able to do so and what Dr Arthur here prescribed and arranged comes into that first category – of a management that represents a holding operation, but not in the nature of a positive act – then he would not be guilty.

. . . [I]t appears there was a discussion as to whether the mother should or should not keep the child. The result of that discussion is shown in the middle of page 3 [of the notes], 'Parents do not wish the baby to survive. Nursing care only.' . . . [T]he houseman who was the specialist in gynaecology, although he had done his paediatric work previously, said that:

> Nursing care only involves dealing with the bodily functions; the child must be kept warm, fed and cherished. I mean fed with an ordinary feed. One has to consider all the options. If pneumonia developed, I would understand nursing care only to mean that the baby should not be treated but kept comfortable, warm and cherished.

. . . By the time the nurses were in fact looking after the child, it had plainly developed pneumonia. By that stage, whichever side is right about the legal effect of what happened, by that stage at all events, it was accepted that the child had reached a stage where, if infection overcame it, it was going to be left to die . . . [In his statement to the police Dr Arthur said 'If a non-treatment course of conduct with mongol children is adopted, it is in accordance with my own practice, which is accepted by modern paediatric thought. If non-treatment is elected it means it would be wrong to treat infection with antibiotics. The withholding of food is accepted by many doctors as part of non-treatment. Some lay people feel that this is distasteful. Sometimes we do feed babies, even if non-treatment is decided upon, if the parents or nurses wish it. But our major aim is to relieve distress in the child. The baby will take water or water and sugar. If it is fed milk it may be that it will inhale it and suffer a distressing condition. Paediatricians may use any of these foods or water. It really contributes little to the ultimate outcome. When non-treatment is decided upon the paediatrician may hope that parents will change their mind after the immediate shock of the birth. If they do not do so the course is continued in the hope that the baby will die peacefully from infection.']

The jury acquitted Dr Arthur.

The view taken by Farquharson J of the law relating to the doctor's duty is difficult, if not impossible, to reconcile with that in *Re B*. Recourse to language such as 'a holding operation' or 'allowing nature to take its course', is at best unhelpful and, at worst, fails to recognise that a doctor may have a duty to act so as, for example, not to 'allow nature to take its course'. In our view, Farquharson J was wrong to draw a clear line between the acts and omissions of Dr Arthur without properly relating it to the issue of duty. Furthermore, it is a matter of some surprise that the judge did not take advantage of the language used by Templeman LJ in *Re B*. This case had been decided shortly before and had itself attracted wide attention.

Before leaving *Arthur* we should remind ourselves that if the criminal law does ultimately set the agenda for the analysis of the scope of the doctor's duty, there is an aspect of the criminal law not mentioned in *Arthur* but worthy of brief comment. The Children and Young Persons Act 1933, s 1, creates the offence of 'wilful neglect' of a child. This provision does not, however, clinch any argument, since it begs the central question of whether to adopt a new regime of management which allows a baby to die is necessarily 'wilful neglect'. A doctor cannot be liable under the Act since he would not in law be regarded as 'ha[ving] responsibility [for the child]', since the section is limited to those with 'parental responsibility'. A parent, however *can* be guilty under s 1 for failing to provide adequate medical treatment (eg, *R v Senior* [1899] 1 QB 283, *R v Lowe* [1973] QB 702, *Oakey v Jackson* [1914] 1 KB 216). The scope of s 1 was established by the House of Lords in *R v Sheppard* [1981] AC 394, [1980] 3 All ER 899. It should be noticed that the failure to provide 'adequate medical aid' must be 'wilful' and must 'cause [the child] unnecessary suffering or injury to health'.

R v Sheppard [1980] 3 All ER 899, [1981] AC 394 (HL)

The appellants were a young couple of low intelligence living in deprived conditions. Following the death of their 16-month-old son from hypothermia and malnutrition, they were charged under s 1(1) of the Children and Young Persons Act 1933 with wilfully neglecting the child in a manner likely to cause it unnecessary suffering or injury to its health. At the trial it was alleged that the appellants had failed to provide the child with adequate medical aid on several occasions, especially during the week immediately preceding his death. The appellants' defence was, in effect, that they had not realised that the child was ill enough to see a doctor, and that although they had observed his loss of appetite and failure to ingest food they had genuinely thought that that was due to some minor upset which would cure itself. The trial judge applying previous authority treated the offence as one of strict liability and directed the jury that the test of the appellants' guilt was to be judged objectively by whether a reasonable parent, with knowledge of the facts that were known to the appellants, would have appreciated that failure to have the child examined was likely to cause unnecessary suffering or injury to health. The appellants were convicted and appealed unsuccessfully against their convictions to the Court of Appeal. On appeal to the House of Lords, by a majority, the House of Lords allowed the appeal (Lords Fraser and Scarman dissenting).

Lord Diplock: [a] failure [to provide a child with such medical aid as is needed] as it seems to me could not be properly described as 'wilful' unless the parent *either* (1) had directed his mind to the question whether there was some risk (though it might fall far short of a probability) that the child's health might suffer unless he were examined by a doctor and provided with such curative treatment as the examination might reveal as necessary, and had made a conscious decision, for whatever reason, to refrain from arranging for such medical examination, *or* (2) had so refrained because he did not care whether the child might be in need of medical treatment or not.

. . . I have referred to the parents' knowledge of the existence of some risk of injury to health rather than of a probability. The section speaks of an act or omission that is 'likely' to cause unnecessary suffering or injury to health. This word is imprecise. It is capable of covering a whole range of possibilities from 'it's on the cards' to 'it's more probable than not', but, having regard to the ordinary parents' lack of skill in diagnosis and to the very serious consequences which may result from failure to provide a child with timely medical attention, it should in my view be understood as excluding only what would fairly be described as highly unlikely . . .

Lord Edmund-Davies: The justice (and, with respect, the common sense) of the matter is surely that, as Professor Glanville Williams has put in his Textbook of Criminal Law (1978, p 88):

> We do not run to a doctor whenever a child is a little unwell. We invoke medical aid only when we think that a doctor is reasonably necessary and may do some good. The requirement of wilfulness means, or should mean, that a parent who omits to call in the doctor to his child is not guilty of the offence if he does not know that the child needs this assistance.

But to that must be added that a parent reckless about the state of his child's health, not caring whether or not he is at risk, cannot be heard to say that he never gave the matter a thought and was therefore not wilful in not calling in a doctor. In such circumstances recklessness constitutes mens rea no less than positive awareness of the risk involved in failure to act . . .

Lord Keith: This appeal is concerned solely with a failure to provide adequate medical care. The word 'adequate', as applied to medical care, may mean no more than 'ordinarily competent'. If it is related to anything, I think it is related to the prevention of unnecessary suffering or injury to health, as mentioned in s 1(1), where in my view the adjective 'unnecessary' qualifies both 'suffering' and 'injury to health'. There could be no question of a finding of neglect against a parent who provided ordinarily competent medical care, but whose child nevertheless suffered further injury to its health, for example paralysis in a case of poliomyelitis, because the injury to health would not in the circumstances have been unnecessary, in the sense that it could have been prevented through the provision by the parent of adequate medical care. Failure to provide adequate medical care may be deliberate, as when the child's need for it is perceived yet nothing is done, negligent, as when the need ought reasonably to have been perceived but was not, or entirely blameless, as when the need was not perceived but was not such as ought to have been perceived by an ordinary reasonable parent. I would say that in all three cases the parent has neglected the child in the sense of the statute, since I am of opinion that in a proper construction of s 1(2)(a) it is to be ascertained objectively and in the light of events whether the parents failed to provide ordinarily competent medical care which as a matter of fact the child needed in order to prevent unnecessary suffering or injury to its health.

Lord Keith appears to regard 'adequate' to be a matter of fact. However, it is really a matter of judgment based on normative criteria. In other words, 'adequate' also connotes 'appropriate'. If this is so, arguably we are no further in determining the extent of parental duty and thus what regime of management is lawful after reading Lord Keith's speech. Likewise, the cases of *Senior, Lowe* and *Oakey v Jackson* (mentioned above), though establishing potential parental liability, throw little light on the problem we are considering since they are all cases where medical treatment was called for on any reasonable view of the facts.

In any event, the *Arthur* case can be consigned to legal history for the oddity it is. The decision of the Court of Appeal in *Re J* is the leading case.

Re J (A Minor) (Wardship: Medical Treatment) [1990] 3 All ER 930, [1991] Fam 33 (CA)

Lord Donaldson MR: Baby J has suffered almost every conceivable misfortune. He was a very premature baby, born after 27 weeks' gestation on 28 May 1990. He weighed only 1.1 kg (2.5lb) at birth. He was not breathing. Almost immediately he was placed on a ventilator and given antibiotics to counteract an infection. He was put on a drip. His pulse rate frequently became very low and for ten days it was touch and go whether he survived.

One month later, on 28 June, the doctors were able to take him off the ventilator, but he was, and still is, a very sick and handicapped baby. There followed recurrent convulsions and episodes when he stopped breathing (apnoea). As a result he was oxygen-dependent until early August. At the end of August the doctors thought that he could be allowed to go home, although the prognosis was gloomy in the extreme. Four days later, on 1 September 1990, he had to be readmitted to hospital because he had choked and become cyanosed.

The subsequent history of J has been traumatic both for him, his parents and those professionally involved in caring for him. On 3 September it was noted that J had become cyanosed when he cried. On 5 September he collapsed suddenly and was again cyanosed. He was without a pulse, but was resuscitated. Two days later he again collapsed and had to be put on a ventilator. Between then and 23 September he was continuously on a ventilator. During that period four attempts were made to wean him from it. The first three failed because he suffered fits which interfered with the efficiency of the ventilator and on one occasion the doctors had to paralyse him in order to make his oxygen level safe. Since 23 September J has been breathing independently and in some ways his condition has slightly improved. However this improvement is from a base line which can only be described as abysmally low.

Needless to say the doctors have been concerned to discover what are likely to be J's long-term disabilities. As a result it is clear that he has suffered very severe brain damage due to shortage of oxygen and impaired blood supply around the time of his birth. This is no one's fault, but stems from his prematurity. Ultrasound scans of his brain were conducted on 22 August and 10 September. They showed a large area of fluid-filled cavities where there ought to have been brain tissue. The body is incapable of making this good. Of the three neo-natalogists who have been concerned with his care, the most optimistic is Dr W. His view is that J is likely to develop serious spastic quadriplegia, that is to say paralysis of both his arms and legs. It is debatable whether he will ever be able to sit up or to hold his head upright. J appears to be blind, although there is a possibility that some degree of sight may return. He is likely to be deaf. He may be able to make sounds which reflect his mood, but he is unlikely ever to be able to speak, even to the extent of saying 'Mum' or 'Dad'. It is highly unlikely that he will develop even limited intellectual abilities. Most unfortunately of all, there is a likelihood that he will be able to feel pain to the same extent as a normal baby, because pain is a very basic response. It is possible that he may achieve the ability to smile and to cry. Finally, as one might expect, his life expectancy has been considerably reduced at most into his late teens, but even Dr W would expect him to die long before then.

This assessment of J's present state and likely future development is not based only on the skills and experience of the doctors caring for him. It is supported by the ultrasound scans to which I have already referred and by other objective scientific testing.

The problem which now has to be faced by all concerned is what is to be done if J suffers another collapse. This may occur at any time, but is not inevitable. In most cases this would be a matter to be discussed and decided by the doctors in consultation with the parents. By this I do not mean that the parents could tell the doctors what to do, but they would have the right to withhold consent to treatment, subject to the right of the doctors to apply to make the child a ward of court and to seek the guidance of the court. In practice it might be expected that the parents would have confidence in the doctors and that the doctors, recognising the agonising dilemma facing the parents, would take all the time that was necessary to explain the very limited options which were available and, if at all possible, would agree with the parents on a course of action or inaction. In the present case there has been no real difference of opinion between the doctors and the parents, but for extraneous reasons into which it is unnecessary to go J has in fact been made a ward of court and, accordingly, the right and duty to give or refuse consent to treatment is vested in the court.

On 11 October Scott Baker J made an order authorising the hospital to treat J within the parameters of the opinion expressed by Dr W in his report of 4 October 1990, subject to amendments to paras 24, 25 and 26 made in the course of his oral evidence. This opinion, as amended and explained in the course of the hearing before this court, was as follows:

24 I am of the opinion that it would not be in [J's] best interests to re-ventilate him [using a ventilation machine] in the event of his stopping breathing, unless to do so seems appropriate to the doctors caring for him given the prevailing clinical situation. However, I think it would be reasonable to suck out his airway to remove any plug of mucous or milk and to give oxygen by his face mask.
25 If he developed a chest infection I would recommend treatment with antibiotics and maintenance of hydration, but not prolonged [manual] ventilation.
26 [Various recommendations to take effect on the assumption that baby J did not in the event have to face a critical condition as a result of his stopping breathing or otherwise].

The Official Solicitor has appealed against this decision. The parents do not formally appeal, but naturally and very reasonably feel that they are in a dilemma. Their solicitor took immense trouble to explain Scott Baker J's decision to them and at that time they were minded to accept it as being a decision taken in the best interests of their son. However, the fact that the Official Solicitor has appealed has caused them to wonder whether they were right.

The Official Solicitor submits that there are two justifications for an appeal. (i) *Re C (a minor) (wardship: medical treatment)* [1989] 2 All ER 782, [1990] Fam 26 gives guidance on the approach which it is appropriate to adopt in relation to the medical treatment of children who are dying and whose deaths can only be postponed for a short while. *Re B (a minor) (wardship: medical treatment)* (1981) 3 All ER 927, [1981] 1 WLR 1421 gives similar guidance in relation to severely, but not grossly, handicapped children with a shortened, but nevertheless substantial, expectation of life. In the Official Solicitor's view, the present case illustrates a different category falling between these two on which guidance should be given. (ii) Whilst Scott Baker J rightly directed himself that he must act in what he considered to be the best interests of the child, in the Official Solicitor's submission he erred in that a court is never justified in withholding consent to treatment which could enable a child to survive a life-threatening condition, whatever the quality of the life which it would experience thereafter. This is the absolutist approach. Alternatively, he submits that the judge erred in that a court is only justified in withholding consent to such treatment if it is certain that the quality of the child's subsequent life would be 'intolerable' to the child, 'bound to be full of pain and suffering' and 'demonstrably . . . so awful that in effect the child must be condemned to die' (see *Re B* 3 All ER 927 at 929, 930, [1981] 1 WLR 1421 at 1424 per Dunn and Templeman LJJ). In this case, in the Official Solicitor's submission, this has not been shown . . .

[Counsel for the Official Solicitor's] first, or absolutist, submission is that a court is never justified in withholding consent to treatment which could enable a child to survive a life-threatening condition, whatever the pain or other side effects inherent in the treatment and whatever the quality of the life which it would experience thereafter. In making this submission, he distinguishes a case such as that of *Re C (a minor) (wardship: medical treatment)* [1989] 2 All ER 782, [1990] Fam 26, where the child was dying and no amount of medical skill or care could do more than achieve a brief postponement of the moment of death. He submits, rightly, that in such a case neither the parents nor the court, in deciding whether to give or to withhold consent, nor the doctors in deciding what treatment they recommend or would be prepared to administer, are balancing life against death. In such a case death is inevitable, not in the sense that it is inevitable for all of us, but in the sense that the child is actually dying. What is being balanced is not life against death, but a marginally longer life of pain against a marginally shorter life free from pain and ending in death with dignity. He also distinguished and excepted from his proposition the case of the child whose faculties have been entirely destroyed, the so-called 'cabbage' case.

In support of his submission counsel for the Official Solicitor draws attention to the decision of this court in *McKay v Essex Area Health Authority* [1982] 2 All ER 771, [1982] QB 1166. . . .

I do not regard this decision as providing us with either guidance or assistance in the context of the present problem. The child was claiming damages and the decision was that no monetary comparison could be made between the two states [of life and death]. True it is that it contains an assertion of the importance of the sanctity of human life, but that is not in issue.

Counsel for the Official Solicitor then turns to the decision of the Supreme Court of British Columbia in *Re Superintendent of Family and Child Service and Dawson* (1983) 145 DLR (3d) 610, which is also reported and referred to in *Re C* sub nom *Re SD* [1983] 3 WWR 618. There the issue was whether a severely brain damaged child should be subjected to a relatively simple kind of surgical treatment which would assure the continuation of his life or whether, as the parents considered was in the child's best interests, consent to the operation should be refused with a view to the child being allowed to die in the near future with dignity rather than to continue a life of suffering. Counsel for the Official Solicitor relies on the first paragraph of the judgment of McKenzie J, but I think that that paragraph read in isolation is capable of being misleading. The full quotation is (145 DLR (3d) 610 at 620-621):

> I do not think that it lies within the prerogative of any parent or of this court to look down upon a disadvantaged person and judge the quality of that person's life to be so low as not to be deserving of continuance. The matter was well put in an American decision – *Re Weberlist* ((1974) 360 NYS 2d 783 at 787), where Justice Asch said: 'There is a strident cry in America to terminate the lives of *other* people – deemed physically or mentally defective . . . Assuredly, one test of a civilization is its concern with the survival of the "unfittest", a reversal of Darwin's formulation . . . In this case, the court must decide what its ward would choose, if he were in a position to make a sound judgment.' This last sentence puts it right. It is not appropriate for an external decision maker to apply his standards of what constitutes a liveable life and exercise the right to impose death if that standard is not met in his estimation. The decision can only be made in the context of the disabled person viewing the worthwhileness or otherwise of his life in its own context as a disabled person – and in that context he would not compare his life with that of a person enjoying normal advantages. He would know nothing of a normal person's life having never experienced it.

I am in complete agreement with McKenzie J that the starting point is not what might have been, but what is. He was considering the best interests of a severely handicapped child, not of a normal child, and the latter's feelings and interests were irrelevant. I am also in complete agreement with his implied assertion of the vast importance of the sanctity of human life. I cavil mildly, although it is a very important point, with his use of the phrase 'the right to impose death'. No such right exists in the court or the parents. What is in issue in these cases is not a right to impose death, but a right to choose a course of action which will fail to avert death. The choice is that of the patient, if of full age and capacity, the choice is that of the parents or court if, by reason of his age, the child cannot make the choice and it is a choice which must be made solely *on behalf* of the child and in what the court or parents conscientiously believe to be his best interests.

In my view the last sentence of the passage which I have quoted from the judge's judgment shows that he was rejecting a particular comparison as a basis for decision rather than denying that there was a balancing exercise to be performed. I do not therefore think that this decision supports the absolutist approach which I would in any event unhesitatingly reject. In real life there are presumptions, strong presumptions and almost overwhelming presumptions, but there are few, if any, absolutes.

I turn, therefore, to the alternative submission of counsel for the Official Solicitor that a court is only justified in withholding consent to treatment which could enable a child to survive a life-threatening condition if it is certain that the quality of the child's subsequent life would be 'intolerable to the child', 'bound to be full of pain and suffering' and 'demonstrably so awful that in effect the child must be condemned to die'. As I have already mentioned, this submission owes much to the decision of this court in *Re B* (1981) [1990] 3 All ER 927, [1981] 1 WLR 1421.

It is I think, important to remember the facts of that case and what was in issue. B was born suffering from Down's syndrome and was a mongol. At birth she also had an intestinal blockage. Nothing could be done to reverse the effect of Down's syndrome, but the intestinal blockage could be cured without great difficulty and, if this was not done, the child would die. The parents with great sorrow came to the conclusion that it was not in the best interests of the child that the intestinal blockage should be relieved, as to do so would lead to their child experiencing 20 to 30 years of life with severe mental and physical handicaps.

From the point of view of the parents, this was an immensely difficult decision and in truth they were in no position to take it. They were suffering from the shock of finding that they had a mongoloid child and they may well have had little or no experience of the quality of life of such a child, viewed from its own point of view. The decision devolved on the court when the local authority made the child a ward.

There was no issue between the doctors that the operation could and, subject to the views of the parents, should be performed. The difference of medical opinion arose out of those views. One surgeon declined to operate saying that he would wish to respect the wishes of the parents and that in the light of 20 years' experience in the profession he thought that the great majority of surgeons would adopt the same attitude. Two other surgeons said that they would operate, subject to obtaining the consent of the court and notwithstanding the expressed wishes of the parents.

The judge originally decided to give the court's consent to the operation, but changed his mind in the light of the arguments adduced by the parents *and* the fact that the parents did not wish the operation to be performed. This court held that whilst the arguments adduced by the parents were of the utmost relevance in deciding where the best interests of the child lay, their wishes (perhaps their evaluation of the child's best interests is a better description) were irrelevant, since the duty of decision had passed from them to the court.

This court then gave consent. Templeman LJ said ([1990] 3 All ER 927 at 929, [1981] 1 WLR 1421 at 1424):

> ... at the end of the day it devolves on this court in this particular instance to decide whether the life of this child is demonstrably going to be so awful that in effect the child must be condemned to die, or whether the life of this child is still so imponderable that it would be wrong for her to be condemned to die. There may be cases, I know not, of severe proved damage where the future is so certain and where the life of the child is so bound to be full of pain and suffering that the court might be driven to a different conclusion, but in the present case the choice which lies before the court is this: whether to allow an operation to take place which may result in the child living for 20 or 30 years as a mongoloid or whether (and I think this must be brutally the result) to terminate the life of a mongoloid child because she also has an intestinal complaint. Faced with that choice I have no doubt that it is the duty of this court to decide that the child must live.

Dunn LJ said ([1990] 3 All ER 927 at 930, [1981] 1 WLR 1421 at 1424-1425):

> One of the difficulties in the case is that there is no prognosis as to the child's future, except that as a mongol her expectation of life is confined to 20 to 30 years. We were told that no reliable prognosis can be made until probably she is about two years old. That in itself leads me to the route by which the court should make its decision, because there is no evidence that this child's short life is likely to be an intolerable one. There is no evidence at all as to the quality of life which the child may expect. As counsel for the Official Solicitor said, the child should be put into the same position as any other mongol child and must be given the chance to live an existence. I accept that way of putting it.

Again I have to cavil at the use of such an expression as 'condemn to die' and 'the child must live' in Templeman LJ's judgment, which, be it noted, was not a reserved judgment. 'Thou shalt not kill' is an absolute commandment in this context. But, to quote the well-known phrase of Arthur Hugh Clough in *The Latest Decalogue*, in this context it is permissible to add 'but need'st not strive officiously to keep alive'. The decision on life and death must and does remain in other hands. What doctors and the court have to decide is whether, in the best interests of the child patient, a particular decision as to medical treatment should be taken which *as a side effect* will render death more or less likely. This is not a matter of semantics. It is fundamental. At the other end of the age spectrum, the use of drugs to reduce pain will often be fully justified, notwithstanding that this will hasten the moment of death. What can never be justified is the use of drugs or surgical procedures with the primary purpose of doing so.

Re B seems to me to come very near to being a binding authority for the proposition that there is a balancing exercise to be performed in assessing the course to be adopted in the best interests of the child. Even if it is not, I have no doubt that this should be and is the law.

This brings me face to face with the problem of formulating the critical equation. In truth it cannot be done with mathematical or any precision. There is without doubt a very strong presumption in favour of a course of action which will prolong life, but, even excepting the 'cabbage' case to which special considerations may well apply, it is not irrebuttable. As this court recognised in *Re B*, account has to be taken of the pain and suffering and quality of life which the child will experience if life is prolonged. Account has also to be taken of the pain and suffering involved in the proposed treatment itself. *Re B* was probably not a borderline case and I do not think that we are bound to, or should, treat Templeman LJ's use of the words 'demonstrably so awful' or Dunn LJ's use of the word 'intolerable' as providing a quasi-statutory yardstick.

For my part I prefer the formulation of Asch J in *Re Werberlist* (1974) 360 NYS 2d 783 at 787 as explained by McKenzie J in the passage from his judgment in *Dawson's* case (1983) 145 DLR (3d) 610 at 620-621 which I have quoted, although it is probably merely another way of expressing the same concept. We know that the instinct and desire for survival is very strong. We all believe in and assert the sanctity of human life. As explained, this formulation takes account of this and also underlines the need to avoid looking at the problem from the point of view of the decider, but instead requires him to look at it from the assumed point of view of the patient. This gives effect, as it should, to the fact that even very severely handicapped people find a quality of life rewarding which to the unhandicapped may seem manifestly intolerable. People have an amazing adaptability. But in the end there will be cases in which the answer must be that it is not in the interests of the child to subject it to treatment which will cause increased suffering and produce no commensurate benefit, giving the fullest possible weight to the child's, and mankind's, desire to survive.

I make no apology for having spent time on the generality of the problem which faces doctors and the courts in cases of this nature. The Official Solicitor invited us to do so and if we can succeed in achieving any degree of clarification, it will be worthwhile in terms of assisting those who have to make these very difficult decisions at short notice and in distressing circumstances. However, I now turn to the instant appeal.

The issue here is whether it would be in the best interests of the child to put him on a mechanical ventilator and subject him to all the associated processes of intensive care, if at some future time he could not continue breathing unaided. Let me say at once that I can understand the doctors wishing to ascertain the court's wishes at this stage, because it is an eventuality which could occur at any time and, if it did, an immediate decision might well have to be made. However, the situation is significantly different from being asked whether or not to consent on behalf of the child to particular treatment which is more or less immediately in prospect. The judge has found that the odds are about even whether the need for artificial ventilation, whether mechanical or manual, will ever arise. If it does arise, the very fact that it has arisen will mean that the more optimistic end of the range of prognoses, pessimistic though the whole range is, will have been falsified. On the other hand, the child's state of health might change at any time for the better as well as for the worse, even though there are distinct limits to what could be hoped for, let alone anticipated.

The doctors were unanimous in recommending that there should be no mechanical reventilation in the event of his stopping breathing, subject only to the qualifications injected by Dr W and accepted by the judge that in the event of a chest infection short term manual ventilation would be justified and that in the event of the child stopping breathing the provisional decision to abstain from mechanical ventilation could and should be revised, if this seemed appropriate to the doctors caring for him in the then prevailing clinical situation.

There can be no criticism of the judge for indorsing this approach on the footing that he was thereby abdicating his responsibility and leaving it to the doctors to decide. He had reviewed and considered the basis of the doctors' views and recommendations in the greatest detail and with the greatest care. Nothing could be more inimical to the interests of the child than the judge should make an order which restricted the doctors' freedom to revise their present view in favour of more active means to preserve the life of the child, if the situation changed and this then seemed to them to be appropriate.

The basis of the doctors' recommendations, approved by the judge, was that mechanical ventilation is itself an invasive procedure which, together with its essential accompaniments, such as the introduction of a naso-gastric tube, drips which have to be resited and constant blood sampling, would cause the child distress. Furthermore, the procedures involve taking active measures which carry their own hazards, not only to life but in terms of causing even greater brain damage. This had to be balanced against what could possibly be achieved by the adoption of such active treatment. The chances of preserving the child's life might be improved, although even this was not certain and account had to be taken of the extremely poor quality of life at present enjoyed by the child, the fact that he had already been ventilated for exceptionally long periods, the unfavourable prognosis with or without ventilation and a recognition that if the question of reventilation ever arose, his situation would have deteriorated still further.

I can detect no error in the judge's approach and in principle would affirm his decision. This is subject to two qualifications. (i) Although all concerned have, as they know, liberty to apply to the judge at any time and he had arranged to review his decision in December, I think that he should have asked for periodic reports meanwhile on J's condition, so that he could, if he thought it appropriate, review the matter before then of his own motion. (ii) I do not think that his order should have been in the form of 'The [local authority] shall direct the relevant health authority to continue to treat . . .' because neither the court in wardship proceedings nor, I think, a local authority having care and control of the baby is able to require the authority to follow a particular course of treatment. What the court can do is to withhold consent to treatment of which it disapproves and it can express its approval of other treatment proposed by the authority and its doctors. There is ample precedent for the judge's formula, but I think that it is wrong and obscures the co-operative nature of the relationship between court and medical authorities. I would prefer 'Approval is given to the continuance of the treatment of . . .'

Taylor LJ: Three preliminary principles are not in dispute. First, it is settled law that the court's prime and paramount consideration must be the best interests of the child. That is easily said but not easily applied. What it does involve is that the views of the parents, although they should be heeded and weighed, cannot prevail over the court's view of the ward's best interests. In the present case the parents, finding themselves in a hideous dilemma, have not taken a strong view so that no conflict arises.

Second, the court's high respect for the sanctity of human life imposes a strong presumption in favour of taking all steps capable of preserving it, save in exceptional circumstances. The problem is to define those circumstances.

Third, and as a corollary to the second principle, it cannot be too strongly emphasised that the court never sanctions steps to terminate life. That would be unlawful. There is no question of approving, even in a case of the most horrendous disability, a course aimed at terminating life or accelerating death. The court is concerned only with the circumstances in which steps should not be taken to prolong life.

Two decisions of this court have dealt with cases at the extremes of the spectrum of affliction. *Re C (a minor) (wardship: medical treatment)* [1989] 2 All ER 782, [1990] Fam 26 was a case in which a child had severe irreversible brain damage such that she was hopelessly and terminally ill. This court held that the best interests of the child required approval of recommendations designed to ease her suffering and permit her life to come to an end peacefully with dignity rather than seek to prolong her life.

By contrast, in the earlier case of *Re B (a minor) (wardship: medical treatment)* (1981) [1990] 3 All ER 927, [1981] 1 WLR 1421, the court was concerned with a child suffering from Down's syndrome, who quite separately was born with an intestinal obstruction. Without an operation this intestinal condition would quickly have been fatal. On the other hand, the operation had a good chance of successfully removing the obstruction, once and for all, thereby affording the child a life expectancy of some 20 to 30 years as a mongol. The parents genuinely believed it was in the child's interests to refrain from operating and allow her to die. The court took a different view . . .

Those two cases thus decide that where the child is terminally ill the court will not require treatment to prolong life; but where, at the other extreme, the child is severely handicapped although not intolerably so and treatment for a discrete condition can enable life to continue for an appreciable period, albeit subject to that severe handicap, the treatment should be given.

I should say that, in my view, the phrase 'condemned to die' which occurs twice in the passage cited from the judgment of Templeman LJ is more emotive than accurate. As already indicated, the court in these cases has to decide, not whether to end life, but whether to prolong it by treatment without which death would ensue from natural causes.

It is to be noted that Templeman LJ did not say, even obiter, that where the child's life would be bound to be full of pain and suffering there would come a point at which the court should rule against prolonging life by treatment. He went no further than to say there may be cases where the court might take that view.

This leads to the arguments presented by counsel for the Official Solicitor. His first submission propounded an absolute test, that, except where the ward is terminally ill, the court's approach should always be to prolong life by treatment if this is possible, regardless of the quality of life being preserved and regardless of any added suffering caused by the treatment itself. I cannot accept this test which in my view is so hard as to be inconsistent at its extreme with the best interests of the child. Counsel for the Official Solicitor submits that the court cannot play God and decide whether the quality of life which the treatment would give the child is better or worse than death. . . .

Despite the court's inability to compare a life afflicted by the most severe disability with death, the unknown, I am of the view that there must be extreme cases in which the court is entitled to say: 'The life which this treatment would prolong would be so cruel as to be intolerable.' If, for example, a child was so damaged as to have negligible use of its faculties and the only way of preserving its life was by the continuous administration of extremely painful treatment such that the child either would be in continuous agony or would have to be so sedated continuously as to have no conscious life at all, I cannot think counsel's absolute test should apply to require the treatment to be given. In those circumstances, without there being any question of deliberately ending the life or shortening it, I consider the court is entitled in the best interests of the child to say that deliberate steps should not be taken artificially to prolong its miserable life span.

Once the absolute test is rejected, the proper criteria must be a matter of degree. At what point in the scale of disability and suffering ought the court to hold that the best interests of the child do not require further endurance to be imposed by positive treatment to prolong its life? Clearly, to justify withholding treatment, the circumstances would have to be extreme. Counsel for the Official Solicitor submitted that if the court rejected his absolute test, then at least it would have 'to be certain that the life of the child, were the treatment to be given, would be intolerably awful'.

I consider that the correct approach is for the court to judge the quality of life the child would have to endure if given the treatment and decide whether in all the circumstances such a life would be so afflicted as to be intolerable to that child. I say 'to that child' because the test should not be whether the life would be tolerable to the decider. The test must be whether the child in question, if capable of exercising sound judgment, would consider the life tolerable. This is the approach adopted by McKenzie J in *Re Superintendent of Family and Child Service and Dawson* (1983) 145 DLR (3d) 610 at 620-621 in the passage cited with approval by Lord Donaldson MR. It takes account of the strong instinct to preserve one's life even in circumstances which an outsider, not himself at risk of death, might consider unacceptable. The circumstances to be considered would, in appropriate cases, include the degree of existing disability and any additional suffering or aggravation of the disability which the treatment itself would superimpose. In an accident case, as opposed to one involving disablement from birth, the child's pre-accident quality of life and its perception of what has been lost may also be factors relevant to whether the residual life would be intolerable to that child.

Counsel for the Official Solicitor argued that, before deciding against treatment, the court would have to be *certain* that the circumstances of the child's future would comply with the extreme requirements to justify that decision. Certainty as to the future is beyond human judgment. The courts have not, even in the trial of capital offences, required certainty of proof. But, clearly, the court must be satisfied to a high degree of probability.

In the present case, the doctors were unanimous that in his present condition, J should not be put back on to a mechanical ventilator. That condition is very grave indeed. I do not repeat the description of it given by Lord Donaldson MR. In reaching his conclusion, the judge no doubt had three factors in mind. First, the severe lack of capacity of the child in all his faculties which even without any further complication would make his existence barely sentient. Second, that, if further mechanical ventilation were to be required, that very fact would involve the risk of a deterioration in B's condition, because of further brain damage flowing from the interruption of breathing. Third, all the doctors drew attention to the invasive nature of mechanical ventilation and the intensive care required to accompany it. They stressed the unpleasant and distressing nature of that treatment. To add such distress and the risk of further deterioration to an already appalling catalogue of disabilities was clearly capable in my judgment of producing a quality of life which justified the stance of the doctors and the judge's conclusion. I therefore agree that, subject to the minor variations to the judge's order proposed by Lord Donaldson MR, this appeal should be dismissed.

Balcombe LJ agreed.

The language adopted by the court in *Re J* makes it clear that the court rejected any absolute notion of the sanctity of life in favour of an enquiry into the patient's quality of life as the means of determining his 'best interests'. That the judges did so cautiously, conscious of the implications of their decision, cannot be denied, but they did so none the less. Three points deserve attention.

First (a minor point), two of the judges curiously purport to apply the 'substituted judgment' test. As we have seen, this has no place where the patient has never been competent so as to express a view or hold values. Taylor LJ, however, talks of whether life would be 'intolerable to *that child*' (our emphasis). By this he clearly intended to direct the decision-maker's attention to what the child would consider intolerable: '[t]he test must be whether the child in question, *if capable of exercising sound judgment*, would consider the life tolerable' (our emphasis). (See also Lord Donaldson MR at 936.) This is an impossible test to apply given the circumstances of the child (see *supra*, ch 4).

Secondly, any reference to 'quality of life' still leaves unanswered the question which 'quality' or 'qualities' are relevant. For the Court of Appeal it would appear that the condition of the patient must be extreme before any consideration of withholding or withdrawing treatment may be contemplated. Arguably, the judges only permit the decision-maker to balance the benefits and burdens of treatment so as to let the patient die in such cases. The judges appear to erect a strong presumption in favour of treatment unless the patient's life will be intolerable or 'demonstrably' awful. It cannot be argued that these terms have any great ring of precision. Indeed, it is not clear whether the judges agree as to how extreme the patient's condition must be. Certainly, it seems that Taylor LJ, by adopting the language of Templeman LJ in *Re B*, would only contemplate letting the patient die in the most extreme circumstances. Lord Donaldson MR (and, perhaps Balcombe LJ also), however, as we saw, rejected the language in *Re B* and, as a consequence, may have 'left the door open' for less extreme cases (per Butler-Sloss LJ in *Airedale NHS Trust v Bland* [1993] 1 All ER 821 at 845).The Court of Appeal in *Bland* did little to make the matter any clearer. It is arguable, however, that both Sir Thomas Bingham MR and Hoffman LJ (like Taylor LJ in *Re J*) opt for a more extreme test emphasising that 'full weight has to be given to the principle of the sanctity of life before deciding that a test of best interests justifies a decision to allow the patient to die' (per Hoffman LJ at 857).

Notwithstanding the above, what appears to emerge is a requirement that the patient must have little or no prospect of any meaningful interaction with others or his environment before a decision to withhold or withdraw treatment can be taken. After all, the Court of Appeal cited with approval the decision of McKenzie J in the British Columbia case of *Dawson* and it is hard to imagine circumstances of more extreme disability than those suffered by Stephen Dawson.

Re Superintendent of Family and Child Service and Dawson (1983) 145 DLR (3d) 610 (BC Sup Ct)

McKenzie J: [Stephen Dawson] is a severely retarded boy approaching seven years, who shortly after birth suffered profound brain damage through meningitis which inflamed the lining of his brain and left him with no control over his faculties, limbs or bodily functions. At the age of five months life-support surgery was performed by implanting a shunt which is a plastic tube which drains excess cerebrospinal fluid from the head to another body cavity from which it is expelled or absorbed.

[He] is legally blind, with atrophied optic nerves, partly deaf, incontinent, cannot hold a spoon to feed himself, cannot stand, walk, talk, or hold objects. [His parents] say that he has no method of communicating with his environment and think he is in pain. The sounds he makes are too soft to be heard from any distance. He is subject to seizures despite anticonvulsant medication. He is restrained by splints which are bandages on his arms to keep his elbows straight so that he cannot chew on his hands and roughly handle his face. Staff carry him from bed to wheelchair, which has a moulded 'insert' to ensure he is held securely and he is belted in with a hip belt.

This description applies to his condition as it existed when he was a patient in Sunnyhill Hospital before the shunt stopped operating. About six weeks ago a blockage in the shunt was detected and the parents gave their consent to remedial surgery but, after a day's reflection, withdrew their consent on the ground that the boy should be allowed to die with dignity rather than continue to endure a life of suffering. They continued to maintain that position . . .

I respect and have given anxious consideration to the views of the parents. In so doing I must give some weight to the fact that they were divorced in mid-1980 after extended matrimonial discord. Also I must give weight to my conclusion based on the evidence that they thought Stephen better dead long before the need for the critical decision arose about replacement of the shunt. Despite the evidence of highly qualified professionals, in whom I place great reliance, they are satisfied Stephen will promptly die if treatment is denied. My finding is that it is by no means a certainty that death will soon follow and a real possibility exists that his life will go on indefinitely but in pain and progressive deterioration. I must reject their assertion that they would consent to the operation if they could be assured that he would thereafter be comfortable and free of pain when at the same time they reject the opinions of competent professionals that such will probably be the case. I believe that their minds are firmly made up and closed shut.

I regret having to make such findings. . . .

I cannot accept their view that Stephen would be better off dead. If it is to be decided that 'it is in the best interests of Stephen Dawson that his existence cease', then it must be decided that, for him, non-existence is the better alternative. This would mean regarding the life of a handicapped child as not only less valuable than the life of a normal child, but so much less valuable that it is not worth preserving. I tremble at contemplating the consequences if the lives of disabled persons are dependent upon such judgments.

To refer back to the words of Templeman LJ I cannot in conscience find that this is a case of severe proved damage 'where the future is so certain and where the life of the child is so bound to be full of pain and suffering that the court might be driven to a different conclusion'. I am not satisfied that 'the life of this child is demonstrably going to be so awful that in effect the child must be condemned to die'. Rather I believe that 'the life of this child is still so imponderable that it would be wrong for her to be condemned to die'.

There is not a simple choice here of allowing the child to live or die according to whether the shunt is implanted or not. There looms the awful possibility that without the shunt the child will endure in a state of progressing disability and pain. It is too simplistic to say that the child should be allowed to die in peace.

It is a matter which ultimately eludes rational analysis whether the condition of Baby J was more extreme, so as to warrant the withholding of treatment, than that of Stephen Dawson. There is, however, one pointer which suggests a difference between the condition of the patients in *Re J* and *Dawson* – that of pain, albeit the difference is not between its presence or absence, but between degrees of pain. You will recall that Stephen Dawson would suffer 'progressing pain' if he were not treated.

As for our third point, this relates to the emphasis placed upon the patient being in pain. The difficulty of identifying pain as the key to determining whether the quality of a patient's life is sufficiently intolerable to justify withdrawing or withholding care is that pain itself is an elusive concept and, more important, it is and should be only one of the factors in assessing 'quality of life'. If 'pain' were elevated to a special status, it would mean that the patient who is free of pain should always be treated if there is even the slightest benefit to be gained thereby (leaving aside what 'benefit' means). You will recall Handler J's concurring opinion in the *Matter of Conroy* (1985) 486 A 2d 1209 (NJ Sup Ct):

> **Handler J:** In my opinion, the Court's objective tests too narrowly define the interests of people like Miss Conroy. While the basic standard purports to account for several concerns, it ultimately focuses on pain as the critical factor. The presence of significant pain in effect becomes the sole measure of such a person's best interests. 'Pain' thus eclipses a whole cluster of other human values that have a proper place in the subtle weighing that will ultimately determine how life should end.
>
> The Court's concentration on pain as the exclusive criterion in reaching the life-or-death decision in reality transmutes the best-interests determination into an exercise of avoidance and nullification rather than confrontation and fulfilment. In most cases the pain criterion will dictate that the decision be one not to withdraw life-prolonging treatment and not to allow death to occur naturally. First, pain will not be an operative factor in a great many cases. '[P]resently available drugs and techniques allow pain to be reduced to a level acceptable to virtually every patient, usually without unacceptable sedation.' *President's Commission Report, supra,* at 50-51. *See id* at 19 n 19 *citing* Saunders, 'Current Views on Pain Relief and Terminal Care' in *The Therapy of Pain* 215 (Swerdlow, ed. 1981) (a hospice reports complete control of pain in over 99% of its dying patients). *See generally id* at 277-95. *See also generally The Management of Terminal Disease* (Saunders, ed 1978); *The Experience of Dying* (Pattison, ed 1977); *Psychopharmacologic Agents for the Terminally Ill and Bereaved* (Goldberg *et al,* eds 1973). Further, as was true in Miss Conroy's case, health care providers frequently encounter difficulty in evaluating the degree of pain experienced by a patient. Finally, '[o]nly a minority of patients – fewer than half of those with malignancies, for example – have substantial problems with pain. . . .' *President's Commission Report, supra* at 278 *citing* Twycross, 'Relief of Pain' in *The Management of Terminal Disease, supra* at 66. Thus, in a great many cases, the pain test will become an absolute bar to the withdrawal of life-support therapy.
>
> The pain requirement, as applied by the Court in its objective tests, effectively negates other highly relevant considerations that should appropriately bear on the decision to maintain or to withdraw life-prolonging treatment. The pain standard may dictate the decision to prolong life despite the presence of other factors that reasonably militate in favor of the termination of such procedures to allow a natural death. The exclusive pain criterion denies relief to that class of people who, at the very end of life, might strongly disapprove of an artificially extended existence in spite of the absence of pain. *See In Re Torres,* 357 NW 332, 340 (Minn 1984) (although a patient 'cannot feel pain,' that patient may have a guardian petition to forego life-sustaining treatment). Thus, some people abhor dependence on others as much, or more, than they fear pain. Other individuals value personal privacy and dignity, and prize independence from others when their personal needs and bodily functions are involved. Finally, the ideal of bodily integrity may become more important than simply prolonging life at its most rudimentary level. Persons, like Miss Conroy, 'may well have wished to avoid . . . [t]he ultimate horror [not of] death but the possibility of being maintained in limbo, in a sterile room, by machines controlled by strangers.' *In Re Torres, supra* 357 NW 2d at 340, quoting Steel, 'The Right to Die: New Options in California,' 93 *Christian Century* [July-Dec 1976].
>
> Clearly, a decision to focus exclusively on pain as the single criterion ignores and devalues other important ideals regarding life and death. Consequently, a pain standard cannot serve as an indirect proxy for additional and significant concerns that bear on the decision to forego life-prolonging treatments. . . .
>
> I share the Court's discomfiture with a standard that does not attempt to identify reasonably verifiable measures of a person's quality of life. However, there is no intrinsic reason why a quality-of-life standard must remain any more vague and undefined than a standard that includes pain. . . .

I would therefore have the Court adopt a test that does not rely exclusively on pain as the ultimately determinative criterion. Rather, the standard should consist of an array of factors to be medically established and then evaluated by the decision-maker both singly and collectively to reach a balance that will justify the determination whether to withdraw or to continue life-prolonging treatment. The withdrawal of life-prolonging treatment from an unconscious or comatose, terminally ill individual near death, whose personal views concerning life-ending treatment cannot be ascertained, should be governed by such a standard.

Several important criteria bear on this critical determination. The person should be terminally ill and facing imminent death. There should also be present the permanent loss of conscious thought processes in the form of a comatose state or profound unconsciousness. Further, there should be the irreparable failure of at least one major and essential bodily organ or system. *See, eg, In Re Quinlan*, 70 NJ 10, 355, A 2d 647 (1976) (respiratory system); *Barber, supra* (same); *In Re Dinnerstein*, 6 Mass App 466, 380 NE 2d 134 (1978) (heart); *Saikewicz, supra* (circulatory system); *Conroy, supra* (swallowing reflex); *Torres, supra* (cerebral cortex and brain-stem); *In Re Hamlin*, 102 Wash 2d 810, 689 P 2d 1372 (1984) (cerebral cortex). Obviously the presence or absence of significant pain is highly relevant.

In addition, the person's general physical condition must be of great concern. The presence of progressive, irreversible, extensive, and extreme physical deterioration, such as ulcers, lesions, gangrene, infection, incontinence and the like, which frequently afflict the bed-ridden, terminally ill, should be considered in the formulation of an appropriate standard. The medical and nursing treatment of individuals *in extremis* and suffering from these conditions entails the constant and extensive handling and manipulation of the body. At some point, such a course of treatment upon the insensate patient is bound to touch the sensibilities of even the most detached observer. Eventually, pervasive bodily intrusions, even for the best motives, will arouse feelings akin to humiliation and mortification for the helpless patient. When cherished values of human dignity and personal privacy, which belong to every person living or dying, are sufficiently transgressed by what is being done to the individual, we should be ready to say: enough.

When the *Bland* case was before the Court of Appeal, all three judges accepted that pain was not the critical factor in the process of weighing so as to determine a patient's best interests.

Sir Thomas Bingham MR: I accept the argument . . . that account may be taken of wider and less tangible considerations. An objective assessment of Mr Bland's best interests . . . would in my opinion give weight to the constant invasions and humiliations to which his inert body is subject; to the desire he would naturally have to be remembered as a cheerful, carefree, gregarious teenager and not an object of pity; to the prolonged ordeal imposed on all members of his family, but particularly on his parents; even, perhaps, if altruism still lives, to a belief that finite resources are better devoted to enhancing life than simply averting death.

Butler-Sloss LJ: [Counsel for the Official Solicitor] argued in *Re J* the fundamentalist or absolutist approach, that the pain and suffering experienced and to be experienced by that child should not displace the sanctity of life, including the preservation of the life of that child, whatever it was to be. This court rejected that approach and placed on the other side of the critical equation the tragic situation of the child concerned and the quality of his life. Lord Donaldson MR did not feel bound to follow the views expresses (obiter) in *Re B (a minor) (wardship: medical treatment)* [1981] 1 WLR 1421 as to the degree of awfulness or intolerability of treatment which might be proposed as providing a quasi-statutory yardstick. He left the door open. Apart from preferring to use a word other than 'cabbage', I respectfully agree with him. . . .

[Counsel for the Official Solicitor's] answer was that severe pain and suffering as experienced by the child in *Re J* is the only factor which can be put on the other side of the equation to the sanctity of life. He reserved his position to argue elsewhere that *Re J* was wrongly decided and there was nothing to place in the balance against the sanctity of life. In his argument to this court the interests of the PVS patient are limited to that sole consideration.

To place pain and suffering in an unique category, the existence of which may justify foregoing the preservation of the sanctity of life, does not appear to me to be justifiable. Two reasons come immediately to mind. First, on a practical level, according to [counsel for the Official Solicitor] the exception of extreme pain can be justified on the basis that it can be objectively verified. The degree of resistance to pain varies enormously from person to person and is intensively subjective however its existence as such may be objectively verified. It is not an absolute state and it will always be a matter of degree as to whether the state of pain of an incompetent patient is sufficiently severe to meet the necessary criterion. If it is to be the only criterion, excluding all other considerations, the lack of clarity in formulating when it comes into play, creates for me a logical problem in accepting it alone on the other side of the equation.

There is however a second and more fundamental objection. The case for the universal sanctity of life assumes a life in the abstract and allows nothing for the reality of Mr Bland's actual existence. There are clearly dangers in departing from the fundamental approach to the preservation of life, but in the American decisions it is not conclusive. Two exceptions are already recognised in English common law, the right of self-determination and the *Re J* situation of extreme pain and suffering. The quality of life has already been recognised as a factor and placed in the equation to allow a life not to be prolonged at all costs. Taylor LJ said in *Re J* [1990] 3 All ER 930 at 945, [1991] Fam 33 at 35: 'Once the absolute test is rejected, the proper criteria must be a matter of degree.' To limit the quality of life to extreme pain is to take a demeaning view of a human being. There must be something more for the humanity of the person of a PVS patient. He remains a person and not an object of concern. In *Re Conroy* (1985) 98 NJ 321 at 396, Handler J supports this approach:

> Clearly, a decision to focus exclusively on pain as the single criterion ignores and devalues other important ideals regarding life and death. Consequently, a pain standard cannot serve as an indirect proxy for additional and significant concerns that bear on the decision to forego life-prolonging treatments.

The concentration exclusively upon pain is to me an unacceptable approach to a patient in Anthony Bland's extreme situation. There are other factors to be placed in the critical equation.

Those other factors have not so far been explored in English decisions but they have been considered extensively in the United States and in a recent case in New Zealand. In *Cruzan v Director, Missouri Dept of Health* (1990) 110 S Ct 2841 at 2885-2886 (a PVS case) Stevens J (in a dissenting opinion) said:

> But Nancy Cruzan's interest in life, no less than any other person, includes an interest in how she will be thought of after her death by those whose opinions mattered to her. There can be no doubt that her life made her dear to her family, and to others. How she dies will affect how that life is remembered.

In *Guardianship of Jane Doe* (1992) 411 Mass 512 the Supreme Judicial Court of Massachusetts (in a PVS case where the patient had always been incompetent) held that incompetent individuals have the same rights as competent individuals to refuse and terminate medical treatment. Abrams J, giving the majority opinion, accepted the rights of the patient to bodily integrity and privacy and upheld the judge's decision to terminate nasoduodenal feeding and hydration. *Re Jobes* (1987) 108 NJ 394 (a PVS patient) following *Re Quinlan* (1976) 70 NJ 10 upheld the principle of self-determination for the incompetent. The views of the family were accepted in each of those cases. Handler J in a concurring opinion considered the best interests test and, after describing the extreme physical condition of Mrs Jobes (very similar to Mr Bland) quoted a passage in his opinion in *Re Conroy* (1985) 98 NJ 321 at 398-399:

> 'The medical and nursing treatment of individuals in extremis and suffering from these conditions entails the constant and extensive handling and manipulation of the body. At some point, such a course of treatment upon the insensate patient is bound to touch the sensibilities of even the most detached observer. Eventually, pervasive bodily intrusions, even for the best of motives, will arouse feelings akin to humiliation and mortification for the helpless patient. When cherished values of human dignity and personal privacy, which belong to every person living or dying, are sufficiently transgressed by what is being done to the individual, we should be ready to say: enough.' Based upon such factors it should be possible to structure critical treatment decisions that are reliable, understandable and acceptable. (See 108 NJ 394 at 443-444.)

Auckland Area Health Board v A-G [1993] 1 NZLR 235 was an extreme example of a Guillain-Barre syndrome, causing a condition somewhat similar to a PVS patient, where the doctors sought a declaration that to withdraw artificial ventilation would not constitute culpable homicide. Thomas J granted the declaration and in doing so considered decisions from a number of common law jurisdictions including the American and our own. He referred (at 245) to

> values of human dignity and personal privacy . . . Human dignity and personal privacy belong to every person, whether living or dying. Yet, the sheer invasiveness of the treatment and the manipulation of the human body which it entails, the pitiful and humiliating helplessness of the patient's state and the degradation and dissolution of all bodily functions invoke these values . . .

The judge based his decision upon the best interests test. Mr Munby [counsel for the Official Solicitor] accepted that there was no difference in principle between the ventilator and the nasogastric tube.

Although the American decisions are often based upon the principle of achieving the right of an incompetent patient to make decisions as if competent through the device of the substituted judgment, in many cases the distinction from best interests is blurred as Handler J pointed out in *Re Jobes* (1987) 108 NJ 394 at 436, and in some cases it is clearly an objective assessment of best interests and the decisions are persuasive support for considerations far wider than the factor of pain to be taken into account in balancing the critical equation.

We all of course recognise that a patient unable to choose cannot himself exercise his right of self-determination and he cannot make the irrational decision he might notionally have made if in possession of his faculties. But not to be able to be irrational does not seem to me to be a good reason to be deprived of a rational decision which could be taken on his behalf in his best interests. Otherwise, if, as I believe they are, other factors as well as pain are relevant considerations, he is put at an unfair disadvantage.

A mentally incompetent patient has interests to be considered and protected, the basic one being the right to be properly cared for by others. He retains the right to have proceedings taken on his behalf, for instance to claim damages for negligence, or to have his estate or other property managed for him, or to respond to actions or proceedings taken against him, such as divorce proceedings. He retains in my view the right to be well regarded by others, and to be well remembered by his family. That right is separate from that of his family to remember him and to have the opportunity to grieve for him when he is dead. He has the right to be respected. Consequently he has a right to avoid unnecessary humiliation and degrading invasion of his body for no good purpose. . . .

The considerations as to the quality of life of Mr Bland now and in the future in his extreme situation are in my opinion rightly to be placed on the other side of the critical equation from the general principle of the sanctity and inviolability of life.

Hoffman LJ: The best interests of the patient in my judgment embrace not only recovery or the avoidance of pain (neither of which apply to this case) but also a dignified death. On this issue I respectfully agree with the dissenting judgments of Handler J in *Re Conroy* (1985) 98 NJ 321 and Brennan and Stevens JJ in *Cruzan v Director, Missouri Dept of Health* (1990) 497 US 261.

The adult cases – We have already made it clear that the legal principles relevant to decisions concerning medical treatment at the end of life are of equal application to babies and to others who are incompetent, whether children or adults. Thus the analysis applied in the case of the severely disabled neonates applies to the senile elderly and terminally ill young adult. English law, however, only has cases on babies. Hence, as regards the application of these principles to others, particularly adults, we must look to other jurisdictions for cases applying them. You will recall our discussion of the important cases of *Conroy* and *Saikewicz* earlier in this chapter. Three other cases in the United States are instructive.

Re Dinnerstein (1978) 380 NE 2d 134 (App Ct Mass)

Justice Armstrong: . . . The patient is a sixty-seven year old woman who suffers from a condition known as Alzheimer's disease. It is a degenerative disease of the brain of unknown origin, described as presenile dementia, and results in destruction of brain tissue and, consequently, deterioration in brain function. The condition is progressive and unremitting, leading in stages to disorientation, loss of memory, personality disorganisation, loss of intellectual function, and ultimate loss of all motor function. The disease typically leads to a vegetative or comatose condition and then to death. The course of the disease may be gradual or precipitous, averaging five to seven years. At this time medical science knows of no cure for the disease and no treatment which can slow or arrest its course. No medical breakthrough is anticipated.

The patient's condition was diagnosed as Alzheimer's disease in July, 1975, although the initial symptoms of the disease were observed as early as 1972. She entered a nursing home in November, 1975, where her (by that time) complete disorientation, frequent psychotic outbursts, and deteriorating ability to control elementary bodily functions made her dependent on intensive nursing care. In February, 1978, she suffered a massive stroke, which left her totally paralysed on her left side. At the present time she is confined to a hospital bed, in an essentially vegetative state, immobile, speechless, unable to swallow without choking, and barely able to cough. Her eyes occasionally open and from time to time appear to fix on or follow an object briefly; otherwise she appears to be unaware of her environment. She is fed through a naso-gastric tube, intravenous feeding having been abandoned because it came to cause her pain. It is probable that she is experiencing some discomfort from the naso-gastric tube, which can cause irritation, ulceration, and infection in her throat and esophageal tract, and which must be removed from time to time, and that procedure itself causes discomfort. She is catheterised and also, of course, requires bowel care. Apart from her Alzheimer's disease and paralysis, she suffers from high blood pressure which is difficult to control; there is risk in lowering it due to a constriction in an artery leading to a kidney. She has a serious, life-threatening coronary artery disease, due to arteriosclerosis. Her condition is hopeless, but it is difficult to predict exactly when she will die. Her life expectancy is no more than a year, but she could go into cardiac or respiratory arrest at any time. One of these, or another stroke, is most likely to be the immediate cause of her death.

In this situation her attending physician has recommended that, when (and if) cardiac or respiratory arrest occurs, resuscitation efforts should not be undertaken. Such efforts typically involve the use of cardiac massage or chest compression and delivery of oxygen under compression through an endotracheal tube into the lungs. An electrocardiogram is connected to guide the efforts of the resuscitation team and to monitor the patient's progress. Various plastic tubes are usually inserted intravenously to supply medications or stimulants directly to the heart. Such medications may also be supplied by direct injection into the heart by means of a long needle. A defibrillator may be used, applying electric shock to the heart to induce contractions. A pacemaker, in the form of an electrical conducting wire, may be fed through a large blood vessel directly to the heart's surface to stimulate contractions and to regulate beat. These procedures, to be effective, must be initiated with a minimum of delay as cerebral anoxia, due to a cutoff of oxygen to the brain, will normally produce irreversible brain damage within three to five minutes and total brain death within fifteen minutes. Many of these procedures are obviously highly intrusive, and some are violent in nature. The defibrillator, for example, causes violent (and painful) muscle contractions which, in a patient suffering (as this patient is) from osteoporosis, may cause fracture of vertebrae or other bones. Such fractures, in turn, cause pain, which may be extreme.

The patient's family, consisting of a son, who is a physician practising in New York City, and a daughter, with whom the patient lived prior to her admission to the nursing home in 1975, concur in the doctor's recommendation that resuscitation should not be attempted in the event of cardiac or respiratory arrest. They have joined with the doctor and the hospital in bringing the instant action for declaratory relief, asking for a determination that the doctor may enter a 'no-code' order [ie an order not to resuscitate] on the patient's medical record without judicial authorisation or, alternatively, if such authorisation is a legal prerequisite to the validity of a 'no-code' order, that that authorisation be given. The probate judge appointed a guardian *ad litem*, who has taken a position in opposition to the prayers of the complaint.

. . . This case does not offer a life-saving or life-prolonging treatment alternative within the meaning of the *Saikewicz* case. It presents a question peculiarly within the competence of the medical profession of what measures are appropriate to ease the imminent passing of an irreversibly, terminally ill patient in light of the patient's history and condition and the wishes of her family. That question is not one for judicial decision, but one for the attending physician, in keeping with the highest traditions of his profession, and subject to court review only to the extent that it may be contended that he has failed to exercise 'the degree of care and skill of the average qualified practitioner, taking into account the advances in the profession'.

The case is remanded to the Probate Court, where a judgment is to enter in accordance with the prayers of the complaint for declaratory relief, declaring that on the findings made by the judge the law does not prohibit a course of medical treatment which excludes attempts at resuscitation in the event of cardiac or respiratory arrest and that the validity of an order to that effect does not depend on prior judicial approval.

Re Spring (1980) 405 NE 2d 115 (Mass Sup Jud Ct)

Braucher J: . . . The ward was born in 1901, had been married for fifty-five years at the time of the hearing, and had one son, the temporary guardian. The ward was suffering from 'end-stage kidney disease', which required him to undergo hemodialysis treatment (filtering of the blood) three days a week, five hours a day. He also suffered from 'chronic organic brain syndrome', or senility, and was completely confused and disoriented. Both the kidney disease and the senility were permanent and irreversible; there was no prospect of a medical breakthrough that would provide a cure for either disease. Apart from the kidney disease and senility the ward's health was good.

Without the dialysis treatment the ward would die; with it he might survive for months. Survival for five years would be not probable, but conceivable. The treatment did not cause a remission of the disease or restore him even temporarily to a normal, cognitive, integrated, functioning existence, but simply kept him alive. He experienced unpleasant side effects such as dizziness, leg cramps, and headaches; on occasion he kicked nurses, resisted transportation for dialysis, and pulled the dialysis needles out of his arm. His disruptive behaviour was controlled through heavy sedation. He would not have suffered any discomfort if the dialysis had been terminated. There was no evidence that while competent he had expressed any wish or desire as to the continuation or withdrawal of treatment in such circumstances, but his wife and son were of the opinion that if competent he would request withdrawal of treatment.

. . . [T]here is something approaching consensus in support of some of the principles elaborated in the *Saikewicz* opinion. A person has a strong interest in being free from nonconsensual invasion of his bodily integrity, and a constitutional right of privacy that may be asserted to prevent unwanted infringements of bodily integrity. Thus a competent person has a general right to refuse medical treatment in appropriate circumstances, to be determined by balancing the individual interest against countervailing State interests, particularly the State interest in the preservation of life. In striking that balance, account is to be taken of the prognosis and of the magnitude of the proposed invasion. The same right is also extended to an incompetent person, to be exercised through a 'substituted judgment' on his behalf. The decision should be that which would be made by the incompetent person, if he were competent, taking into account his actual interests and preferences and also his present and future incompetency. . . .

The present case does not involve State action in the same sense as the *Saikewicz* case, since the patient here was not in State custody. While apparently competent, the patient had acquiesced in hemodialysis treatment, and had received such treatments for several months before his incompetence became apparent. His wife and son filed a petition for the appointment of a guardian and for an order that the treatments be discontinued. Again we hold that the proceeding was properly initiated, and that the judge appropriately decided that the treatments in question should be withheld. Again we disapprove shifting of the ultimate decision-making responsibility away from the duly established courts of proper jurisdiction.

. . . We have pointed out the similarities between the present case and the *Saikewicz* case, which are quite sufficient to bring into play the 'substituted judgment' standard applied in that case. Thus the judge's finding that the ward 'would, if competent, choose not to receive the life-prolonging treatment' was critical. An expression of intent by the ward while competent was not essential. The judge properly relied in part on the opinion of the ward's wife of fifty-five years. That opinion was corroborated by that of the son, and there was every indication that there was a close relationship within the family group, that the wife and son had only the best interests of the ward at heart, and that they were best informed as to his likely attitude. There was no evidence that financial considerations were involved.

You will notice that *Spring* does appear to be an appropriate case for substituted judgment since Earle Spring had been competent before the onset of senility. English courts, as we have seen, are much less attracted by the substituted judgment test. Thus, in a case like *Spring* the court would probably, in the absence of an anticipatory decision, apply the best interests test.

Re John Storar (1981) 420 NE 2d 64 (NY CA)

Wachtler Justice: John Storar was profoundly retarded with a mental age of about eighteen months. At the time of this proceeding he was fifty-two years old and a resident of the Newark Development Center, a state facility, which had been his home since the age of five. His closest relative was his mother, a seventy-seven-year-old widow who resided near the facility. He was her only child and she visited him almost daily.

In 1979 physicians at the Center noticed blood in his urine and asked his mother for permission to conduct diagnostic tests. She initially refused but after discussions with the Center's staff gave her consent. The tests, completed in July 1979, revealed that he had cancer of the bladder. It was recommended that he receive radiation therapy at a hospital in Rochester. When the hospital refused to administer the treatment without the consent of a legal guardian, Mrs Storar applied to the court and was appointed guardian of her son's person and property in August, 1979. With her consent he received radiation therapy for six weeks, after which the disease was found to be in remission.

However in March, 1980 blood was again observed in his urine. The lesions in his bladder were cauterised in an unsuccessful effort to stop the bleeding. At that point his physician diagnosed the cancer as terminal, concluding that after using all medical and surgical means then available, the patient would nevertheless die from the disease.

In May the physicians at the Center asked his mother for permission to administer blood transfusions. She initially refused but the following day withdrew her objection. For several weeks John Storar received blood transfusions when needed. However, on June 19 his mother requested that the transfusions be discontinued.

The Director of the Center then brought this proceeding, pursuant to Section 33.03 of the Mental Health Law, seeking authorisation to continue the transfusions, claiming that without them 'death would occur within weeks'. Mrs Storar cross petitioned for an order prohibiting the transfusions, and named the district attorney as a party. The court appointed a guardian *ad litem* and signed an order temporarily permitting the transfusions to continue, pending the determination of the proceeding.

At the hearing in September the court heard testimony from various witnesses including Mrs Storar, several employees at the Center, and seven medical experts. All the experts concurred that John Storar had irreversible cancer of the bladder, which by then had spread to his lungs and perhaps other organs, with a very limited life span, generally estimated to be between three and six months. They also agreed that he had an infant's mentality and was unable to comprehend his predicament or to make a reasoned choice of treatment. In addition, there was no dispute over the fact that he was continuously losing blood.

The medical records show that at the time of the hearing, he required two units of blood every eight to fifteen days. The staff physicians explained that the transfusions were necessary to replace the blood lost. Without them there would be insufficient oxygen in the patient's blood stream. To compensate for this loss, his heart would have to work harder and he would breathe more rapidly, which created a strain and was very tiresome. He became lethargic and they feared he would eventually bleed to death. They observed that after the transfusions he had more energy. He was able to resume most of his usual activities – feeding himself, showering, taking walks and running – including some mischievous ones, such as stealing cigarette butts and attempting to eat them.

It was conceded that John Storar found the transfusions disagreeable. He was also distressed by the blood and blood clots in his urine which apparently increased immediately after a transfusion. He could not comprehend the purpose of the transfusions and on one or two occasions had displayed some initial resistance. To eliminate his apprehension he was given a sedative approximately one hour before a transfusion. He also received regular doses of narcotics to alleviate the pain associated with the disease.

On the other hand several experts testified that there was support in the medical community for the view that, at this stage, transfusions may only prolong suffering and that treatment could properly be limited to administering pain killers. Mrs Storar testified that she wanted the transfusions discontinued because she only wanted her son to be comfortable. She admitted that no one had ever explained to her what might happen to him if the transfusions were stopped. She also stated that she was not 'sure' whether he might die sooner if the blood was not replaced and was unable to determine whether he wanted to live. However, in view of the fact that he obviously disliked the transfusions and tried to avoid them, she believed that he would want them discontinued.

The court held that the Center's application for permission to continue the transfusions should be denied. It was noted that John Storar's fatal illness had not affected his limited mental ability. He remained alert and carried on many of his usual activities. However, the court emphasised that the transfusions could not cure the disease, involved some pain and that the patient submitted to them reluctantly. The court heard that a person has a right to determine what will be done with his own body and, when he is incompetent, this right may be exercised by another on his behalf. In this case, the court found that John Storar's mother was the person in the best position to determine what he would want and that she 'wants his suffering to stop and believes that he would want this also'.

The Appellate Division affirmed in a brief memorandum.

. . . John Storar was never competent at any time in his life. He was always totally incapable of understanding or making a reasoned decision about medical treatment. Thus it is unrealistic to attempt to determine whether he would want to continue potentially life prolonging treatment if he were competent. As one of the experts testified at the hearing, that would be similar to asking whether 'if it snowed all summer would it then be winter?' Mentally John Storar was an infant and that is the only realistic way to assess his rights in this litigation. . . . [T]here is the additional complication of two threats to his life. There was cancer of the bladder which was incurable and would in all probability claim his life. There was also the related loss of blood which posed the risk of an earlier death, but which, at least at the time of the hearing, could be replaced by transfusions. Thus, as one of the experts noted, the transfusions were analogous to food – they would not cure the cancer, but they could eliminate the risk of death from another treatable cause. Of course, John Storar did not like them, as might be expected of one with an infant's mentality. But the evidence convincingly shows that the transfusions did not involve excessive pain and that without them his mental and physical abilities would not be maintained at the usual level. With the transfusions on the other hand, he was essentially the same as he was before except of course he had a fatal illness which would ultimately claim his life. Thus, on the record, we have concluded that the application for permission to continue the transfusions should have been granted. Although we understand and respect his mother's despair, as we respect the beliefs of those who oppose transfusions on religious grounds, a court should not in the circumstances of this case allow an incompetent patient to bleed to death because someone, even someone as close as a parent or sibling, feels that this is best for one with an incurable disease.

While it may be accepted that the American courts in these adult cases arrived at caring and humane decisions, it can properly be asked whether the cases take us any further in articulating the criteria which determine the extent of a doctor's duty. It may be that the law can do no better. The doctor, however, is left with a somewhat uncertain discretion in weighing where the 'best interests' of the patient lie. The lack of precision demonstrated in the cases coupled with the knowledge that a patient's life or death is at stake would undoubtedly give the English courts cause to pause. Indeed, some members of the House of Lords in *Bland* found the exercise so fraught with difficulty as not to be a proper matter for the judges. It was, they said, a matter for Parliament.

Lord Browne-Wilkinson: Where a case raises wholly new moral and social issues, in my judgment it is not for the judges to seek to develop new, all-embracing, principles of law in a way which reflects the individual judges' moral stance when society as a whole is substantially divided on the relevant moral issues. Moreover, it is not legitimate for a judge in reaching a view as to what is for the benefit of the one individual whose life is in issue to take into account the wider practical issues as to allocation of limited financial resources or the impact on third parties of altering the time at which death occurs.

For these reasons, it seems to me imperative that the moral, social and legal issues raised by this case should be considered by Parliament. The judges' function in this area of the law should be to apply the principles which society, through the democratic process, adopts, not to impose their standards on society. If Parliament fails to act, then judge-made law will of necessity through a gradual and uncertain process provide a legal answer to each new question as it arises. But in my judgment that is not the best way to proceed.

(See also Lord Mustill at 888 and 889.)

II. Challenging 'quality of life'. Lord Goff and Lord Browne-Wilkinson in *Bland* expressly reserved their positions on cases such as *Re J* where balancing factors which touch upon quality of life are required of the court (at 870 and 884). Lord Mustill went further (at 891):

> **Lord Mustill:** The interest of the state in preserving the lives of its citizens is very strong, but it is not absolute. There are contrary interests, and sometimes these prevail; as witness the over-mastering effect of the patient's refusal of treatment, even where this makes death inevitable. It has been suggested, for example in *Re Quinlan* (1976) 70 NJ 10, that the balance may also be tipped, not by the weight of an opposing policy but by the attenuation of the interest in preserving life, where the 'quality' of the life is diminished by disease or incapacity. My Lords, I would firmly reject this argument. If correct it would validate active as well as passive euthanasia, and thus require a change in the law of murder. In any event whilst the fact that a patient is in great pain may give him or her a powerful motive for wanting to end it, to which in certain circumstances it is proper to accede, that is not at all the same as the proposition that because of incapacity or infirmity one life is intrinsically worth less than another. This is the first step on a very dangerous road indeed, and one which I am not willing to take.

And later (at 896):

> I have no doubt that the best interests of Anthony Bland no longer demand the continuance of his present care and treatment. This is not at all to say that I would reach the same conclusion in less extreme cases, where the glimmerings of awareness may give the patient an interest which cannot be regarded as null. The issues, both legal and ethical, will then be altogether more difficult. As Mr Munby has pointed out, in this part of the law the court has moved a long way in a short time. Every step forward requires the greatest caution.

Where does this leave the law as regards patients who are other than permanently insensate, ie not in a persistent vegetative state? In our view, despite the understandable caution of the judges, the House of Lords would endorse the law as expressed at least by Taylor LJ in *Re J*. That is that, if the circumstances of the patient were extreme enough, withholding or withdrawing treatment would be lawful. The court would, however, be anxious to insist on a very high threshold of 'intolerability'. Of course, this is perhaps easier to identify in the case of a very severely disabled new born baby than it is in the case of a senile patient who falls ill. As regards the latter it may be that the anxieties expressed by the judges in *Bland* would mean that they would not contemplate the withholding or withdrawing of treatment.

C. CONCLUDING REMARK

There can be little doubt that the law relating to the treatment of the incompetent at the end of life is less than satisfactory. This should come as no surprise given the pace of technological development. As Lord Mustill put it in *Bland* (at 888): 'the law has been left behind by the rapid advances of medical technology' opening up a 'gap between old law and new medicine'. In the wake of the *Bland* decision the House of Lords in its legislative capacity set up, in the spring of 1993, a Select Committee to investigate the legal, ethical and social issues surrounding treatment decisions at the end of life.

Chapter 17

The end(ing) of life: the competent patient

In this chapter we are concerned with the legal effect of decisions by *competent* patients concerning the end (or ending) of their life. We discussed in Chapter 3 the legal concept of competence and say no more about that here other than to assume the patient is competent according to the appropriate legal test. We will divide our analysis of the law into two parts. *First*, we will consider decisions taken about current treatment to be carried out (or not) while the patient remains competent. *Secondly*, we will consider decisions taken about future treatment to be carried out (or not) at a time when the patient is no longer competent.

Contemporaneous decisions

A. REFUSING TREATMENT

1. The right to refuse

As we saw in Chapter 4, English law recognises the general principle that a competent patient is entitled to refuse treatment, even life-sustaining treatment. As we saw, the courts seem persuaded that there ought to be two exceptions to this: the competent minor *(Re W (A Minor) (Medical Treatment)* [1992] 4 All ER 627 (CA)) and the pregnant woman *(Re S (Adult: Refusal of Medical Treatment)* [1992] 4 All ER 671 (Stephen Brown P)). In Chapter 4 we criticised the creation of these exceptions. Here, we are concerned with the situations falling within the general principle rather than these exceptions.

It suffices for our purposes to refer to the statements of Lord Donaldson MR in *Re T (adult: refusal of medical treatment)* [1992] 4 All ER 649 at 652-3 (CA) and Lords Keith (at 860), Goff (at 866), Browne-Wilkinson (at 881-2) and Mustill (at 889) in *Airedale NHS Trust v Bland* [1993] 1 All ER 821 (HL). In essence they accept, as Lord Keith put it in *Bland*, that ' . . . a person is completely at liberty to decline to undergo treatment, even if the result of his doing so will be that he will die'.

The approach of the English courts reflects that of courts in North America: *Nancy B v Hôtel-Dieu de Québec* (1992) 86 DLR (4th) 385 (Que Sup Ct) (Canada) and, for example, *McKay v Bergstedt* (1990) 801 P 2d 617 (Nev Sup Ct). The *Bergstedt* case is instructive in that it reviews the US cases and thereby rehearses the anxieties found in them, particularly concerning the state's interests in *preserving life* and *preventing suicide* (for an earlier discussion, see *supra*, ch 4).

McKay v Bergstedt (1990) 801 P 2d 617 (Nev Sup Ct)

Steffen J: Kenneth Bergstedt was a thirty-one-year-old mentally competent quadriplegic who sought to vindicate on appeal the lower court's decision confirming his right to die . . .

FACTUAL BACKGROUND
At the tender age of ten, Kenneth suffered the fate of a quadriplegic as the result of a swimming accident. Twenty-one years later, faced with what appeared to be the imminent death of his ill father, Kenneth decided that he wanted to be released from a life of paralysis held intact by the life-sustaining properties of a respirator. Although Kenneth was able to read, watch television, orally operate a computer, and occasionally receive limited enjoyment from wheelchair ambulation, he despaired over the prospect of life without the attentive care, companionship and love of his devoted father.

The limited record before us reflects substantial evidence of facts relevant to the proceedings below and material to the framework upon which the resolution of this appeal is constructed. First, a board-certified neurosurgeon determined that Kenneth's quadriplegia was irreversible. Second, a psychiatrist examined Kenneth and found him to be competent and able to understand the nature and consequences of his decision. Third, Kenneth arrived at his decision after substantial deliberation. Fourth, Kenneth's trusted and devoted father understood the basis for his son's decision and reluctantly approved. Fifth, although Kenneth's quadriplegia was irreversible, his affliction was non-terminal so long as he received artificial respiration.

Kenneth thus petitioned the district court as a non-terminal, competent, adult quadriplegic for an order permitting the removal of his respirator by one who could also administer a sedative and thereby relieve the pain that would otherwise precede his demise. Kenneth also sought an order of immunity from civil or criminal liability for anyone providing the requested assistance. Additionally, he petitioned the court for a declaration absolving him of suicide in the removal of his life-support system.

In ruling, the district court determined that Kenneth was a mentally competent adult fully capable of deciding to forgo continued life connected to a respirator. The court also found that he understood that the removal of his life-support system would shortly prove fatal.

In concluding that Kenneth had a constitutional privacy right to discontinue further medical treatment, the court also ruled that given Kenneth's condition, judicial recognition of the primacy of his individual rights posed no threat to the State's interest in preserving life, adversely affected no third parties, and presented no threat to the integrity of the medical profession. The district court thus concluded that Kenneth was entitled to the relief sought.

DISCUSSION
I
Our research revealed five cases involving decision by competent adults to discontinue the use of life-support systems. Three of the five cases were brought by petitioners who were terminally ill. The other two actions, like the instant case, involved non-terminal, competent adults who were dependent upon artificial life-support systems. Relief was granted in each of the five cases, albeit posthumously in two of the cases where petitioners had died before their appeals were decided.

One of the verities of human experience is that all life will eventually end in death. As the seasons of life progress through spring, summer and fall, to the winter of our years, the expression unknown to youth is often heard evincing the wish to one night pass away in the midst of a peaceful sleep. It would appear, however, that as the scientific community continues to increase human longevity and promote 'the greying of America', prospects for slipping away during peaceful slumber are decreasing. And, for significant numbers of citizens like Kenneth, misfortune may rob life of much of its quality long before the onset of winter.

Because many individuals find themselves facing a terminal condition susceptible to indefinite suspension by medical intervention, the question arises with increasing frequency and fervor concerning the extent to which persons have the right to refuse an artificial extension of life. Courts considering the question have basically agreed that the answer is to be found in the balancing of interests between the person in extremis and the State. On the one hand is the interest of the individual in determining the extent to which he or she is willing to have a devastated life continued artificially or by radical medical treatment. On the other hand, courts agree that the State has several interests of significance that must be weighed in determining whether the rights of the individual should prevail. Those interests have generally been defined as: (1) the interest of the State in preserving the sanctity of all life, including that of the particular patient involved in a given action; (2) the interest of the State in preventing suicide; (3) the interest of the State in protecting innocent third persons who may be adversely affected by the death of the party seeking relief; and (4) the State's interest in preserving the integrity of the medical profession . . .

Under the common law, 'no right is held more sacred, or is more carefully guarded . . . than the right of every individual to the possession and control of his own person, free from all restraint or interference of others, unless by clear and unquestionable authority of law.' *Cruzan v Director, Missouri Department of Health* 110 S Ct 2841, 2846 (1990) (quoting *Union Pacific R Co v Botsford*, 141 US 250, 251 (1891)). Continuing, the *Cruzan* court declared that 'this notion of bodily integrity has been embodied in the requirement that informed consent is generally required for medical treatment'. Id. The corollary embodied in the right of informed consent is the right to refuse the proffered medical treatment or regimen irrespective of consequences. See *Bartling*, 163 Cal App 3d at 194. Obviously, if a patient is powerless to decline medical treatment upon being properly informed of its implications, the requirement of consent would be meaningless. We nevertheless agree with other courts which have held that the right to refuse medical treatment is not absolute. See *Satz v Perlmutter*, 362 So 2d 160, 162 (Fla App 1978); *State v McAfee*, 385 SE 2d at 652; *Cruzan, by Cruzan v Harmon*, 760 SW 2d 408, 421 (Mo 1988) (en banc); *Matter of Farrell*, 529 A 2d at 410. Courts have consistently balanced the fundamental right of the individual to refuse medical treatment against the four State interests enumerated above. See eg, *Bouvia v Superior Court*, 179 Cal App 3d 1127 (Cal Ct App 1986); *Bartling v Super Ct* (Glendale Adven Med), 163 Cal App 3d at 186; *Satz v Perlmutter*, 362 So 2d at 160; *State v McAfee*, 385 SE 2d at 651; *Superintendent of Belchertown v Saikewicz*, 370 NE 2d 417 (Mass 1977); *Cruzan, By Cruzan v Harmon* 110 S Ct at 2841; *Matter of Farrell*, 529 A 2d at 404. . . .

II

Turning, as we must, to the legitimate interests of the State, we now balance those interests against Kenneth's . . . common law right of self-determination, and we do so for decisional purposes despite Kenneth's death.

1. The interest of the State in preserving life. The State's interest in preserving life is both fundamental and compelling. Indeed, it constitutes a basic purpose for which governments are formed. Nevertheless, the State's interest in the preservation of life is not absolute. For example, State-sponsored executions may constitute an exception to the duty to preserve life for a complex of reasons ranging from an emphasis on the value of the lives of innocent victims to the necessity of maintaining an orderly society where the quality of life is of pre-eminent concern. Moreover, as the quality of life diminishes because of physical deterioration, the State's interest in preserving life may correspondingly decrease. However, the State's attenuated interest does not evince a lesser appreciation for the value of life as the physical being deteriorates, but rather a recognition of the fact that all human life must eventually succumb to the aging process or to intervening events or conditions impacting the health of an individual. Moreover, an interest in the preservation of life 'at all costs' is demeaning to death as a natural concomitant of life. Despite its frightening aspects, death has important values of its own. It may come as welcome relief to prolonged suffering. It may end the indignities associated with life bereft of self-determination and cognitive activity. In the mind of some, it may satisfy longings for loved ones preceding them in death. In short, death is a natural aspect of life that is not without value and dignity.

Courts have recognized that persons may reach a condition in life where the individual preference for a natural death may have greater primacy that the State's interest in preserving life through artificial support systems. Although we would have stated it differently, the court in *Matter of Conroy*, 486 A 2d 1209 (NJ 1985), declared that 'in cases that do not involve the protection of the actual or potential life of someone other than the decision-maker, the state's indirect and abstract interest in preserving the life of the competent patient generally gives way to the patient's much stronger personal interest in directing the course of his own life.' Id. at 1223. We do not view the State's interest in preserving the life of a competent patient as either abstract or indirect. It remains, in our view, not only compelling and fundamental, but focused and direct as well. The State's interest in preserving all human life, including that of the particular patient, should not be suspended or minimized under any conditions. We nevertheless agree with the court in *Satz v Perlmutter* that 'there can be no doubt that the State does have an interest in preserving life, but . . . "there is a substantial distinction in the State's insistence that human life be saved where the affliction is curable, as opposed to the State interest where, as here, the issue is not whether, but when, for how long and at what cost to the individual [his] life may be briefly extended".' *Perlmutter*, 362 So.2d at 162 (quoting from *Superintendent of Belchertown v Saikewicz*, 370 N.E.2d 417, 425-26 (Mass 1977)). In *Perlmutter*, however, the competent adult patient was terminally ill with a prognosis of a short remaining life even while connected to a respirator. Kenneth, of course, was not terminally ill despite his dependence on the respirator. The *Perlmutter* ruling is therefore of limited value to the instant case.

In both *Bouvia* and *Bartling* the adult patients were, as here, non-terminal and competent. . . .

Although we may have a difference of opinion over some of the statements . . . from *Bouvia*, we do believe that at some point in the life of a competent adult patient, the present or prospective quality of life may be so dismal that the right of the individual to refuse treatment or elect a discontinuance of artificial life-support must prevail over the interest of the State in preserving life. In instances where the prospects for a life of quality are smothered by physical pain and suffering, only the sufferer can determine the value of continuing mortality. We therefore conclude that in situations involving adults who are: (1) competent; (2) irreversibly sustained or subject to being sustained by artificial life-support systems or some form of heroic, radical medical treatment; and (3) enduring physical and mental pain and suffering, the individual's right to decide will generally outweigh the State's interest in preserving life.

On the assumption that Kenneth would survive the issuance of this opinion, we reviewed his record carefully in an effort to sensitively analyze the circumstances under which he lived and the reasons that prompted him to seek a judicial imprimatur of his decision to disconnect his respirator. It appeared that Kenneth's suffering resulted more from his fear of the unknown than any source of physical pain. After more than two decades of life as a quadriplegic under the loving care of parents, Kenneth understandably feared for the quality of his life after the death of his father, who was his only surviving parent. Although Kenneth completed elementary and high school through private tutoring, study and telephone communication with his teachers, and wrote poetry and otherwise lived a useful and productive life, his physical condition was dire. His quadriplegia left him not only ventilator-dependent, but entirely reliant on others for his bodily functions and needs. His limited sources of entertainment, including reading, watching television and writing poetry through the oral operation of a computer, also required the attentive accommodations of others. Since the death of his mother in 1978, all of these services were provided by his father and attending nurses occasionally called to the home.

It thus appears, and the record so reflects, that Kenneth was preoccupied with fear over the quality of his life after the death of his father. He feared that some mishap would occur to his ventilator without anyone being present to correct it, and that he would suffer an agonizing death as a result. In contemplating his future under the care of strangers, Kenneth stated that he had no encouraging expectations from life, did not enjoy life, and was tired of suffering. Fear of the unknown is a common travail even among those of us who are not imprisoned by paralysis and a total dependency upon others. There is no doubt that Kenneth was plagued by a sense of foreboding concerning the quality of his life without his father.

Someone has suggested that there are few greater sources of fear in life than fear itself. In Kenneth's situation it is not difficult to understand why fear had such an overriding grasp on his view of the quality of his future life. Given the circumstances under which he labored to survive, we could not substitute our own judgment for Kenneth's when assessing the quality of his life. We therefore conclude that Kenneth . . . enjoyed a preeminent right under the common law to withdraw his consent to a continued medical regimen involving his attachment to a respirator. In so ruling, we attach great significance to the quality of Kenneth's life as he perceived it under the particular circumstances that were afflicting him. . . .

2. The interest of the State in preventing suicide. Controversy continues to rage over this semantics-laden issue. Opponents of Kenneth's position describe it in terms of a State-sponsored suicide. Our research reveals no court declaring it so. We nevertheless recognize the controversy as a healthy concern for the value of an individual life.

The dictionary definition of suicide is 'the act or an instance of taking one's own life voluntarily and intentionally; the deliberate and intentional destruction of his own life by a person of years of discretion and of sound mind; one that commits or attempts self-murder.'

Webster's Third New International Dictionary (1968). As we will attempt to show, Kenneth harbored no intent to take his own life, voluntarily or otherwise. He did not seek his own destruction and he most certainly eschewed self-murder, a fact made evident by his petition to the district court for an order declaring that the exercise of his right to decide would not amount to an act of suicide.

It is beyond cavil in one sense, that Kenneth was taking affirmative measures to hasten his own death. It is equally clear that if Kenneth had enjoyed sound physical health, but had viewed life as unbearably miserable because of his mental state, his liberty interest would provide no basis for asserting a right to terminate his life with or without the assistance of other persons. Our societal regard for the value of an individual life, as reflected in our Federal and State constitutions, would never countenance an assertion of liberty over life under such circumstances.

It must nevertheless be conceded, as noted above, that death is a natural end of living. There are times when its beckoning is sweet and benevolent. Most would consider it unthinkable to force one who is racked with advanced, terminal, painful cancer to require a therapy regimen that would merely prolong the agony of dying for a brief season. In allowing such a patient to refuse therapy could it seriously be argued that he or she is committing an act of suicide?

The informed consent doctrine presupposes that persons faced with difficult medical decisions that will, at best, substantially alter the quality of their future lives, may elect to refuse treatment and let the processes of nature take their course. Few would conclude that exercising the right to refuse treatment would be tantamount to suicide. Such persons have not sought to contract the disease or condition that threatens both the quality and duration of their lives. Rather, they have evaluated their circumstances and determined that a future sustained by radical medical treatment or artificial means and entailing a drastic decrease in the quality of their lives, is not a valued alternative despite its effectiveness in extending life or delaying death. Moreover, we see no difference between the patient who refuses treatment and the one who accepts treatment and later refuses its continuance because of a resulting loss in the quality of life.

The primary factors that distinguish Kenneth's type of case from that of a person desiring suicide are attitude, physical condition and prognosis. Unlike a person bent on suicide, Kenneth sought no affirmative measures to terminate his life; he desired only to eliminate the artificial barriers standing between him and the natural processes of life and death that would otherwise ensue with someone in his physical condition. Kenneth survived artificially within a paralytic prison from which there was no hope of release other than death. But he asked no one to shorten the term of his natural life free of the respirator. He sought no fatal potions to end life or hurry death. In other words, Kenneth desired the right to die a natural death unimpeded by scientific contrivances.

Justice Scalia's concurring opinion in *Cruzan* suggests that 'insofar as balancing the relative interests of the State and the individual is concerned, there is nothing distinctive about accepting death through the refusal of "medical treatment," as opposed to accepting it through the refusal of food, or through the failure to shut off the engine and get out of the car after parking in one's garage after work.' *Cruzan*, 110 S Ct at 2862. We respectfully disagree with the learned justice. The distinction between refusing medical treatment and the other scenarios presented by Justice Scalia is the difference between choosing a natural death summoned by an uninvited illness or calamity and deliberately seeking to terminate one's life by resorting to death-inducing measures unrelated to the natural process of dying.

Impliedly, Justice Scalia's last two hypotheticals involved persons who were ambulatory and able to survive without artificial intervention. If they were physically healthy, society's respect for human life demanded that the State prevent, if possible, their deaths by suicide. There was no need to present either person with life-extending medical options, and both enjoyed the prospect of mental rehabilitation that might restore the will to live. There is a significant distinction between an individual faced with artificial survival resulting from heroic medical intervention and an individual, otherwise healthy or capable of sustaining life without artificial support who simply desires to end his or her life. The former adult, if competent, exercises a judgment based upon an assessment of the quality of an artificially maintained life vis-à-vis the quality of a natural death. Conversely, the latter acts from a potentially reversible pessimism or mental attitude concerning only the quality of life.

We are not deciding competing interests between a non-existent right to choose suicide and the interest of the State in preserving life. The State's interest in the preservation of life relates to meaningful life. Insofar as this State's interest is concerned, the State has no overriding interest in interfering with the natural processes of dying among citizens whose lives are irreparably devastated by injury or illness to the point where life may be sustained only by contrivance or radical intervention. In situations such as Kenneth's, only the competent adult patient can determine the extent to which his or her artificially extended life has meaning and value in excess of the death value.

Other courts have consistently agreed that rejecting treatment in the form of artificial life-support systems is not a euphemistic exercise in suicide. See, eg, *Bouvia v Superior Court*, 179 Cal App 2d at 1144; *Bartling v Superior Court*, 163 Cal App 3d at 196; *Floody v Manchester Memorial Hosp*, 482 A 2d 713, 720 (Conn Super Ct 1984); *Satz v Perlmutter*, 362 So 2d at 162-63; *State v McAfee*, 385 SE 2d at 652 (by implication); *Brophy v New England Sinai Hosp*, 497 NE 2d 626, 638 (Mass 1986); *Matter of Farrell*, 529 A 2d at 411; *Matter of Storar*, 420 NE 2d 64, 71 (NY 1981); *Leach v Akron General Medical Center*, P 2d 738, 743 (Wash 1983). However, we do not necessarily agree with the analysis of other courts on the subject. For example, the court in *Bouvia* concluded that 'the trial court seriously erred by basing its decision on the "motives" behind Elizabeth Bouvia's decision to exercise her rights. If a right exists, it matters not what "motivates" its exercise.' *Bouvia*, 179 Cal App 3d at 1145. In the first place, as we have already seen, the 'right' is not absolute. It must be balanced against the previously enumerated interests of the State. Secondly, because the State has an interest in both preserving life and preventing suicide, the circumstances under which the individual seeks to exercise his liberty interest or common law right of refusal must be considered. Part of the complex of circumstances to be considered relates to the attitude or motive of the patient. To a large extent, a patient's attitude or motive may be judged from such factors as severity of physical condition, diagnosis, prognosis, and quality of life. If a competent adult is beset with an irreversible condition such as quadriplegia, where life must be sustained artificially and under circumstances of total dependence, the adult's attitude or motive may be presumed not to be suicidal. In our view, there is a substantial difference between the attitude of a person desiring non-interference with the natural consequences of his or her condition and the individual who desires to terminate his or her life by some deadly means either self-inflicted or through the agency of another.

As medical science continues to develop methods of prolonging life, it is not inconceivable that a person could be faced with any number of alternatives that would delay death and consign him or her to a living hell in which there is hopelessness, total dependence, a complete lack of dignity, and an ongoing cost that would impoverish loved ones. The State's interest in preserving life and preventing what some may erroneously refer to as suicide does not extend so far.

Kenneth did not wish to commit suicide. He desired only to live for as long as the state of his health would permit without artificial augmentation and support. Society had no right to force upon him the obligation to remain alive under conditions that he considered to be anathema. To rule otherwise would place an unwarranted premium on survival at the expense of human dignity, quality of life, and the value that comes from allowing death a natural and timely entrance. . . .

3. The interest of the State in protecting innocent third persons. . . . This State interest was simply not implicated in Kenneth's request.

4. The State's interest in preserving the integrity of the medical profession. In *Matter of Farrell*, the competent adult patient was a thirty-seven-year-old woman who was terminally ill with amyotrophic lateral sclerosis (Lou Gehrig's disease). Although Kathleen Farrell died before her appeal was decided, the *Farrell* court nevertheless determined that 'medical ethics create no tension in this case. Our review of well-established medical authorities finds them in unanimous support of the right of a competent and informed patient such as Mrs Farrell to decline medical treatment.' *Matter of Farrell*, 529 A 2d at 411-12 (discussing authorities). We deem it unnecessary to quote from medical authorities to further support the conclusion reached in *Farrell*. The State has an unquestioned duty to see that the integrity of the medical profession is preserved and that it is never allowed to become an instrument for the selective destruction of lives deemed to have little utility.

Despite the medical profession's healing objectives, there are increasing numbers of people who fall in the category of those who may never be healed but whose lives may be extended by heroic measures. Unfortunately, there are times when such efforts will do little or nothing more than delay death in a bodily environment essentially bereft of quality. Under such conditions or the reasonably likely prospect thereof, the medical profession is not threatened by a competent adult's refusal of life-extending treatment. The President's Commission, established by Congress in 1978, and consisting of doctors, ethicists, lawyers, theologians and others, concluded:

The voluntary choice of a competent and informed patient should determine whether or not life-sustaining therapy will be undertaken, just as such choices provide the basis for other decisions about medical treatment. Health care institutions and professionals should try to enhance patients' abilities to make decisions on their own behalf and to promote understanding of the available treatment options . . . Health care professionals serve patients best by maintaining a presumption in favor of sustaining life, while recognizing that competent patients are entitled to choose to forego any treatments, including those that sustain life.

President's Commission for the Study of Ethical Problems in Medicine and Biomedical and Behavioral Research, Deciding to Forgo Life-Sustaining Treatment, p 3 (US Gov't Printing Office 1983).

We are of the opinion that Kenneth's request to be relieved of his connection to a respirator did not present an ethical threat to the medical profession. Because a competent adult would have enjoyed a qualified . . . common law right to refuse a life-sustaining attachment to a respirator in the first instance, there is no reason why such an adult could not assert the same rights to reject a continuation of respirator-dependency that has proven too burdensome to endure. . .

IV

If Kenneth had survived the date of the issuance of this opinion, we would have confirmed his right to discontinue his artificial life-support system . . .

Young CJ, Rose and Mowbray JJ agreed. Springer J dissented.

It is important to notice that in England the court in *Re T* recognised that the right to refuse life-sustaining treatment applied to all competent adult patients and not merely those who were terminally ill. Cases such as *Re T* and *Bergstedt* raise more starkly the argument that the patient is seeking to commit suicide. The affirmation of the right to refuse treatment in *Re T* indicates that the Court of Appeal must have assumed that Miss T would not have been committing suicide. Curiously, however, the judges did not expressly refer to the point. Subsequently, in *Bland* Lord Goff (at 866) made the point explicitly.

Lord Goff: I wish to add that, in cases of this kind, there is no question of the patient having committed suicide, nor therefore of the doctor having aided or abetted him in doing so. It is simply that the patient has, as he is entitled to do, declined to consent to treatment which might or would have the effect of prolonging his life, and the doctor has, in accordance with his duty, complied with his patient's wishes.

2. Limits on the right to refuse

We have already seen that the cases in the United States seek to place limits on a patient's freedom of decision by reference to various state interests. From *Bergstedt* we have learned that the state's interest in preventing suicide cannot stand as a limitation. As regards the state's interest in preserving life, save in the problematic case of the competent minor, reference to such an interest is incoherent if the law already recognises, as it does, the competent patient's right to make his own decisions including the refusal of life-sustaining treatment. As regards the state's interest in protecting innocent third parties, this is a deeply problematic limit, as we saw in the context of the pregnant woman in cases such as *Re AC* (1990) 573 A 2d 1235 (DC CA) and *Re S*: see ch 4, *supra*.

The last of the state interests mentioned in cases such as *In the Matter of Conroy* (*supra*, ch 4) and *Bergstedt* is that of 'safeguarding the integrity of the medical profession'. In so far as this goes beyond asking them to be involved in suicide and act illegally, the New Jersey Supreme Court in a subsequent case of *Re Farrell* (1987) 529 A 2d 404, stated:

Garibaldi J: Even as patients enjoy control over their medical treatment, health-care professionals remain bound to act in consonance with specific ethical criteria. We realise that these criteria may conflict with some concepts of self-determination. In the case of such a conflict, a patient has no right to compel a health-care provider to violate generally accepted professional standards. Cf *President's Commission Report . . .* at 44. ('A health care professional has an obligation to allow a patient to choose from among medically accepted treatment options . . . or to reject all options. No one, however, has an obligation to provide interventions that would, in his or her judgment, be countertherapeutic.')

The obscure nature of this limitation is illustrated in *Brophy v New England Sinai Hospital* (1986) 497 NE 2d 626. The Supreme Judicial Court of Massachusetts recognised the right of an incompetent patient in a persistent vegetative state to refuse artificial hydration and nutrition albeit that the right had to be exercised by a proxy on the patient's behalf. However, the court did not require the hospital, in which Brophy was, to desist from these interventions.

Liacos J: The hospital argues that it has no constitutional, statutory, or common law right to deny nutrition and hydration to Brophy so as to bring about his death. The probate judge held that the hospital and its medical staff 'should not be compelled to withhold food and water to a patient, contrary to its moral and ethical principles, when such principles are recognised and accepted within a significant segment of the medical profession and the hospital community'. We agree. Neither GL c 111, §70E (1984 ed), the Massachusetts patients' rights statute, the doctrine of informed consent, nor any other provision of law requires the hospital to cease hydration and nutrition upon request of the guardian. There is nothing in *Superintendent of Belchertown State School v Saikewicz*, 373 Mass 728, 370 NE 2d 417 (1977), and its progeny which would justify compelling medical professionals, in a case such as this, to take active measures which are contrary to their view of the ethical duty toward their patients. See *Brandt v St Vincent Infirmary*, 287 Ark 431, 701 SW 2d 103, 106-107 (1985). There is substantial disagreement in the medical community over the appropriate medical action. It would be particularly inappropriate to force the hospital, which is willing to assist in a transfer of the patient, to take affirmative steps to end the provision of nutrition and hydration to him. A patient's right to refuse medical treatment does not warrant such an unnecessary intrusion upon the hospital's ethical integrity in this case.

It is at best curious that a patient's right to refuse an offer of treatment should be subject to his finding a doctor who is prepared to comply with his request. There was another hospital willing to accept Brophy on his terms.

There is one further question concerning the limits of a patient's refusal: can it in law extend to forbidding nurses to carry out the regular activities of washing and changing and otherwise supervising the patient's general hygiene (ie 'nursing care')? In the unlikely event that a patient 'turns his head to the wall' and forbids anyone to have anything to do with him, are the nurses so bound? Would this not be a clear example of a situation where the interests of others, whether health care professionals or other patients whose health might be compromised by complying with the request, would prevail over the patient's? This would mean that the patient could be bathed, cleaned and looked after against his wishes. The justification in law would rest in public policy. The same arguments would not apply, however, where what was being considered was not 'nursing care' (see Law Commission, *Mentally Incapacitated Adults and Decision-Making: Medical Treatment and Research* (Consultation Paper No 129) paragraph 3.25).

B. REQUESTING TREATMENT

The patient, as we have seen, may absolve the doctor from his duty to provide any particular treatment by refusing that treatment. The question which remains is whether the patient may demand that the doctor exceed what would ordinarily be regarded as his duty. Admittedly, the doctor's duty contemplates the exercise of appropriate discretion, but is there a point at which the doctor is not obliged to comply with the requests or demands of his patient?

There are three issues which come to mind. The first is when the patient requests or demands a form of care which the doctor in the exercise of reasonable medical judgment determines is futile, in that it will be of no benefit of any kind to the patient. As in all cases where a doctor has formed a reasonable and responsible clinical judgment that treatment is not called for, the law will not second-guess him by ordering him to provide the treatment (*Re J (A Minor) (Wardship: Medical Treatment)* [1992] 4 All ER 614 (CA) discussed *supra*, ch 4). Of course, if there is some element of benefit but only at considerable cost, it is for the competent patient to be given the choice whether to opt for it or not, but this is not what we are considering here.

The second issue is more problematical. Some would argue that a doctor's duty to his patient is circumscribed by his duty to society. They would draw the implication that a doctor, in deciding whether to offer or provide a particular treatment, should consider the effect that his decision will have on overall resources. The Archbishop of Canterbury, in his Edwin Stevens lecture at the Royal Society of Medicine in 1976 (70 *Proc Roy Soc Med* 80), wrote:

> The doctor has a responsibility – an accountability – to the patient and the patient's family under his immediate care. But he has also a responsibility to the other patients in the long waiting queue. He has a further responsibility – to the Government, or, to put it more personally but none the less accurately, to his fellow tax-payers who provide the resources to keep the National Health Service going. The question arises as to whether some kind of consensus – I had almost said some kind of ethic – can emerge on the distribution of resources as between one part of the Health Service and another. A free-for-all could be disastrous.

What view would a court take? In our view, a court would decide that it is not the responsibility of a doctor caring for a particular patient to consider the interests of others. The fact that the patient is dying is of no consequence here. Only if the treatment is otherwise uncalled for, as being futile, would the doctor be justified in ignoring the patient's request or demand. As Robert Veatch has pointed out in his book *A Theory of Medical Ethics* (1981), it is not for the doctor to do other than care for his patient's interests (see eg pp 281-287). To ask him to do more is to ask him to adopt an impossibly bifurcated moral position. Support for this view may be found in the dictum of Lord Browne-Wilkinson in *Bland* where he said:

> it is not legitimate for a judge in reaching a view as to what is for the benefit of the one individual whose life is in issue to take into account the wider practical issues as to allocation of limited financial resources or the impact on third parties of altering the time at which death occurs.

1. Doctor-assisted death

At the outset we should distinguish between the situation in which a doctor is asked to assist the patient in bringing about his death (aiding and abetting suicide) and where the doctor is asked to kill the patient ('mercy killing'). The current legal position is explained by Professor Glanville Williams in his *Textbook of Criminal Law* (2nd edn 1983, pp 579-80).

A person cannot consent to his own death. The rule is not based upon utilitarian considerations even though these may sometimes buttress it. It is a theocratic survival in our predominantly secular law; and religious ('transcendental') arguments are still its main support.

What is the difference between killing a person with his consent and assisting his suicide?
The first is generally murder, while the second is the statutory offence [under s 2 of the Suicide Act 1961]. The distinction between them is the distinction between perpetrators and accessories. If a doctor, to speed his dying patient's passing, injects poison with the patient's consent, this will be murder; but if the doctor places the poison by the patient's side, and the patient takes it, this will be suicide in the patient and the doctor's guilt will be of the abetment offence under the Suicide Act (not abetment in murder). Although this is the theoretical distinction, a case of consent-killing is occasionally reduced to one of assisting suicide.

The distinction may be thought to have no moral relevance, since the doctor assists the patient's death in both cases. But one or two points may be made. If V asks D to help him to die, D may reasonably say: 'I do not approve of what you propose, and will not do the job for you. But you are entitled to act on your own responsibility; and since you are ill and cannot obtain the means of suicide yourself, I do not mind supplying them to you.' Besides this, the fact that the patient takes the poison with his own hand helps to allay fears that perhaps he did not really consent. Suicide is more clearly an act of self-determination than consent to be killed, and requires greater strength of purpose.

The question may again be asked whether there is any social value in denying the doctor's right to help his patient in this way in terminal cases. Several unsuccessful attempts have been made to change the law, but they have foundered because of the united opposition of the churches and of the medical profession itself. Doctors fear that if they were given the legal power to terminate their patient's lives, although with consent, they would lose the confidence of their patients.

You will notice the reference by Professor Williams to the Suicide Act 1961, s 2(1) provides as follows:

A person who aids, abets, counsels or procures the suicide of another, or an attempt by another to commit suicide, shall be liable on conviction on indictment to imprisonment for a term not exceeding fourteen years.

(a) The current law

Will a doctor who provides a patient with the means to bring about his own death be guilty of an offence under section 2(1) of the Suicide Act 1961? There are two questions to be resolved. First, does the doctor 'aid, abet, counsel or procure' the suicide of the patient? Secondly, does the doctor have the necessary state of mind required under s 2(1)? Both of these questions were considered in the following case, albeit one not involving a doctor.

Attorney General v Able [1984] 1 All ER 277, [1984] QB 795 (QBD)

The executive committee of a society which existed to promote voluntary euthanasia published a booklet entitled 'A Guide to Self-Deliverance' and sold it on request to members of the society aged 25 and over. Some 8,000 copies were distributed in that manner. The booklet's expressed aims were to overcome the fear of dying and to reduce the incidence of unsuccessful suicides. The booklet set out in detail several methods of what it termed 'self-deliverance' but could have deterred some people from committing suicide. The society took the view that the booklet would not encourage suicide and that it was in the public interest to make the advice it contained available to those persons who requested the booklet. The Attorney General, however, took the view that distribution of the booklet constituted an offence under s 2(1) of the Suicide Act 1961, but because he wished to avoid prosecuting members of the society's executive committee, who were respectable persons and had issued the booklet out of genuine and strongly-held beliefs, he applied in civil proceedings for declarations that the future supply of the booklet to persons who were known to be, or were likely to be, considering or intending to commit suicide constituted the offence of aiding, abetting, counselling or procuring the suicide ¬f another, contrary to s 2(1) of the 1961 Act, if after reading the booklet such a person committed or attempted to commit suicide, and constituted an attempt to commit an offence under s 2(1) even where such person after reading the booklet did not commit or attempt suicide. The respondents, who were members of the society's executive committee, submitted that it was inappropriate to grant the declaratory relief sought.

Woolf J: A starting point [for considering whether declaratory relief should be granted] must be the terms of s 2(1) of the 1961 Act itself. The intent of the subsection is clear. Section 1 of the Act having abrogated the criminal responsibility of the suicide, s 2(1) retains the criminal liability of an accessory at or before the fact. The nature of that liability has, however, changed. From being a participant in an offence of another, the accessory becomes the principal offender. This has the result that to attempt to 'aid, abet, counsel or procure the suicide of another, or an attempt by another to commit suicide' can be an offence even if the person concerned does not attempt to commit suicide: see *R v McShane* (1977) 66 Cr App Rep 97 and s 3 of the Criminal Attempts Act 1981. This is of significance in relation to the present issues because if the distribution of the booklet amounts to an offence under s 2(1) of the 1961 Act when the person to whom the booklet is distributed commits suicide or attempts to commit suicide, then the distribution to that person, if there is no attempt to commit suicide, could be an attempt to commit an offence under s 2(1) in the appropriate circumstances.

This being the general effect of s 2(1), the issue can be confined to considering whether distributing the booklet to someone who commits suicide or attempts to commit suicide makes the distributor 'an accessory before the fact' to the suicide or attempted suicide, the position so far as the distributor is concerned being exactly the same as it would be if either suicide or attempted suicide was still a criminal offence. . . .

The editor of *Russell on Crime* . . . provides assistance as to what is the 'bare minimum' which is necessary to constitute a person an accessory before the fact. It is stated (p 151):

> . . . the conduct of an alleged accessory should indicate (a) that he knew that the particular deed was contemplated, and (b) that he approved of or assented to it, and (c) that his attitude in respect of it in fact encouraged the principal offender to perform [and I would here add 'or attempt to perform'] the deed.

In relation to the first minimum requirement, those responsible for publishing the booklet, because of its terms, would almost certainly know that a significant number of those to whom the booklet was intended to be sent would be contemplating suicide. They would not know precisely when, where or by what means the suicide was to be effected, if it took place, but this does not mean they cannot be shown to be accessories. As Lord Parker CJ said in *R v Bainbridge* [1959] 3 All ER 200 at 202, [1960] 1 QB 129 at 134:

> . . . if the principal does not totally and substantially vary the advice or the help and does not wilfully and knowingly commit a different form of felony altogether, the man who has advised or helped, aided or abetted, will be guilty of an accessory before the fact.

As the judge had directed the jury in that case: 'It must be proved he knew the type of crime which was in fact committed was intended.'

In relation to the second requirement, if the recipients of the booklet committed or attempted to commit suicide, the contents of the booklet indicate that the publishers approved or assented to their doing so. To conclude otherwise is inconsistent with the whole object of the booklet, which is to assist those who feel it necessary to resort to self-deliverance.

I turn, therefore, to the final minimum requirement. I have no doubt that, in the case at least of certain recipients of the booklet, its contents would encourage suicide. Ignorance how to commit suicide must by itself be a deterrent. Likewise, the risks inherent in an unsuccessful attempt must be a deterrent. The contents of the booklet provide information as to methods which are less likely to result in an unsuccessful attempt. This assistance must encourage some readers to commit or attempt to commit suicide. This is clearly appreciated by the publishers, thus their care to control the persons to whom the booklet is to be sold and their advice as to the safe keeping of the booklet. . . .

The fact that the supply of the booklet could be an offence does not mean that any particular supply is an offence. It must be remembered that the society is an unincorporated body and there can be no question of the society committing an offence. Before an offence under s 2 can be proved, it must be shown that the individual concerned 'aided, abetted, counselled or procured' a suicide or an attempt at suicide and intended to do so by distributing the booklet. The intention of the individual will normally have to be inferred from facts surrounding the particular supply which he made. If, for example, before sending a copy of the booklet, a member of the society had written a letter, the contents of which were known to the person sending the booklet, which stated that the booklet was required because the member was intending to commit suicide, then, on those facts, I would conclude that an offence had been committed or at least an attempted offence contrary to s 2 of the 1961 Act. However, in the majority of cases, a member requesting the booklet will not make clear his intentions and the supply will be made without knowledge of whether the booklet is required for purposes of research, general information, or because suicide is contemplated. Is it, therefore, enough that in any particular case the person responsible for making the supply would appreciate that there is a real likelihood that the booklet is required by one of the substantial number of members of the society who will be contemplating suicide? It is as to this aspect of the case that there is the greatest difficulty and little assistance from the authorities.

Counsel on behalf of the respondents contends that before a person can be an accessory, there must be a consensus between the accessory and the principal, and there can be no consensus where the alleged accessory does not even know whether the principal is contemplating (in this case) suicide. As, however, is pointed out in Smith and Hogan *Criminal Law* (4th edn, 1978) while counselling implies consensus, procuring and aiding do not. The authors say (p 116):

> . . . the law probably is that: i) 'Procuring' implies causation but not consensus, ii) 'abetting' and 'counselling' imply consensus but not causation and iii) 'aiding' requires actual assistance but neither consensus nor causation.

As a matter of principle, it seems to me that, as long as there is the necessary intent to assist those who are contemplating suicide to commit suicide if they decide to do so, it does not matter that the supplier does not know the state of mind of the actual recipient. The requirement for the necessary intent explains why in those cases where, in the ordinary course of business, a person is responsible for distributing an article, appreciating that some individuals might use it for committing suicide, he is not guilty of an offence. In the ordinary way, such a distributor would have no intention to assist the act of suicide. An intention to assist need not, however, involve a desire that suicide should be committed or attempted.

In this connection, I must refer to *R v Fretwell* (1862) 9 Cox CC 152. In that case the Court of Criminal Appeal decided that the mere provision of the means of committing a crime is not sufficient to make the provider guilty as an accessory. In giving the judgment of the court, Erle CJ said (at 154):

> In the present case the prisoner was unwilling that the deceased should take the poison; it was at her instigation and under the threat of self-destruction that he procured it and supplied it to her; but it was found that he did not administer it to her or cause her to take it. It would be consistent with the facts of the case that he hoped she would change her mind; and it might well be that the prisoner hoped and expected that she would not resort to it.

While I accept that this reasoning does not accord with mine, I do not regard the case as requiring me to come to a different conclusion from that which I have indicated. That case is inconsistent with *National Coal Board v Gamble* [1958] 3 All ER 203, [1959] 1 QB 11 and I regard it as confined to its own facts, for the reasons indicated in Smith and Hogan *Criminal Law* (4th edn, 1978, pp 120, 121).

Counsel for the respondents points out, and this I accept, that in some cases the booklet, far from precipitating someone to commit suicide, might have the effect of deterring someone from committing suicide when they might otherwise have done so. In such circumstances, he submits, it would be quite nonsensical to regard the supply of the booklet as being an attempted offence contrary to s 2 of the 1961 Act. I agree, though I recognise that on one approach the result would be different. The reason why I agree with the submission is because, in such a case, the booklet has not provided any assistance with a view to a contemplated suicide. Such assistance is necessary to establish the actus reus for even the attempted offence.

There will also be cases where, although the recipient commits or attempts to commit suicide, the booklet has nothing to do with the suicide or the attempted suicide; for example, a long period of time may have elapsed between the sending of the booklet and the attempt. In such a case, again, I would agree with counsel for the respondents that there would not be a sufficient connection between the attempted suicide and the supply of the booklet to make the supplier responsible. This does not mean that it has to be shown that the suicide or attempted suicide would not have occurred but for the booklet. However, if 'procuring' alone is relied on, this may be the case. As Lord Widgery CJ stated in *A-G's Reference (No 1 of 1975)* [1975] 2 All ER 684 at 686-687, [1975] QB 773 at 779-780:

> To procure means to produce by endeavour. You procure a thing by setting out to see that it happens and taking the appropriate steps to produce that happening . . . You cannot procure an offence unless there is a causal link between what you do and the commission of the offence . . .

However, you do not need to procure to be an accessory and the same close causal connection is not required when what is being done is the provision of assistance.

I therefore conclude that to distribute the booklet can be an offence. But, before an offence can be established to have been committed, it must at least be proved (a) that the alleged offender had the necessary intent, that is, he intended the booklet to be used by someone contemplating suicide and intended that that person would be assisted by the booklet's contents, or otherwise encouraged to take or to attempt to take his own life; (b) that while he still had that intention he distributed the booklet to such a person who read it; and (c) in addition, if an offence under s 2 of the 1961 Act is to be proved, that such a person was assisted or encouraged by so reading the booklet to take or to attempt to take his own life, otherwise the alleged offender cannot be guilty of more than an attempt.

If these facts can be proved, then it does not make any difference that the person would have tried to commit suicide anyway. Nor does it make any difference, as the respondents contend, that the information contained in the booklet is already in the public domain. The distinguishing feature between an innocent and guilty distribution is that in the former case the distributor will not have the necessary intent, while in the latter case he will.

However, in each case it will be for a jury to decide whether the necessary facts are proved. If they are, then normally the offence will be made out. Nevertheless, even if they are proved, I am not prepared to say it is not possible for there to some exceptional circumstances which means that an offence is not established.

Of course this case is concerned with the publication of a book rather than a doctor providing the means for a particular patient to end his life. The importance of the case, however, lies in Woolf J's identification of what constitutes the elements of the offence which, as you will have seen, he lists at the end of his judgment. The reservation Woolf J expresses concerning proof of the existence of these elements when the case concerned a book issued to the public at large would not trouble a jury in the case of a particular doctor advising or helping a particular patient for a known purpose.

(b) Changing the law

It has been increasingly argued that the law relating to doctor-assisted suicide should be changed. In its present form, it is said, it means that patients are denied control over their own death, when they are unable to help themselves and where the doctor is the only real and reliable source of help. The argument continues that they are thus condemned to suffer, since withdrawal of treatment may not bring about their death, and doctors may be made helpless onlookers (or forced surreptitiously to kill the patient, see *infra*).

The House of Lords' Select Committee on Medical Ethics referred to earlier will perforce have to consider whether a change in the law is called for. Professor Robert Weir puts the arguments for and against what he calls physician-assisted suicide.

R Weir 'The Morality of Physician-Assisted Suicide' (1992) 20 Law, Medicine & Health Care 116

In March, 1989, 12 physicians published an article on the provision of care to hopelessly ill patients. Unfortunately, many of the substantive points in that article received insufficient attention from readers because the authors' call for appropriate, continually adjusted care for terminally ill patients was overshadowed by a portion of the document in which ten of the authors agreed that 'it is not immoral for a physician to assist in the rational suicide of a terminally ill person.' [Wanzer et al 'The Physician's Responsibility Towards Hopelessly Ill Patients: A Second Look' (1989) New Engl J Med 320]

In June, 1990, Jack Kevorkian, a retired pathologist in Michigan, gained international media attention by enabling Janet Adkins, a woman in the early stage of Alzheimer's disease, to terminate her life with the help of his 'suicide machine.' The features of the case were so unusual that physicians, ethicists, and attorneys in health law who were interviewed by journalists were unanimous in judging this particular act of physician-assisted suicide deplorable.

In March, 1991, Timothy Quill, an internist in New York, published a detailed account of the suicide of one of his patients identified only as 'Diane,' a patient with acute myelomonocytic leukemia who requested and received his assistance in killing herself with an overdose of barbiturates. Given the features of this particular case, some of the professionals in medicine, ethics, and law interviewed by the media judged Dr Quill's action to have been morally acceptable, even if against the law in New York.

The issue of physician-assisted suicide (PAS) is not limited to these well-publicized examples. The American Hospital Association estimates that many of the 6,000 daily deaths in the United States are orchestrated by patients, relatives, and physicians, although how many of these deaths are assisted suicides is unknown. In a 1990 *New York Times*-CBS poll, taken two weeks after the initial publicity of the Adkins case, 53 percent of the respondents said that physicians should be allowed to assist a severely ill person in terminating his or her own life. Moreover, PAS is beginning to be addressed as a separate ethical issue in the medical literature, without being lumped together with the related but different issue of voluntary euthanasia.

The legal status of PAS is also being tested in an unprecedented manner. The Hemlock Society, having failed three years ago to get 'The Humane and Dignified Death Act' on the ballot in California, successfully worked with a coalition called Washington Citizens for Death with Dignity to get Initiative 119 on the ballot in Washington in November, 1991. The wording of this initiative, using language that blurs the differences between PAS and voluntary euthanasia, simply asked voters: 'Shall adult patients who are in a medically terminal condition be permitted to request and receive from a physician aid-in-dying?'

Given these events, the time has come for a serious discussion of the morality and legality of physician-assisted suicide. I hope to contribute to that discussion by first analyzing the concept of assisted suicide and describing the diversity of possible legal responses to acts of PAS. I will then provide an ethical analysis of PAS by discussing the cases of Janet Adkins and 'Diane,' sorting out the competing ethical arguments about this issue, and making some recommendations for professional practice and public policy.

The concept of assisted suicide
As is true for all suicides, an assisted suicide involves someone (a person outside a clinical setting, or a patient in a clinical setting) who has suicidal motives, intends to die, does something to cause his or her death, and is non-coerced in deciding to kill himself or herself. However, in contrast to 'normal' suicides, an assisted suicide requires aid from a physician, a relative or friend of the person wanting to commit suicide, or some other person who carries out the role of 'enabler.' The enabler can assist the suicidal person in any number of ways: by supplying information (eg, from the Hemlock Society) on the most effective ways of committing suicide, purchasing a weapon of self-destruction, providing a lethal dose of pills or poison, giving the suicidal person encouragement to carry out the lethal deed, or helping in the actual act of killing (eg, by helping the person take the pills, pull the trigger of a gun, close the garage doors, or turn on the gas). Also in contrast to suicide, an act of assisted suicide is an illegal act in many jurisdictions, punishable by fines and-or short-term imprisonment . . .

The case against physician-assisted suicide
Making a case for an ethical position, especially one that is contrary to traditional moral thinking and current law, requires an analysis of competing arguments and an effort to be as persuasive as possible. I now turn to that dual task by first examining five ethical arguments, some with variant themes, that are sometimes advanced against physician participation in assisted suicide.

(1) The medical profession is committed to healing
The most common argument against PAS has two variants, both of which are based on the view that physicians constitute a unique profession that is defined, at least in part, by a

traditional group morally stipulating standards of care and of behavior by members of the group. One version of this argument involves a direct appeal to the Hippocratic Oath, dating from the fourth century BC. In particular, current opponents of PAS appeal to the portion of the oath that declares: 'I will neither give a deadly drug to anybody if asked for it, nor will I make a suggestion to this effect.'

The second, more general version of this argument emphasizes the centrality of healing in defining who physicians are and what they do in their professional role. For some persons who advocate this view of medicine, the notion that physicians might, even in rare instances, assist patients to commit suicide is automatically and without exception ruled out of bounds for any member of the medical profession. As stated by David Orentlicher, 'Treatment designed to bring on death, by definition, does not heal and is therefore fundamentally inconsistent with the physician's role in the patient-physician relationship.' [(1989) 262 JAMA 1844]

(2) Physicians should not cause death

A related argument asserts that there is no difference between PAS and voluntary euthanasia. Once a physician moves beyond abating life-sustaining treatment, so the argument goes, it does not really matter whether the physician's participation in helping to hasten the patient's death at the patient's request is by prescribing barbiturates or by injecting a lethal agent. Both acts 'encourage doctors to use their skills to kill their patients.' According to Leon Kass, there is little difference between a physician's role as an accomplice to death or as an agent of death: assisting in a patient's death 'is as much in violation of the venerable proscription against euthanasia as were the physician to do it himself.'

(3) Patients should not request physician-assisted suicide

This argument also has two variants, both of which address the moral responsibility of patients in the relationships they have with physicians. One version, the simpler of the two, states that patients should never ask their physicians to help them commit suicide, given that (a) many persons regard suicide as an immoral act and (b) physician participation in enabling that act of self-destruction to occur may constitute criminal action.

The second version of this argument is based on the difference between negative and positive moral rights, as these rights apply to the relationship between a patient and that patient's physician. A decision made by a patient to forgo mechanical ventilation, feeding tubes, or some other life-sustaining treatment involves the *negative* right (or liberty right) of treatment refusal. A correlate of this negative right is the obligation of the patient's physician not to interfere with or thwart that negative right unless the physician has some overriding obligation of another sort.

By contrast, a request by a patient for a physician's assistance in committing suicide can be interpreted as involving a *positive* right (or welfare right), or at least a claim to that effect. The difference is important: the patient does not merely request to be left alone by the physician, but tries to impose a moral obligation on the physician to help the patient accomplish the desired end of self-destruction. That claim, whether based on merit or need, is weak, and certainly need not be regarded as imposing an obligation on the physician who receives it.

(4) Physician-assisted suicide would lead to mistrust and abuses

This view, a form of the 'slippery slope' argument, projects two unfortunate consequences that would follow from the widespread acceptance and/or legalization of PAS. One of these consequences would be damage to the relationship of trust that, one hopes, exists between patients and their physicians. According to David Orentlicher, even a discussion of assisted suicide could damage the patient-physician relationship in two different ways: it could raise questions in the patient's mind about the value the physician attaches to the patient's present life of disability and suffering, and it could raise doubts in the patient's mind about the physician's commitment to provide effective treatment for the patient's current medical conditions. Either way, a physician's willingness even to discuss the possibility of assisted suicide 'might seriously undermine' the patient's trust in the physician.

The other consequences, that of abuses by physicians in assisting patients to commit suicide, would be equally serious. As vividly illustrated by the actions of Jack Kevorkian, some physicians would undoubtedly agree to help patients kill themselves without determining whether a given patient is clinically depressed, whether appropriate other medical opinions have been secured, whether the request for help is necessary, whether alternatives to assisted suicide have been explored, or whether relatives and friends who would be psychologically harmed by an unexpected suicide are aware of what may happen.

The fact that 'Diane's' case was handled in a better manner is of little comfort, according to this argument, since it merely demonstrates that virtually all cases of PAS involve physicians acting alone, with no scrutiny from their peers, the courts, or anybody else.

(5) Physician-assisted suicide is unnecessary

Patients turn to their physicians for help in committing suicide for any number of reasons. Chief among these reasons is a desire to avoid the prolonged pain and suffering, both physical and psychological, often involved in the course of a chronic and/or terminal condition. Frequently having witnessed the long, painful deaths of relatives in hospital settings, patients sometimes ask their physicians to help them avoid the same fate. Concerned that physicians will be unable to control the pain or effectively manage the symptoms of their chronic medical conditions, they conclude that suicide, perhaps requiring assistance from a physician or someone else, is their only alternative.

Such reasoning is wrong, according to advocates of hospice programs. In this argument, the availability of hospice care throughout the country precludes the need for patients to seek suicide, thus making the participation of physicians in assisting suicide unnecessary. Some physicians may, out of ignorance regarding effective pain control, 'agree with patients that their suffering is intolerable and worthy of assisted suicide when in fact the pain may be easily treatable.' A preferable alternative is for physicians to learn how to relieve patients' pain more effectively, manage the symptoms of their conditions more appropriately, and assure them that prolonged suffering need not be the fate that awaits them.

Do these five arguments, taken singly or as a collective argument, make a persuasive case that physicians should never agree to assist their patients in committing suicide? I think not, for the following reasons. Critics of PAS who use the first argument take an undeniably important, defining feature of the medical profession, but emphasize it to the exclusion of other ways of describing who physicians are and what they do professionally. Healing the sick and injured is surely one of the goals of medicine, but not in isolation from other appropriate medical goals. Preventing disease, saving and prolonging lives, relieving pain and suffering, ameliorating disabling conditions, and avoiding undue harm to patients are also important goals that represent defining features of medicine as a profession.

Some of these goals of medicine, it is important to note, are appropriate even when patients cannot be healed – and even when some patients turn to their physicians for help in putting an end to an existence they have come to regard as intolerable. The achievement of these appropriate medical goals is more important than a literal adherence to an ancient oath whose religious and moral framework is of such limited relevance to contemporary medicine that the oath is frequently altered when used in medical school convocations and increasingly replaced entirely by other kinds of oaths, including those written by medical students themselves.

The second argument, the one equating PAS with voluntary euthanasia, is simply misplaced in the debate over PAS. It is true, of course, that euthanasia has for centuries been regarded as contrary to morally responsible medical practice, but the intentional killing of patients is not the ethical issue involved in PAS. Physicians do not cause the deaths of patients in these cases; the patients cause their own deaths, a legal act in all 50 states, subsequent to receiving some type of enabling help from their physicians. Thus critics of PAS who assert that physicians are thereby killing patients are either (a) mistaken about the differences between assisted suicide and voluntary euthanasia or (b) intentionally blurring the differences between these two acts to score points with the emotive language of 'killing'.

The third argument is largely true, in my view, because it appropriately indicates that patients should not make unreasonable demands on physicians. Patients should be hesitant to try to involve their physicians in acts of assisted suicide, just as any of us should refrain from encouraging other persons to participate in actions that may be contrary to their value systems. Equally important, when patients with chronic, progressively deteriorating, or terminal conditions do ask their physicians for help in committing suicide, they should understand that they have no justifiable reason for thinking that their physicians are obligated to render such help. Physician-assisted suicide should be motivated by compassion for a patient, not a misplaced sense of moral obligation.

The last two arguments, the ones stating that PAS is dangerous and unnecessary, are only partially true. Abuses in the name of physician-assisted suicide will undoubtedly take place in the future, as they undoubtedly already do. Whether the abuses will be greater than at present is impossible to say. What is possible to say, however, is that PAS seems to be both necessary and morally justifiable in rare cases and, if handled correctly by morally responsible physicians, need not threaten the foundation of trust that is crucial to patient-physician relationships.

The occasional necessity of PAS is illustrated by the case of 'Diane,' who requested assistance from Timothy Quill in terminating her life even though she was receiving appropriate medical care as a hospice patient. Unfortunately, even hospice care fails, for some patients, to provide them with sufficient personal control over the terminal phase of their lives. 'Diane's' case also suggests that a patient's level of trust in a physician may be increased, not undermined, when a caring physician indicates a reluctant willingness to help the patient bring her or his life to an end.

The case for physician-assisted suicide
Having provided this critical assessment of arguments against PAS, I will now put forth five arguments that may prove to be persuasive in justifying some cases of physician participation in assisted suicide. Taken together, the arguments claim that PAS is occasionally justifiable as a compassionate way for physicians to respond to current medical reality by alleviating patient suffering, optimizing patient control, and minimizing harm to the patient and other persons important to the patient. Taken individually, the arguments suggest that physicians should, in rare cases, consider assisting their patients to commit suicide, for any of five reasons.

(1) To respond to current medical reality
Change is a regular part of medicine, whether the change takes the form of new diagnostic tools, new research discoveries, new victories over old diseases, new diseases, new health problems, new drugs, new life-sustaining technologies, or new concerns over matters pertaining to bio-medical ethics, health economics, and health law. Change is surely a factor in the medical problems that patients bring their physicians, with adult patients now presenting more medical problems that are chronic or degenerative in nature than ever before. Added to this factor is another one: patients are living increasingly longer lives, with the combination of chronic medical conditions and extended life expectancy representing the distinct possibility, for some persons, that remaining alive will be regarded as offering nothing other than more disability, more financial and personal hardship, and more suffering.

The good news is that many adults are now capable, with the help of pharmacological and technological advances in medicine, of having long lives with a remarkable health status that would have been unachievable earlier in this century and unimaginable before that. The bad news is that some adults are caught in an existential situation dominated by intractable pain, severe disability, progressive dementia, a deteriorating neurological condition, a terminal condition, or some combination of these that makes life seem not to be worth living. An unknown number of these persons decide that death is a preferable option to the suffering that life holds for them and, for their own personal reasons, ask their physicians to help them end the suffering.

It is this part of medical reality – the realistic limits of physicians to heal all their patients and effectively relieve suffering – that represents the ethical core of the debate over PAS. Rather than quoting a passage from the Hippocratic Oath about what physicians cannot do for their patients, contemporary physicians should address medical reality as it currently exists in their patients – some with terminal conditions, and an increasing number with chronic and degenerative diseases – and consider again what they might do for that small minority of patients who find their lives to be intolerable and who, perhaps as a last resort, turn to their physicians for help in bringing about death.

(2) To alleviate patient suffering
Virtually anyone who is ill suffers from time to time. For some patients, suffering is primarily physical in nature, with the particular forms of suffering including nausea, dyspnea, fever, hunger, thirst, diarrhea, and pain. For other patients, suffering is partially or perhaps primarily psychological in nature, with individuals experiencing anxiety, depression, denial, loneliness, helplessness, anger, and fear. Much of this suffering, whether physiological or psychological in nature, can be effectively managed with empathic support, medications, various other medical and surgical interventions, nursing care, psychological counseling, stress-reduction techniques and rest.

But for Janet Adkins, 'Diane,' and an unknown number of other patients, the multiple efforts made by themselves, their families and friends, and their physicians to alleviate their suffering ultimately do not work. Janet Adkins, it seems, experienced substantial psychological suffering brought on by thoughts about the losses she had already experienced (she could no longer read literature or play the piano). Additional psychological suffering was undoubtedly created by the anxiety and fear of wondering what her remaining years with Alzheimer's disease would be like for herself and her family.

'Diane' experienced the physical suffering caused by her disease-related bone pain, weakness, infections, fatigue, and fever, but she preferred this suffering to the suffering she would have experienced through hospitalization, chemotherapy, radiation therapy, and bone marrow transplantation. In addition, she seems to have experienced substantial psychological suffering that included anger at an insensitive oncologist, anxiety over losing control of her living and dying, fear about increasing discomfort and dependence, fear about additional pain, and an overwhelming sense of injustice regarding the leukemic condition that struck her soon after she had conquered her other health problems.

The ethical challenge that is presented to physicians by such cases is direct and sharp: should I, having exhausted all other therapeutic possibilities, respond affirmatively to a request for help made by one of my patients? Should I, with the intention of alleviating the life-ruining suffering that my patient is experiencing, be willing to assist the patient in committing suicide? In at least some cases, the appropriate answer is yes.

(3) To optimize patient control

The desire to have control over one's living, dying, and death is a factor in assisted suicide cases that matches the desire for suffering to be ended. Janet Adkins was willing to travel from Portland to Seattle for experimental treatment, then to fly (with her husband) to Detroit to make use of the 'suicide machine' in order to end her life before it was ravaged further by Alzheimer's disease. Although legitimate questions have been raised about her mental status at the time, there seems to be little doubt that, if she was still autonomous in the days before her death, her choice to kill herself was a choice to control her destiny instead of permitting her disease to control her.

The desire for personal control is even clearer in 'Diane's' case. Quill states that 'Diane,' having overcome her earlier medical problems, 'took control of her life' and developed 'a strong sense of independence and confidence.' When she went against Quill's medical advice and the wishes of her family in refusing chemotherapy, she 'articulated very clearly that it was she who would be experiencing all the side effects of treatment.' Later, when 'Diane' knew she was dying, Quill says that it was 'extraordinarily important to "Diane" to maintain control of herself and her own dignity during the time remaining to her.' In describing his own participation in the case, Quill states that he felt he was 'setting her free to get the most out of the time she had left, and to maintain dignity and control on her own terms until her death.'

For physicians in such cases, the option of trying to optimize patient control represents the ultimate challenge of how far one is willing to go to respect the autonomy of patients. If (as seems clear in 'Diane's' case, but not Janet Adkins' case) the patient who requests assistance is autonomous, the patient is therefore capable of making an informed, deliberative, and voluntary decision regarding her or his health care. If personal control over one's living and dying is highly valued by the patient, the decisions made about health care will reflect that value. In extreme cases the desire to remain autonomous and in control sometimes includes a request for help from a physician – a request for help in exercising control over one's final exit.

(4) To minimize harm to the patient and others

The ethical principle of nonmaleficence has considerable importance in medicine. Throughout the history of medicine, physicians have been expected to avoid intentionally or negligently harming their patients. Given that patients are frequently harmed in a variety of ways in clinical contexts, the ethical requirement placed on physicians is that of trying to ensure that patients are not harmed on balance in the course of efforts to heal them or otherwise promote their welfare.

Traditionally, the ultimate harm to befall a patient has been considered to be death. As a consequence, two longstanding moral rules of medical practice have been derived from this professional aversion to having any intentional (or negligent) role in a patient's death: 'do not kill' and 'do not assist another person's death.'

In the great majority of cases, these moral rules continue to apply. However, patients can be harmed in several significant ways short of death, through the invasion of their important interests, the impairment of their mental or psychological welfares, physical injury, and technological abuse. Moreover, most thoughtful persons have some sort of informal ranking or other cataloging of harmful events that could take place in their lives that would represent, to them, a fate worse than death.

Janet Adkins, 'Diane,' and unknown other persons have concluded that remaining alive under terrible, worsening circumstances is a fate worse than death. The important question is whether physicians should have any role in facilitating one harmful event (a patient's self-destruction) in order to help the patient avoid other harms (eg, intractable pain, progressive dementia, loss of personhood, incalculable damage to a family) that the patient regards as worse. In rare cases, the appropriate answer is affirmative, both for the sake of the patient and for persons loved by the patient.

(5) To act out of compassion
What counts as a morally responsible motive for physician participation in assisted suicide? The list of possible motives includes a desire to help the patient, an undervaluing of the quality of the patient's life, a desire to help the family emotionally and financially, a misplaced sense of duty to the patient, a desire for publicity, and so forth.

According to media accounts of the Janet Adkins case, Jack Kevorkian seems to have had several motives, including the desire for publicity in the medical profession. By contrast, Timothy Quill seems not to have been motivated by considerations other than the physical and psychological welfare of his patient and her family.

In my view, the only acceptable motive for physicians to have in enabling a patient to commit suicide is that of compassion. In many instances, of course, compassionate physicians decide, for good moral reasons, not to help patients achieve the sort of self-deliverance that they seek. In other, much less frequent instances, compassionate physicians sometimes decide that the plea for help from a patient for whom life has become intolerable is a request that cannot and should not be rejected. Either moral choice, if motivated by compassion, can be correct, depending on the facts of individual cases.

Justifiable practice and public policy
For PAS to be justifiable, several conditions have to be met. First, a morally responsible physician who is asked to assist in a suicide should determine if the patient is suffering from treatable clinical depression and, if so, recommend treatment for that condition. In addition, the physician should try to determine if the patient's pain and other suffering are, in fact, refractory to treatment.

A second condition is for the physician to determine that assisted suicide is a moral last resort, in the sense that there are no effective medical options available that are acceptable to the patient. No medical treatment is available that will reverse or cure the patient's condition, no life-sustaining treatment is being used that could be abated at the patient's request, and no intervention (even hospice care) seems to provide the relief and release the patient desperately seeks.

A third condition consists of several conversations between the physician and the patient, with at least one of the conversations including one or more of the patient's closest relatives and friends. From the physician's perspective, these conversations, whether done within a few days or over several weeks, should have several purposes: to determine that the patient is autonomous and the decision to commit suicide is rational, to recommend a second medical opinion and other appropriate professional help, to make sure that no acceptable alternatives to assisted suicide are available, to determine that the request for assistance is necessary, and to make sure that the patient's close relatives and friends are informed about the prospective suicide. The consent of the patient's family to the contemplated suicide is not required, but they should at least be aware, in general terms, of what may happen so that the psychological harm they experience will be lessened when they find out that the suicide has taken place.

Even when these conditions are met in individual cases, important questions remain as to how PAS cases should be handled in terms of public policy. How should the law respond when a physician or other person helps an individual do something that is legal in every state, when that legal activity is suicide? Should physicians who decide to assist one or more of their patients in committing suicide be criminally liable, either under a specific state statute or a state homicide law? Should assisted suicide, whether done by physicians or other persons, be decriminalized? Should statutes authorizing PAS in certain cases be limited to cases of terminal illness? Should PAS, along with voluntary euthanasia, be legalized as 'physician aid-in-dying' under certain conditions?

These questions and many others regarding PAS as a matter of public policy require careful analysis and extensive discussion, much more than can be completed here. However, I have some tentative recommendations that might contribute to the discussion. A preferable alternative to the current patchwork of state laws on assisted suicide would be for the National Conference of Commissioners on Uniform State Laws (NCCUSL), working with appropriate medical groups, to develop model legislation on PAS that might be adopted throughout the country, so that physicians practicing in any state could have greater certainty regarding the legality (or illegality) of PAS. My hope is that this new legislation will remove PAS from the criminal statutes in all states, so that physicians who decide for reasons of compassion to engage in PAS will no longer have to be secretive and deceptive with their professional colleagues about having done so.

In my view, the legal restrictions on assisted suicide should be lifted only for physicians. Given the ease with which emotionally unstable, demented, and suicidal individuals could be 'assisted' in their deaths by numerous other persons with questionable motives, the NCCUSL and/or various state legislatures may decide to maintain the legal liability attached to acts of assisted suicide when performed by persons other than physicians.

Physicians, of course, should not be given a legal blank check. Physicians who receive requests for help in committing suicide with regret and sadness, who give serious consideration to such requests only in carefully limited circumstances, and who meet the conditions for morally responsible PAS should not face legal penalties. By contrast, physicians who are irresponsible in taking requests for PAS, who fail to exercise appropriate care in working with patients seeking PAS, and who are careless in providing patients with the means of self-destruction should face penalties for such negligence, perhaps including losing their licenses to practice medicine.

One final point. The case for PAS has been developed with great reluctance, both because I wish such activity by physicians were unnecessary and because I am uncomfortable advocating an ethical position that departs from much traditional thinking about ethics in medicine. However, I am convinced that PAS is sometimes necessary, that it is an alternative not to be automatically rejected by morally responsible physicians, and that it is, in at least some instances, justifiable as the right and compassionate thing to do.

One factor bearing upon pressure for reform in England is the European Convention of Human Rights, in particular Articles 2 and 8. These provide as follows:

Article 2
1. Everyone's right to life shall be protected by law. No one shall be deprived of his life intentionally save in the execution of a sentence of a court following his conviction of a crime for which this penalty is provided by law.
2. Deprivation of life shall not be regarded as inflicted in contravention of this Article when it results from the use of force which is no more than absolutely necessary:
(a) in defence of any person from unlawful violence;
(b) in order to effect a lawful arrest or to prevent the escape of a person lawfully detained;
(c) in action lawfully taken for the purpose of quelling a riot or insurrection.

Article 8
1. Everyone has the right to respect for his private and family life, his home and his correspondence.
2. There shall be no interference by a public authority with the exercise of this right except such as is in accordance with the law and is necessary in a democratic society in the interests of national security, public safety or the economic well-being of the country, for the prevention of disorder or crime, for the protection of health or morals, or for the protection of the rights and freedoms of others.

It could be argued that these provisions prohibit any law which prevents a person exercising a choice, albeit through another (the doctor), to end his life. If the European Court of Human Rights were to accept this argument, English law would have to conform through appropriate legislation. As it happens, a similar argument based upon Section 7 of the Canadian Charter of Rights and Freedoms was considered by the Canadian Supreme Court in the following case.

Rodriguez v British Columbia (Attorney General) (1993) 82 BCLR (2d) 273 (Can Sup Ct)

The petitioner, 42, was suffering from amyotrophic lateral sclerosis, an incurable, progressive disease affecting the nervous system, leading to extensive muscle wasting. Victims of the disease generally die within two to three years of first diagnosis, due to wasting of the muscles used in breathing. Prior to that time, victims experience difficulty with speech, chewing and swallowing. Feeding eventually must be done by stomach tube and the victim requires total care as most bodily functions are lost. Death generally results from starvation or choking. The petitioner wished to avoid the future stress and loss of dignity caused by the prospect of such a death and she proposed to have a physician install an intravenous line containing some effective agent which, at the appropriate time, the petitioner would be able to transfer into her body by activating a switch, ending her life. She applied for an order declaring invalid s 241(b) of the *Criminal Code*, which makes aiding or abetting a suicide a criminal offence. She relied on ss 7, 12 and 15(1) of the *Canadian Charter of Rights and Freedoms*. Her application was dismissed and by a majority (McEachern CJ dissenting) the British Columbia Court of Appeal dismissed her appeal ([1993] 3 WWR 553). She appealed to the Canadian Supreme Court which, by a majority of 5-4, also dismissed her appeal.

Sopinka J: I have read the reasons of the Chief Justice and those of McLachlin J herein. The result of the reasons of my colleagues is that all persons who by reason of disability are unable to commit suicide have a right under the *Canadian Charter of Rights and Freedoms* to be free from government interference in procuring the assistance of others to take their life. They are entitled to a constitutional exemption from the operation of s 241 of the *Criminal Code*, RSC, 1985, c C-46, which prohibits the giving of assistance to commit suicide (hereinafter referred to as assisted suicide). The exemption would apply during the period that this Court's order would be suspended and thereafter Parliament could only replace the legislation subject to this right. I must respectfully disagree with the conclusion reached by my colleagues and with their reasons . . .

I have concluded that the conclusion of my colleagues cannot be supported under the provisions of the *Charter* . . .

I. Section 7

The most substantial issue in this appeal is whether s 241(b) infringes s 7 in that it inhibits the appellant in controlling the timing and manner of her death. I conclude that while the section impinges on the security interest of the appellant, any resulting deprivation is not contrary to the principles of fundamental justice. I would come to the same conclusion with respect to any liberty interest which may be involved.

Section 7 of the *Charter* provides as follows:

> 7. Everyone has the right to life, liberty and security of the person and the right not to be deprived thereof except in accordance with the principles of fundamental justice.

The appellant argues that, by prohibiting anyone from assisting her to end her life when her illness has rendered her incapable of terminating her life without such assistance, by threat of criminal sanction, s 241(b) deprives her of both her liberty and her security of the person. The appellant asserts that her application is based upon (a) the right to live her remaining life with the inherent dignity of a human person, (b) the right to control what happens to her body while she is living, and (c) the right to be free from governmental interference in making fundamental personal decisions concerning the terminal stages of her life. The first two of these asserted rights can be seen to invoke both liberty and security of the person; the latter is more closely associated with only the liberty interest.

(a) Life, Liberty and Security of the Person

The appellant seeks a remedy which would assure her some control over the time and manner of her death. While she supports her claim on the ground that her liberty and security of the person interests are engaged, a consideration of these interests cannot be divorced from the sanctity of life, which is one of the three *Charter* values protected by s 7.

None of these values prevail a priori over the others. All must be taken into account in determining the content of the principles of fundamental justice and there is no basis for imposing a greater burden on the propounder of one value as against that imposed on another.

Section 7 involves two stages of analysis. The first is as to the values at stake with respect to the individual. The second is concerned with possible limitations of those values when considered in conformity with fundamental justice. In assessing the first aspect, we may do so by considering whether there has been a violation of Ms Rodriguez's security of the person and we must consider this in light of the other values I have mentioned . . .

What, then, can security of the person be said to encompass in the context of this case? The starting point for the answer to this question is *R v Morgentaler* [1988] 1 SCR 30 in which this Court struck down *Criminal Code* provisions which had the effect of preventing women access to therapeutic abortion unless they complied with an administrative scheme found to be contrary to principles of fundamental justice.

. . . In my view . . . the judgments of this Court in *Morgentaler* can be seen to encompass a notion of personal autonomy involving, at the very least, control over one's bodily integrity free from state interference and freedom from state-imposed psychological and emotional stress. In *Reference re ss 193 and 195.1(1)(c) of the Criminal Code (Man)*, [1990] 1 SCR 1123 Lamer J (as he then was) also expressed this view, stating at p 1177 that '[s]ection 7 is also implicated when the state restricts individuals' security of the person by interfering with, or removing from the, control over their physical or mental integrity'. There is no question, then, that personal autonomy, at least with respect to the right to make choices concerning one's own body, control over one's physical and psychological integrity, and basic human dignity are encompassed within security of the person, at least to the extent of freedom from criminal prohibitions which interfere with these.

The effect of the prohibition in s 241(b) is to prevent the appellant from having assistance to commit suicide when she is no longer able to do so on her own. She fears that she will be required to live until the deterioration from her disease is such that she will die as a result of choking, suffocation or pneumonia caused by aspiration of food or secretions. She will be totally dependent upon machines to perform her bodily functions and completely dependent upon others. Throughout this time, she will remain mentally competent and able to appreciate all that is happening to her. Although palliative care may be available to ease the pain and other physical discomfort which she will experience, the appellant fears the sedating effects of such drugs and argues, in any event, that they will not prevent the psychological and emotional distress which will result from being in a situation of utter dependence and loss of dignity. That there is a right to choose how one's body will be dealt with, even in the context of beneficial medical treatment, has long been recognized by the common law. To impose medical treatment on one who refuses it constitutes battery, and our common law has recognized the right to demand that medical treatment which would extend life be withheld or withdrawn. In my view, these considerations lead to the conclusion that the prohibition in s 241(b) deprives the appellant of autonomy over her person and causes her physical pain and psychological stress in a manner which impinges on the security of her person. The appellant's security interest (considered in the context of the life and liberty interest) is therefore engaged, and it is necessary to determine whether there has been any deprivation thereof that is not in accordance with the principles of fundamental justice . . .

(b) The Principles of Fundamental Justice
. . . On the one hand, the Court must be conscious of its proper role in the constitutional make-up of our form of democratic government and not seek to make fundamental changes to long-standing policy on the basis of general constitutional principles and its own view of the wisdom of legislation. On the other hand, the Court has not only the power but the duty to deal with this question if it appears that the *Charter* has been violated. The power to review legislation to determine whether it conforms to the *Charter* extends to not only procedural matters but also substantive issues. The principles of fundamental justice leave a great deal of scope for personal judgment and the Court must be careful that they do not become principles which are of fundamental justice in the eye of the beholder *only*.

In this case, it is not disputed that in general s 241(b) is valid and desirable legislation which fulfils the government's objectives of preserving life and protecting the vulnerable. The complaint is that the legislation is over-inclusive because it does not exclude from the reach of the prohibition those in the situation of the appellant who are terminally ill, mentally competent, but cannot commit suicide on their own. It is also argued that the extension of the prohibition to the appellant is arbitrary and unfair as suicide itself is not unlawful, and the common law allows a physician to withhold or withdraw life-saving or life-maintaining treatment on the patient's instructions and to administer palliative care which has the effect of hastening death. The issue is whether, given this legal context, the existence of a criminal prohibition on assisting suicide for one in the appellant's situation is contrary to principles of fundamental justice.

Discerning the principles of fundamental justice with which deprivation of life, liberty or security of the person must accord, in order to withstand constitutional scrutiny, is not an easy task . . .

This Court has often stated that in discerning the principles of fundamental justice governing a particular case, it is helpful to look at the common law and legislative history of the offence in question (*Re BC Motor Vehicle Act* [1985] 2 SCR 486 and *Morgentaler, supra*, and *R v Swain*, [1991] 1 SCR 933). It is not sufficient, however, merely to conduct a historical review and conclude that because neither Parliament nor the various medical associations had ever expressed a view that assisted suicide should be decriminalized, that to prohibit it could not be said to be contrary to the principles of fundamental justice. Such an approach would be problematic for two reasons. First, a strictly historical analysis will always lead to the conclusion in a case such as this that the deprivation is in accordance with fundamental justice as the legislation will not have kept apace with advances in medical technology. Second, such reasoning is somewhat circular, in that it relies on the continuing existence of the prohibition to find the prohibition to be fundamentally just.

The way to resolve these problems is not to avoid the historical analysis, but to make sure that one is looking not just at the existence of the practice itself (ie, the continued criminalization of assisted suicide) but at the rationale behind that practice and the principles which underlie it.

The appellant asserts that it is a principle of fundamental justice that the human dignity and autonomy of individuals be respected, and that to subject her to needless suffering in this manner is to rob her of her dignity. The importance of the concept of human dignity in our society was enunciated by Cory J (dissenting, Lamer CJ concurring) in *Kindler v Canada (Minister of Justice)*, [1991] 2 SCR 779, at p 813. Respect for human dignity underlies many of the rights and freedoms in the *Charter*.

That respect for human dignity is one of the underlying principles upon which our society is based is unquestioned. I have difficulty, however, in characterizing this in itself as a principle of fundamental justice within the meaning of s 7. While respect for human dignity is the genesis for many principles of fundamental justice, not every law that fails to accord such respect runs afoul of these principles. To state that 'respect for human dignity and autonomy' is a principle of fundamental justice, then, is essentially to state that the deprivation of the appellant's security of the person is contrary to principles of fundamental justice because it deprives her of security of the person. This interpretation would equate security of the person with a principle of fundamental justice and render the latter redundant.

I cannot subscribe to the opinion expressed by my colleague, McLachlin J, that the state interest is an inappropriate consideration in recognizing the principles of fundamental justice in this case. This Court has affirmed that in arriving at these principles, a balancing of the interest of the state and individual is required. . . .

Where the deprivation of the right in question does little or nothing to enhance the state's interest (whatever it may be), it seems to me that a breach of fundamental justice will be made out, as the individual's rights will have been deprived for no valid purpose. This is, to my mind, essentially the type of analysis . . . which was carried out in *Morgentaler*. That is, both Dickson CJ and Beetz J were of the view that at least some of the restrictions placed upon access to abortion had no relevance to the state objective of protecting the foetus while protecting the life and health of the mother. In that regard the restrictions were arbitrary or unfair. It follows that before one can determine that a statutory provision is contrary to fundamental justice, the relationship between the provision and the state interest must be considered. One cannot conclude that a particular limit is arbitrary because (in the words of my colleague, McLachlin J) 'it bears no relation to, or is inconsistent with, the objective that lies behind' the legislation without considering the state interest and the societal concerns which it reflects.

The issue here, then, can be characterized as being whether the blanket prohibition on assisted suicide is arbitrary or unfair in that it is unrelated to the state's interest in protecting the vulnerable, and that it lacks a foundation in the legal tradition and societal beliefs which are said to be represented by the prohibition.

Section 241(b) has as its purpose the protection of the vulnerable who might be induced in moments of weakness to commit suicide. This purpose is grounded in the state interest in protecting life and reflects the policy of the state that human life should not be depreciated by allowing life to be taken. This policy finds expression not only in the provisions of our *Criminal Code* which prohibit murder and other violent acts against others notwithstanding the consent of the victim, but also in the policy against capital punishment and, until its repeal, attempted suicide. This is not only a policy of the state, however, but is part of our fundamental conception of the sanctity of human life. The Law Reform Commission expressed this philosophy appropriately in its Working Paper 28, 'Euthanasia, Aiding Suicide and Cessation of Treatment' (1982), at p 36:

> Preservation of human life is acknowledged to be a fundamental value of our society. Historically, our criminal law has changed very little on this point. Generally speaking, it sanctions the principle of the sanctity of human life. Over the years, however, law has come to temper the apparent absolutism of the principle, to delineate its intrinsic limitations and to define its true dimensions.

As is noted in the above passage, the principle of sanctity of life is no longer seen to require that all human life be preserved at all costs. Rather, it has come to be understood, at least by some, as encompassing quality of life considerations, and to be subject to certain limitations and qualifications reflective of personal autonomy and dignity. An analysis of our legislative and social policy in this area is necessary in order to determine whether fundamental principles have evolved such that they conflict with the validity of the balancing of interests undertaken by Parliament.

(i) History of the Suicide Provisions
At common law, suicide was seen as a form of felonious homicide that offended both against God and the King's interest in the life of his citizens. As Blackstone noted in *Commentaries on the Laws of England* (1769), vol 4, at p 189:

> . . . the law of England wisely and religiously considers, that no man hath a power to destroy life, but by commission from God, the author of it; and, as the suicide is guilty of a double offence; one spiritual, in invading the prerogative of the Almighty, and rushing into his immediate presence uncalled for; and the other temporal, against the king, who hath an interest in the preservation of all his subjects; the law has therefore ranked this among the highest crimes, making it a peculiar species of felony, a felony committed on oneself.

This is essentially the view first propounded by Plato and Aristotle that suicide was 'an offence against the gods or the state' (M G Velasquez, 'Defining Suicide' (1987), *3 Issues in Law & Medicine 37*, at p 40).

However, the contrary school of thought has always existed and is premised on notions of both freedom and compassion. The Roman stoics, for example, 'tended to condone suicide as a lawful and rational exercise of individual freedom and even wise in the cases of old age, disease or dishonor' (Velasquez, *supra*, at p 40). A more humane tone was struck by the Chancellor Francis Bacon who would have preferred leaving to the doctors the duty of lessening, or even ending, the suffering of their patients (L Depault, 'Le droit à la mort: rapport juridique' (1974), *7 Human Rights Journal* 464, at p 467). There has never been a consensus with respect to this contrary school of thought.

Thus, until 1823, English law provided that the property of the suicide be forfeited and his body placed at the cross-roads of two highways with a stake driven through it. Burial indignities were also imposed in *ancien régime* France where the body of the suicide was often put on trial before being crucified (G Williams, *The Sanctity of Life and the Criminal Law* (1957), at p 259; Depaule, *supra*, at p 465, citing the *Ordonnance de 1670*, title XXII).

However, given the practical difficulties of prosecuting the successful suicide, most prohibitions centred on attempted suicide; it was considered an offence and accessory liability for assisted suicide was made punishable. In England, this took the form of a charge of accessory before the fact to murder or murder itself until the passage of the *Suicide Act, 1961* (UK), 9 & 10 Eliz. 2 c 60, which created an offence of assisting suicide which reads much like our s 241. In Canada, the common law recognized that aiding suicide was criminal (G W Burbidge, *A Digest of the Criminal Law of Canada* (1890), at p 224) and this was enshrined in the first *Criminal Code*, SC 1892, c 29, s 237. It is, with some editorial changes, the provision now found in s 241.

The associated offence of attempted suicide has an equally long pedigree in Canada, found in the original *Code* at s 238 and continued substantively unaltered until its repeal by SC 1972, c 12, s 16. The fact of this decriminalization does not aid us particularly in this analysis, however. Unlike the situation with the partial decriminalization of abortion, the decriminalization of attempted suicide cannot be said to represent a consensus by Parliament or by Canadians in general that the autonomy interest of those wishing to kill themselves is paramount to the state interest in protecting the life of its citizens. Rather, the matter of suicide was seen to have its roots and its solutions in sciences outside the law, and for that reason not to mandate a legal remedy. Since that time, there have been some attempts to decriminalize assistance to suicide through private members bills, but none has been successful.

(ii) Medical Care at the End of Life
Canadian courts have recognized a common law right of patients to refuse consent to medical treatment, or to demand that treatment, once commenced, be withdrawn or discontinued (*Ciarlariello v Schacter*, [1993] 2 SCR 119). This right has been specifically recognized to exist even if the withdrawal from or refusal of treatment may result in death (*Nancy B v Hôtel-Dieu de Québec* (1992), 86 DLR (4th) 385 (Que SC); *Malette v Shulman* (1990), 72 OR (2d) 417 (CA). . . .

Following Working Paper 28, the Law Reform Commission recommended in its 1983 Report to the Minister of Justice that the *Criminal Code* be amended to provide that the homicide provisions not be interpreted as requiring a physician to undertake medical treatment against the wishes of a patient, or to continue medical treatment when such treatment 'has become therapeutically useless', or from requiring a physician to 'cease administering appropriate palliative care intended to eliminate or to relieve the suffering of a person, for the sole reason that such care or measures are likely to shorten the life expectancy of this person' (Report 20, *Euthanasia, Aiding Suicide and Cessation of Treatment* (1983), at p 35).

The Law Reform Commission had discussed in the Working Paper possibility of the decriminalization of assisted suicide in the following terms, at pp 53-54:

First of all, the prohibition in [s 241] is not restricted solely to the case of the terminally ill patient, for whom we can only have sympathy, or solely to his physician or a member of his family who helps him to put an end to his suffering. The section is more general and applies to a variety of situations for which it is much more difficult to feel sympathy. Consider, for example, a recent incident, that of inciting to mass suicide. What of the person who takes advantage of another's depressed state to encourage him to commit suicide, for his own financial benefit? What of the person who, knowing an adolescent's suicidal tendencies, provides him with large enough quantities of drugs to kill him? The accomplice in these cases cannot be considered morally blameless. Nor can one conclude that the criminal law should not punish such conduct. To decriminalize completely the act of aiding, abetting or counselling suicide would therefore not be a valid legislative policy. But could it be in the case of the terminally ill?

The probable reason why legislation has not made an exception for the terminally ill lies in the fear of the excesses or abuses to which liberalization of the existing law could lead. As in the case of compassionate murder, decriminalization of aiding suicide would be based on the humanitarian nature of the motive leading the person to provide such aid, counsel or encouragement. As in the case of compassionate murder, moreover, the law may legitimately fear the difficulties involved in determining the true motivation of the person committing the act.

Aiding or counselling a person to commit suicide, on the one hand, and homicide, on the other, are sometimes extremely closely related. Consider, for example, the doctor who holds the glass of poison and pours the contents into the patients mouth. Is he aiding him to commit suicide? Or is he committing homicide, since the victim's willingness to die is legally immaterial? There is reason to fear that homicide of the terminally ill for ignoble motives may readily be disguised as aiding suicide.

In its Working Paper, the Commission had originally recommended that the consent of the Attorney General should be required before prosecutions could be brought under s 241(b). However, after negative public response, the Commission retracted this recommendation in its 1983 Report.

It can be seen, therefore, that while the Law Reform Commission of Canada [has] great sympathy for the plight of those who wish to end their lives so as to avoid significant suffering, [it was not] prepared to recognize that the active assistance of a third party in carrying out this desire should be condoned, even for the terminally ill. The basis for this refusal is twofold it seems – first, the active participation by one individual in the death of another is intrinsically morally and legally wrong, and second, there is no certainty that abuses can be prevented by anything less than a complete prohibition. Creating an exception for the terminally ill might therefore frustrate the purpose of the legislation of protecting the vulnerable because adequate guidelines to control abuse are difficult or impossible to develop.

(iii) Review of Legislation in other Countries
A brief review of the legislative situation in other Western democracies demonstrates that in general, the approach taken is very similar to that which currently exists in Canada. Nowhere is assisted suicide expressly permitted, and most countries have provisions expressly dealing with assisted suicide which are at least as restrictive as our s 241. . . .

The relative provision of *Suicide Act, 1961* of the United Kingdom punishes a person who aids, abets, counsels or procures the suicide of another or an attempt by another to commit suicide, and this form of prohibition is echoed in the criminal statutes of all state and territorial jurisdictions in Australia (M Otlowski, Mercy Killing Cases in the Australian Criminal Justice System (1993), 17 *Crim LJ* 10). The UK provision is apparently the only prohibition on assisted suicide which has been subjected to judicial scrutiny for its impact on human rights prior to the present case. In the Application No. 10083/82, *R v United Kingdom*, July 4, 1983, DR 33, p 270, the European Commission of Human Rights considered whether s 2 of the *Suicide Act, 1961* violated either the right to privacy in Article 8 or freedom of expression in Article 10 of the *Convention for the Protection of Human Rights and Fundamental Freedoms*. The applicant, who was a member of a voluntary euthanasia association, had been convicted of several counts of conspiracy to aid and abet a suicide for his actions in placing persons with a desire to kill themselves in touch with his co-accused who then assisted them in committing suicide. The European Commission held (at p 172) that the acts of aiding, abetting, counselling or procuring suicide were excluded from the concept of privacy by virtue of their trespass on the public interest of protecting life, as reflected in the criminal provisions of the 1961 Act, and upheld the applicant's conviction for the offence. Further, the Commission upheld the restriction on the applicant's freedom of expression, recognizing

> the State's legitimate interest in this area in taking measures to protect, against criminal behaviour, the life of its citizens particularly those who belong to especially vulnerable categories by reason of their age or infirmity. It recognizes the right of the State under the Convention to guard against the inevitable criminal abuses that would occur in the absence of legislation, against the aiding and abetting of suicide. [DR p 272.]

Although the factual scenario in that decision was somewhat different from the one at bar, it is significant that neither the European Commission of Human Rights nor any other judicial tribunal has ever held that a state is prohibited on constitutional or human rights grounds from criminalizing assisted suicide.

Some European countries have mitigated prohibitions on assisted suicide which might render assistance in a case similar to that before us legal in those countries. In the Netherlands, although assisted suicide and voluntary active euthanasia are officially illegal, prosecutions will not be laid so long as there is compliance with medically established guidelines. Critics of the Dutch approach point to evidence suggesting that involuntary active euthanasia (which is not permitted by the guidelines) is being practised to an increasing degree. This worrisome trend supports the view that a relaxation of the absolute prohibition takes us down the slippery slope.

. . . As is the case in Europe and the Commonwealth, however, the vast majority of those American states which have statutory provisions dealing specifically with assisted suicide have no intent or malice requirement beyond the intent to further the suicide, and those states which do not deal with the matter statutorily appear to have common law authority outlawing assisted suicide (Shaffer, *supra*, at p 352; and M M Penrose, 'Assisted Suicide: A Tough Pill to Swallow' (1993), 20 *Pepp L Rev* 689, at pp 700-701). It is notable, also, that recent movements in two American states to legalize physician-assisted suicide in circumstances similar to those at bar have been defeated by the electorate in those states. On November 5, 1991, Washington State voters defeated Initiative 119, which would have legalized physician-assisted suicide where two doctors certified the patient would die within six months and two disinterested witnesses certified that the patients choice was voluntary. One year later, Proposition 161, which would have legalized assisted suicide in California and which incorporated stricter safeguards than did Initiative 119, was defeated by California voters (usually thought to be the most accepting of such legal innovations) by the same margin as resulted in Washington – 54 to 46 percent. In both states, the defeat of the proposed legislation seems to have been due primarily to concerns as to whether the legislation incorporated adequate safeguards against abuse (Penrose, *supra*, at pp 708-714).

Overall, then, it appears that a blanket prohibition on assisted suicide similar to that in s 241 is the norm among Western democracies, and such a prohibition has never been adjudged to be unconstitutional or contrary to fundamental human rights. Recent attempts to alter the status quo in our neighbourhood to the south have been defeated by the electorate, suggesting that despite a recognition that a blanket prohibition causes suffering in certain cases, the societal concern with preserving life and protecting the vulnerable rendered the blanket prohibition preferable to a law which might not adequately prevent abuse.

(iv) Conclusion on Principles of Fundamental Justice

What the preceding review demonstrates is that Canada and other Western democracies recognize and apply the principle of the sanctity of life as a general principle which is subject to limited and narrow exceptions in situations in which notions of personal autonomy and dignity must prevail. However, these same societies continue to draw distinctions between passive and active forms of intervention in the dying process, and with very few exceptions, prohibit assisted suicide in situations akin to that of the appellant. The task then becomes to identify the rationales upon which these distinctions are based and to determine whether they are constitutionally supportable.

The distinction between withdrawing treatment upon a patient's request, such as occurred in the *Nancy B* case, on the one hand, and assisted suicide on the other has been criticised as resting on a legal fiction – that is, the distinction between active and passive forms of treatment. The criticism is based on the fact that the withdrawal of life supportive measures is done with the knowledge that death will ensue, just as is assisting suicide, and that death does in fact ensure as a result of the action taken. See, for example, the Harvard Law Review note 'Physician-Assisted Suicide and the Right to Die with Assistance' (1992), 105 *Harv L Rev* 2021, at pp 2030-31.

Other commentators, however, uphold the distinction on the basis that in the case of withdrawal of treatment, the death is natural – the artificial forces of medical technology which have kept the patient alive are removed and nature takes its course. In the case of assisted suicide or euthanasia, however, the course of nature is interrupted, and death results *directly* from the human action taken (E Keyserlingk, *Sanctity of Life or Quality of Life in the Context of Ethics, Medicine and Law* (1979), a study paper for the Law Reform Commission of Canada's Protection of Life Project). The Law Reform Commission calls this distinction 'fundamental' (at p 19 of the Working Paper).

Whether or not one agrees that the active vs passive distinction is maintainable, however, the fact remains that under our common law, the physician has no choice but to accept the patient's instructions to discontinue treatment. To continue to treat the patient when the patient has withdrawn consent to that treatment constitutes battery (*Ciarlariello* and *Nancy B, supra*). The doctor is therefore not required to make a choice which will result in the patient's death as he would be if he chose to assist a suicide or to perform active euthanasia.

The fact that doctors may deliver palliative care to terminally ill patients without fear of sanction, it is argued, attenuates to an every greater degree any legitimate distinction which can be drawn between assisted suicide and what are currently acceptable forms of medical treatment. The administration of drugs designed for pain control in dosages which the physician knows will hasten death constitutes active contribution to death by any standard. However, the distinction drawn here is one based upon intention – in the case of palliative care the intention is to ease pain, which has the effect of hastening death, while in the case of assisted suicide, the intention is undeniably to cause death. The Law Reform Commission, although it recommended the continued criminal prohibition of both euthanasia and assisted suicide, stated, at p 70 of the Working Paper, that a doctor should never refuse palliative care to a terminally ill person only because it may hasten death. In my view, distinctions based upon intent are important, and in fact form the basis of our criminal law. While factually the distinction may, at times, be difficult to draw, legally it is clear. The fact that in some cases, the third party will, under the guise of palliative care, commit euthanasia or assist in suicide and go unsanctioned due to the difficulty of proof cannot be said to render the existence of the prohibition fundamentally unjust.

The principles of fundamental justice cannot be created for the occasion to reflect the court's dislike or distaste of a particular statute. While the principles of fundamental justice are concerned with more than process, reference must be made to principles which are 'fundamental' in the sense that they would have general acceptance among reasonable people. From the review that I have conducted above, I am unable to discern anything approaching unanimity with respect to the issue before us. Regardless of one's personal views as to whether the distinctions drawn between withdrawal of treatment and palliative care, on the one hand, and assisted suicide on the other are practically compelling, the fact remains that these distinctions are maintained and can be persuasively defended. To the extent that there is a consensus, it is that human life must be respected and we must be careful not to undermine the institutions that protect it.

This consensus finds legal expression in our legal system which prohibits capital punishment. This prohibition is supported, in part on the basis that allowing the state to kill will cheapen the value of human life and thus the state will serve in a sense as a role model for individuals in society. The prohibition against assisted suicide serves a similar purpose. In upholding the respect for life, it may discourage those who consider that life is unbearable at a particular moment, or who perceive themselves to be a burden upon others, from committing suicide. To permit a physician to lawfully participate in taking life would send a signal that there are circumstances in which the state approves of suicide.

I also place some significance in the fact that the official position of various medical associations is against decriminalising assisted suicide (Canadian Medical Association,

British Medical Association, Council of Ethical and Judicial Affairs of the American Medical Association, World Medical Association and the American Nurses Association). Given the concerns about abuse that have been expressed and the great difficulty in creating appropriate safeguards to prevent these, it can not be said that the blanket prohibition on assisted suicide is arbitrary or unfair, or that it is not reflective of fundamental values at play in our society. I am thus unable to find that any principle of fundamental justice is violated by s 241(b) . . .

[Sopinka J held that s 12 of the *Charter* prohibiting 'any cruel and unusual treatment or punishment' was not infringed. Further, he assumed that s 15 prohibiting discrimination and providing for the right to equal protection by the law was infringed but was saved by s 1 of the *Charter*.]

IV. Section 1

[S 1 provides that the *Charter* guarantees rights and freedoms subject 'only to such reasonable limits prescribed by law as can be demonstrably justified in a free and democratic society.'] I agree with the Chief Justice that s 241(b) has 'a clearly pressing and substantial legislative objective' grounded in the respect for and the desire to protect human life, a fundamental *Charter* value. I elaborated on the purpose of s 241(b) earlier in these reasons in my discussion of s 7.

On the issue of proportionality, which is the second factor to be considered under s 1, it could hardly be suggested that a prohibition on giving assistance to commit suicide is not rationally connected to the purpose of s 241(b) . . . Section 241(b) protects all individuals against the control of others over their lives. To introduce an exception to this blanket protection for certain groups would create an inequality. As I have sought to demonstrate in my discussion of s 7, this protection is grounded on a substantial consensus among western countries, medical organisations and our own Law Reform Commission that in order to effectively protect life and those who are vulnerable in society, a prohibition without exception on the giving of assistance to commit suicide is the best approach. Attempts to fine tune this approach by creating exceptions have been unsatisfactory and have tended to support the theory of the 'slippery slope'. The formulation of safeguards to prevent excesses has been unsatisfactory and has failed to allay fears that a relaxation of the clear standard set by the law will undermine the protection of life and will lead to abuses of the exception. The recent Working Paper of the Law Reform Commission, quoted above, bears repeating here:

> The probable reason why legislation has not made an exception for the terminally ill lies in the fear of the excesses or abuses to which liberalisation of the existing law could lead. As in the case of 'compassionate murder', decriminalisation of aiding suicide would be based on the humanitarian nature of the motive leading the person to provide such aid, counsel or encouragement. As in the case of compassionate murder, moreover, the law may legitimately fear the difficulties involved in determining the true motivation of the person committing the act. [At p 54.]

The foregoing is also the answer to the submission that the impugned legislation is overbroad. There is no halfway measure that could be relied upon with assurance to fully achieve the legislation's purpose; first, because the purpose extends to the protection of the life of the terminally ill. Part of this purpose, as I have explained above, is to discourage the terminally ill from choosing death over life. Secondly, even if the latter consideration can be stripped from the legislative purpose, we have no assurance that the exception can be made to limit the taking of life to those who are terminally ill and genuinely desire death.

I wholeheartedly agree with the Chief Justice that in dealing with this 'contentious' and 'morally laden' issue. Parliament must be accorded some flexibility. In these circumstances, the question to be answered is, to repeat the words of La Forest J, quoted by the Chief Justice, from *Térreault-Gadoury v Canada (Employment and Immigration Commission)* [1991] 2 SCR 22 at p 44, whether the government can show that it had a reasonable basis for concluding that it has complied with the requirement of minimal impairment. In light of the significant support for the type of legislation under attack in this case and the contentious and complex nature of the issues, I find that the government had a reasonable basis for concluding that it had complied with the requirement of minimum impairment. This satisfies this branch of the proportionality test and it is not the proper function of this Court to speculate as to whether other alternatives available to Parliament might have been preferable.

It follows from the above that I am satisfied that the final aspect of the proportionality test, balance between the restriction and the government objective, is also met. I conclude, therefore, that any infringement of s 15 is clearly justified under s 1 of the *Charter* . . . In the result, the appeal is dismissed, but without costs.

La Forest, Gonthier, Iacobucci and Major JJ agreed with Sopinka J in dismissing the appeal.

McLachlin J: This case raises the question of whether a physically disabled patient may be precluded from obtaining medical assistance in committing suicide by reason of s 241 of the *Criminal Code* R S C 1985, c C-46

. . . I have read the reasons of the Chief Justice. Persuasive as they are, I am of the view that this is not at base a case about discrimination under s 15 of the *Canadian Charter of Rights and Freedoms* , and that to treat it as such may deflect the equality jurisprudence from the true focus of s 15 – to remedy or prevent discrimination against groups subject to stereotyping, historical disadvantage and political and social prejudice in Canadian society. *R v Swain* [1991] 1 SCR 933, at p 992, *per* Lamer CJ. I see this rather as a case about the manner in which the state may limit the right of a person to make decisions about her body under s 7 of the *Charter*. I prefer to base my analysis on that ground.

I have also had the benefit of reading the reasons of my colleague Sopinka J. I am in agreement with much that he says. We share the view that s 241(b) infringes the right in s 7 of the *Charter* to security of the person, a concept which encompasses the notions of dignity and the right to privacy. Sopinka J concludes that this infringement is in accordance with the principles of fundamental justice, because the infringement is necessary to prevent deaths which may not truly be consented to. It is on this point that I part company with him. In my view, the denial to Sue Rodriguez of a choice available to others cannot be justified. The potential for abuse is amply guarded against by existing provisions in the *Criminal Code* , as supplemented by the condition of judicial authorisation, and ultimately, it is hoped, revised legislation. I cannot agree that the failure of Parliament to address the problem of the terminally ill is determinative of this appeal. Nor do I agree that the fact that medically assisted suicide has not been widely accepted elsewhere bars Sue Rodriguez's claim. Since the advent of the *Charter*, this Court has been called upon to decide many issues which formerly lay fallow. If a law offends the *Charter*, this Court has no choice but to so declare.

In my view, the reasoning of the majority in *R v Morgentaler*, [1988] 1 SCR 30, is dispositive of the issues on this appeal. In the present case, Parliament has put into force a legislative scheme which does not bar suicide but criminalizes the act of assisting suicide. The effect of this is to deny to some people the choice of ending their lives solely because they are physically unable to do so. This deprives Sue Rodriguez of her security of the person (the right to make decisions concerning her own body, which affect only her own body) in a way that offends the principles of fundamental justice, thereby violating s 7 of the *Charter*. The violation cannot be saved under s 1. This is precisely the logic which led the majority of this Court to strike down the abortion provisions of the *Criminal Code* in *Morgentaler*. In that case, Parliament had set up a scheme authorising therapeutic abortion. The effect of the provisions was in fact to deny or delay therapeutic abortions to some women. This was held to violate s 7 because it deprived some women of the right to deal with their own bodies as they chose thereby infringing their security of the person, in a manner which did not comport with the principles of fundamental justice. Parliament could not advance an interest capable of justifying this arbitrary legislative scheme, and, accordingly, the law was not saved under s 1 of the *Charter*.

Section 7 of the Charter

. . . It is established that s 7 of the *Charter* protects the right of each person to make decisions concerning his or her body: *Morgentaler*, *supra*. This flows from the fact that decisions about one's body involve 'security of the person' which s 7 safeguards against state interference which is not in accordance with the principles of fundamental justice. Security of the person has an element of personal autonomy, protecting the dignity and privacy of individuals with respect to decisions concerning their own body. It is part of the persona and dignity of the human being that he or she have the autonomy to decide what is best for his or her body. This is in accordance with the fact, alluded to by McEachern CJBC below, that 's 7 was enacted for the purpose of ensuring human dignity and individual control, so long as it harms no one else': (1993) 76 BCLR (2d) 145, at p 164 . . .

. . . The question on this appeal is whether, having chosen to limit the right to do with one's body what one chooses by s 241(b) of the *Criminal Code*, Parliament has acted in a manner which comports with the principles of fundamental justice.

This brings us to the next question: what are the principles of fundamental justice? They are, we are told, the basic tenets of our legal system whose function is to ensure that state intrusions on life, liberty and security of the person are effected in a manner which comports with our historic, and evolving, notions of fairness and justice: *Re BC Motor Vehicle Act, supra*. Without defining the entire content of the phrase 'principles of fundamental justice', it is sufficient for the purposes of this case to note that a legislative scheme which limits the right of a person to deal with her body as she chooses may violate the principles of fundamental justice under s 7 of the *Charter* if the limit is arbitrary. A particular limit will be arbitrary if it bears no relation to, or is inconsistent with, the objective that lies behind the legislation. This was the foundation of the decision of the majority of this Court in *Morgentaler, supra*.

This brings us to the critical issue in the case. Does the fact that the legal regime which regulates suicide denies to Sue Rodriguez the right to commit suicide because of her physical incapacity, render the scheme arbitrary and hence in violation of s 7? Under the scheme Parliament has set up, the physically able person is legally allowed to end his or her life; he or she cannot be criminally penalized for attempting or committing suicide. But the person who is physically unable to accomplish the act is not similarly allowed to end her life. This is the effect of s 241(b) of the *Criminal Code*, which criminalizes the act of assisting a person to commit suicide and which may render the person who desires to commit suicide a conspirator to that crime. Assuming without deciding that Parliament *could* criminalize all suicides, whether assisted or not, does the fact that suicide is not criminal make the criminalization of all assistance in suicide arbitrary?

My colleague Sopinka J has noted that the decriminalization of suicide reflects Parliament's decision that the matter is best left to sciences outside the law. He suggests that it does not reveal any consensus that the autonomy interest of those who wish to end their lives is paramount to a state interest in protecting life. I agree. But this conclusion begs the question. What is the difference between suicide and assisted suicide that justifies making the one lawful and the other a crime, that justifies allowing some this choice, while denying it to others?

The answer to this question depends on whether the denial to Sue Rodriguez of what is available to others can be justified. It is argued that the denial to Sue Rodriguez of the capacity to treat her body in a way available to the physically able is justified because to permit assisted suicide will open the doors, if not the floodgates, to the killing of disabled persons who may not truly consent to death. The argument is essentially this. There may be no reason on the facts of Sue Rodriguez case for denying to her the choice to end her life, a choice that those physically able have available to them. Nevertheless, she must be denied that choice because of the danger that other people may wrongfully abuse the power they have over the weak and ill, and may end the lives of these persons against their consent. Thus, Sue Rodriguez is asked to bear the burden of the chance that other people in other situations may act criminally to kill others or improperly sway them to suicide. She is asked to serve as a scapegoat.

The merits of this argument may fall for consideration at the next stage of the analysis, where the question is whether a limit imposed contrary to the principles of fundamental justice may nevertheless be saved under s 1 of the *Charter* as a limit demonstrably justified in a free and democratic society. But they have no place in s 7 analysis that must be undertaken on this appeal. When one is considering whether a law breaches the principles of fundamental justice under s 7 by reason of arbitrariness, the focus is on whether a legislative scheme infringes a particular person's protected interests in a way that cannot be justified having regard to the objective of this scheme. The principles of fundamental justice require that each person, considered individually, be treated fairly by law. The fear that abuse may arise if an individual is permitted that which she is wrongly denied plays no part at this initial stage. In short, it does not accord with the principles of fundamental justice that Sue Rodriguez be disallowed what is available to others merely because it is possible that other people, at some other time, may suffer, not what she seeks, but an act of killing without true consent. As this Court stated in *Swain, supra*, at p 977, *per* Lamer CJ:

> It is not appropriate for the state to thwart the exercise of the accused's right by attempting to bring societal interests into the principles of fundamental justice and to thereby limit an accused's s 7 rights. Societal interests are to be dealt with under s 1 of the *Charter*, where the Crown has the burden of proving that the impugned law is demonstrably justified in a free and democratic society. In other words, it is my view that any balancing of societal interests against the individual right guaranteed by s 7 should take place within the confines of s 1 of the *Charter*.

I add that it is not generally appropriate that the complainant be obliged to negate societal interests at the s 7 stage, where the burden lies upon her, but that the matter be left for s 1, where the burden lies on the state . . .

The state will always bear the burden of establishing the propriety of an arbitrary legislative scheme, once a complainant has shown it is arbitrary. It will do so at the s 1 stage, where the state bears the onus, and where the public concerns which might save an arbitrary scheme are relevant. This is precisely the way the majority judgments in *Morgentaler* treated the issues that arose there: it is the way I think the Court should proceed in this case.

It is also argued that Sue Rodriguez must be denied the right to treat her body as others are permitted to do, because the state has an interest in absolutely forbidding anyone to help end the life of another. As my colleague Sopinka J would have it: '. . . active participation by one individual in the death of another is intrinsically morally and legally wrong'. The answer to this is that Parliament has not exhibited a consistent intention to criminalize acts which cause the death of another. Individuals are not subject to criminal penalty when their omissions cause the death of another. Those who are under a legal duty to provide the necessaries of life are not subject to criminal penalty where a breach of this duty causes death, if a lawful excuse is made out, for instance the consent of the party who dies, or incapacity to provide: see *Criminal Code*, s 215. Again, killing in self-defence is not culpable. Thus there is no absolute rule that causing or assisting in the death of other is criminally wrong. Criminal culpability depends on the circumstances in which the death is brought about or assisted. The law has long recognised that if there is a valid justification for bringing about someone's death, the person who does so will not be held criminally responsible. In the case of Sue Rodriguez, there is arguably such a justification – the justification of giving here the capacity to end her life which able-bodied people have as a matter of course, and the justification of her clear consent and desire to end her life at a time when, in her view, it makes no sense to continue living it. So the argument that the prohibition on assisted suicide is justified because the state has an interest in absolutely criminalizing any wilful act which contributes to the death of another is of no assistance.

This conclusion meets the contention that only passive assistance – the withdrawal of support necessary to life – should be permitted. If the justification for helping someone to end life is established, I cannot accept that it matters whether the act is 'passive' – the withdrawal of support necessary to sustain life – or 'active' – the provision of a means to permit a person of sound mind to choose to end his or her life with dignity.

Certain of the interveners raise the concern that the striking down of s 241(b) might demean the value of life. But what value is there in life without the choice to do what one wants with one's life, one might counter. One's life includes one's death. Different people hold different views on life and on what devalues it. For some, the choice to end one's life with dignity is infinitely preferable to the inevitable pain and diminishment of a long, slow decline. Section 7 protects that choice against arbitrary state action which would remove it.

In summary, the law draws a distinction between suicide and assisted suicide. The latter is criminal, the former is not. The effect of the distinction is to prevent people like Sue Rodriguez from exercising the autonomy over their bodies available to other people. The distinction, to borrow the language of the Law Reform Commission of Canada, 'is difficult to justify on grounds of logic alone': Working Paper 28, *Euthanasia, Aiding Suicide and the Cessation of Treatment* (1982), at p 53. In short, it is arbitrary. The objective that motivates the legislative scheme that Parliament has enacted to treat suicide is not reflected in its treatment of assisted suicide. It follows that the s 241(b) prohibition violates the fundamental principles of justice and that s 7 is breached.

Section 1 of the Charter
A law which violates the principles of fundamental justice under s 7 of the *Charter* may be saved under s 1 of the *Charter* if the state proves that it is 'reasonable . . . [and] demonstrably justified in a free and democratic society'.

The first thing which the state must show is that the law serves an objective important enough to outweigh the seriousness of the infringement of individual liberties. What then is the objective of the provision of the *Criminal Code* which criminalizes the act of assisting another to commit suicide? It cannot be the prevention of suicide, since Parliament has decriminalized suicide. It cannot be the prevention of the physical act of assisting in bringing about death, since, as discussed above, in many circumstances that act is not a crime. The true objective, it seems, is a practical one. It is the fear that if people are allowed to assist other people in committing suicide, the power will be abused in a way that may lead to the killing of those who have not truly and of their own free will consented to death. It is this concern which my colleague Sopinka J underscores in saying that the purpose of s 241(b) is 'the protection of the vulnerable who might be induced in moments of weakness to commit suicide'.

The justification for s 241(b) embraces two distinct concerns. The first is the fear that unless assisted suicide is prohibited, it will be used as cloak, not for suicide, but for murder.

Viewed thus, the objective of the prohibition is not to prohibit what it purports to prohibit, namely assistance in suicide, but to prohibit another crime, murder or other forms of culpable homicide.

I entertain considerable doubt whether a law which infringes the principles of fundamental justice can be found to be reasonable and demonstrably justified on the sole ground that crimes other than those which it prohibits may become more frequent if it is not present. In Canada it is not clear that such a provision is necessary; there is sufficient remedy in the offences of culpable homicide. Nevertheless, the fear cannot be dismissed cavalierly; there is some evidence from foreign jurisdictions indicating that legal codes which permit assisted suicide may be linked to cases of involuntary deaths of the ageing and disabled.

The second concern is that even where consent to death is given, the consent may not in fact be voluntary. There is concern that individuals will, for example, consent while in the grips of transitory depression. There is also concern that the decision to end one's life may have been influenced by others. It is argued that to permit assisted suicide will permit people, some well intentioned, some malicious, to bring undue influence to bear on the vulnerable person, thereby provoking a suicide which would otherwise not have occurred.

The obvious response to this concern is that the same dangers are present in any suicide. People are led to commit suicide while in the throes of depression and it is not regarded as criminal conduct. Moreover, this appeal is concerned with s 241(b) of the *Criminal Code*. Section 241(a), which prohibits counselling in suicide, remains in force even if it is found that s 241(b) is unconstitutional. But bearing in mind the peculiar vulnerability of the physically disabled, it might be facile to leave the question there. The danger of transitory or improperly induced consent must be squarely faced.

The concern for deaths produced by outside influence or depression centre on the concept of consent. If a person of sound mind, fully aware of all relevant circumstances, comes to the decision to end her life at a certain point, as Sue Rodriguez has, it is difficult to argue that the criminal law should operate to prevent her, given that it does not so operate in the case of others throughout society. The fear is that a person who does not consent may be murdered, or that the consent of a vulnerable person may be improperly procured.

Are these fears, real as they are, sufficient to override Sue Rodriguez' entitlement under s 7 of the *Charter* to end her life in the manner and at the time of her choosing? If the absolute prohibition on assisted suicide were truly necessary to ensure that killings without consent or with improperly obtained consent did not occur the answer might well be affirmative. If, on the other hand, the safeguards in the existing law, supplemented by directives such as those proposed by McEachern CJBC below are sufficient to meet the concerns about false consent, withholding from Sue Rodriguez the choice to end her life, which is enjoyed by able-bodies persons, is neither necessary or justified.

In my view, the existing provisions in the *Criminal Code* go a considerable distance to meeting the concerns of lack of consent and improperly obtained consent. A person who causes the death of an ill or handicapped person without that person's consent can be prosecuted under the provisions for culpable homicide. The cause of death having been established, it will be for the person who administered the cause to establish that the death was really a suicide, to which the deceased consented. The existence of a criminal penalty for those unable to establish this should be sufficient to deter killings without consent or where consent is unclear. As noted above, counselling suicide would also remain a criminal offence under s 241(a). Thus the bringing of undue influence upon a vulnerable person would remain prohibited.

These provisions may be supplemented, but way of a remedy on this appeal, by a further stipulation requiring court orders to permit the assistance of suicide in a particular case. The judge must be satisfied that the consent is freely given with a full appreciation of all the circumstances. This will ensure that only those who truly desire to bring their lives to an end obtain assistance. While this may be to ask more of Ms Rodriguez than is asked of the physically able person who seeks to commit suicide, the additional precautions are arguably justified by the peculiar vulnerability of the person who is physically unable to take her own life.

I conclude that the infringement of s 7 of the *Charter* by s 241(b) has not been shown to be demonstrably justified under s 1 of the *Charter*.

The Respective Roles of Parliament and the Courts

It was strenuously argued that it was the role of Parliament to deal with assisted suicide and that the Court should not enter on the question. These arguments echo the views of the justices of the majority of the Court of Appeal below. Hollinrake JA stated: '... it is my view in areas with public opinion at either extreme, and which involve basically philosophical and not legal considerations, it is proper that the matter be left in the hands of Parliament as historically has been the case' (p 177). Proudfoot JA added: 'On the material available to us, we are in no position to assess the consensus in Canada with respect to assisted suicide . . . I would leave to Parliament the responsibility of taking the pulse of the nation' (p 186).

Were the task before me that of taking the pulse of the nation, I too should quail, although as a matter of constitutional obligation, a court face with a *Charter* breach may not enjoy the luxury of choosing what it will and will not decide. I do not, however, see this as the task which faces the Court in this case. We were not asked to second guess Parliament's objective of criminalizing the assistance of suicide. Our task was the much more modest one of determining whether, given the legislative scheme regulating suicide which Parliament has put in place, the denial to Sue Rodriguez of the ability to end her life is arbitrary and hence amounts to a limit on her security of the person which does not comport with the principles of fundamental justice. Parliament in fact has chosen to legislate on suicide. It has set up a scheme which makes suicide lawful, but which makes assisted suicide criminal. The only question is whether Parliament, having chosen to act in this sensitive area touching the autonomy of people over their bodies, has done so in a way which is fundamentally fair to all. The focus is not on why Parliament has acted, but on the way in which it has acted.

Remedy

I concur generally in the remedy proposed by the Chief Justice in his reasons, although I am not convinced that some of the conditions laid down by his guidelines are essential. In the case at bar, where the plaintiffs own act will trigger death, it may not be necessary to ascertain the consent on a daily basis, nor to a place a limit of 31 days on the certificate. What is required will vary from case to case. The essential in all cases is that the judge be satisfied that if and when the assisted suicide takes place, it will be with the full and free consent of the applicant. I would leave the final order to be made by the chambers judge, having regard to the guidelines suggested by McEachern CJBC below and the exigencies of the particular case.

L'Heureux-Dubé J agreed with McLachlin J's reasons for allowing the appeal.

Lamer CJ would have allowed the appeal on the basis of an infringement of s 15 of the *Charter* which protected the applicant's right to equality and this was not justified under s 1 of the *Charter*.

Cory J agreed with McLachlin J and Lamer CJ and would have allowed the appeal.

This is not the place for a detailed analysis of the constitutional arguments and framework of the Canadian *Charter*. Instead, our interest in the *Rodriguez* case is in the approach of the Supreme Court when faced with the policy issues so as, perhaps, to illustrate how the European Court of Human Rights might approach a challenge to s 2 of the Suicide Act 1961.

The case stands in stark contrast to the approach of the House of Lords in the *Bland* case. All the Justices in *Rodriguez* accept that policy arguments have to be considered by the court in applying the *Charter*. Both Sopinka and McLachlin JJ accept that s 241(b) infringes the patient's right under s 7 of the *Charter*. The different conclusions they reach on the outcome of the case stem, in essence, from their conflicting views as to who has the onus of proving that the infringement is justified ie, who has the better of the policy arguments for and against assisted suicide. Sopinka J sees this as a matter to be determined in large part under s 7 itself, where the onus lies on the individual; while McLachlin J sees this a matter for consideration under s 1 of the *Charter* where a heavy onus lies on the state.

You will notice Sopinka J's reliance upon the arguments that deregulation will permit abuse (ie, the killing of those who do not wish to die) and that this state interest permeates the history of the Canadian provision and that of other countries around the world. In fact, in the one country where physician-assisted suicide is permitted, namely the Netherlands, the evidence does not provide proof of abuse, as we saw earlier, even though some would have us believe otherwise, Sopinka J included. McLachlin J, by contrast, recognises the dangers of abuse but believes that the state has not established that abuse cannot be prevented by permitting physician-assisted suicide in closely controlled circumstances (see below) and by the fact that Canada (as with every other country) makes it the criminal offence of murder to kill someone in such circumstances. It is worth noting that the court was only asked to review the constitutionality of that part of s 241 of the *Criminal Code* which prohibited *assisting* suicide (s 241(b)). No challenge was brought against that part, s 241(a), which prohibits *counselling* suicide.

How then might these arguments and competing approaches help us to understand how s 2 of the 1961 Act would stand up to scrutiny under the European Convention. English judges, of course, can do nothing given the doctrine of parliamentary sovereignty. Unlike the broadly drafted s 7 of the Canadian *Charter*, Article 2 of the Convention is limited to protecting an individual's right to *life*. As a consequence, it may not protect a patient's right to choose how to live or how to die. Indeed, it could be argued that to permit assisting suicide (or euthanasia) infringes Article 2 regardless of the patient's consent (see D Feldman, *Civil Liberties and Human Rights in England and Wales* (1993) at 95-6 and 122-4). (It is doubtful whether Article 5 dealing with 'security of the person' would apply.) It may be that, even if this is correct, it is necessary to look at whether s 2 infringes other rights of the patient protected under the Convention. If it does, the court might either be influenced in its interpretation of Article 2 (and permit physician-assisted suicide with the consent of the patient in properly regulated circumstances) or be required to order the priorities of the rights under the Convention (see, for example, the Irish Supreme Court's decision in *Attorney General v X* [1992] 2 CMLR 277 interpreting the constitutionally protected right to life and right to travel).

The most relevant provision of the Convention is Article 8 which, *inter alia*, protects an individual's right to respect for his private life. Article 8 has been interpreted widely as protecting a range of individual interests. Depriving patients of their choice of how to die may well fall within Article 8(1). However, Article 8(2) permits a breach of the right if it is 'in accordance with the law and is necessary in a democratic society . . . for the protection of health or morals, or for the protection of the rights and freedoms of others'. Could this save s 2 of the Suicide Act 1961? Of course, it is here that the policy arguments addressed in the Supreme Court would surface. In particular, the issue would be whether s 2 was necessary and a proportional response to achieve the purpose underlying it, namely the protection of human life and the prevention of abuse. The European Court of Human Rights allows states a 'margin of appreciation', ie, an element of legislative discretion. Again, a resolution of this issue would reflect the intellectual struggle between the Justices in *Rodriguez*.

You will recall that Sopinka J refers to a decision relating s 2 of the 1961 Act and the European Convention. In that case the European Commission (notice not the Court) rejected an attack on s 2 under Articles 8 and 10 (*R v United Kingdom* (1983) 33 DR 270). But, it is important to notice whose rights were being asserted in this case. It was those of a defendant who had been convicted under s 2 for helping someone commit suicide. The arguments for recognising a patient's right under the Convention are stronger as indeed the Commission itself hints (para 13).

Finally, it is important to notice that the dissenting Justices in *Rodriguez* did not argue for complete deregulation of assisted suicide. The patient's right had to be limited in order to take account of the concerns accepted by all the judges (and found compelling by the majority). These judges proposed a constitutional exemption to the *Criminal Code* following a determination of a court. Lamer CJ deals with this most fully in his judgment adopting, in essence, the approach of McEachern CJ in the British Columbia Court of Appeal. He set out *seven* conditions:

(1) the constitutional exemption may only be sought by way of application to a superior court;

(2) the applicant must be certified by a treating physician and independent psychiatrist, in the manner and at the time suggested by McEachern CJ, [ie not more than 24 hours before the applicant's suicide is assisted] to be competent to make the decision to end her own life, and the physicians must certify that the applicant's decision has been made freely and voluntarily, and at least one of the physicians must be present with the applicant at the time the applicant commits assisted suicide;

(3) the physicians must also certify:
(i) that the applicant is or will become physically incapable of committing suicide unassisted, and (ii) that they have informed him or her, and that he or she understands, that he or she has a continuing right to change his or her mind about terminating his or her life;

(4) notice and access must be given to the Regional Coroner at the time and in the manner described by McEachern CJ [ie not less than 3 clear days before the applicant is examined by a psychiatrist];

(5) the applicant must be examined daily by one of the certifying physicians at the time and in the manner outlined by McEachern CJ [ie to ensure the applicant has not changed her mind];

(6) the constitutional exemption will expire according to the time limits set by McEachern CJ [ie 31 days from the date of the first certificate]; and

(7) the act causing the death of the applicant must be that of the applicant his or herself, and not of anyone else.

Lamer CJ in an addendum to his judgment modified the fourth condition to require, in the case of Ms Rodriguez only, that 24 hours notice be given. He did so because of the evidence of her deteriorating medical condition.

It is likely that if the European Court of Human Rights were to find s 2 of the Suicide Act infringed the Convention, it would permit Parliament to impose similar restrictions on the patient's right so as to prevent abuse and to ensure the patient consented.

2. Mercy killing

(a) The law

The law was restated in *Airedale NHS Trust v Bland* [1993] 1 All ER 821 (HL).

Lord Goff: It is not lawful for a doctor to administer a drug to his patient to bring about his death, even though that course is prompted by a humanitarian desire to end his suffering, however great that suffering may be: see *R v Cox* (1992) 12 BMLR 38 per Ognall J in the Crown Court at Winchester. So to act is to cross the Rubicon which runs between on the one hand the care of the living patient and on the other hand euthanasia – actively causing his death to avoid or to end his suffering. Euthanasia is not lawful at common law.

Lord Mustill: That 'mercy killing' by active means is murder was taken for granted in the directions to the jury in *R v Adams (Bodkin)* [1957] Crim LR 365, *R v Arthur* (1981) Times, 5 November, (Farquharson J) and *R v Cox* [(1992) 12 BMLR 38], was the subject of direct decision by an appellate court in *Barber v Superior Court of Los Angeles County* (1983) 147 Cal App 3d 1006 and has never so far as I know been doubted. The fact that the doctor's motives are kindly will for some, although not for all, transform the moral quality of his act, but this makes no difference in law. It is intent to kill or cause grievous bodily harm which constitutes the mens rea of murder, and the reason why the intent was formed makes no difference at all. . . .

So far as I am aware no satisfactory reason has ever been advanced for suggesting that it makes the least difference in law, as distinct from morals, if the patient consents to or indeed urges the ending of his life by active means. The reason must be that, as in the other cases of consent to being killed, the interest of the state in preserving life overrides the otherwise all-powerful interest of patient autonomy.

(See also Lord Keith at 861.)

The position taken by the judges in *Bland* reflects the tradition of the common law. The law relating to 'mercy killing' generally was examined by the Criminal Law Revision Committee in its 14th Report in 1980 entitled *Offences Against the Person*. The Report is discussed in the following extract.

Roger Leng 'Mercy Killing and the CLRC' (1982) NLJ 76

Recent history of the problem

Prior to 1957 cases of compassionate killing were in theory murder and subject to the death penalty. The rigidity of this position was in a number of ways modified, making it very unlikely that a genuine 'mercy killer' would actually suffer the ultimate penalty. First the mercy killer might benefit from the exercise of prosecutorial discretion. In giving evidence to the Royal Commission on Capital Punishment 1949-53 (The Gowers Commission) the then Director of Public Prosecutions stated that in cases of doubt as between murder and manslaughter his instinct was to choose the lesser charge. Many mercy killings, committed in private with resort to less violent means of death, would fall into this doubtful category. However, the DPP's decision might always be overriden by the magistrates choosing to commit for murder in appropriate cases. Secondly, the Gowers Commission recognised the existence of a significant number of verdicts of acquittal which might be characterised as sympathetic or perverse depending upon one's view of the role of the jury. Thirdly, mercy killings which in fact resulted in murder convictions would almost invariably be subject to commutation of sentence by the Home Secretary, frequently following a recommendation to that effect from the jury. In evidence to the Gowers Commission the Home Office attempted to explain jury recommendations of mercy and concluded that 1071 cases in the period 1900-1949 could be attributed to the 'pitiable circumstances' of the case. It is likely that this figure contained a high proportion of mercy killings. The commutation of the death sentence to 'life' would frequently be followed by early release.

Many bodies and individuals giving evidence to the Gowers Commission favoured legal recognition of the practical position that mercy killers were not dealt with as murderers. The Society of Labour Lawyers (supported by Lord Denning) recommended a provision on the following lines:

> If a person who has killed another proves that he killed that person with the compassionate intention of saving him from physical or mental suffering, he shall not be guilty of murder.

The Commission foresaw difficulties in proving or disproving the necessary motive in court and consequently considered that the provision might be open to abuse. Moreover, the courts would have great difficulty in dealing with cases of actual or potential mixed motive, such as the daughter who killed an invalid father where the motive might be compassion, gain or removal of inconvenience.

The Commission 'reluctantly' rejected the proposal but nevertheless considered that true mercy killers should be excepted from the penalty for murder. This would be accomplished either by the exercise of executive discretion by the Home Secretary or (its preferred alternative) by a binding recommendation from the jury. The proposal was not really coherent. If the mitigation of sentence were to be achieved by Home Secretary's licence he would be faced with precisely the same problem in determining motive but without the jury's advantages in hearing the evidence, observing the demeanour of the defendant, etc. If the decision were to be taken by the jury they would have to apply some criteria, and would surely have to be guided by the judge. Again precisely the same problems of definition and proof would arise.

No change in law or practice directly relating to mercy killing resulted from the Gowers Report. However, as it turned out, the enactment of another of its recommendations, the creation of diminished responsibility by s 2 of the Homicide Act 1957, achieved by a back door what it had declined to recommend openly . . . In 1970 the Home Secretary referred the whole of the law concerning offences against the person, including homicide, to the Criminal Law Revision Committee and it became pertinent to consider whether the practice of the Courts in dealing with the compassionate killer under s 2 should be regularised by the creation of a specific category of homicide. In the CLRC's twelfth report on the *Penalty for Murder*, published in 1972, mention was made of certain tragic cases including compassionate killing where special considerations applied and where it should be made possible by means of a special provision for the judge to make a hospital or probation order or even, where appropriate, to grant a conditional discharge (para 42). This provisional conclusion was prompted by a recognition that whereas some such cases might be dealt with satisfactorily under s 2, in others there might be insufficient evidence of mental abnormality to found that defence but nevertheless the objective circumstances of the victim and the motive of the killer would justify disposal other than as for murder.

This realistic switch of emphasis away from the accused's state of mind to the circumstances and related motives involved in the case was reflected in the bold provisional proposal in the CLRC's 1976 *Working Paper on Offences Against the Person* of a new offence of mercy killing, subject to a maximum sentence of two years' imprisonment. The proposed offence would have applied where a person from compassion unlawfully killed another where the accused with reasonable cause believed that the victim was (i) permanently subject to great bodily pain or suffering, or (ii) permanently helpless from bodily or mental incapacity or (iii) subject to rapid and incurable bodily or mental degeneration.

The CLRC's fourteenth report (1980)
In the Committee's final report on *Offences Against the Person* (1980, par 115) the mercy killing proposal was summarily dropped on the ground that it was too controversial for the exercise in law reform on which the Committee was engaged. This conclusion sits very uneasily with comments made in the same paragraph describing compassionate killing as giving rise to a sentencing problem and pointing out that when an actual case of this nature arises 'no one connected with the case wishes to see the defendant convicted of murder'.

A number of issues require examination. What is the ethical position entailed in recommending a mercy killing defence? Is the CLRC an appropriate body to make such a proposal? How controversial would it be? Is the diminished responsibility defence in present or amended form capable of accommodating the range of killings which by virtue of compassionate motive require to be treated as something less than murder?

The major argument addressed to the CLRC against its original 1976 proposal was that it would mean that the sick and the handicapped would receive less protection from the law than the well and the able-bodied. This is an argument about degrees not absolutes since whether a killing is treated as murder or mercy killing it would remain a serious criminal offence and subject to punishment. Further the objection rests upon an assumption that the potential mercy killer will be deterred more or less according to the punishment which he anticipates. Although the psychological effects of formal deterrents are not susceptible to empirical research the traditional view is that deterrence is more effective in relation to crimes rationally designed to improve the position of the wrong-doer (eg theft) but less effective where the criminal act is prompted by some strong emotion which cannot be rationally suppressed. It is submitted that in true cases of mercy killing the prospect of a particular type of punishment is unlikely to govern the degree of deterrence.

If this is right the major ethical question is not whether killing in certain circumstances should be allowed or partially justified. Rather the real ethical problem focuses on the killer. Having done the totally prohibited act how should he be dealt with?

The Committee was impressed by representations to the effect that as lawyers they had no special qualifications for solving fundamental ethical problems. As a basis for proposing no change this is open to a number of objections. First it was not its task to decide to whom the fundamental ethical question should be addressed. Rightly or wrongly the question of the appropriate legal response to the compassionate killer fell within its general remit. It was its task to answer it within the limits of its own competence. In refusing, it implicitly misstated its own role, which in fact was to propose reform, for which the final responsibility for enactment or non-enactment would rest with Parliament. If Parliament is to fulfil its function of resolving difficult ethical dilemmas it cannot work in a vacuum but must be provided with foundations on which to build a structure of discussion. If the CLRC considered that mercy killing posed problems of sentencing which could not be resolved within the conceptual and practical framework of murder, it was its duty to say so and propose reform leaving it to Parliament to temper the lawyers' view with broader considerations and perhaps reject the proposal.

In stating that the original proposal would be too 'controversial' to be included in its final Report, the CLRC is using 'controversial' in a very limited sense. It clearly does not mean that the actual practice of treating mercy killers as other than murderers is open to such grave objections that it should not be proposed, for this is the very practice which it hopes will continue. What it actually means is that to embody the practice in an unequivocal legal provision would create a terrible fuss and might cause more trouble than it is worth. This hypocrisy will remain politically sensible while it is assumed that in all appropriate cases mercy killers can be dealt with under diminished responsibility. Is this assumption sound?

Mercy killers are not all alike: they occupy a continuum which stretches from the mother, so deranged by constant reminders of her child's suffering that she cannot control her desire to end the child's misery, to the parents who, having rationally weighed up all factors, consider that it is their responsibility to the child to end the suffering. The former clearly falls within the terms of s 2, the latter, on strict application of that provision, does not. Many would consider that the formal legal response to each case should be flexible to allow the judge to sentence in an appropriate manner. The CLRC fondly hopes that the connivances of psychiatrists and judges will continue to accommodate the latter case without the need for legislative change. This hope may be fulfilled but there is evidence that the appeal judges are losing patience with pleas of diminished responsibility in their more extravagant and less legally justified forms. As Lawton LJ [the chairman of the CLRC in 1980] said in *Vinagre* (1979) 69 Cr App Rep 104 'it was never intended that pleas should be introduced on such flimsy grounds . . . cases are tried by the court not by psychiatrists . . . pleas to manslaughter on the ground of diminished responsibility should only be accepted where there is clear evidence of mental imbalance'. Those words were spoken in a different context, and even if applied to a mercy killing would perhaps only entail a shift from plea acceptance to a similar jury verdict. Nevertheless, the statement indicates the strain placed upon the Courts, psychiatrists and the substance of the law by present practice in mercy killing cases and might suggest that it is time that this 'fundamental ethical issue' should cease to be dealt with in an *ad hoc* fashion by the Courts and be resolved by a general statutory provision recognising mercy killing as a ground for mitigation in its own right.

The conclusion of the CLRC (that there be no new offence of 'mercy killing') was not concerned specifically with the position of doctors who compassionately kill their patients. Also, it should be noticed that the defence of 'diminished responsibility' is not a practical option open to a doctor who compassionately kills. The difficulty, therefore, in which doctors find themselves is that the law seems to draw a very clear line between the permissible and the impermissible. But, that line is often blurred or disappears in medical practice. In *Bland* Lord Goff accepted this.

> **Lord Goff:** The law draws a crucial distinction between cases in which a doctor decides not to provide, or to continue to provide, for his patient treatment or care which could or might prolong his life and those in which he decides, for example by administering a lethal drug, actively to bring his patient's life to an end . . .
>
> It is true that the drawing of this distinction may lead to a charge of hypocrisy, because it can be asked why, if the doctor, by discontinuing treatment, is entitled in consequence to let his patient die, it should not be lawful to put him out of his misery straight away, in a more humane manner, by a lethal injection, rather than let him linger on in pain until he dies. But the law does not feel able to authorise euthanasia, even in circumstances such as these, for, once euthanasia is recognised as lawful in these circumstances, it is difficult to see any logical basis for excluding it in others.

Lord Mustill was equally unhappy about the distinction.

> **Lord Mustill:** The conclusion that the declarations can be upheld depends crucially on a distinction drawn by the criminal law between acts and omissions, and carries with it inescapably a distinction between, on the one hand what is often called 'mercy killing', where active steps are taken in a medical context to terminate the life of a suffering patient, and a situation such as the present, where the proposed conduct has the aim for equally humane reasons of terminating the life of Anthony Bland by withholding from him the basic necessities of life. The acute unease which I feel about adopting this way through the legal

and ethical maze is I believe due in an important part to the sensation that however much the terminologies may differ the ethical status of the two courses of action is for all relevant purposes indistinguishable. By dismissing this appeal I fear that your Lordships' House may only emphasise the distortions of a legal structure which is already both morally and intellectually misshapen. Still, the law is there and we must take it as it stands.

Lord Browne-Wilkinson makes the same point.

Lord Browne-Wilkinson: The conclusion I have reached will appear to some to be almost irrational. How can it be lawful to allow a patient to die slowly, though painlessly, over a period of weeks from lack of food but unlawful to produce his immediate death by a lethal injection, thereby saving his family from yet another ordeal to add to the tragedy that has already struck them? I find it difficult to find a moral answer to that question. But it is undoubtedly the law and nothing I have said casts doubt on the proposition that the doing of a positive act with the intention of ending life is and remains murder.

Furthermore, the 'lethal injection' referred to by Lord Browne-Wilkinson may itself be question-begging in practice: the injection of poison is undoubtedly lethal but then so is the injection of morphine or heroin which ends a patient's life albeit that it is the final dose in a course of treatment for pain relief. The example of a case where, all other pain relief having failed, the doctor administered poison at the request of the patient and for entirely compassionate reasons, is *R v Cox*.

R v Cox (1992) 12 BMLR 38 (Winchester CC)

Lillian Boyes, an elderly patient, suffered from an incurable condition. She was terminally ill and *in extremis*. She suffered great pain which could not be controlled by drugs. She repeatedly asked her consultant, Dr Cox and others to kill her. Dr Cox administered a lethal dose of potassium chloride and she died almost immediately. Dr Cox was prosecuted for attempted murder and convicted. The trial judge summed up to the jury in the following terms.

Ognall J: The prosecution allege that Dr Cox attempted to murder Lillian Boyes. They say that he deliberately injected her with potassium chloride in a quantity and in a manner which had no therapeutic purpose and no capacity to afford her any relief from pain and suffering whilst alive. They submit that Dr Cox must have known that and that in truth his conduct in giving that injection was prompted solely and certainly primarily by the purpose of bringing her life to an immediate end.

Proof of murder, members of the jury, would require proof that the doctor's conduct actually caused her death. The prosecution have told you that having regard to Mrs Boyes' condition on that morning, they cannot exclude the possibility though they, no doubt, would say it was remote, that, in fact, she died of natural causes between the actual injection of potassium chloride and her death. That is before the potassium chloride took its effect. It is for that reason, because they cannot exclude that possibility, however remote, that as you know, the charge you have to make up your minds about is not one of murder but of attempted murder, and I am sure you understand.

If it is proved that Dr Cox injected Lillian Boyes with potassium chloride in circumstances which make you sure that by that act he intended to kill her, then he is guilty of the offence of attempted murder. You know, in this case, from the earliest stage that it has been admitted that he did indeed inject her intravenously with two ampoules of undiluted potassium chloride, which no doubt you remember without looking at it ever again, his note at page 70 of the medical records clearly indicates.

According to her younger son Patrick, after that injection she just, and I quote, 'faded away' within minutes. According to Staff Nurse Creasey she died, so she said, in a few minutes. Later, she said about one minute after the injection.

Thus, the giving of the potassium chloride in that form, intravenously, is admitted, as I have said. The only question, therefore, for your consideration, ladies and gentlemen, in arriving at your verdict, is this. Is it proved that in giving that injection Dr Cox intended thereby to kill his patient? In the context of this particular case, what is meant, what do I mean, as a matter of law by proof of an intention to kill? . . .

We all appreciate, do we not, and certainly the evidence you have heard in this case demonstrates it, that some medical treatment, whether of a positive, therapeutic character or solely of an analgesic kind, by which I mean designed solely to alleviate pain and suffering, carries with it a serious risk to the health or even the life of the patient. Doctors, as you know, are frequently confronted with, no doubt, distressing dilemmas. They have to make up their minds as to whether the risk, even to the life of their patient, attendant upon their contemplated form of treatment, is such that the risk is or is not medically justified. Of course, if a doctor genuinely believes that a certain course is beneficial to his patient, either therapeutically or analgesically, even though he recognises that that course carries with it a risk to life, he is fully entitled, nonetheless, to pursue it. If sadly, and in those circumstances the patient dies, nobody could possibly suggest that in that situation the doctor was guilty of murder or attempted murder.

And the problem, you know, is obviously particularly acute in the case of those who are terminally ill and in considerable pain, if not agony. Such was the case of Lillian Boyes. It was plainly Dr Cox's duty to do all that was medically possible to alleviate her pain and suffering even if the course adopted carried with it an obvious risk that as a side effect – note my emphasis, and I will repeat it – even if the course adopted carried with it an obvious risk that as a side effect of that treatment, her death would be rendered likely or even certain.

There can be no doubt that the use of drugs to reduce pain and suffering will often by fully justified notwithstanding that it will, in fact, hasten the moment of death, but please understand this, ladies and gentlemen, what can never be lawful is the use of drugs with the primary purpose of hastening the moment of death.

And so, in deciding Dr Cox's intention, the distinction the law requires you to draw is this. Is it proved that in giving that injection in that form and in those amounts Dr Cox's primary purpose was to bring the life of Lillian Boyes to an end?

If it was, then he is guilty. If, on the other hand, it was or may have been his primary purpose in acting as he did to alleviate her pain and suffering, then he is not guilty, and that is so even though he recognised that in fulfilling that primary purpose he might or even would hasten the moment of her death.

That is the crucial distinction in this case. In shorthand form, the question of primary purpose. It is relatively easy for me to define for you. It is, however, submitted to you that for any doctor it can be, and was in this case, extraordinarily difficult to apply. Certain it is, it must confront you, members of the jury, with a most exacting task in striving to reach, as I know you will, a true verdict according to the evidence.

I have told you that if Dr Cox's primary purpose was to hasten her death, then he is guilty. In using the words 'hasten her death' I do so quite deliberately, members of the jury. It matters not by how much or by how little her death was hastened or intended to be hastened. I am sure you understand. You may recall Staff Nurse Creasey agreeing with [counsel for Dr Cox] that at the time Lillian Boyes received the first injection, not the potassium chloride, but you remember the earlier one of diamorphine and diazepam, that at the time she received that first injection from Dr Cox that morning, she, Staff Nurse Creasey, considered that Lillian Boyes was only hours from death at best and possibly only minutes away.

Of course, there can be no certainty in that regard, but even if that be the case, no doctor can lawfully take any step deliberately designed to hasten that death by however short a period of time.

Of course, members of the jury, to hasten the death, not merely alleviate suffering, it brings it to an end, does it not? A dead person suffers no more. But that is not what I mean by alleviation of suffering, nor, I am confident, what you understand me to mean by it. Alleviation of suffering means the easing of it for so long as the patient survives, not the easing of it in the throes of and because of deliberate purposed killing.

You will remember Professor Blake's evidence. A doctor's duty is to alleviate suffering for so long as the patient survives but, he said, he must never kill in order to achieve relief from suffering. To shorten life intentionally as one's prime purpose, he agreed, is unlawful, even though it may be the only means of alleviating the patient's suffering or pain. . . .

You must understand, members of the jury, that in this highly emotional situation, neither the express wishes of the patient nor of her loving and devoted family can affect the position. You will understand, and I tell you, that Lillian Boyes was fully entitled to decline any further active medical treatment and to specify that thereafter she should only receive painkillers. You remember she did that on 11th August. It is recorded in the notes and there is no doubt that that was universally respected by the doctors and nursing staff thereafter. That was her, Lillian Boyes, absolute right and doctors and nursing staff were obliged to respect her wishes. . . . [Dr Burne, a senior house officer] told you that he had told Lillian

Boyes on that day when she had said 'no more active intervention, please, only painkillers from now on', he had said to her, in effect, these are my words but I hope they reflect what he told you he said to her: 'thus far and no further. We will stop your positive medical treatment. We will confine ourselves to giving you only analgesics, only painkillers, but we cannot accede to your request that we give you something to kill you.'

How then, members of the jury, do you test what the Crown say were Doctor Cox's intentions so as to answer that central question, namely was his primary purpose to bring her life to an end or was it, or may it have been, on the other hand, directed primarily to alleviating her pain and her suffering?

The answer is that you do so by looking at all the circumstances of this case as you find them proved. You will look at Lillian Boyes' medical history, especially in those last days up to the day she died, 16th August and, of course, especially including that day. You will look at the expert evidence from the doctors and others experienced in drugs and toxicology. And you may think it of fundamental importance, it is a matter for you, like all questions of fact, but you may think of fundamental importance to consider the nature of the substance finally injected by Dr Cox in those quantities into Lillian Boyes' body.

If you reach the certain conclusion that potassium chloride injected undiluted and intravenously as it was can only in Dr Cox's mind have been with the purpose of bringing her life to an end, then the charge is made out. Dr Cox, as you know, is a highly-qualified, experienced and respected consultant physician. What did he know of the properties and potential of potassium chloride used in this way? . . .

Let me identify for your assistance, members of the jury, what I understand to be common ground. First, that in the context of this case potassium chloride has no curative properties. Second, that it is not an analgesic. It is not used by the medical profession to relieve pain. Neither this galaxy of talented medical men nor any written medical word has ever suggested otherwise. Third, that injected neat, as I shall put it, into a vein it is a lethal substance. One ampoule would certainly kill. According to Professor Blake the injection here was therefore twice that necessary to cause certain death.

Fourth, that any doctor would know that it would cause certain death and within a very or relatively short period of time. Fifth, that to inject two ampoules into Lillian Boyes intravenously would cause her death within minutes, if not seconds. Sixth, that Dr Toseland gave the unchallenged evidence that there is no clinical use of which he was aware that could account for the use of potassium chloride in this way.

Seventh, that Lillian Boyes was terminally ill. Once she had directed the doctors on the 11th August to abandon any treatment save for painkillers, it is beyond doubt that she had condemned herself to die, and within a relatively short time. To use the graphic phrase of [counsel for Dr Cox], she had signed her own death warrant. . . .

That brings me, members of the jury, to what I shall call a fundamentally important grey area so far as the defence are concerned, and it lies as I understand it, and I hope you agree with me, it lies in the suggested effect of the lethal dose of potassium chloride during the very short time between its administration and the consequential death.

Professor Blake agreed that the probable effect of the injection was to alleviate her suffering only by bringing her life to an end. Notice: only by bringing her life to an end. But, both he and Dr Dixon spoke of the relief of pain in the one, two or five minutes before she succumbed to the effect of that fatal injection. This is a crucial area so far as the defence are concerned. You may think, members of the jury, that you should approach that form of analysis with some care.

First, because that is or may be the effect for those few minutes does not of itself mean that that was Dr Cox's primary purpose. It is highly relevant but not definitive. You must be careful to distinguish effect on the one hand and purpose on the other.

Second, it is, I suppose, members of the jury, a truism that in many cases of death there comes a time when the moribund person is on the very brink of death. It is a distressing subject but we have to look at it and it has been looked at closely in this case, has it not? There comes a time when the moribund, the inevitably dying person is on the very brink of death. You have heard as the jury in this trial evidence of the mechanics of death in this case. The heart begins to fail, the blood pressure is lowered, blood reaches the brain in progressively lower volumes, and as that occurs a deeper and deeper level of unconsciousness supervenes. Finally the heart stops, the brain is completely starved of blood and therefore oxygen and breathing ceases, and at that moment the patient is dead.

In that sense, no doubt you will at once accept that the patient's pain and suffering are indeed progressively reduced as the lethal dose takes effect, until the patient reaches the state described as dead. But, members of the jury, what you will have to ask yourselves, you may think, is this: is that as a matter of common sense and ordinary language saying any more than that even if – notice it – even if you purposely kill someone by drugging them, you incidentally relieve their pain during their death-throes?

So, you may have little hesitation, ladies and gentlemen, if any hesitation, in accepting that as the patient dies and because they are dying their pain and suffering is during that time alleviated. Professor Blake and Dr Dixon told you so. The central question still remains, or course. Given that that injection of potassium chloride had the effect – note my emphasis – of alleviating her suffering as she died, was that or may it have been Dr Cox's primary purpose, or was it an incidental consequence of his proven primary purpose, namely, to hasten her death?

I come back to what Professor Blake said. I quote: 'It is probable that the effect of this injection was to alleviate suffering only by bringing her life to an end. By that means Dr Cox,' he agreed, 'kept his promise to Lillian Boyes that he would ensure that she would die in comfort'. And, of this aspect of the matter Dr Dixon said, 'If no relief can be given other than by shortening life and if the primary purpose of the doctor is to shorten life so that pain is alleviated that is not proper'.

Dr Dixon agreed that having regard to this patient's unique grave condition he, Dr Dixon, knew of no other way of controlling her pain other than by bringing her life to an end. He said that he hoped that if confronted with that situation which, as I understand he was saying mercifully he never had been, he hoped that if he were to be confronted with it he would have had the courage to do what Dr Cox did. . . .

Having regard to all those matters the defence submit that Dr Cox adopted what [counsel for Dr Cox] describes as an unorthodox way but nonetheless a way of relieving pain and suffering. It is submitted for your consideration that however rare, even unique, it may be to describe the administration of potassium chloride in this way in this case it is fully justified and you cannot be sure that in all the circumstances his primary purpose was to kill.

(b) Reforming the law

While the House of Lords in *Bland* approved the decision in *R v Cox* they did so less than enthusiastically. The judges recognised the illogicality of distinguishing between withdrawal of the life-sustaining treatment and taking steps to kill a patient. The judges, however, considered reform of the law to be a matter for Parliament. Lord Goff (at 867) stated:

It is, of course, well known that there are many responsible members of our society who believe that euthanasia should be made lawful; but that result could, I believe, only be achieved by legislation which expresses the democratic will that so fundamental a change should be made in our law, and can, if enacted, ensure that such legalised killing can only be carried out subject to appropriate supervision and control.

All previous attempts to pass legislation in the UK to legalise 'mercy killing' or voluntary euthanasia have failed. Politicians are naturally chary of espousing an issue which promotes such strong emotions on both sides. The likelihood is, therefore, that the law will remain as it is and the doctor faced with a patient *in extremis* and asking to die will have to resort to the 'double speak' of purporting to relieve pain while bringing about death, making sure that the agent bringing about the death is one recognised by other doctors as a pain-reliever.

The Dutch order their affairs differently and offer a unique contrast. Dr John Keown describes what the Dutch have done.

J Keown 'The Law and Practice of Euthanasia in the Netherlands' (1992) 108 LQR 51

I. THE OFFENCE OF KILLING A PERSON AT HIS REQUEST AND THE DEFENCE OF NECESSITY

(a) The offence of killing a person at his request
Killing a person at his request is punished by article 293 of the Penal Code: a person who takes the life of another person at that other person's 'express and serious request'

(*uitdrukkelijk en ernstig verlangen*) is punishable by imprisonment for a maximum of 12 years or by a fine. I shall call this the offence of voluntary euthanasia. It is one of the 'Serious offences against human life' in Title XIX of the Code.

Article 287 provides that a person who intentionally takes another's life without premeditation commits 'homicide' (*doodslag*) and is punishable by imprisonment for a maximum of 15 years. But a person who intentionally and with premeditation takes the life of another is guilty of murder (*moord*) and is punishable by a maximum of life imprisonment: article 289.

Article 294 punishes assisting suicide: a person who 'intentionally incites another to commit suicide, assists in the suicide of another, or procures the means to commit suicide' is punishable, where death ensues, by imprisonment for up to three years or by fine. Suicide itself is not criminal; nor is aiding attempted suicide, evidently because the legislature feared that the imposition of criminal liability might encourage a further attempt.

In short, voluntary euthanasia, or the intentional acceleration of a patient's death at his request as part of his medical care, is prohibited by article 293. The intentional killing of an incompetent person (non-voluntary euthanasia) or of a person against his wishes (involuntary euthanasia) would constitute either 'murder' (contrary to article 289) or 'homicide' (contrary to article 287).

(b) The defence of necessity
(i) The Supreme Court decision of 1984
Notwithstanding the apparently clear terms of article 293, the criminal courts have come to interpret the Code as providing a defence to a charge of voluntary euthanasia under that article and equally to a charge of assisting suicide under article 294. The line of relevant cases stretches from the decision of a District Court (*Arrondissementsrechtbank*) in 1973 to decisions of the Supreme Court (*Hoge Raad*) in 1984 and 1986.

The Supreme Court decision of November 27, 1984, the *Alkmaar* case, involved the killing of an elderly woman, a 'Mrs B,' at her request by her GP. The doctor was acquitted by the Alkmaar District Court but, on an appeal by the prosecution, was convicted by the Court of Appeal at Amsterdam. He then appealed successfully to the Supreme Court which held that the Court of Appeal had wrongly rejected the doctor's defence that he had acted out of necessity. The Supreme Court held that the Court of Appeal had not given sufficient reasons for its decision and that, in particular, it should have investigated whether 'according to responsible medical opinion' measured by the 'prevailing standards of medical ethics' a situation of necessity existed.

The defence of necessity is contained in article 40 of the Penal Code, which provides that a person who commits an offence as a result of 'irresistible compulsion or necessity [*overmacht*] is not criminally liable,' and takes two forms. The first is 'psychological compulsion.' The second is 'emergency' (*noodtoestand*) and applies when the defendant chooses to break the law in order to promote a higher good. Commenting on the latter form of the defence as applied by the Supreme Court to euthanasia, Professor Mulder, an expert on criminal law, explains:

> *Noodtoestand* refers to the situation of the patient's dire distress, wherein an ethical dilemma and conflict of interests arise, resulting in a decision by the physician to break the law in the interest of what is considered a higher good.

The Supreme Court observed in the *Alkmaar* case that whether a situation of necessity existed would depend on the circumstances of the case and that the Appeal Court could have taken into account, for example, the following matters:

> whether and to what extent according to professional medical judgment an increasing disfigurement of the patient's personality and/or further deterioration of her already unbearable suffering were to be expected;
> whether it could be expected that soon she would no longer be able to die with dignity under circumstances worthy of a human being;
> whether there were still opportunities to alleviate her suffering.

The case was referred to the Hague Court of Appeal with a direction that it investigate whether, on the facts, the performance of euthanasia by the doctor 'would, *from an objective medical perspective*, be regarded as an action justified in a situation of necessity.' On September 11, 1986, the Court of Appeal acquitted the accused on the basis that the defence of necessity applied. Having noted that the accused maintained that he had done nothing contrary to medical ethics, the court added that he had, on the basis of his expertise as a physician and his experience as Mrs B's doctor, and after careful consideration of conflicting duties in the light of medical ethics, made a choice which had to be regarded as justified according to 'reasonable' medical opinion.

Advocate-General Feber notes that in its judgment the Hague Court of Appeal raised for discussion, to a greater extent than had previous judicial pronouncements, the extent to which euthanasia could be justified by psychological as opposed to psychiatric suffering, by a normal as opposed to an abnormal psychological reaction to physical deterioration. Mrs B was, he observes, far from being a psychiatric patient: 'her longing for death was a normal reaction to her miserable physical condition.' Feber also notes that the Court of Appeal replaced the Supreme Court's criterion of 'objective' medical opinion with that of 'reasonable' medical opinion.

(ii) *The Supreme Court decision of 1986*
On October 21, 1986, one month after the decision of the Hague Court of Appeal, the Supreme Court delivered a second judgment on euthanasia. This case concerned the prosecution of a doctor who, after repeated requests, euthanatised a 73-year-old friend suffering from advanced multiple sclerosis. The doctor was convicted by the Groningen District Court and her conviction was upheld by the Court of Appeal at Leeuwarden. The Supreme Court, however, allowed her appeal, holding that the Court of Appeal had wrongly failed to consider two defences raised at trial. The first was that the accused acted because of her patient's 'dire distress'; the second that she acted out of 'psychological necessity' because she 'was confronted with the suffering of her patient and found *herself* under duress and could not arrive at any other decision than to grant the assistance requested.' The Supreme Court remitted the case to the Court of Appeal at Arnhem for further investigation; the doctor was convicted.

(iii) *The criteria for lawful euthanasia: a summary*
The criteria laid down by the courts to determine whether the defence of necessity applies in a given case of euthanasia have been summarised by Mrs Borst-Eilers, Vice-President of the Health Council (a body which provides scientific advice to the Government on health issues), as follows:

> 1 The request for euthanasia must come only from the patient and must be entirely free and voluntary.
> 2 The patient's request must be well considered, durable and persistent.
> 3 The patient must be experiencing intolerable (not necessarily physical) suffering, with no prospect of improvement.
> 4 Euthanasia must be a last resort. Other alternatives to alleviate the patient's situation must have been considered and found wanting.
> 5 Euthanasia must be performed by a physician.
> 6 The physician must consult with an independent physician colleague who has experience in this field.

Whether consultation must be with an 'independent' physician is, however, doubtful; in the *Alkmaar* case the defendant GP had merely consulted his assistant. Further, it has been pointed out by Eugene Sutorius, counsel to the Dutch Voluntary Euthanasia Society (DVES), that the Supreme Court has stated that consultation is not always essential. He has explained that, although the Court did not elaborate on this point, in his view, as the purpose of consultation is to obtain a second opinion about the medical aspects of the case, consultation is not necessary when there is no doubt about these aspects and when witnesses are available to verify that the non-medical criteria have been satisfied.

(iv) *Liability for falsifying the death certificate*
Necessity is not, however, a defence to a charge of falsely certifying the cause of death. In a case decided by the Court of the Hague (Penal Chamber) in 1987, the defendant doctor admitted that, having performed euthanasia, he had certified that death was due to natural causes. The Court of Appeal upheld the trial court's decision that death by euthanasia was not death by natural causes and that the doctor could not rely on necessity as a defence to falsifying the death certificate. The Appeal Court declared that it was a matter of great public concern that non-natural deaths should be investigated by officials such as the coroner and prosecutor and that this was especially so in cases of euthanasia in view of the proven danger of abuse.

II. MEDICAL GUIDELINES

The judgment of the Hague Court of Appeal in the *Alkmaar* case gave striking weight to the views of a 'considerable number of medical doctors' against whom, it said, a judge could not 'make a choice in this matter'. In fact, the medical profession, or at least its main representative body the Royal Dutch Medical Association (KNMG), to which some 60 per cent of Dutch doctors belong, has played a significant role in the relaxation of the law and practice of euthanasia.

(a) The KNMG criteria

In 1973 the KNMG issued a provisional statement which said that euthanasia should remain a crime but that if a doctor shortened the life of a patient who was incurably ill and in the process of dying, a court would have to judge whether there was not a conflict of duties which justified the doctor's action. In August 1984, three months before the decision of the Supreme Court in the *Alkmaar* case, the central committee of the KNMG produced a report setting out the criteria which the KNMG felt should be satisfied in cases of euthanasia. As Borst-Eilers has pointed out, there is a close correspondence between these criteria and those laid down by the courts. Subsequently, the KNMG formulated certain 'Guidelines for Euthanasia.'

The Report lists five criteria: 'voluntariness'; 'a well-considered request'; 'a durable death-wish'; 'unacceptable suffering,' and 'consultation between colleagues.' These are reproduced in the Guidelines.

(i) Voluntariness

The Report stresses that the request must be made of the patient's free will and must not be the result of pressure by others. Conceding that it will not always be possible to be completely sure that the request is not influenced by others, the Report says that the doctor should talk privately with the patient and that, after a 'number of conversations,' he must be able to get a 'fairly reliable impression' of the voluntariness of the request. The Guidelines, by contrast, state that there need only be 'a' conversation with the patient to verify voluntariness.

(ii) A well-considered request

To ensure that the request is well-considered the Report urges that the doctor should give the patient a 'clear picture of his medical situation and the appropriate prognosis' and, because a request for euthanasia is 'not uncommonly found to be an expression of fear – such as fear of pain, deterioration, loneliness' the doctor should also examine the extent to which these fears influence the request, and should dispel them as far as possible.

Similarly, the Guidelines state that a doctor must guard against granting a request which arises essentially from 'other problems than the will to terminate life' such as the feeling of being superfluous or a nuisance to the family. A request made on such grounds should first of all be an occasion for a consultation with the patient about alternative solutions; in no case should euthanasia be granted because of problems which could be resolved in another way.

(iii) A durable death wish

The Report declares that requests arising out of 'impulse or a temporary depression' should not be granted but adds that it is not possible to indicate what time span should have elapsed before a request becomes 'durable.' The physician is advised to 'steer mostly by his own compass' but that 'durable,' in the opinion of the committee, does not simply mean more than once.

(iv) Unacceptable suffering

The Guidelines state that the patient must experience his suffering as 'persistent, unbearable, and hopeless' and they add that the relevant case-law indicates that an important consideration is whether the patient will be able to die 'in a dignified manner.'

The Report, however, states that the committee, while aware that the courts indicated that the suffering must be persistent, unbearable and hopeless, declined to support this definition of the criterion because it felt that these concepts overlapped and were unverifiable. It continues that although the degree of suffering is an important criterion, there are only limited possibilities for verification since the unbearable and hopeless character of a person's situation is so dependent on individual standards and values that an objective assessment is difficult.

Suffering, says the Report, can have any of three causes: first, pain; secondly, a physical condition or physical disintegration without pain, and thirdly, suffering without any physical complaint which could be caused either by 'social factors and the like' in a healthy person or by a 'medical-psychiatric syndrome.' Pain, the Report continues, can be controlled to such an extent that, in general, it is not a primary cause of unbearable suffering. And as to suffering caused by social factors, a doctor usually cannot assess the unbearability of the patient's situation or the prospects of its alleviation.

The Report adds that, although the KNMG's 1973 statement had raised the question whether euthanasia was justifiable if the patient were incurably ill and in the process of dying, the committee felt that, quite apart from the fact that the 'dying phase' could not be clearly defined, it was not reasonable to deny a patient who was suffering unbearably the 'right to euthanasia' solely because he was not dying. Consequently, it could no longer support the 'dying phase' as a criterion.

(v) Consultation and reporting

The committee considered consultation with a colleague with experience in this field to be 'indispensable' to promote well-balanced decision-making and the Report recommends that the doctor consult first a colleague with whom he is professionally involved and later an independent doctor.

Finally, having noted that it was 'not unusual' for euthanasia to be reported as natural death in order to protect the relatives and/or the doctor from police investigation, the Report urges that this 'improper' practice be discontinued and stresses the committee's advocacy of due openness in the reporting of death.

(b) Current medical and legal procedures

Procedures followed by doctors who have performed euthanasia vary throughout the country. At one of the leading centres for euthanasia, the Reinier de Graaf Hospital in Delft, the procedure is that the doctor does not certify a natural death but informs the police. The municipal medical examiner (*gemeentelijk lijkschouwer*) comes to inspect the body and a policeman to interview the doctor. Both officials then file reports with the prosecutor who, if satisfied that the legal criteria have been met, gives permission for the corpse to be handed over to the relatives. As Borst-Eilers comments: 'This whole procedure after death need only take a few hours. Only if the public prosecutor suspects that all the criteria have not been met with, he orders further interviews with nurses, members of the family etc.' In November 1990, however, the Minister of Justice and the KNMG agreed that the doctor need only report to the medical examiner, and the Minister of Justice directed prosecutors that on receiving the medical examiner's report they should ask the police to investigate only if there are grounds for suspecting that the appropriate criteria have not been met.

The final decision whether to prosecute is taken at a meeting of the country's five Chief Prosecutors (*Procureurs-Generaal*). The Chief Prosecutors, each of whom is attached to one of the five regional Courts of Appeal, meet every three weeks, together with a representative from the Ministry of Justice, to discuss prosecution policy in relation to crimes in general and to decide, according to the criteria laid down by the courts, whether to prosecute in each notified case of euthanasia. In practice, they simply approve the decision of the local prosecutor.

Subsequently, a Bill was presented to the Dutch Parliament. The Bill, passed in late 1993, formally recognises the legal basis of the current practice but requires the doctor to report the death to the local coroner (see (1993) 307 BMJ 1511).

In England the question of voluntary euthanasia is part of the remit of the House of Lords' Select Committee on Medical Ethics set up in 1993. Clearly, the Committee will have to recommend whether or not to change the law. In doing so they will obviously take account of the Dutch experience, not least the arguments for and against voluntary euthanasia which have been advanced and the data which emerged from the Remmelink Committee (Medical Decisions Concerning the End of Life), which we will see discussed shortly.

The arguments in favour of voluntary euthanasia are materially the same as those we saw earlier in Professor Weir's article concerning doctor-assisted suicide. You will recall that the two principal arguments are the patient's right

of self-determination and the doctor's (and society's) duty to behave with
compassion. In large part the arguments against voluntary euthanasia mirror
those advanced against doctor-assisted suicide. Of course, the significant
differences lie in the role in which the doctor is cast in the case of voluntary
euthanasia (as a death-dealing agent) and the increased opportunity for abuse.
In a wide-ranging discussion focusing upon the legislative initiative in the State
of Washington (Initiative 119), but also drawing on the Dutch experience,
Professor Margaret Battin in an important article examines the arguments
concerning the risk of abuse in some detail.

Margaret Battin 'Voluntary Euthanasia and the Risk of Abuse: Can We Learn Anything from the Netherlands?' (1992) 20 Law, Medicine and Health Care 133

In general, I think it is crucial to be as clear and forthright about the issue of abuse as
possible, even if one supports, as I do, the legalization of aid-in-dying.
   In doing so, one must answer two central questions:
1) Will there be abuse, and if so, precisely what kind?
2) Can abuse of this sort be prevented?
It is to the second of these questions that I will be particularly attentive here. In doing so, I
shall consider only the possible effects of legalizing voluntary, active, physician-performed
euthanasia and physician-assisted suicide, restricted to cases in which such help is requested
by competent, terminally ill patients with less than 6 months to live – that is, I shall be
considering only what Initiative 119 would have legalized – but some of the arguments will
clearly apply to a wider range of possible legislation as well.
   Slippery-slope arguments are designed to address the first of the two questions above:
Will there be abuse, and if so precisely what kind? Since they are predictive empirical
arguments intended to show that permitting a given practice will result in abuse, the
principal strategy available to counter these arguments is to show that they fail to specify
what causal mechanisms will be involved, what back-ground precedents would permit such
erosion, and so on. Thus opponents of legalization warn of abuse in the future, pointing to
alleged current abuse in the Netherlands as evidence; supporters of legalization, on the other
hand, reply that claims about abuse in Holland are unsubstantiated or exaggerated and that
there is little reason to think abuse would occur in the United States. One cannot fear an
analogue of the Nazi holocaust, supporters of the legislation argue, for example, because
even though there are local excrescences of antisemitic, anti-Black, and other racially
prejudiced political activity, it is inconceivable that a country with such strong guarantees of
civil rights could permit a large-scale extermination program. Thus the argument moves
back and forth between opponents and supporters, however erratically; but it remains an
essentially empirical argument about the potential consequences of legalization.
   It is this argument which I would like to enter here. As I have often said elsewhere, I do
not think there is any compelling argument in principle to be made against voluntary active
euthanasia or physician-assisted suicide, at least in specific circumstances, and I believe that
on the contrary control on one's own death as far as possible is a matter of fundamental
human right. However, I also think that the warnings of potential abuse require much more
sensitive and careful examination than either supporters or opponents of such legislation
have generally given them. Indeed, I think it is morally responsible to advocate the
legalization of euthanasia and assisted suicide only if one can conscientiously argue either
that abuse would not occur or that it could be prevented, and it is on this project that I
would like to embark here. Conversely, I also think it is morally responsible to oppose the
legalization of euthanasia and assisted suicide, given the importance of the freedom to be
suppressed, only if one can show with reasonable likelihood that abuse would occur and that
it could not be prevented.
   Thus either way, it is crucial to consider the issue of abuse, and this is an obligation that
no party to the discussion, on either side, ought to evade; the burden of proof in establishing
what the consequences of the proposed legislation would be falls, in this special case, on
both sides. That persons have a basic, fundamental right to control as much as they wish
and as much as is possible the timing and circumstances of their own deaths is a claim that I
shall assume here, but this assumption does not relieve us of the obligation to consider the
risk of abuse. After all, if the risks of abuse are great enough, this may entail that even basic,
fundamental rights of persons should be curtailed. If on the other hand the risks of abuse

turn out to be small or if abuse can be prevented, then it is morally imperative that persons' basic, fundamental right to control as much as possible the circumstances of their own dying be legally recognized.

Will abuse occur?
While euthanasia is presumably practiced clandestinely virtually everywhere else, it is openly practiced only in the Netherlands. Thus our principal source of empirical information about the potential for abuse where euthanasia is effectively legal must come from the Netherlands. To be sure, euthanasia is not fully legal in the Netherlands; it remains a violation of statutory law, punishable in principle by imprisonment, but the lower and supreme courts have developed a series of guidelines under which euthanasia is immune from prosecution. Thus it is effectively legal and openly practiced, and it is supported by a substantial majority of public opinion. Most Dutch hospitals now have protocols governing euthanasia, and many health-care institutions, including nursing homes and hospitals, also have developed publicly stated policies concerning whether they do or do not permit the practice.

The first nationwide study in Holland on euthanasia and other medical decisions at the end of life, prepared by a commission appointed by the Dutch government (the so-called Remmelink Commission), involved detailed interviews with 405 physicians from different disciplines, a questionnaire mailed to the physicians of 7000 deceased persons, and a prospective survey in which physicians interviewed in part I gave information concerning every death in their practice (a total of 2250 deaths) during the six months after the interview. This study found that about 1.8 percent of total deaths per year in the Netherlands are the result of euthanasia with some form of physician involvement and that about 0.3 percent of deaths involve physician-assisted suicide. But it also reported that in 0.8 percent of all deaths 'drugs were administered with the explicit intention to shorten the patient's life, without the strict criteria for euthanasia being fulfilled,' and it is this that has been widely interpreted in the United States to mean that 1000 patients were killed against their will. While this is a clear misinterpretation of the data in the Dutch study, fair treatment of the issue of abuse must take account of both actual and conjectural evidence from Holland.

There are several further matters to be remembered in addressing the issue of abuse. First, judgments about abuse should in principle be comparative, weighing influences on choice, adjusted for the severity of outcome, against influences on other alternative choices. Would choices of euthanasia be more or less abused than, say, choices of high-risk surgery or choices to withhold or withdraw life-sustaining treatment? After all, any of these choices can lead to death, not only choices about euthanasia. Furthermore, judgments about abuse ought not to cloak judgments about outcomes: it cannot be assumed, without further argument, that – in the kind of case at issue here – influences on a choice for euthanasia are potentially abusive while influences on a choice to stay alive are not. It is also to be remembered that there is little theoretical agreement on just what constitutes abuse: is it a distortion of voluntariness, is it the violation of a person's interests, or what?

Finally, it is important to remember that the issue of whether abuse would occur is an issue about the outcomes of policy, not about idiosyncratic acts. In every society and with regard to every kind of social policy, unstable, psychopathic, or otherwise deranged individuals commit acts which clearly constitute abuses: nurses who randomly inject patients with fatal drugs, doctors who perform deliberately damaging, unwarranted operations on patients, anaesthetists who have sex with their patients on their operation tables. Such outlier cases will occur from time to time, regardless of the type of policies in effect. To be sure, one ought not be sanguine about the occurrence of such cases, but the real issue is not so much whether such outlier cases will occur – they will, in any country, with or without legislation – but whether the legislation itself would permit or encourage such cases on a more frequent, more accepted, more 'normal' basis. Thus, the question is whether the policies at issue – the legalization of active euthanasia and of assisted suicide – would engender an abusive pattern of practice, not whether a handful of isolated, marginal cases of abuse would occur from time to time. It is 'normal' patterns of abuse that the slippery slope arguments are properly concerned with: Would family members readily and routinely manipulate patients? Would physicians generally become callous about death? Would institutions regularly force patients into euthanasia or suicide in an effort to save costs? Would prejudice against racial, age, and handicapped groups further infect these practices?

While I have no doubt that some outlier cases of abuse would occur from time to time, I do not think the general answer to these questions is yes. Nor do I think euthanasia choices would be more abused than choices of high-risk surgery or of withholding or withdrawing life-sustaining treatment. Nevertheless, I will assume the contrary for the purposes of this paper, since my real concern here is whether – if such abusive patterns might be tolerated or encouraged by legalizing euthanasia and suicide – there are effective ways of preventing abuse. This is not to assume that human nature is evil or that abuse is humanly inevitable; rather, it is to assume instead that different policies and the incentives and disincentives incorporated in policy can encourage or discourage quite different patterns of practice. Thus the question is, would the legalization of euthanasia and suicide, with or without safeguards such as those proposed by Hemlock [an American society in favour of voluntary euthanasia] or those already in place in Holland, engender abuse? If so, what sort, and can such abuse be prevented even if it would otherwise occur?

Types of possible abuse

Three conceptually distinct types of abuse can be identified among the scenarios that slippery-slope arguments portray: what we might call interpersonal abuse, professional abuse, and institutional abuse. Though they are conceptually distinct, we may expect that in practice they would often be closely intertwined. Although the parallels are not exact, they also invite three rather different sorts of solutions, that is, three rather different sorts of strategies for preventing such abuses from occurring.

1. Interpersonal abuse. Chief among the varieties of interpersonal abuse, one might expect, would be that occurring in familial situations: the resentful or greedy spouse or other family member, who maneuvers a terminally ill patient now perceived as a burden into requesting euthanasia or assistance in suicide. Such pressures might be malevolent, the product of long years of hostility; or, perhaps more likely, they might be the product of the kind of emotional exhaustion familial caregivers often experience in attending to a patient with a lengthy, deteriorative terminal illness. 'All of your suffering could be over soon,' such a family member might be expected to say – not seeing that much of the suffering is not so much the patient's but his or her own. Familial messages supporting euthanasia or suicide can of course be given in an enormous variety of ways, both explicit and inexplicit, verbal and nonverbal, and they can be conveyed by a single individual family member or by a family as a whole.

Familial messages favoring euthanasia or suicide can be comparatively weak, involving suggestion or even the mere raising of the idea; they can be stronger, including what we might variously call recommendation, urging, 'talking into,' pleading, cajoling, remonstrating, and so on; and they can be a great deal stronger, including such tactics as threats, ultimatums, lies, and so on. Not all family life is harmonious, and underlying pathology can often be exacerbated by the stresses a family member's terminal illness brings. 'All right, Granny, it's time to go' is a message we can imagine being conveyed in a large variety of ways, exhibiting an entire range from the faintest suggestions to outright coercion.

2. Professional abuse. If family members will manipulate or pressure patients into choosing death in all the usual ways family members control each other's behavior, it can be further argued, physicians will have an even larger range of methods for doing so. For instance, they may give inaccurate diagnoses or unreliable prognoses. They may scare patients with predictions of pain. They may decline to offer adequate pain control, citing for example the risks of addiction to narcotic drugs, or offer only pain control which is sporadic or has undesirable side effects. They may refuse to offer other treatment which might produce symptom relief. They may 'recommend' premature death in ways that are too persuasive for the patient to resist, or they may recommend it to the family and let the family do the persuasion. Worse still, they may learn to lean on euthanasia as a kind of medical crutch, turning almost automatically to it as the solution for every treatment problem they cannot solve; even worse, they may use it as a cover for their medical mistakes. Perhaps still worse, they will become euthanasia 'enthusiasts', employing euthanasia as part of their own political programs for reforming the medical world.

To understand these claims, it is essential first to see what background assumptions make them plausible, given that it is only voluntary euthanasia and assisted suicide that would be legalized, and then only for competent, terminally ill patients with less than 6 months to live. Yet even given the comparative narrowness of this range of cases, the dire predictions so widely voiced cannot be ignored. For this reason, it is crucial to understand what is distinctive about abuse by doctors, and to some degree by nurses and other care providers as well – that is, what is distinctive about *professional* abuse in contrast to interpersonal, usually familial, abuse of the sort discussed above.

Professional abuse, understood as that range of ways in which professionals, especially physicians, might bring a patient to 'voluntarily' request euthanasia or help in suicide who would not otherwise do so, can exhibit most of the features of interpersonal, domestic abuse

- suggestion, urging, manipulation, and threat aimed at one person by another - but it incorporates an additional feature: the weight of professional authority. It is the physician who holds the power in the physician/patient relationship, not only because the physician has greater knowledge of the physiological process affecting the patient and how to control them, and because the physician's social aura conveys authoritative standing to his or her role, but also because the patient is ill. Especially when it is terminal, illness can place a person in a particularly compromised position: for many patients, illness involves discomfort and pain, anxiety, fear of impending loss of one's relationships, and fear of death. Thus 'professional authority' trades on two factors: the greater weight of the physician and the compromised position of the patient. Both factors invite abuse. The nurse may also be regarded as a medical authority, particularly in situations (eg, home care) where it is the nurse who is the primary or only contact with the patient, but it is the physician whose capacity is greatest for exploiting professional authority.

Given this disparity of power in the physician/patient relationship, physicians are very well aware of their power to influence patient choices - even while preserving the appearance of obtaining informed consent. The Latinate obscurity of medical diagnosis and the overwhelming nature of too much medical information often contribute to this possibility. Thus, many physicians claim they can get patients to agree to nearly anything they propose; it is simply a matter of how the choice is framed. Just as, in the traditional example, the glass of water can be described as half empty or half full, a proposed surgical procedure with a 50/50 predicted outcome, for example, can be described as a probable success or a probable failure; a 'good chance' can mean anything from a 10 or 20 percent chance of success to 80 or 90 percent. Information can be orchestrated to emphasize benefits or to emphasize risks, even when information about both benefits and risks is actually provided. Presumably, thus, physicians would find it easy to frame choices about euthanasia or suicide in similar ways: unfavorably for patients whom they wanted to discourage, but favorably for those whom they hope to maneuver into this choice. Thus, even under legislation which protects only *voluntary* choice by competent patients, it is argued, the physician could manipulate the patient into choosing death when the patient would not otherwise have chosen it or when it is actually contrary to his or her own wishes. In all these cases, the fiction that the patient has given informed consent can be preserved; what is problematic is the way in which the physician presents the information on which the patient's choice is based.

There is a second way in which professional authority can play a substantial role in shaping patient choice. Much of the interaction, as well as the legal support, for the relationship between physician and patient is based on assumptions of *informed consent* - that is, that the patient retains the right to give or withhold consent to treatment and that in making these choices the patient is entitled to adequate information about the alternatives involved. Informed consent must be explicitly documented for specific procedures, eg surgery; it is assumed for a wide range of minor tests and procedures involved in medical care. But reliance on informed consent also reinforces power disparities in the physician/patient role and exacerbates the weight of professional authority: in informed consent, it is the physician who proposes the specific course of treatment and the patient who gets to say yes or no. But in this arrangement, it is the physician who identifies the problem, frames any suggested solution to it, and controls how many alternative solutions are proposed. The patient cannot know whether the problem could be seen in some other way or as some different sort of problem, whether other sorts of solutions could be proposed, whether in making the choice to give or withhold consent he or she is making a choice among all the reasonable alternatives, and, sometimes, whether there really is any problem at all. The agenda is, so to speak, entirely in the control of the physician. This may of course be a reasonable arrangement for consent to medical procedures which do not raise values dilemmas, but it is hardly a defensible arrangement in the case of euthanasia. Euthanasia is, after all, a quintessential 'values' issue: whether a person prefers a chance of extended life in spite of suffering or pain, or whether he or she prefers an earlier, easier end to life in order to avoid suffering and pain. If consent to euthanasia is treated in the way consent to other medical procedures is, it will be the physician's agenda, not the patient's, that is on the table for action, and to which the patient's only option is to agree or disagree. But this, of course, is fertile ground for abuse.

Furthermore, the physician's capacity to shape patient choice in euthanasia, both by selective control of information and by initial formulation of both the problem and the solution presented for consent, may be influenced not only by malevolent but also by paternalistic intentions. To be sure, there are physicians motivated by greed, prejudice, fear of malpractice action for a medical mistake, and so on. But there may also be physicians who genuinely believe that euthanasia would be in the best interests of the patient, given the pain and suffering the physician knows otherwise lies in the patient's future, and who thus may seek to influence patient choice in this direction for the patient's own sake. Of course, whether manipulation of the patient in what the physician perceives to be the patient's own interest is to be counted as abuse depends in the end on theoretical issues about the nature of paternalism and whether abuse is defined as violation of voluntary patient choice or as violation of patient interests, but the possibility of paternalistic manipulation of the patient by the physician must at least be considered among the varieties of possible abuse.

3. *Institutional abuse.* Institutional abuse will no doubt include some of the features of interpersonal abuse and also professional abuse, but it is again conceptually distinct in its central feature: it operates by narrowing the range of actual choices open to the patient. It may seem to closely resemble those forms of professional abuse in which the physician shapes the patient's choice by selectively providing information or proposing one rather than another possible course of action for consent, but it functions in a distinct way: it erects barriers so that certain choices can be made only with difficulty or cannot be made at all. It is not only that choices are shaped, but, more importantly, that only certain choices are possible, while other choices are closed off. There need be nothing clandestine about this, as there may seem to be when the physician withholds specific information or selectively emphasizes some information in order to promote certain choices; in institutional abuse, in contrast with professional abuse, the policies in question are typically open and sometimes widely known, even though they may have manipulative or coercive consequences.

What are the fears, so vocally and variably expressed in the public discussions of euthanasia? They are fears about various sorts of institutions: hospitals, nursing homes, insurance companies, the government. They are fears primarily of policies which are financially motivated, seeking to cut costs in medicine by offering less care, imposing barriers, and withdrawing certain options. They are fears that hospitals will not provide certain types of care or will provide it only to some patients, that nursing homes will let the quality of care and of institutional life deteriorate to the point where it is unbearable, that insurance companies will exclude from coverage many forms of treatment and palliation which might benefit the patient, or that they will exclude some patients from coverage altogether. . . .

Protections against abuse
The picture of possible abuse is a grim one, particularly in a society with a chaotic health care system, but it is, I think, a real risk. Yet I also think it is possible to erect protections against such abuse that can be both stable and effective. Such protections are not foolproof, and the policies and regulations in which they are incorporated are not likely to stop those who operate outside the law in any case. Nevertheless, these protections are adequate, I believe, to prevent the kind of general, large-scale, 'normal' abuse that many forms of the slippery-slope argument predict, and thus render unwarranted the large-scale limitation of patient choice that laws prohibiting euthanasia and assisted suicide represent.

These protections fall into three general categories – policies designed to protect the quality of the patient's choice, policies designed to control professional and institutional distortions of a patient's situation, and policies designed to permit the development of objective indices of abuse. Though they are to be described separately here, they will function best, of course, in concert and interactively. Indeed, I think that all or nearly all of the forms of protections described here will need to be in place to provide reliable prevention of abuse.

Policies designed to protect the quality of the patient's choice
Policies designed to protect the quality of the patient's choice must attempt to look at two things: how the patient reached that choice, and what the content of that choice is. Both raise enormous theoretical issues, requiring answers to two philosophically difficult questions, drawing on two distinct senses of the term 'rational': what must one have done to have made a 'well-chosen' or 'rational' choice? and what characteristics must the 'right' or 'best' choice, that is, the 'rational' choice, display? Nevertheless, we can intuitively discern choices that are badly made in the sense that they are the product of irrational thinking, inadequate information, undue outside influence, and so on; and we can also discern choices that seem to be, given the interests and values of the individual making them, simply bad choices for him or her to have made, regardless of how carefully they were considered. Of course, this raises enormous issues of paternalism, but we can nevertheless discern at least the broad outlines of 'badly made' and 'bad' choices. The two mechanisms discussed below attempt to protect the quality of the patient's decision in both these cases.

Psychological evaluation. Several proposals for amending the proposed aid-in-dying legislation recommend provisions for offering or requiring a psychological evaluation of the patient who requests euthanasia or assistance in suicide. Generally, such evaluations would seek primarily to identify psychopathology or other disturbances of reasoning, especially depression, which might effect the patient's capacity to reach a fully voluntary, autonomous choice; they would thus be designed to protect the patient from choosing badly. Such evaluation might routinely use standard scales of depression, such as the Beck Inventory; it might also involve interviews by the physician involved or by a consulting physician, psychologist, or psychiatrist. Such evaluation should be conducted in private with the patient, away from the influence of family members or other parties who might exert pressures of various subtle sorts. However, it cannot be too easily assumed that any evidence of depression that could be detected in this way is grounds for rejecting a request for euthanasia or assistance in suicide; depression is a natural accompaniment of terminal illness, though more pronounced in some stages of the dying process than in others, and terminal illness, while it may involve some gains in intimacy with one's loved ones, is also a period of continuing loss. The routine use of psychological evaluation adapted for other situations, especially to detect depression, ought not to impose a higher standard for decision-making than for other important decisions in life; instead, it ought to be used just to identify the clearest cases of transient, *reversible* depression which may be affecting patient choice. Thus, psychological evaluation measures used in these situations – for persons diagnosed as terminally ill, with less than six months to live – must be redesigned so that the expression of thoughts about death, considerations of suicide, or the wish to die is not interpreted as *prima facie* evidence of depression and so taken to preclude voluntary choice.

Counseling. As least until recently, most counseling available in the US has been committed to the principle of suicide prevention, and would view any expression of a wish or intention to die as grounds for further treatment. In this sense, most counseling has been directive: it has been concerned to direct clients or patients towards life-affirming choices and constructive ways of resolving their problems, away from death. Furthermore, perhaps as a result of the *Tarasoff* decision [discussed *supra*, ch 9], most psychologists have understood themselves to be obligated to report serious potential harm to third parties or to the patient [*sic*], and hence obligated to take action (for instance by initiating involuntary commitment) with respect to a patient who reports a serious intention to commit suicide. In a large range of cases, these postures are entirely appropriate. But they are not appropriate in the circumstances at issue in terminal illness, especially if the patient has a legally protected right to euthanasia or assistance in suicide; here, what is in order instead is genuinely nondirective counseling, designed to help the patient discover whether his or her request for euthanasia or assistance in suicide is in fact a genuine one, carefully thought through, fully understood, and in keeping with his or her most basic values – that is, whether it is the 'right' or 'best' or 'rational' choice *for this person*. Of course the request might be a 'cry for help' or the product of external manipulation or other abuse, but it might also be a genuine product of the person's most considered, reflective choice. Any counseling offered ought to serve solely to differentiate these two, not to close off one set of options; if not, it is useless in these situations. Suicide-prevention centres and crisis hotlines have . . . been particularly remiss in failing to serve that proportion of the population who may find their services most valuable: persons considering suicide (or euthanasia) as a way of responding to the prospect of deteriorative terminal illness, as well as those with severe permanent disabilities or advanced old age. Such persons, who take themselves to be considering a rational response to difficult circumstances, cannot avail themselves of services whose announced purpose, 'suicide prevention,' makes it clear that they will work to preclude such a choice, or of services whose policies require initiating involuntary commitment for persons viewed as likely to commit suicide. Rather, what is needed is counseling designed to help a patient think through the issues in 'rational suicide,' including requests for assistance or for physician-performed euthanasia. Such suicide-neutral counseling takes the request at face value and seeks to help the patient be sure he or she has considered all consequences, acknowledged his or her own emotions, and recognized all conflicts or affirmations of value such a choice might involve. Indeed, such counseling may well serve to reduce the psychopathology of such situations by allowing more open discussion of them; but it cannot do so if it is committed to pre-shaping choice.

Continuity requirement or waiting period. Some proposals have suggested that a waiting period be required between the initial request for euthanasia or assistance in suicide and the provision of these services. The clear intent behind such proposals is to ensure that the choice is stable and enduring, rather than a fleeting, transitory response to a new setback, and hence that it is an expression of the patient's true, underlying values. Other mechanisms which might be said to provide concrete evidence of the patient's values at earlier periods in life would include such instruments as a Living Will executed before the onset of the terminal illness or at an earlier point during it; some courts have considered records of or testimony about earlier comments made by the patient concerning other persons in similar circumstances. While a short waiting period (say, 24 or 48 hours) may serve as some protection against impetuous decision-making, longer waiting periods (say, a month or two) are not only artificial but have the potential to be cruel, since they postpone that very relief the patient is seeking. Paradoxically, waiting periods may also encourage some patients to make premature requests as a way of getting into the queue early. Living Wills and Durable Power of Attorney documents need not be signed under controlled circumstances, and it is sometimes argued that they do not reliably represent a patient's true choices over time, especially since the patient may be unable to correctly anticipate his or her future situation. Despite the deficiencies of waiting periods and advance directives, nevertheless, some form of protective device designed to ensure both the stability of the choice and its consonance with the patient's own values seems appropriate – provided, of course, that it does not completely preclude any possibility for the patient to change his or her mind. Notice what is *not* recommended here as a protective device: the deliberations of a committee. These can only be deliberations about the content of the patient's choice, not the patient's voluntariness in making that choice, and I do not see that a committee decision on whether the patient may or may not end his or her life protects the quality of the patient's choice. More likely, it serves to protect the institution in which the committee is based.

Policies designed to protect against professional and institutional distortion of a patient's choices
The sorts of policies considered in this section are designed to prevent both intentional and inadvertent distortion of a patient's situation and hence a patient's choices by either the physician or other health care providers or by institutions, including hospitals, nursing homes, home agencies, insurance companies, and governmental agencies.

Prohibition of fees. In remarks published before the vote on Initiative 119, Professor Albert Jonsen warned of a 'flood of persons' who would travel to Washington in order to seek euthanasia. Other voices warned of the development of 'death houses' or 'euthanasia clinics', clearly drawing on the analogy with abortion clinics, and some suggested that unscrupulous physicians would offer inducements to patients to seek such services, perhaps by advertising in the public or medical media. Remote as these predictions might seem to be, there is a simple way to prevent such traffic and the institutional stimulation of such traffic: no physician or other health care provider should be permitted to charge a fee for performing euthanasia or for providing assistance in suicide, or at least no fee beyond minimal compensation for the time actually involved. Advertising such services, at least in any way more elaborate than announcing their availability, should also be prohibited. Euthanasia is not a complex procedure, if reliable information is available to the physician about methods for performing it (as would presumably be the case if the procedure were legalized), though it may be performed in comparatively slow ways that do involve extended time. At least some physicians in the Netherlands, where euthanasia is in effect legal and where medical information about methods to be used is widely available, report that they do not accept fees, even though the procedure may be performed in a hospital or in a home, and even though, at the request of the patient, the procedure is often performed in a way that involves a long, slow induction of sleep followed by coma over a period of several hours, usually to make the transition from life to death easier for the family to watch. Dutch physicians report that they expect to remain with the patient (and the family) throughout this time, though they do not take fees for it. Similarly, to prohibit health care facilities from advertising and from charging fees for euthanasia or any closely related ancillary services, or from charging fees that would provide a profit over expenses, would preclude at least some incentives for euthanasia and for the development of a euthanasia 'trade' or market.

Documentation. A second form of protection against abuse involves extensive documentation of any procedure involving euthanasia or the provision of assistance in suicide. Such documentation, presumably to be part of the patient's medical record, would include the medical history, the prognosis, the nature of the current problem(s), the reasons for the patient's request (both the patient's stated reasons and the physician's perceptions of the patient's reasons, if different), and a record of the physician's discussions with the patient's family, if any. Also to be included in the documentation is a clear expression of the patient's choice: not merely a signed 'informed consent' to the procedure itself, but documentation of the patient's active request. This might of course take many forms – a letter, a tape-recording of the patient's voice, or witnessed statements by observers – but the central element here is documentation of the fact that euthanasia or assistance in suicide is the patient's idea, not that of the physician, the family, or the health care facility.

As a second, equally important component, the documentation should also include a record of treatment alternatives discussed with the patient, including treatment alternatives refused by the patient as well as those accepted, forms of pain relief or symptom control offered the patient, and, also equally important, any forms of treatment potentially effective for the patient's condition but excluded from coverage by insurance policies, by the health care facility's care priorities, by governmental rationing policies, and so on. Thus these three elements of documentation serve to reflect interpersonal, professional, and institutional abuse respectively.

Reporting. The performance of euthanasia or the provision of assistance in suicide should also be reportable to an appropriate external agency. At the moment, of course, there is no such designated agency, but a number of possibilities suggest themselves: for instance, the coroner (since presumably the cause of death, euthanasia, perhaps together with the disease causing the terminal condition, would be entered on the death certificate), or the Centers for Disease Control (as a keeper of mortality statistics), or the National Institutes of Health (as a federal research agency), or Health and Human Services (as the highest level of federal bureaucracy for health issues), etc. However, the natural analog to the Dutch reporting requirement would not be immediately plausible in the US; in the Netherlands, because euthanasia is technically a violation of statutory law and the guidelines developed in lower and supreme court cases serve as a defense to prosecutions for homicide, the physician is obligated to report any occasion of euthanasia to the Ministry of Justice after the fact, where it is reviewed and prosecution undertaken if the guidelines are not met. (As is well known, only a small proportion of Dutch physicians has been doing so, though this number has been increasing in recent years.) However, if in the United States euthanasia and assistance in suicide were legal under statutory law, reporting to the Department of Justice or state-level judicial authorities would not seem immediately plausible, since technically, no crime would have been committed; perhaps, however, a reporting requirement could be inserted in the authorizing law. Whatever the agency to which report is made, what is important in preventing abuse is that detailed information about cases of euthanasia be available for review; the effectiveness of this structure would clearly also be enhanced by a substantial penalty for not reporting.

Indices of abuse. Documentation and reporting of euthanasia cases makes possible what is perhaps the most important mechanism for the control of abuse and the reliable provision of protection to patients. What is central here is the possibility of retroactive inspection on a broad scale of patterns of performance of euthanasia. As in current analyses by John Wennberg at Dartmouth and others of geographical variation in surgical procedures and other statistical assessments of medical practice, the performance of euthanasia and assistance in suicide, if documented and reported, would also be open to objective review. Review, of course, could be made at all levels and for all factors reported: by individual physician, by health care facility, by insurance carrier, by type of terminal condition, by length of association between patient and physician, by types of pain control and symptom palliation provided, by types of alternative treatment denied, by age, race, gender, handicap status, and so on. Thus many quite revealing questions could readily be answered: Do some doctors provide assistance in suicide more frequently than others? Do the patients of some nursing homes request euthanasia more frequently than the patients of others? Are patients covered by some health insurance plans more frequently denied care for certain sorts of conditions, and are these denials listed among their reasons for choosing euthanasia? How often are spend-down provisions among the reasons for such choices? Do black patients 'choose' euthanasia more often than white? Patients with poor educations or lower incomes more often than patients with privileged backgrounds? While such data might not always be easy to interpret, physicians who had become euthanasia enthusiasts, nursing homes providing deliberately intolerable care, and insurance companies forcing patients into euthanasia choices by refusing to cover certain sorts of care could be tentatively identified, and further examination of specific situations then conducted by the appropriate review organizations.

Furthermore, not only would analyses of such data reveal patterns of euthanasia practice and hence probable patterns of euthanasia abuse, but there is already some basis for comparative analysis of such data. The new Remmelink Commission study from the Netherlands provides the first objective glimpse of euthanasia practice in a climate in which it is widely accepted and in which it is legally tolerated: it is now known, as we saw earlier, that about 1.8 percent of all deaths in the Netherlands are the product of euthanasia and that about 0.03 percent of all deaths involve physician-assisted suicide. Additional information about these patients is also available: for example, their average age at the time of euthanasia (62 for men, 68 for women; interestingly, Dutch physicians report very few requests from older patients); their regional location (more in urban areas); and the approximate amount of life forgone (in 70 percent of cases, more than one week; in 8 percent, more than six months). Information is also available about the reasons for their requests of euthanasia: loss of dignity (mentioned in 57 percent of cases), pain (46 percent), 'unworthy dying' (46 percent), being dependent on others (33 percent), and tiredness of life (23 percent). According to this study, in just over 5 percent of cases was pain the only reason. Furthermore, about two-thirds of initial requests for euthanasia do not end up as a serious and persistent request at a later stage of the disease, and of the serious and persistent requests, about two-thirds do not result in euthanasia or assisted suicide since, according to the study, physicians can often offer alternatives.

Information of this sort would provide an initial basis for comparison of US experience with a country in which two relevant characteristics are different. First, the Netherlands is a country in which the practice of euthanasia is widely and generally accepted, both by patients and by physicians; thus, it is a country in which the incidence of euthanasia is, presumably, not distorted by severe social discouragement. Second, it is a country in which the practice of euthanasia is uncoerced by financial considerations on the part of the patient (the Netherlands has an effective national health insurance system which provides all residents with extensive care in the hospital, nursing home, and at home); thus, it is a country in which patient choice is not constricted in at least one way common in the US. Thus, the Dutch experience can provide tentative expectations about what our own experience might be were euthanasia accepted and were it not affected by financial considerations; though of course this is a highly conjectural strategy, examining the practices in the Netherlands can at least initially provide very rough, informal guidelines for scrutinizing our own practice. If we suppose for example that, despite differences between Dutch and American culture, somewhere around 1.8 percent is the 'normal' percentage of persons dying who would choose to do so by euthanasia when that alternative is socially accepted and when it is not coerced by financial considerations, and that a tiny additional fraction would choose physician-assisted suicide, we then have an easy measure for suspecting abuse in our own society. Are, say, 10 or 20 percent of terminally ill Medicaid patients choosing suicide, but not such a high number of privately insured patients? Thirty or 40 percent of the uninsured? About one-fourth of Dutch AIDS patients die by euthanasia; is the proportion higher among AIDS patients here? Is 'pain' the reason for which a large proportion of patients are said to have chosen euthanasia? Since this is the primary reason for only 5 percent of Dutch patients choosing euthanasia, we might well suspect foul play – or its medical and bureaucratic variations, like deliberate neglect or refusal to provide adequate symptom control – if the rates in the US were much higher. Of course, these figures can hardly be treated as rigid norms, and certainly not as either quotas or ceilings; but they can give us some idea of what we might expect were we to permit the practice here, and what would be wildly out of bounds. This is not to assume that the Dutch have got it right, so to speak, and that abuse never occurs in the Netherlands; but inasmuch as there is no documented evidence that abuse is occurring (other than very rare 'outlier' cases), it is reasonable to begin with Dutch experience as a guide to what, if all went well, we might expect in the US. To be sure, these proportions might change as social attitudes change, and would no doubt increase if acceptance for self-determination in dying were to grow; they may of course also change in the Netherlands. And these proportions would of course change dramatically if Robert Kastenbaum's well-known prediction were to come true, that suicide will become the *preferred* mode of dying because it enables a person to control the time, place, and circumstances of doing so. Thus statistical analysis cannot by itself identify patterns of abuse without some further analysis of social values and trends; but it is nevertheless adapted to identify variations in pattern within a culture and across institutional and geographic lines. What the data from the Netherlands now tell us is that we should expect that euthanasia would be quite infrequent – less than 2 percent of all deaths – and that the reasons for which patients choose it do not have to do only with pain. Of the various mechanisms for protecting against abuse, it is the possibility of potential public exposure, incurring the risk of further legal action, that provides the most secure protection, provided of course the penalties for not reporting are substantial as well. It is true that many of the slippery-slope arguments warn of abuse on a vast scale, but they forget that we can easily put in place expert methods for detecting and thus preventing it.

It cannot be doubted that whenever the topic of voluntary euthanasia is breached, rational argument becomes an early casualty. The spectre of Nazism is shamelessly resorted to as an opening gambit by those opposed to any change in the law. The nuances of arguments and the realities of modern medicine tend to be ignored. Against such a background it is unlikely that Parliament, whatever the Select Committee of the House of Lords decides, will legalise voluntary euthanasia for some time to come.

Given the current climate of opinion, we have not considered in this section other forms of euthanasia, ie where the patient has not expressly requested to be killed. The law is clear and reform is unimaginable.

Anticipatory decisions

So far we have been concerned with decisions made by competent patients at the time they are being treated. Now we turn to consider the extent to which a patient while competent may make a decision about possible medical treatment in the future at a time when he is no longer competent by reason for example, of accident or supervening illness.

As before we are concerned with consent to, and refusal of, treatment. For the most part, however, we will concentrate on anticipatory *refusal* although we point out here that every time a consent form for surgery is signed this is, of course, an example of an anticipatory *consent*. Perhaps, if that had been realised earlier, conjecture as to the legal validity of anticipatory decisions generally would have been less.

Re T (Adult: Refusal of Medical Treatment) [1992] 4 All ER 649, (1992) 9 BMLR 46 (CA)

T was injured in a car accident when she was 34 weeks pregnant. She was admitted to hospital and the possibility of her requiring a blood transfusion arose. T had been brought up by her mother, who was a Jehovah's Witness, but she was not herself a member of that religious sect. After a private conversation with her mother, T told the staff nurse that she used to belong to a religious sect which believed blood transfusion to be a sin and a bar to eternal salvation, that she still maintained some beliefs of the sect and that she did not want a blood transfusion. Shortly afterwards she went into labour and because of her distressed condition it was decided that delivery should be by Caesarian section. After being alone with her mother, T again told medical staff that she did not want a blood transfusion and was informed that other solutions to expand the blood could be used and that blood transfusions were not often necessary after a Caesarian section. T then blindly signed a form of refusal of consent to blood transfusions but it was not explained to her that it might be necessary to give a blood transfusion to save her life. After undergoing an emergency Caesarian operation her condition deteriorated and she was transferred to an intensive care unit where, given a free hand, the consultant anaesthetist would unhesitatingly have administered a blood transfusion but felt inhibited from doing so in the light of T's expressed wishes. T was instead put on a ventilator and paralysing drugs were administered. T's father and boyfriend applied to the court for assistance and following an emergency hearing the judge authorised the administration of a blood transfusion to T and declared that, in the circumstances then prevailing, it would not be unlawful for the hospital to do so, despite the absence of her consent, because a blood transfusion appeared manifestly to be in her best interests. At a second hearing the judge held that T had neither consented to nor refused a blood transfusion in the emergency which had arisen and accordingly that it was lawful for the doctors to treat her in whatever way they considered, in the exercise of their clinical judgment, to be in her best interests. T appealed.

In dismissing T's appeal, the Court of Appeal held that on the facts T's refusal of treatment was vitiated by her mother's undue influence [see *supra*, ch 4]. The judges, nevertheless, went on to consider the validity, in principle, of a patient's anticipatory refusal of treatment.

Lord Donaldson MR: There seems to be a view in the medical profession that in . . . emergency circumstances the next of kin should be asked to consent on behalf of the patient and that, if possible, treatment should be postponed until that consent has been obtained. This is a misconception because the next of kin has no legal right either to consent or to refuse consent. This is not to say that it is an undesirable practice if the interests of the patient will not be adversely affected by any consequential delay. I say this because contact with the next of kin may reveal that the patient has made an anticipatory choice which, if clearly established and applicable in the circumstances – two major 'ifs' – would bind the practitioner . . .

The scope and basis of the patient's decision
If the doctors consider that the patient had the capacity to decide and has exercised his right to do so, they still have to consider what was the true scope and basis of that decision. If at the time the issue arises the patient still has capacity to decide, they can not only explore the scope of his decision with the patient, but can seek to persuade him to alter that decision. However this problem will usually arise at that time when this *cannot* be done. In such circumstances what the doctors cannot do is to conclude that if the patient still had had the necessary capacity in the changed situation he would have reversed his decision. This would be simply to deny his right of decision. What they *can* do is to consider whether at the time the decision was made it was intended by the patient to apply in the changed situation. It may well have been so intended, as it was in the Canadian case of *Malette v Shulman* (1990) 72 OR (2d) 417 where the Jehovah's Witness carried a card stating in unequivocal terms that she did not wish blood to be administered to her in *any* circumstances. But it may not have been so intended. It may have been of more limited scope, eg 'I refuse to have a blood transfusion, so long as there is an effective alternative'. Or again it may have been based upon an assumption, eg 'As there is an effective alternative, I refuse to have a blood transfusion'. If the factual situation falls outside the scope of the refusal or if the assumption upon which it is based is falsified, the refusal ceases to be effective. The doctors are then faced with a situation in which the patient has made no decision and, he by then being unable to decide for himself, they have both the right and the duty to treat him in accordance with what in the exercise of their clinical judgment they consider to be his best interests.

Refusal forms
I was surprised to find that hospitals appear to have standard forms of refusal to accept a blood transfusion and was dismayed at the layout of the form used in this case. It is clear that such forms are designed primarily to protect the hospital from legal action. They will be wholly ineffective for this purpose if the patient is incapable of understanding them, they are not explained to him and there is no good evidence (apart from the patient's signature) that he had that understanding and fully appreciated the significance of signing it. With this in mind it is for consideration whether such forms should not be redesigned to separate the disclaimer of liability on the part of the hospital from what really matters, namely the declaration by the patient of his decision with a full appreciation of the possible terms and emphasised by a different and larger type face, by underlining, the employment of coloured print or otherwise.

Informed refusal
As Ward J put it in his judgment, English law does not accept the transatlantic concept of 'informed consent' and it follows that it would reject any concept of 'informed refusal'. What is required is that the patient knew in broad terms the nature and effect of the procedure to which consent (or refusal) was given. There is indeed a duty on the part of doctors to give the patient appropriately full information as to the nature of the treatment proposed, the likely risks (including any special risks attaching to the treatment being administered by particular persons), but a failure to perform this duty sounds in negligence and does not, as such, vitiate a consent or refusal. On the other hand, misinforming a patient, whether or not innocently, and the withholding of information which is expressly or impliedly sought by the patient may well vitiate either a consent or a refusal.

Butler-Sloss LJ: I agree with the reasoning of the Court of Appeal in Ontario in their decision in *Malette v Shulman* (1990) 72 OR (2d) 417 (a blood transfusion given to an unconscious card-carrying Jehovah's Witness). Robins JA said (at 432):

> At issue here is the freedom of the patient as an individual to exercise her right to refuse treatment and accept the consequences of her own decision. Competent adults,

as I have sought to demonstrate, are generally at liberty to refuse medical treatment even at the risk of death. The right to determine what shall be done with one's own body is a fundamental right in our society. The concepts inherent in this right are the bedrock upon which the principles of self-determination and individual autonomy are based. Free individual choice in matters affecting this right should, in my opinion, be accorded very high priority. . . .

The question may arise as to whether the decision to consent to or reject treatment is made by a patient who has the capacity to make the decision, in other words whether he is fit to make it, or whether he has genuinely made the decision. . . .

The patient may make a decision which is limited in scope, and there may also be the situation where no decision is made and in those circumstances the principle of necessity will apply as set out in the speech of Lord Goff of Chieveley in *F v West Berkshire Health Authority (Mental Health Act Commission intervening)* [1989] 2 All ER 545 at 565-566, [1990] 2 AC 1 at 75-76. . . .

There is . . . the question whether she made a decision which was limited in duration and to which she would not have adhered if she had been alerted to dangers of a refusal to accept blood transfusions or similar blood-based treatment. . . .

Limited refusal – the scope of her decision
The judge based his decision upon this point. In my view on the facts as found by the judge this issue does not arise since she was not able to make a genuine decision. But I can see circumstances in which a patient is unwilling to have certain procedures carried out and says so under the impression that in any event the emergency which would bring those procedures into play will not happen. If the patient has been misled or misinformed he may not have given a genuine consent or refusal. This is not to bring in the doctrine of informed consent which is not the law of this country. But on the present facts Miss T did not want a blood transfusion but she did ask whether there was a substitute treatment and was told, erroneously, I believe, that there was. She was also told in order to calm her down that a blood transfusion was most unlikely and she did not have to face, it appears, the possible serious or even fatal consequences of her decision. Had she been making a genuine decision to refuse the treatment, it would be necessary in a case such as this to find out if the patient had received any advice as to the consequences of a refusal to accept treatment. In *Malette v Shulman* (1990) 72 OR (2d) 417 the answer was clear. It may be less clear in other situations.

Staughton LJ: The second reason why an apparent consent or refusal of consent may not be a true consent or refusal is that it may not have been made with reference to the particular circumstances in which it turns out to be relevant. A patient who consents, even in the widest terms, to a dental operation under anaesthetic does not give a true consent to the amputation of a leg. Nor does a patient who refuses consent in some circumstances necessarily give a true refusal of consent to treatment in any quite different circumstances which may arise: an example is to be found in *Werth v Taylor* (1991) 190 Mich App 141. . . .

In *Malette v Shulman* (1990) 72 OR (2d) 417 a Canadian court upheld an award of $20,000 to a patient who had been given a blood transfusion in order to save her life but against her known wishes. I doubt if an English court would have awarded such a sum; but the liability would exist.

Subsequently, three of the judges in the *Bland* case specifically confirmed the legal effect of anticipatory decisions.

Lord Keith: The first point to make is that it is unlawful, so as to constitute both a tort and the crime of battery, to administer medical treatment to an adult, who is conscious and of sound mind, without his consent: see *F v West Berkshire Health Authority (Mental Health Act Commission intervening)* [1989] 2 All ER 545, [1990] 2 AC 1. Such a person is completely at liberty to decline to undergo treatment, even if the result of his doing so will be that he will die. This extends to the situation where the person, in anticipation of his, through one cause or another, entering into a condition such as PVS, gives clear instructions that in such event he is not to be given medical care, including artificial feeding, designed to keep him alive.

Lord Goff: Moreover the same principle [that respect must be given to the patient's wishes] applies where the patient's refusal to give his consent has been expressed at an earlier date, before he became unconscious or otherwise incapable of communicating it; though in such circumstances special care may be necessary to ensure that the prior refusal of consent is still properly to be regarded as applicable in the circumstances which have subsequently occurred.

(See also Lord Mustill at 892.)

The cases show the clear acceptance by the courts of the validity of an anticipatory refusal. The constituent elements of a valid refusal are: (1) that the patient be competent at the time the decision was made; (2) that the patient be free from undue influence; (3) that the patient be sufficiently informed; and (4) that the patient intend his refusal to apply to the circumstances which subsequently arise.

The first two of these elements raise no special problems here. The other two do, however, require further consideration. As regards being 'sufficiently informed', it is important to recognise that the Court of Appeal in *Re T* did not create a doctrine of 'informed refusal'. Instead, the court held that a refusal may be valid provided a patient is aware of the 'nature and effect of the procedure' which he is refusing. There is no need, as Lord Donaldson MR makes clear, for the patient to be aware of other matters such as risks associated with the procedure. However, a patient who is not aware of the relevant risks and alternatives may not satisfy element 4, ie he may not be held to have intended his decision to apply in the circumstances which subsequently arise. Indeed, that was just the case in *Re T* itself where the patient's misunderstanding of the alternatives available to blood transfusions led the court to conclude that Miss T had not contemplated her refusal of treatment as applying if her life were threatened.

This fourth element as developed by Lord Donaldson MR may, therefore, be a Trojan horse. It may allow the courts (and therefore doctors) to undermine the law's apparent commitment to the patient's right of self-determination. If the court wishes, it can, on the basis of the fourth element in *Re T*, require that the patient specifically give his mind to the precise circumstances that have arisen and indicate that, should they arise, he refuses treatment. This may well be a hard criterion to satisfy. The following American case referred to in *Re T* highlights this danger.

Werth v Taylor (1991) 475 NW 2d 426 (Mich CA)

Neff, Presiding Judge: Plaintiffs filed a civil battery claim against defendant Taylor based on his authorization of a blood transfusion for Cindy Werth despite plaintiffs' refusals. Plaintiffs also filed a medical malpractice claim against Taylor and other defendants. The medical malpractice claim is not the subject of this appeal.

The facts are not in dispute. Cindy and her husband Donald are Jehovah's Witnesses. It is unquestioned that they are both devoted adherents to the tenets of their chosen faith. According to Cindy Werth's deposition testimony, one of the most deeply held of these tenets is the belief that it is a sin to receive blood transfusions.

In August 1985, Cindy, the mother of two children, became pregnant with twins. About two months before the expected date of delivery, Cindy went to Alpena General Hospital to preregister. She filled out several forms including a 'Refusal to Permit Blood Transfusion' form. Cindy went into labor on May 8, 1986, and entered Alpena General Hospital on that date. While she was being admitted, Donald signed another 'Refusal to Permit Blood Transfusion' form.

Cindy gave birth to her twins on the evening of May 8, 1986. Following delivery, Cindy was found to be bleeding from her uterus. Around 11:30 pm, Dr Cheryl Parsons was called. She performed a pelvic examination and discovered a great deal of clotting and a fair amount of bleeding. Dr Parsons then discussed performing a dilation of the cervix and curettage of the uterine lining (D & C). As a result, Dr Parsons began discussing with plaintiffs their refusals of blood transfusions.

Following this discussion, Cindy was taken to surgery. In the early hours of May 9, 1986, she was placed under general anesthesia, and Dr Parsons proceeded to perform a D & C. The bleeding, however, continued. Defendant Taylor, an anesthesiologist, was then called to the hospital to examine Cindy. Cindy's blood pressure had risen significantly. At approximately 1:30 am, defendant Taylor observed mottling and cooling of the skin peripherally, premature ventricular activity, oozing of crystalloid material from her eyes, and a fairly rapid and significant fall in blood pressure. These observations prompted defendant Taylor to determine that a blood transfusion was medically necessary to preserve Cindy's life. He ordered the transfusion of packed red blood cells, but before the transfusion was given, Dr Parsons informed him that Cindy was a Jehovah's Witness. Dr Parsons testified that defendant responded by saying something like 'that may be, but she needs the blood.' A blood transfusion was then given.

Plaintiffs thereafter filed their medical malpractice action, alleging negligence by various defendants, including Taylor, and alleging battery against defendant Taylor. . . .

Plaintiffs contend that the trial court erred in granting summary disposition where their refusal of a blood transfusion was made deliberately and voluntarily. . . .

Defendant Taylor, on the other hand, contends that the trial court did not err in granting summary disposition, because plaintiffs did not unequivocally refuse the blood transfusion. He claims that, in the face of a life-threatening emergency, without a fully conscious and contemporaneous refusal, his decision to transfuse blood was appropriate and the court did not err in finding an implicit consent to the procedure authorized by him . . .

Here, the trial court determined that Cindy's refusals were made when she was contemplating merely routine elective surgery and not when life-threatening circumstances were present and concluded that it could not be said that she made the decision to refuse a blood transfusion while in a competent state and while fully aware that death would result from such refusal. The record reflects the unexpected development of a medical emergency requiring blood transfusion to prevent death or serious compromise of the patient's well-being.

The decision of the trial court is supported by one reached by the Supreme Court of Pennsylvania in *In Re Estate of Dorone*, 517 Pa 3, 543 A 2d 452 (1987). In *Dorone*, the patient was a twenty-two-year-old Jehovah's Witness who required a blood transfusion during a cranial operation to relieve an acute subdural hematoma. Without the operation or transfusion, death was imminent. The patient was unconscious, and his parents refused consent to the blood transfusion. The court overruled the parents' refusal, stating:

> Turning to the ultimate decisions the judge rendered, we feel that they were absolutely required under the facts he had before him. Those facts established that medical intervention, which necessarily included blood transfusions, could preserve Mr Dorone's life. When evidence of this nature is measured against third party speculation as to what an unconscious patient would want there can be no doubt that medical intervention is required. Indeed, in a situation like the present, where there is an emergency calling for an immediate decision, nothing less than a fully conscious contemporaneous decision *by the patient* will be sufficient to override evidence of medical necessity. [*Id*, p 9, 534 A 2d 452.]

Here, both plaintiffs signed 'Refusal to Permit Blood Transfusion' forms. Following Cindy's delivery of twins, Dr Parsons discussed these refusals with both plaintiffs. Cindy recalled their conversation as follows:

> She – okay. We told her – she said, 'I understand that you're one of Jehovah's Witnesses and that you won't take blood,' and Don and I both said, 'That's correct,' And she said, 'You mean to tell me if your wife's dying on the table that you're not going to give her blood?' And we said – Don said, 'That's – well, I don't want her to have blood, but I don't want her to die. We want the alternative treatment.'. . .
> She said there would be no problem. It was a routine D & C, there was no problem with the blood . . .
> The idea of a blood transfusion, she made it sound that it wouldn't even be a problem. Blood wouldn't come into the picture. That's how I understood it.

Donald also testified regarding the conversation as follows:

> At the time of the consent form, she gave it to my wife and had her look it over and read it, and she said – she acknowledged us as being one of Jehovah's Witnesses, and then she said, 'Would you accept blood?' And we replied, 'No.' And then she made the remark. 'Even if she was to die, you'd let her die?'
> And at that point, I questioned, I said, 'Well, how serious of a, you know, condition was she?' And the reason why we asked that is because, like I say, in

different situations like there are Witnesses who have gone to hospitals, you know, if there was some type of real emergency, a lot of times they're shipped out or flown out. Different ones have gone to Ann Arbor and other places.

So at that time, I was just kind of questioning, well, how serious was it, you know. First of all, you say it's a routine D & C; then you mention that if she was to die, and so that's why I questioned it, and then she reassured us that there was no problem, nothing to it.

The following colloquy then occurred between defense counsel and Donald:

Q. So you never answered the question.
A. Oh, as far as the idea of dying?
Q. Yes.
A. I said no. The answer was no.
Q. Even if she was to die, you said 'No blood.'
A. Right.
Q. What did your wife say to that?
A. Well, she was right there and that was her feeling also.
Q. But you didn't have the feeling that that was part of the problem or a possibility? It was kind of an academic discussion, that she might die?
A. Well, she said it in a joking manner. It wasn't done as a serious matter. Being with a joking manner, that's why I asked her how serious it was and then she just – 'Oh, there's no problem.'
Q. Okay. So you weren't really biting the bullet because it didn't seem to be part of the problem that she was going to die or there was a risk of her dying.
A. At that point, no.

Dr Parsons testified to the conversation as follows:

I recall discussing with her and her husband the fact that they were Jehovah's Witnesses and that she indicated that this was true. And I said, 'Is it true that you do not want any blood transfusions?' She said 'No.' He looked at me and said, 'Do you think it's that bad?' And I said, 'Not right now.' And I didn't get any further answer from him in terms of whether he felt that if it became that bad he might change his mind. And I left it at that.

She also described Donald's response as 'wishy-washy.'

Following this discussion, Cindy underwent surgery. She was placed under general anesthesia, and Dr Parsons performed a D & C. Cindy did not regain consciousness again until after the operation and transfusion of blood were performed. Defendant Taylor testified that he was aware, before deciding to infuse blood, that Cindy was a Jehovah's Witness. No attempt was made to bring Cindy to consciousness in order to obtain her approval, and defendant Taylor testified that this option was 'fool-hardy.' No attempt was made to discuss his decision with Donald because defendant saw nothing to be gained from it. He did not believe Donald could give or deny permission for a blood transfusion.

We agree with the principle in *Dorone* that it is the patient's fully informed, contemporaneous decision which alone is sufficient to override evidence of medical necessity. . . . It is undisputed that Cindy was unconscious when the critical decision regarding the blood transfusion to avoid her death was being made. Her prior refusals had not been made when her life was hanging in the balance or when it appeared that death might be a possibility if a transfusion were not given. Clearly, her refusals were, therefore, not contemporaneous or informed. Thus, a record could not be developed regarding Cindy's refusal which would leave open an issue upon which reasonable minds could offer.

Our holding in this case is narrow. Without contemporaneous refusal of treatment by a fully informed, competent adult patient, no action lies for battery and summary disposition was proper.

Shepherd and McDonald JJ agreed.

(See also *In the Matter of Alice Hughes* (1992) 611 A 2d 1148 (Sup NJ App Div).)

The situation is not saved by Lord Donaldson MR's assertion in *Re T* that if the patient was not informed of such matters as risks, he would have an action in negligence against his doctor (even though his refusal of treatment would be invalid by not being properly directed to what in fact arose). Any action in negligence against the doctor would, of course, fail even if the doctor were in breach of his duty because the patient would be unable to show that he had suffered any harm. Thus, Lord Donaldson MR takes away with one hand and does not give back with the other. In our view, a patient's right to refuse can only have any real substance if the fourth element we referred to above is not used in such a way so as to undermine the patient's right.

Re T and *Werth* seem to have gone to some lengths to construe the patients' refusals so as to narrow the scope of their application and thereby ignore them. By contrast, the Ontario Court of Appeal in the following case adopted a more sensitive approach.

Malette v Shulman (1990) 67 DLR (4th) 321, [1991] 2 Med LR 162 (Ont CA)

Robins JA: The question to be decided in this appeal is whether a doctor is liable in law for administering blood transfusions to an unconscious patient in a potentially life-threatening situation when the patient is carrying a card stating that she is a Jehovah's Witness and, as a matter of religious belief, rejects blood transfusions under any circumstances.

In the early afternoon of June 30, 1979, Mrs Georgette Malette, then age 57, was rushed, unconscious, by ambulance to the Kirkland and District Hospital in Kirkland Lake, Ontario. She had been in an accident. The car in which she was a passenger, driven by her husband, had collided head-on with a truck. Her husband had been killed. She suffered serious injuries.

On arrival at the hospital, she was attended by Dr David L Shulman, a family physician practicing in Kirkland Lake who served two or three shifts a week in the emergency department of the hospital and who was on duty at the time. Dr Shulman's initial examination of Mrs Malette showed, among other things, that she had severe head and face injuries and was bleeding profusely. The doctor concluded that she was suffering from incipient shock by reason of blood loss, and ordered that she be given intravenous glucose followed immediately by Ringer's Lactate. The administration of a volume expander, such as Ringer's Lactate, is standard medical procedure in cases of this nature. If the patient does not respond with significantly increased blood pressure, transfusions of blood are then administered to carry essential oxygen to tissues and to remove waste products and prevent damage to vital organs.

At about this time, a nurse discovered a card in Mrs Malette's purse which identified her as a Jehovah's Witness and in which she requested, on the basis of her religious convictions, that she be given no blood transfusions under any circumstances. The card, which was not dated or witnessed was printed in French and signed by Mrs Malette. Translated into English, it read:

NO BLOOD TRANSFUSION!

As one of Jehovah's Witnesses with firm religious convictions, I request that no blood or blood products be administered to me under any circumstances. I fully realize the implications of this position, but I have resolutely decided to obey the Bible command: 'Keep abstaining . . . from blood.' (Acts 15:28, 29). However, I have no religious objection to use the nonblood alternatives, such as Dextran, Haemaccel, PVP, Ringer's Lactate or saline solution.

Dr Shulman was promptly advised of the existence of this card and its contents.

Mrs Malette was next examined by a surgeon on duty in the hospital. He concluded, as had Dr Shulman, that, to avoid irreversible shock, it was vital to maintain her blood volume. He had Mrs Malette transferred to the X-ray department for X-rays on her skull, pelvis and chest. However, before the X-rays could be satisfactorily completed, Mrs Malette's condition deteriorated. Her blood pressure dropped markedly, her respiration became increasingly distressed, and her level of consciousness dropped. She continued to bleed profusely and could be said to be critically ill.

At this stage, Dr Shulman decided that Mrs Malette's condition had deteriorated to the point that transfusions were necessary to replace her lost blood and to preserve her life and health. Having made that decision, he personally administered transfusions to her, in spite of the Jehovah's Witness card, while she was in the X-ray department and after she was transferred to the intensive care unit. Dr Shulman was clearly aware of the religious objection to blood manifested in the card carried by Mrs Malette and the instruction that 'NO BLOOD TRANSFUSION!' be given under any circumstances. He accepted full responsibility then, as he does now, for the decision to administer the transfusion . . .

[H]e was not satisfied that the card signed by Mrs Malette expressed her current instructions because, on the information he then had, he did not know whether she might have changed her religious beliefs before the accident; whether the card may have been signed because of family or peer pressure; whether at the time she signed the card she was fully informed of the risks of refusal of blood transfusions; or whether, if conscious, she might have changed her mind in the face of medical advice as to her perhaps imminent but avoidable death.

As matters developed, by about midnight Mrs Malette's condition had stabilized sufficiently to permit her to be transferred early the next morning by air ambulance to Toronto General Hospital where she received no further blood transfusions. She was discharged on August 11, 1979. Happily, she made a very good recovery from her injuries . . .

What then is the legal effect, if any, of the Jehovah's Witness card carried by Mrs Malette? Was the doctor bound to honor the instructions of his unconscious patient or, given the emergency and his inability to obtain conscious instructions from his patient, was he entitled to disregard the card and act according to his best medical judgment?

To answer these questions and determine the effect to be given to the Jehovah's Witness card, it is first necessary to ascertain what rights a competent patient has to accept or reject medical treatment and to appreciate the nature and extent of those rights. . . .

A competent adult is generally entitled to reject a specific treatment or all treatment, or to select an alternate form of treatment, even if the decision may entail risks as serious as death and may appear mistaken in the eyes of the medical profession or of the community. Regardless of the doctor's opinion, it is the patient who has the final say on whether to undergo the treatment. The patient is free to decide, for instance, not to be operated on or not to undergo therapy or, by the same token, not to have a blood transfusion. If a doctor were to proceed in the face of a decision to reject the treatment, he would be civilly liable for his unauthorized conduct notwithstanding his justifiable belief that what he did was necessary to preserve the patient's life or health. . . .

On the facts of the present case, Dr Shulman was clearly faced with an emergency. He had an unconscious, critically ill patient on his hands who, in his opinion, needed blood transfusions to save her life or preserve her health. If there were no Jehovah's Witness card he undoubtedly would have been entitled to administer blood transfusions as part of the emergency treatment and could not have been held liable for so doing. In those circumstances he would have had no indication that the transfusions would have been refused had the patient then been able to make her wishes known and, accordingly, no reason to expect that, as a reasonable person, she would not consent to the transfusions.

However, to change the facts, if Mrs Malette, before passing into unconsciousness, had expressly instructed Dr Shulman, in terms comparable to those set forth on the card, that her religious convictions as a Jehovah's Witness were such that she was not to be given a blood transfusion under any circumstances and that she fully realized the implications of this position, the doctor would have been confronted with an obviously different situation. Here, the patient, anticipating an emergency in which she might be unable to make decisions about her health care contemporaneous with the emergency, has given explicit instructions that blood transfusions constitute an unacceptable medical intervention and are not to be administered to her. Once the emergency arises, is the doctor none the less entitled to administer transfusions on the basis of his honest belief that they are needed to save a patient's life?

The answer, in my opinion, is clearly no. A doctor is not free to disregard a patient's advance instructions any more than he would be free to disregard instructions given at the time of the emergency. The law does not prohibit a patient from withholding consent to emergency medical treatment, nor does the law prohibit a doctor from following his patient's instructions. While the law may disregard the absence of consent in limited emergency circumstances, it otherwise supports the right of competent adults to make decisions concerning their own health care by imposing civil liability on those who perform medical treatment without consent.

The patient's decision to refuse blood in the situation I have posed was made prior to and in anticipation of the emergency. While the doctor would have had the opportunity to dissuade her on the basis of his medical advice, her refusal to accept his advice or her unwillingness to discuss or consider the subject would not relieve him of his obligation to follow her instructions. The principles of self-determination and individual autonomy compel the conclusion that the patient may reject blood transfusions even if harmful consequences may result and even if the decision is generally regarded as foolhardy. Her decision in this instance would be operative after she lapsed into unconsciousness, and the doctor's conduct would be unauthorized. To transfuse a Jehovah's Witness in the face of her explicit instructions to the contrary would, in my opinion, violate her right to control her own body and show disrespect for the religious values by which she has chosen to live her life. . . .

Accepting for the moment that there is no reason to doubt that the card validly expressed Mrs Malette's desire to withhold consent to blood transfusions, why should her wishes not be respected? Why should she be transfused against her will? The appellant's answer, in essence, is that the card cannot be effective when the doctor is unable to provide the patient with the information she would need before making a decision to withhold consent in this specific emergency situation. . . .

In this case, the patient, in effect, issued standing orders that she was to be given 'NO BLOOD TRANSFUSION!' in any circumstances. She gave notice to the doctor and the hospital, in the only practical way open to her, of her firm religious convictions as a Jehovah's Witness and her resolve to abstain from blood. Her instructions plainly contemplated the situation in which she found herself as a result of her unfortunate accident. In light of those instructions, assuming their validity, she cannot be said to have consented to blood transfusions in this emergency. Nor can the doctor be said to have proceeded on the reasonable belief that the patient would have consented had she been in a condition to do so. Given his awareness of her instructions and his understanding that blood transfusions were anathema to her on religious grounds, by what authority could he administer the transfusions? Put another way, if the card evidences the patient's intent to withhold consent, can the doctor none the less ignore the card and subject the patient to a procedure that is manifestly contrary to her express wishes and unacceptable to her religious beliefs? . . .

In the particular doctor-patient relationship which arose in these emergency circumstances it is apparent that the doctor could not inform the patient of the risks involved in her prior decision to refuse consent to blood transfusions in any circumstances. It is apparent also that her decision did not emerge out of a doctor-patient relationship. Whatever the doctor's obligation to provide the information needed to make an informed choice may be in other doctor-patient relationships, he cannot be in breach of any such duty in the circumstances of this relationship. The patient manifestly made the decision on the basis of her religious convictions. It is not for the doctor to second-guess the reasonableness of the decision or to pass judgment on the religious principles which motivated it. The fact that he had no opportunity to offer medical advice cannot nullify instructions plainly intended to govern in circumstances where such advice is not possible. Unless the doctor had reason to believe that the instructions in the Jehovah's Witness card were not valid instructions in the sense that they did not truly represent the patient's wishes, in my opinion he was obliged to honor them. He has no authorization under the emergency doctrine to override the patient's wishes. In my opinion, she was entitled to reject in advance of an emergency a medical procedure inimical to her religious values. . . . On my reading of the record, there was no reason not to regard this card as a valid advance directive. Its instructions were clear, precise and unequivocal, and manifested a calculated decision to reject a procedure offensive to the patient's religious convictions. The instructions excluded from potential emergency treatment a single medical procedure well known to the lay public and within its comprehension. The religious belief of Jehovah's Witnesses with respect to blood transfusions was known to the doctor and, indeed, is a matter of common knowledge to providers of health care. The card undoubtedly belonged to and was signed by Mrs Malette; its authenticity was not questioned by anyone at the hospital and, realistically, could not have been questioned. The trial judge found, '[t]here [was] no basis in evidence to indicate that the card [did] not represent the current intention and instruction of the card holder' [p 268 OR, p 43 DLR]. There was nothing to give credence to or provide support for the speculative inferences implicit in questions as to the current strength of Mrs Malette's religious beliefs or as to the circumstances under which the card was signed or her state of mind at the time. The fact that a card of this nature was carried by her can itself be taken as verification of her continuing and current resolve to reject blood 'fully realiz[ing] the implications of this position'.

In short, the card on its fact set forth unqualified instructions applicable to the circumstances presented by this emergency. In the absence of any evidence to the contrary, those instructions should be taken as validly representing the patient's wish not to be transfused. If, of course, there were evidence to the contrary – evidence which cast doubt on whether the card was a true expression of the patient's wishes – the doctor, in my opinion, would be entitled to proceed as he would in the usual emergency case. In this case, however, there was no such contradictory evidence. Accordingly, I am of the view that the card had the effect of validly restricting the treatment that could be provided to Mrs Malette and constituted the doctor's administration of the transfusions a battery.

Advance directives

A. DEVELOPMENTS IN OTHER COMMON LAW JURISDICTIONS

Legislation designed to give effect to patients' anticipatory decisions first emerged in the United States during the mid-1970s in the form of 'living will' statutes. Subsequent developments involved legislation permitting a patient to appoint an agent, or health care proxy, to make treatment decisions on his behalf after the onset of incompetence. A species of hybrid statute then began to appear combining the two forms, ie living will and durable powers of attorney. Together these developments have become known as 'advance directives'.

President's Commission, *Deciding to Forgo Life-Sustaining Treatment* (1983)

Advance directives

An 'advance directive' lets people anticipate that they may be unable to participate in future decisions about their own health care – an 'instruction directive' specifies the types of care a person wants (or does not want) to receive; a 'proxy directive' specifies the surrogate a person wants to make such decisions if the person is ever unable to do so; and the two forms may be combined. Honoring such a directive shows respect for self-determination in that it fulfils two of the three values that underlie self-determination. First, following a directive, particularly one that gives specific instructions about types of acceptable and unacceptable interventions, fulfils the instrumental role of self-determination by promoting the patient's subjective, individual evaluation of well-being. Second, honoring the directive shows respect for the patient as a person.

An advance directive does not, however, provide self-determination in the sense of active moral agency by the patient on his or her own behalf. The discussion between patient and health care professional leading up to a directive would involve active participation and shared decisionmaking, but at the point of actual decision the patient is incapable of participating. Consequently, although self-determination is involved when a patient establishes a way to project his or her wishes into a time of anticipated incapacity, it is a sense of self-determination lacking in one important attribute: active, contemporaneous personal choice. Hence a decision not to follow an advance directive may sometimes be justified even when it would not be acceptable to disregard a competent patient's contemporaneous choice. Such a decision would most often rest on a finding that the patient did not adequately envision and consider the particular situation within which the actual medical decision must be made.

Advance directives are not confined to decisions to forego life-sustaining treatment but may be drafted for use in any health care situation in which people anticipate they will lack capacity to make decisions for themselves. However, the best-known type of directive – formulated pursuant to a 'natural death' act – does deal with decisions to forego life-sustaining treatment. . . .

Despite a number of unresolved issues about how advance directives should be drafted, given legal effect, and used in clinical practice, the Commission recommends that advance directives should expressly be endowed with legal effect under state law. For such documents to assist decisionmaking, however, people must be encouraged to develop them for their individual use, and health care professionals should be encouraged to respect and abide by advance directives whenever reasonably possible, even without specific legislative authority.

Existing alternative documents. Several forms of advance directives are currently used. 'Living wills' were initially developed as documents without any binding legal effects; they are ordinarily instruction directives. The intent behind the original 'natural death' act was simply to give legal recognition to living wills drafted according to certain established requirements. They are primarily instruction directives, although their terms are poorly enough defined that the physician and surrogate who will carry them out will have to make substantial interpretations. 'Durable power of attorney' statutes are primarily proxy directives, although by limiting or describing the circumstances in which they are to operate they also contain elements of instruction directives. Furthermore, durable powers of attorney may incorporate extensive personal instructions. . . .

Living wills. People's concerns about the loss of ability to direct care at the end of their lives have led a number of commentators as well as religious, educational, and professional groups to promulgate documents, usually refered to as living wills, by which individuals can indicate their preference not to be given 'heroic' or 'extraordinary' treatments. There have been many versions proposed, varying widely in their specificity. Some explicitly detailed directives have been drafted by physicians – outlining a litany of treatments to be forgone or disabilities they would not wish to suffer in their final days. The model living wills proposed by educational groups have somewhat more general language; they typically mention 'life-sustaining procedures which would serve only to artificially prolong the dying process'. One New York group has distributed millions of living wills. The columnist who writes 'Dear Abby' reports receiving tens of thousands of requests for copies each time she deals with the subject. Despite their popularity, their legal force and effect is uncertain. The absence of explicit statutory authorization in most jurisdictions raises a number of important issues that patients and their lawyers or other advisors should keep in mind when drafting living wills.

First, it is uncertain whether health care personnel are required to carry out the terms of a living will; conversely, those who, in good faith, act in accordance with living wills are not assured immunity from civil or criminal prosecution. No penalties are provided for the destruction, concealment, forgery or other misuse of living wills, which leaves them somewhat vulnerable to abuse. The question of whether a refusal of life-sustaining therapy constitutes suicide is unresolved, as are the insurance implications of a patient's having died as a result of a physician's withholding treatment pursuant to a living will.

Yet even in states that have not enacted legislation to recognize and implement advance directives, living wills may still have some legal effect. For example, should a practitioner be threatened with civil liability or criminal prosecution for having acted in accord with such a document, it should at least serve as evidence of a patient's wishes and assessment of benefit when he or she was competent. Indeed, no practitioner has been successfully subjected to civil liability or criminal prosecution for having followed the provisions in a living will, nor do there appear to be any cases brought for having acted against one. . . .

Proxy directives allow patients to control decisionmaking in a far broader range of cases than the instruction directives authorized by most existing natural death acts. . . .

A power of attorney – general or limited – may be employed in making decisions not only about property but about personal matters as well, and in this role powers of attorney might be used to delegate authority to others to make health care decisions. A power of attorney, therefore, can be an advance proxy directive. Using it, a person can nominate another to make health care decisions if he or she becomes unable to make those decisions.

One barrier to this use of a power of attorney, however, is that the usual power of attorney becomes inoperative at precisely the point it is needed; a common-law power of attorney automatically terminates when the principal becomes incapacitated. To circumvent this barrier, many states have enacted statutes creating a power of attorney that is 'durable' – which means that an agent's authority to act continues after his or her principal is incapacitated. As a result, durable power of attorney acts offer a simple, flexible, and powerful device for making health care decisions on behalf of incapacitated patients.

Although not expressly enacted for the problems of incompetent patients' health care decisionmaking, the language of these statutes can accommodate the appointment of a surrogate for that purpose and nothing in the statutes explicitly precludes such a use. The flexibility of the statutes allows directives to be drafted that are sensitive both to the different needs of patients in appointing proxy decisionmakers and to the range of situations in which decisions may have to be made.

The first living will statute was the Natural Death Act 1976 in California (currently, Cal Health and Safety Code section 7185 to 7194.5: for details of the original (unamended) statute, see 1st Edition p 1123). The President's Commission in a 1983 Report discussed critically the California legislation and other early 'living will' statutes.

Deciding to Forgo Life-Sustaining Treatment (1983) (pp 141-5)

Natural death acts. To overcome the uncertain legal status of living wills, 13 states and the District of Columbia have followed the lead set by California in 1976 and enacted statutes that formally establish the requirements for a 'directive to physicians'. The California statute was labeled a 'natural death' act and this term is now used generically to refer to other state statutes. Although well-intended, these acts raise a great many new problems without solving many of the old ones.

No natural death act yet deals with all the issues raised when living wills are used without specific statutory sanction. For instance, the acts differ considerably in their treatment of penalties for failing to act in accord with a properly executed directive or to transfer the patient to a physician who will follow the directive. In some jurisdictions, the statutes consider these failures to be unprofessional conduct and therefore grounds for professional discipline, including the suspension of a license to practice medicine. Other statutes fail to address the issue. Presumably, however, existing remedies such as injunctions or suits for breach of contract or for battery are available to patients or their heirs, although there do not appear to be any instances of such penalties being sought.

Some of the statutes attempt to provide patients with adequate opportunity to reconsider their decision by imposing a waiting period between the time when a patient decides that further treatment is unwanted and the time when the directive becomes effective. Under the California statute, for example, a directive is binding only if it is signed by a 'qualified patient', technically defined as someone who has been diagnosed as having a 'terminal condition'. This is defined as an incurable condition that means death is 'imminent' regardless of the 'life-sustaining procedures' used. A patient must wait 14 days after being told of the diagnosis before he or she can sign a directive, which would require a miraculous cure, a misdiagnosis, or a very loose interpretation of the word 'imminent' in order for the directive to be of any use to a patient. The statute requires that when a directive is signed, the patient must be fully competent and not overwhelmed by disease or by the effects of treatment, but a study of California physicians one year after the new law was enacted found that only about half the patients diagnosed as terminally ill even remain conscious for 14 days. There is an inherent tension between ensuring that dying patients have a means of expressing their wishes about treatment termination before they are overcome by incompetence and ensuring that people do not make binding choices about treatment on the basis of hypothetical rather than real facts about their illness and dying process. If a waiting period is deemed necessary to resolve this tension the time should be defined in a way that does not substantially undercut the objective of encouraging advance directives by people who are at risk of becoming incapacitated.

Although the California statute was inspired in part by the situation of Karen Quinlan, whose father had to pursue judicial relief for a year in order to authorize the removal of her respirator, it would not apply in a case like hers.

> The only patients covered by this statute are those who are on the edge of death *despite the doctors' efforts*. The very people for whom the greatest concern is expressed about a prolonged and undignified dying process are unaffected by the statute because their deaths are not imminent.

The class of persons thus defined by many of the statutes, if it indeed contains any members, at most constitutes a small percentage of those incapacitated individuals for whom decisions about life-sustaining treatment must be made. Although some statutes have not explicitly adopted the requirement that treatments may be withheld or withdrawn only if death is imminent whether or not they are used, this requirement is still found in one of the most recently passed natural death acts. Such a limitation greatly reduces an act's potential.

Some of the patients for whom decisions to forgo life-sustaining treatment need to be made are residents of nursing homes rather than hospitals. Concerned that they might be under undue pressure to sign a directive, the California legislature provided additional safeguards for the voluntariness of their directives by requiring that a patient advocate or ombudsman serve as a witness. The Commission believes that health care providers should make reasonable efforts to involve disinterested parties, not only as witnesses to the signing of a directive under a natural death act, but also as counselors to patients who request such a directive to ensure that they are acting as voluntarily and competently as possible. Yet statutory requirements of this sort may have the effect of precluding use of advance directives by long-term care residents, even though some residents of these facilities might be as capable as any other person of using the procedure in a free and knowing fashion.

Paradoxically, natural death acts may restrict patients' ability to have their wishes about life-sustaining treatment respected. If health care providers view these as the exclusive means for making and implementing a decision to forgo treatment and, worse, if they believe that such a decision cannot be made by a surrogate on behalf of another but only in accordance with an advance directive properly executed by a patient, some dying patients may be subject to treatment that is neither desired nor beneficial. In fact, although 6.5% of the physicians surveyed in California reported that during the first year after passage of the act there they withheld or withdrew procedures they previously would have administered, 10% of the physicians reported that they provided treatment they formerly would have withheld.

In addition there is the danger that people will infer that a patient who has not executed a directive in accordance with the natural death act does not desire life-sustaining treatment to be ended under any circumstances. Yet the person may fail to sign a directive because of ignorance of its existence, inattention to its significance, uncertainty about how to execute one, or failure to foresee the kind of medical circumstances that in fact develop. Unfortunately, even the explicit disclaimer contained in many of these laws – that the act is not intended to impair or supersede any preexisting common law legal rights or responsibilities that patients and practitioners may have with respect to the withholding or withdrawing of life-sustaining procedures – does not in itself correct this difficulty.

First, the declarations about the right of competent patients to refuse 'life-sustaining procedures' take on a rather pale appearance since such procedures are defined by the statutes as those that cannot stop an imminent death. (In other words, competent patients may refuse futile treatments.) Second, it is hard to place great reliance on preexisting common law rights, since had the common law established such rights there would have been no real need for the statutes. Thus, if health care providers are to treat patients appropriately in states that have adopted natural death acts, they will need the encouragement of their attorneys – backed by sensible judicial interpretation of the statutes – to read the acts as authorizing a new, additional means for patients to exercise 'informed consent' regarding life-saving treatment, but not as a means that limits decisionmaking of patients who have not executed binding directives pursuant to the act.

The greatest value of the natural death acts is the impetus they provide for discussions between patients and practitioners about decisions to forgo life-sustaining treatment. This educational effect might be obtained, however, without making the documents binding by statute and without enforcement and punishment provisions.

One particular matter which bedevilled the early American legislation concerns what may be described as the 'triggering event', ie, that event which brings into operation the living will. The President's Commission took the view that living wills 'are not confined to decisions to forgo *life-sustaining* treatment' (our emphasis). This may imply that the onset of incompetence would be enough of itself to trigger the provisions of a living will whatever the directions in the living will might be and whether or not the patient was dying. In fact, however, in all the early statutes in the United States there was an insistence that the patient should be suffering from a terminal illness, or that death be imminent or some such expression. The limitations of the early statutes are discussed in the following extract.

G Gelfand 'Living Will Statutes: The First Decade' (1987) Wisconsin LR 737

Every existing living will act requires that the patient's physical condition or prognosis be 'terminal' or sufficiently poor in order to bring the provisions of a living will into effect. Subtle differences in the way the various statutes define this requirement are crucial because medical treatments may not be withheld unless the declarant's condition qualifies under the statute.

The most significant difference among the various statutory definitions concerns whether the patient's terminal status must be determined irrespective of the effect of the life-supporting treatments. Surprisingly, half of the current living will statutes require that the patient be in a condition where death will occur shortly *whether or not* life-supporting treatments are employed. If the patient will die shortly with or without life-supporting treatment, there is little reason to engage in euthanasia.

Further, if the intent of living will statutes was to permit the 'natural death' of persons who would otherwise linger for years maintained by modern machinery in a vegetative but 'alive' state, then the requirement that death be imminent whether or not treatment is withdrawn nullifies the purpose of such statutes. Even states that have repeatedly 'fine-tuned' their living will statutes through amendments, however, continue to define the necessary patient prognosis as requiring imminent death even with medical treatment. This contradiction between legislative intent and action almost certainly occurs by oversight, as many such statutes are internally inconsistent with regard to this point. In jurisdictions with such inconsistent statutes, a physician presented with a typical and seemingly proper case for the application of a living will – that is, a comatose, terminal individual who can be mechanically maintained with no change in prognosis for years – would have to seek judicial clarification of the statutory definition or risk a homicide prosecution for ending the life of such a patient.

A related question involves the timing of death generally for the purposes of defining a qualified terminally ill patient. A number of statutes require that the patient's condition be such that medical treatments serve only to postpone the moment of dying. This may be the best definition possible, for it conveys more of a sense of the futility of treatment than a time frame for death. Yet such a provision would be far too broad if taken literally. Most medical interventions serve only to postpone the moment of death, even in an otherwise healthy patient.

Other statutes require that death be 'imminent', or that it will occur within a 'short time'. These provisions seem to contain the most appropriate standard since the objective of living will statutes was to allow for the euthanatising of patients with little or no remaining life. However, this standard substitutes a time measure for what is really a more profound question about the futility of medical treatment. If a patient will linger, even for a considerable time, in a vegetative state which medical treatment cannot improve, the intent of living will statutes arguably should be to allow such a patient to die. Perhaps the most satisfactory codification of this intent is found in Alabama's living will statute which allows discontinuance of treatment where 'death is imminent or [the patient's] condition is hopeless'. . . .

Perhaps the most important question, however, concerns the need for such a definition of any kind in the statutes. Political compromise has produced the present requirement that the patient's prognosis be terminal. Yet there may be many cases in which a patient could live for a substantial period, but only if he endures great pain, total physical incapacity, or drastic treatment such as amputation. Since living will statutes reflect a dramatic step toward the recognition of patient autonomy, it can be expected that future provisions will permit the decision to decline treatment in such non-terminal cases.

Given the various criticisms, not least the concern over the limited application of the legislation, a second wave of statutes permitting the creation of durable powers of attorney specifically concerned with health care decisions, emerged. The first and best-known example was again in California: the Durable Power of Attorney Health Care Act 1983 (currently Cal Civil Code sections 2430 to 2445; for text, see 1st Edition, pp 1145-50).

A third generation of statutes emerged subsequently, combining provisions related to living wills with the option of appointing a proxy decision-maker (eg in Florida). Such statutes currently exist in 13 states, complementing or incorporating the living will statutes found in 44 states and powers of attorney acts in 33 states (see *Refusal of Treatment Legislation* (1992) Choice in Dying, NY). Finally, a fourth generation of statutes of a somewhat different nature has emerged which vests decision-making power in the patient's family members in circumstances where the patient has not made an advance directive (eg in Indiana). Twenty states currently have legislation of this sort.

The decision of the Supreme Court of the United States in *Cruzan v Director, Missouri Dept of Health* (1990) 497 US 261 added significant impetus to state legislators in two respects (for a discussion of *Cruzan*'s implications, see A Meisel, 'A Retrospective on *Cruzan*' (1992) 20 Law, Medicine and Health Care 340 and generally the special issue (1991) volume 19 (1-2) of Law, Medicine and Health Care entitled 'Medical Decision-Making and the "Right to Die" after *Cruzan*'). First, the Supreme Court drew no distinction between the withdrawal of other medical treatment and artificial hydration and nutrition. Secondly, a number of the judges took the view that advance directives were beneficial to further patients' choices and, in the case of Justice O'Connor, that the Constitution may actually protect a patient's right to have his wishes respected as reflected in an advance directive. As a consequence, following the *Cruzan* decision, a flurry of legislative activity broke out in the United States, both to amend existing legislation to take account of the artificial hydration and nutrition point (eg in Ohio) and the enactment of new legislation to give effect to a patients' advance directives where previously there had been no such legislation (eg in New York and Massachusetts).

Also, the Federal Government passed the Patient Self-Determination Act 1990 (which came into force in December 1991) which, *inter alia*, requires health care institutions receiving federal funds to advise patients at the time of their admission of their rights under state law to make an advance directive. It also requires institutions to have in effect policies regarding advance directives and to document whether or not a patient has executed one (see discussion in Special Supplement, *Practising the PSDA* (1991) 21 Hastings Center Report).

Legislation has not been limited to the United States. In Australia, both South Australia and the Northern Territory have enacted Natural Death Acts, in 1983 and 1988 respectively (for a discussion, see D Lanham and B Fehlberg, 'Living Wills and the Right to Die with Dignity' (1991) 18 Melbourne University Law Review 329). Victoria has adopted a statutory framework for making anticipatory refusals of treatment and to allow a patient to appoint an agent or proxy (see Medical Treatment Act 1988 (as amended in 1990) discussed by D Lanham and S Woodford, 'Refusal by Agents of Life-Sustaining Medical Treatment' (1992) 18 Melbourne University Law Review 659 and D Lanham, 'The Right to Choose to Die with Dignity' (1990) 14 Criminal Law Journal 401).

In Canada, there are currently two Provinces which have enacted statutes giving effect to advance directives, whether as living wills or as durable powers of attorney (Consent to Treatment Act 1992 and Substitute Decisions Act 1992 (Ontario); The Health Care Directives Act 1992 (Manitoba)). Legislation is proposed in other Provinces, for example, Alberta.

B. ENGLAND

1. Existing law

As regards 'living wills', we have already seen that at common law they have legal effect providing they meet the elements necessary for validity set out in *Re T*. There is, of course, as yet no legislation covering 'living wills' in England.

As regards powers of attorney, the Enduring Powers of Attorney Act 1985 does provide that the grant of a power of attorney may survive the onset of the maker's incompetence. The Act, however, does not cover decisions about medical treatment.

The Living Will: Consent to Treatment at the End of Life (1988) (Working Party Report, Age Concern and Centre of Medical Law and Ethics, King's College) (pp 48-49)

Powers of attorney

As regards powers of attorney, under the Common Law it is arguable that an adult patient could nominate another as his agent so that the other may take decisions concerning the patient's health. There seems, however, to be no reported case in which this has occurred. In any event, any agency would (in the absence of any statutory provision) terminate on the incompetence of the patient.

As for statute law, the agency which a person may create for the management of his affairs under the Powers of Attorney Act 1971, terminates on the incompetence of that person. The Enduring Powers of Attorney Act 1985, however, permits the creation of a power of attorney which, providing certain statutory conditions are met, continues after the creator has become incompetent. Although the Act was designed to give power to deal specifically with the financial affairs of the individual, the question arises whether section 3(1) of the Act, which states that the scope of the general authority of an enduring power of attorney extends to an incompetent's 'property or affairs', thereby covers health care decisions, specifically about treatment. It is most unlikely that a court would so construe the statute in the light of the treatment of what is now Section 95 of the Mental Health Act, 1983 in *Re W (EEM)* [1971] Ch 123. When interpreting the Court of Protection's powers 'with respect to the property and affairs of a patient' in relation to this case Ungoed-Thomas J stated that the court did not have jurisdiction over 'the management of care of the patient's person' . . .

It seems, therefore, that without a specific statutory provision creating an enduring power of attorney in relation to health care decisions, this form of advance directive has no legal validity, unlike for example in California, since the Durable Power of Attorney Health Care Act, 1983.

2. Reforming the law

There are two issues which must be addressed:

(a) Is there a need for legislation to give effect to advance directives?
(b) If law is desirable, what provisions should it contain?

(a) The need for legislation

A study prepared for the Centre of Medical Law and Ethics, King's College London by Charlotta Schlyter examined the attitudes towards advance directives of a group of patients with HIV infection or AIDS and of those caring for them (doctors and nurses).

Advance Directives and AIDS (1992)

The results of this study indicate that there is a substantial degree of dissatisfaction with current practice of medical decision-making about life-sustaining care in all three of the groups studied. Moreover, a great majority of the participants in the study believe that advance directives in some form would be helpful. . . .

Problems in Current Practice

A number of concerns were put forward by participants which related to the ways in which decisions about life-sustaining treatment are currently managed in HIV care. It was feared by some that these shortcomings led to a large number of decisions being taken without any knowledge of, or reference to, the patient's wishes. Three areas of concern emerged.

First, *discussions with patients about life-sustaining treatment did not take place as often as the groups consulted would wish.* The view was put forward during interviews with doctors and under 'other comments' on the questionnaires in all groups that early discussions between doctor and patient was the preferred way in which to ensure patient involvement. Such a discussion, held when the patient was not too ill, would give the patient an opportunity to let the doctor know about his or her personal attitude to life-sustaining treatment. At the same time, the doctor would be able to make sure that the patient was aware of the nature and possible effects of different treatments which were available.

However, in many cases discussions of this kind did not take place. The study showed that only a little less than a third of the people who had symptoms of HIV or AIDS had discussed life-sustaining care with a doctor. Of the remaining two-thirds (who had not done so), 93% said they would like to. During interviews, several doctors and nurses said that discussions were sometimes postponed to a stage when it was too late for communication.

A possible reason why life-sustaining treatment is not often discussed is the fact that the subject is not easy for either party to bring up. For example, a doctor may hesitate to initiate such a discussion for fear that it would make the patient anxious or even depressed. The patient, on the other hand, may be uncertain as to the doctor's reaction to questions about treatments for which there is not any present need.

Where a patient is developing new, serious symptoms, it is likely that many doctors would initiate a discussion with the patient about treatments which may have to be considered. Fifteen out of 35 doctors consulted in this study would initiate such a discussion with a patient who had AIDS at the time of significant deterioration of the patient's condition, or when a new problem developed. However, a doctor may be more reluctant to initiate, or even invite, a discussion where a patient had HIV, but is unlikely to experience any serious illness for a long time.

Therefore, a patient who would like to discuss life-sustaining treatment early on would do best to initiate this him- or herself. This, however, requires that patients are aware that they are entitled to have an input in the course of their care, and that their questions are not met with astonishment. It is possible that some people refrain from mentioning concerns regarding treatment to a doctor not because they do not wish to discuss it, but because they do not think they can influence decisions on what treatments are administered. A number of the doctors consulted mentioned that they considered it normal practice to explain to patients what treatments were available, and let him or her make the choices. Despite this, some nurses claimed to have been asked by patients whether or not it was possible for the patient to influence treatment decisions. It can hardly be expected that patients will take the initiative to express their wishes about treatment, if they are not aware that they are entitled to.

Secondly, *concerns were expressed regarding the way in which participation of persons close to the patient was managed.* A large majority (89%) of the doctors surveyed said that they would 'normally' turn to someone who knows the patient for advice when the patient could not communicate. However, 71% of the doctors said it was not always obvious *who* should be consulted. According to some of the doctors consulted in interviews, it would emerge from the context who should be consulted. It would, for example, be the person who most frequently visited the patient. Others said it would often be the person the patient had put down as 'next-of-kin' or 'contact person' when admitted to the hospital.

A problem with relying on the person put down on the admission form by the patient is that the patient may not have realized that the person named could be consulted about treatment issues, and might otherwise have chosen someone else. If the term 'next-of-kin' has been used on such a form, there is also a risk of confusion about the meaning of this concept. A number of doctors interviewed thought that 'next-of-kin' in this context was specified by law. If this is also what patients believe, they may be likely to name their closest relative. However, many of the persons with HIV/AIDS surveyed did not wish their treatment decisions to be taken by a relative. Of the 91% of persons with HIV/AIDS who said they would like to name a proxy, only 13% would choose a family member, while 37% would name a friend, and 38% a spouse or partner.

Thirdly, *persons with HIV/AIDS may encounter several different doctors during the course of their treatment.* While free of any serious symptoms, their care may be managed by an out-patient doctor or a GP. Patients who get seriously ill will sometimes encounter one or several new doctors in hospital. If the patient is unable to communicate, decisions about treatment may be taken by doctors who have never previously met the patient. Even where life-sustaining care has been discussed with a doctor at an earlier stage, views expressed by the patient will then not be communicated unless the new doctor contacts the earlier one.

Would Advance Directives Help?

A large majority of participants in all three groups were in favour of a more wide-spread use of advance directives, both in the form of living wills, and by the naming of proxies. A variety of benefits with the use of advance directives were envisaged by participants, some of which might help avoid the problems described above.

It was expected by many that *advance directives, if they were to become more common, would encourage and help to initiate discussions about life-sustaining treatment.* If there were more information regarding advance directives, and possibly also forms available for making such directives, these could help reassure a person who had been concerned about treatment at the end of life that theirs was a valid concern shared by others. A discussion with a doctor could be more easily initiated if the patient presented the doctor with a draft living will and asked for comments or advice. Such a discussion would also give the patient an opportunity to establish whether or not his or her doctor was sympathetic to the idea of writing down wishes about treatment in a living will. Where this was not the case, the person might want to consider changing doctors.

A doctor who was told that his or her patient had made an advance directive might ask if the patient wanted to discuss it. A number of doctors put forward the view that once a discussion had been initiated, the patient and the doctor might – provided they had found they had been able to agree, and were able to continue a dialogue – decide that the living will was no longer necessary.

Further, *advance directives could be expected to lead to better practices regarding participation of persons close to the patient in decision making.* If a person has named someone, either in a living will or separately, to be his or her proxy, this will inform the doctor of whom the patient thinks is in the best position to advise the doctor about his or her views. This might be particularly helpful when the patient is visited regularly by a number of different people, for example a partner, parents, relatives, or friends who do not communicate between themselves, and who may also have different views about what the patient would have decided. It would, however, require that doctors be aware that there is no legal obligation on them to consult the next-of-kin unless named by the patient.

An advance directive could also give a doctor a helpful indication of the views of a patient whom he or she has not previously attended. This may, for example, be the case where the patient suddenly becomes very ill, and has to be brought to a hospital at which he or she has never previously been treated. However, advance directives may also be helpful where the patient encounters a new doctor at his or her regular hospital, or where the attending doctor has failed to discuss life-sustaining treatment with the patient while he or she was able to.

This requires that the attending doctor is aware of the existence of the advance directive. This can be achieved in different ways. If the directive is known to another doctor, it may have been attached to the patient's notes. If nobody knows about the directive, or if the patient is in a new hospital, the advance directive could be brought to the doctor's attention by an appointed proxy or another person close to the patient who holds a copy of it. Another, but probably less practical, possibility is that the patient carries a copy of the advance directive.

It can be argued that *the overall benefit of advance directives is that they would enable patients to have more control over what treatment is given.* This was the advantage put forward by the largest number of the nurses in the study (16 out of 28), and a comment made by a number of persons with HIV/AIDS on the questionnaires. Making an advance directive might give the sense to a patient who is able to communicate of being able to influence treatments which are being given at present, as well as care which might be given at a stage where he or she can no longer communicate.

Even where life-sustaining treatment has been discussed with a doctor, having one's wishes documented in a living will, or transmitted to an appointed proxy, might give the patient more hope of having his or her wishes respected. Sixty-three percent of persons with HIV/AIDS in the study, and 78% of those who had AIDS wanted a doctor to be legally bound to comply with a living will. These figures can be seen to indicate that the idea of having some control over what treatment is administered when one can no longer express one's wishes is important.

It is also possible that *advance directives might encourage patients to start a process of thinking about what they feel about life-sustaining treatment.* This aspect was emphasized by the two HIV/AIDS counsellors consulted in the study. It could also help the patient bring up the subject with those close to him or her and friends. Even if the patient did not state a wish until a very late stage, perhaps not until the need for a decision might seem imminent, the chance of the patient making a well-thought-through decision may be better if he or she is not confronted with the idea of influencing the choice of treatment for the first time at that stage.

Finally, *advance directives may be of benefit to persons close to the patient in that it could relieve such persons of the burden of making difficult decisions.* If the patient has written down his or her wishes about life-sustaining care such a person would no longer feel obliged to take a decision regarding matters which they may not have discussed with the patient. They would also be able to satisfy themselves that a decision, if taken according to a living will, is likely to be in accordance with the patient's wishes.

Potential Dangers

As we have seen, it is possible that a more widespread use of advance directives may lead to better practices in decision making about life-sustaining care. However, a number of potential problems or risks which may have to be taken into consideration were put forward by respondents.

For example, one doctor pointed out that although doctors could keep living will forms in their offices, they should be very careful about offering it to a patient without a direct enquiry from the patient about advance directives in order not to harm the relationship between the doctor and the patient. Otherwise, there would be a risk that a patient might feel obliged to make a living will when a form was brought out by an enthusiastic doctor.

In fact, one respondent was concerned that if the living will was initiated by doctors, it could become a weapon at the disposal of doctors who wished to withdraw treatment as early as possible. By pretending that all patients – especially those suffering from the same condition as the patient concerned – opted for making a living will, such a doctor might pressure the patient to reach a certain decision by inflicting feelings of guilt and fear in him or her.

Two doctors in the study were concerned that living wills, instead of stimulating discussions, might replace them. If a doctor was aware that a patient had a living will in which he or she expressed a wish only to receive care which was designed to keep him or her comfortable once terminally ill, the doctor might see it as a pretext for not communicating with the patient to confirm his or her wishes, even where the patient was able to.

The view was also put forward by a number of participants from all groups that a living will should not only enable a person to turn down life-sustaining treatment (which is normally understood to be the purpose of a living will), but also make it possible for a person to state that he or she would wish all treatments which are available and reasonable in the circumstances. The concept of advance directives would otherwise not appeal to those people who were concerned that their treatment would be withdrawn earlier than they would want. This group might also have fears and concerns, and could benefit from writing down their wishes and discussing them with a doctor.

A concern put forward by 13 out of 35 doctors, and eight out of 28 nurses, was that the patient might change his or her mind. This is related to the point made by some that a condition perceived as intolerable by the patient might seem tolerable once it occurs. In the light of these concerns, it may be concluded that a living will should not be made too early. However, a view put forward by, among others, a person with experience of counselling persons with HIV/AIDS at the Royal Free Hospital was that it might be very helpful for a person to make a living will at a stage where he or she is not very ill, but that it must be made clear that a living will was not a 'final' document, but could be changed by the person at a later stage, and should be reconsidered from time to time.

Some respondents pointed out that changes in the relationship between a patient and those close to him or her could be a problem where that person was named as a proxy. According to an HIV/AIDS counsellor at the Salvation Army who was consulted in the study, it was not uncommon for relationships with partners, friends or parents to change at a very late stage. Thus, a person named by the patient early on might not be among those who spend time with the patient at a stage when the proxy would be consulted. This would be a reason for not naming a proxy without also giving some written directions, so that some indications of the patient's wishes remain even if the proxy cannot – or does not want to – be consulted.

A concern brought up by some was the difficulty of deciding when a patient is terminally ill, so as to trigger implementation of the wishes written down in a living will. This is related to the uncertainty of diagnosis mentioned by some. Others, however, described these as uncertainties which were present in the care of very ill and dying patients, whether or not advance directives were being used. Where no indication of the patient's wishes existed, it was regarded as good practice for a doctor to withhold or withdraw treatment he or she thinks would not benefit the patient, where recovery was very unlikely.

Finally, there was widespread concern in all groups regarding the legal status of a living will. A majority of persons with HIV/AIDS who were consulted would prefer advance directives to be legally binding on a doctor. All but seven doctors wanted living wills to be advisory only. In interviews with doctors, and during the discussion with a group of persons with HIV/AIDS at the organization CARA, the question was also discussed as to what might happen if the effect of a living will, or a documented naming of a proxy, was ever to be tested in a court. This legal uncertainty created worries among persons with HIV and AIDS that their advance directives would not be taken into account. Among doctors, there was concern regarding what might happen if a court found them to be guilty of failure to comply with an advance directive (should it be found to be legally binding). A reverse scenario would be that they might face criminal charges for withdrawing treatment in accordance with a living will.

SUMMARY OF CONCLUSIONS

The results of this study indicate that there is a great interest in advance directives in the groups surveyed. Fifty-five out of 64 persons with HIV/AIDS consulted would consider writing a living will, and another seven would 'maybe' do so. Among the doctors consulted, 33 out of 35 thought living wills would be helpful, and the remaining two thought they would be helpful in some circumstances. Twenty-seven out of 28 nurses thought it should be possible to make a living will (one expressed no opinion). The level of interest in and support for the nomination of someone whom the patient wanted to be consulted regarding life-sustaining care was similar.

A common expectation was that a more widespread use of advance directives would stimulate discussions about life-sustaining care between patient and doctor. The results from the study indicate that such discussions do not take place as often as participants would wish. For example, only ten out of 23 persons with AIDS had discussed life-sustaining treatment with a doctor, but of the 13 who had not, all said they would wish to. Also among the respondents who were infected with HIV, but did not have AIDS, a very large group would like to discuss life-sustaining care with a doctor if given the opportunity.

It was also thought that advance directives could change the way in which participation of persons close to the patient was managed. A large majority of the doctors who were consulted (89%) would turn to someone who knows the patient for advice when the patient could not communicate. However, 71% of the doctors said it was not always obvious *who* should be consulted. There appeared to be a widespread, albeit mistaken, belief in all the groups that the law defined who was next-of-kin and that this person had certain decision-making powers about life-sustaining care. This might make many doctors uncertain as to whether or not they could consult a partner or a friend where this seemed more appropriate. All 35 doctors said it would be helpful if the patient had decided in advance who should be consulted in matters relating to life-sustaining care.

Few of those with HIV/AIDS said they would like to name a relative to take decisions about medical care for them. Only eight would name a family member, while 23 would name a spouse or partner and 22 would name a friend. This suggests that those in this position should consider specifying through an advance directive (or otherwise) the person whom they want to act as decision-maker, in order to prevent conflicts among persons close to the patient at a later stage.

The concern most commonly expressed by doctors and nurses about advance directives was that the patient may change his or her mind. This suggests that it must be made clear that a living will is not a final document, but can be changed by the patient either orally or in writing. It should also be pointed out that a proxy appointment can be changed. The concern may be lessened if living wills are made the basis of continuing discussions between doctor and patient. The study indicates that many of the participants did view discussions as a part of the process of making an advance directive. Thus, 84% of respondents with HIV/AIDS said they would like to discuss their living will with their doctors, while more than half of the doctors (66%) would be less likely to take a living will into account if it had not been discussed with a doctor.

Persons with HIV/AIDS and doctors expressed diverging views as to whether or not advance directives should be legally binding. Among persons with HIV/AIDS, 55% wanted the proxy to be the sole decision-maker, and 63% wanted doctors to be legally obliged to comply with a living will. The latter figure was even higher (78%) among persons with AIDS than among those who had HIV but not AIDS. In contrast, only 20% of doctors wanted living wills to be legally binding.

Perhaps the most interesting conclusion is that when it came to the question whether advance directives should have the force of law, a large majority of patients were in favour of their having legal force. By contrast, the doctors in the study were largely opposed. As we have seen, if an advance directive in the form of an enduring power of attorney is to have legal force, legislation would be required. Experience in other countries certainly demonstrates the value of legislation which goes beyond merely recognising living wills. It would follow that if the expression of support for advance directives of patients (assuming the views of those patients in the study are typical) and health care workers are to be reflected in law, legislation would appear to be necessary. Before a final view can be reached, however, let us briefly examine some of the advantages and disadvantages of such legislation.

Advance Directives and AIDS (1992)

Benefits and disadvantages of legislation

There appear to be a number of advantages of regulating advance directives, were these to be more commonly used.

First, a doctor may be expected to take an advance directive more seriously if he or she were legally obliged to follow instructions given in a living will or through a proxy, not only because of fear of the legal consequences of non-compliance, but also because legislation may give advance directives a more 'accepted' status. This is the most likely reason why a majority of the people with HIV/AIDS consulted in the study wished advance directives to be legally binding.

Secondly, a possible advantage for doctors might be that legislation could (and does where it exists) give the doctor immunity from civil or criminal charges for withdrawing or withholding treatment in accordance with a living will or instructions from a proxy.

Third, legislation could contain specific instructions about what directions could be given, and provide definitions relevant to the writing and interpretation of a directive, all of which could lead to increased awareness both for doctors as well as those who make an advance directive.

Finally, legislation could contain safeguards for such things as witnessing and storing of a directive. This might, for example, increase the possibilities of verifying that the directive was actually written by the patient, and that he or she was not being pressured into doing so.

A disadvantage of introducing legislation in the field of medical decision-making is the rigidity it might bring. Legislation may be particularly unhelpful in the case of decision-making about life-sustaining treatment where decisions may have to be taken with a large degree of flexibility to suit each individual case. An example would be a situation where a doctor may feel compelled to comply with a living will because of fear of legal repercussions, despite having strong reasons to suspect that the patient had changed his or her mind since the writing of the will.

Another possible risk is that legislation creates an air of mutual distrust between patients and doctors, thereby possibly discouraging discussions about life-sustaining care.

Moreover, the binding force of a legally endorsed advance directive may in part be illusory, since it will in any event be the doctor who decides when a patient is in a *terminal condition* (which is a criterion common to all legislation on advance directives and widely recognized outside the legislative arena). This dilemma is illustrated in an American case, *Evans v Bellevue Hospital*.* In this case, doctors refused to act in accordance with a durable power of attorney's directive to terminate treatment since they did not find that a patient with toxoplasmosis was terminally ill as defined by the living will.

Is There a Case for Legislation in the UK?

The advantages of legislation in this field are likely to have contributed to the decision to legislate in respect of advance directives in the US, Canada and Australia. It is, however, not to be taken for granted that these same advantages can be used as reasons for enacting legislation on advance directives in the UK.

In the case of the US, legal decisions have had a greater effect on medical decision-making than in the UK, and there is also more reliance on legislation in the area of medical practice. Thus, not to legislate in the area of advance directives might in the US have been regarded as not giving enough support for a widespread use of these documents, and might also have been seen as leaving patients, relatives and doctors in doubt of what constitutes a valid advance directive.

Since this is less likely to be the case in the UK, and since there are, as we saw above, some substantial disadvantages to legislating on advance directives, it should be considered whether some of the above-mentioned benefits could be achieved without the enactment of legislation.

The benefits of having principles laid out as to the contents of advance directives and the circumstances in which they apply should not be ignored, nor should the importance of some mechanism for witnessing a living will in order to prevent abuse. However, certain principles which would apply, such as that which says that treatment which sustains life may be withheld or withdrawn but that no measures aimed solely to hasten death may be undertaken, are already accepted as good medical practice in UK hospitals and by professional bodies. Additional principles, such as that advance directives cannot be considered as long as the patient is able to communicate, and the witnessing requirements, could be set out in guidelines on advance directives.

Moreover, since medical practice in the UK accepts that decisions to end treatment for patients who are terminally ill may be taken in certain circumstances, no legal immunity from criminal charges need be created as long as this practice is respected.

There are, however, some foreseeable reasons why legislation regarding advance directives might have to be considered in the UK. One reason to consider legislation would be if, were advance directives to become more widely used, uncertainty prevented their use. For example, doctors might be reluctant to take into account a living will or a proxy's viewpoint simply because there is no statutory support or requirement to do so, and the legal consequences therefore would appear uncertain to the doctors. Legislation would overcome this problem.

Another reason to consider legislation is if a situation should arise where a court is asked to comment on the legal validity of an advance directive. This could occur if advance directives were to be more commonly used. Whether or not a court actually expressed support for the idea that written directives be legally binding, such a decision could well provoke a call for legislation to clarify matters.

Evans v Bellevue Hospital, N.Y.L.J. (July 28, 1987) at 11 col 1 (N.Y. County, July 27, 1987). The patient, a man with AIDS Related Complex, was suffering from toxoplasmosis and unable to communicate. The patient's power of attorney wanted treatment to be terminated following the patient's wishes in a living will. The hospital respondent refused to withhold treatment, claiming that the patient was not dying from his condition. The living will stated that life-sustaining treatment should be withheld 'when there is no reasonable expectation of recovery or regaining a meaningful quality of life'. The toxoplasmosis was, in fact, treatable. The court held that although there was no recovery from AIDS, there was hope of recovery from the toxoplasmosis. The court asked the patient's power of attorney to present 'clear and convincing' evidence that there was no hope of recovery for the patient. In the absence of such evidence, the court dismissed the application to terminate treatment. Two weeks after the decision, the life-support system was removed under the pretext that the patient would not recover from the toxoplasmosis. He died shortly afterwards.

(b) Framing the legislation

The North American experience would suggest that the optimal form of legislation would have two parts: the first dealing with anticipatory decisions by patients and the second dealing with decision-making through proxies.

(i) ANTICIPATORY DECISIONS

As regards this part of the legislation, the King's College Working Party Report argued as follows.

The Living Will: Consent to Treatment at the End of Life (Working Party Report, Age Concern and Centre of Medical Law and Ethics, King's College) (1988)

There are three principal prerequisites for making the living will perform its function as a prospective expression of autonomy. They are: (1) the phrasing of a declaration should reflect what the person considers to be the circumstances in which it might be used; (2) these circumstances should be identifiable; and (3) the recommendations contained in the declaration should be capable of being implemented within the accepted ethical and legal standards of medical practice.

In order to ensure that these prerequisites can be interpreted in a clinical setting the text of a living will should be precisely drafted. Particular attention needs to be directed to the event which will trigger the living will and to the procedures to be carried out when the time for implementation arrives.

In respect of the *triggering event* three alternatives are possible. The trigger can be incompetence alone, or incompetence with the addition of a particular condition or disability, or incompetence with the addition of terminal illness. Each of these definitions gives rise to particular difficulties. Incompetence alone may cause a living will to be implemented in circumstances which some people would consider inappropriate, for example, a moderate degree of dementia without other disability. Incompetence plus specified conditions or disabilities may lead to problems because of the impossibility of itemising every conceivable triggering clinical circumstance, and the uncertainty in interpreting those which are specified. Incompetence plus terminal illness does not capture all the circumstances under which many people would wish a living will to be instituted. It may also cause problems if clinicians interpret terminal illness restrictively, as occurred in the operation of the California Natural Death Act 1976.

Whichever of these definitions is adopted it should be noted that they apply only to people who are permanently incompetent. It is not uncommon for those who are chronically ill, for example, with dementia, to demonstrate fluctuating competence, and it would be both inappropriate and unworkable to attempt to apply advance directives in such circumstances.

In respect of the *procedures to be adopted* once the living will has come into operation, the more vague the declaration, the less reassured might the patient be that his wishes would be met, and the less able might the doctor be to decide whether or when to implement those wishes. Furthermore, imprecise situations might be thought to oblige both patient and doctor to discuss and agree what they thought each other had in mind. This might require lengthy discussion, which could still be inconclusive. Also, if these discussions were not carefully recorded, they could well be ignored, given the high chance that the doctor who had to decide on the issue when the patient was incompetent would not be the same doctor.

These arguments favour detailed specific instructions, but some would take the view that the declared spirit in which the living will is used in the first place allows those responsible for the patient's care sufficient discretion to implement the living will even in those circumstances in which particular disease states are not specifically mentioned. There might also be a conflict for individuals who found it easy and comforting to sign a readily prepared declaration, whilst at the same time wishing to trust the doctor to attend to them as he saw fit, once it came to be implemented. 'The patient ordinarily trusts his physician not only to act in his best interest during his life but also to see that his death is as comfortable, decent and peaceful an event as possible. This is an implied trust that he may not want to verbalise or discuss.' So, equally, there is a counter-argument favouring more general instructions.

Another issue is whether a prescribed form should be used in drawing up a living will. The American Legal Advisors Committee of Concern for Dying proposed a 'Model Act for the Right to Refuse Treatment' in which the following recommendation was made: 'No specific form or document is included because we believe the individuals' wishes will be more likely to be set forth if their own words are used.' This recommendation assumes that people are capable of expressing their wishes unambiguously. The many versions of the living will in the USA are testimony, however, to the fact that even for those experienced in the field, it is not easy to find an appropriate form of words (although there is broad uniformity of sense). A further difficulty arising from allowing complete individual freedom to write a living will is that there may be a considerable gap between the patient's expectations and medical and legal reality. Patients might well make requests for that which would be medically unsound or legally untenable. In such a case, the doctor responsible for implementing the living will may be exposed to ethical and legal insecurity. Whether a prescribed form is advised or not it is recommended that all those preparing living wills are advised to consult with a professional experienced in the field, most probably their own general practitioner or solicitor, before drawing up the document.

There are therefore advantages and disadvantages to having a prescribed form of declaration. On balance, however, such a form is probably desirable.... .

Practical and procedural matters
Some of the practical and procedural matters which might arise in relation to living wills are discussed briefly below. . . .

(b) *Capacity*
The person making a living will should be a competent adult. Provided competence is defined, the question whether the test is satisfied is a matter for clinical judgment. In the event of

a dispute as to whether the person was competent to execute the document, it is suggested that it should be presumed that he was, i.e. the onus of proving that he was not is upon the person so claiming. Alternatively, it could be a requirement that the witnesses (see (c) below) sign a declaration that the person appears to be of sound mind when the instrument is executed.

(c) *Signature and witnesses*

A living will document, whether of a standard type or in the person's own words, would have to be signed and dated by the person making it. It is a uniform requirement of existing legislation on living wills that there should be witnesses, as a safeguard against coercion. It is suggested that there should be two competent adults, one of whom might be the person's family doctor or a hospital consultant in the case of a hospitalised patient.

A question arises as to whether certain persons, such as creditors or potential beneficiaries, should be excluded from witnessing. It is unlikely that creditors would be selected as witnesses. Perhaps the best solution is that at least one witness must be neither a relative nor a person who would take any part of the estate by will or otherwise on the death of the person involved.

(d) *Notification and recording*

The person making the living will would notify near relatives or friends (if any) of his action, and also his medical practitioner (if not a witness), and legal adviser. The medical practitioner would make a written note in the case records. There would also be a procedure for having the information recorded in any appropriate hospital records.

(e) *Availability of blank forms*

If prescribed living will declaration forms were to be used, consideration should be given to methods of making blank forms readily available, possibly from doctors' surgeries and hospital wards, and from professional legal advisers.

(f) *Notice and implementation*

The means whereby a living will might be brought into effect will vary. Provision should be made for ensuring that the existence of a living will is brought to the attention of the doctor (see (d) above). The most common ways of implementing it would probably be as follows:

(i)   *The patient.* A seriously ill patient, when still conscious and competent, might implement a previously signed living will as a means of substantiating and formalising a request for treatment to be withheld or withdrawn. At a particular juncture in an illness the patient might ask the attending doctors to refer to the living will and to consider implementing it forthwith.

      Alternatively, a patient when already gravely ill could request a copy of a living will for signature and subsequent implementation when the circumstances were deemed to be suitable.

(ii) *A relative or friend.* When a patient has become incompetent and a relative or close friend with knowledge of the patient's living will considered that the time was approaching or had arrived to consider implementing it, an approach could be made to a member of the medical staff.

(iii) *The legal adviser.* If the patient had notified his legal adviser that he had signed a living will form, the legal adviser, either from his own knowledge of the patient's serious condition or by information from others, could suggest to the medical staff that it might be appropriate to implement the living will.

(iv) *The doctor.* The patient's general practitioner or a hospital doctor knowing of a living will in the case records could suggest to the doctor in charge of the patient that the circumstances of implementing the living will might be considered.

(v)   *A nurse, social worker, minister or other person involved in the care of the patient.* Any person with medical knowledge who was aware of the patient's state of health and of the living will could indicate to the medical attendants an opinion that the time might have come to implement the living will.

(g) *Consultation procedure*

When a doctor caring for a patient known to have completed a living will determines (spontaneously or at another's suggestion) that the circumstances might be appropriate to implement the living will, it may be appropriate to notify any next of kin, if possible. If the patient's wishes would be met by implementing the living will and the circumstances were deemed appropriate, it would be advisable to record the relevant facts and opinions in the medical record.

(h) *Revocation*

It is essential to an acceptance of the notion of living wills that it be clear that a person may revoke his living will at any time, by destroying or defacing it, or by asking someone else to do so on his behalf. The living will may be revoked at any time by verbal or written instructions from the signatory to his doctor, legal adviser, or other responsible person. Any legal or medical records must thereupon be amended to take note of the revocation, and any such alteration should be signed and dated. The execution of a living will should also revoke any earlier instrument.

More problematic is the question of revocation when incompetent. The logical expectation is that an incompetent person cannot revoke, as in the case of ordinary wills, for example. However, most of the American legislation permits revocation even after loss of competence. Although at first sight this seems to defeat the object of the exercise, the point is that it would be invidious to refuse treatment which the patient, although confused, is at present requesting. This is a strong argument for accepting revocation despite the person's incompetence. Even if it is thought that the person should only be able to revoke while competent, it should be presumed that he was competent at the time of revocation, so that the onus of proving the contrary is on the person so claiming.

(i) *Time limits*

Should a living will lapse after a specified number of years? On the one hand it might be undesirable if the person's fate should be determined by means of an instrument executed decades ago and now forgotten, while on the other hand the person may fail to recognise the passing of a time limit and therefore fail to reconsider the matter. It would clearly be desirable that the provisions of a living will should be reviewed on a regular basis perhaps every five or ten years. People completing living wills should therefore be advised accordingly, but to make this mandatory would be administratively complex and costly and some people might prefer not to undertake such review at specified times. Therefore it is thought that, on balance, it is better that no obligatory review or time limit is imposed.

(j) *Liability*

A doctor who reasonably and in good faith and after appropriate consultation, acted upon a living will would not be exposed to subsequent civil liability or criminal prosecution. Further, no question of professional misconduct would arise in such circumstances.

If the doctor deliberately disregards the instructions of a living will, consideration should be given as to what if any sanctions should apply and to whether these should go beyond professional censure.

Recourse to fraud, forgery, concealment or destruction in the preparation or implementation of a living will would clearly attract appropriate criminal liability.

(k) *Life assurance*

It would be necessary to make it clear as a matter of law, whether by agreement with assurance companies or by legislation, that the completion or implementation of a living will was to have no effect upon the terms of an existing life assurance policy, particularly as regards any provision excluding cover in the case of suicide (i.e. execution of a living will and then compliance by others with its terms do not amount to suicide).

(l) *Pregnancy*

If a living will comes into operation in relation to a woman who is pregnant, any instructions to forego life-sustaining treatment should be regarded as invalid during the course of the pregnancy.

In its consultation Paper No 129 in 1993, the Law Commission recommended that legislation should be enacted to give effect to a patient's anticipatory decision.

Law Commission, *Mentally Incapacitated Adults and Decision-Making: Medical Treatment and Research* (Consultation Paper No 129, 1993)

3.10 A recent study of the attitudes of patients, nurses and doctors working in the field of HIV and AIDS suggested similar benefits. However, the author argued that there could be substantial disadvantages to detailed legislation on advance directives, and that the publication of guidelines might be a better option in this area of practice. The BMA has also argued that 'mutual respect and common accord is better achieved without legislation'. [*Statement on Advance Directives* (1992)] We see the force of these views. However, legislation in this area would resolve the uncertainty of the law as it stands, which leaves both doctors and patients unclear about their respective positions. The BMA took the view that advance directives did not have legal force, but doubts and concerns regarding the legal status of living wills have certainly been reported. Following the dicta of the House of Lords in *Airedale NHS Trust v Bland* it appears that it may be possible to make an advance directive which is legally binding. Concern both about what is needed to achieve such an effect and about the consequences such document might have is likely to increase.

3.11 If a statutory framework for decision-making for incapacitated adults of the sort proposed in this paper were introduced, it would be difficult to avoid consideration of the extent to which courts and other decision-makers, including doctors, should be bound by relevant decisions made by a patient prior to his incapacity. Legislation could clarify the position and could also provide solutions to a range of ancillary matters. For example, although the BMA argued that a doctor is not bound to comply with an anticipatory decision, it also suggested that if he does comply he could not be found to have been negligent in so doing. Legislation could also make it clear that a doctor who acts in good faith and with reasonable care, in accordance with an advance directive which he believes to be valid, should not be exposed to liability even if the directive is subsequently shown to be invalid. Limitations on the scope of anticipatory decision-making might also be appropriate. Another role of legislation would be to introduce penalties for the wrongful concealment, alteration, falsification or forgery of an advance directive. Finally, in the Ontario case of *Fleming v Reid* [(1991) 82 DLR (4th) 298] it was recognised that the resolution of questions about the clarity or currency of a patient's wishes, their applicability to present circumstances, and whether they have been revised or revoked were all matters for legislation. Therefore we provisionally propose that:

1. Legislation should provide for the scope and legal effect of anticipatory decisions.

3.12 The BMA recommended strongly that advance directives should not be legally binding. It argued that patients might request treatments which are clinically inappropriate, or which distort resource allocation, or which are illegal, such as active euthanasia. However, as the BMA's own statement says, patients cannot insist on the provision of treatments which clinical expertise indicates to be futile for their condition or which diverts resources from other patients, and requests for euthanasia are also legally ineffective. A legally 'binding' advance directive does not enable the patient to make demands which he could not lawfully have made when capable. However, the BMA's main concern was that patients might inadvertently misdirect doctors by an inadequate appreciation of the circumstances or the evolution of new treatments. This concern was shared by some respondents to Consultation Paper No 119 and one possibility would be for legislation to state that anyone providing medical treatment to an incapacitated patient is not bound by an anticipatory decisions which the patient may have made.

3.13 On the other hand, it might be possible to address the anxieties which surround advance directives without depriving anticipatory decisions which are 'clearly established' and 'applicable in the circumstances' of the force which they probably already have under the common law. The BMA was concerned about the patient who is inadequately informed, but it appears to us that directives given in such circumstances would not be 'applicable' in the circumstances about which the patient had not been adequately informed. A decision which is based upon false assumptions would be vitiated. The BMA was also concerned that some patients may informally indicate a change of view from that recorded in an advance directive. However, we consider that, as was said in *Malette v Shulman*, a doctor would be entitled to proceed with treatment if there was evidence which cast doubt whether a directive was a true expression of the patient's wishes. Legislation recognising the patient's 'right of decision' might be acceptable if it also provided a mechanism to which cases could be referred where there was doubt about the validity or applicability of the patient's decision. Legislation might also give protection from liability to a treatment provider who acted reasonably. As a starting point, and in accordance with what appears to be the common law position, we provisionally propose that:

2. If a patient is incapacitated, and subject to the other proposals in Part III of this paper, a clearly established anticipatory decision should be as effective as the contemporaneous decision of the patient would be in the circumstances to which it is applicable.

The form of anticipatory decisions

3.14 If statutory clarification of anticipatory decision-making is considered desirable it would be possible to develop a prescribed form with specified consequences. A working party which considered living wills in 1988 regarded the use of a prescribed form as desirable, since patients might otherwise find it difficult to express their own views unambiguously, or might make requests which were medically unsound or legally untenable. It has also been suggested that doctors might find it difficult to adopt a workable practice if they kept encountering a range of different documents.

3.15 On the other hand, if no prescribed form were introduced, different forms of advance directive could be developed to cater for the concerns of different patients. This approach is demonstrated by the living will developed by the Terrence Higgins Trust and the Centre of Medical Law and Ethics ('the THT Living Will'), which was launched in September 1992. This was specifically designed for people with HIV and AIDS, after extensive consultation with people concerned, service organisations and doctors involved in the area. Its provisions could be adapted to other situations, after similar consultations. Equally, a more general form could be produced as a model, but its use would not be mandatory. This could be done by the Law Commission after appropriate consultation, but we see significant advantages in a more broadly based group undertaking this work. We invite comment on whether a model form should be developed and, if so, by whom.

3.16 In circumstances in which an anticipatory decision would be binding at common law, we would be reluctant to deprive it of validity merely because it is not made in a particular form. The decision of the Court of Appeal in *Re T* suggests that an anticipatory decision may take a variety of forms, including a hospital's standard form of refusal, a 'no blood' card carried by a Jehovah's Witness or a spoken refusal repeated to the patient's doctor, nurse and midwife, in the presence of family members. The BMA suggested that oral remarks which might be made impulsively or when a patient is despondent are unlikely to be indicative of a considered view of stable opinion, and should be in a different category from written advance directives. We agree that an impulsive remark should not be regarded as an anticipatory decision. It would not be 'clearly established' nor would it be 'applicable to' circumstances outside the patient's contemplation, but other decisions expressed orally might be both. We invite views on the practical implications of oral anticipatory decision-making.

3.17 Although a flexible approach to the form of anticipatory decisions may be necessary, we consider that patients should be encouraged to make their views known in a more formal way. One approach, adopted recently by the Manitoba Law Reform Commission, is to provide for 'health care directives' in a statutory scheme, coexisting with the common law. By this means, any directive not made in the prescribed manner would not be prevented from taking effect in accordance with common law principles. In the Manitoba proposals, a decision will be recognised as effective by statute provided that it is made in writing and signed, but an oral direction given immediately before surgery is suggested as an example of a direction which would almost certainly continue to be valid at common law. However, if the effect of informal decisions was left entirely to the common law, this might lead to unnecessary uncertainty and could undermine any restrictions which legislation attempted to impose upon the scope of anticipatory decision-making. For the purposes of any new scheme, we propose that there should be a rebuttable presumption that an anticipatory decision is 'clearly established' until it is revoked, provided that it meets certain statutory requirements. The presumption would not affect questions about the applicability or relevance of the decision. We invite views on whether there should also be a rebuttable presumption that a decision is not 'clearly established' if it is made in a form which does not meet the statutory requirements.

3.18 We envisage that several copies of such a form might be in use. These might be lodged with the patient's General Practitioner, family members or friends. All the copies might be individually signed and witnessed, but photocopies might also be made. In many cases, we consider that a photocopy would be sufficient to establish the existence of an anticipatory decision. We do not consider that an apparent decision should be disregarded simply because the original document is not immediately available. However, if there is any doubt about the validity of the document, the original should be sought. Alternatively there could be an authentication procedure. We invite comment on how copies of a document should be treated.

3.19 Strict formal requirements reduce accessibility, and would increase the number of decisions whose status would be uncertain, because it would not be clear whether or not they were 'clearly established'. However, formalities of execution can serve to minimise undue influence and fraud, provide reliable and permanent evidence of the maker's intentions, and impress the significant consequences of a decision upon the maker. We believe that witnessing is an important safeguard which should be encouraged. An unwitnessed document might still constitute a valid anticipatory decision, especially if a card of some kind is carried as a verification of the patient's 'continuing and current resolve' as in *Malette v Shulman*. However, we consider that there should be no presumption in favour of an unwitnessed document. The proposals in Alberta and Newfoundland require one witness, on the basis that to require two would not be a significantly more effective safeguard. We invite comment on the number of witnesses, if any, and on their qualification. We propose that a person who is the patient's 'medical treatment attorney' should not be able to act as a witness and we invite comment on whether the spouse of such an attorney should also be excluded. Other possible restrictions might exclude the maker's close relatives or those with an interest in his estate, or those expected to provide the medical treatment in question. We provisionally propose that:

> **3. There should be a rebuttable presumption that an anticipatory decision is clearly established if it is in writing, signed by the maker [with appropriate provision for signing at his direction], and witnessed by [one] person who is not the maker's medical treatment attorney.**

3.20 We do not favour a requirement that a witness must be a doctor or solicitor who would certify that the maker had capacity to make the decision. Nevertheless, one of the benefits of advance directives is that a patient can talk the matters involved over with his doctor prior to an incapacity. The BMA very strongly recommended that patients who wish to draft advance directives should do so with medical advice, and that they should be told of the risks as well as the benefits of making such a document. Doctors should share with the patient information about diagnoses, prognoses and realistic treatment options and listen to the patient's views. In addition to helping the doctor overcome any doubt that the person is capable at the time the directive is prepared and signed, such a discussion would give the doctor the opportunity to tell his patient if he objects in principle to the advance directive. This would enable the patient to consult another practitioner, or reconsider his decisions. It has been suggested that the need for the patient to anticipate the eventual medical condition to which his decision may have to apply makes it more likely that an anticipatory decision will be found valid if it is arrived at in consultation with a doctor, and drawn up at a time when the patient and his doctor have the patient's prognosis and treatment options in mind.
3.21 However, where an anticipated situation occurs the patient's general intention may be frustrated, unless he can nominate a 'proxy' who would apply the patient's wishes to the particular situation. The BMA considered that, where treatment options cannot be predicted, a simple statement of the patient's views may be more helpful than a complicated document which tries to cover all possibilities and that a system of 'proxies' could meet new circumstances as they arise, reflecting the patient's true wishes, rather than being tied to the particular words of an advance directive. In other parts of this paper we consider the appointment of substitute decision-makers either by the person concerned while capable, or by someone on his behalf. Patients should certainly be able to record information and views to guide those making decisions for them as well as, or instead of, making anticipatory decisions.

The limits on anticipatory decision-making
3.22 Legislation in the United States and in Australia has been concerned solely with the use of advance directives to refuse treatment in cases of 'terminal illness'. This limitation may overlook the needs of many other patients who wish to exercise control over their medical treatment after they become incapacitated, such as those involved in accidents, and those who wish to express a consent rather than a refusal, or to choose one treatment rather than another. The Saskatchewan Law Reform Commission has proposed legislation which applies only to advance directives taking effect in a 'last illness', but it has been proposed in a number of other Canadian states [sc. Provinces] that patients should be enabled to give directions about all health care decisions taken on their behalf. We agree with the latter approach. No doubt, many decisions will be made to be applicable at the end of life, but we consider that anticipatory decision-making should be possible in any situation where the patient may be incapable of making his own decisions.
3.23 For the same reason, we propose that the scope of anticipatory decisions should not be confined to those who are permanently incapacitated. If it is possible to delay a decision until the patient is able to decide for himself then this should be done, but the patient should be able to exercise control over all the decisions made on his behalf while he is incapable, whether his incapacity is permanent or temporary.

3.24 We recognise that such an approach will generate its own problems. The BMA suggested that an advance directive refusing treatment which is futile, or which most people would reject, will often coincide with good medical practice, but that a mechanism should be available where the directive conflicts with widespread medical opinion. A capable adult patient has an absolute right to refuse medical treatment for reasons which are rational, irrational, unknown or non-existent, and it is possible that the common law right to make anticipatory decisions is just as broad. However, there may be a case for placing some limitations on the scope and effectiveness of such decisions, given that the patient will suffer the consequences only after it is too late for him to change his own mind.

3.25 The first possible limitation relates to the type of treatment which may be refused in such a document. Andrew Grubb has suggested that it would be contrary to public policy to require a doctor to 'abandon' a patient who has refused 'basic care', such as nursing care. Similar considerations may apply to prevent an incapacitated patient being left in great pain because of an earlier refusal of palliative care. In its paper, the BMA recommends that such medical care and pain relief should be given as would appear 'acceptable to the patient and appropriate to the circumstances'. We consider that the acceptability of 'basic care' and pain relief should be judged according to the patient's current needs and wishes (if his wishes can be discerned) without reference to his prior instructions. We would not expect many people to wish to make a directive refusing basic care or pain relief and we do not regard this as a significant infringement of the patient's rights of self-determination. We invite comment on the content of the category of 'basic care'.

3.26 Although some American legislation excludes nutrition and hydration from the category of treatments which can be refused, the BMA considered it should be possible to refuse artificial feeding in an advance directive. We share this view. Artificial feeding is a form of treatment which a patient should be entitled to refuse in an advance directive, and if such a directive is discovered after artificial feeding has been started it should be withdrawn. It should also be withdrawn if the circumstances to which the directive applies, such as persistent vegetative state, can only be reliably diagnosed after some time. It has been accepted by the House of Lords that artificial feeding can lawfully be withdrawn and Lord Keith referred explicitly to a person giving instructions that in certain circumstances he is not to be given medical care, including artificial feeding, designed to keep him alive. We would, however, see spoon-feeding as coming within the category of 'basic care'. We provisionally propose that:

4. An anticipatory decision should be regarded as ineffective to the extent that it purports to refuse pain relief or 'basic care', including nursing care and spoon-feeding.

3.27 Another possible limitation relates to the circumstances in which treatment might be refused. A capable individual may fail to appreciate the value which he might place on his life in a situation he imagines he would find intolerable when thinking about it in advance. For example, an advance directive might refuse all life-sustaining treatment, including anti-biotics, if the maker suffers a serious loss of cognitive function. In the event, the maker of the directive suffers a discrete neurological injury which renders him incapable of understanding information relevant to even the most simple treatments, but he is otherwise healthy and apparently quite happy. If he then develops a life-threatening pneumonia and his doctors follow the instructions given in the directive, the result will be the easily avoidable death of a happy and healthy individual. It is difficult to formulate an appropriate restriction to deal with cases such as this. One approach might be to provide that an anticipatory decision is ineffective if the incapacitated patient 'objects'. Safeguards are certainly required for such a patient, but the incapacitated patient who acquiesces to anything which is done (or not done) may also require protection. The situation described in this paragraph is just one example of the difficult cases which will inevitably arise, whether or not legislation is introduced. We consider that the most appropriate response would be to provide a forum to which the most troubling cases could be referred.

3.28 In cases of doubt or dispute, a judicial forum should be available to determine whether an anticipatory decision is 'clearly established' and 'applicable to the circumstances'. In *Re T*, Ward J was able, in the circumstances of that case, to construe an apparently unequivocal refusal of treatment as not extending to the extreme situation which subsequently arose. Lord Donaldson MR said that a decision may be intended to apply 'so long as there is an effective alternative' to a particular treatment. In the example of the healthy and happy incapacitated person, there might be evidence that the decision was intended to apply where the incapacity occurred in the course of a terminal illness involving distress and pain. The possibility of being incapacitated but healthy and happy, might not have been considered. We recognise the danger that the approach suggested in this paragraph might threaten the patient's right of self-determination if the category of situations to which the decision applies is restricted too much. A genuine attempt to identify the true intentions of the maker is essential. This might be assisted by consultation with the patient's relatives or medical treatment attorney if one has been appointed, or by discussion between the treatment provider and the patient in advance.

3.29 It would also be possible to give a judicial forum the power to override an anticipatory decision even if it was 'clearly established' and 'applicable in the circumstances'. This could either be a general power or could be limited to particular circumstances. For example, there might be a presumption that an anticipatory decision should be respected, but treatment could be authorised when the decision is found to be clearly contrary to the patient's best interests. We are not at present persuaded that there is any need for a power to override, as opposed to a power to determine the scope and validity of, a patient's anticipatory decision, but we invite views on this.

3.30 Legislation which has dealt with this question in other countries has limited the jurisdiction to override anticipatory decisions to specific categories of case. For example, recent legislation in Ontario provides that a person's 'wishes' may be overridden if the Consent and Capacity Review Board is satisfied that the incapable person would probably, if capable, give consent because the likely result of the treatment is significantly better than would have been anticipated in comparable circumstances at the time the decision was made. The Newfoundland Law Reform Commission, on the other hand, considered that it was unnecessary to provide any such explicit mechanism, since the duty to interpret the patient's instructions left enough scope for such considerations to be taken into account. For the same reason we do not propose any specific provision to cover those cases in which there have been advances in treatment which were not anticipated at the time the anticipatory decision was made.

3.31 Another situation in which it has been suggested that an anticipatory decision could be overridden is where a woman refused life-sustaining treatment during the course of a pregnancy. The BMA has argued that the requests of the woman have to be weighed against a moral duty to another human being and the Scottish Law Commission has argued that a terminally ill woman ought to be kept alive for 'longer than strictly necessary' if there is a reasonable chance of thereby saving her unborn child. There are dicta which could be construed as suggesting that a capable patient's current refusal may be overridden if a viable foetus is endangered. However, this is a highly controversial and difficult question which it is not necessary for us to explore here. Whatever the position in relation to a capable patient, we do not think that any greater restriction should be imposed upon any anticipatory decision of a pregnant woman.

Revocation

3.32 It will only be relevant to consider the terms of an anticipatory decision if its maker is incapable of taking the decision to which it relates. However, it is possible that a patient will have sufficient understanding to revoke an advance directive although he lacks the capacity to take the decision to which it relates. Some American legislation permits patients to revoke their advance directives even though they lack the capacity to do so. Our view, however, is that if a patient is found to be incapable of understanding in broad terms what revocation involves, even when given the benefit of the presumption of capacity, he should not be able to make an effective revocation. Since revocation is a legal transaction, rather than a decision whether to give or withhold consent to medical treatment, we consider that the appropriate test of capacity to revoke should be that proposed in Consultation Paper No. 128. Although the test of capacity proposed in that paper is the same as that proposed in this paper, our consultation exercise may suggest that there should be some differences.

3.33 To avoid problems of proof, the Manitoba and Newfoundland Law Reform Commissions considered that the oral revocation of health care directives should not be permitted. A revocation must be written and witnessed, or the directive must be destroyed with the intention of revoking it. The BMA recommended that directives which no longer represent the person's views should be destroyed rather than amended and we agree that the safest way to revoke an advance directive will be to destroy all copies of it. However it is important that patients should be able to change their minds with a minimum of formality. We propose that it should be possible to revoke orally at any time when the maker has the capacity to do so. We invite comment on any practical difficulties this may cause.

Automatic revocation after a fixed period

3.34 The BMA recommended that advance directives should be updated at regular intervals. Five years was suggested. It was said that documents which were unrevised after many years, despite changing circumstances, could only give the most general of indications of the patient's ultimate views. It is clearly desirable that the instructions in an advance directive should be regularly reviewed, but there is a danger that automatic revocation after a fixed period might frustrate the intentions of those making them. We propose that, unless the maker explicitly provides that it is to have limited duration, an unrevoked anticipatory decision should operate for as long as it is applicable. We provisionally propose that:

5. An anticipatory decision may be revoked orally or in writing at any time when the maker has the capacity (according to the test proposed in Part III of Consultation Paper No 128) to do so. There should be no automatic revocation after a period of time.

The protection of treatment providers
3.35 It might be useful to clarify the liability of treatment providers who act in accordance with an anticipatory decision. Under the current law, we consider it unlikely that liability would be incurred for acts reasonably performed in accordance with a patient's valid anticipatory decision. Legitimate doubt may remain, however, in relation to cases where an anticipatory decision is subsequently shown to have been invalid. An example would be where it is later shown that the decision had already been revoked before it was acted on. We provisionally propose that:

6. A treatment provider who acts in accordance with an apparently valid and continuing anticipatory decision should only be liable to any civil or criminal proceedings if he or she does so in bad faith or without reasonable care.

The protection of incapacitated patients
3.36 The effect of concealing, destroying or altering an advance directive, or of producing a document purporting to represent another person's anticipatory decision, might be extremely serious. A suitably drafted offence is needed to discourage such activity. We therefore provisionally propose that:

7. It should be an offence to falsify or forge an advance directive; or to conceal, alter or destroy a directive without the authority of its maker. These offences should apply to a written revocation of an advance directive as they do to the directive itself.

It could be thought, of course, that since the decision in *Re T*, legislation on living wills is unnecessary and consequently the detailed analysis of the Law Commission is gratuitous. You will have noticed, however, that the Law Commission referred to the 'uncertainty of the law', a view we share in the light of the less than clear comments in *Re T* of Lord Donaldson MR.

(ii) ENDURING POWERS OF ATTORNEY

The respective advantages and disadvantages of living wills and enduring powers of attorney were examined by the Working Party of King's College, London in 1988 with a view to establishing how the goal of patient autonomy could be best achieved.

The Living Will: Consent to Treatment at the End of Life (*op cit*)

(a) *Drafting problems*
Existing examples of living will legislation seem to suffer from unsatisfactory drafting. The problem is to strike a balance between terms which are too general and those which are too specific. If the declaration is too general, it might fail to achieve the goal of patient autonomy because a large measure of discretion will inevitably be left with the doctor. If it is too specific, it may not deal with the particular problem which arises. While the drafting could be improved, it seems inevitable that the durable power of attorney must be more advantageous in this respect. Whatever criterion governs the agent's decision-making ... the point is that he will make his decision in the light of the actual circumstances at the time the question arises. Hence a durable power of attorney, or a durable power combined with a living will declaration, must be preferable in this respect to a living will alone.

(b) *Non-medical considerations*

Of less importance, but not entirely without significance, is the question whether non-medical matters can play any part in the decision process. The timing of death can have financial consequences, for example, in the tax context. A living will is unlikely to permit such considerations to be taken into account. This raises the issue of whether the doctor can take such matters into consideration in a case involving no living will or durable power of attorney. For example, would the doctor be acting in the patient's interests if he kept him alive until a particular date for tax reasons, or until a relative gets married or arrives from Australia? To the extent that the doctor could take non-medical matters into account, then a person acting under a power of attorney should also be entitled to do so. In the absence of express provision, however, the point remains unclear. This is a matter which would affect only a small minority of patients, but some consideration should be given to the problem.

(c) *Abuse*

There is always a possibility that a person's free will may be overborne by the exercise of undue influence or pressure. This is so whatever the nature of the transaction, whether it is a living will, an ordinary will, a durable power of attorney or any other power of attorney. As far as contracts, gifts and other dispositions are concerned, the law deals with the problem by allowing the transaction to be set aside in certain circumstances. The requirements of writing, signature and witnesses are directed to minimising the possibility of undue pressure, and are a feature of wills, living wills and powers of attorney. It is not thought that a durable power of attorney is either more or less inherently liable to abuse in this respect.

However, one possible disadvantage of the durable power of attorney is that there is a possibility of abuse at the later stage, when the decision is made. It is not suggested that the agent is likely to act deliberately in bad faith. (If he did, some review procedure might be necessary, as discussed below.) The person in whose favour the power of attorney is executed is likely to be close to the patient. It is not impossible that he might be subconsciously influenced by improper considerations, for example, the prospect of release from the burden of caring for the patient at home. Persons who have an interest (financial or otherwise) in the patient's fate might be prevented from acting as witnesses, but it would be difficult to exclude them from the power of decision-making under a durable power of attorney, because an 'interested party' is the very person most patients would choose.

(d) *Procedure*

It is likely that the procedure for creating a durable power of attorney (see, for example, the Enduring Powers of Attorney Act 1985) will be more cumbersome than the procedure for executing a living will declaration. This is inevitable if the necessary safeguards are to be incorporated. A degree of formality will, however, be required in both cases.

(e) *Lack of suitable agent*

It may be that some people, for example, childless widows or widowers, would have difficulty in finding a trusted person to act. A living will would obviously be more advantageous in such a case, but this does not detract from the advantages of a durable power of attorney for those who do have a trusted friend or relative. One candidate could be a solicitor, but it may be doubted that such a person would have sufficiently intimate knowledge of the patient. For those with limited access to professional legal advice and with no suitable agent, the relative simplicity of a living will may have greater appeal.

(f) *Resources*

The question of resources . . . should not be regarded as a relevant consideration in deciding whether to choose living wills or durable powers of attorney. In any case it is thought that there is little distinction between them in the resources that are likely to be saved.

The above survey indicates that each option has its own advantages and disadvantages, so that it would not desirable to recommend living will legislation to the exclusion of durable power of attorney legislation or vice versa. The remainder of this section deals with the question whether the two options should be separately available, or used in combination, or both.

The advantages of the combined document are twofold:
(i)   any uncertainty resulting from the drafting of the living will declaration (see (a) above) can be resolved by allowing the chosen agent, as opposed to the doctor, to make the decision;

(ii) the statement of wishes contained in the living will declaration provides guidance to the agent (assuming that he is to be guided by the patient's previously expressed wishes, as discussed below).

There is, however, a fundamental problem. If it is recommended that a living will declaration should not be mandatory, ie should take the form of a *request* only, then it is difficult to see what scope there could be for a durable power of attorney. The notion of an agent who has no legal power is unacceptable. It would therefore be impossible to have a combined instrument, part of which was not legally enforceable (the living will) and part of which was (the durable power). Even if the durable power were to be a separate instrument instead of part of the living will instrument, the position would still be unsatisfactory. If the preferred view is that there should be no legal force in a living will, then it should not be possible to achieve legal enforceability via a different route. The conclusion is that a durable power of attorney, either alone or in combination with a living will, can only be recommended, indeed, only makes sense, if the living will is to be legally binding. It is a matter of balancing, on the one hand, the reasons why a living will should be directory rather than mandatory with, on the other hand, the advantages which a durable power has over a living will, which would be lost if the living will is not to be legally binding.

If, in view of the above, it is concluded that the living will should be legally binding, further problems remain, in particular where a combined instrument is not used. It is possible to imagine a person creating more than one living will, or more than one durable power of attorney. The likely solution is, by analogy with the law of wills, that the later document would revoke the earlier either expressly or to the extent of any inconsistency. (See, for example, the Californian Durable Power of Attorney for Health Care Act 1983, which provides that a valid durable power of attorney for health care revokes any prior durable power of attorney for health care.) If a person executed a living will *and* a power of attorney in separate instruments, legislation should clarify whether the later document should revoke the earlier (assuming the order of execution is known), or whether the power of attorney should be construed as designed for the implementation of the living will.

Terms of a durable power of attorney

(a) *Drafting*
As with a living will, the problem is whether the instrument creating the power of attorney should attempt to be specific as to the types of treatment which the agent is empowered to sanction or refuse. Minimum requirements are that the instrument, or at any rate the legislation, should make clear what is the 'triggering event' and what are the criteria for decision-making. These two aspects are discussed below. Of course, the wording of the instrument will vary according to whether the durable power is created in isolation or in combination with a living will declaration. . . .

The conclusion of the President's Commission Report was that 'by combining a proxy directive with specific instructions, an individual could control both the content and the process of decision-making about care in case of incapacity' (pp. 155-160). Although no specific form of document is included, the Model Act attempts to put this into effect by 'permitting the declarant both to define what interventions are refused, and to name an authorised individual to make decisions consistent with the declarant's desires as expressed in the declaration'. Thus Section 1 defines 'competent person', 'medical procedure or treatment' and 'palliative care', and then Section 5 gives the declarant the right to appoint a person to order the administration, withholding or withdrawing of the defined treatments. The trigger is incompetence, and the criterion is 'substituted judgment' (explained below). It seems that these provisions meet the minimum standards of certainty. . . .

Turning to the Californian statute, the Durable Power of Attorney for Health Care 1983, the Act defines 'health care', the 'trigger' is the principal's inability to give informed consent in respect to the particular decision, and the criterion is 'substituted judgment' unless the desires of the principal are unknown, in which case it is 'best interests' (explained below). No particular form of wording is prescribed, except that printed forms sold for use by a person who does not have legal advice must contain a warning notice specified in the Act, and the Act specifies a form of wording which must (in substance) be adopted in the declaration of the witnesses or the notary public, as the case may be.

(b) *The 'triggering event'*
The basic question is whether the durable power of attorney should come into operation merely upon the supervening incompetence of the principal, or whether some further event should be required, for example terminal illness or some other kind of illness. . . .

For present purposes, suffice it to say that the definitions adopted for durable powers of attorney should be the same as those which apply in living wills and to any code of practice dealing with the treatment of competent and incompetent persons.

(c) *The criterion for decision-making by the agent*

This is a matter of choosing between 'substituted judgment' and 'best interests'. The 'substituted judgment' criterion is where the agent's decision is based on the known wishes of the principal, ie the agent makes the decision which the principal would have made but for his incompetence. The 'best interests' test is different, as that requires a decision which, objectively, is deemed to be in the best interests of the principal, even if it is not the decision he would have made.

As far as the treatment of incompetents generally is concerned, it may be that 'best interests' is the preferable test because if a person has never been competent, it is a matter of speculation as to what he or she would have decided if competent [See, for example, discussion of this point in the Canadian case of *Re Eve* [1986] considered in Chapter 4.] However, in the present case we are dealing with people who have been competent, and who are likely to have made their wishes known. For this reason the 'substituted judgment' test is to be preferred. This was the view of the President's Commission Report:

> The Commission believes that, when possible, decision-making for incapacitated patients should be guided by the principle of substituted judgment, which promotes the underlying values of self-determination and well-being better than the best interests standard does. When a patient's likely decision is unknown, however, a surrogate decision-maker should use the best interests standard and choose a course that will promote the patient's well-being as it would probably be conceived by a reasonable person in the patient's circumstances. On certain points, of course, no consensus may exist about what most people would prefer, and surrogates retain discretion to choose among a range of acceptable choices (p 136).

Substituted judgment is the standard applied in the Concern for Dying Model Act and in the Californian Durable Power of Attorney for Health Care Act 1983 which provides that the attorney has a duty to act 'consistent with the desires of the principal as expressed in the durable power of attorney or otherwise made known to the attorney in fact at any time or, if the principal's desires are unknown, to act in the best interests of the principal'.

When the durable power is combined with a living will declaration, the arguments for applying the substituted judgment test are even stronger. However one consequence of adopting this criterion might be that there would be no scope for taking non-medical matters into account (see above). Even if the best interests standards were adopted, it is unclear whether such matters could be considered in the absence of express statutory provision.

Practical and procedural matters

The practical and procedural matters already discussed . . . in relation to living wills, apply equally or very similarly to durable powers of attorney. These will not be dealt with again. However, there are a number of additional matters which are relevant to durable powers of attorney alone.

(a) *Capacity of agent*

As with the principal, the agent should be a competent adult, the test for competence presumably being the same in each case. However in a recent judgment relating to the Enduring Powers of Attorney Act 1985 [*Re K; Re F* [1988] 1 All ER 358], the test of competence applied to the principal was a low one, and lower than that required of the agent. Another question is whether it should be possible to have joint agents in order to provide a further safeguard. In the Law Commission report on the Incapacitated Principal, the notion that joint attorneys should be *compulsory* was rejected. The Enduring Powers of Attorney Act 1985 does, however, *permit* joint agents. It is suggested that this is too cumbersome and that only one should be appointed.

(b) *Witnesses*

Clearly the person in whose favour the power of attorney is executed should not be a witness. Reference has already been made . . . to the difficulty that would arise if potential beneficiaries were to be excluded not merely from witnessing but from acting under the power of attorney.

(c) *Forms*
It has already been suggested that the durable power of attorney must be in writing, signed and witnessed. . . . It does not seem necessary that the document should be in prescribed form. Nor does it seem necessary that there should be a requirement of prior discussion with an informed official, though this would usually be desirable. However, there may be a case for requiring the document to contain explanatory information, for the protection of the principal, in the case where printed power of attorney forms are available to the public at large (see the 1983 Californian Act). It should be noted that the Enduring Powers of Attorney Act 1985 requires both a prescribed form and the incorporation of explanatory information.

(d) *Revocation*
The main issues have already been discussed . . . and the following are additional points, relevant to durable powers of attorney.

The execution of a durable power should revoke any earlier power, and dissolution of marriage should revoke the appointment of the spouse as agent. This is analogous to the law of wills and is also found in the Californian Act of 1983.

In considering whether the principal should be entitled to revoke if he becomes incompetent, the President's Commission Report took the view that he should have power to override the agent as far as life-sustaining treatment is concerned. The Model Act (Section 6) permits revocation without specifying any requirements for continuing capacity.

The Californian Act of 1983 seems to achieve a compromise. On the one hand it provides that the principal can only revoke if he still has capacity (although there is a rebuttable presumption that he does). On the other hand, it further provides that the agent has no authority to consent to or refuse health care necessary to keep the principal alive if the principal objects. In such a case, the matter is governed by the law that would apply if there were no durable power of attorney. This seems to be the most satisfactory solution.

(e) *Limits on the agent's power*
The question arises whether certain matters should be excluded from the agent's sphere of authority. This could be done by limiting his role to 'life-sustaining procedures' (which must be defined) . . . or in some other way. There is much to be said for the provision in the Model Act that he cannot authorise the withholding of palliative care unless the instrument expressly so provides. It is unlikely, however, that there is any justification here for excluding such matters as are excluded in the Californian Act of 1983, for example psychosurgery. The agent should not have any power to make decisions, including consent to abortion, if the principal is pregnant.

There must also be provision for allowing the doctor to give emergency treatment without consulting the agent. (See the Californian Act 1983).

(f) *Delegation by the agent*
If the agent is temporarily or permanently unable or unwilling to act (as to which, see also Disclaimer, below) the question arises as to whether he can delegate. The President's Commission Report (p 151) suggests such a possibility. It is thought, however, that this is undesirable. The principal should be able to choose a 'reserve' . . . but if he does not, the position will be as if no durable power existed if the agent cannot or will not act.

(g) *Disclaimer by the agent*
It would seem impossible to provide that the agent is to be compelled to make a decision. When the time comes he may not wish to take the responsibility. The Californian Act 1983 does not seem to provide for this, but the Enduring Powers of Attorney Act 1985 allows disclaimer by permitting the agent to give notice to the principal while the latter is still competent, or, if he is not, by notice to the court. Disclaimer by notice to the competent principal seems unobjectionable, but a requirement of notice to the court in the present context seems too cumbersome. It is suggested that if the agent declines to act and no reserve has been designated by the principal, then the position will be as if no durable power existed.

(h) *Can the agent's decision be challenged?*
What happens if there is a suspicion of bad faith, or an apparently unreasonable interpretation of the principal's wishes? The President's Commission Report (pp. 152-3) suggests the possibility of an independent review, either 'intrainstitutional' or by way of court proceedings. Certainly the principal's interests must be safeguarded, but the notion of review by the court seems cumbersome. The statute could perhaps provide for review by a body such as the hospital ethics committee, on specified grounds, for example where the agent has not applied the correct criterion . . . to his decision.

(i) *Medical records*
Should the agent be entitled to see the principal's records? He must have the necessary information in order to make a decision, but, on the other hand, the principal's privacy must be respected. Taking the latter point into account, the President's Commission Report suggests that it may be advisable to limit the agent's access to information needed for the particular decision in question. This may not work, since the agent may not know what is relevant until he has looked at everything. The Californian Act 1983 provides that the agent has the same right as the principal to receive information, unless the right is limited in the instrument creating the power. The Model Act is on similar lines. It is thought that this is preferable to the suggestion of the President's Commission.

(j) *Notice to relatives*
The Enduring Powers of Attorney Act 1985 provides that the agent is obliged to notify various relatives when he applies to register the power (which he must do when he believes the principal is or is becoming incompetent). The relatives then have a chance to object on certain grounds, for example that the power is invalid, or the principal is not incompetent. This obviously provides an extra safeguard, but would probably be too cumbersome in the present context, especially if provision is made for a review procedure (see (h) above).

The Law Commission in its Consultation Paper No 129 (*op cit*) concluded its review of enduring powers of attorney by recommending legislation to create what it called 'medical treatment attorneys'.

Mentally Incapacitated Adults and Decision-Making: Medical Treatment and Research (1992) (*op cit*)

5.1 The Scottish Law Commission has proposed that it should be possible to appoint an attorney with power to consent and withhold consent to medical treatment and to require treatment to be discontinued. However, it was considered that binding directions either by the patient or his attorney downgrades the status of doctors, because their 'professional judgments and contributions are ignored and they become mere technicians carrying out the direction of attorneys'. Therefore it was said that doctors should only be required to give due weight to the views expressed and should not be bound by them.
5.2 We do not consider that the requirement to obtain the consent of a patient with the capacity to give it downgrades the doctor's status or reduces him to a mere technician and we have difficulty seeing how the situation would be significantly different where the consent is sought of an attorney acting on the person's behalf. A person with the authority to consent is not a 'sole decision-maker' because, as Lord Donaldson has pointed out, no one can dictate the treatment to be given. Doctors can recommend one treatment in preference to another, while refusing to adopt some other treatment. The person who is authorised to consent can refuse to consent to any treatment offered, but cannot insist on a treatment which the doctor is not prepared to administer. The inevitable and desirable result, said Lord Donaldson MR, is that a choice of treatment is in some measure a joint decision of the doctors and the person authorised to consent.
5.3 Medical treatment attorneys may be appointed in a number of American and Australian States and Canadian provinces and have been proposed in a number of others. Significant support for their introduction has been reported amongst one group of patients, and there was considerable support for their introduction amongst the respondents to Consultation Paper No. 119. We consider that an attorney should be able to consent to or refuse treatment on an incapacitated person's behalf if he has been appointed for that purpose. We provisionally propose that:

1. It should be possible for a person to execute an enduring power of attorney giving another person the authority to give or refuse consent on his or her behalf to some or all medical treatment in relation to which the donor has become incapacitated.

5.4 We consider that, as far as possible, similar provisions should apply to the appointment of medical treatment attorneys as to appointing a person to make personal welfare and financial decisions.

Procedures and Safeguards

The effect of incapacity
5.5 Enduring powers of attorney made under the current law in relation to 'property and affairs' may be, and usually are, effective from the date of execution. In Consultation Paper No. 128 we provisionally proposed that the authority of a personal care attorney should not depend upon the absence of capacity on the part of the donor, since such a stipulation would impose a heavy burden of assessment on the attorney. There are different considerations in relation to medical treatment where there is already an obligation to assess the patient's capacity to give consent before carrying out any treatment. If the person is found to have the capacity to make his own decision, there would be no reason to involve the attorney. Therefore we provisionally propose that:

2. The authority of an attorney in relation to a particular medical treatment decision should operate only where the donor is incapacitated in relation to that decision according to the definition of incapacity proposed in Part II of this paper.

5.6 It follows from this proposal that the donor might have capacity to make certain decisions, at the same time as the attorney has authority to make others in relation to which the donor is incapacitated. It is also possible that a person might be incapacitated in relation to a treatment decision but will have the capacity to appoint a medical treatment attorney to make the decision on his behalf, or to revoke an existing power. Since the giving and revoking of a power is a legal transaction and not a decision about whether to accept or reject medical treatment the test of capacity for this purpose should be that proposed in Part III of Consultation Paper No. 128. We provisionally propose that:

3. A donor under a medical treatment EPA should always retain the power to do any act, including revoking the EPA, in relation to which he or she has capacity at the time. The definition of incapacity for the purpose of the execution or revocation of a medical treatment EPA should be the same as that proposed in Part III of Consultation Paper No 128.

A standard form
5.7 The working party which produced the *Living Will* report proposed that a prescribed form was desirable for the making of anticipatory decisions. This was not thought necessary for 'durable powers of attorney for health care', but it was said that there might be a case for requiring explanatory notes to be included. Partly because of the wide range of possible forms and content we have not proposed a prescribed form for anticipatory decision-making, but there would be less difficulty with requiring the use of a standard form for the appointment of a medical treatment attorney. Attorneys will be in a position of considerable responsibility and an appropriate standard form might ensure that the donor understands the possible consequences of the appointment. A standard form might list particular treatments or situations in relation to which the donor must decide whether the attorney is to have authority. For example, an attorney should not have authority to consent to treatment for mental disorder, or involvement in medical research, unless such authority were granted explicitly. Refusal of life-saving treatment, either in general or in relation to particular situations such as terminal illness, would be another example. We invite views on the content of a standard form.

Execution requirements
5.8 Confirmation of the donor's capacity at the time of execution might be a useful safeguard. Certification of this by a solicitor and a registered medical practitioner was suggested in Consultation Paper No. 128. We invite comments on a similar procedure for medical treatment powers. We provisionally propose that:

4. The donor's capacity to execute a medical treatment EPA should be certified by a solicitor and a registered medical practitioner at the time of execution.

Notification requirements

5.9 In Consultation Paper No 128 we proposed that a donor should name at least two people who should be notified of the execution of the power, and whose acknowledgement is required before the attorney is permitted to act. It may be that such a requirement would be cumbersome in the context of medical treatment powers. Notification which does not take place until the donor becomes incapacitated might take too long. The donor may become incapacitated suddenly, in an accident for example, and treatment decisions might have to be made urgently. A requirement of notification at the time of execution might require the donor to reveal information which he prefers to keep private. Nevertheless, notification might be a useful safeguard and we provisionally propose that:

5. A donor should name in a medical treatment EPA the two (or more) persons who are to be notified of its execution and no action should be taken by an attorney under the power unless and until an acknowledgement has been received from the persons so named.

Assessment by prior appointees

5.10 The donor might wish the attorney's authority to depend upon an independent finding of incapacity, or some other event, and we see no reason why the power should not contain a requirement to this effect. Therefore we provisionally propose that:

6. The donor should be permitted to name someone to confirm his or her incapacity, or to establish any other ground upon which the authority of the attorney depends.

Registration

5.11 In Consultation Paper No 128 we proposed that there should be no requirement that financial or personal powers should be registered when the attorney believes the donor is or is becoming incapacitated. We can see no greater justification for such a requirement in the context of medical treatment powers. Therefore we provisionally propose that:

7. There should be no requirement that a medical treatment EPA be registered with the Court of Protection, or any other authority, when the attorney believes the donor to be or be becoming incapacitated.

Attorneys

5.12 As with attorneys for personal care, we consider that medical treatment attorneys should be individuals. We provisionally propose that:

8. Only individuals should be capable of being appointed medical treatment attorneys.

5.13 It might be valuable to appoint more than one attorney, either as a safeguard so that one may be a check on the other, or so that an attorney is more likely to be available if a decision is required urgently. Disagreement between joint attorneys would result in a failure to either give or refuse consent to the treatment in question so that the treatment could be provided in accordance with the statutory authority. Where joint and several attorneys disagree, and the power does not provide for priority between them, the treatment provider would be entitled to rely on the consent of one. In either case the dispute could be referred to the judicial forum. We considered that it should be possible to appoint alternate personal or financial attorneys, and we consider that it should be possible to appoint alternate medical treatment attorneys also. We provisionally propose that:

9. It should be possible for more than one person to be appointed as medical treatment attorneys, whether to act jointly or jointly and severally. It should also be possible for alternate attorneys to be appointed to act in the event of original attorneys ceasing to act.

5.14 We do not consider that there would be any value in being able to appoint any public official in an official capacity as a treatment attorney. Such a person would not be able to contribute any knowledge of the incapacitated person's circumstances or values to the considerations of the medical team. We therefore provisionally propose that:

10. It should not be possible to appoint public officials in their official capacity as medical treatment attorneys.

5.15 We invite views on whether there should be any other restrictions on appointment as a medical treatment attorney.

The attorney's powers and duties

5.16 We do not propose that a duty to act should be imposed on medical treatment attorneys by statute. If an attorney chooses to give or refuse consent on the donor's behalf we consider that there should be a duty to do so in the donor's best interests considering the same factors as other people involved in the decision. Although the BMA has suggested that the person appointed should apply a substituted judgment approach, acting as a sympathetic interpreter of the patient's own values, rather than attempting to judge the patient's best interest, we prefer to treat the patient's values as a factor to be considered when deciding what his best interests require. The attorney and the treatment provider will have different contributions to make to the decision, based upon their knowledge of different aspects of the person concerned, but we do not see an advantage to requiring each to apply a different standard. Therefore we provisionally propose that:

11. A medical treatment attorney should be under no duty to express a view on behalf of the donor. If an attorney chooses to give or refuse consent to a particular medical treatment, he or she must do so in the best interests of the incapacitated person, taking into account:

(1) the ascertainable past and present wishes and feelings (considered in the light of his or her understanding at the time) of the incapacitated person;

(2) whether there is an alternative to the proposed treatment, and in particular whether there is an alternative which is more conservative or which is less intrusive or restrictive;

(3) the factors which the incapacitated person might be expected to consider if able to do so, including the likely effect of the treatment on the person's life expectancy, health, happiness, freedom and dignity, but not the interests of other people except to the extent that they have a bearing on the incapacitated person's individual interests.

5.17 We do not consider that it is necessary to require the attorney to consult any other person who may have been appointed attorney or manager, in relation to the incapacitated person's financial or personal affairs. Nevertheless we invite views on this.

5.18 A person proposing to provide a treatment in relation to which a medical treatment attorney has been granted authority to give or refuse consent would be under a duty to consult with the attorney, and to give the attorney the opportunity to give or refuse consent. There would be no duty to consult the incapacitated person's 'nearest relative'. We provisionally propose that:

12. If a medical treatment attorney has been appointed, a person proposing to provide a treatment within the scope of the attorney's authority should be under a duty to give the attorney the opportunity to give or refuse consent on the incapacitated person's behalf. There should be no duty to consult the incapacitated person's 'nearest relative' in relation to treatments within the scope of the attorney's authority.

Access to medical records

5.19 We consider that a medical treatment attorney should have the right to make an application for access to the incapacitated person's health care records under the Access to Health Care Records Act 1990 [sc] and under the Data Protection Act 1984, unless the donor specifically excludes this from the powers which the attorney is to have. We therefore provisionally propose that:

13. A medical treatment attorney should be able to exercise the rights of the incapacitated person to apply for access to health records under the Access to Health Care Records Act 1990 and the Data Protection Act 1984, unless this possibility is specifically excluded in the power.

Limitations on the authority of an attorney
5.20 We consider that similar restrictions should apply to the authority of medical treatment attorneys as those proposed in relation to medical treatment proxies appointed by the judicial forum. Therefore we provisionally propose that:

14. A medical treatment attorney should have no authority to refuse pain relief or 'basic care', including nursing care and spoon-feeding.
15. A medical treatment attorney should have no authority to consent to the carrying out of any treatment contrary to a prohibition by the judicial forum, or, unless the power provides otherwise, a valid anticipatory refusal by the donor.
16. A medical treatment attorney should have no authority to consent to the taking of any step for which the approval of the judicial forum or some other person is required (see Part VI).
17. A medical treatment attorney should have no authority to consent to the carrying out of any treatment to which the incapacitated person objects.

The powers of the judicial forum
5.21 In Consultation Paper No. 128, we proposed that the judicial forum should have wide powers to give effect to the intentions of the donor of an EPA for financial affairs or personal care. We invite comment on whether such powers might also be valuable in relation to medical treatment EPAs. We provisionally propose that:

18. The judicial forum should have power to give effect to the wishes of the donor by curing technical defects in the appointment of a medical treatment attorney, or by appointing a replacement for an attorney who is unable or unwilling to act, and, provided that the donor has so directed, by modifying or extending the scope of the powers granted.

Supervision and review of medical treatment EPAs
5.22 The BMA has said that decisions made by a person nominated by the patient have a 'significant determinative value' but that it should be possible to challenge, and if necessary displace, a substitute decision-maker whose actions are 'mischievous'. In the Alberta proposals any interested person may apply to the court to have the decision of an attorney reviewed, and the attorney's authority may be rescinded if the decision is 'unreasonable' having regard to the decision-making criteria. In the Manitoba and Newfoundland proposals it is necessary for the court to be satisfied that an attorney is acting in bad faith or contrary to the known wishes of the patient and in Newfoundland there is an additional ground where the attorney's interpretation of the patient's wishes does not have any 'rational foundation'. These grounds restrict a court's ability to substitute its view for that of the attorney who is assumed to be in the best position to decide for the patient. However, in Victoria, legislation allows any concerned person to apply to the Guardianship and Administration Board if the attorney is not acting in the patient's best interests. We propose that, as in relation to other disputes about an incapacitated patient's medical treatment, the patient's best interests should determine the issue. However in determining whether the proxy is acting in the patient's best interests the patient's views and reasons for choosing the attorney will have to be considered and should be accorded considerable significance. We provisionally propose that:

19. The judicial forum should have wide powers to revoke the appointment of an unsuitable medical treatment attorney, and to substitute its own decision for the decision of a medical treatment attorney who is not acting in the best interests of the incapacitated person.

You will recall the Law Commission's reference in the earlier extract concerning 'anticipatory decisions' to the 'living will' prepared by the Terrence Higgins Trust and the Centre of Medical Law and Ethics at King's College, London. This advance directive is, in fact, a model based upon the hybrid approach which we have seen emerging in North America. Its terms are as follows.

LIVING WILL
DECLARATION

This is an important document. Before completing it, please read the accompanying Explanatory Notes. We recommend that you discuss your Living Will with a doctor, but you do not have to.

YOUR NAME AND ADDRESS

I, [name]

of [address]

make this LIVING WILL to state my wishes in case I become unable to communicate, and cannot take part in decisions about my medical care.

If you consult a doctor about the Living Will (whether before or after you fill it in), please complete this section.

I have discussed this Living Will with the following doctor—

Name of doctor:

Contact address for doctor:

Contact telephone number for doctor:

LIVING WILL
ADVANCE DIRECTIVES

I – MEDICAL TREATMENT IN GENERAL

Three possible health conditions are described below.

For each of the three, either choose "A" or "B" by ticking the appropriate box, or leave both boxes blank if you have no preference. The choice between "A" and "B" is exactly the same in each case.

Treat each case separately. You do not have to make the same choice for each one.

I DECLARE that my wishes concerning medical treatment are as follows:

CASE 1 — Physical Illness

If—

■ I have a physical illness from which there is no likelihood of recovery, *and*
■ it is so serious that my life is nearing its end: ✓

   A. I wish to be kept alive for as long as reasonably possible using whatever forms of medical treatment are available.   ☐

   B. I do not wish to be kept alive by medical treatment. I wish medical treatment to be limited to keeping me comfortable and free from pain.   ☐

CASE 2 — Permanent Mental Impairment

If—

■ my medical function become permanently impaired with no likelihood of improvement, *and*
■ the impairment is so severe that I do not understand what is happening to me, *and*
■ I have a physical illness:

   A. I wish to be kept alive for as long as reasonably possible using whatever forms of medical treatment are available.   ☐

   B. I do not wish to be kept alive by medical treatment. I wish medical treatment to be limited to keeping me comfortable and free from pain.   ☐

CASE 3 — Permanent Unconsciousness

If—

■ I become permanently unconscious with no likelihood of regaining consciousness:

   A. I wish to be kept alive for as long as reasonably possible using whatever forms of medical treatment are available.   ☐

   B. I do not wish to be kept alive by medical treatment. I wish medical treatment to be limited to keeping me comfortable and free from pain.   ☐

LIVING WILL
ADVANCE DIRECTIVES

II – PARTICULAR TREATMENTS OR INVESTIGATIONS

If you have any wishes about particular medical treatments or investigations, you can record them here. You should consult a doctor before writing anything in this space.

I have the following wishes about particular medical treatments or investigations:

III – PRESENCE OF FRIEND OR RELATIVE

You can complete this section if you want wishes you have expressed above to be temporarily disregarded while attempts are made to enable a particular person to be with you. Please note, however, that it may not be possible to contact the person you name, or for him or her to arrive in time.

I wish to be kept alive for as long as is reasonable to enable the following person(s) to be with me before I die, even if this means temporarily disregarding the wishes I have stated earlier in this form—

Name:

Address:

Telephone numbers: (day)   **(evening)**

If you fill in a name in this section, but the wishes you have stated above in section II — *Particular Treatments or Investigations* are so important to you that you do not want them to be disregarded even temporarily, tick this box. This option is fully explained in the notes to this form.

LIVING WILL
HEALTH CARE PROXY

I APPOINT the following person—   **Name:**

Address:

Telephone numbers: (day)   **(evening)**

to take part in decisions about my medical care on my behalf, and to represent my views about them, if I am unable to do so. I wish him or her to be consulted about and involved in those decisions and I wish those caring for me to respect the views he or she expresses on my behalf.

**THIS DOCUMENT REMAINS EFFECTIVE UNTIL I MAKE CLEAR
THAT MY WISHES HAVE CHANGED**

SIGNATURES

Sign and date the form here in the presence of a witness.

Date:

Signature:

IN THE PRESENCE OF—

The witness must sign here after you have signed, and should then print his or her name and address in the spaces provided. Please consult the notes to this form to see who should not be a witness.

Signature of witness:

Name:

Address:

Before we leave the problem of decision-making in the case of incompetent patients we should, perhaps, notice one development rejected by the Law Commission but which has found favour in North America. You will recall we referred earlier to the 'fourth generation' of statutes in North America empowering family members to make decisions on behalf of the incompetent patient. These statutes allow family members to make decisions when the patient has not made an anticipatory decision nor created an enduring power of attorney. In other words, family members are allowed to act as proxies in default of the patient's exercising any choice.

Examples of such legislation are the Ontario Consent to Treatment Act 1992 and the proposed Health Care Instructions Act in Alberta. Commenting on this approach, the Law Commission in its Consultation Paper No 129 (*op cit*) stated:

> 3.68 A few respondents supported the introduction of a duty to seek the consent of relatives or others caring for an incapacitated patient. Recent legislation in Ontario provides that consent may be given or refused by the first person from a list of relatives, who is at least 16 and is available, capable and willing to give or refuse consent. The list includes: the patient's spouse or partner; child; parent; brother or sister; and any other relative.
> 3.69 The difficulty with such schemes is that no statutory list will ever identify the most appropriate relative in every case. While many people might trust their spouses to make decisions for them, fewer will have the same confidence in their nephews. The fact that a person is the patient's next of kin may not be enough if there has been no contact with the patient for twenty years. In the proposals in Alberta, relatives would not have authority to make health care decisions on the incapacitated person's behalf unless they have had personal contact with the patient at some time during the preceding twelve months. Under legislation in New South Wales, except in an emergency the consent of the 'person responsible' is required for all medical treatment other than treatments such as sterilisation which require the consent of the Guardianship Board. The person responsible is the patient's spouse, or if there is no spouse, the person who has care of the patient, unless the patient lives in institutional care, in which case it is the person who cared for him immediately before the admission.
> 3.70 We are not at present persuaded that there is a need to introduce a scheme which gives relatives or carers an automatic authority to consent to, and also to refuse, medical treatment on behalf of an incapacitated person. Although one respondent argued that relatives might only be provided with sufficient information if a treatment provider was required to seek their consent, we believe that an appropriately formulated duty to consult relatives would be a better response to this problem. In New South Wales it has been suggested that incapacitated patients may sometimes not receive treatment because of the formalities required to obtain the consent of the person responsible. The President of the Victorian Guardianship and Administration Board has suggested that if someone automatically has the legal authority to consent it is too easy for doctors just to accept that person's consent without making a proper assessment of the risks involved in a proposed treatment. In Consultation Paper No. 128 we rejected an automatic authority for relatives, and we also do so in the context of medical treatment. The limited authority which we proposed for those who have care of an incapacitated person was intended to be no more than was required to allow the incapacitated person to be appropriately cared for. We do not believe that the interests of the incapacitated person require this to include an authority to give or refuse consent to medical treatment. Therefore we provisionally propose that:
>
> **There should be no duty to obtain the consent of another person to the medical treatment of an incapacitated person simply on the basis of a family relationship.**

Chapter 18

Death

Introduction

Christopher Pallis, *ABC of Brain Stem Death* (1983) (pp 1-4)

Reappraising death

People have been alarmed for centuries at the prospect of being declared dead when they were still living. There was generalised anxiety about the subject 140 years ago, after Edgar Allan Poe had published various short stories, such as *Premature Burial*, in which people had been interred alive. Towards the end of the last century Count Karnice-Karnicki of Berlin patented a coffin of a particular type. If the 'corpse' regained consciousness after burial he or she could summon help from the surface by a system of flags and bells. Recent controversies have revived this longstanding fear of premature or mistaken diagnosis of death.

The need to reappraise death

A dead brain in a body whose heart is still beating is one of the more macabre products of modern technology. During the past 30 years techniques have developed that can artificially maintain ventilation, circulation, and elimination of waste products of metabolism in a body whose brain has irreversibly ceased to function. Such cases begin to appear in all countries as their intensive care facilities reach a certain standard. What we do when confronted with such circumstances raises important questions. Brain death compels doctors (and society as a whole) to re-evaluate assumptions that go back for millennia.

Brain death was described as early as 1959. Renal transplantation was then in its infancy, whole-body irradiation being the only means of modifying the immune response. It is important to emphasise this, because some critics seem to believe that brain death was invented by neurologists to satisfy the demands of transplant surgeons. If transplantation were superseded tomorrow by better methods of treating end-stage renal failure brain dead patients would still be produced in large numbers in well run intensive care units in many parts of the world.

Over half a million people die each year in Great Britain. Whether at home or in hospital, they 'die their own death'. No machines are concerned. Their heart stops and that is the beginning and end of it. Epidemiological data suggest that brain death relates to perhaps 4000 deaths a year – well under 1% of all deaths. These people have sustained acute, irreparable, structural damage, which has plunged them into the deepest coma. The brain damage includes permanent loss of the capacity to breathe. But prompt action by doctors has ensured that ventilation is taken over by a machine before the resulting anoxia can stop the heart. . . .

Concepts and criteria

All talk of the criteria of death – and ipso facto all arguments about better criteria – must be related to some overall concept of what death means. When we consider death the tests we carry out and the decisions we make should be logically derived from conceptual and philosophical premises. There can be no free-floating criteria, unrelated to such premises.

The box [next page] lists several concepts that have prevailed from time to time. In the middle ages, if one entered certain monasteries one ceased to enjoy the limited rights and heavy duties of the outside world. One would be considered 'dead' by civil society. The appropriate criterion for such a concept of death would presumably be a certificate from the father superior of the monastery confirming that one had entered it. Esoteric concepts may be met by esoteric criteria.

Both Hellenic and Judaeo-Christian cultures identified death with the departure of the soul from the body. In 1957 Pope Pius XII, speaking to an international congress of anaesthetists, raised the question of whether one should 'continue the resuscitation process despite the fact that the soul may already have left the body'. I would find it difficult to identify this particular state or to formulate relevant criteria.

Some people have held that the surest notion of death is the biblical one: 'Ashes to ashes, dust to dust'. The appropriate criterion for such a concept would be putrefaction, but no one would argue today that this is necessary before a person can be pronounced dead. We all grasp the difference between 'Is this woman dead?' and 'Has every enzyme stopped working, in every cell of her body?' The controversy is between those who think of death as 'dissolution of the organism as a whole' and those who insist that it can mean only 'dissolution of the whole organism'.

Asked what they mean by death, most people will probably talk about the heart 'having stopped for good'. This is indeed a mechanism of death (and, until brain death appeared on the scene, it was also a universal attribute of a cadaver) but is it really a concept of death? When asked whether an individual is dead whose cardiac function has been permanently taken over by a machine many people begin to realise that a beating heart is not an end in itself but a means to another end: the preservation of the brain. This has been unconsciously perceived by people with little or no knowledge of physiology: we have been hanging and decapitating for centuries.

I conceive of human death as a state in which there is irreversible loss of the capacity for consciousness combined with irreversible loss of the capacity to breathe (and hence to maintain a heartbeat). Alone, neither would be sufficient. Both are essentially brain stem functions (predominantly represented incidentally, at different ends of the brain stem). The concept is admittedly a hybrid one, expressing both philosophical and physiological attributes. It corresponds perhaps to an intermediate stage of current concerns, seeking to maintain a footing on both types of ground. Although seldom explicitly formulated, this view of death is, I believe, widely shared in the West. It is the implicit basis for British practice in diagnosing 'brain death'.

Some people, particularly in the USA, have gone further and proposed a concept of death that would equate it with the loss of personal identity, or with the 'irreversible loss of that which is essentially significant to the nature of man'. 'Cognitive death' is already being evaluated as part of the 'next generation of problems'. I am opposed to 'higher brain' formulations of death because they are the first step along a slippery slope. If one starts equating the loss of higher functions with death, then, which higher functions? Damage to one hemisphere or to both? If to one hemisphere, to the 'verbalising' dominant one, or to the 'attentive' non-dominant one? One soon starts arguing frontal versus parietal lobes.

Concepts

- Entering certain monastic orders in the Middle Ages
- The soul leaving the body
- 'Ashes to ashes; dust to dust'
- Irreversible loss of capacity for consciousness and of capacity to breathe
- Loss of personal identity (the 'higher brain' formulation)

Over the past 100 years modern man has 'secularised his philosophical understanding of his nature' and has sought to find 'more biological formulations of what is meant to be dead'. When we strike existential chords, however, the responses are likely to be implicitly philosophical. If we understand this we will be more tolerant of the diversity of answers people will give when asked, 'What is it that is so central to your humanity that when you lose it you are dead?'

Death: an event or a process?

In 1968 the 22nd World Medical Assembly in Sydney stated: 'Death is a gradual process at the cellular level, with tissues varying in their ability to withstand deprivation of oxygen. But clinical interest lies not in the state of preservation of isolated cells but in the fate of a person. Here the point of death of the different cells and organs is not so important as the certainty that the process has become irreversible, whatever techniques of resuscitation may be employed.' In thus defining death the delegates in Sydney were endorsing – whether they knew it or not – one of the options offered by the *Concise Oxford Dictionary*, which describes death both as 'dying' (a process) and 'being dead' (a state).

It has, of course, been thought for centuries that growth of the hair and nails might continue after the heart had stopped. Surgeons discovered years ago that they could harvest skin 24 hours after irreversible asystole and transplant it. A bone graft or an arterial graft would 'take' even if the tissue had been collected 48 hours after death. In the light of such observations, the classical signs of death (permanent cessation of breathing and of the heartbeat) will be perceived rather differently: they will be seen as major and easily detectable events, triggering a final, rapid sequence of biological changes. They are the usual points of no return in the dissolution of the organism as a whole and proof positive that the process leading to death of the whole organism has indeed become irreversible.

Legal constraints and dictionary definitions have probably delayed acceptance of the notion of death as a process. Fifteen years ago the editorial of a leading American journal talked of the 'end point' of existence 'which ought to be as clear and sharp as in a chemical titration'. In fact the simultaneous destruction of all tissues – death as an event – is rare indeed. The sudden carbonisation of the whole body by a nuclear explosion is the only example that readily comes to mind.

In the heat of the public controversy about brain death two years ago a limerick was written which summed up the simple wisdom that death is a process:

In our graveyards with winter winds blowing
There's a great deal of to-ing and fro-ing
But can it be said
That the buried are dead
When their nails and their hair are still growing?

I think all cultures capable of asking such a question would answer it with an unequivocal 'yes' – whether the premises were true or not.

But there are other points of no return. One type of event epitomises the fact that these may in fact precede cessation of the heartbeat – decapitation. Once the head has been severed from the neck the heart continues to beat. Is that individual alive or dead? If those who hold that a person can be truly dead only when the heart has stopped believe that a decapitated individual is still alive, simply because his heart is still beating, they have a concept of life so different from mine that I doubt if bridges could be built. If, however, they accept that such an individual is dead they should extrapolate this awareness to a similar situation, extended over hours or days (because of a closed circulation). They will be thinking about brain death.

The vegetative state, whole brain death, and death of the brain stem

About 10 years ago [a] picture of an unsuccessfully decapitated chicken appeared in a leading magazine. The forebrain ha[d] been amputated and [lay] on the ground. The brain stem [was] still in situ. The bird, still breathing, was fed with a dropper for several weeks. Was it alive or dead?

The chicken must be considered alive so long as its brain stem is functioning. Let us transfer the argument to a child with hydranencephaly. There is a spinal cord, a brain stem, and perhaps some diencephalic structures but certainly no cerebral hemispheres. The cranial cavity is full of cerebrospinal fluid and transilluminates when a light is applied to it. The child can breathe spontaneously, swallow, and grimace in response to painful stimuli. Its eyes are open. The heart can beat normally for months. No culture would declare that child dead. This emphasises the certainty we instinctively allocate to persisting brain stem function, even in the absence of anything we could describe as cerebration.

These examples may help one grasp the essence of a much more common and important condition: the vegetative state. This is a chronic condition, the result of either cerebral anoxia (which may devastate the cortical mantle of the brain) or of impact injury to the head (which may massively shear the subcortical white matter, disconnecting the cortex from underlying structures). Other pathological processes may also on occasion be responsible. Affected individuals, if adequately nursed, may survive for years. They open their eyes, so that by definition they cannot be described as comatose. But, although awake, they show no behavioural evidence of awareness. Conjugate roving movements of the eyes are common, orientating movements rare. The patients do not speak or initiate purposeful movement of their limbs. Abnormal motor responses to stimulation may often be seen. Like the hydranencephalic child, the patients grimace, swallow, and breathe spontaneously. Their pupillary and corneal reflexes are usually preserved. They have a working brain stem, but show no evidence of meaningful function above the level of the tentorium.

I have described the vegetative state so that I can contrast it with whole brain death. Brain dead individuals show no signs of neural function above the level of the foramen magnum. Even homoeostatic functions, dependent on central neural mechanisms, are affected. The patients are in deep irreversible coma, and have irreversibly lost the capacity to breathe. Brain stem death is the physiological kernel of brain death, the anatomical substratum of its cardinal signs (apnoeic coma with absent brain stem reflexes) and the main determinant of its invariable cardiac prognosis: asystole within hours or days.

[A controversy has developed] in the United States between those who have accepted death as synonymous with 'death of all structures above the foramen magnum', and others tentatively suggesting that death of large parts of both cerebral hemispheres (the vegetative state) might be enough. Very few informed physicians in the United States, it must be emphasised, subscribe to the latter view. A different disagreement smoulders on, meanwhile, both within the United Kingdom and to some extent between British and American neurologists, about whether we can clinically identify death of the brain stem and about what flows from such an identification. When people engaged in one discussion are suddenly parachuted into the other communication is bound, for a while, to be difficult.

Understanding death

Robert Veatch, *Death, Dying, and the Biological Revolution* (1989) (revised edition) (pp 16-17)

Four separate levels in [the definition of death] debate must be distinguished. First, there is the purely formal analysis of the term *death*, an analysis that gives the structure and specifies the framework that must be given content. Second, there is the concept of death which attempts to fill the content of the formal definition. At this level the question is: What is so essentially significant about life that its loss is termed death? Third, there is the question of the locus of death: Where in the organism ought one to look to determine whether death has occurred? Fourth, one must ask the question of the criteria of death: What technical tests must be applied at the locus to determine if an individual is living or dead?

Serious mistakes have been made in slipping from one level of the debate to another and in presuming that expertise on one level necessarily implies expertise on another. These problems began to emerge early in the debate. They can be seen in the historically important Report of the Ad Hoc Committee of the Havard Medical School to Examine the Definition of Brain Death entitled 'A Definition of Irreversible Coma'. The title suggests that the committee members intend simply to report empirical measures that are criteria for predicting an irreversible coma. Yet the name of the committee seems to point more to the question of locus. The committee was established to examine the death of the brain. The implication is that the empirical indications of irreversible coma are also indications of 'brain death'. We now know that to be mistaken even at the empirical level, but the committee's confusions were even more serious. In the first sentence of the report the committee members claim that their 'primary purpose is to define irreversible coma as a new criterion for death'. They have now shifted so that they are interested in 'death'. They must be presuming a philosophical concept of death – that a person in irreversible coma should be considered dead – but they neither argue this nor state it as a presumption.

Even the composition of the Harvard committee signals some uncertainty of purpose. If empirical criteria were the principal concern, the inclusion of nonscientists on the panel was strange. If the philosophical concept of death was the main concern, medically trained people were overrepresented. As it happened, the committee did not deal at all with the conceptual matter of what it really means to be dead, yet that was the important policy issue raised in the shift to a brain-oriented definition of death. The committee and its interpreters have confused the question at different levels.

As for the formal analysis of the term 'death', Veatch offers the following (p 17):

A strictly formal definition of death might be the following: Death means a complete change in the status of a living entity characterised by the irreversible loss of those characteristics that are essentially significant to it.

He points out, however, that (p 17):

> Such a definition would apply equally well to a human being, a nonhuman animal, a plant, an organ, a cell, or even metaphorically to a society or to any temporally limited entity like a research project, a sports event, or a language. To define the death of a human being, we must recognise its essential human characteristics. It is quite inadequate to limit the discussion to the death of the heart or the brain.

A. THE CONCEPT

Veatch *op cit* (pp 19-30) approaches the issue of the concept of death as follows:

> To ask what is essentially significant to a human being is a philosophical question – a question of ethical and other values. Many features have been suggested to be the one that makes human beings unique – their opposable thumbs, their possession of rational souls, their ability to form cultures and manipulate symbol systems, their upright posture, their being created in the image of God, and so on. Any concept of death will depend directly upon how one evaluates these qualities. Four choices seem to me to cover the most plausible approaches.
>
> *Irreversible loss of flow of vital fluids*
> At first it would appear that the irreversible cessation of heart and lung activity would represent a simple and straightforward statement of the traditional understanding of the concept of death in Western culture. Yet upon reflection this cannot be. If patients permanently lose control of their lungs and are supported by mechanical respirators, they are still living persons as long as they continue to get oxygen. If modern technology produced an efficient, compact heart-lung machine capable of being carried on the back or in a pocket, people using such devices would not be considered dead, even though both heart and lungs were permanently nonfunctioning. Some might consider such a technological person an affront to human dignity; some might argue that such a device should never be connected to a human; but even they would, in all likelihood, agree that such people were alive . . .
>
> *Irreversible loss of the soul from the body*
> There is a long-standing tradition, sometimes called vitalism, that holds the essence of humans to be independent of the chemical reactions and electrical forces that account for the flow of the bodily fluids . . .
> The departure of the soul might be seem by believers as occurring at about the time that the fluids stop flowing. But it would be a mistake to equate these two concepts of death, as according to the first fluid stops from natural, if unexplained, causes, and death means nothing more than that stopping of the flow, which is essential to being treated as alive. According to the second view, the fluid stops flowing at the time the soul departs, and it stops because the soul is no longer present. Here the essential thing is the loss of the soul, not the loss of the fluid flow.
>
> *The irreversible loss of the capacity for bodily integration*
> In the debate between those who held a traditional religious notion of the animating force of the soul and those who had the more naturalistic concept of the irreversible loss of the flow of bodily fluids, the trend to secularism and empiricism made the loss of fluid flow more and more the operative concept of death in society. But human intervention in the dying process through cardiac pacemakers, respirators, intravenous medication and feeding, and extravenous purification of the blood has forced a sharper examination of the naturalistic concept of death. It is now possible to manipulate the dying process so that some parts of the body cease to function while other parts are maintained indefinitely . . .
> We now must consider whether concepts of death that focus on the flow of fluids or the departure of the soul are philosophically appropriate. The reason that the question arises as a practical matter is fear of a 'false positive' determination that human life is present. There are several ways of handling doubtful cases. Many would argue that when there is moral or philosophical doubt about whether someone is dead, it would be (morally) safer to act as if the individual were alive. An intermediate position is that we may follow a course of action

whose morality is in doubt if (and only if) it is more likely to be than not. Another position, called probabilism, offers the most leeway, holding that a 'probable opinion' may be followed even though the contrary opinion is also probable or even more probable. In the case under consideration, the probabilist could consider the individual dead even though moral doubt, even perhaps serious doubt, remained. Holders of the more rigorous positions would argue that we should take the morally safer course and consider the person alive even though the heart, lungs, and fluid flow had permanently stopped functioning.

Even the probabilist, however, traditionally has placed restrictions on legitimising actions supported by a probable opinion, for instance, when a life may be saved by taking one of the probable courses of action. This is clearly the sort of case involved in trying to decide whether to treat an individual as dead.

Thus, when modifying our traditional concept of death to pronounce dead some individuals who would under older concepts be considered alive (that is, those with heart and lung but no brain function), the problem of moral doubt must be resolved . . . [T]he . . . most plausible [solution is] to treat the situation as one of perplexed conscience. There are two relevant and important moral principles at stake: preservation of an individual life and preservation of the dignity of an individual by being able to distinguish a dead person from a living one. The introduction of a moral obligation to treat the dead as dead leaves one perplexed. It creates moral pressures in each direction. The defenders of the older concepts, which may lead to false pronouncements of living, must defend their action as well. It seems to me that only when such positive moral pressure is introduced on both sides of the argument can we plausibly overcome the claim that we must take the morally safer course. We must consider that it may be not only right to call persons dead, but also wrong to call them alive. This will still mean minimising the life-saving exception, but at least at this point there will be a positive moral argument for doing so. It is, thus, quite difficult to justify any divergence from the older, more traditional concepts of death, but the case for a neurologically centred concept can be made.

At first it would appear that the irreversible loss of brain activity is the concept of death held by those no longer satisfied with the vitalistic concept of the departure of the soul or the animalistic concept of the irreversible cessation of fluid flow. This is why the name *brain death* is frequently, if ambiguously, given to the new proposals, but the term is unfortunate for two reasons.

First, as we have seen, it is not the heart and lungs as such that are essentially significant but rather the vital functions – the flow of fluids – that we believe according to the best empirical human physiology to be associated with these organs. An 'artificial brain' is not possible at present, but a walking, talking, thinking individual who had one would certainly be considered living. It is not the collection of physical tissues called the brain, but rather their functions – consciousness; motor control; sensory feeling; ability to reason; control over bodily functions including respiration and circulation; major integrating reflexes controlling blood pressure, ion levels, and pupil size; and so forth – that are given essential significance by those who advocate adoption of a new concept of death or clarification of the old one. In short they see the body's capacity for integrating its functions as the essentially significant indication of life. Although there are occasional suggestions that it is the anatomical structure of the brain that is important, now almost any one arguing for a brain-oriented definition of death will accept that it is not technically the death of the brain that is critical, but the irreversible loss of the functions normally carried on by the brain.

Second, as I suggested earlier, we are not interested in the death of particular cells, organs, or organ systems, but in the death of the person as a whole – the point at which the person as a whole undergoes a quantum change through the loss of characteristics held to be essentially significant – and so terms such as brain death or heart death should be avoided. At the public policy level, this has practical consequences. A statute adopted in Kansas in 1970 specifically referred to 'alternative definitions of death' and said that they are 'to be used for all purposes in this state . . .' According to this language, which resulted from talking of brain and heart death, a person in Kansas could simultaneously be dead according to one definition and alive according to another. When a distinction must be made, it should be made directly on the basis of the philosophical significance of the functions mentioned above rather than on the importance of the tissue collection called the brain. For purposes of simplicity I shall use the phrase *the capacity for bodily integration* to refer to the total list of integrating mechanisms possessed by the body. A case for these mechanisms being the ones that are essential to humanness can indeed be made. Humans are more than the flowing of fluids. They are complex, integrated organisms with capacities for internal regulation. With and only with these integrating mechanisms is homo sapiens really human.

There appear to be two general aspects to this concept of what is essentially significant: first, a capacity for integrating one's internal bodily environment (which is done for the most part unconsciously through highly complex homeostatic, feedback mechanisms) and, second, a capacity for integrating one's self, including one's body, with the social environment through consciousness, which permits interaction with other persons. Together these offer a more profound understanding of the nature of the human than does the simple flow of bodily fluids. Whether it is a more profound concept than that which focuses simply on the presence or absence of the soul, it is clearly a very different one. The ultimate test between the two is that of meaningfulness and plausibility. For many in modern secular society, the concept of loss of capacity for bodily integration seems a more meaningful and accurate description of the essential significance of the human and of what is lost at the time of death. According to this view, when individuals lose all of these 'truly vital' capacities we should call them dead and behave accordingly . . .

The irreversible loss of the capacity for consciousness or social interaction
The fourth major alternative for a concept of death draws on the characteristics of the third concept and has often been confused with it. Henry Beecher offers a summary of what he considers to be essential to man's nature: '. . . the individual's personality, his conscious life, his uniqueness, his capacity for remembering, judging, reasoning, acting, enjoying, worrying, and so on.'

Beecher goes on immediately to ask the anatomical question of locus. He concludes that these functions reside in the brain and that when the brain no longer functions, the individual is dead. What is remarkable is that Beecher's list, with the possible exception of 'uniqueness', is composed entirely of functions explicitly related to consciousness and the capacity to relate to one's social environment through interaction with others. All the functions that give the capacity to integrate one's internal bodily environment through unconscious, complex, homeostatic reflex mechanisms – respiration, circulation, and major integrating reflexes – are omitted. In fact, when asked what was essentially significant to man's living, Beecher replied simply, 'Consciousness.'

Thus a fourth possible concept of death is the irreversible loss of the capacity for mental or social functioning. If a group of hypothetical human beings had irreversibly lost the capacity for consciousness or social interaction, they would have lost the essential character of humanness and, according to this definition, they would be dead even if they had capacity for integration of bodily function.

Even if one moves to the so-called higher functions and away from the mere capacity to integrate bodily functions through reflex mechanisms, it is still not clear precisely what is ultimately valued as essential. We must have a more careful specification of mental or social function. Are these two capacities synonymous and, if not, what is the relationship between them? Before taking up that question, I must first make clear what is meant by capacity.

The meaning of capacity
Holders of this concept of death and related concepts of the human essence specifically do not say that individuals must be valued by others in order to be human. This would place life at the mercy of other human beings who may well be cruel or insensitive. Nor does this concept imply that the essence of humanness is the fact of social interaction with others, as this would also place a person at the mercy of others. The infant raised in complete isolation from other human contact would still be human, provided that the child retained the capacity for social interaction. This view of what is essentially significant to humanness makes no quantitative or qualitative judgments. It need not lead to the view that those who have more capacity for social integration are more human. The concepts of life and death are essentially bipolar, threshold concepts. People should either be treated as living or they should not . . .

Specifying mental and social function
Precisely what are the functions considered to be ultimately significant to human life according to this concept? There are several possibilities.

Rationality. The capacity for rationality is one candidate. The human capacity for reasoning is so unique and important that some would suggest it is the critical element in human nature. But certainly infants lack any such capacity, and they are considered living human beings.

Nor is possession of the potential for reasoning what is important. Including potential might resolve the problem of infants, but it does not explain why those who have no potential for rationality (such as the permanently backward psychotic or the senile individual) are considered to be humanly living in a real if not full sense and to be entitled to the protection of civil and moral law.

There is some confusion here because some philosophers are inclined to make a great deal out of labelling some human beings 'persons'. Their view seems to be that among those who are living beings some are persons. Persons are those who can reason, manipulate symbol systems, or otherwise partake in moral discourse. In this narrow, technical sense persons are seen by the proponents of this usage as morally in a different category from other living humans. For them a person apparently is a rights bearing human being by definition while some other humans are not.

I have consistently avoided this usage. Whenever I use the term *person*, it is synonymous with living human beings, and I leave open the question of whether all living humans are equally bearers of rights. In pressing the meaningfulness of the definition of death debate, however, I imply that it is plausible to think of all living human beings as standing in a moral position different from that of those who are dead. To wit, living human beings deserve to be treated differently from those who are dead, as subject to the moral and legal protections of the society such as those granted by the Constitution. They are individuals for whom death behaviours are not yet appropriate. That leaves entirely open the questions of whether there is some subgroup of living humans who have additional moral status and why they would be given that status, whether it be because they have the capacity to reason, to manipulate symbol systems, or to generate claims. It strikes me that it is hard to defend the position that some such subgroup exists, but that is not a problem for a discussion of the definitions of life and death.

Consciousness. Consciousness is a second candidate for that critical function that qualifies one to be treated as living. If the rationalist tradition is reflected in the previous notion, then the empiricist philosophical tradition seems to be represented in the emphasis on consciousness. What may be of central significance is the capacity for experience. This would include the infant and the individual who lacks the capacity for rationality, and it focuses attention on the capacity for sensory awareness, summarised as consciousness. Yet, this is a very individualistic understanding of the human's nature. It describes what is essentially significant to the human life without any reference to other human beings.

Personal identity. A third possibility has been proposed by philosophers Michael B. Green and Daniel Wikler [(1980) 9(2) *Philosophy and Public Affairs* 105] and has been considered by the President's Commission. They argue that it is personal identity that is critical in deciding when a person is dead. Their position is that 'a given person ceases to exist with the destruction of whatever processes there are which normally underlie that person's psychological continuity and connectedness'.

They go on to argue against my position. They suggest that I am making an essentially moral argument for a so-called higher-brain conception of death. In this they are certainly correct. I have repeatedly claimed that all that is at stake in the public policy debate over the definition of death is determining when death behaviours are appropriate.

They claim that this is 'ontological gerrymandering', or arranging a concept of death to fit moral judgments. They argue against doing this by apparently reducing moral judgments to judgments about subjective value. Instead they want what they refer to as an ontological argument for the concept of death, which simply clarifies the concept without going on to reach moral conclusions. They cite as an example the possibility that some society valuing sports might find it congenial to classify the lame as dead. Since it is clearly absurd to do so, they apparently believe that they have demonstrated that the definition of death is not a matter of moral judgment.

Perhaps Green and Wikler have too modest a notion of the ontological status of moral judgments. I would analyse the problem of the lame as follows. The question being debated is a moral one: should lame persons be treated like the dead? The answer is clearly negative, and it is a moral answer. That however, does not make it less ontological. If one believes that moral judgments should be viewed as if they had ontological grounding in reality rather than being merely subjective expressions of a society's values, then one could say of the society that wanted to treat the lame as dead that they have made a mistake. Although they do not value the lame, they are wrong to the extent that they treat them as though they were dead. I would claim they are morally wrong just as Green and Wikler would claim they are conceptually wrong. This has nothing whatsoever to do with the empirical question of whether a society, in fact, values certain of its members. The concept of being dead, for me, can be reduced to being in a state in which one is appropriately treated the way dead people are treated.

Green and Wikler go on to argue that an individual is appropriately considered dead when personal identity (that is, psychological continuity and connectedness) is destroyed. In so far as being dead precipitates what I have called death behaviour, I am sure Green and

Wikler are wrong in equating irreversible loss of personal identity and death. The test case is that of a (possibly hypothetical) individual – call him Jones – who suffers a severe head trauma that leaves him with permanent amnesia. These are, in fact, the kinds of cases Green and Wikler address in their article.

Suppose that Jones eventually recovers consciousness, but it is established that there is a total and irreversible break in psychological continuity and connectedness. He does recover, however, to the point where he can leave the hospital and, after substantial education in language and the skills of living, return to society. The question that Green and Wikler should have difficulty answering in a way that squares with intuitions is whether Jones has died and a new person (say, Smith) has been created. They must say that Jones has died and that a new and different person comes out of the hospital.

I have no problem if they want to claim that according to their theory of personal identity a new person with a new identity emerges, but that question is not really the same as debating whether an individual has died. I am only interested in whether any of the behaviours that society appropriately initiates upon death would be appropriate for Jones. Would, we, for example, read his will and transfer his assets to his beneficiaries, leaving Smith destitute? Would mourning be initiated by relatives who would show no interest in or commitment to Smith, a new and different person who is a stranger? I am convinced that Jones's relatives would have no problem remaining identified with him and that no traditional death behaviours would be appropriate. If Green and Wikler want to say that there is a destruction of personal identity, fine, but they surely cannot say that Jones has died. Anyone who did so would be confusing irreversible loss of personal identity with death.

Social interaction. Social interaction is a fourth candidate. The Western tradition in both its Judeo-Christian and Greek manifestations has long held that the human is essentially a social or political animal. Perhaps the human's capacity or potential for social interaction has such ultimate significance that its loss is considered death. The claim here is a radical one. It is not merely that human life would be boring or miserable lived in total isolation. It is rather that the essence of being human would be lost. I believe that anyone who stands in this tradition must ultimately maintain that it is the capacity for social interaction that is essential for being treated as living.

Is this in any sense different from the capacity for consciousness? Certainly it is conceptually different and places a very different emphasis on the human's essential role. Yet it may well be that the two functions, experience and social interaction, are completely coterminous. For all practical purposes it may make no difference whether we speak of the critical characteristic as capacity for consciousness, or social interaction. Thus even though it is crucial for a philosophical understanding of the human's nature to distinguish between these two functions, it may not be necessary for deciding when an individual has died. Thus, for our purposes we can say that the fourth concept of death is one in which the essential element that is lost is the capacity for consciousness or social interaction or both.

The concept presents one further problem. The Western tradition, which emphasises social interaction, also emphasises, as we have seen, the importance of the body. Consider the admittedly remote possibility that the electrical impulses of the brain could be transferred by recording devices onto magnetic computer tape. Would that tape together with some kind of minimum sensory device be a living human being and would erasure of the tape be considered murder? If the body is really essential, then we might well decide that such a creature would not be a living human being.

This may help explain why Jones, the victim of permanent amnesia, did not die but is still Jones. He still has the same body, to which his family would relate. As long as he did not have another person's identity (the sort of case envisioned in the brain transplant scenarios), I think no one would have difficulty treating the conscious individual with bodily continuity as the same individual. (Whether he is the same person or not is irrelevant.) It also helps explain why we are so repulsed at the thought of a brain transplant. Assuming the consciousness of one person is merged with the body of another, a moral monster would be created, one having all of the components of living people, but containing the bodily trace of one person and the mental trace of another. If continuity of bodily and mental functions is critical then the merging of two produces a chimera. It is not merely the continuation of one person (the one who supplied the mental component) in a new body as some modern day gnostics would have us believe.

Where does this leave us? The earlier concepts of death – the irreversible loss of the soul and the irreversible stopping of the flow of vital body fluids – strike me as quite implausible. The soul as an independent nonphysical entity that is necessary and sufficient for a person to be considered alive is a relic from the era of dichotomised anthropologies. Animalistic fluid flow is simply too base a function to be the human essence. The capacity for bodily integration is more plausible, but I suspect it is attractive primarily because it includes those higher functions that we normally take to be central – consciousness, the ability to think and feel and relate to others. When the reflex networks that regulate such things as blood pressure and respiration are separated from the higher functions, I am led to conclude that it is the higher functions that are so essential that their loss ought to be taken as the death of the individual. While consciousness is certainly important, the human's social nature and embodiment seem to me to be the truly essential characteristics. I therefore believe that death is most appropriately thought of as the irreversible loss of the embodied capacity for social interaction.

As you have just seen Robert Veatch favours the 'irreversible loss of the embodied capacity for social interaction' as the most appropriate concept of death. David Lamb's analysis in his book *Death, Brain Death and Ethics* leads to a somewhat different conclusion.

D Lamb, *Death, Brain Death and Ethics* (1985) (pp 11-16)

[W]hilst it is important to separate the sphere of the philosophical from the medical, it is equally important to stress that in any discussion of death neither party can afford to ignore the contributions of the other. Medical judgments are informed by philosophical presuppositions, whether or not the latter are explicitly formulated. The diagnosis of any illness may be clinical and empirical, but it would be lacking in significance if there were no underlying concepts of health and disease. Whether a patient is classified as dead or alive depends on our understanding of the relevant concept of death. According to Capron and Kass [(1972) 121 Univ Penn LR 87] . . . the departure from the traditional concept of death manifest in the employment of brain-related criteria has brought these extra-medical concepts to the forefront of concern. Whilst traditional criteria, based on the cessation of cardio-respiratory functions, remained congruent with public conceptions of death, the phenomenon of death remained exclusively a matter of medical concern. But once medicine appeared to depart from traditional criteria for determining death, clarification of these extra-medical concepts of death became a matter of urgent concern for those responsible for the management of death. In view of the importance attached to a diagnosis of death in terms of the social, religious, political and ethical consequences, it is essential that this challenge be met and that the concept of death be made explicit. Furthermore, it is essential that criteria and tests for death should be logically derived from the appropriate concept of death.

The concept of death involves a philosophical judgment that a significant change has taken place, which presupposes an idea of the necessary conditions of life. These may range from the faculties involved in social interaction to the capacity to maintain bodily integration. Concepts of death may vary according to cultural patterns, religious traditions and scientific practice . . . . They may include such distinct formulations as 'the separation of soul and body', 'destruction of all physical structures', 'loss of the capacity for social interaction', 'irreversible loss of consciousness', 'loss of bodily integration', and many others. Related to these concepts are appropriate criteria, and tests to ascertain that the criteria have been met. It follows that any shift in the concept of death will necessitate corresponding changes in the criteria and tests for death. However, it does not follow that new criteria and tests mean that a change of concept has taken place. They may indicate nothing more than refinements of previous criteria and tests. For example, the employment of stethoscopes and cardiograms constituted technically better tests for death which did not entail any departure from the traditional cardio-respiratory-based concept of death.

Criteria for death only have meaning if they can be shown to be logically derived from the appropriate concept of death. It is therefore meaningless to use 'free-floating criteria' which are not derived from a clearly-determined concept of death . . . Clarity concerning the concept of death provides a point of reference when deciding upon criteria, but some definitions of death are philosophically inadequate despite the fact that criteria can be logically derived from them. . . . Concepts of death, such as 'entering a monastery' or exclusion from the family, tribe or clan, are widely used and yield appropriate criteria. But they can refer to death only in a metaphorical sense.

The essential point here is that some concepts are more relevant than others. The requirement for a definition of death is a demand for the selection of a concept that is superior to others. For this reason vaguely formulated and indeterminate concepts should be eschewed. Thus a concept of death as 'the loss of that which is essentially significant to the nature of man' is unsatisfactory, since we can say that a patient has lost what is essentially significant but is still alive. This is because concepts like 'essentially significant' are by their very nature undetermined. For if by 'the loss of what is essentially significant' is meant 'the loss of the capacity for social interaction' then various interpretations are possible, from loss of libido to blindness, from senility to dementia, which will provide appropriate criteria. But the question of which, if any, of these states might best fulfil the requirements of the definition cannot be answered without further conceptual guidelines. On what grounds can it be inferred that 'massive brain damage', or 'loss of reproductive function' and so on amount to the 'loss of what is essentially significant'? Furthermore, all of the fore-mentioned criteria may be fulfilled when it is patently obvious that the patient is alive and, in some cases, that his situation is even reversible. If the 'loss of that which is essentially significant' is to have any meaning as a concept of death, then it must be framed so that it involves an irreversible state where the organism as a whole cannot function. Only a concept which specifies the irreversible loss of specified functions (due to the destruction of their anatomical substratum) can avoid the anomalous situation where a patient is said to be alive according to one concept but dead according to another. The only wholly satisfactory concept of death is that which trumps other concepts of death in so far as it yields a diagnosis of death which is beyond dispute. It follows that any criterion which, when fulfilled, leaves it possible for someone to say that the patient is still alive, is unsatisfactory. For this reason concepts relating specifically to psychological functions or moral qualities are wholly inadequate. In fact any criterion which, when fulfilled, leaves it possible for the organism as a whole to continue to function is inadequate. It should not be possible to say that the person is still alive although the criterion has been met, nor to say that the person is dead although the criterion has not been met. . . .

The concept of death that will be proposed and defended in this chapter is the '*irreversible loss of function of the organism as a whole*'. There is confusion between this and 'death of the whole organism'. This is often present – although unformulated – in arguments which maintain that the concept of death should be left undetermined, or that death is a process with no special point at which a non-arbitrary diagnosis can be factually ascertained. . . . Criteria for the 'death of the whole organism' could only be met by tests for putrefaction, since cellular life in certain tissues can continue long after it has ceased in others, and long past the point where the organism as a whole has ceased to function. However, putrefaction has never been seriously advanced as a definition of death by either physicians or philosophers. Consequently, the argument that the concept of death should remain undetermined has no place in a world where practical decisions regarding the criteria of death necessitate an acceptable concept. In contrast criteria for 'irreversible loss of function of the organism as a whole' can be determined with precision, and appropriate diagnostic tests are constantly being developed. . . . The 'irreversible loss of function of the organism as a whole' is a biological concept which yields clinical criteria and tests. It presupposes the irreversible loss of the capacity for consciousness and the irreversible loss of the capacity to breathe, and hence sustain a spontaneous heartbeat. It supersedes ethical and religious-based concepts and its appropriate criterion is the death of the critical system as measured by tests for the irreversible cessation of brainstem function.

Failure to understand the relationship between the concept and criteria for death may lead to serious errors of judgment in practical matters. A patient in a vegetative state, it is argued, may meet a concept of death as 'a worthless existence' but, unless the individual's critical system is dead, it will not satisfy the concept of death formulated above as the 'irreversible loss of function of the organism as a whole'. The latter concept is currently employed in medical practice, if not explicitly formulated. It explains why an anencephalic infant would not be regarded as dead as long as its brainstem remained intact. . . .

For the above reasons it has become commonplace in the literature on brain death to describe the concept of death as a philosophical matter and the development of diagnostic criteria as a task for medical expertise and to warn against conflating definitions of what death is with the problem of when death occurs. The philosophical analysis of death is held to identify what it is that the diagnostic criteria are supposed to determine. . . .

Whilst this distinction is important, it is nevertheless equally important that it should not be drawn too rigidly. Philosophical issues do not exist in complete isolation from technical and scientific issues; they interact and interpenetrate. For this reason a more flexible distinction has been formulated by Bernat, Culver and Gert [(1981) 94(3) Annals of Int Med 389] . . .

> Providing a definition is primarily a philosophical task: the choice of the criteria is primarily medical: and the selection of tests to prove that the criterion is satisfied is solely a medical matter.

This formulation can be illustrated as follows: suppose the concept of death were 'absence of fluid flow', then the criteria would be based on cessation of pulse, heartbeat and respiration, and could be determined by relatively straightforward empirical tests. If, however, the concept were the 'integrated functioning of the organism as a whole', one would have to decide which organ has decisive responsibility for this. If it is a matter of general agreement that the brain has this responsibility, then tests for measuring brain functions will be important. The formulation proposed by Bernat *et al.* has the merit of maintaining the distinction between philosophical discourse regarding the concept of death and medical discourse. Yet it recognises that, whilst philosophical and practical issues can be distinguished at one level, they mutually interact at another level. It is therefore important to be wary of attempts to settle – at the outset of any discussion – which kinds of problems belong exclusively to philosophy and which belong exclusively to medicine. Whilst Veatch's and Korein's [(1978) 315 Annals of NY Acad Sci 19] formulations correctly identify the concept of death as a philosophical issue and the criteria for death as a practical matter, the three-level distinction between concept, criteria and practical tests, which is proposed by Bernat *et al.*, is preferable because it acknowledges the interaction between conceptual issues and the application of criteria in a practical context.

Whether we subscribe to the view of Veatch or Lamb, it is clear that we must look to the brain as the appropriate 'locus' (as Veatch puts it) and not to the heart and lungs. Further we must remind ourselves of Lamb's observation (at p 13) that: 'Only a concept which specifies the irreversible loss of specified functions (due to the destruction of their anatomical substratum) can avoid the anomalous situation where a patient is said to be alive according to one concept but dead according to another.' This entails that the relevant locus chosen must be that which is physiologically responsible for the functions deemed critical to the relevant concept of brain death.

B. THE CRITERIA

What we are concerned with here is the means of identifying the presence or absence of the relevant functions of the locus (ie the whole brain or a part thereof). If the appropriate concept of death is *loss of the capacity for social interaction* then the correct locus of death is the brain. The criterion will then be the permanent and irreversible loss of function of the *higher brain*.

The President's Commission for the Study of Ethical Problems in Medicine and Biomedical and Behavioral Research: 'Medical, Legal and Ethical Issues in the Determination of Death: *Defining Death*', criticises the criterion (pp 38, 40):

The 'higher brain' formulations
When all brain processes cease, the patient loses two important sets of functions. One set encompasses the integrating and coordinating functions, carried out principally but not exclusively by the cerebellum and brainstem. The other set includes the psychological functions which make consciousness, thought, and feeling possible. These latter functions are located primarily but not exclusively in the cerebrum, especially the neocortex. The two 'higher brain' formulations of brain-orientated definitions of death discussed here are premised on the fact that loss of cerebral functions strips the patient of his psychological capacities and properties.

A patient whose brain has permanently stopped functioning will, by definition, have lost those brain functions which sponsor consciousness, feeling, and thought. Thus the higher brain rationales support classifying as dead bodies which meet 'whole brain' standards . . . The converse is not true, however. If there are parts of the brain which have no role in sponsoring consciousness, the higher brain formulation would regard their continued functioning as compatible with death.

The concepts: Philosophers and theologians have attempted to describe the attributes a living being must have to be a person. 'Personhood' consists of the complex of activities (or of capacities to engage in them) such as thinking, reasoning, feeling, human intercourse which make the human different from, or superior to, animals or things. One higher brain formulation would define death as the loss of what is essential to a person. Those advocating the personhood definition often relate these characteristics to brain functioning. Without brain activity, people are incapable of these essential activities. A breathing body, the argument goes, is not in itself a person; and, without functioning brains, patients are merely breathing bodies. Hence personhood ends when the brain suffers irreversible loss of function.

For other philosophers, a certain concept of 'personal identity' supports a brain-orientated definition of death. According to this argument, a patient literally ceases to exist as an individual when his or her brain ceases functioning, even if the patient's body is biologically alive. Actual decapitation creates a similar situation: the body might continue to function for a short time, but it would no longer be the 'same' person. The persistent identity of a person as an individual from one moment to the next is taken to be dependent on the continuation of certain mental processes which arise from brain functioning. When the brain processes cease (whether due to decapitation or to 'brain death') the person's identity also lapses. The mere continuation of biological activity in the body is irrelevant to the determination of death, it is argued, because after the brain has ceased functioning the body is no longer identical with the person.

Critique: Theoretical and practical objections to these arguments led the Commission to rely on them only as confirmatory of other views in formulating a definition of death. First, crucial to the personhood argument is acceptance of one particular concept of those things that are essential to being a person, while there is no general agreement on this very fundamental point among philosophers, much less physicians or the general public. Opinions about what is essential to personhood vary greatly from person to person in our society – to say nothing of intercultural variations.

The argument from personal identity does not rely on any particular conception of personhood, but it does require assent to a single solution to the philosophical problem of identity. Again, this problem has persisted for centuries despite the best attempts by philosophers to solve it. Regardless of the scholarly merits of the various philosophical solutions, their abstract technicality makes them less useful to public policy.

Further, applying either of these arguments in practice would give rise to additional important problems. Severely senile patients, for example, might not clearly be persons, let alone ones with continuing personal identities; the same might be true of the severely retarded. Any argument that classified these individuals as dead would not meet with public acceptance.

Equally problematic for the 'higher brain' formulations, patients in whom only the neocortex or subcortical areas have been damaged may return or regain spontaneous respiration and circulation. Karen Quinlan is a well-known example of a person who apparently suffered permanent damage to the higher centers of the brain but whose lower brain continues to function. Five years after being removed from the respirator that supported her breathing for nearly a year, she remains in a persistent vegetative state but with heart and lungs that function without mechanical assistance. Yet the implication of the personhood and personal identity arguments is that Karen Quinlan, who retains brainstem function and breathes spontaneously, is just as dead as a corpse in the traditional sense. The Commission rejects this conclusion and the further implication that such patients could be buried or otherwise treated as dead persons.

If, however, the preferred concept of death is *loss of bodily integration*, then the correct locus is again the brain. However, here the criterion will be the permanent and irreversible loss of functions of the brain.

For some, particularly in the United States, this 'permanent and irreversible loss of function of the *brain*' means: of the *usable brain*. The President's Commission (*op cit*) writes (pp 32 and 35-6):

One characteristic of living things which is absent in the dead is the body's capacity to organize and regulate itself. In animals, the neural apparatus is the dominant locus of these functions. In higher animals and man, regulation of both maintenance of the internal environment (homeostasis) and interaction with the external environment occurs primarily within the cranium.

External threats, such as heat or infection, or internal ones, such as liver failure or endogenous lung desease, can stress the body enough to overwhelm its ability to maintain organization and regulation. If the stress passes a certain level, the organism as a whole is defeated and death occurs.

This process and its denouement are understood in two major ways. Although they are sometimes stated as alternative formulations of a 'whole brain definition' of death, they are actually mirror images of each other. The Commission has found them to be complementary; together they enrich one's understanding of the 'definition'. The first focuses on the integrated functioning of the body's major organ systems, while recognizing the centrality of the whole brain, since it is neither revivable nor replaceable. The other identifies the functioning of the whole brain as the hallmark of life because the brain is the regulator of the body's integration. . . .

A (more) significant criticism shares the view that life consists of the coordinated functioning of the various bodily systems, in which process the whole brain plays a crucial role. At the same time, it notes that in some adult patients lacking all brain functions it is possible through intensive support to achieve constant temperature, metabolism, waste disposal, blood pressure, and other conditions typical of living organisms and not found in dead ones. Even with extraordinary medical care, these functions cannot be sustained indefinitely – typically, no longer than several days – but it is argued that this shows only that patients with nonfunctional brains are dying, not that they are dead. In this view, the respirator, drugs and other resources of the modern intensive-care unit collectively substitute for the lower brain, just as a pump used in cardiac surgery takes over the heart's function.

This criticism rests, however, on a premise about the role of artificial support vis-a-vis brainstem which the Commission believes is mistaken or at best incomplete. While the respirator and its associated medical techniques do substitute for the functions of the intercostal muscles and the diaphragm, which without neuronal stimulation from the brain cannot function spontaneously, they cannot replace the myriad functions of the brainstem or of the rest of the brain. The startling contrast between bodies lacking *all* brain functions and patients with intact brainstems (despite severe neocortical damage) manifests this. The former lie with fixed pupils, motionless except for the chest movements produced by their respirators. The latter can not only breathe, metabolize, maintain temperature and blood pressure, and so forth, *on their own* but also sigh, yawn, track light with their eyes, and react to pain or reflex stimulation.

It is not easy to discern precisely what it is about patients in this latter group that makes them alive while those in the other category are not. It is in part that in the case of the first category (ie, absence of all brain functions) when the mask created by the artificial medical support is stripped away what remains is not an integrated organism but 'merely a group of artificially maintained sub-systems'. Sometimes, of course, an artificial substitute can forge the link that restores the organism as a whole to unified functioning. Heart or kidney transplants, kidney dialysis, or the iron lung used to replace physically-impaired breathing ability in a polio victim, for example, restore the integrated functioning of the organism as they replace the failed function of a part. Contrast such situations, however, with the hypothetical one of a decapitated body treated so as to prevent the outpouring of blood and to generate respiration: continuation of bodily functions in that case would not have restored the requisites of human life.

However, in the United Kingdom a different view is taken. Christopher Pallis, (*op cit*), explains the English approach (pp 5-9, 17):

From brain death to brain stem death

Historical background

Brain death was first described clinically in 1959 when two French physicians identified a condition they called 'coma dépassé' – literally, a state beyond coma. Twenty of their 23 patients were suffering from primary intercranial disorders and the other three from the cerebral sequelae of cardiorespiratory arrest. All the classic features of brain death are found in the early report. As well as obvious signs indicating death of the nervous system the authors mentioned poikilothermia, diabetes insipidus, a sustained hypotension which proves increasingly difficult to control with pressor amines, and progressive acidosis, initially respiratory and later metabolic. Awed by the potential of resuscitatory techniques the authors described the condition created as both 'une revelation et une rançon'. Those affected were said to have the appearance of 'corpses with a good volume pulse'. Articles published in the early 1960s already hinted that the cerebral circulation was 'blocked' by raised intracranial pressure in most of these cases. These early publications already hint at the presence of cerebral oedema and intracranial hypertension. Within a few years a 'blocked' cerebral circulation was to be recognised as a common concomitant of the condition.

In 1968 the report of the Ad Hoc Committee of the Harvard Medical School brought awareness of brain death to a much wider audience. (Influenced by the French, the committee initially used the term 'irreversible coma' to describe the condition; this has led to confusion as this term was later sometimes used to describe the vegetative state.) The Harvard criteria demanded that the patient should be unreceptive and unresponsive, the most intensely painful stimuli evoking 'no vocal or other response, not even a groan, withdrawal of a limb or quickening of respiration'. No movements were to occur during observation for one hour. Apnoea was to be confirmed by three minutes off the respirator (the centrality of apnoea, properly defined and tested for, had already been appreciated). The Harvard criteria also required that there should be 'no reflexes', the emphasis being on brain stem reflexes. A flat or isoelectric electroencephalogram at high gain was of 'great confirmatory value'. All the tests were to be repeated at least 24 hours later, with no change in the findings.

Harvard criteria

1   Unreceptivity and unresponsivity

2   No movements (observe for 1 h)

3   Apnoea (3 min off respirator)

4   Absence of elicitable reflexes

5   Isoelectric EEG 'of great confirmatory value' (at 5 uV/mm)

All of the above tests shall be repeated at least 24 hours later with no change

---

The report unambiguously proposed that this clinical state should be accepted as death, recognised the moral, ethical, religious, and legal implications, and boldly saw itself as preparing the way 'for better insight into all these matters as well as for better law than is currently applicable'. A year later Beecher, the chairman of the Harvard Committee, stated that this body was 'unanimous in its belief that an electroencephalogram was not essential to a diagnosis of irreversible coma', although it could provide 'valuable supporting data'.

Within three years of this radical yet humane proposal two neurosurgeons from Minneapolis made the challenging suggestions that 'in patients with known but irreparable intracranial lesions' irreversible damage to the brain stem was the 'point of no return'. The diagnosis 'could be based on clinical judgment'.

The Minnesota workers had introduced the notion of aetiological preconditions. (Twenty of their 25 patients had sustained massive craniocerebral trauma and the others were suffering from other primary intracranial disorders.) They emphasised the importance of apnoea to the determination of brain death; in fact they insisted on four minutes of disconnection from the respirator. (I will return to this later. One obviously does not want the tests for brain death, such as the demonstration of apnoea after disconnection, to produce the very brain death one is testing for.) They demanded absent brain stem reflexes, stated that the findings should not change for at least 12 hours, and emphasised that the electroencephalogram was not mandatory for the diagnosis. Their recommendations later became known as the Minnesota criteria, and were to influence thinking and practice in the UK considerably. I am emphasising this because it has been suggested that doctors in the UK have been overcritical of much of American work on this subject.

Minnesota criteria

1   'Known but irreparable intracranial lesion'

2   Non spontaneous movement

3   Apnoea (4 min)

4   Absent brain stem reflexes

5   'All findings unchanged for at least 12 hours'

EEG not mandatory

Since 1971 doctors have sought to identify the necessary and sufficient component (or physiological kernel) of brain death. It was soon realised that absent tendon reflexes (demanded in both the French and Harvard criteria) really implied loss of function of the spinal cord and that this was irrelevant to a diagnosis of brain death. The original insistence of the French on areflexia is strange, for the works of Babinski contain accounts of knee jerks persisting for up to eight minutes after decapitation on the guillotine. Death of the brain and death of the whole nervous system are not the same thing. If the heart beat continues for long enough many patients with dead brains will recover their tendon reflexes or show pathological limb reflexes. The presence or absence of such reflexes, while providing clues whether the spinal cord is alive or dead, tell us nothing about whether the brain stem is functioning or not. Spinal areflexia is in fact the exception in brain death (established by the angiographic demonstration of a non-perfused brain).

The limb reflexes in brain stem death

1   The tendon (stretch) reflexes of the limbs are segmental spinal reflexes

2   Brain stem death may be complicated by spinal shock, causing areflexia

3   After an interval, if the spinal cord is viable, abnormal reflexes will appear below the level of a dead brain stem

4   The reflex pattern in the limbs is of no prognostic value in cases of brain stem death

---

There has also been a systematic attempt to look critically at the meaning of minimal cellular activity above the level of a dead brain stem. It was gradually realised that the cardiac prognosis depended critically on whether the brain stem was functioning or not. If the brain stem was dead the heart would stop quite soon. The pressure of very low voltage residual electroencephalographic activity – seen in a few cases – did not influence the outcome. Such activity usually subsided anyway before asystole supervened. Physicians have therefore been focusing on how to identify irreversible loss of brain stem function.

In retrospect it is interesting that insight into the importance of the brain stem had been achieved as early as 1964, when Professor Keith Simpson, asked by the Medical Protection Society for words to use in a test case, suggested that 'there is life so long as a circulation of oxygenated blood is maintained to live brain stem centers'.

Irreversible loss of brain stem function
The table [below] highlights the implications of the memoranda on brain death issued by the Conference of Medical Royal Colleges and their Faculties in the UK in 1976 and 1979. The first memorandum (which I will call the UK code) emphasises that 'permanent functional death of the brain stem constitutes brain death' and that this should be diagnosed only in a defined context (irremediable structural brain damage) and after certain specified conditions have been excluded. It shows how the permanent loss of brain stem function can be determined clinically and describes simple tests for recognising the condition. The second memorandum identifies brain stem death with death itself. These documents mark a milestone in thinking about brain death and have already influenced practice in most English-speaking countries and in many others.

The basic propositions

Irreversible loss of brain stem function is as valid a yardstick of death as cessation of the heart beat

The loss of brain stem function can be determined operationally (in clinical terms)

The irreversibility of the loss is determined by
• The exclusion of reversible causes of loss of brain stem function
• A context of irremediable structural brain damage

What the proposals imply
Two major strides are necessary before one can accept the propositions implicit in the conference memoranda. The first is the step from 'classical' death to whole brain death. In most countries medical opinion has accepted the basic concept of brain death, although there are still a few influenced by religious or other considerations who oppose it. Leading

spokesmen of all the main Western religions have endorsed it, and publications on the subject are numerous.

Doctors were still taking this first step when they were faced with another challenge: that death of the brain stem was the necessary and sufficient component of whole brain death. It has already been explained . . . how death of the brain stem relates to a given philosophical concept of death (the irreversible loss of the capacity for consciousness and the capacity to breathe). The task is now to convince people that this condition can be identified clinically – and that it is not in conflict with more traditional notions of brain death or of death itself. If we accept the concept of brain stem death it might be wise to change the words we use and no longer speak of 'brain death' when what we mean is brain stem death.

Two important conceptual steps

1   From classical death
→ to total brain death

2   From total brain death
→ to brain stem death

Some neurologists – and many experts in electroencephalography – have been caught off balance by these essentially conceptual, rather than technological, developments. Some of the main proponents of the idea of whole brain death (their first battle won, the role of their electroencephalographs well defined, their areas of expertise widely accepted) have proved reluctant to move a little further.

Functions of the brain stem
As well as being essential for maintaining breathing the brain stem is necessary for the proper functioning of the cortex. It has long been known that small, strategically situated lesions of the brain stem, of acute onset and affecting the paramedian tegmental area bilaterally, might cause prolonged coma because they damage critical parts of the ascending reticular activating system.

The reticular formation constitutes the central core of the brain stem and projects to wide areas of the limbic system and neocortex. Projections from the upper part of the brain stem are responsible for alerting mechanisms. These can be thought of as generating the capacity for consciousness. The content of consciousness (what a person knows, thinks, or feels) is a function of activated cerebral hemispheres. But unless there is a functioning brain stem, 'switching on' the hemispheres, one cannot speak of such a content. There is evidence that brain stem injury in man may massively reduce cerebral oxidative metabolism, cerebral blood flow, or both. Apart from mechanisms essential for respiration, the brain stem contains others which contribute to maintaining blood pressure. All the motor outputs from the hemispheres have to travel through the brain stem, as do all the sensory inputs to the brain (other than sight and smell). . . .

Because the brain stem nuclei are so near one another brain stem function can be clinically evaluated in a unique way. Testing the various cranial nerve reflexes probes the brain stem slice by slice, as if it were salami. Respiratory function can also be assessed very accurately. An acute, massive, and irreversible brain stem lesion (primary or secondary) prevents meaningful functioning of the 'brain as a whole', even if isolated parts of the brain may, for a short while, still emit signals of biological activity.

The difference between functional death (death of the organism as a whole) and total cellular death (death of the whole organism) has already been emphasised. The table [below] summarises the parallel argument in relation to the brain as a whole and the whole brain.

The irreversible cessation of heart beat and respiration implies death of *the patient as a whole*. It does not necessarily imply the immediate death of *every cell in the body*.

The irreversible cessation of brain stem function implies death of *the brain as a whole*. It does not necessarily imply the immediate death of every *cell in the brain*.

Mechanisms of brain stem death
The brain stem may be damaged by a primary lesion or because raised pressure in the supratentorial or infratentorial compartments of the skull has had catastrophic effects on its

blood supply and structural integrity. Direct hypoxic damage affects the cortex more than the brain stem. Brain stem damage in hypoxic encephalopathy is often the result of coning due to cerebral oedema. Several factors may operate in any given case.

A severe head injury may be associated with a pronounced rise of intracranial pressure, even in the absence of a subdural or extradural haemorrhage. Similar rises may be seen after subarachnoid haemorrhage. Intracranial hypertension is also a feature of the cerebral oedema that almost invariably complicates acute anoxic insults to the brain. The initial effects, in such cases, are often complicated by the development of various intracranial 'shifts'. There may be downward-spreading oedema and caudal displacement of the diecephalon and brain stem with stretching of the perforating pontine branches of the basilar artery and secondary haemorrhages in their territory. Or the brain stem may be compressed from uncal herniation into the tentorial opening.

A pressure cone at the level of the foramen magnum may further damage the brain stem. Venous drainage may be compromised. Ischaemic changes may be striking. If ventilation is continued at room temperature in the presence of a dead brain autolysis will occur. The whole brain may liquefy. Fragments of the destroyed cerebella tonsils may become detached and be found even as far away as the roots of the cauda equina.

The severity of the pathological changes may vary widely. Among the factors responsible for such variations are the duration of ventilation after arrest of the cerebral circulation, and the proportion of cases, in some American series, which were not due to primary structural brain damage.

About half the patients in whom brain stem death is diagnosed in the United Kingdom have sustained a recent head injury. Another 30% have had a very recent intracranial haemorrhage (usually subarachnoid, from a ruptured aneurysm). Other primary intracranial conditions are abscess, meningitis, or encephalitis. In cases of cerebral tumour brain stem death may occur after operation or, rarely, when a prior decision has been taken, with the relatives' consent, to put the patient on a ventilator when in terminal coma (with the aim of making organs available for transplantation). Cardiac and respiratory arrest and hypo-perfusion of the brain complicating profound shock are relatively rare causes of brain stem death. They result more often in a vegetative state.

Primary lesions of the brain stem (haemorrhages or infarcts) seldom cause total loss of brain stem function. Restricted lesions (causing restricted deficits) are more common. Massive lesions may occur, however, and result in brain stem death.

Judicial hanging is another cause of lethal, primary brain stem injury. Death in such cases is widely believed to be due to fracture-dislocation of the odontoid, with compression of the upper two segments of the spinal cord. Although such a lesion may be found in some cases, Professor Simpson, Home Office Pathologist when capital punishment was still resorted to in the UK, has informed me that a rupture of the brain stem (between pons and medulla) was more common.

In judicial hanging respiration stops immediately, because of the effect of the brain stem rupture on the respiratory centre. The carotid or vertebral arteries may remain patent. The heart may go on beating for 20 minutes. Circulation continues, and parts of the brain are probably irrigated with blood (of diminishing oxygen saturation) for several minutes. I would guess that an electroencephalogram might, for a short while, continue to show some activity, despite the mortal injury to the brain stem. Is such an individual alive or dead? The very posing of such a question forces one to focus attention on the reversibility or irreversibility of the brain stem lesion and away from extraneous considerations.

Like the stopping of the heart in classical death the irreversible loss of brain stem function is ascertained by simple bedside tests. Their very simplicity seems to render them suspect in a technological age. This is not the case in relation to 'cardiac' death. What is the rationality behind such a double standard?

A heart stops and its inability to function as a pump is diagnosed by an absent pulse, an unrecordable blood pressure, and the absence of audible contractions. McMichael has recently drawn attention to William Harvey's careful observations of what is happening as the hearts of many animals cease to beat. 'The ventricle ceases to beat before the auricles, so that the auricles may be said to outlive it. . . . With all other parts inactive and dead, the right goes on beating, so that life appears to linger longest in this auricle.' But knowledge of this electrophysiological fact – namely, that death of the heart as a whole may in normal individuals without heart disease precede death of the whole heart – has never really altered clinical practice. After clinical asystole has been present for several minutes few doctors would ask for an electrocardiogram to confirm that every part of the heart has really ceased to generate electrical signals. Still fewer would request that the trace be recorded at maximum amplification, using intracardiac probes. And strictly no one would suggest that the clinical findings be corroborated by non-perfusion on coronary angiography, or by biopsy evidence of necrosed cardiac muscle. Yet equivalent procedures have been suggested in relation to brain death.

If the context is known doctors have never objected to equating permanent loss of function with death. 'To live is to function: that is all there is to living' Oliver Wendell Holmes said. The argument is about permanence more than about pathology. And here the evidence can only be empirical. The first patient to speak again after having shown unequivocal evidence of a dead brain stem will create as great a sensation as if the decapitated head of Louix XVI had started berating his executioners.

Aware of the different views held in the United States, Dr Pallis goes on (p 23):

One of the main criticisms of codes based on the clinical identification of a dead brain stem is that they could result in diagnoses of death in some patients who might still show fragments of electroencephalographic activity at maximal amplification. It has been emphasised that 'the prediction of a fatal outcome is not a valid criterion for the accuracy of standards designed to determine that death has already occurred'. I take this to mean that predicting someone is going to die is not the same as saying he is already dead. Superficially, this sounds unexceptionable. But it has meaning only if the words 'fatal outcome', 'dead', and 'death' are unquestioningly (and perhaps even reflexly) used in a doubly traditional sense – that is, either as synonyms for 'asystole', or as shorthand for the eventual development of an electrocephalographic pattern characterised (in 1969) as 'no activity over 2 *u* V when recording from scalp electrode pairs 10 or more centimeters apart, with inter-electrode resistances of under 10,000 ohms (or impedances under 6000 ohms)'.

If one rejects these premises and believes that a person is dead when he has irreversibly lost the capacity for consciousness and the capacity to breathe (irrespective of whether the heart is beating or not, or of whether or not the electroencephalogram may still be showing a few flickers at extreme amplification) this kind of 'critique' assumes a different dimension. It is reduced to the trite conclusion that if a dead brain stem heralds asystole (or the imminent extinction of the electroencephalogram) the differing notions of death are doomed to converge. The words doctors use are indeed important.

How long in fact may cardiac action persist after a diagnosis of brain stem death? Published evidence suggests that in most cases asystole develops within days. Of the 63 patients diagnosed as brain dead in a large Danish series (and maintained on the ventilator) 29 developed asystole within 12 hours, 10 after 12-24 hours, 16 after 24-72 hours, and eight after 72-211 hours. Experience from Great Britain and elsewhere is in line with these observations. A recent case in the USA achieved wide publicity because asystole failed to develop during the two months that followed a diagnosis of brain death. The brain stem would not have been declared dead in this case as early as it was had UK-type criteria been used. Although the necropsy changes were striking it is impossible retrospectively to compute the duration of brain stem death from pathological data alone.

Having seen the medical background and philosophical analysis, how then does the law respond?

The law

A. THE BACKGROUND

It is no surprise that the definition of death did not historically trouble the courts. It was only with the development of medical technology, as we have seen, that the issue became problematic. The following case reflects the time when everything seemed relatively straightforward.

Smith v Smith (1958) 317 SW 2d 275 (Sup Ct Ark)

This case raised the question of whose estate inherited Mr Smith's property. In turn the court had to determine whether Mr and Mrs Smith died simultaneously in the accident.

Harris, Chief Justice: Hugh Smith and Lucy Coleman Smith, his wife, lived at Siloam Springs, Arkansas. They had no children. On April 22, 1947, Mrs Smith executed a will leaving all property to her husband. On November 3, 1952, Mr Smith executed a will leaving all property to his wife. On April 19, 1957, while riding together in an automobile, the Smiths had an accident. Hugh Smith was dead when assistance arrived at the scene, and Lucy Coleman Smith was unconscious, and remained so until her death seventeen days later on May 6th. . . . Let it first be observed that in reading appellant's petition, as a whole, the assertion of the death of Lucy Coleman Smith appears to be predicated on the theory that such demise occurred 'as a matter of medical science', and of course, appellant could not have meant otherwise, for he had already filed the petitions, heretofore mentioned, in the probate court, together with the physician's letter, stating that Mrs Smith was a patient in the hospital, and would be incapacitated for several months. Black's Law Dictionary, 4th Edition, page 488, defines death as follows:

> The cessation of life; the ceasing to exist; defined by physicians as a total stoppage of the circulation of the blood, and a cessation of the animal and vital functions consequent thereon, such as respiration, pulsation, etc.

Admittedly, this condition did not exist, and as a matter of fact, it would be too much of a strain on credulity for us to believe any evidence offered to the effect that Mrs Smith was dead, scientifically or otherwise, unless the conditions set out in the definition existed. . . .

To summarise and conclude, this litigation is determined by two facts. First, Hugh Smith and Lucy Coleman Smith did not die simultaneously . . .

It may be that, judged against the background of philosophical argument and the realities generated by technological advance, the definition adopted by the court is not entirely satisfactory.

B. ENGLAND

In England, there is no statute defining death. Also, there is little English case law concerning the definition of death. The English law, as one might expect, did not historically need to resolve the question of when someone was dead. The first case in which the issue arose was *R v Potter* (1963) Times, 26 July which is discussed by David Meyers in his book *The Human Body and the Law* (2nd edn, 1990) (p 196).

Mr Potter was admitted to the hospital with a severe head injury he had sustained in a fight with the named defendant. He stopped breathing after fourteen hours and was placed on an artificial respirator for twenty-four hours, at the end of which a kidney was removed for transplantation. After this nephrectomy the respirator was shut off and there was no spontaneous respiration or circulation.

Under traditional definitions of death, the victim in *Potter* was not dead until his breathing and circulation came to a persistent and complete halt when the respirator was finally turned off nearly two days after his admission to hospital. Yet if this were the case, the physician who removed the victim's kidney may well have been guilty of a crime (malicious wounding) and a civil wrong (battery), for the removal took place while the victim was still 'alive', without his consent, and was not for his benefit. This seems ridiculous. Nonetheless, the defendant also argued that the actions by the physician, in shutting off the respirator and allowing the patient-victim to die, served to break the chain of causation between the original wrongful act (the assault) and the death, which should release the original wrongdoer from legal liability for the homicide. It would seem that the judge agreed, for the defendant was committed for trial by the Coroner after a jury's finding of manslaughter, yet was convicted only of common assault by the court.

Potter illustrates the most usual circumstance under which this issue may become relevant in law. In the following case, an English court was faced with this issue for the first time.

R v Malcherek, R v Steel [1981] 2 All ER 422, [1981] 1 WLR 690, (CA)

Lord Lane CJ: I start with the applicant Steel. . . . It was on October 10 1977, at about 9 a.m., that Carol Wilkinson was walking to work from her home to the bakery. At some time on that morning between about nine o'clock and half-past-nine, she was savagely attacked by someone who stripped off the greater part of her clothing, and then battered her about the head with a 50 lb stone which was found nearby. She was found shortly afterwards in a field by the road, unconscious. She was taken as rapidly as could be to hospital. She had multiple fractures of the skull and severe brain damage as well as a broken arm and other superficial injuries which need not concern us. She was put almost immediately on a life support machine in the shape of a ventilator. On 12th October the medical team in whose charge she was, after a number of tests, came to the conclusion that her brain had ceased to function and that, accordingly, the ventilator was in effect operating on a lifeless body. The life support machine was switched off and all bodily functions ceased shortly afterwards.

. . . Upon admission to the casualty department of the Bradford Royal Infirmary at about 10.15 a.m. on Monday, October 10, Carol was seen by Dr Nevelos, who found her to be deeply unconscious with no motor activity, her eyes open and the pupils fixed. She was breathing only with the aid of the ventilator. An hour later she was admitted to the intensive care unit of the Royal Infirmary and during the whole of that day she remained deeply unconscious and unresponsive. At 10.00 p.m. the consultant neuro-surgeon, a Mr Price, examined her. He found her to be in a deep coma, unresponding to any stimulus. He carried out a test for electrical activity in the brain which proved negative. The total absence of any motor activity since the girl had been admitted to hospital and the early fixation of the pupils, which I have already mentioned, led him to the conclusion that there had been a devastating impact injury to the brain. The cerebral function monitor showed no activity. Her eyes were too occluded, so it is said, to allow any caloric testing. The suggestion was made by Mr Price that her temperature should be raised and that if by the morning her cerebral function remained as it had been up to date, namely, zero, they should declare her brain to be dead. In fact, in the morning shortly after 10.00 a.m., a cerebral blood flow test was carried out which indicated that there was no blood circulating in the brain. Several electroencephalogram tests were made during that day. None of them had any positive result.

On Wednesday, October 12, two days after the injuries had been inflicted, another electroencephalogram test was made in the morning and another one at 6.00 p.m. but none of those tests showed any signs of electrical activity at all. After that there was a consultation between the doctors who were in charge of the patient, and it was agreed among them that the continued use of the ventilator was without any purpose. At 6.15 p.m. the patient was withdrawn from the ventilator, and at 6.40 p.m. she was declared to be dead. There is an indication, though we are told it was not part of the evidence at the trial, that on post-mortem 50 minutes later it was found that her brain was already in the process of decomposition.

Much of the cross-examination of the medical men was taken up with suggestions that they had failed to conform to certain criteria which have been laid down by the royal medical colleges on the subject of the ascertainment of brain death. The matter which Mr Steer invites this court to take into consideration as possibly differentiating the case of [Steel] from that of [Malcherek] is that he says that two of the suggested tests were not carried out properly, namely the corneal reflex test and the vestibulo-ocular reflex test. The corneal reflex test consists of touching the cornea of the eye with a piece of cotton wool to see if that creates any reaction in the patient and, as we understand it, the vestibulo-ocular reflex test consists of putting ice cold water into the aperture of the ear, again to see if that produces any reflex in the patient. Reasons were given for neither of those tests having been carried out.

The court then discussed the facts of *Malcherek*, the second case.

. . . The victim was Christina Malcherek, his wife, who was then aged 32. It seems that in November 1978 she left Malcherek in order to go and live with her daughters at Poole. There was a non-molestation order in force, directed at Malcherek, but on the evening of March 26 1979 he went to her flat where she was living. There was a quarrel and, to cut a long story short, he stabbed his wife nine times with a kitchen knife. One of the stabs resulted in a deep penetrating wound to Mrs Malcherek's abdomen.

She was taken to Poole General Hospital and there was preliminary treatment in order to try to rectify her very low blood pressure, which was ascertained on admission. The surgical registrar then performed a laparotomy and removed rather more than one and a half litres of blood from the abdomen. There was a section of the intestine which was damaged, and he excised that and joined up the two ends. For several days it seemed as though Mrs Malcherek was making an uneventful recovery. Indeed, she was clearly confidently expected to survive. However, on April 1 she collapsed and the preliminary diagnosis was that she had suffered a massive pulmonary embolism. She was resuscitated and arrangements were made for her admission to the Western Hospital at Southampton, which was equipped to deal with this type of emergency. She arrived there shortly before midnight. A couple of hours later her condition suddenly deteriorated and her heart stopped. She was taken straight away to the operating theatre and given cardiac massage. The surgeon then opened her chest. He found that her heart was distended and not beating. He made an incision into the pulmonary artery and extracted from the pulmonary artery a large clot of blood some twelve inches long, which had plainly formed in one of the veins of the leg (which, we are told, is a common complication of major abdominal surgery), and had then moved on from the leg to the pulmonary artery with the results already described. When the clot was removed the heart started again spontaneously. It will be appreciated that since the heart was not beating for a period of something like 30 minutes there was a grave danger of anoxic damage to the brain. She was returned to the ward and connected to a ventilator. Throughout the Monday she remained on that machine receiving intensive care, but in the afternoon an electroencephalogram showed that there were indeed symptoms of severe anoxic damage to the brain. The prognosis was poor.

The consultant neurologist saw her at 7.00 p.m. She was unresponsive to any stimulus save that her pupils did react to light. He suggested a further electroencephalogram because at that stage it was not clear how much brain damage had been suffered. On the morning of Tuesday, Dr Manners decided to dispense with the ventilator if that could possibly be done. When that was done she was able, first of all, to breathe adequately by herself, but towards midday she suffered a sharp and marked deterioration and the diagnosis was that she had suffered a cerebral vascular accident – possibly a ruptured blood vessel, possibly a clot – causing further brain damage. In any event, by 1.45 p.m. her attempts to breathe were inadequate and she was put back onto the ventilator. There was a continued deterioration and by the following day she was deeply unconscious and seemed to have irreversible brain damage. There was less electrical activity than before when a further electroencephalogram was carried out.

On April 5 the situation had deteriorated still more, and it was quite obvious at 1.15 p.m. on that day, when Dr Lawton made an examination, that her brain was irretrievably damaged. He carried out five of the six royal medical colleges' confirmatory tests. The one he omitted was the 'gag reflex' test, again for reasons which he explained. The patient's relations were consulted and a decision was made to disconnect the ventilator, which was done at 4.30 p.m. A supply of oxygen was fed to her lungs in case she should make spontaneous efforts to breathe but she did not, and shortly after 5.00 p.m. she was certified to be dead.

In these circumstances, as in the earlier case, the judge decided that the question of causation should not be left for the jury's consideration. Consequently, the only issue they had to decide was the one of intent, there being no argument but that Malcherek had in fact inflicted the knife wound or wounds on Mrs Malcherek. In this case the principal and, in effect, the only ground of appeal, as Mr Field-Fisher has told us, is that the judge should have left the issue of causation to the jury.

This is not the occasion for any decision as to what constitutes death. Modern techniques have undoubtedly resulted in the blurring of many of the conventional and traditional concepts of death. A person's heart can now be removed altogether without death supervening; machines can keep the blood circulating through the vessels of the body until a new heart can be implanted in the patient, and even though a person is no longer able to breathe spontaneously a ventilating machine can, so to speak, do his breathing for him, as is demonstrated in the two cases before us. There is, it seems, a body of opinion in the medical profession that there is only one true test of death and that is the irreversible *death of the brain stem* (our emphasis) which controls the basic functions of the body such as breathing. When that occurs it is said the body has died, even though by mechanical means the lungs are being caused to operate and some circulation of blood is taking place.

We have had placed before us, and have been asked to admit, evidence that in each of these two cases the medical men concerned did not comply with all the suggested criteria for establishing such brain death. Indeed, further evidence has been suggested and placed before us that those criteria or tests are not in themselves stringent enough. However, in each of these two cases there is no doubt that whatever test is applied the victim died; that is to say, applying the traditional test, all body functions, breathing and heartbeat and brain function came to an end, at the latest, soon after the ventilator was disconnected.

The question posed for answer to this court is simply whether the judge in each case was right in withdrawing from the jury the question of causation. Was he right to rule that there was no evidence on which the jury could come to the conclusion that the assailant did not cause the death of the victim? The way in which the submissions are put by Mr Field-Fisher on the one hand and Mr Wilfred Steer on the other is as follows: the doctors, by switching off the ventilator and the life support machine, were the cause of death or, to put it more accurately, there was evidence which the jury should have been allowed to consider that the doctors, and not the assailant, in each case may have been the cause of death.

In each case it is clear that the initial assault was the cause of the grave head injuries in the one case and of the massive abdominal haemorrhage in the other. In each case the initial assault was the reason for the medical treatment being necessary. In each case the medical treatment given was normal and conventional. At some stage the doctors must decide if and when treatment has become otiose. This decision was reached, in each of the two cases here, in circumstances which have already been set out in some detail. It is no part of the task of this court to inquire whether the criteria, the royal medical colleges' confirmatory tests, are a satisfactory code of practice. It is no part of the task of this court to decide whether the doctors were, in either of these two cases, justified in omitting one or more of the so called 'confirmatory tests'. The doctors are not on trial: the applicant and the appellant respectively were. . . .

There is no evidence in the present case that at the time of conventional death, after the life support machinery was disconnected, the original wound or injury was other than a continuing, operating and indeed substantial cause of the death of the victim, although it need hardly be added that it need not be substantial to render the assailant guilty. There may be occasions, although they will be rare, when the original injury has ceased to operate at all, but in the ordinary case if the treatment is given bona fide by competent and careful medical practitioners, then evidence will not be admissible to show that the treatment would not have been administered in the same way by other medical practitioners. In other words, the fact that the victim has died, despite or because of medical treatment for the initial injury given by careful and skilled medical practitioners, will not exonerate the original assailant from responsibility for the death. It follows that so far as the ground of appeal in each of these cases relates to the direction given on causation, that ground fails. It also follows that the evidence which it is sought to adduce now, although we are prepared to assume that it is both credible and was not available properly at the trial – and a reasonable explanation for not calling it at the trial has been given – if received could, under no circumstances, afford any ground for allowing the appeal.

The reason is this. Nothing which any of the two or three medical men whose statements are before us could say would alter the fact that in each case the assailant's actions continued to be an operating cause of the death. Nothing the doctors could say would provide any ground for a jury coming to the conclusion that the assailant in either case might not have caused the death. The furthest to which their proposed evidence goes, as already stated, is to suggest, first, that the criteria or the confirmatory tests are not sufficiently stringent and, secondly, that in the present case they were in certain respects inadequately fulfilled or carried out. It is no part of this court's function in the present circumstances to pronounce upon this matter, nor was it a function of either of the juries at these trials. Where a medical practitioner adopting methods which are generally accepted comes bona fine and conscientiously to the conclusion that the patient is for practical purposes dead, and that such vital functions as exist – for example, circulation – are being maintained solely by mechanical means, and therefore discontinues treatment, that does not prevent the person who inflicted the initial injury from being responsible for the victim's death. Putting it in another way, the discontinuance of treatment in those circumstances does not break the chain of causation between the initial injury and the death.

Although it is unnecessary to go further than that for the purpose of deciding the present point, we wish to add this thought. Whatever the strict logic of the matter may be, it is perhaps somewhat bizarre to suggest, as counsel have impliedly done, that where a doctor tries his conscientious best to save the life of a patient brought to hospital in extremis, skilfully using sophisticated methods, drugs and machinery to do so, but fails in his attempt and therefore discontinues treatment, he can be said to have caused the death of the patient.

The Court of Appeal sidestepped the need to adopt as law the notion of brain-stem death, but, as Peter Skegg points out in his book *Law, Ethics and Medicine*, the trial judge in *Malcherek* seems to have done so (at 196).

> The judge at Malcherek's original trial was reported to have said, 'To have kept her on the respirator would have been, in effect, to ventilate a corpse.' This statement, and his ruling that there was no evidence to show that the victim was still alive when the doctors switched off the machine, indicated the trial judge's acceptance of the view that once brain death [semble brain-stem death] is established a person is dead for the purpose of the law of homicide, even though the heart continues to beat.

It should be noted that courts in a number of jurisdictions have in similar circumstances to *Malcherek and Steel* confirmed that court's view on causation without finding it necessary to determine whether the victim was already dead when the ventilator was turned off (*Finlayson v HM Advocate* 1978 SLT (Notes) 60 (Scotland); *R v Kitching and Adams* [1976] 6 WWR 697 (Manitoba) *R v Kinash* [1982] Qld R 648 (Qld)). The third case in England where the issue was raised was, curiously enough, a case in which an issue of copyright turned on whether one of the alleged copyright holders was dead.

Mail Newspapers plc v Express Newspapers plc [1987] FSR 90 (Ch D)

> **Millet J:** Mrs. B had suffered a brain haemorrhage while 24 weeks pregnant. She was being kept on a life-support system in the hope that the baby could be born alive. The evidence suggested that Mrs. B was probably clinically dead, but tests had not been undertaken.
>
> Seven national newspapers obtained and published, without any authority from Mr. B, photographs of the couple's wedding. Thereafter Mr. B entered into an agreement with the plaintiffs granting them exclusive rights to all his archive photographs and undertaking to pose exclusively for the plaintiffs for photographs with his baby within 24 hours of its birth, all rights to those photographs to be owned by the plaintiffs. The plaintiffs wrote to many national newspapers informing them that they held the exclusive rights to Mr. B's photographs and warning them not to publish these. The defendants replied that they intended to use the photographs. The plaintiffs therefore obtained *ex parte* injunctions restraining the defendants from publishing the photographs.
>
> On the *inter partes* hearing of the motion, the defendants argued that the copyright in the photographs vested either in Mrs. B alone or in Mr. and Mrs. B together, and that Mr. B was unable to grant an exclusive licence since Mrs. B was still alive and had not consented. The evidence was that before the wedding Mr. B had asked his fiancee to arrange for the photographs to be taken, but that afterwards Mr. B paid the bill. . . .
>
> The evidence, such as it is, suggests that Mrs. Bell is probably clinically dead, that is to say, that her brain had ceased to function altogether, although she is breathing and her bodily functions are being kept going. Medical tests to determine whether or not Mrs. Bell is clinically dead have not been undertaken, and understandably no one has thought it appropriate to obtain a death certificate.
>
> . . . [I]n submitting to me that the plaintiffs have no real prospect of succeeding at the trial Mr. Shaw was really submitting that Mrs. B is unarguably still alive. The evidence before me does not go nearly far enough to warrant any such conclusion. I have no doubt at all that there is at the very least a serious question to be tried whether Mrs. Bell is alive or dead. Indeed, so far as the evidence before me goes, it supports the conclusion that she is probably already legally dead.

Millet J does not seem to advance the cause of clarity, so necessary in this area, when he uses expressions such as Mrs Bell was 'clinically dead' and, a little later, that she was 'legally dead' implying as a consequence that there are different types of death.

Subsequently, however, the English law seems to have settled the question.

Re A [1992] 3 Med LR 303 (Fam D)

Johnson J: These proceedings concern a boy, A, who was born on April 24, 1990. He and his family come from overseas and there are three other children in the family. A was taken to the Accident & Emergency Department of a hospital near where his family live on January 17 of this year. It was not the first time that he had been taken to a hospital as an emergency because in December he had been taken to hospital suffering from facial bruising and greenstick fractures of both his left femur and tibia and he had been kept in hospital until the beginning of January.

When he arrived at hospital again on January 17 the doctors who examined him could detect no heartbeat. It was said by his mother that he had fallen from a table on to a carpeted floor and had struck his head against a toy of some kind. She also said that some minutes later he had begun to breathe heavily and seemed to be having a convulsion which seemed to last about ten minutes.

On the same day he was transferred to another hospital where extensive attempts at resuscitation were made, but on the following day he was transferred to Guy's Hospital for intensive care and assessment. There the records show that he was found to have bruising on the inside of his right upper ear as well as what is described as a 'probable bruise' behind his left ear. He still had a plaster on his left leg from his earlier admission to hospital. A brain scan showed blood, the presence and distribution of which are said to be typical of non-accidental injury. A was in intensive care. Vigorous attempts were made to improve his situation, but there were no signs of recovery. However, it is plain from the evidence which I have heard that he was not then 'brain-stem dead'.

I have had the advantage of evidence from a consultant paediatric neurologist at Guy's Hospital. She gave her evidence with great clarity and precision. I judged her to be an extremely impressive member of her profession and I have no hesitation in accepting her evidence. A has been under her care ever since he arrived at Guy's Hospital. He has been on a ventilator. Put briefly in lay terms, the brain-stem controls the vital functions of the body. The ventilator enables the body to breathe by introducing oxygen and extracting carbon dioxide and that mechanism enables the heart to keep beating.

On January 20 – that is last Monday – the consultant removed A briefly from the ventilator to see whether he was capable of supporting himself without the ventilator. When she did so she heard slight gasping noises which led her to believe that A was not brain-stem dead according to criteria now generally accepted in medical circles.

The precise definition of death has been the subject of recommendations by both the Royal College of Surgeons and the Royal College of Physicians and a working party of the British Paediatric Association. Applying the criteria laid down by her profession the consultant concluded on January 20 that A was not then brain-stem dead. On the following day she again carried out the tests which are necessary to determine whether the necessary criteria are satisfied. The consultant described those tests to me and she explained to me that each one was satisfied. The tests lasted overall about half an hour.

Describing the criteria and her observations of A, and expressing myself in lay terms, her evidence was to the following effect. A's pupils were fixed and dilated. On movement of the head his eyes moved with his head. What is called the 'doll's eye response' was absent. On his eye being touched with a piece of cotton wool there was no response. On cold water being passed into his ear there was no eye movement in response. On steps being taken, in effect, to cause him to 'gag' there was no reflex reaction, neither was there reaction to pain being applied to his central nervous system. Finally, on his temporary removal from the ventilator to enable the carbon dioxide content of his body to increase there was no respiratory response. All in all, the consultant was satisfied that A was brain-stem dead. . . .

On the same day the consultant had arranged for a colleague consultant paediatric neurologist to carry out the same tests that she had, herself, carried out the previous day with a view to confirming or otherwise the validity of her own professional conclusion. Under professional guidelines it was not necessary for her to seek a second opinion in that way, but she decided that in the particular circumstances of the case it would be a wise thing for her to do. Accordingly, the tests were carried out again on Wednesday of last week, January 22, by this colleague who reached the same conclusion as had been reached by the first consultant.

Both doctors were at pains to exclude other possibilities for A's state, including the possibility of his suffering from extreme hypothermia or some abnormality of his biochemistry. Moreover, they tested for drugs, lest his brain-stem function should have been suppressed by the administration of some drug of which they had not been aware, although he had, in fact, been under the consultant's supervision for three days in Guy's Hospital and they would have been aware had drugs been administered to him. Nonetheless they carried out the necessary checks and satisfied themselves that no such drug was present.

Both doctors concluded that A was brain-stem dead. . . .

It is now Monday, January 27. I have no hesitation at all in holding that A has been dead since Tuesday of last week, January 21.

Even more emphatical was the view expressed by a majority of the Law Lords in *Airedale NHS Trust v Bland* [1993] 1 All ER 821. You will recall that this was the case concerning the legality of the withdrawal of hydration and nutrition from a patient in a persistent vegetative state.

Lord Keith: Anthony Bland has for over three years been in the condition known as persistent vegetative state ("PVS"). It is unnecessary to go into all the details about the manifestations of this state which are fully set out in the judgments of the courts below. It is sufficient to say that it arises from the destruction, through prolonged deprivation of oxygen, of the cerebral cortex, which has resolved into a watery mass. The cortex is that part of the brain which is the seat of cognitive function and sensory capacity. Anthony Bland cannot see, hear or feel anything. He cannot communicate in any way. The consciousness which is the essential feature of individual personality has departed for ever. On the other hand the brain stem, which controls the reflexive functions of the body, in particular heartbeat, breathing and digestion, continues to operate. In the eyes of the medical world and of the law a person is not clinically dead so long as the brain stem retains its function.

Lord Goff: I start with the simple fact that, in law, Anthony is still alive. It is true that his condition is such that it can be described as a living death; but he is nevertheless still alive. This is because, as a result of developments in modern medical technology, doctors no longer associate death exclusively with breathing and heartbeat, and it has come to be accepted that death occurs when the brain, and in particular the brain stem, has been destroyed. . . . The evidence is that Anthony's brain stem is still alive and functioning and it follows that, in the present state of medical science, he is still alive and should be so regarded as a matter of law.

Lord Browne-Wilkinson: Until recently there was no doubt what was life and what was death. A man was dead if he stopped breathing and his heart stopped beating. There was no artificial means of sustaining these indications of life for more than a short while. Death in the traditional sense was beyond human control. Apart from cases of unlawful homicide, death occurred automatically in the course of nature when the natural functions of the body failed to sustain the lungs and the heart.

Recent developments in medical science have fundamentally affected these previous certainties. In medicine, the cessation of breathing or of heartbeat is no longer death. By the use of a ventilator, lungs which in the unaided course of nature would have stopped breathing can be made to breathe, thereby sustaining the heartbeat. Those, like Anthony Bland, who would previously have died through inability to swallow food can be kept alive by artificial feeding. This has led the medical profession to redefine death in terms of brain stem death, i.e., the death of that part of the brain without which the body cannot function at all without assistance. In some cases it is now apparently possible, with the use of the ventilator, to sustain a beating heart even though the brain stem, and therefore in medical terms the patient, is dead; 'the ventilated corpse'.

I do not refer to these factors because Anthony Bland is already dead, either medically or legally. His brain stem is alive and so is he. . . .

Undoubtedly, these views form part of the *ratio decidendi* of the case. It was a necessary step in the reasoning of the Law Lords that Anthony Bland was alive otherwise no question of the doctor's duty as regards treatment would have arisen.

For developments in other common law jurisdictions, see, 1. US: President's Commission, *op cit*, 62-67 (legislative developments), 68-69 (case law), *People v Eulo* (1984) 472 NE 2d 286 (NY CA) and the Uniform Determination of Death Act. Pallis, *op cit*, subjects this Act and its underlying premise of 'whole brain death' to sustained and, in our view, justified criticism (28-29, 30-32); 2. Canada: G Sharpe, *The Law and Medicine in Canada* (2nd edn, 1987); 3. Australia: Report of the Law Reform Commission of Australia, *Human Tissue Transplants* (Report No 7, 1977) and, eg, Death (Definition) Act 1983 of South Australia.

C. APPLYING THE BRAIN-STEM DEATH CRITERION IN ENGLISH LAW

1. The Code of Practice

You will recall that Johnson J in *Re A* referred to the Report of the Conference of Medical Royal Colleges and their Faculties in 1976. As part of the Report there was included a memorandum by way of a Code of Practice.

'Diagnosis of Brain Death' (1976) 2 British Medical Journal 1187

With the development of intensive-care techniques and their wide availability in the United Kingdom it has become commonplace for hospitals to have deeply comatose and unresponsive patients with severe brain damage who are maintained on artificial respiration by means of mechanical ventilators. This state has been recognised for many years and it has been the concern of the medical profession to establish diagnostic criteria of such rigour that on their fulfilment the mechanical ventilator can be switched off, in the secure knowledge that there is no possible chance of recovery.

There has been much philosophical argument about the diagnosis of death which has throughout recorded history been accepted as having occurred when the vital functions of respiration and circulation have ceased. However, with the technical ability to maintain these functions artificially the dilemma of when to switch off the ventilator has been the subject of much public interest. It is agreed that permanent functional death of the brainstem constitutes brain death and that once this has occurred further artificial support is fruitless and should be withdrawn. It is good medical practice to recognise when brain death has occurred and to act accordingly, sparing relatives from the further emotional trauma of sterile hope.

Codes of practice, such as the Harvard criteria [*Report of the Ad Hoc Committee of Harvard Medical School* (1968) 205 JAMA 337] have been devised to guide medical practitioners in the diagnosis of brain death. These have provided considerable help with the problem and they have been refined as the knowledge gained from experience has been collated.

More recently Forrester [(1976) 34 *Health Bulletin* 199] has written on established practice in Scotland and Jennett [(1975) 1 *J of Med Ethics* 63] has made useful observations. The diagnostic criteria presented for brain death here have been written with the advice of the subcommittee of the Transplant Advisory Panel, the working-party of the Royal College of Physicians, the working-party of the Faculty of Anaesthetists, and the Royal College of Surgeons and have been approved by the Conference of Medical Royal Colleges and their Faculties in the United Kingdom. They are accepted as being sufficient to distinguish between those patients who retain the functional capacity to have a chance of even partial recovery and those where no such possibility exists.

Conditions under which the diagnosis of brain death should be considered
1. *The patient is deeply comatose.*
(a)   There should be no suspicion that this state is due to depressant drugs. *Note 1*
(b)   Primary hypothermia as a cause of coma should have been excluded.

(c)   Metabolic and endocrine disturbances which can be responsible for or can contribute to coma should have been excluded. *Note 2*

2. *The patient is being maintained on a ventilator because spontaneous respiration had previously become inadequate or had ceased altogether.*

(a)   Relaxants (neuromuscular blocking agents) and other drugs should have been excluded as a cause of respiratory inadequacy or failure. *Note 3*

3. *There should be no doubt that the patient's condition is due to irremediable structural brain damage. The diagnosis of a disorder which can lead to brain death should have been fully established. Note 4*

Notes

Note 1

Narcotics, hypnotics, and tranquillisers may have prolonged duration of action particularly when some hypothermia exists. The benzodiazepines are markedly cumulative and persistent in their actions and are commonly used as anticonvulsants or to assist synchronisation with mechanical ventilators. It is therefore recommended that the drug history should be carefully reviewed and adequate intervals allowed for the persistence of drug effects to be excluded. This is of particular importance in patients where the primary cause of coma lies in the toxic effects of drugs followed by anoxic cerebral damage.

Note 2

Metabolic and endocrine factors contributing to the persistence of coma must be subject to careful assessment. There should be no profound abnormality of the serum-electrolytes, acid-balance, or blood-glucose.

Note 3

Immobility, unresponsiveness, and lack of spontaneous respiration may be due to the use of neuromuscular blocking drugs and the persistence of their effects should be excluded by elicitation of spinal reflexes (flexion or stretch) or by the demonstration of adequate neuromuscular conduction with a conventional nerve stimulator. Equally, persistent effects of hypnotics and narcotics should be excluded as the cause of respiratory failure.

Note 4

It may be obvious within hours of a primary intra-cranial event such as severe head injury, spontaneous intra-cranial haemorrhage or following neurosurgery that the condition is irremediable. However, when a patient has suffered primarily from cardiac arrest, hypoxia or severe circulatory insufficiency with an indefinite period of cerebral anoxia, or is suspected of having cerebral air or fat embolism then it may take much longer to establish the diagnosis and to be confident of the prognosis. In some patients the primary pathology may be a matter of doubt and a confident diagnosis may only be reached by continuity of clinical observation and investigation.

Diagnostic tests for the confirmation of brain death

All brainstem reflexes are absent:

(i)   The pupils are fixed in diameter and do not respond to sharp changes in the intensity of incident light.

(ii)   There is no corneal reflex.

(iii) The vestibulo-ocular reflexes are absent. *Note (a)*

(iv)   No motor responses within the cranial nerve distribution can be elicited by adequate stimulation of any somatic area.

(v)   There is no gag reflex or reflex response to bronchial stimulation by a suction catheter passed down the trachea.

(vi)   No respiratory movements occur when the patient is disconnected from the mechanical ventilator for long enough to ensure that the arterial carbon dioxide tension rises above the threshold for stimulation of respiration. *Note (b)*

Note (a)

Vestibulo-ocular reflexes. – These are absent when no eye movement occurs during or following the slow injection of 20 ml of ice-cold water into each external auditory meatus in turn, clear access to the tympanic membrane having been established by direct inspection. This test may be contra-indicated on one or other side by local trauma.

Note (b)
Disconnection from the ventilator. – During this test it is necessary for the arterial carbon-dioxide tension to exceed the threshold for respiratory stimulation – that is, the $PaCO_1$ should normally reach 50 mm Hg (6.65 kPa). This is best achieved by measurement of the blood gases; if this facility is available it is recommended that the patient should be disconnected when the $PaCO_2$ reaches 40-45 mm Hg following administration of 5% CO_2 in oxygen through the ventilator. This starting level has been chosen because patients may be moderately hypothermic (35°C-37°C), flaccid, and with a depressed metabolic rate, so that arterial carbon-dioxide tension rises only slowly in apnoea (about 2mm Hg/min). (Hypoxia during disconnection should be prevented by delivering oxygen at 6 litres/min through a catheter into the trachea.) If blood-gas analysis is not available to measure the $PaCO_2$ and PaO_2 the alternative procedure is to supply the ventilator with pure oxygen for ten minutes (pre-oxygenation), then with 5% CO_2 in oxygen for five minutes and to disconnect the ventilator for ten minutes, while delivering oxygen at 6 litres/minute by catheter into the trachea. This establishes diffusion oxygenation and ensures that during apnoea hypoxia will not occur even in ten or more minutes of respiratory arrest. Those patients with preexisting chronic respiratory insufficiency, who may be unresponsive to raised levels of carbon dioxide and who normally exist on an hypoxic drive, are special cases and should be expertly investigated with careful blood-gas monitoring.

Other considerations
1. Repetition of testing
It is customary to repeat the tests to ensure that there has been no observer error. The interval between tests must depend upon the primary pathology and the clinical course of the disease. Note 4 indicates some conditions where it would be unnecessary to repeat them since a prognosis of imminent brain death can be accepted as being obvious.

In some conditions the outcome is not so clear cut and in these it is recommended that the tests should be repeated. The interval between tests depends upon the progress of the patient and might be as long as 24 hours. This is a matter for medical judgement and repetition time must be related to the signs of improvement, stability, or deterioration which present themselves.

2. Integrity of spinal reflexes
It is well established that spinal-cord function can persist after insults which irretrievably destroy brainstem function. Reflexes of spinal origin may persist or return after an initial absence in brain dead patients.

3. Confirmatory investigations
It is now widely accepted that electro-encephalography is not necessary for the diagnosis of brain death. Indeed this view was expressed from Harvard in 1969 [(1969) 281 N Eng J Med 1070] only a year after the publication of their original criteria.

Electroencephalography has its principal value at earlier stages in the care of patients, in whom the original diagnosis is in doubt. When electroencephalography is used, the strict criteria recommended by the Federation of EEG Societies must be followed.

Other investigations such as cerebral angiography or cerebral blood-flow measurements are not required for the diagnosis of brain death.

4. Body temperature
The body temperature in these patients may be low because of depression of central temperature regulation by drugs or by brainstem damage and it is recommended that it should be not less than 35°C before the diagnostic tests are carried out. A low-reading thermometer should be used.

5. Specialist opinion and the status of the doctors concerned
Experienced clinicians in intensive-care units, acute medical wards, and accident and emergency departments should not normally require specialist advice. Only when the primary diagnosis is in doubt is it necessary to consult with a neurologist or neurosurgeon.

Decision to withdraw artificial support should be made after all the criteria presented above have been fulfilled and can be made by any one of the following combination of doctors:
(a)   A consultant who is in charge of the case and one other doctor.
(b)   In the absence of a consultant, his deputy, who should have been registered for 5 years or more *and* who should have had adequate previous experience in the care of such cases, and one other doctor.

An addendum was produced in 1979.

'Memorandum on the diagnosis of death' (1979) 1 British Medical Journal 332

1. In October 1976 the Conference of Royal Colleges and their Faculties (UK) published a report unanimously expressing the opinion that 'Brain Death', when it had occurred, could be diagnosed with certainty. The report has been widely accepted.

The Conference was not at that time asked whether or not it believed that death itself should be presumed to occur when brain death takes place or whether it would come to some other conclusion. The present report examines this point and should be considered as an addendum to the original report.

2. Exceptionally, as a result of massive trauma, death occurs instantaneously or near-instantaneously. Far more commonly, death is not an event, it is a process, the various organs and systems supporting the continuation of life failing and eventually ceasing altogether to function, successively and at different times.

3. Cessation of respiration and cessation of the heart beat are examples of organic failure occurring during the process of dying and since the moment that the heart beat ceases is usually detectable with simplicity by no more than clinical means, it has for many centuries been accepted as the moment of death itself, without any serious attempt being made to assess the validity of this assumption.

4. It is now universally accepted, by the lay public as well as by the medical profession, that it is not possible to equate death itself with cessation of the heart beat. Quite apart from the elective cardiac arrest of open-heart surgery, spontaneous cardiac arrest followed by successful resuscitation is today a commonplace and although the more sensational accounts of occurrences of this kind still refer to the patient being 'dead' until restoration of the heartbeat, the use of the quote marks usually demonstrates that this word is not taken literally, for to most people the one aspect of death that is beyond debate is its irreversibility.

5. In the majority of cases, in which a dying patient passes through the processes leading to the irreversible state we call death, successive organic failures eventually reach a point at which brain death occurs and this is the point of no return.

6. In a minority of cases, brain death does not occur as a result of the failure of other organs or systems but as a direct result of severe damage to the brain itself from, perhaps, a head injury or a spontaneous intracranial haemorrhage. Here the order of events is reversed; instead of the failure of such vital functions as heart beat and respiration eventually resulting in brain death, brain death results in the cessation of spontaneous respiration; this is normally followed within minutes by cardiac arrest due to hypoxia. If, however, oxygenation is maintained by artificial ventilation the heartbeat can continue for some days, and haemoperfusion will for a time be adequate to maintain function in other organs, such as the liver and kidneys.

7. Whatever the mode of its production, brain death represents the state at which a patient becomes truly dead, because by then all functions of the brain have permanently and irreversibly ceased. It is not difficult or illogical in any way to equate this with the concept in many religions of the departure of the spirit from the body.

8. In the majority of cases, since brain death is part of or the culmination of a failure of all vital functions, there is no necessity for a doctor specifically to identify brain death individually before concluding that the patient is dead. In a minority of cases in which it is brain death that causes failure of other organs and systems, the fact that these systems can be artificially maintained even after brain death has made it important to establish a diagnostic routine which will identify with certainty the existence of brain death.

Conclusion

9. It is the conclusion of the Conference that the identification of brain death means that the patient is dead, whether or not the function of some organs, such as a heartbeat, is still maintained by artificial means.

Given the near universal acceptance of the approach adopted in this Code, it is no surprise that the court in *Re A* adopted as the concept of death that which is reflected, at least implicitly, in the Code; adopted the locus (ie brain); and adopted the criteria for determining the presence or absence of the relevant functions and the means of determining clinically these criteria.

2. Non-compliance with Code

Questions concerning compliance or non-compliance with the Code only arise, of course, in those circumstances in which the patient's vital functions are being artificially maintained. Clearly if the patient dies in other circumstances the death will be recognised by the prolonged irreversible absence of vital functions. If the patient is receiving artificial life-support, will non-compliance with the Code have any legal consequences? There are two sets of problems:

(a) the determination of death;
(b) the legality of the doctor's conduct.

It may be useful to divide non-compliance with the Code by looking at the three stages contemplated in the Code.

Stage 1 requires that the doctor exclude patients with certain conditions; see Code (1)(a), (b) and (c) and (2) and (3), *supra.*

Stage 2 requires that the doctor perform the specific clinical 'tests for confirming brain death', *supra.*

Stage 3 requires that the doctor repeat the testing.

(a) The determination of death

The question we are concerned with here is, would a court when presented with evidence of non-compliance with the Code, hold that a patient was not dead when the doctor stated that he was. Undoubtedly, whether a person is dead will always be a question of law for the court. A court in making a determination will make a finding that death occurred on the basis of medical evidence (save in the most obvious circumstances). The medical evidence must *prima facie* include a demonstration that the doctor has complied with the Code. If the doctor's non-compliance occurs at *stage 1* it would be open to the court, on appropriate facts, to find that the patient was not dead at the time certified.

If the non-compliance occurs at *stage 2*, what has to be tested is whether a court would decide that a patient was not dead because, for example, the doctor failed to carry out one or more of the stipulated tests. At first blush, this would seem to be a somewhat recondite point, but we are assuming here, so as to test the analysis, that the precise moment of death is important legally. We take the view that a court, in the absence of evidence of irresponsible behaviour by the doctor, would be reluctant to find that the patient was not dead at the time asserted. But, how can this conclusion be justified in the face of the fact that a person must be presumed to be living until shown to be dead? The justification may be that, although the determination of death is a matter of law, medical evidence is the only material upon which the court can act. We have no doubt that if responsible medical evidence was that the omission of the test(s) was irrelevant on the particular facts the court would not question this. (See *R v Malcherek*, where two tests were not carried out by the doctors and Lord Lane CJ stated: '[r]easons were given for neither of these tests having been carried out'. The court did not cast doubt on the doctors' determination of death.) This would obviously be the case where the test could not physically be carried out but may also be the case in other circumstances where good medical reasons exist for omitting it. It would, of course, be more difficult to sustain this view if none of the prescribed tests had been carried out.

If the non-compliance occurs at *stage 3*, again the only relevant legal question is whether the patient was dead at the time the first set of tests was carried out. If the purpose of the repetition of the tests is *confirmatory*, in view of what has been said before, it must follow that a court would hold that death had occurred no later than the completion of the first set of tests. Of course, if the repeat tests were more than confirmatory, major problems arise not merely concerning repetition of the tests but concerning the validity of the tests themselves. Obviously if a second set of tests are called for why not a third and so on?

Dr Pallis addressed this point in *ABC of Brain Stem Death* (pp 16-17).

> Virtually all codes urge that testing be carried out twice. The recommended intervals between the relevant tests have progressively shortened. There are several reasons why this has happened. Firstly, the objections to ventilating corpses have become more widely accepted. Secondly, when the first and second examinations for brain death were separated by as long as 24 hours several patients would develop asystole before the second examination. Finally, it became widely recognised that provided scrupulous attention was given to the preconditions and exclusions the second examination always confirmed the first. In other words, the more time spent in ascertaining the irremediable nature of the structural brain damage causing the coma the less important does the interval between tests become.
>
> What is the purpose of retesting in a patient with a non-functioning brain stem due to well established, irremediable, structural brain damage? The UK code claims that it is to ensure that there has been no observer error. This is entirely praiseworthy, although no properly documented case has been published where the diagnosis of brain stem death has been revised after repeat testing. In my opinion retesting usually has a different purpose. It ensures that the non-functioning of the brain stem is not just a single observation at one point in time but that it has persisted. For how long? For a period several hundredfold that during which brain stem neurons could survive the total ischaemia of a non-perfused brain. At Hammersmith Hospital we like to separate our tests by two to three hours, which is more than enough to ensure that the findings are irreversible.

One further point which may be noted arises from the final paragraph of the 1976 Code. Although not entirely clearly drafted, the paragraph seems to contemplate that the determination should be made (or confirmed) by medical practitioners of appropriate standing and experience. If this procedure was not complied with, again would a court hold that the patient certified as dead was not dead? Provided the tests were carried out with appropriate skill and the results were not doubted by informed medical opinion, we have no doubt that a court would find the patient was dead certified despite the imprecise compliance.

conduct

(b) The the issue of the doctor's *mens rea* for the purpose of homicide (to we shall return shortly), there seem to be two common features necessary to establish either civil or criminal liability. First, was the doctor's conduct in breach of his duty to his patient? Secondly, if it was, did the breach cause the patient's death?

The doctor's conduct will only be unlawful if the court has found that the patient is not dead either because there has been a failure to comply with the pre-conditions (at stage 1) or an irresponsible performance or failure to perform the tests (at stage 2). To make the issue abundantly clear, we are not here concerned with the doctor's decision in good faith to 'treat for dying' even to the point of withdrawing a patient from a ventilator (see *supra*, ch 16). Here, instead we are concerned with the doctor who by reason of non-compliance with the Code wrongly believes that the patient is dead, and then through his conduct brings about the patient's death, ie, by removing the patient's life-support system.

In these circumstances, we have no doubt that a court would decide that the doctor was both in breach of his legal duty to his patient and that his conduct was a legal cause of death. It follows, therefore, that a doctor could be guilty of gross negligence manslaughter (see *R v Prentice* [1993] 4 All ER 935 (CA)) and could be civilly liable in negligence for the patient's death. Establishing the crime of murder would be more problematic since that requires proof that the defendant intended to kill (ie bring about the death of) another human being. The doctor's belief that the patient was dead would be inconsistent with this state of mind.

D. A SPECIAL CASE – THE ANENCEPHALIC

The anencephalic is a baby born with a fatal neurological condition – anencephaly – involving the absence of all, or most of, the cerebral hemispheres, ie the higher brain. The question is, how should the law respond to the anencephalic baby? This question is of general importance but arises specifically from proposals to harvest the organs of such babies for others while the anencephalic is still breathing.

G Annas 'From Canada with Love: Anencephalic Newborns as Organ Donors' (1987) 17 Hastings Center Report 36

Determining death

The central issue in the debate about using anencephalic infants as organ sources is whether they must be dead, and if so, how death can be determined. Some have argued that since they lack higher brain function anencephalics should not be considered living human beings and thus their organs should be available for immediate use. Although almost all agree that anencephalic infants – unlike nearly every other handicapped newborn – need not be treated to prolong their lives, the majority believe that they are living human beings and that killing them would be murder.

In January 1987, transplant surgeon Calvin Stiller convened an international group, among them Leonard Bailey, in London, to discuss this issue. Diverse views were expressed, including that anencephalic infants be used as organ donors, but only upon pronouncement of death using classical brain death criteria, it would be necessary to put the child on a mechanical ventilator. This intervention permitting him or her to stop breathing naturally would normally result in the child's death; child's breathing becomes more compromised. This intervention, the child's breathing for weeks, or even permitting him or child's life; in the most extreme (but unlikely) scenario, the anencephalic as the strong enough to sustain independent breathing for weeks, or even as the

Arthur Caplan presented the position to the London meeting that anencephalics should be considered a separate category of human ('living but brain absent'), parents should be able to donate their newborns' organs prior to their death. He justifies position on the basis that the anencephalic child can never develop even a 'semblance of personhood', that the 'need for these organs is real', and that (most convincing for Caplan), 'many parents are eager to have their dead or anencephalic child used as a donor in the hope that something good might come of a tragic situation'. He does not believe that existing brain death criteria can be applied, and so is content with less exacting criteria to determine if anencephalic newborns are eligible for organ donation.

Declaring brain death in children

Since the country's first human heart transplant – in which the donor was, in fact, an anencephalic infant – great strides have been made in the mechanics of determining death. There is now general medical, legal, and ethical agreement that an individual is dead either when he or she has irreversible cessation of circulation and respiration, or irreversible cessation 'of all functions of the entire brain, including the brain stem'. However, the medical consultants to the President's Commission concluded in 1981 that because of the 'increased resistance to damage' of their brains, 'physicians should be particularly cautious in applying neurologic criteria to determine death in children younger than five years'.

Responding to that challenge, a Task Force for the Determination of Brain Death in Children was established to develop guidelines for children under five. After years of study and deliberation, the group's report, which has been widely endorsed, was published in June, 1987. The guidelines provide accepted clinical criteria for determining brain death in three categories of children: those over one year of age; those aged two months to one year; and those aged seven days to two months. The criteria are inapplicable to infants under seven days of age; for infants less than two months, in addition to meeting strict clinical criteria, two electroencephalograms separated by at least forty-eight hours are recommended. The guidelines are recommendations only and are not meant as universal requirements. The group did not specifically deal with anencephalic infants, but the basic determination to be made is that the insult to the brain is 'irreversible'. Since anencephalic newborns have no higher brain function, different clinical criteria could be used to determine brain death for them.

New clinical criteria for anencephalics?

This leaves essentially two policy choices: we can abandon attempts to justify use of anencephalic infants as organ donors because there is currently no clinically accepted means to declare brain death in these infants; or we can carry out the research necessary to establish a clinically valid procedure for doing so. The Canadian group has decided to take the second route and experiment on methods to use as organ donors anencephalic newborns who can be validly declared brain-dead on classic criteria. The group has developed a basic protocol that calls for the parents to agree, prior to birth, that: (1) the infant will be resuscitated; (2) periodic testing will be done to determine brain death (removal from the ventilator at six-to-twelve hour intervals for a ten-minute period to determine ability to breathe spontaneously); (3) organ donation is acceptable; and (4) a definite time limit (to be determined by the parents but not more than fourteen days) after which the infant will be removed from the ventilator and permitted to die. Low dose morphine is administered to prevent potential suffering on the part of the infant, although whether anencephalic newborns can suffer is unknown.

This is a true experiment in the sense that there has never been a clinical trial to determine how anencephalic infants do with full ventilator support. They have almost never been so supported, primarily because the condition is quickly and universally fatal. As one pediatric

Anencephalic infants differ from all other organ donors in that they are not routinely resuscitated, intubated, or placed on ventilators and given other support, we cannot justify these interventions as 'treatment' for these infants. Rather, these interventions can only be seen as treatment for the benefit of the ultimate organ recipient, and perhaps as treatment for parents. If we determine that it is never ethically appropriate to prolong an unconsenting person's dying process for the sake of another, then our inquiry is at an end. If we conclude that it may be appropriate to do so (for example, if the harm to the dying child is trivial and the benefit to others is enormous), we can go on to the second step.

This second step would entail research, like that underway in Canada, to determine: how long anencephalic infants can survive with the support available in an intensive care unit; whether they feel pain or have other sensations; the state of their kidneys, liver, and heart, which will determine their general usefulness for transplantation; and whether it is true that the condition of anencephaly can be easily and accurately distinguished from all other abnormalities of infants.

[...] placed on life-support systems initially for their own sake, but solely for the sake of others. Specifically, since anencephalic newborns are not routinely resuscitated, [...]

[...] proper to use dying newborns to help others rather than [...] research is legally and ethically proper? [...] support respiration in [...]

Professor Capron puts the argument against considering anencephalics as dead.

Alexander Morgan Capron 'Anencephalic Donors: Separate the Dead from the Dying' (1987) 17 Hastings Center Report 5

Adding anencephalics to the category of dead persons would be a radical change, both in the social and medical understanding of what it means to be dead and in the social practices surrounding death. Anencephalic infants may be dying, but they are still alive and breathing. Calling them 'dead' will not change physiologic reality or otherwise cause them to resemble those (cold and nonrespirating) bodies that are considered appropriate for post-mortem examinations and burial . . . Physicians do not consider anencephalic infants as dead, but as dying. Their perception is borne out by statistics. One study of liveborn infants with anencephaly, conducted over a thirty-year period, found an equal distribution among males and females. Significantly more males survived the first day of life, but none lived longer than seven days, while female survival was comparable to male after the first day. One female (1.1 percent) survived 14 days:

> The results of this study show that over 40 percent of anencephalic infants can be expected to survive longer than 24 hours (51% males; 34% females), and of these, 35 percent will still be alive on the third day and 5 percent on the seventh day.

For most of the infants in this study, anencephaly was the only neural tube defect, and most of these had no anomalies in other organ systems. Among those infants who also had spina bifida or encephalocele (a protrusion of the brain substance through an opening in the skull), one third had defects in another major organ system.

. . . Although the diagnosis is usually made accurately by neurologists, authors of the thirty-year study just mentioned found that in 'conducting this study, it became obvious that it is important to verify the diagnosis of anencephaly'. They describe several cases of long survival:

> One infant initially coded as anencephaly, who survived over 4 months, had hydranencephaly rather than anencephaly, and another who lived for 12 days actually had amniotic band syndrome mimicking anencephaly.

Misdiagnosis by itself would not appear to be a great enough risk to preclude the use of anencephaly as a category to trigger further action (such as declaration of 'death'). But the observed relationship to – or even overlapping with – other congenital neurological defects underlines the problems that the proposal would create. For example, hydranencephalics have normal brain development early in gestation; as a result of some event (such as an in utero infection) their cerebral hemispheres are destroyed and replaced with fluid. Like anencephalics, hydranencephalics survive depending upon the extent to which their brain stems are able to regulate vegetative functioning, but they usually survive somewhat longer because their skulls are intact and thus their brains are not open to infection.

To further complicate the picture, other neurological conditions, such as certain types of microcephaly, are also inconsistent with long-term survival. Microcephaly – literally, a small head – covers a spectrum of differences . . . indistinguishable . . . hemispheres fail to form. Whatever their clinical differences are *conceptually* indistinguishable . . . lethal neurological . . . microcephalic infants from normal children is their lethal neurological . . . categories, 'dead' . . . anencephalics . . . . of the existence of these other diagnostic categories, situated 'dead' . . .

Because of the existence of these other diagnostic categories, similarly situated 'dead' . . . pressured to expand the 'definition' to sweep in other similarly situated 'dead' . . . babies – Indeed, Dr Alan Shewmon, a pediatric neurologist at UCLA, has pointed out that babies – such as hydranencephalics – who typically live a little longer than anencephalics are actually likely to be *more* attractive sources of organs because of the extra time for development. At present, the regional organ procurement association for California does not accept organs from infants younger than two months of age because of physiologic difficulties (such as the tendency of vessels to clot).

More important, these other diagnostic categories serve as a reminder that the proposals involve a variety of infants who are going to die in a relatively short time. Distinguishing those who will die within a day or two from those (including *some* microcephalics and hydranencephalics as well as the remaining anencephalics) who will die over the following two weeks is inevitably imprecise. The distinctions rest on clinical judgment, not moral principle. . . .

'Defining' anencephalics as dead would place these patients into the same category as patients who lack the capacity to breathe on their own, which has always been taken as a basic sign of life. Perhaps the proponents of this change do not see this as a major alteration because they think the law already lumps together some people who are 'more dead' (those whose hearts have stopped) with others who are merely 'brain dead'. But all persons found to meet the standards of the UDDA [the Uniform Determination of Death Act] are equally dead; it is merely the means of measuring the absence of the integrated functioning of heart, lungs, and brain that differs between those who are and those who are not being treated by methods that can induce breathing and heartbeat.

Defining anencephalics as dead so that they may be used as organ donors could, ironically, actually decrease organ donation. Imagine the effect of the law on the process of seeking organ donations from the relatives of a deceased person. At present, when that situation arises, the person seeking permission can explain that the patient is dead; despite the heaving chest and other appearances of life, if the physicians were to cease the mechanical interventions, it would immediately be apparent that the body is in the same state that we have always recognised as dead. The next-of-kin are told that they do not face a difficult decision over whether to let the patient die; instead they face the reality that their loved one is now a corpse – albeit a corpse with artificially generated heartbeat and breathing – whose organs are still being maintained in a way that would make them useful for transplants. (Remember that only a fraction of persons declared dead on the basis of absence of brain functions are candidates for organ donation.)

If anencephalic babies were also regarded as dead bodies suitable for organ donation, this certainty would be lost. For in these cases, decisions about the extent of treatment remain – indeed, some parents may even wish to try heroic or experimental means to lengthen their child's life. The message to those involved in organ transplantation – both as relatives of potential donors and as physicians, nurses, and others seeking permission for donation – is thus likely to introduce new elements of uncertainty. Is *any* particular patient – and not just an anencephalic baby – *really* dead? Or do the physicians mean only that the outlook for the patient's survival is poor, so why not allow the organs to be taken and bring about death in this (useful) fashion?

Alternatively, perhaps some who favor the anencephalic standard for death *do* mean to change the law radically. A few commentators have argued for many years that the statutes on death should move beyond new means for measuring the traditional state of death and should instead declare that persons who have lost only the higher (neocortical) functions of their brains are also dead. These suggestions have been uniformly rejected by legislators across the country – as well as by most medical, ethical, and legal writers. Yet the inclusion of anencephalics in the 'definition' of death would amount to the first recognition of a 'higher brain' standard – and a first step toward a broader use of this standard – because these babies, despite the massive deficit in their brains, still have some functions (principally at the brain stem level).

To state that such patients are dead would be equivalent to saying that the late Karen Quinlan was 'dead' for the more than ten years that she lived after her respirator was removed. Like the anencephalic babies, Ms. Quinlan and other patients in a persistent vegetative state lack the ability to think, to communicate, and probably even to process any sensations of pain and pleasure (at least in the way that we think of these phenomena). Some people may consider such a life as unrewarding, but that does not justify loose use of language about who is 'dead'. Emotionally, one may be tempted to say that a person in a permanent coma is 'as good as dead' because he or she cannot participate in any of the activities that give life meaning. But such a breathing, metabolising patient does not embody what we mean by dead and is not ready for burial – or organ donation.

A statute that labels anencephalics 'dead' is a bad idea because either it will treat differently another group that is identical on the relevant criteria (the permanently comatose, who are dying and lacking consciousness) or it will lead to a further revision in medical and legal standards under which the permanently comatose would also be regarded as 'dead' although many of them can survive for years with nothing more than ordinary nursing care.

For many people, the prospect of being in a permanent coma is unacceptable; if that occurred, they would want to be allowed to die without further treatment. But that is a separate problem to which society is already responding in other ways. It would be highly controversial – and, indeed, would be rejected by most people – to call people who are in a coma but who still breathe on their own 'dead', especially when the purpose is to allow removal of their vital organs, which *would* then cause their death as that term is now used. That was the nightmarish scenario that took place in the Jefferson Institute in Robin Cook's novel *Coma*.

In 1988, the Working Party of the Medical Royal Colleges on 'Organ Transplantation in Neonates', chaired by Sir Raymond Hoffenberg, considered, *inter alia*, the question of the status of the anencephalic baby. It concluded that:

> 5.1 It is understood that, providing there was professional confidence that brain stem death criteria could be applied to the neonate of a certain gestational age, then there could be no legal or ethical objection to the parents agreeing to, and a surgeon undertaking, organ retrieval.
> 5.2 There is little firm evidence that the well-established criteria used for diagnosing brain stem death in older children and adults can be applied to neonates with beating hearts in the first seven days of life for the purpose of organ removal. The ethics committee of the Child Neurology Society in the United States has concluded that there is insufficient information to diagnose brain death at this age and in that country a joint task force is investigating the matter further and will report soon.
> 5.3 Until acceptable criteria for brain stem death in the first seven days of life are agreed it is the view of the Working Party that the brain stem death criteria used in older children and adults cannot be used to justify the removal of organs from such neonates with beating hearts for transplantation.

In the light of this, the Working Party recommended the following:

> 4.7.3 . . . Tests of brain stem functions are applied in adults because the absence of such function establishes that the brain is dead; they are clearly inapplicable when the forebrain itself is missing. Such infants clearly have a major neurological deficiency incompatible with life for longer than a few hours. A view which commended itself to the Working Party was that organs could be removed from an anencephalic infant when two doctors (who are not members of the transplant team) agreed that spontaneous respiration had ceased. In the adult the diagnosis of brain death plus apnoea is recognised as death. The Working Party felt by analogy that the absence of the forebrain in these infants plus apnoea would similarly be recognised as death.

Index